KU-778-437

LAW OF VALUE-ADDED TAX

IRISH TAXATION INSTITUTE

The Irish Taxation Institute (ITI) is the leading representative body for taxation affairs in Ireland. Our membership work as Registered Tax Consultants, accountants, barristers, lawyers, and other corporate and business professionals. Our mission is to support an efficient, fair and competitive tax system that promotes an understanding of and expertise in taxation and encourages economic and social progress.

Our 6,000 members work with corporate leaders, Government, State agencies, representative groups, professional organisations and the general public. Through our membership of the Confédération Fiscale Européenne, we monitor and influence legislation and tax policy developments in the EU and internationally.

For over 40 years, the ITI has been Ireland's foremost provider of Registered Tax Consultants through our three-year (AITI) and Tax Technicians through our one-year (TMITI) tax qualification courses. Our professional development programme provides continued education, specialist seminars and other support services for members. This ensures Registered Tax Consultants remain professionally competent throughout their working lives.

Through our nationwide branch network and comprehensive committee structure, our members are actively involved in developing and advancing research on taxation, economic and social policy. Drawing on this expert team, ITI produces a comprehensive suite of taxation publications covering the full range of tax topics.

The ITI is governed by a Council made up of senior business executives and managed by a dynamic executive team.

Titles in Print:

A Practitioner's Guide to Revenue Audits
Buying and Selling a Business
Capital Acquisitions Tax
Capital Allowances and Property
  Incentives
Case Law for the Tax Practitioner
Corporation Tax
Direct Tax Acts
Double Taxation Agreements – Vols. 1 & 2
FINAK
From Bóraimhe to Bit – The Art of
  Taxation
Income Tax
Irish Taxation – Law and Practice
Law of Capital Acquisitions Tax
Law of Value-Added Tax
Money Laundering: Guidelines on the
  Money Laundering Legislation for Tax
  Advisers
One Size Fits All? EU Taxation Policy
Pensions: Revenue Law and Practice
PRSI and Levy Contributions
Residential Property Tax Legislation

Stamp Acts
Tax Implications of Marital Breakdown
Taxation of Property Transactions
Taxation Summary
Taxes Consolidation Act 1997:
  The Busy Practitioner's Guide
Taxing Financial Transactions
Taxing GAAP and IFRS
The Law and Practice of Irish Stamp
  Duty
The Taxation of Capital Gains
The 2002 Revenue Audit Code of
  Practice
Trust and Succession Law
Valuation of Shares in Unlisted
  Companies for Tax Purposes
Value-Added Tax
VAT on Property
Who's Afraid of the ECJ? Implications
  of the European Court of Justice
Decision on Ireland's Corporation Tax
  Regime
World Tax Conference Papers 2001

Law of Value-Added Tax

10th edition | Finance Act 2009

Edited by

Breen Cassidy and Jim Somers

Irish Taxation Institute

Irish Taxation Institute
South Block
Longboat Quay
Grand Canal Harbour
Dublin 2

Telephone: +353 1 6631700
Fax: +353 1 6688088
E-mail: info@taxireland.ie
Web: www.taxireland.ie

Irish Taxation Institute and the crest logo are trademarks of the Irish Taxation Institute

Consolidation of legislation and annotations © Irish Taxation Institute 2009

First edition 1977
Seventh edition 2006
Eighth edition 2007
Ninth edition 2008
Tenth edition 2009

All rights reserved. No part of this publication may be reproduced or transmitted in any material form or by any means, including photocopying and recording, without the prior written permission of the copyright holder, application for which should be addressed to the publisher. Such written permission must also be obtained before any part of this publication is stored in any medium by electronic means including in a retrieval system of any nature.

A catalogue record for this book is available from the British Library

The object of this book is to bring together in one volume the text of the Value-Added Tax Acts 2009.

ISBN 978-1-84260-182-2
10 9 8 7 6 5 4 3 2 1

Printed and bound in the UK by Clays Ltd., Popson Street, Bungay, Suffolk, NR 35 1ED

PRIMARY TABLE OF CONTENTS

FOREWORD

I am very pleased to present the tenth edition of the Irish Taxation Institute's *Law of Value-Added Tax*, which has over the years proven to be an indispensible guide to the complexities of Value-Added Tax (VAT) and Vehicle Registration Tax (VRT) legislation affecting Ireland.

Law of Value-Added Tax has been updated for Finance Act 2009 and other relevant legislation including that relating to VRT. Also included are relevant Irish and EU Regulations and Orders, a development of Council Directive 2006/112/EC and the provisions applying to VAT included in general Irish tax law.

To complement these, the editors have provided the full text of Revenue Statements of Practice and Information Leaflets, as well as clear and updated cross-references to Irish and European case law, *Tax Briefings, Irish Tax Review* articles and Revenue precedents.

I would like to extend my sincere thanks to the editors, Breen Cassidy and Jim Somers for their excellent work. A note of thanks goes also to Maria Reade and Mary O'Hare for their assistance to the editors on this publication. I highly recommend this book to practitioners, students and interested readers alike.

JIM RYAN
President
Irish Taxation Institute

Editor's Preface

This publication is the culmination of many months of research. We have formatted it in the order we believe will make it both useful and accessible.

We have placed the Irish Regulations and Orders together in chronological order. We have also placed the European Directives, Regulations and Decisions together in chronological order.

The section "Development of the VAT Acts, 1972-2009" is intended to allow the user to deconstruct the current consolidated version and recreate the consolidated version for each year from 1972 to the present.

The consolidated text of Council Directive No. 2006/112/EC has been included. This Directive repealed the Sixth Directive and many other European Directives.

This year we have included a new section entitled "Development of Council Directive No. 2006/112/EC" which will allow the user to recreate the amended Articles of the consolidated version of the Directive from 2006 to the present.

The section entitled "Law of Vehicle Registration Tax (VRT)", which we added in 2001, has been updated.

The text of Revenue Statements of Practice and Information Leaflets is included with two tables of contents: one listing the documents in chronological order and the second, in alphabetical order.

We would like to thank the Indirect Tax Services Group in Ernst & Young, in particular, Maria Reade and Mary O'Hare, Senior Managers at Ernst & Young, Dublin, for their assistance in researching and collating this publication.

Breen Cassidy

Jim Somers

How to Use this Book

Introduction

VAT is an indirect tax, which is payable on sales (as opposed to a direct tax such as corporation tax or income tax, which are payable on income generated by companies and individuals respectively).

After PAYE, VAT is the largest yielding tax to the Exchequer, and the value of its receipts increases annually.

The VAT system operates such that each party in the chain (e.g., manufacturer, wholesaler, retailer) acts as a VAT collector, in that they take the tax from their customer and remit the excess of VAT they have charged over VAT that has been charged to them to Revenue at the end of each bimonthly VAT period. The payment represents the tax on the added value of the goods and services at each point in the supply chain.

The cornerstone of each Member State's VAT legislation is Council Directive No. 2006/112/EC of 28 November 2006 (w.e.f. 1 January 2007) which repealed the Sixth Council Directive (77/388/EEC of 17 May 1977) on the harmonisation of the laws of the Member States relating to turnover taxes ("the Sixth Directive"). Before an applicant country can accede to the European Union its VAT legislation must be harmonised with the provisions laid down by Council Directive No. 2006/112/EC. Where national legislation differs from Council Directive No. 2006/112/EC the latter usually has primacy. Disputes concerning the interpretation of EU legislation are the domain of the Courts of Justice of the European Communities (ECJ), which is why all relevant rulings have been included in this book.

VAT was introduced in Ireland with effect from 1 November 1972, prior to Ireland's accession to the European Community in 1973. It replaced two sales taxes: turnover tax and wholesale tax. The Value-Added Tax Act 1972 ("VAT Act") is the basis of Irish value-added tax law. The Act, which was substantially amended by the Value-Added Tax (Amendment) Act 1978 (to implement the Sixth Directive), is amended annually by the Finance Act and periodically by European Regulations, and is supported by VAT Regulations and VAT Orders (Statutory Instruments).

For ease of use, this book comprises two main parts:

* Irish legislation, and

* European legislation

Irish Legislation

The first part of the book is dedicated to Irish legislation. The **Consolidated Value-Added Tax Acts 1972 - 2009** section contains, on a section-by-section basis, cross-references to Council Directive No. 2006/112/EC, Regulations and Orders, Revenue e-Briefs, case law, Revenue precedents, Revenue Statements of Practice and Information Leaflets, and references to *Irish Tax Review* articles and Revenue *Tax Briefings*. All amendments to the legislation have been footnoted and cross-referenced to the "Development of the Value-Added Tax Acts" section. Following a review of the precedents on the Revenue website, a number of previously listed items relating to VAT have been deleted. The reason for these deletions, as explained by the Revenue Commissioners, is that the decisions in question, when reviewed, were not considered to constitute precedent or concessionary treatment, but were simply interpretations of the legislation or are now available in other publications. The decisions which Revenue says remain in force are included in this book. Care should be taken when using or availing of these precedents. We have, insofar as is possible, identified those decisions removed from Revenue's list of current precedents.

All extant and revoked **Regulations and Orders** have been included in a section of their own. Regulations and orders have been mingled and are arranged in strict chronological order.

The text of existing **Statements of Practice and Information Leaflets** has been included in a separate section. Two tables of contents accompany them: the first lists the documents in chronological order and the second, in alphabetical order.

The **Other Relevant Legislation** section contains other legislative provisions, which relate to or govern the operation of various sections of the Value-Added Tax Acts 1972 - 2009.

The **Law of Vehicle Registration Tax (VRT)** section contains legislation relating to VRT. This complements VAT legislation, as VRT legislation makes reference in a number of instances to VAT legislation. Finance Act 2003 substantially amended this legislation.

The **Development of the Value-Added Tax Acts 1972 - 2009** section completes this part of the book. It includes the full text of the original Value-Added Tax Act 1972 and every amending provision since 1973, arranged in section order. Using this, the reader will quickly identify how a particular section has been developed over the years.

European Legislation

The second part of the book is devoted to European legislation. It contains a consolidated version of the **Sixth Council Directive** (77/388/EEC) and a consolidated version of **Council Directive 2006/112/EC** of 28 November 2006, which repeals the Sixth Directive with effect from 1 January 2007, followed by the section **Other Directives, Regulations and Decisions**, which deals with other relevant European Council Directives, European Council/Commission Regulations and European Council Decisions. The Sixth Council Directive is cross-referenced to the consolidated Value-Added Tax Acts 1972 - 2009 and relevant case law. Council Directive 2006/112/EC is also cross-referenced to the consolidated Value-Added Tax Acts 1972 – 2009. All amendments to the legislation have been footnoted.

The **Development of Council Directive No. 2006/112/EC** section identifies, on an Article-by-Article basis, the original text and amendments of all those Articles which have been amended.

The final section in this part contains a list of the gold coins referred to in Article 344 of Council Directive 2006/112/EC of 28 November 2006 (formerly Article 26b(A)(ii) of the Sixth Council Directive).

Tables, Glossary and Index

At the front of the book, the **Table of Regulations and Orders** lists 136 Statutory Instruments, while the **Table of Cases** catalogues over 200 Irish and EU cases, updated to include judgments issued in 2009.

Towards the end of the book, you will find, arranged in alphabetical order, a glossary of VAT-related terms.

At the end of the book you will find an index to this book, arranged in alphabetical order. This index contains reference to the relevant Irish and European primary legislation. The references will appear in the following format: "VATAs12" for section 12 of the Value-Added Tax Acts 1972 - 2009, and "6thDirart5" for Article 5 of the Sixth Council Directive (77/388/EEC). References to the Regulations and Orders will appear as "1992SINo.412" for Value-Added Tax (Payment of Tax on Intra-Community Acquisitions of Means of Transport) Regulations 1992 (SI 412 of 1992).

Use of Bold Text

Definitions are highlighted in bold text, as are all amendments to the Value-Added Tax Acts 1972 - 2009 introduced in Finance (No. 2) Act 2008, and Finance Act 2009.

Table of Cases

This index contains details of the name of the case, its relevant number (at the Court of Justice of the European Communities – "the ECJ"), its reference number in *Irish Tax Reports*, its reference number in another jurisdiction or in *Simon's Tax Cases*. A reference is made to the subject matter covered by the case. Cases are cross-referenced to the consolidated Value-Added Tax Acts 1972 - 2009 and to the Sixth Council Directive (77/388/EEC).

For ease of access, cases have been arranged in alphabetical order of the taxpayer's proper or surname. Cases involving countries of the EU are arranged in alphabetical order also. Cases involving individuals or entities and an institution or Member State are arranged in order of the individual's or entity's names. For example:

Finanzamt Osnabruck-Land v Bernhard Langhorst C141/96 is listed as Langhorst, Bernhard v Finanzamt Osnabruck-Land C141/96

Regina v Goodwin and Unstead C3/97 is listed as Goodwin and Unstead v Regina C3/97

Commission Of the European Communities v Ireland C17/84 is listed as Ireland v Communities C17/84

Staatsecretaries van Financiën v Coffeeshop Siberie C158/98 is listed as Coffeeshop Siberie v Staatsecretaries van Financiën C158/98

Name of Case	Case Number	Subject	Irish Legislation Reference	Council Directive Reference
A				
Abbey National plc, Inscape Investment Fund v Commissioners of Customs & Excise	C169/04	Management of special investment funds/Meaning of 'management'	VATA 1st Sch	6th Dir art 13
Abbink, Jan Gerrit	C134/83	Exempted Imports/ Criminal Proceedings	VATA s 15	6th Dir art 14
Akritidis, Savvas v Finanzamt Herne-West	C462/02	Games of chance/ Exemption of/Conditions to/Direct effect	VATA 1st Sch	6th Dir art 13B
Aktiebolaget NN v Skatteverket	C111/05	Place of transaction/ Supply and installation/ Under sea fibre optic cable	VATA s 3	6th Dir art 8
Ambulanter Pflegedienst Kugler GmbH v Finanzamt für Korperschafte 1	C141/00	Medical care/provision by Corporate bodies	VATA 1st Sch	6th Dir art 13
Ampafrance S.A. v Directeur des Services Fiscaux de Maine-et-Loire	C177/99	Recovery/ Entertainment/ Restaurant costs	VATA s 2	6th Dir art 17

Name of Case	Case Number	Subject	Irish Legislation Reference	Council Directive Reference
Danfoss and Astra Zeneca v Skatteministeriet	C371/07	Supplies of services carried out free of charge by a taxable person for purposes other than those of his business	VATA s 5	6th Dir art 6
Debouche, Etienne v Inspecteur der Invoerrechten en Accijinzen Rijswijk	C302/93	Deduction/Right of	VATA s 12	6th Dir arts 3, 17
De Danske Bilimportører v Skatteministeriet	C98/05	Taxable amount/ Registration duty on new motor vehicles	VATA s 10	6th Dir art 11
de Jong, Pieter v Staatssecretaris van Financiën	C20/91	Self-supply/Property/ Taxable amount/Taxable event/Deduction	VATA s 4	6th Dir art 5
Denmark v Commission	C208/88	Travellers' allowances	VATA s 15	6th Dir art 14
Design Concept S.A. and Flanders Expo S.A.	C438/01	Advertising services/ Supplied indirectly	VATA s 5	6th Dir art 9
DFDS A/S v Customs and Excise	C260/95	Travel agent/Taxable person	VATA 1st Sch	6th Dir art 26
D.H. Burke Ltd. v Revenue Commissioners	Irish H.C. Feb. 97	Taxable amount/VAT scheme for retailers	VATA s 10	
Diagnostiko & Therapeftiko Kentro Athinon-Ygeia AE v Ipourgos Ikonomikon	C394/04 C395/04	Activities closely related to hospital and medical care	VATA 1st Sch	6th Dir art 13
Dimosio, Elliniko and Karageorgou, Maria, Petrova, Katina, and Vlachos, Loukas	C78/02, C7902 and C80/02	Taxable person/ Erroneous charge of VAT	VATA s 8	6th Dir art 21
Diners Club Ltd., The v The Revenue Commissioners	Irish H.C. iii ITR 680	Credit cards/Exemption	VATA 1st Sch	6th Dir art 13B
Direct Cosmetics Ltd. (No. 1) v Customs & Excise	C5/84	Taxable amount/ Party-plan selling	VATA s 10	6th Dir art 27
Direct Cosmetics Ltd. (No. 2) v Customs & Excise	C138/86	Taxable amount/ Party-plan selling	VATA s 10	6th Dir art 27
Donner, Andreas Matthias v The Netherlands	C39/82	Imports/Exemption	VATA 1st Sch	6th Dir art 13
Drexl, Rainer	C299/86	Imports	VATA s 15	6th Dir art 23
Dudda, Jürgen v Finanzamt Bergisch Gladback	C327/94	Place of supply	VATA s 5	6th Dir art 9

E

Name of Case	Case Number	Subject	Irish Legislation Reference	Council Directive Reference
Ecotarde SpA v Agenzia delle Entrate – Ufficio di Genova 3	C95/07 and C96/07	Reverse charge procedure/ Right to deduct	VATA s 12	6th Dir arts 17, 21
Eismann Alto Adige Srl v Ufficio Imposta sul Valore Aggento di Bolzano	C217/94	Obligations for payment		6th Dir art 22
Elida Gibbs Ltd. v Customs and Excise	C317/94	Taxable amount/Discount	VATA s 10	6th Dir art 11A
Elmeka NE v Ipourgos Ikonomikon	C181/04 C182/04 C183/04	Chartering of sea-going vessels/Scope of exemption	VATA 1st Sch	6th Dir art 15
Empresa de Desenvolvimento Mineiro SGPS SA (EDM) and Fazenda Pública	C77/01	Meaning of "economic activities"/Meaning of "incidental financial transactions"/Calculation of deductible proportion	VATA ss 2, 12, 1st Sch	6th Dir arts 2, 4, 13B, 17, 19
Enkler, Renate v Finanzamt Hamburg	C230/94	Taxable person	VATA s 8	6th Dir art 4

Name of Case	Case Number	Subject	Irish Legislation Reference	Council Directive Reference
Erin Executor and Trustee Company Limited t/a IPFPUT v Revenue Commissioners	Irish Supreme Court 363 and 369/1994 ITR II/3	Recovery/Leasehold property	VATA s 12	6th Dir art 17
Eurodental Sàrl v Administration de l'enregistrement et des domaines	C240/05	Deduction/Right of/ Intra-Community transactions	VATA s 12	6th Dir art 17
Evangelischer Krankenhausverein Wien v Abgabenberufungskommission and Ikera Warenhandelsgesellschaft mbH v Oberösterreichische Landesregierung	C437/97	Levy	VATA s 2	6th Dir art 33

F

Name of Case	Case Number	Subject	Irish Legislation Reference	Council Directive Reference
Faaborg-Gelting Linien A/S v Finanzamt Flensburg	C231/94	Restaurant services/ Place of supply	VATA s 5	6th Dir art 22
Far, Miguel Amengual v Far, Juan Amengual	C12/98	Property/Right to waive exemption	VATA ss 4, 7	6th Dir art 5
Faxworld Vorgründungsgesellschaft Peter Hünninghausen und Wolfgang Klein GbR and Finanzamt Offenbach am Main-Land	C137/02	Right to deduct	VATA ss 3, 12	6th Dir art 17
FCE Bank plc v Ministero dell' Ecomomia e delle Finanze	C210/04	Concept of taxable person/Fixed establishment	VATA s 8	6th Dir art 4
Federation of Technological Industries and Others v Customs & Excise	C384/04	Anti-avoidance measures/Persons liable to pay tax	VATA s 8	6th Dir arts 21, 22
Feuerbestattungsverein Halle eV v Finanzamt Eisleben	C430/04	Private taxable person in competition with public authority	VATA s 8	6th Dir art 4
Fini H, I/S v Skatteministeriet	C32/03	Ceased economic activity/ Deduction/Right of	VATA s 12	6th Dir arts 4, 17
First Choice Holidays plc. v Customs & Excise	C149/01	Travel agents	VATA 1st Sch	6th Dir art 26
First National Bank of Chicago v Customs & Excise	C172/96	Forex/Exempt	VATA 1st Sch	6th Dir art 13
Fischer, Karlheinz v Finanzamt Donaueschingen	C283/95	Arbitrator/Place of supply	VATA s 5	6th Dir art 9
Floridienne S.A. v Belgium	C142/99	Recovery/ Apportionment/Share dividends to be included	VATA s 12	6th Dir art 17
Fonden Marselisborg Lystbådehavn v Skatteministeriet	C428/02	Letting of premises and sites for parking boats/ Mooring berths	VATA s 11	6th Dir art 13B
Förvaltnings AB Stenholmen and Riksskatteverket	C320/02	Second-hand goods/Live animals	VATA s 10A	6th Dir art 26a
France v Commission	C50/87	Leased buildings deduction/Right of	VATA s 12	6th Dir arts 4, 17
France v Commission	C30/89	Taxable amount/Own resources	VATA s 10	6th Dir art 2
France v Commission	C68/92	Place of supply/ Advertising services	VATA s 5	6th Dir art 9

Name of Case	Case Number	Subject	Irish Legislation Reference	Council Directive Reference
France v Commission	C43/96	Helicopters/Recovery of VAT	VATA s 12	6th Dir art 17
France v Commission	C76/99	Medical supplies/Taking of samples	VATA s 5	6th Dir art 13
France v Commission	C345/99	Recovery/Limitation to vehicles used exclusively for driving instruction	VATA s 12	6th Dir art 17
France v Commission	C404/99	Restaurant service charges	VATA s 5	6th Dir art 2
France v Commission	C40/00	Reintroduction of recovery restrictions	VATA s 12	6th Dir art 17
France v Commission	C243/03	Deduction/Capital goods financed by subsidies	VATA s 12	6th Dir art 17
Freemans plc. v Customs & Excise	C86/99	Taxable amount/Discount accounted for at the time of the supply/Price reduction after the supply takes place	VATA s 10	6th Dir art 11
G				
Gaston Schul Douane Expediteur BV v Inspecteur Der Invoerrechten en Accijnzen	C15/81	Recovery of VAT on imports of second-hand cars	VATA s 12	6th Dir arts 32, 11
Genius Holding BV v Staatssecretaris van Financiën	C342/87	Deduction/Right of	VATA s 12	6th Dir art 20
Gerhard Bockemühl and Förvaltnings AB Stenholmen and Riksskatteverket	C90/02	Deduction/Obligation to possess invoice/9(2)(e) service	VATA s 12	6th Dir art 18
Germany v Commission	C427/98	Money-off coupons	VATA s 10	6th Dir art 11
Germany v Commission	C287/00	Research activities	VATA s 2, 1st Sch	6th Dir arts 2, 13
Germany v Commission of the European Communities	C401/06	Supply of services/Executor of a will	VATA s 5	6th Dir art 9
Ghent Coal Terminal NV v Belgium	C37/95	Deduction/Right of	VATA s 12	6th Dir arts 17, 20
Giant NV v Commune d' Overijse	C109/90	Scope of VAT	VATA s 2	6th Dir art 33
GIL Insurance Ltd. and others v Commissioners of Customs & Excise	C308/01	Tax on insurance premiums/Compatibility with Article 33	VATA s 2	6th Dir arts 33
Gillan Beach Ltd v Ministre de l'Économie, des Finances et de l'Industrie	C114/05	Services connected with boat shows/Article 9(2)(c)	VATA s 5	6th Dir art 9
Glawe Spiel and Unterhaltungsgeraete Aufstellungsgesellschaft mBH and Co. KG v Finanzamt Hamburg Barmbek - Uhlenhorst	C38/93	Taxable amount	VATA s 10	6th Dir art 11A
Gmurzyneska - Bscher Krystyna v Oberfinanzdirektion Köln	C231/89	Imports/Rates of VAT	VATA s 11	6th Dir art 12
Goldsmith (Jewellers) Ltd. v Customs & Excise	C330/95	Taxable amount	VATA s 10	6th Dir art 11
Goritz Intransco International GmbH v Hauptzollamt Düsseldorf	C292/96	Imports	VATA s 2	6th Dir art 2
Gregg, Jennifer and Mervyn v Customs & Excise	C216/97	Medicine/Nursing home	VATA 1st Sch	6th Dir art 13

Name of Case	Case Number	Subject	Irish Legislation Reference	Council Directive Reference
Grendel (R.A.) GmBH v Finanzamt für Korperschaften, Hamburg	C255/81	Restrictions of repayment/Unjust enrichment	VATA s 20	6th Dir art 18
H				
Haderer, Werner v Finanzamt Wilmersdorf	C445/05	Tuition given privately by teachers and covering school or university education/Education provided in the context of courses organised by adult education centres/ No direct contractual link with pupils	VATA 1st Sch	6th Dir art 13A
Halifax plc., Leeds Permanent Development Services Ltd., County Wide property Investments Ltd. v Commissioners of Customs & Excise	C255/02	Economic activity/ Supplies/Abusive practice	VATA ss 2, 8, 12	6th Dir arts 2, 4
Hamann, Knut v Finanzamt Hamburg Eimsbuttel	C51/88	Yachts/Hire of/Place of supply	VATA s 5	6th Dir art 3
Harnas and Helm CV v Staatssecretaris van Financiën	C80/95	Taxable person	VATA s 8	6th Dir art 4
H.A. Solleveld and JE van den Hout-van Eijnsbergen v Straatssecretaris van Financiën	C443/04 C444/04	Medical care/ Paramedical professions/ Definition of	VATA 1st Sch	6th Dir art 13
HE v Bundesfinanzhof (Germany) Finanzamt Bergisch	C25/03	Right to deduct/Use of one room of dwelling for business purposes	VATA s 12	6th Dir art 17
Heerma J. and K. Heerma v Staatssecretaris van Financiën	C23/98	Taxable event/Property let by partner to partnership		6th Dir art 4.1
Heger Rudi GmbH v Finanzamt Graz - Stadt	C166/05	Place of supply/ Transmission of fishing rights	VATA s 5	6th Dir art 9
Heinonen, Sami	C394/97	Imports criminal/ Proceedings	VATA s 15	6th Dir art
Hoffmann, Matthias	C144/00	Cultural bodies/Soloists	VATA 1st Sch	6th Dir art 13A
Hong Kong Trade Development Council v Staatssecretaris van Financiën	C89/81	Government body/ Taxable person	VATA s 8	6th Dir arts 2, 4
Hotel Scandic Gåsabäck AB v Riksskatteverket	C412/03	Application for private use/Consideration less than cost price	VATA ss 2, 3, 5	6th Dir arts 2, 5, 6
Hutchison 3G UK Ltd and others v Commissioners of Customs and Excise	C369/04	Definition of 'economic activity'/Allocation of rights making it possible to use a defined part of the radio-frequency spectrum reserved for telecommunications services	VATA s 8	6th Dir art 4
I				
Ideal Tourisme v Belgium	C36/99	Rate of VAT	VATA s 11	6th Dir art 28
Impresa Construziono Comm. Quirino Mazzalai v Ferrovia del Renon SpA	C111/75	Taxable event/Time of completed supply	VATA s 19	6th Dir art 64
Institute of the Motor Industry v Customs & Excise	C149/97	Trade representative body/Taxable person	VATA 1st Sch	6th Dir art 13A

Name of Case	Case Number	Subject	Irish Legislation Reference	Council Directive Reference
Linneweber, Edith v Finanzamt Gladbeck	C453/02	Games of chance/ Exemption of/Conditions to/Direct effect	VATA 1st Sch	6th Dir art 13B
Lipjes, D. and Staatssecretaris van Financiën	C68/03	Services by intermediaries/Place of supply	VATA s 5	6th Dir art 28b
Lubbock Fine and Company v Customs & Excise	C63/92	Property/Taxable event	VATA s 4	6th Dir art 13B
L.u.P GmbH v Finanzamt Bochum-Mitte	C106/05	Medical care/Conditions for exemption	VATA 1st Sch	6th Dir art 13

M

Name of Case	Case Number	Subject	Irish Legislation Reference	Council Directive Reference
Maatschap M.J.M. Linthorst, KPG Pouwels and Scheres v Inspecteur der Belastingdiest/ Ondermingen Roermond	C167/95	Place of supply	VATA s 5	6th Dir art 9
Madgett (TP) and Baldwin (RM) (T/A Howden Court Hotel) v Customs & Excise	C308/96	Hotel/Tour operators	VATA s 5	6th Dir art 9
Magoora sp. z o. o. v Dyrektor lzby Skrabovej w Krakowie	C414/07	Deduction of VAT on the purchase of fuel for certain vehicles irrespective for the purpose for which they are used	VATA s 12	6th Dir art 17
Maierhofer, Rudolf and Finanzamt Augsburg-Land	C315/00	Letting of immovable property	VATA 6th Sch	6th Dir art 13B
Marks & Spencer plc. v Customs & Excise	UK - 14692 and 14693 and C62/00	Restriction on repayments/Unjust enrichment	VATA s 20	6th Dir art 17
Marks & Spencer plc v The Commissioners of Her Majesty's Revenue and Customs	C309/06	Exemption with refund of tax paid at preceeding stage	VATA s 20	6th Dir arts 12, 28
Marktgemeinde Welden v Finanzamt Augsburg - Stadt	C247/95	Tax payable in advance of supply	VATA s 19	6th Dir art 4
Maye John v Revenue Commissioners	Irish H.C. III ITR 332	Fixtures/Property	VATA ss 4, 12	
Metropol Treuhand Wirtschaftstreuhand GmbH v Finanzlandesdirektion für Steiermark and Michael Stadler v Finanzlandesdirektion für Vorarlberg	C409/99	Car recovery/Right to deduct input VAT/ Exclusions provided for under national laws at the date of entry into force of the directive	VATA s 12	6th Dir art 17
Midland Bank plc v Customs & Excise	C98/98	Recovery	VATA s 12	6th Dir art 17
Mirror Group plc. v Customs & Excise	C409/98	Letting of immovable property/ Undertaking to become a tenant	VATA 1st Sch	6th Dir art 13
MKG-Kraftfahrzeuge-Factory GmbH and Finanzamt Groß-Gerau	C305/01	Factoring	VATA 1st Sch	6th Dir art 13B
Mohr, Jurgen v Finanzamt Bad Segeberg	C215/94	Payment to discontinue activity/Taxable event	VATA s 5	6th Dir arts 2, 11
Mohsche, Gerhard v Finanzamt Munchen III	C193/91	Self-supply	VATA s 5	6th Dir art 6
Mol v Inspecteur der Invoerrechten en Accijnzen	C269/86	Illegal sale of drugs/ Taxable event	VATA s 3	6th Dir art 2

Name of Case	Case Number	Subject	Irish Legislation Reference	Council Directive Reference
Muys en de Winter's Bouw-en Aannemingsbedrijf BV v Staatssecretaris van Financiën	C281/91	Taxable amount/Interest paid to supplier	VATA s 10, 1st Sch	6th Dir arts 11, 13B
N				
Naturally Yours Cosmetics Ltd. v Customs & Excise	C230/87	Taxable amount/Party plan sales	VATA s 10	6th Dir art 11
Navicon SA v Administración del Estado	C97/06	Concept of 'chartering sea-going vessels'/ Compatibility of a national law allowing the exemption for full chartering only	VATA 2ndSch	6th Dir art 15
Nederlandse Spoorwegen NV v Staatssecretaris van Financiën	C126/78	Transport ancillary services	VATA s 2	6th Dir art 11
Netherlands, The v Commission	C16/84	Taxable amount/Trade-ins	VATA s 10	6th Dir art 11
Netherlands, The v Commission	C338/98	Cars recovery	VATA s 12, 17	6th Dir arts 17, 18
Netto Supermarkt GmbH & Co. OHG v Finanzamt Malchin	C271/06	Exports/Conditions for exemption not fulfilled/ Proof of export falsified by the purchaser	VATA 2ndSch	6th Dir art 15
Norbury Developments Ltd. v Customs & Excise	C136/97	Exemption/Waiver of/ Immovable property	VATA s 7	6th Dir art 28
Nordania Finans A/S, BG Factoring A/S v Skatteministeriet	C98/07	Calculation of the deductible proportion/ Exclusion of amounts of turnover attributable to the supplies of capital goods used by the taxable person for the purposes of his business	VATA s 12	6th Dir art 19
Norwich - City of v Customs & Excise	UK Case	Government body/ Taxable person	VATA s 2	6th Dir art 4
O				
Office des produits wallons ASBL v Belgian State	C184/00	Taxable amount/ Subsidies directly linked to the price	VATA s 10	6th Dir art 11
Optigen Ltd, Fulcrum Electronics Ltd, Bond House Systems Ltd v Commissioners of Customs & Excise	C354/03 C355/03 C484/03	Economic activity/ Taxable person/ Deduction/Carousel fraud	VATA ss 2, 8, 12	6th Dir arts 2, 4, 17
ORO Amsterdam Beheer BV & Concerto BV v Inspecteur der Omzetbelasting Amsterdam	C165/88	Deduction/Right of	VATA s 12	6th Dir art 32
P				
Part Service Srl v Ministero dell'Economia e delle Finanze, formerly Ministero delle Finanze	C425/06	Artificial division of the supply into a number of parts/Reduction of the taxable amount/Abusive practice	VATA s 10	6th Dir art 11
Pelzl Erna v Steiermarkische Landesregierung	C338/97 C344/97 C390/97	Scope of VAT	VATA s 2	6th Dir art 33
Pezzulo Molini Pastifici Mangimifici Spa v Ministero delle Finanze	C166/94	Payment on default interest on imports	VATA s 26	6th Dir art 10

Name of Case	Case Number	Subject	Irish Legislation Reference	Council Directive Reference
Shipping & Forwarding Enterprise Safe BV v Staatssecretaris van Financiën	C320/88	Rights over land/ Taxable event	VATA s 4	6th Dir art 5
Sinclair Collis Ltd. v Customs & Excise	C275/01	Letting of installed vending machines	VATA 1st Sch	6th Dir art 13B
Skandia v Forsakringsaktiebolaget	C240/99	Outsourcing	VATA 1st Sch	6th Dir art 13
Skripalle, Werner v Finanzamt Bergisch Gladback	C63/96	Minimum taxable amount	VATA s 10	6th Dir art 27
Société Générale des Grandes Sources d'Eaux Minerales Françaises v Bundesamt für Finanzen	C361/96	Recovery	VATA s 12	6th Dir art 18
Société thermale d'Eugénie-les-Bains v Ministère de l'Économie, des Finances et de l'Industrie	C277/05	Deposits, paid in the context of contracts relating to supplies of services subject to VAT, which are retained by the provider in the event of cancellation	VATA s 2, 5	6th Dir art 2, 6
Sofitam S.A. formerly Satam v Minister responsible for Budget (France)	C333/91	Holding Co./Deduction/ Right of	VATA s 12	6th Dir art 19
Sohl and Sohlke v Hauptzollamt Bremen	C48/98	Negligence	VATA 27	6th Dir art 18
Sosnowska, Alicija v Dyrektor Izby Sakrbowej we Wroclawiu Osrodek Zamiejscowy w Walbrzychu	C25/07	National Legislation determining conditions for repayment of excess VAT	VATA s 20	6th Dir arts 18, 27
Spaarkassernes Datacenter v Skatteministeriet	C2/95	Exemption/Outsourcing for bank	VATA s 1	6th Dir art 13B
Spain v Commission	C124/96	Club membership/Sports	VATA s 1	6th Dir art 13
Spain v Commission	C204/03	Subsidies/Limitation of the right to deduct	VATA s 12	6th Dir art 17
Spar Österreichische Warenhandels AG v Finanzlandesdirektion für Salzburg	C318/96	Scope of VAT/Levy in the nature of VAT/Tax to finance Chambers of Commerce in Austria	VATA s 2	6th Dir art 33
Stadler, Michael v Finanzlandesdirektion für Vorarlberg	C409/99	Cars recovery	VATA s 12	6th Dir art 17
Stadt Sundern v Bundesfinanzhof Finanzamt Arnsberg	C43/04	Concept of 'agricultural service'	VATA ss 8, 12A	6th Dir art 25
Stichting Central Begeleidingsorgaan voor de Intercollegiale Toetsing	C407/07	Exemptions/Services supplied by independent groups	VATA 1st Sch	6th Dir art 13
Stichting "Goed Wonen" v Staatssecretaris van Financiën	C326/99	Property/Rights *in rem*	VATA ss 3, 4, 1st Sch	6th Dir arts 5, 13
Stichting Kinderopvang Enschede v Staatssecretaris van Financiën	C415/04	Intermediary services linked to welfare, social security work and childcare	VATA 1st Sch	6th Dir art 13
Stichting Regionaal Opleidingen Centrum Noord-Kennemerland/West-Friesland (Horizon College) v Staatssecretaris van Financiën	C434/05	Teaching staff employed by one educational establishment made available, for consideration, to another	VATA 1st Sch	6th Dir art 13A

Name of Case	Case Number	Subject	Irish Legislation Reference	Council Directive Reference
Wiener Stadtische Allgemein Versicherungs AG v Tiroler Landesregierung	C344/97	Scope of VAT/Tourism levy	VATA s 2	6th Dir art 33
Wiley v Revenue Commissioners	Irish Case IV ITR 170	Importation free of excise duty	VATA s 20	6th Dir art 17
Wisselinken en Co. BV v Staatssecretaris van Financiën	C93/88 and C94/88	Nature of VAT	VATA s 2	6th Dir art 33
Witzemann, Max v Hauptzollamt München - Mitte	C343/89	Import of counterfeit currency notes	VATA s 2	6th Dir art 2
WLD Worldwide Leather Diffusion Ltd. v Revenue Commissioners	Irish (1994) ITR 165	Registration/Taxable person	VATA s 9	6th Dir art 22

Y

Name of Case	Case Number	Subject	Irish Legislation Reference	Council Directive Reference
Yorkshire Co-operatives Ltd. v Customs & Excise	C398/99	Reduction coupons/ Taxable amount in hands of retailer	VATA s 10	6th Dir art 11

Z

Name of Case	Case Number	Subject	Irish Legislation Reference	Council Directive Reference
Zita Modes Sàrl and Administration de l'Enregistrement et des Domaines	C497/01	Transfer of a business	VATA s 3	6th Dir art 5
Zoological Society of London v Customs & Excise	C267/00	Cultural activities/ Exemption	VATA 1st Sch	6th Dir art 13
Zweckverband zur Trinkwasserversorgung und Abwasserbeseitigung Torgau-Westelbien v Finanzamt Oschatz	C442/05	"Supply of water" or "Water supply"	VATA ss 8, 11	6th Dir arts 4, 12

Table of Regulations and Orders

List of Abbreviations

General

s, ss	Section(s) of the Act
subs, subss	Sub-section(s) of the Act
Sch	Schedule of the Act
para, paras	Paragraph(s) of the Act or of an Order
Ch/Pt	Chapter or Part of the Act
r	Regulation of a Statutory Instrument

Statutes

FA75	Finance Act 1975
IA05	Interpretation Act 2005
PCTA27	Provisional Collection of Taxes Act 1927
TCA97	Taxes Consolidation Act 1997
VATA	Value-Added Tax Act 1972
VATAA78	Value-Added Tax (Amendment) Act 1978
6th Dir art 4	Article 4 of the Sixth Council Directive (77/388/EEC) of 17 May 1977

Statutory Instruments

1992 SINo.412	SI 412 of 1992
ITERs	Income Tax (Employments) Regulations

Case Law

ITR	*Irish Tax Reports*
STC	*Simon's Tax Cases*
C-49/86	Number of case heard at European Court of Justice (ECJ)

Revenue Statements of Practice

SP	Statement of Practice

Narrative

ITR	*Irish Tax Review*

Consolidated
Value-Added Tax Acts
1972 – 2009

VALUE-ADDED TAX ACTS 1972-2009

Section 1

Interpretation

1.   (1)   In this Act, save where the context otherwise requires-

[...][1]

["accountable person"](#) has the meaning assigned to it by section 8;

"accounting year" means a period of 12 months ending on 31 December, but if a taxable person customarily makes up accounts for periods of 12 months ending on another fixed date, then, for such a person, a period of 12 months ending on that particular fixed date;][2]

Annex VII,
a295(1)(4)

["agricultural produce"] has the meaning assigned to it by section 8];[3]

Annex VIII,
a295(1)(5)

["agricultural service"] has the meaning assigned to it by section 8];[4]

['ancillary supply' means a supply, forming part of a composite supply, which is not physically and economically dissociable from a principal supply and is capable of being supplied only in the context of the better enjoyment of that principal supply;][5]

Annex IX

["antiques"] has the meaning assigned to it by section 10A];[6]

"Appeal Commissioners" means persons appointed in accordance with [section 850 of the Taxes Consolidation Act, 1997],[7] to be Appeal Commissioners for the purposes of the Income Tax Acts;

["assignment", in relation to an interest in immovable goods, means the assignment by a person of that interest in those goods or of any part of those goods to another person:

Provided that where that other person at the time of the assignment retains the reversion on that interest in those goods, that assignment shall be a surrender];[8]

"body of persons" means any body politic, corporate, or collegiate, and any company, partnership, fraternity, fellowship and society of persons, whether corporate or not corporate;

["business" means an economic activity, whatever the purpose or results of that activity, and includes any activity of producers, traders or persons supplying services, including mining and agricultural activities and activities of the professions, and the exploitation of tangible or intangible property for the purposes of obtaining income therefrom on a continuing basis;][9]

["capital goods" means developed immovable goods [and includes refurbishment within the meaning of section 12E,][10] and a reference to a capital good includes a reference to any part thereof and the term capital goods shall be construed accordingly;][11]

["clothing" does not include footwear;][12]

"Collector-General" means the Collector-General appointed under [section 851 of the Taxes Consolidation Act, 1997;][13]

Annex IX
a 5

["collectors' items" has the meaning assigned to it by section 10A;][14]

["Community", except where the context otherwise requires, has the same meaning as it has in [Articles 5 to 8 of Council Directive No. 2006/112/EC of 28 November 2006][15], and cognate references shall be construed accordingly,][16]

["completed", in respect of immovable goods, has the meaning assigned to it by section 4B;][17]

['composite supply' means a supply made by a taxable person to a customer comprising two or more supplies of goods or services or any combination of these, supplied in conjunction with each other, one of which is a principal supply;][18]

["contractor", in relation to contract work, means a person who makes or assembles movable goods;

"contract work" means the service of handing over by a contractor to another person of movable goods made or assembled by the contractor from goods entrusted to the contractor by that other person, whether or not the contractor has provided any part of the goods used;][19]

"the customs-free airport" means the land which under the [Customs-free Airport Act 1947][20], for the time being constitutes the Customs-free airport;

"development" in relation to any land, means-

(a)   the construction, demolition, extension, alteration or reconstruction of any building on the land, or

(b)   the carrying out of any engineering or other operation in, on, over or under the land to adapt it for materially altered use,

and "developed" shall be construed correspondingly [, and in this definition 'building' includes, in relation to a transaction, any prefabricated or like structure in respect of which the following conditions are satisfied:

(a)   the structure-

        (i)   has a rigid roof and one or more rigid walls and, except in the case of a structure used for the cultivation of plants, a floor,

(ii)   is designed so as to provide for human access to, and free movement in, its interior,

(iii)   is for a purpose that does not require that it be mobile or portable, and

(iv)   does not have or contain any aids to mobility or portability,

and

(b)   (i)   neither the agreement in respect of the transaction nor any other agreement between the parties to that agreement contains a provision relating to the rendering of the structure mobile or portable or the movement or re-location of the structure after its erection, and

(ii)   and the person for whom the structure is constructed, extended, altered or reconstructed signs and delivers, at the time of the transaction, to the person who constructed, extended, altered or reconstructed the structure a declaration of his intention to retain it on the site on which it is at that time located;][21]

Annex II   ["**electronically supplied services**" includes –

(a)   website supply, web-hosting, distance maintenance of programmes and equipment,

(b)   supply of software and updating of it,

(c)   supply of images, text and information, and making databases available,

(d)   supply of music, films and games, including games of chance and gambling games, and of political, cultural, artistic, sporting, scientific and entertainment broadcasts and events, and

(e)   supply of distance teaching,

a 56(2)   and "**electronic service**" shall be construed accordingly, but where the supplier of a service and his or her customer communicates by means of electronic mail, this shall not of itself mean that the service performed is an electronic service;][22]

[...][23]

["**establishment**"][24] means any fixed place of business, but does not include a place of business of an agent of a person unless the agent has and habitually exercises general authority to negotiate the terms of and make agreements on behalf of the person or has a stock of goods with which he regularly fulfils on behalf of the person agreements for the supply of goods;

a 2(3) ["**excisable products**" means the products referred to in section 104 of the Finance Act, 1992;][25]

"**exempted activity**" means-

(a) a [supply][26] of immovable goods in respect of which pursuant to **[sections 4(6) and 4B(2) and subsections (2) and (6)(b) of section 4C]**[27] tax is not chargeable, and

(b) a [supply of any goods or services][28] of a kind specified in the First Schedule or declared by the Minister by order for the time being in force under section 6 to be an exempted activity;

["**exportation of goods**" means the exportation of goods to a destination outside the Community and, where the context so admits, cognate words shall be construed accordingly;][29]

295(1)(1) ["**farmer**" has the meaning assigned to it by section 8;][30]

295(1)(8) ["**flat-rate addition**" has the meaning assigned to it by section 12A;][31]

295(1)(3) ["**flat-rate farmer**" has the meaning assigned to it by section 12A;][32]

["**footwear**" includes shoes, boots, slippers and the like but does not include stockings, under-stockings, socks, ankle-socks or similar articles or footwear without soles or footwear which is or incorporates skating or swimming equipment;][33]

["**free port**" means the land declared to be a free port for the purposes of the Free Ports Act, 1986 (No. 6 of 1986), by order made under section 2 of that Act;][34]

["**freehold equivalent interest**" means an interest in **[immovable goods, other than a freehold interest,]**[27] the transfer of which constitutes a supply of goods in accordance with section 3;][35]

["**fur skin**" means any skin with the fur, hair or wool attached except skin of woolled sheep or lamb;][36]

"**goods**" means all movable and immovable objects, but does not include things in action or money and references to goods include references to both new and [used][37] goods;

[...][38]

"**hire**", in relation to movable goods, includes a letting on any terms including a leasing;

[...][39]

"**immovable goods**" means land;

a 30 ["**importation of goods**" means the importation of goods from outside the Community into [the State][40] either-

(a) directly, or

(b)   through one or more than one other Member State where value-added tax referred to in [Council Directive No. 2006/112/EC of 28 November 2006][15] has not been chargeable on the goods in such other Member State or Member States in respect of the transaction concerned,

and, where the context so admits, cognate words shall be construed accordingly;][41]

["independently", in relation to a taxable person excludes a person who is employed or who is bound to an employer by a contract of employment or by any other legal ties creating the relationship of employer and employee as regards working conditions, remuneration and the employer's liability;][42]

['individual supply' means a supply of goods or services which is a constituent part of a multiple supply and which is physically and economically dissociable from the other goods or services forming part of that multiple supply, and is capable of being supplied as a good or service in its own right;][43]

"inspector of taxes" means an inspector of taxes appointed under [section 852 of the Taxes Consolidation Act, 1997][44];

a20 ["intra-Community acquisition of goods" has the meaning assigned to it by section 3A;][45]

["joint option for taxation" has the meaning assigned to it by section 4B;

"landlord's option to tax" has the meaning assigned to it by section 7A;][46]

"livestock" means live cattle, [horses,][47] sheep, [goats, pigs and deer][48];

"local authority" has the meaning assigned to it by section 2 (2) of the Local Government Act, 1941, and includes a health board established under the Health Act, 1970;

["margin scheme" has the meaning assigned to it by section 10A;][49]

[...][50]

"the Minister" means the Minister for Finance;

[...][51]

"movable goods" means goods other than immovable goods;

['multiple supply' means two or more individual supplies made by a taxable person to a customer where those supplies are made in conjunction with each other for a total consideration covering all those individual supplies, and where those individual supplies do not constitute a composite supply;][52]

a2(2) ["new means of transport" means motorised land vehicles with an engine cylinder capacity exceeding 48 cubic centimetres or a power exceeding 7.2 kilowatts, vessels exceeding 7.5 metres in length and aircraft with a take-off weight exceeding 1,550 kilogrammes-

(a)   which are intended for the transport of persons or goods, and

(b)   [(i)   which in the case of vessels and aircraft were supplied three months or less after the date of first entry into service and in the case of land vehicles were supplied six months or less after the date of first entry into service, or][53]

       (ii)   which have travelled [6,000 kilometres][54] or less in the case of land vehicles, sailed for 100 hours or less in the case of vessels or flown for 40 hours or less in the case of aircraft,

other than vessels and aircraft of the kind referred to in paragraph (v) of the Second Schedule;][55]

["a person registered for value-added tax" means, in relation to another Member State, a person currently issued with an identification number in that State for the purposes of accounting for value-added tax referred to in [Council Directive No. 2006/112/EC of 28 November 2006][15] and, in relation to the State, means a registered person;][56]

['principal supply' means the supply of goods or services which constitutes the predominant element of a composite supply and to which any other supply forming part of that composite supply is ancillary;][57]

"registered person" means a person who is registered in the register maintained under section 9;

"regulations" means regulations under section 32;

[...][58]

[...][59]

["second-hand goods" has the meaning assigned to it by section 10A;][60]

"secretary" includes such persons as are mentioned in [section 1044 (2) of the Taxes Consolidation Act, 1997][61], and section 55 (1) at the Finance Act, 1920;

"the specified day" means the day appointed by the Minister by order to be the specified day for the purposes of this Act;

a 14   ["supply", in relation to goods, has the meaning assigned to it by section 3 and, in relation to services, has the meaning assigned to it by section 5, and cognate words shall be construed accordingly;][62]

["**surrender**", in relation to an interest in immovable goods, means the surrender by a person (hereafter referred to in this definition as 'the lessee') of an interest in those goods or any part of those goods to the person (hereafter referred to in this definition as 'the lessor') who at the time of the surrender retains the reversion on the interest in those goods and also includes the abandonment of that interest by the lessee and the failure of the lessee to exercise any option of the type referred to in subsection (1)(b) of section 4 in relation to that interest and surrender of an interest also includes the recovery by the lessor of that interest in those goods by ejectment or forfeiture prior to the date that that interest would, but for its surrender, have expired [but in the case of an interest in immovable goods created on or after 1 July 2008, the failure of the lessee to exercise any option of the type referred to in subsection (1)(b) of section 4 in relation to that interest does not constitute a surrender][63;][64]

"**tax**" means value-added tax chargeable by virtue of this Act;

["**taxable dealer**"–

(a)   in relation to supplies of gas through the natural gas distribution system, or of electricity, has the meaning assigned to it by section 3(6A),

(b)   in relation to supplies of movable goods other than a means of transport, has the meaning assigned to it by section 10A, and

(c)   in relation to supplies of means of transport, has the meaning assigned to it by section 12B [and in relation to supplies of agricultural machinery, has the meaning assigned to it by section 12C][65;][66]

"**taxable goods**", in relation to any [supply, intra-Community acquisition or importation,][67] means goods the [supply][26] of which is not an exempted activity;

"**taxable period**" means a period of two months beginning on the first day of January, March, May, July, September or November [provided that the taxable period immediately following that commencing on the 1st day of May, 1973, shall be the period commencing on the 1st day of July, 1973, and ending on the 2nd day of September, 1973, and the next succeeding taxable period shall be the period commencing on the 3rd day of September, 1973, and ending on the 31st day of October, 1973][68];

a 9(1)   ["'**taxable person**'" means a person who independently carries out any business in the State;][69]

"**taxable services**" means services the [supply][26] of which is not an exempted [activity][70];

a 24(2)   ['**telecommunications services**' means services relating to the transmission, emission or reception of signals, writing, images and sounds or information of any nature by wire, radio, optical or other electromagnetic systems and includes-

(a)   the related transfer or assignment of the right to use capacity for such transmission, emission or reception, and

(b)   the provision of access to global information networks;][71]

["**vessel**", in relation to transport, means a waterborne craft of any type, whether self-propelled or not, and includes a hovercraft.][72]

["**works of art**" has the meaning assigned to it by section 10A.][73]

(2)   In this Act references to moneys received by a person include references to-

(a)   money lodged or credited to the account of the person in any bank, savings bank, building society, hire purchase finance concern or similar financial concern, and

(b)   money, other than money referred to in paragraph (a), which, under an agreement, other than an agreement providing for discount or a price adjustment made in the ordinary course of business or an arrangement with creditors, has ceased to be due to the person, and

[(bb)   money due to the person which, in accordance with the provisions of [section 1002 of the Taxes Consolidation Act, 1997][74], is paid to the Revenue Commissioners by another person and has thereby ceased to be due to the person by that other person, and][75]

[(c)   money, which, in relation to money received by a person from another person, has been deducted in accordance with the provisions of-

(i)   [Chapter I of Part I8 of the Taxes Consolidation Act, 1997,][76]

or

(ii)   [Chapter 2 of Part 18 of the Taxes Consolidation Act, 1997,][77]

and has thereby ceased to be due to the first-mentioned person by the other person,][78]

and money lodged or credited to the account of a person as aforesaid shall be deemed to have been received by the person on the date of the making of the lodgement or credit and money which has ceased to be due to a person as aforesaid shall be deemed to have been received by the person on the date of the cesser.

a 5
a 6

[(2A) In this Act, save where the context otherwise requires, a reference to the territory of a Member State has the same meaning as it has

a 7

in Articles 5 to 8 of the Council Directive No. 2006/112/EC of 28 November 2006][15], and references to Member States and cognate references shall be construed accordingly.][79]

(3)   Any reference in this Act to any other enactment shall, except so far as the context otherwise requires, be construed as a reference to that enactment as amended or extended by any subsequent enactment.

(4)   In this Act-

(a)   a reference to a section or Schedule is to a section or Schedule of this Act, unless it is indicated that reference to some other enactment is intended, and

(b)   a reference to a subsection, paragraph or subparagraph is to the subsection, paragraph or subparagraph of the provision (including a Schedule) in which the reference occur, unless it is indicated that reference to some other provision is intended.

Amendments

1   Deleted by VAT Amend. A78...definition of 'accountable person', (w.e.f. 1 March 1979).
2   Inserted by FA08 s83(a)...definitions of 'accountable person' and 'accounting year', (w.e.f. 1 July 2008).
3   Inserted by VAT Amend. A78 s2(c)...definition of 'agricultural produce', (w.e.f. 1 March 1979).
4   Inserted by VAT Amend. A78 s2(c)...definition of 'agricultural service', (w.e.f. 1 March 1979).
5   Inserted by FA06 s93(1)(a)...definition of 'ancillary supply', (w.e.f. 1 November 2006).
6   Inserted by FA95 s119(a)...definition of 'antiques', (w.e.f. 1 July 1995).
7   Substituted by TCA1997 s1100 & Sch 31.
8   Inserted by FA97 s96(a)...definition of 'assignment', (w.e.f. 26 March 1997).
9   Substituted by FA08 s83(b)...definition of 'business', (w.e.f. 1 July 2008).
10   Inserted by F(No. 2)A 08 s99 & Sch6, (w.e.f. 24 December 2008).
11   Inserted by FA s83(c)...definition of 'capital goods', (w.e.f. 1 July 2008).
12   Inserted by FA84 s85(a)...definition of 'clothing', (w.e.f. 1 May 1985).
13   Substituted by TCA97 s1100 & Sch 31.
14   Inserted by FA95 s119(b)...definition of 'collectors' items', (w.e.f. 1 July 1995).
15   Substituted by FA07 s97 & Sch 3, (w.e.f. 1 January 2007)
16   Substituted by EC(VAT) R 1992. r4(a), (w.e.f. 1 January 1993).
17   Inserted by FA s83(d)... definition of 'completed', (w.e.f. 1 July 2008).
18   Inserted by FA06 s93(1)(b)...definition of 'composite supply', (w.e.f. 1 November 2006).
19   Inserted by FA96 s88(a)...definitions of 'contractor' and 'contract work', (w.e.f. 1 January 1996).
20   Substituted by FA08 s141 & Sch 8(3)(a), (w.e.f. 13 March 2008).
21   Extended by FA81 s43...definition of 'development', (w.e.f. 1 November 1972).
22   Inserted by FA03 s113...definition of 'electronically supplied services', (w.e.f. 1 July 2003).
23   Deleted by VAT Amend. A78 s2(a)...definition of 'established', (w.e.f. 1 March 1979).
24   Substituted by VAT Amend. A78 s2(b), (w.e.f. 1 March 1979).
25   Inserted by EC(VAT)R. 1992 r4(b)...definition of 'excisable products', (w.e.f. 1 January 1993).
26   Substituted by VAT Amend. A78 s30(2) & Sch 2, (w.e.f. 1 March 1979).
27   Substituted by F(No. 2)A 08 s99 & Sch 6, (w.e.f. 24 December 2008)
28   Substituted by VAT Amend. A78 s30(2) & Sch 2, (w.e.f. 1 March 1979).
29   Inserted by FA92 s165(a)(i)...definition of 'exportation of goods', (w.e.f. 1 January 1993).
30   Inserted by VAT Amend. A78 s2(c)...definition of 'farmer', (w.e.f. 1 March 1979).
31   Inserted by VAT Amend. A78 s2(c)...definition of 'flat rate addition', (w.e.f. 1 March 1979).
32   Inserted by VAT Amend. A78 s2(c)...definition of 'flat rate farmer', (w.e.f. 1 March 1979).
33   Inserted by FA84 s85(b)...definition of 'footwear', (w.e.f. 1 May 1984).
34   Inserted by FA86 s80...definition of 'free-port', (w.e.f. 27 May 1986).
35   Inserted by FA08 s83(f)...definition of 'freehold equivalent interest' (w.e.f. 1 July 2008).

36 Inserted by FA76 s61 & Sch 1 pt II...definition of 'fur skin' (w.e.f. 1 March 1976).
37 Substituted by FA96 s88(b), (w.e.f. 15 May 1996).
38 Deleted by FA91 s77...definition of 'hotel', (w.e.f. 1 January 1992).
39 Deleted by FA92 s165(a)(ii)...definition of 'harbour authority', (w.e.f. 28 May 1992).
40 Substituted by FA96 s88(c), (w.e.f. 15 May 1996).
41 Inserted by FA92 s165(a)(iii)...definition of 'importation of goods', (w.e.f. 1 January 1993).
42 Inserted by FA08 s83(g)... definition of 'independently', (w.e.f. 1 July 2008).
43 Inserted by FA06 s93(1)(c)...definition of 'individual supply', (w.e.f. 1 November 2006).
44 Substituted by TCA97 s1100 & Sch 31, (w.e.f. 6 April 1997).
45 Inserted by FA92 s165(a)(iv)...definition of 'intra-Community acquisition of goods', (w.e.f. 1 January 1993).
46 Inserted by FA08 s83(h)... definitions of 'joint option for taxation' and 'landlord's option to tax', (w.e.f. 1 July 2008).
47 Inserted by FA90 s98, (w.e.f. 30 May 1990).
48 Substituted by FA87 s39(a)(i), (w.e.f. 9 July 1987).
49 Inserted by FA95 s119(c)...definition of 'margin scheme', (w.e.f. 1 July 1995).
50 Deleted by VAT Amend. A78 s2(a), (w.e.f. 1 March 1978).
51 Deleted by FA08 s141 & Sch 8(3)(a)...definition of 'monthly control statement', (w.e.f. 13 March 2008).
52 Inserted by FA06 s93()(d)...definition of 'multiple supply', (w.e.f. 1 November 2006).
53 Ss(b)(i) substituted by FA94 s91(a), (w.e.f. 1 January 1995).
54 Substituted by FA94 s91(b), (w.e.f. 1 January 1995).
55 Inserted by FA92 s165(a)(vi)... definition of 'new means of transport', (w.e.f. 1 January 1993).
56 Inserted by FA92 s165(a)(vii)...definition of 'a person registered for value added tax', (w.e.f. 1 January 1993).
57 Inserted by FA06 s93(1)(e)...definition of 'principal supply', (w.e.f. 1 November 2006).
58 Deleted by VAT Amend. A78 s2(a), (w.e.f. 1 March 1979).
59 Deleted by VAT Amend. A78 s2(a), (w.e.f. 1 March 1979).
60 Substituted by FA95 s119(d)...definition of 'second-hand goods', (w.e.f. 1 July 1995).
61 Substituted by TCA97 s1100 & Sch 31, (w.e.f. 6 April 1997).
62 Inserted by VAT Amend. A78...definition of 'supply', (w.e.f. 1 March 1979).
63 Inserted by FA08 s83(i), (w.e.f. 1 July 2008).
64 Inserted by FA97 s96(b)...definition of 'surrender', (w.e.f. 26 March 1997).
65 Inserted by FA08 s141 & Sch 8(3), (w.e.f. 13 March 2008).
66 Amended by FA04 s55...definition of 'taxable dealer' (w.e.f. 1 January 2005 (paragraph (a)) and 25 March 2004 (paragraphs (b) and (c))).
67 Substituted by FA92 s165(a)(viii), (w.e.f. 1 January 1993).
68 Inserted by FA73 s90 & Sch 10, (w.e.f. 3 September 1973).
69 Substituted by FA08 s83(j)...definition of 'taxable person', (w.e.f. 1 July 2008).
70 Substituted by FA92 s165(a)(ix), (w.e.f. 1 January 1993).
71 Inserted by FA97 s96(c) ...definition of 'telecommunications service', (w.e.f. 1 July 1997).
72 Inserted by FA92 s165(a)(x)...definition of 'vessel', (w.e.f. 1 January 1993).
73 Inserted by FA95 s119(f)...definition of 'works of art', (w.e.f. 1 July 1995).
74 Substituted by TCA97 s1100 & Sch 31, (w.e.f. 6 April 1997).
75 Ss2(bb) inserted by FA88 s60, (w.e.f. 1 October 1988).
76 Substituted by TCA97 s1100 & Sch 31, (w.e.f. 6 April 1997).
77 Substituted by TCA97 s1100 & Sch 31, (w.e.f. 6 April 1997).
78 Ss2(c) inserted by FA87 s39(a), (w.e.f. 6 June 1987).
79 Ss2A inserted by FA92 s165(b), (w.e.f. 1 January 1993).

Regulations and Orders

| Composite and Multiple Supplies | 2006 SI No. 549 | Finance Act 2006 (Commencement of Sections 93(1), 97(1)(b) and 99(1)(a)) Order 2006 |
| Specified Day 1/11/72 | 1972 SI No. 180 | Value Added Tax (Specified Day) Order, 1972 |

Revenue Statements of Practice and Information Leaflets
Foreign firms doing business in Ireland, VAT treatment of: Information Leaflet dated October 2008

Narrative
Tax Briefing: Issue 52 (VAT Committee Guidelines - Electronically Supplied Services, Guide to Interpretation)

Section 2

Charge of value-added tax

2.   (1)   With effect on and from the specified day a tax, to be called value-added tax, shall, subject to this Act and regulations, be charged, levied and paid-

2(1)(a) & (c),   [(a)   on the supply of goods and services effected within the State for consideration by a taxable person acting as such, other than in the course or furtherance of an exempted activity, and][1]

2(1)(d), a 70   (b)   on goods imported into the State.

[(1A)   Without prejudice to subsection (1), with effect on and from the 1st day of January, 1993, value-added tax shall, subject to this Act and regulations, be charged, levied and paid-

(a)   on the intra-Community acquisition of goods, other than new means of transport, effected within the State for consideration by [an accountable person][2], and

(b)   on the intra-Community acquisition of new means of transport effected within the State for consideration.][3]

(2)   [...][4]

Amendments

1   Ss(1)(a) substituted by FA08 s84, (w.e.f. 1 July 2008).
2   Substituted by FA08 s109 & Sch 4, (w.e.f. 1 July 2008).
3   Ss(1A) inserted by FA92 s166, (w.e.f. 1 January 1993).
4   Deleted by VAT Amend. A78 s30 & Sch 1, (w.e.f. 1 March 1979).

Regulations and Orders

Commencement of VAT 1/11/72	1972 SI No. 180 Value Added Tax (Specified Day) Order, 1972
Commencement of 1978 Act 1/3/79	1978 SI No. 8 Commencement of 1978 Act Value Added Tax (Amendment) Act (Commencement) Order 1979
Free-ports	1987 SI No. 275 Value Added Tax (Free Ports) Regulations, 1987

Revenue e-Briefs

Revenue e-Brief No. 49/2008: Correction: VAT treatment of forfeited deposits and cancellation charges

Revenue Statements of Practice and Information Leaflets

VAT treatment of Forfeited deposits and cancellation charges: Information Leaflet dated September 2008

Case Law

Banca Popolare di Cremona Soc. Coop. arl v Agenzia Entrate Ufficio Cremona	C475/03	Definition of 'Turnover taxes'
Beaulande Raymond v Directeur des Services Fiscaux de Nantes	C208/91	Registration tax v VAT
Bergandi, Gabriel v Directeur Generale Des Impots	C252/86	Scope of VAT/State tax on gaming machines
Bozzi Aldo v Cassa Nazionale Di Previdenza ed Assistenza	C347/90	Scope of VAT
British American Tobacco International Ltd, Newman Shipping & Agency Company NV v Belgian State	C435/03	Supply/Theft from tax warehouse

BUPA Hospitals Ltd, Goldsborough Developments Ltd v Commissioners of Customs & Excise	C419/02	Payment on account/Chargeable Event/ Taxable person/Entitlement to VAT recovery
Careda SA Ferma and Facomara v Administracion General del Estado	C370/95 C371/95 C372/95	Scope of VAT
Coffeeshop Siberie v Staatssecretaris van Financien	C158/98	Sale of drugs/Illegal activities
Empresa de Desenvolvimento Mineiro SGPS SA (EDM) and Fazenda Pública	C77/01	Meaning of 'economic activities'/Meaning of 'incidental financial transactions'/ Calculation of deductible proportion
Evangelischer Krankenhausverein Wien v Abgabenberufungskommission and Ikera Warenhandelsgesekfschaft MBH v Oberosterreichische Lawdesregierung	C437/97	Levy
Germany v Commission	C287/00	Research activities
Giant NV v Commune d' Overijse	C109/90	Scope of VAT
GIL Insurance Ltd and others v Commissioners of Customs and Excise	C308/01	Tax on insurance premiums
Goritz Intransco International GmbH v Hauptzollamt Dusseldorf	C292/96	Imports
Halifax plc, Leeds Permanent Development Services Ltd, County Wide property Investments Ltd v Commissioners of Customs & Excise	C255/02	Economic Activity/Supplies/Abusive practice
Hotel Scandic Gåsabäck AB v Riksskatteverket	C412/03	Application for private use/Consideration less than cost price
Italy v European Commission	C45/95	Outside the Scope
KapHag Renditefonds 35 Spreecenter Berlin-Hellersdorf 3. Tranche GbR and Finanzamt Charlottenburg	C442/01	Scope/Admission of member to a partnership
Kennemer Golf & Country Club v Staatssecretaris van Financiën	C174/00	Services connected with the practice of sport/Non-profit-making organisation
Kretztechnik AG, Außenstelle Linz	C465/03	Supply/Share Issue/Admission of company to stock exchange
Lambert and Others v Directeur des Services Fiscaux de L'orne	C317/86	Scope of VAT/State tax on gaming machines
Levob Verzekeringen BV, OV Bank NV v Staatssecretaris van Financiën	C41/04	Supply and customisation of software
Nederlandse Spoorwegen NV v Staatssecretaris van Financien	C126/78	Transport Ancillary Services
Norwich - City of v Customs and Excise	UK Case	Government body/Taxable Person
Optigen Ltd, Fulcrum Electronics Ltd, Bond House Systems Ltd v Commissioners of Customs & Excise	C354/03 C355/03 C484/03	Economic activity/Taxable person/ Deduction/Carousel fraud
Pelzl Erna and others v Steiermarkische Landesregierung	C338/97 C344/97 C390/97	Scope of VAT
Rousseau, Wilmot SA v Caisse de Compensation de l'organisation Autunome Nationale de l'Industrie et de Commerce (Organic)	C295/84	Scope of VAT
Société thermale d'Eugénie-les-Bains v Ministère de l'Économie, des Finances et de l'Industrie	C277/05	Deposits, paid in the context of contracts relating to supplies of services subject to VAT, which are retained by the provider in the event of cancellation
Spar Osterreichische Warendandels AG v Finanzlandesdirektion Fur Salzburg	C318/96	Scope of VAT levy in the nature of VAT. Tax to finance Chambers of Commerce in Austria.
Stuag Bau-Aktiengesellschaft v Kartner Landesregierung	C390/97	Levy in nature of VAT
Town & County Factors Ltd v Customs and Excise	C498/99	Scope/Taxable Amount
Tulliasiamies and Antti Siilin	C101/00	Nature of VAT/Taxation of imported used cars

University of Huddersfield High Education Corporation v Commissioners of Customs & Excise	C223/03	Economic Activity/Supplies/Abusive practice
Vereniging Happy Family Rustenburgerstraat v Inspecteur der Omzetbelasting	C289/86	Illegal Sales
Victoria Films AS v Riksskatteverket	C134/97	Exemption Authors Temporary Retention of Exemption
Wiener Stadtische Allgemein Versicherungs AG v Tiroler Landesregierung	C344/97	Scope of VAT/Tourism Levy
Wisselink en Co BV v Staatssecretaris van Financien	C93/88 C94/88	Nature of VAT
Witzemann, Max v Hauptzollamt Munchen - Mitte	C343/89	Import of counterfeit currency notes

Revenue Precedents

Topic:	Sporting Activities.
Issue:	Sports - Taxable or not?
Decision:	Sporting activities are not deemed to be carried on in the course of business.
Date:	7/9/95

(withdrawn from the Revenue website in 2002)

Topic:	Application of Zero rate.
Issue:	Computer system supplied within the State for training and testing before being exported by the company out of the State.
Decision:	Authorisation given to zero rate the supply of the computer system to the company.
Date:	3/6/81

Topic:	Application of Zero Rate.
Issue:	A UK company with no presence in Ireland sends PBX system to a factory in this State. A Dublin company supplies component to the foreign company but is delivered directly to the factory in the State. VAT at 21% would normally apply to such a supply. The component is soldered into a finished product and sent back to the UK.
Decision:	Provided the supplier has evidence that the goods have been transferred to OMS then the zero rate can apply.
Date:	16/5/94

Topic:	Sponsorship.
Issue:	Is sponsorship of sporting activities taxable.
Decision:	No - Sport is not viewed as being carried on in the course or furtherance of business.
Date:	1/2/95

(withdrawn from the Revenue website in 2002)

Narrative

Anti-Avoidance, Abuse of Law and VAT: Where are we now?: ITR Nov 2008 Vol. 21 No. 6

VAT Drip-Feed Scheme – Held not to be Automatically "Abusive" in UK High Court Case: ITR Mar 2008: Vol. 21 No. 2

The Cadbury Triangle – Anti Avoidance and the ECJ: ITR Nov 2006 Vol 19 No. 6

ECJ Decision on Intra-Branch Supplies: Ministero dell'Economia e delle Finanze, Agenzia delle Entrate v FCE plc.: ITR July 2006 Vol 19 No. 4

The Halifax Decision: ITR May 2006 Vol 19 No. 3

Halifax, BUPA and University of Huddersfield Cases: ITR Jul 2005: Vol 18 No. 4

Tax Briefing: Issue 59 (Debt Factoring)

VAT on Unlawful & Illegal Activities: ITR Nov 2003: Vol 16 No. 6

Tax Briefing: Issue 43 (VAT Committee Guidelines – Purchasing a New Car Before Moving to Another Member State)

Section 3

[Supply] of goods

3.　　(1)　　　　[In this Act 'supply', in relation to goods, means-][1]

a 14(1)　　　　(a)　　the transfer of ownership of the goods by agreement [[including][2] the transfer of ownership of the goods to a person supplying financial services of the kind specified in subparagraph (i)(e) of the First Schedule, where those services are supplied as part of an agreement of the kind referred to in paragraph (b) in respect of those goods][3],

a 14(2)(c)　　　[(aa)　the sale of movable goods pursuant to a contract under which commission is payable on purchase or sale by an agent or auctioneer who concludes agreements in such agent's or auctioneer's own name but on the instructions of, and for the account of, another person,][4]

a 14(2)(b)　　　(b)　　the handing over of the goods to a person pursuant to an agreement which provides for the renting of the goods for a certain period subject to a condition that ownership of the goods shall be transferred to the person on a date not later than the date of payment of the final sum under the agreement,

a 14(3)
a 15(2)　　　　[(c)　　the handing over by a person (in this paragraph referred to as the developer) to another person of immovable goods which have been developed from goods entrusted to the developer by that other person for the purpose of such development, whether or not the developer has supplied any part of the goods used,][5]

a 14(2)(a)　　　(d)　　the transfer of ownership of the goods pursuant to-

　　　　　　　　(i)　　their acquisition, otherwise than by agreement, by or on behalf of the State or a local authority, or

　　　　　　　　(ii)　their seizure by any person acting under statutory authority,

a 16　　　　　[(e)　　the application (otherwise than by way of disposal to another person) by a person for the purposes of any business carried on by him of the goods, [being movable goods][6] which were developed, constructed, assembled, manufactured, produced, extracted, purchased [,imported or otherwise acquired][7] by him or by another person on his behalf, except where tax chargeable in relation to the application would, if it were charged, be wholly deductible under section 12 [...][8],

a 16　　　　　[(f)　　the appropriation of goods by [an accountable person][9] for any purpose other than the purpose of his business

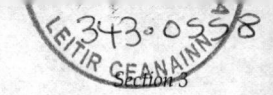

or the disposal of goods free of charge by [an accountable person][9] where -

(i)   tax chargeable in relation to those goods -

(I)   upon their purchase, intra-Community acquisition or importation by [the accountable person][9], or

(II)   upon their development, construction, assembly, manufacture, production, extraction or application under paragraph (e),

as the case may be, was wholly or partially deductible under section 12, or

(ii)   the ownership of those goods was transferred to [the accountable person][9] in the course of a transfer of a business or part thereof and that transfer of ownership was deemed not to be a supply of goods in accordance with subsection (5)(b), and][10]][11]

a 3(1), a 17(1)	[(g) the transfer by a person of goods from his business in the State to the territory of another Member State for the purposes of his business, [or a transfer of a new means of transport by a person in the State to the territory of another Member State,][12] other than for the purposes of any of the following:

(i)   the transfer of the goods in question under the circumstances specified in paragraph (b)[, (cc)][13] or (d) of subsection (6),

a 17(2)(a),
(b) & (c)
(b) & (c)

[(ii)   the transfer of goods to another person under the circumstances specified in paragraph (i) of the Second Schedule and the transfer of the goods referred to in paragraphs (v), (va), (vb) and (x) of the Second Schedule,][14]

a 17(2)(e)

[...][15]

[(iiia) the transfer of goods for the purpose of having a service carried out on them:

a 17(2)(f)

Provided that the goods which were so transferred by the person are, after being worked upon, returned to that person in the State,][16]

(iv)   the temporary use of the goods in question in the supply of a service by him in that other Member State,

a 17(2)(g)

(v)   the temporary use of the goods in question, for a period not exceeding 24 months, in that other

a 17(2)(h)

50020994

Member State, where the importation into that other Member State of the same goods with a view to their temporary use would be eligible for full exemption from import duties.][17]

a 16   [(1A)   Anything which is a supply of goods by virtue of paragraph [(e), (f) or (g)][18] of subsection (1) shall be deemed, for the purposes of this Act, to have been effected for consideration in the course or furtherance of the business concerned:

Provided however, that the following shall not be deemed to have been effected for consideration, that is to say:

(a)   a gift of goods made in the course or furtherance of the business (otherwise than as one forming part of a series or succession of gifts made to the same person) the cost of which to the donor does not exceed a sum specified for that purpose in regulations,

(b)   the gift, in reasonable quantity, to the actual or potential customer, of industrial samples in a form not ordinarily available for sale to the public.][19]

[(1B)   The provision of electricity, gas and any form of power, heat, refrigeration or ventilation shall be deemed, for the purposes of this Act, to be a supply of goods and not a supply of services.][20]

a 15(1)   [(1C)   For the purposes of this Act in the case of immovable goods 'supply' in relation to goods shall be regarded as including—

(a)   the transfer in substance of the right to dispose of immovable goods as owner or the transfer in substance of the right to dispose of **immovable goods.]**[21]

[...][22]

(2)   If three or more persons enter into agreements concerning the same goods and fulfil those agreements by a direct [supply][23] of the goods by the first person in the chain of sellers and buyers to the last buyer, then the [supply][23] to such last buyer shall be deemed, for the purposes of this Act, to constitute a simultaneous [supply][23] by each seller in the chain.

[...][24]

a 14(2)(c)   [(4)   Where an agent or auctioneer makes a sale of goods in accordance with paragraph (aa) of subsection (1) the transfer of those goods to that agent or auctioneer shall be deemed to be a supply of goods to the agent or auctioneer at the time that that agent or auctioneer makes that sale.][25]

(5)   (a)   The transfer of ownership of goods pursuant to a contract of the kind referred to in subsection (1)(b) [by the person supplying financial services of the kind specified in subparagraph (i)(e) of the First Schedule as part of that

contract][26] shall be deemed, for the purposes of this Act, not to be a [supply][23] of the goods.

(b)   The transfer of ownership of goods-

    (i)   as security for a loan or debt, or

    (ii)   where the goods are held as security for a loan or debt, upon repayment of the loan or debt, or

a 19   [(iii)   being the transfer to [an accountable person][9] of a totality of assets, or part thereof, of a business even if that business or part thereof had ceased trading, where those transferred assets constitute an undertaking or part of an undertaking capable of being operated on an independent basis,][27]

shall be deemed, for the purposes of this Act, not to be a [supply][23] of the goods [...][28]

[(c)   Where a person, in this subsection referred to as an **'owner'**

    (i)   supplies financial services of the kind specified in sub-paragraph (i)(e) of the First Schedule in respect of a supply of goods within the meaning of paragraph (b) of subsection (1), [...][29] and

    (ii)   enforces such owner's right to recover possession of those goods,

then the disposal of those goods by such owner [shall be deemed for the purposes of this Act to be a supply of goods to which paragraph (xxiv) of the First Schedule does not apply.][30]][31]

[(d)   The disposal of goods by an insurer who has taken possession of them from the owner of those goods, in this subsection referred to as the "**insured**", in connection with the settlement of a claim under a policy of insurance, being goods—

    (a)   in relation to the acquisition of which the insured had borne tax, and

    (b)   which are of such a kind or were used in such circumstances that no part of the tax borne was deductible by the insured,

shall be deemed for the purposes of this Act not to be a supply of goods.][32]

[(6)   The place where goods are supplied shall be deemed, for the purposes of this Act, to be-

a 32   (a)   in the case of goods dispatched or transported and to which paragraph (d) does not apply, the place where the dispatch or transportation to the person to whom they are supplied begins,

[Provided that where the goods are dispatched or transported from a place outside the Community, the place of supply by the person who imports the goods and the place of any subsequent supplies shall be deemed to be where the goods are imported,][33]

a 36   (b)   in the case of goods which are installed or assembled, with or without a trial run, by or on behalf of the supplier, the place where the goods are installed or assembled,

a 31   (c)   in the case of goods not dispatched or transported, the place where the goods are located at the time of supply,

a 37   [(cc)   in the case of goods supplied on board vessels, aircraft or trains during transport, the places of departure and destination of which are within the Community, the place where the transport began,][34]

a 33, a 34   (d)   notwithstanding paragraph (a) or (b), in the case of goods, other than new means of transport, dispatched or transported by or on behalf of the supplier-

        (i)   (I)   from the territory of another Member State, or

                (II)   from outside the Community through the territory of another Member State into which the said goods have been imported,

                to a person who is not [an accountable person][9] in the State, or

        (ii)   from [...][35] the State to a person in another Member State who is not registered for value-added tax,

the place where the goods are when the dispatch or transportation ends:

[Provided that this paragraph shall not apply to the supply of goods, other than goods subject to a duty of excise, where the total consideration for such supplies does not exceed or is not likely to exceed-

        (A)   in the case of goods to which subparagraph (i) relates, [€35,000][36] in a calendar year, unless the supplier, in accordance with regulations elects that it shall apply, and

        (B)   in the case of goods to which subparagraph (ii) relates, the amount specified in the Member State in question in accordance with [Article 34 of Council Directive No. 2006/112/EC of 28 November 2006][37] unless the supplier elects that it shall apply and registers and accounts for value added tax in that Member State in respect of [such supplies,][38][39][40]

a 38(1)   [(e)   in the case of the supply of gas through the natural gas distribution system, or of electricity, to a taxable dealer, whether in the State, or in another Member State of the Community, or outside the Community, the place where that taxable dealer has established the business concerned or has a fixed establishment for which the goods are supplied, or in the absence of such a place of business or fixed establishment the place where that taxable dealer has a permanent address or usually resides,

a 39   (f)   in the case of the supply of gas through the natural gas distribution system, or of electricity, to a customer other than a taxable dealer, the place where that customer has effective use and consumption of those goods; but if all or part of those goods are not consumed by that customer, then the goods not so consumed shall be deemed to have been supplied to that customer and used and consumed by that customer at the place where that customer has established the business concerned or has a fixed establishment for which the goods are supplied or in the absence of such a place of business or fixed establishment, the place where that customer has a permanent address or usually resides,][41]

a 38(2)   [(6A) In subsection (6) '**taxable dealer**' means [an accountable person][9] whose principal business in respect of supplies of gas through the natural gas distribution system, or of electricity, received by that person, is the supply of those goods for consideration in the course or furtherance of business and whose own consumption of those goods is negligible.][39]

a 18(c)[(7) [(7)   (i)   Where, in the case of a business carried on, or that has ceased to be carried on, by [an accountable person][9], goods forming part of the assets of the business are, under any power exercisable by another person, including a liquidator and a receiver, disposed of by the other person in or towards the satisfaction of a debt owed by [the accountable person][9], or in the course of the winding-up of a company, they shall be deemed to be supplied by [the accountable person][9] in the course or furtherance of his business.

           (ii)   A disposal of goods under this subsection shall include any disposal which is deemed to be a supply of immovable goods under section 4(2).][43]

a 197   [(8)   [Where a person who is not established in the State makes an intra-Community acquisition of goods in the State and makes a subsequent supply of those goods to an accountable person in the State][44], the person to whom the supply is made shall be deemed for the purposes of this Act to have made that supply and the intra-Community acquisition shall be disregarded:

Provided that this provision shall only apply where -

(a)   [the person][44] who is not established in the State has not exercised his option to register in accordance with section 9 by virtue of section 8(3D), and

(b)   the person to whom the supply is made is registered in accordance with section 9.][45]

Amendments

1   Substituted by VAT Amend. A78 s4(a), (w.e.f. 1 March 1979).
2   Substituted by FA07 s76(a), (w.e.f. 1 May 2007)
3   Inserted by FA95 s120(a), (w.e.f. 2 June 1995).
4   Ss(1)(aa) substituted by FA96 s89(a)(i), (w.e.f. 15 May 1996).
5   Ss(1)(c) substituted by FA96 s89(a)(ii), (w.e.f. 1 January 1996).
6   Substituted by FA08 s85(a), (w.e.f. 1 July 2008).
7   Substituted by FA92 s167
8   Deleted by FA92 s167(a)(i)(II), (w.e.f. 1 January 1993).
9   Substituted by FA08 s109 & Sch 4, (w.e.f. 1 July 2008).
10   Ss(1)(f) substituted by FA98 s105, (w.e.f. 27 March 1998).
11   Ss(1)(e) & (f) substituted by VAT Amend. A78 s4(a), (w.e.f. 1 March 1979).
12   Inserted by FA93 s82.
13   Inserted by EC(VAT)R 1992 r5(a)(i), S.I.413 of 1992, (w.e.f. 1 January 1993).
14   Ss(1)(g)(ii) substituted by FA99 s120(a), (w.e.f. 25 March 1999).
15   Deleted by FA96 s89(a)(iii)(I), (w.e.f. 1 January 1996).
16   Ss(1)(g)(iiia) substituted by FA96 s89(a)(iii)(11), (w.e.f. 1 January 1996).
17   Ss(1)(g) inserted by FA92 s167(a)(iii).
18   Substituted by FA92 s167(b), (w.e.f. 1 January 1993).
19   Ss(1A) inserted by FA73 s78, (w.e.f. 3 September 1973).
20   Ss(1B) inserted by VAT Amend. A78 s4, (w.e.f. 1 March 1979).
21   Substituted by F(No. 2)A 08 s68, (w.e.f. 24 December 2008).
22   Deleted by F(No. 2)A 08 s68, w.e.f. (24 December 2008).
23   Substituted by VAT Amend. A78 s30(2).
24   Deleted by FA96 s89(b), (w.e.f. 15 May 1996).
25   Ss(4) substituted by FA96 s89(c), (w.e.f. 15 May 1996).
26   Inserted by FA07 s76(b)(i), (w.e.f. 1 May 2007)
27   Substituted by FA05 s99 (w.e.f. 25 March 2005)
28   Deleted by VAT Amend. A78 s30(1) & Sch 1, (w.e.f. 1 March 1979).
29   Deleted by FA07 s76(b)(ii)(I), (w.e.f. 1 May 2007)
30   Substituted by FA07 s76(b)(ii)(II), (w.e.f. 1 May 2007)
31   Ss(5)(c) inserted by FA99 s120b, (w.e.f. 25 March 1999).
32   Para. (d) inserted by FA01 s182(b), (w.e.f. 21 March 2001).
33   Inserted by EC(VAT)R 1992 r5(b)(i), (w.e.f. 1 January 1993).
34   Ss(6)(cc) inserted by EC(VAT)R 1992 r5(b)(ii), (w.e.f. 1 January 1993).
35   Deleted by EC(VAT)R 1992 r5(b)(iii)(I), (w.e.f. 1 January 1993).
36   Substituted by FA01 s243 (4) & part 4, Sch 5, (w.e.f. 1 January 2002) previously £27,565.
37   Substituted by FA07 s97 & Sch 3, (w.e.f. 1 January 2007)
38   Substituted by FA04 s56(a) (w.e.f. 1 January 2005).
39   Substituted by EC(VAT)R 1992 r5(b)(iii)(II), (w.e.f. 1 January 1993).
40   Ss(6) substituted by FA92 s167(c), (w.e.f. 1 January 1993).
41   Inserted by FA04 s56(a) (w.e.f. 1 January 2005).
42   Inserted by FA04 s56(b) (w.e.f. 1 January 2005).
43   Ss(7) inserted by FA83 s78.
44   Substituted by FA08 s85(c), (w.e.f. 1 July 2008).
45   Ss(8) inserted by EC(VAT)R 1992 r5(c), (w.e.f. 1 January 1993).

Regulations and Orders

Business Gifts Exemption	1979 SI No. 63	Value Added Tax Regulations, 1979
Business Gifts Exemption	2006 SI No. 548	Value-Added Tax Regulations 2006
Contract work	1995 SI No. 363	European Communities (Value Added Tax) Regulations, 1995
Single Market Introduction	1992 SI No. 413	European Communities (Value Added Tax) Regulations, 1992

Revenue e-Briefs

Revenue e-Brief No. 41/2007: Transfer of a business or part of a business.

Revenue e-Brief No. 45/2006: VAT Treatment of Gifts, Promotional Items etc.

Revenue Statements of Practice and Information Leaflets

Distance Sales in the Single Market: Information Leaflet dated October 2008

Foreign firms doing business in Ireland, VAT treatment of: Information Leaflet dated October 2008

Gifts, and VAT: Information Leaflet dated October 2008

Intra-Community supplies: Information Leaflet dated October 2008

Liquidators and Receivers: Information Leaflet dated January 2009

Transfer of a business or Part Thereof: Information Leaflet dated September 2007

Case law

Aktiebolaget NN v Skatteverket	C111/05	Place of transaction/Supply and installation/Under sea fibre optic cable
Auto Lease Holland BV and Bundesamt für Finanzen	C185/01	Place of supply/Refueling of leased vehicle
Colle Parkview Service Station Ltd v BD O'Shea	Irish H.C. No. 390R	Transfer of a business/recovery of VAT
Commerz Credit Bank AG-Europartner v Finanzamt Saarbrucken	C50/91	Transfer of business
Faxworld Vorgründungsgesellschaft Peter Hünninghausen und Wolfgang Klein GbR and Finanzamt Offenbach am Main-Land	C137/02	Right to deduct
Hotel Scandic Gåsabäck AB v Riksskatteverket	C412/03	Application for private use/Consideration less than cost price
Köhler, Antje v Finanzamt Düsseldorf-Nord	C58/04	Supplies on board cruise ships/Stops in a third territory
Kuhne, Heinz v Finanzamt Munchen III	C50/88	Self Supply
Lennartz v Finanzamt Munchen III	C97/90	Taxable Event/Self Supply
Mol v Inspecteur der Invoerrechten en Accijnzen	C269/86	Illegal Sale of Drugs/Taxable Event
Ryborg NC v Rigsadvoraten	C297/89	Criminal Proceedings/Import of untaxed car
Stichting 'Goed Wonen' v Staatssecretaris van Financiën	C326/99	Property/rights *in rem*
Stylo Barratt Shoes Ltd v Inspector of Taxes	Irish S.C.	Transfer of a business
Zita Modes Sàrl and Administration de l'enregistrement et des domaines	C497/01	Transfer of a business

Revenue Precedents

Topic:	Securitisation/Receivables
Issue:	Treatment of lease transactions between taxable persons.
Decision:	In a case, involving sale of lease rentals it was agreed to treat the payment as an advance payment of lease payments.
Date:	15/11/96
Topic:	Registration.
Issue:	The supply and installation of plant in the State is a service requiring a foreign company to register in this State.
Decision:	In a particular case which came to light after the event. On the understanding that the plant was supplied for a single consideration, and there was no separate charge for assembly, and that no installation work was carried out by the company concerned, then VAT registration in the State was not pursued.
Date:	28/10/93

(withdrawn from the Revenue website in 2002)

Topic:	Factoring & Invoice Discounting.
Issue:	Retail shop sells stock to Factor with right to buy back, period 2 months. Is this concessionally included under 3(5)(b)(i) "transfer of ownership of goods as security for a loan or debt".
Decision:	This may be regarded as coming within the law provided that if under any circumstances goods disposed of to any person other than original retailer, VAT would be accounted for on the transaction.
Date:	14/7/89

Topic:	Training flights.
Issue:	VAT rate applicable to supply of fuel to be used in aircraft engaged in training flights.
Decision:	The zero rate of VAT may be applied to duty-free supplies of fuel to aircraft engaged in training flights at Shannon duty-free airport. This applies to fuel supplied on or after 1 July, 1975.
Date:	26/8/75

Topic:	Transfer of a business.
Issue:	Disposal of an hotel to a partnership of 85 investors on whose behalf a holding co. is set up as agent. A separate co. will run hotel.
Decision:	3(5)(b)(iii) applied to disposal subject to receipt from co. operating hotel that it would take responsibility for VAT on behalf of the various investors.
Date:	17/4/85

Topic:	Transfer of a Business.
Issue:	In the context of a multi-national group of companies, a transfer of a business takes place between three companies at the same time the intermediary one of which is not registered.
Decision:	The fact that the intermediary company was unregistered in this State, did not preclude the application of a VAT free transfer under Section 3(5)(b)(iii).
Date:	30/11/95

Topic:	Hiring & Leasing.
Issue:	Request to account for VAT on start up of lease of capital equipment.
Decision:	On application VAT on new leases may be accounted for at commencement of lease and customer invoiced for tax in one lump sum. Concession subject to condition that tax will be accounted for on the invoice basis.
Date:	20/3/74

Topic:	Hiring & Leasing
Issue:	Refund of VAT on respiration monitors.
Decision:	In strict terms, Order No. 15 of 1981 provides for repayment of tax borne or paid on supply or importation of goods. Case in question referred to services. Claim granted.
Date:	19/10/96

(withdrawn from the Revenue website in 2002)

Topic:	Transfer of Business.
Issue:	Transfer of goodwill or other intangible assets.
Decision:	Transfer of goodwill or other intangible assets of an exempt activity to a person engaged in the same activity is regarded as a transaction which is not liable to VAT.
Date:	23/1/90

(withdrawn from the Revenue website in 2002)

Narrative

The EMAG Case and Cross Border Supplies of Goods: ITR July 2006 Vol 19 No. 4

EU Commission Proposals to Counter VAT Avoidance: ITR May 2005: Vol 18 No. 3

Transfer of Business VAT relief - Recent Case Law: ITR Jul 2004: Vol 17 No. 4

EU Accession States – 2004: ITR Jan 2003: Vol 17 No. 1

Transfer of Benefit of Business or Transfer of Assets: ITR July 2003: Vol 16 No. 4

Tax Briefing: Issue 51 (Transfer of a Business)

Transfer of Business Relief – A New VAT Trap: ITR Nov 2001: Vol. 14 No. 6

Tax Briefing: Issue 43 (VAT Committee Guidelines – Construction of Buildings: A Good or Service)

Tax Briefing: Issue 43 (VAT Committee Guidelines – Distance Selling)

Tax Briefing: Issue 42 (VAT Committee Guidelines – Sales of Goods on Board International Means of Transport Following the Abolition of Tax-Free Sales)

Tax Briefing: Issue 42 (VAT Committee Guidelines – Contracts Without Any Supply of Goods by the Customer)

Tax Briefing: Issue 42 (VAT Committee Guidelines – Definition of "Goods Installed or Assembled")

VAT and Electronic Commerce: ITR March 1999: Vol 12 No. 2.

Foreign Firms: VAT issues arising in Ireland: ITR Jan 2000: Vol 13 No. 1

Section 3A

Intra-Community acquisition of goods

a 20, a 68 **3A.**   [(1)   In this Act 'intra-Community acquisition of goods' means the acquisition of-

(a)   movable goods, other than new means of transport, supplied by a person registered for value-added tax in a Member State[, [or by a person obliged to be registered for value-added tax in a Member State,]¹ or by a person who carries on an exempted activity in a Member State,]² [or by a flat-rate farmer in a Member State,]³ to a person in another Member State (other than an individual who is not a taxable person or who is not entitled to elect to be a taxable person[, unless the said individual carries on an exempted activity]⁴) and which have been dispatched or transported from the territory of a Member State to the territory of another Member State as a result of such supply, or

[(b)   new means of transport supplied by a person in a Member State to a person in another Member State and which has been dispatched or transported from the territory of a Member State to the territory of another Member State as a result of being so supplied.]⁵

[(1A)   An intra-Community acquisition of goods shall be deemed not to occur where the supply of those goods is subject to value-added tax referred to in [Council Directive No. 2006/112/EC of 28 November 2006 in the Member State of dispatch under the provisions implementing Articles 4 and 35, first subparagraph of Article 139(3) and Articles 311 to 341 of that Directive in that Member State].⁶]⁷

a 40   (2)   (a)   The place where an intra-Community acquisition of goods occurs shall be deemed to be the place where the goods are when the dispatch or transportation ends.

a 41   (b)   Without prejudice to paragraph (a), when the person acquiring the goods quotes his value-added tax registration number for the purpose of the acquisition, the place where an intra-Community acquisition of goods occurs shall be deemed to be within the territory of the Member State which issued that registration number [, unless the person acquiring the goods can establish that that acquisition has been subject to value added tax referred to in [Council Directive No. 2006/112/EC of 28 November 2006]⁶ in accordance with paragraph (a)]⁸.

(3)   For the purposes of this section-

a 23,

a 68,

a 140

(a)   a supply in the territory of another Member State shall be deemed to have arisen where, under similar circumstances, a supply would have arisen in the State under section 3, and

[(aa)   an activity in another Member State shall be deemed to be an exempted activity where the same activity, if carried out in the State, would be an exempted activity, and

(ab)   a person shall be deemed to be a flat-rate farmer in another Member State where, under similar circumstances, the person would be a flat-rate farmer in the State in accordance with section 12A, and]⁹

(b)   a person shall be deemed to be a taxable person or a person who is entitled to elect to be a taxable person in another Member State where, under similar circumstances, [the person would be an accountable person or entitled to elect to be an accountable person in the State]¹⁰ in accordance with section 8.

a 20   (4)   Where goods are dispatched or transported from outside the Community to a person in the State who is not registered for tax and who is not an individual, and value-added tax referred to in [Council Directive No. 2006/112/EC of 28 November 2006]⁶ is chargeable on the importation of the said goods into another Member State then, for the purposes of subsection (1), the person shall be deemed to be registered for value-added tax in that other Member State and the goods shall be deemed to have been dispatched or transported from that other Member State.

a 42, a 141   (5)   [Paragraph (b) of subsection (2) shall not apply where

(i)   a person quotes the registration number assigned to him in accordance with section 9 for the purpose of making an intra-Community acquisition and the goods are dispatched or transported from the territory of a Member State directly to the territory of another Member State, neither of which are the State,

(ii)   the person makes a subsequent supply of the goods to a person registered for value added tax in the Member State where the dispatch or transportation ends,

(iii)   the person issues an invoice in relation to that supply in such form and containing such particulars as would be required in accordance with section 17(1) if he made the supply of the goods in the State to a person registered for value added tax in another Member State, and containing an explicit reference to the EC simplified triangulation arrangements and indicating that the person in receipt of that supply is liable to account for the value added tax due in that Member State, and

(iv)   in accordance with regulations, the person includes a reference to the supply in the statement referred to in section 19A as if it were an intra-Community supply for the purposes of that section.][11]][12]

Amendments

1   Inserted by FA97 s 97, (w.e.f. 10 May 1997).
2   Inserted by FA93 s83(a), (w.e.f. 17 June 1993).
3   Inserted by EC(VAT)R 1992 r6(a)(i), (w.e.f. 1 January 1993).
4   Inserted by EC(VAT)R 1992 r6(a)(ii), (w.e.f. 1 January 1993).
5   Ss(1)(b) substituted by FA93 s83(b), (w.e.f. 17 June 1993).
6   Substituted by FA07 s97 & Sch 3 (w.e.f. 1 January 2007).
7   Ss(1A) inserted by FA95 s121, (w.e.f. 1 July 1995).
8   Inserted by EC(VAT)R 1992 r6(b), (w.e.f. 1 January 1993).
9   Ss(3)(aa) - (ab) inserted by EC(VAT)R 1992 r6(c), (w.e.f. 1 January 1993).
10 Substituted by FA08 s109 & Sch 4, (w.e.f. 1 July 2008).
11 Ss(5) inserted by EC(VAT)R 1992 r6(d), (w.e.f. 1 January 1993).
12 S3A Inserted by FA92 s168, (w.e.f. 1 January 1993).

Revenue Statements of Practice and Information Leaflets

Exempt persons acquiring goods from other EU Member States: Information Leaflet No. 13/01

Intra-Community Acquisitions of Goods by the State, Local Authorities, etc: Information Leaflet No. 11/01

Postponed accounting and Intra-Community Acquisitions: Information Leaflet dated December 2008

Schemes for Retailers - VAT Treatment of Intra-Community Acquisitions: Information Leaflet dated Mar 1993

Single Market intra-Community transactions in goods by traders from 1/1/93, Value Added Tax: Information Leaflet dated Sept 92

Triangulation in the EU Single Market, VAT treatment of: Information Leaflet dated July 1992

Narrative

Tax Briefing: Issue 43 (VAT Committee Guidelines – Exceeding the Threshold for Acquisitions of Goods)

Tax Briefing: Issue 42 (VAT Committee Guidelines – Article 28c(B)(a): Scope of Exemption)

Foreign Firms: VAT issues arising in Ireland: ITR Jan 2000: Vol 13 No. 1.

Tax Briefing: Issue 27 (Finance Act 1997 Changes: Intra-Community Acquisition of Goods)

Section 3B

Alcohol products

a 211

[3B. (1)   Where alcohol products are supplied while being held under a [suspension arrangement]¹ then any such supply effected while the products are held under that arrangement, other than the last such supply in the State, shall be deemed not to be a supply for the purposes of this Act other than for the purposes of section 12 and any previous-

(a)   intra-Community acquisition, or

(b)   importation,

of such products shall be disregarded for the purposes of this Act.

(2)   Where tax is chargeable on a supply referred to in subsection (1) then, notwithstanding section 19(1), the tax on that supply shall be due at the same time as the duty of excise on the products is due:

Provided that this subsection shall not apply to a supply of the kind referred to in subparagraph (a)(I), (b) or (cc) of paragraph (i) or in paragraph (ia) of the Second Schedule.

(3)   Where, other than in the circumstances set out in section 8(2B) (b), [an accountable person]² makes an intra-Community acquisition of alcohol products and by virtue of such acquisition, [and in accordance with Chapters 1 and 2 of Part 2 of the Finance Act 2001]¹, and any other enactment which is to be construed together with that Chapter, the duty of excise on those products is payable in the State, then, notwithstanding section 19(1A), the tax on the said intra-Community acquisition shall be due at the same time as the duty of excise on the products is due.

(4)   Where tax is chargeable on the importation of alcohol products, which are then placed under a [suspension arrangement]¹ then, notwithstanding section 15(6), the tax on that importation shall be due at the same time as the duty of excise on the products is due.

(5)   Notwithstanding subsections (1) and (1A) of section 10 and section 15 (3), where the provisions of subsection (2), (3) or (4) apply, the amount on which tax is chargeable shall include the amount of the duty of excise chargeable on the products on their release for consumption in the State.

(6)   Notwithstanding any other provision to the contrary contained in this Act, where the provisions of subsection (2), (3) or (4) apply then-

(a)   the tax shall be payable at the same time as the duty of excise is payable on the products,

(b)   the provisions of the statutes which relate to the duties of excise and the management thereof and of any instrument relating to duties of excise made under statute, shall, with any necessary modifications and exceptions as may be specified in regulations, apply to such tax as if it were a duty of excise, and

(c)   the person by whom the tax is payable shall complete such form as is provided for the purposes of this subsection by the Revenue Commissioners.

[(7)   In this section-

'**alcohol products**' has the same meaning as it has in section 73(1) of the Finance Act 2003;

'**suspension arrangement**' means an arrangement under which excisable products are produced, processed, held or moved, excise duty being suspended.]¹]³

Amendments
1   Substituted by FA08 s141 & Sch 8(3)(b), (w.e.f. 13 March 2008).
2   Substituted by FA08 s109 & Sch 4, (w.e.f. 1 July 2008).
3   S3B inserted by FA93 s84, (w.e.f. 1 August 1993).

Revenue Statements of Practice and Information Leaflets
  Alcohol Products at Time of Payment of Excise Duty, Payment of VAT on: Information Leaflet dated October 2008

Narrative
  Tax Briefing: Issue 43 (VAT Committee Guidelines - Article 16(1)(B)(e): Goods likely to be Placed Under Warehousing Arrangements Other Than Customs Warehousing)
  Tax Briefing: Issue 43 (VAT Committee Guidelines - Article 16(1)(B)(e): Goods to Which Arrangements Other Than Customs Warehousing Apply)

Section 4

Special provisions in relation to the supply of immovable goods

4.   (1)   (a)   This section applies to immovable goods-

a135(1)(j)
a 135(1)(k)

         (i)   which have been developed by or on behalf of the person [supplying][1] them, or

         (ii)   in respect of which the person [supplying][1] them was, or would, but for the operation of section 3(5) (b)(iii), have been at any time entitled to claim a deduction under section 12 for any tax borne or paid in relation to a [supply][2] or development of them.

         [(b)   In this section "**interest**", in relation to immovable goods, means an estate or interest therein which, when it was created was for a period of at least ten years or, if it was for a period of less than ten years, its terms contained an option for the person in whose favour the interest was created to extend it to a period of at least ten years, but does not include a mortgage, and a reference to the disposal of an interest includes a reference to the creation of an interest, and an interval of the type referred to in subsection (2A) shall be deemed to be an interest for the purposes of this section.][3]

         [(c)   Where an interest is created and, at the date of its creation, its terms contain one or more options for the person in whose favour the interest was so created to extend that interest, then that interest shall be deemed to be for the period from the date of creation of that interest to the date that that interest would expire if those options were so exercised.][4]

a 12, a 15(2)

   (2)   Subject to […][5], paragraphs (c), (d), (e) and (f) of section 3(1), section 19(2) and subsections (3), (4) and (5), a [supply][2] of immovable goods shall be deemed, for the purposes of this Act, to take place if, but only if, a person having an interest in immovable goods to which this section applies disposes [(including by way of surrender or by way of assignment)][6], as regards the whole or any part of those goods, of that interest or of an interest which derives therefrom.

   [(2A)   Where the surrender of an interest in immovable goods is chargeable to tax, and those goods have not been developed since the date of creation of that interest (hereafter referred to in this subsection as a '**surrendered interest**'), and the person to whom the surrendered interest was surrendered subsequently disposes, as regards the whole or any part of those goods, of an interest or of an interest which derives therefrom on a date before the date on which the surrendered interest would, but for its surrender, have expired, then that disposal shall be deemed to be a supply of immovable goods, for the purposes of this Act, and where the interest (hereafter referred to in this section as a **'subsequent interest'**) disposed of is for a period which extends beyond the date on which the surrendered interest would, but for its surrender, have expired, the disposal of that subsequent interest shall be treated, for the purposes of this Act, as if it were the disposal of an interest for the period equal to the interval between the date of the disposal of the subsequent interest and the date on which the surrendered interest would, but for its surrender, have expired (a period hereafter referred to in this section as an **'interval'**), and where such interval is for a period of less than ten years, that disposal shall be treated as a supply of immovable goods to which subsection (6) applies:

Provided that the person, who disposes of a subsequent interest in which the interval is for a period of less than ten years, may opt, subject to and in accordance with regulations, if any, to have that disposal treated as a supply of immovable goods to which subsection (6) does not apply.

(2B)   Where a person disposes of a subsequent interest in such circumstances that such person retains the reversion on the interest disposed of, then

       (a)   if the subsequent interest expires on or after the date on which the surrendered interest which enabled that person to dispose of a subsequent interest (hereafter referred to in this subsection as **'the surrendered interest'**) would, but for its surrender, have expired, the provisions of subsection (4) shall not apply to that reversion;

       (b)   if the subsequent interest expires prior to the date on which the surrendered interest would, but for its surrender, have expired, the provisions of subsection (4) shall apply to that reversion and that reversion shall be deemed for the purposes of subsection (4) to be for the period between the date of expiry of the subsequent interest and the date on which the surrendered interest would, but for its surrender, have expired.

(2C)   Where the surrender of an interest in immovable goods is chargeable to tax, and those goods have not been developed since that interest was created and the person to whom the interest that was surrendered surrenders possession of those goods or any part thereof, on a date before the date on which the interest that was surrendered would, but for its surrender, have expired, in such circumstances that that surrender of possession does not constitute a supply of goods, that surrender of possession shall be deemed for the purposes of section 3(1)(f), to be an appropriation of the goods or of the part thereof, as the case may be, for a purpose other than the purpose of that person's business except where such surrender of possession is made-

(a)　　in accordance with an agreement for the leasing or letting of those goods where the person surrendering possession is chargeable to tax in respect of the rent or other payment under the agreement, or

(b)　　in connection with a transfer which, in accordance with section 3(5), is deemed, for the purposes of this Act, not to be a supply.][7]

(3)　(a)　[Subject to paragraphs (aa) and (b)][8], where a person having an interest in immovable goods to which this section applies surrenders possession of those goods or of any part thereof in such circumstances that the surrender does not constitute a [supply][2] of the goods for the purposes of subsection (2), the surrender shall be deemed, for the purposes of section 3(1)(f), to be an appropriation of the goods or of the part thereof, as the case may be, for a purpose other than the purpose of his business.

[(aa)　Where a person having an interest in immovable goods to which this section applies surrenders possession of those goods or of any part thereof in such circumstances that the surrender does not constitute a supply of the goods for the purposes of subsection (2), the provisions of paragraph (a) shall not apply when this paragraph and paragraph (ab) take effect pursuant to section 100(2) of the Finance Act 2005.

(ab)　Subject to paragraph (b), where a person having an interest in immovable goods to which this section applies surrenders possession of those goods or any part thereof in such circumstances that the surrender does not constitute a supply of the goods for the purposes of subsection (2), that person shall be liable for an amount, in this paragraph referred to as a deductibility adjustment, which shall be payable as if it were tax due by that person in accordance with section 19 for the taxable period in which the surrender occurred, and that deductibility adjustment shall be calculated in accordance with the following formula:

$$\frac{T \times (Y - N)}{Y}$$

where -

T　　is the amount of tax which the person who surrenders possession of the goods was entitled to deduct in accordance with section 12 in respect of that person's acquisition of the interest in and development of the goods the possession of which is being surrendered,

Y   is 20 or, if the interest when it was acquired by the person who surrenders possession of the goods was for a period of less than 20 years, the number of full years in that interest, and

N   is the number of full years since that person acquired the interest in the immovable goods being surrendered or, if the goods were developed since that interest was acquired, the number of full years since the most recent development:

but if that N is greater than that Y, such deductibility adjustment shall be deemed to be nil.][9]

(b)   This subsection shall not apply to-

(i)   any such surrender of possession made in accordance with an agreement for the leasing or letting of the goods if the person surrendering possession is chargeable to tax in respect of the rent or other payment under the agreement, or

(ii)   a surrender in connection with a transfer which, in accordance with section 3(5), is declared, for the purposes of this Act, not to be a [supply][2].

[(3A)   (a)   Where a person having an interest in immovable goods to which this section applies surrenders possession of those goods or of any part of them by means of a disposal of that interest or of an interest which derives from that interest, and where the value of the interest being disposed of is less than its economic value then for the purposes of this Act such disposal—

(i)   shall be deemed not to be a supply of immovable goods for the purposes of subsection (2), but

(ii)   shall be deemed to be a letting of immovable goods to which paragraph (iv) of the First Schedule applies.

(b)   This subsection does not apply to the disposal of a freehold interest.

(c)   Where a person establishes to the satisfaction of the Revenue Commissioners that the value of an interest in immovable goods being disposed of by such person is less than the economic value of those immovable goods because of an unforeseen change in market conditions affecting the value of that interest since such person acquired and developed those goods, then the Revenue Commissioners may determine that that disposal be treated as a supply of immovable goods for the purposes of subsection (2).

(d)   For the purposes of this subsection –

'**economic value**', in relation to an interest in immovable goods being disposed of, means [the total amount on which tax was chargeable][10] to the person disposing of that interest [in respect of or in relation to][10] that person's acquisition of that interest and [in respect of or in relation to][10] any development of those immovable goods by or on behalf of that person since that acquisition; but if –

(i)   there was no development of those immovable goods by or on behalf of that person since that person's acquisition of that interest, and

(ii)   that person disposes, including by way of surrender or assignment, of an interest (in this subsection referred to as a '**lesser interest**') which is derived from the interest which that person acquired (in this subsection referred to as a '**greater interest**'), and

(iii)   the lesser interest is an interest of not more than 35 years,

then the economic value of the lesser interest shall be deemed to be the amount calculated in accordance with the following formula:

$$E \times \frac{N1}{N2}$$

where –

E   is the economic value of the greater interest,

N1 is the number of full years in the lesser interest, and

N2 is the number of full years in the greater interest, but if the number of full years in the greater interest exceeds 35 or if the greater interest is a freehold interest then N2 shall be deemed to be equal to 35,

but where –

(I)   the disposal of the lesser interest is not a disposal by way of surrender or assignment, and

(II)   the amount so calculated is less than 75 per cent of the economic value of the greater interest,

then the economic value of the lesser interest shall be deemed to be 75 per cent of the economic value of the greater interest;

'**the value of an interest being disposed of**' means the amount on which tax would be chargeable in accordance with section 10 if that disposal were deemed to be a supply of immovable goods in accordance with subsection (2).][11]

(4)   Where a person having an interest in immovable goods to which this section applies disposes, as regards the whole or any part

of those goods, of an interest which derives from that interest in such circumstances that he retains the reversion on the interest disposed of, he shall, in relation to the reversion so retained, be deemed, for the purposes of section 3(1)(f), to have made an appropriation of the goods or of the part thereof, as the case may be, for a purpose other than the purpose of his business.

[(5)   Where a person disposes of an interest in immovable goods to another person and in connection with that disposal a taxable person enters into an agreement with that other person or person connected with that other person to carry out a development in relation to those immovable goods, then-

(a)   the person who disposes of the interest in the said immovable goods shall, in relation to that disposal, be deemed to be a taxable person,

(b)   the disposal of the interest in the said immovable goods shall be deemed to be a supply of those goods made in the course or furtherance of business, and

(c)   the disposal of the interest in the said immovable goods shall, notwithstanding subsection (1), be deemed to be a disposal of an interest in immovable goods to which this section applies.][12]

[(6)   (a)   Tax shall not be charged on the supply of immovable goods-

(i)   which were used in such circumstances so that the person making the supply had no right to deduction under section 12 in relation to tax borne or paid on the acquisition or development of those goods, or

(ii)   which have been occupied before the specified day and had not been developed between that date and the date of the supply.

(b)   Paragraph (a) does not apply to a supply of immovable goods, being goods-

(i)   to which subsection 5 applies, or

(ii)   which were acquired by the person making the supply as a result of a transfer in accordance with section 3(5)(b)(iii) and if tax had been chargeable on such transfer the person making the supply would have had a right to deduction under section 12 in relation to such tax.][13]

(7)   The provisions of section 8(3) shall not apply in relation to a person who makes a [supply][2] of goods to which this section applies

[(8)   (a)   Where tax is chargeable in relation to a supply of immovable goods which is a surrender of an interest

in immovable goods or an assignment of an interest in immovable goods to-

    (i)   [an accountable person][14],

    (ii)   a Department of State or a local authority, or

    (iii)   a person who supplies immovable goods of a kind referred to in paragraph (a) of the definition of 'exempted activity' in section 1 or services of a kind referred to in paragraphs (i), (iv), (ix), (xi), (xia), (xiii) and (xiv) of the First Schedule, in the course or furtherance of business,

then, the person to whom those goods are supplied shall be accountable for and liable to pay the tax chargeable on that supply and the said tax shall be payable as if it were tax due by that person in accordance with section 19 for the taxable period within which the supply to the person took place and for these purposes the person to whom the goods are supplied shall be [an accountable person][14] and the person who made the surrender or assignment shall not be accountable for or liable to pay the said tax.

    (b)   Notwithstanding subsection (2A)(a) of section 8, if the supply referred to in paragraph (a) is to a Department of State or a local authority, that Department of State or local authority shall be accountable for and liable to pay the tax referred to in that paragraph.

    (c)   (i)   A surrender or assignment of immovable goods referred to in paragraph (a) shall be treated as a supply of goods made by the person to whom the goods are supplied.

        (ii)   Upon the surrender or assignment of immovable goods referred to in subparagraph (i), the person who makes the surrender or assignment shall issue a document to the person to whom the surrender or assignment is made indicating the value of the interest being surrendered or assigned and the amount of tax chargeable on that surrender or assignment. **[This subparagraph shall not apply where the person who makes the surrender or assignment is obliged to issue a document in accordance with section 4C(8)(a) to the person to whom that surrender or assignment is made.]**[15]

        (iii)   For the purposes of section 12, that section shall apply as if this paragraph had not been enacted.

(9)   (a)   Where an interest in immovable goods is created in such circumstances that a reversion on that interest (hereafter referred to in this subsection as a **'reversionary interest'**)

is created and retained, then any subsequent disposal to another person of that reversionary interest or of an interest derived entirely therefrom shall be deemed to be a supply of immovable goods to which subsection (6) applies, provided that, since the date the first-mentioned interest was created, those goods have not been developed by, on behalf of, or to the benefit of, the person making such subsequent disposal: but the provisions of this subsection shall not be construed as applying to a disposal of an interest which includes an interval.

(b)   The Revenue Commissioners may make regulations specifying the circumstances or conditions under which development work on immovable goods is not treated, for the purposes of this subsection, as being on behalf of or to the benefit of a person.][16]

[(10) (a)   Where a disposal of an interest in immovable goods is chargeable to tax and the person who acquires that interest is obliged to pay rent to another person (hereafter referred to in this subsection as 'the landlord') under the terms and conditions laid down in respect of that interest, the landlord-

(i)   shall, notwithstanding the provisions of section 8, be deemed not to be [an accountable person][14] in respect of transactions in relation to those immovable goods other than-

(I)   supplies of those immovable goods on which tax is chargeable in accordance with the provisions of this section, or

(II)   supplies of other goods or services effected for consideration by the landlord, or

(III)   post-letting expenses in respect of that interest,

(ii)   shall not be entitled to deduct tax in respect of transactions in relation to those immovable goods other than-

(I)   supplies of those immovable goods on which tax is chargeable in accordance with the provisions of this section other than subsection (4), or

(II)   supplies of other goods or services effected for consideration by the landlord, or

(III)   post-letting expenses in respect of that interest,

         (iii)   shall be deemed, where that landlord is not the person who made the disposal of the interest, to be [an accountable person][14] in respect of post-letting expenses in relation to that interest and shall in relation to those post-letting expenses be entitled to deduct tax, in accordance with section 12, as if those post-letting expenses were for the purposes of the landlord's taxable supplies.

    (b)   For the purposes of this subsection post-letting expenses in relation to an interest in immovable goods are expenses which the landlord incurs-

         (i)   in carrying out services which the landlord is obliged to carry out under the terms and conditions of the written contract entered into on the disposal of the interest which was chargeable to tax but does not include transactions the obligation to perform which is not reflected in the consideration on which tax was charged on the disposal of that interest, or

         (ii)   which directly relate to the collection of rent arising under the contract referred to in subparagraph (i), or

         (iii)   which directly relate to a review of rent where the terms and conditions of the contract referred to in subparagraph (i) provide for such a review, or

         (iv)   which directly relate to the exercise of an option to extend the interest or to exercise a break-clause in relation to that interest where the terms and conditions of the contract referred to in subparagraph (i) provide for such an option or such a break-clause,

but do not include any expenses relating to goods or services of the type specified in section 12(3).][17]

[(11)   Subject to section 4C the other provisions of this section, apart from subsections (9) and (10), shall not apply as regards-

    (a)   a disposal of an interest in immovable goods, or

    (b)   a surrender of possession of immovable goods,

which occurs after 1 July 2008. Subsection (9) shall apply only as respects a reversionary interest created prior to 1 July 2008. Subsection (10) shall apply only as respects an interest which is disposed of prior to 1 July 2008.][18]

Amendments

1   Substituted by VAT Amend. A78 s30(2), (w.e.f. 1 March 1979).

2   Substituted by VAT Amend. A78 s30(2), (w.e.f. 1 March 1979).

3   Ss(1)(b) substituted by FA97 s98(a)(i), (w.e.f. 26 March 1997).
4   Ss(1)(c) Inserted by FA97 s98(a)(ii), (w.e.f. 26 March 1997).
5   Deleted by VAT Amend. A78 s30(1), (w.e.f. 1 March 1979).
6   Inserted by FA97 s98(b), (w.e.f. 26 March 1997).
7   Ss(2A) - (2C) inserted by FA97 s98(c), (w.e.f. 26 March 1997).
8   Substituted by FA05s100(1)(a), (w.e.f. 1 May 2005).
9   Inserted by FA05s100(1)(b), (w.e.f. 1 May 2005).
10 Substituted by FA03 s114, (w.e.f. 28 March 2003).
11 Subsection 3A inserted by FA02 s99, (w.e.f. 25 March 2002).
12 Ss(5) substituted by FA95 s122(a), (w.e.f. 1 July 1995).
13 Substituted by FA05 s100(1)(c) (w.e.f. 25 March 2005).
14 Substituted by FA08 s109 & Sch 4, (w.e.f. 1 July 2008).
15 Inserted by F(No. 2)A 08 s99 & Sch 6, (w.e.f. 24 December 2008).
16 Ss 8 & 9 inserted by FA05 s100(i)(d), (w.e.f. 25 March 2005).
17 Inserted by FA98 s106, (w.e.f. 27 March 1998).
18 Ss11 inserted by FA08 s86, (w.e.f. 13 March 2008).

Regulations and Orders

Property waiver of exemption	1998 SI No. 228	Value Added Tax (Waiver of Exemption) (Amendment) Regulations, 1998
Property waiver of exemption	2003 SI No. 504	Value Added Tax (Waiver of Exemption) (Letting of Immovable Goods) Regulations, 2003
Property - valuation of supply	1998 SI No. 482	Value Added Tax (Valuation of Interests in Immovable Goods) (Amendment) Regulations, 1998
Property	1995 SI No. 184	Finance Act 1994 (Commencement of Sections 93 and 96(a)) Order 1995
Property	2002 SI No. 219	Value-Added Tax (Amendment) (Property Transactions) Regulations, 2002
Valuation of interest	1979 SI No. 63	Value Added Tax Regulations, 1979
Valuation of interest	2006 SI No. 548	Value-Added Tax Regulations 2006

Revenue e-Briefs

Revenue e-Brief No. 37/2008: VAT on property – frequently asked questions

Revenue e-Brief No. 22/2008: VAT on property – changeover to new rules

Revenue e-Brief No. 40/2007: VAT on property review

Revenue e-Brief No. 15/2007: VAT on Property Review Project – Publication of Pro-Forma Text

Revenue e-Brief No. 12/2007: VAT on Property Review Project

Revenue e-Brief No. 54/2006: VAT on Property Review Project

Revenue e-Brief No. 24/2005: Revenue Commissioners' VAT on Property Review Project – Deadline 1st October 2005

Revenue e-Brief No. 27/2004: VAT on Property

Revenue e-Brief No. 12 February 2004, New VAT on Property Multiplier - 2004

Revenue Statements of Practice and Information Leaflets

Building and Associated Services: Information Leaflet dated August 2007

Frequently asked questions: Information Leaflet dated December 2008

Goods and Services supplied to Property Lessees through Landlords ('Service Charges') VAT on: Information Leaflet dated May 1985

Property, development of, increase in de-minimis rule: June 2004

Property Transactions, VAT on; VAT leaflet No. 2, July 1980

Property, VAT on; Finance Act 1997 Changes: A Revenue Guide

Property, (claims for repayment of VAT arising out of the Supreme Court Judgement in the case of Erin Executor for periods prior to 27/3/98), VAT on: Information Leaflet No 3/98

Property, (VAT treatment of post-letting expenses incurred on or after 27/3/98), VAT on: Information Leaflet No 4/98

Property Multiplier: Information Leaflet dated October 2008

Property, reverse charge, application of on a surrender or assignment: June 2004

Property: Summary and checklist: Information Leaflet dated May 2008

Property transactions, VAT and: October 2001

Services connected with foreign property: Information Leaflet dated December 2008

Short-term letting of accommodation to State agencies for use as 'emergency' accommodation, including accommodation provided for asylum seekers and homeless people, and ancillary services: Information Leaflet No. 1/01

Case law

Armbrecht, Dieter v Finanzam Uelzen	C291/92	Taxable Event/Property/Self Supply. Taxable Amount/Deduction
Blasi, Elizabeth v Finanzant Munchen	C346/95	Hotel or long term letting
de Jong, Pieter v Staatssecretaris van Financien	C20/91	Self Supply/Property/Taxable Amount/Taxable Event/Deduction
CSC Financial Services Limited (formerly Continuum Europe Ltd.) v Customs and Excise	C235/00	Transactions in securities/reverse premiums on property
Kerrutt and Another v Finanzamt Monchengladbach - Mitte	C73/85	Property/Taxable person undeveloped land
Lubbock Fine and Company v Customs and Excise	C63/92	Property/Taxable Event
Seeling, Wolfgang v Finanzamt Starnberg	C269/00	Self supply of residential part of property
Stichting 'Goed Wonen' v Staatssecretaris van Financiën	C326/99	Property/rights *in rem*
Urbing (nee Adam) v Administration de l'Enregistrement et des Domaines	C267/99	Property agents

Revenue Precedents

Topic:	Property Transactions
Issue:	Supplemental deed created in exchange for surrender of portion of original property subject of main deed. Rent remained unchanged.
Decision:	The said exchange was disregarded for the purposes of Sec. 4 of the VAT Act. No VAT arises.
Date:	31/8/90

(withdrawn from the Revenue website in 2002)

Topic:	Property Transactions.
Issue:	Reverse Premium - an amount paid by a landlord to a tenant as an inducement to take up a lease.
Decision:	No supply is deemed to have been made.
Date:	3/9/85

Topic:	Property Transactions.
Issue:	In a sale and leaseback situation the entity who leased the property back were allowed deductibility on post-lease development expenditure as the latter related directly to the completion of the development of the property.
Decision:	Deductibility allowed subject to usual criteria and to the fact that the enhanced value was reflected in the value of the interest disposed of.
Date:	11/1/95

Topic:	Property Transactions.
Issue:	Do short term lettings of a taxable property within a VAT group give rise to a self-supply.
Decision:	As there is no supply within a VAT group a self-supply would not arise.
Date:	16/3/94

(withdrawn from the Revenue website in 2002)

Topic:	Property Transactions.
Issue:	Two registered entities sell properties to a State body as trustee who in turn sells to a third party who is VAT-registered. Can the invoices be raised by the first-named to the latter? (one contract involved).
Decision:	It was agreed that the invoices could be raised by the first-named to the last-named, ignoring the State body.
Date:	1/6/95

(withdrawn from the Revenue website in 2002)

Topic: Property Transactions.

Issue: Bakery transferred its trade to a wholly owned subsidiary and allowed it to use premises and equipment without a lease. Parent company later sell freehold interest and equipment to subsidiary, who in turn sell to a third party who will carry on bakery trade.

Decision: Technically the initial surrender of possession gives rise to a self-supply, however the provisions of Section (3)(5)(b)(iii) apply.

Date: 7/7/89

Topic: Property Transactions

Issue: Company with two subsidiaries, one has the freehold reversion, the second has a long leasehold interest. The latter creates long leases to another party whilst the former carries out the redevelopment work and sells the freehold interest to a pension fund. Company with freehold reversion is treated as a taxable person as regards disposal.

Decision: Joint venture registration allowed between the holder of the leasehold interest and the developer who holds the reversion.

Date: 5/2/90

Topic: Property Transactions.

Issue: Lease documents held in escrow pending tenant fitting out unit to landlord's satisfaction/specification.

Decision: The date of supply of taxable leases is the date the signed lease documents are released from escrow.

Date: 7/4/88

Topic: Property Transactions.

Issue: Sale and leaseback transactions.

Decision: Not taxable, subject to conditions. This treatment was extended to unregistered entities. Sec. 4 does not apply.

Date: 7/4/88

(withdrawn from the Revenue website in 2002)

Narrative

Tax Briefing: Issue 69 (FAQs – VAT on Property)

Anticipating the Treatment of Leases under the Proposed New VAT on Property Regime (the Landlord's Viewpoint): ITR Nov 2007: Vol. 20 No. 6

A New Regime for VAT and Property – Four Reasons Why You Should Care: ITR May 2007: Vol. 20 No. 3

VAT and Property: A Terrible Beauty is Born?: ITR March 2007: Vol 20 No. 2

Tax Briefing: Issue 64 (The 10% Rule VAT)

Tax Briefing: Issue 64 (VAT on Property – Registration in Advance of Trading)

Tax Briefing: Issue 64 (VAT Treatment of Sales of Short-Let Properties)

VAT Anti-Avoidance: Section 100 Finance Act 2005. Does it Do Exactly What It Says on the Tin?: ITR Jan 2006: Vol 19 No. 1.

ITI VAT on Property Submission: ITR Nov 2005: Vol 18 No. 6.

VAT Pitfalls: ITR Nov 2005: Vol 18 No. 6.

Tax Briefing: Issue 60 (Finance Act 2005 Changes)

The Economic Value Test - Is it VAT's Darkest Chamber? : ITR Mar 2005: Vol 18 No. 2

VAT and Reversionary Interests in Property: ITR Jan 2005: Vol 18 No. 1.

Development for VAT purposes: ITR Sept 2004: Vol 17 No. 5.

EVT - Economic Value Test for VAT purposes: ITR Jul 2004: Vol 17 No. 4

Tax Briefing: Issue 56 (The 10% Rule/Section 4(8))

Tax Briefing: Issue 55 (Economic Value Test – Freehold Interests and Professional Fees/Multiplier)

VAT on Property – Forbes v Tobin: ITR Mar 2003: Vol 16 No. 2

Tax Briefing: Issue 47 (Multiplier)

VAT and the Finance Act 2002 – New Tax Traps for the Unwary: ITR May 2002: Vol 15 No. 3

Apportionment of Input Tax: ITR Mar 2002: Vol 15 No. 2

VAT and Property: ITR Nov 1998: Vol 11 No. 6.

Ireland's Derogations from the EU Sixth VAT Directive: ITR Sept 1999: Vol. 12 No. 5.

Tax Briefing: Issue 32 (Supreme Court Decision in the case of Erin Executor & Trustee Co.)

Section 4A

Person liable to pay tax in relation to certain supplies of immovable goods

4A. [...]¹

Amendments

1 S(4A) repealed by FA08 s87, (w.e.f. 1 July 2008).

[Section 4B

Supplies of immovable goods

4B.   (1)   In this section–

'**completed**', in respect of immovable goods, means that the development of those goods has reached the state, apart from only such finishing or fitting work that would normally be carried out by or on behalf of the person who will use them, where those goods can effectively be used for the purposes for which those goods were designed, and the utility services required for those purposes are connected to those goods;

'**occupied**', in respect of immovable goods, means–

(a)   occupied and fully in use following completion, where that use is one for which planning permission for the development of those goods was granted, and

(b)   where those goods are let, occupied and fully in such use by the tenant.

(2)   Subject to subsections (3), (5) and (7) **[and section 4C(6)(a)]¹**, tax is not chargeable on the supply of immovable goods–

(a)   that have not been developed **[within 20 years prior to that supply]¹**,

(b)   being completed immovable goods, the most recent completion of which occurred more than 5 years prior to that supply, and those goods have not been developed within that 5 year period,

(c)   being completed immovable goods that have not been developed since the most recent completion of those goods, where that supply–

(i)   occurs after the immovable goods have been occupied for an aggregate of at least 24 months following the most recent completion of those goods, and

(ii)   takes place after a previous supply of those goods on which tax was chargeable and that previous supply–

(I)   took place after the most recent completion of those goods, and

(II)   was a transaction between [...]² persons who were not connected within the meaning of section 7A,

(d)   being a building that was completed more than 5 years prior to that supply and on which development was carried out in the 5 years prior to that supply where–

     (i)   such development did not and was not intended to adapt the building for a materially altered use, and

     (ii)   the cost of such development did not exceed 25 per cent of the consideration for that supply,

   or

(e)   being a building that was completed within the 5 years prior to that supply where–

     (i)   the building had been occupied for an aggregate of at least 24 months following that completion,

     (ii)   that supply takes place after a previous supply of the building on which tax was chargeable and that previous supply–

         (I)   took place after that completion of the building, and

         (II)   was a transaction between [...]² persons who were not connected within the meaning of section 7A,

     and

     (iii)   if any development of that building occurred after that completion–

         (I)   such development did not and was not intended to adapt the building for a materially altered use, and

         (II)   the cost of such development did not exceed 25 per cent of the consideration for that supply.

(3)   Where a person supplies immovable goods to another person and in connection with that supply a taxable person enters into an agreement with that other person or with a person connected with that other person to carry out a development in relation to those immovable goods, then–

   (a)   the person who supplies the goods shall, in relation to that supply, be deemed to be a taxable person,

   (b)   the supply of the said immovable goods shall be deemed to be a supply of those goods to which section 2 applies, and

(c)   subsection (2) does not apply to that supply.

(4)   Section 8(3) does not apply in relation to a person who makes a supply of immovable goods.

(5)   Where a taxable person supplies immovable goods to another taxable person in circumstances where that supply would otherwise be exempt in accordance with subsection (2)[, **subsection (2) or (6)(b) of section 4C**]¹ then tax shall, notwithstanding subsection (2)[, **subsection (2) or (6)(b) of section 4C**]¹, be chargeable on that supply, where the supplier and the taxable person to whom the supply is made enter an agreement in writing **[(no later than the fifteenth day of the month following the month in which the supply occurs)]**¹ to opt to have tax chargeable on that supply (in this Act referred to as a 'joint option for taxation').

(6)   Where a joint option for taxation is exercised in accordance with subsection (5), then–

   (a)   the person to whom the supply is made shall, in relation to that supply, be an accountable person and shall be liable to pay the tax chargeable on that supply as if that person supplied those goods, and

   (b)   the person who made the supply shall not be accountable for or liable to pay the said tax.

(7)   (a)   Where a taxable person supplies immovable goods to another person in circumstances where that supply would otherwise be exempt in accordance with subsection (2), tax shall, notwithstanding subsection (2), be chargeable on that supply where–

      (i)   the immovable goods are buildings designed as or capable of being used as a dwelling,

      (ii)   the person who makes that supply is a person who developed the immovable goods in the course of a business of developing immovable goods or a person connected with that person, within the meaning of section 7A, and

      (iii) the person who developed those immovable goods was entitled to a deduction under section 12 for tax chargeable to that person in respect of that person's acquisition or development of those immovable goods.

   (b)   In the case of a building to which this subsection would apply if the building were supplied by the taxable person at any time during the capital goods scheme adjustment period for that building–

      (i)   section 12E(6) shall not apply, and

      (ii)   notwithstanding section 12E(4) the proportion of total tax incurred that is deductible by that person shall be treated as the initial interval proportion of deductible use.][3]

Amendments

1   Inserted by F(No. 2)A 08 s99 & Sch 6, (w.e.f. 24 December 2008).

2   Deleted by F(No. 2)A 08 s99 & Sch 6, (w.e.f. 24 December 2008).

3   Section 4B inserted by s88, FA08, (w.e.f. 1 July 2008).

Revenue e-Briefs

    Revenue e-Brief No. 37/2008: VAT on property – frequently asked questions

    Revenue e-Brief No. 22/2008: VAT on property – changeover to new rules

Revenue Statements of Practice and Information Leaflets

    Frequently asked questions: Information Leaflet dated December 2008

    Summary and checklist: Information Leaflet dated May 2008

Narrative

    Tax Briefing: Issue 69 (FAQs – VAT on Property)

    Initial Issues Identified in the New VAT on Property Regime : ITR Jul 2008 Vol 21 No. 4

    VAT on Property 2008: ITR Jul 2008 Vol 21 No. 3

[Section 4C

Transitional measures for supplies of immovable goods

4C. (1) This section applies to-

(a) immovable goods which are acquired or developed by a taxable person prior to 1 July 2008[, **being completed immovable goods before 1 July 2008,]**[2] and have not been disposed of by that taxable person prior to that date, until such time as those goods have been disposed of by that taxable person on or after that date, and

(b) an interest in immovable goods within the meaning of [section 4,][3] other than a freehold interest or a freehold equivalent interest, created by a taxable person prior to 1 July 2008 and held by a taxable person on 1 July 2008 **[and the reversionary interest, within the meaning of section 4(9), on that interest until that interest is surrender after 1 July 2008]**[2].

[(1A) **Where an interest to which subsection (1)(b) applies is surrendered, then, for the purposes of the application of section 12E in respect of the immovable goods concerned—**

(a) **the total tax incurred shall include the amount of tax chargeable on the surrender in accordance with subsection (7) and shall not include tax incurred prior to the creation of the surrendered interest, and**

(b) **the adjustment period shall consist of the number of intervals specified in subsection (11)(c)(iv) and the initial interval shall begin on the date of that surrender.]**[4]

(2) In the case of a supply of immovable goods to which subsection (1)(a) applies, being completed immovable goods within the meaning of section 4B-

(a) where the person supplying those goods had no right to deduct under section 12 in relation to the tax chargeable on the acquisition or development of those goods prior to 1 July 2008, and

(b) if any subsequent development of those immovable goods occurs on or after 1 July 2008-

(i) that development does not and is not intended to adapt the immovable goods for a materially altered use, and

(ii) the cost of that development does not exceed 25 per cent of the consideration for that supply,

then, subject to section 4B(3), that supply is not chargeable to tax but a joint option for taxation may be exercised in respect of that supply in accordance with section 4B(5) and that tax is payable in accordance with section 4B(6).

(3)   Where a person referred to in subsection (1)–

    (a)   acquired, developed or has an interest in immovable goods to which this section applies,

    (b)   was entitled to deduct tax, in accordance with section 12 on that person's acquisition or development of those goods, and

    (c)   [makes]³ a letting of those immovable goods to which paragraph (iv) of the First Schedule applies,

then, that person shall calculate an amount in accordance with the formula in section 4(3)(ab), and that amount shall be payable as if it were tax due by that person in accordance with section 19 for the taxable period in which that letting takes place.

(4)   An assignment or surrender of an interest in immovable goods to which subsection (1)(b) applies is deemed to be a supply of immovable goods for the purposes of this Act for a period of 20 years from the creation of the interest [or the most recent assignment]³ of that interest before 1 July 2008, whichever is the later.

(5)   If a person makes a supply of immovable goods to which this section applies and tax is chargeable on that supply and that person was not entitled to deduct all the tax charged to that person on the acquisition or development of those immovable goods that person shall be entitled to make the appropriate adjustment that would apply under section 12E(7)(a) as if the capital goods scheme applied to that transaction.

(6)   In the case of an assignment or surrender of an interest in immovable goods referred to in subsection (4)–

    (a)   tax shall be chargeable if the person who makes the assignment or surrender was entitled to deduct in accordance with section 12 any of the tax chargeable on the acquisition of that interest, or the development of those immovable goods, and

    (b)   tax shall not be chargeable where the person who makes the assignment or surrender had no right to deduction under section 12 on the acquisition of that interest or the development of those immovable goods, but a joint option for taxation of that assignment or surrender may be exercised.

(7)   (a)   Notwithstanding section 10, the amount on which tax is chargeable on a taxable assignment or surrender to which subsection (6) applies shall be the amount calculated in accordance with the formula in paragraph (b) divided

by the rate as specified in section 11(1)(d) expressed in decimal form.

(b) The amount of tax due and payable in respect of a taxable assignment or surrender to which subsection (6) applies is an amount calculated in accordance with the following formula:

$$T \times \frac{N}{Y}$$

where–

T is the total tax incurred referred to in subsection (11)(d) **[except for the amount of tax charged in respect of any development by the person who makes the assignment or surrender following the acquisition of this interest]**[2],

N is the number of full intervals plus one, that remain in the adjustment period referred to in subsection (11)(c), at the time of the assignment or surrender,

Y is the total number of intervals in that adjustment period for the person making the assignment or surrender,

and section 4(8) shall apply to that tax.

(8) (a) Where an interest in immovable goods referred to in subsection (6) is assigned or surrendered **[to a taxable person]**[2] during the adjustment period and tax is payable in respect of that assignment or surrender, then the person who makes the assignment or surrender shall issue a document to the person to whom the interest is being assigned or surrendered containing the following information:

(i) the amount of tax due and payable on that assignment or surrender, and

(ii) the number of intervals remaining in the adjustment period **[as determined in accordance with subsection 11(c)(iv)]**[2].

(b) Where paragraph (a) applies, the person to whom the interest is assigned or surrendered shall be a capital goods owner for the purpose of section 12E in respect of the capital good being assigned or surrendered, and shall be subject to the provisions of that section and for this purpose–

(i) the adjustment period shall be the period referred to in subsection (11)(c) as correctly specified on the document referred to in paragraph (a),

(ii)   the total tax incurred shall be the amount of tax referred to in subsection (11)(d) as correctly specified in the document referred to in paragraph (a), and

(iii)   the initial interval shall be a period of 12 months beginning on the date on which the assignment or surrender occurs.

(9)   (a)   Where a person cancels an election to be an accountable person in accordance with section 8(5A) then, in respect of the immovable goods which were used in supplying the services for which that person made that election, section 12E does not apply if those immovable goods are held by that person on 1 July 2008 and are not further developed after that date.

[...]⁵

(10)   In the application of section 12E to immovable goods and interests in immovable goods to which this section applies, subsections (4), (5) and (6) of that section shall be disregarded in respect of the person who owns those immovable goods or holds an interest in those immovable goods on 1 July 2008 **[but if that person develops the immovable goods and that development is a refurbishment, within the meaning of section 12E, that is completed on or after 1 July 2008, then these subsections shall not be disregarded in respect of that refurbishment]²**.

(11)   For the purposes of applying section 12E **[to immovable goods]³** or interests in immovable goods to which this section applies–

(a)   any interest in immovable goods to which this section applies shall be treated as a capital good,

(b)   any person who has an interest in immovable goods to which this section applies shall be treated as a capital goods owner, but shall not be so treated to the extent that the person has a reversionary interest in those immovable goods if those goods were not **[developed]³** by, on behalf of, or to the benefit of that person,

(c)   the period to be treated as the adjustment period in respect of immovable goods **[or interests in immovable goods]²** to which this section applies is–

(i)   in the case of the acquisition of the freehold interest or freehold equivalent interest in those immovable goods, 20 years from the date of that acquisition,

(ii)   in the case of the creation of an interest in those immovable goods, 20 years or, if the interest when it was created was for a period of less than

20 years, the number of full years in that interest when created, whichever is the **[shorter,]**[3]

(iii)   in the case of the assignment or surrender of an interest in immovable goods **[prior to 1 July 2008,]**[2] the period remaining in that interest at the time of the assignment or surrender of that interest or 20 years, whichever is the **[shorter, or]**[3]

[(iv)   in the case of —

(I)   the surrender or first assignment of an interest in immovable goods on or after 1 July 2008, the number of full years remaining in the adjustment period as determined in accordance with subparagraphs (ii) and (iii), plus one, or

(II)   the second or subsequent assignment of an interest in immovable goods after 1 July 2008, the number of full intervals remaining in the adjustment period as determined in accordance with clause (I), plus one,

and this number shall thereafter be the number of intervals remaining in the adjustment period,][2]

but where the immovable goods have been developed since the acquisition of those immovable goods or the creation of that interest, 20 years from the date of the most recent development of those goods,

(d)   the amount of tax charged, or the amount of tax that would have been chargeable but for the application of sections 3(5)(b)(iii) or 13A, to the person treated as the capital goods owner on the acquisition of, or **[...]**[5] development of, the capital goods shall be treated as the total tax incurred,

(e)   the total tax incurred divided by the number of **[intervals]**[3] in the adjustment period referred to in paragraph (c) shall be treated as the base tax amount,

(f)   each year in the adjustment period referred to in paragraph (c) shall be treated as an interval,

(g)   the first 12 months of the adjustment period referred to in paragraph (c) shall be treated as the initial interval,

(h)   the second year of the adjustment period referred to in paragraph (c) shall be treated as the second interval **[, but in the case of an interest which is assigned or surrendered on or after 1 July 2008, the second interval of**

the adjustment period shall have the meaning assigned to it by section 12E]²,

(i)   each year following the second year in the adjustment period referred to in paragraph (c) shall be treated as a subsequent interval,

(j)   the amount which shall be treated as the total reviewed deductible amount shall be the amount of the total tax incurred as provided for in paragraph (d) less–

    (i)   any amount of the total tax incurred which was charged to the person treated as the capital goods owner but which that owner was not entitled to deduct in accordance with section 12,

    (ii)   any amount accounted for in accordance with section 12D(4) by the person treated as the capital goods owner in respect of a transfer of the goods to that owner prior to 1 July **[2008,]³**

    (iii)   any tax payable **[in respect of those capital goods in accordance with section 3(1)(e) or 4(3)(a)]³** by the person treated as the capital goods **[owner, and]³**

    [(iv)   where an adjustment of deductibility has been made in respect of the capital good in accordance with subsection (3) or section 4(3)(ab), the amount 'T' in the formula in section 4(3)(ab),]²

(k)   the amount referred to in paragraph (d) less the amount referred to in paragraph (j) shall be treated as the non-deductible amount,

and for the purposes of applying paragraphs (f), (h) and (i) **'year'** means each 12 month period in the adjustment period, the first of which begins on the first day of the initial interval referred to in paragraph (g).

(12)   Where a taxable person acquires immovable goods on or after 1 July 2007, then, notwithstanding subsection (10), section 12E(4) shall apply and, notwithstanding subsection (11)(j), the total reviewed deductible amount shall have the meaning assigned to it by section 12E. However this subsection does not apply where a taxable person has made an adjustment in accordance with section 12(4)(f) in respect of those goods.]¹

Amendments

1   S4C inserted by s88, FA08, (w.e.f. 1 July 2008).

2   Inserted by F(No. 2)A 08 s99 & Sch 6, (w.e.f. 24 December 2008).

3   Substituted by F(No. 2)A 08 s99 & Sch 6, (w.e.f. 24 December 2008).

4   Ss(1A) inserted by F(No. 2)A 08 s99 & Sch 6, (w.e.f. 24 December 2008).

5   Deleted by F(No. 2)A 08 s99 & Sch 6, (w.e.f. 24 December 2008).

Revenue e-Briefs
   Revenue e-Brief No. 37/2008: VAT on property – frequently asked questions
   Revenue e-Brief No. 22/2008: VAT on property – changeover to new rules

Revenue Statements of Practice and Information Leaflets
   Frequently asked questions: Information Leaflet dated December 2008
   Summary and checklist: Information Leaflet dated May 2008

Narrative
   Tax Briefing: Issue 69 (FAQs – VAT on Property)
   Tax Briefing: Issue 69 (VAT treatment of Property Developers Renting out Residential Properties)
   Initial Issues Identified in the New VAT on Property Regime : ITR Jul 2008 Vol 21 No. 4
   VAT on Property 2008: ITR Jul 2008 Vol 21 No. 3

Section 5

[Supply] of services

a 24(1),
a 25

5.   [(1)   In this Act '**supply**', in relation to a service, means the performance or omission of any act or the toleration of any situation other than the supply of goods and other than a transaction specified in section 3(5).

(2)   The provision of food and drink, of a kind specified in paragraph (xii) of the Second Schedule, in a form suitable for human consumption without further preparation-

(a)   by means of a vending machine,

(b)   in the course of operating a hotel, restaurant, cafe, refreshment house, canteen, establishment licensed for the sale for consumption on the premises of intoxicating liquor, catering business or similar business, or

(c)   in the course of operating any other business in connection with the carrying on of which facilities are provided for the consumption of the food or drink supplied,

shall be deemed, for the purposes of this Act, to be a supply of services and not a supply of goods.

(3)   Any of the following shall, if so provided by regulations, and in accordance therewith, be deemed, for the purposes of this Act, to be a supply of services by a person for consideration in the course or furtherance of his business-

a 26(1)(a)   [(a)   the use of goods [other than immovable goods]¹ forming part of the assets of a business —

(i)   for the private use of [an accountable person]² or of such person's staff, or

(ii)   for any purposes other than those of [an accountable person's]² business,

where the tax on such goods is wholly or partly deductible,

a 26(1)(b)   (b)   the supply of services carried out free of charge by [an accountable person]² for such person's own private use or that of the staff of such person or for any purposes other than those of such person's business,

a 27   (c)   the supply of services by [an accountable person]² of services for the purposes of such person's business where the tax on such services, were they supplied by [another accountable person]², would not be wholly deductible.]³

[(3A)   Where a person is in receipt of a service, other than a service [specified in paragraphs (f) and (g) of subsection (6) or in the Fourth

Schedule][4], for the purposes of his business and the circumstances are such that value-added tax referred to in [Council Directive No. 2006/112/EC of 28 November 2006][5] is not payable on the supply or, if it is payable, is, in accordance with the laws of the country in which the supplier has his establishment, repayable to or deductible by the person, that person shall be deemed, for the purposes of this Act, to have himself supplied the service for consideration in the course or furtherance of his business and shall be liable for tax on the supply except where such tax, if it were chargeable, would be wholly deductible under section 12.][6]

[(3B)   The use of immovable goods forming part of the assets of a business—

(a)   for the private use of an accountable person or of such person's staff, or

(b)   for any purpose other than those of the accountable person's business,

is a taxable supply of services if—

(i)   that use occurs during a period of 20 years following the acquisition or development of those goods by the accountable person, and

(ii)   those goods are treated for tax purposes as forming part of the assets of the business at the time of their acquisition or development.][7]

a 28   (4)   The supply of services through a person (in this subsection referred to as the agent) who, while purporting to act on his own behalf, concludes agreements in his own name but on the instructions of and for the account of another person, shall be deemed, for the purposes of this Act, to constitute a supply of the services to and simultaneously by the agent.

[(4A)   Where services are supplied by a person and the person is not legally entitled to recover consideration in respect of or in relation to such supply but moneys are received in respect of or in relation to such supply, the services in question shall be deemed, for the purposes of this Act, to have been supplied for consideration and the moneys received shall be deemed to be consideration that the person who supplied the services in question became entitled to receive in respect of or in relation to the supply of those services.][8]

[(4B)   Where a person is indemnified under a policy of insurance in respect of any amount payable in respect of services of a barrister or solicitor, those services shall be deemed, for the purposes of this Act, to be supplied to, and received by, the said person.][9]

a 43   (5)   Subject to subsections (6) and (7), the place where a service is supplied shall be deemed, for the purposes of this Act, to be the place where the person supplying the service [has established his business or][10] has his establishment or (if more than one) the establishment of his which is most concerned with the supply or (if he has no establishment) his usual place of residence.

a 45   (6)   (a)   The place of supply of services connected with immovable goods, including the services of estate agents, architects and firms providing on-site supervision in relation to such goods, shall be deemed, for the purposes of this Act, to be the place where the goods are situated.

a 46   [(b)   Transport services, with the exception of intra-Community transport of goods, shall be deemed, for the purposes of this Act, to be supplied where the transport takes place.][11]

a 52   (c)   The following services shall be deemed, for the purposes of this Act, to be supplied where they are physically performed:

               (i)   cultural, artistic, sporting, scientific, educational, entertainment or similar services.

               [(ii)   ancillary transport activities such as loading, unloading and handling, with the exception of activities ancillary to the intra-Community transport of goods received by a person registered for value-added tax in any Member State,][12]

               (iii)   valuation of movable goods [except where the provisions of subparagraph (iv) of paragraph (f) apply][13],

               (iv)   work on movable goods [including contract work, except where the provisions of subparagraph (iv) of paragraph (f) apply][14].

a 58   [(d)   In confirmation of the provisions contained in the Value-Added Tax (Place of Supply of Certain Services) Regulations, 1985 (S.I. No. 343 of 1985), which regulations are hereby revoked, the place of supply of services consisting of the hiring out of movable goods by a person established outside the Community shall be deemed to be the place where the movable goods are, or are to be, effectively used.][15]

a 58, a 59   [(dd)   Notwithstanding the provisions of subparagraph (v) of paragraph (e), where a person supplies a telecommunications service [, or a telephone card as defined in subsection (6A),][16] [or a radio or television broadcasting service][17] in the course or furtherance of business from outside the Community to a person in the State who is not a person to whom the provisions of subparagraph (ii), (iii) or (iv) of paragraph (e) apply, the place of supply of that service shall be deemed, for the purposes of this Act, to be the State.][18]

a 58   [(ddd) The place of supply of a telecommunications service or of a telephone card as defined in subsection (6A) shall be deemed, for the purposes of this Act, to be the State when that service is supplied by [an accountable person][2] from an establishment in the State and it is received, otherwise than for a business purpose, by a person whose usual place of residence is situated outside the Community, and it is effectively used and enjoyed in the State.][19]

a 58   [(dddd) Notwithstanding the provisions of subsection (5), the place of supply of services consisting of the hiring out of means of transport by a person established in the State shall be deemed to be outside the Community where such means of transport are, or are to be, effectively used and enjoyed outside the Community.][20]

a 56(1)   [(e)   The place of supply of services of any of the descriptions specified in the Fourth Schedule [with the exception of the supply of services referred to in [paragraphs (ddd), (ee) and (eee)][21] in the circumstances specified in those paragraphs respectively and][22] with the exception of services of the description specified in paragraph (ia) of the said Schedule supplied by a person who has his establishment outside the Community, shall be deemed, for the purposes of this Act, to be-

(i)   in case they are received, otherwise than for a business purpose, by a person whose usual place of residence is situated outside the Community, the place where he usually resides,

(ii)   in case they are received, for the purposes of any business carried on by him, by a person-

(I)   who has his establishment outside the Community and has not also an establishment in the Community, or

(II)   who has his establishment in the Community but does not have his establishment or, if he has more than one establishment, his principal establishment in the country in which, but for this subparagraph, the services would be deemed to be supplied, [or][23]

[(III) who has an establishment in the State and his principal establishment in the country in which, but for this subparagraph, the services would be deemed to be supplied,][24]

the place where he has his establishment or, if he has more than one establishment, the establishment of his at which or for the purposes of which the services are most directly used or to be used, as the case may be,

(iii)   in case they are received, for the purposes of any business carried on by him, by a person resident in the Community who has no establishment anywhere, the place where he usually resides,

[(iiia)   in case they are received, otherwise than for a business purpose, by a person in the State (referred to in this subparagraph as the '**recipient**') and are supplied by a person who has his establishment in another Member State of the Community, in circumstances in which value-added tax referred to in [Council Directive No. 2006/112/EC of 28 November 2006 is not payable in that Member State because the recipient held himself out or allowed himself to be held out as a taxable person within the meaning of Article 9(1) and Articles 10 to 13 of that Directive][5] in respect of such supplies, the State,][25]

[(iv)   *in case they are received by a department of State, by a local authority or by a body established by statute, and are supplied-*

(I)   *by a person who has his establishment outside the Community and has not also an establishment in the Community, or*

(II)   *by a person who has his establishment in another Member State of the Community, in circumstances in which value-added tax referred to in [Council Directive No. 2006/112/ EC of 28 November 2006][5] is not payable in that Member State in respect of the supply,*

the State,][26]

(v)   in any other case, the place specified in sub-section (5) that is appropriate to the circumstances.][27]

[(ee)   The place of supply of services of the description specified in paragraph (v) of the Fourth Schedule shall be deemed, for the purposes of this Act, to be the State, when those services are supplied by a person in the course or furtherance of business established in the State and they are received, otherwise than for a business purpose, by a person whose usual place of residence is situated outside the Community, and they are effectively used and enjoyed in the State.][28]

[(eea) Where money transfer services are provided to a person in the State and are effectively used and enjoyed in the State, the place of supply of intermediary services provided in respect of or in relation to such money transfer services to a principal established outside the Community, shall be deemed, for the purposes of this Act, to be the State.][29]

a 57   [(eee) The place of supply of services of the description specified in paragraph (iiic) of the Fourth Schedule shall be deemed, for the purposes of this Act, to be the State when those services are supplied from outside the Community in the course or furtherance of business by a person who has an establishment outside the Community [...][30] and are received, otherwise than for a business purpose, by a person whose usual place of residence is the State.][31]

[(f)   The place of supply of the following services received by a person registered for value-added tax in a Member State shall be deemed, for the purposes of this Act, to be within the territory of the Member State that so registered the person for value-added tax, that is to say:

a 47   (i)   the intra-Community transport of goods,

a 53   (ii)   activities ancillary to the intra-Community transport of goods such as loading, unloading and handling,

            (iii)   services of an [intermediary][32] acting in the name and on behalf of another person in the arrangement of services other than those specified in paragraph (vii) of the Fourth Schedule.

a 55   [(iv)   valuation of or work on movable goods, including contract work, in cases where the goods are dispatched or transported out of the Member State where the valuation or work was physically carried out.][33]

(g)   The place of supply of the following services supplied to persons other than those specified in paragraph (f) shall be deemed for the purposes of this Act to be-

        (i)   the place of departure in the case of-

a 47   (I)   the intra-Community transport of goods,

a 50   (II)   services of an [intermediary][32] acting in the name and on behalf of another person in the arrangement of intra-Community transport of goods, and

a 54   (ii)   the place where they are physically performed in the case of services of an [intermediary][32] acting in the name and on behalf of another person in the arrangement of services other than those specified in subparagraph (i)(II) of this paragraph and paragraph (vii) of the Fourth Schedule.

a 44   [(gg)   Subject to paragraph (f)(iii), the place of supply of services of an intermediary acting in the name and on behalf of another person, other than in cases where that intermediary takes part in the intra-Community transport of goods or in activities ancillary to the intra-Community transport of goods, is the place where the underlying transaction is supplied in accordance with this Act.]³⁴

a 48   (h)   In this subsection-

'intra-Community transport of goods' means transport where the place of departure and the place of arrival are situated within the territories of two different Member States;

'the place of departure' means the place where the transport of goods actually starts, leaving aside distance actually travelled to the place where the goods are;

'the place of arrival' means the place where the transport of goods actually ends.]³⁵

[(6A)   (a)   Subject to paragraph (b), where the supply of a telephone card is taxable within the State and that telephone card is subsequently used outside the Community for the purpose of accessing a telecommunications service, the place of supply of that telecommunications service shall be deemed to be outside the Community and the supplier of that telephone card shall be entitled, in the taxable period within which that supplier acquires proof that that telephone card was so used outside the Community, to a reduction of the tax payable by that supplier in respect of the supply of that telephone card, by an amount calculated in accordance with paragraph (c).

        (b)   Where the supply of a telephone card is taxable in the State and the person liable for the tax on that supply is a person referred to in section 8(2)(a) who -

               (i)   is not entitled to a deduction, in accordance with section 12, of all of the tax chargeable in respect of that supply, or

               (ii)   is entitled to a deduction, in accordance with section 12, of the tax chargeable in respect of that supply because that card was acquired for the purposes of resale,

        and that telephone card is subsequently used outside the Community for the purpose of accessing a telecommunications service, the place of supply of that telecommunications service shall be deemed to be outside the Community and the person who is taxable in respect of that supply of that telephone card shall be entitled, in the taxable period within which that person acquires proof that that telephone card was so used outside the Community, to a reduction of the tax payable in respect of that supply of that telephone card to the extent that that telephone card was so used.

(c)   For the purposes of this subsection the amount of the reduction referred to in paragraph (a) shall be calculated as follows:

$$(A - B) \times \frac{C}{C + 100}$$

where –

A equals the tax inclusive price charged by the supplier for that part of the right contained in the telephone card which was consumed in accessing the telecommunications service which was deemed to be supplied outside the Community,

B equals the tax inclusive price charged to the supplier for that part of the right contained in the telephone card which was consumed in accessing the telecommunications service which was deemed to be supplied outside the Community, and

C is the percentage rate of tax chargeable on the supply of the telephone card at the time of that supply by that supplier.

(d)   Where a telephone card is used to access a telecommunications service, the value of the telephone card so used shall, for the purposes of section 10(2), be disregarded.

(e)   In this subsection 'telephone card' means a card or a means other than money which confers a right to access a telecommunications service and for which, when the card or other means is supplied to a person other than for the purposes of resale, the supplier is entitled to a consideration in respect of the supply and for which the user of that card or other means is not liable for any further charge in respect of the receipt of the telecommunications service accessed by means of that card or other means.][36]

(7)   Provision may be made by regulations for varying, in relation to services generally or of a description specified therein, the rules for determining their place of supply, and for that purpose the Fourth Schedule may be added to or varied.

a 29   [(8)   (a)   The transfer of goodwill or other intangible assets of a business, in connection with the transfer of the business or part thereof, even if that business or that part thereof had ceased trading, [or in connection with a transfer of ownership of goods in accordance with section 3(5)(b) (iii)]³⁷ by

(i)   [an accountable person to a taxable person or]²

(ii)   a person who is not [an accountable person]² to another person,

shall be deemed, for the purposes of this Act, not to be a supply of services.

(b)   For the purposes of this subsection, ['accountable person']² shall not include a person who is [an accountable person]² solely by virtue of subsections (1A) and (2) of section 8.]³⁸]³⁹

Amendments

1   Inserted by FA08 s89(a), (w.e.f. 1 July 2008)
2   Substituted by FA08 s109 & Sch 4, (w.e.f. 1 July 2008).
3   Substituted by FA06 s94, (w.e.f. 31 March 2006).
4   Substituted by FA92 s169(a), (w.e.f. 1 January 1993).
5   Substituted by FA07 s97 & Sch 3 (w.e.f. 1 January 2007).
6   Ss(3A) inserted by FA86 s81, (w.e.f. 27 May 1986).
7   Ss(3B) inserted by FA08 s89(b), (w.e.f. 1 July 2008).
8   Ss(4A) Inserted by FA82 s76, (w.e.f. 1 September 1982).
9   Ss(4B) Inserted by FA89 s54, (w.e.f. 1 March 1989).
10 Inserted by FA95 s123, (w.e.f. 2 June 1995).
11 Ss(6)(b) substituted by FA92 s169(b)(i), (w.e.f. 1 January 1993).
12 Ss(6)(c)(ii) substituted by FA92 s169(b)(ii), (w.e.f. 1 January 1993).
13 Inserted by FA96 s90(a)(i), (w.e.f. 1 January 1996).
14 Inserted by FA96 s90(a)(ii), (w.e.f. 1 January 1996).
15 Ss(6)(d) inserted by FA86 s81, (w.e.f. 27 May 1986).
16 Inserted by FA98 s107(a)(i), (w.e.f. 1 May 1998).
17 Inserted by FA 03 s115(a), (w.e.f. 1 July 2003).
18 Ss(6)(dd) inserted by FA97 s99, (w.e.f. 1 July 1997).
19 Ss(6)(ddd) inserted by FA98 s107(a)(ii), (w.e.f. 1 May 1998).
20 Ss(6)(dddd) inserted by FA99 s121, (w.e.f. 25 March 1999).
21 Substituted by FA 03 s115(b), (w.e.f. 1 July 2003).
22 Inserted by FA98 s107(a)(iii), (w.e.f. 1 May 1998).
23 Inserted by FA90 s100, (w.e.f. 30 May 1990).
24 Ss6(e)(ii)(III) inserted by FA90 s100, (w.e.f. 30 May 1990).
25 Ss6(3)(e)(iiia) inserted by FA01 s183a, (w.e.f. 21 March 2001).
26 Ss6(e)(iv) to be deleted by FA07 s77(1)(a) (w.e.f. date of Ministerial Order not available at time of print)
27 Ss(6)(e) substituted by FA86 s81(b)(ii), (w.e.f. 27 May 1986).
28 Ss(6)(ee) inserted by FA98 s107(a)(iv), (w.e.f. 1 May 1998).
29 Ss(6)(eea) inserted by FA05 s101(a)(i) (w.e.f. 25 March 2005).
30 Deleted by FA05 s101(a)(ii) (w.e.f. 25 March 2005).
31 Ss(6)(eee) inserted by FA 03 s115(c) (w.e.f. 1 July 2003).
32 Substituted by FA07 s 77(1)(b)(i) (w.e.f. 1 January 2008) ... 'agent' replaced with 'intermediary'
33 Ss(6)(f)(iv) inserted by FA96 s90(b), (w.e.f. 1 January 1996).
34 Inserted by FA07 s 77(1)(b)(ii) (w.e.f. 1 January 2008)
35 Ss(6)(f) – (h) inserted by FA92 s169(b)(iii), (w.e.f. 1 January 1993).
36 Ss(6A) inserted by FA98 s107(b), (w.e.f. 1 May 1998).
37 Inserted by FA05 s101(b) (w.e.f. 25 March 2005)
38 Ss 5(8) substituted by FA01 s183(b) (w.e.f. 21 March 2001).
39 S5 substituted by VAT Amend. A78 s5, (w.e.f. 1 March 1979).

Regulations and Orders

Place of supply	1985 SI No. 343	Value Added Tax (Place of Supply of Certain Services) Regulations, 1985
Private or non-busienss use of business assets	2008 SI No. 238	Value-Added Tax (Amendment) Regulations, 2008
Staff catering	1979 SI No. 63	Value Added Tax Regulations, 1979
Staff catering	2006 SI No. 548	Value-Added Tax Regulations 2006

Revenue e-Briefs

Revenue e-Brief No. 34/2008: Value-Added Tax Amendment Regulations 2008 (S.I. No. 238 of 2008)

Revenue e-Brief No. 14/2007 VAT treatment of certain secondments of staff to companies established in the State from related foreign companies.

Revenue e-Brief No. 15/2006: VAT Treatment of Staff Canteens

Revenue Statements of Practice and Information Leaflets

Cultural, Artistic and Entertainment Services Supplied by Non-Established Persons, Treatment of: Information Leaflet No. 3/02

Electronically Supplied Services and Radio and Television Broadcasting Services: Information Leaflet dated October 2008

Foreign firms doing business in Ireland, VAT treatment of: Information Leaflet dated October 2008

Fourth Schedule Services: Information Leaflet dated December 2008

Goods Transport and Ancillary Services between EU countries from 1/1/93, VAT treatment of: Information Leaflet dated October 2008

International Leasing of Means of Transport, VAT treatment of: Information Leaflet dated October 2008

Research services carried out by third level educational bodies: Information Leaflet No. 2/01 (formerly No. 6/01)

Solicitors: Information Leaflet dated December 2008

Veterinary Services: Information Leaflet dated December 2008

Case law

Aro Lease BV/Inspecteur der Belastingdienst Grote Ondernemingen, Amsterdam	C190/95	Place of Supply/leasing of means of transport
Banque Bruxelles Lambert SA v Belgian State	C8/03	Place of supply/Concept of taxable person
Berkholz, Gunter v Finanzamt Hamburg - Mitte Altstadt	C168/84	Place of Supply/Gaming machines on board ferries
Cooperatieve Vereniging Aardapplenbewaarplaats v Staatssecretaris van Financien - Dutch Potato Case.	C154/80	A consideration for Taxable Event
Danfoss and Astra Zeneca v Skatteministeriet	C371/07	Supplies of services carried out free of charge by a taxable person for purposes other than those of his business
Design Concept SA and Flanders Expo SA	C438/01	Advertising services/supplied indirectly
Dudda, Jurgen v Finanzant Bergisch Gladback	C327/94	Place of Supply
Faaborg-Gelting Linien A/S v Finanzamt Flensburg	C231/94	Restaurant services/Place of Supply
France v Commission	C76/99	Medical supplies/Taking of samples
France v Commission	C404/99	Restaurant service charges
France v Commission	C68/92	Place of supply/Advertising Services
Germany v Commission of the European Communities	C401/06	Supply of services/Executor of a will
Gillan Beach Ltd v Ministre de l'Économie, des Finances et de l'Industrie	C114/05	Services connected with boat shows/ Article 9(2)(c)
Hamann, Knut v Finanzamt Hamburg Eimsbuttel	C51/88	Yachts/Hire of/Place of Supply
Heger Rudi GmbH v Finanzamt Graz - Stadt	C166/05	Place of supply/Transmission of fishing rights
Hotel Scandic Gåsabäck AB v Riksskatteverket	C412/03	Application for private use/ Consideration less than cost price
Ireland v Commission	C358/97	Toll Roads
Kollektivavtalsstiftelsen TRR Trygghetsrådet v Statteverket	C291/07	Place of Supply/Consultancy services/recipient engaged in economic and non-economic activities

Leaseplan Luxembourg SA v Belgium	C390/96	Place of Supply
Levob Verzekeringen BV, OV Bank NV v Staatssecretaris van Financiën	C41/04	Supply and customisation of software
Lipjes, D. and Staatssecretaris van Financiën	C68/03	Services by intermediaries/Place of supply
Maatschap M.J.M Linthorst; KGP Pouwels and Scheres v Inspecteur der Belastingdiest/Ondermingen Roermond	C167/95	Place of supply
Madgett (TP) and Baldwin (RM) (T/A Howden Court Hotel) v Customs and Excise	C308/96	Hotel/Tour Operators
Mohr, Jurgen v Finanzamt Bad Segeberg	C215/94	Payment to discontinue activity/Taxable Event
Mohsche, Gerhard v Finanzamt Munchen III	C193/91	Self Supply
Phonographic Performance (Ireland) Ltd v Somers	Ireland IV ITR 314	Taxable Event/Omission of Act/Toleration of situation/Equitable Payments
RAL (Channel Islands) Ltd and Others v Commissioners of Customs & Excise	C452/03	Slot gaming machines/Place of supply
Reiseburo Binder GmBH v Finanzamt Stuttgart-Korperschaften	C116/96	Place of Supply of Transport Services
Société thermale d'Eugénie-les-Bains v Ministère de l'Économie, des Finances et de l'Industrie	C277/05	Deposits, paid in the context of contracts relating to supplies of services subject to VAT, which are retained by the provider in the event of cancellation
Spain v Commission	C124/96	Club Membership/Sports
Syndicat des Producteurs Independents (SPI) v Ministere de l'economie, des finances et de l'industrie	C108/00	Place of Supply of Advertising Services/Supplied by Third Party
Von Hoffman, Bernd v Finanzamt Trier	C145/96	Arbitrator/Place of Supply
W.G. Bradley and Sons v Bourke, Inspector of Taxes	Irish H.C. IV ITR 117	Legal services in insurance

Revenue Precedents

Topic:	Farm Relief Services
Issue:	The provision of relief milking service and relief farm work on a dairy farm are taxable services as provided by Co-operatives.
Decision:	Decisions made that 1. Relief milking services are not taxable and 2. that relief farm work on a dairy farm will be chargeable to VAT as follows. 70 % not taxable as relating to the relief milking. 30 % chargeable at 12.5 %. The treatment was given to the Co-operatives because of the social service being provided by these organisations.
Date:	3/7/92

(withdrawn from the Revenue website in 2002)

Topic:	Milk Recording Services.
Issue:	Co-op. undertaking a milk recording service on behalf of the State.
Decision:	Decision made that one-third of the fee for the milk recording scheme to be taxed. It was regarded that two-thirds of the fee was in respect of non-taxable activities on behalf of the State and the balance as being in respect of taxable supplies by the local Co-op.
Date:	15/9/93

Topic:	Agents.
Issue:	Sale of theatre tickets by a booking agency which are bought in bulk from the theatre at a discount and sold at face value. The difference between the discount amount and the face value of the ticket forms the agency's commission.
Decision:	Commission exempt from VAT as it was regarded as part of the cost involved in supplying those exempt theatre tickets.
Date:	3/3/89

(withdrawn from the Revenue website in 2002)

Topic:	Second VAT Simplification.
Issue:	Contract work carried out in this State for customers in other Member States who provide their own labels and packaging materials that are incorporated in the final product.
Decision:	It was agreed that the contract work would be extended to include packaging and labelling.
Date:	31/7/96

Topic:	Beverages
Issue:	Sale of confectionery with a cup of coffee/tea in a pub.
Decision:	21%, coffee/tea not considered a meal.
Date:	21/8/96

(withdrawn from the Revenue website in 2002)

Topic:	Milk Quotas
Issue:	Sale or lease of a milk quota without land in excess of £20,000 by an unregistered/flat rate farmer.
Decision:	21%, However the farmer will be allowed retain his flat-rate status in all other respects.
Date:	23/5/95

(withdrawn from the Revenue website in 2002)

Narrative

Tax Briefing: Issue 65 (VAT Treatment of Staff Canteens – Role of Commercial Caterer)

VAT and Canteens: The Next Instalment: ITR Mar 2006: Vol 19 No. 2

Tax Briefing: Issue 62 (VAT Treatment of Canteens)

European VAT – Changing Times for International VAT Compliance: ITR Jul 2005: Vol 18 No. 4

VAT on Canteens: Implication of ECJ Judgment in Hotel Scandic Gåsäback AB: ITR Mar 2005: Vol 18 No. 2.

New place of supply of services: a positive step towards a common VAT system: ITR Mar 2004: Vol 17 No. 2

Tax Briefing: Issue 58 (Treatment of Greenhouse Gas Emission)

VAT Canteens: ITR Jan 2004: Vol 17 No. 1

Tax Briefing: Issue 52 (VAT Committee Guidelines - Supplies by Undertakers)

Tax Briefing: Issue 52 (VAT Committee Guidelines - Electronically Supplied Services)

E-Business: Some Recent EU Developments Regarding VAT: ITR July 2002: Vol 15 No. 4

Transfer of Business Relief – A New VAT Trap: ITR Nov 2001: Vol. 14 No. 6

Tax Briefing: Issue 43 (VAT Committee Guidelines – Place of Supply when the Supplier is Registered in the Member State of Establishment of the Client)

Tax Briefing: Issue 43 (VAT Committee Guidelines – Consolidated Document on Transactions, other than Bilateral, Involving Work on Movable Tangible Property)

Tax Briefing: Issue 43 (VAT Committee Guidelines – Construction of Buildings: A Good or Service)

Tax Briefing: Issue 43 (VAT Committee Guidelines – Packages of Services Supplied in Connection with Trade Fairs and Similar Exhibitions)

Tax Briefing: Issue 43 (VAT Committee Guidelines – Article 6: Transfers of Football Players)

Tax Briefing: Issue 43 (VAT Committee Guidelines – Article 9(2)(e): Transfers of Football Players)

Tax Briefing: Issue 43 (VAT Committee Guidelines – Article 9(2)(e): Tracing of Heirs)

Tax Briefing: Issue 43 (VAT Committee Guidelines – Assignment of Broadcasting Rights in Respect of International Football Matches by Organisations Established Abroad)

Tax Briefing: Issue 43 (VAT Committee Guidelines – Application of Articles 9(2)(c) and 28b(f) in Cases of Total or Partial Subcontracting)

Tax Briefing: Issue 42 (VAT Committee – Concept of Agent/Hiring of Movable Tangible Property)

Tax Briefing: Issue 42 (VAT Committee Guidelines – Contracts Without Any Supply of Goods by the Customer)

Tax Briefing: Issue 42 (VAT Committee Guidelines – Translators' and Interpreters' Services)

Tax Briefing: Issue 42 (VAT Committee Guidelines – Services provided to Public Sector Hospitals)

Foreign Firms: VAT issues arising in Ireland: ITR Jan 2000: Vol 13 No. 1

VAT and Cross-border Leasing of Means of Transport: ITR Nov 1999: Vol 12 No. 6.

Ireland's Derogations from the EU Sixth VAT Directive: ITR Sept 1999: Vol 12 No. 5.

VAT and Electronic Commerce: ITR March 1999: Vol 12 No. 2.

Tax Briefing: Issue 30 (EU Supplies)
Tax Briefing: Issue 29 (Staff Canteens)
Tax Briefing: Issue 28 (Veterinary Services)
Tax Briefing: Issue 27 (Finance Act 1997 Changes: Telecommunication Services)

Section 5A

Special scheme for electronic services

[5A. (1)   In this section—

'**electronic services scheme**' means the special arrangements for the taxation of electronically supplied services provided for in [Articles 358 to 369 of Council Directive No. 2006/112/EC of 28 November 2006][1];

'**EU value-added tax**' means value-added tax referred to in [Council Directive No. 2006/112/EC of 28 November 2006][1] and includes tax within the meaning of section 1;

'**identified person**' has the meaning assigned to it by subsection (5);

a 358(4)   '**Member State of consumption**' means the Member State in which the supply of the electronic services takes place according to [Article 57(1) of Council Directive No. 2006/112/EC of 28 November 2006][1];

a 358(3)   '**Member State of identification**' means the Member State which the non-established person chooses to contact to state when his or her activity within the Community commences in accordance with the provisions of the electronic services scheme;

'**national tax number**' means a number (whether consisting of either or both numbers and letters) assigned to a non-established person by his or her own national taxation authorities;

a 358(1)   '**non-established person**' means a person who has his or her establishment outside the Community and has not also an establishment in the Community and who is not otherwise required to be a person registered for value-added tax within the meaning of section 1;

'**scheme participant**' means a non-established person who supplies electronic services into the Community and who opts to use the electronic services scheme in any Member State;

a 358(5)   '**VAT return**' means the statement containing the information necessary to establish the amount of EU value-added tax that has become chargeable in each Member State under the electronic services scheme.

a 359   (2)   Subject to and in accordance with the provisions of this section, a non-established person may opt to apply the electronic services scheme to his or her supplies of electronic services to non-taxable persons within the Community.

(3)   The Revenue Commissioners shall set up and maintain a register, referred to in this section as an '**identification register**',

of non-established persons who are identified in the State for the purposes of the electronic services scheme.

a 360, a 361   (4)   A non-established person who opts to be identified in the State for the purposes of the electronic services scheme shall inform the Revenue Commissioners by electronic means in a manner specified by them, when his or her taxable activity commences and shall, at the same time, furnish them electronically with the following information—

(a)   the person's name and postal address,

(b)   his or her electronic addresses, including website addresses,

(c)   his or her national tax number, if any, and

(d)   a statement that the person is not a person registered, or otherwise identified, for value-added tax purposes within the Community.

a 362   (5)   Where a person has furnished the particulars required under subsection (4), the Revenue Commissioners shall register that person in accordance with subsection (3), allocate to that person an identification number and notify such person electronically of it, and, for the purposes of this section, a person to whom such an identification number has been allocated shall be referred to as an 'identified person'.

a 364, a 367   (6)   An identified person shall, within 20 days immediately following the end of each calendar quarter, furnish by electronic means to the Revenue Commissioners a VAT return, prepared in accordance with, and containing such particulars as are specified in, subsection (7), in respect of supplies made in the Community in that quarter and shall at the same time remit to the Revenue Commissioners, into a bank account designated by them and denominated in euro, the amount of EU value-added tax, if any, payable by such person in respect of such quarter in relation to—

(a)   supplies made in the State in accordance with section 5(6) (eee), and

(b)   supplies made in other Member States in accordance with the provisions implementing [Article 57(1) of Council Directive No. 2006/112/EC of 28 November 2006][1] in such other Member States:

but if the identified person has not made any such electronic supplies to non-taxable persons into the Community within a calendar quarter that person shall furnish a nil VAT return in respect of that quarter.

a 365, a 366   (7)   The VAT return referred to in subsection (6) shall be made in euro and shall contain the following details—

(a) the person's identification number,

(b) for each Member State of consumption where EU value-added tax has become due—

(i) the total value, exclusive of EU value-added tax, of supplies of electronic services for the quarter,

(ii) the amount of the said value liable to EU value-added tax at the applicable rate, and

(iii) the amount of EU value-added tax corresponding to the said value at the applicable rate,

and

(c) the total EU value-added tax due, if any.

a 366 (8) Notwithstanding section 10(9A), where supplies have been made using a currency other than the euro, the exchange rate to be used for the purposes of expressing the corresponding amount in euro on the VAT return shall be that published by the European Central Bank for the last date of the calendar quarter for which the VAT return relates, or, if there is no publication on that date, on the next day of publication.

a 368 (9) Notwithstanding section 12, a scheme participant who supplies services which are deemed in accordance with section 5(6)(eee) to be supplied in the State shall not, in computing the amount of tax payable by him or her in respect of such supplies, be entitled to deduct any tax borne or paid in relation to those supplies but shall be entitled to claim a refund of such tax in accordance with, and using the rules applicable to, Council Directive 86/560/EEC of 17 November 1986, notwithstanding Articles 2(2), 2(3) and 4(2) of that Directive.

(10) A scheme participant who supplies services which are deemed in accordance with section 5(6)(eee) to be supplied in the State shall be deemed to have fulfilled his or her obligations under sections 9, 16 and 19 of this Act if such participant has accounted in full in respect of such supplies in any Member State under the provisions of the electronic services scheme.

(11) For the purposes of this Act, a VAT return required to be furnished in accordance with the electronic services scheme shall, in so far as it relates to supplies made in accordance with section 5(6)(eee), be treated, with any necessary modifications, as if it were a return required to be furnished in accordance with section 19.

a 369 (12) (a) An identified person shall—

(i) keep full and true records of all transactions covered by the electronic services scheme which affect his or her liability to EU value-added tax,

(ii) make such records available, by electronic means and on request, to the Revenue Commissioners,

(iii) make such records available, by electronic means and on request, to all Member States of consumption, and

(iv) notwithstanding section 16, retain such records for each transaction for a period of 10 years from the end of the year when that transaction occurred.

(b) A scheme participant who is deemed to supply services in the State in accordance with section 5(6)(eee) shall be bound by the requirements of subparagraphs (i), (ii) and (iv) in relation to such supplies.

(13) An identified person shall notify the Revenue Commissioners of any changes in the information submitted under subsection (4) and shall notify them if his or her taxable activity ceases or changes to the extent that such person no longer qualifies for the electronic services scheme. Such notification shall be made electronically.

a 363

(14) The Revenue Commissioners shall exclude an identified person from the identification register if —

(a) they have reasonable grounds to believe that that person's taxable activities have ended, or

(b) the identified person —

(i) notifies the Revenue Commissioners that he or she no longer supplies electronic services,

(ii) no longer fulfils the requirements necessary to be allowed to use the electronic services scheme, or

(iii) persistently fails to comply with the provisions of the electronic services scheme.

(15) The Revenue Commissioners may make regulations as necessary for the purpose of giving effect to the electronic services scheme.][2]

Amendments

1   Substituted by FA07 s97 & Sch 3 (w.e.f. 1 January 2007).

2   Section 5A inserted by FA 03 s116, (w.e.f. 1 July 2003).

Regulations and Orders

| Electronic transmission of VAT eServices Returns | 2008 SI No. 339 Taxes (Electronic Transmission of VAT eServices Returns and VIES Statements) Specified Provisions and Appointed Day) Order 2008 |

Revenue Statements of Practice and Information Leaflets

Electronically Supplied Services and Radio and Television Broadcasting Services: Information Leaflet dated October 2008

Narrative

Electronically Supplied Services: ITR May 2003: Vol 16 No. 3

Tax Briefing: Issue 53 (VAT on Electronically Supplied Services – ROS)

E-Business: Some Recent EU Developments Regarding VAT: ITR July 2002: Vol 15 No. 4

Section 6

Exemptions

a 131 **6.** (1) Tax shall not be chargeable in respect of any exempted activity.

(2) (a) The Minister may by order declare the [supply of goods or services][1] of any kind to be an exempted activity.

(b) The Minister may by order amend or revoke an order under this subsection, including an order under this paragraph.

(c) An order under this subsection shall be laid before Dáil Éireann as soon as may be after it is made and, if a resolution annulling the order is passed by Dáil Éireann within the next twenty-one days on which Dáil Éireann has sat after the order is laid before it, the order shall be annulled accordingly, but without prejudice to the validity of anything previously done thereunder.

Amendments

1   Substituted by VAT Amend. A78 s30(2), (w.e.f. 1 March 1979).

Regulations and Orders

Permanent Importation	1985 SI No. 183	European Communities (Exemption from Value Added Tax on the Permanent Importation of Certain goods) Regulations, 1985
Waiver, Investment Gold	1999 SI No. 440	Value Added Tax (Waiver of Exemption on Supplies of and Supplies relating to, Investment Gold) Regulations, 1999

Case law

Cibo Participations SA v Directeur régional des impôts du Nord-Pas-de-Calais	C16/00	Holding Coy taxable person/Recovery of VAT
Cork Communications Ltd. v Brosnan	Irish	Nature of Supply/Communications or Electricity

Section 6A

Special scheme for investment gold

198, a 208,
255, a 325,
353, a 354,
355

[6A. (1) (a) In this section-

'**intermediary**' means a person who intervenes for another person in a supply of investment gold while acting in the name and for the account of that other person;

'**investment gold**' means-

(i)   gold in the form of-

(I)   a bar, or

(II)   a wafer,

of a weight accepted by a bullion market and of a purity equal to or greater than 995 parts per one thousand parts, and

(ii)   gold coins which-

(I)   are of a purity equal to or greater than 900 parts per one thousand parts,

(II)   are minted after 1800,

(III)   are or have been legal tender in their country of origin, and

(IV)   are normally sold at a price which does not exceed the open market value of the gold contained in the coins by more than 80 per cent.

(b)   For the purposes of the definition of investment gold in paragraph (a), gold coins which are listed in the 'C' series of the Official Journal of the European Communities as fulfilling the criteria referred to in that definition in respect of gold coins shall be deemed to fulfil the said criteria for the whole year for which the list is published.

(2)   The provisions of this section shall apply to -

(a)   [investment gold, including investment gold which is represented by securities][1] or represented by certificates for allocated or unallocated gold or traded on gold accounts and including, in particular, gold loans and swaps, involving a right of ownership or a claim in respect of investment gold, and

(b)   transactions concerning investment gold involving futures and forward contracts leading to a transfer of a right of ownership or a claim in respect of investment gold.

(3)   Notwithstanding subsection (1) of section 6, a person who produces investment gold or transforms any gold into investment gold, may, in accordance with conditions set out in regulations, waive such person's right to exemption from tax on a supply of investment gold to another person who is engaged in the supply of goods and services in the course or furtherance of business.

(4)   Where a person waives, in accordance with subsection (3), such person's right to exemption from tax in respect of a supply of investment gold, an intermediary who supplies services in respect of that supply of investment gold may, in accordance with conditions set out in regulations, waive that intermediary's right to exemption from tax in respect of those services.

(5)   (a)   Where a person waives, in accordance with subsection (3), such person's right to exemption from tax in respect of a supply of investment gold, then, for the purposes of this Act, the person to whom the supply of investment gold is made shall, in relation thereto, be [an accountable person][2] and be liable to pay the tax chargeable on that supply as if [such accountable person][2] had made that supply of investment gold for consideration in the course or furtherance of business and the person who waived the right to exemption in respect of that supply shall not be liable to pay the said tax.

        (b)   Where a person is liable for tax in accordance with paragraph (a) in respect of a supply of investment gold, such person shall, notwithstanding the provisions of section 12, be entitled, in computing the amount of tax payable by such person in respect of the taxable period in which that liability to tax arises, to deduct the tax for which such person is liable on that supply, if such person's subsequent supply of that investment gold is exempt from tax.

(6)   (a)   [An accountable person][2] may, in computing the amount of tax payable by such person in respect of any taxable period and notwithstanding section 12, deduct-

                (i)   the tax charged to such person during that period by [other accountable persons][2] by means of invoices, prepared in the manner prescribed by regulations, in respect of supplies of gold to such person,

                (ii)   the tax chargeable during that period, being tax for which such person is liable in respect of intra-Community acquisitions of gold, and

                (iii)   the tax paid by such person, or deferred, as established from the relevant customs documents kept by such person in accordance with section 16(3) in respect of gold imported by such person in that period, where that gold is subsequently transformed into investment gold and such person's subsequent supply of that investment gold is exempt from tax.

(b)   A person may claim, in accordance with regulations, a refund of-

(i)   the tax charged to such person on the purchase of gold, other than investment gold, by such person,

(ii)   the tax chargeable to such person on the intra-Community acquisition of gold, other than investment gold, by such person, and

(iii)   the tax paid or deferred on the importation by such person of gold other than investment gold,

where that gold is subsequently transformed into investment gold and such person's subsequent supply of that investment gold is exempt from tax.

(7)   (a)   [An accountable person]² may, in computing the amount of tax payable by such person in respect of a taxable period and notwithstanding section 12, deduct the tax charged to such person during that period by [other accountable persons]² by means of invoices, prepared in the manner prescribed by regulations, in respect of the supply to the first-mentioned person of services consisting of a change of form, weight or purity of gold where that person's subsequent supply of that gold is exempt from tax.

(b)   A person may claim, in accordance with regulations, a refund of the tax charged to such person in respect of the supply to such person of services consisting of a change of form, weight or purity of gold where such person's subsequent supply of that gold is exempt from tax.

(8)   (a)   [An accountable person]² who produces investment gold or transforms any gold into investment gold may, in computing the amount of tax payable by such person in respect of a taxable period and notwithstanding section 12, deduct -

(i)   the tax charged to such person during that period by [other accountable persons]² by means of invoices, prepared in the manner prescribed by regulations, in respect of supplies of goods or services to the first-mentioned person,

(ii)   the tax chargeable during that period, being tax for which such person is liable in respect of intra-Community acquisitions of goods, and

(iii)   the tax paid by such person, or deferred, as established from the relevant customs documents kept by such person in accordance with section 16(3) in respect of goods imported by such person in that period,

where those goods or services are linked to the production or transformation of that gold, and such person's subsequent supply of that investment gold is exempt from tax.

(b)   A person who produces investment gold or transforms any gold into investment gold may claim, in accordance with regulations, a refund of-

(i)   the tax charged to such person on the purchase by such person of goods or services,

(ii)   the tax chargeable to such person on the intra-Community acquisition of goods by such person, and

(iii)   the tax paid or deferred by such person on the importation of goods by such person,

where those goods or services are linked to the production or transformation of that gold, and such person's subsequent supply of that gold is exempt from tax.

[(9)   Every trader in investment gold shall establish the identity of any person to whom such trader supplies investment gold when the total consideration which such trader is entitled to receive in respect of such supply, or a series of such supplies which are or appear to be linked, amounts to at least 15,000 euros, and such trader shall retain a copy of all documents used to identify the person to whom the investment gold is supplied as if they were records to be kept in accordance with section 16(1A) of this Act.][3]][4]

Amendments

1   Inserted by FA00 s109(a), (w.e.f. 23 March 2000).

2   Substituted by FA08 s109 & Sch 4, (w.e.f. 1 July 2008).

3   Ss9 inserted by FA00 s109(b), (w.e.f. 23 March 2000).

4   S6A inserted by FA99 s122, (w.e.f. 1 January 2000).

Regulations and Orders

Investment gold	1999 SI No. 440	Value Added Tax (Waiver of Exemption on Supplies of, and Supplies relating to , Investment Gold) Regulations 1999
Records of Transactions – Investment gold	2006 SI No. 548	Value-Added Tax Regulations 2006
Refunds, Investment gold	1999 SI No. 441	Value Added Tax (Refund of Tax to Persons making Exempt Supplies of Investment Gold) Regulations 1999
Refunds of tax - Investment gold	2006 SI No. 548	Value-Added Tax Regulations 2006
Records	1999 SI No. 439	Value Added Tax (Records of Transactions in Investment Gold) Regulations, 1999
Waiver of Exemption - Investment gold	2006 SI No. 548	Value-Added Tax Regulations 2006

Narrative

Tax Briefing: Issue 42 (VAT Committee Guidelines – Implementation of Special Scheme for Investment Gold)

Tax Briefing: Issue 42 (VAT Committee Guidelines – Scope of Exemption of Articles 13, 15, 26b and 28c)

Tax Briefing: Issue 39 (Notification of VAT Regulations)

Section 7

Waiver of exemption

a 137
a 391 **7.** (1) [(a)][1] Where, but for the provisions of section 6, tax would be chargeable in respect of the [supply][2] of any of the services [to which paragraph (iv) of the First Schedule relates][3], a person [supplying][4] any such services may, in accordance with regulations, waive his right to exemption from tax in respect thereof. Any such waiver shall extend to all the [services to which the said paragraph (iv) relates][5] that the person [supplies][6].

[Provided that where a person waives his right to exemption from tax in respect of the leasing or letting of goods which are subject to an agreement of the type referred to in section 4(2C)(a) then that waiver shall only apply to the supply of services under that agreement.][7]

[(b) A waiver of exemption from tax under this subsection shall not apply or be extended to any disposal of an interest in immovable goods which is deemed to be a letting of immovable goods to which paragraph (iv) of the First Schedule applies by virtue of section 4(3A)(a)(ii).][1]

[(1A) (a) Notwithstanding subsection (1)(a), a person shall not waive his or her right to exemption from tax on or after the date of passing of the Finance Act 2007 in respect of a letting of immovable goods to which paragraph (iv) of the First Schedule relates which is a letting of all or part of a house, apartment or other similar establishment, to the extent that those immovable goods are used or to be used for residential purposes, including any such letting —

(i) governed by the Residential Tenancies Act 2004,

(ii) governed by the Housing (Rent Books) Regulations 1993 (S.I. No. 146 of 1993),

(iii) governed by section 10 of the Housing Act 1988,

(iv) of a dwelling to which Part II of the Housing (Private Rented Dwellings) Act 1982 applies, or

(v) of accommodation which is provided as a temporary dwelling for emergency residential purposes,

and any waiver of exemption from tax which applies under this section shall not extend to such a letting of immovable goods where those goods are acquired or developed on or after the date of passing of the Finance Act 2007.

(b)   For the purpose of applying paragraph (a), immovable goods are considered to be acquired when a person enters into a binding contract in writing for the acquisition of those goods or of an interest in those goods, or for the construction of those goods, and are considered to be developed when an application for planning permission in respect of the development of those goods as a house, apartment or other similar establishment is received by a planning authority.]⁸

(2)   A waiver of exemption under subsection (1) shall have effect from the commencement of such taxable period as may be agreed between the person making the waiver and the Revenue Commissioners and shall cease to have effect at the end of the taxable period during which it is cancelled in accordance with subsection (3).

[(3)   Provision may be made by regulations for the cancellation, at the request of a person [or in accordance with **[subsection (3), (7) or (9) of section 7B]⁹**]¹⁰, of a waiver made by him under subsection (1) and for the payment by him to the Revenue Commissioners as a condition of cancellation of such sum (if any) as when added to the total amount of tax (if any) due by him in accordance with section 19 in relation to the supply of services by him to which the waiver applied is equal to the total of

(a)   the amount of tax deducted by him in accordance with section 12 in respect of tax borne or paid in relation to the supply of such services,

[(aa)   the amount of tax deducted by him in accordance with section 12, prior to the commencement of the letting of the immovable goods to which the waiver relates, in respect of or in relation to his acquisition of his interest in, or his development of, those immovable goods,]¹¹

(b)   the amount of tax that would be deductible by him in accordance with section 12 if tax had been chargeable on the transfer of ownership of goods to him in respect of which the provisions of section 3(5)(b)(iii) were applied, and those goods were used by him in the supply of such services, and

(c)   the amount of tax that would be deductible by him in accordance with section 12 if tax had been chargeable on the supply to him of goods or services in respect of which the provisions of paragraph (via) of the Second Schedule were applied, and those goods or services were used in relation to the supply of services by him to which the waiver applied.]¹²

(4)   Where exemption has been waived under subsection (1) in respect of the [supply]² of any service, tax shall be charged in relation to the person making such waiver during the period for which such waiver has effect as if the service to which the waiver applies was not specified in the First Schedule.

(5)   (a)   No waiver of exemption from tax in accordance with this section shall commence on or after 1 July 2008.

        (b)   Any waiver of exemption from tax which applies under this section shall not extend to any letting of immovable goods where those goods are acquired or developed on or after 1 July 2008.

        (c)   For the purpose of applying paragraph (b), a waiver of exemption, which is in place on 18 February 2008 in respect of the letting of immovable goods which are undergoing development on that day by or on behalf of the person who has that waiver, may extend to a letting of those immovable goods.]¹³

[(6)   Where a person cancelled his or her waiver of exemption before 1 July 2008 then, for the purposes of applying section 12E, the adjustment period (within the meaning of that section or, as the context may require, the period to be treated as the adjustment period in accordance with section 4C(11)) in relation to any capital good the tax chargeable on that person's acquisition or development of which that person was obliged to take into account when that person made that cancellation, shall be treated as if it ended on the date on which that cancellation had effect.]¹⁴

Amendments

1   Inserted by FA02 s100(a), (w.e.f. 25 March 2002).
2   Substituted by VAT Amend. A78 s30(2), (w.e.f. 1 March 1979).
3   Substituted by FA91 s78, (w.e.f. 1 January 1992).
4   Substituted by VAT Amend. A78 s30(2), (w.e.f. 1 March 1979).
5   Substituted by FA91 s78, (w.e.f. 1 January 1992).
6   Substituted by VAT Amend. A78 s 30(2), (w.e.f. 1 March 1979).
7   Inserted by FA97 s100(a), (w.e.f. 26 March 1997).
8   Inserted by FA07 s78, (w.e.f. 2 April 2007).
9   Substituted by FA09 s21(a), (w.e.f. 3 June 2009).
10 Inserted by FA08 s90(a), (w.e.f. 13 March 2008).
11 Ss (3)(aa) inserted by FA03 s 117, (w.e.f. 28 March 2003).
12 Ss(3) substituted by FA97 s100(a), (w.e.f. 26 March 1997).
13 Ss(5) inserted by FA08 s90(b), (w.e.f. 13 March 2008).
14 Inserted by FA09 s21(b), (w.e.f. 3 June 2009).

Regulations and Orders

| Waiver of Exemption | 2003 SI No. 504 | Value Added Tax (Waiver of Exemption) (Letting of Immovable Goods) Regulations, 2003 |
| Waiver of Exemption | 2006 SI No. 548 | Value-Added Tax Regulations 2006 |

Revenue e-Briefs

Revenue e-Brief No. 20/2007 – VAT treatment of short-term letting of residential property

Case law

Belgocodex S.A v Belgium	C381/97	Waiver/Property
Far, Miguel Amengual v Amengual	C12/98	Property/right to waive exemption
Norbury Developments Ltd v Customs and Excise	C136/97	Exemption/waiver of/Immovable property
Turn – und Sportunion Waldburg v Finanzlandesdirektion für Oberösterreich	C246/04	Property/Option to tax
Vermietungsgesellschaft Objekt Kirchberg SARL v État du grand-duché de Luxembourg	C269/03	Letting of immovable property/Right of option for taxation

Revenue Precedents

Topic:	Property
Issue:	Group registration and waiver of entitlement to exemption.
Decision:	The group is regarded as a single taxable entity.
Date:	13/5/96

Topic:	Short term lettings.
Issue:	Recovery of inputs in relation to restoration work on a castle garden open to the public.
Decision:	Waiver of exemption allowed but only from a current date. Full recovery of inputs in the exceptional circumstances.
Date:	21/7/97

Narrative

Tax Briefing: Issue 33 (Waiver of Exemption (Amendment) Regulations, 1998)

[Section 7A

Option to tax lettings of immovable goods

7A. (1) (a)   Tax shall be chargeable in accordance with this Act on the supply of a service to which paragraph (iv) of the First Schedule relates (in this section referred to as a '**letting**') where, subject to subsections (2) and (4), the supplier (in this section referred to as a '**landlord**') opts to make that letting so chargeable, and a landlord who exercises this option (referred to in this Act as a '**landlord's option to tax**') shall, notwithstanding section 8(3), be an accountable person and liable to account for the tax on that letting in accordance with this Act, and that letting shall not be a supply to which section 6 applies.

(b)   Where a taxable person is entitled to deduct tax on the acquisition or development of immovable goods on the basis that the goods will be used for the purpose of a letting or lettings in respect of which a landlord's option to tax will apply, then–

(i)   that person shall be treated as having exercised the landlord's option to tax in respect of any lettings of those immovable goods, and

(ii)   that option shall be deemed to continue in place until that person makes a letting in respect of which neither of the conditions of paragraph (c) are fulfilled.

(c)   A landlord's option to tax in respect of a letting is exercised by–

(i)   a provision in writing in a letting agreement between the landlord and the person to whom the letting is made (in this section referred to as a '**tenant**') that tax is chargeable on the rent, or

(ii)   the issuing by the landlord of a document to the tenant giving notification that tax is chargeable on the letting.

(d)   A landlord's option to tax in respect of a letting is terminated–

(i)   in the case of an option exercised in accordance with paragraph (b), by making a letting of the immovable goods referred to in that paragraph in respect of which neither of the conditions of paragraph (c) are fulfilled,

(ii)   in the case of an option exercised in accordance with paragraph (c), by–

(I)   an agreement in writing between the landlord and tenant that the option is terminated and specifying the date of termination **[which shall not be earlier than the date of that agreement]**[1], or

(II)   the delivery to the tenant of a document giving notification that the option has been terminated and specifying the date of termination **[which shall not be earlier than the date that notification is received by the tenant]**,[1]

(iii)   when the landlord and tenant become connected persons,

(iv)   when **[the landlord or]**[2] a person connected with the landlord **[occupies]**[3] the immovable goods that are subject to that letting whether that person occupies those goods by way of letting or otherwise, or

(v)   when the immovable goods that are subject to that letting are used or to be used for residential purposes within the meaning of subsection (4).

(2)   (a)   **[Subject to paragraphs (b) and (c), a landlord]**[4] may not opt to tax a letting–

(i)   **[...]**[5] where that landlord and the tenant in respect of that letting are connected persons, or

[(ii)   where the landlord, whether or not connected to the tenant, or a person connected to the landlord, occupies the immovable goods that is subject to that letting whether that landlord or that person occupies those goods by way of letting or otherwise.][3]

(b)   Paragraph (a)(i) **[and subsection (1)(d)(iii)]**[1] shall not apply where the immovable goods which are the subject of the letting are used for the purposes of supplies or activities which entitle the tenant to deduct at least 90 per cent of the tax chargeable on the letting in accordance with section 12. However, where a landlord has exercised a landlord's option to tax in respect of a letting to which paragraph (a)(i) would have applied but for this paragraph, paragraph (a)(i) shall apply from the end of the first accounting year in which the goods are used for the purposes of supplies or activities which entitle the tenant to deduct less than 90 per cent of the said tax chargeable.

[(c)] Paragraph (a)(ii) and subsection (1)(d)(iv) shall not apply where the occupant (being any person including the landlord referred to in that paragraph or that subsection) uses the immovable goods which are the subject of the letting for the purpose of making supplies which entitle that occupant to deduct, in accordance with section 12, at least 90 per cent of all tax chargeable in respect of goods or services used by that occupant for the purpose of making those supplies. However, where a landlord has exercised a landlord's option to tax in respect of a letting to which paragraph (a)(ii) would have applied but for this paragraph, paragraph (a)(ii) shall apply from the end of the first accounting year in which the immovable goods are used for the purpose of making supplies which entitle that occupant to deduct less than 90 per cent of the said tax chargeable.][2]

(3) (a) For the purposes of this section any question of whether a person is connected with another person shall be determined in accordance with the following:

(i) a person is connected with an individual if that person is the individual's spouse, or is a relative, or the spouse of a relative, of the individual or of the individual's spouse,

(ii) a person is connected with any person with whom he or she is in partnership, and with the spouse or a relative of any individual with whom he or she is in partnership,

(iii) subject to clauses (IV) and (V) of subparagraph (v), a person is connected with another person if he or she has control over that other person, or if the other person has control over the first-mentioned person, or if both persons are controlled by another person or persons,

(iv) a body of persons is connected with another person if that person, or persons connected with him or her, have control of that body of persons, or the person and persons connected with him or her together have control of it,

(v) a body of persons is connected with another body of persons —

(I) if the same person has control of both or a person has control of one and persons connected with that person or that person and persons connected with that person have control of the other,

(II)   if a group of 2 or more persons has control of each body of persons and the groups either consist of the same persons or could be regarded as consisting of the same persons by treating (in one or more cases) a member of either group as replaced by a person with whom he or she is connected,

(III)   if both bodies of persons act in pursuit of a common purpose,

(IV)   if any person or any group of persons or groups of persons having a reasonable commonality of identity have or had the means or power, either directly or indirectly, to determine the activities carried on or to be carried on by both bodies of persons, or

(V)   if both bodies of persons are under the control of any person or group of persons or groups of persons having a reasonable commonality of identity,

(vi)   a person in the capacity as trustee of a settlement is connected with–

(I)   any person who in relation to the settlement is a settlor, or

(II)   any person who is a beneficiary under the settlement.

(b)   In this subsection–

'control', in the case of a body corporate or in the case of a partnership, has the meaning assigned to it by section 8(3B);

'relative' means a brother, sister, ancestor or lineal descendant.

(4)   A landlord's option to tax may not be exercised in respect of all or part of a house or apartment or other similar establishment to the extent that those immovable goods are used or to be used for residential purposes, including any such letting–

(a)   governed by the Residential Tenancies Act 2004,

(b)   governed by the Housing (Rent Books) Regulations 1993 (S.I. No. 146 of 1993),

(c)   governed by section 10 of the Housing Act 1988,

(d)   of a dwelling to which Part II of the Housing (Private Rented Dwellings) Act 1982 applies, or

    (e)   of accommodation which is provided as a temporary dwelling for emergency residential purposes,

and a landlord's option to tax, once exercised, shall immediately cease to have effect to the extent that the immovable goods which are the subject of the letting to which the option applies, come to be used for a residential purpose.][6]

Amendments

1   Inserted by F(No. 2)A 08 s99 & Sch 6, (w.e.f. 24 December 2008).
2   Inserted by F(No. 2)A 08 s69, (w.e.f. 24 December 2008).
3   Substituted by F(No. 2)A 08 s69, (w.e.f. 24 December 2008).
4   Substituted by F(No. 2)A 08 s99 & Sch 6, (w.e.f. 24 December 2008).
5   Deleted by F(No. 2)A 08 s99 & Sch 6, (w.e.f. 24 December 2008).
6   S7A inserted by s91, FA08, (w.e.f. 1 July 2008).

Revenue Statements of Practice and Information Leaflets

    Frequently asked questions: Information Leaflet dated December 2008
    Summary and checklist: Information Leaflet dated May 2008

Narrative

    Tax Briefing: Issue 69 (FAQs – VAT on Property)
    Initial Issues Identified in the New VAT on Property Regime : ITR Jul 2008 Vol 21 No. 4
    VAT on Property 2008: ITR Jul 2008 Vol 21 No. 3

[Section 7B

Transitional measures: Waiver of exemption

7B. (1)   This section applies to an accountable person who had waived his or her right to exemption from tax in accordance with section 7 and who had not cancelled that waiver before 1 July 2008 (hereafter in this section referred to as a **'landlord'**).

[(2)   **For the purposes of applying section 12E, the adjustment period (within the meaning of that section or, as the context may require, the period to be treated as the adjustment period in accordance with section 4C(11)) in relation to a capital good the tax chargeable on the landlord's acquisition or development of which that landlord was obliged to take into account when that landlord cancelled his or her waiver of exemption, shall end on the date on which that cancellation had effect.]**[1]

(3)   Where a landlord **[makes or has made]**[2] a letting and, were that letting not already subject to a waiver, that letting would be one in respect of which the landlord would not, because of the provisions of section 7A(2), be entitled to exercise a landlord's option to tax in accordance with section 7A, then the landlord's waiver of exemption shall, subject to subsection (4), immediately cease to apply to that letting, and–

(a)   that landlord shall pay the amount, as if it were tax due by that person in accordance with section 19 for the taxable period in which the waiver ceases to apply to that letting and the amount shall be the sum, if any, which would be payable in accordance with section 7(3) in respect of the cancellation of a waiver as if that landlord's waiver applied only to the immovable goods or the interest in immovable goods subject to that letting to which the waiver has ceased to apply, and

(b)   the amounts taken into account in calculating that sum, if any, shall be disregarded in any future cancellation of that waiver.

(4)   (a)   Subject to paragraph (c), where a landlord has a letting to which subsection (3) would otherwise apply, the provisions of that subsection shall not apply while, on the basis of the letting agreement in place, the tax that the landlord will be required to account for, in equal amounts for each taxable period, in respect of the letting during the next 12 months is not less than the amount calculated at that time in accordance with the formula in subsection (5).

(b)   Where the conditions in paragraph (a) fail to be satisfied because of a variation in the terms of the lease or otherwise or if the tax paid at any time in respect of the letting is less than the tax payable, this subsection shall cease to apply.

(c)   This subsection applies to a letting referred to in paragraph (a)–

(i)   where a landlord has a waiver in place on 18 February 2008 and–

(I)   on 1 July 2008 that letting had been in place since 18 February 2008, or

(II)   the immovable goods subject to the letting are owned by that landlord on 18 February 2008 and are in the course of development by or on behalf of that landlord on that day,

or

(ii)   where a landlord holds an interest, other than a freehold interest or a freehold equivalent interest in the immovable goods subject to the letting, acquired between 18 February 2008 and 30 June 2008 from a person with whom the landlord is not connected, within the meaning of section 7A, in a transaction which is treated as a supply of goods in accordance with section 4.

(5)   The formula to be used for the purposes of subsection (4) is:

$$\frac{A - B}{12 - Y}$$

where–

A   is the amount of tax that would be taken into account for the purposes of section 7(3) in respect of the acquisition or development of the immovable goods, if the waiver were being cancelled at the time referred to in subsection (4),

B   is the amount of tax chargeable on the consideration by the landlord in respect of the letting of those immovable goods and paid in accordance with section 19 that would be taken into account for the purposes of section 7(3) if the waiver were being cancelled at that time, and if that letting were the only one to which that waiver applied, and

Y   is 11, or the number of full years since the later of–

(i)   the date of the first letting of those goods, and

(ii)   the date on which the landlord waived exemption, where that number is less than 11 years.][3]

[(6)   Where a landlord has a letting to which subsection (3) or (4) applies and that landlord becomes a person in a group within the meaning of section 8(8) on or after 1 July 2008 and the person to whom that letting is made is a person in that group, then the person referred to in section 8(8)(a)(i)(I) in respect of that group shall be liable to pay the amount as specified in subsection (3)(a) as if it were tax due in accordance with section 19—

    (a)   in the case of a landlord who became a person in that group before the date of passing of the Finance (No. 2) Act 2008, in the taxable period in which that Act is passed, or

    (b)   in the case of a landlord who became a person in that group after the date of passing of the Finance (No. 2) Act 2008, in the taxable period during which that landlord became a person in that group.][4]

[(7)   (a)   This subsection applies where—

    (i)   on 1 July 2008 a landlord had an interest in relevant immovable goods,

    (ii)   on the relevant date the landlord did not have an interest in any relevant immovable goods, and

    (iii)   that landlord's waiver of exemption had not been cancelled on or before the relevant date in accordance with section 7(3).

    (b)   Where this subsection applies—

    (i)   the landlord's waiver of exemption shall be treated as if it were cancelled in accordance with section 7(3) on the date of the passing of the Finance Act 2009, and

    (ii)   that landlord shall pay an amount, being the amount payable in accordance with section 7(3) in respect of the cancellation of that waiver, as if it were tax due by that landlord for the taxable period beginning on 1 May 2009.

(8)   (a)   This subsection applies where—

    (i)   in the period from 1 July 2008 to the relevant date, a landlord made a supply of relevant immovable goods during the adjustment period (within the meaning of section 12E or, as the context may require, the period to be treated as the adjustment period in accordance with section 4C(11)) in relation to those goods, and

    (ii)   tax was not chargeable on that supply.

(b)   Where this subsection applies, then for the purposes of sections 4B(5), 12E(3)(d) and 12E(7)(b) the supply of the relevant immovable goods is treated as if it was made on the date of the passing of the Finance Act 2009.

(c)   Paragraph (b) shall not apply where —

   (i)   the landlord's waiver of exemption has been cancelled in accordance with subsection (7), or

   (ii)   the landlord cancels his or her waiver of exemption in accordance with section 7(3) before 1 July 2009.

(9)   (a)   This subsection applies where —

   (i)   on or after the date of the passing of the Finance Act 2009 a landlord has an interest in relevant immovable goods,

   (ii)   the landlord ceases, whether as a result of disposing of such goods or otherwise, to have an interest in any such goods, and

   (iii) on the date when that landlord ceases to have any such interest, that landlord's waiver of exemption has not been cancelled in accordance with section 7(3).

(b)   Where this subsection applies —

   (i)   the landlord's waiver of exemption shall be treated as if it were cancelled on the date referred to in paragraph (a)(iii), and

   (ii)   that landlord shall pay an amount, being the amount payable in accordance with section 7(3) in respect of the cancellation of that waiver, as if it were tax due by that landlord for the taxable period in which the waiver of exemption is so treated as cancelled.

(10)   In this section —

'relevant immovable goods' means immovable goods the tax chargeable on the acquisition or development of which a landlord would be obliged to take into account in accordance with section 7(3) in relation to the cancellation of that landlord's waiver of exemption;

'relevant date' means the date immediately before the date of the passing of the Finance Act 2009.][5]

Amendments

1   Substituted by FA09 s22(a), (w.e.f. 3 June 2009).

2   Substituted by F(No. 2)A 08 s99 & Sch 6, (w.e.f. 24 December 2008).

3   S7B inserted by s91, FA08, (w.e.f. 1 July 2008).
4   Inserted by F(No. 2)A 08 s70, (w.e.f. 24 December 2008).
5   Inserted by FA09 s22(b), (w.e.f. 3 June 2009).

Revenue e-Briefs

Revenue e-Brief No. 6/09: Landlord and connected tenant: Deferred payment of waiver cancellation amount on becoming member sofa VAT group

Revenue Statements of Practice and Information Leaflets

Frequently asked questions: Information Leaflet dated December 2008

Summary and checklist: Information Leaflet dated May 2008

Narrative

Tax Briefing: Issue 69 (FAQs – VAT on Property) Initial Issues Identified in the New VAT on Property Regime : ITR Jul 2008 Vol 21 No. 4

VAT on Property 2008: ITR Jul 2008 Vol 21 No. 3

Section 8

Accountable persons

a 192,
a 203
a 9, a 10,

8. [(1) A taxable person who engages in the supply, within the State, of taxable goods or services shall be an accountable person and shall be accountable for and liable to pay the tax charged in respect of such supply. In addition, the person referred to in section 4B(3) and subsections (1A), (2), (2A) and (8) shall be accountable persons. However, a person not established in the State who supplies goods in the State only in the circumstances set out in paragraph (f) or (g) of subsection (1A) or supplies a service in the State only in the circumstances set out in subsections (1B) and (2)(aa) shall not be an accountable person.]¹

a 200

[(1A) (a) Where a person engages in the intra-Community acquisition of goods in the State in the course or furtherance of business he shall be [an accountable person]² and shall be accountable for and liable to pay the tax chargeable.

(b) Subject to subsection (2), and notwithstanding paragraph (a), a person for whose intra-Community acquisitions of goods (being goods other than new means of transport or goods subject to a duty of excise) the total consideration for which has not exceeded and is not likely to exceed [€41,000]³ in any continuous period of 12 months shall not, unless he otherwise elects and then only during the period for which such election has effect, be [an accountable person]²:

Provided that where the provisions of subsection (1) apply to that person, this paragraph shall not apply unless the provisions of subsection (3) also apply to him.

(c) A person who is [an accountable person]² by virtue of this subsection and who is a person referred to in paragraph (a) or (b) of subsection (3) shall be deemed to be [an accountable person]² only in respect of–

(i) intra-Community acquisitions of goods which are made by him, and

(ii) any services of the kind referred to in subsection (2) which are received by him:

Provided that a person may elect that this paragraph shall not apply to him.

(d) A person who is [an accountable person]² by virtue of this subsection and who is a person referred to in subsection (3A) shall be deemed to be [an accountable person]² only in respect of–

(i)   intra-Community acquisitions of goods which are made by him,

(ii)   racehorse training services which are supplied by him, and

(iii)   any services of the kind referred to in subsection (2) which are received by him:

Provided that a person may elect that this paragraph shall not apply to him.

(e)   For the purposes of this subsection, where an intra-Community acquisition is effected in the State by-

(i)   a Department of State or local authority,

(ii)   a body established by statute, or

(iii)   a person for the purpose of any activity [specified in the First Schedule]⁴,

the acquisition shall be deemed to have been effected in the course or furtherance of business.]⁵

a 194   [(f)   Where a person not established in the State supplies goods in the State which are installed or assembled, with or without a trial run, by or on behalf of that person, and where the recipient of the supply of those goods is—

(i)   a taxable person,

(ii)   a Department of State or local authority,

(iii)   a body established by statute,

[...]⁶

then that recipient shall in relation to that supply of those goods be [an accountable person or be deemed to be an accountable person]⁷ and shall be liable to pay the tax chargeable as if that recipient supplied those goods in the course or furtherance of business.]⁸

a 195   [(g)   [Where a person]⁹ not established in the State supplies gas through the natural gas distribution system, or electricity, to a recipient in the State and where such recipient is—

(i)   a taxable person,

(ii)   a Department of State or local authority,

(iii)   a body established by statute, or

[...]¹⁰

then that recipient shall in relation to that supply be [an accountable person or be deemed to be an accountable person][9] and shall be liable to pay the tax chargeable as if that recipient supplied those goods in the course or furtherance of business.][11]

[(1B) (a) This subsection and sections 12(1)(vc) and 17(1C) shall be construed together with Chapter 2 of Part 18 of the Taxes Consolidation Act, 1997.

(b) With effect from 1 September 2008 where a principal **[to whom section 531(1) of the Taxes Consolidation Act 1997 applies]**[12], other than a principal to whom subparagraphs (ii) or (iii) of section 531(1)(b) of the Taxes Consolidation Act 1997 applies, receives services consisting of construction operations (as defined in paragraphs (a) to (f) of section 530(1) of that Act) from a subcontractor, then that principal shall in relation to that supply be an accountable person or deemed to be an accountable person and shall be liable to pay the tax chargeable as if that principal supplied those services in the course or furtherance of business and the subcontractor shall not be accountable for or liable to pay the said tax in respect of such supplies.

(c) This subsection does not apply to services in respect of which the supplier issued or was required to issue an invoice in accordance with section 17 prior to 1 September 2008.][13]

a 196 [(2) (a) Where by virtue of [subparagraph (ii), (iii) [, (iiia)][14] or (iv) of paragraph (e), or paragraph (f), of subsection (6) of section 5][15] a taxable service that, apart from that provision, would be treated as supplied abroad, is deemed to be supplied in the State, the person who receives the service shall, in relation thereto, be [an accountable person][2] and be liable to pay the tax charged as if he had himself supplied the service for consideration in the course or furtherance of his business.][16]

[(aa) Where a person not established in the State supplies a cultural, artistic, entertainment or similar service in the State, then any person, other than a person acting in a private capacity, who receives that service shall—

(i) in relation to it, be [an accountable person][2] or be deemed to be [an accountable person][2], and

(ii) be liable to pay the tax chargeable as if [that accountable person][2] had in fact supplied the service for consideration in the course or furtherance of business;

but where that service is commissioned or procured by a promoter, agent or other person not being a person acting in a private capacity, then that promoter, agent or person shall be deemed to be the person who receives the service.

[...][17]][18]

[(b)   A person who is [an accountable person][2] by virtue of this subsection and who is a person referred to in paragraph (a) or (b) of subsection (3) shall be deemed to be [an accountable person][2] only in respect of–

(i)   any intra-Community acquisitions of goods which are made by him, and

(ii)   services of the kind referred to in this subsection which are received by him:

Provided that a person may elect that this paragraph shall not apply to him.

(c)   A person who is [an accountable person][2] by virtue of this subsection and who is a person referred to in subsection (3A) shall be deemed to be [an accountable person][2] only in respect of–

(i)   any intra-Community acquisitions of goods which are made by him,

(ii)   racehorse training services which are supplied by him, and

(iii)   services of the kind referred to in this subsection which are received by him:

Provided that a person may elect that this paragraph shall not apply to him.][19]

[(d)   (i)   Where a person who owns, occupies or controls land (in this subsection referred to as a '**premises provider**') allows, in the course or furtherance of business, a person not established in the State to supply goods for consideration in the course or furtherance of business (in this subsection referred to as a '**mobile trader**') on that land for a period of less than seven consecutive days, then the premises provider shall, not later than fourteen days before the day when the mobile trader is allowed to supply goods on that land, furnish to the Revenue Commissioners, at the office of the Revenue Commissioners which would normally deal with the examination of the records kept by the premises provider in accordance with section 16, the following particulars —

	(I)	the name and address of the mobile trader,

(II)   the dates on which the mobile trader intends to supply goods on the premises provider's land,

(III)   the address of the land referred to in clause (II), and

(IV)   any other information as may be specified in regulations.

(ii)   Where a premises provider allows, in the course or furtherance of business, a promoter not established in the State to supply on the premises provider's land a cultural, artistic, entertainment or similar service which in accordance with section (2)(aa) is deemed to be supplied by that promoter, then the premises provider shall, not later than fourteen days before such service is scheduled to begin, furnish to the Revenue Commissioners, at the office of the Revenue Commissioners which would normally deal with the examination of the records kept by the premises provider in accordance with section 16, the following particulars—

(I)   the name and address of the promoter,

(II)   details, including the dates, duration and venue, of the event or performance commissioned or procured by the promoter in the provision of that service, and

(III)   any other information as may be specified in regulations.

(iii)   Where a premises provider fails to provide to the Revenue Commissioners true and correct particulars as required in accordance with subparagraph (i) or (ii), then the Revenue Commissioners may, where it appears necessary to them to do so for the protection of the revenue, make such premises provider jointly and severally liable with a mobile trader or promoter, as the case may be, for the tax chargeable in respect of supplies made by that mobile trader or promoter on the premises provider's land, and in those circumstances the Revenue Commissioners shall notify the premises provider in writing accordingly.

(iv)   A premises provider who has been notified in accordance with subparagraph (iii) shall be deemed to be [an accountable person][2] and shall be liable to pay the tax referred to in that subparagraph as if it were tax due in accordance with section 19 by the premises provider for the taxable period within which the supplies are made by the mobile trader or promoter, but the premises provider shall not be liable to pay tax referred to in subparagraph (iii) which the Revenue Commissioners are satisfied was accounted for by a mobile trader or promoter.][20]

a 13   (2A)   (a)   The Minister may, following such consultations as he may deem appropriate, by order provide that the State and every local authority shall [be accountable persons][2] with respect to specified categories of supplies made by them of goods or services and, accordingly, during the continuance in force of any such order but not otherwise, the State and every local authority shall be accountable for and liable to pay tax in respect of any such supplies made by them as if the supplies had been made in the course of business.

[Provided that, where supplies of the kind referred to in, subject to subsection (3E), paragraph (xxiii) of the First Schedule or in paragraph (viic) of the Sixth Schedule are provided by the State or by a local authority, an order under this subsection shall be deemed to have been made in respect of such supplies by the State or by the local authority.][21]

(b)   The Minister may by order amend or revoke an order under this subsection, including an order under this paragraph.

(c)   An order under this subsection shall be laid before Dáil Éireann as soon as may be after it is made and, if a resolution annulling the order is passed by Dáil Éireann within the next twenty-one days on which Dáil Éireann has sat after the order is laid before it, the order shall be annulled accordingly, but without prejudice to the validity of anything previously done thereunder.

a 9(2)   [(2B)   (a)   Where a person is [an accountable person][2] only because of an intra-Community acquisition of a new means of transport, then the person shall not, unless he so elects, be [an accountable person][2] for any purpose of this Act with the exception of subsection (4) of section 19.

(b)   Where

(i)   a person is [an accountable person]² only because of an intra-Community acquisition of excisable products, and

(ii)   by virtue of this acquisition, and in accordance with Chapter II of Part II of the Finance Act, 1992, and any other enactment which is to be construed together with that Chapter, the duty of excise on those products is payable in the State,

the person shall not, unless he so elects, be [an accountable person]² for any purpose of the Act with the exception of subsection (5) of section 19.]²²

a 272, a 281,
a 282, a 283,
a 284, a 288

[(3)   Subject to subsections (1A) and (2), and notwithstanding the provisions of subsection (1)]²³, the following persons shall not, unless they otherwise elect and then only during the period for which such election has effect, [be accountable persons]²-

a 296

[(a)   a farmer, for whose supply in any continuous period of twelve months of-

(i)   agricultural services, other than insemination services, stock-minding or stock-rearing, the total consideration has not exceeded and is not likely to exceed [€37,500]²⁴, or

[(ia)   goods being [bovine]²⁵ semen, the total consideration has not exceeded and is not likely to exceed [€75,000]²⁶ and, in calculating that total consideration, supplies of [bovine]²⁵ semen to⁻

(I)   any other farmer licensed as an artificial insemination centre in accordance with the provisions of the Live Stock (Artificial Insemination) Act, 1947, or

(II)   [an accountable person]² over whom that farmer exercises control,

shall be disregarded, or]²⁷

(ii)   goods of the type specified in paragraph (xia) of the Sixth Schedule to persons who are not engaged in supplying those goods in the course or furtherance of business, the total consideration has not exceeded and is not likely to exceed [€75,000]²⁶, or

(iii)   [services specified in subparagraph (i) and either or both of goods of the type specified in subparagraph (ia) and goods of the type specified in subparagraph (ii) supplied in the circumstances set out in that subparagraph]²⁸, the total consideration has not exceeded and is not likely to exceed [€37,500][24] [or][29]

[(iv)   goods of the type specified in subparagraph (ia) and goods of the type specified in sub-paragraph (ii) supplied in the circumstances set out in that subparagraph, the total consideration has not exceeded and is not likely to exceed [€75,000][26],][30],31

(b)   a person whose supplies of taxable goods or services consist exclusively of-

(i)   supplies [to accountable persons][2] and persons to whom section 13(3) applies of fish (not being at a stage of processing further than that of being gutted, salted and frozen) which he has caught in the course of a sea-fishing business, or

(ii)   supplies of the kind specified in subparagraph (i) and of either or both of the following, that is to say:

(I)   supplies of machinery, plant or equipment which have been used by him in the course of a sea-fishing business, and

[(II)   supplies of other goods and services the total consideration for which is such that such person would not, because of the provisions of paragraph (c) or (e), [be an accountable person][2] if such supplies were the only supplies made by such person,][32

(c)   (i)   subject to subparagraph (ii), a person for whose supply of taxable goods (other than supplies of the kind specified in section 3(6)(d)(i)) and services the total consideration has not exceeded and is not likely to exceed [€75,000][26] in any continuous period of 12 months,

(ii)   subparagraph (i) shall apply if, but only if, not less than 90 per cent. of the total consideration referred to therein is derived from the supply of taxable goods (not being goods chargeable at any of the rates specified in [paragraphs (a), (c) and (d)][33] of subsection (1) of section 11 which were produced or manufactured by him wholly or mainly from materials chargeable at the rate specified in paragraph (b) of that subsection)'

(d)   [...][34

a 281

a 281

(e)   a person, other than a person to whom paragraph (a), (b) or (c) applies, for whose supply of taxable goods and services the total consideration has not exceeded and is not likely to exceed [€37,5000][24] in any continuous period of twelve months:

Provided that-

(i)   where in the case of two or more persons one of whom exercises control over one or more of the other persons, supplies of goods of the same class or of services of the same nature are made by two or more of those persons, the total of the consideration relating to the said supplies shall, for the purposes of the application of paragraphs (c) and (e) in relation to each of the persons aforesaid who made the said supplies be treated as if all of the supplies in question had been made by each of the last-mentioned persons;

[(ia)   where a farmer supplies services or goods of the kind specified in paragraph (a)(i)[, (a)(ia)][35] or (a)(ii), subparagraph (i) of this proviso shall be deemed to apply to those supplies, notwithstanding that the provisions of that subparagraph do not otherwise apply to supplies by a farmer;][36]

[(ii)   the provisions of this subsection shall not apply to a supply of the kind referred to in subsection (2).][37]][38]

[(3A)   Where a person who supplies services consisting of the training of horses for racing, the consideration for which has exceeded [€37,500][24] in any continuous period of 12 months, would, but for the supply of such services, be a farmer, he shall be deemed to be [an accountable person][2] only in respect of the supply of those services [and any intra-Community acquisitions of goods made by him and any services of the kind referred to in subsection (2) received by him][39] and, in the absence of an election, shall, in relation to the supply of any of the goods and services specified in paragraph (a) and subparagraphs (i) and (iii) of paragraph (b) of the definition of **'farmer'** in subsection (9), be deemed not to be [an accountable person][2].][40]

[(3B)   In this section 'control', in relation to a body corporate, means the power of a person to secure, by means of the holding of shares or the possession of voting power in or in relation to that or any other body corporate, or by virtue of any powers conferred by the articles of association or other document regulating that or any other body corporate, that the affairs of the first-mentioned body corporate are conducted in accordance with the wishes of that person, and, in relation to a partnership, means the right to a share of more than one-half of the assets, or of more than one-half of the income, of the partnership.][41]

[(3C) (a) The licensee of any premises (being premises in respect of which a licence for the sale of intoxicating liquor either on or off those premises was granted) shall be deemed to be the promoter of any dance held, during the subsistence of that licence, on those premises and shall be deemed to have received the total money, excluding tax, paid by those admitted to the dance together with any other consideration received or receivable in connection with the dance.

(b) For the purposes of this subsection 'licensee' means-

(i) where the licence is held by the nominee of a body corporate, the body corporate, and

(ii) in any other case, the holder of the licence.][42]

[(3D) (a) The provisions of paragraphs (b), (c) and (e) of subsection (3) shall not apply to a person who is not established in the State.

a 141 (b) A person who is not established in the State shall, unless he opts to register in accordance with section 9, be deemed not to have made an intra-Community acquisition or a supply of those goods in the State where the only supplies by him in the State are in the circumstances set out in section 3(8).][43]

a 13 [(3E) (a) Notwithstanding the provisions of section 6(1) and of subsection (1), and subject to the provisions of subsection (3), where-

(i) a person supplies services which are exempt in accordance with section 6 and paragraph (xxiii) of the First Schedule, or

(ii) the State or a local authority supplies services of the kind referred to in paragraph (xxiii) of the First Schedule,

then an authorised officer of the Revenue Commissioners shall-

(I) where such officer is satisfied that such supply of such services has created or is likely to create a distortion of competition such as to place at a disadvantage a commercial enterprise which is [an accountable person][2] supplying similar-type services, or

(II)   where such officer is satisfied that such supply of such services is managed or administered by or on behalf of another person who has a direct or indirect beneficial interest, either directly or through an intermediary, in the supply of such services,

make a determination in relation to some or all of such supplies as specified in that determination deeming-

(A)   such person, the State or such local authority to be supplying such supplies as specified in that determination in the course or furtherance of business,

(B)   such person, the State or such local authority to be [an accountable person][2] in relation to the provision of such supplies as specified in that determination, and

(C)   such supplies as specified in that determination to be taxable supplies to which the rate specified in section 11(1)(d) refers.

(b)   Where a determination is made under paragraph (a), the Revenue Commissioners shall, as soon as may be after the making thereof, issue a notice in writing of that determination to the party concerned, and such determination shall have effect from such date as may be specified in the notice of that determination:

Provided that such determination shall have effect no sooner than the start of the next taxable period following that in which the notice issued.

(c)   Where an authorised officer is satisfied that the conditions that gave rise to the making of a determination under paragraph (a) no longer apply, that officer shall cancel that determination by notice in writing to the party concerned and that cancellation shall have effect from the start of the next taxable period following that in which the notice issued.

(d)   In this subsection 'authorised officer' means an officer of the Revenue Commissioners authorised by them in writing for the purposes of this subsection.][44]

[(4)   Where, by virtue of subsection (3) or (6), a person has not been [an accountable person]² and a change of circumstances occurs from which it becomes clear that he is likely to become [an accountable person]², he shall be deemed, for the purposes of this Act, to be [an accountable person]² from the beginning of the taxable period commencing next after such change.]⁴⁵

(5)   Provision may be made by regulation for the cancellation, at the request of a person, of an election made by him under this section and for the payment by him to the Revenue Commissioners of such a sum as a condition of cancellation as when added to the net total amount of tax (if any) paid by him in accordance with section 19 in relation to the [supply of [goods or services, other than services of the kind referred to in paragraph (xiii) of the Sixth Schedule,]⁴⁶]⁴⁷ by him in the period for which the election had effect is equal to [the sum of]⁴⁸ the amount of tax repaid to him during such period in respect of tax borne or paid in relation to the [supply of [goods or services, other than services of the kind referred to in paragraph (xiii) of the Sixth Schedule,]⁴⁹]⁵⁰ [and the tax deductible under section 12 in respect of the intra-Community acquisitions made by him during such period.]⁵¹

[(5A)   (a)   Notwithstanding subsection (5), provision may be made by regulation for the cancellation, by the request of a person who supplies services of the kind referred to in paragraph (xiii) of the Sixth Schedule, of an election made by such person under this section and for the payment by such person to the Revenue Commissioners, in addition to any amount payable in accordance with subsection (5), of such an amount (hereafter referred to in this subsection as the 'cancellation amount'), as shall be determined in accordance with paragraph (b), as a condition of cancellation and the cancellation amount shall be payable as if it were tax due in accordance with section 19 for the taxable period in which the cancellation comes into effect.

(b)   (i)   Where the person referred to in paragraph (a)-

(I)   was entitled to deduct tax in accordance with section 12 in respect of the acquisition, purchase or development of immovable goods used by that person in the course of a supply of services of a kind referred to in paragraph (xiii) of the Sixth Schedule, or

(II)   would be entitled to deduct tax in accordance with section 12 in respect of the acquisition, as a result of a transfer to that person, of immovable goods used by that person in the course of a supply of services of a kind referred to in paragraph (xiii) of the Sixth Schedule, if that tax had been chargeable but for the application of the provisions of section 3(5)(b)(iii) on that transfer,

then, in respect of each such acquisition, purchase or development, an amount (hereafter referred to in this subsection as the '**adjustment amount**') shall be calculated in accordance with subparagraph (ii) and the cancellation amount shall be the sum of the adjustment amounts so calculated or, if there is only one such adjustment amount, that amount: but if there is no adjustment amount, the cancellation amount is nil.

(ii) The adjustment amount shall be determined by the formula

$$\frac{A \times (10 - B)}{10}$$

where-

A   is-

(I) the amount of tax deductible in respect of the said acquisition, purchase or development of the said immovable goods, or

(II) the amount of tax that would be deductible in respect of the said acquisition of the said immovable goods if the provisions of section 3(5)(b)(iii) had not applied to the transfer of those immovable goods, and

B   is the number of full years for which the said goods were used by the person in the course of the supply of services of a kind referred to in paragraph (xiii) of the Sixth Schedule: but if the said number of full years is in excess of 10, such adjustment amount shall be deemed to be nil.

(c) For the purposes of paragraph (b) a full year shall be any continuous period of 12 months.][52]

[(d) **This subsection does not apply to immovable goods acquired or developed on or after 1 July 2008.**][12]

[(6) [An accountable person][2], other than a person to whom subsection (5) [or subsection (5A)][53] applies, may, in accordance with regulations, be treated, for the purposes of this Act, as a person who is not [an accountable person][2] if the Revenue Commissioners are satisfied that, in the absence of an election

under subsection (3), he would not be [an accountable person]².]⁵⁴

[(7)   Where any goods or services are provided by a club or other similar organisation in respect of a payment of money by any of its members, then, for the purposes of this Act, the provision of the goods or services shall be deemed to be a supply by the club or other organisation of the goods or services (as the case may be) in the course or furtherance of a business carried on by it and the money shall be deemed to be consideration for the supply.]⁵⁵

a 11   [(8)   (a)   Where the Revenue Commissioners are satisfied that two or more persons [established in the State [, at least one of which is a taxable person,]⁵⁶]⁵⁷ are closely bound by financial, economic and organisational links and [where it seems necessary or appropriate to them for the purpose of efficient and effective administration, including collection, of the tax]⁵⁸ to do so then, [for the purpose of this Act, the said Commissioners may, whether following an application on behalf of those persons or otherwise]⁵⁹ —

[(i)   by notice in writing to each of those persons deem them to be a single taxable person, referred to in this section as a 'group' and the persons so notified shall then be regarded as being in the group for as long as this paragrah applies to them, but the provisions of section 9 shall apply in respect of each of the members of the group, and-

(I)   one of those persons, who shall be notified accordingly by the Commissioners, shall be responsible for complying with the provisions of this Act in respect of the group, and

(II)   all rights and obligations arising under this Act in respect of the transactions of the group shall be determined accordingly, and,]⁶⁰

(ii)   [make each person in the group]⁶¹ jointly and severally liable to comply with all the provisions of this Act and regulations (including the provisions requiring the payment of tax) that apply to each of those persons and subject to the penalties under this Act to which they would be subject if each such person was liable to pay to the Revenue Commissioners the whole of the tax chargeable, apart from regulations under this subsection, in respect of each such person:

Provided that this subsection shall not apply in the case of:

(I)   the supply of immovable goods by any such person to any other such person, or

[(IA)   the requirement to issue an invoice or other document, in accordance with section 17, in respect of supplies to persons other than supplies between persons who are jointly and severally liable to comply with the provisions of this Act in accordance with subparagraph (ii), or

(IB)   the requirement to furnish a statement in accordance with section 19A, or][62]

(II)   the transfer of ownership of goods specified in section 3(5)(b)(iii) from any such person to any other such person, except where, apart from the provisions of this subsection, each of the persons whose activities are deemed to be carried on by that one person is [an accountable person][2].

(b)   The Revenue Commissioners may by notice in writing to each of the persons whose activities are, by virtue of a notification issued in accordance with paragraph (a)(i), deemed to be carried on by one of those persons, and as on and from the date specified in the notice (which date shall not be earlier than the date of issue of the notice) cancel the notification under the said paragraph; and as on and from the date specified in the said notice the provisions of the Act and regulations shall apply to all the persons as aforesaid as if a notification under the said paragraph had not been issued, but without prejudice to the liability of any of the persons for tax or penalties in respect of anything done or not done during the period for which the said notification was in force.

[...][63][64]

[(d)   Where a person in a group (in this subsection referred to as the 'landlord') having acquired an interest in, or developed, immovable goods to which section 4 applies, whether such acquisition or development occurred before or after the landlord became a person in the group, subsequently surrenders possession of those immovable goods, or any part of them, to another person in the group (in this subsection referred to as the 'occupant') where the surrender of possession if it were to a person not in the group would not constitute a supply of immovable goods in accordance with section 4, and either the landlord or the occupant subsequently ceases to be a person in the group (in this subsection referred to as a 'cessation') then, if that landlord **[has not exercised the landlord's option to tax in accordance with section 7A in respect of the letting of those immovable goods at the time of the cessation or]**[12] does not have a waiver of his or her right to exemption from tax in accordance with section 7 still in effect at the time of the cessation —

(i)   the surrender of possession, or

(ii)   if that landlord surrendered possession of those immovable goods more than once to another person in the group, the first such surrender of possession,

shall be deemed to occur when that first such cessation takes place, but if such a landlord's waiver of his or her right to exemption from tax in accordance with section 7 has been cancelled before a surrender of possession of immovable goods to another person in the group ends, that surrender of possession shall be deemed to take place on the date of the said first such cessation.][65]

[(e)   The Revenue Commissioners may make regulations as seem to them to be necessary for the purposes of this subsection.][66]

a 295   [(9)   In this Act-

a 295(1)   **'agricultural produce'** means, in relation to a farmer, goods, other than […][67] live greyhounds, produced by him in the course of an Annex A activity;

'agricultural service' means, in relation to a farmer, any Annex B service supplied by him using his own labour or that of his employees or effected by means of machinery, plant or other equipment normally used for the purposes of an Annex A activity carried on by him;

'Annex A activity' means any activity of a description specified in [Article 295(1) and Annex VII of Council Directive No. 2006/112/EC of 28 November 2006][68]

'Annex B service' means any service of a description specified in [Article 295(1) and Annex VIII of the said Council Directive][68]

[**'farmer'** means a person who engages in at least one Annex A activity and-

(a)   whose supplies consist exclusively of either or both of the following, that is to say:

(i)   supplies of agricultural produce, or

(ii)   supplies of agricultural services, or

(b)   whose supplies consist exclusively of either or both of the supplies specified in paragraph (a) and of one or more of the following, that is to say:

(i)   supplies of machinery, plant or equipment which has been used by him for the purposes of an Annex A activity,

(ii)   supplies of services consisting of the training of horses for racing the total consideration for which has not exceeded and is not likely to exceed [€37,500][24] in any continuous period of 12 months, or

[(iii)   supplies of goods and services other than those referred to in subparagraphs (i) and (ii) or paragraph (a), the total consideration for which is such that such person would not, because of the provisions of paragraph (c) or (e) of subsection (3), be [an accountable person][2] if such supplies were the only supplies made by such person.][69]][70]][71]

Amendments

1   Ss(1) substituted by FA08 s92(a), (w.e.f. 1 July 2008).

2   Substituted by FA08 s109 & Sch 4, (w.e.f. 1 July 2008).

3   Substituted by FA01 s240(4) & part 4, Sch.5 (w.e.f. 1 January 2002), previously IR£32,000.

4   Substituted by FA94 s94(a), (w.e.f. 23 May 1994).

5   Ss(1A) substituted by FA93 s85(a).

6   Deleted by FA08 s92(b)(i), (w.e.f. 1 July 2008).

7   Substituted by FA08 s92(b)(ii), (w.e.f. 1 July 2008).

8   Ss(1A)(f) inserted by FA03 s118(b), (w.e.f. 28 March 2003).

9   Substituted by FA08 s92(c), (w.e.f. 1 July 2008).

10 Deleted by FA08 s92(c)(ii), (w.e.f. 1 July 2008).

11 Ss(1A)(g) inserted by FA04 s58(b), (w.e.f. 1 January 2005).

12 Inserted by F(No. 2)A 08 s 99 & Sch 6, (w.e.f. 24 December 2008).

13 Ss(1B) inserted by FA08 s92(d), (w.e.f. 13 March 2008)

14 Inserted by FA01 s184, (w.e.f. 21 March 2001).

15 Substituted by FA92 s170(2)(c), (w.e.f. 1 January 1993).

16 Ss(2)(a) transposed by FA93 s85(b) from subs (2), (w.e.f. 1 March 1979).

17 Ss(2)(ab) deleted by FA08 s141 & Sch 8(3)(c), (w.e.f. 13 March 2008).

18 Inserted by FA02 s101(b)(i), (w.e.f. 25 March 2002).

19 Ss(2)(b) -(c) inserted by FA93 s85(b)(ii).

20 Inserted by FA02 s101(b)(ii), (w.e.f. 25 March 2002).

21 Inserted by FA95 s124(a), (w.e.f. 1 January 1996).

22 Ss(2B) substituted by EC(VAT)R r7(b), (w.e.f. 1 January 1993).

23 Substituted by FA93 s85(c)(i).

24 Substituted by FA08 s92(e), (w.e.f. 1 May 2008).

25 Substituted by FA99 s123, (w.e.f. 25 March 1999).

26 Substituted by FA08 s92(e), (w.e.f. 1 May 2008).

27 Ss(3)(a)(ia) inserted by FA98 s108(a)(i), (w.e.f. 1 July 1998).

28 Substituted by FA98 s108(a)(ii), (w.e.f. 1 July 1998).

29 Inserted by FA98 s108(a)(iii), (w.e.f. 1 July 1998).

30 Ss(3)(a)(iv) inserted by FA98 s108(a)(iv), (w.e.f. 1 July 1998).

31 Ss(3)(a) substituted by FA97 s101(a), (w.e.f. 1 September 1997).
32 Ss(3)(b)(ii)(II) substituted by FA94 s94(b)(ii), (w.e.f. 1 July 1994).
33 Substituted by FA93 s85(c)(ii), (w.e.f. 1 March 1993).
34 Deleted by FA93 s85(c)(iii).
35 Inserted by FA98 s108(b), (w.e.f. 1 July 1998).
36 Inserted by FA97 s101(b), (w.e.f. 1 September 1997).
37 Substituted by FA93 s85(c)(iv).
38 Ss(3) substituted by FA92 s170(2)(e), (w.e.f. 1 January 1993).
39 Inserted by FA93 s85(d).
40 Ss(3A) inserted by FA82 s77, (w.e.f. 1 September 1982).
41 Ss(3B) inserted by FA84 s86, (w.e.f. 23 May 1984).
42 Ss(3C) inserted by FA92 s170(1)(b), (w.e.f. 28 May 1992).
43 Ss(3D) inserted by EC(VAT)R 1992 r7(c), (w.e.f. 1 January 1993).
44 Ss(3E) inserted by FA95 s124(b), (w.e.f. 1 January 1996).
45 Ss(4) substituted by F(No. 2)A 81 s11, (w.e.f. 20 November 1981).
46 Substituted by FA00 s110(a)(i), (w.e.f. 23 March 2000).
47 Substituted by VATA78 s30(2), (w.e.f. 1 March 1979).
48 Inserted by FA93 s85(e)(i), (w.e.f. 17 June 1993).
49 Substituted by FA00 s110(a)(ii), (w.e.f. 23 March 2000).
50 Substituted by VATA78 s30(2), (w.e.f. 1 March 1979).
51 Inserted by FA93 s85(e)(ii), (w.e.f. 17 June 1993).
52 Ss5A inserted by FA00 s110(b), (w.e.f. 23 March 2000).
53 Inserted by FA00 s110(c), (w.e.f. 23 March 2000).
54 Ss(6) substituted by FA92 s170(2)(f), (w.e.f. 28 May 1992).
55 Ss(7) substituted by VAT Amend. A78 s6, (w.e.f. 1 March 1979).
56 Inserted by FA08 s93(f), (w.e.f. 1 July 2008).
57 Substituted by FA07 s79(b)(i)(I), (w.e.f. 2 April 2007).
58 Substituted by FA06 s94(b), (w.e.f. 31 March 2006).
59 Substituted by FA07 s79(b)(i)(II), (w.e.f. 2 April 2007).
60 Substituted by FA07 s79(b)(i)(III), (w.e.f. 2 April 2007).
61 Substituted by FA07 s79(b)(i)(IV), (w.e.f. 2 April 2007).
62 Inserted by EC(VAT)R r7(d), (w.e.f. 1 January 1993).
63 Deleted by FA07 s79(b)(ii), (w.e.f. 2 April 2007).
64 Ss(8) substituted by FA91 s79, (w.e.f. 29 May 1991).
65 Inserted by FA02 s101(c)(ii), (w.e.f. 25 March 2002).
66 Inserted by FA07 s79(b)(iii) (w.e.f. 2 April 2007).
67 Deleted by FA90 s101, (w.e.f. 1 January 1991).
68 Substituted by FA07 s 97 & Sch 3 (w.e.f. 1 January 2007).
69 Ss(3)(b)(iii) substituted by FA94 s94(d)(ii), (w.e.f. 1 July 1994).
70 Definition of 'farmer' substituted by FA82 s77, (w.e.f. 1 September 1982).
71 Ss(9) substituted by VAT Amend. A78 s6, (w.e.f. 1 March 1979).

Regulations and Orders

Election	1979 SI No. 63	Value Added Tax Regulations, 1979
Election to be a taxable person and cancellation of such election	2006 SI No. 548	Value-Added Tax Regulations 2006
Garden Centres	1997 SI No. 313	Finance Act 1997 (Commencement of Sections 101 and 113) Order 1997
Group Registration	1979 SI No. 63	Value Added Tax Regulations, 1979
Group Registration	2006 SI No. 548	Value-Added Tax Regulations 2006

Revenue e-Briefs

Revenue e-Brief No. 45/2008: VAT – Reverse charge on construction services – Notifications to Principal contractors and subcontractors with a direct debit facility

Revenue e-Brief No. 30/2008: VAT – Reverse charge on construction services – Notifications to Principal contractors and subcontractors

Revenue e-Brief No. 45/2008: VAT – Reverse charge on construction services – New rules for Principal contractors and subcontractors from 1 September 2008

Revenue e-Brief No. 13/2007: Value Added Tax – Changes from 1 March 2007

Revenue Statements of Practice and Information Leaflets

Agricultural Services: Information Leaflet dated December 2008

Dances, VAT on: Information Leaflet dated December 2008

Distance Sales in the Single Market: Information Leaflet dated October 2008

Exempt Persons acquiring Goods from other EU Member States: SP-VAT/13/92

Exempt Persons acquiring Goods from other EU Member States: Information Leaflet No. 13/01

Golf and other sporting activities: Information Leaflet dated October 2008

Horticultural Retailers: Information Leaflet dated December 2008

Intra-Community Acquisition of Goods by the State, Local Authorities etc: SP-VAT/11/92 (replaced by Information Leaflet No. 11/01)

Live Horses: SP-VAT/3/90

Milk Production Partnerships, VAT issues for: Information Leaflet No. 1/04

Promotion of and admission to live theatrical and musical events (including performances by non-established performers, VAT treatment of: Information Leaflet dated December 2008

Racehorse Trainers, Value Added Tax: Information Leaflet dated 1985

Revenue Powers: SP-GEN/1/94

Revenue Powers: SP-GEN/1/99

Sports Facilities: Information Leaflet dated March 2007

Case law

Ampliscientifica Srl and Amplifin SpA v Ministero dell' Economia e delle Finanze, Agenzia delle Entrate	C162/07	Taxable persons/Parent companies and subsidiaries
Apple & Pear Development Council v Customs and Excise	C102/86	Taxable person/Trade Association/voluntary levy
Ayuntamiento de Sevilla v Recaudadores de Tributos de la Zonas Primera & Segunda	C202/90	Taxable persons
Banque Bruxelles Lambert SA v Belgian State	C8/03	Place of supply/Concept of taxable person
BUPA Hospitals Ltd, Goldsborough Developments Ltd v Commissioners of Customs & Excise	C419/02	Payment on account/Chargeable Event/Taxable person/Entitlement to VAT recovery
Camara Municipal do Porto v Fazenda Publica	C446/98	State run car parking
Commune di Carpaneto Piacentino and others v Ufficio Provinciale Imposta sul Valore Aggiunto di Piacenza	C4/89	Taxable Person/Government bodies
Commune di Rivergaro and others v Ufficio Provinciale Imposta sul Valore Aggiunto di Piacenza	C129/88	Taxable Person/Government bodies
Dimosio, Elliniko and Karageorgou, Maria, Petrova, Katina, and Vlachos, Loukas	C78/02, C79/02 and C80/02	Taxable Person - Erroneous charge of VAT
Enkler, Renate v Finanzamt Hamburg	C230/94	Taxable person
FCE Bank plc v Ministero dell' Ecomomia e delle Finanze	C210/04	Concept of taxable person/Fixed establishment
Federation of Technological Industries and Others v Customs & Excise	C384/04	Anti-avoidance measures/Persons liable to pay tax
Feuerbestattungsverein Halle eV v Finanzamt Eisleben	C430/04	Private taxable person in competition with public authority
Halifax plc, Leeds Permanent Development Services Ltd, County Wide property Investments Ltd v Commissioners of Customs& Excise	C255/02	Economic Activity/Supplies/Abusive practice
Harnas and Helm CV v Staatssecretaris van Financien	C80/95	Taxable Person
Hong Kong Trade Development Council v Staatssecretaris van Financien	C89/81	Government Body/Taxable Person
Hutchison 3G UK Ltd and others v Commissioners of Customs and Excise	C369/04	Definition of 'economic activity'/Allocation of rights making it possible to use a defined part of the radio-frequency spectrum reserved for telecommunications services
Isle of Wight and Others v The Commissioners for Her Majesty's Revenue and Customs	C288/07	Activities engaged in by bodies governed by public law/Provision of off-street car-parking

Kollektivavtalsstiftelsen TRR Trygghetsrådet v Statteverket	C291/07	Supplies of services carried out free of charge by a taxable person for purposes other than those of his business
Landesanstalt für Landwirtschaft v Franz Götz	C408/06	Bodies governed by public law/ Transactions of agricultural intervention agencies and staff shops/Significant distortions of competition
Optigen Ltd, Fulcrum Electronics Ltd, Bond House Systems Ltd v Commissioners of Customs & Excise	C354/03 C355/03 C484/03	Economic activity/Taxable person/ Deduction/Carousel fraud
Polysar Investments Netherlands BV v Inspecteur der Inveorrechten en Accijnzen	C60/90	Holding Coy/Taxable Person/ Recovery of VAT
Stadt Sundern v Bundesfinanzhof Finanzamt Arnsberg	C43/04	Concept of 'agricultural service'
T-Mobile Austria GmbH and others v Republik Österreich	C284/04	Definition of 'economic activity'/ Allocation of rights making it possible to use a defined part of the radio-frequency spectrum reserved for telecommunications services
Tolsma RJ v Inspecteur der Omzetbelasting Leeuwarden	C16/93	Taxable person
University of Huddersfield High Education Corporation v Commissioners of Customs & Excise	C223/03	Economic Activity/Supplies/ Abusive practice
van der Steen, J.A. v Inspector van de Belastingdienst Utrecht-Gooi/kantoor Utrecht	C355/06	Company's activities carried out by a natural person as sole director, sole shareholder and sole member of staff
Waterschap Zeeuws Vlaanderen v Staatssecretaris van Financiën	C378/02	Public authority/Supply/Right to adjustment and deduction
Wellcome Trust Ltd v Customs and Excise	C155/94	Taxable person
Zweckverband zur Trinkwasserversorgung und Abwasserbeseitigung Torgau-Westelbein v Finanzamt Oschatz	C442/05	"Supply of water" or "water supply"

Revenue Precedents

Topic:	Property Transactions
Issue:	Company disposes of over 40 units to investors (unregistered) by way of 9,000 year leases. The investors in turn will lease to tenants with 35 year leases. (Most tenants would be registered).
Decision:	To relieve compliance costs - it was agreed that the investors would not be required to register but all VAT obligations would be looked after by the development company.
Date:	26/3/91

(withdrawn from the Revenue website in 2002)

Topic:	Property Transactions
Issue:	Company with two subsidiaries, one has the freehold reversion, the second has a long leasehold interest. The latter creates long leases to another party whilst the former carries out the redevelopment work and sells the freehold interest to a pension fund. Company with freehold reversion is treated as a taxable person as regards disposal.
Decision:	Joint venture registration allowed between the holder of the leasehold interest and the developer who holds the reversion.
Date:	5/2/90

Topic:	Property.
Issue:	Group registration and waiver of entitlement to exemption.
Decision:	The group is regarded as a single taxable entity.
Date:	13/5/96

Topic:	Group treatment.
Issue:	The conditions for group registration require members to be bound by financial, economic and organisational links.
Decision:	(a) VAT grouping allowed where the managed company is passive, and did not have any independent management capabilities.
Date:	16/11/89

(withdrawn from the Revenue website in 2002)

Topic:	Fund Management.
Issue:	Joint and Several Liability.
Decision:	The joint and several liability requirement was relaxed in group situations in IFSC provided group registration conditions were met.
Date:	1/6/91

(withdrawn from the Revenue website in 2002)

Topic:	Jockeys.
Issue:	Jockeys and Jockeys valets were officially brought into tax net from 1 Jan, 1991.
Decision:	Period of grace granted Registration deferred until 1/9/91.
Date:	27/9/91

(withdrawn from the Revenue website in 2002)

Topic:	Golf.
Issue:	VAT liability of commercial golf clubs.
Decision:	Two month period of grace granted to such golf clubs to allow them to effect registration for the first time.
Date:	2/1/96

(withdrawn from the Revenue website in 2002)

Topic:	Property Management & Jt. Expenses.
Issue:	Can a VAT-registered lessee, who holds 13A authorisation of shop and office property, obtain a deduction for VAT charged on services/goods through landlords.
Decision:	Yes, in these circumstances the landlord may register for VAT and recover the VAT suffered on the service charges on an annual basis.
Date:	16/1/98

Topic:	Group Registration.
Issue:	VAT grouping of companies linked either financially or organisationally where their business is not economically linked.
Decision:	In exceptional case a group arrangement allowed for VAT purposes on the basis of economic links even though the actual business of the companies involved were not in themselves economically linked.
Date:	20/2/98

Topic:	Insurance.
Issue:	Grouping for VAT purposes.
Decision:	Revenue accepts that there is no taxable supply of services by an overseas head office to its Irish branch within the same legal entity. Extended to services supplied by affiliate companies in a VAT group via head office based overseas for onward supply to its Irish branch. The concession does not apply to services supplied by affiliate companies via an overseas branch to an Irish head office.
Date:	1/5/91

(withdrawn from the Revenue website in 2002)

Topic:	Aircraft.
Issue:	French airline sells aircraft while it is on ground in Dublin. Are they required to register.
Decision:	No, concessionally, not required to register for VAT.
Date:	13/4/95

Topic:	Flat-Rate Addition.
Issue:	Can individuals who invest in forestry be regarded as "farmers" for VAT purposes?
Decision:	No-investment in forestry is not sufficient to deem a person to come within the meaning of the term "farmer".
Date:	14/9/87

(withdrawn from the Revenue website in 2002)

Topic:	Flat-rate addition.
Issue:	Does turf or peat extracted from own land constitute "agricultural produce".
Decision:	It was considered that for the purposes of the flat-rate addition system turf and peat should be regarded as agricultural produce. This decision was extended to gravel and stone from 10 April, 1987.
Date:	22/6/79

Topic:	Sponsorship.
Issue:	Is sponsorship of sporting activities taxable.
Decision:	No-Sport is not viewed as being carried on in the course or furtherance of business.
Date:	1/2/95

(withdrawn from the Revenue website in 2002)

Topic:	First registration.
Issue:	Whether period of grace could be granted in the requirement to register for sectors which previously had been exempt.
Decision:	A period of grace has been granted to allow the sectors concerned to register for VAT for the first time.
Date:	27/9/91

Topic:	Group registration.
Issue:	VAT grouping of fund management company.
Decision:	In the circumstances of this case and in consideration of previous decisions made concerning the criteria established in relation to group registration it was agreed to allow group registration in this case on the understanding that the managed funds have no independent management capabilities and that the fund management company accepts joint and several liability for all the funds under its control.
Date:	19/07/00

Narrative

RCT & VAT for Principals and Sub-Contractors – An Update: ITR Nov 2008 Vol 21 No. 6

Tax Briefing: Issue 69 (Reverse Charge on Construction Services – New Rules for Principal Contractors and subcontractors from 1st September 2008)

ECJ Decision on Intra-Branch Supplies: Ministero dell'Economia e delle Finanze, Agenzia delle Entrate v FCE plc.: ITR July 2006 Vol 19 No. 4

The Halifax Decision: ITR May 2006 Vol 19 No. 3

Tax Briefing: Issue 60 (VAT Implications for Waste Disposal)

Halifax, BUPA and University of Huddersfield Cases: ITR Jul 2005: Vol 18 No. 4

Tax Briefing: Issue 58 (Supply and Installation of Goods)

Tax Briefing: Issue 43 (VAT Committee Guidelines – Services Supplied by Company Directors)

Ireland's Derogations from the EU Sixth VAT Directive: ITR Sept 1999: Vol 12 No. 5.

Tax Briefing: Issue 43 (VAT Committee Guidelines – Assignment of Broadcasting Rights in Respect of International Football Matches by Organisations Established Abroad)

Tax Briefing: Issue 42 (VAT (Cancellation of Election of Regstration in respect of Sixth Schedule Accommodation) Regulations, 2000)

Tax Briefing: Issue 42 (VAT Committee Guidelines – Services provided to Public Sector Hospitals)

Foreign Firms: VAT issues arising in Ireland: ITR Jan 2000: Vol 13 No. 1.

Tax Briefing: Issue 32 (Treatment of A.I. Services and Sales of Livestock Semen)

Tax Briefing: Issue 30 (EU Supplies)

Tax Briefing: Issue 29 (Foreign Traders and Construction Contracts)

Tax Briefing: Issue 27 (Finance Act 1997 Changes: Garden Centres)

Section 9

Registration

a 213   **9.**   [(1)   The Revenue Commissioners shall set up and maintain a register of persons who may become or who [are accountable persons][4] [or who are persons who dispose of goods which pursuant to section 3(7) are deemed to be supplied by [an accountable person][4] in the course or furtherance of his business]][1]][2].

a 214   [(1A)   The Revenue Commissioners shall assign to each person registered in accordance with subsection (1) a registration number.][3]

      (2)   Every person who on the appointed day or on any day thereafter would be [an accountable person][4] if tax were chargeable with effect as on and from the appointed day shall, within the period of thirty days beginning on the appointed day or on the day thereafter on which the person first becomes [an accountable person][4] or would become such a person if tax were chargeable as aforesaid, furnish in writing to the Revenue Commissioners the particulars specified in regulations and being required for the purpose of registering such person for tax.

     [(2A)   Every person who disposes of goods which pursuant to section 3(7) are deemed to be supplied by [an accountable person][4] in the course or furtherance of his business shall, within fourteen days of such disposal, furnish in writing to the Revenue Commissioners the particulars specified in regulations as being required for the purpose of registering such person for tax.][5]

      (3)   Any person who on the appointed day was registered for the purposes of turnover tax on the basis of particulars furnished in accordance with section 49(2) of the Finance Act, 1963, shall be deemed, unless he notifies the Revenue Commissioners in writing that he does not wish to be so deemed, to have furnished the particulars required by subsection (2).

      (4)   In this section "**the appointed day**" means the day appointed by the Minister by order to be the appointed day for the purpose of this section.

Amendments

1   Inserted by FA 1983 s 80, (w.e.f. 1 September 1983).
2   Sub-section (1) substituted by VAT Amend. Act 1978 s 7, (w.e.f. 1 March 1979).
3   Sub-section (1A) inserted by FA 1992 s 171, (w.e.f. 28 May 1992).
4   Substituted by FA08 s109 & Sch 4, (w.e.f. 1 July 2008).
5   Sub-section (2A) inserted by FA 1983 s 80, (w.e.f. 1 September 1983).

Regulations and Orders

Registration	1972 SI No. 192	Valued Added Tax (Appointed Day) Order 1972
Registration	2006 SI No. 548	Value-Added Tax Regulations 2006
Regulations obligations	1993 SI No. 30	Value Added Tax (Registration) Regulations, 1993

Revenue Statements of Practice and Information Leaflets

Foreign firms doing business in Ireland, VAT treatment of: Information Leaflet dated October 2008

Case law

Breitsohl, Brigitte v Finanzamt Goslar	C400/98	Intending trader
WLD Worldwide Leather Diffusion Ltd v Revenue Commissioners	Irish (1994) ITR 165	Registration/Taxable Person

Revenue Precedents

Topic:	Registration.
Issue:	Is an Irish company acting as an agent for foreign companies obliged to register separately for transactions carried out as agent?
Decision:	In the particular circumstances registration was not required and a company acting as an agent could use its own VAT number to import and claim credit on such goods on behalf of a foreign company.
Date:	21/12/94

Narrative

Foreign Firms: VAT issues arising in Ireland: ITR Jan 2000: Vol 13 No. 1.

Section 10

Amount on which tax is chargeable

a 73, a 78 **10.** [(1) The amount on which tax is chargeable by virtue of section 2(1)(a) shall, subject to this section, be the total consideration which the person supplying goods or services becomes entitled to receive in respect of or in relation to such supply of goods or services, including all taxes, commissions, costs and charges whatsoever but not including value-added tax chargeable in respect of the supply.

a 76, a 83, a 84 [(1A) The amount on which tax is chargeable on the intra-Community acquisition of goods by virtue of section 2(1A) shall, subject to this section, be the total consideration, including all taxes, commissions, costs and charges whatsoever, but not including value-added tax chargeable, in respect of that acquisition.][1]

(2) If the consideration referred to in [subsections (1) or (1A)][2] does not consist of or does not consist wholly of an amount of money, the amount on which tax is chargeable shall be the total amount of money which might reasonably be expected to be charged if the consideration consisted entirely of an amount of money equal to the open market price:

[...][3]

(3) [...][4]

(b) If the consideration actually received in relation to the supply of any goods or services exceeds the amount which the person supplying the goods or services was entitled to receive, the amount on which tax is chargeable shall be the amount actually received, excluding tax chargeable in respect of the supply.

a 90 (c) If, in a case not coming within [subsection (3A)][5], the consideration actually received in relation to the supply of any goods or services is less than the amount on which tax is chargeable or no consideration is actually received, such relief may be given by repayment or otherwise in respect of the deficiency as may be provided by regulations.

[Provided that in any event this paragraph shall not apply in the case of the letting of immovable goods which is a taxable supply of goods in accordance with section 4.][6]

[(d) If, following the issue of an invoice by [an accountable person][7] in respect of a supply of goods or services, the person who issued the invoice allows a reduction or discount in the amount of the consideration due in respect of that supply, the relief referred to in paragraph (c) shall not be given until the person who issued the invoice issues the credit note required in accordance with the provisions of section 17(3)(b) in respect of that reduction or discount.]⁸

a 80   [(3A)   (a)   The Revenue Commissioners may, where they consider it necessary or appropriate to do so to ensure the correct collection of the tax, make a determination that the amount on which tax is chargeable on a supply of goods or services is the open market value of that supply, if they are satisfied that the actual consideration in relation to that supply is –

         (i)   lower than the open market value of that supply where the recipient of that supply has no entitlement to deduct tax under section 12, or is not entitled to deduct all of the tax chargeable on that supply or is a flat-rate farmer,

         (ii)   lower than the open market value of that supply, being an exempted activity, where the supplier engages in the course or furtherance of business in non-deductible supplies or activities as defined in section 12(4)(a), or is a flat-rate farmer, or

         (iii)   higher than the open market value where the supplier engages in the course or furtherance of business in non-deductible supplies or activities as defined in section 12(4)(a), or is a flat-rate farmer,

and that –

         (I)   the supplier and the recipient of that supply are persons connected by financial or legal ties, being persons who are party to any agreement, understanding, promise or undertaking whether express or implied and whether or not enforceable or intended to be enforceable by legal proceedings, or

         (II)   either the supplier or the recipient of that supply exercises control over the other and for this purpose **'control'** has the meaning assigned to it by section 8(3B).

     (b)   A value determined in accordance with this subsection shall be deemed to be the true value of the supply to which it applies, for all the purposes of this Act.

     (c)   The Revenue Commissioners may make regulations as seem to them to be necessary for the purposes of this subsection.

(d)   A determination under this section may be made by an inspector of taxes or such other officer as the Revenue Commissioners may authorise for this purpose.][9]

a 74   (4)   The amount on which tax is chargeable in relation to a supply of goods referred to in paragraph (d)(ii), (e) or (f) of section 3(1) or a supply of services by virtue of regulations made [for the purposes of paragraph (a) or (b) of section 5(3)][10] shall be the cost, excluding tax, of the goods to [the person supplying or acquiring the goods][11] or the cost, excluding tax, of supplying the services, as the case may be [, and the amount on which tax is chargeable in relation to a supply of services by virtue of regulations made for the purposes of section 5(3)(c) shall be the open market price of the services supplied][12].

[Provided that where the supply in question is a supply of immovable goods, (hereafter referred to in this proviso as 'appropriation'), the cost to the person making that appropriation shall include an amount equal to the amount on which tax was chargeable on the supply of those goods to that person, being the last supply of those goods to that person which preceded the appropriation.][13]

a 84   [(4A)   Where goods chargeable with a duty of excise [, other than alcohol products within the meaning of section 3B,][14] are supplied while warehoused, and before payment of the duty, to an unregistered person, the amount on which tax is chargeable in respect of the supply shall be increased by an amount equal to the amount of duty that would be payable in relation to the goods if the duty had become due at the time of the supply.][15]

a 76, a 83   [(4B)   The amount on which tax is chargeable in relation to the supply of goods referred to in section 3(1)(g) shall be the [cost of the goods to the person making the supply or, in the absence of such a cost, the cost price of similar goods in the State, and where an intra-Community acquisition occurs in the State following a supply of goods in another Member State which, if such supply was carried out in similar circumstances in the State would be a supply of goods in accordance with section 3(1)(g), then the amount on which tax is chargeable in respect of that intra-Community acquisition shall be the cost to the person making the supply in that Member State or, in the absence of a cost to that person, the cost price of similar goods in that other Member State][16].][17]

[(4C)   In the case of a supply of goods of the type referred to in section 3(1)(b), where, as part of an agreement of the kind referred to in that provision, the supplier of the goods is also supplying financial services of the kind specified in subparagraph (i)(e) of the First Schedule in respect of those goods, the amount on which tax is chargeable in respect of the supply of the goods in question shall be either-

(a)   the open market price of the goods, or

(b)   the amount of the total consideration as specified in subsection (1) which the person supplying the goods becomes entitled to receive in respect of or in relation to such supply,

whichever is the greater.][18]

[(4D)   (a)   The amount on which tax is chargeable in relation to a supply of services referred to in section 5(3B) in any taxable period shall be an amount equal to one sixth of one twentieth of the cost of the immovable goods used to provide those services, being–

       (i)   the amount on which tax was chargeable to the person making the supply in respect of that person's acquisition or development of the immovable goods referred to in section 5(3B), and

       (ii)   in the case where section 3(5)(b)(iii) applied to the acquisition of the immovable goods, the amount on which tax would have been chargeable but for the application of that section,

       adjusted to correctly reflect the proportion of the use of the goods in that period.

    (b)   The Revenue Commissioners may make regulations specifying methods which may be used–

       (i)   to identify the proportion which correctly reflects the extent to which immovable goods are used for the purposes referred to in section 5(3B), and

       (ii)   to calculate the relevant taxable amount or amounts.][19]

(5)   The amount on which tax is chargeable in relation to services for the tax chargeable on which the recipient is, by virtue of section 8(2), liable shall be the consideration for which the services were in fact supplied to him.

[(5A)   Where,

    (a)   an intra-Community acquisition is deemed to have taken place in the territory of another Member State in accordance with section 3A(2)(a),

    (b)   the intra-Community acquisition has been subject to value-added tax, referred to in [Council Directive No. 2006/112/EC of 28 November 2006][20], in that other Member State, and

    (c)   the intra-Community acquisition is also deemed to have taken place in the State, in accordance with section 3A(2)(b), then the consideration for the intra-Community acquisition to which paragraph (c) relates shall be reduced to nil.][21]

(6)   [Subject to subsection (6A), where][22] a right to receive goods or services [, other than telecommunications services,][23] for an amount stated on any token, stamp, coupon or voucher is granted for a consideration, the consideration shall be disregarded for the purposes of this Act except to the extent (if any) that it exceeds that amount.

[(6A)   Notwithstanding the provisions of subsection (6), where—

(a)   a supplier—

(i)   supplies a token, stamp, coupon or voucher, which has an amount stated on it, to a person who acquires it in the course or furtherance of business with a view to resale, and

(ii)   promises to subsequently accept that token, stamp, coupon or voucher at its face value in full or part payment of the price of goods,

and

(b)   a person who acquires that token, stamp, coupon or voucher, whether from the supplier referred to in paragraph (a) or from any other person in the course or furtherance of business, supplies it for consideration in the course or furtherance of business,

then in the case of each such supply the consideration received shall not be disregarded for the purposes of this Act and when such token, stamp, coupon or voucher is used in payment or part payment of the price of goods, the face value of it shall, for the purposes of section 10(2), be disregarded.][24]

(7)   Provision may be made by regulations for the purpose of determining the amount on which tax is chargeable in relation to one or more of the following:

(a)   supplies of goods and services to which an order under section 8(2A) applies,

(b)   supplies of stamps, coupons, tokens or vouchers when supplied as things in action (not being stamps, coupons, tokens or vouchers specified in subsection (6)),

(c)   [subject to subsection [(6A) or][25] (7A),][26] supplies of goods or services wholly or partly in exchange for stamps, coupons, tokens or vouchers of a kind specified in subsection (6) or paragraph (b),

[...][27]

and such regulations may, in the case of supplies referred to in paragraph (b), provide that the amount on which tax is chargeable shall be nil.

[(7A) (a)   Where a supplier sells a voucher to a buyer at a discount and promises to subsequently accept that voucher at its face value in full or part payment of the price of goods purchased by a customer who was not the buyer of the voucher, and who does not normally know the actual price at which the voucher was sold by the supplier, the consideration represented by the voucher shall, subject to regulations, if any, be the sum actually received by the supplier upon the sale of the voucher.

(b)   Paragraph (a) is for the purpose of giving further effect to [Article 73 of Council Directive No 2006/112/EC of 28 November 2006][20] and shall be construed accordingly.][28]

(8) (a)   Where the value of movable goods (not being goods of a kind specified in paragraph (xii) of the Second Schedule) provided under an agreement for the supply of services exceeds two-thirds of the total consideration under the agreement for the provision of those goods and the supply of the services, other than transport services in relation to them, the consideration shall be deemed to be referable solely to the supply of the goods and tax shall be charged at the appropriate rate or rates specified in section 11 on the basis of any apportionment of the total consideration made in accordance with paragraph (b).

(b)   Where goods of different kinds are provided under an agreement of the kind referred to in paragraph (a), the amount of the consideration referable to the supply of goods of each kind shall be ascertained for the purposes of that paragraph by apportioning the total consideration in proportion to the value of the goods of each kind provided.

(c)   This subsection shall also apply to an agreement for the supply of immovable goods and, accordingly, the references in paragraphs (a) and (b) to an agreement for the supply of services shall be deemed to include a reference to such an agreement.

[(d)   This subsection does not apply in respect of a supply of services to which section 8(1B) applies.][29]

(9) (a)   On the supply of immovable goods and on the supply of services consisting of the development of immovable goods, the value of any interest in the goods disposed of in connection with the supply shall be included in the consideration.

(b)   The value of any interest in immovable goods shall be the open market price of such interest.

[Provided that where a surrender or an assignment of an interest in immovable goods is a supply of immovable goods which is chargeable to tax, the open market price of such interest shall be determined as if the person who surrendered or assigned that interest were disposing of an interest in those goods which that person had created for the period between the date of the surrender or assignment and the date on which that surrendered or assigned interest would, but for its surrender or assignment, have expired.][30]

[(ba)   Subsections (a) and (b) apply in respect of transactions which take place prior to 1 July 2008.][31]

[(c)   Where the Revenue Commissioners wish to ascertain the open market [value][32] of an interest in immovable goods, they may authorise a person to inspect the immovable goods and to report to them the open market [value][32] of such interest in those goods for the purposes of this Act, and a person having custody or possession of those goods shall permit the person so authorised to inspect the goods at such reasonable times as the Revenue Commissioners consider necessary.

(d)   Where the Revenue Commissioners require a valuation to be made by a person named by them, the costs of such valuation shall be defrayed by the Commissioners.][33]

a 91   [(9A)   In relation to the tax chargeable by virtue of section 2(1)(a) or 2(1A), where an amount is expressed in a currency other than the currency of the State the exchange rate to be used shall be -

(a)   unless paragraph (b) applies, the latest selling rate recorded by the Central Bank of Ireland for the currency in question at the time the tax becomes due,

(b)   where there is an agreement with the Revenue Commissioners for a method to be used in determining the exchange rate, the exchange rate obtained using the said method:

Provided that where paragraph (b) applies the method agreed in accordance with that paragraph shall be applied for all transactions where an amount is expressed in a currency other than that of the State until the agreement to use such method is withdrawn by the Revenue Commissioners.][34]

[(10)   In this section-

'**interest**', in relation to immovable goods, and '**disposal**' in relation to any such interest, shall be construed in accordance with section 4(1), provided that for the purposes of determining the open market price of a surrendered or assigned interest in accordance with the proviso to paragraph (b) of subsection (9), an interest in immovable goods shall also mean an estate or interest which, when it was created, was for a period equal to the period referred to in that proviso, regardless of the duration of that period;

'the open market price'-

(a)   in relation to the value of an interest in immovable goods which is not a freehold interest, means the price, excluding tax, which the right to receive an unencumbered rent in respect of those goods for the period of the interest would fetch on the open market at the time that that interest is disposed of, and

(b)   in relation to the supply of any other goods or services or the intra-Community acquisition of goods, means the price, excluding tax, which the goods might reasonably be expected to fetch or which might reasonably be expected to be charged for the services if sold in the open market at the time of the event in question;

['**open market value'**, in relation to a supply of goods or services, means the total consideration excluding tax that a customer, at a marketing stage which is the same as the stage at which the supply of the goods or services takes place, would reasonably be expected to pay to a supplier at arm's length under conditions of fair competition for a comparable supply of such goods or services:

but if there is no such comparable supply of goods or services then 'open market value' means:

(a)   in respect of a supply of goods, an amount that is not less than the purchase price of the goods or of similar goods or, in the absence of a purchase price, the cost price, determined at the time of supply,

(b)   in respect of a supply of services, an amount that is not less than the full cost to the supplier providing the service;][35]

'**unencumbered rent'**, for the purposes of valuing an interest in immovable goods, means the rent at which an interest would be let, if that interest was let on the open market free of restrictive conditions.][36][37]

Amendments
1   Ss(1A) inserted by FA92 s172(a), (w.e.f. 1 January 1993).
2   Substituted by FA92 s172, (w.e.f. 1 January 1993).
3   Deleted by FA95 s125(a), (w.e.f. 1 July 1995).
4   Deleted by FA07 s80(a)(i), (w.e.f. 2 April 2007).
5   Substituted by FA07 s80(a)(ii), (w.e.f. 2 April 2007).
6   Inserted by FA94 s95, (w.e.f. 23 May 1994).
7   Inserted by FA08 s109 & Sch 4, (w.e.f. 1 July 2008).
8   Ss(3)(d) inserted by FA97 s102(a), (w.e.f. 10 May 1997).
9   Inserted by FA07 s80(b), (w.e.f. 2 April 2007).
10 Substituted by FA06 s96(a), (w.e.f. 31 March 2006).
11 Substituted by FA92 s172(e), (w.e.f. 1 January 1992).

12 Inserted by by FA06 s96(b), (w.e.f. 31 March 2006).
13 Inserted by FA97 s102(b), (w.e.f. 26 March 1997).
14 Inserted by FA93 s86, (w.e.f. 1 August 1993).
15 Ss(4A) inserted by FA82 s78, (w.e.f. 1 September 1982).
16 Substituted by FA99 s124, (w.e.f. 25 March 1999).
17 Ss(4B) inserted by FA92 s172(f), (w.e.f. 1 January 1993).
18 Ss(4C) inserted by FA95 s125(b), (w.e.f. 2 June 1995).
19 Ss(4D) inserted by FA08 s93(a), (w.e.f. 1 July 2008).
20 Substituted by FA07 s97 & Sch 3, (w.e.f. 1 January 2007).
21 Ss(5A) inserted by FA92 s172(g), (w.e.f. 1 January 1993).
22 Substituted by FA02 s102(a), (w.e.f. 25 March 2002).
23 Inserted by FA98 s109, (w.e.f. 1 May 1998).
24 Inserted by FA02 s102(b), (w.e.f. 25 March 2002).
25 Inserted by FA02 s102(c), (w.e.f. 25 March 2002).
26 Inserted by FA97 s102(c)(i), (w.e.f. 10 May 1997).
27 Deleted by FA97 s102(c)(ii), (w.e.f. 10 May 1997).
28 Ss(7A) inserted by FA97 s102(d), (w.e.f. 10 May 1997).
29 Inserted by FA08 s93(b), (w.e.f. 1 September 2008).
30 Inserted by FA97 s102(e), (w.e.f. 26 March 1997).
31 Inserted by FA08 s93(c)(i), (w.e.f. 13 March 2008).
32 Substituted by FA08 s93(c)(ii), (w.e.f. 1 July 2008).
33 Inserted by FA05 s102, (w.e.f. 25 March 2005).
34 Ss(9A) inserted by EC(VAT)R 1992 r8, (w.e.f. 1 January 1993).
35 Inserted by FA07 s80(c), (w.e.f. 2 April 2007).
36 Ss(10) substituted by FA97 s102(f), (w.e.f. 26 March 1997).
37 S10 substituted by VAT Amend. A78 s8, (w.e.f. 1 March 1979).

Regulations and Orders

Adjustment bad debts and early determination of hire purchase transactions	2007 SI No. 272	Value-Added Tax (Amendment) Regulations, 2007
Adjustment bad debts discount, etc	1979 SI No. 63	Value Added Tax Regulations, 1979
Adjustment bad debts discount etc	2006 SI No. 548	Value-Added Tax Regulations 2006
Staff Catering	1979 SI No. 63	Value Added Tax Regulations, 1979
Staff Catering	2006 SI No. 548	Value-Added Tax Regulations 2006
Supplies in exchange for stamps, etc.	1979 SI No. 63	Value Added Tax Regulations, 1979
Supplies of Stamps, coupons, tokens,vouchers	1979SI No. 63	Value Added Tax Regulations, 1979
Stamps, coupons, tokens and vouchers	2006 SI No. 548	Value-Added Tax Regulations 2006
Tax inclusive amount	1973SI No. 9	Prices and Charges (Tax-Inclusive Statements) Order 1973
Valuation Interest	1979SI No. 63	Value Added Tax Regulations, 1979
Valuation of interest	2006 SI No. 548	Value-Added Tax Regulations 2006

Revenue e-Briefs

Revenue e-Brief No. 29/2008: Service charges in hotels and restaurants – withdrawal of Revenue concession with effect from 1st September 2008

Revenue e-Brief No. 37/2007: Opticians and VAT – Position with effect from 1 November 2006

Revenue Statements of Practice and Information Leaflets

ECJ Judgements in relation to the VAT treatment of Promotional Schemes: Information Leaflet No. 6/98

Gifts: Information Leaflet dated October 2008

Case law

Argos Distributors Ltd v Customs and Excise	C288/94	Taxable Amount/vouchers
Baz Bausystem AG v Finanzamt Munchen fur Korperschaften	C222/81	Taxable Amount
Belgium v European Commission	C391/85	Taxable Amount

Bertelsmann AG v Finanzamt Wiedenbrück	C380/99	Taxable amount/Delivery costs of bonuses in kind
Boots Company plc v Customs and Excise	C126/88	Taxable Amount/Vouchers
Brandenstein Klaus v Finanzamt Dusseldorf – Mettmann	C323/99	Self supply
Chassures Bally v Ministry of Finance Belgium	C18/92	Taxable Amount/Credit card transactions
D.H. Burke Ltd v Revenue Commissioners	Irish HC Feb 97	Taxable amount/VAT Scheme for retailers
De Danske Bilimportorer v Skatteministeriet	C98/05	Taxable amount/Registration duty on new motor vehicles
Direct Cosmetics Ltd (No 1) v Customs & Excise	C5/84	Taxable Amount/Party plan selling
Direct Cosmetics Ltd (No 2) v Customs and Excise	C138/86	Taxable Amount/Party plan selling
Elida Gibbs Ltd v Customs and Excise	C317/94	Taxable Amount/Discount
France v Commission	C30/89	Taxable Amount/Own Resources
Freemans plc v Customs and Excise	C86/99	Taxable amount/Discount accounted for at the time of the supply/Price reduction after the supply takes place
Germany v Commission	C427/98	Money-off coupons/Taxable amount
Glawe Spiel and Unterhaltungsgeraete Aufstellungsgesellschaft mBH and Co. KG v v Finanzamt Hamburg Barmbek - Uhlenhorst	C38/93	Taxable Amount
Goldsmith (Jewellers) Ltd v Customs and Excise	C330/95	Taxable Amount
Ireland v Commission	C17/84	Taxable Amount Part exchanged goods
Italy v Commission	C278/83	Sparkling Wines Excise Duty
Italy v Commission	C200/85	Imports/Rates
K Line Air Service Europe BV v Eulaerts NV and Belgium	C131/91	Minimum Taxable Amount
Keeping Newcastle Warm Limited and Commissioners of Customs & Excise	C353/00	Taxable amount/Subsidy
Koninklijke Ahold Fiscale eenheid v Staatsecretaris van Financiën	C484/06	Rules concerning rounding of amounts of VAT
Kuwait Petroleum (GB) Ltd v Customs and Excise	C48/97	Taxable Amount/Vouchers
Laughtons Photograph Ltd v Customs and Excise	C139/86	Taxable Amount
Muys en de Winter's Bouw-en Aannemingsbedrijf BV v Staatssecretaris van Financien	C281/91	Taxable Amount/Interest paid to supplier
Naturally Yours Cosmetics Ltd v Customs and Excise	C230/87	Taxable Amount/Party plan sales
Netherlands v Commission	C16/84	Taxable Amount/Trade ins
Office des produits wallons ASBL v Belgian State	C184/00	Taxable amount/Subsidies directly linked to the price
Part Service Srl v Ministero dell'Economia e delle Finanze, formerly Ministero delle Finanze	C425/06	Artificial division of the supply into a number of parts/Reduction of the taxable amount/Abusive practice
Primback Ltd v Customs and Excise	C34/99	Taxable Amount
Skripalle, Werner v Finanzamt Bergisch Gladback	C63/96	Minimum Taxable Amount
Swoboda, Felix v Austrian National Bank	C411/00	Composite/Single Supply of transport services
Town & County Factors Ltd v Customs and Excise	C498/99	Scope/Taxable Amount
Yorkshire Co-operatives Ltd v Customs & Excise	C398/99	Reduction Coupons/Taxable amount in hands of retailer

Revenue Precedents

Topic:	Taxable Amount.
Issue:	Taxable amount re amusement arcade machines.
Decision:	Only the money remaining after disbursement of winnings (i.e. net takings) is taxable.
Date:	14/1/88

(withdrawn from the Revenue website in 2002)

Topic:	Garage Repairs and Maintenance.
Issue:	Two thirds rule applicable to repair and maintenance on motor vehicles and agricultural machinery.
Decision:	Two-thirds rule will not apply to qualifying repair and maintenance services of vehicles and agricultural machinery.
Date:	29/7/83

Topic:	Hotels.
Issue:	Position relating to the levying of tax on facilities provided free of charge to employees in the catering trade.
Decision:	The value for VAT purposes of meals and accommodation. supplied free of charge to the trade may be assessed at £1 per week per employee.
Date:	30/4/76

(withdrawn from the Revenue website in 2002)

Narrative

Part Service Srl: ECJ VAT Decision: ITR May 2008: Vol. 21 No. 3

Claiming Bad Debt Relief – Are You Aware of the New Procedures?: ITR Sept 2007: Vol. 20 No. 5

Tax Briefing; Issue 66 (VAT and Employment Agencies)

Tax Briefing; Issue 60 (VAT Implications for Waste Disposal)

EU Commission Proposals to Counter VAT Avoidance: ITR May 2005: Vol 18 No. 3.

Tax Briefing: Issue 52 (VAT Committee Guidelines – Purchases by Credit Card)

Tax Briefing: Issue 40 (Sale of Vehicle by One Dealer to Another Dealer for Immediate Supply to a Customer)

Tax Briefing: Issue 29 (Staff Canteens)

Tax Briefing: Issue 27 (Finance Act 1997 Changes: Credit Notes, Discount and the "Argos" Case)

Section 10A

Margin scheme goods

1 (b) (6)
26 a (B)

10A. [(1)   In this section-

'**antiques**' means any of the goods specified in paragraph (xvia) of the Sixth Schedule or in paragraph (iii) of the Eighth Schedule;

'**collectors' items**' means any of the goods specified in paragraph (ii) of the Eighth Schedule;

'**margin scheme**' means the special arrangements for the taxation of supplies of margin scheme goods;

['**margin scheme goods**' means any works of art, collectors' items, antiques or second-hand goods supplied within the Community to a taxable dealer -

(a)   by a person, other than a person referred to in paragraph (c), who was not entitled to deduct, under section 12, any tax in respect of that person's purchase, intra-Community acquisition or importation of those goods:

Provided that person is not [an accountable person][1] who acquired those goods from -

(i)   a taxable dealer who applied the margin scheme to the supply of those goods to [that accountable person][1], or

(ii)   an auctioneer within the meaning of section 10B who applied the auction scheme within the meaning of section 10B to the supply of those goods to [that accountable person][1],

or

(b)   by a person in another Member State who was not entitled to deduct, under the provisions implementing [Articles 167, 173, 176, and 177 of Council Directive No. 2006/112/EC of 28 November 2006][2], in that Member State, any value-added tax referred to in that Directive in respect of that person's purchase, intra-Community acquisition or importation of those goods, or

(c)   by another taxable dealer who has applied the margin scheme to the supply of those goods or applied the provisions implementing [Articles 4 and 35, first subparagraph of Article 139(3) and Articles 311 to 325 and 333 to 340 of Council Directive No. 2006/112/EC of 28 November 2006][2], in another Member State to the supply of those goods,

and also includes goods acquired by a taxable dealer as a result of a disposal of goods by a person to such taxable dealer where that disposal was deemed not to be a supply of goods in accordance with [section 3(5)(d)][3]][4]

'**precious metals**' means silver (including silver plated with gold or platinum), gold (including gold plated with platinum), and platinum, and all items which contain any of these metals when the consideration for the supply does not exceed the open market price, as defined in section 10, of the metal concerned;

'**precious stones**' means diamonds, rubies, sapphires and emeralds, whether cut or uncut, when they are not mounted, set or strung;

'**profit margin**' means the profit margin in respect of a supply by a taxable dealer of margin scheme goods and shall be deemed to be inclusive of tax and shall be an amount which is equal to the difference between the taxable dealer's selling price for those goods and the taxable dealer's purchase price for those goods:

Provided that, in respect of that supply, where the purchase price is greater than the selling price, the profit margin shall be deemed to be nil;

'**purchase price**', in relation to an acquisition of margin scheme goods, means the total consideration including all taxes, commissions, costs and charges whatsoever, payable by a taxable dealer to the person from whom that taxable dealer acquired those goods;

'**second-hand goods**' means any tangible movable goods which are suitable for further use either as they are or after repair, other than means of transport, [agricultural machinery (within the meaning of section 12C),][5] works of art, collectors' items, antiques, precious metals and precious stones;

'**selling price**' means the total consideration which a taxable dealer becomes entitled to receive in respect of or in relation to a supply of margin scheme goods including all taxes, commissions, costs and charges whatsoever and value-added tax, if any, payable in respect of the supply;

'**taxable dealer**' means [an accountable person][1] who in the course or furtherance of business, whether acting on that person's own behalf, or on behalf of another person pursuant to a contract under which commission is payable on purchase or sale, purchases or acquires margin scheme goods or the goods referred to in paragraphs (b) and (c)of subsection (4), with a view to resale, or imports the goods referred to in paragraph (a) of subsection (4), with a view to resale, and a person in another Member State shall be deemed to be a taxable dealer where, in similar circumstances, that person would be a taxable dealer in the State under this section;

'**works of art**' means any of the goods specified in paragraph (xvi), or subparagraph (a) of paragraph (xxii), of the Sixth Schedule or in paragraph (i) of the Eighth Schedule.

a 314   (2)   Subject to and in accordance with the provisions of this section, a taxable dealer may apply the margin scheme to a supply of margin scheme goods.

          (3)   Where the margin scheme is applied to a supply of goods, then notwithstanding section 10, the amount on which tax is chargeable by virtue of section 2(1)(a) on that supply shall be the profit margin less the amount of tax included in the profit margin.

a 316   (4)   Subject to such conditions (if any) as may be specified in regulations, a taxable dealer may, notwithstanding subsection (2), opt to apply the margin scheme to all that dealer's supplies of any of the following as if they were margin scheme goods-

          (a)   a work of art, collector's item or antique which the taxable dealer imported, or

          (b)   a work of art which has been supplied to the taxable dealer by its creator or the creator's successors in title, or

          (c)   a work of art which has been supplied to the taxable dealer by [an accountable person][1] other than a taxable dealer, where the supply to that dealer is of the type referred to in section 11(1AA)(b)(ii):

          Provided that where a taxable dealer so opts in accordance with this subsection, such option shall be for a period of not less than two years from the date when such option was exercised.

a 316, a 317   (5)   Where a taxable dealer exercises the option in accordance with subsection (4), in respect of the goods specified at paragraph (a) thereto, then notwithstanding the definition of purchase price in subsection (1), the purchase price for the purposes of determining the profit margin in relation to a supply of those goods shall be an amount equal to the value of those goods for the purposes of importation determined in accordance with section 15 increased by the amount of any tax payable in respect of the importation of those goods.

a 322   (6)   Subject to subsection (7) and notwithstanding section 12, a taxable dealer who exercises the option in respect of the supply of the goods specified in subsection (4) shall not be entitled to deduct any tax in respect of the purchase or importation of those goods.

a 319, a 320   (7)   Where a taxable dealer exercises the option in accordance with subsection (4), that dealer may, notwithstanding the proviso to subsection (4), in respect of any individual supply of the goods

specified in subsection (4), opt not to apply the margin scheme
to that supply, and in such case the right to deduction of the
tax charged on the purchase, intra-Community acquisition or
importation of those goods shall, notwithstanding section 12,
arise only in the taxable period in which the dealer supplies
those goods.

a 318   (8)   (a)   Notwithstanding subsection (3), and subject to and in
                              accordance with regulations (if any)-

                     (i)   where a taxable dealer acquires low value margin
                              scheme goods in job lots or otherwise, the amount
                              of tax due and payable in respect of that dealer's
                              supplies of low value margin scheme goods shall,
                              in respect of a taxable period, be the amount of
                              tax included in that dealer's aggregate margin, or
                              margins, for that period and the amount of tax in
                              each aggregate margin shall be determined by the
                              formula:

$$A \times \frac{B}{B + 100}$$

                     where-

                     A is the aggregate margin for the taxable period in
                     question, and

                     B is the percentage rate of tax chargeable in relation
                     to the supply of those goods,

              and

                     (ii)   where the taxable dealer referred to in paragraph
                              (i) in any taxable period makes supplies which are
                              subject to different rates of tax, that taxable dealer
                              shall calculate separate aggregate margins for that
                              taxable period in respect of the supplies at each of
                              the relevant rates.

              (b)   Subject to, and in accordance with regulations (if any),
                       where a taxable dealer supplies a low value margin
                       scheme good for an amount in excess of [€635][6] then-

                     (i)   notwithstanding the definition of low value margin
                              scheme goods in paragraph (c), the supply of that
                              good shall be deemed not to be a supply of a low
                              value margin scheme good,

                     (ii)   in determining the aggregate margin for the taxable
                              period in which the supply occurs, the taxable
                              dealer shall deduct the purchase price of that good
                              from the sum of the taxable dealer's purchase
                              prices of low value margin scheme goods for that
                              period, and

(iii)   the purchase price of that good shall be used in determining the profit margin in relation to the supply of that good.

(c)   In this subsection-

'**aggregate margin**', in respect of a taxable period, means an amount which is equal to the difference between the taxable dealer's total turnover in that period from supplies of low value margin scheme goods, to which the same rate of tax applies, less the sum of that taxable dealer's purchase prices of low value margin scheme goods to which that rate of tax applies to the supply thereof, in that taxable period:

Provided that where the sum of that dealer's said purchase prices is in excess of the said total turnover, the appropriate aggregate margin shall be deemed to be nil and subject to, and in accordance with, regulations (if any), the amount of the excess shall be carried forward and added to the sum of that dealer's purchase prices for low value margin scheme goods for the purposes of calculating that dealer's appropriate aggregate margin for the immediately following taxable period;

'**low value margin scheme goods**' means margin scheme goods where the purchase price payable by the dealer for each individual item is less than [€635]⁷.

a 323   (9)   Notwithstanding section 17, a taxable dealer shall not, in relation to any supply to which the margin scheme has been applied, indicate separately the amount of tax chargeable in respect of the supply on any invoice or other document in lieu thereof issued in accordance with that section.

(10)   Where the margin scheme is applied to a supply of goods dispatched or transported from the State to a person registered for value-added tax in another Member State, then notwithstanding paragraph (i)(b) of the Second Schedule, the provisions of section 11(1)(b) shall not apply, unless such goods are of a kind specified elsewhere in the Second Schedule.

(11)   Notwithstanding section 3(6)(d), where the margin scheme is applied to a supply of goods dispatched or transported, the place of supply of those goods shall be deemed to be the place where the dispatch or transportation begins.

(12)   Where a taxable dealer applies the margin scheme to a supply of goods on behalf of another person pursuant to a contract under which commission is payable on purchase or sale, the goods shall be deemed to have been supplied by that other person to the taxable dealer when the said taxable dealer supplies those goods.

(13)   Notwithstanding paragraph (xxiv) of the First Schedule, where [an accountable person]¹ acquires goods to which the margin scheme has been applied and that person subsequently supplies those goods, the provisions of that paragraph shall not apply to that supply.]⁸

Amendments

1   Substituted by FA08 s109 & Sch 4, (w.e.f. 1 July 2008).
2   Substituted by FA07 s97 & Sch 3 (w.e.f. 1 January 2007).
3   Inserted by FA07 s81 (w.e.f. 1 May 2007).
4   Substituted by FA99 s125(a), (w.e.f. 1 September 1999).
5   Inserted by FA99 s125(b), (w.e.f. 1 September 1999).
6   Substituted by FA01 s240(4) & part 4, sch.5 (w.e.f. 1 January 2002), previously £500.
7   Substituted by FA01 s240(4) & part 4, sch.5 (w.e.f. 1 January 2002), previously £500.
8   S10A inserted by FA95 s126, (w.e.f. 1 July 1995).

Revenue Statements of Practice and Information Leaflets

The Margin Scheme, VAT treatment of second-hand goods: Information Leaflet dated December 2008

Case law

Förvaltnings AB Stenholmen and Riksskatteverket	C320/02	Second-hand goods/live animals
Jyske Finans A/S v Skatteministeriet	C280/04	Exemption of supplies excluded from the right to deduct/Meaning of taxable dealer

Narrative

Tax Briefing: Issue 30 (Trade Ins and VAT)

Section 10B

Special scheme for auctioneers

333, a 334 **10B.** [(1)   In this section-

'**auctioneer**' means a [an accountable person][1] who, in the course or furtherance of business, acting on behalf of another person pursuant to a contract under which commission is payable on purchase or sale, offers tangible movable goods for sale by public auction with a view to handing them over to the highest bidder;

'**auctioneer's margin**' means an amount which is equal to the difference between the total amount, including any taxes, commissions, costs and charges whatsoever, payable by the purchaser to the auctioneer in respect of the auction of auction scheme goods and the amount payable by the auctioneer to the principal in respect of the supply of those goods and shall be deemed to be inclusive of tax;

'**auction scheme**' means the special arrangements for the taxation of supplies of auction scheme goods;

'**auction scheme goods**' means any works of art, collectors' items, antiques or second-hand goods sold by an auctioneer at a public auction while acting on behalf of a principal who is-

(a)   a person, other than a person referred to in paragraph (c), who was not entitled to deduct, under section 12, any tax in respect of that person's purchase, intra-Community acquisition or importation of those goods:

Provided that person is not [an accountable person][1] who acquired those goods from-

(i)   an auctioneer who applied the auction scheme to the supply of those goods to [that accountable person][1], or

(ii)   a taxable dealer who applied the margin scheme to the supply of those goods to [that accountable person][1], or

[...][2]

[(aaa)   an insurer within the meaning of section 3(5)(d) (inserted by this Act) who took possession of those goods in connection with the settlement of a claim under a policy of insurance and whose disposal of the goods is deemed not to be a supply of the goods in accordance with section 3(5)(d) (inserted by this Act)][3]

(b)   a person in another Member State who was not entitled to deduct, under the provisions implementing [Articles 167, 173, 176 and 177 of Council Directive No. 2006/112/

EC of 28 November 2006][4], in that Member State, any value-added tax referred to in that Directive in respect of that person's purchase, intra-Community acquisition or importation of those goods, or

(c)   a taxable dealer who applied the margin scheme to the supply of those goods or applied the provisions implementing [Articles 4 and 35, first subparagraph of Article 139(3) and Articles 311 to 325 and 333 to 340 of Council Directive No. 2006/112/EC of 28 November 2006][4], in another Member State to the supply of those goods;

'**principal**' means the person on whose behalf an auctioneer auctions goods;

'**purchaser**' means the person to whom an auctioneer supplies auction scheme goods.

a 26a(c)(1)   (2)   Subject to and in accordance with the provisions of this section, an auctioneer shall apply the auction scheme to any supply of auction scheme goods.

a 26a(c)(2)   (3)   Notwithstanding section 10, the amount on which tax is chargeable, by virtue of section 2(1)(a), on a supply by an auctioneer of auction scheme goods shall be the auctioneer's margin less the amount of tax included in that auctioneer's margin.

339, a 340   (4)   Where auction scheme goods are auctioned, the auctioneer shall issue, subject to such conditions (if any) as may be specified in regulations, to both the principal and the purchaser, invoices or documents in lieu thereof setting out the relevant details in respect of the supply of the auction scheme goods.

(5)   Notwithstanding section 17, an auctioneer shall not, in relation to any supply to which the auction scheme has been applied, indicate separately the amount of tax chargeable in respect of the supply on any invoice or other document in lieu thereof issued in accordance with that section.

(6)   Where auction scheme goods are auctioned by an auctioneer on behalf of a principal who is [an accountable person][1], the invoice or document in lieu thereof issued to the principal in accordance with subsection (4) shall be deemed to be an invoice for the purposes of section 17, and the said principal shall be deemed to have issued same.

(7)   Where the auction scheme is applied to a supply of goods dispatched or transported from the State to a person registered for value-added tax in another Member State then, notwithstanding paragraph (i)(b) of the Second Schedule, the provisions of section

11(1)(b) shall not apply, unless such goods are of a kind specified elsewhere in the Second Schedule.

(8)   Notwithstanding section 3(6)(d), where the auction scheme is applied to a supply of goods dispatched or transported, the place of supply of those goods shall be deemed to be the place where the dispatch or transportation begins.

a 335   (9)   Where an auctioneer supplies [auction scheme goods][5] by public auction, the principal shall be deemed to have made a supply of the auction scheme goods in question to the auctioneer when the said auctioneer sells those goods at a public auction.

(10)   Notwithstanding paragraph (xxiv) of the First Schedule, where [an accountable person][1] acquires goods to which the auction scheme has been applied and that person subsequently supplies those goods, the provisions of that paragraph shall not apply to that supply.][6]

Amendments

1   Substituted by FA08 s109 & Sch 4, (w.e.f. 1 July 2008).
2   Deleted by FA07 s82 (w.e.f. 1 May 2007).
3   Ss(1)(aaa) inserted by FA01 s186, (w.e.f. 21 March 2001).
4   Substituted by FA07 s97 & Sch 3, (w.e.f. 1 January 2007).
5   Substituted by FA96 s91, (w.e.f. 15 May 1996).
6   S10B inserted by FA95 s127, (w.e.f. 1 July 1995).

Regulations and Orders

Second hand goods   1988 SI No. 304   Value Added Tax (Furniture, Silver, Glass and Porcelain) Regulations, 1988

Revenue Statements of Practice and Information Leaflets

Auctioneering: Information Leaflet dated December 2008

Narrative

Tax Briefing: Issue 30 (Trade Ins and VAT)

[Section 10C

Travel agent's margin scheme

(1)   In this section–

'bought-in services' means goods or services which a travel agent purchases for the direct benefit of a traveller from another taxable person or from a person engaged in business outside the State;

'margin scheme services' means bought-in services supplied by a travel agent to a traveller;

'travel agent' means a taxable person who acts as a principal in the supply to a traveller of margin scheme services, and for the purposes of this section travel agent includes tour operator;

'travel agent's margin', in relation to a supply of margin scheme services, means an amount which is calculated in accordance with the following formula:

$$A - B$$

where–

A   is the total consideration which the travel agent becomes entitled to receive in respect of or in relation to that supply of margin scheme services including all taxes, commissions, costs and charges whatsoever and value-added tax payable in respect of that supply, and

B   is the amount payable by the travel agent to a supplier in respect of bought-in services included in that supply of margin scheme services to the traveller, but any bought-in services purchased by the travel agent prior to 1 January 2010 in respect of which that travel agent claims deductibility in accordance with section 12 shall be disregarded in calculating the margin,

and if that B is greater than that A the travel agent's margin in respect of that supply shall be deemed to be nil;

'travel agent's margin scheme' means the special arrangements for the taxation of margin scheme services.

(2)   A supply of margin scheme services by a travel agent to a traveller in respect of a journey shall be treated as a single supply.

(3)   The place of supply of margin scheme services is the place where a travel agent has established that travel agent's business, but if those services are provided from a fixed establishment of that travel agent located in a place other than the place where that travel agent has established that travel agent's business, the place of supply of those services is the place where that fixed establishment is located.

(4)   The travel agent's margin scheme shall apply to the supply of margin scheme services in the State.

(5)   Notwithstanding section 10, the amount on which tax is chargeable by virtue of section 2(1)(a) on a supply of margin scheme services shall be the travel agent's margin less the amount of tax included in that margin.

(6)   Notwithstanding sections 12 and 13, a travel agent shall not be entitled to a deduction or a refund of tax borne or paid in respect of bought-in services supplied by that travel agent as margin scheme services.

(7)   Where a travel agent supplies margin scheme services together with other goods or services to a traveller for a total consideration, then that total consideration shall be apportioned by that travel agent so as to correctly reflect the ratio which the value of those margin scheme services bears to that total consideration, and in that case the proportion of the total consideration relating to the value of the margin scheme services shall be subject to the travel agent's margin scheme.

(8)   Margin scheme services shall be treated as intermediary services when the bought-in services are performed outside the Community.

(9)   Where a travel agent makes a supply of margin scheme services that includes some services that are treated as intermediary services in accordance with subsection (8), then the total travel agent's margin in respect of that supply shall be apportioned by that travel agent so as to correctly reflect the ratio which the cost to that travel agent of the bought-in services used in the margin scheme services that are treated as intermediary services in that supply bears to the total cost to that travel agent of all bought-in services used in making that supply of margin scheme services.

(10)   A travel agent being an accountable person who supplies margin scheme services shall include the tax due on that person's supplies of margin scheme services for a taxable period in the return that that person is required to furnish in accordance with section 19(3).

(11)   The Revenue Commissioners may make such regulations as they consider necessary for the purposes of the operation of this section including provisions for simplified accounting arrangements.][1]

Amendments
1   S10C inserted by F(No. 2)A 08 s71, (w.e.f. 1 January 2010).

Narrative
Travel Agents Margin Scheme: ITR Jan 2009: Vol. 22 No. 1

Section 11

Rates of tax

a 96,a 98 **11.** [(1)   Tax shall be charged, in relation to the supply of taxable goods
a 102   or services[, the intra-Community acquisition of goods]¹ and
                 the importation of goods, at whichever of the following rates is
                 appropriate in any particular case-

(a)   **[21.5 per cent]**² of the amount on which tax is chargeable
       other than in relation to goods or services on which tax is
       chargeable at any of the rates specified in paragraphs (b),
       (c), (d), [...]³ and (f),

(b)   zero per cent of the amount on which tax is chargeable
       in relation to goods in the circumstances specified in
       paragraph (i) [or (ia)]⁴ of the Second Schedule or of goods
       or services of a kind specified in paragraphs (iii) to (xx) of
       that Schedule,

(c)   10 per cent of the amount on which tax is chargeable in
       relation to goods or services of a kind specified in the
       Third Schedule,

(d)   [13.5 per cent]⁵ of the amount on which tax is chargeable
       in relation to goods or services of a kind specified in the
       Sixth Schedule, [and]⁶

       [...]⁷

a 297   (f)   [4.8 per cent]⁸ of the amount on which tax is chargeable
                in relation to the supply of livestock and live greyhounds
                and to the hire of horses.]⁹

a 93, a 94(1) [(1A) (a)   The rate at which tax shall be chargeable shall, in relation
                            to tax chargeable under [subsection (1)(a) or (1A) of
                            section 2]¹⁰, be the rate for the time being in force at the
                            time at which the tax becomes due in accordance with
                            [subsection (1), (1A) or (2)]¹¹, as may be appropriate, of
                            section 19.

(b)   Goods or services which are specifically excluded from
       any paragraph of a Schedule shall, unless the contrary
       intention is expressed, be regarded as excluded from
       every other paragraph of that Schedule, and shall not be
       regarded as specified in that Schedule.

a 94(2), a 103 [(1AA) Notwithstanding subsection (1), tax shall be charged at the
                       rate specified in section 11(1)(d) of the amount on which tax is
                       chargeable in relation to-

(a)   the importation into the State of goods specified in the
       Eighth Schedule,

(b)   the supply of a work of art of the kind specified in
       paragraph (i) of the Eighth Schedule, effected-

(i)   by its creator or the creator's successors in title, or

(ii)   on an occasional basis by [an accountable person][12] other than a taxable dealer where-

(I)   that work of art has been imported by [the accountable person][12], or

(II)   that work of art has been supplied to [the accountable person][12] by its creator or the creator's successors in title, or

(III)   the tax chargeable in relation to the purchase, intra-Community acquisition or importation of that work of art by [the accountable person][12] was wholly deductible under section 12,

and

(c)   the intra-Community acquisition in the State by [an accountable person][12] of a work of art of the kind specified in paragraph (i) of the Eighth Schedule where the supply of that work of art to [that accountable person][12] which resulted in that intra-Community acquisition is a supply of the type that would be charged at the rate specified in section 11(1)(d) in accordance with paragraph (b), if that supply had occurred within the State.][13]

[(1AB) Notwithstanding subsection (1), the rate at which tax is chargeable on a supply of contract work shall be the rate that would be chargeable if that supply of services were a supply of the goods being handed over by the contractor to the person to whom that supply is made:

Provided that this subsection shall not apply to a supply of contract work in the circumstances specified in paragraph (xvi) of the Second Schedule.][14]

(1B)   (a)   On receipt of an application in writing from [an accountable person][12], the Revenue Commissioners shall, in accordance with regulations and after such consultation (if any) as may seem to them to be necessary with such person or body of persons as in their opinion may be of assistance to them, make a determination concerning-

(i)   whether an activity of any particular kind carried on by the person is an exempted activity, or

[(ii)   the rate at which tax is chargeable in relation to the supply or intra-Community acquisition by the person of goods of any kind, the supply or intra-Community acquisition of goods in any particular circumstances or the supply by the person of services of any kind.][15]

(b)   The Revenue Commissioners may, whenever they consider it expedient to do so, in accordance with regulations and after such consultation (if any) as may seem to them to be necessary with such person or body of persons as in their opinion may be of assistance to them, make a determination concerning—

    (i)   whether an activity of any particular kind is an exempted activity, or

    [(ii)   the rate at which tax is chargeable in relation to the supply or intra-Community acquisition of goods of any kind, the supply or intra-Community acquisition of goods in any particular circumstances or the supply of services of any kind.][16]

[(c)   A determination under this subsection shall have effect for all the purposes of this Act—

    (i)   in relation to [an accountable person][12] who makes an application for the determination, as on and from the date which shall be specified for the purpose in the determination communicated to [the accountable person][12] in accordance with paragraph (e)(i), and

    (ii)   in relation to any other person, as on and from the date which shall be specified for the purpose in the determination as published in the Iris Oifigiúil.][17]

(d)   The Revenue Commissioners shall not make a determination under this section concerning any matter which has been determined on appeal under this Act or which is for the time being governed by an order under section 6(2) or 11(8), and shall not be required to make such a determination in relation to any of the matters referred to in an application under paragraph (a) if-

    (i)   a previous determination has been published in regard to the matter, or

    (ii)   in their opinion the subject matter of the application is sufficiently free from doubt as not to warrant the making and publication of a determination.

(e)   (i)   A determination under paragraph (a) shall, as soon as may be after the making thereof, be communicated to the person who made the application therefor by the service on him by the Revenue Commissioners of a notice containing particulars of the determination.

    (ii)   A determination under paragraph (a) may and a determination under paragraph (b) shall be published in the Iris Oifigiúil and, in that event,

it shall also be published in at least one daily newspaper published in the State.

(f)   A person, aggrieved by a determination under paragraph (a) made pursuant to an application by him, may, on giving notice in writing to the Revenue Commissioners within the period of twenty-one days beginning on the date of service on him of notice of the determination in accordance with paragraph (e)(i), appeal to the Appeal Commissioners.

(g)   [Any accountable person][12] who, in the course of business, [supplies goods or makes an intra-Community acquisition of goods, or supplies services][18] of a kind or in circumstances specified in a determination under paragraph (a) or (b) may, on giving notice in writing to the Revenue Commissioners within the period of twenty-one days beginning on the date of the publication of the determination in the *Iris Oifigiúil*, appeal to the Appeal Commissioners.][19]

[...][20]

[(3)   (a)   Subject to section 10(8) —

    (i)   in the case of a composite supply, the tax chargeable on the total consideration which [the accountable person][12] is entitled to receive for that composite supply shall be at the rate specified in subsection (1) which is appropriate to the principal supply, but if that principal supply is an exempted activity, tax shall not be chargeable in respect of that composite supply,

    (ii)   in the case of a multiple supply, the tax chargeable on each individual supply in that multiple supply shall be at the rate specified in subsection (1) appropriate to each such individual supply and, in order to ascertain the taxable amount referable to each individual supply for the purpose of applying the appropriate rate thereto, the total consideration which [the accountable person][12] is entitled to receive in respect of that multiple supply shall be apportioned between those individual supplies in a way that correctly reflects the ratio which the value of each such individual supply bears to the total consideration for that multiple supply.

(b)   In the case where a person acquires a composite supply or a multiple supply by means of an intra-Community acquisition, the provisions of this subsection shall apply to that acquisition.

(c)   The Revenue Commissioners may make regulations as necessary specifying—

(i)   the circumstances or conditions under which a supply may or may not be treated as an ancillary supply, a composite supply, an individual supply, a multiple supply or a principal supply,

(ii)   the methods of apportionment which may be applied for the purposes of paragraphs (a) and (b),

(iii)   a [relatively small amount][21], or an element of a supply, which may be disregarded for the purposes of applying this subsection.][22]

[(4)   Where goods for the manufacture of which materials have been supplied by or on behalf of any person are [supplied][23] by the manufacturer to that person and the rate of tax chargeable in relation to the [supply][24] of the goods exceeds that which would be chargeable in relation to a [supply][24] within the State of the materials, the person who [supplies][25] the goods shall, in respect of the [supply][24] of such goods, be liable, in addition to any other liability imposed on him by this Act, to pay tax on the value of the materials [provided][26] to him, at a rate equivalent to the difference between the two aforementioned rates.][27]

[(4A)   Where-

(a)   goods of a kind specified in paragraph (xii) of the Second Schedule are used by a person in the course of the supply by him of taxable services, and

(b)   the goods are provided by or on behalf of the person to whom the services are supplied,

the person who supplies the taxable services shall be liable in respect thereof, in addition to any other liability imposed on him under this Act, to pay tax on the value of the goods so used at the rate specified in [section 11(1)(d)][28].][29]

[...][30]

(6)   Where immovable goods consisting of machinery or business installations are let separately from other immovable goods of which they form part, tax shall be chargeable in respect of the transaction at the rate which would be chargeable if it were a hiring of movable goods of the same kind.

[...][31]

(8)   [(a)   The Minister may by order vary the [Second, Third or Sixth Schedule][32] by adding to or deleting therefrom descriptions of goods or services of any kind or by varying any description of goods or services for the time being specified therein, [...][33] but no order shall be made under this section for the purpose of increasing any of the rates of tax or extending the classes of activities or goods in respect of which tax is for the time being chargeable.][34]

(b)   The Minister may by order amend or revoke an order under this subsection, including an order under this paragraph.

(c)   An order under this subsection shall be laid before Dáil Éireann as soon as may be after it has been made and, if a resolution annulling the order is passed by Dáil Éireann within the next twenty-one days on which Dáil Éireann has sat after the order is laid before it, the order shall be annulled accordingly, but without prejudice to the validity of anything previously done thereunder.

[...]35

Amendments

1   Inserted by FA92 s173(3)(a), (w.e.f. 1 January 1993).
2   Substituted by F(No. 2)A 08 s72, (w.e.f. 1 December 2008).
3   Deleted by FA93 s87(a)(i), (w.e.f. 1 March 1993).
4   Inserted by EC(VAT)R 1992 r9, (w.e.f. 1 January 1993).
5   Substituted by FA03 s119, (w.e.f. 1 January 2003).
6   Inserted by FA93 s87(a)(ii), (w.e.f. 1 March 1993).
7   Deleted by FA93 s87, (w.e.f. 1 March 1993).
8   Substituted by FA05 s103 (w.e.f. 1 January 2005).
9   Ss(1) substituted by FA92 s173(2), (w.e.f. 28 May 1992).
10 Substituted by FA92 s173(3)(b), (w.e.f. 1 January 1993).
11 Substituted by FA92 s173(3)(b), (w.e.f. 1 January 1993).
12 Substituted by FA08 s109 & Sch 4, (w.e.f. 1 July 2008).
13 Ss(1AA) inserted by FA95 s128(a), (w.e.f. 1 July 1995).
14 Ss(1AB) inserted by FA96 s92(b), (w.e.f. 1 March 1996).
15 Ss(1B)(a)(ii) substituted by FA92 s173(3)(c)(i), (w.e.f. 1 January 1993).
16 Ss(1B)(b)(ii) substituted by FA92 s173(3)(c)(ii), (w.e.f. 1 January 1993).
17 Ss(1B)(c) substituted by FA06 s97(1)(a), (w.e.f. 31 March 2006).
18 Substituted by FA92 s173(3)(c)(iii), (w.e.f. 1 January 1993).
19 Ss(1A) - (1B) inserted by FA73 s80, (w.e.f. 3 September 1973).
20 Deleted by FA85 s43, (w.e.f. 1 March 1985).
21 Substituted by FA07 s128 and Sch 4(3), (w.e.f. 2 April 2007).
22 Ss(3) substituted by FA06 s97(1)(b), (w.e.f. 1 November 2006).
23 Substituted by VAT Amend. A78 s30(2), (w.e.f. 1 March 1979).
24 Substituted by VAT Amend. A78 s30(2), (w.e.f. 1 March 1979).
25 Substituted by VAT Amend. A78 s30(2), (w.e.f. 1 March 1979).
26 Substituted by VAT Amend. A78 s30(2), (w.e.f. 1 March 1979).
27 Ss(4) substituted by FA75 s51, (w.e.f. 16 January 1975).
28 Substituted by FA93 s87(b).
29 Ss(4A) substituted by VAT Amend. A78 s9, (w.e.f. 1 March 1979).
30 Deleted by FA95 s128(b), (w.e.f. 2 June 1995).
31 Deleted by FA92 s173(2)(b), (w.e.f. 28 May 1992).
32 Substituted by FA93 s87(c).
33 Deleted by VAT Amend. A78 s30(1), (w.e.f. 1 March 1979).
34 Ss(8)(a) substituted by FA73 s80, (w.e.f. 3 September 1973).
35 Repealed by VAT Amend. A78 s30(1), (w.e.f. 1 March 1979).

Regulations and Orders

Apportionment of consideration	1979 SI No. 63	Valued Added Tax Regulations 1979
Apportionment of consideration	2006 SI No. 548	Value-Added Tax Regulations 2006
Composite and multiple supplies	2006 SI No. 549	Finance Act 2006 (Commencement of Sections 93(1), 97(1)(b) and 99(1)(a)) Order 2006

Candles	1987 SI No. 146	Valued Added Tax (Reduction of Tax) (No. 11) Order 1987
Eurocontrol	1974 SI No. 290	Valued Added Tax (Refund of Tax) (No. 7) Order 1974
European Space Agency	1980 SI No. 239	Valued Added Tax (Refund of Tax) (No. 11) Order 1980
Farmers - Deer	1986 SI No. 412	Imposition of duties (No. 283) (Value Added Tax) Order 1986
Fisherman	1972 SI No. 326	Valued Added Tax (Reduction of Rate) (No. 2.) Order 1972
Rates of VAT	1973 SI No. 238	Valued Added Tax (Refund of Tax) (No. 6) Order 1973
Sea Rescue Services	1973 SI No. 69	Valued Added Tax (Reduction of Rate) (No. 3) Order 1973
Transitional arrangements	1994 SI No. 448	European Communities (Value Added Tax) Regulations, 1994

Revenue e-Briefs

Revenue e-Brief No. 54/2008: VAT rate change – budget 2009

Revenue e-Brief No. 40/2006: Vat Treatment of Goods and Services Sold Together

Revenue e-Brief No. 36/2006: Opticians and VAT

Revenue e-Brief No. 10/2006: Supplies of services to foreign traders who are not established in the State – relief from VAT: [60A Procedure]

Revenue Statements of Practice and Information Leaflets

Agricultural Services: Information Leaflet dated December 2008

Application of the Zero Rate to Sales and other Deliveries of Goods to other EU Member States after 1/1/93: SP-VAT/8/92

Food and Drink: Information Leaflet dated December 2008

Goods and Services Sold Together, VAT Treatment of: Information Leaflet dated December 2008

Live Horses: SP-VAT/3/90

Rates of VAT on Services: SP-VAT/1/92

Retailers, Special Schemes: Information Leaflet dated January 2007

Case law

Cablelink v Inspector of Taxes	Irish S.C. Dec 2003	Separate supplies/ Connections services/TV and radio signals
Fonden Marselisborg Lystbådehavn v Skatteministeriet	C428/02	Letting of premises and sites for parking boats/Mooring berths
Gmurzyneska - Bscher, Krystyna v Oberfinanzdirektion Koln	C231/89	Imports/Rates of VAT
Ideal Tourisme v Belgium	C36/99	Rate of VAT
Swoboda, Felix v Austrian National Bank	C411/00	Composite/Single Supply of transport services
Talacre Beach Caravan Sales Ltd v Commissioners of Customs & Excise	C251/05	Rate of Tax/Classification of supply/Fitted residential caravans
Zweckverband zur Trinkwasserversorgung und Abwasserbeseitigung Torgau-Westelbein v Finanzamt Oschatz	C442/05	"Supply of water" or "Water supply"

Revenue Precedents

Topic:	VAT Rate Increases.
Issue:	Increase in VAT rate.
Decision:	Agreed for a limited period deferment of application of increase in VAT rate to certain bills in exceptional circumstances.
Date:	6/2/91
Topic:	Package rule.
Issue:	The sale of films at a price inclusive of the cost of processing. In such a supply where there is a rate difference between the supply of goods (i.e. the films) and a service (i.e. the processing) the cocktail rule should apply thereby attracting the higher rate of VAT.
Decision:	Decision made on a method of apportionment of the consideration for the film and processing between the standard and lower rate of VAT.
Date:	19/12/90

Topic:	Package rule.
Issue:	Service charge with regard to door to door milk deliveries.
Decision:	Seen as consideration for the supply of milk. Zero rate applies. Section 11 (3) disregarded.
Date:	14/8/79
Topic:	Exports
Issue:	Goods supplied in the State by Irish traders for bulk export for promotion purposes.
Decision:	Such goods were zero-rated subject to the proof of export being retained by the supplier.
Date:	6/5/82
Topic:	Custodial Services.
Issue:	Is supply of custodial services a composite or multiple service.
Decision:	Services supplied by a custodian can be disaggregated and each part considered an independent supply for determining VAT liability.
Date:	9/8/91

(withdrawn from the Revenue website in 2002)

Topic:	T.V. Aerials and Cable Television.
Issue:	VAT Rate on T.V. Aerials.
Decision:	H.C. Judge ruled that aerials are fixtures.
Date:	3/5/85

(withdrawn from the Revenue website in 2002)

Topic:	Medical Services.
Issue:	Psychotherapist.
Decision:	12.5% applies.
Date:	9/1/96

(withdrawn from the Revenue website in 2002)

Topic:	Amusement Services.
Issue:	Kiddies rides - VAT liability on receipts from same.
Decision:	12.5% rate, because of a type supplied in a fairground or amusement park.
Date:	4/11/96

(withdrawn from the Revenue website in 2002)

Topic:	Food.
Issue:	Flavoured syrups/food supplements for babies/infants, supplying Vitamin C and consumed in dosage form.
Decision:	Zero rate as they could not be described as drinks or for use in the taking of drinks for refreshment.
Date:	22/7/82

(withdrawn from the Revenue website in 2002)

Topic:	Medicines.
Issue:	A specific chewing gum to help a person stop smoking.
Decision:	Zero %, as coming within meaning of 2nd Schedule paragraph (xiii).
Date:	17/5/93

(withdrawn from the Revenue website in 2002)

Topic:	Care of the human body.
Issue:	Active balance therapist (alternative/complimentary medicine).
Decision:	12.5% not coming within the meaning of paragraph (iii) 1st Schedule.
Date:	27/11/92

(withdrawn from the Revenue website in 2002)

Topic:	Food
Issue:	Powder product to be mixed with a liquid and drank.
Decision:	Zero%, as it is marketed as a meal replacement and as a result is considered food.
Date:	9/2/95

Topic:	Food.
Issue:	Butter and Chocolate Croissants, Fat content exceeds 2%.
Decision:	Zero%.
Date:	24/8/92

(withdrawn from the Revenue website in 2002)

Topic:	Food.
Issue:	Pastries filled with meat/salad etc.
Decision:	Zero per cent. Pastry deemed incidental to the meat etc, filling (basic food).
Date:	27/4/83

(withdrawn from the Revenue website in 2002)

Topic:	Care of the human body.
Issue:	Hypnotherapist, aromatherapist, reflexologist, homeotherapist, accupuncturist and holistic services.
Decision:	12.5% not coming within the meaning of paragraph (iii) First Schedule.
Date:	21/4/94

(withdrawn from the Revenue website in 2002)

Topic:	Catering.
Issue:	Christmas party night dinner.
Decision:	Entire charge treated as liable to VAT at 12.5% (Dancing facilities can be regarded as incidental to the supply of the meal).
Date:	3/10/95

Topic:	Agricultural Contractors etc.
Issue:	Agricultural consultants - R.E.P.S. Scheme.
Decision:	Liable to VAT at 12.5% on the understanding that it contains advice on matters such as waste control, management of water courses, wells, hedgerows, etc.
Date:	21/3/95

(withdrawn from the Revenue website in 2002)

Topic:	Food.
Issue:	Croissants fat content exceeds 2%.
Decision:	Zero rate allowed.
Date:	31/1/84

(withdrawn from the Revenue website in 2002)

Topic:	Food.
Issue:	Organic Breads containing honey of less than 2% instead of sugar.
Decision:	Zero rate as honey is a natural substitute for sugar.
Date:	11/1/96

(withdrawn from the Revenue website in 2002)

Topic:	Application of Zero rate.
Issue:	Computer system supplied within the State for training and testing before being exported by the company out of the State.
Decision:	Authorisation given to zero rate the supply of the computer system to the company.
Date:	3/6/81

Topic:	Application of Zero Rate.
Issue:	A UK company with no presence in Ireland sends PBX system to a factory in this State. A Dublin company supplies component to the foreign company but is delivered directly to the factory in the State. VAT at 21% would normally apply to such a supply. The component is soldered into a finished product and sent back to the UK.
Decision:	Provided the supplier has evidence that the goods have been transferred to OMS then the zero rate can apply.
Date:	16/5/94

Topic:	Package rule.
Issue:	Combined supply and sowing of seeds for the production of food.

Decision:	The supply of polythene when used in the combined supply and sowing of maize seeds liable to VAT at zero rate regarded as integral part of growing of maize crop.
Date:	12/3/96

(withdrawn from the Revenue website in 2002)

Topic:	Food.
Issue:	Bread rolls and Vienna rolls fat content exceeded 2% limit of the weight of the flour included in the dough.
Decision:	Zero rate. Allow zero rating as fat content was only 2.35% (generally where 5% to 6% by weight of sugar and/or fats added, no account to be taken of such small quantities).
Date:	20/12/79
Topic:	Package rule.
Issue:	Freeze-dried human blood component supplied with saline, a transfer needle and an infusion set in kit form should be subject to the "package rule" as provided for in Section 11(3) of the VAT Act.
Decision:	Confirmed that the supply of the kit in question is exempt from VAT.
Date:	4/11/85
Topic:	Boats.
Issue:	The supply of equipment normally subject to the standard rate of VAT to the owner of an over 15 ton fishing vessel.
Decision:	Zero rating allowed where we are satisfied that the item will be installed in a particular over 15 ton fishing vessel which should be named on the invoice.
Date:	26/2/82

(withdrawn from the Revenue website in 2002)

Topic:	Works of Art.
Issue:	Sculpture (Work of Art).
Decision:	12.5% which also applies to limited editions of original works of art made from the original cast/bust. Does not include mass produced works of art.
Date:	12/12/95

(withdrawn from the Revenue website in 2002)

Topic:	Beverages.
Issue:	Chocolate drink.
Decision:	Zero% as product contains 57% semi-skimmed milk.
Date:	11/11/96

(withdrawn from the Revenue website in 2002)

Topic:	Clothing.
Issue:	Clothing designed for disabled children - sized by height.
Decision:	The zero rate of VAT applies on garments up to and including size 152cm. Garments in excess of 152cm liable to VAT at 21%.
Date:	14/6/89

(withdrawn from the Revenue website in 2002)

Topic:	Medicines.
Issue:	Inhalers (Asthma) (Aerosol and Dry Powder).
Decision:	Zero% comes within meaning of 2nd Schedule. Paragraph (xiii).
Date:	24/1/83

(withdrawn from the Revenue website in 2002)

Topic:	Medicines.
Issue:	Inhaled Anaesthetic Drugs.
Decision:	Zero%, Medicines administered by inhalation similar to asthmatic inhalers.
Date:	2/8/90

(withdrawn from the Revenue website in 2002)

Topic:	Medicines.
Issue:	Throat and Mouth spray.
Decision:	Zero% a licensed medicine for oral consumption paragraph (xiii) 2nd Schedule.

Date: 31/8/95

(withdrawn from the Revenue website in 2002)

Topic: Aircraft.

Issue: Application of zero rate to lease of aircraft to an intermediary company for subsequent onward leasing to qualifying airline.

Decision: Agreed to look through the intermediary, provided it is clear at outset that ultimate lessee is qualifying airline and regard first lease as also qualifying for zero rate in accordance with paragraph (v)(b) Second Schedule.

Date: 4/3/83

Topic: Aircraft.

Issue: Foreign lessor leases government jet to Irish airline for onward leasing. Whether to register foreign lessor for VAT and whether to allow Irish Airline to import aircraft at zero rate.

Decision: Foreign lessor not required to register for VAT Irish Airline allowed to import aircraft at zero rate as if for its airline business.

Date: 4/4/91

Topic: Medicines.

Issue: Antibiotic.

Decision: Zero rate even though it can be administered both orally and by injection.

Date: 24/7/91

Topic: Package Rule.

Issue: Food Hampers which contains both zero, 12.5 and 21 per cent goods.

Decision: Apportionment allowed - provided supplier keeps an accurate record of the goods supplied at the various rates.

Date: 2/3/95

Topic: Package Rule.

Issue: Musical card and a £1 Lottery ticket.

Decision: Apportionment allowed VAT at 21% on value of card.

Date: 21/6/94

Topic: Package rule.

Issue: In a marketing campaign a small bottle of wine is supplied with tubs of spread for an all inclusive price.

Decision: Provided the items in question are listed separately showing the different rates of VAT applying on the invoice the "package rule" is not invoked.

Date: 26/7/94

Topic: Package Rule.

Issue: Rental/laundering of linen such as uniforms, overalls, towels etc.

Decision: Where a particular quantity of specified linen is hired to a customer and there is a separate contract for the laundering of the same linen, 12.5% applies to the laundry charge.

Date: 22/7/86

(withdrawn from the Revenue website in 2002)

Topic: Food.

Issue: Intravenous products.

Decision: Zero rate applies to supply of such products provided they have no pharmacological action and are purely nutritional.

Date: 10/5/85

(withdrawn from the Revenue website in 2002)

Narrative

VAT Rate Simplification – is the end of low rates upon us?: ITR Jan 2008: Vol. 21 No. 1.

The World's greatest Delusion: S11(3) VAT Act 1972: ITR Jan 2007: Vol. 20. No. 1.

VAT on Optical Professional Services: The Story so Far: ITR Jan 2007: Vol. 20. No. 1.

VAT Supplies – To Mix, or Not To Mix: That Is The Question: ITR May 2006: Vol. 19 No. 3.

Tax Briefing: Issue 63 (Composite Meal Packages – VAT)

Single and Multiple Supplies – The Supreme Court's view: ITR Mar 2004: Vol. 17 No. 2.

Single & Multiple Supplies Services: ITR May 2003: Vol. 16 No. 3.

Tax Briefing: Issue 52 (VAT Committee Guidelines – CD-ROMs)

Tax Briefing: Issue 51 (Increase in the Reduced Rate)

Tax Briefing: Issue 46 (Dances, Theatrical and Musical Performances)

Tax Briefing: Issue 45 (Toll Roads and Toll Bridges)

Tax Briefing: Issue 44 (VAT Rates Applicable to Supplies of Goods and Services in the Bloodstock Industry)

Tax Briefing: Issue 43 (VAT Committee Guidelines – Reduced Rates on Medical Equipment and Other Appliances)

Tax Briefing: Issue 42 (Two Thirds Rule: Motor Vehicles)

Tax Briefing: Issue 39 (Commissioned Framed Photographs)

Tax Briefing: Issue 36 (Hot Take-Away Food)

Tax Briefing: Issue 32 (Rates of VAT on Footwear)

Tax Briefing: Issue 27 (Sports Footwear)

Section 12

Deduction for tax borne or paid

a 168, a 179 **12.** [(1)   (a)   In computing the amount of tax payable by him in respect of a taxable period, [an accountable person]¹ may, insofar as the goods and services are used by him for the purposes of his taxable supplies or of any of the qualifying activities, deduct [, subject to making any adjustments required in accordance with section 12D]² –

a 178(a)   (i)   the tax charged to him during the period by [other accountable persons]¹ by means of invoices, prepared in the manner prescribed by regulations, in respect of supplies of goods or services to him,

                       [...]³

a 178(e)   (ii)   in respect of goods imported by him in the period, the tax paid by him or deferred as established from the relevant customs documents kept by him in accordance with section 16(3),

                       [(iia) subject to such conditions (if any) as may be specified in regulations, the tax chargeable during the period, being tax for which he is liable in respect of intra-Community acquisitions of goods,

                       (iib) subject to and in accordance with regulations, in respect of goods supplied under section 3(1)(g) an amount equal to any residual tax included in the consideration for the supply,]⁴

                       [(iic) subject to such conditions (if any) as may be specified in regulations, in respect of goods referred to in section 3B, the tax due in the period in accordance with that section,]⁵

                       (iii) the tax chargeable during the period in respect of goods [other than supplies of goods referred to in section 3(6)(d)]⁶ treated as supplied by him in accordance with section 3(1)(e),

                       [(iiia) the tax charged to him during the period by [other accountable persons]¹ in respect of services directly related to the transfer of ownership of goods specified in section 3(5)(b)(iii),]⁷

                       [(iiib) the tax chargeable during the period, being tax for which he is liable by virtue of section 4A(1), in respect of goods received by him,]⁸

                       [(iiic) the tax chargeable during the period, being tax for which [the accountable person]¹ is liable by virtue of [section 4B(6)(a) or 4(8)][9], in respect of a supply to that person of immovable goods,][10]

[...][11]

[(iiie)   the tax chargeable during the period, being tax or which he is liable by virtue of section 6A(5)(a) in respect of investment gold (within the meaning of section 6A) received by him,][12]

(iv)   the tax chargeable during the period in respect of services treated as supplied by him for consideration in the course or furtherance of his business in accordance with **[section 5(3)(c)]**[13],

(v)   the tax chargeable during the period, being tax for which he is liable by virtue of section 5(3A), in respect of services received by him,

[(va)   the tax chargeable during the period, being tax for which [the accountable person][1] is liable by virtue of section 8(1A)(f) in respect of goods which are installed or assembled; but this subparagraph shall apply only where [the accountable person][1] would be entitled to a deduction of that tax elsewhere under this subsection if that tax had been charged to such person by [another accountable person][1],][14]

[(vb)   the tax chargeable during the period, being tax for which [the accountable person][1] is liable by virtue of section 8(1A)(g) in respect of the supply to such person of gas through the natural gas distribution network, or of electricity; but this subparagraph shall apply only where [the accountable person][1] would be entitled to a deduction of that tax elsewhere under this subsection if that tax had been charged to such person by [another accountable person][1],][15]

[(vc)   the tax chargeable during the period, being tax for which the principal is liable by virtue of section 8(1B) in respect of construction operations services received by that principal; but this subparagraph shall apply only where that principal would be entitled to a deduction of that tax elsewhere under this subsection if that tax had been charged to such principal by another accountable person,][16]

[(vi)   subject to and in accordance with regulations (if any), residual tax referred to in section 12B,][17]

[(via)   the residual tax referred to in section 12C, being residual tax contained in the price charged to him for the purchase of agricultural machinery (within the meaning of section 12C), by means of invoices issued to him during the period by flat-rate farmers,][18]

[(vib) the residual tax referred to in section 12C, being residual tax contained in the price charged to [the accountable person][1] for the purchase of agricultural machinery (within the meaning of section 12C), by means of documents issued to that person during the period in accordance with section 12C(1B),][19]

(vii) the tax chargeable during the period, being tax for which he is liable by virtue of section 8(2), in respect of services received by him, [.....][20]

(viii) [flat-rate addition, which shall be deemed to be tax,][21] charged to him during the period by means of invoices prepared in the manner prescribed by regulations and issued to him in accordance with [section 12A,][22]

[(ix) **subject to subsection (4) and regulations (if any), 20 per cent of the tax charged to that accountable person in respect of the purchase, hiring, intra-Community acquisition or importation of a qualifying vehicle (within the meaning assigned by paragraph (c)), where that vehicle is used primarily for business purposes, being at least 60 per cent of the use to which that vehicle is put, and where that accountable person subsequently disposes of that vehicle the tax deducted by that person in accordance with this subsection shall be treated as if it was not deductible by that person for the purposes of paragraph (xxiv)(c) of the First Schedule:][23]**

[Provided that this paragraph shall not apply to-

(I) [an accountable person][1] referred to in subsection (1A)(c) or (2)(b) of section 8, or

(II) [an accountable person][1] referred to in subsection (1A)(d) or (2)(c) of section 8 unless the tax relates to racehorse training services supplied by him.][24]

(b) In paragraph (a) '**qualifying activities**' means-

(i) transport outside the State of passengers and their accompanying baggage,

[(ia) supplies of goods which, by virtue of section 3(6)(d), are deemed to have taken place in the territory of another Member State:

Provided that the supplier is registered for value added tax in that other Member State,][25] [(ib)   the operation, in accordance with Commission Regulation (EC) No. 2777/2000 of 18 December 2000, of the Cattle Testing or Purchase for Destruction Scheme, by a body who is [an accountable person][1] by virtue of the Value-Added Tax (Agricultural Intervention Agency) Order, 2001(S.I. No. 11 of 2001),][26]

(ii)   services specified in paragraph (i), (ix) [...][27] (d), or (xi), of the First Schedule, supplied-

(I)   outside the Community, or

(II)   directly in connection with the export of goods to a place outside [the Community,][28]

[(iia)   services consisting of the issue of new stocks, new shares, new debentures or other new securities by [the accountable person][1] in so far as such issue is made to raise capital for the purposes of [the accountable person's][1] taxable supplies, and][29]

(iii)   supplies of goods or services outside the State [, other than services consisting of the hiring out of motor vehicles (as defined in subsection (3)(b)) for utilisation in the State,][30] which would be taxable supplies if made in the State.][31]

[(c)   **For the purposes of paragraph (a)(ix) and subsection (4)(ba), a 'qualifying vehicle' means a motor vehicle which, for the purposes of vehicle registration tax is first registered, in accordance with section 131 of Finance Act 1992, on or after 1 January 2009 and has, for the purposes of that registration, a level of CO_2 emissions of less than 156g/km.][32]**

[(1A) (a)   A person who, by election or in accordance with the provisions of section 8(4) is deemed to become [an accountable person][1], shall, in accordance with regulations, be entitled, in computing the amount of tax payable by him in respect of the first taxable period for which he is so deemed to be [an accountable person][1], to treat as tax deductible under subsection (1) such part of the value of the stock-in-trade (within the meaning of section 34) held by him immediately before the commencement of that taxable period as could reasonably be regarded as the amount which he would be entitled to claim under the said subsection (1) if be had been [an accountable person][1] at the time of the delivery to him of such stock-in-trade.

(b)   No claim shall lie under this subsection for a deduction for the tax relating to any stock-in-trade (within the meaning of section 34) if, and to the extent that, a deduction under subsection (1) could be claimed apart from this subsection.

(c)   This subsection shall have effect in relation of taxable periods commencing on or after the 3rd day of September, 1973.][33]

a 183   (2)   If, in relation to any taxable period, the total amount deductible under this section exceeds the amount which, but for this section, would be payable in respect of such period, the excess shall be [refunded to [the accountable person][1] in accordance with section 20(1)][34] [, but subject to [sections 20(1A) and 20(5)][35].][36]

a 176   [(3)   (a)   Notwithstanding anything [in this section, a deduction of tax under this section][37] shall not be made if, and to the extent that, the tax relates to-

[(i)   expenditure incurred by [the accountable person][1] on food or drink, or accommodation other than qualifying accommodation in connection with attendance at a qualifying conference as defined in paragraph (ca), or other personal services, for [the accountable person][1], [the accountable person's][1] agents or employees, except to the extent, if any, that such expenditure is incurred in relation to a supply of services in respect of which [that accountable person][1] is accountable for tax,][38]

[(ia)   expenditure incurred by [the accountable person][1] on food or drink, or accommodation or other entertainment services, where such expenditure forms all or part of the cost of providing an advertising service in respect of which tax is due and payable by [the accountable person][1 ,][39]

(ii)   entertainment expenses incurred by [the accountable person][1 , his agents or his employees,

(iii)   **[subject to subsection (1)(a)(ix)][40]** the [purchase, hiring, intra-Community acquisition, or importation][41] of motor vehicles otherwise than as stock-in-trade [or for the purpose of the supply thereof by a person supplying financial services of the kind specified in subparagraph (i)(e) of the First Schedule in respect of those motor vehicles as part of an agreement of the kind referred to in section 3(1)(b)][42] or for the purposes of a business which consists in whole or part of the hiring of motor vehicles or for use, in a driving school business, for giving driving instruction, [or][43]

(iv)   the purchase [intra-Community acquisition or importation]⁴⁴ of petrol otherwise than as stock-in-trade,

[(iva) the procurement of a supply of contract work where such supply consists of the handing over of goods to which this paragraph applies.]⁴⁵

[...]⁴⁶

(b)   In paragraph (a) of this subsection '**motor vehicles**' means motor vehicles designed and constructed for the conveyance of persons by road and sports motor vehicles, estate cars, station wagons, motor cycles, motor scooters, mopeds and auto cycles, whether or not designed and constructed for the purpose aforesaid, excluding vehicles designed and constructed for the carriage of more than 16 persons (inclusive of the driver), invalid carriages and other vehicles of a type designed for use by invalids or infirm persons.]⁴⁷

[(c)   In subparagraph (i) of paragraph (a), reference to the provision of accommodation includes expenditure by [the accountable person]¹ on a building, including the fitting out of such building, to provide such accommodation.

[(ca)   For the purposes of subparagraph (a)(i) –

'**delegate**' means a taxable person or a taxable person's employee or an agent who attends a qualifying conference in the course or furtherance of that taxable person's business;

'**qualifying accommodation**' means the supply to a delegate of a service consisting of the letting of immovable goods or accommodation covered by paragraph (xiii) of the Sixth Schedule, for a maximum period starting from the night prior to the date on which the qualifying conference commences and ending on the date on which the conference concludes;

'**qualifying conference**' means a conference or meeting in the course or furtherance of business organised to cater for 50 or more delegates, which takes place on or after 1 July 2007 at a venue designed and constructed for the purposes of hosting 50 or more delegates and in respect of which the person responsible for organising the conference issues in writing the details of the conference to each taxable person who attends or sends a delegate, and such details shall include –

(i)   the location and dates of the conference,

(ii)   the nature of the business being conducted,

(iii) the number of delegates for whom the conference is organised, and

(iv) the name, business address and VAT registration number of the person responsible for organising the conference.][48]

(d) In subparagraph (ii) of paragraph (a), '**entertainment expenses**' includes expenditure on a building or facility, including the fitting out of such building or facility, to provide such entertainment.][49]

[(3A) Notwithstanding anything in this section, where-

(a) the provisions of subsection (3) or (8) of section 10A or subsection (3) of section 10B have been applied to a supply of goods to [an accountable person][1] , or

(b) a taxable dealer deducts residual tax, in accordance with subsection (1)(a)(vi), in respect of a supply of a means of transport to [an accountable person][1] ,

[that accountable person][1] shall not deduct, in accordance with subsection (1), any tax in relation to the supply to that person.][50]

a173, a 174, [(4) (a) In this subsection -

a 175   '**deductible supplies or activities**' means the supply of taxable goods or taxable services, or the carrying out of qualifying activities as defined in subsection (1)(b);

'**dual-use inputs**' means [movable][51] goods or services (other than goods or services on the purchase or acquisition of which, by virtue of subsection (3), a deduction of tax shall not be made[, **or services related to the development of immovable goods that are subject to the provisions of section 12E**][52]) which are not used solely for the purposes of either deductible supplies or activities or non-deductible supplies or activities;

'**non-deductible supplies or activities**' means the supply of goods or services or the carrying out of activities other than deductible supplies or activities;

'**total supplies and activities**' means deductible supplies or activities and non-deductible supplies or activities.

(b) Where [an accountable person][1] engages in both deductible supplies or activities and non-deductible supplies or activities then, in relation to that person's acquisition of dual-use inputs for the purpose of that person's business for a period, that person shall be entitled to deduct in accordance with subsection (1) only such proportion of tax, borne or payable on that acquisition, which is calculated in accordance with the provisions of this subsection and regulations, as being attributable to that person's deductible supplies or activities and such proportion of tax is, for the purposes of this subsection, referred to as the '**proportion of tax deductible**'.

[(ba)   **For the purposes of this subsection, the reference in paragraph (b) to 'tax, borne or payable' shall, in the case of an acquisition of a qualifying vehicle (within the meaning assigned by subsection (1)(c)) be deemed to be a reference to '20 per cent of the tax, borne or payable'.][53]**

(c)   For the purposes of this subsection and regulations, the proportion of tax deductible by [an accountable person][1] for a period shall be calculated on any basis which results in a proportion of tax deductible which correctly reflects the extent to which the dual-use inputs are used for the purposes of that person's deductible supplies or activities and has due regard to the range of that person's total supplies and activities.

(d)   The proportion of tax deductible may be calculated on the basis of the ratio which the amount of a person's tax-exclusive turnover from deductible supplies or activities for a period bears to the amount of that person's tax-exclusive turnover from total supplies and activities for that period but only if that basis results in a proportion of tax deductible which is in accordance with paragraph (c).

(e)   Where it is necessary to do so to ensure that the proportion of tax deductible by [an accountable person][1] is in accordance with paragraph (c), [an accountable person][1] shall-

(i)   calculate a separate proportion of tax deductible for any part of that person's business, or

(ii)   exclude, from the calculation of the proportion of tax deductible, amounts of turnover from incidental transactions by that person of the type specified in paragraph (i) of the First Schedule or amounts of turnover from incidental transactions by that person in immovable goods.

(f)   The proportion of tax deductible as calculated by [an accountable person][1] for a taxable period [shall][54] be adjusted in accordance with regulations, if, for the [accounting year][55] in which the taxable period ends, that proportion does not correctly reflect the extent to which the dual-use inputs are used for the purposes of that person's deductible supplies or activities or does not have due regard to the range of that person's total supplies and activities.][56]

[(4A) (a) Where an accountable person deducts tax in relation to the purchase, intra-Community acquisition or importation of a qualifying vehicle in accordance with subsection (1)(a)(ix) and that person disposes of that qualifying vehicle within 2 years of that purchase, acquisition or importation, then that person shall be obliged to reduce the amount of the tax deductible by that person for the taxable period in which the vehicle is disposed of by an amount calculated in accordance with the following formula:

$$\frac{TD \times (4-N)}{4}$$

where—

TD   is the amount of tax deducted by that accountable person on the purchase, acquisition or importation of that vehicle, and

N   is a number that is equal to the number of days from the date of purchase, acquisition or importation of the vehicle by that accountable person to the date of disposal by that person, divided by 182 and rounded down to the nearest whole number,

but if that N is greater than 4 then N shall be 4.

(b) Where an accountable person deducts tax in relation to the purchase, intra-Community acquisition or importation of a qualifying vehicle in accordance with subsection (1)(a)(ix) and the vehicle is subsequently used for less than 60 per cent business purposes in a taxable period, then that person is obliged to reduce the amount of tax deductible by that person for that taxable period by an amount calculated in accordance with the following formula:

$$\frac{TD \times (4-N)}{4}$$

where—

TD   is the amount of tax deducted by that accountable person on the purchase, acquisition or importation of that vehicle, and

N   is a number that is equal to the number of days from the date of purchase, acquisition or importation of the vehicle by that accountable person to the first day of the taxable period in

**which the vehicle is used for less than 60 per cent
business purposes, divided by 182 and rounded
down to the nearest whole number,**
but if that N is greater than 4 then N shall be 4.][57]

[…][58]

Amendments

1   Inserted by FA08 s109 & Sch 4, (w.e.f. 1 July 2008).
2   Inserted by FA01 s188(a), (w.e.f. 21 March 2001).
3   Deleted by FA07 s83(a), (w.e.f. 1 May 2007).
4   Ss(1)(a)(iia) - (iib) inserted by FA92 s174(a), (w.e.f. 1 January 1993).
5   Ss(1)(a)(iic) inserted by FA93 s88(a), (w.e.f. 1 August 1993).
6   Inserted by EC(VAT)R 1992 r10(b), (w.e.f. 1 January 1993).
7   Ss(1)(a)(iiia) inserted by FA91 s81, (w.e.f. 29 May 1991).
8   Ss(1)(a)(iiib) inserted by FA94 s96(a), (w.e.f. date appt. by the Minister).
9   Substituted by FA08 s94(a)(i), (w.e.f. 1 July 2008).
10 Ss(1)(a)(iiic) substituted by FA05 s104(1)(a)(i), (w.e.f. 25 March 2005).
11 Ss(1)(a)(iiid) deleted by FA05 s104(1)(a)(ii), (w.e.f. 25 March 2005).
12 Ss(1)(a)(iiie) inserted by FA99 s128(a), (w.e.f. 1 January 2000).
13 Substituted by F(No. 2)A 08 s99 & Sch 6, (w.e.f. 24 December 2008).
14 Ss(1)(a)(va) inserted by FA04 s60, (w.e.f. 25 March 2004).
15 Ss(1)(a)(vb) inserted by FA04 s60, (w.e.f. 1 January 2005).
16 Ss(1)(a)(vc) inserted by FA08 s94(a)(ii), (w.e.f. 1 September 2008).
17 Ss(1)(a)(vi) substituted by FA95 s129(a), (w.e.f. 1 July 1995).
18 Ss(1)(a)(via) inserted by FA99 s128(b), (w.e.f. 1 January 2000).
19 Ss(1)(a)(vib) inserted by FA00 s12, (w.e.f. 23 March 2000).
20 Deleted by F(No. 2)A 08 s73(a)(i), (w.e.f. 24 December 2008).
21 Substituted by FA93 s88(b), (w.e.f. 17 June 1993).
22 Substituted by F(No. 2)A 08 s73(a)(i), (w.e.f. 24 December 2008).
23 Inserted by F(No. 2)A 08 s73(a)(ii), (w.e.f. 24 December 2008).
24 Inserted by FA93 s88(c), (w.e.f. 17 June 1993).
25 Ss(1)(b)(ia) inserted by EC(VAT)R 1992 r10(a), (w.e.f. 1 January 1993).
26 Para. (ib) inserted by FA01 s188(b), (w.e.f. 8 January 2001).
27 Deleted by FA02 Sch 6, (w.e.f. 25 March 2002).
28 Substituted by FA06 s98(a), (w.e.f. 31 March 2006).
29 Ss(1)(b)(iia) inserted by FA06 s98(b), (w.e.f. 31 March 2006).
30 Inserted by FA98 s111(a), (w.e.f. 27 March 1998).
31 Ss(1) substituted by FA87 s41, (w.e.f. 1 November 1987).
32 Inserted by F(No. 2)A 08 s73(a)(iii), (w.e.f. 24 December 2008).
33 Ss(1a) inserted by FA73 s81, (w.e.f. 3 September 1973).
34 Substituted by FA81 s44, (w.e.f. 28 May 1981).
35 Substituted by FA98 s111(b), (w.e.f. 27 March 1998).
36 Inserted by FA86 s84, (w.e.f. 27 May 1986).
37 Substituted by FA87 s41, (w.e.f. 1 November 1987).
38 Substituted by FA07 s83(b)(i) (w.e.f. 1 July 2007)
39 Ss(3)(a)(ia) inserted by FA94 s96(b)(i), (w.e.f. 23 May 1994).
40 Inserted by F(No. 2)A 08 s73(b), (w.e.f. 24 December 2008).
41 Substituted by FA92 s174(b)(i), (w.e.f. 1 January 1993).
42 Inserted by FA07 s83(b)(ii) (w.e.f. 1 May 2007).
43 Inserted by FA87 s41, (w.e.f. 1 November 1987).
44 Inserted by FA92 s174(b)(ii), (w.e.f. 1 January 1993).
45 Inserted by FA96 s93(b), (w.e.f. 15 May 1996).
46 Deleted by FA87 s41, (w.e.f. 1 November 1987).
47 Ss(3) substituted by VAT Amend. A78 s10, (w.e.f. 1 March 1979).
48 Inserted by FA07 s83(b)(iii), (w.e.f. 1 July 2007).
49 Ss(3)(c) - (d) inserted by FA94 s96(b)(ii), (w.e.f. 23 May 1994).

50 Ss(3A) inserted by FA95 s129(b), (w.e.f. 1 July 1995).
51 Inserted by FA08 s94(b)(i), (w.e.f. 1 July 2008).
52 Inserted by F(No. 2)A 08 s99 & Sch 6, (w.e.f. 24 December 2008).
53 Inserted by F(No. 2)A 08 s73(c), (w.e.f. 24 December 2008).
54 Substituted by FA01 s188(c), (w.e.f. 21 March 2001).
55 Substituted by FA08 s94(b)(ii), (w.e.f. 1 July 2008).
56 Ss(4) substituted by FA00 s112(b), (w.e.f. 23 March 2000).
57 Ss(4A) inserted by F(No. 2)A 08 s73(d), (w.e.f. 24 December 2008).
58 Ss5 deleted by FA08 S94(c), (w.e.f. 1 July 2008).

Regulations and Orders

Apportionment	2006 SI No. 548	Value-Added Tax Regulations 2006
Apportionment of amounts	1979 SI No. 63	Value-Added Tax Regulations, 1979
Apportionment of Input Tax	2000 SI No. 254	Value-Added Tax (Apportionment) Regulations, 2000
Second Hand Motor Vehicles	1988 SI No. 121	Value-Added Tax (Second Hand motor vehicles) Regulations, 1988
Stock relief start-up	1979 SI No. 63	Value-Added Tax Regulations, 1979
Stock relief, start up	2006 SI No. 548	Value-Added Tax Regulations 2006

Revenue e-Briefs

Revenue e-Brief No. 16/2005: VAT Deductibility in relation to share issues – Kretztechnik AG v Finanzamt Linz (Case C-465/03)

Revenue Statements of Practice and Information Leaflets

Conferences – VAT deductibility: Information Leaflet dated October 2008

Deductible tax, VAT on shares not deductible: SP-VAT/2/90

Foreign firms doing business in Ireland, VAT treatment of: Information Leaflet dated October 2008

Motor vehicles, deduction of VAT on certain cars: Information Leaflet dated February 2009

Case law

Ampafrance S.A. v Directeur des Services Fiscaux de Maine-et-Loire	C177/99	Recovery/Entertainment/Restaurant costs
António Jorge Lda v Fazenda Pública	C536/03	Dual use inputs/Deductible proportion
BLP Group v Customs and Excise	C4/94	Shares deduction/Right of
BUPA Hospitals Ltd, Goldsborough Developments Ltd v Commissioners of Customs & Excise	C419/02	Payment on account/Chargeable Event/Taxable person/Entitlement to VAT recovery
Cedilac SA V Ministère de l'Économie, des Finances et de l'Industrie	C368/06	Right to deduct/Carry forward of the excess VAT to the following period or refund
Charles P. and Charles-Tijmens T.S. v Staatssecretaris van Financiën	C434/03	Deduction/Immovable property used for business and private purposes
Cibo Participations SA v Directeur régional des impôts du Nord-Pas-de-Calais	C16/00	Holding Coy Taxable person/Recovery of VAT
Colle Parkview Service Station Ltd v BD O'Shea	Irish H.C. No. 390R	Transfer of a business/Recovery of VAT
Cookies World Vertriebsgesellschaft mbH iL and Finanzlandesdirektion für Tirol	C155/01	Deduction/Exclusions provided for under national law
Debouche, Etienne v Inspecteur der Invoerrechten en Accijinzen Rijswijk	C302/93	Deduction/Right of
Ecotrade SpA vAgenzia delle Entrate – Ufficio di Genova 3	C95/07 and C96/07	Reverse charge procedure/Right to deduct
Empresa de Desenvolvimento Mineiro SGPS SA (EDM) and Fazenda Pública	C77/01	Meaning of 'economic activities'/ Meaning of 'incidental financial transactions'/Calculation of deductible proportion
Erin Executor and Trustee Company Limited t/a IPFPUT v Revenue Commissioners	Irish Supreme Court 363 and 369/1994 ITR VOL II No. 3	Recovery leasehold property/Post letting expenses

Eurodental Sàrl v Administration de l'enregistrement et des domaines	C240/05	Deduction/Right of/Intra-Community transactions
Faxworld Vorgründungsgesellschaft Peter Hünninghausen und Wolfgang Klein GbR and Finanzamt Offenbach am Main-Land	C137/02	Right to deduct
Fini H, I/S v Skatteministeriet	C32/03	Ceased economic activity/ Deduction/Right of
Floridienne SA v Belgium	C142/99	Recovery/Apportionment/Share dividends to be included
France v Commission	C345/99	Cars used by driving schools
France v Commission	C40/00	Reintroduction of recovery restrictions
France v European Commission	C43/96	Means of Transport/Recovery of VAT
France v European Commission	C50/87	Leased buildings/Deduction/ Right of
France v Commission	C243/03	Deduction/Capital goods financed by subsidies
Gaston Schul Douane Expediteur BV v Inspecteur Der Invoerrechtenn EN Accijnzen	C15/81	Recovery of VAT on imports of second hand cars
Genius Holding BV v Staatssecretaris van Financien	C342/87	Deduction/Right of
Gerhard Bockemühl and Förvaltnings AB Stenholmen and Riksskatteverket	C90/02	Deduction/obligation to possess invoice/9(2)(e) service
Ghent Coal Terminal NV v Belgium	C37/95	Deduction/Right of
Halifax plc, Leeds Permanent Development Services Ltd, County Wide property Investments Ltd v Commissioners of Customs& Excise	C255/02	Economic Activity/Supplies/Abusive practice
HE v Bundesfinanzhof (Germany) Finanzamt Bergisch	C25/03	Right to deduct/Use of one room of dwelling for business purposes
Intercommunale voor Zeewaterontzilting "Inzo" v Belgium	C110/94	Intending trader/Deduction/Right of
"Intiem" Leesportefeuille CV v Staatssecretaris van Financien	C165/86	Deduction/Right of
Investrand BV v Staatssecretaris van Financiën	C435/05	Deduction/Right of
Jeunehomme, Lea and Societe Anonyme d'Etude et de EGI Gestion Immobiliere "EGI"v Belgium	C123/87 and C330/87	Deduction/Right of
Kittel, Axel v Belgian State and Recolta Recycling SPRL v Belgian State	C439/04 C440/04	Deduction/Carousel Fraud/Void contract
Kretztechnik AG, Außenstelle Linz	C465/03	Supply/Share Issue/Admission of company to stock exchange
Lennartz v Finanzamt Munchen III	C97/90	Taxable Event/Self Supply
Magoora sp. z.o.o. v Direktor Izby Skrabovej w Krakowie	C414/07	Deduction of VAT on purchase of fuel for certain vehicles irrespective of the purpose for which they are used
Maye John v Revenue Commissioners	Irish H.C. III ITR 332	Fixtures/Property
Metropol Treuhand Wirtschaftstreuhand Gmbh v Finanzlandesdirection fur Steurmark	C409/99	Cars recovery
Midland Bank Plc v Customs and Excise	C98/98	Recovery
Netherlands v Commission	C338/98	Cars Recovery
Nordania Finans A/S, BG Factoring A/S v Skatteministeriet	C98/07	Calculation of the deductible proportion/Exclusion of amounts of turnover attributable to the supplies of capital goods used by the taxable person for the purposes of his business
Optigen Ltd, Fulcrum Electronics Ltd, Bond House Systems Ltd v Commissioners of Customs & Excise	C354/03 C355/03 C484/03	Economic activity/Taxable person/ Deduction/Carousel fraud
ORO Amsterdam Beheer BV & Concerto BV v Inspecteur der Omzetbelasting Amsterdam	C165/88	Deduction/Right of

Polysar Investments Netherlands BV v Inspecteur der Inveorrechten en Accijnzen	C60/90	Holding Coy/Taxable Person/ Recovery of VAT
Regie Dauphinoise - Cabinet A Forest Sarl v Ministre du Budget	C306/94	Apportionment of VAT for recovery
Reisdorf, John v Finanzamt Koln-West	C85/95	Deduction
Rompelman, DA & Rompelman van Deelen, EA v Minister van Financien	C268/83	Intending trader/Recovery by
Royal Bank of Scotland Group plc v The Commissioners for Her Majesty's Revenue and Customs	C488/07	Deduction of input tax/Goods and services used fro taxable and exempt activities
Royscot Leasing Ltd & Others v Customs and Excise	C305/97	Cars/Recovery
Sanofi Winthrop SA v Directeur Service Fiscaux du Val Marne	C181/99	Recovery/Derogation proportionality
Securenta Göttinger Immobilienanlagen und Vermögensmanagement AG v Finanzamt Göttingen	C437/06	Expenditure connected with the issue of shares and atypical silent partnerships/Apportionment of input VAT according to the economic nature of the activity
Societe Generales - des Grandes Sources d'eaux Minerales Francaises v Bundessamt Fur Finanzen	C361/96	Recovery
Sofitam Sa formerly Satam v Minister responsible for Budget (France)	C333/91	Holding Coy Deduction/Right of
Spain v Commission	C204/03	Subsidies/Limitation of the right to deduct
Stadler, Michael v Finanzlandesdirektion fur Vorarlberg	C409/99	Cars recovery
Terra Baubedarf-Handel GmbH and Finanzamt Osterholz-Scharmbeck	C152/02	Right to deduct/Conditions of exercise
United Kingdom v Commission	C33/03	Fuel costs reimbursed by employer/ Recovery of VAT
University of Huddersfield High Education Corporation v Commissioners of Customs & Excise	C223/03	Economic Activity/Supplies/Abusive practice
Waterschap Zeeuws Vlaanderen v Staatssecretaris van Financiën	C378/02	Public authority/Supply/Right to adjustment and deduction
Wellcome Trust Ltd. v Customs and Excise	C155/94	Shares Deduction/Right of

Revenue Precedents

Topic:	Deductible VAT
Issue:	Accommodation non-deductible for VAT-registered persons.
Decision:	Airline Companies allowed deductibility for accommodating passengers in hotels etc. because of flight conditions.
Date:	28/10/83

Topic:	Pension Funds.
Issue:	Right to input credit.
Decision:	Two decisions: (1) Where an employer is responsible under contract for meeting costs of services, and the relevant invoices are issued in his name, he is entitled to input credit. (2) However services supplied to the trustees for the purpose of their business would not be allowable.
Date:	8/6/92

(withdrawn from the Revenue website in 2002)

Topic:	Exported Goods.
Issue:	VAT paid by shipping agents at importation on goods subsequently exported.
Decision:	Input credit can be taken by shipping agent in their next VAT return subject to certain conditions.
Date:	23/2/84

(withdrawn from the Revenue website in 2002)

Narrative

Tour Operators and Travel Agents: ITR Mar 2008: Vol. 21 No. 2

The Halifax Decision: ITR May 2006: Vol. 19 No. 3

VAT Fraud: The ECJ Considers the Liability of the Innocent Trader: ITR Mar 2006: Vol. 19 No. 2.

Tax Briefing: Issue 61 (VAT Deductibility in Relation to New Share Issues – Implications of the ECJ Decision in the Kretztechnik AG Case)

Tax Briefing: Issue 60 (Property - Finance Act 2005 Changes)

Halifax, BUPA and University of Huddersfield Cases: ITR Jul 2005: Vol. 18 No. 4

ECJ Rules VAT is Recoverable on Share Issues: ITR Jul 2005: Vol. 18 No. 4

European VAT – Changing Times for International VAT Compliance: ITR Jul 2005: Vol. 18 No. 4.

Tax Briefing: Issue 59 (Debt Factoring)

VAT Carousel Fraud: ITR Jul 2004: Vol. 17 No. 4.

Recovery of VAT in Europe: a step by step guide: ITR Mar 2004: Vol. 17 No. 2.

Tax Briefing: Issue 54 (Share Acquisitions: VAT Recovery on Professional Expenses)

Tax Briefing: Issue 46 (VAT (Apportionment) Regulations 2000)

Tax Briefing: Issue 43 (VAT Committee Guidelines – Customs Import Documents: Indications Required to Exercise the Right to Deduction of VAT Payable on Import)

Tax Briefing: Issue 42 (VAT (Apportionment) Regulations 2000)

VAT and Cross-border Leasing of Means of Transport: ITR Nov 1999: Vol. 12 No. 6.

VAT and Property: ITR Nov 1998: Vol. 11. No. 6.

Recovery of Foreign VAT: ITR March 1999: Vol. 12 No. 2.

Tax Briefing: Issue 33 (Deduction on Motor Cars and Petrol)

Tax Briefing: Issue 32 (Post-Letting Expenses)

Tax Briefing: Issue 30 (EU Supplies)

Section 12A

Special provisions for tax invoiced by flat-rate farmers

a 295,
a 300,
a 301

12A. [(1)   Where a flat-rate farmer supplies agricultural produce or an agricultural service to a person, the farmer shall, subject to section 17(2), issue to the person an invoice indicating the consideration (exclusive of the flat-rate addition) in respect of the supply and an amount (in this Act referred to as **'a flat-rate addition'**) equal to [5.2 per cent][1] of the said consideration (exclusive of the said addition)[…][2]

[(2)   In this Act **'flat-rate farmer'** means -

(a)   a farmer who is not [an accountable person][3],

(b)   a farmer who is [an accountable person][3] referred to in subsection (1A)(c) or (2)(b) of section 8, or

(c)   a person who, in accordance with section 8(3A), is deemed not to be [an accountable person][3] in relation to the supplies specified in the definition of **'farmer'** in section 8(9).][4][5]

Amendments
1   Substituted by FA07 s84 (w.e.f. 1 January 2007).
2   Deleted by FA92 s175(2), (w.e.f. 1 January 1993).
3   Substituted by FA08 s109 & Sch 4, (w.e.f. 1 July 2008).
4   Ss(2) substituted by FA93 s89(b).
5   S12A inserted by VAT Amend. A78 s11, (w.e.f. 1 March 1979).

Revenue Statements of Practice and Information Leaflets
Farmers and Intra-EU Transactions: Information Leaflet dated December 2008
Milk Production Partnerships, VAT issues for: Information Leaflet No. 1/04
Repayments to Unregistered Persons: Information Leaflet dated October 2008

Case law
Stadt Sundern v Bundesfinanzhof Finanzamt   C43/04   Flat-rate scheme for farmers/
Arnsberg   Agricultural service

Revenue Precedents
Topic:	Flat-Rate Addition.
Issue:	Can Government Departments be regarded as a farmer.
Decision:	Government Departments are entitled to the flat-rate addition on their sales of agricultural produce.
Date:	12/12/86

Narrative
Tax Briefing: Issue 64 (VAT and the Single Farm Payment)
Tax Briefing: Issue 39 (Notification of VAT Regulation)
Tax Briefing: Issue 32 (Treatment of A.I. Services and Sales of Livestock Semen)

Section 12B

Special scheme for means of transport supplied by taxable dealers

12B. [(1)   Where a taxable dealer supplies a means of transport, the residual tax which is deductible in accordance with section 12(1)(a)(vi) shall be deemed to be tax and shall be the amount referred to in subsection (4).

(2)   The entitlement to deduct residual tax referred to in subsection (1) shall arise only where a taxable dealer purchases or acquires [(other than in the circumstances where an owner as referred to in paragraph (c) of subsection (5) of section 3, enforces such owner's right to recover possession of a means of transport)][1] -

    (a)   a means of transport from a person, other than a person referred to in subsection (10), who was not entitled to deduct, under section 12, any tax in respect of that person's purchase, intra-Community acquisition or importation of that means of transport, or

    [(aa)   a means of transport from a person where the disposal of that means of transport by such person to such taxable dealer was deemed not to be a supply of goods in accordance with [section 3(5)(d)][2], or][3]

    (b)   a means of transport other than a new means of transport from a person in another Member State who was not entitled to deduct, under the provisions implementing [Articles 167, 173, 176 and 177 of Council Directive No. 2006/112/EC of 28 November 2006][4] in that Member State, any value-added tax referred to in that Directive in respect of that person's purchase, intra-Community acquisition or importation of that means of transport, or

    (c)   a means of transport from [an accountable person][5] who has exercised the entitlement under section 12(1)(a)(vi) to deduct the residual tax in respect of that person's supply of that means of transport to the said dealer, or

    (d)   a means of transport other than a new means of transport from a taxable dealer in another Member State who has applied the provisions implementing [Articles 4 and 35, first subparagraph of Article 139(3) and Articles 311 to 341 of Council Directive No. 2006/112/EC of 28 November 2006][4] to the supply of that means of transport, in that other Member State.

(3)   In this section -

['taxable dealer' —

    (a)   means an accountable person, who in the course or furtherance of business, whether acting on that person's own behalf, or on behalf of another person pursuant to a contract under which commission is payable on purchase or sale, purchases or acquires means of transport as stock-in-trade with a view to resale, and

(b)   includes a person supplying financial services of the kind specified in subparagraph (i)(e) of the First Schedule who acquires or purchases means of transport for the purpose of the supply thereof as part of an agreement of the kind referred to in section 3(1)(b),

and, for the purpose of this interpretation, a person in another Member State shall be deemed to be a taxable dealer where, in similar circumstances, that person would be a taxable dealer in the State under this section;][6]

'means of transport' means motorised land vehicles with an engine cylinder capacity exceeding 48 cubic centimetres or a power exceeding 7.2 kilowatts, vessels exceeding 7.5 metres in length and aircraft with a take-off weight exceeding 1,550 kilogrammes, which are intended for the transport of persons or goods, other than [agricultural machinery (within the meaning of section 12C), and][7] vessels and aircraft of the kind referred to in paragraph (v) of the Second Schedule.

(4)   The residual tax which may be deducted by a taxable dealer in accordance with section 12(1)(a)(vi) shall be the residual tax deemed to be included in the purchase price payable by such dealer when acquiring a means of transport and shall be determined by the formula-

$$A \times \frac{B}{B + 100}$$

where-

A is the purchase price of the means of transport, and

B is the percentage rate of tax specified-

(a)   in section 11(1)(a) where the means of transport is deemed to be supplied within the State to the taxable dealer, or

(b)   in provisions implementing [Article 93 of Council Directive No. 2006/112/EC of 28 November 2006][4] in another Member State where the means of transport is deemed to be supplied within that Member State to the taxable dealer:

Provided that, subject to subsection (8), where the amount so calculated is in excess of the tax chargeable on the supply by the taxable dealer of the means of transport, the residual tax shall be an amount equal to the amount of tax chargeable on that supply.

(5)   Notwithstanding section 17, where a taxable dealer deducts residual tax referred to in subsection (1) in respect of a supply of a means

of transport, that dealer shall not indicate separately the amount of tax chargeable in respect of that supply on any invoice or other document issued in lieu thereof in accordance with that section.

(6)   Notwithstanding section 3(6)(d), in the case of a supply of a means of transport which is dispatched or transported and where-

(a)   a taxable dealer deducts residual tax referred to in subsection (1) in respect of the supply of that means of transport, or

(b)   a taxable dealer in another Member State has applied the provisions implementing [Articles 4 and 35, first subparagraph of Article 139(3) and Articles 311 to 341 of Council Directive No. 2006/112/EC of 28 November 2006][4] in that other Member State, to the supply of that means of transport,

the place of supply shall be deemed to be the place where the dispatch or transportation begins.

(7)   Where a taxable dealer deducts residual tax referred to in subsection (1) in respect of a supply of a means of transport, then, subject to subsection (8), the provisions of section 11(1)(b) shall not apply in respect of that supply.

(8)   Notwithstanding subsection (7), where a taxable dealer deducts residual tax referred to in subsection (1) in respect of the supply of a new means of transport dispatched or transported by the supplier to a person in another Member State, the provisions of section 11(1)(b) shall apply, and in determining the amount of the residual tax in accordance with subsection (4) the proviso to that subsection shall not apply.

(9)   Where a taxable dealer supplies a means of transport on behalf of another person pursuant to a contract under which commission is payable on purchase or sale, the means of transport shall be deemed to have been supplied by that other person to the taxable dealer when the said taxable dealer supplies that means of transport.

(10)   Notwithstanding paragraph (xxiv) of the First Schedule, the provisions of that paragraph shall not apply to-

(a)   a supply by [an accountable person][5] of a means of transport, other than a motor vehicle as defined in section 12(3)(b), which that person acquired from a taxable dealer who deducted residual tax in respect of the supply of that means of transport to that person, [...][8]

(b)   a supply by [an accountable person][5] other than a taxable dealer of a motor vehicle, as defined in section 12(3)(b), which that person acquired as stock-in-trade or for the purposes of a business which consists in whole or part of the hiring of motor vehicles or for use, in a driving school business, for giving driving instruction, from a taxable dealer who deducted residual tax in respect of the supply [of that motor vehicle to that person, and][9]

[(c)   a supply by a taxable dealer of a means of transport being a motor vehicle as defined in section 12(3)(b) which has been declared for registration in accordance with section 131 of the Finance Act 1992 on that dealer's own behalf, unless it can be shown to the satisfaction of the Revenue Commissioners that, on the basis of the use to which that means of transport has been put by that taxable dealer, the provisions of subsection (11)(b) should not apply to that supply.][10]

[(11)   (a)   Where a means of transport which is a motor vehicle as defined in section 12(3)(b) is declared for registration to the Revenue Commissioners in accordance with section 131 of the Finance Act 1992 by a taxable dealer on that dealer's own behalf and on which deductibility in accordance with section 12 has been claimed by that dealer, then that means of transport shall be treated for the purposes of this Act as if it were removed from stock-in-trade and such removal is deemed to be a supply of that means of transport by that taxable dealer for the purposes of section 3(1)(e) [and, for the avoidance of doubt, the amount of tax chargeable in respect of that supply is included and was always included in the amount deductible in accordance with paragraph (b) and accordingly is not included and was never included in any amount which the taxable person is entitled to deduct in accordance with section 12(1)(a)(iii)][11].

(b)   At the time when a taxable dealer supplies to another person a means of transport which is deemed to have been supplied in accordance with paragraph (a), then that means of transport is deemed to be re-acquired by that dealer as stock-in-trade and, notwithstanding subsection (2), the taxable dealer is entitled to deduct residual tax referred to in subsection (1) and in that case for the purposes of the formula in subsection (4) the residual tax is calculated as if 'A' were equal to the total of —

(i)   the amount on which tax was chargeable on the supply of that means of transport to the dealer,

(ii)   the tax which was chargeable on the supply referred to at subparagraph (i), and

(iii)   the vehicle registration tax accounted for by that dealer in respect of the registration of that means of transport,

and, apart from the cases provided for in paragraph (c), the amount referred to in subparagraph (i) is the amount on which tax was chargeable on the supply of that means of transport in accordance with section 3(1)(e).

(c)   Where a taxable dealer declares a means of transport for registration in the circumstances described in paragraph (a) but does not claim deductibility in accordance with section 12 in respect of that means of transport, then paragraph (b) applies when that dealer supplies that means of transport to another person.][12]][13]

Amendments

1   Inserted by FA99 s130(a)(i), (w.e.f. 25 March 1999).
2   Substituted by FA07 s85, (w.e.f. 1 May 2007).
3   Ss(2)(aa) inserted by FA99 s130(a)(ii), (w.e.f. 25 March 1999).
4   Substituted by FA07 s97 & Sch 3,(w.e.f. 1 January 2007).
5   Substituted by FA08 s109 & Sch 4, (w.e.f, 1 July 2008).
6   Substituted by FA08 s95(a), (w.e.f. 1 July 2008).
7   Inserted by FA99 s130(b), (w.e.f. 1 September 1999).
8   Deleted by FA03 s120(a), (w.e.f. 1 May 2003).
9   Substituted by FA03 s120(a), (w.e.f. 1 May 2003).
10 Ss(10)(c) inserted by FA03 s120(a), (w.e.f. 1 May 2003).
11 Inserted by FA08 s95(b), (w.e.f. 13 March 2008).
12 Ss(11) inserted by FA 03 s120(b), (w.e.f. 1 May 2003).
13 S12B inserted by FA95 s130, (w.e.f. 1 July 1995).

Regulations and Orders

Car, intra-Community Acquisitions	1992 SI No. 412	Value Added Tax (Payment of Tax on Intra-Community Acquisitions of Means of Transport) Regulations, 1992
Car, intra-Community Acquisition	1993 SI No. 248	Value Added Tax (Payment of Tax on intra-Community Acquisition of Certain New Means of Transport) Regulations, 1993
Cars	1996 SI No. 201	Documentation Value Added Tax (Special Scheme for Means of Transport: Documentation) Regulations, 1996
Means of transport, intra-Community acquisitions	2006 SI No. 548	Value-Added Tax Regulations 2006

Revenue Statements of Practice and Information Leaflets

Second-Hand Vehicles, VAT treatment of: Information Leaflet dated Oct 1995

VAT and VRT on transactions involving motor vehicles: Information Leaflet dated January 2009

Vehicles Registered by Distributors or Dealers Prior to Sale, New VAT treatment of: Information Leaflet dated May 2003

Revenue Precedents

Topic:	Farmers.
Issue:	Motor Dealer buying second-hand agricultural machinery and equipment from unregistered farmer claiming residual input credit under 7th Directive mechanism required to issue specially endorsed invoice Special Scheme.
Decision:	Dealer allowed to reclaim the residual VAT and to issue VAT invoices on onward sale of such machinery and equipment. This arrangement applies only in respect of machinery and equipment on which a farmer if he were registered for VAT could claim VAT deductibility.
Date:	26/6/97
(withdrawn from the Revenue website in 2002)	

Narrative

Tax Briefing: Issue 53 (Treatment of Vehicles Registered by Distributors or Dealers Prior to Sale)

Tax Briefing: Issue 36 (Seventh VAT Directive and the Special Scheme for Motor Vehicles)

Tax Briefing: Issue 24 (VAT and Leasing)

Tax Briefing: Issue 22 (Second-hand Vehicles)

Section 12C

Special scheme for agricultural machinery

12C. [(1)   A taxable dealer who purchases agricultural machinery from a flat-rate farmer shall, subject to the provisions of this section and in accordance with sub-paragraph (via)of paragraph (a) of subsection (1) of section 12, be entitled to deduct the residual tax contained in the price payable by such taxable dealer in respect of that purchase.

[(1A)   A taxable dealer who purchases agricultural machinery from a person where the disposal of that agricultural machinery by such person to such taxable dealer was deemed in accordance with [section 3(5)(d)]¹ not to be a supply of goods shall, subject to the provisions of this section and in accordance with subparagraph (vib) of paragraph (a) of subsection (1) of section 12, be entitled to deduct the residual tax contained in the price payable by such taxable dealer in respect of that purchase.

(1B)   A person who disposes of agricultural machinery to a taxable dealer where the disposal of that agricultural machinery by such person to such taxable dealer was deemed in accordance with [section 3(5)(d)]¹ not to be a supply of goods shall issue a document to the taxable dealer to whom the disposal is made and shall indicate on the document-

(a)   that person's name and address,

(b)   the name and address of the taxable dealer,

(c)   the date of issue of the document,

(d)   a description of the agricultural machinery, including details of the make, model and, where appropriate, the year of manufacture, the engine number and registration number of that machinery,

(e)   the consideration for the disposal of the agricultural machinery,

(f)   confirmation that the disposal is deemed in accordance with [section 3(5)(d)]¹ not to be a supply of goods, and

(g)   such other particulars as may be specified by regulations, if any.]²

(2)   A flat-rate farmer who supplies agricultural machinery to a taxable dealer shall, subject to section 17(2A), issue an invoice in respect of that supply.

(3)   The residual tax referred to in subsection (1) shall be determined by the formula-

$$A \times \frac{B}{B + 100}$$

where-

A is the purchase price of the agricultural machinery payable by the taxable dealer, and

B is the percentage rate of tax specified in section 11(1)(a).

(4)   Where a taxable dealer supplies agricultural machinery in respect of which such dealer was entitled to deduct residual tax and where the tax chargeable in respect of that supply is less than the residual tax deducted by that dealer in respect of the purchase of that machinery, then the excess of the residual tax over the tax payable on that supply shall be deemed to be tax chargeable in respect of that supply.

(5)   In this section-

'**agricultural machinery**' means machinery or equipment, other than a motor vehicle as defined in subsection (3) of section 12, which has been used by a flat-rate farmer for the purpose of such farmer's Annex A activity in circumstances where any tax charged on the supply of that machinery or equipment to that farmer would have been deductable by such farmer if such farmer had elected to be [an accountable person][3] at the time of that supply of the machinery or equipment to such farmer;

'**taxable dealer**' means [an accountable person][3] who in the course or furtherance of business, whether acting on that person's own behalf, or on behalf of another person pursuant to a contract under which commission is payable on purchase or sale, purchases agricultural machinery as stock-in-trade with a view to resale [and includes a person supplying financial services of the kind specified in subparagraph (i)(e) of the First Schedule who purchases agricultural machinery for the purpose of the supply thereof as part of an agreement of the kind referred to in section 3(1)(b)][4].[5]

Amendments

1   Substituted by FA07 s86, (w.e.f. 2 April 2007).

2   Ss1A & 1B inserted by FA00 s114, (w.e.f. 23 March 2000).

3   Substituted by FA08 s109 & Sch 4, (w.e.f. 1 July 2008).

4   Inserted by FA08 s96, (w.e.f. 1 July 2008).

5   Inserted by FA99 s131, (w.e.f. 1 September 1999).

Regulations and Orders

Documentation   1999 SI No. 443   Value Added Tax (Agricultural Machinery)(Documentation) Regulations, 1999

Narrative

Tax Briefing: Issue 39 (Notification of VAT Regulation)

Section 12D

Adjustment of tax deductible in certain circumstances

a 19 **[12D.** (1)   For the purposes of this section-

'**full year**' shall be any continuous period of twelve months;

'**interest**' in relation to immovable goods has the meaning assigned to it by section 4.

(2)   Where-

(a)   a person makes a transfer of an interest in immovable goods in accordance with section 3(5)(b)(iii), and

(b)   but for the application of that section, tax would have been chargeable on the transfer, and the person (referred to in this section as a '**transferor**') was entitled to deduct part of the tax charged on the most recent purchase or acquisition of an interest in, or the development of, the immovable goods subject to that transfer,

that transferor shall, for the purposes of section 12, be entitled to increase the amount of tax deductible for the taxable period within which the transfer is made by an amount calculated in accordance with the following formula:

$$\frac{(T - TD) \times (Y - N)}{Y}$$

where-

T is the tax chargeable on that most recent purchase or acquisition of an interest in, or that development of, the immovable goods,

TD is the tax that the transferor was entitled to deduct on that most recent purchase or acquisition of an interest in, or that development of, the immovable goods,

Y is 20 or, if the interest when it was created in the immovable goods being transferred was for a period of less than 20 years, the number of full years in that interest, and

N is the number of full years since the interest was created or, if the goods were developed since that interest was created, the number of full years since the most recent development:

but if that N is greater than that Y, such an amount calculated shall be deemed to be nil.

(3)   Where a transferor acquired an interest in immovable goods as a result of a transfer in accordance with section 3(5)(b)(iii) and the transferor did not develop those immovable goods since the acquisition then, for the purposes of subsection (2), the amount by which that transferor shall be entitled to increase the amount of tax deductible, in accordance with section 12, for the taxable period in which the transferor transfers those goods, shall be calculated in accordance with the following formula:

$$\frac{A \times (Y - N)}{Y}$$

where-

A is the amount which the transferor was required to calculate and reduce his or her deductible amount by, in accordance with subsection (4), when the transferor acquired the interest in those goods,

Y is 20 or, if the interest when it was created in the immovable goods being transferred was for a period of less than 20 years, the number of full years in that interest, and

N is the number of full years since the interest was created 15 or, if the goods were developed since that interest was created, the number of full years since the most recent development:

but if that N is greater than that Y, such an amount calculated shall be deemed to be nil.

(4)   Where a person receives an interest in immovable goods as a result of a transfer and the person would not have been entitled to deduct all the tax that would have been chargeable on the transfer but for the application of section 3(5)(b)(iii), that person shall [calculate an amount which shall be payable as if it were tax due by that person in accordance with section 19 for the taxable period within which the transfer was made, and that amount shall be calculated][1] in accordance with the following formula:

$$\frac{(T1 - TD1) \times (Y - N)}{Y}$$

where-

T1 is the amount of tax that would have been chargeable on the transfer if section 3(5)(b)(iii) did not apply,

TD1 is the amount of tax that would have been deductible by the transferee if section 3(5)(b)(iii) had not applied to the transfer,

Y is 20 or, if the interest when it was created in the immovable goods being transferred was for a period of less than 20 years, the number of full years in that interest, and

N is the number of full years since the interest was created or, if the goods were developed since that interest was created, the number of full years since the most recent development:

but if that N is greater than that Y, such an amount calculated shall be deemed to be nil.][2]

[(5)   This section does not apply to a transfer of an interest in immovable goods which occurs on or after 1 July 2008.][3]

Amendments
1   Substituted by FA02 s104, (w.e.f 25 March 2002).
2   Section 12D inserted by FA01 s191, (w.e.f. 21 March 2001).
3   Inserted by FA08 s97, (w.e.f. 13 March 2008).

[Section 12E

Capital goods scheme

12E. (1)   This section applies to capital goods–

    (a)   on the supply or development of which tax was chargeable to a taxable person, or

    (b)   on the supply of which tax would have been chargeable to a taxable person but for the application of section 3(5) (b)(iii).

a 189   (2)   In this section–

'**adjustment period**', in relation to a capital good, means the period encompassing the number of intervals as provided for in subsection (3)(a) during which adjustments of deductions are required to be made in respect of a capital good;

'**base tax amount**', in relation to a capital good, means the amount calculated by dividing the total tax incurred in relation to that capital good by the number of intervals in the adjustment period applicable to that capital good;

'**capital goods owner**' means–

    (a)   except where paragraph (b) applies, a taxable person who incurs expenditure on the acquisition or development of a capital good,

    (b)   in the case of a taxable person who is a flat-rate farmer, means a taxable person who incurs expenditure to develop or acquire a capital good other than a building or structure designed and used solely for the purposes of a farming business or for fencing, drainage or reclamation of land, and which has actually been put to use in such business;

'**deductible supplies or activities**', has the meaning assigned to it by section 12(4);

'**initial interval**', in relation to a capital good, means a period of 12 months beginning on the date when a capital good is completed or, in the case of a capital good that is supplied following completion, the initial interval for the recipient of that supply is the 12 month period beginning on the date of that supply;

'**initial interval proportion of deductible use**', in relation to a capital good, means the proportion that correctly reflects the extent to which a capital good is used during the initial interval for the purposes of a capital goods owner's deductible supplies or activities;

'**interval**', in relation to a capital good, means the initial, second or subsequent interval in an adjustment period, whichever is appropriate;

'**interval deductible amount**', in relation to a capital good in respect of the second and each subsequent interval, means the amount calculated by multiplying the base tax amount in relation to that capital good by the proportion of deductible use for that capital good applicable to the relevant interval;

'**non-deductible amount**', in relation to a capital good, means the amount which is the difference between the total tax incurred in relation to that capital good and the total reviewed deductible amount in relation to that capital good;

'**proportion of deductible use**', in relation to a capital good for an interval other than the initial interval, means the proportion that correctly reflects the extent to which a capital good is used during that interval for the purposes of a capital goods owner's deductible supplies or activities;

'**reference deduction amount**', in relation to a capital good, means the amount calculated by dividing the total reviewed deductible amount in relation to that capital good by the number of intervals in the adjustment period applicable to that capital good;

'**refurbishment**' means development on a previously completed building, structure or engineering work;

'**second interval**', in relation to a capital good, means the period beginning on the day following the end of the initial interval in the adjustment period applicable to that capital good and ending on the final day of the accounting year during which the second interval begins;

'**subsequent interval**', in relation to a capital good, means each accounting year of a capital goods owner in the adjustment period applicable to that capital good, which follows the second interval;

'**total reviewed deductible amount**', in relation to a capital good, means the amount calculated by multiplying the total tax incurred in relation to that capital good by the initial interval proportion of deductible use in relation to that capital good;

'**total tax incurred**', in relation to a capital good, has the meaning assigned to it by subsection (3)(b).

a 187   (3)   (a)   In relation to a capital good the number of intervals in the adjustment period during which adjustments of deductions are required under this section to be made, is–

           (i)   in the case of refurbishment, 10 intervals,

(ii) in the case of a capital good to which paragraph (c) or (d) of subsection (6) applies, the number of full intervals remaining in the adjustment period applicable to that capital good plus one as required to be calculated in accordance with the formula in subsection (7)(b), and

(iii) in all other cases, 20 intervals.

(b) In this section 'total tax incurred' in relation to a capital good means–

(i) the amount of tax charged to a capital goods owner in respect of that owner's acquisition or development of a capital good,

(ii) in the case of a transferee where a transfer of ownership of a capital good to which section 3(5) (b)(iii) applies–

(I) where such a transfer would have been a supply but for the application of section 3(5)(b)(iii) and that supply would have been exempt in accordance with [section 4B(2) or subsection (2) or (6)(b) of section 4C][1], then the total tax incurred that is required to be included in the copy of the capital good record that is required to be furnished by the transferor in accordance with subsection (10), and

(II) where such a transfer is not one to which clause (I) applies, then the amount of tax that would have been chargeable on that transfer but for the application of sections 3(5)(b)(iii) and 13A,

and

(iii) the amount of tax that would have been chargeable, but for the application of section 13A, to a capital goods owner on that owner's acquisition or development of a capital good.

a 19   (c) Where a capital goods owner acquires a capital good–

(i) by way of a transfer, being a transfer to which section 3(5)(b)(iii) applies other than a transfer to which subsection (10) applies, on which tax would have been chargeable but for the application of section 3(5)(b)(iii), or

(ii) on the supply or development of which tax was chargeable in accordance with section 13A, then, for the purposes of this section, that capital goods owner is deemed to have claimed a deduction in accordance with section 12 of the tax that would have been chargeable–

    (I)   on the transfer of that capital good but for the application of section 3(5)(b)(iii), less than any amount accounted for by that owner in respect of that transfer in accordance with subsection (7)(d), and

    (II)   on the supply or development of that capital good but for the application of section 13A.

    (d)   Where a capital goods owner supplies or transfers by means of a transfer to which section 3(5)(b)(iii) applies a capital good during the adjustment period then the adjustment period for that capital good for that owner shall end on the date of that supply or transfer.

(4)   (a)   Where the initial interval proportion of deductible use in relation to a capital good differs from the proportion of the total tax incurred in relation to that capital good which was deductible by that owner in accordance with section 12, then that owner shall, at the end of the initial interval, calculate an amount in accordance with the following formula:

$$A - B$$

where–

    A   is the amount of the total tax incurred in relation to that capital good which was deductible by that owner in accordance with section 12, and

    B   is the total reviewed deductible amount in relation to that capital good.

    (b)   Where in accordance with paragraph (a)–

    (i)   A is greater than B, then the amount calculated in accordance with the formula in paragraph (a) shall be payable by that owner as if it were tax due in accordance with section 19 for the taxable period immediately following the end of the initial interval, or

    (ii)   B is greater than A, then that owner is entitled to increase the amount of tax deductible for the purposes of section 12 by the amount calculated in accordance with paragraph (a) for the taxable period immediately following the end of the initial interval.

(c)   Where a capital good is not used during the initial interval then the initial interval proportion of deductible use is the proportion of the total tax incurred that is deductible by the capital goods owner in accordance with section 12.

(5)   (a)   (i)   Subject to subsection (6)(b), where in respect of an interval, other than the initial interval, the proportion of deductible use for that interval in relation to that capital good differs from the initial interval proportion of deductible use in relation to that capital good, then the capital goods owner shall, at the end of that interval, calculate an amount in accordance with the following formula:

$$C - D$$

where–

C   is the reference deduction amount in relation to that capital good, and

D   is the interval deductible amount in relation to that capital good.

(ii)   Where in accordance with subparagraph (i)–

(I)   C is greater than D, then the amount calculated in accordance with the formula in subparagraph (i) shall be payable by that owner as if it were tax due in accordance with section 19 for the taxable period immediately following the end of that interval, or

(II)   D is greater than C, then that owner is entitled to increase the amount of tax deductible for the purposes of section 12 by the amount calculated in accordance with the formula in subparagraph (i) for the taxable period immediately following the end of that interval.

(b)   Where for the second or any subsequent interval, a capital good is not used during that interval, the proportion of deductible use in respect of that capital good for that interval shall be the proportion of deductible use for the previous interval.

(6)   (a)   (i)   Where in respect of a capital good for an interval other than the initial interval the proportion of deductible use expressed as a percentage differs by more than 50 percentage points from the initial interval proportion of deductible use expressed as a percentage, then the capital goods owner shall

at the end of that interval calculate an amount in accordance with the following formula:

$$(C - D) \times N$$

where–

C   is the reference deduction amount in relation to that capital good,

D   is the interval deductible amount in relation to that capital good, and

N   is the number of full intervals remaining in the adjustment period at the end of that interval plus one.

(ii) Where in accordance with subparagraph (i)–

    (I)   C is greater than D, then the amount calculated in accordance with the formula in subparagraph (i) shall be payable by that owner as if it were tax due in accordance with section 19 for the taxable period immediately following the end of that interval, or

    (II)   D is greater than C, then that owner is entitled to increase the amount of tax deductible for the purposes of section 12 by the amount calculated in accordance with the formula in subparagraph (i) for the taxable period immediately following the end of that interval.

(iii) The provisions of subparagraph (i) shall not apply to a capital good or part thereof that has been subject to the provisions of paragraphs (c) or (d) during the interval to which subparagraph (i) applies.

(iv) Where a capital goods owner is obliged to carry out a calculation referred to in subparagraph (i) in respect of a capital good, then, for the purposes of the remaining intervals in the adjustment period, the proportion of deductible use in relation to that capital good for the interval in respect of which the calculation is required to be made shall be treated as if it were the initial interval proportion of deductible use in relation to that capital good and, until a further calculation is required under subparagraph (i), all other definition amounts shall be calculated accordingly.

(b)   Where the provisions of paragraph (a) apply to an interval then the provisions of subsection (5) do not apply to that interval.

(c)   Where a capital goods owner who is a landlord in respect of all or part of a capital good terminates his or her landlord's option to tax in accordance with section 7A(1) in respect of any letting of that capital good, then–

    (i)   that owner is deemed, for the purposes of this section, to have supplied and simultaneously acquired the capital good to which that letting relates,

    (ii)   that supply shall be deemed to be a supply on which tax is not chargeable and no option to tax that supply in accordance with section 4B(5) shall be permitted on that supply, and

    (iii) the capital good acquired shall be treated as a capital good for the purposes of this section and the amount calculated in accordance with subsection (7)(b) on that supply shall be treated as the total tax incurred in relation to that capital good.

(d)   Where in respect of a letting of a capital good that is not subject to a landlord's option to tax in accordance with section 7A(1), a landlord subsequently exercises a landlord's option to tax in respect of a letting of that capital good, then–

    (i)   that landlord is deemed, for the purposes of this section, to have supplied and simultaneously acquired that capital good to which that letting relates,

    (ii)   that supply shall be deemed to be a supply on which tax is chargeable, and

    (iii) the capital good acquired shall be treated as a capital good for the purposes of this section, and–

       (I)   the amount calculated in accordance with subsection (7)(a) shall be treated as the total tax incurred in relation to that capital good, and

       (II) the total tax incurred shall be deemed to have been deducted in accordance with section 12 at the time of that supply.

a 19   (7)   (a)   Where a capital goods owner supplies a capital good or transfers a capital good, being a transfer to which section 3(5)(b)(iii) applies, other than a transfer to which subsection (10) applies, during the adjustment period in relation to that capital good, and where–

(i)   tax is chargeable on that supply, or tax would have been chargeable on that transfer but for the application of section 3(5)(b)(iii), and

(ii)   the non-deductible amount in relation to that capital good for that owner is greater than zero or in the case of a supply or transfer during the initial interval, that owner was not entitled to deduct all of the total tax incurred in accordance with section 12,

then that owner is entitled to increase the amount of tax deductible by that owner for the purposes of section 12 for the taxable period in which the supply or transfer occurs, by an amount calculated in accordance with the following formula:

$$\frac{E \times N}{T}$$

where–

E   is the non-deductible amount in relation to that capital good, or in the case of a supply before the end of the initial interval the amount of the total tax incurred in relation to that capital good which was not deductible by that owner in accordance with section 12,

N   is the number of full intervals remaining in the adjustment period in relation to that capital good at the time of supply plus one, and

T   is the total number of intervals in the adjustment period in relation to that capital good.

(b)   Where a capital goods owner supplies a capital good during the adjustment period applicable to that capital good and where tax is not chargeable on the supply and where, either–

(i)   the total reviewed deductible amount in relation to that capital good is greater than zero, or

(ii)   in the case of a supply before the end of the initial interval where the amount of the total tax incurred in relation to that capital good which was deductible by that owner in accordance with section 12 is greater than zero,

then that owner shall calculate an amount which shall be payable as if it were tax due in accordance with section 19 for the taxable period in which the supply occurs in accordance with the following formula:

$$\frac{B \times N}{T}$$

where–

B   is the total reviewed deductible amount in relation to that capital good, or, in the case of a supply to which subparagraph (ii) applies, the amount of the total tax incurred in relation to that capital good which that owner claimed as a deduction in accordance with section 12,

N   is the number of full intervals remaining in the adjustment period in relation to that capital good at the time of supply plus one, and

T   is the total number of intervals in the adjustment period in relation to that capital good.

(c)   Where a capital goods owner supplies or transfers, being a transfer to which section 3(5)(b)(iii) applies, part of a capital good during the adjustment period, then for the remainder of the adjustment period applicable to that capital good–

(i)   the total tax incurred,

(ii)   the total reviewed deductible amount, and

(iii)   all other definition amounts,

in relation to the remainder of that capital good for that owner shall be adjusted accordingly on a fair and reasonable basis.

(d)   Where a transfer of ownership of a capital good occurs, being a transfer to which section 3(5)(b)(iii) applies, but excluding a transfer to which subsection (10) applies, and where the transferee would not have been entitled to deduct all of the tax that would have been chargeable on that transfer but for the application of section 3(5)(b)(iii), then that transferee shall calculate an amount as follows:

$$F - G$$

where–

F   is the amount of tax that would have been chargeable but for the application of section 3(5) (b)(iii), and

G   is the amount of that tax that would have been deductible in accordance with section 12 by that transferee if section 3(5)(b)(iii) had not applied to that transfer, and that amount shall be payable by that transferee as if it were tax due in accordance with section 19 for the taxable period in which the transfer occurs and for the purposes of this section that amount shall be deemed to be the amount of the total tax incurred in relation to that capital good that the transferee was not entitled to deduct in accordance with section 12.

(8) (a) Where a tenant who has an interest other than a freehold equivalent interest in immovable goods is the capital goods owner in respect of a refurbishment carried out on those immovable goods, assigns or surrenders that interest, then that tenant shall calculate an amount in respect of that capital good which is that refurbishment in accordance with the formula in subsection (7)(b), and that amount shall be payable by that tenant as if it were tax due in accordance with section 19 for the taxable period in which the assignment or surrender occurs.

(b) Paragraph (a) shall not apply where–

(i) the total reviewed deductible amount in relation to that capital good is equal to the total tax incurred in relation to that capital good, or in relation to an assignment or surrender that occurs prior to the end of the initial interval in relation to that capital good the tenant was entitled to deduct all of the total tax incurred in accordance with section 12 in relation to that capital good,

(ii) the tenant enters into a written agreement with the person to whom the interest is assigned or surrendered, to the effect that that person shall be responsible for all obligations under this section in relation to the capital good referred to in paragraph (a) from the date of the assignment or surrender of the interest referred to in paragraph (a), as if–

(I) the total tax incurred and the amount deducted by that tenant in relation to that capital good were the total tax incurred and the amount deducted by the person to whom the interest is assigned or surrendered, and

(II) any adjustments required to be made under this section by the tenant were made,

and

(iii) the tenant issues a copy of the capital good record in respect of the capital good referred to in paragraph (a) to the person to whom the interest is being assigned or surrendered.

(c) Where paragraph (b) applies the person to whom the interest is assigned or surrendered shall be responsible for the obligations referred to in paragraph (b)(ii) and shall use the information in the copy of the capital good record issued by the tenant in accordance with paragraph (b)(iii) for the purposes of calculating any tax chargeable or deductible in accordance with this section in respect of that capital good by that person from the date of the assignment or surrender of the interest referred to in paragraph (a).

(d) Where the capital good is one to which subsection (11) applies paragraphs (a), (b) and (c) shall not apply.

(9) Where a capital goods owner–

(a) supplies a capital good during the adjustment period applicable to that capital good, and where tax is chargeable on that supply, or

(b) transfers, other than a transfer to which subsection (10) applies, a capital good during the adjustment period applicable to that capital good and tax would have been chargeable on that transfer but for the application of section 3(5)(b)(iii),

and where, at the time of that supply or transfer, that owner and the person to whom the capital good is supplied or transferred are connected within the meaning of section 7A, and where–

(i) the amount of tax chargeable on the supply of that capital good,

(ii) the amount of tax that would have been chargeable on the transfer of that capital good but for the application of section 3(5)(b)(iii), or

(iii) the amount of tax that would have been chargeable on the supply but for the application of section 13A,

is less than the amount, hereafter referred to as the "adjustment amount", calculated in accordance with the following formula:

$$\frac{H \times N}{T}$$

where–

H is the total tax incurred in relation to that capital good for the capital goods owner making the supply or transfer,

N is the number of full intervals remaining in the adjustment period in relation to that capital good plus one, and

T   is the total number of intervals in the adjustment period in relation to that capital good,

then, that owner shall calculate an amount, which shall be payable by that owner as if it were tax due in accordance with section 19 for the taxable period in which the supply or transfer occurs, in accordance with the following formula:

$$I-J$$

where–

I   is the adjustment amount, and

J   is the amount of tax chargeable on the supply of that capital good, or the amount of tax that would have been chargeable on the transfer of that capital good but for the application of section 3(5)(b)(iii), or the amount of tax that would have been chargeable on the supply but for the application of section 13A.

(10)   Where a capital goods owner transfers a capital good, being a transfer to which section 3(5)(b)(iii) applies and that transfer would have been a supply but for the application of section 3(5)(b)(iii), and where such supply would be exempt in accordance with **[section 4B(2) or subsection (2) or (6)(b) of section 4C]**[1] then–

(a)   the transferor shall issue a copy of the capital good record to the transferee,

(b)   the transferee shall be the successor to the capital goods owner transferring the capital good and shall be responsible for all obligations of that owner under this section from the date of the transfer of that capital good, as if–

(i)   the total tax incurred and the amount deducted by the transferor in relation to that capital good were the total tax incurred and the amount deducted by the transferee, and

(ii)   any adjustments required to be made under this section by the transferor were made,

and

(c)   that transferee as successor shall use the information in the copy of the capital good record issued by the transferor in accordance with paragraph (a) for the purposes of calculating tax chargeable or deductible by that successor in accordance with this section for the remainder of the adjustment period applicable to that capital good from the date of transfer of that capital good.

(11)   If a capital good is destroyed during the adjustment period in relation to that capital good, then no further adjustment under this section shall be made by the capital goods owner in respect of any remaining intervals in the adjustment period in relation to that capital good.

(12)   A capital goods owner shall create and maintain a record (in this section referred to as a 'capital good record') in respect of each capital good and that record shall contain sufficient information to determine any adjustments in respect of that capital good required in accordance with this section.

(13)   The Revenue Commissioners may make regulations necessary for the purposes of the operation of this section, in particular in relation to the duration of a subsequent interval where the accounting year of a capital goods owner changes.][2]

Amendments

1   Substituted by F(No. 2)A 08 s99 & Sch 6, (w.e.f. 24 December 2008).
2   S12E inserted by s98, FA08 (w.e.f. 1 July 2008).

Regulations and Orders

Operation of the capital goods   2008 SI No. 238   Value Added Tax (Amendment) Regulations,
scheme   2008

Revenue e-Briefs

Revenue e-Brief No. 37/2008: VAT on property – frequently asked questions
Revenue e-Brief No. 34/2008: Value-Added Tax Amendment Regulations 2008 (S.I. No. 238 of 2008)
Revenue e-Brief No. 22/2008: VAT on property – changeover to new rules

Revenue Statements of Practice and Information Leaflets

Frequently asked questions: Information Leaflet dated December 2008
Summary and checklist: Information Leaflet dated May 2008

Narrative

Tax Briefing: Issue 69 (FAQs – VAT on Property)
VAT on Property 2008: ITR Jul 2008 Vol 21 No. 3

Section 13

Remission of tax on goods exported, etc.

a 147 **13.**   [(1)   Regulations may make provision for remitting or repaying, subject to such conditions (if any) as may be specified in the regulations or as the Revenue Commissioners may impose, the tax chargeable in respect of the supply of goods, or of such goods as may be specified) in the regulations, in cases where the Revenue Commissioners are satisfied-

(a)   that the goods have been or are to be exported,

(b)   that the goods have been shipped on board an aircraft or ship proceeding to a place outside the State,

(c)   that the goods are, or are to be used in, a fishing vessel used or to be used for the purposes of commercial sea fishing.

[(1A)   The Revenue Commissioners shall, subject to and in accordance with regulations (if any), allow the application of paragraph (b) of subsection (1) of section 11 (hereafter referred to in this section as 'zero-rating') to-

(a)   the supply of a traveller's qualifying goods, and

(b)   the supply of services by a VAT refunding agent consisting of the service of repaying the tax claimed by a traveller in relation to the supply of a traveller's qualifying goods or the procurement of the zero-rating of the supply of a traveller's qualifying goods,

where they are satisfied that the supplier of the goods or services as the case may be-

(i)   has proof that the goods were exported by or on behalf of the traveller by the last day of the third month following the month in which the supply takes place,

(ii)   repays, within such time limit as may be specified in regulations, any amount of tax paid by the traveller and claimed by that person in respect of goods covered by the provisions of paragraph (i),

(iii)   notifies the traveller in writing of any amount (including the mark-up) charged by the supplier for procuring the repayment of the amount claimed or arranging for the zero-rating of the supply [and where an amount so notified is expressed in terms of a percentage or a fraction, such percentage or fraction shall relate to the tax remitted or repayable under this subsection,][1]

(iv)   uses, as the exchange rate in respect of monies being repaid to a traveller in a currency other than the currency of the State, the latest selling rate recorded by the Central Bank of Ireland for the currency in question at the time of the repayment, or where there is an agreement with the Revenue Commissioners for a method to be used in determining the exchange rate, the exchange rate obtained using the said method, and

(v)   has made known to the traveller such details concerning the transaction as may be specified in regulations.

(1B)   Regulations may make provision for the authorisation, subject to certain conditions, [of accountable persons]² or a class [of accountable persons]² for the purposes of zero-rating of the supply of a traveller's qualifying goods or to operate as a VAT refunding agent in the handling of a repayment of tax on the supply of a traveller's qualifying goods and such regulations may provide for the cancellation of such authorisation and matters consequential to such cancellation.

(1C)   A VAT refunding agent acting as such may, in accordance with regulations, treat the tax charged to the traveller on the supply of that traveller's qualifying goods as tax that is deductible by the agent in accordance with paragraph (a) of subsection (1) of section 12, provided that that agent fulfils the conditions set out in subsection (1A) in respect of that supply.]³

(2)   Regulations may make provision for remitting or repaying, subject to such conditions (if any) as may be specified in the regulations or as the Revenue Commissioners may impose, the tax chargeable in respect of the supply of all or any one or more (as may be specified in the regulations) of the following services:

(a)   services directly linked to the export of goods or the transit of goods from a place outside the State to another place outside the State,

(b)   the repair, maintenance and hiring of plant or equipment used in a vessel or an aircraft specified in paragraph (v) of the Second Schedule,

(c)   the repair, maintenance and hiring of a vessel used, or of plant or equipment used in a vessel used, for the purposes of commercial sea fishing.

a 171   (3)   (a)   The Revenue Commissioners shall, in accordance with regulations, repay to a person to whom this subsection applies, deductible tax chargeable in respect of supplies of goods or services to him or in respect of goods imported by him.

(b)   This subsection applies to a person who shows to the satisfaction of the Revenue Commissioners that he carries on a business outside the State and that he supplies no goods or services in the State [other than services for which in accordance with **[paragraph (f) or (g) of subsection (1A), or subsection (1B)(b) or (2), of section 8]**[4] the person who receives them is solely liable for the tax chargeable][5]

(c)   In this subsection '**deductible tax**', in relation to a person to whom this subsection applies, means tax chargeable [(including any flat-rate addition)][6] in respect of goods or services used by him for the purposes of any business carried on by him to the extent that such tax would be deductible by him under section 12 if the business were carried on by him within the State but does not include tax chargeable in respect of goods for supply within the State [[or in respect of motor vehicles (as defined in section 12(3)(b))][7] for hiring out for utilisation within the State][8][…][9]

[(3A) (a)   The Revenue Commissioners shall, in accordance with regulations, repay to a person to whom this subsection applies the residual tax included in the consideration for supply of a new means of transport, where such new means of transport is subsequently dispatched or transported to another Member State

(b)   This subsection applies to a person not entitled to a deduction under section 12 of the tax borne or paid by him on the purchase, intra-Community acquisition or importation of the goods in question.][10]

[(3B) In this section -

'**traveller**' means a person whose domicile or habitual residence is not situated within the Community and includes a person who is normally resident in the Community but who, at the time of the supply of the goods intends to take up residence outside the Community in the near future and for a period of at least 12 consecutive months;

'**traveller's qualifying goods**' means goods, other than goods transported by the traveller for the equipping, fuelling and provisioning of pleasure boats, private aircraft or other means of transport for private use, which are supplied within the State to a traveller and which are exported by or on behalf of that traveller by the last day of the third month following the month in which the supply takes place;

'**VAT refunding agent**' means a person who supplies services, which consist of the procurement of a zero-rating or repayment of tax in relation to supplies of a traveller's qualifying goods.

(3C)   For the purposes of this section, and subject to the direction and control of the Revenue Commissioners, any power, function or duty conferred or imposed on them may be exercised or performed on their behalf by an officer of the Revenue Commissioners.][11]

[...

...][12]][13]

Amendments

1   Inserted by FA99 s132, (w.e.f. 1 May 1999).
2   Substituted by FA08 s109 & Sch 4, (w.e.f. 1 July 2008).
3   Ss(1A) - (1C) inserted by FA97 s106(a), (w.e.f. 1 July 1997).
4   Substituted by F(No. 2)A 08 s 99 & Sch 6, (w.e.f. 24 December 2008).
5   Inserted by FA02 s105 (w.e.f. 25 March 2002).
6   Inserted by FA92 s176(a), (w.e.f. 1 January 1993).
7   Substituted by FA98 s113, (w.e.f. 27 March 1998).
8   Inserted by FA87 s43, (w.e.f. 9 July 1987).
9   Deleted by FA85 s45, (w.e.f. 30 May 1985).
10 Ss(3A) inserted by FA92 s176(b), (w.e.f. 1 January 1993).
11 Ss(3B & 3C) inserted by FA97 s106(b), (w.e.f. 1 July 1997).
12 Deleted by FA82 s82, (w.e.f. 1 September 1982).
13 S13 inserted by VAT Amend. A78 s12, (w.e.f. 1 March 1979).

Regulations and Orders

Refunds, fishing, boats and equipment	1979 SI No. 63	Value Added Tax Regulations, 1979
Refunds, fishing vessels and equipment	2006 SI No. 548	Value-Added Tax Regulations 2006
Refunds to foreign Traders	1979 SI No. 63	Value Added Tax Regulations, 1979
Refunds to foreign traders	2006 SI No. 548	Value-Added Tax Regulations 2006
Retail Export Scheme	2006 SI No. 548	Value-Added Tax Regulations 2006
Tourist, qualifying goods	1998 SI No. 34	Value Added Tax (Retail Export Scheme) Regulations, 1998

Revenue e-Briefs

Revenue e-Brief No 23/2008: 6 month time limit on VAT repayment claims from unregistered foreign traders

Revenue e-Brief No. 5/2007: Change of Address – VAT (Unregistered) Repayments Section

Revenue Statements of Practice and Information Leaflets

Automated Entry Processing for Imports/Exports: SP-VAT/2/91

Tax Free Purchases for non-EU tourists: Information Leaflet dated April 1998

Narrative

Tax Briefing: Issue 27 (Finance Act 1997 Changes: Retail Export Scheme)

Tax Briefing: Issue 23 (Review of VAT Retail Schemes)

Section 13A

Supplies to, and intra-Community acquisitions and imports by, certain taxable persons

a 164 **13A.** [(1)   For the purposes of this section and paragraph (via) of the Second Schedule-

'**authorised person**' means a qualifying person who has been authorised in accordance with subsection (3);

'**qualifying person**' means [an accountable person][1] whose turnover from his supplies of goods made in accordance with [subparagraph (a)(I), (aa) or (b)][2] of paragraph (i) of the Second Schedule[, supplies of contract work where the place of supply is deemed to be a Member State other than the State and supplies of contract work made in accordance with paragraph (xvi) of the Second Schedule][3] amounts to, or is likely to amount to, 75 per cent. of his total annual turnover from his supplies of goods and services:

Provided that the turnover from a supply of goods to [an accountable person][1] which are subsequently leased back from that person is excluded from the total annual turnover for the purposes of establishing whether the person is a qualifying person;

'**qualifying goods**' means all taxable goods excluding motor vehicles within the meaning of section 12(3)(b) and petrol;

'**qualifying services**' means all taxable services excluding the provision of food or drink, accommodation, other personal services, entertainment services or the hire of motor vehicles within the meaning of section 12(3)(b).

(2)   A person who wishes to become an authorised person shall-

(a)   complete such application form as may be provided by the Revenue Commissioners for that purpose,

(b)   certify the particulars shown on such form to be correct, and

(c)   submit to the Revenue Commissioners the completed and certified application form, together with such further information in support of the application as may be requested by them.

170, a 171   (3)   (a)   Where a person has furnished the particulars required under subsection (2), the Revenue Commissioners shall, where they are satisfied that he is a qualifying person, issue to that person in writing an authorisation certifying him to be an authorised person.

(b)   An authorisation issued in accordance with paragraph (a) shall be valid for such period as may be determined by the Revenue Commissioners.

(c)   Where a person who has been authorised in accordance with paragraph (a) ceases to be a qualifying person, he shall, by notice in writing, advise the Revenue Commissioners accordingly not later than the end of the taxable period during which he ceased to be a qualifying person.

(d)   The Revenue Commissioners shall, by notice in writing, cancel an authorisation issued to a person in accordance with paragraph (a) where they are satisfied that he is no longer a qualifying person and such cancellation shall have effect from the date specified in the notice.

(4)   An authorised person shall furnish a copy of the authorisation referred to in subsection (3) to [each accountable person][1] in the State who supplies taxable goods or taxable services to him.

(5)   [An accountable person][1] who supplies goods or services in circumstances where the provisions of paragraph (via) of the Second Schedule apply, shall, in addition to the details to be included on each invoice, credit note or other document required to be issued in accordance with section 17, include on such invoice, credit note or other document a reference to the number of the authorisation issued to the authorised person in accordance with subsection (3).

(6)   In relation to each consignment of goods to be imported by an authorised person at the rate specified in section 11(1)(b) by virtue of paragraph (via) of the Second Schedule the following conditions shall be complied with:

(a)   a copy of the authorisation referred to at subsection (3) shall be produced with the relevant customs entry; and

(b)   the relevant customs entry shall incorporate-

(i)   a declaration by the authorised person, or by his representative duly authorised in writing for that purpose, that he is an authorised person in accordance with this section for the purposes of paragraph (via) of the Second Schedule, and

(ii)   a claim for importation at the rate specified in section 11(1)(b).

(7)   For the purposes of subsections (1)(a)(ii) and (6)(a) of section 4, the tax charged at the rate specified in section 11(1)(b) by virtue of paragraph (via) of the Second Schedule shall be deemed to be tax which is deductible under section 12.

(8)   Where an authorised person is in receipt of a service in respect of which, had the provisions of paragraph (via) of the Second Schedule not applied, tax would have been chargeable at a rate other than the rate specified in section 11(1)(b) and all or part of such tax would not have been deductible by him under section 12, then the authorised person shall, in relation to such service, be liable to pay tax as if he himself had supplied the service for consideration in the course or furtherance of his business to a person who is not an authorised person.

(9)   For the purposes of this section, and subject to the direction and control of the Revenue Commissioners, any power, function or duty conferred or imposed on them may be exercised or performed on their behalf by an officer of the Revenue Commissioners.][4]

Amendments

1   Substituted by FA08 s109 & Sch 4, (w.e.f. 1 July 2008).
2   Substituted by FA01 s192, (w.e.f. 21 March 2001).
3   Inserted by FA96 s95, (w.e.f. 1 January 1996).
4   S13A inserted by FA93 s90, (w.e.f. 1 August 1993).

Regulations and Orders

Export Goods	1984 SI No. 230	Value Added Tax (Exports Goods) Regulations, 1984
Export Goods	1984 SI No. 231	Value Added Tax (Goods Exported in Baggage) Regulations, 1984
Tourist, qualifying goods	1998 SI No. 34	Value Added Tax (Retail Export Scheme) Regulations 1998

Revenue Statements of Practice and Information Leaflets

Zero-Rating of Goods and Services in accordance with Section 13A of the VAT Act: Information Leaflet dated December 2008

Revenue Precedents

Topic:	Section 13A Authorisations.
Issue:	Do receipts from the supply of 4th Schedule services constitute turnover for the purposes of 13A scheme.
Decision:	It was not the intention to discriminate against companies that were essentially exporting companies. It was decided that receipts derived from 4th Schedule supplies outside the State would be ignored when calculating turnover for qualification under new Scheme.
Date:	28/3/95

Narrative

Tax Briefing: Issue 29 (Redraft of Form VAT 13B Authorisation)

Section 14

Determination of tax due by reference to cash receipts

a 10(2) **14.**   [[(1)   A person who satisfies the Revenue Commissioners that-

(a)   taking one period with another, not less than 90 per cent. of such person's turnover is derived from taxable supplies to persons who are not registered persons, or

[(b)   the total consideration which such person is entitled to receive in respect of such person's taxable supplies has not exceeded and is not likely to exceed €1,000,000 in any continuous person of 12 months,]¹

may, in accordance with regulations, be authorised to determine the amount of tax which becomes due by such person during any taxable period (or part thereof) during which the authorisation has effect by reference to the amount of the moneys which such person receives during such taxable period (or part thereof) in respect of taxable supplies.]²

[(1A)   Where an authorisation to which subsection (1) relates has not been cancelled under subsection (2), then-

(a)   the rate of tax due by the person concerned in respect of a supply shall be the rate of tax chargeable at the time the goods or services are supplied,

(b)   if tax on a supply has already been due and payable under any other provisions of this Act prior to the issue of such authorisation, tax shall not be due again in respect of any such supply as a result of the application of subsection (1), and

(c)   if no tax is due or payable on a supply made prior to the issue of such authorisation, tax shall not be due in respect of any such supply as a result of the application of subsection (1).]³

[(1B)   (a)   The Minister may, by order-

(i)   increase the amount specified in subsection (1)(b), or

(ii)   where an amount stands specified by virtue of an order under this paragraph, including an order relating to this subparagraph, further increase the amount so specified.

(b)   An order under paragraph (a) shall be laid before Dáil Éireann as soon as may be after it is made and, if a resolution annulling the order is passed by Dáil Éireann within the next twenty-one sitting days on which Dáil Éireann has sat after the order is laid before it, the order shall be annulled accordingly, but without prejudice to the validity of anything previously done thereunder.]⁴

(2)   The Revenue Commissioners may, in accordance with regulations, cancel an authorisation under [...]⁵ subsection (1), and may, by regulations, exclude from the application of [that subsection]⁶ [...]⁷ any tax due in respect of specified descriptions of supplies of goods or services and any moneys received in respect of such supplies.

[(2A) Where an authorisation has issued to any person in accordance with subsection (1) and that person fails to issue a credit note in accordance with section 17(3)(b) in respect of any supply where the consideration as stated in the invoice issued by that person for that supply is reduced or a discount is allowed, then, at the time when a credit note should have issued in accordance with section 17(7)–

(a)   such tax as is attributable to the reduction or discount shall be treated as being excluded from the application of subsection (1), and

(b)   that person shall be liable for that tax as if it were tax due in accordance with section 19 at that time.]⁸

[(3)   This section shall not apply to tax provided for by subsection (1)(b) [or (1A)]⁹ of section 2.]¹⁰]¹¹

Amendments
1   Substituted by FA07 s87, (w.e.f. 1 March 2007).
2   Ss(1) substituted by FA94 s97(a), (w.e.f. 23 May 1994).
3   Ss(1A) inserted by FA92 s177(1)(b), (w.e.f. 28 May 1992).
4   Ss(1B) inserted by FA95 s131, (w.e.f. 2 June 1995).
5   Deleted by FA94 s97(b)(i), (w.e.f. 23 May 1994).
6   Substituted by FA94 s97(b)(ii), (w.e.f. 23 May 1994).
7   Deleted by FA92 s177(1)(c), (w.e.f. 1 January 1993).
8   Ss(2A) inserted by FA08 s99, (w.e.f. 13 March 2008).
9   Inserted by FA92 s177(2), (w.e.f. 1 January 1993).
10 Ss(3) inserted by FA92 s177(1)(d), (w.e.f. 28 May 1992).
11 S14 substituted by VAT Amend. A78 s13, (w.e.f. 1 March 1979).

Regulations and Orders
Cash receipts basis	1986 SI No. 298	Value Added Tax (Determination of Tax Due by Reference to money Received) Regulations 1986
Cash receipts basis	1992 SI No. 93	Value Added Tax (Determination of Tax Due by Reference to Money Received) Regulations, 1992
Cash receipts basis	1992 SI No. 306	Value Added Tax (Determination of Tax Due by Reference to Money Received) Regulations 1992
Cash Receipts basis	1994 SI No. 259	Value Added Tax (Determination of Tax Due by reference to Money Received) (Amendment) Regulations, 1994
Cash Receipts basis	1997 SI No. 316	Value Added Tax (Eligibility to Determine Tax Due by Reference to Money Received) Order, 1997
Cash Receipts basis	2006 SI No. 548	Value-Added Tax Regulations 2006

Revenue e-Briefs
Revenue e-Brief No. 13/2007: Value Added Tax – Changes from 1 March 2007

Revenue Statements of Practice and Information Leaflets
Moneys Received Basis of Accounting: Information Leaflet dated October 2008

Moneys Received Basis of Accounting: SP-VAT/16/92 (replaced by Information Leaflet dated March 2007)

Revenue Precedents

Topic:	Temporary Exemptions
Issue:	When can a resident of the State be exempt from a further payment of VAT on a motor vehicle temporarily imported?
Decision:	When the State resident is employed in another Member State by an employer established there and that employer makes available to the State resident employee a motor vehicle for use in the course of his employment and the vehicle was acquired VAT paid in the Member State where the employer is established.
Date:	12/3/86

(withdrawn from the Revenue website in 2002)

Narrative

Ireland's Derogations from the EU Sixth VAT Directive: ITR Sept 1999: Vol. 12 No. 5.

Tax Briefing: Issue 30 (Cash Receipts Basis of Accounting for VAT)

Tax Briefing: Issue 29 (Eligibility for Cash Receipts Basis)

a 70, a 71, a 85,
a 86, a 87, a 88,
a 211

Charge of tax on imported goods.

a 60, a 61 **15.**   [[(1)   Tax shall be charged on the importation of goods at whichever
                      of the rates specified in section 11(1) is the appropriate rate in
                      respect of such goods.]¹

              [...]²

a 60, a 61   (3)   The value of imported goods for the purposes of this section
                      shall be their value determined in accordance with the acts
                      for the time being in force adopted by the institutions of the
                      Community relating to the valuation of goods for customs
                      purposes, modified by the substitution of references to the
                      territory of the State for references to the customs territory
                      of the Community, together with any taxes, duties[, expenses
                      resulting from the transport of the goods to another place of
                      destination within the Community, if that destination is known
                      at the time of the importation,]³ and other charges levied
                      either outside or, by reason of importation, within the State
                      (except value-added tax) on the goods and not included in the
                      determination.

              [...]⁴

              (5)   The Revenue Commissioners may, in accordance with
                      regulations, remit or repay, if they think fit, the whole or part of
                      the tax chargeable-

              (a)   on the importation of any goods which are shown to their
                      satisfaction to have been previously exported,

              (b)   on the importation of any goods if they are satisfied that
                      the goods have been or are to be re-exported,

              (c)   on the importation of any goods from the customs free
                      airport by an unregistered person who shows to the
                      satisfaction of the Revenue Commissioners that be has
                      already borne tax on the goods.

       [(5A)   The Revenue Commissioners shall, in accordance with
                regulations, repay the tax chargeable on the importation of
                goods where the goods have been dispatched or transported:

              (a)   to another Member State from outside the Community,
                      and

              (b)   to a person, other than an individual, who is not registered
                      for value-added tax in that other Member State:

                      Provided that this subsection shall only apply
                      where it is shown to the satisfaction of the Revenue
                      Commissioners that the goods in question have been

subject to value-added tax referred to in [Council Directive No. 2006/112/EC of 28 November 2006][5] in that other Member State.][6]

a 60, a 61   (6)   Subject to the foregoing provisions of this section, the provisions of the Customs Consolidation Act, 1876, and of other law in force in the State relating to customs shall apply, with such exceptions and modifications (if any) as may be specified in regulations, to tax referred to in this section as if it were a duty of customs.

a 60, a 61   [(6A) Regulation 26 of the Value- Added Tax Regulations, 1979 (S.I. No. 63 of 1979), is hereby revoked and tax charged under section 2(1)(b) shall, in accordance with the provisions of the Customs Consolidation Act, 1876, and of other law in force in the State relating to customs, as applied to tax by subsection (6) and regulations thereunder, be paid in the manner and at the time that it would have been payable if that regulation had not been made.][7]

(7)   Regulations may-

(a)   make provision for enabling goods imported by registered persons or by such classes of registered persons as may be specified in the regulations for the purposes of a business carried on by them to be delivered or removed, subject to such conditions or restrictions as may be specified in the regulations or as the Revenue Commissioners may impose, without payment of the tax chargeable on the importation, and

(b)   provide that the tax be accounted for by the persons or classes of persons aforesaid in the return, made by them under section 19(3), in respect of the taxable period during which the goods are so delivered or removed.][8]

Amendments

1 Ss(1) substituted by FA92 s178(a), (w.e.f. 28 May 1992).
2 Deleted by FA92 s178(b), (w.e.f. 28 May 1992).
3 Inserted by FA96 s96, (w.e.f. 1 January 1996).
4 Deleted by FA85 s46, (w.e.f. 1 March 1985).
5 Substituted by FA07 s97 & Sch 3 (w.e.f. 1 January 2007).
6 Ss(5A) inserted by FA92 s178(c), (w.e.f. 1 January 1993).
7 Ss(6A) inserted by FA82 s84, (w.e.f. 1 September 1982).
8 S15 substituted by VAT Amend. A78 s14, (w.e.f. 1 March 1979).

Regulations and Orders

Imports	1982 SI No. 279	Valued Added Tax (Imported Goods) Regulations, 1982
Imports	1983 SI No. 129	Value Added Tax (Imported Goods) Regulations, 1983
Imports	1983 SI No. 422	European Communities (Exemption from Import Charges of Certain Vehicles etc. Temporarily Imported), Regulations 1983
Imports personal	1983 SI No. 423	European Communities (Exemption from Import Charges of certain Personal property) Regulations, 1983
Imports	1985 SI No. 183	(Exemption from Value Added Tax on permanent Importation of Certain goods Regulations, 1985

Imports	1985 SI No. 344	Taxable amount Valued Added Tax (Remission and Repayment of Tax on Certain Importation) Regulations, 1985
Imports - temporary	1986 SI No. 264	European Communities (Value Added Tax) (Exemption on Temporary Importation's of Certain Goods) Regulations, 1986
Imports - manufacturers	1992 SI No. 439	Value Added Tax (Imported Goods) Regulations 1992
Imports - warehousing	1992 SI No. 440	Value Added Tax (Imported Goods) (no.2) Regulations, 1992

Case law

Abbink, Jan Gerrit	C134/83	Exempted Imports/Criminal Proceedings
Bergeres - Becque v Chef de Service Interregional des Douanes Bordeaux	C39/85	Imports/Taxable amount
BP Supergas Anonimos Etaira Geniki Emporiki Viomichaniki Kai Antiprossopeion v Greece	C62/93	Recovery on imports
Carciati Giovanni	C833/79	Imports/value
Denmark v European Commission	C208/88	Travellers allowances
Drexl, Rainer	C299/86	Imports
Heinonen, Sami	C394/97	Imports/Criminal Proceedings
Ireland v European Commission	C158/88	Travellers allowances
Ireland v European Commission	C367/88	Travellers allowances
Keller Karl v Revenue Commissioners	Irish HC IV ITR 12S	Import of Cars/Taxable amount
Liberexim BV and Staatssecretaris van Financiën	C371/99	Removal of goods from customs supervision
Profant, Venceslas v Ministere Publique and Ministry of Finance	C249/84	Imports of car to another Member State
Van der Kooy A.J. v Staatssecretaris van Financien	C181/97	Import of boat from overseas province

Narrative

Tax Briefing: Issue 43 (VAT Committee Guidelines – Common form for the application of the Article 15(10) exemption)

Tax Briefing: Issue 43 (VAT Committee Guidelines – Method of calculation of the 175 ECU threshold)

Tax Briefing: Issue 36 (Goods imported by Parcel Post)

Section 15A

Goods in transit

15A. [(1)   Where -

(a)   goods from another Member State were imported into the State on or before the 31st day of December, 1992, and

(b)   the tax referred to in section 2(1)(b) was not chargeable because the goods were, at the time of such importation, placed under one of the arrangements referred to in subparagraph (b) or (c) of paragraph 1 of Article 14, or subparagraph A of paragraph 1 of Article 16, of Council Directive No 77/388/EEC of 17 May 1977, and

(c)   the goods are still subject to such an arrangement on the 1st day of January, 1993,

then, the provisions in force at the time the goods were placed under the arrangement shall continue to apply in relation to those goods until such time as, in accordance with those provisions, the goods to be covered by those arrangements.

(2)   (a)   Notwithstanding the definition of "importation of goods" in section 1, an importation within the meaning of that definition shall be deemed to occur in the following cases:

(i)   where goods have been placed under an internal Community transit operation in another Member State before the 1st day of January, 1993, and the operation terminates in the State on or after that date;

(ii)   where goods referred to in subsection (1) cease to be covered by the arrangements referred to in that subsection;

(iii)   where goods are returned to the State after the 1st day of January, 1993, being goods which were exported from the State before that date and imported into another member State in accordance with any of the arrangements referred to in subsection (1)(b).

(b)   In this subsection "**internal Community transit operation**" means the dispatch or transport of goods under cover of the internal Community transit arrangement referred to in paragraph 3 of Article 1 of Council Regulation (EEC) No 222/77 of 13 December 1976, or under the cover of a T2L or equivalent document provided for in that Regulation and includes the sending of goods by post.

(3)   The tax referred to in section 2(1)(b) shall not be chargeable in the cases referred to in subsection (2) where -

(a)   the goods are dispatched or transported outside the Community.

(b)   the goods are other than a means of transport and are being returned to the State and to the person who exported them from the State, or

(c)   the goods are a means of transport which was acquired or imported before the 1st day of January, 1993, and in respect of which value added tax referred to in Council Directive No 77/388/EEC of 17 May 1977 has been paid in a Member State and that value added tax has not subsequently been refunded because of exportation from that Member State of the means of transport:

Provided that this paragraph shall be deemed to be complied with where it is shown to the satisfaction of the Revenue Commissioners that the first use of the means of transport was prior to the 1st day of January, 1985, or that the tax due does not exceed [€130][1].

(4)   In this section, references to subparagraph (b) or (c) of paragraph 1 of Article 14, and to subparagraph A of paragraph 1 of Article 16, of Council Directive No 77/388/EEC of 17 May 1977 shall be deemed to be references to those provisions of the Directive immediately prior to their amendment by Council Directive 91/680/EEC of 16 December 1991.][2]

Amendments

1   Substituted by FA01 s240(4) & part 4, Sch.5, (w.e.f. 1 January 2002), previously £100.
2   S15A inserted by EC(VAT)R 1992 r11, (w.e.f. 1 January 1993).

Section 15B

Goods in transit (additional provisions)

15B. [(1)   Where-

(a)   goods from a new Member State were imported into the State [before the date of accession][1], and

(b)   the tax referred to in section 2(1)(b) was not chargeable because the goods were, at the time of such importation, placed-

(i)   under an arrangement for temporary importation with total exemption from customs duty, or

(ii)   under one of the arrangements referred to in [Article 156(1) of Council Directive No. 2006/112/EC of 28 November 2006][2], and

(c)   the goods are still subject to such an arrangement on the [date of accession][3],

then, the provisions in force at the time the goods were placed under that arrangement shall continue to apply until the goods leave that arrangement on or after the [date of accession][3].

(2)   (a)   Where-

(i)   goods were placed under the common transit procedure or under another customs transit procedure in a new Member State [before the date of accession][1], and

(ii)   those goods have not left the procedure concerned before the [date of accession][3],

then the provisions in force at the time the goods were placed under that procedure shall continue to apply until the goods leave that procedure on or after the [date of accession][3].

(b)   In this subsection "**common transit procedure**" means the procedure approved by the Council of the European Communities by Council Decision No 87/415/EEC of 15 June 1987, approving the Convention done at Interlaken on the 20th day of May, 1987, between the European Community, the Republic of Austria, the Republic of Finland, the Republic of Iceland, the Kingdom of Norway, the Kingdom of Sweden, and the Swiss Confederation on a common transit procedure, the text of which is attached to that Council Decision.

(3)   Where goods were in free circulation in a new Member State prior to entry into the State, an importation into the State shall be deemed to occur in the following cases:

   (a)   the removal, including irregular removal, within the State of the goods referred to in subsection (1) from the arrangement referred to in subparagraph (i) of paragraph (b) of that subsection;

   (b)   the removal, including irregular removal, within the State of the goods referred to in subsection (1) from the arrangement referred to in subparagraph (ii) of paragraph (b) of that subsection;

   (c)   the termination within the State of any of the procedures referred to in subsection (2).

(4)   An importation into the State shall be deemed to occur when goods, which were supplied within a new Member State [before the date of accession][1] and which were not chargeable to a value added tax in that new Member State, because of their exportation from that new Member State, are used in the State on or after the [date of accession][3], and have not been imported before that date.

(5)   The tax referred to in section 2(1)(b) shall not be chargeable where-

   (a)   the imported goods referred to in subsections (3) and (4) are dispatched or transported outside the enlarged Community.

   (b)   the imported goods referred to in paragraph (a) of subsection (3) are other than means of transport and are being returned to the new Member State from which they were exported and to the person who exported them, or

   (c)   the imported goods referred to in paragraph (a) of subsection (3) are means of transport which were acquired in or imported into a new Member State before the [date of accession][3] in accordance with the general conditions of taxation in force on the domestic market of that new Member State and which have not been subject by reason of their exportation to any exemption from or refund of a value added tax in that new Member State:

   [...][4]

[(5A)   Subsection (5)(c) shall be deemed to be complied with where it is shown to the satisfaction of the Revenue Commissioners that—

   (i)   the date of the first use of the means of transport was before 1 January 1987 in the case of means of transport entering the State from the Republic of Austria, the

Republic of Finland (excluding the Åland Islands) or the Kingdom of Sweden,

(ii)   the date of the first use of the means of transport was before 1 May 1996 in the case of means of transport entering the State from the Czech Republic, the Republic of Estonia, the Republic of Cyprus, the Republic of Latvia, the Republic of Lithuania, the Republic of Hungary, the Republic of Malta, the Republic of Poland, the Republic of Slovenia or [the Slovak Republic,][5]

[(iia)   the date of the first use of the means of transport was before 1 January 1999 in the case of means of transport entering the State from the Republic of Bulgaria or Romania, or][6]

(iii)   the tax due by reason of the importation does not exceed €130.][7]

(6)   The provisions of section 15A shall not apply to goods imported or deemed to be imported from a new Member State.

(7)   (a)   In this section -

["date of accession" means 1 January 1995 in respect of the Republic of Austria, the Republic of Finland (excluding the Åland Islands) and the Kingdom of Sweden or 1 May 2004 in respect of the Czech Republic, the Republic of Estonia, the Republic of Cyprus, the Republic of Latvia, the Republic of Lithuania, the Republic of Hungary, the Republic of Malta, the Republic of Poland, the Republic of Slovenia and the Slovak Republic [or 1 January 2007 in respect of the Republic of Bulgaria and Romania][8];][9]

a 405(3)   "the enlarged Community" means the Community after the accession of the new Member States;

a 405(2)   ["new Member State" means any state referred to in the definition of 'date of accession' with effect from the relevant date.][10]

(b)   A word or expression that is used in this section and is also used in Council Directive No 94/76/EC of 22 December 1994, has, unless the contrary intention appears, the meaning in this section that it has in that Council Directive.][11]

Amendments

1   Substituted by FA04 s 62(a), w.e.f. 1 May 2004).
2   Substituted by FA07 s97 & Sch 3, (w.e.f. 1 January 2007).
3   Substituted by FA04 s62(b), (w.e.f. 1 May 2004).
4   Proviso deleted by FA04 s62(c), (w.e.f. 1 May 2004).
5   Substituted by FA07 s88(a)(i), (w.e.f. 1 January 2007).
6   Inserted by FA07 s88(a)(ii), (w.e.f. 1 January 2007).
7   Ss(5A) inserted by FA04 s62(d), (w.e.f. 1 May 2004).

8 Inserted by FA07 s88(b), (w.e.f. 1 January 2007).
9 Inserted by FA04 s62(e)(i), (w.e.f. 1 May 2004).
10 Substituted by FA04 s62(e)(ii), (w.e.f. 1 May 2004).
11 S15B inserted by EC(VAT)R 1994 r4, (w.e.f. 1 January 1995).

Section 16

Duty to keep records.

a 242 **16.** (1) [Every accountable person][1] shall, in accordance with regulations, keep full and true records of all transactions which affect or may affect his liability to tax [and entitlement to deductibility][2].

a 356 [(1A) Every person who trades in investment gold (within the meaning of section 6A) shall, in accordance with regulations, keep full and true records of that person's transactions in investment gold.][3]

(2) Every person, other than [an accountable person][1], who [supplies goods or services in the course or furtherance of any business][4] shall keep all invoices issued to him in connection with the [supply of goods or services][5] to him for the purpose of such business[...][6]

[(2A) (a) [An accountable person][1] who claims a deduction of tax pursuant to section 12 in respect of qualifying accommodation as defined in section 12(3)(ca) shall retain full and true records in relation to the attendance by the delegate at the relevant qualifying conference, including the details referred to in section 12(3)(ca) issued to [that accountable person][1] by the person responsible for organising that conference.

(b) A person responsible for organising a qualifying conference as defined in section 12(3)(ca) and to which section 12(3)(a)(i) relates shall keep full and true records of each such conference organised by that person.][7]

a 247 (3) Records [...][8] kept by a person pursuant to this section and any books, [invoices, [...][9] copies [...][10] of customs entries][11], credit notes, debit notes, receipts, accounts, vouchers, bank statements or other documents whatsoever which relate to the [supply of goods or services][12], [the intra-Community acquisition of goods][13] [,or the importation of goods][14] by the person and are in the power, possession or procurement of the person and, in the case of any such book, invoice, [...][9] credit note, debit note, receipt, account, voucher or other document which has been issued by the person to another person, any copy thereof which is in the power, possession or procurement of the person shall [, subject to subsection (4),][15] be retained in his power, possession or procurement for a period of six years from the date of the latest transaction to which the [records, invoices, [...][9]][16] or any of the other documents relate:

Provided that this section shall not require the retention of records or invoices or any of the other documents in respect of which the Revenue Commissioners notify the person concerned that retention is not required, nor shall it apply to the books and papers of a company which have been disposed of in accordance with section 305(1) of the Companies Act, 1963.

[(4)   Notwithstanding the retention period specified in subsection (3) the following retention periods shall apply:

(a)   where a person acquires or develops immovable goods to which section 4 applies, the period for which that person shall retain records pursuant to this section in relation to that person's acquisition or development of those immovable goods shall be the duration that such person holds a taxable interest in such goods plus a further period of six years,

(b)   where a person exercises a waiver of exemption from tax in accordance with section 7, the period for which that person shall retain records pursuant to this section shall be the duration of the waiver plus a further period of six years.][17]

[(5)   The requirement to keep records in accordance with this section shall apply to records relating to–

(a)   exercising and terminating a landlord's option to tax,

(b)   a capital good record referred to in section 12E, and

(c)   a joint option for taxation.][18]

Amendments

1   Substituted by FA08 s109 & Sch 4, (w.e.f. 1 July 2008).
2   Inserted by FA08 s100(a), (w.e.f. 13 March 2008).
3   Ss(1A) inserted by FA99 s133, (w.e.f. 1 January 2000).
4   Substituted by VAT Amend. A78 s30(2), (w.e.f. 1 March 1979).
5   Substituted by VAT Amend. A78 s30(2), (w.e.f. 1 March 1979).
6   Deleted by FA92 s179(a), (w.e.f. 1 January 1993).
7   Inserted by FA07 s89, (w.e.f. 2 April 2007)
8   Deleted by FA82 s85, (w.e.f. 1 September 1982).
9   Deleted by FA08 s141 & Sch 8(3)((d), (w.e.f. 13 March 2008).
10   Deleted by FA92 s179(b)(i), (w.e.f. 28 May 1992).
11   Inserted by FA82 s85, (w.e.f. 1 September 1982).
12   Substituted by VAT Amend. A78 s30(2), (w.e.f. 1 March 1979).
13   Inserted by FA92 s179(b)(ii), (w.e.f. 1 January 1993).
14   Inserted by FA82 s85, (w.e.f. 1 September 1982).
15   Inserted by FA03 s121(a), (w.e.f. 28 March 2003).
16   Substituted by FA92 s179(b)(iv), (w.e.f. 1 November 1992).
17   Ss(4) inserted by FA03 s121(b), (w.e.f. 28 March 2003).
18   Ss(5) inserted by FA08 s100(b), (w.e.f. 13 March 2008).

Regulations and Orders

Accounts	1979 SI No. 63	Value Added Tax Regulations, 1979
Accounts	2006 SI No. 548	Value-Added Tax Regulations 2006
Capital Good Record	2008 SI No. 238	Value-Added Tax (Amendment) Regulations, 2008
Documentation Investment Gold	1999 SI No. 443	Value Added Tax (Agricultural Machinery) (Documentation) Regulations,1999
Investment Gold	1999 SI No. 439	Value Added Tax (Records of Transactions in Investment Gold) Regulations, 1999

Revenue e-Briefs

Revenue e-Brief No. 34/2008: Value-Added Tax Amendment Regulations 2008 (S.I. No. 238 of 2008)

Revenue Statements of Practice and Information Leaflets

Revenue Powers: SP-GEN/1/94

Revenue Powers: SP-GEN/1/99

Narrative

Foreign Firms: VAT issues arising in Ireland: ITR Jan 2000 Vol. 13 No. 1.

Section 17

Invoices

a 220 **17.** (1) [An accountable person]¹ who supplies [goods or services]² to [another accountable person]¹ [or to a Department of State or local authority or to a body established by statute or to a person who carries on an exempted activity]³ [or [...]⁴ to a person, other than an individual, in another Member State of the Community]⁵ in such circumstances that tax is chargeable [at any of the rates specified in section 11(1), [or who supplies goods or services to a person in another Member State who is liable to pay value-added tax pursuant to [Council Directive No. 2006/112/EC of 28 November 2006]⁶ on such supply,]⁷ or who supplies goods to a person in another Member State of the Community in the circumstances referred to in section 3(6)(d)(ii),]⁸[...]⁹]¹⁰ shall issue to that [person]¹¹ in respect of each such [supply of goods or services]¹² an invoice in such form and containing such particulars as may be specified by regulations.

[...]¹³

a 232 [(1A) (a) An invoice or other document required to be issued by a person under this section shall, subject to paragraph (b), be deemed to be so issued by that person if the particulars which are required by regulations to be contained in such invoice or other document are recorded, retained and transmitted electronically by a system or systems which ensures the integrity of those particulars and the authenticity of their origin, without the issue of any invoice or other document containing those particulars.

(b) An invoice or other document required to be issued under this section shall not be deemed by paragraph (a) to be so issued unless the person, who is required to issue such invoice or other document, complies with such conditions as are specified by regulations and the system or systems used by that person conforms with such specifications as are required by regulations.

(c) The person who receives a transmission referred to in paragraph (a) shall not be deemed to be issued with an invoice or other document required to be issued under this section unless the particulars which are required by regulations to be contained in such invoice or other document are received electronically in a system which ensures the integrity of those particulars and the authenticity of their origin and unless the system conforms with such specifications as are required by regulations and that person complies with such conditions as are specified by regulations.]¹⁴

[...][15]

[...][16]

(1AB) Where any person issues a document [for the purposes of section 12C(1B)][17] that person shall, in respect of the document, be treated as [an accountable person][1] for the purposes of sections 16 and 18.][18]

[...][19]

[(1C) (a) Where a subcontractor who is an accountable person supplies a service to which section 8(1B) applies, that subcontractor shall issue a document to the principal indicating—

          (i)   that the principal is liable to account for the tax chargeable on that supply, and

          (ii)   such other particulars as would be required to be included in that document if that document was an invoice required to be issued in accordance with subsection (1) but excluding the amount of tax payable.

       (b) Where the principal and the subcontractor so agree, the provisions of subsection (14)(a) may apply to this document as if it were an invoice.][20]

[(2)   A flat-rate farmer who, in accordance with section 12A, is required to issue an invoice in respect of the supply of agricultural produce or an agricultural service shall, in respect of each such supply, issue an invoice in the form and containing such particulars (in addition to those specified in the said section 12A) as may be specified by regulations if the following conditions are fulfilled:

       (a)   the issue of an invoice is requested by a [purchaser][21],

       (b)   the [purchaser][21] provides the form for the purpose of the invoice and enters the appropriate particulars thereon, and

       (c)   the [purchaser][21] gives to the flat-rate farmer a copy of the invoice,

       but may issue the invoice if those conditions or any of them are not fulfilled.][22]

[(2A) A flat-rate farmer who, in accordance with section 12C, is required to issue an invoice in respect of a supply of agricultural machinery shall, in respect of each supply, issue an invoice in the form and containing such particulars as may be specified by regulations if the following conditions are fulfilled:

(a)   the issue of the invoice is requested by the taxable dealer,

(b)   the taxable dealer provides the form for the purpose of the invoice and enters the appropriate particulars thereon, and

(c)   the taxable dealer gives to the flat-rate farmer a copy of the invoice,

but may issue the invoice if those conditions or any one of them are not fulfilled.][23]

a 184   (3)   Where, subsequent to the issue of an invoice by a person [to another person][24] in accordance with subsection (1), the consideration as stated in the invoice is increased or reduced, or a discount is allowed, whichever of the following provisions is appropriate shall have effect:

(a)   if the consideration is increased, the person shall issue [to that other person][25] another invoice in such form and containing such particulars as may be specified by regulations in respect of such increase,

(b)   if the consideration is reduced or a discount is allowed, the person shall issue [to that other person][26] a document (in this Act referred to as a credit note) containing particulars of the reduction or discount in such form and containing such other particulars as may be specified by regulations, [and if that other person is [an accountable person][1], the amount][27] which [the accountable person][1] may deduct under section 12 shall, in accordance with regulations, be reduced by the amount of tax shown on the credit note.

[(3A)   Notwithstanding subsections (5) and (9), where a person issues an invoice in accordance with subsection (1) which indicates a rate of tax and subsequent to the issue of that invoice it is established that a lower rate of tax applied, then-

(a)   the amount of consideration stated on that invoice shall be deemed to have been reduced to nil,

(b)   the provisions of subsection (3)(b) shall have effect, and

(c)   following the issue of a credit note in accordance with the provisions of subsection (3)(b), the person shall issue another invoice in accordance with this Act and regulations made thereunder.][28]

[...][15]

[(3B)   Where, subsequent to the issue of an invoice by a person to another person in accordance with subsection (1) in respect of an amount received by way of a deposit and where section 19(2B) applies, then—

(a)   the amount of the consideration stated on that invoice is deemed to be reduced to nil, and

(b)   the person shall issue to that other person a document to be treated as if it were a credit note containing particulars of the reduction in such form and containing such other particulars as would be required to be included in that document if that document was a credit note, and if that other person is [an accountable person][29] the amount which that other person may deduct under section 12 shall be reduced by the amount of tax shown on the document as if that document were a credit note.][30]

[(4)   Where subsequent to the issue by a flat-rate farmer of an invoice in accordance with subsection (2), the consideration as stated on the invoice is increased or reduced, or a discount is allowed, whichever of the following provisions is appropriate shall have effect:

(a)   in case the consideration is increased, the flat-rate farmer shall issue another invoice (if the conditions referred to in subsection (2) are fulfilled in relation to it) containing particulars of the increase and of the flat-rate addition appropriate thereto and in such form and containing such other particulars as may be specified by regulations and such other invoice shall be deemed, for the purposes of section 12, to be issued in accordance with section 12A, but the said farmer may not issue the invoice if the said conditions or any of them are not fulfilled,

(b)   in case the consideration is reduced or a discount is allowed, the flat-rate farmer shall,[...][31] issue a document (in this section referred to as 'a farmer credit note') containing particulars of the reduction or discount and in such form and containing such other particulars as may be specified by regulations, [and the amount which the person may deduct under section 12 or is entitled to be repaid under section 13 shall,][32] in accordance with regulations, be reduced by an amount equal to the amount of the flat-rate addition appropriate to the amount of the reduction or discount.][33]

(5)   If [an accountable person][1] issues an invoice stating a greater amount of tax than that properly attributable to the consideration stated therein, or issues a credit note stating a lesser amount of tax than that properly attributable to the reduction in consideration or the discount stated therein, he shall be liable to pay to the Revenue Commissioners the excess amount of tax stated in the invoice or the amount of the deficiency of tax stated in the credit note.

[...][15]

(6)   A person who is not a registered person and who, [...][34] issues an invoice stating an amount of tax shall, in relation to the amount of tax stated, be deemed, for the purposes of this Act, to be [an accountable person][1] and shall be liable to pay the amount to the Revenue Commissioners.

[(6A) (a)   If a person, other than a flat-rate farmer, issues an invoice stating an amount of flat-rate addition, he shall be liable to pay to the Revenue Commissioners as tax the amount of flat-rate addition stated and shall, in relation to such amount, be deemed, for the purposes of this Act, to be [an accountable person][1].

       (b)   If a flat-rate farmer issues an invoice stating an amount of flat-rate addition otherwise than in respect of an actual supply of agricultural produce or an agricultural service or in respect of such a supply but stating a greater amount of flat-rate addition than is appropriate to the supply, he shall be liable to pay to the Revenue Commissioners as tax the amount or the excess amount, as the case may be, of the flat-rate addition stated and shall, in relation to such amount or such excess amount, be deemed, for the purposes of this Act, to be [an accountable person][1].

       (c)   If a flat-rate farmer, in a case in which he is required to issue a farmer credit note under subsection (4)(b), fails to issue the credit note within the time allowed by regulations or issues a credit note stating a lesser amount of flat-rate addition than is appropriate to the reduction in consideration or the discount, he shall be liable to pay to the Revenue Commissioners as tax the amount of flat-rate addition which should have been stated on the credit note or the amount of the deficiency of flat-rate addition, as the case may be, and shall, in relation to such amount or such deficiency, be deemed, for the purposes of this Act, to be [an accountable person][1]][35].

(7)   An invoice or credit note shall be issued within such time after the date of [supplying goods or services][36] as may be specified by regulations and an amendment of an invoice pursuant to subsection (4)(b) shall be effected within such time as may be specified by regulations.

[...][15]

(8)   Notwithstanding anything in subsection (7), where payment for the [supply of goods or services][37] [, other than supplies of the kind specified in subparagraph (b) or (c) of paragraph (i) of the Second Schedule][38], is made to a person, either in full or by instalments, before the [supply][39] is completed, the person shall issue an invoice in accordance with subsection (1) [or subsection (2), as may be appropriate,][40] within such time after the date of

actual receipt of the full payment or the instalment as may be specified by regulations.

(9) (a) Notwithstanding anything in subsection (3), where, subsequent to the issue to a registered person of an invoice in accordance with subsection (1), the consideration stated in the invoice is reduced or a discount is allowed in such circumstances that, by agreement between the persons concerned, the amount of tax stated in the invoice is unaltered, paragraph (b) of the said subsection (3) shall not apply in relation to the person by whom the invoice was issued.

[(aa) Paragraph (a) shall not apply [in any case where subsection (3B) applies or][41] where the person who issued the invoice referred to therein was, at the time of its issue, a person authorised, in accordance with section 14 (1), to determine his tax liability in respect of supplies of the kind in question by reference to the amount of moneys received.][42]

(b) In a case to which paragraph (a) applies-

(i) the reduction or discount concerned shall not be taken into account in computing the liability to tax of the person making the reduction or allowing the discount,

(ii) subsection (5) shall not apply, and

(iii) the amount which the person in whose favour the reduction or discount is made or allowed may deduct in respect of the relevant transaction under section 12 shall not be reduced.

(10) Where-

(a) [...][43] agricultural produce or agricultural services are supplied to a registered person by a flat-rate farmer][44] [...][45] and

(b) the person to whom the [[agricultural produce][46] or services are supplied][47] issues to the other person, before the date on which an invoice is issued by that other person, a document (in this Act referred to as a settlement voucher) in such form and containing such particulars as may be specified by regulations, then, for the purposes of this Act-

(i) the person who issues the settlement voucher shall, if the person to whom it is issued accepts it, be deemed to have received from the person by whom the voucher was accepted an invoice containing the particulars set out in the voucher, and

(ii)   the person to whom the settlement voucher is issued shall, if he accepts it, be deemed to have issued to the person from whom the voucher was received an invoice containing the particulars set out in the voucher.

(11)   Where a person who is entitled to receive a credit note under subsection (3)(b) from another person issues to that other person, before the date on which a credit note is issued by that other person, a document (in this subsection referred to as a '**debit note**') in such form and containing such particulars as may be specified by regulations, then, for the purposes of this Act-

(a)   the person who issues the debit note shall, if the person to whom it is issued accepts it, be deemed to have received from the person by whom the note was accepted a credit note containing the particulars set out in such debit note, and

(b)   the person to whom such debit note is issued shall, if he accepts it, be deemed to have issued to the person from whom the debit note was received a credit note containing the particulars set out in such debit note.

[(11A)   Where a person who is entitled to receive a farmer credit note under subsection (4)(b) from another person issues to that other person, before the date on which a farmer credit note is issued by that other person, a document (in this section referred to as 'a farmer debit note') in such form and containing such particulars as may be specified by regulations, then, for the purposes of this Act-

(a)   the person who issues the debit note shall, if the person to whom it is issued accepts it, be deemed to have received from the person by whom the debit note was accepted a farmer credit note containing the particulars set out in such debit note, and

(b)   the person to whom such debit note is issued shall, if he accepts it, be deemed to have issued to the person from whom the debit note was received a farmer credit note containing the particulars set out in such debit note.][48]

(12)   (a)   [An accountable person][1] shall-

(i)   if requested in writing by another person and if the request states that the other person is entitled to repayment of tax under section 20(3), give to that other person in writing the particulars of the amount at tax chargeable [by [the accountable person][1]][49] in respect of the [supply][39] by him of the goods specified in the request or of the [supply][39] by him of the services so specified,

(ii) if requested in writing by another person and if the request states that that other person is entitled to repayment of tax under [section 13][50], give to that other person in writing the particulars specified in regulations for the purposes of subsection (1) in respect of the [goods or][51] services [supplied][52] by [the accountable person][1] to that other person that are specified in the request, and

(iii) if requested in writing by another person and if the request states that that other person is entitled to repayment of tax under section 20(2), give to that other person in writing the particulars of the amount of tax chargeable to the [by [the accountable person][1]][48] in respect of the [supply][39] by him of the radio broadcasting reception apparatus and parts thereof that are specified in the request.

[(ai) A flat-rate farmer shall, if requested in writing by another person and if the request states that the other person is entitled to repayment of the flat-rate addition under section 13, give to that other person in writing the particulars specified in regulations for the purpose of subsection (2) in respect of the goods or services supplied by the flat-rate farmer to that other person that are specified in the request.][53]

(b) A request under paragraph (a) [or (ai)][54] shall be complied with by the person to whom it is given within thirty days after the date on which the request is received by him.

[(13) The provisions of this Act (other than this section) relating to credit notes and debit notes issued under subsections (3) and (11), respectively, of this section shall apply in relation to farmer credit notes and farmer debit notes as they apply in relation to the credit notes and debit notes aforesaid.][55]

a 224   [(14) (a) An invoice required under this section to be issued in respect of a supply by a person, in this subsection referred to as the '**supplier**', is deemed to be so issued by that supplier if that invoice is drawn up and issued by the person to whom that supply is made, in this subsection referred to as the '**customer**', where —

(i) there is prior agreement between the supplier and the customer that the customer may draw up and issue such invoice,

(ii) the customer is a person registered for value-added tax,

(iii) any conditions which are imposed by this Act or by regulations on the supplier in relation to the form, content or issue of the invoice are met by the customer, and

(iv) agreed procedures are in place for the acceptance by the supplier of the validity of the invoice.

(b) An invoice, which is deemed to be issued by the supplier in accordance with paragraph (a), is deemed to have been so issued when such invoice is accepted by that supplier in accordance with the agreed procedures referred to in paragraph (a)(iv).

(c) An invoice required to be issued by a supplier under this section shall be deemed to be so issued by that supplier if -

(i) that invoice is issued by a person who acts in the name and on behalf of the supplier, and

(ii) any conditions which are imposed by this Act or by regulations on the supplier in relation to the form, content or issue of the invoice are met.

(d) Any credit note or debit note issued in accordance with this section which amends and refers specifically and unambiguously to an invoice is treated as if it were an invoice for the purposes of this subsection.

(e) The Revenue Commissioners may make regulations in relation to the conditions applying to invoices covered by this subsection.

a 244 (15) (a) A person who issues, or is deemed to issue, an invoice under this section shall ensure that—

(i) a copy of any invoice issued by such person

(ii) a copy of any invoice deemed to be issued by such person in the circumstances specified in subsection (14), and

(iii) any invoice received by such person,

is stored, and for the purposes of section 16(1) the reference to the keeping of full and true records therein shall be construed accordingly in so far as it relates to invoices covered by this section.

(b) Any invoice not stored by electronic means in a manner which conforms with requirements laid down by the Revenue Commissioners shall be stored within the State, but subject to the agreement of the Revenue

Commissioners and any conditions set by them such invoice may be stored outside the State.][56]

Amendments

1   Substituted by FA08 s109 & Sch 4, (w.e.f. 1 July 2008).
2   Substituted by VAT Amend. A78 s30(2), (w.e.f. 1 March 1979).
3   Inserted by FA 03 s122(a), (w.e.f. 1 January 2004).
4   Deleted by EC(VAT)R 1992 r12, (w.e.f. 1 January 1993).
5   Inserted by FA92 s180(a)(i), (w.e.f. 1 January 1993).
6   Substituted by FA07 s97 & Sch 3, (w.e.f. 1 January 2007).
7   Inserted by FA04, s63, (w.e.f. 25 March 2004).
8   Inserted by FA93 s 91(a), (w.e.f. 17 June 1993).
9   Deleted by FA92 s180(a)(ii), (w.e.f. 1 January 1993).
10 Inserted by FA73 s90, (w.e.f. 3 September 1973).
11 Substituted by FA92 s180(a)(iii), (w.e.f. 1 January 1993).
12 Substituted by VAT Amend. A78 s30(2), (w.e.f. 1 March 1979).
13 Deleted by FA07 s 90(a), (w.e.f. 1 May 2007)
14 Substituted by FA01 s193(a), (w.e.f. 21 March 2001).
15 Deleted by FA07 s 90(b) (w.e.f. 1 May 2007).
16 Deleted by FA08 s101(1)(b), (w.e.f. 1 July 2008).
17 Substituted by FA08 s101(1)(c), (w.e.f. 1 July 2008).
18 Ss(1AA) - (1AB) inserted by FA96 s97(b), (w.e.f. 1 July 1996).
19 Ss(1B) deleted by FA08 s141 & Sch 8(3)(e), (w.e.f. 13 March 2008).
20 Ss(1C) inserted by FA08 s101(1)(a), (w.e.f. 1 September 2008).
21 Substituted by FA92 s180(d), (w.e.f. 1 January 1993).
22 Ss(2) inserted by VAT Amend. A78 s15, (w.e.f. 1 March 1979).
23 Ss(2A) inserted by FA99 s134, (w.e.f. 1 September 1999).
24 Substituted by FA92 s180(e)(i), (w.e.f. 1 January 1993).
25 Substituted by FA92 s180(e)(ii), (w.e.f. 1 January 1993).
26 Substituted by FA92 s180(e)(iii)(I), (w.e.f. 1 January 1993).
27 Substituted by FA92 s180(e)(iii)(xx), (w.e.f. 1 January 1993).
28 Ss(3A) inserted by FA 1993 s 91(b).
29 Substituted by FA08 s101(2), (w.e.f. 1 July 2008).
30 Ss(3B) inserted by FA08 s101(1)(d), (w.e.f. 13 March 2008).
31 Deleted by FA92 s180(f)(i), (w.e.f. 1 January 1993).
32 Substituted by FA92 s180(f)(ii), (w.e.f. 1 January 1993).
33 Ss(4) inserted by VAT Amend. A78 s15, (w.e.f. 1 March 1979).
34 Deleted by FA76 s81, (w.e.f. 1 March 1976).
35 Ss(6A) inserted by VAT Amend. A78 s15, (w.e.f. 1 March 1979).
36 Substituted by VAT Amend. A78 s30(2), (w.e.f. 1 March 1979).
37 Substituted by VAT Amend. A78 s30(2), (w.e.f. 1 March 1979).
38 Inserted by FA92 s180(g), (w.e.f. 1 January 1993).
39 Substituted by VAT Amend. A78 s30(2), (w.e.f. 1 March 1979).
40 Inserted by VAT Amend. A78 s15, (w.e.f. 1 March 1979).
41 Inserted by FA08 s101(1)(e), (w.e.f. 13 March 2008).
42 Ss(9)(aa) inserted by VAT Amend. A78 s15, (w.e.f. 1 March 1979).
43 Deleted by FA03 s122(b), (w.e.f. 1 January 2004).
44 Inserted by VAT Amend. A78 s15, (w.e.f. 1 March 1979).
45 Deleted by FA76 s81, (w.e.f. 1 March 1976).
46 Substituted by FA03 s122(c), (w.e.f. 1 January 2004).
47 Substituted by VAT Amend. A78 s30(2), (w.e.f. 1 March 1979).
48 Ss(11A) inserted by VAT Amend. A78 s15, (w.e.f. 1 March 1979).
49 Substituted by FA06, s127(a) and Sch.2(8), (w.e.f. 31 March 2006)
50 Substituted by VAT Amend. A78 s30(2), (w.e.f. 1 March 1979).
51 Inserted by VAT Amend. A78 s15, (w.e.f. 1 March 1979).
52 Substituted by VAT Amend. A78 s30(2), (w.e.f. 1 March 1979).
53 Ss(12)(ai) inserted by FA92 s180(h)(i), (w.e.f. 1 January 1993).
54 Inserted by FA92 s180(h)(ii), (w.e.f. 1 January 1993).

55 Ss(13) inserted by VAT Amend. A78 s15, (w.e.f. 1 March 1979).

56 Ss(14) and (15) inserted by FA03 s122(d), (w.e.f. 1 January 2004).

Regulations and Orders

Documentation, agricultural machinery	1999 SI No. 443	Value Added Tax (Agricultural Machinery) (Documentation) Regulations, 1999
Electronic Invoicing	1992 SI No. 269	Value Added Tax (Electronic Data Exchange and Storage) Regulations, 1992
Electronic Invoicing	2002 SI No. 504	Value-Added Tax (Electronic Invoicing And Storage) Regulations, 2002
Electronic Invoicing	2006 SI No. 548	Value-Added Tax Regulations 2006
Invoices Credit Notes etc format	1992 SI No. 275	Value Added Tax (Invoices and Other Documents) Regulations, 1992
Invoices Credit Notes etc format	2003 SI No. 723	Value Added Tax (Invoices and Other Documents) (Amendment) Regulations, 2003
Invoices Credit notes - time limits	1992 SI No. 276	Value Added Tax (Time Limits for Issuing Certain Documents) Regulations, 1992
Invoices and credit notes – time limits	2006 SI No. 548	Value-Added Tax Regulations 2006
Invoices and credit notes – content	2006 SI No. 548	Value-Added Tax Regulations 2006
Invoice Credit notes etc.	1998 SI No. 489	Value Added Tax (Invoices and Other Documents) (Amendments) Regulations, 1998
Invoicing provisions – flat rate farmers	2006 SI No. 548	Value-Added Tax Regulations 2006
Monthly Control Statements	1992 SI No. 230	Value Added Tax (Monthly Control Statement) Regulations, 1992
Price alterations Bad Debts	1979 SI No. 63	Value Added Tax Regulations, 1979

Revenue e-Briefs

Revenue e-Brief No. 9/09: Reverse charge on construction services - invoicing

Revenue Statements of Practice and Information Leaflets

Electronic Invoicing (EDI): SP-VAT/9/92

Invoicing, VAT treatment of: Information Leaflet dated October 2008

The Monthly Control Statement: SP-VAT/7/92

Case law

Langhorst, Bernard v Finanzamt Osnabruck - Land	C141/96	Amount of tax payable on credit note issued.
Netherlands v Commission	C338/98	Cars/Recovery
Schmeink and Cofreth, AG & Co v Finanzant Borken and Strobel, Manfred v Finanzamt Esslingen	C454/98	Correction of incorrectly issued invoice

Revenue Precedents

Topic:	Outsourcing.
Issue:	Authorisation to use electronic invoicing between traders in the State who are participating in a purchasing card scheme.
Decision:	It was agreed, for ease of administration, to allow the letter of agreement on the purchasing card scheme to be accepted as simultaneous authorisation provided to all suppliers and purchasers within the scheme to use electronic invoicing.
Date:	12/03/98

Narrative

Implications of VAT Invoicing Regulations for companies: ITR Nov 2004: Vol 17 No. 6.

Tax Briefing: Issue 47 (Issue of Credit Notes Following an Increase in VAT Rate)

Tax Briefing: Issue 46 (New EU Rules on VAT Invoicing)

VAT Invoicing Proposed Directive: ITR Sept 2001: Vol. 14 No. 5

Tax Briefing: Issue 44: (EDI VAT Messages)

Tax Briefing: Issue 24: (Statutory Requirement for Invoices/Purchase Records)

Section 18

Inspection and removal of records

a 273 **18.** [(1)   (a)   For the purposes of this Act and regulations, an authorised officer may at all reasonable times enter any premises or place where he has reason to believe that business is carried on or anything is done in connection with business and-

(i)   may require the person carrying on the business, or any person on those premises or in that place who is employed by the person carrying on the business or who is associated with him in the carrying on of the business, to produce any books, records, accounts or other documents relating to the business or to any other business which he has reason to believe may be, or have been, connected with the said business or have, or have had, trading relations with the said business,

(ii)   may, if he has reason to believe that any of the books, records, accounts or other documents, which he has required to be produced to him under the provisions of this subsection have not been so produced, search in those premises or that place for those books, records, accounts or other documents,

[(iia)   may, if he has reason to believe that a person is carrying or has in his possession any records which may be required as evidence in criminal proceedings in accordance with [section 1078 of the Taxes Consolidation Act, 1997][1], in relation to the tax, request the person to produce any such records, and if that person should fail to do so, the authorised officer or a member of the Garda Síochána may search that person:

Provided that-

(A)   the officer or the member of the Garda Síochána conducting the search shall ensure, as far as practicable, that the person understands the reason for the search,

(B)   the search is conducted with due regard to the privacy of that person,

(C)   the person being searched shall not be searched by an officer or member of the Garda Síochána of the opposite sex, and

(D)   the person being searched shall not be requested to remove any clothing other than headgear or a coat, jacket, glove or a similar article of clothing.][2]

(iii)   may, in the case of any such books, records, accounts or other documents produced to or found by him, take copies of or extracts from them and remove and retain them for such period as may be reasonable for their further examination or for the purposes of any proceedings[...][3] in relation to tax,

(iv)   may, if he has reason to believe that goods connected with taxable supplies[, intra-Community acquisitions][4] or importations are held on those premises or in that place and that particulars of such goods have not been kept and retained, as required by this Act or by regulations, in the books, records, accounts or other documents of the business or of any other business similarly required to keep and retain particulars of those goods, search those premises or that place for the said goods and, on their discovery, examine and take particulars of them,

(v)   may require the person carrying on the business, or any person on those premises or in that place, who is employed by the person carrying on the business or who is associated with him in the carrying on of the business, to give the authorised officer all reasonable assistance[, including providing information and explanations and furnishing documents in connection with the business, as required by the authorised officer][5].

(b)   Nothing in this subsection shall be construed as requiring any person carrying on a profession, or any person employed by any person carrying on a profession, to produce to an authorised officer any documents relating to a client, other than such documents as are material to the tax affairs of the person carrying on the profession, and, in particular, he shall not be required to disclose any information or professional advice of a confidential nature given to a client.][6]

[(1A)   [An accountable person][7] on request from an authorised officer, furnish to that officer, in respect of a specified period, the following information:

(a)   the name and address of each of his customers and the total consideration payable in respect of supplies of goods and services made by him to each customer and the tax thereon [and the value and description of any gifts or promotional items given by him to any person in connection with such supplies or any other payments made by him to any person in connection with such supplies][8], and

(b)   the name, address and registration number of each of his suppliers and the total consideration payable in respect of goods and services supplied to him from each supplier and the tax thereon.

(1B)   In this section '**records**' means any document, or any other written or printed material in any form, including any information stored, maintained or preserved by means of any mechanical or electronic device, whether or not stored, maintained or preserved in a legible form, which a person is required to keep, retain, issue or produce for inspection or which may be inspected under any provision relating to tax.][9]

[…][10]

(3)   A person shall not wilfully obstruct or delay an authorised officer in the exercise of his powers under this section.

(4)   Where, in pursuance of this section, an authorised officer enters any premises, carries out any search or requests production of any documents, he shall, on request, show his authorisation for the purpose of this section to the person concerned.

(5)   In this section 'authorised officer' means an officer of the Revenue Commissioners authorised by them in writing for the purposes of this section.

Amendments
1 Substituted by TCA97 s1100 & Sch31, (w.e.f. 6 April 1997).
2 Ss(1)(iia) inserted by FA92 s181(a)(i), (w.e.f. 1 January 1993).
3 Deleted by FA92 s181(a)(ii), (w.e.f. 28 May 1992).
4 Inserted by FA92 s181(a)(iii), (w.e.f. 1 January 1993).
5 Inserted by FA92 s181(a)(iv), (w.e.f. 28 May 1992).
6 Ss(1) substituted by FA84 s89, (w.e.f. 23 May 1984).
7 Substituted by FA08 s109 & Sch 4, (w.e.f. 1 July 2008).
8 Inserted by FA95 s133, (w.e.f. 2 June 1995).
9 Ss(1A) - (1B) inserted by FA92 s181(b), (w.e.f. 28 May 1992).
10 Deleted by FA84 s89, (w.e.f. 23 May 1984).

Regulations and Orders

| Accounts/Records | 1979 SI No. 63 | Value Added Tax Regulation, 1979 |
| Disclosure of information to Revenue | 1979 SI No. 63 | Value Added Tax Regulations, 1979 |

Revenue Statements of Practice and Information Leaflets
Revenue Powers: SP-GEN/1/94
Revenue Powers: SP-GEN/1/99

Section 19

Tax due and payable

63, a 66, **19.**   (1)   Tax chargeable under section 2(1)(a) shall be due-

a 67, a 68

(a)   in case an invoice is required under section 17 to be issued, at the time of issue of the invoice, or if the invoice is not issued in due time, upon the expiration of the period within which the invoice should have been issued;

(b)   in case a person is liable under subsection (5) or (6) of section 17 to pay an amount of tax by reference to an invoice or credit note issued by him, at the time of issue of such invoice or credit note, [...][1]

a 64   [(bb)   in the case of continuous supplies of telecommunications services, electricity, or gas which has the meaning assigned to it in paragraph (i)(c) of the Sixth Schedule, for which a statement of account issues periodically, supplied to a person other than a person to whom an invoice is required under section 17 to be issued, at the time of issue of the statement of account in respect of those supplies, and in this paragraph 'statement of account' means a balancing statement, or a demand for payment which issues at least once every 3 months, and][2]

(c)   in any other case, at the time the [goods or services are supplied][3]:

[...][4]

a 69   [(1A)   Tax chargeable under section 2(1A) shall be due-

(a)   on the fifteenth day of the month following that during which the intra-Community acquisition occurs;

(b)   in case an invoice is issued before the date specified in paragraph (a) by the supplier in another Member State to the person acquiring the goods, when that invoice is issued.][5]

a 65   (2)   Notwithstanding anything in this Act, the tax chargeable under section 2(1)(a)[, other than tax chargeable in respect of supplies of the kind specified in subparagraph (b) or (c) of paragraph (i) of the Second Schedule,][6] or the relevant part thereof, shall fall due not later than the time when the amount in respect of which it is payable has been received either in full or in part and where the amount is received in full or in part before the [supply of the goods or services][7] to which it relates, a [supply][8] for a consideration equal to the amount received of such part of the goods or services as is equal in value to the amount received, shall be deemed, for the purposes of this

Act, to have taken place at the time of such receipt. [However this subsection does not apply to the tax chargeable in respect of supplies of goods or services where tax is due in accordance with [paragraph (a), (b) or (bb)][9] of subsection (1) by [an accountable person][10] who is not authorised under section 14 to account for tax due by reference to the amount of the moneys received during a taxable period or part thereof.][11]

[(2A)   Where a payment is made prior to the 1st day of July, 1997, in respect of a telecommunications service which is to be supplied by a person in the course or furtherance of business from outside the State on or after that date and the place of supply of that service is deemed by virtue of paragraph (e) of subsection (6) of section 5 to be, at the time of its supply, the State, then that payment shall be deemed, for the purposes of subsection (2), to be made on that date.][12]

[(2B)   Where a person accounts in accordance with subsection (3) for tax referred to in subsection (2) on an amount received by way of a deposit from a customer before the supply of the goods or services to which it relates, and–

     (a)   that supply does not subsequently take place owing to a cancellation by the customer,

     (b)   the cancellation is recorded as such in the books and records of that person,

     (c)   the deposit is not refunded to the customer, and

     (d)   no other consideration, benefit or supply is provided to the customer by any person in lieu of the refund of that amount,

then, the tax chargeable under section 2(1)(a) shall be reduced in the taxable period in which the cancellation is recorded by the amount of tax accounted for on the deposit.][13]

a 250, a 251,   [(3)   (a)   Subject to paragraph (b), [an accountable person][10] shall,
a 252   within 9 days immediately after the tenth day of the month immediately following a taxable period, furnish to the Collector-General a true and correct return prepared in accordance with regulations of the amount of tax which became due by him during the taxable period, not being tax already paid by him in relation to goods imported by him, and the amount, if any, which may be deducted in accordance with section 12 in computing the amount of tax payable by him in respect of such taxable period and such other particulars as may be specified in regulations, and shall at the same time remit to the Collector-General the amount of tax, if any, payable by him in respect of such taxable period.

     [...][14]

[(aa) (i)   In this paragraph:

['**accounting period**' means a period, as determined by the Collector-General from time to time in any particular case, consisting of a number of consecutive taxable periods not exceeding six or such other period not exceeding a continuous period of twelve months as may be specified by the Collector-General:

Provided that-

(I)   where an accounting period begins before the end of a taxable period, the period of time from the beginning of the accounting period to the end of the taxable period during which the accounting period begins shall, for the purposes of this paragraph, be treated as if such period of time were a taxable period, and

(II)   where an accounting period ends after the beginning of a taxable period, the period of time from the beginning of the taxable period during which the accounting period ends to the end of the accounting period shall, for the purposes of this paragraph, be treated as if such period of time were a taxable period,

and any references in this paragraph to a taxable period shall be construed accordingly;][15]

'**authorised person**' means [an accountable person][10] who has been authorised in writing by the Collector-General for the purposes of this paragraph and '**authorise**' and '**authorisation**' shall be construed accordingly.

(ii)   Notwithstanding the provisions of paragraph (a) -

(I)   the Collector-General may, from time to time, authorise in writing [an accountable person][10] for the purposes of this paragraph, unless [the accountable person][10] objects in writing to the authorisation,

and

(II)   an authorised person may, within nine days immediately after the tenth day of the month immediately following an accounting period furnish to the Collector-General a true and correct return prepared in accordance with regulations of the amount of tax which became due by him during the taxable periods which comprise the accounting period, not being tax already paid by him in relation to goods imported by him, and, the amount, if any, which may be deducted in accordance with section 12 in computing the amount of tax payable by him in respect of such taxable periods and such other particulars as may be specified in regulations, and at the same time remit to the Collector-General any amount of tax payable by him in respect of such taxable periods, [and, in the case of an authorised person referred to in subparagraph (iv)(III) that amount shall be the balance of tax remaining to be paid, if any, after deducting from it, the amount of tax paid by him by direct debit in respect of his accounting period,][16] and, where the authorised person concerned so furnishes and remits, he shall be deemed to have complied with the provisions of paragraph (a) in relation to the said taxable periods.

(iii)   For the purposes of issuing an authorisation to [an accountable person][10] the Collector-General shall, where he considers it appropriate, have regard to the following matters-

    (I)   he has reasonable grounds to believe that-

        (A)   the authorisation will not result in a loss of tax, and

        (B)   [the accountable person][10] will meet all his obligations under the authorisation,

and

    (II)   [the accountable person][10] has-

        (A)   been a registered person during all of the period consisting of the six taxable periods immediately preceding the period in which an authorisation would, if it were issued, have effect, and

        (B)   complied with the provisions of paragraph (a).

(iv) An authorisation may-

(I) be issued either without conditions or subject to such conditions as the Collector-General, having regard in particular to the considerations mentioned in subparagraph (iii), considers proper and specifies in writing to [the accountable person][10] concerned when issuing the authorisation,

(II) without prejudice to the generality of the foregoing, require an authorised person to remit to the Collector-General, within nine days immediately after the tenth day of the month immediately following each taxable period (other than the final taxable period) which is comprised in an accounting period, such an amount as may be specified by the Collector-General.

[(III) without prejudice to the generality of the fore-going, require an authorised person to agree with the Collector-General a schedule of amounts of money which he undertakes to pay on dates specified by the Collector-General by monthly direct debit from his account with a financial institution and the total of the amounts specified in that schedule shall be that person's best estimate of his total tax liability for his accounting period and he shall review on an on-going basis whether the total of the amounts specified in that schedule is likely to be adequate to cover his actual liability for his accounting period and where this is not the case or is not likely to be the case, he shall agree a revised schedule of amounts with the Collector-General and adjust his monthly direct debit amounts accordingly.][17]

(v) The Collector-General may, by notice in writing, terminate an authorisation and, where [an accountable person][10] requests him to do so, he shall terminate the authorisation.

(vi) For the purposes of terminating an authorisation the Collector-General shall, where he considers it appropriate, have regard to the following matters:

(I)   he has reasonable grounds to believe that the authorisation has resulted or could result in a loss of tax, or

(II)   [the accountable person][10]-

(A)   has furnished, or there is furnished on his behalf, any incorrect information for the purposes of the issue to him of an authorisation, or

(B)   has not complied with the provisions of paragraph (a) or of this paragraph, including the conditions, if any, specified by the Collector-General under subparagraph (iv) in relation to the issue to him of an authorisation.

(vii)   In relation to any taxable period in respect of which he has not complied with the provisions of paragraph (a), a person whose authorisation is terminated shall be deemed to have complied with paragraph (a) if, within [fourteen][18] days of issue to him of a notice of termination, he furnishes to the Collector-General the return specified in paragraph (a) and at the same time remits to the said Collector-General the amount of tax payable by him in accordance with that paragraph.

(viii)   (I)   An authorisation shall be deemed to have been terminated by the Collector-General on the date that an authorised person-

(A)   ceases to trade (except for the purposes of disposing of the stocks and assets of his business), whether for reasons of insolvency or any other reason,

(B)   being a body corporate, goes into liquidation, whether voluntarily or not, or

(C)   ceases to be [an accountable person][10], dies or becomes bankrupt.

(II)   [An accountable person][10] to whom this subparagraph relates shall, in relation to any taxable period (or part of a taxable period) comprised in the accounting period which was in operation in his case on the date to which clause (I) of this subparagraph relates, be deemed to have complied with paragraph (a) if he furnishes to the Collector-General the return specified in subparagraph (ii) (II) and at the same time remits to the said Collector-General the amount of tax payable by him for the purposes of that subparagraph as if he were an authorised person whose accounting period ended on the last day of the taxable period during which the termination occurred:

Provided that the personal representative of a person who was an authorised person shall be deemed to be [the accountable person][10] concerned.][19]

(b)   A person who disposes of goods which pursuant to section 3(7) are deemed to be supplied by [an accountable person][10] in the course or furtherance of his business-

(i)   shall within 9 days immediately after the tenth day of the month immediately following a taxable period furnish to the Collector-General a true and correct return, prepared in accordance with regulations, of the amount of tax which became due by [such accountable person][10] in relation to the disposal, and such other particulars as may be specified in regulations, and shall at the same time remit to the Collector-General the amount of tax payable in respect of the taxable period in question,

(ii)   shall send to the person whose goods were disposed of a statement containing such particulars as may be specified in regulations, and

(iii)   shall treat the said amount of tax as a necessary disbursement out of the proceeds of the disposal.

(c)   The owner of goods which pursuant to section 3(7) are deemed to be supplied by [an accountable person][10] in the course or furtherance of his business shall exclude from any return, which he is or, but for this subparagraph, would be, required to furnish under this Act, the tax payable in accordance with paragraph (b)][20].

[(d)   (i)   A return required to be furnished by [an accountable person][10] under this subsection may be furnished by [the accountable person][10] or another person acting under [the accountable person's][10] authority for that purpose and a return purporting to be a return furnished by a person acting under [an accountable person's][10] authority shall be deemed to be a return furnished by [the accountable person][10], unless the contrary is proved.

(ii)   Where a return in accordance with paragraph (i) is furnished by a person acting under [an accountable person's][10] authority the provisions of any enactment relating to value-added tax shall apply as if it had been furnished by [the accountable person][10].][21]

[(3A) Where a remittance or, as the case may be, a return and remittance, referred to in paragraph (a), subparagraphs (ii)(II) and (iv)(II) of paragraph (aa) and paragraph (b) of subsection (3) is or are—

(a)   as respects the remittance, made by such electronic means (within the meaning of section 917EA of the Taxes Consolidation Act 1997) as are required by the Revenue Commissioners, and

(b)   as respects the return, made by electronic means and in accordance with Chapter 6 of Part 38 of the Taxes Consolidation Act 1997,

then the said paragraphs (a), (aa) and (b) shall apply and have effect as if '13 days' were substituted for '9 days' or, as the case may be, 'nine days' in each place where it occurs; but where that remittance or return is made after the period provided for in this subsection this Act shall apply and have effect without regard to the provisions of this subsection.][22]

[(4)   (a)   Notwithstanding subsection (3), where-

(i)   a person makes an intra-Community acquisition of a new means of transport, other than a vessel or aircraft, in respect of which he is not entitled to a deduction under section 12, then-

(I)   the tax shall be payable at the time of payment of vehicle registration tax or, if no vehicle registration tax is payable, at the time of registration of the vehicle [or, if section 131 of the Finance Act, 1992, does not provide for registration of the vehicle, at a time not later than the time when the tax is due in accordance with subsection (1A)][23],

(II)   the person shall complete such form as may be provided by the Revenue Commissioners for the purpose of this subsection, and

(III)   the provisions relating to recovery and collection of vehicle registration tax shall apply, with such exceptions and modifications (if any) as may be specified in regulations, to tax referred to in this subparagraph as if it were vehicle registration tax,

and

(ii)   a person makes an intra-Community acquisition of a new means of transport which is a vessel or aircraft, in respect of which he is not entitled to a deduction under section 12, then-

(I)   the tax shall be payable at a time and in a manner to be determined by regulations, and

(II)   the provisions relating to the recovery and collection of a duty of customs shall apply, with such exceptions and modifications (if any) as may be specified in regulations, to tax referred to in this subparagraph as if it were a duty of customs.

(b)   In this subsection-

'**registration of the vehicle**' means the registration of the vehicle in accordance with section 131 of the Finance Act, 1992;

'**vehicle registration tax**' means the tax referred to in section 132 of the Finance Act, 1992.][24]

[(5)   Notwithstanding the provisions of subsection (3), where the provisions of section 8(2B)(b) apply, the tax shall be payable at the time of payment of the duty of excise on the goods and the provisions relating to recovery and collection of that duty of excise shall apply, with such exceptions and modifications (if any) as may be specified in regulations, to tax referred to in this subsection as if it were that duty of excise.][25]

[...][26]

[(6)   Notwithstanding the provisions of subsection (3), in cases where the provisions of section 5A are applied, the tax shall be payable at the time the VAT return is required to be submitted in accordance with section 5A(6).][27]

Amendments

1   Deleted by FA05 s106(a)(i) (w.e.f. 25 March 2005).
2   Inserted by FA05 s106(a)(ii) (w.e.f. 25 March 2005).
3   Substituted by VAT Amend. A78 s30(2), (w.e.f. 1 March 1979).
4   Repealed by VAT Amend. A78 s30(1), (w.e.f. 1 March 1979).
5   Ss(1A) inserted by FA92 s182(a), (w.e.f. 1 January 1993).
6   Inserted by FA92 s182(b), (w.e.f. 1 January 1993).

7   Substituted by VAT Amend. A78 s30(2), (w.e.f. 1 March 1979).
8   Substituted by VAT Amend. A78 s30(2), (w.e.f. 1 March 1979).
9   Substituted by FA05 s106(b) (w.e.f. 25 March 2005).
10 Inserted by FA08 s109 & Sch 4, (w.e.f. 1 July 2008).
11 Inserted by FA02 s106(a), (w.e.f. 1 May 2002).
12 Ss(2A) inserted by FA97 s107(a), (w.e.f. 10 May 1997).
13 Ss(2B) inserted by FA08 s102, (w.e.f. 13 March 2008).
14 Deleted by FA97 s107(b), (w.e.f. 7 November 1996).
15 Substituted by FA95 s134, (w.e.f. 1 September 1996).
16 Amended by FA01 s194(a), (w.e.f. 21 March 2001).
17 Inserted by FA01 s194(b), (w.e.f. 21 March 2001).
18 Substituted by FA02 Sch 6, (w.e.f. 25 March 2002).
19 Ss(3)(aa) inserted by FA89 s58, (w.e.f. 24 May 1989).
20 Ss(3) substituted by FA83 s84, (w.e.f. 1 September 1983).
21 Inserted by FA02 s106(b), (w.e.f. 25 March 2002).
22 Inserted by F(No. 2)A 08 s96 & Sch3, (w.e.f. 1 January 2009).
23 Inserted by FA99 s135, (w.e.f. 25 March 1999).
24 Ss(4) substituted by FA93 s92(b), (w.e.f. 1 September 1993).
25 Ss(5) substituted by FA93 s92(c), (w.e.f. 1 September 1993).
26 Deleted by FA97 s107(c), (w.e.f. 7 November 1996).
27 Ss(6) inserted by FA03 s123, (w.e.f. 1 July 2003).

Regulations and Orders

Advance payment of VAT	1993 SI No. 303	Value Added Tax (Threshold for Advance Payment) Order 1993
Advance payment of VAT	1994 SI No. 342	Value Added Tax (Threshold for Advance payment) (Amendment) Order 1994
Advance VAT	1993 SI No. 345	European Communities (Value Added Tax) Regulations, 1993
Annual Accounts	1996 SI No. 231	Finance Act 1995 (Section 134 (1)) (Commencement) (Order) 1996
INTRASTAT	1993 SI No. 136	European Community (INTRASTAT) Regulations, 1993
Mandatory electronic filing	2008 SI No. 341	Tax Returns and Payments (Mandatory Electronic Filing and Payment of Tax) Regulations 2008
Returns EDI	1992 SI No. 269	Valued Added Tax (Electronic DATA Exchange and Storage) Regulations, 1992
Returns EDI	1998 SI No. 488	Value Added Tax (Electronic DATA Exchange and Storage) (Amendment) Regulations, 1998
Returns	1993 SI No. 247	Value Added Tax (Returns) Regulations, 1993
Returns	1996 SI No. 294	Value Added Tax (Returns) Regulations, 1996
Returns	2002 SI No. 267	Value Added Tax (Returns) Regulations, 2002
Returns	2006 SI No. 548	Value-Added Tax Regulations 2006

Revenue e-Briefs

Revenue e-Brief No. 59/2008: Reduced frequency of tax returns and payments for employers PAYE/PRSI and VAT – extension of newly eligible customers
Revenue e-Brief No. 42/2008: Mandatory electronic filing and payment of tax – new Regulations made
Revenue e-Brief No. 55/2007: Simplified payment and filing arrangements for VAT
Revenue e-Brief No. 38/2007: Payment of tax by direct debit – change of contact details
Revenue e-Brief No. 27/2007: New simplified payment arrangements for VAT
Revenue e-Brief No. 29/2004: New VAT 3 Return

Case law

Balocchi, Maurizio v Ministero delle Finanze dello Stato	C10/92	Payment of VAT before Taxable Event
BUPA Hospitals Ltd, Goldsborough Developments Ltd v Commissioners of Customs & Excise	C419/02	Payment on account/Chargeable Event/Taxable person/Entitlement to VAT recovery

Impresa Construziono Comm. Quirino Mazzalai v Ferrovia del Renon SpA	C111/75	Taxable Event/Time of Completed Supply
Italittica Spa v Ufficio IVA di Trapani	C144/94	Taxable Event/Receipt of payment
Marktgemeinde Welden v Finanzamt Augsburg - Stadt	C247/95	Tax payable in advance of supply

Revenue Precedents

Topic:	Property Transactions.
Issue:	Lease documents held in escrow pending tenant fitting out unit to landlord's satisfaction/specification.
Decision:	The date of supply of taxable leases is the date the signed lease documents are released from escrow.
Date:	7/4/88

Topic:	Credit Card Companies.
Issue:	Breaches in time limit for issue of invoices.
Decision:	Revenue prepared to accept minor breaches, i.e. invoices issued before the end of the calendar month following the month supplies were made, subject to certain conditions.
Date:	4/3/91

Narrative

Tax Briefing: Issue 57 (New VAT 3 Form)

Is the Revenue Commissioners Policy on VAT: "No Loss of Revenue" Cases Costly for Everyone? ITR Jan 2003: Vol 16. No. 1

Tax Briefing: Issue 47 (VAT Returns Made By Agents)

Tax Briefing: Issue 46 (Payment of VAT by Direct Debit)

Tax Briefing: Issue 27 (Finance Act 1997 Changes: Abolition of the "Advance Payment")

Tax Briefing: Issue 27 (Non-Operation of VAT)

Tax Briefing: Issue 24: (Statutory Requirement for Invoices/Purchase Records)

Tax Briefing: Issue 23 (Flexible Annual Accounting – Clarification)

Tax Briefing: Issue 22 (Flexible Annual Accounting)

Section 19A

Statement of intra-Community supplies

a 262,
a 263,
a 264

[19A. (1)   Subject to subsections (2) and (3), [an accountable person][1] shall by the last day of the month immediately following the end of each calendar quarter, furnish to the Revenue Commissioners a statement of his intra-Community supplies in that quarter prepared in accordance with, and containing such other particulars as may be specified in, regulations.

(2)   The Revenue Commissioners shall, on request, authorise [an accountable person][1] to furnish by the last day of each month a statement of his intra-Community supplies in the previous month prepared in accordance with, and containing such other particulars as may be specified in, regulations.

(3)   The Revenue Commissioners may, on request, authorise [an accountable person][1], whose supplies do not exceed or are not likely to exceed, in a calendar year, an amount or amounts specified in regulations, to furnish by the last day of January following that calendar year a statement of such intra-Community supplies prepared in accordance with and containing such other particulars as may be specified in regulations.

(4)   Notwithstanding the provisions of subsections (1), (2) and (3), [an accountable person][1] who made no intra-Community supplies in the relevant period, but who was liable to furnish a statement in respect of a previous period, shall, unless authorised by the Revenue Commissioners, furnish to them within the relevant time limit a statement indicating that he made no such supplies in that period.

(5)   The Revenue Commissioners may, in accordance with regulations, cancel an authorisation under subsection (2) or (3).

[(6)   In this section 'intra-Community supplies' means supplies of goods to a person registered for value-added tax in another Member State.][2]][3]

Amendments

1   Substituted by FA08 s109 & Sch 4, (w.e.f. 1 July 2008)

2   Substituted by FA05 s107 (w.e.f. 25 March 2005).

3   S19A inserted by FA92 s183, (w.e.f. 1 January 1993).

Regulations and Orders

Electronic transmission of VIES statements	2008 SI No. 339 Taxes (Electronic Transmission of VAT eServices Returns and VIES Statements) Specified Provisions and Appointed Day) Order 2008
Statement of intra-Community supplies	2006 SI No. 548 Value-Added Tax Regulations 2006
VIES	1993 SI No. 54 Value Added Tax (Statement of Intra-Community supplies) Regulations 1993

Section 19B

Letter of expression of doubt

[19B. (1) (a) Where [an accountable person][1] is in doubt as to the correct application of any enactment relating to value-added tax (in this section referred to as 'the law') to a transaction which could give rise to a liability to tax by that person or affect that person's liability to tax or entitlement to a deduction or refund of tax, then [that accountable person][1] may, at the same time as the taxable person furnishes to the Collector-General the return due in accordance with section 19 for the period in which the transaction occurred, lodge a letter of expression of doubt with the Revenue Commissioners at the office of the Revenue Commissioners which would normally deal with the examination of the records kept by that person in accordance with section 16, but this section shall only apply if that return is furnished within the time limits prescribed in section 19.

(b) For the purposes of this section 'letter of expression of doubt' means a communication received in legible form which—

(i)   sets out full details of the circumstances of the transaction and makes reference to the provisions of the law giving rise to the doubt,

(ii) identifies the amount of tax in doubt in respect of the taxable period to which the expression of doubt relates,

(iii) is accompanied by supporting documentation as relevant, and

(iv) is clearly identified as a letter of expression of doubt for the purposes of this section,

and reference to an expression of doubt shall be construed accordingly.

(2) Subject to subsection (3), where a return and a letter of expression of doubt relating to a transaction are furnished by [an accountable person][1] to the Revenue Commissioners in accordance with this section, the provisions of section 21 shall not apply to any additional liability arising from a notification to that person by the Revenue Commissioners of the correct application of the law to the said transaction, on condition that such additional liability is accounted for and remitted to the Collector-General by [the

accountable person][1] as if it were tax due for the taxable period in which the notification is issued.

(3)   Subsection (2) does not apply where the Revenue Commissioners do not accept as genuine an expression of doubt in respect of the application of the law to a transaction, and an expression of doubt shall not be accepted as genuine in particular where the Revenue Commissioners –

(a)   have issued general guidelines concerning the application of the law in similar circumstances,

(b)   are of the opinion that the matter is otherwise sufficiently free from doubt as not to warrant an expression of doubt, or

(c)   are of the opinion that [the accountable person][1] was acting with a view to the evasion or avoidance of tax.

(4)   Where the Revenue Commissioners do not accept an expression of doubt as genuine they shall notify [the accountable person][1] accordingly, and [the accountable person][1] shall account for any tax, which was not correctly accounted for in the return referred to in subsection (1), as tax due for the taxable period in which the transaction occurred, and the provisions of section 21 shall apply accordingly.

(5)   [An accountable person][1] who is aggrieved by a decision of the Revenue Commissioners that that person's expression of doubt is not genuine may, by giving notice in writing to the Revenue Commissioners within the period of twenty-one days after the notification of the said decision, require the matter to be referred to the Appeal Commissioners.

(6)   A letter of expression of doubt shall be deemed not to have been made unless its receipt is acknowledged by the Revenue Commissioners and that acknowledgement forms part of the records kept by [the accountable person][1] for the purposes of section 16.

(7)   (a)   For the purposes of this section ['accountable person'][1] includes a person who is not a registered person and is in doubt as to whether he or she is [an accountable person][1] in respect of a transaction and in that case references to a return and records are to be construed as referring to a return that would be due under section 19 and records that would be kept for the purposes of section 16, if that person were in fact [an accountable person][1].

(b)   A person whose expression of doubt concerns whether he or she is [an accountable person][1] shall lodge that expression of doubt for the purposes of applying subsection (2) not later than the nineteenth day of the month following the taxable period in which the transaction giving rise to the expression of doubt occurred.][2]

Amendments

1   Substituted by FA08 s109 & Sch 4, (w.e.f. 1 July 2008).

2   S19B inserted by FA02 s107 (w.e.f. 25 March 2002).

Revenue Statements of Practice and Information Leaflets

   Expression of Doubt: Information Leaflet dated October 2008

Narrative

   Letters of Expression of Doubt: ITR Sept 2002: Vol 15 No. 6

Section 20

Refund of tax

a 183 **20.** [(1) [[Subject to subsections (1A) and (1B)]¹, where]² in relation to a return lodged under section 19 or a claim made in accordance with regulations, it is shown to the satisfaction of the Revenue Commissioners that, as respects any taxable period, the amount of tax, if any, actually paid to the Collector-General in accordance with section 19 together with the amount of tax, if any, which qualified for deduction under section 12 exceeds the tax, if any, which would properly be payable if no deduction were made under the said section 12, they shall refund the amount of the excess less any sums previously refunded under this subsection or repaid under section 12 and may include in the amount refunded any interest which has been paid under section 21.]³

[...]⁴

[(1A) Where the Revenue Commissioners apply the provisions of section 8(8) to a number of persons they may defer repayment of all or part of any tax refundable under subsection (1) to any one or more of the said persons prior to the application of those provisions, where any one or more of the said persons have not furnished all returns and remitted all amounts of tax referred to in section 19(3) at the time of such application.]⁵

[(1B) The Revenue Commissioners may, where it appears requisite to them to do so for the protection of the revenue, require as a condition for making a refund in accordance with subsection (1) the giving of security of such amount and in such manner and form as they may determine:

Provided that the amount of such security shall not, in any particular case, exceed the amount to be refunded.]⁶

(2) Notwithstanding anything in this Act, a refund of the tax paid in respect of radio broadcasting reception apparatus and parts thereof belonging to an institution or society may be made to the institution or society if, but only if-

(a) in the opinion of the Revenue Commissioners, it has for its primary object the amelioration of the lot of blind persons, and

(b) it shows, to the satisfaction of the Revenue Commissioners, that the goods in question are intended for the use of blind persons.

(3) [(a) The Minister may by order provide that a person who fulfils to the satisfaction of the Revenue Commissioners such conditions as may be specified in the order shall be

entitled to be repaid so much, as is specified in the order, of any tax borne or paid by him as does not qualify for deduction under section 12.]⁷

(b)   The Minister may by order amend or revoke an order under this subsection, including an order under this paragraph.

[(bb)   An order under this subsection may, if so expressed, have retrospective effect.]⁸

(c)   An order under this subsection shall be laid before Dáil Éireann as soon as may be after it is made and, if a resolution annulling the order is passed by Dáil Éireann within the next twenty-one days on which Dáil Éireann has sat after the order is laid before it, the order shall be annulled accordingly, but without prejudice to the validity of anything previously done thereunder.

[(4)   (a)   In relation to any taxable period ending before [1 May 2003]⁹, no refund shall, subject to paragraph (b), be made under this section or any other provision of this Act or regulations unless a claim for that refund is made within the period of [six years]⁹ from the end of the taxable period to which the claim relates.

(b)   In relation to any taxable period commencing on or after [1 May 2003]¹⁰, and on or after [1 January 2005]¹⁰, in relation to any other taxable period, no refund shall be made under this section or under any other provision of this Act or regulations unless a claim for that refund is made within the period of [four years]¹⁰ from the end of the taxable period to which that claim relates.]¹¹

a 189(c)   [(5)   [(a)   Where, due to a mistaken assumption in the operation of the tax, whether that mistaken assumption was made by [an accountable person]¹², any other person or the Revenue Commissioners, a person-

(i)   accounted, in a return furnished to the Revenue Commissioners, for an amount of tax for which that person was not properly accountable, or

(ii)   did not, because that person's supplies of goods and services were treated as exempted activities, furnish a return to the Revenue Commissioners and, therefore, did not receive a refund of an amount of tax in accordance with subsection (1), or

(iii)   did not deduct an amount of tax in respect of qualifying activities, as defined in section 12(1)(b), which that person was entitled to deduct, then, in respect of the total amount of tax referred to in subparagraphs (i), (ii) or (iii) (in this subsection referred to as the 'overpaid amount') that person may claim a refund of the overpaid amount and the Revenue Commissioners shall, subject to the provisions of this subsection, refund to the claimant the overpaid amount [unless they determine that the refund of that overpaid amount or part thereof would result in the unjust enrichment of the claimant][13].][14]

[(b)   A person who claims a refund of an overpaid amount under this subsection shall make that claim in writing setting out full details of the circumstances of the case and identifying the overpaid amount in respect of each taxable period to which the claim relates. The claimant shall furnish such relevant documentation to support the claim as the Revenue Commissioners may request.

(c)   (i)   For the purposes of determining whether a refund of an overpaid amount or part thereof would result in the unjust enrichment of a claimant, the Revenue Commissioners shall have regard to—

      (I)   the extent to which the cost of the overpaid amount was, for practical purposes, passed on by the claimant to other persons in the price charged by that claimant for goods or services supplied by that claimant,

      (II)   any net loss of profits which they have reason to believe, based on their own analysis and on any information that may be provided to them by the claimant, was borne by the claimant due to the mistaken assumption made in the operation of the tax, and

      (III)   any other factors that the claimant brings to their attention in this context.

    (ii)   The Revenue Commissioners may request from the claimant all reasonable information relating to the circumstances giving rise to the claim as may assist them in reaching a determination for the purposes of subparagraph (i).

(d)   Where, in accordance with paragraph (c), the Revenue Commissioners determine that a refund of an overpaid amount or part thereof would result in the unjust enrichment of a claimant, they shall refund only so much of the overpaid amount as would not result in the unjust enrichment of that claimant.][15]

(e)   Where, in relation to any claim under paragraph (a), the Revenue Commissioners have withheld an amount of the overpaid amount claimed under paragraph (a) as it would result in the unjust enrichment of the claimant the Revenue Commissioners shall, notwithstanding the provisions of paragraph (a), refund to the claimant that part of the withheld amount [together with any interest payable in accordance with section 21A][16] which the claimant has undertaken to repay to the persons to whom the cost of the overpaid amount was passed on where they are satisfied that the claimant has adequate arrangements in place to identify and repay those persons.

(f)   Where a claimant receives a refund in accordance with paragraph (e) and fails to repay the persons concerned at the latest by the thirtieth day next following the payment by the Revenue Commissioners of that refund, then any amount not so repaid shall, for the purposes of this Act, be treated as if it were tax due by the claimant for the taxable period within which that day falls.][17]

[(6)   Where the Revenue Commissioners refund any amount due under subsection (1) or subsection (5), they may if they so determine refund any such amount directly into an account, specified by the person to whom the amount is due, in a financial institution.][18]

[(7)   The Revenue Commissioners shall not refund any amount of tax except as provided for in this Act, or any order or regulation made under this Act][19]

Amendments

1   Substituted by FA92 s184(1)(a), (w.e.f. 28 May 1992).
2   Substituted by FA86 s87, (w.e.f. 27 May 1986).
3   Ss(1) substituted by FA81 s45, (w.e.f. 28 May 1981).
4   Deleted by FA97 s108, (w.e.f. 7 November 1996).
5   Ss(1A) substituted by FA91 s83, (w.e.f. 29 May 1991).
6   Ss91B) inserted by FA92 s184(1)(b), (w.e.f. 28 May 1992).
7   Ss(3)(a) substituted by FA92 s184(1)(c), (w.e.f. 1 January 1993).
8   Ss(3)(bb) inserted by FA00 s116(a), (w.e.f. 23 March 2000).
9   Substituted by FA03 s124(a), (w.e.f. 1 November 2003).
10 Substituted by FA03 s124(b), (w.e.f. 1 November 2003).
11 Ss(4) substituted by FA98 s114(a), (w.e.f. 27 March 1998).
12 Substituted by FA08 s109 & Sch 4, (w.e.f. 1 July 2008).
13 Substituted by F(No. 2)A 08 s74(a), (w.e.f. 24 December 2008).
14 Ss5(a) substituted by FA00 s116(b), (w.e.f. 23 March 2000).
15 Substituted by F(No. 2)A 08 s74(b), (w.e.f. 24 December 2008).
16 Inserted by FA03 s124(c), (w.e.f. 1 November 2003).
17 Ss(5) substituted by FA98 s114(b), (w.e.f. 27 March 1998).
18 Ss(6) inserted by FA95 s135, (w.e.f. 2 June 1995).
19 Ss(7) inserted by FA03 s124(d), (w.e.f. 1 November 2003).

Regulations and Orders

Claim periods	2003 SI No. 512	Finance Act 2003 (Commencement of Sections 124, 125, 129 and 130(b)) Order 2003
Disabled drivers	1972 SI No. 328	Valued Added Tax (Refund of Tax) (No. 4) Order 1972
Disabled drivers	1980 SI No. 263	Valued Added Tax (Refund of Tax) (No. 13) Order 1980
Disabled drivers	1989 SI No. 351	Value Added Tax (Refund of Tax) (Revocation) Order 1989
Disabled drivers	1989 SI No. 340	Disabled Drivers (Tax Concessions) Regulations 1989
Disabled drivers	1994 SI No. 353	Disabled Drivers and Disabled Passengers (Tax Concessions) Regulations 1994
Disabled drivers	2004 SI No. 469	Disabled Drivers and Disabled Passengers (Tax Concessions) (Amendment) Regulations 2004
Diplomats & Embassies	1996 SI No. 334	Value Added Tax (Refund of Tax) (No. 29) Order 1996
Disabled persons	1979 SI No. 275	Value Added Tax (Refund of Tax) (No. 10) Order 1979
Disabled persons	1981 SI No. 53	Value Added Tax (Reduction of Rate) (No. 5) Order 1981
Disabled persons	1981 SI No. 428	Value Added Tax (Refund of Tax) (No. 15) Order 1981
Euro control (purchases by)	1974 SI No. 290	Value Added Tax (Refund of Tax) (No. 7) Order 1974
European Space Agency (purchases by)	1980 SI No. 239	Value Added Tax (Refund of Tax) (No. 11) Order 1980
Exports - Travellers	1992 SI No. 438	Value Added Tax (Exported Goods) Regulations, 1992
Exports - Travellers	1998 SI No. 34	Value Added Tax (Retail Export Scheme) Regulations, 1998
Farm buildings and drainage	1972 SI No. 267	Value Added Tax (Refund of Tax) (No. 1) Order 1972
Farm building and drainage	1978 SI No. 145	Value Added Tax (Refund of Tax) (No. 8) Order 1978
Farm building and drainage	1984 SI No. 249	Value Added Tax (Refund of Tax) (No. 17) Order 1984
Farmers	1993 SI No. 266	Value Added Tax (Refund of Tax) (No. 25) Order 1993
Fisherman	1972 SI No. 269	Value Added Tax (Refund of Tax (No. 2) Order 1972
Fishermen, vessels	1979 SI No. 63	Value Added Tax Regulations, 1979
Fisherman	1979 SI No. 232	Value Added Tax (Refund of Tax) (Revocation) Order 1979
Fisherman	1983 SI No. 324	Value Added Tax (Refund of Tax) (No. 16) Order 1983
Hospital equipment	1980 SI No. 264	Value Added Tax (Refund of Tax) (No. 14) Order 1980
Medical equipment	1992 SI No. 58	Value Added Tax (Refund of Tax) (No. 23) Order 1992
Medical and Laboratory equipment	1973 SI No. 70	Value Added Tax (Refund of Tax) (No. 5) Order 1973
Medical research equipment	1995 SI No. 38	Value Added Tax (Refund of Tax) (No. 27) Order 1995
Mobile homes	1972 SI No. 327	Value Added Tax (Refund of Tax) (No. 3) Order 1972
Mobile Homes	1980 SI No. 262	Value Added Tax (Refund of Tax) (No. 12) Order 1980
Philanthropic organisation	1987 SI No. 308	Value Added Tax (Refund of Tax) (No. 21) Order 1987
Rate - reduction	1972 SI No. 268	Value Added Tax (Reduction of Rate) (No. 1) Order 1972
Radios and record players	1979 SI No. 59	Value Added Tax (Refund of Tax) (No. 9) Order 1979
Refund of tax	1979 SI No. 63	Value Added Tax Regulations, 1979
Refund of Tax	2006 SI No. 548	Value-Added Tax Regulations 2006
Refund exempt investment	1995 SI No. 442	Value Added Tax (Refund of Tax to Persons making supplies of exempt supplies of Investment Gold) Regulations, 1999
Sea rescue services	1985 SI No. 192	Value Added Tax (Refund of Tax) (No. 18) Order 1985
Touring Coaches	1987 SI No. 10	Value Added Tax (Refund of Tax) (No. 20) Order 1987
Touring Coaches	1988 SI No. 262	Value Added Tax (Refund of Tax) (No. 22) Order 1988
Touring Coaches	1986 SI No. 68	Value Added Tax (Refund of Tax) (No. 19) Order 1986
Touring Coaches	1993 SI No. 134	Value Added Tax (Refund of Tax) (No. 24) Order 1993
Touring Coaches	1994 SI No. 165	Value Added Tax (Refund of Tax) (No. 26) Order 1994
Touring Coaches	1996 SI No. 98	Value Added Tax (Refund of Tax) (No. 28) Order 1996

| Touring Coaches | 1999 SI No. 305 | Value Added Tax (Refund of Tax) (Amendment) Order 1999 |
| Touring Coaches | 2004 SI No. 573 | Value Added Tax (Refund of Tax) (Amendment) Order 2004 |

Revenue e-Briefs

Revenue e-Brief No. 57/2008: 4 year limit on tax repayment claims
Revenue e-Brief No. 37/2007: Opticians and VAT – Position with effect from 1 November 2006
Revenue e-Brief No. 33/2007: Tour operators and VAT
Revenue e-Brief No. 5/2007: Change of Address – VAT (Unregistered) Repayments Section
Revenue e-Brief No. 36/2006: Opticians and VAT

Revenue Statements of Practice and Information Leaflets

Repayments to Unregistered Persons: Information Leaflet dated October 2008

Case law

Grendel (R.A.) GmBH v Finanzamt fur Korperschaften, Hamburg	C255/81	Restrictions of repayment/Unjust Enrichment
Italy v European Commission	C104/86	Unjust enrichment
Marks and Spencer plc v Customs and Excise	UK - 14692 and 14693 and C62/00	Restriction on Repayments/Unjust enrichment
Marks and Spencer plc v Commissioners of Her Majesty's Revenue and Customs	C309/96	Exemption with refund of tax paid at preceding stage
Sosnowska, Alicija v Dyrektor Izby Skarbowej we Wrocławiu Ośrodek Zamiejscowy w Wałbrzychu	C25/07	National legislation determining conditions for repayment of excess VAT
Weissgerber, Gerd v Finanzamt Neustadt an der Weinstrasse	C207/87	Repayment restriction/Unjust enrichment
Wiley v Revenue Commissioners	Irish Case IV ITR 170	Importation free of Excise Duty

Revenue Precedents

Topic: Reliefs from VAT.
Issue: Agent acting on behalf of Community institution.
Decision: Agent allowed remission of VAT subject to limit that would be allowed if the Community Institution had conducted transaction.
Date: 29/10/97
(withdrawn from the Revenue website in 2002)

Narrative

Unjust Enrichment and Finance (No. 2) Act 2008: ITR Jan 2009: Vol. 22 No. 1
Tax Briefing: Issue 67 (Tour Operators and VAT)
Unjust Enrichment: Mistake of Law and Repayment of Tax: ITR Jan 2007 Vol 20 No. 1
Tax Briefing: Issue 65 (Opticians and VAT)
VAT Repayments Revisited – The Foundation for a Hidden Precedent; ITR Nov 204; Vol 17 No. 6.
ECJ Decision in the Marks & Spencers Case: ITR Nov 2002: Vol 15. No. 6
A "Wholly Alien" Case - the Halifax Decision: ITR Jul 2001: Vol 14. No. 4
Ireland's Derogations from the EU Sixth VAT Directive: ITR Sept 1999: Vol. 12 No. 5
Foreign Firms: VAT issues arising in Ireland: ITR Jan 2000: Vol. 13 No. 1.
Tax Briefing: Issue 32 (Change in Repayment System)
Tax Briefing: Issue 30 (Change in system of VAT repayments with effect from 1 July 1998)
Tax Briefing: Issue 29 (Change in Repayment System)
Tax Briefing: Issue 27 (Finance Act 1997 Changes: Abolition of the "Advance Payment")
Tax Briefing: Issue 25 (VAT Reliefs for Diplomats)
Tax Briefing: Issue 23 (Electronic Repayment of VAT)

Section 21

Interest

21.   [(1)   (a)   Where any amount of tax becomes payable under section 19(3) and is not paid, simple interest on the amount shall be paid by [the accountable person]¹, and such interest shall be calculated from the date on which the amount became payable and at a rate of **[0.0274]**² per cent for each day or part of a day during which the amount remains unpaid.

(b)   Where an amount of tax is refunded to a person and where—

(i)   no amount of tax was properly refundable to that person under section 20(1), or

(ii)   the amount of tax refunded is greater than the amount properly refundable to that person under section 20(1),

simple interest shall be paid by that person on any amount of tax refunded to that person which was not properly refundable to that person under section 20(1), from the date the refund was made, at the rate of **[0.0274]**² per cent for each day or part of a day during which the person does not correctly account for any such amount refunded which was not properly refundable.]³

[(1A)   Where the amount of the balance of tax remaining to be paid in accordance with section 19(3)(aa)(ii)(II) by an authorised person referred to in section 19(3)(aa)(iv)(III) (in this subsection referred to as the '**balance**') represents more than 20 per cent of the tax which the authorised person became accountable for in respect of his accounting period, then, for the purposes of this subsection, that balance shall be deemed to be payable on a day (in this subsection referred to as the '**accrual day**') which is 6 months prior to the final day for the furnishing of a return in accordance with section 19(3)(aa)(ii)(II) and simple interest in accordance with this section shall apply from that accrual day, however, where an authorised person can demonstrate to the satisfaction of the Collector-General that the amount of interest payable on the balance, in accordance with this subsection, is greater than the sum of the amounts of interest which would have been payable in accordance with this section if-

(a)   the authorised person was not so authorised,

(b)   the person had submitted a return in accordance with section 19(3)(a) for each taxable period comprising the accounting period, and

(c)   the amounts which were paid by direct debit during a taxable period are deemed to have been paid on the due date for submission of that return for that taxable period,

then that sum of the amounts of interest is payable.][4]

(2)   Subsection (1) shall apply-

(a)   to tax recoverable by virtue of a notice under section 22 as if the tax were tax which the person was liable to pay for the respective taxable period or periods comprised in the notice, and

[(b)   to tax recoverable by virtue of a notice under section 23 as if (whether a notice of appeal under that section is received or not) the tax were tax which the person was liable to pay for the taxable period or, as the case may be, the later or latest taxable period included in the period comprised in the notice][5].

Amendments

1   Substituted by FA08 s109 & Sch 4, (w.e.f. 1 July 2008).

2   Substituted by FA09 s29(4), (w.e.f. 1 July 2009), previously 0.0322%.

3   S(1) substituted by FA02 s 108, (w.e.f. 1 September 2002).

4   S(1A) inserted by FA01 s195, (w.e.f. 21 March 2001).

5   S(2)(b) substituted by FA76 s56, (w.e.f. 27 May 1976).

Regulations and Orders

| Remission of small amount of tax | 1979 SI No. 63 | Value Added Tax Regulations, 1979 |
| Remission of small amount of tax | 2006 SI No. 548 | Value Added Tax Regulations, 2006 |

Narrative

The Principles of VAT - Impact of ECJ Case Law: ITR Jan 2005: Vol 18 No. 1.

Section 21A

Interest on refunds of tax

[21A. (1) For the purposes of this section—

'**claimant**' means a person who submits a valid claim for a refundable amount;

'**overpaid amount**' means an amount which is a refundable amount as a result of a claimant having made a payment of tax;

'**refundable amount**' means an amount which a person is entitled to receive from the Revenue Commissioners in accordance with this Act or any order or regulation made under this Act and which is claimed within the period provided for in subsection 20(4), but such amount does not include interest payable under this section;

'**valid claim**' means a return or a claim, furnished in accordance with this Act or any order or regulation made under it, and which includes all information required by the Revenue Commissioners to establish the refundable amount.

(2) Where a mistaken assumption in the operation of the tax is made by the Revenue Commissioners and as a result a refundable amount is payable to a claimant, interest at the rate set out in subsection (4) or prescribed by order under subsection (7) shall, subject to section 1006A(2A) of the Taxes Consolidation Act 1997, be payable by the Revenue Commissioners on that amount from—

(a) in the case of an overpaid amount, the day that overpaid amount was received by the Revenue Commissioners,

(b) in the case of any other refundable amount, the 19th day of the month following the taxable period in respect of which a claimant would have been entitled to receive a refundable amount but for the mistaken assumption in the operation of the tax by the Revenue Commissioners, but where a return was due in accordance with section 19 from that claimant in respect of that taxable period, the day such return was received,

to the day on which the refundable amount is paid by the Revenue Commissioners to the claimant.

(3) Where, for any reason other than a mistaken assumption in the operation of the tax made by the Revenue Commissioners, a refundable amount is payable to a claimant but is not paid until after the expiry of [93 days][1] from the day the Revenue Commissioners receive a valid claim for that amount, interest at the rate specified in subsection (4) or prescribed by order

under subsection (7) shall, subject to section 1006A(2A) of the Taxes Consolidation Act 1997, be payable by the Revenue Commissioners on that amount from the day on which that [93 days][1] expires to the day on which the refundable amount is paid by the Revenue Commissioners to the claimant.

(4)   Interest payable in accordance with this section shall be simple interest payable at the rate of 0.011 per cent per day or part of a day, or such other rate as may be prescribed by the Minister for Finance by order under subsection (7).

(5)   Interest shall not be payable if it amounts to less than €10.

(6)   (a)   The Revenue Commissioners shall not pay interest in respect of any amount under this Act except as provided for by this section.

        (b)   This section shall not apply in relation to any refund of tax in respect of which interest is payable under or by virtue of any provision of any other enactment.

(7)   (a)   The Minister for Finance may, from time to time, make an order prescribing a rate for the purposes of subsection (4).

        (b)   Every order made by the Minister for Finance under paragraph (a) shall be laid before Dáil Éireann as soon as may be after it is made and, if a resolution annulling the order is passed by Dáil Éireann within the next 21 days on which Dáil Éireann has sat after the order is laid before it, the order shall be annulled accordingly, but without prejudice to the validity of anything previously done under it.

(8)   The Revenue Commissioners may make regulations as necessary governing the operation of this section.][2]

Amendments

1   Substituted by FA07 s121(2), (w.e.f. 2 April 2007).

2   S21A inserted by FA03 s125, (w.e.f. 1 November 2003).

Regulations and Orders

Interest on Refunds   2003 SI No. 512   Finance Act 2003 (Commencement of Sections 124, 125, 129 and 130(b)) Order 2003

Case law

Bank of Ireland Trust Services Ltd v Revenue Commissioners   Irish H.C.   Interest on repayments

Narrative

Throwing away the key to Pandora's Box: ITR Mar 2004: Vol 17. No. 2

Interest on VAT Repayments: ITR Jan 2003: Vol 16. No. 1

Section 22

Estimation of tax due for a taxable period

a 273 **22.** (1) If within the time prescribed by section 19(3) [an accountable person]¹ fails to furnish in accordance with the relevant regulations a return of the tax payable by him in respect of any [period]², then, without prejudice to any other action which may be taken, the Revenue Commissioners may, in accordance with regulations, but subject to section 30, estimate the amount of tax payable by him in respect of that [period]² and serve notice on him of the amount estimated.

[Provided that where the Revenue Commissioners are satisfied that—

(a) the amount so estimated is excessive, they may amend the amount so estimated by reducing it, or

(b) the amount so estimated is insufficient, they may amend the amount so estimated by increasing it,

then, in either case, they shall serve notice on the person concerned of the revised amount estimated and such notice shall supercede any previous notice issued under this subsection.]³

(2) Where a notice is served under subsection (1) on a person, the following provisions shall apply:

(a) the person may, if he claims that he is not [an accountable person]¹, by giving notice in writing to the Revenue Commissioners within the period of [fourteen]⁴ days from the date of the service of the notice, require the claim to be referred for decision to the Appeal Commissioners and their decision shall, subject to section 25, be final and conclusive,

(b) on the expiration of the said period, if no such claim is required to be so referred, or if such a claim is required to be so referred, on final determination against the claim, the estimated tax specified in the notice shall be recoverable in the same manner and by the like proceedings as if the person had furnished, within the prescribed period, a true and correct return, in accordance with regulations, for the [period]² to which the estimate relates, showing as due by him such estimated tax.

(c) if at any time after the service of the notice the person furnishes a return, in accordance with regulations, in respect of the [period]² specified in the notice and pays tax in accordance with the return, together with any interest and costs which may have been incurred in connection with the default, the notice shall, [...]⁵ stand discharged and any excess of tax which may have been paid shall be repaid.

[...]5

(3)   A notice given by the Revenue Commissioners under subsection (1) may extend to two or more taxable periods.

Amendments

1   Substituted by FA08 s109 & Sch 4, (w.e.f. 1 July 2008).
2   Substituted by FA00 s117, (w.e.f. 23 March 2000).
3   Substituted by FA03 s126, (w.e.f. 28 March 2003).
4   Substituted by FA01 s196, (w.e.f. 21 March 2001).
5   Deleted by F(No. 2)A 08 s97 & Sch 4, (w.e.f. 1 March 2009).

Regulations and Orders

Acceptance of assessments	1979 SI No. 63	Value Added Tax Regulations, 1979
Assessments	2000 SI No. 295	Value-Added Tax (Estimation of Tax Payable or Refundable) Regulations, 2000
Estimates and assessments	2006 SI No. 548	Value-Added Tax Regulations 2006
Offset of Repayments	2001 SI No. 399	Taxes (Offset of Repayments) Regulations, 2001
Offset of Repayments	2002 SI No. 471	Taxes (Offset of Repayments) Regulations, 2002

Narrative

Tax Briefing: Issue 42 (VAT (Estimation of Tax Payable and Assessment of Tax Payable or Refundable) Regulations 2000)

Section 22A

Generation of estimates and assessments by electronic, photographic or other process

22A. [For the purposes of this Act and regulations, where an officer of the Revenue Commissioners nominated in accordance with regulations for the purposes of section 22 or an inspector of taxes or an officer of the Revenue Commissioners authorised for the purposes of section 23, or any other officer of the Revenue Commissioners acting with the knowledge of such nominated officer or such inspector or such authorised officer causes to issue, manually or by any electronic, photographic or other process, a notice of estimation or assessment of tax bearing the name of such nominated officer or such inspector or such authorised officer, that estimate or assessment to which the notice of estimation or assessment of tax relates shall be deemed-

(a)   in the case of an estimate made under section 22, to have been made by such nominated officer, and

(b)   in the case of an assessment made under section 23, to have been made by such inspector or such authorised officer, as the case may be, to the best of such inspector's or such authorised officer's opinion.][1]

Amendments

1   S22A inserted by FA99 s136, (w.e.f. 25 March 1999).

Section 23
Assessment of tax due

23. [(1)   Where, in relation to any period [...]¹, [the inspector of taxes, or such other officer as the Revenue Commissioners may authorise to exercise the powers conferred by this section (hereafter referred to in this section as '**other officer**'), has reason to believe]² that an amount of tax is due and payable to [the Revenue Commissioners]³ by a person in any of the following circumstances:

  (a)   the total amount of tax payable by the person was greater than the total amount of tax (if any) paid by him,

  (b)   the total amount of tax refunded to the person in accordance with section 20(1) was greater than the amount (if any) properly refundable to him, or

  (c)   an amount of tax is payable by the person and a refund under section 20(1) has been made to the person,

then, without prejudice to any other action which may be taken, [the inspector or other officer may]⁴, in accordance with regulations but subject to section 30, make an [assessment]⁵ in one sum of the total amount of tax which in [his]⁶ opinion should have been paid or the total amount of tax (including a nil amount) which in accordance with section 20(1) should have been refunded, as the case may be, in respect of [...]⁷ such period and may serve a notice on the person specifying-

  (i)   the total amount of tax so [assessed]⁸,

  (ii)   the total amount of tax (if any) paid by the person or refunded to the person in relation to the said period, and

  (iii)   the total amount so due and payable as aforesaid (referred to subsequently in this section as '**the amount due**')

(2)   Where notice is served on a person under subsection (1), the following provisions shall apply:

  (a)   the person may, if he claims that the amount due is excessive, on giving notice to the [inspector or other officer]⁹ within the period of twenty-one days from the date of the service of the notice, appeal to the Appeal Commissioners, and

  (b)   on the expiration of the said period, if no notice of appeal is received or, if notice of appeal is received, on determination of the appeal by agreement or otherwise, the amount due or the amended amount due as determined in relation to the appeal, shall become due and payable as if the tax were tax which the person was liable to pay for the taxable period during which the period of fourteen days from the date of the service of the notice under subsection (1) expired or the appeal was determined by agreement or otherwise, whichever taxable period is the later.

[(3)   Where a person appeals an assessment under subsection (1), within the time limits provided for in subsection (2), he shall pay to the Revenue Commissioners the amount which he believes to be due, and if-

(a)   the amount paid is greater than 80 per cent of the amount of the tax found to be due on the determination of the appeal, and

(b)   the balance of the amount found to be due on the determination of the appeal is paid within one month of the date of such determination,

interest in accordance with section 21 shall not be chargeable from the date of raising of the assessment.][10]][11]

Amendments

1   Deleted by FA00 s118(a), (w.e.f. 23 March 2000).
2   Substituted by FA85 s47(a)(i), (w.e.f. 30 May 1985).
3   Substituted by FA85 s47(a)(ii), (w.e.f. 30 May 1985).
4   Substituted by FA85 s47(a)(iii), (w.e.f. 30 May 1985).
5   Substituted by FA92 s185(a)(i), (w.e.f. 28 May 1992).
6   Substituted by FA85 s47(a)(iv), (w.e.f. 30 May 1985).
7   Deleted by FA00 s118(b), (w.e.f. 23 March 2000).
8   Substituted by FA92 s185(a)(ii), (w.e.f. 28 May 1992).
9   Substituted by FA85 s47(b), (w.e.f. 30 May 1985)
10 Ss(3) inserted by FA92 s185(b), (w.e.f. 28 May 1992).
11 S23 substituted by VAT Amend. A78 s17, (w.e.f. 1 March 1979).

Regulations and Orders

Acceptance of estimates	1979 SI No. 63	Value Added Tax Regulations 1979
Assessments	2000 SI No. 295	Value-Added Tax (Estimation of Tax Payable or Refundable) Regulations, 2000

Narrative

Tax Briefing: Issue 42 (VAT (Estimation of Tax Payable and Assessment of Tax Payable or Refundable) Regulations 2000)

Section 23A

Security to be given by certain taxable persons

23A. [(1)   The Revenue Commissioners may, where it appears requisite to them to do so for the protection of the revenue, require **[an accountable person]**[1], as a condition of his supplying goods or services under a taxable supply, to give security, or further security, of such amount and in such manner and form as they may determine, for the payment of any tax which is, or may become, due from him from the date of service on him of a notice in writing to that effect.

(2)   Where notice is served on a person in accordance with subsection (1) the person may, on giving notice to the Revenue Commissioners within the period of twenty-one days from the date of the service of the notice, appeal the requirement of giving any security under subsection (1) to the Appeal Commissioners.][2]

Amendments

1   Substituted by FA08 s109 & Sch 4, (w.e.f. 1 July 2008).
2   S23A inserted by FA92 s186, (w.e.f. 28 May 1992).

Section 24

Recovery of tax

24.   [...][1]

Amendments

1   S24 repealed by F(No. 2)A 08 s97 & Sch 4, (w.e.f. 1 March 2009).

Section 25

Appeals

25. (1)   Any person aggrieved by a determination of the Revenue Commissioners in relation to-

   (a)   a liability to tax under subsection (5) or (6) of section 17,

   [(aa)   the treatment of one or more persons as a [single accountable person]¹ in accordance with section 8(8),]²

   [...]³

   [(ac)   a determination under section 8(3E) [or 10 (3A)]⁴,]⁵

   [(ad)   the refusal of an application for authorisation to operate as a VAT refunding agent (within the meaning assigned by section 13(3B)) or the cancellation of any such authorisation,]⁶

   [(ae)   the treatment of a person who allows supplies to be made on land owned, occupied or controlled by that person, as jointly and severally liable with another person, in accordance with section 8(2)(d),

   (af)   the application of section 4(3A)(c),]⁷

   (b)   a charge of tax in accordance with regulations, or

   (c)   a claim for repayment of tax,

   against which an appeal to the Appeal Commissioners is not otherwise provided for under this Act may, on giving notice in writing to the Revenue Commissioners within twenty-one days after the notification to the person aggrieved of the determination, appeal to the Appeal Commissioners.

   [(1A)   Where a person is aggrieved by a decision of the Revenue Commissioners that such person is not [an accountable person]¹ then such person may, on giving notice in writing to the Revenue Commissioners within twenty-one days after the notification of that decision to such person, appeal to the Appeal Commissioners.]⁸

   (2)   The provisions of the Income Tax Acts relating to-

   (a)   the appointment of times and places for the hearing of appeals;

   (b)   the giving of notice to each person who has given notice of appeal of the time and place appointed for the hearing of his appeal;

   (c)   the determination of an appeal by agreement between the appellant and an inspector of taxes or other officer appointed by the Revenue Commissioners in that behalf;

(d) the determination of an appeal by the appellant giving notice of his intention not to proceed with the appeal;

[(dd) the refusal of an application for an appeal hearing;][9]

(e) the hearing and determination of an appeal by the Appeal Commissioners, including the hearing and determination of an appeal by one Appeal Commissioner;

[(ee) the publication of reports of determinations of the Appeal Commissioners;][10]

[(f) the determination of an appeal through the failure of a person who has given notice of appeal to attend before the Appeal Commissioners at the time and place appointed;

(ff) the refusal of an application for the adjournment of any proceedings in relation to an appeal, and the dismissing of an appeal, by the Appeal Commissioners;][11]

(g) the extension of the time for giving notice of appeal, and the readmission of appeals by the Appeal Commissioners;

(h) the rehearing of an appeal by a judge of the Circuit Court and the statement of a case for the opinion of the High Court on a point of law;

[...][12]

(j) the payment of tax which is agreed not to be in dispute in relation to an appeal; and

(k) the procedures for appeal,

[shall, subject to the modifications set out hereunder and to other necessary modifications, apply to a claim under section 22 or an appeal under [section 11(1B), 23 or 23A][13] or this section as if the claim or appeal were an appeal against an assessment to income tax:

(i) a reference to a year of assessment shall include a reference to the [periods][14] concerned,

(ii) a reference to a return of income shall include a reference to a return required to be made under section 19,

(iii) a reference to interest shall include a reference to interest payable under section 21][15].

Amendments

1 Substituted by FA08 s109 & Sch 4, (w.e.f. 1 July 2008).
2 Ss(1)(aa) inserted by FA91 s84, (w.e.f. 29 May 1991).
3 Deleted by FA02 s109(a), (w.e.f. 25 March 2002).
4 Inserted by FA07 s91(a) (w.e.f. 2 April 2007).

5   Ss(1)(ac) inserted by FA95 s137(a), (w.e.f. 1 January 1996).
6   Ss(1)(ad) inserted by FA97 s109, (w.e.f. 1 July 1997).
7   Inserted by FA02 s109(b), (w.e.f. 25 March 2002).
8   Ss(1A) inserted by FA95 s137(b), (w.e.f. 2 June 1995).
9   Ss(2)(dd) inserted by FA95 s137(c), (w.e.f. 2 June 1995).
10 Ss(2)(ee) inserted by FA98 s134(2), (w.e.f. 27 March 1998).
11 Ss(2)(f) - (ff) substituted by FA83 s85, (w.e.f. 8 June 1983).
12 Deleted by FA07 s91(b) (w.e.f. 2 April 2007).
13 Substituted by FA92 s187(b), (w.e.f. 28 May 1992).
14 Substituted by FA00 s119, (w.e.f. 23 March 2000).
15 Substituted by FA83 s85, (w.e.f. 8 June 1983).

Case law
   Valente, Antonio Gomes and Ministerio Publico v Fazenda   C393/98   Right of referral to ECJ
   Publica
Narrative
   The Appeal Who?: ITR March 2007 Vol. 20 No. 2.

Section 26

Penalties generally

26. [(1) A person who does not comply with section 9(2),11(7), 12A, 16, 17, [...]¹ [,19 or 19A]² or any provision of regulations in regard to any matter to which the foregoing sections relate shall be liable to a penalty of **[€4,000]³**.]⁴

(2) A person who is not a registered person and who, on or after the specified day, [...]⁵, issues an invoice in which an amount of tax is stated shall be liable to a penalty of **[€4,000]⁶**.

[(2A) Any person who, otherwise than under and in accordance with section 12A or 17(4)(a), issues an invoice in which an amount of flat-rate addition is stated shall be liable to a penalty of **[€4,000]⁶**.]⁷

(3) Where a person mentioned in subsection (1) or (2) [or (2A)]⁸ is a body of persons, the secretary shall be liable to a separate penalty of **[€4,000]⁶**.

[(3A) A person who does not comply with [subsection (3) of section 18 or with a requirement of an authorised officer under that section]⁹ shall be liable to a penalty of **[€4,000]¹⁰**.]¹¹

[(3AA) Where a person is authorised in accordance with section 10(9)(c) to inspect any immovable goods for the purpose of reporting to the Revenue Commissioners the [open market value]¹² of an interest in those goods and the person having custody or possession of those goods prevents such inspection or obstructs the person so authorised in the performance of his or her functions in relation to the inspection, the person so having custody or possession shall be liable to a penalty of **[€4,000]¹⁰**.]¹³

[(3B) A person who supplies taxable goods or services in contravention of the requirement of security specified in section 23A shall be liable to a penalty of **[€4,000]³** in respect of each such supply.]¹⁴

[...]¹⁵

Amendments

1   Deleted by FA84 s90, (w.e.f. 23 May 1984).

2   Substituted by FA92 s188(a)(i), (w.e.f. 1 January 1993).

3   Substituted by F(No. 2)A 08 s98 & Sch 5, (w.e.f. 24 December 2008), previously €1,520.

4   Ss(1) substituted by FA82 s86, (w.e.f. 1 September 1982).

5   Deleted by FA76 s81, (w.e.f. 1 March 1976).

6   Substituted F(No. 2)A 08 s98 & Sch5, (w.e.f. 24 December 2008), previously €950

7   Ss(2A) inserted by VAT Amend. A78 s18, (w.e.f. 1 March 1979).

8   Inserted by VAT Amend. A78 s18, (w.e.f. 1 March 1979).

9   Substituted by FA84 s90, (w.e.f. 23 May 1984).

10 Substituted by F(No. 2)A 08 s98 & Sch 5, (w.e.f. 24 December 2008), previously €1,265.

11 Ss(3A) inserted by FA73 s83, (w.e.f. 3 September 1973).

12 Substituted by FA08 s103, (w.e.f. 1 July 2008).

13 Ss(3AA) inserted by FA05 s109 (w.e.f. 25 March 2005).

14 Ss(3B) inserted by FA92 s188(f), (w.e.f. 28 May 1992).

15 Subsections (4), (6) and (7) deleted by F(No. 2)A 08 s98 & Sch 5, (w.e.f. 24 December 2008).

Case Law

Pezzulo Molini Pastifici Mangimifici   C166/94   Payment on default interest on Imports
Spa v Ministero delle Finanze

Narrative

The Principles of VAT - Impact of ECJ Case Law: ITR Jan 2005: Vol 18 No. 1.

Section 27

Fraudulent returns, etc.

27.   [...][1]

Amendments
1   Deleted by F(No. 2)A 08 s98 & Sch 5, (w.e.f. 24 December 2008).

Case law

Crystal Oil Ltd v Revenue Commissioners	Irish HC IV ITR 386	Prosecution for evasion of excise duty
Sohl and Sohlke v Hauptzollamt Bremen	C48/98	Negligence

[Section 27A

Penalty for deliberately or carelessly making incorrect returns, etc.

27A. (1)   In this section—

'carelessly' means failure to take reasonable care;

'liability to tax' means a liability to the amount of the difference specified in subsection (11) or (12) arising from any matter referred to in subsection (2), (3), (5) or (6);

'period' means taxable period, accounting period or other period, as the context requires;

'prompted qualifying disclosure', in relation to a person, means a qualifying disclosure that has been made to the Revenue Commissioners or to a Revenue officer in the period between—

(a)   the date on which a person is notified by a Revenue officer of the date on which an investigation or inquiry into any matter occasioning a liability to tax of that person will start, and

(b)   the date that the investigation or inquiry starts;

'qualifying disclosure', in relation to a person, means—

(a)   in relation to a penalty referred to in subsection (4), a disclosure that the Revenue Commissioners are satisfied is a disclosure of complete information in relation to, and full particulars of, all matters occasioning a liability to tax that gives rise to a penalty referred to in subsection (4), and full particulars of all matters occasioning any liability to tax or duty that gives rise to a penalty referred to in section 1077E(4) of the Taxes Consolidation Act 1997, section 134A(2) of the Stamp Duties Consolidation Act 1999 and the application of section 1077E(4) of the Taxes Consolidation Act 1997 to the Capital Acquisitions Tax Consolidation Act 2003, and

(b)   in relation to a penalty referred to in subsection (7), a disclosure that the Revenue Commissioners are satisfied is a disclosure of complete information in relation to, and full particulars of, all matters occasioning a liability to tax that gives rise to a penalty referred to in subsection (7) for the relevant period,

made in writing to the Revenue Commissioners or to a Revenue officer and signed by or on behalf of that person and that is accompanied by—

(i)   a declaration, to the best of that person's knowledge, information and belief, made in writing that all matters contained in the disclosure are correct and complete, and

(ii)   a payment of the tax and duty payable in respect of any matter contained in the disclosure and the interest on late payment of that tax and duty;

'Revenue officer' means an officer of the Revenue Commissioners;

'unprompted qualifying disclosure', in relation to a person, means a qualifying disclosure that the Revenue Commissioners are satisfied has been voluntarily furnished to them —

(a)   before an investigation or inquiry had been started by them or by a Revenue officer into any matter occasioning a liability to tax of that person, or

(b)   where the person is notified by a Revenue officer of the date on which an investigation or inquiry into any matter occasioning a liability to tax of that person will start, before that notification.

(2)   Where a person furnishes a return or makes a claim or declaration for the purposes of this Act or of regulations made under it and, in so doing, the person deliberately, furnishes an incorrect return, or makes an incorrect claim or declaration, then that person shall be liable to a penalty.

(3)   Where a person deliberately fails to comply with a requirement in accordance with this Act or regulations to furnish a return, then that person shall be liable to a penalty.

(4)   The penalty referred to —

(a)   in subsection (2), shall be the amount specified in subsection (11), and

(b)   in subsection (3), shall be the amount specified in subsection (12),

reduced, where the person liable to the penalty cooperated fully with any investigation or inquiry started by the Revenue Commissioners or by a Revenue officer into any matter occasioning a liability to tax of that person, to —

(i)   75 per cent of that amount where paragraph (ii) or (iii) does not apply,

(ii)   50 per cent of that amount where a prompted qualifying disclosure is made by that person, or

(iii)   10 per cent of that amount where an unprompted qualifying disclosure has been made by that person.

(5)   Where a person furnishes a return or makes a claim or declaration for the purposes of this Act or of regulations made under it and, in so doing, the person carelessly, but not deliberately, furnishes an incorrect return or makes an incorrect claim or declaration, then that person shall be liable to a penalty.

(6)   Where a person carelessly but not deliberately fails to comply with a requirement in accordance with this Act or regulations to furnish a return, then that person shall be liable to a penalty.

(7)   (a)   The penalty referred to —

                (i)   in subsection (5) shall be the amount specified in subsection (11), and

                (ii)   in subsection (6) shall be the amount specified in subsection (12),

        reduced to 40 per cent in cases where the excess referred to in subparagraph (I) of paragraph (b) applies and to 20 per cent in other cases.

        (b)   Where the person liable to the penalty cooperated fully with any investigation or inquiry started by the Revenue Commissioners or by a Revenue officer into any matter occasioning a liability to tax of that person, the penalty referred to —

                (i)   in subsection (5) shall be the amount specified in subsection (11), and

                (ii)   in subsection (6) shall be the amount specified in subsection (12),

                reduced —

                (I)   where the difference referred to in subsection (11) or (12), as the case may be, exceeds 15 per cent of the amount referred to in paragraph (b) of subsection (11) or paragraph (b) of subsection (12), to —

                        (A)   30 per cent of that difference where clause (B) or (C) does not apply,

                        (B)   20 per cent of that difference where a prompted qualifying disclosure is made by that person, or

                        (C)   5 per cent of that difference where an unprompted qualifying disclosure is made by that person,

or

(II)   where the difference referred to in subsection (11) or (12), as the case may be, does not exceed 15 per cent of the amount referred to in paragraph (b) of subsection (11) or paragraph (b) of subsection (12) to —

       (A)   15 per cent of that difference where clause (B) or (C) does not apply,

       (B)   10 per cent of that difference where a prompted qualifying disclosure is made by that person, or

       (C)   3 per cent of that difference where an unprompted qualifying disclosure is made by that person.

(8)   Where, for the purposes of this Act or of regulations, a person deliberately or carelessly produces, furnishes, gives, sends or otherwise makes use of, any incorrect invoice, registration number, credit note, debit note, receipt, account, voucher, bank statement, estimate, statement, information, book, document or record, then that person shall be liable to —

    (a)   a penalty of €3,000 where that person has acted carelessly, or

    (b)   a penalty of €5,000 where that person has acted deliberately.

(9)   Where any return, claim or declaration as is mentioned in subsection (2) or (5) was furnished or made by a person, neither deliberately nor carelessly, and it comes to that person's notice that it was incorrect, then, unless the error is remedied without unreasonable delay, the return, claim or declaration shall be treated for the purposes of this section as having been deliberately made or submitted by that person.

(10)   Subject to section 1077D(2) of the Taxes Consolidation Act 1997, proceedings or applications for the recovery of any penalty under this section shall not be out of time by reason that they are commenced after the time allowed by section 30.

(11)   The amount referred to in paragraph (a) of subsection (4) and in paragraph (a)(i) of subsection (7) shall be the difference between —

    (a)   the amount of tax (if any) paid or claimed by the person concerned for the relevant period on the basis of the incorrect return, claim or declaration as furnished or otherwise made, and

(b)   the amount properly payable by, or refundable to, that person for that period.

(12)   The amount referred to in paragraph (b) of subsection (4) and in paragraph (b)(ii) of subsection (7) shall be the difference between—

(a)   the amount of tax (if any) paid by that person for the relevant period before the start by the Revenue Commissioners or by any Revenue officer of any inquiry or investigation where the Revenue Commissioners had announced publicly that they had started an inquiry or investigation or where the Revenue Commissioners have, or a Revenue officer has, carried out an inquiry or investigation in respect of any matter that would have been included in the return if the return had been furnished by that person and the return had been correct, and

(b)   the amount of tax properly payable by that person for that period.

(13)   Where a second qualifying disclosure is made by a person within 5 years of such person's first qualifying disclosure, then as regards matters pertaining to that second disclosure—

(a)   in relation to subsection (4) —

(i)   paragraph (ii) shall apply as if '75 per cent' were substituted for '50 per cent', and

(ii)   paragraph (iii) shall apply as if '55 per cent' were substituted for '10 per cent',

and

(b)   in relation to subparagraph (I) of subsection (7)(b) —

(i)   clause (B) shall apply as if '30 per cent' were substituted for '20 per cent', and

(ii)   clause (C) shall apply as if '20 per cent' were substituted for '5 per cent'.

(14)   Where a third or subsequent qualifying disclosure is made by a person within 5 years of such person's second qualifying disclosure, then as regards matters pertaining to that third or subsequent disclosure, as the case may be —

(a)   the penalty referred to in paragraphs (a) and (b) of subsection (4) shall not be reduced, and

(b)   the reduction referred to in subparagraph (I) of subsection (7)(b) shall not apply.

(15)   A disclosure in relation to a person shall not be a qualifying disclosure where —

(a)   before the disclosure is made, a Revenue officer had started an inquiry or investigation into any matter contained in that disclosure and had contacted or notified that person, or a person representing that person, in this regard, or

(b)   matters contained in the disclosure are matters —

     (i)   that have become known, or are about to become known, to the Revenue Commissioners through their own investigations or through an investigation conducted by a statutory body or agency,

     (ii)   that are within the scope of an inquiry being carried out wholly or partly in public, or

     (iii)   to which the person who made the disclosure is linked, or about to be linked, publicly.

(16)   For the purposes of this section, any return, claim or declaration submitted on behalf of a person shall be deemed to have been submitted by that person unless that person proves that it was submitted without that person's consent or knowledge.

(17)   Where a person mentioned in subsection (2), (3), (5) or (6) is a body of persons the secretary shall be liable to a separate penalty of €1,500 or, in the case of deliberate behaviour, €3,000.

(18)   If a person, in a case in which that person represents that he or she is a registered person or that goods imported by him or her were so imported for the purposes of a business carried on by him or her, improperly procures the importation of goods without payment of tax in circumstances in which tax is chargeable, then that person shall be liable to a penalty of €4,000 and, in addition, that person shall be liable to pay to the Revenue Commissioners the amount of any tax that should have been paid on the importation.

(19)   If a person acquires goods without payment of value-added tax (as referred to in Council Directive No. 2006/112/EC of 28 November 2006) in another Member State as a result of the declaration of an incorrect registration number, that person shall be liable to a penalty of €4,000 and, in addition, that person shall be liable to pay to the Revenue Commissioners an amount equal to the amount of tax which would have been chargeable on an intra-Community acquisition of those goods if that declaration had been the declaration of a correct registration number.

(20)   Where, in pursuance of regulations made for the purposes of section 13(1)(a), tax on the supply of any goods has been remitted or repaid and—

    (a)   the goods are found in the State after the date on which they were alleged to have been or were to be exported, or

    (b)   any condition specified in the regulations or imposed by the Revenue Commissioners is not complied with,

and the presence of the goods in the State after that date or the non-compliance with the condition has not been authorised for the purposes of this subsection by the Revenue Commissioners, then the goods shall be liable to forfeiture and the tax which was remitted or repaid shall be charged upon and become payable forthwith by the person to whom the goods were supplied or any person in whose possession the goods are found in the State and the provisions of sections 960I(1), 960J, 960L and 960N of the Taxes Consolidation Act 1997 shall apply accordingly, but the Revenue Commissioners may, if they think fit, waive payment of the whole or part of that tax.

(21)   (a)   Where goods—

        (i)   were supplied at the rate of zero per cent subject to the condition that they were to be dispatched or transported outside the State in accordance with subparagraph (a), (b) or (c) of paragraph (i) of the Second Schedule and the goods were not so dispatched or transported,

        (ii)   were acquired without payment of value-added tax referred to in Council Directive No. 2006/112/EC of 28 November 2006 in another Member State as a result of the declaration of an incorrect registration number,

        (iii)   were acquired in another Member State and those goods are new means of transport in respect of which the acquirer—

            (I)   makes an intra-Community acquisition in the State,

            (II)   is not entitled to a deduction under section 12 in respect of the tax chargeable on that acquisition, and

            (III)   fails to account for the tax due on that acquisition in accordance with section 19, or

(iv)   are being supplied by an accountable person who has not complied with the provisions of section 9(2), then those goods shall be liable to forfeiture.

(b)   Whenever an officer authorised by the Revenue Commissioners reasonably suspects that goods are liable to forfeiture in accordance with paragraph (a) the goods may be detained by the said officer until such examination, inquiries or investigations as may be deemed necessary by the said officer, or by another authorised officer of the Revenue Commissioners, have been made for the purpose of determining to the satisfaction of either officer whether or not the goods were so supplied or acquired.

(c)   When a determination referred to in paragraph (b) has been made in respect of any goods, or upon the expiry of a period of two months from the date on which the said goods were detained under the said subsection, whichever is the earlier, the said goods shall be seized as liable to forfeiture or released.

(d)   For the purposes of this section 'the declaration of an incorrect registration number' means —

(i)   the declaration by a person of another person's registration number,

(ii)   the declaration by a person of a number which is not an actual registration number which that person purports to be his or her registration number,

(iii)   the declaration by a person of a registration number which is cancelled,

(iv)   the declaration by a person of a registration number which was obtained from the Revenue Commissioners by supplying incorrect information, or

(v)   the declaration by a person of a registration number which was obtained from the Revenue Commissioners for the purposes of acquiring goods without payment of value-added tax referred to in Council Directive No. 2006/112/EC of 28 November 2006, and not for any bona fide business purpose.

(22)   The provisions of the Customs Acts relating to forfeiture and condemnation of goods shall apply to goods liable to forfeiture under subsection (20) or (21) as if they had become liable to

forfeiture under those Acts and all powers which may be exercised by an officer of Customs and Excise under those Acts may be exercised by officers of the Revenue Commissioners authorised to exercise those powers for the purposes of the said subsections and any provisions in relation to offences under those Acts shall apply, with any necessary modifications, in relation to the said subsections.

(23) Where an officer authorised by the Revenue Commissioners for the purposes of this subsection or a member of the Garda Sí ocha´na has reasonable grounds for suspecting that a criminal offence has been committed under the provisions of section 1078 of the Taxes Consolidation Act 1997, in relation to tax, by a person who is not established in the State, or whom that officer believes is likely to leave the State, that officer may arrest that person.][1]

Amendments

1 S27A inserted by F(No. 2)A 08 s98 & Sch 5, (w.e.f. 24 December 2008).

Narrative

New Civil Penalty Regime: ITR Jan 2009: Vol. 22 No. 1

Section 28

Assisting in making incorrect returns, etc.

28.   Any person who assists in or induces the making or delivery, for the purposes of tax, of any return, invoice, [[...]]^1 claim,]^2 credit note, debit note, receipt, account, voucher, bank statement, estimate, statement, information, book, document, record or declaration which he knows to be incorrect shall be liable to a penalty of **[€4,000]**^{3}.

Amendments

1   Substituted by FA08 s141 & Sch 8(3)(g), (w.e.f. 13 March 2008).

2   Inserted by FA92 s190(a), (w.e.f. 1 November 1992).

3   Substituted by F(No. 2)A 08 s98 & Sch 5, (w.e.f. 24 December 2008), previously €950.

Section 29

Proceedings in High Court in respect of penalties

29.   [...]¹

Amendments

1   Deleted by F(No. 2)A 08 s98 & Sch 5, (w.e.f. 24 December 2008).

Section 30

Time limits

30. (1)   Subject to subsection (3) and sections 26(4) and 27(6), proceedings for the recovery of any penalty under this Act may be commenced at any time within six years next after the date on which it was incurred.

[...]¹

(4)   [(a)   (i)   In relation to any taxable period ending before [1 May 2003]², an estimation or assessment of tax under section 22 or 23 may, subject to subparagraph (ii), be made at any time not later than [six years]² after the end of the taxable period to which the estimate or assessment relates or, where the period in respect of which the estimate or assessment is made consists of two or more taxable periods, after the end of the earlier or earliest taxable period comprised in such period.

(ii)   In relation to any taxable period commencing on or after [1 May 2003]³, and on or after [1 January 2005]³, in relation to any other taxable period, an estimation or assessment of tax under section 22 or 23 may be made at any time not later than [four years]³ after the end of the taxable period to which the estimate or assessment relates or, where the period in respect of which the estimate or assessment is made consists of two or more taxable periods, after the end of the earlier or earliest taxable period comprised in such period.

(aa)   Notwithstanding paragraphs (a)(i) and (a)(ii) in a case in which any form of fraud or neglect has been committed by or on behalf of any person in connection with or in relation to tax, an estimate or assessment as aforesaid may be made at any time for any period for which, by reason of the fraud or neglect, tax would otherwise be lost to the Exchequer.]⁴

(b)   In this subsection 'neglect' means negligence or a failure to give any notice, to furnish particulars, to make any return or to produce or furnish any invoice, [...]⁵ credit note, debit note, receipt, account, voucher, bank statement, estimate [or assessment]⁶, statement, information, book, document, record or declaration required to be given furnished made or produced by or under this Act or regulations:

Provided that a person shall be deemed not to have failed to do anything required to be done within a limited time if he did it within such further time, if any, as the Revenue Commissioners may have allowed; and where a person had a reasonable excuse for not doing anything required to be done, he shall be deemed not to have failed to do it if he did it without unreasonable delay after the excuse had ceased.

(5)   (a)   Where a person dies, an estimation [or assessment][6] of tax under section 22 or 23 (as the case may be) may be made on his personal representative for any period for which such an estimation [or assessment][7] could have been made upon him immediately before his death, or could be made upon him if he were living, in respect of tax which became due by such person before his death, and the amount of tax recoverable under any such estimation [or assessment][6] shall be a debt due from and payable out of the estate of such person.

[(b)   No estimation [or assessment][6] of tax shall be made by virtue of this subsection later than three years after the expiration of the year in which the deceased person died, in a case in which the grant of probate or letters of administration was made in that year, and no such estimation [or assessment][6] shall be made later than two years after the expiration of the year in which such grant was made in any other case, but the foregoing provisions of this subsection shall have effect subject to the proviso that where the personal representative-

(i)   after the year in which the deceased person died, lodges a corrective affidavit for the purposes of assessment of estate duty or delivers an additional affidavit under [section 48 of the Capital Acquisitions Tax Consolidation Act 2003][7], or

(ii)   is liable to deliver an additional affidavit under the said [section 48][7], has been so notified by the Revenue Commissioners and did not deliver the said additional affidavit in the year in which the deceased person died,

such estimation [or assessment][6] may be made at any time before the expiration of two years after the end of the year in which the corrective affidavit was lodged or the additional affidavit was or is delivered][8].

Amendments

1   Subsections (2) and (3) deleted by F(No. 2)A 08 s98 & Sch 5, (w.e.f 24 December 2008).

2   Substituted by FA03 s129(a), (w.e.f. 1 November 2003).

3   Substituted by FA03 s129(b), (w.e.f. 1 November 2003).

4   Ss(4)(a) substituted by FA98 s115, (w.e.f. 27 March 1998).
5   Deleted by FA08 s141 & Sch 8(3)(h), (w.e.f. 13 March 2008).
6   Inserted by FA92 s191(b), (w.e.f. 28 May 1992).
7   Substituted by Schedule 3, Capital Acquisitions Tax Consolidation Act 2003, (w.e.f 21 February 2003).
8   Ss(5)(b) substituted by VAT Amend. A78 s20, (w.e.f. 1 March 1979).

Regulations and Orders

Time Limits	2003 SI No. 512	Finance Act 2003 (Commencement of Sections 124, 125, 129 and 130(b)) Order 2003

Section 31

Application of [section 1065 of the Taxes Consolidation Act, 1997]

31.   The provisions of [section 1065 of the Consolidation Act, 1997][1], shall apply to any penalty incurred under this Act.

Amendments
1   Substituted by TCA 1997 s1100 & Sch31, (w.e.f. 6 April 1997).

Section 32

Regulations

32. (1)   The Revenue Commissioners shall make such regulations as seem to them to be necessary for the purpose of giving effect to this Act and of enabling them to discharge their functions thereunder and, without prejudice to the generality of the foregoing, the regulations may make provision in relation to all or any of the following matters-

(a)   the manner in which exemption in respect of certain services may be waived under section 7 and any such waiver may be cancelled, and the adjustments, including a charge of tax, which may be made as a condition of any such cancellation;

[(aa)   the deduction of tax chargeable in respect of intra-Community acquisitions;

(ab)   the manner in which residual tax referred to in section 12(1)(a)(iib) may be calculated and deducted;

(ac)   the manner in which residual tax referred to in section 13(3A) may be calculated and repaid;

(ad)   the repayment, in accordance with section 15(5A), of tax chargeable on the importation of goods;

(ae)   the time and manner in which tax shall be payable in respect of the goods referred to in section 19(4);

(af)   the form of statement required to be furnished in accordance with section 19A, the particulars to be specified therein and the amount or amounts to be applied for the purposes of section 19A(3);

(ag)   the supply of goods [...]^1 in accordance with paragraph (ia) of the Second Schedule;

(ah)   the importation of goods consigned to another Member State in accordance with paragraph (iiib) of the Second Schedule;

(ai)   the circumstances in which a person may elect not to apply the proviso to subsection (6)(d) of section 3;]^2

[(b)   the treatment under section 5(3) of the use and services specified therein as services supplied by a person for consideration in the course of business;]^3

[(ba)   the manner in which the electronic services scheme referred to in section 5A shall operate;]^4

(c)   the particulars required for registration and the manner in which registration may be effected and cancelled;

(d)   the manner in which a person may elect to be [an accountable person][5] and any such election may be cancelled, the treatment of [an accountable person][5] as a person who is [not an accountable person][5][6], and the adjustments, including a charge of tax, which may be made as a condition of any such cancellation or treatment;

[(da)   the conditions for a taxable dealer to opt to apply the margin scheme to certain supplies in accordance with section 10A(4);

(db)   the determination of the aggregate margin in accordance with section 10A(8);

(dc)   the form of the invoice or other document that shall be issued in accordance with section 10B(4);

[(dca) **the manner in which the travel agent's margin scheme referred to in section 10C shall operate;][7]**

(dd)   the manner in which residual tax referred to in section 12(1)(a)(vi) may be deducted;

[(dda) **the manner in which the deduction entitlement referred to in section 12(1)(a)(ix) may be calculated;][7]**

(de)   the particulars to be furnished in relation to antiques as specified in paragraph (xvia) of the Sixth Schedule or paragraph (iii) of the Eighth Schedule;][8]

[(e)   (i)   the manner in which any amount may be apportioned, including the methods of apportionment which may be applied for the purposes of paragraphs (a) and (b) of section 11(3),

       (ii) the circumstances or conditions under which a supply may or may not be treated as an ancillary supply, a composite supply, an individual supply, a multiple supply or a principal supply,

       (iii) a relatively small amount, or an element of a supply, which may be disregarded for the purposes of applying section 11(3);][9]

[...][10]

[(g)   the determination, under section 14, of a person's tax liability for any period by reference to moneys received and the adjustments, including a charge of tax, which may be made when a person becomes entitled to determine his tax liability in the manner aforesaid or, having been so entitled, ceases to be so entitled, or ceases to be [an accountable person][5];][11]

(h)   the keeping [by accountable persons][5] of records and the retention of such records and supporting documents [or other recorded data][12];

[(ha)   the keeping by persons trading in investment gold (within the meaning of section 6A) of records and the retention of such records and supporting documents or other recorded data;

(hb)   the conditions under which a person may waive his right to exemption from tax on the supply of investment gold (within the meaning of section 6A);

(hc)   the conditions under which an intermediary (within the meaning of section 6A) may waive his right to exemption from tax on his supply of services;

(hd)   the conditions under which a person may claim a refund of tax in accordance with subsections (6)(b), (7)(b) and (8)(b) of section 6A, and the manner in which such refund may be claimed;][13]

[(i)   the form of invoice, [...][14] credit note, debit note and settlement voucher, including electronic form, required to be used for the purposes of this Act, the particulars required to be inserted in such documents or electronically recorded and the period within which such documents or electronic data are required to be issued or transmitted and such other conditions in relation to the issue or receipt, in any form, of an invoice, [...][14] credit note, debit note and settlement voucher as may be imposed by the Revenue Commissioners;][15]

(j)   the furnishing of returns and the particulars to be shown thereon;

(k)   the nomination by the Revenue Commissioners of officers to perform any acts and discharge any functions authorised by this Act to be performed or discharged by the Revenue Commissioners;

(l)   the manner in which tax is to be recovered in cases of default of payment;

(m)   the refund of tax in excess of the amount required by law to be borne, or paid to the Revenue Commissioners;

[(ma)   the conditions governing a person's entitlement to interest in accordance with section 21A;][16]

(n)   disclosure to the Revenue Commissioners of such information as they may require for the ascertainment of liability to tax;

(o)   the remission at the discretion of the Revenue Commissioners of small amounts of tax and interest;

[(p)   matters consequential on the death of a registered person or his becoming subject to any incapacity including the treatment of a person of such class or classes as may be specified in the regulations as a person carrying on the business of the deceased or incapacitated person;][17]

(q)   service of notices;

(r)   the acceptance of estimates (whether or not subject to subsequent review) of the amount of tax payable or of any amounts relating to such tax;

(s)   the adjustment of the liability of [an accountable person][5] who supplies [goods or services][18] and of the liability of [an accountable person][5] to whom [goods or services are supplied][19] where goods are returned, the consideration is reduced, a bad debt is incurred or a discount is allowed;

(t)   the valuation of interests in or over immovable goods;

[(ta)   specifying the circumstances or conditions under which development work on immovable goods is not treated as being on behalf of, or to the benefit of, a person;][20]

[(tb)   the operation of the capital goods scheme and in particular the duration of a subsequent interval where the accounting year of a capital goods owner changes;

(tc)   the methods which may be used for the purposes of applying section 10(4D);][21]

(u)   the estimation of tax due for a taxable or other period;

[(uu)   the adjustments to be made by [an accountable person][5] of any apportionment referred to in paragraph (x) or deduction under section 12 previously made, being adjustments by reference to changes, occurring not later than five years from the end of the taxable period to which the original apportionment or deduction relates, in any of the matters by reference to which the apportionment or deduction was made or allowed, and the determination of the taxable period in and from which or in which any such adjustment is to take effect;][22]

(v)   the relief for stock-in-trade held on the specified day;

[(w)   the determination of average build for the purposes of paragraph (xvii) of the Second Schedule;][23]

[(ww) the determination of average foot size for the purposes of paragraph (xix) of the Second Schedule;][24]

a175

[(www) the circumstances, terms and conditions under which a letting of immovable goods constitutes a letting in the short-term guest sector or holiday sector, or under which accommodation is or is not holiday accommodation (within the meaning of paragraph (xiii) of the Sixth Schedule);][25]

(x) the apportionment between tax which may be deducted under section 12 and tax which may not be deducted under that section, the review, by reference to the circumstances obtaining in any period not exceeding one year, of any such apportionment previously made, the charge or repayment of tax consequent on any such review and the furnishing of particulars by [an accountable person][5] to the Revenue Commissioners for the purpose of any such review;

[(xx) the relief (if any) to be given to [an accountable person][5] in respect of tax borne or paid by him on stock-in-trade held by him immediately before the commencement of the first taxable period for which he is deemed to become [an accountable person][5];

(xxx) the manner in which a determination may be made for the purposes of section 11(1B);][26]

[(xxxx) the making of a determination under section 10(3A);][27]

(y) the particulars to be furnished and the manner in which notification is to be given to the Revenue Commissioners by a person who intends to promote a dance, and the manner in which the Revenue Commissioners shall notify the proprietor of any premises in regard to dances proposed to be promoted in such premises.

(2) Regulations under this section may make different provisions in relation to different cases and may in particular provide for differentiation between different classes of persons affected by this Act and for the adoption of different procedures for any such different classes.

[(2A) Regulations under this section for the purposes of section 5(7), [subsection 1(a)(vi) of section 12,][28] subsection (1) or (2) of section 13[, subsection (6) or (7) of section 15 or paragraph (ia) of the Sixth Schedule][29] [or in relation to the [matters specified in [paragraph (w), (ww) or (www) of subsection 1][30]][31]][32] shall not be made without the consent of the Minister for Finance.][33]

[(2B) Regulations under this Act may contain such incidental, supplementary and consequential provisions as appear to the Revenue Commissioners to be necessary for the purposes of giving full effect to—

(a)   [Council Directive No. 2006/112/EC of November 2006],[34]

(b)   Council Directive No. 79/1072/EEC of 6 December 1979,

(c)   Council Directive No. 86/560/EEC of 17 November 1986.][35]

(3)   Every regulation made under this section shall be laid before Dáil Éireann as soon as may be after it is made and, if a resolution annulling the regulation is passed by Dáil Éireann within the next twenty-one days on which Dáil Éireann has sat after the regulation is laid before it, the regulation shall be annulled accordingly, but without prejudice to the validity of anything previously done thereunder.

Amendments

1   Deleted by FA00 s121, (w.e.f. 1 July 1999).
2   Ss(1)(aa) - (ai) inserted by FA92 s192(a), (w.e.f. 1 January 1993).
3   Ss(1)(b) substituted by VAT Amend. A78 s21, (w.e.f. 1 March 1979).
4   Ss(1)(ba) inserted by FA03 s130(a), (w.e.f. 1 July 2003).
5   Substituted by FA08 s109 & Sch 4, (w.e.f. 1 July 2008).
6   Substituted by VAT Amend. A78 s30(2), (w.e.f. 1 March 1979).
7   Inserted by F(No. 2)A 08 s75, (w.e.f. 24 December 2008).
8   Ss(1)(da) - (de) inserted by FA95 s138, (w.e.f. 2 June 1995).
9   Ss(1)(e) substituted by FA06 s99(1)(a), (w.e.f 1 November 2006).
10   Repealed by FA76 s81, (w.e.f. 1 March 1976).
11   Ss(1)(g) substituted by VAT Amend. A78 s21, (w.e.f. 1 March 1979).
12   Inserted by FA86 s88, (w.e.f. 27 May 1986).
13   Ss(1)(ha) - (hd) inserted by FA99 s137, (w.e.f. 25 March 1999).
14   Deleted by FA08 s141 & Sch 8(3)(i), (w.e.f. 13 March 2008).
15   Ss(1)(i) substituted by FA86 s88, (w.e.f. 27 May 1986).
16   Ss(1)(ma) inserted by FA03 s130(b), (w.e.f. 1 November 2003).
17   Ss(1)(p) substituted by VAT Amend. A78 s21, (w.e.f. 1 March 1979).
18   Substituted by VAT Amend. A78 s30(2), (w.e.f. 1 March 1979).
19   Substituted by VAT Amend. A78 s30(2), (w.e.f. 1 March 1979).
20   Ss(1)(ta) Inserted by FA05 s 111(a), (w.e.f. 25 March 2005).
21   Inserted by FA08 s105, (w.e.f. 1 July 2008).
22   Ss(1)(uu) inserted by FA76 s58, (w.e.f. 27 May 1976).
23   Ss(1)(w) inserted by FA84 s91, (w.e.f. 1 May 1984).
24   Ss(1)(ww) inserted by FA85 s48, (w.e.f. 1 March 1985).
25   Ss(1)(www) inserted by FA05 s111(b), (w.e.f. 25 March 2005).
26   Ss(1)(xx) - (xxx) inserted by FA73 s85, (w.e.f. 3 September 1973).
27   Inserted by FA07 s92, (w.e.f. 2 April 2007).
28   Inserted by FA87 s44, (w.e.f. 9 July 1987).
29   Substituted by FA89 s60, (w.e.f. 24 May 1989).
30   Substituted by FA05 s111(c), (w.e.f. 25 March 2005).
31   Inserted by FA85 s48, (w.e.f. 1 March 1985).
32   Inserted by FA84 s91, (w.e.f. 1 May 1984).
33   Ss(2A) substituted by VAT Amend. A78 s21, (w.e.f. 1 March 1979).
34   Substituted by FA07 s97 & Sch 3, (w.e.f. 1 January 2007).
35   Ss(2B) inserted by FA06 s99(1)(b), (w.e.f. 31 March 2006).

Regulations and Orders

Acceptance of estimates	1979 SI No. 63	Value Added Tax Regulations, 1979
Accounts	1979 SI No. 63	Value Added Tax Regulations, 1979
Accounts	2006 SI No. 548	Value-Added Tax Regulations 2006

Adjustment for returned goods discounts and price alterations	1979 SI No. 63	Value Added Tax Regulations, 1979
Adjustment for returned goods discounts and price alterations	2006 SI No. 548	Value-Added Tax Regulations 2006
Apportionment of consideration	1979 SI No. 63	Value Added Tax Regulations, 1979
Apportionment	2006 SI No. 548	Value-Added Tax Regulations 2006
Apportionment of amounts	1979 SI No. 63	Value Added Tax Regulations, 1979
Capital Goods Scheme	2008 SI No. 238	Value-Added Tax (Amendment) Regulations, 2008
Cash Basis	1992 SI No. 306	Value Added Tax (Determination of Tax due by reference to moneys received) Regulations, 1992
Cash Basis	2006 SI No. 548	Value-Added Tax Regulations 2006
Composite and multiple supplies	2006 SI No. 549	Finance Act 2006 (Commencement of Sections 93(1), 97(1)(b) and 99(1)(a)) Order 2006
Death or incapacity of taxable person	1979 SI No. 63	Value Added Tax Regulations, 1979
Death, bankruptcy or liquidation	2006 SI No. 548	Value-Added Tax Regulations 2006
Determining rate of tax	1992 SI No. 278	Value Added Tax (Determination in regards to Tax) Regulations, 1992
Disclosure of Information to the Revenue Commissioners	1979 SI No. 63	Value Added Tax Regulations, 1979
Disclosure of information to the Revenue Commissioners	2006 SI No. 548	Value-Added Tax Regulations 2006
Election	1979 SI No. 63	Value Added Tax Regulations, 1979
Election to be a taxable person and cancellation of such election	2006 SI No. 548	Value-Added Tax Regulations 2006
Electronic Invoicing	2002 SI No. 504	Value-Added Tax (Electronic Invoicing And Storage) Regulations, 2002
Electronic Invoicing	2006 SI No. 548	Value-Added Tax Regulations 2006
Electronic Transmission		Taxes (Electronic Transmission of VAT eServices Returns and VIES Statements (Specified Provisions and Appointed day) Order 2008
Estimates of tax due and assessments of tax payable or refundable	2000 SI No. 295	Value-Added Tax (Estimation of Tax Payable or Refundable) Regulations, 2000
Estimates and assessments	2006 SI No. 548	Value-Added Tax Regulations 2006
Exemption	1979 SI No. 63	Value Added Tax Regulations, 1979
Invoice particulars	1992 SI No. 23	Value Added Tax (Monthly Control Statement) Regulations, 1992
Invoice particulars	1992 SI No. 269	Value Added Tax (Electronic Data Exchange and Storage) Regulations, 1992
Invoice particulars	1992 SI No. 275	Value Added Tax (Invoices and other Documents) Regulations, 1992
Invoice particulars	2003 SI No. 723	Value Added Tax (Invoices and Other Documents) (Amendment) Regulations, 2003
Invoice Time Limits	1992 SI No. 276	Value Added Tax (Time Limits for issuing certain Documents) Regulations, 1992
Invoices and credit notes - content	2006 SI No. 548	Value-Added Tax Regulations 2006
Invoices and credit notes – time limits	2006 SI No. 548	Value-Added Tax Regulations 2006
Mandatory electronic filing	2008 SI No. 341	Tax Returns and Payments (Mandatory Electronic Filing and Payment of Tax) Regulations 2008
Modification of certain provisions	1979 SI No. 63	Value Added Tax Regulations, 1979
Notifications of offices	1979 SI No. 63	Value Added Tax Regulations, 1979
Nomination of officers	2006 SI No. 548	Value-Added Tax Regulations 2006
Particulars of Returns	1993 SI No. 54	Value Added Tax (Statement of intra-Community supplies) Regulations, 1993
Procedures for dances	1979 SI No. 63	Value Added Tax Regulations, 1979
Refund of tax	1979 SI No. 63	Value Added Tax Regulations, 1979
Refund of tax	2006 SI No. 548	Value-Added Tax Regulations 2006

Relief for stock-in-trade held at commencement locality	1979 SI No. 63	Value Added Tax Regulations, 1979
Relief for stock-in-trade held at commencement taxability	2006 SI No. 548	Value-Added Tax Regulations 2006
Registration Particulars	1993 SI No. 30	Value Added Tax (Registration) Regulations, 1993
Registration	2006 SI No. 548	Value-Added Tax Regulations 2006
Remissions of small amounts of tax	1979 SI No. 63	Value Added Tax Regulations, 1979
Remission of small amounts of tax	2006 SI No. 548	Value-Added Tax Regulations 2006
Returns	1979 SI No. 63	Value Added Tax Regulations, 1979
Returns	2006 SI No. 548	Value-Added Tax Regulations 2006
Services of notices	1979 SI No. 63	Value Added Tax Regulations, 1979
Service of notices	2006 SI No. 548	Value-Added Tax Regulations 2006
Supply of certain services	1979 SI No. 63	Value Added Tax Regulations, 1979
Supply of certain services	2006 SI No. 548	Value-Added Tax Regulations 2006
Tax free shops abolition	1999 SI No. 196	Value Added Tax (Supply of Food, Drink and Tobacco Products on board Vessels or Aircraft for onboard Consumption) Regulations 1999
Tax free shops abolition	1999 SI No. 197	European Communities (Value Added Tax) Regulations, 1999
Valuation of interests in immovable goods	1979 SI No. 63	Value Added Tax Regulations, 1979
Valuation of interests in immovable goods	2006 SI No. 548	Value-Added Tax Regulations 2006
Waiver of Exemption	2003 SI No. 504	Value Added Tax (Waiver of Exemption) (Immovable Goods) Regulations, 2003
Waiver of exemption	2006 SI No. 548	Value-Added Tax Regulations 2006

Revenue e-Briefs

Revenue e-Brief No. 57/2006: European Communities (Value-Added Tax) Regulations 2006 (S.I. No. 663 of 2006)

Revenue e-Brief No. 1/2006: Council Regulation (EC) No 1777/2005 of 17 October 2005

Narrative

Tax Briefing: Issue 60 (Property - Finance Act 2005 Changes)

Section 33

Officer responsible in case of body of persons

33. (1)   The secretary or other officer acting as secretary for the time being of any body of persons shall be answerable in addition to the body for doing all such acts as are required to be done by the body under any of the provisions relating to tax.

(2)   Every such officer as aforesaid may from time to time retain out of any money coming into his hands, on behalf of the body, so much thereof as is sufficient to pay the tax due by the body and shall be indemnified for all such payments made in pursuance of this section.

(3)   Any notice required to be given to a body of persons under any of the provisions relating to tax may be given to the secretary or other officer acting as secretary for the time being of such body.

(4)   In this section '**the provisions relating to tax**' means -

(a)   the provisions of this Act and regulations, and

(b)   the provisions relating to tax of any subsequent Act.

Section 34

Relief for stock-in-trade held on the specified day

34. (1)   In computing the amount of tax payable by [an accountable person]¹, the following amounts may, subject to subsections (3) and (4), in addition to the deductions authorised by section 12, be deducted on account of stock-in-trade which has been [supplied]² to, and has not been [supplied]² by, him before the specified day and which is held by him at the commencement of that day, or incorporated in other stock-in-trade held by him at such commencement that is to say:

(a)   in case [the accountable person]¹ was, immediately before the specified day, not registered for turnover tax under the provisions of section 49 of the Finance Act, 1963, nor required under the provisions of that section to furnish the particulars specified for registration, and was met registered for wholesale tax under the provisions of section 4 of the Finance (No. 2) Act, 1966, nor required under the provisions of that section to furnish the particulars specified for registration, an amount equal to the sum of the amounts which he would be liable to pay on account of turnover tax and wholesale tax if,

(i)   he had been accountable for each of those taxes,

(ii)   he had on the day immediately preceding the specified day sold the whole of his stock-in-trade aforesaid in the course of business to a person who was carrying on the same activities as his own and who had not given him, in accordance with section 50 of the Finance Act, 1963, a statement in writing quoting the turnover tax registration number of the person nor given him, in accordance with section 5 of the Finance (No. 2) Act, 1966, a statement in writing quoting the wholesale tax registration number of the person, and

(iii) he had on the said day immediately preceding the specified day received from the person mentioned in subparagraph (ii) payment for the stock-in-trade so deemed to have been sold of an amount equal to the cost to [the accountable person]¹ of such stock or the market value thereof, whichever is the lower, and

(b)   in case, immediately before the specified day [the accountable person]¹ was registered for turnover tax under the provisions of section 49 of the Finance Act, 1963, or required under the provisions of that section to furnish the particulars specified for registration, but was not registered for wholesale tax under the provisions of section 4 of the Finance (No. 2) Act, 1966, nor required under the provisions of that section to furnish the particulars specified for registration, an amount equal to the amount of wholesale tax which he would be liable to pay if,

(i)   he had been [an accountable person][1] for the purposes of wholesale tax,

(ii)   he had on the day immediately preceding the specified day sold the whole of his stock-in-trade aforesaid in the course of business to a person who was carrying on the same activities as his own and who had in accordance with section 50 of the Finance Act, 1963, given him a statement in writing quoting the registration number of the person but had not given him, in accordance with section 5 of the Finance (No. 2) Act, 1966, a statement in writing quoting the wholesale tax registration number of such person, and

(iii)   he had on the said day immediately preceding the specified day received from the person mentioned in subparagraph (ii) payment for the stock-in-trade so deemed to have been sold of an amount equal to the cost to [the accountable person][1] of such stock or the market value thereof, whichever is the lower.

(2)   Where [an accountable person][1] -

(a)   is not such a person as is mentioned in paragraph (a) or (b) of subsection (1) but was such a person at any time during the year ended the day immediately preceding the specified day or

(b)   is such a person as is mentioned in paragraph (a) or (b) of subsection (1) and was such a person during a part of the year ended the day immediately preceding the specified day but was not such a person during another part of that year,

the Revenue Commissioners may allow such deduction or make such restriction in the deduction which would otherwise be allowable as in their opinion is just and reasonable having regard to the nature of the business carried on, the period during the year ended on the day immediately preceding the specified day during which the business was carried on and the period during the said year during which the person was such a person as is mentioned in the said paragraph (a) or (b) of subsection (1).

(3)   A claim for a deduction under this section shall be made in accordance with regulations and the amount authorised to be deducted may be deducted by equal instalments in computing the amount of tax payable in respect of each of the taxable periods beginning on the first day of the first and second taxable periods next following that in which the specified day occurs.

(4)   No deduction shall be granted under this section for any amount which is referable to turnover tax or wholesale tax on immovable goods on the [supply]² of which tax is, by virtue of section 4(6), not chargeable or to wholesale tax on newspapers or periodicals, [or second hand goods]².

(5)   In this section-

'stock-in-trade' mean, in relation to any person, goods which are either-

[(a)   movable goods of a kind that are [supplied]² by the person in the ordinary course of his business being goods which are actually held for [supply]² (otherwise than by virtue of section 3(1)(e)) or which would be so held if they were mature or if their manufacture, preparation or construction were complete, or]³

(b)   materials incorporated in immovable goods of a kind that are [supplied]² by the person in the ordinary course of his business and that have not been [supplied]² by him since the goods were developed, but are actually held for [supply]² or would be so held if their development were complete, or

(c)   consumable materials incorporated in immovable goods by the person in the course of a business consisting of the [supply]² of a service of constructing, repairing, painting or decorating immovable goods where that service has not been completed, or

(d)   materials which have not been incorporated in goods and are such as are used by the person in the manufacture or construction of goods of a kind that are delivered by the person in the ordinary course of his business or, where his ordinary business consists of repairing, painting or decorating immovable goods, are used by him as consumable materials in the course of that business;

materials referred to in paragraph (b) of the paragraph of 'stock-in-trade' shall, for the purposes of subsection (1), be regarded as having been [supplied]² to the same extent as the immovable goods into which they have been incorporated can be regarded as having been [supplied]²;

materials referred to in paragraph (c) of the definition of 'stock-in-trade' shall be regarded as having been [supplied][2] to the extent that the service in relation to which they have been used has been [supplied][2];

'**cost**' means, in relation to stock-in-trade, the total of the money payable by the person for the [supply][2] of the stock, including any addition made for turnover tax or wholesale tax, but excluding any discount or allowance deducted or deductible on payment for the stock.

Amendments

1   Substituted by FA08 Ss109 & Sch 4, (w.e.f. 1 July 2008).
2   Substituted by VAT Amend. A78 s30(2), (w.e.f. 1 March 1979).
3   Substituted by FA76 s59, (w.e.f. 27 May 1976).

Regulations and Orders

Claim form	1979 SI No. 63	Value Added Tax Regulations, 1979
Relief for stock in trade	1979 SI No. 63	Value Added Tax Regulations, 1979
Specified Day 1/11/72	1972 SI No. 180	Value Added Tax (Specified day) Order 1972

Section 35

Special provisions for adjustment and recovery of consideration

35. (1) (a) Notwithstanding the repeal by this Act of the provisions relating to turnover tax and wholesale tax, sums due on account of turnover tax or wholesale tax under a contract entered into before the specified day, together with any additional sums which might be recoverable by virtue of the provisions of section 9 of the Finance (No.2) Act, 1966, section 7 of the Finance (No.2) Act, 1968 section 58 of the Finance Act, 1969, section 51 of the Finance Act, 1970, or section 4 of the Finance (No.2) Act, 1970, shall, in the absence of agreement to the contrary, but subject to subsection (2), be recoverable as if the said provisions relating to turnover tax and wholesale tax had not been repealed.

(b) (i) Subject to subparagraph (ii), where, under an agreement made before the specified day, [an accountable person][1] [supplies goods or services][2] on or after that day in such circumstances that tax is chargeable, the consideration provided for under the agreement shall, in the absence of any agreement to the contrary, be adjusted by excluding therefrom the amount, if any, included on account of turnover tax or wholesale tax or both of those taxes, as the case may be, and including therein an amount equal to the amount of the tax so chargeable, and the consideration as so adjusted shall be deemed to be the consideration provided for under the agreement.

(ii) The consideration provided for under an agreement for the delivery of immovable goods or the rendering of a service consisting of a development made before the specified day shall, in the absence of agreement to the contrary, be deemed, for the purposes of this paragraph, to include an amount of turnover tax and wholesale tax combined equal to the amount of tax chargeable in respect of the transaction.

[...][3]

[(1A) (a) Where, after the making of an agreement for the [supply of goods or services][2] and before the date on which under subsection (1) or (2), as may be appropriate, of section 19 any tax in respect of the transaction [falls due][2], there is a change in the amount of tax chargeable on the [supply][2] in question, then, in the absence of agreement to the contrary, there shall be added to or deducted from the total amount of the consideration and any tax stated separately under the agreement an amount equal to the amount of the change in the tax chargeable.

(b) References in this subsection to a change in the amount of tax chargeable on the [supply of goods or services][2] include references to a change to or from a situation in which no tax is being charged on the [supply][2].][4]

(2) Where, in relation to a [supply of goods or services][2] by [an accountable person][1], the person issues an invoice in which the tax chargeable in respect of the transaction is stated separately, the tax so stated shall, for the purpose of its recovery, be deemed to be part of the consideration for the transaction and shall be recoverable accordingly by the person:

Provided that, if the invoice is issued pursuant to section 17(1), this subsection shall not apply unless it is in the form and contains the particulars specified by regulations.

[(3) (a) Where, under an agreement made before the commencement of section 12A, a flat-rate farmer supplies agricultural produce or an agricultural service after such commencement to any person, the consideration provided for under the agreement shall, in the absence of agreement to the contrary, be increased by an amount equal to the flat-rate addition appropriate to the said consideration.

(b) Where, in relation to a supply of agricultural produce or an agricultural service by a flat-rate farmer, the flat-rate farmer issues an invoice in which the flat-rate addition is stated separately, the flat-rate addition so stated shall, for the purpose of its recovery, be deemed to be part of the consideration for the transaction and shall be recoverable accordingly by the flat-rate farmer.][2]

Amendments
1 Substituted by FA08 s109 & Sch 4, (w.e.f. 1 July 2008).
2 Substituted by VAT Amend. A78 s30(2), (w.e.f. 1 March 1979).
3 Repealed by FA76 s81, (w.e.f. 1 March 1976).
4 Ss(1A) inserted by FA73 s86, (w.e.f. 3 September 1973).

Regulations and Orders

Specified Day 1/11/72   1972 SI No. 180   Value Added Tax (Specified Day) Order 1972

Section 36

Special provisions for deliveries made prior to the specified day

36.   [...][1]

Amendments

1   S36 repealed by VAT Amend. A78 s30(1), (w.e.f. 1 March 1979).

Section 37

Substitution of certain persons for persons not established in the State

37.   [...][1]

Amendments

1   S37 repealed by FA01 s198, (w.e.f. 1 January 2002).

Revenue Statements of Practice and Information Leaflets

Foreign firms doing business in Ireland, VAT treatment of: Information Leaflet dated October 2008

Revenue Precedents

Topic:	Registration.
Issue:	Is an Irish company acting as an agent for foreign companies obliged to register separately for transactions carried out as agent?
Decision:	In the particular circumstances registration was not required and a company acting as an agent could use its own VAT number to import and claim credit on such goods on behalf of a foreign company.
Date:	21/12/94

Narrative

Foreign Firms: VAT issues arising in Ireland: ITR Jan 2000: Vol 13 No. 1.

Section 38

Extension of certain Acts

38. (1)   Section 1 of the Provisional Collection of Taxes Act, 1927, is hereby amended by the insertion of "and value added tax" before "but no other tax or duty".

(2)   Section 1 of the Imposition of Duties Act, 1957, is hereby amended by the insertion in paragraph (gg) (inserted by the Finance Act, 1963) after "turnover tax" of "or value added tax", but no order shall be made under that Act for the purposes of increasing any of the rates of tax or extending the classes of activities or goods in respect of which tax is for the time being chargeable.

(3)   Section 39 of the Inland Revenue Regulation Act, 1890, is hereby amended by the insertion of "value added tax," before "stamp duties".

(4)   The First Schedule to the Stamp Act, 1891, shall have effect as if the following exemption were inserted therein under the heading "Bill of Exchange or Promissory Note":

"Bill drawn on any form supplied by the Revenue Commissioners for the purpose of remitting amounts of value-added tax".

Section 39

Consequential adjustments in regard to capital allowances

39.   [...][1]

Amendments

1   S39 repealed by FA75 s29(3), (w.e.f. 6 April 1975).

Section 40

Increase of excise duty on betting

40.   [...][1]

Amendments

1   This section is not relevant for Value Added Tax

Section 41

Repeals

41.   [...][1]

Amendments

1   This section refers to a previous Sch 5, not the current one. It has no significance in relation to the current Sch 5.

Section 42

Collection of tax

42.   [...]¹

Amendments
1   S42 repealed by F(No. 2)A 08 s97 & Sch 4, (w.e.f. 1 March 2009).

Section 43

Care and management of tax

43.   Tax is hereby placed under the care and management of the Revenue Commissioners.

Section 44

Short title

44.   This Act may be cited as the Value Added Tax Act, 1972.

SCHEDULES
FIRST SCHEDULE
EXEMPTED ACTIVITIES

135(1)(f)   [[(i)   Financial services consisting of-

(a)   the issue, [other than the issue of new stocks, new shares, new debentures or new securities made to raise capital, the][1] transfer or receipt of, or any dealing in, stocks, shares, debentures and other securities, other than documents establishing title to goods,

(b)   the arranging for, or the underwriting of, an issue [of stocks, shares, debentures and other securities, other than documents establishing title to goods,][2]

135(1)(d)   (c)   the operation of any current, deposit or savings account [and the negotiation of, or any dealings in, payments, transfers, debts, cheques and other negotiable instruments excluding debt collection and factoring][3],

135(1)(e)   (d)   the issue, transfer or receipt of, or any dealing in, currency, bank notes and metal coins, in use as legal tender in any country, excluding such bank notes and coins when supplied as investment goods or as collectors' pieces,

135(1)(b)   [(e)   the granting and the negotiation of credit and the management of credit by the person granting it,][4]

135(1)(c)   (f)   the granting of, or any dealing in, credit guarantees or any other security for money and the management of credit guarantees by the person who granted the credit,

135(1)(g)   [(g)   [the management of an undertaking specified in one of the following clauses, and such management may comprise any of the three functions listed in Annex II to Directive 2001/107/EC of the European Parliament and Council (being the functions included in the activity of collective portfolio management) where those functions are supplied by the person with responsibility for the provision of the functions concerned in respect of the undertaking, and which is—][5]

[(I)   a collective investment undertaking as defined in section 172A of the Taxes Consolidation Act, 1997 (as amended by section 59 of the Finance Act, 2000), or][6]

[(Ia)   a special investment scheme within the meaning of section 737 of the Taxes Consolidation Act, 1997, or][7]

(II)   administered by the holder of an authorisation granted pursuant to the European Communities

(Life Assurance) Regulations, 1984 (S.I. No. 57 of 1984), or by a person who is deemed, pursuant to Article 6 of those regulations, to be such a holder, the criteria in relation to which are the criteria specified in relation to an arrangement administered by the holder of a licence under the Insurance Act, 1936, in section 9(2) of the Unit Trusts Act, 1990, or

(III) a unit trust scheme established solely for the purpose of superannuation fund schemes or charities, or

(IV) determined by the Minister for Finance to be a collective investment undertaking to which the provisions of [this subparagraph apply,][8]

[(V) an undertaking which is a qualifying company for the purposes of section 110 of the Taxes Consolidation Act 1997;][9]

[...][10]

(h) services supplied to a person under arrangements which provide for the reimbursement of the person in respect of the supply by him of goods or services in accordance with a credit card, charge card or similar card scheme;][11]

a 132(1)(i), (j) (ii) [children's or young people's education,][12] school or university education, and vocational training or retraining (including the supply of goods and services incidental thereto [, other than the supply of research services][13]), provided by educational establishments recognised by the State, and education, training or retraining of a similar kind [, excluding instruction in the driving of mechanically propelled road vehicles other than vehicles designed or constructed for the conveyance of goods with a capacity of 1.5 tonnes or more,][14] provided by other persons;

a 132(1)(b), (c) [(iii) professional services of a medical nature, other than services specified in paragraph (iiib), but excluding such services supplied in the course of carrying on a business which consists in whole or in part of selling goods;][15]

a 132(1)(b), (c), (e) [(iiia) supply by dental technicians of services of a dental nature and of dentures or other dental prostheses;][16]

a 132(1)(b), (c) [(iiib) professional services of a dental or optical nature;][17]

a 135(1)(i), a 135(2) (iv) letting of immovable goods [(which does not include the service of allowing a person use a toll road or a toll bridge)][18] with the exception of-

(a)   letting of machinery or business installations when let separately from any other immovable goods of which such machinery or installations form part;

[(b)   letting of the kind to which [paragraph (ii) of the Third Schedule or paragraph (xiii) of the Sixth Schedule][19] refers;][20]

[(bi)   provision of facilities of the kind to which paragraph (viia) of the Sixth Schedule refers,][21]

(c)   provision of parking accommodation for vehicles by the operators of car parks; and

(d)   hire of safes;

(1)(b), (c)   (v)   hospital and medical care or treatment provided by a hospital, nursing home, clinic or similar establishment;

[(va)   services closely related to medical care covered by section 61 or 61A of the Health Act 1970 which are undertaken by or on behalf of the Health Service Executive or by home care providers duly recognised by that Executive under section 61A of that Act;][22]

132(1)(h)   (vi)   services for the protection or care of children and young persons, and the provision of goods closely related thereto, provided otherwise than for profit [and the supply of services for the protection or care of children and young persons, and the provision of goods closely related thereto, provided by persons whose activities may be regulated by regulations made under [Part VII or Part VIII of the Child Care Act 1991][23]][24];

132(1)(g)   (vii)   supply of goods and services closely related to welfare and social security by non-profit making organisations;

132(1)(n)   [(viii) promotion of and admissions to live theatrical or musical performances, including circuses, but not including-

(a)   dances [...][25], or

(b)   performances in conjunction with which facilities are available for the consumption of food or drink during all or part of the performance by persons attending the performance;][26]

132(1)(n)   [(viiia) supply of cultural services and of goods closely linked thereto by any cultural body, whether established by or under statute or otherwise, which is recognised as such a body by the Revenue Commissioners for the purposes of this paragraph, not being services to which paragraph (viii) relates;][27]

(ix)   agency services in regard to-

[(a)   the   arrangement   of   passenger   transport   or accommodation for persons, [and]²⁸[...]²⁹]³⁰

[...]³¹

[...]³²

(d)   services specified in paragraph (i),]³³

[excluding [...]³⁴ management and safekeeping services in regard to the services specified in paragraph (i)(a), not being services specified in [subparagraph [(g)]³⁵ of paragraph (i)]³⁶;]³⁷

[...]³⁸

a 135(1)(a)   [(xi)   insurance and reinsurance transactions, including related services performed by insurance brokers and insurance agents and, for the purposes of this paragraph, 'related services' includes the collection of insurance premiums, the sale of insurance, and claims handling and claims settlement services where the supplier of the insurance services delegates the authority to an agent and is bound by the decision of that agent in relation to that claim;]³⁹

a 132(1)(a),
a 135(1)(h)   [(xia)   public postal services (including the supply of goods and services incidental thereto) supplied by An Post including postmasters, or by [designated persons in accordance with the European Communities (Postal Services) Regulations 2000 (S.I. No. 310 of 2000)]⁴⁰;]⁴¹

[...]⁴²

a 132(1)(q)   (xiii)   the national broadcasting and television services, excluding advertising;

a 371,
Annex X(B)(10)   (xiv)   transport of passengers and their accompanying baggage;

a 135(1)(i)   [(xv)   the acceptance of bets subject to excise duty imposed by section 67 of the Finance Act 2002 and of bets exempted from excise duty by section 68 of the Finance Act 2002;]⁴³

[...]⁴⁴

a 135(1)(i)   (xvi)   issue of tickets or coupons for the purpose of a lottery;

[(xvii)   promotion of (other than in the course of the provision of facilities of the kind specified in paragraph (viia) of the Sixth Schedule), or the admission of spectators to, sporting events;]⁴⁵

a 132(1)(d)   (xviii)   collection, storage[, supply, intra-Community acquisition or importation]⁴⁶ of human organs, human blood and human milk;

[(xviiia) supply, intra-Community acquisition and importation of investment gold (within the meaning of section 6A) other than supplies of investment gold to the Central Bank of Ireland;

(xviiib)supply of services of an intermediary (as defined in section 6A) acting in that capacity;][47]

a 371,   (xix)   funeral undertaking;

x X(B)(4)

[...

...][48]

132(1)(l)   (xxii)   supply of services and of goods closely related thereto for the benefit of their members by non-profit making organisations whose aims are primarily of a political, trade union, religious, patriotic, philosophical, philanthropic or civic nature where such supply is made without payment other than the payment of any membership subscription;

132(1)(f)   [(xxiia)supply of services by an independent group of persons (being a group which is an independent entity established for the purpose of administrative convenience by persons whose activities are exempt from or are not subject to tax) for the purpose of rendering its members the services directly necessary for the exercise of their activities and where the group only recovers from its members the exact reimbursement of each member's share of the joint expenses;][49]

132(1)(m)   (xxiii)   provision of facilities for taking part in sporting and physical education activities, and services closely related thereto, provided [...][50] by non-profit making organisations [with the exception of facilities to which paragraph (viib) or (viic) of the Sixth Schedule refers][51];

a 136   (xxiv)   supply of goods [other than [a supply of immovable goods [...][52] or][53] a supply of goods of a kind specified in section 3(1)(g),][54] by a person being goods-

(a)   which were used by him for the purposes of a business carried on by him,

(b)   in relation to the acquisition or application of which he had borne tax, and

(c)   which are of such a kind or were used in such circumstances that no part of the said tax was deductible under section 12;

132(1)(b)   (xxv)   catering services supplied-

(a)   to patients of a hospital or nursing home in the hospital or nursing home, and

(b)   to students of a school in the [school;][55][56]

a 143(1)   [(xxvi)   the importation of gas through the natural gas distribution system, or the importation of electricity.][57]

Amendments

1   Inserted by FA06 s100(a), (w.e.f. 31 March 2006).
2   Substituted by FA06 s100(b), (w.e.f. 31 March 2006).
3   Inserted by FA91 s85, (w.e.f. 29 May 1991).
4   Para(i)(e) substituted by FA95 s139(a), (w.e.f. 2 June 1995).
5   Substituted by FA04s64(a), (w.e.f. 25 March 2004).
6   Substituted by FA02 Sch 6, (w.e.f. 25 March 2002).
7   Para(i)(g)(Ia) inserted by FA99 s138(a), (w.e.f. 25 March 1999).
8   Para(i)(g) substituted by FA91 s85, (w.e.f. 29 May 1991).
9   Inserted by FA04 s64(a)(iii), (w.e.f. 25 March 2004).
10 Deleted by FA91 s85, (w.e.f. 29 May 1991).
11 Para(i) substituted by FA87 s45, (w.e.f. 1 November 1987).
12 Inserted by FA97 s110(a), (w.e.f. 1 May 1997).
13 Inserted by FA01 s85, (w.e.f. 1 September 2001).
14 Inserted by FA90 s106, (w.e.f. 30 May 1990).
15 Para(iii) substituted by FA89 s61, (w.e.f. 1 November 1989).
16 Para(iiia) inserted by FA86 s89, (w.e.f. 1 July 1986).
17 Para(iiib) inserted by FA89 s61, (w.e.f. 1 November 1989).
18 Inserted by FA01 s199(b), (w.e.f. 1 September 2001).
19 Substituted by FA93 s94, (w.e.f. 1 March 1993).
20 Para(iv)(b) inserted by FA91 s85, (w.e.f. 29 May 1991).
21 Para(iv)(bi) inserted by FA92 s194(I)(a), (w.e.f. 1 July 1992).
22 Inserted by FA07 s93, (w.e.f. 2 April 2007).
23 Substituted by FA03 Sch 6, (w.e.f. 28 March 2003).
24 Inserted by FA97 s110(b), (w.e.f. 1 May 1997).
25 Deleted by FA92 s194(I)(b), (w.e.f. 28 May 1992).
26 Para(viii) inserted by FA85 s49, (w.e.f. 1 March 1985).
27 Para(viiia) inserted by FA90 s106, (w.e.f. 30 May 1990).
28 Inserted by FA01 s199(c), (w.e.f. 1 May 2001).
29 Deleted by FA87 s45, (w.e.f. 1 November 1987).
30 Para (ix)(a) deleted by F(No. 2)A 08 s 76, w.e.f 1 January 2010.
31 Deleted by FA01 s199(d)(i), (w.e.f. 1 May 2001).
32 Deleted by FA01 s199(d)(ii), (w.e.f. 1 May 2001).
33 Para(ix)(c) & (d) substituted by FA87 s45, (w.e.f. 1 November 1987).
34 Deleted by FA01 s199(d)(iii), (w.e.f. 1 May 2001).
35 Substituted by FA91 s85, (w.e.f. 29 May 1991).
36 Substituted by FA89 s61, (w.e.f. 1 July 1989).
37 Inserted by FA87 s45, (w.e.f. 1 November 1987).
38 Deleted by FA91 s85, (w.e.f. 1 January 1992).
39 Substituted by FA01 s199(e), (w.e.f. 1 May 2001).
40 Substituted by FA08 s141 & Sch 8(3)(j), (w.e.f. 13 March 2008).
41 Para(xi)(a) inserted by FA91 s85, (w.e.f. 1 January 1992).
42 Deleted by FA87 s45, (w.e.f. 1 November 1987).
43 Substituted by FA05 s112(a), (w.e.f. 25 March 2005).
44 Deleted by FA05 s112(b), (w.e.f. 25 March 2005).
45 Para(xvii) substituted by FA92 s194(I)(c), (w.e.f. 1 July 1992).
46 Substituted by FA92 s194(2)(a), (w.e.f. 1 July 1992).
47 Para(xviiia) & (xviiib) inserted by FA99 s138(b), (w.e.f. 25 March 1999).
48 Deleted by FA90 s106, (w.e.f. 1 January 1991).
49 Para(xxiia) inserted by FA90 s106, (w.e.f. 30 May 1990).
50 Deleted by FA92 s194(I)(e), (w.e.f. 1 July 1992).
51 Inserted by FA95 s139(b), (w.e.f. 1 January 1996).
52 Deleted by FA08 s106, (w.e.f. 1 July 2008).
53 Inserted by FA05 s112(c), (w.e.f. 25 March 2005).
54 Inserted by FA92 s194(2)(b), (w.e.f. 1 January 1993).
55 Substituted by FA04 s64(b), (w.e.f. 1 January 2005).
56 First Schedule substituted by VAT Amend. A78 s24, (w.e.f. 1 March 1979).
57 Para(xxvi) inserted by FA04 s64(c), (w.e.f. 1 January 2005).

Regulations and Orders

Credit cards	1986 SI No. 430	Value Added Tax (Exempted Activities) (No. 1) Order 1986

Revenue e-Briefs

Revenue e-Brief No. 52/2008: VAT Treatment of factoring and invoice discounting

Revenue e-Brief No. 11/2006: VAT Treatment of Financial and Insurance Services

Revenue e-Brief No. 3/2006: VAT liability regarding "back office" services supplied to the Insurance Industry

Revenue e-Brief No. 8/2005: VAT liability regarding "back office" services to the Insurance Industry

Revenue Statements of Practice and Information Leaflets

Exempt Persons acquiring Goods from other EU Member States: SP-VAT/13/92

Exempt Persons acquiring Goods from other EU Member States: Information Leaflet No. 13/01

Factoring: Information Leaflet dated October 2008

Promotion of and admission to live theatrical and musical events (including performances by non-established performers, VAT treatment of: Information Leaflet dated December 2008

Research services carried out by third level educational bodies: Information Leaflet No. 2/01 (formerly No. 6/01)

Shares, VAT not deductible: SP-VAT/2/90

Sports Facilities: Information Leaflet dated October 2008

Case law

Abbey National plc v Commissioners of Customs & Excise	C169/04	Management of special investment funds/Meaning of 'management'
Akritidis, Savvas v Finanzamt Herne-West	C462/02	Games of chance/Exemption of/ Conditions to/Direct effect
Ambulanter Pflegedienst Kugler GmbH v Finanzamt Fur Korperschafte 1	C141/00	Medical care/Provision by Corporate bodies
Arthur Andersen & Co. Accountants c.s. v Staatssecretaris van Financiën	C472/03	Insurance related services/Back office activities/Exemption of
Assurandør-Societetet, acting on behalf of Taksatorringen and Skatteministeriet	C8/01	Independent groups
Bulthuis Griffioen W v Inspecteur der Omzetbelasting Zaandam	C453/93	Medical services/Nursing home
Canterbury Hockey Club and Canterbury Ladies Hockey Club v Commissioners for Her Majesty's Revenue and Customs	C253/07	Services linked to sport
Cantor Fitzgerald International v Commissioners of Customs & Excise	C108/99	Letting of immovable property/ Third party taking over lease for consideration
Card Protection Plan Limited v Customs and Excise	C349/96	Composite supply/Insurance
Christoph-Dornier-Stiftung für Klinische Psychologie and Finanzamt Gießen	C45/01	Pscychotherapeutic treatment/ Provided by foundation governed by public law
CSC Financial Services Ltd v Customs & Excise	C235/00	Transactions in securities/ Negotiation/ Provision of a 'call centre' service
D (a minor) v W (on appeal by Osterreichischer Bundesschatz)	C384/98	Medical expert witnesses
d'Ambrumenil, Peter, Dispute Resolution Services Ltd and Commissioners of Customs and Excise	C307/01	Medical services
DFDS A/S v Customs and Excise	C260/95	Travel agent/Taxable Person
Diagnostiko & Therapeftiko Kentro Athinon-Ygeia AE v Ipourgos Ikonomikon	C394/04 C395/04	Activities closely related to hospital and medical care
Diners Club Ltd The v The Revenue Commissioners	Irish H.C. iii ITR 680	Credit Cards exemption
Donner, Andreas Matthias v Netherlands	C39/82	Imports/Exemption
Eismann Alto Adige Srl v Ufficio Imposta sul Valore Aggento di Bolzano	C217/94	Obligations for Payment
Elmeka NE v Ipourgos Ikonomikon	C181/04 C182/04 C183/04	Chartering of sea-going vessels/ Scope of exemption

Empresa de Desenvolvimento Mineiro SGPS SA (EDM) and Fazenda Pública	C77/01	Meaning of 'economic activities'/ Meaning of 'incidental financial transactions'/Calculation of deductible proportion
First Choice Holidays plc and Commissioners of Customs & Excise	C149/01	Travel Agents
First National Bank of Chicago v Customs and Excise	C172/96	Forex/Exempt
Germany v Commission	C287/00	Research activities
Gregg, Jennifer and Mervyn v Customs and Excise	C216/97	Medicine/nursing home
H.A. Solleveld and JE van den Hout-van Eijnsbergen v Straatssecretaris van Financiën	C443/04 C444/04	Medical care/Paramedical professions/Definition of
Haderer, Werner v Finanzamt Wilmersdorf	C445/05	Tuition given privately by teachers and covering school or university education/Education provided in the context of courses organised by adult education centres/No direct contractual link with pupils
Heerma J and K. Heerma v Staatssecretaris van Financien	C23/98	Taxable Event/Property let by partner to partnership
Hoffmann, Matthias	C144/00	Cultural bodies/soloists
Institute of the Motor Industry (the) v Customs and Excise	C149/97	Trade representative body/Taxable Person
Ireland v Commission	C358/97	Toll Roads
J.C.M Beeher B.V. v Staatssecretaris van Financiën	C-124/07	Supply of services relating to insurance transactions/Insurance brokers and insurance agents
JP Morgan Fleming Claverhouse Investment Trust plc, The Association of Investment Trust Companies v The Commissioners of HM Revenue and Customs	C363/05	Special investment funds/Meaning/ Closed-ended funds
Jyske Finans A/S v Skatteministeriet	C280/04	Exemption of supplies excluded from the right to deduct/Meaning of taxable dealer
Kennemer Golf & Country Club v Staatssecretaris van Financiën	C174/00	Services connected with the practice of sport/Non-profit-making organisation
Kingscrest Associates Ltd, Montecello Ltd v Commissioners of Customs & Excise	C498/03	Meaning of charitable status
Linneweber, Edith v Finanzamt Gladbeck	C453/02	Games of chance/Exemption of/ Conditions to/Direct effect
L.u.P GmbH v Finanzamt Bochum-Mitte	C106/05	Medical care/Conditions for exemption
Mirror Group plc v Commissioners of Customs & Excise	C409/98	Letting of immovable property/ Undertaking to become a tenant
MKG-Kraftfahrzeuge-Factory GmbH and Finanzamt Groß-Gerau	C305/01	Factoring
Sinclair Collis Ltd v Customs and Excise	C275/01	Letting of installed vending machines
Skandia v Forsakringsaktiebolaget	C240/99	Outsourcing
Spaarkassernes Datacenter v Skatteministeriet	C2/95	Exemption/Outsourcing for bank
Stichting Central Begeleiding-sorgaan voor de Intercollegiale Toetsing	C407/07	Exemptions/Services supplied by independent groups
Stichting 'Goed Wonen' v Staatssecretaris van Financiën	C326/99	Property/rights *in rem*
Stichting Kinderopvang Enschede v Staatssecretaris van Financiën	C415/04	Intermediary services linked to welfare, social security work and childcare
Stichting Regionaal Opleidingen Centrum Noord-Kennemerland/West-Friesland (Horizon College) v Staatssecretaris van Financiën	C434/05	Teaching staff employed by one educational establishment made available, for consideration, to another
Temco Europe SA v Belgian State	C284/03	Licence to occupy
Trans Tirreno Express SpA v Ufficio Provinciale IVA Sassari	C283/84	Transport in International Waters

United Kingdom v European Commission	C353/85	Who is Taxable/Taxable Medicine (Services of practitioners in medical & paramedical professions opticians)
United Utilities plc v Commissioners of Customs & Excise	C89/05	Games of chance/Scope of exemption/Activity of call centre
Unterpertinger, Margarete and Pensionsversicherungsanstalt der Arbeiter	C212/01	Doctor/expert report
VDP Dental Laboratory NV v Staatssecretaris van Financiën	C401/05	Scope of exemption/Manufacture and repair of dental protheses
Velker International Oil Company NV Staatssecretaris van Financien	C185/89	Provisioning of Ships
Volker Ludwig v Finanzamt Luckenwalde	C453/05	Concept of transactions consisting in 'the negotiation of credit'
Walderdorff, Gabriele v Finanzamt Waldviertel	C451/06	Leasing and letting of immovable property/Letting of fishing rights
Zoological Society of London v Customs and Excise	C267/00	Cultural Activities/Exemption

Revenue Precedents

Topic:	Tour Operators.
Issue:	Should Tour Operators be treated the same as Travel Agents?
Decision:	Yes. (This followed discussions and agreement with the trade).
Date:	31/3/95

(withdrawn from the Revenue website in 2002)

Topic:	Fund Management
Issue:	Management of a qualifying fund partially subcontracted to Commodity Trading Advisors outside the State.
Decision:	In a particular case Revenue accepted that services were supplied to the Investment Manager outside the State for onward supply to the qualifying funds. Fees payable were not related to services received in the State.
Date:	27/9/96
Topic:	Agency Treasury Companies.
Issue:	Management of ATCs in IFSC
Decision:	To the extent that an ATC is engaged in exempt financial transactions the manager can also be regarded as engaged in exempt financial transactions.
Date:	12/11/95

(withdrawn from the Revenue website in 2002)

Topic:	Group Treatment.
Issue:	Group treatment of management companies and special purpose companies, captive finance companies and captive insurance companies.
Decision:	Group treatment agreed provided the managed entities are passive and not operationally involved in any activities and that the managed entities do not have any independent management capabilities. Relaxation of the joint and several liability requirement extended the managed entities operating in IFSC, provided they have been approved for group treatment.
Date:	16/6/91

(withdrawn from the Revenue website in 2002)

Topic:	Medical Services.
Issue:	Nursing Consultant.
Decision:	Exempt.
Date:	20/3/95
Topic:	Cultural Services.
Issue:	Promotion of certain film festivals in the course of business.
Decision:	Festival company regarded as cultural body for the purposes of (viiia) and exempt for VAT.
Date:	21/11/90

(withdrawn from the Revenue website in 2002)

Topic:	Lottery
Issue:	Commission payable to agents selling lottery cards.

Decision:	Commission exempt. Treatment is made possible through the broader interpretation of the phrase "issue of tickets or coupons for the purpose of a lottery".
Date:	25/5/87

(withdrawn from the Revenue website in 2002)

Topic:	Medical Services.
Issue:	Chiropodists.
Decision:	Exempt, Appeal Commissioner decision.
Date:	30/6/78

(withdrawn from the Revenue website in 2002)

Topic:	Admissions.
Issue:	Admission fees to historic houses and gardens.
Decision:	On foot of appeal case admissions exempt under paragraph (iv) First Schedule.
Date:	22/11/74
Topic:	Medical Services.
Issue:	Company providing medical services.
Decision:	Exempt, as company is run by doctors (medical).
Date:	2/7/92
Topic:	Custodial Services.
Issue:	Global custodial services.
Decision:	On the basis that the taxable element constitutes a negligible part of the total cost of supplying the global custody service, Revenue accept that the service is an exempt financial service. Supply of purely physical service of safekeeping is not exempt.
Date:	16/11/95

(withdrawn from the Revenue website in 2002)

Topic:	Agency services in regard to dealings in shares.
Issue:	Treatment of agency services in relation to issue, transfer or receipt of, or any dealing in stocks and shares.
Decision:	Transfer agency services insofar as they have to do with purchase and redemption of shares, provided as a fully integrated service, qualify as exempt under (i)(a) and or (ix)(d) of First Schedule. Registration services as a separate supply are taxable.
Date:	10/7/95

(withdrawn from the Revenue website in 2002)

Topic:	Business Expansion Scheme.
Issue:	Fees received by solicitors in relation to arranging for issue of shares.
Decision:	Insofar as solicitors actively participate in the arranging for and the issue of specific shares and are involved from the start, their fees are exempt.
Date:	3/7/92

(withdrawn from the Revenue website in 2002)

Topic:	Claims Handling.
Issue:	Is claims handling an insurance service/agency service in relation to insurance.
Decision:	Agent has no authority to conclude contracts either as principal or agent on behalf of insurer. Services are supplied to the insurer and not regarded as exempt activities under paragraph (xi) or (ix) (c) of First Schedule.
Date:	10/10/96

(withdrawn from the Revenue website in 2002)

Topic:	Agency services in relation to financial services.
Issue:	Management of credit card transactions.
Decision:	Provision of management as a total servicing system for credit card transactions is regarded as single composite supply within the meaning of (ix) (d) 1st Schedule.
Date:	11/4/95
Topic:	Funds.
Issue:	Services bought in from overseas by the managers of specified funds.
Decision:	Certain services received from outside the State may qualify for the exemption applying to fund management services, provided Revenue are satisfied that those services form part of the management function.
Date:	28/9/90

(withdrawn from the Revenue website in 2002)

Topic:	Property.
Issue:	Receipts from card games in public house.
Decision:	Exempt - letting
Date:	7/11/86
Topic:	Pension Funds.
Issue:	Breakdown of a fund management service into separate elements, for one overall charge.
Decision:	The service agreement may be regarded as a package of separately identifiable activities and the fee may be apportioned between the separate elements provided that these are identified in the service agreement and that the basis for apportionment is realistic.
Date:	18/2/98

(withdrawn from the Revenue website in 2002)

Topic:	Outsourcing.
Issue:	The supply of administration (back-office) services to specified funds.
Decision:	Where administration services are provided to a fund by an administrator under licence from the IFSC authorisation body, as part of the statutory structure of the fund, then the service may be regarded as part of the exempt management function. Consequently administration in these circumstances becomes a financial service and Fourth Schedule.
Date:	18/2/98

(withdrawn from the Revenue website in 2002)

Topic:	Medical Services.
Issue:	Osteopaths and Chiropractors.
Decision:	Exempt Paragraph (iii) First Schedule.
Date:	30/6/76

(withdrawn from the Revenue website in 2002)

Topic:	Deductible VAT [Input credit].
Issue:	VAT on inputs in relation to the exempt activities of a company that is involved in both taxable and exempt activities is non-deductible.
Decision:	Deductibility allowed on certain inputs deemed attributable to the taxable activities of the company.
Date:	30/6/93

(withdrawn from the Revenue website in 2002)

Topic:	Loss adjusters.
Issue:	Loss adjusters previously exempt brought into tax net with effect from 1/9/94.
Decision:	Appropriate apportionment allowed of the taxable amount in respect of work undertaken before 1/9/94 but not completed (invoiced) before.
Date:	9/8/94

Narrative

Tax Briefing: Issue 70 (VAT Treatment of Factoring and Invoice Discounting)

VAT and Financial Services in the 21st Century: ITR Jul 2007: Vol. 20 No. 4.

Tax Briefing: Issue 59 (Debt Factoring)

VAT and services of medical practitioners - ECJ cases: ITR May 2004: Vol 17 No. 3.

VAT & Short-term Lettings, Easements and Rights over Property: ITR Nov 2003: Vol 16 No. 6

VAT and Agents: ITR Sept 2003: Vol 16 No. 5

VAT and Outsourcing in a Financial Services Context: ITR Jan 2002: Vol 15 No. 1

VAT and Outsourcing in a Financial Services Context: ITR Mar 2002: Vol 15 No. 2

Share Acquisition – Support for VAT Recovery: ITR Nov 2001: Vol 14 No. 6

Tax Briefing: Issue 46 (Emergency Accommodation)

Tax Briefing: Issue 45 (Research Services/Insurance Related Services)

Tax Briefing: Issue 43 (VAT Committee Guidelines – Activities of Public Radio and Television Bodies)

Tax Briefing: Issue 43 (VAT Committee Guidelines – Article 13A(1)(a): Scope of Exemption Applicable to Deliveries by Public Postal Services

Tax Briefing: Issue 42 (VAT Committee Guidelines – Scope of Exemption of Articles 13, 15, 26b and 28c)

Tax Briefing: Issue 27 (Finance Act 1997 Changes: Child Care)

SECOND SCHEDULE

a 146

GOODS AND SERVICES CHARGEABLE AT THE RATE OF ZERO PER CENT

[[(i)   The supply of goods-

    (a)   subject to a condition that they are to be transported directly by or on behalf of the person making the supply-

a 146(1)(a)

        [(I)   outside the Community:

Provided that this subparagraph shall not apply to a supply of goods to a traveller (within the meaning assigned by section 13(3B)) which such traveller exports on behalf of the supplier and such supply shall be deemed to be a supply of the type referred to in subparagraph (f), or][1]

        (II)   to a registered person within the customs-free airport,

a 146(1)(b)

    [(aa)   subject to a condition that they are to be dispatched or transported directly outside the Community by or on behalf of the purchaser of the goods where that purchaser is established outside the State,][2]

a 138(1)

    (b)   dispatched or transported from the State to a person registered for value-added tax in another Member State,

a 138(2)(a)

    (c)   being new means of transport dispatched or transported directly by or on behalf of the supplier to a person in the territory of another Member State,

a 138(2)(b)

    [(cc)   being excisable products dispatched or transported from the State to a person in another Member State when the movement of the goods is subject to the provisions of Chapter II of Part II of the Finance Act, 1992, and any other enactment which is to be construed together with that Chapter, which implement the arrangements specified in paragraph 4 and 5 of Article 7, or Article 16, of the Council Directive No. 92/12/EEC of 25 February 1992,][3]

    (d)   by a registered person within a free port to another registered person within a free port,

    (e)   by a registered person within the customs-free airport to another registered person within the customs-free airport or a free port;

    [(f)   which are a traveller's qualifying goods (within the meaning assigned by subsection (3B) of section 13), provided that the provisions of subsection (1A) of that section and regulations (if any) made thereunder are complied with;][4][5

[(ia)   subject to such conditions and in such amounts as may be specified in regulations,-

(a)   the supply of goods, in a tax-free shop approved by the Revenue Commissioners, to travellers departing the State for a place outside the Community, or

(b)   the supply, other than by means of a vending machine, of food, drink and tobacco products on board a vessel or aircraft to passengers departing the State for another Member State, for consumption on board that vessel or aircraft;][6

(ii)   [...][7

(iii)   the carriage of goods in the State by or on behalf of a person in execution of a contract to transfer the goods to [...][8 a place [outside the Community][9;

a 142   [(iiia) intra-Community transport services involving the carriage of goods to and from the Azores or Madeira;

a 143(d)   (iiib)   subject to and in accordance with regulations, the importation of goods which, at the time of the said importation, are consigned to another Member State;][10

[(iiic) the supply of goods or services to international bodies recognised as such by the public authorities of the host Member State, and to members of such bodies, within the limits and under the conditions laid down by the international conventions establishing the bodies or by the agreements between the headquarters of those bodies and the host Member State of the headquarters;][11

a 148(d)   (iv)   the provision of docking, landing, loading or unloading facilities, including customs clearance, directly in connection with the disembarkation or embarkation of passengers or the importation or exportation of goods;

a 148(c)   [(v)   the supply, modification, repair, [maintenance, chartering and hiring][12 of-

(a)   sea-going vessels of a gross tonnage of more than 15 tons being vessels used or to be used-

(I)   for the carriage of passengers for reward,

(II)   for the purposes of a sea fishing business,

(III)   for other commercial or industrial purposes, or

(IV)   for rescue or assistance at sea, or

a 148(e)　　　　　　　　(b)　　aircraft used or to be used by a transport undertaking operating for reward chiefly on international routes;][13]

a 148(f)　　　[(va)　　the supply, repair, maintenance and hiring of equipment incorporated or used in aircraft to which subparagraph (b) of paragraph (v) relates;][14]

　　　　　　　[(vaa)　subject to and in accordance with regulations, if any, the supply, hiring, repair and maintenance of equipment incorporated or for use in sea-going vessels to which subparagraph (a) of paragraph (v) relates;][15]

a 148(a)　　　[(vb)　　the supply of goods for the fuelling and provisioning of sea-going vessels and aircraft of the kind specified in paragraph (v) [but not including goods for supply on board such vessels or aircraft to passengers for the purpose of those goods being carried off such vessels or aircraft][16];][17]

a 148(g)　　　[(vc)　　the supply of navigation services by the Irish Aviation Authority to meet the needs of aircraft used by a transport undertaking operating for reward chiefly on international routes;][18]

a 153　　　　[(vi)　　services, supplied by an agent acting in the name and on behalf of another person, in procuring-

　　　　　　　　　(a)　　the export of goods [...][19],

　　　　　　　　　(b)　　services specified in paragraphs (iii), [(iiia),][20] (iv), (v) or (x), or

　　　　　　　　　(c)　　the supply of goods or services outside the [Community][21];][22]

　　　　　　　[(via)　subject to and in accordance with section 13A, the supply of qualifying goods and qualifying services to, or the intra-Community acquisition or importation of qualifying goods by, an authorised person in accordance with that section, excluding supplies of goods within the meaning of paragraph (e) or (f) of subsection (1) of section 3;][23]

　　　　　　　[(vib)　the supply of services in procuring a repayment of tax due on the supply of a traveller's qualifying goods (within the meaning assigned by subsection (3B) of section 13) or the application of the provisions of subparagraph (i)(f) of this Schedule to that supply of goods, provided that the provisions of subsection (1A) of that section and regulations (if any) made thereunder are complied with;][24]

　　　　　　　[(vic)　services which are treated as intermediary services in accordance with section 10C(8);][25]

Annex III　　　(vii)　animal feeding stuff, excluding feeding stuff which is packaged, sold or otherwise designated for the use of dogs, cats, cage birds or domestic pets;

nnex III   (viii)   fertiliser (within the meaning of the Fertilisers, Feeding Stuffs and Mineral Mixtures Act, 1955) which is [supplied]²⁶ in units of not less than 10 kilograms and the sale or manufacture for sale of which is not prohibited under section 4 or 6 of the said Act;

         (ix)   services provided by the Commissioners of Irish Lights in connection with the operation of lightships, lighthouses or other navigational aids;

a 152   [(x)   gold supplied to the Central Bank of Ireland;]²⁷

         (xi)   life saving services provided by the Royal National Lifeboat Institution including the organisation and maintenance of the lifeboat service;

nnex III   [(xii)   food and drink of a kind used for human consumption, other than the supply thereof specified in [paragraph (iv) of the Sixth Schedule]²⁸, excluding-

             (a)   beverages chargeable with any duty of excise specifically charged on spirits, beer, wine, cider, perry or Irish wine, and preparations thereof,

           [(b)   other beverages, [drinking water, juice extracted from, and other drinkable products derived from, fruit or vegetables,]²⁹ and syrups, concentrates, essences, powders, crystals or other products for the preparation of beverages, but not including-

                [(I)   **tea and preparations thereof when supplied in non-drinkable form,**

                (II)   **cocoa, coffee and chicory and other roasted coffee substitutes, and preparations and extracts thereof, when supplied in non-drinkable form,]³⁰**

                (III)   milk and preparations and extracts thereof, or

                (IV)   preparations and extracts of meat, yeast, or egg;]³¹

          [(ba)   **tea and preparations thereof when supplied in drinkable form,**

          (bb)   **cocoa, coffee and chicory and other roasted coffee substitutes, and preparations and extracts thereof, when supplied in drinkable form,]³²**

           [(c)   ice cream, ice lollipops, water ices, frozen desserts, frozen yoghurts and similar frozen products, and prepared mixes and powders for making any such product or such similar product;]³³

           (d)   (I)   chocolates, sweets and similar confectionery (including [...]³⁴, glacé or crystallised fruits), biscuits, crackers and wafers of all kinds, and all other confectionery and bakery products [, whether cooked or uncooked,]³⁵ excluding bread,

(II)   in this subparagraph '**bread**' means food for human consumption manufactured by baking dough composed exclusively of a mixture of cereal flour and any one or more of the ingredients mentioned in the following subclauses in quantities not exceeding the limitation, if any, specified for each ingredient-

(1)   yeast or other leavening or aerating agent, salt, malt extract, milk, water, gluten,

(2)   fat, sugar and bread improver, subject to the limitation that the weight of any ingredient specified in this subclause shall not exceed 2 per cent of the weight of flour included in the dough,

(3)   dried fruit, subject to the limitation that the weight thereof shall not exceed 10 per cent of the weight of flour included in the dough,

other than food packaged for sale as a unit (not being a unit designated as containing only food specifically for babies) containing two or more slices, segments, sections or other similar pieces, having a crust over substantially the whole of their outside surfaces, being a crust formed in the course of baking, [frying]³⁶ or toasting, and

[(e)   any of the following when supplied for human consumption without further preparation, namely-

(I)   potato crisps, potato sticks, potato puffs and similar products made from potato, or from potato flour or from potato starch,

(II)   savoury products made from cereal or grain, or from flour or starch derived from cereal or grain, pork scratchings, and similar products,

(III)   popcorn, and

(IV)   salted or roasted nuts whether or not in shells;]³⁷
]³⁸

Annex III   (xiii)   medicine of a kind used for human oral consumption;

Annex III   (xiv)   medicine of a kind used for animal oral consumption, excluding medicine which is packaged, sold or otherwise designated for the use of dogs, cats, cage birds or domestic pets;

Annex III   (xv)   seeds, plants, trees, spores, bulbs, tubers, tuberous roots, corms, crowns and rhizomes, of a kind used for sowing in order to produce food;

Annex III   [(xva) printed books and booklets including atlases but excluding-

           (a)   newspapers, periodicals, brochures, catalogues [, directories][39] and programmes,

           (b)   books of stationery, cheque books and the like,

           (c)   diaries, organisers, yearbooks, planners and the like the total area of whose pages consist of 25 per cent or more of blank spaces for the recording of information,

           (d)   albums and the like, and

           (e)   books of stamps, of tickets or of coupons.][40]

146(1)(d)   [(xvi) the supply of services consisting of work on movable goods acquired or imported for the purpose of undergoing such work within the Community and dispatched or transported out of the Community by or on behalf of the person providing the services;][41]

a144)   [(xvia) the supply of transport services relating to the importation of goods where the value of such services is included in the taxable amount in accordance with section 15(3);][42]

        [(xvii) articles of children's personal clothing of sizes which do not exceed the sizes of those articles appropriate to children of average build of 10 years of age (a child whose age is 10 years or 10 years and a fraction of a year being taken for the purposes of this paragraph to be a child of 10 years of age), but excluding-

           (a)   articles of clothing made wholly or partly of fur skin other than garments merely trimmed with fur skin, unless the trimming has an area greater than one-fifth of the area of the outside material, and

           (b)   articles of clothing which are not described, labelled, marked or marketed on the basis of age or size;][43]

nex III   [(xviii) sanitary towels and sanitary tampons;][44]

        [...][45]

        [(xix) articles of children's personal footwear of sizes which do not exceed the size appropriate to children of average foot size of 10 years of age (a child whose age is 10 years or 10 years and a fraction of a year being taken for the purposes of this paragraph to be a child of 10 years of age), but excluding footwear which is not described, labelled, marked or marketed on the basis of age or size;][46]

Annex III   [(xixa) medical equipment and appliances being -

(a)   invalid carriages, and other vehicles (excluding mechanically propelled road vehicles), of a kind designed for use by invalids or infirm persons,

(b)   orthopaedic appliances, surgical belts, trusses and the like, deaf aids, and artificial limbs and other artificial parts of the body excluding artificial teeth [, corrective spectacles and contact lenses][47],

(c)   walking frames and crutches,

(d)   parts or accessories suitable for use solely or principally with any of the goods specified in subparagraphs (a), (b) and (c) of this paragraph;][48]

[(xx)   (a)   [...],[49]

(b)   wax candles and night-lights which are white and cylindrical, excluding candles and night-lights which are decorated, spiralled, tapered or perfumed.][50]][51]

Amendments

1   Para(i)(a)(I) inserted by FA97 s111(a)(i), (w.e.f. 1 July 1997).
2   Para(i)(aa) inserted by FA99 s139, (w.e.f. 1 July 1999).
3   Para(i)(cc) inserted by EC(VAT)R 1992 r14, (w.e.f. 1 January 1993).
4   Para(i)(f) inserted by FA97 s111(a)(ii), (w.e.f. 1 July 1997).
5   Para(i) substituted by FA92 s195(2)(a), (w.e.f. 1 January 1993).
6   Para(ia) substituted by FA00 s123(a), (w.e.f. 1 July 1999).
7   Repealed by VAT Amend. A78 s30(1), (w.e.f. 1 March 1979).
8   Deleted by FA96 s98(a), (w.e.f. 15 May 1996).
9   Substituted by FA92 195(2)(b), (w.e.f. 1 January 1993).
10 Para(iiia) - (iiib) inserted by FA92 s195(2)(c), (w.e.f. 1 January 1993).
11 Inserted by FA07 s94(a), (w.e.f. 2 April 2007).
12 Substituted by FA07 s94(b), (w.e.f. 2 April 2007).
13 Para(v) substituted by VAT Amend. A78 s25, (w.e.f. 1 March 1979).
14 Para(va) inserted by FA92 s195(1)(a), (w.e.f. 28 May 1992).
15 Para. (vaa) inserted by FA01 s200, (w.e.f. 1 May 2001).
16 Inserted by FA00 s123(b), (w.e.f. 1 July 1999).
17 Para(vb) inserted by FA93 s95(a), (w.e.f. 17 June 1993).
18 Para(vc) inserted by FA98 s116(a), (w.e.f. 1 March 1998).
19 Deleted by FA92 s195(2)(d)(i), (w.e.f. 1 January 1993).
20 Inserted by FA92 s195(2)(d)(ii), (w.e.f. 1 January 1993).
21 Substituted by FA92 s195(2)(d)(iii), (w.e.f. 1 January 1993).
22 Para(vi) substituted by VAT Amend. A78 s25, (w.e.f. 1 March 1979).
23 Para(via) inserted by FA93 s95(b), (w.e.f. 1 August 1993).
24 Para(vib) inserted by FA97 s111(b), (w.e.f. 1 July 1997).
25 Inserted by F(No. 2)A 08 s77(a), (w.e.f. 1 January 2010).
26 Substituted by VAT Amend. A78 s30(2), (w.e.f. 1 March 1979).
27 Para(x) substituted by VAT Amend. A78 s25, (w.e.f. 1 March 1979).
28 Substituted by FA92 s195(1)(b)(i), (w.e.f. 28 May 1992).
29 Substituted by FA07 s94(c), (w.e.f. 2 April 2007).
30 Substituted by F(No. 2)A 08 s77(b), (w.e.f. 24 December 2008).
31 Para(xii)(b) substituted by FA92 s195(1)(b)(ii), (w.e.f. 1 November 1992).
32 Inserted by F(No. 2)A 08 s77(b), (w.e.f. 24 December 2008).
33 Para(xii)(c) substituted by FA92 s195(1)(b)(iii), (w.e.f. 1 July 1992).
34 Deleted by FA87 s46, (w.e.f. 1 July 1987).

35 Inserted by FA92 s195(1)(b)(iv)(I), (w.e.f. 1 July 1992).
36 Inserted by FA92 s95(1)(b)(iv)(II), (w.e.f. 1 July 1992).
37 Para(xii)(e) substituted by FA92 s195(1)(b)(v), (w.e.f. 1 July 1992).
38 Para(xii) substituted by FA85 s50, (w.e.f. 1 March 1985).
39 Inserted by FA00 s123(c), (w.e.f. 23 March 2000).
40 Para(xva) inserted by FA98 s116(b), (w.e.f. 1 May 1998).
41 Para(xvi) substituted by FA96 s98(b), (w.e.f. 1 January 1996).
42 Para(xvia) inserted by FA96 s98(c), (w.e.f. 1 January 1996).
43 Para(xvii) substituted by FA84 s92, (w.e.f. 1 May 1984).
44 Para(xviii) substituted by FA84 s92, (w.e.f. 1 May 1984).
45 Deleted by FA85 s50(b), (w.e.f. 1 March 1985).
46 Para(xix) substituted by FA85 s50, (w.e.f. 1 March 1985).
47 Inserted by FA89 s63, (w.e.f. 1 November 1989).
48 Para(xixa) inserted by Value Added Tax (Reduction of Rate No.5) O81 (SI 53/1981), (w.e.f. 1 March 1981).
49 Deleted by FA88 s63, (w.e.f. 1 March 1988).
50 Para(xx) substituted by FA83 s86, (w.e.f. 1 May 1983).
51 Second Schedule substituted by FA76 s60(b), (w.e.f. 1 March 1976).

Regulations and Orders

Abolition of Duty Free Shops	1999 SI No. 196	European Communities (Value Added Tax) Regulations,1999
Abolition of Duty Shops	1999 SI No. 197	European Communities (Value Added Tax) Regulations, 1999

Revenue Statements of Practice and Information Leaflets

Agricultural Services: Information Leaflet dated December 2008

Application of the Zero Rate to Sales and other Deliveries of Goods to other EU Member States after 1/1/93: SP-VAT/8/92

Clothing, VAT and: Information Leaflet No. 2/05

Footwear: Information Leaflet dated December 2008

Intra-Community supplies: Information Leaflet dated October 2008

Printing and Printed Matter: Information Leaflet dated December 2008

Food and Drink: Information Leaflet dated December 2008

Case law

Austria v Commission	C165/99	Classification of Food
Cimber Air A/S v Skatteministeriet	C382/02	Aircraft/Exemption/Meaning of 'operating chiefly on international routes'
Collée, Albert v Finanzamt Limburg an der Lahn	C146/05	Intra-Community supply/Refusal of exemption/Belated production of evidence of the supply
Navicon SA v Administración del Estado	C97/06	Concept of 'chartering sea-going vessels'/Compatibility of a national law allowing the exemption for full chartering only
Netto Supermarkt GmbH & Co. OHG v Finanzamt Malchin	C271/06	Exports/Conditions for exemption not fulfilled/Proof of export falsified by the purchaser
Teleos PLC and others v Commissioners of Customs & Excise	C409/04	Intra-Community transactions/Evidence/National measures to combat fraud

Revenue Precedents

Topic:	Food.
Issue:	Flavoured syrups/food supplements for babies/infants, supplying Vitamin C and consumed in dosage form.
Decision:	Zero rate as they could not be described as drinks or for use in the taking of drinks for refreshment.
Date:	22/7/82

(withdrawn from the Revenue website in 2002)

Topic: Medicines.

Issue: A specific chewing gum to help a person stop smoking.

Decision: Zero %, as coming within meaning of 2nd Schedule paragraph (xiii).

Date: 17/5/93

(withdrawn from the Revenue website in 2002)

Narrative

Tax Briefing: Issue 43 (VAT Committee Guidelines – Reduced Rates on Medical Equipment and Other Appliances)

Tax Briefing: Issue 42 (VAT Committee Guidelines – Exemption from VAT for persons domiciled or resident outside the European Community)

VAT and Cross-border Leasing of Means of Transport: ITR Nov 1999: Vol 12 No. 6.

Ireland's Derogations from the EU Sixth VAT Directive: ITR Sept 1999: Vol. 12 No. 5.

Tax Briefing: Issue 32 (Rates of VAT on Footwear)

Tax Briefing: Issue 27 (Sports Footwear)

THIRD SCHEDULE

GOODS AND SERVICES CHARGEABLE AT THE RATE SPECIFIED IN SECTION 11(1)(C)

[(i)   Immovable goods being a domestic dwelling for which a contract with a private individual has been entered into before the 25th day of February, 1993, for such supply;

(ii)   services specified in paragraph (xiii) of the Sixth Schedule, under an agreement made before the 25th day of February, 1993, and at charges fixed at the time of the agreement for such supply;

(iii)   services specified in subparagraph (a) of paragraph (xv) of the Sixth Schedule, under an agreement made before the 25th day of February, 1993, and at charges fixed at the time of the agreement for such supply.]^1

Amendments

1   Third Schedule substituted by FA93 s96, (w.e.f. 1 March 1993).

Revenue Statements of Practice and Information Leaflets

Agricultural Services: Information Leaflet dated December 2008

Rates of VAT on Services from 1/3/92: SP-VAT/1/92

FOURTH SCHEDULE

SERVICES THAT ARE TAXED WHERE RECEIVED

a 56(1) [(i)   Transfers and assignments of copyright, patents, licences, trade marks and similar rights;

[(ia) hiring out of movable goods other than means of transport;][1]

(ii) advertising services;

(iii) services of consultants, engineers, consultancy bureaux, lawyers, accountants and other similar services, data processing and provision of information (but excluding services connected with immovable goods);

[(iiia) telecommunications services;][2]

[(iiib) radio and television broadcasting services;

(iiic) electronically supplied services;][3]

(iiicd) the provision of access to, and of transport or transmission through, natural gas and electricity distribution systems and the provision of other directly linked services;][4]

(iv) acceptance of any obligation to refrain from pursuing or exercising in whole or in part, any business activity or any such rights as are referred to in paragraph (i);

(v) banking, financial and insurance services (including re-insurance [and financial fund management functions][5, but not including the provision of safe deposit facilities);

(vi) the provision of staff;

(vii) the services of [intermediaries][6] who act in the name and for the account of a principal when procuring for him any services specified in paragraphs (i) to (vi).][7]

Amendments

1 Para(ia) inserted by FA85 s52, (w.e.f. 30 May 1985).
2 Para(iiia) inserted by FA97 s112, (w.e.f. 1 July 1997).
3 Paras(iiib) and (iiic) inserted by FA03 s131, (w.e.f. 1 July 2003).
4 Para(iiid) inserted by FA04 s65(a), (w.e.f. 1 January 2005).
5 Inserted by FA04s65(b), (w.e.f. 25 March 2004).
6 Substituted by FA07 s95, (w.e.f. 1 January 2008) – Replacing "agents" with "intermediaries."
7 Fourth Schedule substituted by VAT Amend. A78 s27, (w.e.f. 1 March 1979).

Revenue e-Briefs

Revenue e-Brief No. 52/2007: VAT treatment of greenhouse gas emission trading allowances

Revenue e-Brief No. 14/2007 VAT treatment of certain secondments of staff to companies established in the State from related foreign companies.

Revenue Statements of Practice and Information Leaflets

Advertising Services: Information Leaflet dated December 2008

Fourth Schedule Services: Information Leaflet dated December 2008

Revenue Precedents

Topic:	Safekeeping of Assets.
Issue:	Custodial services.
Decision:	These are not 4th Schedule services.
Date:	8/7/96

(withdrawn from the Revenue website in 2002)

Narrative

VAT and Electronic Commerce: ITR March 2000: Vol. 12 No. 2.

FIFTH SCHEDULE

AGRICULTURAL PRODUCTION ACTIVITIES AND SERVICES
[PART 1
Article 295(1) and Annex VII of Council Directive No. 2006/112/EC of 28 November 2006][1]

Annex VII   LIST OF AGRICULTURAL PRODUCTION ACTIVITIES

[I.   CROP PRODUCTION

1.   General agriculture, including viticulture

2.   Growing of fruit (including olives) and of vegetables, flowers and ornamental plants, both in the open and under glass

3.   Production of mushrooms, spices, seeds and propagating materials; nurseries

II.   STOCK FARMING TOGETHER WITH CULTIVATION

1.   General stock farming

2.   Poultry farming

3.   Rabbit farming

4.   Beekeeping

5.   Silkworm farming

6.   Snail farming

III.   FORESTRY

IV.   FISHERIES

1.   Fresh-water fishing

2.   Fish farming

3.   Breeding of mussels, oysters and other molluscs and crustaceans

4.   Frog farming

V.   Where a farmer processes, using means normally employed in an agricultural, forestry or fisheries undertaking, products deriving essentially from his agricultural production, such processing shall also be regarded as agricultural production.

[PART II
Article 295(1) and Annex VIII of Council Directive No. 2006/112/EC of
28 November 2006][1]

Annex VII   **LIST OF AGRICULTURAL SERVICES**

Supplies of agricultural services which normally play a part in agricultural production shall be considered the supply of agricultural services and include the following in particular:

-       field work, reaping and mowing, threshing, baling, collecting, harvesting, sowing and planting

-       packing and preparation for market, for example drying, cleaning, grinding, disinfecting and ensilage of agricultural products

-       storage of agricultural products

-       stock minding, rearing and fattening

-       hiring out, for agricultural purposes, of equipment normally used in agricultural, forestry or fisheries undertakings

-       technical assistance

-       destruction of weeds and pests, dusting and spraying of crops and land

-       operation of irrigation and drainage equipment

-       lopping, tree felling and other forestry services.][2]

Amendments

1   Substituted by FA07 s97 & Sch 3 (w.e.f. 1 January 2007).
2   Fifth Schedule inserted by VAT Amend. A78 s28, (w.e.f. 1 March 1979).

Narrative

Ireland's Derogations from the EU Sixth VAT Directive: ITR Sept 1999: Vol. 12 No. 5.

SIXTH SCHEDULE

GOODS AND SERVICES CHARGEABLE AT THE RATE SPECIFIED IN SECTION 11(1)(d)

[(i) (a) Coal, peat and other solid substances held out for sale solely as fuel,

(b) electricity:

Provided that this subparagraph shall not apply to the distribution of any electricity where such distribution is wholly or mainly in connection with the distribution of communications signals,

(c) Gas of a kind used for domestic or industrial heating or lighting, whether in gaseous or liquid form, but not including [motor vehicle gas within the meaning of section 42(1) of the Finance Act, 1976][1], gas of a kind normally used for welding and cutting metals or gas sold as lighter fuel,

(d) hydrocarbon oil of a kind used for domestic or industrial heating, excluding gas oil [(within the meaning of the Mineral Oil Tax Regulations 2001 (S.I. No. 442 of 2001)][2], other than gas oil which has been duly marked in accordance with Regulation 6(2) of the said Regulations;

(ii) the provision of food and drink of a kind specified in paragraph (xii) of the Second Schedule in a form suitable for human consumption without further preparation-

(a) by means of a vending machine,

(b) in the course of operating a hotel, restaurant, cafe, refreshment house, canteen, establishment licensed for the sale for consumption on the premises of intoxicating liquor, catering business or similar business, or

(c) in the course of operating any other business in connection with the carrying on of which facilities are provided for the consumption of the food or drink supplied;

(iii) the supply, in the course of the provision of a meal, of goods of a kind specified in subparagraph (c), (d) or (e) of paragraph (xii) of the Second Schedule, and fruit juices other than fruit juices chargeable with a duty of excise-

(a) in the course of operating a hotel, restaurant, cafe, refreshment house, canteen, establishment licensed for the sale for consumption on the premises of intoxicating liquor, catering business or similar business, or

(b)   in the course of operating any other business in connection with the carrying on of which facilities are provided for the consumption of the food or drink supplied;

(iv)   the supply of food and drink [(other than bread as defined in subparagraph (d), of paragraph (xii) of the Second Schedule)][3] (other than beverages specified in subparagraph (a) or (b) of paragraph (xii) of the Second Schedule)]which is, or includes, food and drink which-

(a)   has been [heated, enabling][4] it to be consumed at a temperature above the ambient air temperature, or

(b)   has been retained [heated after cooking, enabling][4] it to be consumed at a temperature above the ambient air temperature, or

(c)   is supplied, while still warm after cooking, [...][5] enabling it to be consumed at a temperature above the ambient air temperature,

and is above the ambient air temperature [at the time it is provided to the customer][4];

Annex III   (v)   promotion of and admissions to cinematographic performances;

Annex III   (vi)   promotion of and admissions to live theatrical or musical performances, excluding-

(a)   dances, and

(b)   performances specified in paragraph (viii) of the First Schedule;

Annex III   [(vii)   amusement services of the kind normally supplied in fairgrounds or amusement parks:

Provided that this paragraph shall not apply to-

(I)   services consisting of dances,

(II)   services consisting of circuses,

(III)   services consisting of gaming, as defined in section 2 of the Gaming and Lotteries Act, 1956 (including services provided by means of a gaming machine of the kind referred to in section 43 of the Finance Act, 1975), or

(IV)   services provided by means of an amusement machine of the kind referred to in section 120 of the Finance Act, 1992;][6]

Annex III   [(viia)   the provision by a person other than a non-profit making organisation of facilities for taking part in sporting activities;][7]

323

[(viib) the provision by a member-owned golf club of facilities for taking part in golf to any person, other than an individual whose membership subscription to that club at the time the facilities are used by that individual entitles that individual to use such facilities without further charge on at least 200 days (including the day on which such facilities are used by that individual) in a continuous period of twelve months, where the total consideration received by that club for the provisions of such facilities has exceeded or is likely to exceed [€37,500][8] in any continuous period of twelve months and, for the purpose of this paragraph, the provision of facilities for taking part in golf shall not include the provision of facilities for taking part in pitch and putt;

(viic) the provision by a non-profit making organisation, other than an organisation referred to in paragraph (viib), of facilities for taking part in golf to any person where the total consideration received by that organisation for the provision of such facilities has exceeded or is likely to exceed [€37,500][8] in any continuous period of twelve months and, for the purposes of this paragraph, the provision of facilities for taking part in golf shall not include the provision of facilities for taking part in pitch and putt;][9]

Annex III   (viii) services consisting of the acceptance for disposal of waste material;

Annex III   (ix) admissions to exhibitions, of the kind normally held in museums and art galleries, of objects of historical, cultural, artistic or scientific interest, not being services of the kind specified in paragraph (viiia) of the First Schedule;

(x) services [of a kind][10] supplied in the course of their profession by veterinary surgeons;

(xi) agricultural services consisting of-

(a) field work, reaping, mowing, threshing, baling, harvesting, sowing and planting,

[(ai) stock-minding, stock-rearing, farm relief services and farm advisory services [(other than farm accountancy or farm management services)][11],][12]

(b) disinfecting and ensilage of agricultural products,

(c) destruction of weeds and pests and dusting and spraying of crops and land,

[(d) lopping, tree felling and similar forestry services;][13]

[(xia) nursery or garden centre stock consisting of live plants, live trees, live shrubs, bulbs, roots and the like, not being of a type specified in paragraph (xv) of the Second Schedule, and cut flowers and ornamental foliage not being artificial or dried flowers or foliage;][14]

[(xib) animal insemination services;

(xic) livestock semen;][15]

[(xid) live poultry and live ostriches;][16]

[(xie) miscanthus rhizomes, seeds, bulbs, roots and similar goods used for the agricultural production of bio-fuel;][17]

Annex III [[(xii) printed matter consisting of:

      (a) newspapers and periodicals;

      (b) brochures, leaflets and programmes;

      (c) catalogues, including directories, and similar printed matter;

      (d) maps, hydrographic and similar charts;

      (e) printed music other than in book or booklet form;

but excluding:

      (i) other printed matter wholly or substantially devoted to advertising,

      (ii) the goods specified in subparagraphs (b) to (e) of paragraph (xva) of the Second Schedule, and

      (iii) any other printed matter;][18]

Annex III [(xiii) subject to and in accordance with regulations, if any-

      (a) the letting of immovable goods (other than in the course of the provision of facilities of the kind specified in paragraph (viia))-

          (I) in the hotel or guesthouse sector, or

          (II) being a letting of all or part of a house, apartment or other similar establishment when that letting is provided in the short-term guest sector or holiday sector, or

          (III) in a caravan park, camping site or other similar establishment,

      or

      (b) the provision of holiday accommodation;][19]

(xiv) tour guide services;

(xv) the hiring (in this paragraph referred to as 'the current hiring') to a person of-

      (a) a vehicle designed and constructed, or adapted, for the conveyance of persons by road,

(b) a ship, boat or other vessel designed and constructed for the conveyance of passengers and not exceeding 15 tonnes gross,

(c) a sports or pleasure boat of any description, or

(d) a caravan, mobile home, tent or trailer tent,

under an agreement, other than an agreement of the kind referred to in section 3(1)(b), for any term or part of a term which, when added to the term of any such hiring (whether of the same goods or of other goods of the same kind) to the same person during the period of 12 months ending on the date of the commencement of the current hiring, does not exceed 5 weeks;

[(xva) children's car safety seats,][20]

[(xvi) a work of art being-

(a) a painting, drawing or pastel, or any combination thereof, executed entirely by hand, excluding hand-decorated manufactured articles and plans and drawings for architectural, engineering, industrial, commercial, topographical or similar purposes,

(b) an original lithograph, engraving, or print, or any combination thereof, produced directly from lithographic stones, plates or other engraved surfaces, which are executed entirely by hand, or

(c) an original sculpture or statuary, excluding mass-produced reproductions and works or craftsmanship of a commercial character,

but excluding the supply of such work of art by a taxable dealer in accordance with the provisions of subsection (3) or (8) of section 10A or by an auctioneer within the meaning of section 10B and in accordance with the provisions of subsection (3) of section 10B;][21]

[(xvia) antiques being, subject to and in accordance with regulations, articles of furniture, silver, glass or porcelain, whether hand-decorated or not, specified in the said regulations, which are shown to the satisfaction of the Revenue Commissioners to be more than 100 years old, other than goods specified in paragraph (xvi), but excluding the supply of such antiques by a taxable dealer in accordance with the provisions of subsection (3) or (8) of section 10A or by an auctioneer within the meaning of section 10B and in accordance with the provisions of subsection (3) of section 10B;][22]

(xvii) literary manuscripts certified by the Director of the National Library as being of major national importance and of either cultural or artistic importance;

(xviii) services consisting of-

    (a)   the repair or maintenance of movable goods, or

    (b)   the alteration of [used][23] movable goods, other than [contract work or][24] such services specified in paragraph (v), (va) or (xvi) of the Second Schedule, but excluding the provision in the course of any such repair, maintenance or alteration service of-

        (I)   accessories, attachments or batteries, or

        (II)   tyres, tyre cases, interchangeable tyre treads, inner tubes and tyre flaps, for wheels of all kinds;

(xix) services consisting of the care of the human body, excluding such services specified in the First Schedule, but including services supplied in the course of a health studio business or similar business;

[(xixa) non-oral contraceptive products;][25]

(xx) services supplied in the course of their profession by jockeys;

[(xxa) greyhound feeding stuff, which is packaged, advertised or held out for sale solely as greyhound feeding stuff, and which is supplied in units of not less than 10 kilograms;][26]

(xxi) the supply to a person of photographic prints (other than goods produced by means of a photocopying process), slides or negatives, which have been produced from goods provided by that person;

(xxii) goods being-

    (a)   photographic prints (other than goods produced by means of a photocopying process), mounted or unmounted, but unframed,

    (b)   slides and negatives, and

    (c)   cinematographic and video film,

which record particular persons, objects or events, supplied under an agreement to photograph those persons, objects or events;

(xxiii) the supply by a photographer of-

    (a)   negatives which have been produced from film exposed for the purpose of his business, and

    (b)   film which has been exposed for the purposes of his business;

(xxiv) photographic prints produced by means of a vending machine which incorporates a camera and developing and printing equipment;

(xxv)   services consisting of-

     (a)   the editing of photographic, cinematographic and video film, and

     (b)   microfilming;

(xxvi)   agency services in regard to a supply specified in paragraph (xxi);

(xxvii) instruction in the driving of mechanically propelled road vehicles, not being education, training or retraining of the kinds specified in paragraph (ii) of the First Schedule;

(xxviii) immovable goods;

(xxix)   services consisting of the development of immovable goods and work on immovable goods including the installation of fixtures, where the value of movable goods (if any) provided in pursuance of an agreement in relation to such services does not exceed two-thirds of the total amount on which tax is chargeable in respect of the agreement;

(xxx)   services consisting of the routine cleaning of immovable goods;

Annex III   [(xxxi) food of a kind used for human consumption, other than that included in paragraph (xii) of the Second Schedule, being flour or egg based bakery products including cakes, crackers, wafers and biscuits, but excluding-

     (a)   wafers and biscuits wholly or partly covered or decorated with chocolate or some other product similar in taste and appearance,

     (b)   food of a kind specified in subparagraph (c) or (e) (II) of paragraph (xii) of the Second Schedule, and

     (c)   chocolates, sweets and similar confectionery;][27]][28]

[(xxxii) concrete ready to pour [but excluding the supply of such goods by a taxable dealer in accordance with the provisions of subsection (3) or (8) of section 10A or by an auctioneer within the meaning of section 10B and in accordance with the provisions of subsection (3) of section 10B][29];

(xxxiii) blocks, of concrete, of a kind which comply with the specification contained in the Standard Specification (Concrete Building Blocks, Part 1, Normal Density Blocks) Declaration, 1987 (Irish Standard 20: Part 1: 1987) [but excluding the supply of such goods by a taxable dealer in accordance with the provisions of subsection (3) or (8) of section 10A or by an auctioneer within the meaning of section 10B and in accordance with the provisions of subsection (3) of section 10B][30].][31]][32]

Amendments

1   Substituted by FA93 s97(1)(a), (w.e.f. 1 March 1993).

2   Substituted by FA08 s141& Sch 8(3)(k), (w.e.f. 13 March 2008).
3   Inserted by FA05 s 113(a)(i), (w.e.f. 25 March 2005).
4   Substituted by FA05 s113(a),(w.e.f. 25 March 2005).
5   Deleted by by FA05 s113(a)(iv),(w.e.f. 25 March 2005).
6   Para(vii) substituted by FA94 s101(a), (w.e.f. 1 July 1994).
7   Para(viia) inserted by FA92 s197(3)(a), (w.e.f. 1 July 1992).
8   Substituted by FA08 s107(a), (w.e.f. 1 May 2008).
9   Para(viib) & (viic) inserted by FA95 s140(a), (w.e.f. 1 January 1996).
10 Inserted by FA94 s101(b), (w.e.f. 1 July 1994).
11 Substituted by FA94 s101(c), (w.e.f. 23 May 1994).
12 Para(xi)(ai) inserted by FA92 s197(3)(b), (w.e.f. 1 July 1992).
13 Para(xi)(d) substituted by FA93 s97(1)(b), (w.e.f. 1 March 1993).
14 Para(xia) inserted by FA97 s113, (w.e.f. 1 September1997).
15 Para(xib) & (xic) inserted by FA98 s117(a), (w.e.f. 1 July 1998).
16 Para (xid) inserted by FA98 s117(a), (w.e.f. 1 May 1998).
17 Inserted by FA08 s107(b), (w.e.f. 1 March 2008).
18 Para(xii) substituted by FA98 s117(b), (w.e.f. 1 May 1998).
19 Substituted by FA05 s113(b) (w.e.f. 1 July 2005).
20 Inserted by FA07 s96(b), (w.e.f. 1 July 2007).
21 Para(xvi) substituted by FA95 s140(b), (w.e.f. 1 July 1995).
22 Para(xvia) inserted by FA95 s140(c), (w.e.f. 1 July 1995).
23 Substituted by FA95 s140(d), (w.e.f. 1 July 1995).
24 Inserted by FA96 s99, (w.e.f. 1 January 1996).
25 Inserted by FA08 s107(c), (w.e.f. 13 March 2008).
26 Para(xxa) inserted by FA95 s140(e), (w.e.f. 1 July 1995).
27 Para(xxxi) substituted by FA93 s97(2), (w.e.f. 1 July 1993).
28 Para(xxi) - (xxxi) inserted by FA93 s97(1)(c), (w.e.f. 1 March 1993).
29 Inserted by FA95 s140(f), (w.e.f. 1 July 1995).
30 Inserted by FA95 s140(g), (w.e.f. 1 July 1995).
31 Para(xxxii) & (xxxiii) inserted by FA93 s97(2), (w.e.f. 1 July 1993).
32 Sixth Schedule substituted by FA92 s197(2), (w.e.f. 28 May 1992).

Regulations and Orders

| Antique furniture, silver, glass and porcelain | 2006 SI No. 548 | Value-Added Tax Regulations 2006 |
| Lettings in the short-term guest sector or holiday sector | 2006 SI No. 548 | Value-Added Tax Regulations 2006 |

Revenue e-Briefs

Revenue e-Brief No. 22/2007: Change of VAT rate on children's car safety seats

Revenue Statements of Practice and Information Leaflets

Golf and Other Sporting Activities: Information Leaflet dated October 2008

Horticultural Retailers: Information Leaflet dated December 2008

Photography: Information Leaflet dated December 2008

Promotion of and admission to live theatrical and musical events (including performances by non-established performers, VAT treatment of: Information Leaflet dated December 2008

Sports Facilities: Information Leaflet dated October 2008

Veterinary Services: Information Leaflet dated December 2008

Case law

| Maierhofer, Rudolf and Finanzamt Augsburg-Land | C315/00 | Letting of immovable property |

Narrative

Ireland's Derogations from the EU Sixth VAT Directive: ITR Sept 1999: Vol. 12 No. 5.

Tax Briefing: Issue 39 (Commissioned Framed Photographs)

Tax Briefing: Issue 36 (Take-Away Food)

Tax Briefing: Issue 35 (VAT on Printing and Printed Matter)

Tax Briefing: Issue 32 (Printing and Printed Matter)

SEVENTH SCHEDULE

Amendments

1. Sch 7 Repealed by FA93 s98 w.e.f. 1 March 1993

EIGHTH SCHEDULE

WORKS OF ART, COLLECTORS' ITEMS AND ANTIQUES CHARGEABLE AT THE RATE SPECIFIED IN SECTION 11(1)(d) IN THE CIRCUMSTANCES SPECIFIED IN SECTION 11(1AA)

[(i)   Works of art:

Every work of art being-

(a)   a picture (other than a painting, drawing or pastel specified in paragraph (xvi) of the Sixth Schedule), collage or similar decorative plaque, executed entirely by hand by an artist, other than-

    (I)   plans and drawings for architectural, engineering, industrial, commercial, topographical or similar purposes,

    (II)   hand-decorated manufactured articles, and

    (III)   theatrical scenery, studio back cloths or the like of painted canvas,

(b)   a sculpture cast the production of which is limited to eight copies and supervised by the artist or by the artist's successors in title provided that, in the case of a statuary cast produced before the 1st day of January, 1989, the limit of eight copies may be exceeded where so determined by the Revenue Commissioners,

(c)   a tapestry or wall textile made by hand from original designs provided by an artist, provided that there are not more than eight copies of each,

(d)   individual pieces of ceramics executed entirely by an artist and signed by the artist,

(e)   enamels on copper, executed entirely by hand, limited to eight numbered copies bearing the signature of the artist or the studio, excluding articles of jewellery, goldsmiths' wares and silversmiths' wares, or

(f)   a photograph taken by an artist, printed by the artist or under the artist's supervision, signed and numbered and limited to 30 copies, all sizes and mounts included, other than photographs specified in paragraph (xxii)(a) of the Sixth Schedule;

(ii)   Collectors' items:

Every collectors' item being one or more-

(a)   postage or revenue stamps, postmarks, first-day covers, pre-stamped stationery and the like, franked,

or if unfranked not being of legal tender and not being intended for use as legal tender, or

(b)   collections and collectors' pieces of zoological, botanical, mineralogical, anatomical, historical, archaeological, palaeontological, ethnographic or numismatic interest;

(iii)   Antiques:

Every antique being, subject to and in accordance with regulations, one or more goods which are shown to the satisfaction of the Revenue Commissioners to be more than 100 years old, other than goods specified in paragraph (xvi), (xvia) or (xxii)(a) of the Sixth Schedule or in paragraph (i) or (ii) of this Schedule.][1]

Amendments

1   Eighth Schedule inserted by FA95 s141, (w.e.f. 1 July 1995).

Revenue Statements of Practice and Information Leaflets

   The Margin Scheme, Second-hand Goods: Information Leaflet dated December 2008

Regulations and Orders

REGULATIONS AND ORDERS
IN CHRONOLOGICAL ORDER

Name	*Page*

Name	*Page*

Name

Page

VALUE-ADDED TAX (SPECIFIED DAY) ORDER, 1972

(SI No. 180 of 1972)

I, SEOIRSE Ó COLLA, Minister for Finance, in exercise of the powers conferred on me by section 1(1) of the Value-Added Tax Act. 1972 (No. 22 of 1972), hereby order as follows:

1. This Order may be cited as the Value-Added Tax (Specified Day) Order, 1972.
2. The 1st day of November, 1972, is hereby appointed to be the specified day for the purposes of the Value-Added Tax Act, 1972.

GIVEN under my Official Seal,
this 26th day of July, 1972.
SEOIRSE Ó COLLA,
Minister for Finance.

EXPLANATORY NOTE.

The Value-Added Tax Act, 1972, provides that value-added tax shall be substituted for the present turnover tax and wholesale tax with effect on and from a day to be specified by Order by the Minister for Finance. This Order appoints the 1st day of November, 1972, as the specified day.

VALUE-ADDED TAX (APPOINTED DAY) ORDER, 1972

(SI No. 192 of 1972)

I, SEOIRSE Ó COLLA, Minister for Finance, in exercise of the powers conferred on me by section 9(4) of the Value-Added Tax Act, 1972 (No. 22 of 1972), hereby order as follows:

1.   This Order may be cited as the Value-Added Tax (Appointed Day) Order, 1972.
2.   The 1st day of September, 1972, is hereby appointed to be the appointed day for the purpose of section 9 of the Value-Added Tax Act, 1972.

GIVEN under my Official Seal,
this 10th day of August, 1972.

SEOIRSE Ó COLLA,
Minister for Finance.

EXPLANATORY NOTE.

Section 9 of the Value-Added Tax Act, 1972, provides for the registration of persons who would be accountable for value-added tax if that tax were chargeable as on and from the appointed day. This Order appoints the 1st day of September 1972, as the appointed day.

VALUE-ADDED TAX (REFUND OF TAX) (NO 1) ORDER, 1972

(SI No. 267 of 1972)

> This Order revoked by para 9, Value Added Tax (Refund of Tax)(No.25)
> Order, 1993 (1993 S.I. No. 266) w.e.f. 15 September 1993

I, SEOIRSE Ó COLLA, Minister for Finance, in exercise of the powers conferred on me by section 20(3) of the Value-Added Tax Act, 1972 (No. 22 of 1972), hereby order as follows:

1. This Order may be cited as the Value-Added Tax (Refund of Tax) (No. 1) Order, 1972.

2. (1) In this Order "the Act" means the Value-Added Tax Act, 1972.

    (2) A reference in this Order to a structure includes a reference to a farmyard, a farm road and a concrete path adjacent to farm buildings.

3. A person who establishes to the satisfaction of the Revenue Commissioners that he has borne or paid tax in relation to outlay on the construction, extension, alteration or reconstruction of any building or structure which is designed for use solely or mainly for the purposes of a farming business or on the drainage or reclamation of any land intended for use for the purposes of such a business and who fulfils to the satisfaction of the said Commissioners the conditions which are specified in paragraph 4 of this Order shall be entitled to be repaid so much of such tax as is specified in paragraph 5 of this Order.

4. The conditions to be fulfilled by a person referred to in paragraph 3 of this Order are-

    (a) he shall claim a refund of the tax by completing such claim form as may be provided for the purpose by the Revenue Commissioners and he shall certify the particulars shown on such claim form to be correct;

    (b) he shall, by the production of plans, specifications or other sufficient documentary evidence, establish that the outlay in relation to which his claim for a refund of tax arises was incurred-

        (i) on the construction, extension, alteration or reconstruction of a building or structure which is designed for use solely or mainly for the purposes of a farming business, or

        (ii) on the drainage or reclamation of any land intended for use for the purposes of such a business;

    (c) he shall, by the production of invoices, provided in accordance with section 17(12)(a)(i) of the Act, or by the production of receipts for tax paid on goods imported, establish the amount of tax borne or paid by him in relation to the outlay on the matters specified in clauses (i) and (ii) of subparagraph (b) of this paragraph;

(d) he shall, by the production of a certificate from the Department of Agriculture and Fisheries or such other documentary evidence as may be acceptable to the Revenue Commissioners, establish-

(i) that, in relation to outlay on the matters specified in clause (i) of subparagraph (b) of this paragraph, he was paid a grant under the Farm Building Scheme operated by the said Department, and

(ii) that, in relation to outlay referred to in clause (ii) of subparagraph (b) of this paragraph, he was paid a grant under the Land Project operated by the said Department; and

(e) he shall establish that he is not a person who is registered in the register maintained under section 9 of the Act, nor a person required under the provisions of that section to furnish the particulars specified for registration.

5. The amount of tax to be repaid to a person referred to in paragraph 3 of this Order shall be so much of the amount of tax established in accordance with paragraph 4(c) of this Order to have been borne or paid as the person shows to the satisfaction of the Revenue Commissioners to be referable solely-

(a) to that part of the outlay referred to in paragraph 4 (b) (i) of this Order which relates to the construction, extension, alteration or reconstruction of that part of the building or structure which was designed solely for the purposes of a farming business and has actually been put to use in such a business carried on by him, or

(b) to that part of the outlay referred to in paragraph 4 (b) (ii) of this Order which relates to the drainage or reclamation of any land which has actually been put to use in such a business carried on by him.

GIVEN under my Official Seal,
this 24th day of October, 1972.

SEOIRSE Ó COLLA,
Minister for Finance.

EXPLANATORY NOTE.

This Order enables farmers who are unregistered for value-added tax to be repaid the VAT element in outlay by them on farm buildings and land drainage or reclamation. The relief is confined to outlay in respect of which a grant was paid by the Department of Agriculture and Fisheries.

VALUE-ADDED TAX (REDUCTION OF RATE) (NO 1) ORDER, 1972

(SI No. 268 of 1972)

This Order revoked by s80(f), FA73 with effect from 3 September 1973.

I, SEOIRSE Ó COLLA, Minister for Finance, in exercise of the powers conferred on me by section 11(8) of the Value-Added Tax Act, 1972 (No 22 of 1972), hereby order as follows:

1. This Order may be cited as the Value-Added Tax (Reduction of Rate) (No. 1) Order, 1972.

2. The rate of tax chargeable in relation to the rendering of services of the kind specified in the Schedule to this Order is hereby reduced from 16·37 per cent to 5·26 per cent.

SCHEDULE.

The hiring to a person under a contract in writing, other than a contract of a kind referred to in section 3(1)(b) of the Act, entered into before the 24th day of October, 1972, of movable goods in the possession of the person on the 1st day of November, 1972, of a kind on the delivery of which, if paragraph (xxviii) of Part I of the Third Schedule to the Act were disregarded, tax would be chargeable at the rate of 16·37 per cent.

GIVEN under my Official Seal,
this 24th day of October, 1972.

SEOIRSE Ó COLLA,
Minister for Finance.

EXPLANATORY NOTE.

If the rate of tax chargeable on the delivery of goods of any kind would be 16·37 per cent., this rate would also apply to the hire of such goods. This Order reduces the tax rate chargeable in respect of the hire of any such goods to 5·26 per cent. The reduction in rate will apply only if the goods in question were in the hands of the person to whom hired on 1 November, 1972, under a written contract which was entered into before the date of this Order.

VALUE-ADDED TAX (REFUND OF TAX) (No. 2) ORDER, 1972.

(SI No. 269 of 1972)

> **This Order revoked by Value Added Tax (Refund of Tax)(Revocation) Order, 1979 (1979 S.I. No. 232) with effect from 1 March 1979.**

I, SEOIRSE Ó COLLA, Minister for Finance, in exercise of the powers conferred on me by section 20(3) of the Value-Added Tax Act, 1972 (No. 22 of 1972), hereby order as follows:

1.   This Order may be cited as the Value-Added Tax (Refund of Tax)(No. 2) Order, 1972.

2.   A person who establishes to the satisfaction of the Revenue Commissioners that he has borne or paid tax in relation to the delivery to him of a boat or ship which is designed for use solely or mainly for the purposes of a sea fishing business and who fulfils to the satisfaction of the said Commissioners all the conditions which are specified in paragraph 3 of this Order shall be entitled to be repaid so much of such tax as is specified in paragraph 4 of this Order.

3.   The conditions to be fulfilled by a person referred to in paragraph 2 of this Order are-

    (a)   he shall claim a refund of the tax by completing such claim form as may be provided for the purpose by the Revenue Commissioners and he shall certify the particulars shown on such claim form to be correct;

    (b)   he shall, by the production of sufficient documentary evidence, establish that the outlay in relation to which his claim for a refund of tax arises was incurred in respect of the delivery to him of a ship or boat which was designed for use solely or mainly for the purposes of a sea fishing business;

    (c)   he shall, by the production of an invoice provided in accordance with section 17(12)(a)(i) of the Value-Added Tax Act, 1972, or by the production of a receipt for tax paid on goods imported, establish the amount of tax borne or paid in relation to the outlay referred to in subparagraph (b) of this paragraph;

    (d)   he shall, by the production of a certificate from An Bord Iascaigh Mhara or such other documentary evidence as may be acceptable to the Revenue Commissioners, establish that he received from the said Bord Iascaigh Mhara a grant or loan of money in relation to the outlay referred to in subparagraph (b) of this paragraph; and

    (e)   he shall establish that he is not a person who is registered in the register maintained under section 9 of the Value-Added Tax Act, 1972, nor a person required under the provisions of that section to furnish the particulars specified for registration.

4.   The amount of tax to be repaid to a person referred to in paragraph 2 of this Order shall be so much of the amount of tax established in accordance with paragraph 3(c) of this Order to have been borne or paid as the person shows to the satisfaction of the Revenue Commissioners to be referable solely to outlay referred to in paragraph 3(b) of this Order which relates to the delivery to him of a ship or boat which is designed for use solely or mainly for the purposes of sea fishing and has actually been put to use in a sea fishing business carried on by him.

GIVEN under my Official Seal,
this 24th day of October, 1972.

SEOIRSE Ó COLLA,
Minister for Finance.

EXPLANATORY NOTE.

This Order enables fishermen who are unregistered for value-added tax to be repaid the VAT element in outlay on fishing boats supplied to them. The relief is confined to outlay in respect of which a grant or loan was received from An Bord Iascaigh Mhara.

VALUE-ADDED TAX (REDUCTION OF RATE) (NO 2) ORDER, 1972

(SI No. 326 of 1972)

This Order revoked by s80(f), FA73 with effect from 3 September 1973.

I, SEOIRSE Ó COLLA, Minister for Finance, in exercise of the powers conferred on me by section 11(8) of the Value-Added Tax Act, 1972 (No. 22 of 1972), hereby order as follows:

1.　(1)　This Order may be cited as the Value-Added Tax (Reduction of Rate) (No.2) Order, 1972.

　　(2)　This Order shall come into operation on the 1st day of January, 1973.

2.　The rate of tax chargeable on the delivery or importation of goods specified in the Schedule to this Order is hereby reduced from 16·37 per cent. to 5·26 per cent.

SCHEDULE.

(a)　Textile handkerchiefs.

(b)　Goods of different kinds which are packaged for sale as a unit (hereinafter referred to as the package) and in relation to which all the following conditions are satisfied-

　　(i)　the package consists of goods in relation to the delivery of some of which for a separate consideration tax would be chargeable at the rate of 16·37 per cent. and in relation to the delivery of the remainder of which for such a consideration tax would be chargeable at the rate of 5·26 per cent.,

　　(ii)　the consideration for delivery is referable to the package as a whole and not separately to the different kinds of goods included therein, and

　　(iii)　the total tax-exclusive value of the goods included in the package in relation to the delivery of which for a separate consideration tax would be chargeable at the rate of 16·37 per cent., does not exceed 50 per cent. of the tax-exclusive consideration for the package or 2½ new pence, whichever is the lesser.

GIVEN under my Official Seal,
this 21st day of December, 1972.

SEOIRSE Ó COLLA,
Minister for Finance.

EXPLANATORY NOTE.

This Order, which comes into effect on January 1, 1973, reduces the rate of tax chargeable on textile handkerchiefs from 16·37 per cent. to 5·26 per cent.

The Order also provides that if goods of different kinds some of which are chargeable at the 16.37 per cent. rate and some at the 5·26 per cent. rate are sold as a unit for a single consideration, the lower rate (5·26 per cent.) will apply to the whole consideration for the unit provided the value of the goods chargeable at the 16·37 per cent. rate and included in the unit does not exceed 50 per cent. of the total consideration for the unit or 2½p, whichever is the lesser.

Examples of the goods to which this will apply are breakfast cereal packets and children's lucky bags containing inexpensive toys which, if sold separately, would be liable to the rate of 16·37%.

VALUE-ADDED TAX (REFUND OF TAX) (NO 3) ORDER, 1972

(SI No. 327 of 1972)

This Order revoked by Value Added Tax (Refund of Tax)(No.12) Order, 1980
(1980 S.I. No. 263) with effect from 1 March 1979.

I, SEOIRSE Ó COLLA, Minister for Finance, in exercise of the powers conferred on me by section 20(3) of the Value-Added Tax Act, 1972 (No. 22 of 1972), hereby order as follows:

1. (1)   This Order may be cited as the Value-Added Tax (Refund of Tax) (No. 3) Order, 1972.

    (2)   This Order shall be deemed to have come into operation on the 1st day of November, 1972.

2. (1)   In this Order "the Act" means the Value-Added Tax Act, 1972.

    (2)   A reference in this Order to a caravan includes a reference to a mobile home or any similar structure designed primarily for residential purposes.

3. A person who establishes to the satisfaction of the Revenue Commissioners that he has borne or paid tax in relation to the delivery to or importation by him of a caravan and who fulfills to the satisfaction of the said Commissioners the conditions which are specified in paragraph 4 of this Order shall be entitled to be repaid so much of such tax as is specified in paragraph 5 of this Order.

4. The conditions to be fulfilled by a person referred to in paragraph 3 of this Order are-

    (a)   he shall claim a refund of the tax by completing such claim form as may be provided for the purpose by the Revenue Commissioners and he shall certify the particulars shown in such claim form to be correct;

    (b)   he shall establish that the caravan in relation to which a claim for a refund of tax arises-

        (i)   is used by him as a permanent residence for himself and that neither he nor his spouse, if he is a married man having his spouse living with him, has any other place of abode within the State available for his occupation, or

        (ii)   is, in the case of a local authority, occupied as a residence by a tenant of the local authority;

    (c)   he shall, in the case of a person other than a local authority, by the production of a certificate from the appropriate local authority or such other documentary evidence as may be acceptable to the Revenue Commissioners, establish that the caravan has been rated under the Valuation Acts;

(d)   he shall, by the production of invoices, provided in accordance with section 17(12)(a)(i) of the Act, or by the production of receipts for tax paid on imported goods, establish the amount of tax borne or paid by him in relation to the caravan excluding any amount referable to articles of furniture or equipment which would not be regarded as fixtures if the caravan were regarded as immovable goods at the time of its delivery or importation;

(e)   he shall establish the net tax-exclusive amount of the consideration for the delivery to him of the caravan, or, if the caravan was imported by him, its net tax-exclusive value, exclusive, in either case, of the amount, if any, included in such consideration or value for the delivery or importation of such articles as are referred to in sub-paragraph (d) of this paragraph;

(f)   he shall establish that he is not entitled to a deduction under section 12 of the Act for any portion of the tax specified in subparagraph (d) of this paragraph.

5.   The amount of tax to be repaid to a person referred to in paragraph 3 of this Order shall be so much of the amount of tax specified in paragraph 4 (d) of this Order as the person shows to the satisfaction of the Revenue Commissioners to be in excess of an amount calculated at the rate of 5·26% of 60% of the net tax-exclusive amount of consideration specified in paragraph 4 (e) of this Order or of the net tax-exclusive value so specified.

GIVEN under my Official Seal,
this 21st day of December, 1972.

SEOIRSE Ó COLLA,
Minister for Finance.

EXPLANATORY NOTE.

This Order enables repayment to be made, subject to certain conditions, of portion of the value-added tax paid in relation to a caravan, a mobile home or similar structure, which has been purchased by a person as a residence or, in the case of a local authority, provided for letting as a residence. The refund will have the effect of adjusting the rate of tax to the same effective rate (3·16%) as applies to the construction of permanent buildings.

In the case of a claimant other than a local authority, the title to repayment is conditional on the caravan or mobile home being rated.

VALUE-ADDED TAX (REFUND OF TAX) (NO 4) ORDER, 1972

(SI No. 328 of 1972)

> **This Order revoked by Value Added Tax (Refund of Tax)(No.13) Order, 1980
> (1980 S.I. No. 263) w.e.f. 14 August 1980.**

I, SEOIRSE Ó COLLA, Minister for Finance, in exercise of the powers conferred on me by section 20(3) of the Value-Added Tax Act, 1972 (No. 22 of 1972), hereby order as follows:

1.   (1)   This Order may be cited as the Value-Added Tax (Refund of Tax) (No. 4) order, 1972.

    (2)   This Order shall be deemed to have come into operation on the 1st day of November, 1972.

2.   In this Order "the Act" means the Value-Added Tax Act, 1972.

3.   A person (in this Order referred to as the claimant) who establishes to the satisfaction of the Revenue Commissioners that he has borne or paid tax in relation to the delivery to or importation by him of a new road motor vehicle which has been specially constructed or adapted (whether before or after the date of such delivery or importation) for the use of a disabled person as driver and who fulfils to the satisfaction of the Revenue Commissioners the conditions which are specified in paragraph 4 of this Order shall be entitled to be repaid so much of such tax, together with so much of the tax, if any, borne by him in relation to the adaptation of the motor vehicle for the use specified in this paragraph, as is specified in paragraph 5 of this Order.

4.   The conditions to be fulfilled by a person referred to in paragraph 3 of this Order are-

    (a)   he shall claim a refund of the tax by completing such claim form as may be provided for the purpose by the Revenue Commissioners and he shall certify the particulars shown on such claim form to be correct;

    (b)   he shall, by the production of a certificate from the licensing authority (within the meaning of the Road Vehicles (Registration and Licensing) Order, 1958 (SI No. 15 of 1958)) for the area where the vehicle is registered or other sufficient documentary evidence, establish that by virtue of section 43 of the Finance Act, 1968 (No. 33 of 1968), the duty imposed by section I of the Finance (Excise Duties) (Vehicles) Act, 1952 (No. 24 of 1952), is not charged or levied in respect of the vehicle to which the claim relates;

    (c)   he shall, by the production of invoices, provided in accordance with section 17(12)(a)(i) of the Act, or by the production of receipts for the tax paid on importation of the vehicle, establish-

        (i)   if the vehicle is of a kind specified in paragraph (i) of the Fourth Schedule to the Act-

(I)   the amount of tax which was chargeable at the rate of 30.26 per cent. in relation to the importation or delivery of the vehicle, or, if tax were chargeable at that rate in relation to more deliveries than one of the vehicle, the amount chargeable at that rate on the later or latest such delivery, and

(II)   in a case in which the person who delivered the vehicle to the claimant was not a manufacturer of vehicles of the type delivered, the amount of tax chargeable to such person in respect of such delivery,

(ii)   if the vehicle is not of a kind specified in the said paragraph (i), the amount of tax borne or paid by him in relation to the vehicle, and

(iii)   the amount of tax (if any) chargeable to the person who adapted the vehicle for the use specified in paragraph 3 of this Order in respect of such adaptation;

(d)   he shall establish that he is not entitled to a deduction under section 12 of the Act in respect of any portion of the tax specified in subparagraph (c) of this paragraph.

5.   The amount of tax to be refunded to the claimant shall be the amount (if any) specified in paragraph 4(c)(iii) of this Order together with-

(a)   if the vehicle is of a kind specified in paragraph (i) of the Fourth Schedule to the Act,

(i)   in case the vehicle was imported by the claimant or was delivered to him by a manufacturer of vehicles of the type so delivered, the amount specified in paragraph 4(c)(i)(I) of this Order,

(ii)   in any other case, an amount equal to the aggregate of the product of the amount specified in paragraph 4(c)(i)(1) of this Order and the fraction of which 25 is the numerator and 30·26 is the denominator and the amount specified in paragraph 4(c)(i)(II) of this Order,

(b)   if the vehicle is not of a kind specified in the said paragraph (i), the amount specified in paragraph 4(c)(ii) of this Order.

GIVEN under my Official Seal,
this 21st day of December, 1972.

SEOIRSE Ó COLLA,
Minister for Finance.

EXPLANATORY NOTE.

This Order enables a disabled person to obtain a repayment of the full amount of value-added tax charged in respect of a new motor vehicle which has been specially constructed or adapted for his use. Tax, if any, borne in relation to the adaptation will also be repaid. Repayment is dependent on the person having obtained a remission of the motor vehicle licence duty under section 43 of the Finance Act, 1968, in respect of the vehicle.

PRICES AND CHARGES (TAX-INCLUSIVE STATEMENTS) ORDER, 1973

(SI No. 9 of 1973)

I, PATRICK J. LALOR, Minister for Industry and Commerce, in exercise of the powers conferred on me by section 19(2)(a) of the Prices Act, 1958 (No. 4 of 1958), as amended by the Prices (Amendment) Act, 1972 (No. 20 of 1972), hereby order as follows:

1.　　This Order may be cited as the Prices and Charges (Tax-inclusive Statements) Order, 1973.

2.　　This Order shall come into operation on the 1st day of February, 1973.

3.　　Where, for the purposes of or in connection with the sale by retail by a person of a commodity, the retail price of the commodity is stated orally by the person or by a servant or agent of the person or is stated on the commodity or on any container or wrapper in which the commodity is packed or on a ticket or label attached to the commodity or to such container or wrapper or in a catalogue or advertisement or in a notice or other document (other than an invoice), the price so stated shall be stated as a single amount inclusive of any charge made by the person for any tax payable in respect of the commodity.

4.　　Where, for the purposes of or in connection with the rendering of a service by a person, the charge for the service is stated orally by the person or by a servant or agent of the person or is stated in any catalogue or advertisement or in a notice or other document (other than an invoice), the charge so stated shall be stated as a single amount inclusive of any charge made by the person for any tax payable in respect of the service.

GIVEN under my Official Seal,
this 15th day of January, 1973.

PATRICK J. LALOR,
Minister for Industry and Commerce.

EXPLANATORY NOTE.

This Order requires that all retail prices marked on goods or prices displayed or quoted at the retail level and all charges for services displayed or quoted should be tax-inclusive.

VALUE-ADDED TAX (REDUCTION OF RATE) (NO 3) ORDER, 1973

(SI No. 69 of 1973)

This Order revoked by s80(f), FA73 with effect from 3 September 1973.

I, RICHIE RYAN, Minister for Finance, in exercise of the powers conferred on me by section 11(8) of the Value-Added Tax Act, 1972 (No. 22 of 1972), hereby order as follows:

1.   (1)   This Order may be cited as the Value-Added Tax (Reduction of Rate) (No.3) Order, 1973.

(2)   This Order shall be deemed to have come into operation on the 1st day of November, 1972.

2.   The rate of tax chargeable in relation to the rendering of services of the kind specified in the Schedule to this Order is hereby reduced from 16·37 per cent. or from 5·26 per cent., as the case may be, to zero per cent.

SCHEDULE.

Life saving services provided by the Royal National Lifeboat Institution including the organisation and maintenance of the lifeboat service.

GIVEN under my Official Seal,
this 22nd day of March, 1973.

RICHIE RYAN,
Minister for Finance.

EXPLANATORY NOTE.

This Order applies the zero rate to the lifeboat and allied life-saving services carried on by the Royal National Lifeboat Institution.

The Order has effect from 1st November last.

VALUE-ADDED TAX (REFUND OF TAX) (NO 5) ORDER, 1973

(SI No. 70 of 1973)

This Order revoked by Value Added Tax (Refund of Tax)(No.14) Order, 1980
(1980 S.I. No. 264) with effect from 1 March 1979.

I, RICHIE RYAN, Minister for Finance, in exercise of the powers conferred on me by section 20(3) of the Value-Added Tax Act, 1972 (No. 22 of 1972), hereby order as follows:

1.   (1)   This Order may be cited as the Value-Added Tax (Refund of Tax) (No. 5) Order, 1973.

      (2)   This Order shall be deemed to have come into operation on the 1st day of November, 1972.

2.   In this Order "the Act" means the Value-Added Tax Act, 1972.

3.   This Order applies to the following persons:

      (a)   a body of persons in its capacity as a person operating a hospital

      (b)   a university, college, school or similar educational body in its capacity as a person operating a medical research laboratory;

      (c)   a research institution in its capacity as a person operating a medical research laboratory.

4.   A person to whom this Order applies who establishes to the satisfaction of the Revenue Commissioners that he has borne or paid tax at a rate in excess of 5.26 per cent. in relation to the delivery to or importation by him of any instrument or appliance of a kind commonly used to make a diagnosis, to prevent or treat an illness, to carry out a surgical operation or to carry out scientific research and who fulfils to the satisfaction of the Revenue Commissioners the conditions which are specified in paragraph 5 of this Order shall be entitled to be repaid as much of such tax as is specified in paragraph 6 of this Order.

5.   The conditions to be fulfilled by a person referred to in paragraph 4 of this Order are-

      (a)   he shall claim a refund of the tax by completing such claim form as may be provided for the purpose by the Revenue Commissioners and he shall certify the particulars shown on such form to be correct;

      (b)   he shall establish that he is a person to whom this Order applies and that the instruments or appliances on the delivery or importation of which the tax was borne or paid by him were used by him in the capacity in relation to which this Order applies to him;

      (c)   he shall establish, by the production of invoices, provided in accordance with section 17(12)(a)(i) of the Act, or by the production of receipts for tax paid on imported goods, the amount of tax borne or paid by him in relation to the goods specified in paragraph 4 of this Order;

(d)   he shall establish that he is not entitled to a deduction under section 12 of the Act for any portion of the tax specified in subparagraph (c) of this paragraph.

6.   The amount of tax to be repaid to the claimant shall be so much of the amount of tax specified in paragraph 5(c) of this Order as the person shows to the satisfaction of the Revenue Commissioners to be in excess of-

(a)   5.26 per cent. of the tax-exclusive consideration for the goods to which the amount of tax specified in paragraph 5(c) of this Order applies and which were delivered to him within the State, and

(b)   5.26 per cent. of the tax-exclusive value of any such goods which were imported by him.

GIVEN under my Official Seal,
this 22nd day of March, 1973.

RICHIE RYAN,
Minister for Finance.

EXPLANATORY NOTE.

Under the Value-Added Tax Act, 1972, the 5.26% rate of VAT applies to medical, etc. appliances used solely in professional practice.

Since it is desirable that hospitals and universities, colleges and research institutions operating laboratories for medical, dental, surgical and veterinary research should not have to bear the higher rate of tax on medical and laboratory appliances and instruments, even where they are not of a kind used solely in professional practice but are commonly used by them, this Order provides, in such cases, for the refund of the VAT chargeable in excess of 5.26%.

The Order has effect from 1 November last.

VALUE-ADDED TAX (REFUND OF TAX) (NO 6) ORDER, 1973

(SI No. 238 of 1973)

I, RICHIE RYAN, Minister for Finance, in exercise of the powers conferred on me by section 20(3) of the Value-Added Tax Act, 1972 (No. 22 of 1972), hereby order as follows:

1.   (1)   This Order may be cited as the Value-Added Tax (Refund of Tax) (No 6) Order 1973.

        (2)   This Order shall come into operation on the 3rd day of September, 1973.

2.   The Value-Added Tax (Refund of Tax) (No. 3) Order, 1972 (S.I. No. 327 of 1972), is hereby amended by the substitution for paragraph 5 of the following paragraph:"5.The amount of tax to be repaid to a person referred to in paragraph 3 of this Order shall be so much of the amount of tax specified in paragraph 4 (d) of this Order as the person shows to the satisfaction of the Revenue Commissioners to be in excess of an amount calculated-

        (a)   in case the caravan was delivered to or imported by him before the 3rd day of September, 1973, at the rate of 5·26 per cent. of 60 per cent. of the net tax-exclusive amount of consideration specified in paragraph 4(e) of this Order or of the net tax-exclusive value so specified, and

        (b)   in any other case, at the rate of 6·75 per cent. of 45 per cent. of the net tax-exclusive amount of consideration specified in the said paragraph 4 (e) or of the net tax-exclusive value so specified".

3.   The Value-Added Tax (Refund of Tax) (No. 4) Order, 1972 (S.I. No. 328 of 1972), is hereby amended-

        (a)   by the substitution in paragraph 4(c)(i)(I) for "of 30·26 per cent." of "specified for the time being in section 11(1)(c) of the Act" and, accordingly, the said paragraph 4(c)(i)(I) shall have effect as set out in the Table to this paragraph:

TABLE

        (I)   the amount of tax which was chargeable at the rate specified for the time being in section 11(1)(c) of the Act in relation to the importation or delivery of the vehicle, or, if tax were chargeable at that rate in relation to more deliveries than one of the vehicle, the amount chargeable at that rate on the later or latest such delivery, and

        (b)   by the substitution for clause (ii) of paragraph 5(a) of the following clause-

        "(ii)   in any other case, an amount equal to the aggregate of-

             (I)   the product of the amount specified in paragraph 4(c)(i)(I) of this Order and the fraction of which the numerator is the rate specified in section 11(1)(c) of the Act at which tax was charged in calculating the amount so specified, reduced by the rate specified in section 11(1)(a) of the Act at the time tax at the rate specified in the said section 11(1)(c) was so charged, and the denominator is the rate specified in the said section 11(1)(c) at which tax was so charged, and

(II)   the amount specified in paragraph 4(c)(i)(II) of this Order,".

4.   The Value-Added Tax (Refund of Tax) (No. 5) Order, 1973 (S.I. No. 70 of 1973), is hereby amended-

(a)   by the substitution in paragraph 4 for "5·26 per cent." of "the rate specified for the time being in section 11(1)(a) of the Act" and, accordingly, the said paragraph 4 shall have effect as set out in the Table to this paragraph:

TABLE

4.   A person to whom this Order applies who establishes to the satisfaction of the Revenue Commissioners that he has borne or paid tax at a rate in excess of the rate specified for the time being in section 11(1)(a) of the Act in relation to the delivery to or importation by him of any instrument or appliance of a kind commonly used to make a diagnosis, to prevent or treat an illness, to carry out a surgical operation or to carry out scientific research and who fulfils to the satisfaction of the Revenue Commissioners the conditions which are specified in paragraph 5 of this Order shall be entitled to be repaid so much of such tax as is specified in paragraph 6 of this Order.

and

(b)   by the substitution of the following paragraph for paragraph 6:

"6.   The amount of tax to be repaid to the claimant shall be so much of the amount of tax specified in paragraph 5(c) of this Order as the person shows to the satisfaction of the Revenue Commissioners to be in excess of-

(a)   in case the goods to which the tax specified in paragraph 5(c) relates were delivered to him within the State, an amount equal to the percentage specified in section 11(1)(a) of the Act at the time the goods were so delivered to him of the tax-exclusive consideration for the delivery of goods, and

(b)   in case the goods were imported by him, an amount equal to the percentage specified in the said section 11(1)(a) at the time the goods were so imported of the value (within the meaning of section 15(4)(a) of the Act) of the goods."

GIVEN under my Official Seal,
this 17th day of August, 1973.

RICHIE RYAN,
Minister for Finance.

EXPLANATORY NOTE.

This Order makes consequential amendments in existing Orders under section 20(3) of the Value-Added Tax Act, 1972, arising out of the changes in the rates of value-added tax made by the Finance Act, 1973.

VALUE-ADDED TAX (REFUND OF TAX) (NO 7) ORDER, 1974

(SI No. 290 of 1974)

I, RICHIE RYAN, Minister for Finance, in exercise of the powers conferred on me by section 20(3) of the Value-Added Tax Act, 1972 (No. 22 of 1972), hereby order asfollows :-

1.   This Order may be cited as the Value-Added Tax (Refund of Tax)(No. 7) Order, 1974.

2.   This Order shall be deemed to have come into operation on the 1st day of November, 1972.

3.   In this Order "the Organisation" means the European Organisation for the Safety of Air Navigation (Eurocontrol) established by the International Convention relating to Cooperation for the Safety of Air Navigation signed at Brussels on the 13th day of December, 1960, and references to the Organisation include references to the Permanent Commission for the Safety of Air Navigation comprised in the Organisation and to the Air Traffic Services Agency comprised in the Organisation.

4.   Where the Organisation establishes to the satisfaction of the Revenue Commissioners that, in connection with its official activities it has borne tax on the delivery to it of goods or on the rendering to it of services, and those goods or services are of substantial value, and fulfils to the satisfaction of the said Commissioners all the conditions which are specified in paragraph 5 of this Order it shall be entitled to be repaid the tax so established as having been borne or paid.

5.   (a)   The Organisation shall claim a refund of the tax by completing such claim form as may be provided for the purpose by the Revenue Commissioners and it shall certify the particulars shown on such claim form to be correct.

      (b)   The Organisation shall, by the production of an invoice provided in accordance with section 17(12)(a)(i) of the Value-Added Tax Act, 1972, establish the amount of tax borne in relation to such delivery or rendering.

GIVEN under my Official Seal,
this 26th day of September, 1974.

RICHIE RYAN,
Minister for Finance.

EXPLANATORY NOTE.

This Order enables repayment to be made, subject to certain conditions, of value-added tax paid on purchases of goods and services by the European Organisation for the Safety of Air Navigation (Eurocontrol).

VALUE-ADDED TAX (REFUND OF TAX) (NO 8) ORDER, 1978

(SI No. 145 of 1978)

> This Order revoked by para9, Value Added Tax (Refund of Tax)(No.25) Order, 1993 (1993 S.I. No. 266) w.e.f. 15 September 1993.

I, SEOIRSE Ó COLLA, Minister for Finance, in exercise of the powers conferred on me by section 20(3) of the Value-Added Tax Act, 1972 (No. 22 of 1972), hereby order as follows:

1. (1) This Order may be cited as the Value-Added Tax (Refund of Tax) (No. 8) Order, 1978.

    (2) This Order shall be deemed to have come into operation on the 1st day of November, 1972.

2. The Value-Added Tax (Refund of Tax)(No.1) Order 1972 (SI No.267 of 1972), is hereby amended by the substitution of the following subparagraph for subparagraph (d) of paragraph 4:

    "(d) he shall, by the production of a certificate from the Department of Agriculture, Roinn na Gaeltachta or the Irish Land Commission, as may be appropriate, or such other documentary evidence as may be acceptable to the Revenue Commissioners, establish that, in relation to outlay on any of the matters specified in clauses (i) and (ii) of subparagraph (b) of this paragraph, he was paid a grant by the Department of Agriculture, Roinn na Gaeltachta or the Irish Land Commission;".

GIVEN under my Official Seal,
this 22nd day of May, 1978.

SEOIRSE Ó COLLA,
Minister for Finance.

EXPLANATORY NOTE.

This Order amends the existing Order so as to enable refunds to be made to unregistered farmers of the VAT element in outlay by them on farm buildings and land drainage or land reclamation in respect of which grants were paid by the Department of Agriculture, Roinn na Gaeltachta or by the Irish Land Commission. The Order is effective from 1st November, 1972.

VALUE-ADDED TAX (REDUCTION OF RATE) (NO 4) ORDER, 1978

(SI No. 146 of 1978)

I, SEOIRSE Ó COLLA, Minister for Finance, in exercise of the powers conferred on me by section 11(8) of the Value-Added Tax Act, 1972 (No.22 of 1972), hereby order as follows:

1.   (1)   This Order may be cited as the Value-Added Tax (Reduction of Rate) (No.4) Order, 1978.

      (2)   This Order shall come into operation on the 1st day of July, 1978.

2.   The Second Schedule (inserted by the Finance Act, 1976 (No.16 of 1976)) to the Value-Added Tax Act, 1972, shall be varied by the insertion in paragraph (xx) after subparagraph (c) of the following subparagraph:

"(cc)   wax candles and night-lights which are white and cylindrical, excluding candles and night-lights which are decorated, spiralled, tapered or perfumed,".

GIVEN under my Official Seal,
this 26th day of May, 1978.

SEOIRSE Ó COLLA,
Minister for Finance.

EXPLANATORY NOTE.

This Order, which will come into effect on 1 July, 1978, makes a marginal adjustment to the VAT zero-ratings (which already apply to electricity, gas etc.) by applying the zero rate to plain white wax candles and night-lights.

VALUE-ADDED TAX (AMENDMENT) ACT, 1978 (COMMENCEMENT) ORDER, 1979

(SI No. 8 of 1979)

I, SEOIRSE Ó COLLA, Minister for Finance, in exercise of the powers conferred on me by section 32(3) of the Value-Added Tax (Amendment) Act, 1978 (No. 34 of 1978), hereby order as follows:

1. This Order may be cited as the Value-Added Tax (Amendment) Act, 1978 (Commencement) Order, 1979.

2. The 1st day of March, 1979, is hereby appointed as the day on which sections 1 to 28 and 30 to 32 of the Value-Added Tax (Amendment) Act, 1978, shall come into operation.

GIVEN under my Official Seal,
this 17th day of January, 1979.

SEOIRSE Ó COLLA,
Minister for Finance.

EXPLANATORY NOTE.

This Order brings the Value-Added Tax (Amendment) Act, 1978 into operation on 1 March, 1979.

VALUE-ADDED TAX (REFUND OF TAX) (NO 9) ORDER, 1979

(SI No. 59 of 1979)

I, SEOIRSE Ó COLLA, Minister for Finance, in exercise of the powers conferred on me by section 20(3) of the Value-Added Tax Act, 1972 (No. 22 of 1972), hereby order as follows:-

1.   This Order may be cited as the Value-Added Tax (Refund of Tax)(No.9) Order, 1979.

2.   This Order shall come into operation on the 1st day of March, 1979.

3.   Where a person, other than a manufacturer of goods of the kind in question, registered in accordance with section 9 of the Value-Added Tax Act, 1972 (No.22 of 1972), establishes to the satisfaction of the Revenue Commissioners that-

    (a)   he holds at the commencement of the 1st day of March, 1979, a stock of radio receiving sets that are of the domestic or portable type or of a type suitable for use in road vehicles; or a stock of gramophones, radiogramophones or record players, for supply in the course of a business carried on by him, and

    (b)   he has purchased or imported the goods in question prior to the 1st day of March, 1979, in such circumstances that tax at the rate specified in section 11(1)(c)(ii) of the said Act was borne or paid on the goods either by him or by a previous purchaser or importer of the goods and that the tax did not qualify for deduction under subsection (1) of section 12 of the Act except to the extent specified in the proviso to that subsection,

    he shall, subject to the conditions specified in Article 4 of this Order, be entitled to be repaid such of the following amounts as are appropriate:

    (i)   in a case where the goods in question were imported by or delivered to the person in such circumstances that tax at the rate specified in section 11(1)(c)(ii) of the said Act was charged on the importation or delivery, an amount equal to 30 per cent of the amount on which tax was so charged, and

    (ii)   in any other case, the amount of tax which the Revenue Commissioners are satisfied has been borne on the acquisition of the goods and which does not qualify for deduction under section 12(1)(a) of the Act.

4.   The conditions referred to in Article 3 of this Order are:

    (a)   the person concerned shall claim a refund of the tax by completing such form as may be provided for the purpose by the Revenue Commissioners showing, if requested, the total number of items of each description of goods, the number of different makes and models within each description, the name of the supplier and the number and date of invoice in relation to each item or group of items and the relative amounts of consideration or value at importation and he shall certify the particulars shown on such claim form to be correct,

(b)   the person concerned shall, if requested by the Revenue Commissioners, by the production of invoices issued in accordance with section 17(1) of the Act or by the production of customs documents, establish to them the amount of the consideration or the value at importation, as the case may be, in relation to which a refund is claimed.

GIVEN under my Official Seal,
this 23rd day of February, 1979.

SEOIRSE Ó COLLA,
Minister for Finance.

EXPLANATORY NOTE.

This Order allows traders in radio receivers and record players (other than manufacturers) to claim a refund of VAT in respect of stocks purchased before 1 March, 1979, and held on that date for resale.

VALUE-ADDED TAX REGULATIONS, 1979

(SI No. 63 of 1979)

> This Regulation was revoked by regulation 44, Value-Added Tax
> Regulations, 2006 (2006 S.I. No. 548) w.e.f. 1 November 2006

VALUE-ADDED TAX REGULATIONS, 1979.

The Revenue Commissioners, in exercise of the powers conferred on them by section 32 of the Value-Added Tax Act, 1972 (No.22 of 1972), and, as respects Regulations 26, 28 and 29, with the consent of the Minister for Finance, hereby make the following regulations:

Short title and commencement.

1.   (1)   These Regulations may be cited as the Value-Added Tax Regulations, 1979.

      (2)   These Regulations shall come into operation on the 1st. day of March, 1979.

Interpretation

2.   (1)   In these Regulations-

"the Act" means the Value-Added Tax Act, 1972;

"taxable turnover", in relation to any period, means the total of the amounts on which tax is chargeable for that period at any of the rates specified in section 11(1) of the Act;

"turnover", in relation to any period, means the amount on which tax would be chargeable for that period in accordance with section 10 of the Act if section 6 of the Act were disregarded.

      (2)   In these Regulations-

        (a)   a reference to a regulation is to a regulation of these Regulations, and

        (b)   a reference to a paragraph, subparagraph or clause is to a paragraph, subparagraph or clause of the regulation in which the reference occurs,

        unless it is indicated that reference to some other provision is intended.

Election to be a taxable person.

3.   (1)   A person who, in accordance with section 8(3) of the Act is not a taxable person but who desires to elect to be such a person shall furnish to the Revenue Commissioners the particulars for registration specified in Regulation 6.

      (2)   The furnishing of the particulars referred to in paragraph (1) shall constitute an election to be a taxable person and such election shall have effect as from the end of the taxable period during which such particulars are received by the Revenue Commissioners, or, by agreement between the person and the Revenue Commissioners, as from the end of the next preceding taxable period, until the date on which the person permanently ceases to supply taxable goods or services in the course or

furtherance of business or until the date on which his election is cancelled in accordance with paragraph (3), whichever date is the earlier.

(3)   A person who is a taxable person by reason only of an election in that behalf made in accordance with paragraphs (1) and (2) shall be entitled to have such election cancelled and to be treated, as from the date specified in paragraph (4), as a person who had not made such an election provided he fulfils all of the following conditions; and a person who satisfies the Revenue Commissioners in regard to his turnover in accordance with section 8(6)(a) of the Act may be treated as a person who is not a taxable person provided he fulfils similar conditions:

(a)   he shall notify the Revenue Commissioners in writing that he desires to have his election cancelled or that he desires to be treated as a person who is not a taxable person;

(b)   he shall furnish to the Revenue Commissioners particulars of-

(i)   the total amount of tax paid by him in accordance with section 19(3) of the Act in respect of whichever of the following periods is the lesser:

(I)   all the taxable periods comprised in the period commencing with the beginning of the first taxable period for which his election had effect or he was treated as a taxable person and ending with the termination of the taxable period immediately preceding that during which he notifies the Revenue Commissioners that he wishes to have his election cancelled or be treated as a person who is not a taxable person, or

(II)   the eighteen consecutive taxable periods next before the taxable period during which he so notifies the Revenue Commissioners,

and

(ii)   the total amount of tax refunded to him in accordance with section 20(1) of the Act in respect of whichever of the periods referred to in clause (i) is appropriate;

he shall pay to the Collector-General an amount equal to the excess (if any) of the total amount referred to in clause (ii) of the preceding subparagraph over the total amount referred to in clause (i) of that subparagraph.

[(3A) A person who requests the cancellation of an election made by him or her under section 8 of the Act and who supplies services of the kind referred to in paragraph (xiii) of the Sixth Schedule to the Act is required to fulfil the conditions specified in the Value-Added Tax (Cancellation of Election of Registration in respect of Sixth Schedule Accommodation) Regulations, 2000 and, where applicable, the conditions specified in these Regulations, in order to have such election cancelled.][1]

(4) If the conditions specified in the preceding paragraph have been fulfilled to the satisfaction of the Revenue Commissioners, they shall so notify the person concerned in writing and, on receipt by the person of such notice, his election shall be cancelled or he shall be treated as a person who is not a taxable person with effect as on and from the end of the taxable period during which the conditions have been so fulfilled; and as on and from the end of such taxable period, the person shall be treated as a person who had not elected to be a taxable person or as a person who is not a taxable person.

(5) A person who notifies the Revenue Commissioners during any taxable period (in this paragraph referred to as the final taxable period) of his desire to have his election cancelled or to be treated as a person who is not a taxable person shall not be entitled, under section 20(1) of the Act to any refund of tax, other than a refund referable solely to an error or mistake made by him, in excess of whichever of the following amounts is appropriate-

(a) in a case in which there is an excess of the amount referred to in paragraph (3)(b)(i) over the amount referred to in paragraph (3)(b)(ii), an amount for the final taxable period and for any subsequent taxable period consisting of the amount of such excess, increased by the amounts paid under section 19 (3) of the Act, for the final taxable period and any subsequent taxable periods up to and including the taxable period to which the claim relates and reduced by the total of the refunds under section 20(1) of the Act previously made for any of those taxable periods, and

(b) in any other case, an amount for the final taxable period or for any subsequent taxable period consisting of the excess of the total of the amounts paid under section 19(3) of the Act for the final and all subsequent taxable periods up to and including the taxable period to which the claim relates reduced by the total of the refunds under section 20(1) of the Act previously made for any of those taxable periods.

(6) In the case of a person who, in the absence of an election to be a taxable person, would (in accordance with section 8(3)(a) of the Act) not be such a person, paragraph (3)(b) shall apply as if-

(i)   the amount of tax paid by him in accordance with section 19(3) of the Act in respect of each of the taxable periods comprised in whichever of the periods referred to in clause (i) is appropriate were increased by an amount equal to 1 per cent. of the consideration on which tax was chargeable for each of those taxable periods in respect of transactions specified in section 8(9) of the Act other than in paragraph (d) of the definition of farmer, and

(ii)   the total amount of tax refunded to him in respect of all the taxable periods comprised in the period referred to in clause (ii) were reduced by the total amount of tax which qualified for deduction under section 12 of the Act in respect of those taxable periods and which, in accordance with any order made under section 20(3) of the Act would fall to be refunded to him if he were not a taxable person.

Waiver of exemption.

4.   [...]²

Treatment of two or more taxable persons as a single taxable person.

5.   (1)   If two or more taxable persons desire that all the business activities carried on by each of them shall, in accordance with section 8(8) of the Act be deemed, for the purposes of the Act to be carried on by any one of those persons, each of them shall furnish the following particulars in writing to the Revenue Commissioners:-

(a)   his name, address and registration number;

(b)   the nature of the business activities carried on by him;

(c)   in case the person desires that all the business activities carried on by him should be deemed to be carried on by another person, the name, address and registration number of that other person;

(d)   in case the person desires that all the business activities carried on by another person or two or more other persons should be deemed to be carried on by the first-mentioned person, the name, address and registration number of that other person or of each of those other persons; and

(e)   such other information about the business activities of the person or about the business or financial relationship between him and each of the other persons carrying on the business activities aforesaid as the Revenue Commissioners may, by notice in writing, require.

(2)   The Revenue Commissioners shall, in their absolute discretion, determine-

(a)   whether all the business activities carried on by two or more persons who have furnished the particulars specified in paragraph (1) shall be deemed to be carried on by any one of those persons;

(b)   in case all the business activities referred to in subparagraph (a) are deemed to be carried on by any one of the persons referred to in the said subparagraph (a):-

(i)   the person by whom the said activities are deemed to be carried on;

(ii)   the person or each of the persons all of whose business activities are deemed to be carried on by the person referred to in clause (i);

(c)   the date, not being earlier than the commencement of the taxable period during which the particulars referred to in paragraph (1) are furnished, as from which all of the business activities of the person or persons concerned are deemed to be carried on by one of them, and shall notify each of the persons concerned in writing of the matters so determined.

(3)   Upon the issue of a notification to a person in accordance with paragraph (2) of a determination that all the business activities referred to in the determination are deemed to be carried on by one person, the following provisions shall apply from the date specified in the notification pursuant to paragraph (2)(c) until the notification is cancelled in accordance with paragraph (5):

(a)   in case the person to whom the notification is issued is the person by whom all the business activities referred to in the notification are deemed to be carried on, the provisions of the Act shall, subject to paragraph (4), apply to the person as if all transactions by or between himself and the other person or persons carrying on the said business activities were transactions by himself, and all other rights and obligations under the Act shall be determined accordingly,

(b)   in case the person to whom the notification is issued is not the person by whom all the business activities referred to in the notification are deemed to be carried on, the provisions of the Act shall, subject to paragraph (4), apply to him as if all transactions by or between himself and the person by whom the said business activities are deemed to be carried on (in this subparagraph referred to as the last-mentioned person) were transactions by the last-mentioned person, but the person shall be jointly liable with the last-mentioned person and any other person specified in the notification to comply with all the provisions of the Act and regulations (including the provisions requiring payment of tax) that apply to him and the last-mentioned person and any other person so specified and shall be subject to the penalties under the Act to which he and the last-mentioned person and any other person so specified would be liable if they were liable to pay to the Revenue Commissioners the whole of the tax chargeable, apart from this Regulation, in respect of himself and the last-mentioned person and any other person so specified.

(4)   Notwithstanding anything in paragraph (3), each of the persons all of whose business activities are during any period deemed, in accordance with this Regulation, to be carried on by one of them shall be deemed to be a registered person during the whole of that period, and the provisions of section 17 of the Act shall apply to each of those persons as if a notification under paragraph (3) had not been issued.

(5)   The Revenue Commissioners may, in their absolute discretion, by notice in writing addressed to each of a group of persons all of whose business activities are, by virtue of a notification issued in accordance with paragraph (2), deemed to be carried on by one of those persons, and as on and from the date specified in the notice (which shall not be earlier than the date of the notice) cancel the notification under the said paragraph (2); and as on and from the date specified in the said notice the provisions of the Act and Regulations shall apply to all the persons aforesaid as if a notification under the said paragraph (2) had not been issued, but without prejudice to the liability of any of the persons for tax or penalties in respect of anything done or not done during the period for which the said notification was in force.

Registration.

6.   [...]³

Determination of tax due by reference to cash receipts.

7.   [...]⁴

Adjustments for returned goods, discounts, and price alterations.

8.   (1)   Where, in a case in which section 10(3)(c) of the Act applies and section 17(9) of the Act does not apply, by reason of the return of goods, the allowance of discount, a reduction in price or the default of a debtor, the consideration exclusive of tax actually received by a taxable person in respect of the supply by him of any goods or services is less than the amount on which tax has

become chargeable in respect of such supply, or no consideration is actually received, the following provisions shall apply:

(a)   the amount of the deficiency in respect of any supply shall be ascertained by deducting from the amount of consideration actually chargeable with tax, the amount exclusive of tax, or where a percentage only of the consideration is actually chargeable with tax, a corresponding percentage of the amount actually received, in respect of such supply,

(b)   the sum of the deficiencies, ascertained in accordance with subparagraph (a), incurred in each taxable period and relating to consideration chargeable at each of the various rates of tax (including the zero rate) specified in section 11(1) of the Act shall be deducted from the amounts ascertained in accordance with section 10 of the Act which would otherwise be chargeable with tax at each of those rates and the net amounts as so ascertained shall be the amounts on which tax is chargeable for the taxable period:

Provided that if the sum of the deficiencies as ascertained in accordance with subparagraph (b) in relation to tax chargeable at any of the rates so specified exceeds the amount on which but for this Regulation tax would be chargeable at that rate, or no tax is chargeable at that rate, the tax appropriate to the excess or to the sum of the deficiencies, if no tax is chargeable, shall be treated as tax deductible in accordance with section 12 of the Act,

(c)   the taxable person to whom a credit note is, in accordance with section 17 of the Act, issued by another taxable person in respect of an adjustment under this Regulation shall reduce the amount which would otherwise be deductible under section 12 of the Act for the taxable period during which the credit note is issued (in this Regulation referred to as the tax deduction) by the amount of tax shown thereon or by the amount of tax appropriate to the amount of the reduction of consideration shown thereon whichever is the greater (in this subparagraph referred to as the appropriate tax reduction) and if the appropriate tax reduction exceeds the tax deduction the excess shall be carried forward and deducted from the tax deduction for the next taxable period and so on until the appropriate tax reduction is exhausted.

(2)   Where, in accordance with section 17(4)(b) of the Act a farmer credit note is issued by a flat-rate farmer, the taxable person to whom the credit note is issued shall reduce the amount which would otherwise be deductible under section 12(1)(f) of the Act

for the taxable period during which the farmer credit note is issued (in this Regulation referred to as the flat-rate deduction) by the amount of the flat-rate addition shown thereon (in this subparagraph referred to as the appropriate flat-rate reduction) and, if the appropriate flat-rate reduction exceeds the flat-rate deduction, the excess shall be carried forward and deducted from the flat-rate deduction for the next taxable period and so on until the appropriate flat-rate reduction is exhausted.

Accounts.

9.　(1)　Every taxable person shall keep full and true accounts entered up to date of-

(a)　in relation to consideration receivable from registered persons, the amount receivable from each such person in respect of each transaction for which an invoice is required to be issued under section 17 of the Act together with a cross-reference to the copy of the relevant invoice,

(b)　in relation to consideration receivable from unregistered persons, a daily total of the consideration receivable from all such persons together with a cross-reference to the relevant counter books, copies of sales dockets, cash register tally rolls or other documents which are in use for the purposes of the business,

(c)　in relation to importations, a description of the goods imported together with particulars of the value thereof as determined in accordance with section 15 of the Act, the amount of the consideration relating to the purchase of the goods if purchased in connection with the importation, the amount of tax, if any, paid on importation and a cross-reference to the invoices and customs documents used in connection with the importation,

(d)　in relation to goods, being goods developed, constructed, assembled, manufactured, produced, extracted, purchased or imported by the taxable person or by another person on his behalf and applied by him (otherwise than by way of disposal to another person) for the purposes of any business carried on by him, a description of the goods in question and the cost excluding tax, to the taxable person of acquiring or producing them except where tax chargeable in relation to the application of the goods would, if it were charged, be wholly deductible under section 12 of the Act,

(e)　in relation to goods, being goods which were appropriated by a taxable person for any purpose other than the purpose of his business or disposed of free of charge, where tax chargeable in relation to the goods, upon their acquisition by the taxable person, if they had been so acquired, or upon their development, construction, assembly, manufacture, production, extraction, importation or application in accordance with paragraph (d), as the case may be, was wholly or partly deductible under section 12 of the Act, a description of the goods in question and the cost, excluding tax, to the taxable person, of acquiring or producing them,

(f)   in relation to services regarded in accordance with section 5(3) of the Act as supplied by a person in the course or furtherance of business, a description of the services in question together with particulars of the cost, excluding tax, to the taxable person of supplying the services and of the consideration, if any, receivable by him in respect of the supply,

(g)   in relation to services referred to in section 5(6)(e)(ii) of the Act in respect of which a person is liable to pay tax in accordance with section 8(2) of the Act, a description of the services in question together with particulars of the cost to the person of acquiring the service,

(h)   in the case of services deemed, in accordance with clause (i) or (ii) of subparagraph 5(6)(e) of the Act to be supplied at places outside the State, the name and address of the person to whom the service is supplied, the nature of the service and the amount of the consideration receivable in respect of the supply,

(i)   in relation to discounts allowed or price reductions made to a registered person subsequent to the issue of an invoice to such person, the amount credited to such person and, except in a case in which section 17(9)(a) of the Act applies, a cross-reference to the corresponding credit note,

(j)   in relation to discounts allowed or price reductions made to unregistered persons, a daily total of the amount so allowed together with a cross-reference to the goods returned book, cash book or other record used in connection with the matter,

(k)   in relation to bad debts written off, particulars of the name and address of the debtor, the nature of the goods or services to which the debt relates and the date or dates upon which the debt was incurred,

(l)   in relation to goods and services supplied to the taxable person by another taxable person, the amount of the consideration, the corresponding tax invoiced by the other taxable person and a cross-reference to the corresponding invoice,

(m) in relation to goods and services supplied by unregistered persons, other than goods and services in respect of which flat-rate farmers are required, in accordance with section 12A(1) of the Act to issue invoices, a daily total of the consideration payable to such persons and a cross-reference to the purchases book, cash book, purchases dockets or other records which are in use in connection with the business,

(n) in relation to goods and services supplied by flat-rate farmers but in respect of which such persons are required, in accordance with section 12A(1) of the Act, to issue invoices, the amount of the consideration (exclusive of the flat-rate addition) and of the flat-rate addition invoiced by each such person and a cross-reference to the corresponding invoice,

(o) in relation to discounts or price reductions received from registered persons, subsequent to the receipt of invoices from such persons, except in a case in which section 17(9) (a) of the Act applies, the amount of the discount or price reduction and the corresponding tax received from each such person and a cross-reference to the corresponding credit note,

(p) in relation to discounts or price reductions in relation to goods and services referred to in subparagraph (n), the amount of the discount or price reduction (exclusive of the flat-rate addition) and of the flat-rate addition and a cross-reference to the invoice issued in connection with the goods and services in question,

(q) in relation to discounts or price reductions received other than those referred to in subparagraphs (o) and (p), a daily total of the amounts so received and a cross-reference to the cash book or other record used in connection with such matters,

(r) in relation to dances-

(i)   the date upon which each dance was held and the address of the place at which it was held,

(ii) the charge for admission to each dance,

(iii) the number of persons admitted to each dance,

(iv) the total amount of money received or receivable from the persons admitted to each dance in respect of admission, and

(v)   where goods or services are supplied in connection with a dance and payment of the consideration therefore is a condition of admission to the dance, the amount of such consideration in respect of each dance,

(s)   in respect of supplies of goods specified in paragraph (i) of the Second Schedule to the Act, the name and address of the person to whom the goods are supplied, a description of the goods supplied, the amount of the consideration, a cross-reference to the copy of the relevant invoice and a cross-reference to the relevant Customs and transport documents, and

(t)   in the case of the supply of services in circumstances that, by virtue of any of the provisions of section 5 of the Act, are deemed to be supplied outside the State, the name and address of the person to whom the services are supplied, the amount of the consideration and a cross-reference to the copy of the relevant invoice or other document.

(2)   The accounts kept in accordance with paragraph (1) shall set out separately, the consideration, discounts, price reductions, bad debts and values at importation under separate headings in relation to-

(a)   exempted activities,

(b)   goods and services chargeable at each rate of tax, including the zero rate, and

(c)   goods and services a percentage only of the consideration for the supply of which is chargeable to tax.

(3)   (a)   In relation to a person for the time being authorised in accordance with section 14(1)(a) of the Act to determine the amount of tax which becomes due by him by reference to the amount of moneys which he receives, references in this Regulation to consideration in respect of the supply of goods or services shall be construed as references to the moneys received in respect of such supply, whether made before, on or after the specified day.

(b)   In relation to a person for the time being authorised, in accordance with section 14(1)(b) of the Act, to determine the amount of tax referable to taxable services which becomes due by him by reference to the amount of moneys which he receives in respect of such supply, references in this Regulation to consideration in respect of the supply of services shall be construed as references to the moneys received in respect of such supply, whether made before, on or after the specified day.

(4)   Where the Revenue Commissioners are satisfied that the accounts of a taxable person are kept in such a form as to enable his liability to tax to be computed accurately and verified by them, they may, by notice in writing given to the taxable person, dispense him from keeping accounts in the form prescribed by paragraphs (1) and (2), and any such dispensation may be cancelled by them by notice in writing given to the taxable person.

Invoices and other documents.

10.   [...]⁵

Time limits for certain documents.

11.   [...]⁶

Returns.

12.   [...]⁷

Acceptance of estimates.

13. (1)   The Revenue Commissioners may, if they so think proper and until they otherwise decide, accept estimates, based on procedures approved of by them, of the tax for any taxable period which a person is required to pay by reference to a return furnished in accordance with section 19(3) of the Act and may impose in relation to any such acceptance the condition (which shall be fulfilled by the person) that the person shall, within such period as may be specified, furnish a return in accordance with the said section 19(3) or furnish such further particulars as may be specified to enable the estimates to be reviewed.

    (2)   Where an estimate of the tax payable for any taxable period has been accepted in accordance with paragraph (1), the estimate may be reviewed by reference to the return or other particulars furnished in accordance with the arrangement and any necessary adjustment may be made by way of additional charge of tax or repayment of tax as the circumstances may require.

    (3)   If a person in respect of whom an estimate of the tax payable by him has been accepted for any taxable period fails to furnish the return or other particulars the furnishing of which is a condition of acceptance of the estimate in accordance with paragraph (1), or fails to pay any additional tax found to be payable as a result of a review of an estimate for any taxable period made in accordance with paragraph (2), any additional tax which the Revenue Commissioners have reason to believe may be due may be included in an estimate of tax made in accordance with section 23 of the Act.

    (4)   The provisions of section 21 of the Act shall not apply to any additional charge of tax arising out of a review made in accordance with paragraph (2) if the return or other particulars referred to

in that paragraph are furnished within the time specified in the condition governing the acceptance of the estimate and payment of the additional tax is made not later than the end of the time so specified.

(5)   A review in accordance with paragraph (2) may extend to a period consisting of two or more consecutive taxable periods and any additional tax or repayment of tax arising out of such review shall be regarded as referable to the latest taxable period in such period.

Estimation of tax due.

14.   [...]⁸

Modification of certain provisions.

15. (1)   Section 480 of the Income Tax Act, 1967 (No.6 of 1967), as applied by section 24 of the Act shall so apply subject to the following modifications:

(a)   in subsection (1)-

(i)   the expression "the sum charged" shall be construed as referring to value-added tax payable by the person concerned,

(ii)   the expression "the Collector" shall be construed as referring to the Collector-General,

(iii)   the words "in accordance with the assessments and warrants delivered to him" shall be disregarded,

(iv)   the words "the warrant delivered to him on his appointment" shall be construed as referring to the nomination given to the Collector-General on his being nominated by the Revenue Commissioners as the Collector-General,

(b)   in subsection (4) the words "a distress levied by the Collector" shall be construed as referring to a distress levied by the Collector-General or by a person nominated by the Collector-General to represent him at the execution,

(c)   in subsection (5) references to the Collector or his deputy shall be construed as references to the Collector-General or to a person nominated by him for the purposes of the subsection and the requirement of appraisal of the distress shall be disregarded.

(2)   [Section 962 of the Taxes Consolidation Act, 1997]⁹ , as applied by section 24 of the Act shall so apply subject to the following [modifications in subsection (1), namely, the words "any sum which may be levied on that person in respect of income tax"

shall be construed as referring to value-added tax payable by the person concerned][9].

(3)   [Section 963 of the Taxes Consolidation Act, 1997][9], as applied by section 24 of the Act shall so apply subject to the following modifications:

   (a)   the words "[income tax][9]" in subsection (1) shall be construed as referring to value-added tax,

   (b)   the expression "[the Collector-General or other officer of the Revenue Commissioners, duly authorised to collect the tax][9]" in subsections (1) and (2) and "[the Collector-General or other officer under this section][9]" in subsection (3) shall each be construed as referring to the Collector-General.

(4)   [Section 964(1) of the Taxes Consolidation Act, 1997][9], as applied by section 24 of the Act shall so apply subject to the modification that the references to income tax shall be construed as references to value-added tax.

(5)   [Section 966 of the Taxes Consolidation Act, 1997][9], as applied by section 24 of the Act shall so apply subject to the following modifications:

   (a)   the references in subsections (1) and (5) to [income tax][9] shall be construed as references to value-added tax,

   (b)   in subsection (5) the [references to an inspector and to the Collector-General][9] shall each be construed as a reference to the Collector-General and the words "under an assessment which has become final and conclusive" shall be disregarded.

(6)   [Section 966 of the Taxes Consolidation Act, 1997][9], as applied by section 24 of the Act shall so apply subject to the modification that the expression "[income tax][9]" shall be construed as referring to value-added tax.

Apportionment of amounts.

16.   [...][10]

Refund of tax.

17.   A claim for refund of tax shall be furnished in writing to the Revenue Commissioners and shall-

   (a)   set out the grounds on which the refund is claimed,

   (b)   contain a computation of the amount of the refund claimed, and

   (c)   if so required by the Revenue Commissioners, be vouched by the receipts for tax paid and such other documents as may be necessary to prove the entitlement to a refund of the amount claimed.

Remission of small amounts of tax.

18.   The Revenue Commissioners may, at their discretion, remit the amount of tax, together with interest thereon, payable by a person in respect of goods and services supplied by him during any taxable period, if the total amount of the tax, exclusive of any interest chargeable thereon does not exceed [€20][11].

Valuation of interests in immovable goods.

19.   (1)   Where-

(a)   it is necessary to value an interest in immovable goods for the purposes of section 10(9) of the Act,

(b)   the disposal of such interest consists of or includes the creation of an interest, [and][12]

(c)   a rent is payable in respect of the interest so created,

[...][13]

the value of such rent to be included in the consideration for the purpose of ascertaining the open market price of the interest disposed of shall, in the absence of other evidence of the amount of that price, be-

(i)   three-quarters of the annual amount of the rent multiplied by the number of complete years for which the rent has been created, or

(ii)   the annual amount of the rent multiplied by the fraction of which the numerator is 100 and the denominator is the rate of interest (before deduction of income tax, if any) on the security of the Government which was issued last before the date of the creation of the rent for subscription in the State, and which is redeemable not less than five years after the date of issue (allowance having been made in calculating the interest for any profit or loss which will occur on the redemption of the security),

[...][13]

[However, where the rent payable in respect of the interest so created is less than the unencumbered rent in respect of that interest, the value of the rent to be included in the consideration for the purpose of ascertaining the open market price of the interest disposed of shall be calculated using the unencumbered rent.][14]

(2)   Where a person having an interest in immovable goods (in this paragraph referred to as "the disponor") disposes as regards the whole or any part of those goods of an interest which derives from that interest in such circumstances that he retains the reversion on the interest disposed of (in this paragraph referred to as the reversionary interest), the following provisions shall apply:

(a)   the value of the reversionary interest shall be ascertained by deducting the value of the interest disposed of from the value of the full interest which the disponor had in the goods or the part thereof disposed of at the time the disposition was made, and

[(b)   if, under the terms of the disposition, the interest disposed of is for a period of twenty years or more, or is deemed to be for a period of twenty years or more, the value of the reversionary interest shall be disregarded.][15]

Procedures regarding dances.

Regulation 20 is no longer applicable following the repeal of s11(7), VATA72 by s173(2), FA92 with effect from 28 May 1997

20. (1)   Every person who intends to promote a dance (other than a dance to which the number of persons to be admitted is limited to one hundred and the consideration for admission to which does not exceed twenty pence), or a series of such dances, shall, not later than fourteen days before the date on which the dance, or the first dance of the series, as the case may be, is to be held, send to the Collector-General a notification in writing containing the following particulars:

(a)   the name and address of the person,

(b)   the address of the premises in which the dance or dances is or are to be held,

(c)   the name and address of the proprietor of the premises mentioned in subparagraph (b),

(d)   as respects the dance or each of the series of dances, the date and time of the dance or of each dance within the series of dances and the proposed admission charge, and

(e)   where the person promoting the dance or dances is a body of persons other than a body corporate, the name and address of the individual who will be responsible for payment of the tax.

(2)   On receipt of a notification in accordance with paragraph (1), the Collector-General shall forthwith acknowledge it and shall at the same time send a notice in writing to the proprietor of the premises mentioned in the notification, specifying the dance

or dances so mentioned and stating that notification in respect thereof has been received in accordance with this Regulation.

(3)   The proprietor of any premises shall not promote a dance therein, or allow a dance to be promoted therein by any other person, unless he has received notice from the Revenue Commissioners that they have been notified in accordance with section 11(7)(c) of the Act.

(4)   If any alteration is made or occurs as respects any of the particulars contained in a notification sent to the Collector-General under paragraph (1), the person responsible for sending the notification under that paragraph shall immediately notify the Collector-General in writing of the alteration.

Relief for stock-in-trade held on 1st. November, 1972.

21.   A claim for deduction under section 34(1) of the Act in respect of stock-in-trade held at the commencement of the 1st. day of November, 1972, shall be supported by a statement in writing of all stock-in-trade held at that time setting out details of the stock-in-trade so held under the following headings-

(a)   stocks which have borne turnover tax and wholesale tax on purchase or importation other than-

(i)   second-hand goods;

(ii)   newspapers and periodicals;

(iii)   motor vehicles designed and constructed for the conveyance of persons by road, and sports motor vehicles, estate cars, station wagons, motor cycles, motor scooters, mopeds and auto cycles, whether or not designed and constructed for the purpose aforesaid, excluding vehicles designed and constructed for the carriage of more than sixteen persons (inclusive of the driver), invalid carriages and other vehicles of a type designed for use by invalids or infirm persons;

(iv)   radio receiving sets and television receiving sets which are of the domestic or portable type or which are of a kind suitable for use in road vehicles;

(v)   gramophones, radiogramophones, record reproducers;

(vi)   gramophone records,

(b)   stocks which have borne wholesale tax only on purchase, other than goods of a kind specified in clauses (i) to (vi) of subparagraph (a),

(c)   (i)   goods which suffered turnover tax only on purchase,

       (ii)   second-hand goods which were purchased from persons accountable for turnover tax and on which turnover tax was borne on purchase,

       (iii)   goods of a kind specified at (iii), (iv), (v) and (vi) of subparagraphs (a) and (b),

       (iv)   newspapers and periodicals which suffered turnover tax on purchase, and

  (d)   stocks which do not qualify for relief.

Relief for stock-in-trade held at commencement of taxability.

22. (1)   A claim by a taxable person for a deduction under section 12(1) of the Act of an amount authorised to be so deducted by section 12(1A) of the Act shall be made to the Collector-General and shall be supported by a statement in writing of all stock-in-trade held by him at the commencement of the first taxable period for which he is deemed to be a taxable person (in this Regulation referred to as the relevant day) setting out details of stock-in-trade so held by him under the following headings:

       (a)   stocks supplied to him by taxable persons and in respect of which, if supplied immediately before the relevant day, tax would be chargeable on the full amount of the consideration at the rate specified in section 11(1)(a) of the Act;

       (b)   stocks supplied to him by taxable persons and in respect of which, if supplied immediately before the relevant day, tax would be chargeable on the full amount of the consideration at the rate specified in section 11(1)(c) of the Act;

       (c)   stocks supplied to him by taxable persons and in respect of which, if supplied immediately before the relevant day, tax would be chargeable on the percentage of the total consideration specified in section 11(2)(a) of the Act at the rate specified in section 11(1)(a) of the Act;

       (d)   agricultural produce supplied by flat-rate farmers; and

       (e)   stocks, other than stocks referred to in subparagraph (d), in respect of which, if supplied immediately before the relevant day, tax would not be chargeable or would be chargeable at the zero rate.

  (2) (a)   The deduction in respect of stocks specified in subparagraph (a) or (b) of paragraph (1) shall be ascertained in the following manner:

       (i)   the stocks shall be valued at cost inclusive of tax, or market value, whichever is the lower,

(ii) there shall be deducted from the total value of stocks ascertained in accordance with clause (i) the value of any stocks included therein in respect of which an invoice issued in accordance with subsection (1), (2), (3) or (4) of section 17 of the Act has been or is likely to be received on or after the relevant day,

(iii) the amount of the deduction shall be the amount of tax which would be chargeable if the stocks were supplied immediately before the relevant day by a taxable person in the course or furtherance of business for a consideration inclusive of tax equal to the amount of their value after making the deduction specified in clause (ii) and the tax fell due on the date of supply.

(b) The deduction in respect of stocks specified in subparagraph (c) or (d) of paragraph (1) shall be ascertained in the following manner:

(i) the stocks shall be valued at cost inclusive of tax, or market value, whichever is the lower,

(ii) there shall be deducted from the total value of stocks ascertained in accordance with clause (i) the value of any stocks included therein in respect of which an invoice issued in accordance with subsection (1), (2), (3) or (4) of section 17 of the Act has been or is likely to be received on or after the relevant day,

(iii) the amount of the deduction shall be 1 per cent. of their value after making the deduction specified in clause (ii).

(3) Relief claimed in accordance with this Regulation shall be distinguished if included in a return made in accordance with section 19(3) of the Act.

Determination in regard to tax.

23.   [...]16

Supply of certain services.

[24. (1) Subject to paragraph (2) and in accordance with section 5(3)(b) of the Act, the following services are deemed to be a supply of services by a person for consideration in the course or furtherance of his or her business, that is to say, the supply free of charge of catering services for such person's own private use or that of the staff of such person.

(2)   This Regulation does not apply to any such supplies as are referred to in paragraph (1) if the total cost of providing them has not exceeded and is not likely to exceed the amount specified in section 8(3)(e) of the Act in any continuous period of 12 months, unless the person supplying the services referred to in paragraph (1) elects to be a taxable person in respect of those supplies.][17]

Postponement of payment of tax on goods supplied while warehoused.

25.   (1)   Where goods chargeable with a duty of excise on their manufacture or production are supplied while warehoused to a registered person for the purposes of his business, they may, in accordance with section 13(5) of the Act be removed from warehouse without payment of the tax chargeable on the supply.

(2)   Where goods have been supplied while warehoused to a registered person without payment of the tax chargeable on the supply in accordance with paragraph (1), the tax chargeable in accordance with section 13(5)(b) of the Act in relation to the said supply shall be accounted for by that person together with any tax chargeable on the supply of goods or services by him in a return furnished by him in accordance with these Regulations for the taxable period during which the goods were removed from warehouse.

(3)   Where goods have been supplied while warehoused to a registered person without payment of the tax chargeable on the supply in accordance with paragraph (1) and the tax is not accounted for in a return lodged for the period in question in accordance with paragraph (2), or the person fails to lodge a return due for that period, the tax chargeable in respect of the supply shall become due.

(4)   Where-

(a)   tax due by a person in accordance with paragraph (2) has not been accounted for, or

(b)   tax due by a person in accordance with paragraph (3) has not been paid or accounted for,

the said Commissioners may direct that as from a specified date paragraph (1) shall not apply to that person.

Postponement of payment of tax on goods imported by registered persons.

26.   [...][18]

Repayment of tax on certain importation of goods.

27.   [...][19]

Limitation of application of Customs law to imported goods.

28.   [...][20]

Remission or repayment of tax on fishing vessels and equipment.

29.   (1)   Tax is, in accordance with section 13(1)(c) of the Act, hereby remitted in respect of the supply or importation of fishing nets, and sections thereof, of a kind used by commercial sea-fishermen for the purposes of their occupation and not commonly used for any other purpose.

     (2)   A person who establishes to the satisfaction of the Revenue Commissioners that he has borne or paid tax on-

          (a)   the supply or hire to him, the importation by him or the maintenance or repair for him of a commercial sea-fishing vessel of a gross tonnage of not more than 15 tons, on the acquisition of which he received from An Bord Iascaigh Mhara a grant or loan of money, or

          (b)   the supply or hire to him, the importation by him or the repair, modification or maintenance for him of goods specified in the Schedule to this Regulation for use exclusively in the operation by him of a commercial sea-fishing vessel of a gross tonnage of not more than 15 tons, on the acquisition of which he received from An Bord Iascaigh Mhara a grant or loan of money, or

          (c)   the hire to him, or the repair or maintenance for him of goods specified in the Schedule to this Regulation for use exclusively in the operation by him of a commercial sea-fishing vessel of a gross tonnage of more than 15 tons, whether or not the subject of a grant or loan of money from An Bord Iascaigh Mhara, or

          (d)   the repair or maintenance for him of a fishing net specified in paragraph (1) for use exclusively in the course of a commercial sea-fishing business carried on by him, and who fulfils to the satisfaction of the said Commissioners the conditions specified in paragraph (3) shall be entitled to be repaid the tax borne or paid.

     (3)   The conditions to be fulfilled by a person specified in paragraph (2) are-

          (a)   he shall claim a refund of tax by completing such claim form as may be provided for the purpose by the Revenue Commissioners and he shall certify the particulars shown on such claim form to be correct,

          (b)   he shall, by production of sufficient documentary evidence, establish that the outlay in relation to which his claim for a refund of tax arises was incurred in the operation by him of a vessel specified in paragraph (2) for the purposes of a commercial sea-fishing business,

     (c)   he shall, by production of an invoice provided in accordance with section 17(12)(a)(ii) of the Act or by the production of a receipt for tax paid on goods imported, establish the amount of tax borne or paid in relation to the outlay referred to in paragraph (2),

     (d)   he shall, by the production of a certificate from An Bord Iascaigh Mhara or such other documentary evidence as may be acceptable to the Revenue Commissioners, establish where appropriate that the outlay in relation to which his claim for a refund of tax arises relates to a commercial sea-fishing vessel in respect of which he qualified for financial assistance by grant or loan from An Bord Iascaigh Mhara,

     (e)   he shall establish that he is not a person registered in the register maintained under section 9 of the Act nor a person required under the provisions of that section to furnish the particulars specified for registration.

SCHEDULE

Anchors, autopilots, bilge and deck pumps, buoys and floats, compasses, cranes, echo graphs, echo sounders, electrical generating sets, fish boxes, fish finders, fishing baskets, life boats and life rafts, marine lights, marine engines, net drums, net haulers, net sounders, radar apparatus, radio navigational aid apparatus, radio telephones, refrigeration plant, trawl doors, trawl gallows, winches.

Refund to foreign traders.

[30. (1)   A person to whom section 13(3) of the Act applies is entitled, under the terms of Council Directive No. 79/1072/EEC of 6 December 1979 and Council Directive No. 86/560/EEC of 17 November 1986, to be repaid tax borne by him or her on the purchase of goods or services supplied to him or her in the State or in respect of goods imported into the State by him or her if he or she fulfils to the satisfaction of the Revenue Commissioners the following conditions:

     (a)   in the case of a person having an establishment in another Member State, produces a certificate from the relevant official department of that Member State that he or she is subject, under the laws of that Member State, to value-added tax referred to in Council Directive No. 77/388/EEC of 17 May 1977,

     (b)   in the case of a person not established in the territory of the Community, provides proof, in the form of a written document from the relevant official department of the country in which he or she has an establishment, that he or she is engaged in carrying on an economic activity,

(c)   claims a refund, within 6 months of the end of the calendar year in which the tax became chargeable, by completing and lodging the appropriate claim form, provided for that purpose by the Revenue Commissioners, together with the appropriate documentation as specified in subparagraph (d),

(d)   establishes the amount of tax borne by the production of the invoice issued by the supplier or the relevant import documents,

(e)   establishes that he or she is not entitled to repayment of the tax under any other provision of the Act or Regulations, or any other instrument made under statute that is administered by the Revenue Commissioners.

(2)   A claim for a refund under this Regulation shall relate to invoiced purchases of goods and services or to imports made during a period, within a calendar year, of not less than 3 months or a period of not more than one calendar year, but where that claim relates to the remainder of a calendar year a claim for a refund may relate to a period of less than 3 months.

(3)   A person may not make a claim under this Regulation for an amount that is less than-

(a)   €200 where the claim is in respect of a period of less than one calendar year but not less than 3 months,

(b)   €25 where the claim is in respect of a period that represents a full calendar year or the final part of the calendar year.

(4)   The certificate and written document mentioned in subparagraphs (a) and (b) of paragraph (1), respectively, shall each be taken as evidence of the matters contained therein for the purposes of this Regulation only for a period of one year from the date such certificate or such document was issued by the official authorities in the State in which that person is established.][21]

Exemption of certain business gifts.

31.   For the purposes of section 3(1A)(a) of the Act a gift of goods made in the course or furtherance of business (otherwise than as one forming part of a series or succession of gifts made to the same person) the cost of which to the donor does not exceed [€20][22] exclusive of tax shall not be deemed to have been effected for consideration.

Supplies of stamps, coupons, tokens and vouchers.

32.   The amount on which tax is chargeable by virtue of section 2(1)(a) of the Act in relation to supplies of stamps, coupons, tokens or vouchers specified in section 10(7)(b) of the Act shall be nil where the supplies are made by a person in relation to the operation of a business consisting mainly of the supply of goods or services in exchange for the stamps,

coupons, tokens or vouchers, and the goods or services are of a kind which the person to whom the stamps, coupons, tokens or vouchers are surrendered does not supply except in relation to the operation of such a scheme.

Supplies of goods or services in exchange for stamps, coupons, tokens or vouchers.

33.   The amount on which tax is chargeable by virtue of section 2(1)(a) of the Act in relation to supplies of goods or services to which section 10(7)(c) of the Act relates shall be the cost, excluding tax, to the supplier of producing or acquiring the goods or providing the services, as the case may be, increased by such amount as is reasonable having regard to the open market value of similar goods or services.

Apportionment of consideration.

34.   For the purposes of section 11(3) of the Act-

(a)   the consideration in respect of the provision of board and lodging, otherwise than in the course of carrying on a hotel business, shall be apportioned as to the amount which relates to the supply of services under section 5(2)(c) of the Act and the amount which relates to the letting of immovable goods specified in paragraph (iv) of the First Schedule to the Act;

(b)   where a service consisting of the transport of passengers and the provision of hotel accommodation is supplied for a single consideration, such consideration shall be apportioned as to the amounts which relate to such transport of passengers and such provision of accommodation, respectively.

Disclosure of information to the Revenue Commissioners.

35.   Any person engaged in the supply of goods or services in the course or furtherance of business shall, when required to do so by notice in writing served on him by the Revenue Commissioners, disclose to the Revenue Commissioners such particulars of any goods or services supplied to him as may be required by such notice.

Death or incapacity of taxable person.

36.   If a taxable person dies, becomes bankrupt, or, being a body corporate, goes into liquidation, anything which he would have been liable to do under the Act or these Regulations shall be done by his personal representative, assignee, trustee, committee or liquidator, as the case may be.

Service of notices.

37.   Any notice, notification or requirement which is authorised or required to be given, served, made, sent or issued under the Act or under these Regulations may be sent by post.

Nomination of officers.

38. The Revenue Commissioners may nominate any of their officers to perform any acts and discharge any functions authorised by the Act to be performed or discharged by the Revenue Commissioners.

Revocation.

39. The Value-Added Tax Regulations, 1972 (S.I. No.177 of 1972), and the Value-Added Tax Regulations, 1973 (S.I. No.254 of 1973), are hereby revoked.

GIVEN this 27th day of February, 1979.

M. K. O'CONNOR,
Revenue Commissioner.

The Minister for Finance hereby consents to the making of Regulations 26, 28 and 29 of the foregoing Regulations.

GIVEN under the Official Seal of the Minister for Finance this 27th. day of February, 1979.

SEOIRSE Ó COLLA,
Minister for Finance.

EXPLANATORY NOTE.

These Regulations which come into force on the 1st. of March, 1979, concern the operation of Value-Added Tax. They prescribe procedures in relation to the following matters:

(a)   election for taxability, the waiver of exemption and the treatment of two or more taxable persons as a single taxable person,

(b)   registration and cancellation of registration,

(c)   determination of tax due on basis of moneys received,

(d)   accounts to be kept, including the adjustments to be made in certain circumstances and the issue of invoices, credit notes and debit notes, and the time limits for issuing certain documents,

(e)   returns to be made, payment of tax and postponed payment, the acceptance of estimates, the apportionment of amounts and the estimation of tax due,

(f)   refunds and remissions of tax,

(g)   the valuation of interests in immovable goods,

(h)   the charge of tax in regard to dances,

(i)   relief for stock-in-trade held-

    (I)   on 1 November, 1972,

    (II)   at commencement of taxability,

(j)   determination in regard to tax,

(k)   supply of certain services,

(l)   treatment of certain gifts, trading stamps and goods exchanged therefor.

Amendments

1. Para 3A, Reg 3, inserted by r6, Value Added Tax (Cancellation of Election of Registration in respect of Sixth Schedule Accommodation) Regulations, 2000 w.e.f. 1 September, 2000.

2. Revoked by r4, Value Added Tax (Waiver of Exemption) (Letting of Immovable Goods) Regulations, 2003, w.e.f. 24 October 2003.

3. Revoked by r7, Value Added Tax (Registration) Regulations, 1993.

4. Revoked by r4, Value Added Tax (Determination of Tax Due by Reference to Monies Received) Regulations, 1986.

5. Revoked by r6, Value Added Tax (Invoice and Other Documents) Regulations, 1992, w.e.f. 1 January 1993.

6. Revoked by r7, Value Added Tax (Time Limits for Issuing Certain Documents) Regulations, 1992, w.e.f. 1 January 1993.

7. Revoked by r5, Value Added Tax (Returns) Regulations, 1993.

8. Revoked by r6, Value Added Tax (Estimation and assessment of Tax Due) Regulations, 1992.

9. Substituted by s1100 & sch31, TCA97.

10. Revoked by r8, Value Added Tax (Apportionment) Regulations, 2000.

11. Amended by s240 & sch5, FA01 w.e.f. 1 January 2002. Previously £15.

12. Inserted by r4, Value Added Tax (Amendment) (Property Transactions) Regulations 2002, w.e.f. 25 March 2002.

13. Deleted by r4, Value Added Tax (Amendment) (Property Transactions) Regulations 2002, w.e.f. 25 March 2002.

14. Amended by r4, Value Added Tax (Amendment) (Property Transactions) Regulations 2002, w.e.f. 25 March 2002.

15. Substituted by r3(b), Value Added Tax (Valuation of Interests in Immovable Goods) (Amendment) Regulations, 1998.

16. Revoked by r6, Value Added Tax (Determination in Relation to Tax Due) Regulations, 1992, w.e.f. 1 January 1993.

17. Regulation 24 substituted by r2(a), Value-Added Tax (Amendment) Regulations 2006, w.e.f. 1 May 2006.

18. Repealed by s84, FA82 w.e.f. 1 September 1982.

19. Revoked by Value Added Tax (Remission and Repayment of Tax on Certain Exportations) Regulations, 1985, w.e.f. 25 October 1985.

20. Revoked by Value Added Tax (Imported Goods) Regulations, 1983, w.e.f. 1 September 1982.

21. Regulation 30 substituted by r2(b), Value-Added Tax (Amendment) Regulations 2006, w.e.f. 1 May 2006.

22. Amended by s240 & sch5, FA01 w.e.f. 1 January 2002. Previously £15.

Note

Regulation 15(1) is no longer operable as section 480, Income Tax Act, 1967 was repealed by section 132(2) & Sch. 5, Part II, FA96.'

VALUE-ADDED TAX (REFUND OF TAX) (REVOCATION) ORDER, 1979

(SI No. 232 of 1979)

I, SEOIRSE Ó COLLA, Minister for Finance, in exercise of the powers conferred on me by section 20(3) of the Value-Added Tax Act, 1972 (SI No. 22 of 1972), hereby order as follows:

1.   (1)   This Order may be cited as the Value-Added Tax (Refund of Tax) (Revocation) Order, 1979.

    (2)   This Order shall be deemed to have come into operation on the 1st day of March, 1979.

2.   The Value-Added Tax (Refund of Tax) (No. 2) Order, 1972 (SI No 269 of 1972), is hereby revoked.

GIVEN under my Official Seal,
this 29th day of June, 1979.
SEOIRSE Ó COLLA,
Minister for Finance.

EXPLANATORY NOTE.

This Order revokes the Value-Added Tax (Refund of Tax) (No. 2) Order, 1972, which enabled commercial sea fishermen who were unregistered for VAT to claim repayment of the VAT element in outlay on fishing boats in respect of which they received a grant or loan of money from An Bord Iascaigh Mhara. This relief is now provided for in the context of Regulation 29 of the Value-Added Tax Regulations, 1979 (made under Section 13, of the Value-Added Tax Act, 1972).

VALUE-ADDED TAX (REFUND OF TAX) (NO 10) ORDER, 1979

(SI No. 275 of 1979)

This Order revoked by Value Added Tax (Refund of Tax)(Revocation) Order 1989 (1989 S.I. No. 351) with effect from 19 December 1989.

I, SEOIRSE Ó COLLA, Minister for Finance, in exercise of the powers conferred on me by section 20 (3) of the Value-Added Tax Act, 1972 (No. 22 of 1972), hereby order as follows:

1.   (1)   This Order may be cited as the Value-Added Tax (Refund of Tax) (No. 10) Order, 1979.

     (2)   This Order shall be deemed to have come into operation on the 1st day of June, 1979.

2.   In this Order "the Act" means the Value-Added Tax Act, 1972.

3.   A person who establishes to the satisfaction of the Revenue Commissioners that he has borne or paid tax which became chargeable under the Act on or after the 1st day of June, 1979, in respect of-

    (a)   the supply to or importation by him of-

        (i)   a mechanically propelled road vehicle specially designed and constructed for the transport of severely disabled persons, or

        (ii)   a mechanically propelled road vehicle specially adapted for the transport of severely disabled persons and in respect of which the cost of such adaptation equals or exceeds 30 per cent. of the total consideration excluding tax and excise duty or of the value of the vehicle at importation as appropriate,

    or

    (b)   the adaptation for the transport of severely disabled persons of a mechanically propelled road vehicle, and that the vehicle in question is not intended for use wholly or mainly for the transport of persons to or from hospitals, nursing homes, clinics or similar establishments nor for use for reward and who fulfils to the satisfaction of the said Commissioners the conditions which are specified in paragraph 4 of this Order, shall be entitled to repayment of such tax.

4.   The conditions to be fulfilled by a person referred to in paragraph 3 of this Order are-

    (a)   he shall claim a refund of the tax by completing such claim form as may be provided for the purpose by the Revenue Commissioners and he shall certify the particulars shown on such claim form to be correct;

(b)   he shall by the production of a certificate from a medical practitioner or by the production of such other evidence as may be acceptable to the said Commissioners establish that the person or persons for the transport of whom the vehicle is intended is or are a severely disabled person or persons whose disability is such that the vehicle in question is necessary for his or their transport;

(c)   he shall by the production of invoices, provided in accordance with section 17(12)(a)(i) of the Act, or by the production of receipts for the tax paid on importation of the vehicle, establish the amount of tax borne or paid to which the claim relates;

(d)   he shall establish that he is not entitled to a deduction under section 12 of the Act or a repayment under regulation made under section 13(3) of the Act in respect of any portion of the tax specified in subparagraph (c) of this paragraph.

GIVEN under my Official Seal,
this 3rd day of August, 1979.

SEOIRSE Ó COLLA,
Minister for Finance

EXPLANATORY NOTE

This Order enables a refund of the full amount of VAT to be made in respect of the purchase or importation of vehicles specially constructed for transporting severely disabled persons, or of vehicles converted for that purpose where the cost of conversion is not less than 30% of the outlay exclusive of VAT and excise duty, on the vehicles after conversion. It also enables the refund of VAT borne on the conversion costs only of vehicles for this purpose where the cost of conversion is less than 30% of the price after conversion. This scheme of refunds is to operate from 1 June, 1979.

VALUE-ADDED TAX (REFUND OF TAX) (NO 11) ORDER, 1980

(S.I. No. 239 of 1980)

I, MICHAEL O'KENNEDY, Minister for Finance, in exercise of the powers conferred on me by section 20(3) of the Value-Added Tax Act, 1972 (No. 22 of 1972), hereby order as follows:

1.   This Order may be cited as the Value-Added Tax (Refund of Tax) (No. 11) Order, 1980.

2.   This Order shall be deemed to have come into operation on the 29th day of November, 1976.

3.   In this Order "the Agency" means the European Space Agency established by the Convention for the Establishment of a European Space Agency signed at Paris on the 30th day of May, 1975.

4.   Where the Agency establishes to the satisfaction of the Revenue Commissioners that it has borne tax on the supply to it of goods or services of substantial value which are strictly necessary for the exercise of its official activities and fulfils to the satisfaction of the said Commissioners all the conditions which are specified in paragraph 5 of this Order it shall be entitled to be repaid the tax so established as having been borne.

5.   (a)   The Agency shall claim a refund of the tax by completing such claim form as may be provided for the purpose by the Revenue Commissioners and it shall certify the particulars shown on such claim form to be correct.

       (b)   The Agency shall, by the production of an invoice, provided in accordance with section 17(12)(a)(i) of the Value-Added Tax Act, 1972, establish the amount of tax borne in relation to such supply.

GIVEN under my Official Seal,
this 22nd of July, 1980.

MICHAEL O'KENNEDY,
Minister for Finance.

EXPLANATORY NOTE.

This Order enables repayment to be made, subject to certain conditions, of value-added tax paid on purchases of goods and services by the European Space Agency.

VALUE-ADDED TAX (REFUND OF TAX) (NO 12) ORDER, 1980

(SI No. 262 of 1980)

I, MICHEÁL O CINNÉIDE, Minister for Finance, in exercise of the powers conferred on me by section 20(3) of the Value-Added Tax Act, 1972 (No. 22 of 1972), hereby order as follows:

1. (1)   This Order may be cited as the Value-Added Tax (Refund of Tax) (No. 12) Order, 1980.

    (2)   This Order shall be deemed to have come into operation on the 1st day of March, 1979.

2. (1)   In this Order "the Act" means the Value-Added Tax Act, 1972 (No. 22 of 1972).

    (2)   A reference in this Order to a caravan includes a reference to a mobile home or any similar structure designed primarily for residential purposes.

3. A person who establishes to the satisfaction of the Revenue Commissioners that he has borne or paid tax in relation to the supply to or importation by him of a caravan and who fulfils to the satisfaction of the said Commissioners the conditions which are specified in paragraph 4 of this Order shall be entitled to be repaid so much of such tax as is specified in paragraph 5 of this Order.

4. The conditions to be fulfilled by a person referred to in paragraph 3 of this Order are-

    (a)   he shall claim a refund of the tax by completing such claim form as may be provided for the purpose by the Revenue Commissioners and he shall certify the particulars shown in such claim form to be correct;

    (b)   he shall establish that the caravan in relation to which a claim for a refund of the tax arises-

        (i)   is used by him as a permanent residence for himself and that neither he nor (if he is a married man having his spouse living with him) his spouse has any other place of abode within the State available for his occupation, or

        (ii)   is, in the case of a local authority, occupied as a residence by a tenant of the local authority;

    (c)   he shall, in the case of a person other than a local authority, by the production of a certificate from the appropriate local authority or such other documentary evidence as may be acceptable to the Revenue Commissioners, establish that the caravan has been rated under the Valuation Acts;

    (d)   he shall, by the production of invoices, provided in accordance with section 17(12)(a)(i) of the Act, or by the production of receipts for tax paid on importation, establish the amount of tax

> borne or paid by him in relation to the caravan excluding any amount referable to articles of furniture or equipment which would not be regarded as fixtures if the caravan were regarded as immovable goods at the time of its supply or importation;

(e)   he shall establish the net tax-exclusive amount of the consideration for the supply to him of the caravan, or, if the caravan was imported by him, its net tax-exclusive value, exclusive, in either case, of the amount, if any, included in such consideration or value for the supply or importation of such articles as are referred to in subparagraph (d) of this paragraph;

(f)   he shall establish that he is not entitled to a deduction under section 12 of the Act for any portion of the tax specified in subparagraph (d) of this paragraph.

5.   The amount of tax to be repaid to a person referred to in paragraph 3 of this Order shall be so much of the amount of tax specified in paragraph 4(d) of this Order as the person shows to the satisfaction of the Revenue Commissioners to be in excess of the amount which would have been borne or paid by him if the rate and percentage for the time being referred to in section 11(2)(b) of the Act had applied to the supply or importation in question.

6.   The Value-Added Tax (Refund of Tax) (No.3) Order, 1972 (S.I. No.327 of 1972), is hereby revoked with effect as on and from the 1st day of March 1979.

GIVEN under my Official Seal, this 14th day of August, 1980.

MICHEÁL Ó CINNÉIDE,Minister for Finance.

EXPLANATORY NOTE.

This Order enables repayment to be made, subject to certain conditions, of portion of the value-added tax paid in relation to a caravan, a mobile home or similar structure, which has been purchased by a person as a residence or, in the case of a local authority, provided for letting as a residence. The refund will have the effect of adjusting the rate of tax to the same effective rate (3 per cent as at the date of Order) as applies to the construction of permanent buildings.

In the case of a claimant other than a local authority, the title to repayment is conditional on the caravan or mobile home being rated.

Prior to 1 March 1979 this relief was provided by the Value-Added Tax (Refund of Tax) (No.3) Order, 1972 as amended by the Value-Added Tax (Refund of Tax) (No.6) Order, 1973.

VALUE-ADDED TAX (REFUND OF TAX) (NO 13) ORDER, 1980

(SI No. 263 of 1980)

This Order revoked by Value Added Tax (Refund of Tax)(Revocation) Order
1989, (1989 S.I. No. 351) w.e.f. 19 December 1989.

I, MICHEÁL Ó CINNÉIDE, Minister for Finance, in exercise of the powers conferred on me by section 20(3) of the Value-Added Tax Act, 1972 (No.22 of 1972), hereby order as follows:

1. (1)   This Order may be cited as the Value-Added Tax (Refund of Tax) (No.13) Order, 1980.

    (2)   This Order shall be deemed to have come into operation on the 1st day of March, 1979.

2. In this Order "the Act" means the Value-Added Tax Act, 1972.

3. A person (in this Order referred to as "the claimant") who establishes to the satisfaction of the Revenue Commissioners that he has borne or paid tax in relation to the supply to or importation by him of a new road motor vehicle which has been specially constructed or adapted (whether before or after the date of such supply or importation) for the use of a disabled person as driver and who fulfils to the satisfaction of the Revenue Commissioners the conditions which are specifed in paragraph 4 of this Order shall be entitled to be repaid so much of such tax, together with so much of the tax, if any, borne by him in relation to the adaptation of the motor vehicle for the use specified in this paragraph, as is specified in paragraph 5 of this Order.

4. The conditions to be fulfilled by a person referred to in paragraph 3 of this Order are-

    (a)   he shall claim a refund of the tax by completing such claim form as may be provided for the purpose by the Revenue Commissioners and he shall certify the particulars shown on such claim form to be correct;

    (b)   he shall, by the production of a certificate from the licensing authority (within the meaning of the Road Vehicles (Registration and Licensing) Order, 1958 (S.I. No.15 of 1958)) for the area where the vehicle is registered or other sufficient documentary evidence, establish that by virtue of section 43 of the Finance Act, 1968 (No.33 of 1968), the duty imposed by section 1 of the Finance (Excise Duties)(Vehicles) Act, 1952 (No.24 of 1952), is not charged or levied in respect of the vehicle to which the claim relates;

    (c)   he shall, by the production of invoices, provided in accordance with section 17(12)(a)(i) of the Act, or by the production of receipts for the tax paid on importation of the vehicle, establish-

(i) the amount of tax borne or paid by him in relation to the supply to him or imporation by him of the vehicle, and

(ii) the amount of tax (if any) chargeable to the person who adapted the vehicle for the use specified in paragraph 3 of this Order in respect of such adaptation;

(d) he shall establish that he is not entitled to a deduction under section 12 of the Act in respect of any portion of the tax specified in subparagraph (c) of this paragraph.

5. The amount of tax to be refunded to the claimant shall be the amount specified in paragraph 4(c)(i) of this Order together with the amount (if any) specified in paragraph 4(c)(ii).

6. The Value-Added Tax (Refund of Tax)(No. 4) Order, 1972 (S.I. No.328 of 1972), is hereby revoked with effect as on and from the 1st day of March, 1979.

GIVEN under my Official Seal,
this 14th day of August, 1980.

MICHEÁL Ó CINNÉIDE,
Minister for Finance.

EXPLANATORY NOTE.

This Order enables a disabled person to obtain a repayment of the full amount of value-added tax charged in respect of a new motor vehicle which has been specially constructed or adapted for his use. Tax, if any, borne in relation to the adaptation will also be repaid. Repayment is dependent on the person having obtained a remission of the motor vehicle licence duty under section 43 of the Finance Act, 1968, in respect of the vehicle.

Prior to 1 March 1979 this relief was provided by the Value-Added Tax (Refund of Tax)(No.4) Order, 1972 as amended by the Value-Added Tax (Refund of Tax)(No.6) order, 1973.

VALUE-ADDED TAX (REFUND OF TAX) (NO 14) ORDER, 1980

(SI No. 264 of 1980)

> **Importation means importation from outside the EU, with effect from 1 January 1993.**

I, MICHEÁL Ó CINNÉIDE. Minister for Finance, in exercise of the powers conferred on me by section 20(3) of the Value-Added Tax Act, 1972 (No.22 of 1972), hereby order as follows:-

1. (1)   This Order may be cited as the Value-Added Tax (Refund of Tax) (No.14) Order, 1980.

    (2)   This Order shall be deemed to have come into operation on the 1st day of March, 1979.

2. In this Order "the Act" means the Value-Added Tax Act. 1972.

3. This Order applies to the following persons:

    (a)   a body of persons in its capacity as a person operating a hospital;

    (b)   a university, college, school or similar educational body in its capacity as a person operating a medical research laboratory;

    (c)   a research institution in its capacity as a person operating a medical research laboratory.

4. A person to whom this Order applies who establishes to the satisfaction of the Revenue Commissioners that he has borne or paid tax at a rate in excess of the rate per cent for the time being specified in section 11(1)(a) of the Act in relation to the supply to or importation by him of any instrument or appliance of a kind commonly used to make a diagnosis, to prevent or treat an illness, to carry out a surgical operation or to carry out scientific research and who fulfils to the satisfaction of the Revenue Commissioners the conditions which are specified in paragraph 5 of this Order shall be entitled to be repaid so much of such tax as is specified in paragraph 6 of this Order.

5. The conditions to be fulfilled by a person referred to in paragraph 4 of this Order are-

    (a)   he shall claim a refund of the tax by completing such claim form as may be provided for the purpose by the Revenue Commissioners and he shall certify the particulars shown on such form to be correct;

    (b)   he shall establish that he is a person to whom this Order applies and that the instruments or appliances on the supply or importation of which the tax was borne or paid by him were used by him in the capacity in relation to which this Order applies to him;

(c)   he shall establish, by the production of invoices, provided in accordance with section 17(12)(a)(i) of the Act, or by the production of receipts for tax paid on imported goods, the amount of tax borne or paid by him in relation to the goods specified in paragraph 4 of this Order;

(d)   he shall establish that he is not entitled to a deduction under section 12 of the Act for any portion of the tax specified in subparagraph (c) of this paragraph.

6.   The amount of tax to be repaid to the claimant shall be so much of the amount of tax specified in paragraph 5(c) of this Order as the person shows to the satisfaction of the Revenue Commissioners to be in excess of the amount of tax which would have been borne or paid by him if the rate specified in section 11(1)(a) of the Act had applied to the supply or importation in question.

7.   The Value-Added Tax (Refund of Tax)(No.5) Order, 1973 (S.I. No.70 of 1973) is hereby revoked with effect as on and from the 1st day of March, 1979.

GIVEN under my Official Seal,
this 14th day of August, 1980.

MICHEÁL Ó CINNÉIDE,
Minister for Finance.

EXPLANATORY NOTE.

Under the Value-Added Tax Act, 1972, the low rate of VAT (10 per cent as at the date of Order) applies to medical, etc. appliances used solely in professional practice.

Since it is desirable that hospitals and universities, colleges and research institutions operating laboratories for medical, dental, surgical and veterinary research should not have to bear the higher rate of tax on medical and laboratory appliances and instruments, even where they are not of a kind used solely in professional practice but are commonly used by them, this Order provides, in such cases, for the refund of the VAT chargeable in excess of the low rate.

Prior to 1 March, 1979 this relief was provided by the Value-Added Tax (Refund of Tax)(No.5) Order, 1973 as amended by the Value-Added Tax (Refund of Tax)(No.6) Order, 1973.

EUROPEAN COMMUNITIES (VALUE-ADDED TAX) (MUTUAL ASSISTANCE AS REGARDS THE RECOVERY OF CLAIMS) REGULATIONS, 1980

(SI No. 406 of 1980)

These Regulations revoked by European Communities (Mutual Assistance for the Recovery of Claims relating to Certain Levies, Duties, Taxes and Other Measures) Regulations, 2002 (2002 S.I. No. 462) w.e.f. 25 September 2002.

I, GENE FITZGERALD, Minister for Finance, in exercise of the powers conferred on me by section 3 of the European Communities Act, 1972 (No.27 of 1972), for the purpose of giving effect to Council Directive No. 76/308/EEC of 15 March, 1976 as amended by Council Directive No.79/1071/EEC of 6 December, 1979 and Commission Directive No.77/794/EEC of 4 November, 1977 in so far as they relate to value-added tax, hereby make the following regulations:

1.   These Regulations may be cited as the European Communities (Value-Added Tax) (Mutual Assistance as regards the Recovery of Claims) Regulations, 1980.

2.   (1)   In these Regulations-

"another Member State" means a Member State of the European Communities other than the State;

"the Commission Directive" means Commission Directive No. 77/794/EEC of 4 November, 1977;

"the Council Directive" means Council Directive No. 76/308/EEC of 15 March, 1976, as amended by Council Directive No. 79/1071/EEC of 6 December, 1979.

(2)   A word or expression that is used in these Regulations and is also used in the Council Directive or in the Commission Directive has, unless the contrary intention appears, the meaning in these Regulations that it has in the Council Directive or the Commission Directive, as the case may be.

3.   The amount of value-added tax specified in any request duly made pursuant to the Council Directive by an authority in another Member State for the recovery in the State of any amount claimed by that authority in such Member State pursuant to a claim referred to in Article 2 of the said Directive shall be recoverable in any court of competent jurisdiction by the Minister for Finance and for the purposes of the foregoing the amount shall be regarded as being a debt due to the Minister for Finance, by the person against whom the claim is made by such authority, in respect of a duty or tax under the care and management of the Revenue Commissioners or a simple contract debt due by such person to the aforesaid Minister, as may be appropriate.

4.   The Rules laid down in-

(a)   Articles 4 to 12 and 14 to 17 of the Council Directive, and

(b)   Articles 2 to 21 of the Commission Directive,

shall apply in relation to claims in respect of value-added tax referred to in Article 2 of the Council Directive which arise in another Member State and which are the subject of legal proceedings instituted in pursuance of these Regulations.

5.   In any legal proceedings instituted in pursuance of these Regulations any document which is in the form specified in Annex III to the Commission Directive and which purports to be authenticated in the manner specified in Article 11 of that Directive shall be received in evidence without proof of any seal or signature thereon or that any signatory thereto was the proper person to sign it, and such document shall, until the contrary is shown, be sufficient evidence of the facts therein stated.

6.   (1)   Legal proceedings instituted in pursuance of these Regulations for the recovery of any sum shall be stayed if the defendant satisfies the court that legal proceedings relevant to his liability on the claim to which the proceedings so instituted relate are pending, or are about to be instituted, before a court, tribunal or other competent body in another Member State; but any such stay may be removed if the legal proceedings in such a Member State are not prosecuted or instituted with reasonable expedition.

(2)   In any legal proceedings instituted in pursuance of these Regulations it shall be a defence for the defendant to show that a final decision on the claim to which the proceedings relate has been given in his favour by a court, tribunal or other body of competent jurisdiction in another Member State, and, in relation to any part of a claim to which such legal proceedings relate, it shall be a defence for the defendant to show that such a decision has been given in relation to that part of the claim.

(3)   No question shall be raised in any legal proceedings instituted in pursuance of these Regulations as to the defendant's liability on the claim to which the proceedings relate except as provided in paragraph (2) of this Regulation.

(4)   For the purposes of this Regulation legal proceedings shall be regarded as pending so long as an appeal may be brought against any decision in the proceedings; and for the said purposes a decision against which no appeal lies or against which an appeal lies within a period which has expired without an appeal having been brought shall be regarded as being a final decision.

GIVEN under my Official Seal,
this 23rd day of December, 1980.

GENE FITZGERALD,
Minister for Finance.

EXPLANATORY NOTE.

The Regulations provide for the extension at national level of EEC Directives on mutual assistance between Member States of the Community for the recovery of certain claims to VAT, as required by an amending Council Directive of 6 December, 1979.

EUROPEAN COMMUNITIES (MUTUAL ASSISTANCE IN THE FIELD OF VALUE-ADDED TAX) REGULATIONS, 1980

(SI No. 407 of 1980)

These Regulations revoked by r4, European Communities (Mutual Assistance in the Field of Direct Taxation, Certain Excise Duties and Taxation of Insurance Premiums) Regulations, 2003 (2003 S.I. No. 711) (with effect from 31 December 2003.

I, GENE FITZGERALD, Minister for Finance, in exercise of the powers conferred on me by section 3 of the European Communities Act, 1972 (No.27 of 1972), and for the purpose of giving effect to Council Directive No. 77/799/EEC of 19 December, 1977, as amended by Council Directive No. 79/1070/EEC of 6 December, 1979, in so far as they relate to value-added tax, hereby make the following regulations:

1.   These Regulations may be cited as the European Communities (Mutual Assistance in the Field of Value-Added Tax) Regulations, 1980.

2.   In these Regulations-

"**authorised officer**" means an officer of the Revenue Commissioners authorised in writing by the Revenue Commissioners for the purposes of these Regulations;

"the Council Directive" means Council Directive No. 77/799/EEC of 19 December, 1977, as amended by Council Directive No. 79/1070/EEC of 6 December, 1979.

3.   (1)   The Revenue Commissioners and authorised officers of those Commissioners may disclose to the competent authorities of another Member State any information concerning value-added tax required to be so disclosed by virtue of the Council Directive.

      (2)   Neither the Revenue Commissioners nor an authorised officer of those Commissioners shall disclose any information in pursuance of the Council Directive unless satisfied that the competent authorities of the other Member State concerned are bound by, or have undertaken to observe, rules of confidentiality with respect to the information which are not less strict than those applying to it in the State.

      (3)   Nothing in this section shall permit the Revenue Commissioners or an authorised officer of those Commissioners to authorise the use of information disclosed by virtue of the Council Directive to the competent authorities of another Member State other than for the purposes of taxation or to facilitate legal proceedings for failure to observe the tax laws of that State.

GIVEN under my Official Seal,
this 23rd day of December, 1980.

GENE FITZGERALD,
Minister for Finance.

EXPLANATORY NOTE.

These Regulations provide for the extension at national level of the EEC Council Directive of 19 December 1977 concerning mutual assistance (exchange of information) by the competent authorities of the Member States in the field of direct taxation to VAT, as required by an amending Council Directive of 6 December, 1979.

VALUE-ADDED TAX (REDUCTION OF RATE) (NO 5) ORDER, 1981

(SI No. 53 of 1981)

I, GENE FITZGERALD, Minister for Finance, in exercise of the powers conferred on me by section 11(8) of the Value-Added Tax Act, 1972 (No.22 of 1972), hereby order as follows:

1. (1)   This Order may be cited as the Value-Added Tax (Reduction of Rate) (No.5) Order, 1981.

    (2)   This Order shall come into operation on the 1st day of March, 1981.

2.   The Second Schedule (inserted by the Finance Act, 1976 (No.16 of 1976)) to the Value-Added Tax Act, 1972, shall be varied by the insertion after paragraph (xix) of the following paragraph:

"(xixa) medical equipment and appliances being-

>   (a)   invalid carriages, and other vehicles (excluding mechanically propelled road vehicles), of a kind designed for use by invalids or infirm persons,
>
>   (b)   orthopaedic appliances, surgical belts, trusses and the like, deaf aids, and artificial limbs and other artificial parts of the body excluding artificial teeth,
>
>   (c)   walking frames and crutches,
>
>   (d)   parts or accessories suitable for use solely or principally with any of the goods specified in subparagraphs (a), (b) and (c) of this paragraph;".

3.   The Third Schedule (inserted by the Finance Act, 1976) to the Value-Added Tax Act, 1972, shall be varied by-

    (a)   the deletion of subparagraph (c) of paragraph (xvii), and

    (b)   the substitution of the following subparagraph for subparagraph (f) of that paragraph:

>   "(f)   artificial teeth, splints and other fracture appliances,".

GIVEN under my Official Seal,
this 18th day of February, 1981.

GENE FITZGERALD,
Minister for Finance.

EXPLANATORY NOTE.

This Order, which is expressed to have effect as on and from 1 March, 1981, removes VAT from a variety of goods used by invalid and infirm persons. These goods are listed in Paragraph 2 of the Order.

VALUE ADDED TAX (REFUND OF TAX)(NO.15) ORDER 1981

(SI No. 428 of 1981)

VALUE-ADDED TAX (REFUND OF TAX) (NO.15) ORDER, 1981

I, JOHN BRUTON, Minister for Finance, in exercise of the powers conferred on me by section 20(3) of the Value-Added Tax Act, 1972 (No.22 of 1972), hereby order as follows:

1.   This Order may be cited as the Value-Added Tax (Refund of Tax) (No.15) Order 1981

2.   In this Order –

"the Act" means the Value-Added Tax Act, 1972;

"disabled person" means a person who, as a result of an injury, disease, congenital deformity or physical or mental illness, or defect, suffers from a loss of physical or mental faculty resulting in a specified degree of disablement; and cognate words shall be construed accordingly;

"qualifying goods" means goods other than mechanically propelled road vehicles which are aids or appliances, including parts and accessories, specially constructed or adapted for use by a disabled person and includes goods which, although not so specially constructed or adapted, are of such a kind as might reasonably be treated as so constructed or adapted having regard to the particular disablement of that person;

"specified degree of disablement" means, as regards a disablement to which the provisions of the Social Welfare (Occupational Injuries) Regulations, 1967 (No. 77 of 1967), apply, a degree of disablement which, if assessed in accordance with those provisions, would not be less than 30 per cent, and, as regards any other disablement, a degree of disablement of equivalent extent.

3.   Where a person establishes to the satisfaction of the Revenue Commissioners that –

    (a)   he has borne or paid tax which became chargeable on or after the 1st day of March, 1981, in respect of the supply to or importation by him of qualifying goods, and

    (b)   he fulfills the conditions which are specified in paragraph 4 of this order, and such other conditions as the said Commissioner may impose,

he shall be entitled to payment of the amount of tax so borne or paid.

4.   The conditions to be fulfilled by a person referred to in paragraph 3 of this Order are –

    (a)   he shall claim a refund of the tax by completing such claim form as may be provided for the purpose by the Revenue Commissioners and he shall certify the particulars shown on such claim form to be correct;

(b) (i) in case he is the person for whose use the goods referred to in paragraph 3 of this Order were supplied or imported, he shall, by the production of such evidence as may be acceptable to the said Commissioners, establish that he is a disabled person and that the goods are for the purpose of assisting him to overcome his disability in the performance of essential daily functions or in the exercise of a vocation, and that the goods are so used by him;

(ii) in case he is not the person for whose use the said goods were supplied or imported, he shall, by the production of such evidence as may be acceptable to the said Commissioners, establish that the goods were supplied by him, other than in the course of business, to a particular person who is a disabled person for the purpose of assisting that person to overcome his disability in the performance of essential daily functions or in the exercise of a vocation, and that the goods are so used by that other person;

(c) he shall by the production of invoices, provided in accordance with section 17 (12) (a) (i) of the Act, or by the production of receipts for tax paid on goods imported, establish the amount of tax borne or paid to which the claim related;

(d) he shall establish that he is not entitled to a deduction under section 12 of the Act or a repayment under section 20 (2) of the Act or under a regulation or order, other than this Order, made under the Act in respect of any portion of the tax specified in subparagraph (c) of this paragraph;

(e) he shall establish that the tax specified in subparagraph (c) of this paragraph does not form any part of expenditure incurred by him which has been or will be met, directly or indirectly, by the State, by any board established by statute, or by any public or local authority.

GIVEN under my Official Seal, this 17th day of December, 1981

JOHN BRUTON
Minister for Finance

EXPLANATORY NOTE

(This note is not part of the Instrument and is not a legal interpretation)

This Order enables VAT paid on qualifying goods to be refunded where the goods are purchased for the exclusive use of disabled persons suffering a specified degree of disablement. The Order applies to qualifying goods purchased on or after 1 March, 1981

VALUE-ADDED TAX (IMPORTED GOODS) REGULATIONS, 1982.

(SI No. 279 of 1982)

> These Regulations revoked by p11, Value Added Tax (Imported Goods)
> (No.2) Regulations, 1992, (1992 S.I. No. 440) w.e.f. 1 January 1993.

The Revenue Commissioners, in exercise of the powers conferred on them by section 15 of the Value-Added Tax Act, 1972 (No.22 of 1972), as amended by section 14 of the Value-Added Tax (Amendment) Act, 1978 (No.34 of 1978), and with the consent of the Minister for Finance, hereby make the following Regulations:

1. These Regulations may be cited as the Value-Added Tax (Imported Goods) Regulations, 1982.

2. These Regulations shall come into operation on the 1st day of September, 1982.

3. Notwithstanding the provisions of the Customs Consolidation Act, 1876, and of other law in force in the State relating to customs, tax in the case of imported goods entered for warehousing shall become chargeable at the time when the goods are so entered as if they were goods entered for home use and not at the time of removal from warehouse save that, in the case of goods removed from warehouse by an unregistered person, tax shall, in addition, be chargeable at the time of such removal on the amount of duty payable on the said goods at that time.

4. Section 6 of the Customs and Inland Revenue Act, 1879, and section 25(2) of the Finance Act, 1933 (No. 5 of 1933), shall, in so far at they apply to tax, have effect in relation to goods which are being re-imported into the State after exportation therefrom only if they are re-imported into the State by the person who exported them from the State.

5. Section 11 of the Finance (Miscellaneous Provisions) Act, 1958 (No.28 of 1958), and section 38 of the Finance Act, 1932 (No. 0 of 1932), as amended by section 17 of the Finance Act, 1965 (No.22 of 1965), and the European Communities (Customs) Regulations, 1972 (S.I. No.334 of 1972), shall not apply to tax chargeable at importation.

6. Sections 24 of the Finance Act, 1933 (No.15 of 1933), shall not apply to tax paid on goods imported by registered persons.

7. Section 5(1) of the Customs-Free Airport Act, 1947 (No. 5 of 1947), shall not, in so far as it applies to tax, have effect in relation to goods brought from the customs-free airport (within the meaning of that Act) into any other part of the State if it is established to the satisfaction of the Revenue Commissioners that tax has already been borne or paid on the goods.

8. Section 29(7) of the Finance Act, 1978 (No. 21 of 1978), shall apply in relation to tax payable at importation with the modification that the reference to goods entered for home use shall be deemed to include

a reference to imported goods entered for warehousing and imported goods entered for a process of manufacture and exportation under section 32 of the Finance Act, 1932 (No.20 of 1932), as amended.

9.   Any acts relating to customs adopted, whether before or after the commencement of these Regulations, by the European Communities and which, apart from section 15(6) of the Value-Added Tax Act, 1972, would not apply to tax chargeable at importation shall not apply to such tax.

10. Regulation 28 of the Value-Added Tax Regulations, 1979 (S.I. No. 63 of 1979), is hereby revoked.

GIVEN this 25th day of August, 1982.

S. PÁIRCÉIR,
Revenue Commissioner.

The Minister for Finance hereby consents to the making of the foregoing Regulations.

GIVEN under the Official Seal of the Minister for Finance,
this 25th day of August, 1982.

R. MacSHARRY,
Minister for Finance.

EXPLANATORY NOTE.

These Regulations which have effect on and from the 1st of September, 1982, are concerned with the payment of VAT by registered persons in respect of goods imported by them. The Regulations modify or exclude as appropriate the application to value-added tax of various customs provisions so as to provide, amongst other things, for:

(a)   the application of tax at the time of entry in the case of imported goods entered for warehousing and the application of a further charge of tax, calculated by reference to the duty payable, at the time of removal of imported goods from warehouse in the case of an unregistered person,

(b)   relief from tax in the case of goods re-imported by the person who exported them,

(c)   the application of tax to goods imported for processing and re-export,

(d)   the exclusion of certain customs drawback and repayment provisions,

(e)   relief from tax for goods brought from the customs-free airport into any other part of the State where they have already borne tax,

(f)   provision for arrangements for deferred payment in the case of goods entered for warehousing or for processing and re-export,

(g)   the exclusion from the application to value-added tax of Community customs regulations, and

(h)   the revocation of Regulation 28 of the Value-Added Tax Regulations, 1979.

VALUE-ADDED TAX (IMPORTED GOODS) REGULATIONS, 1983

(SI No. 129 of 1983)

> **These Regulations revoked by Value Added Tax (Imported Goods) Regulations, 1992, w.e.f. 1 January 1993.**

The Revenue Commissioners, in exercise of the powers conferred on them by sections 15 of the Value-Added Tax Act, 1972 (No. 22 of 1972), and with the consent of the Minister for Finance, hereby make the following regulations:

1. These Regulations may be cited as the Value-Added Tax (Imported Goods) Regulations, 1983.

2. These Regulations shall be deemed to have come in operation on the 1st day of April, 1983.

3. In these Regulations "the Act" means the Value-Added Tax Act, 1972.

4. Goods specified in Regulation 5 of these Regulations that are imported by a registered person may be delivered or removed without payment of the tax chargeable on the importation if the person complies with such conditions as the Revenue Commissioners may impose and with the condition that he shows to the satisfaction of the Revenue Commissioners-

    (a) that he is in the business of manufacturing goods in the State,

    (b) that the goods are being imported for the purposes of the business, and

    (c) that the consideration relating to supplies specified in paragraph (i)(a)(I) of the Second Schedule to the Act made by him of goods manufactured by him in the State, taking one taxable period with another, amounts to and is likely to continue to amount to not less than 75 per cent. of the consideration, excluding tax, relating to the total of his supplies of goods manufactured by him.

5. The goods referred to in Regulation 4 of these Regulations are goods imported and entered for the purpose of undergoing a process of manufacture or for the purpose of being incorporated with other goods as a part or ingredient of a manufactured product.

6. Where goods have been imported by a registered person without payment of the tax chargeable on the importation in accordance with Regulation 4 of these Regulations, details of the goods, including the value by reference to each rate of tax including the zero rate shall be included in the return required to be furnished by that person under section 19 of the Act and Regulations thereunder for the taxable period during which the importation took place.

7. Where, in the opinion of the Revenue Commissioners, a person does not, or has ceased to, satisfy a condition referred to or specified in Regulation

4 of these Regulations or has failed to comply with Regulation 6 of these Regulations, they shall send to him by post notification in writing of such opinion and the relief provided for by the said Regulation 4 shall not apply in relation to goods imported by the person during the period from the date on which such notification would be delivered in the ordinary course of post to the time when the person shows to the satisfaction of the Revenue Commissioners that he is complying with the conditions referred to or specified in the said Regulation 4 and with the said Regulation 6.

GIVEN this 17th day of May, 1983.

S. PÁIRCÉIR,
Revenue Commissioner.

The Minister for Finance hereby consents to the making of the foregoing Regulations.

GIVEN under the Official Seal of the Minister for Finance this 3rd day of May, 1983.

ALAN M. DUKES,
Minister for Finance.

EXPLANATORY NOTE.

These Regulations, which have effect as from the 1st of April, 1983, are concerned with the relieving from payment of VAT at importation of raw materials and components for certain manufacturers.

To qualify for the relief an importer must -

(a)   be registered for VAT,

(b)   be in the business of manufacturing goods in the State, and

(c)   export at least 75 per cent. in value of his total manufactured output.

The importations must be accounted for in the normal VAT return by entering details of the goods concerned under the various VAT rates.

Where the foregoing requirements are not, or cease to be met in any case, the Revenue Commissioners are empowered to withhold, or withdraw the relief until such time as the necessary conditions are satisfied.

VALUE-ADDED TAX (REFUND OF TAX) (NO 16) ORDER, 1983

(SI No. 324 of 1983)

I, ALAN M. DUKES, Minister for Finance, in exercise of the powers conferred on me by section 20(3) of the Value Added Tax Act, 1972 (No 22 of 1972), hereby order as follows:

1. (1)

    (2)   This Order may be cited as the Value-Added Tax (Refund of Tax) (No 16) Order, 1983.

          This Order shall be deemed to have come into operation on the 1st day of May, 1983.

2. In this Order-

    (a)

    (b)   "the Act" means the Value-Added Tax Act, 1972;

          "sea-fishing vessel" means a sea-fishing boat which-

          (i)   is registered in accordance with the Merchant Shipping (Registry, Lettering and Numbering of Fishing Boats) (Regulations) Order, 1927 (S.R. & O., No 105 of 1927), and

          (ii)   is registered under the Mercantile Marine Act, 1955 (No.29 of 1955);

    (c)   "hydrocarbon oil" means hydrocarbon oil of a kind specified in paragraph (i)(c) of the Sixth Schedule to the Act.

3. A person who establishes to the satisfaction of the Revenue Commissioners that he has borne or paid tax on the supply to or importation by him of hydrocarbon oil used for combustion in the engine of a sea-fishing vessel in the course of a sea-fishing business carried on by him and who fulfils to the satisfaction of the said Commissioners the conditions which are specified in paragraph 4 of this Order, shall be entitled to be repaid the amount of tax so borne or paid.

4. The conditions to be fulfilled by a person referred to in paragraph 3 of this Order are-

    (a)   he shall claim a refund of the tax concerned by completing such claim form as may be provided for the purpose by the Revenue Commissioners and he shall certify the particulars shown on such claim form to be correct;

    (b)   he shall, by the production of invoices, provided in accordance with section 17(12)(a)(i) of the Act, or by the production of receipts for tax paid on goods imported, establish the amount of tax borne or paid to which the claim relates;

(c)   he shall establish that he is not a person who is registered in the register maintained under section 9 of the Act, nor a person required under the provisions of that section to furnish the particulars specified for registration;

(d)   except where the Revenue Commissioners otherwise allow, the claim for a refund of tax shall be made in respect of hydrocarbon oil used within a period or periods of three months.

GIVEN under my Official Seal,
this 25th day of October, 1983.

ALAN M. DUKES,
Minister for Finance.

EXPLANATORY NOTE.

This Order enables sea-fishermen to reclaim the value-added tax borne or paid by them on the purchase or importation of hydrocarbon oil (marine diesel) for use on a registered sea-fishing vessel.

EUROPEAN COMMUNITIES (EXEMPTION FROM IMPORT CHARGES OF CERTAIN VEHICLES ETC, TEMPORARILY IMPORTED) REGULATIONS, 1983

(SI No. 422 of 1983)

> Council Directive 83/183/EEC of 28 March 1983 as implemented by these Regulations ceased to have effect on 31 December 1992 as regards its provisions on VAT. Importations of vehicles not covered by these Regulations continue to be goverened by Motor Vehicles (Temporary Importation) Regulations, 1970 (1970 S.I. No. 54)

I, ALAN M. DUKES, Minister for Finance, in exercise of the powers conferred on me by section 3 of the European Communities Act, 1972, (No.27 of 1972), and for the purpose of giving effect to Council Directive No. 83/182/EEC of 28 March, 1983, hereby make the following Regulations:

1. These Regulations may be cited as the European Communities (Exemption from Import Charges of Certain Vehicles etc., Temporarily Imported) Regulations, 1983.

2. These Regulations shall come into operation on the 1st day of January, 1984.

3. (a)   In these Regulations-

           "the Community" means the European Economic Community;

           "import charges" means excise duties, value-added tax and any other consumption tax chargeable on imported goods;

           "private vehicle" includes a caravan, pleasure boat, private aircraft, tricycle and bicycle.

    (b)   A word or expression that is used in these Regulations and is also used in Council Directive No. 83/182/EEC of 28 March, 1983, shall, unless the context otherwise requires, have the meaning in these Regulations that it has in that Directive.

4. (1)   These Regulations shall not extend to the temporary importation of private vehicles, or normal spare parts, accessories and equipment for private vehicles imported with the vehicles for private use which have not been acquired or imported in accordance with the general conditions of taxation in force on the domestic market of another Member State or which are subject by reason of their exportation to any exemption from or refund of turnover tax, excise duty or any other consumption tax.

    (2)   For the purpose of this Regulation, paragraph (1) of this Regulation shall be deemed to have been satisfied-

        (a)   where the goods are supplied under diplomatic and consular arrangements, or

        (b)   where the goods are supplied to international organisations recognised as such by the public authorities in the State, and to members of such organisations within the limits and under the conditions laid down by the International Conventions establishing the organisations or by headquarters agreements.

5. (1) Subject to the provisions of these Regulations, where a private vehicle is imported temporarily into the State, the vehicle, and any normal spare parts, accessories and equipment for the vehicle imported into the State with the vehicle, shall be exempt from import charges for a period not exceeding twelve months from the date of such importation or such longer period as the Revenue Commissioners in their discretion may allow in any particular case, provided that-

    (a) the individual importing the vehicle-

        (i) has his normal residence in another Member State; and

        (ii) employs the vehicle for his private use only, and

    (b) the vehicle is not disposed of or hired out in the State or lent to a resident of the State.

(2) Notwithstanding anything to the contrary in paragraph (1)(b) of this Regulation private vehicles belonging to a car hire firm having its head office in the Community-

    (a) may be re-hired to non-residents of the State with a view to being re-exported, if they are in the State as a result of a hire contract which ended in the State; and

    (b) may be returned by an employee of the car-hire firm to the Member State where they were originally hired, even if such employee is resident in the State.

6. (1) A private vehicle imported into the State temporarily for business use shall be exempt from import charges for a period not exceeding twelve months from the date of such importation or such longer period as the Revenue Commissioners in their discretion may allow in any particular case, provided that-

    (a) the individual importing the vehicle-

        (i) has his normal residence in another Member State;

        (ii) does not use the vehicle within the State in order to carry passengers for hire or material reward of any kind, or for the industrial or commercial transport of goods, whether for reward or not;

    (b) the vehicle is not disposed of, hired out or lent in the State; and

    (c) the vehicle has been acquired or imported in accordance with the general conditions of taxation in force on the domestic market of the Member State of normal residence of the user and is not subject, by reason of its exportation, to any exemption from or refund of turnover tax, excise duty or any other consumption tax;

(2)   (a)   The provisions of paragraph (1)(c) of this Regulation shall be presumed to be being complied with in relation to a private vehicle if it bears a standard registration plate of the Member State of registration, (which expression does not include any type of temporary registration plate).

(b)   However, in the case of a private vehicle registered in a Member State where the issue of standard registration plates is not conditional upon compliance with the general conditions of taxation in force on the domestic market, the Revenue Commissioners may require the individual importing the vehicle to show to their satisfaction that any consumption taxes payable in respect of the vehicle have been paid.

7.   (1)   In addition a private vehicle imported temporarily shall be exempt from import charges in the following cases:

(a)   where the vehicle is registered in another Member State being the Member State of normal residence of the user and is used regularly by him for the journey from his residence to his place of work in an undertaking in the State: Exemption under this subparagraph shall not be subject to any time limit;

(b)   where a student residing in the State for the sole purpose of pursuing his studies uses the vehicle in the State and the vehicle is registered in another Member State which is the Member State of his normal residence.

(2)   Grant of the exemptions provided for in paragraph (1) of this Regulation shall be subject to the sole condition that the provisions of paragraphs (a), (b) and (c) of paragraph (1) and paragraph (2) of Regulation 6 are satisfied.

8.   (1)   Saddle-horses imported temporarily into the State shall be exempt for three months from import charges provided that:

(a)   the horses enter the State for the purposes of, or in the course of, horse-riding excursions by their riders;

(b)   exemption is requested not later than the time of their importation; and

(c)   the horses are not hired out, lent, or disposed of to a third party in the State or used for purposes other than that of the excursion.

(2)   Where exemption is requested under this Regulation before the importation of the horse concerned, its rider may be exempted from the requirement to enter the State via a frontier post.

(3)   The Revenue Commissioners may exclude from the benefit of the exemption under this Regulation the temporary importation by residents of the State of horses carried on board means of transport.

9.   (1)   A person who lives in turn in different places situated in two or more Member States shall be regarded for the purposes of these Regulations as having his normal residence in the Member State where his personal ties are if he shows to the satisfaction of the Revenue Commissioners that his family or social commitments require him to return there regularly.

(2)   Individuals shall give proof of their place of normal residence by any appropriate means, such as their identity card or any other valid document.

(3)   Where the Revenue Commissioners have doubts as to the truth or accuracy of a statement as to normal residence made in accordance with paragraph (1) of this Regulation or for the purpose of applying certain specific controls, they may request the individual concerned to furnish them with any information they require or with additional proof.

10.   (1)   In exceptional cases where, despite the furnishing of the additional information referred to in Regulation 9(3) of these Regulations, serious doubts still remain as to the normal residence of an individual the Revenue Commissioners may permit the temporary importation of a private vehicle for business use upon the giving to them of such security as they may specify.

(2)   When the user of the vehicle concerned shows to the satisfaction of the Revenue Commissioners that he has his normal residence in another Member State, the Revenue Commissioners shall release any security given to them within two months following the date on which the evidence is produced.

11.   (1)   While in the State, a vehicle temporarily imported under these Regulations shall not be driven by any person other than the importer, save with the permission of the Revenue Commissioners.

(2)   Vehicles or horses temporarily imported into the State under these Regulations shall cease to be exempt from import charges in the event of the importer ceasing to have his normal residence outside the State, or, at the end of the period for which retention in the State was allowed under these Regulations or on termination of the activities mentioned in Regulation 7(1) of these Regulations as the case may be.

12. (1) All documents relating to the importation of a vehicle or horse temporarily imported into the State under these Regulations shall be kept by the person who imported them with the vehicle or horse when it is in the State and shall be produced on request by an Officer of Customs and Excise or a member of the Garda Síochána.

(2) Any person found in charge or control of a vehicle or horse temporarily imported into the State under these Regulations shall stop the vehicle or horse on request by any Officer of Customs and Excise or any member of the Garda Síochána, and shall answer all such questions as shall be put to him by such Officer or such member for the purpose of verifying that no contravention of these Regulations is taking place.

13. Nothing in these Regulations shall be construed as exempting an importer from compliance with any legal requirement, obligation, restriction or prohibition other than the requirement of paying at the time of importation any import charges which, but for these Regulations, would be chargeable at that time on a vehicle or horse being imported.

14. The Revenue Commissioners shall not accord to imports by private individuals of vehicles or horses from third countries more favourable exemptions than those which are accorded to imports from Member States under these Regulations.

15. (1) Subject to Regulation 5(2) of these Regulations, a person who imports a vehicle or horse temporarily into the State under these Regulations without payment of import charges on the vehicle or horse, as the case may be, shall not dispose of or hire out the vehicle or horse, as the case may be, or lend it to a resident in the State and, if he imports the vehicle for business use, shall not use the vehicle within the State to carry passengers for hire or material reward of any kind or for the industrial or commercial transport of goods whether for reward or not.

(2) A person who imports a vehicle or horse temporarily into the State under these Regulations without payment of import charges on the vehicle or horse, as the case may be, shall, at or before the end of the period for which the vehicle or horse is permitted under these Regulations to remain in the State without such payment, either pay the import charges on the vehicle or horse, as the case may be, to the Revenue Commissioners or export the vehicle or horse, as the case may be, from the State.

16. A person who contravenes a provision of these Regulations shall, without prejudice to any other penalty to which he may be liable, be guilty of an offence and shall be liable, on summary conviction, to a fine not exceeding £500.

17. These Regulations, so far as they relate to value-added tax and the duties of excise on imported goods and the management of those duties, shall be construed together with the Customs Acts and any instrument relating to the customs made under statute.

18. (1) The Motor Vehicles (Temporary Importation) Regulations, 1970, (S.I. No.54 of 1970), shall not apply to private vehicles covered by these Regulations.

(2) Section 29(2) of the Finance Act, 1963 (No.23 of 1963), shall apply in relation to vehicles imported temporarily into the State under these Regulations with the modification that, "in relation to a motor vehicle, a provision of the European Communities (Exemption from Import Charges of Certain Vehicles etc., Temporarily Imported) Regulations, 1983," shall be substituted for "a condition under a regulation under this section".

GIVEN under my Official Seal,
this 30th day of December, 1983.

ALAN M. DUKES,
Minister for Finance

EXPLANATORY NOTE.

These Regulations which come into operation on 1 January, 1984, implement at national level Council Directive 83/182/EEC of 28 March, 1983 which provides for relief from import charges for certain means of transport temporarily imported from another Member State of the European Economic Community.

The provisions of these Regulations, insofar as they apply to the means of transport referred to therein, replace those in the Motor Vehicles (Temporary Importation) Regulations, 1970, (S.I. No.54 of 1970). The provisions of the Motor Vehicles (Temporary Importation) Regulations, 1970 remain in force in respect of other means of transport temporarily imported from other Member States of the European Economic Community and in respect of all means of transport temporarily imported from third countries.

EUROPEAN COMMUNITIES (EXEMPTION FROM IMPORT CHARGES OF CERTAIN PERSONAL PROPERTY) REGULATIONS, 1983

(SI No. 423 of 1983)

Council Directive 83/183/EEC of 28 March 1983 as implemented by these Regulations ceased to have effect on 31 December 1992 as regards its provisions on VAT. The appropriate exemptions are now contained in the European Communities (Exemption from Value Added Tax on the Permanent Importation of Certain Goods) Regulations, 1985, (1985 SI No. 183).

I, ALAN M. DUKES, Minister for Finance, in exercise of the powers conferred on me by Section 3 of the European Communities Act, 1972 (No. 27 of 1972), and for the purpose of giving effect to Council Directive No. 83/183/EEC of 28 March, 1983(1), hereby make the following Regulations:

1.   These Regulations may be cited as the European Communities (Exemption from Import Charges of Certain Personal Property) Regulations, 1983.

2.   These Regulations shall come into operation on the 1st day of January, 1984.

3.   (a)   In these Regulations-

"import charges" means excise duties, value-added tax and any other consumption taxes chargeable on imported goods;

"ECU" means the unit of account as defined in Council Regulation (EEC) No. 3180/78 of 18 December, 1978(2).

(b)   A word or expression that is used in these Regulations and is also used in Council Directive No. 83/183/EEC of 28 March, 1983, shall, unless the context otherwise requires, have the meaning in these Regulations that it has in the Directive.

4.   Subject to the conditions and in the cases hereinafter set out, personal property imported permanently from another Member State by private individuals shall be exempt from import charges.

5.   (1)   The exemption for which Regulation 4 of these Regulations makes provision shall be granted for personal property-

(a)   which has been acquired under the general conditions of taxation in force in the domestic market of one of the other Member States of the Community and which is not the subject, on the grounds of exportation, of any exemption or any refund of turnover tax, excise duty or any other consumption tax,

(b)   which the person concerned has had the use of, in the Member State from which it is being exported, for a period of at least:-

          (i)   six months before the change of residence in the case of motor-driven vehicles (including their trailers), caravans, mobile homes, pleasure boats and private aircraft, and

          (ii)   three months before the change of residence or the setting up of a secondary residence in the case of other property.

(2)   For the purpose of this Regulation, where goods are-

    (a)   supplied under diplomatic or consular arrangements, or

    (b)   supplied to international organisations recognised as such by the public authorities in the State, and to members of such organisations within the limits and under the conditions laid down by the international conventions establishing the organisations or by headquarters agreements,

the conditions specified in paragraph (1)(a) of this Regulation shall be deemed to have been met and the references in paragraph (1)(b) of this Regulation to six months and three months shall be construed as references to twelve months.

(3)   (a)   Proof shall be supplied to the Revenue Commissioners that the conditions specified in paragraph (1) of this Regulation have been satisfied in the case of motor-driven vehicles (including their trailers), caravans, mobile homes, pleasure boats and private aircraft.

    (b)   In the case of other property the Revenue Commissioners shall require such proof only where there are grave suspicions of fraud.

    (c)   The proof referred to in subparagraphs (a) and (b) of this paragraph shall consist of invoices or receipts of purchase or any other documentary evidence the Revenue Commissioners may deem acceptable.

6.   The importation of property may be carried out at one or more times within the periods laid down in Regulations 10 to 13 of these Regulations.

7.   (1)   Property imported under these Regulations shall not be disposed of, hired out or lent during the period of twelve months following its importation free of import charges, except in circumstances duly justified to the satisfaction of and with the permission of the Revenue Commissioners.

    (2)   A person seeking the permission referred to in paragraph (1) of this Regulation shall make prior application therefor to the Revenue Commissioners in writing, setting out the circumstances of the case, and the Revenue Commissioners may, if they see fit, allow disposal, hiring or lending of the property in question

either with or without payment of whatever import charges the property was exempted from under the said Regulation 4.

8.   (1)   (a)   Tobacco products, alcoholic beverages, perfumes and toilet waters contained in the personal luggage of travellers coming from other Member States may be imported without payment of import charges only up to the quantities laid down by the European Economic Community relating to exemption from import charges on imports in international travel.

           (b)   The Revenue Commissioners may allow the importation of up to 18 litres of wine (including sparkling and fortified wine) of an alcoholic strength not exceeding 22% by volume, without payment of import charges, in the case of a private individual who is transferring his normal residence to the State.

    (2)   The exemption from import charges on the importation of riding horses, motor-driven road vehicles (including trailers), caravans, mobile homes, pleasure boats and private aircraft shall be granted only if the private individual transfers his normal residence to the State.

9.   (1)   A person who lives in turn in different places situated in two or more Member States shall be regarded for the purposes of these Regulations as having his normal residence in the Member State where his personal ties are if he shows to the satisfaction of the Revenue Commissioners that his family or social commitments require him to return there regularly.

    (2)   Individuals shall give proof of their place of normal residence by any appropriate means such as their identity card or any other valid document.

    (3)   Where the Revenue Commissioners have doubts as to the truth and accuracy of a statement as to normal residence made in accordance with paragraph (2) of this Regulation, or for the purpose of applying certain specific controls, they may request the individual concerned to furnish them with any information they require or with additional proof.

10.   (1)   The exemption for which Regulation 4 of these Regulations makes provision shall be granted, subject to the conditions laid down in Regulations 5 to 8 of these Regulations, in respect of personal property imported by a private individual when transferring his normal residence.

    (2)   All the property shall be imported not later than twelve months after the transfer of the normal residence, or such longer period as the Revenue Commissioners, in their discretion, may allow in any particular case.

11. (1)   The exemption for which Regulation 4 of these Regulations makes provision shall be granted, subject to the conditions laid down in Regulations 5 to 8 of these Regulations, for personal property imported by a private individual to furnish a secondary residence.

(2)   This exemption shall be granted only where:-

(a)   the person concerned is the owner of the secondary residence or is renting it for a period of at least twelve months;

(b)   the property imported corresponds to the normal furniture of the secondary residence.

(3)   The exemption shall also be granted, subject to the conditions mentioned in paragraph (2) of this Regulation, where, following the relinquishment of a secondary residence, property is imported to the normal residence or to another secondary residence, provided that the property in question has actually been in the possession of the person concerned, and that he has had the use of it, for a period of at least twelve months.

(4)   All the property shall be imported not later than twelve months after the secondary residence has been relinquished or such longer period as the Revenue Commissioners in their discretion may allow in any particular case.

(5)   Regulation 7 of these Regulations shall not apply where property is re-imported.

12. (1)   Notwithstanding Regulation 5(1)(b)(ii) of these Regulations, but without prejudice to the other provisions contained in Regulations 5 to 8 of these Regulations, a person shall on marrying be entitled to exemption from import charges when importing into the State on transfer of normal residence personal property which he acquired or which came into his possession less than three months previously, provided that such importation takes place within a period beginning two months before the marriage date envisaged and ending four months after the actual marriage date, and the person concerned shows to the satisfaction of the Revenue Commissioners that-

(a)   his marriage has taken place, or

(b)   the necessary preliminary formalities for the marriage have been put in hand, as the case may be.

(2)   (a)   Exemption shall also be granted in respect of presents customarily given on the occasion of a marriage which are sent to a person fulfilling the conditions laid down in paragraph (1) of this Regulation by persons having their normal place of residence in another Member State.

(b)   The exemption shall apply to any present of a value not exceeding 200 ECU.

(c)   However, where the value of a present is more than 200 ECU, but less than 1,000 ECU, the Revenue Commissioners may, in their absolute discretion, grant the exemption.

(3)   Where property is imported before the date of the marriage, the Revenue Commissioners may make the granting of exemption dependent on the provision of an adequate guarantee.

(4)   Where the individual fails to provide proof of his marriage within four months of the date given for such marriage, the import charges due on the date of importation shall be payable.

13. (1)   Notwithstanding paragraphs (1) to (3) of Regulation 5 and Regulations 7 and 8(2), but without prejudice to the other provisions contained in Regulation 8, any private individual who has a residence in the State and who acquires by inheritance (causa mortis) the ownership or the beneficial ownership of personal property of a deceased person which is situated within another Member State or the personal representative of any such deceased person who has a residence in the State shall be entitled to exemption from import charges when importing such property into the State, provided that;

(a)   such individual or personal representative provides the Revenue Commissioners with a declaration issued by a notary in the State or by a notary or other competent authority in the Member State of exportation that the property he is importing was acquired by inheritance or that he is the personal representative of the deceased person, as the case may be;

(b)   the property is imported not more than two years after the date on which such individual enters into possession of the property or such personal representative takes control of the property.

(2)   Notwithstanding paragraph 1(b) of this Regulation, the Revenue Commissioners in their discretion may allow such longer period as they see fit, in any particular case.

14.   The Revenue Commissioners shall not accord to imports by private individuals of personal property from third countries more favourable exemptions than those which are accorded to imports from Member States under these Regulations.

15.   These Regulations, so far as they relate to value-added tax and the duties of excise on imported goods and the management of those duties, shall be construed together with the Customs Acts and any instrument relating to the customs made under statute.

16.   A person who contravenes a provision of these Regulations shall, without prejudice to any other penalty to which he may be liable, be guilty of an offence and shall be liable, on summary conviction, to a fine not exceeding £500.

17.   Section 17 of the Finance Act, 1936 (No.31 of 1936), as amended by section 13 of the Finance Act, 1957 (No.20 of 1957), section 18(a) of the Finance Act, 1936 (No.31 of 1936) and section 18(b) of the Finance Act, 1936 (No.31 of 1936), shall not apply to property to which these Regulations apply.

GIVEN under my Official Seal,
this 29th day of December, 1983.

ALAN M. DUKES.

EXPLANATORY NOTE.

These Regulations, which come into operation on 1 January, 1984, implement at national level Council Directive 83/183/EEC of 28 March, 1983 which provides for relief from import charges for goods (personal property)-

(a)   imported in connection with a transfer of normal residence;

(b)   imported in connection with the furnishing or relinquishment of a secondary residence;

(c)   imported on marriage, and

(d)   acquired by inheritance,

where such goods are permanently imported from another Member State of the European Economic Community.

The provisions of these Regulations replace those in Section 17 of the Finance Act, 1936 [No. 31 of 1936] as amended by Section 13 of the Finance Act, 1957 [No. 20 of 1957], Section 18(a) of the Finance Act, 1936 [No. 31 of 1936] and Section 18(b) of the Finance Act, 1936 [No. 31 of 1936] in so far as goods permanently imported from other Member States of the European Economic Community are concerned. The provisions of the Finance Acts referred to above remain in force, for the present, in respect of goods permanently imported from third countries.

VALUE-ADDED TAX (EXPORTED GOODS) REGULATIONS, 1984

(SI No. 230 of 1984)

> **These Regulations revoked by Value Added Tax (Exported Goods) Regulations, 1992 w.e.f. 17 December 1992**

The Revenue Commissioners, in exercise of the powers conferred on them by section 13 (inserted by section 12 of the Value-Added Tax (Amendment) Act, 1978 (No. 34 of 1978)) and section 32 of the Value-Added Tax Act, 1972 (No. 22 of 1972), and with the consent of the Minister for Finance, hereby make the following Regulations:

1. These Regulations may be cited as the Value-Added Tax (Exported Goods) Regulations, 1984.

2. (1) The tax, if any, chargeable on the supply, on or after the 1st day of March, 1984, of goods which are delivered on board a ship or aircraft (other than a private ship or aircraft) proceeding to a place outside the State for export in that ship or aircraft shall be remitted if the Revenue Commissioners are satisfied that-

     (a) the goods were supplied to, and delivered on board the ship or aircraft by or on behalf of, a person who-

          (i) was not normally resident in the State at the time of the supply, or who, if he was normally resident in the State at that time, intended at that time to depart from the State for a period of at least twelve consecutive months, and

          (ii) was not at the time of the supply a member of the crew of any ship, aircraft, train or other conveyance engaged in the transport of passengers or goods into or out of the State,

     (b) the goods do not consist of a mechanically propelled road vehicle or of goods for the equipping, fuelling or provisioning of any means of transport for private use,

     (c) in case the person to whom the goods are supplied was normally resident in a Member State of the European Economic Community at the time of the supply and intended at that time to export the goods to a Member State of that Community, the value of the goods, including tax, exceeded the value, or, if there is more than one, the higher or highest value, standing specified at that time by the Council of the said Community as the limit for exemption from tax of goods in personal baggage of travellers between Member States of the said Community,

    (d)   the goods were exported in that ship or aircraft within two months of the date of their supply, and

    (e)   there is compliance with such other conditions (if any) as the Revenue Commissioners may impose.

(2)   In this Regulation "goods" means any article and includes a group of articles normally supplied as a set.

GIVEN this 6th day of September, 1984.

L. REASON,Revenue Commissioner.

The Minister for Finance hereby consents to the making of the foregoing Regulations.

GIVEN under the Official Seal of the Minister for Finance this 6th day of September, 1984.

ALAN M. DUKES,
Minister for Finance.

EXPLANATORY NOTE

These Regulations, which have effect as from 1 March, 1984, provide for relief from VAT on certain supplies of goods to foreign visitors, and to Irish residents departing the State for more than a year. The goods in question must be shipped by or on behalf of the purchaser on board an aircraft or ship (other than private aircraft or vessels) leaving the State.

VALUE -ADDED TAX (GOODS EXPORTED IN BAGGAGE) REGULATIONS, 1984

(SI No. 231 of 1984)

> These Regulations revoked by Value Added Tax (Exported Goods) Regulations, 1992, with effect from 1 January 1993.

The Revenue Commissioners, in exercise of the powers conferred on them by section 13 (inserted by section 12 of the Value-Added Tax (Amendment) Act, 1978 (No. 34 of 1978)) and section 32 of the Value-Added Tax Act, 1972 (No. 22 of 1972), and with the consent of the Minister for Finance, hereby make the following Regulations:

1. These Regulations may be cited as the Value-Added Tax (Goods Exported in Baggage) Regulations, 1984.

2. (1) The tax, if any, chargeable on the supply on or after the 1st day March, 1984, of goods shall be remitted if the Revenue Commissioners are satisfied that-

   (a) the goods were intended at the time of the supply by the person to whom they were supplied to be exported from the State within two months of such supply in his personal baggage and were so exported,

   (b) the person to whom the goods were supplied-

      (i) was not normally resident in the State at the time of the supply, or, if he was normally resident in the State at that time, intended at that time to depart from the State for a period of at least twelve consecutive months,

      (ii) was not at the time of the supply a member of the crew of a ship, aircraft, train or other conveyance engaged in the transport of passengers or goods into or out of the State,

   (c) in case the person to whom the goods are supplied was normally resident in a Member State of the European Economic Community at the time of the supply and intended at that time to export the goods to a Member State of the Community, the value of the goods, including tax, exceeded the value, or, if there is more than one, the higher or highest value, standing specified at that time by the Council of the said Community as the limit for exemption from tax of goods in personal baggage of travellers between Member States of the said Community, and

   (d) there is compliance with such other conditions (if any) as the Revenue Commissioners may impose.

(2)   In this Regulation "goods" means any article, and includes a group of articles normally supplied as a set.

GIVEN this 6th day of September, 1984.

L. REASON,
Revenue Commissioner.

The Minister for Finance hereby consents to the making of the foregoing Regulations.

GIVEN under the Official Seal of the Minister for Finance this 6th day of September, 1984.

ALAN M. DUKES,Minister for Finance.

EXPLANATORY NOTE

These Regulations, which have effect as from 1 March, 1984, provide for relief from VAT on certain supplies of goods to foreign visitors, and to Irish residents departing the State for more than a year. The goods in question must be exported as personal baggage of the purchaser.

VALUE-ADDED TAX (REFUND OF TAX) (NO 17) ORDER, 1984

(SI No. 249 of 1984)

> This Order revoked by para 9, Value Added tax (Refund of Tax)(No.25) Order 1993 (1993 S.I. No. 266) w.e.f. 15 September 1993.

I, ALAN M. DUKES, Minister for Finance, in exercise of the powers conferred on me by section 20(3) of the Value-Added Tax Act, 1972 (No.22 of 1972), hereby order as follows:

1. (1) This Order may be cited as the Value-Added Tax (Refund of Tax) (No.17) Order, 1984.

    (2) This Order shall be deemed to have come into operation on the 9th day of February, 1983.

2. In this Order "the Principal Order" means the Value-Added Tax (Refund of Tax)(No.1) Order, 1972 (SI No.267 of 1972).

3. The Principal Order is hereby amended by-

    (a) the insertion in subparagraph (b) of paragraph 4 after "evidence" of ", including such particulars as may be required by the said Commissioners of payment of any grant received by him from the Department of Agriculture, Roinn na Gaeltachta or the Irish Land Commission",

    (b) the insertion in paragraph 5 after "paragraph 3 of this Order shall" of ", subject to paragraph 6 of this Order,", and

    (c) the insertion of the following paragraph after paragraph 5:

        "6. A claim for repayment of tax under this Order shall be made only in respect of outlay involving a total amount of tax of more than £100.",

        and the said subparagraph (b) and the said paragraph 5, as so amended, are set out in paragraphs 1 and 2, respectively, of the Table to this paragraph.

TABLE.

1. (b) he shall, by the production of plans, specifications or other sufficient documentary evidence, including such particulars as may be required by the said Commissioners of payment of any grant received by him from the Department of Agriculture, Roinn na Gaeltachta or the Irish Land Commission, establish that the outlay in relation to which his claim for a refund of tax arises was incurred-

        (i) on the construction, extension, alteration or reconstruction of a building or structure which is designed for use solely or mainly for the purposes of a farming business, or

         (ii)   on the drainage or reclamation of any land intended for use for the purposes of such a business.

2.5. The amount of tax to be repaid to a person referred to in paragraph 3 of this Order shall, subject to paragraph 6 of this Order, be so much of the amount of tax established in accordance with paragraph 4(c) of this Order to have been borne or paid as the person shows to the satisfaction of the Revenue Commissioners to be referable solely-

(a)   to that part of the outlay referred to in paragraph 4(b)(i) of this Order which relates to the construction, extension, alteration or reconstruction of that part of the building or structure which was designed solely for the purposes of a farming business and has actually been put to use in such a business carried on by him, or

(b)   to that part of the outlay referred to in paragraph 4(b)(ii) of this Order which relates to the drainage or reclamation of any land which has actually been put to use in such a business carried on by him.

4.   A person who, before the commencement of this Order, has borne or paid tax in relation to outlay referred to in paragraph 3 of the Principal Order shall not be entitled to be repaid tax under the Principal Order by reason only of the making of this Order.

5.   Subparagraph (d) (inserted by the Value-Added Tax (Refund of Tax) (No.8) Order, 1978 (SI No.145 of 1978)), of paragraph 4 of the Principal Order is hereby revoked.

GIVEN under my Official Seal,
this 12th day of October, 1984.

ALAN M. DUKES,
Minister for Finance.

EXPLANATORY NOTE.

This Order extends the existing VAT refund arrangements for unregistered farmers so as to enable refunds to be made in respect of the VAT element in outlay by them on non grant-aided qualifying work in relation to farm buildings and land drainage or reclamation. VAT relief will apply only in respect of claims to repayment in excess of £100. The Order is effective from 9 February 1983.

EUROPEAN COMMUNITIES (EXEMPTION FROM VALUE-ADDED TAX ON THE PERMANENT IMPORTATION OF CERTAIN GOODS) REGULATIONS, 1985

(SI No. 183 of 1985)

I, ALAN M. DUKES, Minister for Finance, in exercise of the powers conferred on me by section 3 of the European Communities Act, 1972 (No. 27 of 1972), and for the purpose of giving effect to Council Directive No. 83/181/EEC of 28 March, 1983, hereby make the following Regulations:

1.   (1)   These Regulations may be cited as the European Communities (Exemption from Value-Added Tax on the Permanent Importation of Certain Goods) Regulations, 1985.

      (2)   These Regulations shall be construed together with the Act and the Customs Acts (other than the provisions thereof specified in Regulation 30 of these Regulations) and any instrument relating to the customs made under statute (other than the instrument specified in the said Regulation 30).

2.   These Regulations shall be deemed to have come into operation on the 1st day of July, 1984.

3.   (1)   In these Regulations-

       "the Act" means the Value-Added Tax Act, 1972 (No.22 of 1972);

       "the Community" means the territory of the Member States where Council Directive No. 77/388/EEC of 17 May, 1977 applies;

       "ECU" means the unit of account as defined in Council Regulation No.3180/78 of 18 December, 1978;

       "importation", in relation to goods, has the meaning assigned to it by Article 7 of the Council Directive No. 77/388/EEC of 17 May, 1977, 2 and cognate words shall be construed accordingly;

       "Member State" means Member State of the European Economic Community;

       "tax" means value-added tax.

      (2)   In Regulations 4, 5 and 6 of these Regulations-

       "alcoholic products" means products (beer, wine, aperitifs with a wine or alcohol base, brandies, liqueurs and spirituous beverages, etc.) falling within headings 22.03 to 22.09 of the Common Customs Tariff;

       "household effects" means personal effects, household linen and furnishings and items of equipment intended for the personal use of the persons concerned or for meeting their household needs;

"personal property" means any property intended for the personal use of the persons concerned or for meeting their household needs, and includes-

(a)   household effects,

(b)   cycles and motor-cycles, private motor vehicles and their trailers, camping caravans, pleasure craft and private aeroplanes,

(c)   household provisions appropriate to normal family requirements, household pets and saddle animals,

(d)   portable instruments of the applied or liberal arts required by the person concerned for the pursuit of his trade or profession, but does not include property whose nature or quantity reflects a commercial interest or property intended for an economic activity within the meaning of Article 4 of Council Directive No. 77/388/EEC of 17 May, 1977;

"value for the purposes of tax chargeable at importation" means the value of imported goods for the purposes of section 15 of the Act as specified in subsections (3) and (4) of that section.

(3)   A word or expression that is used in these Regulations and is also used in Council Directive No. 83/181/EEC of 28 March, 1983, shall, unless the context otherwise requires, have the meaning in these Regulations that it has in that Directive.

4.   (1)   Subject to paragraphs (2) to (8) of this Regulation, tax shall not be charged on goods, being the personal property of any person, other than-

(a)   alcoholic products,

(b)   tobacco and tobacco products,

(c)   commercial means of transport,

(d)   articles for use in the exercise of a trade or profession, excluding portable instruments of the applied or liberal arts,

imported from a country outside the Community by a natural person transferring his normal place of residence to the State and which-

(i)   except in special cases justified by the circumstances, have been in the possession of, and, in the case of durable goods, used by that person for a minimum period of six months before the date on which he ceases to have his normal place of residence outside the Community;

(ii) are intended to be used at his normal place of residence in the State for the purpose for which they were used immediately before such importation;

(iii) have borne either in the country of origin or in the country from which he is departing any customs or fiscal charges to which they are normally liable and are not the subject, on the grounds of exportation, of any exemption from or refund of such charges;

(iv) are the personal property of that person, being a person whose normal place of residence has been outside the Community for a continuous period of at least 12 months, or who shows to the satisfaction of the Revenue Commissioners that his intention was to reside outside the Community for a continuous period of at least 12 months;

(v) except in special cases justified by the circumstances, are entered for customs purposes, for permanent importation within 12 months of the date of establishment in the State by that person of his normal place of residence.

(2) In the case of goods which are-

(a) supplied under diplomatic or consular arrangements, or

(b) supplied to international organisations recognised as such by the public authorities in the State, or to members of such organisations within the limits and under the conditions laid down by the international conventions establishing the organisations or by headquarters agreements,

the reference in subparagraph (i) of paragraph (1) of this Regulation to six months shall be construed as a reference to twelve months, and the conditions specified in subparagraph (iii), of the said paragraph shall be deemed to have been complied with.

(3) Goods the subject of relief under paragraphs (1) or (2) of this Regulation may be imported in several separate consignments within the period specified in subparagraph (v) of the said paragraph (1).

(4) Until 12 months have elapsed from the date of the declaration for their final importation, goods which have been imported tax-free under this Regulation may not be lent, given as security, hired out or transferred, whether for a consideration or free of charge, except in circumstances duly justified to the satisfaction of, and with the prior sanction of the Revenue Commissioners.

(5) Any lending, giving as security, hiring out or transfer before the expiry of the period referred to in paragraph (4) of this

Regulation shall entail payment of the relevant tax on the goods concerned, at the rate applying on the date of such loan, giving as security, hiring out or transfer, on the basis of the type of goods and the value for the purposes of tax chargeable at importation as ascertained or accepted on that date by the Revenue Commissioners.

(6) (a) Relief under this Regulation shall also apply in respect of personal property permanently imported before the person concerned establishes his normal place of residence in the State, provided that he gives an undertaking in writing to the Revenue Commissioners that he will actually establish his normal place of residence in the State within a period of 6 months after the importation. Such undertaking shall be accompanied by security, the form and amount of which shall be determined by the Revenue Commissioners.

(b) For the purpose of subparagraph (a) of this paragraph the period specified in paragraph (1)(i) of this Regulation shall be calculated from the date of the importation of the personal property into the State.

(7) (a) Subject to subparagraphs (b) and (c) of this paragraph, where the person concerned leaves the country situated outside the Community where he had his normal place of residence and, because of occupational commitments, does not simultaneously establish his normal place of residence in the State, although having the intention of ultimately doing so, relief under this Regulation shall apply in respect of the personal property which he transfers into the State for this purpose.

(b) Relief in respect of the personal property referred to in subparagraph (a) of this paragraph shall be granted in accordance with the conditions laid down in this Regulation on the basis that:

(i) the periods specified in paragraphs (1)(i) and (v) of this Regulation shall be calculated from the date of importation;

(ii) the period specified in paragraph (4) of this Regulation shall be calculated from the date when the person concerned actually establishes his normal place of residence in the State.

(c) Relief under this paragraph shall not be given unless the person concerned gives an undertaking in writing to the Revenue Commissioners that he will actually establish his normal place of residence in the State within such period as may be specified by the Revenue Commissioners having regard to the circumstances. Such undertaking shall, if the Revenue Commissioners so require, be accompanied by security, the form and amount of which shall be determined by the Revenue Commissioners.

(8)   Where, owing to exceptional political circumstances, a person has to transfer his normal place of residence from a country situated outside the Community to the State, the Revenue Commissioners may in their absolute discretion waive or modify the requirements of paragraph (1) of this Regulation, in so far as it refers to use of the goods prior to and subsequent to importation, subparagraph (b) of that paragraph, the conditions of the said paragraph relating to commercial means of transport and to articles for use in the exercise of a trade or profession and the requirements of paragraph (4) of this Regulation.

5.   (1)   Subject to paragraphs (3) to (7) of this Regulation, tax shall not be charged on the importation of trousseaux and household effects, whether or not new, belonging to a person transferring his or her normal place of residence from a country outside the Community to the State on the occasion of his or her marriage.

(2)   (a)   Subject to subparagraphs (b) and (c) of this paragraph, relief under this Regulation shall also apply to presents customarily given on the occasion of a marriage which are sent to a person fulfilling the conditions laid down in paragraph (1) of this Regulation by person sharing their normal place of residence in a country situated outside the Community.

    (b)   The exemption shall apply to presents of a unit value not exceeding [€200][1].

    (c)   However, where the value of a present is more than [€200][2], but less than [€1,000][3], the Revenue Commissioners may, in their absolute discretion, grant the exemption.

(3)   Relief in respect of the goods referred to in paragraph (1) of this Regulation shall be conditional on the goods having borne, either in the country of origin or in the country from which the person concerned is departing, any customs or fiscal charges to which they are normally liable.

(4)   Relief under this Regulation shall apply only to a person:

    (a)   whose normal place of residence has been outside the Community for a continuous period of at least twelve months, or where it is shown to the satisfaction of the Revenue Commissioners that the intention of the person concerned was clearly to reside outside the Community for a continuous period of at least 12 months, and

    (b)   who produces evidence of the marriage.

(5)   Relief under this Regulation shall not apply to alcoholic products, tobacco or tobacco products.

(6)   Save in exceptional cases justified by the circumstances, relief under this Regulation shall be granted only in respect of goods permanently imported-

   (a)   not earlier than two months before the date fixed for the wedding; in such case the Revenue Commissioners may make the granting of relief dependent on the provision of security in such form and of such amount as the Revenue Commissioners may determine, and

   (b)   not later than four months after the date of the wedding.

(7)   Goods the subject of relief under this Regulation may be imported in several separate consignments within the period specified in paragraph (6) of this Regulation.

(8)   Until 12 months have elapsed from the date of the declaration for their final importation, goods which have been imported tax-free under this Regulation may not be lend, given as security, hired out or transferred, whether for a consideration or free of charge, except in circumstances duly justified to the satisfaction of, and with the prior sanction of the Revenue Commissioners.

(9)   Any lending, giving as security, hiring out or transfer before the expiry of the period referred to in paragraph (8) of this Regulation shall entail payment of the relevant tax on the goods concerned, at the rate applying on the date of such loan, giving as security, hiring out or transfer, on the basis of the type of goods and the value for the purposes of tax chargeable at importation ascertained or accepted on that date by the Revenue Commissioners.

6.   (1)   Subject to paragraphs (2) and (3) of this Regulation, tax shall not be charged on personal property of a deceased person imported from a country outside the Community by a person, being an individual resident in the State who either has acquired by inheritance (causa mortis) the ownership or the beneficial ownership of such property or who is the personal representative of such deceased person, if-

   (a)   such individual or personal representative provides the Revenue Commissioners with a statutory declaration or a corresponding declaration made under the laws of the country of exportation that the property he is importing was acquired by inheritance or that he is the personal representative of the deceased person, as the case may be,

   (b)   the property is imported not more than two years, or such longer period, in special cases, as the Revenue

Commissioners may determine, after the date on which such individual enters into possession of the property or such personal representative takes control of the property, and

(c)   the property is personal property other than-

(i)   alcoholic products,

(ii)   tobacco or tobacco products,

(iii)   commercial means of transport,

(iv)   articles for use in the exercise of a trade or profession, other than portable instruments of the applied or liberal arts, which were required for the exercise of the trade or profession of the deceased,

(v)   stocks of raw materials and finished or semi-finished products,

(vi)   livestock and stocks of agricultural products exceeding the quantities appropriate to normal family requirements.

(2)   Goods the subject of relief under this Regulation may be imported in several separate consignments within the period provided for in subparagraph (b) of paragraph (1) of this Regulation.

(3)   Paragraph (1) of this Regulation shall apply mutatis mutandis to personal property acquired by inheritance by a body of persons engaged in a non-profit making activity and established in the State.

7.   Tax shall not be charged on articles of clothing, scholastic materials or household effects imported for their personal use during the period of their studies by persons not normally resident in the State who are enrolled in an educational establishment in the State in order to attend full-time educational courses.

8.   Tax shall not be charged on the importation of goods (other than alcoholic products, perfumes, toilet waters, tobacco and tobacco products) not exceeding a total value of [€10][4] which-

(a)   are delivered to a consignee by letter or parcel post in a single postal delivery,

(b)   are despatched to him by a single consignor, and

(c)   do not form part of grouped consignments from the same consignor to the same consignee.

9.   (1)   Subject to paragraph (2) to (5) of this Regulation, tax shall not be charged on-

(a)   machinery, plant or equipment imported by a person on cessation of his business activity abroad in order to carry on a similar activity within the State:

Provided that the following conditions are complied with in relation to the goods, namely, the goods have been used in his business for a period of at least 12 months or such shorter period as the Revenue Commissioners consider reasonable prior to the date on which the business ceased to operate in the country of departure, are intended for the same purposes after transfer and are for use in the State in an agricultural activity or in an activity in respect of which he would be a taxable person in accordance with section 8 of the Act; or

(b)   livestock imported by a farmer on the transfer to the State of an activity carried on in an agricultural holding:

Provided that the following conditions are complied with in relation to the livestock, namely, the livestock were owned by the farmer for at least 12 months or such shorter period as the Revenue Commissioners consider reasonable prior to the importation and are intended to be used for farming after importation and their number is appropriate to the nature and size of the farming enterprise being undertaken by the person in the State.

(2)   Paragraph (1) of this Regulation shall not apply to importations by persons established outside the State the transfer of whose business to the State is consequent upon or is for the purpose of merging with, or being absorbed by, a person or persons in the State in circumstances in which a new activity is not, or is not intended to be, commenced.

(3)   Notwithstanding the provisions of paragraph (1) of this Regulation, relief may be granted in respect of machinery, plant or equipment imported from another Member State by charitable or philanthropic organisations at the time of the transfer of their principal place of business to the State if the goods were not exempt under Article 15(12) of Council Directive No. 77/388/EEC of 17 May, 1977.

(4)   Relief under this Regulation shall not apply to-

(a)   means of transport which are not used in the production process of the business concerned nor, in the case of a service business, used directly in the provision of the service;

(b)   food supplies intended for human consumption or for animal feed;

(c)   fuel and stocks of raw materials or finished or semi-finished products;

(d)   livestock in the possession of dealers.

(5)   Except in special cases justified by the circumstances, relief under this Regulation shall be granted only in respect of machinery, plant or equipment imported before the expiry of a period of 12 months from the date when the importer ceased his activities in the country of departure.

(6)   Where the Revenue Commissioners are satisfied that there are special circumstances justifying it, they may grant relief under this Regulation notwithstanding that the conditions specified in paragraph (1) or (2), as may be appropriate, of this Regulation are not complied with.

10.   (1)   Subject to paragraphs (2) to (6) of this Regulation tax shall not be charged on the importation of agricultural, stock-farming, bee-keeping, horticultural or forestry products from land situated in Northern Ireland and occupied and operated by farmers having their principal farms in the State adjacent to the land frontier of the State.

(2)   In paragraph (1) of this Regulation "stock-farming products" means such products obtained from animals reared or acquired in the State or imported in accordance with the general tax arrangements applicable in the State.

(3)   Relief under this Regulation shall also apply to pure-bred horses of not more than 6 months of age and born outside the State of an animal covered in the State and then exported temporarily to give birth.

(4)   Relief under this Regulation shall apply only to products which have not undergone any treatment other than that which normally follows their harvesting or production.

(5)   Relief under this Regulation shall apply only in respect of products imported by the farmer concerned or expressly on his behalf.

(6)   Relief under this Regulation shall apply, mutatis mutandis, to the products of fishing or fish-farming activities carried out in the lakes or waterways bordering or crossing the land frontier of the State by persons established in the State, and to the products of hunting activities carried out on such lakes or waterways by persons established in the State.

11.   (1)   Subject to paragraph (2) of this Regulation, tax shall not be charged on the importation from Northern Ireland of seeds, fertilizers and products for the treatment of soil and crops and intended for use on land situated in the State and operated by farmers having their principal farms in Northern Ireland adjacent to the land frontier of the State.

(2)   Relief under this Regulation shall apply only to the quantities of seeds, fertilisers or other products-

(a)   required for the purpose of operating the land concerned;

(b)   imported directly into the State by the farmer or expressly on his behalf.

12. (1)   Subject to the provisions of this Regulation, tax shall not be charged on the importation of the following goods:

(a)   live animals specially prepared and sent free of charge for laboratory use,

(b)   biological or chemical substances-

(i)   which are imported free of charge from another Member State, or

(ii)   which are imported from countries outside the Community subject to the limits and conditions laid down in Article 60(1)(b) of Council Regulation No. 918/83/EEC of 28 March, 1983, setting up a Community system of reliefs from customs duty.

(c)   therapeutic substances of human origin, being human blood and its derivatives (whole human blood, dried human plasma, human albumin and fixed solutions of human plasma protein, human immunoglobulin and human fibrinogen);

(d)   blood-grouping reagents whether of human, animal, plant or other origin used for blood-type grouping and for the detection of blood incompatibilities;

(e)   tissue-typing reagents whether of human, animal, plant or other origin used for the determination of human tissue-types;

(f)   pharmaceutical products for human or veterinary medical use by persons or animals participating in international sports events, within the limits necessary to meet their requirements during their stay in the State.

(2) (a)   Relief under subparagraphs (a) or (b) of paragraph (1) of this Regulation shall apply only to animals and biological and chemical substances intended for-

(i)   public establishments, or departments of public establishments, principally engaged in education or scientific research, or

(ii)   private establishments principally engaged in education or scientific research and approved by the Revenue Commissioners for the purposes of this Regulation.

(b)   Relief under subparagraphs (c), (d) or (e) of paragraph (1) of this Regulation shall apply only to-

    (i)   goods that-

        (I)   are intended for institutions or laboratories approved by the Revenue Commissioners for the purposes of this Regulation for use exclusively for non-commercial medical or scientific purposes,

        (II)   are accompanied by a certificate of conformity of a duly authorised body in the country of departure, and

        (III)   are in containers bearing a special label identifying them,

    and

    (ii)   special packaging essential for the transport of therapeutic substances of human origin or blood-grouping or tissue-typing reagents, and

    (iii)   solvents and accessories needed for their use and included in consignments of the goods.

13.   (1)   Subject to paragraphs (2) to (7) of this Regulation, and to any limit as to quantity or value that the Revenue Commissioners may impose in order to remedy any abuse and to combat major distortions of competition tax shall not be charged on the importation of-

    (a)   basic human necessities obtained free of charge by State organisations or by charitable or philanthropic organisations approved by the Revenue Commissioners for distribution free of charge to needy persons,

    (b)   goods sent free of charge by a person or organisation established abroad, and without any commercial intent on the part of the sender, to State organisations or charitable or philanthropic organisations approved by the Revenue Commissioners, for the purposes of fund-raising at occasional charity events for the benefit of needy persons,

    (c)   equipment and office materials sent free of charge by a person or organisation established abroad, and without any commercial intent on the part of the sender, to charitable or philanthropic organisations approved by the Revenue Commissioners, for use solely for the purpose of meeting their operating needs or carrying out their stated charitable or philanthropic aims.

    (2)   Relief under this Regulation shall not apply to-

(a)   alcoholic products,

(b)   tobacco or tobacco products,

(c)   motor vehicles other than ambulances.

(3)   Relief under this Regulation shall be granted only to organisations the accounting procedures of which enable the Revenue Commissioners to supervise their operations and which provide such guarantees as the Revenue Commissioners may consider necessary.

(4)   (a)   Goods the subject of relief under paragraph (1) of this Regulation shall not be lent, hired out or otherwise disposed of, whether for consideration or free of charge, for purposes other than those laid down in the said paragraph except in circumstances duly justified to the satisfaction of and with the prior sanction of the Revenue Commissioners.

    (b)   Goods and equipment may be lent, hired out or transferred to an organisation entitled to benefit from relief under paragraph (1) of this Regulation where the latter body uses the goods and equipment for purposes specified in subparagraphs (a) and (b) of the said paragraph.

    (c)   Goods the subject of relief under this Regulation which are lent, hired out or transferred otherwise than in accordance with subparagraph (a) or (b) of this paragraph shall be subject to payment of tax at the rate applying on the date of the loan, hiring out or transfer, on the basis of the type of goods and equipment and the value for the purposes of tax chargeable at importation ascertained or accepted on that date by the Revenue Commissioners.

(5)   Organisations referred to in paragraph (1) of this Regulation which cease to fulfil the conditions giving entitlement to relief under that paragraph, or which propose to use goods and equipment imported without payment of tax for purposes other than those provided for by the said paragraph (1), shall so inform the Revenue Commissioners.

(6)   Goods remaining in the possession of organisations which cease to fulfil the conditions giving entitlement to relief under this Regulation shall be liable to the relevant tax payable on importation at the rate applying on the date on which those conditions cease to be fulfilled, on the basis of the type of goods and equipment and the value for the purposes of tax chargeable at importation as ascertained or accepted on that date by the Revenue Commissioners.

(7)   Goods used by an organisation benefiting from relief under this Regulation for purposes other than those provided for in

paragraph (1) of this Regulation shall be liable to the relevant tax payable on importation at the rate applying on the date on which they are put to such other use on the basis of the type of goods and equipment and the value for the purposes of tax chargeable at importation ascertained on that date by the Revenue Commissioners.

14. (1)   Subject to paragraphs (2) to (6) of this Regulation, tax shall not be charged on the importation of-

        (a)   articles specially designed for the education, employment or social advancement of blind or other physically or mentally handicapped persons which are-

            (i)   imported by institutions or organisations principally engaged in the education of or the provision of assistance to handicapped persons, and approved by the Revenue Commissioners for the purposes of this Regulation, and

            (ii)   donated to such institutions or organisations free of charge and with no commercial intent on the part of the donor;

        (b)   specific spare parts, components or accessories specifically for such articles as aforesaid and tools for use for the maintenance, checking, calibration and repair of the said articles:

Provided that such spare parts, components, accessories or tools are imported at the same time as the said articles or, if imported subsequently, that they can be identified as being intended for articles previously imported tax-free or which would be eligible for tax-free importation at the time when such entry is requested for the said spare parts, components or accessories and tools.

    (2)   Goods the subject of relief under this Regulation shall not be used for purposes other than the education, employment or social advancement of blind or other physically or mentally handicapped persons.

    (3)   (a)   Goods the subject of relief under paragraph (1) of this Regulation may be lent, hired out or transferred, whether for a consideration or free of charge, by the institutions or organisations referred to in the said paragraph on a non-profit making basis to other such institutions or organisations with whom they are associated.

        (b)   No loan, hiring out or transfer of goods the subject of relief under this Regulation may be effected under conditions other than those provided for in subparagraph (a) except in special cases justified by the circumstances and with the prior sanction of the Revenue Commissioners:

Provided that-

(i)   goods may be lent, hired out or transferred to an institution or organisation itself entitled to benefit from relief under this Regulation where the latter body uses the article for purposes specified in paragraph (1) of this Regulation,

(ii)   goods the subject of relief under this Regulation which are lent, hired out or transferred otherwise than in accordance with the preceding provisions of this subparagraph shall be subject to payment of tax, at the rate applying on the date of the loan, hiring out or transfer, on the basis of the type of goods and the value for the purposes of tax chargeable at importation ascertained or accepted on that date by the Revenue Commissioners.

(4)   Institutions or organisations referred to in paragraph (1) of this Regulation which cease to fulfil the conditions giving entitlement to relief under the said paragraph or which propose to use such goods for purposes other than those provided for by the said paragraph shall so inform the Revenue Commissioners.

(5)   Goods remaining in the possession of institutions or organisations which cease to fulfil the conditions giving entitlement to relief under paragraph (1) of this Regulation shall be liable to tax at the rate applying on the date on which those conditions cease to be fulfilled, on the basis of the type of goods and the value for the purposes of tax chargeable at importation ascertained or accepted on that date by the Revenue Commissioners.

(6)   Goods used by an institution or organisation benefiting from relief under this Regulation for purposes other than those provided for in paragraph (1) of this Regulation shall be liable to tax payable on importation at the rate applying on the date on which they are put to such other use on the basis of the type of goods and the value for the purposes of tax chargeable at importation ascertained or accepted on that date by the Revenue Commissioners.

15.   (1)   Subject to paragraphs (2) to (8) of this Regulation, tax shall not be charged on-

(a)   goods, other than building materials or equipment intended for rebuilding disaster areas, imported by State organisations, or charitable or philanthropic organisations, approved of by the Revenue Commissioners for the purposes of this Regulation-

(i)   for distribution free of charge to victims of natural disasters affecting the territory of any Member State of the Community, or

(ii)   for making available free of charge to the victims of such disasters, while remaining the property of the importer,

or

(b)   goods imported by disaster-relief agencies in order to meet their needs during the period of their activity in connection with such disasters.

(2)   The granting of relief under paragraph (1) of this Regulation shall be subject to a decision by the Commission of the European Communities, acting at the request of the State or other Member States concerned in accordance with an emergency procedure entailing the consultation of the other Member States:

Provided that, pending notification of the Commission's decision, the Revenue Commissioners may grant relief under paragraph (1) subject to an undertaking by the organisation concerned to pay the relevant tax if relief is not granted.

(3)   Entitlement to relief under this Regulation may be granted only to disaster-relief organisations the accounting procedures of which enable the Revenue Commissioners to supervise their operations and which provide such security as the Revenue Commissioners may consider necessary.

(4)   The organisations benefiting from relief under paragraph (1) of this Regulation shall not lend, hire out or transfer, whether for a consideration or free of charge, the goods referred to in that paragraph under conditions other than those laid down in that paragraph except in special cases justified by the circumstances and with the prior sanction of the Revenue Commissioners:

Provided that-

(a)   goods may be lent, hired out or transferred to an organisation itself entitled to benefit from relief under this Regulation where the latter body uses the goods for purposes specified in paragraph (1) of this Regulation, and

(b)   goods the subject of relief under this Regulation which are lent, hired out or transferred otherwise than in accordance with the preceding provisions of this subparagraph shall be subject to prior payment of tax, at the rate applying on the date of the loan, hiring out or transfer, on the basis of the type of goods and the value for the purposes of tax chargeable at importation ascertained or accepted on that date by the Revenue Commissioners.

(5)   The goods referred to in paragraph (1)(a)(ii) of this Regulation, after they cease to be used by disaster victims, may not be lent, hired out or transferred, whether for a consideration or free of

charge, except in special cases justified by the circumstances and with the prior sanction of the Revenue Commissioners:

Provided that-

(a)   goods may be lent, hired out or transferred to an organisation itself entitled to benefit from relief pursuant to the said paragraph (1) or, if appropriate, to an organisation entitled to benefit from relief pursuant to Regulation 13(1)(a) of these Regulations where such organisations use them for purposes specified in the said paragraph (1) or Regulation 13(1)(a),

(b)   goods the subject of loan, hiring out or transfer otherwise than in accordance with subparagraph (i) of this proviso shall be subject to payment of tax, at the rate applying on the date of the loan, hiring out or transfer, on the basis of the type of goods and the value for the purposes of tax chargeable at importation ascertained or accepted on that date by the Revenue Commissioners.

(6)   Organisations referred to in paragraph (1) of this Regulation which cease to fulfil the conditions giving entitlement to relief or which propose to use such goods for purposes other than those provided for by that paragraph shall so inform the Revenue Commissioners.

(7)   In the case of goods remaining in the possession of organisations which cease to fulfil the conditions giving entitlement to relief under this Regulation when these are transferred to an organisation itself entitled to benefit from relief pursuant to this Regulation or, if appropriate, to an organisation entitled to relief pursuant to Regulation 13 of these Regulations, the appropriate relief shall be granted, if the organisation uses the goods in question for purposes which confer the right to such relief. In other cases, the goods shall be liable to the relevant tax at the rate applying on the date on which those conditions cease to be fulfilled, on the basis of the type of goods and the value for the purposes of tax chargeable at importation ascertained or accepted on that date by the Revenue Commissioners.

(8)   Goods used by an organisation benefiting from relief under this Regulation for purposes other than those provided for in paragraph (1) of this Regulation shall be liable to the relevant tax at the rate applying on the date on which they are put to such other use, on the basis of the type of goods and the value for the purposes of tax chargeable at importation ascertained or accepted on that date by the Revenue Commissioners.

16. (1)   Tax shall not be charged on the importation of-

(a)   decorations conferred by foreign governments on persons normally resident in the State,

(b)   cups, medals and similar articles of an essentially symbolic nature awarded in a foreign county to persons normally resident in the State in connection with their activities in fields such as the arts, science, sport, the public service, or in recognition of merit at a particular event and imported by such persons, or

(b)   cups, medals and similar articles of an essentially symbolic nature awarded in a foreign country to or other persons established in a foreign country for presentation in the State for the same purposes as those specified in subparagraph (b) of this paragraph:

Provided that satisfactory evidence as to the facts is produced to the Revenue Commissioners by the importer and the operations involved are not in any way of a commercial character.

(2) (a)   Without prejudice, where relevant, to the provisions applicable to the international movement of travellers, tax shall not be charged on the importation of-

(i)   goods imported by

(I)   persons normally resident in the State, being goods presented to them as gifts by the host authorities, during the course of an official visit paid in a foreign country, or

(II)   persons not normally resident in and paying an official visit in the State, being goods intended to be offered as gifts on that occasion to the host authorities; or

(ii)   goods sent as gifts, in token of friendship or goodwill, by an official body, public authority or group carrying on an activity in the public interest which is located in another country, to an official body, public authority or group carrying on an activity in the public interest which is located in the State and approved by the Revenue Commissioners for the purposes of this Regulation to receive such goods free of tax.

(b)   Relief under subparagraph (a) of this paragraph shall apply only to goods, other than alcoholic products, tobacco and tobacco products, which

(i)   are offered on an occasional basis,

(ii)   do not, by their nature, value or quantity, reflect any commercial interest, and

(iii)   are not used for commercial purposes.

(3)   (a)   Within the limits and subject to the conditions laid down by the Revenue Commissioners tax shall not be charged on the importation of-

(i)   gifts to reigning monarchs and heads of State, or

(ii)   goods to be used or consumed by reigning monarchs and foreign heads of State, or by persons officially representing them, during their official stay in the State.

(b)   Subparagraph (a) of this paragraph shall apply also to persons enjoying prerogatives at international level analogous to those enjoyed by reigning monarchs or heads of State.

17.   (1)   Without prejudice to Regulation 19(1)(a)(i) of these Regulations and subject to paragraphs (2) and (3) of this Regulation, tax shall not be charged on the importation of samples of goods of negligible value which can be used only to solicit orders for goods of the type they represent.

(2)   The Revenue Commissioners may, if they think fit, require that, in order to qualify for relief, articles be rendered permanently unusable by being torn, perforated, or clearly and indelibly marked, or by any other process, provided such operation does not destroy their character as samples.

(3)   In this Regulation "samples of goods" means any article representing a type of goods whose manner of presentation and quantity, for goods of the same type or quality, rule out its use for any purpose other than that of seeking orders.

18.   (1)   (a)   Subject to subparagraph (b) of this paragraph, tax shall not be charged on the importation of printed advertising matter such as catalogues, price lists, directions for use or brochures relating to-

(i)   goods for sale or hire, or

(ii)   transport, commercial insurance or banking services offered, by a person established outside the State.

(b)   Relief under subparagraph (a) of this paragraph shall apply only to printed advertisements which fulfil the following conditions:

(i)   printed matter shall clearly display the name of the underta

king which produces, sells or hires out the goods, or which offers the services, to which it refers,

(ii)   each consignment shall contain no more than one document or a single copy of each document if it is made up of several documents; however, tax shall not be charged on the importation of consignments comprising several copies of the same document if their total gross weight does not exceed 1 kilogram, and

(iii)   printed matter shall not be the subject of grouped consignments from the same consignor to the same consignee.

(2)   Tax shall not be charged on the importation of articles for advertising purposes, of no intrinsic commercial value, sent free of charge by suppliers to their customers which, apart from their advertising function, are not capable of being used.

19.   (1)   (a)   Subject to paragraphs (2) to (5), tax shall not be charged on the importation of-

(i)   small representative samples of goods intended for a trade fair or similar event,

(ii)   goods imported solely in order to be demonstrated or in order to demonstrate machines and apparatus displayed at a trade fair or similar event,

(iii)   materials such as paints, varnishes and wallpaper, of such value and quantity as are appropriate for the purposes of building, fitting-out and decorating of a temporary stand at a trade fair or similar event, and which are incapable of further use, or

(iv)   printed matter, catalogues, prospectuses, price lists, advertising posters, calendars, whether or not illustrated, unframed photographs and other articles supplied free of charge in order to advertise goods displayed at a trade fair or similar event.

(b)   In subparagraph (a) of this paragraph "trade fair or similar event" means:

(i)   exhibitions, fairs, shows and similar events connected with trade, industry, agriculture or handicrafts;

(ii)   exhibitions and events held mainly for charitable purposes;

(iii)   exhibitions and events held mainly for scientific, technical, handicraft, artistic, educational or cultural or sporting purposes, for religious reasons or for reasons of worship, trade union activity or tourism, or in order to promote international understanding,

(iv) meetings of representatives of international organisations or collective bodies, and

(v) official or commemorative ceremonies and gatherings,

but not exhibitions staged for private purposes in commercial stores or premises to sell goods.

(2) Paragraph (1)(a)(i) of this Regulation shall apply only to samples which:

(a) are imported free of charge as such or are obtained at the exhibition from goods imported in bulk;

(b) are used only for distribution free of charge to the public at the exhibition for use or consumption by the persons to whom they are offered;

(c) are identifiable as advertising samples of low unitary value;

(d) are not readily marketable and, where appropriate, are packaged in such a way that the quantity of the item involved is less than the smallest quantity of the same item normally sold on the market;

(e) in the case of foodstuffs and beverages not packaged in the manner specified in subparagraph (d) of this paragraph, are intended for consumption during the exhibition;

(f) in their total value and quantity, are appropriate to the nature of the exhibition, the number of visitors, and the extent of the exhibitor's participation.

(3) Paragraph (1)(a)(ii) of this Regulation shall apply only to goods which are:

(a) consumed or destroyed during the exhibition, and

(b) appropriate, in their total value and quantity, to the nature of the exhibition, the number of visitors, and the extent of the exhibitor's participation.

(4) Paragraph (1)(a)(iv) of this Regulation shall apply only to printed matter and articles for advertising purposes which:

(a) are intended solely for distribution free of charge to the public at the exhibition;

(b) in their total value and quantity, are appropriate to the nature of the exhibition, the number of visitors, and the extent of the exhibitor's participation.

(5)   Clauses (i) and (ii) of paragraph (1)(a) of this Regulation shall not apply to-

(a)   alcoholic products,

(b)   tobacco or tobacco products, or

(c)   fuels, whether solid, liquid or gaseous.

20. (1)   Subject to paragraphs (2) to (7) of this Regulation, tax shall not be charged on the importation of goods imported for examination, analysis or tests to determine their composition, quality or other technical characteristics for purposes of information or industrial or commercial research.

(2)   Subject to the provisions of paragraph (5) of this Regulation, paragraph (1) of this Regulation shall apply to goods only if they are completely used up or destroyed in the course of the examination, analysis or test for which they are imported.

(3)   This Regulation shall not apply to goods used in examinations, analyses or tests which in themselves constitute sales promotion operations.

(4)   This Regulation shall apply only to the quantities of goods which are strictly necessary for the purpose for which they are imported. These quantities shall in each case be determined by the Revenue Commissioners, taking into account the said purpose.

(5)   (a)   This Regulation shall apply to goods which are not completely used up or destroyed during examination, analysis or testing if the products remaining are, with the agreement and under the supervision of the Revenue Commissioners:

(i)   completely destroyed or rendered commercially valueless on completion of the examination, analysis or testing concerned,

(ii)   surrendered to the State without causing it any expense and comply with such other conditions (if any) as the Revenue commissioners may determine, or

(iii)   in duly justified circumstances, exported.

(b)   In subparagraph (a) of this paragraph "products remaining" means products resulting from the examinations, analyses or tests or goods not actually used.

(6)   Save where paragraph (5)(a) applies, products remaining at the end of the examinations, analyses or tests referred to in paragraph (1) shall be subject to the relevant tax, at the rate applying on the date of completion of the examinations, analyses or tests

concerned, on the basis of the type of goods and the value for the purposes of tax chargeable at importation ascertained or accepted on that date by the Revenue Commissioners; however, the person concerned may, with the agreement and under the supervision of the Revenue Commissioners, convert products remaining to waste or scrap, in which case the appropriate amount of tax shall be that applying to such waste or scrap at the time of conversion.

(7)   The period within which the examinations, analyses or tests referred to in this Regulation are to be carried out and the administrative formalities completed in order to ensure the use of the goods concerned for the purposes intended shall be determined in each case by the Revenue Commissioners.

21.   Tax shall not be charged on the importation of trademarks, patterns or designs or their supporting documents or on applications for patents for invention or the like for submission to the bodies competent to deal with the protection of copyrights or the protection of industrial or commercial patent rights.

22.   Tax shall not be charged on the importation of:

(a)   documentation, being leaflets, brochures, books, magazines, guidebooks, posters, whether or not framed, unframed photographs and photographic enlargements, maps, whether or not illustrated, window transparencies and illustrated calendars for distribution free of charge whose principal purpose is to encourage the public to visit foreign countries, in particular in order to attend cultural, tourist, sporting, religious or trade or professional meetings or events and which contain not more than 25 per cent. of private commercial advertising and the general nature of whose promotional aims is evident,

(b)   foreign hotel lists and yearbooks published by official tourist agencies,

or under their auspices, and timetables for foreign transport services that are for distribution free of charge and contain not more than 25 per cent. of private commercial advertising, or

(c)   reference material supplied to accredited representatives or correspondents appointed by official national tourist agencies and not intended for distribution such as yearbooks, lists of telephone or telex numbers, hotel lists, fairs catalogues, specimens of craft goods of negligible value, and literature on museums, universities, spas or other similar establishments.

23.   Tax shall not be charged on the importation of-

(a)   documents sent free of charge to the public service of the State,

(b)   publications of foreign governments and publications of official international bodies for distribution free of charge,

(c)   ballot papers for elections organised by bodies set up outside the State,

(d)   objects to be submitted as evidence or for like purposes to the courts or other official agencies of the State,

(e)   specimen signatures and printed circulars concerning signatures sent as part of customary exchanges of information between public services or banking establishments,

(f)   official printed matter sent to the Central Bank of Ireland,

(g)   reports, statements, notes, prospectuses, application forms and other documents drawn up by companies whose headquarters are outside the State and sent to the bearers or subscribers of securities issued by such companies,

(h)   recorded media, such as punched cards, sound recordings, microfilms and the like, which contain information sent free of charge to the addressee where such relief does not give rise to abuses or to major distortion of competition,

(i)   files, archives, printed forms and other documents to be used in international meetings, conferences or congresses, and reports on such gatherings,

(j)   plans, technical drawings, traced designs, descriptions and other similar documents imported with a view to obtaining or fulfilling orders outside the State or to participating in a competition held in the State,

(k)   documents to be used in examinations held in the State by institutions set up outside the State,

(l)   printed forms to be used as official documents in the international movement of vehicles or goods, within the framework of international conventions,

(m)   printed forms, labels, tickets and similar documents sent by transport undertakings or by undertakings of the hotel industry located outside the State to travel agencies set up in the State,

(n)   printed forms and tickets, bills of lading, way-bills and other commercial or office documents which have been used,

(o)   official printed forms from national or international authorities and printed matter conforming to international standards sent for distribution by associations of another country to corresponding associations located in the State,

(p)   photographs, slides and stereotype mats for photographs, whether or not captioned, sent to press agencies or newspaper or magazine publishers,

(q)   visual and auditory materials of an educational, scientific or cultural character specified in the Schedule to these Regulations which are produced by the United Nations or one of its specialised agencies, whatever the use for which they are intended,

(r)   collectors' pieces and works of art of an educational, scientific or cultural character which are not intended for sale and which are imported by museums, galleries and other institutions approved of by the Revenue Commissioners for the purposes of this Regulation and on condition that the articles in question are imported free of charge or, if they are imported against payment, are not supplied by a taxable person.

24.   Tax shall not be charged on the importation of-

(a)   materials such as rope, straw, cloth, paper, cardboard, wood and plastics used in the stowage and protection, including heat protection, of imported goods during their transportation to the State, where such materials are not normally re-usable and where the consideration for their supply forms part of the taxable amount as defined in Article 11 of the Sixth Council Directive No. 77/388/EEC of 17 May 1977,

(b)   litter, fodder and feeding stuffs put on board means of transport used to convey animals to the territory of the State for distribution to the said animals during the journey.

25.   (1)   Subject to paragraphs (2) to (4) of this Regulation, tax shall not be charged on the importation of-

(a)   fuel contained in the standard tanks of private and commercial motor vehicles, including motor cycles,

(b)   fuel contained in portable tanks carried by private motor vehicles and motor cycles, with a maximum of 10 litres per vehicle,

(c)   lubricants carried in motor vehicles and required for their normal operation during the journey in question.

(2)   In paragraph (1) of this Regulation-

"commercial motor vehicle" means any motorised road vehicle which by its type of construction and equipment is designed for and capable of transporting, whether for payment or not:

(a)   more than nine persons including the driver, or

(b)   goods,

and any road vehicle for a special purpose other than transport as such;

"private motor vehicle" means any motor vehicle not covered by the definition in (a);

"standard tanks" means the tanks permanently fixed by the manufacturer to all motor vehicles of the same type as the vehicle in question and whose permanent fitting enables fuel to be used directly, both for the purposes of propulsion and, where appropriate, for the operation of a refrigeration system;

gas tanks fitted to motor vehicles designed for the direct use of gas as a fuel shall also be considered to be standard tanks.

(3)   Fuel the subject of relief under paragraph (1) of this Regulation shall not be used in a vehicle other than that in which it was imported nor be removed from that vehicle and stored, except during necessary repairs to that vehicle, or transferred for a consideration or free of charge by the importer.

(4)   Non-compliance with the provisions of paragraph (3) shall give rise to application of tax on the goods at the rate in force on the date of such non-compliance, on the basis of the type of goods and the value for the purposes of tax chargeable at importation ascertained or accepted on that date by the Revenue Commissioners.

26.   Tax shall not be charged on the importation of-

(a)   goods for use by organisations approved by the Revenue Commissioners for the purposes of this Regulation for the construction, upkeep or ornamentation of cemeteries and tombs of, and memorials to, war victims of a foreign country who are buried in the State,

(b)   coffins containing bodies and urns containing the ashes of deceased persons, and flowers, funeral wreaths and other ornamental objects normally accompanying them, or

(c)   flowers, wreaths and other ornamental objects imported by persons resident in another Member State of the Community attending a funeral in or visiting the State to decorate graves if such importations do not reflect, either by their nature or their quantity, any commercial intent.

27.   (1)   The value in Irish currency of the ECU to be applied in each year for the purposes of these Regulations shall be calculated by reference to the official rate of exchange between the currencies obtaining on the first working day of October of the previous year.

(2)   The amounts in Irish currency arrived at by converting the amounts of ECU shall be rounded off to the nearest IR£.

(3)   The said value applying in a particular year shall continue in force in the following year, if, without taking into account the rounding off aforesaid, the difference between the values applicable to those years is less than 5 per cent of the earlier year's value.

28.   Nothing in these Regulations shall be construed as affecting-

(a)   the privileges and immunities granted under cultural, scientific or technical cooperation agreements concluded between the State and other countries;

(b)   the special exemptions justified by the nature of frontier traffic which are granted under frontier arrangements concluded between the State and other countries.

29.   Nothing in these Regulations shall be construed as exempting an importer from compliance with any legal requirement, obligation, restriction or prohibition other than the requirement of payment of tax on goods which, but for these Regulations, would be chargeable to tax on importation.

30.   The following provisions shall not apply in relation to goods relieved from tax by virtue of these Regulations:

section 17 of the Finance Act, 1936 (No.31 of 1936), as amended by section 13 of the Finance Act, 1957 (No.20 of 1957),

paragraphs (a), (b), (d) and (e) of section 18 of the Finance Act, 1936 (No.31 of 1936),

section 18 of the Finance Act, 1938 (No. 25 of 1938),

section 17 of the Finance Act, 1946 (No. 15 of 1946),

Relief from Customs Duties (Fairs, Exhibitions, and Similar Events) Order, 1965 (S.I. No.143 of 1965),

section 76 of the Finance Act, 1974 (No.27 of 1974), and

Council Regulation No. 918/83/EEC of 28 March, 1983.

31.   A person who, after the date of the making of these Regulations, contravenes a provision thereof, shall be guilty of an offence and shall, without prejudice to any other penalty to which he may be liable, be liable, on summary conviction, to a fine not exceeding [€630][5].

GIVEN under my Official Seal,
this 28th day of June, 1985.

ALAN M. DUKES,
Minister for Finance.

SCHEDULE.
Goods referred to in Regulation 23(q)

Visual and auditory materials of an educational, scientific or cultural character

Common Tariff Number	Customs Heading Description
37.04	Sensitized plates and film, exposed but not developed, negative or positive:
	A. Cinematograph film:

ex II. Other positives, of an educational, scientific or cultural character

3x 37.05   Plates, unperforated film and perforated film (other than cinematograph film), exposed and developed, negative or positive, of an educational, scientific or cultural character

37.07   Cinematograph film, exposed and developed, whether or not incorporating sound track or consisting only of sound track, negative or positive:

ex A. Newsreels (with or without sound track) depicting events of current news value at the time of importation, and imported up to a limit of two copies of each subject for copying purposes.

ex B. Other:

- Archival film material (with or without sound track) intended for use in connection with newsreel films

- Recreational films particularly suited for children and young people

- Other films of an educational, scientific or cultural character

49.11   Other printed matter including printed pictures and photographs:

ex B. Other:

- Microcards or other information storage media required in computerized information and documentation services, of an educational, scientific or cultural character.

- Wall charts designed solely for demonstration and education

ex 90.21   Instruments, apparatus or models, designed solely for demonstrational purposes (for example, in education or exhibition), unsuitable for other uses:

- Patterns, models and wall charts of an educational, scientific or cultural character, designed solely for demonstration and education

- Mock-ups or visualisations of abstract concepts such as molecular structures or mathematical formulae

92.12   Gramophone records and other sound or similar recordings, matrices for the production of records, prepared record blanks, film for mechanical sound recording, prepared tapes, wires, strips and like articles of a kind commonly used for sound or similar recording

ex B. Recorded

- Of an educational, scientific or cultural character

Various

- Holograms for laser projection

- Multi-media kits

- Materials for programmed instruction, including materials in kit form, with the corresponding printed materials.

EXPLANATORY NOTE.

These Regulations give effect to EEC Council Directive No. 83/181/EEC of 28 March 1983 which determined the scope of Article 14(1)(d) of Directive 77/388/EEC (the 6th VAT Directive) as regards exemption from VAT on the final importation of certain goods. The Regulations provide for VAT exemptions for a comprehensive list of importations, many of which are already covered, wholly or partly, by existing legislation or practice.

The Regulations provide, for example, for exemption from VAT, subject to various conditions, on the importation of personal property from outside the Community (there are already Regulations in force covering intra-Community importations of this kind). The importation of scholastic outfits, materials and household effects of students coming to study on a full-time basis are also

VAT-exempt, subject to conditions, as are imports of negligible value, imports of certain goods on the transfer of undertakings to the State, imports of certain agricultural products, imports of certain therapeutic substances, medicines, laboratory animals and biological or chemical substances, imports of certain goods for charitable or philanthropic organisations, imports of certain goods in the context of international relations, imports of certain goods for the promotion of trade, goods imported for examination, analysis or test purposes and a number of other miscellaneous exemptions.

The EEC Directive referred to above came into force on 1 July 1984 and the Regulations are also effective from that date.

Amendments
1   Amended by s240 & sch5, FA01, w.e.f. 1 January 2002. Previously 200ECU
2   Amended by s240 & sch5, FA01, w.e.f. 1 January 2002. Previously 200ECU
3   Amended by s240 & sch5, FA01, w.e.f. 1 January 2002. Previously 1000ECU
4   Amended by s240 & sch5, FA01, w.e.f. 1 January 2002. Previously 10ECU
5   Amended by s240 & sch5, FA01, w.e.f. 1 January 2002. Previously £500

VALUE-ADDED TAX (REFUND OF TAX) (NO 18) ORDER, 1985

(SI No. 192 of 1985)

I, ALAN M. DUKES, Minister for Finance, in exercise of the powers conferred on me by section 20(3) of the Value-Added Tax Act, 1972 (No 22 of 1972), hereby order as follows:

1. (1)   This Order may be cited as the Value-Added Tax (Refund of Tax) (No 18) Order, 1985.

    (2)   This Order shall be deemed to have come into operation on the 1st day of January, 1979.

2.   In this Order-

   "the Act" means the Value-Added Tax Act, 1972, (No 22 of 1972);

   "the Irish Water Safety Association" means the body established under the Irish Water Safety Association (Establishment) Order, 1980 (SI No 244 of 1980).

3.   A body of persons which establishes to the satisfaction of the Revenue Commissioners that it has borne or paid tax in relation to the supply or hire to it, the importation by it or the repair, modification or maintenance for it of a boat or similar craft of a gross tonnage of 15 tons or less, designed and constructed, or adapted, for the purpose of rescue or assistance at sea, of equipment for use in or in conjunction with any such boat or craft, or of a building or structure for housing or operating such boat, craft or equipment, and which fulfils to the satisfaction of the said Commissioners the conditions specified in paragraph 4 of this Order shall be entitled to be repaid such tax.

4.   The conditions to be fulfilled by a body of persons referred to in paragraph 3 of this Order are:

   (a)   it shall claim a refund of the tax by completing such form as may be provided for the purpose by the Revenue Commissioners and shall certify the particulars shown on such form to be correct;

   (b)   it shall, by the production of documentary evidence establish that the outlay in relation to which the claim for a refund of tax arises was incurred in respect of the supply or hire to it, the importation by it or the repair, modification or maintenance for it of a boat or similar craft of a gross tonnage of 15 tons or less designed and constructed, or adapted, for the purpose of rescue or assistance at sea, of equipment for use in or in conjunction with such boat or craft, or of a building or structure for housing or operating such boat, craft or equipment;

   (c)   it shall, by the production of invoices provided in accordance with section 17(12)(a)(i) of the Act, or by the production of a receipt for tax paid on importation, establish the amount of tax borne or paid in relation to the outlay referred to in subparagraph (b) of this paragraph;

(d)   subject to paragraph 5 of this Order, it shall, by the production of documentary evidence from the Irish Water Safety Association, establish to the satisfaction of the Revenue Commissioners that it provides services of rescue or assistance at sea and that the nature and extent of such services meet the requirements of the said Association in relation to the organisation and functioning of bodies of persons providing services of rescue or assistance at sea;

(e)   it shall establish to the satisfaction of the Revenue Commissioners that the boat or craft, the equipment, and the building or structure specified in paragraph 3 of this Order are not used for any purpose other then in relation to rescue or assistance at sea or the training of persons in connection therewith;

(f)   it shall establish that it is not a person who is registered in the register maintained under section 9 of the Act, nor a person required under the provisions of that section to furnish the particulars specified for registration;

(g)   except where the Revenue Commissioners otherwise allow, the claim for a refund of tax shall be made only in respect of outlay incurred within a period of twelve months or more.

5.   The provisions of this Order, other than paragraph 4(d), shall apply to claims for refund of tax made by the Irish Water Safety Association.

6.   The secretary, or other officer acting as secretary for the time being, of a body of persons which makes a claim for refund of tax under this Order shall be answerable in addition to the body for doing all such acts as are required to be done by the body in relation to the making of such a claim.

GIVEN under my Official Seal,
this 1st day of July, 1985.

ALAN M. DUKES,
Minister for Finance.

EXPLANATORY NOTE.

This Order enables VAT to be repaid, subject to certain conditions, in respect of small rescue craft, ancillary equipment and special boat buildings, to qualifying groups who provide a sufficient standard of sea rescue and assistance services. The Order also applies to similar equipment used by the Irish Water Safety Association. The Order applies retrospectively to qualifying purchases made from 1 January 1979.

VALUE-ADDED TAX (PLACE OF SUPPLY OF CERTAIN SERVICES) REGULATION 1985

(SI No. 343 of 1985)

> **These Regulations revoked by s5(6)(d) VATA72 (as inserted by s81(b)(i), FA86), with effect from 27 May 1986.**

The Revenue Commissioners, in exercise of the powers conferred on them by sections 5 of the Value-Added Tax Act, 1972 (No.22 of 1972), and with the consent of the Minister for Finance, hereby make the following Regulations:

1.   These Regulations may be cited as the Value-Added Tax (Place of Supply of Certain Services) Regulations, 1985.

2.   These Regulations shall come into operation on the 25th day of October, 1985.

3.   For the purposes of the Value-Added Tax Act, 1972, the place of supply of services consisting of the hiring out of movable goods by a person established outside the European Economic Community shall be deemed to be the place where the movable goods are, or are to be, effectively used.

GIVEN this 24th day of October, 1985.

L. REASON,
Revenue Commissioner.

The Minister for Finance hereby consents to the making of the foregoing Regulations.

GIVEN under the Official Seal of the Minister for Finance, this 24th day of October, 1985.

ALAN M. DUKES,
Minister for Finance.

EXPLANATORY NOTE

These Regulations, which enter into force on 25 October, 1985, concern the operation of Value-Added Tax in relation to certain services supplied to persons in this country from outside the area of the European Economic Community.

The services in question are the hiring out of movable goods, and the Regulations provide that the place of supply of such services for VAT purposes will be deemed to be the place where the goods are effectively used.

VALUE-ADDED TAX (REMISSION AND REPAYMENT OF TAX ON CERTAIN IMPORTATIONS) REGULATIONS, 1985

(SI No. 344 of 1985)

This Regulation was revoked by regulation 44, Value-Added Tax Regulations, 2006 (2006 S.I. No. 548) w.e.f. 1 November 2006

The Revenue Commissioners, in exercise of the powers conferred on them by sections 15 of the Value-Added Tax Act, 1972 (No. 22 of 1972), hereby make the following regulations:

1.   These Regulations may be cited as the Value-Added Tax (Remission and Repayment of Tax on Certain Importations) Regulations, 1985.

2.   These Regulations shall come into operation on the 25th day of October, 1985.

3.   In these Regulations "the Act" means the Value-Added Tax Act, 1972.

4.   (1)   Tax is hereby remitted in accordance with section 15(5)(a) of the Act on the importation of goods by a person, not being a taxable person, where the Revenue Commissioners are satisfied that the goods were exported by the person in circumstances not qualifying for relief from tax, if any, previously paid or borne and that the goods have undergone work which has been carried out exclusively in another Member State of the Community, and in circumstances in which value-added tax referred to in Council Directive No. 77/388/EEC of 17 May, 1977, was charged in respect of all of the work without the right to deduction or refund.

       (2)   (a)   A person who establishes to the satisfaction of the Revenue Commissioners that he has paid tax on the importation of goods which were subsequently exported and which, during the whole of the period from the date of importation to the date of exportation, were on hire, lease or loan to him or were used by him solely in connection with the supply of taxable services shall, in accordance with section 15(5)(b) of the Act, be entitled to repayment of tax subject to the limitations provided for in subparagraph (b) if he fulfils the following conditions to the satisfaction of the Revenue Commissioners:

               (i)   he shall establish that he is not a taxable person;

               (ii)   he shall claim a refund by completing such claim form as may be provided for the purpose by the Revenue Commissioners and he shall certify the particulars shown on such claim form to be correct;

               (iii)   he shall establish that the goods have been exported;

(iv)   he shall, by the production of receipts for tax paid on importation of the goods to which the claim relates, establish the amount of such tax;

(v)   he shall by the production of the appropriate form, duly certified, or by other sufficient documentary evidence, establish that the goods to which the claim relates are the same goods as those on which the tax was paid by him;

and

(vi)   he shall establish that he is not entitled to repayment of the tax under any other provision of the Act or Regulations or of any other Act or instrument made under statute administered by the Revenue commissioners.

(b)   The amount of tax which shall be repaid-

(i)   in the case of goods which were on hire, lease or loan to the claimant, shall be the excess, if any, of the tax paid on the importation of the goods over the tax which would have been chargeable on the hiring or leasing of the goods if the transaction had been chargeable to tax;

(ii)   in the case of goods imported in connection with the supply of taxable services by the person by whom or for whom the goods were imported, shall be the excess, if any, of the tax paid on importation over the tax which would have been chargeable on such supply if the supply had been chargeable to tax.

5.   Regulation 27 of the Value-Added Tax Regulations, 1979 (S.I. No.63 of 1979), is hereby revoked.

GIVEN this 24th day of October, 1985.

L. REASON,
Revenue Commissioner.

EXPLANATORY NOTE.

These Regulations, which enter into force on 25 October, 1985, concern relief from Value-Added Tax on-

(a)   goods re-imported after having undergone work in another Member State of the European Economic Community;

(b)   goods imported on hire, lease or loan, or for use in connection with the supply of taxable services, and subsequently exported.

Where goods are exported by a non-taxable person to another Member State and undergo repair, maintenance, etc., exclusively in that State with a charge to VAT there which is non-recoverable, the re-importation of the goods will be exempt from Irish VAT.

Where goods are imported by a non-taxable person on hire, lease or loan, or for use by him solely in connection with the supply of taxable services, and are subsequently exported, provision is made for a measure of relief from the VAT charged at importation.

Subject to specified conditions, the relief, by way of repayment, will be the excess, if any, of the VAT paid at importation over the tax attributable to the hiring or leasing of the goods or to the supply of any taxable services in connection with which they are used.

These Regulations supersede the provisions of Regulation 27 of the Value-Added Tax Regulations, 1979, which is now revoked.

VALUE-ADDED TAX (EXEMPTED ACTIVITIES) (NO 1) ORDER, 1985

(SI No. 430 of 1985)

I, ALAN M. DUKES, Minister for Finance, in exercise of the powers conferred on me by section 6(2) of the Value-Added Tax Act, 1972 (No 22 of 1972), hereby make the following Order:

1. This Order may be cited as the Value-Added Tax (Exempted Activities) (No 1) Order, 1985.

2. The First Schedule to the Value-Added Tax Act, 1972, is hereby amended by the insertion after paragraph (xi) of the following paragraph:

    "(xia) services supplied to a person under arrangements which provide for the reimbursement of the person in respect of the supply by him of goods or services in accordance with a credit card, charge card or similar card scheme;".

GIVEN under my Official Seal this 20th day of December, 1985.

ALAN M. DUKES,
Minister for Finance.

EXPLANATORY NOTE.

This Order concerns the arrangements whereby credit card companies reimburse traders for goods and services supplied to cardholders. It provides that such service shall be exempted activity for VAT purposes.

VALUE-ADDED TAX (REFUND OF TAX) (No 19) ORDER, 1986

(SI No. 68 of 1986)

> This Order revoked by para 7, Value Added Tax (Refund of Tax)(No 24) Order, 1993 (1993 S.I. No. 134) with effect from 21 May, 1993

I, JOHN BRUTON, Minister for Finance, in exercise of the powers conferred on me by section 20(3) of the Value-Added Tax Act, 1972 (No 22 of 1972), hereby order as follows:

1. (1)   This Order may be cited as the Value-Added Tax (Refund of Tax) (No 19) Order, 1986.

    (2)   This Order shall be deemed to have come into operation on the 1st day of March, 1986.

2. In this Order "the Act" means the Value-Added Tax Act, 1972.

[3. A person who establishes to the satisfaction of the Revenue Commissioners that he has borne or paid tax in relation to the acquisition, including the hiring (other than the hiring for a period of less than 6 consecutive months), by him of a passenger road motor vehicle not more than 24 months old, being-

    (a)   a single-deck touring coach having dimensions as designated by the manufacturer of not less than 3,350 millimetres in height, not less than 10,000 millimetres in length and not less than 1,400 millimetres in floor height, or

    (b)   a double-deck touring coach having dimensions as designated by the manufacturer of not more than 4,300 millimetres in height and not less than 10,000 millimetres in length, for use by him for the purposes of the business referred to in subparagraph (b) of paragraph 4 of this Order, and who fulfils to the satisfaction of the said Commissioners the conditions that are specified in the said paragraph 4 and such other conditions as the said Commissioners may impose, shall be entitled to be repaid so much of such tax as is specified in paragraph 5 of this Order.]1

4. The conditions to be fulfilled by a person referred to in paragraph 3 of this Order are-

    (a)   he shall claim a refund of the tax by completing such claim form as may be provided for the purpose by the Revenue Commissioners and he shall certify the particulars shown on such form to be correct;

    (b)   he shall, by the production of such evidence as the Revenue Commissioners may require, establish that he is engaged in the business of carriage of persons, including tourists, by road under contracts for group transport;

    (c)   he shall, by the production of invoices, provided in accordance with section 17(12)(a)(i) of the Act, or by the production of receipts for the tax paid on importation of the vehicle, establish the amount of tax borne or paid by him in relation to the acquisition by him of the vehicle;

(d)   he shall establish that he is not entitled to a deduction under section 12 of this Act in respect of any portion of the tax specified in subparagraph (c) of this paragraph.

5.   The amount of tax to be repaid under this Order shall be so much of the amount of tax specified in paragraph 4(c) of this Order as is shown to the satisfaction of the Revenue Commissioners to be in excess of the amount which would have been borne or paid if the rate and percentage for the time being specified in section 11(1)(c) of the Act had applied in relation to the acquisition in question.

GIVEN under my Official Seal this 27th day of March, 1986.

JOHN BRUTON,
Minister for Finance.

EXPLANATORY NOTE.

This Order enables VAT in excess of the rate specified in Section 11(1)(c) of the Value-Added Tax Act, 1972 (10 per cent as at the date of Order) to be repaid, subject to certain conditions, in respect of the acquisition of new touring coaches of certain dimensions, to persons engaged in the transport by road of persons, including tourists.

Amendments
1   Para3 substituted by Value Added Tax (Refund of Tax) (No. 22) Order 1988

EUROPEAN COMMUNITIES (VALUE-ADDED TAX) (EXEMPTION ON TEMPORARY IMPORTATION OF CERTAIN GOODS) REGULATIONS, 1986

(SI No. 264 of 1986)

> These regulations gave effect to Seventeenth Council Directive (85/362/EEC) of 16 July 1985. This directive ceased to have effect as to relations between Member States on 31 December 1992.

I, JOHN BRUTON, Minister for Finance, in exercise of the powers conferred on me by section 3 of the European Communities Act, 1972 (No 27 of 1972), and for the purposes of giving effect to Council Directive No 85/362/EEC of 16 July, 19851 hereby make the following Regulations:

1. (1) These Regulations may be cited as the European Communities (Value-Added Tax) (Exemption on Temporary Importation of Certain Goods) Regulations, 1986.

    (2) These Regulations shall be deemed to have come into operation on the 1st day of January, 1986.

    (3) These Regulations shall be construed together with the Act and the Customs Acts and any instrument relating to customs made under statute.

    (4) Means of transport, pallets and containers are excluded from the scope of these Regulations.

    (5) In these Regulations-

    "the Act" means the Value-Added Tax Act, 1972 (No 22 of 1972);

    "the Community" means the territory of the Member States of the European Economic Community where Council Directive No 77/388/EEC of 17 May, 1972 applies;

    "Member State" means a Member State of the Community;

    "person" means a natural or legal person;

    "tax" means value-added tax;

    "temporary importation exemption" means the arrangements whereby goods, which are intended to remain temporarily in the territory of the State and to be re-exported, may be imported with exemption from tax in accordance with the conditions laid down by these Regulations.

    (6) A word or expression that is used in these Regulation and is also used in Council Directive No 85/362/EEC of 16 July, 1985 shall, unless the context otherwise requires, have the meaning in these Regulations that it has in that Directive.

(7) A reference to a Regulation is to a Regulation of these Regulations and a reference to a paragraph, subparagraph or clause is to a paragraph, subparagraph or clause of the provision in which the reference occurs, unless it is indicated that reference to some other provision is intended.

2. The Revenue Commissioners shall, subject to the provisions of these Regulations and such conditions as the said Commissioners may impose, grant temporary importation exemption for goods temporarily imported into the State from another Member State, provided that they are satisfied that such goods-

(a) are intended to be re-exported from the State without alteration;

(b) satisfy the conditions laid down in Articles 9 and 10 of the Treaty establishing the European Economic Community or, in the case of goods falling under the Treaty establishing the European Coal and Steel Community, are in free circulation;

(c) have been acquired subject to the rules governing the application of tax in the Member State of exportation and have not benefited by virtue of their exportation, from any relief from tax;

(d) belong to a person established outside the State; and

(e) are not consumable goods.

3.

(1) Subject to paragraph (2), goods imported into the State from an other Member State which do not qualify for temporary importation exemption under Regulation 2 shall qualify for such exemption if, had they been imported from outside the Community, they would qualify for such exemption under any of the Regulations 14 to 29.

(2) Temporary importation exemption shall not be granted in any case where-

(a) the goods meet the conditions laid down in Article 9 and 10 of the Treaty establishing the European Economic Community;

(b) the goods were not acquired pursuant to the rules governing the application of tax in the Member State of exportation or, by virtue of being exported, benefited from exemption from tax; and

(c) the importer is a non-taxable person or is a taxable person not entitled to deduction of tax in full.

4. The Revenue Commissioners shall, subject to the provisions of these Regulations and such conditions as the said Commissioners may impose, grant temporary importation exemption for goods imported temporarily into the State from a country outside the Community where the goods qualify for such exemption under any of the Regulations 14 to 29.

5. (1)   Subject to paragraph (2), the Revenue Commissioners may require security to be given at the time of granting temporary importation exemption to ensure payment of any tax which may become due if a chargeable event within the meaning of Regulation 12 should occur, and where such security is required-

   (a)   the person to whom temporary importation exemption has been granted may choose whether it shall be given by-

      (i)   making a cash deposit in Irish pounds,

      (ii)   a guarantor who has his normal residence or an establishment in the State and who is approved by the Revenue Commissioners, or

      (iii)   any other guarantee acceptable to the Revenue Commissioners;

   (b)   it shall not exceed the amount of tax that would have been due on the value of the goods at the time of their importation if they had been declared for home use at that time.

   (2)   No security shall be required-

   (a)   for goods covered by the procedure provided for in Council Regulation (EEC) No 3/84 of 19 December, 1983;

   (b)   for goods imported either from another Member State or from a country outside the Community in the cases referred to in Annex 1 of Commission Regulation (EEC) No 1751/84 of 13 June, 1984 and Articles 3 and 33 of Council Regulation (EEC) No 3599/82 of 21 December, 1982.

6.   The provisions of Commission Regulation (EEC) No 1751/84 other than Articles 22, 23, 29 and 30 of the said Regulation shall apply to importations under these Regulations as if the tax were a customs duty or charge or levy to which Council Regulation (EEC) No 3599/82 applied and such a duty, charge or levy applied to importations from other Member States as well as to importations from countries outside the Community.

7.   The Revenue Commissioners may refuse to grant temporary importation exemption in cases where-

   (a)   they consider it impossible to identify the goods or to verify their use in the State;

   (b)   the guarantees considered necessary are not provided by the person requesting such exemption; or

   (c)   the person requesting the exemption has previously made improper use of such exemption or has committed a serious infringement of customs or fiscal legislation.

8.   (1)   The Revenue Commissioners may require persons to whom they have granted temporary importation exemption to make available for inspection at times and places that are reasonable the goods which are the subject of such exemption together with all relevant documents.

      (2)   The Revenue Commissioners may revoke temporary importation exemption if they find that a person to whom such exemption has been granted has not satisfied the provisions of these Regulations.

9.   (1)   The Revenue Commissioners shall fix the period during which goods may remain in the State under temporary importation exemption arrangements under these Regulations but, without prejudice to the limits laid down in Regulations 16, 17, 18, 20, 23, 28 and 30, the maximum duration of this period shall be 24 months.

      (2)   Notwithstanding paragraph (1), the Revenue Commissioners may, in exceptional circumstances and at their absolute discretion, on request by the person to whom temporary importation exemption has been granted extend, within reasonable limits and subject to the provisions of these Regulations, the periods referred to in paragraph (1).

10.   The Revenue Commissioners shall on request by any person authorise the transfer of the temporary importation exemption to that person, where he satisfies the conditions laid down in these Regulations and assumes all the obligations imposed on the person to whom the temporary importation exemption was first granted, in particular those arising from the fixing of the period during which the goods in question may remain under the said exemption.

11.   Where goods, in respect of which temporary importation exemption applies, are supplied, tax shall not be chargeable provided that the purchaser is a person established outside the State and the goods continue to remain eligible for the said exemption.

12.   (1)   Temporary importation exemption shall terminate, but tax shall not become chargeable, if goods to which the said exemption applies are-

            (a)   re-exported from the State;

            (b)   placed with a view to their subsequent re-exportation-

                  (i)   under warehouse arrangements,

                  (ii)   in a free zone, or

                  (iii) under transit arrangements provided for or permitted under Community law; or

            (c)   destroyed under customs control, or are provided to the satisfaction of the Revenue Commissioners to have been totally destroyed or irretrievably lost and incapable of use thereafter.

(2)   (a)   Temporary importation exemption shall terminate and tax shall, subject to paragraph (b), become chargeable-

        (i)   when, in exceptional cases and cases covered by Regulation 15, the Revenue Commissioners authorise goods, in respect of which temporary importation exemption has been granted, to be declared for home use,

        (ii)   when goods which are recoverable in the form of waste products resulting from duly authorised destruction are declared for home use, or

        (iii)   when the goods referred to in Regulation 30 are declared for home use.

(b)   Where goods are released for home use and the importer is a non-taxable person or a taxable person not entitled to deduct the tax in full, tax shall be deemed to have become chargeable at the time when the goods entered the State.

(3)   If any of the conditions, under which temporary importation exemption was granted, ceases to be fulfilled in circumstances other than those specified in paragraph (1), the exemption shall terminate and tax shall become chargeable either at the time when the condition ceased to be fulfilled, or at the time when the goods entered the State if it is established that the condition was never fulfilled.

13.   (1)   Temporary importation exemption shall not be granted for goods temporarily imported from countries outside the Community with partial or total relief from customs duties under the provisions of Title III of Regulation (EEC) No 3599/82.

    (2)   For goods which are eligible for partial relief from customs duties, tax shall become chargeable at the time of entry of the goods into the State, and adjustment of such tax shall not be required following payment of customs duties chargeable where the importer is a taxable person entitled to deduct the full amount of tax due in respect of the imported goods.

14.   (1)   In this Regulation "professional equipment" means equipment and accessories (including spare parts subsequently imported for the repair of the said equipment) needed for the exercise of his trade or profession by a person established outside the State for the purpose of performing in the State a particular job of work, inasmuch as such equipment is of a kind described in Annex IV of Commission Regulation (EEC) No 1751/84.

    (2)   Temporary importation exemption shall be granted for professional equipment which is-

(a)   owned by a person established outside the State;

(b)   imported by a person established outside the State; and

(c)   to be used exclusively by the person importing the said equipment, or under his supervision:

Provided that-

(i)   the condition referred to in subparagraph (c) shall not apply to cinematographic equipment imported for the purpose of producing films under a co-production contract concluded with a person established in the State;

(ii)   in the case of joint radio or television programme productions, professional equipment may be the subject of a hire-contract or similar contract to which a person established in the State is party.

15.   (1)   In this Regulation "event" means-

(a)   a trade, industrial, agricultural or craft exhibition, fair or similar show or display;

(b)   an exhibition or meeting which is organised primarily to promote a charitable purpose;

(c)   an exhibition or meeting which is organised primarily to promote any branch of learning, art, craft, sport or scientific, technical, educational, cultural, trade union or tourist activity, or to promote friendship between peoples or to promote religious knowledge or worship;

(d)   a meeting of representatives of international organisations or international groups of organisations;

(e)   a ceremony or meeting of an official or commemorative character;

other than exhibitions organised for private purposes in shops or business premises with a view to sale of the goods imported.

(2)   Temporary importation exemption shall be granted for-

(a)   goods intended for display or to be the subject of a demonstration at an event;

(b)   goods intended for use at an event for the purpose of presenting imported products, including-

(i)   goods necessary for the demonstration of imported machinery or apparatus on exhibition,

(ii)   equipment, including electrical fittings, used for constructing and decorating the temporary stands of a person established outside the State,

(iii)   advertising material and demonstration and other equipment intended for use in publicising imported goods on exhibition, including sound recordings, films and transparencies, together with the apparatus required in connection with their use;

(c)   equipment, including interpreting installations, sound-recording apparatus and educational, scientific or cultural films, intended for use at international meetings, conferences and symposia;

(d)   live animals intended for exhibition at, or participation in, an event;

(e)   products obtained during an event from goods, machinery, apparatus or animals imported temporarily.

16.   (1)   In this Regulation "teaching aid" means any aid intended for the exclusive purpose of teaching or vocational training and, in particular, models, instruments, apparatus, machines and accessories thereof, insofar as such aids are of a kind described in Annex V of Commission Regulation (EEC) No 1751/84.

(2)   Subject to paragraphs (3) and (4), temporary importation exemption shall be granted for-

(a)   teaching aids;

(b)   spare parts and accessories for such aids;

(c)   tools especially designed for the maintenance, checking, calibration or repair of such aids.

(3)   The exemption referred to in paragraph (2) shall be granted provided that the goods referred to in that paragraph-

(a)   are imported by public or private teaching or vocational training establishments which are essentially non-profit making and have been approved by the Revenue Commissioners for the purposes of this Regulation, and are used under the supervision and responsibility of such establishments;

(b)   are used for non-commercial purposes;

(c)   are imported in reasonable quantities, having regard to their intended purposes; and

(d)   remain, throughout their stay in the State, the property of a person who is established outside the State.

(4)   The period during which such teaching aids may be granted the said exemption shall not exceed six months.

17. (1) In this Regulation "scientific equipment" means instruments, apparatus, machines and accessories thereof used solely for the purpose of scientific research or education.

     (2) Subject to paragraphs (3) and (4), temporary importation exemption shall be granted for -

          (a) scientific equipment and accessories;

          (b) spare parts for equipment referred to under (a);

          (c) tools specially designed for the maintenance, checking, calibration or repair of scientific equipment used in the State exclusively for purposes of scientific research or teaching.

     (3) The exemption referred to in paragraph (2) shall be granted provided that the scientific equipment, accessories, spare parts and tools-

          (a) are imported by scientific or teaching establishments which are essentially non-profit making and have been approved by the Revenue Commissioners for the purposes of this Regulation, and are used under the supervision and responsibility of such establishments;

          (b) are used for non-commercial purposes;

          (c) are imported in reasonable numbers having regard to their intended purposes; and

          (d) remain, throughout their stay in the State, the property of a person who is established outside the State.

     (4) The period during which such scientific equipment may be granted the said exemption shall not exceed six months.

18. (1) Subject to paragraph (2), temporary importation exemption shall be granted for medical, surgical and laboratory equipment intended for hospitals and other medical institutions, provided that the said equipment-

          (a) has been dispatched on an occasional basis, on loan and free of charge; and

          (b) is intended for diagnostic or therapeutic purposes.

     (2) The period during which medical, surgical and laboratory equipment may be granted the said exemption shall not exceed six months.

19. (1) Temporary importation exemption shall be granted for materials for use in connection with countering the effects of disasters affecting the State, provided that such materials-

          (a) have been imported on loan and free of charge; and

(b)   are intended for State bodies or bodies approved by the Revenue Commissioners for the purposes of this Regulation.

20.   (1)   In this Regulation "packings" means-

    (a)   holders used, or to be used, as external or internal coverings for goods;

    (b)   holders on which goods are, or are to be, rolled, wound or attached; but excluding packing materials such as straw, paper, glass, wool and shavings when imported in bulk.

    (2)   Subject to paragraphs (3) and (4), temporary importation exemption shall be granted for packings provided that where-

    (a)   the packings are imported filled, they are declared as being for re-exportation empty or filled; or

    (b)   the packings are imported empty, they are declared as being for re-exportation filled.

    (3)   Packings admitted under temporary importation exemption shall not be used, even as an exception, between two points located within the State except with a view to the export of goods, and in the case of packings imported filled, this prohibition shall apply only from the time that they are emptied.

    (4)   The period during which packings may be granted such exemption shall not exceed six months where they are imported filled or three months where they are imported empty.

21.   (1)   In this Regulation-

"personal effects" means any clothing and other new or used articles intended for the personal use of the traveller,

"personal luggage" has the meaning assigned to it by Council Directive 69/169/EEC of 28 May, 1969.

    (2)   Temporary importation exemption shall be granted in respect of the personal effects which travellers are carrying on their person or in their personal luggage for the duration of their stay in the State.

22.   Temporary importation exemption shall be granted in respect of-

    (a)   samples which are representative of a particular category of goods and which are intended to be displayed or used for demonstration purposes with a view to obtaining orders for similar goods;

    (b)   films demonstrating the nature or the operation of foreign equipment or products, provided that they are not intended for public showing for charge;

(c)　　tourist publicity material of a kind described in Annex VI of Commission Regulation (EEC) No 1751/84;

(d)　　goods of any kind which are to be subjected to tests, experiments or demonstrations, including the tests and experiments required for type-approval procedures, but excluding any tests, experiments or demonstrations constituting a gainful activity;

(e)　　goods of any kind to be used to carry out tests, experiments or demonstrations, but excluding any tests, experiments or demonstrations constituting a gainful activity.

23.　(1)　　In this Regulation-

"welfare material" means material intended for cultural, educational, recreational, religious or sporting activities by seafarers, inasmuch as such material is of a kind described in Annex VII of Commission Regulation (EEC) No 1751/84,

"seafarers" means all persons transported on board a vessel and responsible for tasks relating to the operation or servicing of the vessel at sea,

"cultural or social establishments" means hostels, clubs and recreational premises for seafarers which are managed by official bodies or religious or other non-profit making organisations, and places of worship where religious services are held regularly solely or mainly for the benefit of seafarers.

(2)　　Temporary importation exemption shall be granted in respect of welfare material for seafarers, provided that the material is-

(a)　　brought ashore from a vessel for use on land by the crew of that vessel for a period not exceeding that of the vessel's stay in port; or

(b)　　imported for use in cultural or social establishments for a period not exceeding six months.

24.　　Temporary importation exemption shall be granted for equipment used, under the supervision and responsibility of a public authority, for the building, repair or maintenance of infrastructure of common importance in the area adjoining the land frontier of the State.

25.　　Temporary importation exemption shall be granted for-

(a)　　live animals of any species imported for dressage, training or breeding purposes or in order to be given veterinary treatment;

(b)　　live animals of any species imported for grazing purposes.

26.　　Temporary importation exemption shall be granted for-

(a)　　positive cinematograph films, printed and developed, intended for protection prior to commercial use;

(b)   films, magnetic tapes and wires which are intended to be provided with a sound track, dubbed or copied;

(c)   carrier material for recorded sound and data-processing, including punched cards, made available free of charge to a person, whether or not established in the State.

27.   Temporary importation exemption shall be granted for-

(a)   moulds, dies, blocks, drawings, sketches and other similar articles intended for a person established in the State, where at least 75 per cent of the production resulting from their use is exported from the territory of the Community;

(b)   measuring, checking and testing instruments and other similar articles intended for a person established in the State for use in a manufacturing process, where at least 75 per cent of the production resulting from their use is exported from the territory of the Community;

(c)   special tools and instruments made available free of charge to a person established in the State for use in the manufacture of goods which are to be exported in their entirety, on condition that such special tools and instruments remain the property of the person who made them available.

28.   (1)   Temporary importation exemption shall be granted for replacement means of production made temporarily available free of charge to the importer on the initiative of the supplier of similar means of production to be subsequently imported for release for home use or for means of production re-installed after repair.

(2)   The period during which such means of production may remain under the said exemption may not exceed six months.

29.   The Revenue Commissioners shall grant temporary importation exemption where they are satisfied that the goods concerned have no economic effect.

30.   (1)   Notwithstanding that the definition of "temporary importation exemption" in Regulation 1(5) includes the provision that the goods concerned are intended to remain temporarily in the State and to be re-exported, temporary importation exemption shall, subject to these Regulations, be granted in respect of the following goods, whether imported from another Member State or from outside the Community-

(a)   second-hand goods imported with a view to their sale by auction;

(b)   goods, imported under a contract of sale, which are to be subjected to satisfactory acceptance tests;

(c) consignments on approval or made-up articles of fur, precious stones, carpets and articles of jewellery, provided that their particular characteristics prevent their being imported as samples;

(d) works of art and other goods, intended for decoration but not generally for utility purposes, which are imported for the purposes of exhibition with a view to possible sale, being-

(i) paintings, drawings and pastels, including copies, executed entirely by hand, excluding hand-decorated manufactured wares and industrial drawings,

(ii) lithographs, prints and engravings, signed and numbered by the artist, obtained from lithographic stones, plates or other engraved surfaces, executed entirely by hand,

(iii) original sculptures and statuary, excluding mass-produced reproductions and handicrafts of a commercial nature,

(iv) tapestries and wall textiles made by hand from original designs provided by artists, provided that there is not more than one example of each, and

(v) original ceramics and mosaics on wood.

(2) The period during which the said exemption may be granted shall not exceed six months in the case of goods referred to in paragraph (1)(a), (1)(b) and (1)(d) and four weeks in that of paragraph (1)(c).

(3) For the purposes of this Regulation, where goods specified in paragraph (1) cease to be eligible for temporary importation exemption by reason of their sale in the State, the amount on which tax shall be chargeable shall be the price paid by the first purchaser of the goods in the State.

31. Authorisations in respect of temporary importation exemptions granted prior to the commencement of these Regulations and which are not provided for under the said Regulations may, if the Revenue Commissioners think fit, continue for a period not exceeding twenty four months from the said date.

32. The following enactments shall not apply in relation to goods in respect of which temporary importation exemption has been granted by virtue of these Regulations:

Section 12 of the Finance (Customs Duties) (No.4) Act, 1932 (No.34 of 1932),

Section 17 of the Finance Act, 1946 (No.15 of 1946), the Relief from Customs Duties (Fairs, Exhibitions and Similar Events) Order, 1956 (SI No.148 of 1956),

the Relief from Customs Duties (Professional Equipment Order), 1965 (SI No.143 of 1965),

the Relief from Customs Duties (Packings) Order, 1965 (SI No.223 of 1965),

and Council Regulation (EEC) No 3599/82.

33. A person who, after the commencement of these Regulations, contravenes a provision thereof, shall be guilty of an offence and shall, without prejudice to any other penalty to which he may be liable, be liable, on summary conviction, to a fine not exceeding £500.

GIVEN under my Official Seal,
this 28th day of July 1986.

JOHN BRUTON,
Minister for Finance.

EXPLANATORY NOTE.

These Regulations give effect to EEC Council Directive No 85/362/EEC of 16 July 1985. The Directive is based on a mandatory requirement in Article 14(1) (c) of the Sixth VAT Directive (77/388/EEC) and sets down the scope of the exemptions from VAT for goods declared to be under temporary importation arrangements and which qualify for exemptions from customs duties.

The Regulations provide relief from the payment of VAT, subject to conditions, for most goods imported on a temporary basis into Ireland from another Member State of the EEC. Consumable goods and means of transport are excluded from the provisions of the Regulations. Exceptionally, temporary importation exemption is also being provided for certain goods, including certain second-hand goods and specific works of art, imported on a temporary basis with a view to possible sale. Exemption from VAT is also provided for certain specific temporary importations of goods from countries outside the EEC. The goods affected include certain professional equipment, teaching aids, scientific equipment, medical, surgical and laboratory equipment etc. The VAT exemption for these goods parallels a customs duty exemption for similar importations provided by Council Regulation (EEC) No 3599/82.

The Revenue Commissioners may require security to be given in the case of most importations under these Regulations. An importer can choose the type of security he wishes to provide (cash, bond or other security) so long as it is in a form acceptable to the Revenue Commissioners.

VALUE-ADDED TAX (DETERMINATION OF TAX DUE BY REFERENCE TO MONEYS RECEIVED) REGULATIONS, 1986

(SI No. 298 of 1986)

These Regulations revoked by r13, Value Added Tax (Determination of Tax by Reference to Moneys Received) Regulations, 1992 (1992 S.I. No. 306) with effect from 28 October 1992.

The Revenue Commissioners, in exercise of the powers conferred on them by section 32 of the Value-Added Tax Act, 1972 (No 22 of 1972), hereby make the following regulations:

Short title and commencement.

1.   These Regulations may be cited as the Value-Added Tax (Determination of Tax Due by reference to Moneys Received) Regulations, 1986.

Definitions.

2.   (1)   In these Regulations-

"the Act" means the Value-Added Tax Act, 1972;

"taxable turnover", in relation to any period means the total of the amounts on which tax is chargeable for that period at any of the rates specified in section 11(1) of the Act;

"turnover", in relation to any period, means the amount on which tax would be chargeable for that period in accordance with section 10 of the Act if section 6 of the Act were disregarded.

(2)   In these Regulations a reference to a paragraph, subparagraph or clause is to a paragraph, subparagraph or clause of the provision in which the reference occurs unless it is indicated that reference to some other provision is intended.

Determination of tax due by reference to moneys received.

3.   (1)   A person who desires that, in accordance with section 14(1)(a) of the Act, the amount of tax which becomes due by him during any taxable period (or part thereof), other than tax due in relation to supplies referred to in paragraph (5), should be determined by reference to the amount of moneys which he receives during such taxable period in respect of the supply of taxable goods or services, whether made before, on or after the specified day, shall give notice in writing to the Revenue Commissioners of his desire that the tax should be so determined and shall at the same time, unless he has already done so, furnish the following particulars to the Revenue Commissioners-

(a)   the nature of the business activities carried on by him;

(b)   the percentage of his taxable turnover, if any, which related to supplies of taxable goods and services to unregistered persons-

    (i)   in the period of 12 months ended on the last day of the taxable period prior to the giving of the notice, or

    (ii)   in the period from the commencement of his business activities to the last day of the taxable period referred to in clause (i), whichever is the shorter;

(c)   his estimate of the percentage of his taxable turnover which will relate to supplies of taxable goods and services to unregistered persons in the period of 12 months commencing with the beginning of the taxable period during which the notice is given,

(d)   the amount due to him on the last day of the taxable period prior to the giving of the notice in respect of the goods and services supplied by him.

(2)   Where a change occurs in any of the particulars furnished in accordance with paragraph (1), the taxable person shall, within thirty days immediately following the date of the change, furnish to the Revenue Commissioners particulars of the change.

(3)   (a)   The Revenue Commissioners shall, if the inspector of taxes is satisfied that not less than 90 per cent. of the taxable turnover of the person is likely to be derived from the supply of taxable goods or services to unregistered persons, by notice in writing, authorise the person to determine the amount of tax which becomes due by him during any taxable period (or part thereof) during which the authorisation has effect by reference to the amount of the moneys which he receives during such taxable period from the supply, whether made before, on or after the specified day, of taxable goods or services:

    (b)   An authorisation given under subparagraph (a) shall have effect while the person is a taxable person from the commencement of the taxable period during which it is given until the commencement of the taxable period during which it is cancelled in accordance with paragraph (9).

(4)   (a)   A person who desires that, in accordance with section14(1)(b) of the Act, the amount of tax referable to taxable services which becomes due by him during any taxable period (or part thereof), other than tax due in relation to supplies referred to in paragraph (5), should be determined by reference to the amount of the moneys which he receives during such taxable period (or part thereof) in respect of

the supply of taxable services, whether made before, on or after the specified day, shall give notice in writing to the Revenue Commissioners of his desire that the tax should be so determined, and the Revenue Commissioners shall, by notice in writing given to the person, authorise the tax to be determined accordingly.

(b) An authorisation given in accordance with subparagraph (a) shall have effect while the person is a taxable person from the commencement of the taxable period during which it is given until the commencement of the taxable period during which it is cancelled in accordance with paragraph (9).

(5) An authorisation under paragraph (3) or (4) shall not apply to tax chargeable on any supply of goods or services where the person to whom or to whose order the supply is made is a connected person.

(6) Where a person, who for any period is authorised in accordance with paragraph (3) to determine the amount of tax which becomes due by him by reference to the amount of the moneys which he has received from the supply of taxable goods or services, ceases to be so authorised or ceases to be a taxable person, the tax payable by him for the taxable period during which any such cesser occurs shall be adjusted as follows:

(a) the excess, if any, of the total amount due to him at the end of the first-mentioned period for goods and services supplied by him over the total amount due to him at the commencement of that period for goods and services supplied by him shall be apportioned between amounts by reference to which tax is to be determined and amounts by reference to which tax is not to be determined at each of the various rates of tax (including the zero rate) specified in section 11(1) of the Act in the same proportions as the amounts of consideration by reference to which tax was to be determined and amounts by reference to which tax did not fall to be determined at each of those rates of tax bear to each other in the period consisting of six consecutive taxable periods (or the total number of taxable periods for which he was authorised as aforesaid, if less than six) next before the taxable period in which the cesser occurs,

(b) the portions of the excess referred to in subparagraph (a) on which tax is chargeable at the various rates, as ascertained by apportionment in accordance with that subparagraph, shall be treated as consideration in respect of which tax at the said rates fell to be determined during the taxable period during which the cesser occurs and tax shall be chargeable accordingly.

(7)   Where a person who for any period is authorised in accordance with paragraph (4) to determine the amount of tax referable to taxable services which becomes due by him by reference to the amount of the moneys which he has received for the supply of taxable services ceases to be so authorised or ceases to be a taxable person, the tax payable by him for the taxable period during which any such cesser occurs shall be adjusted as follows:

(a)   the excess, if any, of the total amount due to him at the end of the first-mentioned period for services supplied by him over the total amount due to him at the commencement of that period for services supplied by him shall be apportioned between amounts by reference to which tax is to be determined and amounts by reference to which tax is not to be determined at each of the various rates (including the zero rate) specified in section 11(1) of the Act in the same proportions as the amounts of consideration for the supplying of services by reference to which tax was to be determined and amounts by reference to which tax did not fall to be determined at each of those rates of tax bear to each other in the period consisting of six consecutive taxable periods (or the total number of taxable periods for which he was authorised as aforesaid if less than six) next before the taxable period in which the cesser occurs,

(b)   the portions of the excess referred to in subparagraph (a), which are referable to the supplying of services chargeable at the various rates, as ascertained by apportionment in accordance with that subparagraph, shall be treated as consideration in respect of which tax at the said rates fell to be determined during the taxable period during which the cesser occurs, and tax shall be chargeable accordingly.

(8)   An authorisation under this Regulation shall not affect the amount on which tax is chargeable in any of the circumstances referred to in subsections (2) to (9) of section 10 of the Act or tax chargeable on supplies referred to in paragraph (5).

(9)   (a)   The Revenue Commissioners shall cancel an authorisation given The Revenue Commissioners in accordance with paragraph (3) or (4)-

(i)   if the person to whom the authorisation was given requests the cancellation by notice in writing given to the Revenue Commissioners,

(ii)   if, in the case of a person authorised in accordance with paragraph (3), the inspector of taxes ceases to be satisfied that, taking one taxable period with another, the person derives not less than 90 per cent. of his taxable turnover from the supply of taxable goods or services to unregistered persons, or

(iii) if, on a review of any period consisting of three or more consecutive taxable periods, the inspector of taxes is satisfied that, in relation to supplies by a person authorised in accordance with paragraph (3) or (4), the amount of tax due by the person in respect of the amount of moneys which he has received in the period is less than 80 per cent. of the amount of tax which would be due in the period in relation to the said supplies if no authorisation under this Regulation had been issued.

(b) An authorisation under this Regulation may be cancelled by notice in writing given by the Revenue Commissioners to the person who was the subject of the authorisation, and such cancellation shall have effect for the purposes of section 14 of the Act from the commencement of the taxable period during which notice was given or from the commencement of such later taxable period as may be specified in the notice.

(10) No adjustment of liability as provided for in paragraph (6) or (7) shall be made if the cesser of authorisation as aforesaid was occasioned by the death of the taxable person, or if the period immediately preceding the date of the cesser during which he was authorised in accordance with the relevant paragraph exceeded six years.

(11) For the purposes of this Regulation any question of whether a person is connected with another person shall be determined in accordance with the following provisions:

(a) a person is connected with an individual if that person is the individual's husband or wife, or is a relative, or the husband or wife of a relative, of the individual or of the individual's husband or wife;

(b) a person is connected with any person with whom he is in partnership and with the husband or wife or a relative of any individual with whom he is in partnership;

(c) subject to paragraphs (d), and (e), a person is connected with another person if he has control over that other person or if the other person has control over the first-mentioned person or if both persons are controlled by another person or persons;

(d) a body corporate is connected with another person if that person or persons connected with him have control of it or the person and persons connected with him together have control of it;

(e) a body corporate is connected with another body corporate-

(i) if a person has control of one and persons connected with him or he and persons connected with him have control of the other, or

(ii) if a group of two or more persons has control of each body corporate and the groups either consist of the same persons or could be regarded as consisting of the same persons by treating (in one or more cases) a member of either group as replaced by a person with whom he is connected;

(f) "relative" means brother, sister, ancestor or lineal descendant.

(12) In this Regulation "control" in relation to a body corporate, means the power of a person to secure, by means of the holding of shares or the possession of voting power in or in relation to that or any other body corporate, or by virtue of any powers conferred by the articles of association or other document regulating that or any other body corporate, that the affairs of the first-mentioned body corporate are conducted in accordance with the wishes of that person, and, in relation to a partnership, means the right to a share or more than one-half of the assets, or of more than one-half of the income, of the partnership.

4. Regulation 7 of the Value-Added Tax Regulations, 1979 (SI No.63 of 1979), is hereby revoked.

GIVEN this 2nd day of September, 1986.

L. REASON,
Revenue Commissioner.

EXPLANATORY NOTE.

These Regulations amend the terms and conditions relating to the operation of the moneys received basis of accounting for VAT formerly contained in Regulation 7 of the Value-Added Tax Regulations, 1979. The new Regulations extend the definition of connected persons, transactions between which are excluded from the moneys received basis of accounting. They also give to an Inspector of Taxes the power to withdraw the moneys received basis where in a particular case he is satisfied that it has not proved to be a reliable measure of the true liability. The new Regulations also contain some other minor changes from the former Regulation 7 which is now repealed.

IMPOSITION OF DUTIES (NO. 283) (VALUE-ADDED TAX) ORDER, 1986

(SI No. 412 of 1986)

This Order revoked by s39(b), FA87 with effect from 9 July 1987

The Government, in exercise of the powers conferred on them by section 1 of the Imposition of Duties Act, 1957 (No. 7 of 1957), and section 38(2) of the Value-Added Tax Act, 1972 (No. 22 of 1972), hereby order as follows.

1. This Order may be cited as the Imposition of Duties (No. 283) (Value-Added Tax) Order, 1986.

2. This Order shall come into operation on the 1st day of January, 1987.

3. Section 1(1) of the Value-Added Tax Act, 1972 is hereby amended by the substitution in the definition of "livestock" of ", pigs and deer" for "and pigs".

4. This Order and the Value-Added Tax Acts, 1972 to 1986, shall be construed together.

GIVEN under the Official Seal of the Government, this day of 11th December, 1986.

GARRET FITZGERALD.
The Taoiseach.

EXPLANATORY NOTE.

The effect of this Order is to reduce the rate of VAT on the supply and importation of live deer from 25 per cent to 2.4 per cent.

VALUE-ADDED TAX (REFUND OF TAX) (No 20) ORDER, 1987

(SI No. 10 of 1987)

> This Order revoked by Value Added Tax (Refund of Tax)(No.23) Order 1992, (1992 S.I. No. 58) with effect from 29 January 1992.

I, JOHN BRUTON, Minister for Finance, in exercise of the powers conferred on me by section 20(3) of the Value-Added Tax Act, 1972 (No 22 of 1972), hereby order as follows:

1.   This Order may be cited as the Value-Added Tax (Refund of Tax) (No.20) Order, 1987.

2.   In this Order-

"the Act" means the Value-Added Tax Act, 1972 (No.22 of 1972);

"qualifying goods" means any new instrument or new appliance, excluding means of transport-

(a)   in relation to which the amount on which tax is chargeable by virtue of the Act is £20,000 or more,

(b)   which has been designed and manufactured for use solely in medical research or in diagnosis, prevention, or treatment of illness,

(c)   which has been the subject of a recommendation by the Minister for Health that, having regard to the requirements of the health services in the State, a refund of tax under this Order would be appropriate;

"qualifying body" means any body of persons engaged in the operation of a hospital.

3.   Where a person establishes to the satisfaction of the Revenue Commissioners that-

(a)   he has borne or paid tax which became chargeable on or after the 1st day of April, 1986, in respect of the supply to, or importation by, him of qualifying goods,

(b)   he is a qualifying body or, if he is not such a body, the qualifying goods have been, or are to be, donated by him to a qualifying body,

(c)   no part of the funds used, or to be used, in the purchase of the qualifying goods was, or is to be, provided, directly or indirectly, by the State, or by any board established by statute, or by any public or local authority, or by the qualifying body which has purchased the qualifying goods or to which they have been, or are to be, donated, or by any body of persons associated with such qualifying body in the operation of a hospital, or by any other body of persons operating a hospital,

and

(d)   in respect of the supply or importation of qualifying goods, he is
        not entitled to repayment of the tax under any other provision of
        the Act or under any instrument made under statute administered
        by the Revenue Commissioners, and the person completes such
        claim form as may be provided for the purpose by the Revenue
        Commissioners and certifies the particulars shown on such claim
        form to be correct, he shall be entitled to be repaid so much of
        such tax as is specified in paragraph 4 of the Order.

4.   The amount of tax to be repaid under this Order shall be so much of
        the amount of tax specified in paragraph 3(a) of this Order as is shown
        to the satisfaction of the Revenue Commissioners to be in excess of the
        amount which would have been borne or paid if the rate and percentage
        for the time being specified in section 11(1)(c) of the Act had applied in
        relation to the goods.

GIVEN under my Official Seal,
this 15th day of January, 1987.

JOHN BRUTON,
Minister for Finance.

EXPLANATORY NOTE.

The effect of this Order will be to reduce the rate of Value-Added Tax from 25
per cent to 10 per cent on qualifying medical equipment purchased through
voluntary donations.

VALUE-ADDED TAX (FREE PORTS) REGULATIONS, 1987

(SI No. 275 of 1987)

This Regulation was revoked by regulation 44, Value-Added Tax
Regulations, 2006 (2006 S.I. No. 548) w.e.f. 1 November 2006

The Revenue Commissioners, in exercise of the powers conferred on them by sections 15 of the Value-Added Tax Act, 1972 (No.22 of 1972), and with the consent of the Minister for Finance, hereby make the following Regulations:

1.   These Regulations may be cited as the Value-Added Tax (Free Ports) Regulations, 1987.

2.   These Regulations shall be deemed to have come into operation on the 24th day of July, 1987.

3.   In these Regulations-

"the Act" means the Value-Added Tax Act, 1972;

"control" has the meaning ascribed to it by section 8(3B) (inserted by the Finance Act, 1984 (No 9 of 1984)) of the Act.

4.   (1)   Subject to paragraph (2) of this Regulation, goods that are imported by a registered person may be delivered, or removed, directly to a free port without payment of the tax chargeable on the importation if that person complies with-

    (a)   the condition that he shows to the satisfaction of the Revenue Commissioners that-

        (i)   he is a person who has, under section 4 of the Free Ports Act, 1986 (No. 6 of 1986), been granted a licence authorising him to carry on within that free port any trade, business or manufacture and

        (ii)   the goods are being imported for the purposes of his trade, business or manufacture in that free port,

    and

    (b)   such other conditions as the Revenue Commissioners may impose.

    (2)   This Regulation shall not apply to the importation of food, drink, motor vehicles or petrol except where tax on the importation of those goods would, if it were paid, be wholly deductible under section 12 of the Act.

5.   (1)   Without prejudice to paragraph (2) of this Regulation, goods, which have been imported by a registered person without payment of the tax chargeable on the importation in accordance with Regulation 4 of these Regulations, may not be removed from the free port concerned to any other part of the State (other than into another free port or the customs-free airport), in circumstances in which such removal is not in relation to a supply

of those goods or, if it is in relation to a supply of those goods, is in relation to a supply to a person who exercises control over the registered person, or over whom the registered person exercises control, or over whom and the registered person another person exercises control.

(2)   (a)   The removal of goods, precluded by paragraph (1) of this Regulation, may be allowed, with the prior agreement in writing of the Revenue Commissioners, in such exceptional cases as may be determined by them in their absolute discretion.

        (b)   Where, by virtue of this paragraph, the removal of goods is allowed, tax which would, but for these Regulations, have been payable on the importation of the goods, shall be payable at the time of the removal by the registered person specified in paragraph (1) of this Regulation.

6.   Where goods have been imported by a registered person without payment of the tax chargeable on the importation in accordance with Regulation 4 of these Regulations, details of the goods, including the value by reference to each rate of tax (including the zero rate) shall, if so required, be included in the return for the taxable period during which the importation took place required to be furnished by that person under section19 of the Act and the regulations made thereunder.

7.   Where, in the opinion of the Revenue Commissioners, a person does not, or has ceased to, satisfy a condition referred to, or specified, in Regulation 4 of these Regulations, or has failed to comply with Regulation 5 or 6 of these Regulations, the Revenue Commissioners shall send to such person by post notification of their opinion and the relief provided for by the said Regulation 4 shall not apply in relation to goods imported by that person during the period from the date on which such notification would be delivered in the ordinary course of post until the time when the person concerned shows to the satisfaction of the Revenue Commissioners that he intends to comply with the conditions referred to, or specified, in the said Regulation 4 and with the said Regulations 5 and 6.

GIVEN this 7th day of October, 1987.

L. REASON,
Revenue Commissioner.

The Minister for Finance hereby consents to the making of the foregoing Regulations.

GIVEN under the Official Seal of the Minister for Finance, this 7th day of October, 1987.

RAY MAC SHARRY,
Minister for Finance.

EXPLANATORY NOTE.

These Regulations, which have effect from 24 July, 1987, are concerned with the relieving from payment of VAT at importation of goods for use in a free port established in accordance with the Free Ports Act, 1986.

To qualify for the relief an importer must-

(a)   be registered for VAT,

(b)   be licensed to carry on business in the free port, and

(c)   import the goods for the purposes of his business in the free port.

The relief does not extend to imports of food, drink, motor vehicles or petrol except in circumstances where, but for these Regulations, tax paid on such imports would have been deductible by the VAT registered importer. Goods on which the relief has been allowed on import may not be merely transferred to another premises of the same business (or associate business) in the State except in special cases.

The importations must be accounted for in the normal VAT return by entering details of the goods concerned under the various VAT rates.

Where the requirements of the Regulations are not, or cease to be, met in any case, the Revenue Commissioners are empowered to withhold, or withdraw the relief until such time as they are satisfied that the importer intends to comply with such requirements.

VALUE-ADDED TAX (REFUND OF TAX) (NO 21) ORDER, 1987

(SI No. 308 of 1987)

From 1 January 1993 'export' means export to a country outside the EU.

I, RAY MACSHARRY, Minister for Finance, in exercise of the powers conferred on me by section 20(3) of the Value-Added Tax Act, 1972 (No 22 of 1972), hereby order as follows:

1.　(1)　This Order may be cited as the Value-Added Tax (Refund of Tax) (No. 21) Order, 1987.

　　(2)　This Order shall be deemed to have come into operation on the 1st day of July, 1987.

2.　In this Order-

　　(a)　"the Act" means the Value-Added Tax Act, 1972;

　　(b)　"qualifying body" means any non-profit making body of persons with aims of a philanthropic nature, engaged in humanitarian, charitable or teaching activities abroad;

　　(c)　"qualifying goods" means goods which, within four months of their supply in, or importation into, the State, have been exported, by or on behalf of a qualifying body, for use in its humanitarian, charitable or teaching activities abroad.

3.　A person, who establishes to the satisfaction of the Revenue Commissions that-

　　(a)　he is a qualifying body, or that he is acting on behalf of a qualifying body,

　　(b)　the goods to which the claim relates are qualifying goods,

　　(c)　he has borne or paid tax on the supply to, or importation by, him of those qualifying goods,

　　and who fulfils, to the satisfaction of the said Commissioners, the conditions specified in paragraph 4 of this Order, shall be entitled to be repaid such tax.

4.　The conditions to be fulfilled by a person referred to in paragraph 3 of this Order are that he shall-

　　(a)　claim a refund of the tax by completing such claim form as may be provided for the purpose by the Revenue Commissioners, and certify the particulars shown on such claim form to be correct,

　　(b)　establish the amount of tax borne or paid to which the claim relates by the production of invoices or other documents, provided in accordance with section 17(12)(a)(i) of the Act, or by the production of receipts for tax paid on goods imported,

(c)   establish that he is not entitled to remission, repayment or deduction of the tax under any other provision of the Act, or under any instrument made under statute administered by the Revenue Commissioners in respect of the supply or importation of the qualifying goods.

GIVEN under my Official Seal,
this 8th day of December, 1987.

RAY MACSHARRY,
Minister for Finance

EXPLANATORY NOTE.

This Order provides relief from VAT, subject to conditions for goods purchased for export by philanthropic organisations for use in their activities abroad. The Order gives effect to Article 15(12) of EEC Council Directive 77/388/EEC of 17th May 1977.

VALUE-ADDED TAX (SECOND-HAND MOTOR VEHICLES) REGULATIONS, 1988

(SI No. 121 of 1988)

> These Regulations revoked by r9, Value Added Tax (Special Scheme for Means of Transport; Documentation) Regulations, 1996, (1996 S.I. No. 201) with effect from 1 July 1996.

The Revenue Commissioners, in exercise of the powers conferred on them by sections12(1) of the Value-Added Tax Act, 1972 (No 22 of 1972), and with the consent of the Minister for Finance, hereby make the following Regulations:

1.   These Regulations may be cited as the Value-Added Tax (Second-hand Motor Vehicles) Regulations, 1988.

2.   These Regulations shall be deemed to have come into operation on the 1st day of November, 1987.

3.   (1)   In these Regulations-

"the Act" means the Value-Added Tax Act, 1972;

"qualifying vehicle" means a second-hand mechanically propelled vehicle, designed and constructed for the conveyance by road of persons or goods, which is acquired in the State for resale in the State.

(2)   In these Regulations, a reference to a Regulation is to a Regulation of these Regulations and a reference to a paragraph, subparagraph or clause is to a paragraph, subparagraph or clause of the provision in which the reference occurs, unless it is indicated that reference to some other provision is intended.

4.   (1)   Section 12(1)(a)(vi) (inserted by the Finance Act, 1987 (No 10 of 1987)) of the Act shall have effect subject to, and insofar as is provided for in, these Regulations.

(2)   For the purposes of giving effect by these Regulations to the said section12(1)(a)(vi), each of the following terms in that section shall have the meaning ascribed to it in this Regulation, that is to say-

"the amount of tax, as defined" means the amount obtained by multiplying the consideration payable in each case by a fraction, the numerator of which is the number of percentage points for the time being specified in section 11(1)(a) of the Act and the denominator of which is the said number of percentage points and one hundred;

"specified second-hand goods or categories of second-hand goods" means qualifying vehicles.

5.   A taxable person may not deduct an amount of tax in accordance with section12(1)(a)(vi) of the Act unless the following conditions, and such other conditions as the Revenue Commissioners may, from time to time, impose, are fulfilled-

(a)   he is in possession of an invoice and a declaration issued in accordance with Regulation 6 in respect of the supply to him of the qualifying vehicle concerned,

(b)   such deduction is made in computing the amount of tax payable by him in respect of the taxable period in which the qualifying vehicle is resold by him: provided that such taxable period commences not later than the last day of the period of three hundred and sixty five days next following the date on which the qualifying vehicle is acquired by him,

(c)   the amount of such deduction is not in excess of the amount of tax chargeable on the resale by him of the said vehicle: provided that in relation to the calculation of such amount of tax chargeable, the proviso to section 10(2) of the Act, if it were to apply, were, for the purposes of this Regulation, disregarded.

6.   A person who supplies a qualifying vehicle to a taxable person shall-

(a)   on the date of such supply, or within the ten days next following that date, issue to the taxable person, who acquires that vehicle, an invoice in respect of that supply, which sets out the following particulars:

(i)   the name and address of the person who is supplying the vehicle to which the invoice relates,

(ii)   the name, address and tax registration number of the said taxable person,

(iii)   the date upon which the invoice is issued,

(iv)   the date upon which the vehicle to which the invoice relates is supplied,

(v)   a description of the vehicle, including details of the make, model, engine number, registration number and year of manufacture,

(vi)   the total consideration for the supply, and

(vii)   the signature or acknowledgement of the person by whom the invoice is issued,

(b)   sign or acknowledge a declaration to the effect that-

(i)   he is not a taxable person,

or

(ii)   he is a taxable person and-

(I) the said qualifying vehicle was used by him for the purposes of a business carried on by him,

(II) he has borne tax on the acquisition or application of the vehicle, and

(III) the vehicle is of such a kind or was used in such circumstances that no part of the said tax was deductible under section 12 of the Act,

and the taxable person to whom the qualifying vehicle is supplied shall provide the form for the purpose of the said invoice and said declaration, enter the appropriate particulars thereon, and give a copy of the invoice and declaration to the supplier of the vehicle.

7. Every taxable person shall, in relation to a qualifying vehicle which he has acquired in the circumstances specified in section 12(1)(a)(vi) of the Act, keep full and true records, entered up to date, of the acquisition and resale of the said vehicle, together with cross-references between all such records.

GIVEN this,
9th day of June, 1988.

L. REASON,
Revenue Commissioner.

The Minister for Finance hereby consents to the making of the foregoing Regulations.

GIVEN under the Official Seal of the Minister for Finance, this 9th day of June, 1988.

RAY MACSHARRY,
Minister for Finance.

EXPLANATORY NOTE.

These Regulations, which have effect from 1 November 1987, provide, subject to conditions, for VAT relief in relation to the acquisition, for the purposes of resale, by taxable persons from non-taxable persons (or from taxable persons in certain circumstances) of certain second-hand road motor vehicles.

VALUE-ADDED TAX (REFUND OF TAX) (NO 22) ORDER, 1988

(SI No. 262 of 1988)

> **This Order revoked by para7, Value added Tax(Refund of Tax)(No 24) Order, 1993 (1993 S.I. No. 134).**

I, RAY MAC SHARRY, Minister for Finance, in exercise of the powers conferred on me by section 20(3) of the Value-Added Tax Act, 1972 (No.22 of 1972), hereby order as follows:

1.   (1)   This Order may be cited as the Value-Added Tax (Refund of Tax) (No.22) Order, 1988.

    (2)   This Order shall be deemed to have come into operation on the 1st day of October, 1988.

2.   The Value-Added Tax (Refund of Tax) (No.19) Order, 1986 (SI No.68 of 1986), is hereby amended by the substitution of the following paragraph for paragraph 3:

    "3.   A person who establishes to the satisfaction of the Revenue Commissioners that he has borne or paid tax in relation to the acquisition, including the hiring (other than the hiring for a period of less than 6 consecutive months), by him of a passenger road motor vehicle not more than 24 months old, being-

    (a)   a single-deck touring coach having dimensions as designated by the manufacturer of not less than 3,350 millimetres in height, not less than 10,000 millimetres in length and not less than 1,400 millimetres in floor height, or

    (b)   a double-deck touring coach having dimensions as designated by the manufacturer of not more than 4,300 millimetres in height and not less than 10,000 millimetres in length, for use by him for the purposes of the business referred to in subparagraph (b) of paragraph 4 of this Order, and who fulfils to the satisfaction of the said Commissioners the conditions that are specified in the said paragraph 4 and such other conditions as the said Commissioners may impose, shall be entitled to be repaid so much of such tax as is specified in paragraph 5 of this Order.".

Given under my Official Seal,
this 11th day of October 1988.

RAY MAC SHARRY,
Minister for Finance.

EXPLANATORY NOTE.

This Order provides for an extension of the existing VAT refund scheme for luxury touring coaches.

VALUE-ADDED TAX (FURNITURE, SILVER, GLASS AND PORCELAIN) REGULATIONS, 1989

(SI No. 304 of 1989)

> **This Regulation was revoked by regulation 44, Value-Added Tax Regulations, 2006 (2006 S.I. No. 548) w.e.f. 1 November 2006**

The Revenue Commissioners, in exercise of the powers conferred on them by section32 of, and paragraph (ia) of the Sixth Schedule to, the Value-Added Tax Act, 1972 (No 22 of 1972), as amended by the Finance Act, 1989 (No 10 of 1989), and with the consent of the Minister for Finance, hereby make the following Regulations:

1.   These Regulations may be cited as the Value-Added Tax (Furniture, Silver, Glass and Porcelain) Regulations, 1989.

2.   (1)   In these Regulations-

"the Act" means the Value-Added Tax Act, 1972;

"qualifying goods" means articles of the kind specified in Regulation 3 which are more than 100 years old, where such evidence, as specified in Regulation 4, is produced which satisfies the Revenue Commissioners that the articles concerned are more than 100 years old.

(2)   In these Regulations a reference to a Regulation is to a Regulation of these Regulations.

3.   (1)   Paragraph (ia)(d) (inserted by the Finance Act, 1989 (No.10 of 1989)) of the Sixth Schedule to the Act shall have effect subject to and in accordance with these Regulations.

(2)   For the purposes of giving effect by these Regulations to the said paragraph (ia)(d), the following articles of furniture, silver, glass and porcelain are hereby specified to be the articles to which the said paragraph (ia)(d) of these Regulations apply, that is to say:

(a)   in the case of furniture, any article being movable goods which have been manufactured wholly or mainly from wood, metal (other than silver), marble or other stone, or any combination thereof, and which were designed for use as furnishings, fitments or decoration for private, commercial or public buildings, or for gardens, and to which subparagraphs (a), (b) and (c) of paragraph (ia) of the Sixth Schedule to the Act do not relate;

(b)   in the case of silver, any article manufactured wholly or mainly from silver, not being jewellery, coins, medals, ingots or bars;

(c)   in the case of glass, any article manufactured wholly or mainly from glass, including mirrors, chandeliers and leaded or stained glass windows;

(d)   in the case of porcelain, any article being a cup, saucer, bowl, plate, dish, jug, vase, pot, urn or similar goods, or a statue or statuary (other than an article to which paragraph (ia)(c) of the Sixth Schedule to the Act relates), manufactured wholly or mainly from porcelain, china, terracotta, clay, ceramics or similar materials, or any combination thereof.

4.   Evidence that qualifying goods are more than 100 years old shall consist of-

(a)   a certificate issued by a member of the association known as the Irish Antique Dealers' Association, or of an equivalent trade association recognised by the Revenue Commissioners for the purpose of issuing such a certificate, or

(b)   a certificate issued on behalf of the National Museum of Ireland, or

(c)   a statutory declaration by a person recognised, for the purpose of making such a declaration, as a connoisseur by the Revenue Commissioners in respect of articles of the types concerned, or

(d)   in the case of imported goods, a certificate, declaration or other document made under the laws of the country of exportation which in the opinion of the Revenue Commissioners correspond to any of the foregoing provisions of this Regulation, or

(e)   an invoice issued in accordance with Regulation 6 or a certification made in accordance with Regulation 7.

5.   A non-taxable person who supplies qualifying goods to a taxable person who is acquiring such goods for resale shall on the date of such supply, or within the ten days next following that date, issue to the taxable person who acquires the goods an invoice in respect of that supply, which sets out the following particulars:

(a)   the name and address of the person who is supplying the goods to which the invoice relates,

(b)   the name, address, and tax registration number of the said taxable person,

(c)   the date upon which the invoice is issued,

(d)   the date upon which the goods to which the invoice relates are supplied,

(e)   a description of the goods including details of the quantity, type, apparent material of construction, possible origin and identifying features,

(f)   the consideration for the supply, and

(g)   the signature or acknowledgement of the person by whom the invoice is issued,

and the taxable person to whom the qualifying goods are supplied shall provide the form for the purpose of the said invoice, enter the appropriate particulars thereon, and give a copy of the invoice to the supplier of the goods.

6.   A taxable person who supplies qualifying goods to another taxable person shall include on the invoice concerned, which he is required to issue in accordance with section 17(1) of the Act, a declaration to the effect that the goods are more than 100 years old.

7.   A taxable person who supplies qualifying goods to a non-taxable person shall, for the purposes of Regulation 8, certify in writing in respect of each such supply that the said goods are more than 100 years old.

8.   Every taxable person shall, in relation to qualifying goods which he has acquired or supplied, keep full and true records, entered up to date, of the acquisition and resale of such goods, together with cross-references between all such records, the relevant invoices issued in accordance with Regulations 5 and 6, and the certification made in accordance with Regulation 7.

GIVEN this 17th day of November, 1989.

F. CASSELLS.
Revenue Commissioner.

The Minister for Finance hereby consents to the making of the foregoing Regulations.

GIVEN under the Official Seal of the Minister for Finance, this 17th day of November, 1989.

ALBERT REYNOLDS,
Minister for Finance.

EXPLANATORY NOTE.

These Regulations provide, subject to conditions, for the reduction from 25 to 10 per cent. in the rate of VAT on the supply and importation of certain articles of furniture, silver, glass and porcelain more than 100 years old. The reduction is operational from 1 November, 1989.

DISABLED DRIVERS (TAX CONCESSIONS) REGULATIONS, 1989

(SI No. 340 of 1989)

> These Regulations revoked by r19, Disabled Drivers and
> Disabled Passengers (Tax Concessions) Regulations, 1994,
> (1994 S.I. No. 353) with effect from 1 December 1994.

I, ALBERT REYNOLDS, Minister for Finance, in exercise of the powers conferred on me by section 92 of the Finance Act, 1989 (No 10 of 1989), and after consultation with the Minister for Health and the Minister for the Environment, hereby make the following Regulations:

1.   (1)   These Regulations may be cited as the Disabled Drivers (Tax Concessions) Regulations, 1989, and shall come into operation on the 21st day of December, 1989.

       (2)   A person may apply under these Regulations in respect of a vehicle purchased by him on or after the 24th day of May, 1989.

2.   (1)   In these Regulations-

         "adapted", in relation to motor vehicles, does not include adaptations of production line models which are available from the manufacturer or assembler thereof as an optional extra, and "adaptation" shall be construed accordingly;

         "licensing authority" has the same meaning as it has for the purposes of the Finance (Excise Duties) (Vehicles) Act, 1952 (No 24. of 1952);

         "motor vehicle" has the same meaning as it has in paragraph 3 (a) of the Imposition of Duties (No.236) (Excise Duties on Motor Vehicles, Televisions and Gramophone Records) Order, 1979 (SI No.57 of 1979);

         "the Order of 1979" means the Imposition of Duties (No.236) (Excise Duties on Motor Vehicles, Televisions and Gramophone Records) Order, 1979 (SI No.57 of 1979);

         "the Order of 1984" means the Imposition of Duties (No.272) (Excise Duties on Motor Vehicles) Order, 1984 (SI No.353 of 1984).

       (2)   In these Regulations a reference to a Regulation or Schedule is to a Regulation of, or Schedule to, these Regulations and a reference to a paragraph or subparagraph is to a paragraph or subparagraph of the provision in which the reference occurs.

3.   For the purpose of section 92(2)(a) of the Finance Act, 1989 (No.10 of 1989), the eligibility on medical grounds of persons, being severely and permanently disabled persons, shall be assessed by reference to any one or more of the following medical criteria:

(a)   persons who are wholly or almost wholly without the use of both legs;

(b)   persons wholly without the use of one of their legs and almost wholly without the use of the other leg such that they are severely restricted as to movement of their lower limbs;

(c)   persons without both hands or without both arms;

(d)   persons without one or both legs;

(e)   persons having the medical condition of dwarfism and who have serious difficulties of movement of the lower limbs.

4.   Without prejudice to Regulation 5, either or both repayment and remission, as appropriate, of any tax or excise duty by virtue of these Regulations shall be conditional on the applicant for such repayment or remission obtaining, in each case either-

(a)   a primary medical certificate duly completed in the form prescribed in the First Schedule as evidence of qualifying disablement, signed and dated by the appropriate Director of Community Care and Medical Officer of Health, or

(b)   a certificate duly completed in the form prescribed in the Second Schedule to which Regulation 6 relates,

and complying with the relevant provisions of Regulations 7 to 12.

5.   (1)   Any person who is deemed, by virtue of section 92(3)(b) of the Finance Act, 1989, to be a person who possesses a primary medical certificate shall not be entitled to a repayment of tax or excise duty unless the person has complied with the requirements, other than the medical requirements, set out in these Regulations and which relate to the tax or excise duty concerned.

     (2)   A person to whom paragraph (1) relates shall, for the purposes of Regulations 8 and 9, be deemed to have produced to the Revenue Commissioners and the licensing authority concerned a primary medical certificate.

6.   (1)   On the nomination of the Minister for Health and for such period of time as is specified by him, the Minister for Finance shall appoint three medical practitioners to be a board to a known as the Disabled Drivers Medical Board of Appeal (in these Regulations referred to as "the Board").

     (2)   A person who is aggrieved by a decision of a Director of Community Care and Medical Officer of Health in respect of primary medical certification may appeal to the Board within 28 days, or such longer period as it may allow, of the person first being informed of that decision.

     (3)   Where the Board adjudicates in favour of the disabled driver or passenger concerned, as the case may be, it shall issue a medical

certificate in the form prescribed in the Second Schedule which shall be signed on behalf of the Board by a member thereof.

(4)   Whenever the Minister for Health so requests, the Minister for Finance shall remove any named person from the Board.

(5)   Every vacancy on the Board shall be filled by the appointment by the Minister for Finance of a medical practitioner nominated for that purpose, and for such period of time as is specified, by the Minister for Health.

7.   A person applying for the repayment or remission of any excise duty or tax by virtue of section 92 of the Finance Act, 1989, shall produce to the Revenue Commissioners or the licensing authority concerned, as appropriate, a certificate duly completed in accordance with and in the form prescribed in the Third Schedule.

8.   (1)   On application to the Revenue Commissioners and on production, duly completed, to them of a certificate in the form prescribed in the First or Second Schedule and of a certificate in the form prescribed in the Third Schedule, the Revenue Commissioners shall remit any additional excise duty chargeable upon adaptation of a motor vehicle for passenger carrying purposes and, subject to paragraph (2) and Regulations 10 to 12, repay-

(a)   the excise duty and value-added tax in respect of a motor vehicle used by, and

(b)   the excise duty relating to hydrocarbon oil used for combustion in the engine of the motor vehicle so used by, a severely and permanently disabled person-

(i)   as a driver, where the disablement is of such a nature that the person concerned could not drive the motor vehicle unless it is specially constructed or adapted to take account of that disablement, or

(ii)   as a passenger, where the motor vehicle has been specially constructed or adapted to take account of the passenger's disablement, and where the vehicle is so adapted, the cost of such adaptation excluding tax consists of not less than 30 per cent. of the value of the vehicle excluding tax and excise duty:

Provided that where the cost (excluding tax) of adaptation of a vehicle for use by a severely and permanently disabled person as a passenger consists of less than 30 per cent. of the value before adaptation of the vehicle excluding tax and excise duty, excise duty shall be remitted in respect of the additional excise duty chargeable upon adaptation of the vehicle only, and value-added tax shall be repaid in respect of the cost of the adaptation only.

(2)   The excise duty on hydrocarbon oil purchased by a person to whom subparagraph (i) or (ii) of paragraph (1) relates and used for combustion in the engine of a motor vehicle concerned, not being a motor vehicle to which the proviso to paragraph (1) relates shall, subject to such proof as the Revenue Commissioners consider appropriate in the circumstances, be repaid to an annual maximum at the highest rate applicable for the time being in respect of not more than 600 gallons of hydrocarbon oil.

9.   On application to the appropriate licensing authority and on production, duly completed, to them of a certificate in the form prescribed in the First or Second Schedule and of a certificate in the form prescribed in the Third Schedule the licensing authority shall, subject to Regulation 11, remit the excise duty which would, but for this provision, be payable under section 1 of the Finance (Excise Duties) (Vehicles) Act, 1952 (being the duty commonly known as road tax).

10.   Subject to Regulation 12, the amount of excise duty and value-added tax repayable by the Revenue Commissioners, other than in respect of hydrocarbon oil, to any person under these Regulations in any period of 2 years shall not exceed in total-

(a)   where the relevant vehicle is for use by a severely and permanently disabled person as a driver, £7,500, or

(b)   where the relevant vehicle is for use by a severely and permanently disabled person as a passenger, £9,000.

11.   The repayment or remission, as the case may be, of excise duty or tax in respect of a motor vehicle for use by a severely and permanently disabled person-

(a)   as a driver, shall not be made where the engine size is in excess of 2,000 cubic centimetres, or

(b)   as a passenger, shall not be made where the engine size is in excess of 4,000 cubic centimetres.

12.   (1)   The repayment or remission, as the case may be, by the Revenue Commissioners of any excise duty or tax by virtue of the provisions of these Regulations to any severely and permanently disabled person shall not be made to that person unless-

(a)   he has given to the Revenue Commissioners an undertaking that if, within 2 years from the date of purchase (in this Regulation referred to as "the original date of purchase") of the motor vehicle in question, he intends to dispose of that vehicle by sale or otherwise, he will before disposing of the vehicle notify the Revenue Commissioners of his intention, and

(i)   in case the intended disposal is to another person who would be entitled to claim repayment or remission if the original date of purchase were the date of the intended disposal, that other person has complied with subparagraph (b) in so far as it relates to him,

(ii)   in any other case, pays to the Commissioners an amount equal to the excise duty and value-added tax repaid to him by the Commissioners in respect of that vehicle by virtue of these Regulations, less an amount, to be determined by the Commissioners by reference to paragraph 19 (as amended by the Order of 1984) of the Order of 1979, to take account of the age and value of the vehicle at the date of its disposal,

and

(b)   he has complied with any and every previous undertaking to like effect given by him to the Commissioners and, in the case to which subparagraph (a)(i) relates, that other person has given a similar undertaking to the Commissioners in respect of the remainder of the 2 years left from the original date of purchase.

(2)   Nothing in these Regulations shall be construed as permitting a person, under Regulation 8(2), to claim repayment annually in respect of more than 600 gallons of hydrocarbon oil.

Regulation 4(a)

FIRST SCHEDULE
MEDICAL CERTIFICATE

Issued for the purposes of section 92 of the Finance Act, 1989, and the Disabled Drivers (Tax Concessions) Regulations, 1989.

Name of applicant :

Mr./Mrs./Miss/Ms.*..

Normal address :

....

....

....

I,..., Director of Community Care and Medical Officer of Health for the Health Board area, hereby certify that in my opinion the person named above is a severely and permanently disabled person who meets one or more of the medical criteria set out in the Regulations entitled the Disabled Drivers (Tax Concessions) Regulations, 1989.

Particulars of the appellant's disablement are as follows**:

(a)   wholly or almost without the use of both legs;

(b)   wholly without the use of one leg and almost wholly without the use of the other leg such that

the applicant is severely restricted as to movement of the lower limbs;

(c)   the applicant is a person without both hands or without both arms;

(d)   the applicant is a person without one or both legs;

(e)   the applicant has the medical condition of dwarfism and has serious difficulties of movement of the lower limbs;

Date:..................................

....

(Signature)

Director of Community Care and Medical Officer of Health, Health Board.

**Tick as appropriate and cross out particulars that do not apply

*Delete as appropriate

Regulation 4(b)

SECOND SCHEDULE
MEDICAL CERTIFICATE

Issued, on appeal, for the purposes of section 92 of the Finance Act, 1989, and the Disabled Drivers (Tax Concessions) Regulations, 1989.

Name of applicant :

Mr./Mrs./Miss/Ms.*..

Normal address :

....

....

....

The Disabled Drivers Medical Board of Appeal hereby certifies that in its opinion the person named above is a severely and permanently disabled person who meets one or more of the medical criteria set out in the Regulations entitled the Disabled Drivers (Tax Concessions) Regulations, 1989.

Particulars of the applicant's disablement are as follows**:

(a)   wholly or almost without the use of both legs;

(b)   a wholly without the use of one leg and almost wholly without the use of the other leg such that the applicant is severely restricted as to movement of the lower limbs;

(c)   the applicant is a person without both hands or without both arms;

(d)   the applicant is a person without one or both legs;

(e)   the applicant has the medical condition of dwarfism and has serious difficulties of movement of the lower limbs;

Date:....................................

....

(Signature)

For and on behalf of the Disabled Drivers Medical Board of Appeal and a member of that Board.

**Tick as appropriate and cross out particulars that do not apply

*Delete as appropriate

Regulation 7

THIRD SCHEDULE
DISABLED DRIVERS (TAX CONCESSIONS) REGULATIONS, 1989
CERTIFICATE

Issued for the purposes of applications for either or both repayments and remissions of any excise duty or tax by virtue of section 92 of the Finance Act, 1989, and the Disabled Drivers (Tax Concessions) Regulations, 1989.

PART I(To be completed by the applicant before Part II is completed).

I,...*, who normally reside a t...*, hereby declare as follows**:

[Note: To be completed where applicant is applying as a disabled driver.]
Vehicle, registration number (if available)......................................,
engine number..and chassis
number......................................is registered in my name, is intended for my personal use as driver and has been specially constructed or adapted to take account of my disablement. I am unable to drive any vehicle not specially adapted for my use. I am the holder of a valid current driving licence for the class to which the vehicle belongs.

[Note: To be completed where applicant is applying as a disabled passenger.]
Vehicle, registration number (if available)................................, engine number......................... and chassis number................................, has been specially constructed or adapted to take account of my disablement for my use as passenger but not as a driver.

Date:...................................

....

(Signature)

*Name and address of applicant.

**Cross out paragraph that does not apply.

PART II(To be completed by a member of the Garda Síochána)

I have examined vehicle, registration number (if available) ....
............., engine number .... and chassis number ....
........................., and find that it is specially constructed or adapted for use by the above as disabled driver/passenger* to take account of the disablement. The vehicle is specially adapted as follows**:

Vehicle for Disabled Driver			**Vehicle for Disabled Passenger**		
	YES	NO		YES	NO
Construction: specially constructed			Construction: Specially constructed		
Steering: power assisted (but see note) electronic joystickremote (hand) controlremote (foot) controlknob or clamp on wheel			Vehicle structure :roof raised (for person(s) seated in wheelchair (s))door widenedfloor lowered		
Gears: motorised gear stick extensionclutch pedel extension			Passenger accommodation: swivel conversion seat adjustmentspecial seatsaccommodation for stretcher(s)		
Brakes, Accelerator:pedal extension rod or cable (for hand operation)additional servo-assistance extension for left foot operation			Other accommodation aids: special head restraintspecial safety harnessspecial child safety seatspecial backrestseatbelt adaptor(s)		
Ignition, Lights, Signalling:special console			Assistance for boarding, alighting:extension rampcar hoistpower door actuation		
Driver's seat:swivel conversionraised seataccess for wheelchair (in Lieu of seat)					
Engine size: .... (not exceeding 2,000 cc)			Engine size: .... (not exceeding 4,000 cc)		
Other:(specify)***			Other: (specify)***		

[Note Optional extras, such as power steering and automatic gearbox, which are available from the manufacturer or assembler on production line models do not constitute special adaptations.]

*The person named as a disabled driver in Part I is the holder of a valid current driving licence for the class to which the vehicle belongs.

Date:...................................

Signed: ....

Rank:.................................

Garda Station (Stamp):

*Delete as appropriate.

**Tick and fill in as appropriate.

***If there is not enough room here, please indicate that another page has been used and date, sign and stamp that page the same as for above.

Given under my Official Seal, this 14th day of December, 1989.

ALBERT REYNOLDS,
Minister for Finance.

EXPLANATORY NOTE

These Regulations, which come into operation on 21st December 1989, set out the medical criteria, certification procedures, repayment limits and other matters necessary for the purposes of giving effect to section 92 of the Finance Act, 1989 which provides for tax concessions for disabled drivers.

VALUE-ADDED TAX (REFUND OF TAX)
(REVOCATION) ORDER, 1989

(SI No. 351 of 1989)

I, ALBERT REYNOLDS, Minister for Finance, in exercise of the powers conferred on me by section 20(3) of the Value-Added Tax Act, 1972 (No. 22 of 1972), hereby order as follows:

1.   (1)   This Order may be cited as the Value-Added Tax (Refund of Tax) (Revocation) Order, 1989.

    (2)   This Order shall come into operation on the 21st day of December, 1989.

2.   The Value-Added Tax (Refund of Tax) (No.10) Order, 1979 (S.I. No.275 of 1979) and the Value Added Tax (Refund of Tax) (No.13) Order, 1980 (S.I. No.263 of 1980), are hereby revoked.

GIVEN under my Official Seal,
this 19th day of December, 1989.

ALBERT REYNOLDS,
Minister for Finance.

EXPLANATORY NOTE.

This Order provides for the revocation of VAT Refund Orders No. 10 (S.I. No 275 of 1979) and 13 (S.I. No 263 of 1980). This revocation is consequent on the coming into effect on 21 December 1989 of the Disabled Drivers (Tax Concessions) Regulations 1989 (S.I. No 340 of 1989), which provide for new arrangements for refunds of VAT and excise duty to disabled drivers.

VALUE-ADDED TAX (REFUND OF TAX) (NO 23) ORDER, 1992

(SI No. 58 of 1992)

I, BERTIE AHERN, Minister for Finance, in exercise of the powers conferred on me by section20(3) of the Value-Added Tax Act, 1972 (No 22 of 1972), hereby order as follows:

1.   (1)   This Order may be cited as the Value-Added Tax (Refund of Tax) (No 23) Order, 1992.

      (2)   This Order shall be deemed to have come into operation on the 29th day of January, 1992.

2.   In this Order-

      "the Act" means the Value-Added Tax Act, 1972 (No. 22 of 1972), and every enactment which is to be construed together with that Act;

      "qualifying goods" means any new instrument or new appliance, excluding means of transport-

      (a)   in relation to which the amount on which tax is chargeable by virtue of the Act is [€25,390][1] or more,

      (b)   which has been designed and manufactured for use solely in medical research or in diagnosis, prevention, or treatment of illness,

      (c)   which has been the subject of a recommendation by the Minister for Health that, having regard to the requirements of the health services in the State, a refund of tax under this Order would be appropriate;

      "qualifying body" means any body of persons engaged in the operation of a hospital.

3.   Where a person establishes to the satisfaction of the Revenue Commissioners that-

      (a)   he has borne or paid tax which became chargeable on or after the 29th day of January, 1992, in respect of the supply to, or importation by, him of qualifying goods,

      (b)   he is a qualifying body or, if he is not such a body, the qualifying goods have been, or are to be, donated by him to a qualifying body,

      (c)   no part of the funds used, or to be used, in the purchase of the qualifying goods was, or is to be, provided, directly or indirectly, by the State, or by any board established by or under statute, or by any public or local authority, or by the qualifying body which has purchased the qualifying goods or to which they have been, or are to be, donated, or by any body of persons associated with such qualifying body in the operation of a hospital, or by any other body of persons operating a hospital, and

(d)   in respect of the supply or importation of qualifying goods, he is not entitled to repayment of the tax under any provision of the Act or under any instrument other than this Order made under statute administered by the Revenue Commissioners,

and the person completes such claim form as may be provided for the purpose by the Revenue Commissioners and certifies the particulars shown on such claim form to be correct, he shall be entitled to be repaid the full tax so borne or paid.

4.   The Value-Added Tax (Refund of Tax) (No.20) Order, 1987 (SI No.10 of 1987), is hereby revoked.

GIVEN under my Official Seal,
this 31st day of March, 1992.

BERTIE AHERN,
Minister for Finance.

EXPLANATORY NOTE.

The effect of this Order is to allow a full refund of the value-added tax paid on qualifying medical equipment purchased through voluntary donations with effect from 29 January, 1992. The Order replaces the Value-Added Tax (Refund of Tax) (No 20) Order, 1987 which provided only for partial relief on the same goods.

Amendments
1   Amended by s240 & sch5, FA01, w.e.f. 1 January 2002. Previously £20,000

VALUE-ADDED TAX (DETERMINATION OF TAX DUE BY REFERENCE TO MONEYS RECEIVED) (AMENDMENT) REGULATIONS, 1992

(SI No. 93 of 1992)

> These Regulations revoked by r13, Value Added Tax (Determination of Tax Due by Reference to Moneys Received) Regulations, 1992, (1992 S.I. No. 306) with effect from 28 October 1992.

The Revenue Commissioners, in exercise of the powers conferred on them by sections 14 of the Value-Added Tax Act, 1972 (No. 22 of 1972), hereby make the following Regulations:

1. These Regulations may be cited as the Value-Added Tax (Determination of Tax Due by reference to Moneys Received) (Amendment) Regulations, 1992.

2. Regulation 3 of the Value-Added Tax (Determination of Tax Due by reference to Moneys Received) Regulations, 1986 (SI No. 298 of 1986) is hereby amended by the substitution of the following paragraph for paragraph (10):

    "(10) Where an adjustment of liability as provided for in paragraph (6) or (7) is to be made by reason of the cesser in a taxable period of an authorisation under paragraph (3), in no case shall an aforementioned adjustment be made by reason of that cesser for any taxable period which ends on a date which is more than six years before the date of cessation of the taxable period immediately preceding that in which the aforementioned cesser took place, and in no case shall an adjustment be made for any taxable period if that adjustment would, apart from this paragraph, be made by reason only of a cesser resulting from the death of the taxable person.".

GIVEN this 16th day of April, 1992.

F. CASSELLS,
Revenue Commissioner.

EXPLANATORY NOTE.

These Regulations amend the Value-Added Tax (Determination of Tax Due by reference to Moneys Received) Regulations, 1986 (SI No.298 of 1986) which deal with the terms and conditions relating to the operation of the moneys received basis of accounting for VAT. The amendment substitutes a new paragraph for paragraph (10) of Regulation 3 of the Principal Regulations which deals with the adjustment of liability following a change in the basis of accounting. The amendment means that an adjustment is required in all cases of a change from the moneys received to the invoice basis of accounting. This adjustment will be calculated by reference either to the position at the time of authorisation for use of the moneys received basis of accounting or to the position that existed six years previous to the change of basis, whichever is the later. As at present, no adjustment will be required where the cessation of use of the moneys received basis of accounting results from the death of the taxable person.

VALUE-ADDED TAX (MONTHLY CONTROL STATEMENT) REGULATIONS, 1992

(SI No. 230 of 1992)

> This Regulation was revoked by regulation 44, Value-Added Tax Regulations, 2006 (2006 S.I. No. 548) w.e.f. 1 November 2006

The Revenue Commissioners, in exercise of the powers conferred on them by sections 17 of the Value-Added Tax Act, 1972 (No 22 of 1972), hereby make the following Regulations:

1. These Regulations may be cited as the Value-Added Tax (Monthly Control Statement) Regulations, 1992.

2. These Regulations shall come into operation on the 1st day of November, 1992.

3. In these Regulations-

    "the Act" means the Value-Added Tax Act, 1972;

    "monthly control statement" means the monthly control statement which is

    required to be issued in accordance with section 17(1B) of the Act.

4. Every monthly control statement issued by a taxable person shall set out the following particulars:

    (a) the name, address and registration number of the person by whom the goods referred to in the statement were supplied,

    (b) the name and address of the person to whom the goods referred to in the statement were supplied,

    (c) the date of issue of the statement,

    (d) the calendar month to which the statement refers,

    (e) in relation to supplies of goods for which an invoice, credit note, debit note or settlement voucher was issued in accordance with section 17 of the Act, the total amount of the consideration inclusive of tax shown on each of those documents,

    (f) in relation to supplies of goods for which an invoice, credit note, debit note or settlement voucher was not issued,

        (i) the date of each such supply,

        (ii) a description of the goods supplied,

        (iii) the consideration, exclusive of tax, for each supply,

        (iv) the rate or rates of tax and amount of tax at each rate chargeable to the person who has supplied the goods,

(g)   in relation to any adjustment of the consideration for the supplies referred to in paragraph (e) or (f) agreed between the supplier of the goods and the taxable person and for which a credit note was not issued under section 17 of the Act,

     (i)   the amount of such adjustment,

     (ii)   the date of such adjustment,

(h)   where, in respect of the supply referred to in paragraph (e) or (f), any payment has been or will be made by the person by whom the goods were supplied,

     (i)   the amount of such payment or payments,

     (ii)   the date or dates when such payment or payments were or will be made,

     (iii)   the person or persons to whom such payment or payments have been or will be made,

and

     (i)   in relation to any gifts or promotional items given in connection with the supplies referred to in paragraph (e) or (f),

     (i)   a description of such gifts or promotional items,

     (ii)   the value of such gifts or promotional items,

     (iii)   the date of provision of such gifts or promotional items.

5.   A monthly control statement required to be issued in accordance with section 17(1B) of the Act shall be issued not later than the last day of the month following the month during which goods are supplied.

6.   Every person issuing a monthly control statement shall keep a copy thereof and references in these regulations to any such statement, other than references to its issue, shall include references to a copy thereof.

GIVEN this 13th day of August, 1992.

F. CASSELLS,
Revenue Commissioner.

EXPLANATORY NOTE.

These Regulations specify the details which must be included in the monthly control statement which, in accordance with section 17(1B) of the Value-Added Tax Act, suppliers of taxable goods to other taxable persons must issue if the supplier's turnover of taxable goods exceeds £2 million per annum. The Regulations also specify the period within which the monthly control statement must be issued and provide that a copy of the statement must be retained by the supplier. The Regulations have effect from 1 November, 1992.

VALUE-ADDED TAX (ELECTRONIC DATA EXCHANGE AND STORAGE) REGULATIONS, 1992

(SI No. 269 of 1992)

> These Regulations revoked by para 5, Value-Added Tax (Electronic Invoicing And Storage) Regulations, 2002 (2002 S.I. No. 504) w.e.f. 5 November 2002.

The Revenue Commissioners, in exercise of the powers conferred on them by subsection(1A) (as amended by the Finance Act, 1992 (No.9 of 1992)) of section 17 and section 32 of the Value-Added Tax Act, 1972 (No.22 of 1972), hereby makes the following Regulations:

1. These Regulations may be cited as the Value-Added Tax (Electronic Data Exchange and Storage) Regulations, 1992.

2. (1) In these Regulations-

"the Act" means the Value-Added Tax Act, 1972 (No. 22 of 1972);

"message" means an invoice, credit note, debit note or settlement voucher, required to be issued in accordance with section 17 of the Act;

"file" means a computer record consisting of a number of messages;

"registration number", in relation to a person, means the number assigned to the person for the purposes of registration under section 9 of the Act;

"transmission file" means a file that is constructed in a definitive format for electronic transmission to a particular trading partner;

"transmission sequence number" means a number, being one of a series of numbers which is unique to particular trading partners, generated sequentially at the time of preparation of a transmission file;

"trading partners" means any two taxable persons engaged in the electronic exchange of messages;

"transaction log" means a record of transmission sequence numbers between particular trading partners.

(2) In these Regulations-

(a) a reference to a Regulation is to a Regulation of these Regulations, and

(b) a reference to a paragraph, subparagraph or clause is to a paragraph, subparagraph or clause of the provision in which the reference occurs, unless it is indicated that reference to some other provision is intended.

[2A.   Where an amount or consideration is specified for the purposes of these Regulations, then such amount or consideration shall be expressed in a denomination of the currency of the State and be identified by the use of the symbol appropriate to the denomination so expressed.]1

3.   (1)   Where, by virtue of section 17(1A) of the Act, a taxable person proposes to issue or receive messages by electronic means, he shall apply in writing to the Revenue Commissioners to be authorised to so issue and receive messages and shall at the same time furnish to the Revenue Commissioners-

   (a)   the following particulars:

      (i)   his name and address,

      (ii)   his registration number,

      (iii) the name, address and registration number of each of his trading partners, and

      (iv)   the date from which he intends, if authorised by the Revenue Commissioners, to issue or receive messages by electronic means, being a date not less than one month after the date he so applies to the Revenue Commissioners,

   and

   (b)   a declaration that the electronic data exchange system, to be used by him is capable of satisfying the requirements specified in subparagraphs (a), (b), (c), (d), (e) and (f) of Regulation 4(1).

   (2)   Where a change occurs in any of the particulars furnished in accordance with clauses (i), (ii) and (iii) of subparagraph (a) of paragraph (1) the taxable person shall furnish to the Revenue Commissioners particulars of the change within thirty days following the date of the change.

4.   (1)   Where the Revenue Commissioners consider that it is expedient in the interests of the efficient administration of the tax, they shall authorise in writing, where appropriate from a specified or ascertainable date, a taxable person who has furnished the particulars required in accordance with paragraphs (1) and (2) of Regulation 3 to issue or receive messages by electronic means, to or from another taxable person who has also been so authorised, subject to the condition that the electronic data exchange system to be used by the trading partners concerned is capable of-

   (a)   producing, retaining and storing a record of such messages in such form and containing such particulars as are required in accordance with section 17 of the Act and regulations under the Act,

(b)   reproducing on paper any file, message, transmission file or any other document required to be produced, retained or stored in accordance with regulations under the Act,

(c)   generating transmission sequence numbers,

(d)   precluding the repeated issue of any particular transmission sequence number,

(e)   precluding the omission of any particular number in the sequence of issue of transmission sequence numbers, and

(f)   maintaining records required to be retained or stored in accordance with paragraph (2) in such manner as will allow their retrieval by reference either to the date or the transmission sequence number of the transmission.

(2)   A taxable person who is authorised in accordance with paragraph (1) to issue or receive messages by electronic means shall, in addition to the documents required to be issued, retained and stored in accordance with the Act and regulations under the Act, issue, retain and store the following documents:

(a)   in the case of an authorised issuer, a record capable of being reproduced on paper, made at the time of construction of a transmission file and issued to a trading partner, containing the following particulars:

    (i)   the name, address and registration number of the issuer,

    (ii)   the name, address and registration number of the recipient,

    (iii)   the date of transmission of the transmission file,

    (iv)   the transmission sequence number, and

    (v)   for each type of message in the transmission file the following particulars:

        (I)   the total number of messages in the file,

        (II)   the total consideration, exclusive of tax, in respect of which the messages were issued by him,

        (III)   the amount of the said consideration liable to tax at each rate including the zero rate,

        (IV)   the amount of tax appropriate to the said consideration at each rate, and

        (V)   the total consideration for exempt supplies, if any, in the file;

(b)   in the case of an authorised recipient, a record, capable of being reproduced on paper, made at the time of receipt of a transmission file, the file having been converted from the issuer's transmission file format to the recipient's own file format, and containing the following particulars:

    (i)   the name, address and registration number of the issuer,

    (ii)   the name, address and registration number of the recipient,

    (iii)   the date of transmission of the transmission file,

    (iv)   the transmission sequence number, and

    (v)   for each type of message in the file the following particulars:

        (I)   the total number of messages in the file,

        (II)   the total consideration, exclusive of tax in respect of which the messages were received by him,

        (III)   the amount of the said consideration liable at each rate including the zero rate,

        (IV)   the amount of tax appropriate to the said consideration at each rate, and

        (V)   the total consideration for exempt supplies, if any, in the file;

(c)   in the case of an authorised issuer and an authorised recipient, a summary document produced at the end of each calendar month by each of them of a transmission file, containing the following particulars:

    (i)   the name, address and registration number of the issuer,

    (ii)   the name, address and registration number of the recipient,

    (iii)   the calendar month to which the document relates, and

    (iv)   in respect of that month the following particulars:

        (I)   each transmission sequence number,

        (II)   the total consideration, exclusive of tax, to which the document relates,

        (III)   the amount of the consideration liable at each rate of tax including the zero rate,

(IV)   the amount of tax appropriate to the said consideration at each rate,

(V)   the total consideration for exempt supplies, if any,

and

(v)   in the case of the authorised issuer, the sequence numbers of faulty or failed transmissions;

(d)   in the case of an authorised recipient, a document produced by him and issued to a trading partner giving details of any discrepancy between the documents specified in paragraphs (a) and (b);

(e)   in all cases, a transaction log.

5.   An authorisation issued under Regulation 4 may be withdrawn by the Revenue Commissioners where-

(a)   the condition specified in paragraph (1) of Regulation 4 ceases to be met,

(b)   the requirements of paragraph (2) of Regulation 4 are not being carried out,

(c)   the provisions of Regulation 3 have not been complied with, or

(d)   they consider that such an authorisation is no longer expedient in the interests of the efficient administration of the tax.

GIVEN this 22nd day of September, 1992.

F. J. CASSELLS.
Revenue Commissioner.

EXPLANATORY NOTE.

These Regulations specify the requirements that must be fulfilled by taxable persons who wish to issue or receive invoices, credit notes etc. by electronic means in accordance with Section17(1A) of the Act.

Amendments

1   Inserted by r2, Value Added Tax (Electronic Data Exchange and Storage) (Amendment) Regulations, 1998, w.e.f. 1 January 1999.

VALUE-ADDED TAX (INVOICES AND OTHER DOCUMENTS) REGULATIONS, 1992

(SI No. 275 of 1992)

> This Regulation was revoked by regulation 44, Value-Added Tax Regulations, 2006 (2006 S.I. No. 548) w.e.f. 1 November 2006

The Revenue Commissioners, in exercise of the powers conferred on them by sections 17 of the Value-Added Tax Act, 1972 (No 22 of 1972), hereby make the following Regulations:

1. (1) These Regulations may be cited as the Value-Added Tax (Invoices and other Documents) Regulations, 1992.

    (2) These Regulations shall come into operation on the 1st day of January, 1993.

2. In these Regulations-

    "the Act" means the Value-Added Tax Act, 1972;

    "registration number", in relation to a person, means the number assigned to the person for the purpose of registration under section 9 of the Act;

    "value-added tax registration number in another Member State" means the registration number issued to a person by the authorities of another Member State of the Community for the purposes of value-added tax referred to in Council Directive No 77/388/EEC of 17 May, 1977.

[2A. Where an amount or consideration is specified for the purposes of these Regulations, then such amount or consideration shall be expressed in a denomination of the currency of the State and be identified by the use of the symbol appropriate to the denomination so expressed.]1

3. [(a) Every invoice issued by a taxable person in accordance with section 17(1) of the Act shall set out the following particulars:

    (i)   the date of issue of the invoice,

    (ii) a sequential number, based on one or more series, which uniquely identifies the invoice,

    (iii) the full name, address and the registration number of the person who supplied the goods or services to which the invoice relates,

    (iv) the full name and address of the person to whom the goods or services have been supplied,

    (v)   in the case of a reverse charge supply, being a supply of goods or services to a person in another Member State who is liable to pay value-added tax under Council Directive No. 77/388/EEC of 17 May 1977 on such supply, the value-added tax identification number of that person in that Member State and an indication that a reverse charge applies,

(vi)   in the case of a supply of goods, other than a reverse charge supply, to a person registered for value-added tax in another Member State, the person's value-added tax identification number in that Member State and an indication that the invoice relates to an intra-Community supply of goods,

(vii)   the quantity and nature of the goods supplied or the extent and nature of the services rendered,

(viii)   the date on which the goods or services were supplied or, in the case of supplies specified in section 17(8) of the Act, the date on which the payment on account was made, insofar as that date can be determined and differs from the date of issue of the invoice,

(ix)   in respect of the goods or services supplied:

   (I)   the unit price exclusive of tax,

   (II)   any discounts or price reductions not included in the unit price, and

   (III)   the consideration exclusive of tax,

(x)   in respect of goods or services supplied, other than reverse charge supplies,

   (I)   the consideration exclusive of tax per rate of tax, and

   (II)   the rate of tax chargeable,

(xi)   the tax payable in respect of the supply of the goods or services, except in the case of a reverse charge supply or where section 10A(9), 10B(5) or 12B(5) of the Act applies, and

(xii)   in the case where a tax representative is liable to pay the value-added tax in another Member State, the full name and address and the value-added tax identification number of that representative.][2]

(b)   Every invoice issued by a flat-rate farmer in accordance with section 17(2) of the Act shall be signed or acknowledged by him and shall set out the following particulars:

   (i)   the name and address of the person who supplied the goods or services to which the invoice relates,

   (ii)   the name, address and registration number of the person to whom the goods or services were supplied,

(iii) in the case of a supply of goods to a person registered for value-added tax in another Member State the name, address and value-added tax registration number in that Member State of the person to whom the goods or services have been supplied,

(iv) the date of issue of the invoice,

(v) the date on which the goods or services were supplied,

(vi) a description of the goods or services supplied,

(vii) the quantity or volume of the goods supplied,

(viii) the consideration, exclusive of the flat-rate addition, for the supply, and

(ix) the rate and amount of the flat-rate addition.

(c) Every invoice issued by a taxable person in accordance with section 17(3) of the Act shall set out the following particulars:

(i) the name, address and registration number of the person who supplied the goods or services to which the invoice relates,

(ii) the name and address of the person to whom the goods or services were supplied,

(iii) in the case of a supply of goods to a person, other than an individual who does not engage in the supply of goods or services in the course or furtherance of business, in another Member State:

(I) the name,

(II) the address, and

(III) where the person is a person registered for value-added tax in that other Member State, the value-added tax registration number in that Member State,

of the person to whom the goods or services have been supplied,

(iv) the date of issue of the invoice,

(v) the amount, exclusive of tax, of the increase in consideration for the supply,

(vi) the rate or rates of tax and amount of tax at each rate, appropriate to the increase in consideration chargeable in respect of the supply of goods or services, and

(vii) a cross-reference to every other invoice issued by the taxable person in respect of the total consideration for the supply of the goods or services.

(d)   Every invoice issued by a flat-rate farmer in accordance with section 17(4) of the Act shall be signed or acknowledged by him and shall set out the following particulars:

    (i)   the name and address of the person who supplied the goods or services to which the invoice relates,

    (ii)   the name, address and registration number of the person to whom the goods or services were supplied,

    (iii)   in the case of a supply of goods to a person registered for value-added tax in another Member State the name, address and value-added tax registration number in that Member State of the person to whom the goods or services have been supplied,

    (iv)   the date of issue of the invoice,

    (v)   the amount, exclusive of the flat-rate addition, of the increase in consideration for the supply of goods or services,

    (vi)   the rate and amount of the flat-rate addition,

    (vii)   a cross-reference to every other invoice issued by the flat-rate farmer in respect of the total consideration for the supply of goods or services.

(e)   Every credit note issued by a taxable person in accordance with section 17(3) of the Act shall set out the following particulars:

    (i)   the name, address and registration number of the person issuing the credit note,

    (ii)   the name and address of the person to whom the credit note is issued,

    (iii)   in the case of a supply of goods to a person, other than an individual who does not engage in the supply of goods or services in the course or furtherance of business, in another Member State:

        (I)   the name,

        (II)   the address, and

        (III)   where the person is a person registered for value-added tax in that other Member State, the value-added tax registration number in that Member State,

    of the person to whom the goods or services have been supplied,

    (iv)   the date of issue of the credit note,

    (v)   the reason why the credit note is being issued and a cross-reference to the corresponding invoice,

       (vi)   the amount of the consideration, exclusive of tax, in respect of which the credit note is being issued, and

       (vii)   the relevant rate or rates of tax, current on the date upon which the credit note is issued, and the amount of tax at each rate appropriate to the consideration for which credit is being given.

(f)   Every farmer credit note issued in accordance with section 17(4) of the Act shall set out the following particulars:

       (i)   the name and address of the person issuing the credit note,

       (ii)   the name, address and registration number of the person to whom the credit note is being issued,

       (iii)   in the case of a supply of goods to a person registered for value-added tax in another Member State the name, address and value-added tax registration number in that Member State of the person to whom the goods or services have been supplied,

       (iv)   the date of issue of the credit note,

       (v)   the reason why the credit note is being issued and a cross-reference to the corresponding invoice,

       (vi)   the amount of the consideration exclusive of the flat-rate addition in respect of which the credit note is being issued, and

       (vii)   the rate and amount of the flat-rate addition.

[(g)   Every invoice issued by a customer in accordance with section 17(14) of the Act in respect of goods or services supplied to that customer shall set out the details specified in Regulation 3(a).][3]

(h)   Every settlement voucher issued in accordance with section 17(10) of the Act in respect of agricultural produce or agricultural services supplied to a registered person by a flat-rate farmer shall be signed and acknowledged by the flat-rate farmer and shall set out the following particulars:

       (i)   the name and address of the person who supplied the goods or services to which the settlement voucher relates,

       (ii)   the name, address and registration number of the person to whom the goods or services have been supplied,

       (iii)   the date of issue of the settlement voucher,

       (iv)   the date on which the goods or services were supplied,

       (v)   a description of the goods or services supplied,

       (vi)   the quantity or volume of goods supplied,

> > (vii)   the amount of the consideration, exclusive of the flat-rate addition, for the supply, and
>
> > (viii)   the rate and amount of the flat-rate addition.

> (i)   Every debit note issued in accordance with section 17(11) of the Act shall set out the following particulars:

> > (i)   the name, address and registration number of the person issuing the debit note,
>
> > (ii)   the name, address and registration number of the person to whom the debit note is being issued,
>
> > (iii)   the date of issue of the debit note,
>
> > (iv)   the reason why the debit note is being issued and a cross-reference to the corresponding invoice or settlement voucher,
>
> > (v)   the amount of the consideration, exclusive of tax, in respect of which the debit note is being issued, and
>
> > (vi)   the relevant rate or rates of tax and the amount of tax at each rate appropriate to the consideration shown on the debit note.

> (j)   Every farmer debit note issued in accordance with section 17(11A) of the Act shall be signed or acknowledged by the flat-rate farmer and shall set out the following particulars:

> > (i)   the name, address and registration number of the person issuing the debit note,
>
> > (ii)   the name and address of the person to whom the debit note is being issued,
>
> > (iii)   the date of issue of the debit note,
>
> > (iv)   the reason why the debit note is being issued and a cross-reference to the corresponding invoice or settlement voucher,
>
> > (v)   the amount of the consideration, exclusive of the flat-rate addition, in respect of which the debit note is being issued, and
>
> > (vi)   the rate and the amount of the flat-rate addition appropriate to the consideration shown on the debit note.

> [(k)   A person, other than a flat-rate farmer, issuing an invoice in accordance with section 17(3) of the Act or a credit note, settlement voucher or debit note in accordance with section 17 of the Act shall also comply with the following conditions in respect of every invoice, credit note, settlement voucher or debit note so issued:

(i)   it shall be identified by a sequential number, based on one or more series, which uniquely identifies it,

(ii)   in the case of a reverse charge supply, it shall show the value-added tax identification number of the person who is liable to pay the value-added tax, and an indication that a reverse charge applies,

(iii)   in respect of goods or services supplied, it shall show the unit price exclusive of tax and any discounts or price reductions not included in the unit price, and

(iv)   in respect of goods or services supplied, other than reverse charge supplies, it shall show the consideration exclusive of tax per rate of tax, and the rate of tax applicable.][4]

[3A.   An invoice, credit note, settlement voucher or debit note issued by a taxable person in accordance with section 17 of the Act relating to an intra-Community supply of a new means of transport (within the meaning given by section 1 of the Act) shall set out details necessary to identify the goods as a new means of transport.

3B.   Every invoice issued by a taxable person in accordance with section 10A(9) or 10B(5) of the Act shall indicate that the margin scheme or auction scheme has been applied.

3C.   The amount of tax included on an invoice or other document issued in accordance with section 17 of the Act shall be expressed in euro.

3D.   (1)   Notwithstanding these Regulations, the Revenue Commissioners may allow invoices, credit notes, settlement vouchers or debit notes to be issued under simplified arrangements in accordance with Article 22(9)(d) of Council Directive No. 77/388/EEC of 17 May 1977 but only if they include the following particulars:

(a)   the date of issue,

(b)   identification of the supplier,

(c)   identification of the type of goods or services supplied,

(d)   the tax due or the information needed to calculate it, and

(e)   such other details as the Revenue Commissioners may require and to which paragraph (2) of this Regulation relates.

(2)   The Revenue Commissioners shall publish in the Iris Oifigiúil the details to be included in the documents referred to in paragraph (1) of this Regulation and the circumstances under which they qualify for the simplified arrangements.][5]

4.   Any person issuing in accordance with section 17 of the Act an invoice, credit note, settlement voucher or debit note shall keep an exact copy thereof and references in these Regulations to any such document include references to a copy thereof.

[...]⁶

6.   Regulation 10 of the Value-Added Tax Regulations, 1979 (SI No 63 of 1979) is hereby revoked.

GIVEN this 29th day of September, 1992.

F. CASSELLS
Revenue Commissioner.

EXPLANATORY NOTE.

These Regulations specify the form of and the particulars to be contained in invoices, credit notes, and other documents which are required to be issued by taxable persons in accordance with section 17 of the Act. They revoke and replace Regulation 10 of the Value-Added Tax Regulations, 1979, (SI 63 of 1979).

Amendments

1   Reg.2A inserted by r2, Value Added Tax (Invoices and Other Documents) (Amendments) Regulations 1998, w.e.f. 1 January 1999.

2   Regulation 3(a) substituted by r3(a), Value Added Tax (Invoices and Other Documents) (Amendment) Regulations, 2003, w.e.f. 1 January 2004.

3   Regulation 3(g) substituted by r3(b) Value Added Tax (Invoices and Other Documents) (Amendment) Regulations, 2003, w.e.f. 1 January 2004.

4   Regulation 3(k) inserted by r3(c) Value Added Tax (Invoices and Other Documents) (Amendment) Regulations, 2003, w.e.f. 1 January 2004.

5   Regulations 3A – 3D inserted by r4 Value Added Tax (Invoices and Other Documents) (Amendment) Regulations, 2003, w.e.f. 1 January 2004.

6   Regulation 5 revoked by r5 Value Added Tax (Invoices and Other Documents) (Amendment) Regulations, 2003, w.e.f. 1 January 2004.

VALUE-ADDED TAX (TIME LIMITS FOR ISSUING CERTAIN DOCUMENTS) REGULATIONS, 1992.

(S.I. No. 276 of 1992)

> This Regulation was revoked by regulation 44, Value-Added Tax Regulations, 2006 (2006 S.I. No. 548) w.e.f. 1 November 2006

The Revenue Commissioners, in exercise of the powers conferred on them by sections 17 of the Value-Added Tax Act, 1972 (No.22 of 1972), hereby make the following Regulations:

1. (1)   These Regulations may be cited as the Value-Added Tax (Time Limits for Issuing Certain Documents) Regulations, 1992.

    (2)   These Regulations shall come into operation on the 1st day of January, 1993.

2. In these Regulations "the Act" means the Value-Added Tax Act, 1972.

3. An invoice, required to be issued in accordance with sections 12A or 17(1) of the Act, shall be issued within fifteen days next following the month during which the goods or services were supplied.

4. An invoice, required to be issued in accordance with sections 17(3)(a) or 17(4)(a) of the Act, shall be issued within fifteen days next following the day upon which the increased consideration is paid or the increase in consideration is agreed between the parties, whichever day is the earlier.

5. A credit note, required to be issued in accordance with sections 17(3)(b) or 17(4)(b) of the Act, shall be issued-

    (a)   in the case of a decrease because of an allowance of a discount, within fifteen days of the date of receipt of the money to which the discount relates, or

    (b)   in any other case, within fifteen days next following the day on which the decrease in consideration is agreed between the parties.

6. An invoice, required pursuant to section 17(8) of the Act, to be issued in respect of a payment for a supply of goods or services before the supply is completed shall be issued within fifteen days next following the month during which the payment was received.

7. Regulation 11 of Value-Added Tax Regulations, 1979 (S.I. No.63 of 1979) is hereby revoked.

GIVEN this 29th day of September, 1992.

F. CASSELLS,
Revenue Commissioner.

EXPLANATORY NOTE.

These Regulations set out the time limits within which invoices and credit notes must be issued for VAT purposes. They revoke and replace Regulation 11 of the Value-Added Tax Regulations, 1979 (S.I.63 of 1979).

VALUE-ADDED TAX (ESTIMATION AND ASSESSMENT OF TAX DUE) REGULATIONS, 1992

(SI No. 277 of 1992)

This Regulation was revoked by Value-Added Tax (Estimation of Tax Payable and Assessment of Tax Payable or Refundable) Regulations, 2000 (2000SI.No.295) w.e.f. 25 September 2000.

The Revenue Commissioners, in exercise of the powers conferred on them by sections 22 of the Value-Added Tax Act 1972 (No.22 of 1972) hereby make the following Regulations:

1. These Regulations may be cited as the Value-Added Tax (Estimation and Assessment of Tax Due) Regulations, 1992.

2. These Regulations shall come into operation on the 1st day of January, 1993.

3. In these Regulations "**the Act**" means the Value-Added Tax Act, 1972.

4. (1) An estimation of tax due for a taxable period for the purposes of section 22 of the Act may be made by an officer of the Revenue Commissiones, authorised by them in that behalf. The authorised officer shall sign a list containing the relevant particulars of the persons to whom the estimates relate and enter on the list the date of such signing and the list shall be retained by the Revenue Commissioners for a period of not less than ten years from the date of such signing.

    (2) The relevant particulars are-

    (a) the name, address and registration number of each person in respect of whom an estimate or two or more estimates is or are made,

    (b) the taxable period to which each estimate relates, and

    (c) the amount of tax estimated to be payable in respect of each taxable period referred to in subparagraph (b) of this paragraph.

5. (1) An assessment of tax due or refundable for a taxable period or other period consisting of two or more taxable periods for the purposes of section 23 of the Act may be made by an inspector of taxes or such other officer as the Revenue Commissioners may authorise in that behalf. The inspector of taxes or other authorised officer shall sign a list containing the relevant particulars of the persons to whom the assessments relate and enter on the list the date of such signing and the list shall be retained by the Revenue Commissioners for a period of not less than ten years from that date of such signing.

(2)   The relevant particulars are-

(a)   the name, address and registration number of each person in respect of whom an assessment or two or more assessments is or are made,

(b)   the period consisting of one taxable period or two or more consecutive taxable periods to which each assessment relates,

(c)   the total amount of tax which it is assessed should have been paid or the total amount of tax (including a nil amount) which in accordance with section 20(1) of the Act should have been refunded, as the case may be, in respect of the taxable period or periods comprised in each period referred to in subparagraph (b) of this paragraph,

(d)   the total amount of tax (including a nil amount) paid by the person or refunded to the person, as the case may be, in respect of the taxable period or periods concerned, and

(e)   the net amount due in respect of the taxable period or periods comprised in each period referred to in subparagraph (b) of this paragraph.

6.   Regulation 14 of the Value-Added Tax Regulations, 1979 (SI No.63 of 1979) is hereby revoked.

GIVEN this 29th day of September, 1992.

F. CASSELLS,
Revenue Commissioner.

EXPLANATORY NOTE.

These Regulations set out the manner in which estimates and assessments of tax due or refundable may be made by an officer of the Revenue Commissioners and the particulars of such estimates and assessments which must be retained by the Revenue Commissioners. They revoke and replace Regulation 14 of the Value-Added Tax Regulations 1979 (SI No 63 of 1979).

VALUE-ADDED TAX (DETERMINATION IN REGARD TO TAX) REGULATIONS, 1992

(SI No. 278 of 1992)

This Regulation was revoked by regulation 44, Value-Added Tax
Regulations, 2006 (2006 S.I. No. 548) w.e.f. 1 November 2006

The Revenue Commissioners, in exercise of the powers conferred on them by
sections 11 of the Value-Added Tax Act, 1972 (No.22 of 1972), hereby make the
following Regulations:

1. These Regulations may be cited as the Value-Added Tax (Determination
    in Regard to Tax) Regulations, 1992.

2. These Regulations shall come into operation on the 1st day of January,
    1993.

3. In these Regulations-

    "the Act" means the Value-Added Tax Act, 1972;

    "a determination" means a determination made for the purposes of
    section 11(1B) of the Act.

4. A determination shall be in writing, shall contain the particulars of the
    determination, shall be signed by the officer making the determination
    and shall bear the date upon which it is so signed.

5. Determinations concerning two or more matters may be included in the
    same document.

6. Regulation 23 of the Value-Added Tax Regulations, 1979 (SI No. 63 of
    1979) is hereby revoked.

GIVEN this 29th day of September, 1992.

F. CASSELLS.
Revenue Commissioner.

EXPLANATORY NOTE.

These Regulations set out the form and content of a determination made by
the Revenue Commissioners for the purposes of Section 11(1B) of the Act.
They revoke and replace Regulation 23 of the Value-Added Tax Regulations,
1979 (S.I. 63 of 1979).

VALUE-ADDED TAX (DETERMINATION OF TAX DUE BY REFERENCE TO MONEYS RECEIVED) REGULATIONS, 1992

(SI No. 306 of 1992)

> This Regulation was revoked by regulation 44, Value-Added Tax Regulations, 2006 (2006 S.I. No. 548) w.e.f. 1 November 2006

The Revenue Commissioners, in exercise of the powers conferred on them by sections 14 of the Value-Added Tax Act, 1972 (No.22 of 1972) hereby make the following Regulations:

1. These Regulations may be cited as the Value-Added Tax (Determination of Tax Due by Reference to Moneys Received) Regulations, 1992.

2. (1) In these Regulations-

    "the Act" means the Value-Added Tax Act, 1972;

    "moneys received basis of accounting" means the method of determining, in accordance with section 14(1) of the Act, the amount of tax which becomes due by a taxable person;

    "turnover from taxable supplies", in relation to any period, means the total of the amounts on which tax is chargeable for that period at any of the rates specified in section 11(1) of the Act.

    (2) In these Regulations-

    (a) a reference to a Regulation is to a Regulation of these Regulations, and

    (b) a reference to a paragraph or subparagraph is to a paragraph or subparagraph of the provision in which it occurs, unless it is indicated that reference to some other provision is intended.

3. For the purposes of [section 14(1)(a)]¹ of the Act and for the purposes of these Regulations supplies to [persons who are not registered persons]² shall be deemed to include any supplies to a taxable person where the said taxable person is not entitled to claim, under section 12 of the Act, a full deduction of the tax chargeable in relation to the said supply.

[4. (1) An application by a taxable person (hereafter referred to in this Regulation as the 'applicant') for authorisation to use the moneys received basis of accounting shall be made in writing to the Revenue Commissioners and shall include-

    (a) the applicant's name and address;

    (b) the number assigned, if any, to the applicant for the purposes of registration under section 9 of the Act (the VAT registration number);

    (c) the nature of the business activities carried on by the applicant.

(2)   An applicant who claims eligibility under section 14(1)(a) of the Act shall include in any application made in accordance with this Regulation particulars of-

    (a)   the percentage of the applicant's turnover from taxable supplies, if any, which related to supplies to persons who are not registered persons-

        (i)   in the period of 12 months ended on the last day of the taxable period prior to the application, or

        (ii)   in the period from the commencement of his business activities to the last day of the taxable period referred to in clause (i) of this subparagraph,

    whichever is the shorter; and,

    (b)   the applicant's estimate of the percentage of the said applicant's turnover from taxable supplies which will relate to supplies to persons who are not registered persons in the period of 12 months commencing with the beginning of the taxable period during which the application is made.

(3)   An applicant who claims eligibility under section 14(1)(b) of the Act shall include in any application made in accordance with this Regulation particulars of-

    (a)   the amount of the applicant's turnover from taxable supplies in the period of 12 months ended on the last day of the taxable period prior to the application; and

    (b)   the applicant's estimate of the said applicant's turnover from taxable supplies in the period of 12 months commencing with the beginning of the taxable period during which the application is made.][3]

5.   (1)   The Revenue Commissioners shall, if they consider that a person satisfies the requirements of section 14(1) of the Act, authorise the person, by notice in writing, to use the moneys received basis of accounting.

    (2)   An authorisation given under paragraph (1) shall have effect from the commencement of the taxable period during which it is given or from such other date as may be specified in the authorisation.

6.   An authorisation to use the moneys received basis of accounting given by the Revenue Commissioners before the coming into force of these Regulations shall be deemed to have been issued in accordance with Regulation 5.

7.   (1)   An authorisation under Regulation 5 shall not apply to tax chargeable on any supply where the person to whom or to whose order the supply is made is a connected person.

(2)   For the purposes of this Regulation any question of whether a person is connected with another person shall be determined in accordance with the following provisions:

(a)   a person is connected with an individual if that person is the individual's husband or wife, or is a relative, or the husband or wife of a relative, of the individual or of the individual's husband or wife;

(b)   a person is connected with any person with whom he is in partnership, and with the husband or wife or a relative of any individual with whom he is in partnership;

(c)   subject to subparagraphs (d) and (e), a person is connected with another person if he has control over that other person, or if the other person has control over the first-mentioned person, or if both persons are controlled by another person or persons;

(d)   a body corporate is connected with another person if that person, or persons connected with him, have control of it, or the person and persons connected with him together have control of it;

(e)   a body corporate is connected with another body corporate-

(i)   if a person has control of one and persons connected with him or he and persons connected with him have control of the other, or

(ii)   if a group of two or more persons has control of each body corporate and the groups either consist of the same persons or could be regarded as consisting of the same persons by treating (in one or more cases) a member of either group as replaced by a person with whom he is connected;

(f)   in this paragraph "relative" means brother, sister, ancestor or lineal descendant.

(3)   In this Regulation "control", in relation to a body corporate or in relation to a partnership, has the meaning assigned to it by section 8(3B) of the Act.

8.   An authorisation under Regulation 5 shall not affect the amount on which tax is chargeable in any of the circumstances referred to in subsections (2) to (9) of section 10 of the Act or tax chargeable on supplies referred to in Regulation 7.

9.   [(1)   A taxable person authorised in accordance with Regulation 5 shall notify the Revenue Commissioners in writing whenever, for any period of four consecutive calendar months during the validity of such authorisation, the following occurs:

(a)   the percentage of the taxable person's turnover from taxable supplies to persons who are not registered persons is less than 90 per cent; and

(b)   the taxable person's turnover from taxable supplies is such that in the twelve months immediately following such four months period it is likely to exceed £250,000,

and notification in accordance with this Regulation shall be made within 30 days of the end of such four month period.]⁴

(2)   Where a taxable person fails to notify the Revenue Commissioners in accordance with paragraph (1), the authorisation under Regulation 5 shall be deemed to be cancelled in accordance with Regulation 10. Such cancellation shall have effect for the purposes of section 14 of the Act from the commencement of the taxable period during which the taxable person should have notified the Revenue Commissioners in accordance with paragraph (1).

10.   (1)   The Revenue Commissioners shall cancel an authorisation under Regulation 5:

(a)   if the person so authorised requests the cancellation by notice in writing given to the Revenue Commissioners, or

(b)   they consider that the person no longer satisfies the requirements of sction 14(1) of the Act.

(2)   An authorisation under Regulation 5 shall be cancelled by notice in writing given by the Revenue Commissioners to the person who was the subject of the authorisation. Without prejudice to Regulation 9, such cancellation shall have effect for the purposes of section 14 of the Act from the commencement of the taxable period during which notice is given or from the commencement of such later taxable period as may be specified in the notice.

11.   (1)   (a)   Where a person, who for any period is authorised under Regulation 5 and such authorisation was issued prior to 28 May, 1992, ceases to be so authorised or ceases to be a taxable person, the tax payable by him for the taxable period during which such cessation occurs shall be adjusted in accordance with subparagraphs (b) and (c).

(b)   An amount shall be established and apportioned between each rate of tax specified in section 11(1) of the Act in accordance with the following formula-

$$\frac{(B - A) \times C}{D}$$

where-

A is the total amount due to the person at the beginning of the authorised period for goods and services supplied by him,

B is the total amount due to the person at the end of the authorised period for goods and services supplied by him,

C is the chargeable amount in respect of taxable supplies at each such rate of tax in the 12 months prior to the date of cessation or in the authorised period, whichever is the shorter, and

D is the chargeable amount in respect of total taxable supplies in the 12 months prior to the date of cessation or in the authorised period, whichever is the shorter:

Provided that-

(i) no adjustment of liability shall be made where A is greater than B, and

(ii) the apportionment between the various rates of tax may be made in accordance with any other basis which may be agreed between the taxable person and the Revenue Commissioners.

(c)   The amount so apportioned at each rate shall be a tax-inclusive amount and the tax therein shall be payable during the taxable period in which the cessation occurs.

(2)   (a)   Where a person, who for any period is authorised under Regulation 5 and such authorisation was issued on or after 28 May, 1992, ceases to be so authorised or ceases to be a taxable person, the tax payable by him for the taxable period during which the cessation occurs shall be adjusted in accordance with subparagraphs (b) and (c).

(b)   The total amount due to the person at the end of the authorised period for goods and services supplied by him shall be apportioned between each rate of tax specified in section 11(1) of the Act in accordance with the following formula-

$$B \times \frac{C}{D}$$

where B, C and D have the same meaning as in subparagraph (b) of paragraph (1):

Provided that the apportionment between the various rates of tax may be made in accordance with any other basis which may be agreed between the taxable person and the Revenue Commissioners.

(c)   The amount so apportioned at each rate shall be a tax-inclusive amount and the tax therein shall be payable during the taxable period in which the cessation occurs.

(3)   No adjustment of liability as provided for in this Regulation shall be made if the cessation referred to in subparagraph 11(1)(a) or 11(2)(a) was occasioned by the death of the taxable person.

(4)   For the purposes of this Regulation-

(a)   "the authorised period" means the period during which the person was authorised to apply the moneys received basis of accounting:

Provided that where the person was authorised to apply the moneys received basis of accounting for more than six years the authorised period shall be deemed to be for a period of six years ending on the date on which the cancellation of the authorisation has effect.

    (b)   "the tax therein" shall be established at the rates specified in section 11(1) of the Act-

        (i)   applicable on the date the authorised period ends or,

        (ii)   applicable at the time the relevant goods and services were supplied where such details can be established to the satisfaction of the Revenue Commissioners.

12.   For the purposes of these Regulations and subject to the direction and control of the Revenue Commissioners, any power, function or duty conferred or imposed on the Revenue Commissioners may be exercised or performed on their behalf by an officer of the Revenue Commissioners.

13.   The Value-Added Tax (Determination of Tax Due by reference to Moneys Received) Regulations, 1986 (SI No.298 of 1986) and the Value-Added Tax (Determination of tax Due by reference to Moneys Received) (Amendment) Regulations, 1992 (SI No.93 of 1992) are hereby revoked.

GIVEN this 28th day of October, 1992.

F. CASSELLS,
Revenue Commissioner.

EXPLANATORY NOTE.

These Regulations set out the terms and conditions relating to the operation of the moneys received basis of accounting formerly contained in SI 298 of 1986. The new Regulations take account of the amendment to section 14 of the Principal Act contained in the Finance Act 1992.

Amendments

1 Substituted by r3, Value Added Tax (Determination of Tax Due by Reference to Moneys received) Regulations, 1994.

2 Substituted by r3, Value Added Tax (Determination of Tax Due by Reference to Moneys received) Regulations, 1994.

3 Substituted by r4, Value Added Tax (Determination of Tax Due by Reference to Moneys received) Regulations, 1994.

4 Substituted by r5, Value Added Tax (Determination of Tax Due by Reference to Moneys received) Regulations, 1994.

VALUE-ADDED TAX (PAYMENT OF TAX ON INTRA-COMMUNITY ACQUISITIONS OF MEANS OF TRANSPORT) REGULATIONS, 1992

(SI No. 412 of 1992)

> These Regulations revoked by r5, Value Added tax (Payment of Tax on intra-Community Acquisition of Certain New Means of Transport) Regulations, 1993, (1993 S.I. No. 248) w.e.f. 1 September 1993.

The Revenue Commissioners, in exercise of the powers conferred on them by sections 19(4) of the Value-Added Tax Act, 1972 (No. 22 of 1972), hereby make the following Regulations:

1. These Regulations may be cited as the Value-Added Tax (Payment of Tax on Intra-Community Acquisitions of Means of Transport) Regulations, 1992.

2. These Regulations shall come into operation on the 1st day of January, 1993.

3. (1)   In these Regulations-

    "the Act" means the Value-Added Tax Act, 1972;

    "new aircraft" means a new means of transport other than a motorised land vehicle or a vessel;

    "new motorised land vehicle" means a new means of transport other than a vessel or an aircraft;

    "new vessel" means a new means of transport other than a motorised land vehicle or an aircraft;

    "registration of the vehicle" means the registration of the vehicle in accordance with section 131 of the Finance Act, 1992;

    "vehicle registration office" means an office established by the Revenue Commissioners at which declarations under section 131 of the Finance Act, 1992 may be made for the purpose of registration of vehicles;

    "vehicle registration tax" means the duty of excise referred to in section 132 of the Finance Act, 1992;

    (2)   In these Regulations-

    (a)   a reference to a Regulation is to a Regulation of these Regulations, and

    (b)   a reference to a paragraph is to a paragraph of the provision in which the reference occurs

    unless it is indicated that reference to some other provision is intended.

4. Where a person makes an intra-Community acquisition of a new motorised land vehicle, in respect of which he is not entitled to a deduction of tax under section 12 of the Act, the person shall-

    (a)   complete such form as may be provided by the Revenue Commissioners for the purpose of this Regulation,

    (b)   provide such further documentation in support of the details provided on the form as the Revenue Commissioners may request,

    (c)   certify that the particulars and documentation provided are true and accurate,

    (d)   at the time of registration of the vehicle, present the completed form and supporting documentation referred to in paragraphs (a) and (b) at the vehicle registration office and pay the tax due at that office, and

    (e)   if requested to do so, make the vehicle available for inspection by an officer of the Revenue Commissioners.

5. Where a person makes an intra-Community acquisition of a new aircraft or a new vessel, in respect of which he is not entitled to a deduction of tax under section 12 of the Act, the person shall-

    (a)   complete such form as may be provided by the Revenue Commissioners for the purpose of this Regulation,

    (b)   provide such further documentation in support of the details provided on the form as the Revenue Commissioners may request,

    (c)   certify that the particulars and documentation provided are true and accurate,

    (d)   not later than three days after the due date furnish, to the Collector of Customs and Excise for the area in which he is resident, the completed form and supporting documentation referred to in paragraphs (a) and (b) and at the same time pay to that Collector the amount of tax due, at that office, and

    (e)   if requested to do so, make the means of transport available for inspection in the State by an officer of the Revenue Commissioners.

6. Where a taxable person makes an intra-Community acquisition of a means of transport other than in the circumstances set out in Regulations 4 and 5, the tax shall be payable in accordance with the provisions of section 19(3) of the Act.

GIVEN this 18th day of December, 1992.

F. CASSELLS,
Revenue Commissioner.

EXPLANATORY NOTE.

These Regulations set out the procedures to be followed in relation to the payment of value-added tax on the intra-Community acquisition of new means of transport by private individuals and other persons not entitled to deduct the tax chargeable on the goods.

EUROPEAN COMMUNITIES (VALUE-ADDED TAX) REGULATIONS, 1992

(SI No. 413 of 1992)

I, BERTIE AHERN, Minister for Finance, in exercise of the powers conferred on me by section 3 of the European Communities Act, 1972 (No. 27 of 1972), and for the purpose of giving effect to Council Directive No 77/388/EEC of 17 May 1977 (a) (as last amended by Council Directive No 92/111/EEC of 14 December, 1992 amending Directive 77/388/EEC and introducing simplification measures with regard to value-added tax) hereby make the following Regulations:

1. (1)   These Regulations may be cited as the European Communities (Value-Added Tax) Regulations, 1992.

    (2)   These Regulations shall be construed together with the Value-Added Tax Acts, 1972 to 1992.

2. These Regulations shall come into operation on the 1st day of January, 1993.

3. In these Regulations-

"the Principal Act" means the Value-added Tax Act, 1972;

"the Act of 1978" means the Value Added Tax (Amendment) Act, 1978;

"the Act of 1992" means the Finance Act, 1992.

4. Section 1 of the Principal Act is hereby amended in subsection (1)-

    (a)   by the substitution of the following definition for the

definition of "Community":

"'Community', except where the context otherwise requires, has the same meaning as it has in Article 3 of Council Directive No 77/3881 EEC of 17 May, 1977 (as last amended by council Directive No 92/111/EEC of 14 December 1992), and cognate references shall be construed accordingly,",

and

    (b)   by the insertion after the definition of "establishment" of the following definition:

"'excisable products' means the products referred to in section 104 of the Finance Act, 1992;".

5. Section 3 of the Principal Act is hereby amended-

    (a)   in paragraph (g) (inserted by the Act of 1992) of subsection (1):

        (i)   by the insertion in subparagraph (i) after "paragraph (b)" of ", (cc)", and

        (ii)   by the insertion of the following subparagraph after subparagraph (iii):

"(iiia) the transfer of goods for the purpose of having a service carried out on them,",

(b)   in subsection (6) (inserted by the Act of 1992):

(i)   by the addition of the following proviso to paragraph (a):

"Provided that where the goods are dispatched or transported from a place outside the Community, the place of supply by the person who imports the goods and the place of any subsequent supplies shall be deemed to be where the goods are imported,",

(ii)   by the insertion of the following paragraph after paragraph (c):

"(cc)   in the case of goods supplied on board vessels, aircraft or trains during transport, the places of departure and destination of which are within the community, the place where the transport began,",

and

(iii)   in paragraph (d):

(I)   by the deletion in subparagraph (ii) of "a taxable person in", and

(II)   by the substitution of the following proviso for the proviso to the paragraph:

"Provided that this paragraph shall not apply to the supply of goods, other than goods subject to a duty of excise, where the total consideration for such supplies does not exceed or is not likely to exceed-

(A)   in the case of goods to which subparagraph (i) relates, £27,000 in a calendar year, unless the supplier, in accordance with regulations elects that it shall apply, and

(B)   in the case of goods to which subparagraph (ii) relates, the amount specified in the Member State in question in accordance with Article 28b. B(2) (inserted by Council Directive No 91/680/EEC of 16 December 1991) of Council Directive No 77/388/EEC of 17 May 1977 unless the supplier elects that it shall apply and registers and accounts for value-added tax in that Member State in respect of such supplies.",

and

(c)   by the addition of the following subsection after subsection (7) (inserted by the Finance Act, 1983):

"(8)   Where a taxable person who is not established in the State makes an intra-Community acquisition of goods in the State and makes a subsequent supply of those goods to a taxable person in the State, the person to whom the supply is made shall be deemed for the purposes of this Act to have made that supply and the intra-Community acquisition shall be disregarded:

Provided that this provision shall only apply where-

(a)   the taxable person who is not established in the State has not exercised his option to register in accordance with section 9 by virtue of section 8(3D), and

(b)   the person to whom the supply is made is registered in accordance with section 9.".

6.   Section 3A (inserted by the Act of 1992) of the Principal Act is hereby amended-

(a)   in paragraph (a) of subsection (1)-

(i)   by the insertion after "in a Member State" of "or by a flat-rate farmer in a Member State," and

(ii)   by the insertion after "who is not entitled to elect to be a taxable person" of ", unless the said individual carries on an exempted activity",

(b)   in paragraph (b) of subsection (2) by the insertion after "that registration number" of ", unless the person acquiring the goods can establish that that acquisition has been subject to value-added tax referred to in Council Directive No 77/388/EEC of 17 May 1977 in accordance with paragraph (a).",

(c)   in subsection (3) by the insertion of the following paragraphs after paragraph (a):

"(aa)   an activity in another Member State shall be deemed to be an exempted activity where the same activity, if carried out in the State, would be an exempted activity, and

(ab)   a person shall be deemed to be a flat-rate farmer in another Member State where, under similar circumstances, the person would be a flat-rate farmer in the State in accordance with section 12A, and",

and

(d)   by the addition of the following subsection after subsection (4):

"(5)   Paragraph (b) of subsection (2) shall not apply where-

(i)   a person quotes the registration number assigned to him in accordance with section 9 for the purpose of making an intra-Community acquisition and the goods are dispatched or transported from the territory of a Member State directly to the territory of another Member State, neither of which are the State,

(ii)   the person makes a subsequent supply of the goods to a person registered for value-added tax in the Member State where the dispatch or transportation ends,

(iii)   the person issues an invoice in relation to that supply in such form and containing such particulars as would be required in accordance with section 17(1) if he made the supply of the goods in the State to a person registered for value-added tax in another Member State, and containing an explicit reference to the EC simplified triangulation arrangements and indicating that the person in receipt of that supply is liable to account for the value-added tax due in that Member State, and

(iv)   in accordance with regulations, the person includes a reference to the supply in the statement referred to in section 19A as if it were an intra-Community supply for the purposes of that section.".

7.   Section 8 of the Principal Act is hereby amended-

(a)   in subsection (1A) by the insertion after "goods" of "in the State",

(b)   by the substitution of the following subsection for subsection (2B) (inserted by the Act of 1992):

"(2B) (a)   Where a person is a taxable person only because of an intra-Community acquisition of a new means of transport, then the person shall not, unless he so elects, be a taxable person for any purposes of this Act with the exception of subsection (4) of section 19.

      (b)   Where

(i)   a person is a taxable person only because of an intra-Community acquisition of excisable products, and

(ii)   by virtue of this acquisition, and in accordance with Chapter II of Part II of the Finance Act, 1992, and any other enactment which is to be construed together with that Chapter, the duty of excise on those products is payable in the State, the person shall not, unless he so elects, be a taxable person for any purposes of the Act with the exception of subsection (5) of section 19.",

(c)   by the insertion of the following subsection after subsection (3C) (inserted by the Act of 1992):

"(3D) (a)   The provisions of paragraphs (b), (c) and (e) of subsection (3) shall not apply to a person who is not established in the State.

(b)   A person who is not established in the State shall, unless he opts to register in accordance with section 9, be deemed not to have made an intra-Community acquisition or a supply of those goods in the State where the only supplies by him in the State are in the circumstances set out in section 3 (8).",

and

(d)   in subsection (8) (inserted by the Finance Act, 1991) by the insertion of the following paragraphs after paragraph I of the proviso to paragraph (a):

"(IA)   the requirement to issue an invoice or other document, in accordance with section 17, in respect of supplies to persons other than supplies between persons who are jointly and severally liable to comply with the provisions of this Act in accordance with subparagraph (ii), or

(IB)   the requirement to furnish a statement in accordance with section 19A, or".

8.   Section 10 (inserted by the Act of 1978) of the Principal Act is hereby amended by the insertion of the following subsection after subsection (9):

"(9A) In relation to the tax chargeable by virtue of section 2(1)(a) or 2(IA), where an amount is expressed in a currency other than the currency of the State the exchange rate to be used shall be-

(a)   unless paragraph (b) applies, the latest selling rate recorded by the Central Bank of Ireland for the currency in question at the time the tax becomes due,

(b)   where there is an agreement with the Revenue Commissioners for a method to be used in determining

the exchange rate, the exchange rate obtained using the said method:

Provided that where paragraph (b) applies the method agreed in accordance with that paragraph shall be applied for all transactions where an amount is expressed in a currency other than that of the State until the agreement to use such method is withdrawn by the Revenue Commissioners.".

9.   Section II of the Principal Act is hereby amended in subsection (1) (inserted by the Act of 1992) by the insertion in paragraph (b) after "paragraph (i)" of "or (ia)".

10.   Section 12 of the Principal Act is hereby amended in paragraph (b) of subsection (1) (inserted by the Finance Act, 1987)-

(a)   by the insertion of the following subparagraph after subparagraph (i):

"(ia)   supplies of goods which, by virtue of section 3(6)(d), are deemed to have taken place in the territory of another Member State:

Provided that the supplier is registered for value-added tax in that other Member State,",

and

(b)   by the insertion in subparagraph (iii) after "goods" of "(other than supplies of goods referred to in section 3(6)(d))".

11.   The Principal Act is hereby amended by the insertion of the following section after section 15:

"15A. (1)   Where-

(a)   goods from another Member State were imported into the State on or before the 31st day of December, 1992, and

(b)   the tax referred to in section 2(1)(b) was not chargeable because the goods were, at the time of such importation, placed under one of the arrangements referred to in subparagraph (b) or (c) of paragraph 1 of Article 14, or subparagraph A of paragraph 1 of Article 16, of Council Directive No 77/388/EEC of 17 May 1977, and

(c)   the goods are still subject to such an arrangement on the 1st day of January, 1993, then, the provisions in force at the time the goods were placed under the arrangement shall continue to apply in relation to those goods until such time as, in accordance with those provisions, the goods cease to be covered by those arrangements.

(2)   (a)   Notwithstanding the definition of 'importation of goods' in section 1, an importation within the meaning of that definition shall be deemed to occur in the following cases:

       (i)   where goods have been placed under an internal Community transit operation in another Member State before the 1st day of January, 1993, and the operation terminates in the State on or after that date;

      (ii)   where goods referred to in subsection (1) cease to be covered by the arrangements referred to in that subsection;

     (iii)   where goods are returned to the State after the 1st day of January, 1993, being goods which were exported from the State before that date and imported into another Member State in accordance with any of the arrangements referred to in subsection (1) (b).

     (b)   In this subsection 'internal Community transit operation' means the dispatch or transport of goods under cover of the internal Community transit arrangement referred to in paragraph 3 of Article 1 of Council Regulation (EEC) No.222/77 of 13 December 1976, or under the cover of a T2L or equivalent document provided for in that Regulation and includes the sending of goods by post.

(3)   The tax referred to in section 2(1)(b) shall not be chargeable in the cases referred to in subsection (2) where-

     (a)   the goods are dispatched or transported outside the Community,

     (b)   the goods are other than a means of transport and are being returned to the State and to the person who exported them from the State, or

     (c)   the goods are a means of transport which was acquired or imported before the 1st day of January, 1993, and in respect of which value-added tax referred to in Council Directive No 77/388/EEC of 17 May 1977 has been paid in a Member State and that value-added tax has not subsequently been refunded because of exportation from that Member State of the means of transport:

Provided that this paragraph shall be deemed to be complied with where it is shown to the satisfaction of the Revenue Commissioners that the first use of the means of transport was prior to the 1st day of January, 1985, or that the tax due does not exceed £100.

(4)   In this section, references to subparagraph (b) or (c) of paragraph 1 of Article 14, and to subparagraph A of paragraph 1 of Article 16, of Council Directive No 77/388/EEC of 17 May 1977 shall be deemed to be references to those provisions of the Directive immediately prior to their amendment by Council Directive 91/680/EEC of 16 December 1991.".

12.   Section 17 of the Principal Act is hereby amended in subsection (1) by the deletion after "to another taxable person or" of "goods".

13.   Section 19 of the Principal Act is hereby amended by the insertion of the following subsection after subsection (4) (inserted by the Act of 1992):

"(5)   Notwithstanding the provisions of subsection (3), where the provisions of section 8 (2B) (b) apply, the tax shall be payable at the time of payment of the duty of excise on the goods as if it were that duty of excise."

14.   The Second Schedule (inserted by the Finance Act, 1976) to the Principal Act is hereby amended by the insertion of the following subparagraph in paragraph (i) (inserted by the Act of 1992) after subparagraph (c):

"(cc)   being excisable products dispatched or transported from the State to a person in another Member State when the movement of the goods is subject to the provisions of Chapter II of Part II of the Finance Act, 1992, and any other enactment which is to be construed together with that Chapter, which implement the arrangements specified in paragraph 4 and 5 of Article 7, or Article 16, of Council Directive No 92/12/EEC of 25 February 1992(b),".

GIVEN under my Official Seal,
this 22nd day of December, 1992.

BERTIE AHERN,
Minister for Finance.

EXPLANATORY NOTE.

These Regulations, which have effect from 1 January 1993, implement EC Council Directive 92/111/EEC relating to the introduction of the transitional arrangements for the levying and collection of VAT in the Single Market. The Regulations supplement the detailed measures already introduced in the Finance Act, 1992 (No.9 of 1992).

VALUE-ADDED TAX (EXPORTED GOODS) REGULATIONS, 1992

(SI No. 438 of 1992)

These Regulations revoked by Value Added Tax (Retail Export Scheme)
Regulations, 1998 (1998 S.I. No. 34) w.e.f. 1 March 1998.

The Revenue Commissioners, in exercise of the powers conferred on them by sections 13(1) of the Value-Added Tax Act, 1972 (No. 22 of 1972) and with the consent of the Minister for Finance, hereby make the following Regulations:

1. (1) These Regulations may be cited as the Value-Added Tax (Exported Goods) Regulations, 1992.

    (2) These Regulations shall come into operation on the 1st day of January, 1993.

2. (1) In these Regulations-

    "goods" means any article, and includes a group of articles normally supplied as a set;

    "qualifying goods" means goods other than mechanically propelled road vehicles or goods for the equipping, fuelling or provisioning of any means of transport for private use;

    "qualifying person" means any person who, at the time of the supply to him of qualifying goods-

    (a) was not normally resident in the Community or, if he was normally resident in the Community at that time, intended at the time to depart from the Community for a period of at least twelve consecutive months, and

    (b) was not a member of the crew of a ship, aircraft or other conveyance engaged in the transport of passengers or goods into or out of the Community.

    (2) In these Regulations-

    (a) a reference to a Regulation is to a Regulation of these Regulations, and

    (b) a reference to a paragraph or subparagraph is to a paragraph or subparagraph of the provision in which the reference occurs,

    unless it is indicated that reference to some other provision is intended.

3. The tax, if any, chargeable on the supply of qualifying goods-

    (1) to a qualifying person who intended at the time of the supply to export the said goods in his personal baggage, or

    (2) which are delivered, by or on behalf of a qualifying person, on board a ship or aircraft (other than a private ship or aircraft)

proceeding to a place outside the Community for export in that ship or aircraft,

shall be remitted, provided that the said goods are exported within two months of the date of their supply and subject to the conditions set out in Regulation 4.

4. (1)   The supplier of the qualifying goods shall-

   (a)   satisfy himself that the person to whom the goods are being supplied is a qualifying person,

   (b)   issue to the qualifying person at the time of the supply of the qualifying goods an invoice in respect of that supply setting out the following particulars:

      (i)   the name, address and tax registration number of the supplier,

      (ii)   the name and address of the qualifying person,

      (iii)   the date upon which the invoice is issued,

      (iv)   a description of and the quantity of the qualifying goods,

      (v)   the consideration for the supply,

      (vi)   an indication of the basis on which the supplier satisfied himself in accordance with subparagraph (1)(a), including details of any relevant document inspected, and

      (vii)   the signature or acknowledgement of the qualifying person,

   and

   (c)   retain in his records a copy of the said invoice together with documentary proof of export of the goods in accordance with paragraphs (2) or (3).

   (2)   Where the provisions of paragraph (1) of Regulation 3 apply, the qualifying person shall return to the supplier of the qualifying goods the invoice issued in accordance with subparagraph (1)(b) on which the export of the goods is duly certified by-

   (a)   a customs officer in the State, or

   (b)   where the goods have been exported via another Member State of the Community, a customs officer in that Member State, or

   (c)   an equivalent official in the country to which the said goods have been exported,

   or in such other manner as the Revenue Commissioners may deem acceptable for that purpose.

(3)   Where the provisions of paragraph (2) of Regulation 3 apply, the supplier shall obtain documentary evidence, certified by a customs officer in the State, that the qualifying goods have been exported.

5.   The Value-Added Tax (Exported Goods) Regulations, 1984 (SI No. 230 of 1984) and the Value-Added Tax (Goods Exported in Baggage) Regulations, 1984 (SI No. 231 of 1984) are hereby revoked.

GIVEN this 17th day of December, 1992.

F. CASSELLS,
Revenue Commissioner.

The Minister for Finance hereby consents to the making of the foregoing Regulations.

GIVEN under my Official Seal this 24th day of December, 1992.

BERTIE AHERN,
Minister for Finance.

EXPLANATORY NOTE.

These Regulations provide for relief from VAT on certain supplies of goods to foreign visitors, and to Irish residents departing the Community for more than a year. The goods in question must be exported as personal baggage of the purchaser or must be shipped by or on behalf of the purchaser on board an aircraft or ship (other than private aircraft or vessels) leaving the Community.

This relief was formerly provided for in SI.230 and SI.231 of 1984, which are revoked and replaced by these Regulations.

VALUE-ADDED TAX (IMPORTED GOODS) REGULATIONS, 1992

(SI No. 439 of 1992)

> This Regulation was revoked by regulation 44, Value-Added Tax
> Regulations, 2006 (2006 S.I. No. 548) w.e.f. 1 November 2006

The Revenue Commissioners, in exercise of the powers conferred on them by sections 15(7) of the Value-Added Tax Act, 1972 (No.22 of 1972) and with the consent of the Minister for Finance, hereby make the following Regulations:

1. These Regulations may be cited as the Value-Added Tax (Imported Goods) Regulations, 1992.

2. These Regulations shall come into operation on the 1st day of January, 1993.

3. (1)   In these Regulations-

    "the Act" means the Value-Added Tax Act, 1972.

    "qualifying goods" means goods imported and entered for the purpose of undergoing a process of manufacture or for the purpose of being incorporated with other goods as a part or ingredient of a manufactured product.

    (2)   In these Regulations a reference to a Regulation is to a Regulation of these Regulations, unless it is indicated that reference to some other provision is intended.

4. Qualifying goods that are imported by a registered person may, subject to compliance with the requirements of these Regulations, be delivered or removed without payment of the tax chargeable on the importation where the person shows to the satisfaction of the Revenue Commissioners-

    (a)   that he is in the business of manufacturing goods in the State,

    (b)   that the goods are being imported for the purposes of the business, and

    (c)   that the consideration relating to supplies specified in subparagraphs (i)(a)(I), (i)(b) or (i)(c) of the Second Schedule to the Act made by him of goods manufactured by him in the State, taking one taxable period with another, amounts to and is likely to continue to amount to not less than 75 per cent. of the consideration, excluding tax, relating to the total of his supplies of goods manufactured by him.

5. A person who wishes to import qualifying goods without payment of the tax chargeable on their importation, in accordance with Regulation 4, shall apply in writing to the Revenue Commissioners for authorisation to do so. He shall complete such form as is provided for that purpose by the Revenue Commissioners and he shall certify the particulars shown on such form to be correct. He shall in addition provide such

further documentation in support of the application as the Revenue Commissioners may request.

6. Where they consider that a person satisfies the requirements of Regulation 4, the Revenue Commissioners shall authorise that person, by notice in writing, to have qualifying goods delivered or removed without payment of the tax chargeable on the importation of those goods.

7. Registered persons who, before the coming into force of these Regulations, have been authorised by the Revenue Commissioners to deliver or remove goods without payment of the tax chargeable on the importation in accordance with the Value-Added Tax (Imported Goods) Regulations, 1983 (SI No.129 of 1983) shall be deemed to have been authorised in accordance with Regulation 6.

8. In relation to each consignment of goods to be imported by a person authorised under Regulation 6 without payment of the tax chargeable on the importation, the following conditions shall be complied with-

    (a) the authorisation or, by agreement with a customs officer in the State, a copy thereof shall be produced with the relevant customs entry, and

    (b) the relevant customs entry shall incorporate

        (i) a declaration by the authorised person, or by his representative duly authorised by him in writing for this purpose, that the goods are raw materials and components for use in the authorised person's manufacturing business, and

        (ii) a claim for VAT-free importation.

9. Where goods have been imported by a person without payment of the tax chargeable on the importation in accordance with these Regulations, the tax so chargeable shall be accounted for by the authorised person in the return required to be furnished by him under section 19 of the Act for the taxable period during which the importation took place.

10. (1) A person authorised in accordance with Regulation 6 shall notify the Revenue Commissioners in writing where he no longer satisfies the requirements of Regulation 4. Such notification shall be made within 30 days of the person no longer satisfying the requirements of Regulation 4.

    (2) Where a person fails to notify the Revenue Commissioners in accordance with paragraph (1) of this Regulation, the authorisation under Regulation 6 shall be deemed to be cancelled in accordance with Regulation 11. Such cancellation shall have effect from the date on which the person no longer satisfies the requirements of Regulation 4.

11.   (1)   The Revenue Commissioners shall cancel an authorisation under Regulation 6 where they consider that the person no longer satisfies the requirements of Regulation 4.

      (2)   An authorisation under Regulation 6 shall be cancelled by notice in writing given by the Revenue Commissioners to the person who was the subject of the authorisation. Such cancellation shall have effect from the date of the notice or from such later date as may be specified in the notice.

12.   The Value-Added Tax (Imported Goods) Regulations, 1983 (SI No.129 of 1983) are hereby revoked.

GIVEN this 17th day of December, 1992.

F. CASSELLS,
Revenue Commissioner.

The Minister for Finance hereby consents to the making of the foregoing Regulations.

GIVEN under my Official Seal this 24th day of December, 1992.

BERTIE AHERN,
Minister for Finance.

EXPLANATORY NOTE.

These Regulations set out the terms and conditions for relief from payment of VAT on importation of raw materials and components by manufacturers whose exports or intra-Community supplies exceed 75 per cent. in value of their total manufactured output.

This relief was formerly provided for in S.I. 129 of 1983 which is revoked and replaced by these Regulations.

VALUE-ADDED TAX (IMPORTED GOODS) (NO 2)
REGULATIONS, 1992

(SI No. 440 of 1992)

> This Regulation was revoked by regulation 44, Value-Added Tax
> Regulations, 2006 (2006 S.I. No. 548) w.e.f. 1 November 2006

The Revenue Commissioners, in exercise of the powers conferred on them by section 15 of the Value-Added Tax Act, 1972 (No.22 of 1972), and with the consent of the Minister for Finance, hereby make the following Regulations:

1.   These Regulations may be cited as the Value-Added Tax (Imported Goods) (No.2) Regulations, 1992.

2.   These Regulations shall come into operation on the 1st day of January, 1993.

3.   In these Regulations-

    (a)   a reference to a Regulation is to a Regulation of these Regulations, and

    (b)   a reference to a paragraph is to a paragraph of the provision in which it occurs, unless it is indicated that reference to some other provision is intended.

4.   Without prejudice to Regulation 9, the provisions of the Customs Consolidation Act, 1876 as amended relating to the warehousing of imported goods, section 11 of the Finance (Miscellaneous Provisions) Act, 1958 (No.28 of 1958), and section 38 of the Finance Act, 1932 (No.20 of 1932), as amended by section 17 of the Finance Act, 1965 (No.22 of 1965), and the European Communities (Customs) Regulations, 1972 (SI No.334 of 1972), shall not apply to tax chargeable at importation.

5.   Section 6 of the Customs and Inland Revenue Act, 1879, and section 25(2) of the Finance Act, 1933 (No.15 of 1933), shall, insofar as they apply to tax, have effect in relation to goods which are being re-imported into the State after exportation therefrom only if they are re-imported into the State by the person who exported them from the State.

6.   Section 24 of the Finance Act, 1933 (No.15 of 1993), shall apply to tax chargeable at importation only insofar as the tax is not deductable under section 12 of the Act.

7.   Without prejudice to Regulation 9, section 5(1) of the Customs-Free Airport Act, 1947 (No 5 of 1947), shall not, insofar as it applies to tax, have effect in relation to goods brought from the Customs-free airport (within the meaning of that Act) into any other part of the State where it is established to the satisfaction of the Revenue Commissioners that the goods are Community goods or that the tax has already been borne or paid on the goods.

8.   Section 29(7) of the Finance Act, 1978 (No.21 of 1978), shall apply in relation to tax payable at importation with the modification that the

reference to goods entered for home use shall be deemed to include a reference to imported goods entered for free circulation [...][1]

9.   Legislation relating to customs adopted by the European Communities concerning the placing of goods under-

(a)   arrangements for temporary importation with total exemption from customs duty,

(b)   external transit arrangements,

(c)   temporary storage arrangements,

(d)   free zone or free warehouse arrangements,

(e)   customs warehousing arrangements,

(f)   inward processing (suspension) arrangements,[...][1]

(g)   arrangements for the admission of goods into territorial waters in connection with drilling or production platforms, [or

(h)   arrangements for processing under customs control.][2]

shall only apply in relation to tax chargeable at importation where, and for such time as, goods are held under those arrangements for the purpose of compliance with and implementation of the Community rules relating to customs.

10.   Without prejudice to Regulation 9, legislation relating to customs adopted by the European Community concerning suspension of customs duties, reduction in customs duties, or repayment or remission of customs duties shall not apply to tax chargeable at importation.

11.   The Value-Added Tax (Imported Goods) Regulations, 1982 (SI No.279 of 1982) are hereby revoked.

GIVEN this 21st day of December, 1992.

F. CASSELLS,
Revenue Commissioner.

The Minister for Finance hereby consents to the making of the foregoing Regulations.

GIVEN under my Official Seal, this 24th day of December, 1992.

BERTIE AHERN,
Minister for Finance.

EXPLANATORY NOTE.

These Regulations modify or exclude as appropriate the application to VAT payable at importation of various customs provisions insofar as they relate to-

(a)   application of VAT to goods imported for warehousing or for processing or re-export,

(b)   relief from VAT on goods re-imported by the person who exported them,

(c)   the exclusion of certain customs drawback and repayment provisions,

(d)   relief from VAT on certain goods brought from the customs-free airport into any other part of the State,

(e)   provision for arrangements for deferred payment of VAT payable on importation,

(f)   application of the EC customs legislation to VAT payable at importation.

These Regulations revoke and replace SI No.279 of 1982.

Amendments
1   Deleted by SI 628 of 2001 (w.e.f. 19 December 2001)
2   Inserted by SI 628 of 2001 (w.e.f. 19 December 2001)

VALUE-ADDED TAX (REGISTRATION) REGULATIONS, 1993

(SI No. 30 of 1993)

> This Regulation was revoked by regulation 44, Value-Added Tax Regulations, 2006 (2006 S.I. No. 548) w.e.f. 1 November 2006

The Revenue Commissioners, in exercise of the powers conferred on them by sections 9 of the Value-Added Tax Act, 1972 (No.22 of 1972) hereby make the following Regulations:-

1.   These Regulations may be cited as the Value-Added Tax (Registration) Regulations, 1993.

2.   In these Regulations "the Act" means the Value-Added Tax Act, 1972.

3.   A taxable person, or a person who in accordance with section 8(3) of the Act desires to elect to be a taxable person, shall register for tax by completing such form as is provided for that purpose by the Revenue Commissioners and he shall certify the particulars shown on such form to be correct.

4.   Where a change occurs in any of the particulars furnished in the form referred to in Regulation 3 of these Regulations-

   (a)   the registered person,

   (b)   if the registered person is dead, his personal representative, or

   (c)   if the registered person is a body of persons which is in liquidation or is otherwise being wound up, the liquidator or any other person who is carrying on business during such liquidation or, as the case may be, winding up,

   shall, within thirty days immediately following the date of the change, furnish to the Revenue Commissioners particulars of the change.

5.   A person who is registered in accordance with section 9 of the Act and who ceases-

   (a)   to supply taxable goods or services, and

   (b)   to make intra-Community acquisitions,

   in the State shall notify the Revenue Commissioners in writing of such cessation. Such written notification must be furnished by the end of the taxable period following that in which the cessation occurred.

6.   The Revenue Commissioners may, by notice in writing, cancel the registration of a person who does not become, or who ceases to be, a taxable person, and such cancellation shall have effect as on and from the date of the notice, or as on and from such date as may be specified in the notice.

7.   Regulation 6 of the Value-Added Tax Regulations, 1979 (SI No 63 of 1979) is hereby revoked.

GIVEN this 5th day of February, 1993.

D. B. QUIGLEY,
Revenue Commissioner.

EXPLANATORY NOTE.

These Regulations set out the procedures to be followed in relation to value-added tax registration and also in relation to subsequent deregistration. They revoke and replace Regulation 6 of the Value-Added Tax Regulations, 1979 (SI No.3 of 1979).

VALUE-ADDED TAX (STATEMENT OF INTRA-COMMUNITY SUPPLIES) REGULATIONS, 1993

(SI No. 54 of 1993)

This Regulation was revoked by regulation 44, Value-Added Tax
Regulations, 2006 (2006 S.I. No. 548) w.e.f. 1 November 2006

The Revenue Commissioners, in exercise of the powers conferred on them by sections 19A (inserted by the Finance Act, 1992 (No.9 of 1992)) and 32 of the Value-Added Tax Act, 1972 (No.22 of 1972), hereby make the following Regulations:

1. These Regulations may be cited as the Value-Added Tax (Statement of Intra-Community Supplies) Regulations, 1993.

2. These Regulations shall be deemed to have come into operation on the 1st day of January, 1993.

3. (1) In these Regulations-

    "the Act" means the Value-Added Tax Act, 1972;

    "correction statement" means a statement of corrective details furnished in relation to a statement previously supplied;

    "intra-Community supplies" has the meaning assigned to it by section 19A(6) of the Act;

    "statement" means a statement of intra-Community supplies required to be furnished to the Revenue Commissioners by a taxable person in accordance with section 19A of the Act;

    "working day" means a day other than-

    (a)   a Saturday or Sunday,

    (b)   a day that is a public holiday (within the meaning of the Holidays (Employees) Act, 1973 (No.25 of 1973)), or

    (c)   any other day when the offices of the Revenue Commissioners are closed to the public.

    (2) In these Regulations-

    (a)   a reference to a Regulation is to a Regulation of these Regulations, and

    (b)   a reference to a paragraph or subparagraph is to a paragraph or subparagraph of the provision in which it occurs,

    unless it is indicated that reference to some other provision is intended.

4. (1) Subject to Regulation 5 a taxable person who is required in accordance with section 19A of the Act to furnish a statement of intra-Community supplies shall complete to the satisfaction of

the Revenue Commissioners such forms as are provided for that purpose by them.

(2)   Where for any reason a taxable person becomes aware of an error in a statement furnished in accordance with paragraph (1) he shall, within five working days, furnish a correction statement on the form provided for that purpose by the Revenue Commissioners.

5.   (1)   Notwithstanding the provisions of Regulation 4, a taxable person may, on written application to the Revenue Commissioners, be authorised by them to finish a statement or correction statement on a document or in a manner other than by use of the forms referred to in Regulation 4.

(2)   Where a taxable person is authorised in accordance with paragraph (1), the statement or correction statement shall be furnished in a format specified by the Revenue Commissioners and shall include all the particulars that would have been provided had the person completed the relevant form referred to in Regulation 4.

6.   In furnishing a statement or correction statement in accordance with Regulation 4 or 5 a taxable person shall, in respect of the period covered by the statement-

(a)   make a separate entry in respect of his intra-Community supplies to each person registered for value-added tax in another Member State,

(b)   include in each entry referred to in subparagraph (a) the indicator "P" where the intra-Community supplies include-

     (i)   goods which have been returned by him to that person having undergone contract work in the State, or

     (ii)   goods dispatched or transported by him to that person for the purposes of having contract work carried out on the goods,

(c)   in the case of intra-Community supplies referred to in paragraph (b)(ii), omit in the entry any indication of the value of the goods, and

(d)   make a separate entry including the indicator "T" in respect of any supplies of the type referred to in section 3A(5)(iii) of the Act to each person registered for value-added tax in another Member State,

and shall also furnish such other particulars of his intra-Community supplies as are requested on the appropriate form.

7.   (1)   (a)   A statement or correction statement may be prepared and

furnished to the Revenue Commissioners by a person other than the taxable person where that person has been authorised by the taxable person to act on his behalf in that regard.

(b)   Where a statement or correction statement is prepared and furnished to the Revenue Commissioners by virtue of subparagraph (a), the provisions of the Act shall apply as if it had been prepared and furnished to the Revenue Commissioners by the taxable person.

(2)   A statement or correction statement purporting to be prepared and furnished to the Revenue Commissioner by or on behalf of any taxable person shall, for all the purpose of the Act, be deemed to have been prepared and finished to the Revenue Commissioners by that taxable person, on by his authority, as the case may be, unless the contrary is proved.

(3)   A taxable person who authorises another person in accordance with paragraph (1) shall notify the Revenue Commissioners in writing of such authorisation.

(4)   A taxable person shall, on cancelling an authorisation referred to in paragraph (1), advise the Revenue Commissioners in writing of the cancellation within five working days of such cancellation.

(5)   The Revenue Commissioners may by notice in writing exclude a taxable person from the provisions of this Regulation.

8.   (1)   Subject to paragraph (2) and save as may be otherwise permitted by the Revenue Commissioners under these Regulations, every statement and correction statement shall be completed otherwise than in handwriting by means of typing or other similar process.

(2)   Every statement and correction statement shall be signed and dated by the taxable person or the person authorised by him in accordance with paragraph (1) of Regulation 7.

(3)   Where a taxable person has been authorised in accordance with Regulation 5 to furnish a statement or correction statement by electronic means or through magnetic media, any such statement shall have the same effect as if it were a signed statement or correction statement, as the case may be.

9.   (1)   A taxable person may, on written application to the Revenue Commissioners, be authorised by the Commissioners to submit an annual statement in accordance with section 19A(3) of the Act where the taxable person's supplies of goods and services do not exceed or are not likely to exceed [€85,000][1] in a calendar year, and his intra-Community supplies do not exceed or are not likely to exceed [€15,000][2] in that calendar year and provided

such intra-Community supplies do not include the supply of new means of transport.

(2)   A taxable person authorised to submit a return in accordance with section 19(3)(aa) of the Act may, on written application to the Revenue Commissioners, be authorised by the Commissioners to submit an annual statement in accordance with section 19A(3) of the Act where the taxable person's supplies of goods and services do not exceed or are not likely to exceed [€200,000][3] in a calendar year, and his intra-Community supplies do not exceed or are not likely to exceed [€15,000][4] in that calendar year and provided such intra-Community supplies do not include the supply of new means of transport.

10.   An authorisation under subsection (2) or (3) of section 19A of the Act shall be cancelled by notice in writing given by the Revenue Commissioners to the person who was the subject of the authorisation and any such cancellation shall have effect from the date of the notice or from such later date as may be specified in the notice.

11.   The provisions of Regulations 4,5,6,7 and 8 shall apply to a statement or correction statement furnished on a monthly or annual basis as the case may be:

Provided that the taxable person referred to in paragraph (1) of Regulation 9 shall not be obliged to furnish details of the value of his intra-Community supplies or to comply with subparagraphs (b) or (d) of paragraph (1) of Regulation 6.

GIVEN this 26th day of February, 1993.

D. B. QUIGLEY,
Revenue Commissioner.

EXPLANATORY NOTE.

These Regulations set out the particulars required to be included by taxable persons on statements of their intra-Community supplies. The Regulations also specify the means by which such statements may be returned to the Revenue Commissioners and the frequency of such returns.

Amendments

1   Amended by s240 & sch5, FA01, w.e.f. 1 January 2002. Previously £60,000

2   Amended by s240 & sch5, FA01, w.e.f. 1 January 2002. Previously £12,000

3   Amended by s240 & sch5, FA01, w.e.f. 1 January 2002. Previously £150,000

4   Amended by s240 & sch5, FA01, w.e.f. 1 January 2002. Previously £12,000

VALUE-ADDED TAX (REFUND OF TAX) (NO 24) ORDER, 1993

(SI No. 134 of 1993)

> This Order revoked by para6, Value-Added Tax (Refund of Tax) (No. 26) Order 1994 (1994 S.I. No. 165) with effect from 1 June 1994.

I, BERTIE AHERN, Minister for Finance, in exercise of the powers conferred on me by section 20(3) of the Value-Added Tax Act, 1972 (No.22 of 1972), hereby order as follows:

1.   This Order may be cited as the Value-Added Tax (Refund of Tax) (No.24) Order, 1993.

2.   (1)   In this Order-

"the Act" means the Value-Added Tax Act, 1972;

"qualifying vehicle" means-

    (a)   a single-deck touring coach having dimensions as designated by the manufacturer of not less than 3,350 millimetres in height, not less than 10,000 millimetres in length and not less than 1,400 millimetres in floor height, and which is not more than two years old, or

    (b)   a double-deck touring coach having dimensions as designated by the manufacturer of not more than 4,300 millimetres in height and not less than 10,000 millimetres in length, and which is not more than two years old;

"qualifying person" means a person who is engaged in the business of carriage for reward of persons, including tourists, by road under contracts for group transport.

    (2)   In this Order a reference to a paragraph or subparagraph is to a paragraph or subparagraph of this Order, unless it is indicated that reference to some other provision is intended.

3.   (1)   Unless the option in subparagraph (2) is availed of, a qualifying person who has borne or paid tax on-

    (a)   the purchase, or hiring to him (other than hiring for a period of less than six consecutive months), within the State,

    (b)   the intra-Community acquisition in the State, or

    (c)   the importation into the State,

of a qualifying vehicle shall, subject to the conditions specified in paragraph 4, be repaid so much of such tax as is specified in paragraph 5.

    (2)   Where a qualifying person is a taxable person and makes an intra-Community acquisition of a qualifying vehicle in the State he may, at the time the tax becomes payable in accordance

with section 19(3) of the Act, reduce the amount payable on the acquisition by the amount specified in paragraph 5(2).

(3)   The provisions of subparagraph (1) or (2) shall apply only where a qualifying person is not entitled to a deduction or repayment, under any other provision of the Act or regulations made thereunder or of any other Act or Instrument made under statute administered by the Revenue Commissioners, of any portion of the tax paid or payable in respect of the qualifying vehicle.

4.   The conditions to be fulfilled by a person in order to obtain a repayment of tax under this Order by virtue of being a qualifying person are as follows:

(a)   the person shall claim a repayment of the tax, by completing such form as is provided for that purpose by the Revenue Commissioners, and shall certify the particulars shown on such form to be correct;

(b)   the person shall establish to the satisfaction of the Revenue Commissioners that he is a qualifying person;

(c)   the person shall produce-

    (i)   in the case of a purchase or hire within the State of a qualifying vehicle, an invoice, issued to that person in accordance with section 17(12)(a)(i) of the Act, establishing the amount of tax paid on the purchase or hire, or

    (ii)   in the case of an intra-Community acquisition in the State of a qualifying vehicle, an official receipt or other document establishing the amount of tax paid on the intra-Community acquisition together with the invoice issued to that person by the supplier in the Member State of supply, or

    (iii)   in the case of an importation into the State of a qualifying vehicle, an official receipt or other document establishing the amount of tax paid on the importation and indicating the number of the relevant customs entry;

(d)   the person is not a person to whom a notice has been issued under paragraph 6 and which has not been revoked.

5.   (1)   The amount of tax to be repaid in accordance with paragraph 3(1) shall be so much of the amount of tax borne or paid at the rate specified in section 11(1)(a) of the Act which is shown to the satisfaction of the Revenue Commissioners to be in excess of the amount which would have been borne or paid if the rate for the time being specified in section 11(1)(d) of the Act had applied to the purchase, hiring, intra-Community acquisition or importation in question.

(2)   The reduction referred to in paragraph 3(2) shall be equal to the amount of the tax that would fall to be repaid under subparagraph (1) if paragraph 3(1) had applied.

6.   (1)   The Revenue Commissioners may, where it appears requisite to them to do so for the protection of the revenue, by notice in writing exclude a taxable person from the provisions of paragraph 3(2).

(2)   A notice under this paragraph shall be revoked where it appears to the Revenue Commissioners that it is no longer requisite for the protection of the revenue to exclude the taxable person concerned from the provisions of paragraph 3(2).

7.   The Value-Added Tax (Refund of Tax) (No.19) Order, 1986 (SI No.68 of 1986), and the Value-Added Tax (Refund of Tax) (No.22) Order, 1988 (SI No.262 of 1988), are hereby revoked.

GIVEN under my Official Seal,
this 21st day of May, 1993.

BERTIE AHERN,
Minister for Finance.

EXPLANATORY NOTE.

This Order replaces S.I. Nos.68 of 1986 and 262 of 1988. It retains the schemes set out in those Orders whereby VAT in excess of the reduced rate (12.5 per cent as at the date of the Order) can be repaid, subject to certain conditions, to unregistered coach operators in respect of the tax paid on touring coaches of certain dimensions.

The Order also introduces a mechanism whereby a coach operator who is a taxable person (but without deductability in respect of his coach tour activities) may reduce the amount of tax payable on his intra-Community acquisition of a touring coach by an amount equal to the amount which would have been repaid had he not been a taxable person.

EUROPEAN COMMUNITIES (INTRASTAT) REGULATIONS, 1993

(SI No. 136 of 1993)

I, ALBERT REYNOLDS, T.D., Taoiseach, in exercise of the powers conferred on me by section 3 of the European Communities Act, 1972 (No.27 of 1972), and for the purpose of giving full effect to Council Regulation (EEC) No. 3330/91 of 7 November 1991, Commission Regulation (EEC) No. 3046/92 of 22 October 1992, Commission Regulation (EEC) No. 2256/92 of 31 July 1992 and Commission Regulation (EEC) No. 3590/92 of 11 December 1992, hereby make the following Regulations:

1. These Regulations may be cited as the European Communities (Intrastat) Regulations, 1993.

2. These Regulations shall come into operation on the 22 day of May, 1993.

3. (1) [In these Regulations-

    'authorised officer' means an officer of the Revenue Commissioners authorised by them in writing to exercise the powers of an authorised officer referred to in these Regulations;

    'basic Regulation' means Regulation (EC) No. 638/2004 of the European Parliament and of the Council of 31 March 2004;

    'Community Regulations' means the basic Regulation and Commission Regulation (EC) No. 1982/2004 of 18 November 2004;

    'Member State' means a Member State of the European Community;

    'Intrastat system' means the Intrastat system referred to in the basic Regulation in so far as that system applies to trade between Member States pursuant to Articles 5 to 14 of that Regulation;

    'officer of statistics' has the meaning assigned to it by the Statistics Act 1993 (No. 21 of 1993);

    'records' means any document or other written or printed material in any form as well as information (including statistical information) stored, maintained or preserved by means of any mechanical or electronic device, whether or not stored, maintained or preserved in a legible form;

    'trader' means a person referred in Article 7 (1) of the basic Regulation.][1]

4. (1) The statistical information required by the Intrastat system which a trader is responsible for providing in respect of each month in accordance with the provisions of the Community Regulations shall be furnished to the Revenue Commissioners, on forms provided by them for that purpose, by or on behalf of that trader not later than the 10th working day immediately

following the end of the month concerned and the said forms shall be completed in accordance with, as appropriate:-

(a)   the terms of the manual entitled "VIES and INTRASTAT Traders Manual" published by the Revenue Commissioners in October, 1992, (hereafter in this Regulation referred to as the "relevant manual") and any document published by them for the time being amending the relevant manual, or

(b)   the terms of any subsequent edition of the relevant manual published by the Revenue Commissioners that is the current such edition (hereafter in this Regulation referred to as a "replacement manual") and any document published by them for the time being amending the replacement manual.

(2)   A document referred to in subparagraph (a) or (b) of paragraph (1) of this Regulation is referred to hereafter in this Regulation as a "supplement".

(3)   The Revenue Commissioners may, on written application being made to them by a trader, authorise the furnishing of the statistical information referred to in paragraph (1) of this Regulation by or on behalf of that trader in a manner other than by use of the forms referred to in the said paragraph (1) and the manner to be so authorised shall be one that is specified in the relevant manual, a replacement manual or a supplement.

(4)   A trader to whom on authorisation as aforesaid has been given shall furnish or cause to be furnished on his behalf the statistical information referred to in paragraph (1) of this Regulation to the Revenue Commissioners in the manner specified in the authorisation not later than the 10th working day immediately following the end of the month concerned and the information so furnished shall include all the particulars that would have been provided had the trader, or the person acting on his behalf, completed the forms referred to in the said paragraph (1).

(5)   The furnishing of statistical information in accordance with paragraph (4) of this Regulation shall have the same effect as if the statistical information was furnished on the forms referred to in paragraph (1) of this Regulation.

(6)   A trader who fails to comply with paragraph (1) or (4) of this Regulation shall be guilty of an offence under these Regulations.

(7)   Prima facie evidence of the relevant manual, a replacement manual or a supplement may be given in proceedings for an offence under these Regulations by the production of a copy of the relevant manual, replacement manual or supplement purporting to be published by the Revenue Commissioners together with a

certificate purporting to be signed by an officer of the Revenue Commissioners certifying that the relevant manual, replacement manual or supplement, as the case may be, contains the relevant matters as respects the obligations of the trader concerned (who shall be named in the certificate) under paragraph (1) or (4), as the case may be, of this Regulation.

(8)   In proceedings for an offence under these Regulations:-

(a)   it shall be presumed until the contrary is proved that no authorisation has been given by the Revenue Commissioners under paragraph (3) of this Regulation, and

(b)   prima facie evidence of such an authorisation may be given by the production of a document purporting to be a written application by the trader concerned for the authorisation and of a document purporting to be a copy of the authorisation granted by the Revenue Commissioners.

(9)   A certificate referred to in paragraph (7) of this Regulation shall:-

(a)   indicate the rank or position in the Office of the Revenue Commissioners of the officer who has signed it.

(b)   be admitted in evidence without proof of the signature of that officer.

(10)   (a)   Notice of the publication of the relevant manual shall be published in the Iris Oifigiúil as soon as may be after the commencement of these Regulations.

(b)   Notice of the publication of a replacement manual or a supplement shall be published in the Iris Oifigiúil as soon as may be after the publication of the replacement manual or supplement, as the case may be.

(c)   A notice under this paragraph shall indicate that a member of the public shall be entitled to be supplied by the Revenue Commissioners free of charge with a copy of the relevant manual, replacement manual or supplement, as the case may be, on request being made by him therefor.

(d)   Prima facie evidence of the publication of a notice under this paragraph may

be given in proceedings for an offence under these Regulations by the production of a copy of the Iris Oifigiúil purporting to contain the notice.

(11)   The Revenue Commissioners shall supply to a member of the public, free of charge, a copy of the relevant manual, replacement manual or supplement on request being made by him therefor.

[5. (1) The Taoiseach shall make a specification from time to time of thresholds below which parties are exempted from providing any Intrastat information in accordance with Article 10 of the basic Regulation.[2]

(2) (a) A specification by the Taoiseach for the purposes of paragraph (1) shall be published in the Iris Oifigiúil as soon as may be after it is made.

(b) Until the contrary is shown, evidence of a specification for the purposes of paragraph (1) may be given in proceedings for an offence under these Regulations by the production of a copy of the Iris Oifigiúil purporting to contain the specification.][3]

6. A trader who, in purported compliance with Regulation 4 of these Regulations, furnishes or causes or permits to be furnished to the Revenue Commissioners information which is false, misleading or incomplete in any respect shall be guilty of an offence under these Regulations.

7. (1) An authorised officer may at all reasonable times enter any premises or place where he reasonably believes records relating to goods to which the intrastat system applies are kept and may require any person on those premises or in that place to produce to him the said records or such of them as he specifies and may search for, inspect and take copies of, or extracts from, the said records and may remove the said records from those premises or that place for further inspection.

(2) A person who obstructs, hinders or interferes with an authorised officer in the exercise of the powers conferred on him by paragraph (1) of this Regulation or who refuses without lawful excuse to produce to such an officer records which he is required by such an officer to produce under the said paragraph shall be guilty of an offence under these Regulations.

8. (1) All records received or kept by a trader relating to goods in respect of which he is responsible for furnishing statistical information to the Revenue Commissioners under Regulation 4 of these Regulations shall be preserved by him for a period of not less than 2 years from the end of the month to which they relate.

(2) A trader shall produce or cause to be produced to an authorised officer upon request by that officer the records referred to in paragraph (1) of this Regulation or such of them as that officer specifies.

(3) A trader who fails to comply with paragraph (1) of this Regulation or with a request under paragraph (2) of this Regulation shall be guilty of an offence under these Regulations.

9.   An officer of statistics shall:

    (a)   have access to, and, on request, be given by the Revenue Commissioners copies of, the statistical information furnished to the Revenue Commissioners by or on behalf of traders under Regulation 4 of these Regulations,

    (b)   on request, be given such information by the Revenue Commissioners as they deem fit to give relating to goods to which the Intrastat system applies and which has come into their possession through the exercise by an authorised officer of his powers under Regulation 7 or 8 of these Regulations.

10.   (1)   Statistical information furnished by or on behalf of a trader under Regulation 4 of these Regulations shall not, save with the consent of that trader or for the purposes of a prosecution under these Regulations, be shown or communicated to any person other than an officer of the Revenue Commissioners or an officer of statistics in the course of his official duties.

    (2)   As far as practicable statistics derived from statistical information furnished by or on behalf of a trader under Regulation 4 of these Regulations shall not be published or disseminated in a manner that would result directly or indirectly in the disclosure of details relating to any business of that trader but nothing in this paragraph shall be held to impose a duty owed to a trader to avoid such a disclosure.

11.   (1)   A trader who by act or omission fails to comply with a provision of the Community Regulations shall be guilty of an offence under these Regulations.

    (2)   A person who is guilty of an offence under these Regulations shall be liable on summary conviction to a fine of [€1,265][4].

    (3)   Where a trader is convicted of an offence under Regulation 4 of these Regulations he shall, if the failure in respect of which he is convicted of the offence is continued after conviction, be guilty of a further offence on every day on which the failure continues and for each such offence he shall be liable on summary conviction to a fine of [€60][5].

    (4)   Proceedings for an offence under these Regulations may be brought and prosecuted by the Revenue Commissioners.

12.   (1)   Where an offence under these Regulations is committed by a body corporate and is proved to have been committed with the consent or connivance of or to be attributable to any neglect on the part of a person being a director, manager, secretary or other similar officer of the body corporate, or a person who was purporting to act in any such capacity, that person as well as the body corporate shall be guilty of an offence and shall be liable

to be proceeded against and punished as if he were guilty of the first-mentioned offence.

(2) Where the affairs of a body corporate are managed by its members, paragraph (1) of this Regulation shall apply in relation to the acts and defaults of a member in connection with his functions of management as if he were a director of the body corporate.

13. (1) Subject to the provisions of this Regulation, in proceedings for an offence under these Regulations a certificates signed by an officer of the Revenue Commissioners which certifies that he has inspected the relevant records of the Revenue Commissioners and that it appears from them that the trader concerned (who shall be named in the certificate):-

   (a) was required under Regulation 4 of these Regulations to provide statistical information of a kind and at a time or times specified in the certificate, and failed to do so, or

   (b) failed, in a manner specified in the certificate, to do a stated act or furnish stated records or particulars in accordance with any of the provisions of these Regulations, shall be prima facie evidence that the trader concerned was so required to provide statistical information as aforesaid or, as the case may be, failed to do a stated act or furnish stated records or particulars as aforesaid.

(2) A certificate referred to in paragraph (1) of this Regulation shall:-

   (a) indicate the rank or position in the Office of the Revenue Commissioners of the officer who has signed it,

   (b) be admitted in evidence without proof of the signature of that officer.

(3) If in proceedings against a person for an offence under these Regulations it is proposed to tender in evidence a certificate referred to in paragraph (1) of this Regulation the prosecution shall cause to be served on the person not less than 21 days before the commencement of the trial of the offence a copy of the certificate together with a notice informing the person:-

   (a) that it is proposed to tender the certificate in evidence in the proceedings,

   (b) that the certificate shall not, without the leave of the Court, be admitted in evidence if the person serves on the solicitor for the prosecution not later than 7 days before the commencement of the trial of the offence a notice objecting to the admissibility of the certificate.

   (c) that if the person serves a notice as aforesaid and the facts stated in the certificate are required to be proved, wholly or partly, by oral evidence at the trial of the offence the person shall be liable to pay to the prosecution the costs and witness expenses incurred in so proving the said facts unless, in the opinion of the Court, the person had good grounds for serving the said notice.

(4)   (a)   A certificate referred to in paragraph (1) of this Regulation shall not, without the leave of the Court, be admitted in evidence if the defendant concerned has served on the solicitor for the prosecution a notice referred to in paragraph (3)(b) of this Regulation within the period mentioned in that provision.

        (b)   If the defendant concerned has served a notice as aforesaid and the facts stated in the certificate are required to be proved, wholly or partly, by oral evidence at the trial of the offence in question the Court shall, unless it is of the opinion that the defendant had good grounds for serving the said notice, order him to pay to the prosecution the costs and witness expenses incurred in so proving the said facts.

14.   The Revenue Commissioners may, in their discretion, mitigate any fine incurred under these Regulations, or stay or compound any proceedings for recovery thereof, and may also, after judgement, further mitigate or entirely remit such a fine.

GIVEN under my Official Seal,
this 21st day of May, 1993.

ALBERT REYNOLDS,
Taoiseach.

Notes
1   Amended by r3, European Communities (Intrastat) (Amendment) Regulations 2005.

2   The assimilation thresholds in Ireland, with effect from 1 January 2003, are: dispatches €635,000, arrivals €191,000 by notice, Iris Oifigiúil 19 November 2002.

3   Amended by r4, European Communities (Intrastat) (Amendment) Regulations 2005.

4   Amended by s240 & sch5, FA01, w.e.f. 1 January 2002. Previously £1,000

5   Amended by s240 & sch5, FA01, w.e.f. 1 January 2002. Previously £50

This regulation gave effect to, among others, EC Regulation 3046/92. EC Regulation 3046/92, with the exception of Reg. 22 therein, was repealed by EC Regulation 1901/2000.

The CSO, which deals with the intra-Community trade statistics, is currently in the process of drafting a new set of Regulations to give effect to EC Regulation 1901/2000.

VALUE-ADDED TAX (RETURNS) REGULATIONS, 1993

(SI No. 247 of 1993)

> These Regulations revoked by r5, Value Added Tax (Returns) Regulations, 1996 (1996 S.I. No. 294) with effect from 8 October 1996.

The Revenue Commissioners, in exercise of the powers conferred on them by sections 19 of the Value-Added Tax Act, 1972 (No.22 of 1972), hereby make the following Regulations:

1. These Regulations may be cited as the Value-Added Tax (Returns) Regulations, 1993.

2. In these Regulations "the Act" means the Value-Added Tax Act, 1972.

3. A taxable person who is required in accordance with section 19(3)(a) of the Act to furnish a return, shall complete such form as is issued to him for that purpose by the Collector-General in respect of the taxable period in question and he shall certify the particulars shown on that form to be correct.

    Provided that where the form issued to the said taxable person by the Collector-General specifies supplementary trading details to be furnished in respect of preceding taxable periods as well as the taxable period in question, such supplementary trading details shall be part of the return which is required to be furnished in respect of that taxable period.

4. A taxable person who is required in accordance with section 19(3)(aa) of the Act to furnish a return, shall complete such form as is issued to him for that purpose by the Collector-General and he shall certify the particulars shown on that form to be correct.

5. Regulation 12 of the Value-Added Tax Regulations, 1979 (SI No.63 of 1979), is hereby revoked.

GIVEN this 27th day of August, 1993.

C. C. MAC DOMHNAILL,
Revenue Commissioner.

EXPLANATORY NOTE.

These Regulations require a taxable person to furnish the details requested on the VAT return issued to him in accordance with Section 19(3) of the Act. They revoke and replace Regulation 12 of the Value-Added Tax Regulations, 1979 (SI No.63 of 1979).

VALUE-ADDED TAX (PAYMENT OF TAX ON INTRA-COMMUNITY ACQUISITIONS OF CERTAIN NEW MEANS OF TRANSPORT) REGULATIONS, 1993

(SI No. 248 of 1993)

This Regulation was revoked by regulation 44, Value-Added Tax Regulations, 2006 (2006 S.I. No. 548) w.e.f. 1 November 2006

The Revenue Commissioners, in exercise of the powers conferred on them by sections 19(4) of the Value-Added Tax Act, 1972 (No. 22 of 1972), hereby make the following Regulations:

1.   These Regulations may be cited as the Value-Added Tax (Payment of Tax on Intra-Community Acquisitions of Certain New Means of Transport) Regulations, 1993.

2.   These Regulations shall come into operation on the 1st day of September, 1993.

3.   In these Regulations-

"the Act" means the Value-Added Tax Act, 1972;

"new aircraft" means a new means of transport other than a motorised land vehicle or a vessel;

"new vessel" means a new means of transport other than a motorised land vehicle or an aircraft.

4.   Where a person makes an intra-Community acquisition of a new aircraft or a new vessel, in respect of which he is not entitled to a deduction of tax under section 12 of the Act, the person shall-

(a)   complete such form as may be provided by the Revenue Commissioners for the purpose of this Regulation,

(b)   provide such further documentation in support of the details provided on the form as the Revenue Commissioners may request,

(c)   certify that the particulars and documentation provided are true and accurate,

(d)   not later than three days after the due date furnish, to the Collector of Customs and Excise for the area in which he is resident, the completed form and supporting documentation referred to in paragraph (a) and (b) of this Regulation and at the same time pay to that Collector the amount of tax due, and

(e)   if requested to do so, make the new aircraft or the new vessel, as appropriate, available for inspection in the State by an officer of the Revenue Commissioners.

5.   The Value-Added Tax (Payment of Tax on Intra-Community Acquisitions of Means of Transport) Regulations, 1992 (SI No.412 of 1992), are hereby revoked.

GIVEN this 27th day of August, 1993.

C. C. MAC DOMHNAILL,
Revenue Commissioner.

EXPLANATORY NOTE.

These Regulations set out the procedures to be followed in relation to the payment of value-added tax on the intra-Community acquisition of new aircraft and new vessels by private individuals and other persons not entitled to deduct the tax chargeable on the goods. They revoke and replace SI No.412 of 1992.

VALUE-ADDED TAX (REFUND OF TAX) (NO 25) ORDER, 1993

(SI No. 266 of 1993)

I, BERTIE AHERN, Minister for Finance, in exercise of the powers conferred on me by section 20(3) of the Value-Added Tax Act, 1972 (No.22 of 1972), hereby order as follows:

1.   This Order may be cited as the Value-Added Tax (Refund of Tax) (No.25) Order, 1993.

2.   (1)   In this Order-

"the Act" means the Value-Added Tax Act, 1972;

"flat-rate farmer" has the meaning assigned to it by section 12A(2) of the Act;

"qualifying person" means a flat-rate farmer who has borne or paid tax in relation to outlay on the construction, extension, alteration or reconstruction of any building or structure which is designed for use solely or mainly for the purposes of a farming business, or on the fencing, drainage or reclamation of any land intended for use for the purposes of such a business;

"registered person" means a flat-rate farmer who is a taxable person referred to in subsection (1A)(c) or (2)(b) of section 8 of the Act and who is included on the register of taxable persons maintained by the Revenue Commissioners pursuant to section 9 of the Act;

"structure" includes a farmyard, a farm road and a concrete path adjacent to farm buildings;

"unregistered person" means a flat-rate farmer other than a registered person.

    (2)   In this Order a reference to a paragraph is to a paragraph of this Order, unless it is indicated that reference to some other provision is intended.

3.   An unregistered person who establishes to the satisfaction of the Revenue Commissioners that he is a qualifying person, and who fulfils to the satisfaction of the said Commissioners the conditions which are specified in paragraph 4, shall be entitled to be repaid so much of such tax as is specified in paragraph 7.

4.   The conditions to be fulfilled by an unregistered person are as follows:

    (a)   he shall claim a repayment of the tax by completing such claim form as may be provided for that purpose by the Revenue Commissioners and he shall certify the particulars shown on such claim form to be correct;

    (b)   he shall produce-

(i)   the invoices or other documents, issued or given to him for the purposes of section 17 of the Act, or

(ii)   the receipts for tax paid on goods imported,

showing the tax borne or paid by him which is the subject of the refund claim;

(c)   he shall, if requested to do so by the Revenue Commissioners, produce the plans, specifications or other documentary evidence in relation to-

(i)   the construction, extension, alteration or reconstruction of a building or structure which is designed for use solely or mainly for the purposes of a farming business, or

(ii)   the fencing, drainage or reclamation of any land intended for use for the purposes of such a business,

in respect of which his claim for a refund of tax is being made; and

(d)   he shall have complied with all the obligations imposed on him by the Act, the Income Tax Acts, the Corporation Tax Acts or the Capital Gains Tax Act, and any instruments made thereunder, in relation to-

(i)   the payment or remittance of the taxes, interest and penalties required to be paid or remitted thereunder, and

(ii)   the delivery of returns.

5.   A registered person who is a qualifying person shall, subject to the conditions which are specified in paragraph 6, be entitled to reclaim so much of such tax as is specified in paragraph 7 as if such tax were deductible tax under section 12 of the Act.

6.   The conditions to be fulfilled by a registered person are as follows:

(a)   he shall reclaim the tax in the return which he is obliged to furnish in accordance with section 19(3) of the Act and he shall certify the particulars shown on the relevant return form to be correct;

(b)   he shall retain all the documents referred to in subparagraphs (b) and (c) of paragraph 4 which are relevant to his claim as if they were records to be kept in accordance with section 16 of the Act; and

(c)   he shall have complied with all the obligations imposed on him by the Act, the Income Tax Acts, the Corporation Tax Acts or the Capital Gains Tax Act, and any instruments made thereunder, in relation to-

(i)   the payment or remittance of the taxes, interest and penalties required to be paid or remitted thereunder, and

(ii)   the delivery of returns.

7.   The amount of tax to be repaid in accordance with paragraph 3 or reclaimed in accordance with paragraph 5 shall, subject to paragraph 8, be the tax borne or paid which the qualifying person shows to the satisfaction of the Revenue Commissioners to be referable solely to outlay which relates to-

    (a)   the construction, extension, alteration or reconstruction of that part of the building or structure which was designed solely for the purposes of a farming business and has actually been put to us in such a business carried on by him, or

    (b)   the fencing, drainage or reclamation of any land which has actually been put to use in such a business carried on by him.

8.   A claim for repayment of tax under subparagraph (a) of paragraph 4 shall be made only in respect of outlay involving a total amount of tax of more than [€125]1.

9.   The Value-Added Tax (Refund of Tax) (No.1) Order, 1972 (S.I. No.267 of 1972), the Value-Added Tax (Refund of Tax) (No.8) Order, 1978 (S.I. No.145 of 1978) and the Value-Added Tax (Refund of Tax) (No.17) Order, 1984 (S.I. No.249 of 1984), are hereby revoked.

GIVEN under my Official Seal,
this 15th day of September, 1993.

BERTIE AHERN,
Minister for Finance.

EXPLANATORY NOTE.

This Order replaces SI No.267 of 1972, SI No.145 of 1978 and SI No.249 of 1984. It retains the scheme provided for in those Orders for the refund of VAT paid by farmers on the construction of farm buildings, fencing, drainage and reclamation of farm land. The previous scheme applied only to farmers who were not registered for VAT. However, under Single Market rules farmers may have to register for VAT because of intra-Community acquisitions or certain services received from abroad; the new Order ensures that these farmers can still obtain the benefit of the VAT refund.

The Order also updates the documentary evidence required in support of a refund claim and makes the granting of a refund conditional on the claimant's tax affairs being in order.

Notes
1   Amended by s240 & sch5, FA01, w.e.f. 1 January 2002. Previously £100

VALUE-ADDED TAX (THRESHOLD FOR ADVANCE PAYMENT) ORDER, 1993

(SI No. 303 of 1993)

I, BERTIE AHERN, Minister for Finance, in exercise of the powers conferred on me by section19(6)(h) (inserted by section 92(c) of the Finance Act, 1993 (No.13 of 1993)) of the Value-Added Tax Act, 1972 (No.22 of 1972), hereby order as follows:

1.   This Order may be cited as the Value-Added Tax (Threshold for Advance Payment) Order, 1993.

2.   In this Order-

   "the Act" means the Value-Added Tax Act, 1972 (No.22 of 1972);

   "threshold" means a threshold for the purposes of section 19(6) of the Act;

   "due date" means a due date for the purposes of section 19(6) of the Act.

3.   The threshold to be applied for the purposes of section 19(6) of the Act to the due date which is the 1st day of December, 1993, and to each successive due date thereafter, shall be [£1,000,000]1.

GIVEN under my Official Seal,
this 26th day of October, 1993.

BERTIE AHERN,
Minister for Finance.

EXPLANATORY NOTE.

Section 19(6) of the VAT Act requires that an advance payment of VAT be made in December 1993, and subsequent years, by taxable persons whose net annual VAT liability exceeds a threshold. The Order increases this threshold from £120,000 to £300,000.

Amendments
1. Threshold increased by Value-Added Tax (Threshold for Advanced Payment) (Amendment) Order, 1994, w.e.f. 10 Dec 1994.

EUROPEAN COMMUNITIES (VALUE-ADDED TAX) REGULATIONS, 1993

(SI No. 345 of 1993)

WHEREAS the Sixth Council Directive of 17 May, 1977 on the harmonisation of the laws of the Member States relating to turnover taxes - Common system of value added tax: uniform basis of assessment (Council Directive No. 77/388/EEC), as last amended by Council Directive No. 92/111/EEC of 14 December, 1992, establishes rules as to when value added tax becomes chargeable on supplies of goods, supplies of services and intra-Community acquisitions of goods;

AND WHEREAS paragraph 5 of Article 22 of Council Directive No. 77/388/EEC permits Member States to require of taxable persons an interim payment of value added tax;

AND WHEREAS, in its judgment of 20 October, 1993 in Case C-10/92 Maurizio Balocchi v Ministero delle Finanze dello Stato, the Court of Justice of the European Communities held that, while interim payments were permissible, they could not be used to require a taxable person to make payment where the value added tax had not become chargeable;

NOW, I, BERTIE AHERN, Minister for Finance, in exercise of the powers conferred on me by section 3 of the European Communities Act, 1972 (No. 27 of 1972), and for the purpose of giving further effect to Council Directive No. 77/388/EEC of 17 May, 1977, as last amended by Council Directive No. 92/111/EEC of 14 December, 1992, hereby make the following Regulations:

1.　　(1)　　These Regulations may be cited as the European Communities (Value-Added Tax) Regulations, 1993.

　　　　(2)　　These Regulations shall be construed together with the Value-Added Tax Acts 1972 to 1993.

2.　　In these Regulations-

"advance payment" means the advance payment referred to in section 19(6) of the Principal Act;

"due date" means the due date referred to in section 19(6) of the Principal Act;

"November liability" means-

(a)　　the amount of tax which would be payable in accordance with section 19(3) of the Principal Act, or

(b)　　nil, where an amount of tax would be repayable in accordance with section 20(1) of the Principal Act,

　　　　if the November period were to be treated as a taxable period;

"November period" means the month of November immediately preceding a due date;

"the Principal Act" means the Value-added Tax Act, 1972.

3.   Notwithstanding the provisions of section 19(6) of the Principal Act, for the purposes of the application of the said section 19(6) and of these Regulations, all references in the said section 19(6) to the 1st day of December shall be construed as references to the 10th day of December.

4.   Subject to his complying with Regulation 5, a taxable person who is liable to pay an advance payment in accordance with section 19(6) of the Principal Act may opt, as an alternative, to pay his November liability and in such circumstances all the provisions of the said section 19(6) shall apply to the November liability as if it were the advance payment.

5.   Where a taxable person desires to avail of the option provided for in Regulation 4, he shall, by the due date, notify the Collector-General accordingly in writing and declare his November liability to the Collector-General in writing.

GIVEN under my Official Seal,
this 24th day of November, 1993.

BERTIE AHERN,
Minister for Finance.

EXPLANATORY NOTE.

Section19(6) of the VAT Act, as modified by S.I. No. 303 of 1993, requires that an advance payment of VAT be made in December 1993, and in December in subsequent years, by any taxable person whose total net annual VAT liability exceeds a threshold of £300,000 in the 12 months ending in the preceding June.

These Regulations provide that the taxable persons concerned may opt to make the advance payment on the basis of their actual November liability rather than on the basis provided for in the Act (i.e. one-twelfth of their total net VAT for the relevant year).

VALUE-ADDED TAX (REFUND OF TAX) (NO 26) ORDER, 1994

(SI No. 165 of 1994)

> This Order revoked by para6, Value Added Tax (Refund of Tax) (No.28) Order 1996 (1996 S.I. No. 98) with effect from 4 April 1996.

I, BERTIE AHERN, Minister for Finance, in exercise of the powers conferred on me by section 20(3) of the Value-Added Tax Act, 1972 (No.22 of 1972), hereby order as follows:

1.   This Order may be cited as the Value-Added Tax (Refund of Tax) (No.26) Order, 1994.

2.   (1)   In this Order-

"the Act" means the Value-Added Tax Act, 1972;

"qualifying person" means a person who-

(a)   is engaged in the business of carriage for reward of persons by road under contracts for group transport, and

(b)   has complied with all the obligations imposed on the person by the Act, the Income Tax Acts, the Corporation Tax Acts or the Capital Gains Tax Acts, and any instruments made thereunder, in relation to-

(i)   the payment or remittance of the taxes, interest and penalties required to be paid or remitted thereunder, and

(ii)   the delivery of returns;

"qualifying vehicle" means-

(a)   a single-deck touring coach having dimensions as designated by the manufacturer of not less than 3,350 millimetres in height, not less than 10,000 millimetres in length and not less than 1,400 millimetres in floor height, or

(b)   a double-deck touring coach having dimensions as designated by the manufacturer of not more than 4,300 millimetres in height and not less than 10,000 millimetres in length.

(2)   In this Order a reference to a paragraph or subparagraph is to a paragraph or subparagraph of this Order, unless is it indicated that reference to some other provision is intended.

3.   (1)   Unless the provisions in subparagraph (2) apply, a qualifying person who has borne or paid tax on-

(a)   the supply to such person or hiring (other than hiring for a period of less than six consecutive months) to such person, or

(b)   the intra-Community acquisition or importation by such person,

of a qualifying vehicle used by such person in the State for the carriage for reward of persons by road under contracts for group transport shall, subject to the conditions specified in paragraph 4, be repaid the full tax so borne or paid provided that-

(i)   the supply, intra-Community acquisition or importation of the vehicle which gave rise to such tax occurred when the vehicle was not more than two years old, or

(ii)   the hiring or leasing of the vehicle (other than hiring or leasing for a period of less than six consecutive months) which gave rise to such tax was on the basis of a contract for such hire or lease first entered into when the vehicle was not more than two years old.

(2)   Where a qualifying person is a taxable person and makes an intra-Community acquisition, in respect of which tax is chargeable, of a qualifying vehicle which at the time of the said intra-Community acquisition was not more than two years old and which is used by the qualifying person in the State for the carriage for reward of persons by road under contracts for group transport, the qualifying person shall, subject to the conditions specified in paragraph 5, be entitled to reclaim an amount of tax equivalent to the tax chargeable on the said intra-Community acquisition as if such amount of tax were deductible tax under section 12 of the Act.

(3)   The provisions of subparagraph (1) or (2) shall apply only where-

(a)   the supply, hire or leasing, intra-Community acquisition or importation referred to in subparagraph (1) or (2) occurred on or after the 27th day of January, 1994, and

(b)   the qualifying person is not entitled to a deduction or repayment-

(i)   by any other provision of the Act or regulations made thereunder, or

(ii)   under any other enactment administered by the Revenue Commissioners of any portion of the tax paid or payable in respect of the qualifying vehicle.

4.   The conditions to be fulfilled by a person in order to obtain a repayment of tax under this Order in accordance with subparagraph (1) of paragraph 3 are as follows:

(a)   the person shall claim a repayment of the tax, by completing such form as is provided for that purpose by the Revenue Commissioners, and shall certify the particulars shown on such form to be correct;

(b)   that the person is a qualifying person shall be established to the satisfaction of the Revenue Commissioners by that person;

(c)   the person shall produce-

(i)   in the case of a supply to that person of a qualifying vehicle, an invoice, issued to that person in accordance with section 17(12)(a)(i) of the Act, establishing the amount of tax borne by that person on that supply, or

(ii)   in the case of the hire or lease of a qualifying vehicle, a copy of the agreement or contract specific to the vehicle in question and, in respect of each repayment claim, an invoice, issued to that person in accordance with section 17(12)(a)(i) of the Act, establishing the amount of tax borne by that person, or

(iii)   in the case of an intra-Community acquisition of a qualifying vehicle, an official receipt or other document establishing the amount of tax paid by that person on the intra-Community acquisition, together with the invoice issued to that person by the supplier in the Member State of supply, or

(iv)   in the case of an importation of a qualifying vehicle, an official receipt or other document establishing the amount of tax paid by that person on the importation and indicating the number of the relevant customs entry.

5.   In order to reclaim an amount of tax under this Order in accordance with subparagraph (2) of paragraph 3, a taxable person shall reclaim the tax in the return which such person is obliged to furnish in accordance with section 19(3) of the Act and such person shall certify the particulars shown on the relevant return form to be correct.

6.   The Value-Added Tax (Refund of Tax) (No 24) Order, 1993 (SI No 134 of 1993) is hereby revoked.

GIVEN under my Official Seal,
this 1st day of June, 1994.

BERTIE AHERN,
Minister for Finance.

EXPLANATORY NOTE.

This Order replaces SI No.134 of 1993. The Order provides for a full repayment of VAT to exempt coach operators, subject to certain conditions, in respect of the tax paid on touring coaches of certain age and dimensions.

VALUE-ADDED TAX (DETERMINATION OF TAX DUE BY REFERENCE TO MONEYS RECEIVED) (AMENDMENT) REGULATIONS, 1994

(SI No. 259 of 1994)

> This Regulation was revoked by regulation 44, Value-Added Tax Regulations, 2006 (2006 S.I. No. 548) w.e.f. 1 November 2006

The Revenue Commissioners, in exercise of the powers conferred on them by sections 14 of the Value-Added Tax Act, 1972 (No. 22 of 1972), hereby make the following Regulations:

1. (1) These Regulations may be cited as the Value-Added Tax (Determination of Tax Due by Reference to Moneys Received) (Amendment) Regulations, 1994.

   (2) The Principal Regulations and these Regulations shall be construed together as one and may be cited together as the Value-Added Tax (Determination of Tax Due by Reference to Moneys Received) Regulations, 1992 and 1994.

2. In these Regulations-

   "the Act" means the Value-Added Tax Act, 1972;

   "the Principal Regulations" means the Value-Added Tax (Determination of Tax Due by Reference to Moneys Received) Regulations 1992 (S.I. No. 306 of 1992).

3. Regulation 3 of the Principal Regulations is hereby amended-

   (1) by the substitution of "section 14(1)(a)" for "section 14(1)", and

   (2) by the substitution of "persons who are not registered persons" for "unregistered persons".

4. The Principal Regulations are hereby amended by the substitution of the following Regulation for Regulation 4:

   "4. (1) An application by a taxable person (hereafter referred to in this Regulation as the 'applicant') for authorisation to use the moneys received basis of accounting shall be made in writing to the Revenue Commissioners and shall include-

   (a) the applicant's name and address;

   (b) the number assigned, if any, to the applicant for the purposes of registration under section 9 of the Act (the VAT registration number);

   (c) the nature of the business activities carried on by the applicant.

(2)   An applicant who claims eligibility under section 14(1) (a) of the Act shall include in any application made in accordance with this Regulation particulars of-

(a)   the percentage of the applicant's turnover from taxable supplies, if any, which related to supplies to persons who are not registered persons-

(i)   in the period of 12 months ended on the last day of the taxable period prior to the application, or

(ii)   in the period from the commencement of his business activities to the last day of the taxable period referred to in clause (i) of this subparagraph,

whichever is the shorter; and,

(b)   the applicant's estimate of the percentage of the said applicant's turnover from taxable supplies which will relate to supplies to persons who are not registered persons in the period of 12 months commencing with the beginning of the taxable period during which the application is made.

(3)   An applicant who claims eligibility under section 14(1) (b) of the Act shall include in any application made in accordance with this Regulation particulars of-

(a)   the amount of the applicant's turnover from taxable supplies in the period of 12 months ended on the last day of the taxable period prior to the application; and

(b)   the applicant's estimate of the said applicant's turnover from taxable supplies in the period of 12 months commencing with the beginning of the taxable period during which the application is made.".

5.   The Principal Regulations are hereby amended by the substitution of the following paragraph for paragraph (1) of Regulation 9:

"(1)   A taxable person authorised in accordance with Regulation 5 shall notify the Revenue Commissioners in writing whenever, for any period of four consecutive calendar months during the validity of such authorisation, the following occurs:

(a)   the percentage of the taxable person's turnover from taxable supplies to persons who are not registered persons is less than 90 per cent; and

(b)   the taxable person's turnover from taxable supplies is such that in the twelve months immediately following such four months period it is likely to exceed £250,000,

and notification in accordance with this Regulation shall be made within 30 days of the end of such four month period.".

GIVEN this 8th day of August, 1994.

D. B. QUIGLEY,
Revenue Commissioner.

EXPLANATORY NOTE.

Section 97 of the Finance Act, 1994 amended the moneys received basis of accounting for VAT to allow taxable persons with a turnover of not more than £250,000 to use that method of accounting for VAT. These Regulations amend the Value-Added Tax (Determination of Tax Due by Reference to Moneys Received) Regulations, 1992 (S.I. No.306 of 1992) to take account of that extended eligibility. A minor technical amendment to Regulation 3 of those Regulations is also being made.

VALUE-ADDED TAX (THRESHOLD FOR ADVANCE PAYMENT) (AMENDMENT) ORDER, 1994

(SI No. 342 of 1994)

This Order revoked by s114, FA97, w.e.f. 7 November 1997.

I, BERTIE AHERN, Minister for Finance, in exercise of the powers conferred on me by section 19(6)(h) (inserted by section 92 (c) of the Finance Act, 1993 (No 13 of 1993)) of the Value-Added Tax Act, 1972 (No 22 of 1972), hereby order as follows:

1.   This Order may be cited as the Value-Added Tax (Threshold for Advance Payment) (Amendment) Order, 1994.

2.   In this Order-

"the Act" means the Value-Added Tax Act, 1972 (No 22 of 1972);

"due date" means a due date (as construed by reference to the European Communities (Value-Added Tax) Regulations, 1993 (SI No 345 of 1993)) for the purposes of section19(6) of the Act;

"threshold" means a threshold for the purposes of section 19(6) of the Act.

3.   The threshold to be applied for the purposes of section 19(6) of the Act to the due date which is the 10th day of December, 1994, and to each successive due date thereafter, shall be £1,000,000 and, accordingly, for the purposes of section 19(6)(h)(i)(II) of the Act the threshold of £300,000 specified in Article 3 of the Value-Added Tax (Threshold for Advance Payment) Order, 1993 (SI No 303 of 1993), is hereby increased to £1,000,000.

GIVEN under my Official Seal,
this 14th day of November, 1994.

BERTIE AHERN,
Minister for Finance.

EXPLANATORY NOTE.

Section 19(6) of the VAT Act, together with SI No.345 of 1993, requires that an advance payment of VAT be made in December 1993, and subsequent years by any taxable person whose total net annual VAT liability exceeds a threshold.

The Order amends SI No.303 of 1993 to further increase this threshold from £300,000 to £1,000,000 in respect of the advance payment to be made in December 1994 and in subsequent years.

DISABLED DRIVERS AND DISABLED PASSENGERS (TAX CONCESSIONS) REGULATIONS, 1994

(SI No. 353 of 1994)

I, BERTIE AHERN, Minister for Finance, in exercise of the powers conferred on me by section 92 (as amended by section 17 of the Finance (No.2) Act, 1992 (No. 28 of 1992)) of the Finance Act, 1989 (No.10 of 1989), and after consultation with the Minister for Health and the Minister for the Environment, hereby make the following Regulations:

1.   These Regulations may be cited as the Disabled Drivers and disabled Passengers (Tax Concessions) Regulations, 1994, and shall come into operation on the 1st day of December, 1994.

2.   (1)   In these Regulations-

"adapted", in relation to a vehicle, does not include adaptations of production line models which are available from the manufacturer or assembler thereof as an optional extra, and "adaptation" shall be construed accordingly;

"authorised person" means a person authorised under section 136 of the Finance Act, 1992 (No.9 of 1992);

"Board medical certificate" means a certificate duly completed in the form prescribed in the Second Schedule and issued by the Disabled Drivers Medical Board of Appeal or a certificate duly completed in the form prescribed in the Second Schedule to the Disabled Drivers (Tax Concessions) Regulations, 1989 (S.I. No. 340 of 1989), and so issued under those Regulations;

"conversion" has the meaning assigned to it in section 130 of the Finance Act, 1992;

"disabled driver" means a severely and permanently disabled person who possesses a certificate of the kind referred to in paragraph (a) or (b) of Regulation 4 and whose disablement is of such a nature that the person concerned could not drive a vehicle unless it is specially constructed or adapted to take account of that disablement;

"disabled passenger" means a severely and permanently disabled person who possesses a certificate of the kind referred to in paragraph (a) or (b) of Regulation 4 and for whom a vehicle has been specially constructed or adapted to the extent prescribed in Regulation 10(1)(a), to take account of that passenger's disablement;

"disabled person" means a person who is severely and permanently disabled, fulfilling one or more of the medical criteria set out in Regulation 3;

"licensing authority" has the meaning assigned to it in section 130 of the Finance Act, 1992;

"purchased" does not include any form of lease arrangement;

"qualifying organisation" means a philanthropic organisation which is not funded primarily by-

(a)   the State,

(b)   any board established by statute, or

(c)   any public or local authority,

which organisation is chiefly engaged, in a voluntary capacity on a non-commercial basis, in the care and transport of severely and permanently disabled persons and which is recognised as such, for the purposes of these Regulations, by the Revenue Commissioner;

"registered" has the meaning assigned to it in section 130 of the Finance Act, 1992;

"residual value-added tax" means an amount determined by the Revenue Commissioners as being equivalent to the amount of value-added tax which would be included in the open market selling price of a vehicle if it were sold by an authorised person at the time specified in these Regulations;

"residual vehicle registration tax" means an amount determined by the Revenue Commissioners as being equivalent to the amount of vehicle registration tax which would be chargeable if that vehicle were liable for such tax at the time specified in these Regulations;

"vehicle" has the meaning assigned to it in section 130 of the Finance Act, 1992.

(2)   In these Regulations a reference to a Regulation or Schedule is to a Regulation of, or Schedule to, these Regulations and a reference to a paragraph or subparagraph is to a paragraph or subparagraph of the provision in which the reference occurs.

Medical criteria

3.   For the purposes of section 92(2)(a) of the Finance Act, 1989, the eligibility on medical grounds of disabled persons who are severely and permanently disabled shall be assessed by reference to any one or more of the following medical criteria:

(a)   persons who are wholly or almost wholly without the use of both legs;

(b)   persons wholly without the use of one of their legs and almost wholly without the use of the other leg such that they are severely restricted as to movement of their lower limbs;

(c)   persons without both hands or without both arms;

(d)   persons without one or both legs;

(e)   persons wholly or almost wholly without the use of both hands or arms and wholly or almost wholly without the use of one leg;

(f)   persons having the medical condition of dwarfism and who have serious difficulties of movement of the lower limbs.

4.   Without prejudice to Regulation 5, a claim for repayment or remission under these Regulations shall be allowed only where the person who makes the claim, or in connection with whom the claim is made, is in possession of either-

(a)   a primary medical certificate duly completed in the form prescribed in the First Schedule as evidence of qualifying disablement, signed, dated and endorsed with the official stamp by the appropriate Director of Community Care and Medical Officer of Health, or

(b)   a Board medical certificate duly completed in the form prescribed in the Second Schedule as evidence of qualifying disablement, signed and dated by a member of the Disabled Drivers Medical Board of Appeal:

Provided that compliance with this Regulation may be waived by the Revenue Commissioners in the case of a claim made by a qualifying organisation.

[4A. (1)   A Director of Community Care and Medical Officer of Health shall not consider an application under these Regulations for a primary medical certificate where a determination has been made by the Disabled Drivers Medical Board of Appeal within the period of 6 months prior to the date of the making of the application unless the application is accompanied by a medical certificate from a registered medical practitioner indicating that the practitioner has formed the opinion that the person concerned is severely and permanently disabled as respects one or more of the criteria specified in Regulation 3.

(2)   Each subsequent application by that person for a primary medical certificate shall be accompanied by a medical certificate from a registered medical practitioner indicating that the practitioner has formed the opinion that the medical condition of the person concerned has materially disimproved since the previous application.][1]

5.   Any person who is deemed, by virtue of section 92(3)(b) of the Finance Act, 1989, to be a person who possesses a primary medical certificate shall be deemed to have satisfied the Revenue Commissioners and the licensing authority concerned that that person is a disabled driver or a disabled passenger as the case may be.

[*Medical Board of Appeal*

6.   (1)   (a)   Subject to paragraph (2) and Regulation 19 (3), on the nomination of the Minister for Health and Children, [the Minister for Finance shall appoint a minimum of 5 medical practitioners][2] to the Disabled Drivers Medical Board of Appeal (in this Regulation referred to as the 'Board') for a period of 4 years in each case and any such practitioner may be reappointed by the Minister for Finance on the nomination of the Minister for Health and Children for a further such period or periods.

(b)   [One of the appointed medical practitioners][3] shall be appointed by the Minister for Finance to be the chairperson of the Board.

(c)   Three members of the Board shall constitute a quorum for a meeting of the Board.

(d)   In the absence of the chairperson from a meeting of the Board, the members present shall elect one of their number to chair that meeting.

(e)   The Board shall be independent in the exercise of its functions.

[...][4]

(3)   Whenever the Minister for Health and Children so requests, for reasons stated in writing, the Minister for Finance shall remove any named person from the Board.

(4)   (a)   A person who is dissatisfied by a decision of a Director of Community Care and Medical Officer of Health in respect of primary medical certification may appeal to the Board within 28 days of the person first being informed of that decision, or such longer period as the Board may allow, and the person concerned shall be informed of the right to so appeal.

(b)   An appeal under subparagraph (a) shall be accompanied by a copy of the decision so appealed.

(5)   The Board shall inform the appellant in writing of its decision and

(a)   where the Board determines that the appellant meets one or more of the criteria specified in Regulation 3, it shall issue a Board Medical Certificate,

(b)   where the Board determines that the appellant does not meet the criteria specified in Regulation 3, it shall refuse the appeal.

(6)   Where a person has previously made an appeal to the Board, a subsequent appeal to the Board shall be accompanied by a copy of

the refusal of the Director of Community Care and Medical Officer of Health of the application made under Regulation 4A and by a copy of the determination of the Board previously so made.][5]

7.   Where a licensing authority or the Revenue Commissioners have reason to believe that the person named on a primary medical certificate or a Board medical certificate or who was deemed to have satisfied the said authority or Commissioners under the terms of Regulation 5, does not fulfil any one of the criteria set out in Regulation 3, they shall refer such person to the Board who shall cancel the primary medical certificate or Board medical certificate in question, if they consider it appropriate to do so.

Reliefs for disabled drivers

8.   (1)   Where a person satisfies the Revenue Commissioners that that person is a disabled driver and has borne or paid value-added tax, vehicle registration tax or residual vehicle registration tax in respect of a vehicle or in respect of the adaptation of a vehicle which-

(a)   is specially constructed or adapted to take account of that person's disablement,

(b)   is purchased by that person,

(c)   is registered in the name of that person, and

(d)   is fitted with an engine whose capacity is not greater than 2,000 cubic centimetres,

that person shall be entitled to be repaid the said amounts of tax and residual vehicle registration tax, subject to the limit specified in Regulation 9 for the purposes of this Regulation:

Provided that the Revenue Commissioners shall repay residual vehicle registration tax only where the person concerned has purchased the vehicle in question from an authorised person.

(2)   Where at the time of registration of a vehicle in the name of a person who satisfies the Revenue Commissioners that that person is a disabled driver and the vehicle in question complies with the provisions set out at subparagraphs (a), (b) and (d) of paragraph (1), the Revenue Commissioners shall remit the vehicle registration tax payable, subject to the limit specified in Regulation 9 for the purposes of this Regulation.

(3)   Where, after these Regulations come into force, a person becomes a severely and permanently disabled person who fulfils one of the medical criteria set out in Regulation 3 after that person has purchased a vehicle which complies with the provisions set out at subparagraphs (c) and (d) of paragraph (1), and the vehicle is specially adapted to take account of that person's disablement, that person shall be entitled to be repaid-

(a)   the amount of residual value-added tax and residual vehicle registration tax appropriate to the vehicle at the time such person lodges a claim with the Revenue Commissioners, and

(b)   the value-added tax charged in respect of the adaptation of that vehicle,

subject to the limit specified in Regulation 9 for the purposes of this Regulation.

(4)   Where a person receives a repayment or remission under paragraph (1) or (2), that person shall undertake-

(a)   to use the vehicle in question for a period of 2 years from the date of purchase, and to inform the Revenue Commissioners immediately if any circumstances arise during that period where the vehicle is sold or otherwise disposed of by that person, and

(b)   to abide by the provisions of Regulation 15.

(5)   Where a person receives a repayment or remission under paragraph (3), that person shall undertake-

(a)   to use the vehicle in question for a period of 2 years from the date on which the Revenue Commissioners receive the application for the repayment, and to inform the Revenue Commissioners immediately if any circumstances arise during that period where the vehicle is sold or otherwise disposed of by that person, and

(b)   to abide by the provisions of Regulation 15.

9.   The total amount to be repaid and remitted under Regulation 8 or under paragraph (3) and, in so far as it relates to that paragraph, paragraph (4) of Regulation 12 shall not exceed [€9,525][6] in respect of any vehicle.

Reliefs for disabled passengers

10.   (1)   Where a person satisfies the Revenue Commissioners that that person is a severely and permanently disabled passenger or a family member of such a disabled passenger residing with and responsible for the transportation of that disabled passenger and such person has borne or paid value-added tax, vehicle registration tax or residual vehicle registration tax in respect of a vehicle or in respect of the adaptation of a vehicle which-

(a)   has been specially constructed or adapted for use by that disabled passenger, and where the vehicle is so adapted, the cost of such adaptation excluding value-added tax consists of not less than the amount specified for the purpose in section 92(1) of the Finance Act, 1989:

Provided that in calculating the cost of adaptation of such vehicle, if the Revenue Commissioners so approve, there shall be included-

(i)   the cost of conversion of that vehicle, excluding the additional vehicle registration tax incurred in such conversion, and

(ii)   the purchase cost excluding value-added tax of any adaptations previously fitted to another vehicle adapted for use by that disabled passenger, and refitted to the vehicle in question,

(b)   has been purchased by the disabled passenger or by the said family member of that disabled passenger for the purpose of transporting that person, and

(c)   is fitted with an engine whose capacity is not greater than 4,000 cubic centimetres,

the person who has borne or paid the said amounts of tax and residual vehicle registration tax shall be entitled to be repaid same, subject to the limit specified in Regulation II for the purposes of this Regulation:

Provided that the Revenue Commissioners shall repay residual vehicle registration tax only where the said person has purchased the vehicle in question from an authorised person.

(2)   Where at the time of registration of a vehicle by a severely and permanently disabled passenger or by a family member of a severely and permanently disabled passenger residing with and responsible for the transportation of that disabled person and the vehicle in question complies with the provisions set out at subparagraphs (a), (b) and (c) of paragraph (1), the Revenue Commissioners shall remit the vehicle registration tax payable, subject to the limit specified in Regulation 11 for the purposes of this Regulation.

(3)   Where, after these Regulations come into force, a person becomes a severely and permanently disabled person who fulfils one of the medical criteria set out in Regulation 3 after that person or a family member of that person residing with and responsible for the transportation of that person has purchased a vehicle which complies with the provision set out at paragraph (1)(c) and the vehicle is adapted to the extent outlined in paragraph (1)(a) for the disabled person's use as a passenger, the person who has purchased the vehicle shall be entitled to be repaid-

(a)   the amount of residual value-added tax and residual vehicle registration tax appropriate to the vehicle at the time such person lodges a claim with the Revenue Commissioners, and

(b)   the value-added tax charged in respect of the adaptation of that vehicle,

subject to the limit specified in Regulation 11 for the purposes of this Regulation.

(4)   (a)   Where a person receives a repayment or remission under paragraph (1) or (2)

of this Regulation that person shall undertake-

(i)   to use the vehicle in question for the transportation of the disabled passenger in question, for a period of 2 years from the date of purchase, and to inform the Revenue Commissioners immediately if any circumstances arise during that period where the vehicle is sold or otherwise disposed of by that person, and

(ii)   to abide by the provisions of Regulation 15.

(b)   Where a person receives a repayment or remission under paragraph (3) that person shall undertake-

(i)   to use the vehicle in question for the transportation of the disabled passenger in question, for a period of 2 years from the date on which the Revenue Commissioners receive the application for repayment, and to inform the Revenue Commissioners immediately if any circumstances arise during that period where the vehicle is sold or otherwise disposed of by that person, and

(ii)   to abide by the provisions of Regulation 15.

(c)   Where the Revenue Commissioners accept a claim under this Regulation in respect of the transport of a disabled passenger, they shall not accept a claim (other than in the circumstances to which Regulation 15 applies) relating to any further vehicle in respect of the transport of the same passenger for a period of 2 years from the date of purchase of the vehicle for which the claim was accepted where such claim was made under the provisions of paragraph (1) or (2), and a period of 2 years from the date of receipt of the application by the Revenue Commissioners, where such application was made under the provisions of paragraph (3).

(d)   Where the Revenue Commissioners have accepted a claim for repayment of vehicle registration tax in respect of the transport of a disabled person as passenger under the Disabled Drivers (Tax Concessions) Regulations, 1989, they shall not accept a claim relating to any further vehicle in respect of the transport of the same passenger for a period of 2 years from the date of purchase of the vehicle for which the claim was accepted:

Provided that the Revenue Commissioners may waive this provision in exceptional circumstances subject to the refund of a portion of the repayment, calculated in accordance with the formula set out in Regulation 15(1).

(5)   (a)   In exceptional circumstances, the Revenue Commissioners may waive the condition concerning residency of a claimant under Regulation 10.

        (b)   The Revenue Commissioners shall waive the conditions concerning both family membership and residency of a claimant under Regulation 10 in the case of a claim lodged by a person appointed by the President of the High Court to act on behalf of a disabled passenger who is a Ward of Court.

11.   The total amount to be repaid and remitted under Regulation 10 shall not exceed [€15,875][6] in respect of any vehicle.

Reliefs for qualifying organisations

12.   (1)   Where a qualifying organisation satisfies the Revenue Commissioners that it has borne or paid value-added tax, vehicle registration tax or residual vehicle registration tax in respect of a vehicle or in respect of the adaptation of a vehicle which, subject to paragraph (2)-

        (a)   is specially constructed or adapted for the transport of disabled persons, and where the vehicle is so adapted the cost of such adaptation, excluding value-added tax, consists of not less than the amount specified for the purpose in subsection 92(1) of the Finance Act, 1989:

            Provided that in calculating the cost of adaptation of such vehicle, if the Revenue Commissioners so approve, there shall be included-

            (i)   the cost of conversion of that vehicle, excluding the additional vehicle registration tax incurred in such conversion, and

            (ii)   the purchase cost excluding value-added tax of any adaptations previously fitted to another vehicle adapted for use by that qualifying organisation, and refitted to the vehicle in question,

        (b)   is purchased by that organisation,

        (c)   is registered in the name of that organisation, and

        (d)   is fitted with an engine whose capacity is not greater than 4,000 cubic centimetres, that organisation shall be entitled to be repaid the said amounts of tax and residual vehicle registration tax, subject to the limit specified in Regulation 13 for the purposes of this paragraph:

Provided that the Revenue Commissioners shall repay residual vehicle registration tax only where the said organisation has purchased the vehicle in question from an authorised person.

(2)   Where the vehicle referred to in paragraph (1) has been specially constructed or adapted for the transport of 5 or more disabled persons, the provisions of subparagraph (1)(d) and of Regulation 13 shall not apply where the seating capacity in the vehicle for passengers who are not disabled persons is not greater than twice the seating capacity for disabled passengers.

(3)   Where a qualifying organisation satisfies the Revenue Commissioners that it has borne or paid value-added tax, vehicle registration tax or residual vehicle registration tax in respect of a vehicle or in respect of the adaptation of a vehicle which-

(a)   is specially constructed or adapted to take account of the disablement of a disabled person as driver,

(b)   is purchased by that organisation,

(c)   is registered in the name of that organisation, and

(d)   is fitted with an engine whose capacity is not greater than 2,000 cubic centimetres,

that organisation shall be entitled to be repaid the said amounts of tax and residual vehicle registration tax, subject to the limit specified in Regulation 9 for the purposes of this paragraph:

Provided that the Revenue Commissioners shall repay residual vehicle registration tax only where the said organisation has purchased the vehicle in question from an authorised person.

(4)   Where, at the time of registration of a vehicle by a qualifying organisation, the Revenue Commissioners are satisfied that the vehicle in question complies with the provisions set out at subparagraphs (a), (b) and (d) of paragraph (1) or set out at subparagraphs (a), (b) and (d) of paragraph (3), as appropriate, they shall remit the vehicle registration tax payable.

(5)   The Revenue Commissioners shall give a repayment or remission under this Regulation only where they are satisfied that the vehicle in question is a reasonable requirement of the organisation making the claim, having regard, inter alia, to the number of disabled persons being transported by that organisation, and the number and capacity of vehicles already owned by that organisation.

(6)   Where an organisation receives a repayment or remission under paragraph (1) or (3) that organisation shall undertake-

(a)   to use the vehicle in question for a period of 2 years from the date of purchase, and to inform the Revenue Commissioners immediately if any circumstances arise during that period where the vehicle is sold or otherwise disposed of by that organisation, and

(b)   to abide by the provisions of Regulation 15.

(7)   The Revenue Commissioners shall consult the National Rehabilitation Board in respect of each organisation which applies to them under these Regulations.

(8)   Where the Revenue Commissioners have reasonable cause to believe that a qualifying organisation should no longer be entitled to the benefit of these Regulations, they shall consult the National Rehabilitation Board and may withdraw the concessions from such organisation.

13.   The total amount to be repaid and remitted under paragraph (1) and, in so far as it relates to that paragraph, paragraph (4) of Regulation 12 shall not exceed [€15,875][6] in respect of any vehicle.

Passenger vehicles qualifying more than once

14.   Where a repayment or remission has been granted under Regulation 10 or 12 in respect of a vehicle which is subsequently purchased for the transport of a different disabled passenger or by a different qualifying organisation, and the adaptations remain in the vehicle at the time of such subsequent purchase, the requirements set out at Regulation 10(1) (a) or 12 (1)(a), as the case may be, shall be deemed to be fulfilled.

Refunds to the Revenue Commissioners

15.   (1)   Where a beneficiary of a repayment or remission under Regulation 8 or 10 in respect of a vehicle (in this Regulation referred to as "the first-mentioned vehicle")-

(a)   sells it or otherwise disposes of it within 2 years of the date of purchase or, in the case of a person referred to in Regulation 8(3) or 10(3), within 2 years of the date on which the Revenue Commissioners receive the application for repayment, or

(b)   claims a repayment or remission under the same Regulation in respect of a subsequent vehicle purchased by that person within 2 years of purchasing the first-mentioned vehicle, or, in the case of a person referred to in Regulation 8(3) or 10(3), within 2 years of the date on which the Revenue Commissioners receive the application for repayment,

such person shall refund to the Revenue Commissioners a portion of the amount which was either or both repaid and remitted on the first-mentioned vehicle, calculated by the

Revenue Commissioners according to the following formula:

$$A \times \frac{B}{(C + D)}$$

where:

A is the open market selling price of the first-mentioned vehicle on the date of its sale or disposal or on the date of purchase of the subsequent vehicle, whichever is applicable,

B is the total amount repaid or remitted in respect of the first-mentioned vehicle and any adaptations thereto,

C is the open market selling price of the first-mentioned vehicle at the time of its purchase by the beneficiary, and

D is the cost including value-added tax of any adaptations to the first-mentioned vehicle on which repayment was claimed by the beneficiary.

(2)   The refund referred to in paragraph (1) shall be paid to the Revenue Commissioners within one month of the sale or disposal of the first-mentioned vehicle, but where the circumstances referred to at paragraph (1)(b) apply, not later than the time of the repayment or remission of any tax in respect of the subsequent vehicle.

(3)   Where a qualifying organisation which receives a repayment or remission under Regulation 12 in respect of a vehicle sells it or otherwise disposes of it within 2 years of the date of purchase such organisation shall refund to the Revenue Commissioners a portion of the amount which was either or both repaid and remitted on the vehicle, calculated by the Revenue Commissioners according to the following formula:

$$A \times \frac{B}{(C + D)}$$

where:

A is the open market selling price of the vehicle on the date of its sale or disposal,

B is the total amount repaid or remitted in respect of the vehicle and any adaptations thereto,

C is the open market selling price of the vehicle at the time of its purchase by the organisation, and

D is the cost including value-added tax of any adaptations to the vehicle on which repayment was claimed by the organisation.

(4)   The refund referred to in paragraph (3) shall be paid to the Revenue Commissioners within one month of the sale or disposal of the vehicle in question.

(5)   The Revenue Commissioners shall not repay or remit any tax or residual vehicle registration tax under Regulation 8, 10 or 12 in respect of any vehicle unless the provisions of paragraph (2) or (4), as the case may be, have been fulfilled.

(6)   In exceptional cases, and subject to such conditions as they consider necessary in each such case, the Revenue Commissioners may reduce the amount of the refund required under this Regulation.

Fuel repayments

16.   (1)   The excise duty paid on any fuel used for combustion in the engine of a vehicle on which repayment or remission of tax, or residual vehicle registration tax has been granted in accordance with these Regulations shall be repaid by the Revenue Commissioners where the use of the fuel was related to the transportation of the disabled person or persons concerned whether as driver or passenger.

(2)   Where the repayment or remission of tax or residual vehicle registration tax was made under Regulation 8 or 10, the repayment of excise duty on fuel referred to in paragraph (1) shall be limited to the duty on an annual maximum of 600 gallons per beneficiary.

(3)   Where the repayment or remission of tax or residual vehicle registration tax was made under Regulation 12, the repayment of excise duty on fuel referred to in paragraph (1) shall be limited to the duty on an annual maximum of 900 gallons per vehicle.

(4)   The excise duty paid on any fuel used for combustion in the engine of a vehicle which would have qualified for repayment or remission of value-added tax, vehicle registration tax or residual vehicle registration tax in accordance with these Regulations but for the fact that the vehicle was purchased prior to the coming into effect of these Regulations, shall be repaid by the Revenue Commissioners where the use of the fuel was related to the transportation of the disabled person or persons concerned whether as driver or passenger, and the provisions of paragraphs (2) and (3) shall apply with any necessary modifications.

Road Tax

17.   The licensing authority shall remit the excise duty which would, but for this provision, be payable under section 1 of the Finance (Excise Duties) (Vehicles) Act, 1952 (No. 24 of 1952) (being the duty known as road tax), on any vehicle which qualifies for relief under regulation 8, 10 or 12.

General

18.   (1)   A person or organisation wishing to avail of the provisions of Regulation 8, 10 or 12 shall complete the Declaration in the Third Schedule in respect of each vehicle involved, and such claim form as may be provided for the purpose by the Revenue Commissioners and present them to the Revenue Commissioners, together with such documentary evidence as they shall require.

(2)   A person or organisation wishing to avail of the provisions of Regulation 17 shall apply to the appropriate licensing authority and produce to it evidence that the vehicle has qualified for relief under Regulation 8, 10 or 12, and, in the case of an applicant who has qualified for relief under Regulation 8, a valid current driving licence.

Revocation and transitional provisions, etc.

19.   (1)   The Disabled Drivers (Tax Concessions) Regulations, 1989 (S.I. No.340 of 1989), are hereby revoked.

(2)   Any primary medical certificate or other certificate issued under the Regulations revoked by paragraph (1) shall be deemed to be a valid certificate for the purposes of these Regulations, and such certificate and person named thereon shall be subject to the provisions of Regulation 7.

(3)   Notwithstanding paragraph (1), the Board appointed under Regulation 6 of the Disabled Drivers (Tax Concessions) Regulations, 1989, shall continue for the period of its appointment as if appointed under these Regulations and Regulation 6(1) of these Regulations shall be construed accordingly.

Regulation 4(a)

FIRST SCHEDULE

PRIMARY MEDICAL CERTIFICATE

Issued for the purposes of section 92 of the Finance Act, 1989, and the Disabled Drivers and Disabled Passengers (Tax Concessions) Regulations, 1994.

Name of applicant :

Mr./Mrs./Miss/Ms.*...

Normal address :

....

....

....

I,.., Director of Community Care and Medical Officer of Health for the....................................... Health Board area, hereby certify that in my opinion the person named above is a severely and permanently disabled person who meets one or more of the medical criteria set out in the Disabled Drivers and Disabled Passengers (Tax Concessions) Regulations, 1994.

Particulars of the applicant's disablement are as follows:**

(a)   the applicant is wholly or almost wholly without the use of both legs;

(b)   the applicant is wholly without the use of one leg and almost wholly without the use of the other leg such that the applicant is severely restricted as to movement of the lower limbs;

(c)   the applicant is without both hands or without both arms;

(d)   the applicant is without one or both legs;

(e)   the applicant is wholly or almost wholly without the use of both hands or arms and wholly or almost wholly without the use of one leg;

(f)   the applicant has the medical condition of dwarfism and has serious difficulties of movement of the lower limbs.

Date:.....................................

....(Signature)

Director of Community Care and Medical Officer of Health,

....Health Board.

```
Official
Stamp
```

*Delete as appropriate.

**Tick as appropriate and cross out particulars that do not apply.

Regulation 4(b)

SECOND SCHEDULE

BOARD MEDICAL CERTIFICATE

Issued, on appeal, for the purposes of section 92 of the Finance Act, 1989, and the Disabled Drivers and Disabled Passengers (Tax Concessions) Regulations, 1994.

Name of applicant :

Mr./Mrs./Miss./Ms.*...

Normal address:

....

....

....

The Disabled Drivers Medical Board of Appeal hereby certifies that in its opinion the person named above is a severely and permanently disabled person who meets one or more of the medical criteria set out in the Disabled Drivers and Disabled Passengers (Tax Concessions) Regulations, 1994.

Particulars of the applicant's disablement are as follows:**

(a)   the applicant is wholly or almost wholly without the use of both legs;

(b)   the applicant is wholly without the use of one leg and almost wholly without the use of the other leg such that the applicant is severely restricted as to movement of the lower limbs;

(c)   the applicant is without both hands or without both arms;

(d)   the applicant is without one or both legs;

(e)   the applicant is wholly or almost wholly without the use of both hands or arms and wholly or almost wholly without the use of one leg;

(f)   the applicant has the medical condition of dwarfism and has serious difficulties of movement of the lower limbs.

Date:..............................

....

(Signature)

For and on behalf of the Disabled Drivers Medical Board of Appeal and a member of that Board.

*Delete as appropriate.

**Tick as appropriate and cross out particulars that do not apply.

Regulation 18

THIRD SCHEDULE
DISABLED DRIVERS AND DISABLED PASSENGERS (TAX
CONCESSIONS) REGULATIONS, 1994.
(Every applicant must complete Part I, II or III, as appropriate).
PART I.
DECLARATION BY A DISABLED DRIVER.

NAME OF DISABLED DRIVER:...

ADDRESS:

....

....

....

I hereby declare as follows:

Vehicle, registration number (if available) ....,

Engine number...and

chassis number... ,

is registered or about to be registered in my name, is intended for my personal
use as driver and has been specially constructed or adapted to take account
of my disablement. I am unable to drive any vehicle not specially adapted for
my use. I am the holder of a valid current driving licence for the class to which
the vehicle belongs.

Signed:.. (applicant)

Date:................

WARNING: ANY PERSON WHO MAKES A FALSE DECLARATION WILL
INCUR SEVERE PENALTIES.

PART II
DECLARATION BY OR ON BEHALF OF A DISABLED PASSENGER.

NAME OF DISABLED PASSENGER.* ....

ADDRESS:

....

....

....

Where a family member is applying in respect of the transport of the abovementioned person:

NAME OF FAMILY MEMBER APPLYING ....

ADDRESS:

....

....

....

....

I hereby declare as follows:

Vehicle, registration number (if available) ....,

Engine number...and

Chassis number..

has been specially constructed or adapted to take account of the disablement of the passenger mentioned above and has been purchased for the purpose of transporting the passenger in question.

Signed:..(applicant)

Date:...

WARNING: ANY PERSON WHO MAKES A FALSE DECLARATION WILL INCUR SEVERE PENALTIES.

PART III.

DECLARATION ON BEHALF OF A QUALIFYING ORGANISATION.

NAME OF ORGANISATION...

ADDRESS...

....

....

I hereby declare as follows:

Vehicle, registration number (if available) ....,

Engine number...and

chassis number..,

either

has been specially constructed or adapted to take account of the disablement of .... (specify the number) severely and permanently disabled passengers, being cared for and transported by this organisation*

or

has been specially constructed or adapted for the use of a disabled person as driver*

Signed:.. (applicant)

Position in organisation (e.g. Chairman, Secretary etc.) ....

Date:....................................

WARNING: ANY PERSON WHO MAKES A FALSE DECLARATION WILL INCUR SEVERE PENALTIES.

*Tick whichever is appropriate.

GIVEN under my Official Seal, this 24th day of November, 1994.

BERTIE AHERN,
Minister for Finance.

EXPLANATORY NOTE.

These Regulations, which come into operation on the 1st day of December, 1994, set out the medical criteria, certification procedures, repayment limits and other matters necessary for the purposes of giving effect to section 92 of the Finance Act, 1989 which provides for tax concessions for disabled drivers and disabled passengers.

Amendments

1   Regulation 4A inserted by para 2(a) S.I. No. 469 of 2004, w.e.f. 23 July 2004.

2   Substituted by para 2(a), S.I. No. 566 of 2005, w.e.f. 13 September 2005.

3   Substituted by para 2, S.I. No. 178 of 2005, w.e.f. 7 April 2005.

4   Deleted by para 2(b), S.I. No. 566 of 2005, w.e.f. 13 September 2005.

5   Regulation 6 substituted by para 2(b) S.I. No. 469 of 2004, w.e.f. 23 July 2004.

6   Substituted by FA01 s240 and Sch 5, w.e.f. 1 Januray 2002.

EUROPEAN COMMUNITIES (VALUE-ADDED TAX) REGULATIONS, 1994

(SI No. 448 of 1994)

I, RUAIRÍ QUINN, Minister for Finance, in exercise of the powers conferred on me by section 3 of the European Communities Act, 1972 (No.27 of 1972), and for the purpose of giving effect to Council Directive No. 94/76/ EC of 22 December 1994 (amending Council Directive No. 77/388/EEC by the introduction of transitional measures applicable, in the context of the enlargement of the European Union on 1 January 1995, as regards value-added tax) hereby make the following Regulations:

1.　(1)　These Regulations may be cited as the European Communities (Value-Added Tax) Regulations, 1994.

　　(2)　These Regulations shall be construed together with the Value-Added Tax Acts 1972 to 1994.

2.　These Regulations shall come into operation on the 1st day of January, 1995.

3.　In these Regulations "the Principal Act" means the Value-Added Tax Act, 1972.

4.　The Principal Act is hereby amended by the insertion of the following section after section 15A:

"Goods in transit (additional provisions).

　　15B　(1)　Where-

　　　　(a)　goods from a new Member State were imported into the State on or before the 31st day of December, 1994, and

　　　　(b)　the tax referred to in section 2(1)(b) was not chargeable because the goods were, at the time of such importation, placed-

　　　　　　(i)　under an arrangement for temporary importation with total exemption from customs duty, or

　　　　　　(ii)　under one of the arrangements referred to in clauses (a), (b), (c) and (d) of subparagraph B of paragraph 1 of Article 16, of Council Directive No. 77/388/EEC of 17 May 1977, and

　　　　(c)　the goods are still subject to such an arrangement on the 1st day of January, 1995,

　　　　then, the provisions in force at the time the goods were placed under that arrangement shall continue to apply until the goods leave that arrangement on or after the 1st day of January, 1995.

(2)   (a)   Where-

    (i)   goods were placed under the common transit procedure or under another customs transit procedure in a new Member State on or before the 31st day of December, 1994, and

    (ii)   those goods have not left the procedure concerned before the 1st day of January, 1995,

then the provisions in force at the time the goods were placed under that procedure shall continue to apply until the goods leave that procedure on or after the 1st day of January, 1995.

(b)   In this subsection 'common transit procedure' means the procedure approved by the Council of the European Communities by Council Decision No. 87/415/EEC of 15 June 1987, approving the Convention done at Interlaken on the 20th day of May, 1987, between the European Community, the Republic of Austria, the Republic of Finland, the Republic of Iceland, the Kingdom of Norway, the Kingdom of Sweden and the Swiss Confederation on a common transit procedure, the text of which is attached to that Council Decision.

(3)   Where goods were in free circulation in a new Member State prior to entry into the State, an importation into the State shall be deemed to occur in the following cases:

(a)   the removal, including irregular removal, within the State of the goods referred to in subsection (1) from the arrangement referred to in subparagraph (i) of paragraph (b) of that subsection;

(b)   the removal, including irregular removal, within the State of the goods referred to in subsection (1) from the arrangement referred to in subparagraph (ii) of paragraph (b) of that subsection;

(c)   the termination within the State of any of the procedures referred to in subsection (2).

(4)   An importation into the State shall be deemed to occur when goods, which were supplied within a new Member State on or before the 31st day of December, 1994, and which were not chargeable to a value-added tax in that new Member State, because of their exportation from that

new Member State, are used in the State on or after the 1st day of January, 1995, and have not been imported before that date.

(5)   The tax referred to in section 2(1)(b) shall not be chargeable where-

    (a)   the imported goods referred to in subsections (3) and (4) are dispatched or transported outside the enlarged Community,

    (b)   the imported goods referred to in paragraph (a) of subsection (3) are other than means of transport and are being returned to the new Member State from which they were exported and to the person who exported them, or

    (c)   the imported goods referred to in paragraph (a) of subsection (3) are means of transport which were acquired in or imported into a new Member State before the 1st day of January, 1995 in accordance with the general conditions of taxation in force on the domestic market of that new Member State and which have not been subject by reason of their exportation to any exemption from or refund of a value-added tax in that new Member State:

    Provided that this paragraph shall be deemed to be complied with where it is shown to the satisfaction of the Revenue Commissioners that the first use of the means of transport was prior to the 1st day of January, 1987, or that the tax due does not exceed £100.

(6)   The provisions of section 15A shall not apply to goods imported or deemed to be imported from a new Member State.

(7)   (a)   In this section-

    "the enlarged Community" means the Community after the accession of the new Member States;

    "new Member State" means the Republic of Austria, the Republic of Finland (excluding the Aland Islands) or the Kingdom of Sweden.

    (b)   A word or expression that is used in this section and is also used in Council Directive No. 94/76/ EC of 22 December 1994 has, unless the contrary intention appears, the meaning in this section that it has in that Council Directive.".

GIVEN under my Official Seal,
this 22nd day of December, 1994.

RUAIRÍ QUINN,
Minister for Finance.

EXPLANATORY NOTE.

These Regulations insert a new section 15B into the VAT Act. The new section deals with the transitional arrangements applicable for the taxation of trade between Austria, Finland and Sweden, and Ireland, in the context of such countries' accession to the European Union on I January, 1995. In effect the Regulations introduce transitional measures which ensure that VAT at the point of entry applies to goods from Austria, Finland and Sweden which are dispatched prior to 1 January, 1995 and placed under a tax suspended import procedure in the State, but are not cleared through that procedure until after 1 January, 1995.

VALUE-ADDED TAX (REFUND OF TAX) (NO. 27) ORDER, 1995

(SI No. 38 of 1995)

I, RUAIRÍ QUINN, Minister for Finance, in exercise of the powers conferred on me by section 20(3) of the Value-Added Tax Act, 1972 (No. 22 of 1972), hereby order as follows:

1.   (1)   This Order may be cited as the Value-Added Tax (Refund of Tax) (No.27) Order, 1995.

       (2)   This Order shall be deemed to have come into operation on the 27th day of January, 1994.

2.   In this Order-

"**the Act**" means the Value-Added Tax Act, 1972 (No.22 of 1972), and every enactment which is to be construed together with that Act;

"**qualifying body**" means-

(a)   a research institution, or

(b)   a university, college, school or similar educational body,

which conducts medical research in a laboratory;

"**qualifying goods**" means any new instrument or new appliance, excluding means of transport-

(a)   in relation to which the amount on which tax is chargeable by virtue of the Act is [€25,390][1] or more,

(b)   which has been designed and manufactured for use in medical research, and

(c)   which has been the subject of a recommendation by the Health Research Board that, having regard to the requirements of medical research in the State, a refund of tax under this Order would be appropriate.

3.   Where a person establishes to the satisfaction of the Revenue Commissioners that-

(a)   such a person has borne or paid tax which became chargeable on or after the 27th day of January, 1994, in respect of the supply of goods to, the intra-Community acquisition of goods by, or the importation of goods by, such person where such goods are qualifying goods,

(b)   such person is a qualifying body or, if such person is not a qualifying body, the qualifying goods have been, or are to be, donated by such person to a qualifying body,

(c)   no part of the funds used, or to be used, in the purchase of the qualifying goods was, or is to be, provided, directly or indirectly, by the State, or by any board established by or under statute, or by any public or local authority, or by the qualifying body which has purchased the qualifying goods or to which they have been, or are to be, donated, or by any body of persons associated with such qualifying body in the operation of a medical research laboratory or by any other body of persons operating a medical research laboratory, and

(d)   such person is not entitled, under any provision of the Act or under any instrument other than this Order made under statute administered by the Revenue Commissioners, to a deduction or repayment of the tax borne or paid in respect of the supply of goods to, the intra-Community acquisition of goods by or the importation of goods by such person where such goods are qualifying goods,

and the person completes such claim form as may be provided for the purpose by the Revenue Commissioners and certifies the particulars shown on such claim form to be correct, such person shall be entitled to be repaid the full tax so borne or paid.

GIVEN under my Official Seal,
this 15th day of February, 1995.

RUAIRÍ QUINN,
Minister for Finance.

EXPLANATORY NOTE

The effect of this Order is to allow a full refund of the value-added tax paid on qualifying equipment for medical research purchased through voluntary donations with effect from 27th January, 1994.

Amendments
1   Amended by s240 & sch5, FA01, w.e.f. 1 January 2002. Previously £20,000.

FINANCE ACT, 1994 (COMMENCEMENT OF SECTIONS 93 AND 96(A)) ORDER, 1995

(SI No. 184 of 1995)

I, RUAIRÍ QUINN, Minister for Finance, in exercise of the powers conferred on me by section 166(9)(d) of the Finance Act, 1994 (No. 13 of 1994), hereby order as follows:

1. This Order may be cited as the Finance Act, 1994 (Commencement of Sections 93 and 96(a)) Order, 1995.

2. The 7th day of July, 1995 is hereby appointed as the date on which section 93 of the Finance Act, 1994 (No.13 of 1994), shall take effect.

GIVEN under my Official Seal, this 7th day of July, 1995.

RUAIRÍ QUINN,
Minister for Finance.

EUROPEAN COMMUNITIES (VALUE-ADDED TAX) REGULATIONS, 1995

(SI No. 363 of 1995)

> These Regulations revoked by s100, FA96, as all of the changes contained therein were replicated in FA96.

I, RUAIRÍ QUINN, Minister for Finance, in exercise of the powers conferred on me by section 3 of the European Communities Act, 1972 (No.27 of 1972), and for the purpose of giving effect to provisions of Council Directive No. 95/7/EC of 10 April 1995, hereby make the following regulations:

1.　(1)　These Regulations may be cited as the European Communities (Value-Added Tax) Regulations, 1995.

　　(2)　These Regulations shall be construed together with the Value-Added Tax Acts, 1972 to 1995.

2.　These Regulations shall come into operation on the 1st day of January, 1996.

3.　In these Regulations-

"the Principal Act" means the Value-Added Tax Act, 1972;

"the Act of 1978" means the Value-Added Tax (Amendment) Act, 1978;

"the Act of 1992" means the Finance Act, 1992.

4.　Section 1 of the Principal Act is hereby amended by the insertion after the definition of "Community" of the following definitions:

"contractor', in relation to contract work, means a person who makes or assembles movable goods;

"contract work" means the service of handing over by a contractor to another person of movable goods made or assembled by the contractor from goods entrusted to the contractor by that other person, whether or not the contractor has provided any part of the goods used;".

5.　Section 3 of the Principal Act is hereby amended in subsection (1)-

　　(a)　by the substitution of the following paragraph for paragraph (c):

　　　　"(c)　the handing over by a person (in this paragraph referred to as the developer) to another person of immovable goods which have been developed from goods entrusted to the developer by that other person for the purpose of such development, whether or not the developer has supplied any part of the goods used,",

　　and

　　(b)　in paragraph (g)-

　　　　(i)　by the deletion of subparagraph (iii), and

　　　　(ii)　by the addition of the following proviso to subparagraph (iiia):

"Provided that the goods which were so transferred by the person are, after being worked upon, returned to that person in the State,".

6.   Section 5 (inserted by the Act of 1978) of the Principal Act is hereby amended-

(a)   in paragraph (c) of subsection (6)-

(i)   by the insertion in subparagraph (iii) after "movable goods" of "except where the provisions of subparagraph (iv) of paragraph (f) apply,", and

(ii)   by the insertion in subparagraph (iv) after "movable goods" of ", including contract work, except where the provisions of subparagraph (iv) of paragraph (f) apply",

and

(b)   in paragraph (f) of subsection (6), by the insertion of the following subparagraph after subparagraph (iii):

"(iv)   valuation of or work (including contract work) on movable goods, in cases where the goods are dispatched or transported out of the Member State where the valuation or work was physically carried out.".

7.   Section 11 of the Principal Act is hereby amended by the insertion of the following subsection after subsection (1AA):

"(1AB) Notwithstanding subsection (1), the rate at which tax is chargeable on a supply of contract work shall be the rate that would be chargeable if that supply of services were a supply of the goods being handed over by the contractor to the person to whom that supply is made:

Provided that this subsection shall not apply to a supply of contract work in the circumstances specified in paragraph (xvi) of the Second Schedule.".

8.   Section 15 (inserted by the Act of 1978) of the Principal Act is hereby amended in subsection (3) by the insertion after "duties" of ", expenses resulting from the transport of the goods to another place of destination within the Community, if that destination is known at the time of the importation,".

9.   The Second Schedule to the Principal Act is hereby amended by the insertion of the following paragraph after paragraph (xvi):

"(xvia) the supply of transport services relating to the importation of goods where the value of such services is included in the taxable amount in accordance with section 15(3);".

10.   The Sixth Schedule (inserted by the Act of 1992) to the Principal Act is hereby amended in subparagraph (b) of paragraph (xviii) by the insertion after "other than" of "contract work or".

GIVEN under my Official Seal,
this 21st day of December, 1995.

RUAIRÍ QUINN
Minister for Finance.

EXPLANATORY NOTE

These Regulations transpose into the VAT Act, 1972 certain provisions of Council Directive No. 95/7/EC, which amends the Council Directive No. 77/388/EEC. The areas affected are contract work, valuation of and work on movable goods and transport costs following importation. These Regulations come into effect on 1 January, 1996.

VALUE-ADDED TAX (REFUND OF TAX) (NO.28) ORDER, 1996

(SI No. 98 of 1996)

I, RUAIRÍ QUINN, Minister for Finance, in exercise of the powers conferred on me by section 20(3) (amended by section 184(1)(c) of the Finance Act, 1992 (No.9 of 1992)) of the Value-Added Tax Act, 1972 (No.22 of 1972), hereby order as follows:

1. (1)   This Order may be cited as the Value-Added Tax (Refund of Tax) (No.28) Order, 1996.

    (2)   This Order shall be deemed to have come into operation on the 23rd day of January, 1996.

2. (1)   In this Order-

          "the Act" means the Value-Added Tax Act, 1972 (No.22 of 1972);

          "qualifying person" means a person who-

          (a)   is engaged in the business of carriage for reward of tourists by road under contracts for group transport, and

          (b)   has complied with all the obligations imposed on the person by the Act, the Income Tax Acts, the Corporation Tax Acts or the Capital Gains Tax Acts, and any instruments made thereunder, in relation to-

                (i)   the payment or remittance of the taxes, interest and penalties required to be paid or remitted thereunder, and

                (ii)   the delivery of returns;

          "qualifying vehicle" means-

          (a)   a single-deck touring coach having dimensions as designated by the manufacturer of not less than [2,700 millimetres in height,][1] not less than 8,000 millimetres in length, not less than [775 millimetres in floor height][2] and with an underfloor luggage capacity of not less than 3 cubic metres, or

          (b)   a double-deck touring coach having dimensions as designated by the manufacturer of not more than 4,300 millimetres in height and not less than 10,000 millimetres in length.

    (2)   In this Order a reference to a paragraph or subparagraph is to a paragraph or subparagraph of this Order, unless is it indicated that reference to some other provision is intended.

3. (1)   Unless the provisions in subparagraph (2) are applied, a qualifying person who has borne or paid tax on-

    (a)   the supply to such person or the hiring or leasing (other than hiring or leasing for a period of less than six consecutive months) to such person, or

    (b)   the intra-Community acquisition or importation by such person,

of a qualifying vehicle which is for use by such person in the State in the business of the carriage for reward of tourists by road under contracts for group transport shall, subject to the conditions specified in paragraph 4, be repaid the full tax so borne or paid provided that-

    (i)   the supply, intra-Community acquisition or importation of the vehicle which gave rise to such tax occurred when the vehicle was not more than two years old, or

    (ii)   the hiring or leasing of the vehicle (other than hiring or leasing for a period of less than six consecutive months) which gave rise to such tax was on the basis of a contract for such hire or lease first entered into when the vehicle was not more than two years old.

(2)   A qualifying person who is a taxable person and who becomes liable for tax in the State in respect of the intra-Community acquisition of a qualifying vehicle may, in lieu of claiming repayment under subparagraph (1), elect to deduct the tax chargeable in respect of that acquisition in the return which such person is obliged to furnish, concerning that acquisition, in accordance with section 19(3) (inserted by section 84 of the Finance Act, 1983 (No. 15 of 1983)) of the Act.

(3)   The provisions of this paragraph shall apply only where-

    (a)   the supply, hire, lease, intra-Community acquisition or importation, as the case may be, referred to in subparagraph (1) or (2) occurred on or after the date specified in paragraph 1(2), and

    (b)   the qualifying person is not entitled to a deduction or repayment-

    (i)   by any other provision of the Act or regulations made thereunder, or

    (ii)   under any other enactment administered by the Revenue Commissioners,

of any portion of the tax paid or payable in respect of the qualifying vehicle.

4.   The conditions to be fulfilled by a person in order to obtain a repayment of tax under this Order in accordance with subparagraph (1) of paragraph 3 are that the person shall:

(a)   complete such form as is provided for that purpose by the Revenue Commissioners, and shall certify the particulars shown on such form to be correct;

(b)   establish to the satisfaction of the Revenue Commissioners that that person is a qualifying person;

(c)   produce-

   (i)   in the case of a supply to that person of a qualifying vehicle, an invoice, issued to that person in accordance with section 17(12)(a)(i) (amended by section 30(2) of, and the Second Schedule to, the Value-Added Tax (Amendment) Act, 1978 (No.34 of 1978)) of the Act, establishing the amount of tax borne by that person on that supply,

   (ii)   in the case of the hire or lease of a qualifying vehicle, a copy of the hiring agreement or leasing agreement, as may be appropriate, and, in respect of each repayment claim, an invoice, issued to that person in accordance with the said section 17(12)(a)(i) establishing the amount of tax borne by that person,

   (iii)   in the case of an intra-Community acquisition of a qualifying vehicle, an official receipt or other document establishing the amount of tax paid by that person in respect of the intra-Community acquisition, together with the invoice issued to that person by the supplier in the Member State of supply, or

   (iv)   in the case of an importation of a qualifying vehicle, an official receipt or other document establishing the amount of tax paid by that person on the importation and indicating the number of the relevant customs entry.

5.   This Order shall not apply to vehicles used or intended to be used primarily for the provision of public transport services.

6.   The Value-Added Tax (Refund of Tax) (No. 26) Order, 1994 (S.I. No. 165 of 1994) is hereby revoked.

GIVEN under my Official Seal,
this 4th day of April, 1996.

RUAIRÍ QUINN,
Minister for Finance.

EXPLANATORY NOTE

This Order replaces S.I. No. 165 of 1994. The Order provides for a full repayment of VAT to exempt coach operators, subject to certain conditions, in respect of the tax paid on touring coaches of certain age and dimensions.

Amendments

1   Substituted by para2, Value added Tax (Refund of Tax)(Amendment) Order 1999, w.e.f. 1 April 1999.

2   Substituted by para2, Value-Added Tax (Refund of Tax)(Amendment) Order 2004, w.e.f. 27 September 2004.

VALUE-ADDED TAX (SPECIAL SCHEME FOR MEANS OF TRANSPORT: DOCUMENTATION) REGULATIONS, 1996

(SI No. 201 of 1996)

> This Regulation was revoked by regulation 44, Value-Added Tax Regulations, 2006 (2006 SI No. 548) w.e.f. 1 November 2006

The Revenue Commissioners, in exercise of the powers conferred on them by sections 12 of the Value-Added Tax Act, 1972 (No.22 of 1972), and with the consent of the Minister for Finance, hereby make the following Regulations:

1.   These Regulations may be cited as the Value-Added Tax (Special Scheme for Means of Transport: Documentation) Regulations, 1996.

2.   These Regulations shall come into operation on the 1st day of July, 1996.

3.   In these Regulations -

"the Act of 1995" means the Finance Act, 1995 (No.8 of 1995);

"taxable dealer" has the meaning assigned to it by section 12B(3) (inserted by the Act of 1995) of the Principal Act;

"means of transport" has the meaning assigned to it by section 12B(3) (inserted by the Act of 1995) of the Principal Act;

"the Principal Act" means the Value-Added Tax Act, 1972;

"residual tax" has the meaning assigned to it by section 12B(4) (inserted by the Act of 1995) of the Principal Act.

4.   (1)   A taxable dealer shall deduct residual tax in accordance with section 12(1)(a)(vi) of the Principal Act in respect of the acquisition or purchase of a means of transport from a person specified in paragraph (a) or (b) of subsection (2) of section 12B of that Act, subject to the following conditions:

(a)   that the dealer prepares a document which sets out all the particulars specified in paragraph (2) of this Regulation, in respect of the transaction in question,

(b)   that the document referred to at subparagraph (a) of this paragraph is signed and dated by the person who is supplying the means of transport concerned, acknowledging the accuracy of the details therein and declaring that that person is a person of the type referred to in either paragraph (a) or (b) of subsection (2) of section 12B of the Principal Act, and

(c)   that the dealer gives to the person who is supplying the means of transport concerned a copy of the completed document referred to at subparagraphs (a) and (b) of this paragraph within 15 days of the date of the acquisition or purchase of that means of transport.

(2)   The particulars in respect of the means of transport concerned which are to be included in the document referred to in paragraph (1) of this Regulation are as follows:

(a)   the name and address of the person who is supplying that means of transport;

(b)   the name and address of the taxable dealer who is purchasing or acquiring that means of transport;

(c)   the date upon which the supply of that means of transport takes place;

(d)   a description of that means of transport, including details of the make, model, engine number, registration number and year of manufacture; and

(e)   the total consideration for the supply of that means of transport.

5.   A taxable dealer shall deduct residual tax in accordance with section 12(1)(a)(vi) of the Principal Act in respect of the acquisition or purchase of a means of transport from a person specified in paragraph (c) of subsection (2) of section 12B of that Act, subject to the condition that such dealer shall be in possession of an invoice issued by that person in accordance with the provisions of sections 12B(5) and 17(1) of that Act.

6.   A taxable dealer shall deduct residual tax in accordance with section 12(1)(a)(vi) of the Principal Act in respect of the acquisition or purchase of a means of transport from a person specified in paragraph (d) of subsection (2) of section 12B of that Act, subject to the condition that such dealer shall be in possession of an invoice issued by that person which indicates that the supply by that person was subject to value-added tax in accordance with the provisions implementing Article 26a or 28o of Council Directive 77/388/EEC of 17 May 1977 in the Member State in which the supply took place.

7.   An invoice issued in accordance with the provisions of sections 12B(5) and 17(1) of the Principal Act shall show the following endorsement:

"Special Scheme - this invoice does not give the right to an input credit of VAT".

8.   A taxable dealer shall keep full and true records, entered up to date, of the acquisition and disposal of a means of transport, in respect of which that dealer has deducted residual tax in accordance with section 12(1)(a)(vi) of the Principal Act, together with appropriate cross-references between all such records.

9.   The Value-Added Tax (Second-hand Motor Vehicles) Regulations 1988 (SI No. 121 of 1988) are hereby revoked.

GIVEN under my hand,
this 27th day of June, 1996.

D.B. QUIGLEY,
Revenue Commissioner.

The Minister for Finance hereby consents to the making of the foregoing Regulations.

GIVEN under the Official Seal of the Minister for Finance, this 27th day of June, 1996.

RUAIRÍ QUINN
Minister for Finance

EXPLANATORY NOTE

These Regulations specify the documentation required by a taxable dealer to deduct residual tax in respect of certain means of transport. They revoke and replace S.I.No.121 of 1988.

FINANCE ACT, 1995 (SECTION 134 (1)) (COMMENCEMENT) ORDER, 1996

(SI No. 231 of 1996)

I, RUAIRÍ QUINN, Minister for Finance, in exercise of the powers conferred on me by section 134(2) of the Finance Act, 1995 (No.8 of 1995), hereby order as follows:

1.   This Order may be cited as the Finance Act, 1995 (Section 134(1)) (Commencement) Order, 1996.

2.   The 1st day of September, 1996 is hereby appointed as the day on which section 134(1) of the Finance Act, 1995 (No.8 of 1995) shall take effect.

GIVEN under my Official Seal, this 1st day of August, 1996.

RUAIRÍ QUINN,
Minister for Finance.

EXPLANATORY NOTE

This Order appoints the 1st day of September, 1996 as the date for coming into operation of section 134(1) of the Finance Act, 1995. This section amends section 19(3)(aa) of the VAT Act to allow the Collector-General to nominate a trader's own accounting period as the basis for the annual return, if the trader so wishes.

VALUE-ADDED TAX (RETURNS) REGULATIONS, 1996

(SI No. 294 of 1996)

> These Regulations revoked by Value-Added Tax (Returns)
> Regulations, 2002 (2002 SI No. 267)

The Revenue Commissioners, in exercise of the powers conferred on them by sections 19 of the Value-Added Tax Act, 1972 (No.22 of 1972), hereby make the following Regulations:

1. (1) These Regulations may be cited as the Value-Added Tax (Returns) Regulations, 1996.

    (2) These Regulations shall be deemed to have come into operation on the 1st day of September, 1996.

2. In these Regulations "the Act" means the Value-Added Tax Act, 1972 (No.22 of 1972).

3. A taxable person who is required in accordance with section 19(3)(a) of the Act to furnish a return shall complete such form as is issued to the person for that purpose by the Collector-General in respect of the taxable period concerned and he or she shall sign a declaration on the form to the effect that the particulars shown thereon are correct:

    Provided that where the form aforesaid provides for the inclusion of supplementary trading details in respect of any period, those details shall be deemed to be part of such a return as aforesaid in respect of the taxable period concerned.

4. A taxable person who is required in accordance with section 19(3)(aa) of the Act to furnish a return shall complete such form as is issued to the person for that purpose by the Collector-General and he or she shall sign a declaration on the form to the effect that the particulars shown thereon are correct.

5. The Value-Added Tax (Returns) Regulations, 1993 (S.I. No. 247 of 1993), are hereby revoked.

GIVEN this 8th day of October, 1996.

D. B. QUIGLEY
Revenue Commissioner.

EXPLANATORY NOTE

These Regulations require a taxable person to supply the details requested on the VAT return issued to him or her under section 19(3) of the Act. Recent changes in VAT primary law permit traders who account annually for VAT to align the period covered by their annual VAT return with their annual commercial accounting period. For these traders this annual return covers both the tax payment and the associated trading details for the period. Traders who account for their VAT bi-monthly must also make an annual return of trading details and the Regulations have the effect of extending the same flexibility as regards this annual return to these traders. The Regulations also revoke and replace the Value-Added Tax (Returns) Regulations, 1993 (S.I. No.247 of 1993).

VALUE-ADDED TAX (REFUND OF TAX) (NO. 29) ORDER, 1996

(SI No. 334 of 1996)

I, Ruairí Quinn, Minister for Finance, in exercise of the powers conferred on me by section 20(3) (as amended by section 184(1)(c) of the Finance Act, 1992 (No.9 of 1992)) of the Value-Added Tax Act, 1972 (No.22 of 1972), hereby order as follows:

1.   This Order may be cited as the Value-Added Tax (Refund of Tax) (No.29) Order, 1996.

2.   This Order shall come into operation on the 1st day of December, 1996.

3.   (1)   In this Order -

    (a)   **"the Act of 1967"** means the Diplomatic Relations and Immunities Act, 1967 (No.8 of 1967);

    (b)   **"the Act"** means the Value-Added Tax Act, 1972 (No.22 of 1972);

    (c)   **"the Act of 1992"** means the Finance Act, 1992 (No.9 of 1992);

    (d)   **"excisable products"** has the meaning assigned to it by section 104 of the Act of 1992;

    (e)   **"qualifying person"** means-

        (i)   the head of a diplomatic mission of a sending State, as defined in Article 1(a) of the First Schedule to the Act of 1967,

        (ii)   a member of the diplomatic staff of a diplomatic mission, as defined in Article 1(d) of the First Schedule to the Act of 1967,

        (iii)   a member of the administrative and technical staff of a diplomatic mission, as defined in Article 1(f) of the First Schedule to the Act of 1967,

        (iv)   the head of a consular post, as defined in Article 1(1)(c) of the Second Schedule to the Act of 1967,

        (v)   a consular officer, as defined in Article 1(1)(d) of the Second Schedule to the Act of 1967, or

        (vi)   a consular employee as defined in Article 1(1)(e) of the Second Schedule to the Act of 1967,

who is not a national of, or permanently resident in, the State and who is accepted by the Minister for Foreign Affairs as being entitled to privileges and immunities under the Act of 1967.

(2)   In this Order a reference to a paragraph is to a paragraph of this Order and a reference to a subparagraph is to a subparagraph of the provision in which the reference occurs, unless it is indicated that reference to some other provision is intended.

4.   The provisions of this Order shall apply only where the Minister for Foreign Affairs is satisfied that -

(a)   the sending State of the qualifying person extends a satisfactory level of reciprocal relief to corresponding personnel representing Ireland in that State,

(b)   the supply of goods and services for which relief is claimed under this Order is reasonable and appropriate to the circumstance of each case, and

(c)   the person claiming relief under this Order has respected the laws and regulations of the State.

5.   A qualifying person who is a person specified in paragraph 3(1)(e)(i) or 3(1)(e)(iv), shall, subject to the conditions specified in paragraph 8, be repaid the tax borne or paid by such person on-

(a)   the purchase or lease of the premises of a diplomatic mission as defined in Article 1(i) of the First Schedule to the Act of 1967 or a consular premises as defined in Article 1(1)(j) of the Second Schedule to the Act of 1967, including construction work, alteration, decoration and work of maintenance and repair carried out thereto,

(b)   the purchase or lease of a principal residential premises, including construction work, alteration, decoration and work of maintenance and repair carried out thereto,

(c)   the supply of, and repair to, household goods being non-perishable goods relating to the running of the premises referred to in subparagraphs (a) and (b) and used at or in such premises,

(d)   the supply of, and repair to, business goods being goods other than those specified elsewhere in this paragraph which are necessary for the purposes of carrying out the official duties of such qualifying person,

(e)   the supply of a motor vehicle which qualifies for a refund or remission of Vehicle Registration Tax under section 134(1)(g) of the Act of 1992 and the supply of a bicycle:

Provided that in the case of a motor vehicle if the qualifying person intends to dispose of such motor vehicle by sale or otherwise within two years of the date of purchase, that person shall notify the Minister for Foreign Affairs of such intention, and, where so instructed by that Minister, shall refund to the Revenue Commissioners an amount determined by them deemed to be the amount of tax included in the open market selling price of the vehicle at the time of such determination,

(f)   the hire of a motor vehicle which is necessary for the purposes of carrying out the official duties of such qualifying person,

(g)   the hire, transport and storage of the goods specified in subparagraphs (c) and (d),

(h)   the supply of excisable products which qualify for a refund or remission of excise duty under section 113 of the Act of 1992,

(i)   the supply of electricity and of gas to the premises referred to in subparagraphs (a) and (b), and of goods and services directly related to those supplies, and

(j)   the supply of telecommunication services provided to the premises referred to in subparagraphs (a) and (b) and of goods and services directly related to those supplies.

6.   A qualifying person who is a person specified in paragraph 3(1)(e)(ii) or 3(1)(e)(v) shall, subject to the conditions specified in paragraph 8, be repaid the tax borne or paid by such person on -

(a)   the purchase or lease of a principal residential premises, including construction work, alteration, decoration and work of maintenance and repair carried out thereto,

(b)   the supply of, and repair to, household goods being non-perishable goods relating to the running of the premises referred to in subparagraph (a) and used at or in such premises,

(c)   the supply of, and repair to, business goods being goods which are necessary for the purposes of carrying out the official duties of such qualifying person, other than goods specified elsewhere in this paragraph or the supply of electricity, gas and telecommunication services and goods and services directly related thereto,

(d)   the supply of a motor vehicle which qualifies for a refund or remission of Vehicle Registration Tax under section 134(1)(g) of the Act of 1992 and the supply of a bicycle:

Provided that in the case of a motor vehicle if the qualifying person intends to dispose of such motor vehicle by sale or otherwise within two years of the date of purchase, that person shall notify the Minister for Foreign Affairs of such intention, and, where so instructed by that Minister, shall refund to the Revenue Commissioners an amount determined by them deemed to be the amount of tax included in the open market selling price of the vehicle at the time of such determination,

(e)   the hire of a motor vehicle which is necessary for the purposes of carrying out the official duties of such qualifying person,

(f)   the hire, transport and storage of the goods specified in subparagraphs (b) and (c), and

(g)   the supply of excisable products which qualify for a refund or remission of excise duty under section 113 of the Act of 1992.

7.   A qualifying person who is a person specified in paragraph 3(1)(e)(iii) or 3(1)(e)(vi) shall, subject to the conditions specified in paragraph 8, be repaid the tax borne or paid by such person on -

(a)   the purchase or lease of a principal residential premises, including construction work, alteration, decoration and work of maintenance and repair carried out thereto,

(b)   the supply of, and repair to, household goods being non-perishable goods relating to the running of the premises referred to in subparagraph (a) and used at or in such premises,

(c)   the supply of, and repair to, business goods being goods which are necessary for the purposes of carrying out the official duties of such qualifying person, other than goods specified elsewhere in this paragraph or the supply of electricity, gas and telecommunication services and goods and services directly related thereto,

(d)   the supply of a motor vehicle which qualifies for a refund or remission of Vehicle Registration Tax under section 134(1)(g) of the Act of 1992 and the supply of a bicycle:

Provided that in the case of a motor vehicle if the qualifying person intends to dispose of such motor vehicle by sale or otherwise within two years of the date of purchase, that person shall notify the Minister for Foreign Affairs of such intention, and, where so instructed by that Minister, shall refund to the Revenue Commissioners an amount determined by them deemed to be the amount of tax included in the open market selling price of the vehicle at the time of such determination,

(e)   the hire of a motor vehicle which is necessary for the purposes of carrying out the official duties of such qualifying person, and

(f)   the hire, transport and storage of the goods specified in subparagraphs (b) and (c).

8.   The conditions to be fulfilled by a qualifying person in order to obtain a repayment of tax under this Order are as follows:

(a)   the person shall complete such claim form as may be provided for the purpose by the Revenue Commissioners and shall certify the particulars shown on such claim form to be correct,

(b)   the person shall establish the amount of tax borne or paid by such person by the production of invoices or other documents, provided in accordance with section 17(12)(a)(i) of the Act.

9.   Where the total of the tax chargeable and the amount on which tax is chargeable in relation to a supply of any individual good or service referred to in this Order is [€315][1] or more, the amount of tax chargeable may be remitted in accordance with paragraph 10.

10.   A qualifying person shall apply for remission of tax in accordance with paragraph 9 by completing such application form as may be provided for the purpose by the Revenue Commissioners and shall certify the particulars shown on such application form to be correct.

11.   Where a qualifying person satisfies the requirements for remission of tax under this Order in respect of a supply of goods or services the Revenue Commissioners shall authorise that supply without payment of the tax chargeable and notify the applicant accordingly and such notification shall be valid for three months from the date of its issue.

12.   The notification referred to in paragraph 11 shall be:

(a)   tendered by the qualifying person to the supplier of the goods or services, and

(b)   retained by the supplier as:

(i)   the authority under which such supplier may supply the goods or services to the qualifying person free of tax and

(ii)   a record to be kept in accordance with section 16 of the Act.

13.   A repayment of tax under this Order shall be made only in respect of claims involving a total amount of tax of more than [€315][2]:

Provided that the Revenue Commissioners may, at their discretion, waive application of this paragraph in the particular circumstances of a case.

14.   Nothing in this Order shall apply so as to affect a right to relief of tax prescribed in any other enactment.

GIVEN under my Official Seal, this 12 day of November, 1996.

RUAIRÍ QUINN
Minister for Finance.

EXPLANATORY NOTE

This Order provides relief from VAT for certain goods and services purchased by accredited diplomatic personnel serving in Ireland.

Amendments
1   Amended by s240 & sch5, FA01, w.e.f. 1 January 2002. Previously £250.
2   Amended by s240 & sch5, FA01, w.e.f. 1 January 2002. Previously £100.

FINANCE ACT, 1997 (COMMENCEMENT OF SECTIONS 101 AND 113) ORDER, 1997

(SI No. 313 of 1997)

I, Charlie McCreevy, Minister for Finance, in exercise of the powers conferred on me by section 166(10)(f) of the Finance Act, 1997 (No.22 of 1997), hereby order as follows:

1.   This Order may be cited as the Finance Act, 1997 (Commencement of Sections 101 and 113) Order, 1997.

2.   The 1st day of September, 1997, is hereby appointed as the date on which sections 101 of the Finance Act, 1997 (No.22 of 1997), shall take effect.

GIVEN under my Official Seal, this 14th day of July, 1997.

Charlie McCreevy
Minister for Finance.

EXPLANATORY NOTE

This Order appoints the 1st day of September, 1997 as the date for coming into operation of sections 101 of the Finance Act, 1997. Section 101 amends section 8(3)(a) of the VAT Act to provide that a farmer whose supplies of horticultural products to final consumers exceed or are likely to exceed £40,000 per annum, or whose supplies of a combination of retail agricultural products and agricultural services exceed or are likely to exceed £20,000 per annum is obliged to register and account for VAT on such supplies. It also amends the proviso to section 8(3) of the VAT Act to prevent farmers engaged in the supply of retail horticultural products or agricultural services from separating these activities into smaller units in order to remain under the VAT registration limit. Section 113 amends the Sixth Schedule to the VAT Act to provide for the application of the 12.5 per cent rate of VAT to certain horticultural products.

VALUE-ADDED TAX (ELIGIBILITY TO DETERMINE TAX DUE BY REFERENCE TO MONEYS RECEIVED) ORDER, 1997

(SI No. 316 of 1997)

I, Charlie McCreevy, Minister for Finance, in exercise of the powers conferred on me by section 14(1B) (inserted by section 131 of the Finance Act, 1995 (No. 8 of 1995)) of the Value-Added Tax Act, 1972 (No. 22 of 1972), hereby order as follows:

1.   This Order may be cited as the Value-Added Tax (Eligibility to Determine Tax Due by Reference to Moneys Received) Order, 1997.

2.   The amount specified in section 14(l)(b) (inserted by section 97(a) of the Finance Act, 1994 (No. 13 of 1994)) of the Value-Added Tax Act, 1972 (No. 22 of 1972), is hereby increased to £500,000.

GIVEN under my Official Seal, this 17th day of July, 1997.

Charlie McCreevy
Minister for Finance.

EXPLANATORY NOTE

Section 14(l)(b) of the VAT Act allows a taxable person with a turnover of not more than £250,000 to use the moneys received basis of accounting for VAT. The Order increases that turnover amount to £500,000.

VALUE-ADDED TAX (RETAIL EXPORT SCHEME) REGULATIONS, 1998

(SI No. 34 of 1998)

This Regulation was revoked by regulation 44, Value-Added Tax Regulations, 2006 (2006 SI No. 548) w.e.f. 1 November 2006

The Revenue Commissioners, in exercise of the powers conferred on them by subsections 13(1), 13(1A) (inserted by the Finance Act, 1997 (No.22 of 1997)) and section 32 of the Value-Added Tax Act, 1972 (No.22 of 1972), and with the consent of the Minister for Finance, hereby make the following Regulations:

1. (1) These Regulations may be cited as the Value-Added Tax (Retail Export Scheme) Regulations, 1998.

   (2) These Regulations shall come into operation on the first day of March, 1998.

2. (1) In these Regulations

   "the Act" means the Value-Added Tax Act, 1972;

   "traveller" and "traveller's qualifying goods" have the meanings assigned to them, respectively, by subsection 13(3B) (inserted by the Finance Act, 1997 (No.22 of 1997)) of the Act.

   (2) In these Regulations-

   (a) a reference to a Regulation is to a Regulation of these Regulations, and

   (b) a reference to a paragraph or subparagraph is to a paragraph or subparagraph of the Regulation in which the reference occurs,

   unless it is indicated that reference to some other Regulation is intended.

3. The application of the rate of zero per cent, specified in subsection 11(1)(b) of the Act, to a supply of goods or services specified in subsection 13(1A) of the Act shall be subject to the following conditions-

   (a) that the supplier keeps a record of the details of documentary proof inspected by him or her confirming that the purchaser was a traveller;

   (b) that at the time of supply, the supplier issues an invoice to the traveller showing the following details:

   (i) the name, address and tax registration number of the supplier,

   (ii) the name and address of the traveller,

   (iii) the date upon which the invoice is issued,

   (iv) a description of the goods supplied,

      (v)   the amount payable by the traveller at the time of the sale of the goods,

      (vi)   the tax charged, if any, and

      (vii)   the exchange rate or method to be used in determining the exchange rate, if repayment of the tax is to be made to the traveller

      by the supplier in a currency other than the currency of the State;

(c)   that the traveller duly signs the completed invoice, referred to at subparagraph (b), in duplicate;

(d)   that the notification of the charges made by the supplier, referred to in subsection 13(1A)(iii) of the Act, is made at the latest

      (i)   where the goods are exported by the traveller, at the time of the handing over of the goods in question to the traveller,

      (ii)   where the goods are exported on behalf of the traveller, at the time when the goods in question are supplied to the traveller,

      and where an amount is charged to the traveller for procuring a repayment of tax or arranging for the zero-rating of the supply, such amount does not exceed the amount notified in accordance with the said subsection 13(1A)(iii);

(e)   that the time limit for making a repayment to the traveller, referred to in subsection 13(1A)(ii) of the Act, is not later than the twenty-fifth working day following the receipt by the supplier of the traveller's claim to repayment;

(f)   that the supplier keeps a copy of the invoice issued in accordance with subparagraph (b), duly signed by the traveller, and keeps a record in relation to each invoice of-

      (i)   the net amount (being the amount of tax charged to the traveller minus any commission or fee charged by the supplier to the traveller in respect of the transaction in question) repaid by the supplier to the traveller in respect of the supply in question, expressed in the currency in which the repayment was made,

      (ii)   where appropriate, the exchange rate used,

      (iii)   the date and method of such repayment, and

(iv)   proof in accordance with Regulation 4, that the goods were exported by or on behalf of the traveller.

4.   (1)   In the case where the goods are exported by the traveller, the proof of export of the goods required shall be the invoice issued in accordance with Regulation 3(b) in respect of that supply, duly certified-

(a)   by an officer of the Revenue Commissioners assigned to a customs office in the State, or

(b)   where the goods have been exported via another Member State of the Community, by a customs officer in that Member State, or

(c)   in such other manner as the Revenue Commissioners may deem acceptable for the purpose.

(2)   In the case where the goods are exported on behalf of the traveller, the proof of export of the goods shall take the form of documentary evidence of export, duly certified by an officer of the Revenue Commissioners assigned to a customs office in the State, or, in the case where the goods are exported from another Member State of the Community, duly certified by a customs officer in that Member State.

5.   The Value-Added Tax (Exported Goods) Regulations, 1992 (S.I. No.438 of 1992), are hereby revoked.

GIVEN this 4th day of February, 1998.

D. B. QUIGLEY,
Revenue Commissioner.

The Minister for Finance hereby consents to the making of the foregoing Regulations.

GIVEN under the Official Seal of the Minister for Finance, this 9th day of February, 1998.

CHARLIE McCREEVY,
Minister for Finance.

EXPLANATORY NOTE

These Regulations provide the conditions for granting relief from VAT on goods bought by visiting (non EU) tourists or by Irish residents who are departing the EU with the intention of taking up residence outside the EU. The goods must be exported in the purchaser's personal luggage or put on board a ship or aircraft which is travelling to a non-EU destination, by the end of the third month following the month of purchase. The purchaser must get the benefit of the relief by 25 working days after lodging a valid claim, at the latest, and he/she must be made aware of the specified details concerning the transaction.

VALUE-ADDED TAX (WAIVER OF EXEMPTION) (AMENDMENT) REGULATIONS, 1998

(SI No. 228 of 1998)

> This Regulation was revoked by regulation 44, Value-Added Tax Regulations, 2006 (2006 SI No. 548) w.e.f. 1 November 2006

The Revenue Commissioners, in exercise of the powers conferred on them by section 7 of the Value-Added Tax Act, 1972 (No.22 of 1972), hereby make the following Regulations:

1. These Regulations may be cited as the Value-Added Tax (Waiver of Exemption) (Amendment) Regulations, 1998.

2. These Regulations shall be deemed to have come into effect on the 26th day of March, 1997.

3. Regulation 4 of the Value-Added Tax Regulations, 1979 (S.I. No.63 of 1979), is hereby amended-

   (a)   by the insertion of the following paragraphs after paragraph (2):

   "(2A)   Where a taxable person makes an exempt letting of immovable goods referred to in paragraph (iv) of the First Schedule to the Act, and those immovable goods were acquired or developed by him for the purpose of his taxable supplies, then, notwithstanding the provisions of paragraph (2), that taxable person may apply to the Revenue Commissioners to waive his right to exemption in respect of that letting from a date earlier than the commencement of the current taxable period referred to in subparagraph (d) of paragraph (1).

   (2B)   An application under paragraph (2A) shall be made in writing to the Revenue Commissioners and shall include the following:

   (a)   the name, address and registration number of the taxable person making the application,

   (b)   the tenant's name, address and registration number,

   (c)   details of the letting agreement,

   (d)   the date from which the taxable person desires that the waiver shall have effect.

   (2C)   A waiver of exemption shall be backdated only where the tenant would have been entitled to deduct, in accordance with section 12 of the Act, all the tax that would have been chargeable in respect of the letting if the waiver had applied from the date specified in accordance with subparagraph (d) of paragraph (2B) to the date specified in paragraph (2E).

(2D) Where the Revenue Commissioners are satisfied that the provisions of paragraph (2C) apply, they shall, subject to paragraph (2F), notify the applicant that the waiver may by back-dated in respect of the letting for which back-dating of a waiver was sought specifying the date to which the waiver shall be back-dated.

(2E) Where a waiver is back-dated in respect of a specific letting, the taxable person shall be deemed to have waived his exemption in respect of all exempt lettings referred to in paragraph (iv) of the First Schedule to the Act which he supplies, from a date, not being earlier than the commencement of the current taxable period, specified by the Revenue Commissioners in the notification issued in accordance with paragraph (2D).

(2F) A waiver may not be back-dated to a date prior to the 26th day of March, 1997.

(2G) Any tax chargeable on the letting of immovable goods resulting from the back-dating of a waiver prior to the date specified in paragraph (2E) shall, for the purposes of the Act, be deemed to have been due and paid by the taxable person in accordance with section 19 of the Act and deducted by the tenant in accordance with section 12 of the Act.

(2H) For the purposes of these Regulations-

"back-dating" in relation to a waiver means the waiving of a right to exemption from tax in respect of an exempt letting of immovable goods to which paragraph (iv) of the First Schedule to the Act refers, from a date earlier than the current taxable period referred to in subparagraph (d) of paragraph (1), and cognate words shall be construed accordingly;

"registration number" in relation to a person, means the number assigned to the person for the purposes of registration under section 9 of the Act.",

and

(b) in subparagraph (b)(ii) of paragraph (3) by the substitution of "the total of the amounts of tax referred to at paragraphs (a), (b) and (c) of subsection (3) of section 7 of the Act" for "the total amount of tax refunded to him in accordance with section 20(1) of the Act".

GIVEN this 30th day of June, 1998.

D. B. QUIGLEY,
Revenue Commissioner.

EXPLANATORY NOTE

These Regulations amend Regulation 4 of the Value-Added Tax Regulations, 1979 to provide for the back-dating of a waiver of exemption for VAT on short term lettings of immovable property in specified circumstances. They also amend Regulation 4 to take account of the VAT on property changes contained in the Finance Act, 1997 to section 7(3) of the VAT Act which deals with the calculation of the amount due on the cancellation of a waiver.

VALUE-ADDED TAX (VALUATION OF INTERESTS IN IMMOVABLE GOODS) (AMENDMENT) REGULATIONS, 1998

(SI No. 482 of 1998)

This Regulation was revoked by regulation 44, Value-Added Tax Regulations, 2006 (2006 SI No. 548) w.e.f. 1 November 2006

The Revenue Commissioners, in exercise of the powers conferred on them by section 32 of the Value-Added Tax Act, 1972 (No.22 of 1972), hereby make the following Regulations:

1. These Regulations may be cited as the Value-Added Tax (Valuation of Interests in Immovable Goods) (Amendment) Regulations, 1998.

2. In these Regulations "**unencumbered rent**" has the meaning assigned to it by subsection (10) (as amended by section 102 of the Finance Act, 1997 (No.22 of 1997)) of section 10 of the Value-Added Tax Act, 1972 (No.22 of 1972).

3. Regulation 19 of the Value-Added Tax Regulations, 1979 (S.I. No.63 of 1979), is hereby amended-

    (a) by the addition of the following proviso to paragraph (1):

    "Provided that the provisions of this paragraph shall not apply where the rent payable in respect of the interest so created is less than the unencumbered rent in respect of that interest.",

    and

    (b) in paragraph (2) by the substitution of the following subparagraph for subparagraph (b):

    "(b)   if under the terms of the disposition, the interest disposed of is for a period of twenty years or more, or is deemed to be for a period of twenty years or more, the value of the reversionary interest shall be disregarded.".

GIVEN this 11th day of December, 1998.

Josephine Feehily
Revenue Commissioner

EXPLANATORY NOTE

These Regulations amend Regulation 19 of the Value-Added Tax Regulations, 1979 to provide that where the rent payable in respect of an interest in immovable goods is less than the unencumbered rent, the provisions of Regulation 19(1) do not apply. They also confirm that where an interest is created for twenty years or more, in all cases, the value of the reversionary interest is disregarded.

VALUE-ADDED TAX (ELECTRONIC DATA EXCHANGE AND STORAGE) (AMENDMENT) REGULATIONS, 1998

(SI No. 488 of 1998)

> This Regulation was revoked by regulation 44, Value-Added Tax Regulations, 2006 (2006 S.I. No. 548) w.e.f. 1 November 2006

The Revenue Commissioners, in exercise of the powers conferred on them by sections 17 of the Value-Added Tax Act, 1972 (No. 22 of 1972), hereby make the following regulations:

1.   (1)   These Regulations may be cited as the Value-Added Tax (Electronic Data Exchange and Storage) (Amendment) Regulations, 1998.

     (2)   These Regulations shall come into operation on the 1st day of January, 1999.

2.   The Value-Added Tax (Electronic Data Exchange and Storage) Regulations, 1992 (S.I. No. 269 of 1992), are hereby amended by the insertion of the following Regulation after Regulation 2:

     "2A.   Where an amount or consideration is specified for the purposes of these Regulations, then such amount or consideration shall be expressed in a denomination of the currency of the State and be identified by the use of the symbol appropriate to the denomination so expressed."

GIVEN this 18th day of December, 1998

Josephine Feehily
Revenue Commissioner

EXPLANATORY NOTE

These Regulations amend the Value-Added Tax (Electronic Data Exchange and Storage) Regulations, 1992, to provide that amounts or considerations specified in VAT invoices and other documents must be expressed in a denomination of the State's currency and the appropriate symbol must be used to identify which denomination is being used. The Regulations do not prevent a person showing the amount or consideration in both denominations, if desired, provided the appropriate symbols are included.

VALUE-ADDED TAX (INVOICES AND OTHER DOCUMENTS) (AMENDMENT) REGULATIONS, 1998

(SI No. 489 of 1998)

> This Regulation was revoked by regulation 44, Value-Added Tax Regulations, 2006 (2006 S.I. No. 548) w.e.f. 1 November 2006

The Revenue Commissioners, in exercise of the powers conferred on them by sections 17 of the Value-Added Tax Act, 1972 (No.22 of 1972), hereby make the following regulations:

1.   (1)   These Regulations may be cited as the Value-Added Tax (Invoices and Other Documents) (Amendment) Regulations, 1998.

   (2)   These Regulations shall come into operation on the 1st day of January, 1999.

2.   The Value-Added Tax (Invoices and Other Documents) Regulations, 1992 (S.I. No.275 of 1992), are hereby amended by the insertion of the following Regulation after Regulation 2:

   "2A.   Where an amount or consideration is specified for the purposes of these Regulations, then such amount or consideration shall be expressed in a denomination of the currency of the State and be identified by the use of the symbol appropriate to the denomination so expressed.".

GIVEN this 18th day of December, 1998

Josephine Feehily
Revenue Commissioner

EXPLANATORY NOTE

These Regulations amend the Value-Added Tax (Invoices and Other Documents) Regulations, 1992 to provide that amounts or considerations specified in VAT invoices and other documents must be expressed in a denomination of the State's currency and the appropriate symbol must be used to identify which denomination is being used. The Regulations do not prevent a person from showing the amount or consideration in both denominations, if desired, provided the appropriate symbols are included.

EUROPEAN COMMUNITIES (VALUE-ADDED TAX) REGULATIONS, 1999

(S.I. No. 196 of 1999)

I, Charlie Mc Creevy, Minister for Finance, in exercise of the powers conferred on me by section 3 of the European Communities Act, 1972 (No. 27 of 1972), and for the purpose of giving effect to certain provisions of Council Directive No. 77/388/EEC of 17 May 1997 on the harmonization of the laws of the Member States relating to turnover taxes - Common system of value-added tax: uniform basis of assessment, in consequence of the cessor of Article 28k thereof, hereby make the following Regulations:

1.   (1)   These Regulations may be cited as the European Communities (Value-Added Tax) Regulations, 1999.

       (2)   These Regulations shall be construed together with the Value-Added Tax Acts, 1972 to 1999.

2.   These Regulations shall come into operation on the 1st day of July, 1999.

3.   In these Regulations "**the Principal Act**" means the Value-Added Tax Act, 1972 (No.22 of 1972).

4.   Section 32 of the Principal Act is hereby amended in paragraph (ag) (inserted by the Finance Act, 1992 (No.9 of 1992)) of subsection (1) by the deletion of "**by tax-free shops**".

5.   The Second Schedule to the Principal Act is hereby amended -

    (a)   by the substitution of the following paragraph for paragraph (ia) (inserted by the Finance Act, 1994 (No. 13 of 1994)):

        "(ia)   subject to such conditions and in such amounts as may be specified in regulations-

            (a)   the supply of goods, in a tax-free shop approved by the Revenue Commissioners, to travellers departing the State for a place outside the Community, or

            (b)   the supply, other than by means of a vending machine, of food, drink and tobacco products on board a vessel or aircraft to passengers departing the State for another Member State, for consumption on board that vessel or aircraft,",

    and

    (b)   by the insertion in paragraph (vb) (inserted by the Finance Act, 1993 (No. 13 of 1993)) after "paragraph (v)" of "but not including goods for supply on board such vessels or aircraft to passengers for the purpose of those goods being carried off such vessels or aircraft".

Given under the Official Seal of the Minister for Finance

CHARLIE McCREEVY
Minister for Finance

EXPLANATORY NOTE

(This note is not part of the Instrument and does not purport to be a legal interpretation).

These Regulations amend the VAT Act, 1972, so as to give effect to the abolition of duty-free sales to passengers making intra-EU journeys after 30 June, 1999. From then on sales of goods to such passengers will be liable to VAT at the appropriate rate. However, certain food, drink and tobacco products supplied to passengers for consumption on board a vessel or an aircraft during an intra-EU journey will continue to be liable to VAT at the zero rate.

Duty-free sales will, however, continue to apply in respect of journeys outside the Community.

VALUE-ADDED TAX (SUPPLY OF FOOD, DRINK AND TOBACCO PRODUCTS ON BOARD VESSELS OR AIRCRAFT FOR ONBOARD CONSUMPTION) REGULATIONS, 1999

(S.I. No. 197 of 1999)

> **This Regulation was revoked by regulation 44, Value-Added Tax Regulations, 2006 (2006 S.I. No. 548) w.e.f. 1 November 2006**

The Revenue Commissioners, in exercise of the powers conferred on them by paragraph (ia) of the Second Schedule to, and section 32 of the Value-Added Tax Act, 1972 (No.22 of 1972) (as amended by the European Communities (Value-Added Tax) Regulations, 1999), hereby make the following Regulations:

1.   These Regulations may be cited as the Value-Added Tax (Supply of Food, Drink and Tobacco Products on board Vessels or Aircraft for onboard Consumption) Regulations, 1999.

2.   These Regulations shall come into operation on the 1st day of July, 1999.

3.   In these Regulations -

"**the Principal Act**" means the Value-Added Tax Act, 1972;

"**the Act of 1992**" means the Finance Act, 1992 (No.9 of 1992):

"**excisable products**" has the meaning assigned to it by -

(a)   paragraphs (a) to (e) and (i),

or

(b)   on and from the commencement of section 112 of the Finance Act, 1999 (No. 2 of 1999), paragraphs (a) to (f),

of section 104 of the Act of 1992.

4.   The conditions which apply for the purposes of paragraph (ia) of the Second Schedule to the Principal Act are that the food, drink and tobacco products shall be supplied -

(a)   in the case of excisable products, in such form, manner and quantities as may be permitted by the Revenue Commissioners in respect of relief from excise duty, and

(b)   in the case of food and drink other than drink to which paragraph (a) applies -

(i)   from outlets, on board vessels or aircraft, approved by the Revenue Commissioners, and

(ii)   in such form and quantity as renders it suitable to be consumed by passengers while on board such vessels or aircraft.

GIVEN this 30th day of June, 1999

Josephine Feehily
Revenue Commissioner

EXPLANATORY NOTE

(This note is not part of the Instrument and does not purport to be a legal interpretation)

After 30 June, 1999 sales of goods to passengers making intra-EU journeys will be liable to VAT at the appropriate rate. However, certain food, drink and tobacco products supplied to passengers for consumption on board a vessel or aircraft during an intra-EU journey will continue to be liable at the zero rate of VAT subject to the conditions specified in these Regulations.

VALUE-ADDED TAX (REFUND OF TAX) (AMENDMENT) ORDER, 1999

(S.I. No. 305 of 1999)

I, Charlie McCreevy, Minister for Finance, in exercise of the powers conferred on me by section 20(3) (as amended by section 184(1)(c) of the Finance Act, 1992 (No.9 of 1992)) of the Value-Added Tax Act, 1972 (No.22 of 1972), hereby order as follows:

1. (1) This Order may be cited as the Value-Added Tax (Refund of Tax) (Amendment) Order, 1999.

    (2) This Order shall be deemed to have come into operation on the 1st day of April, 1999.

2. Paragraph (2)(1) of the Value-Added Tax (Refund of Tax) (No.28) Order, 1996 (S.I. No.98 of 1996), is hereby amended by the substitution in the definition of "qualifying vehicle" of "2,7000 millimetres in height" for "3,000 millimetres in height and of "950 millimetres in floor height" for "1,000 millimetres in floor height".

Given under my Official Seal this 27 day of September, 1999.

Charlie McCreevy
Minister for Finance

EXPLANATORY NOTE

(This note is not part of the instrument and does not purport to be a legal interpretation).

S.I. No.98 of 1996 provides for a full repayment of VAT incurred by exempt coach operators on touring coaches of certain dimensions. This Order amends the S.I. to allow touring coaches of lesser dimensions in height and floor height to qualify for the repayment.

VALUE-ADDED TAX (RECORDS OF TRANSACTIONS IN INVESTMENT GOLD) REGULATIONS, 1999.

(S. I. No. 439 of 1999)

This Regulation was revoked by regulation 44, Value-Added Tax
Regulations, 2006 (2006 S.I. No. 548) w.e.f. 1 November 2006

The Revenue Commissioners, in exercise of the powers conferred on them by
section 16 (1A) (inserted by section 133 of the Finance Act, 1999 (No. 2 of 1999))
and section 32 of the Value-Added Tax Act, 1972 (No. 22 of 1972), hereby make the
following Regulations:

1.   (1)   These Regulations may be cited as the Value-Added Tax (Records
             of Transactions in Investment Gold) Regulations, 1999.

      (2)   These Regulations shall come into operation on the 1st day of
             January, 2000.

2.   In these Regulations:

      "Principal Act" means the Value-Added Tax Act, 1972 (No. 22 of 1972);

      "intermediary services" means services supplied by an intermediary.

3.   Every person who trades in investment gold shall keep full and true
      records entered up to date of-

      (a)   in relation to supplies of investment gold, the name of each
             person to whom the investment gold is supplied, the amount
             receivable from each such person in respect of such supplies and
             a cross-reference to the relevant invoices or documents which
             issued in respect of such supplies,

      (b)   in relation to purchases of investment gold, the name of each
             person from whom the investment gold is purchased, the
             purchase price of the investment gold and a cross-reference
             to the relevant invoices or documents which were received in
             respect of such purchases,

      (c)   in relation to importations of investment gold, the value of the
             investment gold determined in accordance with section 15 of the
             Principal Act in respect of each importation, the purchase price
             of the investment gold imported and a cross-reference to the
             invoices and customs documents used in connection with such
             importations,

      (d)   in relation to intra-Community acquisitions of investment gold,
             the name of the person from whom the investment gold is
             acquired, the purchase price of the investment gold and a cross-
             reference to the relevant invoices which were received in respect
             of such acquisitions,

      (e)   in relation to the supply of intermediary services, the name
             of each person to whom the service is supplied, the amount

receivable in respect of the supply and a cross-reference to the relevant invoices or documents which issued in respect of the supply of such services,

(f)   in relation to intermediary services received, the name of the intermediaries, the amount payable in respect of the supply of the services and a cross-reference to the relevant invoices or documents which were received in respect of such services,

(g)   in relation to discounts allowed or price reductions made to a person subsequent to the issue of an invoice or other document to such person, the amount credited to such person and, except in a case to which section 17(9)(a) of the Principal Act applies, a cross-reference to the corresponding credit note,

(h)   in relation to bad debts written off, particulars of the name and address of the debtor, a description of the supply of investment gold to which the debt relates and the date or dates upon which the debt was incurred,

(i)   in relation to discounts or price reductions received from taxable persons subsequent to the receipt of invoices from such persons, except in a case to which section 17(9)(a) of the Principal Act applies, the amount of the discount or price reduction and corresponding tax received from each such person and a cross-reference to the corresponding invoice, and

(j)   in relation to discounts or price reductions received from persons who are not taxable persons, the amount of the discount or price reduction and a cross-reference to the document which was received in respect of such discount or price reduction.

4.   Regulation 9(1) of the Value-Added Tax Regulations, 1979 (S.I. No.63 of 1979) shall not apply in relation to transactions in investment gold.

GIVEN this 24th day of December, 1999.

Josephine Feehily
Revenue Commissioner

VALUE-ADDED TAX (WAIVER OF EXEMPTION ON SUPPLIES OF, AND SUPPLIES RELATING TO, INVESTMENT GOLD) REGULATIONS, 1999

(S.I. No. 440 of 1999)

This Regulation was revoked by regulation 44, Value-Added Tax Regulations, 2006 (2006 S.I. No. 548) w.e.f. 1 November 2006

The Revenue Commissioners, in exercise of the powers conferred on them by subsections (3) and (4) of section 6A (inserted by section 122 of the Finance Act, 1999 (No.2 of 1999)), and section 32, of the Value-Added Tax Act, 1972 (No.22 of 1972), hereby make the following Regulations:

1. (1)   These Regulations may be cited as the Value-Added Tax (Waiver of Exemption on Supplies of, and Supplies relating to, Investment Gold) Regulations, 1999.

    (2)   These Regulations shall come into operation on the 1st day of January, 2000.

2. In these Regulations-

    "Act of 1999" means the Finance Act, 1999 (No.2 of 1999);

    "Principal Act" means the Value-Added Tax Act, 1972, (No.22 of 1972);

    "registration number", in relation to a person, means the number assigned to the person for the purposes of registration under section 9 of the Principal Act;

    "value-added tax registration number in another Member State" means the registration number issued to a person by the authorities of another Member State of the Community for the purposes of value-added tax referred to in Council Directive No. 77/388/EEC of 17 May, 1977.

3. A person who produces investment gold or transforms any gold into investment gold and who, in accordance with section 6A(3) of the Principal Act, wishes to waive his or her right to exemption from tax on supplies of investment gold to another person who is engaged in the supply of goods and services in the course or furtherance of business, shall apply to the Revenue Commissioners for authorisation to do so and shall furnish to them the following particulars-

    (a)   his or her name, address and registration number (if any), and

    (b)   a declaration stating that he or she produces investment gold or transforms any gold into investment gold and that he or she supplies or intends to supply investment gold to other persons engaged in the supply of goods and services in the course or furtherance of business.

4. Where they are satisfied that it is appropriate to do so for the proper administration of the tax, the Revenue Commissioners shall, within three weeks of receipt of the application for authorisation, authorise the applicant to waive, where he or she so wishes and in accordance with

section 6A(3) of the Principal Act, his or her right to exemption from tax on a supply of investment gold.

5.   A person, authorised in accordance with Regulation 4, who waives, in accordance with section 6A(3) of the Principal Act, his or her right to exemption from tax in respect of a supply of investment gold to another person shall, in relation to that supply, issue to that other person an invoice showing the following particulars-

(a)   his or her name, address and registration number,

(b)   the name, address and registration number (if any) of the person to whom the investment gold is being supplied,

(c)   in the case of a supply of investment gold to- (i) a person in another Member State, that person's value-added tax registration number (if any) in that Member State,(ii) a person outside the Community, an indication of the type of business being carried on by that person,

(d)   the date of issue of the invoice,

(e)   the date of supply of the investment gold,

(f)   a description of the investment gold including, where applicable, form, weight, quantity, purity and any other distinguishing features,

(g)   the total consideration, exclusive of tax, receivable in respect of the supply,

(h)   the rate or rates of tax and the amount of tax at each rate chargeable in respect of the supply of the investment gold,

(i)   an endorsement stating "The right to exemption from tax has been waived in respect of this supply and the person to whom the investment gold is being supplied is liable for the tax chargeable on the supply in accordance with section 6A(5) of the Value-Added Tax Act 1972" or words to the like effect.

6.   Where a person is authorised to waive, in accordance with Regulation 4, his or her right to exemption from tax on supplies of investment gold, an intermediary, who supplies services in respect of those supplies of investment gold and who wishes to waive his or her right to exemption from tax in respect of those services, shall apply to the Revenue Commissioners for authorisation to do so and shall furnish to them the following particulars:

(a)   his or her name, address and registration number (if any), and

(b)   a declaration stating that he or she supplies services in respect of the supply of investment gold.

7.   Where they are satisfied that it is appropriate to do so for the proper administration of the tax, the Revenue Commissioners shall, within three weeks of receipt of the application for authorisation, authorise the

intermediary referred to in Regulation 6, to waive, in accordance with section 6A(4) of the Principal Act, his or her right to exemption from tax, on the supply of a service in respect of the supply of investment gold for which the supplier of such investment gold has waived his or her right to exemption from tax in accordance with section 6A(3) of the Principal Act.

8.   An intermediary, authorised in accordance with Regulation 7, who waives, in accordance with section 6A(4) of the Principal Act, his or her right to exemption from tax on the supply of a service in respect of the supply of investment gold to another person shall, in relation to that supply, issue to that other person an invoice showing the following particulars-

(a)   his or her name, address and registration number,

(b)   the name, address and registration number (if any) of the person on whose name and account he or she is acting in respect of the supply of investment gold, and where that person is in another Member State, that person's value-added tax registration number (if any) in that Member State,

(c)   the date of issue of the invoice,

(d)   the date of the supply of the services,

(e)   the total consideration, exclusive of tax, receivable in respect of the supply of the services,

(f)   the rate or rates of tax and the amount of tax at each rate chargeable in respect of the supply of the services,

(g)   a description of the services being supplied in respect of the supply of investment gold, and

(h)   an endorsement stating "The right to exemption from tax has been waived in respect of this supply" or words to the like effect.

9.   Where the right to exemption from tax has been waived, in respect of a supply of investment gold or the supply of services relating to the supply of investment gold, that waiver shall be irrevocable for that supply.

10   The Revenue Commissioners may revoke any authorisation referred to in Regulation 4 or 7 where it appears necessary for them to do so for the proper administration of the tax and, accordingly, such authorisation shall cease to have effect from such date as may be notified by them to the holder of the authorisation.

GIVEN this 24th day of December, 1999.

Josephine Feehily
Revenue Commissioner

VALUE -ADDED TAX (REFUND OF TAX TO PERSONS MAKING EXEMPT SUPPLIES OF INVESTMENT GOLD) REGULATIONS, 1999

(S.I. No. 441 of 1999)

This Regulation was revoked by regulation 44, Value-Added Tax Regulations, 2006 (2006 S.I. No. 548) w.e.f. 1 November 2006

The Revenue Commissioners, in exercise of the powers conferred on them by subsections (6)(b), (7)(b) and (8)(b) of section 6A (inserted by section 122 of the Finance Act, 1999 (No. 2 of 1999)), and section 32 of the Value-Added Tax Act, 1972 (No.22 of 1972), hereby make the following Regulations:

1. (1)   These Regulations may be cited as the Value-Added Tax (Refund of Tax to Persons making Exempt Supplies of Investment Gold) Regulations, 1999.

   (2)   These Regulations shall come into operation on the 1st day of January, 2000.

2. In these Regulations "the Principal Act" means the Value-Added Tax Act, 1972, (No.22 of 1972).

3. A person who is entitled, in accordance with subsection (6)(b), (7)(b) or (8)(b) of section 6A of the Principal Act, to claim a refund of the tax charged, paid or deferred in the circumstances specified in those subsections, shall claim such refund of tax-

   (a)   by completing such claim form as may be provided for that purpose by the Revenue Commissioners and certifying that the particulars shown on such claim form are correct,

   (b)   by establishing the amount of tax borne by production, where requested to do so by the Revenue Commissioners, of invoices or import documents, and

   (c)   by establishing that such person is not entitled to repayment of the tax under any other provision of the Principal Act, any Regulations made thereunder or of any other Act or instrument made under statute administered by the Revenue Commissioners.

GIVEN this 24th day of December, 1999.

Josephine Feehily
Revenue Commissioner

VALUE-ADDED TAX (AGRICULTURAL MACHINERY) (DOCUMENTATION) REGULATIONS, 1999

(S. I. No. 443 of 1999)

This Regulation was revoked by regulation 44, Value-Added Tax Regulations, 2006 (2006 S.I. No. 548) w.e.f. 1 November 2006

The Revenue Commissioners, in exercise of the powers conferred on them by section 32 of the Value-Added Tax Act, 1972 (No.22 of 1972), hereby make the following regulations:

1. (1)   These Regulations may be cited as the Value-Added Tax (Agricultural Machinery) (Documentation) Regulations, 1999.

    (2)   These Regulations shall come into operation on the 1st day of March, 2000.

2. In these Regulations -

    "the Principal Act" means the Value-Added Tax Act, 1972 (No.22 of 1972);

    "the Act of 1999" means the Finance Act, 1999 (No.2 of 1999);

    "agricultural machinery" has the meaning assigned to it by section 12C (inserted by the Act of 1999) of the Principal Act;

    "flat-rate farmer" has the meaning assigned to it by section 12A as amended (inserted by section 11 of the Value-Added Tax (Amendment) Act, 1978 (No. 34 of 1978)) of the Principal Act;

    "taxable dealer" has the meaning assigned to it by the said section 12C.

3. Each invoice issued by a flat-rate farmer in accordance with section 17(2A) (inserted by the Act of 1999) of the Principal Act shall be signed by him and shall include the following, that is to say: (a) his name and address;(b) the name and address of the taxable dealer to whom the agricultural machinery was supplied and the registration number assigned to him under subsection (1A) (inserted by section 171 of the Finance Act, 1992 (No.9 of 1992)) of section 9 of the Principal Act;(c) the date on which the supply of the agricultural machinery took place;(d) the date of issue of the invoice; (e) a description of the agricultural machinery, including details of the make, model and, where appropriate, the year of manufacture, the engine number and registration number thereof;(f) the consideration for the supply of the agricultural machinery, and (g) a declaration that the agricultural machinery was used by him for the purposes of his farming activities.

4. (1)   Each invoice issued by a flat-rate farmer in accordance with section 17(2A) (inserted by the Act of 1999) of the Principal Act shall be issued within the period of fifteen days immediately following the month in which the agricultural machinery was supplied.

(2)   A flat-rate farmer shall keep copies of all invoices to which paragraph (1) applies.

5.   A taxable dealer shall keep - (a) a full and proper record of all acquisitions and disposals of agricultural machinery by him, the entries in relation to which shall be made at the time of any such acquisition or disposal, or as soon as may be thereafter, and(b) all invoices received in respect of agricultural machinery acquired by him and copies of all invoices in respect of agricultural machinery disposed of by him.

GIVEN under my hand, this 23rd day of December, 1999.

Josephine Feehily,
Revenue Commissioner.

EXPLANATORY MEMORANDUM

(This note is not part of the Instrument and does not purport to be a legal interpretation.)

These Regulations give the details which must be included on invoices issued (under section 17(2A) of the VAT Act) by flat-rate farmers in respect of supplies of agricultural machinery made by them to taxable dealers.

VALUE-ADDED TAX (CANCELLATION OF ELECTION OF REGISTRATION IN RESPECT OF SIXTH SCHEDULE ACCOMMODATION) REGULATIONS, 2000

(S.I. No. 253 of 2000)

This Regulation was revoked by regulation 44, Value-Added Tax Regulations, 2006 (2006 S.I. No. 548) w.e.f. 1 November 2006

The Revenue Commissioners, in exercise of the powers conferred on them by sections 8 and 32 of the Value-Added Tax Act, 1972 (No. 22 of 1972), make the following Regulations:

1. (1) These Regulations may be cited as the Value-Added Tax (Cancellation of Election of Registration in respect of Sixth Schedule Accommodation) Regulations, 2000.

   (2) These Regulations shall come into operation on 1 September 2000.

2. In these Regulations "**Principal Act**" means the Value-Added Tax Act, 1972.

3. In these Regulations -

   (a) a reference to a Regulation is to a Regulation of these Regulations, and

   (b) a reference to a paragraph is to a paragraph of the Regulation in which the reference occurs,

   unless it is indicated that reference to some other provision is intended.

4. A person who requests the cancellation of an election made by him or her under section 8 of the Principal Act and who supplies services of the kind referred to in paragraph (xiii) of the Sixth Schedule to that Act shall notify the Revenue Commissioners in writing that he or she wishes to have his or her election cancelled and shall furnish to the Revenue Commissioners any further details as may be required by them.

5. (1) A person shall be treated as a person who had not elected to be a taxable person with effect from the end of a taxable period as specified by the Revenue Commissioners which shall be no earlier than the end of the taxable period in which the notification in accordance with Regulation 4 was submitted, and the Revenue Commissioners shall so notify the person concerned accordingly.

   (2) The person referred to in paragraph (1) shall furnish a return in accordance with section 19(3) of the Principal Act, and remit any tax payable, in respect of the taxable period in which the cancellation comes into effect and at the same time pay to the Revenue Commissioners in addition to any amount payable in accordance with section 8(5) of that Act, the cancellation amount

provided for in section 8(5A) of that Act as if it were tax due in accordance with section 19 of that Act.

6. Regulation 3 of the Value-Added Tax Regulations, 1979 (SI. No. 63 of 1979), is amended by the insertion of the following paragraph after paragraph 3 of that Regulation:

"(3A) A person who requests the cancellation of an election made by him or her under section 8 of the Act and who supplies services of the kind referred to in paragraph (xiii) of the Sixth Schedule to the Act is required to fulfil the conditions specified in the Value-Added Tax (Cancellation of Election of Registration in respect of Sixth Schedule Accommodation) Regulations, 2000 and, where applicable, the conditions specified in these Regulations, in order to have such election cancelled.".

GIVEN this 11th day of August, 2000.

Josephine Feehily.
Revenue Commissioner.

EXPLANATORY NOTE

(This note is not part of the instrument and does not purport to be a legal interpretation.)

These Regulations set out the procedure whereby a person who elects to register for VAT in respect of the letting out of accommodation covered by paragraph (xiii) of the Sixth Schedule to the VAT Act may cancel that registration.

VALUE-ADDED TAX (APPORTIONMENT) REGULATIONS, 2000

(S.I. No. 254 of 2000)

> This Regulation was revoked by regulation 44, Value-Added Tax Regulations, 2006 (2006 S.I. No. 548) w.e.f. 1 November 2006

The Revenue Commissioners, in exercise of the powers conferred on them by sections 12 and 32 of the Value-Added Tax Act, 1972 (No. 22 of 1972), make the following Regulations:

1. These Regulations may be cited as the Value-Added Tax (Apportionment) Regulations, 2000.

2. These Regulations shall come into operation on 1 September 2000.

3. In these Regulations

    "Principal Act" means the Value-Added Tax Act, 1972;

    "accounting period" means a period of 12 months ending on 31 December 2000 and on each 31 December thereafter, but if a taxable person customarily makes up accounts for periods of 12 months ending on another fixed date, an accounting period is a period of 12 months ending on that fixed date;

    "authorised officer" means a person authorised for the purposes of section 18 of the Principal Act;

    "final accounting period" means the period from the end of the previous accounting period to the date that a person ceases to be a taxable person;

    "review period" means a period consisting of all the taxable periods which end during an accounting period.

4. In these Regulations -

    (a) a reference to a Regulation is to a Regulation of these Regulations, and

    (b) a reference to a paragraph is to a paragraph of the Regulation in which the reference occurs,

    unless it is indicated that reference to some other provision is intended.

5. (1) Where a taxable person deducts, in accordance with subsections (1) and (4) of section 12 of the Principal Act, a proportion of the tax borne or payable on the taxable person's acquisition of dual-use inputs for a taxable period that proportion of tax deductible by that person for a taxable period shall be -

    (a) the proportion which -

    (i) correctly reflects the extent to which the dual-use inputs are used for the purposes of that person's deductible supplies or activities, and

(ii)   has due regard to the range of that person's total supplies and activities,

for that taxable period,

(b)   the proportion which was calculated as being the proportion of tax deductible for the review period immediately preceding the taxable period in question,

(c)   the proportion which that person estimates will -

(i)   correctly reflect the extent to which the dual-use inputs will be used for the purposes of that person's deductible supplies or activities, and

(ii)   have due regard to the range of that person's total supplies and activities,

for the review period in which that taxable period ends, or

(d)   any other proportion of tax deductible which is arrived at in accordance with paragraph (3) of this Regulation.

(2)   Where a taxable person estimates a proportion of tax deductible for a taxable period in accordance with paragraph (1)(c), then the taxable person shall submit, at the same time as the return required to be furnished in accordance with section 19(3) of the Principal Act for the taxable period in question, details setting out the basis for that estimate to the office of the Revenue Commissioners which would normally deal with the examination of the records kept by that person in accordance with section 16 of the Principal Act.

(3)   If an authorised officer is satisfied that the proportion of tax deductible estimated in accordance with paragraph (1)(c) does not correctly reflect the extent to which the dual-use inputs will be used for the purposes of the taxable person's deductible supplies or activities and does not have due regard to the range of that person's total supplies and activities for the review period in which the taxable period ends, then that officer may direct that taxable person to use a proportion of tax deductible in accordance with subparagraph (a) or (b) of paragraph (1) or any other appropriate proportion which that officer agrees with that person.

6.   (1)   A taxable person who deducts, in accordance with subsections (1) and (4) of section 12 of the Principal Act, a proportion of the tax borne or payable on the taxable person's acquisition of dual-use inputs shall, at the end of each review period, calculate the proportion of tax deductible for that review period and shall, if necessary, in accordance with paragraph (2), adjust the amount of tax deducted in that review period to ensure that it correctly reflects the extent to which the dual-use inputs were used for the

purposes of that person's deductible supplies or activities and had due regard to the range of that person's total supplies and activities for that review period.

(2)   Any necessary adjustment under paragraph (1) shall be made by way of an increase or decrease, as the circumstances may require, in the amount of tax deductible by the taxable person, for -

    (a)   the taxable period next following the end of the review period, or

    (b)   such later taxable period which is agreed between the taxable person and an authorised officer,

but if the adjustment relates to that person's final accounting period any necessary adjustment shall be made by way of an increase or decrease in the amount of tax deductible for the taxable period in which that final accounting period ends.

(3)   Any adjustment in accordance with paragraph (2) shall be made in the return required to be furnished in accordance with section 19(3) of the Principal Act for -

    (a)   the taxable period next following the end of the review period, or

    (b)   such later taxable period which is agreed between the taxable person and an authorised officer,

but if the adjustment relates to that person's final accounting period any necessary adjustment shall be made in the return required to be furnished in accordance with section 19(3) of the Principal Act for the taxable period in which that final accounting period ends.

(4)   Any increase or decrease in the amount of tax deductible resulting from an adjustment of tax deductible made in accordance with this Regulation, shall be disregarded in calculating the proportion of tax deductible for the review period in which that adjustment was made.

7.   Where a taxable person adjusts, in accordance with Regulation 6, the amount of tax deductible for a review period and subsequent to that adjustment it is established that that adjustment was incorrect, then the provisions of section 21 of the Principal Act shall not apply to any additional liability for tax arising out of the correction of that adjustment but only if-

    (a)   that person, or any person acting on his or her behalf, did not act fraudulently or negligently in relation to that adjustment,

    (b)   that person submitted, by the due date for submission of the return referred to in Regulation 6(3), details setting out the basis on which the adjustment was made to the office of the Revenue Commissioners which would normally deal with the examination of the records kept by that person in accordance with section 16 of the Principal Act, and

(c)   that additional liability is not the subject of an assessment of tax under section 23 of the Principal Act.

8.   Regulation 16 of the Value-Added Tax Regulations, 1979 (SI. No. 63 of 1979), is hereby revoked with effect as on and from 1 September, 2000.

GIVEN this 11th day of August, 2000.

Josephine Feehily
Revenue Commissioner

EXPLANATORY NOTE

(This note is not part of the instrument and does not purport to be a legal interpretation.)

These Regulations deal with the proportion of tax deductible by a person for a taxable period in relation to his or her acquisition of dual-use inputs for the purposes of his or her business. They also provide for the adjustment of the amount of tax deducted in respect of a review period. They replace Regulation 16 of the Value-Added Tax Regulations, 1979 (SI. No. 63 of 1979).

TAXES (ELECTRONIC TRANSMISSION OF CERTAIN REVENUE RETURNS) (SPECIFIED PROVISIONS AND APPOINTED DAY) ORDER, 2000

(S.I. No. 289 of 2000)

The Revenue Commissioners in exercise of the powers conferred on them by section 917E (inserted by section 209 of the Finance Act, 1999 (No. 2 of 1999)) of the Taxes Consolidation Act, 1997 (No. 39 of 1997), order as follows:

1. This Order may be cited as the Taxes (Electronic Transmission of Certain Revenue Returns) (Specified Provisions and Appointed Day) Order, 2000.

2. Each of the provisions set out in the Schedule to this Order is specified for the purpose of Chapter 6 of Part 38 of the Taxes Consolidation Act, 1997.

3. The 28th day of September 2000 is appointed as the day appointed by this Order in relation to returns to be made under each of the provisions specified in accordance with paragraph 2.

SCHEDULE

Section 19(3)(a) (as amended by the Finance Act, 1983 (No. 15 of 1983))

of the Value Added Tax Act, 1972 (No. 22 of 1972).

Section 19(3)(aa) (inserted by the Finance Act, 1989 (No. 10 of 1989))

of the Value Added Tax Act, 1972.

Regulation 22(1) of the Income Tax (Employments) Regulations,

1960 (S.I. No. 28 of 1960).

Regulation 25(6) of the Income Tax (Employments) Regulations, 1960.

Regulation 31 of the Income Tax (Employments) Regulations, 1960.

Regulation 31A (inserted by the Income Tax (Employments)

Regulations, 1989 (S.I. No. 58 of 1989) of the Income

Tax (Employments) Regulations, 1960.

Given this 20th day of September 2000.

FRANK M. DALY,
Revenue Commissioner.

Explanatory Note

(This note is not part of the Instrument and does not purport to be a legal interpretation.)

This Order -

    (a)   by specifying certain provisions of the tax code under which certain tax returns are made, applies the legislation governing electronic tax returns contained in Chapter 6 of Part 38 of the Taxes Consolidation Act, 1997, to tax returns required to be made under the provisions so specified, and

(b)   by appointing a day, namely 28 September 2000, in relation to such returns, ensures that the legislation referred to only applies to any such return required to be made on or after 29 September 2000.

Chapter 6 of Part 38 of the Taxes Consolidation Act, 1997 (inserted by section 209 of the Finance Act, 1999) provides the legislative framework for making electronic tax returns. The legislation only applies to a tax return where the provision under which the return is made is specified in an order by the Revenue Commissioners. Where a provision is so specified the legislation applies to returns made under that provision after the day appointed in the order in relation to the provision concerned. The reason for this procedure is to allow the Revenue Commissioners to manage the roll-out of the system for receiving electronic tax returns. This system will be extended to further tax returns as the necessary development work in relation to the electronic receipt of particular returns is completed.

The returns which are made under the provisions specified in this Order are -

Traders' VAT - 3 returns.

Employers' PAYE/PRSI remittance forms.

Part 1 of form P45 - certificate sent by an employer to the inspector of taxes when an employee leaves an employment.

VALUE-ADDED TAX (ESTIMATION OF TAX PAYABLE AND ASSESSMENT OF TAX PAYABLE OR REFUNDABLE) REGULATIONS, 2000

(S.I. No. 295 of 2000)

> **This Regulation revoked by r44, Value-Added Tax Regulations 2006 (S.I. No. 548 of 2006) with effect from 1 November 2006.**

The Revenue Commissioners, in exercise of the powers conferred on them by sections 22, 23 and 32 of the Value-Added Tax Act, 1972 (No. 22 of 1972), make the following Regulations:

1. These Regulations may be cited as the Value-Added Tax (Estimation of Tax Payable and Assessment of Tax Payable or Refundable) Regulations, 2000.

2. These Regulations shall come into operation on 25 September 2000.

3. In these Regulations "Principal Act" means the Value-Added Tax Act, 1972.

4. (1) An estimation of tax payable for a period for the purposes of section 22 of the Principal Act may be made by an officer of the Revenue Commissioners authorised by them in that behalf.

    (2) A notice served in accordance with section 22 of the Principal Act shall contain the following particulars -

    (a) the name, address and registration number of the person in respect of whom an estimate is made,

    (b) the period to which the estimate relates, and

    (c) the amount of tax estimated to be payable in respect of the period referred to in subparagraph (b) of this paragraph.

5. (1) An assessment of tax payable or refundable for a period for the purposes of section 23 of the Principal Act may be made by an inspector of taxes or such other officer as the Revenue Commissioners may authorise in that behalf.

    (2) A notice served in accordance with section 23 of the Principal Act shall contain the following particulars -

    (a) the name, address and registration number of the person in respect of whom an assessment is made,

    (b) the period to which the assessment relates,

    (c) the total amount of tax which it is assessed should have been paid or the total amount of tax (including, where appropriate, a nil amount) which in accordance with section 20(1) of the Principal Act should have been refunded, as the case may be, in respect of the period referred to in subparagraph (b) of this paragraph,

     (d)   the total amount of tax (including, where appropriate, a nil amount) paid by the person or refunded to the person, as the case may be, in respect of the period concerned, and

     (e)   the net amount due in respect of the period referred to in subparagraph (b) of this paragraph.

6.   The Value-Added Tax (Estimation and Assessment of Tax Due) Regulations, 1992 (S.I. No. 277 of 1992), are revoked.

7.   (1)   All officers who immediately before the commencement of these Regulations stood authorised for the purposes of any provision of the Regulations revoked by Regulation 6 of these Regulations shall be deemed to be authorised for the purposes of the corresponding provision of these Regulations.

     (2)   All estimates or assessments of tax and notices of estimation or assessment of tax made or issued under the Regulations revoked by Regulation 6 of these Regulations and in force immediately before the commencement of these Regulations shall continue in force as if made or issued under these Regulations.

GIVEN this 25 day of September, 2000.

Josephine Feehily
Revenue Commissioner.

EXPLANATORY NOTE

(This note is not part of the Instrument and does not purport to be a legal interpretation).

These Regulations provide for the making of estimates of tax payable for any period, and for the making of assessments of tax payable or refundable for any period, by an officer of the Revenue Commissioners. They revoke the Value-Added Tax (Estimation and Assessment of Tax Due) Regulations, 1992 (S.I. No. 277 of 1992).

VALUE-ADDED TAX (AGRICULTURAL INTERVENTION AGENCY) ORDER, 2001

(S.I. No. 11 of 2001)

I, Charlie McCreevy, Minister for Finance, in exercise of the powers conferred on me by section 8(2A) (as amended by section 124 of the Finance Act, 1995 (No. 8 of 1995)) of the Value-Added Tax Act, 1972 (No. 22 of 1972), order as follows:

1. This Order may be cited as the Value-Added Tax (Agricultural Intervention Agency) Order, 2001.

2. This Order shall be deemed to have come into operation on 8 January 2001.

3. The bodies who may become taxable persons by virtue of section 8(2A) (a) of the Value-Added Tax Act, 1972 (No. 22 of 1972) shall (to the extent that such bodies act as an agricultural intervention agency) be taxable persons as respects the categories of supplies specified in the Schedule, where acting as such an intervention agency.

SCHEDULE

Transactions in respect of agricultural products carried out pursuant to regulations on the common organisation of the market in those products.

GIVEN under my Official Seal,

this 27 day of January, 2001.

Charlie McCreevy TD
Minister for Finance.

TAXES (OFFSET OF REPAYMENTS) REGULATIONS, 2001

(S.I. No. 399 of 2001)

> These Regulations revoked by r8, Taxes (Offset of Repayments) Regulations 2002 (S.I. No. 471 of 2002) with effect from 2 October 2002.

ARRANGEMENT OF REGULATIONS

PART 1
General

1. Citation and commencement.

2. Interpretation.

PART 2
Offsetting

3. Order of priority of offset against tax liabilities.

4. Special arrangements regarding corporation tax, income tax and capital gains tax.

5. Chronological order of priority of liabilities.

6. Nomination of liabilities by taxpayer.

7. Offset of interest.

The Revenue Commissioners, in exercise of the powers conferred on them by section 1006A of the Taxes Consolidation Act, 1997 (No. 39 of 1997), make the following Regulations:

PART 1
General

Citation and commencement

1. (1)   These Regulations may be cited as the Taxes (Offset of Repayments) Regulations, 2001.

    (2)   These Regulations shall come into operation on 14 September 2001.

Interpretation

2. (1)   In these Regulations, unless the context otherwise requires—

    "Acts", **"claim"**, **"liability"** and **"overpayment"** have each the same meaning as they have, respectively, in the principal section;

"**Collector-General**" means the person appointed under section 851 of the Principal Act;

"**estimate**" means an estimate of tax made in accordance with the provisions of–

(a)   section 989 of the Principal Act,

(b)   Regulation 13 of the Income Tax (Relevant Contracts) Regulations, 2000 (S.I. No. 71 of 2000), or

(c)   section 22 of the Value-Added Tax Act, 1972 (No. 22 of 1972);

"**current estimate**", in relation to any particular time, means an estimate in respect of either an income tax month or a taxable period, as the case may be, the due date for which is immediately prior to that time or the income tax month or taxable period immediately preceding that month or period;

"**due date**", in relation to a liability, means the date on which the liability is due and payable under the appropriate provision of the Acts and, in relation to an estimate, the date on which the period for the payment of the tax for the income tax month or taxable period, as the case may be, expires;

"**liability at enforcement**" means a liability which, at the time at which the repayment is to be made in respect of the claim or overpayment–

(a)   was certified in a certificate issued, and not withdrawn, under section 962 of the Principal Act,

(b)   was the subject of proceedings initiated, and not withdrawn, as a debt due to the Minister for Finance, in any court of competent jurisdiction, or

(c)   was entered as a specified amount in a notice of attachment issued, and not revoked, under section 1002 of the Principal Act;

"**Principal Act**" means the Taxes Consolidation Act, 1997 (No. 39 of 1997);

"**principal section**" means section 1006A of the Principal Act;

"**taxhead**" means–

(a)   tax deductible under Chapter 2 of Part 18 of the Principal Act and any regulations made under it,

(b)   income tax deductible under Chapter 4 of Part 42 of the Principal Act and any regulations made under it,

(c)   corporation tax,

(d)   income tax (other than that referred to in paragraph (b) of this definition),

(e)   capital gains tax,

(f)   value-added tax,

(g)   inheritance tax and gift tax,

(h)   stamp duties,

(i)   residential property tax,

(j)   vehicle registration tax, or

(k)   excise duties,

as the case may be.

(2)   In these Regulations —

(a)   A reference to a Regulation is to a Regulation of these Regulations, unless it appears that reference to some other provision is intended;

(b)   a reference to a paragraph is to the paragraph of the provision in which the reference occurs, unless it appears that reference to some other provision is intended.

(3)   Subject to paragraph (1), a word or expression that is used in these Regulations and is also used in any provision of the Acts has, except where the context otherwise requires, the same meaning in these Regulations as it has in that provision.

PART 2
Offsetting

Order of priority of set-off against liabilities

3.   Subject to Regulations 4, 5, 6 and 7, the amount of any repayment in respect of a claim or overpayment made by any person, which is, by virtue of subsection (2) of the principal section, to be set against any liability of that person, shall be set against —

(a)   firstly, any liability, other than a current estimate or a liability at enforcement, in the following sequence:

(i)   a liability arising under the same taxhead in respect of which the claim or overpayment is made,

(ii)   a liability arising under the Value-Added Tax Act, 1972, and the enactments amending or extending that Act,

(iii)   a liability arising under Chapter 4 of Part 42 of the Principal Act and the regulations made under it,

(iv)   a liability arising under Chapter 2 of Part 18 of the Principle Act and the regulations made under it,

(v)   a liability arising under the Corporation Tax Acts,

     (vi)   a liability arising under any provision (other than Chapter 4 of Part 42 of the Principal Act) of the Income Tax Acts,

     (vii)   a liability arising under the Capital Gains Tax Acts,

     (viii)   a liability arising under Part VI of the Finance Act, 1983 (No. 15 of 1983), and the enactments amending or extending that Part,

     (ix)   a liability arising under the Capital Acquisitions Tax Act, 1976 (No. 8 of 1976), and the enactments amending or extending that Act,

     (x)   a liability arising under the Stamp Duties Consolidation Act, 1999 (No. 31 of 1999), and the enactments amending or extending that Act,

     (xi)   a liability arising under Chapter IV of Part II of the Finance Act, 1992 (No. 9 of 1992),

     (xii)   a liability arising under the statues relating to the duties of excise and to the management of those duties,

     and

  (b)   secondly, any liability, being a liability at enforcement, in the sequence set out in paragraph (a).

Special arrangements regarding corporation tax, income tax and capital gains tax

4.   Notwithstanding Regulation 3 but subject to Regulations 5, 6 and 7, in any case where a repayment in respect of a claim or overpayment made by any person, is under a taxhead referred to in paragraph (c), (d) or (e) of the definition of "**taxhead**", the amount of the repayment, which is, by virtue of subsection (2) of the principal section, to be set against any liability of that person, shall be set against—

  (a)   firstly, any liability, other than a current estimate or a liability at enforcement, in the following sequence:

     (i)   a liability arising under the same taxhead in respect of which the claim or overpayment is made,

     (ii)   a liability arising under the Corporation Tax Acts,

     (iii)   a liability arising under any provision (other than Chapter 4 of Part 42 of the Principal Act) of the Income Tax Acts,

     (iv)   a liability arising under the Capital Gains Tax Acts,

     (v)   a liability arising under the Value-Added Tax Act, 1972, and the enactments amending or extending that Act,

     (vi)   a liability arising under Chapter 4 of Part 42 of the Principal Act and the regulations made under it,

(vii)   a liability arising under Chapter 2 of Part 18 of the Principle Act and the regulations made under it,

(viii) a liability arising under Part VI of the Finance Act, 1983, and the enactments amending or extending that Part,

(ix)   a liability arising under the Capital Acquisitions Tax Act, 1976, and the enactments amending or extending that Act,

(x)   a liability arising under the Stamp Duties Consolidation Act, 1999, and the enactments amending or extending that Act,

(xi)   a liability arising under Chapter IV of Part II of the Finance Act, 1992,

(xii)   a liability arising under the statues relating to the duties of excise and to the management of those duties,

and

(b)   secondly, any liability, being a liability at enforcement, in the sequence set out in paragraph (a).

Chronological order of priority of liabilities

5.   For the purposes of Regulation 3 or 4, where, at any time, a repayment is to be set against more than one liability arising under a taxhead, it shall be set against any liability due for an earlier period or event in priority to a later period or event, as the case may be.

Nomination of liabilities by taxpayer

6.   Notwithstanding Regulation 3 or 4, a person may, at any time but not later than 30 days after the issue of a notice to him or her under subsection (2A) of the principal section, by notice in writing to the Collector-General request that the repayment concerned be set against liabilities in an order nominated by the person and the Collector-General shall arrange accordingly.

Offset of interest

7.   For the purposes of these regulations, interest due and payable in relation to any liability to tax, duty, levy or other charge arising under the Acts in respect of any period or event, shall be deemed to be due and payable in respect of that period or event, as the case may be.

Given this 27th day of August, 2001

Frank M. Daly
Revenue Commissioner

EXPLANATORY NOTE

(This note is not part of the Instrument and does not purport to be a legal interpretation.)

These Regulations are being made under subsection (4) of section 1006A (inserted by the Finance Act, 2000 and amended by the Finance Act 2001) of the Taxes Consolidation Act, 1997. That section empowers the Revenue to offset repayments due to a person against outstanding liabilities of the person.

The purpose of the Regulations is to set out an order of priority for such offsets.

Liabilities will be divided into 2 priority categories as follows:

1.   Liabilities other than current estimates and liabilities at enforcement, and

2.   Liabilities at enforcement.

Within each category, but subject to one special case, a repayment will be set off in the following sequence–

    (a)   the taxhead giving rise to the repayment,

    (b)   value-added tax,

    (c)   employers PAYE,

    (d)   relevant contracts tax,

    (e)   corporation tax,

    (f)   income tax, other than at (c),

    (g)   capital gains tax,

    (h)   residential property tax,

    (i)   inheritance/gift taxes,

    (j)   stamp duties,

    (k)   vehicle registration tax, and

    (l)   excise duties

The special case is where the repayment arises in the corporation tax, income tax, capital gains tax grouping. In such a case liabilities within that same grouping are dealt with first before reverting to the order referred to above.

The taxpayer will have the option to request the Collector-General, at any time but not later than 30 days after the issue of the notice of offset, to vary the offset as nominated by him/her.

Within a taxhead a claim or overpayment will be offset against older liabilities before younger ones.

For the purpose of offsetting against interest owed by the taxpayer, the "**age**" of the interest is determined by the "**age**" of the tax, etc. giving rise to it.

VALUE-ADDED TAX (IMPORTED GOODS) (AMENDMENT) REGULATIONS, 2001

(S.I. No. 628 of 2001)

> **This Regulation was revoked by regulation 44, Value-Added Tax Regulations, 2006 (2006 S.I. No. 548) w.e.f. 1 November 2006**

The Revenue Commissioners, in exercise of the powers conferred on them by sections 15 and 32 of the Value-Added Tax Act, 1972 (No. 22 of 1972), and with the consent of the Minister for Finance, make the following regulations:

1. These Regulations may be cited as the Value-Added Tax (Imported Goods) (Amendment) Regulations, 2001.

2. These Regulations shall come into operation on the date of consent of the Minister for Finance.

3. In these Regulations "Regulations of 1992" means the Value-Added Tax (Imported Goods) (No. 2) Regulations, 1992 (S.I. No. 440 of 1992).

4. Regulation 8 of the Regulations of 1992 is amended by deleting "or for processing under customs control".

5. Regulation 9 of the Regulations of 1992 is amended -

    (a) by deleting "or" in paragraph (f), and,

    (a) by inserting the following after paragraph (g):

    "or

    (h) arrangements for processing under customs control,".

6. These Regulations shall not apply to goods which, on the date when these Regulations come into operation, are under arrangements for processing under customs control and on the importation of which tax chargeable has been paid.

GIVEN this 17th day of December, 2001

Josephine Feehily
Revenue Commissioner

The Minister for Finance hereby consents to the making of the foregoing Regulations. GIVEN under my Official seal this 19th day of December 2001.

Charlie McCreevy
Minister for Finance

EXPLANATORY NOTE

(This note is not part of the Instrument and does not purport to be a legal interpretation.)

These Regulations ensure that VAT at importation is suspended in respect of goods placed under arrangements for processing under customs control.

VALUE-ADDED TAX (AMENDMENT) (PROPERTY TRANSACTIONS) REGULATIONS 2002

(S.I. No. 219 of 2002)

> This Regulation was revoked by regulation 44, Value-Added Tax Regulations, 2006 (2006 S.I. No. 548) w.e.f. 1 November 2006

The Revenue Commissioners, in exercise of the powers conferred on them by section 32 of the Value-Added Tax Act 1972 (No. 22 of 1972) make the following regulations:

1. These Regulations may be cited as the Value-Added Tax (Amendment) (Property Transactions) Regulations 2002.

2. In these Regulations the "Regulations of 1979" means the Value-Added Tax Regulations 1979 (S.I. No. 63 of 1979).

3. Regulation 4 of the Regulations of 1979 is amended–

    (a) in paragraph (1)–

        (i) by deleting "or (x)",

        (ii) in subparagraph (b) by inserting "and" after "registration number;",

        (iii) by deleting subparagraph (c), and

        (iv) by renumbering subparagraph (d) as subparagraph (c),

    (b) in paragraph (2)–

        (i) by substituting "(c)" for "(d)",

        (ii) by substituting "paragraph (iv) of the First Schedule" for "the paragraph or paragraphs referred to in subparagraph (c) of the said preceding paragraph", and

        (iii) by substituting "paragraph (iv) of the First Schedule were not so specified" for "the paragraph or paragraphs referred to in paragraph (1)(c) were not specified in the said First Schedule",

    (c) in paragraph (2A) by substituting "subparagraph (c) of paragraph (1). However, no application under this paragraph may be made in respect of any disposal of an interest in immovable goods which is deemed to be a letting of immovable goods to which paragraph (iv) of the First Schedule applies by virtue of section 4(3A)(a)(ii) of the Act." for "subparagraph (d) of paragraph (1).",

    (d) in paragraph (2H) in the definition of "back-dating", by substituting "(c)" for "(d)",

    (e) in paragraph (3)–

        (i) by deleting "or (x)",

      (ii)   by substituting the following for subparagraph (a):

             "(a)   he shall notify the Revenue Commissioners in writing that he desires to have the waiver of his right to exemption cancelled;",

      (iii)   by substituting the following for subparagraph (b)(i):

             "(i)   the tax paid by him in accordance with section 19(3) of the Act in respect of or in relation to the supply of services by him to which the waiver applied for all taxable periods comprised in the period commencing with the beginning of the first taxable period for which his waiver had effect and ending with the termination of the taxable period immediately preceding that during which he notifies the Revenue Commissioners that he desires to have his waiver cancelled, and",

      (iv)   in subparagraph (b)(ii)–

             (I)   by inserting "deducted or deductible by him" after "the total amount of tax", and,

             (II)   by deleting ", or in case such total amount is referable partly to services specified in the paragraphs referred to in the notification aforesaid and partly to the supply of goods or other services, the amount included in such total amount which is referable to the services specified",

and

      (v)   by substituting the following subparagraph for subparagraph (c):

             "(c)   he shall pay to the Collector-General an amount equal to the excess (if any) of the tax referred to in subparagraph (b)(ii) over the tax referred to in subparagraph (b)(i).",

  (f)   in paragraph (4) by deleting "specified in the paragraph or paragraphs",

     and

  (g)   by deleting paragraph (6) with effect from 1 November 2002.

4.   With effect from 25 March 2002, Regulation 19 of the Regulations of 1979 is amended in paragraph (1)–

  (a)   in subparagraph (b) by inserting "and" after "of an interest,",

  (b)   in subparagraph (c) by deleting "and",

  (c)   by deleting subparagraph (d),

  (d)   by deleting ", whichever is the lower",

and

(e)   by substituting the following for the proviso:

"However, where the rent payable in respect of the interest so
created is less than the unencumbered rent in respect of that
interest, the value of the rent to be included in the consideration
for the purpose of ascertaining the open market price of the
interest disposed of shall be calculated using the unencumbered
rent.".

GIVEN the 24 May 2002
JOSEPHINE FEEHILY.
Revenue Commissioner.

EXPLANATORY NOTE

(This note is not part of the Instrument and does not purport to be a legal
interpretation.)

These Regulations amend and update Regulations 4 and 19 of the Value-
Added Tax Regulations, 1979.

Regulation 4 is amended to provide that a person cannot backdate his or
her waiver of a right to exemption from VAT in relation to certain lettings
of immovable goods. The review period in relation to the cancellation of a
waiver of exemption is deleted with effect from 1 November 2002. There are
also several amendments to reword provisions and update cross-references.

Regulation 19 is amended to remove the condition regarding the five year
rent review and to allow either of two methods of valuing a leasehold interest
in immovable goods. The proviso to paragraph (1) is also reworded for the
purpose of improved clarity.

VALUE-ADDED TAX (RETURNS) REGULATIONS, 2002

(S.I. No. 267 of 2002)

> This Regulation was revoked by regulation 44, Value-Added Tax
> Regulations, 2006 (2006 S.I. No. 548) w.e.f. 1 November 2006

The Revenue Commissioners, in exercise of the powers conferred on them by sections 19 and 32 of the Value-Added Tax Act 1972 (No. 22 of 1972), hereby make the following Regulations:

1. (1)   These Regulations may be cited as the Value-Added Tax (Returns) Regulations 2002.

    (2)   These Regulations are deemed to have come into operation on the 25 March 2002.

2. In these Regulations "Principal Act" means the Value-Added Tax Act 1972 (No. 22 of 1972).

3. Where a taxable person is required to furnish a return in accordance with paragraph (a) or (b) (inserted by section 84 of the Finance Act 1983) of section 19(3) of the Principal Act, then that person, or another person acting under that person's authority, shall complete such form as is issued for that purpose by the Collector-General in respect of the taxable period concerned and either the taxable person or the other person acting under that person's authority, as appropriate, shall sign a declaration on the form to the effect that the particulars shown on it are correct, and if that form provides for the inclusion of supplementary trading details in respect of any period, those details shall be deemed to be part of the return in respect of the taxable period concerned.

4. Where a taxable person is authorised to furnish a return in accordance with section 19(3)(aa) (inserted by section 58 of the Finance Act 1989) of the Principal Act, then that person, or another person acting under that taxable person's authority, shall complete such form as is issued for that purpose by the Collector-General and either that taxable person or another person acting under that person's authority, as appropriate, shall sign a declaration on the form to the effect that the particulars shown on it are correct.

5. The Value-Added Tax (Returns) Regulations 1996 (S.I. No. 294 of 1996) are revoked.

GIVEN under my hand, 4th June 2002.

JOSEPHINE FEEHILY
Revenue Commissioner.

EXPLANATORY NOTE

(This note is not part of the Instrument and does not purpose to be a legal interpretation.)

These Regulations allow a taxable person or another person acting under the taxable person's authority to furnish the details requested on the VAT return issued by the Collector-General under section 19 of the Act. The Regulations revoke and replace the Value-Added Tax (Returns) Regulations, 1996.

EUROPEAN COMMUNITIES (MUTUAL ASSISTANCE FOR THE RECOVERY OF CLAIMS RELATING TO CERTAIN LEVIES, DUTIES, TAXES AND OTHER MEASURES) REGULATIONS, 2002

(S.I. No. 462 of 2002)

I, CHARLIE McCREEVY, Minister for Finance, in exercise of the powers conferred on me by section 3 of the European Communities Act 1972 (No. 27 of 1972) and for the purpose of giving effect to Council Directive No. 76/308/EEC of 15 March 1976, as amended by Council Directive No. 79/1071/EEC of 6 December 1979, Council Directive No. 92/12/EEC of 25 February 1992, and Council Directive No. 2001/44/EC of 15 June 2001, hereby make the following regulations:

Citation

1.   These Regulations may be cited as the European Communities (Mutual Assistance for the Recovery of Claims relating to Certain Levies, Duties, Taxes and Other Measures) Regulations 2002.

Interpretation

2.   (1)   In these Regulations -

"claim" means any of the claims to which Regulation 3 applies;

"claimant" means the competent authority of a Member State which makes a request for assistance concerning a claim;

['Commission Directive' means Commission Directive No. 2002/94/EC of 9 December 2002 as amended by Commission Directive 2004/79/EC of 4 March 2004 and Commission Directive 2006/84/EC of 23 October 2006;][1]

"Council Directive" means Council Directive No. 76/308/EEC of 15 March 1976 as amended by Council Directive No. 79/1071/EEC of 6 December 1979, Council Directive No. 92/12/EEC of 25 February 1992, and Council Directive No. 2001/44/EC of 15 June 2001;

"excise duties" means any excise duty in a Member State on-

(a)   manufactured tobacco,

(b)   alcohol and alcoholic beverages, or

(c)   mineral oils;

"export duties" means -

(a)   customs duties and charges having equivalent effect on exports, and

(b)   export charges laid down within the framework of-

(i)   the common agricultural policy, or

          (ii)   specific arrangements applicable to certain goods resulting from the processing of agricultural products,

        which are imposed by, or apply within, a Member State;

"import duties" means -

    (a)   customs duties and charges having equivalent effect on imports, and

    (b)   import charges laid down within the framework of -

          (i)   the common agricultural policy, or

          (ii)   specific arrangements applicable to certain goods resulting from the processing of agricultural products,

        which are imposed by, or apply within, a Member State;

"Member State" means a Member State of the European Communities other than the State;

"taxes on income and capital" means those taxes set out in Article 1(3) of Council Directive 77/799/EEC of 19 December 1977 (as amended by the 1994 Act of Accession, in so far as it relates to Member States) read in conjunction with article 1(4) of that Directive which are imposed by, or apply within, a Member State;

"taxes on insurance premiums" means those taxes set out in the sixth indent to Article 3 of the Council Directive, read in conjunction with the seventh indent of the Council Directive, which are imposed by, or apply within, a Member State;

"value-added tax", in relation to a Member State, means the tax referred to in Council Directive No. 77/388/EEC of 17 May 1977.

(2)   A word or expression that is used in these Regulations and is also used in the Council Directive has, unless the contrary intention appears, the meaning in these Regulations that it has in the Council Directive.

(3)   A word or expression that is used in these Regulations and is also used in the Tax Acts has, subject to paragraph (2) and unless the contrary intention appears, the meaning in these Regulations that it has in the Tax Acts.

(4)   In these Regulations -

    (a)   a reference to a Regulation is to a Regulation of these Regulations, and

(b)   a reference to a paragraph or subparagraph is to the paragraph or subparagraph of the provision in which the reference occurs,

unless it is indicated that reference to some other provision is intended.

Claims covered

3.   This Regulation applies to a claim made by a claimant relating to-

(a)   refunds, interventions and other measures forming part of the system of total or partial financing of the European Agricultural Guidance and Guarantee Fund (EAGGF), including sums to be collected in connection with these actions;

(b)   levies and other duties provided for under the common organisation of the market for the sugar sector;

(c)   import duties;

(d)   export duties;

(e)   value added tax;

(f)   excise duties;

(g)   taxes on income and capital;

(h)   taxes on insurance premiums;

(i)   interest, administrative penalties and fines, and costs incidental to a claim referred to in paragraphs (a) to (h), with the exclusion of any fine or penalty in respect of which the act or commission giving rise to the fine or penalty if committed in the State would have been of a criminal nature.

Exchange of information

4.   (1)   In this Regulation "relevant authority", in relation to a request for information under this Regulation, means -

(a)   the Minister for Agriculture and Food, in the case of claims to which Regulation 3 applies which are referred to in paragraph (a) or (b), or, in so far as relates to any claim referred to in either of those paragraphs, paragraph (i), of that Regulation, and

(b)   the Revenue Commissioners, in the case of any other claim to which Regulation 3 applies.

(2)   Subject to paragraph (3), a relevant authority may, at the request of a competent authority of a Member State, disclose to the competent authority any information in relation to a claim which is required to be disclosed by virtue of the Council Directive.

(3)   (a)   A relevant authority shall not disclose any information for the purposes of the Council Directive which would, in the opinion of the relevant authority, be liable to prejudice the security of the State or be contrary to public policy.

(b)   A relevant authority shall not be obliged to disclose any information for the purposes of the Council Directive -

(i)   that the relevant authority concerned would not be able to obtain for the purposes of recovering a similar claim in the State, or

(ii)   that would, in the opinion of the relevant authority, be materially detrimental to any commercial, industrial or professional secrets.

(4)   In obtaining the information referred to in paragraph (2), it shall be lawful for the relevant authority concerned to make use of the provisions of any enactment or instrument made under statute relating to the recovery of a similar claim in the State.

(5)   Nothing in this Regulation shall permit the relevant authority concerned to authorise the use of information disclosed by virtue of the Council Directive to the competent authorities of a Member State other than for the purposes of the recovery of a claim or to facilitate legal proceedings in relation to the recovery of such a claim.

Recovery of claims

5.   (1)   The Collector-General shall, in accordance with the provisions of these Regulations, collect the amount of a claim specified in any request duly made in accordance with the Council Directive by a claimant.

(2)   When the Collector-General duly receives a request from a claimant for the recovery of a claim, the Collector-General shall make demand in writing of the amount stated in the claim made by the claimant from the person against whom the claim is made.

(3)   For the purposes of these Regulations, the amount of any claim made by a claimant shall be deemed due and payable not later than 7 days from the date on which the Collector-General makes demand of the amount in accordance with paragraph (2).

(4)   The provisions of any enactment relating to the collection or recovery of income tax (other than sections 960, 961, 970, 971, 1000, 1003, 1004 and 1006B, and Chapter 4 of Part 42, of the Taxes Consolidation Act 1997) and the provisions of any rule of court so relating for those purposes shall, with any necessary modifications, apply in relation to the recovery of a claim referred

to in paragraph (1) as they apply in relation to income tax, and for this purpose the amount of the claim shall be deemed to be an amount of income tax.

(5)   For the purposes of these Regulations, the amount of the claim referred to in paragraph (1) shall be regarded as a debt due to the Minister for Finance, by the person against whom the claim is made by the claimant, in respect of a tax or duty under the care and management of the Revenue Commissioners.

(6)   Any reference in this Regulation to the amount of the claim shall include any interest payable in respect of that claim under Regulation 6.

(7)   The amount of any claim payable to the Collector-General under these Regulations -

    (a)   shall be payable without any deduction of income tax, and

    (b)   shall not be allowed as a deduction in computing any income, profits or losses for any of the purposes of the Tax Acts (except in so far as any relief is due in respect of the amount of the claim under Part 35 of the Taxes Consolidation Act 1997).

(8)   On payment of an amount under these Regulations, the Collector-General shall furnish the person concerned with a receipt in respect of that payment.

Interest

6. [(1)   The amount of any claim payable in accordance with Regulation 5(1) shall carry interest from the date when the amount of the claim becomes due and payable in accordance with Regulation 5(3) until payment, and the amount of such interest shall be determined by the formula —

$$(T \times D) \times 0.0273\%$$

where —

T is the amount of the claim payable in accordance with Regulation 5(1), and

D is the number of days (including part of a day) in the period beginning on the date when the amount of the claim becomes due and payable in accordance with Regulation 5(3) and ending on the date of payment of the claim.]'

(2)   Subsections (2) to (4) of section 1080 of the Taxes Consolidation Act 1997 shall apply in relation to interest payable in relation to the claim referred to in paragraph (1) as they apply in relation to interest payable under section 1080 of that Act in relation to tax charged by any assessment.

Application of rules

7.   The rules laid down in Articles 4 to 12 and 14 to 17 of the Council Directive (to the extent that they are not otherwise given effect to by these Regulations) and [Articles 2 to 28 of the Commission Directive][2] shall apply in relation to claims made by claimants and which are the subject of recovery in accordance with these Regulations.

Stay on proceedings

8.   (1)   Subject to paragraph (5), any action taken by the Revenue Commissioners or the Collector-General to recover the amount of any claim, whether by way of legal proceedings or other action, shall be stayed if -

(a)   in the case of court proceedings, the defendant satisfies the court that court proceedings relevant to that person's liability on the claim to which the proceedings so instituted relate are pending before a court, tribunal or other competent body in a Member State, or

(b)   in any other case, the person against whom the other action is being taken satisfies the Revenue Commissioners that court proceedings relevant to that person's liability on the claim to which the action relates are pending before a court, tribunal or other competent body in a Member State.

(2)   In any legal proceedings instituted under these Regulations it shall be a defence for the defendant to show that a final decision on the claim to which the proceedings relate has been given in the defendant's favour by a court, tribunal or other body of competent jurisdiction in a Member State, and, in relation to any part of a claim to which such legal proceedings relate, it shall be a defence for the defendant to show that such a decision has been given in relation to that part of the claim.

(3)   No question shall be raised in any legal proceedings instituted in pursuance of these Regulations as to the liability on the claim to which the proceedings relate of the person against whom the claim is made, [except as provided in paragraph (2)][2].

(4)   For the purposes of this Regulation, legal proceedings shall be regarded as pending so long as an appeal may be brought against any decision in the proceedings; and for these purposes a decision against which no appeal lies, or against which an appeal lies within a period which has expired without an appeal having been brought, shall be regarded as a final decision.

(5)   Paragraph (1) shall not apply where a claimant in accordance with the Council Directive so requests, and where the claimant so requests no action shall lie against the State (including the Revenue Commissioners, the Collector-General, any officer of the Revenue Commissioners and any agent of the Revenue Commissioners) in

any court by reason of the Revenue Commissioners, the Collector-General or any such officer or agent recovering, or taking any action to recover, the amount of, or part of the amount of, any claim the subject of such a request.

Remittance of claims

9.   Any amount recovered under these Regulations on foot of a claim made by a claimant under the Council Directive (including any interest under Regulation 6) shall be remitted to that claimant.

Application of Council Directive to certain Irish tax, etc. due

10.   (1)   In this Regulation-

"tax" means any tax, duty, levy or charge referred to in Article 2 of the Council Directive which is under the care and management of the Revenue Commissioners;

"agricultural levy" means any levy or other measure referred to in Article 2 of the Council Directive for which the Minister for Agriculture and Food is responsible;

"interest on unpaid tax", in relation to an amount of unpaid tax, means the amount of interest that has accrued to the date on which a certificate under this Regulation is signed in respect of the unpaid tax under any provision whatever providing for the charging of interest in respect of that tax, including interest on an undercharge of tax which is attributable to fraud or neglect, as specified in the certificate.

(2)   For the purpose of the Council Directive and for the avoidance of doubt, a demand by the Revenue Commissioners or the Minister for Agriculture and Food, as the case may be, for payment of an amount of tax (including, where appropriate, interest on unpaid tax) or agricultural levy where the amount demanded remains unpaid after expiration of the period for payment set out in the demand shall be an instrument permitting enforcement of the debt.

Delegation of powers and functions

11.   (1)   The Minister for Agriculture and Food may nominate, in writing, any of his or her officers to perform any acts and discharge any functions authorised by these Regulations to be performed or discharged by the Minister.

(2)   The Revenue Commissioners may nominate, in writing, any of their officers to perform any acts and discharge any functions authorised by these Regulations to be performed or discharged by them.

(3)   The Revenue Commissioners may nominate, in writing, any of their officers to perform any acts and discharge any functions authorised by these Regulations to be performed or discharged by the Collector-General.

Repeal and revocations

12.   (1)   Section 108 of the Finance Act 2001 is repealed.

(2)   The European Communities (Agriculture and Customs) (Mutual Assistance as regards the Recovery of Claims) Regulations 1980 (S.I. No. 73 of 1980) and the European Communities (Value-Added Tax) (Mutual Assistance as regards the Recovery of Claims) Regulations 1980 (S.I. No. 406 of 1980) are revoked.

GIVEN under my Official Seal, 25th September 2002.

CHARLIE McCREEVY,
Minister for Finance.

EXPLANATORY NOTE

The Regulations provide for the implementation of EC Directives on mutual assistance between Member States of the Community on the provision of information in respect of, and the recovery in the State of, claims made by other Member States in respect of debts due to that State from -

- refunds, interventions and other measures forming part of the system of financing the European Agricultural Guidance and Guarantee Fund (EAGGF);

- levies and other duties provided for under the common organisation of the market for the sugar sector;

- import duties;

- export duties;

- value-added tax;

- excise duties on manufactured tobacco, alcohol and alcoholic beverages and mineral oils;

- taxes on income and capital;

- taxes on insurance premiums; and

- interest, administrative penalties and fines, and costs incidental to these claims with the exclusion of any sanction in respect of which the act or commission giving rise to the sanction if committed in the State would be criminal in nature.

Amendments
1   Substituted by S.I. No. 249 of 2007, w.e.f. 1 January 2007.
2   Substituted by S.I. No. 344 of 2003, w.e.f. 24 July 2003.

TAXES (OFFSET OF REPAYMENTS) REGULATIONS 2002

(S.I. No. 471 of 2002)

ARRANGEMENT OF REGULATIONS

PART 1

General

1.   Citation.

2.   Interpretation.

PART 2

Offsetting

3.   Order of priority of offset against liabilities.

4.   Special arrangements regarding corporation tax, income tax and capital gains tax.

5.   Chronological order of priority of liabilities.

6.   Nomination of liabilities by taxpayer.

7.   Offset of interest.

PART 3

Miscellaneous

8.   Revocation.

The Revenue Commissioners, in exercise of the powers conferred on them by section 1006A of the Taxes Consolidation Act 1997 (No. 39 of 1997), make the following regulations:

PART 1

General

Citation

1.   These Regulations may be cited as the Taxes (Offset of Repayments) Regulations 2002.

Interpretation

2.   (1)   In these Regulations, unless the context otherwise requires–

"Acts", "claim", "liability", "overpayment" and "tax" have each the same meaning as they have, respectively, in the principal section;

"Collector-General" means the person appointed under section 851 of the Principal Act;

"estimate" means an estimate of tax made in accordance with the provisions of–

(a)   section 989 of the Principal Act,

(b)   Regulation 13 of the Income Tax (Relevant Contracts) Regulations 2000 (S.I. No. 71 of 2000), or

(c)   section 22 of the Value-Added Tax Act 1972 (No. 22 of 1972);

"current estimate", in relation to any particular time, means an estimate in respect of either an income tax month or a taxable period, as the case may be, the due date for which is immediately prior to that time or the income tax month or taxable period immediately preceding that month or period;

"due date", in relation to a liability, means the date on which the liability is due and payable under the appropriate provision of the Acts and, in relation to an estimate, the date on which the period for the payment of the tax for the income tax month or taxable period, as the case may be, expires;

"liability at enforcement" means a liability which, at the time at which the repayment is to be made in respect of the claim or overpayment -

(a)   was certified in a certificate issued, and not withdrawn, under section 962 of the Principal Act,

(b)   was the subject of proceedings initiated, and not withdrawn, as a debt due to the Minister for Finance, in any court of competent jurisdiction, or

(c)   was entered as a specified amount in a notice of attachment issued, and not revoked, under section 1002 of the Principal Act;

"Principal Act" means the Taxes Consolidation Act 1997 (No. 39 of 1997);

"principal section" means section 1006A of the Principal Act;

"taxhead" means-

(a)   tax deductible under Chapter 2 of Part 18 of the Principal Act and any regulations made under it,

(b)   income tax deductible under Chapter 4 of Part 42 of the Principal Act and any regulations made under it,

(c)   corporation tax,

(d)   an amount to be collected as income tax by the Collector-General in accordance with the provisions of the European Communities (Mutual Assistance for the Recovery of Claims relating to Certain Levies, Duties, Taxes and Other Measures) Regulations 2002 (S.I. No. 462 of 2002),

      (e)   income tax (other than that referred to in paragraphs (b) and (d) of this definition),

      (f)   capital gains tax,

      (g)   value-added tax,

      (h)   inheritance tax and gift tax,

      (i)   stamp duties,

      (j)   residential property tax,

      (k)   vehicle registration tax, or

      (l)   excise duties,

as the case may be.

(2)   In these Regulations -

      (a)   a reference to a Regulation is to a Regulation of these Regulations, unless it appears that reference to some other provision is intended;

      (b)   a reference to a paragraph is to the paragraph of the provision in which the reference occurs, unless it appears that reference to some other provision is intended.

(3)   Subject to paragraph (1), a word or expression that is used in these Regulations and is also used in any provision of the Acts has, except where the context otherwise requires, the same meaning in these Regulations as it has in that provision.

PART 2
Offsetting

Order of priority of offset against liabilities

3.   Subject to Regulations 4, 5, 6 and 7, the amount of any repayment in respect of a claim or overpayment made by any person, which is, by virtue of subsection (2) of the principal section, to be set against any liability of that person, shall be set against–

    (a)   firstly, any liability, other than a current estimate or a liability at enforcement, in the following sequence:

      (i)   a liability arising under the same taxhead in respect of which the claim or overpayment is made,

      (ii)   a liability arising under the Value-Added Tax Act 1972 and the enactments amending or extending that Act,

      (iii)   a liability arising under Chapter 4 of Part 42 of the Principal Act and the regulations made under it,

      (iv)   a liability arising under Chapter 2 of Part 18 of the Principal Act and the regulations made under it,

(v)   a liability arising under the Corporation Tax Acts,

(vi)   a liability arising under any provision (other than Chapter 4 of Part 42 of the Principal Act) of the Income Tax Acts,

(vii)   a liability arising under the Capital Gains Tax Acts,

(viii)   a liability arising under Part VI of the Finance Act 1983 (No. 15 of 1983) and the enactments amending or extending that Part,

(ix)   a liability arising under the [Capital Acquisitions Tax Consolidation Act 2003 (No. 1 of 2003)][1] and the enactments amending or extending that Act,

(x)   a liability arising under the Stamp Duties Consolidation Act 1999 (No. 31 of 1999) and the enactments amending or extending that Act,

(xi)   a liability arising under Chapter IV of Part II of the Finance Act 1992 (No. 9 of 1992),

(xii)   a liability arising under the statutes relating to the duties of excise and to the management of those duties,

(b)   secondly, any liability, being a liability at enforcement, in the sequence set out in paragraph (a), and

(c)   finally, against any amount referred to in paragraph (d) of the definition of "taxhead".

Special arrangements regarding corporation tax, income tax and capital gains tax

4.   Notwithstanding Regulation 3 but subject to Regulations 5, 6 and 7, in any case where a repayment in respect of a claim or overpayment made by any person, is under a taxhead referred to in paragraph (c), (e) or (f) of the definition of "taxhead", the amount of the repayment, which is, by virtue of subsection (2) of the principal section, to be set against any liability of that person, shall be set against–

(a)   firstly, any liability, other than a current estimate or a liability at enforcement, in the following sequence:

(i)   a liability arising under the same taxhead in respect of which the claim or overpayment is made,

(ii)   a liability arising under the Corporation Tax Acts,

(iii)   a liability arising under any provision (other than Chapter 4 of Part 42 of the Principal Act) of the Income Tax Acts,

(iv)   a liability arising under the Capital Gains Tax Acts,

(v)   a liability arising under the Value-Added Tax Act 1972 and the enactments amending or extending that Act,

(vi)   a liability arising under Chapter 4 of Part 42 of the Principal Act and the regulations made under it,

(vii)   a liability arising under Chapter 2 of Part 18 of the Principal Act and the regulations made under it,

(viii) a liability arising under Part VI of the Finance Act 1983 and the enactments amending or extending that Part,

(ix)   a liability arising under the [Capital Acquisitions Tax Consolidation Act 2003] and the enactments amending or extending that Act,

(x)   a liability arising under the Stamp Duties Consolidation Act 1999 and the enactments amending or extending that Act,

(xi)   a liability arising under Chapter IV of Part II of the Finance Act 1992,

(xii)   a liability arising under the statutes relating to the duties of excise and to the management of those duties,

(b)   secondly, any liability, being a liability at enforcement, in the sequence set out in paragraph (a), and

(c)   finally, against any amount referred to in paragraph (d) of the definition of "taxhead".

Chronological order of priority of liabilities

5.   For the purposes of Regulation 3 or 4, where, at any time, a repayment is to be set against more than one liability arising under a taxhead, it shall be set against any liability due for an earlier period or event in priority to a later period or event, as the case may be.

Nomination of liabilities by taxpayer

6.   Notwithstanding Regulation 3 or 4, a person may, at any time but not later than 30 days after the issue of a notice to him or her under subsection (2A) of the principal section, by notice in writing to the Collector-General request that the repayment concerned be set against liabilities (other than any amount referred to in paragraph (d) of the definition of "taxhead") in an order nominated by the person and the Collector-General shall arrange accordingly.

Offset of interest

7.   For the purposes of these Regulations, interest due and payable in relation to any liability to tax in respect of any period or event shall be deemed to be due and payable at the same time as the tax in respect of that period or event, as the case may be.

PART 3
Miscellaneous

Revocation

8.   The Taxes (Offset of Repayments) Regulations 2001 (S.I. No. 399 of 2001) are revoked.

GIVEN under my hand, 2 October 2002.

Michael O'Grady,
Revenue Commissioner.

EXPLANATORY NOTE

(This note is not part of the Instrument and does not purport to be a legal interpretation.)

These Regulations are being made under subsection (3) of section 1006A (inserted by the Finance Act, 2000 and amended by the Finance Acts of 2001 and 2002) of the Taxes Consolidation Act, 1997. That section empowers the Revenue Commissioners to offset repayments due to a person against outstanding liabilities of the person.

They replace the existing regulations (Taxes (Offset of Repayments) Regulations, 2001 (S.I. No. 399 of 2001)) which set out an order of priority for such offsets.

Under the repealed regulations, liabilities were divided into 2 priority categories as follows:

(1)   liabilities other than current estimates and liabilities at enforcement, and

(2)   liabilities at enforcement.

Within each category, but subject to one special case, a repayment was set off in the following sequence-

(a)   the taxhead giving rise to the repayment,

(b)   value-added tax,

(c)   employers PAYE,

(d)   relevant contracts tax,

(e)   corporation tax,

(f)   income tax, other than at (c),

(g)   capital gains tax,

(h)   residential property tax,

(i)   inheritance/gift taxes,

(j)   stamp duties,

(k)   vehicle registration tax, and

(l)   excise duties.

The special case is where the repayment arises in the corporation tax, income tax, capital gains tax grouping. In such a case liabilities within that same grouping are dealt with first before reverting to the order referred to above.

A third category of liability is now being introduced, that is, amounts which the Collector-General is to collect in accordance with the provisions of the European Communities (Mutual Assistance for the Recovery of Claims relating to Certain Levies, Duties, Taxes and Other Measures) Regulations 2002 (S.I. No.462 of 2002)). A repayment may be set off against a liability in this category, when there are no outstanding liabilities in the other two categories.

The taxpayer will have the option to request the Collector-General, at any time but not later than 30 days after the issue of the notice of offset, to vary the offset as nominated by him/her. However, this right does not extend to liabilities in the new category referred to in the preceding paragraph.

Within a taxhead a claim or overpayment will be offset against older liabilities before younger ones.

For the purpose of offsetting against interest owed by the taxpayer, the "age" of the interest is determined by the "age" of the tax, etc. giving rise to it.

Amendments
1   Substituted by s141 and Sch 8(6), FA 2008, w.e.f. 13 March 2008.

VALUE-ADDED TAX (ELECTRONIC INVOICING AND STORAGE) REGULATIONS, 2002

(S.I. No. 504 of 2002)

> **This Regulation was revoked by regulation 44, Value-Added Tax Regulations, 2006 (2006 S.I. No. 548) w.e.f. 1 November 2006**

The Revenue Commissioners, in exercise of the powers conferred on them by sections 17 and 32 of the Value-Added Tax Act 1972 (No. 22 of 1972) hereby make the following regulations:

1.   These Regulations may be cited as the Value-Added Tax (Electronic Invoicing and Storage) Regulations 2002.

2.   (1)   In these Regulations-

"Act" means the Value-Added Tax Act 1972 (No. 22 of 1972);

"Electronic Commerce Act" means the Electronic Commerce Act 2000 (No. 27 of 2000);

"advanced electronic signature" means an electronic signature which is -

(a)   uniquely linked to the signatory,

(b)   capable of identifying the signatory,

(c)   created using means that are capable of being maintained by the signatory under his or her sole control, and

(d)   linked to the data to which it relates in such a manner that any subsequent change of the data is detectable;

"electronic signature" means data in electronic form which are attached to or logically associated with a message and which serve as a method of authentication;

"electronic data interchange" means the electronic transfer, from computer to computer, of commercial and administrative data using an agreed standard to structure a message;

"electronic record" means a record required to be kept for the purposes of section 16 of the Act which is generated, transmitted and stored electronically;

"message" means an invoice, credit note, debit note, settlement voucher or document issued or received in accordance with section 17 of the Act and which is transmitted electronically;

"registration number" in relation to a person, means the number assigned to the person for the purposes of registration under section 9 of the Act;

"trading partners" means any two persons engaged by prior agreement in the electronic exchange of messages;

"transmission" means the transfer or making available of a message to a trading partner by electronic means;

"unique identification number" means a sequential number which is based on one or more series and which uniquely identifies a message transmitted between trading partners.

(2)   In these Regulations "signatory", "signature-creation data", "signature-creation device", "signature-verification-data", and "signature-verification device" have the meanings assigned to them by the Electronic Commerce Act.

(3)   In these Regulations-

(a)   a reference to a Regulation is to a Regulation of these Regulations, and

(b)   a reference to a paragraph, subparagraph or clause is to a paragraph, subparagraph or clause of the provision in which the reference occurs,

unless it is indicated that reference to some other provision is intended.

3.   (1)   A message issued or received by electronic means by a taxable person shall be deemed to be so issued or received for the purposes of section 17(1A) of the Act if each such message -

(a)   is transmitted between trading partners using an electronic data interchange system which satisfies the requirements specified in paragraphs (2) and (3), or

(b)   is transmitted between trading partners using an advanced electronic signature and an associated system which satisfy the requirements specified in paragraphs (2) and (3).

(2)   The electronic data interchange system or the advanced electronic signature and associated system used by the taxable person referred to in paragraph (1) shall be capable of -

(a)   producing, retaining and storing, and making available to an officer of the Revenue Commissioners on request, electronic records and messages in such form and containing such particulars as may be required in accordance with sections 16 and 17 of the Act and Regulations made under the Act,

(b)   causing to be reproduced on paper any electronic record or message required to be produced, retained or stored in accordance with sections 16 and 17 of the Act and Regulations made under the Act,

(c)   allocating a unique identification number for each message transmitted, and

(d)   maintaining electronic records in such manner as will allow their retrieval by reference to the name of a trading partner or the date or the unique identification number, of the message.

(3)   The electronic data interchange system or the advanced electronic signature and associated system used by the taxable person referred to in paragraph (1) shall-

    (a)   preclude the repeated transmission of a message,

    (b)   preclude the omission of any message from the electronic record,

    (c)   verify the origin or receipt of a message by a trading partner, and

    (d)   guarantee the integrity of the contents of a message, or of an electronic record related to that message, during transmission and during the period provided for in section 16 for the retention of records, invoices or any other documents specified in the Act or in Regulations made under the Act.

(4)   (a)   A taxable person who issues or receives messages by electronic means in accordance with paragraph 3(1) shall retain and store such messages or copies of such messages as appropriate and electronic records related to those messages and in addition shall retain and store electronically the following data:

        (i)   details of the form of encryption, electronic signature, signature creation data or device, signature verification data or device, or any other method used to ensure the integrity of the records and messages transmitted, retained and stored and the authenticity of their origin,

        (ii)   details of where and in what format the information required in accordance with clause (i) is stored and how it can be accessed.

    (b)   A taxable person who issues or receives messages by electronic means shall-

        (i)   provide details on request to an officer of the Revenue Commissioners on where and how an electronic record or message is stored on that taxpayer's system and how it can be accessed by that officer,

        (ii)   allow such access to electronic records or messages for inspection by an officer of the Revenue Commissioners at all reasonable times, and

(iii)   reproduce any such electronic record or message on paper on request by an officer of the Revenue Commissioners including details required to be retained and stored under subparagraph (a).

4.   A taxable person may transmit messages by means other than those referred to in Regulation 3(1) where-

(a)   he or she is satisfied that such messages are recorded, retained and transmitted in accordance with section 17(1A) of the Act,

(b)   the requirements of paragraphs (2), (3) and (4) of Regulation 3 are met, and

(c)   he or she notifies the Revenue Commissioners accordingly, and until 31 December 2005 such notification shall be made prior to the commencement of the transmission of such messages.

5.   The Value-Added Tax (Electronic Data Exchange and Storage) Regulations 1992 (S.I. No. 269 of 1992) are revoked.

GIVEN under my hand, 5th November 2002.

JOSEPHINE FEEHILY
Revenue Commissioner.

EXPLANATORY NOTE

(This note is not part of the Instrument and does not purport to be a legal interpretation.)

Section 17(1A) of the VAT Act provides, inter alia, that an invoice or other document required to be issued by a person under section 17 of the Act is not deemed to be so issued by that person unless the person complies with conditions specified by regulations and the system or systems used by the person conforms with such specifications as are required by regulations.

Section 17 (1A) also provides that a person in receipt of an electronic transmission will not be deemed to be in receipt of an invoice or other document unless the system used by that person conforms with specifications as are required by regulations and the person complies with conditions specified by regulations.

These Regulations lay down these conditions and systems specifications and partially implement Council Directive 2001/115/EC of 20 December, 2001 insofar as invoices sent by electronic means are concerned.

The Regulations revoke the Value-Added Tax (Electronic Data Exchange and Storage) Regulations 1992 (S.I. No. 269 of 1992).

EUROPEAN COMMUNITIES (MUTUAL ASSISTANCE FOR THE RECOVERY OF CLAIMS RELATING TO CERTAIN LEVIES, DUTIES, TAXES AND OTHER MEASURES) (AMENDMENT) REGULATIONS 2003

(S.I. No. 344 of 2003)

I, CHARLIE McCREEVY, Minister for Finance, in exercise of the powers conferred on me by section 3 of the European Communities Act 1972 (No. 27 of 1972) and for the purposes of giving effect to Commission Directive 2002/94/EC of 9 December 2002, hereby make the following regulations:

1.   These Regulations may be cited as the European Communities (Mutual Assistance for the Recovery of Claims relating to Certain Levies, Duties, Taxes and Other Measures) (Amendment) Regulations 2003.

2.   The European Communities (Mutual Assistance for the Recovery of Claims relating to Certain Levies, Duties, Taxes and Other Measures) Regulations 2002 (S.I. No. 462 of 2002) are amended –

   (a)   in Regulation 2 (1) by substituting the following for the definition of "Commission Directive":

   "'**Commission Directive**' means Commission Directive No. 2002/94/EC of 9 December 2002;",

   (b)   in Regulation 7 by substituting "Articles 2 to 28 of the Commission Directive" for "Articles 2 to 21 of the Commission Directive",

   and

   (c)   in Regulation 8(3) by substituting "except as provided in paragraph (2)" for "except as provided in paragraph (3)".

GIVEN under my Official Seal,
24th July 2003.

CHARLIE McCREEVY,
Minister for Finance.

EXPLANATORY NOTE

(This note is for information purposes only and does not form part of the Statutory Instrument)

These Regulations provide for the amendment of the European Communities (Mutual Assistance for the Recovery of Claims relating to Certain Levies, Duties, Taxes and Other Measures) Regulations, 2002. These regulations ensure that references to the Commission Directive in European Communities (Mutual Assistance for the Recovery of Claims relating to Certain Levies, Duties, Taxes and Other Measures) Regulations, 2002 (S.I. No. 462 of 2002) are references to Commission Directive 2002/94/EC which replaces an earlier Commission Directive (77/794/EEC) which sets out the detailed rules for implementing Council Directive 76/308/EEC. The rules as set out in Articles 2 to 28 of the Commission Directive detail how the competent authorities of the Member States interact with each other in regard to requests for information, requests for recovery and the accompanying paperwork.

VALUE-ADDED TAX (WAIVER OF EXEMPTION) (LETTING OF IMMOVABLE GOODS) REGULATIONS 2003

(S.I. No. 504 of 2003)

> This Regulation was revoked by regulation 44, Value-Added Tax Regulations, 2006 (2006 S.I. No. 548) w.e.f. 1 November 2006

The Revenue Commissioners, in exercise of the powers conferred on them by sections 7 and 32(1)(a) of the Value-Added Tax Act 1972 (No. 22 of 1972), hereby make the following regulations:

1.   These Regulations may be cited as the Value-Added Tax (Waiver of Exemption) (Letting of Immovable Goods) Regulations 2003.

2.   (1)   In these Regulations–

"**Act**" means the Value-Added Tax Act 1972 (No. 22 of 1972);

"**back-dating**" in relation to a waiver, means the waiving of a right to exemption from tax in respect of an exempt letting of immovable goods to which paragraph (iv) of the First Schedule to the Act refers, from a date earlier than the current taxable period referred to in Regulation 3(1)(c), and cognate words shall be construed accordingly;

"**cancellation request period**" means the taxable period during which a request for the cancellation of a waiver is made in accordance with Regulation 3(7);

"**registration number**" in relation to a person, means the number assigned to the person for the purposes of registration under section 9 of the Act;

"**specified letting**" means an exempt letting of immovable goods to which paragraph (iv) of the First Schedule to the Act applies;

"**waiver**" means the waiver by a person of his or her right to exemption from tax on a specified letting.

(2)   In these Regulations–

(a)   a reference to a Regulation is to a Regulation of these Regulations, unless it is indicated that reference to some other Regulations is intended,

(b)   a reference to a paragraph or subparagraph is a reference to a paragraph or subparagraph of the provision in which the reference occurs, unless it is indicated that reference to some other provision is intended.

3.   (1)   A person who, in accordance with section 7(1) of the Act wishes to waive his or her right to exemption from tax on the supply of a specified letting, shall furnish in writing to the Revenue Commissioners the following particulars–

(a)   his or her name and address,

     (b)   his or her registration number (if any), and

     (c)   the taxable period, from the commencement of which he or she desires that the waiver should have effect, not being earlier than the current taxable period.

(2)   The Revenue Commissioners shall acknowledge receipt of the particulars referred to in paragraph (1) and shall specify the taxable period (in this paragraph referred to as the 'start period') not being earlier than the taxable period referred to in paragraph (1)(c), from the commencement of which the waiver of exemption has effect. From the start period to the date on which the person permanently ceases to supply taxable goods or services (including services to which the waiver of exemption applies), or until his or her waiver is cancelled in accordance with paragraph (8), the Act applies to him or her as if the specified letting were not an exempt activity.

(3)   Where a taxable person makes a specified letting and the immovable goods which are the subject of the letting were acquired or developed by him or her for the purpose of his or her taxable supplies, then, notwithstanding paragraph (2), that person may apply to the Revenue Commissioners to backdate the waiver of his or her right to exemption in respect of that letting. However, no application under this paragraph may be made in respect of any disposal of an interest in immovable goods which is deemed to be a letting of immovable goods to which paragraph (iv) of the First Schedule to the Act applies by virtue of section 4(3A)(a)(ii) of the Act.

(4)   An application under paragraph (3) shall be made in writing to the Revenue Commissioners and shall include the following–

     (a)   the name, address and registration number of the taxable person making the application,

     (b)   the tenant's name, address and registration number,

     (c)   details of the letting agreement, and

     (d)   the date from which the taxable person desires that the waiver shall have effect.

(5)   A waiver of exemption shall be backdated only where the tenant would have been entitled to deduct, in accordance with section 12 of the Act, all the tax that would have been chargeable in respect of the letting if the waiver had applied from the date specified in accordance with paragraph (6)(a)(i) to the date notified in accordance with paragraph (6)(a)(ii).

(6)   Where the Revenue Commissioners are satisfied that an applicant has complied with paragraph (4) and that paragraph (5) applies–

(a)   they shall notify the applicant–

(i)   that the waiver may be back-dated in respect of the letting for which back-dating of a waiver was sought specifying the date to which the waiver shall be back-dated being a date not earlier than 26 March 1997, and

(ii)   of the date from which he or she is deemed, for the purposes of the Act, to have waived his or her right to exemption in respect of all specified lettings which he or she supplies, such date not being earlier than the commencement of the taxable period during which the notification issued, and

(b)   any tax chargeable on the letting of immovable goods resulting from the back-dating of a waiver prior to the date notified under subparagraph (a)(ii) is deemed to have been due and paid by the taxable person in accordance with section 19 of the Act and deducted by the tenant in accordance with section 12 of the Act.

(7)   A person who, in accordance with paragraph (1), waives his or her right to exemption in respect of a specified letting shall be entitled to have such waiver cancelled and to be treated, as from the date specified in paragraph (8), as a person who had not so waived provided he or she–

(a)   applies to the Revenue Commissioners in writing to have the waiver of his or her right to exemption cancelled,

(b)   furnishes particulars to the Revenue Commissioners of–

(i)   the tax paid by him or her in accordance with section 19(3) of the Act in respect of or in relation to the supply of services by him or her to which the waiver applied for all taxable periods comprised in the period commencing with the beginning of the start period and ending with the termination of the taxable period immediately preceding the cancellation request period, and

(ii)   the total amount of tax deducted or deductible by him or her referred to in paragraphs (a), (b) and (c) of subsection (3) (inserted by section 100 of the Finance Act 1997 (No. 22 of 1997)) of section 7 of the Act in respect of all of the taxable periods comprised in the period referred to in clause (i), together with the total amount of tax deducted by him or her referred to in paragraph (aa) (inserted by section 117 of the Finance Act 2003 (No. 3 of 2003)) of the said subsection (3),

and

(c)   pays to the Collector-General an amount equal to the excess (if any) of the tax referred to in subparagraph (b)(ii) over the tax referred to in subparagraph (b)(i).

(8)   Where a person wishing to have his or her waiver cancelled, complies with paragraph (7) to the satisfaction of the Revenue Commissioners, they shall so notify the person in writing. On receipt by the person of the notification, his or her waiver shall be cancelled with effect from the end of the taxable period during which he or she is so notified and from the end of that taxable period the person shall be treated as a person who had not waived his or her right to exemption.

(9)   A person who applies for the cancellation of his or her waiver in accordance with paragraph (7) is not entitled, under section 20(1) of the Act, to any refund of tax (other than a refund referable solely to some error or mistake made by him or her) for the cancellation request period or any subsequent taxable periods, in relation to the letting to which the waiver relates, in excess of an amount calculated in accordance with the following sum:

A + B

where-

A is the excess of the amount referred to in paragraph 7(b)(i) over the amount referred to in paragraph 7(b)(ii), but where there is no such excess A is equal to zero,

and

B is the sum of the amounts of tax paid under section 19(3) of the Act, in relation to the letting to which the waiver relates, for the cancellation request period and any subsequent taxable periods until the waiver is cancelled.

4.   Regulation 4 of the Value-Added Tax Regulations 1979 (S.I. No. 63 of 1979) is revoked.

GIVEN under my hand,
24 October 2003

JOSEPHINE FEEHILY
Revenue Commissioner

EXPLANATORY NOTE

(This note is not part of the Instrument and does not purport to be a legal interpretation.)

These Regulations provide the conditions and procedures which a person must comply with in order to waive his or her right to exemption from tax on the letting of immovable goods or to cancel that waiver.

These Regulations replace Regulation 4 of the Value-Added Tax Regulations 1979.

FINANCE ACT 2003 (COMMENCEMENT OF SECTIONS 124, 125, 129 AND 130(B)) ORDER 2003

(S.I. No. 512 of 2003)

I, Charlie McCreevy, Minister for Finance, in exercise of the powers conferred on me by section 171(10)(e) of the Finance Act 2003 (No.3 of 2003), hereby order as follows:

1.   This Order may be cited as the Finance Act 2003 (Commencement of Sections 124, 125, 129 and 130(b)) Order 2003.

2.   The 1st day of November 2003 is appointed as the day on which sections 124, 125, 129 and 130(b) of section 130 of the Finance Act 2003 shall take effect.

GIVEN under my Official Seal,
this 31 day of October, 2003.

CHARLIE McCREEVY,
Minister for Finance.

EXPLANATORY NOTE – Sections 124, 125, 129, 130(b)

(This note is not part of the instrument and does not purport to be a legal interpretation).

This order appoints the 1st day of November, 2003 as the date for coming into effect of the provisions of sections 124, 125, 129 and 130(b) of the Finance Act 2003.

Section 124   amends the legislative basis for making refunds of VAT by providing for a four year time limit within which a refund of tax can be made by Revenue for taxable periods after 1 May 2003. However, as an interim measure where a claim relates to a taxable period before 1 May 2003, the existing six year limit for making a claim for refund of tax will apply up to 31 December 2004.

Section 125 provides the framework for the payment of interest on VAT refunds.

Section 129 amends the legislative basis by providing a four year time limit for the making of estimates and assessments for underpayment of VAT for taxable periods after 1 May 2003. However, as an interim measure where an estimate or assessment relates to a taxable period before 1 May 2003, the existing six year limit for the making of estimates and assessments will apply up to 31 December 2004.

Section 130(b) provides for the making of regulations in connection with the new interest scheme.

EUROPEAN COMMUNITIES (MUTUAL ASSISTANCE IN THE FIELD OF DIRECT TAXATION, CERTAIN EXCISE DUTIES AND TAXATION OF INSURANCE PREMIUMS) REGULATIONS, 2003

(S.I. No. 711 of 2003)

> These Regulations revoked by r11, European Communities (Mutual Assistance in the Field of Direct Taxation, Certain Excise Duties and Taxation of Insurance Premiums) Regulations, 2005 (2005 S.I. No. 367)

I, CHARLIE Mc CREEVY, Minster for Finance, in exercise of the powers conferred on me by section 3 of the European Communities Act 1972 (No. 27 of 1972) and for the purpose of giving effect to Council Directive 77/799/EEC of 19 December 1977, as amended by Council Directive No. 79/1070/EEC of 6 December 1979, Council Directive No. 92/12/EEC of 25 February 1992 and Council Directive 2003/93/EC of 7 October 2003, hereby make the following regulations:

1. (1)   These Regulations may be cited as the European Communities (Mutual Assistance in the Field of Direct Taxation, Certain Excise Duties and Taxation of Insurance Premiums) Regulations 2003.

    (2)   These Regulations come into operation on 31 December 2003.

2. In these Regulations -

    "**authorised officer**" means an officer of the Revenue Commissioners authorised in writing by the Revenue Commissioners for the purpose of these Regulations;

    "**the Council Directive**" means Council Directive 77/799/EEC of 19 December 1977, as amended by Council Directive No. 79/1070/EEC of 6 December 1979, Council Directive No. 92/12/EEC of 25 February 1992 and Council Directive 2003/93/EC of 7 October 2003.

3. (1)   The Revenue Commissioners and authorised officers of those Commissioners may disclose to the competent authorities of another Member State any information required to be to be so disclosed by virtue of the Council Directive.

    (2)   Neither the Revenue Commissioners nor an authorised officer of those Commissioners shall disclose any information in pursuance of the Council Directive unless satisfied that the competent authorities of the other Member State concerned are bound by, or have undertaken to observe, rules of confidentiality with respect to the information which are not less strict than those applying to it in the State.

    (3)   Nothing in this Regulation permits the Revenue Commissioners or an authorised officer of those Commissioners to authorise the use of information disclosed by virtue of the Council Directive to the competent authority of another Member State other than

for the purposes of taxation or to facilitate legal proceedings for failure to observe the tax laws of that State.

4.   (1)   Section 107 of the Finance Act 2001 is repealed.

(2)   The European Communities (Mutual Assistance in the Field of Direct Taxation) Regulations 1978 (S.I. No. 334 of 1978) and the European Communities (Mutual Assistance in the Field of Value-Added Tax) Regulations 1980 (S.I. No. 407 of 1980) are revoked.

GIVEN under my Official Seal,
18th December 2003.

CHARLIE McCREEVY,
Minister for Finance.

EXPLANATORY NOTE

(This note is not part of the instrument and does not purport to be a legal instrument)

These Regulations provide for an extension at national level of the EEC Council Directive of 19 December 1977 concerning mutual assistance (exchange of information) by the competent authorities of Member States, as required by an amending Council Directive of 7 October 2003. These Regulations also consolidate and give effect, in one set of regulations, to Council Directive 77/799/EEC as amended.

VALUE-ADDED TAX (INVOICES AND OTHER DOCUMENTS) (AMENDMENT) REGULATIONS, 2003

(S.I. No. 723 of 2003)

> This Regulation was revoked by regulation 44, Value-Added Tax Regulations, 2006 (2006 S.I. No. 548) w.e.f. 1 November 2006

The Revenue Commissioners, in exercise of the powers conferred on them by sections 17 and 32 of the Value-Added Tax Act 1972 (No. 22 of 1972), and for the purpose of giving further effect to Council Directive 2001/115/EC of 20 December 2001, make the following regulations:

1. (1)   These Regulations may be cited as the Value-Added Tax (Invoices and Other Documents)(Amendment) Regulations 2003.

    (2)   These Regulations come into operation on 1 January 2004.

2. In these Regulations "**Principal Regulations**" means the Value-Added Tax (Invoices and Other Documents) Regulations 1992 (S.I. No. 275 of 1992).

3. Regulation 3 of the Principal Regulations is amended–

    (a)   by substituting the following for paragraph (a):

    "(a)   Every invoice issued by a taxable person in accordance with section 17(1) of the Act shall set out the following particulars:

    (i)   the date of issue of the invoice,

    (ii)   a sequential number, based on one or more series, which uniquely identifies the invoice,

    (iii) the full name, address and the registration number of the person who supplied the goods or services to which the invoice relates,

    (iv)   the full name and address of the person to whom the goods or services have been supplied,

    (v)   in the case of a reverse charge supply, being a supply of goods or services to a person in another Member State who is liable to pay value-added tax under Council Directive No. 77/388/EEC of 17 May 1977 on such supply, the value-added tax identification number of that person in that Member State and an indication that a reverse charge applies,

    (vi)   in the case of a supply of goods, other than a reverse charge supply, to a person registered for value-added tax in another Member State, the person's value-added tax identification number in that Member State and an indication that the invoice relates to an intra-Community supply of goods,

(vii)   the quantity and nature of the goods supplied or the extent and nature of the services rendered,

(viii)   the date on which the goods or services were supplied or, in the case of supplies specified in section 17(8) of the Act, the date on which the payment on account was made, insofar as that date can be determined and differs from the date of issue of the invoice,

(ix)   in respect of the goods or services supplied:

(I)   the unit price exclusive of tax,

(II)   any discounts or price reductions not included in the unit price, and

(III)   the consideration exclusive of tax,

(x)   in respect of goods or services supplied, other than reverse charge supplies,

(I)   the consideration exclusive of tax per rate of tax, and

(II)   the rate of tax chargeable,

(xi)   the tax payable in respect of the supply of the goods or services, except in the case of a reverse charge supply or where section 10A(9), 10B(5) or 12B(5) of the Act applies, and

(xii)   in the case where a tax representative is liable to pay the value-added tax in another Member State, the full name and address and the value-added tax identification number of that representative.",

(b)   by substituting the following for paragraph (g):

"(g)   Every invoice issued by a customer in accordance with section 17(14) of the Act in respect of goods or services supplied to that customer shall set out the details specified in Regulation 3(a).",

and

(c)   by inserting the following after paragraph (j):

"(k)   A person, other than a flat-rate farmer, issuing an invoice in accordance with section 17(3) of the Act or a credit note, settlement voucher or debit note in accordance with section 17 of the Act shall also comply with the following conditions in respect of every invoice, credit note, settlement voucher or debit note so issued:

(i)   it shall be identified by a sequential number, based on one or more series, which uniquely identifies it,

(ii)   in the case of a reverse charge supply, it shall show the value-added tax identification number of the person who is liable to pay the value-added tax, and an indication that a reverse charge applies,

(iii)   in respect of goods or services supplied, it shall show the unit price exclusive of tax and any discounts or price reductions not included in the unit price, and

(iv)   in respect of goods or services supplied, other than reverse charge supplies, it shall show the consideration exclusive of tax per rate of tax, and the rate of tax applicable.".

4.   The Principal Regulations are amended by inserting the following after Regulation 3:

"3A.   An invoice, credit note, settlement voucher or debit note issued by a taxable person in accordance with section 17 of the Act relating to an intra-Community supply of a new means of transport (within the meaning given by section 1 of the Act) shall set out details necessary to identify the goods as a new means of transport.

3B.   Every invoice issued by a taxable person in accordance with section 10A(9) or 10B(5) of the Act shall indicate that the margin scheme or auction scheme has been applied.

3C.   The amount of tax included on an invoice or other document issued in accordance with section 17 of the Act shall be expressed in euro.

3D.   (1)   Notwithstanding these Regulations, the Revenue Commissioners may allow invoices, credit notes, settlement vouchers or debit notes to be issued under simplified arrangements in accordance with Article 22(9)(d) of Council Directive No. 77/388/EEC of 17 May 1977 but only if they include the following particulars:

(a)   the date of issue,

(b)   identification of the supplier,

(c)   identification of the type of goods or services supplied,

(d)   the tax due or the information needed to calculate it, and

(e)   such other details as the Revenue Commissioners may require and to which paragraph (2) of this Regulation relates.

(2)   The Revenue Commissioners shall publish in the Iris Oifigiúil the details to be included in the documents referred to in paragraph (1) of this Regulation and the circumstances under which they qualify for the simplified arrangements.".

5.   Regulation 5 of the Principal Regulations is revoked.

Given this 22 day of December 2003

JOSEPHINE FEEHILY
Revenue Commissioner

EXPLANATORY NOTE

(This note is not part of the Instrument and does not purport to be a legal document.)

These Regulations specify the form and particulars to be contained in VAT invoices, credit notes and other documents which are required to be issued by taxable persons in accordance with section 17 of the VAT Act and implement the outstanding parts of Council Directive 2001/115/EC of 20 December 2001.

They revoke Regulation 5 of the VAT (Invoices and Other Documents) Regulations 1992 (S.I. No. 275 of 1992).

DISABLED DRIVERS AND DISABLED PASSENGERS (TAX CONCESSIONS) (AMENDMENT) REGULATIONS 2004

(S.I. No. 469 of 2004)

I, Charlie McCreevy, Minister for Finance, in exercise of the powers conferred on me by section 92 (as amended by section 17 of Finance (No. 2) Act 1992 (No. 28 of 1992)) of the Finance Act 1989 (No. 10 of 1989), and after consultation with the Minister for Health and Children (as adapted by the Health (Alteration of Name of Department and Title of Minister) Order 1997 (S.I. No.308 of 1997)) and the Minister for the Environment, Heritage and Local Government (as adapted by the Environment and Local Government (Alteration of Name of Department and Title of Minister) Order 2003 (S.I. No. 233 of 2003)) hereby make the following regulations:

1. These Regulations may be cited as the Disabled Drivers and Disabled Passengers (Tax Concessions) (Amendment) Regulations 2004.

2. The Disabled Drivers and Disabled Passengers (Tax Concessions) Regulations 1994 (S.I. No. 353 of 1994) are amended -

    (a) by inserting the following after Regulation 4:

    "4A. (1) A Director of Community Care and Medical Officer of Health shall not consider an application under these Regulations for a primary medical certificate where a determination has been made by the Disabled Drivers Medical Board of Appeal within the period of 6 months prior to the date of the making of the application unless the application is accompanied by a medical certificate from a registered medical practitioner indicating that the practitioner has formed the opinion that the person concerned is severely and permanently disabled as respects one or more of the criteria specified in Regulation 3.

    (2) Each subsequent application by that person for a primary medical certificate shall be accompanied by a medical certificate from a registered medical practitioner indicating that the practitioner has formed the opinion that the medical condition of the person concerned has materially disimproved since the previous application."

    and

    (b) by substituting for Regulation 6 the following:

"Medical Board of Appeal.

6.   (1)   (a)   Subject to paragraph (2) and Regulation 19 (3), on the nomination of the Minister for Health and Children, the Minister for Finance shall appoint 5 medical practitioners to the Disabled Drivers Medical Board of Appeal (in this Regulation referred to as the 'Board') for a period of 4 years in each case and any such practitioner may be reappointed by the Minister for Finance on the nomination of the Minister for Health and Children for a further such period or periods.

       (b)   One of the 5 appointed medical practitioners shall be appointed by the Minister for Finance to be the chairperson of the Board.

       (c)   Three members of the Board shall constitute a quorum for a meeting of the Board.

       (d)   In the absence of the chairperson from a meeting of the Board, the members present shall elect one of their number to chair that meeting.

       (e)   The Board shall be independent in the exercise of its functions.

   (2)   Each vacancy on the Board shall be filled by the appointment by the Minister for Finance of a medical practitioner, nominated for that purpose by the Minister for Health and Children, for the remainder of the period of the former member's appointment to which the vacancy relates.

   (3)   Whenever the Minister for Health and Children so requests, for reasons stated in writing, the Minister for Finance shall remove any named person from the Board.

   (4)   (a)   A person who is dissatisfied by a decision of a Director of Community Care and Medical Officer of Health in respect of primary medical certification may appeal to the Board within 28 days of the person first being informed of that decision, or such longer period as the Board may allow, and the person concerned shall be informed of the right to so appeal.

       (b)   An appeal under subparagraph (a) shall be accompanied by a copy of the decision so appealed.

   (5)   The Board shall inform the appellant in writing of its decision and

       (a)   where the Board determines that the appellant meets one or more of the criteria specified in Regulation 3, it shall issue a Board Medical Certificate,

> (b)   where the Board determines that the appellant does not meet the criteria specified in Regulation 3, it shall refuse the appeal.
>
> (6)   Where a person has previously made an appeal to the Board, a subsequent appeal to the Board shall be accompanied by a copy of the refusal of the Director of Community Care and Medical Officer of Health of the application made under Regulation 4A and by a copy of the determination of the Board previously so made.".

GIVEN under my Official Seal,

This 23rd day of July 2004.

CHARLIE MCCREEVY
Minister for Finance

VALUE-ADDED TAX (REFUND OF TAX)(AMENDMENT) ORDER 2004

(S.I. No. 573 of 2004)

I, Charlie McCreevy, Minister for Finance, in exercise of the powers conferred on me by section 20(3) (as amended by section 184(1)(c) of the Finance Act 1992 (No. 9 of 1992)) of the Value-Added Tax Act 1972 (No. 22 of 1972), hereby order as follows:

1.   This Order may be cited as the Value-Added Tax (Refund of Tax) (Amendment) Order 2004.

2.   Paragraph (2)(1) of the Value-Added Tax (Refund of Tax)(No.28) Order 1996 (S.I. No.98 of 1996) (as amended by S.I. No. 305 of 1999), is hereby amended by the substitution in the definition of "qualifying vehicle" of "775 millimetres in floor height" for "950 millimetres in floor height".

GIVEN under my Official Seal,

this 27th day of September, 2004.

CHARLIE MCCREEVY TD
Minister for Finance.

EXPLANATORY NOTE

(This note is not part of the Instrument and does not purport to be a legal interpretation).

S.I. No. 98 of 1996 provides for a full repayment of VAT incurred by exempt coach operators on touring coaches of certain dimensions. This Order amends the S.I. to allow touring coaches of lower floor height to qualify for the repayment.

EUROPEAN COMMUNITIES (MUTUAL ASSISTANCE FOR THE RECOVERY OF CLAIMS RELATING TO CERTAIN LEVIES, DUTIES, TAXES AND OTHER MEASURES) (AMENDMENT) REGULATIONS 2004

(S.I. No. 851 of 2004)

I, BRIAN COWEN, Minister for Finance, in exercise of the powers conferred on me by section 3 of the European Communities Act 1972 (No. 27 of 1972) and for the purpose of giving effect to Commission Directive 2004/79/EC of 4 March 2004, hereby make the following regulations:

1.　(1)　These Regulations may be cited as the European Communities (Mutual Assistance for the Recovery of Claims relating to Certain Levies, Duties, Taxes and Other Measures) (Amendment) Regulations 2004.

　　(2)　These Regulations are deemed to have come into operation on 1 May 2004.

2.　The European Communities (Mutual Assistance for the Recovery of Claims relating to Certain Levies, Duties, Taxes and Other Measures) Regulations 2002 (S.I. No. 462 of 2002) are amended in Regulation 2(1) by substituting for the definition of "Commission Directive" (inserted by the European Communities (Mutual Assistance for the Recovery of Claims relating to Certain Levies, Duties, Taxes and Other Measures) (Amendment) Regulations 2003 (S.I. No. 344 of 2003)) the following:

"Commission Directive" means Commission Directive No. 2002/94/EC of 9 December 2002 as amended by Commission Directive 2004/79/EC of 4 March 2004;".

GIVEN under my Official Seal,
15 December 2004.

BRIAN COWEN,
Minster for Finance.

EXPLANATORY NOTE

(This note is not part of the instrument and does not purport to be a legal interpretation)

These regulations provide for the amendment of the European Communities (Mutual Assistance for the Recovery of Claims relating to Certain Levies, Duties, Taxes and Other Measures) Regulations 2002 to facilitate the admission of the 10 new EU Member States. These regulations ensure that references to Commission Directive in the European Communities (Mutual Assistance for the Recovery of Claims relating to Certain Levies, Duties, Taxes and Other Measures) Regulations 2002, are references to Commission Directive 2002/94/EC as amended by Commission Directive 2004/79/EC. The effect of the change contained in Commission Directive 2004/79/EC is to add the 10 new Member States to the list of Member States in a form for returning information to the Commission contained in the annex to Commission Directive 2002/94/EC.

DISABLED DRIVERS AND DISABLED PASSENGERS (TAX CONCESSIONS) (AMENDMENT) REGULATIONS 2005

(S.I. No. 178 of 2005)

I, Brian Cowen, Minister for Finance, in exercise of the powers conferred on me by section 92 (as amended by section 17 of Finance (No. 2) Act 1992 (No. 28 of 1992)) of the Finance Act 1989 (No. 10 of 1989), and after consultation with the Minister for Health and Children (as adapted by the Health (Alteration of Name of Department and Title of Minister) Order 1997 (S.I. No.308 of 1997)) and the Minister for the Environment, Heritage and Local Government (as adapted by the Environment and Local Government (Alteration of Name of Department and Title of Minister) Order 2003 (S.I. No. 233 of 2003)), hereby make the following regulations:

1. These Regulations may be cited as the Disabled Drivers and Disabled Passengers (Tax Concessions) (Amendment) Regulations 2005.

2. Regulation 6 (inserted by the Disabled Drivers and Disabled Passengers (Tax Concessions) (Amendment) Regulations 2004 (S.I. No. 469 of 2004)) of the Disabled Drivers and Disabled Passengers (Tax Concessions) Regulations 1994 (S.I. No. 353 of 1994) is amended -

    (a)   in paragraph (1) (a), by substituting "the Minister for Finance shall appoint 5 medical practitioners and may appoint a further 5 medical practitioners" for "the Minister for Finance shall appoint 5 medical practitioners", and

    (b)   in paragraph (1) (b), by substituting "One of the appointed medical practitioners" for "One of the 5 appointed medical practitioners".

Given under my official seal,

This 7th day of April 2005

Brian Cowen

Minister for Finance.

EXPLANATORY NOTE

(This note is not part of the instrument and does not purport to be a legal interpretation).

These Regulations allow the Minister for Finance to appoint an additional five medical practitioners to the Medical Board of Appeal for the Disabled Drivers and Disabled Passengers (Tax Concessions) Scheme.

This means that the Minister for Finance may now appoint up to ten medical practitioners to the Board.

FINANCE ACT 2005 (COMMENCEMENT OF SECTIONS 100 AND 104(1)(B)) ORDER 2005

(S.I. No. 225 of 2005)

I, Brian Cowen, Minister for Finance, in exercise of the powers conferred on me by section 100(2) and 104(2) of the Finance Act 2005 (No.5 of 2005), hereby order as follows:

1.   This Order may be cited as the Finance Act 2005 (Commencement of Sections 100 and 104(1)(b)) Order 2005.

2.   The 1st day of May 2005 is appointed as the day on which paragraphs (a) and (b) of subsection (1) of section 100 and paragraph (b) of subsection (1) of section 104 of the Finance Act 2005 shall take effect.

Given under my official seal,

This 28th day of April, 2005.

Brian Cowen
Minister for Finance.

EXPLANATORY NOTE

(This note is not part of the instrument and does not purport to be a legal interpretation).

This order appoints the 1st day of May, 2005 as the date for coming into effect of the provisions of paragraphs (a) and (b) of subsection (1) of section 100 and paragraph (b) of subsection (1) of section 104 of the Finance Act 2005.

Section 100 provides for a change in the rules regarding the VAT treatment of certain property transactions. Paragraph (a) is a technical amendment. Paragraph (b) provides for the termination of the existing rules when the new rules come into effect. It also provides for a clawback of a proportion of deductibility which the taxpayer was previously entitled to claim, if a property is diverted into exempt short-term letting. The clawback arises when the letting commences. Section 104 paragraph (b) provides for a credit of a proportion of the same deductibility when the property is subsequently disposed of.

VALUE-ADDED TAX (SHORT-TERM GUEST SECTOR OR HOLIDAY SECTOR) REGULATIONS 2005

(S.I. No. 321 of 2005)

This Regulation was revoked by regulation 44, Value-Added Tax Regulations, 2006 (2006 S.I. No. 548) w.e.f. 1 November 2006

The Revenue Commissioners, in exercise of the powers conferred on them by section 32 and the Sixth Schedule to the Value-Added Tax Act 1972 (No. 22 of 1972), and with the consent of the Minister for Finance, hereby make the following regulations:

1.   (1)   These Regulations may be cited as the Value-Added Tax (Short-Term Guest Sector or Holiday Sector) Regulations 2005.

(2)   These Regulations come into operation on 1 July 2005.

2.   A letting which constitutes a letting which is provided in the short-term guest sector or holiday sector for the purposes of paragraph (xiii)(a) (II) of the Sixth Schedule to the Value-Added Tax Act 1972 (No. 22 of 1972) is a letting of all or part of a house, apartment or other similar establishment to a tourist, holidaymaker or other visitor for a period which does not exceed or is unlikely to exceed 8 consecutive weeks, but is not a letting

(a)   governed by the Housing (Rent Books) Regulations 1993 (S.I. No.146 of 1993),

(b)   of a dwelling to which Part II of the Housing (Private Rented Dwellings) Act 1982 (No. 6 of 1982) applies, or

(c)   of accommodation which is provided as a temporary dwelling for emergency residential purposes.

GIVEN under my hand, 25 June 2005.

Josephine Feehily
Revenue Commissioner.

The Minister for Finance consents to the making of the foregoing Regulations.
GIVEN under the Official Seal
of the Minister for Finance, 29 June 2005.

Brian Cowen
Minister for Finance.

EXPLANATORY NOTE

(This note is not part of the Instrument and does not purport to be a legal interpretation.)

These Regulations specify what lettings are treated as being in the short-term guest or holiday sector for the purpose of applying the reduced rate of VAT.

EUROPEAN COMMUNITIES (MUTUAL ASSISTANCE IN THE FIELD OF DIRECT TAXATION, CERTAIN EXCISE DUTIES AND TAXATION OF INSURANCE PREMIUMS) REGULATIONS, 2005

(S.I. No. 367 of 2005)

I, BRIAN COWEN, Minister for Finance, in exercise of the powers conferred on me by section 3 of the European Communities Act 1972 (No. 27 of 1972) and for the purpose of giving effect to Council Directive 77/799/EEC of 19 December 1977, as amended by Council Directive 79/1070/EEC of 6 December 1979, Council Directive 92/12/EEC of 25 February 1992, Council Directive 2003/93/EC of 7 October 2003, Council Directive 2004/56/EC of 21 April 2004 and Council Directive 2004/106/EC of 16 November 2004, hereby make the following regulations:

1.   These Regulations may be cited as the European Communities (Mutual Assistance in the Field of Direct Taxation, Certain Excise Duties and Taxation of Insurance Premiums) Regulations 2005.

2.   (1)   In these Regulations "**authorised officer**" means a person appointed as an authorised officer under Regulation 9;

['Council Directive' means Council Directive 77/799/EEC of 19 December 1977 as amended by Council Directive 79/1070/ EEC of 6 December 1979, Council Directive 92/12/EEC of 25 February 1992, Council Directive 2003/93/EC of 7 October 2003, Council Directive 2004/56/EC of 21 April 2004, Council Directive 2004/106/EC of 16 November 2004 and Council Directive 2006/98/EC of 20 November 2006;][1]

"**instrument**" means any instrument or decision which emanates from the competent authorities of the requesting Member State and concerns the application in its territory of legislation referable to taxes that are the subject of the Council Directive and which contains the information referred to in Article 8a (2) of the Council Directive;

"**Member State**" means a Member State of the European Communities.

    (2)   A word or expression that is used in these Regulations and that is also used in the Council Directive, has, unless the context otherwise requires, the same meaning in these Regulations as it has in the Council Directive.

    (3)   In these Regulations, unless otherwise indicated -

        (a)   a reference to a Regulation is a reference to a Regulation of these Regulations;

        (b)   a reference to a paragraph is to the paragraph of the Regulation in which the reference occurs.

3.   The Revenue Commissioners are the competent authority in the State for the purposes of the Council Directive and shall, save where

Regulation 6 applies, comply with the requirements imposed by the Council Directive on competent authorities in a Member State.

4. (1)   Where the Revenue Commissioners are notifying an addressee of all instruments and decisions that emanate from the administrative authorities of the requesting Member State in accordance with Article 8a of the Council Directive, such instruments and decisions shall be either delivered to the addressee, sent or left -

(a)   in a case where the addressee is a company, at the company's registered office or place of business,

(b)   in any other case, at the addressee's usual or last known place of abode or place of business, or

(c)   if the addressee is an individual, at his or her place of employment.

(2)   An instrument to which paragraph (1) refers may be served by registered post addressed -

(a)   in a case where the addressee is a company, to the addressee at either of the places specified in paragraph (l) (a), or

(b)   in any other case, to the addressee at any of the places specified in paragraph (1)(b) or (1)(c).

5. (1)   Nothing shall prevent the Revenue Commissioners from authorising any authorised officer to participate in the conduct of simultaneous controls with a view to the exchange of information by the Commissioners where, in the opinion of the Commissioners the following conditions are satisfied -

(a)   the tax situation of one or more persons liable to tax is of common or complimentary interest to the Revenue Commissioners and to the competent authorities of one or more Member States other than the State, and

(b)   the conduct of simultaneous controls would be more effective than a control carried out by the competent authorities of one Member State (including the State).

(2)   Where in any case the Revenue Commissioners are of opinion that the conditions in paragraph (1) are satisfied, they shall -

(a)   identify the person liable to tax who in their opinion should be subject to the simultaneous control,

(b)   notify the competent authorities of the Member States of that person and provide reasons for so identifying that person, and

(c)   specify the period of time during which it is proposed that such simultaneous controls should be conducted.

(3)   Where the Revenue Commissioners receive a proposal for the conduct of simultaneous controls from the competent authorities of a Member State other than the State, they shall -

    (a)   where they are of opinion that the conditions in paragraph (1) are satisfied, advise the competent authorities that they will authorise the conduct of a control, or

    (b)   where they are of opinion that the conditions in paragraph (1) are not satisfied, advise the competent authorities of their opinion and the reasons for forming that opinion.

(4)   In this Regulation:

"**control**" in relation to a person means where the person is chargeable to tax -

    (a)   in the State, the making of enquiries or the taking of such actions as are within the powers conferred on an officer of the Revenue Commissioners under Chapter 4 of Part 38 of the Taxes Consolidation Act 1997 (No. 37 of 1997) as the officer considers necessary to satisfy himself or herself as to any liability to tax of the person or the amount of the liability, or

    (b)   in a Member State other than the State, the making of enquiries or the taking of such actions by the competent authorities of that Member State as are within the powers of that competent authority as that competent authority considers necessary to satisfy itself as to any liability to tax of the person or the amount of the liability;

"**simultaneous controls**" in relation to a person means that the controls referred in the definition of control are carried out at or about the same time.

6.   Regulations 4 and 5 do not apply in respect of excise duties.

7.   The Revenue Commissioners shall not disclose any information in pursuance of the Council Directive unless satisfied that the competent authorities of the other Member State concerned are bound by, or have undertaken to observe, rules of confidentiality with respect to the information which are not less strict than those applying to it in the State.

8.   Nothing in these Regulations permits the Revenue Commissioners to authorise the use of information disclosed by virtue of the Council Directive to the competent authority of another Member State other than for the purposes of taxation or to facilitate legal proceedings for failure to observe the tax laws of that State.

9.   (1)   The Revenue Commissioners may appoint such and so many of their officers as they shall determine to be authorised officers for the purposes of these Regulations.

(2)   An authorised officer may, for the purposes of these Regulations, exercise a power conferred under Chapter 4 of Part 38 of the Taxes Consolidation Act 1997 on an officer of the Revenue Commissioners within the meaning of that Act.

(3)   An authorised officer, when exercising any power conferred on him or her by these Regulations, shall, if so requested by any person affected, produce evidence in writing of his or her appointment as an authorised officer.

10.   The Revenue Commissioners may delegate to their officers any of the functions to be performed by the Revenue Commissioners under the Council Directive in relation to exchange of information.

11.   The European Communities (Mutual Assistance in the Field of Direct Taxation, Certain Excise Duties and Taxation of Insurance Premiums) Regulations 2003 (S.I. No. 711 of 2003) are revoked.

GIVEN under my Official Seal,

Minister for Finance.

EXPLANATORY NOTE

(This note is not part of the instrument and does not purport to be a legal interpretation)

These Regulations provide for an extension at national level of the EEC Council Directive of 19 December 1977 concerning mutual assistance (exchange of information) by the competent authorities of Member States, as required by an amending Council Directive 2004/56/EC of 21 April 2004. The amending Directive expands the rules for administrative co-operation concerning mutual assistance. In particular, it obliges the competent authorities of a Member State, at the request of the competent authorities of another Member State, to notify to a person in the requested Member State an instrument concerning tax in the requesting Member State. There is also provision that allows Member States to take part in the conduct of simultaneous controls with a view to exchange of information whenever they would appear to be more effective than controls conducted by one Member State alone. The Regulations also take account of the derogation provided for in Article 4 of Council Directive 2004/1 06/ EC which allows for the exclusion of excise duties from the provisions of the amending Directive.

These Regulations also consolidate and give effect, in one set of regulations, to Council Directive 77/799/EEC as amended.

Amendment

2   Substituted by r2, European Communities (Mutual Assistance in the Field of Direct Taxation, Certain Excise Duties and Taxation of Insurance Premiums)(Amendment) Regulations 2007, w.e.f 1 January 2007.

DISABLED DRIVERS AND DISABLED PASSENGERS (TAX CONCESSIONS) (AMENDMENT)(NO. 2) REGULATIONS 2005

(S.I. No. 566 of 2005)

I, Brian Cowen, Minister for Finance, in exercise of the powers conferred on me by section 92 (as amended by section 17 of Finance (No. 2) Act 1992 (No. 28 of 1992)) of the Finance Act 1989 (No. 10 of 1989), and after consultation with the Minister for Health and Children (as adapted by the Health (Alteration of Name of Department and Title of Minister) Order 1997 (S.I. No. 308 of 1997)) and the Minister for the Environment, Heritage and Local Government (as adapted by the Environment and Local Government (Alteration of Name of Department and Title of Minister) Order 2003 (S.I. No. 233 of 2003)), hereby make the following regulations:

1. These Regulations may be cited as the Disabled Drivers and Disabled Passengers (Tax Concessions)(Amendment)(No. 2) Regulations 2005.

2. Regulation 6 (inserted by the Disabled Drivers and Disabled Passengers (Tax Concessions)(Amendment) Regulations 2004 (S.I. No. 469 of 2004)) of the Disabled Drivers and Disabled Passengers (Tax Concessions) Regulations 1994 (S.I. No. 353 of 1994) is amended -

    (a)   in paragraph (1)(a) (as amended by the Disabled Drivers and Disabled Passengers (Tax Concessions)(Amendment) Regulations 2005 (S.I. No. 178 of 2005)) by substituting "the Minister for Finance shall appoint a minimum of 5 medical practitioners" for "the Minister for Finance shall appoint 5 medical practitioners and may appoint a further 5 medical practitioners", and

    (b)   by deleting paragraph (2).

3. Nothing in these Regulations shall read as affecting an appointment made by the Minister for Finance to the Medical Board before the making of these Regulations.

GIVEN under my Official Seal,
13th September 2005.

Brian Cowen
Minister for Finance.

EXPLANATORY NOTE

(This note is not part of the instrument and does not purport to be a legal interpretation).

These Regulations amend the principal regulations on the tax concessions scheme for disabled drivers and disabled passengers. Formerly the number of appointments to the Medical Appeal Board for the Scheme was limited to 10; these Regulations remove that limitation. They also remove the restriction on an appointee's tenure to the remaining term of the appointee that he or she replaces.

EUROPEAN COMMUNITIES (INTRASTAT) (AMENDMENT) REGULATIONS 2005

(S.I. No. 675 of 2005)

I, Bertie Ahern, Taoiseach, in exercise of the powers conferred on me by section 3 of the European Communities Act 1972 (No. 27 of 1972) and for the purpose of giving further effect to Regulation (EC) No. 638/2004 of the European Parliament and of the Council of 31 March 2004 and Commission Regulation (EC) No. 1982/2004 of 18 November 2004, hereby make the following regulations:

1. These Regulations may be cited as the European Communities (Intrastat) (Amendment) Regulations 2005.

2. In these Regulations "Principal Regulations" means the European Communities (Intrastat) Regulations 1993 (S.I. No. 136 of 1993), as amended by Schedule 5 to the Finance Act 2001 (No. 7 of 2001) and the European Communities (Intrastat) (Amendment) Regulations 2002 (S.I. No. 466 of 2002).

3. Regulation 3 of the Principal Regulations are amended by substituting the following for paragraph (1):

    "(1)   In these Regulations -

    '**authorised officer**' means an officer of the Revenue Commissioners authorised by them in writing to exercise the powers of an authorised officer referred to in these Regulations;

    '**basic Regulation**' means Regulation (EC) No. 638/2004 of the European Parliament and of the Council of 31 March 2004;

    '**Community Regulations**' means the basic Regulation and Commission Regulation (EC) No. 1982/2004 of 18 November 2004;

    '**Member State**' means a Member State of the European Community;

    '**Intrastat system**' means the Intrastat system referred to in the basic Regulation in so far as that system applies to trade between Member States pursuant to Articles 5 to 14 of that Regulation;

    '**officer of statistics**' has the meaning assigned to it by the Statistics Act 1993 (No. 21 of 1993);

    '**records**' means any document or other written or printed material in any form as well as information (including statistical information) stored, maintained or preserved by means of any mechanical or electronic device, whether or not stored, maintained or preserved in a legible form;

    '**trader**' means a person referred in Article 7 (1) of the basic Regulation.".

4.   The Principal Regulations are amended by substituting the following for Regulation 5:

"5.   (1)   The Taoiseach shall make a specification from time to time of thresholds below which parties are exempted from providing any Intrastat information in accordance with Article 10 of the basic Regulation.

(2)   (a)   A specification by the Taoiseach for the purposes of paragraph (1) shall be published in the Iris Oifigiúil as soon as may be after it is made.

(b)   Until the contrary is shown, evidence of a specification for the purposes of paragraph (1) may be given in proceedings for an offence under these Regulations by the production of a copy of the Iris Oifigiúil purporting to contain the specification.".

GIVEN under my Official Seal,
17 October 2005.

BERTIE AHERN
Taoiseach.

EXPLANATORY NOTE

These Regulations amend S.I. No. 136 of 1993 so as to include Regulation (EC) No. 638/2004 of the European Parliament and of the Council and Commission Regulation (EC) No. 1982/2004.

VALUE-ADDED TAX (AMENDMENT) REGULATIONS 2006

(S.I. No. 198 of 2006)

> This Regulation was revoked by regulation 44, Value-Added Tax Regulations, 2006 (2006 SI No. 548) w.e.f. 1 November 2006

The Revenue Commissioners, in exercise of the powers conferred on them by sections 5(3), 13(3) and 32 of the Value-Added Tax Act 1972 (No. 22 of 1972) make the following regulations:

1. (1) These Regulations may be cited as the Value-Added Tax (Amendment) Regulations 2006.

    (2) These Regulations come into operation on 1 May 2006.

2. The Value-Added Tax Regulations 1979 (S.I. No. 63 of 1979) are amended-

    (a) by substituting the following for Regulation 24:

    "24. (1) Subject to paragraph (2) and in accordance with section 5(3)(b) of the Act, the following services are deemed to be a supply of services by a person for consideration in the course or furtherance of his or her business, that is to say, the supply free of charge of catering services for such person's own private use or that of the staff of such person.

    (2) This Regulation does not apply to any such supplies as are referred to in paragraph (1) if the total cost of providing them has not exceeded and is not likely to exceed the amount specified in section 8(3)(e) of the Act in any continuous period of 12 months, unless the person supplying the services referred to in paragraph (1) elects to be a taxable person in respect of those supplies.",

    and

    (b) by substituting the following for Regulation 30:

    "30 (1) A person to whom section 13(3) of the Act applies is entitled, under the terms of Council Directive No. 79/1072/EEC of 6 December 1979 and Council Directive No. 86/560/EEC of 17 November 1986, to be repaid tax borne by him or her on the purchase of goods or services supplied to him or her in the State or in respect of goods imported into the State by him or her if he or she fulfils to the satisfaction of the Revenue Commissioners the following conditions:

(a)   in the case of a person having an establishment in another Member State, produces a certificate from the relevant official department of that Member State that he or she is subject, under the laws of that Member State, to value-added tax referred to in Council Directive No. 77/388/EEC of 17 May 1977,

(b)   in the case of a person not established in the territory of the Community, provides proof, in the form of a written document from the relevant official department of the country in which he or she has an establishment, that he or she is engaged in carrying on an economic activity,

(c)   claims a refund, within 6 months of the end of the calendar year in which the tax became chargeable, by completing and lodging the appropriate claim form, provided for that purpose by the Revenue Commissioners, together with the appropriate documentation as specified in subparagraph (d),

(d)   establishes the amount of tax borne by the production of the invoice issued by the supplier or the relevant import documents,

(e)   establishes that he or she is not entitled to repayment of the tax under any other provision of the Act or Regulations, or any other instrument made under statute that is administered by the Revenue Commissioners.

(2)   A claim for a refund under this Regulation shall relate to invoiced purchases of goods and services or to imports made during a period, within a calendar year, of not less than 3 months or a period of not more than one calendar year, but where that claim relates to the remainder of a calendar year a claim for a refund may relate to a period of less than 3 months.

(3)   A person may not make a claim under this Regulation for an amount that is less than-

(a)   €200 where the claim is in respect of a period of less than one calendar year but not less than 3 months,

           (b) €25 where the claim is in respect of a period that represents a full calendar year or the final part of the calendar year.

    (4)   The certificate and written document mentioned in subparagraphs (a) and (b) of paragraph (1), respectively, shall each be taken as evidence of the matters contained therein for the purposes of this Regulation only for a period of one year from the date such certificate or such document was issued by the official authorities in the State in which that person is established.".

Given under my hand,
19 April 2006

Josephine Feehily
Revenue Commissioner.

EXPLANATORY NOTE

(This note is not part of the Instrument and does not purport to be a legal interpretation.)

These Regulations substitute two new regulations for Regulations 24 and 30 of the 1979 Regulations. Regulation 24 deals with catering services supplied free of charge for a person's own private use or that of his or her staff, and Regulation 30 deals with the refund of tax to foreign traders as provided for under the Eighth and Thirteenth VAT Directives.

VALUE-ADDED TAX REGULATIONS 2006

(SI No. 548 of 2006)

Commencement and Interpretation

VALUE-ADDED TAX REGULATIONS 2006

The Revenue Commissioners, in exercise of the powers conferred on them by section 32 of the Value-Added Tax Act 1972 (No. 22 of 1972), and as respects Regulations 5, 25, 31, 32, 33, 35 and 37 with the consent of the Minister for Finance, hereby make the following regulations:

Commencement and Interpretation

Citation and commencement

1.   (1)   These Regulations may be cited as the Value-Added Tax Regulations 2006.

      (2)   These Regulations come into operation on 1 November 2006.

Interpretation

2.   In these Regulations —

"**Act**" means the Value-Added Tax Act 1972;

"**registration number**", in relation to a person, means the number assigned to the person for the purposes of registration under section 9 of the Act;

[...][1]

"**value-added tax identification number in another Member State**" means the identification number issued to a person by the authorities of another Member State for the purposes of value-added tax referred to in the [VAT Directive;][2]

["**VAT Directive**" means Council Directive 2006/112/EC of 28 November 2006 on the common system of value-added tax.]³

[**Accountable Person**]²

Election to be [an accountable person]² and cancellation of such election

3. (1) In this Regulation —

"**application form**" means such form as is provided by the Revenue Commissioners for the purpose of enabling a person to apply to elect to be [an accountable person]²;

"**end-date**" means the last day of the taxable period immediately preceding the request period;

"**relevant taxable periods**" means the taxable periods comprised in whichever of the periods referred to in paragraph (5)(b)(i) is appropriate;

"**request period**" means the taxable period during which a person notifies the Revenue Commissioners that he or she requests the cancellation of an election;

"**start-date**" means —

    (a)   (i)   in the case of [an accountable person] referred to in paragraph (4)(b), the date that person was first treated as [an accountable person]², or

          (ii)   in any other case, the beginning of the taxable period immediately following the taxable period during which the application form is received by the Revenue Commissioners, or

    (b)   by agreement between the person concerned and the Revenue Commissioners, the beginning of the taxable period during which the application form is received.

(2) A person who, in accordance with section 8(3) of the Act, is not [an accountable person]² but who wishes to elect to be such a person is required to register for tax by completing the application form.

(3) The submission of the application form referred to in paragraph (2) constitutes an election to be [an accountable person]². Such election is effective from the start-date until the date the election is cancelled in accordance with paragraph (7).

(4) (a) A person who is [an accountable person]² by reason only of an election made in accordance with paragraphs (2) and (3) is entitled to have such election cancelled, subject to fulfilling the requirements of paragraph (5).

    (b) [An accountable person]² who satisfies the Revenue Commissioners that in accordance with section 8(6) of the Act he or she may be treated as a person who is not [an accountable person]², is entitled to have his or her registration as [an accountable person]² cancelled subject to fulfilling the requirements of paragraph (5), and for the purposes of this Regulation such a request shall be treated as if it were a request to have an election cancelled.

(5)   The person who wishes to have his or her election cancelled is required to —

(a)   apply to the Revenue Commissioners in writing to have his or her election cancelled,

(b)   furnish particulars to the Revenue Commissioners of —

(i)   the total amount of tax paid by him or her in accordance with section 19(3) of the Act on the supply by him or her of goods or services, other than services consisting of the letting of immovable goods referred to in paragraph (xiii) of the Sixth Schedule to the Act, in respect of whichever of the following periods is the shorter:

(I)   all the taxable periods comprised in the period commencing with the start-date and ending with the end-date, or

(II)   the 18 consecutive taxable periods up to the end-date,

(ii)   the total amount of tax refunded to him or her in accordance with section 20(1) of the Act in respect of tax borne or paid in relation to the supply by him or her of goods or services, other than services consisting of the letting of immovable goods referred to in paragraph (xiii) of the Sixth Schedule to the Act, in respect of the relevant taxable periods, and

(iii)   the tax deductible under section 12 of the Act in respect of the intra-Community acquisition of goods, if any, made by him or her in the same relevant taxable periods,

and

(c)   furnish a return in accordance with section 19(3) of the Act for the request period, and at the same time pay to the Collector-General —

(i)   any tax payable in respect of goods and services supplied by him or her during the request period, and

     (ii)   an amount equal to the excess (if any) of the sum of the tax referred to in clause (ii) and (iii) of subparagraph (b) over the tax referred to in clause (i) of that subparagraph;

but if that person supplied qualifying goods and services in accordance with section 13A of the Act during the relevant taxable periods, he or she may include in the amount referred to in subparagraph (b)(i) the tax that would have been chargeable had the supplies not been zero-rated under that section.

(6) Where a person who supplies services consisting of the letting of immovable goods referred to in paragraph (xiii) of the Sixth Schedule to the Act wishes to have his or her election cancelled, he or she is required to –

    (a)   apply to the Revenue Commissioners in writing to have his or her election cancelled, and

    (b)   furnish a return in accordance with section 19(3) of the Act and at the same time pay to the Collector-General-

        (i)   any tax payable in respect of those services supplied during the request period, and

        (ii)   the cancellation amount provided for in section 8(5A) of the Act as if it were tax due in accordance with section 19 of the Act in addition to any amount payable in accordance with section 8(5) of the Act.

(7) Where the Revenue Commissioners are satisfied that the requirements of paragraph (5) and, where appropriate, paragraph (6) are fulfilled by the person concerned, they shall-

    (a)   in writing notify that person accordingly, and

    (b)   cancel that person's election to be [an accountable person][2] with effect from the end of the taxable period during which those requirements have been fulfilled.

(8) A person who requests the cancellation of his or her election to be [an accountable person][2] is not entitled, under section 20(1) of the Act, to any refund of tax, other than a refund referable solely to an error or mistake made by him or her, for the request period or any subsequent taxable periods in excess of an amount calculated in accordance with the following formula:

$$A + B$$

where –

    A   is the excess of the amount referred to in clause (i) of paragraph (5)(b) over the sum of the amounts referred to in clause (ii) and (iii) of that paragraph, but where there is no such excess A is equal to zero, and

B   is the sum of the amounts of tax paid under section 19(3) of the Act for the request period and any subsequent taxable periods until the election is cancelled.

(9)   In the case of a farmer who, had he or she made no election to be [an accountable person][2], would not be [an accountable person][2] by virtue of section 8(3)(a) of the Act, paragraph (5)(b)(i) applies as if—

(a)   the amount of tax paid by him or her in accordance with section 19(3) of the Act in respect of each of the relevant taxable periods were increased by an amount equal to the flat-rate addition, which that farmer would be required (in accordance with section 12A of the Act) to indicate on an invoice in respect of the supply of agricultural produce or of an agricultural service if that farmer had not elected to be [an accountable person][2] and

(b)   the total amount of tax refunded to him or her in respect of all the relevant taxable periods comprised in the period included in the calculation in clause (i) were reduced by the total amount of tax which qualified for deduction under section 12 of the Act in respect of those taxable periods and which, in accordance with any order made under section 20(3) of the Act, would fall to be refunded to him or her if he or she were not [an accountable person][2].

Waiver of exemption

4.   (1)   In this Regulation—

"**back-dating**" in relation to a waiver, means the waiving of a right to exemption from tax in respect of an exempt letting of immovable goods to which paragraph (iv) of the First Schedule to the Act refers, from a date earlier than the current taxable period referred to in paragraph (2)(c), and "**back-dated**" shall be construed accordingly;

"**cancellation request period**" means the taxable period during which a request for the cancellation of a waiver of exemption is made in accordance with paragraph (10);

"**specified letting**" means an exempt letting of immovable goods to which paragraph (iv) of the First Schedule to the Act applies other than a letting of immovable goods to which paragraph (iv) of the First Schedule to the Act applies by virtue of section 4(3A) (a)(ii) of the Act;

"**waiver**" means the waiver by a person of his or her right to exemption from tax on a specified letting.

(2)   A person who, in accordance with section 7(1) of the Act wishes to waive his or her right to exemption from tax on the supply of a

specified letting, is required to furnish in writing to the Revenue Commissioners the following particulars —

(a)   his or her name and address,

(b)   his or her registration number (if any), and

(c)   the taxable period, from the commencement of which he or she desires that the waiver should have effect, not being earlier than the current taxable period.

(3)   When the Revenue Commissioners receive the particulars referred to in paragraph (2) they shall —

(a)   acknowledge receipt of them to the person concerned, and

(b)   specify the taxable period (in this Regulation referred to as the "**start period**") not being earlier than the taxable period referred to in paragraph (2)(c), from the commencement of which the waiver of exemption has effect,

and, accordingly, the Act applies to that person in respect of all specified lettings which that person supplies as if those lettings were not an exempt activity, from the start period until his or her waiver is cancelled in accordance with paragraph (11).

(4)   Where —

(a)   [an accountable person]² makes a specified letting, and

(b)   the immovable goods which are the subject of that letting were acquired or developed by him or her for the purpose of his or her taxable supplies,

then, notwithstanding paragraph (3), that person may apply to the Revenue Commissioners to backdate the waiver of his or her right to exemption in respect of that letting.

(5)   An application under paragraph (4) is required to be made in writing to the Revenue Commissioners and to include the following:

(a)   the name, address and registration number of [the accountable person]² making the application,

(b)   the tenant's name, address and registration number,

(c)   details of the letting agreement, and

(d)   the date from which [the accountable person]² desires that the waiver shall have effect.

(6)   A waiver of exemption shall be backdated only where the tenant would have been entitled to deduct, in accordance with section of the Act, all the tax that would have been chargeable in respect of the letting if the waiver had applied from the date

specified in accordance with paragraph (7) to the date on which the Revenue Commissioners issue the notification referred to in paragraph (7).

(7)   Where the Revenue Commissioners are satisfied that an applicant has complied with paragraph (5) and that paragraph (6) applies, then they shall notify the applicant that the waiver may be back- dated in respect of the letting for which back-dating of a waiver was sought specifying the date to which the waiver is to be back- dated being a date not earlier than 26 March 1997.

(8)   Where the Revenue Commissioners backdate a waiver at the request of the applicant in respect of a specific letting, that applicant shall be deemed to have waived his or her right to exemption in respect of all his or her specified lettings from the start of the taxable period in which the Revenue Commissioners issue the notification referred to in paragraph (7).

(9)   Any tax chargeable prior to the date the Revenue Commissioners issue the notification referred to in paragraph (7) which becomes chargeable on the letting of immovable goods as a result of the back-dating of a waiver is deemed to have been due and paid by the applicant in accordance with section 19 of the Act and deducted by the tenant in accordance with section 12 of the Act.

(10)   A person who waives his or her right to exemption in respect of a specified letting is entitled to have such waiver cancelled provided he or she —

   (a)   applies to the Revenue Commissioners in writing to have the waiver of his or her right to exemption cancelled,

   (b)   furnishes particulars to the Revenue Commissioners of —

      (i)   the tax due and accounted for by him or her, in accordance with section 19 of the Act, in relation to the supply of services by him or her to which the waiver applied for all taxable periods comprised in the period commencing with —

         (I)   in the case of a back-dated waiver the start of the period in which the Revenue Commissioners issued the notification referred to in paragraph (7), or

         (II)   in any other case, the start period referred to in paragraph (3)(b),

      and ending with the last day of the taxable period immediately preceding the cancellation request period, and

(ii)   the total amount of tax deducted or deductible by him or her referred to at paragraphs (a), (b) and (c) of subsection (3) of section 7 of the Act in respect of all of the taxable periods comprised in the appropriate period referred to in clause (i), together with the total amount of tax deducted by him or her referred to in paragraph (aa) of the said subsection (3),

and

(c)   pays to the Collector-General an amount equal to the excess (if any) of the tax referred to in subparagraph (b) (ii) over the tax referred to in subparagraph (b)(i).

(11)   Where a person complies with paragraph (10) to the satisfaction of the Revenue Commissioners, his or her waiver shall be cancelled with effect from the end of the taxable period during which he or she so complies. The Revenue Commissioners shall notify the person of such cancellation in writing and from the end of that taxable period the person shall be treated as a person who had not waived his or her right to exemption.

(12)   A person who applies for the cancellation of his or her waiver in accordance with paragraph (10) is not entitled, under section 20(1) of the Act, to any refund of tax, other than a refund referable solely to some error or mistake made by him or her, for the cancellation request period or any subsequent taxable periods, in relation to all the lettings to which the waiver relates, in excess of an amount calculated in accordance with the following formula:

$$A + B$$

where—

A   is the excess of the amount referred to in paragraph 10(b)(i) over the amount referred to in paragraph 10(b)(ii), but where there is no such excess A is equal to zero, and

B   is the sum of the amounts of tax paid under section 19(3) of the Act, in relation to all the lettings to which the waiver relates, for the cancellation request period and any subsequent taxable periods until the waiver is cancelled.

Lettings in the short-term guest sector or holiday sector

5.   A letting which constitutes a letting which is provided in the short-term guest sector or holiday sector for the purposes of paragraph (xiii)(a) (II) of the Sixth Schedule to the Act is a letting of all or part of a house, apartment or other similar establishment to a tourist, holidaymaker or other visitor for a period which does not exceed or is unlikely to exceed 8 consecutive weeks, but is not a letting

    (a)   governed by the Housing (Rent Books) Regulations 1993 (S.I. No. 146 of 1993),

    (b)   of a dwelling to which Part II of the Housing (Private Rented Dwellings) Act 1982 (No. 6 of 1982) applies, or

    (c)   of accommodation which is provided as a temporary dwelling for emergency residential purposes.

Groups

6.   (1)   Where 2 or more persons want to be regarded as being in a group so as to satisfy the Revenue Commissioners that they are in a group in accordance with section 8(8) of the Act, each of them is required to complete such forms as are provided for that purpose by the Revenue Commissioners.

    (2)   The Revenue Commissioners shall —

        (a)   determine whether a notification, under section 8(8) of the Act, should be issued to such persons, and

        (b)   specify the date from which the notification applies where they determine that such notification should issue.

Registration

7.   (1)   [An accountable person][2] is required —

        (a)   to register for tax by completing such form as is provided for that purpose by the Revenue Commissioners, and

        (b)   to certify that the particulars shown on such form are correct.

    (2)   Where a change occurs in any of the particulars furnished in the form referred to in paragraph (1), then —

        (a)   the registered person,

        (b)   if the registered person has died, his or her personal representative, or

        (c)   if the registered person is a body of persons which is in liquidation or is otherwise being wound up, the liquidator or any other person who is carrying on the business during such liquidation or, as the case may be, winding up,

    is required to furnish to the Revenue Commissioners particulars of the change within 30 days immediately following the date of the change.

    (3)   A person who is registered in accordance with section 9 of the Act and who ceases —

        (a)   to supply taxable goods or services, and

        (b)   to make intra-Community acquisitions,

in the State is required to notify the Revenue Commissioners in writing of such cessation. Such written notification is required to be furnished by the end of the taxable period following that in which the cessation occurred.

(4)   The Revenue Commissioners may, by notice in writing, cancel the registration of a person who does not become, or who ceases to be, [an accountable person]² and such cancellation has effect as on and from the date of the notice, or as on and from such date as may be specified in the notice.

Record Keeping

Accounts

8.   (1)   [The full and true records of all transactions which affect or may affect the accountable person's liability to tax and entitlement to deductibility, which every accountable person is required to keep in accordance with section 16 of the Act, shall be entered up to date and include—

(a)   in relation to consideration receivable from registered persons—

(i)   the amount receivable from each such person in respect of each transaction for which an invoice or other document is required to be issued under section 17 of the Act, and

(ii)   a cross-reference to the copy of the relevant invoice or other document,

(b)   in relation to consideration receivable from unregistered persons—

(i)   a daily total of the consideration receivable from all such persons,

(ii)   a cross-reference from that daily total to the relevant books or other documents which are in use for the purposes of the business, and

(iii)   where the accountable person uses an electronic cash register or point of sale system the complete record of each entry on that register or system, uniquely identified by sequential number, date and time of such entry,]²

(c)   in relation to consideration receivable from persons registered for value-added tax in another Member State—

(i)   the amount receivable from each such person in respect of each transaction for which an invoice is required to be issued under section 17 of the Act, and

(ii)   a cross-reference to the copy of the relevant invoice,

(d)   in relation to intra-Community acquisitions of goods, in respect of which [the accountable person][2] is liable to pay the tax chargeable—

    (i)   the amount of the consideration relating to those acquisitions, and

    (ii)   a cross-reference to the relevant invoice,

(e)   in relation to importations of goods, a description of those goods together with—

    (i)   particulars of their value as determined in accordance with section 15 of the Act,

    (ii)   the amount of the consideration relating to the purchase of the goods if purchased in connection with the importation,

    (iii)   the amount of tax, if any, paid on importation, and

    (iv)   a cross-reference to the invoices and customs documents used in connection with the importation,

(f)   in relation to goods supplied in accordance with section (3)(1)(e) of the Act, being goods developed, constructed, assembled, manufactured, produced, extracted, purchased, imported or otherwise acquired by [the accountable person][2] or by another person on his or her behalf, and applied by [the accountable person][2] (otherwise than by way of disposal to another person) for the purposes of any business carried on by him or her—

    (i)   a description of the goods in question, and

    (ii)   the cost, excluding tax, to [the accountable person][2] of acquiring or producing them except where tax chargeable in relation to the application of the goods would, if it were charged, be wholly deductible under section 12 of the Act,

(g)   in relation to goods supplied in accordance with section (3)(1)(f) of the Act, being goods appropriated by [an accountable person][2] for any purpose other than the purpose of his or her business or disposed of free of charge, where tax chargeable in relation to the goods—

    (i)   on their purchase, intra-Community acquisition or importation by [the accountable person][2], or on their development, construction, assembly, manufacture, production, extraction, or application in accordance with section 3(1)(e) of the Act, as the case may be, was wholly or partly deductible under section 12 of the Act, or

(ii)   where the ownership of those goods was transferred to [the accountable person]² in the course of a transfer of a totality of assets, or part thereof, of a business and that transfer of ownership was deemed not to be a supply of goods in accordance with section 3(5)(b) of the Act,

a description of the goods in question and the cost, excluding tax, to [the accountable person]², of acquiring or producing them,

(h)   in relation to services deemed to be supplied by a person in the course or furtherance of business in accordance with section 5(3) of the Act —

(i)   a description of the services in question, and

(ii)   particulars of the cost, excluding tax, to [the accountable person]² of supplying the services and of the consideration, if any, receivable by him or her in respect of the supply,

(i)   in the case of the supply of services in circumstances that, by virtue of any of the provisions of section 5 of the Act, are deemed to be supplied outside the State —

(i)   the name and address of the person to whom the services are supplied,

(ii)   the nature of the services,

(iii)   the amount of the consideration receivable in respect of the supply, and

(iv)   a cross-reference to the copy of the relevant invoice or other document,

(j)   in the case of the receipt of goods and services in the State in respect of which the recipient of those goods and services is liable to pay the tax chargeable —

(i)   a description of the goods and services in question, and

(ii)   a cross-reference to the relevant invoice,

(k)   in relation to discounts allowed or price reductions made to a registered person subsequent to the issue of an invoice to such person —

(i)   the amount credited to such person, and

(ii)　　except in a case in which section 17(9)(a) of the Act applies, a cross-reference to the corresponding credit note,

(l)　　in relation to discounts allowed or price reductions made to unregistered persons—

(i)　　a daily total of the amount so allowed, and

(ii)　　a cross-reference to the goods returned book, cash book or other record used in connection with the matter,

(m)　　in relation to bad debts written off, —

(i)　　particulars of the name and address of the debtor,

(ii)　　the nature of the goods or services to which the debt relates,

(iii)　　the date or dates on which the debt was incurred, and

(iv)　　the date or dates on which the debt was written off,

(n)　　in relation to goods and services supplied to [the accountable person][2] by [another accountable person][2]—

(i)　　the amount of the consideration payable,

(ii)　　the corresponding tax invoiced by the [other accountable person][2], and

(iii)　　a cross-reference to the corresponding invoice,

(o)　　in relation to goods and services supplied to [the accountable person][2] by unregistered persons, other than a means of transport supplied under the special scheme in accordance with Regulation 31 and goods and services in respect of which flat-rate farmers are required in accordance with section 12A(1) of the Act to issue invoices—

(i)　　a daily total of the consideration payable to such persons, and

(ii)　　a cross-reference to the purchases book, cash book, purchases dockets or other records which are in use in connection with the business,

(p)　　in relation to goods and services supplied to [the accountable person][2] by flat-rate farmers who are required, in accordance with section 12A(1) of the Act, to issue invoices—

(i)　　the amount of the consideration payable (exclusive of the flat-rate addition) and the amount of the flat-rate addition invoiced by each such farmer, and

(ii)   a cross-reference to the corresponding invoice,

(q)   in relation to agricultural machinery supplied to [the accountable person]² by flat-rate farmers who are required, in accordance with section 12C(2) of the Act, to issue invoices, a full and true record entered up to date of all acquisitions and disposals of agricultural machinery by him or her,

(r)   in relation to discounts or price reductions received from registered persons, subsequent to the receipt of invoices from such persons, except in a case in which section 17(9) (a) of the Act applies —

(i)   the amount of the discount or price reduction, and the corresponding tax received from each such person, and

(ii)   a cross-reference to the corresponding credit note,

(s)   in relation to discounts or price reductions in relation to goods and services supplied to [the accountable person]² by flat- rate farmers who are required, in accordance with section 12A(1) of the Act, to issue invoices —

(i)   the amount of the discount or price reduction (exclusive of the flat-rate addition) and the amount of the corresponding flat-rate addition, and

(ii)   a cross-reference to the invoice issued in connection with the goods and services in question,

(t)   in relation to discounts or price reductions received other than those referred to in subparagraphs (r) and (s) —

(i)   a daily total of the amounts so received, and

(ii)   a cross-reference to the cash book or other record used in connection with such [matters,]²

[(u)   in relation to each capital good in respect of which a capital goods owner is required to create and maintain a capital good record in accordance with section 12E(12) of the Act —

(i)   the total tax incurred,

(ii)   the amount of the total tax incurred which is deductible in accordance with section 12 of the Act,

(iii)   the date on which the adjustment period begins,

(iv)   the number of intervals in the adjustment period,

(v)   the initial interval proportion of deductible use,

(vi)   the total reviewed deductible amount,

(vii)   the proportion of deductible use for each interval,

(viii) details of any adjustments required to be made in accordance with section 12E, and

(ix)   details of any sale or transfer of the capital good or details of any assignment or surrender of a lease where section 12E(8)(b) applies in relation to that capital good,

and

(v)   in respect of supplies of goods specified in paragraph (i) of the Second Schedule to the Act—

(i)   the name and address of the person to whom the goods are supplied,

(ii)   a description of the goods supplied,

(iii)   the amount of the consideration,

(iv)   a cross-reference to the copy of the relevant invoice, and

(v)   a cross-reference to the relevant Customs and transport documents.][2]

(2)   The accounts kept in accordance with paragraph (1) are required to set out separately, the consideration, discounts, price reductions, bad debts and values at importation under separate headings in relation to—

(a)   exempted activities, and

(b)   goods and services chargeable at each rate of tax including the zero rate.

(3)   In relation to a person authorised in accordance with section 14(1) of the Act to determine the amount of tax which becomes due by such person by reference to the amount of moneys which he or she receives, references in this Regulation to consideration in respect of the supply of goods or services are construed as references to such moneys received in respect of such supply.

Invoices and other documents

9. (1)   In this Regulation **"reverse charge supply"** means a supply of goods or services to a person in another Member State who is liable to pay value-added tax under the [VAT Directive][2] on such supply.

(2)   The following particulars are specified for purposes of subsection (1) of section 17 of the Act and are required to be included in every invoice issued or deemed to be issued by [an accountable person][2]:

(a)   the date of issue of the invoice,

(b)   a sequential number, based on one or more series, which uniquely identifies the invoice,

(c)   the full name, address and the registration number of the person who supplied the goods or services to which the invoice relates,

(d)   the full name and address of the person to whom the goods or services were supplied,

(e)   in the case of a reverse charge supply the value-added tax identification number of the person to whom the supply was made and an indication that a reverse charge applies,

(f)   in the case of a supply of goods, other than a reverse charge supply, to a person registered for value-added tax in another Member State, the person's value-added tax identification number in that Member State and an indication that the invoice relates to an intra-Community supply of goods,

(g)   the quantity and nature of the goods supplied or the extent and nature of the services rendered,

(h)   the date on which the goods or services were supplied or, in the case of supplies specified in section 17(8) of the Act, the date on which the payment on account was made, in so far as that date differs from the date of issue of the invoice,

(i)   in respect of the goods or services supplied:

    (i)   the unit price exclusive of tax,

    (ii)   any discounts or price reductions not included in the unit price, and

    (iii)   the consideration exclusive of tax,

(j)   in respect of the goods or services supplied, other than reverse charge supplies:

    (i)   the consideration exclusive of tax per rate of tax, and

    (ii)   the rate of tax chargeable,

(k)   the tax payable in respect of the supply of the goods or services, except –

    (i)   in the case of a reverse charge supply, or

    (ii)   where section 10A(9), 10B(5) or 12B(5) of the Act applies,

and

(l)   in the case where a tax representative is liable to pay the value-added tax in another Member State, the full name and address and the value-added tax identification number of that representative.

(3)   An invoice, credit note or debit note issued by [an accountable person][2] in accordance with section 17 of the Act relating to an intra- Community supply of a new means of transport (within the meaning given by section 1 of the Act) is required to include details necessary to identify the goods as a new means of transport.

(4)   Every invoice issued by [an accountable person][2] in accordance with section 17(3)(a) of theAct in respect of an increase in consideration, is required to include the particulars specified in subparagraphs (a) to (f) of paragraph (2) and shall indicate:

(a)   the amount, exclusive of tax, of the increase in consideration for the supply,

(b)   the rate or rates of tax and the amount of tax at each rate appropriate to that increase in consideration, and

(c)   a cross-reference to every other invoice issued by [the accountable person][2] in respect of the total consideration for the supply.

(5)   Every credit note or debit note issued by a person in accordance with subsection (3)(b) or (11) of section 17 of the Act is required to include the following particulars:

(a)   the date of issue of the note,

(b)   a number which uniquely identifies the note,

(c)   the name, address and registration number of the person issuing the note,

(d)   the name, address and registration number of the person to whom the note is being issued,

(e)   in the case of a supply to a person who is registered for value-added tax in another Member State, the person's value-added tax identification number in that Member State,

(f)   the reason why the note is being issued and a cross-reference to the invoice which was issued for the supply in respect of which the consideration was reduced,

(g)   the amount of the consideration, exclusive of tax in respect of which the note is being issued, and

(h)   the rate or rates of tax current when the invoice referred to in subparagraph (f) was issued and the amount of tax at each rate as appropriate to the consideration shown on the note.

(6)   Every invoice issued by [an accountable person][2] in accordance with section 10A(9) or 10B(5) of the Act is required to indicate that the margin scheme or auction scheme, as appropriate, has been applied.

(7)   The amount of tax included on an invoice or other document issued in accordance with section 17 of the Act is required to be expressed in euro.

(8)   (a)   Notwithstanding this Regulation, the Revenue Commissioners may allow invoices, credit notes, settlement vouchers or debit notes to be issued under simplified arrangements in accordance with [Article 238 of the VAT Directive][2] but only if they include the following particulars:

(i)   the date of issue,

(ii)   identification of the supplier,

(iii)   identification of the type of goods or services supplied,

(iv)   the tax due or the information needed to calculate it, and

(v)   such other details as the Revenue Commissioners may require.

(b)   The Revenue Commissioners shall publish in the Iris Oifigiúil the details to be included in the documents referred to in subparagraph (a) and the circumstances under which they qualify for the simplified arrangements.

(9)   Any person issuing (other than by electronic means in accordance with Regulation 10(2)(a)) an invoice, credit note or debit note in accordance with section 17 of the Act is required to keep an exact copy of it and references in this Regulation to any such document include references to that copy.

[(10)   Where a document containing –

(a)   a schedule of dates on which rent in respect of a letting of immovable goods which is chargeable to tax is due (in this paragraph referred to as 'due dates') under a letting agreement, and

(b)   the particulars specified in paragraph (2), is issued prior to the earliest of those due dates listed in that schedule, then that document shall be treated as an invoice issued in accordance with section 17(1) of the Act and shall be deemed to be so issued in respect of each rent payment listed in that schedule on the due date for that rent payment.

(11)   Where the rate of tax changes during the period covered by the document referred to in paragraph (10) then that document shall be amended to provide for the new rate of tax and the corresponding amounts of tax due for the periods following the date of that change in the tax rate.][3]

Electronic invoicing

10.   (1)   In this Regulation–

"**advanced electronic signature**" means an electronic signature which is–

(a)   uniquely linked to the signatory,

(b)   capable of identifying the signatory,

(c)   created using means that are capable of being maintained by the signatory under his or her sole control, and

(d)   linked to the data to which it relates in such a manner that any subsequent change of the data is detectable;

"**electronic data interchange**" means the electronic transfer, from computer to computer, of commercial and administrative data using an agreed standard to structure a message;

"**electronic record**" means a record required to be kept for the purposes of section 16 of the Act which is generated, transmitted and stored electronically;

"**electronic signature**" means data in electronic form which are attached to or logically associated with a message and which serve as a method of authentication;

"**message**" means an invoice, credit note, debit note, settlement voucher or document issued or received in accordance with section 17 of the Act and which is transmitted electronically;

"**signatory**", "**signature-creation data**", "**signature-creation device**", "**signature-verification-data**", and "**signature- verification device**" have the meanings assigned to them by the Electronic Commerce Act 2000 (No. 27 of 2000);

"**trading partners**" means any 2 persons engaged by prior agreement in the electronic exchange of messages;

"**transmission**" means the transfer or making available of a message to a trading partner by electronic means;

"**unique identification number**" means a sequential number which is based on one or more series and which uniquely identifies a message transmitted between trading partners.

(2)   (a)   A message issued or received by electronic means by [an accountable person][2] is deemed to be so issued or received

for the purposes of section 17(1A) of the Act if each such message:

(i)   is transmitted between trading partners using an electronic data interchange system which satisfies the requirements specified in subparagraphs (b) and (c), or

(ii)   is transmitted between trading partners using an advanced electronic signature and an associated system which satisfy the requirements specified in subparagraphs (b) and (c).

(b)   The electronic data interchange system or the advanced electronic signature and associated system used by [the accountable person][2] referred to in subparagraph (a) is required to be capable of–

(i)   producing, retaining and storing, and making available to an officer of the Revenue Commissioners on request, electronic records and messages in such form and containing such particulars as may be required in accordance with sections 16 and 17 of the Act and Regulations made under the Act,

(ii)   causing to be reproduced on paper any electronic record or message required to be produced, retained or stored in accordance with sections 16 and 17 of the Act and Regulations made under the Act,

(iii)   allocating a unique identification number for each message transmitted, and

(iv)   maintaining electronic records in such manner that allows their retrieval by reference to the name of a trading partner or the date of the message or the unique identification number of the message.

(c)   The electronic data interchange system or the advanced electronic signature and associated system used by [the accountable person][2] referred to in subparagraph (a) is required to–

(i)   preclude the repeated transmission of a message,

(ii)   preclude the omission of any message from the electronic record,

(iii)   verify the origin or receipt of a message by a trading partner, and

(iv)   guarantee the integrity of the contents of a message, or of an electronic record related to that message, during transmission and during the period provided for in section 16 for the retention of records, invoices or any other documents specified in the Act or in Regulations made under the Act.

(3)   [An accountable person][2] may transmit messages by means other than those referred to in paragraph (2)(a) where —

(a)   he or she is satisfied that such messages are recorded, retained and transmitted in accordance with section 17(1A) of the Act,

(b)   the requirements of subparagraphs (b) and (c) of paragraph (2) and paragraph (4) are met, and

(c)   he or she notifies the Revenue Commissioners accordingly.

(4)   (a)   [An accountable person][2] who issues or receives messages by electronic means in accordance with paragraph (2)(a) is required to —

(i)   retain and store such messages or copies of such messages, as appropriate, together with electronic records relating to those messages, and

(ii)   retain and store electronically the following data:

(I)   details of the form of encryption, electronic signature, signature creation data or device, signature verification data or device, or any other method used to ensure the integrity of the records and messages transmitted, retained and stored and the authenticity of their origin,

(II)   details of where and in what format the information required in accordance with subclause (I) is stored and how it can be accessed.

(b)   [An accountable person][2] who issues or receives messages by electronic means is required to —

(i)   provide details on request to an officer of the Revenue Commissioners on where and how an electronic record or message is stored on that taxpayer's system and how it can be accessed by that officer,

(ii)   allow such access to electronic records or messages for inspection by an officer of the Revenue Commissioners at all reasonable times, and

(iii)   reproduce any such electronic record or message on paper on request by an officer of the Revenue Commissioners including details required to be retained and stored under subparagraph (a).

Invoicing provisions for flat-rate farmers

11.   (1)   In this Regulation **"agricultural machinery"** and **"taxable dealer"** have the same meanings, respectively, as they have in section 12C of the Act.

(2)   Every invoice issued by a flat-rate farmer in respect of agricultural produce or an agricultural service in accordance with section 17(2) of the Act is required to be acknowledged by that farmer and to include the following particulars:

(a)   the date of issue of the invoice,

(b)   the full name and address of the flat-rate farmer who supplied the goods or services to which the invoice relates,

(c)   the full name, address and registration number of the person to whom the goods or services have been supplied,

(d)   in the case of a supply of agricultural produce or an agricultural service to a person registered for value-added tax in another Member State, the person's value-added tax identification number in that Member State,

(e)   the quantity and nature of the goods supplied or the extent and nature of the services rendered,

(f)   the date on which the goods or services were supplied,

(g)   the consideration, exclusive of the flat-rate addition, for the supply, and

(h)   the rate and amount of the flat-rate addition appropriate to the consideration shown on the invoice.

(3)   Every invoice issued by a flat-rate farmer in respect of a supply of agricultural machinery in accordance with section 17(2A) of the Act is required to be acknowledged by that farmer and to include, in addition to the particulars specified in subparagraphs (a) to (c) and (f) of paragraph (2) —

(a)   a description of the agricultural machinery, including details of the make, model and where appropriate, the year of manufacture, the engine number and registration number thereof,

(b)   the consideration for the supply of the agricultural machinery, and

(c)   a declaration by that farmer that the agricultural machinery was used by him or her for the purposes of his or her farming activities.

(4)   Every invoice issued by a flat-rate farmer in respect of an increase in consideration in accordance with section 17(4)(a) of the Act is required to be acknowledged by that farmer and to include, in addition to the particulars specified in subparagraphs (a) to (d) of paragraph (2) –

(a)   indicate the amount, exclusive of the flat-rate addition, of the increase in consideration for the supply,

(b)   indicate the rate and amount of the flat-rate addition, and

(c)   include a cross-reference to every other invoice issued by the flat-rate farmer in respect of the total consideration for the supply.

(5)   Every farmer credit note or farmer debit note issued by a flat-rate farmer in accordance with subsection (4)(b) or (11A) of section 17 of the Act is required to include the following particulars:

(a)   the date of issue of the note,

(b)   the full name, address and registration number (if any) of the person issuing the note,

(c)   the full name, address and registration number (if any) of the person to whom the note is being issued,

(d)   in the case of a supply to a person who is registered for value-added tax in another Member State, the person's value-added tax identification number in that Member State,

(e)   the reason why the note is being issued and a cross-reference to the invoice which was issued for the supply in respect of which the consideration was reduced, or settlement voucher as appropriate,

(f)   the amount of the consideration exclusive of the flat-rate addition in respect of which the note is being issued, and

(g)   the rate and amount of the flat-rate addition as appropriate to the consideration shown on the note.

(6)   Every settlement voucher issued in accordance with section 17(10) of the Act in respect of agricultural produce or agricultural services supplied to a registered person by a flat-rate farmer is required to be acknowledged by that farmer and to include the following particulars:

(a)   the date of issue of the settlement voucher,

(b)   the full name and address of the flat-rate farmer who supplied the produce or services to which the voucher relates,

(c)   the full name, address and registration number for the person to whom the produce or services have been supplied,

(d)   a description, including quantity, of the produce or services supplied,

(e)   the date on which the produce or services were supplied,

(f)   the consideration, exclusive of the flat-rate addition, for the supply, and

(g)   the rate and amount of the flat-rate addition appropriate to the consideration shown on the voucher.

(7)   A taxable dealer is required to keep all invoices received in respect of agricultural machinery acquired by him or her and copies of all invoices in respect of agricultural machinery disposed of by him or her.

(8)   Any person issuing (other than by electronic means in accordance with Regulation 10(2)(a)) an invoice, credit note, settlement voucher or debit note in accordance with section 17 of the Act is required to keep an exact copy of it and references in this Regulation to any such document include references to that copy.

Time limits for issuing invoices and credit notes

12.   The following are the time limits specified for issuing invoices and credit notes for the purpose of section 17(7) of the Act–

(a)   within the 15 days following the end of the month during which the goods or services were supplied, in the case of an invoice required to be issued in accordance with section 12A, 12C or 17(1) of the Act,

(b)   within the 15 days following the day on which the increased consideration is paid or the day on which the increase in consideration is agreed between the parties, whichever day is the earlier, in the case of an invoice required to be issued in accordance with subsection (3)(a) or (4)(a) of section 17 of the Act,

(c)   in the case of a credit note required to be issued in accordance with subsection (3)(b) or (4)(b) of section 17 of the Act:

(i)   where a decrease is due to a discount, within the 15 days of the date of receipt of the money to which the discount relates, or

(ii)   in any other case, within the 15 days of the day on which the decrease in consideration is agreed between the parties,

and

(d)   within the 15 days following the end of the month during which the payment was received in the case of an invoice required to be issued in respect of a payment for a supply of goods or services before the supply is completed in accordance with section 17(8) of the Act.

Returns

13.   (1)   Where [an accountable person][2] is required to furnish a return in accordance with paragraph (a) or (b) of section 19(3) of the Act, then that person, or another person acting under that person's authority-

(a)   shall complete such form as is issued for that purpose by the Revenue Commissioners in respect of the taxable period concerned, and

(b)   either [the accountable person][2], or the other person acting under that person's authority shall sign a declaration on the form to the effect that the particulars shown on it are correct,

and if that form provides for the inclusion of supplementary trading details in respect of any period, those details are deemed to be part of the return in respect of the taxable period concerned.

(2)   Where [an accountable person][2] is authorised to furnish a return in accordance with section 19(3)(aa) of the Act, then that person, or another person acting under [that accountable person's][2] authority —

(a)   shall complete such form as is issued for that purpose by the Revenue Commissioners, and

(b)   either [the accountable person][2], or the other person acting under that person's authority shall sign a declaration on the form to the effect that the particulars shown on it are correct.

(3)   The obligation of [an accountable person][2] to make a return is fulfilled by that person if the information required in such a return is transmitted electronically in accordance with Chapter 6 of Part 38 of the Taxes Consolidation Act 1997.

Statement of intra-Community supplies

14.   (1)   In this Regulation —

"**correction statement**" means a statement of corrective details furnished in relation to a statement previously supplied;

"**intra-Community supplies**" has the meaning assigned to it by section 19A(6) of the Act;

"**statement**" means a statement of intra-Community supplies required to be furnished to the Revenue Commissioners by [an accountable person][2] in accordance with section 19A of the Act;

"**working day**" means a day other than —

    (a)   a Saturday or Sunday,

    (b)   a day that is a public holiday (within the meaning of the Organisation of Working Time Act 1997 (No. 20 of 1997)), or

    (c)   any other day when the offices of the Revenue Commissioners are closed generally to the public.

(2)   (a)   Subject to paragraph (3), [an accountable person][2] who is required in accordance with section 19A of the Act to furnish a statement of intra-Community supplies shall complete to the satisfaction of the Revenue Commissioners such forms as are provided for that purpose by them.

    (b)   Where for any reason [an accountable person][2] becomes aware of an error in a statement furnished in accordance with subparagraph (a), that person is required, within 5 working days, to furnish a correction statement on the form provided for that purpose by the Revenue Commissioners.

(3)   Notwithstanding paragraph (2), [an accountable person][2] may, on written application to the Revenue Commissioners, be authorised by them to furnish a statement or correction statement on a document or in a manner other than by use of the forms referred to in paragraph (2). In this case the relevant statement is required to —

    (a)   be furnished in a format specified by the Revenue Commissioners, and

    (b)   include all the particulars that would have been provided had the person completed the forms referred to in paragraph (2).

(4)   In furnishing a statement or correction statement in accordance with paragraph (2) or (3), [an accountable person][2] is required to —

(a) make a separate entry in respect of his or her intra-Community supplies to each person registered for value- added tax in another Member State, and

(b) make a separate entry including the indicator "T" in respect of any supplies of the type referred to in section 3A(5)(iii) of the Act to each person registered for value- added tax in another Member State,

in respect of the period covered by the statement and to furnish such other particulars of his or her intra-Community supplies as are requested on the appropriate form.

(5) (a) A statement or correction statement may be prepared and furnished to the Revenue Commissioners by a person other than [the accountable person][2] where that person has been authorised by [the accountable person][2] to act on his or her behalf in that regard. The Act applies to such a statement as if it had been prepared and furnished to the Revenue Commissioners by [the accountable person][2].

(b) A statement or correction statement purporting to be prepared and furnished to the Revenue Commissioners by or on behalf of [any accountable person][2] is, for all the purposes of the Act, deemed to have been prepared and furnished to the Revenue Commissioners by [that accountable person][2], or on his or her authority, as the case may be, unless the contrary is proved.

(c) [An accountable person][2] who authorises another person in accordance with subparagraph (a) is required to notify the Revenue Commissioners in writing of such authorisation.

(d) [An accountable person][2] is required, on cancelling an authorisation referred to in subparagraph (a), to advise the Revenue Commissioners in writing of the cancellation within 5 working days of such cancellation.

(e) The Revenue Commissioners may by notice in writing exclude [an accountable person][2] from the provisions of this paragraph.

(6) (a) Subject to subparagraph (b) and unless otherwise permitted by the Revenue Commissioners under this Regulation, every statement and correction statement is required to be completed by means of typing or other similar process.

(b) Every statement and correction statement is required to be signed and dated by —

(i) [the accountable person][2], or

(ii) the person authorised by [the accountable person][2] in accordance with paragraph (5)(a).

(c)　Where [an accountable person][2] has been authorised in accordance with paragraph (3) to furnish a statement or correction statement by electronic means or through magnetic media, any such statement has the same effect as if it were a signed statement or correction statement, as the case may be.

(7)　(a)　[An accountable person][2] may, on written application to the Revenue Commissioners, be authorised by them to submit an annual statement in accordance with section 19A(3) of the Act where —

　　(i)　his or her supplies of goods and services do not exceed or are not likely to exceed €85,000 in a calendar year, and

　　(ii)　his or her intra-Community supplies do not exceed or are not likely to exceed €15,000 in that calendar year,

but only if such intra-Community supplies do not include the supply of new means of transport.

(b)　[An accountable person][2] authorised to submit a return in accordance with section 19(3)(aa) of the Act may, on written application to the Revenue Commissioners, be authorised by them to submit an annual statement in accordance with section 19A(3) of the Act where —

　　(i)　his or her supplies of goods and services do not exceed or are not likely to exceed €200,000 in a calendar year, and

　　(ii)　his or her intra-Community supplies do not exceed or are not likely to exceed €15,000 in that calendar year,

but only if such intra-Community supplies do not include the supply of new means of transport.

(8)　The cancellation of an authorisation referred to in section 19A(2) or 19A(3) of the Act shall be by notice in writing given by the Revenue Commissioners to the person who was the subject of the authorisation and any such cancellation has effect from the date of the notice or from such later date as may be specified in the notice.

(9)　Paragraphs (2) to (6) apply to a statement or correction statement furnished on a monthly or annual basis, as the case may be. However, [the accountable person][2] referred to in paragraph 7(a) is not obliged to furnish details of the value of his or her intra-Community supplies or to comply with paragraph (4)(b).

Tax due and payable

Determination of tax due by reference to moneys received

15.   (1)   In this Regulation—

"**moneys received basis of accounting**" means the method of determining, in accordance with section 14(1) of the Act, the amount of tax which becomes due by [an accountable person][2];

"**turnover from taxable supplies**", in relation to any period, means the total of the amounts on which tax is chargeable for that period at any of the rates specified in section 11(1) of the Act.

(2)   For the purposes of section 14(1)(a) of the Act and this Regulation, supplies to persons who are not registered persons shall be deemed to include any supplies to [an accountable person][2] where the [said accountable person][2] is not entitled to claim, under section 12 of the Act, a full deduction of the tax chargeable in relation to the said supply.

(3)   (a)   An application by [an accountable person][2] (referred to in this Regulation as the "**applicant**") for authorisation to use the moneys received basis of accounting is required to be made in writing to the Revenue Commissioners and to include—

(i)   the applicant's name and address,

(ii)   the applicant's VAT registration number (if any),

(iii)   the nature of the business activities carried on by the applicant.

(b)   An applicant who claims eligibility under section 14(1)(a) of the Act is required to include in the application made in accordance with this paragraph particulars of—

(i)   the percentage of the applicant's turnover from taxable supplies, if any, which related to supplies to persons who are not registered persons—

(I)   in the period of 12 months ended on the last day of the taxable period prior to the application, or

(II)   in the period from the commencement of his or her business activities to the last day of the taxable period referred to in subclause (I), whichever is the shorter, and

(ii)   the applicant's estimate of the percentage of his or her turnover from taxable supplies which will relate to supplies to persons who are not registered persons in the period of 12 months commencing with the beginning of the taxable period during which the application is made.

(c)   An applicant who claims eligibility under section 14(1)(b) of the Act is required to include in the application made in accordance with this paragraph particulars of —

     (i)   the amount of the applicant's turnover from taxable supplies in the period of 12 months ended on the last day of the taxable period prior to the application, and

     (ii)   the applicant's estimate of his or her turnover from taxable supplies in the period of 12 months commencing with the beginning of the taxable period during which the application is made.

(4)   The Revenue Commissioners shall, if they consider that a person satisfies the requirements of section 14(1) of the Act, authorise the person, by notice in writing, to use the moneys received basis of accounting subject to this Regulation. An authorisation given for the purposes of section 14(1) of the Act shall have effect from the commencement of the taxable period during which it is given or from such other date as may be specified in the authorisation.

(5)   (a)   An authorisation of any person for the purposes of section 14(1) of the Act does not apply to tax chargeable on any supply where the person to whom or to whose order the supply is made is a person connected to that authorised person.

        (b)   For the purposes of this paragraph any question of whether a person is connected with another person shall be determined in accordance with the following:

     (i)   a person is connected with an individual if that person is the individual's spouse, or is a relative, or the spouse of a relative, of the individual or of the individual's spouse;

     (ii)   a person is connected with any person with whom he or she is in partnership, and with the spouse or a relative of any individual with whom he or she is in partnership;

     (iii)   subject to subparagraphs (iv) and (v), a person is connected with another person if he or she has control over that other person, or if the other person has control over the first-mentioned person, or if both persons are controlled by another person or persons;

(iv)   a body corporate is connected with another person if that person, or persons connected with him or her, have control of it, or the person and persons connected with him or her together have control of it;

(v)   a body corporate is connected with another body corporate—

(I)   if the same person has control of both or a person has control of one and persons connected with that person or that person and persons connected with that person have control of the other, or

(II)   if a group of 2 or more persons has control of each body corporate and the groups either consist of the same persons or could be regarded as consisting of the same persons by treating (in one or more cases) a member of either group as replaced by a person with whom he or she is connected;

(vi)   in this subparagraph "**relative**" means brother, sister, ancestor or lineal descendant.

(c)   In this paragraph "**control**", in relation to a body corporate or in relation to a partnership, has the meaning assigned to it by section 8(3B) of the Act.

[(5A)   Tax chargeable in respect of the supply of goods within the meaning of section 3(1)(b) of the Act is excluded from the application of section 14(1) of the Act.

(5B)   Tax chargeable in respect of the supply of goods or services [referred to in section 8(1B)(b) of the Act or][3] in any of the circumstances referred to in subsections (2) to (9) of section 10 of the Act is excluded from the application of section 14(1) of the Act.][4]

(6)   An authorisation for the purposes of section 14(1) of the Act does not affect the amount on which tax is chargeable under the Act.

(7)   (a)   [An accountable person][2] authorised for the purposes of section 14(1) of the Act is required to notify the Revenue Commissioners in writing if, for any period of 4 consecutive calendar months during the validity of such authorisation, he or she no longer satisfies the requirements of that section and such notification shall be made within 30 days of the end of such 4 month period.

(b)   Where [an accountable person]² fails to notify the Revenue Commissioners in accordance with subparagraph (a), the authorisation for the purposes of section 14(1) of the Act is deemed to be cancelled in accordance with paragraph (8). Such cancellation has effect for the purposes of section 14 of the Act from the commencement of the taxable period during which [the accountable person]² should have notified the Revenue Commissioners in accordance with subparagraph (a).

(8)   (a)   The Revenue Commissioners shall cancel an authorization to which section 14(1) of the Act and paragraph (4) relates if either:

       (i)   the person so authorised makes a request to them in writing to have the authorisation cancelled, or

       (ii)   they consider that the person no longer satisfies the requirements of section 14(1) of the Act.

(b)   The Revenue Commissioners shall cancel the authorisation to which section 14(1) of the Act and paragraph (4) relates by issuing a notice in writing to the authorised person. Without prejudice to paragraph (7)(b), such cancellation has effect from the commencement of the taxable period during which notice is given or from the commencement of such later taxable period as may be specified in the notice.

(9)   (a)   Where a person who for any period is authorised under section 14(1) of the Act ceases to be so authorised or ceases to be [an accountable person]², the tax payable by him or her for the taxable period during which the cessation occurs shall be adjusted in accordance with this paragraph.

(b)   The total amount due to the person at the end of the authorised period for goods and services supplied by him or her shall be apportioned between each rate of tax specified in section 11(1) of the Act in accordance with the following formula —

$$A \times \frac{B}{C}$$

where –

A   is the total amount due to the person at the end of the authorised period for goods and services supplied by him or her during the authorised period,

B   is the taxable amount in respect of taxable supplies at each rate of tax in the 12 months prior to the date of cessation or in the authorised period, whichever is the shorter, and

C   is the taxable amount in respect of total taxable supplies in the 12 months prior to the date of cessation or in the authorised period, whichever is the shorter,

but the apportionment between the various rates of tax may be made in accordance with any other basis which may be agreed between [the accountable person][2] and the Revenue Commissioners.

(c)   The amount so apportioned at each rate is a tax-inclusive amount and the tax therein shall be treated as tax due for the taxable period in which the cessation occurs.

(d)   No adjustment of liability as provided for in this paragraph shall be made if the cessation referred to in subparagraph (a) was occasioned by the death of [the accountable person][2].

(e)   For the purposes of this paragraph—

"the authorised period" means the period during which the person was authorised to apply the moneys received basis of accounting, but where the person was authorised to apply the moneys received basis of accounting for more than 6 years the authorised period is deemed to be for a period of 6 years ending on the date on which the cancellation of the authorisation has effect;

"the tax therein" shall be established at the rates specified in section 11(1) of the Act—

(i)   applicable on the date the authorised period ends, or

(ii)   applicable at the time the relevant goods and services were supplied where such details can be established to the satisfaction of the Revenue Commissioners.

Adjustments for returned goods, discounts, and price alterations

16.   (1)   Paragraphs (2) to (4) apply where, in a case in which section 10(3) (c) of the Act applies and section 17(9) of the Act does not apply, [by reason of the allowance of discount, a reduction in price or the return of goods other than the return of goods in an early determination of a hire purchase agreement][5]-

(a)   the consideration exclusive of tax actually received by [an accountable person][2] in respect of the supply by him or her of any goods or services is less than the amount on which tax has become chargeable in respect of such supply, or

(b)   no consideration is actually received.

(2)   The amount of the deficiency in respect of any supply shall be ascertained by deducting from the amount on which tax has become chargeable in respect of such supply, the consideration actually received exclusive of tax.

(3)   (a)   Subject to subparagraph (b), the sum of the deficiencies ascertained in accordance with paragraph (2), incurred in each taxable period and relating to consideration chargeable at each of the various rates of tax (including the zero rate) specified in section 11(1) of the Act, shall be deducted from the amounts ascertained in accordance with section 10 of the Act which would otherwise be chargeable with tax at each of those rates and the net amounts as so ascertained shall be the amounts on which tax is chargeable for the taxable period during which the deficiencies are ascertained.

     (b)   For the purposes of subparagraph (a), where the sum of the deficiencies as ascertained in accordance with subparagraph (a) in relation to tax chargeable at any of the rates so specified in section 11(1) of the Act exceeds the amount on which, but for this Regulation—

       (i)   tax would be chargeable at that rate, or

       (ii)   no tax is chargeable at that rate,

then, the tax appropriate to the excess or to the sum of the deficiencies, if no tax is chargeable, shall be treated as tax deductible in accordance with section 12 of the Act for that taxable period.

(4)   (a)   Where, in accordance with section 17 of the Act, a credit note is issued by [an accountable person][2] in respect of an adjustment under this Regulation, then [the accountable person][2] to whom the credit note is issued shall reduce the amount which would otherwise be deductible under section 12 of the Act for the taxable period during which the credit note is issued (in this paragraph referred to as the "**tax deduction**") by the appropriate amount of tax shown thereon (in this paragraph referred to as the "**tax reduction**").

     (b)   Where the tax reduction exceeds the tax deduction, then the excess shall be carried forward and deducted from the tax deductible under section 12 of the Act for the next taxable period and so on until the tax reduction is exhausted.

(5)   (a)   Where, in accordance with section 17(4)(b) of the Act, a farmer credit note is issued by a flat-rate farmer, then [the accountable person][2] to whom the credit note is issued shall reduce the amount which would otherwise

be deductible under section 12(1)(a)(viii) of the Act for the taxable period during which the farmer credit note is issued (in this paragraph referred to as the "**flat-rate deduction**") by the amount of the appropriate flat-rate addition shown thereon (in this paragraph referred to as the "**flat-rate reduction**").

(b)   Where the flat-rate reduction exceeds the flat-rate deduction, the excess shall be carried forward and deducted from the amount deductible under section 12(1)(a)(viii) of the Act for the next taxable period and so on until the flat-rate reduction is exhausted.

[*Adjustments for bad debts and for early determination of hire purchase transactions*

16A. (1)   In this Regulation —

"**determination**" means the termination of a hire purchase agreement and the return of the goods which are subject to that agreement on a prior date to the date fixed for such termination under that agreement;

"**part payment**" means the amount of money or the value of goods traded in by the customer which amount or value is shown in the hire purchase agreement as representing that part of the sale price of goods which is not being financed under the terms of the hire purchase agreement;

"**sale price**" means the price shown in the hire purchase agreement which is inclusive of tax, and vehicle registration tax where appropriate, and which is the price for which the goods would be sold to a customer if their purchase were not financed in whole or in part under a hire purchase agreement.

(2)   In a case in which section 10(3)(c) of the Act applies by reason of the default of a debtor, where–

(a)   the consideration exclusive of tax actually received by [an accountable person][2] in relation to the supply by him or her of any goods or services is less than the amount on which tax was chargeable in respect of such supply, or

(b)   no consideration is actually received,

then, subject to the conditions in paragraph (3), relief in respect of the tax attributable to the deficiency (in this Regulation referred to as a "**bad debt**") may be claimed in accordance with this Regulation.

[(3)   An accountable person who has accounted for tax in respect of a supply covered by paragraph (2) may subsequently claim bad debt relief for the tax attributable to the bad debt, where —

(a)   that accountable person has taken all reasonable steps to recover the bad debt,

(b)   the bad debt is allowable as a deduction under section 81(2)(i) of the Taxes Consolidation Act 1997 (No. 39 of 1997) in cases where the accountable person is chargeable to tax under Case I or II of Schedule D of that Act,

(c)   the bad debt has been written off in the financial accounts of that accountable person and the requirements of Regulation 8(1)(m) in respect of that debt have been fulfilled by that accountable person, and

(d)   the person from whom the debt is due is not connected with that accountable person, and the question of whether a person is connected with that accountable person shall be determined in accordance with section 7A(3) of the Act.][2]

(4)   The amount of the relief which [an accountable person][2] may claim in respect of a supply covered by paragraphs (2) and (3), which is not a supply within the meaning of section 3(1)(b) of the Act, is calculated in accordance with the following formula:

$$A \times \frac{B}{100 + B}$$

where —

A   is the amount which is outstanding from the debtor in relation to the taxable supply, and

B   is the percentage rate of tax, specified in section 11(1) of the Act, which was applied to the supply in question.

(5)   (a)   The amount of the relief which [an accountable person][2] may claim in respect of a supply covered by paragraphs (2) and (3), which is a supply within the meaning of section 3(1)(b) of the Act (in this Regulation referred to as a **"supply of the goods under the hire purchase agreement"**), is calculated in accordance with the following formula:

$$(C - D) \times \frac{(E - F)}{C}$$

where —

C   is the sum of all the amounts scheduled for payment by instalment under the hire purchase agreement,

D   is the total amount paid by the customer against the instalments scheduled for payment under the hire purchase agreement up to and including the date on which the bad debt is written off in the financial accounts of [the accountable person][2],

E   is an amount equal to the amount of tax accounted for by [the accountable person][2] on the supply of the goods under the hire purchase agreement, and

F   is an amount equal to the tax attributable to a part payment shown in the hire purchase agreement calculated in accordance with subparagraph (b).

(b)   The tax attributable to a part payment shall be calculated in accordance with the following formula:

$$G \times \frac{E}{H}$$

where—

G   is an amount equal to the part payment,

E   is an amount equal to the amount of tax accounted for by [an accountable person][2] on the supply of the goods under the hire purchase agreement, and

H   is the sale price of the goods.

(6)   In a case in which section 10(3)(c) of the Act applies by reason of the return of the goods by a customer to his or her supplier as part of a determination, relief in respect of the supply of the goods under the hire purchase agreement may, subject to section 10(3)(d) of the Act, be claimed in accordance with paragraph (7).

(7)   The amount of the relief which [an accountable person][2] may claim in respect of a supply of the goods referred to in paragraph (6) is established by—

(a)   calculating the tax attributable to the part payment in accordance with the formula in paragraph (5)(b), and

(b)   calculating, in accordance with the following formula, the tax attributable to the sum of the total amount paid by the customer against the instalments scheduled for payment under the hire purchase agreement and any amount paid by the customer as part of the determination:

$$J \times \frac{(E - K)}{C}$$

where—

J   is the total amount paid by the customer against the instalments scheduled for payment under the hire purchase agreement up to and including the prior date agreed under the determination plus any amount paid by the customer as part of the determination,

> E   is an amount equal to the amount of tax accounted for by [the accountable person][2] on the supply of the goods under the hire purchase agreement,
>
> K   is an amount equal to the amount of tax attributable to the part payment shown in the hire purchase agreement calculated in accordance with paragraph (5)(b), and
>
> C   is the sum of all the amounts scheduled for payment by instalment under the hire purchase agreement,
>
> subtracting the sum of the amounts calculated in accordance with subparagraphs (a) and (b) from the tax accounted for by [the accountable person][2] on the supply of the goods under the hire purchase agreement.

(8)   Notwithstanding paragraphs (4), (5) and (7), [the accountable person][2] may, subject to the prior agreement of the Revenue Commissioners, use any other method of calculating the relief that correctly reflects the tax appropriate to the amount outstanding.

(9)   [An accountable person][2] is entitled to claim the total amount of relief calculated in accordance with paragraphs (4), (5), (7) or (8), as if that amount were tax deductible in accordance with section 12 of the Act for the taxable period in which a claim is made.][1]

Estimates and assessments

17. (1)   A notice of an amount of tax estimated in accordance with section 22 of the Act shall contain the following:

     (a)   the name, address and registration number of the person whose tax liability is estimated,

     (b)   the period to which the estimate relates, and

     (c)   the amount of tax estimated to be payable in respect of the period referred to in subparagraph (b).

(2)   A notice of an amount of tax assessed in accordance with section 23 of the Act shall contain the following:

     (a)   the name, address and registration number of the person whose tax liability or refund is assessed,

     (b)   the period to which the assessment relates (in this paragraph referred to as the '**assessment period**'),

     (c)   an assessment of the total amount of tax which should have been paid or the total amount of tax (including, where appropriate, a nil amount) which in accordance with section 20(1) of the Act should have been refunded, as the case may be, in respect of the assessment period,

(d)   the total amount of tax (including, where appropriate, a nil amount) paid by the person or refunded to the person, as the case may be, in respect of the assessment period, and

(e)   the net amount due in respect of the assessment period.

Apportionment

18.   [(1)   In this Regulation—

"**authorised officer**" means a person authorised for the purposes of section 18 of the Act;

"**final accounting year**" means the period from the end of the previous accounting year to the date that a person ceases to be an accountable person;

"**review period**" means a period consisting of all the taxable periods which end during an accounting year.]²

(2)   (a)   Where [an accountable person]² deducts, in accordance with subsections (1) and (4) of section 12 of the Act, a proportion of the tax borne or payable on [the accountable person's]² acquisition of dual-use inputs for a taxable period, then that proportion of tax deductible by that person for a taxable period is—

(i)   the proportion which—

(I)   correctly reflects the extent to which the dual-use inputs are used for the purposes of that person's deductible supplies or activities, and

(II)   has due regard to the range of that person's total supplies and activities,

for that taxable period,

(ii)   the proportion which was calculated as being the proportion of tax deductible for the review period immediately preceding the taxable period in question,

(iii)   the proportion which that person estimates will—

(I)   correctly reflect the extent to which the dual-use inputs will be used for the purposes of that person's deductible supplies or activities, and

(II)   have due regard to the range of that person's total supplies and activities,

for the review period in which that taxable period ends, or

(iv)   any other proportion of tax deductible which is arrived at in accordance with paragraph (2)(c).

(b)   Where [an accountable person]² estimates a proportion of tax deductible for a taxable period in accordance with subparagraph (a)(iii), then [the accountable person]² is required to submit, at the same time as the return required to be furnished in accordance with section 19(3) of the Act for the taxable period in question, details setting out the basis for that estimate to the office of the Revenue Commissioners which would normally deal with the examination of the records kept by that person in accordance with section 16 of the Act.

(c)   If an authorised officer is satisfied that the proportion of tax deductible, estimated in accordance with sub-paragraph (a)(iii) –

    (i)   does not correctly reflect the extent to which the dual-use inputs will be used for the purposes of [the accountable person's]² deductible supplies or activities, and

    (ii)   does not have due regard to the range of that person's total supplies and activities for the review period in which the taxable period ends,

then that officer may direct [that accountable person]² to use a proportion of tax deductible in accordance with clause (i) or (ii) of subparagraph (a) or any other appropriate proportion which that officer agrees with that person.

(3)   (a)   [An accountable person]² who deducts, in accordance with subsections (1) and (4) of section 12 of the Act, a proportion of the tax borne or payable on [the accountable person's]² acquisition of dual-use inputs is required, at the end of each review period–

    (i)   to calculate the proportion of tax deductible for that review period, and

    (ii)   to adjust, if necessary in accordance with subparagraph (b), the amount of tax deducted in that review period to ensure that it correctly reflects the extent to which the dual-use inputs were used for the purposes of that person's deductible supplies or activities and had due regard to the range of that person's total supplies and activities for that review period.

(b)   Subject to subparagraph (c), any necessary adjustment under subparagraph (a) is required to be made by way of an increase or decrease, in accordance with the circumstances, in the amount of tax deductible by [the accountable person]², for —

    (i)   the taxable period immediately following the end of the review period, or

    (ii)   such later taxable period which is agreed between [the accountable person]² and an authorised officer.

[(c)   Where the adjustment under subparagraph (b) relates to the final accounting year of the accountable person concerned, then any necessary adjustment is required to be made by way of an increase or decrease in the amount of tax deductible for the taxable period in which that final accounting year ends. Any such adjustment is required to be made in the return to be furnished in accordance with section 19(3) of the Act in respect of the appropriate taxable period.]²

(d)   Any increase or decrease in the amount of tax deductible resulting from an adjustment of tax deductible made in accordance with this paragraph, is to be disregarded in calculating the proportion of tax deductible for the review period in which that adjustment was made.

(4)   Where [an accountable person]² adjusts in accordance with paragraph (3) the amount of tax deductible for a review period and subsequent to that adjustment it is established that that adjustment was incorrect, then section 21 of the Act does not apply to any additional liability for tax arising out of the correction of that adjustment but only if —

(a)   that person, or any person acting on his or her behalf, did not act fraudulently or negligently in relation to that adjustment,

(b)   that person submitted, by the due date for submission of the return referred to in paragraph (3)(c), details setting out the basis on which the adjustment was made to the office of the Revenue Commissioners which would normally deal with the examination of the records kept by that person in accordance with section 16 of the Act, and

(c)   that additional liability is not the subject of an assessment of tax under section 23 of the Act.

Valuation of interests in immovable goods

19.   (1)   Where —

(a)   it is necessary to value an interest in immovable goods for the purposes of section 10(9) of the Act,

(b)   the disposal of such interest consists of or includes the creation of an interest, and

(c)   a rent is payable in respect of the interest so created,

then, the value of such rent to be included in the consideration for the purpose of ascertaining the open market price of the interest disposed of shall, in the absence of other evidence of the amount of that price, be determined in accordance with paragraph (2).

(2)   For the purposes of paragraph (1) the value of the rent concerned is to be determined as follows:

    (a)   three-quarters of the annual amount of the rent multiplied by the number of complete years for which rent has been created, or

    (b)   the annual amount of the rent multiplied by the fraction of which the numerator is 100 and the denominator is the rate of interest (before deduction of income tax, if any) on the security of the Government which was issued last before the date of the creation of the rent for subscription in the State, and which is redeemable not less than 5 years after the date of issue (allowance having been made in calculating the interest for any profit or loss which will occur on the redemption of the security),

but if the rent payable in respect of the interest so created is less than the unencumbered rent in respect of that interest, then the value of the rent to be included in the consideration for the purpose of ascertaining the open market price of the interest disposed of shall be calculated using the unencumbered rent.

(3)   Where a person having an interest in immovable goods (in this paragraph referred to as the "**disponor**") disposes as regards the whole or any part of those goods of an interest which derives from that interest in such circumstances that he or she retains the reversion on the interest disposed of (in this paragraph referred to as the "**reversionary interest**"), the following provisions apply:

    (a)   the value of the reversionary interest shall be ascertained by deducting the value of the interest disposed of from the value of the full interest which the disponor had in the goods or the part thereof disposed of at the time the disposition was made, and

    (b)   if, under the terms of the disposition, the interest disposed of is for a period of 20 years or more or is deemed to be for a period of 20 years or more, the value of the reversionary interest shall be disregarded.

Stamps, coupons, tokens and vouchers

20.   (1)   The amount on which tax is chargeable by virtue of section 2(1)(a) of the Act in relation to supplies of stamps, coupons, tokens or vouchers specified in section 10(7)(b) of the Act shall be nil where

the supplies are made by a person in relation to the operation of a business consisting mainly of the supply of goods or services in exchange for the stamps, coupons, tokens or vouchers, and the goods or services are of a kind which the person to whom the stamps, coupons, tokens or vouchers are surrendered does not supply except in relation to the operation of such a scheme.

(2)   The amount on which tax is chargeable by virtue of section 2(1)(a) of the Act in relation to supplies of goods or services to which section 10(7)(c) of the Act relates shall be the consideration which was disregarded for the purpose of the Act in accordance with section 10(6) of the Act.

Apportionment of consideration

21.   (1)   In this Regulation **"remaining individual supply"** means an individual supply which is not disregarded.

(2)   (a)   Subject to paragraphs (3) and (4), an individual supply or supplies in a multiple supply may be disregarded by [an accountable person][2] for the purpose of the application of section 11(3)(a)(ii) of the Act where the total tax exclusive cost to [the accountable person][2] of such supply or supplies does not exceed 50 per cent of the total tax exclusive consideration which [the accountable person][2] becomes entitled to receive for that multiple supply or €1, whichever is the lesser.

(b)   Notwithstanding subparagraph (a), an individual supply of a beverage suitable for human consumption on which tax is chargeable at a rate other than the rate specified in section 11(1)(b) of the Act shall not be disregarded.

(3)   Where a multiple supply consists of an individual supply or supplies which [an accountable person][2] disregards in accordance with paragraph (2) and one remaining individual supply, then the total consideration which [the accountable person][2] is entitled to receive for that multiple supply shall be treated as an amount chargeable at the rate specified in section 11(1) of the Act appropriate to that remaining individual supply.

(4)   Where a multiple supply consists of an individual supply or supplies which [an accountable person][2] disregards in accordance with paragraph (2) and more than one remaining individual supply, then the taxable amount referable to the disregarded individual supply as ascertained in accordance with section 11(3)(a)(ii) of the Act shall be treated as an amount chargeable to tax

(a)   where there is more than one rate applicable to those remaining individual supplies, at the lowest of those rates, and

(b)   in any other case, at the rate applicable to the remaining individual supplies.

[*The operation of the capital goods scheme*

21A. (1)   (a)   For the purposes of section 12E of the Act where a capital goods owner changes the end date of his or her accounting year during a subsequent interval of the adjustment period for a capital good, then the duration of that subsequent interval shall be a period of 12 months from the start date of that subsequent interval and in such circumstances, starting from and including the first day following the end of that subsequent interval, the remaining subsequent intervals in the adjustment period shall be consecutive periods of 12 months.

(b)   Notwithstanding subparagraph (a), where the change in the end date of the accounting year results in that accounting year ending—

(i)   more than 12 months from the start date of the subsequent interval in which that change takes place, then the capital goods owner may extend the period of that subsequent interval to the end date of that accounting year, or

(ii)   less than 12 months from the start date of the subsequent interval in which that change takes place, then the capital goods owner may extend the period of that subsequent interval to the end date of the following accounting year.

(2)   (a)   Where—

(i)   a capital good is transferred in accordance with section 12E(10) of the Act during a subsequent interval of the adjustment period for that capital good, and

(ii)   the accounting year of the transferee differs from the accounting year of the transferor,

then that subsequent interval shall be a period of 12 months from the start date of that subsequent interval in which the transfer takes place and in such circumstances, starting from and including the first day following the end of the subsequent interval during which the transfer takes place, the remaining subsequent intervals in the adjustment period shall be consecutive periods of 12 months.

(b)   Notwithstanding subparagraph (a), in cases where the accounting year of the transferee ends-

(i)   more than 12 months from the start of the subsequent interval in which the transfer takes place, then the transferee may extend that subsequent interval to the last day of that accounting year, or

(ii)   less than 12 months from the start of the subsequent interval in which the transfer takes place, then the transferee may extend that subsequent interval to the last day of the following accounting year.

The supply of services comprising the use of business assets for private or non-business purposes

21B. (1)   In this Regulation 'private use proportion' means the proportion which correctly reflects the extent to which immovable goods are used for private or non-business purposes in the relevant taxable period.

(2)   Where section 5(3B) of the Act applies the private use proportion shall be calculated in accordance with the following formula:

$$\frac{A}{B}$$

where —

A   is equal to the floor area of that part of the immovable goods that is used for private or non-business purposes in the relevant taxable period, and

B   is equal to the total floor area of those immovable goods.

(3)   The amount on which tax is chargeable in relation to the supply of services referred to in section 5(3B) of the Act in any taxable period shall be calculated in accordance with the following formula:

$$\frac{C \times D}{20 \times 6}$$

where —

C   is the amount on which tax is chargeable on the acquisition or development of the immovable goods,

D   is the private use proportion calculated in accordance with the formula in paragraph (2).

(4)   The rate of tax applicable to the supply of services referred to in paragraph (3) is the rate specified in section 11(1)(a) of the Act.][6]

Refunds, remissions and relief

Refund of tax

22.   A claim for refund of tax shall be made in writing to the Revenue Commissioners and shall–

    (a)   set out the grounds on which the refund is claimed,

    (b)   contain a computation of the amount of the refund claimed, and

    (c)   if so required by the Revenue Commissioners, be vouched by the receipts for tax paid and such other documents as may be necessary to prove the entitlement to a refund of the amount claimed.

Refund to foreign traders

23.   (1)   A person to whom section 13(3) of the Act applies is entitled, under the terms of Council Directive No. 79/1072/EEC of 6 December 1979 and Council Directive No. 86/560/EEC of 17 November 1986, to be repaid tax borne by him or her on the purchase of goods or services supplied to him or her in the State or in respect of goods imported into the State by him or her if he or she fulfils to the satisfaction of the Revenue Commissioners the following conditions:

    (a)   in the case of a person having an establishment in another Member State, produces a certificate from the relevant official department of that Member State that he or she is subject, under the laws of that Member State, to value-added tax referred to in the [VAT Directive][2],

    (b)   in the case of a person not established in the territory of the Community, provides proof, in the form of a written document from the relevant official department of the country in which he or she has an establishment, that he or she is engaged in carrying on an economic activity,

    (c)   claims a refund, within 6 months of the end of the calendar year in which the tax became chargeable, by completing and lodging the appropriate claim form, provided for that purpose by the Revenue Commissioners, together with the appropriate documentation as specified in subparagraph (d),

    (d)   establishes the amount of tax borne by the production of the invoice issued by the supplier or the relevant import documents,

    (e)   establishes that he or she is not entitled to repayment of the tax under any other provision of the Act or Regulations, or any other instrument made under statute that is administered by the Revenue Commissioners.

(2)   A claim for a refund under this Regulation shall relate to invoiced purchases of goods and services or to imports made during a period, within a calendar year, of not less than 3 months or a period of not more than one calendar year, but where that claim relates to the remainder of a calendar year a claim for a refund may relate to a period of less than 3 months.

(3)   A person may not make a claim under this Regulation for an amount that is less than-

(a)   €200 where the claim is in respect of a period of less than one calendar year but not less than 3 months,

(b)   €25 where the claim is in respect of a period that represents a full calendar year or the final part of the calendar year.

(4)   The certificate and written document mentioned in subparagraphs (a) and (b) of paragraph (1), respectively, shall each be taken as evidence of the matters contained therein for the purposes of this Regulation only for a period of one year from the date such certificate or such document was issued by the official authorities in the State in which that person is established.

Remission of small amounts of tax

24.   The Revenue Commissioners may, at their discretion, remit the amount of tax, together with interest thereon, payable by a person in respect of goods and services supplied by him or her during any taxable period, if the total amount of the tax, exclusive of any interest chargeable thereon does not exceed €20.

Remission or repayment of tax on fishing vessels and equipment

25.   (1)   In accordance with section 13(1)(c) of the Act, tax is remitted in respect of the supply or importation of fishing nets, and sections of fishing nets, used or to be used for the purposes of commercial sea-fishing.

(2)   A person who—

(a)   establishes to the satisfaction of the Revenue Commissioners that he or she has borne or paid tax on any goods or services specified in paragraph (3), and

(b)   fulfils to the satisfaction of the Revenue Commissioners the conditions specified in paragraph (4),

is entitled to be repaid the tax so borne or paid.

(3)   The goods and services to which paragraph (2) relate are—

(a)   the supply or hire to that person, the importation by that person or the maintenance or repair for that person of a commercial sea-fishing vessel of a gross tonnage of not more than 15 tons, on the acquisition of which he or she received from An Bord Iascaigh Mhara a grant or loan of money,

(b)   the supply or hire to that person, the importation by that person or the repair, modification or maintenance for that person, of goods of the kind specified in the Table to this Regulation for use exclusively in the operation by that person of a commercial sea-fishing vessel of a gross tonnage of not more than 15 tons, on the acquisition of which he or she received from An Bord Iascaigh Mhara a grant or loan of money, or

(c)   the repair or maintenance for that person of a fishing net specified in paragraph (1) for use exclusively for the purposes of his or her commercial sea-fishing business.

(4)   The conditions to be fulfilled are that the person specified in paragraph (2) —

(a)   claims a refund of tax by completing such claim form as may be provided for that purpose by the Revenue Commissioners,

(b)   produces sufficient documentary evidence to establish that the outlay in relation to which his or her claim for a refund of tax arises was incurred in the operation by him or her of a vessel specified in paragraph (3) for the purposes of a commercial sea-fishing business,

(c)   produces either an invoice provided in accordance with section 17(12)(a)(ii) of the Act or a receipt for tax paid on goods imported to establish the amount of tax borne or paid in relation to the outlay referred to in paragraph (3),

(d)   produces a certificate from An Bord Iascaigh Mhara, or such other documentary evidence acceptable to the Revenue Commissioners, to establish that the outlay in relation to which his or her claim for a refund of tax arises relates to a commercial sea-fishing vessel in respect of which he or she qualified for financial assistance by grant or loan from An Bord Iascaigh Mhara,

(e)   is not, or is not required to be, registered for tax in accordance with section 9 of the Act.

TABLE

Anchors, autopilots, bilge and deck pumps, buoys and floats, compasses, cranes, echo graphs, echo sounders, electrical generating sets, fish boxes, fish finders, fishing baskets, life boats and life rafts, marine lights, marine engines, net drums, net haulers, net sounders, radar apparatus, radio navigational aid apparatus, radio telephones, refrigeration plant, trawl doors, trawl gallows, winches.

Relief for stock-in-trade held at commencement of taxability

26. (1)   [An accountable person][2] who makes a claim for a deduction under section 12(1) of the Act of an amount which he or she is entitled to deduct in accordance with section 12(1A) of the Act, is required

    (a)   to keep detailed records of all stock-in-trade held at the commencement of the first taxable period for which he or she is deemed to be [an accountable person][2] (in this Regulation referred to as the "**relevant day**"), and

    (b)   to so keep those records under the headings set out in paragraph (2).

  (2)   The following are the headings for the purposes of paragraph (1):

    (a)   stocks supplied to [the accountable person][2] concerned by [other accountable persons][2] and in respect of which, if supplied immediately before the relevant day, tax would be chargeable on the full amount of the consideration at the rate specified in section 11(1)(a) of the Act,

    (b)   stocks supplied to [the accountable person][2] concerned by [other accountable persons][2] and in respect of which, if supplied immediately before the relevant day, tax would be chargeable on the full amount of the consideration at the rate specified in section 11(1)(d) of the Act,

    (c)   agricultural produce supplied by flat-rate farmers, and

    (d)   stocks, other than stocks referred to in subparagraph (c), in respect of which, if supplied immediately before the relevant day, tax would not be chargeable or would be chargeable at the zero rate.

  (3)   (a)   The total amount of the deduction to which [the accountable person][2] concerned is entitled in respect of stocks specified in subparagraph (a) or (b) of paragraph (2) shall be calculated by the formula:

$$(A - B) \times \frac{C}{100 + C}$$

where —

A   is the value of stocks specified in subparagraph (a) or (b) of paragraph (2), as the case may be, which is calculated on the basis of cost inclusive of tax, or market value, whichever is the lower,

B   is the value of the stocks referred to in A in respect of which an invoice issued in accordance with section 17 of the Act has been, or is likely to be, received on or after the relevant day, and

> C   is the percentage rate of tax, applicable on the day before the relevant day, as specified in section 11(1)(a) of the Act in respect of stocks referred to in paragraph (2)(a) and section 11(1)(d) of the Act in respect of stocks referred to in paragraph (2)(b).

> (b)   The deduction to which [the accountable person][2] concerned is entitled in respect of stocks specified in paragraph (2)(c) shall be determined by the formula:

$$(D - E) \times F$$

where —

> D   is the value of stocks specified in paragraph (2)(c) which is calculated on the basis of cost inclusive of tax, or market value, whichever is the lower,

> E   is the value of the stocks referred to in D in respect of which an invoice issued in accordance with section 17 of the Act has been, or is likely to be, received on or after the relevant day, and

> F   is the percentage rate of flat-rate addition applicable on the day before the relevant day, specified in section 12A(1) of the Act.

(4)   A detailed record must be kept of the relief, claimed under this Regulation, which is included in a return made in accordance with section 19(3) of the Act.

Exemption of certain business gifts

27.   For the purposes of section 3(1A)(a) of the Act a gift of goods made in the course or furtherance of business (otherwise than as one forming part of a series or succession of gifts made to the same person) the cost of which to the donor does not exceed €20 exclusive of tax shall be deemed not to have been effected for consideration.

Special schemes

Investment gold - records of transactions

28.   (1)   In this Regulation "**intermediary services**" means services supplied by an intermediary.

(2)   Every person who trades in investment gold is required to keep full and true records entered up to date of —

> (a)   in relation to supplies of investment gold, the name of each person to whom the investment gold is supplied, the amount receivable from each such person in respect of such supplies and a cross-reference to the relevant invoices or documents which issued in respect of such supplies,

(b)   in relation to purchases of investment gold, the name of each person from whom the investment gold is purchased, the purchase price of the investment gold and a cross-reference to the relevant invoices or documents which were received in respect of such purchases,

(c)   in relation to importations of investment gold, the value of the investment gold determined in accordance with section 15 of the Act in respect of each importation, the purchase price of the investment gold imported and a cross-reference to the invoices and customs documents used in connection with such importations,

(d)   in relation to intra-Community acquisitions of investment gold, the name of the person from whom the investment gold is acquired, the purchase price of the investment gold and a cross-reference to the relevant invoices which were received in respect of such acquisitions,

(e)   in relation to the supply of intermediary services, the name of each person to whom the service is supplied, the amount receivable in respect of the supply and a cross-reference to the relevant invoices or documents which issued in respect of the supply of such services,

(f)   in relation to intermediary services received, the name of the intermediaries, the amount payable in respect of the supply of the services and a cross-reference to the relevant invoices or documents which were received in respect of such services,

(g)   in relation to discounts allowed or price reductions made to a person subsequent to the issue of an invoice or other document to such person, the amount credited to such person and, except in a case to which section 17(9)(a) of the Act applies, a cross-reference to the corresponding credit note,

(h)   in relation to discounts or price reductions received [from accountable persons]² subsequent to the receipt of invoices from such persons, except in a case to which section 17(9) (a) of the Act applies, the amount of the discount or price reduction and corresponding tax received from each such person and a cross-reference to the corresponding credit note,

(i)   in relation to discounts or price reductions received from persons who are not taxable persons, the amount of the discount or price reduction and a cross-reference to the document which was received in respect of such discount or price reduction, and

(j)   in relation to bad debts written off, particulars of the name and address of the debtor, a description of the supply of investment gold to which the debt relates, the date or dates upon which the debt was incurred and the date or dates on which the debt was written off.

(3)   Regulation 8(1) does not apply in relation to transactions in investment gold.

Investment gold - waiver of exemption

29. (1)   A person who produces investment gold or transforms any gold into investment gold and who, in accordance with section 6A(3) of the Act, wishes to waive his or her right to exemption from tax on supplies of investment gold to another person who is engaged in the supply of goods and services in the course or furtherance of business, is required to apply to the Revenue Commissioners for authorisation to do so and to furnish them with the following particulars—

(a)   his or her name, address and registration number (if any), and

(b)   a declaration stating that he or she produces investment gold or transforms any gold into investment gold and that he or she supplies or intends to supply investment gold to other persons engaged in the supply of goods and services in the course or furtherance of business.

(2)   Where they are satisfied that it is appropriate to do so for the proper administration of the tax, the Revenue Commissioners shall authorise the applicant to waive in accordance with section 6A(3) of the Act, his or her right to exemption from tax on a supply of investment gold.

(3)   A person, authorised in accordance with paragraph (2) in respect of a supply of investment gold to another person shall, in relation to that supply, issue to that other person an invoice showing the following particulars—

(a)   the date of issue of the invoice,

(b)   a sequential number, based on one or more series, which uniquely identifies the invoice,

(c)   his or her full name, address and registration number,

(d)   the full name, address and registration number of the person to whom the investment gold is being supplied,

(e)   in the case of a supply of investment gold to—

(i)   a person in another Member State, that person's value-added tax identification number (if any) in that Member State,

(ii)   a person outside the Community, an indication of the type of business being carried on by that person,

(f)   a description of the investment gold including, where applicable, form, weight, quantity, purity and any other distinguishing features,

(g)   the date of supply of the investment gold,

(h)   the total consideration, exclusive of tax, receivable in respect of the supply,

(i)   the rate or rates of tax and the amount of tax at each rate chargeable in respect of the supply of the investment gold, and

(j)   an endorsement stating "The right to exemption from tax has been waived in respect of this supply and the person to whom the investment gold is being supplied is liable for the tax chargeable on the supply in accordance with section 6A(5) of the Value-Added Tax Act 1972" or words to that effect.

(4)   Where a person is authorised to waive, in accordance with paragraph (2), his or her right to exemption from tax on supplies of investment gold, an intermediary, who supplies services in respect of those supplies of investment gold and who wishes to waive his or her right to exemption from tax in respect of those services, is required to apply to the Revenue Commissioners for authorisation to do so and to furnish them with the following particulars —

(a)   his or her name, address and registration number (if any), and

(b)   a declaration stating that he or she supplies services in respect of the supply of investment gold.

(5)   Where they are satisfied that it is appropriate to do so for the proper administration of the tax, the Revenue Commissioners shall authorise the intermediary referred to in paragraph (4) to waive, in accordance with section 6A(4) of the Act, his or her right to exemption from tax, on the supply of a service in respect of the supply of investment gold for which the supplier of such investment gold has waived his or her right to exemption from tax in accordance with section 6A(3) of the Act.

(6)   An intermediary, authorised in accordance with paragraph (5) in respect of the supply of investment gold to another person shall, in relation to that supply, issue to that other person an invoice showing the following particulars —

(a)   the date of issue of the invoice,

(b)   a sequential number, based on one or more series, which uniquely identifies the invoice,

(c)   his or her full name, address and registration number,

(d)   the full name, address and registration number (if any) of the person on whose name and account he or she is acting in respect of the supply of investment gold, and where that person is in another Member State, that person's value-added tax identification number (if any) in that Member State,

(e)   a description of the services being supplied in respect of the supply of investment gold,

(f)   the date of the supply of the services,

(g)   the total consideration, exclusive of tax, receivable in respect of the supply of the services,

(h)   the rate of tax and the amount of tax chargeable in respect of the supply of the services, and

(i)   an endorsement stating "The right to exemption from tax has been waived in respect of this supply" or words to that effect.

(7)   Where the right to exemption from tax has been waived, in respect of a supply of investment gold or the supply of services relating to the supply of investment gold, that waiver shall be irrevocable for that supply.

Investment gold - refunds of tax

30.   A person who is entitled, in accordance with subsection (6)(b), (7)(b) or (8)(b) of section 6A of the Act, to claim a refund of the tax charged, paid or deferred in the circumstances specified in those subsections, shall claim such refund of tax —

(a)   by completing such claim form as may be provided for that purpose by the Revenue Commissioners and certifying that the particulars shown on such claim form are correct,

(b)   by establishing the amount of tax borne by production, where requested to do so by the Revenue Commissioners, of invoices or import documents, and

(c)   by establishing that such person is not entitled to repayment of the tax under any other provision of the Act, any Regulations made thereunder or of any other Act or instrument made under statute administered by the Revenue Commissioners.

Special scheme for means of transport

31.   (1)   In this Regulation —

"**taxable dealer**" and "**means of transport**" have the meanings assigned to them by section 12B(3) of the Act;

"**residual tax**" has the meaning assigned to it by section 12B(4) of the Act.

(2)   A taxable dealer shall deduct residual tax in accordance with section 12(1)(a)(vi) of the Act in respect of the acquisition or purchase of a means of transport from a person specified in paragraph (a), (aa) or (b) of section 12B(2) of the Act, subject to the following conditions:

    (a)   that the dealer prepares a document which sets out all the particulars specified in paragraph (3) in respect of the transaction in question,

    (b)   that the document referred to at subparagraph (a) is signed and dated by the person who is supplying the means of transport concerned, acknowledging the accuracy of the details therein and declaring that that person is a person of the type referred to in paragraph (a), (aa) or (b) of section 12B(2) of the Act, and

    (c)   that the dealer gives to the person who is supplying the means of transport concerned a copy of the completed document referred to at subparagraphs (a) and (b) within 15 days of the date of the acquisition or purchase of that means of transport.

(3)   The particulars in respect of the means of transport concerned which are to be included in the document referred to in paragraph (2) are as follows:

    (a)   the name and address of the person who is supplying that means of transport,

    (b)   the name and address of the taxable dealer who is purchasing or acquiring that means of transport,

    (c)   a description of that means of transport, including details of the make, model, engine number, registration number and year of manufacture,

    (d)   the date on which the supply of that means of transport takes place, and

    (e)   the total consideration for the supply of that means of transport.

(4)   A taxable dealer shall deduct residual tax in accordance with section 12(1)(a)(vi) of the Act in respect of the acquisition or purchase of a means of transport from a person specified in section 12B(2)(c) of the Act, subject to the condition that such dealer is in possession of an invoice issued by that person in accordance with sections 12B(5) and 17(1) of the Act.

(5)   A taxable dealer shall deduct residual tax in accordance with section 12(1)(a)(vi) of the Act in respect of the acquisition or purchase of a means of transport from a person specified in section 12B(2)(d) of that Act, subject to the condition that such dealer is in possession of an invoice issued by that person which indicates that the supply by that person was subject to

value-added tax in accordance with the provisions implementing [Articles 4 and 35, the first paragraph of Article 139(3) and Articles 311 to 341 of the VAT Directive][2] in the Member State in which the supply took place.

(6)   An invoice issued in accordance with sections 12B(5) and 17(1) of the Act shall show the endorsement "Special Scheme — this invoice does not give the right to an input credit of VAT" or words to that effect.

(7)   A taxable dealer shall keep full and true records entered up to date of the acquisition and disposal of a means of transport, in respect of which that dealer has deducted residual tax in accordance with section 12(1)(a)(vi) of the Act, together with appropriate cross-references between all such records.

Antique furniture, silver, glass and porcelain

32.   (1)   (a)   For the purposes of paragraph (xvia) of the Sixth Schedule to the Act the following articles of furniture, silver, glass and porcelain are specified to be the antiques to which the said paragraph applies:

(i)   in the case of furniture, any article being movable goods which have been manufactured wholly or mainly from wood, metal (other than silver), marble or other stone, or any combination thereof, and which were designed for use as furnishings, fitments or decoration for private, commercial or public buildings, or for gardens, and which is not covered by paragraph (xvi) of the Sixth Schedule to the Act,

(ii)   in the case of silver, any article manufactured wholly or mainly from silver, not being jewellery, coins, medals, ingots or bars,

(iii)   in the case of glass, any article manufactured wholly or mainly from glass, including mirrors, chandeliers and leaded or stained glass windows,

(iv)   in the case of porcelain, any article being a cup, saucer, bowl, plate, dish, jug, vase, pot, urn or similar goods, or a statue or statuary (other than an article to which paragraph (xvi)(c) of the Sixth Schedule to the Act relates), manufactured wholly or mainly from porcelain, china, terracotta, clay, ceramics or similar materials, or any combination thereof.

(b)   Evidence that the antiques referred to in subparagraph (a) are more than 100 years old shall consist of —

(i)   a certificate issued by a member of the Irish Antique Dealers' Association, or of an equivalent trade association recognised by the Revenue Commissioners for the purpose of issuing such a certificate,

(ii)   a certificate issued by or on behalf of the National Museum of Ireland,

(iii)   a statutory declaration made by a person recognised, for the purpose of making such a declaration, as a connoisseur by the Revenue Commissioners in respect of articles of the types concerned,

(iv)   in the case of imported goods, a certificate, declaration or other document issued or made under the laws of the country of exportation which in the opinion of the Revenue Commissioners correspond to a certificate issued under clause (i) or (ii) or a statutory declaration made under clause (iii), or

(v)   an invoice issued in accordance with paragraph (4) or a certification made in accordance with paragraph (5).

(2)   Antiques which meet the requirements of paragraph (1) and which are not supplied —

(a)   by a taxable dealer in accordance with subsection (3) or (8) of section 10A of the Act, or

(b)   by an auctioneer within the meaning of section 10B and in accordance with subsection (3) of that section,

shall be referred to as "**Sixth Schedule antiques**" for the purpose of this Regulation.

(3)   A non-taxable person who supplies Sixth Schedule antiques to [an accountable person][2] who is acquiring such antiques for resale shall, on the date of such supply or within 10 days of that date, issue to [the accountable person][2] who acquires the antiques a document in respect of that supply and the taxable dealer to whom the antiques are supplied shall provide the form for that purpose, setting out the following particulars:

(a)   the date of issue of the document,

(b)   the name and address of the person who is supplying the goods to which the document relates,

(c)   the name, address, and registration number of the [said accountable person][2],

(d)   a description of the goods including details of the quantity, type, apparent material of construction, possible origin and identifying features,

(e)   the date on which the goods to which the document relates are supplied,

(f)   the consideration for the supply, and

(g)   the acknowledgement of the person by whom the document is issued,

and [the accountable person]² shall give a copy of the document to the supplier of the goods.

(4)   [An accountable person]² who supplies Sixth Schedule antiques to [another accountable person]² shall include on the invoice concerned, which he or she is required to issue in accordance with section 17(1) of the Act, a declaration to the effect that the antiques are more than 100 years old.

(5)   [An accountable person]² who supplies Sixth Schedule antiques to a non-taxable person shall, for the purposes of paragraph (6), certify in writing in respect of each such supply that the said antiques are more than 100 years old.

(6)   [Every accountable person]² shall, in relation to antiques which he or she has acquired or supplied, keep full and true records entered up to date, of the acquisition and resale of such goods, together with cross-references between all such records, the relevant document issued in accordance with paragraph (3), the relevant invoice issued in accordance with paragraph (4) and the certification made in accordance with paragraph (5).

Retail Export Scheme

33.   (1)   In this Regulation "**traveller**" and "**traveller's qualifying goods**" have the meanings assigned to them by section 13(3B) of the Act.

(2)   The application of the rate of zero per cent to a supply of goods or services specified in section 13(1A) of the Act is subject to the following conditions:

(a)   that the supplier keeps a record of the details of documentary proof inspected by him or her confirming that the purchaser was a traveller,

(b)   that at the time of supply, the supplier issues an invoice to the traveller showing the following details:

(i)   the date on which the invoice is issued,

(ii)   the name, address and registration number of the supplier,

(iii)   the name and address of the traveller,

(iv)   a description of the goods supplied,

(v)   the amount payable by the traveller at the time of the sale of the goods,

(vi)   the tax charged, if any, and

(vii)   the exchange rate or method to be used in determining the exchange rate, if repayment of the tax is to be made to the traveller by the supplier in a currency other than the euro,

(c)   that the traveller signs the completed invoice referred to at subparagraph (b),

(d)   that the notification of the charges made by the supplier, referred to in section 13(1A)(iii) of the Act, is made at the latest—

(i)   where the goods are exported by the traveller, at the time of the handing over of those goods to the traveller,

(ii)   where the goods are exported on behalf of the traveller, at the time when those goods are supplied to the traveller,

and where an amount is charged to the traveller for procuring a repayment of tax or arranging for the zero-rating of the supply, such amount does not exceed the amount notified in accordance with the said section 13(1A)(iii),

(e)   that the time limit for making a repayment to the traveller, referred to in section 13(1A)(ii) of the Act, is not later than the twenty-fifth working day following the receipt by the supplier of the traveller's claim to repayment,

(f)   that the supplier keeps a copy of the invoice issued in accordance with subparagraph (b), signed by the traveller, and keeps a record in relation to each invoice of–

(i)   the net amount (being the amount of tax charged to the traveller minus any commission or fee charged by the supplier to the traveller in respect of the transaction in question) repaid by the supplier to the traveller in respect of the supply in question, expressed in the currency in which the repayment was made,

(ii)   where appropriate, the exchange rate used,

(iii)   the date and method of such repayment, and

      (iv)   proof in accordance with paragraph (3) that the goods were exported by or on behalf of the traveller.

(3)   Where the goods–

    (a)   are exported by the traveller, the proof of export of the goods required shall be the invoice issued in accordance with paragraph 2(b) in respect of that supply, certified–

      (i)   by an officer of the Revenue Commissioners assigned to a customs office in the State,

      (ii)   where the goods have been exported via another Member State of the Community, by a customs officer in that Member State, or

      (iii)   in such other manner as the Revenue Commissioners may deem acceptable for the purpose,

    (b)   are exported on behalf of the traveller, the proof of export of the goods shall take the form of documentary evidence of export, certified–

      (i)   by an officer of the Revenue Commissioners assigned to a customs office in the State, or

      (ii)   where the goods are exported from another Member State of the Community, by a customs officer in that Member State.

Miscellaneous supplies

Supply of certain services

34.   (1)   Subject to paragraph (2) and in accordance with section 5(3)(b) of the Act, the following services are deemed to be a supply of services by a person for consideration in the course or furtherance of his or her business, that is to say, the supply free of charge of catering services for such person's own private use or that of the staff of such person.

    (2)   This Regulation does not apply to any such supplies as are referred to in paragraph (1) if the total cost of providing them has not exceeded and is not likely to exceed the amount specified in section 8(3)(e) of the Act in any continuous period of 12 months, unless the person supplying the services referred to in paragraph (1) elects to be [an accountable person][2] in respect of those supplies.

Free ports

35.   (1)   In this Regulation **"control"** has the meaning assigned to it by
             section 8(3B) of the Act.

      (2)   (a)   Subject to subparagraph (b), goods that are imported by
                    a registered person may be delivered or removed directly
                    to a free port without payment of the tax chargeable on
                    the importation if that person—

                    (i)   shows to the satisfaction of the Revenue
                           Commissioners that—

                           (I)   he or she has been granted a licence under
                                  section 4 of the Free Ports Act 1986 (No. 6
                                  of 1986) authorising him or her to carry on
                                  within that free port any trade, business or
                                  manufacture, and

                           (II)   the goods are being imported for the
                                  purposes of his or her trade, business or
                                  manufacture in that free port,

                    and

                    (ii)   complies with such other conditions as the
                           Revenue Commissioners may impose.

             (b)   This paragraph does not apply to the importation of
                    food, drink, motor vehicles or petrol except where tax on
                    the importation of those goods would, if it were paid, be
                    wholly deductible under section 12 of the Act.

      (3)   (a)   Except in accordance with subparagraph (b), goods
                    which have been imported without payment of the tax
                    in accordance with paragraph (2) may not be removed
                    from the free port concerned to any other part of the State
                    (other than into another free port or the customs-free
                    airport), unless such removal is in relation to a supply
                    of those goods and is not a supply between the supplier
                    and—

                    (i)   a person who exercises control over the supplier,

                    (ii)   a person over whom the supplier exercises control,
                           or

                    (iii) a person over whom the supplier and another
                           person exercise control.

             (b)   Goods in a free port whose removal from that free port
                    is precluded by subparagraph (a) may be so removed
                    with the prior agreement in writing of the Revenue
                    Commissioners in such exceptional cases as may be
                    determined by them. Where such removal is allowed, tax
                    which would, but for this Regulation, have been payable

on the importation of the goods, is payable at the time of that removal by the supplier.

Intra-Community acquisitions - certain new means of transport

36. (1)   In this Regulation —

"**new aircraft**" means a new means of transport other than a motorised land vehicle or a vessel;

"**new vessel**" means a new means of transport other than a motorised land vehicle or an aircraft.

(2)   Where a person makes an intra-Community acquisition of a new aircraft or a new vessel, in respect of which he or she is not entitled to a deduction of tax under section 12 of the Act, the person is required to —

(a)   complete such form as may be provided by the Revenue Commissioners for the purpose of this paragraph,

(b)   provide such further documentation in support of the details provided on the form as the Revenue Commissioners may request,

(c)   certify that the particulars and documentation provided are true and accurate,

(d)   not later than 3 days after the arrival of the aircraft or vessel, furnish to the Revenue Commissioners the completed form and supporting documentation referred to in subparagraphs (a) and (b) and at the same time pay to the Revenue Commissioners the amount of tax due, and

(e)   if requested to do so, make the new aircraft or the new vessel, as appropriate, available for inspection in the State by an officer of the Revenue Commissioners.

Imported goods

37. (1)   Without prejudice to paragraph (3), section 5(1) of the Customs-Free Airport Act 1947 (No. 5 of 1947) shall not, in so far as it applies to tax, have effect in relation to goods brought from the Customs-free airport (within the meaning of that Act) into any other part of the State where it is established to the satisfaction of the Revenue Commissioners that those goods are Community goods or that the tax has already been borne or paid on those goods.

(2)   Section 29(7) of the Finance Act 1978 (No. 21 of 1978) applies in relation to tax payable at importation with the modification that the reference to goods entered for home use shall be deemed to include a reference to imported goods entered for free circulation.

(3)   Legislation relating to customs adopted by the European Communities concerning the placing of goods under —

(a)   arrangements for temporary importation with total exemption from customs duty,

(b)   external transit arrangements,

(c)   temporary storage arrangements,

(d)   free zone or free warehouse arrangements,

(e)   customs warehousing arrangements,

(f)   inward processing (suspension) arrangements,

(g)   arrangements for processing under customs control, or

(h)   arrangements for the admission of goods into territorial waters in connection with drilling or production platforms,

shall only apply in relation to tax chargeable at importation where, and for such time as, goods are held under those arrangements for the purpose of compliance with and implementation of the Community rules relating to customs.

(4)   Without prejudice to paragraph (3), legislation relating to customs adopted by the European Communities concerning suspension of customs duties, reduction in customs duties, or repayment or remission of customs duties does not apply to tax chargeable at importation.

[(5)   In accordance with section 15 of the Act, where goods are reimported by the person who exported them, in the state in which they were exported, being goods which are exempt from customs duties on such re-importation, then those goods shall be exempt from value-added tax.]³

Supplies for onboard consumption

38.   (1)   In this Regulation "**excisable products**" means the alcoholic products referred to in paragraphs (a) to (e), and the tobacco products referred to in paragraph (f), of section 104, (inserted by the Finance Act 1999 (No. 2 of 1999)) of the Finance Act 1992 (No. 9 of 1992).

(2)   The conditions which apply for the purposes of paragraph (ia) of the Second Schedule to the Act are that the food, drink and tobacco products must be supplied —

(a)   in the case of excisable products, in such form, manner and quantities as may be permitted by the Revenue Commissioners in respect of relief from excise duty, and

(b)   in the case of food and drink other than drink to which paragraph (a) applies —

(i)   from outlets on board vessels or aircraft approved by the Revenue Commissioners, and

(ii)   in such form and quantity as renders it suitable to be consumed by passengers while on board such vessels or aircraft.

Administration and general

Determination in regard to tax

39. (1)   In this Regulation a **"determination"** means a determination made for the purposes of section 11(1B) of the Act.

     (2)   A determination shall —

     (a)   be in writing,

     (b)   contain the particulars of the determination,

     (c)   be signed by the officer making the determination, and

     (d)   specify the date as on and from which the determination has effect.

     (3)   Determinations concerning 2 or more matters may be included in the same document.

Disclosure of information to the Revenue Commissioners

40. Any person engaged in the supply of goods or services in the course or furtherance of business shall, when required to do so by notice in writing served on such person by the Revenue Commissioners, disclose to the Revenue Commissioners such particulars of any goods or services supplied to him or her as may be required by such notice.

Death, bankruptcy or liquidation

41. If [an accountable person][2] dies, becomes bankrupt or, being a body corporate, goes into liquidation, anything which he or she would have been liable to do under the Act or these Regulations shall be done by his or her personal representative, assignee, trustee, committee or liquidator, as the case may be.

Service of notices

42. Any notice, notification or requirement that is authorised or required to be given, served, made, sent or issued under the Act or under these Regulations may be sent by post.

Nomination of officers

43. Any functions authorised by the Act to be performed or discharged by the Revenue Commissioners may be performed or discharged by officers nominated by the Revenue Commissioners for that purpose.

Revocations

44.   The Regulations set out in the Schedule to these Regulations are revoked.

SCHEDULE

Value-Added Tax Regulations 1979 (S.I. No. 63 of 1979)

Value-Added Tax (Remission and Repayment of Tax on Certain Importations) Regulations 1985 (S.I. No. 344 of 1985)

Value-Added Tax (Free Ports) Regulations 1987 (S.I. No. 275 of 1987)

Value-Added Tax (Furniture, Silver, Glass and Porcelain) Regulations 1989 (S.I. No. 304 of 1989)

Value-Added Tax (Monthly Control Statement) Regulations 1992 (S.I. No. 230 of 1992)

Value-Added Tax (Invoices and other Documents) Regulations 1992 (S.I. No. 275 of 1992)

Value-Added Tax (Time Limits for Issuing Certain Documents) Regulations 1992 (S.I. No. 276 of 1992)

Value-Added Tax (Determination in Regard to Tax) Regulations 1992 (S.I. No. 278 of 1992)

Value-Added Tax (Determination of Tax Due by Reference to Moneys Received) Regulations 1992 (S.I. No. 306 of 1992)

Value-Added Tax (Imported Goods) Regulations 1992 (S.I. No. 439 of 1992)

Value-Added Tax (Imported Goods) (No. 2) Regulations 1992 (S.I. No. 440 of 1992)

Value-Added Tax (Registration) Regulations 1993 (S.I. No. 30 of 1993)

Value-Added Tax (Statement of Intra-Community Supplies) Regulations 1993 (S.I. No. 54 of 1993)

Value-Added Tax (Payment of Tax on Intra-Community Acquisitions of Certain New Means of Transport) Regulations 1993 (S.I. No. 248 of 1993)

Value-Added Tax (Determination of Tax Due by Reference to Moneys Received) (Amendment) Regulations 1994 (S.I. No. 259 of 1994)

Value-Added Tax (Special Scheme for Means of Transport: Documentation) Regulations 1996 (S.I. No. 201 of 1996)

Value-Added Tax (Retail Export Scheme) Regulations 1998 (S.I. No. 34 of 1998)

Value-Added Tax (Waiver of Exemption) (Amendment) Regulations 1998 (S.I. No. 228 of 1998)

Value-Added Tax (Valuation of Interests in Immovable Goods) (Amendment) Regulations 1998 (S.I. No. 482 of 1998)

Value-Added Tax (Electronic Data Exchange and Storage) (Amendment) Regulations 1998 (S.I. No. 488 of 1998)

Value-Added Tax (Invoices and Other Documents) (Amendment) Regulations 1998 (S.I. No. 489 of 1998)

Value-Added Tax (Supply of Food, Drink and Tobacco Products on board Vessels or Aircraft for onboard Consumption) Regulations 1999 (S.I. No. 197 of 1999)

Value-Added Tax (Records of Transactions in Investment Gold) Regulations 1999 (S.I. No. 439 of 1999)

Value-Added Tax (Waiver of Exemption on Supplies of, and Supplies relating to, Investment Gold) Regulations 1999 (S.I. No. 440 of 1999)

Value-Added Tax (Refund of Tax to Persons making Exempt Supplies of Investment Gold) Regulations 1999 (S.I. No. 441 of 1999)

Value-Added Tax (Agricultural Machinery) (Documentation) Regulations 1999 (S.I. No. 443 of 1999)

Value-Added Tax (Cancellation of Election of Registration in respect of Sixth Schedule Accommodation) Regulations 2000 (S.I. No. 253 of 2000)

Value-Added Tax (Apportionment) Regulations 2000 (S.I. No. 254 of 2000)

Value-Added Tax (Estimation of Tax Payable and Assessment of Tax Payable or Refundable) Regulations 2000 (S.I. No. 295 of 2000)

Value-Added Tax (Imported Goods) (Amendment) Regulations 2001 (S.I. No. 628 of 2001)

Value-Added Tax (Amendment) (Property Transactions) Regulations 2002 (S.I. No. 219 of 2002)

Value-Added Tax (Returns) Regulations 2002 (S.I. No. 267 of 2002)

Value-Added Tax (Electronic Invoicing and Storage) Regulations 2002 (S.I. No. 504 of 2002)

Value-Added Tax (Waiver of Exemption) (Letting of Immovable Goods) Regulations 2003 (S.I. No. 504 of 2003)

Value-Added Tax (Invoices and other Documents) (Amendment) Regulations 2003 (S.I. No. 723 of 2003)

Value-Added Tax (Short-Term Guest Sector or Holiday Sector) Regulations 2005 (S.I. No. 321 of 2005)

Value-Added Tax (Amendment) Regulations 2006 (S.I. No. 198 of 2006).

GIVEN under my Official Seal
this 26 October 2006

Brian Cowen
Minister for Finance

EXPLANATORY NOTES

Commencement and Interpretation

1.   Citation and commencement

This Regulation contains the provisions relating to title and commencement.

2.   Interpretation

This is a definitions Regulation.

Taxable Person

3.   Election to be a taxable person and cancellation of such election

This is a modernisation of Regulation 3 of the 1979 Regulations (S.I. No. 63 of 1979) and incorporates the relevant part of Regulation 3 of Value-Added Tax (Registration) Regulations 1993 (S.I. No. 30 of 1993) and the provisions of the Value-Added Tax (Cancellation of Election of Registration in respect of Sixth Schedule Accommodation) Regulations 2000 (S.I. No. 253 of 2000).

This Regulation deals with the procedures relating to an election to be a taxable person, the cancellation of such election and the cancellation of a registration at the request of a taxable person whose turnover falls below the registration thresholds. No new obligations have been imposed by this Regulation.

4.   Waiver of exemption

This is a modernisation of the Value-Added Tax (Waiver of Exemption) (Letting of Immovable Goods) Regulations 2003 (S.I. No. 504 of 2003).

This Regulation deals with the conditions and procedures which a person must comply with if he or she wishes to waive his or her right to exemption from tax on the short-term letting of immovable goods. It also deals with the provisions relating to the backdating and the cancellation of that waiver. No new obligations have been imposed by this Regulation.

5.   Lettings in the short-term guest sector or holiday sector

This is a re-statement of the Value-Added Tax (Short-Term Guest Sector or Holiday Sector) Regulations 2005 (S.I. No. 321 of 2005).

This Regulation specifies what lettings are treated as being in the short-term guest sector or holiday sector for the purpose of applying the reduced rate of VAT. No changes have been made to this Regulation.

6.   Groups

This is a modernisation of Regulation 5 of the 1979 Regulations (S.I. No. 63 of 1979).

This Regulation caters for the formalities to be observed where a number of linked companies wish to be grouped for VAT purposes. Many of the details in Regulation 5 of the 1979 Regulations, which was entitled "Treatment of two or more taxable persons as a single taxable person", have been deleted as they are provided for in section 8(8) of the Act. No new obligations have been imposed by this Regulation.

7.   Registration

This is a modernisation of the Value-Added Tax (Registration) Regulations 1993 (S.I. No. 30 of 1993).

This Regulation sets out the procedures to be followed in relation to registration. It also covers cancellation of a registration when the taxable person ceases to trade. No new obligations have been imposed by this Regulation.

Record Keeping

8.   Accounts

This is a modernisation of Regulation 9 of the 1979 Regulations (S.I. No. 63 of 1979).

This Regulation deals with the type of records and accounts that are required to be kept by taxable persons. Some of the amendments to this Regulation are to cater for requirements necessitated by changes in the law since 1979, such as the need to keep records in relation to intra-Community acquisitions, reverse charge transactions and "supply and install" transactions. In addition this Regulation requires a taxable person to keep a record of the date or dates on which a debt is written off.

9.   Invoices and other documents

This is a modernisation of the Value-Added Tax (Invoices and other Documents) Regulations 1992 (S.I. No. 275 of 1992) as amended by the Value-Added Tax (Invoices and other Documents) (Amendment) Regulations 2003 (S.I. No. 723 of 2003), but excluding the provisions for flat-rate farmers which have now been included in a separate Regulation (see Regulation 11 below).

This Regulation deals with the provisions relating to the issuing of invoices, credit notes, debit notes etc. It also provides for a mechanism for simplified invoicing arrangements. No new obligations have been imposed on the taxable person in this Regulation.

10.   Electronic invoicing

This is a modernisation of the Value-Added Tax (Electronic Invoicing and Storage) Regulations 2002 (S.I. No. 504 of 2002).

This Regulation deals with the issuing of invoices and other documents by electronic means and sets out the conditions and the system specifications required in order for those invoices etc. to be valid for VAT purposes. No new obligations have been imposed on the taxable person in this Regulation.

11.   Invoicing provisions for flat-rate farmers

This is a modernisation of the flat-rate farmer provisions in the Value-Added Tax (Invoices and other Documents) Regulations 1992 (S.I. No. 275 of 1992) as amended by the Value-Added Tax (Invoices and other Documents) (Amendment) Regulations 2003 (S.I. No. 723 of 2003) and also includes the invoicing provisions relating to agricultural machinery in the Value-Added Tax (Agricultural Machinery) (Documentation) Regulations 1999 (S.I. No. 443 of 1999).

This Regulation deals with the provisions relating to the issuing of invoices, credit notes, debit notes etc. by flat-rate farmers for agricultural produce and services and agricultural machinery. No new obligations have been imposed by this Regulation.

12.   Time limits for issuing invoices and credit notes

This is a modernisation of the Value-Added Tax (Time Limits for Issuing Certain Documents) Regulations 1992 (S.I. No. 276 of 1992).

This Regulation sets out the time limits for the issue of invoices and credit notes. No new obligations have been imposed by this Regulation.

13.   Returns

This is a modernisation of the Value-Added Tax (Returns) Regulations 2002 (S.I. No. 267 of 2002) and incorporates the provisions of Taxes (Electronic Transmission of Certain Revenue Returns) (Specified Provisions and Appointed Day) Order 2000 (S.I. No. 289 of 2000) insofar as they apply to VAT.

This Regulation requires a taxable person to furnish the details requested on a VAT return. Those details may be furnished by the taxable person or another person acting under the authority of that taxable person. No new obligations have been imposed on the taxable person in this Regulation.

14.   Statement of intra-Community supplies

This is a modernisation of the Value-Added Tax (Statement of Intra-Community Supplies) Regulations 1993 (S.I. No. 54 of 1993).

This Regulation sets out the particulars required on statements of intra-Community supplies (VIES). The Regulation also specifies the means by which such statements may be returned to the Revenue Commissioners and the frequency of such returns. No new obligations have been imposed by this Regulation.

Tax Due And Payable

15.   Determination of tax due by reference to moneys received

This is a modernisation of the Value-Added Tax (Determination of Tax Due by Reference to Moneys Received) Regulations 1992 (S.I. No. 306 of 1992) as amended by the Value-Added Tax (Determination of Tax Due by Reference to Moneys Received) (Amendment) Regulations 1994 (S.I. No. 259 of 1994).

This Regulation sets out the terms and conditions relating to the operation of the moneys received basis of accounting. No new obligations have been imposed by this Regulation.

16.   Adjustments for returned goods, discounts, and price alterations

This is a modernisation of Regulation 8 of the Value-Added Tax Regulations 1979 (S.I. No. 63 of 1979).

This Regulation deals with the adjustments to be made where the consideration received is less than the chargeable amount for any supply, e.g. in the case of discounts, price reductions etc. or in the case of bad debts. No new obligations have been imposed by this Regulation.

17.   Estimates and assessments

This is a modernisation of the Value-Added Tax (Estimation of Tax Payable and Assessment of Tax Payable or Refundable) Regulations 2000 (S.I. No. 295 of 2000).

This Regulation deals with estimates and assessments of tax due and payable in accordance with sections 22 and 23 of the Act. No new obligations have been imposed by this Regulation.

18.   Apportionment

This is a modernisation of the Value-Added Tax (Apportionment) Regulations 2000 (S.I. No. 254 of 2000).

This Regulation deals with the proportion of tax deductible in relation to inputs which are used for both taxable and non-taxable transactions and the adjustment of that proportion over a review period. No new obligations have been imposed by this Regulation.

19.   Valuation of interests in immovable goods

This is a modernisation of Regulation 19 of the Value-Added Tax Regulations 1979 (S.I. No. 63 of 1979) as amended by Value-Added Tax (Valuation of Interests in Immovable Goods) (Amendment) Regulations 1998 (S.I. No. 482 of 1998) and Regulation 4 of Value-Added Tax (Amendment) (Property Transactions) Regulations 2002 (S.I. No. 219 of 2002).

This Regulation deals with the method of calculating the capital value of a lease of ten years or more. No new obligations have been imposed by this Regulation.

20.   Stamps, coupons, tokens and vouchers

This is a modernisation of Regulations 32 and 33 of the Value-Added Tax Regulations 1979 (S.I. No. 63 of 1979). Those two Regulations have now been amalgamated into one Regulation.

This Regulation deals with the amount chargeable on supplies of certain stamps, coupons, tokens or vouchers and the amount chargeable when they are redeemed. The substance of the Regulation is new and provides that the taxable amount of the goods when redeemed is the consideration which was disregarded in accordance with section 10(6) of the Act. This reflects the ECJ jurisprudence in this area.

21.   Apportionment of consideration

This Regulation replaces Regulation 34 of the Value-Added Tax Regulations 1979 (S.I. No. 63 of 1979).

The substance of the Regulation is new. It deals with the circumstances and conditions under which a taxable person may disregard an individual supply or supplies in a multiple supply and the manner in which the consideration for such a multiple supply must be treated as regards the rate or rates of taxation to apply.

Refunds, remissions and relief

22.   Refund of tax

This is a re-statement of Regulation 17 of the Value-Added Tax Regulations 1979 (S.I. No. 63 of 1979).

This Regulation sets out the procedures for claiming a refund of tax. No changes have been made to this Regulation.

23.   Refund to foreign traders

This is a re-statement of the part of Value-Added Tax (Amendment) Regulations 2006 (S.I. No. 198 of 2006) which updated Regulation 30 of the Value-Added Tax Regulations 1979 (S.I. No. 63 of 1979).

This Regulation deals with the refund of tax to foreign traders as provided for under the Eighth and Thirteenth VAT Directives. No changes have been made to this Regulation.

24.   Remission of small amounts of tax

This is a re-statement of Regulation 18 of the Value-Added Tax Regulations 1979 (S.I. No. 63 of 1979).

This Regulation provides for the remission of negligible amounts of tax at the discretion of the Revenue Commissioners. No changes have been made to this Regulation.

25.   Remission or repayment of tax on fishing vessels and equipment

This is a modernisation of Regulation 29 of the Value-Added Tax Regulations 1979 (S.I. No. 63 of 1979).

This Regulation sets out the conditions under which an unregistered person can qualify for a refund of tax on commercial sea-fishing vessels and equipment. No new obligations have been imposed by this Regulation.

26.   Relief for stock in trade held at commencement of taxability

This is a modernisation of Regulation 22 of the Value-Added Tax Regulations 1979 (S.I. No. 63 of 1979).

This Regulation deals with relief for stock-in-trade at the commencement of taxability and sets out how the deduction in respect of such stock must be calculated and recorded. This Regulation has been simplified by the use of formulae, but no new obligations have been imposed.

27.   Exemption of certain business gifts

This is a re-statement of Regulation 31 of the Value-Added Tax Regulations 1979 (S.I. No. 63 of 1979).

This Regulation provides for an exemption from VAT for business gifts of negligible value. No changes have been made to this Regulation.

Special Schemes

28.   Investment gold – records of transactions

This is a modernisation of the Value-Added Tax (Records of Transactions in Investment Gold) Regulations 1999 (S.I. No. 439 of 1999).

This Regulation deals with the type of records and accounts that are required to be kept by taxable persons who trade in investment gold. The only change of substance made to this Regulation is the requirement for the taxable person to keep a record of the date or dates on which a bad debt is written off. This is in line with a similar requirement inserted into Regulation 8 of these Regulations.

29.   Investment gold – waiver of exemption

This is a modernisation of the Value-Added Tax (Waiver of Exemption on Supplies of, and Supplies relating to, Investment Gold) Regulations 1999 (S.I. No. 440 of 1999)

This Regulation deals with the conditions and procedures for waiving exemption on supplies of investment gold or related intermediary services. No new obligations have been imposed by this Regulation.

30.   Investment gold – refunds of tax

This is a re-statement of the Value-Added Tax (Refund of Tax to Persons making Exempt Supplies of Investment Gold) Regulations 1999 (S.I. No. 441 of 1999).

This Regulation sets out the conditions for a refund of tax on the purchase, intra-Community acquisition or importation of gold. No changes have been made to this Regulation.

31.   Special scheme for means of transport

This is a modernisation of the Value-Added Tax (Special Schemes For Means Of Transport: Documentation) Regulations 1996 (S.I. No. 201 of 1996).

This Regulation specifies the documentation required by a taxable dealer to deduct residual tax in respect of certain second-hand means of transport. No new obligations have been imposed by this Regulation.

32.   Antique furniture, silver, glass and porcelain

This is a modernisation of the Value-Added Tax (Furniture, Silver, Glass and Porcelain) Regulations 1989 (S.I. No. 304 of 1989).

This Regulation specifies the types of antique furniture, silver, glass and porcelain to which the reduced rate of VAT can apply in accordance with paragraph (xvia) of the Sixth Schedule to the VAT Act. No new obligations have been imposed by this Regulation.

33.   Retail Export Scheme

This is a modernisation of the Value-Added Tax (Retail Export Scheme) Regulations 1998 (S.I. No. 34 of 1998).

This Regulation sets out the conditions for granting relief of VAT in accordance with section 13 of the Act on goods purchased in the State by non-EU residents or by Irish residents who are taking up residence outside the EU. No new obligations have been imposed by this Regulation.

Miscellaneous Supplies

34.   Supply of certain services

This is a re-statement of the part of Value-Added Tax (Amendment) Regulations 2006 (S.I. No. 198 of 2006) which updated Regulation 24 of the Value-Added Tax Regulations 1979 (S.I. No. 63 of 1979).

This Regulation deals with the supply by a taxpayer free of charge of certain catering services for the taxpayer's own private or personal use or that of his or her staff and reflects the Finance Act 2006 changes to section 5 of the VAT Act. No changes have been made to this Regulation.

35.   Free ports

This is a modernisation of the Value-Added Tax (Free Ports) Regulations 1987 (S.I. No. 275 of 1987).

This Regulation sets out the conditions for the relief of VAT at import of goods for use in a free port. No new obligations have been imposed by this Regulation.

36.   Intra-Community acquisitions – certain new means of transport

This is a modernisation of the Value-Added Tax (Payment of Tax on Intra-Community Acquisitions of Certain New Means of Transport) Regulations 1993 (S.I. No. 248 of 1993).

This Regulation sets out the procedures to be followed in relation to the payment of VAT on the intra-Community acquisition of new aircraft and new vessels by private individuals and other persons not entitled to deduct the tax chargeable on the goods. No new obligations have been imposed by this Regulation.

37.   Imported goods

This is a modernisation of the Value-Added Tax (Imported Goods) (No. 2) Regulations 1992 (S.I. No. 440 of 1992).

This Regulation deals with the application of certain customs rules to VAT at import. No new obligations have been imposed by this Regulation.

38.   Supplies for onboard consumption

This is a modernisation of the Value-Added Tax (Supply of Food, Drink and Tobacco Products on board Vessels or Aircraft for onboard Consumption) Regulations 1999 (S.I. No. 197 of 1999).

This Regulation provides the conditions under which certain food, drink and tobacco products supplied to passengers for consumption on board a vessel or aircraft during an intra-EU journey qualify for the zero rate of VAT. No new obligations have been imposed by this Regulation.

Administration and General

39.   Determination in regard to tax

This is a modernisation of the Value-Added Tax (Determination in Regard to Tax) Regulations 1992 (S.I. No. 278 of 1992).

This Regulation sets out the form and content of a determination made by the Revenue Commissioners for the purposes of Section 11(1B) of the Act. The changes to this Regulation reflect the Finance Act 2006 changes made to that section.

40.   Disclosure of information to the Revenue Commissioners

This is a re-statement of Regulation 35 of the Value-Added Tax Regulations 1979 (S.I. No. 63 of 1979).

This Regulation requires a person in business to disclose information to the Revenue Commissioners when requested by them to do so. No changes have been made to this Regulation.

41.   Death, bankruptcy or liquidation

This is a re-statement of Regulation 36 of the Value-Added Tax Regulations 1979 (S.I. No. 63 of 1979).

This Regulation specifies who must undertake the liabilities of the taxable person where that taxable person dies or becomes bankrupt or, in the case of a company, goes into liquidation. No changes have been made to this Regulation other than to the title.

42.   Service of notices

This is a re-statement of Regulation 37 of the Value-Added Tax Regulations 1979 (S.I. No. 63 of 1979).

This Regulation provides that the issue of any notice under the Act may be sent by post. No changes have been made to this Regulation.

43.   Nomination of officers

This is a modernisation of Regulation 38 of the Value-Added Tax Regulations 1979 (S.I. No. 63 of 1979).

This Regulation allows the Revenue Commissioners to delegate certain functions. No changes of substance have been made to this Regulation.

44.   Revocation

This Regulation lists in a schedule all the Regulations revoked by these Regulations.

Amendments
1   Deleted by S.I. No. 238 of 2008, w.e.f. 2 July 2008.
2   Substituted by S.I. No. 238 of 2008, w.e.f. 2 July 2008.
3   Inserted by S.I. No. 238 of 2008, w.e.f. 2 July 2008.
4   Inserted by S.I. No. 272 of 2007, w.e.f. 11 June 2007.
5   Substituted by S.I. No. 272 of 2007, w.e.f. 11 June 2007.
6   Ss21A and 21B inserted by S.I. No. 238 of 2008, w.e.f. 2 July 2008

FINANCE ACT 2006 (COMMENCEMENT OF SECTIONS 93(1), 97(1)(b) AND 99(1)(a)) ORDER 2006

(SI No. 549 of 2006)

I, Brian Cowen, Minister for Finance, in exercise of the powers conferred on my by sections 93(2), 97(2) and 99(2) of the Finance Act 2006 (No. 6 of 2006), hereby order as follows:

1.   This Order may be cited as the Finance Act 2006 (Commencement of sections 93(1), 97(1)(b) and 99(1)(a)) Order 2006.

2.   The 1st day of November 2006 is appointed as the day on which sections 93(1), 97(1)(b) and 99(1)(a) of the Finance Act 2006 (No. 6 of 2006) come into operation.

GIVEN under my Official Seal
26 October 2006

Brian Cowen
Minister for Finance

EXPLANATORY NOTES

Commencement and Interpretation

(This note is not part of the instrument and does not purport to be a legal interpretation).

This Order appoints the 1st day of November 2006 as the date for coming into effect of the provisions specified in the Order. Each of these sections amends the VAT Act 1972.

Section 93(1) amends section 1 of the VAT Act 1972 to provide definitions for VAT purposes of five types of supply comprising two or more elements which attract VAT at different rates.

Section 97(1)(b) provides the framework in section 11 of the VAT Act 1972 for the calculation of the rate or rates of tax on the types of supply mentioned above.

Section 99(1)(a) amends section 32 of the VAT Act 1972 to provide for the making of regulations by the Revenue Commissioners in connection with the operation of the new rules.

EUROPEAN COMMUNITIES (VALUE-ADDED TAX) REGULATIONS 2006

(SI No. 663 of 2006)

> **This Regulation was revoked by s97, Finance Act 2007 w.e.f. 1 January 2007 and deemed never to have had effect**

I, Brian Cowen, Minister for Finance, in exercise of the powers conferred on me by section 3 of the European Communities Act 1972 (No. 27 of 1972), and for the purpose of giving effect to Council Directive No. 2006/112/EC of 28 November 2006 and Council Directive No. 2006/98/EC of 27 November 2006, hereby make the following regulations:

1.   (1)   These Regulations may be cited as the European Communities (Value-Added Tax) Regulations 2006.

     (2)   These Regulations shall be construed together with the Value-Added Tax Acts 1972 to 2006.

2.   These Regulations come into operation on 1 January 2007.

3.   In these Regulations "Principal Act" means the Value-Added Tax Act 1972 (No. 22 of 1972).

4.   Section 1 of the Principal Act is amended by inserting the following subsection after subsection (2A) (inserted by the Finance Act 1992 (No. 9 of 1992)):

     "(2B) In this Act any reference to Council Directive No. 77/388/EEC (however expressed) or to any Directive amending that Directive shall be read as a reference to Council Directive No. 2006/112/EC of 28 November 2006 and any reference to an Article, paragraph or subparagraph in Council Directive No. 77/388/EEC shall be read as a reference to the corresponding Article, paragraph or subparagraph in accordance with the correlation table in Annex XII to Council Directive No. 2006/112/EC of 28 November 2006."

5.   Section 15B (inserted by the Finance Act 2004 (No. 8 of 2004)) of the Principal Act is amended–

     (a)   in subsection (5A)–

           (i)   by substituting "the Slovak Republic," for "the Slovak Republic, or" in subparagraph (ii), and

           (ii)   by inserting the following after subparagraph (ii):

           "(iia)   the date of the first use of the means of transport was before 1 January 1999 in the case of means of transport entering the State from the Republic of Bulgaria or Romania, or",

     and

(b)   in the definition of "date of accession" in subsection (7)(a) by inserting "or 1 January 2007 in respect of the Republic of Bulgaria and Romania" after "Slovak Republic".

GIVEN under my Official Seal,
this 20th day of December 2006.

BRIAN COWEN
Minister for Finance.

EXPLANATORY NOTE

(This note is not part of the Instrument and does not purport to be a legal interpretation).

These Regulations cater for the entry into force of Council Directive 2006/112/EC of 28 November 2006 (OJ No. L 347 of 11 December 2006) and Council Directive 2006/98/EC of 27 November 2006 (OJ No. L 363 of 20 December 2006).

Council Directive 2006/112/EC replaces the Sixth VAT Directive. Consequently, these Regulations provide for the updating of the references to the Sixth Directive in the VAT Act.

Council Directive 2006/98/EC (OJ No. L 363 of 20 December 2006) deals with the accession to the EU of the Republic of Bulgaria and Romania. These Regulations amend the application of transitional VAT measures to goods in transit between the two new accession countries (i.e. the Republic of Bulgaria and Romania) and Ireland on 1 January 2007.

EUROPEAN COMMUNITIES (MUTUAL ASSISTANCE FOR THE RECOVERY OF CLAIMS RELATING TO CERTAIN LEVIES, DUTIES, TAXES AND OTHER MEASURES) (AMENDMENT) REGULATIONS, 2007

(S.I. No. 249 of 2007)

I, BRIAN COWEN, Minister for Finance, in exercise of the powers conferred on me by section 3 of the European Communities Act 1972 (No. 27 of 1972) and for the purpose of giving effect to Commission Directive 2006/84/EC of 23 October 2006, and giving further effect to Commission Directive No. 2002/94/EC of 9 December 2002, hereby make the following regulations:

1.　(1)　These Regulations may be cited as the European Communities (Mutual Assistance for the Recovery of Claims relating to Certain Levies, Duties, Taxes and Other Measures) (Amendment) Regulations 2007.

　　(2)　These Regulations are deemed to have come into operation on 1 January 2007.

2.　The European Communities (Mutual Assistance for the Recovery of Claims relating to Certain Levies, Duties, Taxes and Other Measures) Regulations 2002 (S.I. No. 462 of 2002) are amended —

　　(a)　in Regulation 2(1) by substituting the following for the definition of "Commission Directive" (inserted by the European Communities (Mutual Assistance for the Recovery of Claims relating to Certain Levies, Duties, Taxes and Other Measures) (Amendment) Regulations 2004 (S.I. No. 851 of 2004)):

　　　"'Commission Directive' means Commission Directive No. 2002/94/EC of 9 December 2002 as amended by Commission Directive 2004/79/EC of 4 March 2004 and Commission Directive 2006/84/EC of 23 October 2006; ".

　　(b)　in Regulation 6 by substituting the following for paragraph (1):

　　　"(1)　The amount of any claim payable in accordance with Regulation 5(1) shall carry interest from the date when the amount of the claim becomes due and payable in accordance with Regulation 5(3) until payment, and the amount of such interest shall be determined by the formula —

$$(T \times D) \times 0.0273\%$$

where —

T　is the amount of the claim payable in accordance with Regulation 5(1), and

D　is the number of days (including part of a day) in the period beginning on the date when the amount of the claim becomes due and payable in accordance with Regulation 5(3) and ending on the date of payment of the claim.".

GIVEN under my Official Seal,

21 May 2007

BRIAN COWEN,

Minister for Finance.

EXPLANATORY NOTE

(This note is not part of the instrument and does not purport to be a legal interpretation.)

These regulations transpose Commission Directive 2006/84/EC by amending the European Communities (Mutual Assistance for the Recovery of Claims relating to Certain Levies, Duties, Taxes and Other Measures) Regulations 2002 to facilitate the admission of Bulgaria and Romania to the European Union. These regulations ensure that references to Commission Directive in the European Communities (Mutual Assistance for the Recovery of Claims relating to Certain Levies, Duties, Taxes and Other Measures) Regulations 2002, are references to Commission Directive 2002/94/EC as amended, by amending Directives including Commission Directive 2006/84/EC of 23 October 2006 which deals with the admission of Bulgaria and Romania to the European Union.

The regulation also amends the European Communities (Mutual Assistance for the Recovery of Claims relating to Certain Levies, Duties, Taxes and Other Measures) Regulations 2002, to ensure that the rate of interest charged on an amount subject to recovery under S.I. 462 of 2002 shall be computed in accordance with the formula set out in the regulations. This brings the rate of interest and the computation of such interest in line with that that applies to other outstanding taxes and duties.

EUROPEAN COMMUNITIES (MUTUAL ASSISTANCE IN THE FIELD OF DIRECT TAXATION, CERTAIN EXCISE DUTIES AND TAXATION OF INSURANCE PREMIUMS) (AMENDMENT) REGULATIONS 2007

(S.I. No. 250 of 2007)

I, BRIAN COWEN, Minister for Finance, in exercise of the powers conferred on me by section 3 of the European Communities Act 1972 (No. 27 of 1972) and for the purpose of giving effect to Council Directive 2006/98/EC of 20 November 2006, hereby make the following regulations:

1.   (1)   These Regulations may be cited as the European Communities (Mutual Assistance in the Field of Direct Taxation, Certain Excise Duties and Taxation of Insurance Premiums) (Amendment) Regulations 2007.

    (2)   These Regulations are deemed to have come into operation on 1 January 2007.

2.   The European Communities (Mutual Assistance in the Field of Direct Taxation, Certain Excise Duties and Taxation of Insurance Premiums) Regulations 2005 (S.I. No. 367 of 2005) are amended in Regulation 2(1) by substituting the following for the definition of "Council Directive":

" 'Council Directive' means Council Directive 77/799/EEC of 19 December 1977 as amended by Council Directive 79/1070/ EEC of 6 December 1979, Council Directive 92/12/EEC of 25 February 1992, Council Directive 2003/93/EC of 7 October 2003, Council Directive 2004/56/EC of 21 April 2004, Council Directive 2004/106/EC of 16 November 2004 and Council Directive 2006/98/EC of 20 November 2006;".

GIVEN under my Official Seal,

21 May 2007

BRIAN COWEN,

Minister for Finance.

EXPLANATORY NOTE

(This note is not part of the instrument and does not purport to be a legal interpretation.)

These regulations provide for the amendment of the European Communities (Mutual Assistance in the Field of Direct Taxation, Certain Excise Duties and Taxation of Insurance Premiums) Regulations 2005 (S.I. 367 of 2005), in connection with the admission of Bulgaria and Romania to the European Union. These Regulations ensure that references to the term "Council Directive" in the European Communities (Mutual Assistance in the Field of Direct Taxation, Certain Excise Duties and Taxation of Insurance Premiums)

Regulations 2005 are references to the original Council Directive 77/799/EEC, as amended by all amending Directives, including Council Directive 2006/98/EC of 20 November 2006 which is concerned with the admission of Bulgaria and Romania to the European Union.

VALUE-ADDED TAX (AMENDMENT) REGULATIONS 2007

(S.I. No. 272 of 2007)

The Revenue Commissioners, in exercise of the powers conferred on them by sections 10(3)(c), 14(2) and 32 of the Value-Added Tax Act 1972 (No. 22 of 1972), make the following regulations:

1.   These Regulations may be cited as the Value-Added Tax (Amendment) Regulations 2007.

2.   The Value-Added Tax Regulations 2006 (S.I. No. 548 of 2006) are amended –

   (a)   in Regulation 15 by inserting the following after paragraph (5):

   "(5A)   Tax chargeable in respect of the supply of goods within the meaning of section 3(1)(b) of the Act is excluded from the application of section 14(1) of the Act.

   (5B)   Tax chargeable in respect of the supply of goods or services in any of the circumstances referred to in subsections (2) to (9) of section 10 of the Act is excluded from the application of section 14(1) of the Act.",

   (b)   in Regulation 16(1) by substituting "by reason of the allowance of discount, a reduction in price or the return of goods other than the return of goods in an early determination of a hire purchase agreement" for "by reason of the return of goods, the allowance of discount, a reduction in price or the default of a debtor", and

   (c)   by inserting the following after Regulation 16:

   "Adjustments for bad debts and for early determination of hire purchase transactions

   16A.   (1)   In this Regulation –

   "determination" means the termination of a hire purchase agreement and the return of the goods which are subject to that agreement on a prior date to the date fixed for such termination under that agreement;

   "part payment" means the amount of money or the value of goods traded in by the customer which amount or value is shown in the hire purchase agreement as representing that part of the sale price of goods which is not being financed under the terms of the hire purchase agreement;

   "sale price" means the price shown in the hire purchase agreement which is inclusive of tax, and vehicle registration tax where appropriate, and which is the price for which the goods would be sold to a customer if their purchase were not financed in whole or in part under a hire purchase agreement.

(2)   In a case in which section 10(3)(c) of the Act applies by reason of the default of a debtor, where–

(a)   the consideration exclusive of tax actually received by a taxable person in relation to the supply by him or her of any goods or services is less than the amount on which tax was chargeable in respect of such supply, or

(b)   no consideration is actually received,

then, subject to the conditions in paragraph (3), relief in respect of the tax attributable to the deficiency (in this Regulation referred to as a "bad debt") may be claimed in accordance with this Regulation.

(3)   A taxable person who has accounted for tax in respect of a supply covered by paragraph (2) may subsequently claim bad debt relief for the tax attributable to the bad debt, where–

(a)   that taxable person has taken all reasonable steps to recover the bad debt,

(b)   the bad debt is allowable as a deduction for the purposes of section 81(2)(i) of the Taxes Consolidation Act 1997 (No. 39 of 1997) and has been written off as such in the financial accounts of that taxable person and the requirements of Regulation 8(1)(m) in respect of that debt have been fulfilled, and

(c)   the person from whom the debt is due is not connected with that taxable person, and the question of whether a person is connected with that taxable person shall be determined in accordance with Regulation 15(5)(b).

(4)   The amount of the relief which a taxable person may claim in respect of a supply covered by paragraphs (2) and (3), which is not a supply within the meaning of section 3(1)(b) of the Act, is calculated in accordance with the following formula:

$$A \times \frac{B}{100 + B}$$

where–

A is the amount which is outstanding from the

debtor in relation to the taxable supply, and

B is the percentage rate of tax, specified in section 11(1) of the Act, which was applied to the supply in question.

(5) (a) The amount of the relief which a taxable person may claim in respect of a supply covered by paragraphs (2) and (3), which is a supply within the meaning of section 3(1)(b) of the Act (in this Regulation referred to as a "supply of the goods under the hire purchase agreement"), is calculated in accordance with the following formula:

$$(C - D) \times \frac{(E - F)}{C}$$

where —

C is the sum of all the amounts scheduled for payment by instalment under the hire purchase agreement,

D is the total amount paid by the customer against the instalments scheduled for payment under the hire purchase agreement up to and including the date on which the bad debt is written off in the financial accounts of the taxable person,

E is an amount equal to the amount of tax accounted for by the taxable person on the supply of the goods under the hire purchase agreement, and

F is an amount equal to the tax attributable to a part payment shown in the hire purchase agreement calculated in accordance with subparagraph (b).

(b) The tax attributable to a part payment shall be calculated in accordance with the following formula:

$$G \times \frac{E}{H}$$

where —

G is an amount equal to the part payment,

E is an amount equal to the amount of tax accounted for by the taxable person on the supply of the goods under the hire purchase agreement, and

H is the sale price of the goods.

(6)   In a case in which section 10(3)(c) of the Act applies by reason of the return of the goods by a customer to his or her supplier as part of a determination, relief in respect of the supply of the goods under the hire purchase agreement may, subject to section 10(3)(d) of the Act, be claimed in accordance with paragraph (7).

(7)   The amount of the relief which a taxable person may claim in respect of a supply of the goods referred to in paragraph (6) is established by —

(a)   calculating the tax attributable to the part payment in accordance with the formula in paragraph (5)(b), and

(b)   calculating, in accordance with the following formula, the tax attributable to the sum of the total amount paid by the customer against the instalments scheduled for payment under the hire purchase agreement and any amount paid by the customer as part of the determination:

$$J \times \frac{(E - K)}{C}$$

where —

J is the total amount paid by the customer against the instalments scheduled for payment under the hire purchase agreement up to and including the prior date agreed under the determination plus any amount paid by the customer as part of the determination,

E is an amount equal to the amount of tax accounted for by the taxable person on the supply of the goods under the hire purchase agreement,

K is an amount equal to the amount of tax attributable to the part payment shown in the hire purchase agreement calculated in accordance with paragraph (5)(b), and

C is the sum of all the amounts scheduled for payment by instalment under the hire purchase agreement,

subtracting the sum of the amounts calculated in accordance with subparagraphs (a) and (b) from the tax accounted for by the taxable person on the supply of the goods under the hire purchase agreement.

(8)   Notwithstanding paragraphs (4), (5) and (7), the taxable person may, subject to the prior agreement of the Revenue Commissioners, use any other method of calculating the relief that correctly reflects the tax appropriate to the amount outstanding.

(9)   A taxable person is entitled to claim the total amount of relief calculated in accordance with paragraphs (4), (5), (7) or (8), as if that amount were tax deductible in accordance with section 12 of the Act for the taxable period in which a claim is made.".

GIVEN under my hand,

11 June 2007

JOSEPHINE FEEHILY

Revenue Commissioner.

EXPLANATORY NOTE

(This note is not part of the Instrument and does not purport to be a legal interpretation.)

These Regulations amend Regulations 15 and 16 of Value-Added Tax Regulations 2006 (S.I. No. 548 of 2006) and insert a new Regulation 16A into those Regulations.

The amendment to Regulation 15 excludes certain transactions from the operation of the cash receipts basis of accounting for VAT.

The amendment to Regulation 16 deletes the reference to bad debts and the return of goods in an early termination of a hire purchase agreement from that Regulation as relief in such circumstances is now provided for in the new Regulation 16A.

Regulation 16A sets out the conditions to be fulfilled and the procedures to be followed to qualify for bad debt relief for VAT already accounted for in respect of all supplies including supplies of goods under hire purchase agreements. It also provides for relief for VAT already accounted for in respect of a supply of goods under a hire purchase agreement that is terminated early where those goods are returned to the hire purchase company.

VALUE-ADDED TAX (AMENDMENT) REGULATIONS 2008

(S.I. No. 238 of 2008)

The Revenue Commissioners, in exercise of the powers conferred on them by sections 10, 12E, 15 and 32 of the Value-Added Tax Act 1972 (No. 22 of 1972) and, as respects paragraphs (*j*) and (*k*) of Regulation 3 of the following Regulations, with the consent of the Minister for Finance, make the following regulations:

1.   These Regulations may be cited as the Value-Added Tax (Amendment) Regulations 2008.

2.   In these Regulations "Regulations of 2007" means the Value-Added Tax (Amendment) Regulations 2007 (S.I. No. 272 of 2007).

3.   The Value-Added Tax Regulations 2006 (S.I. No. 548 of 2006) are amended —

    (a)   in each provision specified in the first column of Schedule 1 to these Regulations for the words set out in the second column of that Schedule at that entry (in each place where those words occur in the provision concerned) there is substituted the words set out at the corresponding entry in the third column of that Schedule,

    (b)   in Regulation 2 —

        (i)   by deleting the definition of "Sixth Council Directive",

        (ii)   in the definition of "value-added tax identification number in another Member State" by substituting "VAT Directive;" for "Sixth Council Directive.", and

        (iii)   by inserting the following after the definition of "value-added tax identification number in another Member State":

        "VAT Directive" means Council Directive 2006/112/EC of 28 November 2006 on the common system of value-added tax.",

    (c)   in Regulation 8(1) —

        (i)   by substituting the following for the matter preceding paragraph (*c*):

        "The full and true records of all transactions which affect or may affect the accountable person's liability to tax and entitlement to deductibility, which every accountable person is required to keep in accordance with section 16 of the Act, shall be entered up to date and include —

            (a)   in relation to consideration receivable from registered persons —

                (i)   the amount receivable from each such person in respect of each transaction for which an invoice or other document is required to be issued under section 17 of the Act, and

(ii) a cross-reference to the copy of the relevant invoice or other document,

(b) in relation to consideration receivable from unregistered persons—

(i) a daily total of the consideration receivable from all such persons,

(ii) a cross-reference from that daily total to the relevant books or other documents which are in use for the purposes of the business, and

(iii) where the accountable person uses an electronic cash register or point of sale system the complete record of each entry on that register or system, uniquely identified by sequential number, date and time of such entry,",

(ii) in paragraph (t) by substituting "matters," for "matters, and", and

(iii) by substituting the following for subparagraph (u):

"(u) in relation to each capital good in respect of which a capital goods owner is required to create and maintain a capital good record in accordance with section 12E(12) of the Act—

(i) the total tax incurred,

(ii) the amount of the total tax incurred which is deductible in accordance with section 12 of the Act,

(iii) the date on which the adjustment period begins,

(iv) the number of intervals in the adjustment period,

(v) the initial interval proportion of deductible use,

(vi) the total reviewed deductible amount,

(vii) the proportion of deductible use for each interval,

(viii)   details of any adjustments required to be made in accordance with section 12E, and

(ix)   details of any sale or transfer of the capital good or details of any assignment or surrender of a lease where section 12E(8)(*b*) applies in relation to that capital good,

and

(v)   in respect of supplies of goods specified in paragraph (i) of the Second Schedule to the Act—

(i)   the name and address of the person to whom the goods are supplied,

(ii)   a description of the goods supplied,

(iii)   the amount of the consideration,

(iv)   a cross-reference to the copy of the relevant invoice, and

(v)   a cross-reference to the relevant Customs and transport documents.",

(d)   in Regulation 9—

(i)   by substituting—

(I)   in paragraph (1) "VAT Directive" for "Sixth Council Directive", and

(II)   in paragraph (8)(*a*) "Article 238 of the VAT Directive" for "Article 22(9)(*d*) of the Sixth Council Directive",

and

(ii)   by inserting the following after paragraph (9):

"(10)   Where a document containing—

(a)   a schedule of dates on which rent in respect of a letting of immovable goods which is chargeable to tax is due (in this paragraph referred to as 'due dates') under a letting agreement, and

(b)   the particulars specified in paragraph (2),

is issued prior to the earliest of those due dates listed in that schedule, then that document shall be treated as an invoice issued in accordance with section 17(1) of the Act and shall be deemed to be so issued in respect of each rent payment listed in that schedule on the due date for that rent payment.

(11)   Where the rate of tax changes during the period covered by the document referred to in paragraph (10) then that document shall be amended to provide for the new rate of tax and the corresponding amounts of tax due for the periods following the date of that change in the tax rate.",

(e)   in Regulation 15(5B) (inserted by the Regulations of 2007) by inserting "referred to in section 8(1B)(b) of the Act or" after "services",

(f)   in Regulation 16A (inserted by the Regulations of 2007) by substituting the following for paragraph (3) —

"(3)   An accountable person who has accounted for tax in respect of a supply covered by paragraph (2) may subsequently claim bad debt relief for the tax attributable to the bad debt, where —

(a)   that accountable person has taken all reasonable steps to recover the bad debt,

(b)   the bad debt is allowable as a deduction under section 81(2)(*i*) of the Taxes Consolidation Act 1997 (No. 39 of 1997) in cases where the accountable person is chargeable to tax under Case I or II of Schedule D of that Act,

(c)   the bad debt has been written off in the financial accounts of that accountable person and the requirements of Regulation 8(1)(*m*) in respect of that debt have been fulfilled by that accountable person, and

(d)   the person from whom the debt is due is not connected with that accountable person, and the question of whether a person is connected with that accountable person shall be determined in accordance with section 7A(3) of the Act.",

(g)   in Regulation 18 —

(i)   by substituting the following for paragraph (1) —

"(1) In this Regulation —

"authorised officer" means a person authorised for the purposes of section 18 of the Act;

"final accounting year" means the period from the end of the previous accounting year to the date that a person ceases to be an accountable person;

"review period" means a period consisting of all the taxable periods which end during an accounting year.",

and

(ii)   by substituting the following for paragraph (3)(c) —

"(c)   Where the adjustment under subparagraph (b) relates to the final accounting year of the accountable person concerned, then any necessary adjustment is required to be made by way of an increase or decrease in the amount of tax deductible for the taxable period in which that final accounting year ends. Any such adjustment is required to be made in the return to be furnished in accordance with section 19(3) of the Act in respect of the appropriate taxable period.",

(h)   by inserting the following after Regulation 21:

"**The operation of the capital goods scheme**

21A.   (1)   (a)   For the purposes of section 12E of the Act where a capital goods owner changes the end date of his or her accounting year during a subsequent interval of the adjustment period for a capital good, then the duration of that subsequent interval shall be a period of 12 months from the start date of that subsequent interval and in such circumstances, starting from and including the first day following the end of that subsequent interval, the remaining subsequent intervals in the adjustment period shall be consecutive periods of 12 months.

(b)   Notwithstanding subparagraph (a), where the change in the end date of the accounting year results in that accounting year ending —

(i)   more than 12 months from the start date of the subsequent interval in which that change takes place, then the capital goods owner may extend the period of that subsequent interval to the end date of that accounting year, or

(ii)   less than 12 months from the start date of the subsequent interval in which that change takes place, then the capital goods owner may extend the period of that subsequent interval to the end date of the following accounting year.

(2) (a) Where—

   (i) a capital good is transferred in accordance with section 12E(10) of the Act during a subsequent interval of the adjustment period for that capital good, and

   (ii) the accounting year of the transferee differs from the accounting year of the transferor,

   then that subsequent interval shall be a period of 12 months from the start date of that subsequent interval in which the transfer takes place and in such circumstances, starting from and including the first day following the end of the subsequent interval during which the transfer takes place, the remaining subsequent intervals in the adjustment period shall be consecutive periods of 12 months.

(b) Notwithstanding subparagraph (a), in cases where the accounting year of the transferee ends-

   (i) more than 12 months from the start of the subsequent interval in which the transfer takes place, then the transferee may extend that subsequent interval to the last day of that accounting year, or

   (ii) less than 12 months from the start of the subsequent interval in which the transfer takes place, then the transferee may extend that subsequent interval to the last day of the following accounting year.

The supply of services comprising the use of business assets for private or non-business purposes

21B. (1) In this Regulation 'private use proportion' means the proportion which correctly reflects the extent to which immovable goods are used for private or non-business purposes in the relevant taxable period.

(2) Where section 5(3B) of the Act applies the private use proportion shall be calculated in accordance with the following formula:

$$\frac{A}{B}$$

where—

A is equal to the floor area of that part of the immovable goods that is used for private or non-business purposes in the relevant taxable period, and

B   is equal to the total floor area of those immovable goods.

(3)   The amount on which tax is chargeable in relation to the supply of services referred to in section 5(3B) of the Act in any taxable period shall be calculated in accordance with the following formula:

$$\frac{C \times D}{20 \times 6}$$

where —

C   is the amount on which tax is chargeable on the acquisition or development of the immovable goods,

D   is the private use proportion calculated in accordance with the formula in paragraph (2).

(4)   The rate of tax applicable to the supply of services referred to in paragraph (3) is the rate specified in section 11(1)(a) of the Act.",

(i)   in Regulation 23(1)(a) by substituting "VAT Directive" for "Sixth Council Directive",

(j)   in Regulation 31(5) by substituting "Articles 4 and 35, the first paragraph of Article 139(3) and Articles 311 to 341 of the VAT Directive" for "Article 26a or 28o of the Sixth Council Directive", and

(k)   in Regulation 37 by inserting the following after paragraph (4):

"(5)   In accordance with section 15 of the Act, where goods are re-imported by the person who exported them, in the state in which they were exported, being goods which are exempt from customs duties on such re-importation, then those goods shall be exempt from value-added tax.".

4.   For convenience of reference, in the table of contents, cross headings and shoulder notes accompanying the printed version of the Value-Added Tax Regulations 2006 and specified in the first column of Schedule 2 to these Regulations for the words set out in the second column of that Schedule at that entry there is substituted the words set out at the corresponding entry in the third column of that Schedule.

Schedule 1
Miscellaneous Amendments Relating to the Amendment of the Definition of Taxable Person

Amendments to Value-Added Tax Regulations 2006

S.I. No. 548 of 2006	Words to be replaced	Words to be inserted
3(1)	a taxable person	an accountable person
3(2)	a taxable person	an accountable person
3(3)	a taxable person	an accountable person
3(4)(*a*)	a taxable person	an accountable person
3(4)(*b*)	A taxable person	An accountable person
3(4)(*b*)	a taxable person	an accountable person
3(7)	a taxable person	an accountable person
3(8)	a taxable person	an accountable person
3(9)	a taxable person	an accountable person
4(4)	a taxable person	an accountable person
4(5)	the taxable person	the accountable person
7(1)	A taxable person	An accountable person
7(4)	a taxable person	an accountable person
8(1)(*d*)	the taxable person	the accountable person
8(1)(*f*)	the taxable person	the accountable person
8(*g*)	a taxable person	an accountable person
8(*g*)	the taxable person	the accountable person
8(*h*)	the taxable person	the accountable person
8(*n*)	the taxable person	the accountable person
8(*n*)	another taxable person	another accountable person
8(*n*)	other taxable person	other accountable person
8(*o*)	the taxable person	the accountable person
8(*p*)	the taxable person	the accountable person
8(*q*)	the taxable person	the accountable person
8(*s*)	the taxable person	the accountable person
9(2)	a taxable person	an accountable person
9(3)	a taxable person	an accountable person
9(4)	a taxable person	an accountable person
9(4)(*c*)	the taxable person	the accountable person
9(6)	a taxable person	an accountable person
10(2)	a taxable person	an accountable person
10(2)	the taxable person	the accountable person
10(3)	A taxable person	An accountable person
10(4)	A taxable person	An accountable person

S.I. No. 548 of 2006	Words to be replaced	Words to be inserted
13(1)	a taxable person	an accountable person
13(1)	the taxable person	the accountable person
13(2)	a taxable person	an accountable person
13(2)	that taxable person's	that accountable person's
13(2)	the taxable person	the accountable person
13(3)	a taxable person	an accountable person
14(1)	a taxable person	an accountable person
14(2)	a taxable person	an accountable person
14(3)	a taxable person	an accountable person
14(4)	a taxable person	an accountable person
14(5)	the taxable person	the accountable person
14(5)	any taxable person	any accountable person
14(5)	that taxable person	that accountable person
14(5)	A taxable person	An accountable person
14(5)	a taxable person	an accountable person
14(6)	the taxable person	the accountable person
14(6)	a taxable person	an accountable person
14(7)	A taxable person	An accountable person
14(9)	the taxable person	the accountable person
15(1)	a taxable person	an accountable person
15(2)	a taxable person	an accountable person
15(2)	said taxable person	said accountable person
15(3)	a taxable person	an accountable person
15(7)	A taxable person	An accountable person
15(7)	a taxable person	an accountable person
15(7)	the taxable person	the accountable person
15(9)	a taxable person	an accountable person
15(9)	the taxable person	the accountable person
16(1)	a taxable person	an accountable person
16(4)	a taxable person	an accountable person
16(4)	the taxable person	the accountable person
16(5)	the taxable person	the accountable person
16A(2)	a taxable person	an accountable person
16A(4)	a taxable person	an accountable person
16A(5)	a taxable person	an accountable person
16A(5)	the taxable person	the accountable person
16A(7)	a taxable person	an accountable person
16A(7)	the taxable person	the accountable person
16A(8)	the taxable person	the accountable person

S.I. No. 548 of 2006	Words to be replaced	Words to be inserted
16A(9)	A taxable person	An accountable person
18(2)	a taxable person	an accountable person
18(2)	the taxable person's	the accountable person's
18(2)	the taxable person	the accountable person
18(2)	that taxable person	that accountable person
18(3)	A taxable person	An accountable person
18(3)	the taxable person's	the accountable person's
18(3)	the taxable person	the accountable person
18(4)	a taxable person	an accountable person
21(2)	a taxable person	an accountable person
21(2)	the taxable person	the accountable person
21(3)	a taxable person	an accountable person
21(3)	the taxable person	the accountable person
21(4)	a taxable person	an accountable person
26(1)	A taxable person	An accountable person
26(1)	a taxable person	an accountable person
26(2)	the taxable person	the accountable person
26(2)	other taxable persons	other accountable persons
26(3)	the taxable person	the accountable person
28(2)(*h*)	from taxable persons	from accountable persons
28(2)(*h*)	not taxable persons	not accountable persons
32(3)	a taxable person	an accountable person
32(3)	the taxable person	the accountable person
32(3)	said taxable person	said accountable person
32(4)	A taxable person	An accountable person
32(4)	another taxable person	another accountable person
32(5)	A taxable person	An accountable person
32(6)	Every taxable person	Every accountable person
34(2)	a taxable person	an accountable person
41	a taxable person	an accountable person

Schedule 2
Miscellaneous Changes to Table of Contents, Cross Headings and Shoulder Notes in Printed Version of Value-Added Tax Regulations 2006

(included for convenience of reference)

S.I. No. 548 of 2006	Words to be replaced	Words to be inserted
Cross heading "TAXABLE PERSON" in the Table of Contents	TAXABLE PERSON	ACCOUNTABLE PERSON
Title to Regulation 3 in Table of Contents	a taxable person	an accountable person
Cross heading "*Taxable Person*" before Regulation 3	*Taxable person*	*Accountable person*
Shoulder note to Regulation 3	a taxable person	an accountable person

GIVEN under my hand,
2 July 2008

MICHAEL O'GRADY
Revenue Commissioner.

The Minister for Finance consents to the making of paragraphs (*j*) and (*k*) of Regulation 3 of the foregoing Regulations.

GIVEN under my Official Seal,
2 July 2008

BRIAN LENIHAN
Minister for Finance.

EXPLANATORY NOTE

(This note is not part of the Instrument and does not purport to be a legal interpretation.)

These Regulations amend the Value-Added Tax Regulations 2006 (S.I. No. 548 of 2006)—

- to correct all references to taxable person and accountable person following the amendments to these terms in Finance Act 2008 (the changes are outlined in two Schedules to the Regulations),

- to update all references to the Sixth Directive which was repealed by Council Directive 2006/112/EC of 28 November 2006 (Regulations 2, 9, 23 and 31 of the 2006 VAT Regulations),

- to provide that records of transactions that affect a person's entitlement to deductibility are required to be kept, to clarify the type of records required to be kept by businesses whose customers are unregistered persons and to set out the details required in a capital good record (Regulation 8 of the 2006 VAT Regulations),

- to provide that a document containing a schedule of dates on which rent is payable will be treated as a VAT invoice provided it contains all the information required for a VAT invoice (Regulation 9 of the 2006 VAT Regulations),

- to exclude from the cash basis of accounting the tax chargeable on construction services supplied by subcontractors to principal contractors and in respect of which tax the principal contractor must account on a reverse charge basis (Regulation 15 of the 2006 VAT Regulations),

- to ensure that persons who are not liable to tax under the TCA 1997 are entitled to make a claim for bad debt relief in respect of VAT (Regulation 16A of the 2006 VAT Regulations),

- to substitute "accounting year" for "accounting period" wherever it occurs following the amendment to section 12(4) of the Act in Finance Act 2008 (Regulation 18 of the 2006 VAT Regulations), and

- to insert a provision in relation to exempting goods that are re-imported by the person who exported them so as to align it with the Customs rules (Regulation 37 of the 2006 VAT Regulations).

Two new Regulations are also inserted into the Value-Added Tax Regulations 2006 as follows—

Regulation 21A in relation to the capital goods scheme to deal with a change in accounting year during an adjustment period, and

Regulation 21B in relation to the private or non-business use of business assets.

TAXES (ELECTRONIC TRANSMISSION OF VAT eSERVICES RETURNS AND VIES STATEMENTS) (SPECIFIED PROVISIONS AND APPOINTED DAY) ORDER 2008

(S.I. No. 339 of 2008)

The Revenue Commissioners, in exercise of the powers conferred on them by section 917E (inserted by section 209 of the Finance Act 1999 (No. 2 of 1999)) of the Taxes Consolidation Act 1997 (No. 39 of 1997), order as follows:

1. This Order may be cited as the Taxes (Electronic Transmission of VAT eServices Returns and VIES Statements) (Specified Provisions and Appointed Day) Order 2008.

2. Each of the provisions set out in the Schedule to this Order is specified for the purposes of Chapter 6 of Part 38 of the Taxes Consolidation Act 1997.

3. The 25th day of August 2008 is appointed in relation to returns and statements to be made under the provisions specified in accordance with Article 2 of this Order.

SCHEDULE

Section 5A(6) of the Value-Added Tax Act 1972 (No. 22 of 1972).

Subsections (1), (2), (3) and (4) of section 19A of the Value-Added Tax Act 1972.

Paragraph (2) of Regulation 14 of the Value-Added Tax Regulations 2006 (S.I. No. 548 of 2006).

GIVEN this 21 day of August 2008

MICHAEL O'GRADY
Revenue Commissioner

EXPLANATORY NOTE

(This note is not part of the Instrument and does not purport to be a legal interpretation)

This Order applies the legislation governing the electronic filing of tax information to VAT eServices Returns and Statements of intra-Community Supplies (VIES Statements).

The order also appoints a day, namely the 25th of August 2008, in relation to such returns and statements which ensures that the electronic filing legislation will apply to VAT eServices Returns and VIES Statements which are due to be made on or after 26th of August 2008.

Chapter 6 of Part 38 of the Taxes Consolidation Act 1997 provides the legislative framework whereby tax related information required to be provided to the Revenue Commissioners may be supplied electronically. The legislation only applies to information where the provision under which the information is supplied is specified in an order made by the Revenue Commissioners. Where a provision is so specified the legislation only applies to information that is required to be supplied under that provision after the day appointed in the Order in relation to the provision concerned. The reason for this procedure is to allow the Revenue Commissioners to manage the roll-out of the system for receiving tax related information electronically.

TAX RETURNS AND PAYMENTS (MANDATORY ELECTRONIC FILING AND PAYMENT OF TAX) REGULATIONS 2008

(S.I. No. 341 of 2008)

ARRANGEMENT OF REGULATIONS

The Revenue Commissioners in exercise of the powers conferred on them by section 917EA (inserted by section 164 of the Finance Act 2003 (No. 3 of 2003)) of the Taxes Consolidation Act 1997 (No. 39 of 1997) make the following regulations:

Citation and commencement

1.   (1)   These Regulations may be cited as the Tax Returns and Payments (Mandatory Electronic Filing and Payment of Tax) Regulations 2008.

      (2)   These Regulations come into operation on 1 September 2008.

Interpretation and general

2.   (1)   In these Regulations—

             "Acts" has the same meaning as it has in section 917D of the Principal Act;

"capacity" means access to the technology, including both hardware and software, by which either or both a specified return or the payment of any specified tax liabilities may be made by electronic means;

"Commissioners" means the Revenue Commissioners;

"Large Cases Division" means the division of the Office of the Revenue Commissioners known as Large Cases Division;

"Principal Act" means the Taxes Consolidation Act 1997;

"return" has the same meaning as it has in section 917D of the Principal Act.

(2)   (a)   Any return which a person is or may be required by the Acts to give to the Commissioners and which is specified for the purposes of Chapter 6 of Part 38 of the Principal Act by order made by the Commissioners under section 917E of that Act is specified as a specified return.

       (b)   Any liabilities to tax, including interest on unpaid tax, arising under any provision of the Acts, the payment of which is or will be accounted for, directly or indirectly, in a specified return, including any payment which is treated under the Acts as a payment on foot of, or on account of, any liabilities to tax, is specified as specified tax liabilities.

       (c)   Each person referred to in Schedules 1 and 2 is specified as a specified person for the purposes of paragraphs (a) and (b) of subsection (3) of section 917EA of the Principal Act and these Regulations.

Persons required to make returns and payments by electronic means from
1 January 2009

3.   (1)   Subject to paragraph (3), where, on or after 1 January 2009, any specified return falls due to be made by or on behalf of a specified person to whom Schedule 1 relates, then the return shall be made by electronic means and in accordance with Chapter 6 of Part 38 of the Principal Act.

     (2)   Subject to paragraph (3), where, on or after 1 January 2009, a payment of any specified tax liabilities falls due to be made by or on behalf of a specified person to whom Schedule 1 relates, then the payment shall be made by such electronic means as are required by the Commissioners.

     (3)   Where the specified person is a person to whom paragraph (1) or (2) relates and is a person whose tax affairs are dealt with by Large Cases Division, then the provisions of these Regulations shall only apply where the person has been notified in writing to that effect by the Commissioners.

Persons required to make returns and payments by electronic means from
1 January 2010

4.   (1)   Subject to paragraph (3), where, on or after 1 January 2010, any specified return falls due to be made by or on behalf of a specified person to whom Schedule 2 relates, then the return shall be made by electronic means and in accordance with Chapter 6 of Part 38 of the Principal Act.

      (2)   Subject to paragraph (3), where, on or after 1 January 2010, a payment of any specified tax liabilities falls due to be made by or on behalf of a specified person to whom Schedule 2 relates, then the payment shall be made by such electronic means as are required by the Commissioners.

      (3)   The requirements placed by paragraphs (1) and (2) upon a specified person to whom paragraph 2 of Schedule 2 relates shall continue to apply, notwithstanding that the obligation on that person to append audited accounts to its annual return (under any provision of the Companies Acts) may no longer apply.

Repayment of tax by electronic means

5.   Where a repayment of any specified tax liabilities falls due to be made by the Commissioners —

      (a)   on or after 1 January 2009 to a specified person referred to in Schedule 1, or

      (b)   on or after 1 January 2010 to a specified person referred to in Schedule 2,
      the repayment shall be made by electronic means.

Exclusion of certain specified persons

6.   (1)   A specified person may, by notifying the Commissioners in writing, request to be excluded from the provisions of these Regulations on the grounds that the person does not have the capacity to make a specified return or to pay the specified tax liabilities by electronic means and the notification shall include all information relevant to the consideration by the Commissioners of the request.

      (2)   Where the Commissioners receive a notification from a specified person in accordance with paragraph (1) or where the Commissioners otherwise consider it appropriate, they may exclude the person from the provisions of these Regulations only if they are satisfied that, in all of the circumstances, the person could not reasonably be expected to have the capacity to make a specified return or to make a payment in respect of specified tax liabilities by electronic means.

(3)   A decision to exclude a specified person from the provisions of these Regulations by the Commissioners in accordance with paragraph (2) shall be made within 30 days of receipt of the notification from the specified person, and the Commissioners shall notify the specified person in writing of the decision.

Right of appeal to the Appeal Commissioners

7.   (1)   A person aggrieved by a failure of the Commissioners to exclude such person from the provisions of these Regulations in accordance with Regulation 6(2) may, by notice in writing to the Commissioners before the end of the period of 30 days beginning with the day on which notice of the decision was given to the person, apply to have such person's request to be excluded from the provisions of these Regulations heard and determined by the Appeal Commissioners.

      (2)   The Appeal Commissioners shall hear and determine an appeal made to them under paragraph (1) as if it were an appeal against an assessment to income tax, and the provisions of the Income Tax Acts relating to appeals shall apply accordingly.

      (3)   On the hearing of an appeal made under this Regulation, the Appeal Commissioners shall have regard only to those matters to which the Commissioners may or are required to have regard under these Regulations.

Provisions to amend exclusions

8.   (1)   If, at any time after a decision by the Commissioners in accordance with Regulation 6(2) or a determination by the Appeal Commissioners in accordance with Regulation 7(2) to exclude a specified person from the provisions of these Regulations, the Commissioners decide that, due to a material change in all of the circumstances, the specified person should not be so excluded, they shall notify the specified person in writing of that decision.

      (2)   The decision referred to in paragraph (1) shall be deemed to be a failure to exclude the specified person from the provisions of these Regulations and Regulation 7 shall apply accordingly.

Time at which payments and repayments made by electronic means are taken to be made

9.   For the purpose of these Regulations —

      (a)   the time at which a payment of any specified tax liabilities by or on behalf of a specified person shall be taken as having been made shall be the later of the due date for that payment or the time at which the Commissioners receive authorisation to debit the amount of the payment from the account of the specified person in a financial institution, and

(b)   the time at which a repayment of any specified tax liabilities to a specified person shall be taken as having been made shall be the time at which the Commissioners give authorisation to credit the amount of the repayment to the account of the specified person in a financial institution.

Presumptions

10.   For the purposes of any dispute arising as to the time at which either or both a payment or a repayment of any specified tax liabilities to which these Regulations apply is to be taken as having been made, a certificate signed by an officer of the Commissioners which certifies that he or she has examined the relevant records and that it appears from them that the time at which the payment or the repayment is to be taken as having been made, is the time so specified in the certificate, shall be evidence until the contrary is proven that the payment or the repayment was made at the time so certified.

SCHEDULE 1

SPECIFIED PERSONS FOR THE PURPOSES OF REGULATION 3

1.   A Minister of the Government.

2.   The Attorney General.

3.   The Comptroller and Auditor General.

4.   The Revenue Commissioners.

5.   The Public Appointments Service.

6.   The Commissioners of Public Works in Ireland.

7.   The Houses of the Oireachtas Commission.

8.   A company or other body whose tax affairs are dealt with by Large Cases Division at any time on or after 1 January 2009.

SCHEDULE 2

SPECIFIED PERSONS FOR THE PURPOSES OF REGULATION 4

1.   A person referred to in Schedule 13 to the Principal Act, other than one referred to in Schedule 1 to these Regulations.

2.   A company which, at any time on or after 1 January 2010, is required under any provisions of the Companies Acts to append audited accounts to its annual return, other than one referred to in Schedule 1 to these Regulations.

GIVEN under my hand,
22 August 2008

MICHAEL O'GRADY
Revenue Commissioner.

EXPLANATORY NOTE

Tax Returns and Payments (Mandatory Electronic Filing and Payment of Tax) Regulations 2008

These Regulations are made by the Revenue Commissioners under the provisions of section 917EA of the Taxes Consolidation Act 1997. This section was inserted by section 164 of the Finance Act 2003 and was made subject to a commencement order by the Minister for Finance. This order was signed on 28 July 2008.

The Regulations provide for mandatory electronic filing and paying of certain tax returns and tax liabilities by Government Departments and Offices State Bodies and larger companies. These obligations are being introduced in 2 phases. Government Departments, certain named Government Offices and bodies whose tax affairs are dealt with by Large Cases Division of the Revenue Commissioners come within phase 1, with effect from 1 January 2009, while all other State agencies and companies who are obliged under the Companies Act to produce audited accounts come within phase 2, with effect from 1 January 2010.

In essence, any tax return to be made to the Revenue Commissioners, which can be made electronically under the provisions of Chapter 6 of Part 38 of the Taxes Consolidation Act 1997, is covered by these Regulations as well as the payment of all associated tax liabilities. Companies in phase 2 will continue to be obliged to pay and file electronically even if they subsequently become exempt from the obligation to produce audited accounts.

The Regulations also provide that, in all cases where a repayment is due to be made by the Revenue Commissioners, it will be made electronically.

The Revenue Commissioners may, on application, exclude a person from the obligations to pay and file electronically if they are satisfied that the person does not have the capacity to do so and in this context "capacity" is defined to mean access to the requisite technology, both hardware and software. A person aggrieved at a failure by the Revenue Commissioners to exclude them from the requirements may appeal that failure to the Appeal Commissioners. An excluded person may, if circumstances change, have that exclusion revoked and that decision may also be appealed to the Appeal Commissioners.

Finally, provision is made to determine the time at which payments and repayments made by electronic means are to be taken as having been made.

The bodies to which these Regulations apply are set out in Schedules 1 and 2 to these Regulations.

EUROPEAN COMMUNITIES (TAX EXEMPTION FOR CERTAIN NON-COMMERCIAL GOODS IMPORTED IN THE PERSONAL LUGGAGE OF TRAVELLERS FROM THIRD COUNTRIES) REGULATIONS 2008

(S.I. No. 480 of 2008)

I, BRIAN LENIHAN, Minister for Finance, in exercise of the power conferred on me by section 3 of the European Communities Act 1972 (No. 27 of 1972) and for the purpose of giving effect to Council Directive 2007/74/EC of 20 December 2007, hereby make the following regulations:

Citation, Commencement and Interpretation

1. (1)   These Regulations may be cited as the European Communities (Tax Exemption for Certain Non-Commercial Goods Imported in the Personal Luggage of Travellers from Third Countries) Regulations 2008.

    (2)   These Regulations come into operation on 1 December 2008.

2. (1)   In these Regulations—

    "cigarillos" means cigars of a maximum weight of 3 grams each;

    "crewmember" means a member of the crew of a means of transport used, other than for private pleasure-flying or private pleasure-sea-navigation, to travel to the State from a third country or from a territory where the Community provisions on value-added tax or excise duty, or both do not apply;

    "non-commercial character" in relation to imports, means imports that—

    (a)   take place occasionally,

    (b)   consist exclusively of goods for the personal or family use of the traveller, or of goods intended as presents,

    where the nature and quantity of the goods are not such as to indicate that they are being imported for commercial purposes;

    "personal luggage" means the whole of the luggage which a traveller is able to present to the customs authorities upon arrival in the State, as well as luggage which the traveller presents later to the same authorities, subject to proof that such luggage was registered as accompanied luggage at the time of the traveller's departure with the company which has been responsible for conveying the traveller. Fuel, other than mineral oil in the standard tank of a mechanically propelled vehicle and a quantity of fuel not exceeding 10 litres contained in a portable container, is not personal luggage;

    "private pleasure-flying" means the use of an aircraft by its owner or the natural or legal person who enjoys its use either through hire or through any other means, for purposes other than commercial and in particular other than for the carriage of passengers or goods or for the supply of services for consideration or for the purposes of public authorities;

"private pleasure-sea-navigation" means the use of a seagoing vessel by its owner or the natural or legal person who enjoys its use either through hire or through any other means, for purposes other than commercial and in particular other than for the carriage of passengers or goods or for the supply of services for consideration or for the purposes of public authorities;

"territory where the Community provisions on value-added tax or excise duty, or both do not apply" means any territory, other than the Isle of Man or a territory of a third country, where Directives 2006/112/EC or 92/12/EEC, or both do not apply;

"third country" means any country, which is not a Member State of the European Union. However, Monaco shall not be regarded as a third country and San Marino shall not be regarded as a third country in respect of excise duty;

"traveller" means an air traveller or a sea traveller arriving, other than by private pleasure-flying or private pleasure-sea-navigation, in the State from a third country or a territory where the Community provisions on value-added tax or excise duty, or both do not apply;

"% vol" means alcoholic strength by volume which is the ratio, expressed as a percentage, of the volume of alcohol present in a product to the total volume of the product at a temperature of 20° Celsius.

(2)   A word or expression that is used in these Regulations and is also used in Council Directive 2007/74/EC has, unless the contrary intention appears, the same meaning in these Regulations that it has in that Directive.

Travellers

3.   Goods, the importation of which is regarded as being of a non-commercial character, imported in the personal luggage of a traveller shall—

(a)   subject to Regulation 4, be exempt from value-added tax, and

(b)   subject to Regulations 5, 6 and 7, be exempt from value-added tax and excise duty.

4.   (1)   Goods, other than those to which Regulation 5, 6 or 7 applies, shall be exempt from value-added tax where—

(a)   in the case of travellers other than those to whom paragraph (b) applies, the total value of the goods does not exceed €430, or

(b)   in the case of a traveller under 15 years of age, the total value of the goods does not exceed €215.

(2)   For the purposes of applying the monetary thresholds specified in paragraph (1), the value of an individual item may not be split up.

(3)   The value of the personal luggage of a traveller, which is imported temporarily or is re-imported following its temporary export, and the value of medicinal products required to meet the personal needs of a traveller shall not be taken into consideration for the purposes of applying the exemptions specified in paragraph (1).

5.   (1)   Tobacco products specified in this paragraph shall be exempt from value-added tax and excise duty subject to the following quantitative limits per traveller:

(a)   200 cigarettes;

(b)   100 cigarillos;

(c)   50 cigars;

(d)   250 grams smoking tobacco.

(2)   Each amount specified in subparagraphs (a) to (d) of paragraph (1) shall represent 100 per cent of the total allowance for tobacco products for a traveller.

(3)   The exemption may be applied by a traveller to any combination of the tobacco products specified in subparagraphs (a) to (d) of paragraph (1) provided that the aggregate of the percentages made up from the individual allowances does not exceed 100 per cent.

6.   (1)   Alcohol products specified in this paragraph shall be exempt from value-added tax and excise duty subject to the following quantitative limits per traveller:

(a)   (i)   1 litre of alcohol or alcoholic beverages of alcoholic strength exceeding 22% vol, or

(ii)   1 litre of undenatured ethyl alcohol of 80% vol and over, or

(iii)   2 litres of alcohol or alcoholic beverages of an alcoholic strength not exceeding 22% vol;

(b)   4 litres of still wine; and

(c)   16 litres of beer.

(2)   Each amount specified in clause (i) to (iii) of paragraph (1)(a) shall represent 100 per cent of the total allowance for those alcohol products.

(3)   The exemption under paragraph (1)(a) may be applied by a traveller to any combination of the alcohol products in clauses (i) to (iii), provided that the aggregate of the percentages made up from the individual allowances does not exceed 100 per cent.

7.   Fuel imported in the standard tank of a mechanically propelled vehicle and a quantity of fuel not exceeding 10 litres contained in a portable container, shall be exempt from value-added tax and excise duty.

Crewmembers

8.   Goods, the importation of which is regarded as being of a non-commercial character, imported in the luggage of a crewmember disembarking from a ship or aircraft shall —

(a)   subject to Regulation 9, be exempt from value-added tax, and

(b)   subject to Regulations 10 and 11, be exempt from value-added tax and excise duty.

9.   (1)   Goods, other than those to which Regulation 10 or 11 applies, shall be exempt from value-added tax where their total value does not exceed €430.

(2)   For the purposes of applying the monetary threshold specified in paragraph (1), the value of an individual item may not be split up.

(3)   The value of medicinal products required to meet the personal needs of a crewmember shall not be taken into consideration for the purposes of applying the exemption specified in paragraph (1).

10.   (1)   Tobacco products specified in this paragraph shall be exempt from value-added tax and excise duty subject to the following quantitative limits per crewmember:

(a)   40 cigarettes;

(b)   20 cigarillos;

(c)   10 cigars;

(d)   50 grams smoking tobacco.

(2)   Each amount specified in subparagraph (a) to (d) of paragraph (1) shall represent 100 per cent of the total allowance for tobacco products for a crewmember.

(3)   The exemption may be applied by a crewmember to any combination of the tobacco products specified in subparagraphs (a) to (d) of paragraph (1) provided that the aggregate of the percentages made up from the individual allowances does not exceed 100 per cent.

11. (1)   Alcohol products specified in this paragraph shall be exempt from value-added tax and excise duty subject to the following quantitative limits per crewmember:

(a)   (i)   0.35 litres of alcohol or alcoholic beverages of alcoholic strength exceeding 22% vol, or

(ii)   0.5 litres of alcohol or alcoholic beverages of an alcoholic strength not exceeding 22% vol;

(b)   0.75 litres of still wine; and

(c)   4 litres of beer.

Additional provisions

12. The exemptions under Regulations 5, 6, 10 and 11 shall not apply to persons under 17 years of age.

13. These Regulations shall apply where a traveller's journey has involved transit through the territory of a third country or a territory where the Community provisions on value-added tax or excise duty, or both do not apply, unless such traveller can establish that the goods transported in his or her baggage have been acquired subject to the general conditions governing taxation on the domestic market of a Member State and do not qualify for any refunding of value-added tax or excise duty. Overflying without landing shall not be regarded as transit.

GIVEN under my Official Seal,
25 November 2008

BRIAN LENIHAN.
Minister for Finance.

EXPLANATORY NOTE

(This is not part of the Instrument and does not purport to be a legal interpretation.)

These Regulations give effect to Council Directive No. 2007/74/EC of 20 December 2007 which allows for the exemption from excise duty and value-added tax of certain goods imported in the personal luggage of persons travelling from third countries. All goods which are admitted exempt from excise duty and/or value-added tax under these Regulations are also admitted free of customs duties in accordance with the provisions of Article 45 (as replaced by Article 1 paragraph 4 of Council Regulation (EC) No. 274/2008) of Council Regulation (EEC) No. 918/83.

List of
Statements of Practice
& Information Leaflets

STATEMENTS OF PRACTICE & INFORMATION LEAFLETS
In chronological order

VAT Treatment of Goods and Services Sold Together (Value-Added Tax Information Leaflet No. 3/06) *[Replaced by Value-Added Tax Information Leaflet July 2007]*

VAT Treatment of Dances (Value-Added Tax Information Leaflet No. 4/06) *[Replaced by Value-Added Tax Information Leaflet April 2007]*

Gifts, self-supplies, Industrial Samples, Replacement Goods, Promotional Schemes, Gift Vouchers, Gift Tokens (Value-Added Tax Information Leaflet No. 5/06) *[Replaced by Value-Added Tax Information Leaflet October 2008]*

Solicitors (Value-Added Tax Information Leaflet January 2007) *[Replaced by Value-Added Tax Information Leaflet December 08]*

Special Scheme for Retailers (Value-Added Tax Information Leaflet January 2007) *[Replaced by Value-Added Tax Information Leaflet December 08]*

Repayments to Unregistered Persons (Value-Added Tax Information Leaflet January 2007) *[Replaced by Value-Added Tax Information Leaflet October 08]*

Advertising Services (Value-Added Tax Information Leaflet March 2007) *[Replaced by Value-Added Tax Information Leaflet December 08]*

Building and Associated Services (Value-Added Tax Information Leaflet March 2007) *[Replaced by Value-Added Tax Information Leaflet August 2007]*

Distance Sales (Value-Added Tax Information Leaflet March 2007) *[Replaced by Value-Added Tax Information Leaflet October 08]*

Expression of Doubt (Value-Added Tax Information Leaflet March 2007) *[Replaced by Value-Added Tax Information Leaflet October 08]*

Moneys Received Basis of Accounting (Value-Added Tax Information Leaflet March 2007) *[Replaced by Value-Added Tax Information Leaflet October 08]*

Margin Scheme – Second-Hand Goods (Value-Added Tax Information Leaflet March 2007) *[Replaced by Value-Added Tax Information Leaflet June 2007]*

Sports Facilities (Value-Added Tax Information Leaflet March 2007) *[Replaced by Value-Added Tax Information Leaflet October 08]*

Veterinary Services (Value-Added Tax Information Leaflet March 2007) *[Replaced by Value-Added Tax Information Leaflet December 08]*

Zero-rating of goods and services (Value-Added Tax Information Leaflet March 2007) *[Replaced by Value-Added Tax Information Leaflet December 08]*

Dances (Value-Added Tax Information Leaflet April 2007) *[Replaced by Value-Added Tax Information Leaflet December 08]*

Alcohol Products (Value-Added Tax Information Leaflet June 2007) *[Replaced by Value-Added Tax Information Leaflet October 08]*

Conferences –VAT Deductibility (Value-Added Tax Information Leaflet June 2007) *[Replaced by Value-Added Tax Information Leaflet October 08]*

Footwear (Value-Added Tax Information Leaflet June 2007) *[Replaced by Value-Added Tax Information Leaflet December 08]*

Hire Purchase Transactions (Value-Added Tax Information Leaflet June 2007) *[Replaced by Value-Added Tax Information Leaflet December 08]*

Margin Scheme (Value-Added Tax Information Leaflet June 2007) *[Replaced by Value-Added Tax Information Leaflet December 08]*

Theatrical & Musical Events (Value-Added Tax Information Leaflet June 2007) *[Replaced by Value-Added Tax Information Leaflet December 08]*

Agricultural Services (Value-Added Tax Information Leaflet June 2007) *[Replaced by Value-Added Tax Information Leaflet December 08]*

eServices & Broadcasting (Value-Added Tax Information Leaflet July 2007) *[Replaced by Value-Added Tax Information Leaflet October 08]*

EU Intra-Community Acquisitions (Value-Added Tax Information Leaflet July 2007) *[Replaced by Value-Added Tax Information Leaflet December 08]*

EU Intra-Community Supplies (Value-Added Tax Information Leaflet July 2007) *[Replaced by Value-Added Tax Information Leaflet October 08]*

STATEMENTS OF PRACTICE & INFORMATION LEAFLETS

In alphabetical order

Accommodation, 'Emergency' Accommodation, Including Accommodation Provided for Asylum Seekers and Homeless People, and Ancillary Services	No. 1/01
Advertising Services	SP-VAT/03/92 *[Replaced by Mar 2007]*
Advertising Services	Mar 2007 *[Replaced by Dec 2008]*
Advertising Services	Dec 2008
Agricultural Services	SP-VAT/05/92 *[Replaced No. 23/01]*
Agricultural Services	No. 23/01 *[Replaced by Jul 2007]*
Agricultural Services	Jul 2007 *[Replaced by Dec 2008]*
Agricultural Services	Dec 2008
Alcohol Products, Payment of VAT at Time of Payment of Excise Duty	SP-VAT/03/93 *[Replaced by Jun 2007]*
Alcohol Products	Jun 2007 *[Replaced by Oct 2008]*
Alcohol Products	Oct 2008
Auctioneers, and Auction and Agency sales, VAT treatment of	No. 5/98 *[Replaced by Aug 2007]*
Auctioneering	Aug 2007 *[Replaced by Dec 2008]*
Auctioneering	Dec 2008
Building and Associated Services, VAT Treatment of	No. 2/99 (updated 01.01.2003) *[Replaced by Mar 2007]*
Building and Associated Services	March 2007 *[Replaced by Aug 2007]*
Building and Associated Services	Aug 2007
Cars, Vehicles Registered by Distributors or Dealers Prior to Sale, New VAT treatment of	May 2003
Charities, Value Added Tax in the Case of	Jun 1999
Clothing, VAT and	No. 2/05
Conferences, VAT Deductibility	Jun 2007 *[Replaced by Oct 2008]*
Conferences, VAT Deductibility	Oct 2008
Construction Contractors: Construction Services new rules	Jun 2008
Construction Contractors: Reverse Charge	Jun 2008
Cultural, Artistic And Entertainment Services Supplied By Non-Established Persons, VAT Treatment of	No. 3/02
Dances, VAT on	SP-VAT/06/92 *[Replaced by No. 20/01]*
Dances, VAT on	No. 20/01 *[Replaced by No. 4/06]*
Dances, VAT on	No. 4/06 *[Replaced by Apr 2007]*
Dances, VAT on	April 2007 *[Replaced by Dec 2008]*
Dances	Dec 2008
Deductible tax (Input credit)	SP-VAT/02/90

Deposits: Changes to Treatment for VAT purposes on forfeited deposits and cancellation charges	Sept 2008
Distance Sales in Single Market	SP-VAT 14/92 *[Replaced by No. 08/01]*
Distance Sales in the Single Market	No. 8/01 *[Replaced by Mar 2007]*
Distance Sales in EU	March 2007 *[Replaced by Oct 2008]*
Distance Sales	Oct 2008
Doubt, Expression of, A Letter of	No. 2/02 *[Replaced by Mar 2007]*
Doubt, Expression of	March 2007
Doubt, Expression of, A Letter of	No. 2/02 *[Replaced by Mar 2007]*
Doubt, Expression of	March 2007
Duty-Free Sales, Tax-Free Purchases for non-EU Tourists	Apr 1998
Duty-Free Sales to Travellers on Intra-Community Journeys, Abolition of	SP-VAT 01/99
Electricity Market	Nov 2007
Electronically Supplied Services and Radio and Television Broadcasting Services	No. 2/03 *[Replaced by Jul 2007]*
e-Services and Broadcasting	Jul 2007 *[Replaced by Oct 2008]*
e-Services and Broadcasting	Oct 2008
Exempt Persons Acquiring Goods from other EU Member States, Financial Institutions, Insurance Companies, Theatres, Providers of Passenger Transport and other exempt persons	No. 13/01
Expression of Doubt	Mar 2007 *[Replaced by Oct 2008]*
Expression of Doubt	Oct 2008
Factoring	Oct 2008
Farmers and Intra-EU Transactions	No. 12/01 *[Replaced by Aug 2007]*
Farmers and Intra-EU Transactions	Aug 2007 *[Replaced by Dec 2008]*
Farmers and Intra-EU Transactions	Dec 2008
Farmers, Flat Rate and the Single Market	SP-VAT/02/93 *[Replaced by No. 12/01]*
Food and Drink, Rates of VAT on from 1/11/1992	SP-VAT 10/92 *[Replaced by No. 19/01]*
Food and Drink, Rates of VAT on	No. 19/01 *[Replaced by Jul 2007]*
Food and Drink	Jul 2007 *[Replaced by Dec 2008]*
Food and Drink	Dec 2008
Footwear, Value-Added Tax and	No. 1/98 *[Replaced by No. 31/01]*
Footwear, Value-Added Tax and	No. 31/01 *[Replaced by Jun 2007]*
Footwear	Jun 2007 *[Replaced by Dec 2008]*
Footwear	Dec 2008
Foreign Firms Doing Business in Ireland	No. 1/99 *[Replaced by Aug 2007]*
Foreign Firms Doing Business in Ireland	Aug 2007 *[Replaced by Oct 2008]*
Foreign Suppliers Doing Business in Ireland	Oct 2008
Fourth Schedule Services, liability of Recipients on Certain Services Received from Abroad	SP-VAT/01/90 *[Replaced by SP-VAT/05/94]*

Fourth Schedule Services	SP-VAT/05/94 *[Replaced by No. 9/01]*
Fourth Schedule Services	No. 9/01 *[Replaced by No. 1/05]*
Fourth Schedule Services	No. 1/05 *[Replaced by Jul 2007]*
Fourth Schedule Services	Jul 2007 *[Replaced by Dec 2008]*
Fourth Schedule Services	Dec 2008
Gifts, VAT and	SP-VAT/03/94 *[Replaced by No. 14/01]*
Gifts, VAT and	No. 14/01 *[Replaced by No. 5/06]*
Gifts, VAT and	No. 5/06 *[Replaced by Oct 2008]*
Gifts and Promotional Items	Oct 2008
Golf and Other Sporting Activities, Changes in the VAT Treatment of	SP-VAT/01/95 *[Replaced by Aug 2007]*
Golf	Aug 2007 *[Replaced by Oct 2008]*
Golf	Oct 2008
Goods, Intra-Community Supplies	No. 26/01 *[Replaced by Jul 2007]*
Goods, Intra-Community Supplies	Jul 2007 *[Replaced by Oct 2008]*
Goods, Intra-Community Supplies	Oct 2008
Goods and Services Sold Together, VAT Treatment of	No. 3/06 *[Replaced by Jul 2007]*
Goods and Services Sold Together	Jul 2007 *[Replaced by Dec 2008]*
Goods and Services Sold Together	Dec 2008
Hire Purchase Transactions	Jun 2007 *[Replaced by Dec 2008]*
Hire Purchase Transactions	Dec 2008
Horticultural Retailers	SP-VAT/01/97 *[Replaced by No. 24/01]*
Horticultural Retailers	No. 24/01 *[Replaced by Jul 2007]*
Horticultural Retailers	Jul 2007 *[Replaced by Dec 2008]*
Horticultural Retailers	Dec 2008
Horses, live	SP-VAT/03/90
Imports/Exports, Automated Entry Processing for	SP-VAT/02/91
Invoicing, Electronic (EDI)	SP-VAT 09/92
Invoicing, VAT Treatment of	No. 1/06 *[Replaced by Oct 2008]*
Invoicing, VAT Treatment of	Oct 2008
Leasing of Means of Transport, VAT Treatment of International	No. 3/99 *[Replaced by Aug 2007]*
Leasing (International) of Means of Transport	Aug 2007 *[Replaced by Oct 2008]*
Leasing (International) of Means of Transport	Oct 2008
Letting, Post-letting Expenses, Claims for repayment of VAT arising out of the Supreme Court Judgement in the case of Erin Executor and Trustee Company Limited, for periods prior to 27 March, 1998	No. 3/98
Letting, Post-letting expenses incurred on or after 27 March, 1998, VAT treatment of	No. 4/98
Milk Production Partnerships, VAT Issues for	No. 1/04

Moneys Received Basis of Accounting, changes Relating to the	SP-VAT/02/92
Moneys Received Basis of Accounting	SP-VAT/16/92 *[Replaced by No. 22/01]*
Moneys Received or "Cash" Basis of Accounting	No. 22/01 *[Replaced by Mar 2007]*
Moneys Received Basis of Accounting	March 2007 *[Replaced by Oct 2008]*
Moneys Received Basis of Accounting	Oct 2008
Monthly Control Statement	SP-VAT/07/92
Motor Vehicles: Deduction of VAT on certain cars	Feb 2009
Motor Vehicles: VAT and VRT on Transactions involving Motor Vehicles	Jan 2009
Musical and Theatrical Events (Including Performances by Non-Established Performers), Live, VAT Treatment of the promotion of and Admission to	No. 2/06 *[Replaced by Jun 2007]*
Musical and Theatrical Events (Including Performances by Non-Established Performers), Live, VAT Treatment of the promotion of and Admission to	Jun 2007 *[Replaced by Dec 2008]*
Non Taxable Entities Acquiring Goods between EC Countries after 1/1/93	SP-VAT/11/92 *[Replaced by No. 11/01]*
Photography	Dec 2008
Plant and Machinery	Oct 1998 *[Replaced by Dec 2008]*
Plant and Machinery	Dec 2008
Postponed Accounting and Intra-Community Acquisitions	SP-VAT 15/92 *[Replaced by No. 07/01]*
Postponed Accounting and Intra-Community Acquisitions	No. 7/01 *[Replaced by Jul 2007]*
Postponed Accounting and Intra-Community Acquisitions	Jul 2007 *[Replaced by Dec 2008]*
Postponed Accounting and Intra-Community Acquisitions	Dec 2008
Printing and Printed Matter	No. 10/01 *[Replaced by Aug 2007]*
Printing and Printed Matter	Aug 2007 *[Replaced by Dec 2008]*
Printing and Printed Matter	Dec 2008
Promotional Schemes, European court of Justice (ECJ) Judgements in relation to the VAT Treatment of	No. 6/98 *[Replaced by No. 14/01]*
Property: Frequently Asked Questions	Dec 2008
Property: Section 4(8) VAT Act 1972	Jun 2004
Property: Services vis Foreign Property	Dec 2007 *[Replaced by Dec 2008]*
Property: Services vis Foreign Property	Dec 2008
VAT; Summary and Checklist	May 2008
Property: The 10% Rule	Jun 2004
Property: VAT Multiplier	Jun 2004 *[Replaced by Oct 2008]*
Property: VAT Multiplier	Oct 2008
Rate Change – Budget 2009	Oct 2008
Rates of VAT on Services from 1 March 1991	SP-VAT/01/91

Rates of VAT on Services from 1 March 1992	SP-VAT/01/92
Relief from Customs Duty and VAT on goods to be used by Monarchs or Heads of State and individuals with Diplomatic status (Diplomatic Privilege)	Aug 2007
Relief from Customs Duty and VAT on goods to be used by Monarchs or Heads of State and individu-als with Diplomatic status (Diplomatic Privilege)	Sept 2008
Relief from Customs Duty and VAT on honorary decorations, awards and goodwill presents	Aug 2007
Relief from Customs Duty and VAT on the importation of articles for the Blind	Aug 2007
Relief from Customs Duty and VAT on the importation of articles for the Handicapped and Disabled	Aug 2007
Relief from Customs Duty and VAT on the importation of certain substances of a therapeutic or medical-related nature	Aug 2007
Relief from Customs Duty and VAT on the importation of Coffins, Funerary Urns and Ornamental Funeral Articles	Aug 2007
Relief from Customs Duty and VAT on the importation of consignments sent to Organisations protecting copyrights or industrial and commercial patent rights	Aug 2007
Relief from Customs Duty and VAT on the importation of goods for Charitable and Humanitarian Organisations	Aug 2007
Relief from Customs Duty and VAT on the importation of goods for Disaster Victims	Aug 2007
Relief from Customs Duty and VAT on the importation of goods for examination, analysis or test purposes	Aug 2007
Relief from Customs Duty and VAT on the importation of litter, fodder and feeding stuffs for animals during their transport	Aug 2007
Relief from Customs Duty and VAT on the importation of materials for the construction, upkeep or ornamentation of Memorials to, or Cemeteries for, War Victims	Aug 2007
Relief from Customs Duty and VAT on the importation of miscellaneous documents and articles	Aug 2007
Relief from Customs Duty and VAT on the importation of pharmaceutical products	Aug 2007

Relief from Customs Duty and VAT on the importation of student goods	Aug 2007 *[Replaced by Oct 2008]*
Relief from Customs Duty and VAT on the importation of student goods	Oct 2008
Repayments to Unregistered Persons	SP-VAT/02/94 *[Replaced by No. 18/01]*
Repayments to Unregistered Persons	No. 18/01 *[Replaced by Jan 2007]*
Repayments to Unregistered Persons	Jan 2007 *[Replaced by Oct 2008]*
Repayments to Unregistered Persons	Oct 2008
Research Services Carried out by Third Level Educational Bodies	No. 2/01
Retail Export Scheme	SP-VAT/09/94
Retail Export Scheme (Tax-Free Shopping for Tour-ists)	Apr 1998 *[Replaced by Jul 2008]*
Retail Export Scheme (Tax-Free Shopping for Tour-ists)	Jul 2008
Retailers Special Schemes	Jan 2007 *[Replaced by Dec 2008]*
Retailers Special Schemes	Dec 2008
Second Hand Goods, VAT Treatment of (The Margin Scheme)	Dec 1994 *[Replaced by No. 17/01]*
Second-hand Goods - The Margin Scheme, VAT Treatment of	No. 17/01 *[Replaced by Mar 2007]*
Second-Hand Goods – Margin Scheme	March 2007 *[Replaced by Jun 2007]*
Second-Hand Goods – Margin Scheme	Jun 2007 *[Replaced by Dec 2008]*
Second-Hand Goods – Margin Scheme	Dec 2008
Second-Hand Vehicles, VAT Treatment of	Oct 1995
Service Changes in Hotels and Restaurants (With-drawal of Concession)	Oct 2008
Solicitors, VAT and	April 1988 *[Replaced by No. 15/01]*
Solicitors, VAT and	No. 15/01 *[Replaced by Jan 2007]*
Solicitors, VAT and	Jan 2007 *[Replaced by Dec 2008]*
Solicitors, VAT and	Dec 2008
Sporting Activities and Golf, Changes in the VAT Treatment of	SP-VAT/01/95
Sports Facilities	SP-VAT/04/92 *[Replaced by Mar 2007]*
Sports Facilities	March 2007 *[Replaced by Oct 2008]*
Sports Facilities	Oct 2008
State Bodies etc. Acquiring goods from other EU Member States, Government Departments, Local Authorities, Health Boards, Hospitals, Educational Bodies, and other Non-Taxable Entities	No. 11/01
State Procurement	Aug 2007 *[Replaced by Jan 2009]*
State Procurement	Jan 2009
Telecommunications Services, VAT on	No. 7/98
Theatrical and Musical Events (Including Performances by Non-Established Performers), Live, VAT Treatment of the promotion of and Admission to	No. 2/06 *[Replaced by Jun 2007]*
Theatrical and Musical Events	Jun 2007 *[Replaced by Dec 2008]*

Theatrical and Musical Events	[Dec 2008]
Transfer of a Business or Part Thereof	No. 1/02 *[Replaced by Sept 2007]*
Transfer of a Business or Part Thereof	Sept 2007
Transport, Goods and, Ancillary Service, Intra-Community	SP-VAT 12/92 *[Replaced by No. 16/01]*
Transport, Goods and, Ancillary Services between EU Countries, VAT Treatment of	No. 16/01 *[Replaced by Aug 2007]*
Transport of Goods and Ancillary Services within the EU	Aug 2007 *[Replaced by Oct 2008]*
Transport of Goods and Ancillary Services within the EU	Oct 2008
Veterinary Services	SP-VAT/03/91 *[Replaced by Mar 2007]*
Veterinary Services	March 2007 *[Replaced by Dec 2008]*
Veterinary Services	Dec 2008
Zero Rate, Sales and Deliveries of Goods to other EC Member States after 1 January 1993, Application of the	SP-VAT/08/92
Zero-rating, Goods and Services in Accordance with Section 13A of the VAT Act	SP-VAT/01/93
Zero-rating, Goods and Services in Accordance with Section 13A of the VAT Act	No. 21/01 *[Replaced by Mar 2007]*
Zero-rating of Goods and Services	March 2007 *[Replaced by Dec 2008]*
Zero-rating of Goods and Services - Section 13A	Dec 2008

STATEMENT OF PRACTICE SP-VAT/02/90

DEDUCTIBLE TAX

(INPUT CREDIT)

1.   At a recent meeting of the EC VAT Committee in Brussels, it was agreed that any expenses incurred in relation to buying or selling shares relate to an exempt activity and therefore do not qualify for input credit.

2.   Accordingly no input credit may be allowed in respect of any costs directly attributable to the buying or the selling of shares.

3.   No change in practice is envisaged in relation to

   (a)   supplies to non EC customers (sections 12(1) and 13(3) of VAT Act 1972, as amended), or

   (b)   transfer of a business or part thereof (Section 3(5)(b)(iii) of VAT Act 1972, as amended).

STATEMENT OF PRACTICE SP-VAT/03/90

LIVE HORSES

General

1. With effect from 1 January 1991, the supply (sale), importation and leasing of horses will become liable to VAT at the rate of 2.3%. This means that the exemption which live horses have enjoyed since September 1973, will come to an end, and horses will be treated in the same way for VAT purposes as cattle, goats, sheep, pigs and deer. In effect the breeding and rearing of horses will be regarded as a farming activity and VAT at 2.3% will be applied to the sale price of horses.

2. While all imports of horses will become liable to VAT at 2.3% from 1 January 1991, (see paragraphs 7, 18 and 23), insofar as transactions within the State are concerned, only supplies and leasings of horses which are made by a taxable person, in the course or furtherance of business, will come within the scope of the tax. For example, a taxable person who sells his child's riding pony will not be regarded as making a supply in the course of business, whereas a VAT registered breeder of childrens' ponies would. Likewise VAT payable on the purchase or importation of horses by taxable persons for non-business use may not be offset against output tax.

3. The term "live horses" has not been defined but it may be taken to cover all horses, including thoroughbreds, draught horses, foals, ponies, asses, mules and hinnies. In the practical administration of the tax the Revenue Commissioners will be prepared to regard the sale of nominations in stallions and part-ownership and shares in stallions and mares as supplies (sales) of horses also.

4. The existing treatment of dead animals will not be affected by the change. Dead horses will continue to qualify for the zero rate, although the separate supply of hides, skins and horsehair will remain liable at 23%. The sale of live horses for slaughter will not qualify for the zero rate unless, of course, sold for export by the supplier.

5. Horses will not be regarded as "means of transport" for the purpose of determining the place of supply of horse leasing services (see paragraph 16).

6. The Taxable Amount: Supplies (sales) within the State

The amount on which VAT is chargeable is "...the total consideration which the person supplying goods or services becomes entitled to receive in respect of or in relation to such supply of goods or services, including all taxes, commissions, costs and charges whatsoever, but not including value added tax, chargeable in respect of the supply". It is emphasised that the amount which is taxable is the amount excluding VAT which a taxable person becomes entitled to receive. If an auctioneer knocks down a horse to a bidder for £9,600 and adds, say £500 for commission and, say, a further £400 for other fees, giving a total of £10,500 excluding VAT he will have a liability of £241.50 (2.3% of £10,500). The amount actually payable to the Revenue will be the difference between this liability and the credits or deductions allowable (see paragraphs 8, 9 and Appendix II). Although the auctioneer is the person responsible for paying the tax to the Revenue, in practice he will pass the tax on to the buyer.

7. **The Taxable Amount: Imports**

For the purposes of assessing the VAT payable at importation the value of the imported horses will be their value for customs purposes, determined on a delivery-to-State basis together with any taxes, duties or other charges levied outside or inside the State (excluding VAT - see paragraphs 12.5 and 12.11 of "Guide to the Value Added Tax").

As a general rule where the horse has been recently purchased prior to import, VAT will be payable on the purchase price. Horses imported for sale by auction in cases where the auctioneer is acting as importer for that auction will be valued at the average value for that particular sale the previous year. For horses imported in other circumstances the importer will be required to furnish a declared value which should reflect the open market value of the animal. It is a requirement of law that the cost of transport and insurance of the horses be included in all cases. (Inquiries concerning the question of valuations at importation should be made to C & E Division 6, Castle House).

8. **Relief from VAT on Purchases and Imports**

A taxable person who is registered and accounting for VAT is entitled to claim a deduction (or credit) in his next following VAT return in respect of most goods and services purchased or imported for the purposes of the business for which he is taxable once he is in possession of a proper VAT invoice or a stamped copy of the customs entry, as appropriate. The invoice does not have to be paid before claiming the deduction. The only tax for which a deduction may not be taken is tax relating to expenditure on hotel, etc. expenses, entertainment expenses, the purchase or hire of cars and other passenger vehicles and petrol and on goods or services for exempt or private activities. No deduction is allowable in respect of purchases relating to exempted activities. Where a person has both taxable and exempt supplies his input tax will have to be apportioned, usually, on the basis of the ratio which taxable turnover bears to total turnover. Horse-racing, hunting etc. are not regarded as business activities, therefore, VAT incurred on training, racing, etc. expenses is not deductible.

9. **Farmers (Including Stud Farmers)**

For VAT purposes a farmer is a person who engages in agricultural production on land which he owns or occupies, and who does not engage in non-agricultural activities except on a moderate scale (i.e. from which he derives annual turnover of less than £15,000 - see Chapter 20 of VAT

Guide). A farmer is not obliged to register for VAT but may elect to do so. Farmers who elect to register are subject to the normal requirements of the VAT system, and are obliged to keep records and submit returns in the same way as other registered persons. With effect from 1 January 1991, a VAT registered farmer who sells or leases horses will be obliged to account for VAT on the transactions at 2.3%. A stud farmer is a farmer for VAT purposes.

The effect of treating the breeding, rearing and supply (sale) of horses as a farming activity means that:

(1)   Persons engaged in these activities will be treated as farmers for VAT purposes, subject to the above requirements;

(2)   sales of horses by unregistered farmers to VAT registered purchasers will qualify for the 2.3% flat-rate addition to prices.

The VAT element in expenditure incurred by unregistered farmers in the erection or alteration of farm buildings or in the draining or reclamation of land may be reclaimed subject to conditions (see paragraphs 19.4/19.6 of VAT Guide).

10.   Sales of Horses by Unregistered Farmers

A farmer who does not elect to register for VAT is entitled under the VAT system to a flat-rate addition (at present 2.3%) to the prices at which he sells his produce to VAT registered purchasers. This flat-rate addition (together with the scheme of refund of VAT on expenditure relating to farm buildings and land reclamation - see paragraph 9 above) is intended to compensate the unregistered farmer for VAT borne on most of his purchases. With effect from 1 January 1991, horses will come within the scope of the flat-rate addition system which works as follows:

	£
An unregistered farmer sells a horse to a VAT registered breeder for, say,	10,000
The flat-rate addition at 2.3% is	230
The price paid to the farmer is	10,230

The breeder provided he is in possession of an invoice which he must prepare showing separately the purchase price and the 2.3% addition may claim back £230 in his next VAT return.

11.   Sales of Horses by VAT Registered Farmers

Farmers who elect to register for VAT although under no obligation to do so will be liable for VAT at 2.3% on their sales or leasings of horses as from 1 January 1991. The flat-rate addition will not apply to sales by registered farmers. Purchases of horses made by them from unregistered farmers will be subject to the treatment described in paragraph 10.

See Appendix I for the rates of VAT applicable to a range of goods and services appropriate to the industry.

12. Sales of Horses through Auctioneers and Bloodstock Agents

The sale of horses through auctioneers and other agents will be treated from 1 January 1991, in the same way as the sale of other livestock, i.e. cattle, sheep, pigs, goats and deer. The horses for sale will be treated as being simultaneously bought and sold by the auctioneer or agent. The effect will be to cause the commission and other fees receivable by the auctioneer or agent in respect of such sale to be treated as taxable at the same rate as the sale of horse, that is at 2.3%.

If the seller is an unregistered farmer the auctioneer or agent will be entitled to set off against his own VAT liability a deduction equal to the flat rate addition, that is 2.3% of the VAT exclusive purchase price. An example of how the arrangement works is given in Appendix II. If the seller is a VAT registered farmer the auctioneer or agent will be entitled to claim against the tax payable on the sale the 2.3% invoiced to him by such farmer. Auctioneers and bloodstock agents will be obliged to register if their annual turnover exceeds £32,000.

13. Syndicates

Sales of nominations in stallions and sales of shares and part-ownership in stallions and mares will be treated in the same way as sales of horses, that is, VAT will be chargeable at the 2.3% rate on the amount receivable by a taxable person. A stallion syndicate will not itself be regarded as a taxable person for VAT purposes and VAT incurred in connection with the administration of a syndicate will not be recoverable by the syndicate or its members. Members of the syndicates as co-owners of the stallions will be treated for VAT purposes in accordance with each member's individual VAT status as regards any sales of nominations. For example:

(1)   An unregistered farmer will have no liability on sale of his nomination, but would be entitled to the flat-rate addition to the sale price where the nomination is sold to a taxable breeder;

(2)   A taxable person will be liable at 2.3% on his receipts from sale of nominations.

14. Horses Applied to Non-Business Use

Where a taxable owner or breeder transfers to racing, show-jumping, hunting etc. horses which he has bred, purchased or imported in connection with his taxable business, such transfers will be deemed to be taxable supplies and will attract liability to VAT on the basis of the cost of the animals, excluding VAT, to the supplier. VAT incurred thereafter on training and racing expenses is not deductible. Once a horse has been transferred to training for racing etc., and VAT accounted for, any further transactions will not give rise to a VAT liability unless the animal is re-applied to business use by a taxable person as a stallion or brood-mare or sold at auction.

15. Racehorse Training

The training of horses for racing is already liable to VAT at the rate of 23%. The amount on which tax is chargeable is that part of the total fee which relates to training only, i.e., normally 10% of the trainer's gross fee. Racehorse training services are treated for VAT purposes as being in effect a separate business from farming. This position will not be affected by the new provisions. (See VAT Guide - paragraphs 20.22/20.24 and leaflet entitled "Racehorse Trainers").

16. Leasing of Horses: Services Received from Abroad

Leasing of horses will be liable at 2.3%.

This service, although supplied from Ireland, will, in certain circumstances, be treated as supplied abroad and not subject to Irish VAT if the lessee is resident or established outside the State.

Conversely, this service, although supplied from abroad, will be treated as supplied in Ireland an subject to Irish VAT if the lessee is resident or established in Ireland and the service is received for business purposes. In these circumstances the lessee will be responsible for paying over the tax.

A "flat-rate" farmer, obliged to register for VAT solely on account of his liability on services received from abroad (leasing, advertising, consultancy etc.), may retain his "flat-rate" farmer status insofar as his farming activities are concerned, as described in paragraph 9. The matter is explained in greater detail in a leaflet entitled "Liability of Recipients on certain Services received from Abroad".

17. Sales of Horses by Foreign Farmers

The flat rate addition will not apply to sales by farmers from outside the State to VAT registered persons in the State. Therefore in the case of horses imported for sale at the bloodstock auction sales there can be no question of a flat-rate addition to the purchase price. The import of such horses will be liable at 2.3% (but see next paragraph).

18. Horses imported for Sale by Auction

Horses imported for sale in the State will be liable to VAT in the usual way. VAT will be payable at time of importation unless the importer has been approved under the scheme for Deferred Payment under which payment may be deferred until the fifteenth day of the month following the month in which payment became due (see paragraph 22).

Where horses are imported for sale by auction, VAT registered auctioneers may avail themselves of the deferred payment scheme and undertake such importation without payment of VAT at time of importation using deferred payment facilities. The auctioneer by special arrangement undertakes liability for the VAT payable at importation which he may in due course offset against his VAT liability. The auctioneer must account for VAT at 2.3% on the ultimate sale of the horse unless of course, the horse is sold for export when the zero rate will apply. If the horse is not sold at auction the auctioneer must account for VAT at 2.3% unless the horse is re-exported.

19. Exports

Horses sold for export are liable to VAT at the zero rate. In order to qualify for the zero rate it is a requirement that the horses be transported outside the State directly by or on behalf of the seller who is required to retain proof of export, that is, a stamped copy of the Single Administrative Document (SAD - see Chapter 13 of VAT Guide).

20. Horses sold by approved Auctioneers to Overseas Purchasers

Under an arrangement peculiar to the bloodstock industry a sale to an overseas purchaser can be zero rated even though the horse may not be exported immediately. The arrangement may be operated by auctioneers who have been approved by the Revenue Commissioners for that purpose and who have undertaken responsibility for its administration. Under the arrangement a horse sold with an export undertaking may be zero rated provided the horse is exported within 24 months of the date of supply or, in the case of yearlings purchased after 1 September of any year, is exported within 28 months of purchase. If the horse is subsequently sold in the State or not exported within the required time limits VAT will have to be accounted for by the original vendor (i.e. the auctioneer).

Auctioneers wishing to participate in the scheme should apply to their local tax office and must be prepared to abide by the conditions imposed by the Revenue Commissioners.

21. Relief from Import VAT for Certain Permanent Importers of Horses

A horse acquired by a private (non-taxable) person whether as a gift or otherwise from a private (non-taxable) person in another Member State of the E.C., may qualify for relief at importation in respect of the residual part of the value added tax paid in the exporting Member State. (Inquiries on this and other matters concerning permanent importations and certain re-importations - see paragraph 26 - should be made to C & E Division 4, Castle House.)

There is provision for relief from VAT at importation in the case of pure-bred foals of not more than six months of age born outside the State of an animal covered in the State and then exported temporarily to give birth.

(Inquiries on this relief should be made to C & E Division 1, Dublin Castle.)

22. Deferred Payment of Import VAT

Provision exists for deferment of payment of VAT at importation to the 15 day of the month following the month of importation. The essential feature of the scheme is that Collectors of Customs and Excise, with the authority of the importer or his agent, initiate payment by the issue of a direct debit voucher drawn on the importer's or agent's bank. Details are contained in Public Notice 1183D (Rev 1) which is available from any Custom House.

Importers or agents who are not approved for deferred payment or who do not fulfil all the conditions of the scheme will be required to pay VAT at the time of importation.

23. Temporary Importation of Horses

The various reliefs from payment of VAT, subject to conditions, for horses temporarily imported into the State are as follows:

	Circumstances of importation	Period of relief	Security required	Documentary requirement
(1)	EC Carnet Racehorses only Other horses	6 months 2 years	No	Carnet Entry Sheet Carnet Entry Sheet
(2)	ATA Carnet for exhibition at, or participation	1 year in an event.	No	Importation counterfoil
(3)	Horses for exhibition at, or participation in an event.	2 years	Yes	Form No. 1047
(4)	Horses imported for dressage, training or breeding purposes, or for veterinary treatment.	2 years	Yes	Form No. 1047
(5)	Horses imported for grazing purposes.	2 years	No	Oral declaration plus inventory
(6)	Second-hand horses imported for sale by auction.	6 months	Yes	Form No. 1047

With the exception of imports under cover of the ATA Carnet (see (2) above) relief from import VAT is available for horses in free circulation owned by non-State residents which are imported, for any purpose, from other Member States provided the horses were acquired under the normal VAT provisions of the Member State of exportation and did not benefit from relief by virtue of exportation.

VAT relief is also available for horses owned by either State or non-State residents imported in the circumstances set out in (2) to (5) above from EEC or non EEC countries. However, in cases (3) to (5), relief is not available for horses imported from another Member State which are owned by State residents who are not taxable persons or, if taxable, are not entitled to deduction of tax in full, where (i) the horses are in free circulation and (ii) the horses were not acquired under the normal VAT provisions of the Member States of exportation or benefited for VAT relief by virtue of exportation.

Second-hand horses should be taken to mean "horses which had been applied for racing or other non-business use which usage has now come to an end". These animals may be temporarily imported for sale by auction only where ownership remains outside the State.

In relation to (3) to (5) above the Revenue Commissioners may, in exceptional circumstances and at their absolute discretion, on application of the person to whom relief has been granted, extend the time limit allowed from 2 years to 2 years and 8 months.

In relation to (1) above, the Revenue Commissioners may, at the request of the beneficiary, extend the period of validity of the E.C. Movement Carnet on the basis of the expected duration and nature of the operation planned. (Inquiries concerning temporary importations should be made to C & E Division 1, Dublin Castle.)

24. Re-Importation of Horses

Horses which are re-imported after having been temporarily abroad may be re-imported by the person who exported them without payment of VAT provided they have not been subjected to any process while abroad. For example, a colt sent to Epsom to run in the Derby would not be subject to VAT on its return. However, a mare sent for service to a stallion in the U.K. on its return in foal would be liable to VAT on the basis of the cost of nomination, insurance, transport, etc.

25. Foreign Breeders suffering Irish VAT

The position regarding foreign breeders suffering Irish VAT is no different from that of foreign business persons generally. Such person may, subject to conditions, claim repayment of Irish VAT on most goods and services purchased in Ireland (see Chapter 19.24 of VAT Guide). It should, however, be noted that foreign racehorse owners would not, as a general rule, be entitled to relief for Irish VAT on expenditure connected with their horse racing activities since these would not normally be regarded as business activities.

26. Registration for VAT

Applications for registration should be made to the local tax office (see VAT Guide for addresses and telephone numbers).

APPENDIX I

RATES OF VAT (This list is not exhaustive)

Accommodation of horses	if letting only of paddocks, stables letting, minding, etc. supplied by unregistered farmers letting, minding, etc. supplied by others	-exempt - not taxable - 23%
Boxes, horse		- 23%
Bridles		- 23%
Exports of horses		- zero
Farriers' services	- repair and maintenance of hooves - supply and fitting of shoes	- 10% - 23%
Feeding and keeping of horses	by unregistered farmers Other	- not taxable - 10%
Horses	supply of live horses by - unregistered farmers - other - hiring/leasing by unregistered farmers - other - exports - dead horses - hides - horsehair	 - not taxable - 2.3% - not taxable - 2.3% - zero - zero - 23% - 23%
Imports of horses	- permanent - temporary	- 23% - see para.
Insurance and agency services relating thereto	- Intra – E.C. - Outside – E.C.	- exempt - zero
Jockeys' services		- 23%
Livery	- see feeding and keeping	
Nominations	- by unregistered farmers - other mares in the ownership of foreigners imported for service by stallions owned by taxable persons and afterwards exported	- not taxable - 2.3% - zero
Pedigree Research		- 23%
Pony Trekking		- 23%
Prize money		- not taxable
Racing admissions		- exempt
Racehorse training		- 23%
Repair services		- 10%

Riding schools		- exempt
Show jumping admissions		- exempt
Stabling of horses	- see accommodation	
Stables, Erection of		- 10%
Swimming pools for horses	- lettings	- exempt
Tack		- 23%
Transport	- within the State - international	- 23% - zero
Valets' services		- 23%

APPENDIX II

Sale of a horse by an unregistered farmer through an auctioneer (or bloodstock agent) to another unregistered farmer.

The accepted bid price excluding VAT, is 10,000 guineas (£10,500).
The auctioneer's commission is 5% which is charged entirely to the vendor.

The auctioneer is deem to have bought the horse from the farmer for	9,600.00
Flat Rate addition at 2.3%	220.80
The auctioneer is deemed to have sold the horse for VAT at 2.3%	10,500.00
The auctioneer's liability is 2.3% of £10,500 less (i.e. 2.3% of £900)	241.20
The purchasing farmer pays the auctioneer £10,741.50 that is £10,500 plus 2.3%	20.70

The selling farmer is paid £9,820.80 that £9,600 plus 2.3%

STATEMENT OF PRACTICE SP-VAT/01/91

RATES OF VAT ON SERVICES FROM 1 MARCH, 1991

General

1. (i)   On and from 1 March, 1991 the rate of VAT on most goods and services at present liable at 10 per cent will become 12.5 per cent. The goods and services in question are:-

   (a)   admissions to certain exhibitions,

   (b)   adult clothing and footwear including materials for their manufacture,

   (c)   agricultural services,

   (d)   cabaret admissions,

   (e)   car driving instruction,

   (f)   care of the human body; hairdressing, health studio services,

   (g)   cinema admissions,

   (h)   fuel for power and heating; coal, peat, timber, electricity, gas,

   (i)   heating oil,

   (j)   general repair and maintenance services of movable goods,

   (k)   photographic services,

   (l)   restaurant/hotel meals,

   (m)   spectacles and contact lenses,

   (n)   telephone services,

   (o)   waste disposal,

   (p)   works of art; literary manuscripts; most antiques.

   (ii)   A number of supplies will continue to be liable at the 10 per cent rate. These include buildings and building work, concrete blocks, ready mix concrete, newspapers, hotel lettings, short-term hiring of cars, boats, caravans and tour guide services.

2.   Goods and services at present liable at 23 per cent will become 21 per cent (effective 1 March, 1991).

List of Services

3.   An illustrative list is attached of the principal services which will be affected together with examples of those which will not and an indication of the rate of VAT which will apply on and from 1 March, 1991. The list is NOT comprehensive. Information concerning the VAT

rating of unlisted services and other information may be obtained from the Revenue Commissioners (VAT), Castle House, South Great George's Street, Dublin 2 (Tel. 01-6792777 Ext. 2440, 2441, 2442, and 2443) or from local Tax Offices.

Rates of VAT on certain services on and from 1 March, 1991

Subject to 2/3rds rule - see paragraph 15.11 of "Guide to Value-Added Tax"

(This list is NOT comprehensive)

	%
Accommodation (letting of rooms, etc.) -	
- by hotels, as defined	10
Accountants (see also par. 20.21 of "Guide")	21
Actuaries	21
Addressing envelopes	21
Advertising	21
Agents, commission	21
Agricultural Contracting see pars. 20.19, 20.20 of Guide	
Agricultural Machinery -	
- hire (and sale)	21
- Repair, maintenance (excl. supply of accessories and tyres, tubes, batteries)	12.5
Alarms -	
- in buildings (supply and fit or fit only)	10
- in vehicles (supply, supply and fit, or fit only)	21
- other (supply, supply and fit, or fit only)	21
Alterations (to secondhand goods)	12.5
Amusements see "Entertainment"	
Anodising	21
Arcades, amusement	21
Architects	21
Artists services (e.g. portrait painting)	12.5
Batteries, all, including supply in the course of repair	21
Battery charging and battery repair	12.5
Beauty salon services (21% on sales of cosmetics etc.)	12.5
Bed & Breakfast -	
- by hotels, as defined (sleeping accommodation only),	10
- meals	12.5
Biscuits -	
- with meal	12.5
- other (including vending machines)	21
Bicycle -	
- repairs	12.5
- long-term hire and sale	21
- short-term hire	10
Blinds and curtain making	21
Boiler cleaning	10
Book Binding	0, 21
Building services	10
Boning/de-boning meat	0

Cable TV	21
Cafes	12.5
21% on alcohol and soft drinks	
Canteens (see par. 21.11 - 21.16 of Guide)	12.5
Car Accessories, supply, supply and fit or fit only of phones, alarms, batteries, tyres etc.	21
Caravans -	
- short-term hire	10
- other hire and sale (new and used)	21
- repair	12.5
Car Hire -	
- long	21
- short	10
Car parking	21
Car phones (supply, supply and fit, or fit only)	21
Car repair and maintenance	12.5
Car wash	12.5
Carpet cleaning	10, 12.5
Carpet laying (see "alterations" and also par. 15.7 of Guide)	10, 21
Catering	12.5
(21 on alcohol and soft drinks see Chapter 21 of Guide)	
Chimney Cleaning	10
Chips (cooked)	12.5
Chiropody	Exempt
Cinema admissions	12.5
Circus admissions	Exempt
Cleaning -	
- immovable goods	10
- other	12.5
Coin or token - operated machines -	
- Launderettes	12.5
- car park	21
- car wash	12.5
- juke boxes	21
- weighing scales	21
- amusement machines	21
- video games	21
- food and drink vending machines (see Chapter 21 of Guide)	12.5, 21
- other vending machines	21
Cold Storage	21
Communal TV charges	21
Computer Programmes	21
Confectionery -	
- with meals	12.5
- hot take aways	12.5
- other	21
Consultancy (See par. 20.21 of Guide)	21
Couriers	21
Contract Cleaning -	
- immovable goods	10
- other	12.5

Curing (animal skins)	21
Curtain Cleaning	12.5
Curtain Making	21
Cutting to shape (timber, mirrors)	21
Dances (see par. 5.16 of Guide)	21
Dental Technicians	Exempt
Design Services	21
Driving Lessons (vehicles less than 1.5 tonnes) -	12.5
- otherwise	Exempt
De-boning	0
Dry Cleaning	12.5
Drying (e.g. Timber) manufacture	21
Dyeing	12.5
Ear piercing	12.5
Electricity	12.5
Electroplating	21
Employment Agencies	21
Engraving	21
Entertainment -	
- Cabaret type including shows with which food and drink are supplied (supplies of alcohol and soft drinks - 21%) 12.5	
- cinema admissions	12.5
- circus admissions	Exempt
- dances	21
- admission to sporting events	Exempt
- theatre admissions	Exempt
- amusement machines	21
- exhibition admissions	12.5
- fairground entertainment (some exempt and 21)	12.5
- juke boxes	21
Etching -	21
- original work of art	12.5
Farm Accountancy	12.5
Farm management	12.5
Film processing	12.5
Fitting services	21
Food and Drink (see separate leaflet)	0, 12.5, 21
French Polishing (of used goods)	12.5
Fruit Juices -	
- freshly squeezed juices (non manufactured)	0
- with meal	12.5
- other	21
Furniture -	
- hire and sale	21
- repair, restoration	12.5
- upholstering	21 (New); 12.5 (Old)
Gas Conversion (vehicles)	12.5
Galvanising (new goods)	21
Glazing	10

Goods Transport	21
Grain Drying and Storage	21
Grain Grinding, Mixing	21
Guest Houses See Chapter 21 of Guide	
Hairdressing	12.5
Haulage	21
Health Studio	12.5
Hire of Goods	2.3, 10, 21
Hotels See Chapter 21 of Guide	
Inspection Services	21
Installation Services -	
- movable goods	21
- immovable goods	10
Juke Boxes (to play)	21
Key Cutting	21
Laminating	21
Laundering	12.5
Law Searchers	21
Lettings -	
- by hotels (as defined)	10(meals 12.5)
Linen Hire	21
Mailing Services (addressing and distributing envelopes etc.)	21
Management Services (see par. 20.21 of Guide)	21
Manicuring	12.5
Massage	12.5
Meals see Chapter 21 of Guide	
Microfilming	12.5
Mounting (coins on to rings)	21
Office, factory cleaning -	
- immovable	10
- movable	12.5
Packaging Services (wrapping, strapping)	21
Patents	21
Painting -	
- of fixtures	10
- of portraits, etc.	12.5
- fittings (free-standing goods)	21
Pest Control	10, 12.5, 21
Photocopying	21
Photography	12.5
Polishing -	
- fixtures	10
- second hand goods	12.5
- new goods (e.g. furniture)	21
Printing -	
- books	0, 21
- magazines	10, 21
- newspapers -	
- most daily, weekly, fortnightly	10
- other	21

Picture Framing	21
Puncture Repairs	12.5
Reconditioning	12.5
Recording Studios	21
Refrigeration Services	21
Repairs -	
- movable goods	12.5
- immovable goods	10
Restaurants see Chapter 21 of Guide	
Restoration Services	10, 12.5
Re-surfacing	10, 12.5
Re-upholstering	12.5
Rustproofing	
- old goods	10,12.5
- new goods	21
Sand Blasting (of buildings)	10
Sauna Service -	
- hotel	10
- elsewhere	Exempt
Security Services	21
Self-operating services see coin-operated machines	
Sharpening Services	12.5
Shoe Repairs	12.5
Signwriting -	21
- on fixtures	12.5
Snooker	21
(Spectators and competition admissions exempt)	
Soft Drinks	21
Solicitors (Some services 12.5)	21
Stamping (e.g. of precious metals)	21
Storage	21
Storage and Drying of Grain	21
Surveyors (12.5 and Exempt some activities)	21
Take Aways see Chapter 21 of Guide	
Tanning (hides)	21
Telecommunication services	12.5
Telephones -	
- hire/leasing of equipment	21
- installation of systems in buildings as fixtures	10
- installation in vehicles	21
- rental of handsets	12.5
Tents -	
- long-term hire and sale	21
- short-term hire	10
Testing	21
Tour Guides	10
Towel Hire	21
Training (taxable)	21
TV Rental including repairs	21
Typesetting	21

Typing Services	21
Tyres -	
- sale of goods	21
- re-treading, re-moulding (service)	12.5
Repair	12.5
Upholstering	
- old	12.5
- new, free standing	21
Upholstery Cleaning	12.5
Valuation	21
Van Conversions	21
(alteration of secondhand vans 12.5%)	
Vending machines see separate leaflet	
Video Games	21
Waste Disposal	12.5
Waste Food	0
Water softening	21
Wedding Cakes, Baking	21
Weighing Machines, use of	21
Woodworm/dry rot service	10,12.5,21

STATEMENT OF PRACTICE SP-VAT/02/91

AUTOMATED ENTRY PROCESSING FOR IMPORTS/EXPORTS

1. The Automated Entry Processing system (AEP) for the processing of Customs entries came into effect on 1 April 1991. Under the new system, Customs entries may now be made directly into the Customs computer network. This means that the information formerly inscribed on the Single Administrative Document (SAD) may now be transmitted electronically to Customs.

2. As a consequence of the new system, certified SADs will no longer be available to support claims for deduction or refund of VAT paid on imports or, for the purposes of verifying exportation of goods. Instead, the following arrangements will apply:

    *   Imports

        In relation to claims for deduction or refund of VAT paid on imports traders must have evidence of payment of the VAT i.e.

        *   Monthly Customs & Excise statement for traders who are on the Deferred Payment/FACT Schemes (traders should claim input credits/refunds strictly in accordance with the net VAT amount on the deferred statements i.e. the amount of VAT which has been debited to their bank accounts.), or

        *   Official receipt issued by Customs & Excise where payment is made direct to Customs & Excise by the trader other than by the Deferred Payment/FACT Schemes, or

        *   Invoice from Customs Clearance Agent. This should show clearly the entry number and the amount and rate of VAT paid on behalf of the trader. Alternatively, a copy of the SAD showing the entry no. may be attached to the invoice.

        Each claim for deduction or refund of VAT paid on imports must also be supported by the suppliers' invoice(s) which must be cross referenced to the appropriate debit(s), on the monthly C&E statement, or to the C&E receipt etc. Normal commercial documentation e.g. delivery dockets, proof of payment to supplier etc., where appropriate, should also be retained.

        In addition, traders/customs clearance agents may attach copy SADs showing the entry nos. to their deferred statements, receipts or invoices.

    *   Exports

        With regard to exports each transaction must be supported by the sales invoice cross referenced to the normal commercial documents (delivery dockets, bills of lading, proof of payment from customer etc.).

Where necessary traders may be required to support their claim that goods have been exported, by production of documentation from the Customs Authorities of the country to which the goods were exported.

Further information concerning the trader's VAT accounting as affected by the new arrangements is available from the Revenue Commissioners, Indirect Taxes Branch, Dublin Castle, Dublin 2 (Tel. 01-6792777 Ext. 2440, 2441, 2442, 2443) or from local tax offices.

STATEMENT OF PRACTICE SP-VAT/01/92

RATES OF VAT ON SERVICES FROM 1 MARCH 1992

General

1. (i) On and from 1 March, 1992 the rate of VAT on certain goods and services at present liable at 12.5 per cent will become 16 per cent. The goods and services in question are:

   — adult clothing and footwear including materials for their manufacture,

   — auto LPG,

   — car driving instruction,

   — hairdressing and certain other personal services,

   — farm auctioneering and solicitor services relating to sales of agricultural land,

   — farm accountancy and farm management services,

   — general repair and maintenance services (other than building work), including car repairs,

   — photographic services,

   — services of jockeys,

   — corrective spectacles and contact lenses,

   — telecommunications,

   — works of art; literary manuscripts; most antiques.

   (ii) A number of supplies will continue to be liable at the 10 per cent and 12.5 per cent rates. The 10 per cent supplies include buildings and building work, concrete blocks, ready mix concrete, newspapers, hotel lettings, short-term hiring of cars, boats, caravans and tour guide services. The 12.5 per cent supplies include fuel for power and heating, electricity, restaurant and hotel meals, cinema admissions, certain live entertainment, admissions to certain exhibitions, waste disposal, general agricultural services and veterinary services.

List of Services

2. An illustrative list is attached of the principal services which will be affected together with those which will be liable at other rates from 1 March, 1992. The list is NOT comprehensive. Information concerning the VAT rating of unlisted services and other information may be obtained from the Revenue Commissioners (VAT), Castle House, South Great George's Street, Dublin 2 (Tel. 01-6792777 Ext. 2440, 2441, 2442, and 2443) or from local Tax Offices.

Issued by the Revenue Commissioners.
March, 1992.

Rates of VAT on certain services on and from 1 March, 1992

Subject to 2/3rds rule - see paragraph 15.11 of "Guide to Value-Added Tax"

(This list is NOT comprehensive)

Accommodation (letting of rooms, etc.) -	10
- hotels, guest houses and similar establishments	10
- accommodation which is held out as being holiday accommodation or accommodation for visitors or travellers	10
Accountants -	21
- farm accountancy	16
Actuaries	21
Addressing envelopes	21
Advertising	21
Agents, commission	21
Agricultural Contracting	0,12.5,21
Agricultural Machinery -	
- hire (and sale)	21
- repair, maintenance (excl. supply of accessories and tyres, tubes, batteries)	16
Alarms -	
- in buildings (supply and fit or fit only)	10
- in vehicles (supply, supply and fit, or fit only)	21
- other (supply, supply and fit, or fit only)	21
Alterations (to secondhand goods)	16
Amusements see Entertainment	
Anodising	21
Arcades, amusement	21
Archaeologists	16, 21
Architects	21
Artists services (e.g. portrait painting)	16
Auctioneers -	21
- vegetables, fruit, eggs, dead poultry	0
- live cattle, horses, greyhounds, sheep, goats, pigs and deer	2.7
- farm auctioneering	16
Batteries, all, including supply in the course of repair	21
Battery charging and battery repair	16
Beauty Salon services	16
(21% on sales of Beauty salon services cosmetics etc.)	
Bed & Breakfast -	
- by hotels, guest houses etc. (see Accommodation)	10
- meals	12.5
Biscuits -	
- with meal	12.5
- other (including vending machines)	21
Bicycle -	
- repairs	16
- long-term hire and sale	21
- short-term hire	10

Blinds and curtain making	21
Boiler maintenance	10
Book Binding	0, 21
Building services	10
Boning/de-boning meat	0
Cable TV	21
Cafes	12.5
(21% on alcohol and soft drinks)	
Camp sites (lettings)	10
Canteens (see par. 21.11 -21.16 of Guide)	12.5
Car Accessories, supply, supply and fit or fit only of phones, alarms. batteries, tyres etc.	21
Caravans -	
- short-term hire	10
- other hire and sale (new and used)	21
- repair	16
Caravan parks (lettings)	10
Car Hire -	
- long	21
- short	10
Car parking	21
Car phones (supply, supply and fit, or fit only)	21
Car repair and maintenance	16
Car wash	16
Carpet cleaning	16
Carpet laying (see "alterations' and also par. 15.7 of Guide)	10, 21
Catering	12.5
(21% on alcohol and soft drinks see Chapter 21 of Guide)	
Chimney Cleaning	10
Chips (cooked)	12.5
Chiropody	Exempt
Cinema admissions	12.5
Circus admissions	Exempt
Cleaning	
- contract	16
- immovable goods	10
Coin or token - operated machines -	
- launderettes	16
- carpark	21
- car wash	16
- juke boxes	21
- weighing scales	21
- amusement machines	21
- video games	21
- food and drink vending machines (see Chapter 21 of guide)	12.5, 21
- other vending machines	21
Cold Storage	21
Communal TV charges	21
Computer Programmes	21

Confectionery -	
- with meals	12.5
- hot take aways	12.5
- other	21
Consultancy (see par. 20.21 of Guide)	21
Couriers	21
Contract Cleaning (routine)	16
Curing (animal skins)	21
Curtain Cleaning	16
Curtain Making	21
Cutting to shape (timber, mirrors)	21
Dances	21
Dental Technicians	Exempt
Design Services	21
Digging and Excavating (other than development)	16
Driving Lessons (vehicles less than 1.5 tonnes)	16
- otherwise	Exempt
De-boning	0
Dry Cleaning	16
Drying (e.g. Timber)	21
Dyeing	16
Ear piercing	16
Electricity	12.5
Electroplating	21
Employment Agencies	21
Engraving	21
Entertainment -	
- cabaret type including shows with which food and drink are supplied	12.5
(supplies of alcohol and soft drinks - 21%)	
- cinema admissions	12.5
- circus admissions	Exempt
- dances	21
- admission to sporting events	Exempt
- theatre admissions	Exempt
- amusement machines	21
- exhibition admissions	12.5
- fairground entertainment	12.5, 21
- juke boxes	21
Etching	21
- original work of art	16
Farm Accountancy	16
Farm Management	16
Farmhouse Accommodation	10
Film processing	16
Fitting services	21
Food and Drink (see separate leaflet)	0,12.5,21
French Polishing (of used goods)	16
Fruit Juices -	
- freshly squeezed juices (non manufactured)	0

- with meal	12.5
- other	21
Furniture -	
- hire and sale	21
- repair, restoration	16
- upholstering	21 (new);
	16 (old)
Galvanising (new goods)	21
Gas Conversion (vehicles)	16
Glazing	10
Goods Transport (0 international)	21
Grain Drying and Storage	21
Grain Grinding, Mixing	21
Guest Houses (Accommodation)	10
- meals	12.5
Hairdressing	16
Haulage (0 for international)	21
Health Studio	16,21
Hire of Goods	2.7,10,21
Holiday Cottages	10
Hotels (accommodation)	10
- meals	12.5
Inspection Services	21
Installation Services -	
- movable goods	21
- immovable goods	10
Jockeys	16
Juke Boxes (to play)	21
Key Cutting	21
Laminating	21
Landscaping and land reclamation and drainage	10
Laundering	16
Law Searchers	21
Linen Hire	21
Mailing Services (addressing and distributing envelopes etc.)	21
Management Services (see par. 20.21 of Guide)	21
Manicuring	16
Massage	16
Meals see Chapter 21 of Guide	
Microfilming	16
Motels	10
Mounting (coins on to rings)	21
Office, factory cleaning (routine)	16
- other	10
Packaging Services (wrapping, strapping)	21
Patents	21
Painting -	
- of fixtures	10
- of portraits, etc.	16
- fittings (free-standing goods)	16,21

STATEMENT OF PRACTICE SP-VAT/02/92

CHANGES RELATING TO THE MONEYS RECEIVED BASIS OF ACCOUNTING

1.   The Value Added Tax (Determination of Tax Due by Reference to Moneys Received) (Amendment) Regulations 1992, which were made by the Revenue Commissioners on 16 April 1992, amended the existing regulation as regards the adjustment of liability following a change in the basis of accounting for VAT.

2.   Previously, where persons ceased to account for VAT on the moneys received (or 'cash receipts') basis of accounting, they were required to adjust their liability for VAT to take account of any increase in their debtors during the period for which they accounted on that basis. However, where they had been accounting on the moneys received basis for longer than six years no such adjustment was required.

3.   From 16 April 1992 this adjustment will be required in all cases of cessation on the moneys regardless of the period of time involved. However, persons who have been accounting on the moneys received basis for longer than six years will be required to adjust their liability to take account of any increase in their debtors only in relation to the six years prior to the change.

4.   There will be no change in the position where the cessation of use of the moneys received basis results from the death of the taxable person. No adjustment is required in such cases.

STATEMENT OF PRACTICE SP-VAT/07/92

THE MONTHLY CONTROL STATEMENT

General

1. Section 17(1B) of the Value-Added Tax Act 1972 obliges a taxable person to issue a monthly control statement to each taxable person to whom he or she supplies goods. The obligation only applies where a person's taxable turnover in respect of supplies of goods to other taxable persons exceeds £2 million in the previous period of twelve months. Where the grouping provisions of section 8(8) are applicable, the £2 million threshold will apply to the supplies of the group as a whole.

Operative date

2. The obligation to issue a monthly control statement applies in relation to goods supplied after 1 November, 1992. The Revenue Commissioners will exercise flexibility in relation to the commencement date where traders need additional time to clarify the implications of the new requirement and to install and test new reporting systems (see paragraph 10).

Details to be included on the monthly control statement

3. The details to be included in the monthly control statement are set out in the Value-Added Tax (Monthly Control Statement) Regulations (S.I. No. 230 of 1992) which were made by the Revenue Commissioners on 13 August 1992. The details are

    (a)   the name, address and registration number of the person by whom the goods referred to in the statement were supplied;

    (b)   the name and address of the person to whom the goods referred to in the statement were supplied;

    (c)   the date of issue of the statement;

    (d)   the calendar month to which the statement refers;

    (e)   in relation to supplies of goods for which an invoice, credit note, debit note or settlement voucher was issued in accordance with section 17 of the VAT Act, the total amount of the consideration inclusive of tax shown on each of those documents;

    (f)   in relation to supplies of goods for which an invoice, credit note, debit note or settlement voucher was not issued,

        (i)   the date of each such supply,

        (ii)   a description of the goods supplied,

        (iii) the consideration, exclusive of tax, for each supply,

        (iv)   the rate or rates of tax and amount of tax at each rate chargeable to the person who has supplied the goods;

(g)   in relation to any adjustment of the consideration for the supplies referred to in paragraph (e) or (f) agreed between the supplier of the goods and the taxable person and for which a credit note was not issued under section 17 of the VAT Act,

     (i)   the amount of such adjustment,

     (ii)   the date of such adjustment;

(h)   where, in respect of the supply referred to in paragraph (e) or (f), any payment has been or will be made by the person issuing the monthly control statement,

     (i)   the amount of such payment or payments,

     (ii)   the date or dates when such payment or payments were or will be made,

     (iii)   the person or persons to whom such payment or payments have been or will be made;

    and

(i)   in relation to any gifts or promotional items given in connection with the supplies referred to in paragraph (e) or (f),

     (i)   a description of such gifts or promotional items,

     (ii)   the value of such gifts or promotional items,

     (iii)   the date of provision of such gifts or promotional items.

Time limit for issuing the monthly control statement

4.   The monthly control statement must be issued not later than the last day of the month following the month during which the goods were supplied.

Document to be retained

5.   Every person who receives a monthly control statement is obliged to retain the document for six years. The person issuing a monthly control statement is obliged to retain an exact copy of the statement for a similar period. Subject to agreement with the local tax office copies of the monthly control statements can be stored on non-paper media such as microfiche or computer tape or disc.

Use of commercial statements

6.1   Where a trader issues a statement to his or her customers for commercial reasons this statement will be accepted by the Revenue Commissioners as fulfilling the legal requirement of the monthly control statement, provided the commercial statement includes the required details as set out in paragraph 3 above. If the commercial statement contains details additional to those indicated in paragraph 3 (e.g. details of payments received from customers) it can still serve as the monthly control statement.

6.2   While the legislation requires a monthly statement, traders who use a different accounting period e.g. a four week cycle, can issue the statement based on this period.

6.3   Where the commercial statement contains some, but not all, of the required details, the Revenue Commissioners will accept the listing of additional details on a separate document provided that the commercial statement contains a specific cross reference to the separate documentation in the following or similar terms "For the purpose of complying with section 17(1B) of the VAT Act additional details are contained in document number .... date........."

All supplies to be included

7.1   The monthly control statement must include details of all supplies made to the taxable person to whom the statement is being issued. Thus both credit sales and cash sales must be recorded on the statement.

7.2   Where a trader carries on a cash business e.g. where a large number of customers are supplied on a regular basis by a van sales person who issues the VAT invoice, this invoice may substitute for the monthly control statement provided it is clearly indicated that this invoice covers all supplies (irrespective of whether they are being charged for or not). Where more than one supply is made to a particular customer in any month, each invoice issued must state clearly that it is in respect of all supplies to that customer since the date of the last invoice.

All payments to be included

8.   The monthly control statement should include details of any amounts paid by the person issuing the monthly control statement in relation to the supplies referred to on that statement (see paragraph 3(h) above). Such payments could take the form for example of payments under long term agreements, discounts, "hello money" etc. Where the person issuing the statement makes a payment which relates to supplies over a number of periods the payment may be included in the statement for the month during which the payment was made.

Gift and Promotional Items

9.1   The statement should include details of gifts and promotional items given by the supplier to the trader or any other person in respect of the supplies. The statement should show a description, value and date of

- goods for resale supplied free, details of which have not been included in an invoice;

- capital or expense items supplied without charge e.g. a cold room or a freezer;

- gifts or benefits given to the trader, (including an employee of the trader or any other person) in respect of the goods supplied e.g. televisions, holidays etc.. (However, details of these gifts need not be sent with the statement. They may be kept in a separate list provided that they are available for inspection by the local VAT inspector and that a reference to the existence of such a list is made on the monthly statement). Details of gifts of goods the aggregate cost of which in a given twelve month period does not exceed £600, need not be included in the statement. If, however, a trader does not wish to keep such details on a twelve month basis, he may opt for a monthly basis. In those cases, details of gifts which do not exceed £50 in any one month need not be included in the statement.

9.2   Items which are given for advertising purposes by the supplier and are used on the purchaser's premises e.g. beer mats, ash trays, etc. need not be included on the statement. Similarly details of sponsorship of sporting events and sponsorship of prizes, with the exception of the provision of goods for resale, need not be included in the statement.

Modifications

10.   Any trader who wishes to present the information in a format or manner different to that outlined in the Regulations and described in paragraph 3 and 4 of this Statement of Practice, or who wishes to seek a deferral of the implementation date should apply to the local office. Revenue officers will be designated in each tax office to deal with applications and enquiries in relation to the monthly control statement.

Issued by the Revenue Commissioners.
October, 1992.

STATEMENT OF PRACTICE SP-VAT/08/92

APPLICATION OF THE ZERO RATE TO SALES AND DELIVERIES OF GOODS TO OTHER EC MEMBER STATES AFTER 1 JANUARY 1993

General
1. Currently exports of goods to destinations outside the State qualify for the zero rate of VAT. The existing procedures will continue to apply for exports to countries outside the EC after 1 January 1993. However, under the new European Community (EC) VAT arrangements applicable from that date revised arrangements will be introduced in relation to the zero rating of goods supplied to other Member States of the EC. This Statement of Practice outlines the new requirements to enable such supplies to be zero rated.

Essential Conditions for Zero Rating
2. An Irish trader, registered for VAT may zero rate the supply of goods to a customer in another Member State provided that:

    I.   the customer is registered for VAT in another Member State,

    II.   the customer's VAT registration number is obtained and retained in the supplier's records (see paragraph 7),

    III. this number, together with the supplier's VAT registration number, is quoted on the sales invoice,

    IV.   the goods are despatched or transported to another EC Member State.

    If these four conditions are not met the seller will be accountable for VAT at the appropriate Irish rate. If a supplier is not able to satisfy the Revenue Commissioners that particular consignments of goods have been sold and delivered to a VAT registered person in another Member State, the supplier will be liable for the payment of Irish VAT on the transaction.

Evidence of Despatch to Another Member State and of Removal of the Goods from the State
3. The precise commercial documentation required to confirm despatch and removal of the goods from the State will depend on the particular circumstances involved.

4. In many cases the supplier will arrange transportation of the goods and the normal commercial documentation related to the supply and transportation of the goods will be available (e.g. order document, delivery docket, supplier's invoice, transport document/bill of lading, evidence of transfer of foreign currency for payment, etc.). In such cases the trader should retain this documentation.

5.   Where transport of the goods is arranged by the customer, or the goods are taken away by the customer using his or her own transport, the seller will need to be satisfied that the goods are dispatched or transported to another Member State. The normal documentary evidence should be retained in relation to the sale itself but, in addition, the supplier should obtain and retain documentary evidence from the customer that the goods were received in another Member State. The type of documentation acceptable will include transport documents, copies of warehouse receipts, delivery dockets, etc. It might also be prudent for the supplier to record details (e.g. vehicle registration nos.) of the means of transport used by the customer.

6.   Special care should be taken by the supplier to ensure that the four conditions outlined in paragraph 2 will be met for sales and deliveries of goods to other Member States.

Examples of where a doubt could arise include:

- customer is not previously known to the supplier,

- customer will arrange to collect and transport the goods,

- customer's transport arrives at supplier's premises without advance notice or correspondence,

- payment in cash,

- type or quantity of goods being purchased are not consistent with commercial practice bearing in mind the purported destination of the goods.

Cases where one or more of these various factors combine together must be treated with particular caution. Where a doubt arises, the supplier should charge Irish VAT. If the conditions for zero rating are subsequently established the customer will be entitled to recover the VAT paid from the supplier.

Verification of Customers' VAT numbers

7.   For zero rating to apply there must be a supply of goods to a person registered in another Member State. The fiscal authorities in each Member State are arranging to put in place a computerised system that will make it possible for traders to verify the VAT numbers of their customers in other Member States. However, use of the verification system is not obligatory and traders who are familiar with their customers, and are aware of their bona fides from trading with them over a period of time, will not be expected or required to use the verification system. Instead they are advised to contact their EC customers and ask them to confirm in writing their VAT registration numbers. (An example of the type of form that might be used for this purpose is attached as Appendix I.)

8.   An Irish trader who has doubts about the validity of a VAT number quoted will be able to use the verification system to establish whether a particular number is valid. The system is primarily intended to be used in such circumstances and is not intended for routine checks. Pending

the establishment of the VIES/INTRASTAT Office in Dundalk (probably in December 1992), verification queries will be dealt with by the VIMA Office in Dublin, Telephone (01) 6792777, Ext. 2334, 2373, 2357 or Fax (01) 6792636.

Requirement to Take all Reasonable Steps

9. Any supplier who takes all reasonable steps to confirm that the conditions for zero rating are met will not be penalised if it subsequently transpires that a problem has arisen in connection with particular consignments. However, the tax due will be demanded from the supplier in any case where he or she has failed to do so.

Fraudulent Claims for Zero Rating

10. There are severe penalties for making fraudulent claims for zero rating:

I. seizure and forfeiture of zero rated goods which have not been despatched or transported outside the State (subsections (9A) and (10) of section 27 of the VAT Act),

II. arrest of a person suspected of a criminal offence who is not established in the State, or whom an authorised Revenue Officer or a Garda has reason to believe may leave the State (subsection (11) of section 27 of the VAT Act),

III. civil and criminal penalties, ranging from £1,200 to £10,000 and imprisonment for a period of up to five years (sections 26, 27 and 28 of the VAT Act and section 94 of the Finance Act 1983).

Appendix I

Dear Customer,

VAT/TVA/IVA/MWSt/BTW

To comply with new EC regulations, we will, from January 1993, have to show your VAT/Sales Tax Number on our invoices.

To help us with this, could you please fill in the box below with your VAT/Sales Tax Number and return it to us as soon as possible. Please ensure that the country prefix is included.

N.B. If you are not registered for VAT, please tick

In addition, to help us update our records, please forward your:

Telephone No. ....

Fax No. ....

Thank you.

Yours faithfully,

STATEMENT OF PRACTICE SP-VAT/09/92

ELECTRONIC INVOICING (EDI)

General

1. A taxable person who supplies goods and services to another taxable person must issue to that other taxable person a VAT invoice. Up to now this requirement could be satisfied only by issue of a paper invoice. However the Revenue Commissioners have recently made regulations which provide for the issue of invoices, credit notes, debit notes and settlement vouchers by electronic means.

Authorisation

2. A taxable person proposing to issue or receive invoices/credit notes, etc. acceptable for the purposes of the VAT system by electronic means must be authorised by the local VAT inspector to do so and must meet the following requirements:

    Each taxable person must:

    *   apply in writing to the local VAT office for authorisation to issue or receive messages by electronic means at least one month in advance of the intended start up date stating -

        *   his or her name, address and registration number,

        *   the name, address and registration number of each taxable person to whom or from whom he or she will be issuing or receiving messages electronically,

        *   the date from which he or she intends to issue or receive messages being not later than one month after the date of application, and

    *   make a declaration in writing that the EDI system to be used is capable of meeting the criteria which have been laid down by law (see next paragraph).

Capacity of the System

3. The system must be capable of:

    I.   producing, retaining and storing a record of the messages transmitted or received in such form and containing such particulars as are required by the VAT Act and Regulations. For the purposes of the EDI regulation "message" means an invoice, credit note, debit note or settlement voucher required to be issued in accordance with section 17 of the VAT Act (see Chapter 10 of the Guide to the Value Added Tax),

    II.   reproducing on paper a record of any messages transmitted by or stored in the system,

    III. generating a sequential series of numbers unique to each two trading partners who are engaged in the electronic exchange of messages. Each batch of messages from the sender must carry a unique number which must be verified by the recipient as the next logical number from that sender. The system must have in-built safeguards to preclude the possibility of the same number issuing twice or the omission of any particular number in the sequence of numbers,

IV.   maintaining records required to be retained or stored in accordance with paragraph 4 below in such manner as will allow their retrieval by reference either to the date or the transmission sequence number of the batch of messages.

Keeping of Records
4.   On receipt of authorisation the taxable person can proceed to transmit or receive messages by electronic means. The existing provisions of VAT law as regards issue, retention and storage of records apply to electronic records in the same way as they apply to paper records. However a taxable person who is authorised to issue or receive messages by electronic means must also issue, or, in the case of the recipient construct, retain and store the following additional documents:

(a)   a batch control record (that is a summary of all the messages included in each transmission) containing the following particulars:

   (i)   the name, address and registration number of the issuer,

   (ii)   the name, address and registration number of the recipient,

   (iii)   the date of preparation of the message,

   (iv)   the transmission sequence number, and

   (v)   for each type of message in the transmission the following particulars:

      (I)   the total number of messages,

      (II)   the total consideration, exclusive of tax, in respect of which the messages were issued or received,

      (III)   the amount of the consideration liable to tax at each rate including the zero rate,

      (IV)   the amount of tax appropriate to the consideration at each rate, and

      (V)   the total consideration for exempt supplies, if any;

(b)   *a summary document produced at the end of each month by both issuer and recipient containing the following particulars:

   (i)   the name, address and registration number of the issuer,

   (ii)   the name, address and registration number of the recipient,

(iii)   the calendar month to which the document relates, and

(iv)   in respect of that month the following particulars:

    (I)   each transmission sequence number,

    (II)   the total consideration, exclusive of tax, to which the document relates,

    (III)   the amount of the consideration liable at each rate of tax including the zero rate,

    (IV)   the amount of tax appropriate to the said consideration at each rate,

    (V)   the total consideration for exempt supplies, if any, and

(v)   in the case of the authorised issuer, the sequence numbers of faulty or failed transmissions;

(c)   in the case of an authorised recipient, a document produced by him and issued to a trading partner giving details of any discrepancy between the batch control document issued by the sender and that constructed by the recipient;

(d)   in all cases, a transmission log i.e. a record of transmission sequence numbers between each trading partner.

*NOTE: Section 17(1B) of the Value Added Tax Act 1972, obliges a taxable person to issue a monthly control statement to each taxable person to whom he or she supplies goods. The monthly summary document referred to above may not be accepted as a monthly control statement for the purposes of section 17(1B) unless all the details required by the VAT (Monthly Control Statement) Regulations 1992, are included in that document. A separate Statement of Practice on the monthly control statement is now available.

Receipt of Transmitted Messages

5.   On receipt of a transmission the recipient should

- verify that the transmission is from an authorised sender,

- verify that the sequence number is the next logical number from that sender,

- recalculate the message totals and VAT liability for each rate of VAT (including zero rate)

- compare the calculated values with the batch control record.

In the event of discrepancies between the control documents, a discrepancy report must be sent to the issuer and, after correction as necessary, the entire transmission must be reissued with a new sequence number. Discrepancy reports must be retained as part of both the issuer's and recipient's business records.

In the event of a transmission being corrupted in any way, or in the event of the receiver being unable to read the transmission, the supplier must repeat the transmission.

The received messages must be retained in the sequence in which they have been transmitted and must be kept in strict numerical order.

Acceptance of an Invoice

6.   Acceptance of a transmission does not necessarily indicate acceptance of an invoice within the transmission. When received, invoices are normally validated against the original order or contract. An invalid invoice in the transmission may result in the invoice being rejected. Where correction of an invoice results in rejection of the invoice, a credit note must be transmitted by the sender followed by a re-issue of the corrected invoice, etc. in a subsequent transmission.

New Trading Partners

7.   Where a taxable person, already authorised to issue or receive messages by electronic means, wishes to take on a new partner, he or she should write to the local VAT office giving the name, address and registration number of the proposed new partner. That partner should, at the same time, formally apply in accordance with paragraph 2 for the appropriate authorisation.

Changes in Conditions

8.   Where any change occurs in the particulars furnished by a taxable person at the time of the application for authorisation, details of the change must be notified to the local VAT office within 30 days of the change.

Withdrawal of Authorisation

9.   An authorisation to issue or receive messages by electronic means may be withdrawn where the conditions in paragraphs 3, 4 and 5 above are not being fulfilled or where it is considered that it is no longer expedient to allow an authorisation to continue.

STATEMENT OF PRACTICE SP-VAT/09/94

RETAIL EXPORT SCHEME

1. Introduction

Subject to certain restrictions and limitations, relief from VAT is allowed in respect of purchases in the State of goods which are exported from the European Union by visitors from outside the EU. Relief applies to goods taken away by the purchaser at the time of sale, and exported from the EU in his personal baggage. It applies also to goods which are placed by, or on behalf of the, purchaser on board a ship or aircraft for, transportation out of the EU. The goods in question must be exported within three months from the end of the month in which they are purchased. For example goods sold during the month of January must he exported by 30 April. Relief is not allowed on services (e.g. hotel accommodation, meals, car hire etc.).

2. Visitors from other Member States

The Retail Export Scheme does not apply to visitors from other Member States of the European Union. Following the abolition of fiscal frontiers on 1 January, 1993, VAT is no longer payable at the point of entry into the Member States of the European Union on goods which have been acquired by private individuals in other Member States. This means that EU visitors to Ireland do not have a VAT liability in their own Member States on goods which they have purchased in Ireland. Accordingly, relief is not available in respect of purchases in the State by EU visitors. Subject to paragraph 3, relief is available only in respect of goods which are leaving the European Union.

3. Residents of the EU leaving the Community

As a concession, the Commission of the EU has decided that relief from VAT can also be given to EU residents, including therefore Irish residents, who are going to live in a non-EU country for at least a year. Satisfactory evidence of this must, however, be furnished.

4. How relief is granted

The granting of relief by an individual trader is optional. A trader is not obliged to participate in the scheme but may do so if he wishes. A participating trader may choose between the methods of relief at (a) (b) and (c) below. If the trader uses methods (a) or (b) he must have documentary proof of the export of the goods. Lacking such documentary proof he himself will be liable for the VAT.

(a)   The trader need not charge the VAT to the purchaser. He must then rely on the purchaser to send back documentary proof of export, otherwise, the trader will he liable to VAT on the sale in question.

(b)   The trader may charge VAT to the purchaser and subsequently refund it to him when he receives from the purchaser documentary proof of export.

(c)   The trader may operate the relief scheme through one of the VAT refunding agencies (see paragraph 7).

5.   Obligations of participating traders

A participating trader is required to satisfy himself that the person to whom the goods are being supplied is entitled to relief from VAT. This can be by means of inspection of the customer's passport, travel tickets etc.

The trader must also issue to the purchaser an invoice which shows the following particulars:

— trader's name, address and VAT number;

— the name and address of the customer;

— the date of issue;

— a description of and the quantity of the goods;

— the purchase price;

— an indication of the basis on which the trader satisfied himself of the person's entitlement to relief, including details of the relevant documents inspected;

— the trader's signature.

The trader must keep a copy of this invoice together with the documentary proof that the goods have been exported from the EU.

6.   Obligations of purchasers

A purchaser of goods under the relief scheme must provide the supplier with documentary evidence that the goods have in fact been exported. Normally this proof will be the purchase invoice stamped by Customs authorities of the EU Member State from which the goods eventually leave the EU. For example, a visitor who purchases goods in Ireland and then travels to the UK before leaving the EU must have the relevant invoices stamped by the UK Customs authorities. The Irish Customs authorities will stamp invoices only for visitors who are leaving the EU directly from Ireland.

If, however, the purchaser is either unable to have the invoice stamped by the relevant Member State Customs authorities, or does not avail himself of the services of a VAT-refunding agency (see paragraph 7), he should have the documentation stamped in his own country by any person of official status - for example, by Customs, the Police, or a Notary Public - before returning it to the trader.

7.   **VAT Refunding Agencies**

Many retailers choose to operate this relief scheme through one of the agencies which undertake to make refunds to purchasers in respect of the VAT paid. Invoices for total purchases up to a value of £200 may be lodged with these agencies which are usually located at the main departure points from the State (these invoices may be for a single item costing up to £200 or a number of items whose total value does not exceed £200). Purchasers may, of course, present such invoices direct to Customs for stamping, if so desired. Details of the agencies and of the terms and conditions under which they operate are available from the retailers concerned.

Supplies of second-hand goods, works of art, collectors' items or antiques sold under the special margin scheme may only benefit from this relief using the methods outlined at paragraphs 4(a) and (b). Because the margin scheme does not permit the issue of invoices showing VAT separately goods sold under the margin scheme will not attract refunds through the refund agencies. Traders operating through the refunding agencies must therefore charge VAT on the full sales price, which can subsequently be recouped by the visitor on departure.

The VAT refunding agencies are independent entities. The Revenue Commissioners make no endorsement of any such agencies and cannot accept any responsibility for problems encountered by traders or purchasers in dealings with them. Persons who experience delays in receiving their refunds or who are unhappy with the conditions applied by the agencies should write to the trader or to the VAT refunding agency concerned.

8.   **Purchases over £200**

Invoices for purchases over £200 and all purchases not processed through a VAT refunding agency must be presented to the relevant Customs authorities for stamping. If so required by the Customs authorities the goods in question must be produced for inspection. If it is not possible to obtain the necessary Customs certification one of the arrangements listed in paragraph 6 may be applied.

9.   **Exports by trader**

The arrangements under which the zero rate of VAT applies to purchases which are exported or posted out of the EU by the trader, continue to apply.

10.   **Enquiries**

Trader enquiries concerning the operation of the relief should be made to the local VAT Office.

VALUE-ADDED TAX INFORMATION LEAFLET
(OCTOBER 1995)

VAT TREATMENT OF SECOND-HAND VEHICLES

1.   INTRODUCTION

1.1   From 1 July, 1995, there are a number of changes in the VAT treatment of second-hand motor vehicles. These changes arise out of the implementation of the EU Seventh VAT Directive (94/5/EEC) in the Finance Act, 1995. This information leaflet sets out details of the new system.

1.2   The main areas to note are:

- the abolition of the trade-in rule;

- the definition of qualifying second-hand vehicles for the purpose of the new scheme;

- the right to deduction of residual VAT in respect of the purchase (including by way of trade-in) of a qualifying second-hand vehicle;

- the calculation of residual VAT and, where necessary, the clawback;

- the invoice/settlement voucher required to substantiate the deduction of the residual tax;

- the invoicing rule for the sale of a qualifying vehicle to another taxable person;

- the VAT rate to be used and the invoicing rule for the sale of a qualifying vehicle to a person in another Member State;

- the date of effect of the changes.

2.   TRADE-IN

2.1   The VAT rules with regard to trade-ins have been abolished with effect from 1 July, 1995. Prior to that date, when a vehicle was traded-in against the purchase of a new vehicle, VAT was chargeable on the amount of the cash settlement only. The subsequent sale of the traded-in vehicle was taxable on the consideration payable on that sale.

2.2   From 1 July, 1995, if a dealer accepts a vehicle as a trade-in against the purchase of another vehicle, say a new vehicle, both the sale of the new vehicle and the acceptance of the trade-in are treated as two separate transactions for the purpose of accounting for VAT.

- In respect of the sale of the new vehicle the dealer must account for VAT on the full consideration s/he is entitled to receive on that sale, i.e. the total of the cash settlement plus the value of the trade-in and this total should equal the amount that s/he would sell that new vehicle for in cash;

- the trade-in is treated as the purchase of a second-hand vehicle by the dealer and a VAT deduction may be claimed by the dealer. If the dealer receives a VAT invoice from the person supplying the trade-in, s/he claims the deduction in the normal way. Otherwise, if it is qualifying vehicle (see paragraph 3), the dealer claims a deduction of the residual VAT included in the purchase price (see paragraph 4).

It should be noted that this is also the position where the dealer accounts for VAT on the cash basis.

3.   WHAT IS A QUALIFYING VEHICLE?

3.1 A motor dealer may deduct the residual VAT included in the purchase price of any qualifying vehicle which s/he buys, whether as a straight sale or as a trade-in. A qualifying vehicle is a vehicle bought by the dealer as stock- in-trade for resale from one of the following:

- a private individual in Ireland or in another Member State of the European Union;

- a business in Ireland or in another Member State of the European Union which could not claim a VAT credit on its purchase of the vehicle or which is not obliged to issue a VAT invoice in respect of the sale of the vehicle;

- another motor dealer in Ireland who claimed residual VAT on the purchase of the vehicle;

- a motor dealer in another Member State selling the vehicle under the special scheme for taxation of second-hand goods in that other Member State.

3.2 Essentially, the vehicles on which a dealer can claim deduction of residual VAT are those which are sold or traded in to the dealer by a person who was not entitled to deduct any VAT in relation to the original purchase of that vehicle. However, a dealer may also claim deduction of residual VAT on a vehicle which is sold or traded-in to her/him by another dealer who took a deduction of residual VAT on the original purchase of that vehicle.

4.   THE DEDUCTION OF RESIDUAL VAT

4.1 Residual VAT is deductible in the VAT period in which the vehicle is purchased. To claim the residual VAT, the motor dealer should add the amount of the residual VAT (see paragraph 4.3) to the amount of VAT charged on any other deductible purchases and enter that total on the VAT3 return for that period.

4.2 The amount of the residual VAT is calculated at the rate of VAT chargeable on the supply of motor vehicles in the Member State where the person selling the vehicle to the dealer is based. (If the dealer purchases the vehicle from an Irish source, the rate used for the calculation is the Irish VAT rate. If the dealer purchases the vehicle from a UK source, the rate used for the calculation is the UK VAT rate.) The purchase price is always treated as VAT inclusive.

4.3   If the qualifying vehicle is bought from an individual or business in Ireland, where the current VAT rate is 21%, the residual VAT is calculated as follows:

Assume purchase price   = €10,000

Residual VAT = €10,000 x $\frac{21}{121}$ = € 1,736

4.4   If the qualifying vehicle is bought from an individual or business in the UK for an amount equivalent to €10,000, the residual VAT, which is based on the UK VAT rate (currently 17.5%), is calculated as follows:

$$€10,000 \times \frac{17.5}{117.5} = € 1,489$$

5.   THE CLAWBACK

5.1   The amount of residual VAT deducted by the dealer in respect of the purchase of a qualifying vehicle must not be more than the amount of VAT charged by the dealer on the subsequent sale of that vehicle. Effectively, if a qualifying vehicle is sold for less than it was bought for, an adjustment must be made in the VAT return covering the period of the sale, to reduce the amount originally claimed. (If the vehicle is sold in the same VAT period in which it was bought, then the amount claimed should be reduced accordingly in that period.) The adjustment is called a 'clawback' and is the difference between the amount of residual VAT claimed on the purchase of that vehicle in the period of the purchase and the (lower) amount due on its subsequent sale. The dealer accounts for the VAT on the sale in the normal way, but reduces the figure for VAT on purchases in that period to account for the clawback.

5.2   The clawback can best be illustrated by example:

Qualifying vehicle purchased for €10,000
Residual VAT claimed in VAT3 for period of purchase   = €1,736

Sold for €9,000 including VAT
VAT on sale accounted for in VAT 3 for period of sale   = €1,562

Amount of clawback which must be deducted from
VAT on purchases in VAT 3 for period of sale   = € 174

5.3   To allow the industry time to adjust its practices, the Revenue Commissioners have agreed that the clawback will not apply to vehicles taken into stock prior to 1 November, 1995.

5.4   Where a dealer sells more than one qualifying vehicle to a customer in a single transaction (e.g. in a dealer-to-dealer transaction), the amount of the residual VAT deducted in respect of all the vehicles included in the transaction can be added together and compared with the amount of VAT due on that sale for the purpose of calculating whether a clawback is due.

6.   INVOICING/SETTLEMENT VOUCHER REQUIRED

6.1   Where a motor dealer claims residual VAT on the purchase of a qualifying vehicle, s/he must be able to support that claim by an invoice or settlement voucher, completed in accordance with the appropriate Regulations.

6.2   Where the vehicle is bought from a person other than a dealer, a settlement voucher should be prepared by the dealer. It should show:

a)   the name and address of the supplier;

b)   the name and address of the dealer;

c)   the date of the supply;

d)   the make, model, engine number, registration number and year of manufacture of the vehicle;

e)   the total price of the vehicle; and

f)   a declaration signed and dated by the supplier of the vehicle that the details on the voucher are accurate and the vehicle is a qualifying vehicle.

6.3   The dealer must give the supplier a copy of the completed settlement voucher within 15 days of the purchase.

6.4   Where a dealer buys a qualifying vehicle from another dealer established within the State, the invoice issued by that other dealer, suitably endorsed (see paragraph 7.1), is required to support the claim to residual tax.

6.5   Where a dealer buys a vehicle from a dealer in another Member State, it will be supplied either under the special scheme for the taxation of second-hand goods in that member State, or under the normal zero-rated intra-Community supply rules. If it is supplied under a second-hand goods scheme, the purchase price will contain residual VAT, which the dealer can deduct as set out in paragraph 4.4. To support this deduction the dealer must have an invoice issued by the supplier in the other Member State which does not show VAT separately and which is endorsed by the supplier to the effect that the vehicle has been sold under the margin scheme/second-hand goods scheme in the Member State.

6.6   If the vehicle is zero-rated under the intra-Community rules, it means that the dealer in the other Member State is not supplying the vehicle under the special scheme and the vehicle is not, therefore, a qualifying vehicle. The dealer in Ireland will not be entitled to claim residual VAT on the transaction, but must put it through the normal intra-Community acquisition mechanism for VAT. In that case, the invoice from the supplier should show the VAT number of both parties and should indicate that the supply is zero-rated. (Revenue Commissioners' Information Leaflet 7/01 is available on this subject.)

7.   THE SALE OF A QUALIFYING VEHICLE TO A TAXABLE PERSON (INCLUDING TO ANOTHER DEALER)

7.1   Where a dealer sells a vehicle on which s/he has claimed residual VAT, s/he may not issue a VAT invoice for the customer to claim input credit. Therefore, where a qualifying vehicle is sold to another taxable person, the invoice issued must not show VAT separately and must include the following endorsement:

"Special Scheme – this invoice does not give the right to an input credit of VAT".

7.2   This rule applies even when the customer is another motor dealer. However, in that case, even though the customer is not receiving a VAT invoice, s/he is entitled to deduct the residual VAT in the transaction because the vehicle is a qualifying vehicle (see paragraph 3.1).

7.3   Because of the impact of this rule on the car leasing sector, its introduction was postponed until 1 January, 1996. Up to that date, it was acceptable for a motor dealer to issue a normal VAT invoice in respect of the sale of a vehicle on which s/he had claimed deduction of residual VAT.

7.4   The restriction on passing on credit by means of a VAT invoice is a requirement of the Seventh Directive. However, it is always open to the dealer and his customer to agree that the sale of a particular qualifying vehicle will not be dealt with under the scheme outlined in this leaflet. In that case, the dealer can issue a VAT invoice, but if s/he does so s/he cannot take the residual VAT deduction on the purchase of the vehicle. S/he is effectively taking the vehicle out of the special scheme, so, if s/he has already claimed the deduction for that vehicle in a previous VAT period, s/he must reduce his/her deductibility for the current period by the full amount which s/he had previously claimed for that vehicle.

8.   THE SALE OF A QUALIFYING VEHICLE TO ANOTHER MEMBER STATE

8.1   Where a qualifying vehicle is 'new' in VAT terms (i.e. less than six months old or has travelled less than 6,000 km), and is sold to a person in another Member State, the sale should be zero-rated, either directly, if the vehicle is transported by the dealer, or by refund on obtaining proof of transport to the other Member State (i.e. proof of registration of the vehicle there). In this case, there is no obligation to operate the clawback rule at paragraph 5.

8.2   If a qualifying vehicle is not "new" (see above), and is sold to a person in another Member State, Irish VAT is payable on the supply as if it was sold to a customer in the State. If that customer is a VAT-registered person, the rules concerning the invoice (see paragraph 7.1) apply. However, in that case, the dealer and the customer can agree to have the sale zero-rated subject to the normal conditions of intra Community supplies. In that case, the Irish dealer is effectively selling the vehicle under the "normal" VAT rules, not under the special scheme, and has to treat the sale as outlined in paragraph 7.4. The dealer is not entitled to deduction of any residual VAT in respect of his purchase and must make the appropriate adjustment in his current VAT return if he had previously claimed a residual VAT credit for that vehicle.

9. RECORDS

The Revenue Commissioners will require an audit trail from the purchase of a qualifying vehicle to the sale of that vehicle with cross-reference to the relevant supporting documentation. Where residual VAT has been claimed and the vehicle has not been sold, adequate stock records should be available to substantiate this.

10. DATE OF EFFECT

The special scheme had effect from 1 July, 1995. However, as stated at paragraphs 5.3 and 7.3, the date of effect of the clawback and the invoicing rules were phased in to allow the industry adopt new procedures.

11. WITHDRAWAL OF OLD SCHEME

Under the terms of the Second Hand Motor Vehicles Regulations 1988 (S.I. 121 of 1988), a motor dealer was entitled to deduct the residual tax included in the purchase price of certain vehicles. On 1 January, 1994, this scheme was extended to purchases from other Member States. The Finance Act, 1995 replaced this scheme, and the trade- in rules, from 1 July, 1995.

VALUE ADDED TAX INFORMATION LEAFLET NO. 3, MAY 1998

VAT ON PROPERTY
CLAIMS FOR REPAYMENT OF VAT ARISING OUT OF THE SUPREME COURT JUDGEMENT IN THE CASE OF ERIN EXECUTOR AND TRUSTEE COMPANY LIMITED, FOR PERIODS PRIOR TO 27 MARCH, 1998

Introduction

1. The Supreme Court in the Erin Executor and Trustee Company Ltd. case held that section 4(4) of the VAT Act does not take a property out of the VAT net and that a landlord is, therefore, entitled to deduct VAT on post-letting expenses. Section 106 of the Finance Act 1998 amended section 4 of the VAT Act to take account of this judgement. There is a separate information leaflet dealing with the new legislation which has effect from 27 March, 1998.

2. This information leaflet sets out how claims for repayment of VAT on post-letting expenses arising out of the judgement for periods prior to 27 March, 1998 should be dealt with. It should be noted that this right to deductibility has been qualified in the Finance Act, 1998 and the separate information leaflet *VAT on Property - Post-letting expenses, VAT Information Leaflet No. 4 1998*, should be consulted in respect of periods from 27 March, 1998 onwards.

What is deductible?

3. The questions before the Court were-

    "(1)   Whether we [the Appeal Commissioners] were correct in law upon the above facts in holding that the appellant was not entitled to input credit by way of deduction under section 12 of the Value Added Tax Act, 1972 in respect of tax paid on expenses incurred by it either as general overheads or administrative costs of its business or in the maintenance, further development and management of specific properties where the same were incurred subsequent to the creation of the longterm lettings?

    (2)   Whether we [the Appeal Commissioners] were correct in law upon the above facts in holding that the appellant was not entitled to input credit by way of deduction under section 12 of the Value Added Tax Act, 1972 in respect of tax paid on expenses incurred by it either as general overheads or administrative costs of its business or in the maintenance or further development and management of specific properties which were required (sic) by IPFPUT [Erin] with sitting tenants and which have subsequently been partly developed?

    (3)   Whether we [the Appeal Commissioners] were correct in law upon the above facts in holding that the appellant was not entitled to input credit by way of deduction under section 12 of the Value Added Tax Act, 1972 in respect of tax paid on expenses

incurred by it either as general overheads or administrative costs of the business or in the maintenance and management of specific properties which the appellant had acquired with sitting tenants and in respect of which no subsequent development has been carried out?

(4)   Whether we [the Appeal Commissioners] were correct in law in holding that section 4(4) of the said Act of 1972 as is construed and applied by the respondent was not incompatible with or ultra vires the provisions of the said Council Directive 77/388/EEC?"

4.   The answer to the first three questions was no and question 4 was not considered by the Court. The extent to which additional tax is now deductible must be considered in the context of the Supreme Court's decision concerning the first three questions. The judgement also implied that a subsequent supply of a property was chargeable to tax. The new legislation effective from 27 March, 1998 provides that such subsequent supplies are generally exempt. Revenue has decided that it will not retrospectively seek to treat such supplies as taxable. Consequently, Revenue will not refund VAT on expenses incurred in connection with such supplies. Nevertheless, as the implication of the judgement is that such supplies were taxable, a landlord could insist on claiming deductibility on expenses relating to such supplies. Where a landlord insists on deductibility, Revenue will require payment of VAT on the appropriate supply. However, while Revenue will not normally treat such supplies as taxable, they reserve the right to do so in cases where avoidance schemes are evident.

5.   In accordance with the Supreme Court judgement VAT on post-letting expenses incurred by a landlord in respect of a property following a taxable supply of an interest in that property may now be deducted, subject to paragraphs 8 and 9 below, for periods prior to 27 March, 1998. Deductible expenses would include costs relating to rent reviews and rent collection, maintenance of the property and general overheads such as accountancy and office expenses. Expenses directly related to a subsequent disposal of the landlord's interest in the property,(such as the sale of the freehold with sitting tenants) are not deductible as these expenses related to a non-taxable disposal. Similarly, if the tenant surrendered his or her interest in the property and the landlord created a new interest in the property under the VAT rules applicable prior to 26 March, 1997, VAT on expenses relating to the subsequent disposal is not deductible as that disposal was not chargeable to VAT.

6.   A landlord who acquired a property with sitting tenants is also affected by the judgement. Although this type of landlord has not made a taxable supply of the property, the Court has held that he or she is entitled to deduct VAT on post-letting expenses, where the creation of the lease was chargeable to VAT. Again, input tax will be allowed on expenses the landlord incurred in relation to the lease to the original tenants. General overheads will also be deductible, but see paragraph 8 below. If any of

the sitting tenants was not party to the original taxable supply, input tax will not be deductible in relation to expenses relating to the letting to those tenants. This could have arisen if the original tenant surrendered his or her interest in the property and the landlord created a new interest in the property under the VAT rules applicable prior to 26 March 1997.

7. VAT on expenses relating to the acquisition of a property with sitting tenants will be allowed to the extent that the creation of the tenants' interest was subject to VAT. Therefore, in a situation where part of the property is occupied by tenants who acquired their interest as a result of a taxable supply and part of the property is not, then apportionment of the input credit will be required.

Apportionment

8. Where a landlord paid VAT on general overheads and administrative costs he or she will be entitled to deduct VAT to the extent that these costs relate to taxable supplies. In most cases affected by the Erin judgement the landlord will have both deductible and non-deductible VAT. Some apportionment of VAT on general overheads or administrative costs will be required in these cases. The most common apportionment method is based on taxable turnover over total turnover. The turnover method will be unlikely to give a fair result in relation to post letting expenses having regard to the effect of the capitalised value in the first year of the lease with no taxable turnover in the following years. A more equitable result would be one based on a break-down of the rent roll or of the area of the properties let, between those lettings which were subject to a taxable supply and those lettings which were not. Agreement on apportionment should be reached with the appropriate tax office. However, whatever method is used this method must be applied for all periods.

Claims

9. Any claim for a repayment of VAT on post-letting expenses following the Erin judgement should be submitted to the appropriate tax office. Claims should be prepared on an annual basis by way of a supplementary VAT return. Claims may be made for periods up to ten years prior to the date of submission of the claim. It should be noted that the 1998 Finance Act reduces from ten years to six years the time limit within which a claim for a refund of VAT generally may be made. However, as an interim measure anyone claiming a refund for taxable periods prior to 1 May, 1998 can still avail themselves of the ten year limit up to 1 May, 1999. Claims must be supported by proper VAT invoices and computations of the make-up of the claim. These supporting documents should be retained and may be subject to examination. While the provisions of section 20(5) with regard to unjust enrichment could apply to the repayment of VAT on post-letting expenses, Revenue will not invoke these provisions in regard to claims arising out of the Erin judgement.

Direct taxes

10.   To the extent that this VAT has already been claimed as a deduction in the landlord's accounts adjustments will need to be made to his or her direct tax liability for the years/periods in question.

Queries

11.   Any queries about claims for repayment of VAT arising out of the judgement in the case of Erin Executor and Trustee Company Ltd. should be addressed to the appropriate tax office.

Revenue Commissioners.
May, 1998.

VALUE-ADDED TAX INFORMATION LEAFLET
NO. 4, AUGUST 1998

VAT TREATMENT OF POST-LETTING EXPENSES INCURRED ON OR AFTER 27 MARCH, 1998

Introduction
1.   The Supreme Court, in the case of Erin Executor and Trustee Company Ltd., held that a landlord was entitled to deduct VAT on post-letting expenses incurred in relation to a property which had been the subject of a taxable supply of immovable goods for VAT purposes. Section 106 of the Finance Act 1998 amends section 4 of the VAT Act to provide for the effects of the judgement. This information leaflet explains the changes to section 4 of the VAT Act and sets out the circumstances in which VAT on post-letting expenses is deductible with effect from 27 March, 1998.

2.   This leaflet deals with situations that arise following the creation of a taxable leasehold interest in developed property. The creation of the interest is taxable on the capitalized value of the lease. The landlord is also liable to VAT on a self-supply of the reversionary interest on that lease in accordance with section 4(4) of the VAT Act. Where the lease created is for a period of twenty years or more the value of the reversionary interest is disregarded. The Supreme Court held that the application of section 4(4) to the reversionary interest did not take the property out of the VAT net and accordingly a landlord was entitled to VAT deductibility on post-letting expenses in relation to that property.

3.   Following the Supreme Court judgement, the law has been amended to provide for the treatment of subsequent supplies of an interest in property (see paragraphs 4 to 8 of this leaflet). In general, subsequent supplies will be exempt from VAT unless the property has been redeveloped. In addition, the law now specifies the circumstances in which post-letting expenses are deductible for VAT purposes. Two situations are dealt with in this leaflet. What happens when the landlord is the person who created the taxable interest? (see paragraphs 9 and 10 of this leaflet). What happens when the landlord acquired the property after the taxable interest was created? (see paragraph 11 of the leaflet).

      Post-letting expenses are defined in paragraphs 13 to 19 of this leaflet.

Subsequent supplies
4.   Prior to the judgement it was the view of Revenue that where the creation of an interest in immovable goods was taxable, section 4(4) took the property out of the VAT net. This meant that subsequent supplies of an interest in that property by the landlord were generally outside the scope of VAT. However, if the property was redeveloped or was subject to a taxable surrender of that interest, a subsequent supply of an interest in that property was taxable.

5. As the Supreme Court has held that a self-supply under section 4(4) does not take the property out of the VAT net, it is necessary to provide for the VAT treatment of subsequent supplies of the property. The new section 4(9) provides for the exemption of these supplies. There are essentially two types of supply involved. The first involves the transfer of the reversionary interest, say by the sale of the freehold, during the term of the taxable interest and the second involves the disposal of an interest in the property following the expiry of the term of the lease. The changes in section 4(9) provide that, if the property concerned has not been developed since the creation of the taxable interest, subsequent supplies of the property are exempt in both situations just outlined.

6. The first case can best be illustrated by an example:

Example 1

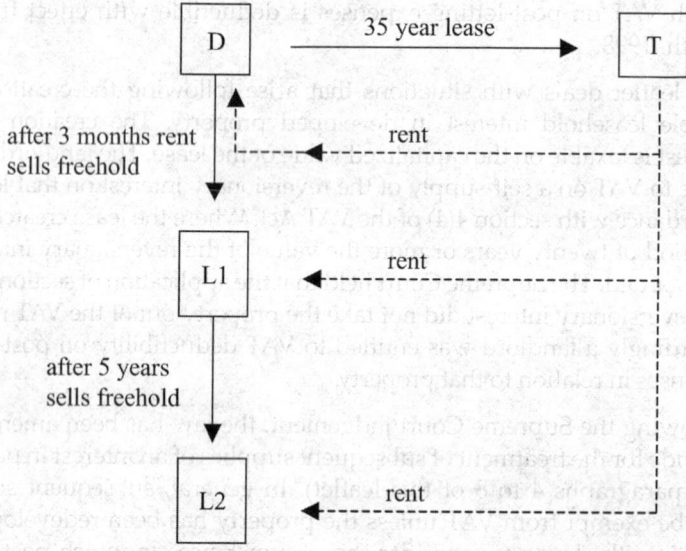

In this example D, the property developer, develops the property and creates a 35 year lease in favour of T, the tenant. The value of the lease is capitalised and VAT is accounted for. As the lease is for 35 years the value of the reversionary interest is disregarded. After 3 months D sells the freehold to L1, an investor. This sale is exempt from VAT. After 5 years L1 sells the freehold to L2, again this sale is exempt from VAT. As both sales of the freehold are exempt from VAT, any costs connected to these sales are not deductible (see, however, paragraph 11 regarding the treatment of postletting expenses).

7. The second category involves supplies following the expiry of the term of the interest.

    This can be illustrated as follows:

    Example 2

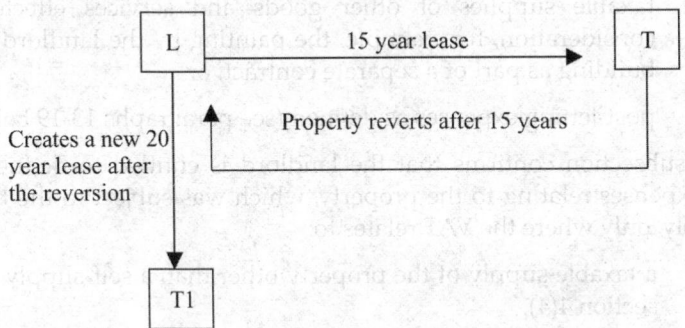

    In this example L creates a fifteen year lease in favour of T. VAT is accounted for on the supply of the interest and the self-supply of the reversion. After fifteen years the property reverts to L. Following the reversion L creates a subsequent lease for twenty years to T1. This subsequent lease is exempt provided, of course, the property has not been developed since the first lease was created. As a consequence, VAT incurred on any costs associated with the new 20 year lease to T1 is not deductible.

8. Section 4(9), therefore, clarifies the treatment of subsequent supplies by the landlord after the creation of a taxable interest. It should be borne in mind that this subsection does not deal with subsequent supplies of an interest in the property following a surrender of that interest by the tenant. The VAT treatment of those transactions was amended in the Finance Act, 1997 and is explained in the booklet called *VAT on Property - Finance Act 1997 Changes - A Revenue Guide*, which is available from local tax offices.

VAT treatment of post-letting expenses from 27 March, 1998

9. The new subsection 4(10) of the VAT Act provides for the deductibility of VAT on post-letting expenses. It ensures that where the creation of an interest in immovable goods was subject to tax, the landlord is entitled to deduct VAT on post-letting expenses as defined (see paragraphs 13 to 19) over the term of the interest. The subsection specifically provides that where the landlord did not create the taxable interest, (L1 or L2 in example 1), he or she shall be deemed to be a taxable person in respect of the postletting expenses even though he or she was not the person who made the taxable supply of the immovable goods.

    The subsection also defines the post-letting expenses that are deductible.

10. Section 4(10)(a) deals with two categories of landlord. The first category is the landlord who creates the taxable interest and who in accordance with the Supreme Court judgement remains a taxable person in respect

of that property. This subsection provides that the landlord is a taxable person in relation to that property in respect of:

(a)   taxable supplies of that property, for example, a taxable disposal of an interest in the property or a self-supply of the property,

(b)   taxable supplies of other goods and services effected for consideration, for example, the painting by the landlord of the building as part of a separate contract, or

(c)   post-letting expenses as defined (see paragraphs 13-19 below).

The subsection confirms that the landlord is entitled to deduct VAT on expenses relating to the property, which was subject to the taxable supply, only where the VAT relates to:

(i)   a taxable supply of the property other than a self-supply under section 4(4),

(ii)   a taxable supply of other goods and services effected for consideration, or

(iii)   post letting expenses as defined (see paragraphs 13-19 below).

This subsection, therefore, limits the circumstances in which VAT is deductible in relation to a property which was the subject of a taxable supply. It confirms the basic principles of VAT law which provide that a taxable person is entitled to claim only input tax which directly relates to a taxable supply. Therefore, VAT on expenses such as legal fees in relation to, say, the sale of a freehold by D to L1 in example 1, is not deductible as these expenses directly relate to an exempt supply.

11.   The second category of landlord dealt with in section 4(10)(a) is the landlord who acquires the property with sitting tenants. This case can best be illustrated by an example:

Example 3

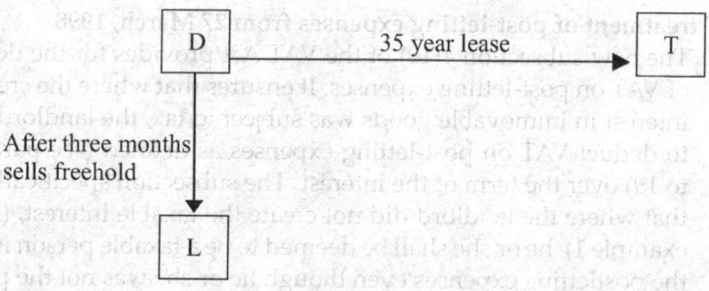

In this example, the developer (D) creates a 35 year lease in favour of the tenant (T). The value of the lease is capitalised and VAT accounted for. As the lease is for 35 years the value of the reversionary interest is disregarded. After three months D sells the freehold to L, the landlord.

This supply is exempt and VAT is not deductible on expenses relating to the supply. The landlord takes on the developer's rights and obligations under the contract. The tenant will now pay the rent to the landlord.

In this example the landlord (L) has not made any taxable supply and would not normally be entitled to claim back VAT on expenses incurred. However, as VAT has been accounted for on the value of the lease on its creation, this subsection deems the landlord to be a taxable person and entitled to deduct VAT in respect of post-letting expenses as defined.

12.   Where a landlord is deemed to be a taxable person in the circumstances outlined above, he or she should contact the appropriate tax office to register for VAT. If the landlord is already a taxable person because he or she makes taxable supplies and is registered for VAT, the VAT on post-letting expenses can be claimed under his or her VAT return.

Definition of post-letting expenses
13.   Paragraph (b) of subsection 4(10) defines post-letting expenses in relation to a taxable lease. There are essentially two categories of deductible post-letting expenses. The first are expenses which the landlord incurs in carrying out services which he or she is obliged to carry out under the terms and conditions of the lease. In effect, these expenses directly relate to the taxable supply of the interest to the tenant. However, to qualify for deduction, the value of these obligations must have been reflected in the value of the lease for VAT purposes. This will normally be the case as the level of the rent will reflect the terms and conditions of the lease and the value of the supply for VAT purposes will therefore reflect this.

14.   While section 4(10)(b)(i) refers to expenses incurred in carrying out services, Revenue will allow deductibility on the provision of supplies of goods of the type specified in section 3(1B) of the VAT Act, i.e. the supply of electricity, gas, and any form of power, heat, refrigeration or ventilation. To qualify for deductibility those supplies must, of course, be provided under the terms and conditions of the lease.

15.   VAT on expenses that the landlord incurs which he or she is obliged to carry out under the terms of the lease but which are not reflected in the rent charged is not deductible under the provisions of this section. However, under "the landlord's concession", which has been in place since 1985, landlords have been able to deduct the VAT on these expenses and pass on a VAT credit to their taxable tenants. Where expenses such as cleaning, security, electricity, etc. are provided by the landlord on a reimbursement basis from the tenants, the landlord's concession can still apply to these expenses. However, as the landlord will now be a taxable person in respect of post-letting expenses, the landlord's concession can be processed through the landlord's VAT return and a separate VAT registration is not required. Where reimbursable expenses are passed through the landlord, he or she should issue to each tenant, once a year, an invoice showing VAT charged to the tenant on these services. The VAT deductible and payable by the landlord should be incorporated in the appropriate VAT return.

16. Of course, where a landlord is actually supplying such services directly and for consideration, he or she is a taxable person in the normal way. VAT is chargeable on such service charges and the expenses which the landlord incurs in supplying those services is deductible subject to the normal rules.

17. The second category of deductible post-letting expenses are expenses which the landlord incurs in:

   (a)   collecting the rent payable by the tenant,

   (b)   carrying out a rent review,

   (c)   the exercise of an option to extend the term of the lease or the exercise of a break clause to terminate the lease.

General overheads

18. Revenue have decided, following consultation with trade interests, to allow deductibility on a landlord's general overheads. Under this concessional treatment the following category of expenses will also be treated as post-letting expenses:

   "general overheads of a landlord's business to the extent that the landlord's letting of immovable property was taxable as a supply of immovable goods under section 4 of the VAT Act"

   These expenses will include items such as office expenses and audit fees. For the purpose of this concession general overheads do not include any goods or services which are provided by the landlord to the tenant. Effectively general overheads are expenses that the landlord incurs in relation to his or her own business. Where the landlord's entire lettings of immovable property was taxable as a supply of goods all general overheads relating to the lettings are deductible.

19. However, the concession does not extend to expenses a landlord incurs in relation to an exempt supply of property. Where a landlord acquires a property with sitting tenants, where the lease to these tenants was taxable, expenses relating to the acquisition of the property are not treated as general overheads for the purpose of this concession. Therefore VAT on expenses, such as legal fees, relating to such acquisition are not deductible.

Apportionment

20. Where a landlord has a mixed portfolio of lettings, some which were taxable as a supply of goods and some which were not, apportionment of VAT on general overheads will be required. Apportionment of input credit is usually based on the proportion of taxable turnover to total turnover. However, given the nature of property transactions a more appropriate method may be one based on a break-down of the rent roll between lettings which were subject to a taxable supply and those that were not. Any apportionment method should be agreed with the relevant tax office.

Date of effect

21.   These changes have effect as on and from 27 March 1998.

Queries

22.   Any queries about this issue should be addressed to the appropriate tax office.

Revenue Commissioners.
August, 1998.

VALUE-ADDED TAX INFORMATION LEAFLET NO. 7/98

VAT ON TELECOMMUNICATIONS SERVICES

General

1. Several provisions in the 1997 and 1998 Finance Acts relate to changes in the VAT rules concerning international telecommunications services.

2. Prior to 1 July, 1997, the place where telecommunications services were deemed to be supplied was the place where the supplier had established his/her business. Therefore, a supply of telecommunications services from a supplier in, say, the US to a customer in the EU escaped VAT altogether because the place of liability to tax was outside the scope of EU VAT. This meant that although such services were entirely consumed within the EU, they were not subject to EU VAT. The opposite case also applied as EU suppliers of telecommunications services to customers outside the EU were obliged to account for VAT on those services, even though they were entirely consumed outside the EU. This resulted in distortion of competition to the disadvantage of the EU suppliers. To combat this, all Member States have sought and received identical derogations from Article 9(1) of the Sixth VAT Directive.

3. The arrangements set out in this leaflet explain how the derogation is applied in Ireland. The new rules deal primarily with international telecommunications suppliers.

4. Under the terms of the derogation, as from 1 July, 1997, VAT is chargeable on supplies of telecommunications services used within the EU, even if the supplier is established outside the EU. There are various rules which determine where and by whom this VAT must be accounted for. Also, certain supplies by EU suppliers to non-EU established customers are now taken out of the VAT net.

5. The main features of Irish VAT law and practice can now be summarised as follows:

the term "telecommunications service" has been defined for VAT purposes (see paragraph 8);

- telecommunications services have been added to the Fourth Schedule of the VAT Act (see Statement of Practice SP - VAT 5/94- Fourth Schedule Services) with the result that

   a customer in the State, other than a private individual, who buys telecommunications services from outside the EU or from another Member State must self-account for and pay the VAT on those services and

   a service provider established in the State whose customers are business persons outside the State may supply those customers without VAT;

- an EU service provider who supplies a service to a private individual in another Member State must account for the VAT in his/her own Member State;

- a non-EU service provider who supplies a service to private individuals in this State must register and account for the VAT here;

- a service provider established here must account for VAT here on services which he/she provides to private individuals who, although resident outside the EU, use the services while they are here. Such a service provider is not liable for VAT on the services which the non-EU resident uses outside the EU.

6. The derogation includes certain anti-avoidance rules concerning pre-payments, which have the effect of applying the new rules to payments made prior to 1 July, 1997, in respect of services supplied after that date.

7. The following chart (Chart A) illustrates how the new rules are being operated throughout the EU.

Chart A

Liability to VAT on supplies of telecommunications services.

	Status and place of establishment or residence of customer	Supplier in Ireland	Supplier in OMS	Supplier outside EU
(1)	business customer in Ireland	Supplier accounts for Irish VAT	Customer accounts for Irish VAT	Customer accounts for Irish VAT
(2)	private individual in Ireland	Supplier accounts for Irish VAT	Supplier accounts for OMS VAT	Supplier must register and account for Irish VAT
(3)	business customer in OMS	Customer accounts for OMS VAT	Supplier/ customer accounts for OMS VAT[1]	Customer accounts for OMS VAT
(4)	private individual in OMS	Supplier accounts for Irish VAT	Supplier accounts for OMS VAT[2]	Supplier must register and account for OMS VAT
(5)	outside EU, whether business customer or private individual	Outside the scope of Irish VAT - No VAT payable (but see column 6)	Outside the scope of Irish VAT	Outside the scope of EU VAT
(6)	private individual resident outside EU but avails of service while in Ireland	Supplier accounts for Irish VAT	Outside the scope of Irish VAT	Outside the scope of Irish VAT when mobile services, cards etc. are involved

OMS = other Member State of the EU

1   If supplier and customer in the same Member State, supplier pays VAT.

If supplier and customer in different Member States, customer pays VAT in his/her Member State.

2   Supplier pays VAT in his/her Member State, even if customer in a different State.

Scope of the tax

8.   The scope of the term "telecommunications services" has been defined in the VAT Act as

"services relating to the transmission, emission or reception of signals, writing, images and sounds or information of any nature by wire, radio, optical or other electromagnetic systems, including the transfer or assignment of the right to use capacity for such transmission, emission or reception".

9.   In general, the services concerned are those which consist of making available the means of telecommunication. The types of service covered by the definition include the following:

* telephone calls, telephone calls delivered by cellular phones, paging, the transmission element of Electronic Data Interchange, teleconferencing and call-back services;

* switching, completion of another provider's calls, the provision of leased lines and circuits or global networks;

* telex, facsimile, multi-messaging;

* e-mail and access to the internet;

* satellite transmission services, covering transponder rental/hire and both space segments and earth segments, which includes uplinks and downlinks via land earth stations, coastal stations, outside broadcasting units, or similar.

Added value services, for which the customer pays a charge in addition to the telecommunications service access charge, are not included in the definition. Each added value service is to be treated according to the VAT rules appropriate to the service in question e.g. advertising service (see SP VAT 3/92 - Advertising Services).

It should be noted that, by common agreement among all Member States, the definition does not cover the service of broadcasting, which remains taxable by reference to the place where the supplier has established his/her business or has a fixed establishment.

Who is liable?

10.   Persons who are liable to pay VAT in the State in respect of telecommunications services are the following:

(i)   telecommunications suppliers established in the State (see para 13) whose customers are

* established or resident in the State, (whether business customers or other) or

- private individuals in another Member State of the EU, or

- private individuals resident outside the EU and are availing of the service while in the State, on or after 1 May 1998

if the annual turnover of the supplier exceeds or is likely to exceed £20,000;

(ii)   telecommunications suppliers established outside the EU whose customers are private individuals in the State, regardless of the size of the supplier's turnover;

(iii)   business customers, who receive telecommunications supplies from outside the State (either from another Member State or from outside the EU), regardless of the value of the supply received.

The categories mentioned in subparagraphs (ii) and (iii) above are liable for the VAT involved in respect of supplies made/received on or after 1 July 1997. Persons who are not already registered for VAT, and who now find themselves obliged to register and account for VAT on telecommunications services should contact the Central Registration Information Office at Arus Brugha, 9/15 Upper O'Connell Street, Dublin 2 for the appropriate form and information about the registration procedure.

11.   Where a telecommunications supplier established in another Member State supplies services to private individuals in this State, that supplier is liable to VAT on those services in the Member State where he or she is established.

12.   Where a telecommunications supplier is established in the State and all the customers are either established outside the EU (and using the service outside the EU), or are business customers in another Member State, the supplier is deemed not to be supplying taxable services here. Therefore, unless that supplier is registered for VAT in respect of other activities, he or she would not normally be in a position to register for VAT here. However, such a supplier can recover VAT paid on the business inputs by applying to VAT Repayments Section, Ennis (see Statement of Practice SP-VAT/2/94 -Repayments to Unregistered Persons).

The Supplier

13.   The place of establishment of a supplier is the place where the supplier has established the business or has an establishment, or, if he or she has more than one establishment, the one which is most concerned with the supply in question. If the supplier has established the business in several countries, and there is doubt about which establishment is most concerned with a particular supply, he or she should consult the local Inspector of Taxes. In general terms, a supplier is regarded as making supplies from the location where he or she has the technical and staff resources sufficient to make those supplies. (However, a supplier whose establishment is outside the EU but who supplies private individuals within the State must register here and account for the VAT on those supplies.)

The customer

14.   The status and place of establishment or residence of the customer and, in certain circumstances, the place of use and enjoyment must be taken into account in deciding where the service is to be taxed.

As regards status, the customer is either a private individual, a business customer or a public body. Farmers who are not registered for VAT are treated as business customers in respect of telecommunications services they receive from abroad for the purpose of their farming activities. Although they must register and account for VAT on these telecommunications services, they are entitled to retain their unregistered status for their farming activities.

Public bodies i.e. Government Departments, local authorities and other statutory bodies must self-account for VAT in respect of telecommunication services received from suppliers outside the State where EU VAT has not been charged.

The Member State or country of establishment or residence of the customer can be identified in several ways, for example

- the country where the customer uses the service (e.g. a fixed line in a particular location)

- the country where the customer is billed for the service.

Normally it will be possible to identify which country is the appropriate one for the purposes of deciding where an international telecommunications service should be taxed (or if tax is due at all). However, if there is a doubt, for example if a business customer received a fixed line service or a mobile phone service in one country but is invoiced for it at an establishment in another country, the parties concerned should contact their local Inspector of Taxes to confirm whether, and where, tax is payable.

Effect of the rules on certain services

15.   (a)   Mobile phone services

Irish suppliers of mobile phone services are liable to VAT on services provided to business and private customers established or resident in the State, for their usage of the service anywhere in the world.

If an Irish supplier of mobile phone services makes supplies to business customers established in another Member State of the EU, those services are not subject to Irish VAT but the customers are liable to VAT in the Member State where they are established.

Similarly, any business customers who are established here and supplied with mobile phone services in Ireland from suppliers outside the State and who use their mobile phones for business purposes must account for the VAT on those services here.

They are entitled to deductibility of that VAT under the normal deductibility rules.

(b)   Phone cards

There are several variations of cards which can be used to procure telecommunications services, and the VAT treatment can vary, depending on the transaction involved. The following paragraphs indicate the VAT treatment of the cards currently available. Suppliers marketing new cards are advised to check on the correct VAT treatment in advance.

(i)   Pre-paid phone cards

Pre-paid phone cards are specifically legislated for in the Finance Act, 1998. The following rules apply in the case of

- physical cards denominated in terms of units of service;
- physical cards denominated in money amounts;
- other tokens including personal identification numbers (P.I.Ns) which give the customer a right to access a telecom network without incurring a further charge at the time when that network is accessed (note - in this case it is possible that the customer may not receive a physical card or token at the time of sale - merely an allocation of a PIN, for which the payment is made).

For the purpose of clarity, the term 'pre-paid phone card' will be used to cover all the above possibilities.

The place and time of taxation are, respectively, the place and time of supply of the pre-paid phone card itself. Pre-paid phone cards sold in Ireland attract VAT at 21%. The Finance Act 1998 contains a provision to ensure there is not double taxation when a telecom service is provided on foot of a pre-paid phone card on which the VAT has already been accounted for.

A company which sells pre-paid phone cards either as a wholesaler or retailer is normally liable to VAT on those sales as if it was in the business of supplying any taxable fourth schedule service (see Statement of Practice SP - VAT 5/94 – Fourth Schedule Services). However, the Revenue are prepared to accept arrangements whereby a company which supplies pre-paid phone cards to retailers within the State can account for VAT by reference to the full retail value of the card so no liability attaches to the retailer. Retailers should not, however, assume this arrangement applies in the case of all pre-paid phone card sales and should check with their suppliers. Any telecommunications supplier wishing to avail of this arrangement should apply to the local Inspector of Taxes.

The Finance Act, 1998, makes provision for the repayment of VAT to a taxable person who, in the course of business, sells pre-paid phone cards *which are subsequently used outside the EU* to access a telecommunications network. (The repayment does not apply to cards used within the EU.) The repayment is allowed *to the extent that* the card is used outside the EU. This means that, in the case where a customer uses the same card both in the EU and also outside it, part of the VAT which was accounted for at the time of the sale of the card can be refunded to the taxable person, to the extent that the card was used outside the EU. The taxable person (telecommunications supplier or retailer)can make the appropriate adjustment in the VAT 3 return for the period in which the telecommunications supplier's records of the place of use of the card become available.

The formula for calculating the VAT deduction is as follows:

$$(A-B) \times \frac{C}{C + 100}$$

where

A　　equals the tax inclusive price charged by the company (telecommunications supplier or retailer) which sold the card for that part of the value of the card which was used up in accessing the telecommunications service in a country outside the EU, and

B　　equals the tax inclusive price charged to the company which sold the card for that part of the value of the card which was used up in accessing the telecommunications service in a country outside the EU, and

C　　is the percentage rate of tax chargeable on the supply of the card at the time of that supply by that supplier (currently 21).

Where pre-paid phone cards are supplied through a number of suppliers e.g. a telecommunications supplier and a retailer each supplier can claim a VAT refund based on the formula provided the appropriate proof of use outside the EU is available.

The following examples illustrate how a VAT refund may be calculated in various circumstances:-

1)   retail selling price of phone card = IR£10.0

2)   records/accounts show that IR£2.5 in value of phone calls (i.e. 25 per cent) accessed outside EU

3)   retailer has a 10 per cent mark-up.

Example 1 – Supplier to retailer to final consumer.

Supplier – Formula (A-B) x $\dfrac{C}{C+100}$ = (2.3 - nil) x $\dfrac{2}{21+100}$ = 39p

VAT refund to Supplier = 39p

Retailer – Formula (A-B) x $\dfrac{C}{C+100}$ = (2.5 - 2.3) x $\dfrac{2}{21+100}$ = 4p

VAT refund to Retailer = 4p

The combined refunds of 43p equals VAT at 21 per cent included in the value of IR£2.50 which reflects the value of the card accessed outside the EU.

Example 2   **– Supply of pre-paid phone card by a company which supplies to retailers but which accounts for VAT on the full retail value of the card and no VAT liability is attached to the retailer.**

Supplier – Formula (A-B) x $\dfrac{C}{C+100}$ = (2.5 - nil) x $\dfrac{2}{21+100}$ = 43p

VAT Refund to Supplier = 43p

As in the previous example the VAT refund equals the VAT at 21 per cent included in the value of IR£2.50. (i.e. value of card accessed outside EU) but the full refund is made to the supplier of the pre-paid phone card who is accounting on the gross retail value of the card.

Repayment is also available to taxable or exempt bodies who incur VAT under the reverse-charge mechanism on purchases of pre-paid phone cards from abroad, if the subsequent use of the cards takes place outside the EU. This can be claimed as a deduction on the VAT 3 return in the period when the record of the use of the cards becomes available.

Example 3 —   Retailer who accounts for VAT under the reverse-charge mechanism on purchase of pre-paid phone cards from abroad.

	IR£
Price to retailer from foreign supplier	7.5
- self accounts for VAT at 21 per cent in this State	1.6
VAT incl. price	9.1
Retailer sells (assuming 10 per cent mark-up)	8.3
-VAT at 21 per cent	1.7
VAT incl. price	10.0

Retailer entitled to refund of VAT to the extent that phone card was used outside EU (i.e. 25 per cent of 1.7) = 43p.

Example 4 —   Exempt body which accounts for VAT under the reverse-charge mechanism on purchase of pre-paid phone cards from abroad.

	IR£
Price to exempt body from foreign supplier	7.5
- self accounts for VAT at 21 per cent in this State	1.6
VAT incl. price	9.1

Exempt body uses card outside EU (for business purposes or not), to the extent of 25 per cent.

Exempt body entitled to refund of VAT to the extent of 25 per cent (i.e. 25 per cent of 1.6) = 40p

It is emphasised that a person claiming repayment of VAT for the non-EU use of a pre-paid phone card must have the appropriate proof that the card was used outside the EU and the extent of such use. This must be retained in the records and may be required for inspection.

(ii)   Telephone charge cards or post-paid PIN cards

These are cards which are sold to customers for telephone use in advance of payment. The charge card operates on the basis of a PIN which is keyed in as part of the dialling sequence. The customer is subsequently invoiced in respect of the use of the card, frequently by incorporating the appropriate amount into the normal telephone bill covering the telephone services to his or her establishment or residence. While these cards are marketed as a convenience for persons travelling abroad, they can also be used within the State. When the card is used abroad, the customer dials a free-phone number allocated to the country where he or she is making the call, and this puts him or her in contact with the network which issued the card and which will later issue the invoice. That network then connects the customer to the required number.

For VAT purposes these transactions are treated as telecommunications services supplied to the customer at the location of the customer's establishment or residence, regardless of where the customer is physically located when using the card. The VAT treatment is the same as that for other invoiced telecom services, as outlined in this leaflet.

(c)　　Internet

Access to the Internet is regarded as a telecommunications service for VAT purposes. Therefore, a person who supplies access to the Internet in return for subscription or fee by the customer is treated as a supplier of telecommunications services. If the customer is charged for access to specialised services via the Internet, these extra charges are not regarded as part of the charge for the telecommunications service. The VAT treatment of such extra charges follows the normal VAT rules regarding supplies of services, i.e. the nature of the service supplied dictates which VAT rule applies.

(d)　　Leased Lines

The provision of access to lines or networks is treated as a telecommunications service, including access under long or short-term lease arrangements.

Further Information

Any additional queries should be addressed to your local Inspector of Taxes.

EXPLANATORY LEAFLET (JUNE 1999)

VALUE ADDED TAX IN THE CASE OF CHARITIES

PART 1.

Does Value Added Tax (VAT) Apply to Charities ?

Yes, there is no general exemption in respect of Value Added Tax for organisations which have been granted charitable tax exemption. There are, however, specific reliefs from VAT in certain circumstances and, where appropriate, such reliefs may also be availed of by charities (see Part 2 of this leaflet).

Must a Charity register and account for VAT ?

Charities are not, in the normal course, regarded as supplying goods or services in the course or furtherance of a business and as such are neither obliged nor entitled to register and account for VAT on their income. They are not therefore entitled to a repayment of VAT incurred on their purchases other than in the specific circumstances provided for in Part 2 of this leaflet. Charities carrying on a trade e.g. the sale of publications, operating a restaurant etc. are however obliged to register for VAT in respect of such trading activities subject to the threshold for registration, currently €51,000 for the sale of goods, being exceeded.

It should be noted that a Charity or any other group engaged in non-commercial activity which acquires or is likely to acquire more than €41,000 worth of goods from another EU Member State in any period of twelve months is obliged to register and account for VAT in respect of such intra-Community acquisition(s). Registration does not give VAT deduction rights to the charity. Similarly, a charity is obliged to register and account for VAT on certain services received from abroad irrespective of the level of expenditure involved. These services are typically the services of consultants, lawyers, accountants etc. Further details in this regard can be obtained from your local tax office.

If, as a charity, you are required to register for VAT you must complete form STR (in the case of an unincorporated body) or form TR2 (in the case of a limited company) which is obtainable from the Taxes Central Registration Office, Arus Brugha, 9/15 Upper O'Connell St, Dublin 1 Tel: 01-8746821 or from your local tax office.

PART 2.

Specific reliefs from VAT and which may relate to charitable activities

1.   Organisations involved in the transport of severely and permanently physically disabled persons

Repayment of VAT paid may be claimed in relation to the purchase and adaptation of vehicles for use by organisations for the transport of severely and permanently disabled persons. A qualifying organisation means a philanthropic organisation which is not funded primarily by the State, by any board established by statute, or by any public or local authority. The organisation must be chiefly engaged, in a voluntary capacity and on a non-commercial basis, in the care and transport of severely and permanently physically disabled persons and is recognised as such by the Revenue Commissioners.

There is provision for the repayment or reduction of Vehicle Registration Tax (VRT) under this heading also.

2.   Radios for the blind

Section 20(2) VAT Act 1972 provides for repayment of VAT paid in respect of radio broadcasting reception apparatus intended for use by blind persons. The repayment is only made to the institution/society if it shows to the satisfaction of the Revenue Commissioners that:

- its primary object is the amelioration of the lot of blind persons; and,

- the goods in question are intended for the use of blind persons.

Repayment claim form VAT 59 refers.

3.   Appliances for use by Disabled Persons

Statutory Instrument No. 428/81 provides for repayment of VAT on certain aids and appliances purchased by or on behalf of a disabled person which assist that disabled person in the performance of essential daily functions or in the exercise of a vocation e.g. stair-lifts.

Repayment claim form VAT 61A refers.

4.   Sea rescue craft and equipment

Statutory Instrument No. 192/85 enables VAT on certain small reserve craft (15 tons gross tonnage or less), ancillary equipment and special boat buildings and also on the hire, repair and maintenance of these craft, to be repaid to qualifying sea rescue groups.

Repayment claim form VAT 70 refers.

5.   Humanitarian Goods for Export

Statutory Instrument No. 308/87 provides relief from VAT for goods purchased for exportation by philanthropic organisations for humanitarian, charitable or teaching activities abroad e.g. Apostolic Societies, Chernobyl Children Projects etc.

Repayment claim form VAT 73 refers.

6.   Donated medical equipment

Statutory Instrument No. 58/92 provides for repayment of VAT suffered by a hospital or a donor on the purchase of new medical instruments and appliances (excluding means of transport) which are funded by voluntary donations. The VAT refund may be claimed by whomever suffers the tax i.e. the hospital or the donor, as appropriate, but not, of course, both. The principal conditions are that the instrument or appliance must:

- cost €25,000 or more (exclusive of VAT);

- be designed and manufactured for use solely in medical research or in diagnosis, prevention or treatment of illness;

- not have been part-funded by the State, and

- be the subject of a recommendation by the Minister for Health that, having regard to the requirements of the health services in the State, a refund of the VAT would be appropriate.

Repayment claim form VAT 72 refers.

7.   Donated Research Equipment

Statutory Instrument No. 38/95 provides for repayment of VAT, incurred in the purchase or importation of any new instrument or appliance (excluding means of transport) through voluntary donations, to a research institution or a university, school or similar educational body engaged in medical research in a laboratory. The principal conditions are that the instrument or appliance must:

- cost €25,000 or more (exclusive of VAT);

- be designed and manufactured for use in medical research;

- not have been part-funded by the State, and

- be the subject of a recommendation by the Health Research Board that, having regard to the requirements of medical research in the State, a refund of the VAT would be appropriate.

Repayment claim form VAT 72A refers.

Addresses for further Contact

Repayment of VAT	Claim Form	Contact Address
1. Vehicle purchased by an organisation for the transport of severely and permanently disabled persons	DD O	Central Repayments Office Revenue Commissioners Coolshannagh Monaghan Tel: 047-82800 Fax: 047-82782
2. Radios for the Blind	VAT 59	VAT Repayments (Unregistered Section) Accountant General's Office Revenue Commissioners Government Offices Kilrush Road
3. Appliances for use by disabled persons	VAT 61A	Ennis Co. Clare
4. Sea rescue craft and equipment	VAT 70	Tel: 065-6841200
5. Humanitarian Goods for Export	VAT 73	Fax: 065-6840394
6. Donated Medical Equipment	VAT 72	
7. Donated Research Equipment	VAT 72A	

Issued June, 1999
Office of the Revenue Commissioners
Charities Section
Government Offices
Nenagh
Co. Tipperary

STATEMENT OF PRACTICE (SP - VAT 01/99)

ABOLITION OF DUTY-FREE SALES TO TRAVELLERS ON INTRA-COMMUNITY JOURNEYS

1.   Introduction

As and from 30 June, 1999, duty-free sales to travellers on intra-Community journeys will be abolished. This means that such travellers will no longer be able to purchase goods free of excise duty and VAT. Such purchases - with the exception of food, drink and tobacco products for on-board consumption - will now be subject to normal rates of excise duty and VAT. Duty-free sales will, however, continue for passengers travelling to destinations outside the EU.

The information contained in this Statement of Practice is primarily aimed at economic operators engaged in the supply of, or retail selling of, goods to intra-Community travellers in airports and on board ships and aircraft, but it will also inform travellers regarding the new arrangements.

2   (a)   What goods may no longer qualify as duty-free?

- All goods sold or supplied in airports to travellers embarking on intra-Community journeys.

- All goods sold or supplied to passengers or crew members on intra-Community journeys, other than food, drink and tobacco products for on-board consumption during the journey.

- Supplies of provisions and merchandise to ships and aircraft intended for "take-away" sale or supply to passengers or crew.

2   (b)   What goods may continue to be sold duty-free?

- All goods sold or supplied to passengers travelling to destinations outside the EU.

- Small quantities of food, drink and tobacco products sold or supplied to passengers on intra-Community journeys for consumption on board. (See also paragraph 5.)

3.   What journeys will be affected by the change?

All direct intra-Community journeys will be affected by the change.

The fact that the vessel or aircraft passes through international waters/airspace or through the territorial waters or airspace of another EU Member State or non-EU country does not affect the tax liability, provided that the route is a direct one between two EU ports/airports.

However, if the vessel or aircraft stops off in a non-EU country or an area outside the EU fiscal area to enable passengers to embark or disembark, the route is deemed to be one to or from a non-EU country. The present rules on duty-free sales to passengers travelling to countries outside the EU will continue to apply to such routes.

4. **Who will be affected by the change?**

- Passengers and crews on intra-Community journeys buying goods for take-away.

- Operators of "duty-free" outlets, both land-based and on ships and aircraft.

- Suppliers of dutiable and taxable products to ships and aircraft for sale on board for take-away.

As and from 1 July, 1999, the traditional duty-free crew allowances relating to goods for take-away (or bringing ashore) will be discontinued. The on-board consumption of duty-free goods available to passengers on intra-Community journeys can, from a Revenue viewpoint, be equally availed of by crew members under the same general limitations and conditions.

5. **What can be sold duty-free for consumption on board?**

Food, drink and tobacco products sold or provided for consumption on board vessels or aircraft during an intra-Community journey can be supplied duty-free from a bar, restaurant or kiosk or from a bar trolley in the case of aircraft . The number of such on-board sales outlets and their location and operation will be subject to Revenue prior approval. However, sales of food, drink and tobacco products from other shops (e.g. supermarkets) or vending machines will not be duty-free.

To avoid abuse, the duty-free sale of goods for consumption on board will be subject to certain conditions, as follows:

i.　　*Alcoholic beverages* are to be served in approved outlets, with sales being restricted as follows:

- Spirits may only be sold as poured drinks or in miniature bottles; poured measures of duty-free spirits must be dispensed from a different size bottle (i.e.1.125 litre) to that sold on board duty-paid (namely, 70 cl or 1 litre).

- Wine may be sold in full bottles, half-bottles or quarter bottles; however, full bottles and half-bottles must be opened (i.e. uncorked) before being handed over to the customer.

- Beer must be sold as poured drinks or in opened cans or bottles.

ii.　　*Tobacco products* are to be sold in approved outlets, with sales being restricted to the following quantities to any one customer:

Cigarettes: in a single packet of 20 or smaller,

or

Cigars: in a single packet of 5 or less,

or

Cigarillos: in a single packet of 10 or less,

or

Tobacco: in a single packet of 25 gms. or less.

* **Note**: All sales of tobacco products on board aircraft operating a no-smoking policy will be regarded as not for consumption on board and must always be duty-paid.

iii   *Other food and drink* are to be sold in quantities and in a manner suitable for immediate consumption on board, e.g. meals served in a restaurant and fruit, bars of chocolate, snacks, cans of soft drinks, etc. sold from an approved outlet.

6.   Treatment of take-away sales on intra-Community journeys

(a)   Excise Duty

All take-away sales of excisable products must be duty-paid. The EU rules which apply to the charging of excise duty specify that the duty rate to be applied will be the rate in force in the Member State where the goods are released for consumption (in practice, initially, at the place and time of loading). In the case of excisable products loaded in the Member State of departure of a ferry or airline on an intra-Community journey, sales of such goods will continue to bear these rates up to the point of arrival in the territorial waters or airspace of the Member State of destination. Sales beyond this point will attract excise duty liability in the Member State of destination and will have to be accounted for to the tax authorities of that Member State. Provision exists for the reimbursement of the excise duty originally borne on the goods concerned in the Member State of departure.

In the case of sea traffic between Ireland, UK and France, the limit of territorial waters commences 12 nautical miles from the coastline. In the case of air traffic, the limit will be deemed to be 20 minutes prior to landing of the aircraft.

In practical terms, a fundamental decision for operators is whether or not to close shops/outlets for business within the territorial limits of the Member State of destination. If the decision is made to close shops, liability to excise duty on stocks, already duty-paid at the rates of the Member State of loading/departure, will not arise in the Member State of destination throughout the journey across the sea/air territory of the latter State, on both the outward and return journeys. For example in the case of a ferry, Irish duty-paid excisable goods loaded at Dunlaoghaire may be sold at the **Irish** duty rate up to 12 nautical miles from the UK coastline on the outward journey.

If the shop is closed at this point and no further sales of these goods take place on both the outward and return journeys through UK territorial waters, liability to UK excise duty will not be incurred. Sales of this stock may re-commence at **Irish** duty rates without incurring UK duty liability once the ferry proceeds beyond the UK 12-mile limit on its return voyage to Dunlaoghaire.

If, on the other hand, sales of this Irish duty-paid stock take place within the 12-mile outward or return journeys across UK territorial waters, liability to **UK** excise duty arises and must be accounted for to the UK authorities. In this case, the UK duty liability will apply in respect of sales made up to the Irish 12 nautical miles limit.

(b)   VAT

VAT is chargeable and must be accounted for in the Member State of departure. For example, goods sold on board a vessel or aircraft on a journey from Ireland to the UK will be subject to **Irish** VAT. On the return journey from the UK to Ireland, goods sold on board will be subject to **UK** VAT. The territorial limit rules for excise duty do not apply for VAT.

In the case of travel by air, each flight is regarded for VAT purposes as a separate journey. However, in cases where an aircraft has a short stopover in one Member State en route to another, and the flight number remains unchanged for both legs of the journey, the stopover will be disregarded and the VAT regime to apply will be that of the Member State of the first place of departure. (See paragraph 9 as regards air passengers transiting through a Member State en route to a destination outside the EU.)

7.   When can sales on board vessels or aircraft take place?

There is no Revenue restriction on when sales from on-board shops, bars, restaurants or kiosks can take place once the voyage or flight has commenced. However, attention is again drawn to the special rules applicable to sales of excisable goods within the territorial sea or air limits of the country of destination as outlined in paragraph 6(a).

8.   What happens if ships or aircraft stop-off at a non-EU country during an intra-Community journey?

Take-away sales of duty-free products will be allowed on journeys where vessels or aircraft stop-off at a non-EU country or a place outside the Community's fiscal territory (e.g. Channel Islands, Canary Islands) provided passengers have the opportunity to disembark and make purchases during such stop-offs.

Passengers finally disembarking in Ireland following such a stop-off are restricted to the normal travellers' allowances for passengers arriving from outside the EU and must pass through normal Customs controls on arrival, i.e. the Red or Green Channel as appropriate.

9.   **Treatment of airline passengers transiting through a second EU airport en route to a final non-EU destination**

Passengers on such routes in possession of a single through ticket are regarded as being on an extra-Community journey, as far as Revenue are concerned. They may avail of duty-free shopping either at the first Community airport of departure or at the final airport of departure from the Community, (e.g. on a through ticket from Dublin via Frankfurt to Sydney the passenger may purchase duty-free at Dublin, and at Frankfurt if the local airport authorities so permit).

10.   **What will be the main effect on the operation of duty-free shops at airports?**

Shops in airports handling both intra- and extra-Community flights will need to distinguish, in sales and accounting, between sales to passengers travelling to destinations outside the EU (duty-free) and sales to passengers travelling to other Member States (not duty-free). The determination of whether a sale is duty-free or not will be made at the point of payment (i.e. at the check-out), where the passenger's ticket will provide evidence of duty-free entitlement.

These shops will be approved as tax warehouses with special approval conditions to take account of this trade.

Accounting for the excise duty and VAT will be on the basis of the total dutiable/VATable sales over the appropriate accounting period. Deferment of the excise duty will be available, subject to provision of the usual security.

11.   **Treatment of duty-free stocks held on changeover**

From the end of business on 30 June, 1999, arrangements will be made for the assessment of excise duty liability on stocks of goods held in shops on board ferries and at regional airports dealing only with intra-Community sales, as these will have changed in status from duty-free to duty-paid on 1 July, 1999. This assessment of excise duty will not apply to airport shops handling both intra- and extra-Community traffic, since the liability in the latter shops will be determined at the point of payment at the check-outs.

In the case of ferries, the duty liability will apply to stocks held on vessels in Irish ports and arriving in Irish territorial waters on 1 July, 1999 which have not been otherwise accounted for.

12.   Registration with Revenue

(a)   *Excise*

Revenue will require all commercial operators who sell or supply excisable goods for take-away on intra-Community journeys to be registered as Registered Excise Traders (RET). Applications to register and any associated accounting enquiries should be addressed to the local Collector of Customs & Excise. Where an operator or carrier does not have an Irish business address or residence, he or she will be required to appoint a fiscal representative as agent in handling these tax matters.

(b)   *VAT*

A trader who is not established in the State, who sells goods for take-away to passengers on board aircraft or vessels during an intra-Community journey departing from the State, will have to register for VAT in the State. There is no registration threshold applicable to such traders. They should contact the Taxes Central Registration Office, Aras Brugha, 9/15 Upper O'Connell Street, Dublin 1 and complete the appropriate registration form (TR1 or TR2).

An Irish trader who sells goods for take-away to passengers on board aircraft or vessels during intra-Community journeys departing from other Member States may have to register for VAT in each of those Member States, subject to the registration thresholds, if any, applicable in the Member States concerned. VAT must be accounted for in the Member State of departure of the transport.

13.   Documentation required

Under EU law (Council Directive 92/12/EEC), excise duty-paid goods loaded on a ship or aircraft on an intra-Community journey and intended for sale to passengers for take-away are required to be covered by a prescribed Accompanying Document.

A simplified procedure, based on the use of commercial documentation, may however apply. The main condition in granting this simplification is an undertaking from the operator that goods loaded duty-paid in one Member State will not be sold within the territorial limits of another Member State. Under such an undertaking, goods remaining intact on board while within territorial limits will be treated as "in transit" subject to Customs control. This simplified procedure cannot apply where such goods are sold within the territorial limits of another Member State.

14.   Stock accounts of excisable goods to be maintained

Revenue will require periodic returns of stock positions of excisable goods in respect of each airport shop, ferry and airline bar stores, distinguishing between duty-paid and duty-free goods, showing receipts, disposals and balances as necessary. Normally, the standard stock reports used by the operators will be adequate for verification or checking purposes. Such accounts must be made available to Revenue officers on demand at all reasonable times. Officers must also be permitted to carry out physical stock checks in duty-free shops or other locations stocking duty-free goods at all reasonable times.

15.   VAT transfers

Goods transferred by a person from his business in the State, for the purposes of onward supply to passengers on board a vessel or aircraft during an intra-Community journey, are not regarded as supplies of goods. Accordingly such transfers do not trigger an intra-Community supply from the State. VIES and Intrastat declarations need not be completed in the circumstances.

16.   VAT position of unsold stocks

A person who holds a stock of unsold goods on arrival in one Member State, from another Member State, will not have to make an intra-Community acquisition for VAT purposes in that Member State of arrival, provided that such stock is subsequently used by that person for supply to passengers for take-away on intra-Community journeys.

17.   VAT treatment in relation to provisioning

From 1 July, 1999, VAT at the appropriate rate is chargeable on the supply of provisions or merchandise to traders involved in the onward supply of those goods to airline or ferry passengers for take-away. However, in the case of supplies of food, drink and tobacco products which are for consumption on board during an international journey, the zero rate of VAT may apply. Suppliers who wish to supply such goods for on-board consumption to airlines and ferries at the zero rate must have sufficient records to substantiate the application of the zero rate.

18.   Contact points for further help in relation to VAT and Excise

Any queries on this Statement of Practice should be addressed to:

VAT	Excise
VAT Administration Branch, 3rd Floor, Stamping Building, Dublin Castle, Dublin, 2.	Excise Procedures Branch B, Room 317, 3rd Floor, Castle House, South Great George's Street, Dublin, 2.
Phone (01) 6748859, (01) 6748858, (01) 6748861 or (01) 6748862.	Phone (01) 6748351 or (01) 6748744.

Revenue Commissioners,
Dublin Castle.

June, 1999.

VALUE-ADDED TAX INFORMATION LEAFLET NO. 1/01

**'EMERGENCY' ACCOMMODATION, INCLUDING
ACCOMMODATION PROVIDED FOR ASYLUM SEEKERS AND
HOMELESS PEOPLE, AND ANCILLARY SERVICES**

1. **Introduction**

   This information leaflet outlines the appropriate VAT treatment of the short-term letting of accommodation to State agencies such as the Directorate for Asylum Seekers Services (to be renamed the 'Reception and Integration Agency' during 2001), Local Authorities and Health Boards, for use as 'emergency' accommodation, including accommodation provided for asylum seekers and homeless people. This leaflet also outlines the appropriate VAT treatment of the provision of ancillary services, such as catering, laundry, cleaning and security.

2. **Short-Term Letting of 'Emergency' Accommodation**

   The position in relation to the short-term letting of accommodation for use as 'emergency' accommodation, is as follows:

   (a) *State-owned accommodation*
   The provision of accommodation in State-owned property is outside the scope of VAT.

   (b) *Self-catering accommodation (e.g. apartments or houses)* Short-term letting of self-catering accommodation, let otherwise than as holiday accommodation, is VAT exempt. When let as 'emergency' accommodation, it continues to be exempt. The owner of the accommodation may choose to waive his/her exemption (see paragraph 4).

   (c) *Hotel or guesthouse accommodation*

   Accommodation in a hotel or guesthouse activity, provided by taxable persons, is taxable (at the 12½% VAT rate). However, if the hotel or guesthouse is contracted to a State agency as being provided exclusively as 'emergency' accommodation and it is not available for letting to the general public, the owner has the option either:

   (i) to continue to treat the property as a hotel or guesthouse (this means that the activity continues to be taxable), or

   (ii) to elect to treat the provision of accommodation as a letting of immovable goods other than by a hotel or guesthouse, but as 'emergency accommodation' (Revenue accepts that this means that the activity is VAT exempt).

   If the owner elects to change the status of his/her supplies from taxable to exempt, as outlined at (ii) above, and if first, the property has been developed since 1 November 1972 and second, the owner was entitled to recover VAT on the acquisition or development of the property, the change in status of the supplies from taxable to exempt constitutes a self-supply. The effect of this is that the owner must account for VAT on the cost of acquiring or developing the property. In practice, Revenue deals with this by clawing back the VAT claimed by the owner on the acquisition or development of the property.

If the status of the supplies is changed from taxable to exempt, as outlined at (ii) above, and they subsequently revert to being taxable (as could happen if, say, the accommodation ceases to be provided exclusively for asylum seekers/homeless people), there is no mechanism to undo the self-supply provisions. This means that any VAT clawed back by Revenue is not recoverable by the hotel or guesthouse owner when he/she again becomes liable to account for VAT on the provision of accommodation.

If only a part of the hotel or guesthouse accommodation is provided as 'emergency' accommodation and the remaining part is available for letting to the general public, all of the lettings, whether for the general public or for 'emergency' cases, are taxable (at the 12½% VAT rate).

3.   Ancillary Services

Ancillary services such as catering, laundry, cleaning and security, provided by taxable persons are liable to VAT at the appropriate rate. For example, catering, laundry and routine cleaning services are liable to VAT at 12½% while security services are liable at 20%.

Where a hotel or guesthouse owner has elected to treat his/her supply of accommodation as exempt 'emergency accommodation', the supply of ancillary services in connection with the provision of that accommodation would only become liable to VAT if the annual taxable turnover from such services exceeds £20,000 (assuming, of course, that this person makes no other taxable supplies). All suppliers of exempt 'emergency accommodation' should keep a breakdown in their income and expenditure records between amounts relating to the exempt supply of accommodation and those relating to the supply of ancillary services.

4.   Waiver of Exemption

A property owner who is engaged in exempt lettings may apply to the Revenue Commissioners to waive his/her right to exemption, in accordance with the relevant VAT legislation.

By waiving the right to exemption, the property owner must charge VAT, at 20%, on all of his/her short-term property lettings. He/she is however allowed VAT credit, at the appropriate rate, on inputs but only during the period for which he/she is registered for VAT.

The application to waive the entitlement to exemption must be in writing and must include the following:

(a)   the property owner's name, address and VAT registration number;

(b)   details of the letting agreement;

(c)   the date from which the property owner wishes the waiver to take effect which, in circumstances such as this, cannot be earlier than the commencement of the period in which the application is made.

5.   Cancellation of Waiver of Exemption

A property owner who is engaged in exempt lettings and who has waived his/her right to exemption, may subsequently cancel the waiver of exemption, in accordance with the relevant VAT legislation. If the property owner cancels the waiver of exemption, he/she is obliged to repay any excess of VAT input credits received over VAT payments made during the period of the waiver, or the previous ten years, whichever is the shorter.

6.   Further Information

Further information on this issue may be obtained from your local Inspector of Taxes, or from:

VAT Administration Branch
Indirect Taxes-Policy & Legislation Division
Stamping Building
Dublin Castle
Dublin 2
tel: 01-6745000 fax: 01-6795236 e-mail: vat@revenue.ie

Issued by the Office of the Revenue Commissioners
Dublin Castle
Dublin 2
February 2001

VALUE-ADDED TAX INFORMATION LEAFLET NO. 2/01
(FORMERLY NO. 6/01)

RESEARCH SERVICES CARRIED OUT BY THIRD LEVEL EDUCATIONAL BODIES

1.   Introduction

1.1.   Section 199 of the Finance Act 2001 amended the First Schedule to the VAT Act, which deals with exempt supplies. The effect of the amendment is that from 1 September 2001 the supply of research services by educational bodies is no longer an entirely exempt activity, but, in certain circumstances, is subject to VAT. Where VAT applies, it is normally chargeable at the standard rate, apart from supplies to the European Commission under the EU Commission Framework programmes, which are entitled to the zero rate.

1.2.   Following the Finance Act 2001 amendment, paragraph (ii) of the First Schedule to the VAT Act now exempts "school or university education .... including the supply of goods or services incidental thereto, *other than the supply of research services*". Prior to the insertion of the words in italics, all research carried out by educational bodies was treated as exempt because it was regarded as incidental to their primary function of education. Therefore, such bodies did not charge VAT on any of their research activities and they were not entitled to deduct VAT on their inputs in relation to such activities.

2.   The purpose of this leaflet

2.1.   This leaflet explains the impact of this change on the various types of research carried out by educational bodies. It gives guidance on how an educational body can go about determining what constitutes the supply of taxable research and what remains exempt as a purely educational activity.

2.2.   Attention is drawn to the transitional arrangements, as set out in paragraph 7 below, which apply to the new provisions.

2.3.   Should doubt or difficulty arise in relation to the taxable status of any particular case or activity, individual organisations should contact their local Inspector of Taxes for advice.

3.   The effect of the amendment

3.1.   With the introduction of these new provisions, educational bodies who engage in research activities and receive payment associated with those activities must consider the VAT implications of the transaction. To come within the charge for VAT according to the VAT Act, 1972, there must be a 'supply of services for consideration'. There are various principles derived from European Court of Justice decisions that define what is a supply for consideration, and these are outlined briefly in Appendix 1. The key principles are:

- there must be a direct link between the goods or services supplied and the payment received,

- there must be a legal relationship between the supplier and the recipient,

- the service must be "consumed" by an identifiable customer or customers.

3.2. Various activities which are often carried out by third level educational bodies cannot be considered as part of their educational function and are, hence, never covered by the exemption applying to "school or university education ...... including the supply of goods or services incidental thereto". These activities are taxable when supplied for consideration by a third level educational body. Examples of such activities may be:

- management consultancy and business efficiency advice;

- collection and recording of statistics, with or without accompanying collation, analysis and interpretation,

- market research and opinion polling; writing computer programmes;

- routine testing and analysis of materials, components and processes.

3.3. Any other research activities carried out by a third level educational body which comply with the three key principles outlined by the European Court of Justice will generally be taxable.

3.4. Where a third level educational body carries out a research activity which is not subject to VAT, any subsequent commercial exploitation of the results of such research by the third level body would be a separate taxable activity.

4. Types of funding

4.1. The type of funding for research is a key determination of whether a transaction constitutes a supply for consideration. The funding received by third level educational bodies for research can be categorised as follows for VAT purposes:

- Funding from the European Commission under their Framework Programmes

- Fees for contract work for a client which produces a specific result.

- Funding for non-specific research in a particular area of study.

5. The application of VAT to various types of funding for research

5.1. Supplies of research to the European Commission under the Fifth and any following Framework Programmes are taxable from 1 September 2001. The decision concerning the taxable status of transactions under the Framework Programme was issued by the Commission, and applies throughout the EU. The reasons given by the Commission to explain why research contracts issued under this programme are taxable are shown in Appendix 2. However, the rate applied in this particular case is the zero rate because, under EU law, any taxable supply of a good or service to the European Commission is zero-rated. In general, taxable supplies of research are normally subject to the standard rate (currently 20 per cent.).

5.2. Research funded from national sources which constitutes a supply for consideration is taxable at the standard rate. This could include research carried out on a consultancy, outsourcing, or contract basis for State agencies.

5.3. Research funded from various national sources where it falls into the third category in paragraph 4, i.e., funding that is not directly linked to the supply of specific research, should, in general, remain outside the VAT net.

6.   Pointers to help to determine VAT status of research carried out by educational institutions:

The usefulness of the following questions is to assist in deciding whether a research activity constitutes a supply for consideration:

- Is there a direct link between the service provided and the consideration received? An indicator of a direct link could be the use of a contract rather than grant of a subsidy, a donation or a letter of agreement for funding. If no direct link exists, then there is no supply for consideration, and hence no VAT liability.

- Is there a legal relationship between the supplier and the recipient pursuant to which there is reciprocal performance and remuneration received by the supplier of the service (which constitutes the value actually given in return for the service supplied to the recipient)? Such a relationship is a strong indicator that a supply for consideration has taken place.

- What type of research is being carried out? Is it the type of research known as 'basic research', i.e., research that is carried out for the purpose of creating, improving of enhancing knowledge or information about a particular discipline or activity, the output of which is available to a reasonably wide range of groups or individuals and is not produced solely for the benefit of whoever funds the research? Or, is it the type of research known as 'applied research'? This tends to take the results of basic research which have a commercial potential and further refine them to realise that potential. Its purpose is to produce results which can be commercially exploited, usually by whoever commissions and funds the research. Applied research is more likely than basic research to be a supply for consideration.

- What is the objective of the educational body in carrying out the research? Is it only to improve its standing in the research world or improve knowledge in a particular field? If so, it is likely that the results of the research would not be handed back to the funding body. The primary motivation could be educational.

- What is the objective of the funding body in funding each piece of research? Is it the production of specific results or deliverables, which could be commercially exploited, or the generation of knowledge in a general area of study or in the public interest?

- If the research produces specific results, who gets ownership rights of these? If they remain with the third level educational body which carried out the research, there is no supply to the funding body. However, if the third level body were to commercially exploit such results, such exploitation would be taxable.

7. Transitional arrangements

7.1. Special arrangements apply to contracts in place prior to the date the amendment comes into force (1 September 2001):

- Supplies of research under contracts entered into prior 1 July 2001 may continue to be treated as exempt. In order for the exemption to apply, a signed written contract must be in place prior to 1 July 2001, with supporting documentation (e.g., tendering documents, etc.) available for inspection.

- Supplies of research under contracts entered into post-1 July 2001 are taxable from 1 September 2001.

7.2. Where a contract contains an 'option to renew' clause, a new contract shall be deemed to be created upon exercise of this option. Accordingly, the VAT implications must be considered for any contract renewal after 30 June 2001.

8. Apportionment of input tax

8.1. Educational bodies will be entitled to reclaim VAT on any inputs relating to their taxable research business. However, as many of the inputs, for example, capital equipment, premises, and information technology, will be used both for their taxable supplies and their educational activities, VAT on inputs must be apportioned between deductible and non-deductible VAT, under Section 12(4) of the VAT Act. Those bodies should have appropriate recording systems to allow them comply with the VAT system in relation to this issue.

8.2. Revenue will shortly publish a separate guide to the apportionment of input tax which will be of information to educational bodies who make taxable supplies of research in addition to their exempt activities.

9.   Place of supply

9.1.   A taxable research activity is a consultancy service and under the third paragraph of the Fourth Schedule to the VAT Act, 1972, is taxable where received. A separate Statement of Practice (SP-VAT/5/94) on Fourth Schedule services is available and should be consulted where appropriate.

10.   The application of Section 13A of the VAT Act

10.1.   The normal Section 13A rules apply to supplies of taxable research services to companies authorised under that Section. Again, a separate Statement of Practice is available (SP-VAT/1/93 – Zero-rating of goods and services in accordance with section 13A of the VAT Act), and should be consulted where appropriate.

11.   Enquiries

11.1.   For further information please contact your local Inspector of Taxes, or VAT Administration, Stamping Building, Dublin Castle, Dublin 2. (Tel: 01-6475000 Extns. 48858, 48859, 48861. 48862, Fax: 01-6795236, E–mail: vat@revenue.ie).

Revenue
August, 2001.

Appendix 1

Principles derived from European Court of Justice decisions that define what constitute a supply for consideration

- There must be a **direct link** between the goods or services supplied and the consideration received. Any benefits arising from the supply must be conferred directly onto the person providing the consideration. It is not a supply for consideration if the person providing the consideration only indirectly receives the benefit, e.g. if the benefits actually accrue to the industry or group as a whole. (*Apple and Pear Development Council Case 102/86*). The link between the goods or services supplied and the fee paid must be such that a relationship can be established between the level of the benefits which the recipient obtains from the services provided and the amount of consideration. (*Tolsma Case 16/93*).

- There must be a '**legal relationship** between the provider of the service and the recipient pursuant to which there is reciprocal performance, the remuneration received by the provider of the service constituting the value actually given in return for the service supplied to the recipient'. (*Tolsma Case 16/93*).

- There must be **consumption of a service** in order for the consideration to be subject to VAT. VAT is a tax on consumption of goods or services - there must be a supply of a good or service for consumption by identifiable customers or the provision of a benefit capable of being regarded as a cost component of the activity of another person in the commercial chain (*Mohr Case 215/94 and Landboden-Agrardienste GmbH Case 384/95*).

Appendix 2

In 1997 the European Commission provided the following list of reasons to explain why the Commission now regard research under the Framework Programmes as constituting a taxable supply of services:

- Call for tender: With the intention to build up know-how in certain fields of technology, the Commission publishes programme particulars in the Official Journal and calls on interested parties to submit a tender for a project that could achieve the specified results. Apparently many participants in research projects design their activities and projects in anticipation of a likely tender.

- Selection: The Commission never funds all eligible projects. Depending on the programme particulars only one or a certain number of projects are chosen, usually those which are likely to produce the intended research results (patents, know-how, etc.). With view to the funding there is actually competition between the bids.

- Legal Form: The winning joint-venture signs a contract with the Commission. The Commission has opted for a contract as a legal instrument governing the research project as it allows for much tighter control than a grant of a subsidy.

- Activity: The contract obliges the participant to undertake a detailed research project, with a view to obtain specified results, to protect the research results and to either exploit the results commercially themselves or to grant licenses.

- Consideration: The Commission undertakes to cover, subject to the maximum amount fixed in the contract, 50% of the expenses incurred by the contractor in execution of its contractual obligation.

- Termination: If it turns out, at any time in the execution of the project, that the project will not produce the intended results, the Commission has the right to terminate the contract.

- The property: Each of the contractors will keep the property rights on its own research results (single or joint ownership). They are, however, obliged to grant to each other royalty free licenses for commercial exploitation.

- Royalty free licenses for the Commission: The Commission's own joint research centres may ask for a royalty free license on all research results obtained in execution of the contract. They may use the licenses even in their own commercial operations. It is understood that the remuneration paid by the Commission covers for this aspect as well.

- Transfer of Property: Provided that a contracting party fails to protect and to exploit intellectual and commercial property derived from the project, the property will pass on to the Commission.

- Publication and Publicity: The contractors have to provide project reports and other useful material to the Commission. The Commission may publish the reports or disseminate data on exploitable results. The contractor is obliged to participate, on the request of the Commission, in trade fairs and to give presentations.

VALUE-ADDED TAX INFORMATION LEAFLET NO. 11/01

GOVERNMENT DEPARTMENTS, LOCAL AUTHORITIES, HEALTH BOARDS, HOSPITALS, EDUCATIONAL BODIES, AND OTHER NON-TAXABLE ENTITIES ACQUIRING GOODS FROM OTHER EU MEMBER STATES

1.   General

1.1.   Government Departments, local authorities, health boards, public hospitals, educational establishments and other similar bodies are treated as non-taxable entities for VAT purposes. This means that they may pay VAT on any goods purchased or imported but generally speaking, they cannot recover these VAT payments. They are not required to register for VAT in respect of supplies of goods by them but may be required to register and account for VAT in respect of goods received from other Member States of the EU.

This information leaflet updates and replaces Statement of Practice SP-VAT/11/92.

2.   "Non-Taxable entities" - Who is affected?

2.1.   "Non-taxable entities" include State bodies (such as Government Departments, local authorities, health boards, etc.), educational establishments (such as schools, universities, VECs, etc.), public hospitals, charities, sports bodies and church bodies - in fact all groups of persons (other than private individuals) engaged in any type of non-commercial activity.

3.   Obligations of non-taxable entities to register for VAT

3.1.   A non-taxable entity that acquires, or is likely to acquire, more than £32,000 (€40,631.62) (€41,000 from 1 January, 2002) worth of goods from other EU Member States in any period of 12 months is obliged to register for VAT in respect of those acquisitions. Such a non-taxable entity should register for VAT by completing form TR1 or TR2 which can be obtained from, and which should be returned to the Taxes Central Registration Office (TCRO).

3.2.   Registration is not required where the £32,000 (€40,631.62) threshold for acquisitions is not exceeded or likely to be exceeded. In these cases goods acquired from other Member States are charged the VAT applicable in the supplier's Member State but are not charged Irish VAT when the goods enter the State. Non-taxable entities below the threshold may, however, elect to register if they so wish.

4.   Special rules for certain goods

4.1.   It should be noted that intra-Community acquisitions of new means of transport, (i.e. motor vehicles, boats and planes) are always subject to VAT when they are brought into the State, even when the annual threshold is not exceeded. There are special rules for paying VAT on these items and, in certain cases, on excisable goods also.

5.   VAT registration number

5.1.   On registration, the local Inspector of Taxes will issue a VAT number to the non-taxable entity. This number should be made available to all suppliers in other Member States to enable those suppliers to zero rate their supplies on despatch to Ireland.

6.   Obligations when registered

6.1.   All VAT registered persons are obliged:

- to calculate VAT due on their intra-Community acquisitions of goods,

- to complete the periodic VAT return showing their VAT liability,

- to send the completed return to the Collector-General, together with the tax due, within the prescribed time limit,

- to keep proper records of their acquisitions from other Member States so as to enable their VAT liability to be determined,

- to make these records available for inspection by Revenue, on request.

A separate leaflet, which explains how to complete the VAT 3 return, is available from the Collector-General's Division.

7.   Invoices

7.1.   Non-taxable persons, once registered for VAT who acquire goods from taxable persons in other Member States should be issued with an invoice by their supplier. This invoice will form the basis for determining the VAT due on the acquisition.

8.   How to calculate the VAT due on intra-Community acquisitions

8.1.   VAT becomes due on the date of issue of the invoice or, if no invoice issues, on the fifteenth of the month following the acquisition. The rate of VAT applicable is the rate that applies to the supply of the same goods in Ireland. The VAT is assessed on the price charged for the goods. The following example serves to illustrate the arrangement.

8.2.   **Example:**

Local authority acquires a computer from a German company. The supply in Germany is zero-rated because the local authority has provided its VAT registration number to the German company and the goods have been despatched or transported to Ireland.

Computer delivered   29.4.'01

Invoice issued   10.5.'01

Invoiced amount   €200,000

VAT on acquisition at 20%   €40,000

No entitlement to recover the VAT

VAT (€40,000) payable to Collector-General (with May/June VAT return) by 19.07.01.

9.   Rate of Exchange

9.1.   Where acquiring goods from a country, which is not part of the Euro zone the rate of exchange to be used for VAT purposes is the rate applicable when the tax becomes due.

10.   No entitlement to recover VAT paid

10.1.   Non-taxable entities which are required to register for VAT in respect of intra-Community acquisitions are not entitled to recover VAT paid on those acquisitions. This is similar to the situation where the non-taxable entity pays VAT on goods purchased in the State or at point of entry, without entitlement to deduction.

11.   Received services

11.1.   Non-taxable entities are required to account for VAT in respect of certain services received by them VAT free from abroad. There is no threshold for registration purposes. The services affected include advertising, consultancy services and hiring of goods other than means of transport. (A detailed information leaflet No. 9/01 entitled Fourth Schedule services on this subject is available on request). Non-taxable entities, already registered for VAT because they receive such services, are, regardless of the level of their intra-Community acquisitions of goods, liable to Irish VAT on those acquisitions.

12.   Intrastat

12.1.   Non-taxable entities which acquire more than £150,000 (€190,460.71) (€190,500 from 1 January 2002) worth of goods per annum from other Member States are required to make a monthly statistical return in respect of these acquisitions. Details of this requirement are contained in the VIES and Intrastat Traders Manual, which is available from the VIMA Office.

13.   Imports from Non-EU countries

13.1.   VAT on imports of goods from outside the EU is payable at point of entry and Customs documentation is required. Non-taxable entities should note that the imports of goods from outside the EU are not to be included when calculating the £32,000 (€40,631.62) (€41,000 from 1

January, 2002) registration threshold (referred to in paragraph 4 above) – this threshold relates only to goods acquired from other Member States. Customs documentation in relation to imports from outside the EU is required.

14. Further information

14.1. Further information may be obtained from VAT Administration, Stamping Building, Dublin Castle, Dublin 2 (Tel 67485000, Extns 48858, 48859, 48861, 48862 or from local Inspectors of Taxes.

November 2001

VALUE-ADDED TAX INFORMATION LEAFLET NO. 13/01

FINANCIAL INSTITUTIONS, INSURANCE COMPANIES, THEATRES, PROVIDERS OF PASSENGER TRANSPORT AND OTHER EXEMPT PERSONS ACQUIRING GOODS FROM OTHER EU MEMBER STATES

1.   General

1.1.   Financial institutions, insurance companies, theatres, providers of passenger transport and other persons engaged in exempt activities are not liable to VAT insofar as their exempted activities are concerned. This means that they pay VAT on any goods purchased or imported but are not required to register in respect of exempt supplies made by them.

1.2.   Since the abolition of fiscal frontiers on 1 January, 1993, VAT is no longer payable on goods brought in from other EU Member States. Instead revised arrangements were introduced to deal with such goods. This information leaflet outlines these arrangements insofar as they apply to exempt persons.

2.   Exempt Persons - Who is affected?

2.1.   "Exempt persons" are those persons who supply exempt goods and services. Typically these include bodies such as financial institutions, insurance companies and persons who supply educational, medical and welfare services as well as funeral undertakers, theatrical and certain sports promoters. A more detailed list may be found in Appendix A of the "Guide to the Value-Added Tax 1999".

3.   Obligations of exempt persons to register for VAT

3.1.   Where an exempt person acquires or is likely to acquire more than £32,000 (€40,631.62) (€41,000 from 1 January, 2002) worth of goods (other than new means of transport or excisable goods) from other EU Member States in any period of 12 months, that person is obliged to register for VAT in respect of those intra-Community acquisitions. The exempt person should register for VAT by completing form TR1 or TR2 which can be obtained from, and which should be returned to, the Taxes Central Registration Office (T.C.R.O) 9/15 Upper O'Connell St., Dublin 1.

3.2.   Registration is not required where the €40,631.62 threshold for intra-Community acquisitions is not exceeded. In those cases, goods acquired from other Member States will be chargeable to VAT in the supplier's Member State but will not be charged Irish VAT when the goods enter the State. Exempt persons below the threshold may, however, elect to register if they so wish.

4.   Special rules for certain goods

4.1.   Intra-Community acquisitions of new means of transport, i.e. new motor vehicles, boats and planes, are always liable to Irish VAT, even when the annual threshold is not exceeded. There are special rules for paying VAT on these goods and, in certain cases, on excisable goods also.

5.   VAT registration number

5.1.   On registration, the local Inspector of Taxes issues a VAT number to the exempt person. This number should be made available by the exempt person to all his or her suppliers of goods in other Member States to enable those suppliers to zero rate their supplies on despatch to the State.

6.   Obligations when registered

6.1.   Exempt persons, once registered for VAT, are obliged

- to calculate VAT due on their intra-Community acquisitions of goods,

- to complete the periodic VAT return showing their VAT liability,

- to send the completed return to the Collector-General, together with any tax payable, within the prescribed time limit,

- to keep proper records of their acquisitions from other Member States to enable their VAT liability to be determined,

- to make those records available for inspection by Revenue on request.

Advice on how to complete the VAT 3 return, is available from the Collector-General's Division.

7.   Invoices

7.1.   Once registered for VAT exempt persons who acquire goods from taxable persons in other Member States should be issued with an invoice by their supplier. This invoice will form the basis for determining the VAT due on the acquisition.

8.   How to calculate the VAT due on intra-Community acquisitions

8.1.   VAT becomes due on the date of issue of the invoice or, if no invoice issues, on the fifteenth day of the month following the month in which the acquisition is made. The rate of VAT applicable is the rate that applies to the supply of the same goods in the State. The VAT is calculated on the price charged for the goods. The following example illustrates the arrangements:-

8.2. **Example:**

An insurance company in the State acquires a computer from a German company. The supply in Germany is zero-rated because the insurance company has provided its VAT registration number to the German company and the goods have been transported to the State.

Computer delivered	29.4.'01
Invoice issued	12.5.'01
Invoiced amount	€100,000
VAT on acquisition at 20%	€20,000

No input credit allowed.

VAT (€20,000) payable to Collector-General (with May/June VAT return) by 19 .07.01.

9. **Rate of Exchange**

9.1. Where acquiring goods from a country, which is not part of the Euro zone the rate of exchange to be used is the rate applicable when the tax becomes due.

10. **Deductibility**

10.1. Where exempt persons are required to register solely because of their intra-Community acquisitions, they are not entitled to a deduction in respect of VAT paid on those acquisitions. Exempt persons already registered for VAT because they engage in both taxable and exempt activities are entitled to deductibility in respect of inputs relating to those taxable activities, e.g. a bank which is primarily involved in exempt activities but which also carries on a taxable activity such as leasing of movable goods. Such persons may also be entitled to full or partial deductibility in respect of VAT due on intra-Community acquisitions. A full deduction of the VAT on the intra-Community acquisitions will arise if the acquisitions are wholly attributable to the person's taxable activities. No input credit is allowable if the intra-Community acquisitions relate solely to the person's exempt activities. If the intra-Community acquisitions are common to both types of activity i.e. dual use inputs, the input credit should be apportioned in accordance with the persons current apportionment arrangements.

11. **Inter-company transfers**

11.1. A transfer of goods from one branch of a business to another within the State is not a supply for VAT purposes. However, under the Single Market VAT arrangements, a transfer of goods from a business in one Member State to another Member State for the purposes of the business, is deemed to be an intra-Community supply in the Member State of despatch and an intra-Community acquisition in the Member State of arrival. The rules relating to intra-Community acquisitions apply in such cases in the same way as if the goods had been purchased.

11.2. Where, for example, the UK head office of a wholly exempt insurance company transfers a computer to its Irish branch, the transfer is a supply in the UK and an intra-Community acquisition in the State. If the Irish branch's acquisitions exceed or are likely to exceed £32,000 (€40,631.62) (€41,000 from 1 January 2002) in any period of 12 months, it is obliged to register and account for VAT in the State at the standard rate on the current market value of the computer. If the threshold is not exceeded and the Irish branch has not elected to register, the supply is liable to VAT in the UK.

11.3. In the converse case of a transfer of a computer from an Irish branch to the UK head office, the same rules apply in determining where the charge of VAT will arise. In that case, the Irish branch, being an exempt person, will have borne VAT on the purchase of the computer with no right of deduction. In order to avoid double taxation, the Irish branch will be allowed to take an appropriate VAT deduction at the time of the transfer of the computer. The amount of the tax which may be deducted will not be the amount paid on the original purchase of the computer but the amount of tax contained in the value of the computer at the time of transfer known as the "residual tax". The following example shows the calculation of the residual tax:

(a)   Assume computer purchased in Ireland in 1999 for €500,000 plus 21% VAT i.e. a total of €605,000. The VAT paid at that stage was not deductible.

(b)   At time of transfer assume the open market value of the computer is €200,000 and VAT rate applying is 20%.

(c)   The residual tax contained in the market value of the computer is calculated as follows:

$$\frac{€200,000 \times 100}{120} = €166,666 @ 20\% = €33,333$$

This residual VAT of €33,333 will be allowed as a deduction to the Irish branch.

12.   Fourth Schedule services

12.1. Exempt persons are required to account for VAT in respect of certain services received by them from abroad for business purposes regardless of their value. The services affected include advertising, consultancy and financial services. (An information leaflet No. 09/01 entitled Fourth Schedule Services is available). Exempt persons already registered for VAT because they receive such services, are, regardless of the level of their intra-Community acquisitions of goods, liable to Irish VAT on those acquisitions.

13.   INTRASTAT

13.1. Persons, including exempt persons, who acquire more than £150,000 (€190,460.71) (€190,500 from 1 January 2002) worth of goods per annum from other Member States will also be required to make a monthly statistical return in respect of those acquisitions. Details of this requirement are contained in the VIES and INTRASTAT Traders Manual, which is available from the VIMA Office.

14.   Imports from non-EU countries

14.1. Exempt persons should note that the imports of goods from outside the EU are not to be included when calculating the £32,000 (€40,631.62) registration threshold. This threshold relates only to goods acquired from other Member States. Such imports of goods from outside the EU are liable to Irish VAT at the point of importation and customs documentation continues to be required.

15.   Further Information

15.1. Further information may be obtained from VAT Administration, Stamping Building, Dublin Castle, Dublin 2 (Tel 6745000, Extns 48858, 48859, 48861, 48862) or from local Inspectors of Taxes.

November 2001

VALUE-ADDED TAX INFORMATION LEAFLET NO. 3/02

VAT TREATMENT OF CULTURAL, ARTISTIC AND ENTERTAINMENT SERVICES SUPPLIED BY NON-ESTABLISHED PERSONS

Introduction

1.   The purpose of this information leaflet is to outline changes to the VAT treatment of cultural, artistic and entertainment services supplied by non-established persons in the State which apply from 25 March 2002.

What are 'cultural, artistic and entertainment' services?

2.   The 'cultural, artistic and entertainment' services affected by the changes in VAT treatment include concerts, music recitals, theatrical performances, art exhibitions, dance exhibitions, comedy shows, and similar services.

What is a 'non-established' person?

3.   In practice, a non-established person is regarded as being either an individual who is not normally resident in this State or who does not have a business establishment here, or a company which does not have a business establishment here. For example, a promoter who does not have a business establishment here is regarded as being a nonestablished promoter.

4.   For the purposes of this information leaflet, non-established persons supplying cultural, artistic and entertainment services will be referred to as 'non-established performers'.

Changes with effect from 25 March 2002

5.   Prior to 25 March 2002, a non-established performer supplying taxable goods or services in this State was obliged to register and account for Irish VAT on his/her sales, regardless of the level of sales involved. However, Revenue could deem a person connected with the supplies (for example, the concert promoter or the owner of the concert venue) to be actually making the supplies and thus liable to account for any VAT due. Alternatively, the performer could appoint a 'fiscal representative' in the State to account for any VAT due.

6.   With effect from 25 March 2002, a non-established performer is not liable for VAT on his or her taxable supplies of cultural, artistic and/ or entertainment services. Instead, the promoter, agent or other person who commissions the performance or event is automatically liable for the VAT due. (However, deferral of the application of these new provisions is available in certain circumstances and under which the nonestablished performer remains liable to VAT. See paragraphs 18-19 for details.)

7. For ease of reference in this information leaflet, the promoter, agent or other person who commissions the performance or event will be referred to as the 'promoter' and the performance or event will be referred to simply as the 'performance'.

8. The promoter must account for VAT on all supplies in respect of the performance, regardless of the level of turnover concerned. The normal turnover thresholds which apply to goods and services provided by persons who are established in this State do not therefore apply.

Non-established promoter: provider of the premises may be liable

9. Where a non-established promoter arranges for the supply of cultural, artistic, entertainment or similar services, the provider of the premises in which the performance is to take place has certain obligations to Revenue.

10. For the purposes of these provisions, the 'provider of the premises' is a person who *'owns, occupies or controls'* the venue in which the performance is to take place. In a situation where a non-established promoter is engaged by the owner of a venue, the owner would be the sole provider of the premises. However, in a situation where a non-established promoter is engaged by a third party who has hired the venue from its owner, there could be two providers of the premises: first, the owner of the venue; and second, the third party, who by virtue of having hired the venue, is likely to have gained a temporary right to occupy it.

11. The provider of the premises (whether the owner or a third party, or both jointly) is obliged to give the following information to Revenue:

    • the name and address of the promoter, and

    • details, such as the dates, duration and venue of the performance.

12. The provider of the premises should send this information, not later than 14 days before the performance is scheduled to begin, to Revenue's Special Enquiry Branch, contact details for which are as follows:

    Special Enquiry Branch
    Chief Inspector of Taxes
    Office of the Revenue Commissioners
    Plaza Complex
    Belgard Road
    Tallaght
    Dublin 24
    Tel: 01-6470700
    Fax: 01-6341981
    e-mail: seb@revenue.ie

13. Where this information is not furnished to Revenue, the provider of the premises may be made jointly and severally liable with the non-established promoter for the VAT liability in respect of the performance.

In practice, this could mean that if the nonestablished promoter fails to account for any VAT due, the provider of the premises (whether the owner or a third party, or both jointly) may become liable for the entire amount of VAT due in respect of the performance.

Non-established trader: obligation to register for Irish VAT

14.   Any trader who is not established in this State but who is engaged in selling taxable goods here is obliged to register and account for Irish VAT on his/her sales. This obligation to register and account for Irish VAT exists, regardless of the level of sales made or the number of days spent here by the non-established trader in making those sales. An example of a non-established trader engaged in selling taxable goods here would be one who sells merchandise (such as souvenirs, CDs, tapes, videos etc.) at a concert.

Non-established trader: provider of the premises may be liable

15.   Where a provider of a premises (whether the owner or a third party) allows a nonestablished trader to supply goods for a period of less than seven consecutive days on the premises in which the performance is to be held, that provider of the premises must give the following information to Revenue:

- the name and address of the non-established trader,

- the dates on which the non-established trader intends to trade on the premises, and

- the address of the premises.

16.   The provider of the premises should send this information, not later than 14 days before the performance is scheduled to begin, to Revenue's Special Enquiry Branch, contact details for which are supplied in paragraph 12.

17.   Where this information is not furnished to Revenue, the provider of the premises may be made jointly and severally liable with the non-established trader for his/her VAT liability in respect of his/her supplies of goods in the premises concerned. In practice, this could mean that if the non-established trader fails to account for any VAT due, the provider of the premises (whether the owner or a third party, or both jointly) may become liable for the entire amount of VAT due in respect of the non-established trader's sales here.

Possible deferral of the application of these new provisions

18.   If a promoter has received funding from the Arts Council at any time since 25 March 1999, he/she may apply to Revenue to defer the application of the new provisions to a time not later than 1 March 2003. The effect of deferring these provisions is that it is the non-established performer, not the promoter, who remains liable for the VAT due on the supply of the services performed by him/her. However, with effect from 1 March 2003, the new provisions will apply automatically.

19. All applications for deferral of the new provisions should be sent to Revenue's Special Enquiry Branch, contact details for which are supplied in paragraph 12. These applications must be sent to Special Enquiry Branch well in advance of the performance being held. In practice, Revenue would expect to receive such applications at least 14 days in advance of the performance date. Any applications sent after the performance has been held will not be accepted.

Legislation

20. These changes form part of a package of measures which were introduced in order to comply with Council Directive 2000/65/EC which removed the right of an EU Member State to oblige a non-established person to appoint a 'fiscal representative' in the State to account for any VAT due by that non-established person. This directive was enacted into national legislation by section 198 of Finance Act 2001 which repealed section 37 of the VAT Act, 1972, together with section 101 of Finance Act 2002 which amended section 8 of the VAT Act, 1972.

Further information

21. Further information on this matter generally may be obtained from your local Inspector of Taxes or from the following:

VAT Interpretation Branch
Indirect Taxes – Policy & Legislation Division
Office of the Revenue Commissioners
Stamping Building
Dublin Castle
Dublin, 2
Tel: 01-6475000
Fax: 01-6795236
e-mail: vat@revenue.ie

Special Enquiry Branch
Chief Inspector of Taxes
Office of the Revenue Commissioners
Plaza Complex
Belgard Road
Tallaght
Dublin 24
Tel: 01-6470700
Fax: 01-6341981
e-mail: seb@revenue.ie

22. Further information on the obligations of non-established traders is available in our VAT information leaflet 'VAT Treatment of Foreign Firms Doing Business in Ireland'. This information leaflet was published in 1999 and is currently in the process of being updated. An up-to-date version will soon be available on our website.

Issued by the Office of the Revenue Commissioners
Dublin Castle
Dublin 2
September 2002

VAT INFORMATION LEAFLET (MAY 2003)

NEW VAT TREATMENT OF VEHICLES REGISTERED BY DISTRIBUTORS OR DEALERS PRIOR TO SALE

1. Under the terms of section 120 of the Finance Act 2003, the VAT and VRT treatment of vehicles registered by distributors or dealers in their own name will change on 1 May 2003.

    Vehicles to which the new rules apply

2. The only vehicles involved are those of the type, which, outside of the motor trade, are non-deductible vehicles for VAT purposes. These are the vehicles classified for Vehicle Registration Tax (VRT) purposes as category A vehicles (cars in general) and motor cycles.

    Vehicle registered on or after 1 May 2003

3. Where on or after 1 May 2003 a distributor or dealer (referred to in this statement, for convenience, as "dealer") registers a category A vehicle or a motor cycle in the name of the distributorship/dealership, etc, the vehicle is treated as removed from stock in trade. This removal results in a 'self-supply' for VAT purposes. This means that a dealer who has taken deductibility for VAT on the purchase or importation of the vehicle must account for VAT on that vehicle in the VAT return for the period in which the vehicle is registered in the dealer's name as if the vehicle were sold at cost price.

    Vehicle subsequently sold on

4. When the vehicle is subsequently sold to a customer, the dealer will be entitled to make a claim on the VAT 3 return for a residual input credit. This means that the vehicle is treated as if it were bought into stock from outside the trade, for sale as a second hand vehicle. The basis for calculating the residual VAT is the VAT-inclusive cost price plus VRT (see calculation at paragraph 6). This residual VAT available for credit cannot exceed the amount of VAT due on the sale of the vehicle.

5. As the residual input credit is only available at the time of the sale of the vehicle to a customer, both the claim for the VAT credit and the VAT on the sale of the vehicle will be accounted for in the same VAT return. The effect of this mechanism is that the residual input credit will be offset against the output VAT on the sale, and the dealer will actually pay VAT only on the difference between the cost price (inclusive of VAT and VRT) and the sale price. However, the dealer cannot claim more residual credit than the VAT due on the sale. If the cost price (inclusive of VAT and VRT) is greater than the sale price the residual input credit is limited to an amount equal to the VAT on the sale price.

Calculation of the amount of the residual input credit

6. The residual input credit is calculated according to the formula normally used for the calculation of residual input credit for second hand motor vehicles, with slight variation, as follows:

$$A \times \frac{B}{B + 100}$$

Where –

A is the cost price (inclusive of VAT and VRT) and
B is the percentage rate of VAT.

Example:

Assume the cost price of a vehicle qualifying for the new treatment by the dealer is as follows:

Cost of vehicle to the dealer excluding VAT and VRT	€11,465
VAT (amount of liability in respect of self supply)	2,408
VRT	5,625
Cost price (inclusive of VAT and VRT)	€19,498
Vehicle Sold for	€21,000

The Value Added Tax due on the sale is accounted for as follows:

VAT due on the sale (21,000 ÷121) × 21 =	€3,644.62
Residual credit* due (19,498 ÷121) × 21=	€3,383.95
Net VAT due on sale of demo vehicle	€260.67

* The residual credit cannot exceed the VAT due on the sale

VRT Refund Scheme for Vehicles in demonstration to be abolished

7. As a consequence of the changes in the Finance Act 2003 the current VRT refund scheme for demonstration vehicles will be abolished in respect of vehicles registered on or after 1 May 2003. Any vehicle which is already registered and in demonstration before that date will be treated under the old rules, i.e. the VRT refund will be payable under the normal conditions, but the scheme outlined above and detailed in Section 120 of the Finance Act 2003 will not apply.

May 2003

VALUE-ADDED TAX LEAFLET (JUNE 2004)

SECTION 4 (8) VAT ACT 1972

Circumstances where the reverse charge applies:

Where VAT is chargeable on a surrender of a leasehold interest or on an assignment of a leasehold interest to any of the following classes of person:

(a)   a taxable person (for VAT purposes),

(b)   a Department of State or a local authority, or

(c)   a person supplying goods of a kind referred to in paragraph (a) of the definition of 'exempted activity' in section 1 of the VAT Act, 1972 [property, the supply of which is not chargeable to VAT], or

(d)   a person supplying services of a kind referred to in paragraphs (i), (iv), (ix), (xi), (xia), (xiii) and (xiv) of the First Schedule to the VAT Act, 1972, in the course or furtherance of business,

then, for VAT purposes, these persons are deemed to supply those goods in the course or furtherance of business and they, rather than the person making the surrender/assignment, will be liable to pay the VAT on the surrender/assignment. They must declare the VAT liability in their VAT return and where they are taxable persons they may be entitled to claim a deduction (or input credit) for the VAT, in accordance with Section 12 of the VAT Act 1972.

Example 1

Joe, a builder and taxable person, is the lessee under a 35 year lease of an office and yard (developed since 1/11/1972). He assigns the lease to Melanie, another taxable person, who operates a garden centre. In the normal course, Melanie will account for VAT on the value of the assignment, even though she is the customer in the transaction.

Circumstances where the reverse charge does not apply:

The reverse charge does not apply and VAT must be applied in the normal way by the person making the supply/assignment in all other circumstances where VAT is chargeable on a surrender/assignment of a leasehold interest.

It is not possible to compile a comprehensive list of those persons who should be charged VAT on such surrenders or assignments, however, the following is a non-exhaustive list:

(a)   Private persons

(b)   School Bodies

(c)   Doctors or Dentists

(d)   Certain Hospital Authorities

(e)   Bookmakers

(f)   The National Lottery

(g)   Undertakers

Example 2

Fred, a florist and taxable person, has a 35-year lease of a unit (developed since 1/11/1972) in a Shopping Centre. He assigns his lease to Larry, a bookmaker. In this case, Fred must account for VAT on the supply. He will therefore invoice Larry.

Example 3

Suzy, an accountant and a taxable person, has a 20-year lease of a ground floor office. The property was developed since 1/11/1972. Donal, the landlord, who resides in the upper section of the property, agrees to take a surrender of the lease. He will use it to expand his residence and will not use it for business purposes. Suzy must account for VAT on the surrender.

June 2004

VALUE-ADDED TAX LEAFLET (JUNE 2004)

VAT AND PROPERTY – THE 10% RULE

1. Introduction

The so-called 10% rule is a simplification rule designed to assist in determining whether the creation of an interest in property is taxable. The rule provides where relatively insignificant amounts of extension, alteration or demolition work have been carried out to the property prior to its disposal the property will be regarded as not having been developed. The rule has been in place since 1973 and has been operated without difficulty in the vast majority of appropriate property transactions. It provides the necessary clarity to determine whether or not the supply of a property may be regarded as taxable.

The rule is of course merely a simplification measure and has no statutory authority. It was pointed out in a 2001 High Court case (Forbes and Tobin) that the rule cannot be relied on by a purchaser where the vendor insists that the property has been developed even though the vendor may not have incurred expenditure in excess of 10% (or the de minimis amount) of the sale value in carrying out the development of the property.

The Revenue Commissioners have reviewed the 10% rule and have decided to issue the following guidelines to bring greater clarity to the application of the rule. At the same time the maximum expenditure permitted within the rule is being increased from €100,000 to €300,000.

It should be remembered that once a property is regarded as developed after 1 November 1972 it remains developed irrespective of the amounts of expenditure incurred thereafter by its owner or subsequent owners. The taxability or otherwise of such a property depends on the normal rules for taxability and the 10% de-minimis rule has no relevance as regards any further disposal of the property. (See example D).

2. Legislation

Section 1 of the VAT Act 1972 as amended defines development as

"**development**" in relation to any land, means-

(a)   the construction, demolition, extension, alteration or recon-struction of any building on the land, or

(b)   the carrying out of any engineering or other operation in, on, over or under the land to adapt it for materially altered use,

and "**developed**" shall be construed correspondingly

3. Meaning of Extension, Alteration or Demolition where there is no essential change of use for the purposes of the 10% Rule in determining the taxable status of a property.

1) In determining whether or not a property was developed after 31 October 1972, or subsequent to its acquisition after that date (if not already developed), relatively small and routine outlay on extensions, alterations or demolitions carried out periodically (which did not adapt the property for materially altered use) for the purposes of the persons taxable activities may be ignored notwithstanding that a vat credit or deduction may have been claimed in relation to such outlay. In practical terms this may be taken as meaning that, where there is no essential change in the use of the property or where the expenditure was not carried out to adapt the property for such a change, such outlay may be ignored if it is reasonably clear that its cost would not exceed 10 per cent of the total amount on which tax would be chargeable if the work in question were treated as a development, or €300,000 whichever is the lesser.

2) The carrying out of any engineering or other operation in, on, over or under the land to adapt it for materially altered use, is always regarded as development and the 10 per cent rule, as outlined in (1) above, does not apply in determining whether or not a supply of immovable goods so developed is subject to Value Added Tax.

Examples

	Properties undeveloped for VAT purposes at the time of acquisition by the supplier			Property developed at time of acquisition
	Example A Retail Shop	Example B Factory Building	Example C Field/Site	Example D Office Building
Being sold for (or capitalised value of rent)	€1,000,000	€8,000,000	€1,500,000	€3,000,000
Outlay on alterations subsequent to acquisition by the supplier	€90,000	€700,000	€90,000	€275,000

What are the VAT implications?

Example A, a shopkeeper purchased a retail shop in 1986. The retail shop was undeveloped for VAT purposes at the time of acquisition by the shopkeeper. Since the acquisition the shopkeeper incurred outlay of €90,000 on various alterations. The retail shop is now being sold for €1,000,000.

The property which has not been adapted for materially altered use would be regarded as not having been developed subsequent to its acquisition by the shop-keeper, because the outlay on subsequent alteration did not exceed €300,000 and is also less than 10% of the selling price. Consequently, the supply would be regarded as outside the scope of VAT.

Example B, a manufacturing company purchased a factory building in 1996. The factory was undeveloped for VAT purposes at the time of acquisition by the manufacturing company. Since the acquisition the manufacturing company incurred outlay of €700,000 on various alterations. The factory building is now being sold for €8,000,000.

The property, which, although it has not been adapted for materially altered use, would be regarded as developed by the manufacturing company because the outlay (of €700,000) on subsequent alteration exceeded €300,000. Consequently, the manufacturing company is liable to tax on the supply, provided all the other requirements for taxability are satisfied. VAT would be chargeable by reference to the full supply value of €8,000,000.

Example C, an investor purchased a field in 2001. The field was undeveloped for VAT purposes at the time of acquisition by the investor. Since the acquisition the investor incurred outlay of €90,000 involving the laying of roads, sewers and service cables over the entire area of the field. The field is now being sold for €1,500,000.

The field, has been adapted for materially, altered use, involving the carrying out of an engineering or other operation in, on, over or under the land. Consequently, the investor making the supply would be liable to tax on its supply, provided all the other requirements for taxability are satisfied. This is so because the development involved the carrying out of an engineering or other operation in, on, over or under the land to adapt it for materially altered use and this type of development is not covered by the 10% rule as outlined in this memo. VAT would be chargeable by reference to the full supply value of €1,500,000.

Example D, an accountancy firm purchased an office building in 1999. The office building was developed in 1999 by a developer who supplied it to the accountancy firm. Since the acquisition the accountancy firm incurred outlay of €275,000 on various alterations. The office building is now being sold for €3,000,000.

The office building was developed after 1 November 1972. It remains developed for VAT purposes irrespective of the amounts of expenditure incurred thereafter by the accountancy firm. The taxability or otherwise of such a property depends on the normal rules for taxability and the 10% de-minimis rule has no relevance as regards any further disposal of the property. VAT would be chargeable by reference to the full supply value of €3,000,000.

VAT Interpretation Branch,
Indirect Taxes Division.

22 June, 2004.

VALUE-ADDED TAX INFORMATION LEAFLET NO. 1/04

VAT ISSUES FOR MILK PRODUCTION PARTNERSHIPS

Introduction

1.   The purpose of this information leaflet is to outline the principal features of the Value-Added Tax (VAT) system as it relates to farmers establishing and registering a Milk Production Partnership under regulation 8 of the European Communities (Milk Quota) Regulations 2000.

2.   Any farmers thinking about establishing a Milk Production Partnership might find it useful to read this information leaflet in conjunction with Revenue's information leaflet, Taxation Issues for Milk Production Partnerships, which deals with the Income Tax, Capital Gains Tax, Capital Acquisitions Tax and Stamp Duty issues.

For VAT purposes, who is a farmer?

3.   For VAT purposes, a "farmer" is a person who engages in agricultural production activities on land he/she owns or occupies in the State.

4.   Generally speaking, for VAT purposes, 'agricultural production' refers to the production of agricultural goods (e.g. crop production; general stock farming; poultry farming; forestry; and fisheries) and/or the supply of agricultural services (e.g. sowing and planting; crop spraying; harvesting; stock minding, rearing and fattening; and tree felling).

Milk Production Partnership - for VAT purposes, a separate farming entity to the individual partners

5.   On the basis that the Milk Production Partnership is a registered farm partnership under regulation 8 of the European Communities (Milk Quota) Regulations 2000, it is Revenue's view that, for VAT purposes:

   • the partnership may be regarded as being a farmer, and

   • it is a separate entity to the individuals who came together to establish that partnership.

Milk Production Partnership - obligation to register for VAT

6.   As a separate farming entity to the individual partners, the partnership is obliged to register for VAT if its turnover from certain supplies exceeds, or is likely to exceed, the relevant threshold for those supplies in a continuous twelve month period.

7.   The supplies in question, together with the relevant turnover thresholds are as follows:

   (a)   supplies of agricultural services (other than insemination services, stock minding or stock rearing) which exceed, or are likely to exceed, €25,500

(b)   supplies of livestock semen, other than to other farmers licensed as an A.I. centre, or to a person over whom the farmer exercises control, which exceed, or are likely to exceed, €51,000

(c)   supplies of retail horticultural products which exceed, or are likely to exceed, €51,000

Note: Where the partnership's supplies consist of the services referred to in (a), as well as the goods referred to in (b) or (c), the relevant threshold is €25,500.

(d)   intra-Community acquisitions which exceed, or are likely to exceed, €41,000

(e)   Fourth Schedule services, regardless of their value

(f)   supplies of taxable goods, other than agricultural goods, which exceed or are likely to exceed €51,000

(g)   supplies of taxable services, other than agricultural services, which exceed or are likely to exceed €25,500.

8.   If the partnership is obliged to register in respect of its Fourth Schedule services (paragraph (e) refers), it must also account for VAT in respect of its intra-Community acquisitions (paragraph (d) refers), regardless of the value of the intra-Community acquisitions.

9.   If the partnership is obliged to register in respect of either its intra-Community acquisitions or its Fourth Schedule services, such registration is effectively 'ring-fenced' to the intra-Community acquisitions and/or the Fourth Schedule services. The partnership is not obliged to register in respect of its farming activities.

10.   Racehorse training services are taxable services (paragraph (g) refers). However, the minding and rearing of horses is regarded as a farming activity. If the partnership is obliged to register in respect of its racehorse training services, such registration is effectively 'ring-fenced' to the training element of these services and the partnership is not obliged to register in respect of the farming element. Revenue will accept, as a general but not invariable rule, that where the partnership is minding and rearing racehorses, as well as training them, that approximately ten per cent of the total turnover relates to the training element.

11.   Of course, where the partnership is obliged to register for VAT in respect of supplies of any other goods or services, as outlined in paragraphs (a), (b), (c), (f) and (g) above, the partnership must account for VAT in respect of all of its activities, including farming and racehorse training.

Milk Production Partnership - option to register for VAT

12.   A partnership which is not obliged to register for VAT may opt to do so.

13.   If a partnership which has opted to register for VAT wishes subsequently to cancel its registration, it may do so by arrangement with its local Revenue district. However, this may give rise to recovery by Revenue of

all or some of the net VAT repaid to the partnership during the period for which it opted to register.

Transfer of ownership of movable assets, such as livestock, machinery and feedstuff

14.   Teagasc indicates that it is normal to transfer ownership of assets such as livestock, machinery and feedstuff from the individual partners to the partnership. For VAT purposes, the transfer of ownership of such goods would fall into one of four scenarios, as follows:

(i)   Transfer from a farmer who is not, nor obliged to be, VAT-registered to a VAT-registered farming partnership

(ii)   Transfer from a farmer who is not, nor obliged to be, VAT-registered to a farming partnership which is not, nor obliged to be, VAT-registered

In the above two scenarios, as the farmer is not, nor obliged to be, VAT-registered, the transfer would not be liable to VAT.

(iii)   Transfer from a VAT-registered farmer to a VAT-registered farming partnership

In this scenario, in the circumstances of the arrangements for the Milk Production Partnerships, the transfer of ownership of these goods may be regarded as being in connection with the transfer of the farming business from the individual farmer to the farming partnership. On this basis, this transfer may be deemed not to be a supply of goods, in accordance with section 3(5)(b)(iii) of the VAT Act, 1972. The effect of this is that the transfer of ownership of these goods would not be liable to VAT.

(iv)   Transfer from a VAT-registered farmer to a farming partnership which is not, nor obliged to be, VAT registered

In this scenario, the transfer of these goods may be liable to VAT.

Licencing of the use of immovable assets, such as farm-land and farm-buildings, and intangible assets, such as milk quotas

15.   Teagasc indicates that in most farm partnerships, immovable assets such as farm-land and farm-buildings, and intangible assets, such as milk quotas, remain in the ownership of the individual partners and a licence for their use is granted to the partnership, for the purposes of the carrying on by the partnership of its farming business.

16.   On the basis that the licence for use of such immovable assets and intangible assets is granted by one of the individual partners to the partnership, or to another partner on a personal basis - with the qualification that this 'personal basis' relates only to that person's position as a partner carrying on the business of farming within the farming partnership - then, in the circumstances of the arrangements for setting up the Milk Production Partnerships, the initial granting of the

licence for the use of these assets may be regarded as being in connection with the transfer of the farming business from the individual farmer to the farming partnership. On this basis, the granting of the licence may be deemed not to be a supply of services, in accordance with section 5(8) of the VAT Act 1972. The effect of this is that the granting of the licence would not be liable to VAT.

17. However, subsequent to the setting up of the partnership, should one of the individual partners acquire additional assets, such as land or milk quotas, and should that partner grant a licence to the partnership for the use of these additional assets, this licence may be liable to VAT.

18. In the course of exercising its right to use the farm-land and farm-buildings, should a VAT-registered partnership carry out substantial amounts of extension, alteration or demolition work to this property, the property may be regarded as being developed, for VAT purposes. Consequently, any subsequent disposal of this property by its owner or occupier may be liable to VAT.

'Flat-rate addition'

19. Farmers who are not registered for VAT are not entitled to recover the VAT charged to them on their farming expenses (e.g. farm machinery, electricity etc). Generally speaking, such farmers are compensated for these VAT charges by means of a flat-rate amount (currently 4.4 per cent) which is added to the prices at which they sell their products and services to other VAT-registered persons (e.g. marts, agricultural co-operatives and meat factories). This compensatory amount is referred to as a 'flat-rate addition'. Farmers who are not registered for VAT, thus who are entitled to the payment of this flat-rate addition, are referred to as 'flat-rate farmers'.

For example:

A flat-rate farmer sells a quantity of milk produced from his/her dairy herd to a VAT-registered agricultural co-operative for €1,000.
The flat-rate addition at 4.4 per cent is €44.
The farmer charges the co-operative €1,044.

20. In the practical administration of the tax, there are special arrangements in relation to sales of livestock. Flat-rate farmers are required to sign declaration forms confirming their status as flat-rate farmers entitled to payment of the flat-rate addition on sales of livestock. A declaration form must be provided on a once-off basis by each flat-rate farmer to each VAT-registered person (e.g. mart, meat factory, abattoir) to whom that farmer sells livestock.

21. Where a Milk Production Partnership is a flat-rate farmer, it is obliged to provide a completed declaration form to each VAT-registered person (e.g. mart, meat factory, abattoir) to whom the partnership sells livestock. Any declaration forms signed previously by an individual partner, in his/her capacity as a separate flat-rate farmer, are of no relevance to the partnership.

VAT refunds on farm buildings and land drainage works

22. Generally speaking, a flat-rate farmer is entitled to a refund of VAT incurred by him/her in respect of expenditure on farm buildings and land drainage works for the purposes of his/her farming business.

23. Claims for refund must be completed on the appropriate form (Form VAT 58). Single claims amounting to less than €125 are not admissible. However, such claims may be represented with other claims from the same claimant once the combined value of the total claim exceeds €125.

24. Where the flat-rate farmer is registered for VAT in respect of intra-Community acquisitions and/or Fourth Schedule services only, he/she is still entitled to a refund of VAT incurred in respect of such works. However, rather than making a separate claim for refund, the refund must be claimed as a deduction from the amount of VAT payable by that farmer with his/her periodic VAT return.

25. Where a Milk Production Partnership is a flat-rate farmer, it is entitled to make claims for refund. However, for the claim to be valid, the expenditure on farm buildings and land drainage works must have been carried out for the purposes of its farming business and the documentation supporting the claim (e.g. invoices and receipts) must be made out in the name and for the account of the partnership. Any documentation in the name and for the account of one of the individual partners, in his/her capacity as a separate entity to the partnership, is of no relevance to the partnership.

Further information

26. For further information on the VAT issues referred to in this information leaflet, you might like to read the following publications:

Guide to Value-Added Tax, January 2003
VAT and Property Transactions
VAT no. 12/01: Farmers and Intra-EU Transactions
VAT no. 18/01: Repayments to Unregistered Persons
VAT no. 23/01: Agricultural Services
VAT no. 24/01: Horticultural Retailers
VAT no. 1/02: Transfer of a Business or Part Thereof
VAT no. 2/04: Fourth Schedule Services

27. These publications are available on Revenue's website at www.revenue. ie. Paper copies of these leaflets may be obtained from Revenue's Forms and Leaflets Services by phoning our Lo-Call number: 1890 30 67 06 (This service is available on a 24 hour basis, 7 days a week. All calls are charged at local rates).

28. For further information on any VAT matter, whether a general enquiry or an enquiry relating to a specific transaction, you should contact your local Revenue district.

Issued by:
VAT Interpretation Branch
Indirect Taxes Division
Revenue Legislation Services
Revenue Commissioners
Dublin Castle
Dublin 2
October 2004

VALUE-ADDED TAX INFORMATION LEAFLET NO. 2/05

VAT AND CLOTHING

1. **Introduction**

    This Information Leaflet sets out the VAT treatment of supplies of clothing for children and adults. This leaflet updates and replaces the Information Leaflet 'VAT on Footwear and Clothing' issued in September 1987 insofar as it relates to VAT on Clothing. An updated Information Leaflet 'VAT and Footwear – No. 31/01' issued in November 2001.

2. **Clothing liable at the zero rate of VAT**

    VAT law provides that the zero rate of VAT applies to

    > "articles of children's personal clothing of sizes which do not exceed the sizes of those articles appropriate to children of average build of 10 years of age (a child whose age is 10 years or 10 years and a fraction of a year being taken for the purposes of this paragraph to be a child of 10 years of age), but excluding –
    >
    > (a)   articles of clothing made wholly or partly of fur skin other than garments merely trimmed with fur skin, unless the trimming has an area greater than one-fifth of the area of the outside material, and
    >
    > (b)   articles of clothing which are not described, labelled, marked or marketed on the basis of age or size;"

    It is important to note that the zero rate of VAT applies only to articles of children's clothing which are described, labelled, marked or marketed for children below 11 years of age. The fact that these sizes may not fit a particular child under that age does not determine the VAT rating of a garment for that child. In addition to normal garments, clothing includes such articles as laces, belts, wigs, headbands, armbands and braces.

3. **Clothing liable at the standard rate of VAT**

    Articles of clothing, other than the articles of children's clothing referred to in paragraph 2, are chargeable to VAT at the standard rate, currently 21 per cent.

    Any articles of clothing which are not described, labelled, marked or marketed on the basis of age, or size appropriate to children of average build of 10 years of age, are chargeable to VAT at 21 per cent, even where these are marketed as children's wear. Examples might include scarves and gloves with no age or size markings.

    Any articles of clothing that are made wholly or partly of natural fur are chargeable to VAT at 21 per cent. This includes children's clothing unless the fur is merely trimming which has an area of one fifth or less of the area of the outside material.

Clothing imported from outside the EU is liable to VAT at the rate that applies to the supply of these goods in the State.

4.   **Measurements for children's clothing**

The sizes of children's clothing are indicated principally in accordance with the following sizing conventions:

(a)   The age of child for whom an article is designed. The maximum age sizes for clothing appropriate to children of average build of less than 11 years of age are '10 Years', or '9 – 11 Years'. It should be noted that clothing marked to fit ranges beyond 10 – 11 years (for example, 10 – 12) will not normally qualify for zero rating.

(b)   The body measurements which an article is designed to fit. The maximum measured sizes for clothing appropriate to children of average build of less than 11 years of age are

    i. To fit up to and including chest (body measurement) size 32"

    ii. To fit up to and including waist (body measurement) size 26"

(c)   The following international measurements can be applied as the equivalent of the imperial measurements used in this leaflet:

International Clothing Measurements		
Ireland/U.K.	**Europe**	**U.S.**
26 inches	65 cm	6
32 inches	80 cm	10

(d)   The Leeds numeric code for certain boy's tailored garments (for example, school blazers). The maximum Leeds numeric code sizing for clothing appropriate to children of average build of less than 11 years of age is size 8, which is equivalent to 30" chest measurement, or size 30.

(e)   Other numeric codes (for example, "size 32" which corresponds to a chest measurement of 32")

(f)   Other maximum measurements may apply where appropriate.

(g)   As an exception to the general rule, a trader who is engaged in selling certain garments which are clearly within the body measurements to which the zero rate applies but which are disqualified from zero rating because of another marking (for example, chest 31" to fit age 11) may submit his case to Revenue for special consideration.

Please note that these measurements only apply to children's clothing. Clothing other than children's clothing is liable at the standard rate, regardless of size.

More than one of the above sizing conventions may be displayed on a garment. In the practical administration of the tax, the size for VAT purposes will be determined by

(a)   The age specification, where it is one of the sizes,

(b)   Where the age specification is not one of the sizes shown, the body measurement specification will generally be regarded as the size for VAT purposes.

As an aid for determining the VAT liability of clothing, Appendix A below sets out the appropriate maximum measurements qualifying for zero rating under the main sizing conventions. The sizes set out are expressed in terms of whichever of these conventions is appropriate. In most cases no distinction is made between boys and girls sizes.

5.   **Supplies associated with clothing**

Supplies of goods and services associated with clothing will also have a VAT liability.

(a)   Dressmaking and tailoring are liable to VAT at zero per cent where the supply of the clothing concerned is also zero-rated. Otherwise, these services are liable at 21 per cent.

(b)   Repairs and alterations, even where carried out by a dressmaker or tailor, are liable to VAT at 13.5 per cent.

(c)   The hiring of clothes is liable to VAT at 21 per cent.

(d)   The supply of a knitting pattern in book form is liable to VAT at zero per cent, provided that it consists of at least 8 pages, has a separate cover, and is bound, stitched or stapled. Otherwise the 21 per cent rate applies.

6.   **Second-hand clothing**

The sale of second-hand clothing by a taxable person is liable to VAT at the same rates as new clothing.

7.   **Enquiries**

For further information on any VAT matter, whether a general enquiry or an enquiry relating to a specific transaction, you should contact your local Revenue district.

Revenue Legislation Services,
Dublin Castle.

May 2005

APPENDIX I

Listing of clothing measurements and VAT rates

The following items of clothing are liable to zero per cent VAT in all circumstances:

Baby Clothes	Baby Bibs (incl. dribblers and feeders)	Baby bootees
Christening robes and shawls	Communion outfits (accessories 21%)	Fancy dress outfits for children
Nappies and diapers (babies only)	Pram suits	Romper suits

The following items of clothing are liable to zero per cent VAT only if they are described, labelled, marked and marketed for children under 11 years of age, or for children up to and including ages 9 – 11 or 10 – 11:

Aprons	Armbands (safety) [see wristbands-21%]	Braces
Garters	Handkerchiefs (textile only)	Hair bands (fabric) [non fabric and hair slides-21%]
Hats/headgear [see fur – 21%]	Leg (incl. ankle) warmers	Laces
Ribbons	Scarves	Swim wear
Ties		

The following items of clothing are liable to zero per cent VAT only if they are described, labelled, marked and marketed for children under 11 years of age, or for children up to and including ages 9 – 11 or 10 – 11, and they are for body measurements up to and including 32" or 80 cm chest, or up to and including size 32.

[However, as an exception to the general rule boys tailored blazers, coats, jackets, school uniforms, suits and waistcoats will qualify for zero rating up to and including Leeds size 8 (size 30) only.]:

Anoraks	Bathrobes	Windcheaters/rain coats
Blazers	Blouses/blousons	Beachrobes
Cardigans	Cat suits	Capes
Dresses (incl. pinafores)	Frocks	Coats
Gowns – bath and dressing	Housecoats	Gabardine coats
Jerseys and jumpers	Leotards	Jackets
Overalls (incl. dungarees)	Overcoats	Nightdresses
Slips	Sweatshirts and other tops	Pyjamas
T-shirts	Track suits – as for suits	Suit jackets (trousers rated separately)
Waistcoats		Underwear – vests/upper body

The following items of clothing are liable to zero per cent VAT only if they are described, labelled, marked and marketed for children under 11 years of age, or for children up to and including ages 9 – 11 or 10 – 11, and they are for body measurements up to and including 26" or 65 cm waist, or up to and including 32" or 80 cm hips:

Jeans	Kilts	Shorts
Skirts	Slacks	Tights
Trousers (incl. suit trousers)	Underwear – Briefs/lower body	

The following items of clothing are liable to zero per cent VAT only if they are described, labelled, marked and marketed for children under 11 years of age, or for children up to and including ages 9 – 11 or 10 – 11, and subject to the conditions set out:

Belts up to and including for 26" or 65 cm waist

Gloves up to and including 7.5 cm palm size. Does not include e.g. oven, gardening or boxing gloves not intended clothes.

Shirts up to and including 13" neck or size 6

Socks up to and including shoe size 3½

Stockings up to and including shoe size 3½

ITEMS OF CLOTHING OF ALL SIZES NOT SPECIFIED ABOVE ARE LIABLE TO VAT AT 21%

The following items are liable to 21 per cent VAT in all circumstances:

Badges	Buckles	Buttons
Costume jewellery	Hair nets	Fasteners
Fur clothing (except trimming – see section 3 above)	Hair bands – non fabric	Handbags
	Knitting wool	Hair slides
Handkerchiefs – non-textile	Thread	Motifs (iron-on etc.)
Headgear – fur hats	Yarn	Tie pins
Swimming arm-bands and rings		Zips
Wristbands (not treated as armbands)		

VALUE-ADDED TAX INFORMATION LEAFLET (AUGUST 2007)

BUILDING AND ASSOCIATED SERVICES

1. **Introduction**

    The building industry consists of traders at a number of different levels who are required to register for, and account for, VAT on their services. These include property developers, building contractors, suppliers of materials and self-employed tradesmen. This Information Leaflet describes how VAT is applied to the various supplies of goods and services associated with the building industry.

2. **Building and other contractors**

    All contractors operating in the building industry carry on taxable businesses and are obliged to register for VAT if their annual turnover exceeds or is likely to exceed the specified limit (€35,000 as from 1 March 2007) in any 12-month period.

    This also applies to self-employed tradesmen operating in the industry, including those involved in general building, electrical, plumbing, plastering, heating, painting, roofing and flooring. However, it is important to note that the nature of the contract and relationship between a principal contractor and a self-employed tradesman will be taken into account when determining the tax treatment. For example, a tradesman who has changed his/her status from employee to self-employed contractor may still be treated as an employee if the contractual position indicates that an employer–employee relationship still exists. In certain circumstances, a person may be a contractor on one contract and an employee on another contract. For further information, traders should contact the Revenue District responsible for their tax affairs.

    Non-resident contractors who have no business establishment in Ireland must register for VAT for work they carry out in the State irrespective of the turnover, even if the job is a 'once-off' contract. Please note, all non-resident contractors are dealt with by Dublin City Centre Revenue District.

    VAT-registered contractors are entitled to deduct VAT properly invoiced to them by their suppliers and where this results in an excess over VAT payable by them in a particular VAT period, they may claim a repayment on their VAT 3 return form.

3. **Application of the 13.5% rate**

    The 13.5% rate of VAT applies to most activities carried on by building contractors and most other contractors operating in the building sector. It applies to house building and construction work generally; to building renovation and demolition; to building maintenance and repair; to the installation of plumbing, heating and electrical services; and to the supply, installation, maintenance and repair of fixtures. The 13.5% rate also applies to the supply and placing in a fixed position of garden sheds, greenhouses and similar structures, subject to certain conditions.

Please note, the 13.5% rate applies to the supply only of ready to pour concrete and concrete blocks. However, the 21% rate applies to the supply only of all other building materials, including the supply of Scaffolding, the hire of Scaffolding, and to the hire and erection of Scaffolding

4.   Fixtures

Fixtures are goods which have become attached to buildings in such a way that they cannot be removed without substantial damage being caused to the goods themselves or to the building to which they are attached. In the case of houses, fixtures could, as a general rule, be said to include the basic structural items normally to be found in a new, unfurnished, standard house. Fixtures would not however include carpets and other floor coverings (unless they are stuck down over their entire surface), cookers, hobs, gas and electric fires and the like. It is important to note that, apart from ready to pour concrete and concrete blocks, the supply only of goods does not qualify for the 13.5% rate of VAT even though the goods may ultimately become fixtures.

For example, the supply only of kitchen units to a builder is chargeable at 21% even though the units, when installed in a building by the builder, may be chargeable at 13.5% (see paragraph 8 below on the 'two-thirds rule'). The builder, of course, is entitled to a full deduction for the tax charged to him or her on the units, subject to the usual conditions. The installation only or the maintenance and repair of fixtures is normally taxable at 13.5% (please see list of examples below).

5.   Fixtures which qualify for the 13.5 % rate

Appendix 1 provides examples of goods which are regarded as qualifying for the 13.5% rate of VAT once they have been permanently installed as fixture (subject to the 'two-thirds rule' not being breached).

6.   Fittings

As distinct from fixtures, fittings are goods that, though often attached to buildings, can be removed without substantial damage being caused to the goods themselves or to the building to which they are attached. Their supply, supply and fitting, and fitting only, is therefore subject to the 21% rate.

Examples are listed in APPENDIX 2.

The supply, or supply and fitting for a single inclusive charge, of these goods is chargeable to VAT at 21%. For example the supply and fitting of a kitchen cooker for an inclusive charge is liable at 21%. If, however, it was necessary to re-wire for a power supply point and a separate charge was raised for such work, the 13.5% rate would apply to that separate charge. The connection only of the cooker to an existing power supply would however be subject to 21%. The plumbing of a washing machine is 21%.

7. Invoicing and accounting for VAT

When supplying goods or services to a VAT registered customer, a VAT registered contractor or supplier whether operating on the 'monies received' or the 'invoice' basis of accounting must issue a VAT invoice by the fifteenth day of the month following the month during which the goods or services were supplied. Please refer to paragraph 8 for instructions relating to the receipt of deposits and stage payments.

In the case of the contractor or supplier operating on the 'invoice' basis any VAT charged must be accounted for in the return for the period in which the invoice issued, or ought to have issued, in the case of a delayed invoice.

In the case of the contractor or supplier operating on the 'monies received' basis any VAT due must be accounted for in the return for the period in which the payment was received.

In dealings with unregistered customers (except Departments of State, Local Authorities, Statutory Bodies, or persons carrying on an exempted activity) it is not necessary to issue a VAT invoice.

8. Deposits and progress payments

Overall payment for a building contract may be split up between smaller payments at different times during the contract, especially where the services are supplied over an extended period of time. A contractor or supplier cannot wait until the job is completed, but must account for VAT on each payment as it is received. These payments are liable to VAT at the same rate as the overall contract.

A deposit, which is retained towards final payment under the contract, is treated in the same way as a progress payment or installment. All are treated for VAT purposes as advance payments towards final completion of the contract. VAT must be accounted for on all such payments by reference to the date of payment, as it is deemed that services have been supplied to the value of the payment on that date. **If a VAT invoice is required (see Paragraph 7 above) then one must be prepared and issued – Contractor's Progress Accounts or certificates from an architect, engineer etc. cannot substitute for a VAT invoice.** In addition, please note VAT cannot be claimed on foot of architects certificates/progress claims, etc. – ideally, these should include the statement 'This is not a VAT invoice'.

(See examples below for treatment of progress claims/installments/ advance payments.)

Examples

1. Builder on invoice basis - customer registered for VAT

	VAT inclusive	Date
Progress claim issued	€200,000	5-1-0X
Part Payment received	€180,000	20-2-0X
Invoice now to issue	€180,000	Due to issue between 20-2-0X and 15-3-0X (but no later)
Invoice issued (say)		1-3-0X
VAT Return Jan/Feb	€0.00	
VAT Return Mar/Apr	€21,410 *	Includes invoice of 1-3-0X)

Customer reclaims VAT in March/April VAT return on foot of VAT invoice issued in March

2. Builder on 'monies received' basis – customer registered for VAT

	VAT inclusive	Date
Progress claim issued	€200,000	5-1-0X
Part Payment received	€180,000	20-2-0X
Invoice now to issue	€180,000	Due to issue between 20-2-0X and 15-3-0X (but no later)
Invoice issued (say)		1-3-0X
VAT Return Jan/Feb	€21.410 *	Account by reference to date of payment
VAT Return Mar Apr	€0.00	

Customer reclaims VAT in March/April VAT return on foot of VAT invoice issued in March.

3. Builder on either basis – customer not registered for VAT

	VAT inclusive	Date
Progress claim issued	€200,000	5-1-0X
Part Payment received	€180,000	20-2-0X
No VAT invoice required	€180,000	
VAT Return Jan/Feb	€21.410 *	Account by reference to date of payment

* VAT element of €180,000 payment inclusive of VAT @ 13.5% – [€180,000 divided by 113.5] multiplied by 13.5.

The following sets out in very general terms how VAT applies at the various stages of building contracts. The rate of VAT on building jobs is generally 13.5%, including the installation of fixtures. The rate of VAT on supply of goods, including the installation of fittings, is 21%.

9.   VAT on a typical building job

The following table sets out in very general terms how VAT applies at the various stages of building contracts. The rate of VAT on building jobs is generally 13.5%, including the installation of fixtures. The rate of VAT on supply of goods, including the installation of fittings, is 21%.

Sequence of Events	VAT Liability
(i) Tender	Not governed by VAT law, but care should be taken to quote the correct rate of VAT. A sub-contractor who incorrectly quotes 13.5% VAT on a tender will be held liable at 21% even if he/she cannot subsequently recover the difference from a main contractor or customer.
(ii) Award of Contract	Not governed by VAT law.
(iii) Deposit (or payment in advance)	For VAT purposes, deposits or advance payments are treated as payments for work already done, and VAT must be accounted for by reference to the date on which the payment is received. However, where a contractor who is operating on the invoice basis of accounting receives a deposit or advance payment from another VAT registered trader then the contractor must account for VAT by reference to the date the invoice is issued or ought to be issued (not later than the fifteenth day of the month following the date of payment). A deposit or advance payment is liable to VAT at the same rate that applies to the overall contract.
(iv) Contractor's progress claim.	Tax not payable at time of issue. This should include a statement 'This is not a VAT invoice'.
(v) Progress payment to contractor	Treated similarly to (iii) above.
(vi) Certificate from architect, engineer, etc.	Certificate does not rank as a VAT invoice.
(vii) Final payment to contractor (excluding retention money)	As in (iii) above, VAT must be accounted for by reference to the date on which payment is received, if the contractor is operating on the 'monies received' basis of accounting. If both the supplier and the customer are registered for VAT, and the supplier is operating on the invoice basis of accounting, then the supplier must issue a VAT invoice, and account for VAT by reference to the date on which the invoice issued or ought to have issued.

Sequence of Events	VAT Liability
(viii) Retention money	(a) In dealings with unregistered customers VAT is payable at the time the money is received, where the contractor is on the monies received basis. (b) In dealings between VAT registered persons a VAT invoice must be issued when the guarantee period expires. A contractor operating on the monies received basis of accounting will not account for VAT until he/she has received the money.

10. **The two-thirds rule**

The rate of VAT applying to services, including building services, depends on the 'two-thirds rule'. This provides that a transaction is liable for VAT as a sale of goods at the appropriate rate, and not as a service, if the VAT exclusive cost of the goods used in providing the service exceeds two-thirds of the total VAT exclusive charge to the customer. The two-thirds rule does not usually affect building services in which the labour element is substantial. It would be likely to come into operation in the case of a service consisting of the supply and installation of, say, a transformer or a strong room. The possibility of its application should never be overlooked and contractors should consult their local Revenue District if there is any doubt about the correct liability to VAT. Sub-contractors may find that the 21% rate may apply to their portion of a main contract even though the main contract may itself be liable at the 13.5% rate.

11. **Changes in VAT rates**

Where changes are made to the rates of VAT the rate applying to a particular payment will depend on whether that payment was made before or after the change came into effect. The rate applicable to a deposit, advance payment or progress payment in a contract where both parties are registered for VAT is:

- In the case of contractors operating on the 'monies received' basis of accounting, the rate in force at the time of the payment.

- In the case of contractors operating on the invoice basis of accounting, the rate in force at the time the invoice is issued or ought to have issued, whichever is the earlier.

Where the customer is not registered for VAT, then all contractors must account for VAT at the rate in force at the time of payment.

Where a contract is made for a fixed price including a current rate of VAT, and before the date on which the tax becomes due there is a change in VAT rate, then in the absence of agreement to the contrary the increase or decrease in the rate may be added to or deducted from the price.

12.   Do-it-yourself (D.I.Y.)

Building materials, with the exception of ready to pour concrete and concrete blocks (to which the 13.5 % rate applies) are liable at 21% VAT. There is no provision for the repayment of any VAT to private individuals who do their own building work. Specifically, there is no provision for repayment of any excess of VAT charged at 21% on building materials over the 13.5% rate which would be chargeable if the work was done by a contractor registered for VAT.

13.   Self-supplies or supplies to connected persons

Where a sole trader carries out building work for himself/herself the transaction is treated as a self-supply and VAT is not recoverable on the costs incurred in making the supply/carrying out the work.

Where a limited company carries out work for a director or for any connected persons VAT is chargeable by reference to the market value of the work carried out.

14.   Property transactions

As a general rule property does not attract a liability to VAT unless all the following conditions are satisfied:-

- the property must have been developed in whole or in part after 31 October 1972;
- the vendor must have a taxable interest in the property;
- the vendor must dispose of a taxable interest in the property;
- the disposal must have been made in the course or furtherance of business;
- the circumstances must be such that the person disposing of the interest was entitled to a tax credit for any tax suffered in relation to the development or the acquisition of his or her interest;
- the consideration in relation to the disposal of a leasehold interest must be at least equal to the 'economic value' of those goods.

All these matters and others, including the valuation of interests, together with assignments and surrenders are discussed in the Revenue booklet 'VAT and Property Transactions' which may be obtained from any Revenue District.

Further information

Enquiries regarding any issue contained in this Information Leaflet should be addressed to the Revenue District responsible for your tax affairs. Contact details for all Revenue Districts can be found on our website under Contact Details.

VAT Appeals & Communications Branch,
Indirect Taxes Division,
Stamping Building
Dublin Castle.

Appendix 1

The following are examples of goods which are regarded as qualifying for the 13.5% rate of VAT once they have been permanently installed as fixtures (subject to the two-thirds rule not being breached).

- Advertising structures
- Air-conditioning equipment
- Airdomes
- Attic insulation
- Attic ladders
- Baths
- Blinds – (certain types, for example where rail is countersunk into the ceiling or parapet)
- Built-in kitchen units
- Built-in wardrobes and presses
- Burglar alarms
- Canopies (at filling stations)
- Central heating systems
- Cold rooms (excluding free-standing type)
- Counters (excluding free-standing type)
- Curtain rails (fixed)
- Double glazing
- Electrical wiring (down to and including lampholders, power points and fuse boards)
- Fencing posts
- Fire escapes
- Fireplaces
- Floor covering stuck down over its entire surface
- Foam insulation (injected into cavity walls)
- Gates
- Generators
- Headstones (fixed)
- Immersion heaters
- Lifts and associated machinery
- Milking parlour equipment (fixed)
- Mirrored tiles (and similar fixed wall-coverings)

- PABX telephone systems
- Partitioning (fixed)
- Pelmets (fixed)
- Prefabricated buildings (subject to conditions)
- Recessed light (excluding light tubes and lamps)
- Roller shutters
- Sewerage treatment plants
- Sinks
- Sliding door equipment
- Slurry tanks (fixed)
- Storage heaters/radiators
- Storage tanks (for oil or water for heating systems)
- Strong room (in banks)
- Switch equipment
- Traffic signaling equipment
- Weighbridges
- Window cleaning rails (for cradle)
- Window guard (wire mesh)
- Wooden floors (permanently fixed)

Appendix 2

The following list provides examples of fittings, as opposed to fixtures. Fittings are goods which, though often attached to buildings, can be removed without substantial damage being caused to the goods themselves or to the building to which they are attached. Their supply and installation is therefore subject to the 21% rate.

- Blinds (most types)
- Curtains
- Stand alone electric and gas fires
- Exhibition stands
- Fitted carpets and lino, (other than floor covering stuck down over its entire surface)
- Free-standing shop counters
- Kitchen cookers (most types)
- Lighting (other than recessed lighting)
- Mirrors

- Most shelving
- Refrigeration units, including deep freezes
- Safes (certain)
- Scaffolding (supply, hire, and hire and erection of)
- Seating, including cinema and church seating whether or not secured to the floor
- Snooker tables and other games tables
- Washing machines and dishwashers, including plumbed-in machines
- Wooden flooring ('floating' – not permanently fixed)

August 2007

This information leaflet which sets out the current practice at the date of its issue is intended for guidance only and does not purport to be a definitive legal interpretation of the provisions of the Value-Added Tax Act 1972 (as amended).

VALUE-ADDED TAX INFORMATION LEAFLET (AUGUST 2007)

RELIEF FROM CUSTOMS DUTY AND VAT ON HONORARY DECORATIONS, AWARDS AND GOODWILL PRESENTS

1. Introduction

Honorary decorations, awards and goodwill presents may be imported from non-European Community (EC) countries free from payment of Customs duty and VAT. This leaflet describes the goods involved, the relief available and the procedures involved at importation.

2. Relief Available

Where it can be established that there is no commercial implication the following awards shall be admitted free from payment of Customs Duty and VAT:

i.   Decorations conferred by governments of non-EC countries on persons whose normal place of residence is in the EC;

ii.   Cups, medals and similar articles of an essentially symbolic nature which, having been awarded in a non-EC country to persons having their normal place of residence in the EC as a tribute to their activities in fields such as the arts, the sciences, sport or the public service or in recognition for merit at a particular event, are imported into the EC by such persons themselves;

iii.   Cups, medals and similar articles of an essentially symbolic nature which are given free of charge by authorities or persons established in a non-EC country to be presented in the EC for the same purposes as referred to in paragraph (ii); and

iv.   Awards, trophies and souvenirs of a symbolic nature and of limited value intended for distribution free of charge to persons normally resident in non-EC countries at business conferences or similar international events. Their nature, unitary value or other features, must not be such as might indicate that they are being imported for commercial reasons.

In addition, goods intended as gifts which:

i.   are offered on an occasional basis; and

ii.   do not by their nature, value or quantity, reflect any commercial intent; and

iii.   are not used for commercial purposes

may be imported free from payment of Customs Duty and VAT in the following circumstances:

a.   they are received by official visitors from their host authorities in non-EC countries; or

b.   they are imported by official visitors to the EC who intend to offer them on that occasion as gifts to host authorities;

c.   they are sent as gifts, in a token of friendship or goodwill, by an official body, public authority or group, carrying on an activity in the public interest which is located in a non-EC country, to an official body, public authority or group carrying on an activity in the public interest which is located in the EC and approved by Revenue to receive such articles free of duty. In such cases, the importer must apply in writing to Customs Procedures Branch, Nenagh for initial authorisation to import the goods.

3.   Procedure at importation

Where goods are forwarded by post, the declaration on the parcel should be endorsed:

1.   "Honorary Decorations or Awards: Exemption from import charges claimed " or

2.   "Goodwill Presents: Exemption from import charges claimed"

The documentary evidence referred to in paragraph 4 should be attached to the outside of the parcel and marked 'Customs Documents'.

Where goods are imported other than by post the goods should be presented to Revenue accompanied by an import declaration (SAD), with a claim to relief from Customs Duty and VAT thereon. For the purposes of completion of the SAD, the legal references are:

1.   Article 86 of Regulation (EEC) No. 918/83 for Customs Duty; Article 56 of Directive 83/181/EEC for VAT

2.   Article 87 of Regulation (EEC) No. 918/83 for Customs Duty; Article 57 of Directive 83/181/EEC for VAT

To claim this relief from Customs Duty and VAT one of the following codes must be entered in box 37 b of the SAD:

    Code C27   Honorary decorations or awards.

    Code C28   Goodwill presents – presents received in the context of international relations.

The entry should be accompanied by the documentary evidence outlined in paragraph 4.

4.   Documentary Evidence

The following documentary evidence should be presented to Revenue at the time of importation:

1.   Documentation from the organisation or host in the non-EC country outlining the circumstances of the award, gift or otherwise, in support of the importers claim to relief; and

2.   In the case of gifts as described at (c) above, a letter of authorisation from Customs Procedures Branch, Nenagh.

5.   Further Information

Enquiries regarding any issue contained in this Information Leaflet should be addressed to the Revenue District responsible for your tax affairs.

Customs Division,
Customs Procedures Branch,
Government Offices,
Nenagh,
Co. Tipperary.

August 2007
Legal Disclaimer

While every effort is made to ensure that the information given in this guide is accurate, it is not a legal document. Responsibility cannot be accepted for any liability incurred or loss suffered as a consequence of relying on any matter published herein.

VALUE-ADDED TAX INFORMATION LEAFLET (AUGUST 2007)

RELIEF FROM CUSTOMS DUTY AND VAT ON THE IMPORTATION OF ARTICLES FOR THE BLIND

1. **Introduction**

    Articles for the Blind may be imported free from payment of Customs Duty and VAT. This leaflet describes the goods involved, the relief available and the procedures involved at importation.

2. **Relief Available**

    Goods specially designed for the educational, scientific or cultural advancement of blind persons as listed in Annex I shall be admitted free from payment of Customs Duty and VAT.

    In addition, the Goods listed in Annex II may also be imported free of Customs Duty and VAT provided they are imported by either:

    i.   The blind person him/herself for his/her own use; or

    ii.   Institutions or organisations concerned with the education of or provision of assistance to the blind approved by the Department of Enterprise, Trade and Employment to receive such articles duty free.

    Spare Parts, components and their accessories including spare parts and tools specially designed for their maintenance, inspection, calibration or repair, used for the purpose of said articles also qualify for relief. Where these items are not imported at the same time as the said articles the Revenue Official at the point of importation will need to establish that:

    i.   They can be identified as being intended for articles originally imported free from Customs Duty and VAT; and

    ii.   The articles originally imported are still entitled to the relief.

    Note: VAT relief is conditional upon the goods having been donated free of charge.

3. **Procedure at importation**

    Where goods are forwarded by post, the declaration on the parcel should be endorsed:

    "Goods for Blind: Exemption from import charges claimed.".

    The documentary evidence referred to in paragraph 4 should be attached to the outside of the parcel and marked 'Customs Documents'.

    Where goods are imported other than by post, the goods should be presented to Revenue accompanied by an import declaration (SAD), with a claim to relief from Customs Duty and VAT thereon. To claim this relief from Customs Duty and VAT one of the following codes must be entered in box 37 b of the SAD:

Code C21   Goods described in Annex I.

Code C22   Goods described in Annex II where the goods are imported by blind persons themselves for their own use.

Code C23   Goods described in Annex II where the goods are imported for the blind by certain approved institutions or organisations.

In each case, the entry should be accompanied by the documentary evidence outlined in paragraph 4.

For the purposes of completion of the SAD, the legal references are:

Article 70 and 71 of Regulation (EEC) No. 918/83 for Customs Duty;

Article 46 of Directive 83/181/EEC for VAT

4.   Documentary Evidence

The following documents should be presented to Revenue at the time of importation:

i.   Evidence that the importer is blind. If not registered with the National Council for the Blind, a qualifying certificate of visual impairment from an ophthalmic surgeon;

ii.   A letter from the Department of Enterprise, Trade and Employment approving the importer to receive the goods duty free; and

ii.   A letter from the supplier confirming the goods are sent free of charge.

5.   Disposal of Goods

i.   In general goods may only be lent, hired out or transferred, whether for payment or free of charge, to an establishment or organisation that qualifies under the conditions listed above provided Revenue has received prior notification. In all other cases loan, hiring out or transfer shall be subject to prior payment of import charges at the rate applying on the date of the loan, hiring out or transfer on the customs value ascertained by Revenue.

ii.   However, goods imported by institutions or organisations eligible for the relief as described above may be lent, hired out or transferred whether for payment or free of charge, on a non-profit making basis to blind persons with whom they are concerned without payment of the corresponding charges.

iii.   Institutions and organisations which qualified for relief shall inform their local Revenue office of the following situations:

    a.   Where they no longer meet the conditions which entitled them to the relief; or

b.   Where the goods are being used for purposes other than that which entitled them to the relief.

In such cases, Revenue shall apply the rate of duty applicable to the goods in the cases of a) on the date the conditions ceased to be fulfilled or b) on the date the goods were put to another use.

6.   Further Information

Enquiries regarding any issue contained in this Information Leaflet should be addressed to the Revenue District responsible for your tax affairs.

Customs Division,
Customs Procedures Branch,
Government Offices,
Nenagh,
Co. Tipperary.

August 2007
Legal Disclaimer

While every effort is made to ensure that the information given in this guide is accurate, it is not a legal document. Responsibility cannot be accepted for any liability incurred or loss suffered as a consequence of relying on any matter published herein.

ANNEX I

Other printed matter, including printed pictures and photographs:

CN code	Description
4911	
4911 10	Trade advertising material, commercial catalogues and the like:
ex 4911 10 90	- - Other:
	- In relief for the blind and partially sighted
4911 91	- Other:
	- - Pictures, prints and photographs:
	- - - Other:
ex 4911 91 91	- - - - Pictures and designs:
	- In relief for the blind and partially sighted
ex 4911 91 99	- - - - Photographs:
	- In relief for the blind and partially sighted

4911 99   - - Other:

ex 4911 99 90   - - - Other:
                                 - In relief for the blind and partially sighted

ANNEX II

CN code	Description
4802	Uncoated paper and paperboard, of a kind used for writing, printing or other graphic purposes, and punch card-stock and punch tape paper, in rolls or sheets, other than paper of heading No 4801 or 4803; hand-made paper and paperboard:
	- Other paper and paperboard not containing fibres obtained by mechanical process or of which not more than 10% by weight of the total fibre content consists of such fibres:
ex 4802 52 00	- - Weighting 40 g/m² or more but not more than 150 g/m² - Braille paper
4802 53	- - Weighting more than 150 g/m²:
ex 4802 53 90	- - - Other: - Braille paper
4802 60	- Other paper and paperboard of which more than 10% by weight of the total fibre content consists of fibres obtained by a mechanical process:
ex 4802 60 90	- - Other: - Braille paper
4805	Other uncoated paper and paperboard, in rolls or sheets:
4805 60	- Other paper and paperboard, weighting 150 g/m² or less:
ex 4805 60 90	- Other: - Braille paper
4805 70	- Other paper and paperboard, weighting more than 150 g/m² but less than 225 g/m² :

ex 4805 70 90	- - Other:
	- Braille paper

4805 80   **- Other paper and paperboard, weighting 225 g/m² or more:**

ex 4805 80 90	- - Other:
	- Braille paper

4823   Other paper, paperboard, cellulose wadding and webs of cellulose fibres, cut to size or shape; other articles of paper pulp, paper, paperboard, cellulose wadding or webs of cellulose fibres:

     - Other paper and paperboard, of a kind used for writing, printing or other graphic purposes:

4823 59   - - Other:

ex 4823 59 90	- - Other:
	- Braille paper

ex 6602 00 00   **- White canes for the blind and partially sighted**

ex 8469   Typewriters and word-processing machines:
     - Adapter for use by the blind and partially sighted

ex 8471   Automatic data-processing machines and units thereof; magnetic or optical readers, machines for transcribing data onto data media in coded form and machines for processing such data, not elsewhere specified or included:

     - Equipment for the mechanical production of Braille and recorded material for the blind

ex 8519   Turntables (record-decks), record-players, cassette-players and other sound reproducing apparatus, not incorporating a sound recording device:

     - Record-players and cassette players specially designed or adapted for the blind and partially sighted

ex 8524   **Records, tapes and other recorded media for sound or other similarly recorded phenomena, including matrices and masters for the production of records, but excluding products of Chapter 37:**

– Talking books
– Magnetic tapes and cassettes for the production of Braille and
  talking books

9013	Liquid crystal devices not constituting articles provided for more specifically in other headings; lasers, other than laser diodes; other optical appliances and instruments, not specified or included elsewhere in this chapter:
ex 9013 80 00	– Other devices, appliances and instruments:
	– Televisions enlargers for the blind and partially sighted
9021	Orthopaedic appliances, including crutches, surgical belts and trusses; splints and other fracture appliances; artificial parts of the body; hearing aids and other appliances which are worn or carried, or implanted in the body, to compensate for a defect or disability:
9021 90	– Other:
ex 9021 90 90	– – Other:
	– Electonic orientator and obstacle detector appliances for the blind and partially sighted – Television enlargers for the blind and partially sighted – Electronic reading machines for the blind and partially sighted
9023 00	Instruments, apparatus and models, designed for demonstrational purposes (for example, in education or exhibitions), unsuitable for other uses:
ex 9023 00 90	– Other:
	- Teaching aids and apparatus specifically designed for the use of the blind and partially sighted
ex 9102	Wrist-watches, pocket-watches and other watches, including stop-watches, other than those of heading No. 9101: – Braille watches with cases other than of precious metals
9504	Articles for funfair, table or parlour games, including pintables, billiards, special tables for casino games and automatic bowling alley equipment:

9504 90   – Other:

ex 9504 90 90   – – Other:

                           – Tables games and accessories specially adapted for the use of
                           the blind and partially sighted

Various   All other articles specially designed for the education, scientific or
                           cultural advancement of the blind and partially sighted'

VALUE-ADDED TAX INFORMATION LEAFLET (AUGUST 2007)

RELIEF FROM CUSTOMS DUTY AND VAT ON THE IMPORTATION OF ARTICLES FOR THE HANDICAPPED AND DISABLED

1.   Introduction

Articles for the Handicapped and Disabled may be imported from non-European Community (EC) countries free from payment of Customs Duty and VAT. This leaflet describes the goods involved, the relief available and the procedures involved at importation.

2.   Relief Available

Goods specially designed for the education, employment or social advancement of physically or mentally handicapped persons other than the blind shall be admitted free from payment of Customs Duty and VAT provided they are imported by either:

i.   Handicapped persons themselves for their own use; or

ii.   Institutions or organisations that are primarily engaged in the education of or the provision of assistance to handicapped persons and are authorised by the Department of Enterprise, Trade and Employment to receive such goods duty free.

Note: VAT relief is conditional upon the goods having been donated free of charge.

3.   Procedure at importation

Where goods are forwarded by post, the declaration on the parcel should be endorsed:

"Goods for the Disabled: Exemption from import charges claimed".

The documentary evidence referred to in paragraph 4 should be attached to the outside of the parcel and marked 'Customs Documents'.

Where goods are imported other than by post they should be presented to Revenue accompanied by an import declaration (SAD), with a claim to relief from Customs Duty and VAT thereon. To claim this relief from Customs Duty and VAT one of the following codes must be entered in box 37 b of the SAD:

Code C24   Goods intended for handicapped and disabled persons imported by themselves for their own use.

Code C25   Goods intended for handicapped and disabled persons imported by certain approved institutes and organisations.

In each case the entry should be accompanied by the documentary evidence outlined in paragraph 4.

For the purposes of completion of the SAD, the legal references are:

Article 72 of Regulation (EEC) No. 918/83 for Customs Duty;
Article 46 of Directive 83/181/EEC for VAT

4.   Documentary Evidence

Documentary Evidence of the importer's disability must be provided together with a letter from the supplier confirming that the goods are specially designed for the purposes outlined at paragraph 1 and that they are being imported free of charge. A letter from the Department of Enterprise, Trade and Employment approving the importer to receive the goods duty free must also be provided.

5.   Disposal of Goods

i.   In general goods may only be lent, hired out or transferred, whether for payment or free of charge, to an establishment or organisation that qualifies under the conditions listed above provided Revenue has received prior notification. In all other cases loan, hiring out or transfer shall be subject to prior payment of import charges at the rate applying on the date of the loan, hiring out or transfer on the customs value ascertained by Revenue.

ii.   However, goods imported by institutions or organisations eligible for the relief as described above may be lent, hired out or transferred whether for payment or free of charge, on a non-profit making basis to handicapped or disabled persons with whom they are concerned without payment of the corresponding charges.

iii.   Institutions and organisations which qualified for relief shall inform their local Revenue office of the following situations:

   a.   Where they no longer meet the conditions which entitled them to the relief; or

   b.   Where the goods are being used for purposes other than that which entitled them to the relief.

In such cases Revenue shall apply the rate of duty applicable to the goods in the cases of a) on the date the conditions ceased to be fulfilled or b) on the date the goods were put to another use.

6.   Further Information

Enquiries regarding any issue contained in this Information Leaflet should be addressed to the Revenue District responsible for your tax affairs.

Customs Division,

Customs Procedures Branch,
Government Offices,
Nenagh,
Co. Tipperary.

August 2007
Legal Disclaimer

While every effort is made to ensure that the information given in this guide is accurate, it is not a legal document. Responsibility cannot be accepted for any liability incurred or loss suffered as a consequence of relying on any matter published herein.

VALUE-ADDED TAX INFORMATION LEAFLET (AUGUST 2007)

RELIEF FROM CUSTOMS DUTY AND VAT ON THE IMPORTATION OF CERTAIN SUBSTANCES OF A THERAPEUTIC OR MEDICAL-RELATED NATURE

1.   **Introduction**

Certain substances of a Therapeutic or Medical-related nature may be imported from non-European Community (EC) countries without payment of Customs Duty and VAT. This leaflet describes the substances involved, the relief available and the procedures involved at import.

2.   **Relief Available**

Therapeutic substances of human origin, blood-grouping reagents and tissue-typing reagents, together with any special packaging essential for their transport or solvents and accessories needed for their use, may be imported free from payment of Customs Duty and VAT on the following conditions:

a.   They are intended for institutions or laboratories approved by Revenue, for use exclusively for non-commercial medical or scientific purposes;

b.   They are accompanied by a certificate of conformity issued by a duly authorised body in the non-EC country of departure; and

c.   They are in containers bearing a special label identifying them.

3.   **Definitions**

Therapeutic substances of human origin – means human blood and its derivatives (whole human blood, dried human plasma, human albumin and fixed solutions of human plasmic protein, human immunoglobulin and human fibrinogen);

Blood-grouping reagents – means all reagents, whether of human, animal, plant or other origin used for blood-type grouping and for the detection of blood incompatibilities. (A reagent is a substance used to produce a chemical reaction); and

Tissue-typing reagents – means all reagents whether of human, animal, plant or other origin used for the determination of human tissue-types.

4.   **Prior Approval Required**

Importers claiming the relief should apply to Customs Procedures Branch, Government Offices, St. Conlons Rd., Nenagh, for initial approval before any importation is undertaken.

5.   **Procedure at importation**

Where goods are forwarded by post, the importer needs to ensure that the declaration on the parcel is endorsed as follows by the person sending the goods:

"Therapeutic Substances & Reagents: Exemption from import charges claimed".

The documentary evidence referred to below should be attached to the outside of the parcel and marked 'Customs Documents'.

Where goods are imported other than by post, they should be presented to Revenue accompanied by an import declaration (SAD) containing a claim to relief from Customs Duty and VAT. For the purposes of completion of the SAD, the legal references are:

Article 61 of Regulation (EEC) No. 918/83 for Customs Duty;

Article 36 of Directive 83/181/EEC for VAT

Code C16 should be entered in box 37 b of the SAD in order to avail of the relief from Customs Duty and VAT. The entry should be accompanied by the documentary evidence outlined in paragraph 6.

6. **Documentary Evidence**

   The following documentary evidence should be presented to Revenue at the time of importation:

   a.   A letter of authorisation from Customs Procedures Branch, Nenagh;

   b.   A letter of declaration from the importer that the goods are exclusively for non commercial medical or scientific purposes; and

   c.   A certificate of conformity issued by a duly authorised body in the third country of departure.

7. **Further Information**

   Enquiries regarding any issue contained in this Information Leaflet should be addressed to the Revenue District responsible for your tax affairs.

Customs Division,
Customs Procedures Branch,
Government Offices,
Nenagh,
Co. Tipperary.

August 2007

[1] Basic Necessities – means those goods required to meet the immediate needs of human beings, e.g., food, medicine, clothing and bedclothes.

Legal Disclaimer

While every effort is made to ensure that the information given in this guide is accurate, it is not a legal document. Responsibility cannot be accepted for any liability incurred or loss suffered as a consequence of relying on any matter published herein.

VALUE-ADDED TAX INFORMATION LEAFLET (AUGUST 2007)

RELIEF FROM CUSTOMS DUTY AND VAT ON THE IMPORTATION OF COFFINS, FUNERARY URNS AND ORNAMENTAL FUNERAL ARTICLES

1. **Introduction**

    Coffins, Funerary Urns and Ornamental Funeral Articles from non-European Community (EC) countries may be imported free from payment of Customs Duty and VAT. This leaflet describes the goods involved, the relief available and the procedures involved at importation.

2. **Relief Available**

    The following shall be admitted free from payment of Customs Duty and VAT:

    a. Coffins containing bodies and urns containing the ashes of deceased persons, as well as flowers*, funeral wreaths* and other ornamental objects normally accompanying them; and

    b. Flowers*, wreaths* and other ornamental objects brought by persons resident in non-EC countries attending a funeral or coming to decorate graves in the EC, provided the importations do not reflect, by their nature or their quantity, any commercial intent.

3. **Procedure at importation**

    Caskets containing remains and urns containing ashes may be landed and cleared without a SAD declaration or examination.

    Caskets and urns, when accompanied, are not required to be reported but are treated in the same way as private effects. In practice, they are usually reported.

    If they are reported on the carriers manifest, a written request or baggage sufferance form is to be submitted to effect clearance.

4. **Documentary Evidence**

    Remains for first interment or re-interment: a certificate from the Civil Registrar or other authority of the place where the death occurred stating that the body is being removed for interment or re-interment.

    Urns containing ashes: a certificate of cremation issued by the crematorium.

    ***Fresh Flowers:** a 'Phyto Sanitary Certificate' is required. This is issued in the country of export by our Department of Food and Agriculture equivalent there.

5.   Further Information

Enquiries regarding any issue contained in this Information Leaflet should be addressed to the Revenue District responsible for your tax affairs.

Customs Division,
Customs Procedures Branch,
Government Offices,
Nenagh,
Co. Tipperary.

August 2007
Note
Further to, but completely separate from, the customs requirements set out in this leaflet there are other formalities involved in bringing a body to Ireland for burial or cremation. Further information should be sought from the coroner's office. Details are also available on http://www.citizensinformation.ie/categories/death/sudden-or-unexplained-death/coroners

Legal Disclaimer

While every effort is made to ensure that the information given in this guide is accurate, it is not a legal document. Responsibility cannot be accepted for any liability incurred or loss.

VALUE-ADDED TAX INFORMATION LEAFLET (AUGUST 2007)

RELIEF FROM CUSTOMS DUTY AND VAT ON THE IMPORTATION OF CONSIGNMENTS SENT TO ORGANISATIONS PROTECTING COPYRIGHTS OR INDUSTRIAL AND COMMERCIAL PATENT RIGHTS

1.   Introduction

Consignments sent from non-European Community (EC) countries to organisations protecting Copyrights or Industrial and Commercial Patent Rights may be imported free from payment of Customs Duty and VAT. This leaflet describes the goods involved, the relief available and the procedures involved at importation.

2.   Relief Available

Trademarks, patterns or designs and their supporting documents, as well as applications for patents for invention or the like, to be submitted to the bodies competent to deal with the protection of copyrights or the protection of industrial or commercial patent rights shall be admitted free from payment of import charges.

3.   Procedure at importation

Where goods are forwarded by post, the declaration on the parcel should be endorsed:

> "Patent, Copyright Protection: Exemption from Import charges claimed".

Where goods are imported other than by post the goods should be presented to Revenue accompanied by an import declaration (SAD), with a claim to relief from import charges thereon. For the purposes of completion of the SAD, the legal references are:

Article 107 of Regulation (EEC) No. 918/83 for Customs Duty;
Article 77 of Directive 83/181/EEC for VAT

Code C34 should be entered in box 37 b of the SAD in order to avail of the relief from Customs Duty and VAT.

4.   Further Information

Enquiries regarding any issue contained in this Information Leaflet should be addressed to the Revenue District responsible for your tax affairs.

Customs Division,
Customs Procedures Branch,
Government Offices,
Nenagh,
Co. Tipperary.

August 2007

Legal Disclaimer

While every effort is made to ensure that the information given in this guide is accurate, it is not a legal document. Responsibility cannot be accepted for any liability incurred or loss suffered as a consequence of relying on any matter published herein.

VALUE-ADDED TAX INFORMATION LEAFLET (AUGUST 2007)

RELIEF FROM CUSTOMS DUTY AND VAT ON THE IMPORTATION OF GOODS FOR CHARITABLE AND HUMANITARIAN ORGANISATIONS

1.   **Introduction**

     Goods for Charitable and Humanitarian organisations from non-European Community (EC) countries may be imported free from payment of Customs Duty and VAT. This leaflet describes the goods involved, the relief available and the procedures involved at importation.

2.   **Relief Available**

     The following goods may be imported free from payment of Customs Duty and VAT:

     a.   Basic necessities [1] imported by State organisations or Charitable or Humanitarian organisations for distribution free of charge to people in need;

     b.   Goods sent free of charge by a person or organisation established outside of the EC, where there is no commercial intent on the part of the sender, to State organisations or Charitable or Humanitarian organisations to be used for fund-raising at occasional charity events for the benefit of needy persons; and

     c.   Equipment and office materials sent free of charge by a person or organisation established outside of the EC, where there is no commercial intent on the part of the sender, to Charitable or Humanitarian organisations to be used solely for the purpose of meeting their operating needs or carrying out their charitable aims.

     Note: Relief is not allowed on alcoholic products, tobacco and tobacco products and motor vehicles other than ambulances.

3.   **Procedure at importation**

     Where goods are forwarded by post, the declaration on the parcel should be endorsed:

     "Goods for Charitable Purposes: Exemption from import charges claimed".

     The documentary evidence outlined in paragraph 4 should be attached to the outside of the parcel and marked 'Customs Documents'.

     Where goods are imported other than by post the goods should be presented to Revenue accompanied by an import declaration (SAD), with a claim to relief from import charges thereon. For the purposes of completion of the SAD, the legal references are:

Article 65 of Regulation (EEC) No. 918/83 for Customs Duty;
Article 40 of Directive 83/181/EEC for VAT

Code C20 should be entered in box 37 b of the SAD in order to avail of the relief from Customs Duty and VAT. The entry should be accompanied by the documentary evidence outlined in paragraph 4.

4.   Documentary Evidence

Written confirmation from the importer for each of the situations outlined above is required as follows:

a.   A declaration from the importer confirming that the goods are for distribution free of charge to people in need;

b.   Letter from the sender of the goods confirming that they are sent free of charge with no commercial intent on their behalf and a declaration from the importer confirming that the goods are for fund-raising at occasional charity events for the benefit of needy people; and

c.   Letter from sender confirming the equipment is sent free of charge without any commercial intent on the part of the sender and a declaration from the charity/organisation that the goods are to be used solely for the purpose of meeting their operating needs or carrying out their charitable aims.

5.   Disposal of Goods

Goods may only be lent, hired out or transferred to an establishment or organisation that qualifies under the conditions listed above provided Revenue has received prior notification. In all other cases loan, hiring out or transfer shall be subject to prior payment of import charges at the rate applying on the date of the loan, hiring out or transfer on the customs value ascertained by Revenue.

Institutions and Organisations who qualified for relief shall inform their local Revenue office of the following situations:

a.   Where they no longer meet the conditions which entitled them to the relief; or

b.   Where the goods are being used for purposes other than that which entitled them to the relief.

In such cases Revenue shall apply the rate of duty applicable to the goods in the cases of (a) on the date the conditions ceased to be fulfilled or (b) on the date the goods were put to another use.

6.   Further Information

Enquiries regarding any issue contained in this Information Leaflet should be addressed to the Revenue District responsible for your tax affairs.

Customs Division,
Customs Procedures Branch,
Government Offices,
Nenagh,
Co. Tipperary.

August 2007

[1] Basic Necessities – means those goods required to meet the immediate needs of human beings, e.g., food, medicine, clothing and bedclothes.

Legal Disclaimer

While every effort is made to ensure that the information given in this guide is accurate, it is not a legal document. Responsibility cannot be accepted for any liability incurred or loss suffered as a consequence of relying on any matter published herein.

VALUE-ADDED TAX INFORMATION LEAFLET (AUGUST 2007)

RELIEF FROM CUSTOMS DUTY AND VAT ON THE IMPORTATION OF GOODS FOR DISASTER VICTIMS

1. **Introduction**

   Goods for the Disaster Victims may be imported from non-European Community (EC) countries free from payment of Customs Duty and VAT. This leaflet describes the goods involved, the relief available and the procedures involved at importation.

2. **Relief Available**

   Goods imported by State organisations, Charitable or Humanitarian organisations approved by Revenue, or Disaster-relief agencies in order to meet their needs during the period of their activity shall be admitted free from payment of import charges provided they are intended:

   a. For distribution free of charge to victims of disasters affecting the territory of one of more Member States; or

   b. To be made available free of charge to the victims of such disasters, while remaining the property of the organisation in question.

   The granting of the relief is subject to approval by the European Commission in consultation with the Member States and shall where necessary lay down the scope and the conditions of the relief.

   Note: There is no Relief for materials and equipment intended for rebuilding disaster areas.

3. **Procedure at importation**

   Where goods are forwarded by post, the declaration on the parcel should be endorsed:

   "Goods for use of Disaster Victims: Exemption from import charges claimed".

   The documentary evidence referred to below should be attached to the outside of the parcel and marked 'Customs Documents'.

   Where goods are imported other than by post the goods should be presented to Revenue accompanied by an import declaration (SAD), with a claim to relief from import charges thereon. For the purposes of completion of the SAD, the legal references are:

   Article 79 of Regulation (EEC) No. 918/83 for customs duty; Article 49 of Directive 83/181/EEC for VAT

   Code C26 should be entered in box 37 b of the SAD in order to avail of the relief from Customs Duty and VAT. The entry should be accompanied by the documentary evidence outlined in paragraph 4.

4. Documentary Evidence

Organisations requesting such relief should apply in writing to Customs Procedures Branch, Nenagh, Co. Tipperary, for referral to the European Commission for decision. Pending receipt of approval from the Commission, Revenue at the point of importation may suspend the relevant Customs Duty and VAT charges subject to an undertaking by the importing Organisation to pay such charges if relief is not granted.

5. Disposal of Goods

a. Goods may only be lent, hired out or transferred, to an organisation that qualifies under the conditions listed above provided Revenue has received prior notification. In all other cases loan, hiring out or transfer shall be subject to prior payment of import charges at the rate applying on the date of the loan, hiring out or transfer on the customs value ascertained by Revenue.

b. Organisations which qualified for relief shall inform their local Revenue office of the following situations:

i. Where they no longer meet the conditions which entitled them to the relief; or

ii. Where the goods are being used for purposes other than that which entitled them to the relief

In such cases, Revenue shall apply the rate of duty applicable to the goods in the cases of (i) on the date the conditions ceased to be fulfilled or (ii) on the date the goods were put to another use.

6. Further Information

Enquiries regarding any issue contained in this Information Leaflet should be addressed to the Revenue District responsible for your tax affairs.

Customs Division,
Customs Procedures Branch,
Government Offices,
Nenagh,
Co. Tipperary.

August 2007

Legal Disclaimer

While every effort is made to ensure that the information given in this guide is accurate, it is not a legal document. Responsibility cannot be accepted for any liability incurred or loss suffered as a consequence of relying on any matter published herein.

VALUE-ADDED TAX INFORMATION LEAFLET (AUGUST 2007)

RELIEF FROM CUSTOMS DUTY AND VAT FOR GOODS IMPORTED
FOR EXAMINATION, ANALYSIS OR TEST PURPOSES

1.   **Introduction**

Goods imported for Examination, Analysis or Test purposes may
be imported from non-European Community (EC) countries free
from payment of Customs Duty and VAT. This leaflet describes the
goods involved, the relief available and the procedures involved at
importation.

2.   **Relief Available**

Goods, which are to undergo examination, analysis or tests to determine
their compositions, quality or other technical characteristics for
purposes of information or industrial or commercial research, shall be
imported free from payment of Customs Duty and VAT on the following
conditions:

a.   The goods are completely used up or destroyed in the course
of the examination, analysis or testing. Where they are not, the
local Revenue Office can agree under their supervision that the
goods are:

i.   Completely destroyed or rendered commercially valueless
on completion of the examination, analysis or testing; or

ii.   Surrendered to the State without causing it any expense,
where this is possible under national law; and

iii. In duly justified circumstances, exported outside of the
EC.

b.   The local Revenue Office should also determine the types of
records to be maintained and the period within which the
examinations, analysis or tests must be carried out based on
information received from the importer and the type of goods
involved.

c.   Products remaining* should be subject to the relevant Customs
Duty and VAT charges on the date of completion of the
examination, analysis or tests. Alternatively, Revenue may agree,
where the importers request to convert products remaining to
waste or scrap, to charge Customs Duty and VAT at the rate
applicable to the waste or scrap on the date of conversion.

*Products remaining means products resulting from the examination,
analysis or tests or goods not actually used

3.   **Procedure at importation**

Where goods are forwarded by post, the declaration on the parcel should be endorsed:

"Goods for Examination, Analysis or Test purposes: Exemption from import charges claimed"

The documentary evidence referred to in paragraph 4 should be attached to the outside of the parcel and marked 'Customs Documents'.

Where goods are imported other than by post the goods should be presented to Revenue accompanied by an import declaration (SAD), with a claim to relief from import charges thereon. For the purposes of completion of the SAD, the legal references are:

Article 100 of Regulation (EEC) No. 918/83 for Customs Duty;
Article 70 of Directive 83/181/EEC for VAT

Code C33 should be entered in box 37 b of the SAD in order to avail of the relief from Customs Duty and VAT. The entry should be accompanied by the documentary evidence outlined in paragraph 4.

4.   **Documentary Evidence**

The importer should apply in writing to Customs Procedures Branch, Nenagh for a letter of authorisation to import the goods in question.

5.   **Further Information**

Enquiries regarding any issue contained in this Information Leaflet should be addressed to the Revenue District responsible for your tax affairs.

Customs Division,
Customs Procedures Branch,
Government Offices,
Nenagh,
Co. Tipperary.

August 2007

Legal Disclaimer

While every effort is made to ensure that the information given in this guide is accurate, it is not a legal document. Responsibility cannot be accepted for any liability incurred or loss suffered as a consequence of relying on any matter published herein.

VALUE-ADDED TAX INFORMATION LEAFLET (AUGUST 2007)

RELIEF FROM CUSTOMS DUTY AND VAT ON THE IMPORTATION
OF LITTER, FODDER AND FEEDING STUFFS FOR ANIMALS
DURING THEIR TRANSPORT

1.   **Introduction**

Litter, Fodder and Feeding stuffs for animals during their transport
from non-European Community (EC) countries may be imported free
from payment of Customs Duty and VAT. This leaflet describes the
goods involved, the relief available and the procedures involved at
importation.

2.   **Relief Available**

Litter, fodder and feeding stuffs of any description put on board the means
of transport used to convey animals from a non-EC country to the EC for
the purpose of distribution to the said animals during their journey may
be imported free from payment of Customs Duty and VAT.

3.   **Procedure at importation**

The import declaration (SAD), with a claim to relief from Customs
Duty and VAT thereon should be presented to Revenue at the point
of importation. For the purposes of completion of the SAD, the legal
references are:

Article 111 of Regulation (EEC) No. 918/83 for Customs Duty;
Article 81 of Directive 83/181/EEC for VAT

Code C38 should be entered in box 37 b of the SAD in order to avail of
the relief from Customs Duty and VAT.

4.   **Prohibitions**

Imports of hay, straw and peat moss litter from non-EC countries are
prohibited except under general authorisation or licence from the
Minister for Agriculture, Fisheries and Food as part of the arrangements
to prevent the spread of Foot and Mouth Disease.

Further information in relation to prohibitions and restrictions can be
obtained from International and Trade Security Branch, Nenagh.

5.   **Further Information**

Enquiries regarding any issue contained in this Information Leaflet
should be addressed to the Revenue District responsible for your tax
affairs.

Customs Division,
Customs Procedures Branch,
Government Offices,
Nenagh,
Co. Tipperary.

August 2007

Legal Disclaimer

While every effort is made to ensure that the information given in this guide is accurate, it is not a legal document. Responsibility cannot be accepted for any liability incurred or loss suffered as a consequence of relying on any matter published herein.

VALUE-ADDED TAX INFORMATION LEAFLET (AUGUST 2007)

RELIEF FROM CUSTOMS DUTY AND VAT ON THE IMPORTATION OF MATERIALS FOR THE CONSTRUCTION, UPKEEP OR ORNAMENTATION OF MEMORIALS TO, OR CEMETERIES FOR, WAR VICTIMS

1.   Introduction

Materials for the Construction, Upkeep or Ornamentation of Memorials to, or Cemeteries for, War Victims may be imported from non-European Community (EC) countries free from payment of Customs Duty and VAT. This leaflet describes the goods involved, the relief available and the procedures involved at importation.

2.   Relief Available

Goods of every description, imported by organisations authorised for this purpose by the competent authority, e.g., the local planning authorities, to be used for the construction, upkeep or ornamentation of cemeteries and tombs of, and memorials to, war victims of non-EC countries who are buried in the EC shall be admitted free from payment of Customs Duty and VAT.

3.   Procedure at importation

Where goods are forwarded by post, the declaration on the parcel should be endorsed:

"Materials for Upkeep of Cemeteries: Exemption from import charges claimed".

The documentary evidence referred to below should be attached to the outside of the parcel and marked 'Customs Documents'.

Where goods are imported other than by post the goods should be presented to Revenue accompanied by an import declaration (SAD), with a claim to relief from import charges thereon.

For the purposes of completion of the SAD, the legal references are:

Article 117 of Regulation (EEC) No. 918/83 for Customs Duty;
Article 87 of Directive 83/181/EEC for VAT

Code C40 should be entered in box 37 b of the SAD in order to avail of the relief from Customs Duty and VAT.

4.   Documentary Evidence

A letter from the body that has authorised the work e.g., the local planning authority, should accompany the importation.

5.   Further Information

Enquiries regarding any issue contained in this Information Leaflet should be addressed to the Revenue District responsible for your tax affairs.

Customs Division,
Customs Procedures Branch,
Government Offices,
Nenagh,
Co. Tipperary.

August 2007

Legal Disclaimer

While every effort is made to ensure that the information given in this guide is accurate, it is not a legal document. Responsibility cannot be accepted for any liability incurred or loss suffered as a consequence of relying on any matter published herein.

VALUE-ADDED TAX INFORMATION LEAFLET (AUGUST 2007)

RELIEF FROM CUSTOMS DUTY AND VAT ON THE IMPORTATION
OF MISCELLANEOUS DOCUMENTS AND ARTICLES

1. **Introduction**

   Miscellaneous Documents and Articles may be imported from non-European Community (EC) countries free from payment of Customs Duty and VAT. This leaflet describes the goods involved, the relief available and the procedures involved at importation.

2. **Relief Available**

   The following shall be admitted free from payment of Customs Duty and VAT:

   a.   Documents sent free of charge to the public services of Member States of the EC;

   b.   Publications of foreign governments or of official international bodies intended for distribution free of charge;

   c.   Ballot papers for elections organised by bodies set up in non-EC countries;

   d.   Objects to be submitted as evidence or similar to the courts or other official agencies of the Member States;

   e.   Specimen signatures and printed circulars concerning signatures set as part of customary exchanges of information between public services or banking establishments;

   f.   Official printed matter sent to the central banks of the Member States;

   g.   Reports, statements, notes, prospectuses, application forms and other documents drawn up by companies registered in a non-EC country and sent to the bearers or subscribers of securities issued by such companies;

   h.   Recorded media (sound recordings, microfilms, etc.) used for the transmission of information sent free of charge to the addressee, in so far as duty-free admission does not give rise to abuses or to major distortions of competition;

   i.   Files, archives, printed forms and other documents to be used in international meetings, conferences or congresses, and reports on such gatherings;

   j.   Plans, technical drawings, traced designs, descriptions and other similar documents imported with a view to obtaining or fulfilling orders in third countries or to participating in a competition held in the EC;

k. Documents to be used in examinations held in the EC by institutions set up in non-EC countries;

l. Printed forms to be used as official documents in the international movement of vehicles or goods, within the framework of international conventions;

m. Printed forms, labels, tickets and similar documents sent by transport undertakings or by undertakings of the hotel industry in a non-EC country to travel agencies set up in the EC;

n. Printed forms and tickets, bills of lading, way-bills and other commercial or office documents which have been used;

o. Official printed forms from non-EC country or international authorities, and printed matter conforming to international standards sent for distribution by non-EC country associations to corresponding associations located in the EC;

p. Photographs, slides and stereotype mats for photographs, whether or not captioned, sent to press agencies or newspaper or magazine publishers;

q. Tax and similar stamps proving payment of charges in non-EC countries.

The following shall be admitted free from payment of VAT:

r. Collectors' pieces and works of art of an educational, scientific or cultural character which are not intended for sale and which are imported by museums, galleries and other institutions approved by Revenue for the purpose of duty-free admission of these goods.

The exemption is granted only on condition that the articles in question are imported free of charge, or if they are imported for payment, that they are not supplied by a taxable person.

There may be relief from Customs Duty under Educational, Scientific and Cultural Materials.

3. **Prior Approval Required**

Importers claiming the relief referred to at paragraphs 2 (r) should apply to Customs Procedures Branch, Government Offices, St. Conlon's Rd., Nenagh, Co. Tipperary for initial approval before any importation is undertaken.

4. **Procedure at importation**

Where goods are forwarded by post, the declaration on the parcel should be endorsed:

"Miscellaneous Documents and Articles: Exemption from import charges claimed".

Where required, the documentary evidence outlined in paragraph 5 should be attached to the outside of the parcel and marked 'Customs Documents'.

Where goods are imported other than by post the goods should be presented to Revenue accompanied by an import declaration (SAD), with a claim to relief from import charges thereon. For the purposes of completion of the SAD, the legal references are:

Article 109 of Regulation (EEC) No. 918/83 for Customs Duty;
Article 79 of Directive 83/181/EEC for VAT.

Code C36 should be entered in box 37 b of the SAD in order to avail of the relief from Customs Duty and VAT.

5.   Documentary Evidence

In cases where the importer is importing goods under (r) she/he must apply in writing to Customs Procedures Branch, Nenagh for a letter of authorisation to import the goods in question.

6.   Further Information

Enquiries regarding any issue contained in this Information Leaflet should be addressed to the Revenue District responsible for your tax affairs.

Customs Division,
Customs Procedures Branch,
Government Offices,
Nenagh,
Co. Tipperary.

August 2007

Legal Disclaimer

While every effort is made to ensure that the information given in this guide is accurate, it is not a legal document. Responsibility cannot be accepted for any liability incurred or loss suffered as a consequence of relying on any matter published herein.

VALUE-ADDED TAX INFORMATION LEAFLET (AUGUST 2007)

RELIEF FROM CUSTOMS DUTY AND VAT ON THE IMPORTATION OF PHARMACEUTICAL PRODUCTS

1. **Introduction**

   Certain Pharmaceutical products for human or veterinary medical use may be imported from non-European Community (EC) countries without payment of Customs Duty and VAT. This leaflet describes the goods and products involved, the relief available and the procedures involved at import.

2. **Relief Available**

   Relief is available in respect of pharmaceutical products for human or veterinary medical use by persons or animals coming from third countries to participate in international sports events organised in the customs territory of the Community provided they are within the quantitative limits necessary to meet the importer's requirements for their stay in the EC.

3. **Prior Approval Required**

   Importers claiming the relief should apply to Customs Procedures Branch, Government Offices, St. Conlon's Rd., Nenagh, for initial approval before any importation is undertaken.

4. **Procedure at importation**

   Where goods are forwarded by post, the importer needs to ensure that the declaration on the parcel is endorsed:

   'Pharmaceutical Products, Sport Events: Exemption from import charges claimed'.

   The documentary evidence referred to in paragraph 5 should be attached to the outside of the parcel and marked 'Customs Documents'.

   Where goods are imported other than by post the goods should be presented to Revenue accompanied by an import declaration (SAD), containing a claim to relief from Customs Duty and VAT. For the purposes of completion of the SAD, the legal reference is:

   Article 64 of Regulation (EEC) No. 918/83 for Customs Duty;
   Article 39 of Directive 83/181/EEC for VAT.

   The following codes should be entered in box 37 b of the SAD in order to avail of the relief from Customs Duty and VAT:

   C19 for imports of Pharmaceutical products for human or veterinary medical use.

   The entry should be accompanied by the documentary evidence outlined in paragraph 5.

5.   **Documentary Evidence**

In the case of imports described above the importer must have a letter from a doctor/vet confirming the need for the products and this should be presented to Revenue at the time of importation.

6.   **Further Information**

Enquiries regarding any issue contained in this Information Leaflet should be addressed to the Revenue District responsible for your tax affairs.

Customs Division,
Customs Procedures Branch,
Government Offices,
Nenagh,
Co. Tipperary.

August 2007

Legal Disclaimer

While every effort is made to ensure that the information given in this guide is accurate, it is not a legal document. Responsibility cannot be accepted for any liability incurred or loss suffered as a consequence of relying on any matter published herein.

VALUE-ADDED TAX INFORMATION LEAFLET (SEPTEMBER 2007)

TRANSFER OF BUSINESS OR PART THEREOF

1.   Introduction

1.1   The VAT Act provides that where a transfer of ownership of goods takes place in the course of the transfer of a business or part of a business from one taxable person to another taxable person, that transfer is deemed not to be a supply for VAT purposes. Similar provisions apply as regards the transfer between qualifying entities of goodwill or other intangible assets.

1.2   These provisions are important trade facilitation measures aimed at reducing compliance costs for traders involved in this type of transaction. However, traders are advised that when they are involved in a transfer of this type, particularly as an acquirer of a business or part thereof, they should check with their Revenue District office before paying any VAT invoiced by the vendor. Where a transfer of business is involved it is important to note that any VAT paid by a purchaser to a vendor in these circumstances will not be deductible as no supply is deemed to have taken place.

2.   What the law says

Sections 3(5)(b)(iii), 5 (8), 12 D of the Value Added Tax Act 1972 (as amended), refer. The corresponding provisions are in Articles 19 and 29 of the EU VAT Directive 2006. The precise wording of these provisions are contained in Appendix II.

3.   What is the transfer of business or part thereof?

There is no definition of a transfer of a business or part thereof in VAT law. However, the component parts of the transfer of a business can normally be broken down into the transfer of some or all of the following: Employees, premises, plant and machinery, stock, goodwill, intellectual property, and debtors.

4.   Circumstances in which the transfer rules apply

4.1   The transfer, in order to qualify for the transfer of business rules, must be made to another person in circumstances where that other person intends to apply those goods or services for the purposes of a taxable business and where that amalgam of assets constitutes an undertaking or part of an undertaking capable of being operated on an independent basis. It is not a requirement of Irish VAT law that the transfer must constitute a transfer of a business as a going concern.

4.2   EU case law indicates that it must be the intention of the transferee to carry on the business. In practice, a person who transfers a business or part of a business to another person where all or parts of the assets are intended to be used:-

1.   to carry on the same or a similar taxable business,

2.   for the purposes of the acquirer's own taxable business, following the cessation of the transferor's business or

3.   to carry on a different taxable business in the premises using the assets acquired

is not required to account for VAT on the transfer of such a business or part of a business.

Once-off-sales of business assets do not qualify as VAT-free supplies. For example, the sale of an oil tanker by a garage-owner who also delivers home heating oil is not a VAT-free supply under Section 3(5)(b)(iii) of the VAT Act. However, the sale of the entire home-heating oil distribution business which also includes an oil tanker would qualify as a VAT-free sale.

4.4   The absence of any one of the component parts of the business will therefore not preclude the application of the provisions to the transaction.

4.5   It should be noted that, in relation to the transfer of goodwill and other intangible assets the term 'taxable person' does not include a person registered only for the purposes of intra-Community acquisitions, received Fourth Schedule services, received cultural, artistic, entertainment or similar services or who receives goods for installation or assembly by a non-established trader.

4.6   Where a person acquiring a business or part of a business has applied for but has not yet received a VAT registration number, the vendor should apply the provisions of Section 3(5)(b)(iii).

5.   Licence to operate a public house

The transfer of a public house business, with accompanying assets, between two taxable persons, qualifies for the relief. Revenue are prepared to treat the sale or transfer of a pub licence without accompanying assets from one taxable person to another taxable person as coming within the ambit of Section 3(5)(b)(iii).

6.   Transfer of an interest in a partnership or co-ownership

6.1   In the case of a partnership carrying on a taxable activity where a partner exits the partnership and sells out to a new partner, then Section 3(5)(b)(iii) applies.

6.2   In the case of a taxable co-ownership, Revenue is prepared to change its current treatment under which the sale by a co-owner of his/her interest in a co-ownership is regarded as a taxable supply. Revenue will in future regard such a supply as the transfer of a business to which Sections 3(5)(b)(iii) applies.

7.   Transfer of a business to a non-established customer

The transfer of a business to a customer who is not registered or entitled to register for VAT in the State is not covered by the relief. The transfer of the goods may benefit from the EU intra-Community supply or export provisions while the transfer or rights to intellectual property may qualify for zero rating under the Fourth Schedule to the VAT Act. The transfer of goodwill in itself or the sale of debtors are not classified as Fourth Schedule Services. It is open to the customer to apply for refund of VAT under the provisions of the Eighth and Thirteenth VAT Directives.

8.   **Milk Quota**

The transfer of intangible assets between farmers and between non-taxable persons is not chargeable to VAT. A transfer of a milk or beet quota between farmers does not give rise to a VAT liability. The transfer of business rules apply where the business has ceased trading.

9.   **Transfers of property as part of a transfer of business or part thereof**

9.1   The transfer of property in connection with the transfer of business qualifies for the relief.

9.2   Where a taxpayer owns a building which he/she lets on a short-term basis to a business which uses it for warehousing, for example, and he disposes of the building with the tenant in situ to another taxable person, then Section 3(5)(b)(iii) would heretofore not have applied. However, in future Revenue will accept that the concept of 'undertaking' and 'business' could include the exploitation of tangible and intangible property for the purposes of obtaining income therefrom on a continuing basis and that the transfer of a let property is a transfer capable of qualifying for the relief. This, however, will only apply when the person acquiring the letting business is a taxable person in respect of the 'business' being acquired. For example, if the person acquires a letting business where there are short-term lettings and that person does not waive their exemption in respect of those lettings, then Section 3(5)(b)(iii) will not apply to such a transfer. Similarly, where a person acquires a letting business where the vendor has let out on long leases, the purchaser is not a taxable person in respect of the lettings and therefore the sale will not come within Section 3(5)(b)(iii).

9.3   Transfers of property to or by a person not entitled to full deductibility

Section 12D of the VAT Act provides for special measures to deal with transfers of business which include property or interests in property where either the transferor or transferee or both are not entitled to full deductibility on acquisition or development of the property. It deals with transfers of an interest of 10 years or more in property in the context of a transfer of a business where one of the parties involved is not entitled to full deductibility. The purpose of the section is to limit by means of a clawback the opportunity for a taxable person who is not entitled to deduct all the VAT on his/her inputs, to obtain, using the transfer of business rules, an interest in property VAT-free. The provision also reduces the extent of any trapped VAT by means of add-backs where the transferor was not entitled to full deductibility on the acquisition.

Further information on this subject is available in the Revenue Guide to VAT and Property Transactions (PDF, 345KB).

10. Records

10.1 Where a business is transferred in accordance with 3(5)(b)(iii) and the transferee will operate the business under a different VAT number, the transferor will normally be required to retain is his/her possession all records for at least 6 years from the date of the last transaction, unless Revenue notify the person that retention is not required.

Credit Notes issued after a transfer of business

10.2 Where a transferor of a business issues an invoice to a customer and, subsequent to the transfer of the business, the goods are proved to be faulty and returned (or where a discount or rebate is due to the customer against the price originally charged for the goods), then technically speaking, the transferor is obliged to issue a credit note in respect of this transaction in accordance with **Sections 10(3)(d) and 17(3)(b) of the VAT Act 1972, together with regulation 16 VAT Regulations, 2006.**

However, on a concessional basis and on condition that the transferor had no tax liabilities outstanding in respect of the business or part thereof which had been transferred in accordance with **Section 3(5)(b)(iii)**, Revenue are prepared to allow the transferee, rather than the transferor, to issue a credit note in respect of the transaction in question.

Costs incurred fulfilling outstanding obligations, e.g., warranties after a transfer of business

10.3 Where a transferor of the business supplies goods issued under warranty and, subsequent to the transfer of a business, the customer returns the goods to the transferee for repair/replacement, again technically speaking, the transferee is not entitled to recover VAT incurred on expenditure relating to the fulfillment of the warranty on the basis that this expenditure does not relate to any taxable supplies made by the transferee.

However, on a concessional basis and on condition that the transferor had no tax liabilities outstanding in respect of the business or part thereof which had been transferred in accordance with **Section 3(5) (b)(iii)**, Revenue are be prepared to allow the transferee to claim input credit in respect of expenditure incurred by him/her in relation to the fulfilment of the warranties issued by the transferor.

Bad debts determined after a transfer of business

10.4 Where, as part of the transfer of the business in accordance with **Section 3(5)(b)(iii)**, the transferor of a business transfers debts which, subsequent to the transfer, are determined to be 'bad debts' (i.e., wholly irrecoverable debts) an adjustment in respect of the VAT already accounted for by the transferor in respect of these bad debts remains a matter for the transferor. The transferee is not entitled to make any adjustment to his/her VAT liability in respect of these debts

11.   VAT Credit in relation to services supplied

Section 12 (1) (a) (iiia) of the VAT Act provides that input credit is allowable in respect of services in connection with a transfer of goods in accordance with Section 3 (5) (b) (iii). In practice, input credit may also be taken in respect of services in connection with the transfer of goodwill or other intangible assets in accordance with Section 5 (8) where the parties to the transaction are taxable persons. Such credit may be taken by the transferor or transferee as appropriate.

Further Information

Further information in the form of questions and answers is contained in Appendix I. Enquiries regarding any issue contained in this Information Leaflet should be addressed to the Revenue District responsible for your tax affairs. Contact details for all Revenue Districts can be found on the Contact Details Page.

VAT Appeals and Communications Branch,
Indirect Taxes Division,
Dublin Castle.

September 2007

Appendix I

Transfer of Business or Part of a Business – Questions and Answers

The following sets out a number of questions and answers on the operation of the transfer of business exemption provided in Sections 3(5)(b)(iii) and 5(8).

Question 1

Where a business is transferred, the assets that may be transferred can normally be sub-divided as follows: premises, employees, plant and machinery, stock, goodwill, intellectual property, and debtors. The classic transfer of a business will comprise all seven. Some businesses may not have some of these items, for example, there may be no plant, machinery or stock where the business is a service business. Where part of a business is transferred and incorporated into the business of the purchaser it may be difficult to decide whether the exemption applies.

On what basis does Revenue consider that the relief applies if some parts of the classic seven items are transferred with some of such items being retained?

Example

In a sale of business assets the following items are retained or, as the case may be, sold by a taxable person:

Retained by Vendor	Sold by Vendor
Premises	Plant and Machinery
Debtors	Goodwill
Employees	

The purchaser, another taxable person, incorporates the plant and machinery and the goodwill into his taxable business. Will transfer of business exemption apply? If the situation is uncertain, what features will the Revenue look for to qualify or disqualify such a transaction from the exemption?

Response to Question 1

It is considered that the tax treatment in the scenario posed is covered adequately in paragraph 4.1 of this information leaflet. In order to qualify for the exemption, the transfer must be made to another person where that other person intends to use the goods or services supplied for the purposes of a taxable business and where the goods or services constitute an amalgam of assets capable of assisting in the realisation of the business. It is not a requirement that the transfer must constitute a transfer of a business as a going concern. The issue in the scenario posed is whether or not the goodwill assists in the realisation of the purchaser's business. If it does not, the transfer of the plant and machinery could be viewed as the simple sale of an asset and subject to VAT. However, it is more than likely that the transfer of plant and machinery and goodwill would meet the criteria set out in paragraph 4.1 of this information leaflet.

Question 2

In the transfer of a business or part of a business qualifying for the exemption does Revenue require any identity between the business formerly carried on by the vendor and the business subsequently carried on by the purchaser?

Response to Question 2

Again, it is considered that this question is covered adequately in paragraph 4.1 of this information leaflet. Similarity between the former business carried on by the vendor and the business carried on by the purchaser is not a prerequisite for qualification for the exemption.

Question 3

Where the business or part of a business of an Irish taxable person is transferred to a taxable person in another Member State does the transfer of business exemption apply?

Example

X Limited, an Irish company, carries on a computer software business in Ireland but trading mainly with companies located in Scotland where a cluster of high-tech companies use the products of X Limited. The goodwill is therefore located in Scotland. X Limited sells the computer software business to Y Limited, a company located in Hungary. Y buys the intellectual property, goodwill and the debtors of X Limited with the intention of carrying on the business. Will this be a transfer of a business for VAT purposes?

Response to Question 3

In general, a person who, otherwise as an employee of another person, engages in the supply, within the State, of taxable goods or services in the course or furtherance of business is a taxable person for the purposes of Irish VAT law – Section 8 of the Value Added Tax Act 1972, as amended, refers.

In the scenario posed what is envisaged is the sale by an Irish- registered company, X Limited (assumed to be a service company involved in the supply of custom-made software rather than just the sale of goods) of its business to another company, Y Limited, which is not registered or established in Ireland. Thus, the sale of the goodwill and the intellectual property by X Limited are not covered by Section 5(8) of the Value-Added Tax Act 1972, as amended, as it is not a transfer by a taxable person to another taxable person.

The sale of the intellectual property is a Fourth Schedule service taxable where received on Y Limited, the Hungarian company. In so far as the goodwill is concerned, a supply that is described simply as 'goodwill' cannot be considered as falling within the Fourth Schedule rules, which cover intellectual property. Consequently, a simple sale of the goodwill is covered by the normal place of establishment rules and is liable to Irish VAT at 21%, with Y Limited being able to claim a refund under the Eight VAT Directive. However, goodwill is often used to describe part of another supply of services such as permission to use a logo, etc., in which case Revenue would treat its supply as a Fourth Schedule service.

The sale of debtors is not a supply of goods or services. Any goods going with the transfer of the business would not be covered by Section 3(5)(b)(iii) of the Value-Added Tax Act 1972, as amended, as this would not be a supply of goods from one taxable person to another. Accordingly, the normal place of supply of goods rules would apply, thus making the supply of the goods a zero-rated intra-Community acquisition if Y Limited is registered for VAT in Hungary.

Question 4

Where a taxpayer carries on the business of making short-term lettings for warehousing purposes of a building, can the transfer of the building plus the goodwill of the business amount to a transfer of the business?

Response to Question 4

The warehousing of goods, which involves the provision of ancillary services such as security, maintenance of inventory as well as storage, is a taxable activity in itself and would not be regarded as short-term letting.

The ECJ judgement in the Zita Modes case (C-479/01) stated that an amalgam of assets must constitute an undertaking or part of one capable of carrying on an independent economic activity (Irish VAT law contains the phrase 'capable of being operated on an independent basis'). That judgement also confirmed that it must be the intention that the transferee will carry on the business. As such, the transfer of the building by a warehousing business plus the goodwill could qualify for exemption under Section 3(5)(b)(iii) of the Value-Added Tax Act 1972, as amended.

If the warehouse operator doesn't own the building in which the warehousing business is carried on but short-term lets it from a landlord, and as part of a transfer of the business assigns the lease or creates a sub-lease to the new owner, then the transfer would be outside the scope of VAT.

Where a taxpayer owns a building and short-term lets it to a business which uses it for warehousing, for example, then, in line with Revenue's existing treatment, Section 3(5)(b)(iii) of the Value-Added Tax Act 1972, as amended, would heretofore not have applied. However, the concept of undertaking (Zita Modes) and 'business' could include the exploitation of tangible or intangible property for the purposes of obtaining income therefrom on a continuing basis. Accordingly, in future Revenue will accept that the transfer of a let property is a transfer capable of coming within Section 3(5)(b)(iii) of the Value-Added Tax Act 1972, as amended. This, however, will apply only when the person acquiring the letting business is a taxable person in respect of the 'business' being acquired. For example, if the person acquires a letting business where there are short-term lettings and that person does not waive their exemption in respect of those lettings, then Section 3(5)(b)(iii) of the Value-Added Tax Act 1972, as amended, will not apply to such a transfer. Similarly, where a person acquires a letting business where the vendor has let out on long leases, the purchaser is not a taxable person in respect of the lettings and therefore the sale will not come within Section 3(5)(b)(iii) of the Value-Added Tax Act 1972, as amended.

Question 5

Where a development company with sites, development contracts, partially completed buildings and buildings that are let on long leases transfers its operation, will the transfer of business exemption apply?

Response to Question 5

It is assumed that the reference is to a property development company. It is not clear from the question, however, if the sites are stock in trade or capital assets held as investments. If the sites were stock in trade, the sale would not constitute the transfer of a business unless it was part of a larger transaction that amounted to the transfer of a business. Where the sites are capital assets, held as investments, it is unlikely that the transfer of business relief would apply since the mere holding of land as an investment would not be regarded as a business. However, where the sites form part of the assets of a business or part of a business that is capable of being operated on an independent basis, then the relief could apply.

In the circumstances, it is not possible to provide a conclusive answer to this question. The question as to whether the transfer of business exemption would apply in individual cases such as the one outlined would be considered based on the full and particular circumstances of the case concerned.

Question 6

Where a co-owner in a partnership (registered for VAT as a partnership) operating a construction business with, say, a 40% share in the partnership, transfers his interest in the partnership to a third party who then becomes a partner with the continuing partner, will the transfer of the share in the partnership qualify for the transfer of business exemption in respect of that transfer?

Example

Jones and Smith are the limited partners in a limited partnership with Murphy as general partner. Jones has a 30% stake, Smith a 25% stake and Murphy a 45% stake. The partnership is engaged in the construction and letting of commercial buildings. Some of the properties held are let on long leases and to taxable persons and some are undeveloped and partially developed sites. If Smith sells his 25% stake to Greene will the transfer of business exemption apply on the basis that Greene registers for VAT as part of the limited partnership?

If the answer is that the exemption does not apply, would the answer be different if the limited partnership had been exclusively engaged in another business such as, for example, the manufacture and sale of furniture?

Response to Question 6

In the case of partnership where a partner exits the partnership and sells out to a new partner, then Section 3(5)(b)(iii) of the Value-Added Tax Act 1972, as amended, will apply.

In the case of a co-ownership, Revenue is prepared to change its current treatment under which the sale by a co-owner of his/her interest in the co-ownership is regarded as a sale of an interest in property. Revenue will now regard such a sale as the sale of a business to which Section 3(5)(b)(iii) of the Value-Added Tax Act 1972, as amended, can apply.

Question 7

One of the reasons practitioners feel obliged to obtain a ruling from the Revenue on transfers of business is the fear that the inspector for the vendor and the inspector for the purchaser may take opposing views on whether the exemption applies. Can anything be done to remove this source of anxiety?

Response to Question 7

Revenue would expect that the inspector for the vendor and the inspector for the purchaser should take the same view on the question of the application or otherwise of the exemption. The problem that arises for Revenue is that the facts provided from purchaser and vendor often differ, and this leads to possible different interpretations. Moreover, queries on the matter are often made very close to (or sometimes on) the day of the sale and an immediate decision is sought.

VAT is a self-assessment tax. Perhaps the best possible way to deal with the fear of different interpretations arising on the transfer of a business is for the respective solicitors acting for the purchaser and vendor to include a clause in the sale contract that the transfer in question is or is not a transfer that is in accordance with Section 3(5)(b)(iii) of the Value-Added Tax Act 1972, as amended. The contract can then be inspected by Revenue at a future audit, etc. The solicitors and the vendor and purchaser are, after all, the people with all the information pertaining to the transfer.

In general, though, Revenue is prepared to state that it will not seek to have the application of Section 3(5)(b)(iii) of the Value-Added Tax Act 1972, as amended, set aside where a vendor has obtained an assurance that the purchaser intends to use the assets acquired for a taxable purpose.

Question 8

Does the transfer of a pub licence in isolation (i.e., with no other accompanying assets) come within the ambit of Section 3(5)(b)(iii) of the Value-Added Tax Act 1972, as amended?

Response to Question 8

Technically, such a transfer would not qualify as the licence, in itself, does not constitute an undertaking or part of an undertaking capable of being operated on an independent basis; the licence is no more or less than an entitlement or right to carry on a licensed pub trade. Nonetheless, Revenue is prepared to treat the sale or transfer of a pub licence from one taxable person to another taxable person as coming within the ambit of Section 3(5)(b)(iii) of the Value-Added Tax Act 1972, as amended. However, the transfer of the licence to a person who is not fully taxable for VAT purposes will continue to be subject to VAT at the standard rate of 21%.

Question 9

X Limited, an Irish company, carries on a fully taxable business. X Limited sells the business to Y Limited, including all stock and goodwill, with the employees also transferring. As part of the transfer, X Limited creates long leases in the properties in which the trade is carried on to Y Limited. Would the creation of the otherwise VAT-able leases be free of VAT pursuant to Ssection 3(5)(b)(iii) of the Value-Added Tax Act 1972, as amended?

Response to Question 9

The Zita Modes judgement stated that an amalgam of the assets transferred must constitute an undertaking or part of one capable of carrying on an independent economic activity (Irish VAT law refers to 'capable of being operated on an independent basis'.). It is not necessary that all the assets of the business be transferred. Revenue can see no distinction between a case in which a trader decides to hold on to part of the assets (e.g., a part of a business) and one in which he retains a free-hold but creates a long lease to the purchaser of the business. Accordingly, provided what is transferred constitutes an amalgam of assets capable of being operated on an independent basis, Revenue would regard the transfer in the scenario posed in the question as coming within the ambit of Section 3(5)(b)(iii) of the Value-Added Tax Act, 1972, as amended.

Appendix II
Relevant Legislation
EU VAT Directive 2006

Corresponding provisions in EU law are in Article 19 of the EU VAT Directive 2006 as follows:-

- 'In the event of a transfer, whether for consideration or not as a contribution to a company, of a totality of assets or part thereof, Member States may consider that no supply of goods has taken place and that the person to whom the goods have been transferred to is treated as the successor to the transferor....'.

Article 29 of the Directive states that, as follows:

- 'Article 19 shall apply in like manner to the supply of services'.

Value-Added Tax Act 1972, as amended.

Section 3(5)(b)(iii):-

'(b)   The transfer of ownership of goods -

(iii)   being a transfer to a taxable person of a totality of assets or part thereof, of a business even if that business or part thereof had ceased trading, where those transferred assets constitute an undertaking or part of an undertaking capable of being operated on an independent basis, shall be deemed, for the purposes of this Act, not to be a supply of the goods ....'

Section 5(8)(a):-

'(a)   The transfer of goodwill or other intangible assets of a business, in connection with the transfer of the business or part thereof, even if that business or that part thereof had ceased trading, or in connection with a transfer of ownership of goods in accordance with Section 3(5)(b)(iii) –

    i   a taxable person to another taxable person or a flat-rate farmer, or

    ii   a person who is not a taxable person to another person,

shall be deemed, for the purposes of this Act, not be a supply of services.

(b)   For the purposes of this subsection, 'taxable person' shall not include a person who is a taxable person solely by virtue of subsections (1A) and (2) of Section 8'.

Section 12 D of VAT Act 1972, as amended

12D Adjustment of tax deductible in certain circumstances

[(1)   For the purposes of this section –

'full year' shall be any continuous period of 12 months;

'interest' in relation to immovable goods has the meaning assigned to it by Section 4.

(2)   Where –

    a.   a person makes a transfer of an interest in immovable goods in accordance with Section 3(5)(b)(iii), and

    b.   but for the application of that section, tax would have been chargeable on the transfer, and the person (referred to in this section as a 'transferor') was entitled to deduct part of the tax charged on the most recent purchase or acquisition of an interest in, or the development of, the immovable goods subject to that transfer,

that transferor shall, for the purposes of Section 12, be entitled to increase the amount of tax deductible for the taxable period within which the transfer is made by an amount calculated in accordance with the following formula:

$$(T - TD) \times \frac{(Y - N)}{Y}$$

where—

T   is the tax chargeable on that most recent purchase or acquisition of an interest in, or that development of, the immovable goods,

TD is the tax that the transferor was entitled to deduct on that most recent purchase or acquisition of an interest in, or that development of, the immovable goods,

Y   is 20 or, if the interest when it was created in the immovable goods being transferred was for a period of less than 20 years, the number of full years in that interest, and

N   is the number of full years since the interest was created or, if the goods were developed since that interest was created, the number of full years since the most recent development:

but if that N is greater than that Y, such an amount calculated shall be deemed to be nil.

(3)   Where a transferor acquired an interest in immovable goods as a result of a transfer in accordance with Section 3(5)(b)(iii) and the transferor did not develop those immovable goods since the acquisition then, for the purposes of subsection (2), the amount by which that transferor shall be entitled to increase the amount of tax deductible, in accordance with Section 12, for the taxable period in which the transferor transfers those goods, shall be calculated in accordance with the following formula:

$$A \times \frac{(Y - N)}{Y}$$

where—

A   is the amount which the transferor was required to calculate and reduce his/her deductible amount by, in accordance with subsection (4), when the transferor acquired the interest in those goods,

Y   is 20 or, if the interest when it was created in the immovable goods being transferred was for a period of less than 20 years, the number of full years in that interest, and

N   is the number of full years since the interest was created or, if the goods were developed since that interest was created, the number of full years since the most recent development:

but if that N is greater than that Y, such an amount calculated shall be deemed to be nil.

(4)   Where a person receives an interest in immovable goods as a result of a transfer and the person would not have been entitled to deduct all the tax that would have been chargeable on the transfer but for the application of Section 3(5)(b)(iii), that person shall [calculate an amount which shall be payable as if it were tax due by that person in accordance with Section 19 for the taxable period within which the transfer was

made, and that amount shall be calculated] in accordance with the following formula:

$$(T1 - TD1) \times \frac{(Y - N)}{Y}$$

where—

T1   is the amount of tax that would have been chargeable on the transfer if Section 3(5)(b)(iii) did not apply,

TD1   is the amount of tax that would have been deductible by the transferee if Section 3(5)(b)(iii) had not applied to the transfer,

Y   is 20 or, if the interest when it was created in the immovable goods being transferred was for a period of less than 20 years, the number of full years in that interest, and

N   is the number of full years since the interest was created or, if the goods were developed since that interest was created, the number of full years since the most recent development:

but if that N is greater than that Y, such an amount calculated shall be deemed to be nil.]

VALUE-ADDED TAX INFORMATION LEAFLET (APRIL 2008)

RELIEF FROM PAYMENT OF CUSTOMS DUTY AND VAT ON IMPORTATION FROM NON-EUROPEAN COMMUNITY COUNTRIES OF TROUSSEAUX AND HOUSEHOLD EFFECTS AND WEDDING PRESENTS GIVEN ON THE OCCASION OF A MARRIAGE

Combined Notice and Form of Declaration

1.   General

In addition to the relief's set out in Notice No. 1875 - Transfer of Residence, a private individual whose normal place of residence has been outside the European Community (EC) for a continuous period of at least twelve months and who is transferring such residence to the State may, **on marrying**, import without payment of Customs Duty and VAT, trousseaux and household effects (whether or not new) belonging to him/her, subject to compliance with the conditions and procedure set out in this Notice.

"Household effects" means personal effects, household linen, furnishings and items of equipment intended for the personal use of the persons concerned or for meeting their household needs.

2.   Conditions

1.   Importation must take place within a period beginning two months before the marriage date envisaged and ending four months after the actual marriage date;

2.   The person concerned must provide documentary evidence —

   1.   that the marriage has taken place or that the necessary preliminary formalities have been put in place (as the case may be), such as wedding certificate or marriage licence, hotel or church reservations etc. Where an individual fails to provide proof of his/her marriage within four months of the date given for such marriage, the Customs duty and/or VAT due on the goods concerned on the date of importation must be paid; and

   2.   that he/she had his/her normal place of residence outside the EC for the required period. The documentary evidence required is set out in Paragraph 4 of Notice No. 1875; and

3.   The exemption, insofar as it applies to VAT, will be granted only for trousseaux and household effects which have borne either in the country of origin or the country from which the person concerned is departing, any customs or fiscal charges to which they are normally liable and which are not the subject, on the grounds of exportation, of any exemption from or refund of the charges involved.

3.   **Wedding Presents**

In addition to the relief allowed under paragraph 1 of this Notice, exemption will also be granted in respect of presents customarily given on the occasion of a marriage which are received by a person fulfilling the conditions laid down in paragraphs 1 and 2 above from persons having their normal residence outside the EC. The exemption applies to presents of a unit value not exceeding approximately €1000.

4.   **Requirement of a Guarantee**

Where goods are imported before the date of the marriage, an adequate guarantee may be required before exemption is granted.

5.   **Restriction on Exemption**

Alcoholic products, tobacco and tobacco products are not eligible for importation free of import charges under the provisions of this Notice.

6.   **Restriction on Disposal of Goods**

Property imported under these provisions may not be lent, given as security, hired out or transferred in the State within a period of twelve months from the date of acceptance of the import declaration unless payment of the relevant charges is made.

7.   **Procedure at Importation**

The procedure outlined in Notice No. 1875 applies generally to goods imported under the provisions of this Notice. However, the declaration in the Appendix attached must also be completed in respect of goods to which this Notice applies and those goods should be listed and enumerated therein.

Where a wedding present is sent by parcel post to a person transferring residence to the State on marriage by a person whose normal residence is outside the EC, a declaration is to be made by the sender on the Customs Declaration Form affixed to the parcel, as follows:

"WEDDING GIFT FOR PERSON TRANSFERRING RESIDENCE ON MARRIAGE - EXEMPT FROM CUSTOMS DUTY/VAT"

8.   **Further Information**

Enquiries regarding any issue contained in this Information Leaflet should be addressed to the Revenue District responsible for your tax affairs. .

Customs Division,

Notice No. 1821

April 2008

Legal Disclaimer

While every effort is made to ensure that the information given in this guide is accurate, it is not a legal document. Responsibility cannot be accepted for any liability incurred or loss suffered as a consequence of relying on any matter published herein.

VALUE-ADDED TAX INFORMATION LEAFLET (APRIL 2008)

RELIEF FROM CUSTOMS DUTY AND VAT ON IMPORTATION OF GOODS FROM NON-EUROPEAN COMMUNITY (EC) COUNTRIES FOR DISPLAY OR USE AT EXHIBITIONS, FAIRS, MEETINGS OR SIMILAR EVENTS

Part 1. General

1. General

This Notice sets out the arrangements for the importation of goods from non-(EC) countries, without payment of Customs Duty and VAT, for display or use at exhibitions, fairs, meetings or similar events.

Where the imported goods are to remain in the EC, they should be imported under the procedure at Part 2 of this Notice - "Permanent Imports". Where they are intended for re-export, they should be imported under the procedure at Part 3 - "Temporary Imports".

2. Events for which Relief is Given

Relief from Customs Duty and VAT is given for goods imported for display or demonstration at:

1. A trade, industrial, agricultural or craft exhibition, fair or similar show or display; or

2. An exhibition or meeting which is primarily organised to promote a charitable purpose; or

3. An exhibition or meeting which is primarily organised to promote any branch of learning, art, craft, sport or scientific, technical, educational, cultural, trade union or tourist activity, to promote religious knowledge or worship, or to promote friendship between peoples; or

4. A meeting of representatives of international organisations or international groups of organisations; or

5. A representative meeting of an official or commemorative character.

Relief does not apply in respect of exhibitions organised for private purposes in shops or business premises with a view to sale of the goods imported.

Part 2. Permanent Importations

3. Scope of the Relief

Relief is available for the following goods:

1. Small representative samples of goods (excluding alcoholic beverages, tobacco, tobacco products and fuels) intended for a trade fair or similar event, provided that:

    1.   They are imported free of charge or are obtained at the event from goods imported in bulk;

    2.   They are used only for distribution free of charge to the public at the event for use or consumption by the persons to whom they are offered;

    3.   They are identifiable as advertising samples of low value;

    4.   They are not readily marketable and, where appropriate, are packaged in such a way that the quantity of the item involved is less than the smallest quantity of the same item normally sold on the market; and

    5.   In the case of foodstuffs and beverages not packaged as mentioned in (iv), above, they are intended for consumption during the exhibition

2.   Goods (excluding alcoholic beverages, tobacco, tobacco products and fuels) imported solely in order to be demonstrated or in order to demonstrate machines and apparatus displayed at an event, provided the imported goods are consumed or destroyed during the exhibition. In the case of relief from Customs Duty, the machines and apparatus must be manufactured outside the EC;

3.   Materials such as paints, varnishes, wallpaper etc., sufficient for the purpose of building, fitting out and decorating the temporary stand(s) of exhibitors at a trade fair or similar event, and which are incapable of further use. In the case of relief from Customs Duty, the stand(s) must be occupied by representatives of countries established outside the EC;

4.   Printed matter, catalogues, prospectuses, price lists, advertising posters, calendars, whether or not illustrated, unframed photographs and other articles supplied free of charge in order to advertise goods displayed at a trade fair or similar event, provided that such printed matter and advertising articles are intended solely for distribution free of charge to the public at that event. In the case of relief from Customs Duty, the goods being advertised must be manufactured outside the EC; and

5.   Files, archives, printed forms and other documents to be used in international meetings, conferences or congresses, and reports of such gatherings.

In the case of goods mentioned at (a), (b) and (d) above, their total respective values and quantities must be appropriate to the nature of the event, the numbers of visitors and the extent of the exhibitor's participation.

Goods subject to an import prohibition or restriction may not be imported, except under licence or authorisation issued by the appropriate Authority and presented at importation.

4.   Procedure at Importation

Except where they are imported under cover of an ATA Carnet, the goods should be presented to Customs accompanied by an import declaration Single Administrative Document (SAD), with a claim to relief from import charges thereon. For the purposes of completion of the SAD, the appropriate legal references are:

Article 95 of Regulation (EEC) No. 918/83 for Customs Duty; and Article 65 of Directive 83/181/EEC for VAT.

Where an electronic customs declaration is made, code C32 should be entered in Box 37 b of the SAD in order to avail of the relief from Customs Duty and VAT. Revenue may require security to be provided in one of the forms specified in paragraph 7(a).

5.   Post-Importation Procedure

A record of the use and disposal of the goods imported under these provisions must be kept by the importer and made available for inspection by Revenue. This record should include full particulars of the name, date and place of the event. Where security has been provided, the importer should present the record to Revenue within one month of the termination of the event or within six months of the date of importation, whichever is the earlier, in order to have the security refunded, cancelled or adjusted.

If any goods entered for permanent importation are not, in fact, distributed or consumed in accordance with the relevant provisions and within the time specified above, they must be produced to Revenue for examination and exportation or payment of the appropriate Customs Duty and VAT.

PART 3. TEMPORARY IMPORTS

6.   Scope of Relief

Relief is available for the following goods:

1.   Goods intended for display or demonstration at an event;

2.   Goods intended for use in connection with the display of imported products at an event, including:

    1.   Goods necessary for the purpose of demonstrating imported machinery or apparatus to be displayed;

    2.   Construction and decoration material, including electrical fittings, for the temporary stands of persons established outside the EC; and

    3.   Advertising and demonstration material and other equipment which is publicity material for the imported goods displayed, such as sound and image recordings, films and transparencies, together with the apparatus necessary for their use.

3.   Equipment, including interpretation equipment, sound and image recording apparatus and films of an educational, scientific or cultural character, intended for use at international meetings, conferences and congresses;

4.   Live animals intended for exhibition at, or participation in, an event; and

5.   Products obtained during an event from goods, machinery, apparatus or animals imported temporarily.

7.   Conditions

The following conditions must be observed:

1.   **Security** – Security must be provided in the form of -

    1.   A valid ATA Carnet (see Notice No. 1007); or

    2.   A cash deposit (refundable when the goods are re-exported); or

    3.   A bond (or, as a temporary measure, a Cover Note) either from an approved insurance company or a bank licensed by the Central Bank to carry out insurance business. Application for approval to use a bond or Cover Note should be made to Revenue at the proposed place of importation, from whom full information as to procedure and all the necessary forms may be obtained;

2.   **Period allowed** – The goods must be re-exported within the time limit authorised by Revenue at importation. The prescribed maximum period of temporary importation permitted is 24 months. However, where the goods are covered by an ATA Carnet, they must be re-exported within the period of validity of the Carnet;

3.   **Identification** – The goods must be capable of being identified at re-exportation. For this purpose marks or seals may be applied to them at importation by Revenue;

4.   **Export control** – The goods must be re-exported under Revenue control; and

5.   **Prohibited or restricted goods** – Goods subject to a national or Community prohibition or restriction may not be imported, except under licence or authorisation issued by the appropriate Authority and presented at importation.

8.   Procedure at Importation

The goods should be presented to Revenue at importation in all cases. However, the procedure will differ depending on whether or not an ATA Carnet is used.

1.   **Cases involving an ATA Carnet**

Where an ATA Carnet is used, the itemised lists on the reverse of the relevant importation voucher should be completed, indicating clearly the items which are being imported. The Revenue Official will stamp and sign the importation voucher and counterfoil and remove the importation voucher. The Revenue Official will insert the final date for re-exportation of the goods (which will not be later than the date on which the Carnet's validity expires) and return the Carnet to the importer.

2.   **Cases NOT involving an ATA Carnet**

In all such cases, Forms C&E 1047 (Rev. 1) should be completed in duplicate and the required security provided. The Revenue Official will stamp and sign both copies of Form C&E 1047 (Rev.1), fix the time limit during which the goods may remain under temporary importation arrangements, insert the final date for re-exportation on the Form and return one copy to the importer.

9.   **Procedure at Re-Exportation**

The goods and documentation should be presented to Revenue at the Export Station in sufficient time to allow for Revenue examination before the period for temporary importation expires. However, the procedure will differ depending on whether or not an ATA Carnet is used.

1.   **Cases involving an ATA Carnet**

Where an ATA Carnet is used, particulars of the goods should be declared on the reverse of the re-exportation voucher bearing the same identifying number as the importation voucher on which the goods were declared at importation. If everything is in order the re-exportation voucher and counterfoil will be stamped and signed by Revenue. The voucher will be detached and the Carnet returned to the importer.

2.   **Cases NOT involving an ATA Carnet**

When goods imported on Form C&E 1047 (Rev.1) are re-exported, the importer's copy of the Form with Part III completed should be presented to Revenue. Where all the goods are correctly re-exported, the Form will be retained by Revenue and arrangements will be made to refund the deposit or release the security as appropriate.

10.   **Transfer of Authorisation**

Temporary importation facilities may be transferred to another person subject to certain conditions. Requests for such transfers should be made to Revenue at the place of importation.

11.   Partial Relief from Customs Duty

Goods, which do not meet all the conditions set out in this Notice may, in certain circumstances, qualify for temporary importation with partial relief from Customs Duty. This involves payment of a percentage of the full amount of Customs Duty in respect of each month the goods remain in the EC.

Prior approval is required from Revenue. All enquiries should be addressed to the Revenue District responsible for your tax affairs.

Note: Relief from VAT is not allowable in these cases.

12.   Further Information

Enquiries regarding any issue contained in this Information Leaflet should be addressed to the Revenue District responsible for your tax affairs.

Customs Division.

Notice No. 567

April 2008

Legal Disclaimer

While every effort is made to ensure that the information given in this guide is accurate, it is not a legal document. Responsibility cannot be accepted for any liability incurred or loss suffered as a consequence of relying on any matter published herein.

VALUE-ADDED TAX INFORMATION LEAFLET (APRIL 2008)

RELIEF FROM CUSTOMS DUTY AND VAT ON GOODS WHICH ARE IMPORTED FROM OUTSIDE THE EUROPEAN COMMUNITY HAVING BEEN INHERITED

1. **General**

    The personal property of a deceased person which is imported into the State by, or on behalf of, a person resident in the State or a person or body of persons established in the State and engaged in a non-profit making activity, who either acquired the ownership or the beneficial ownership of such property or is the personal representative resident in the State of the deceased person may be imported without payment of Customs Duty and VAT.

2. **Definitions**

    "Personal property of a deceased person" means any property, which was intended for the personal use of the deceased person concerned or for meeting his household needs. It does not include property, which by reason of its nature or quantity reflect any commercial interest or is intended for any economic activity with the exception of portable instruments of the applied or liberal arts, which were required for the exercise of the trade or profession of the deceased.

    The term "applied or liberal arts" includes artists, sculptors and professions such as doctors, barristers and solicitors.

3. **Restrictions on Relief**

    No relief from Customs Duty or VAT is granted for: -

    1. Alcoholic products;

    2. Tobacco or tobacco products;

    3. Articles for use in the exercise or a trade or profession, other than portable instruments of the applied or liberal arts which were required for the exercise of the trade or profession of the deceased;

    4. Stocks of raw materials and finished or semi-finished products; and

    5. Livestock and stock of agricultural products exceeding the quantities appropriate to normal family requirements.

4. **Time limit**

    The property must be imported not later than two years after the date on which such property enters into the possession of the person who acquired it by inheritance or the personal representative takes control of it.

5. **Documentary evidence required**

    The documentary evidence required to support a claim to relief from import charges shall consist of:

1.   evidence of the death of the person as a result of whose death the property was acquired by inheritance such as a death certificate or a true copy thereof;

2.   a copy of the will concerned duly made by the deceased person showing that the property in question was bequeathed to the beneficiary, together with proof (whether appended to the will or otherwise) that the will has been duly submitted to the relevant authority in the jurisdiction concerned for the purpose of the administration of the estate of that deceased person, or where the deceased person died intestate, a declaration issued by a notary or other competent authority in the country where the deceased died or a notary in the State that the property was acquired by inheritance by the person concerned or any other documentary evidence that Revenue may deem acceptable;

3.   and where any such will, certificate, declaration or document is in a language other than English or Irish, a translation thereof into English or Irish duly certified, to the satisfaction of Revenue, to be a true translation, must be provided.

6.   **Importation of motor vehicles of a deceased person acquired by inheritance, without payment of Vehicle Registration Tax (VRT)**

Relief from Vehicle Registration Tax (VRT) will be allowed in respect of a motor vehicle which is the personal property of a deceased person which is brought into the State by, or on behalf of, a person resident in the State or a person or body of persons established in the State and engaged in a non-profit making activity, who either acquired the ownership or the beneficial ownership of such property or is the personal representative resident in the State of the deceased person subject to compliance with the provisions in place at the time.

Further information regarding relief from VRT may be obtained from your **Regional VRO**.

7.   **Procedure at Importation**

Form C&E 1080 is to be completed by the importer/owner of the goods and all the articles to be imported are to be listed and enumerated thereon and on such additional sheets as may be necessary. The application must be presented to the appropriate Revenue official **at the place and time of importation**. If more than one importation is required to bring all the goods into the State and if, on the occasion of the first importation, the inventory listing all the goods to be imported is presented, then only a copy of that inventory need be presented on the occasion(s) of the subsequent importation(s). Where the contents of any package listed are not shown on the inventory, a separate inventory, signed by the importer, containing such information is to be presented.

Documentary evidence, such as the death certificate of the person as a result of whose death the property was acquired by inheritance, or a true copy thereof, a copy of the Will, or a declaration issued by a notary or other competent authority must be produced with the application for relief to show that the property concerned was acquired by inheritance.

Part III of Form No. 1080 provides for two declarations to be completed at the time of importation. The first declaration includes a claim for relief from relevant charges in respect of the property being imported and is to be made by the importer or by the person or firm (e.g. Customs Clearance Agent, shipping company etc.) whom the importer has authorised to act on his/her behalf. The second declaration relates to the loading of the vehicle or container in which the goods are packed and is to be completed in all cases by the carrier of the goods (i.e. by the haulier or transport company responsible for delivering the goods to the place of unloading or by the importer where the goods are packed and transported by him/her).

Articles of gold or silver plate (other than those which are electroplated) which are being imported should be accompanied by a declaration that the goods are for private use and not for sale or exchange, on either Form No. C.U. 56 or Form C&E 136 (where the owner is accompanying the goods).

8. Prohibited and Restricted Goods

Certain goods may not be imported/brought into the State or may be imported/brought into the State only under licence. The principal items are firearms, ammunition, explosives, dangerous drugs and indecent or obscene material. A comprehensive list of prohibited and restricted items is contained in the Customs and Excise Tariff of Ireland.

9. Other Legal Requirements

The relief from Customs Duty and VAT (and VRT where relevant) on goods acquired by inheritance does not exempt the importer/owner from compliance with any legal requirement, obligation, restriction or prohibition other than the requirement of paying at the time of importation/transfer the import charges which would otherwise be payable on the property.

10. Further Information

Enquiries regarding any issue contained in this Information Leaflet should be addressed to the Revenue District responsible for your tax affairs.

Customs Division.

Notice No. 1837

April 2008

Legal Disclaimer

While every effort is made to ensure that the information given in this guide is accurate, it is not a legal document. Responsibility cannot be accepted for any liability incurred or loss suffered as a consequence of relying on any matter published herein.

VALUE-ADDED TAX INFORMATION LEAFLET (APRIL 2008)

RELIEF FROM CUSTOMS DUTY AND VAT ON IMPORTATION OF PUBLICITY MATERIAL FROM NON-EUROPEAN COMMUNITY COUNTRIES

Part 1 – General

1.   **General**

This notice sets out the arrangements for the importation of tourist publicity material, without payment of Customs Duty and VAT.

Where the imported goods are to remain in the European Community (EC), they should be imported under the procedure at Part 2 of this Notice – "Permanent Imports".

Where they are intended for re-export, they should be imported under the procedure at Part 3 – "Temporary Imports".

Part 2 – Permanent Imports

2.   **Scope of the Relief**

The following material may be permanently imported without payment of Customs Duty and VAT:

1.   Documentation (leaflets, brochures, books, magazines, guide-books, posters whether or not framed, unframed photographs and photographic enlargements, maps whether or not illustrated, window transparencies and illustrated calendars) the principal purpose of which is to encourage the public to visit foreign countries, in particular in order to attend cultural, tourist, sporting, religious, trade or professional meetings or events, provided that:

   1.   the material is intended to be distributed free of charge;

   2.   the literature contains not more than 25% of private commercial advertising matter. If this percentage exceeds 25%, relief from **Customs Duty** (but not VAT) will still be allowed provided that any additional advertising is exclusively for EC firms;

   3.   the general nature of its promotional aims is evident;

2.   foreign hotel lists and yearbooks published by the official tourist agencies, or under their auspices, and timetables for foreign transport services, provided that –

   1.   the literature is intended to be distributed free of charge;

   2.   the literature contains not more than 25% of private commercial advertising matter. If this percentage exceeds 25%, relief from **Customs Duty** (but not VAT) will still

be allowed provided that any additional advertising is exclusively for EC firms; and

3.   reference material supplied to accredited representatives or correspondents appointed by official national tourist agencies and not intended for distribution, viz. yearbooks, lists of telephone or fax numbers, hotel lists, fairs catalogues, specimens of craft goods of negligible value and literature on museums, universities, spas or other similar establishments.

3.   Procedure at Importation

Where goods are forwarded by post, the declaration on the parcel should be endorsed:

"Publicity material: exemption from import charges claimed".

Where goods are imported other than by post the goods should be presented to Revenue accompanied by an import declaration Single Administrative Document (SAD), with a claim to relief from import charges thereon. For the purposes of completion of the SAD, the legal references are:

Article 108 of Regulation (EEC) No. 918/83 for Customs Duty; and Article 78 of Directive 83/181/EEC for VAT

Where an electronic customs declaration is made, code C35 should be entered in Box 37 b of the SAD in order to avail of the relief from Customs Duty and VAT.

Part 3 – Temporary Imports

4.   Scope of the Relief

The following articles may be imported temporarily without payment of Customs Duty and VAT:

1.   Material intended for display in the offices of the accredited representatives or correspondents appointed by the official national tourist agencies or in other places approved by Revenue; including pictures and drawings, framed photographs and photographic enlargements, art books, paintings, engravings or lithographs, sculptures, tapestries and other similar works of art;

2.   Display material (show-cases, stands and similar articles) including electrical and mechanical equipment required for operating such display;

3.   Documentary films, records, tape recordings and other sound recordings intended for use in performances at which no charge is made, but excluding those whose subjects lend themselves to commercial advertising and those which are on general sale in the State;

4.   A reasonable number of flags;

5.   Dioramas, scale models, lantern-slides, printing blocks, photographic negatives; and

6.   Specimens, in reasonable numbers, of articles of national handicrafts, local costumes and similar articles of folklore.

5.   Conditions

The following conditions must be observed:

1.   **Security** – Security must be provided in the form of –

    1.   a valid ATA Carnet (see Notice No. 1007); or

    2.   a cash deposit (refundable when the goods are re-exported); or

    3.   a bond (or, as a temporary measure, a Cover Note) either from an approved insurance company or a bank licensed by the Central Bank to carry out insurance business. Application for approval to use a bond or Cover Note should be made to Revenue at the proposed place of importation, from whom full information as to procedure and all the necessary forms may be obtained;

2.   **Period allowed** – The goods must be re-exported within the time limit authorised by Revenue at importation. The prescribed maximum period of temporary importation is 24 months. However, where an ATA Carnet covers the goods, they must be re-exported within the period of validity of the Carnet;

3.   **Identification** – The goods must be capable of being identified at re-exportation. For this purpose marks or seals may be applied to them at importation by Revenue;

4.   **Export Control** – The goods must be re-exported under Revenue control; and

5.   **Goods imported by Parcel Post** – Where the goods are imported by Parcel Post the sender's declaration should bear conspicuously the words "Publicity material" in addition to the other particulars required. When the parcel arrives, the procedure at paragraph 6 will apply.

6.   Procedure at Importation

The goods should be presented to Revenue at importation.

Where an ATA Carnet is used, the itemised lists on the reverse of the relevant importation voucher should be completed, indicating clearly the items which are being imported. The Revenue official will stamp and sign the importation voucher and counterfoil and remove the importation voucher. S/he will insert the final date for re-exportation of the goods (which will not be later than the date on which the Carnet's validity expires) and return the Carnet to the importer.

In all other cases, Form C&E No. 1047 (Rev 1) should be completed in duplicate and the required security provided.

The Revenue official will stamp and sign both copies of Form C&E 1047 (Rev 1), fix the time limit during which the goods may remain under temporary importation arrangements, insert the final date for re-exportation on the Form and return one copy to the importer.

7. Procedure at Re-Exportation

The goods and documentation should be presented to Revenue at the Export Station in sufficient time to allow for examination before the period for temporary importation expires.

Where an ATA Carnet is used, particulars of the goods should be declared on the reverse of the re-exportation voucher bearing the same identifying number as the importation voucher on which the goods were declared at importation. If everything is in order the re-exportation voucher and counterfoil will be stamped and signed by Revenue. The voucher will be detached and the Carnet returned to the importer.

Where goods imported on Form C&E 1047 (Rev 1) are re-exported, a copy of the Form with Part III completed should be presented to Revenue. Where all the goods are correctly re-exported, the Form will be retained by Revenue and arrangements will be made to refund the deposit or release the security as appropriate.

8. Transfer of Authorisation

Temporary importation facilities may be transferred to another person subject to certain conditions. Requests for such transfers should be made to Revenue at the place of importation.

9. Partial Relief from Customs Duty

Goods that do not meet all the conditions set out in this Notice for temporary importation without payment of import charges may, in certain circumstances, qualify for temporary importation with partial relief from Customs Duty. This involves payment of a percentage of the full amount of Customs Duty in respect of each month the goods remain in the EC. Prior approval is required from Revenue. All enquiries should be addressed to the Revenue District responsible for your tax affairs.

Note: Relief from VAT is not allowable in these cases.

10. Further Information

Enquiries regarding any issue contained in this Information Leaflet should be addressed to the Revenue District responsible for your tax affairs.

Customs Division.

Notice No. 1095

April 2008 Edition

Legal Disclaimer

While every effort is made to ensure that the information given in this guide is accurate, it is not a legal document. Responsibility cannot be accepted for any liability incurred or loss suffered as a consequence of relying on any matter published herein.

VALUE-ADDED TAX INFORMATION LEAFLET (MAY 2008)

VAT ON PROPERTY – SUMMARY OF NEW RULES

The new VAT on Property Guide deals with the new rules for applying VAT to property transactions that are effective from 1 July 2008. These rules are briefly summarised below.

1.   **Supplies of property**

The new rules provide that VAT must be charged @13.5% on the supply, in the course of an economic activity, of a developed property while the property is considered "new". The supply can be either the sale of the freehold or the creation or assignment of a very long lease (e.g. a lease for 99 years), which is referred to in the guide as a freehold equivalent interest.

Two rules, the two and five year rules, determine if a property is "new" –

- The first supply of a completed property within five years of its completion is considered to be the supply of a new property and is subject to VAT.

- The second and subsequent supply of a property is considered to be the supply of a new property and subject to VAT but only if it takes place within two years of occupation.

The supply of an "old" property (i.e. one no longer considered "new") is exempt from VAT.

2.   **Supply of residential property**

VAT is always chargeable on the supply of a residential property by a developer/builder - the two and five-year rules do not apply in such cases.

3.   **Supply of property in connection with a contract to develop the property**

A supply of property in connection with a contract to develop the property is subject to VAT, whether the property is developed or not and even it the person making the supply is not carrying on an economic activity.

4.   **Joint option to charge VAT on supply of "old" property**

Where the supply of property is exempt from VAT, the seller and buyer may opt to charge VAT on the supply. Where they do so, the purchaser accounts for the VAT on the supply.

5.   **Letting of property**

The letting of property is exempt from VAT. A landlord may opt to charge VAT @ 21% on rents from a letting. A landlord who does so is entitled to deduct VAT incurred on the acquisition or development of the property or on the portion of the property to which the option relates.

Unlike the old waiver of exemption rules, the option to tax applies to a specific letting. In other words, the landlord has the right to opt (or not to opt) in relation to each letting. However, the option to tax does not apply to –

- a letting of residential property, or
- a letting between connected parties – the guide includes a full definition of who are connected parties.

A landlord can exercise an option to tax a letting or terminate an existing option to tax a letting at any time. Doing either has implications under the capital goods scheme – see below.

6.   Capital goods scheme

6.1   The new rules introduce a Capital Goods Scheme (CGS). The CGS provides for the adjustment of VAT incurred on the acquisition, development or refurbishment costs or a property over the "VAT-life" of a property. The purchaser will be entitled to deduct the VAT when it is charged to the extent that a property is to be used for taxable purposes. The purpose of the CGS is to take account of changes in the use to which the property is put over its "VAT-life" and to ensure fairness and proportionality in the VAT system.

The "VAT-life" of a property is generally twenty years but the "VAT-life" of a refurbishment is ten years. The VAT deducted initially is adjusted annually over the "VAT-life" of the property.

The CGS does not have any impact in respect of properties that are used for the entire "VAT-life" for either fully taxable or fully exempt purposes.

6.2   **CGS and supplies of property**

The CGS has special rules that deal with the supply of properties during their "VAT-life".

It is important to note that the exempt supply of an "old" property during its "VAT-life" will mean a claw-back of some of the VAT deducted in respect of the acquisition or development costs of the property. This can be avoided by using the joint option to charge VAT on the supply. Similarly if VAT is charged on the supply of a property during its "VAT-life" (either because the property is considered "new" or because of an option to tax the supply of an "old" property), the seller will be entitled to deduct some of the VAT incurred on the acquisition or development costs that the seller was not previously entitled to deduct.

6.3   **CGS and landlord's option to tax lettings**

The exercising or terminating of a landlord's option to tax a letting during the "VAT-life" of a property has CGS implications. Where the option is exercised during the "VAT-life" of a property that had previously been subject to an exempt letting, the landlord is entitled to deduct some of the VAT incurred on the acquisition or development costs of the property that the landlord was not previously entitled to deduct. Where an option is terminated during the "VAT-life" of a property, there is a claw-back of some of the VAT that the landlord deducted on the acquisition or development costs of the property. Both of these adjustments arise at the time the option is exercised or terminated.

6.4   CGS record

The CGS applies to all new properties (developed) on or after 1 July 2008 or properties refurbished on or after 1 July 2008. For all such properties, a "capital good record" must be set up and maintained. This record should contain all of the information relating to the scheme including how much VAT was deducted on the acquisition or development and details of any adjustments under the scheme, etc.

7.   Transitional rules – freeholds and leaseholds

Transitional rules apply to the supply of properties that were taxable under the old rules and which are supplied on or after 1 July 2008. The rules for such properties mirror the new rules above, i.e. the two and five year rules apply.

The two and five year rules also apply to certain leasehold interests, which are assigned or surrendered on or after 1 July 2008. These are leases for a period of 10 years or more, but not freehold equivalents. Under the old rules the VAT charged on the creation of these leases was based on the capitalised value of the lease. Where an assignment or surrender of such a leasehold interest occurs on or after 1 July 2008, it is subject to VAT. The taxable amount is calculated by reference to VAT charged on the creation or previous assignment of the lease and the number of years remaining in the "VAT-life" of the lease.

The CGS rules for dealing with changes in the use of a property during the "VAT-life" of the property do not apply to freehold or leasehold properties that are subject to the transitional arrangements. This means that no adjustment is required if the taxable use of a transitional property (or a transitional leasehold interest in property) changes from one year to the next[1]. However, where the sale of a transitional freehold occurs or the assignment or surrender of a transitional leasehold interest occurs, the CGS rules as outlined above apply. (Claw-back of some VAT if supply exempt, VAT credit if taxable and not entitled to full deductibility.)

---

[1] The exception to this rule is if an exempt letting of a transitional property occurs after 1 July 2008.

8.   Transitional rules - waiver of exemption

There are also rules to deal with transitional properties that were rented prior to 1 July 2008 where the landlord has a waiver of exemption in place. The existing waiver of exemption may continue in place for the majority of these properties on or after 1 July 2008. The waiver of exemption may also be cancelled under the old rules. There are special cancellation rules that apply in respect of waivers of exemption in the case of lettings between connected parties.

9. What to do now – checklist & further information

The Guide to VAT on Property sets out in detail the rules that apply to the various types of property transactions. Concern has been expressed that tax practitioners, accountants and solicitors need to review all of their clients' property portfolios before 1 July 2008 to ensure compliance with the new VAT on property rules.

In the vast majority of cases no action is needed in respect of existing properties. The key transactions that need to be reviewed are lettings between connected persons where the waiver of exemption has been exercised. In all other cases, action is only required where the transitional property is being disposed of or let. Care has to be taken in respect of the transactions that are currently being negotiated. If the transaction is completed before 1 July 2008 the old rules apply; if the transaction is completed on or after 1 July 2008 the new rules apply. The transitional rules generally apply to properties that were subject to the old rules prior to 1 July 2008 and are subsequently disposed of on or after 1 July 2008. The checklist below is to facilitate agents in the changeover to the new rules.

Checklist for Agents

What have you to do for 1 July 2008?

1. For clients who own and occupy properties for the purpose of their business – generally nothing

2. For clients who have a leasehold interest that was taxed as a supply of goods under the old rules – generally nothing.

3. For clients who are landlords and charge VAT on their rents (as they have waived their exemption in respect of the letting of property) – check whether any of the lettings are to connected persons (See 5 below)

4. Where the lettings are to unconnected tenants or in the circumstances mentioned in 5 below, the old rules continue to apply to these lettings.

5. Where the lettings are to connected tenants –

    (a) If the tenant is entitled to deduct at least 90% of the VAT charged on the rents, (4) above applies;

    (b) If the tenant is **not** entitled to deduct at least 90% of the VAT charged then the waiver of exemption is cancelled under the old cancellation rules with effect from 1 July 2008. In such circumstances, in the July/August 2008 VAT return, the landlord must account for the claw-back of the excess of the VAT claimed in respect of property over the aggregate of the VAT paid on the rents to 30 June 2008;

(c)   **But** if the VAT payable on the rent over a twelve year period is greater than or equal to the VAT claimed on the initial acquisition or development of the property then (4) above applies;

(d)   **And** if the VAT on the rents does not meet the conditions set out at (c) the landlord can benefit from (4) if the VAT on the rent for the rest of the twelve-year period is increased to meet the condition at (c).

6.   If a client is in the process of selling or entering into a lease agreement before 1 July 2008 the old rules will apply if the sale or lease is entered into before 1 July 2008. If negotiations are under way and the supply takes place on or after 1 July the new rules apply.

7.   If a client has a property on hands at 1 July 2008 and the property is sold on or after 1 July 2008, it is subject to the new rules (2/5 year rule, etc).

8.   If a client surrenders or assigns a leasehold interest on or after 1 July 2008 that was taxed as supply of goods under the old rules and the client was entitled to deduct any of the VAT then the assignment or surrender is subject to VAT on an amount based on a CGS calculation.

VALUE-ADDED TAX INFORMATION LEAFLET (JUNE 2008)

CONSTRUCTION SERVICES: NEW VAT RULES FOR PRINCIPAL CONTRACTORS AND SUB-CONTRACTORS FROM 1ST SEPTEMBER 2008

Introduction

From 1 September 2008, there will be major changes in how principal contractors and sub-contractors in the construction industry account for VAT. Principal contractors and sub-contractors will need to know how to operate the new system and be prepared for the change.

Who is affected?

The new system applies to principal contractors and sub-contractors involved in construction operations to which Relevant Contracts Tax (RCT) applies (but excluding haulage for hire).

RCT applies when a principal contractor is obliged to deduct tax @35% from payments to a sub-contractor or would have to do so but for the fact that the principal contractor holds a *Relevant Payments Card* (RCT 47) for that sub-contractor. Public bodies, including Local Authorities, who receive construction services are principal contractors for RCT purposes and the person who contracts to provide such services to a public body is regarded as a sub-contractor.

What is the change?

Prior to 1 September 2008 the charge that a sub-contractor makes to a principal contractor includes VAT on that service. The principal pays the sub-contractor and the sub-contractor passes on the VAT to the Revenue Commissioners.

From 1 September 2008 the charge the sub-contractor makes to a principal contractor does not include VAT. Instead the principal contractor calculates the VAT on the amount charged by the sub-contractor and pays the VAT directly to the Revenue Commissioners through his/her VAT return.

Does the new system apply to all services supplied by a sub-contractor?

No. VAT on construction services that are not subject to RCT will continue to be taxed under the normal VAT system. For example, a builder who builds an extension for a private individual, or an electrician who installs a new alarm system in a shop should charge and account for VAT on the supply. The reverse charge does not apply to these supplies.

As many construction service providers are involved in different types of contracts (e.g. a builder may be acting as principal in one contract, as a sub-contractor in another and supplying services that are not subject to RCT under another contract) it is important to be aware of how the system operates.

System before 1ˢᵗ September 2008

The position up to 1 September 2008 is as follows:

- A VAT registered sub-contractor invoices the principal contractor for construction services provided.

- The invoice shows the consideration plus the VAT rate(s) and the amount of VAT at the relevant rate(s).

- The principal contractor pays the sub-contractor for the services. This payment includes VAT.

- Unless the principal contractor holds a Relevant Payments Card for the sub-contractor, the principal contractor deducts RCT @ 35% from the full payment including VAT.

- The sub-contractor includes the VAT on the construction services in its VAT return to Revenue.

- Where entitled to do so the principal claims an input credit for the VAT incurred in its VAT return.

System after 1st September 2008

Invoice (No VAT)

Sub-contractor

Principal

Payment (No VAT)　　　VAT

Revenue

From the 1st September 2008 the principal accounts for the VAT on services received from a sub-contractor under what is known as the reverse charge.

- The charge for services by the subcontractor does not include VAT on the services.

- The VAT registered sub-contractor issues an invoice to the principal, which shows all the same information as appears on a VAT invoice, except the VAT rate and VAT amount. The invoice should include the VAT registered number of the sub-contractor.

- The invoice should also contain the statement "VAT ON THIS SUPPLY TO BE ACCOUNTED FOR BY THE PRINCIPAL CONTRACTOR".[1]

- The principal contractor pays the sub-contractor for the services. This payment should not include VAT.

- If RCT is to be deducted, it should be calculated on the VAT exclusive amount.

- The principal contractor should include the VAT on the services received from the sub-contractor in its VAT return for the period in which the supply is made as VAT on Sales (T1).[2]

- Where entitled to do so, the principal can claim a simultaneous input credit in its VAT return for the period.[3]

---

[1] If agreed by both the principal contractor and the sub-contractor the principal may issue the invoice.

[2] In the case of a payment in advance of completion of the supply, the principal will include the VAT on the payment in its VAT return for the period in which the payment is made.

[3] Principal contractor for RCT purposes includes Local Authorities, Government Departments and boards established by or under statute. Many of these bodies would not be entitled to VAT input credit.

Examples

The following examples illustrate the effects of the change. The services in question are invoiced in September/October 2008.

Example 1

A Ltd

A Ltd is renovating a factory building for a manufacturing company. A Ltd invoices the manufacturing company in October 2008 as follows:

Construction services	€740,740
VAT @13.5%	€100,000
Total	€840,740

These services do not come within the reverse charge since A Ltd is not a sub-contractor to the manufacturing company for RCT purposes.

B, a building contractor, supplies services to A Ltd. A Ltd is the principal contractor and B is the sub-contractor. A Ltd does not hold a Relevant Payments Card for B.

B incurred €13,000 VAT on purchases in September/October 2008 for the purposes of his business.

B charges A Ltd €600,000 in September 2008 for the building services. B does not charge any VAT on this amount. A Ltd accounts for the VAT on the construction services from B. VAT chargeable on the services @13.5% = €81,000.

As the construction services provided by the sub-contractor to the principal were invoiced during September/October 2008 the VAT on these services is accounted for by reverse charge.

- In its September/October 2008 VAT return A Ltd includes VAT €181,000 as VAT on Sales (i.e. VAT on its own sales of €100,000 plus reverse charge VAT €81,000 on services received from B).

- A Ltd can claim input credit for €81,000 reverse charge VAT in the same return.

- A Ltd should pay Revenue €100,000.

- A Ltd would deduct RCT from the payment due to B (amount deducted €600,000 @ 35% = €210,000)

September/October 2008 VAT Return - A Ltd - Principal contractor

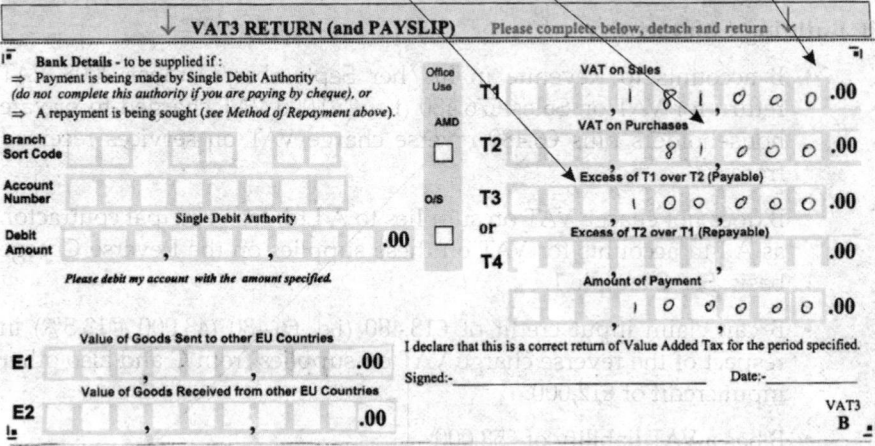

- B does not account for VAT on the services supplied to A Ltd. As B only does work for a principal contractor his VAT on Sales figure is Nil.

- B is entitled to his input credit of €13,000.

- He is entitled to a repayment of €13,000.

September/October 2008 VAT Return - B, Sub-contractor.

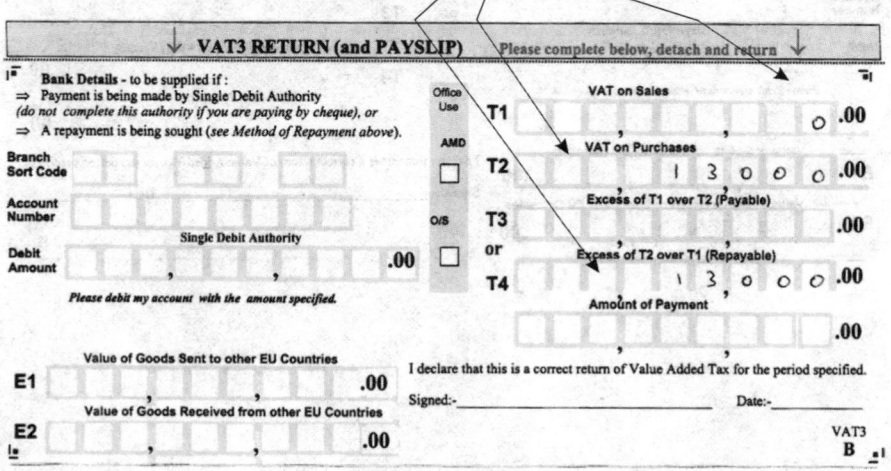

Example 2

The facts are as in Example 1 but B also does building work for private householders in September/October 2008. RCT does not apply to this work. He accounts for VAT €70,000 in respect of these supplies.

C is a subcontractor, who has his own electrical business, but who does occasional work for B. C's only supplies in this period are made to B. C is registered for VAT. He charges B €48,000. C has incurred VAT of €1,000 for which he is entitled to input credit.

B is a principal contractor in respect of the electrical services he receives from C. A Ltd: See Example 1.

B, Building Contractor

- B accounts to Revenue in his/her September/October 2008 VAT return for VAT on Sales €76,480 (i.e. €70,000 VAT charged to private householders plus €6,480 reverse charge VAT on services received from C).

- B does not charge VAT on supplies to A Ltd, his principal contractor, as A Ltd accounts for VAT on these supplies on the Reverse Charge basis. See Example 1.

- B can claim input credit of €18,480 (i.e. €6,480 (48,000 @13.5%) in respect of the reverse charge VAT on supplies from C and also other input credit of €12,000.

- B has a VAT liability of €58,000

September/October 2008 VAT Return - B, Principal/sub-contractor

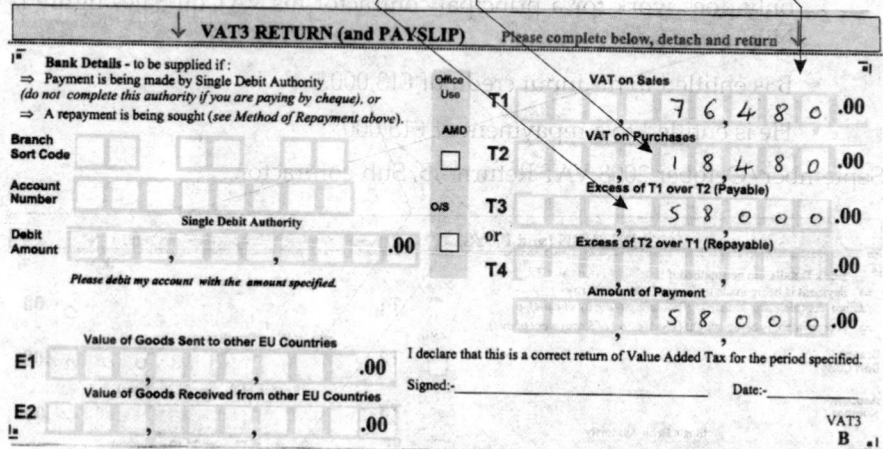

C, Electrical Contractor

- C will not account for VAT on any supplies as C only provided services to a principal contractor. VAT on Sales is Nil.

- C can claim input credit for VAT incurred of €1,000.

- C is due a repayment of €1,000.

September/October 2008 VAT Return - C, Sub-contractor.

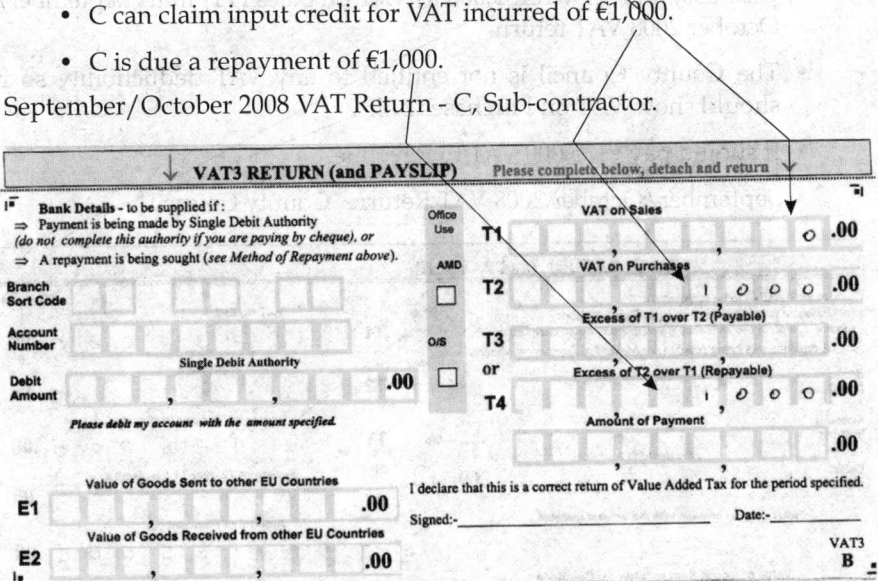

Government Departments, Local Authorities and Public Bodies

From 1 September 2008 Government Departments, Local Authorities and Public bodies who are principal contractors for the purposes of RCT and who receive construction services must be registered for VAT. They should no longer pay any VAT over to sub-contractors and instead should account for the VAT on services received from sub-contractors directly to Revenue through their VAT return. As these bodies are generally not carrying on any taxable activities they would not normally be entitled to claim any deduction for VAT incurred.

Example 3

A County Council contracts for the building of a road with D Ltd which charges €1,000,000 for its services in September/October 2008. For RCT purposes the County Council is a principal contractor and the construction company is a sub-contractor.

- The construction company should invoice the County Council for €1,000,000 (it does not charge VAT).

- The County Council should calculate the VAT (€1,000,000 @ 13.5% = €135,000) and show €135,000 as VAT on Sales (T1) in its September/October 2008 VAT return.

- The County Council is not entitled to any VAT deductibility so it should show VAT on Purchases Nil.

- It should pay €135,000 VAT to Revenue.

- September/October 2008 VAT Return - County Council

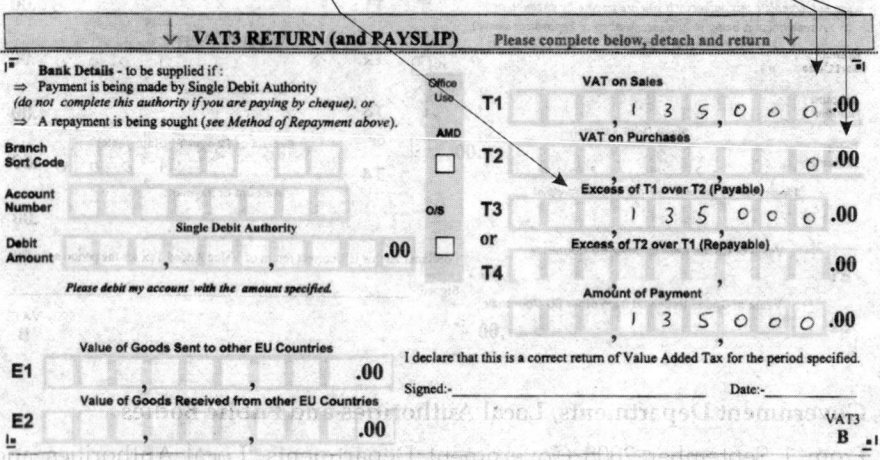

"Two-Thirds Rule"

Where the VAT exclusive cost of goods supplied in the course of providing a service exceeds two thirds of the total VAT exclusive charge for the supply, the rate of VAT applicable is the rate that applies to the goods.

The two-thirds rule does not apply where the reverse charge applies.

Supply of goods only

The reverse charge will not apply to a supply of goods where that supply is not part of a construction service that is subject to RCT.

Commencement

The new system will apply with effect from 1 September 2008. It will not apply to any invoice that is issued before that date or that should have been issued before that date.

Records

Both principal contractors and sub-contractors should ensure that their records and accounting systems can deal with the new system.

Sub-contractors established outside the State.

A sub-contractor who is established outside the State, and whose only supplies in the State are to principals, is no longer required to be VAT registered in the State. S/he will however need to register for VAT for the purposes of claiming any refund of VAT. A sub-contractor who is established outside the State but who also provides construction services to customers other than principal contractors must register for VAT irrespective of the level of his/her turnover.

Further information

Further information is also available on the Revenue web site (www.revenue.ie.)

VALUE-ADDED TAX INFORMATION LEAFLET (JUNE 2008)

CONSTRUCTION SERVICES: REVERSE CHARGE VAT IN THE CONSTRUCTION INDUSTRY ON SERVICES SUBJECT TO RELEVANT CONTRACTS TAX (RCT)

Introduction

From **1 September 2008**, there will be major changes in how principal contractors and subcontractors in the construction industry account for VAT.

The overall VAT cost to principal contractors & subcontactors will not change.

Principal contractors and subcontractors will need to know how to operate the new system and be prepared for the change.

Position before 1 September 2008

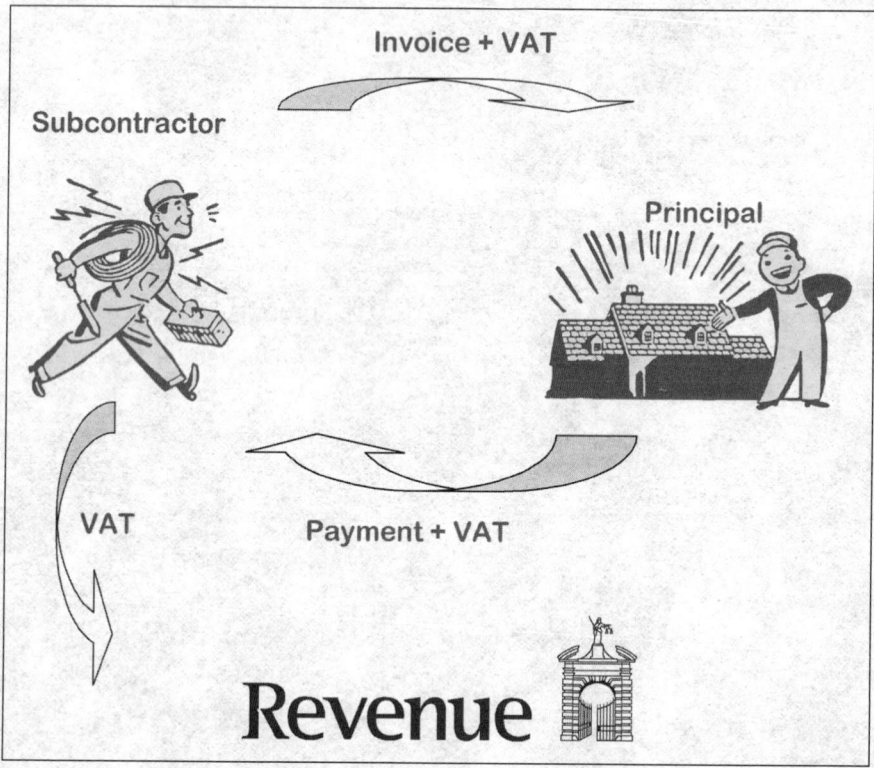

- **The subcontractor charges VAT to the principal.**
- **The principal contractor pays the VAT to the subcontractor.**
- **The subcontractor passes it on to the Revenue Commissioners.**

Position after 1 September 2008

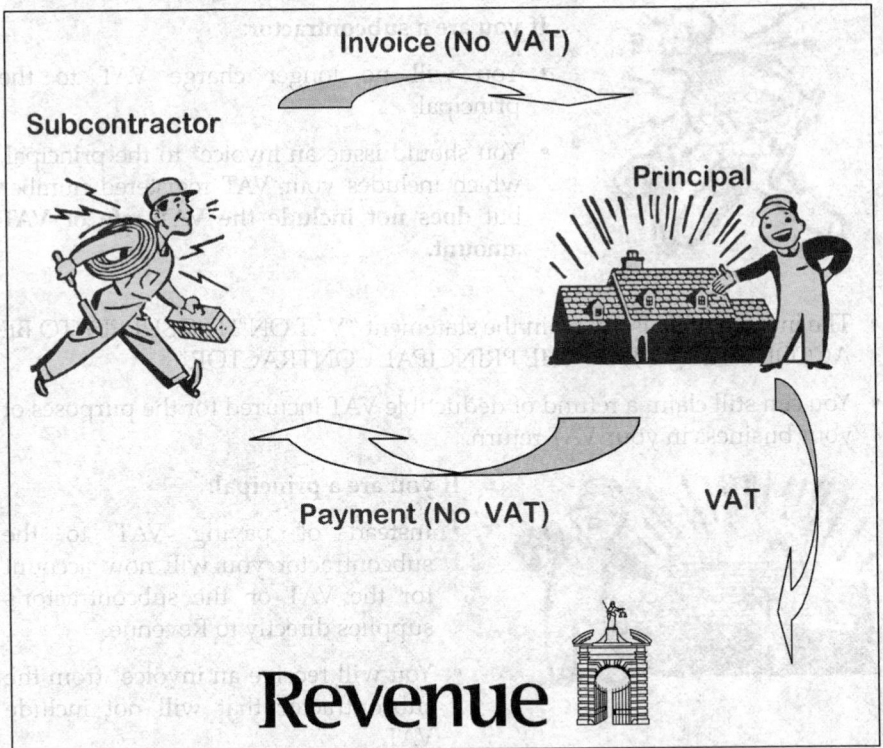

- The subcontractor will not charge VAT to the principal contractor.
- The principal contractor will calculate the VAT on the amount charged by the subcontractor.
- The principal contractor will account for the VAT directly to Revenue in his/her VAT return.
- The principal contractor can normally claim a deduction for this VAT in his/her VAT return.

What services are affected?

All construction services (other than haulage) to which RCT applies. If RCT applies, reverse charge applies.

If you are a subcontractor:

- You will no longer charge VAT to the principal.

- You should issue an invoice* to the principal, which includes your VAT registered number but **does not include the VAT rate or VAT amount.**

- The invoice will also contain the statement "VAT ON THIS SUPPLY TO BE ACCOUNTED FOR BY THE PRINCIPAL CONTRACTOR"

- You can still claim a refund of deductible VAT incurred for the purposes of your business in your VAT return.

If you are a principal:

- Instead of paying VAT to the subcontractor you will now account for the VAT on the subcontractor's supplies directly to Revenue.

- You will receive an invoice* from the subcontractor that will not include VAT.

- You should calculate the VAT on the supply and account for the VAT due by including it in your VAT return with your VAT on sales.

- You can claim a simultaneous deduction for this VAT in your return under VAT on purchases.

- If RCT is to be deducted, it should be calculated on the **VAT exclusive** amount.

Where can I get more information?

A more detailed information leaflet is available on the Revenue website at **www.revenue.ie** or contact your local Revenue Office.

This leaflet is intended to describe the subject in general terms. As such, it does not attempt to cover every issue which may arise in relation to the subject. It does not purport to be a legal interpretation of the statutory provisions and consequently, responsibility cannot be accepted for any liability incurred or loss suffered as a result of relying on any matter published herein.

*If agreed between the principal and the subcontractor, the principal may issue this invoice

VALUE-ADDED TAX INFORMATION LEAFLET (JULY 2008)

RETAIL EXPORT SCHEME (TAX-FREE SHOPPING FOR TOURISTS)

This information notice replaces the leaflet on Tax Free Purchases for non-EU Tourists issued by Revenue in April 1998, which should now be treated as withdrawn. Any changes in this leaflet to previous practices should be regarded as coming into effect as and from 1 July 2008. This notice, which sets out the current practice at the date of its issue, is intended for guidance only and does not purport to be a definitive legal interpretation of the provisions of the Value-Added Tax Act 1972 (as amended).

- Introduction – how the Scheme works
- Useful terms and definitions
- Documents required as proof that a person is a tourist/traveller
- Details that a retailer or agent must keep for each sale of goods
- VAT refund agents
- How to certify that goods have been exported from Ireland
- Fees charged for procuring a VAT refund
- Time limits for refunds of VAT to tourists/travellers
- Exchange rates used in calculating VAT refunds
- Supplies of goods at a zero per cent rate of VAT
- Legislation on which the Retail Export Scheme is based
- Enquiries from Irish traders

Introduction – how the Scheme works

The Retail Export Scheme allows certain people who purchase goods in Ireland to get a refund of the Value-Added Tax paid. Subject to the more detailed instructions contained in the rest of this leaflet, the Scheme works as follows:

- How can a person get a refund of VAT?
- People who qualify for refund of VAT
- People who do NOT qualify for refund of VAT under the scheme
- Purchases that are eligible for refund of VAT
- Monetary limits for refunds
- Refund paid by a retailer
- Refund paid by a VAT refund agent
- Who should be contacted with questions about the scheme

How can a person get a refund of VAT?

In order for a refund to apply, a person who qualifies under the Scheme (a tourist or other traveller) must purchase goods in Ireland, and then take them to a location outside the E.U. The scheme does not apply to all goods - See: Purchases that are eligible for refund of VAT. That such a transaction has taken place will be certified by Customs Officers at the last point of departure from the E.U. If a refund is due, it will be paid directly to the tourist/traveller by the retailer who made the supply, or by a VAT Refund agent. Irish Revenue does not make any refunds directly to tourists/ travellers under this scheme. It is important to note that not all retailers participate in the scheme – For further details see: Supplies of goods at a zero per cent rate of VAT.

People who qualify for refund of VAT

Any person who comes within the definition of a traveller in the 'Useful terms and definitions' section of this leaflet – for practical purposes this generally means tourists visiting Ireland from countries outside the European Union (E.U.), other non-resident travellers, and also Irish or E.U. citizens who are leaving to take up residence outside the E.U. for at least 12 consecutive months.

People who do NOT qualify for refund of VAT under the scheme

People normally resident in Ireland or other E.U. countries do not qualify, including

- Tourists from other E.U. countries.

- Tourists from outside the E.U. who are not leaving the E.U. directly from Ireland generally do not qualify, but see the section dealing with certification of exports for exceptions to this rule.

- Foreign nationals resident in Ireland going home (e.g. for holidays) who intend to return to Ireland.

- Irish (or E.U.) citizens taking up residence abroad for less than 12 consecutive months.

- Irish (or E.U.) citizens who, having taken up residence outside the E.U. for 12 consecutive months, return on a visit (e.g. for holidays or business).

Supplies of goods to the above categories of people may be zero-rated for VAT where they are dispatched by the supplier to an address outside the E.U. – see the section dealing with zero-rated supplies for more details.

Purchases that are eligible for refund of VAT

Any purchases that come within the definition of 'traveller's qualifying goods' – in effect, refunds can be obtained on purchases of goods, such as souvenirs, gifts etc., bought for non-business purposes, which the tourist/ traveller brings with himself/herself when leaving the E.U. (and not later than three months from the month of purchase). No refund can be obtained for goods that remain in Ireland, or for services such as hotel accommodation, car-hire or restaurant meals.

Monetary limits for refunds

Unlike many other E.U. countries, Ireland does not apply a lower limit for VAT refunds. A tourist/traveller is entitled to get the VAT back regardless of the value of the goods purchased. However, in respect of individual items whose value (including VAT) exceeds €635.00 the process of obtaining proof that the goods are being exported is more stringent, and any individual items whose value (including VAT) exceeds €2,000.00 must be presented to Customs for inspection (see the section dealing with certification of exports for details).

Refund paid by a retailer

If a retailer operates the scheme by way of a VAT refund agent, this will be indicated to the customer. If a retailer operates the scheme in its own name, then the tourist/traveller will need to provide documentary proof of his or her status, and in particular the tourist/traveller must sign the required declarations in that section. A receipt will be issued in respect of each purchase. The receipt for the goods should be presented to a Customs Officer at the airport, or placed into a mail slot or 'drop-box' designated for this purpose. Customs may then check to ensure that the goods are being exported – it is important that the goods are easily available for inspection if required. The receipt will be returned by Customs to the retailer (or to the VAT refund agent, where appropriate), who will then refund the VAT (less any fee charged for processing the refund) directly to the tourist/traveller.

Not all retailers operate the Retail Export or Tax-Free Shopping Scheme. A tourist/traveller should check this before making purchases, as they may encounter practical difficulties in obtaining a refund of VAT where the Scheme is not operated. In any event, goods may be supplied free of VAT if the retailer dispatches them on behalf of the customer to a place outside the E.U.

Refund paid by a VAT refund agent

VAT refund agents are private companies that work on behalf of the tourist/ traveller to get a refund of VAT. Where a VAT refund agent is used, the tourist/ traveller should follow the specific procedures for obtaining a refund set out by the agent, which may differ form those used by retailers (see above). The tourist/traveller will need to provide specific information, and in particular, must sign the required declarations.

Who should be contacted with questions about the scheme

If you are a retailer, or a VAT refund agent, and you have any enquiries relating to the operation of the Retail Export Scheme or your tax affairs generally, you should contact your local Revenue District Office.

If you are a tourist or traveller and you have any enquiries with regard to specific refunds of VAT, you should address these directly to the retailer or VAT refund agent with whom you have been dealing.

Any general enquiries, suggestions or observations concerning the operation of the Retail Export Scheme should be sent to the VAT Interpretation Branch, Revenue Commissioners, Stamping Building, Dublin Castle, Dublin 2; or by e-mail to vat@revenue.ie.

Useful terms and definitions

There are certain words and phrases that have a particular meaning in the context of the Scheme. These are:

Export: An export of goods takes place where the goods are transported directly to a place outside the VAT territory of the European Union, by or on behalf of either the seller or the purchaser.

Retail sales: Any sales of goods by a supplier directly to a customer, which are not intended for subsequent re-sale by that customer in the course of business.

Retailer: Any person who makes supplies directly to non-business customers. This includes sales of goods through the Internet or any similar means as long as the customer takes delivery of the goods in the State. In practice, most VAT refund agents are treated as retailers for the operation of VAT free shopping (see below).

Traveller (referred to in this leaflet as tourist/traveller): A traveller is a person whose domicile or habitual residence is not situated within the E.U. and includes a person who is normally resident in the E.U. but who, at the time of the supply of the goods intends to take up residence outside the E.U. in the near future and for a period of at least 12 consecutive months.

Traveller's qualifying goods: These are goods [other than goods transported by the traveller for the equipping, fuelling and provisioning of pleasure boats, private aircraft or other means of transport for private use] which are supplied within the State to a traveller and which are exported by or on behalf of that traveller by the last day of the third month following the month in which the supply takes place.

VAT refunding/refund agent: A person who supplies services which consist of the procurement of a zero rating or repayment of tax in relation to supplies of a traveller's qualifying goods, in return for a fee charged to the traveller. Although referred to as agents, they themselves are usually part of the supply chain, and actually purchase the goods from the retailer, and make a simultaneous retails sale of the goods to the tourist/traveller. The voucher or similar agreement signed by the traveller can give evidence of a sale of the goods by the retailer to the refund agent, and an onward sale by the agent to the traveller.

Zero-rated: The application of a zero per cent rate of VAT to supplies of goods or services.

Documents required as proof that a person is a tourist/traveller

Any retailer or VAT refund agent who wants to refund VAT must keep a record of the details of documentary proof inspected by him/her confirming that the purchaser is a tourist/traveller. This documentary proof will typically include passports; flight tickets and evidence of the place of residence, and the details that the retailer will need to record consist of:

- The date of arrival of the traveller in the European Union.
- The intended date of departure of the traveller from the European Union.

- The number of the traveller's passport.

- The permanent address of the traveller outside the European Union.

- A signed declaration that the traveller is not resident within the E.U. at the time of the purchase, or if resident, that he/she intends to take up residence outside the E.U. within the next three months, for a period of at least twelve consecutive months.

- A signed declaration that the traveller intends to take the goods outside of the E.U. when he/she departs from its territory.

- If a tourist/traveller makes a purchase from a retailer and does not provide the required information to the retailer* then he/she may still obtain a refund provided that:

- The receipt was stamped by Customs on leaving Ireland.

- Full details as set out above, along with the stamped receipt, are provided to the retailer by the tourist/traveller.

- Copies of all relevant documents (flight tickets, passports etc.) are also provided.

* Whether because the retailer does not operate the Scheme, or the tourist/ traveller is unaware of the Scheme at the time of purchase, or for any other reason

The retailer in this situation should allow the refund, subject to the rules of the Scheme regarding time limits etc., and claim a corresponding credit in the VAT return for the period in question. If the retailer is in any doubt as to the validity of the claim, he/she should refer the matter to the local Revenue District Office.

Details that a retailer or agent must keep for each sale of goods

Once a retailer or VAT refund agent has confirmed that a person to whom he/she is supplying goods is a tourist/traveller, the retailer must issue an invoice, receipt or similar record (including electronic records, if appropriate) containing details of the transaction. These details consist of:

- The name, address and VAT number of the retailer

- The name and permanent address of the traveller

- The date of the transaction

- A description of the goods supplied

- The amount of the purchase, and the amount of the VAT charged

- The signature of the traveller

- The rate of exchange, or the method to be used to determine the rate, if the refund is to be made in a currency other than the Euro.

In relation to each VAT-free transaction, the retailer must keep

- A copy of the above invoice, receipt or record issued to the traveller;

And a record of

- The net amount actually refunded to the traveller
- The actual exchange rate used
- The date and method of the repayment.

VAT refund agents

VAT refund agents will provide tourists/travellers with a refund of VAT incurred on purchases in accordance with the rules of the Scheme. These refund agents may act as principals in the supply of goods, or as agents of the tourist/traveller. Although the end result is the same, i.e. the tourist/traveller gets a refund of VAT; the process whereby the refund is provided may differ between agents. It is important that the full requirements necessary to obtain a refund are clearly set out by the agent in advance of any purchase of goods, and explained fully to the tourist/traveller.

VAT refund agents acting as retailers

In general, VAT refund agents will operate in the same manner as retailers, and the requirements of the Scheme will apply to them as if they were retailers. This is because VAT refund agents usually involve themselves in the supply of goods to tourists/travellers as principals, rather than as agents per se. That is, they actually buy the goods from the original retailer, and then resell them to the traveller. The voucher or similar document issued by the VAT refund agent and completed by the tourist/traveller and the retailer is retained as the record in respect of each such transaction.

VAT refund agents operating in accordance with Section 13(1A)(b)

Although this is less common, Irish legislation also provides for the operation of VAT refund agents, not as retailers, but as agents who will facilitate the traveller in getting a refund of VAT due to him/her. A person operating as a VAT refund agent in accordance with this legislation does not actually supply any goods to a traveller, but procures the repayment of VAT or the application of a zero percent rate of VAT in relation to the supply of goods to the traveller. Section 13(1A)(b) of the VAT Act provides for the zero rating of "the supply of services by a VAT refunding agent consisting of the service of repaying the tax claimed by a traveller in relation to the supply of a traveller's qualifying goods or the procurement of the zero-rating of the supply of a traveller's qualifying goods...". Section 13(1A)(b) also provides for the issuing of regulations requiring the approval or authorization of VAT refund agents by Revenue, and for allowing the agent to deduct VAT charged to the traveller. These regulations, however, have not been issued, so at present VAT refund agents cannot be formally approved by Revenue; and all claims for refunds of VAT must be made in the name of the traveller rather than the agent.

In order to obtain a refund of VAT for the traveller, a VAT refund agent acting in accordance with Section 13(1A)(b) must obtain proof from the traveller that the goods have been exported, provide that proof to the retailer, obtain the VAT refund from the retailer in the name of the traveller, and furnish the refund to the traveller. From the amount of the refund the agent will retain the fee for the transaction, which is also zero-rated provided that the fee charged for obtaining the refund is notified to the traveller in advance. This fee may be expressed as a percentage or fraction of the total refund due.

How to certify that goods have been exported from Ireland

Certification by Customs Officers

The role of Customs is to certify that goods have actually been exported in accordance with the terms of the Retail Export Scheme/Tax-free shopping. This certification may involve Officers stamping the voucher (from a VAT Refund Agent) or the receipt (from a retailer) relating to each purchase of goods. All such receipts or vouchers should be presented to Customs for stamping.

If no Customs Officers are available, the receipts or vouchers may be placed in a specially designated 'drop-box' or mail slot. All these vouchers and receipts will be examined before being stamped. If appropriate, Customs will then inspect the goods – tourists/travellers should be in a position to produce the goods to Customs, if requested to do so. Vouchers and receipts that have been stamped may be forwarded by Customs to the appropriate refund agent or retailer, who will then refund the VAT to the traveller. If Customs Officers are not satisfied regarding the validity of any voucher or receipt, it will be returned unstamped to the tourist/traveller.

Some refund agents may have an office or post at the departures area of an airport. Where this is the case, the agent will provide full details to tourists/travellers, who should then present the vouchers appropriate to these agents at the offices or posts, rather than to Customs Officers. The Refund agent will make the arrangements necessary to refund the VAT according to their own procedures.

It is important to note that procedures may vary between E.U. Member States. A traveller who intends departing the EU from another country should check the requirements of Customs regarding the Tourist VAT Refund Scheme in that country.

Certification at the final point of departure from the E.U.

In order for a refund of VAT to be allowed, Customs must be satisfied that the tourist/traveller has complied with the conditions of the Retail Export Scheme with regard to the export of goods from the E.U. This should be certified at the final point of departure from the E.U., which may not be the country where the goods were purchased. For example, a traveller who departs the E.U. on a flight from London should have any vouchers or receipts certified by UK Customs.

However, even if Ireland is not the last point of departure from the E.U., Irish Customs Officers will nevertheless certify a refund of VAT for goods purchased in Ireland subject to evidence that the tourist/traveller has a ticket for a destination outside of the E.U. valid not later than the end of the third month from the date on which the goods were purchased, and the usual proof that the tourist/traveller is a qualifying person.

Certification by officials in the tourist/traveller's country of residence

If a tourist/traveller is unable to get certification of export from Customs on leaving the State, he/she may still obtain a refund by getting a person of similar standing in his/her own country to certify (by means of an official stamp or otherwise) that the goods have been transported to that country. Such persons include a Customs official, a law-enforcement officer, a Notary Public and a Commissioner for Oaths. The tourist/traveller should then return the receipt or voucher to the retailer or VAT refund agent. It is important to note that the certification or stamping of the document is the basis for allowing the remission of VAT both on the supply of goods and on any fees charged in respect of the supply. Any retailers or VAT refund agents who wish to operate the VAT free shopping scheme on the basis of documents stamped abroad must obtain the prior agreement of their local Revenue District Office.

Special procedures for high-value goods

In the case of individual goods costing €2,000.00 or more (including VAT), each item must be presented to Customs, along with the receipt/voucher, before any VAT refund will be approved. Receipts or vouchers for such items that are left in the 'drop-box', or handed in to Refund Agents, will NOT be subsequently stamped by Customs. It is important that travellers who wish to obtain refunds in respect of these items allow enough time, following check-in, to attend at Customs with the item.

For individual items costing between €635.00 and €2,000.00 (including VAT), Customs Officers will certify that refund is due subject to the VAT Refund Agent or the retailer presenting each receipt or voucher to customs, along with the usual proofs that both the goods and the tourist/traveller qualify under the Retail Export Scheme.

Fees charged for procuring a VAT refund

All refunds are subject to a fee charged by either the VAT Refund Agent or the retailer, which will be deducted from the amount of VAT before the refund is made to the tourist/traveller. This fee may be expressed as a monetary amount, or as a percentage or fraction of the total refund due, and is at the discretion of the agent or retailer. The fee is zero-rated provided that it was notified to the tourist/traveller on or before the time at which the goods were originally supplied to him/her, i.e. the time of sale. If it can be clearly shown that the tourist/traveller was referred by the agent or retailer to an easily available document or website containing a scale of chargeable fees, then this will be considered as notification, and it will not be necessary to notify him/her of the specific fee for each transaction.

Time limits for refunds of VAT to tourists/travellers

The retailer or refund agent must refund any VAT to the tourist/traveller not later than the twenty-fifth working day following the receipt of a claim for repayment accompanied by proof that the goods were exported.

Exchange rates used in calculating VAT refunds

Where a refund is being made in a currency other than the Euro, then the question of exchange rates arises. The rate of exchange generally used on such transactions is either the official rate of exchange as published by the Central Bank of Ireland for the date on which the refund is given, or the official monthly average rate of exchange as published by the Central Bank of Ireland for the month in which the refund was given. Other internationally recognised exchange rate sources may also be used, subject to the agreement of the local Revenue District.

Supplies of goods at a zero per cent rate of VAT

Goods can be sold VAT-free (zero percent rate) if they are exported by or on behalf of the supplier - that is, where the retailer or VAT refund agent posts or dispatches the goods to an address outside the E.U. This is subject to proof in the form of postal or shipping documents showing that the goods have left the E.U.

If the goods are exported by or on behalf of the tourist/traveller, then the supplier does not have proof of export at the time of supply, and the supply should not be zero-rated. If the supplier nonetheless chooses to zero-rate a sale to a tourist/traveller (for example where payment is by credit card), the supplier must account for the VAT due on the sale in the VAT return for the period following the sale unless, at that stage, he/she is in possession of documentary proof that the goods have been exported.

A supplier who zero-rates a sale, and subsequently accounts for the VAT in the next return may claim an adjustment in the following VAT return to account for this if he/she subsequently receives proof that the goods were exported within the three months limit. It is important to note that the traveller has no liability to pay VAT following a zero rated sale, even if he/she fails to provide the necessary proofs of export. The liability to account for VAT on the sale remains with the supplier, whose entitlement to apply the zero rating to a particular sale is retracted if the conditions attached to the scheme are not complied with.

Legislation on which the Retail Export Scheme is based

Section 13 of the VAT Act 1972 (as amended) provides that the zero rating is appropriate to the supply of a traveller's qualifying goods, and to the supply of the services of a VAT refund agent, subject to the conditions which are set out in this leaflet.

The Regulations which put this into effect are contained in Regulation 33 of the 2006 VAT Regulations, which sets out details of the proofs required to be kept that a person is a traveller and that the goods have been exported; and also details of the time limits and fees relevant to the refund of VAT to travellers.

Paragraphs (i)(a)(I) and (i)(f) of the Second Schedule to the VAT Act provide that the supply of qualifying goods to a traveller will not be entitled to be zero rated unless made subject to Section 13 and the Regulations set out above.

The corresponding provisions of European legislation are contained in Article 147 of the VAT Directive 2006/112/EC.

Enquiries from Irish traders

Any queries regarding your tax affairs as a trader established in Ireland should be addressed to your local Revenue District.

This information leaflet which sets out the current practice at the date of its issue is intended for guidance only and does not purport to be a definitive legal interpretation of the provisions of the Value-Added Tax Act 1972 (as amended).

VALUE-ADDED TAX INFORMATION LEAFLET (AUGUST 2008)

RELIEF FROM CUSTOMS DUTY AND VAT (IMPORT DUTIES) ON GOODS RE-IMPORTED INTO THE EUROPEAN UNION

PART I GENERAL

1. Introduction

Goods exported outside the European Community (EC) and subsequently re-imported into the EC may qualify for relief from Customs Duty and/or VAT on re-importation. If the returned goods are parts or accessories belonging to machines, instruments, apparatus or other products previously exported, they may also qualify for relief. This leaflet describes the relief available and the procedures involved at importation.

2. Law

Articles 185 to 187 of Regulation (EEC) No. 2913/92 (Community Customs Code) and Articles 844 to 855 of Regulation (EEC) No. 2454/93 (Customs Code Implementing Provisions) govern relief from Customs Duty on re-importation.

Similarly, Article 143 (e) of Council Directive 2006/112/EC and Regulation 37 of the Value-Added Tax Regulations 2006 (SI 548 of 2006) as amended by Regulation 3 (k) of Value-Added Tax (Amendment) Regulations 2008 (SI 238 of 2008) provide for relief from VAT but only in relation to goods which are being re-imported by the same person who exported them.

3. Conditions

In order to benefit from the relief from payment of Customs Duty and/ or VAT as described, the following conditions must apply:

1. **Time limit** - The goods must, as a general rule, be re-imported within three years from the date of export. However, Customs may allow this period to be exceeded to take account of special circumstances. Goods re-imported outside the authorised time limits are subject to any duties and restrictions applicable at the time of re-importation.

2. **Goods previously imported for a particular purpose** - In the case of goods which had originally been imported at a reduced or nil rate of customs duty because of their use for a particular purpose, e.g. end-use, relief is subject to their being re-imported for the same purpose. Where the goods will not be used for the same purpose, the duty normally chargeable is reduced by the amount, if any, originally charged when the goods were first released for free circulation (if the amount originally charged exceeds that chargeable when the goods are being re-imported, no refund is allowed).

3.   **Inward Processing** – In the case of re-importation of compensating products originally exported after Inward Processing, the amount of duty chargeable on re-importation is the amount that would have been charged if the goods had been entered for free circulation on the date of the original exportation.

4.   **Same-state goods** – Normally, goods (including goods exported under the outward processing procedure) are not eligible for relief under the re-importation provisions unless they are re-imported in the same state as they were exported. However, exceptions to this rule are outlined in paragraph 4.

4.   Treatment Abroad

As a general rule, goods do not qualify for duty-free re-importation if they have been subjected to treatment abroad. However, goods, which have received treatment, deemed necessary to keep them in good condition, or which have received handling which altered their appearance only, can qualify. In addition, goods after exportation found to be defective or unsuitable for their intended use and were treated while abroad can also qualify for relief, provided:

1.   that the treatment was applied solely to repair them or to restore them to good condition; or

2.   that their unsuitability for their intended use became apparent only after such treatment had commenced.

Where the value of the goods at exportation is increased by the treatment or handling while abroad, Duty is payable on re-importation in accordance with the provisions relating to Outward Processing. However, where it is shown to the satisfaction of Customs that such treatment became necessary due to unforeseen circumstances abroad, relief will be allowed, provided the treatment did not exceed that which was strictly necessary to enable the goods to be continued to be used in the same way as at the time of export even if this treatment resulted in an increase in the value of the goods.

5.   Procedure at Re-Importation

Where goods are forwarded to him/her by post, the importer needs to ensure that the declaration on the parcel is endorsed:

"Returned Goods: Exemption from import charges claimed".

The documentary evidence referred to at paragraph 6 should be attached to the outside of the parcel and marked 'Customs Documents'.

Where goods are imported other than by post the goods should be presented to Revenue accompanied by an import declaration (SAD), with a claim to relief from import charges thereon.

To claim this relief one of the following codes must be entered in box 37 b of the SAD:

Code F01	Relief from import duties for returned goods (Article 185 of the Code)
Code F02	Relief from import duties for returned goods (Special circumstances provided for in Article 844, 1: agriculture goods)
Code F03	Relief from import duties for returned goods (Special circumstances provided for in Article 846, 2:repair or restoration)

Please note the relevant procedure code should be entered in box 37 a of the SAD. This may be confirmed at the following link - Procedure Codes (Appendix 18, AEP, Electronic Services, www.revenue.ie)

Also the related original Export SAD should be declared by entering 1Q27 in box 44/1 along with the Export SAD number in box 44/2 of the re-importation SAD.

The documentary evidence referred to at paragraph 6 is also required.

6.   **Documentary Evidence**

The importer must provide evidence to satisfy Customs that the re-imported goods are those, which were exported. Where the goods were originally exported from this country, an original copy of the export declaration, or a certified photocopy authenticated by Customs will normally be required. For goods originally exported from another Member State, the copy of the export declaration (or certified photocopy) or Form INF 3 (see paragraph 7) completed by the competent authorities in the exporting Member State is usually required. The importer may present alternative evidence to the export declaration or the INF 3 if it is available. Customs at the office of re-importation may require additional evidence over and above the copy of the export declaration or the INF 3, in particular for the purpose of identifying the re-imported goods.

Where an ATA carnet has been issued in the EU for the goods, this would also be acceptable evidence. In such cases, goods may be released for free circulation with relief being allowed even if the period of validity of the ATA Carnet has expired provided that they are being re-imported within a period of three years from the date of exportation.

7.   **Information Sheet INF 3**

The form INF 3 is normally used when the exporter believes that it is probable that the goods will be re-imported into a Member State other than the Member State of exportation.

Supplies of Information Sheets INF 3, consisting of one original and two copies are available from your Regional Customs and Excise Office. The INF 3 will be issued and endorsed at an exporter's request provided the Customs officer concerned is satisfied that the particulars thereon relate to the goods which have been exported or are being exported. The original and one copy of the INF 3 will be returned to the exporter for presentation at the time of re-importation.

Where necessary, the INF 3 may be issued in respect of a proportion only of the goods being exported. Also, a number of INF 3's may be issued to cover the total quantity of the goods exported or being exported. The latter situation could arise, where, for example, the goods are intended to be re-imported into a number of Member States.

Under the verification procedure for the INF 3, the customs authorities in the Member States of re-importation may seek verification of the issue of, and the information contained in, the information sheet from the Customs authorities in the Member State of exportation.

PART II – CAP GOODS

In general the provisions of part I apply to CAP goods. The following additional provisions also apply to such goods.

8. **Prior approval by Revenue and the Department of Agriculture, Fisheries and Food**

   CAP goods (whether originally exported from the State or another Member State) may not be re-imported without the prior approval of Revenue and the Department of Agriculture, Fisheries and Food. Importers who intend to re-import such goods should make applications to CAP, Transit and Own Resources Branch, Government Offices, St. Conlon's Road, Nenagh, Co. Tipperary (067-63134/63409) and to the Department of Agriculture, Fisheries and Food, Johnstown Castle Estate, Wexford (Tel: 053-9163400) enclosing all available documentary evidence from commercial and official sources, indicating the reason the goods are being returned, the intended purpose of the returned goods, and stating the proposed date and place of re-importation of the goods. Traders are advised to liaise fully with Customs Officers throughout the re-importation process.

9. **Time Limit**

   CAP goods, which have benefited from export refunds may, subject to such refunds being repaid, only be granted relief from import charges if re-imported within 12 months of the date of exportation. Customs may allow this period to be exceeded where exceptional circumstances justify this. CAP goods which have not qualified for export refunds may benefit from relief if re-imported within three years. However, the three year period may be exceeded with Customs permission in order to take account of special circumstances. Goods re-imported outside the authorised time limits are subject to the same duties and restrictions as if they were being imported for the first time.

10. **Goods on which Export Refunds were Paid or Claimed**

    These goods qualify for relief from import charges if the refunds are repaid or withheld provided the re-importation became necessary in any of the following circumstances:-

    • where the goods could not be entered for home use in the country to which they were consigned because of any laws in force in that country;

- where the goods were returned by the consignee because they were defective or not in accordance with the provisions of the contract relating to them;

- where the goods could not be used for the purpose intended because of circumstances not brought about by the exporter as follows:

    1. goods returned to the EU following damage occurring before delivery to the consignee, either to the goods themselves, or to the means of transport on which they were carried;

    2. goods originally exported for the purposes of consumption or sale in the course of a trade fair or similar occasion and which have not been so consumed or sold;

    3. goods which could not be delivered to the consignee on account of his physical or legal incapacity to honour the contract under which the goods were exported;

    4. goods, which, because of natural, political or social disturbances, could not be delivered to their consignee or which reached him after the mandatory delivery date stipulated in the contract under which the goods were exported;

    5. products covered by the common organisation of the market in fruit and vegetables, exported and sent for sale on consignment, but which were not sold in the market of the third country of destination.

11.   Information Sheet INF 3

Where CAP goods are re-imported into a Member State other than the Member State from which exported, entry for free circulation must be accompanied by a certificate on form INF 3 issued by the competent authorities of the Member State of exportation, in addition to any other documentary evidence necessary in the circumstances of the re-importation. The certificate must bear one of the following endorsements inserted by the competent authorities of the Member State of exportation:

"No refunds or other amounts granted on exportation"; or

"Refunds and other amounts granted on exportation repaid for..... (quantity)"; or

"Entitlement to payment of refunds or other amounts on exportation cancelled for ...(quantity)".

12.   Form RG1

Where CAP goods originally exported from the State are re-imported into the state, a claim to relief from import charges under the re-importation provisions must be supported by Form RG1, available from and issued by the Department of Agriculture, Fisheries and Food in addition to the export declaration (copy 3 SAD) and evidence of rejection of the goods under the circumstances outlined in paragraph 10. The form must bear one of the following endorsements inserted by the Department of Agriculture, Fisheries and Food:

"No refunds or other amounts granted on exportation"; or

"Refunds and other amounts granted on exportation repaid for..... (quantity)"; or

"Entitlement to payment of refunds or other amounts on exportation cancelled for ...(quantity)".

13. **Adjustment of licences/certificates**

Where CAP goods have been exported under an export licence or advance fixing certificate are re-imported, it must be proved that the relevant Community provisions in regard to licenses/export refunds have been complied with. The importer must produce to Customs, at the time of re-importation, a duly completed certificate from the Department of Agriculture, Fisheries and Food on form RG1 to this effect.

14. **Further Information**

Enquiries regarding any issue contained in this Notice should be addressed to the Revenue District responsible for your tax affairs. Contact details for all Revenue Districts can be found on the Contact Details Page.

Customs Division,
Customs Procedures,
Government Offices,
Nenagh,
Co. Tipperary

Notice No. 1438

August 2008 Edition

While every effort is made to ensure that the information given in this leaflet is accurate, it is not a legal document. Responsibility cannot be accepted for any liability incurred or loss suffered as a consequence of relying on any matter published herein.

VALUE-ADDED TAX INFORMATION LEAFLET (SEPTEMBER 2008)

VAT TREATMENT OF FORFEITED DEPOSITS AND CANCELLATION CHARGES

1.   Introduction

1.1.   Following the ruling issued by the European Court of Justice (ECJ) in case C-277/05 Sociéte thermale d'Eugenie-Les-Bains, Revenue has revised its VAT treatment of:

(a)   a deposit, received by a supplier in respect of an order or request for a taxable supply of goods or services, when it is forfeit following a customer cancellation and where the supply has not taken place, and

(b)   a cancellation charge levied by a supplier where an order or request for a supply is cancelled by the customer and the supply does not take place.

1.2.   This Notice now advises of the change in Revenue policy and procedures which has been implemented by measures in the Finance Act 2008 amending the Value Added Tax Act 1972 (VAT Act) and outlines the treatment of repayment claims for prior years.

2.   ECJ Ruling - Sociéte thermale d'Eugenie-Les-Bains (STELB)

2.1.   STELB provides hotel and restaurant facilities in France. It received deposits paid in advance by customers when reserving accommodation. Following an audit by the French tax authorities, the company was deemed liable for VAT in respect of the deposits which had been paid to it by customers and which it had retained following cancellation of the reservations. The case was appealed through the appeal system and was eventually referred to the ECJ for a preliminary ruling.

2.2.   The ECJ ruled "a sum paid as a deposit, in the context of a contract relating to the supply of hotel services which is subject to value added tax, is to be regarded, where the client exercises the cancellation option available to him and that sum is retained by the hotelier, as a fixed cancellation charge paid as compensation for the loss suffered as a result of client default and which has no direct connection with the supply of any service for consideration and, as such, is not subject to that tax".

2.3.   The Court observed that in situations where the performance of the contract follows its normal course and a taxable supply takes place, the deposit is applied towards the price of the services supplied and is therefore subject to VAT.

3.   Effect of Ruling in Ireland

3.1.   The ruling affects the VAT treatment of forfeited deposits, owing to a cancellation by the customer, not only in the hotel services sector but also in relation to the supply of other services and goods.

3.2.   A charge levied by a supplier when a customer makes a cancellation ("cancellation charge") and a supply does not take place, is to be treated as falling outside the scope of VAT by virtue of it being regarded as compensation and not a payment in respect of a taxable supply.

4.   Position in Ireland prior to ECJ ruling

4.1.   Payment of a deposit is a prepayment for the supply of the goods or services to which it relates, and the supply of those goods or services for a consideration equal to the amount of the prepayment is deemed to have taken place. Where such supplies are taxable, tax is chargeable on the deposit under Article 65 of Directive 2006/112/EC (the VAT Directive) and section 19(2) of the Value Added Tax Act 1972, as amended.

4.2.   Relief from VAT was not available in respect of a forfeited deposit.

5.   Position in Ireland following the ECJ ruling

5.1.   There is no change in the tax treatment of a deposit when it is paid. The payment is a prepayment made in advance of the supply to which it relates and taxed as set out in paragraph 4.1.

5.2.   However, where the amount of a deposit paid to a supplier is retained owing to a cancellation by the customer and:

- a supply does not subsequently take place,

- the cancellation is recorded as such in the books and records of the supplier,

- the deposit is not refunded to the customer, and

- no other consideration, benefit or supply is provided to the customer by any person in lieu of that amount,

the supplier may reclaim any VAT already accounted for on such amount in the VAT return for the period in which the deposit is forfeit. Section 102 of the Finance Act 2008 inserted section 19(2B) in the VAT Act to clarify taxpayers' entitlements following the ECJ ruling. While the provision came into effect on 13 March 2008 (the date of passing of the Finance Act 2008) taxpayers are entitled to claim similar treatment for earlier years, subject to the 4 year time-limit for repayment claims

5.3.   If a VAT invoice has issued in respect of the deposit retained by the supplier at 5.2 the consideration on the invoice is reduced to nil. The supplier should issue a document, to be treated as a credit note, containing particulars of the reduction. The deductible amount in respect of the transaction is, therefore, reduced to nil. The relevant legislative provisions are contained in sections 17(3B) and 17(9)(aa) of the VAT Act, as inserted by section 101(1)(d) and amended by section 101(1)(e), respectively, of the Finance Act 2008.

5.4.   Where a supplier levies a charge on a customer in the event of the customer cancelling an order or request for a supply of goods or services and the supply does not take place, VAT is not due on the "cancellation charge" as set out in paragraph 3.2 above.

6. Claims for Refund of VAT paid on Forfeited Deposits/Cancellation Charges in prior years

6.1. Claims for a refund of VAT accounted for on forfeited deposits referred to in paragraph 1.1 in prior years should be submitted to your district tax office.

6.2. The normal statutory period of four years applies to receipt of refund claims in accordance with section 20 (Refund of tax) of the VAT Act.

6.3. Where a refundable amount is payable under this article, interest calculated from the tax period(s) to which the claim relates (the period in which the deposit was forfeit as in paragraph 5.2 or the cancellation charge was paid as in paragraph 5.4 above), up to the date of the refund payment, will be paid under the provisions of section 21A(2) (interest on refunds of tax) of the VAT Act.

7. Adjustment for Income/Corporation Tax

7.1. Taxpayers who had reduced their liability for income tax or corporation tax to take account of VAT paid on retained deposits will need to adjust their income tax/corporation tax liability for the relevant years/accounting periods arising from the repayment of any such VAT.

7.2. For ease of administration, rather than re-opening prior years of assessment/accounting periods to give effect to these adjustments, the amount of the VAT repayment plus interest (if any) to be claimed for the years in question should be reduced by the amount of the additional liability arising to Income Tax or Corporation Tax.

8. Information to accompany claims

Claimants should:

(a) submit evidence of the terms on which deposits were paid and retained, and

(b) certify that such deposits were not applied to any other taxable supply.

9. Queries

Queries about this Notice should be addressed to your local Revenue District.

10. Application

This notice comes into operation with immediate effect.

VALUE-ADDED TAX INFORMATION LEAFLET (SEPTEMBER 2008)

RELIEF FROM CUSTOMS DUTY AND VAT ON GOODS TO BE USED BY MONARCHS OR HEADS OF STATE AND INDIVIDUALS WITH DIPLOMATIC STATUS (DIPLOMATIC PRIVILEGE)

1. **Introduction**

   Certain goods to be used by Monarchs or Heads of State or those individuals with Diplomatic status (Diplomatic Privilege) may be imported from non-European Union (EU) countries without payment of Customs Duty and VAT. This leaflet describes the goods and products involved, the relief available and the procedures involved at import.

2. **Relief Available**

   The following goods may be imported free from payment of Customs Duty and VAT:

   1. Gifts to reigning Monarchs and Heads of State;

   2. Goods to be used or consumed by reigning Monarchs and Heads of State of non-EU countries or persons officially representing them, during their official stay in the EU on condition the relief is reciprocal; and

   3. Goods to be used or consumed by diplomats during their official stay in the EU.

   The Department of Foreign Affairs, Protocol Section, Tel 01 4780822, will confirm an individual's diplomatic status.

   Note: Irish Diplomats working abroad lose their diplomatic status when they return to Ireland. Therefore, they must apply for relief under the provisions of Transfer of Residence (please see Public Notice (PN) 1875).

3. **Further Information**

   Enquiries regarding any issue contained in this Information Leaflet should be addressed to the Revenue District responsible for your tax affairs. Contact details for all Revenue Districts can be found on the Contact Details Page.

   Customs Division,
   Customs Procedures Branch,
   Government Offices,
   Nenagh,
   Co. Tipperary.

   September 2008

Legal Disclaimer

While every effort is made to ensure that the information given in this guide is accurate, it is not a legal document. Responsibility cannot be accepted for any liability incurred or loss suffered as a consequence of relying on any matter published herein.

VALUE-ADDED TAX INFORMATION LEAFLET (SEPTEMBER 2008)

RELIEF FROM CUSTOMS DUTY AND VAT WHEN TRANSFERRING BUSINESS ACTIVITIES FROM A COUNTRY OUTSIDE THE EUROPEAN UNION

1. **General**

    Capital goods and other equipment belonging to undertakings established outside the European Union (EU) which definitively cease their activity and move to the State in order to carry on a similar activity here, may be imported free of import charges, subject to compliance with the conditions and procedure set out in this notice.

    Where the undertaking transferred is an agricultural holding, its livestock may also be admitted free of import charges.

    The exemption does not apply to importations by undertakings established outside the State the transfer of whose business to the State is consequent upon or is for the purpose of merging with, or being absorbed by, an undertaking established in the State, without a new activity being set up. In this context, a new activity must consist of an effective change in the current activities of an undertaking i.e. the new activity must not have been carried out previously by the undertaking already established in the State with which the foreign undertaking has merged or been absorbed by.

    Note: The exemption applying to capital goods and to other equipment does not extend to VAT in the case of:

    a. persons engaged in a liberal profession, provided such persons are authorised to engage in their profession in the State; and

    b. bodies engaged in a non-profit making activity who transfer this activity to the State.

2. **Definitions**

    "Import charges" means Common Customs Tariff (CCT)/Customs Duty, charges under the Common Agricultural Policy (CAP) or on processed agricultural products and value-added tax (VAT) chargeable on imported goods.

    "Liberal profession" includes professions such as that of a doctor, advocate, notary, etc.

    "Undertaking" means an independent economic unit of production or of the service industry.

3. **Conditions**

    1. Relief is limited to capital goods and other equipment which:

        1. Except in special cases justified by the circumstances, have actually been used in the undertaking for a period of at least 12 months prior to the date on which the

undertaking ceased to operate in the country from which it has transferred its activities;

2. Are intended to be used for the same purposes after the transfer;

3. Are, in relation to relief from VAT, for use in the State in an agricultural activity or in an activity in respect of which it will be accountable for VAT. Accordingly, VAT relief will not extend to goods for use in exempt activities such as banking, insurance, medicine, education – further information on exempt activities may be obtained from your Local Revenue Office. Alternatively, a detailed listing of the rates of VAT applicable to your products is available - VAT rates;

4. Are appropriate to the nature and size of the undertaking; and;

5. Are imported before the expiry of a period of 12 months from the date when the undertaking ceased its activities in the country of departure, except in special cases justified by the circumstances

2. In the case of livestock imported by a farmer on the transfer to the State of an activity carried out in an agricultural holding, relief will be allowed provided the livestock were owned by the farmer for at least 12 months or such shorter period as Revenue considers reasonable prior to the importation and are intended to be used for farming after importation and their number is appropriate to the nature and size of the farming enterprise being undertaken by the person in the State.

3. Capital goods and other equipment which have been admitted duty-free may not be lent, given as security, hired out or transferred, whether for a consideration or free of charge, within one year from the date of importation unless payment of the import charges (other than VAT) has been made. The import charges (other than VAT) payable will be calculated by reference to the rates of duties applying on the date of such loan, giving as security, hiring out or disposal on the basis of the type of goods and the customs value ascertained or accepted on that date by Revenue.

4. **Documentary Evidence Required**

The documentary evidence required to support a claim to relief from import charges shall consist of –

1. Evidence of transfer of business activities such as proof of the sale of the undertaking's premises to show that the undertaking has ceased activity outside the State, proof of acquisition or construction of a permanent business premises in the State, any

State or local authority approval or consent relating to such acquisition or construction or the carrying on of a similar activity in the State; or

2.   Evidence that the goods concerned have been used in the undertaking for the specified period such as sales invoices or receipts of purchase (in the case of a motor vehicle the vehicle registration and insurance certificate(s)); or

3.   Any other evidence that Revenue may deem acceptable.

5.   No Relief for Certain Goods

Exemption shall not be granted in respect of:

1.   Means of transport which are not used in the production process of the business nor, in the case of a service business, used directly in the provision of the service;

2.   Food supplies of all kinds intended for human consumption or for animal feed;

3.   Fuel and stocks of raw materials or finished or semi-finished products; and

4.   Livestock in the possession of dealers.

6.   Relief from Vehicle Registration Tax on vehicles brought into the State on transfer of business activities

Relief from vehicle registration tax will be allowed in respect of motor vehicles being brought permanently into the State as part of the capital goods and other equipment of a business undertaking that definitively ceases its activity outside the State and moves to the State in order to carry out a similar activity here.

The relief does not extend to vehicles brought into the State by business undertakings the transfer of which to the State is consequent upon or is for the purpose of merging with, or being absorbed by, a business undertaking established in the State, in circumstances in which a new activity is not, or is not intended to be, commenced.

7.   Procedure at importation

Form c&e 1078 is to be completed by the importer (owner) of the goods and all the goods, equipment and/or livestock to be imported are to be listed and enumerated thereon and on such additional sheets as may be necessary. The total value, approximately of all the articles enumerated on the list must be shown thereon. The form must be presented to a Revenue official **at the time of importation**. Where total exemption is not applicable (e.g. where VAT is payable) a SAD (import entry) must also be presented. If more than one importation is required to bring all the goods into the State and if, on the occasion of the first importation, the inventory listing all the goods to be imported is presented, then only a copy of that inventory need be presented on the occasion(s) of the subsequent importation(s). Where the contents of any package listed are not shown on the list, a separate list, signed by the importer, containing such information is to be presented.

The documentary evidence of the transfer of the business activity and use of the goods for the requisite period, as set out in paragraph 4 above, must be lodged with the import declaration(s)/entry.

Part III of Form No. 1078 provides for two declarations to be completed at the time of importation. The first declaration includes a claim for relief from relevant charges in respect of the goods/equipment/ livestock being imported and is to be made by the importer or by the person or firm (e.g. Customs Clearance Agent, shipping company etc.) whom the importer has authorised to act on his/her behalf. The second declaration relates to the loading of the vehicle or container in which the goods are packed and is to be completed, except in cases where a SAD is required to be presented, by the carrier of the goods (i.e. by the haulier or transport company responsible for delivering the goods to the place of unloading or by the importer where the goods are packed and transported by him/her).

Where a SAD is presented it should be endorsed along the following lines:

"Exemption from import charges excluding VAT claimed – Capital goods and other equipment (or livestock, as the case may be) imported on a transfer of a business undertaking".

8.   **Removal for Examination at Owner's Premises**

Except in the case of very small consignments which a Revenue Official is satisfied can be examined at the place of importation, any necessary examination of property imported on transfer of a business activity will normally be carried out, at the written request of the owner or his/ her agent at the owner's premises or other suitable premises where the goods can be fully unloaded from the vehicle or other container in which transported. The importer, or his/her agent, must also make arrangements for the removal of the goods to the place of examination and he/she will be required to pay any expense which arises in connection with the attendance of a Revenue official at such place.

9.   **Prohibited/Restricted Goods**

Certain goods may not be imported/brought into the State or may be imported/brought into the State only under licence. The principal items are firearms, ammunition, explosives, and dangerous drugs, indecent or obscene books. A full list of prohibited and restricted items is contained in the Customs and Excise Tariff of Ireland.

10.   **Other Legal Requirements**

The relief from import charges under the transfer of business provisions does not exempt the importer/owner from compliance with any legal requirement, obligation, restriction or prohibition other than the requirement of paying at the time of importation/transfer the import charges and/or vehicle registration tax which would otherwise be payable on the goods.

11.   Transfer of Personal Property

The terms of Notice No. 1875 - Transfer of Residence which relates to relief from Customs Duty and VAT available to individuals in respect of personal property imported/brought into the State on a transfer of residence to the State, are not affected by this Notice.

15.   Further Information

Enquiries regarding any issue contained in this Information Leaflet should be addressed to the Revenue District responsible for your tax affairs. Contact details for all Revenue Districts can be found on the **Contact Details Page**.

Customs Division.
Notice No. 1775
September 2008

Legal Disclaimer

While every effort is made to ensure that the information given in this guide is accurate, it is not a legal document. Responsibility cannot be accepted for any liability incurred or loss suffered as a consequence of relying on any matter published herein.

VALUE-ADDED TAX INFORMATION LEAFLET (SEPTEMBER 2008)

RELIEF FROM CUSTOMS DUTY AND VAT WHEN TRANSFERRING RESIDENCE FROM A COUNTRY OUTSIDE THE EUROPEAN UNION

1. **General**

    This Notice outlines the circumstances in which persons transferring their normal residence from outside the European Union (EU) to Ireland may obtain relief from Customs Duty and VAT in respect of their personal property (including the personal property of members of their household).

    It should be noted that relief from Customs Duty, VAT and Vehicle Registration Tax (VRT) on motor vehicles brought into Ireland under the Transfer of Residence provisions are not covered by this Notice. Details of this relief are set out in Leaflet VRT 3 - Tax Relief on Transfer of Residence.

2. **Exceptions**

    No relief from Customs Duty and VAT is granted for alcoholic products or tobacco products forming part of the personal property of individuals transferring residence other than the normal duty free allowances available to travellers, please see information for travellers arriving in Ireland from countries outside the European Union who have purchased goods in those countries for personal use.

    Neither is relief granted for articles for use in the exercise of a trade or profession other than portable instruments of the applied or liberal arts (which includes artists, sculptors, and professions such as doctors, barristers and solicitors.

    Property, which, by reason of its nature and/or quantity, reflects any commercial interest, is not eligible for relief under these provisions. However, a person who is transferring his/her business activities to the State may be eligible for relief in the circumstances outlined in Notice No. 1775 - Transfer of Business Activities

3. **Conditions**

    In order to qualify for the relief the following conditions must be observed:

    1. The goods must have been obtained duty and tax-paid in the country of purchase (there are certain exceptions in the case of diplomats and members of international organisations recognised by the Minister for Foreign Affairs - details are available from Revenue);

    2. The goods must have been in the possession of and used by the person transferring residence for a minimum period of six months (12 months in the case of goods acquired duty-free by

diplomats and members of international organisations) at his/her former normal place of residence prior to the date of transfer of residence;

3. The person transferring residence must have had his/her place of normal residence outside the EU for a continuous period of at least twelve months prior to the transfer. However, relief may also be granted if it can be established that the intention was clearly to reside outside the EU for a continuous period of at least 12 months;

4. Importation of the goods must take place within six months before or twelve months after the date of the transfer. Where the importation takes place before the transfer of residence, the person concerned must give an undertaking to actually take up residence in the State within six months of the importation; and

5. The goods may not be hired out, lent, sold or otherwise disposed of for twelve months after their importation unless import charges are paid.

4.   Procedure at Importation

A Form c&e 1076 (Rev 1) must be completed by the importer/owner of the goods and all the items imported should be listed on this form. Additional sheets giving a full inventory of the items may be attached. Articles of used clothing, toiletries and accessories belonging to the importer or the members of his/her family living with him/her need not be shown on the inventory.

There are three declarations, which are required to be made on the Form:

1. A declaration by the applicant that s/he has complied with the conditions necessary for the grant of relief;

2. A declaration at import by the importer or his/her agent (Customs Clearance Agent, Shipping Company, etc.); and

3. A declaration by the transport company responsible for delivering the goods to the place of unloading or by the importer where the goods are packed and transported by him/her.

The completed Form should be presented to Revenue at the time and place of importation. Where all the goods listed on the inventory are not being imported on one single occasion, a copy of the inventory must be presented for any further importations.

Documentary evidence of residence abroad, transfer of residence and ownership and use of the imported goods will be required in addition to the declarations on Form c&e 1076 (Rev. 1). Examples of the documentary evidence required are:

1. Sales invoices or receipts of purchase or other similar documentation which clearly establish, where relevant, that all taxes and duties payable on the goods have been paid and were not refunded;

2. Documentation relating to the purchase, rental or lease of property, employment or occupational information such as proof of employment or cessation of employment or other evidence of day-to-day living abroad; and

3. Documentation relating to the disposal of property in the country of departure and rental/purchase of property in Ireland, employment or occupational information such as documentation or statements from present employers.

Articles of gold or silver plate (other than those which are electroplated) which are being imported should be accompanied by a declaration that the goods are for private use and not for sale or exchange, on either Form CU 56 or Form c&e 136 (where the owner is accompanying the goods).

5. Customs Examination

Revenue may decide to examine the goods. Except for very small consignments, which can be examined with ease at the place of importation, examinations are normally carried out at the owner's private residence or other place suitable for examination where the goods can be fully unloaded. This facility can be arranged at the written request of the importer or his/her agent. Removal of the goods to the place of examination and the payment of any expenses arising from the attendance of the Revenue official for the examination is the responsibility of the importer or his/her agent.

6. Prohibited or Restricted Goods

Certain goods may not be imported/brought into the State or may only be imported/brought into the State under licence. These items include firearms, ammunition, explosives, dangerous drugs and indecent or obscene material. A full list of prohibited or restricted goods is contained in the Customs and Excise Tariff of Ireland.

7. Other Legal Requirements

This Notice deals only with the conditions for relief from Customs Duty and VAT on goods imported on transfer of residence. This does not exempt the person transferring residence from complying with any other legal requirement, obligation, prohibition or restriction.

8. Further Information

Enquiries regarding any issue contained in this Information Leaflet should be addressed to the Revenue District responsible for your tax affairs. Contact details for all Revenue Districts can be found on the Contact Details Page.

Customs Division.
Notice No. 1875
September 2008

Legal Disclaimer

While every effort is made to ensure that the information given in this guide is accurate, it is not a legal document. Responsibility cannot be accepted for any liability incurred or loss suffered as a consequence of relying on any matter published herein.

VALUE-ADDED TAX INFORMATION LEAFLET (OCTOBER 2008)

ALCOHOL PRODUCTS

Introduction

1. Special rules apply to the payment of VAT on alcohol products when supplied while being held under duty suspension arrangements. In general, VAT is not chargeable on the supply of alcohol products while held under such arrangements but the final supply forms the basis for the charge to VAT which is payable along with the excise duty at the time the good are removed from duty suspension, Section 3B of the VAT Act 1972 (as amended) refers.

Scope

2. The alcohol products concerned are spirits, wine, other fermented beverages, intermediate beverages, beer, cider and perry which are supplied while held under a duty suspension arrangement or which have been the subject of an EU intra-Community acquisition or importation into a duty suspension arrangement in the State.

3. Supplies of alcohol products outside a duty suspension arrangement (i.e. goods supplied after excise duty has been paid) continue to be dealt with under the normal VAT arrangements and are not affected by the provisions outlined in this leaflet.

Alcohol Products supplied while held under Duty Suspension Arrangements

4. In the case of alcohol products from any source (imports, EU intra-Community acquisitions or home produced) which are supplied while held under a duty suspension arrangement, only the last such supply will form the basis for VAT liability and any previous supply, EU intra-Community acquisition or importation, will be disregarded. The VAT due on the last supply will not be chargeable on the VAT invoice issued at the time of supply but rather will be payable with the excise duty by the owner at the time of the removal of the goods from the duty suspension. Accordingly, where alcohol products are supplied while held under a duty suspension arrangement, VAT should not be charged by the supplier or shown on any invoice issued in respect of the supply.

Goods held under duty suspension arrangements which are the subject of an EU intra-Community supply or export.

5. Where alcohol products are supplied while held under a duty suspension arrangement and the goods leave the State as a result of such a supply, the normal VAT rules will continue to apply. For example, if the goods are supplied to a VAT registered trader in another EU Member State the supply will be zero rated. Likewise, if the goods are exported, the supply will be zero rated.

Home produced alcohol products which have not been the subject of a supply.

6. VAT is not payable on removal from the tax warehouse of home manufactured alcohol products which have not been the subject of a supply while under duty suspension. It should be noted in this context that the removal of alcohol products from one tax warehouse to another without a transfer of ownership taking place does not constitute a supply of the goods for VAT purposes.

7. Where a company supplies a consignment of its home manufactured alcohol products to a company with which it is grouped for VAT purposes, that supply, and any subsequent similar supplies between members of that VAT group, is disregarded for VAT purposes. The companies concerned will be required to produce, to the warehouse officer, a letter from the Revenue District responsible for their tax affairs confirming the grouping arrangement between them, and sales within the group will then be disregarded for the purpose of these arrangements.

EU Intra-Community Acquisitions of Alcohol Products

8. VAT chargeable on the EU intra-Community acquisition of alcohol products is payable at the same time as the excise duty is paid i.e. on removal of the goods from a tax warehouse for home consumption. It should be noted that in this case the VAT is not accounted for under the postponed accounting arrangements that apply to EU intra-Community acquisitions generally. If, following an EU intra-Community acquisition, the alcohol products in question are supplied while held under a duty suspension arrangement, the rules set out above apply and the EU intra-Community acquisition should be disregarded for VAT purposes.

Importations of Alcohol Products from outside the EU

9. VAT at point of entry is not chargeable on imported alcohol products being entered for an excise duty suspension arrangement (tax warehousing). Instead, the VAT due on the importation is payable with the excise duty on removal of the goods from duty suspension. If, following importation, the alcohol products in question are supplied while held under duty suspension, the rules set out above apply and the importation should be disregarded for VAT purposes.

Taxable Amount

10. In relation to EU intra-Community acquisitions and supplies, the amount on which VAT is chargeable is the invoiced price of the goods increased by the amount of the excise duty payable. In the case of importations, the taxable amount is the value for customs purposes increased by the amount of customs duty and excise duty payable.

Deferred Payment

11. The legislation relating to the collection of excise duty also applies to the collection of VAT under these arrangements. This means that where a

trader has the facility to defer payment of excise duty, payment of VAT can also be deferred to the same date.

Persons Authorised under Section 13A of the VAT Act

12.   Persons authorised to receive goods at the zero rate of VAT in accordance with section 13A of the VAT Act will not be required to pay the VAT due on removal by them of alcohol products from a tax warehouse or other duty suspension arrangement. This does not affect their liability to pay excise duty.

Forms to be Used

13.   The following forms should be used for payment of the excise duties and VAT:

    1.   excise duty entry (C&E 1087) for EU intra-Community acquisitions where the excise duty and VAT is being paid on arrival in the State;

    2.   SAD (import entry) for imports where the excise duty and VAT is being paid on arrival in the State;

    3.   home consumption warrant (C&E 1115) in respect of deliveries from warehouse for home consumption.

14.   In connection with point (c), it should be noted in particular that it is not permitted for warehouse keepers to produce single bulk warrants on behalf of a number of owners of goods - a separate warrant for each owner must be presented.

Deductibility for VAT Return

15.   Subject to the normal rules governing VAT deductibility, a trader is entitled to deduct the VAT charged under these arrangements in the VAT return for the period in which the liability arises (i.e. the period in which the VAT is paid with the excise duty). The evidence that the trader must retain in support of his claims to deductibility is as follows:

    1.   in the cases referred to in paragraphs 13(a) and (b) above, a monthly customs and excise statement where the trader uses the deferred payment/FACT schemes, or an official receipt in other cases;

    2.   in the case referred to in paragraph 13(c) above, a copy of the home consumption warrant signed and stamped by the warehouse officer.

Further information

16.   Enquiries regarding any issue contained in this Information Leaflet should be addressed to the Revenue District responsible for the taxpayer's affairs. Contact details for all Revenue Districts can be found on the Contact Details Page.

This leaflet is issued by:

VAT Appeals & Communications Branch ,
Indirect Taxes Division,
Stamping Building
Dublin Castle.

October 2008

This information leaflet which sets out the current practice at the date of its issue is intended for guidance only and does not purport to be a definitive legal interpretation of the provisions of the Value-Added Tax Act 1972 (as amended).

VALUE-ADDED TAX INFORMATION LEAFLET (OCTOBER 2008)

CONFERENCES – VAT DEDUCTIBILITY

Entitlement to deduct VAT incurred on accommodation in connection with attendance at qualifying conferences.

1.   Introduction

This information leaflet sets out the changes introduced by the Finance Act 2007 in respect of the entitlement to deduct input VAT incurred on attendance at certain business conferences with effect from 1 July 2007.

Prior to the enactment of the new provisions an accountable person could not claim a deduction for VAT incurred on costs for accommodation even where such expenditure was incurred in the course or furtherance of business. The new provisions allow an accountable person to deduct VAT incurred on accommodation in connection with the attendance by him or her or by his or her representative at a 'qualifying conference' as defined. A deduction may be made where the accommodation is provided at the conference venue or at a different location.

The entitlement to deduct input VAT relates solely to VAT incurred on costs of accommodation and does not include VAT incurred on expenditure on food or drink. In accordance with normal VAT rules, deductibility is allowed only where expenditure is incurred which is attributable to taxable supplies by a business.

2.   Definitions

'Delegate' means an accountable person or an accountable person's employee or agent who attends a qualifying conference in the course or furtherance of that person's taxable business.

'Qualifying conference' means a conference or meeting in the course of furtherance of business organised to cater for fifty or more delegates. It must take place on or after 1 July 2007 at a venue designed and constructed for the purposes of hosting fifty or more delegates. The person responsible for organising the conference must issue in writing the details of the conference to each accountable person who attends or sends a delegate. These details must include-

1.   the location and dates of the conference;

2.   the nature of the business being conducted;

3.   the number of delegates for whom the conference is organised, and

4.   the name, business address and VAT registration number of the person responsible for organising the conference.

'Qualifying accommodation' means the supply to a delegate of a service consisting of the letting of immovable goods or accommodation covered in paragraph (xiii) of the Sixth Schedule, for a maximum period starting from the night prior to the date on which the qualifying conference commences and ending on the date on which the qualifying conference concludes.

Effectively, the accommodation covered is that normally provided in a hotel or guesthouse and the maximum period for which deductions or refunds of VAT on accommodation may be claimed is from the night prior to the date the conference begins to the date the conference concludes. In this regard VAT incurred in respect of accommodation for the night the conference ends may be claimed. Where a delegate attends for only part of the duration of the conference, entitlement to deduct the VAT incurred on the accommodation is reduced accordingly. The following examples illustrate the position.

Example 1

A delegate attends a two-day conference which begins on a Thursday morning and concludes at midday on Friday. The delegate arrives at the venue on Wednesday evening and obtains accommodation for three nights. The three-night stay would be viewed as qualifying accommodation and so the VAT incurred on that accommodation would be deductible.

Example 2

A delegate attends part of a two-day conference which begins on a Thursday morning and concludes at midday Friday. The delegate attends on Thursday only. The delegate arrives at the venue on Wednesday evening and obtains accommodation for three nights. Only two of those three nights accommodation would be viewed as qualifying accommodation. The VAT incurred on the accommodation for those two nights only would be deductible.

Example 3

A delegate attends a two-day conference starting on Thursday morning and ending midday on Friday. The delegate arrives on Wednesday and obtains accommodation from Wednesday to Saturday night inclusive. In these circumstances the three nights from Wednesday to Friday are qualifying accommodation. The Saturday night is not and the VAT charge in respect of the Saturday night accommodation is not deductible.

3.   Claims by accountable persons established in Ireland

Claims for VAT input credit under this provision should be made on the VAT return in the normal way. Expenditure on accommodation is treated as an overhead cost and VAT charged on it is deductible insofar as it can be attributed to taxable supplies made by a business. Illustrative examples are as follows.

Example 4

A delegate to a conference is engaged in a totally deductible business, e.g. a salesperson in a computer manufacturing company. The subject matter of the conference is selling techniques. In this case the VAT incurred on qualifying accommodation related to that conference would be fully deductible by the manufacturing company.

Example 5

A delegate to a conference is engaged in a non-deductible activity e.g. insurance, which is exempt from VAT. In this case no deductibility would arise in respect of the VAT incurred in respect of accommodation related to that delegate's attendance at a conference.

Example 6

A delegate engaged in financial services, for example, a business involving partially taxable/partially exempt supplies attends a qualifying conference covering banking (a non-deductible activity) and leasing (a deductible activity). In this case the VAT on the accommodation charges associated with attending the qualifying conference must be apportioned between the amount deductible and that which is non-deductible. There are various practical methods for apportioning the VAT and the accountable person may use whatever apportionment method he or she normally uses in relation to overhead costs. Further information on apportionment rules is provided in the leaflet entitled Value-Added Tax: A Guide to Apportionment of Input Tax.

Example 7

If an accountable person attends a conference on a topic which is unrelated to that person's accountable business, the accommodation charges associated with attending that conference are attributable to non-taxable activities and are not deductible for VAT purposes.

4.   Claims by businesses established abroad

Claims for refunds of VAT incurred by delegates from abroad on qualifying accommodation in Ireland may also be made by accountable persons established abroad in accordance with the Eighth or Thirteenth VAT Directives. The Eighth Directive caters for refunds to accountable persons established in other EU Member States. The Thirteenth Directive caters for refunds to businesses established outside the EU. Entitlement to repayment will arise where the business established abroad is such that it would be taxable if carried on in the State. Claims may be submitted with the appropriate documentation to the following: Office of the Revenue Commissioners, Strategic Planning Division, VAT Unregistered Repayments, 3rd Floor, River House, Charlotte Quay, Limerick. (Telephone Lo-call 1890 252449 or 0035 36 1212799, Fax 00353 61 402125), e-mail: unregvat@revenue.ie

5.   Invoices and other documentation

5.1   A VAT refund can be claimed only on foot of a valid VAT invoice for accommodation. This would be issued in the normal way to the accountable person by a hotel or by a VAT registered conference organiser. The accommodation charge must be invoiced to the accountable person. It must not be invoiced to an agent or employee. In addition the accommodation charge must be separately identified from any other goods or services provided e.g. food, drink, etc.

5.2   In addition to having a valid VAT invoice the accountable person must retain in his or her records details in writing, provided by the organiser of the qualifying conference, as set out in paragraph 2. The legislation does not define a conference organiser. The term can refer to anyone who is involved in organising a conference whether this is, for example, the hotel hosting the conference, or a professional conference organiser. In this regard the legislation provides that a conference organiser does not also have to be the accommodation provider. The important thing from the claimant's point of view is to ensure that the written details referred to in paragraph 2 are made available to him or her by the organiser.

5.3   Claims under the Eighth and Thirteenth Directives by businesses established outside of the State will only be accepted as valid if accompanied by a valid invoice and by the details set out in paragraph 2.

6.   Records

VAT legislation requires that accountable persons must retain all records that affect their VAT liabilities for a period of six years. This six-year rule also applies to the details, set out in paragraph 2, which must be issued to the accountable person by the conference organiser. The organiser, whether or not he or she is an accountable person, is also required to retain these details as part of his or her own records.

7.   Further information

Enquiries regarding any issue contained in this Information Leaflet should be addressed to the Revenue District responsible for the taxpayer's affairs. Contact details for all Revenue Districts.

This leaflet is issued by:

VAT Appeals & Communications Branch,
Indirect Taxes Division,
Stamping Building,
Dublin Castle.

October 2008

This information leaflet which sets out the current practice at the date of its issue is intended for guidance only and does not purport to be a definitive legal interpretation of the provisions of the Value-Added Tax Act 1972 (as amended).

VALUE-ADDED TAX INFORMATION LEAFLET (OCTOBER 2008)

DISTANCE SALES IN EU

What are distance sales?

Distance selling in the EU occurs when a supplier in one EU Member State sells goods to a person in another Member State who is not registered for VAT and the supplier is responsible for the delivery of the goods. It includes mail order sales, phone or tele-sales or physical goods ordered over the internet.

Under the distance selling arrangements, sales to customers in other Member States who are not registered for VAT are liable to VAT in the Member State of the supplier provided that the threshold appropriate to the Member State of the customer is not breached (see **Thresholds** below). Where sales exceed the threshold in any particular Member State, the supplier must register and account for VAT in that Member State.

Distance sales to the State

Where the value of distance sales to persons in this State by a supplier in another Member State exceeds or is likely to exceed €35,000 in a calendar year, that supplier must register for VAT in this State and must account for VAT at the appropriate Irish rates. If the threshold is not exceeded, the supplier may, nevertheless, opt to register and account for VAT in this State on his or her distance sales.

Distance sales from the State

An Irish supplier who makes distance sales to customers in other Member States who are not registered for VAT, is liable to Irish VAT on such sales until the value of the sales reaches the threshold applying in that other Member State. Once the value of the supplier's sales exceeds the threshold in the other Member State, the supplier is obliged to register in that Member State and account for VAT at the rates applicable there. If the appropriate threshold is not exceeded, the supplier may, nevertheless, opt to account for VAT in the Member State to which the distance sales are made.

It should be noted that a supplier who is engaged in distance sales to several Member States is required to register in each Member State in which the value of the distance sales exceeds the appropriate threshold.

Thresholds

Under the EU VAT arrangements, Member States were required to adopt a distance sales threshold of either €35,000 or €100,000. Ireland has opted for €35,000.

The value of distance sales of excisable goods should not be taken into account for the purposes of determining whether or not the threshold has been exceeded. If the threshold, excluding the value of excisable goods, is not exceeded the supplier may continue to account for VAT in the Member State from which supplies are made.

Any supplier who makes distance sales of excisable goods e.g. alcohol, tobacco and oil to another Member State must register and account for VAT in that

Member State, since distance sales of excisable goods are always subject to VAT in the Member State to which they are dispatched.

Goods excluded from the distance selling arrangements

Sales of new means of transport are excluded from the distance selling arrangements. These sales are always intra-Community acquisitions and the person acquiring the new means of transport must pay VAT in the Member State of destination.

Obligations of traders

If a foreign supplier is obliged to register for VAT in the State because the annual value of his or her distance sales to the State exceeds or is likely to exceed €35,000 s/he must register for VAT. Applications for registration are made using Forms TR1/TR2, which are available on the Revenue website under Registration Forms.

Once registered for VAT the distance seller will be obliged to;

- calculate VAT due on the value of his or her distance sales,

- complete the periodic VAT 3 return, showing the VAT liability,

- send the completed return to the Collector-General, together with payment of any VAT due, within the prescribed time limit (Returns made be made using Revenue's ROS online services via the Revenue website),

- keep proper records so as to enable the VAT liability to be determined,

- make those records available for inspection by Revenue on request.

If an Irish supplier is obliged to register for VAT in another Member State because the value of his or her distance sales to that Member State exceeds the relevant threshold, s/he should contact the fiscal authority of the Member State concerned who will provide details of the requirements for registration.

Intrastat - distance sales from the State

A supplier who is registered for VAT in the State and also registered in another Member State because of his or her distance sales to that Member State must include the value of such sales in the INTRASTAT Box E1 of the Irish VAT 3 return. However, a person who is registered for VAT in Ireland should **not** include the value of distance sales to other Member States in Box E1 where s/he is not registered for VAT in those Member States.

Intrastat - distance sales to the State

A supplier, registered in another Member State who is also registered in the State because of his or her distance sales to the State, should include the value of such sales in the INTRASTAT Box E2 of the Irish VAT return.

Internet

Sales of goods ordered via the internet but physically supplied are considered to be distance sales for VAT purposes. However digitised goods, that is goods for downloading by the customer via the internet are considered to be services, within the meaning of the Fourth Schedule for VAT purposes.

Further information

Enquiries regarding any issue contained in this Information Leaflet should be addressed to the Revenue District responsible for the taxpayer's affairs. Contact details for all Revenue Districts are available on the revenue website at: Contact Details

VAT Appeals & Communications Branch,
Indirect Taxes Division,
Stamping Building,
Dublin Castle.

October 2008

This information leaflet which sets out the current practice at the date of its issue is intended for guidance only and does not purport to be a definitive legal interpretation of the provisions of the Value-Added Tax Act 1972 (as amended).

VALUE-ADDED TAX INFORMATION LEAFLET (OCTOBER 2008)

ELECTRICITY MARKET

VAT Treatment under the Single Electricity Market (SEM)

1.   Background

1.1   A Single Electricity Market (SEM) for the entire island of Ireland has been introduced with effect from 1 November 2007. The SEM is a pool-based mechanism for the sale and purchase of wholesale electricity across the island of Ireland. Entities that generate electricity for sale (generators) sell their electricity through the pool, and entities that sell electricity direct to the final consumer (suppliers) buy their electricity from the pool, at the prevailing pool price for any given half-hour trading period. The pool price is determined based on the prices at which generators are prepared to sell their electricity in any given trading period and looking at the predicted demand for that trading period. Financial settlement of the trades in the pool will take place in accordance with the rules set out in the Trading and Settlement Code for the SEM.

1.2   The SEM is jointly regulated by the Commission for Energy Regulation (in the Republic of Ireland) and The Northern Ireland Authority for Utility Regulation (in Northern Ireland). To operate the market, a Single Electricity Market Operator (SEMO) has been established. The SEMO is a joint venture between EirGrid who is licensed as market operator in the Republic of Ireland and SONI Ltd who is licensed as market operator in Northern Ireland. The SEMO will:

- administer the mandatory pooling arrangements created by the SEM Trading and Settlement Code;

- manage market operations in both jurisdictions;

- have a physical presence in both the Republic of Ireland and Northern Ireland, and

- be responsible for calculating the price of electricity and recording all transactions within the SEM between generators and suppliers of electricity.

1.3.   The introduction of the SEM necessitated joint approval by the Revenue Commissioners in the Republic of Ireland and Her Majesty's Revenue & Customs (HMRC) in the UK on how VAT is to be operated in relation to generation and supply of electricity on the island of Ireland. Following discussions between the Revenue Commissioners and HMRC and consultation with relevant stakeholders, agreement has now been reached on the operation of VAT in the SEM. This Information Leaflet sets out the agreed VAT treatment.

2.   VAT registration - participants

Participants (generators and suppliers) in the SEM will be registered for VAT on the basis of their place of establishment in either the Republic of Ireland or Northern Ireland.

3.   VAT registration - SEMO

3.1   The role of the SEMO results in it supplying services to SEM participants that are subject to VAT. The SEMO is registered for VAT as a joint venture, in both the Republic of Ireland and the UK, in respect of these services. The normal VAT rules relating to the supply of services apply to the services supplied by the SEMO and those services are subject to the rates of VAT applicable in Ireland and the UK, as appropriate.

3.2.   In the context of its operation of the SEM pool, the SEMO receives supplies of goods and services. These supplies are subject to the normal VAT legislation in force in the Republic of Ireland or the UK, as appropriate.

4.   Supplies of electricity through the Pool

General

4.1   The role of the SEMO is restricted to the operation of the pool and it does not take ownership of any of the electricity supplied between participants. As part of that role, the SEMO is responsible for calculating the price of the electricity supplied between the participants.

4.2   At the end of each settlement period the SEMO will provide each participant with a settlement document, which will include the VAT amount that is due to be paid by that participant to the Revenue Commissioners or to HMRC depending on the jurisdiction in which the participant is established. The settlement document will be acceptable to both the Revenue Commissioners and HMRC as the equivalent of a VAT invoice, and there will be no further requirement on participants to issue VAT invoices regarding the supply of electricity through the pool.

4.3   Participants operating within the pool will use these SEMO settlement documents as the basis for accounting for the output tax due on their supplies or recovering the input tax on purchases, as appropriate.

4.4   Information held by the SEMO will be available to the Revenue Commissioners and HMRC on request.

5.   Cross-border supplies

5.1   Operation of the SEM will involve cross-border supplies of electricity. In the case of the cross-border supply of electricity from a generator to a supplier, the obligation to account for VAT rests with the recipient who is obliged to self account, on a reverse charge basis, for the VAT due on the supply at the appropriate rate (13.5% where the recipient is established in the Republic of Ireland; 17.5% where the recipient is established in the UK). However, the nature of the pooling arrangements in the SEM means that both generators and suppliers will be unable to positively identify the cross-border element of their respective sales and purchases. Of necessity, therefore, the liability of recipient companies to account for VAT on the reverse charge basis in relation to cross-border supplies will be estimated by the SEMO. The production of electricity on the island of

Ireland at present is such that, in overall terms, the cross-border element will be from Northern Ireland to the Republic of Ireland.

5.2.   For the initial 14 months of operation of the Pool, the SEMO will provide both Revenue authorities with the estimated data to be used for this purpose. This will be based on the projections (used in setting up the SEM) of electricity:

- generated and supplied in Northern Ireland;

- generated and supplied in the Republic of Ireland;

- generated in Northern Ireland and supplied to the Republic of Ireland, and

- generated in the Republic of Ireland and supplied in Northern Ireland.

5.3   For each subsequent year estimates will be based on the actual trading for the previous year. At year-end the estimates may be compared against the actual energy flows and the rate of VAT applied to settlement documents for that year adjusted as appropriate. Ad hoc year-end settlement documents may be issued to participants reflecting any adjustments in the amount of VAT.

6.   Settlement documents

6.1   All SEM transactions will be considered part of the supply of electricity and subject to VAT at the rate in force in either the Republic of Ireland or UK, as appropriate. A "blended" calculation (being VAT at 13.5%/17.5% as appropriate on the domestic element of the supply with no VAT due on the balance as this will be subject to a reverse charge by the relevant participants) will be applied by the SEMO based on the estimated cross border flows and applied to relevant supplies in accordance with the Trading and Settlement Code. An example of a blended computation is contained in Appendix 1 of this Information Leaflet. The settlement document will show the VAT due to be paid to the relevant jurisdiction. The example at Appendix 2 of this Leaflet outlines the entries that are required on the VAT returns of relevant participants.

6.2   The SEMO will also, as a temporary measure, issue an additional summary document (bi-monthly to relevant participants in the Republic of Ireland and monthly to participants in Northern Ireland) identifying the total value of cross-border supplies during the period in question. This information will enable participants to meet their intra-EU VAT accounting obligations, including application of the reverse charge by those receiving cross-border supplies. With the system now live since 1 November 2007, the SEMO will, as a priority, work towards including this information as part of the normal settlement document.

7.   **Supplies of electricity outside the Pool**

Any trading of electricity outside of the Pool, in which the SEMO is not involved in any part of the transaction, will be subject to the VAT legislation in force in the Republic of Ireland or the UK, as appropriate.

8   SEMO supplies to participants

Invoices issued by the SEMO for its own services, as distinct from settlement documents issued in respect of the sale and purchase of electricity, will be subject to the VAT legislation in the Republic of Ireland or the UK, dependant on the VAT registration (Irish or UK, as appropriate) under which it is issued. Generally, these services will be supplied by the SEMO within the relevant jurisdiction – it is not anticipated that a cross border supply of such services will arise. Thus, supplies to a Northern Ireland participant will be supplied under the SEMO's UK VAT registration, while supplies to a Republic of Ireland participant will be supplied under the SEMO's Irish VAT registration. In the unlikely event that cross-border supplies of the SEMO's services arise, the VAT position will depend on the nature of the supplies and the VAT treatment will follow the normal place of supply rules.

9   Retention of Records

The time limit for retention of records will be six years for both the SEMO and the SEM participants.

10   Contracts for Differences

10.1   A feature of the SEM is that it is anticipated that Contracts for Differences (CFDs) may arise.

10.2   A Contract for Difference is an agreement through which parties can effectively fix the price of a price-volatile commodity, by reference to the difference between the fixed contract price and the market price. That difference is paid after the trading period. In this way the parties can hedge their exposure to price fluctuations.

10.3.   In the context of the SEM, generators and suppliers may enter into CFDs, which will specify a fixed or indexed price for electricity (strike price) at which the parties have agreed to sell and buy electricity. Where in any trading period the pool price exceeds the strike price the generator pays the supplier the difference between the two. Similarly, where the strike price exceeds the pool price in any trading period the supplier will pay any difference to the generator.

10.4   CFDs are completely outside the pool trading and settlement arrangements, under which the sale of the electricity itself takes place. CFDs are exempt from VAT on the basis that they are considered to be a financial transaction and are not connected with the supply of electricity. Thus, it will be necessary for participants who trade in CFDs to apportion the VAT input credit to take account of their exempt income. The apportionment should be agreed with the participant's local Revenue District.

11   Further Information

Enquiries regarding any issue contained in this Information Leaflet should be addressed to the Revenue District responsible for the taxpayer's affairs.

This leaflet is issued by

VAT Appeals and Communications Branch,
Indirect Taxes Division,
Dublin Castle.

October 2008

Appendix 1 - Computation of blended calculation

The diagram below illustrates the flow of electricity, (expressed in € millions), in and out of the SEM pool. The figures in brackets shows the electricity expressed as a percentage of total generation and total supply.

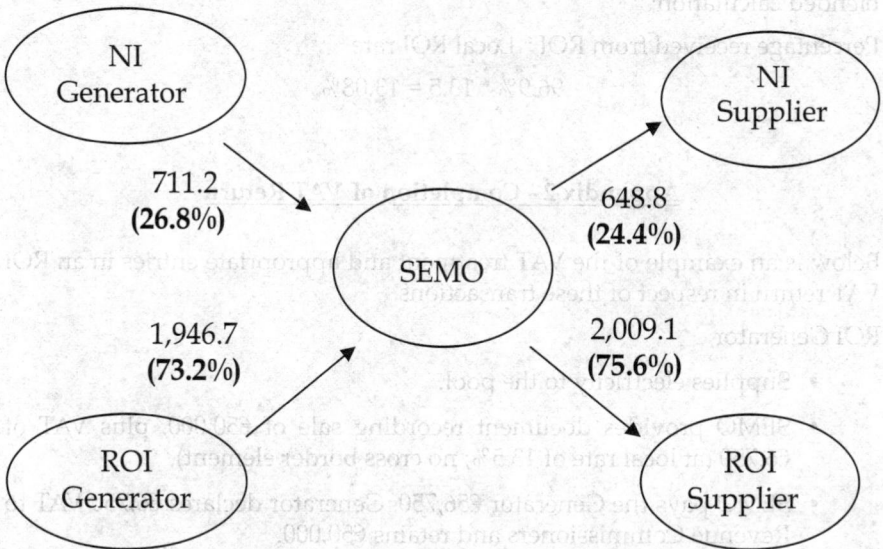

Total Generated = 2657.9m

NI Generator

Assuming that all electricity generated in NI goes first to NI suppliers, the NI generators' position is as follows:

Generates:	711.2
To NI:	648.8
To ROI:	62.4

The amount of cross border supply (to ROI) represents 8.77% of the total amount generated in NI. Therefore 91.23% generated represents local supply. Effectively this means that 91.23% is taxed at 17.5% (local UK rate) and 8.77% is zero-rated as an intra-Community supply. In order to tax the whole amount generated as one, a blended calculation is carried out as follows:

Percentage supplied to NI * Local UK Rate
91.23% * 17.5 = 15.97%

Therefore, the total amount generated by a NI generator is liable to VAT at the blended calculation of 15.97%.

ROI Supplier

Following the same logic as above, an ROI supplier receives 96.9% (1946.7/2009.1) of its electricity from ROI generators and 3.1% from NI generators. Effectively, this means 96.9% of electricity is taxed at 13.5% and 3.1% zero-rated under the reverse charge mechanism. See below for the blended calculation:

Percentage received from ROI * Local ROI rate

$$96.9\% * 13.5 = 13.08\%$$

Appendix 2 - Completion of VAT Return

Below is an example of the VAT treatment and appropriate entries in an ROI VAT return in respect of these transactions.

ROI Generator

- Supplies electricity to the pool.

- SEMO provides document recording sale of €50,000, plus VAT of €6,750 (at local rate of 13.5%; no cross border element).

- SEMO pays the Generator €56,750. Generator declares €6,750 VAT to Revenue Commissioners and retains €50,000.

> VAT Return
>
> Box T1: €6,750
> Net VAT Payable: €6,750

- Return of Trading Details required annually.*

ROI Supplier

- Purchases electricity from the pool.

- Invoiced by the SEMO for purchase of €40,000 plus VAT of €5,232 (at blended calculation of 13.08%, shown in Appendix 1).

- SEMO also provides a document showing the total value of energy supplied, split between local and cross border acquisitions according to the estimated percentage split; 96.9% local and 3.1% cross-border.

- Supplier pays the SEMO €45,232.

- Supplier calculates VAT on reverse charge element, [€40,000 * 3.1% = €1,240 @13.5% = €167.4]. This amount is declared as output tax in Box T1 and is also added to the actual VAT amount incurred.

```
┌─────────────────────────────────────┐
│  VAT Return                          │
│                                      │
│  Box T1: €167.40                     │
│  Box T2: €5,399.40                   │
│  Box E2: €1,240 [€40,000 * 3.1%]     │
│  Net VAT Deducted: €5,232            │
└─────────────────────────────────────┘
```

- Return of Trading Details required annually.*

* ROI participants will be required to submit a return of trading details annually on form VAT 3G(A). Details of the VAT-exclusive values for sales, purchases, importations and intra-Community acquisitions and intra-Community supplies made by participant in the period covered by the return must be included. This is an existing requirement for all taxable persons and there is no additional burden for participants in the SEM.

VALUE-ADDED TAX INFORMATION LEAFLET (OCTOBER 2008)

eSERVICES & BROADCASTING

Introduction

This document explains the different measures regarding the value-added-tax arrangements applicable to radio and television broadcasting services and certain electronically supplied services, to ensure that where these services are consumed in the EU then they should be taxed in the EU, and not taxed if they are consumed outside the EU.

- Electronically supplied services (eServices)
- Place of supply rules for eServices
- Special scheme for eServices
- Broadcasting Services

Please note that **broadcasting services do not come within the scope** of the definition of electronically supplied services (eServices).

These measures deal with the place of supply rules for these services, and include an **optional** special scheme for non-EU suppliers supplying digital products into the EU.

1.   Electronically Supplied Services (eServices)

What are electronically supplied services?

1.1   An 'electronically supplied service' is one that is delivered over the Internet (or an electronic network which is reliant on the Internet or similar network for its provision) and is heavily dependent on information technology for its supply - i.e. the service is essentially automated, involving minimal human intervention and in the absence of information technology does not have viability. An indicative list of such services is, as follows:

- **Digitised products** (such as software and changes to or upgrades of software);
- **Services** which provide or support a business or personal presence on an electronic network (for example, a website);
- **Services automatically generated from computer,** via the Internet or an electronic network, in response to specific data input by the customer;
- **Other services** which are automated and dependent on the Internet or an electronic network for their provision.

In general, the use of the Internet or other electronic networks by parties to communicate with respect to transactions or to facilitate trading does not, any more than the use of a phone or fax, affect the normal VAT rules that apply. For example, where parties simply use the Internet to convey information in the course of a business transaction (e.g. email), this does not change the nature of that transaction. This differs from a supply that is completely dependent on the

Internet in order to be carried out (e.g. searching and retrieving information from a database with no human intervention).

Detailed examples of electronically supplied services

1.2   Tables giving examples of transactions that are either included or excluded from the definition of 'electronically supplied services', are reproduced in Appendices 1 & 2.

1.3   Supplies that are regarded as being electronically supplied (appendix 1) are treated in accordance with the rules laid down in EU Directive 2002/38/EC which was transposed into national law with effect from 1 July 2003. Supplies that are regarded as not being electronically supplied (appendix 2) are treated in accordance with other place of supply rules.

1.4   Particular care should be taken where a service includes both electronic and other elements. Such composite or multiple transactions must generally be considered on a case-by-case basis. Where any doubt remains reference should be made to the local Revenue District.

The VAT rate

1.5   Electronically supplied services are taxable at the standard rate in each EU Member State, unless an exemption applies in a EU Member State. For example, if the 'traditional' forms of supply of gambling is exempt in a EU Member State, it would also be exempt in that EU Member State if it is supplied as an electronically supplied service.

2.   Place of Supply Rules For Electronic Services

Business-to-Business (B2B)

2.1   The new Business-to-Business (B2B) place of supply rules apply to all such supplies where the recipient is established in a EU Member State for electronically supplied services.

The rules provide that the place of supply is the place where the customer has established his or her business. The reverse charge rule applies, under which the customer must account for the VAT.

Business-to-Consumer (B2C)

2.2   The Business-to-Consumer (B2C) place of supply rules for electronically supplied services provides that, where a non-EU business supplies to a private consumer in any EU Member State, the place of supply is the place where the consumer normally resides. For example, if a Canadian business supplies electronic services to an Irish consumer the place of supply (and of taxation) is Ireland.

2.3   Suppliers of these services are liable to register and account for VAT in every EU Member State where they have private customers. However, an optional special scheme is available whereby **non-EU businesses can register in one EU Member State** only - this is covered in section 4.

2.4   The B2C place of supply rule for electronically supplied services supplied by an EU business to a private consumer in the EU, is still the EU Member State in which the supplier is established.

B2B: Verification of business status

2.5   **How can a supplier verify their customer's business status?**

For B2B supplies within the EU the evidence required at the time of the transaction would normally be the customer's VAT registration number and country identification code prefix. The number must conform to the format for the registration person's EU Member State (VAT numbers can be checked online in the VIES database.)

It is possible to verify Irish VAT registration numbers with the VIMA Office that can be contacted at vimahelp@revenue.ie. Other EU Member States may have similar systemsto check the validity of VAT registration numbers.

Under normal trading practices businesses will often know their business customers and, in such cases, they will not therefore need to routinely check all VAT numbers quoted, provided that the numbers conform to the correct country format.

If you are unable to confirm that the customer is in business or if there remains any doubt about the use of a VAT registration number, VAT should be charged as appropriate on all supplies to that customer including supplies that have already been made.

The position in relation to various supplies is summarised in the table below.

Table 2.1 - place of supply rules for electronic services

Supplied from	Supplied to	Place of Supply
Business in Ireland	Business in Ireland	Ireland
Business in Ireland	Business in other EU State	Other EU State
Business in Ireland	Business outside EU	Outside EU (no VAT)
Business in Ireland	Private consumer in Ireland	Ireland
Business in Ireland	Private consumer in other EU State	Ireland
Business in Ireland	Private consumer outside EU	Outside EU (no VAT)
Business in other EU State	Business in Ireland	Ireland
Business in other EU State	Private consumer in Ireland	Other EU State
Business outside EU	Business in Ireland	Ireland
Business outside EU	Private consumer in Ireland	Ireland

3.   Special Scheme for Electronic Services

A special scheme, introduced to reduce the compliance burden and administrative costs for taxable persons, is in operation.

Broad outline of the special scheme

3.1   The special scheme enables the non-EU supplier to choose a EU Member State in which to register for and pay VAT, regardless of the EU Member State in which the suppliers private consumer resides. Once registered the supplier makes VAT returns to that EU Member State, declaring the VAT due on all the on-line sales to consumers within the EU. The rate of VAT is the standard rate in the country in which the consumer resides. A special on-line return form is provided under which the supplier must provide a breakdown of all electronic supplies to customers in each EU Member State. Payment is made to a designated account in the EU Member State of registration. That EU Member State re-distributes the VAT receipts to other Member States in accordance with the amounts due as declared by the supplier.

3.2   For example, an Australian business supplies on-line digital products to private B2C in Ireland, France and Germany. It opts to register for the special scheme in Ireland. It charges Irish VAT to its Irish customers, French VAT to its French customers and German VAT to its German customers. It registers electronically in Ireland, puts all the details on a single quarterly electronic return and pays all the VAT due to the Irish Revenue each quarter. The Irish Revenue retains the Irish VAT and distributes the French and German VAT to those countries.

What businesses are eligible to use the special scheme?

3.3   A business is eligible to use the special scheme if that business:

- supplies electronically supplied services to private consumers who reside in the EU,
- is not established within the EU, and
- is not otherwise registered (or required to be registered) for VAT in any EU Member State.

How does the scheme operate in Ireland?

3.4   The Revenue Commissioners have set up a register of non-EU suppliers who opt to register in this country under the scheme. Registration is only be accessible through the Revenue Online System (ROS). Suppliers must supply certain details (specified below) to ROS in order to register under the scheme. A section on ROS, especially for non-EU customers, facilitates applicants in the registration process.

3.5   A supplier registered under the scheme is allocated an identification number (the special VAT number for electronic services supplies) and a digital certificate by ROS. Suppliers on the Irish register use their digital certificates to access the system via ROS. Suppliers must submit special VAT returns and pay Revenue the VAT due in respect of their supplies in all EU Member States including Ireland within 20 days of the end of each calendar quarter. Payment must be made in € to a bank account designated by the Revenue Commissioners.

Registration - information needed and procedures

3.6   The non-EU supplier must furnish the following information to Revenue in order to register under the scheme:

- Name and postal address
- Electronic addresses including website addresses
- National tax number, if any
- A statement that the supplier is not registered for VAT within the EU
- The date from which the supply of electronically supplied services to EU consumers commences.

3.7 The information must be supplied electronically, on the registration form available on ROS. When registration is confirmed, Revenue will email the applicant his or her special VAT number, together with details on how the digital certificate is to be retrieved.

3.8 Must a business be making supplies before registering?

Not necessarily. On registration, the supplier must state the date from which the supply of electronically supplied services to EU consumers commences. For example, a supplier could register in August on the basis that the supplies would start from 1 September. Note however that nil returns must be submitted if there are no supplies in a calendar quarter.

3.9 **Must a business make supplies in Ireland in order to register here?**

No. Businesses who only make, or intend making, supplies under the special scheme to customers in other EU Member States may register for the special scheme in Ireland if they so wish. The VAT due in those other EU Member States will be paid to the Revenue Commissioners, who will distribute it to the relevant tax authorities.

The procedure for submitting VAT returns and making payments

3.10 The special VAT returns are due for each calendar quarter (30 September, 31 December, 31 March and 30 June) and must be submitted by the 20th of the month at the end of the quarter to which the return relates. For example, the return for the calendar quarter ending on 30 September 2007 must be submitted by 20 October 2007. The VAT due in respect of supplies in all EU Member States must be paid at the same time as the return, into a bank account designated by the Revenue Commissioners. Nil returns must also be submitted.

3.11 The special VAT return must show the following information:

- The non-EU supplier's identification number.
- For each EU Member State where VAT is due, the total value (excluding VAT), the applicable VAT rate and the amount of VAT due at each applicable rate in respect of electronically supplied services for the quarter.
- The total VAT payable in all EU Member States.

3.12 The special VAT returns must be filed electronically on ROS for the special scheme, using the digital certificates for access. Suppliers should give both their VAT number and details on the relevant quarterly period to the bank when making payments. Receipts for moneys received will be issued to the supplier via the ROS system.

VAT on purchases

3.12 A person from outside the EU who makes supplies in Ireland under the scheme is not entitled to deduct input VAT using the VAT return. However, the supplier is entitled to claim a refund under the terms of the 13th Directive in respect of VAT paid on goods or services used for the purposes of taxable activities falling under the special scheme. Claims in respect of the VAT paid in Ireland should be made to the Revenue Commissioners under the standard 13th Directive procedures. For further information contact unregvat@revenue.ie

Records

3.13 Suppliers registered for the special scheme must keep records of all transactions affecting their VAT liability - for example, the value and date of the transaction, the customer's name and location, etc. These records must be kept for 10 years and must be made available electronically, on request, to the tax authorities in the EU Member State where the supplier is registered for the special scheme and to each EU Member State where the supplier's customers reside.

Changes in details supplied or business circumstances

3.14 Suppliers under the scheme are required to notify Revenue if there are any changes in the details provided under paragraph 3.6 above (name and address, websites, etc.) or if their taxable activity changes to the extent that they are no longer eligible to use the special scheme. For example, if the supplier begins to supply goods or services in the EU, he/she will be liable to register for VAT under the normal rules and will cease to be eligible for the scheme.

3.15 Revenue may exclude from the scheme suppliers who fail to comply with the provisions of the scheme.

Suppliers not registered for the special scheme in Ireland

3.16 Non-EU businesses who supply electronic services to consumers in Ireland and are registered for the special scheme in another EU Member State must pay the Irish VAT due to the tax authorities in that other EU Member State, under the terms of their Special Scheme. Such businesses must also keep records of the Irish (and other) transactions.

3.17 Non-EU businesses who supply electronic services to consumers in Ireland and are not registered for the special scheme in any EU Member State must register in Ireland and account for the Irish VAT in respect of those supplies, under the normal VAT rules. These businesses must also register and account for VAT in each and every other EU Member State where supplies are made.

4.   Radio and Television Broadcasting Services

The new place of supply rules

4.1   The new place of supply rules provide that these services are taxed in the EU Member State of consumption. In particular,

- Where businesses supply radio and television broadcasting services to businesses in the EU, the place of supply is where the customer has established his or her business. The reverse charge rule applies, under which the business customer will account for the VAT. This is similar to the B2B rule for electronic services - see paragraph 2.1

- Where non-EU businesses supply radio and television broadcasting services to private consumers in Ireland, the place of taxation is Ireland and the supplier must register and account for the VAT here. This is similar to the B2C rule for electronic services - see paragraph 2.2. However, there is no optional special scheme for non-EU suppliers of radio and TV broadcasting services.

Some examples

4.2   Accountable persons - for example VAT registered pubs and clubs - who buy in broadcasting services from suppliers established in other EU Member States or outside the EU (by means of a satellite dish and decoder), are taxed in Ireland under the reverse charge procedure. This is a change to the current rule, which says the place of taxation is where the supplier is established.

4.3   Private individuals in Ireland who pay for broadcasting services supplied by non-EU suppliers (e.g. 'pay per view') are taxable in Ireland under the new rules. The non-EU supplier is obliged to register and account for VAT in Ireland in respect of all his or her supplies to private individuals in the State.

Appendix 1

Examples of services regarded as being electronically supplied

Example 1: Web site supply, web-hosting and distance maintenance of programmes and equipment

- Website hosting and webpage hosting
- Automated, online distance maintenance of programmes
- Remote systems administration
- Online data warehousing (i.e. where specific data is stored and retrieved electronically)
- Online supply of on-demand disc space

Example 2: Software and updating thereof

- Accessing or downloading software (e.g. procurement/accountancy programmes, anti-virus software) plus updates.

- Bannerblockers (software to block banner adverts showing).
- Download drivers, such as software that interfaces PC with peripheral equipment (e.g. printers).
- Online automated installation of filters on websites.
- Online automated installation of firewalls.

Example 3: Images

- Accessing or downloading desktop themes
- Accessing or downloading photographic or pictorial images or screensavers

Example 4: Text and information

- The digitised content of books and other electronic publications
- Subscription to online newspaper and journals
- Weblogs and website statistics
- Online news, traffic information and weather reports
- Online information generated automatically by software from specific data input by the customer, such as legal and financial data (e.g. continually updated stock market data)
- The provision of advertising space (e.g. banner ads on a website/ webpage)

Example 5: Making databases available

- Use of search engines and Internet directories.

Example 6: Music

- Accessing or downloading of music onto PCs, mobile phones, etc.
- Accessing or downloading of jingles, excerpts, ringtones, or other sounds.

Example 7: Films

- Accessing or downloading of films.

Example 8: Broadcasts and events - political, cultural, artistic, sporting, scientific and entertainment

- Web-based broadcasting that is only provided over the internet or similar electronic network and is not simultaneously broadcast over a traditional radio or television network (as opposed to example 4, appendix 2).

Example 9: Games, including games of chance and gambling games

- Downloads of games onto PCs, mobile phones, etc.
- Accessing automated on-line games which are dependent on the internet, or other similar electronic networks, where players are remote from one another.

Example 10: Distance teaching

• Teaching that is automated and dependent on the Internet or similar electronic network to function, including virtual classrooms (as opposed to example 2, appendix 2).

• Workbooks completed by pupil on-line and marked automatically, without human intervention

Example 11: items not explicitly listed in examples 1-5

• Online auction services (to the extent that they are not already considered to be web-hosting services under example 1) that are dependent on automated databases and data input by the customer requiring little or no human intervention (e.g. online marketplace or online shopping portal) (as opposed to example 3, appendix 2).

• Internet Service Packages (ISPs) in which the telecommunications component is an ancillary and subordinate part (i.e. a package that goes beyond mere Internet access, comprising various elements (e.g. content pages containing news, weather, travel information; games fora; web-hosting; access to chat-lines etc.))

Appendix 2

Examples of services not regarded as being electronically supplied

Example 1

A supply of

• A good, where the order and processing is done electronically

• A CDROM, floppy disc or similar tangible media

• Printed matter such as a book, newsletter, newspaper or journal

• A CD or audio cassette

• A video cassette or DVD

• A game on CDROM or DVD

Rationale: these are supplies of goods.

Example 2

A supply of

• services of lawyers and financial consultants, etc. who advise clients through email

• interactive teaching services where the course content is delivered by a teacher over the Internet or an electronic network (i.e. via remote link)

Rationale: this is a supply of service that relies on substantial human intervention and the internet or electronic network is only used as a means of communication.

Example 3

A supply of

- Physical repair services of computer equipment
- Off-line data warehousing services
- Advertising services, such as in newspapers, on posters and on television
- Telephone helpdesk services
- Teaching services involving correspondence courses such as postal courses
- Conventional auctioneers' services reliant on direct human intervention, irrespective of how bids are made (e.g. in person, via internet or telephone) (as opposed to example 11, appendix 1).

Rationale: these are supplies of services that are not delivered over the Internet and rely on substantial human intervention.

Example 4

A supply of a radio and television broadcasting service provided over the Internet or similar electronic network, simultaneous to the same broadcast being provided over traditional radio or television network (as opposed to example 8, appendix 1).

Rationale: this is a supply of a radio and television broadcasting service, which is covered by the penultimate indent of Article 9(2)(e).

Example 5

A supply of

- Videophone services (i.e. telephone services with a video component)
- Access to the internet and World Wide Web
- Telephony (i.e. telephone service provided through the internet)

Rationale: these are supplies of telecommunication services and are covered by the place of supply rules for such services under the ninth indent of Article 9(2)(e).

Further Information

Enquiries regarding any issue contained in this Information Leaflet should be addressed to the Revenue District responsible for your tax affairs. (Contact details for all Revenue Districts).

This leaflet is issued by

**VAT Appeals and Communications Branch,
Indirect Taxes Division,
Dublin Castle.**

October 2008

This information leaflet which sets out the current practice at the date of its issue is intended for guidance only and does not purport to be a definitive legal interpretation of the provisions of the Value-Added Tax Act 1972 (as amended).

VALUE-ADDED TAX INFORMATION LEAFLET (OCTOBER 2008)

EXPRESSION OF DOUBT

1.   **General**

Section 19B of the Value-Added Tax Act, 1972, allows a person who is in doubt about the application of VAT law to a transaction to lodge a 'letter of expression of doubt' with Revenue. If the expression of doubt is accepted by Revenue as genuine, interest will not apply to any VAT found to be due following Revenue's examination of the application of VAT law to the transaction. This provision does not affect the taxpayer's right to contact Revenue in the normal way for advice on the VAT treatment of any transaction. It is also important to note that the expression of doubt facility does not displace or override the normal obligations of an accountable persons in regard to the VAT code.

2.   **How is a letter of expression of doubt used?**

A person who wishes to use this provision must submit a letter of expression of doubt (which can be in the form of electronic communication or letter) on time (see paragraph 5) to the Revenue District that normally deals with the tax affairs of the accountable person. The VAT return in respect of the period in which the transaction occurs must be lodged separately and on time with the Office of the Collector-General in the normal way.

The Revenue District will issue an acknowledgement of receipt of the letter of expression of doubt. If the expression of doubt is not accepted as genuine the person will be so advised in writing, within 14 days of its receipt, by the Revenue District. The taxpayer then should submit a supplementary VAT return to the Collector-General with any additional VAT liability due, for the period in which the transaction took place. As interest will be payable on any additional liability in these circumstances arrangements should be made to submit the supplementary return without delay. If the expression of doubt is accepted as genuine the Revenue District will make a ruling as soon as possible as to the correct VAT treatment of the transaction. Where additional VAT liability is identified it must be included in the VAT return for the period in which the ruling is given as if it were tax due for that period. No interest will apply in such circumstances to the VAT due on that transaction, provided that the return is submitted and VAT paid by the relevant due date.

3.   **Details to be included in the letter of expression of doubt**

A letter of expression of doubt must be clearly identified as such and must:

- set out full details of the circumstances of the transaction in doubt,

- provide the basis on which doubt is being expressed,

- identify the amount of tax or deductibility in doubt in respect of the taxable period to which the expression of doubt relates (see paragraph 7 in relation to recurring transactions),

- make reference to the provisions of the law giving rise to the doubt,

- be accompanied by any relevant supporting documentation, and

- state whether relevant professional advice has been taken on the matter.

4.   **Time limit for submission of a letter of expression of doubt**

A letter of expression of doubt must be submitted to the Revenue District responsible for a trader's tax affairs at the time the VAT return for the period in which the transaction occurred is submitted to the Collector-General. An expression of doubt will not be accepted unless the VAT return is lodged by the due date (i.e. 19th of the month following the end of the taxable period – see also paragraph 11).

5.   **What must be included in the VAT return if an expression of doubt is being lodged?**

The transaction giving rise to the doubt should be included or excluded in the VAT return on the basis of the treatment which the accountable person or agent feels is correct. For example, if an accountable person is lodging an expression of doubt about a rating issue but considers that a rate lower than the standard rate applies, then he/she may account for VAT on the return at the lower rate but lodge the expression of doubt with the Revenue District at the same time. If an accountable person has a doubt about whether a transaction is taxable at all, (or exempt from VAT), then this transaction may be excluded from the return but details should be included in the letter of expression of doubt. Again, if an accountable person considers that he/she is entitled to deductibility as regards any transaction then a VAT credit may be claimed in the return subject to a letter of expression of doubt being furnished.

6.   **What is the position regarding the issue of a VAT invoice?**

Where an accountable person lodges an expression of doubt in relation to the tax treatment of a transaction in respect of which a VAT invoice must issue, the VAT details on the invoice must be consistent with the tax treatment that the taxpayer decides to adopt (see paragraph 5). In this regard it should be noted that the outcome of the expression of doubt could be that additional VAT is payable in respect of the transactions in question.

7.   **What is the position regarding recurring transactions?**

Transactions which give rise to a letter of expression of doubt can be recurring. These recurring transactions can arise in two different situations. Firstly, where the same type of transaction recurs during a taxable period. Secondly, where the same type of transaction recurs during a taxable period subsequent to the taxable period in respect of which a letter of expression of doubt has been lodged. The second situation will only arise where Revenue has not yet given a ruling on the transaction in question.

In the first instance, it is necessary only to submit one example of the documentation on the type of transaction involved with the letter of expression of doubt. However, the full amount of the VAT in doubt in the total of all the recurring transactions during that period must be mentioned in the letter of expression of doubt.

In the second instance, where sample documentation has already been submitted with the first letter of expression of doubt and Revenue's ruling is awaited, it is only necessary in the subsequent letters of expression of doubt to refer to the first letter of expression of doubt, but the amount of tax in doubt in each return must be identified in each subsequent letter.

8. **Circumstances when a letter of an expression of doubt is not accepted as genuine**

A letter of expression of doubt will not be accepted where -

- Revenue has issued general guidelines such as the Guide to Value-Added Tax, Statements of Practice, Information Leaflets, Notes for Guidance, FOI Precedents Database or VAT Rates Database about the application of the law in similar circumstances.

- Revenue is of the opinion that the matter is sufficiently free from doubt as not to warrant an expression of doubt, or

- Revenue is of the opinion that the accountable person was acting with a view to the evasion or avoidance of tax.

Where Revenue does not accept that a letter of expression of doubt is genuine the accountable person will be informed in writing of the reason or reasons for the non-acceptance of the letter by Revenue.

9. **Appeal**

A person aggrieved by a decision of Revenue that a letter of expression of doubt is not genuine may appeal to the Appeal Commissioners by giving notice in writing to his/her Revenue District within twenty-one days from the date of the decision. Of course, where an accountable person is aggrieved by a Revenue ruling regarding the VAT treatment of the transaction which is the subject of the letter of expression of doubt, he/she can appeal this in the normal way.

10. **Interest**

Where Revenue accepts that a genuine expression of doubt has been lodged by an accountable person, interest charges will not apply to any additional liability arising from the matter in doubt provided the additional liability is included in the return for the taxable period in which Revenue's ruling on the VAT treatment of the transaction in question is issued as if it were tax due for that period.

However, interest charges will arise in situations where Revenue does not accept an expression of doubt as genuine. Interest will apply from the day after the due date for submission of the return for the period in which the transaction occurred, not from the date of the Revenue decision.

Interest will also apply in situations where the Appeal Commissioners uphold a decision of Revenue that a particular letter of expression of doubt is not genuine. Interest in these situations will apply from the day after the due date for submission of the return for the period in which the transaction occurred. Where –

- a genuine expression of doubt is lodged,

- Revenue (or, where appropriate, the Appeal Commissioners) determine that VAT is due on a transaction or that VAT claimed by a taxpayer was not, in fact, deductible on a transaction, and

- VAT is not paid (or accounted for) by the due date for the VAT return covering the taxable period in which the Revenue ruling is issued, interest will apply from the day after the due date for submission of the return for the period in which the Revenue ruling is issued.

11.   Can a person not registered for VAT avail of this facility?

The legislation also provides that a person not registered for VAT who is in doubt as to whether he/she is an accountable person may avail of the expression of doubt mechanism. In these circumstances the person must lodge the letter of expression of doubt not later than the nineteenth day of the month following the taxable period in which the transaction giving rise to the doubt occurred.

12.   Documents to be retained/records kept

The accountable person must keep the Revenue acknowledgement of his or her expression of doubt as part of his or her records. A letter of expression of doubt shall be deemed not to have been made unless its receipt is acknowledged by Revenue and that acknowledgement forms part of the records kept by the accountable person for the purposes of section 16 of the VAT Act. An accountable person should contact the local Revenue District in the event that an acknowledgement of the letter of expression of doubt is not received.

13.   Further information

Enquiries regarding any issue contained in this Information Leaflet should be addressed to the Revenue District responsible for the taxpayer's affairs. Contact details for all Revenue Districts can be found on the Contact Details Page

VAT Appeals & Communications Branch ,
Indirect Taxes Division,
Stamping Building
Dublin Castle.

October 2008

VALUE-ADDED TAX INFORMATION LEAFLET (OCTOBER 2008)

FACTORING

VAT treatment of factoring following European Court of Justice ruling in the MKG-Kraftfahrzeuge-Factory GmbH (case C-305/01).

This leaflet, originally publishing in Taxbriefing Issue 59, has been superceded by VAT Treatment of Factoring and Invoice Discounting as published in eBrief 52/2008.

Introduction

This article examines the effect of the MKG European Court of Justice ruling on various transactions, principally true and quasi-factoring, and invoice discounting. These terms are often used imprecisely which can sometimes mislead, so it is important to ascertain the nature of the transaction itself and not how it is described in order to determine the VAT treatment.

In brief, the Court held that true factoring in which a business purchases debts assuming the risk of the debtors' default is an economic activity for the purposes of Articles 2 and 4 of the Sixth Directive which does not come within the exemption for certain financial transactions and is therefore a taxable activity with the right to deduct VAT on inputs.

The concept of making a supply for the purposes of VAT is not necessarily identical with the performance of an obligation for the purposes of the law of contract. The nature and reality of the supply must be looked at, as the true construction of a contractual document may not always answer the VAT treatment, although it is usually helpful.

In this context it may be useful to quote from Laws J. of the UK Queen's Bench Division, in the case of Customs and Excise Commissioners v Reed Personnel Services Ltd. (1995) STC 588.

- 'in principle, the nature of a VAT supply is to be ascertained from the whole facts of the case'
- 'many of the cases which have caused difficulty in the VAT field, requiring resolution by the higher courts, have concerned situations involving three parties'
- 'the concept of VAT supply is not coterminous with the concept of contractual duty'.

These quotes are particularly apt in interpreting this judgement, which raises very difficult issues in its application.

VAT treatment of debt factoring

Article 13(B) of the Sixth VAT Directive provides for exemption for transactions concerning debts and other negotiable instruments, but excluding debt collection and factoring. This exemption is transposed into paragraph (i) (c) of the First Schedule to the VAT Act 1972, as amended.

Revenue had always accepted that pure debt collection, including a charge for debt collection or administration provided in accordance with a debt factoring contract, did not come within the terms of the exemption and was a taxable activity with the right to deduction. However, Revenue regarded true factoring as being a financing operation, being essentially the granting of credit by the debt factor and, as such, exempt without the right to deduction.

As indicated above the European Court of Justice considered the treatment of true factoring for VAT purposes in the case of *MKG-Kraftfahrzeuge - Factory GmbH, case C-305/01*. Revenue is implementing the judgement but understands that there may be a need to provide guidance for practitioners and taxpayers as to how it will interpret the judgement.

Where the factoring arrangements mirror the scenario outlined in the judgement Revenue accepts that these are taxable activities with the right to deductibility. However, difficulties arise as to whether certain transactions are debt factoring for the purposes of the Sixth Directive.

What is debt factoring?

The judgement related essentially to true factoring, which is where the factor purchases debts owed to his client without enjoying a right of recourse against the client if the debtors default and which in turn invoices its clients in respect of commission. This activity was held to be a taxable economic activity.

The Court ruled that:

'....a business which purchases debts, assuming the risk of the debtors default, and which in return, invoices its clients in respect of commission pursues an economic activity for the purposes of Articles 2 and 4 of that directive, so that it has the status of taxable person and thus enjoys the right to deduct tax under Article 17 thereof'.

In arriving at its conclusion the court observed (paragraphs 77 and 78) that:

'the term debt collection must be interpreted as encompassing all forms of factoring. In accordance with its objective character, the essential aim of factoring is the recovery and collection of debts owed to a third party. Therefore, factoring must be regarded as constituting merely a variant of the more general concept of debt collection, whatever the manner in which it is carried out.

Moreover, the term debt collection refers to clearly circumscribed financial transactions, designed to obtain payment of a pecuniary debt, which are clearly different in nature from the exemptions set out in the first part of Article 13 B(d)(3) of the Sixth Directive'.

True and Quasi-Factoring

The case which was the subject of the judgement related to a true factoring agreement however reference was made also to quasi-factoring.

Both of these types of agreement are similar to the extent that the services the factor provides are essentially the same i.e. managing and recovery of the debts owed to their clients. As stated at paragraph 13 of the judgement, quoting from the German guidelines 'the activities carried out by the factor for the client in cases of quasi-factoring are the grant of credit, assessment of debtor solvency, management of debtor accounts, preparation of analyses and statistical material and debt collection. This involves the provision of a number of principal services.'

In the case of true factoring there may not be a grant of credit but all the other aspects of factoring, i.e., assessment of debtor solvency, management of debtor accounts etc. would be expected. The essential distinction between true factoring and quasi-factoring is that true factoring is done on a non-recourse basis (the factor assumes the risk of the debtors' default) and quasi-factoring is carried out on a recourse basis (the factor has recourse against the original supplier in the event of non-payment by the debtor).

From the judgement in relation to true factoring and from what was stated in the judgement in relation to quasi factoring both are considered to be taxable activities with VAT deductibility allowed in relation to inputs attributed directly to the factoring services.

The Court considered at paragraph 54 that:

'first of all there is no valid justification for treating true factoring and quasi-factoring differently from the point of view of VAT, given that in both cases the factor makes supplies to the client for consideration and accordingly pursues an economic activity. Any other interpretation would draw an arbitrary distinction between those two categories of factoring and would make the business concerned bear, in the course of certain of its economic activities, the cost of the VAT without giving it the possibility of deducting that cost in accordance with Article 17 of the Sixth Directive'

It is important to bear in mind that it is the actual activity carried out which determines the VAT treatment, as the term factoring may be used in agreements to describe a variety of different services. As indicated in paragraph 64 of the judgement, it is necessary to have regard to the objective character of the transaction in question in applying the exemption provided for in Article 13.

Revenue's view of what constitutes debt factoring

Revenue's interpretation of the judgement is that for a transaction to be debt factoring and therefore to come within the terms of the judgement, there must be a clear nexus between the factor and the debtor. The factor, as envisaged by the ECJ judgement, must have the possibility of collecting the debts itself.

It has been suggested that an arrangement, involving the **contractual** purchasing of the debt but with the **actual** collection being outsourced back to the vendor, who would then act as agent for the purchaser, comes within the scope of the judgement. Revenue accept that the purchaser of the debts, by relieving the vendor of the risk of default, is carrying on an economic activity but regards this as an exempt financial service. The purchaser of the debts is the recipient of a debt collection service from the vendor. The purchaser of the debts is not engaged in debt factoring or debt collection. The debt collection service provided by the vendor as agent for the purchaser is a taxable service but the VAT on that supply is not deductible in the hands of the purchaser.

The granting of credit

The question of interest charged in relation to the granting of credit, although part of the MKG case, was not addressed by the Court. Revenue is of the view that where, as part of a factoring agreement, the factor grants its client credit and charges interest on this advance the grant of credit constitutes an exempt supply. The granting of credit element of the factoring agreement must not be regarded as ancillary to a 'debt collection' service but rather as another principal supply which is exempt under the provision of the First Schedule.

VAT deductibility

VAT deductibility arises in both true and quasi-factoring transactions as described above where the factor provides services in relation to the management and recovery of its clients debts.

Where there is a granting of credit for which interest is charged an apportionment of the factor's inputs will be required.

In deriving a correct apportionment, any interest accruing to the factor should be included in the denominator (the Revenue Guide to Apportionment of input tax may be useful in this regard).

Naturally, where an undertaking is involved in both factoring and invoice discounting operations or purchase of debts without provision of a factoring service then there will also be an apportionment and the practitioner should discuss this with the appropriate local Revenue official.

Invoice Discounting

Invoice discounting is not factoring and does not mirror the true factoring model which was the subject of the ECJ judgement. From an economic point of view, factoring and invoice discounting can appear to be similar economic services. They target similar business needs and are often services offered by the same providers.

However, a factoring agreement completely discharges the customer from managing his debts, an invoice discounting agreement does not. This is the essential difference between the two. **The invoice discounter does not provide the customer with an actual debt collection service (see paragraphs 77 & 78 of the ECJ judgment quoted above).** On the contrary, the principal service being provided with invoice discounting is the provision of credit, which is an exempt activity. The invoice discounter has no involvement in the collection of the debts or the sales ledger and credit control function.

Revenue is of the view that such transactions remain exempt, as was the practice until now, and that the ECJ ruling does not affect the existing VAT treatment. Invoice discounting is not considered to be a variant of debt collection.

Further queries

Queries regarding the general application of the principles laid down in the MKG judgement as outlined here should be referred to:

VAT Interpretation Branch (Property and Financial Services),
Indirect Taxes Division,
Dublin Castle.

Telephone: 01 6748648 or 01 6748353.

Queries regarding specific cases should be addressed to the Revenue office dealing with the case.

VALUE-ADDED TAX INFORMATION LEAFLET (OCTOBER 2008)

FOREIGN SUPPLIERS DOING BUSINESS IN IRELAND

This information leaflet which sets out the current practice at the date of its issue is intended for guidance only and does not purport to be a definitive legal interpretation of the provisions of the Value-Added Tax Act 1972 (as amended).

1.   **General**

In this leaflet the term 'foreign supplier' refers to a supplier of goods or service who does not have a fixed place of business in this State. Suppliers not established in the State are frequently involved in supplying goods or services here. Such suppliers may also be involved in the purchase here of goods and services for their own businesses and end up paying Irish VAT on their purchases. The VAT treatment of such suppliers differs in certain ways from that applicable to suppliers established in the State and the purpose of this leaflet is to clarify the various issues affecting such non-established suppliers.

2.   **Non-established suppliers supplying goods/services in Ireland**

2.1   Non-established suppliers supplying taxable goods or services here are generally obliged to register and account for Irish VAT. The turnover thresholds for VAT registration which apply to Irish suppliers do not apply and such suppliers must register regardless of the level of their turnover.

2.2   Non-established suppliers are required to register where they:-

- import goods into the State;

- supply goods within the State (but please see paragraph 5);

- supply goods on board vessels, aircraft or trains leaving the State for another Member State;

- engage in distance selling of goods to a person who is not a taxable person in the State (see paragraph 3);

- engage in the supply of services connected with immovable goods located in the State, including the services of builders, plumbers and the like, estate agents, architects (other than sub-contractors engaged in construction services) and firms providing cleaning and security services and on site supervision in relation to property (see paragraph 4);

- engage in the transport of goods or ancillary transport activities within the State (other than intra-Community transport services), and intra-Community transport services beginning in the State for an customer who is not registered for VAT;

- engage in cultural, artistic, sporting, scientific entertainment or similar services in the State (however see paragraph 10 in relation to cultural, artistic and entertainment services supplied to person acting in other than a private capacity, an agent or promoter);

- engage in the valuation of movable goods within the State, including contract work;

- engage (in the case of suppliers established outside the EU), in the hire of movable goods for effective use within the State;

- engage in the supply of a telecommunications service, or telephone cards, or radio or television broadcasting services from outside the EU to a private individual in the State in certain circumstances;

- engage in the supply of electronic services from outside the EU to a private individual whose usual place of residence is the State. These services include the following:

  - website supply, web-hosting, distance maintenance of programmes and equipment

  - supply of software and the updating of it,

  - supply of images, text and information, and making databases available,

  - supply of music, films and games, including games of chance and gambling games and of political, cultural, artistic, sporting, scientific and entertainment broadcasts and events,

  - supply of distance teaching.

3.   Non-established suppliers making distance sales to Ireland

3.1   Distance sales covers mail order sales and phone or tele-sales made to persons in the State who are not taxable persons, by a supplier registered in another EU Member State where such supplier is responsible for delivery of the goods.

3.2   Where the value of distance sales to the State by a supplier in another EU Member State exceeds €35,000 in a calendar year that supplier must register for VAT in the State and must account for VAT at the appropriate Irish rates. If the threshold is not exceeded, the supplier may opt to register and account for VAT in the State on his or her distance sales.

3.3   Non-established suppliers making distance sales of excisable goods (spirits, tobacco etc.) to the State are obliged to register for VAT in the State irrespective of the level of turnover.

4.   Building Sub-contractors

From 1 September 2008 non-established traders engaged in construction services, including plumbers, electricians and the like, as sub-contractors are not required or entitled to account for VAT on such services supplied to a principal contractor. VAT is accounted for by the principal contractor.

VAT on construction services that are not subject to Relevant Contracts Tax will continue to be taxed in the normal way and the non-established contractor must register and account for VAT. For example, a builder who builds an extension for a private individual, or an electrician who installs a new alarm system in a shop should charge and account for VAT on the supply. The reverse charge does not apply to these supplies.

As many construction service providers are involved in different types of contracts (e.g. a builder may be acting as principal in one contract, as a sub-contractor in another and supplying services that are not subject to RCT under another contract) it is important to be aware of how the system operates. Please refer to VAT Information Leaflet on Construction Services-New VAT rules for principal contractors and sub-contractors from September 2008.

Where Relevant Contracts Tax is deducted it should be calculated on the VAT exclusive amount. Application for repayment of this tax can be made to Revenue. Further details regarding this tax can be obtained by contacting the **Office of the Revenue Commissioners, Government Offices, St. Conlan's Road, Nenagh, Co. Tipperary Telephone** 00353 67 33533, **email**: intclaims@revenue.ie

5.   **Supply and installation/assembly**

Where a non-established supplier supplies goods in the State which are installed or assembled, with or without a trial run, by or on behalf of that person and where the recipient of those goods in the State is one of the persons listed hereunder, then there is no requirement on the non-established supplier to register for VAT.

- a VAT registered person

- a Government Department or a local authority

- a body established by statute

- an exempt person.

In such circumstances the customer must register and self-account for the VAT due. Typical examples of qualifying supplies are the supply, installation and assembly of exhibition stands, movable shop counters, computer systems or electrical generators.

6.   **Non-established suppliers supplying gas through the natural gas system or electricity.**

Where a trader not established in the State supplies gas through the natural system or electricity to a recipient in the State where the recipient in the State is;

- an accountable person

- a Department of State or a local authority

- a body established by statute then that recipient is required to register and account for VAT and the supplier is not required to register for VAT

7.   Hiring/Leasing of means of transport

Where means of transport are hired/leased in the State by a lessor established in another EU Member State (who has no staff or establishment in this State), the lessor is not obliged to register for VAT in the State. VAT will be accounted for by the lessor in his/her EU Member State of establishment. A lessor established outside the EU, hiring means of transport in the State, is required to register for VAT in the State.

8.   Non-established suppliers purchasing goods/services in the State

8.1   The general position is that a supplier who is engaged in business outside the State and who is not engaged in a business in the State which would require him/her to register for VAT may claim repayment of Irish VAT on most business purchases in Ireland. Claims for a refund must be made within six months of the end of the calendar year on which the VAT became chargeable. A separate Information Leaflet titled 'Repayments to Unregistered Persons' is available on this matter.

8.2   All enquiries relating to repayments to foreign firms not registered for VAT in the State should be made to Office of the Revenue Commissioners, VAT Unregistered Repayments, 3rd Floor, River House, Charlotte Quay, Limerick. (Telephone Lo-call 1890 252449 or 00353 61 212799, Fax 00353 61 402125, email unregvat@revenue.ie Claim forms can be obtained from that office or from the Revenue website www.revenue.ie

9.   Zero rating of services supplied to non-established suppliers (VAT 60A Procedure)

9.1   Non-established suppliers who are not obliged to register for VAT in the State and who are in receipt of taxable services from Irish traders **on a regular and continuous basis** may apply to have those services relieved from VAT. In this way, the necessity of applying to the Revenue Commissioners for VAT repayments is avoided.

9.2   Application for relief is made by way of Form VAT 60A. Suppliers established in EU Member States must submit a certificate of taxable status with their applications. Traders established outside of the EU must provide proof of economic activity issued by the competent authority of his/her own State. Form VAT 60A is available from the **Office of the Revenue Commissioners, VAT Unregistered Repayments, 3rd Floor, River House, Charlotte Quay, Limerick. (Telephone Lo-call 1890 252449 or 00353 61 212799, Fax 00353 61 402125, email unregvat@revenue.ie**

9.3   The relief is subject to periodic review, is valid for two years, but may be renewed on application. **The relief does not apply to supplies of taxable goods.**

10.   Stock supplied from another Member State and held in Ireland for onward supply to a customer in the State

Where a non-established supplier sends stock from another EU Member State to Ireland for the use of customers then the non-established supplier is not obliged to register for VAT. The VAT will be accounted for by means of EU intra-Community acquisition by the customer when the stock is drawn off. The warehouse keeper must in all cases be independent of, that is not an employee or agent of, the supplier.

11. Agents

In many cases, non-established suppliers have agents or representatives in this country who take orders and transmit them to their principals abroad. In some cases the principals send back the orders directly to the customer and, in other cases, to the agent or representative for distribution. Where orders are sent to its agent or representative for distribution the non-established suppliers must register even if the agent holds only a small stock of goods and irrespective of the level turnover. Agents or representatives of non-established suppliers will normally to be registered on their own account. Such agents should not quote their own VAT numbers in connection with the importation of goods by their principals or account for VAT in respect of the intra-Community acquisition of such goods.

12. Cultural, artistic, entertainment or similar services supplied in the State by non-established persons

12.1 Where a person not established in the State supplies cultural, artistic, entertainment or similar services in the State or person to a promoter or agent other than a private individual then there is no obligation on the non-established person to register and account for VAT. The person who received the service for business purposes or the promoter or agent who procured the service is the person who must self-account for any VAT due.

12.2 Premises provider for non-established promoter

Where a premises provider allows a promoter not-established in the State to provide cultural, artistic, entertainment or similar services on the premises providers land then the premises provider is obliged to notify and furnish Revenue with certain information including the name and address of the promoter and details of the event not later than fourteen days before the event (see VAT Information Leaflet 'Theatrical and Musical Events').

12.3 Premises provider – mobile traders

Mobile traders not established in the State supplying goods in the State are obliged to register for VAT irrespective of their turnover level. A premises provider who allows such a person not established in the State to supply goods for consideration on that land for a period of less than seven days, is obliged to notify and furnish Revenue with certain information including the name and address of the mobile trader and the dates of supply not later than fourteen days before the mobile trader is allowed on to the land to supply the goods. The mobile traders are obliged to register for VAT in such circumstances.

13.   Registration for VAT

13.1   Where registration for VAT is required, the office in the local Revenue District in which the supplies are being made is the appropriate office to which they completed VAT application should be addressed. In the absence of there being an identifiable district then applications should be addressed to Dublin City Centre Revenue District Office, 9-10 Upper O'Connell Street, Dublin 1. Where a non-resident construction contractor is required to register for VAT (see paragraph 4 above) he/she should in all cases contact this Revenue District office to register all countrywide non-established construction contractors.

13.2   Application forms TR1 - Tax Registration form for Sole Traders, Trusts and Partnerships or TR2 - Tax Registration form for Companies should be used for VAT registration. Form TR1 applies to sole traders, trusts and partnerships while form TR2 applies to limited companies. Both forms are available from the Revenue website at www.revenue.ie

14.   Requirement of Security

Revenue may request VAT registered persons supplying taxable goods or services to provide security for the tax which becomes due as a result of sales made in the State. The security may be in the form of a bond issued by a bank licensed to carry on a banking business in the State or, alternatively, may be in cash, bank draft or in money order form.

15.   Obligations of non-established suppliers to keep records

A non-established supplier who supplies taxable goods or services in the State and who is registered for Irish VAT is subject to the same obligations as an Irish established traders in relation to the keeping in this country of the appropriate accounts and records required for the purposes of the tax and producing them at its place of business in this State to any authorised officer of the Revenue Commissioners when requested. Where the records are normally kept outside the State and their maintenance in the State would create serious difficulties, the appropriate Revenue District office may be prepared, subject to appropriate safeguards, to consider applications for the relaxation of certain of the requirements. There will be no relaxation of the requirement that the non-established supplier must produce the records for examination in the State if requested.

16.   Importation of goods from outside the EU by a non-established supplier

Where a non-established supplier imports goods in his/her own name that supplier is obliged to register for VAT in the State. The supplier will have a VAT liability for the onward supply of those goods. VAT borne at importation may be reclaimed.

17. Goods consigned from outside the EU by non-established suppliers direct to Irish customers

17.1 In the case of goods consigned by non-established suppliers direct to Irish customers from outside the EU including postal packets exceeding €650 in value it is primarily a matter for the importer or his/her agent (usually the shipping company or a customs clearance firm) to present the necessary entry documents to Customs. Any VAT (or duty) payable is a matter for the importer.

17.2 In the case of parcel post importation's exceeding IR €260 but not exceeding €650 in value, the goods are assessed by Customs and any VAT payable is collected from the consignee by An Post. In the case of parcel post importations not exceeding IR €260 in value, where the consignee is registered for Irish VAT his/her registration number should be shown on the Customs declaration form affixed to or accompanying the parcel. This declarations form must show the nature and value of the goods enclosed in the parcel.

17.3 The VAT due in respect of the importation of these goods will be deferred but must be accounted for in the VAT return for the period.

18. Payment of tax by foreign sender (F.D.D.)

Under the system known internationally as Franc de Droits (F.D.D.) it may be possible for a sender in a non EU country to pay the tax and duty on goods imported by post into the State to the postal authorities in the country of despatch. The VAT will be transferred to the Customs authorities in this country through An Post to whom enquiries in the matter should be made.

There is no requirement on the non-established supplier to register for VAT in the State in respect of such supplies.

Further Information

Enquiries regarding any issue contained in this Information Leaflet should be addressed to the Revenue District responsible for the taxpayer's affairs. Contact details for all Revenue Districts can be found by on the Contact Details page.

This leaflet is issued by

**VAT Appeals and Communications Branch,
Indirect Taxes Division,
Dublin Castle.**

October 2008

VALUE-ADDED TAX INFORMATION LEAFLET (OCTOBER 2008)

GIFTS, PROMOTIONAL ITEMS ETC.

Introduction

As well as dealing with the VAT treatment of gifts, this information leaflet covers self-supplies, industrial samples, replacement goods, promotional schemes, gift vouchers and tokens etc. It replaces Information Leaflet 14/01.

Gifts

Problems frequently arise when goods are supplied on a promotional basis either on their own or in conjunction with other supplies. A gift for VAT purposes is legislated for in Article 16 of the 2006 VAT Directive and section 3(1A) of the VAT Act and Regulation 27 of the Value-Added Tax Regulations 2006. A gift only arises where no consideration is received for it by the supplier. However, if there is a requirement for the customer to pay a consideration in connection with the receipt of goods, even if the supplier describes part of that goods as a "gift", or as being "free", (for example "buy one, get one free", a free bar of chocolate with the purchase of a jar of coffee, a CD/promotional item with a newspaper/magazine), it does not come within the terms of a gift for VAT purposes. Where there is consideration it is always referable to all the items supplied.

As a general rule, gifts of taxable goods made in the course or furtherance of a business are liable to VAT unless their cost to the donor, excluding VAT, is €20 or less. Where gifts are taxable the taxable amount is their cost to the donor, excluding VAT. In the case of gifts costing more than €20 no allowance can be made for the amount below which gifts are not taxable. Accordingly, the person who makes a gift of goods costing €20 excluding VAT, has no liability, while the same person making a gift of goods costing €21, excluding VAT, has a liability for tax on €21. The rate of tax depends on the goods involved.

A VAT-registered person is generally entitled to an input credit or deduction in his/her VAT return for VAT charged to him/her in respect of the importation, purchase or intra-Community acquisition of goods to be given away as gifts, subject to the usual conditions. In the case of goods on the acquisition of which only certain persons are entitled to a deduction (petrol, cars etc.) only those persons entitled to deduction have a liability to account for VAT on such goods when they are given away as gifts. If, for example, a supermarket were to give away a car as a gift or promotional item, it would not be liable to account for VAT on such a gift since it would not have been entitled to a deduction in respect of the acquisition of the car.

The gifts concession does not apply if the gift forms part of a series or succession of gifts made to the same person (for example, the gift to a person each week or month of a piece of crockery consisting of a part of a complete china set).

Gifts are to be distinguished from self-supplies. A trader who supplies himself/herself or his/her family with goods from stock (e.g. where a record dealer takes one of his CDs for his/her own use) is not entitled to the benefit of the gifts relief.

Advertising goods

Gifts in the nature of advertising, such as trophies bearing the name of the donor, or gifts to employees for long service, outstanding sales and the like, are treated in the same way as other gifts.

Certain goods given free of charge for business use to trade customers may continue to be supplied tax free even though in excess of €20 in value. Examples are advertising 3 mirrors, glasses or beer mats, bearing the donor's name, supplied to a hotel or public house, display stands supplied to a grocer or a showcase supplied to a jeweller.

Industrial samples

The gift, in reasonable quantity, to an actual or potential customer of industrial samples in a form not ordinarily available for sale to the public is not taxable in any circumstances, regardless of the value of the goods.

'Money-off' Schemes

These are schemes under which a manufacturer (or a distributor or wholesaler) redeems a money-off voucher, issued in his/her name, which has been accepted by a retailer as part payment for a sale. Reimbursement made by the manufacturer to the retailer on redemption of the money-off coupon from the retailer reduces the taxable amount on which the manufacturer must account for VAT. Accordingly, the manufacturer is entitled to deduct the amount reimbursed for the voucher from his/her taxable amount. This reimbursement to the retailer by the manufacturer should be treated as 'third party consideration' forming part of the total consideration for the supply and taxed accordingly in the hands of the retailer. The 2006 EU VAT Directive (Article 73 provides that third party consideration is taxable. Section 10 (1) of the VAT Act provides that the amount on which tax is chargeable is 'the total consideration which the person supplying goods becomes entitled to receive' in respect of a supply. This includes third party consideration.

'Cash-back' Schemes

These are schemes under which a manufacturer (or a distributor or wholesaler) undertakes to refund cash to a retail customer on the making of specific purchases. The customer sends a voucher back to the manufacturer (indicating proof of a qualifying 4 purchase) and the manufacturer sends money to the value of the voucher directly back to the customer.

The manufacturer's taxable amount is reduced by the amount reimbursed to the retail customer. The manufacturer must retain adequate records of refunds made and keep such records available for inspection.

Gift Tokens and Book tokens

The chargeable amount in the case of goods or services supplied in exchange for tokens is the amount stated on the token as well, of course, as any money paid in addition to that amount.

The sale of gift tokens, book tokens, vouchers, etc. is not liable to tax except where, and to the extent that, the amount charged exceeds the value shown on the tokens (for example, a combined gift token/greeting card). However, when tokens, vouchers etc having a face value are supplied to an intermediary with a view to re-sale to private consumers, and are to be used to exchange goods, these tokens become liable to VAT at the standard rate on the consideration received at the time of their sale by the principal to the intermediary involved. In turn the intermediary must also account for VAT on the onward sale of the vouchers. In these cases, the charge to VAT does not arise at the time the tokens are being redeemed but instead arises on the sale of the voucher.

Vouchers Sold at a Discount

In some cases, a supplier of goods may sell vouchers at a discount to companies who purchase them to distribute them free to their staff, or to resell to the public. The supplier undertakes to accept a voucher in full or part payment of goods purchased by a customer who was not the buyer of the voucher.

Subject to the conditions set out below, the taxable amount attributable to a voucher in the circumstances outlined is the sum of money obtained by the supplier of the goods from the sale of the voucher and not the face value of that voucher.

There is no VAT on the initial transaction involving the sale of the voucher as the consideration is disregarded. VAT becomes chargeable only when the voucher is presented in exchange for goods or services. For this reason, this is allowed only in cases where a proper audit trail is maintained by the trader to the satisfaction of his/her local Revenue District.

Accordingly, a trader operating such a scheme must be able to demonstrate to the local Revenue District that a system in place so that, when a voucher is being redeemed, the original purchaser of that voucher can be clearly identified and the amount of any discount granted to that original purchaser can be determined.

Replacement goods

Replacement goods supplied free of charge in accordance with warranties or guarantees on original goods are not taxable.

Cash Basis

Traders who account on the cash basis and who exchange vouchers, etc. for cash must include the value of such vouchers as cash in their taxable receipts.

Further information

Enquiries regarding any issue contained in this Information Leaflet should be addressed to the Revenue District responsible for the taxpayer's affairs. Contact details for all Revenue Districts can be found on the Contact Details Page

VAT Appeals & Communications Branch ,
Indirect Taxes Division,
Stamping Building
Dublin Castle.

October 2008

This information leaflet which sets out the current practice at the date of its issue is intended for guidance only and does not purport to be a definitive legal interpretation of the provisions of the Value-Added Tax Act 1972 (as amended).

VALUE-ADDED TAX INFORMATION LEAFLET (OCTOBER 2008)

GOLF

This information leaflet which sets out the current practice at the date of its issue is intended for guidance only and does not purport to be a definitive legal interpretation of the provisions of the Value-Added Tax Act 1972 (as amended).

1. **Introduction**

    Membership fees, annual subscriptions from members of member-owned golf clubs are exempt, as are capital levies paid by members. However, certain non-member golf turnover such as income from green fees of member-owned golf clubs are liable for VAT. In addition, all income from State/local authority and commercially owned courses are taxable.

    Golf facilities includes driving ranges and par 3 golf but not 'Pitch and Putt'.

2. **Member-owned clubs**

    Where the total annual taxable income (i.e. green fee and other golf turnover) from the provision of facilities for taking part in golf in a member-owned golf course exceeds the specified limit (€37,500 in any continuous period of twelve months), it will be liable for VAT at 13.5%.

    Taxable income includes green fees, other pay-as-you-play income, short-term membership subscriptions and corporate subscriptions. The excess in competition fees paid by a non-member over the amount paid by a member is regarded as a green-fee and is also taxable.

    Individual membership subscriptions for member-owned golf clubs are exempt from VAT as also are the fees charged to Pavilion or Social members.

    For VAT purposes a member is defined as a person who, having paid the annual subscriptions, is entitled to play golf on the course without further payment for at least 200 days per year. If a member makes an additional payment for a further benefit (e.g. the right to play on days not covered by the terms of his membership), that payment is liable for VAT.

3. **Election to register**

    A golf club can elect to account for VAT in respect of its non-member golf turnover if it is below the specified limit. An application for such an election should be submitted to your local Revenue District.

4. **State/local authority owned and commercial golf courses**

4.1 State or local authority owned golf courses are also required to register and account for VAT. If a local authority operates a number of courses the specified limit relates to the combined golf turnover of all its courses. While one VAT registration will cover all golf courses operated by a local authority, the body in question may opt for separate registration for each course if this is more convenient.

4.2   Commercial golf courses are required to register and account for VAT where the total turnover exceeds or is likely to exceed €37,500. All income, including any membership fees, annual subscriptions and levies are subject to VAT.

4.3   Income received by such golf clubs, including from share issue, which confers an entitlement on purchasers to avail of the facilities of the club are taxable.

5.   Apportionment of inputs

Where a golf club is made taxable in respect of its non-member golf income it may deduct VAT on its inputs to the extent of its taxable activities. As the income from the golf club will be derived from both taxable (e.g. bar receipts, non-member green fees etc.) and exempt activities (e.g. membership fees), it will be entitled to apportion VAT incurred on its expenditure for the purposes of claiming input credit. Expenses directly related to taxable activities will be allowed full deductibility of VAT, while expenses directly related to exempt activities will not be allowed any deductibility. Apportionment will arise in the case of dual-use inputs where activities with an element of both taxable and exempt are involved.

Examples illustrating the changes in relation to registration and accounting for VAT by member-owned golf clubs are given in Appendix I.

6.   Sporting facilities provided by non-profit making bodies

The provision of facilities for taking part in other sports and services closely related there to by non-profit making organisations is exempt from VAT. However, the Revenue Commissioners may determine that the provision of such facilities by the State, a local authority or a non-profit making organisation is liable for VAT at 13.5% where the annual turnover for such activities exceeds or is likely to exceed the specified limit, if:

1.   the exemption of those services creates or is likely to create a distortion of competition which puts a commercial supplier of similar services at a disadvantage, or

2.   the service is actually a commercial enterprise

Where the Revenue Commissioners are satisfied that such conditions apply they will issue a determination in writing to the body concerned giving notice of the decision.

Further Information

For further information on VAT and other Sporting Activities, please refer to VAT Information Leaflet 'Sporting Facilities'. Enquiries regarding any issue contained in this Information Leaflet should be addressed to the Revenue

District responsible for the taxpayer's affairs. Contact details for all Revenue Districts can be found on the Contact Details page.

This leaflet is issued by

VAT Appeals and Communications Branch,
Indirect Taxes Division,
Dublin Castle.

October 2008

Appendix I

Summary of VAT Position in the Case of Member-Owned Golf Clubs (Assume non-golf turnover = A, and non-member golf turnover = B)

Example: 1

Already registered for VAT in respect of its turnover from non-golf activities: if its non-member golf turnover exceeds or is likely to exceed the specified limit it must account for VAT at 13.5% on such turnover, in addition to accounting for VAT on its turnover from non-golf activities.

Hence, already registered for A, and B exceeds the specified limit; VAT on B must be accounted for in addition to A.

Example: 2

It is not obliged to account for VAT on its non-member golf turnover if less than the specified limit but it must continue to account for VAT on its non-golf turnover.

Hence, already registered for A, and B less than the specified limit; not obliged to account for VAT on B. but must account for VAT on A.

Example: 3

Not already registered for VAT, in respect of its turnover from non-golf activities, because that turnover is below the threshold for registration: if its non-member golf turnover exceeds or is likely to exceed the specified limit, it must register and account for VAT on both its non-golf turnover and its non-member golf turnover,

Hence, not registered for A, and B exceeds the specified limit; must register, and account for VAT on both A and B.

Example: 4

If its non-member golf turnover is less than the threshold, it is not required to register, even though the combined total of non-golf and non-member golf turnover exceeds the specified limit.

Hence, not registered for A, and B less than the specified limit; not required to register, even if A + B exceeds the specified limit.

VALUE-ADDED TAX INFORMATION LEAFLET (OCTOBER 2008)

INTRA-COMMUNITY SUPPLIES

- Introduction
- Supplies of goods to other Member States
- Evidence of despatch to another Member State and removal of the goods from the State
- Verification of customers' VAT numbers
- Requirement to take all reasonable steps
- Fraudulent claims for zero-rating
- Sale of new vehicles to persons in other EU Member States
- What is a new means of transport?
- Triangular transactions
- Certain transfers are not supplies
- Branch to branch transfers of goods
- VIES returns
- Intrastat returns
- Further information

1. **Introduction**

    The terms 'intra-Community supply' and 'intra-Community acquisition' relate to goods supplied by a business in one EU Member State to a business in another which have been dispatched or transported from the territory of one Member State to another as a result of such supply. (The terms also apply to new means of transport supplied by a person in one Member State to a person, including a private individual, in another Member State and transferred to that Member State. This is dealt with in 'Certain transfers are not supplies').

2. **Supplies of goods to other Member States**

    The supply of goods by a VAT-registered trader in one EU Member State to a VAT registered trader in another EU Member State, with some exceptions, is referred to as an intra-Community supply. A VAT-registered trader in the State may zero rate the supply of goods to a customer in another EU Member State if:-

    - the customer is registered for VAT in that other EU Member State,
    - the customer's VAT registration number (including country prefix) is obtained and retained in the supplier's records
    - this number, together with the supplier's VAT registration number, is quoted on the sales invoice
    - the goods are dispatched or transported to that other Member State.

If these four conditions are not met the supplier is liable for VAT at the appropriate Irish rate. If the supplier is not able to satisfy Revenue that particular consignments of goods have been sold and delivered to a VAT registered person in another Member State, the supplier becomes liable for the payment of Irish VAT on the transaction. **Where any of the above four conditions are not satisfied the supplier should charge Irish VAT.** If the conditions for zero-rating are subsequently established the customer is entitled to recover the VAT paid from the supplier. The supplier can then make an adjustment in his/her VAT return for the period.

3.   **Evidence of despatch to another Member State and removal of the goods from the State**

The precise commercial documentation required to confirm despatch and removal of the goods from the State depends on the particular circumstances involved.

In many cases a supplier arranges transportation of the goods and the normal commercial documentation related to the supply and transportation of the goods is available (e.g. order document, delivery docket, supplier's invoice, transport document/bill of lading, evidence of transfer of foreign currency for payment, etc.). In such cases the supplier should retain this documentation.

Where transport of the goods is arranged by the customer, or the goods are taken away by the customer using his or her own transport, the supplier needs to be satisfied that the goods are dispatched or transported to another Member State. The normal documentary evidence should be retained in relation to the sale itself but, in addition, the supplier should obtain and retain documentary evidence from the customer that the goods were received in another Member State. The type of documentation acceptable includes transport documents, copies of warehouse receipts, delivery dockets, etc. It might also be prudent for the supplier to record details of the means of transport (e.g. vehicle registration nos.) used by the customer.

Special care should be taken by the supplier to ensure that the four conditions outlined in 'Supplies of goods to other Member States' are met for sales and deliveries of goods to other Member States. Some examples of where a doubt can arise are where:

- customer is not previously known to the supplier
- customer arranges to collect and transport the goods
- customer's transport arrives at supplier's premises without advance notice or correspondence
- payment is made in cash
- type or quantity of goods being purchased are not consistent with commercial practice bearing in mind the purported destination of the goods.

Cases where one or more of these various factors combine together must be treated with particular caution. Where a doubt arises, the supplier should charge Irish VAT. If the conditions for zero-rating are subsequently established the customer is entitled to recover the VAT paid from the supplier.

4. Verification of customers' VAT numbers

For zero-rating to apply there must be a supply of goods to a person registered for VAT in another Member State. The fiscal authorities in each Member State have put in place a computerised system that makes it possible for traders to verify the VAT numbers of their customers in other Member States. However, use of the verification system is not obligatory and traders who are familiar with their customers, and are aware of their bona fides from trading with them over a period of time, are not expected or required to use the verification system. Instead they are advised to contact their EU customers and ask them to confirm in writing their VAT registration numbers.

An Irish trader who has doubts about the validity of a VAT number quoted may use the verification system to establish whether or not a particular number is valid. The system is primarily intended to be used in such circumstances and is not intended for routine checks. Verification of queries is dealt with by the VIMA Office, Government Offices, Millennium Centre, Dundalk, Co. Louth, Phone No: (042) 9353700 or LoCall 1890 251010 or by email at vimahelp@revenue.ie

It is possible to verify the format only and for some Member States, the details, on any given VAT Number in the EU by referring to the EU Commission database.

5. Requirement to take all reasonable steps

Any supplier who takes all reasonable steps to confirm that the conditions for zero-rating are met will not be penalised if it subsequently transpires that a problem has arisen in connection with particular consignments. However, the tax due will be demanded from the supplier in any case where he or she has failed to take all reasonable steps.

6. Fraudulent claims for zero-rating

There are severe penalties for making fraudulent claims for zero-rating:

- Seizure and forfeiture of zero-rated goods which have not been dispatched or transported outside the State (subsections (9A) and (10) of section 27 of the VAT Act).

- A person who acquires goods VAT free in another Member State as a result of making a declaration of an incorrect VAT registration number shall be liable to a penalty of €630 plus an amount equal to the amount of tax which would have be chargeable.

- Arrest of a person suspected of a criminal offence who is not established in the State, or whom an authorised Revenue Officer or a Garda has reason to believe may leave the State (subsection (11) of section 27 of the VAT Act).

- Civil and criminal penalties, ranging up to €126,970 and imprisonment for a period of up to five years (sections 26, 27 and 28 of the VAT Act, and section 1078 of the TCA 1997).

7.   **Sale of new vehicles to persons in other EU Member States**

Sales of new means of transport, i.e. motor vehicles, boats, aircraft, etc., are always intra-Community supplies/acquisitions and any person acquiring a new means of transport must always pay VAT in the EU Member State of arrival.

For a dealer selling a new means of transport to a person registered for VAT in another EU Member State, the VAT treatment is the same as that which applies to goods generally.

In the case of the sale of a new vehicle, for example, to a private individual in another EU Member State, VAT is ultimately payable in the EU Member State of destination. If the private individual collects the vehicle in the State, VAT should be charged by the dealer. However, once the customer satisfies the dealer that VAT has been paid in his/her own EU Member State, the dealer should refund the VAT charged to the customer and adjust his/her VAT liability accordingly. The dealer should retain documentary proof. The normal level of proof required would be a copy of the receipt of VAT payment or proof of registration of the vehicle in the other EU Member State.

8.   **What is a new means of transport?**

Definitions of 'new means of transport' for VAT purposes.

Means of Transport	Specification	Definition
Motor Vehicle	Over 48cc or over 7.2 kw power	6 months old or less, or travelled 6,000 km or less
Marine vessel	over 7.5 metres in length	3 months old or less, or sailed for 100 hours or less
Aircraft	over 1,550 kg take-off weight	3 months old or less, or flown for 40 hours or less

9.   **Triangular transactions**

Triangulation in the Single Market involves two supplies of goods between three VAT-registered traders in three different EU Member States e.g. where a trader in one Member State orders goods from a trader in a second Member State, to be delivered to a trader in a third Member State. To reduce the administrative and compliance burdens both on traders and the relevant revenue authorities with regard to registration and accounting, a simplification measure known as triangulation is in operation in such cases. A technical notice on the VAT treatment of triangulation in the Single Market is available on request.

10.   **Certain transfers are not supplies**

For VAT purposes, certain transfers to other Member States are not treated as intra-Community supplies/acquisitions. These include goods for installation or assembly by the supplier, (in this case the customer must self-account for VAT) transfers for the purposes of having contract work carried out and transfer with a view to their temporary use in another Member State.

11.   Branch to branch transfers of goods

For VAT purposes, branch to branch (with some exceptions) and similar transfers of goods between business persons in different EU Member States are treated as being intra-Community supplies and acquisitions.

12.   VIES returns

When an Irish VAT-registered trader makes zero-rated supplies of goods to a trader in another EU Member State, summary details of those supplies must be returned to Revenue on a quarterly or monthly basis. This return, known as the VIES return, is to enable the authorities in each EU Member State to ensure that intra-Community transactions are properly recorded and accounted for.

13.   Intrastat returns

Traders engaged in intra-Community trade are also obliged to make a periodic INTRASTAT return, for statistical purposes, where the value of goods acquired by them from other Member States exceeds €191,000 per annum or the value of goods supplied by them to other EU Member States exceeds €635,000 per annum.

Further Information

Enquiries regarding any issue contained in this Information Leaflet should be addressed to the Revenue District responsible for the taxpayer's affairs.

This leaflet is issued by

**VAT Appeals and Communications Branch,
Indirect Taxes Division,
Dublin Castle.**

October 2008

This information leaflet which sets out the current practice at the date of its issue is intended for guidance only and does not purport to be a definitive legal interpretation of the provisions of the Value-Added Tax Act 1972 (as amended).

VALUE-ADDED TAX INFORMATION LEAFLET (OCTOBER 2008)

INVOICING

1.   Introduction

This information leaflet sets out the current rules relating to the issue of invoices, credit notes and other documents for VAT purposes, and outlines the importance of these documents in the operation of the VAT system.

2.   Importance of Invoices and Credit Notes

2.1   The information given on invoices and credit notes normally establishes the VAT liability of the supplier of goods or services and the entitlement of the customer to a deduction, where applicable, for the VAT charged. It is vital, therefore, that these documents are properly drawn up and carefully retained. The checking of these documents forms a most important part of the periodic examination, which Revenue officers may make of a trader's VAT position.

2.2   VAT law contains specific requirements for the issue and retention of invoices, credit notes and related documents. Failure to comply with these requirements leaves a trader liable to penalties. Traders who issue invoices and credit notes, and persons to whom these documents are issued, should ensure that the documents accurately represent the transactions to which they refer.

3.   Who must issue a VAT Invoice?

3.1   An accountable person (that is, a person registered for VAT) who supplies goods or services is obliged to issue a VAT invoice where the supply is made to any of the following:

- another taxable person,

- a Government Department,

- a local authority,

- a body established by statute,

- a person who caries on an activity which is exempt from VAT,

- a person, who is not an individual, in another EU Member State,

- a person in another EU Member State where a reverse charge applies, that is, where the VAT is not accountable for by the supplier in Ireland but is accountable for by the customer in the other EU Member State, and

- a person in another EU Member State under the distance selling rules. Distance selling occurs when a supplier in one EU Member State sells goods to a person in another EU Member State who is not registered for VAT and the supplier is responsible for the delivery of the goods. It includes mail order sales and phone or tele-sales but does not include sales of new means of transport or excisable goods.

3.2   It should be noted that an accountable person is required, if requested in writing, to issue a VAT invoice in respect of a transaction with an unregistered person in the State who is entitled to a repayment of the VAT. An accountable person is not required to issue a VAT invoice to an unregistered person otherwise, but may do so if he or she so wishes.

4.   Information required on VAT Invoice

4.1   The VAT invoice issued must show:

- the date of issue of the invoice,

- a sequential number, based on one or more series, which uniquely identifies the invoice,

- the full name, address and VAT registration number of the person who supplied the goods or services to which the invoice relates,

- the full name and address of the person to whom the goods or services were supplied,

- in the case of a reverse charge supply, the VAT identification number of the person to whom the supply was made and an indication that a reverse charge applies,

- in the case of the supply of goods, other than a reverse charge supply, to a person registered for VAT in another EU Member State, the person's VAT identification number in that Member State and an indication that the invoice relates to an intra-Community supply of goods,

- the quantity and nature of the goods supplied or the extent and nature of the services supplied,

- the date on which the goods or services were supplied or, where payment in full, or by instalments, for goods or services is made before the completion of the supply, the date on which the payment on account was made in so far as that date differs from the date of issue of the invoice.

- the unit price, exclusive of tax, of the goods or services supplied, any discounts or price reductions not included in the unit price, and the consideration for the supply exclusive of VAT,

- except where a reverse charge applies, the amount of the consideration exclusive of VAT taxable at each rate (including zero rate) of VAT and the rate of tax chargeable,

- the VAT payable in respect of the supply, except where a reverse charge applies or where the Margin Scheme, Special Scheme for Auctioneers or Special Scheme for second-hand Motor Vehicles applies (see paragraph 16), and

- in the case where a tax representative is liable to pay VAT in another EU Member Sate, the full name and address and value-added tax identification number of the representative.

4.2   As indicated in paragraph 4.1, the unit price has to be shown on an invoice. This applies to countable goods and services. For services this could be, for example, an hourly rate or a price for standard services. If the supply of a particular service cannot readily be broken down into countable elements, then, the total tax-exclusive price for the specific service will be accepted as the unit price.

4.3   An invoice issued by an accountable person relating to an Intra-Community supply of a new means of transport must include details necessary to identify the goods as a new means of transport. In the case of motor vehicles, "new" means that the vehicle has been supplied 6 months or less after the date of first entry into service or that it has travelled 6,000 kilometres or less.

4.4   Where a person is engaged in EU triangular transactions, the person must also include an explicit reference to the EU simplified triangulation arrangements on the invoice. Triangulation involves two supplies of goods between three VAT-registered traders in three different EU Member States, e.g. where a trader in one Member State orders goods from a trader in a second Member State, to be delivered to a trader in a third Member State.

5.   Increase in Invoiced Amounts – Supplementary Invoices

5.1   Because the amount of VAT shown on an invoice affects the VAT liability of both the VAT-registered supplier and the VAT-registered customer, any change in the amount of VAT payable or deductible on an invoice must be properly vouched.

5.2   If, subsequent to the issue of an invoice, the amount charged is increased, the supplier must issue a supplementary invoice on which the increase in the charge and the appropriate VAT rate is shown.

6.   Decrease in Invoiced Amounts – Credit Notes

6.1   Where, because of an allowance or discount or similar adjustment, the amount of VAT payable as shown on an invoice is subsequently reduced, the person who issued the invoice should issue a credit note (but see paragraph 7.1). This note should state the amount of the reduction in the price and the appropriate VAT. The supplier may then reduce, by the amount credited, his or her liability for the accounting period in which the credit note is issued, and the recipient must increase his or her liability by the same amount. All credit notes must contain a reference to the corresponding invoices.

6.2   Where the supplier is accounting for VAT on the moneys received basis, a credit note showing VAT must always be issued. No reduction in the supplier's VAT liability may be made on this account. The VAT deduction or credit available to the customer on the basis of the original invoice is reduced as a result of the issue of the credit note.

7.   Where a Credit Note is not required

7.1   A VAT-registered supplier on the invoice/sales basis and a VAT-registered customer may agree in respect of a transaction not to make any change in the VAT shown on the original invoice. In such circumstances, even if the price charged is reduced subsequently, there is no obligation to issue a credit note in respect of the VAT and the amount of VAT originally invoiced is allowed to stand.

7.2 The arrangements mentioned in paragraph 7.1 above apply in the circumstances where the discount or other reduction is taken on the goods or services only. If the customer takes the discount or other reduction on the VAT as well as on the price, the supplier must always issue a credit note. If the supplier is accounting for VAT on the invoiced sales basis, the supplier must then adjust his or her VAT liability downwards and the customer must adjust his or her VAT liability upwards. Moreover, a VAT-registered supplier who is on the moneys received basis of accounting must always issue a credit note.

8.   Incorrect Rate of VAT charged – Credit Note and Revised Invoice required

8.1 Where a person issues a VAT invoice that shows a rate of VAT, which is subsequently found to be higher than the rate correctly applicable, the person must issue a credit note cancelling the invoice and must then issue a revised invoice. This may arise, for example, in relation to an intra-Community supply where the supplier charges VAT initially (e.g. because of being unsure that the goods will leave the State) and subsequently is satisfied that the goods should have been zero-rated. However, the rule is not confined to intra-Community supplies; it is equally applicable in the case of internal supplies where tax is charged at the standard rate when a reduced rate is in fact applicable.

9.   Information required on Credit Notes

The credit note must show:

- the date of issue of the note,

- a number, which uniquely identifies the note,

- the full name, address and VAT registration number of the person issuing the note,

- the full name, address and VAT registration number of the person to whom the note is being issued,

- in the case of a supply to a person who is registered for value-added tax in another EU Member State, the person's VAT identification number in that Member State,

- the reason why the note is being issued and a cross-reference to the invoice which was issued for the supply in respect of which the consideration was reduced,

- the amount of the consideration, exclusive of tax, in respect of which the note is being issued, and

- the rate or rates of tax in force when the related invoice was issued and the amount of tax at each rate as appropriate to the consideration shown on the note.

10.   Settlement Vouchers and Debit Notes

Settlement vouchers and debit notes are often used in commercial transactions instead of invoices and credit notes. Settlement vouchers and debit notes must contain the VAT registration number of the person issuing them and the VAT registration number of the supplier, in addition to all the other details required to be shown by an accountable person on invoices and credit notes. It is also a condition that the supplier of goods or services is prepared to accept such documents. If accepted, the supplier is subject to the same obligations as if he or she had issued an invoice or credit note.

11.   Self-billing and outsourcing arrangements

11.1   Where a person supplies goods or services to a customer who is registered for VAT, the customer may issue the required invoice provided –

- there is prior agreement between the supplier and the customer that the customer may draw up and issue the invoice,

- all conditions relating to the content or issue of the invoice are met by the customer, and

- agreed procedures are in place for the acceptance by the supplier of the validity of the invoice.

An invoice issued under these arrangements is regarded as having been issued when the supplier accepts it in accordance the agreed procedures referred to above.

11.2   A supplier may outsource the issuing of invoices. When an invoice is issued under outsourcing arrangements it is regarded as having been issued by the supplier if –

- the invoice is issued by a person who acts in the name and on behalf of the supplier, and

- all conditions relating to the content or issue of the invoice are met.

11.3   Self-billing and outsourcing can also apply to credit notes and debit notes.

12.   Invoices, etc. issued in Foreign Currency

12.1   Invoices issued for VAT purposes in amounts expressed in foreign (non-€ denominated) currency should contain the corresponding figures in € and must contain the actual VAT amount in €. The copy of the invoice that has to be retained must show the same figures. This rule also applies to credit notes, debit notes and settlement vouchers.

12.2   The latest selling rate recorded by the Central Bank at the time the VAT becomes due should be used when converting foreign currency invoices. The Central Bank rates for most major currencies appear on a daily basis in the newspapers. It is possible, by agreement with Revenue, to use an alternative method of determining the exchange rate, for example, the rate determined on a calendar month basis under the monthly rate of exchange system for customs valuation purposes. Such agreements are subject to the condition that the agreed method must be used in respect of all the trader's foreign currency transactions. Traders who wish to avail of this facility should write to their local Revenue District responsible for their tax affairs indicating the exchange rate method they propose to use and obtain appropriate agreement.

13. Time limit for issuing VAT Invoices and Credit Notes

13.1 In general, where a VAT invoice has to be issued, it must be issued within 15 days of the end of the month in which the goods or services are supplied. In the case of a supplementary invoice, the invoice must be issued within 15 days following either the day on which the increased in consideration is paid or the day on which the increase in consideration is agreed between the parties concerned, whichever is the earlier.

13.2 Situations may arise where payment in full, or by instalments, for goods or services supplied to a VAT-registered person is made before the completion of the supply. In such cases the person receiving payment must issue an invoice within 15 days following the end of the month following that during which each payment was received. This rule does not apply in the case of intra-Community supplies of goods.

13.3 In the case of credit notes, where a decrease is due to a discount, the note must be issued within 15 days following the date of receipt of the money to which the discount relates. In any other case, the credit note must be issued within 15 days on which the decrease in consideration is agreed between the parties concerned.

13.4 Failure to issue an invoice or credit note in time leaves the person concerned liable to penalties.

14. Incorrect Amounts on VAT Invoices and Credit Notes

A VAT-registered trader who issues an invoice showing a greater amount of VAT than is correct for the transaction is nonetheless liable for the whole amount of VAT shown on the invoice. If a trader issues a credit note showing a lesser amount of VAT than is proper, the trader is liable for the deficiency. In either case the trader may also be liable to penalties.

15. Invoices issued by Unregistered Persons

Where a trader not registered for VAT issues an invoice showing an amount of VAT, that trader is liable for the VAT shown on the invoice. Such a person also leaves himself liable to penalties. This rule does not apply to an unregistered farmer who issues an invoice under the special arrangements for flat-rate farmers (see paragraph 18).

16. Margin Scheme goods/Special Scheme for Auctioneers/Special Scheme for second-hand Motor Vehicles

16.1 In so far the amount on which VAT is chargeable is concerned, special schemes operate in relation to sales by dealers and auctioneers of second-hand movable goods, works of art, collectors items and antiques. The principal feature of the schemes is that dealers and auctioneers effectively pay VAT only on their margin in certain circumstances. Where a supply of goods is made under either of these schemes, the invoice must indicate that the appropriate scheme applies.

16.2   A special scheme also operates in relation to the VAT treatment of second-hand motor vehicles. It provides for the right to deduct residual VAT in respect of the purchase of a qualifying second-hand vehicle, including by way of trade-in. A separate VAT Information Leaflet on the VAT treatment of second-hand vehicles is available.

17.   Hire Purchase Transactions

17.1   Where a supply of goods is subject to a hire-purchase agreement, the supplier is obliged to issue the VAT invoice to the financial institution concerned instead of to the customer. The invoice must contain the name and address of the financial institution, in addition to the standard information required on a VAT invoice.

17.2   The financial institution must issue a VAT invoice to a taxable person for the purposes of enabling the customer to claim VAT deductibility. If a hire-purchase agreement contains all the details required on a VAT invoice then that document will be accepted as a VAT invoice. The document must include the name, address and VAT registration number of the supplier, the name and address of both the financial institution and the customer, and must show separately the amount of tax that appeared on the corresponding invoice received by the financial institution. The document must be issued within 22 days following the month of supply of the goods.

17.3   Where a financial institution receives a VAT credit note in a hire-purchase agreement, after goods have been supplied and invoiced to a customer, the institution must then issue to the customer a document corresponding to that credit note. The document must contain the details required on a normal VAT credit note, and the amount shown on the document in respect of tax is the amount by which the customer's entitlement to a VAT deduction is to be reduced.

17.4   The financial institution is responsible for the full VAT amount contained on the document that serves as a VAT invoice. If the amount allowed as a credit to the customer is in excess of the amount shown on the supplier's invoice, the institution is liable for the excess.

18.   Flat-rate Farmers

18.1   Flat-rate farmers supplying agricultural produce or services, or supplying agricultural machinery to an accountable dealer, are required to issue an invoice (flat-rate invoice) for these supplies in accordance with sections 12A and 12C, respectively, of the Value-Added Tax Act 1972 if:

- the issue of the invoice is requested by the purchaser,

- the purchaser provides the form for the invoice and enters the appropriate particulars on it, and

- the purchaser gives the flat-rate farmer a copy of the invoice.

A flat-rate farmer may nevertheless choose to issue the invoice even if any of these conditions are not fulfilled.

18.2   Every invoice issued by a flat-rate farmer in respect of agricultural produce or an agricultural service is required to be acknowledged by that farmer and to include the following particulars:

1.   the date of issue of the invoice,

2.   the full name and address of the flat-rate farmer who supplied the goods or services to which the invoice relates,

3.   the full name, address and registration number of the person to whom the goods or services have been supplied,

4.   in the case of a supply of agricultural produce or an agricultural service to a person registered for value-added tax in another Member State, the person's value-added tax identification number in that Member State,

5.   the quantity and nature of the goods supplied or the extent and nature of the services rendered,

6.   the date on which the goods or services were supplied,

7.   the consideration, exclusive of the flat-rate addition, for the supply, and

8.   the rate and amount of the flat-rate addition appropriate to the consideration shown on the invoice.

18.3   Where after the issue of a flat-rate invoice the consideration is increased or reduced, then -

- if the consideration is increased, a further invoice for the additional amount must be issued, subject to the same conditions as regards the preparation of the invoice by the purchaser, etc., and

- if the consideration is reduced, the farmer must issue a farmer credit note if the customer is a taxable person and the taxable person must make a corresponding adjustment in the amount of flat-rate credit claimed as a deduction.

18.4   If a person, other than a flat-rate farmer, issues a flat rate invoice, that person is liable for the amount of the flat-rate addition and, for the purposes of payment of the amount, is treated as a taxable person.

18.5   If a flat-rate farmer issues an invoice for a fictitious transaction or for an inflated amount for a genuine transaction, he or she is liable for the amount of the flat-rate addition or the excess amount, as appropriate. For the purposes of payment of the amount in question, the flat-rate farmer will be treated as taxable person.

18.6   If a flat-rate farmer is obliged to issue a farmer credit note but fails to do so within the relevant time limit, he or she is liable for the amount of the flat-rate addition that should have been stated on the note. If he or she issues a farmer credit stating a lesser sum of flat-rate addition than is appropriate to the reduction in consideration or discount, he or she is liable for the amount of the deficiency of the flat-rate addition. In either of these cases the flat-rate farmer is treated as a taxable person for the purposes of payment of the amount due. He or she is also liable to penalties.

19.   Simplified Invoicing

19.1   Simplified arrangements for issuing invoices, credit notes, settlement vouchers or debit notes may be allowed -

- when commercial, technical or administrative practices in a particular business sector make it difficult to comply with general invoicing requirements, or

- if the amount of the invoice is minor.

19.2   Under a simplified arrangement the relevant documents must include the following details:

- the date of issue,

- the identification of the supplier, including the supplier's VAT number,

- the identification of the types of goods or services supplied, and

- the tax due or the information needed to calculate the tax due.

19.3   Revenue has agreed simplified invoicing arrangements in the Corporate Purchasing Card sector and may negotiate similar agreements in other sectors. In the case of the Corporate Purchasing Card sector, it has been agreed that:

- the Evidence for VAT Deduction Report is recognised as a VAT Invoice and contains the information necessary to form a valid invoice.

- such reports can be used as the basis for claiming input credit.

- input credit can be claimed by reference to the transaction date rather than the date of issue of the report.

- commodity codes as agreed with Revenue can be used to describe goods and services.

- such reports can be either in paper or electronic format.

19.4   Credit Card companies, which have Corporate Purchasing Card schemes, must satisfy their customers that the simplified VAT invoicing procedure in operation by the company has been approved by the Revenue Commissioners.

19.5   Applications for approval of simplified invoicing arrangements should be made to VAT Interpretation Branch, Indirect Taxes Division, Revenue Commissioners, Dublin Castle, Dublin 2 via the applicant's Revenue District.

20. Electronic Invoicing

20.1 It is open to traders to operate an electronic invoicing system provided the particulars to be contained in such invoices or other documents are recorded, retained and transmitted electronically by a system that ensures the integrity of those particulars and the authenticity of their origin.

20.2 Invoices, etc maybe transmitted between trading partners using either an electronic data interchange (EDI) system, or an advanced electronic signature (AES) and associated system, which satisfy the requirements set out below. An accountable person may also use a different electronic system to the EDI or AES systems, provided the requirements in question are met and the person notifies the Revenue Commissioners accordingly.Up to 31 December 2005, it was necessary for traders to notify Revenue prior to the commencement of the transmission of electronic invoices, etc.

20.3 The electronic system in use must be capable of –

- producing, retaining and storing, and making available to a Revenue officer on request, electronic records and messages in such form and containing such particulars as are required for VAT purposes,

- reproducing paper copies of such records or messages,

- allocating a unique identification number for each message transmitted, and

- maintaining the electronic records in such manner as allows their retrieval by reference to a trading partner or the unique identification number of the message.

20.4 The system in use must also –

- preclude the repeated transmission of a message and the omission of a message from the electronic record,

- verify the origin or receipt of a message from a trading partner, and

- guarantee the integrity of the contents of a message or an electronic record related to that message during transmission and during the period for the retention of records for VAT purposes.

21. Retention of, and Inspection of, Records

21.1 Every accountable person must retain all books, records and documents relevant to the business, including invoices, credit notes, settlement vouchers and debit notes (and copies of any such documents issued to another person). These business records must be preserved in their original form* for 6 years from the date of the latest transaction to which they refer, unless the written permission of the Revenue District has been obtained for their retention for a shorter period. This rule applies equally to electronic records and messages. In addition, a taxable person keeping electronic records must retain and store particulars such as details of the form of encryption, electronic signature, etc used and the format in which they are stored and how they can be accessed.

*Invoices that have been issued in paper form must be retained in paper form. Electronic retention of invoices is only acceptable where they were originally issued electronically.

21.2   Authorised Revenue officers have extensive powers in regard to the inspection of records, and failure by traders or their employees or associates to co-operate with the officers is an offence. These officers will have proof of their identity. They will check the trader's VAT returns against the trader's records and will crosscheck invoices, etc, against the suppliers' and customers' records. Returns of VAT will also be checked against the trading accounts for Income Tax and Corporation Tax purposes.

22.   **Further Information**

Enquiries regarding any issue contained in this Information Leaflet should be addressed to the Revenue District responsible for your tax affairs. Contact details for all Revenue Districts can be found on the Contact Details Page.

This leaflet has been issued by:

VAT Appeals & Communications Branch,
Indirect Taxes Division,
Stamping Building
Dublin Castle.

October 2008

This information leaflet which sets out the current practice at the date of its issue is intended for guidance only and does not purport to be a definitive legal interpretation of the provisions of the Value-Added Tax Act 1972 (as amended).

VALUE-ADDED TAX INFORMATION LEAFLET (OCTOBER 2008)

LEASING (INTERNATIONAL) OF MEANS OF TRANSPORT

- Introduction
- The ARO judgement
- Meaning of Establishment
- Illustration of the VAT treatment of means of transport
- What are Means of Transport?
- Deductibility
- Leasing to a passenger transport undertaking in another EU Member State
- Leasing to lessees outside the EU
- Effective use and enjoyment
- Further Information
- Appendix I
- Appendix II

1. Introduction

This leaflet sets out the VAT treatment of international leasing of means of transport having regard to the decisions of the European Court of Justice (ECJ).

The principle established by the rulings of the ECJ is that where a lessor in one Member State hires or leases vehicles to customers in another Member State the place of supply is the Member State where the lessor has established its business.

The information leaflet clarifies the meaning of 'established' in the context of the ARO case and sets out the VAT treatment of the leasing of cars and other means of transport supplied by a lessor established in one country to a customer in another.

2. The ARO judgement

The judgement dealt with car leasing from the Netherlands into Belgium. The lessor (ARO Lease BV) was established in the Netherlands. It had no administrative or physical presence in Belgium but it had 800 (out of 6,800) of its vehicles leased to customers in Belgium. Both the Dutch and the Belgian tax authorities sought to collect VAT on the leases to Belgian customers.

The ECJ held that

'a leasing company established in one Member State does not supply services from a fixed establishment in another Member State if it makes passenger cars available in the second State under leasing agreements to customers established there, if its customers have entered into contact with it through self-employed intermediaries established in the second State, if they have chosen their cars from dealers established in the second State, if the leasing company has acquired the cars in the second State, in which they are registered, and has made them available to its customers under leasing agreements drawn up and signed at its main place of business, and if the customers bear maintenance costs and pay road tax in the second State, but the leasing company does not have an office or any premises on which to store the cars there'.

In short, the judgement described the precise circumstances of the ARO case and said that in those circumstances, the place of supply and of taxation is the Member State of the lessor.

The question of whether the hire or lease of vehicles by an undertaking in one Member State to customers in another Member State constituted a 'fixed establishment' was further addressed in the ECJ case of Lease Plan Luxembourg SA and the Belgian State (Case C-390/96). On this point the Court ruled:

'that an undertaking established in one Member State which hires out or leases a number of vehicles to clients established in another Member State **does not possess a fixed establishment in that other State merely by engaging in that hiring out or leasing'**.

3. Meaning of Establishment

The EU VAT Directive 2006 does not define 'established' or 'establishment' but establishment has been defined for the purposes of Irish VAT law.

'Establishment' means

'any fixed place of business, but does not include a place of business of an agent of a person unless the agent has and habitually exercises general authority to negotiate the terms of and makes agreements on behalf of the person or has a stock of goods with which he regularly fulfils on behalf of the person agreements for the supply of goods'.

The question of determining the place of establishment depends on the facts of each case. Neither ARO nor Lease Plan was deemed to have an establishment in the Member State in which the vehicles were hired out.

The Court found that independent garages which facilitated the leasing company's customers in arranging provision of the leased vehicles did not constitute an establishment of the lessor. However, the relationship between the supplier of the goods, any agent who acts on behalf of the lessor and the lessor will have to be examined in order to determine whether the lessor is established in the State.

Accordingly, where:

- leasing arrangements are entered into by a lessor established in another EU Member State by means of agreements drawn up and signed, and management decisions taken in that Member State in which it has established its business,

- the vehicles are made available under those leasing arrangements to customers in the State and

- the lessor has no staff, or fixed establishment or a structure adequate, in terms of human and technical resources, to supply the services in the State,

the leasing services is regarded as supplied in the other EU Member State.

Where a lessor established in another EU Member State leases vehicles to customers here and has either an establishment here or a structure adequate, in terms of human and technical resources, to supply the services in question, the services are regarded as supplied in the State and the lessor is liable for Irish VAT.

4. **Illustration of the VAT treatment of means of transport**

The leasing of means of transport involving domestic and international suppliers is best demonstrated in a series of charts, as follows:-

- Chart A - describes the treatment of leasing of cars.

- Chart B - describes the treatment of leasing of deductible means of transport to VAT registered lessees.

- Chart C - describes the leasing of rail-cars, buses, aircraft etc. to passenger transport undertakings.

5. **What are Means of Transport?**

Although 'new means of transport' is defined in section 1 of the VAT Act, 1972 and 'means of transport' is defined for the purposes of the special scheme for second-hand cars in section 12B, in general terms, including for the purposes of a leasing transaction a broader definition is applied. 'Means of transport' is taken to mean motor vehicles and other equipment and devices, which might be pulled or drawn by such vehicles, and are normally used for carrying out a transport contract, as well, of course, as vessels and aircraft.

6. **Deductibility**

Section 13 (3) of the VAT Act 1972 provides that a lessor established outside the State is able to get a VAT refund on means of transport (apart from motor cars - see definition at Appendix II) purchased here for the purpose of leasing out to customers here. An accountable person in another Member State, which has leasing services supplied to it by a lessor established in the State on an ongoing basis and which is entitled to reclaim the VAT chargeable on those leasing services under the 8th Directive, may apply to the Revenue Commissioners to have the services treated as subject to the zero rate under the VAT 60A procedure.

Any relief so granted is subject to periodic review. The relief does not apply to supplies of goods. (Application Form VAT 60A is available from VAT Repayments (Unregistered) Section, River House, Charlotte Quay, Limerick.

7. **Leasing to a passenger transport undertaking in another EU Member State**

As indicated in Chart C, Revenue allows a refund of VAT in relation to the leasing of means of transport to passenger transport undertakings in other Member States on the basis that the undertakings are engaged in passenger transport outside the State (i.e. transport effected entirely outside Ireland or transport between Ireland and another country) and provided they meet the 8th Directive requirements. The 60A procedure referred to at paragraph 6 above may apply.

8. **Leasing to lessees outside the EU**

Section 5 (6) (dddd) of the VAT Act 1972 provides that the place of supply of the leasing of means of transport by a lessor in the State is outside the EU where the means of transport are to be effectively used and enjoyed outside the EU. This means that the leasing of, for example, railway rolling stock for use in the United States by a lessor established in Ireland is not subject to Irish VAT. The lessor is of course entitled to deduction of his or her inputs relating to this activity in the normal way or to a refund under the 13th Directive.

9. **Effective use and enjoyment**

Effective use and enjoyment is not defined in the VAT Act. This provision is based on Article 58 of the VAT Directive 2006. The purpose of this provision is to allow Member States to treat services which are consumed outside the EU as outside the scope of EU VAT.

If there is any doubt about whether the use and enjoyment takes place outside the EU a lessor should charge VAT. In addition while the use and enjoyment of a means of transport at the start of the leasing agreement may be outside the EU, a lessor is responsible for ensuring that the correct VAT treatment is applied to the leasing service for the full period of the lease. Therefore, if during the period of the lease agreement the lessee transfers the means of transport to a Member State, VAT should be charged on the leasing service when the conditions of section 5(6) (dddd) no longer apply.

Further Information

Enquiries regarding any issue contained in this Information Leaflet should be addressed to the Revenue District responsible for the taxpayer's affairs. Contact details for all Revenue Districts are available on the revenue website at: Contact Details.

Claims for repayment of VAT under the 8th and 13th Directive should be addressed to:

VAT (Unregistered) Repayments Section,
River House,
Charlotte Quay,
Co. Limerick,
Tel. 061 212 700.

VAT Appeals & Communications Branch,
Indirect Taxes Division,
Stamping Building,
Dublin Castle.

October 2008

Appendix I

Chart A - Leasing of Means of Transport

Motor Vehicles (Cars, motor cycles and other vehicles as defined in section 12 (3) (b) of the Value-Added Tax Act, 1972).[1] - VAT Treatment

Place of establishment of Lessor	Lessee established or resident in	Place of taxation of Leasing Services	Deductibility		On Lease rental charged to VAT - registered lessee
			On acquisition of the Vehicle by the Lessor		On Lease rental charged to VAT - registered lessee
			Sourced in Ireland	Sourced in OMS	
Ireland	OMS	Ireland	Yes [2]	OMS/8th Directive rules apply	No
OMS	Ireland	OMS	No. Section 13 (3) (c) of VAT Act	OMS/8th Directive rules apply on purchase of car in OMS. ICA on arrival in the State. VAT payable not deductible. (Section 13 (3) (c))	OMS rules apply
Outside the EU	Ireland	Ireland [3]	Yes (lessor is obliged to register for VAT in the State)	OMS rules apply on purchase of car in OMS. ICA on arrival in the State. Deductible	No
Ireland	Outside the EU	Outside EU Section 5(6)(dddd) [4]	Yes	OMS/8th Directive rules apply. ICA on arrival in the State. Deductible.	N/A

OMS = Other Member State
ICA = Intra-Community acquisition

[1]   'motor vehicles' means motor vehicles designed and constructed for the conveyance of persons by road and sports motor vehicles, estate cars, station wagons, motor cycles, motor scooters, mopeds and auto cycles, whether or not designed and constructed for the purpose aforesaid, excluding vehicles designed and constructed for the carriage of more than 16 persons (inclusive of the driver), invalid carriages and other vehicles of a type designed for use by invalids or infirm persons.

[2]   OMS rules apply on intra-Community acquisition of the vehicle in the OMS.

[3]   or if effectively used outside the State, the place where the vehicles are effectively used

[4]   Section 5 (6) (dddd) introduced in Finance Act, 1999 (see paragraph 9) if effectively used and enjoyed outside the EU.

Chart B - Leasing of Means of Transport

Leasing of deductible Means of Transport (Vans/lorries etc. to VAT-Registered persons). - VAT Treatment

Place of establishment of Lessor	Lessee established or resident in	Place of taxation of Leasing Service	Deductibility		
			On acquisition of the Vehicle by the Lessor		On Lease rental charged to VAT - registered lessee
			Sourced in Ireland	Sourced in OMS	
Ireland	OMS	Ireland	Yes [1]	OMS/8th Directive rules apply	Yes (8th Directive)
OMS	Ireland	OMS	Yes under 8th Directive rules	OMS/8th Directive rules apply. ICA on arrival in the State. VAT payable is deductible. (Section 13 (3) (c))	OMS rules apply
Outside the EU	Ireland	Ireland [2]	Yes (lessor is obliged to register for VAT in the State)	OMS rules apply on purchase of car in OMS. ICA on arrival in the State. Deductible	Yes
Ireland	Outside the EU	Outside EU Section 5(6) (dddd) [3]	Yes	OMS/8th Directive rules apply. ICA on arrival in the State. Deductible.	N/A

OMS = Other Member State
ICA = Intra-Community acquisition

[1] OMS rules apply on intra-Community acquisition of the vehicle in the OMS

[2] or if effectively used outside the State, the place where the vehicles are effectively used.

[3] Section 5 (6) (dddd) introduced in Finance Act, 1999 (see paragraph 9) if effectively used and enjoyed outside the EU.

Chart C - Leasing of Means of Transport

Leasing of Means of Transport to Passenger Transport Undertakings (rail - cars, buses, aircraft etc.). - VAT Treatment

Place of establishment of Lessor	Lessee established or resident in	Place of taxation of Leasing Service	Deductibility		
			On acquisition of the Vehicle by the Lessor		On Lease rental charged to VAT - registered lessee
			Sourced in Ireland	Sourced in OMS	
Ireland	OMS	Ireland	**Yes** [1]	OMS/8th Directive rules apply	**Yes** [2]
OMS	Ireland	OMS	Yes under 8th Directive rules	OMS/8th Directive rules apply on purchase. ICA on arrival in the State. Deductible	OMS rules apply
Outside the EU	Ireland	Ireland [3]	Yes (lessor is obliged to register for VAT in the State)	OMS/8th Directive rules on purchase. ICA on arrival in the State. Deductible	**No** [2]
Ireland	Outside the EU	Outside EU Section 5(6) (dddd) [4]	Yes	OMS/8th Directive rules apply.	N/A

OMS = Other Member State
ICA = Intra-Community acquisition

[1] OMS rules apply on intra-Community acquisition of the vehicle in the OMS.

[2] Deductible to the extent that the lessee is an undertaking engaged in passenger transport services outside the State (see paragraph 8).

[3] or if effectively used outside the State, the place where the vehicles are effectively used

[4] Section 5 (6) (dddd) introduced in Finance Act, 1999 (see paragraph 9) if effectively used and enjoyed outside the EU.

Appendix II

Value Added Tax Act, 1972 - Section 12 (3)(b)

'Motor vehicles' means motor vehicles designed and constructed for the conveyance of persons by road and sports motor vehicles, estate cars, station wagons, motor cycles, motor scooters, mopeds and auto cycles, whether or not designed and constructed for the purpose aforesaid, excluding vehicles designed and constructed for the carriage of more than 16 persons (inclusive of the driver), invalid carriages and other vehicles of a type designed for use by invalids or infirm persons.

This information leaflet which sets out the current practice at the date of its issue is intended for guidance only and does not purport to be a definitive legal interpretation of the provisions of the Value-Added Tax Act 1972 (as amended).

VALUE-ADDED TAX INFORMATION LEAFLET (OCTOBER 2008)

MONEYS RECEIVED BASIS OF ACCOUNTING

1. **General**

    This Information Leaflet sets out which VAT-registered traders may opt to account for VAT on the basis of moneys received from their customers instead of the normal method based on the issue of invoices to their customers, and how such traders may apply to operate this scheme.

2. **Description of moneys received basis**

    VAT is normally accounted for on the invoice basis, i.e. VAT is payable on the total sales invoiced in the relevant period regardless of whether or not the trader has been paid for the supply in that period. However, certain traders can opt for the moneys received (cash) basis of accounting, under which the trader is not required to account for VAT until payment for the supply is actually received.

3. **Traders who may opt for moneys received basis**

    The traders who may opt to account for VAT in this way are:

    *   VAT-registered traders whose supplies of goods or services are almost exclusively (at least 90%) made to unregistered persons. This would apply in practice mainly to retail outlets, public houses, restaurants, hairdressers and any similar type of business, or

    *   VAT-registered traders whose annual turnover (exclusive of VAT) does not exceed or is not likely to exceed €1,000,000 (with effect from 1st March 2007).

It should be noted that the use of this basis of accounting in no way removes from a VAT-registered trader his or her obligations as regards the issue of invoices and other documents, the maintenance of records, lodgment of returns etc.

The supply of goods and services to a person who is not entitled to full deduction of the VAT charged in respect of that supply may be treated as a supply to an unregistered person, for the purposes of determining whether a person qualifies to use the cash basis (i.e. for the purpose of the 90% rule).

Examples of such supplies are:

*   the supply of a car;

*   provision of accommodation or entertainment services;

*   the supply of goods to an exempt body;

*   the supply of goods to a person who is registered for VAT solely in respect of his intra-Community acquisitions or Fourth Schedule services **provided that in each case** the person in receipt of the supply is not entitled to a **full** deduction of the VAT charged.

4.   Excluded transactions

Transactions between connected persons are excluded from the moneys received basis of accounting. VAT on any transactions between such persons must be paid by reference to the normal invoice/sales basis. VAT on property transactions must always be accounted for on the invoice basis.

5.   Application and authorisation

A taxable person who wishes to account on the cash basis, should apply in writing for authorisation to his or her local Revenue District setting out the following details:

- name and address;
- VAT registration number, where appropriate;
- the nature of the person's business activities;
- the percentage of turnover from taxable supplies, if any, which related to supplies tounregistered persons for whichever of the following periods is the shorter:

   ° the period of 12 months ended on the last day of the taxable period prior to the application, or

   ° the period from the commencement of business activities to the last day of the taxable period prior to the application;

- an estimate of the percentage of the turnover from taxable supplies to unregistered persons for the 12 months from the start of the taxable period during which the application is made;

- level of annual turnover, if under €1,000,000.

An authorization to account for VAT on the cash basis has effect from the start of the period during which it is given, or from a subsequent date if so specified.

Persons who are applying for VAT registration for the first time, and find that they are eligible for this basis of accounting should indicate in the appropriate box on the application form (TR1 or TR2) whether or not they wish to use the moneys received basis.

6.   VAT liability on moneys received

A trader who has opted to account on the moneys received basis is liable for VAT at the rate applicable at the time the goods or services are supplied and not at the rate applicable when payment is received, if a change in rate has taken place in the interim.

Moneys received by a VAT-registered trader include any sums:

- credited to the trader's account in a bank, building society or other financial concern,

- received by another person on the trader's behalf, or

- paid to Revenue by a third party to the trader's account in accordance with the Commissioners' power of attachment,

- deducted as Professional Services Withholding Tax by an accountable person. See **professional Services Withholding Tax** below).

- deducted as Relevant Contract Tax deducted by a principal contractor or a sub-contractor. See **Relevant Contract Tax** below.

A VAT-registered trader is also deemed to have received money if liability in respect of a business transaction is settled by setting off against it a credit due in respect of some other transaction. Care must be taken when money is received through an agent that any amount withheld by the agent to cover fees, expenses etc., is included in the taxable amount.

7.   **Professional Services Withholding Tax**

Income Tax withheld from payments for professional services is deemed, for VAT purposes, to have been part of the consideration received by the trader.

8.   **Relevant Contract Tax**

Relevant Contract Tax deducted from payments for relevant contracts is deemed, for VAT purposes, to have been part of the consideration received by the sub-contractor.

9.   **Credit card transactions**

In the case of credit card transactions the taxable amount is the marked selling price, that is, the amount actually charged to the customer by the supplier. Amounts withheld by credit card companies from their settlements with traders are part of the taxable amount and should not be disregarded.

10.   **Credit notes**

A VAT-registered trader accounting for VAT on the basis of moneys received must issue to a VAT-registered customer a credit note showing VAT if there is a discount or price reduction allowed subsequent to the issue of an invoice. The effect of the credit note is to reduce the VAT deduction available to the customer on the basis of the original invoice. This has no effect on the liability of the person issuing the credit note since he or she is calculating liability by reference to the moneys actually received.

The cash receipts basis of accounting does not apply to a transaction where a supplier on the cash receipts basis grants a discount to a customer after issuing an invoice, but subsequently fails a credit note.

11.   **Review of eligibility and cancellation of authorisation**

Where an accountable person is authorised to account for VAT on the moneys received basis and, for a period of four consecutive months his or her turnover from taxable supplies to unregistered persons is less than 90% of total turnover, the accountable person should notify the local Revenue District accordingly by the end of the following month and indicate the actual percentage of such supplies. If the change in the level of such supplies to unregistered persons is of a marginal or temporary nature, the authorisation may be allowed to continue.

Where an accountable person is authorised to operate the cash receipts basis because his/her annual turnover is less than €1,000,000, that person must apply to have that authorisation cancelled where it is clear that the turnover will exceed the limit in any continuous period of twelve months.

Where an accountable person fails to notify the local Revenue District as in paragraph 11.1 above, the authorisation will be deemed to have been automatically cancelled with effect from the start of the VAT accounting period within which the notification should have been made.

Cancellation of an authorisation will have effect from the start of the VAT accounting period during which the person is notified of such cancellation by the local Revenue District or from the start of a later VAT accounting period if specified in the notice.

12. Changing from moneys received basis to invoice/sales basis

Where an accountable person who for any period is authorized to account for VAT on the monies received basis ceases to be so authorized, or ceases to be an accountable person, liability for VAT at the time of the change, or cessation, must be adjusted. Where the authorisation was issued for a period of more than 6 years the authorized period, for the purposes of this adjustment, is deemed to be for a period of 6 years. The adjustment is calculated as follows:

The total amount due to the person at the end of the authorized period shall be apportioned between each rate of VAT in accordance with the following formula:

$$(\textbf{A} \text{ multiplied by } \textbf{B}) \text{ divided by } \textbf{C}$$

Where:-

A is the total amount due to the person at the end of the authorized period for goods and services supplied during the authorized period.

B is the taxable amount in respect of taxable supplies at each rate of tax in the twelve months prior to the date of cessation or in the authorized period, whichever is the shorter.

C is the total amount taxable in respect of total taxable supplies in the twelve months prior to the date of cessation or in the authorized period, whichever is the shorter.

However, the apportionment between the various rates of tax may be made in accordance with any other basis agreed between an accountable person and the local Revenue District. The amount so apportioned at each rate is a tax-inclusive amount and the tax included is to be treated as tax due for the period in which the cessation of the monies received basis occurs. No adjustment of liability is made where the cessation is occasioned by the death of an accountable person.

13. **Changing from invoice/sales basis to moneys received basis**

Where a VAT-registered trader already accounting for VAT on the invoice basis obtains permission to change to the moneys received basis, that trader is liable for VAT on any moneys received on and after the approved date of the change, excluding any payments on which VAT has already been accounted for in respect of goods and services supplied while accounting on the invoice basis.

14. **Further information**

Enquiries regarding any issue contained in this Information Leaflet should be addressed to the Revenue District responsible for the taxpayer's affairs. Contact details for all Revenue Districts can be found on the Contact Details Page

VAT Appeals & Communications Branch ,
Indirect Taxes Division,
Stamping Building,
Dublin Castle.

October 2008

This information leaflet which sets out the current practice at the date of its issue is intended for guidance only and does not purport to be a definitive legal interpretation of the provisions of the Value-Added Tax Act 1972 (as amended).

VALUE-ADDED TAX INFORMATION LEAFLET (OCTOBER 2008)

VAT MULTIPLIER

(For Information only)

VAT multiplier to be used when valuing an interest in immovable goods from 1990 to 30/06/2008.

DATE ISSUE	REDEMPTION YIELD	MULTIPLIER
21 May 1991	9.30 per cent	10.75
24 January 1992	9.11 per cent	10.98
14 June 1993	7.37 per cent	13.57
15 October 1993	6.87 per cent	14.56
17 August 1994	8.56 per cent	11.68
15 May 1995	8.52 per cent	11.74
19 April 1996	6.93 per cent	14.43[1]
17 September 1997	6.26 per cent	15.97
11 May 1999	4.26 per cent	23.47[2]
29 January 2002	5.14 per cent	19.45
1 March 2003	3.377 per cent	29.61
1 February 2004	4.702 per cent	21.27

(1) The operative date for the multiplier of 14.43 is the 26 March, 1997

(2) The operative date for the multiplier of 23.47 is the 30 June, 1999

VALUE-ADDED TAX INFORMATION LEAFLET (OCTOBER 2008)

RATE CHANGE – BUDGET 2009

Increase in the standard rate of VAT from 21% to 21.5% from 1 December, 2008

- General
- Which VAT rate must the trader apply? - general rule
- The effect of the change of VAT rate on contracts with fixed interval payments
- Invoices
- Credit notes
- Advance Payments received before 1 December 2008
- Contracts existing on 1 December 2008
- Continuous supplies of utilities
- Budget account sales, hire-purchase sales and other credit sales
- Stock on hands on 1 December 2008
- Accounting for VAT
- Further Information

General

1.　The standard rate of VAT will be increased from 21% to 21.5% with effect from 1 December, 2008. This rate applies, for example, to supplies of motor vehicles, petrol, electrical supplies, furniture, carpets, adult footwear and clothing. The purpose of this leaflet is to outline the implications of the change for VAT-registered traders.

　　Note: Zero rated goods, such as basic foodstuffs, children's clothing and children's footwear and oral medicines, and goods and services subject to VAT at the 13.5% rate such as catering, new houses, construction services and solid fuel are not affected by the change.

Which VAT rate must the trader apply?- general rule

2.1　The general position is that traders accounting for VAT on the invoice basis should apply the rate of VAT in force at the time they issue or are obliged to issue a VAT invoice , whichever is the earlier. In the case of transactions with private individuals, a trader should apply the rate in force at the time of the supply.

2.2　Although traders who account for VAT on the cash basis are not liable for VAT on their supplies until they receive payment where they supply goods or services before 1 December 2008 but receive payment on or after 1 December 2008 they should account for VAT on those supplies at the 21% rate. Such traders should account for

VAT at 21.5% on goods and services supplied on or after 1 December 2008.

The effect of the change of VAT rate on contracts with fixed interval payments

3.1 When payments for continuous supplies due at fixed intervals over an agreed time-frame become due before 1 December 2008, they may be treated as being taxable at the 21% rate of VAT if invoiced before 1 December 2008. This applies even if the interval over which the supplies take place spans the time both before and after that date. For example, rental of office equipment or a television for the interval from 1 October 2008 to 31 December 2008 may be treated as taxable entirely at 21% if the payment is due before 1 December 2008 and the invoice for that fixed payment is issued before that date. If such an invoice is issued on or after 1 December 2008, the rate is 21.5%.

Invoices

4.1 VAT invoices issued by a VAT-registered person (who is not on the cash basis) to another VAT-registered person on or after 1 December 2008 should show VAT at the 21.5% rate. This is so, even if the goods or services were supplied before that date. A supplementary VAT invoice issued in respect of an increase in the charge should accordingly show the rate applicable at the time of its issue.

4.2 A trader on the cash basis who is required to issue a VAT invoice to another VAT registered person should show the VAT rate which applies on the date of the supply, not on the date of receipt of payment (see paragraph 2.2)

4.3 VAT liability in respect of goods or services supplied to an unregistered person is normally determined by the date of supply and not the date of issue of the invoice, if any. Goods or services which are actually supplied to unregistered persons prior to 1 December 2008 are taxable at the 21% rate even though they may be invoiced on or after 1 December.

4.4 For invoices relating to utilities please refer to paragraph 8.

Credit notes

5.1 Any VAT credit note or debit note relating to a supply of goods or services which contains a VAT adjustment and which is issued to a VAT-registered person, a Public Body or an exempt person on or after 1 December 2008 should show VAT at the rate in force at the time the original invoice was issued.

5.2 Any credit note or debit note relating to a supply of goods or services which is issued to an unregistered person on or after 1 December 2008 should show or include VAT at the rate in force at the time of the supply.

5.3 For credit notes relating to utilities, please refer to paragraph 8.

Advance Payments received before 1 December 2008

6.1   An advance payment, including a deposit, received from a VAT-registered person before 1 December 2008 in respect of goods or services not supplied until that date is subject to VAT at 21% if the invoice relating to that payment is issued or required to be issued before 1 December 2008. However, if the invoice relating to that payment is issued or required to be issued on or after 1 December 2008, the payment is taxable at 21.5%. In the case of traders accounting for VAT on the cash basis, an advance payment received before 1 December is taxable at 21%. Any advance payment received from an unregistered person is taxable at the 21% rate if received before 1 December 2008 and 21.5% if received on or after that date.

Contracts existing on 1 December 2008

7.1   Where a contract to supply goods or services is entered into before 1 December 2008 and the contract is not completed until after that date, then the agreed VAT inclusive price may be subject to an appropriate adjustment on account of the change in the VAT rate, unless there is agreement to the contrary between the contracting parties.

7.2   When, for example, a trader were to contract in October 2008 to make blinds for a house for €1,000 and the rate of VAT is increased with effect from 1 December 2008 ,then, in the absence of an agreement to the contrary, the trader can increase the agreed price to include the extra VAT , assuming the blinds have not been supplied or paid for before 1 December. The trader is, of course, liable to VAT at the increased rate on the supply.

Continuous supplies of utilities

8.1   In the case of continuous supplies of utilities (i.e. gas, electricity, telecommunications) to non-business and other unregistered customers the rate applicable is the rate in force at the time the bill issues to the consumer, provided that the company issues a bill at least every three months. Of those, the only continuous supplies chargeable at the standard rate are telecommunications supplies. (Supplies of gas and electricity, both subject to the 13.5% rate, so this change does not affect them.) The VAT rate applying to supplies to business customers is the rate applicable on the date of issue of the invoice or bill.

8.2   Telecommunications services billed before 1 December are taxable at 21% and telecommunications services billed on or after 1 December are taxable at 21.5%.

8.3   Any credit note or debit note covering a supply of telecommunications services which is issued to non-business or other unregistered customers after 1 December 2008 relating to a bill issued before 1 December 2008 should show the rate applicable on the date of issue of the bill itself, i.e. the 21% rate.

Budget account sales, hire-purchase sales and other credit sales

9.1   These sales are chargeable to VAT as follows –

- at the rate in force at the time of the sale by the finance house, in the case of sales to unregistered persons, or

- at the rate in force at the time of issue of the invoice by the finance house in the case of sales to VAT-registered traders.

Stock on hands on 1 December 2008

10.1   Persons who are registered for VAT on 1 December 2008 should account for VAT at the 21.5% rate on stock supplied after that date even though they may have purchased their stock with VAT at the 21% rate before that date. Such persons will already have been entitled to a credit for VAT on the purchase of that stock, subject to the usual conditions.

Accounting for VAT

11.1   Traders should bear in mind when completing their VAT return for the November/December 2008 taxable period that they must account for VAT at the rates appropriate to the particular months.

11.2   When completing the Return of Trading Details for the year the same row should be used for both the old and the new rates.

Further Information

12.1   Enquiries regarding any issue contained in this information leaflet should be addressed to the Revenue District responsible for the taxpayer's affairs.

12.2   This information leaflet is a non-statutory guidance note aimed at informing traders about straightforward scenarios. It cannot be relied on by businesses where an interpretation put on this leaflet could have an unintended effect.

VAT Appeals and Communications Branch
New Stamping Building
Dublin Castle

October, 2008

VALUE-ADDED TAX INFORMATION LEAFLET (OCTOBER 2008)

RELIEF FROM CUSTOMS DUTY AND VAT ON THE IMPORTATION OF STUDENT GOODS

1. **Introduction**

   The personal belongings of students from non-European Union (EU) countries who come to the EU to study may be imported without payment of Customs Duty and VAT. This leaflet describes the relief available, the associated conditions and the procedures involved at import.

2. **Relief Available**

   Students who come to stay in the EU for the purpose of studying here, may import their personal belongings (i.e. outfits, scholastic materials and household effects) free from the payment of Customs Duty and VAT under the following conditions:

   1. The student must be enrolled in an educational establishment in order to attend a full-time course there; and

   2. The goods must belong to the student and are intended only for his/her personal use during the period of his/her studies; and

   3. The goods represent those normally required;

      1. to furnish a student's room; and

      2. for the purpose of their studies.

   The relief may be granted more than once per school year.

3. **Definitions**

   Pupil or Student – means any person enrolled in an educational establishment in order to attend full-time the courses offered therein.

   Outfit – means underwear or household linen as well as clothing, whether or not new.

   Scholastic materials – means objects and instruments (including calculators and personal computers) normally used by pupils or students for the purposes of their studies.

4. **Documentary Evidence**

   A letter from the Educational establishment, confirming that the importer has enrolled in a full-time course there, is required for presentation to Revenue at the time of importation. Revenue may require the importer to provide a further letter from the Educational establishment confirming the necessity of the goods.

5. **Procedure at importation**

   Where goods are forwarded to the student by post, the importer needs to ensure that the declaration on the parcel is endorsed as follows by the person sending the goods:

"Scholastic Materials: Exemption from import charges claimed".

The documentary evidence as outlined at paragraph 4 should be attached to the outside of the parcel and marked 'Customs Documents'.

Where goods are imported other than by post they should be presented to Revenue accompanied by an import declaration (SAD), containing a claim to relief from Customs Duty and VAT. For the purposes of completion of the SAD, the legal references are:

Article 25 of Regulation (EEC) No. 918/83 for Customs Duty;

Article 20 of Directive 83/181/EEC for VAT

Code C06 should be entered in box 37 b of the SAD in order to avail of the relief from Customs Duty and VAT. The import declaration should be accompanied by the documentary evidence outlined in paragraph 4.

6.   Further Information

Enquiries regarding any issue contained in this Information Leaflet should be addressed to the Revenue District responsible for your tax affairs. Contact details for all Revenue Districts can be found on the Contact Details Page.

Customs Division,
Customs Procedures Branch,
Government Offices,
Nenagh,
Co. Tipperary.

October 2008

[1] Basic Necessities – means those goods required to meet the immediate needs of human beings, e.g. food, medicine, clothing and bedclothes.

Legal Disclaimer

While every effort is made to ensure that the information given in this guide is accurate, it is not a legal document. Responsibility cannot be accepted for any liability incurred or loss suffered as a consequence of relying on any matter published herein.

VALUE-ADDED TAX INFORMATION LEAFLET (OCTOBER 2008)

REPAYMENTS TO UNREGISTERED PERSONS

Introduction and enquiries

This information leaflet sets out the various schemes for repayment of VAT to persons who are not registered for VAT in the State. It updates and replaces Information Leaflet 18/01.

Except where stated otherwise in the following paragraphs, all claims and enquiries relating to repayments to unregistered persons should be made to the **Office of the Revenue Commissioners, Strategic Planning Division, VAT Unregistered Repayments, 3rd Floor, River House, Charlotte Quay, Limerick. (Telephone Lo-call 1890 252449 or 00353 61 212799, Fax 00353 61 402125, email unregvat@revenue.ie)**. Similarly, except where stated otherwise, all claim forms referred to in this leaflet may be obtained from that Office, on request, or downloaded from the VAT Forms menu on this website.

Foreign businesses paying Irish VAT

The general position is that, under the terms of the 8th or 13th EU VAT Directives, a person who is engaged in business outside the State, and who is not engaged in business in the State, may claim repayment of Irish VAT on most business purchases in Ireland. The main conditions governing repayment are:

- the claimant must produce a certificate of taxable status confirming that s/he is VAT-registered in another Member State of the EU. However, where the claimant is carrying on business outside of the European Union s/he must provide written proof of economic activity issued by the competent authority of his/her own state;

- the goods/services giving rise to the claim must be goods/services in respect of which tax would be deductible if the claimant's business was carried on in Ireland, and must not include goods for supply within the State or motor vehicles for hiring out for utilisation within the State;

- the business for which the goods/services were purchased must be a business which would be taxable if carried on in Ireland;

- application for repayment is made by way of Form VAT 60EC - Application for Refund of Value-Added Tax (VAT) by a taxable person not established in Ireland (8th Directive) and Form VAT 60OEC - Application for Refund of Value Added Tax (VAT) by a taxable person not established in Ireland (13th Directive);

- Claims to repayment must be lodged within six months of the end of the year in which the tax paid became chargeable.

Zero-rating of services supplied to foreign traders (VAT 60A Procedure)

Foreign traders in receipt of taxable **services** from Irish traders on a regular and continuous basis may apply to have those services relieved from VAT. In this way, the necessity of applying to Revenue for VAT repayments is avoided.

Application for relief is made by way of Form VAT 60A - Application by a Foreign Trader who is not established in Ireland for relief from Value-Added Tax (VAT) on charges for Services supplied to it by Irish Supplier(s). Traders established in EU Member States must submit a certificate of taxable status with their applications confirming that they are VAT-registered in another Member State of the EU. Traders established outside of the EU must provide proof of economic activity issued by the competent authority of their own State.

This relief is subject to periodic review. Generally, it is made available and is valid for a two-year period, but may be renewed on application. **The relief does not apply to supplies of taxable goods.**

Farm buildings or structures, land drainage and land reclamation

Farmers who are not registered for VAT may reclaim VAT paid by them in relation to the construction, extension, alteration or reconstruction of farm buildings and structures or on land drainage and land reclamation. Claims for such repayment should be made on Form VAT 58 - Claim by Unregistered Farmer for Refund of Value-Added Tax (VAT) under the Value Added Tax (Refund of Tax) (No. 25) Order, 1993.

Farmers who are registered for VAT only in respect of their intra-Community acquisitions or certain services received from abroad are similarly entitled to repayment but must claim this refund as a deduction or input credit in their VAT return.

Applications for repayment must be submitted within four years from the end of the taxable period to which the claim relates.

Sea fishing vessels and equipment

The purchase, intra-Community acquisition, importation, hire, maintenance and repair of sea-fishing vessels of a gross tonnage of not more than 15 tons are liable to VAT. An unregistered fisherman may claim repayment of such VAT provided the fishing vessel concerned has been the subject of a grant or loan from An Bord Iascaigh Mhara.

An unregistered fisherman may also claim repayment of VAT on the purchase, intra-Community acquisition, importation, hire, maintenance and repair of specified fishing equipment. If the vessel for which the equipment is intended is not more than 15 tons (gross tonnage), it is a condition that the vessel must have been the subject of a grant or loan from An Bord Iascaigh Mhara. Repayment in respect of equipment for a vessel of more than 15 tons (gross tonnage) may be claimed whether of not the vessel was the subject of a grant or loan.

The following are specified fishing equipment:

- Anchors, autopilots, bilge and deck pumps, buoys and floats, compasses, cranes, echo graphs, echo sounders, electrical generating sets, fish boxes, fish finders, fishing baskets, life boats and life rafts, marine lights, marine engines, net drums, net hauliers, net sounders, radar apparatus, radio navigational aid apparatus, radio telephones, refrigeration plant, trawl doors, trawl gallows and winches.

Application for repayment should be made on Form VAT 58A available from the **Central Repayments Office, The Plantation, Monaghan (Telephone. 00353 47 81425)** and should be returned to this address. Applications for repayment must be submitted within four years from the end of the taxable period to which the claim relates.

There is no provision for relief on other equipment or materials purchased for the carrying out of repair or maintenance work by an unregistered fisherman himself or by any other unregistered person.

Marine diesel

An unregistered fisherman may claim repayment of VAT paid on the purchase, intra-Community acquisition or importation of marine diesel. Mineral oil tax on such marine diesel may also be reclaimed by both VAT-registered and unregistered fishermen. Claims for repayment of VAT and mineral oil tax should be made on claim Form C & E No. 1131/VAT 5813, which may be obtained from the local Revenue District or Central Repayments Office. Applications for repayment should be made to the **Central Repayments Office, Revenue Commissioners, The Plantation, Monaghan (Telephone: 00353 47 81425)**.

Applications for repayment of VAT must be submitted within four years from the end of the taxable period to which the claim relates. Claims for repayment of mineral oil tax are to be made in respect of mineral oil used within a period of not less than one and not more than six calendar months. The time limit for mineral oil tax claims is four months following the end of the claim period. Claims lodged outside the prescribed time limit may not be paid except in exceptional circumstances.

VAT charged at point of importation by customs

Repayment of VAT charged at import where the VAT was not legally owed, e.g. VAT overpaid due to miscalculation, may be made by the **Central Repayments Office, Revenue Commissioners, The Plantation, Monaghan (Telephone: 00353 47 81425)**.

Application must first be made to the local Revenue District where the VAT was charged.

Applications for repayment must be submitted within four years from the end of the taxable period to which the claim relates.

Sea rescue craft, equipment, etc.

Qualifying groups may reclaim VAT incurred on outlay on small sea rescue craft (15 tons gross tonnage or less), ancillary equipment and special boat buildings used exclusively in connection with rescue or assistance at sea or with the training of persons for such purposes. Application for repayment should be made on Form VAT 70 - Claim for Refund of Value-Added Tax (VAT) on Sea Rescue Boat or Craft/Equipment/Boathouse under the Value-Added Tax (Refund of Tax) (No. 18) Order, 1985.

Applications for repayment must be submitted within four years from the end of the taxable period to which the claim relates.

Disabled Persons

Repayment may be claimed for VAT paid in relation to vehicles for use (a) by severely and permanently disabled persons as drivers or passengers, or (b) by organisations for the transport of severely and permanently disabled persons. There is also provision for the repayment of, and in certain circumstances, the remission of Vehicle Registration Tax in respect of such vehicles.

Application forms and public notices relating to the relief are available from the **Central Repayments Office, Disabled Drivers Section, Revenue Commissioners, Coolshannagh, Co. Monaghan (Telephone: 00353 47 38010).**

Applications for repayment must be submitted within four years from the end of the taxable period to which the claim relates.

Disabled persons - Aids and Appliances

Disabled persons may reclaim VAT paid on certain aids and appliances. The relief is also available in certain circumstances to persons other than disabled persons who purchase such goods for handing over to a particular disabled person. Applications for repayment should be made on Form VAT 61A - Claim for Refund of Value-Added Tax (VAT) chargeable on aids and appliances for use by Disabled Persons under the Value-Added Tax (Refund of Tax) (No. 15) Order, 1981.

Applications for repayment must be submitted within four years from the end of the taxable period to which the claim relates.

Radios for the blind

An institution or society having for its primary object the amelioration of the lot of blind persons may claim repayment of the VAT paid by it on the purchase or importation of radio sets which are intended for the use of blind persons. Application for repayment should be made on Form VAT 59 - Claim by an Institution/Society for Refund of Value-Added Tax (VAT) paid in respect of radio broadcasting reception apparatus intended for use by blind persons under section 20(2) of the Value-Added Tax Act, 1972.

Applications for repayment must be submitted within four years from the end of the taxable period to which the claim relates.

Residential caravans and mobile homes

VAT in excess of 13.5% which has been paid on the supply or importation of a caravan, mobile home, or similar structure, which is purchased by a person as a residence or, in the case of a local authority, provided for letting as a residence may be reclaimed. Application for repayment should be made on Form VAT 62.

Applications for repayment must be submitted within four years from the end of the taxable period to which the claim relates.

Irish companies providing certain services outside the State

In certain circumstances a person who conducts a business from within the State, but who does not supply goods or services in the State, may claim a refund of deductible VAT on outlay on goods or services. For example, an Irish bank or insurance company providing services outside the EU, which are not taxable in this country, may be entitled to claim relief as a 'foreign' business. Applications for refunds should be made on Form VAT 60E - Claim for Refund of Value-Added Tax (VAT) by an Unregistered Person established in the State in respect of outlay on "Qualifying Activities".

Applications for repayment must be submitted within four years from the end of the taxable period to which the claim relates.

Touring Coaches

Subject to certain conditions, persons who are engaged in the business of the carriage for reward of tourists by road, under contracts for group transport, may reclaim VAT incurred on the purchase, intra-community acquisition, lease/hire of touring coaches. Application for repayments should be made on Form VAT 71 - Claim for Refund of Value-Added Tax (VAT) on Certain Touring Coaches under the Value Added Tax (Refund of Tax) (No. 28) Order, 1996 (as amended).

Applications for repayment must be submitted within four years from the end of the taxable period to which the claim relates.

Donated medical equipment

Repayment of VAT incurred on the purchase or importation of new medical instruments and appliances (excluding means of transport), which is purchased through voluntary donations, may be claimed by hospitals or donors, as appropriate, subject to conditions. The principal conditions are that the instrument or appliance must be:

- €25,390 or more in value (exclusive of tax),

- designed and manufactured for use solely in medical research or in diagnosis, prevention or treatment of illness,

- such that no part of the funds used in the purchase of the goods is provided directly or indirectly by the State, a State body or any public or local authority, and

- subject to a recommendation by the Minister for Health and Children that having regard to the requirements of the health services in the State, a refund of tax would be appropriate.

Applications for repayments should be made on Form VAT 72 - Claim for Refund of Value-Added Tax (VAT) on certain Medical Instruments and Appliances under the Value-Added Tax (Refund of Tax) (No. 23) Order, 1992.

Applications for repayment must be submitted within four years from the end of the taxable period to which the claim relates.

Donated Research Equipment

Repayment of VAT incurred in the purchase or importation of any new instrument or appliance (excluding means of transport), which is purchased through voluntary donations, may be claimed by a research institution or a university, school or similar educational body engaged in medical research in a laboratory. The principal conditions are that the instrument or appliance be:-

* €25,390 or more in value (exclusive of tax),

* designed and manufactured for use in medical research,

* such that no part of the funds used in the purchase of the goods is provided, directly or indirectly, by the State, a State body or any public or local authority, and

* subject to a recommendation by the Health Research Board that, having regard to the requirements of medical research in the State, a refund of tax would be appropriate.

Application for repayment should be made on Form VAT 72A - Claim for Refund of Value-Added Tax (VAT) on certain Medical Research Equipment under the Value-Added Tax (Refund of Tax) (No. 27) Order, 1995.

Applications for repayment must be submitted within four years from the end of the taxable period to which the claim relates.

Humanitarian goods

Philanthropic organisations may reclaim VAT paid on the supply in, or importation into, the State of goods which are exported or re-exported for use in the organisations' humanitarian, charitable or teaching activities abroad.

Application for repayment should be made on Form VAT 73 - Claim for Refund of Value-Added Tax (VAT) on Humanitarian Goods for Export under the Value-Added Tax (Refund of Tax) (No. 21) Order, 1987.

Applications for repayment must be submitted within four years from the end of the taxable period to which the claim relates.

Irish businesses paying foreign VAT

Traders who are registered for the purposes of Irish VAT and who pay VAT in another Member State of the EU are normally entitled to claim a repayment of tax from the relevant Member State subject to conditions. Certificates of taxable status for traders established in this State who wish to apply for such repayments are available from the **Office of the Revenue Commissioners, Strategic Planning Division, VAT Unregistered Repayments, 3rd Floor, River House, Charlotte Quay, Limerick. (Telephone Lo-call 1890 252449 or 00353 61 212799, Fax 00353 61 402125, email unregvat@revenue.ie).** Application for certificates of status may also be applied for on Form VAT 66A - Application for Irish Certificate of Taxable Status for the purpose of claiming refund of VAT in other Member States of the European Union.

Investment gold

Where exempt supplies of investment gold are made, the VAT incurred on the supply, transformation, change of form and on the goods and services linked to the production of or transformation into investment gold may be refunded in certain circumstances.

Application for repayment should be made on Form VAT 6A - Claim for Refund of Value-Added Tax (VAT) incurred on gold under Section 6A, VAT Act, 1972.

Applications for repayment must be submitted within four years from the end of the taxable period to which the claim relates.

Further information

Enquiries regarding any issue contained in this Information Leaflet should be addressed to the Revenue District responsible for the taxpayer's affairs. Contact details for all Revenue Districts can be found on the Contact Details Page.

VAT Appeals & Communications Branch ,
Indirect Taxes Division,
Stamping Building
Dublin Castle.

October 2008

VALUE-ADDED TAX INFORMATION LEAFLET (OCTOBER 2008)

SERVICE CHARGES IN HOTELS AND RESTAURANTS - WITHDRAWAL OF CONCESSION

Introduction

Revenue has, for a number of years, operated a concession (see Appendix 1) whereby service charges in hotels and restaurants were not regarded as part of the taxable amount if they were distributed in full to staff. This concession operates widely throughout the hotel and restaurant sector, and was presented as a way of ensuring that staff in this sector could receive gratuities intended for them, but included on the bill presented to a customer, without these gratuities being subject to VAT. It was conditional on the hotels or restaurants not converting any part of the charges for their own benefit.

The European Court of Justice has found that any amount which a supplier (restaurant, hotel, etc.) is entitled to receive forms part of the taxable amount [1]. Therefore, service and other charges that are included on the bill presented to the customer are liable to VAT.

Withdrawal of Concession

Revenue is withdrawing the concession with effect from 1st September 2008. From that date hotels and restaurants must account for VAT on all amounts included on bills to customers. Hotels and restaurants may continue to operate within the terms of the concession until 31st August 2008.

Voluntary payments (tips) made by customers and not included in the bill presented to the customer will continue to be outside the scope of VAT.

Rate of VAT

From 1st September 2008 all service charges included in hotel and restaurant bills will be liable to VAT @ 13.5%.

Further Information

Enquiries regarding any issue contained in this Information Leaflet should be addressed to the Revenue District responsible for the taxpayer's affairs.

VAT Appeals and Communications Branch,
Indirect Taxes Division,
Dublin Castle.

October 2008

Appendix 1

Terms of the concession:

The terms of this concession were as follows:

"Where a hotel, etc. bill or price list indicates, or bears a clear statement that it includes, a specified percentage addition to cover service charges, such service charges may, concessionally, be ignored for VAT purposes, subject to what follows:

1.   the whole of these service charges must be distributed to the staff;

2.   if it is a hoteliers practice, in accordance with an agreement with his staff, to withhold some part of the service charge receipts during one period and to distribute the amount withheld during another period the amount withheld may be ignored provided that it is, in fact, fully distributed within the agreed period and is in addition to whatever salaries/wages may be due to the staff by virtue of the agreement. Service charges which are used to finance, wholly or partly, contractual salaries/wages due to employees are liable to VAT;

3.   where, apart from the circumstances described at (b) above, a hotelier, etc. distributes less than the full amount of the service charge, the full amount is taxable. No adjustment may be made for the amount actually distributed. In this connection amounts withheld to cover breakages, etc. may be regarded as having been distributed; and

4.   where, apart from the circumstances described at (b) above, a hotelier, etc. distributes more than the amount of the service charge indicated on or included in the bill or price list the excess will not be relieved from VAT liability."

Footnote 1: Case C-404, Commission of the European Communities v French Republic

This information leaflet which sets out the current practice at the date of its issue is intended for guidance only and does not purport to be a definitive legal interpretation of the provisions of the Value-Added Tax Act 1972 (as amended).

VALUE-ADDED TAX INFORMATION LEAFLET (OCTOBER 2008)

SPORTS FACILITIES

General

The provision by a person other than a non-profit making organisation, of facilities for taking part in sporting activities are taxable and liable to VAT at the rate of 13.5%.

The provision of facilities for taking part in sporting and physical education activities, and services closely related thereto, provided by non-profit making organisations, with the exception of subparagraphs (a) and (b) below, are exempt from VAT.

1. The provision by a member-owned golf club of facilities for taking part in golf to any person who is not a member of the club where the total consideration received by the club exceeds the specific limit (€37,500 from 1/5/08) in any continuous period of twelve months.

2. The provision by any other non-profit making organisation of facilities for taking part in golf to any person who is not a member of the club where the total consideration received by the club exceeds the specific limit in any continuous period of twelve months.

In the case of the services referred to in subparagraphs (a) and (b) above VAT is chargeable at 13.5%.

It should be noted that the provision of facilities for taking part in 'Pitch & Putt' by non-profit-making organisations does not come within the scope of these exceptions and is accordingly exempt.

Where sporting facilities are hired out by sports clubs or sporting organisations the receipts are generally exempted from VAT on the grounds that the provision of the facility is not considered to be in the course or furtherance of business.

Determination under Section 8(3E) VAT Act

Where non-profit making organisations, the State, or a Local Authority, provides facilities for taking part in sporting and physical education activities, in excess of the appropriate specified limit, and the Revenue Commissioners are satisfied that-

1. the exemption of the service puts a commercial rival at a competitive disadvantage, or;

2. the services are actually operating behind a 'not-for-profit' façade;

the Revenue Commissioners shall issue a determination in relation to some or all of the services provided specifying that the service or services are deemed to be taxable for the purpose of VAT. Where a determination is issued, VAT is chargeable at 13.5%. Where a distortion of competition no longer exists the Revenue Commissioners may cancel the determination.

Please note that in order for Revenue to consider making a determination of this nature it must be satisfied that the sporting facilities are being provided at a commercial rate to the general public. It is not considered to be a commercial transaction where a Club arranges for a charge to be levied on an individual member or group of members of the same Club or Organisation to use the facilities.

Persons Liable

Only those persons providing sporting facilities on a commercial basis plus those covered by the exceptions listed at paragraphs 1 or 2 above, are liable to VAT.

Applications for registration are made using Form TR1 or TR2, which is available on request to the Revenue District responsible for your tax affairs, and it also available on the Revenue website: under the Businesses section.

What is a non profit making organisation?

In deciding what is a non-profit making organisation the Revenue Commissioners will have regard, for example, to the organisation's constitution or articles of association as to whether or not it is precluded from distributing profits. In practice, most private member golf, tennis or similar clubs will continue to qualify for exemption insofar as the provision of sporting facilities for members is concerned.

Promotion of and Admissions to Sporting Events

VAT liability applies only to charges made for facilities for participation in sporting activities. There is no change insofar as spectators are concerned. Admission to sporting events, as well as receipts arising from promotion of sporting events by non-profit making organisations, are exempt.

What are Sports Facilities?

'Sports facilities' means any grounds or premises designed or adapted for playing sport. This includes bowling alleys, driving ranges, gymnasia, golf courses, lands let for fishing or shooting, snooker halls, skating rinks, squash courts, swimming pools and tennis courts. Leisure complexes which normally comprise a gymnasium or swimming pool, together with ancillary facilities such as jacuzzi, sauna or steam room are also included.

'Sporting facilities' does **not** include the following:

1. facilities provided for activities which do not amount to a sport, for example, board or card games, computer or video games or amusement machines;

2. provision of equipment only, for example, the hire of golf clubs as a charge separate from green fees. In these circumstances the rate of VAT appropriate to the hire of equipment will apply. However, where hire of equipment is incidental to the provision of the sports facilities without separate charge, for example, shoes provided for persons using indoor bowling facilities, the charge will be deemed to relate to the sporting facilities and so qualify for the 13.5% rate.

Advertising and Sponsorship

Receipts from advertising and sponsorship by Sporting Clubs are not treated as taxable turnover.

Further information

Enquiries regarding any issue contained in this Information Leaflet should be addressed to the Revenue District responsible for the taxpayer's affairs. Contact details for all Revenue Districts can be found on the Contact Details Page.

VAT Appeals & Communications Branch,
Indirect Taxes Division,
Stamping Building,
Dublin Castle.

October 2008

VALUE-ADDED TAX INFORMATION LEAFLET (OCTOBER 2008)

TRANSPORT OF GOODS AND ANCILLARY
SERVICES WITHIN THE EU

Revenue Legislation Services

This information leaflet which sets out the current practice at the date of its issue is intended for guidance only and does not purport to be a definitive legal interpretation of the provisions of the Value-Added Tax Act 1972 (as amended).

1.   General

Special rules apply to the transport of goods between EU Member States. These rules are set out in this information leaflet and for convenience the treatment is summarized in Appendix 1 to this leaflet.

2.   EU intra-Community goods transport services supplied by persons registered for VAT in the State

2.1   Where a person registered for VAT in the State supplies EU intra-Community goods transport services, that is, the transport of goods from one EU Member State to another, to a customer registered for VAT in the State, the supplier is liable to Irish VAT and must account for it in the normal way (same as internal transport services).

2.2   Where a person registered for VAT in the State supplies such services to customers registered for VAT in another EU Member State no Irish VAT liability arises for the supplier. The customers are, however, obliged to account for VAT in their own Member States as if the customers themselves had supplied the services.

2.3   If a customer is not registered for VAT (e.g. a private individual) the supply of intra-Community goods transport services is taxable in the place of departure i.e. where the transport of the goods begins. In the case of the transport of goods on behalf of a private individual from Ireland to the UK. liability to VAT arises in Ireland because that is the place of departure; in the case of haulage on behalf of a private individual from the UK to Ireland liability arises in the UK. Suppliers of intra-Community goods transport services to unregistered persons should note that if they are providing services which are taxable in another Member State they are subject to the rules relating to VAT in that other Member State.

3.   Domestic transport services supplied as part of EU intra-Community transport services

3.1   Where a domestic goods transport service (i.e. where transport begins and ends in the State) is supplied to a person registered for VAT in another Member State and that service forms part of an intra-Community goods transport service, no Irish VAT liability arises for the supplier and the customer should account for VAT in his/her own Member State as if s/he had supplied the service. In effect the supplier treats the supply as if it were an intra-Community transaction.

3.2   An example of this would be where a shipping company, registered for VAT in the U.K. is contracted to transport goods from London to Athlone. The shipping company transports the goods from London to Dublin and then employs an Irish transporter to transport the goods from Dublin to Athlone. In this example the Irish transporter will invoice the U.K. shipping company free of VAT. The U.K. company accounts for the VAT on this transaction in the U.K. on the reverse charge basis.

3.3   The Irish transporter must obtain and retain for subsequent inspection documentary evidence to confirm that the service provided by him/her is part of an overall intra-Community transport service.

3.4   It should be noted that this arrangement does not apply to wholly domestic goods transport services, even where these are supplied to a person registered for VAT in another Member State. Neither does it apply to a domestic goods transport service supplied as part of intra-Community goods transport services supplied to Irish VAT-registered customers by transporters registered for VAT in the State. In both these cases Irish VAT is chargeable.

4.   **Domestic and EU intra-Community transport services supplied in connection with transport of goods into and out of the EU(Imports and Exports)**

4.1   Expenses incurred in the transport of imported goods to their place of destination within the EU should be included in the value for VAT at point of entry, if known and taxed accordingly. The effect of this is that the internal EU transport costs will attract the same rate of VAT as that chargeable on the goods at importation.

4.2   Where the costs of transport within the EU are included in the value for VAT at importation and charged with VAT accordingly the transport service itself is then zero-rated.

4.3   A haulier providing zero-rated transport services in these circumstance is obliged to obtain and retain for subsequent inspection, documentary evidence that the transport costs were included in the value for VAT at importation.

4.4   If the onward transport costs are not known at the time of importation and therefore not included in the value for tax at point of entry, then the transport service may be liable at a positive rate (see Appendix I).

4.5   Transport services supplied in connection with goods which are to be exported out of the EU are not affected by this provision. Such services will continue to be zero-rated provided, of course, that the transporter is in a position to satisfy the Inspector of Taxes that the zero-rating correctly applies and that s/he holds documentary evidence that the transportation in question is part of an export transportation service.

5.   **Ancillary services in Ports and Airports**

5.1   Services ancillary to intra-Community goods transport (i.e. loading, unloading, handling etc) supplied in port areas or in airports to meet the direct needs of ships or aeroplanes is zero-rated. This zero-rating applies for example to loading, unloading and handling of cargo in the port or airport, limited storage in the port or airport (no more than five days) while awaiting the onward transport of the goods. A more comprehensive list of the services affected is contained in Appendix III.

5.2   The zero-rating referred to in paragraph 5.1 **does not** apply to services ancillary to intra-Community goods transport supplied beyond the direct needs of ships and aeroplanes, such as breaking down of containers, packing or repacking and similar handling services supplied in connection with the onward distribution of goods, etc. Long term storage and warehousing of goods also continues to be taxable in the normal way.

5.3   Ancillary services in connection with intra-Community goods transport supplied outside of ports and airports are taxable by reference to the normal rules applying to transport services. Where supplied to an Irish VAT-registered or to an unregistered customer they are liable to Irish VAT. Where supplied to a customer registered for VAT in another Member State VAT liability arises in that other Member State in the customer's hands.

5.4   Services ancillary to the import and export of goods into and out of the EU will continue to be zero-rated in the normal way.

6.   **Intermediary services supplied by Irish VAT-registered persons**

6.1   The treatment of intermediary services (e.g. shipping agents) in connection with intra-Community goods transport and ancillary services is the same as that which applies to the services themselves. Such agency services supplied to VAT-registered persons are taxed by reference to the Member State of registration of the customer. In the case of such agency services supplied to unregistered persons, liability arises in the Member State where the transport begins or the ancillary service is carried out.

7.   **VAT status of immediate customer**

Suppliers of goods transport services should note that it is the VAT status of the immediate customer for the haulage or ancillary service that determines the VAT treatment of the supply. For example, where a supplier of goods transport services is contracted by a freight forwarder to transport goods belonging to a third party to another Member State, it is the VAT status of the freight forwarder that determines the treatment of the supply rather than the VAT status of the owner of the goods.

8.   **Verification of customers' VAT numbers**

8.1   As outlined above, the VAT status of the customer is the key element in determining the VAT treatment of intra-Community goods transport and ancillary services. Traders are advised to contact their EU customers and ask them to confirm in writing their VAT registration number. (An example of the type of letter that might be used for this purpose is attached in Appendix II). The customers VAT Number must be shown on the invoice issued by a transport operator in connection with intra-Community transport.

8.2 Where a trader who has doubts about the validity of a VAT number quoted he/she may contact Revenue at vimahelp@revenue.ie to establish whether a particular number is valid. The system is primarily intended to be used in such circumstances and is not intended for routine checks. Use of the verification system is not obligatory and traders who are aware of their customers' bona fides from trading with them over a period of time are not expected or required to use the verification system. A trader may also contact the EU Commission website at http://ec.europa.eu/taxation_customs/vies/vieshome.do?selectedLanguage=EN in this regard.

9.   Customers registered for VAT in the State

9.1 Customers registered for VAT in the State receiving intra-Community goods transport and related services from suppliers registered for VAT in the State are charged Irish VAT at the standard rate which may be deducted in accordance with the normal VAT rules relating to deductibility.

9.2 Customers registered for VAT in the State receiving such services from suppliers who are not registered in Ireland but are registered in another Member State are not charged VAT by their suppliers. However, these customers must account for Irish VAT in respect of such services as if the customers themselves had supplied the services. This is done by declaring a liability to VAT at the standard rate in the VAT return. Customers entitled to full or partial deduction of VAT charged to them simultaneously take a deduction of all or some of the tax, as appropriate. Customers who are not entitled to deduction in full or in part of the tax must pay the tax for which they are liable when sending the VAT return to the Collector-General.

9.3 The same procedure will be followed by customers registered for VAT in other Member States who receive intra-Community goods transport services from suppliers registered for VAT in Ireland

10   VAT at importation; treatment of onward transport costs

10.1 Where the onward costs are known at the time of importation, whether shown separately or not, they are included in the amount which is subject to VAT at the point of entry and taxable at the rate applicable to the supply of the goods in the State. Where, for example, goods are imported into Ireland for onward movement to another Member State, or vice versa, then if the value of the haulage is included in the amount subject to VAT at the point of entry the haulage service is zero-rated.

Further Information

Further information in the form of questions and answers is contained in Appendix I. Enquiries regarding any issue contained in this Information

Leaflet should be addressed to the Revenue District responsible for the taxpayer's affairs. Contact details for all Revenue Districts can be found on the Contact Details page.

This leaflet is issued by

**VAT Appeals and Communications Branch,
Indirect Taxes Division,
Dublin Castle**.

October 2008

Appendix 1
Intra EU Goods Transport Treatment in Single Market

Intra EU Goods Transport Treatment in Single Market			
Haulier	**Customer**	**Circumstances**	**VAT Position**
Person registered for VAT in Ireland	Person registered for VAT in Ireland	Intra-EU Transport	Haulier charges Irish VAT.*
Person registered for VAT in Ireland	Person registered for VAT in other EU Member State	Intra-EU Transport	Haulier charges no Irish VAT. Customer liable to VAT in other Member State under the reverse charge rule.
Person registered for VAT in Ireland	Not registered for VAT(e.g. private individual)	Intra-EU Transport from Ireland	Haulier charges Irish VAT because the transport begins in Ireland
Person registered for VAT in Ireland	Not registered for VAT(e.g. private individual)	Intra-EU Transport to Ireland	Liable to VAT in the other Member State because that is where the transport begins. Irish hauler register for VAT in the other Member State subject to the VAT rules in that other Member State.
Person registered for VAT in other EU Member State	Person registered for VAT in Ireland	Intra-EU Transport to or from Ireland	Haulier does not charge any VAT. Customer must account for Irish VAT* under the reverse charge rule.
Person registered for VAT in other EU Member State	Not registered for VAT(e.g. private individual)	Intra-EU Transport from Ireland	Liability to Irish VAT arises because the transport begins in Ireland. Haulier must register and charge customer Irish VAT.
Person registered for VAT in other EU Member State	Not registered for VAT(e.g. private individual)	Intra-EU Transport to Ireland	No liability to Irish VAT. Haulier charges the customer VAT in the other Member Stat eat the rate applicable there because that is where the transport begins.
Person registered for VAT in Ireland	Registered for VAT or private individual	Import of goods to Ireland where Ireland is the final destination	Where costs of transport are included in the value for VAT at importation then the transport service is zero-rated.
Person registered for VAT in Ireland	Registered for VAT or private individual	Import of goods to Ireland where another EU Member State is the final destination	Intra-Community transport service. However, if the value of the haulage is included in the amount subject to VAT at the point of entry, then the haulage service is zero-rated.
Person registered for VAT in other EU Member State	Registered for VAT or private individual	Import of goods into other EU Member States where Ireland is the final destination	Intra-Community transport service. However, if the value of the haulage is included in the amount subject to VAT at the point of entry, then the haulage service is zero-rated.

Note: In most cases Irish VAT can be claimed as a credit by a VAT-registered trader

Appendix II

Example: Confirm in writing your VAT registration number

Dear Customer,

VAT/TVA/IVA/MWSt/BTW

To comply with EU regulations, we must show your VAT/Sales Tax Number on our invoices.

To help us with this, could you please fill in the box below with your VAT/ Sales Tax Number and return it to us as soon as possible. Please ensure that the country prefix is included.

N.B. If you are not registered for VAT, please tick

In addition, to help us update our records, please forward your:

Telephone No. ....

Fax No. ....

Address ....

E. mail ....

Thank you.

Yours faithfully,

Appendix III

Ancillary transport services to which the zero-rate applies when supplied in ports and airports

- River and harbour pilotage
- Mooring and unmooring
- Stevedoring
- Landing
- Stowing
- Loading
- Restowing
- Cranage
- Tonnage dues
- Cargo dues
- Towage

VALUE ADDED TAX INFORMATION LEAFLET (DECEMBER 08)

ADVERTISING SERVICES

General

The supply of advertising services in the State is a taxable activity liable to VAT at the rate of 21.5%. Persons who supply advertising services in the course or furtherance of business and whose annual turnover in a 12 month period exceeds, or is likely to exceed the specified limit €37,500, are obliged to register and account for VAT.

Scope

The scope of the term 'advertising services' has not been defined in VAT law. However, as a matter of practice, advertising services include all services actually carried out by advertising agencies which have the aim of promoting a product, a business or a person, for example, media publicity, promotional launches and other publicity events.

Place of Supply

As a general rule the place of supply of services is the place where the person supplying the services has established an advertising services business. However, as an exception to this general rule and in common with other services listed in the Fourth Schedule to the VAT Act, the place of supply of advertising services is determined by the status and location of the recipient of the services.

Advertising services supplied by an advertising agent established in Ireland to any person in Ireland or to any non-business person within the EU are deemed to be supplied in Ireland and are liable to Irish VAT. Services supplied by Irish suppliers to business persons (whether they are registered for VAT or not) outside Ireland are deemed to be supplied at the place where the customer has a business establishment. Similarly, services received in Ireland by Irish business persons (whether they are registered for VAT or not) from overseas suppliers are deemed to be supplied in Ireland and are liable to Irish VAT.

Taxable Amount

The amount chargeable to VAT is the total consideration paid by the client in respect of the total service supplied.

Input Credit

Credit or deduction for VAT charged on expenditure incurred in providing advertising services is allowable except for expenditure relating to the following:

* the provision of food, drink, accommodation or other personal services for the accountable person, his agents or employees (for example, hotel costs);

* entertainment expenses;

* purchase or hire of cars or other road passenger vehicles;

- purchase of petrol;

- expenditure relating to exempt or non-business activities.

Where an advertising agency incurs VAT on food, drink, accommodation or other entertainment services, where such expenditure forms part of an advertising service in respect of which VAT is due and payable by the accountable person, the advertising agency may not claim credit in respect of the VAT incurred. VAT charged by the advertising agency to the client in respect to the advertising service itself is deductible, subject to the normal rules.

Further information

Enquiries regarding any issue contained in this Information Leaflet should be addressed to the Revenue District responsible for the taxpayer's affairs. Contact details for all Revenue Districts can be found on the Contact Details Page.

VAT Appeals & Communications Branch,
Indirect Taxes Division,
Stamping Building,
Dublin Castle.

December 2008

This information leaflet which sets out the current practice at the date of its issue is intended for guidance only and does not purport to be a definitive legal interpretation of the provisions of the Value-Added Tax Act 1972 (as amended).

VALUE ADDED TAX INFORMATION LEAFLET (DECEMBER 08)

AGRICULTURAL SERVICES

1.　Introduction

1.1　A farmer who supplies agricultural services in addition to carrying on a farming business is obliged to register and account for VAT if the receipts from such agricultural services exceed or are likely to exceed €37,500 in any 12 month period. In this context the term 'agricultural services' does not include insemination services, stock-minding or stock rearing, all of which may be excluded for the purposes of calculating the €37,500 threshold.

Farmers supplying agricultural services consisting only of insemination services, stock-minding or stock-rearing are not obliged to register for VAT but may opt to do so.

1.2　Agricultural services, as described, are treated for VAT purposes in the same way as other non-farming activities engaged in by farmers. For the purposes of determining whether or not a person is obliged to register, receipts from insemination services and stock-minding and stock-rearing may be disregarded. However, once a person becomes registered for VAT, all taxable receipts must be taken into account in determining liability, including receipts from farming and non-farming activities, (if any), in addition to receipts from the agricultural services. A list of typical agricultural services and the appropriate rates of VAT is attached at Appendix 1.

1.3　Application for registration should be made to the Revenue District responsible for your tax affairs.

It should be noted that once registered for VAT, the farmer ceases to be a 'flat-rate' farmer.

Accordingly, the flat-rate addition to prices does not apply to his/her sales to other VAT-registered persons. Instead, credit for VAT borne on inputs is obtained directly in the returns which s/he becomes obliged to make in the same way as other VAT-registered persons.

2.　Obligations of VAT-registered Farmers

2.1　VAT-registered farmers are obliged to:

1.　keep records which are sufficiently detailed to enable their liability as declared by themselves to be confirmed;

2.　issue invoices containing specified particulars in respect of taxable supplies to other accountable persons. If the consideration shown on an invoice is subsequently reduced and a tax adjustment is actually made, a credit note must be issued where the customer is a VAT-registered person, showing the amount of tax by which the liability has been reduced;

3.   submit a return on the appropriate form, normally every two months, of their supplies and taxable purchases together with a remittance for any tax due. This form is issued to registered persons before the end of each taxable period.

3.   Determination of Liability

3.1   A VAT-registered farmer is liable to pay VAT at the appropriate rate on taxable goods and services supplied by him/her. A VAT-registered farmer determines his/her VAT liability for each taxable period by calculating the total tax due on his/her sales of goods or services for the period and subtracting the deductible tax invoiced to him/her or paid on imports from non EU countries in the period - the difference is the amount which s/he pays. If the deductible tax exceeds the tax chargeable the difference is refunded.

4.   Taxable Amount

The amount on which an accountable person is liable, is the total amount which the person is entitled to receive for the goods or services supplied, including commissions, costs and charges, and all taxes (other than VAT).

5.   Accounting for VAT

The normal basis of accounting for VAT is the invoice or sales basis. However, a person may, subject to certain conditions (see paragraph 7) account for VAT on the 'moneys received' basis.

6.   Invoice Basis

A VAT-registered person using the invoice or sales basis of accounting will be liable to pay VAT by reference to his/her supplies as follows: - in the case of transactions with persons who are not registered for VAT s/he is liable at the rate in force at the time the goods or services are supplied; - in the case of transactions with other VAT-registered persons s/he is obliged to issue invoices and is liable to VAT at the rate of tax in force at the time s/he issues, or ought to issue an invoice.

7.   Moneys received Basis

7.1   Certain registered persons, including farmers, may use the moneys received basis of accounting instead of the more usual sales/invoice basis. Persons qualifying are

1.   persons whose annual turnover does not exceed and is not likely to exceed €1,000,000,

2.   persons supplying goods and services almost exclusively (at least 90 per cent) to unregistered persons.

7.2   Farmers wishing to avail themselves of this facility must specify this when applying for registration.

8.   Deduction for VAT charged on Purchases

8.1   A VAT-registered farmer is entitled to take a credit or deduction (i.e. set off against his/her liability) for VAT properly invoiced to him/her or paid on imports or intra- Community acquisitions in respect of most goods and services used in connection with his/her taxable activities. S/he is not required to pay the supplier before taking the credit.

8.2   Expenditure, in respect of which a credit or deduction may not be taken, is expenditure relating to:-

1.   the provision of food, drink, accommodation (other than accommodation in connection with certain conferences) or other personal services for the person, his/her agents or employees;

2.   entertainment expenses;

3.   purchase or hire of cars or other road passenger vehicles;

4.   purchase of petrol;

5.   contract work involving the handing over of goods when such goods are themselves not deductible;

6.   an exempt (for example, letting of premises for a period of less than 10 years) or nonbusiness activity, and

7.   VAT borne prior to registration.

8.3   A credit or deduction may be taken in respect of diesel, car repairs and maintenance, and car parts (for example, a set of tyres), subject to the condition that they are used for the purposes of a taxable business.

Appendix I

VAT Rates on Typical Agricultural Services

(The list is not exhaustive)

Agricultural services and their corresponding VAT rate

Supply	Rate (%)
Ploughing, harrowing, discing, rolling	13.5
Combined supply and sowing/planting of seeds/plants etc. for the production of food, including animal feed	zero
Combined supply and sowing/planting of other seeds, plants, etc.	13.5
Sowing/planting only of all seeds/plants	13.5
Combined supply and spreading of fertilisers	zero
Spreading only of fertilisers	13.5
Spraying/dusting of crops (whether or not chemicals are supplied by contractor)	13.5
Harvesting, reaping, mowing, baling	13.5
Silage making (including supply of silage additive and polythene cover)	13.5
Transport, storage	21.5
Stock minding and rearing	13.5
Stock-insemination	13.5
General consultancy and advisory services (including tax and general financial advisory services)	21.5
Farm management and accountancy services	21.5
Farm advisory services	13.5
Hiring of agricultural or other equipment	21.5
Farm relief services	13.5
Land drainage and land reclamation including removal of weed, scrub, bracken, pests, etc. and the supply and spreading of fertilisers and seeds under inclusive contract	13.5
Pruning, tree felling, hedge trimming	13.5
Landscaping (excluding architectural design services and the like)	13.5
Letting of farm buildings (short-term for period of less than 10 years)	exempt
Agricultural products – packing and preparation for market, cleaning, grinding and disinfecting	21.5

Where services liable at different rates are supplied for an inclusive charge the higher or highest rate involved normally applies to the entire charge.

Further information

Enquiries regarding any issue contained in this document should be addressed to the Revenue District responsible for your tax affairs.

This document is issued by

VAT Appeals and Communications Branch,
Indirect Taxes Division,
Dublin Castle.

December 2008

This information leaflet which sets out the current practice at the date of its issue is intended for guidance only and does not purport to be a definitive legal interpretation of the provisions of the Value-Added Tax Act 1972 (as amended).

VALUE ADDED TAX INFORMATION LEAFLET (DECEMBER 08)

AUCTIONEERING

1. **Introduction**

   This Leaflet deals with the VAT treatment of sales made under the special scheme for auctioneers as well as other Auction and Agency sales. A separate VAT Information Leaflet entitled 'Margin Scheme' dealing with the supply of works of art, collectors' items, antiques and second-hand goods by accountable dealers is available and should be read in conjunction with this leaflet.

2. **Sales of movable goods**

   Auctioneers selling movable goods are regarded for VAT purposes as buying and selling the goods simultaneously and are, therefore, principals in their own right. Accordingly, all auctioneers of movable goods are governed by the normal VAT rules i.e. the auctioneer is obliged to register if the annual turnover from sales of taxable goods exceeds or is likely to exceed €75,000 and the usual rules relating to the issue of invoices/settlement vouchers apply.

3. **Sales of immovable goods**

   Auctioneers engaged in connection with the selling of immovable goods are regarded as supplying a service and are liable for VAT on the commissions they receive at the standard 21.5% rate of VAT.

4. **Special scheme for Auctioneers**

   4.1 Section 10(B) Vat Act 1972 provides for the application of a scheme to certain works of art, collectors' items, antiques or movable second-hand goods which are sold by an auctioneer at a public auction. This scheme provides that where those goods are sold by an auctioneer, the auctioneer is liable for VAT on the profit margin. The arrangement is referred to as the "auction scheme" and the goods concerned are referred to as "auction scheme goods".

   4.2 **Auction Scheme goods**

   The auction scheme applies to works of art, collectors' items, antiques or movable secondhand goods passed to an auctioneer for sale by public auction by a person who is:-

   - a private individual, exempt person or a person who is otherwise not entitled to input credit on the acquisition of the goods, or

   - a person who is an insurance company which took possession of the goods in connection with the settlement of a claim under a policy of insurance from a person who was not entitled to input credit in respect of the goods, or

- an accountable dealer who has already applied the margin scheme to his or her supply of the goods (as described in VAT Information Leaflet 'Margin Scheme').

Effectively, this means that neither the person who passed the goods to the auctioneer nor the auctioneer him/herself was entitled to claim a VAT input credit on the transaction. The auctioneer should take reasonable precautions to ensure that the goods qualify as auction scheme goods, as set out in the bullets points above.

4.3   Auctioneer's margin

The auctioneer's margin is the difference between what the auctioneer receives from the purchaser and what he/she pays to the person who passed the goods to him/her for sale, and it is tax inclusive.

For example, the auctioneer receives €525 from the purchaser on sale of the goods and passes €500 to the seller. The auctioneer's margin in this instance is €25 tax inclusive.

4.4   Taxable amount

The taxable amount is the auctioneer's margin less the amount of VAT included in that margin. The following examples illustrate the position, assuming that

'A' is the seller of the goods,

'B' is the auctioneer, and

'C' is the purchaser of the goods from the auctioneer.

Example (a) here reflects normal practice

Sale proceeds (gross) from C to B =	€525
less commission charged to seller A =	€25
Seller A's net proceeds =	€500
Auctioneer's margin including tax at 21.5% =	€25
Tax included in the margin (at 21.5%) =	$\dfrac{€25 \times 21.5}{121.5}$
	= €4.42
Taxable Amount =	€25
less €4.42 =	€20.58

However, there may be situations where an auctioneer charges commission to both the seller and the purchaser. Where this occurs, the auctioneer's margin and the taxable amount are calculated as follows (example b):-

Example (b)

Sale proceeds (gross) from C to B =	€550
less commission charged to seller A =	€25
Total	€525
less commission charged to buyer C=	€25
Seller A's net proceeds =	€500
Margin, including tax at 21.5% =	€50
Tax included in the margin (at 21.5%) =	$\dfrac{€50 \times 21.5}{121.5}$
=	€8.84
Taxable Amount =	€50
less €8.84 =	€41.16

4.5 VAT rates

Generally, the normal VAT rules apply. The rate applicable is the rate applying to a sale of goods as new but there are some exceptions under the auction scheme. The exceptions are works of art and antiques, which are normally liable at the rate of 13.5 per cent but which become liable at the 21.5 per cent rate when sold under the auction/margin scheme. For technical reasons to do with the wording of the VAT Act 'concrete, ready to pour' and 'concrete blocks' also fall into this category and would become liable at 21.5 per cent in the unlikely event of an auction sale of these products.

4.6 Time of supply

For VAT accounting purposes, where the goods are passed to an auctioneer for sale, the time of supply to the auctioneer is regarded as having taken place when the auctioneer **sells** the goods to a purchaser at a public auction. The auctioneer is obliged to issue both to the purchaser and the vendor written details of the transaction.

4.7 Invoices

An auctioneer should not show on the invoice issued by him/her to the purchaser, the amount of VAT for which s/he is accountable in respect of auction scheme goods. Any such invoice should be clearly endorsed – **'Auction Scheme - this invoice does not give the right to an input credit of VAT'**.

If the principal is required under normal VAT rules to issue an invoice, the invoice issued by the auctioneer to the purchaser will fulfill this requirement.

4.8 Supply of goods to other EU Member States

Where an auctioneer supplies auction scheme goods to a VAT registered person in another EU Member State, the supply cannot be zero-rated as an intra-Community supply. Irish VAT included in the margin must be accounted for as if it was an auction scheme sale within the State. In this connection, the Member State of dispatch is deemed to be the legal place of supply. The foreign purchaser is not entitled to a repayment of such VAT.

4.9   Onward supply of Auction Scheme Goods

Auction scheme goods purchased from an auctioneer by an accountable person in connection with his or her business activities are treated in the same way as the other assets of his or her business and are fully liable to VAT on disposal.

4.10 Droit de Suite

Royalty payments due by the seller to artists under the recently implemented European Communities (Artist's Resale Right) Regulations 2006, known as Droit de Suite/Artists re-sale rights, do not effect the liability of the auctioneer who remains taxable on his/her margin.

5.   Agricultural produce (including fish)

These are not generally margin scheme or auction scheme goods.

5.1   Live cattle, sheep, goats, pigs and deer

These animals are generally sold through livestock marts, or by auctioneers or livestock dealers. Sales by marts, auctioneers or dealers are liable to VAT at the livestock rate. This rate is currently 4.8 per cent and is chargeable on the final accepted VAT exclusive bid or selling price plus such commissions or fees, if any, as are charged to the purchaser. Marts, auctioneers or dealers are obliged to register for VAT if their annual turnover exceeds or is likely to exceed €75,000.

5.2   Unregistered Farmers

If a farmer is not registered for VAT, the auctioneer must pay him or her an amount called a flat-rate addition. The addition is currently equal to 5.2 per cent on to the price paid to the farmer. The auctioneer is entitled to set off this addition against his or her liability of 4.8 per cent VAT on the sale of the animals.

Example:

VAT exclusive sale price to purchaser	€10,000
VAT @ (4.8%)	€480
Total paid by purchaser	€10,480
Commission on fees charged by auctioneer to farmer	€1,000
Net price paid to farmer	€9,000
Flat-rate addition of 5.2%	€468
Total paid to farmer	€9,468

VAT payable by auctioneer	€480
Less flat-rate addition	€468
Net VAT paid by auctioneer	€12

In order to qualify for the flat-rate addition, the farmer must sign a once-off declaration to the effect that s/he is not registered for VAT. The declaration must be retained by the auctioneer. If the farmer does not sign the declaration, he or she will be required instead to sign a settlement voucher or invoice made out by the auctioneer in respect of each separate sale, before the 5.2 per cent addition can be paid. To claim the 5.2 per cent deduction, the auctioneer must be in possession of that invoice, which must show details of the transaction and separately show the purchase price and the 5.2 per cent addition.

5.3 Registered farmers

In the case of livestock sold on behalf of registered farmers the auctioneer is entitled to claim the 4.8 per cent VAT invoiced to him/her by such farmers against the tax payable by him/her on the sale. Livestock is liable to VAT at the rate of 4.8 per cent.

5.4 Foreign buyers

Livestock sold within the State to export companies is taxable in the same way as livestock sold to other buyers. Sales of livestock to persons registered for VAT in other EU Member States and which are dispatched or transported from this State are zero rated provided that the essential conditions for zero-rating are met.

Livestock purchased within the State by non-EU buyers, including non-EU farmers, from a VAT-registered person, for example, a VAT-registered mart or export company, is taxable but the tax is refundable to the foreign buyer, subject to conditions. Claims for repayment should be made to

VAT Unregistered Repayments,
3rd Floor,
River House,
Charlotte Quay,
Limerick.

Telephone Lo-call **1890 252449** or from outside the Republic of Ireland **00353 61 212799**,
Fax: **00353 61 402125**,
email: unregvat@revenue.ie

5.5 Vegetables, fruit, eggs and dead poultry

These goods qualify for the zero rate of VAT and the auctioneer has a VAT liability on his or her commission or other charges albeit at the zero rate. He or she is entitled to claim the 5.2 per cent VAT input credit in respect of sales made on behalf of unregistered farmers, as outlined at paragraph 5.2 above.

5.6   Fish

Dead fish are liable at the zero rate of VAT and the auctioneer has a VAT liability on his or her commission or other charges at the zero rate. The rules outlined at paragraph 5.1 above apply, also, to sales of fish sold on behalf of unregistered fish farmers and unregistered fresh water fisherman.

5.7   Live Poultry and Live Ostriches

Live poultry and live ostriches are liable at 13.5 per cent. The rules outlined at paragraph 5.2 above apply, also, to sales of poultry and ostriches sold on behalf of farmers.

5.8   Flowers

Flowers are liable at 13.5 per cent and the auctioneer is liable to account for VAT at this rate on the final accepted bid plus any commission or fees charged to the purchaser. The rules outlined at paragraph 5.2 above apply, also, to sales of flowers sold on behalf of farmers.

5.9   Taxable consideration

Auctioneers selling agricultural produce are generally obliged to register for VAT if their annual turnover exceeds or is likely to exceed €75,000. VAT is chargeable on 'the total consideration which the person supplying the goods or services becomes entitled to receive in respect of or in relation to such supply of goods or services, including all taxes, commissions, costs and charges whatsoever, but not including value-added tax chargeable in respect of the supply'.

6.   Bloodstock, i.e. live horses

Horses are treated similarly to other livestock in so far as the sale by auctioneers and the flat-rate addition are concerned. However other special rules apply, as follows:-

6.1   Horses imported for sale by auction

Where horses are imported from outside of the EU for sale by auction, VAT-registered auctioneers may avail of the deferred payment scheme and undertake such importation without payment of VAT at the time of importation using deferred payment facilities. The auctioneer, by special arrangement with Revenue, undertakes liability for the VAT payable at importation. This however may in due course be disregarded provided the auctioneer accounts for VAT at 4.8 per cent on the ultimate sale of the horse, unless of course, the horse is sold for export or to a VAT registered person in another Member State of the EU and the horse is in fact dispatched or transported from the State. If the horse is not sold at auction the auctioneer must account for VAT at 4.8 per cent on the import value unless, again, the horse is re-exported.

6.2   Horses sold by Approved Auctioneers to foreign (non-established) Purchasers

Under a special arrangement for the bloodstock industry, a sale to a foreign(non-established) purchaser can be zero-rated even though the horse may not immediately be exported or dispatched to a registered person in another Member State. The arrangement may be operated by auctioneers who have been approved by the Revenue Commissioners for that purpose and who have undertaken responsibility for its administration. Under the arrangement a horse sold with an export undertaking or under a similar intra-Community arrangement may be zero-rated provided the horse is exported or dispatched from the State within 24 months of the date of supply or, in the case of yearlings purchased after 1 September of any year, is exported within 28 months of purchase. If the horse is subsequently sold in the State or not exported or dispatched from the State within the required time limits, VAT will have to be accounted for by the original vendor (i.e. the auctioneer).

Auctioneers wishing to participate in the scheme should apply to their local Revenue District and must be prepared to abide by the conditions set down by the Revenue Commissioners.

7.　Motor vehicles

A special scheme applies to auction sales of motor vehicles. This is detailed in a separate VAT Information Leaflet entitled 'Motor Vehicles'.

8.　Property (immovable goods)

Auctioneers dealing with immovable goods continue to be regarded as supplying a service, and are liable for VAT on their commissions plus charges at the standard rate. The auctioneer who charges a commission or fee, exclusive of VAT, of say, €5,000 in respect of the sale of a house is liable for VAT on this amount at 21.5 per cent. If in addition, he or she is entitled to recover an amount to cover expenses e.g. subsistence, travel, telephone, this amount forms part of the taxable consideration and is taxable at the same rate.

9.　Further Information

Enquiries regarding any issue contained in this Information Leaflet should be addressed to the Revenue District responsible for taxpayer's affairs. Contact details for all Revenue Districts can be found on the Contact Details page.

VAT Appeals and Communications Branch,
Indirect Taxes Division,
Dublin Castle.

December 2008

VALUE ADDED TAX INFORMATION LEAFLET (DECEMBER 08)

DANCES

Introduction

The promotion of dances is a taxable activity liable to VAT at the standard rate, currently 21.5 per cent. Dances are treated as an ordinary part of the activities carried on by an accountable person in the course or furtherance of business. There are special arrangements for dances held on licensed premises.

General Rules

Where a dance is held on premises licensed for the sale of intoxicating liquor, the licensee is deemed to be the promoter of the dance. The licensee is deemed to have received the total amount payable in respect of admissions, is liable to account for the tax chargeable and, if not already registered, is obliged to register if annual receipts from taxable activities exceed or are likely to exceed €37,500.

Where a dance is held on premises which are not licensed for the sale of intoxicating liquor, the promoter of the dance is accountable for the VAT chargeable, subject to the normal VAT rules. The promoter is obliged to register and account for VAT where his or her annual receipts from taxable activities (including the promotion of dances) exceed or are likely to exceed €37,500.

Dances in Licensed Premises

Scope

Dances that are promoted in the course or furtherance of business come within the scope of VAT liability. 'Dances' includes all **public** dances, that is, functions or gatherings which include dancing, and which are open to the public on payment of an admission charge, or on pre-purchase of a ticket (for example, cabarets, supper dances, discos, socials, and dances run by sports clubs). It does not include **private** dinner dances, where admission is **not** open to the public, for example, wedding receptions. Dinner dances held in hotels or other licensed premises for fund-raising purposes and not in the course or furtherance of business (for example benefit dances organised by charities or clubs on an occasional basis) are also outside of the scope of the provisions. In these latter cases the hotelier or licensee is not regarded as the promoter of the dance and is, therefore, liable only in respect of the receipts relating to the services supplied - for example, meals, drinks, etc.

Dances promoted by non-licensees

Where a person other than the licensee promotes public dances on the licensee's premises liability for the VAT chargeable remains with the licensee. The promoter is not the person accountable for VAT in these circumstances. Accordingly, the licensee would need to ensure that s/he takes appropriate steps to ensure that s/he is in a position to make the appropriate returns and pay over the tax chargeable to the Collector-General. In this regard, since the promoter's records are subject to examination by Revenue officers, the licensee might consider agreeing with the promoter on right of access to the promoter's relevant records.

Taxable Amount

The amount on which tax is chargeable is the total consideration received in connection with the dance. This includes the amounts paid by those admitted to the dance together with any other consideration received in connection with the dance. As already mentioned, the obligation to account for the tax is the responsibility of the licensee, notwithstanding such amounts may be received or receivable by a promoter or other person.

Where persons are admitted to dances for amounts less than the face-value of the ticket or where no admission is charged (complimentary tickets) the normal VAT rules apply and only the amount actually payable will attract liability.

Deductible VAT

A VAT-registered licensee is entitled to take credit or deduction against his or her VAT liability for the VAT charged on goods and services purchased in connection with the dance. It is a requirement of the VAT system that to take credit or deduction, the VAT registered person must be in possession of proper VAT invoices made out to him or her. Subject to this requirement, the licensee would be able to take credit for VAT charged and invoiced on the printing of tickets, spot prizes, advertising, light, heat, bands or groups, and other qualifying expenditure connected with the dance.

Deductions are not allowable unless the invoices are made out in the name of the licensee. Where the expenses are incurred by and the charges are invoiced to somebody other than the licensee, deduction against the licensee's liability will not be allowed.

Dinner Dances

Receipts from admissions to dinner dances are liable at the standard rate, currently 21.5 per cent, including the dinner element included in the charge. If there are separate charges 4 for the dinner and the dance and the payment of the charge for dinner is not a condition of admission to the dance, the dinner charge is liable at the reduced rate, currently 13.5 per cent, and the charge for admission to the dance is liable at the standard rate, currently 21.5 per cent.

Further Information

Enquiries regarding any issue contained in this Information Leaflet should be addressed to the Revenue District responsible for the taxpayer's affairs. Contact details for all Revenue Districts are available on the revenue website at: Contact Details

VAT Appeals & Communications Branch,
Indirect Taxes Division,
Stamping Building,
Dublin Castle.

December 2008

This information leaflet which sets out the current practice at the date of its issue is intended for guidance only and does not purport to be a definitive legal interpretation of the provisions of the Value-Added Tax Act 1972 (as amended).

VALUE ADDED TAX INFORMATION LEAFLET (DECEMBER 2008)

FARMERS & INTRA-EU TRANSACTIONS

1.   Introduction

This document sets out the VAT arrangements that apply to intra-EU transactions involving farmers.

2.   Definition of farmer for VAT purposes

2.1   For VAT purposes a farmer means a person who engages in at least one of the agricultural production activities in the State listed in appendix 1 and whose supplies consist exclusively of either or both

    1.   agricultural produce (other than bovine semen and nursery stock - see paragraph 3.1 b), or

    2.   agricultural services (other than agricultural contracting services - see paragraph 3.1 a), or

whose supplies consist exclusively of either or both agricultural produce (but see (a) above) and/or agricultural services (but see (b) above) and of one or more of the following:-

- machinery, plant or equipment which s/he has used for his/her farming activity;

- racehorse training services for which the annual turnover does not exceed and is not likely to exceed €37,500;

- goods, other than those referred to above, for which the annual turnover does not exceed and is not likely to exceed €75,000 or services, other than those referred to above, for which the annual turnover does not exceed and is not likely to exceed €37,500.

2.2   In brief therefore, a person who engages in agricultural production, and whose turnover from non-agricultural activities does not exceed the appropriate annual threshold, is a flat-rate farmer i.e. a farmer who is not obliged to register for VAT in respect of his/her farming activities.

3.   Obligation to register

3.1   A farmer is obliged to register where:-

    1.   his/her annual turnover from agricultural contracting activities other than insemination services, stock minding and stock rearing exceeds or is likely to exceed €37,500.

    2.   his/her annual turnover from sales of bovine semen other than to other farmers licensed as an A.I. centre or supplies to a person over whom the farmer exercises control, exceeds or is likely to exceed €75,000.

    3.   his/her annual turnover from retail sales of horticultural products exceeds or is likely to exceed €75,000.

4.   his/her annual turnover from supplies of agricultural services, other than insemination services, stock minding or rearing, and either or both bovine semen or nursery stock exceeds or is likely to exceed €37,500.

5.   s/he is in receipt of Fourth Schedule services from abroad (see appendix 3).

6.   his/her annual turnover from sales of bovine semen and retail sales of nursery stock exceeds or is likely to exceed €75,000.

7.   his/her annual turnover from intra-Community acquisitions exceeds or is likely to exceed €41,000.

8.   his/her annual turnover from taxable goods or services, other than any exclusions mentioned above exceeds or is likely to exceed the appropriate thresholds.

4.   Option to register

4.1   A farmer who is not obliged to register may elect to do so.

4.2   If a farmer is obliged to register under paragraph 3.1 (e) or (g) above such registration is effectively 'ring fenced' to the intra-Community acquisitions or the Fourth Schedule services. S/he is not obliged to register in respect of his/her farming activities.

4.3   Where s/he registers in respect of racehorse training this registration may also be isolated and s/he is not required to register in respect of his/her farming activities. In general Revenue will accept that where a racehorse trainer is also a farmer, that the training element is only 10 per cent of the total turnover.

5.   Flat-rate farmers

5.1   A flat-rate farmer is a farmer who is not registered for VAT in respect of his/her farming activities. In order to compensate for VAT paid on supplies to him/her, such a farmer is entitled to a flat-rate addition (at present 5.2%) to the prices at which his/her agricultural produce or agricultural services are supplied to VAT-registered persons including marts, agricultural co-operatives and meat factories. A flat-rate farmer is also entitled to reclaim VAT incurred in respect of the construction, extension, alteration or reconstruction of farm buildings, and land drainage, from the VAT Repayment (Unregistered) Section.

5.2   Flat-rate farmers have no Irish VAT liability in respect of purchases in other Member States provided the €41,000 threshold is not exceeded. Instead, VAT is charged in the Member State of purchase at the rate applicable there. **Farmers who exceed the acquisitions threshold** are liable to Irish VAT regardless of whether or not they have paid VAT in the Member State of purchase. Therefore, to avoid double taxation, farmers whose purchases in other Member States exceed or are likely to exceed €41,000 per annum must register and account for VAT here.

6.   Sales of agricultural produce by flat-rate farmers to persons who are registered for VAT in other Member States

6.1   The flat-rate addition which applies to supplies of agricultural produce within the State also applies to supplies made to VAT-registered traders in other Member States.

6.2   The VAT-registered person in the other Member State who buys the goods should, in order to obtain a refund of the flat-rate addition, be in possession of an invoice showing separately the purchase price of the goods and the flat-rate addition. This invoice, which is normally prepared by the purchaser, must be signed by the flat-rate farmer who must retain a copy of the invoice. A flat-rate farmer who is registered in respect of intra-Community acquisitions and/or because of Fourth Schedule services received from abroad only (see paragraph 4.2) should treat such sales in the same way and should not include his/her VAT number on the invoice. The purchaser of the goods in the other Member State may reclaim the flat-rate addition from Office of the Revenue Commissioners, VAT Unregistered Repayments, 3rd Floor, River House, Charlotte Quay, Limerick. (Telephone Lo-call 1890 252449 or 00353 61 212799, fax +353 61 402125 or email unregvat@revenue.ie.) It is necessary to complete the appropriate claim form (VAT 60 EU) and submit it together with a certificate of taxable status and the supporting invoice. Claim forms can be obtained from that office or from the Revenue website.

7.   'Distance sales'

7.1   Special rules obtain in the case of 'distance sales'. Distance sales are where a supplier in one EU Member State sells goods to a person in another Member State who is not an accountable person for VAT and the supplier is responsible for the delivery of the goods. Farmers should be aware of these rules because the practical effect is that they may have to register for VAT in another Member State.

7.2   Briefly, the position is that a flat-rate farmer who makes distance sales in excess of an annual threshold to another Member State is obliged to register for and charge VAT in that other Member State. Under EU VAT arrangements, Member States are required to adopt a distance sales threshold of either €35,000 (or the equivalent in national currency) or €100,000 (or equivalent). Farmers should contact the tax authorities in the other EU Member States to establish the appropriate limit there.

8.   Purchases by flat-rate farmers of goods from other Member States

8.1   A flat-rate farmer who is obliged to register for and pay VAT in respect of intra-Community acquisitions (and certain services received from abroad, if any - see paragraph 9) can, (unless s/he elects to be accountable in respect of all his/her activities) retain flat-rate farmer status in all other respects. Even if his/her acquisitions do not exceed the €41,000 threshold a farmer may opt to register in respect of intra-Community acquisitions (see paragraph 4.2).

8.2   A flat-rate farmer who is registered in respect of intra-Community acquisitions may purchase goods in other Member States free of VAT, subject to the normal Single Market rules, by quoting his/her VAT number to the supplier. The farmer is obliged to pay Irish VAT on such acquisitions through the periodic VAT return. A farmer registered in this way will not have any entitlement to recovery of VAT paid (but see paragraphs 5.1 and 10).

9.   Certain services received from abroad

9.1   A flat-rate farmer receiving 'Fourth Schedule' services from abroad is also required to register for VAT in respect of these services regardless of their cost to him/her. There is no threshold in respect of such services.

9.2   The services concerned include hire of equipment and machinery, accountancy and legal services, and consultancy services. A full list of the services concerned is contained in appendix 3. A farmer who is obliged to register for and pay VAT because of the receipt of these services must also account for VAT on all his/her intra-Community acquisitions, regardless of their value, but can, (unless s/he elects to be taxable in respect of all his/her activities) nevertheless, retain his/her flat-rate farmer status in all other respects. A farmer registered in this way will not have an entitlement to recovery of VAT paid (but see paragraphs 5.1 and 10). The requirement to register in respect of such services does not affect the farmer's flat-rate status but it does make him/her liable to VAT in respect of intra-Community acquisitions of goods, even if the €41,000 threshold is not exceeded (see paragraphs 8.1 and 8.2).

10.   Refunds on farm building work, etc.

Under an existing Refund Order, a flat-rate farmer may recover the VAT paid by him/her in respect of farm structures and land drainage by completing claim form VAT 58 and returning it, with the supporting invoices, to VAT Repayments Section (see contact details in paragraph 6.2). Where a flat-rate farmer is registered for VAT in respect of intra-Community acquisitions and/or certain services received from abroad (see paragraphs 8 and 9) s/he is still entitled to a refund under the Order. However this refund must be claimed as a deduction through periodic VAT returns and not be means of the VAT 58 form.

11.   Livestock brought into the State from another Member State

11.1 Temporary importation schemes apply in relation to imports from non-Community countries but livestock brought into the State from other Member States are normally treated as intra-Community acquisitions which are liable to VAT in the State once the threshold is exceeded (see paragraphs 8 and 9). This will not be the case, however, in the circumstances set out in paragraph 11.2.

11.2 Where livestock are brought into the State from another Member State for the purpose of having a service or treatment carried out on them (e.g. veterinary services) an intra-Community acquisition does not arise. Instead the service is liable to Irish VAT. In addition, an intra-Community acquisition does not arise in relation to livestock brought into the State where the livestock would qualify for temporary importation without payment of VAT if they were imported into the State from outside the EU. This normally means that transfer of ownership does not take place and that the livestock remain in the State for less than two years.

12. Livestock sent from the State temporarily to another Member State

The principles set down in paragraphs 11.1 and 11.2 apply in reverse with regard to livestock sent temporarily from the State to another Member State. In the case of such temporary transfers, the person who dispatches the livestock from the State must maintain a record showing details of the goods and the name, address and VAT number (if any) of the person to whom they are sent.

13. Intra-Community goods transport services

13.1 Farmers who regularly receive such services may wish to study VAT Information Leaflet 'Goods Transport and Ancillary Services within the EU'.

13.2 In general, a farmer who is not registered for VAT will be charged VAT by the haulage company at the appropriate rate, in the Member State of departure of the transport. For example, Irish VAT at the 21.5% standard rate will apply if goods are being transported from Ireland to France. No entitlement to recovery of such VAT arises for the farmer (but see paragraph 5.1).

13.3 If the farmer is registered for VAT only in respect of intra-Community acquisitions or received services s/he will not be entitled to any recovery of VAT charged by the haulier (but see paragraph 5.1). If the transport service is being received from a haulier in another Member State the farmer should ensure that his/her VAT number is made available to that haulier so as to avoid double taxation. The farmer must then pay VAT in respect of the service as if it were s/he who supplied the service in the same way as s/he accounts for VAT on received services (see paragraph 9). Again there is no entitlement to recovery of this VAT for the farmer.

Where a farmer is registered for VAT in respect of all his/her farming supplies s/he is entitled to a VAT credit on his/her VAT return.

14. New means of transport

14.1 here are special rules concerning the intra-Community acquisition of new means of transport. The person acquiring the new means of transport must always account for VAT in the Member State of destination of the goods.

Definitions of 'new means of transport' for VAT purposes.

Means of Transport	Specification	Definition
Motor Vehicle	over 48 cc or over 7.2. kw power	6 months old or less, or travelled 6,000 km or less
Boat	over 7.5 metres in length	3months old or less, or sailed for 100 hrs. or less
Aircraft	over 1,550 kg take-off weight	3 months old or less, or flown for 40 hrs. or less

14.3 If a flat-rate farmer acquires a new motor vehicle in another Member State, VAT must be paid on this vehicle at the time of its registration in the State. In the case of intra-Community acquisitions of new boats and aircraft, the VAT due must be paid to the local Collector of Customs & Excise on arrival of the boat or aircraft in the State. However, the acquisition of a new means of transport will not affect the flat-rate status of the farmer and the value of the new means of transport will not be included in the value of intra-Community acquisitions for the purpose of determining whether a farmer is required to register for VAT in respect of those acquisitions.

14.4 Agricultural plant and machinery, including tractors, are not regarded as a new means of transport for VAT purposes and are taxed under the normal rules for intra-Community transactions i.e. acquisitions of plant and machinery are treated as intra-Community acquisitions for the purpose of determining whether a farmer must register (see paragraph 8).

Appendix 1

Article 295 and Annex VII of Council Directive No. 2006/112/EC of 28 November 2006 - List of agricultural production activities

- Crop Production

    - General agriculture, including viticulture.

    - Growing of fruit (including olives) and of vegetables, flowers and ornamental plants, both in the open and under glass.

    - Production of mushrooms, spices, seeds and propagating materials; nurseries.

- Stock Farming together with Cultivation

    - General stock farming

    - Poultry farming

    - Rabbit farming

    - Beekeeping

    - Silkworm farming

    - Snail farming

- Forestry

- Fisheries

    - Fresh-water fishing

    - Fish farming

    - Breeding of mussels, oysters and other molluscs and crustaceans

    - Frog farming

Where a farmer, processes, using means normally employed in an agricultural, forestry or fisheries undertaking, products deriving essentially from his agricultural production, such processing shall also be regarded as agricultural production.

Appendix 2

Article 295 and Annex VIII of Council Directive No. 2006/112/EC of 28 November 2006 - list of agricultural services

Supplies of agricultural services which normally play a part in agricultural production shall be considered the supply of agricultural services, and include the following in particular:

- field work, reaping and mowing, threshing, baling, collecting, harvesting, sowing and planting.

- packing and preparation for market, for example drying, cleaning, grinding, disinfecting and ensilage of agricultural products.

- storage of agricultural products.

- stock minding, rearing and fattening.
- hiring out, for agricultural purposes, of equipment normally used in agricultural, forestry or fisheries undertakings.
- technical assistance.
- destruction of weeds and pests, dusting and spraying crops and land.
- operation of irrigation and drainage equipment.
- lopping, tree felling and other forestry services.

Appendix 3

The complete list of the Fourth Schedule services referred to in paragraph 9 is as follows:-

1. transfers and assignments of copyright, patents, licences, trade marks and similar rights

2. hiring out movable goods other than means of transport (but see note hereunder

3. advertising services

4. services of consultants, engineers, consultancy bureaux, lawyers, accountants and other similar services, data processing and provision of information (but excluding services connected with immovable goods)

5. telecommunications services

6. radio and television broadcasting services

7. electronically supplied services

8. the provision of access to, and of transport or transmission through, natural gas and electricity distribution systems and the provision of directly linked services

9. acceptance of any obligation to refrain from pursuing or exercising in whole or in part, any business activity or any such rights as are referred to in paragraph (a)

10. banking, financial and insurance services (including re-insurance and financial fund management functions but not including the provision of safe deposit facilities)

11. the provision of staff

12. the services of intermediaries who act in the name and for the account of a principal when procuring for him any services specified in paragraphs (a) to (k)

Note: Subparagraph (b) does not apply to movable goods hired out by lessors established outside the EU. These are excluded by a specific provision of VAT Law which, in effect, makes such lessors accountable for VAT in Ireland in the normal way.

Further Information

Enquiries regarding any issue contained in this Information Leaflet should be addressed to the Revenue District responsible for the taxpayer's affairs. (Contact details for all Revenue Districts.)

This leaflet is issued by

VAT Appeals and Communications Branch,
Indirect Taxes Division,
Dublin Castle.

December 2008

VALUE ADDED TAX INFORMATION LEAFLET (DECEMBER 2008)

FOOD & DRINK

1.   General

1.1   This Information Leaflet sets out the rates of VAT on supplies of food and drink.

1.2   Most food and drink sold by retail shops is chargeable to VAT at the zero-rate. This includes most basic foodstuffs, for example, bread, butter, tea, sugar, meat, milk, vegetables etc.. Certain items of food and drink are specifically excluded from the scope of the zero-rate. These are taxable at the rates of 13.5% or 21.5%. Food liable at the 13.5% rate includes flour or egg based bakery products e.g. cakes, crackers, certain wafers and biscuits. Food and drink liable at the 21.5% rate includes sweets, chocolates, confectionery, crisps, ice-cream and soft drinks.

In addition food and drink liable at the 21.5 % rate includes:-

- frozen desserts, frozen yogurts and similar frozen products, and prepared mixes and powders for making any such product or similar products;

- uncooked confectionery;

- savoury snack products made from cereal or grain, fried bread segments, pork scratchings, and similar products and

- soft drinks and alcohol.

2.   Food and drink supplied in the course of operating a catering business (including Vending Machines, Take-Aways, and Supermarkets).

2.1   Food and drink normally chargeable to VAT at the zero-rate becomes liable to VAT at 13.5% when supplied in the course of operating hotels, restaurants, cafes, canteens, public houses, caterers and other similar businesses or by means of vending machines.

2.2   Food and drink normally liable to VAT at the rate of 21.5% becomes **liable at 13.5% when supplied in the course of provision of a meal by any of the specified classes of business (see preceding paragraph) excluding alcohol, soft drinks and vegetable juice**.

2.3   Alcohol, soft drinks, bottled waters and health drinks are liable to VAT at 21.5% **in all circumstances**.

2.4   **All** hot take-away food is liable at 13.5% irrespective of the rate which would apply if it were supplied otherwise (but see paragraph 4.1).

2.5   Vending machine sales of **zero-rated** food and drink are liable at 13.5%. Food and drink other than zero-rated food and drink sold by means of a vending machine are taxable at the appropriate rates e.g. cakes 13.5%, confectionary 21.5%.

2.6   **Zero-rated** food and drink remains free of VAT so long as it is not supplied by means of a vending machine or in the course of operating any of the specified classes of business (see paragraph 2.1 above).

2.7   Cold take-away food and drink supplied by supermarkets, etc. are taxable at the zero, 13.5 or 21.5% rate, as appropriate (see paragraph 4.1).

3.   **Summary**

The rates of VAT appropriate to the supply of food and drink through the various outlets are set out below. A tabular summary is attached (Appendix I).

4.   **Retail shops including supermarkets**

4.1   Food and drink supplied by retail shops is liable at the zero, 13.5% or 21.5% rate as appropriate. The supply of freshly baked bread which may have retained some heat after baking but which has not been maintained heated and which is supplied in the course of a grocery business is liable at the rate appropriate to the same food when cold. However, hot food, including hot cooked chickens is liable to VAT at the 13.5% rate.

4.2   Supermarkets which operate restaurants or café's are generally regarded as carrying on a separate restaurant business. Food and drink supplied in the course of the restaurant business is normally liable at 13.5%. This includes fruit juices, ice cream, and confectionery supplied in the course of the provision of a meal (but the supply of such foods for taking away is liable at 21.5%). As already stated alcohol, bottled waters and soft drinks other than fruit juices are always liable at 21.5%.

4.3   Food and drink sold by means of vending machines is liable at 13.5% or 21.5%, as appropriate. The zero-rate never applies and food and drink which might otherwise be zero-rated is liable at 13.5% when sold by means of vending machines. The sale of zero rated food and drink by means of a vending machine is considered to be a service for VAT purposes.

5.   **Hotels, Restaurants, Cafés, Canteens, Public Houses, Caterers and Similar Businesses**

5.1   Food and drink, including fruit juices, supplied with a meal, but **excluding alcohol, bottled waters, soft drinks and vegetable juice** is liable at 13.5%. This is so even if the food or drink would have been liable at 21.5 % if supplied otherwise (for example, fruit juice or ice cream, liable at 21.5%, is liable at 13.5% when supplied in the course of the provision of a meal).

5.2   Alcohol, bottled waters and soft drinks are liable at 21.5% in all circumstances.

5.3   Staff meals, when taxable, are liable at 13.5%.

5.4   Receipts from admissions to dinner dances are liable at 21.5% including the dinner element in the charge. If there are separate charges for the dinner and the dance and payment of the charge for dinner is not a condition of admission to the dance the dinner charge is liable at 13.5% and the charge for admission to the dance is liable at 21.5% (see separate VAT Information Leaflet Dances).

6.   Take-aways: Traders whose business consists entirely of take-aways

6.1   Food and drink supplied will be taxable as follows:

* Hot take-away food and drink 13.5%.

* Cold take-away food and drink zero %. (e.g. sandwich/cold milk) or 13.5%. (e.g. cold apple tart) or 21.5% (e.g. chocolate bar), as appropriate.

* Alcohol, bottled waters and soft drinks 21.5%.

6.2   If cold take-away zero-rated food or drink is supplied with hot take-away food for an inclusive price (for example, coleslaw with hot chicken) the entire charge is liable at 13.5%. Soft drinks supplied with hot take-away food for an inclusive price are liable at 21.5%. It will be open to the proprietor of a take-away business to charge separately for the different constituents of a take-away meal and to pay tax accordingly.

6.3   The term hot take-away food and drink should be understood as including cooked food which is supplied while hot for the purpose of consumption while hot, that is, at a temperature above the ambient air temperature. It includes items such as burgers which consist of hot meat enclosed in a cold bun, cooked chickens and similar food. The term does not include freshly baked bread which may be hot at the time of purchase.

7.   Take-aways: Traders whose business does not consist entirely of take-aways

Although, strictly, zero-rated food supplied in the course of operating a hotel, restaurant, public house, canteen or similar business is liable at 13.5%, application may be made to the Revenue District responsible for your tax affairs to have the take-away activities treated concessionally as a separate activity and, to the extent that the take-away's consist of zero-rated food, relieved accordingly.

8.   Waste food

8.1   Waste food of all kinds which is sold as animal food may be regarded as qualifying for the zero-rate of VAT.

8.2   Waste oils sold for reprocessing are liable to VAT at the 21.5% rate.

9.   Location Catering

This service is liable at 13.5% but alcohol, bottled waters and soft drinks supplied are liable at 21.5%.

10.   Catering on off-shore oil rigs outside territorial waters and on foreign-going ships and aircraft

The zero-rate effectively applies.

11. Catering in schools and hospitals

Catering services are exempt from VAT where supplied

1. to **patients** of a hospital or nursing home in the hospital or nursing home; and

2. to **students** of a school in the school.

Further information

Enquiries regarding any issue contained in this Information Leaflet should be addressed to the Revenue District responsible for the taxpayer's affairs. Contact details for all Revenue Districts can be found on the Contact Details page.

VAT Appeals and Communications Branch,
Indirect Taxes Division,
Dublin Castle.

December 2008

Appendix I

Food and Drink: Rates of VAT

Type of Food or Drink	How supplied				
	With meals in hotels, restaurants, canteens, pubs etc.	By hotel other than with meals	By means of vending machines	By retail stores(see note)	By 'take-away' only business
All food and drink **except** alcohol and soft drinks	13.5%	13.5%, 21.5%	13.5%, 21.5%	0%, 13.5%, 21.5%	0%, 13.5%, 21.5%
Zero-rated food	13.5%	13.5%	13.5%	0% (cold), 13.5% (hot)	0% (cold), 13.5% (hot)
Cakes, biscuits (other than chocolate covered biscuits)	13.5%	13.5%	13.5%	13.5%	13.5%
Chocolates, confectionary, chocolate biscuits, crisps, ice cream	13.5%	21.5%	21.5%	21.5%	21.5%
Alcohol, bottled waters and soft drinks including health drinks	21.5%	21.5%	21.5%	21.5%	21.5%
Fruit Juices including freshly squeezed juices	13.5%	21.5%	21.5%	21.5%	21.5%
'Take-aways' - hot		13.5%		13.5%	13.5%
'Take-aways' - cold		0%, 13.5%, 21.5%		0%, 13.5%, 21.5%	0%, 13.5%, 21.5%
'Take-aways' - hot and cold for inclusive price		13.5%, 21.5%		13.5%, 21.5%	13.5%, 21.5%
Chips (cooked)	13.5%	13.5%		13.5%	13.5%
Dinner Dances	21.5% (see para 5.4 of leaflet)				
Service Charges	13.5%				

Note: Retail Stores including supermarkets – see paragraph 4 of leaflet.

This information leaflet which sets out the current practice at the date of its issue is intended for guidance only and does not purport to be a definitive legal interpretation of the provisions of the Value-Added Tax Act 1972 (as amended).

VALUE ADDED TAX INFORMATION LEAFLET (DECEMBER 2008)

FOOTWEAR

1. **General**

   The supply of footwear other than certain children's personal footwear (see paragraphs 3 to 5 below), is chargeable to VAT at the 21.5% rate. Paragraph (xix) of Second Schedule to the VAT Act 1972 (amended) refers.

2. **Meaning of footwear for VAT purposes**

   The term 'footwear', for VAT purposes, should be understood as meaning shoes, boots, slippers etc. including fur footwear but not socks, stockings etc.. Neither does the term include roller blades, roller skates and the like.

3. **Meaning of children's personal footwear**

   VAT law provides that the zero rate applies to articles of children's personal footwear of sizes which do not exceed the average foot size appropriate to children under 11 years of age, which are described, labelled, marked or marketed on the basis of age or size.

   It is therefore important to note that the legal basis for the relief of VAT of certain children's footwear requires that the footwear in question is both:-

   - designed specifically for the use of children and

   - of a size no larger than the average size applicable to children under 11 years of age.

   In the practical administration of the tax, the supply of baby and infant footwear, and footwear which has been specifically designed for children in sizes up to and including size 5½ (38 continental or other equivalent) qualifies for the zero rate.

   Children's footwear, the sizes of which exceed 5½ (38 continental or other equivalent) and adult's footwear, irrespective of size is taxable at 21.5%.

4. **Certain styles common to children and adults**

   It is accepted that there may be a difficulty in respect of a small number of styles of shoes and boots which are not designed as either adults' or children's footwear, and **which are manufactured in the full range of sizes from the smallest children's size* to large adult sizes.** Revenue are prepared, concessionally, to accept that the zero rate may apply to sizes up to and including size 5½ for these specific styles.

   Footwear ranges not starting at the smallest children's size*, e.g. ranges starting at large size 1 or 2, are taxable at 21.5% **in all sizes** unless it can be shown that they were designed for the use of children, in which case the size 5½ cut-off will apply.

5.   **Sports leisure footwear (trainers)**

Sports leisure footwear (trainer type footwear) is normally designed in three separate ranges, i.e. for men, for women, and for children. Accordingly, men's and women's ranges are taxable in all sizes and children's ranges are zero-rated (except for any sizes exceeding 5½). Where a particular range of such footwear is available in a single style common to adults and children, and where it is also available in the full range of sizes from smallest children's size* to large adult sizes, then it may also benefit from the concession outlined at paragraph 5 above.

*Smallest to be taken as the usual smallest size in non-infant children's ranges.

Articles of children's personal footwear which are not described, labelled, marked or marketed on the basis of age or size do not qualify for the zero rate.

6.   **Sports footwear**

Revenue are prepared to continue with their concessional treatment of football boots and other sports footwear as being articles of 'personal footwear' and they therefore may benefit from the concession outlined at paragraph 5 above. However roller blades, roller-skates, etc. will continue to be taxable at 21.5% in all sizes.

7.   **Orthopaedic footwear**

The zero rate of VAT applies to the supply of orthopaedic footwear specially made or specially adapted for a particular patient on the basis of a prescription issued by a medical doctor.

8.   **Second-hand footwear**

Second-hand footwear is liable at the same rate as it would be if new, i.e. zero or 21.5%.

9.   **Hire of footwear**

The hiring of footwear is a service and taxable at 21.5% VAT irrespective of the type of footwear involved.

10.   **Repair of footwear**

The repair of footwear is taxable at 13.5% VAT.

11.   **Imports and EU acquisitions of footwear**

Imports and EU intra-Community acquisitions of footwear are taxable on resale at the zero or 21.5% rates, as appropriate. EU intra-Community acquisitions must be shown correctly on VAT returns.

12.   **Further information**

Enquiries regarding any issue contained in this Information Leaflet should be addressed to the Revenue District responsible for the taxpayer's affairs. Contact details for all Revenue Districts can be found on the Revenue website at Contact Details

This leaflet is issued by:

VAT Appeals and Communications Branch,
Indirect Taxes Division,
Dublin Castle.

December 2008

This information leaflet which sets out the current practice at the date of its issue is intended for guidance only and does not purport to be a definitive legal interpretation of the provisions of the Value-Added Tax Act 1972 (as amended).

VALUE ADDED TAX INFORMATION LEAFLET (DECEMBER 2008)

FOURTH SCHEDULE SERVICES

1. This information leaflet sets out the VAT treatment of the services listed in the Fourth Schedule to the VAT Act, 1972 (as amended). These are set out in full in Paragraph 3 and a brief guide to them is set out in Paragraph 24.

Place of Supply of Fourth Schedule Services

2. The general rule in relation to the place of supply of services is that they are taxable at the place where the supplier is established. However, certain services are taxable where physically performed or where property is located. Normally, it is the suppliers who account for VAT due. However, there are certain types of services which, because they are generally intellectual or intangible in nature and easily traded internationally, are treated differently when supplied across national boundaries for the purposes of the customer's business. When they are received from outside the State for business purposes or supplied to a business outside the State, it is the recipient of the service who accounts for any VAT due. It should be noted that where both the supplier and the customer are established in the one State, then the general rule applies i.e. the supplier accounts for any VAT due.

3. The legal provisions are contained in Section 5(6)(e) and the Fourth Schedule to the VAT Act 1972(as amended). The corresponding provisions of the VAT Directive 2006 are contained in Article 52 (a), (b) and (c).

List of Fourth Schedule Services

3. The services are as follows:

    1. Transfers and assignments of copyright, patents, licences, trade marks and similar rights; (1A) hiring out of movable goods other than means of transport

    2. advertising services;

    3. services of consultants, engineers, consultancy bureau, lawyers, accountants and other similar services, data processing and provision of information (but excluding services connected with immovable goods);

        *   (3A) Telecommunications services;

        *   (3B) Radio and television broadcasting services;

        *   (3C) Electronically supplied services;

        *   (3D) The provision of access to, and of transport or transmission through, natural gas and electricity distribution systems and the provision of other directly linked services;

4. acceptance of any obligation to refrain from pursuing or exercising in whole or in part, any business activity or any such rights as are referred to in paragraph (i);

5. banking, financial and insurance services (including re-insurance and financial fund management functions, but not including the provision of safe deposit facilities);

6. the provision of staff;

7. the services of intermediaries who act in the name and for the account of a principal when procuring for him any services specified in paragraphs (i) to (vi).

Fourth Schedule Services received from outside the State

4. Persons registered for VAT in the normal course of business who receive any of the taxable services listed in the Fourth Schedule from outside the State must account in Box T1 in their periodic VAT returns, along with their other VAT liabilities, on the invoiced amounts at the appropriate rate as if they had themselves made the supply. They must furnish their VAT number to the supplier. They are entitled to a credit for such VAT accounted for, in Box T2 of the return. Please see paragraphs 12 to 15 for details of entitlement to deductibility.

5. VAT-exempt persons (e.g. bookmakers, banks, insurance companies), and persons whose activities are outside the scope of VAT, such as charitable organizations, who receive taxable Fourth Schedule Services for business purposes from outside the State, must register and account for Irish VAT on these received services. It might be noted that persons in the State which receive Fourth Schedule services from a person established in another EU Member State where VAT is not charged in that EU Member State because the Irish recipient held himself/herself out to the supplier to be an accountable person, are required to self-account for Irish VAT on those received services. They will receive periodic VAT returns from the Office of the Collector General and must account for VAT in Box T1 of the return on the amounts charged to them, as if they had supplied them themselves from within the State. Where such persons receive taxable Fourth Schedule services for the purposes of an exempt business are not entitled to a VAT credit in the VAT return.

6. Government Departments, local authorities and bodies established by statute who receive Fourth Schedule Services from outside the State must register and account for the VAT on these services unless, in cases where they are supplied from another EU Member State, VAT is chargeable by the supplier in that Member State. It may be noted that Section 77 (1)(a) of the Finance Act 2007 provides for a change in the treatment of Fourth Schedule Services received by Government Departments, local authorities, and bodies established by statute. However, this change

is subject to a commencement order being made by the Minister for Finance. Such an order has not yet been made.

7.   A turnover threshold does not apply to persons in receipt of Fourth Schedule Services. Accordingly, all persons who receive such services from outside the State for business purposes must register and account for VAT.

8.   An individual receiving Fourth Schedule Services for private (non-business) purposes is not obliged to register or account for Irish VAT in respect of the receipt of those services. Those services will be taxed in the country of the supplier.

Implications of registering for VAT in respect of received Fourth Schedule Services

9.   Exempt persons retain their non-accountable status in respect of their non-accountable activities, even where they are obliged to register and account for received Fourth Schedule Services. Flat-rate farmers, fishermen and race-horse trainers who register in respect of Fourth Schedule Services are entitled to retain their unregistered status in respect of their farming or fishing activities.

10.   Businesses which supply taxable goods or services and are not already registered for VAT because they are below the threshold for registration and who, for business purposes, receive Fourth Schedule Services from outside the State, are obliged to register and account for VAT on those services, irrespective of their value. However, once registered for Fourth Schedule Services they are required to account for VAT on all their activities.

Rates of VAT

11.   The rate at which VAT is chargeable on Fourth Schedule Services is the same as that which applies to similar services supplied within the State, generally liable at the standard rate 21.5 per cent. The amount on which VAT is chargeable is the amount payable to the foreign supplier at the rate of exchange (if not in €) applicable on the date of the invoice. The receipt of certain services such as banking, financial and insurance will not give rise to a VAT liability. The supply of distance teaching electronically retains the VAT classification that applies to it when supplied directly.

Claim for credit on VAT Return

12.   A person who is registered for VAT in the State is entitled to claim a credit for VAT accounted for on received Fourth Schedule Services for the purpose of his/her taxable activities. Thus, the entries on the VAT return, T1 for accounting and T2 for credit, are self-cancelling and no net VAT is actually paid over in respect of the transaction.

13.   A person who is obliged to register for VAT solely in respect of Fourth Schedule Services is not entitled to any VAT credit or deduction in respect of the VAT accounted for on receipt of those services.

14. Persons whose activities are engaged in partly taxable, partly exempt activities in the State will be entitled to a VAT credit only to the extent that the services are for use in the taxable activities of the business.

15. Persons whose activities are outside the scope of the tax or whose activities are exempt from VAT are not entitled to any VAT credit.

Supply of Fourth Schedule Services to a business customer outside the State

16. When an Irish business supplies a taxable Fourth Schedule service to a business customer established in another EU Member State or outside the EU, there is no liability to Irish VAT i.e. they are effectively zero rated. In such cases the place of supply is deemed to be the place of establishment of the recipient. Where the customer is established in another EU Member State, VAT is accounted for in that Member State. Where the customer is in business in another Member State but is not registered for VAT, the Irish supplier of Fourth Schedule Services should still apply the effective zero rate of VAT to the supply.

17. When an Irish business supplies goods or services outside the State only they are not required to register for VAT but are entitled to a repayment of input VAT in accordance with Section 12(1)(b) of the VAT Act. In practice, an Irish business whose supplies consist only of Fourth Schedule Services outside the State is permitted to register for VAT and to reclaim input VAT by means of the VAT return, subject to the normal restrictions.

Evidence of the business status of the recipient

18. Where the service is supplied to a VAT registered customer in another Member State, the supplier must ascertain the VAT Number of the customer and that number, and an indication that the reverse charge applies must be included on the relevant invoice issued by the supplier along with the suppliers' own VAT Number and the usual information. It is possible to verify the format of a VAT Number at the EU Commission or whether a VAT Number is appropriate to a particular trader by contacting the VIMA Office at vimahelp@revenue.ie.

Fourth Schedule Services supplied to a private individual in EU

19. Fourth Schedule Services supplied to private individuals are subject to Irish VAT, even if the individual resides in another EU Member State.

Fourth Schedule services supplied to customers resident or established outside the EU

20. Fourth Schedule services supplied to customers resident or established outside the EU are not subject to Irish VAT whether received for private or business purposes.

Fourth Schedule Services - summary table

21.   The person liable to pay Irish VAT in respect of Fourth Schedule Services

Country of establishment of supplier	Country in which customer established	Status of Customer	Place of supply	Person liable to pay Irish VAT
Ireland	Ireland	Business or Private	Ireland	Supplier
Ireland	Other EU State	Business	Other EU State	No Irish VAT
Ireland	Other EU State	Private	Ireland	Supplier
Ireland	Outside EU	Business or Private		No Irish VAT * - **
Other EU State	Ireland	Business	Ireland	Customer
Other EU State	Ireland	Private	Other EU State	No Irish VAT
Outside EU	Ireland	Business	Ireland	Customer
Outside EU	Ireland	Private	Outside EU	No Irish VAT * - **

* Telecommunications

Where telecommunications services are supplied to a private customer and the effective use and enjoyment of these services takes place within the State, the place of taxation is Ireland and VAT registration by the supplier is required.

** Electronically Supplied Services (e-Services)

The 'business to consumer' place of supply rule for e-services provides that, where a non-EU business supplies such services to a private consumer in any Member State, the place of supply will be the place where the consumer normally resides. For example, if a Canadian business supplies electronic services to an Irish consumer, the place of supply (and of taxation) is the State. See VAT Information Leaflet - e-Services and Broadcasting.

Traders with more than one establishment

22.   A trader may have a number of establishments within the EU or indeed outside the EU. The place where the service is deemed to be received for VAT purposes is the establishment of the trader at which, or for the purposes of which, the services are most directly used or to be used, as the case may be.

Certain Fourth Schedule services supplied in connection with property

23.   It should be noted that services of consultants, lawyers, accountants and other similar services listed at Paragraph (iii) of the Fourth Schedule are not treated as Fourth Schedule Services where they are connected with property. Property includes roads, buildings, walls and fences.

24.   Examples of property related services are:

   • Services in connection with the supply or letting of property or a license relating to property

- Services supplied in the course of construction, alteration, demolition, repair or maintenance of any building.

- Services of estate agents, auctioneers, valuers, architects, surveyors, engineers and similar professional people relating to land and buildings. This includes the management, conveyancing, survey or valuation of property by a solicitor, surveyor or loss adjuster or on-site supervision of property.

Such services are taxable by reference to the place where the property is located.

Fourth Schedule services which are not related to property include:

- The hire of movable goods or plant and machinery on their own.

- The supply or secondment of staff other than as part of a contract by the supplier to undertake the work for which the staff are employed.

- A general assessment of the property market with a view to investment.

Guide to the services covered in the Fourth Schedule

25.   The following provides a more detailed breakdown of the list of services covered in the Fourth Schedule.

   1.   Transfers and assignments of copyright, patents, licences, trade marks and similar rights;

   This relates to rights to intellectual property in return for royalties and covers, for example, the transfer of rights in respect of text, publications, music, software, film, television or radio recordings, images, photographs in return for royalties or other form of payment. It does not include a right granted, for example, to a supplier of goods or services to enter a premises to carry on his/her business. The supply of standarised software (e.g. games) other than electronically is a supply of goods and VAT must be accounted for as an intra-community acquisition of goods or at the point of importation when coming from outside the EU.

   1.   hiring out of movable goods other than means of transport;

   This includes the hiring of plant and machinery, industrial and commercial equipment. It should be noted that the place of supply of the hiring out of movable goods to a customer in the State by a person established outside the EU is considered to be the place where the movable goods are effectively used and VAT registration in the State is required. Please note, the hiring out of means of transport is taxable where the lessor has established his/her business – please see VAT Information Leaflet - Leasing (International) of Means of Transport.

2.   **advertising services;**

This includes the provision of promotional services, product endorsement, publicity, advertising space or time in the media.

3.   **services of consultants, engineers, consultancy bureau, lawyers, accountants and other similar services, data processing and provision of information (but excluding services connected with immovable goods);**

* **Consultants:**
  - This includes the provision of professional advice such as business analysis, research and development, software maintenance, other than site-specific services related to property. While scientific services are taxable by reference to the place where they are physically performed, services such a laboratory analysis which forms the basis of a professional assessment of goods by the laboratory, are considered as the services of a consultant.

* **Engineers:**
  - This includes design of products or systems. It does not include repair services or services connected with property.

* **Lawyers:**
  - This includes services provided by solicitors and barristers. It does not include conveyancing services relating to property, but it does include the general administration of an estate even if that estate includes property. The services of arbitrators are not considered to be the services of a lawyer or similar services.

* **Accountants:**
  - The services of a bookkeeper or administration services are not considered to be Fourth Schedule services. Payroll services are likewise not considered to be Fourth Schedule services.

* **Other Similar Services:**
  - The provision of similar services to those provided by consultants, engineers, lawyers, and accountants etc. by professionals are generally covered under this. Examples include creative design services, management services, services of loss adjusters, assessors, surveyors provided they are not supplied in connection with property. Services which are cultural, artistic, sporting, scientific or entertainment services are generally excluded (please see 'Consultants' above for further details of certain scientific type services). Educational services are also generally excluded but electronically supplied distance teaching is considered to be a Fourth Schedule service.

- **Data Processing:**
  - This can be loosely described as the provision of information in a particular format through the processing of supplied data.

- **Provision of Information:**
  - This includes the supply of information of any nature in any form, such as customer support services, commercial data and on-line information.

It should be noted again that any of the above listed services do not retain their Fourth Schedule status where supplied in connection with property. See paragraphs 23 & 24 .

8. **telecommunications services;**

   This means services relating to the transmission, emission or reception of signals, writing, images and sounds of information of any nature by wire, radio, optical or other electromagnetic systems and includes

   - the related transfer or assignment of the right to use capacity for such transmission, emission or reception, and

   - the provision of access to global information networks

9. **radio and television broadcasting services;**

   This includes, for example, radio and television signal received by VAT registered pubs and clubs who buy in those broadcasting services from suppliers established in other Member States or outside the EU.

10. **electronically supplied services;**
    This includes, for example,

    - website support, web-hosting, distance maintenance of programmes and equipment

    - supply of software and updating of it

    - supply of images, text and information, and making databases available,

    - supply of music, films and games, including games of chance and gambling games, and of political, cultural, artistic, sporting, scientific and entertainment broadcasts and events

    - supply of distance teaching.

It should be noted that where a supplier and his/her customer communicates by means of electronic mail, this shall not of itself mean that the service performed is an electronic service. Please see VAT Information Leaflet - e-Services and Broadcasting.

11. **the provision of access to, and of transport or transmission through, natural gas and electricity distribution systems and the provision of other directly linked services;**

Charges incurred for services consisting of access to and transmission through gas and electricity distribution systems are taxed where the business customer using these services is located. The treatment also applies for other directly linked services such as grid management, monitoring etc

4. **acceptance of any obligation to refrain from pursuing or exercising in whole or in part, any business activity or any such rights as are referred to in paragraph (i);**

This includes entering into an agreement not to exercise a right of the type referred to in paragraph (i) above.

5. **banking, financial and insurance services (including re-insurance and financial fund management functions, but not including the provision of safe deposit facilities);**

This includes exempt financial services of a kind listed in the First Schedule of the VAT Act as well as taxable financial services such as financial and investment advice, safe-keeping services, factoring, rent and debt collection, and other taxable financial services.

6. **the provision of staff;**

This involves the supply or secondment of staff where the staff are placed under the direct control of the other party as employees and the supplier is not contracted to undertake the work for which the staff are being employed.

7. **the services of intermediaries who act in the name and for the account of a principal when procuring for him any services specified in paragraphs (i) to (vi);**

This includes services of agents such as copyright agents and advertising agents in procuring for their principals any of the services listed in the Fourth Schedule.

Further Information

Enquiries regarding any issue contained in this Information Leaflet should be addressed to the Revenue District responsible for the taxpayer's affairs. Registration forms TR1 - Tax Registration form for Sole Traders, Trusts and Partnerships and TR2 - Tax Registration form for Companies are available, along with general information on VAT and other taxes from the Revenue website at www.revenue.ie. Contact details for all Revenue Districts can be found on the Revenue website at Contact Details.

This leaflet is issued by:

VAT Appeals and Communications Branch,
Indirect Taxes Division,
Dublin Castle.

December 2008

Appendix 1 - List of EU Member States

- AT - Austria
- BE - Belgium
- BU - Bulgaria
- CY - Cyprus
- CZ - Czech Republic
- DE - Germany
- DK - Denmark
- EE - Estonia
- EL - Greece
- ES - Spain
- FI - Finland
- FR - France
- GB - United Kingdom
- HU - Hungary
- IE - Ireland
- IT - Italy
- LT - Lithuania
- LU - Luxembourg
- LV - Latvia
- MT - Malta
- NL - Netherlands
- PL - Poland
- PT - Portugal
- RM - Romania
- SE - Sweden
- SL - Slovenia
- SK - Slovakia

This information leaflet which sets out the current practice at the date of its issue is intended for guidance only and does not purport to be a definitive legal interpretation of the provisions of the Value-Added Tax Act 1972 (as amended).

VALUE ADDED TAX INFORMATION LEAFLET (DECEMBER 2008)

GOODS AND SERVICES SOLD TOGETHER. SECTION 11(3) OF THE VAT ACT AS AMENDED

1. **Introduction**

   Section 11(3) of the VAT Act provides for rules on how the supply of a package comprising two or more elements, each potentially attracting VAT at different rates, is treated for VAT purposes. This provision came into operation on 1 November 2006. Regulation 21 of the Value-Added Tax Regulations 2006 (S.I. No. 548 of 2006 (PDF, 430KB)), covers certain specific areas and supplements the primary legislation in the VAT Act. This information leaflet sets out the VAT treatment of goods and services sold together.

2. **General**

   As a general rule, the consideration payable in respect of goods or services supplied as a package is apportioned between each of the individual elements in the supply. VAT applies to these elements at the rate that would apply to them if they were each sold separately. However, in relation to certain categories of supplies referred to as **composite supplies**, VAT is chargeable at the rate applicable to the principal element in the supply.

3. **Definitions**

   Section 1 of the VAT Act provides definitions of different types of supply. Although there are five definitions, two main categories are of relevance for the purpose of applying the appropriate VAT treatment namely a "multiple supply" and a "composite supply":

   - a **multiple supply** is defined as being two or more supplies made in conjunction with each other to a customer for a total consideration covering all those where each of those supplies are physically and economically dissociable from each other. In this arrangement each of the supplies made in conjunction with others is treated as an **individual supply** and is taxable/exempt in its own right;

   - a **composite supply** has one principal element referred to as a **principal supply** with the other elements of that supply being described as **ancillary supplies**. These always accompany the principal supply and the main feature of an ancillary supply is that it would not make sense from an economic or practical point of view to supply it other than in the context of that principal supply.

4. **How the rates of VAT are applied**

4.1 Section 11(3) of the VAT Act provides for how tax is to be applied in the case of a multiple supply or a composite supply as defined in the Act.

   - In the case of a multiple supply, each constituent element of the transaction is treated as an individual supply for VAT rating purposes.

The accountable person must apportion the consideration payable by the customer between all the constituent elements supplied, thereby ensuring that the appropriate rate of VAT is applied to each portion of the consideration payable. In this regard the VAT Act requires that the total consideration be apportioned in a way that correctly reflects an accurate ratio of the values involved. The accountable person must be able to demonstrate, on request, to the satisfaction of Revenue that the result of the apportionment calculation is reasonable. Acceptable apportionment methods would include, for example, splitting the consideration according to the ratios of the cost of supplying each element, or according to the market value of each element.

- In the case of a composite supply there is one principal element or supply to which any other element or elements are ancillary. A single rate of VAT applies to the entire transaction at the rate applicable to the principal supply.

4.2 In the majority of transactions it will be clear what is the appropriate category for each supply. However, cases inevitably arise where it is not so clear. In such cases the following criteria, illustrated by examples, are relevant in deciding on the nature of a particular supply i.e. whether it is a **multiple supply** consisting of a number of **individual supplies** taxable at different rates or a **composite supply** taxable at a single rate or exempt as appropriate.

4.3 A feature of an **individual supply**, which by definition always forms part of a **multiple supply**, is that it is physically and economically dissociable from the other elements of that multiple supply. This means that each element the customer is being supplied with must be a distinct element of the overall supply. It must amount to more than a mere enhancement of a principal supply. In the language of the ECJ it must be capable of constituting "an aim in itself". An indicator that it is an individual supply is that it would be possible and sensible to supply the item or element separately in its own right. The following are examples of a multiple supply:

- The sale of food hampers which contain goods which if sold separately would be taxable at the zero, 13.5 and 21.5 per cent rate. Under the new rules each of the differently rated elements is taxed as an individual supply at the rate appropriate to it. The consideration must be apportioned so as to reflect the taxable amount applicable to each VAT rate. (This accords with the concessionary treatment of these supplies under the old rules.)

- A meal made up of food together with a soft drink or wine is sold for a single price. The food is liable to VAT at the rate of 13.5% whereas the soft drink or wine is liable at the 21.5% rate. Such a meal is taxed as a multiple supply as each of the parts of the meal are physically and economically dissociable from one another. Accordingly, the total consideration payable should be apportioned so that the food element is taxed at the 13.5% rate and the drink element is taxed at the 21.5%

rate. (This accords with the concessionary treatment of these supplies under the old rules applying prior to November 2006.)

- A car repair service is provided at the same time as the fitting of a set of tyres for a single consideration. As the supply of car tyres does not normally form part of a routine car service, the repair service and the supply of tyres would be regarded as a multiple supply. Both supplies are physically and economically dissociable from each other. In these circumstances the consideration should be apportioned so that the service is taxed at the 13.5% rate and the tyres at the 21.5% rate.

4.4 The **composite supply** rule applies where there is a principal element as well as an ancillary element or elements being supplied and where the ancillary elements would not realistically be sold on their own without the principal element. Such ancillary supplies are not physically and economically dissociable from the principal supply. The VAT rate applicable to the total consideration is the rate applicable to the principal supply. Again, in the words of the ECJ, a supply must be regarded as ancillary "if it does not constitute for customers an aim in itself, but a means of better enjoying the principal service supplied." In addition, when considering if a transaction is a composite supply or not, due regard should be given to the essential features of the transaction, e.g. would it make sense or would it be practical to supply an ancillary element on its own, what are the terms of the contract, the intention of the parties involved, the pricing arrangements, etc. Also, a supply that is a composite supply, from an economic point of view, should not be artificially split to gain a tax advantage. In this regard the existence of separate contracts, or the furnishing of two or more invoices is not always indicative of two individual supplies having taken place.

The following are some examples of a composite supply:

- The supply of a mobile phone (21.5% VAT) with an instruction booklet (zero % VAT). The instruction booklet is clearly for the better enjoyment of the mobile phone and is clearly ancillary to it. The rate applicable to the principal supply is 21.5% and this rate applies to the entire supply regardless of how the consideration for the supply is allocated by the supplier.

- The purchase or lease of computers programmed to perform a specific function coupled with specific training on how to operate and access the system as an integral part of the overall deal. The leasing of the equipment (21.5% VAT) is the principal supply and the provision of the training (exempt from VAT) is ancillary. Accordingly the 21.5% rate applies to the overall transaction.

5. **Regulations**

Regulation 21 of the VAT Regulations 2006 (S.I. No. 548 of 2006), covers the situation where the cost to the supplier of an individual supply or supplies in a multiple supply does not exceed 50 per cent of the total tax exclusive consideration which a taxable person is entitled to receive or €1 whichever is the lesser (de minimis rule). In that case, as a simplification measure the Regulation provides that the accountable person may choose to disregard such individual supply or supplies for the purpose of applying the appropriate rate. This means that even where more than one individual supply in a multiple supply has a tax exclusive cost of less than €1, the maximum value of all the supplies that can be disregarded is €1 (for this purpose the value of any individual supply cannot be split).

For the rule to apply, the multiple supply must contain at least one individual supply which is not disregarded. An individual supply which is not disregarded is referred to in the Regulation as a "remaining individual supply". The Regulation does not permit the supply of beverages to be disregarded.

Where the accountable person chooses to disregard one or more individual supplies in a multiple supply the following rules apply:

- where there is only one remaining individual supply after an individual supply or supplies have been disregarded then the rate of tax chargeable on the total consideration for the multiple supply is the rate applicable to that remaining individual supply,

- where there is more than one remaining individual supply after an individual supply or supplies have been disregarded then the rate of tax chargeable on the total consideration for the multiple supply is the rate applicable to those remaining individual supplies or the lowest rate, if there is more than one rate applicable to those remaining individual supplies.

6. **Examples of certain cases**

- The hire and cleaning of linen is treated as a multiple supply. Each element of this supply is taxed individually and the overall consideration is apportioned between the various elements at the appropriate rates.

Simplifications already agreed prior to November 2006 in certain areas will continue to apply. Examples are:

- The supply of biscuit assortments where the chocolate biscuits are 15% or less of the total weight may be treated as a composite supply of biscuits liable at the 13.5%.

- The supply of a potted plant may continue to be taxed at the rate appropriate to the plant i.e. 13.5% where the value of the pot is less than 20% of the tax exclusive price of the plant and the pot.

Other

7. **Discounts:** Where a trader gives a price discount on a multiple supply, the details of how that discount is apportioned between the various individual elements of the supply must be recorded at the time of sale, and available for inspection by the local Revenue District. A trader who does not have electronic point of sale systems (EPOS) which can record the appropriate break-down of how the discount applies to the

various elements in the supply must agree the apportionment with the local Revenue District (see in particular Tax Briefing 63 May 2006, page 10).

8.   **Gifts and Promotional Items:** Problems frequently arise when goods are supplied on a promotional basis either on their own or in conjunction with other supplies. A gift for VAT purposes is legislated for in Article 16 of Council Directive 2006/112/EC and section 3(1A) of the VAT Act and Regulation 27 of the Value-Added Tax Regulations 2006. A gift only arises where no consideration is received for it by the supplier. In such cases, where the cost of the gift is below €20, there is no output VAT due by the supplier, although input VAT is deductible.

However, if there is a requirement for the customer to pay a consideration in connection with the receipt of an item, even if the supplier describes part of that item as a **"gift"**, or as being **"free"**, (for example "buy one, get one free", a free bar of chocolate with the purchase of a jar of coffee, a CD/promotional item with a newspaper/magazine), it does not come within the terms of a gift for VAT purposes. Where there is consideration it is always referable to all the items supplied.

As regards "buy one, get one free" offers the VAT analysis is that the consideration is referable to the supply of both items. There is no issue regarding which rate applies. As regards the free bar of chocolate (at 21.5% rate) with a jar of coffee (0% rate), assuming the bar of chocolate does not come within the de minimis rule (see paragraph 5) the VAT analysis is that the consideration is referable to both items, resulting in a multiple supply. As regards the supply of newspapers, magazines and periodicals when they are supplied together with, for example, a CD or other promotional item Revenue regards all such supplies as multiple supplies for consideration in the course or furtherance of business. In these circumstances the promotional item should not be treated as a gift. The total consideration payable must be apportioned as outlined in paragraph 4 for a multiple supply. However, the de minimis rule provided for by regulation may apply (see paragraph 5).

9.   **Manufacturers' Warranties/Additional Insurance:** Under the existing rules insurance forming an integral part of the supply of goods, typically a manufacturer's guarantee or warranty, attracts the rate of VAT applicable to the goods. Additional insurance, sold with goods, where it is paid over in full to the insurance company is regarded as being exempt from VAT.

10.   **Opticians:** Following a decision by the Appeal Commissioner, Revenue accepts that where a dispensing service is supplied by an optician with corrective spectacles or contact lenses that constitutes a multiple supply consisting of two individual supplies namely:

1.   A taxable supply of goods,

2.   An exempt supply of professional services of an optical nature referred to as 'dispensing services'.

11. **Cable television**: In a Supreme Court case regarding the supply of a broadcasting service and an installation service it was ruled that these are two distinct supplies. Some of the factors taken into account by the Court in reaching that decision included the facts that two separate amounts were invoiced for the two distinct services and the installation work was physically and temporally distinguishable from the broadcasting service. The Supreme Court took into consideration the ECJ case law on the question.

The two supplies involved form a multiple supply as the installation is capable of being supplied in its own right e.g. to a builder/developer prior to the sale of a property to individual buyers. As such Revenue considers that the supply of installation services does not fall to be treated as ancillary or as capable of being supplied only in the context of the better enjoyment of the broadcasting service.

12. **"Two-thirds" rule:** In accordance with section 10(8) of the Act, where a contract for the supply of services also involves the supply of goods (apart from food), the total consideration is deemed to be referable to the goods, where the VAT-exclusive cost of the goods exceeds two-thirds of the total contract price (excluding transport costs). In these circumstances the taxable person is liable to account for VAT on the total consideration at the rate applying to the goods.

13. **Records:** In accordance with section 16 of the VAT Act, records and documents relating to all transactions which affect or may affect an accountable person's liability to VAT must be retained for the appropriate time period. A trader using the electronic point of sale (EPOS) system should ensure it is programmed to record how the various VAT rates have been applied to a multiple supply. Where a taxpayer chooses to disregard a supply in accordance with the regulations referred to in paragraph 5 or where an agreed special methodology referred to in paragraph 7 is used the records must clearly show how the consideration is apportioned.

14. **Further Information**

Enquiries regarding any issue contained in this Information Leaflet should be addressed to the Revenue District responsible for the taxpayer's affairs. Contact details for all Revenue Districts can be found on the Contact Details Page.

VAT Appeals & Communications Branch ,
Indirect Taxes Division,
Stamping Building
Dublin Castle.

December 2008

VALUE ADDED TAX INFORMATION LEAFLET (DECEMBER 2008)

GOODS: INTRA-COMMUNITY ACQUISITIONS

1.   **Introduction**

This document sets out the VAT treatment of EU intra-Community acquisitions of goods by taxable persons, and it outlines the postponed accounting system for such acquisitions.

The terms 'intra-Community supply' and 'intra-Community acquisition' relate to goods supplied by a business in one EU Member State to a business in another which have been dispatched or transported from the territory of one Member State to another as a result of such supply. (The terms also apply to new means of transport supplied by a person in one Member State to a person, including a private individual, in another Member State and transferred to that Member State. This is dealt with in paragraph 10).

2.   **Acquisitions from other Member States**

2.1   The VAT treatment of EU intra-Community acquisitions is as follows:

1.   The supply will be zero-rated in the Member State of dispatch as an EU intra-Community supply.

2.   The accountable customer becomes liable for VAT on the acquisition of goods at the appropriate rate in his/her own Member State.

3.   The accountable customer declares a liability for VAT in the VAT return.

4.   Where an accountable person is entitled to full deductibility (input credit), the VAT payable on the intra-Community acquisition is deducted in the same VAT period, thus effectively cancelling out the VAT liability.

5.   An accountable customer accounts for VAT on any subsequent supply of the goods in the appropriate VAT return.

2.2   The mechanism by which an accountable person in the State accounts for the VAT charge arising in respect of goods acquired from another Member State is termed 'Postponed Accounting'.

2.3   The VAT 3 return requires an accountable person to declare summary VAT details. It includes two statistical boxes in respect of intra-Community transactions that must be completed (E1 and E2). The annual return of trading details is a more comprehensive document which requires a breakdown of the annual trading figures according to VAT rate.

3.   **Postponed Accounting with full deductibility**

3.1   A person registered for VAT in the State can buy goods in another Member State at the zero rate provided the goods are dispatched or transferred to this State. The accountable person is required to account for VAT on any intra-Community acquisition of the goods on arrival in the State, at the appropriate Irish VAT rate, in Box T1 of the VAT3 return for the period in which the goods are acquired. Where an accountable person is entitled to full deductibility, a simultaneous input credit may be taken in Box T2 of the same VAT3 return, thus cancelling the liability (see appendix - example 1). The treatment of accountable persons who are not entitled to full deductibility is dealt with in paragraphs 4 to 5 below.

- If the goods acquired are subsequently supplied, liability on that supply will arise in the normal way in the period in which the supply is made (see appendix - example 1).

4.   Partially exempt persons

4.1   As outlined above, accountable persons with full deductibility can take a simultaneous credit for any VAT liability on intra-Community acquisitions. However, a number of accountable persons registered for VAT may not have full input tax deductibility e.g. a bank which is primarily involved in exempt activities but also carries on a taxable activity such as leasing of movable goods. Where such persons acquire goods in another Member State, they are liable to VAT on the acquisition of these goods but they are only entitled to a deduction in accordance with an accountable person's existing apportionment arrangements (determined by the exempt/taxable status). The making of intra-Community acquisitions does not affect the person's existing input tax deductibility entitlements. The accountable person is required to account for VAT on any intra-Community acquisition, at the appropriate Irish VAT rate, in Box T1 of the VAT3 return, for the period in which the goods were acquired. However the extent to which this VAT may be simultaneously deducted (Box T2 on the VAT3 return) varies.

4.2   A full deduction of the VAT on the intra-Community acquisition arises if the goods are wholly attributable to a person's taxable activities. No deduction of the VAT is allowable if the intra-Community acquisition relates to a person's exempt activities. If the intra-Community acquisition is used for both types of activity i.e. dual use inputs, the tax should be deducted in accordance with The accountable person's existing apportionment arrangements (see appendix - example 2).

5.   Persons required to register solely because of intra-Community acquisitions

Wholly exempt bodies (e.g. insurance companies and building societies) and (b) other non-taxable entities (e.g. public authorities and universities) are required to register for VAT if their intra-Community acquisitions exceed or are likely to exceed €41,000 in any continuous period of 12 months and they must account for VAT on their intra-Community acquisitions, through their VAT return, (Box T1), at the rate applicable to the supply of such goods within the State. They are not entitled to any deduction in relation to the intra-Community acquisitions or indeed any other VAT that they have borne on purchases or imports (see appendix - example 3).

Persons who become registered for VAT for their intra-Community acquisitions and who supply taxable goods or services within the State are required to account for VAT on their supplies.

6.   **EU intra-Community acquisitions by farmers**

Farmers are also obliged to register for VAT where their intra-Community acquisitions exceed or are likely to exceed €41,000 in any continuous period of twelve months. However, farmers registered in respect of their acquisitions may opt to retain their flat-rate status for the purpose of obtaining the 5.2 per cent flat-rate addition on their agricultural supplies to registered persons.

7.   **Racehorse trainers**

Similarly, a flat-rate farmer who is registered for VAT in respect of racehorse training, who is obliged to account for VAT on intra-Community acquisitions may retain flat-rate farmer status for all agricultural purposes, other than racehorse training.

8.   **Retail Schemes**

Traders who calculate their VAT liability by reference to a retail scheme should specifically ensure that goods for resale acquired in another Member State are always accounted for at the correct rate and that they include the intra- Community acquisition at the correct VAT rate in the scheme as purchases for resale. The VAT rate applicable to an intra-Community acquisition is always that which applies to the supply of the same goods here.

9.   **How to calculate the VAT due on intra-Community acquisitions**

VAT becomes due on the fifteenth of the month following the acquisition or if the supplier in the other Member State issues an invoice before that date, the date when the invoice is issued. The rate of VAT applicable is the rate that applies to the supply of the same goods in the State. The VAT is assessed on the price charged for the goods. If the supplier's invoice is in foreign currency, the rate of exchange applicable when the tax becomes due should be used. Tax is payable by the 19th day of the month following the period during which the tax became due. The following example serves to illustrate the arrangements:

A local authority acquires a computer from a German company. The supply in Germany is zero-rated because the local authority has provided its VAT registration number to the German company and the goods have been dispatched or transported to Ireland.

• Computer delivered 29/1/09

• Invoice issued 12/3/09

• Invoiced amount €200,000

• VAT on acquisition at 21.5% €43,000

- No input credit allowed.

- VAT (€43,000) payable to Collector-General with VAT returns for the period.

10. Intra-Community acquisitions of new means of transport

10.1 The purchase of new means of transport in other Member States by private individuals and accountable persons is subject to VAT in the country of destination.

10.2 In the case of private individuals and accountable persons who are not entitled to a VAT deduction, VAT on the acquisition of a new means of transport is normally payable with the Vehicle Registration Tax (VRT) or, if no VRT is payable, at the time of registration of the vehicle. In the case of new vessels and aircraft, VAT becomes payable not later than three days after the date of arrival in the State.

10.3 Accountable persons who are entitled to a VAT deduction on the acquisition of a new means of transport must account for the VAT through their VAT return.

11. Intra-Community Transport of Goods

The special arrangements relating to the intra-Community Transport of Goods are dealt with in a separate VAT Information Leaflet.

12. INTRASTAT returns

Traders acquiring more than €191,000 worth of goods per annum from other Member States or supplying goods in excess of €635, 000 per annum to other Member States are also obliged to submit a periodic INTRASTAT return.

13. Branch to branch transfers

For VAT purposes, branch to branch (with some exceptions) and similar transfers of goods between business persons in different EU Member States are also treated as being intra-Community supplies and acquisitions.

14. Certain transfers not supplies

14.1 For VAT purposes, certain transfers to other Member states are not treated as intra-Community supplies/acquisitions.

14.2 These include goods for installation or assembly by the supplier (in this case the supplier is obliged to register and account for VAT in the State), transfers for the purposes of having contract work carried out on them and transfers with a view to their temporary use in another Member State.

Appendix

Example 1

A company with full deductibility acquires a computer in the UK. for €80,000. Supply is zero-rated in the UK. The company sells the computer in the State during the same taxable period for €100,000 plus VAT. These are the only transactions in the period.

Acquisition of computer €80,000 @ 21.5% €17,200 include in Box T1 of VAT 3

Simultaneous input credit €80,000 @ 21.5% €17,200 include in Box T2 of VAT3

Subsequent supply of computer in the State €100,000 @ 21.5% €21,500 include in Box T1 of VAT3.

Net VAT payable €21,500 include in Box T3 on VAT3.

Example 2

An Irish bank (60% taxable/40% exempt activities) acquires a computer in the UK which is a dual use input to be used for both its taxable and exempt activities in this State for €80,000. Supply is zero-rated in the UK.

Acquisition of computer €80,000 @ 21.5% €17,200 include in Box T1 of VAT 3.

Simultaneous input credit on 60% of €80,000 @ 21.5% €10,320 include in Box T2 of VAT 3.

Net VAT payable €6,880 include in Box T3 of VAT 3.

Example 3

An insurance company or university acquires a computer in the U.K. for €80,000. Supply is zero-rated in the UK.

Acquisition of computer €80,000 @ 21.5% €17,200 include in Box T1 of VAT 3

No input credit

Net VAT payable €17,200 include in Box T3 of VAT 3.

Further information

Enquiries regarding any issue contained in this document should be addressed to the Revenue District responsible for the taxpayer's affairs. (Contact details for all Revenue Districts.)

This leaflet is issued by

VAT Appeals and Communications Branch,
Indirect Taxes Division,
Dublin Castle.

December 2008

This information leaflet which sets out the current practice at the date of its issue is intended for guidance only and does not purport to be a definitive legal interpretation of the provisions of the Value-Added Tax Act 1972 (as amended).

VALUE ADDED TAX INFORMATION LEAFLET (DECEMBER 2008)

HIRE PURCHASE TRANSACTIONS

1.   Introduction

1.1   The Finance Act 2007 amends the VAT treatment of hire purchase transactions. The amendments allow finance houses to become entitled to bad debt relief in respect of such transactions. Under the new provisions, with effect from 1 May 2007, finance houses involved in hire purchase transactions are accountable persons in respect of the supply of the underlying goods concerned and on the subsequent sale of such goods if repossessed by them. This leaflet provides guidance in relation to the Finance Act amendments and also information on bad debt relief in general.

2.   Summary of New Provisions

2.1   Arising from the changes in the Finance Act 2007 there is a supply by the dealer of the goods to the finance house and the supply from the finance house to the customer who acquires the goods under the hire purchase agreement. These two supplies occur simultaneously. The finance house continues to be exempt from VAT on its finance charges.

2.2   The new legislation provides that the transfer of ownership of goods from the dealer to the finance house is a taxable supply. The dealer must issue a VAT invoice to the finance house. (The special documentary procedure for hire purchase transactions in operation since 1996 no longer applies).

2.3   The finance house makes a taxable supply when the goods are handed over to the customer. Accordingly, it must account for the VAT on that supply, and may claim deductibility in respect of the VAT chargeable in relation to that supply. (The handing over of the goods to the customer has always been a taxable supply but prior to Finance Act 2007 that supply was treated as a supply by the dealer directly to the customer.)

2.4   Where the customer defaults on the hire purchase payments the finance house is entitled to claim bad debt relief in respect of the VAT element of the outstanding payments. This should be calculated on a pro-rata basis as outlined in paragraph 19 below.

2.5   Where the hire purchase agreement is terminated early and the goods are handed back to the finance company then the finance company can claim relief in respect of the VAT element of the outstanding payments in accordance with paragraph 20 below.

2.6   If the finance house repossesses goods before the hire purchase agreement has run its course, and subsequently sells those goods, that sale is a taxable supply on which the finance house must account for VAT.

3.   Invoices

3.1   A finance house must issue a VAT invoice in respect of a supply of goods under a hire purchase agreement where the supply is to an accountable person. However, if the hire purchase document contains all the details required by regulation for a VAT invoice then that document will be accepted as a VAT invoice.

3.2   Where the supply by the finance house consists of qualifying goods as defined in section 13A of the VAT Act and that supply is to a taxable customer who holds a section 13A authorisation then the VAT invoice/ hire purchase document will show the zero rate of VAT together with the usual authorisation number. It should be noted that motor vehicles do not come within the meaning of qualifying goods and therefore the supply is not zero-rated.

4.   Taxable amount

4.1   The taxable amount of goods supplied by the finance house to the customer is usually the same as that of the supply of those goods from the dealer to the finance house. This is because the finance house does not apply a profit margin to the value of the supply of the goods from the dealer. Therefore, (apart from the situation outlined in paragraph 9 above), the tax on the purchase from the dealer by the finance house and the tax on the supply of the goods by the finance house will be the same amount.

4.2   In the case of a new motor vehicle the amount on which VAT is chargeable in respect of the supply by the dealer does not include Vehicle Registration Tax (VRT). In the case of the supply by the finance house to its customer, the amount of the VRT is treated for VAT purposes as a disbursement on behalf of the customer and accordingly is not included in the taxable amount.

4.3   Interest charges are treated as consideration for the supply of credit and are not part of the taxable amount for the goods. These charges are exempt from VAT.

5.   Transfer of ownership at the end of the hire purchase agreement

5.1   The transfer of ownership of the goods from the finance house to the customer at the end of the hire purchase agreement is not a supply for VAT purposes.

6.   Payments of instalments by the customer

6.1   No VAT liability arises for the finance house at the time the instalments are received by it during the term of the hire purchase agreement. The VAT will have been accounted for when the goods were handed over to the customer. The interest element of the instalments is treated for

VAT purposes as consideration for the exempt supply of credit. The cash receipts basis of accounting for VAT does not apply to hire purchase transactions.

7.   Entitlement to deductibility

7.1   Finance houses which supply goods on hire purchase terms are entitled to full deductibility in respect of the purchase by them of those goods for onward supply. As regards dual-use inputs used by the finance house for both deductible and non-deductible supplies, the finance house is entitled to deduct only the proportion of input tax which correctly reflects the extent to which those inputs are used for the taxable supplies.

8.   Cases where a customer defaults on repayments

The conditions under which bad debt relief is allowed are set out in Regulations. In general, a taxable person must be in a position to demonstrate that:

1.   The consideration due for the supply is treated as a bad debt only after the taxable person has taken all reasonable steps to recover the debt.

2.   The bad debt is allowable as a deduction for the purposes of the Taxes Consolidation Act 1997 and has been written off as such in the financial accounts of the taxable person and the requirements of Regulation 8(1)(m) of the Value-Added Tax Regulations 2006 in respect of that debt have been fulfilled.

3.   The debt is not due from a person connected with the taxable person within the meaning of Regulation 15(5)(b) of the Value-Added Tax Regulations 2006.

The VAT bad debt relief should be calculated in accordance with the VAT analysis of the transactions outlined in paragraphs 18 and 19 below.

9.   Bad debt relief for a supply, other than a supply under hire purchase

9.1   Before dealing with bad debt relief in respect of a supply under a hire purchase agreement it may be helpful to first outline the general method for calculating bad debt relief. This is calculated in accordance with the following formula (First Formula):

$$\frac{A \times B}{100 + B}$$

where:

A: is the amount which is outstanding from the debtor in relation to the taxable supply

B: is the percentage rate of VAT applicable to the supply

Example 1

Bad debt relief for a supply, other than a supply under hire purchase:

Sale Price of the Goods:	€24,200
[B]VAT rate:	21.5%
VAT amount accounted for on the supply:	€4,282
Amount received from debtor:	€14,520
[A]Amount outstanding from debtor:	€9,680

Therefore the VAT adjustment for bad debt relief, using the First Formula, is as follows:

$$\frac{€9,680 \times 21.5}{100 + 21.5}$$

Bad debt relief = €1,713

10.   Bad debt relief for a supply made under a hire purchase agreement

10.1   Relief from VAT on bad debts arises only in respect of the VAT element of hire purchase transactions. A hire purchase agreement is made up of different elements, comprising payment in respect of the goods, VAT, VRT (in the case of motor vehicles) and credit charges. In the normal course, the value of each of these elements should be available in the records of the finance house. Bad debt relief should be calculated in accordance with the following formula (Second Formula):

$$\frac{(C - D) \times (E - F)}{C}$$

where:

C is the sum of all the amounts scheduled for payment by instalment under the hire purchase agreement,

D is the total amount paid by the customer against the instalments scheduled for payment under the hire purchase agreement up to and including the date on which the bad debt is written off in the financial accounts of the accountable person,

E is an amount equal to the amount of tax accounted for by the taxable person on the supply of the goods under the hire purchase agreement, and

F is an amount equal to the tax attributable to a part payment referred to in the hire purchase agreement calculated in accordance with the Third Formula. However, if there is no part payment F is equal to zero.

The result of this calculation gives the amount of the VAT bad debt relief which can be claimed. The following examples will help to clarify the position:

Example 2

Hire Purchase of equipment where no part payment is made and the customer defaults after three years:

Sale Price of the Goods:	€24,200
VAT rate:	21.5%
[E] VAT accounted for:	€4,282
Hire Purchase term:	5 years
Credit charges over 5 years:	€4,800
[C] Total of instalments scheduled for payment:	€29,000
Annual instalment Payment:	€5,800
[D] Total paid by instalment in the first 3 years:	€17,400
[C–D] Amount outstanding:	€11,600

Therefore the VAT adjustment for bad debt relief, using the Second Formula, is as follows:

$$\frac{(€29,000 - €17,400) \times (€4,282)}{€29,000}$$

Bad debt relief = €1,713

Example 3

Hire purchase of a new means of transport where no part payment is made and the customer defaults after 3 years:

Sale Price of the Goods:	€32,266
VRT (say 24% of €32,266):	€7,743
VAT inclusive price (32,266 – 7,743):	€24,523
[E] VAT accounted for:	€4,339
Hire Purchase term	5 years
Credit charges over 5 years	€6,453
[C] Total of instalments scheduled for payment:	€38,719
Annual instalment Payment:	€7,744
[D] Total paid by instalment in the first 3 years:	€23,232
[C–D] Amount outstanding:	€15,487

Therefore the VAT adjustment for bad debt relief, using the Second Formula, is as follows:

$$\frac{(€38,719 - €23,232) \times (€4,339 - 0)}{€38,719}$$

Bad debt relief = €1,735

Example 4

Hire purchase of new means of transport involving a part payment (such as a trade-in or a cash payment/deposit) where the customer defaults after 3 years:-

[H] Sale Price of the Goods :	€32,266
VRT (say 24% of €32,266) :	€7,743
VAT inclusive price (32,266 – 7,743) :	€24,523
[E] VAT accounted for :	€4,339
[G] Part Payment :	€5,000
[F] Tax attributable to the part payment :	€672
Hire Purchase term :	5 years
Credit charges over 5 years :	€5,453
[C]Total of instalments scheduled for payment :	€32,719
Annual instalment Payment :	€6,544
[D] Total paid by instalment in the first 3 years :	€19,632
[C–D] Amount outstanding :	€13,087

As this example includes a part payment it is necessary to calculate the tax attributable to that part payment in order to establish a value for F so that the Second Formula can be completed. The tax attributable to the part payment is calculated in accordance with the following formula (Third Formula):

$$\frac{G \times E}{H}$$

$$\frac{€5,000 \times €4,339}{€32,266}$$

F is therefore equal to €672

Therefore the VAT adjustment for bad debt relief, using the Second Formula, is as follows:

$$\frac{(€32,719 - €19,632) \times (€4,339 - €672)}{€32,719}$$

Bad debt relief =   €1,540

11.   Early Determinations

11.1   Under the Consumer Credit Act 1995 a customer is entitled to end the hire purchase agreement on a date earlier than the date fixed in the agreement for termination of that agreement. This is referred to as a determination. The customer may in these circumstances have to pay an additional amount as part of that determination. Where early determination of the hire purchase agreement occurs and the full amount payable on the original agreement is not paid and no transfer of title from the finance house to the customer takes place, the finance house will be entitled to relief in respect of the excess VAT already accounted for. The relief should be calculated on a pro-rata basis in accordance with the following formula (Fourth Formula):

$$\frac{J \times (E - K)}{C}$$

where:

J: is the total amount paid by the customer against the instalments scheduled for payment under the hire purchase agreement up to and including the prior date agreed under the determination plus any amount paid by the customer as part of the determination,

E: is an amount equal to the amount of tax accounted for by the accountable person on the supply of the goods under the hire purchase agreement,

K: is an amount equal to the amount of tax attributable to the part payment shown in the hire purchase agreement calculated in accordance with the Third Formula (however, if there is no part payment K is equal to zero), and

C: is the sum of all the amounts scheduled for payment by instalment under the hire purchase agreement.

Example 5

Early determination of hire purchase agreement after 1 year, where a deposit is paid, an amount is paid as part of that determination and the goods are returned to the finance company:

Sale Price of the Goods:	€24,200
VAT rate:	21.5%
[E] VAT accounted for:	€4,282
[G] Part Payment:	€5,000
[K] Tax attributable to the part payment:	€884
Hire Purchase term:	5 years
Credit charges over 5 years:	€3,840
[C]Total of instalments scheduled for payment:	€23,040
Annual instalment Payment:	€4,608
[J*]Total paid by instalment in the first year:	€4,608
[J*] Amount paid as part of the determination:	€4,412
Total amount paid:	€14,020

*One element of the value of J

If the customer opts to end the hire purchase agreement after one year and return the goods to the finance company he or she is obliged under the hire purchase agreement to pay at least half of the hire purchase price and so must pay a further €1,912.

The tax attributable to the part payment

Before calculating the relief that can be claimed in this case it is necessary to first calculate the tax attributable to the part payment. This is calculated as follows using the Third Formula:

$$\frac{G \times E}{H}$$

$$\frac{€5,000 \times €4,282}{€24,200}$$

Tax attributable to the part payment is therefore equal to €884

This figure is also needed in order to establish a value for K so that the Fourth Formula can be completed.

The tax attributable to the remaining payments made by the customer

It is now necessary to calculate the tax attributable to the amount paid by the customer against the instalments scheduled for payment under the hire purchase agreement plus any amount paid by the customer as part of the determination.

This is calculated as follows using the Fourth Formula:

$$\frac{€6,520 \times (4,282 - 884)}{€23,040} = €961$$

The total VAT due in relation to the payments made by the customer is therefore equal to €1,845 (i.e. €884 + €961)

VAT accounted for on the handing over of the goods was equal to €4,282

Therefore the relief for the determination of the hire purchase agreement is equal to €2,437 (i.e. €4,282 – €1,845).

Relief under this paragraph cannot be claimed until the credit note, required to be issued in accordance with section 10(3)(d) of the Act, has been issued.

11.2   Relief under paragraph 20 does not arise where early determination of the hire purchase agreement occurs and the transfer of title from the finance house to the customer takes place.

12.   Sale of repossessed goods

12.1   Where a finance house repossesses goods which have been subject to a hire purchase contract which terminates early, or on which the customer defaults, such repossession is not a taxable event as the title had not been transferred from the finance house to the customer. (In such cases relief is available as outlined in paragraphs 19 and 20 above.) However, the subsequent sale by the finance house of those goods is taxable. The taxable amount is the consideration received by the finance house for that sale of those goods.

13.   Hire Purchase transactions in respect of second-hand means of transport

13.1   The provisions regarding residual input credit allowed to taxable dealers under section 12B of the VAT Act apply to finance houses involved in the sale on hire purchase of second-hand means of transport. The finance house may deduct the residual tax deemed to be included in the value of the means of transport when acquired by it and must account for VAT on the subsequent supply of that means of transport.

14.   EU Intra-Community acquisitions

14.1   Arising from changes in the Finance Act 2008 a finance house is required to account for VAT on the Intra-Community Acquisition of goods acquired by it where those goods are funded through a hire purchase agreement.

15.   Further information

Enquiries regarding any issue contained in this Information Leaflet should be addressed to the Revenue District responsible for the taxpayer's affairs. Contact details for all Revenue Districts can be found on the Contact Details Page.

VAT Appeals & Communications Branch,
Indirect Taxes Division,
Stamping Building,
Dublin Castle.

December 2008

VALUE ADDED TAX INFORMATION LEAFLET (DECEMBER 2008)

HORTICULTURAL RETAILERS

1.   **Introduction**

All retailers of horticultural products, including garden centres and flat-rate farmers whose annual retail sales of horticultural products and other goods exceed or are likely to exceed the VAT registration threshold €75,000 are obliged to register and account for VAT. 'Horticultural products' for this purpose means non-food products of a type listed at paragraph 2. 'Other goods' means goods other than agricultural produce.

2.   **Rates**

Plants, trees, bulbs, roots and seeds used for growing food are taxable at the zero rate. The reduced rate of 13.5% applies to:

- live plants, including instant lawn turf
- live trees
- live shrubs
- bulbs, roots and the like
- seeds
- cut flowers
- ornamental foliage.

Artificial flowers, dried flowers and dried foliage are taxable at the standard rate currently 21.5%. Cut trees (for example, Christmas trees), are also liable at the standard rate.

The supply of pots is subject to VAT at the 21.5% rate. The supply of potted plants is normally taxable at the 13.5% rate. However, where the value of the pot is 20% or greater than the tax exclusive price of the plant and the pot, its supply becomes taxable at 21.5%.

3.   **Obligation to Register**

3.1   Farmers and garden centres supplying horticultural products to the general public must register and account for VAT on all their business activities subject to the VAT registration threshold of €75,000.

3.2   A retailer of horticultural products cannot avoid registering for VAT by splitting his/her business into a number of separate smaller units, each selling less than the annual registration limit. The various units will be grouped as a single business for VAT purposes.

3.3   In addition, where a person supplies a combination of retail horticultural produce and agricultural services, the registration threshold is €37, 500. This is the normal VAT registration threshold which applies where a person supplies both goods and services.

3.4   Businesses such as florists benefit from the reduced VAT rate of 13.5% on the horticultural produce of a type listed at paragraph 2.

Further information

Enquiries regarding any issue contained in this Information Leaflet should be addressed to the Revenue District responsible for the taxpayer's affairs. Contact details for all Revenue Districts are available on the revenue website at: Contact Details

VAT Appeals & Communications Branch,
Indirect Taxes Division,
Stamping Building,
Dublin Castle.

December 2008

This information leaflet which sets out the current practice at the date of its issue is intended for guidance only and does not purport to be a definitive legal interpretation of the provisions of the Value-Added Tax Act 1972 (as amended).

VALUE ADDED TAX INFORMATION LEAFLET (DECEMBER 08)
PHOTOGRAPHY

1.   General

1.1   The supply of a wide range of photographic goods such as prints, negatives and exposed film is subject to VAT at the 13.5% rate. The supply of certain services such as the editing of film and microfilming is also subject to the 13.5% rate of VAT. Certain other supplies in the photographic sector are subject to the 21.5% rate of VAT including the supply of digitized products on disc or downline by computer. This Information Leaflet sets out the rates of VAT appropriate to the different photographic and associated supplies.

2.   Photographic goods and services classified at the 13.5% rate of VAT

2.1   Paragraphs (xxi) to (xxvi) of the 6th Schedule to the VAT Act are the provisions which apply the 13.5% rate to certain photographic supplies. These are set out in Appendix II to this Information Leaflet.

2.2   Paragraph (xxi) covers the supply of photographs (including enlargements and reprints), slides, negatives, cine film and video films where these are produced from materials provided by the customer. It includes the normal case where photographs etc. are supplied by developing and printing from a customers roll of film. It includes printed photos supplied as a result of digital photography processing. It does not include photocopying or digitized products supplied on disc or down-line by computer, which are subject to 21.5% VAT.

2.3   Paragraph (xxii) (a), (b) and (c) cover the supply on a commissioned basis of photographs, mounted (including in albums) or unmounted, but unframed. An example of this is commissioned wedding photographs supplied in an album. Also classified here are slides, negatives and cine and video films supplied on the same basis. Supplies of photocopies are excluded as are digitized images supplied on disc or downline.

2.4   Paragraph (xxiii) (a) and (b) covers the supply of negatives and exposed film by professional photographers, ie. uncommissioned photographs accepted by newspapers from photographers.

2.5   Paragraph (xxiv) covers photographs supplied from automatic photo vending booths.

2.6   Paragraph (xxv) covers the services of editing of film and microfilming.

2.7   Paragraph (xxvi) covers agency services (e.g. by chemists) in regard to the developing of film.

3.   Photographic goods and services classified at the 21.5% rate.

3.1   The supply or hire of other photographic goods is subject to VAT at the standard 21.5% rate. These goods include photographic, cine and video equipment and materials, photographic frames, unused rolls and cassettes of film, discs, batteries. The supply of digitised photographs or film on disc or downline by computer is subject to the 21.5% rate. Also subject to the 21.5% rate are photographs, slides, negatives, prerecorded video tapes and cine films other than where supplied in the particular circumstances referred to in paragraph 2 above.

4.   Photographic goods and services classified at the zero rate of VAT

4.1   Printed books and booklets, with certain exceptions, are classified at the zero rate of VAT. Please refer to VAT Information Leaflet Printing and Printed Matter. A book consisting of non-commissioned printed photographs may qualify for the zero rate , subject to those conditions. It should be noted that a photographic album is not considered as a book for VAT purposes.

5.   Digitised products supplies on disc or electronically

5.1   The VAT Act, reflecting the terms of the 2006 EU VAT Directive does not provide for the application of the reduced rate of VAT to the supply of digitized photographs on disc or downline by computer. Such supplies are subject to VAT at the standard 21.5% rate of VAT.

5.2   Where such images are supplied on disc or downline to a business outside the State they are subject to an effective zero rate. VAT is accounted for by the recipient by reference to the rules in his/her country of establishment. Please refer to VAT Information leaflet Fourth Schedule Services.

6.   Works of art

6.1   The 8th Schedule to the VAT Act relates to photographs taken by an artist, printed by the artist or under the artist's supervision, signed and numbered and limited to 30 copies, all sizes and mounts included. The 13.5% rate applies to

1.   the importation into the State of such works of art

2.   the supply of such a works of art, effected by its creator or the creator's successor in title, or on an occasional basis by an accountable person other than a taxable dealer where —

1.   that work of art has been imported by the accountable person, or

2.   that work of art has been supplied to the accountable person by its creator or the creator's successors in title, or

3.   the tax chargeable in relation to the purchase, intra-Community acquisition or importation of that work of art by [the accountable person was wholly deductible under section 12, and

3.   the intra-Community acquisition in the State by an accountable person of such a work of art where the supply of that work

of art to that accountable person which resulted in that intra-Community acquisition is a supply of the type that would be charged at the 13.5% rate in accordance with the above supply, if that supply had occurred within the State.

6.2   The supply of photographic works of art, other than as outlined in the above paragraph and commissioned photographs, is subject to VAT at the standard 21.5% rate.

6.3   copy of Section 11(1A) and the 8th Schedule to the VAT Act are set out in Appendix II to this leaflet.

7   Event, press, PR and sports photography

7.1   Where such work is commissioned and handed over in hard copy or on cinematographic or video film the 13.5% rate applies. The supply of negatives and exposed film by professional photographers, including uncommissioned photographs accepted by newspapers from photographers also qualifies for the lower 13.5% rate. It should be noted that the supply of such work on disc or downline is subject to the 21.5% rate of VAT.

7.2   The supply if digitized images on disc or downline to a business outside the State is subject to an effective zero rate of VAT and is taxable in the hands of the recipient by reference to the rule in their country of establishment. Please refer to VAT Information Leaflet Fourth Schedule Services.

8.   Wedding and Portrait photography

8.1   A wedding album is not considered to be a book for VAT purposes. On a concessionary basis Revenue accepts that the supply of commissioned wedding or portrait photographs in frames or in albums qualifies for the reduced 13.5% rate, subject to the cost of the skeleton album or frame, excluding VAT, not exceeding two-thirds of the total charge of the completed product, excluding VAT. This concession extends to standard albums where the exposed photographs are inserted into the album manually and to 'contemporary' albums where the photographic prints are bonded into the pages of the album by another process.

9.   Royalties

9.2   The assignment of rights in photographic images is a services and where such rights are assigned to a business in another State the fees are taxable at an effective zero rate in this State and subject to VAT in the hands of the recipient of the right by reference to the rules in the recipients own country of establishment. Please refer to VAT Information Leaflet on Fourth Schedule Services.

10.   Examples

10.1   A list indicating the rates of VAT to be charged on supplies in the photographic industry is set out in Appendix I to this leaflet.

11.   Further information

11.1   Enquiries regarding any issue contained in this Information Leaflet should be addressed to the Revenue District responsible for your tax affairs. Contact details for all Revenue Districts can be found Contact Details page.

This leaflet is issued by

VAT Appeals and Communications Branch,
Indirect Taxes Division,
Dublin Castle.

December 2008

Appendix I

Agency services in regard to —prints, slides, negatives (see "Chemists") —digitised images supplied on disc or downline		13.5% 21.5%
Albums,		photograph
–	unused	21.5%
–	complete with commissioned photographs	13.5%
–	other	21.5%
Books on photography– Booths, photographic		Zero 13.5%
Cameras–		
–	sale and hire	21.5%
–	importation	21.5%
–	repair, maintenance, etc.	13.5%
Chemists, printing and developing service through —prints, slides, negatives, film —images supplied on disc or downline		13.5% 21.5%
Cinematographic film–		
–	supply of unexposed film	21.5%
–	commissioned film	13.5%
–	editing of	13.5%
–	other	21.5%
Colouring (old films, photographs, etc.)		13.5%
Composites (see "montages")		
Developers (goods) Digital photography processing-product supplied:– Printed photos– Disc On-line Discs –blank —with photographic images Downline supplies of photographic or moving images		21.5% 13.5% 21.5% 21.5% 21.5% 21.5% 21.5%
Diazo-copying		21.5%
Editing of photographic, cinematographic and video film		13.5%
Enlargements from goods provided by customer		13.5%
Film–		
–supply of unexposed film		21.5%
–see also "cinematographic film" and "editing"		
Fixers (goods)		21.5%
Framing, of photographs and other goods		21.5%
Gums		21.5%

Appendix II

Extract from 6th Schedule to the VAT Act—supplies at 13.5% VAT

(xxi)   the supply to a person of photographic prints (other than goods produced by means of a photocopying process), slides or negatives, which have been produced from goods provided by that person;

(xxii) goods being—

    (a)   photographic prints (other than goods produced by means of a photocopying process), mounted or unmounted, but unframed,

    (b)   slides and negatives, and

    (c)   cinematographic and video film,

    which record particular persons, objects or events, supplied under an agreement to photograph those persons, objects or events;

(xxiii) the supply by a photographer of—

    (a)   negatives which have been produced from film exposed for the purpose of his business, and

    (b)   film which has been exposed for the purposes of his business;

(xxiv) photographic prints produced by means of a vending machine which incorporates a camera and developing and printing equipment;

(xxv)   services consisting of—

    (a)   the editing of photographic, cinematographic and video film, and

    (b)   microfilming;

(xxvi) agency services in regard to a supply specified in paragraph (xxi);

Section 11(1AA) VAT Act

13.5% VAT Rate applicable to 8th Schedule goods in certain circumstances
(1AA) Notwithstanding subsection (1), tax shall be charged at the rate specified in section 11(1)(*d*) (**13.5%**) of the amount on which tax is chargeable in relation to—

(a)   the importation into the State of goods specified in the Eighth Schedule, VAT Information Leaflet – Photography – December 2008 10

(b)   the supply of a work of art of the kind specified in paragraph (i) of the Eighth Schedule, effected—

    (i)   by its creator or the creator's successors in title, or

    (ii) on an occasional basis by an accountable person other than a taxable dealer where—

        (I)   that work of art has been imported by [the accountable person, or

(II)   that work of art has been supplied to [the accountable person by its creator or the creator's successors in title, or

(III)   the tax chargeable in relation to the purchase, intra-Community acquisition or importation of that work of art by the accountable person was wholly deductible under section 12,

and

(c)   the intra-Community acquisition in the State by an accountable person of a work of art of the kind specified in paragraph (i) of the Eighth Schedule where the supply of that work of art to that accountable person which resulted in that intra-Community acquisition is a supply of the type that would be charged at the rate specified in section 11(1)(d) (13.5%) in accordance with paragraph (b), if that supply had occurred within the State.

Extract from 8th Schedule to the VAT Act

EIGHTH SCHEDULE WORKS OF ART, COLLECTORS' ITEMS AND ANTIQUES CHARGEABLE AT THE RATE SPECIFIED IN SECTION 11(1)(d) IN THE CIRCUMSTANCES SPECIFIED IN SECTION 11(1AA)

[(i) Works of art:

Every work of art being—

.... (f) a photograph taken by an artist, printed by the artist or under the artist's supervision, signed and numbered and limited to 30 copies, all sizes and mounts included, other than photographs specified in paragraph (xxii)(a) of the Sixth Schedule;

VALUE ADDED TAX INFORMATION LEAFLET (DECEMBER 08)

PLANT & MACHINERY

The hire without an operator of any machine is chargeable to VAT at the rate appropriate to a sale of the machine when new. However, the provision with an operator of any of the machines specified below is chargeable to VAT at the 13.5% rate of VAT.

- Excavators/Traxcavators/Diggers
- Trench cutters with loader attachment
- Bulldozers
- Graders
- Scrapers
- Road Rollers
- Vibrating Rollers
- Hand Vibrating Rollers
- Macadam laying and spreading machines
- Verge Trimmers
- Hedge Cutters
- Sludge disposal units
- Sludge pumps/tankers
- Excavators with rock breaker
- Kango hammers
- Compactors
- Tar spraying machines

The provision **with an operator** of other items of plant and machinery is chargeable at the standard 21.5% rate of VAT.

Further information

Enquiries regarding any issue contained in this Information Leaflet should be addressed to the Revenue District responsible for the taxpayer's affairs. Contact details for all Revenue Districts can be found on the Contact Details Page

VAT Appeals & Communications Branch,
Indirect Taxes Division,
Stamping Building,
Dublin Castle.

December 2008

VALUE ADDED TAX INFORMATION LEAFLET (DECEMBER 08)

PRINTING & PRINTED MATTER

1.   Introduction

This leaflet aims to provide a brief guide to the scope of each of the three rates of VAT (zero, 13.5% and 21.5%) in relation to the supply of printed matter. The general position is that books are zero rated, newspapers and periodicals are subject to 13.5% and stationery and other printed matter are liable at the standard rate of 21.5%.

2.   Printing

2.1   Printing includes all forms of reproduction i.e. lithography; off-set; heliography; photogravure; engraving; duplicating; embossing; photography etc. in letters of any alphabet, figures, shorthand or other symbols, braille characters, musical notations, pictures or diagrams.

2.2   The rate chargeable for printing depends on the publication/product being printed. For example, the printing of books qualifies for the zero rate while the printing of newspapers and periodicals attracts VAT at the 13.5% rate.

3.   Zero-rated printed matter

3.1   The zero-rate of VAT applies to printed books and booklets including atlases. It also covers children's picture, drawing and colouring books, and books of music. Annual publications, even a periodical which is published once a year as a special edition which does **not** replace, for example, the standard monthly edition are liable to VAT at zero %.

3.2   In order to qualify for the zero rate, a publication must meet the four requirements listed hereunder:-

1.   it must consist essentially of textual or pictorial matter,

2.   it must have a distinctive cover, that is at least the outside of the front cover must be devoid of text,

3.   it must comprise not less than four leaves (eight pages) exclusive of the cover, and

4.   it must be bound (loose-leaf or otherwise), or stitched or stapled.

3.3   Parts of large works published over a limited and pre-determined period including a related binder supplied free of charge are **not** regarded as periodicals, and provided they qualify as printed books or booklets or will qualify as such when the series is completed, are zero-rated.

4.   Printed matter liable at the 13.5% rate

*   **All newspapers and periodicals are liable at the 13.5% rate.** This includes sectoral publications (sports/entertainment, fashion/health/beauty, mens/womens, computers/cars etc.).

- Holiday/tourist brochures, prospectuses, leaflets, programmes, catalogues (including directories) and similar printed matter. Similarly newspapers which deal with sectoral issues (e.g. sports papers) attract the lower rate.

- Maps, hydrographic and similar charts, and sheet music not in book or booklet form.

5.   Printed matter liable at the standard rate of VAT

5.1   All printed matter not falling within the zero-rated or the 13.5% rated categories is automatically liable at the standard rate of 21.5%.

5.2   Essentially this covers all stationery and the like, advertising and other printed matter. This includes;

- books of stationery, cheque books and the like

- calendars, greeting cards, business cards, identification cards

- diaries, organisers, yearbooks, planners and the like the total area of whose pages consist of 25% or more of blank pages for the insertion or recording of information

- albums and the like

- books of tokens, of tickets or of coupons

- other printed matter devoted wholly or substantially devoted to advertising.

5.3   Examples of other printed material attracting the standard rate are posters, beer mats etc. A detailed list is given in Appendix 1.

5.4   It should be noted that the supply of **all** publications in other formats e.g. CD's and audio cassette tapes is liable to VAT at 21.5%.

6.   Internet

When printed matter is purchased and downloaded via the internet it is considered to be a service within the meaning of electronically supplied services in the Fourth Schedule to the VAT Act, 1972 (as amended). This will have implications for non-EU suppliers where the customer is a private consumer. For further information on this, including the optional special scheme which allows EU businesses to register in an EU Member State only please consult VAT Information Leaflet 'e-Services and Broadcasting'. **All** digitised publications regardless of their rate when printed (e.g. a book liable at zero rate) are treated as a supply of services rather than goods and are classified at the 21.5% rate.

7.   Goods Sold Together

7.1   Where printed material is supplied with other goods for a single price it may be considered to be:

- A composite supply, made up of a principal supply and one or more ancillary supplies.

- A multiple supply, made up of more than one individual supply.

In the case of a composite supply, the rate of VAT applicable to the entire supply is that applicable to the principal supply. This would arise where the ancillary elements would not realistically be sold on their own without the principal element (e.g. a computer manual sold with a computer).

In the case of multiple supply, VAT is chargeable at the rates applicable to each individual supply. A multiple supply exists where each individual constituent is physically and economically dissociable from the other i.e. is capable of constituting an aim in itself (e.g. a newspaper with a CD).

Where the cost to the supplier of an individual supply (say, a CD) does not exceed the lesser of 50% of the total tax exclusive consideration chargeable or €1, the supplier may choose to disregard the relevant individual supply (the CD) for the purpose of applying the appropriate VAT rate.

7.2 For further details on goods sold together please see Revenue's VAT Information Leaflet 'Goods and Services Sold Together'.

8. **Acquisitions from other Member States of the EU and Imports**

The rates which apply to publications printed within the State apply similarly to publications acquired by traders from other Member States of the EU and to those imported from outside the EU. Also, Government Departments, local authorities, health boards, public hospitals, educational establishments, charities, trade unions, political parties and other similar bodies **must** account for VAT on the intra-Community acquisition of printed matter where their intra-Community acquisitions exceed €41,000 in any period of 12 months. Private individuals purchasing publications from other EU Member States are not liable for Irish VAT as VAT will already have been charged in the supplying Member State.

9. **Types of publications:**

VAT Rates: A list in alphabetical order of the VAT ratings of the various types of publications is given at Appendix I.

Further information

Enquiries regarding any issue contained in this Information Leaflet should be addressed to the Revenue District responsible for the taxpayer's affairs. Contact details for all Revenue Districts can be found on the Contact Details Page

VAT Appeals & Communications Branch ,
Indirect Taxes Division,
Stamping Building,
Dublin Castle.

December 2008

Appendix 1

Types of Publications, VAT Rates

An alphabetical listing of the various types of publications and the VAT rates applicable

Type of Publication	VAT Rates
Account Books	21.5%
Advertising printed matter (wholly or substantially dedicated to)	21.5%
Albums	21.5%
Annual Reports	0%
Annuals	0%
Atlases	0%
Audio Cassette Books	21.5%
Beer Mats	21.5%
Bingo books	21.5%
Books, booklets (other than catalogues) including books consisting wholly or mainly of reproductions of paintings	0%
Bookmarks etc. (included with books)	0%
Bookmarks etc. (not included with books)	21.5%
Braille Books	0%
Brochures	13.5%
Calendars	21.5%
Cards e.g. business, greeting.	21.5%
Catalogues	13.5%
Charts, hydrographic and similar	13.5%
Cheque Books	21.5%
Children's Drawing & Painting Books	0%
Children's Picture Books including 'cut out' and 'stand up' types.	0%
Comics	13.5%
Computer manuals	0%
Copy Books	21.5%
Coupons, books of	21.5%
Diaries (however, see paragraph 5.2).	21.5%
Diaries/Organisers/Planners	21.5%
Dictionaries	0%
Directories	13.5%
Dust Covers (included with books)	0%
Encyclopedias	0%
Examination Papers (certain)	0%
Exercise Books	21.5%
Fixture Lists	13.5%
Forms	21.5%
Globes	21.5%
Hymn Books	0%
Hymn sheets	13.5%
Invitation Cards	21.5%
Journals (Diary)	21.5%
Journals (Research)*	13.5%
Leaflets including flyers	13.5%

Type of Publication	VAT Rates
Magazines	13.5%
Maps	13.5%
Missals	0%
Missalettes (Mass Leaflets)	13.5%
Music, books of music, other than in book or booklet form	0%
Music copy book	21.5%
Newspapers	13.5%
Note Books	21.5%
Parts of large works published over pre-determined period including related binder supplied free of charge	0%
Picture Books i.e. books of pictures (other than catalogues)	0%
Periodicals	13.5%
Photocopying	21.5%
Posters	21.5%
Postcards including books of postcards	21.5%
Prayer Books	0%
Printed music other than in book or booklet form	13.5%
Programmes	13.5%
Prospectuses	13.5%
Puzzle books excluding periodicals	0%
Sheet Music	13.5%
Stationery	21.5%
Stamps, Books of postal stamps.	exempt
Telephone Directories	13.5%
Tickets, Books of	21.5%
Timetables	13.5%
Tokens, Books of	21.5%
Trade Catalogues/Promotional Literature	13.5%

* Where journals are normally paid for by annual subscription, have their pages sequentially numbered by reference to the completed work and are supplied with a binder or are bound for no extra cost in book form at the end of the year, they are regarded as qualifying for the zero rate.

This information leaflet which sets out the current practice at the date of its issue is intended for guidance only and does not purport to be a definitive legal interpretation of the provisions of the Value-Added Tax Act 1972 (as amended).

VALUE ADDED TAX INFORMATION LEAFLET (DECEMBER 08)

VAT ON PROPERTY - FREQUENTLY ASKED QUESTIONS

This collection of replies to frequently asked questions in relation to the new VAT on property provisions has been prepared by Revenue in response to questions that were submitted by the representative bodies on the TALC Indirect Taxed Sub-Committee. It is expected that the number of questions and answers will be added to over time as further issues arise.

1. At the end of April 2008 the Revenue posted the New VAT on Property Guide. On 6 May 2008 the Revenue posted a slightly different version of the New VAT on Property Guide. Can the Revenue explain the difference between the new version and the old version?

    There were two changes:

    *   page 20, para 3.5 - addition of sentence 'However....required'

    *   page 31, para 4.11 - addition of ...'or a legacy lease (see Chapter 3.7)'

2. Under Section 7A(1)(d)(iii) it is provided that a landlord's option to tax is terminated where the landlord and the tenant become connected persons after the lease has been granted. Upon a strict reading of the legislation this applies whether or not the tenant has the ability to recover at least 90% of VAT on input costs.

    Where a landlord and tenant become connected the landlord's option to tax is terminated. However, if the tenant is entitled to at least 90% deductibility in relation to the VAT on rents, the option to tax may remain in place. Similarly if the tenant sub-lets the property to a person who is connected to the landlord, the landlord's option is terminated. However, if the person connected to the landlord is entitled to at least 90% deductibility in relation to the VAT on rents, the option to tax may remain in place. Accordingly, in Example 17 VAT on Property Guide, the termination of the option would not arise if 'C' has at least 90% VAT recovery entitlement.

3. Section 5(3B) provides for a blanket period of twenty years following the acquisition or development of the goods by the accountable person. This does not take account of the fact that the adjustment period will be twenty intervals and not twenty years, the adjustment period for a refurbished property is ten intervals and the adjustment period for a legacy lease or a property acquired under transfer of business rules could be any period but will inevitably be less than twenty years.

    The provisions in Section 5(3B) deal with diversion to non-business or private use. These rules are independent of the CGS. The rules for adjusting deductibility in Section 12E relate to diversions to exempt use. Twenty years is the period over which the taxpayer must account for the VAT where a deduction has been taken and the property is subsequently diverted to a non-business use in accordance with Section 5(3B). The amount on which VAT is chargeable as a result of this supply is based on this same twenty-year period in accordance with Section 10(4D). See also Regulation 21B of S.I. No. 548 of 2006 - VAT Regulations 2006 (inserted by S.I. No. 238 of 2008 - VAT (Amendment) Regulations 2008).

4. **The final paragraph of Chapter 3.18 VAT on Property Guide confirms that the existing practice as regards 'shared services' (i.e. where a landlord passes on VAT on such services to tenant) is continued for legacy lease after 1 July 2008. Is this practice also extended to new leases created after 1 July 2008?**

    Yes this practice extends to such leases.

5. **Where a tenant carries out a refurbishment in say year fifteen of a twenty-year lease and the lease expires at the end of the twenty years without being renewed, is the tenant responsible for a capital goods adjustment in respect of the refurbishment when the lease expires?**

    In the case described above there is no obligation on the tenant to make an adjustment since the lease simply expires. It is not assigned or surrendered. It should be noted that Revenue will examine cases where a tenant carries out a significant refurbishment approaching the end of the lease to see if in fact the refurbishment is for the benefit of the landlord and the issue of entitlement to input credit of the landlord, etc., would need to be considered.

6. **What is the VAT treatment of a premium/reverse premium payable by the tenant to his landlord on the surrender/assignment of a legacy lease on/after 1 July?**

    The payment of a reverse premium to the landlord by the tenant on the surrender of a 'legacy' lease is not taxable: it is considered outside the scope of VAT. The consideration for the assignment/surrender of a legacy lease is based on the CGS amount as per Section 4C(7). The position of premiums generally is set out in paragraph 4.11 of the VAT on Property Guide.

7. **Where after 30 June a landlord makes a letting by way of an occupational lease to a tenant and exercises the landlord's option to tax, what is the VAT treatment if the tenant then makes a sub letting of part only of the original property to a person connected with the landlord where the sub tenant does not have at least 90% VAT recoverability? Is the landlord's option to tax terminated for the entire of the property let by the landlord or only in respect of part of it, namely the part occupied by the connected sub tenant?**

    Only the part occupied is effected by the termination of the option to tax. Section 12E(6)(c) has the effect of clawing-back the proportion of the landlord's deduction that relates to the part occupied by the connected tenant.

7a. **What is the position as regards charging VAT on such an occupational lease if, for example, 25% of the property was sub-let to a connected person with less than 90% recovery. The claw-back would be based on 25% of the VAT recovered by the landlord. Would the landlord only charge VAT on 75% of the rent paid under the occupational lease?**

Yes, the landlord would only charge VAT based on 75% of the rent charge to the main (unconnected) tenant. Please note that the apportionment of the rent between the taxable and exempt use would have to be made on a fair and reasonable basis. For example, if the ground floor represented 25% of the floor space but was more valuable in terms of the amount of rent receivable this would affect the amount of the claw-back under section 12E(6)(c) and the corresponding amount of the rent subject to VAT.

8. **Section 4C(11) provides that the adjustment period for an assigned or surrendered legacy leasehold interest in the hands of the assignee or person who makes the surrender is 20 years. The capital goods scheme operates by intervals. Can the Revenue explain how the capital goods scheme will work in relation to an assigned or surrendered legacy lease?**

Where a legacy lease is assigned/surrendered from 1 July onwards, the person who is assigning or surrendering the lease calculates the number of intervals remaining in the adjustment. This is calculated from Section 4C(11)(c).

The adjustment period for the new owner (assignee/landlord) is advised by the assignor/surrendering tenant per section 4C(8)(b)(i), which will be the number of intervals remaining (being the number of intervals remaining in the latter's adjustment period, including that in which the assignment/surrender takes place).

Section 4C(8)(b) provides that that the assignee/landlord is a capital goods owner for the purposes of Section 12E. The initial interval runs for a full twelve months from the date on which the assignment and surrender occurs. The second interval (as per Section 12E) will end on the date of the end of the accounting year of the capital goods owner. (Example 1 in Appendix A illustrates how this operates in practice)

9. **In Section 12E(3)(a) the adjustment periods for various classes of capital goods are set out. This sub section does not refer to shorter adjustment periods which will apply in the case of capital goods to which the transfer of business applies and legacy leases. The words 'in all other cases 20 years' give cause for concern. Can the Revenue confirm that different periods than those set out in Section 12E(3) can apply in the case of properties transferred under transfer of business rules and legacy leases?**

The adjustment period for legacy leases for the person who holds the interest on 1 July is provided for in Section 4C(11). For a person to whom a lease is assigned or surrendered post 1 July the adjustment period is provided for in Section 4C(8)(b)(i).

In relation to a transfer of business there are two separate scenarios. If a transfer of business occurs during the period where the property is considered 'new' then the adjustment period is 20 intervals as per Section 12E(3)(a)(iii) for the transferee and the 'total tax incurred' is the amount of tax that would have been chargeable on the transfer but for the application of Section 3(5)(b)(iii) as per section 12E(3)(b)(ii).

If the transfer occurs outside the period where the property is considered 'new' then Section 12E(10) provides that transferee will effectively 'step into the shoes' of the transferor and must make adjustments for the remainder of the adjustment period as provided for in Section 12E(10)(c). Where the transferee's accounting year ends on a different date to the transferor's, the transferee may align the end of the CGS intervals with his or her end of accounting year. See Regulation 21A of S.I. No. 548 of 2006 - VAT Regulations 2006 (inserted by S.I. No. 238 of 2008 - VAT (Amendment) Regulations 2008).

10. **Can a body that is considered outside the scope of VAT, such as local authority avail of the option to tax the sale of a transitional property under Section 4C(2)?**

A local authority, or any other person or entity to the extent that their activities are outside the scope of VAT, cannot avail of the option to tax since they are not a 'taxable person' and therefore do not come within the provisions of Section 4C which only applies to immovable goods acquired or developed by a taxable person. Similarly the CGS will not apply to such a person since it only applies to taxable persons.

11. **When a person leaves a VAT Group and is either the landlord or the tenant of a person who remains a member, can the landlord avoid a deductibility adjustment by opting to tax the letting?**

Yes, subject to the connected persons rule in Section 7A.

12. **Does a CGS positive adjustment apply where a landlord has a short term letting pre 1 July 2008 without a waiver and opts to tax the letting on or after 1 July 2008?**

A CGS positive adjustment is not provided for in these circumstances as transitional properties are not subject to the change of use provisions in Section 12E.

13. **More clarification is needed regarding the meaning of 'freehold equivalent' - What is the position of a lease for 50 years, for 70 years, for 80 years that do not fall foul of the '50% rule'?**

The length of the lease is not of great importance. The amount of the payment and the nature of the payment(s) is the most significant issue. However, as a very general rule of thumb, leases of 75 years duration or longer are likely to be considered as 'freehold equivalent'.

14. What is the position for a waived letting between connected persons (where the connected tenant is not entitled to at least 90% deducibility) where the VAT on the rents prior to 1 July satisfies the minimum test in the 12-year rule?

In such cases the landlord simply continues to charge VAT on the rents. The landlord must however ensure that the VAT on the rents continues to satisfy the minimum amount provided for in the 12-year rule.

15. What is the position for a waived letting between connected persons (where the connected tenant is not entitled to at least 90% deducibility) where the VAT on the rents prior to 1 July is less than the minimum amount provided for in the 12-year rule?

In such cases the waiver is cancelled with effect from 1 July. However, the landlord may increase the rents so that the VAT on the rents is at least equal to the minimum amount provided for the 12-year rule on 1 July. Rents will not have to apply on a monthly or bimonthly basis in order to satisfy the 12-year rule. However rent payable from 1 July 2008 should, irrespective of the period for which it is payable, be at such a level that when 'annualised' the 12-year rule will be satisfied. The VAT on the rents, which meets the minimum amount1, must be accounted for in the July/Aug VAT return.

It is important to note that the 12-year rule is subject to the landlord paying the resulting VAT liabilities on time. It is not a requirement that the tenant must have paid the VAT to the landlord. Note – bad debt relief does not apply in such a case. See Regulation 16A of S.I. No. 548 of 2006 - VAT Regulations 2006 (inserted by S.I. No. 272 of 2007 - VAT (Amendment) Regulations 2007 as amended by S.I. No. 238 of 2008 - VAT (Amendment) Regulations 2008).

16. Will there be flexibility with the practical application of the CGS in regard to the first and second interval? For some businesses, the partial exemption calculation is a major task performed once a year - the application of the CGS would require partial exemption calculations throughout the year. Would it be acceptable to allow some flexibility in the timing of calculating the initial interval adjustment?

In practice this major task of calculating the partial exemption calculation is likely to be dealt with in Large Cases Division (LCD) and should be taken up by each business with LCD. In the majority of cases the proportion of taxable use should be readily identifiable by direct attribution. See paragraph 6.9 of the VAT on Property Guide. Revenue appreciate the practical application of the CGS may give rise in certain circumstances to some issues and some flexibility will be considered as these issues come to light.

For example, if the minimum VAT as calculated by the formula is €12,000 per year, the minimum amount for each taxable period is €2,000. Therefore €2,000 must be accounted for the in July/Aug VAT return.

17.   **Example 3 in the VAT on Property Guide would appear to relate to repairs not development. Can Revenue clarify the example?**

Expenditure on repairs and renewals does not fall to be taken into account when calculating development expenditure. Example 3 in future editions of the Guide will be amended to enhance clarity.

18.   **Has the exclusion for supplies of immovable goods in the grouping provisions being removed?**

The exclusion has not been removed. The grouping provisions do not apply to the supply of immovable goods.

19.   **Can a person who carries on an exempt business avail of the joint option for taxation and is such a person subject to the CGS?**

Any person who carries on a business in the State (even an exempt business) is a 'taxable person'. The joint option for taxation is allowed when the sale is between taxable persons. The CGS applies to properties where VAT was chargeable on the acquisition or development of that property to a **taxable person.** This should not be confused with a person or body who is involved in activities that are outside the scope of VAT. (See Q10).

20.   **In relation to Section 12E(8) – are paragraphs (b)(i) and (b)(ii) separate exclusions?**

The conditions for the non-application of Section 12E(8)(a) set out in (i), (ii) and (iii) of Section 12E(8)(b) are not separate - they are cumulative. The taxpayer must satisfy the three conditions in order to avoid the CGS adjustment.

21.   **Does Section 12E(8) apply to 'legacy leases'?**

Yes. It is separate to the tax charge that arises on the assignment or surrender of a legacy lease under Section 4C.

22.   **Can Revenue confirm that, where a long lease that is subject to VAT is granted before 1 July 2008 (passing EVT, etc.) and the landlord then disposes of the reversionary interest in that lease after 1 July 2008 in circumstances where S.4(9) applies, the landlord will not suffer any CGS adjustment on that disposal of the reversion?**

A CGS adjustment will not apply in these circumstances.

23.   **Is VAT chargeable on the sale of commercial or residential 'transitional' property post cancellation of waiver after payment of cancellation sum?**

Generally no VAT due on sale but see Tax Briefing 64 in respect of sales by a developer/builder - otherwise no change in treatment intended under new rules.

24.   **When does development constitute 'refurbishment'? Is it subject to the 25% rule?**

Refurbishment is a concept within the CGS. Whenever a person carries out a development on a previously completed building, this constitutes a refurbishment and essentially 'creates' a capital good. The adjustment period for a refurbishment is ten intervals, the first of which begins when that refurbishment is completed.

If a property is sold, the 25% test and the materially altered test apply to determine whether or not a property is 'new'. For example, suppose a property was acquired in 1985 without VAT and developed at a cost of €1,000,000 + VAT €135,000 in Apr 2007 (the development was completed 5 July 2007). A further development was carried out in Jan 2008 (completed 18 Mar 2008) at a cost of €200,000 + VAT €27,000. Both developments constitute refurbishment and 'create' two separate capital goods with ten intervals for each capital good. The adjustment period for the first capital good (development completed 5 July 2007) begins on 5 July 2007. The adjustment period for the second capital good (development completed 18 Mar 2008) begins on 18 Mar 2008.

If the property is subsequently sold, it is necessary to determine whether or not the sale is taxable or exempt. This means looking at all development carried out in the five years before the sale occurs. The property is sold in Feb 2009 for €4,000,000. The total cost of the development (neither of which materially altered the property) in the previous five years is €1,200,000. Since this is more than 25% of the consideration for sale the sale is taxable.

If the property had been sold for €6,000,000 the cost of the development would not breach the 25% rule and so the sale would be exempt. In order to avoid a CGS claw-back (separate claw-back for each capital good), the joint option for taxation would have to be exercised.

Note – if the property is not sold there are simply two capital goods - each with an adjustment period of ten intervals. Neither of these capital goods is subject to the annual adjustment provisions under the CGS since the development which 'created' them was completed prior to 1 July 2008.

25. **If a developer disposes of a holiday cottage after 1 July 2008, what are the VAT implications for the developer and the investor? Is the investor entitled to recover VAT on the purchase price and let the property to the management company as the letting of a holiday cottage is a taxable activity?**

The position for such arrangements post 1 July 2008 is as follows. The developer charges VAT to the investor on the sale of the holiday home. As there is no distinction between long and short leases under the new system for VAT on property the granting of the lease from the investor to the management company is an exempt supply of a service. There is no entitlement to deductibility for the purchaser. However, the investor can choose to register for VAT and exercise the landlord's option to tax in accordance with Section 7A and opt to tax the letting to the management company (assuming that the investor and the management company are not connected, or if connected the tenant is entitled to at least 90% deductibility). The investor must then charge VAT on the periodic rents to the management company at 21.5% over the term of the lease. The management company who are engaged in the provision of holiday accommodation are obliged to charge VAT at 13.5% (para (xiii)(b) Sixth Schedule) on the moneys received for providing the holiday homes to its customers.

26. **Can a waiver of exemption be backdated to a letting that commences prior to 1 July 2008?**

Yes, providing all the normal criteria as provided for in Regulation 4(4) VAT Regulations 2006 are applicable, e.g. tenant must be entitled to full deductibility, a waiver may be backdated in respect of an **individual letting.** The backdated waiver will not extend to any of the landlord's other lettings.

27. **Where a property, in which there is a short-term letting that is subject to a waiver, is sold and the sale is subject to VAT Revenue have traditionally allowed the amount of VAT charged on the sale be included in the 'tax paid' for the purposes of the cancellation adjustment. Will this practice continue for waivers that are cancelled after 1 July?**

Yes, this practice will continue where VAT is chargeable on the sale of a property and the waiver is subsequently cancelled.

28. **A landlord creates a 25-year letting in a property on or after 1 July and the landlord's option to tax is exercised. Two years later the landlord sells the property. Can the transfer of business relief in Section 3(5) (b)(iii) apply to such a situation where the purchaser will continue to apply the landlord's option to tax?**

Yes the transfer of business relief can apply where a landlord sells a property in which there is a sitting tenant and where the purchaser (landlord 2) will continue with the landlord's option to tax and charge VAT on the rents to the sitting tenant.

29. **A landlord has two properties that are let short-term and are subject to a waiver of exemption on 1 July 2008. In December 2008 the landlord wises to cancel his or her waiver of exemption. Can he or she cancel in respect of just one of the properties?**

No, the normal waiver cancellation rules as contained in Regulation 4 of S.I. No. 548 of 2006 - VAT Regulations 2006 apply and the cancellation amount must be calculated in respect of both properties.

30. **What is the VAT treatment of a premium/reverse premium payable by a landlord to a tenant or a tenant to a landlord on or after 1 July in respect of leases created prior to 1 July?**

There are essentially four possible scenarios -

1. Long lease created prior to 1 July on which VAT was chargeable when created.

2. Long lease created prior to 1 July on which VAT was **not** chargeable when created.

3. Short lease created prior to 1 July where waiver of exemption did not apply (i.e. exempt lease).

4. Short lease created prior to 1 July where waiver of exemption did apply (i.e. landlord charges VAT at 21.5% on the rents).

In respect of (1) the VAT chargeable on the assignment or surrender of the lease is restricted to the amount specified in Section 4C(7). (See question 6 above)

In respect of (2) and (3) no VAT is chargeable on the assignment or surrender of the lease in such cases.

In respect of (4) VAT is chargeable at 21.5% the payment on the assignment or surrender of the lease is linked to the taxable waived letting.

Note – the treatment of premiums and reverse premiums on leases created on or after 1 July is explained in paragraph 4.11 VAT on Property Guide.

Appendix A

Example 1 – CGS intervals for legacy leases

Mr X grants Ms Y a 35-year lease on 1 July 2000. VAT is charged on the capitalised value of the lease of €1million. Ms Y is still the tenant (and so has the 'interest' in the property on 1 July 2008.) The adjustment period for the legacy lease for the person who holds the legacy on 1 July 2008, i.e. Mr Y, is 20 years from 1 July 2000. (This is determined from Section 4C(11)(c).

On the 15 April 2012 Ms Y assigns the lease to Mr J. The assignment is taxable, on the reverse charge basis, as it occurs within the 20-year adjustment period.

VAT charged on the assignment is calculated as follows –

$$\frac{T \times N}{Y}$$

$$\frac{€1,000,000 \times 9}{20}$$

$$= €450,000$$

The assignment is reverse charged which means that Mr J is liable to account for VAT of €450,000 on the supply in his Mar/Apr 2012 VAT return. Mr Y must issue a document to Mr J which contains-

- The amount of tax due on the assignment (€450,000)

- The number of intervals remaining in the adjustment period at the time of the assignment2, which is in this case is 9 intervals.

Section 4C(8)(b) deems Mr J to be a capital goods owner for the purposes of Section 12E. Therefore, the interest that he owns is subject to the annual adjustments and all the other rules in the CGS. The number of intervals in the adjustment period for the person to whom a legacy lease is assigned or surrendered after 1 July 2008, is determined by Section 4C(8)(b)(i). For Mr J it is 9 intervals. The initial interval for Mr J begins on 15/14/2012 and end on 14/4/2013. Mr J's accounting year ends on 31/12. The second interval for the interest will begin on 15/4/2013 end on 31/12/2013. Mr J must make any adjustments required under the CGS until the end of the adjustment period (9 intervals) the last of which will end on 31/12/2020.

VALUE ADDED TAX INFORMATION LEAFLET (DECEMBER 08)

VAT ON SERVICES CONNECTED WITH FOREIGN PROPERTY

Services Connected with Foreign Immovable Property

1.   Introduction

The VAT treatment of a service that is supplied in relation to a foreign* immovable** property depends on the nature of the service and the extent of its connection with the property. While many services have a connection with property in the ordinary meaning of the words, certain services which are closely linked to particular properties are treated differently. These services are regarded, for VAT purposes, as connected with the property, and in respect of these a person supplying the services is normally required to register and account for VAT where the property is located. In the case of other services, the VAT treatment depends on the place where the supplier of the service has established a business or, in certain circumstances, where the customer has established a business or is resident.

The principal questions that this leaflet answers, for a supplier established in Ireland, are:

What services are regarded as being liable to VAT where an immovable property is located?

What services, connected with immovable property, are liable to Irish VAT?

And

Whether a person who supplies these services can recover VAT incurred in Ireland.

*This leaflet is primarily concerned with foreign property. Where reference is also made to Irish property, this will be clearly indicated.

** Any reference to 'property' in this leaflet means 'immovable property' as defined in Section 2 of the leaflet.

2.   What is immovable property?

For the purposes of this leaflet, immovable property means land; and any buildings or fixtures attached to the land including tenements, hereditaments, houses and buildings, walls, fences and any other permanent structures or fixtures; land covered by water; and any estate, right or interest in or over land.

[Machinery that is not installed as a fixture is regarded as movable goods, and does not come within the definition of immovable property for the purposes of this leaflet.]

Foreign immovable property includes any of the above located outside of the territory of the State; and more specifically includes any of the following: holiday homes, time-share properties, investment properties and hotels.

3.   Services liable to VAT where immovable property is located

3.1   Services are not liable to Irish VAT if they are regarded, for VAT purposes, as connected with a foreign immovable property. When determining whether such connection exists, it is necessary to examine the nature of the service. A service may be regarded, for VAT purposes, as connected with the property when it is supplied in relation to a particular property, and is not a service related to property in general. Any fees charged in respect of such a service are liable to VAT by reference to the location of the property – where the property is located abroad, the fees will not be subject to Irish VAT.

3.2   Services that are regarded, for VAT purposes, as connected with foreign immovable property include those that have a direct physical link with the property, and require the presence of personnel or facilities there. These include:

- The surveying of a site or property;

- Security or supervision on a site or property;

- The construction, development, repair, maintenance (including decoration), demolition, conversion or alteration of a property.

Services of this nature are generally supplied by:

- Surveyors

- Architects

- Engineers

- Decorators

- Interior designers

- Security companies

- Site supervisors

- Property management companies

3.3   Services are also regarded for VAT purposes as directly connected with a foreign immovable property if they involve:

- The sale of a property;

- The assignment or surrender of any interest in the property (e.g. a lease);

- The granting of any right or licence in relation to the property;

- The letting, including short-term holiday letting, of a property

These services are usually provided by

- Auctioneers;

- Solicitors or other legal professionals.

- Estate agents;

- Any other agents connected with the transaction;

- Tour operators.

3.4　It should be noted that estate agents, architects etc., may also provide services that are not regarded, for VAT purposes, as connected with specific immovable properties. For example, estate agents may provide general marketing services in relation to foreign developments, and architects may provide designs to be used as a template for the construction of houses in several different countries. See Paragraph 4 for details of the treatment of services of this nature.

4.　Services liable to VAT where the supplier (or customer) is located

Services that have no direct physical link with a foreign immovable property, and do not involve the transfer of any interest in the property, are not generally regarded, for VAT purposes, as connected with a property. These services include:

- General advertising of property;

- Marketing of property, including the holding of exhibitions. However where negotiation of contracts for the sale of properties takes place at an exhibition, any deposit or similar fee paid in respect of such a contract is regarded as being connected with the property;

- The securing of purchasers where this does not form part of the process of negotiating for the sale of specific properties;

- Advice and information relating to land prices or property markets which do not relate to specific properties;

- Feasibility studies of the commercial potential of development etc. in a geographical area;

- Any other general consultancy or advice service in relation to foreign property.

These services are liable to Irish VAT if the supplier is established in the State. However, where any of the services listed above are also included in the Fourth Schedule to the VAT Act, where such services are supplied to customers established outside the State, and are used by them for business purposes, they are liable to VAT by reference to the place of establishment of the customer – effectively, they may be zero-rated for Irish VAT purposes. These include the provision of legal advice, the provision of information, advertising and marketing. A supplier of these Fourth Schedule services may still register for VAT in Ireland, even if he/she has no other taxable activities in the State. An Information Leaflet on the subject of Fourth Schedule Services is available on the Revenue website.

5.　VAT Registration for persons supplying services in relation to foreign immovable property

A trader who is established in Ireland and who supplies services that are regarded, for VAT purposes, as connected with a foreign immovable property (i.e. regarded for VAT purposes as taxable where the property is located) may incur VAT in Ireland in the course of supplying these services. To recover this VAT, he/she should register for VAT, and claim it back by way of the VAT Return. This applies even if the person makes no supplies in Ireland, and would not otherwise be entitled to register for VAT.

In these cases, registration applications will be accepted subject to the proof that the trader does in fact supply services that are regarded as taxable abroad in respect of which he/she would have been entitled to recover VAT had he/she supplied the same services in Ireland.

Traders who are already registered in respect of the provision of services in the State, such as estate agents who provide services in Ireland and also services regarded, for VAT purposes, as connected with foreign property, should similarly recover all VAT incurred in relation to all those services in their normal VAT return.

6.   **Legislation**

Section 5(5) of the VAT Act 1972 (as amended) sets out the general rule that the place of supply of a service is the place where the person supplying the service has his/her establishment.

Section 5(6)(a) of the Act sets out the special provision that the place of supply of services connected with immovable goods, including the services of estate agents, architects and firms providing on-site supervision, is where the immovable goods are situated.

Section 5(6)(e) provides that the place of supply of certain services (listed in the Fourth Schedule to the VAT Act), when those services are received for business purposes, is the place where the customer has an establishment or, if the customer has more than one establishment, the establishment where the services are most directly used.

Section 12(1)(b)(iii) provides that a person who supplies services outside the State is entitled to recover VAT incurred (in Ireland) in relation to these services to the extent that he/she would have been entitled to recover the VAT if the services had been supplied in Ireland.

7.   **Specific Services/Examples**

7.1   **Property exhibition held in Ireland**

In all circumstances, where an **admission fee** is charged to a property exhibition, this is subject to Irish VAT at 21.5%. Any person charging such a fee should register and account for VAT, subject to the usual registration thresholds. The following examples are dealt with on the basis that no admission fee is charged:

- (a) **An exhibition is staged by a person selling, or supplying an interest in, immovable property abroad:** Where the person staging the exhibition is also the person supplying the interest in foreign property, no taxable supply is taking place in Ireland. If the person is established in Ireland, he/she may register for VAT and thus reclaim any VAT incurred in holding the exhibition by way of the usual VAT return.

- (b) **An exhibition is staged on behalf of a person selling, or supplying an interest in, immovable property abroad:** Where the person staging the exhibition does not own the property, he/she is providing a marketing service to the owner of the property. If the owner is established in Ireland, then this marketing service is liable to Irish VAT at 21.5%. The owner of the property in this case may register for VAT, and reclaim any VAT charged to him/her. If the owner is not established in Ireland, then the person staging the exhibition should charge VAT at zero %, as services of this nature are liable to tax where the customer is established in accordance with the Fourth Schedule to the VAT Act 1972 (as amended).

Any actual sale or negotiation of contracts in respect of foreign property taking place at an exhibition is liable to VAT by reference to the location of the property, and not where the sale takes place. Accordingly there is no Irish VAT due on deposits, arrangement fees or similar fees paid in respect of these sales.

7.2 Estate Agent acting for developer of foreign immovable property

Any services provided by an estate agent established in Ireland that are regarded, for VAT purposes, as connected with the sale of a foreign property are liable to VAT by reference to the location of the property. The fees charged are therefore not liable to Irish VAT. (The agent may be required to register for tax where the property is located, subject to the rules in that State). The estate agent, however, may register for VAT in Ireland for the purpose of reclaiming any VAT incurred in the course of arranging the sale. If the estate agent is already registered in Ireland, then he/she should reclaim any VAT through the VAT return as though it was incurred in the course of his/her domestic activities. An estate agent not established in the State may be entitled to recover VAT incurred under the 8th or 13th VAT Directives, and should contact the Unregistered VAT Repayments Section, River House, Charlotte's Quay, Limerick in this regard.

7.3 Services of a solicitor in connection with immovable property

Where the solicitor's services are supplied in connection with the transfer of an interest in property, including the drawing up of a contract in relation to such a transfer, they are liable to VAT where the property is located. If the property is located in a country other than Ireland, the solicitor may be required to register for VAT (or an equivalent tax) in that country.

Fees charged by a solicitor established in Ireland in respect of services not regarded, for VAT purposes, as connected with property are generally liable to VAT as follows:

1. If the client is established or resident in Ireland, then Irish VAT applies.

2.   If the client is established in the E.U., and the client is acting in a private capacity, Irish VAT applies.

3.   If the client is established in the E.U. and is acting in a business capacity, the services are zero rated, i.e. no VAT is charged by the Irish solicitor, and the client accounts for the VAT in his/her own country as if he/she had made the supply.

4.   If the client is established outside the E.U., the services are zero rated for VAT.

7.3.1 Solicitor acting for a company with immovable property in different countries

Where a company engages a solicitor established in Ireland to act on its behalf in relation to transactions involving property that it owns in different countries, the VAT treatment depends on the nature of the transaction.

If, for example, the **company wishes to mortgage any or all immovable property**, including property located in Ireland, this transaction is not considered to be a service connected with property in the terms of paragraph 4 above, and therefore legal services supplied in connection with this transaction are taxable subject to the general rules governing legal services; i.e. if the company is established in Ireland, then Irish VAT applies; if the company is established outside Ireland, then the supply can be zero-rated for VAT. It should be noted that if the company has an establishment in Ireland and also in another country, the VAT treatment would depend on which establishment most directly uses the services supplied.

If, on the other hand, the company wishes to dispose of any immovable property, any legal work done by the solicitor directly in connection with the disposal of individual properties is liable to VAT where the properties are located, and the solicitor may be required to register for VAT in each country. In a situation where the actual disposal is carried out by **local solicitors under the instruction of the Irish solicitor**, it is only the services of these local solicitors that are regarded as being liable to VAT where the property is located. The services of the Irish solicitor in providing instruction to the local solicitors, or in providing other services such as legal advice regarding the sale, procurement of valuations, etc., are liable to VAT subject to the general rules set out in paragraph 7.3.

7.3.2 Solicitor acting for estates

Legal services supplied to a private (non-business) client in connection with the **general administration of an estate** are liable to VAT by reference to the place of establishment of the solicitor – if the solicitor is established in Ireland, and the client is established in Ireland or in another Member State of the E.U. then Irish VAT applies. However, if the client is established or resident outside the E.U., the fees can be zero-rated for VAT. The general administration of the estate may include services provided in relation to property, but not regarded, for VAT purposes, as connected with it, such as defending legal claims made against the estate in respect of the title to any land.

However, services supplied by a solicitor connected with the disposal of **any property** that forms part of the estate are in all cases liable to VAT by reference to the location of the property. If a person resident outside the country is the beneficiary of an estate that includes land or other property in Ireland, and that person engages a solicitor established in Ireland to sell or let the property, then the solicitor's fees are liable to Irish VAT. Similarly, if the land in the above example is located in another country, then the fees charged are liable to VAT by reference to the rules in place in that country, and no Irish VAT applies to the Irish solicitors' fees.

Where a solicitor established in Ireland supplies legal services to a client resident outside the E.U., and these consist in part of services regarded, for VAT purposes, as connected with the property as set out above, and in part of services which are not so connected, this should be treated as a **multiple supply**, and the fee should be split to show those services liable to Irish VAT separately from those which are zero-rated.

7.4 Property management companies

Where a company established in Ireland is engaged to manage immovable properties outside the State, these services are liable to VAT by reference to the location of the property. In this context, 'management' includes (but is not limited to)

• Supervision and maintenance of the property;

• Administration of rents, service charges and insurance charges;

• Control or administration of lettings.

A company providing these services may register for VAT in Ireland for the purpose of reclaiming any VAT incurred here in the course of providing the services.

Further Information

Enquiries regarding any issue contained in this Information Leaflet should be addressed to the Revenue District responsible for the taxpayer's affairs. Contact details for all Revenue Districts.

This leaflet is issued by:

**VAT Appeals and Communications Branch
Indirect Taxes Division,
Dublin Castle.**

December 2008

VALUE ADDED TAX INFORMATION LEAFLET (DECEMBER 08)

RETAILERS SPECIAL SCHEMES

1. **Introduction**

   Revenue's special schemes for retailers are designed to assist them account for VAT on their retail transactions. The purpose of this leaflet is to update Revenue's Schemes for retailers to take into account inflation and technological changes in the retail sector. A separate scheme applies to chemists/pharmacists.

2. **Purpose of Schemes**

   Some retailers who account for VAT on a cash receipts basis may encounter difficulty in determining the amounts of their sales of goods at different rates of tax. Where all sales are inclusive of tax and the retailer has no facility at check-out point for identifying sales of goods at the different rates of VAT, the special schemes are available to allow the retailer to segregate their total receipts for the purpose of calculating the VAT due.

   The schemes cater for different classes of retailers with small to large turnovers and relate to sales chargeable at the zero, 13.5% and 21.5% VAT rates.

   In order to calculate the tax due in a taxable period a retailer must know the amount of purchases at the different rates of VAT and the total retail sales for the respective period. The retailer uses this information to apportion the trading receipts to calculate the VAT due on sales.

3. **Who may use the Schemes?**

   The schemes may be used only by retailers who:

   - sell goods chargeable at two or more VAT rates, and

   - do not have facilities for segregating receipts at point of sale into the different rates and cannot reasonably be expected to do so (see **Electronic point of sale (EPOS)/Scanning equipment below**), and

   - sell goods in the form in which they buy them, i.e. without applying any further process in their production/manufacture.

4. **Who may NOT use the Schemes?**

   The Schemes **may not be used** in the following circumstances:

   - Where a retailer uses **Electronic Point of Sale (EPOS)** equipment capable of accurately recording sales at the various applicable VAT rates.

   - Where a retailer is selling second-hand goods under the Margin Scheme (see Information Leaflet: VAT Treatment of Second-hand Goods The Margin Scheme.)

- **Where a retailer has receipts from the provision of services.** Where a retailer has combined receipts from services and the sale of goods, the receipts and inputs in respect of the services should be separated out. The balance of the receipts from retail sales should then be segregated between the various VAT rates by using the appropriate scheme.

- Where a retailer is selling goods that the retailer has processed. For example, the purchase of materials for making sandwiches where such an activity forms part of, say, a supermarket café business. The purchases and receipts from such sales should be treated separately.

- Where a retailer is supplying hot take-away food. The retailer must exclude purchases of zero-rated food that is chargeable to VAT at the 13.5% rate. The receipts from sales of this food must also be excluded from the total receipts for the purposes of the appropriate retailers scheme.

- Where a retailer has agreed an otherwise acceptable method of segregating sales at each VAT rate with the Local Revenue District.

5. Electronic point of sale/Scanning equipment

Traders whose point of sale equipment (typically by means of scanning bar codes) is capable of accurately recording sales at the various VAT rates should use the data produced by the system when completing their VAT returns.

VAT analysis based on till readings, which require the operator of the till to segregate sales into different VAT rates, is not normally acceptable. In such circumstances the traders concerned should use the appropriate Retail Scheme as outlined in this leaflet.

6. Environmental Levy (Plastic Bags Tax)

Where a retailer suppliers plastic bags on which the Environmental Levy is chargeable the total receipts from the levy should be excluded from the sales figures used in the retailer's scheme.

7. Record keeping

Retailers using any of the special schemes in this leaflet must retain their scheme workings for each VAT period. This, of course, is in addition to keeping those records required by regulations to be retained by taxable persons (please see the Revenue Guide to Value-Added Tax, July 2008 for details).

8. Different Schemes for Different Retailers

There are 3 different Schemes for retailers plus the Special Scheme for Chemists. The types of business and the appropriate and alternative Schemes are as follows:

The appropriate scheme dependent on turnover and the alternative scheme where appropriate

Annual Turnover (VAT inclusive)	Appropriate Scheme	Alternative Scheme
Under €500,000	Scheme 1	Scheme 2, 3
€500,000 to €1,500,000	Scheme 2	Scheme 3
Over €1,500,000	Scheme 3	No Alternative

9.   Review and Audit

The use of the schemes by retailers is not obligatory. Retailers should check and ensure that over a number of taxable periods the estimated sales figures at each rate of tax indicate a realistic mark-up when compared to the purchases at each rate over the same period. Schemes 2 and 3 involve the calculation of an **average or weighted mark-up** for each VAT rate and an example of this calculation is included at Appendix 1. As part of an audit, the Revenue Auditor will check that the VAT returns reflect the mark-ups and product mix of the retailer and may raise assessments where it appears that the returns do not do so accurately. Retailers are advised to retain copies of the calculations of the average or weighted mark-ups used by them in the Schemes and to carry out a review of the calculations periodically such as at the accounts year end. Please note the calculation of VAT on sales through the operation of the schemes is subject to periodic review by Revenue.

Further information

Enquiries regarding any issue contained in this Information Leaflet should be addressed to your local Revenue District. Contact details for all Revenue Districts.

VAT Appeals and Communications Branch,
Indirect Taxes Division,
Dublin Castle.

December 2008

Scheme 1 - For Retailers with Annual Turnover less than €500,000

Receipts from sales in the taxable period are to be apportioned in the same ratio as purchases, importations, and intra-Community acquisitions of goods for resale in the same period. In this example the purchases figures include importations inclusive of VAT charged at point of import and the tax-inclusive values of intra-Community acquisitions (ICAs).

Example:

Total sales including tax in the taxable period: €60,000

Total purchases, importations, ICAs (tax-inclusive) in the taxable period	VAT Rate
€24,000	zero
€15,000	13.5%
€9,000	21.5%

Total Tax-inclusive purchases €48,000

Proportion of turnover €60,000 chargeable at each VAT rate:

Rate	Proportion	Turnover tax inclusive	Tax included	Tax Exclusive
zero%	$\frac{24,000 \times 60,000}{48,000}$	€30,000	Nil	€30,000
13.5%	$\frac{15,000 \times 60,000}{48,000}$	€18,750	€2,230	€16,520
21.5%	$\frac{9,000 \times 60,000}{48,000}$	€11,250	€1,990	€9,260

When this exercise is completed the retailer should then complete the VAT return to show at the TI box the aggregate of:

- VAT on supplies as computed above, and

- VAT due on intra-Community acquisitions.

Notes on Scheme 1 - Calculation of Tax-Inclusive Purchases

For the purposes of Scheme 1 it is necessary to calculate the total VAT-INCLUSIVE value of purchases of stock-in-trade. This will include the following:

1. Purchases from registered persons

The figure to be taken is the invoice value of the goods inclusive of VAT.

2. Imports from non-EU countries

In the case of such imports the figure to be taken is the customs entry value of the goods inclusive of VAT paid at the point of import.

3. Intra-Community acquisitions

For goods imported from other EU Member States (intra-Community acquisitions) the figure to be taken is the invoiced value of the goods plus VAT due on the intra-Community acquisition at the Irish rate of VAT applicable to the goods in question.

4. Purchases from unregistered suppliers

No tax will be shown on invoices from these suppliers but the amount invoiced may be treated as inclusive of VAT.

5. Purchases from farmers

For unregistered farmers, the amount to be included in the scheme workings is the amount inclusive of the flat-rate addition. For a registered farmer the amount to be included in the scheme workings is the total amount paid inclusive of VAT at the appropriate rates.

6. Goods liable to duty of excise.

Any duty of excise paid on acquisition or importation of goods must always be included when calculating the VAT-inclusive price even though they may not have been shown on the supplier's invoice.

Scheme 2 - For Retailers with Annual Turnover less than €1,500,000

Receipts from sales in the taxable period are segregated by estimating the value of sales at the 2 positive rates (purchases plus average or weighted mark up) and treating the balance as chargeable at the zero rate.

In this example the purchases figures include importations exclusive of VAT charged at point of import and the tax-exclusive values of intra-Community acquisitions (ICAs).

Example:

Total Sales including tax in the taxable period: €87,000

Purchases for resale

Purchases for resale	VAT exclusive @ zero rate	VAT exclusive @ 13.5% rate	VAT exclusive @ 21.5% rate
	€14,000	€36,360	€7,200

The total sales figure €87,000 is apportioned as follows:

- **Step 1:** Mark up standard-rated VAT-exclusive purchases, importations and ICAs at the average or weighted mark up.

- **Step 2:** Mark up low-rated VAT-exclusive purchases, importations and ICAs at the average or weighted mark up.

- **Step 3:** Add VAT to marked up 21.5% and 13.5% figures and deduct the total from gross sales to arrive at the balance which represents zero-rated sales.

Step 1. Resale purchases at 21.5%

VAT-exclusive purchases	€7,200
Add Mark up (say 50%)	€3,600
VAT-exclusive Sale price	€10,800
Add VAT @ 21.5%	€2,322
VAT-inclusive sale price	€13,122

Step 2. Resale purchases at 13.5%

VAT-exclusive purchases	€36,360
Add Mark up (say 35%)	€12,726
VAT-exclusive Sale price	€49,086
Add VAT @ 13.5%	€6,626
VAT-inclusive sale price	€55,712

Step 3. To arrive at zero-rated sales

Total Sales: VAT inclusive	€87,000
Less Estimated Sales at 21.5% and 13.5% (13,122 + 55,712)	(68,834)
Balance VAT-inclusive sales at zero rate	€ 3,600

When this exercise is completed the retailer should then complete the VAT return to show at the TI box the aggregate of

- VAT on supplies as computed above, and
- VAT due on intra-Community acquisitions.

Notes on Scheme 2

1. A variant of this Scheme may be agreed with the local Revenue District in the case of retailers where purchases of goods at the standard rate occurs at a seasonal time, e.g. Christmas supplies purchased by Stationers, Tobacconists, etc.

2. The mark-up figures shown in the example are for illustrative purposes only. Mark-ups will vary and depend on various factors such as the type and location of the business. Retailers should apply the average or weighted rate of mark-up applicable to the 21.5 per cent. and 13.5 per cent goods. (Please see Appendix 1 for an example of the calculation of average or weighted mark-up). The mark-up used should be reviewed each year.

3. Retailers using this scheme should ensure that the sales figures at the zero per cent has a realistic relationship to purchases at the same rate.

4. Imports from non-EU countries, intra-Community acquisitions, purchases from unregistered suppliers and purchases from farmers are to be dealt with in accordance with the notes on scheme 1.

Scheme 3 - For Retailers with Annual Turnover exceeding €1,500,000

Receipts in the taxable period are apportioned by reference to marked-up purchases, importations, and intra-Community acquisitions (ICAs) for resale in that period and in the preceding five taxable periods (or the number of periods since trading commenced if less than 5). In this example the purchases figures include importations exclusive of VAT charged at point of import and the VAT exclusive values of ICAs.

Example:

Total sales including VAT in the Taxable period: €300,000

Rate of VAT	Purchases for period (plus 5 previous periods tax-exclusive)	Mark-up	Purchases marked up to selling price tax-exclusive	Tax Added	Purchases marked up to selling price tax-inclusive
zero	€362,750	€108,825	€471,575	Nil	€471,575
13.5%	129,750	€45,412	€175,162	€23,647	€198,809
21.5%	€44,750	€13,425	€58,175	€12,507	€70,682
				Total	€741,066

The total sales figure €300,000 is apportioned as follows

Example:

Total sales including VAT in the taxable period: €300,000

Chargeable At	Calculation	Amount Tax-Inclusive	Tax included	Amount Tax-Exclusive
Zero	$\dfrac{€471,575 \times €300,000}{€741,066}$	€190,904	Nil	€190,904
13.5%	$\dfrac{€198,809 \times €300,000}{€741,066}$	€80,482	€9,572	€70,910
21.5%	Balance €300,000 less (€190,904 + €80,482)	€28,614	€5,063	€23,550

When this exercise is completed the retailer should then complete the VAT return to show at the TI box the aggregate of

- VAT on supplies as computed above, and

- VAT due on intra-Community acquisitions

Appendix 1

Average or Weighted Mark-ups

Retailers determine the mark-up that they apply to the various goods supplied by them. Accordingly, a retailer using Scheme 2 or 3 should be in a position to prove the accuracy of the mark-ups used in the chosen scheme workings. When commencing to trade each retailer should carry out the following exercise to determine the appropriate mark-ups to be used in the scheme workings. This exercise should be carried out again at the end of each accounting period.

The average or weighted mark-up is calculated as follows:

- **Step 1** - Break down the business (if all receipts liable at one rate e.g. pub with no pub grub) into its constituent parts categorising the different types of goods sold.

- **Step 2** - Take a representative period of normal trading, and establish what percentage of trading is reflected by purchases in each of the categories.

- **Step 3** - Determine the average rate of mark-up in each category. This is done by comparing the supplier's prices (exclusive of VAT) with the retailer's selling price exclusive of VAT.

- **Step 4** - The average mark-up within each category will reflect itself into the overall rate of mark-up for each rate of VAT. An example may help to illustrate the principle.

Example – average or weighted mark-ups.

Establish the average rate of mark-up on standard-rate goods of a retailer who sells petrol, groceries, hardware, drink, and electrical appliances.

Isolate the purchases in each category and calculate the percentage of standard-rate purchases comprised in that category.

The average rate of mark-up on standard goods

Category	% of purchases
Petrol	9%
Grocery	24%
Hardware	10%
Bar	39%
Electrical Appliances	18%
Total	100%

Ascertain the average mark-up for each category.*

The average mark-up for each category

Category	Average Mark-up
Petrol	8%
Grocery	17%
Hardware	50%
Bar	100%
Electrical Appliances	15%

Apply the mark-up to the corresponding % of turnover for each category.*

The mark-up to the corresponding % of turnover for each category

Category	% of purchases by Average Mark-up	%
Petrol	9 x 8% =	0.72
Grocery	24 x 17% =	4.08
Hardware	10 x 50% =	5.00
Bar	39 x 100% =	39.00
Electrical Appliances	18 x 15% =	2.70
Average mark-up		51.5%

*Please note the mark-ups listed above are for illustrative purposes only.

This information leaflet which sets out the current practice at the date of its issue is intended for guidance only and does not purport to be a definitive legal interpretation of the provisions of the Value-Added Tax Act 1972 (as amended).

VALUE ADDED TAX INFORMATION LEAFLET (DECEMBER 08)

SECOND-HAND GOODS – MARGIN SCHEME

1. Introduction

1.1 This leaflet sets out the VAT treatment of works of art, collectors' items and antiques, and second-hand movable goods, in particular the system known as the 'margin scheme'.

1.2 **This leaflet does not apply to sales of second-hand vehicles and second-hand agricultural machinery.** Special schemes applying to transactions involving second-hand motor vehicles and second-hand agricultural machinery are described in a separate Information Leaflet.

2. Margin scheme

2.1 The margin scheme was introduced as a means of reducing the likelihood of double taxation in the context of the sale of second-hand goods.

2.2 It operates by allowing dealers in certain second-hand goods, works of art, antiques and collectors' items to pay VAT on the difference between the sale price and the purchase price of the goods.

2.3 The scheme is at the option of the dealers concerned. If the dealer chooses not to operate the margin scheme then the normal VAT rules apply.

3. Margin Scheme Invoice

An invoice issued by an accountable dealer in respect of a supply under the margin scheme must not show VAT separately. Any such invoice should be clearly endorsed **'Margin Scheme - this invoice does not give the right to an input credit of VAT'.**

4. Who are accountable dealers?

Accountable dealers are persons who deal in margin scheme goods as set out in paragraph 5, either on their own behalf or on commission for others.

5. What are margin scheme goods?

Goods which qualify for the margin scheme are:

- second-hand movable goods;
- certain works of art, collectors items and antiques as described in Appendices I & III,
- specified precious metals and precious stones other than those described in Appendix II.

5.2 For the purposes of the margin scheme, second-hand goods are, broadly speaking, movable goods which are suitable for use either as they are or after repair.

5.3 Second-hand motor vehicles and second-hand agricultural machinery do not qualify for the margin scheme. These are covered by their own special schemes and are dealt with in a separate Information Leaflet. (However see paragraph 14.9 regarding car dismantlers).

6.   The sources of margin scheme goods

6.1   Margin scheme goods are the goods referred to in paragraph 5, purchased for resale, by dealers from specific sources in the EU, as follows:-

- private individuals, or

- exempt bodies (e.g. bank, insurance company, etc.) or accountable persons who were not entitled to any input credit for VAT on purchase of the goods. (Goods purchased from accountable persons with partial deductibility in respect of those goods cannot however be included in the margin scheme, or

- another dealer operating the margin scheme for the supply in question, or

- a person who is an insurance company which took possession of the goods in connection with the settlement of a claim under a policy of insurance from a person who was not entitled to input credit in respect of the goods.

6.2   Effectively, therefore, this means that the margin scheme applies to the sale of goods by a dealer which were acquired by him/her from persons who could not have issued a VAT invoice or, in the case of purchases from other dealers under the scheme, where the dealer issued an invoice which does not show VAT separately.

6.3   The margin scheme can also be applied to certain works of art, collectors' items or antiques which would not normally qualify for inclusion in the scheme because of their source, i.e. imported from outside the EU.

6.4   These items are listed in Appendix I (items 2 and 3), and in Appendix III (item 2), which also includes special rules relating to what is termed the "extended margin scheme".

7.   How the margin scheme operates

7.1   The margin scheme provides that VAT is payable on the sale of margin scheme goods by reference to the difference between the sale price and the purchase price of the goods. This is illustrated as follows:

Dealer's sale price of goods	€500
less dealer's purchase price	€300
Dealer's Margin	€200

The dealer's margin is a tax-inclusive amount. For supplies liable at the standard rate, at present 21.5%, the VAT payable is:

$$\frac{(€200 \times 21.5)}{121.5} = €35.39$$

7.2   The margin for the purposes of this scheme is the difference between the sale price and purchase price of the goods. This margin should not be reduced by deducting the cost of repairs, accessories, overheads, etc.

7.3   Where the sale price is less than the purchase price, the margin is regarded as being nil and there is no VAT due on the sale. It should be noted that in such cases the dealer is not entitled to a refund of VAT in respect of the loss nor can it be offset against profits from other transactions. (However see paragraph 14 for special simplified arrangements for low-value goods).

8.   **Rates**

The general rule is that the rate applicable to a margin scheme supply is the rate applicable to a normal supply. However, there are some exceptions to this rule and these are itemised in Appendix I. In the case of those goods the standard 21.5% rate applies when they are sold under the margin scheme, even though a different rate applies when they are sold under normal VAT rules.

9.   **Deductibility**

A dealer operating the margin scheme cannot claim deductibility for any VAT included in the purchase price of margin scheme goods.

10.   **Invoices**

10.1   Where an invoice is issued by an accountable dealer in respect of goods supplied under the margin scheme **this invoice must not show VAT separately.** Any such invoice should be clearly endorsed 'Margin Scheme - this invoice does not give the right to an input credit of VAT'.

10.2   This means that an accountable person is not entitled to deductibility in respect of any VAT included in the purchase price of goods sold to him/her under the margin scheme.

10.3   However see paragraph 13 below for option to apply the normal rules, where an accountable dealer is selling margin scheme goods to an accountable person.

11.   **Goods bought from other Member States of the EU**

11.1   Where a dealer sells margin scheme goods that were bought from the persons mentioned in paragraph 6.1 above in another Member State he/she should apply the margin scheme in the same way as if the goods were bought in the State i.e. VAT is payable on the dealer's margin and there is no VAT deductibility. If the goods have been bought from a person mentioned at (3) of paragraph 6.1 in another Member State the normal VAT rules in relation to the intra-Community acquisition of goods **do not** apply. **Any VAT included in the price charged in the other Member State is not deductible and would not, as a general rule be shown separately on the invoice.**

12.   **Sales of goods to other Member States of the EU**

Irish VAT is always payable on sales under the margin scheme to persons (including accountable persons) in other Member States. However the VIES reporting requirements do not apply to such sales. **As at paragraph 10 above, VAT must not be shown separately on the sales invoice.**

13.   **Normal VAT rules**

13.1   The margin scheme is generally advantageous to dealers because it reduces their VAT liability. The dealer can, of course, opt to apply the normal VAT rules to any supply. This is more likely to occur where s/he is selling to a customer who is an accountable person and who requires a VAT invoice in order to recover his/her VAT inputs.

13.2   'Normal VAT rules' mean that VAT is chargeable on the full selling price, instead of on the margin, and a VAT-registered customer is entitled to be issued with a VAT invoice in relation to the supply. **The dealer him/ herself may not however claim any VAT credit in relation to his/her purchase.**

14.   Simplified arrangements for low-value goods (Globalisation)

14.1   Simplified arrangements for the calculation of the margin must be applied to low-value margin scheme goods.

14.2   Low-value margin scheme goods are defined as goods where the purchase price of each individual item is less than €635. Individual items subsequently sold for an amount in excess of €635 cease to qualify for the simplified arrangements.

14.3   The simplified arrangements provide that a dealer accounts for VAT on his/her global profit margin. The global margin is the difference between the value of sales and purchases of all low-value margin scheme goods at each VAT rate in each taxable period.

14.4   Goods purchased from accountable persons with partial deductibility in respect of those goods cannot be included in a globalisation arrangement.

14.5   Where the total purchases exceed the sales in any taxable period the dealer is not entitled to a refund of VAT nor should the deficit be set off against any other liability for that period. Instead, the negative margin should be carried forward and added to the purchases of low-value margin scheme goods in calculating the global margin for the next taxable period. This can be illustrated by an example:

Taxable Period 1   €
Sales   3,000
Purchases   2,000
Margin   1,000 including VAT at 21.5%

$(1,000 \times 21.5)/121.5 = €176.95$ VAT payable

Taxable Period 2
Sales   2,000
Purchases   3,000
Negative margin   1,000 No VAT payable

Taxable Period 3
Sales   3,000
Purchases   1,500
Negative margin for period   2 1,000
Margin   500

$(500 \times 21.5)/121.5 = €88.47$ VAT payable

This example assumes that all goods sold qualify for globalisation.

14.6 **Where the global accounting procedure is applied to goods chargeable at different VAT rates, a separate margin must be calculated for each rate.** Where a negative amount arises in calculating the global margin at any tax rate that amount should be carried forward and used in calculating the global margin at that rate for the next period.

14.7 Where a low-value margin scheme item is subsequently sold for more than €635 it no longer qualifies for globalisation. Instead, the sale should be dealt with under the margin scheme. This means that the purchase price of the item should be deducted from the total purchases of low-value margin scheme goods in the period in which the sale takes place.

14.8 Occasionally, a dealer may wish to sell a low-value margin scheme item under the normal VAT rules, e.g. if his/her customer is an accountable person who requires a VAT invoice. In that case again, as above, the purchase price of the item should be deducted from the total purchases of low-value margin scheme goods in the period in which the sale takes place. Normal VAT rules, as at paragraph 13 above will then apply.

14.9 The globalisation arrangements may be used by car dismantlers subject to the conditions outlined above. While the margin scheme cannot be applied to secondhand motor vehicles, it can be applied to dismantlers who are essentially purchasing a collection of used parts which are no longer physically capable to use as a motor vehicle.

15. Records

15.1 An accountable dealer must keep records in sufficient detail to allow the margin to be calculated in respect of individual transactions and global margin (at each VAT rate to be calculated in the case of global accounting transactions. In addition, if an accountable dealer applies both the normal scheme and the margin scheme (including the globalisation arrangements), he/she must keep separate records in relation to each scheme.

Further information

Enquiries regarding any issue contained in this Information Leaflet should be addressed to the Revenue District responsible for the taxpayer's affairs. Contact details for all Revenue Districts can be found on the Contact Details Page.

VAT Appeals & Communications Branch ,
Indirect Taxes Division,
Stamping Building
Dublin Castle.

December 2008

Appendix I

Second-Hand Goods, Works of Art and Antiques which are normally liable for VAT at 13.5%, but which would be liable at the standard rate of 21.5% on the Dealer's Margin, if sold under this Scheme

1.   **Second-hand goods:**

   • ready to pour concrete

   • concrete blocks which comply with the specification contained in the Standard Specification (Concrete Building Blocks, Part 1, Normal Density Blocks) Declaration, 1987 (Irish Standard 20 : Part 1 : 1987)

2.   **Works of Art, defined as follows:**

   • paintings, drawings or pastels or any combination thereof, executed entirely by hand but excluding hand-decorated manufactured articles, and plans and drawings for architectural, engineering, industrial, commercial, topographical or similar purposes;

   • original lithographs, engravings or prints or any combination thereof, produced directly from lithographic stones, plates or other engraved surfaces, which are executed entirely by hand;

   • original sculptures or statuary, excluding mass produced reproductions and works of craftsmanship of a commercial character.

3.   **Antiques, defined as follows:**

   Antiques being, subject to and in accordance with regulations, articles of furniture, silver, glass or porcelain, whether hand-decorated or not, specified in the said regulations, which are shown to the satisfaction of Revenue to be more than 100 years old other than the goods described in Appendix III.

Appendix II

Definition of Precious Stones and Precious Metals (excluded from the margin scheme)

•   **Precious Stones**

   These are diamonds, rubies, sapphires and emeralds, whether cut or uncut, when they are not mounted, set or strung.

•   **Precious Metals**

   These are:-

   • silver (including silver plated with gold or platinum),

   • gold (including gold plated with platinum),

   • platinum, and

   • all items which contain any of these metals when the sale price does not exceed the open market price of the metal concerned.

Appendix III

Extended margin scheme

1. Application

The margin scheme can be applied by a dealer in respect of **all** of his/ her sales of the following goods and the goods described in Appendix I (items 2 & 3) even when such goods would not normally be eligible for the margin scheme because of their source:-

1. works of art, collectors items or antiques which s/he has imported from outside the EU,

2. works of art supplied to him/her by the creator or the creator's successors in title,

3. works of art supplied to him/her by an accountable person, other than a dealer, where the supply of such works of art by that taxable person is liable for VAT at the 13.5 per cent rate.

4. All the above goods sold under the margin scheme are liable for VAT at the 21.5 per cent rate. However, see also the Rates Guide at Appendix IV which covers the circumstances under which a different rate could be applied on the acquisition of works of art by dealers or individuals.

2. Goods liable at 21.5 per cent when sold under the margin scheme

2.1 Works of art

- a picture, collage or similar decorative plaque executed entirely by hand by an artist. (Excluded from this are plans and drawings for architectural, engineering etc. purposes; hand-decorated manufactured articles, and theatrical scenery, studio back cloths or the like of painted canvas,

- sculpture cast, the production of which is **limited** to eight copies, and supervised by the artist or his/her successors in title. (That limit may however be exceeded, on approval by Revenue, in the case of a statuary cast produced before 1 January, 1989.),

- a tapestry or wall textile made by hand from original designs provided by an artist, provided that there are no more than eight copies of each,

- individual pieces of ceramics executed entirely by an artist, and signed by the artist,

- enamels on copper, executed entirely by hand, limited to eight numbered copies bearing the signature of the artist or the studio. (Articles of jewellery, goldsmith's wares and silversmith's wares are excluded from this.),

- a photograph taken by an artist, printed by the artist or under the artist's supervision, signed and numbered and limited to thirty copies, all sizes and mounts included. (Photographic prints mounted or unmounted but unframed which record particular persons, objects or events supplied under an agreement to photograph those persons, objects or events remain liable at 13.5 per cent.)

2.2   Collectors' items

Every collectors' item being one or more of the following:-

- postage or revenue stamps, postmarks, first-day covers, pre-stamped stationery and the like, franked, or if unfranked not being of legal tender and not being intended for use as legal tender, or

- collections and collectors' pieces of zoological, botanical, mineralogical, anatomical, historical, archaeological, palaeontological, ethnographic or numismatic interest.

2.3   Antiques

Every antique being one or more goods which are shown to the satisfaction of Revenue to be more than one hundred years old other than works of art and collectors items described above and the goods defined in Appendix I even if over one hundred years old. They can however be included in the margin scheme and the extended margin scheme.

3.   Option by dealer

If a dealer opts to apply this extended margin scheme to the above goods, s/he must opt in for a period of at least two years.

4.   How a dealer opts to apply

The dealer opts to apply the scheme simply by not claiming a VAT input credit on the purchase or importation of the goods in question. S/he is not required to notify a Revenue Officer, but s/he must keep adequate records.

5.   How a dealer opts out

A dealer operating the extended margin scheme may at any time in respect of any individual supply, apply the normal VAT rules. If he/she does this, he/she cannot claim a VAT input credit on the purchase or importation of the goods in question until the taxable period in which he/she is accounting for the sale. This is because he/she will not know until the point of sale whether he/she is accounting for this transaction under the normal rules, or under the margin scheme. In this way, all stock-on-hand is treated the same way, as regards VAT input credit, until the point of sale.

Appendix IV

Rates Guide, i.e. rates of VAT applicable to the sale of Works of Art.

1.   Works of art are divided into two groups. Those listed in the Sixth Schedule to the VAT Act (paintings, drawings, engravings, sculptures)

which are normally liable at 13.5 per cent, and those listed in the Eighth Schedule (other types of pictures done by hand, tapestries, ceramics, enamels and some photographs) which are normally liable at 21.5 per cent but are liable at 13.5 per cent in **certain circumstances** (principally imports from outside the EU and a supply by the original artist). This is part of the rates strategy in the EU 7th VAT Directive designed to encourage the flow of works of art into the EU. The rates are listed hereunder:-

- **Group A:** works of art as defined in the Sixth Schedule to the VAT Act normally liable at 13.5 per cent (precise definition of these works of art is given at Appendix I)

- **Group B:** works of art defined in the Eighth Schedule to the VAT Act liable at 13.5 per cent in certain circumstances instead of 21.5 per cent as heretofore (precise definition of these works of art is given at Appendix III).

The effect of the Directive is to allow these groups to be taxable at different rates of VAT, depending on the circumstances under which the goods in question are acquired by the dealer as follows:-

Different rates of VAT applicable depending on the circumstances under which the goods in question are acquired

Circumstances	Group A	Group B
Import from outside EU by art dealer:	13.5%	13.5%
Import from outside EU by taxable person:	13.5%	13.5%
Import from outside EU by an individual:	13.5%	13.5%
Normal supply by art dealer	13.5%	21.5%
Normal supply by creator/successor	13.5%	13.5%

Normal supply by taxable person not art dealer:-

Circumstances	Group A	Group B
(a) if s/he imported, acquired from creator or got full deductibility	13.5%	13.5%
(b) otherwise (e.g. partial deductibility, or none at all because acquired under margin scheme)	13.5%	21.5%
Margin scheme supply by art dealer	21.5%	21.5%
Auction by auctioneer	21.5%	21.5%
Intra-Community acquisition by art dealer	13.5%	21.5%

Intra-Community acquisition by taxable person not a dealer:-

Circumstances	Group A	Group B
(a) if s/he acquires it from a creator/successor in another Member State, or a person in another Member State who imported, acquired from creator or got full deductibility	13.5%	13.5%
(b) if s/he acquires it from another source (e.g. a dealer in another Member State)	13.5%	21.5%

2.   Examples of the above would be:

- **An individual** can import a tapestry (Group B) from outside the EU at 13.5 per cent, but would be charged 21.5 per cent on the supply of a tapestry by an Irish dealer.

- **A dealer** could import a tapestry (Group B) from outside the EU at 13.5 per cent, but would be liable at 21.5 per cent on intra-Community acquisition.

This information leaflet which sets out the current practice at the date of its issue is intended for guidance only and does not purport to be a definitive legal interpretation of the provisions of the Value-Added Tax Act 1972 (as amended).

VALUE ADDED TAX INFORMATION LEAFLET (DECEMBER 08)

SECTION 13A ZERO RATING OF GOODS AND SERVICES

Introduction

Section 13A of the Value-Added Tax Act 1972, (as amended), provides for the zero-rating of supplies of qualifying goods and services to, and intra-Community acquisitions and imports from outside the European Union by certain accountable persons. In general, the accountable persons who qualify are those primarily engaged in making zero-rated intra-Community supplies of goods, exporting goods outside the European Union (referred to as 'exports' in this leaflet) or in making supplies of certain contract work.

The **Qualifying Persons** section of this leaflet outlines the conditions that must be satisfied by an accountable person if that person is to be a qualifying person for Section 13A purposes.

The **Qualifying Goods and Services** section lists the goods and services that qualify for zero-rating when supplied to qualifying persons.

Qualifying Persons

- A qualifying person under Section 13A of the Value-Added Tax Act 1972, (as amended), is an accountable person whose turnover from zero-rated intra-Community supplies of goods, exports and supplies of certain contract work exceeds, or is likely to exceed, 75% of his or her total annual turnover. Total annual turnover comprises turnover from the supply of all goods and services, including exempt supplies. However, the turnover from sales which involve the subsequent lease-back of the goods sold is excluded from annual turnover for the purposes of determining whether an accountable person qualifies under Section 13A.

- In certain cases it may also be possible for an accountable person in a start-up situation to qualify for the zero-rating facility on an interim basis. In such a case it is necessary to establish, to the satisfaction of the relevant Revenue District, that the person's turnover from zero-rated intra-Community supplies of goods, exports and certain supplies of contract work will exceed 75% of the person's total turnover in the first year of trading. In such cases, the application for authorisation to avail of the zero-rating facility should be supported by a statement from the IDA or a similar State agency. This statement should give details of the person's anticipated total annual turnover and annual turnover from zero-rated intra-Community supplies, export and certain supplies of contract work.

Group Registrations

A VAT-registered group (i.e. where a number of companies are treated as a single taxable person for VAT purposes) may only be authorised under Section 13A of the Value-Added Tax Act 1972, as amended, where at least 75% of the group's total annual turnover is derived from zero-rated intra-Community supplies of goods or exports and certain supplies of contract work. Sales between individual group members are ignored for this purpose. The turnover from sales outside the group, which involve the subsequent lease back by any member of the group of the goods sold, is also excluded for the purposes of determining whether the group qualifies for the scheme. Individual members of VAT groups may not obtain Section 13A authorisations unless the group as a whole is a qualifying person.

Authorisation Procedure

1. Applications for authorisation should be made on Form VAT 13A, which is available from the Revenue District responsible for your tax affairs, or may be downloaded from the Revenue website under VAT Forms.

2. The Revenue District responsible for your tax affairs will issue an authorisation where it is satisfied that the applicant is a qualifying person.

3. The authorisation will take effect two weeks after the date of its issue. This is to allow the authorised person sufficient time to forward copies of the authorisation to his/her suppliers. Accordingly, a qualifying person should apply in good time before the desired date of effect of the authorisation.

4. If an authorised person ceases to be a qualifying person the local Revenue District must be notified immediately.

Purchases within the State

1. **Authorised person**

   On receipt of the authorisation, the authorised person is obliged to send a copy of the authorisation to all persons in the State making supplies to him/her. It should be noted in particular that, apart from the exception mentioned in the **Qualifying goods and services** section below, once a person has been authorised, the zero-rating facility must be used in the case of all qualifying supplies, intra-Community acquisitions or imports from outside the European Union. If a supplier charges VAT incorrectly on a qualifying supply to the authorised person, the authorised person is not entitled to claim the amount as a deduction when completing his/her VAT return. Any such incorrect charging of VAT is a matter for resolution between the authorised person and the supplier in question. The original invoice should be cancelled by a credit note and a correct invoice should then be issued by the supplier.

2. It is recognised that it may be inconvenient to operate the zero-rating facility in relation to petty cash or other minor purchases. Accordingly, an exception may be made to the position outlined at **Authorised person** above where the VAT on the individual transaction is less than €40.

3. **Supplier to an authorised person**

   A supplier, once s/he has received a copy of an authorisation from an authorised person, must zero-rate all qualifying supplies from the effective date of the authorization (see **Qualifying goods and services** below) to the authorised person, and must quote the authorisation number on VAT invoices issued in respect of such supplies. If there is any doubt in relation to an authorisation, the Revenue District which issued the authorisation should be contacted to confirm its validity. When making zero-rated supplies under the scheme, the supplier should ensure that the supply is in fact made to the person named on the authorisation. Particular attention should also be paid to the commencement date and the expiry date of the authorisation as zero-rating applies only during the period of validity of the authorisation.

4.   **Supplier of canteen services to an authorised person**

A supplier of services consisting of the provision of food and drink is not entitled to zero rate this supply to an authorised person. Accordingly, where the authorised person is liable to account for VAT on canteen services supplied to staff, a claim may be made in the VAT return for an input credit in respect of the VAT charged on the food and drink supplied.

Intra-Community Acquisitions

To obtain goods from another Member State without payment of VAT in that Member State, the VAT registration number must continue to be quoted to the foreign supplier. The Section 13A authorisation means that the authorised person must account for VAT on the intra-Community acquisition at the zero rate.

Imports

In order to import qualifying goods VAT free from outside the European Union, the authorised person should make a declaration on the relevant customs entry (SAD) that s/he is an authorised person under Section 13A of the Value-Added Tax Act 1972, as amended, and quote his/her authorisation number. When requested by a Revenue officer, a copy of the authorisation should be produced in support of the declaration.

Alcohol Products

A person who is authorised in accordance with Section 13A of the Value Added Tax Act 1972, as amended, may have the zero-rate applied to the import from outside of the European Union, or the intra-Community acquisition, of alcohol products. The authorised person must also make a declaration on the relevant excise form confirming that (s)/he is authorised in accordance with Section 13A. When requested by a Revenue official, a copy of the authorisation should be produced in support of the declaration.

Qualifying goods and services

The zero-rating procedure applies to all goods and services (qualifying goods and services), with the following exceptions:

- the supply or hire of any passenger motor vehicle,

- the supply of petrol,

- the provision of food, drink, accommodation (other than qualifying accommodation in connection with attendance at a qualifying conference), entertainment or other personal services.

Self-supplies or exempt use

Where an authorised person applies qualifying goods or services, which have been obtained at the zero rate, to an exempt or non-business use, the authorised person must, in respect of such application, account for and pay VAT on the cost price to him/her of those goods or services. For example, if an authorised person purchases goods for, say, €10,000 at the zero rate and the supply of those goods is normally liable at the 21.5% rate, the authorised person must, if s/he applies the goods to a non-business use, pay VAT of €2,150 with his/her VAT return. The authorised person has no entitlement to claim an input credit in respect of such VAT.

Further information

Enquiries regarding any issue contained in this Information Leaflet should be addressed to the Revenue District responsible for your tax affairs. Contact details for all Revenue Districts.

This leaflet is issued by:

VAT Appeals & Communications Branch ,
Indirect Taxes Division,
Stamping Building
Dublin Castle.

December 2008

This information leaflet which sets out the current practice at the date of its issue is intended for guidance only and does not purport to be a definitive legal interpretation of the provisions of the Value-Added Tax Act 1972 (as amended).

VALUE ADDED TAX INFORMATION LEAFLET (DECEMBER 08)

SOLICITORS

1. **Introduction**

   This information leaflet sets out the treatment of solicitors in relation to VAT. It updates and replaces information leaflets of the same title issued in prior years.

2. **Which solicitors have to register for VAT?**

   All independent solicitors (that is, solicitors who are not employees) are obliged to register for VAT, if their annual turnover from the supply of taxable services exceeds or is likely to exceed €37,500 (from 1/5/08). 'Turnover' consists of professional fees together with 'all taxes (excluding VAT itself), commissions, costs and charges whatsoever' which a solicitor is entitled to receive. State Solicitors are not obliged to register in respect of their activities as State Solicitors. However, they are obliged to register if their annual turnover from other professional activities exceeds or is likely to exceed €37,500 (from 1/5/08). Applications for registration are made using Form TR1, which is available on the Revenue website - under Forms for Businesses.

3. **Obligations of VAT-registered solicitors**

   VAT-registered solicitors are obliged to;

   - keep sufficiently detailed records to enable their liability as declared by themselves to be confirmed;

   - issue invoices in respect of taxable services supplied to other VAT-registered persons; [If the consideration payable in respect of the supply of taxable services which is shown on an invoice is subsequently reduced, a credit note must be issued if the client is a VAT-registered person. Copies of invoices and credit notes must be retained.]

   - submit, every two months, a return of their outputs and purchases together with a remittance for any tax due. Solicitors may have the choice of paying VAT on the basis of services supplied or moneys received.

4. **Records to be kept**

   Details of the records which solicitors are obliged to keep are given in the Revenue *Guide to Value-Added Tax*. The records need to be in such a form and contain such information as is necessary to confirm that the amounts entered in a solicitor's VAT return or series of VAT returns are correct. The records need to distinguish by VAT rate between taxable, exempt and non-taxable output and taxable inputs.

5. **Confidentiality & Examination of Records**

   The general supervision of the operation of the VAT system by Revenue is effected by means of periodic visits by Revenue officers to taxpayers' premises.

Examination of records is normally carried out by Revenue officers from the Revenue District dealing with the solicitor's tax affairs. The purpose of examination is to ensure that records are maintained in accordance with the VAT Acts and Regulations and that the records systems used are adequate to give the correct VAT payable by, or repayable to, the taxpayer. Examination covers both a check of the returns which have been made against the actual records, an examination of the records kept and a check of invoices issued and received.

Please see Appendix 1 which details the Memorandum of Understanding between the Revenue Commissioners and the Law Society of Ireland concerning the Audit of the tax returns of Solicitors and Solicitors Practices.

6. Rates of VAT

Almost all services supplied by solicitors are liable to VAT at 21.5 per cent. The principal exceptions are the following:

Exempt

- collection of insurance premiums

- letting of solicitor's own premises (short-term)

Zero per cent

- services connected with property situated outside the State (see paragraph 12(a))

- Fourth Schedule services (see paragraph 12(b))

not taxable

- Directors' fees; Commissioner for Oaths fees; Notary Public fees

7. Taxable Amount

7.1   The amount on which a solicitor is liable, and the amount by reference to which a solicitor is or is not obliged to register, is the amount of his/her professional fees together with 'all taxes (other than VAT), commissions, costs and charges whatsoever' which the solicitor is entitled to receive in respect of or in relation to the supply of his or her services. Outlays made by a solicitor on behalf of a client are not regarded as part of the solicitor's charges and are not, therefore, taxable. Expenses incurred by a solicitor in the course of, and for the purposes of, carrying out his or her professional services are regarded as part of the solicitor's charges and are taxable.

7.2   Those outlays which are not liable to VAT in the hands of a solicitor include:

- Advertising

- Company Registration, etc. Fees including Company Seals

- Counsels' Fees (see note in paragraph 7.3)

- Court Fees and Fines

- Deposits (such as house deposits paid by clients)
- Land Registry Fees
- Photographs of Court Exhibits
- Registration of Deeds Fees
- Search Fees
- Stamp Duty and other duties and taxes
- Surveyors' and Estate Agents' Fees
- Valuation Services (by actuaries and Valuation Office)
- Witnesses' Fees and Expenses.

7.3   Where it is practicable for these outlays to be invoiced directly by the supplier to the client (although transmitted through the solicitor) the solicitor may not be involved at all, but it is most important for the solicitor to ensure that all invoices relating to such transactions are in the name of the client. If they are not, the client, if he or she is a VAT-registered person and there is an amount of VAT invoiced, will not be entitled to a deduction for the tax. (**NOTE re Counsels' fees**: When Counsel has received payment of fees he or she will issue to the instructing solicitor, at the solicitor's request, a combined VAT invoice/receipt drawn up in the name of the client).

7.4   Those expenses which are regarded as part of a solicitor's charges for professional services and which are liable to VAT include:

- Courier Fees.
- Hire of consultation rooms from Incorporated Law Society (exempt if charged out separately by solicitor).
- Hotel costs, photocopying, postage, summons serving fees, telephone, town agent fees, travelling costs.

8.   Deduction for VAT charged on purchases

8.1   A VAT-registered solicitor is entitled to take a credit or deduction (i.e. set off against his or her liability) for most VAT properly invoiced to him or her by suppliers. The solicitor does not have to have paid the suppliers to be entitled to the credit.

8.2   The only expenditure in respect of which a tax credit may not be taken is expenditure relating to:

- the provision of food, drink, accommodation or other personal services for the solicitor or his or her agents or employees (for example, hotel costs);
- entertainment expenses;
- the purchase, hire or leasing of a car or other road passenger vehicle;
- the purchase of petrol;

- an exempt (for example short-term letting of premises) or non-business activity;

- VAT incurred prior to registration.

8.3   A credit or deduction may be taken in respect of diesel, LPG, car repairs and maintenance, and car parts (for example, a set of tyres), subject to the condition that they are used for the purposes of a taxable business.

9.   Accounting for Tax

The normal basis of accounting is the invoice or sales basis. A VAT-registered solicitor using this basis of accounting is liable to pay VAT by reference to services supplied. VAT is not chargeable on services, which are **completed** before the date of registration no matter when the relevant invoice is issued. Services that are not completed before the date of registration will not be chargeable to VAT to the extent that they are paid for (that is, that the solicitor's office account has been credited) before that date.

10.   Moneys Received Basis of Accounting

10.1   An alternative basis of accounting is the moneys received or "cash" basis. This is available to solicitors whose annual turnover does not exceed and is not likely to exceed €635,000, or, as on and from 1 March 2007, €1 million, or where not less than 90% of the turnover is derived from unregistered persons. To avail of the moneys received basis, a solicitor needs to indicate this specifically on form TR1 when applying for VAT registration or at a later time if he or she wishes to change the basis of accountability from invoice to monies received basis.

10.2   A solicitor who opts to use the moneys received basis is liable for tax **at the rate in force at the time the services are supplied** on all moneys received in each VAT period excluding moneys received in respect of exempt services and payments on which VAT has already been accounted for if previously on the invoice basis of accounting. Monies received in respect of services supplied during the period prior to registration are not taxable.

10.3   Moneys received by a VAT-registered person include any sums:

- credited to the person's account in a bank or other financial concern,

- received by a solicitor on behalf of the person, or

- paid to Revenue by a third party to his/her account in accordance with certain provisions of the Tax Acts.

A VAT-registered person is also deemed to have received money if liability in respect of a business transaction is settled by setting off against it a credit due in respect of some other transaction. Care must be taken when money is received through an agent that any amount withheld by the agent to cover fees, expenses, etc., is included in the taxable amount.

10.4   Moneys received are treated as being inclusive of VAT and only the tax-exclusive content is taxable. If, for example, a solicitor accounting on the moneys received basis were to receive, say, €10,000 in a taxable period, the solicitor's liability would be €1769, that is €8,230 at 21.5 per cent.

11.   Withholding Tax - Professional Services

Income Tax withheld from payments for professional services is deemed, for VAT purposes, to have been received by the solicitor. If, for example, payment of an amount due to a solicitor is reduced from €1,215 (€1,000 + €215 VAT) to €1,015 (€200 withheld for Income Tax (20% of the net)) the solicitor is for VAT purposes deemed to have received €1,215 and must account for VAT on the full amount of €1,215.

12.   Foreign Services

Council Directive 2006/112/EC on the common system of VAT contains rules for determining the place of supply of services. These may be briefly summarised as follows in relation to 'foreign' services supplied by a solicitor:

1.   Legal services relating to immovable property are deemed to be supplied where the property is situated. Accordingly, a solicitor acting for a client in relation to the purchase, say, of a property in Northern Ireland is not liable to Irish VAT but may have a liability in respect of U.K. VAT;

2.   other legal services supplied to persons not resident or not established in Ireland will be liable to Irish VAT only if they are supplied to EU resident clients for non-business purposes (i.e. to private individuals).

Further information

Enquiries regarding any issue contained in this Information Leaflet should be addressed to the Revenue District responsible for your the taxpayer's affairs. Contact details for all Revenue Districts can be found on the Contact Details Page.

VAT Appeals & Communications Branch ,
Indirect Taxes Division,
Stamping Building
Dublin Castle.

December 2008

APPENDIX 1

Memorandum of Understanding between the Revenue Commissioners and the Law Society of Ireland concerning the Audit of the tax returns of Solicitors and Solicitors Practices

1. The Purpose of this Memorandum of Understanding

The purpose of this memorandum of understanding is to clarify certain procedural matters that may arise in the audit of the tax returns (Income tax, Capital Gains tax, VAT, PAYE/PRSI, 3rd Party returns etc.) of solicitors and solicitors' practices.

2. Audit Focus

The primary purpose of the Revenue audit of solicitors or solicitors' practices is the audit of the tax returns of the individual solicitor or partnership, or both, as the situation demands. In carrying out these audits Revenue officials will not be collecting, collating or verifying client information.

However, Revenue audit programmes include verifying or cross checking tax related financial information on transactions from one taxpayers business records to those of another taxpayer. Similar checks are carried out in all businesses.

3. Information or professional advice of a confidential nature given to clients is not sought by Revenue Auditors

Confidential information which does not have a bearing on the tax liability of any solicitor is not sought by Revenue officials.

Revenue officials fully recognise the concept of legal advice privilege (Footnote 1) and litigation privilege (footnote 2).

Revenue officials are entitled to access the names and addresses of clients subject to the exclusions as described at footnote (footnote 3).

Tax legislation obliges solicitors to give authorised Revenue officials access to books, records and other documents, information and explanations for the purposes of verifying the tax liabilities of any individual solicitor or practice. Revenue officials are also entitled to reasonable assistance in this regard.

4. Special Cases

In addition to paragraph 3, in certain limited situations, where there are exceptionally sensitive issues, a solicitor may request that either the name and address of the client, or certain aspects of the case, should not be disclosed. Revenue officials will agree to conduct the audit without the client's name and address or the issues being revealed, provided the non disclosure does not restrict the audit process, and that sufficient meaningful information is supplied to the Revenue official to enable the tax issues to be verified.

Bearing in mind the confidentiality obligations on Revenue officials, it is expected that situations where this clause might be invoked will be exceptional.

Where there is disagreement regarding disclosure in these circumstances, the solicitor may request a review by the Principal Officer to whom the Revenue official reports or a review by the internal/external reviewers in accordance with Statement of Practice S.P. Gen 2/99 (Revised January 2005).

5.   **Access to books, records, documents and information and explanations relating to tax.**

Revenue officials will seek access to books, records, documents and information and explanations relating to tax so as to verify the amounts of professional income and other income earned within a specified period, and also to verify the correct accounting for VAT and the correct operation of PAYE/PRSI.

Broadly in general terms, access is sought, where appropriate, to the following:

- The underlying records (cash book, cheque journal, etc.), the accounts linking papers which link the underlying records to the annual accounts, including Trial Balance, Nominal Ledger, Journal entries, Bank account reconciliation, client Ledger balances reconciliation and reconciliation of opening and closing accounts balances.

- Records relating to fees receivable and profits earned, the timing of earnings, valuations of debtors and work in progress, timely transfer of costs to office account, treatment of clients outlay, treatment of office and personal expenditure, reconciliation of clients balances with balances in clients bank accounts.

- Access is sought to individual client's ledger accounts, correspondence, information and explanations so as to verify figures in the accounts, the status or timing of some transactions such as the source or destination of sums passing through the client ledger accounts, the commencement and ending of separate steps in litigation or other services giving rise to payment of fees, the valuation of work in progress, the determination of bad debts and other income or expense related transactions.

- Records and documents relevant to VAT.

- Records of employee emoluments relevant to PAYE/PRSI.

- all bank accounts (current, loan, deposit etc.) - client accounts, office accounts (including paid cheques) and private accounts.

- Computations of taxable profits and distribution of profits among the partners.

- Documents relating to various claims to relief and allowances.

- The correct accounting for any relevant tax under any provisions of the Taxes Acts.

The above is an indicative list only and other records etc. may be required depending on the circumstances of any particular case.

Access is sought only to such practice correspondence that is likely to assist in verifying issues such as checking the timing of transfer of fees to office account, valuation of debtors and work in progress, verifying creditors and other income or expense related transactions. Where files are sought the solicitor may remove from the files, where relevant, items attracting legal advice privilege, litigation privilege and details of tax advice given to clients.

Where there is disagreement regarding disclosure in these circumstances the solicitor may request a review by the Principal Officer to whom the Revenue official reports or a review by the internal/external reviewers in accordance with Statement of Practice S.P. Gen 2/99 (Revised January 2005).

Review

It is agreed that this Memorandum of Understanding will be reviewed as necessary, and in any event after two years in operation.

Position re Non-Production of Records to Date

It is accepted by Revenue that the non-production of records in the course of an audit which commenced prior to 28 February 2002, on the basis that the solicitor was of the view that privilege applied, will not count as non co-operation for the purposes of penalty mitigation.

Note 1: Legal Advice Privilege: The basic rule is that communications between a lawyer in his professional capacity and his client are privileged from production if they are confidential and for the purposes of seeking or giving legal advice to the client. It does not apply to legal assistance which covers many tasks which a solicitor carries out for clients.

Note 2: Litigation Privilege The basic rule here is that communications, after litigation has been commenced or after litigation has been contemplated, between (a) a lawyer and his client, (b) a lawyer and his non professional agent or (c) a lawyer and third party, for the sole or dominant purpose of such litigation (whether for seeking or giving advice in relation to it, or for obtaining evidence to be used in it, or for obtaining information leading to such obtaining), are privileged from production.

Note 3: Exceptional Circumstances In addition to the privilege items outlined in the preceding footnotes account will also be taken of Mr. Justice Kelly's dicta in Miley v Flood [HC 2000 No. 310 J.R. (Kelly J) 24 January 2001]; "...... a solicitor is not entitled to maintain a claim to privilege in respect of the identity of his client. A dilution of this general principle arises where (a) the naming of the client would incriminate or (b) where the identity of the client is so bound up with the nature of the advice sought , that to reveal the clients identity would be in fact to reveal that advice".

Disclaimer

Neither the Law Society nor the Revenue Commissioners accept any responsibility for any errors, omissions or inaccuracies herein nor for any loss arising to anyone as a consequence of acting or refraining from acting in reliance on the information herein contained. Readers are advised to obtain professional advice and guidance as appropriate.

This information leaflet which sets out the current practice at the date of its issue is intended for guidance only and does not purport to be a definitive legal interpretation of the provisions of the Value-Added Tax Act 1972 (as amended).

VALUE ADDED TAX INFORMATION LEAFLET (DECEMBER 08)

THEATRICAL & MUSICAL EVENTS

1. **Definitions**

1.1 In this Information Leaflet, certain terms have specific meanings assigned to them, as follows:

- **'Admission'**: The allowing of an audience into an event. Admission includes the selling of tickets and the taking of money at the entrance, so that the person who sells a ticket for an event is deemed to be providing admission, and is treated for VAT accordingly.

- **'Food and drink'**: This includes all types of food, hot or cold, and all drinks, including water, and soft drinks. By concession, Revenue is prepared to extend the exemption from VAT to include events where certain types of food and drink are available (see Appendix 1).

- **'Live theatrical or musical event (event)'**: A play, musical, concert, recital, dramatic presentation, dance presentation, cabaret, comedy act or similar event performed before a live audience.

- **'Performance'**: The time when the performers are actually on stage or otherwise providing the entertainment for the audience.

- **'Performer(s)'**: The actors, musicians, dancers and comedians etc. who entertain the audience. Also includes a group, such as a theatre company, which has the actual performers as employees.

- **'Premises-provider'**: A person who owns, occupies or controls the venue (including land in the case of an open-air outdoor event) in which an event is to take place.

- **'Promotion'**: The financing or organizing of an event, including publicizing and other ventures to increase sales or public awareness.

- **'Self-promoting performer'**: A performer who finances, organizes and publicizes the performance and/or event.

- **'Ticket agent/ticket seller'**: A person engaged by the promoter to distribute and sell tickets for an event, normally reimbursed by way of a charge to the customer included in the ticket price and/or by commission charged to the promoter.

2. **Legislation - relevant sections of the VAT Act**

2.1 The law provides for an exemption from VAT for the following:

'**promotion of and admissions to live theatrical or musical performances, including circuses, but not including**

1. **dances, or**

2. **performances in conjunction with which facilities are available for the consumption of food or drink during all or part of the performance by persons attending the performance'.**

[Paragraph (viii) of the First Schedule to the VAT Act 1972 (as amended)]

2.2   The law further provides that the following are liable to VAT at 13.5 per cent:

'**promotion of and admissions to live theatrical or musical performances, excluding**

1. dances, and

2. performances specified in paragraph (viii) of the First Schedule;'

2.3   **[Paragraph (vi) of the Sixth Schedule to the VAT Act 1972 (as amended)].**

The promotion of and admissions to dances are liable at the standard rate of 21.5 per cent. Where a dance is held on licensed premises, the law also specifies who is responsible for accounting for VAT:

'**The licensee of any premises (being premises in respect of which a licence for the sale of intoxicating liquor either on or off those premises was granted) shall be deemed to be the promoter of any dance held, during the subsistence of that licence, on those premises and shall be deemed to have received the total money, excluding tax, paid by those admitted to the dance together with any other consideration received or receivable in connection with the dance'.**

[Section 8 (3C)(a) of the VAT Act 1972 (as amended)]

3.   **Summary**

3.1   **Background**

The exemption from VAT for live theatrical and musical events was introduced in 1985. In the intervening two decades a certain amount of confusion has arisen concerning the type of events to which it applies. Following a number of requests for clarification it was decided to issue this leaflet to restate the law and provide guidance regarding its application.

This Information Leaflet sets out the VAT treatment of the different services involved in the staging of live theatrical and musical events. These services include promoting the event, distributing and selling tickets, providing security and catering, the sale of concessions within the venue, the sale of goods within the venue, the performing of the artists, and the granting of admission. Each of these subjects is dealt with in detail in the main body of the leaflet and a brief synopsis of their treatment for VAT is set out below.

3.2   **Ticket prices, promoter's fees and ticket agent's commission**

The law provides that promoter's fees and admission charges for a live event are liable to 13.5 per cent VAT if food or drink is available at the event (Paragraph 5 - Events which are liable to VAT at 13.5%). If no food or drink is available, then promoter's fees and admission charges are exempt from VAT (Paragraph 4 - Events which come within the scope of the exemption from VAT). Non-resident promoters are obliged to register for and charge VAT in Ireland (Paragraph 9 - Treatment of non-established performers and traders). Commission fees, credit card handling charges and any other charges made by ticket selling agents form part of the price of the ticket, and are liable to VAT at the same rate (Paragraph 15 - Sales of tickets by ticket agents and distributors).

In conjunction with the law, a concession currently operates (Appendix II – The Theatres' Concession) in respect of venues where food or drink is provided, and must be consumed, in a part of the venue completely separate from the performance. In addition, as a result of the consultation process undertaken for this leaflet, a new concessionary treatment is being offered by Revenue in respect of the supply of certain types of food and drink at events (See Appendix I for full details). In effect, the supply of crisps, sweets, soft drinks and water will not make an otherwise exempt event liable to VAT. Only the supply of substantial snacks, hot food or alcoholic drink will be considered when deciding if an event is exempt or liable to VAT.

3.3 Performer's fees

Any fee charged by a performer is subject to VAT at 21.5 per cent. A performer who is registered for VAT will issue a VAT invoice for the amount of his/her fee and charge VAT at 21.5 per cent on the full amount of that fee. A non-resident performer will normally not be required to register for VAT in Ireland. In the case of performances by non-resident performers, the person who hired the performer, normally the promoter, will account for the VAT (Paragraph 9 - Treatment of non-established performers and traders). If the actual performers are employees of a production company, then the amount received by that company is regarded as the performance fee, rather than the salary paid to the performers. Where a performer promotes his/her own performance, then the fee paid may be split as between the promotion activities and the performance (Paragraph 13 - The withdrawal of the '50% (50/50) rule' for non-established performers with effect from 1st January 2007).

3.4 Security, catering and similar services

These services are all liable to VAT at the appropriate rates (Paragraph 7 - Traders operating within a venue). If a company supplying these services is not established in Ireland it must register and account for VAT.

3.5 Traders selling goods or services within a venue

Goods and services sold in the course of an event are liable to VAT in the usual way. Non-resident traders are obliged to register for VAT prior to trading. Concessions that permit traders to sell goods or services within a venue are liable to VAT at 21.5 per cent on the full amount received in respect of the granting of the concession (Paragraph 8 - VAT rates for ticket sales and other supplies associated with an event).

4.   Events which come within the scope of the exemption from VAT

4.1   The exemption from VAT covers promotion charges and admission fees for all live events at venues where there are no facilities available for consumption of substantial snacks, hot food or alcoholic drink (Appendix 1 - New concession regarding the supply of certain kinds of food and drink) during all or part of the performance by persons attending. Promotion of and admission to any live theatrical or musical event will be exempt where:

- No substantial snacks, hot food or alcoholic drink are supplied to persons attending the event during any part of the performance.

- No substantial snacks, hot food or alcoholic drink are available for purchase during any part of the event at the venue in which the performance is taking place.

- No substantial snacks, hot food or alcoholic drink can be taken by persons attending the event or on their behalf into the venue where the performance is taking place.

4.2   Events to which the exemption applies generally include outdoor concerts and performances, and plays, concerts and similar events in theatres and concert halls, and any other halls or similar establishments where substantial snacks, hot food or alcoholic drink are not permitted to be consumed during all or part of the performance

The diagram below shows the VAT treatment of the supplies that go to make up an exempt event.

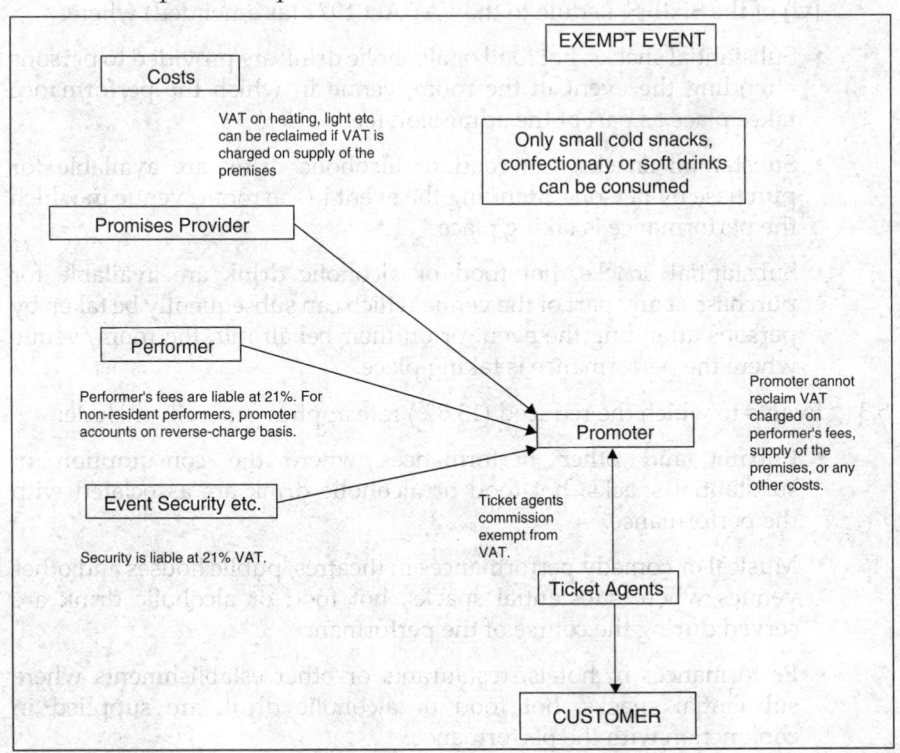

If no substantial snacks, hot food or alcoholic drink are available at the event, then the ticket sales are exempt from VAT. This means that the promoter is not able to recover VAT charged by performers, security etc. in connection with the event.

5.   Events which are liable to VAT at 13.5%

5.1   The exemption does not cover promotion of or admission to events where facilities are available for the consumption of substantial snacks, hot food or alcoholic drink during all or part of the performance by persons attending the performance. This exclusion from exemption also applies where a separate charge is made for the food and drink.

5.2   The **13.5 % rate of VAT** applies to events where there are facilities for the consumption* of substantial snacks, hot food or alcoholic drink during the performance by persons attending the performance. VAT at this rate must be accounted for on money received for tickets, and any fee charged by the promoter in relation to these events. However, this VAT may be offset by the right of the promoter and the ticket agent to recover any VAT charged to them in connection with the staging of the event, such as VAT on the performer's fee, security, hire of equipment etc.

The expression 'facilities for the consumption of food or drink' does not imply a formal sit-down venue. If people attending an event can obtain food or drink and consume it, then it must be accepted that facilities are available to do so.

Accordingly, VAT is chargeable at 13.5% on promotion and admission charges in respect of any live theatrical or musical event under Paragraph (vi) of the Sixth Schedule to the VAT Act 1972 (as amended) where:

- Substantial snacks, hot food or alcoholic drink are provided to persons attending the event in the room/venue in which the performance takes place as part of the admission fee.

- Substantial snacks, hot food or alcoholic drink are available for purchase by persons attending the event in the room/venue in which the performance is taking place.

- Substantial snacks, hot food or alcoholic drink are available for purchase at any part of the venue which can subsequently be taken by persons attending the event or on their behalf into the room/venue where the performance is taking place.

5.3   Events to which the reduced (13.5%) rate applies generally include:

- Cabaret and other performances where the consumption of substantial snacks, hot food or alcoholic drink are associated with the performance.

- Musical or comedy performances in theatres, public houses and other venues where substantial snacks, hot food or alcoholic drink are served during the course of the performance.

- Performances in hotels, restaurants or other establishments where substantial snacks, hot food or alcoholic drink are supplied in conjunction with the performance.

- Outdoor concerts where substantial snacks, hot food or alcoholic drink are available within the confines of the venue.

5.4   The diagram below illustrates the VAT treatment of the supplies that go to make up a taxable event.

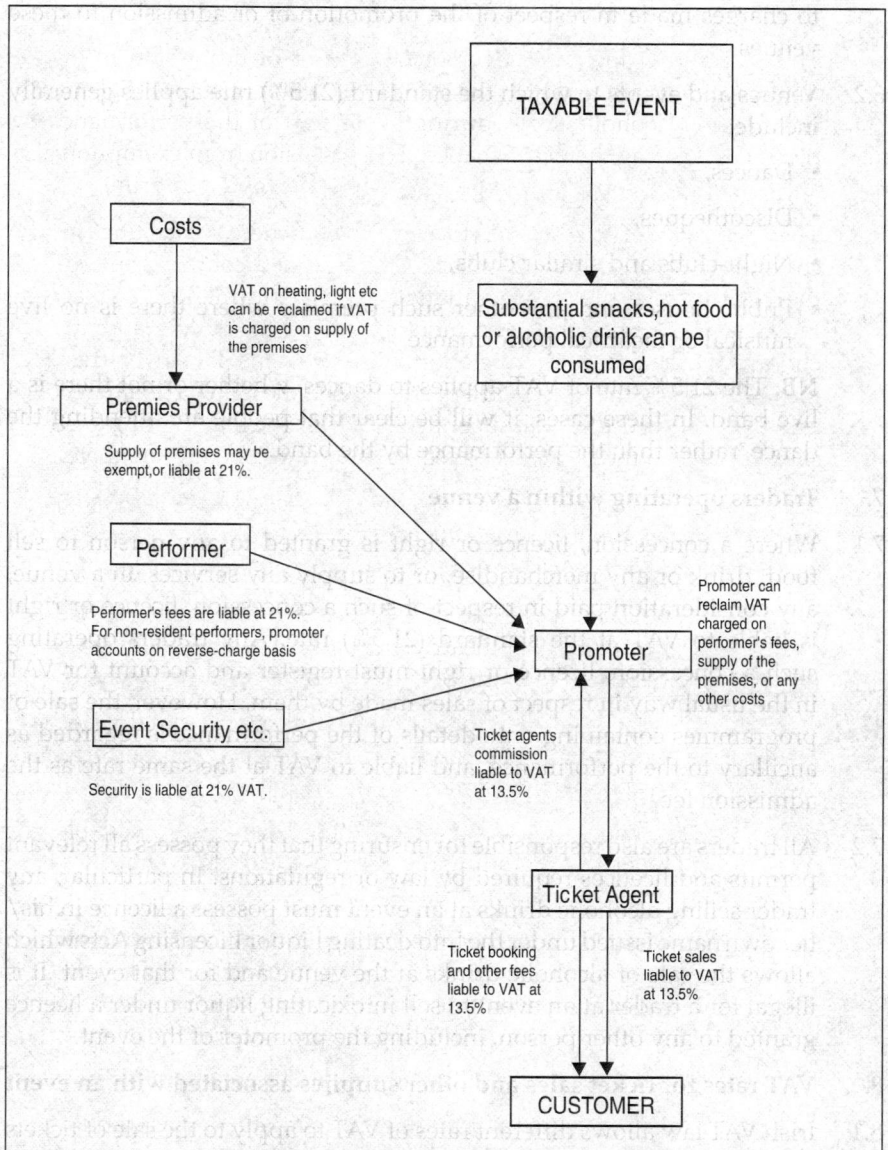

If substantial snacks, hot food or alcoholic drink are available at the event, then the ticket sales are liable to VAT at 13.5%. This allows the promoter to recover VAT charged by performers, security etc. in connection with the event. Since much of the VAT charged to the promoter is at the 21.5% rate, the promoter may actually be in a net VAT repayment position - i.e. the VAT charged to the promoter in respect of costs may exceed the VAT due on ticket sales.

6.   Events which are liable to VAT at 21.5%

6.1   Neither the exemption nor the reduced rate applies to the promotion of or admission to venues where the entertainment, if any, is not a live theatrical or musical performance. The standard rate of VAT applies to charges made in respect of the promotion of or admission to these venues.

6.2   Venues and events to which the standard (21.5%) rate applies generally include:

- Dances,

- Discotheques,

- Night-clubs and similar clubs,

- Public houses and any other such premises where there is no live musical or theatrical performance.

NB: The 21.5% rate of VAT applies to dances, whether or not there is a live band. In these cases, it will be clear that people are attending the dance, rather than the performance by the band.

7.   Traders operating within a venue

7.1   Where a concession, licence or right is granted to any person to sell food, drink or any merchandise, or to supply any services, in a venue, any consideration paid in respect of such a concession, licence or right is liable to VAT at the standard (21.5%) rate. Any traders operating such a concession, licence or right must register and account for VAT in the usual way in respect of sales made by them. However, the sale of programmes containing only details of the performance is regarded as ancillary to the performance, and liable to VAT at the same rate as the admission fee.

7.2   All traders are also responsible for ensuring that they possess all relevant permits and licences required by law or regulations. In particular, any trader selling alcoholic drinks at an event must possess a licence in his/ her own name issued under the Intoxicating Liquor Licensing Acts which allows the sale of alcoholic drinks at the venue and for that event. It is illegal for a trader at an event to sell intoxicating liquor under a licence granted to any other person, including the promoter of the event.

8.   VAT rates for ticket sales and other supplies associated with an event

8.1   Irish VAT law allows different rates of VAT to apply to the sale of tickets for different kinds of events. There are also different rates which apply to other services associated with events, and these rates are set out in the table below.

Different rates of VAT apply to the sale of tickets for different kinds of events. There are also different rates which apply to other services associated with events, and these rates are set out in this table.

Examples of the services and charges associated with events	Only small cold snacks, confectionary or soft drinks can be consumed. The VAT Rate applicable	Substantial snacks, hot food or alcoholic drink can be consumed. The VAT Rate applicable
Ticket Prices	Exempt	13.5%
Ticket Booking Fees	Exempt	13.5%
Ticket Agent's Commission	Exempt	13.5%
Promoter's Fees	Exempt	13.5%
Performer's Fees	21.5%	21.5%
Security	21.5%	21.5%
Catering	13.5%	13.5%
Concessions*	21.5%	21.5%

Where the promoter or premises-provider charges traders for the right to sell goods and services at the venue

8.2   As can be seen, the VAT rate that applies to the admission fees for live theatrical or musical events also extends to other fees and charges connected with the issuing of tickets and promotion of the events. These include:

- The booking fees or handling fees charged for issuing a ticket;

- The commissions charged by ticket agents;

- The fees charged by promoters to performers who have hired them to organise events;

- The fees charged by promoters to venue owners for sourcing performers.

9.   Treatment of non-established performers and traders

The provisions which refer to the supply of services by non-established performers are included below.

9.1   Relevant sections of the VAT Act

The law provides that

'where a person not established in the State supplies a cultural, artistic, entertainment or similar service in the State, then any person, other than a person acting in a private capacity, who receives that service shall

- *in relation to it, be an accountable person or be deemed to be an accountable person, and*

- *be liable to pay the tax chargeable as if that accountable person had in fact supplied the service for consideration in the course or furtherance of business;*

but where that service is commissioned or procured by a promoter, agent or other person not being a person acting in a private capacity, then that promoter, agent or person shall be deemed to be the person who receives the service;'

9.2   [Section 8(2)(aa) of the VAT Act 1972 (as amended)]

In addition Section 8(2)(d) of the VAT Act 1972 (as amended) provides that a 'premises provider' (being a person who owns, occupies or controls land) who allows non-established traders or promoters to operate on the land, has certain obligations with regard to the VAT liability of these non-established traders or promoters.

9.3   In the case of non-established traders supplying goods for a period of less than 7 consecutive days on the land, the premises provider must, not later than 14 days before the day on which the non-established trader is allowed to trade on the land, notify the local Revenue District of the name and address of the trader, the dates on which the trader intends to supply goods, and the address of the land.

9.4   In the case of non-established promoters supplying a cultural, artistic, entertainment, or similar service, the premises provider must, not later than 14 days before the day on which the service is scheduled to begin, notify the local Revenue District of the name and address of the promoter, and the dates, duration and venue of the event or performance.

9.5   Where a premises provider fails to provide true and correct information as required, then he/she may be made jointly and severally liable with the non-established trader or promoter for the VAT due in respect of the supplies made by them.

10.   What VAT obligations have non-established traders?

10.1   Where non-established performers or any other non-established traders make sales of merchandise such as CDs, posters, t-shirts etc at a venue in the State, they are obliged to register and account for VAT on all such sales and all other supplies made by them.

11.   Non-established traders - What liability has the provider of the premises?

11.1   Where a person who owns, occupies or controls premises (whether the owner or a third party) allows a non-established trader to supply goods for a period of less than seven consecutive days on the premises in which a performance is to be held, the provider of the premises must give the following information to Revenue:

• The name and address of the non-established trader.

• The dates on which the non-established trader intends to trade on the premises

• The address of the premises

The provider of the premises must give this information to the officer in the Revenue District responsible for his/her tax affairs not later than 14 days before the performance is scheduled to begin.

11.2   Where this information is not given to Revenue as set out above, the provider of the premises may be made jointly and severally liable with the non-established trader for the VAT liability in respect of the supplies of goods in the premises concerned. In practice, this means that if the non-established trader fails to register and account for any VAT due in respect of sales made in the State, the provider of the premises, whether the owner or a third party or both jointly, will become liable for the entire amount of VAT due.

12.   Non-established performers - who accounts for VAT on performances?

12.1   A non-established performer is an individual who is not normally resident in the State or who does not have a business establishment here. It also may be a performance company which does not have a business establishment here. Section 8(2)(aa) of the VAT Act as set out in paragraph 9.1 above provides that a non-established performer is not obliged to register and account for VAT in respect of live theatrical or musical performances in the State. Instead, the promoter, agent or other person (including non-established promoters etc – Paragraph 12.2) who commissions the performance or event is automatically obliged to account for the VAT due. This applies even where the turnover from the performance does not exceed registration thresholds.

12.2   What VAT obligations have non-established promoters?

Non-established promoters supplying services in Ireland must register and account for VAT on taxable supplies made by them, and also in respect of any payments made by them to non-established performers *. In practice this means that registration is required in all circumstances, except only where the non-established promoter is promoting only a performance by a performer registered for VAT in Ireland, and this performance features in an event which comes under the exemption from VAT.

This applies even where the payments are the subject of a separate contract covering a number of performances in different countries, or where the performer issues an invoice from an establishment outside the State in respect of the performance. If the place of supply of the performance is Ireland, then the VAT liability for payments to the performer arises in Ireland.

12.3   Non-established promoters – what liability has the provider of premises?

Where a non-established promoter arranges for the supply of live musical or theatrical entertainment, the person who owns, occupies or controls the premises in which the performance is to take place has certain obligations to Revenue.

The provider of the premises must give the following information to Revenue:

• The name and address of the non-established promoter.

• Details such as the dates, duration and venue of the performance.

12.4 The provider of the premises must give this information to the officer in the Revenue District responsible for his/her tax affairs not later than 14 days before the performance is scheduled to begin.

12.5 Where this information is not given to Revenue as set out above, the provider of the premises may be made jointly and severally liable with the non-established promoter for the VAT liability in respect of the performance. In practice, this means that if the non-established promoter fails to register and account for any VAT due, the provider of the premises, whether the owner or a third party or both jointly, will become liable for the entire amount of VAT due.

13. The withdrawal of the "50% (50/50) rule" for non-established performers with effect from 1st January 2007

13.1 The '50% rule' was an administrative procedure whereby Revenue, on a concessional basis, allowed promoters/performers/venue owners (as appropriate) to account for VAT on performances by non-established performers as follows:

'50% of the gross income @ 21.5% was treated as being the amount of tax payable by the performer on his/her performance at the event. There were no input credits available against this amount. There were no further reductions available.'

Following the change to Section 8 (2) (aa) of VAT Act 1972 (as amended) this concession no longer applies.

14. Treatment of performers who promote their own performances

14.1 Where a performer promotes, either by him/herself or with others, an event in which he/she is performing, any payment received must be apportioned as between the performance and the promotion. Any such apportionment will depend on the individual circumstances, and the performer must demonstrate to the satisfaction of Revenue that the apportionment is a correct one. Where the actual performers are employees of the promoter or another company, the promoter or other company is liable for VAT on the performance.

14.2 If a performer can show evidence of real work carried out in the promotion of the event, Revenue is prepared to accept that a portion of the payment received by a self-promoting performer may be treated as being in respect of the promotion, up to a maximum of 40 per cent of the total, which is either exempt or liable to VAT according to the nature of the event. The remainder, at least 60 per cent, is treated as being in respect of the performance, and liable to VAT at the standard (21.5%) rate.

15. Sales of tickets by ticket agents and distributors

15.1 A promoter of an event may use a ticket agent to sell tickets for events. Promoters and ticket agents may also use a network of distributors, such as local music stores, to ensure a broad distribution of tickets. The actual sale of a ticket by a promoter, a ticket agent or distributor is the supply to the customer of the right to admission to an event.

15.2   Accordingly, for an event that does not come within the scope of the exemption, the agent or distributor who sells a ticket is liable to account for VAT on the full sale price (the face value of the ticket and all booking charges and fees whatsoever, including any commission charged to the promoter) at the rate appropriate to the event.

15.3   The agent or distributor should issue a VAT invoice for the commission on the sale. The person to whom the agent or distributor forwards the balance of the ticket price (e.g. another agent or the promoter) must issue a VAT invoice on receipt of the money, and account for VAT on the amount received.

The diagram below illustrates the VAT treatment of the sale of tickets for a taxable event by ticket agents and distributors.

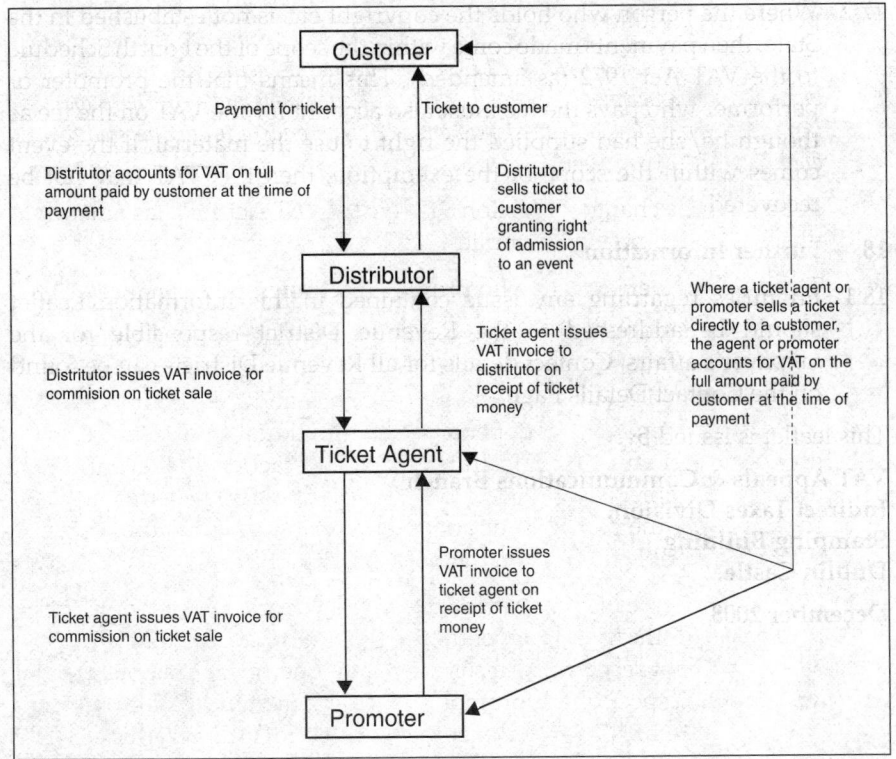

16.   **The treatment of advance ticket sales**

16.1   Payments received in advance of the supply of goods or services are always liable to VAT at the time the payment is made. This also applies to sales of tickets for live theatrical and musical events, where these are sold prior to the date on which the event takes place.

16.2   With effect from 1st January 2007, ticket sales in advance are liable to VAT by reference to the date on which the ticket is sold and VAT must be accounted for in the taxable period in which the sale is made, and not when the event takes place. The rate of VAT that applies is always the rate current at the time of sale of the ticket.

16.3 If an event is cancelled, and the promoter, ticket-agent or distributor refunds the full amount of the ticket, including VAT, to the purchaser, a claim may be made in the next VAT return for a repayment of any VAT previously submitted.

It should be noted that advance payments by promoters to performers are also liable to VAT at the time of payment.

17. Royalties, licence fees etc. paid by promoters or performers

17.1 Certain performances consist of or contain material which is subject to copyright or similar intellectual property protection. Any fee charged by a person registered for VAT in Ireland in respect of the right to use this material is liable to VAT at 21.5 per cent.

17.2 Where the person who holds the copyright etc. is not established in the State, then payments made come within the scope of the Fourth Schedule to the VAT Act 1972 (as amended). This means that the promoter or performer who pays the fee must also account for the VAT on the fee as though he/she had supplied the right to use the material. If the event comes within the scope of the exemption, then this VAT may not be recovered.

18. Further Information

18.1 Enquiries regarding any issue contained in this Information Leaflet should be addressed to the Revenue District responsible for the taxpayer's affairs. Contact details for all Revenue Districts can be found on the Contact Details Page.

This leaflet is issued by:

VAT Appeals & Communications Branch ,
Indirect Taxes Division,
Stamping Building
Dublin Castle.

December 2008

Appendix I. New concession regarding the supply of certain kinds of food and drink

Previously, where food and/or drink were available at any event, the promotion and admission fees were in all cases liable to VAT. However, in recognition of certain practical difficulties, and to ensure consistency of treatment, Revenue is prepared to concessionally disregard the supply of certain items of food and drink when considering the VAT treatment of events.

Revenue will allow the exemption to continue to apply to events where certain cold snack foods, confectionary and soft drinks can be consumed during the performance. This means that promotion charges and the sales of tickets for these events will not now be subject to VAT, whereas previously the availability of any food and drink would have denoted a VAT liability. The items of food and drink to which this concession refers are as follows:

Food

- **Confectionary:**
  - Packets of sweets
  - Bars (e.g. chocolate)
  - Chewing gum
  - Lollipops etc.
- **Savoury snacks:**
  - Crisps and similar snacks
  - Peanuts
  - Popcorn (incl. heated)
- **Fruit**

Drink

- **Soft Drinks:**
  - Carbonated (fizzy) drinks
  - Fruit juices
  - Milk
  - 'Smoothies' and other milk or yoghurt based drinks
  - 'Slushies' and similar ice drinks.
- **Water:**
  - Still bottled water
  - Sparkling bottled water
- **Hot drinks :**
  - Tea
  - Coffee
  - Hot Chocolate

Sales of any other kind of food and drink including sandwiches, wraps, hot snacks, meals and alcoholic drink are not included in this concession. The sale of such items would have the effect of bringing the event within the scope of VAT.

Appendix II. The "Theatres' Concession" – food or drink supplied in a separate room

Many theatres allow the supply of food and drink during an interval or intermission in a performance. Revenue concessionally allowed the exemption from VAT to continue to apply to these events on the following conditions:

- The food and drink was only available in a room separate from the auditorium in which the performance was taking place,

- The performance was not visible from the room where the food or drink is available,

- Patrons were not permitted to take the food or drink into the auditorium where the performance was taking place before, during or after the interval.

While this concession was originally only granted in respect of theatres, Revenue has extended it to include other types of performances in other venues. Accordingly, in the case of any event, where substantial snacks, hot food or alcoholic drink (See Appendix I above) are available to the audience at any stage during the performance, then the event remains within the exemption if it is the stated and enforced policy of the management that the following conditions are adhered to:

- Substantial snacks, hot food or alcoholic drink are only available in a separate part of the venue from that in which the performance takes place,

- The performance is not visible from the area where the substantial snacks, hot food or alcoholic drink are available,

- Patrons are not permitted to take substantial snacks, hot food or alcoholic drink into the part of the venue where the performance takes place at any time during the performance.

The availability of substantial snacks, hot food or alcoholic drink under any other circumstances would have the effect of bringing the event within the scope of VAT.

VALUE ADDED TAX INFORMATION LEAFLET (DECEMBER 08)

VETERINARY SERVICES

1.　Introduction

Services of a kind supplied in the course of their profession by veterinary surgeons are liable to VAT at 13.5%. Such services need not necessarily be provided by veterinary surgeons. This leaflet sets out the general implications of applying VAT to these services.

2.　General

2.1　A person who supplies taxable services in the course or furtherance of business in excess of specified limits (€37,500) in any continuous period of twelve months is an accountable person and is required to register for VAT.

2.2　An accountable person is liable to pay VAT at the appropriate rate on taxable goods and services supplied by him/her. An accountable person calculates VAT liability on a two-monthly basis by calculating the total tax due on sales of goods or services for the period and subtracting the deductible tax invoiced during the period - the difference is the amount of liability.

3.　Which suppliers of veterinary services must register for VAT?

3.1　All veterinary surgeons and other persons supplying veterinary services (veterinary professionals) working independently are obliged to register for VAT if their annual turnover exceeds or is likely to exceed the specified limits (as above). Veterinary surgeons who are members of partnerships, or who operate as members of veterinary practices, are not regarded as independent persons for VAT purposes. In these circumstances, the combined receipts of all persons contributing to the partnership or practice are aggregated and are subject to the registration thresholds.

3.2　Applications for registration are made using Form TR1, which is available on the Revenue website under Forms/Forms for Businesses.

4.　Veterinary Professionals Carrying on Farming or Other Businesses

4.1　A veterinary professional who is registered, or is obliged to register, because of the supply of veterinary services, and who is also engaged in other business activities, for example, farming or racehorse training, is liable to VAT on all his/her activities. As a general rule, a farmer is not obliged to register although he/she may opt to do so. However, when taxable activities, other than racehorse training, are carried on in addition to the farming activities, the turnover from all of the activities including farming are taxable. Therefore, a farmer supplying veterinary services is liable to VAT on receipts both from veterinary services and farming activities.

5.   Obligations of VAT Registered Persons

5.1   VAT registered persons are obliged to:

- keep records which are sufficiently detailed to enable their liability as declared by themselves to be confirmed;

- issue invoices containing specified particulars in respect of taxable supplies to other accountable persons.

- submit a return on the prescribed form every two months of their supplies and taxable purchases together with a remittance of tax due

6.   Accounting for VAT

6.1   The normal basis of accounting for VAT is the invoice or sales basis. However, veterinary professionals may, subject to conditions. Please see: **Moneys Received Basis of Accounting for Tax.**

7.   Invoice Basis

7.1   A VAT registered veterinary professional using the invoice or sales basis of accounting will be liable to pay VAT by reference to his/her supplies as follows:-

- in the case of transactions with persons who are not registered for VAT s/he is liable at the rate in force at the time of supply;

- in the case of transactions with other VAT registered persons he/she is obliged to issue invoices and is liable to VAT at the rate of tax in force at the time he/she issues or ought to issue an invoice.

8.   Moneys Received Basis of Accounting for Tax

8.1   Certain registered persons, as follows, may use the moneys received basis of accounting instead of the usual sales basis:

- persons engaged in the supply of taxable services where the turnover does not exceed €1,000,000, and

- persons selling goods almost exclusively (at least 90% to unregistered persons).

8.2   Transactions between connected persons, and property transactions, are excluded from the moneys received basis of accounting.

8.3   This facility is available to veterinary surgeons but they must specify this on Form TR1 when applying for VAT registration.

9.   Withholding Tax

9.1   Income Tax withheld from payments to a veterinary professional which cover taxable supplies is deemed for VAT purposes to have been received by the veterinary professional. If, for example, in the case of taxable supplies, payment of an amount due to a veterinary professional is reduced from €1135.00 (€1000 + €135.00 VAT) to €935.00 (€200 withheld for Income Tax) the veterinary professional is, for VAT purposes, deemed to have received €1135.00 (€1000 + €135.00) and is liable for the VAT element therein. Please see the example below.

Example

Veterinary fees =   €1000.00
VAT at 13.5% =   €135.00

Calculation of withholding tax

VAT exclusive sum =   €1000.00
Withholding tax at 20% =   €200.00
Net =   €800.00
VAT on the €1000 fees 13.5% =   €135.00
Total receivable by veterinary professional =   €935.00
Amount payable to Collector-General by the veterinary professional in respect of VAT = €135.00

10.   Deduction for VAT Charged on Purchases

10.1   A VAT registered veterinary professional is entitled to take a credit or deduction (i.e. set off against VAT liability) for most VAT properly invoiced on supplies.

10.2   However, a credit or deduction may not be taken on expenditure on the following:

- the provision of food, drink, or other personal services for the person, his agents or employees (for example, hotel costs);

- accommodation other than accommodation in connection with a qualifying conference as defined in legislation

- entertainment expenses;

- purchase or hire of cars or other road passenger vehicles;

- purchase of petrol;

- an exempt or non-business activity, and

- VAT borne prior to registration.

10.3   Where a person carries on both taxable activities and other activities (for example, inspection of meat in factories as a State employee) only the expenses appropriate to his/her taxable activities qualify as deductible.

11.   Rates of VAT

11.1   **The following are examples of the rates of VAT applicable to supplies made by veterinary professionals. The list is not exhaustive.**

The rates of VAT applicable to supplies made by veterinary professionals

Supplies made by veterinary professionals	Rates of VAT applicable
A.I. Services - (subject to the 2/3rds rule please see below)	13.5%
Attendance at track meetings	13.5%
Consultancy	13.5%
Greyhounds (supply of)	4.8%

Supplies made by veterinary professionals (Cont'd)	Rates of VAT applicable
Livestock (live cattle, sheep, goats, horses, pigs and deer - supply of)	4.8%
Other live animals (supply of)	21.5%
Treatment of illness or disease - (subject to the 2/3rds rule)	13.5%
TB testing	13.5%
Supply only of medicine - Oral	0%
Supply only of medicine - non oral	21.5%
Dehorning of cattle	13.5%
Hoof paring	13.5%
Shodding of horses	21.5%

12. Supply of Goods in Addition to Supply of Services

12.1 Veterinary professionals who supply medicines or other products as part of the veterinary service are liable to VAT at 13.5%, subject to the two-thirds rule (please see paragraph 13 below). This is so even if the goods are, separately, liable at 21.5% or 0%. On the other hand, if goods are left by the veterinary professionals to be administered by the client and separate charges are made and recorded for the separate supplies, this is regarded as a separate supply of goods, taxable at the rate applicable to the goods - 21.5% or 0% as appropriate.

13. The Two-Thirds Rule

13.1 The rate of tax applying to all services, including veterinary services, is determined by the 'two-thirds rule'. This provides that a transaction is liable to VAT as a sale of goods at the appropriate rate and not as a service if the value of the goods (that is, their cost, excluding VAT, to the supplier) administered in providing the service exceeds two-thirds of the total charge to the customer.

Example 1: Two-thirds Rule

Total charge to client = €100
Cost of non oral medicines administered = €70: (this exceeds 2/3rds of €100)
Veterinary services are liable on this transaction at 21.5% (rate for non-oral medicines).

Example 2: Two-thirds Rule

Total charge to client = €200
Cost of oral medicines administered = €150: (this exceeds 2/3rds of €200)
Veterinary services are liable on this transaction at 0% (rate for oral medicines).

14. Place of supply of veterinary services

14.1 Veterinary services are deemed to be carried out by reference to the place of establishment of the supplier. Veterinary surgeons whose only place of establishment is outside the state are therefore not required to register for Vat.

15.　Further information

15.1　Enquiries regarding any issue contained in this Information Leaflet should be addressed to the Revenue District responsible for your tax affairs. Contact details for all Revenue Districts.

VAT Appeals & Communications Branch,
Indirect Taxes Division,
Stamping Building,
Dublin Castle.

December 2008

This information leaflet which sets out the current practice at the date of its issue is intended for guidance only and does not purport to be a definitive legal interpretation of the provisions of the Value-Added Tax Act 1972 (as amended).

VALUE ADDED TAX INFORMATION LEAFLET (JANUARY 2009)

LIQUIDATORS & RECEIVERS

1.   General

1.1   What is a liquidator?

Under the provisions of the Companies Acts, 1963 to 2001, a company may be wound up either by order of the Court or, voluntarily, by resolution of the company. The liquidation of a company is the process by which a company is legally dissolved. The main distinction between the two types of winding up is that while a compulsory liquidation is undertaken under the supervision of the High Court (the court appoints a liquidator to act on its behalf), a voluntary liquidation is normally carried out with little or no reference to the courts, with members or creditors playing a more active role. The principal duties of a liquidator, either Court appointed or voluntary, are to inquire into the company's affairs, realise its assets, pay its debts and distribute any surplus to its members.

1.2   Following the winding-up order or resolution, the liquidator is appointed and every creditor is required to prove his or her debt. In a "members' voluntary winding-up" the company appoints the liquidator. In a "creditors' voluntary winding-up" both the creditors and the company have the right to nominate a liquidator. .

1.3   Where the winding-up is by order of the High Court, the Court appoints the liquidator, usually on the nomination of the petitioner. The order takes affect from the date of the presentation of the petition, with the effect that all disposals by the company after the presentation are rendered void and ineffective, unless the Court otherwise directs.

1.4   What is a receiver?

A receiver is a person appointed pursuant to a debenture (loan agreement) or a High Court order, whose main task is to take control of those of the compay's assets that have been mortgaged or charged by the company in favour of a debenture holder (lender), to sell such assets and apply the proceeds to discharge the debt owing to the debenture holder.

1.5   A receiver can only liquidate the assets covered in the debenture. The primary duty of the receiver is to the debenture holder that appointed him/her (note that this is different from a liquidator who must act in the interest of all creditors). The precise action of the receiver will depend on the nature of the debenture but the situation will often arise that the company will continue trading while the receiver is involved in the operation of the company to realise and dispose of the assets covered by the debenture.

1.6   There are certain obligations on receivers in relation to payment of the company's outstanding tax debts (and Revenue enjoys a preferential position in certain instances) but this depends on whether the debenture is based on a fixed charge or a floating charge. The receiver is also responsible for payment of current tax liabilities if he/she decides to run the company for a period. In some instances the company may be able to continue trading even after the receiver has realised the debenture assets and left the company. In any event, however, the appointment of a receiver will usually have a significant impact on the operation of a company and, where the company has outstanding tax liabilities, concerns arise that these tax debts may not be recovered.

2.   VAT position of liquidators/receivers

2.1   Section 3(7) of the VAT Act 1972 (as amended) provides that goods, being business assets of an accountable person, when disposed of under any powers exercised by another person, including a liquidator or receiver or official assignee, in settlement of a debt, are deemed to be supplied by that accountable person in the course or furtherance of his/her business. It also provides that the obligations imposed in respect of the payment of VAT on the disposal of goods by a liquidator apply in all cases of the winding-up of a company. This provision extends to a voluntary winding-up and to any other winding-up in which the liquidator might not be disposing of the goods in the satisfaction of the debts due. While the provision deems the accountable person to supply the goods, it is the liquidator or receiver who registers for VAT. (see paragraph 3 below). This requires the liquidator or receiver to make VAT returns and to account for any VAT due on the supply by them of goods owned by the accountable person. This applies whether or not the business of the accountable person continues to be carried on. Section 9(2A) of the VAT Act provides that a liquidator/receiver must register for VAT within 14 days of the disposal of goods. Section 19(3)(b) and (c) of the Act sets out the VAT liability of liquidators/receivers while regulation 41 of the VAT Regulations, 2006 provides that any obligations under the VAT which a trader in liquidation was obliged to do, shall be done by the liquidator. The legal text and the relevant extracts from the Notes for Guidance are set out in Appendix I to this leaflet.

2.2   To whom does Section 3(7) apply?

The provision applies to receivers appointed to sell the business in whole or in part or to trade towards the most substantial recovery of the debt owed to the charge holder. In the case of receivers appointed under a fixed charge, the receiver is taxable on the fixed charge only (see paragraph 7 below). It also applies to liquidators, appointed compulsorily or voluntarily by virtue of either a fixed (specific) or floating (general) charge over one or more of the assets. The provision is not limited to liquidators and receivers but extends to goods disposed of by a person acting under any power towards the satisfaction of a debt owed or in the course of the winding up of a company. The disposal need not be in satisfaction of a specific debt.

2.3   It does not apply to an official assignee in connection with bankrupts (see paragraph 17 below). Neither does it apply to the supply by the State or a local authority of goods acquired compulsorily by it or the supply of goods by a a sheriff or other person acting under statutory authority (see paragraph 18 below).

2.4   Where a liquidator or receiver carries on the business, as distinct from taking control of the company towards the satisfaction of a debt or for the purposes of winding up of the company, the liquidator or receiver must register for VAT in his/her own right (see paragraph 3 below).

2.5   A liquidator/receiver is not be obliged or entitled to register for VAT where the supplies would not be taxable. For example, where the goods to be disposed of consist entirely of a non-taxable transfer of a business or a motor vehicle on which no credit had been allowed, then application for VAT registration will not be accepted.

Since Section 3(7) applies to the supply of goods only, the sale of services, such as copyrights, licences and other intangible assets by a liquidator/receiver must be accounted for under the accountable person's own VAT number.

3.   Registration for VAT.

3.1   Subject to the exceptions listed below, although the VAT registered person, or a person who ought to have been VAT registered, is deemed to have supplied the goods, a liquidator or receiver must register in and account , in respect of each separate liquidation or receivership, for VAT due on those supplies, irrespective of their value.

(Subsection 9 (2A) of the VAT Act 1972 (as amended) requires that a person, such as a receiver or liquidator who disposes of goods forming part of the assets of an accountable person, and in respect of which VAT is payable, must, within 14 days of such disposal, apply for registration for the purpose of accounting for tax).

3.2   The assets which give rise to the liability for VAT on disposal must have passed into the control of the liquidator/receiver before registration is granted

3.3   Application for registration should be made on form TR2. The Company Name should be entered in the Name Field with "in liquidation" or "in Receivership" appended, e.g. REDCAR SALES LTD IN LIQUIDATION or REDCAR SALES LTD IN RECEIVERSHIP

The Liquidator/Receiver/Assignee name and address should be entered as the Official Address e.g.

Per P Murphy Liquidator, P Murphy & Co., Main Street, Dublin

or

Per P. Murphy, Receiver, P Murphy & Co., Main Street, Dublin.

A new VAT number will be allocated to each such registration.

3.4   It must be established that assets which give rise to liability on disposal have passed into the control of the liquidator/receiver/assignee. Registration will be refused if there are no taxable assets for disposal.

3.5   The liquidator/receiver/assignee should be registered for VAT in the Revenue District responsible for the taxable person's affairs. A separate registration number to that of the taxable person will be allocated.

3.6   When an existing liquidator or receiver resigns or is replaced the existing registration should be amended to reflect the new name and address details. A new registration number should not be allocated. However where the appointment of a receiver is followed by the appointment of a liquidator, the latter must be registered under a new registration number.

4.   Group registration

4.1   If a company in liquidation or receivership was, prior to liquidation or receivership, registered as a member of a group for VAT purposes, then liquidators or receivers may apply for a corresponding group registration. It is the remitter which will account for VAT in the VAT return for the group.

5.   Non-taxable supplies

5.1   A liquidator or receiver is not an accountable person in respect of the supply of business assets of persons who are not properly VAT registered persons.

5.2   Goods disposed of by a liquidator or receiver which are the assets of a VAT registered person are not taxable in the following circumstances:-

The transfer of goods being a transfer of a totality of the assets or part thereof, of a business, even if that business or part thereof had ceased trading, where those transferred assets constitute an undertaking, or part of an undertaking, capable of being operated on an independent basis.

Business goods in respect of which the company in liquidation or receivership was not entitled to a VAT deduction (e.g. Cars acquired other than as stock in trade or acquisitions of property in certain instances)

Goods returned to a supplier under reservation of title arrangements. If these goods were invoiced to the company in liquidation or receivership and a VAT deduction was taken, the supplier is obliged to issue a VAT credit note. This will have the effect of cancelling the deduction.

6.   Property transactions

6.1   Since goods sold by a receiver or liquidator are deemed to be supplied by the company in receivership or liquidation disposals of immovable goods which are assets of a company are deemed to be an economic activity and subject to the same rules as if the company had itself supplied the property. In other words the supply of freehold or freehold equivalent interests in "new" properties is subject to VAT. The joint option to tax can be availed of and the transitional rules, for properties which were taxable under the pre 1 July, 2008 VAT rules and which are supplied on or after that date, apply. The appropriate Capital Goods Scheme rules will also apply. [Information on the treatment of VAT and property transactions is set out in the VAT on Property Guide, April 2008.]

6.2.   Where such a transfer of ownership takes place in the course of the 'transfer of a business' rules (a transfer of a totality of the assets, or part thereof, even if that business had ceased trading, where those transferred assets constitute an undertaking or part of an undertaking capable of being operated on an independent basis) to another accountable person, that transfer is deemed not to be a supply for VAT purposes. This means that no VAT is chargeable. There are special rules within the Capital Goods Scheme to deal with such transactions. There are basically two main rules dealing with the transferee to enable him or her to operate the scheme.One applies where the transfer occurs during the period when the sale of the property would have been taxable but for the transfer of business relief (i.e. while the property was considered "new"). The second rule applies when the transfer of the property occurs outside this period i.e. when if it were supplied other than as part of a transfer of a business, the sale would have been exempt. There are also rules dealing with the transferor [see the VAT on Property Guide, (April, 2008)].

6.3   Where a company had financed its acquisition of a property by means of a standard legal mortgage, the mortgagor will retain a legal interest in the property. If the company defaults on its repayments and the property is part of the assets of the company's business and is repossessed and disposed of by the mortgagee, then there is considered to be a transfer of the property between the mortgagor and the mortgagee. The mortgagee must account for any VAT due on the disposal of the property by it, using the special VAT number appropriated to it for such purposes.

6.4   Since Section 3(7) applies to goods only, a liquidator/receiver is not taxable in respect of the transfer of a leasehold interest in property other than an effective freehold interest. It is the company itself which must account for any VAT due on such supplies.

7.   Supplies of services

7.1   The liquidator or receiver is not liable to VAT for the supply of services by the company in the course of liquidation or receivership. The company is, however, liable on transactions not covered by the terms of the receiver or liquidator's appointment.

7.2   The transfer of goodwill or other intangible assets of a business, in connection with the transfer of a business or part thereof, even if that business or part thereof had ceased trading, or in connection with a transfer of goods, as outlined in the first indent of paragraph 5.2 above, to a taxable person, is not a supply. In circumstances where the supply of intangible assets is taxable, it is the company which must account for the VAT due.

7.3   The liquidator or receiver is liable for VAT on his/her charge to the company for professional services rendered by him/her and such VAT is deductible by the Company, subject to the normal rules.

8.   Obligations of liquidators and receivers under VAT law

8.1   Liquidators and receivers are obliged under Sn19(3)(b) of the VAT Act 1972 (as amended) to account for VAT on the disposal of the business assets and to make a VAT return at the end of each taxable period. The liquidator/receiver should send to the accountable person whose goods are disposed of, a statement containing such particulars as may be specified in regulations and shall treat the amount of tax as a necessary disbursement out of the proceeds of the disposal. The owner of the goods disposed of by a liquidator or receiver is entitled to exclude from any VAT return required to be made by him/her the tax for which the person disposing of the goods is required to account.

9.   Receivers appointed under a fixed (specific)charge

9.1   In the case of receiverships in which a receiver is appointed under a fixed (specific) charge, the receiver is taxable on the disposal of the specific asset only. A company accounting on the cash basis of accounting is itself (not the receiver) liable on moneys received in respect of transactions (supplies of goods and services), whether pre or post receivership. The company is, in any event, liable on transactions not covered by the terms of the receiver's appointment.

10.   Carrying on the business

10.1   Where a liquidator or receiver is authorised to continue to trade and does so, as opposed to merely taking control of the company for the purposes of the satisfaction of a debt owed by the taxable person or the winding up of the company, then the liquidator or receiver is required to register and account for VAT in respect of goods and services, subject to the threshold limits.

11.   VAT due

11.1   The amount of VAT on which liquidators and receivers are accountable in respect of goods disposed of by them to unregistered persons is the VAT content, at the appropriate rate(s), in the amount received from the disposal. The proceeds of all such disposals are regarded as being VAT inclusive. The usual rules apply concerning disposals to a taxable person, whereby VAT must be charged and accounted for on the consideration charged and the amount of VAT must be shown separately on a VAT invoice.

11.2   Where no money is paid in respect of a disposal of goods (eg. In the case of goods distributed in specie among creditors or shareholders), an amount equivalent to the VAT at the appropriate rate(s) on the open market value of the goods, is payable.

12.   VAT deductible

12.1   Claims for VAT deductions should be segregated between pre and post liquidation/receivership transactions as follows:-

Deductible VAT Incurred by a liquidator or receiver on goods or services supplied to him/her in connection with a liquidation or receivership should, subject to the normal restrictions, be claimed in the VAT returns that he/she is required to make in respect of goods disposed of by him/her. Claims for VAT charged on a liquidator's/ receiver's professional services may be included in these returns also. The liquidator's/receiver's charges are considered as overheads of the company in liquidation/receivership and are deductible to the extent of the company's entitlement to a deduction for inputs prior to his/her appointment.

VAT adjustments arising out of pre receivership/liquidation transactions should be claimed under the company's original VAT number and not the VAT number of the company in liquidation or receivership.

13. Bad debts

13.1 Relief for bad debts is allowable, subject to the usual conditions. Claims for relief should be made on a supplementary VAT return under the company's original VAT number.

14. Invoices, credit notes, settlement vouchers.

14.1 Liquidators and receivers should issue invoices and credit notes on the same basis as accountable persons, the name and address of the person issuing the document being "Company X in liquidation/receivership per A.B" (as appropriate), the VAT number on the document being the number allocated for that purpose.

14.2 Goods returned to a company in liquidation or receivership should be treated as having been bought back by the liquidator or receiver. If the person returning the goods does not issue a VAT invoice, the liquidator should issue a settlement voucher and take an appropriate deduction in his/her return.

15. Statement by liquidator or receiver to the owner of the goods

15.1 A copy of the invoice issued to the purchasers of the goods disposed of suffices for this purpose.

16. Examiners

16.1 An examiner is a person, appointed by a company or the Court, who assesses the affairs of a company put under the protection of the Court in certain circumstances, to consider whether the company is capable of rescue and to prepare a plan for the rescue of the company, its undertakings or substantial parts thereof. On application to it, the Court may make an order empowering the examiner to dispose of the company's assets if he/she considers that this would facilitate the achievement of his/her objectives. The provisions of Section 3(7) of the VAT Act therefore apply to any such disposals by an examiner.

16.2 One implication of the appointment of an examiner is that debts may not be executed against the company. Accordingly all Revenue enforcement activity has to be suspended while the examiner is in place. To stop the tax debt continuing to grow, Revenue usually requests the Court to direct the examiner to pay current tax debts while the company is in examinership.

16.3 The Court invariably seeks Revenue's views on the proposals being formulated by the Examiner. In addition Revenue, (Collector General Insolvency Section, Dublin) along with other creditors, is entitled to vote on whether or not to accept the proposals being put forward. Revenue's position will depend on the circumstances of the case (e.g. previous tax collection history, whether there will be a change of directors etc.).

17.   Official Assignee

17.1 Where a business person other than a company gets into financial difficulties and is unable to meet liabilities a creditor may apply to the Courts to have the defaulter adjudicated bankrupt. When the Court grants the application the bankrupt must cease business and may not dispose of assets. These become vested in the Official Assignee of the Court. Sn3(1)(d) of the VAT Act provides that the transfer of the goods to their acquisition by the Assignee is a taxable event and the bankrupt is liable. The Official Assignee, being an Officer of the State, is not a taxable person and any disposal of assets by him/her is not subject to VAT.

18.   Disposals by the State, local authority, sheriff, etc. after compulsory acquisition

18.1 Section 3(1)(d) of the VAT Act 1972 (as amended) provides that the transfer of goods is a supply of goods on which VAT is accountable by the taxpayer where these goods are acquired compulsorily by the State, including a local authority or are seized from a person by a Sheriff or other person acting under statutory authority. Such public bodies are not liable to VAT on their onward disposal of the goods.

Further information

Enquiries regarding any issue contained in this Information Leaflet should be addressed to the Revenue District responsible for your tax affairs. Contact details for all Revenue Districts can be found by clicking here .

This VAT Information Leaflet is issued by

VAT Appeals and Communications Branch
Indirect Taxes Division,
Dublin Castle

January 2009

APPENDIX 1

VAT law and Notes for Guidance on liquidators/receivers

VAT Act 1972 (as amended) — Sn3(7)

(i)   Where, in the case of a business carried on, or that has ceased to be carried on, by an accountable person, goods forming part of the assets of the business are, under any power exercisable by another person, including a liquidator and a receiver, disposed of by the other person in or towards the satisfaction of a debt owed by the accountable person, or in the course of the winding up of a company, they shall be deemed to be supplied by the accountable person in the course or furtherance of his business.

(ii)   A disposal of goods under this subsection shall include any disposal which is deemed to be a supply of immovable goods under section 4(2).

Consolidated Notes for Guidance — Sn3(7)

Subsection (7)(i) deems goods which formed part of the business assets of an accountable person, which are disposed of under powers exercised by another person, to be supplied

"by the accountable person"

and

"in the course or furtherance of his/her business".

This subsection deals with sales of an accountable person's assets by a liquidator or a receiver as well as other persons (such as a mortgagee) who might dispose of goods forming part of the assets of an accountable person in settlement of a debt.

It also provides that the obligations imposed in respect of the payment of VAT on the disposal of goods by a liquidator apply in all cases of the winding-up of a company. The main effect is to extend the section to cover a voluntary winding-up and any other winding-up in which the liquidator might not be disposing of the goods in the satisfaction of the debts due.

VAT Act 1972 (as amended) — Sn9(2A)

(2A)   Every person who disposes of goods which pursuant to section 3(7) are deemed to be supplied by a taxable person in the course or furtherance of his business shall, within fourteen days of such disposal, furnish in writing to the Revenue Commissioners the particulars specified in regulations as being required for the purpose of registering such person for tax.

Consolidated Notes for Guidance — Sn9(2A)

Subsection (2A) requires that a person such as a receiver or liquidator who disposes of goods forming part of the assets of an accountable person, and in respect of which VAT is payable, must within 14 days of such disposal apply for registration for the purpose of accounting for tax.

VAT Act 1972 (as amended) — Sn19(3)(b) and (c)

(b) A person who disposes of goods which pursuant to section 3(7) are deemed to be supplied by an accountable person in the course or furtherance of his business —

    (i) shall within 9 days immediately after the tenth day of the month immediately following a taxable period furnish to the Collector-General a true and correct return, prepared in accordance with regulations, of the amount of tax which became due by such accountable person in relation to the disposal, and such other particulars as may be specified in regulations, and shall at the same time remit to the Collector-General the amount of tax payable in respect of the taxable period in question,

    (ii) shall send to the person whose goods were disposed of a statement containing such particulars as may be specified in regulations, and

    (iii) shall treat the said amount of tax as a necessary disbursement out of the proceeds of the disposal.

(c) The owner of goods which pursuant to section 3(7) are deemed to be supplied by a accountable person in the course or furtherance of his business shall exclude from any return, which he is or, but for this subparagraph, would be, required to furnish under this Act, the tax payable in accordance with paragraph (b).

Consolidated Notes for Guidance 2008 — Sn19(3)(b) and (c) — Liability of Liquidators and Receivers

Paragraph (b) deals with the liability of liquidators and receivers. Effectively the liquidators or receivers of an accountable person's business must account for VAT on the disposal of the business assets.

Subparagraph (i) provides that a person such as a liquidator or receiver who disposes of goods forming part of the assets of an accountable person must furnish a return at the end of each two-month taxable period and pay any tax due in respect of such sales;

subparagraph (ii) provides that the person referred to in (i) must send to the accountable person whose goods are disposed of such details as may be specified by regulations;

subparagraph (iii) treats the tax due as a necessary disbursement out of the proceeds of the disposal.

Paragraph (c) provides that the owner of the goods disposed of by a liquidator or receiver will be entitled to exclude from any VAT return required to be made by him/her the tax for which the person disposing of the goods is required to account.

Regulation 41, VAT Regulations 2006

If a taxable person, being a body corporate, goes into liquidation, anything which he she would have been liable to do under the Act or these Regulations shall be done by assignee, trustee, committee or liquidator, as appropriate.

VALUE-ADDED TAX INFORMATION LEAFLET (JANUARY 2009)

VAT AND VRT ON TRANSACTIONS INVOLVING MOTOR VEHICLES

Introduction

Motor vehicles sold in Ireland are liable to Value-Added Tax (VAT) at the standard rate, currently 21.5%. In addition, when a motor vehicle is being registered in Ireland, it is liable to Vehicle Registration Tax (VRT). The rate of VRT varies between vehicle types, and is mainly dependant on the level of CO_2 emissions. VRT is payable on new unregistered vehicles, and also on vehicles brought into Ireland from other countries.

The VAT and VRT procedures involved when buying and selling motor vehicles may vary depending on the status of the buyers or sellers. These may be motor dealers, traders buying or selling their own business vehicles, motor auctions, private individuals, etc. There are also special procedures for transactions involving second-hand vehicles, or vehicles being transported between countries as part of a purchase or sale. As well as vehicle sales, VAT is also due on any work on motor vehicles, such as repair and maintenance, and on the hire and leasing of vehicles.

How VAT and VRT should be paid in different transactions, and the circumstances in which these taxes may be reclaimed, are set out in this guide. Contact details for any further questions are available in the Enquiries section.

What this guide contains

This guide sets out details of how VAT and VRT should be paid and accounted for when buying or selling new or second-hand motor vehicles. It does not contain rates of VRT, or procedures for registration of vehicles. These are available by contacting the local Vehicle Registration Office (VRO), or on the Revenue website.

Also included are:

- Guidelines regarding the treatment of other transactions involving motor vehicles, such as hiring and repair/maintenance.

- The special VAT schemes for second-hand means of transport and agricultural machinery

- Particulars of the VAT/VRT treatment of vehicles registered by distributors or dealers in their own names.

For reasons of clarity, the term 'motor vehicles' is used in preference to the more general 'means of transport', as this leaflet is directed mainly at the motor trade and private purchasers in respect of motorised land vehicles. Where a means of transport other than a motor vehicle is referred to this will be explicitly stated in the relevant part of the leaflet. A glossary of the specialist terms used in this leaflet is available at the section on Useful Terms and Definitions.

This guide replaces previous publications, 'VAT treatment of Second Hand Motor Vehicles', 'VAT Treatment of International Leasing of Means of Transport 3/99' and 'New VAT Treatment of Vehicles registered by Distributors or Dealers prior to Sale'. This guide is broken down into **eight** sections, as described below.

1.   Vehicles bought or sold by an authorised motor dealer

- New motor vehicles bought and sold by an authorised motor dealer

- Second-hand motor vehicles bought and sold by an authorised motor dealer

- Vehicles purchased as stock-in-trade from foreign sellers by an authorised motor dealer

- Registration of vehicles by dealers/distributors in their own names

- Scheme for agricultural machinery and vehicles purchased by dealers

2.   Purchase and sale of second-hand motor vehicles under Special Scheme rules

- What second-hand vehicles qualify for the Special Scheme?

- Calculation and deduction of residual VAT on second-hand vehicles in the Special Scheme

- Clawback of residual VAT following the sale of a qualifying second-hand vehicle in the Special Scheme

- Invoicing – the purchase of a qualifying second-hand vehicle in the Special Scheme

- Invoicing - the sale of a qualifying second-hand vehicle in the Special Scheme

- Treatment of qualifying second-hand vehicles when taken out of the Special Scheme

- The sale of a new means of transport, that is also a qualifying second-hand vehicle, to another EU Member State

- Requirement to keep records for the purchase and sale of vehicles in the Special Scheme

3.   Vehicles bought or sold by a person other than an authorised motor dealer

- Vehicles purchased from foreign sellers by Irish VAT-registered traders (including motor dealers without TAN numbers)

- Vehicles purchased from foreign sellers by private individuals

- Motor vehicles supplied by private individuals

- Motor vehicles supplied by dealers without TAN numbers

- Motor vehicles supplied by traders who are not motor dealers

4.   Hiring and leasing of vehicles

- Short-term and long-term hire

- Insurance, damage waivers, maintenance etc.

- Accessories supplied with a hired vehicle

- Recovery of VAT charged on hire/leasing payments

- Recovery of VAT & VRT by hire/lease providers

5.   Work on vehicles, including repair and maintenance

- Servicing, repair and maintenance

- Alterations and conversions

- Painting (including logos)

6.   Recovery of tax on the purchase of motor vehicles

- Recovery of VAT by motor dealers

- Recovery of VAT & VRT by driving schools

- Recovery of VAT by other VAT-registered traders

- Recovery of VAT under hire-purchase agreements

- Recovery of VAT and/or VRT by purchasers not registered for VAT

7.   Useful terms and definitions

8.   Enquiries

Vehicles bought or sold by an authorised motor dealer

A motor dealer who wishes to deal or trade in unregistered or foreign-registered vehicles must apply for authorisation to do so. Once authorised, a dealer will be issued with a **TAN (Trader Account Number)** by the local Revenue District. Details of the application process and requirements are available on the Revenue website. Authorisation and possession of a TAN number only affects the way in which the dealer operates Vehicle Registration Tax (VRT). For further information on the operation of VRT by traders without a TAN number, see Motor vehicles supplied by dealers without TAN numbers. Dealers' obligations with regard to Value-Added Tax (VAT) are the same whether or not they have a TAN number.

New Motor Vehicles bought and sold by an authorised motor dealer

For the purposes of this leaflet, a new motor vehicle should generally be regarded as one which has not been owned by any person other than the manufacturer, distributor(s) and authorised dealer(s), and/or has not been registered by any of these in their own name(s). This is not the same as a 'new means of transport', which is a technical term that applies where vehicles are brought in to Ireland from other EU countries (see sections on vehicles brought into the State by motor dealers, other traders and private individuals).

- Vehicle Registration Tax (VRT) charges on new vehicles bought and sold by an authorised motor dealer

- Value-Added Tax (VAT) charges on new vehicles bought and sold by an authorised motor dealer

- VAT on new vehicles sold to VAT-registered customers outside the State by an authorised motor dealer

- VAT on new vehicles sold to private customers outside the State by an authorised motor dealer

Vehicle Registration Tax (VRT) charges on new vehicles bought and sold by an authorised motor dealer

An authorised motor dealer, who holds a new motor vehicle as stock-in-trade, is not required to register the vehicle in his or her own name. However, the dealer is obliged to ensure that the vehicle is registered before the customer takes delivery of it. In the course of a sale, the dealer therefore generally collects the VRT amount from the customer and registers the vehicle in the customer's name. This can be done by using the Revenue On-line System (ROS), or at any Vehicle Registration Office (VRO office). Once a vehicle is registered, it can then be supplied to the customer with registration plates fitted.

An easy way of calculating the VRT liability on any vehicle is to use the VRT Calculator on the Revenue website. The VRO office will confirm the amount of VRT payable. It should be noted that VRT is calculated on the Open Market Selling Price (OMSP) of a vehicle, rather than the actual purchase price.

N.B.: Only authorised motor dealers are entitled to hold unregistered vehicles. If a person other than an authorised dealer obtains a motor vehicle that is not registered in the State, the vehicle must then be registered in his or her own name, and the VRT must be paid at that time.

Value-Added Tax (VAT) charges on new vehicles bought and sold by an authorised motor dealer

In general, VAT is due (at the standard rate, currently 21.5 per cent) on the full purchase price received by a dealer for any vehicle. However, in the sale of an unregistered vehicle by an authorised dealer, Revenue will accept that the portion of the purchase price that represents the VRT liability is paid by the dealer in the name and on the account of the purchaser; i.e., the customer pays the VRT, and the dealer simply administers the payment from the money handed to him or her. Accordingly, the VAT liability on the sale of a new vehicle by an authorised motor dealer is generally calculated on the VRT-exclusive amount received from the customer. (This also applies in the case of a second-hand or used vehicle brought into the State by an authorised dealer, and sold by him or her prior to being registered in Ireland.) In the case of the sale of a registered vehicle, a VAT liability arises on the full VRT-inclusive amount received, and no adjustment is allowed.

VAT on new vehicles sold to VAT-registered customers outside the State by an authorised motor dealer

Sales of new vehicles to VAT registered traders in other Member States of the EU where the vehicles are dispatched to that other Member State by or on behalf of the Irish vendor should generally be treated as intra-Community supplies, and zero-rated for VAT. The dealer must retain proof that the vehicle was transported outside the State. New vehicles exported by the dealer outside the EU should also generally be zero rated for VAT, and the dealer must retain proof that the vehicle was transported outside the EU (The zero-rate does not apply in any circumstances to second-hand or used vehicles sold by Irish vendors under the Special scheme for second-hand vehicles – these are liable to Irish VAT.)

VAT on new vehicles sold to private customers outside the State by an authorised motor dealer

In the case of the sale of a new vehicle which is also a new means of transport to a private individual in another EU Member State, VAT is ultimately payable by the private individual in that other Member State. Nonetheless, the Irish dealer should charge Irish VAT on the sale of the vehicle. The purchaser will then be liable to account again for VAT in his or her own Member State. Once the customer satisfies the dealer that VAT has been paid, and the vehicle registered with the licensing authorities in that Member State, the dealer should refund the Irish VAT to the customer. The dealer must obtain documentary proof from the customer that VAT has been paid, and the vehicle registered, in the other EU Member State, and he or she can then claim an adjustment in the VAT return to account for the refund of VAT.

If an Irish dealer supplies a vehicle in the circumstances set out above, he or she may elect not to charge VAT if the vehicle is dispatched by the dealer to a place in another EU Member State; and the customer is known to the dealer. In this situation, the dealer is relying on the customer returning documents confirming registration of the vehicle in another Member State. If such proof has not been provided by the date on which the VAT return for the period is due, the Irish dealer must account for VAT on the transaction.

Second-Hand Motor Vehicles bought and sold by an authorised motor dealer

For this section, a second-hand or used vehicle may be regarded as a motor vehicle, agricultural machine, etc. that has had at least one previous owner, including the current owner, but not including a motor dealer who held the vehicle, etc. as stock-in-trade. Most transactions by motor dealers involving second-hand vehicles will also come within the scope of the Special Scheme for Second-Hand Vehicles, which should be consulted in conjunction with this section.

* VRT due on second-hand motor vehicles
* VAT due on sales of second-hand motor vehicles
* VAT on second-hand vehicles sold to customers outside the State
* VAT treatment of 'trade-ins'

VRT due on second-hand motor vehicles

Where an authorised motor dealer holds a second-hand motor vehicle as stock-in-trade, he/she is not required to register the vehicle in his/her own name, but it must be registered in the name of the eventual purchaser. In general, there is no VRT due on Irish second-hand vehicles; i.e. vehicles that were previously registered in the State. When such a vehicle is sold, the dealer's only obligation with regard to registration is to forward the documentation for the change of owner (the Single Registration Certificate) to Vehicle Licensing (Motor Tax Unit), Department of Environment, Heritage and Local Government, Shannon, Co. Clare. There is, however, a VRT charge on second-hand vehicles brought into the State from any other country. This VRT must be paid before the vehicle can be registered in Ireland.

VAT due on sales of second-hand motor vehicles

In the case of Irish-registered second-hand vehicles, VAT is due on the price received for the vehicle. Under no circumstances can any portion of the price, e.g. the VRT element, be separated from the rest of the sale price when calculating the VAT liability, which is due (at the standard rate, currently 21.5 per cent) on the full sale price received by a dealer for a second-hand vehicle.

Where an authorised dealer brings a second-hand vehicle into the State that has been registered in another country, he/she is not obliged to register the vehicle in Ireland until it is being sold. At that stage, the dealer is obliged to ensure that the vehicle is registered in Ireland in the name of the purchaser (or the nominated person, where the purchaser is a company) before the vehicle is released to the purchaser. In this situation Revenue generally accepts that the portion of the sale price that represents the VRT liability is paid by the dealer in the name and on the account of the purchaser, i.e. the customer pays the VRT, and the dealer simply administers the payment from the money handed to him or her.

Accordingly, the VAT liability on the sale by an authorised motor dealer of a second-hand vehicle, brought into the State from another country, is generally calculated on the VRT-exclusive amount received from the customer. (This also applies in the case of a new vehicle sold by an authorised dealer prior to being registered in Ireland.)

In the case of the sale of a second-hand vehicle by any person other than an authorised dealer, a VAT liability arises on the full VRT-inclusive amount received, and no adjustment is allowed.

VAT on second-hand vehicles sold to customers outside the State

Most sales of second-hand vehicles by a VAT registered dealer in Ireland to VAT registered traders in other Member States of the EU will come within the scope of the Special Scheme for second-hand motor vehicles. These sales are liable to Irish VAT, and cannot be zero-rated.

Some sales of second-hand vehicles by a VAT registered dealer in Ireland to VAT registered traders in other Member States of the EU do not come within the scope of the Special Scheme for second-hand motor vehicles. These sales should be zero-rated for VAT as intra-Community supplies.

In the case of the sale of a second-hand vehicle to a private individual in another EU Member State, whether under the Special Scheme or not, the dealer should charge Irish VAT.

Second-hand vehicles exported by an Irish dealer to a place outside the EU should generally be zero rated for VAT. Documentary proof of export must be retained. However, exported second-hand vehicles being sold under the Special Scheme for second-hand motor vehicles are liable to Irish VAT, and cannot be zero-rated.

VAT treatment of 'trade-ins'

If a dealer accepts a vehicle as a trade-in against the purchase of another vehicle, this is treated as two separate transactions for the purpose of accounting for VAT: the sale of a vehicle by the dealer, and the purchase of the 'trade-in' by the dealer.

In respect of the sale of the vehicle the dealer accounts for VAT on the full consideration she or he is entitled to receive on that sale, i.e. the value of the trade-in plus any other payment made in respect of the purchase of the vehicle.

The dealer treats the trade-in as the simple purchase of a second-hand vehicle. If the dealer receives a VAT invoice from the person supplying the trade-in (i.e. the trade-in is from a VAT-registered person who was entitled to reclaim VAT on the vehicle) the VAT charged may be reclaimed in the normal way. Otherwise, if it is a qualifying vehicle the Special scheme for second-hand vehicles will generally apply, and the dealer may claim a deduction of the residual VAT included in the purchase price.

Each qualifying vehicle purchased from a private individual by way of trade-in must be accompanied by a signed declaration that the person selling (i.e. trading-in) the vehicle was not registered for VAT, and did not claim back VAT on the vehicle. (Where a person claimed a refund of VAT or VRT under the scheme for disabled drivers he or she may nonetheless sign the declaration as if no VAT had been reclaimed.) If the person trading-in the vehicle was registered for VAT, but was nonetheless not entitled to reclaim VAT on the purchase of the vehicle, the declaration should reflect this.

Vehicles purchased as stock-in-trade from foreign sellers by an authorised motor dealer

Where an authorised motor dealer purchases a vehicle from a supplier outside the State, the procedures for paying and reclaiming VAT will vary depending on the status of the supplier, and the way in which the transaction is carried out. In general terms, authorised dealers are entitled to recover VAT on any vehicle purchased as stock-in-trade from any person outside the State. Authorised dealers are not required to register any stock in trade vehicle for VRT purposes until the onward sale of the vehicle takes place (this applies to both new and second-hand vehicles, and whether or not the vehicles were previously registered in any other jurisdiction).

N.B.: Vehicles purchased from suppliers outside the EU are referred to as imports, and may be liable to Customs duty as well as VAT (see below). Vehicles purchased from suppliers within the EU are referred to as 'intra-Community acquisitions', and are not liable to Customs duty, but may be liable to VAT.

In this section, the term 'second-hand vehicle' applies generally to pre-owned vehicles. However, it does not include a pre-owned vehicle brought in to the State that was either supplied less than 6 months after entering into service, or has travelled 6,000 kilometers or less. Such vehicles, even if they were previously owned and registered in another country, are categorised as 'new means of transport', and do not come within the Special Scheme for second-hand motor vehicles. New means of transport bought and sold within the State are not subject to any such restrictions, and may be included in the Special Scheme.

- Second-hand vehicles purchased by an authorised motor dealer from a dealer in another country operating the Special or Margin Scheme, including motor auctioneers
- Second-hand vehicles purchased by an authorised motor dealer from a VAT-registered person in another country other than a dealer
- Second-hand vehicles purchased by an authorised motor dealer from a private person in another country
- New vehicles (New Means of Transport) purchased by an authorised motor dealer from a VAT-registered person in another country
- New vehicles (New Means of Transport) purchased by an authorised motor dealer from a private person in another country
- Vehicles imported into the EU by an authorised motor dealer as a result of purchase

Second-hand vehicles purchased by an authorised motor dealer from a dealer in another country operating the Special or Margin Scheme, including motor auctioneers

Vehicles purchased from a motor dealer operating under a Special or Margin Scheme in another EU Member State are liable to VAT in that country; e.g. a vehicle purchased from a dealer operating the Margin Scheme in the U.K. is liable to U.K. VAT at 17.5%. This is included in the purchase price as residual VAT, and as such can be recovered by the Irish dealer. To support any claim for residual VAT the dealer must have an invoice issued by the supplier in the other Member State which does not show VAT separately and which is endorsed by the supplier to the effect that the vehicle has been sold under the margin scheme/second-hand goods scheme in that Member State.

N.B.: To avoid confusion, it is essential to note that the term 'qualifying vehicle' applies in Irish law only. Where a vehicle is purchased from a dealer in another Member State of the EU, the use of this term alone is not sufficient indication that the vehicle is within the Special or Margin Scheme. A full statement that the invoice does not give rise to a right to input credit is required. When the Irish dealer sells a vehicle on which he or she has claimed residual VAT, the vehicle must be sold on under the Special Scheme, and the end purchaser will not have any entitlement to reclaim VAT on the vehicle.

Occasionally, a foreign dealer may sell a vehicle outside of the Special or Margin Scheme. In this case, the foreign dealer must issue a zero-rated VAT invoice in respect of the vehicle, quoting the purchaser's VAT number. The purchasing dealer then accounts for VAT in the VAT return for that period, and can claim a simultaneous credit. When selling on a vehicle that was purchased outside of the Scheme the Irish trader may issue a normal VAT invoice if the customer is registered for VAT, and the customer may reclaim the VAT charged, subject to the usual conditions.

A motor auctioneer is deemed to buy and sell the vehicles that pass through the auction. The auctioneer may operate the Special or Margin Scheme in his or her own country, or may sell the vehicles outside of the Scheme, as a VAT registered trader. In either case, the rules set out above will apply equally to an auctioneer. It is important that any vehicle purchased from an auctioneer is accompanied by the correct documentation in order for the purchaser to be entitled to get a refund of VAT.

Second-hand vehicles purchased by an authorised motor dealer from a VAT-registered person in another country other than a dealer

Second-hand vehicles which are purchased as stock in trade by a VAT registered dealer from a VAT registered supplier other than a motor dealer (or a person operating the margin scheme) in another EU Member State are treated as intra-Community acquisitions. That is, the supplier of the vehicle must issue a zero-rated VAT invoice in respect of the vehicle, quoting the purchasing dealer's VAT number. The purchasing dealer then accounts for VAT in the VAT return for that period, and can claim a simultaneous credit. If this vehicle is subsequently sold by the Irish dealer, s/he must charge VAT on the sale and, where appropriate, issue a normal VAT invoice, and allow the purchaser to claim a credit for the VAT charged.

If the sale of the vehicle takes place in the other Member State, and the supplier charges VAT on the sale rather than zero-rating it, then it may be possible for the Irish dealer to recover the VAT charged once the vehicle has been moved to Ireland. This is subject to the rules in the other Member State, but would normally require the Irish dealer to provide proof to the supplier that the vehicle had been transported to Ireland. The supplier would then issue a credit note and reissue the invoice without VAT.

When selling on a vehicle that was purchased from a VAT registered person other than a dealer, the Irish dealer may issue a normal VAT invoice if the customer is registered for VAT, and the customer may reclaim the VAT charged, subject to the usual conditions.

Second-hand vehicles purchased by an authorised motor dealer from a private person in another country

Where an Irish dealer purchases a second-hand vehicle from a private person in another EU Member State, there will be residual or trapped VAT contained in the price. The purchasing dealer may recover the residual VAT, at the rate that applies in the Member State where the vehicle was registered. In order to claim this residual VAT, the purchasing dealer must prepare a settlement voucher, to include:

- The name and address of the seller;
- The name and address of the dealer;
- The date of the supply;
- The make, model, engine number, registration number and year of manufacture of the vehicle;

- The total price of the vehicle;

- A declaration signed and dated by the seller of the vehicle that the details on the voucher are accurate; and

- A declaration signed and dated by the seller of the vehicle that he/she is not a VAT-registered person, and/or was not entitled to claim relief in respect of VAT on the vehicle.

This settlement voucher is required to support the dealer's claim to residual VAT. The dealer must give the seller a copy of the completed settlement voucher within 15 days of the purchase. When the Irish dealer sells a vehicle on which he or she has claimed residual VAT, the vehicle must be sold on under the Special Scheme, and the end purchaser will not have any entitlement to reclaim VAT on the vehicle.

New vehicles (New Means of Transport) purchased by an authorised motor dealer from a VAT-registered person in another country

A 'new means of transport' is a technical term which may be used to describe a motor vehicle that has travelled less than 6,000 km or was supplied less than 6 months since it first entered into service (see full definition). Where an Irish authorised dealer purchases a new means of transport from a person in another EU country, he or she generally accounts for Irish VAT on the vehicle. The VAT-registered foreign supplier issues a zero-rated VAT invoice in respect of the vehicle, quoting the purchasing dealer's VAT number. The purchasing dealer then accounts for VAT in his or her next VAT return, and can claim a simultaneous credit.

If the sale of the vehicle takes place in another Member State, and the supplier charges VAT on the sale rather than zero-rating it, then the Irish dealer can generally recover the VAT charged once the vehicle has been moved to Ireland. The Irish trader will normally be required to provide proof to the supplier that the vehicle has been transported to Ireland, allowing the supplier to issue a credit note and reissue the invoice at zero per cent VAT. This procedure is subject to the rules in force in the other Member State.

When selling on a new means of transport that was purchased from a VAT registered person other than a dealer, the Irish dealer may issue a normal VAT invoice if the customer is registered for VAT, and the customer may reclaim the VAT charged, subject to the usual conditions.

New vehicles (New Means of Transport) purchased by an authorised motor dealer from a private person in another country

Where a dealer purchases a new means of transport from a private person in another country, he or she must always account for Irish VAT on the vehicle even though the supplier cannot charge VAT. The purchasing dealer simply accounts for VAT on the purchase price in the VAT return following the purchase, and can claim a simultaneous credit.

When selling on a new means of transport purchased from a private person in another country, the Irish dealer must issue a normal VAT invoice if the customer is registered for VAT, and the customer may reclaim the VAT charged, subject to the usual conditions.

Vehicles imported into the EU as a result of purchase by an authorised motor dealer

Vehicles purchased from suppliers outside the EU are referred to as imports. These are liable to Customs Duty and to VAT at the point where they first enter the EU Customs are responsible for taxes and duties on imported goods, and all VAT and duty is payable to Customs. A VAT registered dealer can reclaim this VAT in his or her VAT return. Customs duty cannot be recovered.

Registration of vehicles by dealers/distributors in their own names

There are a number of different reasons why a dealer would want to register a vehicle in the name of the dealership (a self-registered vehicle). These include where a vehicle is used by the business other than as stock in trade, or where it is used as a demonstration model. In the case of a vehicle on which VAT is not normally deductible (see 'Commercial and non-Commercial Vehicles'), registering it in the name of the dealership is regarded as a 'self-supply' of the vehicle, and the VAT treatment changes. [It is important to note that, in the normal course of events, where a dealer sells a vehicle it must be registered in the name of the purchaser (or in the case of a company car, a person nominated by the company). Following the sale of a vehicle, it cannot be (or remain) registered in the name of the dealer.]

Self-supply of vehicles registered in the name of a dealer/distributor

Where a dealer (and/or distributor) registers a non-deductible vehicle in the name of the dealership the vehicle is treated as removed from stock-in-trade. This removal results in a 'self-supply' for VAT purposes. This means that a dealer, who had taken deductibility for VAT on the purchase or importation of the vehicle, must pay back the VAT claimed on that vehicle. This must be done in the VAT return for the period in which the vehicle was registered in the dealer's name. The amount of VAT is calculated as if the vehicle were sold at cost price at the time of registration.

Subsequent sale of a vehicle registered in the name of a dealer/distributor

When a vehicle that was self-registered is subsequently sold to a customer, the vehicle is treated as if it were brought back into stock for sale as a second hand vehicle, and it must then be sold through the Special Scheme for second-hand motor vehicles. This means that the dealer will be entitled to make a claim on his/her VAT return for the residual VAT.

Calculation of the amount of the residual input credit on a vehicle registered in the name of a dealer/distributor

The basis for calculating the residual VAT is the VAT-inclusive cost price plus VRT. This is calculated according to the formula normally used for the calculation of residual input credit for second hand motor vehicles with a slight variation, as follows:

$$A \times [B/(B+100)]$$

Where

- A is the original cost price (inclusive of VAT and VRT) and

- B is the percentage rate of VAT

Where a self-registered vehicle is brought back into stock both the claim for the residual VAT and the VAT on the sale of the vehicle will be accounted for in the same VAT return. The effect of this mechanism is that the residual VAT credit will be offset against the output VAT on the sale, and the dealer will actually pay VAT only on the difference between the cost price (inclusive of VAT and VRT) and the sale price. However, the dealer cannot claim more residual VAT than the VAT due on the sale. If the cost price (inclusive of VAT and VRT) is greater than the sale price the residual input credit is limited to an amount equal to the VAT on the sale price. As the vehicle is being sold through the Special Scheme, no deductibility is allowed on foot of the invoice issued (except if the vehicle is purchased by another dealer operating the Special Scheme).

Example VAT due on sale of a demonstration vehicle:

Where a vehicle is to be used as a demonstration model, the dealer (and/ or distributor) is obliged to register the vehicle in his or her own name (also referred to as self-registration). The VAT and VRT treatment of such vehicles changed with effect from 1 May 2003. The vehicles involved are those of the type, which, outside of the motor trade, are non-deductible vehicles for VAT purposes. These include the vehicles classified for VRT purposes as 'category A' vehicles (cars in general) and motorcycles.

A new vehicle was purchased by a motor dealer for €11,465 (exclusive of VAT and VRT), registered by the dealer, used for demonstration purposes, and later sold for €21,000. The VAT liability is calculated as follows:

Net cost of vehicle to dealer:	€11,465
VAT (liability on self-supply):	€2,465
VRT:	€5,625
Total cost price (incl. VAT and VRT):	€19,555

Following use as a demo model, the vehicle was subsequently sold for €21,000.00. The net VAT due on sale of the vehicle is calculated as follows:

VAT due on sale: (21,000 x 21.5)/121.5	=	€3,716.04
Residual credit* due: (19,555 x 21.5)/121.5	=	€3,460.34
Net VAT due on sale of demo vehicle:		€255.70

*The amount of residual credit claimed cannot exceed the amount of VAT due on the sale of the vehicle.

Scheme for agricultural machinery and vehicles purchased by dealers

Agricultural machinery is defined as equipment or machinery used by a flat-rate farmer in the course of his or her normal farming activities (as defined in the Fifth Schedule to the VAT Act). This definition covers commercial vehicles used in the course of the farming business.

This scheme, which came into effect on 1 September 1999, provides VAT arrangements for purchases, by dealers, of agricultural machinery from flat-rate farmers. The scheme provides that dealers in agricultural machinery can deduct the residual tax contained in the purchase price of second-hand agricultural machinery bought from any of the above mentioned persons and issue a VAT invoice on the subsequent sale of the goods. The Finance Act 2000 extended the scheme to agricultural machinery that had been repossessed by a hire purchase company, and later sold to a taxable dealer.

The Finance Act 2002 further extended the scheme to agricultural machinery that had been surrendered to an insurance company in connection with the settlement of a claim under a policy of insurance, and later sold to a taxable dealer.

- Calculation and deduction of residual VAT on agricultural machinery
- Restriction on recovery of residual VAT on agricultural machinery
- Invoicing for sales of agricultural machinery

Calculation and deduction of residual VAT on agricultural machinery

Residual VAT is deductible in the VAT period in which the vehicle is purchased, along with any other VAT incurred by the taxable dealer, by way of the VAT return for that period. The amount of the residual VAT is calculated at the rate of VAT chargeable on the supply of agricultural machinery. The purchase price paid by the dealer is always treated as VAT inclusive. The residual VAT is calculated using the following formula:

$$(A \times B)/(B + 100)$$

Where

A is the price paid by the dealer for the purchase of the agricultural machinery, and B is the percentage rate of VAT

Example

Where a flat-rate farmer sells a second-hand tractor to a taxable dealer for €10,000, the residual tax is calculated as follows:

Purchase price   = €10,000
Residual VAT = (€10,000 x 21.5)/121.5   = € 1,769

Restriction on recovery of residual VAT on agricultural machinery

The residual tax claimed by the dealer on the purchase of the machinery cannot be greater than the tax chargeable on the subsequent supply. If the dealer sells the machinery for less than the purchase price paid, he or she must pay the same amount of tax as that claimed on the purchase. An adjustment must therefore be made in the VAT return covering the period of the sale to increase the amount of VAT due on the sale to match the amount of residual VAT originally claimed.

Example

A dealer who buys a second-hand tractor from a flat-rate farmer for €5,000, and sells it for €3,000 VAT exclusive, must account as follows:

Tractor purchased for   = €5,000

Residual VAT claimed in VAT3 for period of purchase   =   €884

Sold for €3,000 excluding VAT

VAT liability on sale =   €645

Dealer must increase the VAT due on sales in his/her VAT return by €239 to account for difference.

Invoicing for sales of agricultural machinery

A flat-rate farmer must issue an invoice in relation to a supply of agricultural machinery to the taxable dealer. However, the document will usually actually be prepared by the taxable dealer and accepted by the flat rate farmer. and shall include the following particulars:

1. The flat-rate farmer's full name and address,

2. The full name, address and VAT registration number of the taxable dealer,

3. The date of issue of the invoice,

4. A description of the agricultural machinery, including details of the make, model and, where appropriate, the year of manufacture, the engine number and registration number of that machinery,

5. The date on which the agricultural machinery was supplied,

6. The consideration for the supply of the agricultural machinery,

7. A declaration by the farmer that the agricultural machinery was used for the purposes of his or her farming activities.

Where the person disposing of repossessed or surrendered agricultural machinery is an insurance company * and such disposals are deemed not to be a supply of goods, they shall issue a document to the taxable dealer, which shall include the following particulars:

1. The insurance company's full name and address,

2. The full name, address and VAT registration number of the taxable dealer,

3. The date of issue of the invoice,

4. A description of the agricultural machinery, including details of the make, model and, where appropriate, the year of manufacture, the engine number and registration number of that machinery,

5. The date on which the agricultural machinery was supplied,

6. The consideration for the supply of the agricultural machinery,

7. Confirmation that the disposal is deemed in accordance with Section 3(5)(d) of the VAT Act 1972 (as amended) not to be a supply of goods.

*Disposal of machinery following repossession by a hire-purchase company is considered to be a supply of goods (with effect from 1 May 2007) and is liable to VAT.

Purchase and sale of second-hand motor vehicles under Special Scheme rules

Where a motor dealer (whether authorised or not) purchases a second-hand motor vehicle from a person who was not entitled to reclaim VAT on his or her original purchase of the vehicle, the dealer is still obliged to charge VAT on the resale of the vehicle. Therefore, the original VAT charged on the vehicle is regarded as 'trapped' or 'residua'. However, a Special Scheme for second-hand motor vehicles has been put in place to allow to recover some or all of this trapped or residual VAT. The rules and procedures relating to this Scheme are set out below. Any dealer who wishes to operate the Scheme must follow all the relevant rules, particularly with regard to the invoicing requirements under the Scheme.

What second-hand vehicles qualify for the special scheme?

Vehicles that qualify for the scheme are ones which are

1.   sold (or traded-in) to the dealer by a person who was not entitled to deduct any VAT in relation to the original purchase of the vehicle, or

2.   sold (or traded-in) by another dealer who took a deduction of residual VAT on the original purchase of the vehicle.

These are referred to in Irish law as 'qualifying vehicles'.

Qualifying vehicles are bought by the dealer as stock-in-trade for resale, from one of the following:

1.   A private individual in Ireland or in another Member State of the European Union;

2.   A business in Ireland or in another Member State of the European Union which could not claim a VAT credit on its purchase of the vehicle or which is not obliged to issue a VAT invoice in respect of the sale of the vehicle;

3.   A business which is an exempt insurance company which took possession of the goods in connection with the settlement of a claim under a policy of insurance from a person who was not entitled to input credit in respect of the goods.

In the case of each of the categories (1) to (3) above, each qualifying vehicle purchased by a dealer must be accompanied by a signed declaration that the person selling or trading-in the vehicle was not registered for VAT, and/or was not entitled to claim back VAT on the vehicle. However, a vehicle may still qualify under the scheme where the dealer purchased the vehicle from a person who claimed a refund of VAT or VRT under the scheme for disabled drivers.

Other vehicles that qualify under the scheme include those purchased from:

4.   A business which is a hire-purchase provider and has claimed residual VAT on the vehicle;

5.   Another motor dealer in Ireland who claimed residual VAT on the purchase of the vehicle;

6.   A motor dealer in another Member State selling the vehicle under the special scheme/margin scheme for taxation of second-hand goods in that other Member State.

In the case of each of the categories (4) and (5) above, each qualifying vehicle purchased by a dealer must be accompanied by a valid Special Scheme invoice endorsed "Special Scheme – this invoice does not give the right to an input credit". In the case of category (6) above, each vehicle must be accompanied by a valid Special Scheme or Margin Scheme invoice issued in accordance with the legislation in that Member State.

N.B.: To avoid confusion, it is essential to note that the term 'qualifying vehicle' applies in Irish law only. Where a vehicle is purchased from a dealer in another Member State of the EU, the use of this term alone is not sufficient indication that the vehicle is within the Special or Margin Scheme. A full statement that the invoice does not give rise to a right to input credit is required.

Calculation and deduction of residual VAT on second-hand vehicles in the Special Scheme

A motor dealer may deduct the residual VAT included in the purchase price of any qualifying vehicle which s/he buys, whether as a straight purchase or as a trade-in (subject to correct procedures having been followed – see Invoicing – the purchase of a qualifying vehicle in the Special Scheme). Residual VAT is deductible in the VAT period in which the vehicle is purchased by way of the VAT return for that period.

The amount of the residual VAT is calculated on the basis that the purchase price is VAT inclusive. The rate at which the VAT should be calculated is the rate at which it is chargeable on the supply of motor vehicles in the EU Member State where the person selling the qualifying vehicle to the Irish dealer is based. That is, if the dealer purchases the vehicle from an Irish source, the rate used for the calculation is the Irish VAT rate of 21.5%. If the dealer purchases the vehicle from a UK source, the rate used for the calculation is the UK VAT rate, currently 17.5%.

Example 1 – A Qualifying second-hand vehicle purchased from an Irish vendor

If the qualifying vehicle is bought from an individual or business in Ireland, where the current VAT rate is 21.5%, the residual VAT is calculated as follows:

Purchase price   =   €10,000

Residual VAT = (€10,000 × 21.5)/121.5   =   € 1,769

Example 2 – A Qualifying second-hand vehicle purchased from a U.K. vendor

If the qualifying vehicle is bought from an individual or business in the UK, the residual VAT calculation is based on the UK VAT rate, currently 17.5%, as follows:

Euro equivalent of Sterling purchase price   =   €10,000

Residual VAT = (€10,000 x 17.5)/117.5   =   € 1,489

Clawback of residual VAT following the sale of a qualifying second-hand vehicle in the Special Scheme

A 'clawback' is the term used for an adjustment required when the price paid for a qualifying vehicle is greater than the price obtained when the dealer sells that vehicle. For each vehicle, the amount of residual VAT deductible by the dealer must not be more than the amount of VAT charged by the dealer on the subsequent sale.

Example:

Qualifying vehicle purchased in January for €10,000

Residual VAT claimed in VAT 3 for January/February   =   €1,769

Vehicle sold in May for €9,000 including VAT

VAT on sale accounted for in VAT 3 for May/June   =   €1,592

Amount of clawback which must be deducted from VAT

on purchases in VAT return for May/June = €1769 - €1592   =   €177

Effectively, if a qualifying vehicle is sold for less than it was bought for (or less than was given on a trade-in), an adjustment must be made in the VAT return covering the period of the sale to reduce the amount originally claimed. The dealer accounts for the VAT on the sale in the normal way, but reduces the figure for VAT on purchases in that period to account for the clawback. (This also applies if the vehicle is sold in the same VAT period in which it was bought).

The adjustment must be made on each individual transaction, and in respect of the tax period in which the vehicle is sold. However, where a dealer sells more than one qualifying vehicle to a customer in a single transaction (e.g. in a dealer-to-dealer transaction), the amount of the residual VAT deducted in respect of all the vehicles included in the transaction can be added together and compared with the amount of VAT due on that sale for the purpose of calculating whether a clawback is due.

A temporary measure allowing for the deferral of payment of residual VAT due to be clawed-back for 2008 was introduced in December 2008. Full details are available in Chapter 12b-04 of the VAT Manual.

Invoicing – the purchase of a qualifying second-hand vehicle in the Special Scheme

Where a motor dealer claims residual VAT on the purchase of a qualifying vehicle, he or she must be able to support that claim by an invoice or settlement voucher, completed in accordance with the appropriate VAT Regulations.

1.   Where a dealer buys a qualifying vehicle from another dealer established within the State, a valid Special Scheme invoice issued by that other dealer, endorsed "Special Scheme – this invoice does not give the right to an input credit", is required to support the claim to residual VAT.

2. Where a dealer buys a qualifying vehicle from a person who is not another dealer, the purchasing dealer shall prepare a settlement voucher. It must include:

    • The name and address of the seller;

    • The name and address of the dealer;

    • The date of the supply;

    • The make, model, engine number, registration number and year of manufacture of the vehicle;

    • The total price of the vehicle;

    • A declaration signed and dated by the seller of the vehicle that the details on the voucher are accurate; and a declaration signed and dated by the seller of the vehicle that he/she is not a VAT-registered person, and/or was not entitled to claim relief in respect of VAT on the original purchase vehicle*. If the seller is a VAT-registered person who nonetheless was not entitled to claim VAT on the purchase of the vehicle, the declaration should reflect this.

This settlement voucher is required to support the dealer's claim to residual VAT. The dealer must give the seller a copy of the completed settlement voucher within 15 days of the purchase.

*(Where a person claimed a refund of VAT or VRT under the scheme for disabled drivers he or she may nonetheless sign the declaration as if no VAT had been reclaimed.)

3. Where a dealer buys a qualifying vehicle from a dealer in another Member State, it will be supplied either under a Special Scheme or a Margin Scheme for the taxation of second-hand goods in that Member State. The purchase price will contain residual VAT, which the Irish dealer can deduct as set out in Calculation and deduction of residual VAT on second-hand vehicles in the Special Scheme.

To support this deduction the dealer must have an invoice issued by the supplier in the other Member State which does not show VAT separately and which is endorsed by the supplier to the effect that the vehicle has been sold under the margin scheme/second-hand goods scheme in that Member State.

N.B.: To avoid confusion, it is essential to note that the term 'qualifying vehicle' applies in Irish law only. Where a vehicle is purchased from a dealer in another Member State of the EU, the use of this term alone is not sufficient indication that the vehicle is within the Special or Margin Scheme. A full statement that the invoice does not give rise to a right to input credit is required. In particular, the Irish dealer must ensure that a vehicle on which he or she claimed residual VAT was not in fact zero-rated by the seller as an intra-Community supply. In such a situation, the Irish dealer would be obliged to pay back the residual VAT claimed, and account for VAT on the acquisition of the vehicle.

For vehicles brought in under the normal zero-rated intra-Community supply rules, see Vehicles purchased as stock-in-trade from foreign sellers by an authorised motor dealer.

Invoicing - the sale of a qualifying second-hand vehicle in the Special Scheme

Where a dealer sells a vehicle on which he or she has claimed residual VAT, he or she cannot issue a VAT invoice that allows the customer to claim input credit (this restriction is a legal requirement under European law). Therefore, where a qualifying vehicle is sold to another taxable person, the invoice issued must not show VAT separately and must include the following endorsement:"Special Scheme – this invoice does not give the right to an input credit of VAT".

This rule applies even when the customer is another motor dealer in the State. However, in that case, even though the purchasing dealer is not receiving a normal VAT invoice, he or she is entitled to deduct the residual VAT in the transaction under the Special Scheme because the vehicle is a qualifying vehicle.

If a qualifying vehicle is sold to a person in another Member State, Irish VAT is charged in the same way as it would be if the vehicle was sold to a customer in the State. If that customer in the other Member State is a VAT-registered person, the dealer must issue an invoice under the Special Scheme containing the endorsement set out above.

Treatment of qualifying second-hand vehicles when taken out of the Special Scheme

In order to allow a VAT-registered customer to reclaim VAT, a dealer may choose to take a vehicle out of the Scheme, having already claimed residual VAT. In this case, the dealer must repay any residual VAT previously claimed, by making an adjustment in the VAT return for the period when the vehicle was taken out of the scheme for the full amount of VAT claimed. The dealer may then issue a normal VAT invoice on selling the vehicle, allowing the customer to recover VAT.

When supplying a vehicle taken out of the Scheme to a VAT-registered trader in Ireland, the dealer must issue a normal VAT invoice, including the rate and amount of VAT on the sale. If the customer is a VAT-registered trader in another Member State, the invoice should be zero-rated, and quote the customer's VAT number.

Similarly, if a vehicle purchased by a dealer in Ireland from a dealer in another Member State is accompanied by a zero-rated VAT invoice under the intra-Community rules, it means that the dealer in the other Member State is not supplying the vehicle under the special scheme and the vehicle is not, therefore, a qualifying vehicle. The dealer in Ireland will not be entitled to claim residual VAT on the transaction, but must put it through the normal intra-Community acquisition mechanism for VAT. In that case, in accordance with normal rules, the invoice from the supplier should show the VAT number of both parties and should indicate that the supply is zero-rated.

For all private customers, Irish VAT at 21.5 per cent should be charged.

The sale of a new means of transport, that is also a qualifying second-hand vehicle, to another EU Member State

Legislation specifies that a vehicle that was supplied less than six months after it first entered into service or has travelled less than 6,000 km is a 'new means of transport' for VAT purposes. It is important to note that the term applies to any vehicle that satisfies either one of the criteria above – for example, a vehicle that was supplied 10 months after it first entered into service, but has travelled only 5,000 km is still a new means of transport, as is a vehicle that has travelled 10,000 km but was supplied only 5 months after first entry into service. For a full definition, see Useful Terms and Definitions.

New means of transport are liable to VAT in the country where they are to be used (generally the country where they are, or should be, registered) rather than where the supplier is established.

A qualifying vehicle may also be a new means of transport if a customer trades in (or sells to a garage) a vehicle that was supplied less than six months after first entry into service or has travelled less than 6000 km. The onward sale of such a vehicle to a person in another Member State will be liable to Irish VAT at the standard rate, currently 21.5%, if the sale takes place in Ireland. If the customer then transports the vehicle to another Member State, registers it there with the vehicle licensing authorities, and pays VAT, then the Irish VAT may be refunded subject to proof that the vehicle is registered and VAT was paid in that other EU Member State.

A dealer who gives a VAT refund following the sale of a new means of transport (that is also a qualifying vehicle) to a private customer in another EU Member State may claim a deduction for the VAT charged in the VAT return for the period. In this situation, there is no obligation to operate the clawback rule – i.e. the VAT adjustment claimed may exceed the amount of residual VAT claimed on the vehicle.

Requirement to keep records for the purchase and sale of vehicles in the Special Scheme

The Revenue Commissioners require an audit trail from the purchase of a qualifying vehicle to the sale of that vehicle with cross-reference to the relevant supporting documentation. Where residual VAT has been claimed and the vehicle has not been sold, adequate stock records should be available to substantiate this. It is important for traders to note that if documentation is missing or incorrectly completed, this may affect the right of the trader to claim a refund of VAT.

Vehicles Bought or Sold by a Person Other Than an Authorised Motor Dealer

Vehicles purchased from foreign sellers by Irish VAT-registered traders (including dealers without TAN numbers)

Where a VAT-registered trader, other than an authorised motor dealer, purchases a vehicle from a supplier outside the State, the procedures for paying and reclaiming VAT will vary depending on the status of the supplier, and the way in which the transaction is carried out. In general terms, VAT-registered traders may recover VAT incurred on the purchase of any commercial vehicle for business use. In addition, motor dealers without TAN numbers are also entitled to recover residual VAT on any qualifying second-hand vehicles purchased as stock-in-trade. Any person other than an authorised dealer who brings a vehicle into the State is obliged to register it for VRT purposes by the end of the day following its arrival in the State (this applies to both new and second-hand vehicles, and whether or not the vehicles were previously registered in any other jurisdiction). An easy way of calculating the VRT liability on any vehicle is to use the VRT Calculator on the Revenue website. The VRO office will confirm the amount of VRT payable. It should be noted that VRT is calculated on the Open Market Selling Price (OMSP) of a vehicle, rather than the actual purchase price.

N.B.: Vehicles purchased from suppliers outside the EU are referred to as imports, and may be liable to Customs duty as well as VAT (see below). Vehicles purchased from suppliers within the EU are referred to as 'intra-Community acquisitions', and are not liable to Customs duty, but may be liable to VAT.

In this section, the term 'second-hand vehicle' applies generally to pre-owned vehicles. However, it does not include a pre-owned vehicle brought into the State that was either supplied less than 6 months after entering into service, or has travelled 6,000 kilometers or less. Such vehicles, even if they were previously owned and registered in another country, are categorised as 'new means of transport', and do not come within the Special Scheme for second-hand motor vehicles. New means of transport bought and sold within the State are not subject to any such restrictions, and may be included in the Special Scheme.

- Second-hand vehicles purchased by a VAT-registered trader from a dealer operating the Special or Margin Scheme in another country

- Second-hand vehicles purchased by a VAT-registered trader from a VAT-registered person in another country other than a dealer

- Second-hand vehicles purchased by a VAT-registered trader from a private person in another country

- New vehicles (New Means of Transport) purchased by a VAT-registered trader from a VAT-registered person in another country

- New vehicles (New Means of Transport) purchased by a VAT-registered trader from a private person in another country

- Vehicles imported into the EU as a result of purchase by an Irish VAT-registered trader

Second-hand vehicles purchased by a VAT-registered trader from a dealer operating the Special or Margin Scheme in another country

Second-hand vehicles purchased from a motor dealer operating under a Special or Margin Scheme for sales of goods in another EU Member State are liable to VAT in that country; e.g. a vehicle purchased from a dealer operating the Margin Scheme in the U.K. is subject to U.K. VAT at 17.5%. This VAT forms part of the purchase price. Any invoice issued under a Special or Margin Scheme will contain an endorsement to the effect that no part of the

VAT charged may be reclaimed. Therefore, a VAT registered trader (other than a motor dealer) will normally not be entitled to recover any VAT on a vehicle purchased from a dealer in another Member State operating under a Special or Margin Scheme. However, if the trader subsequently sells any such vehicle, he or she will be obliged to charge VAT on the sale, despite not having any entitlement to reclaim VAT on the purchase.

A motor dealer does not have to be authorised or have a TAN number in order to avail of the Special Scheme for Second-Hand Vehicles in Ireland. If such a motor dealer purchases a vehicle as stock in trade from a dealer abroad operating a Special or Margin Scheme, then he or she is entitled to recover the residual VAT contained in the purchase price. To support any claim for residual VAT the Irish dealer must have an invoice issued by the supplier in the other Member State which does not show VAT separately and which is endorsed by the supplier to the effect that the vehicle has been sold under the margin scheme/second-hand goods scheme in that Member State.

Any subsequent sale of the vehicle by the Irish dealer must also be under the Special Scheme in Ireland, unless he or she takes the vehicle out of the Scheme and repays the residual VAT.

N.B.: To avoid confusion, it is essential to note that the term 'qualifying vehicle' applies in Irish law only. Where a vehicle is purchased from a dealer in another Member State of the EU, the use of this term alone is not sufficient indication that the vehicle is within the Special or Margin Scheme. A full statement that the invoice does not give rise to a right to input credit is required. When the Irish dealer sells a vehicle on which he or she has claimed residual VAT, the vehicle must be sold on under the Special Scheme, and the end purchaser will not have any entitlement to reclaim VAT on the vehicle.

Occasionally, a foreign dealer may sell a vehicle outside of the Special or Margin Scheme. In this case, the foreign dealer must issue a zero-rated VAT invoice in respect of the vehicle, quoting the purchaser's VAT number. The purchaser then accounts for VAT in his or her next VAT return, and can claim a simultaneous credit. When selling on a vehicle that was purchased outside of the Scheme, the Irish trader may issue a normal VAT invoice if the customer is registered for VAT, and the customer may reclaim the VAT charged, subject to the usual conditions.

A motor auctioneer is deemed to buy and sell the vehicles that pass through the auction. The auctioneer may operate the Special or Margin Scheme in his or her own country, or may sell the vehicles outside of the Scheme, as a VAT registered trader. In either case, the rules set out above will apply equally to an auctioneer. It is important that any vehicle purchased from an auctioneer is accompanied by the correct documentation in order for the purchasing dealer to be entitled to get a refund of VAT.

Second-hand vehicles purchased by a VAT-registered trader from a VAT-registered person in another country other than a dealer

Second-hand vehicles which are purchased by an Irish VAT-registered trader from a VAT-registered supplier in another EU Member State are 'intra-Community acquisitions'. That is, the supplier of the vehicle must issue a zero-rated VAT invoice in respect of the vehicle, quoting the purchasing trader's VAT number. The purchasing trader then accounts for VAT in his or her next VAT return, and can claim a simultaneous credit. If this vehicle is subsequently sold by the Irish trader, the seller must charge VAT on the sale and issue a normal VAT invoice and the purchaser may claim a credit for the VAT charged.

If the sale of the vehicle takes place in the other Member State, and the supplier charges VAT on the sale rather than zero-rating it, then the Irish trader may nonetheless recover the VAT charged once the vehicle has been moved to Ireland. The Irish trader must provide proof to the supplier that the vehicle has been transported to Ireland, and the supplier should then issue a credit note and reissue the invoice at zero per cent VAT.

When selling on a vehicle that was purchased from a VAT-registered person other than a dealer, the Irish trader may issue a normal VAT invoice if the customer is registered for VAT, and the customer may reclaim the VAT charged, subject to the usual conditions.

Second-hand vehicles purchased by a VAT-registered trader from a private person in another country

Where an Irish VAT–registered trader purchases a second-hand vehicle from a private person in another country there are generally no VAT implications on arrival of the vehicle in Ireland. The trader has not been charged VAT, and has no entitlement to recover any VAT.

However, where an unauthorised dealer operating the Special Scheme for Second-Hand Vehicles purchases a second-hand vehicle from a private person in another EU Member State, there will be residual or trapped VAT contained in the price. The purchasing dealer may recover the residual VAT, at the rate that applies in the Member State where the vehicle was registered.

In order to claim this residual VAT, the purchasing dealer must prepare a settlement voucher, to include:

- The name and address of the seller;
- The name and address of the dealer;
- The date of the supply;
- The make, model, engine number, registration number and year of manufacture of the vehicle;
- The total price of the vehicle;
- A declaration signed and dated by the seller of the vehicle that the details on the voucher are accurate; and
- A declaration signed and dated by the seller of the vehicle that he/she is not a VAT-registered person, and/or was not entitled to claim relief in respect of VAT on the vehicle.

This settlement voucher is required to support the dealer's claim to residual VAT. The dealer must give the seller a copy of the completed settlement voucher within 15 days of the purchase. When the Irish dealer sells a vehicle on which he or she has claimed residual VAT, the vehicle must be sold on under the Special Scheme, and the end purchaser will not have any entitlement to reclaim VAT on the vehicle.

New vehicles (New Means of Transport) purchased by a VAT-registered trader from a VAT-registered person in another country

A 'new means of transport' is a technical term which may be used to describe a motor vehicle that has travelled less than 6,000 km or was supplied less than 6 months since it first entered into service (see full definition). Where an Irish VAT-registered trader, including an unauthorised dealer, purchases a new means of transport from a person in another EU country he or she must account for Irish VAT on the vehicle. The VAT-registered foreign supplier issues a zero-rated VAT invoice in respect of the vehicle, quoting the purchaser's VAT number. The irish purchaser then accounts for VAT in his or her next VAT return, and can claim a simultaneous credit.

If the sale of the vehicle takes place in the other Member State, and the supplier charges VAT on the sale rather than zero-rating it, then the Irish trader may nonetheless recover the VAT charged once the vehicle has been moved to Ireland. The Irish trader must provide proof to the supplier that the vehicle has been transported to Ireland, and the supplier should then issue a credit note and reissue the invoice at zero per cent VAT. The Irish trader must then self-account for the VAT on the supply.

When selling on a new means of transport that was purchased from a VAT registered person other than a dealer, the Irish trader must issue a normal VAT invoice if the customer is registered for VAT, and the customer may reclaim the VAT charged, subject to the usual conditions.

New vehicles (New Means of Transport) purchased by a VAT-registered trader from a private person in another country

A 'new means of transport' is a technical term which may be used to describe a motor vehicle that has travelled less than 6,000 km or was supplied less than 6 months since it first entered into service (see full definition). Where a VAT-registered trader, including an unauthorised dealer, purchases a 'new means of transport' from a private person in another country, this is regarded as an 'intra-Community acquisition' of the vehicle. The trader must account for Irish VAT on the vehicle even though the supplier cannot charge VAT. The purchasing trader simply accounts for VAT in the VAT return following the purchase, and may be able to claim a simultaneous credit if the vehicle is purchased as stock-in-trade, or is 'commercial'.

The private person in another country who sells a new means of transport to an Irish VAT-registered trader may be entitled to reclaim the VAT charged to them on the original purchase of the vehicle, subject to the rules applying in their own country. This will normally be dependent on proof that VAT has been paid on the vehicle in Ireland.

When selling on a new means of transport purchased from a private person in another country, the Irish trader may issue a normal VAT invoice if the customer is registered for VAT, and the customer may reclaim the VAT charged, subject to the usual conditions.

Vehicles imported into the EU as a result of purchase by an Irish VAT-registered trader

Vehicles purchased from suppliers outside the EU are referred to as imports. These are liable to Customs Duty and to VAT at the point where they first enter the EU Customs are responsible for taxes and duties on imported goods, and all VAT and duty is payable to Customs. A VAT registered dealer can reclaim this VAT in his or her VAT return. Customs duty cannot be recovered.

Vehicles purchased from foreign sellers by private individuals

Any vehicle purchased abroad and brought in to the country by a private individual is liable to VRT, and will be liable to VAT if it is a 'new means of transport'. In this section, the term 'second-hand vehicle' applies generally to pre-owned vehicles. However, it does not include a pre-owned vehicle brought in to the State that was either supplied less than 6 months after entering into service, or has travelled 6,000 kilometers or less. Such vehicles, even if they were previously owned and registered in another country, are categorised as 'new means of transport', and are always liable to VAT in Ireland.

An easy way of calculating the VRT liability on any vehicle is to use the VRT Calculator on the Revenue website. The VRO office will confirm the amount of VRT payable. It should be noted that VRT is calculated on the Open Market Selling Price (OMSP) of a vehicle, rather than the actual purchase price.

- Second-hand vehicles purchased by a private individual from a VAT-registered trader, including a motor dealer, in another country
- Second-hand vehicles purchased by a private individual from a private individual in another country
- New vehicles (New Means of Transport) purchased by a private individual from a VAT-registered person, including a motor dealer, in another country
- New vehicles (New Means of Transport) purchased by a private individual from a private individual in another country
- Vehicles imported into the EU as a result of purchase by a private individual

Second-hand vehicles purchased by a private individual from a VAT-registered trader, including a motor dealer, in another country

Where a private individual purchases a second-hand vehicle from a motor dealer or any VAT-registered trader in another country, the price will generally include any VAT or other tax chargeable in that country. This VAT cannot be reclaimed. There is no VAT liability in Ireland. The vehicle must be registered by the end of the day following the day on which it arrives in Ireland. This must be done at the local VRO office (MS Word, 51KB). The VRT liability can be calculated using the VRT Calculator on the Revenue website.

Second-hand vehicles purchased by a private individual from a private individual in another country

Where a private individual in Ireland purchases a second-hand vehicle (but not a 'new means of transport' – see below) from a private person in another country, there is no VAT element included in the price, nor is there any VAT liability in Ireland. The vehicle must be registered by the end of the day following the day on which it arrives in Ireland. This must be done at the local VRO office (MS Word, 51KB). The VRT liability can be calculated using the VRT Calculator on the Revenue website.

New vehicles (New Means of Transport) purchased by a private individual from a VAT-registered person, including a motor dealer, in another country

A 'new means of transport' is a technical term which may be used to describe a motor vehicle that has travelled less than 6,000 km or was supplied less than 6 months since it first entered into service (see full definition). It is important to note that the operative date in determining whether a means of transport comes within the time limits is the date on which it was purchased by the current owner. The distance travelled, however, is calculated by reference to when the vehicle arrives in Ireland.

For example;

• If a person purchases a 4-month old car in the U.K., and brings it into Ireland when it is 7 months old, then at the time of supply it was less than 6 months old. Regardless of the distance travelled, this vehicle is a new means of transport, and is liable to Irish VAT.

• If a person purchases a 7-month old car in the U.K., which, at the time of supply in the U.K. had travelled only 5,000 kilometres, but had travelled 6001 kilometres in total by the time it arrived in Ireland, the vehicle is not a new means of transport.

Where a private individual purchases a new means of transport from a VAT-registered person in another country it must be registered by the end of the day following the day on which it arrives in Ireland. This must be done at the local VRO office (MS Word, 51KB). The VRT liability can be calculated using the VRT Calculator on the Revenue website. The vehicle is also liable to Irish VAT on registration, and this VAT is payable to the VRO office. The VRT is calculated on the Open Market Selling Price (OMSP) of a vehicle, rather than the actual purchase price. The value for calculating VAT is the price charged for the vehicle, converted to Euro where necessary.

If the seller also charged VAT or an equivalent tax on the sale of the vehicle in the other country, then this can normally be reclaimed from the foreign supplier, once the vehicle is registered and VAT has been paid in Ireland. The purchaser must send proof of registration and payment of Irish VAT to the foreign supplier, who will then arrange repayment of the foreign VAT (or equivalent tax) subject to the regulations in that country. However, it is important to note that the refund of VAT from the foreign supplier is subject to the laws and regulations in force in that country, which may differ significantly from the Irish laws. This means that in certain circumstances a person bringing a vehicle into Ireland, and therefore obliged to pay VAT in Ireland, may be unable to obtain a refund of VAT paid in another country. This will result in VAT being paid twice on the same vehicle. It is essential that any person who intends to purchase a new vehicle in another EU country, with the intention of bringing it into Ireland, ensures that he or she will be able to obtain a refund of any VAT paid in the other country, as there is no provision whereby VAT properly charged in Ireland can be refunded to a private individual.

For example, Revenue has been advised that the current position in the U.K. is that a dealer will not refund VAT on a vehicle purchased there and subsequently registered in Ireland -

• If, at the time of purchase in the UK, the dealer was not notified that the vehicle was going to be brought out of the country;

• If the vehicle was not brought out of the UK within two months of purchase;

• If the original invoice shows a UK address for the purchaser.

Similar positions may be held in other EU countries, and details should be obtained from the relevant tax authorities in those countries.

New vehicles (New Means of Transport) purchased by a private individual from a private individual in another country

A 'new means of transport' is a technical term which may be used to describe a motor vehicle that has travelled less than 6,000 km or was supplied less than 6 months since it first entered into service (see full definition). It is important to note that the operative date in determining whether a means of transport comes within the time limits is the date on which it was purchased by the current owner. The distance travelled, however, is calculated by reference to when the vehicle arrives in Ireland.

For example;

• If a person purchases a 4-month old car in the U.K., and brings it into Ireland when it is 7 months old, then at the time of supply it was less than 6 months old. Regardless of the distance travelled, this vehicle is a new means of transport, and is liable to Irish VAT

• If a person purchases a 7-month old car in the U.K., which, at the time of supply in the U.K. had travelled only 5,000 kilometres, but had travelled 6001 kilometres in total by the time it arrived in Ireland, the vehicle is not a new means of transport.

Where a private person purchases a new means of transport from a private person in another country, there is no VAT chargeable on that transaction.

When the vehicle is brought into Ireland, it must be registered by the end of the day following the day on which it arrives. This must be done at the local VRO office (MS Word, 51KB). The VRT liability can be calculated using the VRT Calculator on the Revenue website. The vehicle is also liable to Irish VAT on registration, and this VAT is payable to the VRO office. The VRT is calculated on the Open Market Selling Price (OMSP) of a vehicle, rather than the actual purchase price. The value for calculating VAT is the price charged for the vehicle, converted to Euro where necessary.

Vehicles imported into the EU as a result of purchase by a private individual

Vehicles purchased from suppliers outside the EU are referred to as imports. Where a private individual purchases a vehicle from a person outside the EU, he or she is liable to Customs Duty and to VAT at the point where the vehicle first enters the EU. These must be paid to Customs before the vehicle will be released. It should be noted that the value of the vehicle for Customs purposes may include freight costs.

The vehicle must be registered, and VRT paid, by the end of the day following the day on which it clears Customs. This must be done at the local VRO office (MS Word, 51KB). The VRT liability can be calculated using the VRT Calculator on the Revenue website. The VRT is calculated on the Open Market Selling Price (OMSP) of a vehicle, rather than the actual purchase price. While a vehicle is normally also liable to Irish VAT on registration, proof that VAT has been paid to Customs will be accepted.

Motor vehicles supplied by private individuals

Private individuals are not registered for VAT, and do not use vehicles owned by them in the course or furtherance of a business. Therefore, they are not entitled or obliged to charge VAT on the sale of any such vehicles. This applies even where the individual had an entitlement under a special repayment scheme to recover VAT on the purchase of the vehicle (see Recovery of VAT and/or VRT by Purchasers not Registered for VAT). Private individuals resident in the State are not entitled to hold unregistered vehicles. Any vehicle offered for sale by a private individual should be already registered, and VRT should not be an issue.

Motor vehicles supplied by dealers without TAN numbers

The possession of a Trader Account Number (TAN) only affects the way in which the dealer operates VRT. The VAT obligations remain unchanged for dealers whether or not they have a TAN number, and such dealers may also avail of any of the special VAT schemes referred to in this leaflet. A dealer without a TAN number may not defer the registration of vehicles that are held as stock-in-trade. Where such a dealer acquires a vehicle that is not registered in the State (either new or second-hand - see also Vehicles purchased from foreign sellers by Irish VAT-registered traders), and the vehicle is not sold on by the end of the next working day, then the dealer remains the owner of the vehicle, and must register it in his/her own name. This registration is treated as a self-supply of the vehicle, as if the vehicle was taken out of stock by the dealer for his/her own use or for use as a demonstration model (see Registration of vehicles by dealers/distributors in their own names).

This means that, while a dealer, with or without a TAN number, is entitled to recover any VAT charged on the acquisition of a vehicle as stock-in-trade, following self-registration the dealer will be liable to repay any VAT claimed by him/her, and any subsequent sale of the vehicle must come under the Special Scheme for Second-Hand Vehicles set out in Special scheme for second-hand motor vehicles. It should also be noted that when such a vehicle is sold, under no circumstances may any portion of the sale price be regarded as attributable to VRT and stripped out from the sale price prior to calculating the VAT.

Motor vehicles supplied by traders who are not motor dealers

Ordinary VAT registered traders who are not motor dealers may acquire motor vehicles (such as vans, trucks and company cars) for their own business use, and which they later resell. These vehicles are not acquired as stock-in-trade, but for the purpose of carrying on the normal activities of the business.

If the trader was entitled to recover VAT on the acquisition of the vehicle (see Recovery of Tax on the Purchase of Motor Vehicles) then the subsequent resale of the vehicle is liable to VAT on the full amount received for the vehicle. If the trader was not entitled to recover VAT on the acquisition of the vehicle, then the subsequent sale of the vehicle is not liable to VAT. This applies generally to non-deductible vehicles, such as passenger motorcars. However, it also applies where a VAT registered trader is reselling a commercial vehicle that he or she purchased at a time prior to registration for VAT (e.g. the trader was below the turnover threshold for registration at the time of purchase). In this case, the trader may be required to show that he or she did not recover VAT on the original purchase.

Hiring and Leasing of Vehicles

- Short-term and long-term hire

- Insurance, damage waivers, maintenance etc.

- Accessories supplied with a hired vehicle

- Recovery of VAT charged on hire/leasing payments

- Recovery of VAT & VRT by hire/lease providers

Short-term and long-term hire

Short-term hire is an agreement for the hire of a motor vehicle to a person, not exceeding a total of 5 weeks hire in any 12-month period. This is liable to VAT at 13.5%. The hiring of a motor vehicle for more than 5 weeks in any twelve-month period is liable to VAT at 21.5%.

N.B.: It is important to note, when determining the rate of VAT, that the 5 weeks hire do not have to be consecutive, and that the agreement does not have to relate to a specific vehicle. The hiring of the same vehicle, or of a number of vehicles of the same kind, for a single period or a number of non-consecutive periods totalling more than five weeks in any 12 months, is 'long-term hire' and is liable to VAT at 21.5%.

Insurance, damage waivers, maintenance etc.

The amount that is liable to VAT is the full amount that the hiring or leasing company is entitled to receive under the contract. This includes any amounts paid by the customer in respect of insurance, accidental damage waivers, cleaning, maintenance, etc., all of which are liable to VAT at the same rate as the main contract for hire of the vehicle. (Payments specifically for petrol are always liable at 21.5 per cent.) However, if the customer enters into an insurance policy with an insurance company or intermediary at the time of hiring, and the exact amount of the insurance payment is collected by the hire/leasing company on behalf of the insurance company or intermediary, then, and only in these circumstances, this amount may be treated as being an exempt payment in respect of insurance.

Accessories supplied with a hired vehicle

Where vehicle accessories, such as global positioning systems, roof-boxes etc. are supplied with hired or leased vehicles then the rate of VAT that applies to the main contract for hire of the vehicle (13.5% for short-term, 21.5% for long-term) will apply to any extra charge in respect of the accessory. This is the case even where a separate charge is made for these accessories.

Recovery of VAT charged on hire/leasing payments

Any traders registered for VAT are entitled to recover any VAT charged to them on the acquisition of 'commercial' vehicles (e.g. vans, trucks, crew-cabs etc.) insofar as these are used for business purposes. This includes the right to recover any VAT charged on the hire, leasing or hire-purchase of vehicles.

VAT-registered traders generally may not recover VAT incurred on the hire, leasing or purchase of vehicles for use in their businesses where these vehicles are classed as Category A for VRT purposes, i.e. non-commercial passenger cars or motorcycles. However, a trader may be entitled to recover VAT on vehicles for use as stock-in-trade, or in a driving school or car-hire business - see Recovery of Tax on the Purchase of Motor Vehicles for further details.

Recovery of VAT & VRT by hire/lease providers

A company that operates a business hiring or leasing out cars or other vehicles is entitled to claim back VAT on any vehicles purchased or hired by it for onward hiring to customers. In other words, vehicles purchased for hiring out are treated in the same way as stock-in-trade. The hire company must charge and account for VAT on any subsequent sale or disposal of vehicles that were used for hiring out.

Vehicle hire companies may also recover a portion of the VRT charged on the registration of certain non-commercial (category A) cars and motorcycles purchased for onward hiring or leasing. Details of the requirements and procedures for repayments are contained in Statement of Practice SP1/97 - Repayment of Vehicle Registration Tax in respect of Vehicles acquired for leasing or hiring or providing instructions in the driving of Vehicles (PDF, 62KB) . There is also a Statement of Practice SP1/98 - Repayment of Vehicle Registration Tax in respect of Motor Vehicles used solely for hiring to others under short term self-drive contracts (PDF, 159KB). dealing specifically with traders engaged in short-term hire. Further information and application forms can also be obtained from:

The Central Repayments Office,
Freepost,
M: TEK II Building, Armagh Road,
Monaghan,
Co. Monaghan.
Phone: Lo-Call 1890-60 60 61, also 047-62100, or by Fax at 047-62199.

Work on Vehicles, Including Repair and Maintenance

In the context of this section only, a new motor vehicle is one that has not been registered (in any country) at the time that a service, repair, alteration, conversion or paint-job is carried out. This is different from the definition of new means of transport used in the parts of this leaflet dealing with buying and selling vehicles.

- Servicing, repair and maintenance
- Alterations and conversions
- Painting (including logos)

Servicing, repair and maintenance

Any service, maintenance or repair that is carried out on any vehicle, whether new or second-hand, is liable to VAT at 13.5%. This rate also covers the supply of most parts essential to the service, maintenance or repair, even if the supply of these parts would normally be liable at 21.5%. However, the 13.5% cannot be applied to the supply of certain parts and accessories, which are always liable at 21.5%. The list below sets out the parts, or types of parts, the supply of which is always liable to VAT at 21.5% (this list is not exhaustive – items similar to those mentioned at (1) and (2) will also be liable at 21.5%):

1. Accessories such as radios/CD players, speakers, car-phones, GPS and similar navigation systems, alarms, seat covers and floor mats;

2. Attachments such as spoilers, body kits, roof racks, tow bars and fake exhausts;

3. Batteries;

4. Tyres, tyre cases, interchangeable tyre treads, inner tubes and tyre flaps, for wheels of all kinds.

The two-thirds' rule (see * The two-thirds' rule) is not applied in the case of the bona fide service, repair or maintenance of motor vehicles. The 13.5% VAT rate still applies to the labour and other goods supplied in the course of the service, repair or maintenance, regardless of the value of the goods supplied at 21.5%. The repair or maintenance of any accessories and attachments that were fitted previously is also liable at 13.5%, and again the two-thirds rule does not apply. For example, the supply and fitting of a GPS to a vehicle is liable at 21.5%, but the subsequent repair or maintenance of the GPS is liable at 13.5%.

It is important to note that the supply and fitting of the parts or accessories set out above is not regarded, in itself, as repair or maintenance, or as the alteration of the vehicle (see Alterations and conversions). For a job consisting solely of the fitting of an accessory, the 21.5% rate of VAT applies to both the supply of the part, and any associated labour costs. For example, in the case of the repair or fitting of a spoiler in the course of the repair or maintenance of a vehicle, the part is liable at 21.5%, and the labour at 13.5%. In the case of the fitting of a new body kit in circumstances other than repair or maintenance, both the parts and the labour are liable at 21.5%. The 21.5% VAT rate also applies to all other parts supplied outside the context of service, maintenance or repair, including all over-the-counter sales.

Vehicle recovery services such as the towing, securing and temporary storage of vehicles are generally liable at 21.5%. If a vehicle is recovered and repaired as part of a single contract, any amount charged separately for the recovery is liable at 21.5%, even if the repair work is liable at 13.5%. Long term storage and 'garaging' of vehicles is also liable at 21.5%.

Alterations and conversions

The alteration of a vehicle involves changing the physical characteristics of the vehicle, but not changing its essential nature. Alterations are liable to VAT at 21.5% on new vehicles, and at 13.5% on second-hand vehicles, subject to the two-thirds' rule (see * The two-thirds' rule). The following work on a vehicle constitutes alteration (this list is not exhaustive – operations similar to those set out below will also be liable at 13.5% if carried out on second-hand vehicles):

- The fitting of a sunroof;

- The conversion of a vehicle from a commercial jeep or van to a car;

- The conversion of a vehicle from a van to a minibus;

- The conversion of a vehicle from one fuel system to another, e.g. from petrol to LPG

However, where a trader builds up a vehicle using parts that have been supplied by the customer, then this is liable to VAT at 21.5% in all cases, being regarded as similar to the supply of a new vehicle. An example is where a coachbuilder builds an ambulance using a chassis supplied by a customer, and delivers the finished or nearly finished ambulance back to the customer after it has been worked on.

It should be noted that the conversion or alteration of a vehicle post-registration might involve a change in the VRT category of the vehicle – for example, a small van may be converted from Category B (commercial) to Category A (passenger) by the insertion of seats, footwells, rear windows, etc. In the case of any vehicle altered or converted in this manner, the person who has possession of the vehicle at the time must notify the local VRO office and, if necessary, it will be reclassified, and additional VRT may be payable. Where the conversion has been carried out by, for example, a garage or mechanic, it is their responsibility to notify the VRO office that the conversion has been carried out.

The VRO office will subsequently notify the Department of Environment, Heritage and Local Government Vehicle Licensing Unit of the change in the vehicle category, and the registration certificate will be updated accordingly.

* The two-thirds' rule provides that the supply of goods made as part of the supply of a service is liable at the same rate as the supply of services (13.5% in this case) unless the VAT exclusive cost of the goods to the supplier exceeds two-thirds of the total VAT exclusive charge to the customer. In other words, if the VAT exclusive cost of a sun-roof itself exceeds two-thirds of the total VAT exclusive cost of supplying and fitting the sun-roof, then it is treated as a supply of goods liable at 21.5% VAT.

Painting (including logos)

The rate of VAT on painting depends on whether the vehicle is new at the time the work is carried out. Again, in this context, a new vehicle is one that has not been registered at the time that the work is carried out. If a vehicle manufacturer or distributor arranges for the paint colour to be changed or repaired, or for a logo to be included, on any vehicle prior to its first registration, then any extra cost to the customer is regarded as part of the purchase price of the vehicle, and is liable to VAT at 21.5%. In the case of a second-hand vehicle (subsequent to purchase and registration), then Revenue are concessionally prepared to accept that this constitutes a form of maintenance and is liable to VAT at 13.5%. A paint shop or similar trader may only charge the 13.5% rate if they have sufficient proof that any vehicle was registered at the time that the work was carried out. Otherwise the 21.5% rate must be charged. If the colour of a vehicle is changed subsequent to registration, the owner should notify the Vehicle Licensing (Motor Tax Unit), Department of Environment, Heritage and Local Government, Shannon, Co. Clare in order that the details on the registration certificate of the vehicle may be updated.

Recovery of Tax on the Purchase of Motor Vehicles

Recovery of VAT by Motor Dealers

Motor dealers who are registered for VAT are entitled to recover any VAT properly incurred and invoiced on the purchase of vehicles for use as stock-in-trade, including vehicles acquired from abroad.

In addition, in the case of commercial vehicles (i.e. generally other than VRT Category A vehicles or motor cycles) the dealer is entitled to recover some or all of the VAT included in the invoice if the vehicle is to be used in the course of the dealer's business, even if it is not purchased as stock-in-trade.

The amount of VAT that can be recovered will reflect the extent to which the vehicle is used for the business.

Restrictions on the recovery of VAT for non-commercial vehicles (i.e. generally VRT Category A vehicles and motor-cycles) purchased for use as demonstration models or otherwise self-registered by the dealer are dealt with in Registration of vehicles by dealers/distributors in their own names.

Motor dealers are also entitled to recover some or all of the VAT incurred on expenses such as the repair, maintenance or servicing of vehicles.

Paperwork and Documentation

As with all claims for the recovery of VAT, the issuing and retention of documentation is of great importance. A motor dealer may purchase a vehicle from a number of different sources, and the paperwork requirements and procedures will vary accordingly. There are relatively few documents involved, the most important being the VAT invoice, the Special Scheme VAT invoice and the declaration, to be signed by certain sellers, that they had no entitlement to recover VAT. A motor dealer who fails to get and retain correct documentation for each purchase will not be entitled to recover VAT on the purchase of the vehicle, although he or she will still be liable to VAT on the subsequent resale.

If a dealer buys a motor vehicle from a VAT-registered supplier in the State (other than another dealer using the Special Scheme for second-hand motor vehicles) the supplier must issue a VAT invoice, dated by reference to the date of transfer of ownership of the vehicle to the dealer. VAT is liable at 21.5% on the full sale price. If the vehicle is to be used as stock-in-trade, or is a commercial vehicle to be used in the business, the dealer is entitled to reclaim the VAT charged, and will include it in the 'T2' box in the next VAT return, to set off against any VAT liability he or she may have.

With regard to a vehicle purchased from a foreign VAT-registered supplier who is not using the Special or Margin Scheme for sales, the dealer will give the foreign supplier his or her VAT registration number, and the supplier will issue an invoice charging zero per cent VAT. The dealer must then 'self-account' for VAT on the transaction – he or she must calculate the VAT due on the vehicle at 21.5% of the sale price, and include this in the 'T1 box' on the VAT return. If the vehicle is to be used as stock-in-trade, or is a commercial vehicle to be used in the business, then a cancelling amount may be included in the 'T2 box'.

If a dealer buys a second-hand vehicle from a private individual (e.g. by way of a trade-in), or from another dealer using the Special Scheme, the dealer can claim a deduction of the residual VAT. There is specific documentation required with regard to the Special Scheme for Second-Hand Vehicles. A dealer must ensure that all this documentation is correct before claiming a deduction for VAT. Full details of the documentation required are set out in Invoicing – the purchase of a qualifying second-hand vehicle in the Special Scheme and Invoicing - the sale of a qualifying second-hand vehicle in the Special Scheme.

Recovery of VAT & VRT by Driving Schools

Driving training schools (which must charge 13.5% VAT on driving lessons) can recover VAT on all vehicles purchased to be used by them for the purpose of tuition. In addition, driving schools may recover a portion of the VRT charged on the registration of certain non-commercial vehicles (generally category A cars and motorcycles). Details of the requirements and procedures for repayments are contained in Statement of Practice SP1/97 - Repayment of Vehicle Registration Tax in respect of Vehicles acquired for leasing or hiring or providing instructions in the driving of Vehicles (PDF, 62KB). Further information and application forms can also be obtained from:

The Central Repayments Office,
Freepost,
M: TEK II Building, Armagh Road,
Monaghan,
Co. Monaghan.
Phone: Lo-Call 1890-60 60 61, also 047-38010, or by Fax at 047-82782.

Recovery of VAT by Other VAT-Registered Traders

The general rule for VAT-registered traders is that they are entitled to recover any VAT charged to them on purchases made for business purposes. However, in the case of motor vehicles, there are some limitations to this entitlement. Any VAT-registered trader is generally entitled to reclaim VAT charged on the purchase of a motor vehicle for use in his or her business if the vehicle comes within the definitions of Category B or Category C vehicles for the purposes of VRT. If such a vehicle is used exclusively for business purposes, a full refund of the VAT is allowed. The refund should be claimed in the next VAT return following the purchase of the vehicle. If the vehicle is used partly for business and partly for non-business use, then the trader will recover a portion of the VAT incurred to reflect the amount of business use. If the vehicle is purchased from a dealer operating the special scheme set out in Special Scheme for second-hand motor vehicles, then the purchaser has no right to recover any VAT charged. In this case, the invoice will clearly indicate that no recovery of VAT is allowed.

VAT registered traders are also entitled to recover some or all of the VAT incurred on expenses such as the purchase of diesel (but not petrol), road tolls, and the repair or servicing of vehicles.

Up to the end of 2008, a trader was not able to recover any VAT on non-commercial or Category A vehicles [which includes cars (saloons, estates, hatchbacks, convertibles, coupes, MPVs, Jeeps, etc.) and minibuses with less than 12 permanently fitted passenger seats], even where they were 'company cars' or otherwise used for business purposes. Nor was there any entitlement to reclaim VAT on motorcycles, motor scooters or any similar vehicles. The only traders entitled to reclaim VAT on the purchase of any of these vehicles were motor dealers who purchased them as stock-in-trade; driving schools that purchased them for teaching purposes; car-hire companies that purchased them for hiring out; and financial services companies selling vehicles by hire-purchase arrangements, or leasing vehicles.

However, this position was changed with effect from 1 January 2009. With effect from that date, any VAT-registered trader other than those mentioned above is entitled to recover some of the VAT charged on the purchase or hire of vehicles coming within VRT Category A, subject to certain conditions, including:

- This provision only applies to vehicles registered from 1 January 2009;

- A maximum of 20% of the VAT incurred can be reclaimed. In the case of hire or leasing charges, a maximum of 20% of the VAT on the monthly leasing charges may be reclaimed;

- VAT can only be reclaimed for vehicles that have a level of CO_2 emissions of less than 156g/km (i.e. CO_2 emission bands A, B and C);

- At least 60% of the vehicle's use must be for business purposes;

- If the business is exempt from VAT (e.g. taxi, limousine and other passenger transport) then no VAT can be reclaimed. Partly exempt businesses can reclaim some, but not all, of the 20%;

- If VAT is reclaimed on a vehicle purchased under this provision, some or all of the VAT must be repaid to Revenue if the vehicle is disposed of (by sale or otherwise) within two years;

- There is no need to charge VAT on the disposal of the vehicle, even though VAT was reclaimed under this provision;

- If the vehicle is sold or traded-in to a motor-dealer, the special scheme for second-hand vehicles will apply, and the dealer can reclaim any residual VAT.

Full details of how the recovery of this VAT can be achieved, including examples, are available in the information leaflet Deduction of VAT for Certain Business Cars.

Recovery of VAT under Hire-Purchase Agreements

A hire-purchase agreement is one whereby a customer hires a vehicle from a provider (usually a bank or finance company) for a specified period of time, with an option to purchase the vehicle after the period of hire. An agreement is drawn up providing for regular repayments of equal amounts. Generally, the actual legal transfer of ownership of the vehicle occurs with the last payment. For VAT purposes, however, the supply of the vehicle takes place at the time that it is handed over by the supplier to the customer. That is, a customer who is registered for VAT receives a VAT invoice (from the hire-purchase provider) for the value of the vehicle, not including any finance charges that might apply. If the vehicle is a commercial one then the VAT registered customer is entitled to recover the full amount of the VAT at the time that he or she takes delivery of the vehicle. The actual legal transfer of ownership of the vehicle (at the time of the final payment) is therefore ignored for VAT purposes. If a second-hand vehicle is sold by hire-purchase arrangement, then, subject to the conditions set out, the hire-purchase provider may avail of the special scheme for motor dealers set out in Special Scheme for second-hand motor vehicles. In this situation, the bank, finance company etc., may recover any residual or trapped VAT, and will issue a special invoice with the onward supply of the vehicle. A customer acquiring such a vehicle will not be entitled to recover any VAT charged to him/her. The VAT treatment of hire-purchase providers changed with effect from 1 May 2007. An information leaflet setting out the new treatment is available on the Revenue website at Hire Purchase Transactions.

Recovery of VAT and/or VRT by Purchasers not Registered for VAT

A person who is not registered for VAT and who buys a motor vehicle is generally not entitled to recover any VAT charged. However, in certain circumstances VAT may be repaid, as set out below:

- Repayment of VAT on touring coaches

- Repayment of tax on motor vehicles for use by or for disabled persons

Repayment of VAT on touring coaches

The transport of passengers is an exempt activity, and a person carrying on this activity cannot register for or reclaim VAT. However, in accordance with regulations set out in Statutory Instrument 98/1996 (VAT Refund Order No. 28) a coach operator can reclaim VAT on the purchase, lease or hire of touring coaches, where the coaches are used

- To carry tourists,

- Under contracts for group transport, and

- The coaches come within the following specifications:

    - Single-deck touring coaches having dimensions as designated by the manufacturer of not less than 2,700 millimetres in height, not less than

8,000 millimetres in length, not less than 775 millimetres in floor height and with an underfloor luggage capacity of not less than 3 cubic metres; or

- Double-deck touring coaches having dimensions as designated by the manufacturer of not more than 4,300 millimetres in height and not less than 10,000 millimetres in length.

Repayment claims should be entered on form VAT 71 - Claim for Refund of Value-Added Tax (VAT) on Certain Touring Coaches under the Value Added Tax (Refund of Tax) (No. 28) Order, 1996 (as amended) (PDF, 57KB) , and submitted to the following address:

VAT Unregistered Repayments,
Revenue Commissioners,
Floor 3 River House,
Charlotte's Quay,
Limerick.

Form VAT 71 - Claim for Refund of Value-Added Tax (VAT) on Certain Touring Coaches under the Value Added Tax (Refund of Tax) (No. 28) Order, 1996 (as amended) (PDF, 57KB) can be obtained from the Revenue website or by contacting the repayments section at unregvat@revenue.ie

Repayment of tax on motor vehicles for use by or for disabled persons

There is provision for the repayment, subject to conditions, of VAT, VRT and fuel excise duty in respect of vehicles used by drivers or for passengers with disabilities. Registration of motor vehicles for the transport of drivers and passengers with disabilities without the payment of Vehicle Registration Tax may be allowed - the appropriate Form (DD1) - Tax Relief in Relation to Vehicles Purchased for Use by People with Disabilities (PDF, 32KB) is available from the Revenue website or can be obtained by contacting the repayments section at:

The Central Repayments Office,
Freepost,
M: TEK II Building,
Armagh Road,
Monaghan,
Co. Monaghan.

The form can also be ordered by phone from Lo-Call 1890-60 60 61, also 047-38010, or by Fax at 047-82782. Once relief from VRT is granted, the Central Repayments Office will also arrange for repayment of VAT incurred on the purchase of the vehicle. Excise duty on fuel used in motor vehicles for the transport of drivers and passengers with disabilities can also be reclaimed - the appropriate Form DD3 - Claim for Repayment of Excise Duty on Fuel used in Motor Vehicles for the Transport of Drivers & Passengers with Disabilities (PDF, 57KB) is available on the Revenue website or can be obtained by contacting the repayments office at the above numbers.

Useful Terms and Definitions

- Agricultural Machinery

- Commercial and Non-Commercial Vehicles
- Importation
- Intra-Community Acquisitions and Supplies
- Member State
- Motor Dealer
- New Means of Transport
- New Motor Vehicle
- Private Individual
- Qualifying Vehicles
- Registration for VRT
- Residual VAT
- Second-Hand or Used Motor Vehicle
- Self-registered vehicles
- Special Scheme for Second-Hand Motor Vehicles
- Trade-In
- Value Added Tax (VAT)
- Vehicle Registration Tax

Agricultural Machinery

Agricultural machinery is equipment or machinery used by a farmer entitled to the flat-rate addition in the course of his or her normal farming activities as defined in the Fifth Schedule to the VAT Act. This definition also covers commercial vehicles used in the course of the farming business: See Scheme for agricultural machinery purchased by dealers.

Commercial and non-Commercial Vehicles

The term 'commercial vehicle' does not occur in VAT law, and therefore there is no strict definition of the term. Nonetheless, when a trader intends to purchase a vehicle, the questions are often asked "Is it a commercial vehicle?", and "can I get my VAT back on it?" Traders are entitled to recover VAT on a number of different types of vehicles (to the extent that the vehicles are used for business purposes). It is these which are often referred to as 'commercial vehicles', and this term denotes vehicles that are deductible for VAT, i.e., any trader registered for VAT may reclaim the VAT charged to him or her on the purchase or hire of the vehicle.

Whether a trader can reclaim VAT on the purchase of a vehicle depends on four things:

1. Is the trader registered for VAT and generally entitled to claim it back?

2. Is the vehicle to be used for the purposes of a VAT-registered business?

3. Is the vehicle of a category that allows a repayment to be made?

4.　　Was VAT charged on the sale of the vehicle?

We will assume that the answer to questions (1) and (2) is 'Yes', and deal with questions (3) and (4) below.

Vehicle Categories

VAT legislation does not generally allow a repayment of VAT to any person who purchases (other than as stock-in-trade) any motor vehicle designed or constructed for carrying people by road. Nor is any VAT repayment allowed in respect of sports motor vehicles, estate cars, station wagons, motor cycles, motor scooters, mopeds and auto cycles whether or not they are designed and constructed for carrying people by road. However, repayment may be allowed in respect of vehicles designed and constructed for the carriage of more than 16 persons (inclusive of the driver), invalid carriages and other vehicles of a type designed for use by invalids and infirm persons.

For practical purposes, an attempt has been made to match the VAT legislation to the VRT registration categories. Motor vehicles are divided into a number of different categories for VRT purposes. Vehicles may be liable to different rates of VRT and different registration procedures depending on the category. Vehicles used for commercial purposes will generally come within Categories B and C, and will be liable to VRT at lower rates than Category A vehicles. Further details of the VRT Categories are available on the Revenue website.

Vehicles within VRT Categories B & C, such as vans, lorries, pick-ups and crew-cabs are generally deductible for VAT, and these are often referred to as commercial vehicles for VAT purposes. However, buses or minibuses suitable for carrying between 12 and 16 persons (including the driver) are not generally deductible for VAT, although they come within Category C. (Buses or minibuses are not usually deductible in any case, as they are normally used for the exempt activity of carrying passengers. However, for example, a company that purchased a bus, suitable for carrying more than 16 persons, to transport its own staff between worksites would be entitled to reclaim some or all of the VAT.)

Vehicles that come within VRT Category A [which includes cars (saloons, estates, hatchbacks, convertibles, coupes, MPVs, Jeeps, etc.) and minibuses with less than 12 permanently fitted passenger seats] are not generally deductible, and neither are motorcycles, motor scooters or similar vehicles of all kinds. The only traders entitled to reclaim VAT on these vehicles are those who purchase them as stock-in-trade (see Recovery of VAT by Motor Dealers), for use in a driving school (see Recovery of VAT & VRT by Driving Schools), or for use in a car hire business (see Hiring and Leasing of Vehicles).

Vehicles that come within VRT Category D, and other vehicles not in Categories A, B, or C may be deductible, depending on whether the purchasers are registered for VAT and the uses to which the vehicles are put.

Purchasing & selling commercial vehicles

Where a dealer (or other VAT-registered trader) sells a commercial vehicle to a VAT-registered purchaser, the purchaser will normally seek to recover the VAT element of the purchase price. A trader may only reclaim VAT charged to him or her on the purchase of a commercial vehicle if the seller issues a VAT invoice that allows a VAT deduction (a 'normal' VAT invoice).

If a motor dealer sells any vehicle, that would otherwise be deductible, through the 'Special Scheme for second-hand motor vehicles' then the dealer must issue an invoice containing an endorsement specifically disallowing any right for the purchaser to deduct VAT. If a dealer issues a 'normal' invoice in respect of a vehicle in the Special Scheme, this has the effect of taking the vehicle out of the Scheme, and the dealer will need to make an adjustment for any residual VAT previously claimed.

Where a VAT-registered trader sells a vehicle, by way of trade-in or otherwise, on which VAT has been claimed back, the trader must issue a VAT invoice, and account for VAT on the sale (see Motor vehicles supplied by traders who are not motor dealers).

Importation

Importing a vehicle means bringing it into the State from any place outside the European Union. VAT is due on imports at the point where they enter the EU, and is normally paid directly to Customs before the goods are released. Imports include vehicles that enter the EU in another country and are trans-shipped from there to Ireland.

Intra-Community Acquisitions

An intra-Community acquisition is a transaction that results in a person in Ireland being obliged to account for Irish VAT on a vehicle purchased or otherwise acquired from a person in another EU Member State. This happens in the case of:

1.   Any 'new means of transport' supplied by any person, including a private individual, in another Member State and dispatched or transported by them, or by the purchaser, into the State. This includes a 'new means of transport' that enters the EU as an import in a Member State other than Ireland, but is transported on to Ireland. A 'new means of transport' is always liable to VAT in the country where it is to be used, regardless of where, by whom and from whom it is purchased.

2.   Any other means of transport supplied by a VAT registered person in any other Member State and dispatched or transported by them to a person carrying on business in Ireland, but NOT INCLUDING any such vehicle sold under the Special Scheme or Margin Scheme for second-hand goods in that Member State. These are liable to VAT in the country where the supplier is located.

An Information leaflet on intra-Community acquisitions is available on the Revenue website.

Intra-Community Supplies

An intra-Community supply is a transaction that allows a VAT-registered trader in Ireland to charge 0% VAT on the supply of a vehicle to another EU Member State. This applies where a vehicle is dispatched or transported to a VAT-registered trader carrying on business in the other Member State, but NOT INCLUDING any such vehicle sold under the Special Scheme for second-hand vehicles. These are liable to VAT in Ireland. Where a 'new means of transport' is supplied by any person, including a private individual, in Ireland and dispatched or transported by them or by the purchaser to another Member State, then there is a liability to VAT in that Member State as an intra-Community acquisition there. The purchaser will be entitled, on proof that VAT was paid in the other country, to a refund of any Irish VAT paid on the purchase of the vehicle.

An Information leaflet on intra-Community Supplies is available on the Revenue website.

Member State

A Member State is a country that is a full member of the European Union (EU), and therefore part of the European VAT system.

Motor Dealer

A Motor dealer is a person who has a business in the buying and selling of cars. Motor Dealers will generally be registered for VAT (taxable dealer), and may also be authorised to trade in unregistered vehicles (authorised dealer).

- **Taxable Dealer:** A Taxable Dealer is a VAT-registered person whose business is the buying and selling of motor vehicles and/or agricultural machinery on his or her own behalf, or on behalf of others. Dealers must register for VAT when their turnover exceeds, or is likely to exceed, €75,000 (increased from €70,000 w.e.f. 12/05/08) in any 12-month period. A person can be a taxable dealer for VAT purposes without being an Authorised Dealer (see next paragraph) for VRT purposes.

- **Authorised Dealer:** An Authorised Dealer is a motor dealer who is granted authorisation to deal or trade in unregistered or foreign-registered vehicles. These dealers are issued with a **TAN (Trader Account Number)** by the local Revenue District. Details of the application process and requirements for the authorisation of motor dealers are available on the Revenue website, which also contains a Guide to Methods of Payment for VRT Traders. Authorisation and possession of a TAN number only affects the way in which the dealer operates VRT, not VAT.

New Means of Transport

The term 'new means of transport' refers to vehicles which are less than a specified age, or have travelled less than a specified distance. It is a concept in European VAT law, and is significant only when calculating VAT liability for vehicles transported into a Member State from another Member State or non-EU country. It is important to note that a vehicle can have been owned by one or more persons, or registered in one or more countries, and still be taxable as a 'new means of transport' if it is moved from one country to another. The following vehicles are 'new means of transport':

- A **motorised land vehicle** with an engine cylinder capacity of 48 cubic centimetres or a power exceeding 7.2 kilowatts which was supplied 6 months or less after the date of first entry into service; or has travelled 6,000 kilometres or less.

- A **vessel** exceeding 7.5 metres in length which was supplied 3 months or less after the date of first entry into service; or has sailed for 100 hours or less

- An **aircraft** with a take-off weight exceeding 1550 kilogrammes which is intended for the transport of persons or goods and which was supplied 3 months or less after the date of first entry into service; or has flown for 40 hours or less.

In the case of motor vehicles, the 'date of first entry into service' is generally the date on which the vehicle was registered, unless the registration was delayed for any reason.

If a vehicle with any of the specifications set out above is brought into Ireland, then the person bringing it in is liable to pay Irish VAT. This is normally paid at the same time as the vehicle is registered in Ireland.

It is important to note that the operative date of supply, when determining whether a means of transport comes within the time limits, is the date on which it was purchased by the current owner. The distance travelled, however, is calculated by reference to when the vehicle arrives in Ireland. For example;

1. If a person purchases a 4-month old car in the U.K., and brings it into Ireland when it is 7 months old, then at the time of supply it was less than 6 months old. Regardless of the distance travelled, this vehicle is a new means of transport, and is liable to Irish VAT

2. If a person purchases a 7-month old car in the U.K., which, at the time of supply in the U.K. had travelled only 5,000 kilometres, but had travelled 6001 kilometres in total by the time it arrived in Ireland, the vehicle is not a new means of transport.

New Motor Vehicle

Unlike the technical term 'new means of transport', there is no definition in VAT law for the standard concept of a new motor vehicle, as distinct from a used or second-hand vehicle. For the purposes of this leaflet, a new motor vehicle should generally be regarded as one which has not been owned by any person other than the manufacturer, distributor(s) and authorised dealer(s). However, where a dealer has registered a vehicle in his or her own name and subsequently sells that vehicle, it must be treated as a second-hand vehicle and sold through the special scheme, even if there have been no other owners.

For the purposes of the section of this leaflet dealing with Work on vehicles, including repair & maintenance only, a new vehicle is one that has not been registered (in any country) at the time that a service, repair, alteration, conversion or paint-job is carried out.

Private Individual

For the purposes of this leaflet, a private individual is a person who is acting in a non-business capacity in relation to the purchase or sale of a vehicle. This includes people who are not in the motor trade or any other trade involving the purchase or sale of vehicles. It also includes any person who may be in such a trade but who is buying or selling his or her own personal vehicle. For example, a VAT-registered self-employed haulier bringing in a car from the U.K. for his own personal use will be treated as a private individual for that transaction.

Qualifying Vehicles

A qualifying vehicle is one that qualifies for a deduction of residual VAT under the Special Scheme for second-hand motor vehicles. Essentially, a qualifying vehicle under the Scheme is

1. one that is sold or traded-in to the dealer by a person who was not entitled to deduct any VAT in relation to the original purchase of that vehicle; or

2. a vehicle which is sold or traded-in by another dealer who took a deduction of residual VAT on his or her purchase of that vehicle.

A dealer who purchases a qualifying vehicle may claim the residual VAT on the vehicle, and on selling the vehicle must issue an invoice containing an endorsement disallowing any deduction of VAT to the purchaser.

Registration for VRT

Each EU Member State (and every other jurisdiction) maintains a register of motor vehicles. In the context of this leaflet, registration for VRT means the registering of a vehicle with a Vehicle Registration Office in the State, including the payment of any VRT. A vehicle is regarded as unregistered in the State even if it has been registered in another jurisdiction.

Residual VAT

Residual VAT is the portion of the price paid by a motor dealer for a car that represents unrecoverable VAT paid by a previous owner. For example, if a private individual buys a car, he or she is not entitled to reclaim any VAT. If this car is then traded in or sold to a dealer, the dealer may calculate the VAT on the basis of the price paid for the car, and claim the 'trapped' or residual VAT from Revenue. Residual VAT may only be reclaimed by a dealer where a vehicle is to be sold under the Special Scheme for second-hand motor vehicles.

Second-Hand or Used Motor Vehicle

As with 'new motor vehicle', there is no definition in VAT law for a second-hand, or used, vehicle. For the purposes of this leaflet a second-hand or used vehicle may be regarded as a motor vehicle, agricultural machine, etc. that has had at least one previous owner, including the current owner, but not including a motor dealer who held the vehicle, etc. as stock-in-trade. However, where a dealer has registered a vehicle in his or her own name and subsequently sells that vehicle, it must be treated as a second-hand vehicle and sold through the special scheme, even if there have been no other owners. It is important to note that a vehicle may be used or second-hand and still come within the definition of 'new means of transport' above.

Self-registered Vehicles

A self-registered vehicle is one that has been registered for VRT in the name of the dealer or distributor. This happens where a vehicle is used as a demonstration model by a dealer, or where it is otherwise taken out of stock-in-trade. If a vehicle is sold, or provided for the use of a person other than the dealer or distributor, it should not be self-registered, but should be registered in the name of the purchaser or user. When a vehicle, other than a commercial vehicle, is self-registered, any VAT reclaimed on the purchase of the vehicle must be returned to Revenue. If the vehicle is subsequently sold, it must be sold through the Special Scheme for second-hand motor vehicles. The dealer can reclaim an amount of residual VAT equal to the amount of VAT charged on the sale.

Special Scheme for Second-Hand Motor Vehicles

The Special Scheme for Second-Hand Vehicles allows a dealer to reclaim the notional or residual VAT in the price of a car he or she purchases from a private individual, and sets out the rules governing the subsequent sale of the vehicle. This is dealt with fully in the section of this leaflet titled Purchase and sale of second-hand motor vehicles under the Special Scheme rules.

Trade-in

A trade-in is the sale of a vehicle to a dealer to reduce the cost of the purchase of a (usually more expensive) vehicle from the dealer. For VAT purposes, these are treated as two separate transactions – a sale of the trade-in to the dealer, and the subsequent purchase of another vehicle.

Value Added Tax (VAT)

Value Added Tax is chargeable on the supply of goods and services. All traders who exceed the relevant turnover thresholds are required to register for and charge VAT. A liability to VAT also arises in the case of a new means of transport brought into the State, which is payable on registration of the vehicle, along with the VRT.

Vehicle Registration Tax (VRT)

Vehicle Registration Tax is chargeable on the registration of a motor vehicle in the State. All motor vehicles in the State, other than those brought in temporarily by visitors, must be registered with the Revenue Commissioners before being licensed for road tax purposes.

Enquiries

Enquiries regarding the topics covered in this leaflet should be addressed as follows:

- Value Added Tax (VAT) queries should be addressed to the local Revenue District office. The contact details for your district, and other useful addresses, telephone, fax numbers and email addresses can be found on the Contact Details section of the Revenue website.

- Vehicle Registration Tax (VRT) queries should be addressed to the local Vehicle Registration Office (VRO). A list of contact details for the VROs (MS Word, 51KB) is available on the Revenue website.

- Contact details for specific queries regarding topics covered in this leaflet will be set out in the relevant section of the leaflet.

Enquiries or comments regarding the leaflet itself should be addressed to:

VAT Appeals & Communications Branch,
Indirect Taxes Division
Stamping Building,
Dublin Castle,
Dublin 2.

This Guide is issued by:
VAT Appeals & Communications Branch,
Dublin Castle.

December, 2008

This information leaflet which sets out the current practice at the date of its issue is intended for guidance only and does not purport to be a definitive legal interpretation of the provisions of the Value-Added Tax Act 1972 (as amended).

VALUE-ADDED TAX INFORMATION LEAFLET (JANUARY 2009)

PROCUREMENT OF GOODS AND SERVICES BY THE STATE, LOCAL AUTHORITIES AND BODIES ESTABLISHED BY STATUTE

This information leaflet which sets out the current practice at the date of its issue is intended for guidance only and does not purport to be a definitive legal interpretation of the provisions of the Value-Added Tax Act 1972 (as amended). This leaflet should be read in conjunction with the Revenue VAT Guide July 2008, and VAT Information Leaflet Foreign Suppliers Doing Business in Ireland.

1.   The purpose of this leaflet

1.1   The purpose of this leaflet is to set out the circumstances in which the State, local authorities and bodies governed by public law are to be charged VAT by the supplier on goods or services procured by them is obliged to register and account for VAT on goods or services procured by them.

2.   Scope of the terms 'the State, local authorities and bodies established by statute'.

2.1   The State, local authorities and bodies established by statute includes Government Departments, state sponsored bodies, An Garda Siochana, the Defence Forces, the Health Services Executive, public hospitals, enterprise boards, educational establishments (such as universities, institutes of technology, schools, VECs), local authorities including regional authorities, harbour authorities – in practice, the State and emanations of the State. These are not normally required to register for VAT in respect of supplies of goods or services by them but may be required to register and account for VAT in respect of goods and services received by them. For ease of reference in this leaflet they are referred to as public bodies.

3.   Circumstances in which the supplier will be obliged to register for, charge and account for VAT on supplies to public bodies.

3.1   VAT is a tax on consumer spending and in the normal course is charged, collected and accounted for to Revenue by VAT registered traders on their supplies of goods and services in the State. Foreign traders who have an establishment in the State from which they supply goods are required to register for VAT. Traders supplying goods from a business in the State are obliged to register, charge and account for VAT where their annual turnover exceeds or is likely to exceed €75,000 but may register if under this amount if they so wish. Foreign traders who import goods from outside the EU for supply in the State are also obliged to register, charge and account for VAT. In such circumstances a public body will not have to self account for the VAT due but will merely pay the VAT along with the price of the goods to the supplier who will account to Revenue for the VAT due. Traders established in another member State of the EU who make intra-Community supplies to public bodies in the State are not required to register. Rather VAT is self accounted for by the public body. (see paragraph 7 below).

3.2   The general rule for services is that the supplier is obliged to register and account for VAT by reference to the place where s/he has her/his establishment. Because of the nature of certain services, when they are supplied across national boundaries this general rule will not apply and the supplier may be required to register and account for VAT in Ireland or the public body may be obliged to self account for the VAT. In other circumstances such as construction services received from either a trader established in the State it is the public body which will be required to account for the VAT due. The circumstances in which a public body is required to register and self account for VAT this are listed at paragraph 4 below and dealt with in detail in subsequent paragraphs.

4.   **Circumstances where public bodies are obliged to register and self-account for VAT**

4.1   A public body is obliged to register and self-account for VAT in the following circumstances:-

- where it is in receipt of Fourth Schedule services from abroad (see paragraph 5 of this leaflet);

- where it acquires, or is likely to acquire more than €41,000 worth of goods from other EU Member States (intra-Community acquisitions) (refer to paragraph 9 of this leaflet);

- where it is in receipt of goods which are supplied and installed/ assembled (other than fixtures) by a non-established supplier;

- where it is in receipt of cultural, entertainment, artistic or similar services from a person not established in the State.

- where it is in receipt, as a principal contractor, of construction services supplied by a sub-contractor (see Paragraph 6 of this leaflet).

4.2   Where a public body is registered for VAT in respect of either the receipt of Fourth Schedule services, received cultural services or goods which are installed/assembled then it is obliged to account on all the received services and goods listed above and on intra-Community acquisitions, irrespective of the threshold.

4.3   Once registered for VAT, it will, in addition be obliged to self-account for VAT on receipt of valuation of or work on movable goods (including contract work) in cases where the goods are dispatched or transported out of the Member State where the valuation or work was physically performed. In addition, it will be obliged to self-account on intra-Community transport services supplied by a carrier not registered for VAT in the State. There is no entitlement to a refund of input VAT for public bodies registered for the purpose of accounting for VAT on received goods or services.

4.4   Where, exceptionally a public body is required to register and account for VAT on supplies of taxable goods or services by them, they will be entitled to a VAT credit in their return for VAT incurred on related inputs.

5.   Fourth Schedule Services

5.1   This paragraph should be read in conjunction with VAT Information Leaflet 'Fourth Schedule Services'.

5.2   Where a public body is in receipt of Fourth Schedule services from a supplier in another Member State in circumstances in which VAT is not payable in that Member State in respect of the supply, or from a supplier outside the EU, it is obliged to account for VAT on the total invoiced value. The complete list of Fourth Schedule services is as follows:-

1.   transfers and assignments of copyright, patents, licences, trade marks and similar rights;

2.   hiring out of movable goods other than means of transport;

3.   advertising services;

4.   services of consultants, engineers, consultancy bureaux, lawyers, accountants and other similar services, data processing and provision of information (but excluding services connected with immovable goods);

5.   telecommunications services;

6.   radio and television broadcasting services;

7.   electronically supplied services;

8.   the provision of access to, and of transport or transmission through, natural gas and electricity distribution systems and the provision of other directly linked services;

9.   acceptance of any obligation to refrain from pursuing or exercising in whole or in part, any business activity or any such rights as are referred to in the first indent above.

10.   banking, financial and insurance services (including re-insurance and financial fund management functions, but not including the provision of safe deposit facilities);

11.   the provision of staff;

12.   the services of intermediaries who act in the name and for the account of a principal when procuring for him any services specified in the first six indents above.

The Finance Act 2007 provided for a change in the treatment of Fourth Schedule services received by Government Departments, local authorities and bodies established by statute, subject to a Commencement Order being made. This Order has not yet been made.

6.   Public Bodies receiving construction services

6.1   From 1 September 2008 public bodies are required to register and self-account for VAT in their return on construction services received by them as principal contractors.

6.2   The new system applies to principal contractors and sub-contractors involved in construction operations to which Relevant Contracts Tax (RCT) applies (but excluding haulage for hire).

6.3   RCT applies when a principal contractor is obliged to deduct tax @ 35% from payments to a sub-contractor or would have to do so but for the fact that the principal contractor holds a Relevant Contracts Card (RCT 47) for that sub-contractor. Public bodies, including local authorities, who receive construction services are principal contractors for RCT purposes and the person who contracts to provide such services to a public body is regarded as a sub-contractor.

6.4   From 1 September 2008 the principal public body acting as a principal contractor accounts for the VAT on services received from a sub-contractor under what is known as the reverse charge.

- The charge for services by the sub-contractor does not include VAT on the services.

- The VAT registered sub-contractor or a non-established sub-contractor who is not registered for VAT issues an invoice to the principal, which shows all the same information as appears on a VAT invoice, except the VAT rate and the VAT amount. The invoice should include the VAT registration number of the sub-contractor.

- The invoice should contain the statement "VAT ON THIS SUPPLY TO BE ACCOUNTED FOR BY THE PRINCIPAL CONTRACTOR". (Note 1)

- The public body, as a principal contractor, pays the sub-contractor for the services. This payment should not include VAT.

- If RCT is to be deducted, it should be calculated on the VAT-exclusive amount.

- The principal contractor should include the VAT on the services received from the sub-contractor in his/her VAT return for the period in which the supply is made as VAT on Sales (T1). (Note 2)

- Where entitled to do so, the principal can claim a simultaneous input credit in his/her VAT return for the period. (Note 3)

Note 1: If agreed by both the principal contractor and the sub-contractor the principal may issue the invoice.

Note 2: In the case of a payment in advance of completion of the supply, the principal will include the VAT on the payment in his/her VAT return for the period in which the payment is made.

Note 3: Principal contractor for RCT purposes includes local authorities, Government Departments and boards established by or under statute. Many of these bodies would not be entitled to VAT input credit.

7.   Intra-Community acquisitions of goods

7.1   A public body which is otherwise registered for VAT or which acquires or is likely to acquire more than €41,000 worth of goods from other EU Member States in any continuous period of twelve months is obliged to account for VAT at the appropriate rate in respect of those acquisitions. The public body should furnish details of its VAT number in the State to the supplier who will then apply a zero rate of VAT to the intra-Community supply from his/her Member State. VAT must then be self-accounted for on the intra-Community acquisition of the goods here in the VAT return for the taxable period. Further detail is included in VAT Information Leaflet 'EU intra-Community Acquisitions'.

7.2   It should be noted that intra-Community acquisitions of new means of transport (i.e. motor vehicles, boats, planes) are always subject to VAT when they are bought into the State, even where the non-taxable entity is not otherwise registered for VAT. There are special rules for paying VAT on new means of transport and, in certain cases, on excisable goods also. Further detail is included in VAT Information Leaflet 'EU intra-Community Acquisitions'.

8.   Cultural artistic, entertainment or similar services

8.1   Where a person not established in the State supplies cultural, artistic, entertainment or similar services to a public body in the State then the person, other than a person acting in a private capacity, who receives that service, must self-account for any VAT due. If it is a promoter or agent who receives the service then he/she will self-account for the VAT due. However, where a public body is in direct receipt of the services from a person not established in the State then it will be obliged to self-account for VAT due.

8.2   Where a public body owns a premises and allows a promoter not established in the State to supply cultural, artistic, entertainment or similar services on those premises, it must, not later than fourteen days before the event or performance is scheduled to begin, notify the appropriate Revenue District of the name and address of the promoter and details of the performance. Where these details are not furnished to the appropriate Revenue District, the public body may be made jointly and severally liable, with the promoter, for VAT due.

9.   Intra-Community transport of goods

9.1   This paragraph should be read in conjunction with VAT Information Leaflet 'Transport of Goods and Ancillary Services within the EU'.

9.2   Where a public body is in receipt of intra-Community goods transport services from a haulier established in the State then it is the haulier's responsibility to account for the VAT due. Where, however, the haulier is established in another member State then it is the public body which must self-account for VAT in the State under the reverse charge rule.

9.3   In the case of transport of goods in the State, other than as part of the intra-Community transport of goods, the VAT must be accounted for by the haulier.

10.   Repair, valuation and contract work

10.1   Where goods are dispatched or transported to another Member State, where the valuation of, or work on, movable goods, including contract work is physically carried out, the supplier should apply a zero rate of VAT to his/her charge for the service in his/her own Member State and the public body must self-account for Irish VAT at the appropriate rate on the invoiced value of the service, on the return of the goods to the State. The public body must provide the supplier with its VAT number for inclusion on the invoice.

10.2   **Contract work** means the service of handing over by a contractor to another person of movable goods made or assembled by the contractor from goods entrusted to the contractor by that other person, whether or not the contractor has provided any part of the goods used.

11.   Importation of goods

11.1   Goods imported by public bodies into the State from outside the European Union are subject to VAT at the point of entry, at the appropriate rate (a special deferral scheme, however, applies to imports by Government Departments).

11.2   It should be noted however that VAT due on importations of goods by parcel post will be not be payable at the time of importation where the value of each such consignment is €260 or less. However VAT must be accounted for in box TI of the VAT 3 return for the period. The importers VAT number should be quoted on the customs declaration form or on the wrappers of the green label packets.

12.   Invoices

12.1   Traders supplying taxable goods or services to Public Bodies are obliged to issue VAT invoices. They are likewise obliged to issue VAT credit notes and VAT debit notes where appropriate. However see 6.4 for invoices for received construction services.

12.2   VAT normally becomes due on the date of issue of a VAT invoice, or if no invoice issues, on the 15th day of the month following the receipt of the goods or services. In the case of EU intra-Community acquisitions VAT becomes due on the 15th day of the month following that during which the acquisition takes place or in case an invoice is issued before this date, at the time when the invoice is issued. In general, the rate applicable is that which applies to the supply of such goods or services in the State. (There is one exception to this in the case of the intra-Community acquisition of certain works of art, collectors items and antiques). VAT is generally chargeable on received supplies, including EU intra-Community acquisitions on the invoiced amount. In the case of imports VAT is chargeable on the invoiced amount plus insurance and freight charges.

12.3   In the case of payment made in advance of the completion of a supply on foot of an invoice from a sub-contractor for construction services, a principal contractor should account for VAT in its return in the period in which the payment is made.

12.4   In the case of a change in VAT rates traders have the same obligations in relation to the VAT rate to be charged on VAT invoices, VAT credit and VAT debit notes issued in respect of supplies to Public Bodies as applies to sales to VAT registered persons. The VAT treatment of supplies in relation to fixed interval payments, advance payments, existing contracts, continuous supplies of utilities, budget account sales, hire-purchase and other credit sales is similar to such supplies to VAT registered persons. Increase in standard rate of VAT from 21% to 21.5% from 1 Dec 2008.

13.   Rate of VAT

13.1   Public bodies are not, in the normal course, entitled to reclaim input VAT. Being registered for accounting for VAT in respect of received services (construction services, Fourth Schedule services etc.) or goods (intra-Community supplies) does not give an entitlement to a VAT credit. Therefore VAT is a cost to public bodies and differing rates indicated on tenders for similar supplies will need to be examined.

13.2   Rates can vary depending on the circumstances, for example photographic goods are normally subject to the 13.5% rate but other rates may be applicable, depending on the circumstances. Information on this particular subject is available in the VAT Information leaflet Photography.

13.2   The correct rate of VAT appropriate to any supply can be ascertained by consulting the VAT Rates Subject Index , the VAT Guides, leaflets and other VAT information available on the Revenue website or their local Revenue District.

13.3   The current standard rate of VAT is 21.5%. A lower rate of 13.5% also exists as does a zero rate and a livestock rate of 4.8%. It should be noted that banking, financial and insurance services mentioned at item number 10 of paragraph 5.2-10 above are included in the exemptions from VAT. In general, the rate applicable to intra-Community acquisitions is that which applies to the supply of such goods in the State. (There is one exception to this in the case of the intra-Community acquisition of certain works of art, collectors items and antiques).

14.   Rate of exchange

Where acquiring goods or services from an EU Member State which is not part of the EURO zone the rate of exchange to be used is the rate applicable when the tax becomes due, which is normally on the fifteenth day of the month following that in which the intra-Community acquisition occurs. The rate of exchange can be, however, as with imports from outside the EU which are expressed in a foreign currency, that determined on a calendar month basis under the monthly rates of exchange system for customs valuation purposes. Information on monthly rates of exchange is available from any Customs office.

15. No entitlement to recover VAT

Public bodies which are registered for VAT only in respect of accounting for VAT on received goods or services are not entitled to recover the VAT they have accounted for.

16. VAT Number

A VAT number will be issued on application to a Public Body where it engages in the receipt of taxable goods or services as outlined above. Any VAT due for any other such received taxable goods or services will be accounted for by reference to this number. Where there is no VAT to be accounted for in any taxable period then a nil VAT return must be filed. It is open to a body to apply to have its VAT number cancelled where it considers that will not engage in any further taxable events.

17. Intrastat

Public bodies which acquire more than €191,000 worth of goods per annum from other Member States are required to make a monthly statistical return in respect of these acquisitions. Details of this requirement are contained in the VIES and Intrastat Traders Manual, which is available from the VIMA Office at vimahelp@revenue.ie

Further information

Enquiries regarding any issue contained in this Information Leaflet should be addressed to the Revenue District responsible for the taxpayer's affairs. Contact details for all Revenue Districts can be found on the Contact Details page.

This leaflet is issued by

VAT Interpretation Branch,
Indirect Taxes Division,
Dublin Castle.

January 2009

VALUE ADDED TAX INFORMATION LEAFLET (FEBRUARY 2009)

MOTOR VEHICLES – DEDUCTION OF VAT ON CERTAIN CARS

Entitlement to Partial VAT Deductibility for Certain Business Cars

General

Finance (No. 2) Act 2008 provides that an accountable person is entitled, subject to the normal deductibility rules, to deduct up to 20% of the VAT incurred in respect of the purchase, hiring, intra-Community acquisition or importation of certain cars by businesses.

Scope

The provision applies to motor vehicles, as defined in section 12(3)(b) of the VAT Act, which are first registered for VRT purposes on or after 1 January 2009 and which have a level of CO_2 emissions of less than 156g/km (i.e. CO_2 emission bands A, B and C).

The motor vehicles covered by this provision are listed in Paragraph 10.8 of the VAT Guide 2008, and for the purposes of this leaflet are referred to as 'cars'. The car must be used primarily for business purposes. 'Business purposes' is defined as at least 60% business use. In addition, a car must be used for business purposes for a period of 2 years or more.

If circumstances change after the purchase, acquisition or importation of a car i.e. the car is disposed of within 2 years, or it is used for less than 60% business purposes, and VAT credit has been claimed, then the accountable person is required to make an adjustment in the relevant taxable period.

What is business use?

For the purpose of this provision, business use means use for either taxable activities, exempt activities or a mixture of both, **but does not include private use**.

What is meant by 60% business use?

A car, which is used for business purposes for a five-day working week, can be regarded as having been used for 60% business purposes for that week. To demonstrate that a car is being used for 60% business use, businesses can refer to current requirements in relation to the use of company cars and benefit-in-kind calculations. **No VAT credit can be claimed on cars where intended private use is greater than 40%.**

Accountable persons who have claimed VAT credit on the purchase, hiring, intra-Community acquisition or importation of a car are required to ensure that the car continues to be used for at least 60% business purposes. For practical purposes and in line with the claw-back rules, the 60% business use rule is to be examined every 6 months (up to 2 years) from the purchase, intra-Community acquisition or importation of a car. Any adjustment which may need to be made, as a result of a car no longer being used for 60% business use, is to be done in the Revenue VAT return for the next taxable period following the 6-month period.

How much VAT can be deducted?

This is best illustrated by examples. It is presumed in all cases that the car is used for least 60% business purposes.

Example A – Taxpayer's business use of the car is for wholly taxable activities

In this case the taxpayer can avail of the maximum 20% deductibility.

VAT on the purchase of the car	= €4,000
VAT deductible	= €800

In the case of leasing VAT deductibility is based on 20% of the monthly leasing charges.

Example B – Taxpayer's business use of the car is for wholly exempt activities

In this case the taxpayer is not entitled to any deductibility. An accountable person is entitled to deduct VAT charged on his or her inputs only when those inputs are attributable to the supply of taxable goods or services or qualifying activities.

Example C – Taxpayer's business use of the car is for a mixture of both taxable and exempt activities

Where a business uses the car for both its taxable and exempt supplies, VAT deductible is apportioned in the ratio of exempt versus taxable supplies

Example:

Assume 70% of car use is for taxable supplies and 30% is for exempt supplies.

VAT on the purchase of a car	= €4,000
VAT deductible is 70% of €800	= €560

If VAT on the lease of the car is €100 per month, then €14 is deductible i.e. 20% of the €70 eligible for deductibility.

What happens if a car which had qualified for deductibility is disposed of within 2 years?

Where an accountable person disposes of a car within 2 years of purchase a clawback will arise. This means that the accountable person must repay all or some of the VAT deducted depending on the period of time the car was used, in the taxable period during which the car was disposed. The clawback rules apply as follows:

Disposal **within 6 months** from date of purchase, acquisition or importation of the car	Clawback of all VAT deducted
Disposal in the period **6 to12 months** from date of purchase, acquisition or importation of the car	75% clawback of VAT deducted
Disposal in the period **12 to18 months** from date of purchase, acquisition or importation of the car	50% clawback of VAT deducted
Disposal in the period **18 to 24 months** from date of purchase, acquisition or importation of the car	25% clawback of VAT deducted
Disposal **after 24 months** from date of purchase, acquisition or importation of the car	No clawback

The clawback is calculated according to the following formula:

$$\frac{TD \times (4-N)}{4}$$

TD   is the amount of tax deducted by that accountable person on the purchase, acquisition or importation of that car, and

N   is a number that is equal to the number of days from the date of purchase, acquisition or importation of the car by that accountable person to the date of disposal by that person, divided by 182 (representing 6 months) and rounded down to the nearest whole number,

Example A – Car disposed of after 3 months (90 days)

     TD   =   €800

     N   = $\frac{90}{182}$ = 0.49 and therefore rounded down to 0

Using the formula:

$$\frac{800 \times (4 - 0)}{4} = \frac{3200}{4} = €800$$

In this case the full amount deducted i.e. €800 is to be accounted for to Revenue as tax due in VAT return for the next taxable period after 6 months from the date of purchase, intra-Community acquisition or importation of the car.

Example B – Car disposed of after 20 months (600 days)

     TD   =   €800

     N   = $\frac{600}{182}$ = 3.29, and therefore is rounded down to 3

Using the formula:

$$\frac{800 \times (4 - 3)}{4} = \frac{800}{4} = €200$$

In this case, the amount of €200 is to be accounted for to Revenue as tax due in VAT return for the next taxable period after the fourth 6-month period from the date of purchase, intra-Community acquisition or importation of the car.

What happens if a car does not meet the business use criteria subsequent to purchase?

Similar to the rules applying to the disposal of a car, there is a clawback of all or part of the amount deducted if a car is no longer used for business purposes, or is used for less than 60% business purposes, at any time within 2 years of purchase, intra-Community acquisition or importation of the car.

The clawback rules apply as follows:

Business use discontinues (or is used for less than 60% business use) **within 6 months** from date of purchase, acquisition or importation of the car	Clawback of all VAT deducted
Business use discontinues (or is used for less than 60% business use) in the period **6 to12 months** from date of purchase, acquisition or importation of the car	75% clawback of VAT deducted
Business use discontinues (or is used for less than 60% business use) in the period **12 to18 months** from date of purchase, acquisition or importation of the car	50% clawback of VAT deducted
Business use discontinues (or is used for less than 60% business use) in the period **18 to 24 months** from date of purchase, acquisition or importation of the car	25% clawback of VAT deducted
Business use discontinues (or is used for less than 60% business use) **after 24 months** from date of purchase, acquisition or importation of the car	No clawback

The clawback is calculated in accordance with the following formula:

$$\frac{TD \times (4\text{-}N)}{4}$$

TD   is the amount of tax deducted by that accountable person on the purchase, acquisition or importation of that car, and

N   is a number that is equal to the number of days from the date of purchase, acquisition or importation of the car by that accountable person to the first day of the taxable period in which the car is used for less than 60% business purposes, divided by 182 (representing 6 months) and rounded down to the nearest whole number,

Example A – Business use discontinues (or is used for less than 60% business use) after 180 days

TD   =   €800

N   = $\frac{180}{182}$ = 0.99, and therefore rounded down to 0

Using the formula:

$$\frac{800 \times (4 - 0)}{4} = \frac{3200}{4} = €800$$

In this case the full deductible amount of €800 is to be repaid to Revenue in the next VAT return.

Example B – Business use discontinues (or is used for less than 60% business use) after 15 months (450 days)

TD = €800

N = $\frac{450}{182}$ = 2.47, and therefore is rounded down to 2

Using the formula:

$$\frac{800 \times (4-2)}{4} = \frac{1600}{4} = €400$$

In this case, the amount of €400 is to be repaid to Revenue in the next VAT return.

Is VAT chargeable on the sale of a car which has qualified for this partial VAT deductibility provision?

No, the subsequent sale of a car by the taxable person who was entitled to the partial deductibility provision described in this leaflet will be exempt from VAT. The operation of the special scheme for motor vehicles applies where that sale is to a taxable dealer within the meaning of Section 12B.

Further information

Enquiries regarding any issue contained in this Information Leaflet should be addressed to the Revenue District responsible for your tax affairs.

This VAT Information Leaflet is issued by

VAT Appeals and Communications Branch
Indirect Taxes Division
Dublin Castle

February 2009

Other Relevant Legislation

OTHER IRISH LEGISLATION RELEVANT TO VALUE ADDED TAX

Provisional Collection of Taxes Act, 1927

(Number 7 of 1927)

AN ACT TO GIVE STATUTORY EFFECT FOR A LIMITED PERIOD TO RESOLUTIONS
OF THE COMMITTEE ON FINANCE OF DÁIL ÉIREANN IMPOSING, RENEWING,
VARYING, OR ABOLISHING TAXATION, AND TO MAKE PROVISION WITH RESPECT
TO PAYMENTS, DEDUCTIONS, ASSESSMENTS, CHARGES, AND OTHER THINGS
MADE OR DONE ON ACCOUNT OF ANY TEMPORARY TAX IN ANTICIPATION OF
THE RENEWAL OF THE TAX BY THE OIREACHTAS.

[19th March, 1927.]

BE IT ENACTED BY THE OIREACHTAS OF SAORSTÁT EIREANN AS FOLLOWS:-

Section 1

Definition

1.   In this Act-

the expression **"Committee on Finance"** means the Committee on
Finance of Dáil Éireann when and so long as such Committee is a
committee of the whole House;.

[the expression **"new tax"** when used in relation to a resolution under
this Act means a tax which was not in force immediately before the date
on which the resolution is expressed to take effect or, where no such
date is expressed, the passing of the resolution by Dáil Éireann;][1]

the expression **"permanent tax"** means a tax which was last imposed or
renewed without any limit of time being fixed for its duration;

the expression **"temporary tax"** means a tax which was last imposed or
renewed for a limited period only;

the expression **"normal expiration"** when used in relation to a
temporary tax means the end of the limited period for which the tax
was last imposed or renewed;

the word **"tax"** includes duties of customs, duties of excise, income
tax [...][2] [...][3] [and value added tax][4] [and capital gains tax][5] [...][6] [and
corporation tax][7] [...][8] [and residential property tax][9] [and stamp duties][10]
[and parking levy][11] but no other tax or duty.

Section 2

Certain resolutions to have statutory effect

2.   Whenever a resolution (in this Act referred to as a resolution under this
Act) is passed by [Dáil Éireann][12] resolving-

(a)   that a new tax specified in the resolution be imposed, or

(b)   that a specified permanent tax in force [immediately before
the date on which the resolution is expressed to take effect or,

where no such date is expressed, the passing of the resolution by Dáil Éireann][13] be increased, reduced, or otherwise varied, or be abolished, or

(c)　　that a specified temporary tax in force [immediately before the date on which the resolution is expressed to take effect or, where no such date is expressed, the passing of the resolution by Dáil Éireann][13] be renewed (whether at the same or a different rate and whether with or without modification) as from the date of its normal expiration or from an earlier date or be discontinued on a date prior to the date of its normal expiration,

and the resolution contains a declaration that it is expedient in the public interest that the resolution should have statutory effect under the provisions of this Act, the resolution shall, subject to the provisions of this Act, have statutory effect as if contained in an Act of the Oireachtas.

Section 3

Application of general taxing enactments

3.　(1)　Whenever a new tax is imposed by a resolution under this Act and such resolution describes the tax as a duty of customs or as a duty of excise or as an income tax [...][14], the enactments which [immediately before the date on which the resolution is expressed to take effect or, where no such date is expressed, the passing of the resolution by Dáil Éireann][13] were in force in relation to customs duties generally, or excise duties generally, or income tax generally, [...][15] (as the case may require) shall, subject to the provisions of this Act, apply to and have full force and effect in respect of such new tax so long as the resolution continues to have statutory effect.

　　(2)　Whenever a permanent tax is increased, reduced, or other wise varied by a resolution under this Act, all enactments which were in force with respect to that tax [immediately before the date on which the resolution is expressed to take effect or, where no such date is expressed, the passing of the resolution by Dáil Éireann][13] shall, so long as the resolution continues to have statutory effect and subject to the provisions of this Act, have full force and effect with respect to the tax as so increased, reduced, or otherwise varied.

　　(3)　Whenever a temporary tax is renewed (whether at the same or a different rate and whether with or without modification) by a resolution under this Act, all enactments which were in force with respect to that tax [immediately before the date on which the resolution is expressed to take effect or, where no such date is expressed, the passing of the resolution by Dáil Éireann][13] shall, so long as the resolution continues to have statutory effect and subject to the provisions of this Act, have full force and effect with respect to the tax as renewed by the resolution.

Section 4

Duration of statutory effect of resolution

4.　　[A resolution under this Act shall cease to have statutory effect in or upon the happening of whichever of the following events first occurs, that is to say:

　　[(a)　　subject to section 4A of this Act, if a Bill containing provisions to the same effect (with or without modifications) as the resolution is not read a second time by Dáil Éireann-

　　　　(i)　　where Dáil Éireann is in recess on any day between the eighty-second and the eighty-fourth day after the resolution is passed by Dáil Éireann, within the next five sitting days of the resumption of Dáil Éireann after that recess,

　　　　(ii)　　in any other case, within the next eighty-four days after the resolution is passed by Dáil Éireann,][16]

　　(b)　　if those provisions of the said Bill are rejected by Dáil Éireann during the passage of the Bill through the Oireachtas;

　　(c)　　the coming into operation of an Act of the Oireachtas containing provisions to the same effect (with or without modification) as the resolution;

　　(d)　　[subject to section 4A of this Act][17] the expiration of a period of four months from the date on which the resolution is expressed to take effect or, where no such date is expressed, from the passing of the resolution by Dáil Éireann][18].

Section 4A

Effect of dissolution of Dáil Éireann

[4A.　　Where Dáil Éireann, having passed a resolution under this Act, has been dissolved on the date the resolution was so passed or within four months of that date, then the period of dissolution shall be desregarded for the purposes of calculating any period to which paragraph (a) or (d) of section 4 of this Act relates.][19]

Section 5

Repayment of certain payments and deductions

5.　　(1)　　Whenever a resolution under this Act ceases to have statutory effect by reason of the happening of any event other than the coming into operation of an Act of the Oireachtas containing provisions to the same effect (with or without modification) as the resolution, all moneys paid in pursuance of the resolution shall be repaid or made good and every deduction made in pursuance of the resolution shall be deemed to be an unauthorised deduction.

(2)   [...][20]

(3)   Whenever an Act of the Oireachtas comes into operation containing provisions to the same effect with modifications as a resolution under this Act and such resolution ceases by virtue of such coming into operation to have statutory effect, all moneys paid in pursuance of such resolution which would not be payable under such Act shall be repaid or made good and every deduction made in pursuance of such resolution which would not be authorised by such Act shall be deemed to be an unauthorised deduction.

Section 6

Certain payments and deductions deemed to be legal

6.   (1)   Any payment or deduction on account of a temporary tax to which this section applies made within two months after the expiration of such tax in respect of a period or event occurring after such expiration shall, if such payment or deduction would have been a legal payment or deduction if the tax had not expired, be deemed to be a legal payment or deduction subject to the conditions that-

(a)   if a resolution under this Act renewing the tax (with or without modification) is not passed by [Dáil Éireann][21] within two months after the expiration of the tax, the amount of such payment or deduction shall be repaid or made good on the expiration of such two months, and

(b)   if (such resolution having been so passed) an Act of the Oireachtas renewing the tax (with or without modification) does not come into operation when or before such resolution ceases to have statutory effect, the amount of such payment or deduction shall be repaid or made good on such cesser, and

(c)   if (such Act having been so passed) the tax is renewed by such Act with such modifications that the whole or some portion of such payment or deduction is not a legal payment or deduction under such Act, the whole or such portion (as the case may be) of such payment or deduction shall be repaid or made good on the coming into operation of such Act.

(2)   This section applies only to a temporary tax which was last imposed or renewed for a limited period not exceeding eighteen months and was in force immediately before the end of the financial year next preceding the financial year in which the payment or deduction under this section is made.

Section 7

Repeal

7.   The Provisional Collection of Taxes Act, 1913, is hereby repealed.

Section 8

Short title

8.   This Act may be cited as the Provisional Collection of Taxes Act, 1927.

Amendments
1   Substituted by s139(a) FA02, w.e.f. 25 March 2002.
2   Words 'and super-tax' deleted by s86, FA74 w.e.f. '74/'75 and later years.
3   Words 'and also turnover tax' deleted by, VATA s41.
4   Inserted by, s38 VATA .
5   Inserted by s50, CGTA75.
6   Words 'and wealth tax' deleted by s38, FA78.
7   Inserted by s6, CTA76.
8   Repealed by s 118, CAT Consolidation Act 2003. Previously "and gift and inheritance tax."
9   Inserted by s114(1), FA83.
10   Inserted by s100, FA86.
11   Inserted by s2(2), FA (No. 2) 2008, w.e.f. 1 January 2009.
12   Substituted by s85(1)(a), FA74, w.e.f. 23 October 1974.
13   Substituted by s139(b) FA02, w.e.f. 25 March 2002.
14   Words 'or as a super-tax' deleted by s86 & sch2 Pt1, FA74, w.e.f. '74/'75, and later years.
15   Words 'or super-tax generally' deleted by s86 & sch2 Pt1, FA74, w.e.f. '74/'75 and later years.
16   Para(a) substituted by s2(a)(i), Appropriation Act 1991.
17   Inserted by s2(a)(ii), Appropriation Act 1991.
18   Section 4 substituted by s85(1)(b), FA74, w.e.f. 23 October 1974.
19   Section 4A substituted by s250, FA92.
20   Deleted by s85(1)(c), FA74, w.e.f. 23 October 1974.
21   Substituted by s85(1)(d), FA74, w.e.f. 23 October 1974.

Finance Act 1928

(Number 11 of 1928)

Section 34

Care and management of taxes and duties

34. (1) All taxes and duties imposed or continued by this Act are hereby placed under the care and management of the Revenue Commissioners.

(2) Any information acquired, whether before or after the passing of this Act, by the Revenue Commissioners in connection with any tax or duty under their care and management may be used by them for any purpose connected with any other tax or duty under their care and management.

European Communities Act, 1972

(No. 27 of 1972)

AN ACT TO MAKE IMPROVEMENTS WITH RESPECT TO MEMBERSHIP OF
THE STATE OF THE EUROPEAN COMMUNITIES.

(16 December 1972)

BE IT ENACTED BY THE OIREACHTAS AS FOLLOWS:

Section 1

Definitions

1.   (1)   In this Act-

"**the European Communities**" means the European Economic
Community, the European Coal and Steel Community and the
European Atomic Energy Community;

"**the treaties governing the European Communities**" means-

(a)   "**the ECSC Treaty**", that is to say, the Treaty establishing
the European Coal and Steel Community, signed at Paris
on the 18th day of April, 1951,

(b)   "**the EEC Treaty**", that is to say, the Treaty establishing
the European Economic Community, signed at Rome on
the 25th day of March, 1957,

(c)   "**the Euratom Treaty**", that is to say, the Treaty establishing
the European Atomic Energy Community, signed at Rome
on the 25th day of March, 1957,

(d)   the Convention on certain Institutions common to the
European Communities, signed at Rome on the 25th day
of March, 1957,

(e)   the Treaty establishing a single Council and a single
Commission of the European Communities, signed at
Brussels on the 8th day of April, 1965,

(f)   the treaty amending certain Budgetary Provisions of the
Treaties establishing the European Communities and
of the Treaty establishing a single Council and a single
Commission of the European Communities, signed at
Luxembourg on the 22nd day of April, 1970,

(g)   the Treaty relating to the accession of Ireland to the
European Economic Community and to the European
Atomic Energy Community, signed at Brussels on the
22nd day of January, 1972,

(h)   the decision, of the 22nd day of January, 1972, of the
Council of the European Communities relating to the

accession of Ireland to the European Coal and Steel Community,

as supplemented or amended by treaties or other acts of which the dates of entry into force are dates met later than the 1st day of January, 1973 [, and

(i)   the Treaty amending certain financial provisions of the Treaties establishing the European Communities and of the Treaty establishing a single Council and a single Commission of the European Communities, signed at Brussels on the 22nd day of July, 1975][1] [and

(j)   the Treaty relating to the accession of the Hellenic Republic to the European Economic Community and to the European Atomic Energy Community, signed at Athens on the 28th day of May, 1979, and

(k)   the decision, of the 24th day of May, 1979, of the Council of the European Communities relating to the accession of the Hellenic Republic to the European Coal and Steel Community,][2] [and

(l)   the Treaty amending, with regard to Greenland, the Treaties establishing the European Communities, signed at Brussels on the [13th][3] day of March, 1984][4] [and

(m)   the Treaty concerning the accession of the Kingdom of Spain and the Portuguese Republic to the European Economic Community and to the European Atomic Energy Community, signed at Lisbon and Madrid on the 12th day of June, 1985, and

(n)   the decision, of the 11th day of June, 1985, of the Council of the European Communities relating to the accession of the Kingdom of Spain and the Portuguese Republic to the European Coal and Steel Community,][5] [and

(o)   the following provisions of the Single European Act (done at Luxembourg on the 17th day of February, 1986, and at The Hague on the 28th day of February, 1986), namely, Article 3.1; Title II; Articles 31 and 32; and, in so far as they relate to the said Article 3. 1, the said Title II and the said Articles 31 and 32, Articles 33 and 34][6] [and

(p)   the following provisions of the Treaty on European Union, namely, Titles II, III and IV; in Title VII, Articles L, M and P, and the other provisions of that Title in so far as they relate to any of the treaties governing the European Communities as defined by this subsection; together with the Protocols (whether expressed to be annexed to the Treaty establishing the European Community, or to the said Treaty on European Union and the Treaties establishing the European Communities), done at Maastricht on the 7th day of February, 1992,][7] [and

(q)   the Act amending the Protocol on the Statute of the European Investment Bank, empowering the Board of Governors to establish a European Investment Fund, signed at Brussels on the 25th day of March, 1993, together with the Treaty amending certain provisions of the Protocol on the Statute of the European Investment Bank, signed at Brussels on the 10th day of July, 1975,][8] [and

(r)   the Treaty concerning the accession of the Kingdom of Norway, the Republic of Austria, the Republic of Finland and the Kingdom of Sweden to the European Union signed at Corfu on the 24th day of June, 1994, in so far as that Treaty relates to the European Communities.][9] [and

(s)   the following provisions of the Treaty of Amsterdam amending the Treaty on European Union, the Treaties establishing the European Communities and certain related Acts, namely, Articles 1.13 and 2 to 12 together with the annexed Protocols whether expressed to be annexed to–

   (i)   the Treaty on European Union and to the Treaty establishing the European Community,

   (ii)   the Treaty establishing the European Community, or

   (iii)   the Treaty on European Union and the Treaties establishing the European Community, the European Coal and Steel Community and the European Atomic Energy Community,

signed at Amsterdam on the 2nd day of October, 1997.][10] [and

(t)   the following provisions of the Treaty of Nice amending the Treaty on European Union, the Treaties establishing the European Communities and certain related Acts, namely, Articles 1.15 and 2 to 10 together with the annexed Protocols whether expressed to be annexed to–

   (i)   the Treaty on European Union and to the Treaties establishing the European Communities,

   (ii)   the Treaty on European Union, to the Treaty establishing the European Community and to the Treaty establishing the European Atomic Energy Community, or

   (iii)   the Treaty establishing the European Community,

signed at Nice on the 26th day of February 2001][11] [and

(u) the Treaty concerning the accession of the Czech Republic, the Republic of Estonia, the Republic of Cyprus, the Republic of Latvia, the Republic of Lithuania, the Republic of Hungary, the Republic of Malta, the Republic of Poland, the Republic of Slovenia and the Slovak Republic to the European Union done at Athens on the 16th day of April 2003, in so far as that Treaty relates to the European Communities.][12]

[and

(v) the Treaty concerning the accession of the Republic of Bulgaria and Romania to the European Union signed at Luxembourg on the 25th day of April 2005, in so far as that Treaty relates to the European Communities.][13]

(2) (a) In the foregoing subsection "treaties or other acts of which the dates of entry into force are dates not later than the 1st day of January, 1973" does not include a treaty or other act of which the date of entry into force is later than the 22nd day of January, 1972, unless the Government have, not later than the 1st day of January, 1973, by order declared that this section applies to it.

(b) Where an order under this section is proposed to be made, a draft thereof shall be laid before each House of the Oireachtas and the order shall not be made until a resolution approving of the draft has been passed by each such House.

Section 2

General provision

2. [(1)][8] From the 1st day of January, 1973, the treaties governing the European Communities and the existing and future acts adopted by the institutions of those Communities [and by bodies competent under the said treaties][7] shall be binding on the State and shall be part of the domestic law thereof under the conditions laid down in those treaties.

[(2) Without prejudice to subsection (1) of this section, from the coming into force of the EEA Agreement, the provisions of that Agreement and the acts to be adopted by institutions established by that Agreement which, pursuant to the treaties governing the European Communities, will be binding on the State and an integral part of the legal order of those Communities, shall have the force of law in the State on the conditions laid down in those treaties and in that Agreement.][8]

Section 3

Power to make regulations

3.   (1)   A Minister of State may make regulations for enabling section 2 of this Act to have full effect.

(2)   Regulations under this section may contain such incidental, supplementary and consequential provisions as appear to the Minister making the regulations to be necessary for the purposes of the regulations (including provisions repealing, amending or applying, with or without modification, other law, exclusive of this Act).

[(3)   Regulations under this section may–

(a)   make provision for offences under the regulations to be prosecuted on indictment, where the Minister of the Government making the regulations considers it necessary for the purpose of giving full effect to–

(i)   a provision of the treaties governing the European Communities, or

(ii)   an act, or provision of an act, adopted by an institution of the European Communities or any other body competent under those treaties,

and

(b)   make such provision as that Minister of the Government considers necessary for the purpose of ensuring that penalties in respect of an offence prosecuted in that manner are effective and proportionate, and have a deterrent effect, having regard to the acts or omissions of which the offence consists, provided that the maximum fine (if any) shall not be greater than €500,000 and the maximum term of imprisonment (if any) shall not be greater than 3 years.][14]

(4)   Regulations under this section may be made before the 1st day of January, 1973, but regulations so made shall not come into operation before that day.

[(5)   In this section–

'maximum fine' means the maximum fine to which a person shall be liable on conviction on indictment of an offence;

'maximum term of imprisonment' means the maximum term of imprisonment to which a person shall be liable on conviction on indictment of an offence.][15]

[3A.   Every regulation to which subsection (3) (inserted by section 2(a) of the European Communities Act 2007) of section 3 of this

Act applies shall be laid before each House of the Oireachtas as soon as may be after it is made and, if a resolution annulling the regulation is passed by either such House within the next 21 days on which that House sits after the regulation is laid before it, the regulation shall be annulled accordingly but without prejudice to the validity of anything previously done thereunder.][15]

Section 4
Effect and confirmation of regulations

4.   [(1)   (a)   Regulations under this Act shall have statutory effect.

              (b)   If the [Joint Committee on Foreign Affairs][16] recommends to the Houses of the Oireachtas that any regulations under this Act be annulled and a resolution annulling the regulations is passed by both such Houses within one year after the regulations are made, the regulations shall be annulled accordingly and shall cease to have statutory effect, but without prejudice to the validity of anything previously done thereunder.

          (2)   (a)   If when regulations under this Act are made, or at any time within one year thereafter and while the regulations have statutory effect, Dáil Éireann stands adjourned for a period of more than ten days and if, during the adjournment, at least one-third of the members of Dáil Éireann by notice in writing to the Ceann Comhairle require Dáil Éireann to be summoned, the Ceann Comhairle shall summon Dáil Éireann to meet on a day named by him being neither more than twenty-one days after the receipt by him of the notice nor less than ten days after the issue of the summons.

              (b)   If when regulations under this Act are made, or at any time within one year thereafter and while the regulations have statutory effect, Seanad Éireann stands adjourned for a period of more than ten days and if, during the adjournment, at least one-third of the members of Seanad Éireann by notice in writing to the Cathaoirleach require Seanad Éireann to be summoned, the Cathaoirleach shall summon Seanad Éireann to meet on a day named by him being neither more than twenty-one days after the receipt by him of the notice nor less than ten days after the issue of the summons.

              (c)   Paragraphs (a) and (b) of this subsection shall not apply to regulations in relation to which a resolution for their annulment has been refused by either House of the Oireachtas.][17]

Section 5

Report to Houses of Oireachtas

5.   The Government shall make a report twice yearly to each House of the Oireachtas on developments in the European Communities.

Section 6

Short title

6.   This Act may be cited as the European Communities Act, 1972.

Amendments

1   Inserted by European Communities (Amendment) Act, 1977.
2   Inserted by European Communities (Amendment) Act, 1979.
3   Amended by European Communities (Amendment) Act, 1993.
4   Inserted by European Communities (Amendment) Act, 1985.
5   Inserted by European Communities (Amendment) (No. 2) Act, 1985.
6   Inserted by European Communities (Amendment) Act, 1986.
7   Inserted by European Communities (Amendment) Act, 1992.
8   Inserted by European Communities (Amendment) Act, 1993.
9   Inserted by European Communities (Amendment) Act, 1994.
10 Inserted by European Communities (Amendment) Act, 1998.
11 Inserted by European Communities (Amendment) Act, 2002.
12 Inserted by European Communities (Amendment) Act, 2003.
13 Inserted by European Communities (Amendment) Act 2006.
14 Substituted by European Communities Act, 2007
15 Inserted by European Communities Act 2007
16 Inserted by European Communities (Amendment) Act, 1993.
17 Inserted by European Communities (Amendment) Act, 1973.

Finance Act 1975

(Number 6 of 1975)

Section 29

Adjustment of capital allowances by reference to value-added tax

29. (1)   In computing any deduction, allowance or relief, for any of the purposes of-

(a)   Part XIII to XVIII, inclusive, of the Income Tax Act, 1967,

(b)   section 22 of the Finance Act, 1971,

(c)   the Finance (Taxation of Profits of Certain Mines) Act, 1974, or

(d)   section 22 of the Finance Act, 1974,

the cost to a person of any machinery or plant, or the amount of any expenditure incurred by him, shall not take account of any amount included in such cost or expenditure for value-added tax in respect of which the person may claim-

(i)   a deduction under section 12 of the Value-Added Tax Act, 1972, or

(ii)   a refund of value-added tax under an order under section 20(3) of that Act.

(2)   In calculating, for any of the purposes of Part XVI of the Income Tax Act, 1967, the amount of sale, insurance, salvage or compensation moneys to be taken into account in computing a balancing allowance or balancing charge to be made to or on a person, no account shall be taken of the amount of value-added tax (if any) chargeable to the person in respect of those moneys.

(3)   Section 39 of the Value-Added Tax Act, 1972, is hereby repealed.

Finance Act 1983

(Number 15 of 1983)

Section 22

Obligation to show tax reference number on receipts, etc.

22.   (1)   In this section-

"**business**" means-

(a)   a profession, or

(b)   a trade consisting solely of the supply (which word has in this paragraph the same meaning as in the Value-Added Tax Acts, 1972 to 1983) of a service and includes, in the case of a trade part of which consists of the supply of a service, that part, and also includes, in the case of a trade the whole or part of which consists of the supply of a service which incorporates the supply of goods in the course of the supply of that service, that trade or that part, as the case may be;

"**specified person**", in relation to a business, means-

(a)   in case the business is carried on by an individual, that individual, and

(b)   in case the business is carried on by a partnership, the precedent partner;

"**tax reference number**", in relation to a specified person, means each of the following:

(a)   the Revenue and Social Insurance (RSI) Number stated on any certificate of tax-free allowances issued to that person by an inspector, not being a certificate issued to an employer in respect of an employee of that employer,

(b)   the reference number stated on any return of income form or notice of assessment issued to that person by an inspector, and

(c)   the registration number of that person for the purposes of value-added tax.

(2)   The specified person in relation to a business shall ensure that his tax reference number or, if he has more than one tax reference number, one of his tax reference numbers or, if he has not got a tax reference number, his full names and his address is or are stated on any document (being an invoice, credit note, debit note, receipt, account, statement of account, voucher or estimate relating to an amount of £5 or more) issued on or after the 1st day of September, 1983, in the course of that business.

(3)   Schedule 15 to the Income Tax Act, 1967, is hereby amended by the insertion in column (3) thereof of "Finance Act, 1983, section 22".

Section 23

Publication of names of tax defaulters

23.   (1)   In this section "**the Acts**" means-

(a)   the Tax Acts,

(b)   the Capital Gains Tax Acts,

(c)   the Value-Added Tax Act, 1972, and the enactments amending or extending that Act,

(d)   the Capital Acquisitions Tax Act, 1976, and the enactments amending or extending that Act,

(e)   the statutes relating to stamp duty and to the management of that duty, and

(f)   *Part VI,*

and any instruments made thereunder.

[(2)   The Revenue Commissioners shall, as respects each relevant period (being the period beginning on the 1st day of January, 1997, and ending on the 30th day of June, 1997, and each subsequent period of three months beginning with the period ending on the 30th day of September, 1997), compile a list of names and addresses and the occupations or descriptions of every person-

(a)   upon whom a fine or other penalty was imposed by a court under any of the Acts during that relevant period,

(b)   upon whom a fine or other penalty was otherwise imposed by a court during that relevant period in respect of an act or omission by the person in relation to tax, or

(c)   in whose case the Revenue Commissioners, pursuant to an agreement made with the person in that relevant period, refrained from initiating proceedings for recovery of any fine or penalty of the kind mentioned in paragraphs (a) and (b) and, in lieu of initiating such proceedings, accepted, or undertook to accept, a specified sum of money in settlement of any claim by the Revenue Commissioners in respect of any specified liability of the person under any of the Acts for-

(i)   payment of any tax,

(ii)   payment of interest thereon, and

        (iii)   a fine or other monetary penalty in respect thereof.]¹

[(3)   Notwithstanding any obligation as to secrecy imposed on them by the Acts or the Official Secrets Act, 1963-

        (a)   the Revenue Commissioners shall, before the expiration of three months from the end of each relevant period, cause each such list referred to in subsection (2) in relation to that period to be published in Iris Oifigiúil, and

        (b)   the Revenue Commissioners may, at any time, cause any such list referred to in subsection (2) to be publicised in such manner as they shall consider appropriate.]²

(4)   Paragraph (c) of subsection (2) does not apply in relation to a person in whose case-

        (a)   the Revenue Commissioners are satisfied that, before any investigation or inquiry had been commenced by them or by any of their officers into any matter occasioning a liability referred to in the said paragraph of the person, the person had voluntarily furnished to them complete information in relation to and full particulars of the said matter, or

        [(aa)   the provisions of section 72 of the Finance Act, 1988, or section 3 of the Waiver of Certain Tax, Interest and Penalties Act, 1993, apply, or]³

        (b)   the specified sum referred to in the said *paragraph (c)* does not exceed £10,000 or was paid on or before the 31st day of December, 1983.

(5)   Any such list as is referred to in *subsection (2)* shall specify in respect of each person named in the list such particulars as the Revenue Commissioners think fit-

        (a)   of the matter occasioning the fine or penalty of the kind referred to in *subsection (2)* imposed on the person or, as the case may be, the liability of that kind to which the person was subject, and

        (b)   of any interest, fine or other monetary penalty, and of any other penalty or sanction, which that person was liable, or which was imposed on him by a court, and which was occasioned by the said matter.

(6)   In this section "**tax**" means income tax, capital gains tax, corporation tax, value-added tax, gift tax, inheritance tax, residential property tax and stamp duty.

Section 94

Revenue offences

94.   (1)   In this Part-

"the Acts" means

(a)   the Customs Acts,

(b)   the statutes relating to the duties of excise and to the management of those duties,

(c)   the Tax Acts,

(d)   the Capital Gains Tax Acts,

(e)   the Value-Added Tax Act, 1972, and the enactments amending or extending that Act,

(f)   the Capital Acquisitions Tax Act, 1976, and the enactments amending or extending that Act,

(g)   the statutes relating to stamp duty and to the management of that duty, and

(h)   Part VI,

and any instruments made thereunder and any instruments made under any other enactment and relating to tax;

['**an authorised officer**' means an officer of the Revenue Commissioners authorised by them in writing to exercise any of the powers conferred by the Acts;][4]

"**tax**" means any tax, duty, levy or charge under the care and management of the Revenue Commissioners.

(2)   A person shall, without prejudice to any other penalty to which he may be liable, be guilty of an offence under this section if, after the date of the passing of this Act, he-

(a)   knowingly or wilfully delivers any incorrect return, statement or accounts or knowingly or wilfully furnishes any incorrect information in connection with any tax,

(b)   knowingly aids, abets, assists, incites or induces another person to make or deliver knowingly or wilfully any incorrect return, statement or accounts in connection with any tax,

(c)   claims or obtains relief or exemption from, or repayment of, any tax, being a relief, exemption or repayment to which, to his knowledge, he is not entitled,

(d)   knowingly or wilfully issues or produces any incorrect invoice, receipt, instrument or other document in connection with any tax, [(dd)   (i)   fails to make any deduction required to be made by him under section 32(1) of the Finance Act, 1986,

    (ii)   fails, having made the deduction, to pay the sum deducted to the Collector-General within the time specified in that behalf in section 33(3) of that Act, or

    (iii)   fails to pay to the Collector-General an amount on account of appropriate tax (within the meaning of Chapter IV of Part I of that Act) within the time specified in that behalf in section 33(4) of that Act,][5]

[(ddd) (i)   fails to make any deduction required to be made by him under section 18(5) of the Finance Act, 1989, or

    (ii)   fails, having made the deduction, to pay the sum deducted to the Collector-General within the time specified in paragraph 1(3) of the First Schedule to that Act.][6]

(e)   knowingly or wilfully fails to comply with any provision of the Acts requiring

    (i)   the furnishing of a return of income, profits or gains, or of sources of income, profits or gains, for the purposes of any tax,

    (ii)   the furnishing of any other return, certificate, notification, particulars, or any statement or evidence, for the purposes of any tax,

    (iii)   the keeping or retention of books, records, accounts or other documents for the purposes of any tax, or

    (iv)   the production of books, records, accounts or other documents, when so requested, for the purposes of any tax,

[(ee)   knowingly or wilfully, and within the time limits specified for their retention, destroys, defaces, or conceals from an authorised officer-

    (i)   any documents, or

    (ii)   any other written or printed material in any form, including any information stored, maintained or preserved by means of any mechanical or electronic device, whether or not stored, maintained or preserved in a legible form, which a person is obliged by any provision of the Acts to keep, to issue or to produce for inspection.][7]

(f)   fails to remit any income tax payable pursuant to Chapter IV of Part V of the Income Tax Act, 1967, and the regulations thereunder, or section 7 of the Finance Act, 1968, and the said regulations, or value-added tax within the time specified in that behalf in relation to income tax or value-added tax, as the case may be, by the Acts, or

(g)   obstructs or interferes with any officer of the Revenue Commissioners, or any other person, in the exercise or performance of powers or duties under the Acts for the purposes of any tax.

(3)   A person guilty of an offence under this section shall be liable-

[(a)   on summary conviction, to a fine not exceeding £1,000, which may be mitigated to not less than one fourth part thereof or, at the discretion of the court, to imprisonment for a term not exceeding 12 months or to both the fine and the imprisonment, or][8]

(b)   on conviction on indictment, to a fine not exceeding £10,000 or, at the discretion of the court, to imprisonment for a term not exceeding 5 years or to both the fine and the imprisonment.

(4)   Section 13 of the Criminal Procedure Act, 1967, shall apply in relation to an offence under this section as if, in lieu of the penalties specified in subsection (3) of the said section 13, there were specified therein the penalties provided for by subsection (3)(a) of this section, and the reference in subsection (2)(a) of the said section 13 to the penalties provided for in the said subsection (3) shall be construed and have effect accordingly.

(5)   Where an offence under this section is committed by a body corporate and the offence is shown to have been committed with the consent or connivance of any person who, when the offence was committed, was a director, manager, secretary or other officer of the body corporate, or a member of the committee of management or other controlling authority of the body corporate, that person shall also be deemed to be guilty of the offence and may be proceeded against and punished accordingly.

(6)   In any proceedings under this section, a return or statement delivered to an inspector or other officer of the Revenue Commissioners under any provision of the Acts and purporting to be signed by any person shall be deemed, until the contrary is proved, to have been so delivered, and to have been signed, by that person.

(7)   Notwithstanding the provisions of any other enactment, proceedings in respect of an offence under this section may be instituted within 10 years from the date of the commission of the offence or incurring of the penalty (as the case may be).

(8)   Section 1 of the Probation of Offenders Act, 1907, shall not apply in relation to offences under this section.

(9)   The provisions of sections 128(4), 500(4), 501(3), 502(3), 506 and 507 of the Income Tax Act, 1967, and sections 26(6) and 27(7) of the Value-Added Tax Act, 1972, shall, with any necessary modifications, apply for the purposes of this section as they apply for the purposes of those provisions, including, in the case of such of those provisions as were applied by the Capital Gains Tax Act, 1975, the Corporation Tax Act, 1976, or Part VI, the purposes of those provisions as so applied.

Amendments

1   Substituted by s158(a), FA97 for 1997 and subsequent years.

2   Substituted by s158(b), FA97 for 1997 and subsequent years.

3   Substituted by s3(7) Waiver of Certain Taxes, Interest and Penalties Act, 1993.

4   Inserted by s243(a)(i), FA92.

5   Inserted by s40(2), FA86.

6   Inserted by s18 & Sch1 para3(2), FA89.

7   Inserted by s132(i) & Sch5 PtI para13(2), FA92.

8   Substituted by s243(b), FA92.

Finance Act 1986

(Number 13 of 1986)

Section 113

Use of electronic data processing

113. (1) In this section-

"**the Acts**" means-

(a) the Tax Acts,

(b) the Capital Gains Tax Acts,

[(c) the Value-Added Tax Act, 1972,][1]

(d) the Capital Acquisitions Tax Act, 1976, and the enactments amending or extending that Act, and

(e) Part VI of the Finance Act, 1983,

and any instruments made thereunder;

"**records**" means documents which a person is obliged by any provision of the Acts to keep, to issue or to produce for inspection, and any other written or printed material;

"**tax**" means income tax, corporation tax, capital gains tax, value-added tax or residential property tax, as the case may be.

(2) Subject to the agreement of the Revenue Commissioners, records may be stored, maintained, transmitted, reproduced or communicated, as the case may be, by any electronic, photographic or other process approved of by the Revenue Commissioners, and in circumstances where the use of such process has been agreed by them and subject to such conditions as they may impose.

(3) Where, in pursuance of subsection (2), records are preserved by electronic, photographic or other process, a statement contained in a document produced by any such process shall, subject to the rules of court, be admissible in evidence in any proceedings, whether civil or criminal, to the same extent as the records themselves.

(4) Notwithstanding anything in the Tax Acts, duplicates of assessments need not be made, transmitted or delivered.

(5) The entering by an inspector or other authorised officer of details of an assessment and the tax charged therein in an electronic, photographic or other record from which the Collector-General may extract such details by electronic, photographic or other process shall constitute transmission of such details by the inspector or other authorised officer to the Collector-General.

(6)   In any proceedings in the Circuit Court, the District Court or the High Court for or in relation to the recovery of any tax, a certificate signed by the Collector-General or other authorised officer certifying that, before the institution of proceedings, a stated sum of tax as so transmitted became due and payable by the defendant-

    (a)   (i)   under an assessment which had become final and conclusive,

          (ii)   under the provisions of section 429(4) (inserted by the Finance Act, 1971) of the Income Tax Act, 1967, or

          (iii) under the provisions relating to the specified amount of tax within the meaning of section 30 of the Finance Act, 1976,

    and

    (b)   that demand for the payment of the tax has been duly made, shall be prima facie evidence, until the contrary has been proved, of those facts and a certificate certifying as aforesaid and purporting to be signed by the Collector-General or other authorised officer may be tendered in evidence without proof and shall be deemed, until the contrary is proved, to have been signed by the Collector-General or other authorised officer.

Section 115

Liability to tax, etc., of holder of fixed charge on book debts of company

115.   (1)   Subject to the other provisions of this section, where a person holds a fixed charge (being a fixed charge which is created on or after the passing of this Act) on the book debts of a company (within the meaning of the Companies Act, 1963), such person shall, if the company fails to pay any relevant amount for which it is liable, become liable to pay such relevant amount on due demand, and on neglect or refusal of payment may be proceeded against in like manner as any other defaulter:

    Provided that-

    (a)   this section shall not apply-

          (i)   unless the holder of the fixed charge has been notified in writing by the Revenue Commissioners that a company has failed to pay a relevant amount for which it is liable and that, by reason of this section, the holder of the fixed charge-

(I)   may become liable for payment of any relevant amount which the company subsequently fails to pay, and

(II)   where subparagraph (iii) does not apply, has become liable for the payment of the relevant amount that the company has failed to pay,

(ii)   to any amounts received by the holder of the fixed charge from the company before the date on which the holder is notified in writing by the Revenue Commissioners in accordance with subparagraph (i), and

(iii)   where, within 21 days of the passing of the Finance Act, 1995, or of the creation of the fixed charge, whichever is the later, the holder of the fixed charge furnishes to the Revenue Commissioners a copy of the prescribed particulars of the charge delivered or to be delivered to the registrar of companies in accordance with the provisions of section 99 of the Companies Act, 1963, to any relevant amount which the company was liable to pay before the date on which the holder is notified in writing by the Revenue Commissioners in accordance with subparagraph (i),

and

(b)   the amount or aggregate amount which the person shall be liable to pay in relation to a company in accordance with this section shall not exceed the amount or aggregate amount which that person has, while the fixed charge on book debts in relation to the said company is in existence, received, directly or indirectly, from that company in payment or in part payment of any debts due by the company to that person.

(1A)   The Revenue Commissioners may, at any time and by notice in writing given to the holder of the fixed charge, withdraw, with effect from a date specified in the notice, a notification issued by them in accordance with the provisions of subsection (1):

Provided that such withdrawal shall not-

(i)   affect in any way any liability of the holder of the fixed charge under this section which arose prior to such withdrawal, or

(ii)   preclude the issue under subsection (1) of a subsequent notice to the holder of the fixed charge.

(1B)   The Revenue Commissioners may nominate any of their officers to perform any acts and discharge any functions authorised by this section to be performed or discharged by the Revenue Commissioners.][2]

(2)   In this section **"relevant amount"** means any amount which the company is liable to remit-

(a)   under Chapter IV of Part V of the Income Tax Act, 1967, and

(b)   under the Value-Added Tax Act, 1972.

Amendments
1   Subs1(c) substituted by s99, FA93.
2   Subs (1) - (1B) inserted by s174, FA95, w.e.f.6 April 1995.

Finance Act 1989

(Number 10 of 1989)

Section 92

Tax concession for disabled drivers, etc.

92. (1)   Notwithstanding anything to the contrary contained in any enactment, the Minister for Finance may, after consultation with the Minister for Health and the Minister for the Environment, make regulations providing for-

(a)   the repayment of excise duty and value-added tax and the remission of road tax in respect of a motor vehicle used by, and

(b)   the repayment of excise duty relating to hydrocarbon oil used for combustion in the engines of vehicles, to be specified in the regulations, by, a severely and permanently disabled person-

(i)   as a driver, where the disablement is of such a nature that the person concerned could not drive any vehicle unless it is specially constructed or adapted to take account of that disablement, or

(ii)   as a passenger, where the vehicle has been specially constructed or adapted to take account of the passenger's disablement, and where the vehicle is adapted, the cost of such adaptation consists of not less than [20 per cent.][1] of the value of the vehicle excluding tax and excise duty, or such lesser percentage in respect of certain cases as may be specified by regulations in respect of the repayment of any tax relating to adaptation costs only.

(2)   Regulations under this section shall provide for-

(a)   the criteria for eligibility for the remission of the taxes specified in subsection (1), including such further medical criteria in relation to disabilities as may be considered necessary,

(b)   subject to subsection (3) (b), the procedures to be used in relation to the primary medical certification of a disabled person and to appeals against such certification,

(c)   the procedures in relation to the certification of vehicles to which the regulations relate,

(d)   the amount of value-added tax and excise duty repayable in respect of a vehicle to which the regulations relate,

(e)   the maximum engine size or sizes to which the regulations relate,

(f)   the limits on the frequency of renewal of a vehicle, for the purposes of obtaining a refund of tax or excise duty, and

(g)   in the case of the driver concerned, evidence that the vehicle is for his personal use and evidence of his driving capacity,

and the regulations may provide for such other matters as the Minister for Finance considers necessary or expedient for the purposes of giving effect to this section.

(3)   (a)   Upon the first coming into operation of regulations under this section, section 43(1) of the Finance Act, 1968, shall cease to have effect.

(b)   Any person who, at the passing of this Act, was the registered owner of a motor vehicle, being a motor vehicle in respect of which such person was entitled to and had received a refund of tax or excise duty by reference to section 43(1) of the Finance Act, 1968, shall be deemed to be a person who possesses a primary medical certificate which, subject to compliance with the non-medical requirements set out in the regulations, entitles him to a similar repayment of tax or excise duty by reference to this section.

(4)   Regulations made under this section shall be laid before Dáil Éireann as soon as may be after they are made, and if a resolution annulling the regulations is passed by Dáil Éireann within the next subsequent 21 days on which Dáil Éireann has sat after the regulations have been so laid, the regulations shall be annulled accordingly, but without prejudice to the validity of anything previously done thereunder.

(5)   In this section-

"**medical practitioner**" means a medical practitioner registered under the Medical Practitioners Act, 1978;

"**primary medical certification**" means medical certification by a medical practitioner who is the holder of a post in a health board, being the post commonly known as the post of Director of Community Care and Medical Officer of Health, in the area in which the person to whom the certification relates ordinarily resides and "**primary medical certificate**" shall be construed accordingly.

Amendments
1   Substituted by s124, FA91.

Finance Act 1992

(Number 9 of 1992)

Obligation to keep certain records

231. Part I of the Finance Act, 1968, is hereby amended by the substitution of the following section for section 6:

"6.   (1)   In this section–

'**linking documents**' means documents that are drawn up in the making up of accounts and which show details of the calculations linking the records to the accounts;

'**records**' includes accounts, books of account, documents and any other data maintained manually or by any electronic, photographic or other process, relating to–

(*a*)   all sums of money received and expended in the course of the carrying on or exercising of a trade, profession or other activity and the matters in respect of which the receipt and expenditure take place,

(*b*)   all sales and purchases of goods and services where the carrying on or exercising of a trade, profession or other activity involves the purchase or sale of goods or services,

(*c*)   the assets and liabilities of the trade, profession or other activity referred to in *paragraph (a)* or *(b)*, and

(*d*)   all transactions which constitute an acquisition or disposal of an asset for capital gains tax purposes.

(2)   (*a*)   Every person who, on his own behalf or on behalf of any other person, carries on or exercises any trade, profession or other activity the profits or gains of which are chargeable under Schedule D, or who is chargeable to tax under Schedule D or Schedule F in respect of any other source of income, or who is chargeable to capital gains tax in respect of chargeable gains, shall keep, or cause to be kept on his behalf, such records as will enable true returns to be made, for the purposes of income tax and capital gains tax, of such profits or gains or chargeable gains.

(*b*)   The records shall be kept on a continuous and consistent basis, that is to say the entries therein shall be made in a timely manner and be consistent from one year to the next.

(*c*)   Where accounts are made up to show the profits or gains from any such trade, profession or activity or in relation to a source of income, of any person, that person shall retain, or cause to be retained on his behalf, linking documents.

(d)   Where any such trade, profession or other activity is carried on in partnership, the precedent partner, within the meaning of section 69 of the Income Tax Act, 1967, shall, for the purposes of this section, be deemed to be the person carrying on that trade, profession or other activity.

(3)   Records required to be kept or retained by virtue of this section, shall be kept–

(a)   in written form in an official language of the State, or

(b)   subject to section 113(2) of the Finance Act, 1986, by means of any electronic, photographic or other process.

(4)   Linking documents and records kept pursuant to the preceding provisions of this section shall be retained by the person required to keep the records for a period of 6 years after the completion of the transactions, acts or operations to which they relate or, in the case of a person who fails to comply with section 10 (1) of the Finance Act, 1988, requiring the preparation and delivery of a return on or before the specified return date for a year of assessment, until the expiry of a period of 6 years from the end of the year of assessment in which a return has been delivered showing the profits or gains or chargeable gains derived from the said transactions, acts or operations:

Provided that, this subsection shall not–

(a)   require the retention of linking documents and records in respect of which the inspector notifies in writing the person who is required to retain them that retention is not required, or

(b)   apply to the books and papers of a company which have been disposed of in accordance with section 305(1) of the Companies Act, 1963.

(5)   Any person who fails to comply with the provisions of *subsection (2), (3)* or *(4)* in respect of any records or linking documents in relation to a return for any year of assessment shall be liable to a penalty of £1,200:

Provided that a penalty shall not be imposed under this subsection if it is proved that no person is chargeable to tax in respect of the profits or gains for that year of assessment.

Number 24 of 1993

WAIVER OF CERTAIN TAX, INTEREST AND PENALTIES ACT, 1993

AN ACT TO WAIVE CERTAIN TAX AND INTEREST AND PENALTIES ON CERTAIN TAX, TO AMEND THE PROVISIONS OF THE INCOME TAX ACT, 1967, BY AMENDING SECTION 512 AND SCHEDULE 15 TO THAT ACT AND BY SUBSTITUTING A NEW PROVISION FOR SECTION 516 OF THAT ACT, TO PROVIDE FOR THE FURNISHING OF CERTAIN INFORMATION BY FINANCIAL INSTITUTIONS TO INSPECTORS OF THE REVENUE COMMISSIONERS AND TO PROVIDE FOR CONNECTED MATTERS.

[14th July, 1993]

BE IT ENACTED BY THE OIREACHTAS AS FOLLOWS:

Section 1

Interpretation

1.   (a)   In this Act, except where the context otherwise requires–

"**arrears of tax**", subject to section 2 (5) (a), has the meaning assigned to it by section 3 (2);

"**Chief Special Collector**" has the meaning assigned to it by section 7 (3);

"**the declared amounts**" has the meaning assigned to it by section 2 (3) (a) (iii);

"**estimate**" means an estimate of, or an assessment to, tax made in accordance with the provisions of–

     (i)   section 7 or 8 of the Finance Act, 1968,

     (ii)   section 17 of the Finance Act, 1970, and the regulations made thereunder, or

     (iii)   section 22 or 23 of the Value-Added Tax Act, 1972,

as the case may be;

"**functions**" includes powers and duties;

"**inspector**" means an inspector of taxes appointed under section 161 of the Income Tax Act, 1967;

"**the Minister**" means the Minister for Finance;

"**relevant interest**" means interest payable in accordance with the specified provisions;

"**the relevant period**" means any period ending on or before the 5th day of April, 1991;

"**relevant tax**" has the meaning assigned to it by section 2 (2);

"**settlement amount** "has the meaning assigned to it by section 2 (3) (b);

"**the specified period**" means the period beginning with the passing of this Act and ending on the [21st day of December]¹;

"**the specified provisions**" means any provision of the Acts (within the meaning of section 2 or 3, as the case may be) pursuant to which a person may be liable–

(i)   to interest in respect of tax (within the aforesaid meaning) which is unpaid, including interest on an undercharge of such tax which is attributable to fraud or neglect, or

(ii)   to a fine or other penalty in respect of an offence or default.

(b)   References in this Act to tax (within the meaning of section 2 or 3, as the case may be) being due and payable by a person include references to such tax which would have been due and payable by him if any return, statement or declaration (being a return, statement or declaration, as the case may be, which should have, but had not, been made by him in accordance with any provision of the Acts (within the aforesaid meaning)) had been so made and if that tax had been contained in an assessment made on the person or in an estimate issued to the person.

Section 2
Waiver of certain tax and related interest and penalties.

2.   (1)   In this section–

"**the Acts**" means–

(a)   the Income Tax Acts (other than Chapter IV of Part V of the Income Tax Act, 1967, and section 17 of the Finance Act, 1970),

(b)   the Capital Gains Tax Acts,

(c)   section 16 of the Finance Act, 1983,

(d)   the Health Contributions Act, 1979, and

(e)   the Youth Employment Agency Act, 1981,

and any instruments made thereunder;

"**income**" means total income from all sources as estimated in accordance with the provisions of the Income Tax Acts after deducting from the income so much of any deduction allowed by virtue of the provisions referred to in section 33 of the Finance Act, 1975, as is to be deducted from or set off against that income in charging it to income tax;

"**tax**" means any tax, levy or contributions payable in accordance with any provision of the Acts.

(2)   This section applies to an individual who, for the relevant period, was in receipt of income or had chargeable gains in respect of which any tax (referred to in this Act as "relevant tax") due and payable by him in accordance with any provision of the Acts has not been paid:

Provided that–

(a)   this section shall not apply to an individual if, before the 25th day of May, 1993 (hereafter in this proviso referred to as "the designated date"), he had been notified in writing by an inspector–

(i)   that the inspector intended to make any enquiries or take any actions as are specified in section 15 of the Finance Act, 1988, in relation to the liability to tax of the individual for the relevant period, or

(ii)   that any matter which occasions or may occasion a liability or further liability to tax of the individual for the relevant period is under investigation or enquiry by the inspector,

and such enquiries or actions, or investigation or enquiry, as the case may be, had not been concluded on or before the designated date, and for the purposes of this paragraph the aforesaid enquiries or actions, or investigation or enquiry, shall be deemed not to have been concluded unless an agreement has been reached between the individual and the inspector as to the liability to tax of the individual for the relevant period,

(b)   relevant tax shall not include any sum–

(i)   which, before the designated date, was certified in a certificate issued, and not withdrawn, under section 485 of the Income Tax Act, 1967,

(ii)   which, before the designated date, was the subject of proceedings initiated, and not withdrawn, as a debt due to the Minister, in any court of competent jurisdiction,

(iii) which was tax contained in an assessment which was on the designated date the subject of an appeal to which the provisions of Part XXVI of the Income Tax Act, 1967, apply,

(iv) which, before the designated date, was entered as a specified amount in a notice of attachment issued, and not revoked, under section 73 of the Finance Act, 1988,

(v)   which was not paid on or before the designated date by virtue of an arrangement or scheme the main purpose, or one of the main purposes, of which was the avoidance of liability to tax,

(vi)   which, following enquiries made, or action taken, by an inspector pursuant to section 15 of the Finance Act, 1988, or any other investigation by an inspector, had been agreed before the designated date by an individual and an inspector as being the individual's tax liability,

(vii)   being tax in respect of income or chargeable gains which arose from, or by reason of, an illegal source or activity (other than the evasion of tax or the non-compliance with the provisions relating to exchange control), or

(viii)   paid or remitted in accordance with the provisions of section 3 in respect of arrears of tax.

(3)   An individual to whom this section applies shall–

(a)   within the specified period give a declaration in writing to the Chief Special Collector which–

(i)   is made and signed by the individual,

(ii)   is in a form prescribed by the Revenue Commissioners and approved of by the Minister,

(iii)   contains, in relation to the individual, a full and true statement of the respective amounts (referred to in this Act as "the declared amounts") of–

(I)   the income, and

(II)   the chargeable gains,

referred to in subsection (2), and

(iv)   declares that neither the declared amounts nor any part of those amounts arose from, or by reason of, an unlawful source or activity (other than the evasion of tax or the non-compliance with the provisions relating to exchange control), and

(b)   not earlier than the giving of the declaration referred to in paragraph (a) but on or before the 14th day of January, 1994, remit to the Chief Special Collector an amount (referred to in this Act as "the settlement amount") equal to 15 per cent. of the declared amounts.

(4)   On receipt by him of the declaration referred to in subsection (3) and the settlement amount, the Chief Special Collector shall give to the individual concerned–

(a) a certificate, in a form prescribed by the Revenue Commissioners and approved of by the Minister, stating, in relation to that individual–

(i) his name and address,

(ii) the settlement amount paid by him, and

(iii) the respective amounts of the declared amounts, and

(b) evidence, in a form prescribed by the Revenue Commissioners and approved of by the Minister, that such a certificate has been given.

(5) Notwithstanding any other provision of the Acts but subject to section 4, where an individual to whom this section applies complies with the provisions of subsection (3)–

(a) his liability to relevant tax in respect of the declared amounts–

(i) shall be deemed to be satisfied by the settlement amount, and

(ii) shall not be arrears of tax,

(b) any amount of relevant interest which the individual may have become liable for in relation to relevant tax in respect of the declared amounts shall be waived, and

(c) proceedings shall not be initiated or continued for the recovery of any fine or penalty to which the individual may be liable under any of the specified provisions in relation to relevant tax in respect of the declared amounts, nor shall the Revenue Commissioners seek or demand from the individual payment of any sum in lieu of such fine or penalty.

Section 3

Waiver of certain interest and penalties in respect of certain tax.

3. (1) (a) In this section–

"**the Acts**" means–

(i) the Acts within the meaning of section 2,

(ii) Chapter IV of Part V of the Income Tax Act, 1967,

(iii) section 17 of the Finance Act, 1970,

(iv) the Corporation Tax Acts,

(v)   Part V of the Finance Act, 1920, and the enactments amending or extending that Part,

(vi)   the Value-Added Tax Act, 1972, and the enactments amending or extending that Act,

(vii)   the Capital Acquisitions Tax Act, 1976, and the enactments amending or extending that Act,

(viii) the Stamp Act, 1891, and the enactments amending or extending that Act, and

(ix)   Part VI of the Finance Act, 1983, and the enactments amending or extending that Part,

and any instruments made thereunder;

"the due date" means, in relation to an amount of tax, the date on which a person becomes liable to interest under any of the specified provisions in respect of the late payment of that tax;

"tax" means any tax, duty, levy or contributions payable in accordance with any provision of the Acts.

(b)   The reference in subsection (2) to an amount of tax due and payable shall, in a case where tax is assessed or estimated in an assessment or estimate against which an appeal has been made, be construed as a reference to the amount of tax which becomes due and payable on the determination of the appeal (within the meaning of section 550 (2A) (c) of the Income Tax Act, 1967) or, pending such determination, the tax as assessed or estimated.

(2)   This section applies to a person who had not paid or remitted before the due date an amount of tax (in this Act referred to as "arrears of tax") due and payable by him, or chargeable, in accordance with any provision of the Acts in respect of or during the relevant period.

(3)   Where a person to whom this section applies has unpaid arrears of tax on the passing of this Act, he shall on or before the 14th day of January, 1994, and subject to the provisions of subsection (6), pay or remit those arrears of tax.

(4)   Notwithstanding any other provision of the Acts but subject to the provisions of subsection (5) and section 4, where a person has paid or remitted, on or before the 14th day of January, 1994, his arrears of tax–

(a)   any amount of relevant interest to which the person may be liable in relation to arrears of tax and which is unpaid at the date of the payment or remittance referred to in subsection (3) shall be waived,

(b)   any amount of relevant interest in relation to arrears of tax which is paid by the person on or after the 26th day of May, 1993, shall be refunded to him, and

(c)   proceedings shall not be initiated or continued for the recovery of any fine or penalty to which the person may be liable under any of the specified provisions in relation to arrears of tax, nor shall the Revenue Commissioners seek or demand from the person payment of any sum in lieu of such fine or penalty.

(5)   This section shall not apply to any interest, fine or other penalty that–

(a)   in the case of a fine or other penalty, is imposed by a court under any of the Acts,

(b)   in the case of interest, is ordered by a court in any proceedings for the recovery of tax or interest to be paid by a person, or

(c)   in any case, is included in a specified sum such as is referred to in subsection (2) (c) of section 23 of the Finance Act, 1983, where the full amount of the specified sum was not paid on or before the 25th day of May, 1993.

(6)   (a)   Where a payment or remittance in accordance with the provisions of subsection (3) is made by an individual who also remits a settlement amount, then, without prejudice to the amount of that payment or remittance, so much of that payment or remittance as is referable to value-added tax may be remitted to the Chief Special Collector.

(b)   Where, in accordance with paragraph (a), an individual makes a remittance to the Chief Special Collector, the individual by whom the remittance is made shall on the earlier of–

(i)   the date of payment, or

(ii)   a date within the specified period,

give a declaration in writing to the Chief Special Collector which–

(I)   is made and signed by the individual,

(II)   is in a form prescribed by the Revenue Commissioners and approved of by the Minister, and

(III)   contains, in relation to that individual, a full and true statement of the amount of value-added tax comprised in the arrears of tax.

(c)   On receipt by him of the declaration referred to in paragraph (b) and the remittance referred to in paragraph (a), the Chief Special Collector shall give to the individual by whom the remittance is made–

   (i)   a certificate, in a form prescribed by the Revenue Commissioners and approved of by the Minister, stating, in relation to that individual–

      (I)   his name and address, and

      (II)   the amount of the said remittance, and

   (ii)   evidence, in a form prescribed by the Revenue Commissioners and approved of by the Minister, that such a certificate has been given.

(7)   Section 23 (4) of the Finance Act, 1983, is hereby amended by the substitution of the following paragraph for paragraph (aa) (inserted by section 72 of the Finance Act, 1988):

"(aa) the provisions of section 72 of the Finance Act, 1988, or section 3 of the Waiver of Certain Tax, Interest and Penalties Act, 1993, apply, or".

Section 4
Non-application of sections 2 (5) and 3 (4).

4.   (1)   The provisions of sections 2 (5) and 3 (4) shall not apply, and those provisions shall be deemed never to have applied, to a person where–

   (a)   such person fails–

      (i)   if he is an individual, for the year of assessment 1992-93, or

      (ii)   in any other case, for any accounting period ending in the year beginning on the 1st day of January, 1993, and ending on the 31st day of December, 1993,

   to duly deliver a return of income on or before the specified date in relation to that return, or

   (b)   (i)   a declaration given by such person to the Chief Special Collector under subsection (3) (a) of section 2–

      (I)   did not contain a full and true statement of the kind referred to in subparagraph (iii) of the said subsection, or

(II)　is proven to be false in so far as the requirements of subparagraph (iv) of the said subsection are concerned,

or

(ii)　a declaration given by him to the Chief Special Collector under subsection (6) (b) of section 3 did not contain a full and true statement of the kind referred to in subparagraph (III) of the said subsection, or

(c)　the amount paid or remitted by him in respect of arrears of tax was less than the arrears of tax due and payable by him,

and any certificate issued to that person pursuant to section 2 (4) or section 3 (6) (c) shall be null and void.

(2)　Where, by virtue of this section, section 2 (5) does not apply and is deemed never to have applied to an individual, the amount paid by him as the settlement amount shall be treated as a payment on account of relevant tax.

(3)　(a)　In subsection (1) "return of income" and "specified date" have the meanings assigned to them by section 48 of the Finance Act, 1986.

(b)　The provisions of subsection (1) (b) of section 48 of the Finance Act, 1986, shall apply for the purposes of subsection (1) (a) of this section as they apply for the purposes of that section.

Section 5

Enquiries or action by inspection or other officers.

5.　(1)　Where, in relation to any liability to tax (within the meaning of section 2 or 3, as the case may be) of an individual for the relevant period, being tax which has been remitted to the Chief Special Collector, an inspector or other officer of the Revenue Commissioners commences to make such enquiries, or take such action, as are within his powers, or gives a notice in writing to an individual of his intention to make such enquiries or take such action in relation to such liability to tax and the individual produces to the inspector or other officer, not later than 30 days from the commencement of the said enquiries or the taking of the said action, or the giving of the notice as aforesaid, a certificate referred to in section 2 (4) or 3 (6) (c), as the case may be, in respect of such liability to tax given to him by the Chief Special Collector, the inspector or other officer shall, on production to him of the said certificate and on validation of that certificate in accordance with the provisions of paragraph (a) of the proviso to section 7 (4), be precluded from continuing with or commencing the said enquiries or continuing with or commencing the said action unless, on application by him to the Appeal Commissioners, he shows to the satisfaction of those Commissioners that–

(a)   enquiries made or action taken in relation to the liability to tax (within the aforesaid meaning) of the individual for any period commencing on or after the 6th day of April, 1991, indicate, or

(b)   there are other reasonable grounds which indicate,

that a declaration made by the individual to the Chief Special Collector under section 2 (3) (a) or 3 (6) (b) did not contain a full and true statement of the declared amounts or the amount of value-added tax comprised in the [arrears of tax, as the case may be, or that the declaration made by the individual under section 2(3)(a)(iv) is false][2].

(2)   (a)   An application by the inspector or other officer under subsection (1) shall be made by him by notice in writing to the Appeal Commissioners within 30 days of the receipt by him from the individual concerned of the certificate referred to in section 2 (4) or 3 (6) (c), as the case may be, given to that individual by the Chief Special Collector, and a copy of the application shall be furnished as soon as practicable by the inspector or other officer to the individual concerned.

(b)   An application under subsection (1) shall, with any necessary modifications, be heard by the Appeal Commissioners as if it were an appeal against an assessment to income tax.

(c)   Any action required to be taken by the individual and any further action proposed to be taken by the inspector or other officer pursuant to the inspector's or other officer's enquiry or action shall be suspended pending decision by the Appeal Commissioners on the application.

(d)   Where, on the hearing of the application by an inspector or other officer under subsection (1), the Appeal Commissioners–

(i)   decide that there are no reasonable grounds to suggest that the declaration made by the individual to the Chief Special Collector under section 2 (3) (a) or 3 (6) (b) did not contain a full and true statement of the declared amounts or the amount of value-added tax comprised in the arrears of tax, as the case may be, then the individual shall not be required to take any action pursuant to the inspector's or other officer's enquiry or action and the inspector or other officer shall be prohibited from pursuing his enquiry or action, or

(ii)   decide that there are such reasonable grounds, then the inspector or other officer may continue with his enquiry or action.

Section 6

Demands or other requests for payment.

6.   Where, in relation to an individual

(a)   the Revenue Commissioners, the Collector-General or any of their or his officers authorised in that behalf, have demanded or otherwise requested the payment of any tax–

(i)   in respect of which a settlement amount has been remitted to the Chief Special Collector, or

(ii)   which is value-added tax in respect of which a remittance has been made to the Chief Special Collector in accordance with section 3 (6) (a), and

(b)   the individual has been given a certificate as is referred to in section 2 (4) or 3 (6) (c) in respect of such tax,

the individual shall produce to the Revenue Commissioners, the Collector-General or the authorised officer, as the case may be, within 30 days of–

(i)   the date of the making of the demand or request, or

(ii)   if later, the date he received the certificate,

the evidence referred to in section 2 (4) (b) or section 3 (6) (c), as the case may be, and the demand or request shall be withdrawn and the amount of tax specified in the demand or request shall be discharged:

Provided that, where subsection (5) of section 2 and subsection (4) of section 3 do not apply by virtue of the provisions of section 4–

(i)   the amount of tax discharged shall be reinstated, and

(ii)   any additional assessments or estimates necessary to give effect to this proviso shall be made.

Section 7

Confidentiality.

7.   (1)   In this section–

"**declaration of confidentiality**" means the declaration of confidentiality contained in the Schedule to this Act;

"**special collection function**" means any function or duty related to–

(a)   the receipt and retention of declarations referred to in section 2 (3) (a) or 3 (6) (b),

(b)   the receipt, recording and lodgement of–

(i)   settlement amounts, or

(ii)   so much of any payment or remittance referred to in section 3 (6) (a) as is referable to value-added tax, or

(c)   the issue and recording of certificates referred to in section 2 (4) or 3 (6) (c),

which could result in the person or persons discharging that function or performing that duty acquiring, or having access to, any information in respect of such declarations, amounts or certificates, and a reference to the discharge of a special collection function shall be construed as a reference to the discharge of such a function or performance of such a duty;

"**special collector**" means any officer or employee of the Revenue Commissioners who–

(a)   has been nominated by the Revenue Commissioners to discharge a special collection function, and has not had his nomination revoked, and

(b)   has   made   and   subscribed   the   declaration   of confidentiality.

(2)   (a)   Special collection functions may only be discharged by special collectors.

(b)   Every person nominated by the Revenue Commissioners to be a special collector shall, upon making and subscribing to the declaration of confidentiality, become a special collector.

(c)   Declarations of confidentiality shall be made before a peace commissioner or other person duly authorised to take and receive statutory declarations.

(3)   (a)   Special collection functions shall be under the control and direction of a special collector, to be known as and is referred to

in this Act as "the Chief Special Collector", who is designated to be such by the Revenue Commissioners.

(b)   Whenever there is no Chief Special Collector, the Revenue Commissioners shall designate as soon as is practicable thereafter a special collector to be the Chief Special Collector and all other special collectors shall observe and follow the orders, instructions and directions of the Chief Special Collector in relation to any special collection function:

Provided that nothing in paragraph (b) shall be construed so as to affect the proviso to subsection (6).

(c)   For the purposes of the receipt of any declaration, amount or remittance, or the issue of any certificate or evidence, in accordance with section 2 or 3, references to the Chief Special Collector shall be construed as including a reference to any other special collector acting on behalf of the Chief Special Collector in that matter.

(d)   If and so long as the Chief Special Collector is unable through illness, absence or other cause to fulfil his duties, another special collector designated in that behalf by the Revenue Commissioners shall act as Chief Special Collector, and any reference in this Act to the Chief Special Collector shall be construed as including, where appropriate, a reference to a special collector designated under this paragraph.

(4)   A special collector shall be deemed to have contravened his declaration of confidentiality if he discloses, or causes to be disclosed, to a person who is not a special collector, any information which he could have acquired, or had access to, only by virtue of being a special collector:

Provided that a special collector shall not be deemed to have contravened his declaration of confidentiality where

(a)   having been requested to validate a certificate or evidence referred to in section 2 (4) or 3 (6) (c) by an officer of the Revenue Commissioners to whom that certificate or evidence has been produced for the purposes of section 5 or 6, as the case may be, he informs that officer whether or not that certificate or evidence, as the case may be, was given by a special collector,

(b)   he provides to the Minister or the Revenue Commissioners such information, in the form of aggregates and in that form only, as the Minister or the Commissioners, as the case may be, may request in relation to–

(i)   the total amount of–

(I)   the declared amounts,

(II)   settlement amounts, or

(III) such amounts of any payments or remittances referred to in section 3 (6) (a) as are referable to value-added tax remitted to the Chief Special Collector,

and

(ii) the total respective numbers of individuals who remitted amounts to the Chief Special Collector in respect of income, chargeable gains or value-added tax,

or

(c) he provides to the Comptroller and Auditor General or the Accounting Officer of the Revenue Commissioners such information as the Comptroller and Auditor General or that Accounting Officer, as the case may be, may request and reasonably require to ensure that any special collection function has been discharged in accordance with this Act.

(5) Any information acquired by the Comptroller and Auditor General or the Accounting Officer of the Revenue Commissioners by virtue of paragraph (c) of the proviso to subsection (4) shall be used by the Comptroller and Auditor General or that Accounting Officer, as the case may be, only for the purpose of ensuring that any special collection function has been discharged in accordance with this Act:

Provided that the foregoing provisions of this subsection shall not prevent the Comptroller and Auditor General from carrying out his functions, including exercising his reporting duty to Dáil Éireann.

(6) The Revenue Commissioners may make such nominations as are required for the purposes of this section and may at any time also revoke any such nomination:

Provided that the Revenue Commissioners may only revoke at any time the nomination of the special collector who is the Chief Special Collector where they also designate, with effect from that time, a special collector to be his successor as Chief Special Collector.

Section 8

Remittances.

8. Any remittance made to the Chief Special Collector under section 2 (3) (b) or 3 (6) (a) shall—

(a) where it is made otherwise than in cash, be made payable to the Revenue Commissioners, and

(b) be lodged to the General Account of the Revenue Commissioners in the Central Bank of Ireland as soon as prompt recording, and secure transmission to that account, of that remittance permits.

Section 9

Penalty for failure to comply with section 2(3)(a) or 3(6)(b).

9. (1) Where an individual, being an individual to whom section 2 applies, or a person to whom section 3 applies–

   (a) (i) has knowingly or wilfully failed to comply with any provision of the Acts requiring–

      (I) the furnishing of a return of income, profits or gains, or of sources of income, profits or gains, for the purposes of any tax,

      (II) the furnishing of any other return, certificate, notification, particulars, or any statement or evidence, for the purposes of any tax, or

   (ii) has knowingly or wilfully delivered any incorrect return, statement or accounts or knowingly or wilfully furnished any incorrect information in connection with any tax,

   in respect of the relevant period, and

   (b) (i) fails to give a declaration required by section 2 (3) (a), or

   (ii) gives such a declaration as aforesaid or a declaration under section 3 (6) (b) which is false or fails to comply with the requirements of subparagraph.(iii) or (iv) of the said section 2 (3) (a) or subparagraph (III) of the said section 3 (6) (b) to the extent that any of the said subparagraphs apply to him,

   he shall, without prejudice to any other penalty to which he may be liable, be guilty of an offence and shall be liable–

      (I) on summary conviction where the amount of the specified difference is–

         (A) less than £1,200, to a fine not exceeding 25 per cent. of the amount of the specified difference or, at the discretion of the court, to a term of imprisonment not exceeding 12 months or to both,

         (B) equal to or greater than £1,200, to a fine not exceeding £1,200 or, at the discretion of the court, to a term of imprisonment not exceeding 12 months or to both,

or

(II)   on conviction on indictment where the amount of the specified difference is–

(A)   less than £5,000, to a fine not exceeding 25 percent. of the amount of the specified difference or, at the discretion of the court, to a term of imprisonment not exceeding 2 years or to both,

(B)   equal to or greater than £5,000 but less than £10,000, to a fine not exceeding 50 per cent. of the amount of the specified difference or, at the discretion of the court, to a term of imprisonment not exceeding 3 years or to both,

(C)   equal to or greater than £10,000 but less than £25,000, to a fine not exceeding the amount of the specified difference or, at the discretion of the court, to a term of imprisonment not exceeding 4 years or to both,

(D)   equal to or greater than £25,000 but less than £100,000, to a fine not exceeding twice the amount of the specified difference or, at the discretion of the court, to a term of imprisonment not exceeding 8 years or to both,

(E)   equal to or greater than £100,000, to a fine not exceeding twice the amount of the specified difference and to a term of imprisonment not exceeding 8 years.

(2)   Subsections (4), (6), (7) and (8) of section 94 of the Finance Act, 1983, shall, with any necessary modifications, apply and have effect for the purposes of this section as they apply and have effect for the purposes of that section.

(3)   In this section–

"**the Acts**" and "**tax**" have the meanings assigned to them, respectively, by section 2 or 3, as appropriate;

"the specified difference" means the difference between–

(a)   the amount of tax payable for the relevant period by the individual, and

(b)   the amount which would have been so payable if–

      (i)   any return, certificate, notification or particulars or any statement of evidence, referred to in subsection (1) (a) (i), not furnished by him, had, in fact, been so furnished and the details therein had been correct, or

      (ii)   any incorrect return, statement or accounts, or any incorrect information, referred to in subsection (1) (a) (ii), in connection with any tax had, in fact, been correct.

Section 10

Amendment of section 512 (mitigation and application of fines and penalties) of Income Tax Act, 1967.

[...]³

Section 11

Penalty for false statement made to obtain allowance.

[...]³

Section 12

Amendment of Schedule 15 to Income Tax Act, 1967.

[...]³

Section 13

Furnishing of certain information of financial institutions.

[...]³

Section 14

Care and management.

14.   Subject to section 7 (3) (a), all matters relating to this Act are hereby placed under the care and management of the Revenue Commissioners.

Section 15

Short title, construction and collective citation.

15.   (1)   This Act may be cited as the Waiver of Certain Tax, Interest and Penalties Act, 1993.

(2)   This Act shall be construed–

(a)   so far as relating to income tax and sur-tax, together with the Income Tax Acts,

(b)   so far as relating to corporation profits tax, together with Part V of the Finance Act, 1920, and the enactments amending or extending that Part,

(c)   so far as relating to corporation tax, together with the Corporation Tax Acts,

(d)   so far as relating to capital gains tax, together with the Capital Gains Tax Acts,

(e)   so far as relating to value-added tax, together with the Value Added Tax Acts, 1972 to 1993,

(f)   so far as relating to stamp duty, together with the Stamp Act, 1891, and the enactments amending or extending that Act,

(g)   so far as relating to capital acquisitions tax, together with the Capital Acquisitions Tax Act, 1976, and the enactments amending or extending that Act,

(h)   so far as relating to residential property tax, together with Part VI of the Finance Act, 1983, and the enactments amending or extending that Part,

(i)   so far as relating to income levy, together with section 16 of the Finance Act, 1983, and the enactments amending or extending that section,

(j)   so far as relating to health contributions, together with the Health Contributions Act, 1979, and the enactments amending or extending that Act, and

(k)   so far as relating to employment and training levy, together with the Youth Employment Agency Act, 1981, and the enactments amending or extending that Act.

(3)   The collective citation "the Value-Added Tax Acts, 1972 to 1993" shall include this Act in so far as it relates to value-added tax.

(4)   Any reference in this Act to any other enactment shall, except so far as the context otherwise requires, be construed as a reference to that enactment as amended by or under any other enactment including this Act.

(5)   In this Act, a reference to a section is to a section of this Act, unless it is indicated that reference to some other enactment is intended.

(6)   In this Act, a reference to a subsection, paragraph or subparagraph is to the subsection, paragraph or subparagraph of the provision in which the reference occurs, unless it is indicated that reference to some other provision is intended.

Schedule

Section 7

Form of declaration of confidentiality to be made by special collectors

"I, A.B., do solemnly declare that I have read and understand section 7 of the Waiver of Certain Tax, Interest and Penalties Act, 1993, and that I will not disclose, or cause to be disclosed, to a person who is not a special collector (within the meaning of that section) any information which I acquire, or have access to, in the course of discharging special collection functions (within the meaning of the said section) save where the disclosure of such information is deemed, by virtue of the proviso to subsection (4) of the said section 7, not to be a contravention of this declaration."

Amendments
1. Substituted by s163, FA94.
2. Substituted by s25, Criminal Assets Bureau Act, 1996.
3. Ss10-13 repealed by s1098 and Sch 30, TCA1997.

Finance Act 1995

(Number 8 of 1995)

Section 172

Duties of a relevant person in relation to certain revenue offences

172. (1)   In this section-

"**the Acts**" means-

    (a)   the Customs Acts,

    (b)   the statutes relating to the duties of excise and to the management of those duties,

    (c)   the Tax Acts,

    (d)   the Capital Gains Tax Acts,

    (e)   the Value-Added Tax Act, 1972, and the enactments amending or extending that Act,

    (f)   the Capital Acquisitions Tax Act, 1976, and the enactments amending or extending that Act,

    (g)   the statutes relating to stamp duty and to the management of that duty,

and any instruments made thereunder and any instruments made under any other enactment and relating to tax;

"**appropriate officer**" means any officer nominated by the Revenue Commissioners to be an appropriate officer for the purposes of this section;

"**company**" means any body corporate;

"**relevant person**", in relation to a company, means a person who-

    (a)   (i)   is an auditor to the company appointed in accordance with section 160 of the Companies Act, 1963 (as amended by the Companies Act, 1990), or

            (ii)   in the case of an industrial and provident society or a friendly society, is a public auditor to the society for the purposes of the Industrial and Provident Societies Acts, 1893 to 1978, and the Friendly Societies Acts, 1896 to 1977,

    or

    (b)   with a view to reward assists or advises the company in the preparation or delivery of any information, declaration, return, records, accounts or other document which he or she knows will be, or is likely to be, used for any purpose of tax:

Provided that a person who would, but for this proviso, be treated as a relevant person in relation to a company shall not be so treated if the person assists or advises the company solely in the person's capacity as an employee of the said company, and a person shall be treated as assisting or advising the company in that capacity where the person's income from assisting or advising the company consists solely of emoluments to which Chapter IV of Part V of the Income Tax Act, 1967, applies;

"**relevant offence**" means an offence committed by a company which consists of the company-

(a) knowingly or wilfully delivering any incorrect return, statement or accounts or knowingly or wilfully furnishing or causing to be furnished any incorrect information in connection with any tax,

(b) knowingly or wilfully claiming or obtaining relief or exemption from, or repayment of, any tax, being a relief, exemption or repayment to which there is no entitlement,

(c) knowingly or wilfully issuing or producing any incorrect invoice, receipt, instrument or other document in connection with any tax,

(d) knowingly or wilfully failing to comply with any provision of the Acts requiring the furnishing of a return of income, profits or gains, or of sources of income, profits or gains, for the purposes of any tax:

Provided that an offence under this paragraph committed by a company shall not be a relevant offence if the company has made a return of income, profits or gains to the Revenue Commissioners in respect of an accounting period falling wholly or partly into the period of 3 years immediately preceding the accounting period in respect of which the offence was committed;

"**tax**" means tax, duty, levy or charge under the care and management of the Revenue Commissioners.

(2) If, having regard solely to information obtained in the course of examining the accounts of a company, or in the course of assisting or advising a company in the preparation or delivery of any information, declaration, return, records, accounts or other document for the purposes of tax, as the case may be, a person who is a relevant person in relation to the company becomes aware that the company has committed, or is in the course of

committing, one or more relevant offences, the person shall, if the offence or offences are material-

(a)   communicate particulars of the offence or offences in writing to the company without undue delay and request the company to-

(i)   take such action as is necessary for the purposes of rectifying the matter, or

(ii)   notify an appropriate officer of the offence or offences,

not later than 6 months after the time of communication, and

(b)   (i)   unless it is established to the person's satisfaction that the necessary action has been taken or notification made, as the case may be, under paragraph (a), cease to act as the auditor to the company or to assist or advise the company in such preparation or delivery as is specified in paragraph (b) of the definition of relevant person, and

(ii)   shall not so act, assist or advise before a time which is-

(I)   3 years after the time at which the particulars were communicated under paragraph (a), or

(II)   the time at which it is established to the person's satisfaction that the necessary action has been taken or notification made, as the case may be, under paragraph (a),

whichever is the earlier:

Provided that nothing in this paragraph shall prevent a person from assisting or advising a company in preparing for, or conducting, legal proceedings, either civil or criminal, which are extant or pending at a time which is 6 months after the time of communication under paragraph (a).

(3)   Where a person, being in relation to a company a relevant person within the meaning of paragraph (a) of the definition of relevant person, ceases under the provisions of this section to act as auditor to the company, then the person shall deliver-

(a)   a notice in writing to the company stating that he or she is so resigning, and

(b)   a copy of the notice to an appropriate officer not later than 14 days after he or she has delivered the notice to the company.

(4)   A person shall be guilty of an offence under this section if the person-

(a)   fails to comply with subsection (2) or (3), or

(b)   knowingly or wilfully makes a communication under subsection (2) which is incorrect.

(5)   Where a relevant person is found guilty of an offence under this section the person shall be liable-

(a)   on summary conviction to a fine of £1,000 which may be mitigated to not less than one-fourth part thereof, or

(b)   on conviction on indictment, to a fine not exceeding £5,000 or, at the discretion of the court, to imprisonment for a term not exceeding 2 years or to both the fine and the imprisonment.

(6)   Section 13 of the Criminal Procedure Act, 1967, shall apply in relation to this section as if, in lieu of the penalties specified in subsection (3) of the said section 13, there were specified therein the penalties provided for by subsection (5)(a) of this section, and the reference in subsection (2)(a) of the said section 13 to the penalties provided for in the said subsection (3) shall be construed and have effect accordingly.

(7)   Notwithstanding the provisions of any other enactment, proceedings in respect of this section may be instituted within 6 years from the time at which a person is required under subsection (2) to communicate particulars of an offence or offences in writing to a company.

(8)   It shall be a good defence in a prosecution for an offence under subsection (4)(a) in relation to a failure to comply with subsection (2) for an accused (being a person who is a relevant person in relation to a company) to show that he or she was, in the ordinary scope of professional engagement, assisting or advising the company in preparing for legal proceedings and would not have become aware that one or more relevant offences had been committed by the company if he or she had not been so assisting or advising.

(9)   If a person who is a relevant person takes any action required by subsection (2) or (3), no duty to which the person may be subject shall be regarded as contravened and no liability or action shall lie against the person in any court for so doing.

(10)   The Revenue Commissioners may nominate an officer to be an appropriate officer for the purposes of this section and the name of an officer so nominated and the address to which copies of

notices under subsection (2) or (3) shall be delivered shall be published in the Iris Oifigiúil.

(11)   This section shall have effect as respects a relevant offence committed by a company in respect of tax which is-

(a)   assessable by reference to accounting periods, for any accounting period beginning after the 30th day of June, 1995,

(b)   assessable by reference to years of assessment, for the year of assessment 1995-96 and subsequent years,

(c)   payable by reference to a taxable period, for a taxable period beginning after the 30th day of June, 1995,

(d)   chargeable on gifts or inheritances taken on or after the 30th day of June, 1995,

(e)   chargeable on instruments executed on or after the 30th day of June, 1995, or

(f)   payable in any other case, on or after the 30th day of June, 1995.

Section 174

Amendment of section 115 (liability to tax, etc., of holder of fixed charge on book debts of company) of Finance Act, 1986

174.   Section 115 of the Finance Act, 1986, is hereby amended by the substitution of the following subsections for subsection (1):

"(1)   Subject to the other provisions of this section, where a person holds a fixed charge (being a fixed charge which is created on or after the passing of this Act) on the book debts of a company (within the meaning of the Companies Act, 1963), such person shall, if the company fails to pay any relevant amount for which it is liable, become liable to pay such relevant amount on due demand, and on neglect or refusal of payment may be proceeded against in like manner as any other defaulter:

Provided that-

(a)   this section shall not apply-

(i)   unless the holder of the fixed charge has been notified in writing by the Revenue Commissioners that a company has failed to pay a relevant amount for which it is liable and that, by reason of this section, the holder of the fixed charge-

(I)   may become liable for payment of any relevant amount which the company subsequently fails to pay, and

(II)   where subparagraph (iii) does not apply, has become liable for the payment of the relevant amount that the company has failed to pay,

(ii)   to any amounts received by the holder of the fixed charge from the company before the date on which the holder is notified in writing by the Revenue Commissioners in accordance with subparagraph (i), and

(iii)   where, within 21 days of the passing of the Finance Act, 1995, or of the creation of the fixed charge, whichever is the later, the holder of the fixed charge furnishes to the Revenue Commissioners a copy of the prescribed particulars of the charge delivered or to be delivered to the registrar of companies in accordance with the provisions of section 99 of the Companies Act, 1963, to any relevant amount which the company was liable to pay before the date on which the holder is notified in writing by the Revenue Commissioners in accordance with subparagraph (i),

and

(b)   the amount or aggregate amount which the person shall be liable to pay in relation to a company in accordance with this section shall not exceed the amount or aggregate amount which that person has, while the fixed charge on book debts in relation to the said company is in existence, received, directly or indirectly, from that company in payment or in part payment of any debts due by the company to that person.

(1A)   The Revenue Commissioners may, at any time and by notice in writing given to the holder of the fixed charge, withdraw, with effect from a date specified in the notice, a notification issued by them in accordance with the provisions of subsection (1):

Provided that such withdrawal shall not-

(i)   affect in any way any liability of the holder of the fixed charge under this section which arose prior to such withdrawal, or

(ii)   preclude the issue under subsection (1) of a subsequent notice to the holder of the fixed charge.

(1B)   The Revenue Commissioners may nominate any of their officers to perform any acts and discharge any functions authorised by this section to be performed or discharged by the Revenue Commissioners.".

Section 175

Power to obtain information

175. (1) For the purposes of the assessment, charge, collection and recovery of any tax or duty placed under their care and management, the Revenue Commissioners may, by notice in writing, request any Minister of the Government to provide them with such information in the possession of the Minister in relation to payments for any purposes made by the Minister, whether on his own behalf or on behalf of any other person, to such persons or classes of persons as the Revenue Commissioners may specify in the notice and a Minister so requested shall provide such information as may be specified.

(2) The Revenue Commissioners may nominate any of their officers to perform any acts and discharge any functions authorised by this section to be performed or discharged by the Revenue Commissioners.

Section 177

Tax clearance certificates in relation to public sector contracts

177. (1) In this section-

"**the Acts**" means-

(a) the Tax Acts,

(b) the Capital Gains Tax Acts,

(c) the Value-Added Tax Act, 1972, and the enactments amending or extending that Act,

and any instruments made thereunder;

"**the scheme**" means a scheme of the Department of Finance for the time being in force for requiring persons to show, by means of tax clearance certificates, compliance with the obligations imposed by the Acts in relation to the matters specified in subsection (2) before the award to them of contracts that are specified in a circular of the Department of Finance entitled 'Tax Clearance Procedures - Public Sector Contracts', numbered F 49/29/84 and issued on the 30th day of July, 1991, or any such circular amending or replacing that circular;

"**tax clearance certificate**" shall be construed in accordance with subsection (2).

(2)   Subject to the provisions of this section, where a person who is in compliance with the obligations imposed on the person by the Acts in relation to -

(a)   the payment or remittance of any taxes, interest or penalties required to be paid or remitted under the Acts to the Revenue Commissioners, and

(b)   the delivery of any returns required to be made under the Acts,

applies to the Collector-General in that behalf for the purposes of the scheme, the Collector-General shall issue to the person a certificate (in this section referred to as "a tax clearance certificate") stating that the person is in compliance with the obligations aforesaid.

(3)   A tax clearance certificate shall not be issued to a person unless-

(a)   the person, and any partnership of which the person is or was a member, in respect of the period of the person's membership thereof,

(b)   in a case where the person is a partnership, each person who is a member of the partnership, and

(c)   in a case where the person is a company, each person who is either the beneficial owner of, or able directly or indirectly, to control, more than 50 per cent. of the ordinary share capital of the company,

is in compliance with the obligations imposed on the person and each other person (including any partnership) by the Acts in relation to the matters specified in paragraphs (a) and (b) of subsection (2).

(4)   Where a person (hereafter in this subsection referred to as "**the first-mentioned person**") applies for a tax clearance certificate in accordance with subsection (2) and the business activity to which the application relates was previously carried on by, or was previously carried on as part of a business activity carried on by, another person (hereafter in this subsection referred to as "the second-mentioned person") and-

(a)   the second-mentioned person is a company which is connected within the meaning of section 16(3) of the Finance (Miscellaneous Provisions) Act, 1968, with the first-mentioned person or would have been such a company but for the fact that the company has been wound up or dissolved without being wound up, or

(b)   the second-mentioned person is a company and the first-mentioned person is a partnership and-

(i)   a member of the partnership is or was able, or

(ii)   where more than one such member is a shareholder of the company, those members acting together are or were able,

directly or indirectly, either on his, her or their own, or with a connected person or connected persons within the meaning of the said section 16(3), to control more than **50 per cent** of the ordinary share capital of the company, or

(c)   the second-mentioned person is a partnership and the first-mentioned person is a company and-

(i)   a member of the partnership is or was able, or

(ii)   where more than one such member is a shareholder of the company, those members acting together are or were able,

directly or indirectly, either on his, her or their own, or with a connected person or connected persons within the meaning of the said section 16(3) to control more than **50 per cent** of the ordinary share capital of the company,

then, a tax clearance certificate shall not be issued to the first-mentioned person unless, in relation to the business activity to which the application relates, the second-mentioned person is in compliance with the obligations imposed on that person by the Acts in relation to the matters specified in [paragraphs (a) and (b) and subsection (2)][1]:

Provided that this subsection shall not apply to a business the transfer of which was effected before the 9th day of May, 1995, or a business the transfer of which is or was effected after that date if a contract for the transfer was made before that date.

(5)   Subsections (4), (5) and (6) of section 242 of the Finance Act, 1992, shall, with any necessary modifications, apply to an application for a tax clearance certificate under this section as they apply to an application for a tax clearance certificate under that section.

(6)   A tax clearance certificate shall be valid for the period specified therein.

(7)   This section shall come into operation on the 1st day of July, 1995.

Amendments
1   Substituted by s132(1), FA96, w.e.f.6 April 1996.

Finance Act 1997

(Number 22 of 1997)

Section 114

Revocation (Part III)

114. The European Communities (Value-Added Tax) Regulations, 1993 (S.I. No. 345 of 1993), and the Value-Added Tax (Threshold for Advance Payment) (Amendment) Order, 1994 (S.I. No. 342 of 1994), shall be deemed to have been revoked with effect from the 7th day of November, 1996.

Section 159

Evidence of authorisation

159. (1)   In this section, except where the context otherwise requires-

"**the Acts**" means -

(a)   (i)   the Customs Acts,

(ii)   the statutes relating to the duties of excise and to the management of those duties,

(iii) the Tax Acts,

(iv)   the Capital Gains Tax Acts,

(v)   the Value-Added Tax Act, 1972, and the enactments amending or extending that Act,

(vi)   the Capital Acquisitions Tax Act, 1976, and the enactments amending or extending that Act,

(vii) the statutes relating to stamp duty and to the management of that duty,

and any instruments made thereunder or under any other enactment and relating to tax, and

(b)   the European Communities (Intrastat) Regulations, 1993 (S.I. No. 136 of 1993);

"**authorised officer**" means an officer of the Revenue Commissioners who is authorised, nominated or appointed under any provision of the Acts, to exercise or perform any functions under any of the specified provisions, and "authorised" and "authorisation" shall be construed accordingly;

"**functions**" includes powers and duties;

"**identity card**", in relation to an authorised officer, means a card which is issued to the officer by the Revenue Commissioners and which contains-

(a)   a statement to the effect that the officer-

   (i)   is an officer of the Revenue Commissioners, and

   (ii)   is an authorised officer for the purposes of the specified provisions,

(b)   a photograph and signature of the officer,

(c)   a hologram showing the logo of the Office of the Revenue Commissioners,

(d)   the facsimile signature of a Revenue Commissioner, and

(e)   particulars of the specified provisions under which the officer is authorised;

"specified provisions", in relation to an authorised officer, means either or both the provisions of the Acts under which the authorised officer-

(a)   is authorised and which are specified on his or her identity card, and

(b)   exercises or performs functions under the Customs Acts or any statutes relating to the duties of excise and to the management of those duties;

"tax" means any tax, duty, levy, charge under the care and management of the Revenue Commissioners.

(2)   Where, in the exercise or performance of any functions under any of the specified provisions in relation to him or her, an authorised officer is requested to produce or show his or her authorisation for the purposes of that provision, the production by the authorised officer of his or her identity card-

(a)   shall be taken as evidence of authorisation under that provision, and

(b)   shall satisfy any obligation under that provision which requires the authorised officer to produce such authorisation on request.

(3)   This section shall come into operation on such day as the Minister for Finance may appoint by order.

Taxes Consolidation Act 1997

(Number 39 of 1997)

PART 1

Interpretation

Application to certain taxing statutes of Age of Majority Act, 1985

7. (1)   Notwithstanding subsection (4) of section 2 of the Age of Majority Act, 1985 (in this section referred to as "the Act of 1985"), subsections (2) and (3) of that section shall, subject to subsection (2), apply for the purposes of the Income Tax Acts and any other statutory provision (within the meaning of the Act of 1985) dealing with the imposition, repeal, remission, alteration or regulation of any tax or other duty under the care and management of the Revenue Commissioners, and accordingly section 2(4)(b)(vii) of the Act of 1985 shall cease to apply.

    (2)   Nothing in subsection (1) shall affect a claimant's entitlement to a deduction under section 462 or 465.

PART 6

Chapter 8A
Interpretation

[172A. (1)   (a)   In this Chapter and in Schedule 2A–

'**American depositary receipt**' has the same meaning as in section 207 of the Finance Act, 1992;

['**approved body of persons**' has the same meaning as in section 235;][1]

['**approved minimum retirement fund**' has the same meaning as in section 784C;

'**approved retirement fund**' has the same meaning as in section 784A;][2]

'**auditor**', in relation to a company, means the person or persons appointed as auditor of the company for the purposes of the Companies Acts, 1963 to 1990, or under the law of the territory in which the company is incorporated and which corresponds to those Acts;

'**authorised withholding agent**', in relation to a relevant distribution, has the meaning assigned to it by section 172G;

['**collective investment undertaking**' means–

(i)   a collective investment undertaking within the meaning of section 734,

(ii)   an undertaking for collective investment within the meaning of section 738, [...][3]

(iii) an investment undertaking within the meaning of section 739B (inserted by the Finance Act, 2000, [or][4]

[(iv) a common contractual fund within the meaning of section 739I (inserted by the Finance Act 2005),][4]

not being an offshore fund within the meaning of section 743;][5]

['**designated broker**' has the same meaning as in section 838;][2]

'**dividend withholding tax**', in relation to a relevant distribution, means a sum representing income tax on the amount of the relevant distribution at the standard rate in force at the time the relevant distribution is made;

['**electronic dividend voucher**' means a statement in electronic format that satisfies the requirements of section 172I(1A)(a);

'**electronic number**' means a unique number on an electronic dividend voucher;][6]

'**excluded person**', in relation to a relevant distribution, has the meaning assigned to it by section 172C(2);

'**intermediary**' means a person who carries on a trade which consists of or includes–

(i)   the receipt of relevant distributions from a company or companies resident in the State, or

(ii)   the receipt of amounts or other assets representing such distributions from another intermediary or intermediaries,

on behalf of other persons;

['**ISI Number**', in relation to a security issued by a company, means that security's unique International Securities Identification Number (ISIN) issued by the Irish Stock Exchange Limited or by an equivalent authority in a relevant territory;][6]

'**non-liable person**', in relation to a relevant distribution, means the person beneficially entitled to the relevant distribution, being an excluded person or a qualifying non-resident person;

'**pension scheme**' means an exempt approved scheme within the meaning of section 774 or a retirement annuity contract or a trust scheme to which section 784 or 785 applies;

['**PRSA administrator**' has the same meaning as in section 787A;

'**PRSA assets**' has the same meaning as in section 787A;][7]

'**qualifying employee share ownership trust**' means an employee share ownership trust which the Revenue Commissioners have approved of as a qualifying employee share ownership trust in accordance with Schedule 12 and which approval has not been withdrawn;

['**qualifying fund manager**' has the same meaning as in section 784A;][2]

'**qualifying intermediary**', in relation to a relevant distribution, has the meaning assigned to it by section 172E;

'**qualifying non-resident person**', in relation to a relevant distribution, has the meaning assigned to it by section 172D(3);

['**qualifying savings manager**' has the same meaning as in section 848B (inserted by the Finance Act, 2001);][2]

['**recipient ID code**', in relation to the recipient of a dividend, means the unique code on an electronic dividend voucher that identifies that recipient;][6]

'**relevant distribution**' means–

(i)   a distribution within the meaning of paragraph 1 of Schedule F in section 20(1), other than such a distribution made to a Minister of the Government in his or her capacity as such Minister, and

(ii)   any amount assessable and chargeable to tax under Case IV of Schedule D by virtue of section 816;

'**relevant person**', in relation to a relevant distribution, means–

(i)   where the relevant distribution is made by a company directly to the person beneficially entitled to the distribution, the company making the relevant distribution,

and

(ii)   where the relevant distribution is not made by the company directly to the person beneficially entitled to the relevant distribution but is made to that person through one or more than one qualifying intermediary, the qualifying intermediary from whom the relevant distribution, or an amount or other asset representing the relevant distribution, is receivable by the person beneficially entitled to the distribution;

'**relevant territory**' means–

(i)   a Member State of the European Communities other than the State, [...]⁸

(ii)   not being such a Member State, a territory with the government of which arrangements having the force of law by virtue of [section 826(1)]⁹ **[have been made, or]**¹⁰

[(iii)   **not being a territory referred to in subparagraph (i) or (ii), a territory with the government of which arrangements have been made which on completion of the procedures set out in section 826(1) will have the force of law;]**¹¹

['**special portfolio investment account**' has the same meaning as in section 838;]²

['**special savings incentive account**' has the same meaning as in section 848M (inserted by the Finance Act, 2001);]²

'**specified person**', in relation to a relevant distribution, means the person to whom the relevant distribution is made, whether or not that person is beneficially entitled to the relevant distribution;

'**tax**', in relation to a relevant territory, means any tax imposed in that territory which corresponds to income tax or corporation tax in the State;

'**tax reference number**' has the same meaning as in section 885.

(b)   In this Chapter and in Schedule 2A, references to the making of a relevant distribution by a company, or to a relevant distribution to be made by a company, or to the receipt of a relevant distribution from a company do not include, respectively, references to the making of a relevant distribution by a collective investment undertaking, or to a relevant distribution to be made by a collective investment undertaking, or to the receipt of a relevant distribution from a collective investment undertaking.

(2)   For the purposes of this Chapter, the amount of a relevant distribution shall be an amount equal to–

(a)   where the relevant distribution consists of a payment in cash, the amount of the payment,

(b)   where the relevant distribution consists of an amount which is treated under section 816 as a distribution made by a company, the amount so treated,

(c)   where the relevant distribution consists of an amount which is assessable and chargeable to tax under Case IV of Schedule D by virtue of section 816, the amount so assessable and chargeable, and

(d)   where the relevant distribution consists of a non-cash distribution, not being a relevant distribution to which paragraph (b) or (c) applies, an amount which is equal to the value of the distribution,

and a reference in this Chapter to the amount of a relevant distribution shall be construed as a reference to the amount which would be the amount of the relevant distribution if no dividend withholding tax were to be deducted from the relevant distribution.

(3)   Schedule 2A shall have effect for the purposes of supplementing this Chapter.][12]

PART 23

Chapter 2
Miscellaneous
Transactions to avoid liability to tax

811. (1)   (a)   [In this section and section 811A-][13]

"**the Acts**" means-

(i)   the Tax Acts,

(ii)   the Capital Gains Tax Acts,

(iii)   the Value-Added Tax Act, 1972, and the enactments amending or extending that Act,

(iv)   the [Capital Acquisitions Tax Consolidation Act 2003][14], and the enactments amending or extending that Act,

(v)   Part VI of the Finance Act, 1983, and the enactments amending or extending that Part, and

(vi)   the statutes relating to stamp duty,

and any instruments made thereunder;

"**business**" means any trade, profession or vocation;

"**notice of opinion**" means a notice given by the Revenue Commissioners under subsection (6);

"tax" means any tax, duty, levy or charge which in accordance with the Acts is placed under the care and management of the Revenue Commissioners and any interest, penalty or other amount payable pursuant to the Acts;

"tax advantage" means-

(i)   a reduction, avoidance or deferral of any charge or assessment to tax, including any potential or prospective charge or assessment, or

(ii)   a refund of or a payment of an amount of tax, or an increase in an amount of tax, refundable or otherwise payable to a person, including any potential or prospective amount so refundable or payable, arising out of or by reason of a transaction, including a transaction where another transaction would not have been undertaken or arranged to achieve the results, or any part of the results, achieved or intended to be achieved by the transaction;

"tax avoidance transaction" has the meaning assigned to it by subsection (2);

"tax consequences", in relation to a tax avoidance transaction, means such adjustments and acts as may be made and done by the Revenue Commissioners pursuant to subsection (5) in order to withdraw or deny the tax advantage resulting from the tax avoidance transaction;

"transaction" means-

(i)   any transaction, action, course of action, course of conduct, scheme, plan or proposal,

(ii)   any agreement, arrangement, understanding, promise or undertaking, whether express or implied and whether or not enforceable or intended to be enforceable by legal proceedings, and

(iii) any series of or combination of the circumstances referred to in paragraphs (i) and (ii),

whether entered into or arranged by one person or by 2 or more persons-

(I)   whether acting in concert or not,

(II)   whether or not entered into or arranged wholly or partly outside the State, or

(III) whether or not entered into or arranged as part of a larger transaction or in conjunction with any other transaction or transactions.

(b)   In subsections (2) and (3), for the purposes of the hearing or rehearing under subsection (8) of an appeal made under subsection (7) or for the purposes of the determination of a question of law arising on the statement of a case for the opinion of the High Court, the references to the Revenue Commissioners shall, subject to any necessary modifications, be construed as references to the Appeal Commissioners or to a judge of the Circuit Court or, to the extent necessary, to a judge of the High Court, as appropriate.

[(c)   For the purposes of this section and section 811A, all appeals made under section 811(7) by, or on behalf of, a person against any matter or matters specified or described in the notice of opinion of the Revenue Commissioners that a transaction is a tax avoidance transaction, if they have not otherwise been so determined, shall be deemed to have been finally determined when–

    (i)   there is a written agreement, between that person and an officer of the Revenue Commissioners, that the notice of opinion is to stand or is to be amended in a particular manner,

    (ii)   (I)   the terms of such an agreement that was not made in writing have been confirmed by notice in writing given by the person to the officer of the Revenue Commissioners with whom the agreement was made, or by such officer to the person, and

        (II)   21 days have elapsed since the giving of the notice without the person to whom it was given giving notice in writing to the person by whom it was given that the firstmentioned person desires to repudiate or withdraw from the agreement, or

    (iii)   the person gives notice in writing to an officer of the Revenue Commissioners that the person desires not to proceed with an appeal against the notice of opinion.][15]

(2)   For the purposes of this section and subject to subsection (3), a transaction shall be a **"tax avoidance transaction"** if having regard to any one or more of the following–

    (a)   the results of the transaction,

    (b)   its use as a means of achieving those results, and

    (c)   any other means by which the results or any part of the results could have been achieved, the Revenue Commissioners form the opinion that-

(i)   the transaction gives rise to, or but for this section would give rise to, a tax advantage, and

(ii)   the transaction was not undertaken or arranged primarily for purposes other than to give rise to a tax advantage,

and references in this section to the Revenue Commissioners forming an opinion that a transaction is a tax avoidance transaction shall be construed as references to the Revenue Commissioners forming an opinion with regard to the transaction in accordance with this subsection.

(3)   (a)   Without prejudice to the generality of subsection (2), in forming an opinion in accordance with that subsection and subsection (4) as to whether or not a transaction is a tax avoidance transaction, the Revenue Commissioners shall not regard the transaction as being a tax avoidance transaction if they are satisfied that-

(i)   notwithstanding that the purpose or purposes of the transaction could have been achieved by some other transaction which would have given rise to a greater amount of tax being payable by the person, the transaction-

(I)   was undertaken or arranged by a person with a view, directly or indirectly, to the realisation of profits in the course of the business activities of a business carried on by the person, and

(II)   was not undertaken or arranged primarily to give rise to a tax advantage,

or

(ii)   the transaction was undertaken or arranged for the purpose of obtaining the benefit of any relief, allowance or other abatement provided by any provision of the Acts and that the transaction would not result directly or indirectly in a misuse of the provision or an abuse of the provision having regard to the purposes for which it was provided.

(b)   In forming an opinion referred to in paragraph (a) in relation to any transaction, the Revenue Commissioners shall have regard to-

(i)   the form of that transaction,

(ii)   the substance of that transaction,

(iii)   the substance of any other transaction or transactions which that transaction may reasonably be regarded as being directly or indirectly related to or connected with, and

(iv)   the final outcome and result of that transaction and any combination of those other transactions which are so related or connected.

(4)   Subject to this section, the Revenue Commissioners as respects any transaction may at any time-

    (a)   form the opinion that the transaction is a tax avoidance transaction,

    (b)   calculate the tax advantage which they consider arises, or which but for this section would arise, from the transaction,

    (c)   determine the tax consequences which they consider would arise in respect of the transaction if their opinion were to become final and conclusive in accordance with subsection (5)(e), and

    (d)   calculate the amount of any relief from double taxation which they would propose to give to any person in accordance with subsection (5)(c).

(5)   (a)   Where the opinion of the Revenue Commissioners that a transaction is a tax avoidance transaction becomes final and conclusive, they may, notwithstanding any other provision of the Acts, make all such adjustments and do all such acts as are just and reasonable (in so far as those adjustments and acts have been specified or described in a notice of opinion given under subsection (6) and subject to the manner in which any appeal made under subsection (7) against any matter specified or described in the notice of opinion has been finally determined, including any adjustments and acts not so specified or described in the notice of opinion but which form part of a final determination of any such appeal) in order that the tax advantage resulting from a tax avoidance transaction shall be withdrawn from or denied to any person concerned.

    (b)   Subject to but without prejudice to the generality of paragraph (a), the Revenue Commissioners may-

        (i)   allow or disallow in whole or in part any deduction or other amount which is relevant in computing tax payable, or any part of such deduction or other amount,

(ii)   allocate or deny to any person any deduction, loss, abatement, relief, allowance, exemption, income or other amount, or any part thereof, or

(iii)   recharacterize for tax purposes the nature of any payment or other amount.

(c)   Where the Revenue Commissioners make any adjustment or do any act for the purposes of paragraph (a), they shall afford relief from any double taxation which they consider would but for this paragraph arise by virtue of any adjustment made or act done by them pursuant to paragraphs (a) and (b).

(d)   Notwithstanding any other provision of the Acts, where

(i)   pursuant to subsection (4)(c), the Revenue Commissioners determine the tax consequences which they consider would arise in respect of a transaction if their opinion that the transaction is a tax avoidance transaction were to become final and conclusive, and

(ii)   pursuant to that determination, they specify or describe in a notice of opinion any adjustment or act which they consider would be, or be part of, those tax consequences,

then, in so far as any right of appeal lay under subsection (7) against any such adjustment or act so specified or described, no right or further right of appeal shall lie under the Acts against that adjustment or act when it is made or done in accordance with this subsection, or against any adjustment or act so made or done that is not so specified or described in the notice of opinion but which forms part of the final determination of any appeal made under subsection (7) against any matter specified or described in the notice of opinion.

(e)   For the purposes of this subsection, an opinion of the Revenue Commissioners that a transaction is a tax avoidance transaction shall be final and conclusive-

(i)   if within the time limited no appeal is made under subsection (7) against any matter or matters specified or described in a notice or notices of opinion given pursuant to that opinion, or

(ii)   as and when all appeals made under subsection (7) against any such matter or matters have been finally determined and none of the appeals has been so determined by an order directing that the opinion of the Revenue Commissioners to the effect that the transaction is a tax avoidance transaction is void.

(6)   (a)   Where pursuant to subsections (2) and (4) the Revenue Commissioners form the opinion that a transaction is a tax avoidance transaction, they shall immediately on forming such an opinion give notice in writing of the opinion to any person from whom a tax advantage would be withdrawn or to whom a tax advantage would be denied or to whom relief from double taxation would be given if the opinion became final and conclusive, and the notice shall specify or describe-

     (i)   the transaction which in the opinion of the Revenue Commissioners is a tax avoidance transaction,

     (ii)   the tax advantage or part of the tax advantage, calculated by the Revenue Commissioners which would be withdrawn from or denied to the person to whom the notice is given,

     (iii)   the tax consequences of the transaction determined by the Revenue Commissioners in so far as they would refer to the person, and

     (iv)   the amount of any relief from double taxation calculated by the Revenue Commissioners which they would propose to give to the person in accordance with subsection (5)(c).

   (b)   Section 869 shall, with any necessary modifications, apply for the purposes of a notice given under this subsection or subsection (10) as if it were a notice given under the Income Tax Acts.

(7)   Any person aggrieved by an opinion formed or, in so far as it refers to the person, a calculation or determination made by the Revenue Commissioners pursuant to subsection (4) may, by notice in writing given to the Revenue Commissioners within 30 days of the date of the notice of opinion, appeal to the Appeal Commissioners on the grounds and, notwithstanding any other provision of the Acts, only on the grounds that, having regard to all of the circumstances, including any fact or matter which was not known to the Revenue Commissioners when they formed their opinion or made their calculation or determination, and to this section-

   (a)   the transaction specified or described in the notice of opinion is not a tax avoidance transaction,

   (b)   the amount of the tax advantage or the part of the tax advantage, specified or described in the notice of opinion which would be withdrawn from or denied to the person is incorrect,

(c)   the tax consequences specified or described in the notice of opinion, or such part of those consequences as shall be specified or described by the appellant in the notice of appeal, would not be just and reasonable in order to withdraw or to deny the tax advantage or part of the tax advantage specified or described in the notice of opinion, or

(d)   the amount of relief from double taxation which the Revenue Commissioners propose to give to the person is insufficient or incorrect.

(8)   The Appeal Commissioners shall hear and determine an appeal made to them under subsection (7) as if it were an appeal against an assessment to income tax and, subject to subsection (9), the provisions of the Income Tax Acts relating to the rehearing of an appeal and to the statement of a case for the opinion of the High Court on a point of law shall apply accordingly with any necessary modifications; but on the hearing or rehearing of the appeal-

(a)   it shall not be lawful to enquire into any grounds of appeal other than those specified in subsection (7), and

(b)   at the request of the appellants, 2 or more appeals made by 2 or more persons pursuant to the same opinion, calculation or determination formed or made by the Revenue Commissioners pursuant to subsection (4) may be heard or reheard together.

(9)   (a)   On the hearing of an appeal made under subsection (7), the Appeal Commissioners shall have regard to all matters to which the Revenue Commissioners may or are required to have regard under this section, and-

(i)   in relation to an appeal made on the grounds referred to in subsection (7)(a), the Appeal Commissioners shall determine the appeal, in so far as it is made on those grounds, by ordering, if they or a majority of them-

(I)   consider that the transaction specified or described in the notice of opinion or any part of that transaction is a tax avoidance transaction, that the opinion or the opinion in so far as it relates to that part is to stand,

(II)   consider that, subject to such amendment or addition thereto as the Appeal

Commissioners or the majority of them deem necessary and as they shall specify or describe, the transaction, or any part of it, specified or described in the notice of opinion, is a tax avoidance transaction, that the transaction or that part of it be so amended or added to and that, subject to the amendment or addition, the opinion or the opinion in so far as it relates to that part is to stand, or

(III)   do not so consider as referred to in clause (I) or (II), that the opinion is void,

(ii)   in relation to an appeal made on the grounds referred to in subsection (7)(b), they shall determine the appeal, in so far as it is made on those grounds, by ordering that the amount of the tax advantage or the part of the tax advantage specified or described in the notice of opinion be increased or reduced by such amount as they shall direct or that it shall stand,

(iii)   in relation to an appeal made on the grounds referred to in subsection (7)(c), they shall determine the appeal, in so far as it is made on those grounds, by ordering that the tax consequences specified or described in the notice of opinion shall be altered or added to in such manner as they shall direct or that they shall stand, or

(iv)   in relation to an appeal made on the grounds referred to in subsection (7)(d), they shall determine the appeal, in so far as it is made on those grounds, by ordering that the amount of the relief from double taxation specified or described in the notice of opinion shall be increased or reduced by such amount as they shall direct or that it shall stand.

(b)   This subsection shall, subject to any necessary modifications, apply to the rehearing of an appeal by a judge of the Circuit Court and, to the extent necessary, to the determination by the High Court of any question or questions of law arising on the statement of a case for the opinion of the High Court.

(10)   The Revenue Commissioners may at any time amend, add to or withdraw any matter specified or described in a notice of opinion by giving notice (in this subsection referred to as "**the notice of amendment**") in writing of the amendment, addition or withdrawal to each and every person affected thereby, in so far as the person is so affected, and subsections (1) to (9) shall

apply in all respects as if the notice of amendment were a notice of opinion and any matter specified or described in the notice of amendment were specified or described in a notice of opinion; but no such amendment, addition or withdrawal may be made so as to set aside or alter any matter which has become final and conclusive on the determination of an appeal made with regard to that matter under subsection (7).

(11)   Where pursuant to subsections (2) and (4) the Revenue Commissioners form the opinion that a transaction is a tax avoidance transaction and pursuant to that opinion notices are to be given under subsection (6) to 2 or more persons, any obligation on the Revenue Commissioners to maintain secrecy or any other restriction on the disclosure of information by the Revenue Commissioners shall not apply with respect to the giving of those notices or to the performance of any acts or the discharge of any functions authorised by this section to be performed or discharged by them or to the performance of any act or the discharge of any functions, including any act or function in relation to an appeal made under subsection (7), which is directly or indirectly related to the acts or functions so authorised.

(12)   The Revenue Commissioners may nominate any of their officers to perform any acts and discharge any functions, including the forming of an opinion, authorised by this section to be performed or discharged by the Revenue Commissioners, and references in this section to the Revenue Commissioners shall with any necessary modifications be construed as including references to an officer so nominated.

(13)   This section shall apply as respects any transaction where the whole or any part of the transaction is undertaken or arranged on or after the 25th day of January, 1989, and as respects any transaction undertaken or arranged wholly before that date in so far as it gives rise to, or would but for this section give rise to-

(a)   a reduction, avoidance or deferral of any charge or assessment to tax, or part thereof, where the charge or assessment arises by virtue of any other transaction carried out wholly on or after a date, or

(b)   a refund or a payment of an amount, or of an increase in an amount, of tax, or part thereof, refundable or otherwise payable to a person where that amount or increase in the amount would otherwise become first so refundable or otherwise payable to the person on a date,

which could not fall earlier than the 25th day of January, 1989.

[811A. (1)   (a)   In this section references to tax being payable shall, except where the context requires otherwise, include references to tax being payable by a person to withdraw from that person so much of a tax advantage as is a refund of, or a payment of, an amount of tax, or an increase in an amount of tax, refundable, or otherwise payable, to the person.

(b) For the purposes of this section the date on which the opinion of the Revenue Commissioners that a transaction is a tax avoidance transaction becomes final and conclusive is–

  (i) where no appeal is made under section 811(7) against any matter or matters specified or described in the notice of that opinion, 31 days after the date of the notice of that opinion, or

  (ii) the date on which all appeals made under section 811(7) against any such matter or matters have been finally determined and none of the appeals has been so determined by an order directing that the opinion of the Revenue Commissioners to the effect that the transaction is a tax avoidance transaction is void.

(c) This section shall be construed together with section 811 and shall have effect notwithstanding any of the provisions of section 811.

[(1A) Without prejudice to the generality of any provision of this section or section 811, sections 955(2)(a) and 956(1)(c), as construed together with section 950(2), shall not be construed as preventing an officer of the Revenue Commissioners from-

(a) making any enquiry, or

(b) taking any action,

at any time in connection with this section or section 811.

(1B) Where the Revenue Commissioners have received from, or on behalf of, a person, on or before the relevant date (within the meaning of subsection (3)(c)) a notification (referred to in subsection (3) and (6) as a '**protective notification**') of full details of a transaction, then the Revenue Commissioners shall not form the opinion that the transaction is a tax avoidance transaction pursuant to subsections (2) and (4) of that section after the expiry of the period of 2 years commencing at–

(a) the relevant date, or

(b) if earlier, the date on which the notification was received by the Revenue Commissioners,

but this subsection shall not be construed as preventing an officer of the Revenue Commissioners from making any enquiry at any time in connection with this section or section 811.

(1C)   Where the Revenue Commissioners have not received from, or
on behalf of, a person, on or before the relevant date (within
the meaning of subsection (3)(c)) a notification (referred to
in subsection (3) and (6) as a **'protective notification'**) of full
details of the transaction, then section 811 shall apply as respects
that transaction, if it is a transaction specified or described in
a notice of opinion given by the Revenue Commissioners, as if
the following clauses were substituted for clauses (I) and (II) of
subsection (9)(a)(i):

'(I)   consider that there are grounds on which the transaction
specified or described in the notice of opinion or any part
of that transaction could reasonably be considered to be a
tax avoidance transaction, that the opinion or the opinion
in so far as it relates to that part is to stand,

(II)   consider that, subject to such amendment or addition
thereto as the Appeal Commissioners or the majority
of them deem necessary and as they shall specify or
describe, there are grounds on which the transaction,
or any part of it, specified or described in the notice of
opinion, could reasonably be considered to be a tax
avoidance transaction, that the transaction or that part
of it be so amended or added to and that, subject to the
amendment or addition, the opinion or the opinion in so
far as it relates to that part is to stand, or',

and the provisions of section 811 shall be construed
accordingly.]¹⁶

(2)   Where, in accordance with adjustments made or acts done by
the Revenue Commissioners under section 811(5), on foot of
their opinion (as amended, or added to, on appeal where
relevant) that a transaction is a tax avoidance transaction having
become final and conclusive, an amount of tax is payable by
a person that would not have been payable if the Revenue
Commissioners had not formed the opinion concerned, then,
subject to subsection (3)–

(a)   the person shall be liable to pay an amount (in this section
referred to as the **'surcharge'**) equal to [20 per cent.]¹⁷ of
the amount of that tax and the provisions of the Acts,
including in particular section 811(5) and those provisions
relating to the collection and recovery of that tax, shall
apply to that surcharge, as if it were such tax, and

(b)   for the purposes of liability to interest under the Acts on
tax due and payable, the amount of tax, or parts of that
amount, shall be deemed to be due and payable on the
day or, as respects parts of that amount, days specified in
the notice of opinion (as amended, or added to, on appeal

where relevant) in accordance with section 811(6)(a)(iii) construed together with subsection (4)(a) of this section,

and the surcharge and interest shall be payable accordingly.

(3)   (a)   Subject to subsection (6), neither a surcharge nor interest shall be payable by a person in relation to a tax avoidance transaction finally and conclusively determined to be such a transaction if the Revenue Commissioners have received from, or on behalf of, that person, on or before the relevant date (within the meaning of paragraph (c)), notification (referred to in this subsection and subsection (6) as a '**protective notification**') of full details of that transaction.

        (b)   Where a person makes a protective notification, or a protective notification is made on a person's behalf, then the person shall be treated as making the protective notification–

            (i)   solely to prevent any possibility of [the application of subsection (1C) to the transaction concerned or][16] a surcharge or interest becoming payable by the person by virtue of subsection (2), and

            (ii)   wholly without prejudice as to whether any opinion that the transaction concerned was a tax avoidance transaction, if such an opinion were to be formed by the Revenue Commissioners, would be correct.

        (c)   Regardless of the type of tax concerned–

            (i)   where the whole or any part of the transaction, which is the subject of the protective notification, is undertaken or arranged on or after [19 February 2008][17], then the relevant date shall be–

                (I)   the date which is 90 days after the date on which the transaction commenced, or

                (II)   if it is later than the said 90 days, [19 May 2008][17],

            (ii)   where–

                (I)   the whole of the transaction is undertaken or arranged before [19 February 2008][17], and would give rise to, or would but for section 811 give rise to, a reduction, avoidance, or deferral of any charge or assessment to tax, or part thereof, and

                (II)   that charge or assessment would arise only by virtue of one or more other transactions carried out wholly on or after [19 February 2008][17],

then the relevant date shall be the date which is 90 days after the date on which the first of those other transactions commenced, or

(iii) where–

(I) the whole of the transaction is undertaken or arranged before [19 February 2008][17], and would give rise to, or would but for section 811 give rise to, a refund or a payment of an amount, or of an increase in an amount of tax, or part thereof, refundable or otherwise payable to a person, and

(II) that amount or increase in the amount would, but for section 811, become first so refundable or otherwise payable to the person on a date on or after [19 February 2008][17],

then the relevant date shall be the date which is 90 days after that date.

(d) Notwithstanding the receipt by the Revenue Commissioners of a protective notice, paragraph (a) shall not apply to any interest, payable in relation to a tax avoidance transaction finally and conclusively determined to be such a transaction, in respect of days on or after the date on which the opinion of the Revenue Commissioners in relation to that transaction becomes final and conclusive.

(4) (a) The determination of tax consequences, which would arise in respect of a transaction if the opinion of the Revenue Commissioners, that the transaction was a tax avoidance transaction, were to become final and conclusive, shall, for the purposes of charging interest, include the specification of–

(i) a date or dates, being a date or dates which is or are just and reasonable to ensure that tax is deemed to be due and payable not later than it would have been due and payable if the transaction had not been undertaken, disregarding any contention that another transaction would not have been undertaken or arranged to achieve the results, or any part of the results, achieved or intended to be achieved by the transaction, and

(ii)   the date which, as respects such amount of tax as is due and payable by a person to recover from the person a refund of or a payment of tax, including an increase in tax refundable or otherwise payable, to the person, is the day on which the refund or payment was made, set off or accounted for,

and the date or dates shall be specified for the purposes of this paragraph without regard to-

(I)   when an opinion of the Revenue Commissioners that the transaction concerned was a tax avoidance transaction was formed,

(II)   the date on which any notice of that opinion was given, or

(III) the date on which the opinion (as amended, or added to, on appeal where relevant) became final and conclusive.

(b)   Where the grounds of an appeal in relation to tax consequences refer to such a date or dates as are mentioned in paragraph (a), subsection (7) of section 811 shall apply, in that respect, as if the following paragraph were substituted for paragraph (c) of that subsection:

'(c)   the tax consequences specified or described in the notice of opinion, or such part of those consequences as shall be specified or described by the appellant in the notice of appeal, would not be just and reasonable to ensure that tax is deemed to be payable on a date or dates in accordance with subsection (4)(a) of section 811A'

and the grounds of appeal referred to in section 811(8)(a) shall be construed accordingly.

(5)   A surcharge payable by virtue of subsection (2)(a) shall be due and payable on the date that the opinion of the Revenue Commissioners that a transaction is a tax avoidance transaction becomes final and conclusive and interest shall be payable in respect of any delay in payment of the surcharge as if the surcharge were an amount of that tax by reference to an amount of which the surcharge was computed.

(6)   (a)   A protective notification shall–

   (i)   be delivered in such form as may be prescribed by the Revenue Commissioners and to such office of the Revenue Commissioners as–

      (I)   is specified in the prescribed form, or

      (II)   as may be identified, by reference to guidance in the prescribed form, as the office to which the notification concerned should be sent, and

   (ii)   contain–

      (I)   full details of the transaction which is the subject of the protective notification, including any part of that transaction that has not been undertaken before the protective notification is delivered,

      (II)   full reference to the provisions of the Acts that the person, by whom, or on whose behalf, the protective notification is delivered, considers to be relevant to the treatment of the transaction for tax purposes, and

      (III)   full details of how, in the opinion of the person, by whom, or on whose behalf, the protective notification is delivered, each provision, referred to in the protective notification in accordance with clause (II), applies, or does not apply, to the transaction.

(b)   Without prejudice to the generality of paragraph (a), the specifying, under–

   (i)   section 19B of the Value-Added Tax Act 1972,

   (ii)   section 46A of the Capital Acquisitions Tax Consolidation Act 2003,

   (iii)   section 8 of the Stamp Duties Consolidation Act 1999, or

   (iv)   section 955(4) of this Act,

of a doubt as to the application of law to, or the treatment for tax purposes of, any matter to be contained in a return shall not be regarded as being, or being equivalent to, the delivery of a protective notification in relation to a transaction for [the purposes of subsections (1B) and (3)].[17]

(c)   Where the Revenue Commissioners form the opinion that a transaction is a tax avoidance transaction and believe that a protective notification in relation to the transaction has not been delivered by a person in accordance with subsection (6)(a) by the relevant date (within the meaning of subsection (3)(c)) then, in giving notice under section 811(6)(a) to the person of their opinion in relation to the transaction, they shall give notice that they believe that a protective notification has not been so delivered by the person and section 811 shall be construed, subject to any necessary modifications, as if–

    (i)   subsection (7) of that section included as grounds for appeal that a protective notification in relation to the transaction was so delivered by the person, and

    (ii)   subsection (9) of that section provided that an appeal were to be determined, in so far as it is made on those grounds, by ordering that a protective notification in relation to the transaction was so delivered or that a protective notification in relation to the transaction was not so delivered.

[(6A)   **The Revenue Commissioners may nominate any of their officers to perform any acts and discharge any functions authorised by this section to be performed or discharged by the Revenue Commissioners, and references in this section to the Revenue Commissioners shall with any necessary modifications be construed as including references to an officer so nominated.]**[18]

(7)   This section shall apply–

    (a)   as respects any transaction where the whole or any part of the transaction is undertaken or arranged on or after [19 February 2008][17], and

    (b)   as respects any transaction, the whole of which was undertaken or arranged before that date, in so far as it gives rise to, or would but for section 811 give rise to–

        (i)   a reduction, avoidance, or deferral of any charge or assessment to tax, or part thereof, where the charge or assessment arises only by virtue of another transaction or other transactions carried out wholly on or after [19 February 2008][17], or

        (ii)   a refund or a payment of an amount, or of an increase in an amount of tax, or part thereof, refundable or otherwise payable to a person where, but for section 811, that amount or increase in the amount would become first so refundable or otherwise payable to the person on or after [19 February 2008.][17]][19]

PART 35

Chapter 1
Principal reliefs

Agreements for relief from double taxation

826. [(1)   Where–

(a)   the Government by order declare that arrangements specified in the order have been made with the government of any territory outside the State in relation to–

(i)   affording relief from double taxation in respect of–

(I)   income tax,

(II)   corporation tax in respect of income and chargeable gains (or, in the case of arrangements made before the enactment of the Corporation Tax Act 1976, corporation profits tax),

(III) capital gains tax,

(IV)   any taxes of a similar character,

imposed by the laws of the State or by the laws of that territory, and

(ii)   in the case of taxes of any kind or description imposed by the laws of the State or the laws of that territory–

(I)   exchanging information for the purposes of the prevention and detection of tax evasion, or

(II)   granting relief from taxation under the laws of that territory to persons who are resident in the State for the purposes of tax,

and that it is expedient that those arrangements should have the force of law, and

(b)   the order so made is referred to in Part 1 of Schedule 24A,

then, subject to this section and to the extent provided for in this section, the arrangements shall, notwithstanding any enactment, have the force of law as if each such order were an Act of the Oireachtas on and from the date of–

(A)   the insertion of Schedule 24A into the Principal Act by paragraph (b), or

(B)   the insertion of a reference to the order into Part 1
        of Schedule 24A,

whichever is the later.

(1A)   Where–

(a)   the Government by order declare that arrangements
        specified in the order have been made with the government
        of any territory outside the State in relation to affording
        relief from double taxation of air transport undertakings
        and their employees in respect of all taxes which are or
        may become chargeable on profits, income and capital
        gains imposed by the laws of the State or the laws of that
        territory, and that it is expedient that those arrangements
        should have the force of law, and

(b)   the order so made is referred to in Part 2 of Schedule 24A,

then, subject to this section and to the extent provided for in this
section, the arrangements shall, notwithstanding any enactment,
have the force of law as if each such order were an Act of the
Oireachtas on and from the date of–

(i)   the insertion of Schedule 24A into the Principal
        Act by paragraph (b), or

(ii)   the insertion of a reference to the order into Part 2
        of Schedule 24A, 15

whichever is the later.

(1B)   Where–

(a)   the Government by order declare that arrangements
        specified in the order have been made with the government
        of any territory outside the State in relation to–

(i)   exchanging information for the purposes of the
        prevention and detection of tax evasion in the case
        of taxes of any kind or description imposed by the
        law of the State or the laws of that territory,

(ii)   such other matters relating to affording relief
        from double taxation as the Government consider
        appropriate,

and that it is expedient that those arrangements should
have the force of law, and

(b)   the order so made is specified in Part 3 of Schedule 24A,

then, subject to this section, the arrangements shall, notwithstanding any enactment, have the force of law as if each
such order were an Act of the Oireachtas on and from the
date of the insertion of a reference to the order into Part 3 of
Schedule 24A.][20]

(2)   Schedule 24 shall apply where arrangements which have the force of law by virtue of this section provide that tax payable under the laws of the territory concerned shall be allowed as a credit against tax payable in the State.

(3)   Any arrangements to which the force of law is given under this section may include provision for relief from tax for periods before the passing of this Act or before the making of the arrangements and provisions as to income or chargeable gains which is or are not subject to double taxation, and subsections (1) and (2) shall apply accordingly.

(4)   For the purposes of subsection (1), arrangements made with the head of a foreign state shall be regarded as made with the government of that state.

(5)   Any order made under this section may be revoked by a subsequent order, and any such revoking order may contain such transitional provisions as appear to the Government to be necessary or expedient.

(6)   Where an order is proposed to be made under this section, a draft of the order shall be laid before Dáil Éireann and the order shall not be made until a resolution approving of the draft has been passed by Dáil Éireann.

(7)   Where any arrangements have the force of law by virtue of this section, the obligation as to secrecy imposed by any enactment shall not prevent the Revenue Commissioners or any authorised officer of the Revenue Commissioners from disclosing to any authorised officer of the government with which the arrangements are made such information as is required to be disclosed under the arrangements.

(8)   The necessary apportionments as respects corporation tax shall be made where arrangements having the force of law by virtue of this section apply to the unexpired portion of an accounting period current at a date specified by the arrangements, and any such apportionment shall be made in proportion to the number of months or fractions of months in the part of the relevant accounting period before that date and in the remaining part of the relevant accounting period respectively.

(9)   The Revenue Commissioners may from time to time make regulations generally for carrying out the provisions of this section or any arrangements having the force of law under this section and may in particular, but without prejudice to the generality of the foregoing, by those regulations provide–

        (a)   for securing that relief from taxation imposed by the laws of the territory to which any such arrangements relate does not enure to the benefit of persons not entitled to such relief, and

(b)   for authorising, in cases where tax deductible from any periodical payment has, in order to comply with any such arrangements, not been deducted and it is discovered that the arrangements do not apply to that payment, the recovery of the tax by assessment on the person entitled to the payment or by deduction from subsequent payments.

PART 37

Administration

Evidence of authorisation

858. (1)   In this section, except where the context otherwise requires-

"the Acts" means -

(a)   (i)   the Customs Acts,

(ii)   the statutes relating to the duties of excise and to the management of those duties,

(iii)   the Tax Acts,

(iv)   the Capital Gains Tax Acts,

(v)   the Value-Added Tax Act, 1972, and the enactments amending or extending that Act,

(vi)   the [Capital Acquisitions Tax Consolidation Act 2003][14], and the enactments amending or extending that Act,

(vii)   the statutes relating to stamp duty and to the management of that duty,

and any instruments made thereunder or under any other enactment and relating to tax, and

(b)   the European Communities (Intrastat) Regulations, 1993 (S.I. No. 136 of 1993);

"authorised officer" means an officer of the Revenue Commissioners who is authorised, nominated or appointed under any provision of the Acts to exercise or perform any functions under any of the specified provisions, and "authorised" and "authorisation" shall be construed accordingly;

"functions" includes powers and duties;

"identity card", in relation to an authorised officer, means a card which is issued to the officer by the Revenue Commissioners and which contains-

(a)   a statement to the effect that the officer-

(i)   is an officer of the Revenue Commissioners, and

(ii)   is an authorised officer for the purposes of the specified provisions,

(b)   a photograph and signature of the officer,

(c)   a hologram showing the logo of the Office of the Revenue Commissioners,

(d)   the facsimile signature of a Revenue Commissioner, and

(e)   particulars of the specified provisions under which the officer is authorised;

"specified provisions", in relation to an authorised officer, means either or both the provisions of the Acts under which the authorised officer-

(a)   is authorised and which are specified on his or her identity card, and

(b)   exercises or performs functions under the Customs Acts or any statutes relating to the duties of excise and to the management of those duties;

"tax" means any tax, duty, levy or charge under the care and management of the Revenue Commissioners.

(2)   Where, in the exercise or performance of any functions under any of the specified provisions in relation to him or her, an authorised officer is requested to produce or show his or her authorisation for the purposes of that provision, the production by the authorised officer of his or her identity card-

(a)   shall be taken as evidence of authorisation under that provision, and

(b)   shall satisfy any obligation under that provision which requires the authorised officer to produce such authorisation on request.

(3)   This section shall come into operation on such day as the Minister for Finance may appoint by order.

Anonymity of authorised officers in relation to certain matters

859.   (1)   In this section-

"authorised officer" means an officer of the Revenue Commissioners nominated by them to be a member of the staff of the body;

"the body" has the meaning assigned to it by section 58;

"proceedings" includes any hearing before the Appeal Commissioners (within the meaning of the Revenue Acts);

"the Revenue Acts" means-

(a)   the Customs Acts,

(b)   the statutes relating to the duties of excise and to the management of those duties,

(c)   the Tax Acts,

(d)   the Capital Gains Tax Acts,

(e)   the Value-Added Tax Act, 1972, and the enactments amending or extending that Act,

(f)   the [Capital Acquisitions Tax Consolidation Act 2003][14], and the enactments amending or extending that Act,

(g)   the statutes relating to stamp duty and the management of that duty,

(h)   Chapter IV of Part 11 of the Finance Act, 1992, and

(i)   Part VI of the Finance Act, 1983,

and any instruments made thereunder or under any other enactment and relating to tax;

"**tax**" means any tax, duty, levy or charge under the care and management of the Revenue Commissioners.

(2)   Notwithstanding any requirement made by or under any enactment or any other requirement in administrative and operational procedures, including internal procedures, all reasonable care shall be taken to ensure that the identity of an authorised officer shall not be revealed.

(3)   In particular and without prejudice to the generality of subsection (2):

(a)   where, for the purposes of exercising or performing his or her powers or duties under the Revenue Acts in pursuance of the functions of the body, an authorised officer may apart from this section be required to produce or show any written authority or warrant of appointment under those Acts or otherwise to identify himself or herself, the authorised officer shall-

(i)   not be required to produce or show any such authority or warrant of appointment or to so identify himself or herself, for the purposes of exercising or performing his or her powers or duties under those Acts, and

(ii)   be accompanied by a member of the Garda Síochána who shall, on request by a person affected, identify himself or herself as a member of the Garda Síochána and shall state that he or she is accompanied by an authorised officer;

(b)   where, in pursuance of the functions of the body, an authorised officer exercises or performs in writing any of his or her powers or duties under the Revenue Acts or any provision of any other enactment, whenever passed, which relates to Revenue, such exercise or performance of his or her powers or duties shall be done in the name of the body and not in the name of the individual authorised officer involved, notwithstanding any provision to the contrary in any of those enactments;

(c)   in any proceedings arising out of the exercise or performance, in pursuance of the functions of the body, of powers or duties by an authorised officer, any documents relating to such proceedings shall not reveal the identity of any authorised officer, notwithstanding any requirements to the contrary in any provision, and in any proceedings the identity of such officer other than as an authorised officer shall not be revealed other than to the judge or the Appeal Commissioner, as the case may be, hearing the case;

(d)   where, in pursuance of the functions of the body, an authorised officer is required, in any proceedings, to give evidence and the judge or the Appeal Commissioner, as the case may be, is satisfied that there are reasonable grounds in the public interest to direct that evidence to be given by such authorised officer should be given in the hearing and not in the sight of any person, he or she may so direct.

Claims for repayment, interest on repayments and time limits for assessment

[865. (1)   (a)   In this section and section 865A–

the '**Acts**' means the Tax Acts and the Capital Gains Tax Acts and instruments made thereunder;

'**chargeable period**' has the meaning assigned to it by section 321;

'**correlative adjustment**' means an adjustment of profits under the terms of arrangements entered into by virtue of [section 826(1)]⁹;

'**tax**' means any tax, including interest thereon, paid by a person under or in accordance with any provision of the Acts;

'**valid claim**' shall be construed in accordance with paragraph (b).

(b)   For the purposes of subsection (3)–

[(i)   where a person furnishes a statement or return which is required to be delivered by the person in accordance with any provision of the Acts for a chargeable period, such a statement or return shall be treated as a valid claim in relation to a repayment of tax where-

(I)   all the information which the Revenue Commissioners may reasonably require to enable them determine if and to what extent a repayment of tax is due to the person for that chargeable period is contained in the statement or return, and

(II)   the repayment treated as claimed, if due-

(A)   would arise out of the assessment to tax, made by the inspector within the meaning of section 950 (in this clause referred to as the 'inspector') at the time the statement or return was furnished, on foot of the statement or return, or

(B)   would have arisen out of the assessment to tax, that would have been made by the inspector at the time the statement or return was furnished, on foot of the statement or return if an assessment to tax had been made by the inspector at that time,][21]

(ii)   where all information which the Revenue Commissioners may reasonably require, to enable them determine if and to what extent a repayment of tax is due to a person for a chargeable period, is not contained in such a statement or return as is referred to in subparagraph (i), a claim to repayment of tax by that person for that chargeable period shall be treated as a valid claim when that information has been furnished by the person, and

(iii)   to the extent that a claim to repayment of tax for a chargeable period arises from a correlative adjustment, the claim shall not be regarded as a valid claim until the quantum of the correlative adjustment is agreed in writing by the competent authorities of the two Contracting States.

(2)   Subject to the provisions of this section, where a person has, in respect of a chargeable period, paid, whether directly or by deduction, an amount of tax which is not due from that person or which, but for an error or mistake in a return or statement

made by the person for the purposes of an assessment to tax, would not have been due from the person, the person shall be entitled to repayment of the tax so paid.

(3)   The Revenue Commissioners shall not make a repayment of the tax referred to in subsection (2) unless a valid claim has been made to them for that purpose.

[(3A)   (a)   Subject to paragraph (b), subsection (3) shall not prevent the Revenue Commissioners from making, to a person other than a chargeable person (within the meaning of section 950), a repayment in respect of tax deducted, in accordance with Chapter 4 of Part 42 and the regulations made thereunder, from that person's emoluments for a year of assessment where, on the basis of the information available to them, they are satisfied that the tax so deducted, and in respect of which the person is entitled to a credit, exceeds the person's liability for that year.

(b)   A repayment referred to in paragraph (a) shall not be made at a time at which a claim to the repayment would not be allowed under subsection (4).][22]

(4)   Subject to subsection (5), a claim for repayment of tax under the Acts for any chargeable period shall not be allowed unless it is made–

(a)   in the case of claims made on or before 31 December 2004, under any provision of the Acts other than subsection (2), in relation to any chargeable period ending on or before 31 December 2002, within 10 years,

(b)   in the case of claims made on or after 1 January 2005 in relation to any chargeable period referred to in paragraph (a), within 4 years, and

(c)   in the case of claims made–

(i)   under subsection (2) and not under any other provision of the Acts, or

(ii)   in relation to any chargeable period beginning on or after 1 January 2003,

within 4 years,

after the end of the chargeable period to which the claim relates.

(5)   Where a person would, on due claim, be entitled to a repayment of tax for any chargeable period under any provision of the Acts other than this section, and–

(a)   that provision provides for a shorter period, within which the claim for repayment is to be made, which ends before the relevant period referred to in subsection (4), then this section shall apply as if that shorter period were the period referred to in subsection (4), and

(b)   that provision provides for a longer period, within which the claim for repayment is to be made, which ends after the relevant period referred to in subsection (4), then that provision shall apply as if the longer period were the period referred to in subsection (4).

(6)   Except as provided for by this section, section 865A or by any other provision of the Acts, the Revenue Commissioners shall not–

(a)   repay an amount of tax paid to them, or

(b)   pay interest in respect of an amount of tax paid to them.

(7)   Where any person is aggrieved by a decision of the Revenue Commissioners on a claim to repayment by that person, in so far as that decision is made by reference to any provision of this section, the provisions of section 949 shall apply to such decision as if it were a determination made on a matter referred to in section 864.

[(8)   Where the Revenue Commissioners make a repayment of tax referred to in subsection (2), they may if they so determine repay any such amount directly into an account, specified by the person to whom the amount is due, in a financial institution.][23]

Interest on repayments

865A. (1)   Where a person is entitled to a repayment of tax for a chargeable period and that repayment, or part of the repayment, arises because of a mistaken assumption made by the Revenue Commissioners in the application of any provision of the Acts, that repayment or that part of the repayment shall, subject to section 1006A(2A), carry interest for each day or part of a day for the period commencing with the day after the end of the chargeable period or, as the case may be, the end of each of the chargeable periods for which the repayment is due or the date on which the tax was paid (whichever is the later) and ending on the day on which the repayment is made.

(2)   Where, for any reason other than that mentioned in subsection (1), a repayment of tax or a part of a repayment is due to a person for a chargeable period, that repayment or the part of the repayment shall, subject to section 1006A(2A), carry interest for the period beginning on the day which is [93 days][24] after the day on which the claim to repayment becomes a valid claim and ending on the day the repayment is made.

(3)   (a)   Interest payable in accordance with this section shall be simple interest payable at the rate of 0.011 per cent per day or part of a day.

(b)　The Minister for Finance may, from time to time, make an order prescribing a rate for the purpose of paragraph (a).

(c)　Every order made by the Minister for Finance under paragraph (b) shall be laid before Dáil Éireann as soon as may be after it is made and, if a resolution annulling the order is passed by Dáil Éireann within the next 21 days on which Dáil Éireann has sat after the order is laid before it, the order shall be annulled accordingly, but without prejudice to the validity of anything previously done under it.

(4)　(a)　Interest shall not be payable under this section if it amounts to less than €10.

(b)　Income tax shall not be deductible on payment of interest under this section and such interest shall not be reckoned in computing income, profit or gains for the purposes of the Tax Acts.

(5)　(a)　This section shall not apply in relation to any repayment or part of a repayment in respect of which interest is payable under any other provision of the Acts.][25]

Use of information relating to other taxes and duties

872.　(1)　Any information acquired, whether before or after the passing of this Act, in connection with any tax or duty under the care and management of the Revenue Commissioners may be used by them for any purpose connected with any other tax or duty under their care and management.

(2)　The Revenue Commissioners or any of their officers may, for any purpose in connection with the assessment and collection of income tax, corporation tax or capital gains tax, make use of or produce in evidence any returns, correspondence, schedules, accounts, statements or other documents or information to which the Revenue Commissioners or any of their officers have or has had or may have lawful access for the purposes of the Acts relating to any tax, duty, levy or charge under the care and management of the Revenue Commissioners.

PART 38

Chapter 3
Other obligations and returns

Use of electronic data processing

[887.　(1)　In this section—

"**the Acts**" means—

(a)　the Tax Acts,

(b)   the Capital Gains Tax Acts,

(c)   the Value-Added Tax Act, 1972, and the enactments amending or extending that Act,

(d)   the [Capital Acquisitions Tax Consolidation Act 2003][14], and the enactments amending or extending that Act, and

(e)   Part VI of the Finance Act, 1983,

and any instrument made under any of these enactments;

'record' means any document which a person is obliged by the Acts to keep, to issue or to produce for inspection, and any other written or printed material.

(2)   For the purposes of the Acts, but subject to section 17 of the Value-Added Tax Act, 1972, a record may be stored, maintained, transmitted, reproduced or communicated, as the case may be, by any electronic, photographic or other process that-

(a)   provides a reliable assurance as to the integrity of the record from the time when it was first generated in its final form by such electronic, photographic or other process,

(b)   permits the record to be displayed in intelligible form and produced in an intelligible printed format,

(c)   permits the record to be readily accessible for subsequent reference in accordance with paragraph (b), and

(d)   conforms to the information technology and procedural requirements drawn up and published by the Revenue Commissioners in accordance with subsection (3).

(3)   The Revenue Commissioners shall from time to time draw up and publish in Iris Oifigiuil the information technology and procedural requirements to which any electronic, photographic or other process used by a person for the storage, maintenance, transmission, reproduction and communication of any record shall conform.

(4)   The authority conferred on the Revenue Commissioners by this section to draw up and publish requirements shall be construed as including the authority exercisable in a like manner to revoke and replace or to amend any such requirements.

(5)   (a)   Every person who preserves records by any electronic, photographic or other process, when required to do so by a notice in writing from the Revenue Commissioners, shall, within such period as is specified in the notice, not being less than 21 days from the date of service of the notice, supply to the Revenue Commissioners full particulars relating to the process used by that person,

including full particulars relating to software (within the meaning of section 912).

(b)   A person who fails or refuses to comply with a notice served on the person under paragraph (a) shall be liable to a penalty of **[€3,000]**[26].

(6)   (a)   Subject to paragraph (b), where records are kept by a person (being a person who is obliged by the Acts to keep such records) by any electronic, photographic or other process which does not conform with the requirements referred to in paragraphs (a) to (d) of subsection (2), then the person shall be deemed to have failed to comply with that obligation and that person shall be liable to the same penalties as the person would be liable to if the person had failed to comply with any obligation under the Acts in relation to the keeping of records.

(b)   Paragraph (a) shall not apply where the person referred to in that paragraph complies with any obligation under the Acts in relation to the keeping of records other than in accordance with the provisions of subsection (2).

(7)   Where records are preserved by any electronic, photographic or other process, information contained in a document produced by any such process shall, subject to the rules of court, be admissible in evidence in any proceedings, whether civil or criminal, to the same extent as the records themselves.

(8)   The Revenue Commissioners may nominate any of their officers to discharge any function authorised by this section to be discharged by the Revenue Commissioners.][27]

Chapter 4
Revenue Powers

Power to require production of accounts and books

900. **[(1)**   In this section and in section 901–

'**authorised officer**' means an officer of the Revenue Commissioners authorised by them in writing to exercise the powers conferred by this section, or as the case may be, section 901;

'**books, records or other documents**' includes–

(a)   accounts (including balance sheets) relating to a trade or profession and where the accounts have been audited, a copy of the auditor's certificate,

(b)   books, accounts, rolls, registers, papers and other documents, whether–

(i)   comprised in bound volume, loose-leaf binders or other loose-leaf filing system, loose-leaf ledger sheets, pages, folios or cards, or

(ii)   kept on microfilm, magnetic tape or in any non-legible form (by the use of electronics or otherwise) which is capable of being reproduced in a legible form,

(c)   every electronic or other automatic means, if any, by which any such thing in non-legible form is so capable of being reproduced, and

(d)   documents in manuscript, documents which are typed, printed, stencilled or created by any other mechanical or partly mechanical process in use from time to time and documents which are produced by any photographic or photo-static process;

'**judge**' means a judge of the High Court;

'**liability**' in relation to a person, means any liability in relation to tax to which the person is or may be, or may have been, subject, or the amount of such liability;

'**tax**' means any tax, duty, levy or charge under the care and management of the Revenue Commissioners.

(2)   Subject to this section, an authorised officer may serve on a person a notice in writing, requiring the person, within such period as may be specified in the notice, not being less than 21 days from the date of the service of the notice, to do either or both of the following, namely–

    (a)   to deliver to, or to make available for inspection by, the authorized officer such books, records or other documents as are in the person's possession, power or procurement and as contain, or may (in the authorised officer's opinion formed on reasonable grounds) contain, information relevant to a liability in relation to the person,

    (b)   to furnish to the authorized officer, in writing or otherwise, such information, explanations and particulars as the authorised officer may reasonably require, being information, explanations and particulars that are relevant to any such liability, and which are specified in the notice.

(3)   A notice shall not be served on a person under subsection (2) unless the person has first been given a reasonable opportunity to deliver, or as the case may be, to make available to the authorized officer concerned the books, records or other documents in question, or to furnish the information, explanations and particulars in question.

[(4)   Nothing in this section shall be construed as requiring any person to disclose to an authorised officer –

   (a)   information with respect to which a claim to legal professional privilege could be maintained in legal proceedings,

   (b)   information of a confidential medical nature, or

   (c)   professional advice of a confidential nature given to a client (other than advice given as part of a dishonest, fraudulent or criminal purpose).][28]

(5)   Where, in compliance with the requirements of a notice served on a person under subsection (2), the person makes available for inspection by an authorised officer, books, records or other documents, the person shall afford the authorised officer reasonable assistance, including information, explanations and particulars, in relation to the use of all the electronic or other automatic means, if any, by which the books, records or other documents, in so far as they are in a non-legible form, are capable of being reproduced in a legible form, and any data equipment or any associated apparatus or material.

(6)   Where, under subsection (2), a person makes books, records or other documents available for inspection by the authorised officer, the authorised officer may make extracts from or copies of all or any part of the books, records or other documents.

(7)   A person who refuses or fails to comply with a notice served on the person under subsection (2) or fails to afford the assistance referred to in subsection (5) shall be liable to a penalty of [€4,000][29].][30]

Power to require delivery of books and papers relating to tax

901. [(1)   An authorised officer may make an application to a judge for an order requiring a person, to do either or both of the following, namely–

   (a)   to deliver to the authorized officer, or to make available for inspection by the authorised officer, such books, records or other documents as are in the person's power, possession or procurement and as contain, or may (in the authorised officer's opinion formed on reasonable grounds) contain, information relevant to a liability in relation to the person,

   (b)   to furnish to the authorised officer such information, explanations and particulars as the authorised officer may reasonably require, being information, explanations and particulars that are relevant to any such liability,

and which are specified in the application.

(2)   Where the judge, to whom an application is made under subsection (1), is satisfied that there are reasonable grounds for the application being made, that judge may, subject to such conditions as he or she may consider proper and specify in the order, make an order requiring the person to whom the application relates–

(a)   to deliver to the authorised officer, or to make available for inspection by the authorised officer, such books, records or other documents, and

(b)   to furnish to the authorised officer such information, explanations and particulars,

as may be specified in the order.

[(3)   Nothing in this section shall be construed as requiring any person to disclose to an authorised officer –

(a)   information with respect to which a claim to legal professional privilege could be maintained in legal proceedings,

(b)   information of a confidential medical nature, or

(c)   professional advice of a confidential nature given to a client (other than advice given as part of a dishonest, fraudulent or criminal purpose).][31]][32]

[(4)   Where in compliance with an order made under subsection (2), a person makes available for inspection by an authorised officer, books, records or other documents, the person shall afford the authorised officer reasonable assistance, including information, explanations and particulars, in relation to the use of all the electronic or other automatic means, if any, by which the books, records or other documents, in so far as they are in a non-legible form, are capable of being reproduced in a legible form, and any data equipment or any associated apparatus or material.

(5)   Where in compliance with an order made under subsection (2), a person makes books, records or other documents available for inspection by the authorised officer, the authorised officer may make extracts from or copies of all or any part of the books, records or other documents.][33]

Power to obtain from certain persons particulars of transactions with and documents concerning tax liability of taxpayer

902. [(1)   In this section and in section 902A–

'**authorised officer**' means an officer of the Revenue Commissioners authorised by them in writing to exercise the powers conferred by this section, or as the case may be, section 902A;

'books, records or other documents' and **'liability'**, in relation to a person, have, respectively, the meaning assigned to them by section 900(1).

(2)   Notwithstanding any obligation as to secrecy or other restriction upon disclosure of information imposed by or under statute or otherwise, and subject to this section, an authorized officer may for the purpose of enquiring into a liability in relation to a person (in this section referred to as **'the taxpayer'**) serve on any other person (not being a financial institution within the meaning of section 906A) a notice in writing requiring that other person, within such period as may be specified in the notice, not being less than 30 days from the date of the service of the notice, to do either or both of the following, namely–

(a)   to deliver to, or make available for inspection by, the authorised officer, such books, records or other documents as are in the other person's power, possession or procurement and as contain, or may (in the authorised officer's opinion formed on reasonable grounds) contain, information relevant to a liability in relation to the taxpayer,

(b)   to furnish to the authorized officer, in writing or otherwise, such information, explanations and particulars as the authorised officer may reasonably require, being information, explanations and particulars that are relevant to any such liability,

and which are specified in the notice.

(3)   A notice shall not be served on a person under subsection (2) unless the authorised officer concerned has reasonable grounds to believe that the person is likely to have information relevant to the establishment of a liability in relation to the taxpayer.

(4)   The persons who may be treated as a taxpayer for the purposes of this section include a company which has been dissolved and an individual who has died.

(5)   A notice under subsection (2) shall name the taxpayer in relation to whose liability the authorised officer is enquiring.

(6)   Where an authorised officer serves a notice under subsection (2), a copy of such notice shall be given by the authorised officer to the taxpayer concerned.

(7)   Where, under subsection (2), a person has delivered any books, records or other documents and those books, records or other documents are retained by the authorised officer, the person shall, at all reasonable times and subject to such reasonable conditions as may be determined by the authorised officer, be entitled to inspect those books, records or other documents and to obtain copies of them.

(8)   Where, under subsection (2), a person makes books, records or other documents available for inspection by the authorised officer, the authorized officer may make extracts from or copies of all or any part of the books, records or other documents.

[(9)   Nothing in this section shall be construed as requiring any person to disclose to an authorised officer—

(a)   information with respect to which a claim to legal professional privilege could be maintained in legal proceedings,

(b)   information of a confidential medical nature, or

(c)   professional advice of a confidential nature given to a client (other than advice given as part of a dishonest, fraudulent or criminal purpose).][34]

(10)   Where, in compliance with the requirements of a notice under subsection (2), a person makes available for inspection by an authorised officer, books, records or other documents, the person shall afford the authorised officer reasonable assistance, including information, explanations and particulars, in relation to the use of all the electronic or other automatic means, if any, by which the books, records or other documents, in so far as they are in non-legible form, are capable of being reproduced in a legible form and any data equipment or any associated apparatus or material.

(11)   A person who fails or refuses to comply with a notice served on the person under subsection (2) or to afford the assistance referred to in subsection (10) shall be liable to a penalty of [€4,000][29], but nothing in section 1078 shall be construed as applying to such failure or refusal.][35]

Application to High Court: information from third party

902A. [(1)   In this section–

'the Acts' has the meaning assigned to it by section 1078(1);

'judge' means a judge of the High Court;

'a taxpayer' means any person including a person whose identity is not known to the authorised officer, and a group or class of persons whose individual identities are not so known.

(2)   An authorised officer may make an application to a judge for an order requiring a person (other than a financial institution within the meaning of section 906A) to do either or both of the following, namely–

(a)   to deliver to the authorised officer, or to make available for inspection by the authorised officer, such books, records or other documents as are in the person's power, possession or procurement and as contain, or may (in the authorised officer's opinion formed on reasonable grounds) contain, information relevant to a liability in relation to a taxpayer,

(b)   to furnish to the authorised officer such information, explanations and particulars as the authorised officer may reasonably require, being information, explanations and particulars that are relevant to any such liability,

and which are specified in the application.

(3)   An authorised officer shall not make an application under subsection (2) without the consent in writing of a Revenue Commissioner, and without being satisfied–

(a)   that there are reasonable grounds for suspecting that the taxpayer, or, where the taxpayer is a group or class of persons, all or any one of those persons, may have failed or may fail to comply with any provision of the Acts,

(b)   that any such failure is likely to have led or to lead to serious prejudice to the proper assessment or collection of tax (having regard to the amount of a liability in relation to the taxpayer, or where the taxpayer is a group or class of persons, the amount of a liability in relation to all or any one of those persons, that arises or might arise from such failure), and

(c)   that the information–

(i)   which is likely to be contained in the books, records or other documents to which the application relates, or

(ii)   which is likely to arise from the information, explanations and particulars to which the application relates,

is relevant to the proper assessment or collection of tax.

(4)   Where the judge, to whom an application is made under subsection (2), is satisfied that there are reasonable grounds for the application being made, that judge may, subject to such conditions as he or she may consider proper and specify in the order, make an order requiring the person to whom the application relates –

(a)   to deliver to the authorised officer, or to make available for inspection by the authorised officer, such books, records or other documents, and

(b)   to furnish to the authorised officer such information, explanations and particulars,

as may be specified in the order.

(5)   The persons who may be treated as a taxpayer for the purposes of this section include a company which has been dissolved and an individual who has died.

[(6)   Nothing in this section shall be construed as requiring any person to disclose to an authorised officer—

(a)   information with respect to which a claim to legal professional privilege could be maintained in legal proceedings,

(b)   information of a confidential medical nature, or

(c)   professional advice of a confidential nature given to a client (other than advice given as part of a dishonest, fraudulent or criminal purpose).][36]

[(6A)   Where in compliance with an order made under subsection (4), a person makes available for inspection by an authorised officer, books, records or other documents, the person shall afford the authorised officer reasonable assistance, including information, explanations and particulars, in relation to the use of all the electronic or other automatic means, if any, by which the books, records or other documents, in so far as they are in a non-legible form, are capable of being reproduced in a legible form, and any data equipment or any associated apparatus or material.

(6B)   Where in compliance with an order made under subsection (4), a person makes books, records or other documents available for inspection by the authorised officer, the authorised officer may make extracts from or copies of all or any part of the books, records or other documents.][37]

(7)   Every hearing of an application for an order under this section and of any appeal in connection with that application shall be held in camera.][38]

Inspection of documents and records

905. (1)   In this section-

"**authorised officer**" means an officer of the Revenue Commissioners authorised by them in writing to exercise the powers conferred by this section;

"**property**" means any asset relating to a tax liability;

["**records**" means any document or any other written or printed material in any form, and includes any information stored, maintained or preserved by means of any mechanical or electronic device, whether or not stored, maintained or preserved in a legible form—

(i)   which relates to a business carried on by a person, or

(ii) which a person is obliged by any provision relating to tax to keep, retain, issue or produce for inspection or which may be inspected under any provision relating to tax;][39]

"tax" means any tax, duty, levy or charge under the care and management of the Revenue Commissioners;

"tax liability" means any existing liability to tax or further liability to tax which may be established by an authorised officer following the exercise or performance of his or her powers or duties under this section.

(2) (a) An authorised officer may at all reasonable times enter any premises or place where the authorised officer has reason to believe that-

    (i) any trade, profession or other activity, the profits or gains of which are chargeable to tax, is or has been carried on,

    (ii) anything is or has been done in connection with any trade, profession or other activity the profits or gains of which are chargeable to tax,

    (iii) any records relating to-

        (I) any trade, profession, other source of profits or gains or chargeable gains,

        (II) any tax liability, or

        (III) any repayments of tax in regard to any person,

        are or may be kept,

    (iv) any property is or has been located, and the authorised officer may-

        (A) require any person who is on those premises or in that place, other than a person who is there to purchase goods or to receive a service, to produce any records or property,

        (B) if the authorised officer has reason to believe that any of the records or property which he or she has required to be produced to him or her under this subsection have not been produced, search on those premises or in that place for those records or property,

        (C) examine any records or property and take copies of or extracts from any records,

(D)   remove any records and retain them for a reasonable time for the purposes of their further examination or for the purposes of any legal proceedings instituted by an officer of the Revenue Commissioners or for the purposes of any criminal proceedings, and

(E)   examine property listed in any records.

(b)   An authorised officer may in the exercise or performance of his or her powers or duties under this section require any person whom he or she has reason to believe-

(i)   is or was carrying on any trade, profession or other activity the profits or gains of which are chargeable to tax,

(ii)   is or was liable to any tax, or

(iii)   has information relating to any tax liability

to give the authorised officer all reasonable assistance, including providing information and explanations or furnishing documents and making available for inspection property as required by the authorised officer in relation to any tax liability or any repayment of tax in regard to any person.

[(c)   **Nothing in this section shall be construed as requiring any person to disclose to an authorised officer —**

(i)   **information with respect to which a claim to legal professional privilege could be maintained in legal proceedings,**

(ii)   **information of a confidential medical nature, or**

(iii)   **professional advice of a confidential nature given to a client (other than advice given as part of a dishonest, fraudulent or criminal purpose).]**[40]

[...][41]

[(e)   An authorised officer shall not, without the consent of the occupier, enter any premises, or that portion of any premises, which is occupied wholly and exclusively as a private residence, except on production by the officer of a warrant issued under subsection (2A).][42]

[...][43]

[(2A)   (a)   In this subsection 'the Acts' has the meaning assigned to it by section 1078(1).

(b)   Without prejudice to any power conferred by subsection (2), if a Judge of the District Court is satisfied by information on oath that there are reasonable grounds for suspecting-

    (i)   that a person may have failed or may fail to comply with any provision of the Acts,

    (ii)   that any such failure is likely to have led or to lead to serious prejudice to the proper assessment or collection of tax (having regard to the amount of any tax liability that arises or might arise from such failure), and

    (iii)   that records, which are material to the proper assessment or collection of tax are likely to be kept or concealed at any premises or place,

the Judge may issue a search warrant.

(c)   A search warrant issued under this subsection shall be expressed and shall operate to authorise an authorised officer accompanied by such other named officers of the Revenue Commissioners and such other named persons as the authorised officer considers necessary, at any time or times within one month of the date of issue of the warrant, to enter (if need be by force) the premises or other place named or specified in the warrant, to search such premises or other place, to examine anything found there, to inspect any records found there and, if there are reasonable grounds for suspecting that any records found there are material to the proper assessment or collection of tax, or that the records may be required for the purpose of any legal proceedings instituted by an officer of the Revenue Commissioners [...]⁴³, remove such records and retain them for so long as they are reasonably required for the purpose aforesaid.]⁴⁴

(3)   A person who does not comply with any requirement of an authorised officer in the exercise or performance of the authorised officer's powers or duties under this section shall be liable to a penalty of [€4,000]²⁶.

(4)   An authorised officer when exercising or performing his or her powers or duties under this section shall on request show his or her authorisation for the purposes of this section.

Authorised officers and Garda Síochána

906.   Where an authorised officer (within the meaning of section 903, 904 or 905, as the case may be) in accordance with section 903, 904 or 905 enters any premises or place, the authorised officer may be accompanied by a member or members of the Garda Síochána, and any such member may arrest without warrant any person who obstructs or interferes with the

authorised officer in the exercise or performance of his or her powers or duties under any of those sections.

Information to be furnished by financial institutions.

[906A. (1)	In this section and in sections 907 and 908 —

"**the Acts**" has the meaning assigned to it by section 1078(1);

"**authorised officer**" means an officer of the Revenue Commissioners authorised by them in writing to exercise the powers conferred by this section, or, as the case may be, section 907 or 908;

"**books, records or other documents**" includes —

(a)	any records used in the business of a financial institution, or used in the transfer department of a financial institution acting as registrar of securities, whether —

(i)	comprised in bound volume, loose-leaf binders or other loose-leaf filing system, loose-leaf ledger sheets, pages, folios or cards, or

(ii)	kept on microfilm, magnetic tape or in any non-legible form (by the use of electronics or otherwise) which is capable of being reproduced in a legible form,

(b)	every electronic or other automatic means, if any, by which any such thing in non-legible form is so capable of being reproduced,

(c)	documents in manuscript, documents which are typed, printed, stenciled or created by any other mechanical or partly mechanical process in use from time to time and documents which are produced by any photographic or photostatic process, and

(d)	correspondence and records of other communications between a financial institution and its customers;

"**connected person**" has the same meaning as in section 10; but an individual (other than in the capacity as a trustee of a settlement) shall be connected with another individual only if that other individual is the spouse of or a minor child of the first-mentioned individual;

"**deposit**" and "**interest**" have, respectively, the meaning assigned to them by section 256(1);

["**financial institution**" means —

[(a)	a person who holds or has held a licence under section 9 of the Central Bank Act 1971, or a person who holds or has held a licence or other similar authorisation under the law of any other Member State of the European Communities which corresponds to a licence granted under that section,][45]

(b)   a person referred to in section 7(4) of the Central Bank Act, 1971, or

(c)   a credit institution (within the meaning of the European Communities (Licensing and Supervision of Credit Institutions) Regulations, 1992 (S.I. No. 395 of 1992)) which has been authorised by the Central Bank of Ireland to carry on business of a credit institution in accordance with the provisions of the supervisory enactments (within the meaning of those Regulations);][46]

"**liability**" in relation to a person means any liability in relation to tax to which the person is or may be, or may have been, subject, or the amount of such liability;

"**tax**" means any tax, duty, levy or charge under the care and management of the Revenue Commissioners.

(2)   Notwithstanding any obligation as to secrecy or other restriction upon disclosure of information imposed by or under statute or otherwise, and subject to this section, an authorised officer may, for the purpose of enquiring into a liability in relation to a person (in this section referred to as the '**taxpayer**'), serve on a financial institution a notice in writing requiring the financial institution, within such period as may be specified in the notice, not being less than 30 days from the date of the service of the notice, to do either or both of the following, namely —

(a)   to make available for inspection by the authorised officer such books, records or other documents as are in the financial institution's power, possession or procurement and as contain, or may (in the authorised officer's opinion formed on reasonable grounds) contain, information relevant to a liability in relation to the taxpayer,

(b)   to furnish to the authorised officer, in writing or otherwise, such information, explanations and particulars as the authorised officer may reasonably require, being information, explanations and particulars that are relevant to any such liability,

and which are specified in the notice.

(3)   Where, in compliance with the requirements of a notice under subsection (2), a financial institution makes available for inspection by an authorised officer, books, records or other documents, it shall afford the authorised officer reasonable assistance, including information, explanations and particulars, in relation to the use of all the electronic or other automatic means, if any, by which the books, records or other documents,

in so far as they are in a non-legible form, are capable of being reproduced in a legible form and any data equipment or any associated apparatus or material.

(4) An authorised officer shall not serve a notice on a financial institution under subsection (2) without the consent in writing of a Revenue Commissioner and without having reasonable grounds to believe that the financial institution is likely to have information relevant to a liability in relation to the taxpayer.

(5) Without prejudice to the generality of subsection (2), the books, records or other documents which a financial institution may be required by notice under that subsection to deliver or to make available and the information, explanations and particulars which it may likewise be required to furnish, may include books, records or other documents and information, explanations and particulars relating to a person who is connected with the taxpayer.

(6) The persons who may be treated as a taxpayer for the purposes of this section include a company which has been dissolved and an individual who has died.

(7) A notice served under subsection (2) shall name the taxpayer in relation to whose liability the authorised officer is enquiring.

(8) Where an authorised officer serves a notice under subsection (2), a copy of such notice shall be given by the authorised officer to the taxpayer concerned.

(9) Where, in compliance with a notice served under subsection (2), a financial institution makes books, records or other documents available for inspection by an authorised officer, the authorised officer may make extracts from or copies of all or any part of the books, records or other documents.

(10) A financial institution which fails or refuses to comply with a notice issued under subsection (2) or which fails or refuses to afford reasonable assistance to an authorised officer as required under subsection (3), shall be liable to a penalty of [€19,045][47] and, if the failure or refusal to comply with such notice continues after the expiry of the period specified in the notice served under subsection (2), a further penalty of [€2,535][47] for each day on which the failure or refusal continues.][48]

Application to Appeal Commissioners: information from financial institutions.

[907. (1) In this section "**a taxpayer**" means any person including—

(a) a person whose identity is not known to the authorised officer, and a group or class of persons whose individual identities are not so known, and

(b)   a person by or in respect of whom a declaration has been made under section 263(1) declaring that the person is beneficially entitled to all or part of the interest in relation to a deposit.

(2)   An authorised officer may, subject to this section, make an application to the Appeal Commissioners for their consent, under subsection (5), to the service by him or her of a notice on a financial institution requiring the financial institution to do either or both of the following, namely —

    (a)   to make available for inspection by the authorised officer, such books, records or other documents as are in the financial institution's power, possession or procurement as contain, or may (in the authorised officer's opinion formed on reasonable grounds) contain, information relevant to a liability in relation to a taxpayer,

    (b)   to furnish to the authorised officer such information, explanations and particulars as the authorised officer may reasonably require, being information, explanations and particulars that are relevant to any such liability,

and which are specified in the application.

(3)   An authorised officer shall not make an application under subsection (2) without the consent in writing of a Revenue Commissioner, and without being satisfied —

    (a)   that there are reasonable grounds for suspecting that the taxpayer, or where the taxpayer is a group or class of persons, all or any one of those persons, may have failed or may fail to comply with any provision of the Acts,

    (b)   that any such failure is likely to have led or to lead to serious prejudice to the proper assessment or collection of tax (having regard to the amount of a liability in relation to the taxpayer, or where the taxpayer is a group or class of persons, the amount of a liability in relation to all or any one of those persons, that arises or might arise from such failure), and

    (c)   that the information —

        (i)   which is likely to be contained in the books, records or other documents to which the application relates, or

        (ii)   which is likely to arise from the information, explanations and particulars to which the application relates,

is relevant to the proper assessment or collection of tax.

(4)   Without prejudice to the generality of subsection (2), the authorised officer may make an application under that subsection to the Appeal Commissioners for their consent, under subsection (5), to the service by him or her of a notice on a financial institution in respect of the matters referred to in paragraphs (a) and (b) of subsection (2) in so far as they relate to a person who is connected with the taxpayer.

(5)   Where the Appeal Commissioners determine that in all the circumstances there are reasonable grounds for the application being made, they may give their consent to the service by the authorised officer concerned of a notice on the financial institution, requiring the financial institution —

(a)   to make available for inspection by the authorised officer, such books, records or other documents, and

(b)   to furnish to the authorised officer such information, explanations and particulars,

of the kind referred to in subsection (2) as may, with the Appeal Commissioners' consent, be specified in the notice.

(6)   The persons who may be treated as a taxpayer for the purposes of this section include a company which has been dissolved and an individual who has died.

(7)   Where the Appeal Commissioners have given their consent in accordance with this section, the authorised officer shall, as soon as practicable, but not later than 14 days from the time that such consent was given, serve a notice on the financial institution concerned and stating that —

(a)   such consent has been given, and

(b)   the financial institution should, within a period of 30 days from the date of the service of the notice, comply with the requirements specified in the notice.

[(7A)   Where in compliance with the requirements of a notice served under subsection (7), a financial institution makes available for inspection by an authorised officer, books, records or other documents, the financial institution shall afford the authorised officer reasonable assistance, including information, explanations and particulars, in relation to the use of all the electronic or other automatic means, if any, by which the books, records or other documents, in so far as they are in a non-legible form, are capable of being reproduced in a legible form, and any data equipment or any associated apparatus or material.

(7B)   Where in compliance with the requirements of a notice served under subsection (7), a financial institution makes books, records or other documents available for inspection by the authorised officer, the authorised officer may make extracts from or copies of all or any part of the books, records or other documents.][49]

(8) (a) Subject to paragraph (b), an application by an authorised officer under subsection (2) shall, with any necessary modifications, be heard by the Appeal Commissioners as if it were an appeal against an assessment to income tax.

(b) Notwithstanding section 933(4), a determination by the Appeal Commissioners under this section shall be final and conclusive.

(9) A financial institution which fails to comply with a notice served on the financial institution by an authorised officer in accordance with this section shall be liable to a penalty of [€19,045][47] and, if the failure continues after the expiry of the period specified in subsection (7)(b), a further penalty of [€2,535][47] for each day on which the failure so continues.][50]

Application to High Court seeking order requiring information: financial institutions.

[908. (1) In this section—

"judge" means a judge of the High Court;

"a taxpayer" means any person including—

(a) a person whose identity is not known to the authorised officer, and a group or class of persons whose individual identities are not so known, and

(b) a person by or in respect of whom a declaration has been made under section 263(1) declaring that the person is beneficially entitled to all or part of the interest in relation to a deposit.

(2) An authorised officer may, subject to this section, make an application to a judge for an order requiring a financial institution, to do either or both of the following, namely—

(a) to make available for inspection by the authorised officer, such books, records or other documents as are in the financial institution's power, possession or procurement as contain, or may (in the authorised officer's opinion formed on reasonable grounds) contain information relevant to a liability in relation to a taxpayer,

(b) to furnish to the authorised officer such information, explanations and particulars as the authorised officer may reasonably require, being information, explanations and particulars that are relevant to any such liability,

and which are specified in the application.

(3)   An authorised officer shall not make application under subsection (2) without the consent in writing of a Revenue Commissioner, and without being satisfied —

(a)   that there are reasonable grounds for suspecting that the taxpayer, or, where the taxpayer is a group or class of persons, all or any one of those persons, may have failed or may fail to comply with any provision of the Acts,

(b)   that any such failure is likely to have led or to lead to serious prejudice to the proper assessment or collection of tax (having regard to the amount of a liability in relation to the taxpayer, or where the taxpayer is a group or class of persons, the amount of a liability in relation to all or any one of them, that arises or might arise from such failure), and

(c)   that the information —

(i)   which is likely to be contained in the books, records or other documents to which the application relates, or

(ii)   which is likely to arise from the information, explanations and particulars to which the application relates,

is relevant to the proper assessment or collection of tax.

(4)   Without prejudice to the generality of subsection (2), the authorised officer may make an application under that subsection to the judge for an order in respect of the matters referred to in paragraphs (a) and (b) of that subsection in so far as they relate to a person who is connected with the taxpayer.

(5)   Where the judge, to whom an application is made under subsection (2), is satisfied that there are reasonable grounds for the application being made, the judge may, subject to such conditions as he or she may consider proper and specify in the order, make an order requiring the financial institution —

(a)   to make available for inspection by the authorised officer, such books, records or other documents, and

(b)   to furnish to the authorised officer such information, explanations and particulars,

as may be specified in the order.

(6)   The persons who may be treated as a taxpayer for the purposes of this section include a company which has been dissolved and an individual who has died.

[(6A)   Where in compliance with an order made under subsection (5), a financial institution makes available for inspection by an authorised officer, books, records or other documents, the financial institution shall afford the authorised officer reasonable assistance, including information, explanations and particulars, in relation to the use of all the electronic or other automatic means, if any, by which the books, records or other documents, in so far as they are in a non-legible form, are capable of being reproduced in a legible form, and any data equipment or any associated apparatus or material.

(6B)   Where in compliance with an order made under subsection (5), a financial institution makes books, records or other documents available for inspection by the authorised officer, the authorised officer may make extracts from or copies of all or any part of the books, records or other documents.]⁵¹

(7)   Every hearing of an application for an order under this section and of any appeal in connection with that application shall be held in camera.

(8)   Where a judge makes an order under this section, he or she may also, on the application of the authorised officer concerned, make a further order prohibiting, for such period as the judge may consider proper and specify in the order, any transfer of, or any dealing with, without the consent of the judge, any assets or moneys of the person to whom the order relates that are in the custody of the financial institution at the time the order is made.

(9)   (a)   Where–

           (i)   a copy of any affidavit and exhibits grounding an application under subsection (2) or (8) and any order made under subsection (5) or (8) are to be made available to the taxpayer, or the taxpayer's solicitor or to the financial institution or the financial institution's solicitor, as the case may be, and

           (ii)   the judge is satisfied on the hearing of the application that there are reasonable grounds in the public interest that such copy of an affidavit, exhibits or order, as the case may be, should not include the name or address of the authorised officer,

      such copy, or copies or order shall not include the name or address of the authorised officer.

     (b)   Where, on any application to the judge to vary or discharge an order made under this section, it is desired to cross-examine the deponent of any affidavit filed by or on behalf of the authorised officer and the judge is satisfied that there are reasonable grounds in the public interest to so order, the judge shall order either or both of the following—

(i)   that the name and address of the authorised officer shall not be disclosed in court, and

(ii)   that such cross-examination shall only take place in the sight and hearing of the judge and in the hearing only of all other persons present at such cross-examination.][52]

Revenue offence: power to obtain information from financial institutions.

[908A. (1)   In this section—

["the Acts" means the Waiver of Certain Tax, Interest and Penalties Act, 1993, together with the meaning assigned to it by section 1078(1) and;][53]

"authorised officer" means an officer of the Revenue Commissioners authorised by them in writing to exercise the powers conferred by this section;

"books, records or other documents" includes—

(a)   any records used in the business of a financial institution, or used in the transfer department of a financial institution acting as registrar of securities, whether—

(i)   comprised in bound volume, loose-leaf binders or other loose-leaf filing system, loose-leaf ledger sheets, pages, folios or cards, or

(ii)   kept on microfilm, magnetic tape or in any non-legible form (by the use of electronics or otherwise) which is capable of being reproduced in a legible form, and

(b)   documents in manuscript, documents which are typed, printed, stencilled or created by any other mechanical or partly mechanical process in use from time to time and documents which are produced by any photographic or photostatic process;

"judge" means a judge of the Circuit Court or of the District Court;

["financial institution" means—

[(a)   a person who holds or has held a licence under section 9 of the Central Bank Act 1971, or a person who holds or has held a licence or other similar authorisation under the law of any other Member State of the European Communities which corresponds to a licence granted under that section,][54]

(b)   a person referred to in section 7(4) of the Central Bank Act, 1971, or

(c)   a credit institution (within the meaning of the European Communities (Licensing and Supervision of Credit Institutions) Regulations, 1992 (S.I. No. 395 of 1992)) which has been authorised by the Central Bank of Ireland to carry on business of a credit institution in accordance with the provisions of the supervisory enactments (within the meaning of those Regulations);][46]

"liability" in relation to a person means any liability in relation to tax to which the person is or may be, or may have been, subject, or the amount of such liability;

["**offence**" means an offence falling within any provision of the Acts;][55]

"tax" means any tax, duty, levy or charge under the care and management of the Revenue Commissioners.

[(2)   (a)   In this subsection '**documentation**' includes information kept on microfilm, magnetic tape or in any non-legible form (by use of electronics or otherwise) which is capable of being reproduced in a permanent legible form.

(b)   If, on application made by an authorised officer, with the consent in writing of a Revenue Commissioner, a judge is satisfied, on information given on oath by the authorised officer, that there are reasonable grounds for suspecting—

(i)   that an offence, which would result (or but for its detection would have resulted) in serious prejudice to the proper assessment or collection of tax, is being, has been, or is about to be committed (having regard to the amount of a liability in relation to any person which might be, or might have been, evaded but for the detection of the relevant facts), and

(ii)   that there is material in the possession of a financial institution specified in the application which is likely to be of substantial value (whether by itself or together with other material) to the investigation of the relevant facts,

the judge may make an order authorising the authorised officer to inspect and take copies of any entries in the books, records or other documents of the financial institution, and any documentation associated with or relating to an entry in such books, records or other documents, for the purposes of investigation of the relevant facts.][56]

(3)   An offence the commission of which, if considered alone, would not be regarded as resulting in serious prejudice to the proper assessment or collection of tax for the purposes of this section may nevertheless be so regarded if there are reasonable grounds for suspecting that the commission of the offence forms part of a course of conduct which is, or but for its detection would be, likely to result in serious prejudice to the proper assessment or collection of tax.

(4)   Subject to subsection (5), a copy of any entry in books, records or other documents of a financial institution shall in all legal proceedings be received as prima facie evidence of such an entry, and of the matters, transactions, and accounts therein recorded.

(5)   A copy of an entry in the books, records or other documents of a financial institution shall not be received in evidence in legal proceedings unless it is further proved that—

    (a)   in the case where the copy sought to be received in evidence has been reproduced in a legible form directly by either mechanical or electronic means, or both such means, from a financial institution's books, records or other documents maintained in a non-legible form, it has been so reproduced;

    (b)   in the case where the copy sought to be received in evidence has been made (either directly or indirectly) from a copy to which paragraph (a) would apply—

        (i)   the copy sought to be so received has been examined with a copy so reproduced and is a correct copy, and

        (ii)   the copy so reproduced is a copy to which paragraph (a) would apply if it were sought to have it received in evidence,

    and

    (c)   in any other case, the copy has been examined with the original entry and is correct.

(6)   Proof of the matters to which subsection (5) relates shall be given—

    (a)   in respect of paragraph (a) or (b)(ii) of that subsection, by some person who has been in charge of the reproduction concerned, and

    (b)   in respect of paragraph (b)(i) of that subsection, by some person who has examined the copy with the reproduction concerned, and

(c)   in respect of paragraph (c) of that subsection, by some person who has examined the copy with the original entry concerned,

and may be given either orally or by an affidavit sworn before any commissioner or person authorised to take affidavits.][57]

Application to High Court seeking order requiring information: associated institutions.

[908B. (1)   In this section —

"**the Acts**" has the meaning assigned to it by section 1078(1);

"**associated institution**", in relation to a financial institution, means a person that —

(a)   is controlled by the financial institution (within the meaning of section 432), and

(b)   is not resident in the State;

"**authorised officer**" means an officer of the Revenue Commissioners authorised by them in writing to exercise the powers conferred by this section;

"**books, records or other documents**" includes —

(a)   any records used in the business of an associated institution, or used in the transfer department of an associated institution acting as registrar of securities, whether —

(i)   comprised in bound volume, looseleaf binders or other loose-leaf filing system, loose-leaf ledger sheets, pages, folios or cards, or

(ii)   kept on microfilm, magnetic tape or in any non-legible form (by the use of electronics or otherwise) which is capable of being reproduced in a legible form,

(b)   every electronic or other automatic means, if any, by which any such thing in non-legible form is so capable of being reproduced,

(c)   documents in manuscript, documents which are typed, printed, stencilled or created by any other mechanical or partly mechanical process in use from time to time and documents which are produced by any photographic or photostatic process, and

(d)   correspondence and records of other communications between an associated institution and its customers;

"**financial institution**" means—

[(a)   a person who holds or has held a licence under section 9 of the Central Bank Act 1971, or a person who holds or has held a licence or other similar authorisation under the law of any other Member State of the European Communities which corresponds to a licence granted under that section,][58]

(b)   a person referred to in section 7(4) of the Central Bank Act 1971, or

(c)   a credit institution (within the meaning of the European Communities (Licensing and Supervision of Credit Institutions) Regulations 1992 (S.I. No. 395 of 1992)) which has been authorised by the Central Bank and Financial Services Authority of Ireland to carry on business of a credit institution in accordance with the provisions of the supervisory enactments (within the meaning of those Regulations);

"**judge**" means a judge of the High Court;

"**liability**" in relation to a person means any liability in relation to tax which the person is or may be, or may have been, subject, or the amount of such liability;

"**tax**" means any tax, duty, levy or charge under the care and management of the Revenue Commissioners;

"**a taxpayer**" means any person including a person whose identity is not known to the authorised officer, and a group or class of persons whose individual identities are not so known.

(2)   An authorised officer may, subject to this section, make an application to a judge for an order requiring a financial institution to do either or both of the following, namely—

(a)   to make available for inspection by the authorised officer, such books, records or other documents as are in the power, possession or procurement of an associated institution, in relation to the financial institution, as contain, or may (in the authorised officer's opinion formed on reasonable grounds) contain information relevant to a liability in relation to a taxpayer, or

(b)   to furnish to the authorised officer such information, explanations and particulars held by, or available from, the financial institution or an associated institution, in relation to the financial institution, as the authorised officer may reasonably require, being information, explanations or particulars that are relevant to any such liability,

and which are specified in the application.

(3)   An authorised officer shall not make an application under subsection (2) without the consent in writing of a Revenue Commissioner, and without being satisfied—

(a)   that there are reasonable grounds for suspecting that the taxpayer, or where the taxpayer is a group or class of persons, all or any one of those persons, may have failed or may fail to comply with any provision of the Acts,

(b)   that any such failure is likely to have led or to lead to serious prejudice to the proper assessment or collection of tax (having regard to the amount of a liability in relation to the taxpayer, or where the taxpayer is a group or class of persons, the amount of a liability, in relation to all or any one of them, that arises or might arise from such failure), and

(c)   that the information—

(i)   which is likely to be contained in the books, records or other documents to which the application relates, or

(ii)   which is likely to arise from the information, explanations and particulars to which the application relates,

is relevant to the proper assessment or collection of tax.

(4)   Where the judge, to whom an application is made under subsection (2), is satisfied that there are reasonable grounds for the application being made, then the judge may, subject to such conditions as he or she may consider proper and specify in the order, make an order requiring the financial institution—

(a)   to make available for inspection by the authorised officer, such books, records or other documents, and

(b)   to furnish to the authorised officer such information, explanations and particulars,

as may be specified in the order.

(5)   The persons who may be treated as a taxpayer for the purposes of this section include a company which has been dissolved and an individual who has died.

(6)   Where in compliance with an order made under subsection (4) a financial institution makes available for inspection by an authorised officer, books, records or other documents, then the financial institution shall afford the authorised officer reasonable assistance, including information, explanations and particulars, in relation to the use of all the electronic or other automatic means, if any, by which the books, records or other documents, in so far as they are in a non-legible form, are capable of being

reproduced in a legible form, and any data equipment or any associated apparatus or material.

(7)   Where in compliance with an order made under subsection (4) a financial institution makes books, records or other documents available for inspection by the authorised officer, then the authorised officer may make extracts from or copies of all or any part of the books, records or other documents.

(8)   Every hearing of an application for an order under this section and of any appeal in connection with that application shall be held in camera.][59]

[Search warrants

[908C. (1)   In this section—

'**the Acts**' means the Waiver of Certain Tax, Interest and Penalties Act 1993 together with the meaning assigned to it in section 1078(1);

'**authorised officer**' means an officer of the Revenue Commissioners authorised by them in writing to exercise the powers conferred by this section;

'**commission**', in relation to an offence, includes an attempt to commit the offence;

'**computer**' includes any electronic device capable of performing logical or arithmetical operations on data in accordance with a set of instructions;

'**computer at the place which is being searched**', includes any other computer, whether at that place or at any other place, which is lawfully accessible by means of that computer;

'**information in non-legible form**' means information which is kept (by electronic means or otherwise) on microfilm, microfiche, magnetic tape or disk or in any other non-legible form;

'**material**' means any books, documents, records or other things (including a computer);

'**offence**' means an offence under the Acts;

'**place**' includes any building (or part of a building), dwelling, vehicle, vessel, aircraft or hovercraft and any other place whatsoever;

'**record**' includes any information in non-legible form which is capable of being reproduced in a permanently legible form.

(2)   If a judge of the District Court is satisfied by information given on oath by an authorised officer that there are reasonable grounds for suspecting—

(a)   that an offence is being, has been or is about to be committed, and

(b) (i) that material which is likely to be of value (whether by itself or together with other information) to the investigation of the offence, or

(ii) that evidence of, or relating to the commission of, the offence,

is to be found in any place,

the judge may issue a warrant for the search of that place, and of any thing and any persons, found there.

(3) A warrant issued under this section shall be expressed and shall operate to authorise the authorised officer, accompanied by such other named officers of the Revenue Commissioners and such other named persons as the authorised officer considers necessary—

(a) to enter, at any time or times within one month from the date of issuing of the warrant (if necessary by the use of reasonable force), the place named in the warrant,

(b) to search, or cause to be searched, that place and any thing and any persons, found there, but no person shall be searched except by a person of the same sex unless express or implied consent is given,

(c) to require any person found there—

(i) to give his or her name, home address and occupation to the authorised officer, and

(ii) to produce to the authorised officer any material which is in the custody or possession of that person,

(d) to examine, seize and retain (or cause to be examined, seized and retained) any material found there, or in the possession of a person present there at the time of the search, which the authorised officer reasonably believes—

(i) is likely to be of value (whether by itself or together with other information) to the investigation of the offence, or

(ii) to be evidence of, or relating to the commission of, the offence, and

(e) to take any other steps which may appear to the authorised officer to be necessary for preserving any such material and preventing interference with it.

(4) The authority conferred by subsection (3)(d) to seize and retain (or to cause to be seized and retained) any material includes—

(a) in the case of books, documents or records, authority to make and retain a copy of the books, documents or records, and

(b)   where necessary, authority to seize and, for as long as necessary, retain, any computer or other storage medium in which records are kept and to copy such records.

(5)   An authorised officer acting under the authority of a warrant issued under this section may–

(a)   operate any computer at the place which is being searched or cause any such computer to be operated by a person accompanying the authorised officer, and

(b)   require any person at that place who appears to the authorised officer to be in a position to facilitate access to the information held in any such computer or which can be accessed by the use of that computer–

(i)   to give to the authorised officer any password necessary to operate it,

(ii)   otherwise to enable the authorised officer to examine the information accessible by the computer in a form in which the information is visible and legible, or

(iii)   to produce the information in a form in which it can be removed and in which it is, or can be made, visible and legible.

(6)   A person who–

(a)   obstructs or attempts to obstruct the exercise of a right of entry and search conferred by virtue of a warrant issued under this section,

(b)   obstructs the exercise of a right so conferred to examine, seize and retain material,

(c)   fails to comply with a requirement under subsection (3) (c) or gives to the authorised officer a name, address or occupation that is false or misleading, or

(d)   fails to comply with a requirement under subsection (5)(b),

is guilty of an offence and is liable on summary conviction to a fine not exceeding [€5,000][60] or imprisonment for a term not exceeding 6 months or to both the fine and the imprisonment.

(7)   Where an authorised officer enters, or attempts to enter, any place in the execution of a warrant issued under subsection (2), the authorised officer may be accompanied by a member or members of the Garda Síochána, and any such member may arrest without warrant any person who is committing an offence under subsection (6) or whom the member suspects, with reasonable cause, of having done so.

(8)   Any material which is seized under subsection (3) which is required for the purposes of any legal proceedings by an officer

of the Revenue Commissioners or for the purpose of any criminal proceedings, may be retained for so long as it is reasonably required for the purposes aforesaid.

Order to produce evidential material

[**908D.** (1)   In this section–

'**the Acts**' means the Waiver of Certain Tax, Interest and Penalties Act 1993 together with the meaning assigned to it in section 1078(1);

'**authorised officer**' means an officer of the Revenue Commissioners authorised by them in writing to exercise the powers conferred by this section;

'**commission**', in relation to an offence, includes an attempt to commit the offence;

'**computer**' includes any electronic device capable of performing logical or arithmetical operations on data in accordance with a set of instructions;

'**information in non-legible form**' means information which is kept (by electronic means or otherwise) on microfilm, microfiche, magnetic tape or disk or in any other non-legible form;

'**material**' means any books, documents, records or other things (including a computer);

'**offence**' means an offence under the Acts;

'**record**' includes any information in non-legible form which is capable of being reproduced in a permanently legible form.

(2)   If a judge of the District Court is satisfied by information given on oath by an authorised officer that there are reasonable grounds for suspecting–

(a)   that an offence is being, has been or is about to be committed, and

(b)   that material–

(i)   which is likely to be of value (whether by itself or together with other information) to the investigation of the offence, or

(ii)   which constitutes evidence of, or relating to the commission of, the offence,

is in the possession or control of a person specified in the application, the judge may order that the person shall–

(I)   produce the material to the authorised officer for the authorised officer to take away, or

(II)   give the authorised officer access to it,

either immediately or within such period as the order may specify.

(3)   Where the material consists of or includes records contained in a computer, the order shall have effect as an order to produce the records, or to give access to them, in a form in which they are visible and legible and in which they can be taken away.

(4)   An order under this section–

(a)   in so far as it may empower an authorised officer to take away books, documents or records, or to be given access to them, shall also have effect as an order empowering the authorised officer to take away a copy of the books, documents or, as the case may be, records (and for that purpose the authorised officer may, if necessary, make a copy of them),

(b)   shall not confer any right to production of, or access to, any document subject to legal privilege, and

(c)   shall have effect notwithstanding any other obligation as to secrecy or other restriction on disclosure of information imposed by statute or otherwise.

(5)   Any material taken away by an authorised officer under this section may be retained by the authorised officer for use as evidence in any criminal proceedings.

(6)   (a)   Information contained in books, documents or records which were produced to an authorised officer, or to which an authorised officer was given access, in accordance with an order under this section, shall be admissible in any criminal proceedings as evidence of any fact therein of which direct oral evidence would be admissible unless the information–

(i)   is privileged from disclosure in such proceedings,

(ii)   was supplied by a person who would not be compellable to give evidence at the instance of the prosecution,

(iii)   was compiled for the purposes of, or in contemplation of, any–

(I)   criminal investigation,

(II)   investigation or inquiry carried out pursuant to or under any enactment,

       (III)   civil or criminal proceedings, or

       (IV)   proceedings of a disciplinary nature,

or unless the requirements of the provisions mentioned in paragraph (b) are not complied with.

(b)   References in sections 7 (notice of documentary evidence to be served on accused), 8 (admission and weight of documentary evidence) and 9 (admissibility of evidence as to credibility of supplier of information) of the Criminal Evidence Act 1992 to a document or information contained in it shall be construed as including references to books, documents and records mentioned in paragraph (a) and the information contained in them, and those provisions shall have effect accordingly with any necessary modifications.

(7)   A judge of the District Court may, on the application of an authorised officer, or of any person to whom an order under this section relates, vary or discharge the order.

(8)   A person who without reasonable excuse fails or refuses to comply with an order under this section is guilty of an offence and liable on summary conviction to a fine not exceeding [€5,000][60] or imprisonment for a term not exceeding 6 months or to both the fine and the imprisonment.][61]

Power to obtain information from Minister of the Government

910. [(1)   For the purposes of the assessment, charge, collection and recovery of any tax or duty placed under their care and management, the Revenue Commissioners may, by notice in writing, request any Minister of the Government or any body established by or under statute to provide them with such information in the possession of that Minister or body in relation to payments for any purposes made by that Minister or by that body, whether on that Minister's or that body's own behalf or on behalf of any other person, to such persons or classes of persons as the Revenue Commissioners may specify in the notice and a Minister of the Government or body of whom or of which such a request is made shall provide such information as may be so specified.][62]

(2)   The Revenue Commissioners may nominate any of their officers to perform any acts and discharge any functions authorised by this section to be performed or discharged by the Revenue Commissioners.

[(3)   Where information is to be provided to the Revenue Commissioners in accordance with subsection (1) it shall be provided, where the Revenue Commissioners so require, in an electronic format approved by them.][63]

Computer documents and records

912. (1)   In this section–

"**the Acts**" means -

(a)   the Customs Acts,

(b)   the statutes relating to the duties of excise and to the management of those duties,

(c)   the Tax Acts,

(d)   the Capital Gains Tax Acts,

(e)   the Value -Added Tax Act, 1972, and the enactments amending or extending that Act,

(f)   the [Capital Acquisitions Tax Consolidation Act 2003][14], and the enactments amending or extending that Act, and

(g)   Part V1 of the Finance Act, 1983,

and any instruments made thereunder;

"**data**" means information in a form in which it can be processed;

"**data equipment**" means any electronic, photographic, magnetic, optical or other equipment for processing data;

"**processing**" means performing automatically logical or arithmetical operations on data, or the storing, maintenance, transmission, reproduction or communication of data;

"**records**" means documents which a person is obliged by any provision of the Acts to keep, issue or produce for inspection, and any other written or printed material;

"**software**" means any sequence of instructions used in conjunction with data equipment for the purpose of processing data or controlling the operation of the data equipment.

(2)   Any provision under the Acts which–

(a)   requires a person to keep, retain, issue or produce any records or cause any records to be kept, retained, issued or produced, or

(b)   permits an officer of the Revenue Commissioners-

(i)   to inspect any records,

(ii)   to enter premises and search for any records, or

(iii)   to take extracts from or copies of or remove any records,

shall, where the records are processed by data equipment, apply to the data equipment together with any associated software, data, apparatus or material as it applies to the records.

(3)   An officer of the Revenue Commissioners may in the exercise or performance of his or her powers or duties require-

(a)   the person by or on whose behalf the data equipment is or has been used, or

(b)   any person having charge of, or otherwise concerned with the operation of, the data equipment or any associated apparatus or material,

to afford him or her all reasonable assistance in relation to the exercise or performance of those powers or duties.

Information for tax authorities in other territories

[**912A.** (1)   In this section-

['**foreign tax**' means a tax chargeable under the laws of a territory in relation to which arrangements (in this section referred to as 'the arrangements') having the force of law by virtue of section 826, 898P(2) or section 106 of the Capital Acquisitions Tax Consolidation Act 2003 apply;][64]

'**liability to foreign tax**', in relation to a person, means any liability in relation to foreign tax to which the person is or may be, or may have been, subject, or the amount of any such liability.

(2)   For the purposes of complying with provisions with respect to the exchange of information contained in the arrangements, sections 900, 901, 902, 902A, 906A, 907 and 908 shall, subject to subsection (3), have effect-

(a)   as if references in those sections to tax included references to foreign tax, and

(b)   as if references in those sections to liability, in relation to a person, included references to liability to foreign tax, in relation to a person.

(3)   Where sections 902A, 907 and 908 have effect by virtue only of this section, they shall have effect as if-

(a)   there were substituted ' "**a taxpayer**" means a person;' for the definition of 'a taxpayer' in subsection (1) of each of those sections, and

(b)   the references in those sections to-

(i)   tax, were references to foreign tax, and

(ii)   any provision of the Acts, were references to any provision of the law of a territory in accordance with which foreign tax is charged or collected.][65]

[912B. (1) In this section–

'authorised officer' means an officer of the Revenue Commissioners authorised by them in writing to exercise the powers conferred by this section;

'specified offence' means any offence under–

(a) the Customs Acts, including any offence under section 1078 or 1078A in so far as those sections relate to customs, and any instruments made thereunder and any instruments made under any other enactment and relating to customs,

(b) the statutes relating to the duties of excise and to the management of those duties, including any offence under section 1078 or 1078A in so far as those sections relate to excise, and any instruments made thereunder,

(c) (i) subsection (1A) and paragraphs (c), (d) and (ii) of subsection (2) of section 1078, and

(ii) section 1078A,

in so far as it is an offence relating to Chapter 2 of 20 Part 18 and any instruments made under that Chapter, or

(d) (i) subsection (1A) and paragraphs (c) and (d) of subsection (2) of section 1078, and

(ii) section 1078A,

in so far as it is an offence relating to the Value-Added Tax Act 1972, and the enactments amending or extending that Act and any instruments made thereunder,

which is an arrestable offence within the meaning of section 2 of the Criminal Law Act 1997.

(2) This section shall apply to a specified offence only.

(3) Where a member of the Garda Síochána arrests without warrant, whether in a Garda station or elsewhere, a person whom he or she, with reasonable cause, suspects of committing or of having committed a specified offence and the person has been taken to and detained in a Garda station, or if the person is arrested in a Garda station, has been detained in the station, pursuant to section 4 of the Criminal Justice Act 1984, an authorised officer or officers (but not more than 2 such officers) may, if and for so long as the officer or officers is, or are, accompanied by a member of the Garda Síochána, attend at, and participate in, the questioning of a person so detained in connection with the investigation of the specified offence, but only if the member of the Garda Síochána requests the authorised officer or officers to do so and the member is satisfied that the attendance at, and

participation in, such questioning of the authorised officer or officers is necessary for the proper investigation of the specified offence concerned.

(4)   An authorised officer who attends at, and participates in, the questioning of a person in accordance with subsection (3) may not commit any act or make any omission which, if committed or made by a member of the Garda Síochána, would be a contravention of any regulation made under section 7 of the Criminal Justice Act 1984.

(5)   An act committed or omission made by an authorised officer who attends at, and participates in, the questioning of a person in accordance with subsection (3) which, if committed or made by a member of the Garda Síochána, would be a contravention of any regulation made under section 7 of the Criminal Justice Act 1984 shall not of itself render the authorised officer liable to any criminal or civil proceedings or of itself affect the lawfulness of the custody of the detained person or the admissibility in evidence of any statement made by him or her.][66]

Chapter 6
Electronic Transmission of returns, profits etc and of other Revenue items

Interpretation

[917D. (1)   In this Chapter-

'**the Acts**' means-

(a)   the statutes relating to the duties of excise and to the management of those duties,

(b)   the Tax Acts,

(c)   the Capital Gains Tax Acts,

(d)   the Value-Added Tax Act, 1972, and the enactments amending or extending that Act,

(e)   the [Capital Acquisitions Tax Consolidation Act 2003][14], and the enactments amending or extending that Act, and

(f)   the [Stamp Duties Consolidation Act 1999,][67], and the enactments amending or extending that Act,

and any instruments made under any of the statutes and enactments referred to in paragraphs (a) to (f);

'**approved person**' shall be construed in accordance with section 917G;

'**approved transmission**' shall be construed in accordance with section 917H;

'**authorised person**' has the meaning assigned to it by [section 917G(3)(b);][67];

['**digital signature**' in relation to a person, means an advanced electronic signature (within the meaning of the Electronic Commerce Act, 2000) provided to the person by the Revenue Commissioners solely for the purpose of making an electronic transmission of information which is required to be included in a return to which this Chapter applies and for no other purpose and a qualified certificate (within the meaning of that Act) provided to the person by the Revenue Commissioners or a person appointed in that behalf by the Revenue Commissioners;][68]

['**electronic identifier**', in relation to a person, means–

(a)   the person's digital signature, or

(b)   such other means of electronic identification as may be specified or authorised by the Revenue Commissioners for the purposes of this Chapter;][69]

'**hard copy**', in relation to information held electronically, means a printed out version of that information;

['**return**' means any return, claim, application, notification, election, declaration, nomination, statement, list, registration, particulars or other information which a person is or may be required by the Acts to give to the Revenue Commissioners or any Revenue officer;][70]

'**revenue officer**' means the Collector-General, an inspector or other officer of the Revenue Commissioners (including an inspector or other officer who is authorised under any provision of the Acts (however expressed) to receive a return or to require a return to be prepared and delivered);

'**tax**' means any income tax, corporation tax, capital gains tax, value-added tax, gift tax, inheritance tax, excise duty or stamp duty.

(2)   [...][71]

(3)   Any references in this Chapter to the making of a return include references in any provision of the Acts to-

(a)   the preparing and delivering of a return;

(b)   the sending of a return;

(c)   the furnishing of a return or of particulars;

(d)   the delivering of a return;

(e)   the presentation of a return;

(f)   the rendering of a return;

(g)   the giving of particulars or of any information specified in any provision; and

(h)   any other means whereby a return is forwarded, however expressed.][72]

Application

[917E.   This Chapter shall apply to a return if-

(a)   the provision of the Acts under which the return is made is specified for the purpose of this Chapter by order made by the Revenue Commissioners, and

(b)   the return is required to be made after the day appointed by such order in relation to returns to be made under the provision so specified.][73]

Mandatory electronic filing and payment of tax

[917EA. (1)   In this section-

'**electronic means**' includes electrical, digital, magnetic, optical, electromagnetic, biometric, photonic means of transmission of data and other forms of related technology by means of which data is transmitted;

'**repayment of tax**' includes any amount relating to tax which is to be paid or repaid by the Revenue Commissioners;

'**specified person**' means any person, group of persons or class of persons specified in regulations made under this section for the purposes of either or both paragraphs (a) and (b) of subsection (3);

'**specified return**' means a return specified in regulations made under this section;

'**specified tax liabilities**' means liabilities to tax including interest on unpaid tax specified in regulations made under this section.

(2)   Section 917D shall apply for the purposes of regulations made under this section in the same way as it applies for the purposes of this Chapter.

(3)   The Revenue Commissioners may make regulations-

(a)   requiring the delivery by specified persons of a specified return by electronic means where an order under section 917E has been made in respect of that return,

(b)   requiring the payment by electronic means of specified tax liabilities by specified persons, and

(c)   for the repayment of any tax specified in the regulations to be made by electronic means.

(4)   Regulations made under this section shall include provision for the exclusion of a person from the requirements of regulations made under this section where the Revenue Commissioners are satisfied that the person could not reasonably be expected to have the capacity to make a specified return or to pay the specified tax liabilities by electronic means, and allowing a person, aggrieved by a failure to exclude such person, to appeal that failure to the Appeal Commissioners.

(5)   Regulations made under this section may, in particular and without prejudice to the generality of subsection (3), include provision for-

(a)   the electronic means to be used to pay or repay tax,

(b)   the conditions to be complied with in relation to the electronic payment or repayment of tax,

(c)   determining the time when tax paid or repaid using electronic means is to be taken as having been paid or repaid,

(d)   the manner of proving, for any purpose, the time of payment or repayment of any tax paid or repaid using electronic means, including provision for the application of any conclusive or other presumptions,

(e)   notifying persons that they are specified persons, including the manner by which such notification may be made, and

(f)   such supplemental and incidental matters as appear to the Revenue Commissioners to be necessary.

(6)   The Revenue Commissioners may nominate any of their officers to perform any acts and discharge any functions authorised by regulation made under this section to be performed or discharged by the Revenue Commissioners.

(7)   Where a specified person-

(a)   makes a return which is a specified return for the purposes of regulations made under this section, or

(b)   makes a payment of tax which is specified tax liabilities for the purposes of regulations made under this section,

in a form other than that required by any such regulation, the specified person shall be liable to a penalty of €1,520 and, for the purposes of the recovery of a penalty under this subsection, section 1061 applies in the same manner as it applies for the purposes of the recovery of a penalty under any of the sections referred to in that section.

(8)   Every regulation made under this section shall be laid before Dáil Éireann as soon as may be after it is made and, if a resolution

annulling the regulation is passed by Dáil Éireann within the next 21 days on which Dáil Éireann has sat after the regulation is laid before it, the regulation shall be annulled accordingly but without prejudice to the validity of anything previously done under the regulation.][74]

Electronic transmission of returns

[917F. (1)   Notwithstanding any other provision of the Acts, the obligation of any person to make a return to which this Chapter applies shall be treated as fulfilled by that person if information is transmitted electronically in compliance with that obligation, but only if-

(a)   the transmission is made by an approved person or an authorised person,

(b)   the transmission is an approved transmission,

[(c)   the transmission bears the electronic identifier of that person, and][75]

(d)   the receipt of the transmission is acknowledged in accordance with section 917J.

(2)   In subsection (1), the reference to the information which is required to be included in the return includes any requirement on a person to-

(a)   make any statement,

(b)   include any particulars, or

(c)   make or attach any claim.

(3)   Where the obligation of any person to make a return to which this Chapter applies is treated as fulfilled in accordance with subsection (1) then, any provision of the Acts which-

(a)   requires that the return include or be accompanied by any description of declaration whatever by the person making the return, apart from a declaration of an amount,

(b)   requires that the return be signed or accompanied by a certificate,

(c)   requires that the return be in writing

(d)   authorises the return to be signed by a person acting under the authority of the person obliged to make the return,

(e)   authorises the Revenue Commissioners to prescribe the form of a return or which requires a return to be in or on any prescribed form, or

(f)   for the purposes of any claim for exemption or for any allowance, deduction or repayment of tax under the Acts which is required to be made with the return, authorises the Revenue Commissioners to prescribe the form of a claim,

shall not apply.

(4)   Where the obligation of any person to make a return to which this Chapter applies is treated as fulfilled in accordance with subsection (1) then, the time at which any requirement under the Acts to make a return is fulfilled shall be the day on which the receipt of the information referred to in that subsection is acknowledged in accordance with section 917J.

[(5)   Where an approved transmission is made by-

(a)   an approved person on behalf of another person, or

(b)   an authorised person on behalf of another person (not being the person who authorised that person),

a hard copy of the information shall be made and authenticated in accordance with section 917K.][76]

(6)   (a)   Where the obligation of any person to make a return to which this Chapter applies is treated as fulfilled in accordance with subsection (1) then, any requirement that-

(i)   the return or any claim which is to be made with or attached to the return should be accompanied by any document (in this subsection referred to as a 'supporting document') other than the return or the claim, and

(ii)   the supporting document be delivered with the return or the claim,

shall be treated as fulfilled by the person subject to the requirement if the person or the approved person referred to in subsection (1)(a) retains the document for inspection on request by a revenue officer.

(b)   Any person subject to the requirement referred to in paragraph (a) shall produce any supporting documents requested by a revenue officer within 30 days of that request.

(c)   The references in this subsection to a document include references to any accounts, certificate, evidence, receipts, reports or statements.][77]

Approved persons

[917G. (1) A person shall be an approved person for the purposes of this Chapter if the person is approved by the Revenue Commissioners for the purposes of transmitting electronically information which is required to be included in a return to which this Chapter applies (in this section referred to as '**the transmission**') and [complies with the condition specified in subsection 15(3)(a) in relation to authorised persons and the condition specified in subsection (3)(b) in relation to the making of transmissions and the use of [electronic identifiers]⁷⁵]⁷⁸.

(2) A person seeking to be approved under this section shall make application in that behalf to the Revenue Commissioners [by such means as the Revenue Commissioners may determine]⁷⁹ for the purposes of this section.

[(3) The conditions referred to in subsection (1) are that-

(a) the person notifies the Revenue Commissioners in a manner to be determined by the Revenue Commissioners of the persons (each of whom is referred to in this section as an '**authorised person**'), in addition to the person, who are authorised to make the transmission, and

(b) the person and each person who is an authorised person in relation to that person in making the transmission complies with the requirements referred to in subsections (2) and (3) of section 917H.]⁸⁰

(4) A person seeking to be approved under this section shall be given notice by the Revenue Commissioners of the grant or refusal by them of the approval and, in the case of a refusal, of the reason for the refusal.

(5) An approval under this section may be withdrawn by the Revenue Commissioners by notice in writing or by such other means as the Revenue Commissioners may decide with effect from such date as may be specified in the notice.

(6) (a) A notice withdrawing an approval under the section shall state the grounds for the withdrawal.

(b) No approval under this section may be withdrawn unless an approved person or an authorised person has failed to comply with one or more of the requirements referred to in section 917H(2).

(7) A person who is refused approval under this section or whose approval under this section is withdrawn may appeal to the Appeal Commissioners against the refusal or withdrawal.

(8) The appeal under subsection (7) shall be made by notice to the Revenue Commissioners before the end of the period of 30

days beginning with the day on which notice of the refusal or withdrawal was given to the person.

(9)   The Appeal Commissioners shall hear and determine an appeal made to them under subsection (7) as if it were an appeal against an assessment to income tax, and the provisions of the Tax Acts relating to appeals shall apply accordingly.][81]

Approved transmissions

[917H. (1)   Where an approved person transmits electronically information which is required to be included in a return to which this Chapter applies the transmission shall not be an approved transmission unless it complies with the requirements of this section.

[(2)   The Revenue Commissioners shall publish and make known to each approved person and each authorised person any requirement for the time being determined by them as being applicable to-

(a)   the manner in which information which is required to be included in a return to which this Chapter applies is to be transmitted electronically, and

(b)   the use of a person's [electronic identifier][75].

(3)   The requirements referred to in subsection (2) include-

(a)   requirements as to the software or type of software to be used to make a transmission,

(b)   the terms and conditions under which a person may make a transmission, and

(c)   the terms and conditions under which a person may use that person's [electronic identifier][75].][82]][83]

[(4)   For the purposes of subsection (3), the Revenue Commissioners may determine different terms and conditions in relation to different returns or categories of a return, different categories of persons and different returns or categories of a return made by different categories of persons.][69]

[...][84]

Acknowledgement of electronic transmissions

[917J. For the purposes of this Chapter, where an electronic transmission of information which is required to be included in a return to which this Chapter applies is received by the Revenue Commissioners, the Revenue Commissioners shall send an electronic acknowledgement of receipt of that transmission to the person from whom it was received.][85]

Hard copies

[917K. (1)   A hard copy shall be made in accordance with this subsection only if-

(a)   the hard copy is made under processes and procedures which are designed to ensure that the information contained in the hard copy shall only be the information [transmitted to be transmitted][86] in accordance with section 917F(1),

(b)   the hard copy is in a form approved by the Revenue Commissioners which is appropriate to the information so transmitted, and

(c)   the hard copy is authenticated in accordance with subsection (2).

(2)   For the purposes of this Chapter, a hard copy made in accordance with subsection (1) shall be authenticated only if the hard copy is signed by the person who would have been required to make the declaration, sign the return or furnish the certificate, as the case may be, but for paragraph (a), (b) or (d) of section 917F(3).][87]

Exercise of powers

[917L. (1)   This section shall apply where the obligation of any person to make a return to which this Chapter applies is treated as fulfilled in accordance with section 917F(1).

(2)   Where this section applies the Revenue Commissioners and a revenue officer shall have all the powers and duties in relation to the information contained in the transmission as they or that officer would have had if the information had been contained in a return made by post.

(3)   Where this section applies the person whose obligation to make a return to which this Chapter applies is treated as fulfilled in accordance with section 917F(1) shall have all the rights and duties in relation to the information contained in the transmission as the person would have had if that information had been contained in a return made by post.][88]

Proceedings

[917M. (1)   This section shall apply where the obligation of any person to make a return to which this Chapter applies is treated as fulfilled in accordance with section 917F(1).

(2)   In this section, '**proceedings**' means civil and criminal proceedings, and includes proceedings before the Appeal Commissioners or any other tribunal having jurisdiction by virtue of any provision of the Acts.

(3)   Where this section applies a hard copy certified by a revenue officer to be a true copy of the information transmitted electronically in accordance with section 917F(1) shall be treated [for the purposes of the Acts][89] as if the hard copy-

(a)   were a return or, as the case may be, a claim made by post, and

(b)   contained any declaration, certificate or signature required by the Acts on such a return or, as the case may be, such a claim.

(4)   For the purposes of any proceedings under the Acts, unless a Judge or any other person before whom proceedings are taken determines at the time of the proceedings that it is unjust in the circumstances to apply this provision, any rule of law restricting the admissibility or use of hearsay evidence shall not apply to a representation contained in a document recording information which has been transmitted in accordance with section 917F(1) in so far as the representation is a representation as to-

(a)   the information so transmitted,

(b)   the date on which, or the time at which, the information was so transmitted, or

(c)   the identity of the person by whom or on whose behalf the information was so transmitted.][90]

Miscellaneous

[917N. The Revenue Commissioners may nominate any of their officers to perform any acts and discharge any functions authorized by this Chapter to be performed or discharged by the Revenue Commissioners.][91]

PART 39

Chapter 1
Income Tax and Corporation Tax

Transmission to Collector-General of particulars of sums to be collected

[928. (1)   In this section—

'assessment' and 'Revenue officer' have, respectively, the same meanings as in Chapter 1A of Part 42;

'tax' means income tax, corporation tax, capital gains tax, value-added tax, excise duty, stamp duty, gift tax and inheritance tax.

(2)   After assessments to tax have been made, the inspectors or other Revenue officers shall transmit particulars of the sums

to be collected to the Collector-General or to a Revenue officer nominated in writing under section 960B for collection.

(3)   The entering by an inspector or other Revenue officer of details of an assessment to tax and of the tax charged in such an assessment in an electronic, digital, magnetic, optical, electromagnetic, biometric, photonic, photographic or other record from which the Collector-General or a Revenue officer nominated in writing under section 960B may extract such details by electronic, digital, magnetic, optical, electromagnetic, biometric, photonic, photographic or other process shall constitute transmission of such details by the inspector or other Revenue officer to the Collector-General or to the Revenue officer nominated in writing under section 960B.][92]

PART 40

Chapter 1
Appeals against income tax and corporation tax assessments

Prohibition on alteration of assessment except on appeal.

932. Except where expressly authorised by the Tax Acts, an assessment to income tax or corporation tax shall not be altered before the time for hearing and determining appeals and then only in cases of assessments appealed against and in accordance with such determination, and if any person makes, causes, or allows to be made in any assessment any unauthorised alteration, that person shall incur a penalty of [€60][47].

Appeals against assessment.

933. (1)   (a)   A person aggrieved by any assessment to income tax or corporation tax made on that person by the inspector or such other officer as the Revenue Commissioners shall appoint in that behalf (in this section referred to as "**other officer**") shall be entitled to appeal to the Appeal Commissioners on giving, within 30 days after the date of the notice of assessment, notice in writing to the inspector or other officer.

(b)   Where on an application under paragraph (a) the inspector or other officer is of the opinion that the person who has given the notice of appeal is not entitled to make such an appeal, the inspector or other officer shall refuse the application and notify the person in writing accordingly, specifying the grounds for such refusal.

(c)   A person who has had an application under paragraph (a) refused by the inspector or other officer shall be entitled to appeal against such refusal by notice in writing to the

Appeal Commissioners within 15 days of the date of issue by the inspector or other officer of the notice of refusal.

(d)   On receipt of an application under paragraph (c), the Appeal Commissioners shall request the inspector or other officer to furnish them with a copy of the notice issued to the person under paragraph (b) and, on receipt of the copy of the notice, they shall as soon as possible-

    (i)   refuse the application for an appeal by giving notice in writing to the applicant specifying the grounds for their refusal,

    (ii)   allow the application for an appeal and give notice in writing accordingly to both the applicant and the inspector or other officer, or

    (iii)   notify in writing both the applicant and the inspector or other officer that they have decided to arrange a hearing at such time and place specified in the notice to enable them determine whether or not to allow the application for an appeal.

(2)   (a)   The Appeal Commissioners shall from time to time appoint times and places for the hearing of appeals against assessments and the Clerk to the Appeal Commissioners shall give notice of such times and places to the inspector or other officer.

    (b)   The inspector or other officer shall give notice in writing to each person who has given notice of appeal of the time and place appointed for the hearing of that person's appeal; but-

    (i)   notice under this paragraph shall not be given in a case in which subsection (3)(b) applies either consequent on an agreement referred to in that subsection or consequent on a notice referred to in subsection (3)(d), and

    (ii)   in a case where it appears to the inspector or other officer that an appeal may be settled by agreement under subsection (3), he or she may refrain from giving notice under this paragraph or may by notice in writing and with the agreement of the appellant withdraw a notice already given.

    (c)   Where, on application in writing in that behalf to the Appeal Commissioners, a person who has given notice of appeal to the inspector or other officer in accordance with subsection (1)(a) satisfies the Appeal Commissioners that the information furnished to the inspector or other officer is such that the appeal is likely to be determined on the first occasion on which it comes before them for hearing, the Appeal Commissioners may direct the inspector or other officer to give the notice in writing first mentioned in paragraph (b) and the inspector or other officer shall comply forthwith with such direction, and accordingly subparagraph (ii) of that paragraph shall not apply to that notice of appeal.

(3) (a) This subsection shall apply to any assessment in respect of which notice of appeal has been given, not being an assessment the appeal against which has been determined by the Appeal Commissioners or which has become final and conclusive under subsection (6).

(b) Where, in relation to an assessment to which this subsection applies, the inspector or other officer and the appellant come to an agreement, whether in writing or otherwise, that the assessment is to stand, is to be amended in a particular manner or is to be discharged or cancelled, the inspector or other officer shall give effect to the agreement and thereupon, if the agreement is that the assessment is to stand or is to be amended, the assessment or the amended assessment, as the case may be, shall have the same force and effect as if it were an assessment in respect of which no notice of appeal had been given.

(c) An agreement which is not in writing shall be deemed not to be an agreement for the purposes of paragraph (b) unless—

(i) the fact that an agreement was come to, and the terms agreed on, are confirmed by notice in writing given by the inspector or other officer to the appellant or by the appellant to the inspector or other officer, and

(ii) 21 days have elapsed since the giving of that notice without the person to whom it was given giving notice in writing to the person by whom it was given that the first-mentioned person desires to repudiate or withdraw from the agreement.

(d) Where an appellant desires not to proceed with the appeal against an assessment to which this subsection applies and gives notice in writing to that effect to the inspector or other officer, paragraph (b) shall apply as if the appellant and the inspector or other officer had, on the appellant's notice being received, come to an agreement in writing that the assessment should stand.

(e) References in this subsection to an agreement being come to with an appellant and the giving of notice to or by an appellant include references to an agreement being come to with, and the giving of notice to or by, a person acting on behalf of the appellant in relation to the appeal.

(4) All appeals against assessments to income tax or corporation tax shall be heard and determined by the Appeal Commissioners, and their determination on any such appeal shall be final and conclusive, unless the person assessed requires that that person's appeal shall be reheard under section 942 or unless under the Tax Acts a case is required to be stated for the opinion of the High Court.

(5) An appeal against an assessment may be heard and determined by one Appeal Commissioner, and the powers conferred on the Appeal Commissioners by this Part may be exercised by one Appeal Commissioner.

(6) (a) In default of notice of appeal by a person to whom notice of assessment has been given, the assessment made on that person shall be final and conclusive.

(b) Where a person who has given notice of appeal against an assessment does not attend before the Appeal Commissioners at the time and place appointed for the hearing of that person's appeal, the assessment made on that person shall, subject to subsection (8), have the same force and effect as if it were an assessment in respect of which no notice of appeal had been given.

(c) Where on the hearing of an appeal against an assessment-

(i) no application is or has been made to the Appeal Commissioners before or during the hearing of the appeal by or on behalf of the appellant for an adjournment of the proceedings on the appeal or such an application is or has been made and is or was refused, and

(ii) (I) a return of the appellant's income for the relevant year of assessment or, as the case may be, a return under section 884 has not been made by the appellant, or

(II) such a return has been made but-

(A) all the statements of profits and gains, schedules and other evidence relating to such return have not been furnished by or on behalf of the appellant,

(B) information requested from the appellant by the Appeal Commissioners in the hearing of the appeal has not been supplied by the appellant,

(C)   the terms of a precept issued by the Appeal Commissioners under section 935 have not been complied with by the appellant, or

(D)   any questions as to an assessment or assessments put by the Appeal Commissioners under section 938 have not been answered to their satisfaction,

the Appeal Commissioners shall make an order dismissing the appeal against the assessment and thereupon the assessment shall have the same force and effect as if it were an assessment in respect of which no notice of appeal had been given.

(d)   An application for an adjournment of the proceedings on an appeal against an assessment, being an application made before or during the hearing of the appeal, shall not be refused before the expiration of 9 months from the earlier of-

         (i)   the end of the year of assessment or, as the case may be, accounting period to which the assessment appealed against relates, and

         (ii)   the date on which the notice of assessment was given to the appellant.

(e)   Paragraph (c) shall not apply if on the hearing of the appeal the Appeal Commissioners are satisfied that sufficient information has been furnished by or on behalf of the appellant to enable them to determine the appeal at that hearing.

(7)   (a)   A notice of appeal not given within the time limited by subsection (1) shall be regarded as having been so given where, on an application in writing having been made to the inspector or other officer in that behalf within 12 months after the date of the notice of assessment, the inspector or other officer, being satisfied that owing to absence, sickness or other reasonable cause the applicant was prevented from giving notice of appeal within the time limited and that the application was made thereafter without unreasonable delay, notifies the applicant in writing that the application under this paragraph has been allowed.

     (b)   Where on an application under paragraph (a) the inspector or other officer is not so satisfied, he or she shall by notice

in writing inform the applicant that the application under this paragraph has been refused.

(c)   Within 15 days after the date of a notice under paragraph (b) the applicant may by notice in writing require the inspector or other officer to refer the application to the Appeal Commissioners and, in relation to any application so referred, paragraphs (a) and (b) shall apply as if for every reference in those paragraphs to the inspector or other officer there were substituted a reference to the Appeal Commissioners.

(d)   Notwithstanding paragraph (a), an application made after the expiration of the time specified in that paragraph which but for that expiration would have been allowed under paragraph (a) may be allowed under that paragraph if at the time of the application-

    (i)   there has been made to the inspector or other officer a return of income or, as the case may be, a return under section 884, statements of profits and gains and such other information as in the opinion of the inspector or other officer would enable the appeal to be settled by agreement under subsection (3), and

    (ii)   the income tax or corporation tax charged by the assessment in respect of which the application is made has been paid together with any interest on that tax chargeable under section 1080.

(e)   Where on an application referred to in paragraph (d) the inspector or other officer is not satisfied that the information furnished would be sufficient to enable the appeal to be settled by agreement under subsection (3) or if the tax and interest mentioned in paragraph (d)(ii) have not been paid, the inspector or other officer shall by notice in writing inform the applicant that the application has been refused.

(f)   Within 15 days after the date of a notice under paragraph (e) the applicant may by notice in writing require the inspector or other officer to refer the application to the Appeal Commissioners and, in relation to an application so referred, if-

    (i)   the application is one which but for the expiration of the period specified in paragraph (a) would have been allowed under paragraph (c) if the application had been referred to the Appeal Commissioners under that paragraph,

(ii)   at the time the application is referred to the Appeal Commissioners the income tax or corporation tax charged by the assessment in respect of which the application is made, together with any interest on that tax chargeable under section 1080, has been paid, and

(iii)   the information furnished to the inspector or other officer is such that in the opinion of the Appeal Commissioners the appeal is likely to be determined on the first occasion on which it comes before them for hearing,

the Appeal Commissioners may allow the application.

(8)   In a case in which a person who has given notice of appeal does not attend before the Appeal Commissioners at the time and place appointed for the hearing of that person's appeal, subsection (6)(b) shall not apply if-

(a)   at that time and place another person attends on behalf of the appellant and the Appeal Commissioners consent to hear that other person,

(b)   on an application in that behalf having been made to them in writing or otherwise at or before that time, the Appeal Commissioners postpone the hearing, or

(c)   on an application in writing having been made to them after that time the Appeal Commissioners, being satisfied that, owing to absence, sickness or other reasonable cause, the appellant was prevented from appearing before them at that time and place and that the application was made without unreasonable delay, direct that the appeal be treated as one the time for the hearing of which has not yet been appointed.

(9)   (a)   Where action for the recovery of income tax or corporation tax charged by an assessment has been taken, being action by means of the institution of proceedings in any court or the issue of a certificate under **[section 960L]**[92], neither subsection (7) nor subsection (8) shall apply in relation to that assessment until that action has been completed.

(b)   Where, in a case within paragraph (a), an application under subsection (7)(a) is allowed or, on an application under subsection (8)(c), the Appeal Commissioners direct as provided in that subsection, the applicant shall in no case be entitled to repayment of any sum paid or borne by the applicant in respect of costs of any such court proceedings or, as the case may be, of any fees or expenses charged by the county registrar or sheriff executing a certificate under **[section 960L]**[92].

Procedure on appeals.

934. (1)   The inspector or such other officer as the Revenue Commissioners shall authorise in that behalf (in this section referred to as **"other officer"**) may attend every hearing of an appeal, and shall be entitled-

    (a)   to be present during all the hearing and at the determination of the appeal,

    (b)   to produce any lawful evidence in support of the assessment, and

    (c)   to give reasons in support of the assessment.

(2)   (a)   On any appeal, the Appeal Commissioners shall permit any barrister or solicitor to plead before them on behalf of the appellant or the inspector or other officer either orally or in writing and shall hear-

    (i)   any accountant, being any person who has been admitted a member of an incorporated society of accountants, or

    [(ii)   any person who has been admitted a member of the Irish Taxation Institute.][93]

    (b)   Notwithstanding paragraph (a), the Appeal Commissioners may permit any other person representing the appellant to plead before them where they are satisfied that such permission should be given.

(3)   Where on an appeal it appears to the Appeal Commissioners by whom the appeal is heard, or to a majority of such Appeal Commissioners, by examination of the appellant on oath or affirmation or by other lawful evidence that the appellant is overcharged by any assessment, the Appeal Commissioners shall abate or reduce the assessment accordingly, but otherwise the Appeal Commissioners shall determine the appeal by ordering that the assessment shall stand.

(4)   Where on any appeal it appears to the Appeal Commissioners that the person assessed ought to be charged in an amount exceeding the amount contained in the assessment, they shall charge that person with the excess.

(5)   Unless the circumstances of the case otherwise require, where on an appeal against an assessment which assesses an amount which is chargeable to income tax or corporation tax it appears to the Appeal Commissioners-

    (a)   that the appellant is overcharged by the assessment, they may in determining the appeal reduce only the amount which is chargeable to income tax or corporation tax,

(b)   that the appellant is correctly charged by the assessment, they may in determining the appeal order that the amount which is chargeable to income tax or corporation tax shall stand, and

(c)   that the appellant ought to be charged in an amount exceeding the amount contained in the assessment, they may charge the excess by increasing only the amount which is chargeable to income tax or corporation tax.

[(6)   Where an appeal is determined by the Appeal Commissioners, the inspector or other officer shall, unless either–

(a)   the person assessed requires that that person's appeal shall be reheard under section 942, or

(b)   under the Tax Acts a case is required to be stated for the opinion of the High Court,

give effect to the Appeal Commissioners' determination and thereupon, if the determination is that the assessment is to stand or is to be amended, the assessment or the amended assessment, as the case may be, shall have the same force and effect as if it were an assessment in respect of which no notice of appeal had been given.]⁹⁴

(7)   Every determination of an appeal by the Appeal Commissioners shall be recorded by them in the prescribed form at the time the determination is made and the Appeal Commissioners shall within 10 days after the determination transmit that form to the inspector or other officer.

Power to issue precepts.

935. (1)   Where notice of appeal has been given against an assessment, the Appeal Commissioners may, whenever it appears to them to be necessary for the purposes of the Tax Acts, issue a precept to the appellant ordering the appellant to deliver to them, within the time limited by the precept, a schedule containing such particulars for their information as they may demand under the authority of the Tax Acts in relation to–

(a)   the property of the appellant,

(b)   the trade, profession or employment carried on or exercised by the appellant,

(c)   the amount of the appellant's profits or gains, distinguishing the particular amounts derived from each separate source, or

(d)   any deductions made in determining the appellant's profits or gains.

(2)   The Appeal Commissioners may issue further precepts whenever they consider it necessary for the purposes of the Tax Acts, until complete particulars have been furnished to their satisfaction.

(3)   A precept may be issued by one Appeal Commissioner.

(4)   A person to whom a precept is issued shall deliver the schedule required within the time limited by the precept.

(5)   Any inspector or such other officer as the Revenue Commissioners shall authorise in that behalf may at all reasonable times inspect and take copies of or extracts from any such schedule.

Objections by inspector or other officer to schedules.

936. (1)   The inspector or such other officer as the Revenue Commissioners shall authorise in that behalf (in this section referred to as "**other officer**") may, within a reasonable time to be allowed by the Appeal Commissioners after examination by the inspector or other officer of any schedule referred to in section 935, object to that schedule or any part of that schedule, and in that case shall state in writing the cause of his or her objection according to the best of his or her knowledge or information.

(2)   In every such case the inspector or other officer shall give notice in writing of his or her objection to the person chargeable in order that that person may, if that person thinks fit, appeal against the objection.

(3)   A notice under subsection (2) shall be under cover and scaled, and addressed to the person chargeable.

(4)   No assessment shall be confirmed or altered until any appeal against the objection has been heard and determined.

Confirmation and amendment of assessments.

937. Where-

(a)   the Appeal Commissioners see cause to disallow an objection to a schedule by the inspector or such other officer as the Revenue Commissioners shall authorise in that behalf, or

(b)   on the hearing of an appeal, the Appeal Commissioners are satisfied with the assessment, or if, after the delivery of a schedule, they are satisfied with the schedule and have received no information as to its insufficiency,

they shall confirm or alter the assessment in accordance with the schedule, as the case may require.

Questions as to assessments or schedules.

938. (1)   Whenever the Appeal Commissioners are dissatisfied with a schedule or require further information relating to a schedule, they may at any time and from time to time by precept put any questions in writing concerning the schedule, or any matter which is contained or ought to be contained in the schedule, or concerning any deductions made in arriving at the profits or gains, and the particulars thereof, and may require true and particular answers in writing signed by the person chargeable to be given within 7 days after the service of the precept.

(2)   The person chargeable shall within the time limited either answer any such questions in writing signed by that person, or shall present himself or herself to be examined orally before the Appeal Commissioners, and may object to and refuse to answer any question; but the substance of any answer given by that person orally shall be taken down in writing in that person's presence and be read over to that person and, after that person has had liberty to amend any such answer, he or she may be required to verify the answer on oath to be administered to him or her by any one of the Appeal Commissioners, and the oath shall be subscribed by the person by whom it is made.

(3)   Where any clerk, agent or servant of the person chargeable presents himself or herself on behalf of that person to be examined orally before the Appeal Commissioners, the same provisions shall apply to his or her examination as in the case of the person chargeable who presents himself or herself to be examined orally.

Summoning and examination of witnesses.

939. (1)   (a)   The Appeal Commissioners may summon any person whom they think able to give evidence as respects an assessment made on another person to appear before them to be examined, and may examine such person on oath.

         (b)   The clerk, agent, servant or other person confidentially employed in the affairs of a person chargeable shall be examined in the same manner, and subject to the same restrictions, as in the case of a person chargeable who presents himself or herself to be examined orally.

(2)   The oath shall be that the evidence to be given, touching the matter in question, by the person sworn shall be the truth, the whole truth and nothing but the truth, and the oath shall be subscribed by the person by whom it is made.

(3)   A person who after being duly summoned-

(a)   neglects or refuses to appear before the Appeal Commissioners at the time and place appointed for that purpose,

(b)   appears but refuses to be sworn or to subscribe the oath, or

(c)   refuses to answer any lawful question touching the matters under consideration,

shall be liable to a penalty of [€3,000][95]; but the penalty imposed in respect of any offence under paragraph (b) or (c) shall not apply to any clerk, agent, servant or other person referred to in subsection (1)(b).

Determination of liability in cases of default.

940.   Where-

(a)   a person has neglected or refused to deliver a schedule in accordance with a precept of the Appeal Commissioners,

(b)   any clerk, agent or servant of, or any person confidentially employed by, a person chargeable, having been summoned, has neglected or refused to appear before the Appeal Commissioners to be examined,

(c)   the person chargeable or that person's clerk, agent or servant or any person confidentially employed by the person chargeable has declined to answer any question put to him or her by the Appeal Commissioners,

(d)   an objection has been made to a schedule and the objection has not been appealed against, or

(e)   the Appeal Commissioners decide to allow any objection made by the inspector or such other officer as the Revenue Commissioners shall authorise in that behalf,

the Appeal Commissioners shall ascertain and settle according to the best of their judgment the sum in which the person chargeable ought to be charged.

Statement of case for High Court.

941.   (1)   Immediately after the determination of an appeal by the Appeal Commissioners, the appellant or the inspector or such other officer as the Revenue Commissioners shall authorise in that behalf (in this section referred to as "other officer"), if dissatisfied with the determination as being erroneous in point of law, may declare his or her dissatisfaction to the Appeal Commissioners who heard the appeal.

(2)   The appellant or inspector or other officer, as the case may be, having declared his or her dissatisfaction, may within 21

days after the determination by notice in writing addressed to the Clerk to the Appeal Commissioners require the Appeal Commissioners to state and sign a case for the opinion of the High Court on the determination.

(3)   The party requiring the case shall pay to the Clerk to the Appeal Commissioners a fee of [€25]⁴⁷ for and in respect of the case before that party is entitled to have the case stated.

(4)   The case shall set forth the facts and the determination of the Appeal Commissioners, and the party requiring it shall transmit the case when stated and signed to the High Court within 7 days after receiving it.

(5)   At or before the time when the party requiring the case transmits it to the High Court, that party shall send notice in writing of the fact that the case has been stated on that party's application, together with a copy of the case, to the other party.

(6)   The High Court shall hear and determine any question or questions of law arising on the case, and shall reverse, affirm or amend the determination in respect of which the case has been stated, or shall remit the matter to the Appeal Commissioners with the opinion of the Court on the matter, or may make such other order in relation to the matter, and may make such order as to costs as to the Court may seem fit.

(7)   The High Court may cause the case to be sent back for amendment and thereupon the case shall be amended accordingly, and judgment shall be delivered after it has been amended.

(8)   An appeal shall lie from the decision of the High Court to the Supreme Court.

[(9)   If the amount of the assessment is altered by the order or judgment of the Supreme Court or the High Court, then–

    (a)   if too much tax has been paid, the amount overpaid shall be refunded with interest in accordance with section 865A, or

    (b)   if too little tax has been paid, the amount unpaid shall be deemed to be arrears of tax (except in so far as any penalty is incurred on account of arrears) and shall be paid and recovered accordingly.]⁹⁴

Appeals to Circuit Court.

942. (1)   Any person aggrieved by the determination of the Appeal Commissioners in any appeal against an assessment made on that person may, on giving notice in writing to the inspector or such other officer as the Revenue Commissioners shall authorise in that behalf (in this section referred to as "**other officer**") within 10 days after such determination, require that the appeal shall be reheard by the judge of the Circuit Court (in this section referred to as "**the judge**") in whose circuit is situate, in the case of-

(a)   a person who is not resident in the State,

(b)   the estate of a deceased person,

(c)   an incapacitated person, or PT

(d)   a trust,

the place where the assessment was made and, in any other case, the place to which the notice of assessment was addressed, and the Appeal Commissioners shall transmit to the judge any statement or schedule in their possession which was delivered to them for the purposes of the appeal.

(2)   At or before the time of the rehearing of the appeal by the judge, the inspector or other officer shall transmit to the judge the prescribed form in which the Appeal Commissioners' determination of the appeal is recorded.

(3)   The judge shall with all convenient speed rehear and determine the appeal, and shall have and exercise the same powers and authorities in relation to the assessment appealed against, the determination, and all consequent matters, as the Appeal Commissioners might have and exercise, and the judge's determination shall, subject to section 943, be final and conclusive.

(4)   Section 934(2) shall, with any necessary modifications, apply in relation to a rehearing of an appeal by a judge of the Circuit Court as it applies in relation to the hearing of an appeal by the Appeal Commissioners.

(5)   The judge shall make a declaration in the form of the declaration required to be made by an Appeal Commissioner as set out in Part 1 of Schedule 27.

[(6)   Where an appeal is determined by the judge, the inspector or other officer shall, unless under the Tax Acts a case is required to be stated for the opinion of the High Court, give effect to the judge's determination and thereupon, if the determination is that the assessment is to stand or is to be amended, the assessment or the amended assessment, as the case may be, shall have the same force and effect as if it were an assessment in respect of which no notice of appeal had been given.]⁹⁴

[...]⁹⁶

(8)   Where following an application for the rehearing of an appeal by a judge of the Circuit Court in accordance with subsection (1) there is an agreement within the meaning of paragraphs (b), (c) and (e) of section 933(3) between the inspector or other officer

and the appellant in relation to the assessment, the inspector shall give effect to the agreement and, if the agreement is that the assessment is to stand or is to be amended, the assessment or the amended assessment, as the case may be, shall have the same force and effect as if it were an assessment in respect of which no notice of appeal had been given.

(9)   Every rehearing of an appeal by the Circuit Court under this section shall be held in camera.

[...]⁹⁶

Extension of section 941.

943. (1)   Section 941 shall, subject to this section, apply to a determination given by a judge pursuant to section 942 in the like manner as it applies to a determination by the Appeal Commissioners, and any case stated by a judge pursuant to section 941 shall set out the facts, the determination of the Appeal Commissioners and the determination of the judge.

(2)   The notice in writing required under section 941(2) to be addressed to the Clerk to the Appeal Commissioners shall, in every case in which a judge is under the authority of this section required by any person to state and sign a case for the opinion of the High Court on the determination, be addressed by such person to the county registrar.

(3)   The fee required under section 941(3) to be paid to the Clerk to the Appeal Commissioners shall in any case referred to in subsection (2) be paid to the county registrar.

Communication of decision of Appeal Commissioners.

944. (1)   Where the Appeal Commissioners have entertained an appeal against an assessment for any year of assessment or any accounting period and, after hearing argument on the appeal, have postponed giving their determination either for the purpose of considering the argument or for the purpose of affording to the appellant an opportunity of submitting in writing further evidence or argument, the Appeal Commissioners may, unless they consider a further hearing to be necessary, cause their determination to be sent by post to the parties to the appeal.

(2)   Where the determination of an appeal by the Appeal Commissioners is sent to the parties by post under this section, a declaration of dissatisfaction under section 941(1) or a notice requiring a rehearing under section 942(1) may be made or given in writing within 12 days after the day on which the determination is so sent to the person making the declaration or giving the notice.

Publication of determinations of Appeal Commissioners.

[944A. The Appeal Commissioners may make arrangements for the publication of reports of such of their determinations as they consider appropriate, but they shall ensure that any such report is in a form which, in so far as possible, prevents the identification of any person whose affairs are dealt with in the determination.][97]

Chapter 2
Appeals against capital gains tax assessments

Appeals against assessments.

945. (1)   A person aggrieved by any assessment under the Capital Gains Tax Acts made on the person by the inspector or other officer mentioned in section 931(1) shall be entitled to appeal to the Appeal Commissioners on giving, within 30 days after the date of the notice of assessment, notice in writing to the inspector or other officer, and in default of notice of appeal by a person to whom notice of assessment has been given the assessment made on such person shall be final and conclusive.

       (2)   The provisions of the Income Tax Acts relating to-

           (a)   the appointment of times and places for the hearing of appeals,

           (b)   the giving of notice to each person who has given notice of appeal of the time and place appointed for the hearing of that person's appeal,

           (c)   the determination of an appeal by agreement between the appellant or the appellant's agent and an inspector of taxes or other officer mentioned in section 931(1),

           (d)   the determination of an appeal by the appellant giving notice of the appellant's intention not to proceed with the appeal,

           (e)   the hearing, determination or dismissal of an appeal by the Appeal Commissioners, including the hearing, determination or dismissal of an appeal by one Appeal Commissioner,

           (f)   the assessment having the same force and effect as if it were an assessment in respect of which no notice of appeal had been given where the person who has given notice of appeal does not attend before the Appeal Commissioners at the time and place appointed,

           (g)   the extension of the time for giving notice of appeal and the readmission of appeals by the Appeal Commissioners and the provisions which apply where action by means of court proceedings has been taken,

(h)   the rehearing of an appeal by a judge of the Circuit Court and the statement of a case for the opinion of the High Court on a point of law, [and][98]

[...][99]

(j)   the procedures for appeal,

shall, with any necessary modifications, apply to an appeal under any provision of the Capital Gains Tax Acts providing for an appeal to the Appeal Commissioners as if the appeal were an appeal against an assessment to income tax.

Regulations with respect to appeals.

946. (1)   The Revenue Commissioners may make regulations–

(a)   for the conduct of appeals against assessments and decisions on claims under the Capital Gains Tax Acts;

(b)   entitling persons, in addition to those who would be so entitled apart from the regulations, to appear on such appeals;

(c)   regulating the time within which such appeals or claims may be brought or made;

(d)   where the market value of an asset on a particular date or an apportionment or any other matter may affect the liability to capital gains tax of 2 or more persons, enabling any such person to have the matter determined by the tribunal having jurisdiction to determine that matter if arising on an appeal against an assessment, and prescribing a procedure by which the matter is not determined differently on different occasions;

(e)   authorising an inspector or other officer of the Revenue Commissioners, notwithstanding the obligation as to secrecy imposed by the Income Tax Acts or any other Act, to disclose–

(i)   to a person entitled to appear on such an appeal, the market value of an asset as determined by an assessment or decision on a claim, or

(ii)   to a person whose liability to tax may be affected by the determination of the market value of an asset on a particular date or an apportionment or any other matter, any decision on the matter made by an inspector or other officer of the Revenue Commissioners.

(2)   Regulations under this section may contain such supplemental and incidental provisions as appear to the Revenue Commissioners to be necessary.

(3)   Every regulation made under this section shall be laid before Dáil Éireann as soon as may be after it is made and, if a resolution annulling the regulation is passed by Dáil Éireann within the next 21 days on which Dáil Éireann has sat after the regulation is laid before it, the regulation shall be annulled accordingly, but without prejudice to the validity of anything previously done thereunder.

Chapter 3

Miscellaneous

Appeals against determination under sections 98 to 100.

947. (1)   Where it appears to the inspector that the determination of any amount on which a person may be chargeable to income tax or corporation tax by virtue of section 98, 99 or 100 may affect the liability to income tax or corporation tax of other persons, the inspector shall give notice in writing to those persons as well as to the first-mentioned person of the determination the inspector proposes to make and of the rights conferred on them by this section.

(2)   Any person to whom such a notice is given may within 21 days after the date on which it is given object to the proposed determination by notice in writing given to the inspector, and section 933(7) shall apply, with any necessary modifications, in relation to any such notice as it applies in relation to a notice of appeal under section 933.

(3)   (a)   Subject to paragraph (b), where notices have been given under subsection (1) and no notice of objection is duly given under subsection (2), the inspector shall make the determination as proposed in his or her notices and the determination shall not be called in question in any proceedings.

(b)   This subsection shall not operate to prevent any person to whom notice has not been given under subsection (1) from appealing against any such determination of the inspector which may affect that person's liability to income tax or corporation tax, as the case may be.

(4)   Where a notice of objection is duly given, the amount mentioned in subsection (1) shall be determined in the like manner as an appeal and shall be so determined by the Appeal Commissioners.

(5)   All persons to whom notices have been given under subsection (1) may take part in any proceedings under subsection (4) and in any appeal arising out of those proceedings and shall be bound by the determination made in the proceedings or on appeal, whether or not they have taken part in the proceedings, and their successors in title shall also be so bound.

(6)   A notice under subsection (1) may, notwithstanding any obligation as to secrecy or other restriction on the disclosure of information, include a statement of the grounds on which the inspector proposes to make the determination.

(7)   An inspector may by notice in writing require any person to give, within 21 days after the date of the notice or within such longer period as the inspector may allow, such information as appears to the inspector to be required for deciding whether to give a notice under subsection (1) to any person.

Appeals against amount of income tax deducted under Schedule E.

948. (1)   Any person charged to income tax under Schedule E may appeal to the Appeal Commissioners against the amount of tax deducted from that person's emoluments for any year.

(2)   The Appeal Commissioners shall hear and determine an appeal to them under subsection (1) as if it were an appeal to them against an assessment to income tax, and the provisions of the Income Tax Acts relating to the rehearing of an appeal and to the statement of a case for the opinion of the High Court on a point of law shall, with the necessary modifications, apply accordingly.

Appeals against determinations of certain claims, etc.

949. (1)   Any person aggrieved by any determination by the Revenue Commissioners, or such officer of the Revenue Commissioners (including an inspector) as they may have authorised in that behalf, on any claim, matter or question referred to in section 864 may, subject to section 957 and on giving notice in writing to the Revenue Commissioners or the officer within 30 days after notification to the person aggrieved of the determination, appeal to the Appeal Commissioners.

(2)   The Appeal Commissioners shall hear and determine an appeal to them under subsection (1) as if it were an appeal against an assessment to income tax and the provisions of section 933 with respect to such appeals, together with the provisions of the Tax Acts relating to the rehearing of an appeal and to the statement of a case for the opinion of the High Court on a point of law, shall apply accordingly with any necessary modifications.

(3)   Where-

(a)   a right of appeal to the Appeal Commissioners is given by any provision of the Tax Acts or the Capital Gains Tax Acts other than section 1037, and

(b)   such provision, while applying the provisions of the Tax Acts relating to appeals against assessments, does not apply the provisions of those Acts relating to the rehearing of appeals, such provision shall be deemed to apply those provisions relating to the rehearing of appeals.

(4)   In a case in which-

(a)   a notice of appeal is not given within the time limited by subsection (1), or

(b)   a person who has given notice of appeal does not attend before the Appeal Commissioners at the time and place appointed for the hearing of the person's appeal,

subsections (5) and (7) to (9) of section 933 shall apply with any necessary modifications.

[Chapter 1A

Interpretation

Interpretation

960A. (1)   In Chapters 1A, 1B and 1C, unless the contrary is expressly stated—

'Acts' means—

(a)   the Tax Acts,

(b)   the Capital Gains Tax Acts,

(c)   the Value-Added Tax Act 1972, and the enactments amending and extending that Act,

(d)   the statutes relating to the duties of excise and to the management of those duties and the enactments amending and extending those statutes,

(e)   the Stamp Duties Consolidation Act 1999 and the enactments amending and extending that Act,

(f)   the Capital Acquisitions Tax Consolidation Act 2003 and the enactments amending and extending that Act,

(g)   Parts 18A and 18B (inserted by the Finance (No. 2) Act 2008),

and any instruments made under any of those Acts;

'assessment' means any assessment to tax made under any provision of the Acts, including any amended assessment, additional assessment, correcting assessment and any estimate made under section 990 or under Regulation 13 or 14 of the RCT Regulations and any estimate made under section 22 of the Value-Added Tax Act 1972;

'emoluments' has the same meaning as in section 983;

'income tax month' has the same meaning as in section 983;

'PAYE Regulations' means regulations made under section 986;

'RCT Regulations' means the Income Tax (Relevant Contracts) Regulations 2000 (S.I. No. 71 of 2000);

'Revenue officer' means any officer of the Revenue Commissioners;

'tax' means any income tax, corporation tax, capital gains tax, value-added tax, excise duty, stamp duty, gift tax, inheritance tax or any other levy or charge which is placed under the care and management of the Revenue Commissioners and includes —

(a)   any interest, surcharge or penalty relating to any such tax, duty, levy or charge,

(b)   any clawback of a relief or an exemption relating to any such tax, duty, levy or charge, and

(c)   any sum which is required to be deducted or withheld by any person and paid or remitted to the Revenue Commissioners or the Collector-General, as the case may be, under any provision of the Acts;

'tax due and payable' means tax due and payable under any provision of the Acts.

Discharge of Collector-General's functions.

960B. The Revenue Commissioners may nominate in writing any Revenue officer to perform any acts and to discharge any functions authorised by Chapters 1B and 1C to be performed or discharged by the Collector-General other than the acts and functions referred to in subsections (1) to (4) of section 960N, and references in this Part to 'Collector-General' shall be read accordingly.

Chapter 1B

Collection of tax, etc.

Tax to be due and payable to Revenue Commissioners.

960C. Tax due and payable under the Acts shall be due and payable to the Revenue Commissioners.

Tax to be debt due to Minister for Finance.

960D. Tax due and payable to the Revenue Commissioners shall be treated as a debt due to the Minister for Finance for the benefit of the Central Fund.

Collection of tax, issue of demands, etc.

960E. (1) Tax due and payable to the Revenue Commissioners by virtue of section 960C shall be paid to and collected by the Collector-General, including tax charged in all assessments to tax, particulars of which have been given to the Collector-General under section 928.

(2) The Collector-General shall demand payment of tax that is due and payable but remaining unpaid by the person from whom that tax is payable.

(3) Where tax is not paid in accordance with the demand referred to in subsection (2), the Collector-General shall collect and levy the tax that is due and payable but remaining unpaid by the person from whom that tax is payable.

(4) On payment of tax, the Collector-General may provide a receipt to the person concerned in respect of that payment and such receipt shall consist of whichever of the following the Collector-General considers appropriate, namely —

(a) a separate receipt in respect of each such payment, or

(b) a receipt for all such payments that have been made within the period specified in the receipt.

Moneys received for capital acquisitions tax and stamp duties and not appropriated to be recoverable.

960F. (1) Any person who —

(a) having received a sum of money in respect of gift tax, inheritance tax or stamp duties, does not pay that sum to the Collector-General, and

(b) improperly withholds or detains such sum of money,

shall be accountable to the Revenue Commissioners for the payment of that sum to the extent of the amount so received by that person.

(2) The sum of money referred to in subsection (1) shall be treated as a debt due to the Minister for Finance for the benefit of the Central Fund and section 960I shall apply to any such sum as if it were tax due and payable.

Duty of taxpayer to identify liability against which payment to be set, etc.

960G. (1) Subject to subsection (2), every person who makes a payment of tax to the Revenue Commissioners or to the Collector-General shall identify the liability to tax against which he or she wishes the payment to be set.

(2) Where payment of tax is received by the Revenue Commissioners or the Collector-General and the payment is accompanied by a

pay slip, a tax return, a tax demand or other document issued by the Revenue Commissioners or the Collector-General, the payment shall, unless the contrary intention is or has been clearly indicated, be treated as relating to the tax referred to in the document concerned.

(3)   Where a payment is received by the Revenue Commissioners or the Collector-General from a person and it cannot reasonably be determined by the Revenue Commissioners or the Collector-General from the instructions, if any, which accompanied the payment which liabilities the person wishes the payment to be set against, then the Revenue Commissioners or the Collector-General may set the payment against any liability due by the person under the Acts.

Offset between taxes.

960H. (1)   In this section —

'claim' means a claim that gives rise to either or both a repayment of tax and a payment of interest payable in respect of such a repayment and includes part of such a claim;

'liability' means any tax due and payable which is unpaid and includes any tax estimated to be due and payable;

'overpayment' means a payment or remittance (including part of such a payment or remittance) which is in excess of the amount of the liability against which it is credited.

(2)   Where the Collector-General is satisfied that a person has not complied with the obligations imposed on the person in relation to either or both —

(a)   the payment of tax that is due and payable, and

(b)   the delivery of returns required to be made,

then the Collector-General may, in a case where a repayment is due to the person in respect of a claim or overpayment —

(i)   where paragraph (a) applies, or where paragraphs (a) and (b) apply, instead of making the repayment, set the amount of the repayment against any liability, and

(ii)   where paragraph (b) only applies, withhold making the repayment until such time as the returns required to be delivered have been delivered.

(3)   (a)   Where a person (referred to in this subsection as the 'first-mentioned person') has assigned, transferred or sold a right to a claim or overpayment to another person (referred to in this subsection as the 'second-mentioned

person') and subsection (2)(a) applies, then the Collector-General shall, in a case where a repayment would have been due to the first-mentioned person in respect of the claim or overpayment if he or she had not assigned, transferred or sold his or her right to the claim or overpayment, instead of making the repayment to the second-mentioned person, set that claim or overpayment against tax that is due and payable by that first-mentioned person.

(b)   Where the first-mentioned person and the second-mentioned person are connected persons within the meaning of section 10, then the balance, if any, of the repayment referred to in paragraph (a) shall be set against tax due and payable by the second-mentioned person.

(4)   Where the Collector-General has set or withheld a repayment by virtue of subsection (2) or (3), then he or she shall give notice in writing to that effect to the person or persons concerned and, where subsection (2)(ii) applies, interest shall not be payable under any provision of the Acts from the date of such notice in respect of any repayment so withheld.

(5)   The Revenue Commissioners may make regulations for the purpose of giving effect to this section and, without prejudice to the generality of the foregoing, such regulations may provide for the order of priority of the liabilities to tax against which any claim or overpayment is to be set in accordance with subsection (2) or (3) or both.

(6)   Every regulation made under this section is to be laid before Dáil Éireann as soon as may be after it is made and, if a resolution annulling the regulation is passed by Dáil Éireann within the next 21 days on which Dáil Éireann has sat after the regulation is laid before it, the regulation shall be annulled accordingly, but without prejudice to the validity of anything previously done under the regulation.

(7)   The Taxes (Offset of Repayments) Regulations 2002 (S.I. No. 471 of 2002) shall have effect as if they were made under subsection (5) and had complied with subsection (6).

Chapter 1C

Recovery provisions, evidential rules, etc.

Recovery of tax by way of civil proceedings.

960I. (1)   Without prejudice to any other means by which payment of tax may be enforced, any tax due and payable or any balance of such tax may be sued for and recovered by proceedings taken by the Collector-General in any court of competent jurisdiction.

(2)   All or any of the amounts of tax due from any one person may be included in the same summons.

(3)   The rules of court for the time being applicable to civil proceedings commenced by summary summons, in so far as they relate to the recovery of tax, shall apply to proceedings under this section.

(4)   The acceptance of a part payment or a payment on account in respect of tax referred to in a summons shall not prejudice proceedings for the recovery of the balance of the tax due and the summons may be amended accordingly.

(5)   (a)   Proceedings under this section may be brought for the recovery of the total amount which an employer is liable, under Chapter 4 and the PAYE Regulations, to pay to the Collector-General for any income tax month without —

            (i)   distinguishing the amounts for which the employer is liable to pay by reference to each employee, and

            (ii)   specifying the employees in question.

       (b)   For the purposes of the proceedings referred to in paragraph (a), the total amount shall be one single cause of action or one matter of complaint.

       (c)   Nothing in this subsection shall prevent the bringing of separate proceedings for the recovery of each of the several amounts which the employer is liable to pay by reference to any income tax month and to the employer's several employees.

(6)   For the purposes of subsection (5), any amount of tax —

       (a)   estimated under section 989, or

       (b)   estimated under section 990 or any balance of tax so estimated but remaining unpaid,

is deemed to be an amount of tax which any person paying emoluments was liable, under Chapter 4 and the PAYE Regulations, to pay to the Collector- General.

Evidential and Procedural rules.

960J. (1)   In proceedings for the recovery of tax, a certificate signed by the Collector-General to the effect that, before the proceedings were instituted, any one or more of the following matters occurred:

       (a)   the assessment to tax, if any, was duly made,

       (b)   the assessment, if any, has become final and conclusive,

(c)   the tax or any specified part of the tax is due and outstanding,

(d)   demand for the payment of the tax has been duly made,

shall be evidence until the contrary is proved of such of those matters that are so certified by the Collector-General.

(2)   (a)   Subsection (1) shall not apply in the case of tax to which Chapter 4 applies.

(b)   In proceedings for the recovery of tax to which Chapter 4 applies, a certificate signed by the Collector-General that a stated amount of income tax under Schedule E is due and outstanding shall be evidence until the contrary is proved that the amount is so due and outstanding.

(3)   In proceedings for the recovery of tax, a certificate purporting to be signed by the Collector-General certifying the matters or any of the matters referred to in subsection (1) or (2) may be tendered in evidence without proof and shall be deemed until the contrary is proved to have been duly signed by the person concerned.

(4)   If a dispute relating to a certificate referred to in subsection (1), (2) or (3) arises during proceedings for the recovery of tax, the judge may adjourn the proceedings to allow the Collector-General or the Revenue officer concerned to attend and give oral evidence in the proceedings and for any register, file or other record relating to the tax to be produced and put in evidence in the proceedings.

Judgments for recovery of tax.

960K. (1)   In this section 'judgment' includes any order or decree.

(2)   Where, in any proceedings for the recovery of tax, judgment is given against a person and a sum of money is accepted from the person against whom the proceedings were brought on account or in part payment of the amount of which the judgment was given, then —

(a)   such acceptance shall not prevent or prejudice the recovery under the judgment of the balance of that amount that remains unpaid,

(b)   the judgment shall be capable of being executed and enforced in respect of the balance as fully in all respects and by the like means as if the balance were the amount for which the judgment was given,

(c)   the law relating to the execution and enforcement of the judgment shall apply in respect of the balance accordingly, and

(d)   a certificate signed by the Collector-General stating the amount of the balance shall, for the purposes of the enforcement and execution of the judgment, be evidence until the contrary is proved of the amount of the balance.

Recovery by sheriff or county registrar.

960L. (1)   Where any person does not pay any sum in respect of tax for which he or she is liable under the Acts, the Collector-General may issue a certificate to the county registrar or sheriff of the county in which the person resides or has a place of business certifying the amount due and outstanding and the person from whom that amount is payable.

(2)   (a)   For the purposes of this subsection— which the judgment was given, then—

'electronic' has the meaning assigned to it by the Electronic Commerce Act 2000 and an 'electronic certificate' shall be construed accordingly;

'issued in non-paper format' includes issued in facsimile.

(b)   A certificate to be issued by the Collector-General under this section may—

(i)   be issued in an electronic or other format, and

(ii)   where the certificate is issued in a non-paper format, be reproduced in a paper format by the county registrar or sheriff or by persons authorised by the county registrar or sheriff to do so.

(c)   A certificate issued in a non-paper format in accordance with paragraph (b) shall—

(i)   constitute a valid certificate for the purposes of this section,

(ii)   be deemed to have been made by the Collector-General, and

(iii)   be deemed to have been issued on the date that the Collector-General caused the certificate to issue.

(d)   (i)   Where a certificate issued by the Collector-General is reproduced in a non-paper format in accordance with paragraph (b)(ii) and—

(I)   the reproduction contains, or there is appended to it, a note to the effect that it is a copy of the certificate so issued, and

(II)   the note contains the signature of the county registrar or sheriff or of the person authorised under paragraph (b)(ii) and the date of such signing,

then the copy of the certificate with the note so signed and dated shall, for all purposes, have effect as if it was the certificate itself.

(ii)   A signature or date in a note, on a copy of, or appended to, a certificate issued in a non-paper format by the Collector-General, and reproduced in a paper format in accordance with paragraph (b)(ii), that—

(I)   in respect of such signature, purports to be that of the county registrar or sheriff or of a person authorised to make a copy, shall be taken until the contrary is shown to be the signature of the county registrar or sheriff or of a person who at the material time was so authorised, and

(II)   in respect of such date, shall be taken until the contrary is shown to have been duly dated.

(3)   (a)   Immediately on receipt of the certificate, the county registrar or sheriff shall proceed to levy the amount certified in the certificate to be in default by seizing all or any of the goods, animals or other chattels within his or her area of responsibility belonging to the defaulter.

(b)   For the purposes of paragraph (a), the county registrar or sheriff shall (in addition to the rights, powers and duties conferred on him or her by this section) have all such rights, powers and duties as are for the time being vested in him or her by law in relation to the execution of a writ of fieri facias in so far as those rights, powers and duties are not inconsistent with the additional rights, powers and duties conferred on him or her by this section.

(4)   A county registrar or sheriff executing a certificate under this section shall be entitled—

(a)   if the sum certified in the certificate is in excess of €19,050, to charge and (where appropriate) to add to that sum and (in any case) to levy under the certificate such fees and expenses, calculated in accordance to the scales appointed by the Minister for Justice, Equality and Law Reform under section 14(1)(a) of the Enforcement of Court Orders Act 1926 and for the time being in force, as the county registrar or sheriff would be entitled so to charge or add and to levy if the certificate were an execution order, within the meaning of the Enforcement of Court Orders Act 1926 (in this section referred to as an 'execution order'), of the High Court,

(b) if the sum referred to in the certificate to be in default exceeds €3,175 but does not exceed €19,050, to charge and (where appropriate) to add to that sum and (in any case) to levy under the certificate such fees and expenses, calculated according to the scales referred to in paragraph (a), as the county registrar or sheriff would be entitled so to charge or add and to levy if the certificate were an execution order of the Circuit Court, and

(c) if the sum certified in the certificate to be in default does not exceed €3,175 and (where appropriate) to add to that sum and (in any case) to levy under the certificate such fees and expenses, calculated according to the scales referred to in paragraph (a), as the county registrar or sheriff would be entitled so to charge or add and to levy if the certificate were an execution order of the District Court.

Taking by Collector-General of proceedings in bankruptcy.

960M. (1) The Collector-General may in his or her own name apply for the grant of a bankruptcy summons under section 8 of the Bankruptcy Act 1988 or present a petition for adjudication under section 11 of that Act in respect of tax (except corporation tax) due and payable or any balance of such tax.

(2) Subject to this section, the rules of court for the time being applicable and the enactments relating to bankruptcy shall apply to proceedings under this section.

Continuance of pending proceedings and evidence in proceedings.

960N. (1) Where the Collector-General has instituted proceedings under section 960I(1) or 960M(1) for the recovery of tax or any balance of tax and, while such proceedings are pending, such Collector-General ceases for any reason to hold that office, the proceedings may be continued in the name of that Collector-General by any person (in this section referred to as the 'successor') duly appointed to collect such tax in succession to that Collector-General or any subsequent Collector-General.

(2) In any case where subsection (1) applies, the successor shall inform the person or persons against whom the proceedings concerned are pending that those proceedings are being so continued and, on service of such notice, notwithstanding

any rule of court, it shall not be necessary for the successor to obtain an order of court substituting him or her for the person who has instituted or continued proceedings.

(3)   Any affidavit or oath to be made by a Collector-General for the purposes of the Judgment Mortgage (Ireland) Act 1850 or the Judgment Mortgage (Ireland) Act 1858 may be made by a successor.

(4)   Where the Collector-General duly appointed to collect tax in succession to another Collector-General institutes or continues proceedings under section 960I(1) or 960M(1) for the recovery of tax or any balance of tax, then the person previously appointed as Collector-General shall for the purposes of the proceedings be deemed until the contrary is proved to have ceased to be the Collector-General appointed to collect the tax.

(5)   Where a Revenue officer nominated in accordance with section 960B has instituted proceedings under section 960I(1) or 960M(1) for the recovery of tax or the balance of tax, and while such proceedings are pending, such officer dies or otherwise ceases for any reason to be a Revenue officer—

(a)   the right of such officer to continue proceedings shall cease and the right to continue proceedings shall vest in such other officer as may be nominated by the Revenue Commissioners,

(b)   where such other officer is nominated he or she shall be entitled accordingly to be substituted as a party to the proceedings in the place of the first-mentioned officer, and

(c)   where an officer is so substituted, he or she shall give notice in writing of the substitution to the defendant.

(6)   In proceedings under section 960I(1) or 960M(1) taken by a Revenue officer nominated in accordance with section 960B, a certificate signed by the Revenue Commissioners certifying the following facts—

(a)   that a person is an officer of the Revenue Commissioners,

(b)   that he or she has been nominated by them in accordance with section 960B, and

(c)   that he or she has been nominated by them in accordance with subsection (5)(a),

shall be evidence unless the contrary is proved of those facts.

(7)   In proceedings under sections 960I(1) or 960M(1) taken by a Revenue officer nominated in accordance with section 960B, a certificate signed by the Revenue Commissioners certifying the following facts—

(a)   that the plaintiff has ceased to be an officer of the Revenue Commissioners nominated by them in accordance with section 960B,

(b)   that another person is a Revenue officer,

(c)   that such other person has been nominated by them in accordance with section 960B, and

(d)   that such other person has been nominated by them to take proceedings to recover tax,

shall be evidence until the contrary is proved of those facts.

Winding-up of companies: priority for taxes.

960O. (1)   In this section—

'Act of 1963' means the Companies Act 1963;

'Act of 1972' means the Value-Added Tax Act 1972;

'relevant date' has the same meaning as in section 285 of the Act of 1963;

'relevant period' means—

(a)   in paragraph (a)(i) of subsection (4) and in paragraphs (b) and (c) of that subsection, the 12 month period next before the date that is 14 days after the end of the income tax month in which the relevant date occurred;

(b)   in subparagraphs (ii) to (v) of subsection (4)(a), the 12 month period referred to in the relevant subsection;

'relevant subsection' means subsection (2)(a)(iii) of section 285 of the Act of 1963.

(2)   For the purposes of section 98 of the Act of 1963 and the relevant subsection, the amount referred to in the relevant subsection is deemed to include corporation tax and capital gains tax.

(3)   (a)   Any value-added tax, including interest payable on that value-added tax in accordance with section 21 of the Act of 1972, for which a company is liable for taxable periods (within the meaning of that Act) which ended within the period of 12 months next before the relevant date are to be included among the debts which under section 285 of the Act of 1963 are to be paid in priority to all other debts in the winding up of the company.

        (b)   For the purposes of section 98 of the Act of 1963, paragraph (a) is deemed to be included in section 285 of that Act.

(4)   (a)   For the purposes of section 98 of the Act of 1963 and the relevant subsection, the amount referred to in the relevant subsection is deemed to include—

(i)   so much as is unpaid of an authorised employer's PAYE liability,

(ii)   amounts of tax deducted under section 531(1) that relate to a period or periods falling in whole or in part within the relevant period,

(iii)   amounts of tax recoverable under Regulation 14 of the RCT Regulations that relate to a period or periods falling in whole or in part within the relevant period,

(iv)   amounts of tax to which section 989 applies that relate to a period or periods falling in whole or in part within the relevant period,

(v)   amounts of tax to which section 990 applies that relate to a period or periods falling in whole or in part within the relevant period.

(b)   In the case of any amount referred to in subparagraphs (ii) to (v) of paragraph (a) for a period falling partly within and partly outside the relevant period, the total sum or amount is to be apportioned according to the respective lengths of the periods falling within the relevant period and outside of that period so as to determine the amount of tax that relates to the relevant period.

(c)   For the purposes of paragraph (a)(i) 'authorised employer's PAYE liability', in relation to an employer authorised under Regulation 29 of the PAYE Regulations, means the amount determined by the formula—

$$(A + B - C) + D$$

where—

A is any amount which, apart from Regulation 29 of the PAYE Regulations, would otherwise have been an amount due at the relevant date in respect of sums that the employer is liable under Chapter 4 and the PAYE Regulations (other than Regulation 29 of those Regulations) to deduct from emoluments paid by the employer during the relevant period,

B is any amount which, apart from Regulation 29 of the PAYE Regulations, would otherwise have been an amount due at the relevant date in respect of sums that were not so deducted but which the employer was liable, in accordance with section 985A and any regulations under that section, to remit to the Collector-General in respect of notional payments made by the employer during the relevant period,

C   is any amount which the employer was liable under Chapter 4 and the PAYE Regulations to repay during the relevant period, and

D   is any interest payable under section 991 in respect of the amounts referred to in the meanings of A and B.

Bankruptcy: priority for taxes.

960P. (1)   In this section —

'Act of 1972' means the Value-Added Tax Act 1972;

'Act of 1988' means the Bankruptcy Act 1988;

'relevant period', in relation to the distribution of the property of a bankrupt, arranging debtor or person dying insolvent, means the period of 12 months before the date on which the order for adjudication of the person as a bankrupt was made, the petition of arrangement of the person as a debtor was filed or, as the case may be, the person died insolvent.

(2)   For the purposes of subsection (1)(a) of section 81 of the Act of 1988, the amount referred to in that subsection is deemed to include capital gains tax.

(3)   The priority attaching to the taxes to which section 81 of the Act of 1988 applies shall also apply to —

(a)   any value-added tax, including interest payable on value-added tax in accordance with section 21 of the Act of 1972, for which a person is liable for taxable periods (within the meaning of that Act) which have ended within the relevant period,

(b)   so much as is unpaid of an employer's PAYE liability for the relevant period,

(c)   amounts of tax deducted under section 531(1) which relate to a period or periods falling in whole or in part within the relevant period,

(d)   amounts of tax recoverable under Regulation 14 of the RCT Regulations which relate to a period or periods falling in whole or in part within the relevant period,

(e)   amounts of tax to which section 989 applies which relate to a period or periods falling in whole or in part within the relevant period,

(f)   amounts of tax to which section 990 applies which relate to a period or periods falling in whole or in part within the relevant period.

(4)   In the case of any amount referred to in paragraphs (c) to (f) of subsection (3) for a period falling partly within and partly

outside the relevant period, the total sum or amount is to be apportioned according to the respective lengths of the periods falling within the relevant period and outside of that period in order to determine the amount of tax which relates to the relevant period.

(5)   In subsection (3)(b) 'employer's PAYE liability for the relevant period' means the amount determined by the formula —

$$(A + B - C) + D$$

where —

A   is all sums which an employer was liable under Chapter 4 and the PAYE Regulations to deduct from emoluments paid by the employer during the relevant period,

B   is all sums that were not so deducted but which an employer was liable, in accordance with section 985A and regulations under that section, to remit to the Collector-General in respect of notional payments made by the employer during the relevant period,

C   is any amounts which the employer was liable under Chapter 4 and the PAYE Regulations to repay during the relevant period, and

D   is any interest payable under section 991 in respect of the sums referred to in the meanings of A and B.][100]

PART 42

Chapter 5

Miscellaneous Provisions

Liability to tax, etc. of holder of fixed charge on book debts or company

1001. (1)   In this section, **"relevant amount"** means any amount which the company is liable to remit under -

(a)   Chapter 4 of this Part, and

(b)   the Value-Added Tax Act, 1972.

(2)   Subject to this section, where a person holds a fixed charge (being a fixed charge created on or after the 27th day of May, 1986) on the book debts of a company (within the meaning of the Companies Act, 1963), such person shall, if the company fails to pay any relevant amount for which it is liable, become liable to pay such relevant amount on due demand, and on neglect or refusal of payment may be proceeded against in the like manner as any other defaulter.

(3)   This section shall not apply-

     (a)   unless the holder of the fixed charge has been notified in writing by the Revenue Commissioners that a company has failed to pay a relevant amount for which it is liable and that by virtue of this section the holder of the fixed charge-

         (i)   may become liable for payment of any relevant amount which the company subsequently fails to pay, and

         (ii)   where paragraph (c) does not apply, has become liable for the payment of the relevant amount which the company has failed to pay,

     (b)   to any amounts received by the holder of the fixed charge from the company before the date on which the holder is notified in writing by the Revenue Commissioners in accordance with paragraph (a), and

     [(c)   where within 21 days of the creation of the fixed charge the holder of the fixed charge furnishes in writing to the Revenue Commissioners the following details in relation to the charge:

         (i)   the name of the company on whose book debts the charge has been created;

         (ii)   the registration number of the company as issued by the Companies Registration Office to that company;

         (iii)   the tax registration number of the company as issued by the Revenue Commissioners to that company;

         (iv)   the date the fixed charge was created; and

         (v)   the name and address of the holder of the fixed charge;

     to any relevant amount which the company was liable to pay before the date on which the holder is notified in writing by the Revenue Commissioners in accordance with paragraph (a).][101]

(4)   The amount or aggregate amount which a person shall be liable to pay in relation to a company in accordance with this section shall not exceed the amount or aggregate amount which the person has, while the fixed charge on book debts in relation to the company is in existence, received directly or indirectly from that company in payment or in part payment of any debts due by the company to the person.

(5)   The Revenue Commissioners may, at any time and by notice in writing given to the holder of the fixed charge, withdraw with effect from a date specified in the notice a notification issued by them in accordance with subsection (3); but such withdrawal shall not-

(a)   affect in any way any liability of the holder of the fixed charge under this section which arose before such withdrawal, or

(b)   preclude the issue under subsection (3) of a subsequent notice to the holder of the fixed charge.

(6)   The Revenue Commissioners may nominate any of their officers to perform any acts and discharge any functions authorised by this section to be performed or discharged by the Revenue Commissioners.

Deduction from payments due to defaulters of amounts due in relation to tax

1002. (1)   (a)   In this section, except where the context otherwise requires-

"**the Acts**" means -

(i)   the Customs Acts,

(ii)   the statutes relating to the duties of excise and to the management of those duties,

(iii)   the Tax Acts,

[(iiia) Part 18A,][102]

(iv)   the Capital Gains Tax Acts,

(v)   the Value-Added Tax Act, 1972, and the enactments amending or extending that Act,

(vi)   the [Capital Acquisitions Tax Consolidation Act 2003][14], and the enactments amending or extending that Act, and

(vii)   the Stamp Act, 1891, and the enactments amending or extending that Act,

[(viii) Part 18B,][103]

and any instruments made thereunder;

"**additional debt**", in relation to a relevant person who has received a notice of attachment in respect of a taxpayer, means any amount which, at any time after the time of the receipt by the relevant person of the notice of attachment but before the end of the relevant period in relation to the notice, would be a debt due by the relevant person to the taxpayer if a notice of attachment were received by the relevant person at that time;

"debt", in relation to a notice of attachment given to a relevant person in respect of a taxpayer and in relation to that relevant person and taxpayer, means, subject to paragraphs (b) to (e), the amount or aggregate amount of any money which, at the time the notice of attachment is received by the relevant person, is due by the relevant person (whether on that person's own account or as an agent or trustee) to the taxpayer, irrespective of whether the taxpayer has applied for the payment (to the taxpayer or any other person) or for the withdrawal of all or part of the money;

"deposit" means a sum of money paid to a financial institution on terms under which it will be repaid with or without interest and either on demand or at a time or in circumstances agreed by or on behalf of the person making the payment and the financial institution to which it is made;

"emoluments" means anything assessable to income tax under Schedule E;

['financial institution' means —

(a) **a person who holds or has held a licence under section 9 of the Central Bank Act 1971, or a person who holds or has held a licence or other similar authorisation under the law of any other Member State of the European Communities which corresponds to a licence granted under that section,**

(b) **a person referred to in section 7(4) of the Central Bank Act 1971,**

(c) **a credit institution (within the meaning of the European Communities (Licensing and Supervision of Credit Institutions) Regulations 1992 (S.I. No. 395 of 1992)) which has been authorised by the Central Bank and Financial Services Authority of Ireland to carry on business of a credit institution in accordance with the provisions of the supervisory enactments (within the meaning of those Regulations), or**

(d) **a branch of a financial institution which records deposits in its books as liabilities of the branch;]**[104]

"**further return**" means a return made by a relevant person under subsection (4);

"**interest on unpaid tax**", in relation to a specified amount specified in a notice of attachment, means interest that has accrued to the date on which the notice of attachment is given under any provision of the Acts providing for the charging of interest in respect of the unpaid tax, including interest on an undercharge of tax which is attributable to fraud or neglect, specified in the notice of attachment;

"**notice of attachment**" means a notice under subsection (2);

"**notice of revocation**" means a notice under subsection (10);

"**penalty**" means a monetary penalty imposed on a taxpayer under a provision of the Acts;

"**relevant period**", in relation to a notice of attachment, means, as respects the relevant person to whom the notice of attachment is given, the period commencing at the time at which the notice is received by the relevant person and ending on the earliest of-

(i) the date on which the relevant person completes the payment to the Revenue Commissioners out of the debt, or the aggregate of the debt and any additional debt, due by the relevant person to the taxpayer named in the notice, of an amount equal to the specified amount in relation to the taxpayer,

(ii) the date on which the relevant person receives a notice of revocation of the notice of attachment, and

(iii) where the relevant person or the taxpayer named in the notice-

(I) is declared bankrupt, the date the relevant person or the taxpayer is so declared, or

(II) is a company which commences to be wound up, the relevant date within the meaning of section 285 of the Companies Act, 1963, in relation to the winding up;

"**relevant person**", in relation to a taxpayer, means a person whom the Revenue Commissioners have reason to believe may have, at the time a notice of attachment is received by such person in respect of a taxpayer, a debt due to the taxpayer;

"**return**" means a return made by a relevant person under subsection (2)(a)(iii);

"**specified amount**" has the meaning assigned to it by subsection (2)(a)(ii);

"**tax**" means any tax, duty, levy or charge which in accordance with any provision of the Acts is placed under the care and management of the Revenue Commissioners;

"**taxpayer**" means a person who is liable to pay, remit or account for tax to the Revenue Commissioners under the Acts.

(b)   Where a relevant person is a financial institution, any amount or aggregate amount of money, including interest on that money, which at the time the notice of attachment is received by the relevant person is a deposit held by the relevant person-

    (i)   to the credit of the taxpayer for the taxpayer's sole benefit, or

    (ii)   to the credit of the taxpayer and any other person or persons for their joint benefit,

shall be regarded as a debt due by the relevant person to the taxpayer at that time.

(c)   Any amount of money due by the relevant person to the taxpayer as emoluments under a contract of service shall not be regarded as a debt due to the taxpayer.

(d)   Where there is a dispute as to an amount of money which is due by the relevant person to the taxpayer, the amount in dispute shall be disregarded for the purposes of determining the amount of the debt.

(e)   In the case referred to in paragraph (b), a deposit held by a relevant person which is a financial institution to the credit of the taxpayer and any other person or persons (in this paragraph referred to as "**the other party or parties**") for their joint benefit shall be deemed (unless evidence to the contrary is produced to the satisfaction of the relevant person within 10 days of the giving of the notices specified in subsection (2)(e)) to be held to the benefit of the taxpayer and the other party or parties to the deposit equally, and accordingly only the portion of the deposit so deemed shall be regarded as a debt due by the relevant person to the taxpayer at the time the notice of attachment is received by the relevant person and, where such evidence is produced within the specified time, only so much of the deposit as is shown to be held to the benefit of the taxpayer shall be regarded as a debt due by the relevant person to the taxpayer at that time.

(2)   (a)   Subject to subsection (3), where a taxpayer has made default whether before or after the passing of this Act in paying, remitting or accounting for any tax, interest on unpaid tax, or penalty to the Revenue Commissioners, the Revenue Commissioners may, if the taxpayer has not made good the default, give to a relevant person in relation to the taxpayer a notice in writing (in this section referred to as **"the notice of attachment"**) in which is entered-

(i)   the taxpayer's name and address,

(ii)   (I)   the amount or aggregate amount, or

(II)   in a case where more than one notice of attachment is given to a relevant person or relevant persons in respect of a taxpayer, a portion of the amount or aggregate amount,

of the taxes, interest on unpaid taxes and penalties in respect of which the taxpayer is in default at the time of the giving of the notice or notices of attachment (the amount, aggregate amount, or portion of the amount or aggregate amount, as the case may be, being referred to in this section as **"the specified amount"**), and

(iii)   a direction to the relevant person-

(I)   subject to paragraphs (b) and (c), to deliver to the Revenue Commissioners, within the period of 10 days from the time at which the notice of attachment is received by the relevant person, a return in writing specifying whether or not any debt is due by the relevant person to the taxpayer at the time the notice is received by the relevant person and, if any debt is so due, specifying the amount of the debt, and

(II)   if the amount of any debt is so specified, to pay to the Revenue Commissioners within the period referred to in clause (I) a sum equal to the amount of the debt so specified.

(b)   Where the amount of the debt due by the relevant person to the taxpayer is equal to or greater than the specified amount in relation to the taxpayer, the amount of the debt specified in the return shall be an amount equal to the specified amount.

(c)   Where the relevant person is a financial institution and the debt due by the relevant person to the taxpayer is part of a deposit held to the credit of the taxpayer and any other person or persons to their joint benefit, the return shall be made within a period of 10 days from-

     (i)   the expiry of the period specified in the notices to be given under paragraph (e), or

     (ii)   the production of the evidence referred to in paragraph (e)(ii).

(d)   A relevant person to whom a notice of attachment has been given shall comply with the direction in the notice.

(e)   Where a relevant person which is a financial institution is given a notice of attachment and the debt due by the relevant person to the taxpayer is part of a deposit held by the relevant person to the credit of the taxpayer and any other person or persons (in this paragraph referred to as **"the other party or parties"**) for their joint benefit, the relevant person shall on receipt of the notice of attachment give to the taxpayer and the other party or parties to the deposit a notice in writing in which is entered-

     (i)   the taxpayer's name and address,

     (ii)   the name and address of the person to whom a notice under this paragraph is given,

     (iii)   the name and address of the relevant person, and

     (iv)   the specified amount,

     and which states that-

       (I)   a notice of attachment under this section has been received in respect of the taxpayer,

       (II)   under this section a deposit is deemed (unless evidence to the contrary is produced to the satisfaction of the relevant person within 10 days of the giving of the notice under this paragraph) to be held to the benefit of the taxpayer and the other party or parties to the deposit equally, and

       (III)   unless such evidence is produced within the period specified in the notice given under this paragraph-

(A)   a sum equal to the amount of the deposit so deemed to be held to the benefit of the taxpayer (and accordingly regarded as a debt due to the taxpayer by the relevant person) shall be paid to the Revenue Commissioners, where that amount is equal to or less than the specified amount, and

(B)   where the amount of the deposit so deemed to be held to the benefit of the taxpayer (and accordingly regarded as a debt due to the taxpayer by the relevant person) is greater than the specified amount, a sum equal to the specified amount shall be paid to the Revenue Commissioners.

(3)   An amount in respect of tax, interest on unpaid tax or a penalty, as respects which a taxpayer is in default as specified in subsection (2), shall not be entered in a notice of attachment unless-

(a)   a period of [14 days][105] has expired from the date on which such default commenced, an

(b)   the Revenue Commissioners have given the taxpayer a notice in writing (whether or not the document containing the notice also contains other information being communicated by the Revenue Commissioners to the taxpayer), not later than 7 days before the date of the receipt by the relevant person or relevant persons concerned of a notice of attachment, stating that if the amount is not paid it may be specified in a notice or notices of attachment and recovered under this section from a relevant person or relevant persons in relation to the taxpayer.

(4)   If, when a relevant person receives a notice of attachment, the amount of the debt due by the relevant person to the taxpayer named in the notice is less than the specified amount in relation to the taxpayer or no debt is so due and, at any time after the receipt of the notice and before the end of the relevant period in relation to the notice, an additional debt becomes due by the relevant person to the taxpayer, the relevant person shall within 10 days of that time-

(a)   if the aggregate of the amount of any debt so due and the additional debt so due is equal to or less than the specified amount in relation to the taxpayer-

> (i)   deliver a further return to the Revenue Commissioners specifying the additional debt, and
>
> (ii) pay to the Revenue Commissioners the amount of the additional debt,
>
> and so on for each subsequent occasion during the relevant period in relation to the notice of attachment on which an additional debt becomes due by the relevant person to the taxpayer until-
>
>> (I)   the aggregate amount of the debt and the additional debt or debts so due equals the specified amount in relation to the taxpayer, or
>>
>> (II) paragraph (b) applies in relation to an additional debt, and

(b)   if the aggregate amount of any debt and the additional debt or debts so due to the taxpayer is greater than the specified amount in relation to the taxpayer-

> (i)   deliver a further return to the Revenue Commissioners specifying such portion of the latest additional debt as when added to the aggregate of the debt and any earlier additional debts is equal to the specified amount in relation to the taxpayer, and
>
> (ii) pay to the Revenue Commissioners that portion of the additional debt.

(5)   Where a relevant person delivers, either fraudulently or negligently, an incorrect return or further return that purports to be a return or further return made in accordance with this section, the relevant person shall be deemed to be guilty of an offence under section 1078.

(6)   (a)   Where a notice of attachment has been given to a relevant person in respect of a taxpayer, the relevant person shall not, during the relevant period in relation to the notice, make any disbursements out of the debt, or out of any additional debt, due by the relevant person to the taxpayer except to the extent that any such disbursement-

> (i)   will not reduce the debt or the aggregate of the debt and any additional debts so due to an amount that is less than the specified amount in relation to the taxpayer, or
>
> (ii) is made pursuant to an order of a court.

(b) For the purposes of this section, a disbursement made by a relevant person contrary to paragraph (a) shall be deemed not to reduce the amount of the debt or any additional debts due by the relevant person to the taxpayer.

(7) (a) Sections 1052 and 1054 shall apply to a failure by a relevant person to deliver a return required by a notice of attachment within the time specified in the notice or to deliver a further return within the time specified in subsection (4) as they apply to a failure to deliver a return referred to in section 1052.

(b) A certificate signed by an officer of the Revenue Commissioners which certifies that he or she has examined the relevant records and that it appears from those records that during a specified period a specified return was not received from a relevant person shall be evidence until the contrary is proved that the relevant person did not deliver the return during that period.

(c) A certificate certifying as provided by paragraph (b) and purporting to be signed by an officer of the Revenue Commissioners may be tendered in evidence without proof and shall be deemed until the contrary is proved to have been so signed.

(8) Where a relevant person to whom a notice of attachment in respect of a taxpayer has been given-

(a) delivers the return required to be delivered by that notice but fails to pay to the Revenue Commissioners within the time specified in the notice the amount specified in the return or any part of that amount, or

(b) delivers a further return under subsection (4) but fails to pay to the Revenue Commissioners within the time specified in that subsection the amount specified in the further return or any part of that amount,

the amount specified in the return or further return or the part of that amount, as the case may be, which the relevant person has failed to pay to the Revenue Commissioners may, if the notice of attachment has not been revoked by a notice of revocation, be sued for and recovered by action or other appropriate proceedings at the suit of an officer of the Revenue Commissioners in any court of competent jurisdiction.

(9) Nothing in this section shall be construed as rendering any failure by a relevant person to make a return or further return required by this section, or to pay to the Revenue Commissioners the amount or amounts required by this section to be paid by the

relevant person, liable to be treated as a failure to which section 1078 applies.

(10) (a) A notice of attachment given to a relevant person in respect of a taxpayer may be revoked by the Revenue Commissioners at any time by notice in writing given to the relevant person and shall be revoked forthwith if the taxpayer has paid the specified amount to the Revenue Commissioners.

(b) Where in pursuance of this section a relevant person pays any amount to the Revenue Commissioners out of a debt or an additional debt due by the relevant person to the taxpayer and, at the time of the receipt by the Revenue Commissioners of that amount, the taxpayer has paid to the Revenue Commissioners the amount or aggregate amount of the taxes, interest on unpaid taxes and penalties in respect of which the taxpayer is in default at the time of the giving of the notice or notices of attachment, the first-mentioned amount shall be refunded by the Revenue Commissioners forthwith to the taxpayer.

(11) Where a notice of attachment or a notice of revocation is given to a relevant person in relation to a taxpayer, a copy of such notice shall be given by the Revenue Commissioners to the taxpayer forthwith.

(12) (a) Where in pursuance of this section any amount is paid to the Revenue Commissioners by a relevant person, the relevant person shall forthwith give the taxpayer concerned a notice in writing specifying the payment, its amount and the reason for which it was made.

(b) On the receipt by the Revenue Commissioners of an amount paid in pursuance of this section, the Revenue Commissioners shall forthwith notify the taxpayer and the relevant person in writing of such receipt.

(13) Where in pursuance of this section a relevant person pays to the Revenue Commissioners the whole or part of the amount of a debt or an additional debt due by the relevant person to a taxpayer, or any portion of such an amount, the taxpayer shall allow such payment and the relevant person shall be acquitted and discharged of the amount of the payment as if it had been paid to the taxpayer.

(14) Where in pursuance of this section a relevant person is prohibited from making any disbursement out of a debt or an additional debt due to a taxpayer, no action shall lie against the relevant person in any court by reason of a failure to make any such disbursement.

(15)   Any obligation on the Revenue Commissioners to maintain secrecy or any other restriction on the disclosure of information by the Revenue Commissioners shall not apply in relation to information contained in a notice of attachment.

(16)   A notice of attachment in respect of a taxpayer shall not be given to a relevant person at a time when the relevant person or the taxpayer is an undischarged bankrupt or a company being wound up.

(17)   The Revenue Commissioners may nominate any of their officers to perform any acts and discharge any functions authorised by this section to be performed or discharged by the Revenue Commissioners.

Poundage and certain other fees due to sheriffs or county registrars

1006. (1)   In this section-

"**the Acts**" means-

(a)   the Tax Acts,

[(aa)   Part 18A,][102]

(b)   the Capital Gains Tax Acts,

(c)   the Value-Added Tax Act, 1972, and the enactments amending or extending that Act,

(d)   the [Capital Acquisitions Tax Consolidation Act 2003][14], and the enactments amending or extending that Act, and

(e)   Part VI of the Finance Act, 1983, and the enactments amending or extending that Part,

[(f)   Part 18B,][103]

and any instruments made thereunder;

"**certificate**" means a certificate issued under [section 960L][92];

"**county registrar**" means a person appointed to be a county registrar under section 35 of the Court Officers Act, 1926;

"**defaulter**" means a person specified or certified in an execution order or certificate on whom a relevant amount specified or certified in the order or certificate is leviable;

"**execution order**" has the same meaning as in the Enforcement of Court Orders Act, 1926;

"**fees**" means the fees known as poundage fees payable under section 14(1) of the Enforcement of Court Orders Act, 1926, and orders made under that section for services in or about the execution of an execution order directing or authorising the execution of an order of a court by the seizure and sale of a person's property or, as may be appropriate, the fees corresponding to those fees payable under [**section 960L**][92] for the execution of a certificate;

"**interest on unpaid tax**" means interest which has accrued under any provision of the Acts providing for the charging of interest in respect of unpaid tax, including interest on an undercharge of tax which is attributable to fraud or neglect;

"**relevant amount**" means an amount of tax or interest on unpaid tax;

"**tax**" means any tax, duty, levy or charge which, in accordance with any provision of the Acts, is placed under the care and management of the Revenue Commissioners;

references, as respects an execution order, to a relevant amount include references to any amount of costs specified in the order.

(2)   Where -

(a)   an execution order or certificate specifying or certifying a defaulter and relating to a relevant amount is lodged with the appropriate sheriff or county registrar for execution,

(b)   the sheriff or, as the case may be, the county registrar gives notice to the defaulter of the lodgment or of his or her intention to execute the execution order or certificate by seizure of the property of the defaulter to which it relates, or demands payment by the defaulter of the relevant amount, and

(c)   the whole or part of the relevant amount is paid to the sheriff or, as the case may be, the county registrar or to the Collector-General, after the giving of that notice or the making of that demand,

then, for the purpose of the liability of the defaulter for the payment of fees and of the exercise of any rights or powers in relation to the collection of fees for the time being vested by law in sheriffs and county registrars-

(i)   the sheriff or, as the case may be, the county registrar shall be deemed to have entered, in the execution of the execution order or certificate, into possession of the property referred to in paragraph (b), and

(ii)   the payment mentioned in paragraph (c) shall be deemed to have been levied, in the execution of the execution order or certificate, by the sheriff or, as the case may be, the county registrar,

and fees shall be payable by the defaulter to such sheriff or, as the case may be, country registrar accordingly in respect of the payment mentioned in paragraph (c).

Offset between taxes

1006A. [........]^106

Appropriation of payments

1006B. [........]^107

PART 47

Chapter 1
Income tax and corporation tax penalties

Recovery of penalties

1061. (1)   Without prejudice to any other mode of recovery of a penalty under the [preceding provisions of this Part, Chapter 4 of Part 38]^108 or under section 305, 783, 789 or 886, an officer of the Revenue Commissioners authorized by them for the purposes of this subsection may sue in his or her own name by civil proceedings [for the recovery of the penalty in any court of competent jurisdiction as a liquidated sum, and, where appropriate, section 94 of the Courts of Justice Act 1924 shall apply accordingly.]^109

(2)   Where an officer who has commenced proceedings pursuant to this section, or who has continued the proceedings by virtue of this subsection, dies or otherwise ceases for any reason to be an officer authorised for the purposes of subsection (1)–

(a)   the right of such officer to continue the proceedings shall cease and the right to continue them shall vest in such other officer so authorised as may be nominated by the Revenue Commissioners,

(b)   where such other officer is nominated under paragraph (a), he or she shall be entitled accordingly to be substituted as a party to the proceedings in the place of the first-mentioned officer, and

(c)   where an officer is so substituted, he or she shall give notice in writing of the substitution to the defendant.

(3)   In proceedings pursuant to this section, a certificate signed by a Revenue Commissioner certifying that–

(a)   a person is an officer of the Revenue Commissioners, and

(b)   he or she has been authorised by them for the purposes of subsection (1),

shall be evidence of those facts until the contrary is proved.

(4)   In proceedings pursuant to this section, a certificate signed by a Revenue Commissioner certifying that–

(a)   the plaintiff has ceased to be an officer of the Revenue Commissioners authorised by them for the purposes of subsection (1),

(b)   another person is an officer of the Revenue Commissioners,

(c)   such other person has been authorised by them for the purposes of subsection (1), and

(d)   he or she has been nominated by them in relation to the proceedings for the purposes of subsection (2),

shall be evidence of those facts until the contrary is proved.

(5)   In proceedings pursuant to this section, a certificate certifying the facts referred to in subsection (3) or (4) and purporting to be signed by a Revenue Commissioner may be tendered in evidence without proof and shall be deemed until the contrary is proved to have been so signed.

(6)   Subject to this section, [the rules of Court]¹¹⁰ for the time being applicable to civil proceedings shall apply to proceedings pursuant to this section.

[(7)   This section shall not apply in respect of any acts or omissions arising after the passing of the Finance (No. 2) Act 2008.]¹¹¹

Mitigation and application of fines and penalties

1065. (1)   (a)   The Revenue Commissioners may in their discretion mitigate any fine or penalty, or stay or compound any proceedings for the recovery of any fine or penalty, and may also, after judgment, further mitigate the fine or penalty, and may order any person imprisoned for any offence to be discharged before the term of his or her imprisonment has expired.

(b)   The Minister for Finance may mitigate any such fine or penalty either before or after judgment.

(2)   Notwithstanding subsection (1)–

(a)   where a fine or penalty is mitigated or further mitigated, as the case may be, after judgment, the amount or amounts so mitigated shall, subject to paragraph (b), not be greater than 50 per cent of the amount of the fine or penalty, and

(b)   in relation to an individual, being an individual referred to in section 2(2) of the Waiver of Certain Tax, Interest and Penalties Act, 1993, or a person referred to in section 3(2) of that Act, who–

        (i)   fails to give a declaration required by section 2(3) (a) of that Act, or

        (ii)   gives a declaration referred to in subparagraph (i) or a declaration under section 3(6)(b) of that Act which is false or fails to comply with the requirements of subparagraph (iii) or (iv) of section 2(3)(a) of that Act or subparagraph (III) of section 3(6)(b) of that Act to the extent that any of those subparagraphs apply to that person,

no mitigation shall be allowed.

(3)   Moneys arising from fines, penalties and forfeitures, and all costs, charges and expenses payable in respect of or in relation to such fines, penalties and forfeitures, shall be accounted for and paid to the Revenue Commissioners or as they direct.

[Chapter 3A

Determination of Penalties and Recovery of Penalties

Interpretation

1077A. In this Chapter —

    'the Acts' means —

    (a)   the Tax Acts,

    (b)   the Capital Gains Tax Acts,

    (c)   Parts 18A and 18B,

    (d)   the Value-Added Tax Act 1972, and the enactments amending or extending that Act,

    (e)   the Capital Acquisitions Tax Consolidation Act 2003, and the enactments amending or extending that Act,

    (f)   the Stamp Duties Consolidation Act 1999, and the enactments amending or extending that Act,

    (g)   the statutes relating to the duties of excise and to the management of those duties

    and any instrument made thereunder and any instrument made under any other enactment relating to tax;

    'relevant court' means the District Court, the Circuit Court or the High Court, as appropriate, by reference to the jurisdictional limits for civil matters laid down in the Courts of Justice Act 1924, as amended, and the Courts (Supplemental Provisions) Act 1961, as amended;

    'Revenue officer' means an officer of the Revenue Commissioners,

'tax' means any tax, duty, levy or charge under the care and management of the Revenue Commissioners.

Penalty notifications and determinations.

1077B. (1)   Where —

     (a)   in the absence of any agreement between a person and a Revenue officer that the person is liable to a penalty under the Acts, or

     (b)   following the failure by a person to pay a penalty the person has agreed a liability to,

     a Revenue officer is of the opinion that the person is liable to a penalty under the Acts, then that officer shall give notice in writing to the person and such notice shall identify —

        (i)   the provisions of the Acts under which the penalty arises,

        (ii)   the circumstances in which that person is liable to the penalty, and

        (iii)   the amount of the penalty to which that person is liable,

     and include such other details as the Revenue officer considers necessary.

   (2)   A Revenue officer may at any time amend an opinion that a person is liable to a penalty under the Acts and shall give due notice of such amended opinion in like manner to the notice referred to in subsection (1).

   (3)   Where a person to whom a notice issued under subsection (1) or (2) does not, within 30 days after the date of such a notice —

     (a)   agree in writing with the opinion or amended opinion contained in such notice, and

     (b)   make a payment to the Revenue Commissioners of the amount of the penalty specified in such a notice,

     then a Revenue officer may make an application to a relevant court for that court to determine whether —

        (i)   any action, inaction, omission or failure of, or

        (ii)   any claim, submission or delivery by,

     the person in respect of whom the Revenue officer made the application gives rise to a liability to a penalty under the Acts on that person.

(4)   A copy of any application to a relevant court for a determination under subsection (3) shall be issued to the person to whom the application relates.

(5)   This section applies in respect of any act or omission giving rise to a liability to a penalty under the Acts whether arising before, on or after the passing of the Finance (No. 2) Act 2008 but shall not apply in respect of a penalty paid, or amounts paid in respect of a penalty, before the passing of that Act.

Recovery of penalties.

1077C. (1)   Where a relevant court has made a determination that a person is liable to a penalty —

(a)   that court shall also make an order as to the recovery of that penalty, and

(b)   without prejudice to any other means of recovery, that penalty may be collected and recovered in like manner as an amount of tax.

(2)   Where a person is liable to a penalty under the Acts, that penalty is due and payable from the date —

(a)   it had been agreed in writing (or had been agreed in writing on that person's behalf) that the person is liable to that penalty,

(b)   the Revenue Commissioners had agreed or undertaken to accept a specified sum of money in the circumstances mentioned in paragraph (c) or (d) of section 1086(2) from that [person][112], or

(c)   a relevant court has determined that the person is liable to that penalty.

(3)   This section applies in respect of any act or omission giving rise to a liability to a penalty under the Acts whether arising before, on or after the passing of the Finance (No. 2) Act 2008.

Proceedings against executor, administrator or estate.

1077D. (1)   Where before an individual's death —

(a)   that individual had agreed in writing (or it had been agreed in writing on his or her behalf) that he or she was liable to a penalty under the Acts,

(b)   that individual had agreed in writing with an opinion or amended opinion of a Revenue officer that he or she was liable to a penalty under the Acts (or such opinion or amended opinion had been agreed in writing on his or her behalf),

(c)   the Revenue Commissioners had agreed or undertaken
        to accept a specified sum of money in the circumstances
        mentioned in paragraph (c) or (d) of section 1086(2)
        from that individual, or

(d)   a relevant court has determined that the individual was
        liable to a penalty under the Acts,

then the penalty shall be due and payable and, subject to
subsection (2), any proceedings for the recovery of such penalty
under the Acts which have been, or could have been, instituted
against that individual may be continued or instituted against
his or her executor, administrator or estate, as the case may
be, and any penalty awarded in proceedings so continued or
instituted shall be a debt due from and payable out of his or
her estate.

(2)   Proceedings may not be instituted by virtue of subsection
        (1) against the executor or administrator of a person at a time
        when by virtue of subsection (2) of section 1048 that executor
        or administrator is not assessable and chargeable under that
        section in respect of tax on profits or gains which arose or
        accrued to the person before his or her death.][113]

Chapter 4
Penalties, Revenue offences, Interest on
overdue Tax and other Sanctions

Revenue offences

1078. (1)   In this Part-

"the Acts" means-

(a)   the Customs Acts,

(b)   the statutes relating to the duties of excise and to the
        management of those duties,

(c)   the Tax Acts,

[(ca)   Part 18A,][102]

(d)   the Capital Gains Tax Acts,

(e)   the Value-Added Tax Act, 1972, and the enactments
        amending or extending that Act,

(f)   the [Capital Acquisitions Tax Consolidation Act 2003][14],
        and the enactments amending or extending that Act,

(g)   the statutes relating to stamp duty and to the management
        of that duty, and

(h)   Part VI of the Finance Act, 1983,

[(i)   Part 18B][103]

and any instruments made thereunder and any instruments made under any other enactment and relating to tax;

"**authorised officer**" means an officer of the Revenue Commissioners authorised by them in writing to exercise any of the powers conferred by the Acts;

"**tax**" means any tax, duty, levy or charge under the care and management of the Revenue Commissioners.

[(1A)   (a)   In this subsection—

'**facilitating**' means aiding, abetting, assisting, inciting or inducing;

'**fraudulent evasion of tax by a person**' means the person—

(a)   evading or attempting to evade any payment or deduction of tax required under the Acts to be paid by the person or, as the case may be, required under the Acts to be deducted from amounts due to the person, or

(b)   claiming or obtaining, or attempting to claim or obtain, relief or exemption from, or payment or repayment of, any tax, being relief, exemption, payment or repayment, to which the person is not entitled under the Acts,

where, for those purposes, the person deceives, omits, conceals or uses any other dishonest means including—

(i)   providing false, incomplete or misleading information, or

(ii)   failing to furnish information, to the Revenue Commissioners or to any other person.

(b)   For the purposes of this subsection and subsection(5) a person (in this paragraph referred to as the '**first-mentioned person**') is reckless as to whether or not he or she is concerned in facilitating—

(i)   the fraudulent evasion of tax by a person, being another person, or

(ii)   the commission of an offence under subsection (2) by a person, being another person,

if the first-mentioned person disregards a substantial risk that he or she is so concerned, and for those purposes '**substantial risk**' means a risk of such a nature and degree that, having regard to all the circumstances and the extent of the information available to the first-mentioned person, its disregard by that person involves culpability of a high degree.

(c)   A person shall, without prejudice to any other penalty to which the person may be liable, be guilty of an offence under this section if the person–

    (i)   is knowingly concerned in the fraudulent evasion of tax by the person or any other person,

    (ii)   is knowingly concerned in, or is reckless as to whether or not the person is concerned in, facilitating–

        (I)   the fraudulent evasion of tax, or

        (II)   the commission of an offence under subsection (2) (other than an offence under paragraph (b) of that subsection),

        by any other person, or

    (iii)   is knowingly concerned in the fraudulent evasion or attempted fraudulent evasion of any prohibition or restriction on importation for the time being in force, or the removal of any goods from the State, in contravention of any provision of the Acts.][114]

[(1B)   A person is guilty of an offence under this section if he or she, with the intention to deceive–

    (a)   purports to be, or

    (b)   makes any statement, or otherwise acts in a manner, that would lead another person to believe that he or she is,

an officer of the Revenue Commissioners.][115]

(2)   A person shall, without prejudice to any other penalty to which the person may be liable, be guilty of an offence under this section if the person–

    (a)   knowingly or wilfully delivers any incorrect return, statement or accounts or knowingly or wilfully furnishes any incorrect information in connection with any tax,

    (b)   knowingly aids, abets, assists, incites or induces another person to make or deliver knowingly or wilfully any incorrect return, statement or accounts in connection with any tax,

    (c)   claims or obtains relief or exemption from, or repayment of, any tax, being a relief, exemption or repayment to which, to the person's knowledge, the person is not entitled,

    (d)   knowingly or wilfully issues or produces any incorrect invoice, receipt, instrument or other document in connection with any tax,

      (e)   (i)   fails to make any deduction required to be made by the person under section 257(1),

           (ii)   fails, having made the deduction, to pay the sum deducted to the Collector-General within the time specified in that behalf in section 258(3), or

           (iii) fails to pay to the Collector-General an amount on account of appropriate tax (within the meaning of Chapter 4 of Part 8) within the time specified in that behalf in section 258(4),

      [(f)   fails to pay to the Collector-General appropriate tax (within the meaning of section 739E) within the time specified in that behalf in section 739F,][116]

      (g)   [fails without reasonable excuse][117] to comply with any provision of the Acts requiring-

           (i)   the furnishing of a return of income, profits or gains, or of sources of income, profits or gains, for the purposes of any tax,

           (ii)   the furnishing of any other return, certificate, notification, particulars, or any statement or evidence, for the purposes of any tax,

           (iii) the keeping or retention of books, records, accounts or other documents for the purposes of any tax, or

           (iv) the production of books, records, accounts or other documents, when so requested, for the purposes of any tax,

      (h)   knowingly or wilfully, and within the time limits specified for their retention, destroys, defaces or conceals from an authorised officer-

           (i)   any documents, or

           (ii)   any other written or printed material in any form, including any information stored, maintained or preserved by means of any mechanical or electronic device, whether or not stored, maintained or preserved in a legible form, which a person is obliged by any provision of the Acts to keep, to issue or to produce for inspection,

      [(hh) knowingly or wilfully falsifies, conceals, destroys or otherwise disposes of, or causes or permits the falsification, concealment, destruction or disposal of, any books, records or other documents-

      (i)   which the person has been given the opportunity to deliver, or as the case may be, to make available in accordance with section 900(3), or

      (ii)   which the person has been required to deliver or, as the case may be, to make available in accordance with a notice served under section 900, 902, 906A or 907, or an order made under section 901, 902A or 908,][118]

    (i)   fails to remit any income tax payable pursuant to Chapter 4 of Part 42, and the regulations under that Chapter, or value-added tax within the time specified in that behalf in relation to income tax or value-added tax, as the case may be, [by the Acts,][116]

  [(ii)   (i)   fails to deduct tax required to be deducted by the person under section 531(1), or

        (ii)   fails, having made that deduction, to pay the sum deducted to the Collector-General within the time specified in that behalf in section 531(3A),

      or][119]

    (j)   obstructs or interferes with any officer of the Revenue Commissioners, or any other person, in the exercise or performance of powers or duties under the Acts for the purposes of any tax.

(3)   A person convicted of an offence under this section shall be liable-

    (a)   on summary conviction to a fine of [€5,000][120] which may be mitigated to not less than one fourth part of such fine or, at the discretion of the court, to imprisonment for a term not exceeding 12 months or to both the fine and the imprisonment, or

    (b)   on conviction on indictment, to a fine not exceeding [€126,970][121] or, at the discretion of the court, to imprisonment for a term not exceeding 5 years or to both the fine and the imprisonment.

[(3A) Where a person has been convicted of an offence referred to in subparagraph (i), (ii) or (iv) of subsection (2)(g), then, if an application is made, or caused to be made to the court in that regard, the court may make an order requiring the person concerned to comply with any provision of the Acts relating to the requirements specified in the said subparagraph (i), (ii) or (iv), as the case may be.][122]

[(3B) A person shall, without prejudice to any other penalty to which the person may be liable, be guilty of an offence under this section if the person fails or refuses to comply with an order referred to in subsection (3A) **[within a period of 30 days commencing on the day the order is made]**[123]**.]**[124]

(4)   Section 13 of the Criminal Procedure Act, 1967, shall apply in relation to an offence under this section as if, in place of the penalties specified in subsection (3) of that section, there were specified in that subsection the penalties provided for by subsection (3)(a), and the reference in subsection (2)(a) of section 13 of the Criminal Procedure Act, 1967, to the penalties provided for in subsection (3) of that section shall be construed and apply accordingly.

(5)   Where an offence under this section is committed by a body corporate and the offence is shown [to have been committed with the consent or connivance of or to be attributable to any recklessness (as provided for by subsection (1A)(b)) on the part of][125] any person who, when the offence was committed, was a director, manager, secretary or other officer of the body corporate, or a member of the committee of management or other controlling authority of the body corporate, that person shall also be deemed to be guilty of the offence and may be proceeded against and punished accordingly.

(6)   In any proceedings under this section, a return or statement delivered to an inspector or other officer of the Revenue Commissioners under any provision of the Acts and purporting to be signed by any person shall be deemed until the contrary is proved to have been so delivered and to have been signed by that person.

(7)   Notwithstanding any other enactment, proceedings in respect of an offence under this section may be instituted within 10 years from the date of the commission of the offence or incurring of the penalty, as the case may be.

(8)   Section 1 of the Probation of Offenders Act, 1907, shall not apply in relation to offences under this section.

(9)   Sections 987(4) and 1052(4), subsections (3) and (7) of section 1053, **[subsections (9) and (17) of section 1077E,]**[126] and sections 1068 and 1069 **[, and section 27A(16) of the Value Added Tax Act 1972,]**[127] shall, with any necessary modifications, apply for the purposes of this section as they apply for the purposes of those sections, including, in the case of such of those sections as are applied by the Capital Gains Tax Acts, the Corporation Tax Acts, or Part VI of the Finance Act, 1983, the purposes of those sections as so applied.

[**Concealing facts disclosed by documents.**

1078A. (1) Any person who–

(a) knows or suspects that an investigation by an officer of the Revenue Commissioners into an offence under the Acts or the Waiver of Certain Tax, Interest and Penalties Act 1993 is being, or is likely to be, carried out, and

(b) falsifies, conceals, destroys or otherwise disposes of material which the person knows or suspects is or would be relevant to the investigation or causes or permits its falsification, concealment, destruction or disposal, is guilty of an offence

(2) Where a person–

(a) falsifies, conceals, destroys or otherwise disposes of material, or

(b) causes or permits its falsification, concealment, destruction or disposal,

in such circumstances that it is reasonable to conclude that the person knew or suspected–

(i) that an investigation by an officer of the Revenue Commissioners into an offence under the Acts or the Waiver of Certain Tax, Interest and Penalties Act 1993 was being, or was likely to be, carried out, and

(ii) that the material was or would be relevant to the investigation,

the person shall be taken, for the purposes of this section, to have so known or suspected, unless the court or the jury, as the case may be, is satisfied having regard to all the evidence that there is a reasonable doubt as to whether the person so knew or suspected.

(3) A person guilty of an offence under this section is liable–

(a) on summary conviction to a fine not exceeding [€5,000][120], or at the discretion of the court, to imprisonment for a term not exceeding 6 months or to both the fine and the imprisonment, or

(b) on conviction on indictment, to a fine not exceeding €127,000 or, at the discretion of the court, to imprisonment for a term not exceeding 5 years or to both the fine and the imprisonment.

Presumptions.

1078B. (1)   In this section–

'**return, statement or declaration**' means any return, statement or declaration which a person is required to make under the Acts or the Waiver of Certain Tax, Interest and Penalties Act 1993.

(2)   The presumptions specified in this section apply in any proceedings, whether civil or criminal, under any provision of the Acts or the Waiver of Certain Tax, Interest and Penalties Act 1993.

(3)   Where a document purports to have been created by a person it shall be presumed, unless the contrary is shown, that the document was created by that person and that any statement contained therein, unless the document expressly attributes its making to some other person, was made by that person.

(4)   Where a document purports to have been created by a person and addressed and sent to a second person, it shall be presumed, unless the contrary is shown, that the document was created and sent by the first person and received by the second person and that any statement contained therein–

(a)   unless the document expressly attributes its making to some other person, was made by the first person, and

(b)   came to the notice of the second person.

(5)   Where a document is retrieved from an electronic storage and retrieval system, it shall be presumed unless the contrary is shown, that the author of the document is the person who ordinarily uses that electronic storage and retrieval system in the course of his or her business.

(6)   Where an authorised officer in the exercise of his or her powers under subsection (2A) of section 905 **[or subsection (3) of section 908C]**[128] has removed records (within the meaning of that section) from any place, gives evidence in proceedings that to the best of the authorised officer's knowledge and belief, the records are the property of any person, the records shall be presumed unless the contrary is proved, to be the property of that person.

(7)   Where in accordance with subsection (6) records are presumed in proceedings to be the property of a person and the authorised officer gives evidence that, to the best of the authorised officer's knowledge and belief, the records are records which relate to any trade, profession, or, as the case may be, other activity, carried on by that person, the records shall be presumed unless the contrary is proved, to be records which relate to that trade, profession, or, as the case may be, other activity, carried on by that person.

(8)   In proceedings, a certificate signed by an inspector or other officer of the Revenue Commissioners certifying that a return, statement or declaration to which the certificate refers is in the possession of the Revenue Commissioners in such circumstances as to lead the officer to conclude that, to the best of his or her knowledge and belief it was delivered to an inspector or other officer of the Revenue Commissioners, it shall be presumed unless the contrary is proved, to be evidence that the said return, statement, or declaration was so delivered.

(9)   In proceedings, a certificate, certifying the fact or facts referred to in subsection (8) and purporting to be signed as specified in that subsection, may be tendered in evidence without proof and shall be deemed until the contrary is proved to have been signed by a person holding, at the time of the signature, the office or position indicated in the certificate as the office or position of the person signing.

(10) References in this section to a document are references to a document in written, mechanical or electronic format and, for this purpose 'written' includes any form of notation or code whether by hand or otherwise and regardless of the method by which, or the medium in or on which, the document concerned is recorded.

Provision of information to juries.

1078C. (1)   In a trial on indictment of an offence under the Acts or the Waiver of Certain Tax, Interest and Penalties Act 1993, the trial judge may order that copies of any or all of the following documents shall be given to the jury in any form that the judge considers appropriate:

(a)   any document admitted in evidence at the trial,

(b)   the transcript of the opening speeches of counsel,

(c)   any charts, diagrams, graphics, schedules or agreed summaries of evidence produced at the trial,

(d)   the transcript of the whole or any part of the evidence given at the trial,

(e)   the transcript of the closing speeches of counsel,

(f)   the transcript of the trial judge's charge to the jury,

(g)   any other document that in the opinion of the trial judge would be of assistance to the jury in its deliberations including, where appropriate, an affidavit by an accountant or other suitably qualified person, summarising, in a form which is likely to be comprehended by the jury, any transactions by the accused or other persons which are relevant to the offence.

(2)   If the prosecutor proposes to apply to the trial judge for an order that a document mentioned in subsection (1)(g) shall be given to the jury, the prosecutor shall give a copy of the document to the accused in advance of the trial and, on the hearing of the application, the trial judge shall take into account any representations made by or on behalf of the accused in relation to it.

(3)   Where the trial judge has made an order that an affidavit by an accountant or other person mentioned in subsection (1)(g) shall be given to the jury, the accountant, or as the case may be, the other person so mentioned–

   (a)   shall be summoned by the prosecution to attend at the trial as an expert witness, and

   (b)   may be required by the trial judge, in an appropriate case, to give evidence in regard to any relevant procedures or principles within his or her area of expertise.][129]

Duties of relevant person in relation to certain revenue offences

1079. (1)   In this section–

"**the Acts**" means–

   (a)   the Customs Acts,

   (b)   the statutes relating to the duties of excise and to the management of those duties,

   (c)   the Tax Acts,

   [(ca)   **Part 18A,**][102]

   (d)   the Capital Gains Tax Acts,

   (e)   the Value-Added Tax Act, 1972, and the enactments amending or extending that Act,

   (f)   the [Capital Acquisitions Tax Consolidation Act 2003][14], and the enactments amending or extending that Act,

   (g)   the statutes relating to stamp duty and to the management of that duty,

   and any instruments made thereunder and any instruments made under any other enactment and relating to tax;

"**appropriate officer**" means any officer nominated by the Revenue Commissioners to be an appropriate officer for the purposes of this section;

"**company**" means any body corporate;

"**relevant person**", in relation to a company and subject to subsection (2), means a person who–

(a)   (i)   is an auditor to the company appointed in accordance with section 160 of the Companies Act, 1963 (as amended by the Companies Act, 1990), or

        (ii)   in the case of an industrial and provident society or a friendly society, is a public auditor to the society for the purposes of the Industrial and Provident Societies Acts, 1893 to 1978, and the Friendly Societies Acts, 1896 to 1977,

or

(b)   with a view to reward, assists or advises the company in the preparation or delivery of any information, declaration, return, records, accounts or other document which he or she knows will be or is likely to be used for any purpose of tax;

"**relevant offence**" means an offence committed by a company which consists of the company-

(a)   knowingly or wilfully delivering any incorrect return, statement or accounts or knowingly or wilfully furnishing or causing to be furnished any incorrect information in connection with any tax,

(b)   knowingly or wilfully claiming or obtaining relief or exemption from, or repayment of, any tax, being a relief, exemption or repayment to which there is no entitlement,

(c)   knowingly or wilfully issuing or producing any incorrect invoice, receipt, instrument or other document in connection with any tax, or

(d)   knowingly or wilfully failing to comply with any provision of the Acts requiring the furnishing of a return of income, profits or gains, or of sources of income, profits or gains, for the purposes of any tax, but an offence under this paragraph committed by a company shall not be a relevant offence if the company has made a return of income, profits or gains to the Revenue Commissioners in respect of an accounting period falling wholly or partly in the period of 3 years preceding the accounting period in respect of which the offence was committed;

"**tax**" means any tax, duty, levy or charge under the care and management of the Revenue Commissioners.

(2)   For the purposes of paragraph (b) of the definition of "**relevant person**", a person who but for this subsection would be treated as a relevant person in relation to a company shall not be so treated if the person assists or advises the company solely in the

person's capacity as an employee of the company, and a person shall be treated as assisting or advising the company in that capacity where the person's income from assisting or advising the company consists solely of emoluments to which Chapter 4 of Part 42 applies.

(3)　If, having regard solely to information obtained in the course of examining the accounts of a company, or in the course of assisting or advising a company in the preparation or delivery of any information, declaration, return, records, accounts or other document for the purposes of tax, as the case may be, a person who is a relevant person in relation to the company becomes aware that the company has committed, or is in the course of committing, one or more relevant offences, the person shall, if the offence or offences are material-

(a)　communicate particulars of the offence or offences in writing to the company without undue delay and request the company to-

(i)　take such action as is necessary for the purposes of rectifying the matter, or

(ii)　notify an appropriate officer of the offence or offences,

not later than 6 months after the time of communication, and

(b)　(i)　unless it is established to the person's satisfaction that the necessary action has been taken or notification made, as the case may be, under paragraph (a), cease to act as the auditor to the company or to assist or advise the company in such preparation or delivery as is specified in paragraph (b) of the definition of "**relevant person**", and

(ii)　shall not so act, assist or advise before a time which is the earlier of-

(I)　3 years after the time at which the particulars were communicated under paragraph (a), and

(II)　the time at which it is established to the person's satisfaction that the necessary action has been taken or notification made, as the case may be, under paragraph (a).

(4)　Nothing in paragraph (b) of subsection (3) shall prevent a person from assisting or advising a company in preparing for, or conducting, legal proceedings, either civil or criminal, which are extant or pending at a time which is 6 months after the time of communication under paragraph (a) of that subsection.

(5)   Where a person, being in relation to a company a relevant person within the meaning of paragraph (a) of the definition of **"relevant person"**, ceases under this section to act as auditor to the company, then, the person shall deliver-

    (a)   a notice in writing to the company stating that he or she is so resigning, and

    (b)   a copy of the notice to an appropriate officer not later than 14 days after he or she has delivered the notice to the company.

(6)   A person shall be guilty of an offence under this section if the person-

    (a)   fails to comply with subsection (3) or (5), or

    (b)   knowingly or wilfully makes a communication under subsection (3) which is incorrect.

(7)   Where a relevant person is convicted of an offence under this section, the person shall be liable-

    (a)   on summary conviction, to a fine of [€1,265][47] which may be mitigated to not less than one-fourth part of such fine, or

    (b)   on conviction on indictment, to a fine not exceeding [€6,345][47] or, at the discretion of the court, to imprisonment for a term not exceeding 2 years or to both the fine and the imprisonment.

(8)   Section 13 of the Criminal Procedure Act, 1967, shall apply in relation to this section as if, in place of the penalties specified in subsection (3) of that section, there were specified in that subsection the penalties provided for by subsection (7)(a), and the reference in subsection (2)(a) of section 13 of the Criminal Procedure Act, 1967, to the penalties provided for in subsection (3) of that section shall be construed and apply accordingly.

(9)   Notwithstanding any other enactment, proceedings in respect of this section may be instituted within 6 years from the time at which a person is required under subsection (3) to communicate particulars of an offence or offences in writing to a company.

(10)   It shall be a good defence in a prosecution for an offence under subsection (6) (a) in relation to a failure to comply with subsection (3) for an accused (being a person who is a relevant person in relation to a company) to show that he or she was in the ordinary scope of professional engagement assisting or advising the company in preparing for legal proceedings and would not have become aware that one or more relevant offences had been

committed by the company if he or she had not been so assisting or advising.

(11)   Where a person who is a relevant person takes any action required by subsection (3) or (5), no duty to which the person may be subject shall be regarded as having been contravened and no liability or action shall lie against the person in any court for having taken such action.

(12)   The Revenue Commissioners may nominate an officer to be an appropriate officer for the purposes of this section, and the name of an officer so nominated and the address to which copies of notices under subsection (3) or (5) shall be delivered shall be published in Iris Oifigiúil.

(13)   This section shall apply as respects a relevant offence committed by a company in respect of tax which is-

(a)   assessable by reference to accounting periods, for any accounting period beginning after the 30th day of June, 1995,

(b)   assessable by reference to years of assessment, for the year 1995-96 and subsequent years of assessment,

(c)   payable by reference to a taxable period, for a taxable period beginning after the 30th day of June, 1995,

(d)   chargeable on gifts or inheritances taken on or after the 30th day of June, 1995,

(e)   chargeable on instruments executed on or after the 30th day of June, 1995, or

(f)   payable in any other case, on or after the 30th day of June, 1995.

Chapter 6
Other sanctions

Publication of names of tax defaulters

1086. (1)   In this section -

"the Acts" means -

(a)   the Tax Acts,

(b)   the Capital Gains Tax Acts,

(c)   the Value-Added Tax Act, 1972, and the enactments amending or extending that Act,

(d)   the [Capital Acquisitions Tax Consolidation Act 2003]¹⁴, and the enactments amending or extending that Act, [(e)   the Stamp Duties Consolidation Act, 1999, and the enactments amending or extending that Act,][130]

(f)   Part VI of the Finance Act, 1983,

[(g)   the Customs Acts,

(h)   the statutes relating to the duties of excise and to the management of those duties,][131]

and any instruments made thereunder;

['**tax**' means any tax, duty, levy or charge under the care and management of the Revenue Comissioners.][132]

(2)   The Revenue Commissioners shall, as respects each relevant period (being the period beginning on the 1st day of January, 1997, and ending on the 30th day of June, 1997, and each subsequent period of 3 months beginning with the period ending on the 30th day of September, 1997), compile a list of the names and addresses and the occupations or descriptions of every person-

(a)   on whom a fine or other penalty was imposed [**or determined**][111] by a court under any of the Acts during that relevant period,

(b)   on whom a fine or other penalty was otherwise imposed [**or determined**][111] by a court during that relevant period in respect of an act or omission by the person in relation to tax, [...][133]

(c)   in whose case the Revenue Commissioners, pursuant to an agreement made with the person in that relevant period, refrained from initiating proceedings for the recovery of any fine or penalty of the kind mentioned in paragraphs (a) and (b) and, in place of initiating such proceedings, accepted or undertook to accept a specified sum of money in settlement of any claim by the Revenue Commissioners in respect of any specified liability of the person under any of the Acts for-

(i)   payment of any tax,

[(ii)   except in the case of tax due by virtue of paragraphs (g) and (h) of the definition of 'the Acts', payment of interest on that tax, and

(iii)   a fine or other monetary penalty in respect of that tax including penalties in respect of the failure to deliver any return, statement, declaration, list or other document in connection with the tax, or][134]

[(d)   in whose case the Revenue Commissioners, having initiated proceedings for the recovery of any fine or penalty of the kind mentioned in paragraph (a) and (b), and whether or not a fine or penalty of the kind mentioned in those paragraphs has been imposed **[or determined]**[111] by a court, accepted or undertook to accept, in that relevant period, a specified sum of money in settlement of any claim by the Revenue Commissioners in respect of any specified liability of the person under any of the Acts for–

(i) payment of any tax,

[(ii) except in the case of tax due by virtue of paragraphs (g) and (h) of the definition of 'the Acts', payment of interest on that tax, and

(iii) a fine or other monetary penalty in respect of that tax including penalties in respect of the failure to deliver any return, statement, declaration, list or other document in connection with the tax.][135]][136]

[(2A) For the purposes of subsection (2), the reference to a specified sum in paragraphs (c) and (d) of that subsection includes a reference to a sum which is the full amount of the claim by the Revenue Commissioners in respect of the specified liability referred to in those paragraphs. Where the Revenue Commissioners accept or undertake to accept such a sum, being the full amount of their claim, then –

(a) they shall be deemed to have done so pursuant to an agreement, made with the person referred to in paragraph (c), whereby for the recovery of any fine or penalty of the kind mentioned in paragraphs (a) and (b) of subsection (2), and

(b) that agreement shall be deemed to have been made in the relevant period in which the Revenue Commissioners accepted or undertook to accept that full amount.][95]

(3) Notwithstanding any obligation as to secrecy imposed on them by the Acts or the Official Secrets Act, 1963-

(a) the Revenue Commissioners shall, before the expiration of 3 months from the end of each relevant period, cause each such list referred to in subsection (2) in relation to that period to be published in Iris Oifigiúil, and

[(b) the Revenue Commissioners may, at any time after each such list referred to in subsection (2) has been published as provided for in paragraph (a), cause any such list to be publicised or reproduced, or both, in whole or in part, in such manner, form or format as they consider appropriate.][137]

(4) [Paragraph (c) and (d)][138] of subsection (2) shall not apply in relation to a person in whose case-

[(a)   the **Revenue Commissioners are satisfied that, before any investigation or inquiry had been started by them or by any of their officers into any matter occasioning a liability referred to in those paragraphs, the person had voluntarily furnished to them a qualifying disclosure (within the meaning of section 1077E, section 27A of the Value-Added Tax Act 1972 or section 134A of the Stamp Duties Consolidation Act 1999, as the case may be) in relation to and full particulars of that matter,]**[95]

(b)   section 72 of the Finance Act, 1988, or section 3 of the Waiver of Certain Tax, Interest and Penalties Act, 1993, [applied,][139]

(c)   the specified sum referred to in [paragraph (c) or (d), as the case may be,][140] of subsection (2) does not exceed [€30,000][141], or][139]

[(d)   the amount of fine or other penalty included in the specified sum referred to in paragraph (c) or (d), as the case may be, of subsection (2) does not exceed 15 per cent of the amount of tax included in that specified sum.][142]

[(4A) (a)   In this subsection-

'**the consumer price index number**' means the All Items Consumer Price Index Number compiled by the Central Statistics Office;

'**the consumer price index number relevant to a year**' means the consumer price index number at the mid-December before the commencement of that year expressed on the basis that the consumer price index at mid-December 2001 was 100;

'**the Minister**' means the Minister for Finance.

(b)   The Minister shall, in the year 2010 and in every fifth year thereafter, by order provide, in accordance with paragraph (c), an amount in lieu of the amount referred to in subsection (4)(c), or where such an order has been made previously, in lieu of the amount specified in the last order so made.

(c)   For the purposes of paragraph (b) the amount referred to in subsection (4)(c) or in the last previous order made under the said paragraph (b), as the case may be, shall be adjusted by-

(i)   multiplying that amount by the consumer price index number relevant to the year in which the adjustment is made and dividing the product by the consumer price index number relevant to the

year in which the amount was previously provided for, and

(ii)   rounding the resulting amount up to the next €1,000.

(d)   An order made under this subsection shall specify that the amount provided for by the order-

(i)   takes effect from a specified date, being 1 January in the year in which the order is made, and

(ii)   does not apply to any case in which the specified liability referred to in paragraphs (c) and (d) of subsection (2) includes tax, the liability in respect of which arose before, or which relates to periods which commenced before, that specified date.][143]

[(4B)   Paragraphs (a) and (b) of subsection (2) shall not apply in relation to a person in whose case—

(a)   the amount of a penalty determined by a court does not exceed 15 per cent of, as appropriate—

(i)   the amount of the difference referred to in subsection (11) or (12), as the case may be, of section 1077E,

(ii)   the amount of the difference referred to in subsection (11) or (12), as the case may be, of section 27A of the Value-Added Tax Act 1972, or

(iii)   the amount of the difference referred to in subsection (7), (8) or (9), as the case may be, of section 134A of the Stamp Duties Consolidation Act 1999,

(b)   the aggregate of the—

(i)   the tax due in respect of which the penalty is computed,

(ii)   except in the case of tax due by virtue of paragraphs (g) and (h) of the definition of 'the Acts', interest on that tax, and

(iii)   the penalty determined by a court, does not exceed €30,000, or

(c)   there has been a qualifying disclosure.][113]

(5)   Any list referred to in subsection (2) shall specify in respect of each person named in the list such particulars as the Revenue Commissioners think fit-

(a)   of the matter occasioning the fine or penalty of the kind referred to in subsection (2) imposed [or determined][113]

on the person or, as the case may be, the liability of that kind to which the person was subject, and

(b)   of any interest, fine or other monetary penalty, and of any other penalty or sanction, to which that person was liable, or which was imposed **[or determined]**[113] on that person by a court, and which was occasioned by the matter referred to in paragraph (a).

[(5A)   Without prejudice to the generality of paragraph (a) of subsection (5), such particulars as are referred to in that paragraph may include-

(a)   in a case to which paragraph (a) or (b) of subsection (2) applies, a description, in such summary form as the Revenue Commissioners may think fit, of the act, omission or offence (which may also include the circumstances in which the act or omission arose or the offence was committed) in respect of which the fine or penalty referred to in those paragraphs was imposed **[or determined]**[113], and

(b)   in a case to which paragraph (c) or (d) of subsection (2) applies, a description, in such summary form as the Revenue Commissioners may think fit, of the matter occasioning the specified liability (which may also include the circumstances in which that liability arose) in respect of which the Revenue Commissioners accepted, or undertook to accept, a settlement, in accordance with those paragraphs.][144]

PART 48

Miscellaneous and supplemental

Disclosure of information to Ombudsman

1093. Any obligation to maintain secrecy or other restriction on the disclosure or production of information (including documents) obtained by or furnished to the Revenue Commissioners, or any person on their behalf, for taxation purposes, shall not apply to the disclosure or production of information (including documents) to the Ombudsman for the purposes of an examination or investigation by the Ombudsman under the Ombudsman Act, 1980, of any action (within the meaning of that Act) taken by or on behalf of the Revenue Commissioners, being such an action taken in the performance of administrative functions in respect of any tax or duty under the care and management of the Revenue Commissioners.

Tax clearance certificates in relation to certain licences

1094. (1)   In this section-

"**the Acts**" means-

(a)   the Tax Acts,

(b)   the Capital Gains Tax Acts, and

(c)   the Value-Added Tax Act, 1972, and the enactments amending or extending that Act,

and any instruments made thereunder;

"**beneficial holder of a licence**" means the person who conducts the activities under the licence and, in relation to a licence issued under the Auctioneers and House Agents Act, 1947, includes the authorised individual referred to in section 8(4), or the nominated individual referred to in section 9(1), of that Act;

"**licence**" [means a licence, permit or authorisation][145], as the case may be, of the kind referred to in-

(a)   the proviso (inserted by section 156 of the Finance Act, 1992) to section 49(1) of the Finance (1909-1910) Act, 1910,

(b)   the further proviso (inserted by section 79(1) of the Finance Act, 1993) to section 49(1) of the Finance (1909-1910) Act, 1910,

(c)   the proviso (inserted by section 79(2) of the Finance Act, 1993) to section 7(3) of the Betting Act, 1931,

(d)   the proviso (inserted by section 79(3) of the Finance Act, 1993) to section 19 of the Gaming and Lotteries Act, 1956,

(e)   the proviso (inserted by section 79(4)(a) of the Finance Act, 1993) to subsection (1) of section 8 of the Auctioneers and House Agents Act, 1947,

(f)   the proviso (inserted by section 79(4)(b) of the Finance Act, 1993) to subsection (1) of section 9 of the Auctioneers and House Agents Act, 1947 (an auction permit under that section being deemed for the purposes of this section to be a licence),

(g)   the proviso (inserted by section 79(4)(c) of the Finance Act, 1993) to subsection (1) of section 10 of the Auctioneers and House Agents Act, 1947,

[(h)   section 101 of the Finance Act, 1999[,]][145][146]

(j)   section 93 of the Consumer Credit Act, 1995[,][145]

[(k)   subsection (2A) (inserted by section 106 of the Finance Act, 2000) of section 62 of the National Cultural Institutions Act, 1997[,]][145][147] [(l)   subsection (1A) (inserted by section 172 of the Finance Act, 2001) of section 2 of the Intoxicating Liquor (National Concert Hall) Act, 1983[,]¹⁴⁵]¹⁴⁸

[(m)   subsection (3) (inserted by the Finance Act, 2002) of section 122 of the Finance Act, 1992, and

(n)   subsection (1A) (inserted by the Finance Act, 2002) of the Finance (1909-10) Act, 1910;]¹⁴⁹

['market value', in relation to any property, means the price which such property might reasonably be expected to fetch on a sale in the open market on the date on which the property is to be valued;]¹⁵⁰

"specified date" means the date of commencement of a licence sought to be granted under any of the provisions referred to in paragraphs [paragraphs (a) to (n)]¹⁴⁵ of the definition of "licence" as specified for the purposes of a tax clearance certificate under subsection (2);

"tax clearance certificate" shall be construed in accordance with subsection (2).

(2)   Subject to subsection (3), the Collector-General shall, on an application to him or her by the person who will be the beneficial holder of a licence due to commence on a specified date, issue a certificate (in this section referred to as a "tax clearance certificate") for the purposes of the grant of a licence if-

(a)   that person and, in respect of the period of that person's membership, any partnership of which that person is or was a partner,

(b)   in a case where that person is a partnership, each partner,

(c)   in a case where that person is a company, each person who is either the beneficial owner of, or able directly or indirectly to control, more than 50 per cent of the ordinary share capital of the company,

has or have complied with all the obligations imposed on that person or on them by the Acts in relation to-

(i)   the payment or remittance of the taxes, interest and penalties required to be paid or remitted under the Acts, and

(ii)   the delivery of returns.

(3)   Subject to subsection (4), where a person (in this section referred to as "the first-mentioned person") will be the beneficial holder of a licence due to commence on a specified date and another person (in this section referred to as "the second-mentioned person") was the beneficial holder of the licence at any time during the year ending on that date, and-

(a)   the second-mentioned person is a company connected (within the meaning of section 10 as it applies for the purposes of the Tax Acts) with the first-mentioned person or would have been such a company but for the fact that the company has been wound up or dissolved without being wound up,

(b)   the second-mentioned person is a company and the first-mentioned person is a partnership in which-

(i)   a partner is or was able, or

(ii)   where more than one partner is a shareholder, those partners together are or were able,

directly or indirectly, whether with or without a connected person or connected persons (within the meaning of section 10 as it applies for the purposes of the Tax Acts), to control more than 50 per cent of the ordinary share capital of the company, or

(c)   the second-mentioned person is a partnership and the first-mentioned person is a company in which-

(i)   a partner is or was able, or

(ii)   where more than one partner is a shareholder, those partners together are or were able,

directly or indirectly, whether with or without a connected person or connected persons (within the meaning of section 10 as it applies for the purposes of the Tax Acts), to control more than 50 per cent of the ordinary share capital of the company,

then, a tax clearance certificate shall not be issued by the Collector-General under subsection (2) unless, in relation to the activities conducted under the licence, the second-mentioned person has complied with the second-mentioned person's obligations under the Acts as specified in subsection (2).

[(3A)   Where-

(a)   the first-mentioned person will be the beneficial holder of a licence due to commence on a specified date on foot of a certificate granted or to be granted under section 2(1) (as amended by section 23 of the Intoxicating Liquor Act, 1960) of the Licensing (Ireland) Act, 1902,

(b)   the second-mentioned person was the beneficial holder of the last licence issued prior to the specified date in respect of the premises for which the certificate referred to in paragraph (a) was granted, and

(c)   the acquisition of the premises by the said first-mentioned person was for a consideration of less than market value at the date of such acquisition, then, subsection (3) shall apply as if-

    (i)   the reference to the year ending on that date were a reference to 5 years ending on that date, and

    (ii)   the reference to the activities conducted under the licence was a reference to the activities conducted by the second-mentioned person under the last licence held by the said person prior to the specified date.][151]

(4)   Subsection (3) shall not apply to a transfer of a licence effected before the 24th day of April, 1992, or to such transfer effected after that date where a contract for the sale or lease of the premises to which the licence relates was signed before that date.

[(5)   An application for a tax clearance certificate under this section shall be made to the Collector-General in a form prescribed by the Revenue Commissioners or in such other manner as the Revenue Commissioners may allow.][152]

(6)   Where an application for a tax clearance certificate under this section is refused by the Collector-General, he or she shall as soon as is practicable communicate in writing such refusal and the grounds for such refusal to the person concerned.

(7)   (a)   Where an application under this section to the Collector-General for a tax clearance certificate is refused, the person aggrieved by the refusal may, by notice in writing given to the Collector-General within 30 days of the refusal, apply to have such person's application heard and determined by the Appeal Commissioners; but no right of appeal shall exist by virtue of this section in relation to any amount of tax or interest due under the Acts.

    (b)   A notice under paragraph (a) shall be valid only if-

        (i)   that notice specifies-

            (I)   the matter or matters with which the person is aggrieved, and

            (II)   the grounds in detail of the person's appeal as respects each such matter,

        and

        (ii)   any amount under the Acts which is due to be remitted or paid, and which is not in dispute, is duly remitted or paid.

(c)   The Appeal Commissioners shall hear and determine an appeal made to them under this subsection as if it were an appeal against an assessment to income tax and, subject to paragraph (d), the provisions of the Income Tax Acts relating to such an appeal (including the provisions relating to the rehearing of an appeal and to the statement of a case for the opinion of the High Court on a point of law) shall apply accordingly with any necessary modifications.

(d)   On the hearing of an appeal made under this subsection, the Appeal Commissioners shall have regard to all matters to which the Collector-General is required to have regard under this section.

[(8)   A tax clearance certificate to be issued by the Collector-General under this section may–

(a)   be issued in electronic format, and

(b)   with the agreement in writing of the applicant, be published in a secure electronic medium and be accessed by persons authorised by the applicant to do so.

(9)   A tax clearance certificate shall be valid for the period specified in the certificate.][153]

Tax clearance certificates: general scheme

[**1095.** (1)   In this section -

'**the Acts'** means–

(a)   the Tax Acts,

(b)   the Capital Gains Tax Acts, and

(c)   the Value-Added Tax Act, 1972, and the enactments amending or extending that Act,

and any instruments made thereunder;

'**licence'** has the same meaning as in section 1094;

'**tax clearance certificate'** shall be construed in accordance with subsection (3).

(2)   The provisions of this section shall apply in relation to every application by a person to the Collector-General for a tax clearance certificate other than an application for such a certificate made–

(a)   in relation to a licence, or

(b)   pursuant to the requirements of–

(i)   section 847A (inserted by the Finance Act, 2002),

(ii)   the Standards in Public Office Act, 2001, or

           (iii)   Regulation 6 of the Criminal Justice (Legal Aid) (Tax Clearance Certificate) Regulations 1999 (S.I. No. 135 of 1999).

(3)   Subject to this section, where a person who is in compliance with the obligations imposed on the person by the Acts in relation to–

      (a)   the payment or remittance of any taxes, interest or penalties required to be paid or remitted under the Acts, and

      (b)   the delivery of any returns to be made under the Acts,

applies to the Collector-General in that behalf the Collector-General shall issue to the person a certificate (in this section referred to as a '**tax clearance certificate**') stating that the person is in compliance with those obligations.

(4)   A tax clearance certificate shall not be issued to a person unless–

      (a)   that person and, in respect of the period of that person's membership, any partnership of which that person is or was a partner,

      (b)   in a case where that person is a partnership, each partner, and

      (c)   in a case where that person is a company, each person who is either the beneficial owner of, or able directly or indirectly to control, more than 50 per cent of the ordinary share capital of the company,

is in compliance with the obligations imposed on the person and each other person (including any partnership) by the Acts in relation to the matters specified in paragraphs (a) and (b) of subsection (3).

(5)   Where a person who applies for a tax clearance certificate in accordance with subsection (3) (in this section referred to as '**the first-mentioned person**') carries on a business activity which was previously carried on by, or was previously carried on as part of a business activity by, another person (in this section referred to as '**the second-mentioned person**') and–

      (a)   the second-mentioned person is a company connected (within the meaning of section 10 as it applies for the purposes of the Tax Acts) with the first-mentioned person or would have been such a company but for the fact that the company has been wound up or dissolved without being wound up,

      (b)   the second-mentioned person is a company and the first-mentioned person is a partnership in which–

(i)   a partner is or was able, or

(ii)   where more than one partner is a share-holder, those partners together are or were able,

directly or indirectly, whether with or without a connected person or connected persons (within the meaning of section 10 as it applies for the purposes of the Tax Acts), to control more than 50 per cent of the ordinary share capital of the company, or

(c)   the second-mentioned person is a partnership and the first-mentioned person is a company in which–

(i)   a partner is or was able, or

(ii)   where more than one partner is a share-holder, those partners together are or were able,

directly or indirectly, whether with or without a connected person or connected persons (within the meaning of section 10 as it applies for the purposes of the Tax Acts), to control more than 50 per cent of the ordinary share capital of the company,

then, a tax clearance certificate shall not be issued by the Collector-General under subsection (3) to the first-mentioned person unless, in relation to that business activity, the second-mentioned person is in compliance with the obligations imposed on that person by the Acts in relation to the matters specified in paragraphs (a) and (b) of subsection (3).

(6)   Subsections (5) to (9) of section 1094 shall apply to an application for a tax clearance certificate under this section as they apply to an application for a tax clearance certificate under that section.][154]

Amendments
1   Inserted by s30(a), FA00.
2   Inserted by s43(a), FA01.
3   Deleted by s44(a)(i), FA05.
4   Inserted by s44(a), FA05.
5   Substituted by s59, FA00.
6   Inserted by s38, FA07.
7   Inserted by s47(1)(a), FA05.
8   Deleted by s33, F(No. 2)A 2008.
9   Substituted by s35 and Sch. 2, FA07.
10 Substituted by s33, F(No. 2)A 2008.
11 Inserted by s33, F(No. 2)A 2008.
12 s172A inserted by s27(a), FA99.
13 Substituted by s126(a)(i), FA06.
14 Substituted by Sch 3, Capital Acquisitions Tax Consolidation Act 2003.
15 Inserted by s126(a)(ii), FA06.
16 Inserted by s140, FA08.
17 Substituted by s140, FA08.
18 Inserted by s95, F(No. 2)A 2008.
19 s811A inserted by s126(b), FA06.

20 Substituted by s35(1)(a), FA07.

21 Substituted by s24(1)(c)(i), FA05.

22 Inserted by s24(1)(c)(ii), FA05.

23 Inserted by s127 & Sch2(1)(s), FA06.

24 Substituted by s121, FA07.

25 Substituted by s17(a), FA03. Ss 865 and 865A have only been included as they form part of the general package of measures regarding repayments and interest on repayments covering direct and indirect taxes.

26 Substituted by s98 and Sch 5, F(No. 2)A 2008, (previously €1,265).

27 Substituted by s232(a), FA01.

28 Substituted by s92(b), F(No. 2)A 2008.

29 Replaced by s98 and Sch 5, F(No. 2)A 2008, (previously €1,900).

30 s900 substituted by s207(a), FA99.

31 Substituted by s92(c), F(No. 2)A 2008.

32 s901 substituted by s207(b), FA99.

33 Inserted by s132(a), FA02.

34 Substituted by s92(d), F(No. 2)A 2008.

35 s902 substituted by s207(c), FA99.

36 Substituted by s92(e), F(No. 2)A 2008.

37 Inserted by s132(b) FA02.

38 s902A inserted by s207(d), FA99.

39 Substituted by s132(d) FA02.

40 Substituted by s92(f), F(No. 2)A 2008.

41 s905(2)(d), deleted by s209(f)(i), FA99.

42 Substituted by s124, FA07.

43 Deleted by s124, FA07.

44 s905(2A) inserted by s207(f)(ii), FA99.

45 Substituted by s92(g), F(No. 2)A 2008.

46 Substituted by s68(c), FA00.

47 Replaced by s240 & Sch 5, FA01

€ 10	previously	£ 10
€ 25	previously	£ 20
€ 60	previously	£ 50
€ 950	previously	£ 750
€ 1,265	previously	£ 1,000
€ 2,535	previously	£ 2,000
€ 6,345	previously	£ 5,000
€ 12,700	previously	£ 10,000
€ 19,045	previously	£ 15,000

48 s906A inserted by s207(g), FA99.

49 Inserted by s132(e), FA02.

50 s907 substituted by s207(h), FA99.

51 Inserted by s132(f), FA02.

52 s908 substituted by s207(i), FA99.

53 Inserted by s132(g)(i)(I), FA02.

54 Substituted by s92(h), F(No. 2)A 2008.

55 Substituted by s132(g), FA02.

56 Substituted by s88, FA04.

57 s908A inserted by s207(j), FA99.

58 Substituted by s92(i), F(No. 2)A 2008.

59 s908B inserted by s87, FA04.

60 Substituted by s138, FA08.

61 s908C, 908D inserted by s124(c), FA07.

62 Substituted by s208, FA99.

63 Inserted by s123(c), FA07.

64 Substituted by s144(2), FA05.

65 s912A inserted by s38(b), FA03.

66 Inserted by s134, FA08.

67 Substituted by s141 & Sch8(1)(q), FA08.

68 Substituted by s235(a)(i)(I), FA01.

69 Inserted by s22, FA05.
70 Substituted by s235(a)(i)(II), FA01.
71 Deleted by s235(a)(ii), FA01.
72 s917D inserted by s209, FA99.
73 s917E inserted by s209, FA99.
74 s917EA inserted by s164, FA03.
75 Substituted by s22, FA05.
76 Substituted by s235(b)(ii), FA01.
77 s917F inserted by s209, FA99.
78 Substituted by s235(c)(i), FA01.
79 Substituted by s235(c)(ii), FA01.
80 Substituted by s235(c)(iii), FA01.
81 s917G inserted by s209, FA99.
82 Substituted by s235(d), FA01.
83 s917H inserted by s209,FA99.
84 s917I deleted s235(e),FA01.
85 s917J inserted by s209, FA99.
86 Substituted by s235(f), FA01.
87 s917K inserted by s209, FA99.
88 s917L inserted by s209, FA99.
89 Substituted by s235(m), FA01.
90 s917M inserted by s209, FA99.
91 s917N inserted by s209, FA99.
92 Substituted by s97 and Schedule 4, F(No. 2)A 2008.
93 Substituted by s128 & Sch 4, FA07.
94 Substituted by s20, FA07.
95 Substituted by s98 and Sch 5, F(No. 2)A 2008, (previously €950).
96 Deleted by s147 and Sch 6(1)(o), FA05.
97 Inserted by s134(a), FA98.
98 Inserted by s20, FA07.
99 Deleted by s20, FA07.
100 Ss960A-960P inserted by s97 and Sch4(1)(b).
101 Substituted by s120, FA07.
102 Inserted by s2, F(No. 2)A 2008.
103 Inserted by s3, F(No. 2)A 2008.
104 Substituted by s92(j), F(No. 2)A 2008.
105 Substituted by s238, FA01.
106 S1006A repealed by s97 and Sch 4, F(No. 2)A 2008.
107 S1006B repealed by s97 and Sch 4, F(No. 2)A 2008.
108 Substituted by s130(c), FA02.
109 Substituted by s162(a), FA03.
110 Substituted by s162(b), FA03.
111 Inserted by s98 and Sch 5, F(No. 2)A 2008.
112 Substituted by s30(2), FA09.
113 Inserted by s98 and Sch 5, F(No. 2)A 2008.
114 Inserted by s142(a), FA05.
115 Inserted by s126, FA07.
116 Substituted by s142(b), FA05.
117 Substituted by s133(a), FA02.
118 Inserted by s211(a), FA99.
119 Inserted by s142(b)(iii), FA05.
120 Substituted by s138, FA08.
121 Substituted by FA01, Sch 5, Part 1.
122 Inserted by s211(c), FA99.
123 Inserted by s92(k), F(No. 2)A 2008.
124 Inserted by s133(b), FA02.

125 Substituted by s142(c), FA05.

126 Inserted by s98 and Sch 5, F(No. 2)A 2008.

127 Substituted by s98 and Sch 5, F(No. 2)A 2008.

128 Inserted by s99 and Sch 6, F(No. 2)A 2008.

129 S1078A,1078B and 1078C inserted by s161, FA03.

130 Substituted by s126(1)(a)(i), FA02.

131 Inserted by s126(1)(a)(i), FA02.

132 Substituted by s126(1)(a)(ii), FA02.

133 Deleted by s162, FA00.

134 Substituted by s126(1)(b)(i), FA02.

135 Substituted by s126(1)(b)(ii), FA02.

136 Inserted by s162(a)(ii), FA00.

137 Substituted by s126(1)(c), FA02.

138 Inserted by s162(c)(i), FA00.

139 Substituted by s126(1)(d), FA02.

140 Inserted by s162(c)(ii), FA00.

141 Substituted by s143(1)(a), FA05.

142 Inserted by s126(1)(d), FA02.

143 Inserted by s143(1)(b), FA05.

144 Inserted by s162(d), FA00.

145 Substituted by s127(a)(i), FA02.

146 Substituted by s212(a)(i), FA99.

147 Inserted by s163, FA00.

148 Inserted by s234, FA01.

149 Inserted by s127(a)(i), FA02.

150 Inserted by s212(a)(ii), FA99.

151 Inserted by s212(b), FA99.

152 Substituted by s127(a)(ii), FA02.

153 Inserted by s127(a)(iii), FA02.

154 s1095 replaced by s127(b), FA02.

Electronic Commerce Act, 2000

(Number 27 of 2000)

AN ACT TO PROVIDE FOR THE LEGAL RECOGNITION OF ELECTRONIC CONTRACTS, ELECTRONIC WRITING, ELECTRONIC SIGNATURES AND ORIGINAL INFORMATION IN ELECTRONIC FORM IN RELATION TO COMMERCIAL AND NON-COMMERCIAL TRANSACTIONS AND DEALINGS AND OTHER MATTERS, THE ADMISSIBILITY OF EVIDENCE IN RELATION TO SUCH MATTERS, THE ACCREDITATION, SUPERVISION AND LIABILITY OF CERTIFICATION SERVICE PROVIDERS AND THE REGISTRATION OF DOMAIN NAMES, AND TO PROVIDE FOR RELATED MATTERS.

[10th July, 2000]

BE IT ENACTED BY THE OIREACHTAS AS FOLLOWS:

PART I

PRELIMINARY AND GENERAL

Short title and commencement

1. (1) This Act may be cited as the Electronic Commerce Act, 2000.

    (2) This Act shall come into operation on such day or days as the Minister, after consultation with the Minister for Enterprise, Trade and Employment, may appoint by order or orders, either generally or with reference to any particular purpose or provision, and different days may be so appointed for different purposes or different provisions.

Interpretation

2. (1) In this Act, unless the context otherwise requires—

    "accreditation" means an accreditation under section 29(2);

    "addressee", in relation to an electronic communication, means a person or public body intended by the originator to receive the electronic communication, but does not include a person or public body acting as a service provider in relation to the processing, receiving or storing of the electronic communication or the provision of other services in relation to it;

    "advanced electronic signature" means an electronic signature—

    (a) uniquely linked to the signatory,

    (b) capable of identifying the signatory,

    (c) created using means that are capable of being maintained by the signatory under his, her or its sole control, and

    (d) linked to the data to which it relates in such a manner that any subsequent change of the data is detectable;

"**certificate**" means an electronic attestation which links signature verification data to a person or public body, and confirms the identity of the person or public body;

"**certification service provider**" means a person or public body who issues certificates or provides other services related to electronic signatures;

"**Directive**" means the European Parliament and Council Directive 1999/93/EC of 13 December, 1999;

"**electronic**" includes electrical, digital, magnetic, optical, electromagnetic, biometric, photonic and any other form of related technology;

"**electronic communication**" means information communicated or intended to be communicated to a person or public body, other than its originator, that is generated, communicated, processed, sent, received, recorded, stored or displayed by electronic means or in electronic form, but does not include information communicated in the form of speech unless the speech is processed at its destination by an automatic voice recognition system;

"**electronic contract**" means a contract concluded wholly or partly by means of an electronic communication;

"**electronic signature**" means data in electronic form attached to, incorporated in or logically associated with other electronic data and which serves as a method of authenticating the purported originator, and includes an advanced electronic signature;

"**excluded law**" means a law referred to in section 10;

"**information**" includes data, all forms of writing and other text, images (including maps and cartographic material), sound, codes, computer programmes, software, databases and speech;

"**information system**" means a system for generating, communicating, processing, sending, receiving, recording, storing or displaying information by electronic means;

"**legal proceedings**" means civil or criminal proceedings, and includes proceedings before a court, tribunal, appellate body of competent jurisdiction or any other body or individual charged with determining legal rights or obligations;

"**Minister**" means the Minister for Public Enterprise;

"**originator**", in relation to an electronic communication, means the person or public body by whom or on whose behalf the electronic communication purports to have been sent or generated before storage, as the case may be, but does not include a person or public body acting as a service provider in relation to the generation, processing, sending or storing of that electronic communication or providing other services in relation to it;

"person" does not include a public body;

"prescribed" means prescribed by regulations made under section 3;

"public body" means–

(a)   a Minister of the Government or a Minister of State,

(b)   a body (including a Department of State but not including a non-government organisation) wholly or partly funded out of the Central Fund or out of moneys provided by the Oireachtas or moneys raised by local taxation or charges, or

(c)   a commission, tribunal, board or body established by an Act or by arrangement of the Government, a Minister of the Government or a Minister of State for a non-commercial public service or purpose;

"qualified certificate" means a certificate which meets the requirements set out in Annex I and is provided by a certification service provider who fulfils the requirements set out in Annex II;

"secure signature creation device" means a signature creation device which meets the requirements set out in Annex III;

"'signatory" means a person who, or public body which, holds a signature creation device and acts in the application of a signature by use of the device either on his, her or its own behalf or on behalf of a person or public body he, she or it represents;

"signature creation data" means unique data, such as codes, passwords, algorithms or private cryptographic keys, used by a signatory or other source of the data in generating an electronic signature;

"signature creation device" means a device, such as configured software or hardware used to generate signature creation data;

"signature verification data" means data, such as codes, passwords, algorithms or public cryptographic keys, used for the purposes of verifying an electronic signature;

"signature verification device" means a device, such as configured software or hardware used to generate signature verification data.

(2)   In the application of this Act, "writing", where used in any other Act or instrument under an Act (and whether or not qualified by reference to it being or being required to be under the hand of the writer or similar expression) shall be construed as including

electronic modes of representing or reproducing words in visible form, and cognate words shall be similarly construed.

(3)　　In this Act–

(a)　a reference to a section is a reference to a section of this Act, unless it is indicated that a reference to some other enactment is intended,

(b)　a reference to a subsection, paragraph or subparagraph is a reference to a subsection, paragraph or subparagraph of the provision in which the reference is made, unless it is indicated that a reference to some other provision is intended,

(c)　a reference to an enactment shall, except to the extent that the context otherwise requires, be construed as a reference to that enactment as amended by or under any other enactment, and

(d)　a reference to an Annex by number is a reference to the Annex so numbered to the Directive and included in the Schedule to this Act.

(4)　　Where in any legal proceedings the question of whether–

(a)　a body is a non-government organisation, or

(b)　a body, commission, tribunal or board is or was established by an Act or by arrangement of the Government, a Minister of the Government or a Minister of State for a non-commercial service or purpose,

is in issue then, for the purpose of establishing whether it is or is not a public body as defined in subsection (1), a document signed by the Minister, a Minister of the Government or a Minister of State declaring that–

(i)　he or she is the appropriate Minister for determining whether the body is or is not a non-government organisation, and that in fact it is or is not such an organisation, or

(ii)　he or she is the appropriate Minister for determining whether the body, commission, tribunal or board was or was not so established for a non-commercial service or purpose, and that in fact it was or was not so established,

is sufficient evidence of those facts, until the contrary is shown, and the Minister, Minister of the Government or Minister of State may make such a declaration.

Regulations

3.　(1)　The Minister may make regulations prescribing any matter or thing referred to in this Act as prescribed or to be prescribed, or in relation to any matter referred to in this Act as the subject of regulation.

(2)   Regulations under this section may contain such incidental, supplementary and consequential provisions as appear to the Minister to be necessary or expedient for the purposes of the regulations or for giving full effect to this Act.

Laying of orders and regulations before Houses of Oireachtas

4.   Every order (other than an order made under section 1(2)) or regulation made by the Minister under section 3 shall be laid before each House of the Oireachtas as soon as may be after it is made and, if a resolution annulling the order or regulation is passed by either such House within the next subsequent 21 days on which that House has sat after the order or regulation is laid before it, the order or regulation shall be annulled accordingly but without prejudice to the validity of anything previously done under it.

Expenses of Minister

5.   Expenses incurred by the Minister in the administration of this Act shall, to such extent as may be sanctioned by the Minister for Finance, be paid out of moneys provided by the Oireachtas.

Prosecution of offences

6.   (1)   Summary proceedings for offences under this Act or a regulation made under section 3 may be brought and prosecuted by the Minister or a person or public body prescribed by the Minister for that purpose.

(2)   Notwithstanding section 10(4) of the Petty Sessions (Ireland) Act, 1851, summary proceedings for an offence under this Act or a regulation made under section 3 may be commenced at any time within 12 months from the date on which evidence that, in the opinion of the person or public body by whom the proceedings are brought, is sufficient to justify the bringing of the proceedings, comes to that person's or public body's knowledge.

(3)   For the purpose of subsection (2), a document signed by or on behalf of the person or public body bringing the proceedings as to the date on which the evidence referred to in that subsection came to his, her or its knowledge is prima facie evidence thereof and in those or any other legal proceedings a document purporting to be issued for the purpose of this subsection and to be so signed is taken to be so signed and shall be admitted as evidence without further proof of the signature of the person or public body purporting to sign it.

Offences by bodies corporate

7.   Where an offence under this Act has been committed by a body corporate and is proved to have been committed with the consent or connivance of, or to be attributable to any neglect on the part of, a person being a director, shadow director (as defined in section 3(1) of the Companies Act, 1990), manager, secretary or other officer of the body corporate, or a person who was purporting to act in any such capacity, that person, as well as the body corporate, shall be guilty of an offence and be liable to be proceeded against and punished as if he or she were guilty of the first-mentioned offence.

Penalties

8.   A person or public body guilty of an offence under this Act for which no penalty other than by this section is provided shall be liable–

(a)   on summary conviction, to a fine not exceeding £1,500 or, at the discretion of the court, to imprisonment for a term not exceeding 12 months, or to both the fine and the imprisonment, or

(b)   on conviction on indictment, to a fine not exceeding £500,000 or, at the discretion of the court, to imprisonment for a term not exceeding 5 years, or to both the fine and the imprisonment.

PART 2

LEGAL RECOGNITION AND NON-DISCRIMINATION IN RESPECT OF ELECTRONIC SIGNATURES, ORIGINALS, CONTRACTS AND RELATED MATTERS

Legal Recognition of Electronic Communications and Information in Electronic Form

Electronic form not to affect legal validity or enforceability

9.   Information (including information incorporated by reference) shall not be denied legal effect, validity or enforceability solely on the grounds that it is wholly or partly in electronic form, whether as an electronic communication or otherwise.

Excluded laws

10.   (1)   Sections 12 to 23 are without prejudice to–

(a)   the law governing the creation, execution, amendment, variation or revocation of–

(i)   a will, codicil or any other testamentary instrument to which the Succession Act, 1965, applies,

(ii)   a trust, or

(iii)   an enduring power of attorney,

(b)   the law governing the manner in which an interest in real property (including a leasehold interest in such property) may be created, acquired, disposed of or registered, other than contracts (whether or not under seal) for the creation, acquisition or disposal of such interests,

(c)   the law governing the making of an affidavit or a statutory or sworn declaration, or requiring or permitting the use of one for any purpose, or

(d)   the rules, practices or procedures of a court or tribunal,

except to the extent that regulations under section 3 may from time to time prescribe.

(2)   Where the Minister is of the opinion that–

(a)   technology has advanced to such an extent, and access to it is so widely available, or

(b)   adequate procedures and practices have developed in public registration or other services, so as to warrant such action, or

(c)   the public interest so requires,

he or she may, after consultation with such Minister or Ministers as in the Minister's opinion has or have a sufficient interest or responsibility in relation to the matter, by regulations made under section 3, for the purpose of encouraging the efficient use of electronic communication facilities and services in commerce and the community generally while at the same time protecting the public interest, extend the application of this Act or a provision of this Act to or in relation to a matter specified in subsection (1) (including a particular aspect of such a matter) subject to such conditions as he or she thinks fit, and the Act as so extended shall apply accordingly.

(3)   Without prejudice to the generality of subsection (2), the regulations may apply to a particular area or subject, or for a particular time, in the nature of a trial of technology and procedures.

Certain laws not to be affected

11.   Nothing in this Act shall prejudice the operation of–

(a)   any law relating to the imposition, collection or recovery of taxation or other Government imposts, including fees, fines and penalties,

(b)   the Companies Act, 1990 (Uncertificated Securities) Regulations, 1996 (S.I. No. 68 of 1996) or any regulations made in substitution for those regulations,

(c)   the Criminal Evidence Act, 1992, or

    (d)   the Consumer Credit Act, 1995, or any regulations made thereunder and the European Communities (Unfair Terms in Consumer Contracts) Regulations, 1995 (S.I. No. 27 of 1995).

Writing

12.   (1)   If by law or otherwise a person or public body is required (whether the requirement is in the form of an obligation or consequences flow from the information not being in writing) or permitted to give information in writing (whether or not in a form prescribed by law), then, subject to subsection (2), the person or public body may give the information in electronic form, whether as an electronic communication or otherwise.

      (2)   Information may be given as provided in subsection (1) only–

          (a)   if at the time the information was given it was reasonable to expect that it would be readily accessible to the person or public body to whom it was directed, for subsequent reference,

          (b)   where the information is required or permitted to be given to a public body or to a person acting on behalf of a public body and the public body consents to the giving of the information in electronic form, whether as an electronic communication or otherwise, but requires–

              (i)   the information to be given in accordance with particular information technology and procedural requirements, or

              (ii)   that a particular action be taken by way of verifying the receipt of the information,

              if the public body's requirements have been met and those requirements have been made public and are objective, transparent, proportionate and non-discriminatory, and

          (c)   where the information is required or permitted to be given to a person who is neither a public body nor acting on behalf of a public body– if the person to whom the information is required or permitted to be given consents to the information being given in that form.

      (3)   Subsections (1) and (2) are without prejudice to any other law requiring or permitting information to be given–

          (a)   in accordance with particular information technology and procedural requirements,

          (b)   on a particular kind of data storage device, or

          (c)   by means of a particular kind of electronic communication.

(4)   This section applies to a requirement or permission to give information whether the word "give", "send", "forward", "deliver", "serve" or similar word or expression is used.

(5)   In this section, "give information" includes but is not limited to–

   (a)   make an application,

   (b)   make or lodge a claim,

   (c)   make or lodge a return,

   (d)   make a request,

   (e)   make an unsworn declaration,

   (f)   lodge or issue a certificate,

   (g)   make, vary or cancel an election,

   (h)   lodge an objection,

   (i)   give a statement of reasons,

   (j)   record and disseminate a court order,

   (k)   give, send or serve a notification.

Signatures

13.   (1)   If by law or otherwise the signature of a person or public body is required (whether the requirement is in the form of an obligation or consequences flow from there being no signature) or permitted, then, subject to subsection (2), an electronic signature may be used.

     (2)   An electronic signature may be used as provided in subsection (1) only–

        (a)   where the signature is required or permitted to be given to a public body or to a person acting on behalf of a public body and the public body consents to the use of an electronic signature but requires that it be in accordance with particular information technology and procedural requirements (including that it be an advanced electronic signature, that it be based on a qualified certificate, that it be issued by an accredited certification service provider or that it be created by a secure signature creation device) – if the public body's requirements have been met and those requirements have been made public and are objective, transparent, proportionate and non-discriminatory, and

        (b)   where the signature is required or permitted to be given to a person who is neither a public body nor acting on behalf of a public body – if the person to whom the signature is required or permitted to be given consents to the use of an electronic signature.

(3)   Subsections (1) and (2) are without prejudice to any other provision of this Act or law requiring or permitting an electronic communication to contain an electronic signature, an advanced electronic signature, an electronic signature based on a qualified certificate, an electronic signature created by a secure signature creation device or other technological requirements relating to an electronic signature.

Signatures required to be witnessed

14. (1)   If by law or otherwise a signature to a document is required to be witnessed (whether the requirement is in the form of an obligation or consequences flow from the signature not being witnessed) that requirement is taken to have been met if–

(a)   the signature to be witnessed is an advanced electronic signature, based on a qualified certificate, of the person or public body by whom the document is required to be signed,

(b)   the document contains an indication that the signature of that person or public body is required to be witnessed, and

(c)   the signature of the person purporting to witness the signature to be witnessed is an advanced electronic signature, based on a qualified certificate.

(2)   An advanced electronic signature based on a qualified certificate may be used as provided in subsection (1) only–

(a)   where the signature required or permitted to be witnessed is on a document to be given to a public body or to a person acting on behalf of a public body and the public body consents to the use of an electronic signature of both the person attesting the document and witnessing the signature but requires that the document and signatures be in accordance with particular information technology and procedural requirements (including that a qualified certificate on which the signature or signatures are based be issued by an accredited certification service provider)— if the public body's requirements are met and those requirements have been made public and are objective, transparent, proportionate and non-discriminatory, and

(b)   where the document on or in respect of which the signature is to be witnessed is required or permitted to be given to a person who is neither a public body nor acting on behalf of a public body — if the person to whom it is required or permitted to be given consents to the use of an advanced electronic signature based on a qualified certificate for that purpose.

Consumer law to apply

15.   All electronic contracts within the State shall be subject to all existing consumer law and the role of the Director of Consumer Affairs in such legislation shall apply equally to consumer transactions, whether conducted electronically or non-electronically.

Documents under seal

16.   (1)   If by law or otherwise a seal is required to be affixed to a document (whether the requirement is in the form of an obligation or consequences flow from a seal not being affixed) then, subject to subsection (2), that requirement is taken to have been met if the document indicates that it is required to be under seal and it includes an advanced electronic signature, based on a qualified certificate, of the person or public body by whom it is required to be sealed.

(2)   An advanced electronic signature based on a qualified certificate may be used as provided in subsection (1) only–

(a)   where the document to be under seal is required or permitted to be given to a public body or to a person acting on behalf of a public body and the public body consents to the use of an electronic signature but requires that it be in accordance with particular information technology and procedural requirements (including that a qualified certificate on which it is based be issued by an accredited certification service provider)– if the public body's requirements have been met and those requirements have been made public and are objective, transparent, proportionate and non-discriminatory, and

(b)   where the document to be under seal is required or permitted to be given to a person who is neither a public body nor acting on behalf of a public body– if the person to whom it is required or permitted to be given consents to the use of an advanced electronic signature based on a qualified certificate.

Electronic originals

17.   (1)   If by law or otherwise a person or public body is required (whether the requirement is in the form of an obligation or consequences flow from the information not being presented or retained in its original form) or permitted to present or retain information in its original form, then, subject to subsection (2), the information may be presented or retained, as the case may be, in electronic form, whether as an electronic communication or otherwise.

(2)   Information may be presented or retained as provided in subsection (1) only–

(a)   if there exists a reliable assurance as to the integrity of the information from the time when it was first generated in its final form, whether as an electronic communication or otherwise,

(b)   where it is required or permitted that the information be presented– if the information is capable of being displayed in intelligible form to a person or public body to whom it is to be presented,

(c)   if, at the time the information was generated in its final form, it was reasonable to expect that it would be readily accessible so as to be useable for subsequent reference,

(d)   where the information is required or permitted to be presented to or retained for a public body or for a person acting on behalf of a public body, and the public body consents to the information being presented or retained in electronic form, whether as an electronic communication or otherwise, but requires that it be presented or retained in accordance with particular information technology and procedural requirements– if the public body's requirements have been met and those requirements have been made public and are objective, transparent, proportionate and non-discriminatory, and

(e)   where the information is required or permitted to be presented to or retained for a person who is neither a public body nor acting on behalf of a public body– if the person to whom the information is required or permitted to be presented or for whom it is required or permitted to be retained consents to the information being presented or retained in that form.

(3)   Subsections (1) and (2) are without prejudice to any other law requiring or permitting information to be presented or retained–

(a)   in accordance with particular information technology and procedural requirements,

(b)   on a particular kind of data storage device, or

(c)   by means of a particular kind of electronic communication.

(4)   For the purposes of subsections (1) and (2)–

(a)   the criteria for assessing integrity is whether the information has remained complete and unaltered, apart from the addition of any endorsement or change which arises in the normal course of generating, communicating, processing, sending, receiving, recording, storing or displaying, and

(b)   the standard of reliability shall be assessed in the light of the purpose for which and the circumstances in which the information was generated.

Retention and production

18.   (1)   If by law or otherwise a person or public body is required (whether the requirement is in the form of an obligation or consequences flow from the information not being retained or produced in its original form) or permitted to retain for a particular period or produce a document that is in the form of paper or other material on which information may be recorded in written form, then, subject to subsection (2), the person or public body may retain throughout the relevant period or, as the case may be, produce, the document in electronic form, whether as an electronic communication or otherwise.

(2)   A document may be retained throughout the period, or produced, by the person or public body as provided in subsection (1) only–

(a)   if there exists a reliable assurance as to the integrity of the information from the time when it was first generated in its final form as an electronic communication,

(b)   in the case of a document to be produced– if the information is capable of being displayed in intelligible form to the person or public body to whom it is to be produced,

(c)   in the case of a document to be retained – if, at the time of the generation of the final electronic form of the document, it was reasonable to expect that the information contained in the electronic form of the document would be readily accessible so as to be useable for subsequent reference,

(d)   where the document is required or permitted to be retained for or produced to a public body or for or to a person acting on behalf of a public body, and the public body consents to the document being retained or produced in electronic form, whether as an electronic communication or otherwise, but requires that the electronic form of the document be retained or produced in accordance with particular information technology and procedural requirements— if the public body's requirements have been met and those requirements have been made public and are objective, transparent, proportionate and nondiscriminatory, and

(e)   where the document is required or permitted to be retained for or produced to a person who is neither a public body nor acting on behalf of a public body— if the person for or to whom the document is required or permitted to be retained or produced consents to it being retained or produced in that form.

(3)   Subsections (1) and (2) are without prejudice to any other law requiring or permitting documents in the form of paper or other material to be retained or produced–

(a)   in accordance with particular information technology and procedural requirements,

(b)   on a particular kind of data storage device, or

(c)   by means of a particular kind of electronic communication.

(4)   For the purposes of subsections (1) and (2)–

(a)   the criteria for assessing integrity is whether the information has remained complete and unaltered, apart from the addition of any endorsement or change which arises in the normal course of generating, communicating, processing, sending, receiving, recording, storing or displaying, and

(b)   the standard of reliability shall be assessed in the light of the purpose for which the information was generated and the circumstances in which it was generated.

Contracts

19.   (1)   An electronic contract shall not be denied legal effect, validity or enforceability solely on the grounds that it is wholly or partly in electronic form, or has been concluded wholly or partly by way of an electronic communication.

(2)   In the formation of a contract, an offer, acceptance of an offer or any related communication (including any subsequent amendment, cancellation or revocation of the offer or acceptance of the offer) may, unless otherwise agreed by the parties, be communicated by means of an electronic communication.

Acknowledgement of receipt of electronic commu nications

20.   (1)   Subject to any other law, where the originator of an electronic communication indicates that receipt of the electronic communication is required to be acknowledged but does not indicate a particular form or method of acknowledgement,

then, unless the originator and the addressee of the electronic communication agree otherwise, the acknowledgement shall be given by way of an electronic communication or any other communication (including any conduct of the addressee) sufficient to indicate to the originator that the electronic communication has been received.

(2)   Where the originator of an electronic communication indicates that receipt of the electronic communication is required to be acknowledged, the electronic communication, in relation to the establishing of legal rights and obligations between parties, shall, until the acknowledgement is received by the originator and unless the parties otherwise agree, be treated as if it had never been sent.

(3)   Where the originator of an electronic communication has indicated that receipt of the electronic communication is required to be acknowledged but has not stated that the electronic communication is conditional on the receipt of acknowledgement and the acknowledgement has not been received by the originator within the time specified or agreed or, if no time has been specified or agreed, within a reasonable time, then the electronic communication, in relation to the establishing of legal rights and obligations between parties, shall, unless the parties otherwise agree, be treated as if it had never been sent.

Time and place of dispatch and receipt of electronic communications

21. (1)   Where an electronic communication enters an information system, or the first information system, outside the control of the originator, then, unless otherwise agreed between the originator and the addressee, it is taken to have been sent when it enters such information system or first information system.

(2)   Where the addressee of an electronic communication has designated an information system for the purpose of receiving electronic communications, then, unless otherwise agreed between the originator and the addressee or the law otherwise provides, the electronic communication is taken to have been received when it enters that information system.

(3)   Where the addressee of an electronic communication has not designated an information system for the purpose of receiving electronic communications, then, unless otherwise agreed between the originator and the addressee, the electronic communication is taken to have been received when it comes to the attention of the addressee.

(4)   Subsections (1), (2) and (3) apply notwithstanding that the place where the relevant information system is located may be different from the place where the electronic communication is

taken to have been sent or received, as the case may be, under those subsections.

(5)   Unless otherwise agreed between the originator and the addressee of an electronic communication, the electronic communication is taken to have been sent from and received at, respectively, the place where the originator and the addressee have their places of business.

(6)   For the purposes of subsection (5), but subject to subsection (7)–

    (a)   if the originator or addressee has more than one place of business, the place of business is the place that has the closest relationship to the underlying transaction or, if there is no underlying transaction, the principal place of business, and

    (b)   if the originator or addressee does not have a place of business, the place of business is taken to be the place where he or she ordinarily resides.

(7)   If an electronic communication is or is in connection with a notification or other communication required or permitted by or under an Act to be sent or given to, or served on, a company at its registered office, the registered office is taken to be the place of business of the company in connection with that electronic communication for the purpose of subsection (5).

Admissibility

22.   In any legal proceedings, nothing in the application of the rules of evidence shall apply so as to deny the admissibility in evidence of–

    (a)   an electronic communication, an electronic form of a document, an electronic contract, or writing in electronic form–

        (i)   on the sole ground that it is an electronic communication, an electronic form of a document, an electronic contract, or writing in electronic form, or

        (ii)   if it is the best evidence that the person or public body adducing it could reasonably be expected to obtain, on the grounds that it is not in its original form, or

    (b)   an electronic signature–

        (i)   on the sole ground that the signature is in electronic form, or is not an advanced electronic signature, or is not based on a qualified certificate, or is not based on a qualified certificate issued by an accredited certification service provider, or is not created by a secure signature creation device, or

(ii)   if it is the best evidence that the person or public body adducing it could reasonably be expected to obtain, on the grounds that it is not in its original form.

Defamation law to apply

23.   All provisions of existing defamation law shall apply to all electronic communications within the State, including the retention of information electronically.

General

Electronic form not required

24.   Nothing in this Act shall be construed as—

(a)   requiring a person or public body to generate, communicate, produce, process, send, receive, record, retain, store or display any information, document or signature by or in electronic form, or

(b)   prohibiting a person or public body engaging in an electronic transaction from establishing reasonable requirements about the manner in which the person will accept electronic communications, electronic signatures or electronic forms of documents.

Prohibition of fraud and misuse of electronic signatures and signature creation devices

25.   person or public body who or which—

(a)   knowingly accesses, copies or otherwise obtains possession of, or recreates, the signature creation device of another person or a public body, without the authorisation of that other person or public body, for the purpose of creating or allowing, or causing another person or public body to create, an unauthorised electronic signature using the signature creation device,

(b)   knowingly alters, discloses or uses the signature creation device of another person or a public body, without the authorisation of that other person or public body or in excess of lawful authorisation, for the purpose of creating or allowing, or causing another person or public body to create, an unauthorised electronic signature using the signature creation device,

(c)   knowingly creates, publishes, alters or otherwise uses a certificate or an electronic signature for a fraudulent or other unlawful purpose,

(d)   knowingly misrepresents the person's or public body's identity or authorisation in requesting or accepting a certificate or in requesting suspension or revocation of a certificate,

(e)   knowingly accesses, alters, discloses or uses the signature creation device of a certification service provider used to issue certificates, without the authorisation of the certification service provider or in excess of lawful authorisation, for the purpose of creating, or allowing or causing another person or a public body to create, an unauthorised electronic signature using the signature creation device, or

(f)   knowingly publishes a certificate, or otherwise knowingly makes it available to anyone likely to rely on the certificate or on an electronic signature that is verifiable with reference to data such as codes, passwords, algorithms, public cryptographic keys or other data which are used for the purposes of verifying an electronic signature, listed in the certificate, if the person or public body knows that–

  (i)   the certification service provider listed in the certificate has not issued it,

  (ii)   the subscriber listed in the certificate has not accepted it, or

  (iii) the certificate has been revoked or suspended, unless its publication is for the purpose of verifying an electronic signature created before such revocation or suspension, or giving notice of revocation or suspension,

is guilty of an offence.

Activities partly outside the State

26.   The provisions of section 25 extend to activities that took place partly outside the State.

Investigative procedures

27.   (1)   Where, on the sworn information of an officer of the Minister or a member of the Garda Síochána not below the rank of Inspector, a judge of the District Court is satisfied that there are reasonable grounds for suspecting that evidence of or relating to an offence under this Act is to be found at a place specified in the information, the judge may issue a warrant for the search of that place and any persons found at that place.

       (2)   A warrant issued under this section shall authorise a named officer of the Minister or member of the Garda Síochána, alone or accompanied by such member or other members of the Garda Síochána and such other persons as may be necessary–

(a)　to enter, within 7 days from the date of the warrant, and if necessary by the use of reasonable force, the place named in the warrant,

(b)　to search the place and any person reasonably suspected of being connected with any activities of the place found thereon, and

(c)　to seize anything found there, or anything found in the possession of a person present there at the time of the search, which that officer or member reasonably believes to be evidence of or relating to an offence under this Act and, where the thing seized is or contains information or an electronic communication that cannot readily be accessed or put into intelligible form, to require the disclosure of the information or electronic communication in intelligible form.

(3)　An officer of the Minister or member of the Garda Síochána acting in accordance with a warrant issued under this section may require any person found at the place where the search is carried out to give the officer or member the person's name and address.

(4)　A person who or public body which–

(a)　obstructs or attempts to obstruct an officer of the Minister or member of the Garda Síochána acting in accordance with a warrant issued under subsection (1),

(b)　fails or refuses to comply with a requirement under this section, or

(c)　gives a name or address which is false or misleading, is guilty of a summary offence.

(5)　An officer of the Minister or member of the Garda Síochána may retain anything seized under subsection (2)(c) which he or she has reasonable grounds for believing to be evidence of an offence under this Act, for use as evidence in relation to proceedings in relation to any such offence, for such period as is reasonable or, if proceedings are commenced in which the thing is required to be used in evidence, until the conclusion of the proceedings.

(6)　In this section, "place" includes any dwelling, any building or part of a building and any vehicle, vessel or structure.

Confidentiality of deciphering data

28.　Nothing in this Act shall be construed as requiring the disclosure or enabling the seizure of unique data, such as codes, passwords, algorithms, private cryptographic keys, or other data, that may be necessary to render information or an electronic communication intelligible.

PART 3

CERTIFICATION SERVICES

Accreditation and supervision of certification service providers

29. (1)   A person or public body is not required to obtain the prior authority of any other person or public body to provide certification or other services relating to electronic signatures.

(2)   (a)   The Minister, after consultation with the Minister for Enterprise, Trade and Employment, may by regulations made under section 3 establish a scheme of voluntary accreditation of certification service providers for the purpose of the Directive and to enhance levels of certification service provision in the State, and may designate accreditation authorities and prescribe such matters relating to their designation as the Minister thinks appropriate for the purpose.

(b)   A person or public body who or which provides certification or other services in the State relating to electronic signatures ay apply as prescribed to the accreditation authority designated under paragraph (a) to participate in any scheme of voluntary accreditation established pursuant to that paragraph.

(c)   The regulations may prescribe–

(i)   the rights and obligations specific to the provision of certification services of participants in a scheme of voluntary accreditation, and

(ii)   the manner in which the accreditation authority designated under paragraph (a) shall elaborate and supervise compliance with those rights and obligations in accordance with the Directive and, in particular, Annex II.

(d)   A participant in a scheme referred to in paragraph (a) shall not exercise a right under the scheme without the prior permission of the accreditation authority.

(3)   The Minister shall prescribe a scheme of supervision of certification service providers established in the State who issue qualified certificates to the public.

(4)   (a)   The Minister may, after consultation with the Minister for Enterprise, Trade and Employment, by order, designate persons or public bodies for the purposes of determining whether secure signature creation devices conform with the requirements of Annex III.

(b)   The Minister may, by order, amend or revoke an order under this subsection, including an order under this paragraph.

(5)   No civil action shall lie or be maintained against a person or public body designated under or for the purposes of subsection (2), (3) or (4) in respect of any determination made or thing done by the person or public body, in good faith, in the performance or purported performance of a function under a scheme referred to in subsection (2) or (3) or for which he, she or it is designated under subsection (4).

Liability of certification service providers

30. (1)   A certification service provider who provides a service to the public of issuing certificates and who as a part of that service issues a certificate as a qualified certificate or guarantees such a certificate, shall be liable for any damage caused to a person who, or public body which, reasonably relies on the certificate unless the certification service provider proves that he, she or it has not acted negligently.

(2)   It shall be the duty of every certification service provider who provides to the public a service of issuing certificates and who issues a certificate as a qualified certificate or guarantees such a certificate, to take reasonable steps to ensure–

(a)   the accuracy of all information in the qualified certificate as at the time of issue and that the certificate contains all the details required by Annex I to be so contained in a qualified certificate,

(b)   that, at the time of the issue of the certificate, the signatory identified in the certificate held the signature creation device corresponding to the signature verification device given or identified in the certificate, and

(c)   that the signature creation device and the signature verification device act together in a complementary manner, in cases where the certification service provider generates both.

(3)   A certification service provider who provides a service to the public of issuing certificates and who as a part of that service issues a certificate as a qualified certificate, or guarantees such a certificate, is liable for any damage caused to a person who, or public body which, reasonably relies on the certificate, for the certification service provider's failure to register or publish notice of the revocation or suspension of the certificate as prescribed, unless the certification service provider proves that he, she or it has not acted negligently.

(4)   A certification service provider who provides a service to the public of issuing certificates and who as a part of that service issues a certificate as a qualified certificate, or guarantees such a certificate, may indicate in the qualified certificate limits on the uses of the certificate (including a limit on the value of transactions for which the certificate can be used) and, if the limits are clear and readily identifiable as limitations, the certification service provider shall not be liable for damages arising from a contrary use of a qualified certificate which includes such limits on its uses.

PART 4

DOMAIN NAME REGISTRATION

Registration of domain names

31.   (1)   The Minister may, by regulations made for the purpose of easy comprehension, fairness, transparency, avoidance of deception, promotion of fair competition and public confidence under section 3 after consultation with the Minister for Enterprise, Trade and Employment and such other persons and public bodies, if any, as the Minister thinks fit, including the body known as the Internet Corporation for Assigned Names and Numbers, authorise, prohibit or regulate the registration and use of the ie domain name in the State.

      (2)   Without prejudice to the generality of subsection (1), the regulations may prescribe–

             (a)   designated registration authorities,

             (b)   the form of registration,

             (c)   the period during which registration continues in force,

             (d)   the manner in which, the terms on which and the period or periods for which registration may be renewed,

             (e)   the circumstances and manner in which registrations may be granted, renewed or refused by the registration authorities,

             (f)   the right of appeal and appeal processes,

             (g)   the fees, if any, to be paid on the grant or renewal of registration and the time and manner in which such fees are to be paid,

             (h)   such other matters relating to registration as appear to the Minister to be necessary or desirable to prescribe.

(3)   A person who contravenes or fails to comply with a regulation made pursuant to this section is liable on summary conviction to a fine not exceeding £500.

(4)   In this section, "ie domain name" means the top level of the global domain name system assigned to Ireland according to the two-letter code in the International Standard ISO 3166-1 (Codes for Representation of Names of Countries and their Subdivision) of the International Organisation for Standardisation.

SCHEDULE

ANNEXES TO DIRECTIVE OF THE EUROPEAN PARLIAMENT AND OF THE COUNCIL ON A COMMUNITY FRAMEWORK FOR ELECTRONIC SIGNATURES

ANNEX I

Requirements for qualified certificates

Qualified certificates must contain:

(a)   an indication that the certificate is issued as a qualified certificate;

(b)   the identification of the certification-service-provider and the State in which it is established;

(c)   the name of the signatory or a pseudonym, which shall be identified as such;

(d)   provision for a specific attribute of the signatory to be included if relevant, depending on the purpose for which the certificate is intended;

(e)   signature-verification data which correspond to signature-creation data under the control of the signatory;

(f)   an indication of the beginning and end of the period of validity of the certificate;

(g)   the identity code of the certificate;

(h)   the advanced electronic signature of the certification-service-provider issuing it;

(i)   limitations on the scope of use of the certificate, if applicable; and

(j)   limits on the value of transactions for which the certificate can be used, if applicable.

ANNEX II

Requirements for certification-service-providers issuing qualified certificates

Certification-service-providers must:

(a)   demonstrate the reliability necessary for providing certification services;

(b)   ensure the operation of a prompt and secure directory and a secure and immediate revocation service;

(c)   ensure that the date and time when a certificate is issued or revoked can be determined precisely;

(d)   verify, by appropriate means in accordance with national law, the identity and, if applicable, any specific attributes of the person to which a qualified certificate is issued;

(e)   employ personnel who possess the expert knowledge, experience and qualifications necessary for the services provided, in particular competence at managerial level, expertise in electronic signature technology and familiarity with proper security procedures; they must also apply administrative and managerial procedures which are adequate and correspond to recognised standards;

(f)   use trustworthy systems and products which are protected against modification and ensure the technical and cryptographic security of the processes supported by them;

(g)   take measures against forgery of certificates, and, in cases where the certification-service-provider generates signature-creation data, guarantee confidentiality during the process of generating such data;

(h)   maintain sufficient financial resources to operate in conformity with the requirements laid down in the Directive, in particular to bear the risk of liability for damages, for example by obtaining appropriate insurance;

(i)   record all relevant information concerning a qualified certificate for an appropriate period of time, in particular for the purpose of providing evidence of certification for the purposes of legal proceedings. Such recording may be done electronically;

(j)   not store or copy signature-creation data of the person to whom the certification-service-provider provides key management services;

(k)   before entering into a contractual relationship with a person seeking a certificate to support his electronic signature, inform that person by a durable means of communication of the precise terms and conditions regarding the use of the certificate, including any limitations on its use, the experience of a voluntary accreditation scheme and procedures for complaints and dispute settlement. Such information, which may be transmitted electronically, must be in writing and in readily understandable language. Relevant parts of this information must also be made available on request to third-parties relying on the certificate;

(l)   use trustworthy systems to store certificates in a verifiable form so that:

— only authorised persons can make entries and changes,

— information can be checked for authenticity,

— certificates are publicly available for retrieval in only those cases for which the certificate-holder's consent has been obtained, and

— any technical changes comprising these security requirements are apparent to the operator.

ANNEX III

Requirements for secure signature-creation devices

1. Secure signature-creation devices must, by appropriate technical and procedural means, ensure at the least that:

    (a)   the signature-creation-data used for signature generation can practically occur only once, and that their secrecy is reasonably assured;

    (b)   the signature-creation-data used for signature generation cannot, with reasonable assurance, be derived and the signature is protected against forgery using currently available technology;

    (c)   the signature-creation-data used for signature generation can be reliably protected by the legitimate signatory against the use of others.

2. Secure signature-creation devices must not alter the data to be signed or prevent such data from being presented to the signatory prior to the signature process.

Interpretation Act 2005

(Number 23 of 2005)

AN ACT RESPECTING THE INTERPRETATION AND APPLICATION OF ACTS AND OF STATUTORY INSTRUMENTS MADE UNDER ACTS AND PROVIDING FOR THE REPEAL OF CERTAIN ENACTMENTS RELATING TO THOSE MATTERS.

[17th October, 2005]

BE IT ENACTED BY THE OIREACHTAS AS FOLLOWS:

PART I

PRELIMINARY AND GENERAL

Short title and commencement

1.   (1)   This Act may be cited as the Interpretation Act 2005.

(2)   This Act comes into operation on 1 January 2006.

Interpretation

2.   (1)   In this Act–

"**Act**" means–

(a)   an Act of the Oireachtas, and

(b)   a statute which was in force in Saorstát Éireann immediately before the date of the coming into operation of the Constitution and which continued in force by virtue of Article 50 of the Constitution;

"**enactment**" means an Act or a statutory instrument or any portion of an Act or statutory instrument;

"**repeal**" includes revoke, rescind, abrogate or cancel;

"**statutory instrument**" means an order, regulation, rule, bye-law, warrant, licence, certificate, direction, notice, guideline or other like document made, issued, granted or otherwise created by or under an Act and references, in relation to a statutory instrument, to "made" or to "made under" include references to made, issued, granted or otherwise created by or under such instrument.

(2)   For the purposes of this Act, an enactment which has been replaced or has expired, lapsed or otherwise ceased to have effect is deemed to have been repealed.

Repeals and savings

3. (1) The following Acts are repealed:

    (a) the Interpretation Act 1889;

    (b) the Interpretation Act 1923;

    (c) the Interpretation Act 1937;

    (d) the Interpretation (Amendment) Act 1993.

    (2) (a) The repeal by this Act of an Act which assigns a meaning to a word or expression in another enactment does not affect the meaning so assigned if–

        (i) in the absence of that meaning in this Act, or

        (ii) by the application to the other enactment of the meaning assigned by this Act to the same or a similar word or expression,

        the other enactment would be changed in intent or become unclear or absurd.

    (b) The repeal by this Act of an Act which provides for any matter (other than a matter to which paragraph (a) relates) in another enactment does not affect the matter so provided for if–

        (i) in the absence of that matter being provided for in this Act, or

        (ii) by the application to the other enactment of a matter provided for by this Act which corresponds to a matter provided for in the repealed Act concerned,

        the other enactment would be changed in intent or become unclear or absurd.

Application

4. (1) A provision of this Act applies to an enactment except in so far as the contrary intention appears in this Act, in the enactment itself or, where relevant, in the Act under which the enactment is made.

    (2) The provisions of this Act which relate to other Acts also apply to this Act unless the contrary intention appears in this Act.

PART 2

MISCELLANEOUS RULES

Construing ambiguous or obscure provisions, etc.

5. (1) In construing a provision of any Act (other than a provision that relates to the imposition of a penal or other sanction)–

(a) that is obscure or ambiguous, or

(b) that on a literal interpretation would be absurd or would fail to reflect the plain intention of–

(i) in the case of an Act to which paragraph (a) of the definition of "Act" in section 2(1) relates, the Oireachtas, or

(ii) in the case of an Act to which paragraph (b) of that definition relates, the parliament concerned,

the provision shall be given a construction that reflects the plain intention of the Oireachtas or parliament concerned, as the case may be, where that intention can be ascertained from the Act as a whole.

(2) In construing a provision of a statutory instrument (other than a provision that relates to the imposition of a penal or other sanction)–

(a) that is obscure or ambiguous, or

(b) that on a literal interpretation would be absurd or would fail to reflect the plain intention of the instrument as a whole in the context of the enactment (including the Act) under which it was made,

the provision shall be given a construction that reflects the plain intention of the maker of the instrument where that intention can be ascertained from the instrument as a whole in the context of that enactment.

Construing provisions in changing circumstances

6. In construing a provision of any Act or statutory instrument, a court may make allowances for any changes in the law, social conditions, technology, the meaning of words used in that Act or statutory instrument and other relevant matters, which have occurred since the date of the passing of that Act or the making of that statutory instrument, but only in so far as its text, purpose and context permit.

Supplemental provision to sections 5 and 6

7. (1) In construing a provision of an Act for the purposes of section 5 or 6, a court may, notwithstanding section 18(g), make use of all matters that accompany and are set out in–

(a)   in the case of an Act of the Oireachtas, the signed text of such law as enrolled for record in the Office of the Registrar of the Supreme Court pursuant to Article 25.4.5° of the Constitution,

(b)   in the case of an Act of the Oireachtas of Saorstát Éireann, the signed text of such law as enrolled for record in the office of such officer of the Supreme Court of Saorstát Éireann as Dáil Éireann determined pursuant to Article 42 of the Constitution of the Irish Free State (Saorstát Éireann),

(c)   in the case of any other Act, such text of that Act as corresponds to the text of the Act enrolled in the manner referred to in paragraph (a) or (b).

(2)   For the purposes of subsection (1), it shall be presumed, until the contrary is shown, that a copy of the text of an Act that is required to be judicially noticed is a copy of the text to which subsection (1) relates.

Reading provisions together as one and summary proceedings for offences

8.   Where–

(a)   an Act or portion of an Act (whenever passed)–

(i)   provides that summary proceedings for offences under it may be prosecuted by a specified person, and

(ii)   is subsequently read together as one with any provision of another Act,

and

(b)   an offence is created under that provision which can be prosecuted in a summary manner but no express power is given to the specified person to so prosecute,

then, the specified person may bring summary proceedings for an offence under that other provision unless some other person is authorised by that other Act to bring such proceedings.

References in enactments to Parts, etc.

9.   (1)   A reference in an enactment to a Part, Chapter, section, Schedule or other division, by whatever name called, shall be read as a reference to a Part, Chapter, section, Schedule or other division of the enactment in which the reference occurs.

(2)   A reference in an enactment to a subsection, paragraph, subparagraph, clause, subclause, article, subarticle or other division, by whatever name called, shall be read as a reference

to a subsection, paragraph, subparagraph, clause, subclause, article, subarticle or other division of the provision in which the reference occurs.

Enactment always speaking

10.   An enactment continues to have effect and may be applied from time to time as occasion requires.

References in enactments to examples

11.   If under the heading–

(a)   in the Irish language "Sampla" or "Samplaí", or

(b)   in the English language "Example" or "Examples",

an enactment includes at the end of a provision or in a schedule relating to such provision an example of the operation of the provision, then the example–

(i)   is not to be read as exhaustive of the provision, and

(ii)   may extend, but does not limit, the meaning of the provision.

Deviation from form

12.   Where a form is prescribed in or under an enactment, a deviation from the form which does not materially affect the substance of the form or is not misleading in content or effect does not invalidate the form used.

PART 3

CITATION AND OPERATION OF ENACTMENTS

Judicial notice

13.   An Act is a public document and shall be judicially noticed.

Citation and references to amended enactments

14.   (1)   An Act may be cited in any enactment or other document–

(a)   by the long title or short title of the Act,

(b)   where appropriate, by the consecutive number of the Act in the calendar year and by the calendar year in which it was passed, or

(c)   where the Act was passed prior to the enactment of the Constitution of the Irish Free State (Saorstát Eireann) Act 1922, by its regnal year and chapter number and, where there was more than one parliamentary session in the same regnal year, by reference to the session concerned.

(2)   A citation of or a reference to an enactment shall be read as a citation of or reference to the enactment as amended (including as amended by way of extension, application, adaptation or other

modification of the enactment), whether the amendment is made before, on or after the date on which the provision containing the citation or reference came into operation.

(3) In citing–

(a) an Act by its short title, or

(b) any other enactment by its citation (if any),

a comma immediately before a reference to a year and a comma immediately after such a reference that is not required for the purpose of punctuation may be omitted.

Date of passing of Acts of Oireachtas

15. (1) The date of the passing of an Act of the Oireachtas is the date of the day on which the Bill for the Act is signed by the President.

(2) Immediately after the Bill for an Act of the Oireachtas is signed by the President, the Clerk of Dáil Éireann shall endorse on the Act immediately after the long title the date of the passing of the Act, and that date shall be taken to be part of the Act.

Commencement

16. (1) Subject to subsection (2), every provision of an Act comes into operation on the date of its passing.

(2) Where an Act or a provision of an Act is expressed to come into operation on a particular day (whether the day is before or after the date of the passing of the Act and whether the day is named in the Act or is to be fixed or ascertained in a particular manner), the Act or provision comes into operation at the end of the day before the particular day.

(3) Subject to subsection (4), every provision of a statutory instrument comes into operation at the end of the day before the day on which the statutory instrument is made.

(4) Where a statutory instrument or a provision of a statutory instrument is expressed to come into operation on a particular day (whether the day is before or after the date of the making of the statutory instrument and whether the day is named in the instrument or is to be fixed or ascertained in a particular manner), the statutory instrument or provision comes into operation at the end of the day before the particular day.

Exercise of statutory powers before commencement of Act

17. Where an Act or a provision of an Act is expressed to come into operation on a day subsequent to the date of the passing of the Act, the following provisions apply:

(a)   if the day on which the Act or the provision comes into operation is to be fixed or ascertained in a particular manner, the statutory instrument, act or thing whereby the day is fixed or ascertained may, subject to any restriction imposed by the Act, be made or done at any time after the passing of the Act;

(b)   if, for the purposes of the Act or the provision, the Act confers a power to make a statutory instrument or do any act or thing, the making or doing of which is necessary or expedient to enable the Act or provision to have full force and effect immediately on its coming into operation, the power may, subject to any restriction imposed by the Act, be exercised at any time after the passing of the Act.

PART 4

MEANING AND CONSTRUCTION OF WORDS AND EXPRESSIONS

General rules of construction

18.   The following provisions apply to the construction of an enactment:

(a)   *Singular and plural.* A word importing the singular shall be read as also importing the plural, and a word importing the plural shall be read as also importing the singular;

(b)   *Gender.*

   (i)   A word importing the masculine gender shall be read as also importing the feminine gender;

   (ii)   In an Act passed on or after 22 December 1993, and in a statutory instrument made after that date, a word importing the feminine gender shall be read as also importing the masculine gender;

(c)   *Person.* "Person" shall be read as importing a body corporate (whether a corporation aggregate or a corporation sole) and an unincorporated body of persons, as well as an individual, and the subsequent use of any pronoun in place of a further use of "person" shall be read accordingly;

(d)   *Adopted child.* A reference, however expressed, to a child of a person shall be read as including–

   (i)   in an Act passed after the passing of the Adoption Act 1976 a reference to a child adopted by the person under the Adoption Acts 1952 to 1998 and every other enactment which is to be construed together with any of those Acts, or

   (ii)   in an Act passed on or after 14 January 1988 (the commencement of section 3 of the Status of Children Act 1987), a child to whom subparagraph (i) relates or a child adopted outside the State whose adoption is recognised by virtue of the law for the time being in force in the State;

(e)   *Distance.* A word or expression relating to the distance between two points and every reference to the distance from or to a point shall be read as relating or referring to such distance measured in a straight line on a horizontal plane;

(f)   *Series description.* Where a consecutive series is described by reference to the first and last in the series, the description shall be read as including the first and the last in the series;

(g)   *Marginal and shoulder notes, etc.* Subject to section 7, none of the following shall be taken to be part of the enactment or be construed or judicially noticed in relation to the construction or interpretation of the enactment:

         (i)   a marginal note placed at the side, or a shoulder note placed at the beginning, of a section or other provision to indicate the subject, contents or effect of the section or provision,

         (ii)   a heading or cross-line placed in or at the head of or at the beginning of a Part, Chapter, section, or other provision or group of sections or provisions to indicate the subject, contents or effect of the Part, Chapter, section, provision or group;

(h)   *Periods of time.* Where a period of time is expressed to begin on or be reckoned from a particular day, that day shall be deemed to be included in the period and, where a period of time is expressed to end on or be reckoned to a particular day, that day shall be deemed to be included in the period;

(i)   *Time.* Where time is expressed by reference to a specified hour or to a time before or after a specified hour, that time shall be determined by reference to the Standard Time (Amendment) Act 1971;

(j)   *Offences by corporations.* A reference to a person in relation to an offence (whether punishable on indictment or on summary conviction) shall be read as including a reference to a body corporate.

Construction of statutory instruments

19.   A word or expression used in a statutory instrument has the same meaning in the statutory instrument as it has in the enactment under which the instrument is made.

Interpretation provisions

20. (1)   Where an enactment contains a definition or other interpretation provision, the provision shall be read as being applicable except in so far as the contrary intention appears in–

    (a)   the enactment itself, or

    (b)   the Act under which the enactment is made.

    (2)   Where an enactment defines or otherwise interprets a word or expression, other parts of speech and grammatical forms of the word or expression have a corresponding meaning.

Interpretation of words and expressions in Schedule

21. (1)   In an enactment, a word or expression to which a particular meaning, construction or effect is assigned in Part 1 of the Schedule has the meaning, construction or effect so assigned to it.

    (2)   In an enactment which comes into operation after the commencement of this Act, a word or expression to which a particular meaning, construction or effect is assigned in Part 2 of the Schedule has the meaning, construction or effect so assigned to it.

PART 5

POWERS AND DUTIES

Powers under enactments

22. (1)   A power conferred by an enactment may be exercised from time to time as occasion requires.

    (2)   A power conferred by an enactment on the holder of an office as that holder shall be deemed to be conferred on, and may accordingly be exercised by, the holder for the time being of that office.

    (3)   A power conferred by an enactment to make a statutory instrument shall be read as including a power, exercisable in the like manner and subject to the like consent and conditions (if any), to repeal or amend a statutory instrument made under that power and (where required) to make another statutory instrument in place of the one so repealed.

Duties under enactments

23. (1)   A duty imposed by an enactment shall be performed from time to time as occasion requires.

(2)   A duty imposed by an enactment on the holder of an office as that holder shall be deemed to be imposed on, and shall accordingly be performed by, the holder for the time being of that office.

Rules of court

24.   Where an enactment confers a new jurisdiction on a court or extends or varies an existing jurisdiction of a court, the authority having for the time being power to make rules or orders regulating the practice and procedure of the court has, and may at any time exercise, power to make rules or orders for regulating the practice and procedure of that court in the exercise of the jurisdiction so conferred, extended or varied.

Service by post

25.   Where an enactment authorises or requires a document to be served by post, by using the word "serve", "give", "deliver", "send" or any other word or expression, the service of the document may be effected by properly addressing, prepaying (where required) and posting a letter containing the document, and in that case the service of the document is deemed, unless the contrary is proved, to have been effected at the time at which the letter would be delivered in the ordinary course of post.

PART 6

AMENDMENT OF ENACTMENTS, ETC.

Repeals and substitutions

26.   (1)   Where an enactment repeals another enactment and substitutes other provisions for the enactment so repealed, the enactment so repeazes in force until the substituted provisions come into operation.

(2)   Where an enactment ("former enactment") is repealed and reenacted, with or without modification, by another enactment ("new enactment"), the following provisions apply:

(a)   a person appointed under the former enactment shall continue to act for the remainder of the period for which the person was appointed as if appointed under the new enactment;

(b)   a bond, guarantee or other security of a continuing nature given by a person under the former enactment remains in force, and data, books, papers, forms and things prepared or used under the former enactment may continue to be used as before the repeal;

(c)   proceedings taken under the former enactment may, subject to section 27(1), be continued under and in conformity with the new enactment in so far as that may be done consistently with the new enactment;

(d)   if after the commencement of this Act–

    (i)   any provision of a former enactment, that provided for the making of a statutory instrument, is repealed and re-enacted, with or without modification, as a new provision, and

    (ii)   such statutory instrument is in force immediately before such repeal and re-enactment,

    then the statutory instrument shall be deemed to have been made under the new provision to the extent that it is not inconsistent with the new enactment, and remains in force until it is repealed or otherwise ceases to have effect;

(e)   to the extent that the provisions of the new enactment express the same idea in a different form of words but are in substance the same as those of the former enactment, the idea in the new enactment shall not be taken to be different merely because a different form of words is used;

(f)   a reference in any other enactment to the former enactment shall, with respect to a subsequent transaction, matter or thing, be read as a reference to the provisions of the new enactment relating to the same subject-matter as that of the former enactment, but where there are no provisions in the new enactment relating to the same subject-matter, the former enactment shall be disregarded in so far as is necessary to maintain or give effect to that other enactment.

Effect of repeal of enactment

27. (1)   Where an enactment is repealed, the repeal does not–

(a)   revive anything not in force or not existing immediately before the repeal,

(b)   affect the previous operation of the enactment or anything duly done or suffered under the enactment,

(c)   affect any right, privilege, obligation or liability acquired, accrued or incurred under the enactment,

(d)   affect any penalty, forfeiture or punishment incurred in respect of any offence against or contravention of the enactment which was committed before the repeal, or

(e)   prejudice or affect any legal proceedings (civil or criminal) pending at the time of the repeal in respect of any such right, privilege, obligation, liability, offence or contravention.

(2)   Where an enactment is repealed, any legal proceedings (civil or criminal) in respect of a right, privilege, obligation or liability acquired, accrued or incurred under, or an offence against or contravention of, the enactment may be instituted, continued or enforced, and any penalty, forfeiture or punishment in respect of such offence or contravention may be imposed and carried out, as if the enactment had not been repealed.

SCHEDULE
INTERPRETATION OF PARTICULAR WORDS AND EXPRESSIONS
PART 1

"affidavit", in the case of a person for the time being allowed by law to declare instead of swearing, includes declaration;

"British statute" means an Act of the Parliament of the former United Kingdom of Great Britain and Ireland;

"Circuit Court" means the Circuit Court as established and for the time being maintained by law;

"commencement", when used in relation to an enactment, means the time at which the enactment comes into operation;

"Constitution" means the Constitution of Ireland enacted by the people on 1 July 1937, as amended;

"Dáil Éireann" means the House of the Oireachtas to which that name is given by section 1 of Article 15 of the Constitution;

"District Court" means the District Court as established and for the time being maintained by law;

"financial year", in relation to an exchequer financial year, means the period which is coextensive with a calendar year;

"Government" means the Government mentioned in Article 28 of the Constitution;

"Great Britain" does not include the Channel Islands or the Isle of Man;

"High Court" means the High Court as established and for the time being maintained by law pursuant to Article 34 of the Constitution;

"land" includes tenements, hereditaments, houses and buildings, land covered by water and any estate, right or interest in or over land;

"local financial year" means a period which is coextensive with a calendar year;

"midnight" means, in relation to a particular day, the point of time at which the day ends;

"Minister of the Government" means a member of the Government having charge of a Department of State;

"**month**" means a calendar month;

"**oath**", in the case of a person for the time being allowed by law to affirm or declare instead of swearing, includes affirmation or declaration;

"**Oireachtas**" means the National Parliament provided for by Article 15 of the Constitution;

"**ordnance map**" means a map made under the powers conferred by the Survey (Ireland) Acts 1825 to 1870;

"**President**" means the President of Ireland or any Commission, or other body or authority, for the time being lawfully exercising the powers and performing the duties of the President;

"**pre-union Irish statute**" means an Act passed by a Parliament sitting in Ireland at any time before the coming into force on 1 January 1801 of the Act entitled "An Act for the Union of Great Britain and Ireland";

"**rateable valuation**" means the valuation under the Valuation Act 2001 of the property concerned;

"**rules of court**" means rules made by the authority for the time being having power to make rules regulating the practice and procedure of the court concerned;

"**Saorstát Éireann statute**" means an Act of the Oireachtas of Saorstát Éireann;

"**Seanad Éireann**" means the House of the Oireachtas to which that name is given by section 1 of Article 15 of the Constitution;

"**statutory declaration**" means a declaration made under the Statutory Declarations Act 1938;

"**Supreme Court**" means the Supreme Court as established and for the time being maintained by law pursuant to Article 34 of the Constitution;

"**swear**", in the case of a person for the time being allowed by law to affirm or declare instead of swearing, includes affirm and declare;

"**week**" means the period between midnight on any Saturday and midnight on the following Saturday;

"**week-day**" means a day which is not a Sunday;

"**writing**" includes printing, typewriting, lithography, photography, and other modes of representing or reproducing words in visible form and any information kept in a non-legible form, whether stored electronically or otherwise, which is capable by any means of being reproduced in a legible form;

"**year**", when used without qualification, means a period of 12 months beginning on the 1st day of January in any year.

PART 2

"**Companies Acts**" means the Companies Acts 1963 to 2001 and every other enactment which is to be read together with any of those Acts;

"**full age**", in relation to a person, means the time when the person attains the age of 18 years or sooner marries, or any time after either event;

"functions" includes powers and duties, and references to the performance of functions include, with respect to powers and duties, references to the exercise of the powers and the carrying out of the duties;

"Member State" means, where the context so admits, a Member State of the European Communities or of the European Union;

"Minister of State" means a person appointed under section 1 of the Ministers and Secretaries (Amendment) (No. 2) Act 1977 to be a Minister of State;

"public holiday" means a public holiday determined in accordance with the Organisation of Working Time Act 1997;

"Social Welfare Acts" means the Social Welfare (Consolidation) Act 1993 and every other enactment which is to be read together with that Act;

"working day" means a day which is not a Saturday, Sunday or public holiday.

Law of Vehicle
Registration Tax

LAW OF VEHICLE REGISTRATION TAX

Acts/Regulations

Finance Act 1992

(Number 9 of 1992)

Interpretation

130. In this Chapter, save where the context otherwise requires —

["**ambulance**" means a vehicle which is specially designed, constructed or adapted, and is primarily used following registration, for the conveyance of injured or seriously ill person to a hospital on a stretcher and which is permanently fitted to accommodate and hold in position one or more standard stretchers;][1]

"**the Act of 1952**" means the Finance (Excise Duties) (Vehicles) Act, 1952;

"**authorised person**" means a person authorised under section 136;

"**bus**" means a vehicle which is designed, constructed or adapted for the conveyance of persons and so as to provide seating accommodation in permanent fixtures for more than [11 passengers][2] and for the purposes of this definition —

(a)   each separate such seat in the vehicle which is 40 centimetres or more in width when measured lengthwise on the front of the seat shall be reckoned as providing seating accommodation for one person, and

(b)   each continuous such seat (which expression includes 2 or more separate seats which are divided by such means as to allow them to be used as one continuous seat) shall be reckoned as providing seating accommodation for one person in respect of each 40 centimetres of the width of the seat when measured lengthwise on the front of the seat;

["**category A vehicle**" means a vehicle other than a category D vehicle, [a crew cab, a motor caravan,][3] a motor-cycle or a listed vehicle -

(a)   which is designed, constructed or adapted solely or mainly for the carriage of the driver alone or the driver and one or more other persons, or

(b)   which is of not more than 3 tonnes unladen weight and has, to the rear of the driver's seat, a roofed area -

(i)   which is fitted with one or more side windows, or

(ii)   in which openings, suitable for the fitting of side windows, are or were incorporated and are not closed and sealed in accordance with such conditions as may be prescribed, or

(iii)   in which one or more seats have been fitted or in which are provided fixtures or other devices for the purpose of fitting one or more seats, or

(iv)   in which the floor is constructed or fitted otherwise than in accordance with such conditions as may be prescribed;][4]

["category B vehicle" means a vehicle (other than a category A vehicle, a category D vehicle, [a pick-up][5] a motor-cycle or a listed vehicle) which—

[(a)   in the case of a crew cab, is less than 3,500 kilograms gross vehicle weight, or][6]

(b)   in the case of a motor caravan, is not more than 3,000 kilograms unladen weight, or

(c)   is not more than 2,519 kilograms gross vehicle weight or not more than 2.449 metres wheelbase:

but if a vehicle is of not more than 1,600 kilograms unladen weight and the roofed area of the vehicle to the rear of the driver's seat has a load volume of more than 2 cubic metres when measured in such manner as the Commissioners may approve, the vehicle shall not be regarded as a category B vehicle;][7],

["category C vehicle" means a vehicle other than a category A vehicle, a category B vehicle, a category D vehicle or a motor-cycle;][8]

["category D vehicle" means one of the following vehicles, namely, an invalid carriage, a refuse cart, a sweeping machine, a watering machine used exclusively for cleansing public streets and roads, an ambulance, a road roller, a fire engine, a fire-escape, a vehicle used exclusively for transport (whether by carriage or traction) of road construction machinery used only for the construction or repair of roads and a vehicle used exclusively for the transport (whether by carriage or traction) of life boats and their gear or any equipment for affording assistance in the preservation of life and property in cases of shipwreck or distress at sea;][9]

"certificate" means a certificate of registration issued under section 131(5);

"the Commissioners" means the Revenue Commissioners;

"conversion" means the modification of a category B vehicle in such a manner as to make it a category A vehicle or the modification of a category C vehicle in such manner as to make it a category A vehicle or a category B vehicle [or the modification of a category D vehicle in such manner as to make it a category A vehicle, a category B vehicle or a category C vehicle][10] and cognate words shall be construed accordingly;

["CO2 emissions" means the level of carbon dioxide (CO_2) emissions for a vehicle measured in accordance with the provisions of Council Directive 80/1268/EEC of 16 December 1980 (as amended) and listed in Annex VIII of Council Directive 70/156/EEC of 6 February 1970 (as amended) and displayed in accordance with the provisions of Council Directive 1999/94/EC of 13 December 1999 (as amended) and contained in the relevant EC type-approval certificate or EC certificate of conformity or any other appropriate documentation which confirms compliance with any measures taken to give effect in the State to any act of the European Communities relating to the approximation of the laws of Member States in respect of type-approval for the type of vehicle concerned;]¹¹

["**crew cab**" means a vehicle that comprises a cab, with seating for a driver and a minimum of 3 and a maximum of 6 other persons, and an area to the rear of the cab that is designed, constructed or adapted exclusively for the carriage of goods and which area —

(i)   is completely and permanently separated from the cab by a rigid partition that is fixed in such manner as may be prescribed by the Commissioners, and

(ii)   has a floor length that is not less than 45 per cent of the wheelbase when measured in such manner as may be prescribed by the Commissioners;]¹²

"**cylinder capacity of an engine**" means the cylinder capacity of an engine calculated in accordance with regulations for the time being in force under section 1(3) of the Act of 1952, for the purpose of a rate of duty specified in the Schedule to that Act;

"**deal**" means offer for hire, lease or sale in the State one or more unregistered vehicles or converted vehicles prior to the entry of the prescribed particulars thereof in the register, and cognate words shall be construed accordingly;

["**listed vehicle**" means one of the following vehicles, namely, a hearse, a bus, a special purpose vehicle, an agricultural tractor, a two-wheeled tractor, an armoured fighting vehicle, or a vehicle (not including a motor-cycle) which is shown to the satisfaction of the Commissioners to be more than 30 years old at the time of registration;]¹³

"**licensing authority**" means the council of a county or the corporation of a county borough which licenses a vehicle under section 1 of the Act of 1952;

"**manufacture**" means the making or assembling in the State of a vehicle and includes conversion and cognate words shall be construed accordingly;

["**mechanically propelled vehicle**" means a vehicle that:

(a)   has been designed and constructed for road use,

(b)   is, at the time of declaration for registration, in compliance with any measures taken to give effect in the State to any act of the European Communities relating to the approximation of the laws of Member States in respect of type-approval for the type of vehicle concerned,

(c)   is intended or adapted for propulsion by a mechanical means, or by an electrical means or by a partly mechanical and a partly electrical means, and

(d)   is capable of achieving vehicle propulsion at the time of registration, to the satisfaction of the Commissioners, including [a motor-cycle][14] but not including a tramcar or other vehicle running on permanent rails or a vehicle including a cycle with an attachment for propelling it by mechanical power not exceeding 400 kilogrammes in weight unladen adapted and used for invalids;][15]

"the Minister" means the Minister for Finance;

["motor caravan" means a vehicle which is shown to the satisfaction of the Commissioners to be designed, constructed or adapted to provide temporary living accommodation which has an interior height of not less than 1.8 metres when measured in such manner as may be approved by the Commissioners and, in respect of which vehicle, as such design, construction or adaptation incorporates the following permanently fitted equipment -

(a)   a sink unit

(b)   cooking equipment of not less than a hob with 2 rings or such other cooking equipment as may be prescribed, and

(c)   any other equipment or fittings as may be prescribed;][16]

["motor-cycle" means a mechanically propelled vehicle being a bicycle, tricycle or quadricycle propelled by an engine or motor or with an attachment for propelling it by mechanical power, whether or not the attachment is being used, a moped, a scooter and an autocycle.][17]

"owner" means —

(a)   in relation to a vehicle (other than a vehicle specified in paragraph (b)), the person by whom the vehicle is kept,

(b)   in relation to a vehicle which is the subject of a hire-purchase agreement or a lease, the person in possession of the vehicle under the agreement or lease;

"the Order of 1979" means the Imposition of Duties (No.236) (Excise Duties on Motor Vehicles, Televisions and Gramophone Records) Order, 1979 (S.I. No.57 of 1979);

"the Order of 1984" means the Imposition of Duties (No.273) (Excise Duty on Motor-cycles) Order, 1984 (S.I. No.354 of 1984);

["pick-up" means a vehicle that comprises a cab, with a single row of seating for a driver and a maximum of two other persons, and an uncovered area to the rear of the cab that is designed, constructed or adapted exclusively for the carriage of goods and which area —

(i)   is completely and permanently separated from the cab by a rigid partition that is fixed in such manner as may be prescribed by the Commissioners, and

(ii)   has a floor length that is not less than 45 per cent of the wheelbase when measured in such manner as may be prescribed by the Commissioners;][18]

"prescribed" means prescribed by regulations made by the Commissioners under section 141;

"**the register**" means the register of vehicles established and maintained by the Commissioners under section 131 and "registered" and other cognate words shall be construed accordingly;

"**special purpose vehicle**" means a vehicle which is designed, constructed or adapted solely or mainly for a purpose other than the carriage of persons or goods;

"**vehicle**" means a mechanically propelled vehicle.

Vehicle built from chassis or monocoque or assembly

[**130A.** For the purposes of this Chapter, an unregistered vehicle includes a vehicle –

(a)   built up from a chassis, or

(b)   built using a monocoque or an assembly serving an equivalent purpose to a chassis,

which chassis or monocoque or assembly is either new and unused or is derived from another unregistered vehicle.][19]

Delegation of certain powers of the Revenue Commissioners

[**130B.** (1)   For the purposes of this Chapter, and subject to the direction and control of the Commissioners, any power, function or duty conferred or imposed on them may, subject to subsection (2), be exercised or performed on their behalf by an officer of the Commissioners.

(2)   Any power, function or duty conferred or imposed on the Commissioners by –

(a)   paragraph (c) of subsection (1) of section 131

(b)   paragraphs (c) and (d) of subsection (2) of section 133, or

(c)   subsections (2) and (3) of section 136

may be exercised or performed on their behalf, and subject to their direction and control, by an officer of the Commissioners authorised by them in writing for the purposes of that section.][20]

Registration of vehicles by Revenue Commissioners

131. (1)   (a)   The Commissioners shall establish and maintain a register of all vehicles in the State (in this Chapter referred to subsequently as "**the register**").

(b)   The Commissioners may enter in the register such particulars in relation to a vehicle and its ownership and connected matters as they consider appropriate.

[(ba) (i)   **In respect of a vehicle which is within any particular category of vehicle that is prescribed** for the purposes of this paragraph or is within any other class of vehicle that is prescribed, the Commissioners may, as a condition of registration, require confirmation in accordance with this paragraph that such vehicle —

(i)   is a mechanically propelled vehicle as defined in section 130, and

(ii)   complies with any matter prescribed for the purposes of subparagraph (ii)(II).

(ii)   The Commissioners may appoint one or more than one individual or body (in this paragraph referred to as a 'competent person') to carry out a pre-registration examination of a vehicle to which subparagraph (i) relates —

(I)   to determine whether or not each vehicle duly examined under this paragraph is a mechanically propelled vehicle for the purposes of section 130, and

(II)   to ascertain whether or not such other prescribed matters (being matters required to be ascertained) have been complied with as are necessary —

(A)   for the registration of the vehicle concerned, and

(B)   for the proper operation of vehicle registration tax.

(iii)   Where in respect of a vehicle the Commissioners require confirmation as provided for by subparagraph (i), then they shall not register the vehicle without the production of a statement issued by a competent person that the vehicle —

(i)   is a mechanically propelled vehicle, and

(ii)   complies with any matter prescribed for the purposes of subparagraph (ii)(II) and which relates to the vehicle.

(iv)   The fee to be charged by the competent person for the examination of a vehicle shall be agreed with the Commissioners. Different fees may be so agreed in respect of different types of examination and different categories or other classes of vehicles. The fee shall be paid by the person presenting the vehicle concerned for pre-registration examination. The fee shall be credited against the vehicle registration tax payable in respect of the registration of the vehicle but no other fees, charges or costs incurred by the person presenting the vehicle for examination shall be so credited.

(v)   A competent person shall comply with any instructions and directions given by the Revenue Commissioners to such person for the purposes of this paragraph.

(vi)   The Commissioners may revoke the appointment of a competent person.][21]

(c)   The Commissioners may amend an entry in or delete an entry from the register.

(d)   The register may be established and maintained in a form that is not legible if it is capable of being converted into a legible form.

[(e)   (i)   The Commissioners shall, in accordance with such conditions (if any) as they may prescribe, establish a separate register, in this Chapter referred to as **"the zz register"**, for vehicles which are in the State temporarily and solely for the use of persons established outside the State, and in relation to which such persons applying in writing to the person maintaining the zz register for registration and furnish to him the prescribed particulars.

(ii)   There may be entered in the zz register such particulars in relation to a vehicle and its ownership and connected matters as the Commissioners consider appropriate.

(iii)   The person maintaining the zz register may amend an entry in or delete an entry from it

(iv)   The zz register may be established and maintained in a form that is not legible if it is capable of being converted into a legible form.

(f)   In this subsection **"persons established outside the State"** shall have the meaning assigned to it by regulations made by the Minister for the purposes of section 135

(g)   The Commissioners may appoint persons resident or carrying on business in the State to maintain the zz register on their behalf

(h)   There shall be assigned to each vehicle entered in the zz register an identification mark containing the letters zz and a unique number and the mark shall be displayed on the vehicle at all times while it is in the State.

(i)   A vehicle bearing an identification mark assigned to it under paragraph (h) shall be deemed, for the purposes of section 135(a), to be a vehicle temporarily brought into the State and shall be subject to such conditions, restrictions and limitations as may be prescribed by the Minister for purposes of section 135(a).][22]

(2)   (a)   The prescribed particulars of each vehicle that, on or after the 1st day of January, 1993, is not a registered vehicle shall be declared to the Commissioners for the purposes of registration.

      (b)   A vehicle in relation to which the prescribed particulars have been furnished under this subsection shall be deemed to be a registered vehicle.

      [(c)   Where the prescribed particulars of a registered vehicle are altered after registration of the vehicle, the altered particulars shall be declared to the Commissioners for the purpose of amending the entry in the register relating to the vehicle.][23]

(3)   (a)   Where a registered vehicle is converted, the prescribed particulars shall be declared to the Commissioners for the purpose of the entry in the register of particulars in relation to the conversion and the Commissioners may enter in the register such particulars in relation to the conversion as they consider appropriate.

      (b)   The owner of a vehicle which has been converted shall deliver to the Commissioners with the declaration under paragraph (a) in relation to the conversion the certificate in relation to the vehicle and the Commissioners shall enter on the certificate such particulars in relation to the conversion as they consider appropriate.

(4)   A person shall not have in his possession or charge after the 1st day of January, 1993, an unregistered vehicle or a converted vehicle as respects which the prescribed particulars in relation to the conversion have not been declared to the Commissioners unless the person is an authorised person or the vehicle is the subject of an exemption under section 135 in force for the time being [or is a vehicle referred to in section 143(3) or is exempt from registration under section 135A.][24]

[(5)   (a)   The Commissioners shall assign in the prescribed manner a unique identification mark to each vehicle entered in the register and, following the issue of a licence under section 1 of the Act of 1952, the Minister for the Environment and Local Government shall issue to the owner of each such vehicle a certificate of registration in the prescribed form.

(b)   Notwithstanding the provisions of paragraph (a), a certificate of registration may be issued where a licence under the Act of 1952 is not issued and the Minister for the Environment and Local Government or a licensing authority, as appropriate, is satisfied that the vehicle has not or will not in the future be used in any public place within the meaning of section 64 of the Finance Act 1976.][25]

[(5A)   At the request of the owner of a vehicle, the Commissioners may, subject to such conditions (if any) as they may specify, assign to the vehicle an identification mark chosen by the owner on payment of such fees as may be prescribed.][26]

(6)   (a)   There shall be displayed in the prescribed manner on each registered vehicle in the State the identification mark assigned to it under subsection (5).

        (b)   An identification mark assigned to a vehicle under subsection (5) shall not be displayed on any other vehicle.

        (c)   A mark which purports to be but is not an identification mark assigned to a vehicle under subsection (5) shall not be displayed on a vehicle.

        (d)   A person (other than an authorised person) shall not have in his possession or charge a vehicle in respect of which there is a contravention of paragraph (a).

        (e)   A person shall not have in his possession or charge a vehicle in respect of which there is a contravention of paragraph (b) or (c).

(7)   The Minister for the Environment shall have access to and may inspect and examine the register and—

        (a)   may take, or be supplied by the Commissioners with, such information from the register as he considers appropriate for the purpose of his functions, and

        (b)   take, or be supplied by the Commissioners with, copies of the register or of such extracts from the register as he considers appropriate for the purpose of his functions.

(8)   The Roads Act, 1920, is hereby amended, with effect from the 1st day of January, 1993, by the substitution of the following section for section 6:

        "6.   (1)   On the first application to a licensing authority for a licence in respect of a vehicle under section 1 of the Finance (Excise Duties) (Vehicles) Act, 1952, the authority shall not issue the licence unless and until the authority is satisfied that the vehicle has been registered in the register maintained under section 131 of the Finance Act, 1992.

(2)   For the purposes of this section, a certificate of registration under the said section 131 or such other (if any) evidence as the Minister for the Environment may, with the consent of the Minister for Finance, direct shall be sufficient evidence of the registration of the vehicle in the register aforesaid.".

[(9)   The Commissioners may, at the request of a person who shows to their satisfaction that he has reasonable grounds for making the request and subject to such conditions (if any), and upon payment of such fee, as they may specify furnish to the person -

(a)   such information from the register, or

(b)   copies of such entries in the register or of such parts of such entries in the register.

as they consider appropriate.]²⁷

Evidence of computer stored records in court proceedings

[131A. (1)   In this section-

"**copy record**" means any copy of an original record or a copy of that copy made in accordance with either of the methods referred to in subsection (2) and accompanied by the certificate referred to in subsection (4), which original record or copy of an original record is in the possession of the Commissioners;

"**original record**" means any document, record or record of an entry in a document or record or information stored by means of any storage equipment whether or not in a legible form, made or stored by the Commissioners for the purposes of or in connection with this Chapter and regulations made thereunder and which is in the possession of the Commissioners;

"**provable record**" means an original record or a copy record and in the case of an original record or a copy record stored in any storage equipment, whether or not in a legible form, includes the production or reproduction of the record in a legible form;

"**storage equipment**" means any electronic, magnetic, mechanical, photographic, optical or other devise used for storing information.

(2)   The Commissioners may, where by reason of-

(a)   the deterioration of, or

(b)   the inconvenience in storing, or

(c)   the technical obsolescence in the manner of keeping,

any original record or any copy record, make a legible copy of the record or store information concerning that record otherwise than in a legible form so that the information is capable of being used to make a legible copy of the record, and the Commissioners may thereupon destroy the original record or the copy record:

Provided that any authorisation required by the National Archives Act, 1986, for such destruction has been granted.

(3)   The legible copy of a record made in accordance with subsection (2) or the information concerning such record stored in accordance with subsection (2) shall be deemed to be an original record for the purposes of this section.

(4)   In any proceedings a certificate signed by an officer of the Commissioners stating that a copy record has been made in accordance with the provisions of subsection (2) shall be *prima facie* evidence, until the contrary has been proved, of the fact of the making of such a copy record and that it is a true copy.

(5)   In any proceedings a document purporting to be a certificate under subsection (4) shall be deemed, until the contrary has been proved, to be such a certificate without proof of the signature of the person purporting to sign the certificate or that such person was a proper person to so sign.

(6)   A provable record shall be admissible in evidence in any proceedings and shall be *prima facie* evidence, until the contrary has been proved, of any fact therein stated or event thereby recorded:

Provided that the court is satisfied of the reliability of the system used to make or compile-

(a)   in the case of an original record, that record, and

(b)   in the case of a copy record, the original on which it was based.

(7)   In any proceedings a certificate signed by an officer of the Commissioners stating that a full and detailed search has been made for a record of an event in every place where such records are kept and that no such record has been found shall be *prima facie* evidence, until the contrary has been proved, that the event did not happen:

Provided that the court is satisfied-

(a)   of the reliability of the system used to compile or make or keep such records,

(b)   that, if the event had happened, a record would have been made of it, and

(c)   that the system is such that the only reasonable explanation for the absence of such a record is that the event did not happen.

[...][28]][29]

Charge of excise duty

132. (1)   In addition to any other duty which may be chargeable, subject to the provisions of this Chapter and any regulations thereunder, with effect on and from the 1st day of January, 1993, a duty of excise, to be called vehicle registration tax, shall be charged, levied and paid [at whichever of the rates specified in subsection (3) is appropriate][30] on —

(a)   the registration of a vehicle, and

(b)   a declaration under section 131(3).

[(2)   Vehicle registration tax shall become due and be paid at the time of the registration of a vehicle or the making of the declaration under section 131(3), as may be appropriate, by —

(a)   **an authorised person in accordance with section 136(5)(b),**

(b)   **the person who registers the vehicle,**

(c)   **the person who has converted the vehicle where the prescribed particulars in relation to the conversion have not been declared to the Commissioners in accordance with section 131(3),**

(d)   **the person who is in possession of the vehicle that is a converted vehicle which has not been declared to the Commissioners in accordance with section 131(4),**

and where under paragraphs (a) to (d), more than one such person is, in any case, liable for the payment of a vehicle registration tax liability, then such persons shall be jointly and severally liable.][31]

[(3)   The duty of excise imposed by subsection (1) shall be charged, levied and paid-

[(a)   in case the vehicle the subject of the registration or declaration concerned is a category A vehicle —

(i)   by reference to the Table to this subsection, or

(ii)   where —

(I)   the level of CO_2 emissions cannot be confirmed by reference to the relevant EC type-approval certificate or EC certificate of conformity, and

(II)   the Commissioners are not satisfied of the level of CO_2 emissions by reference to any other document produced in support of the declaration for registration,

at the rate of an amount equal to the highest percentage specified in the Table to this subsection of the value of the vehicle or €720, whichever is the greater,][32]

(c)   in case it is a category B vehicle, at the rate of an amount equal to 13.3 per cent of the value of the vehicle or [€125][33], whichever is the greater,

(d)   in case it is a category C vehicle, at the rate of [€50][34],

(e)   in case it is a category D vehicle, at the rate of nil per cent of the value of the vehicle,

(f)   subject to subsection (4), in case it is a motor-cycle –

    (i)   if it is propelled by an internal combustion engine the cubic capacity of which does not exceed 350 cubic centimetres, at the rate of [[€2][35] per cubic centimetre][36] of such capacity,

    (ii)   if it is propelled by an internal combustion engine the cubic capacity of which exceeds 350 cubic centimetres, at the rate of [[€2][37] per cubic centimetre][36] in respect of the first 350 cubic centimetres of such capacity and [[€1][38] per cubic centimetre][39] in respect of each additional cubic centimetre of such capacity, and

    (iii)   if it is propelled by means other than an internal combustion engine, at the rate at which it would be charged, levied and paid if the motor-cycle were propelled by an internal combustion engine of the same power output.][40]

[TABLE

CO_2 Emissions (CO_2 g/km)	Percentage payable of the value of the vehicle
0 g/km up to and including 120 g/km	14% or €280 whichever is the greater
More than 120 g/km up to and including 140 g/km	16% or €320 whichever is the greater
More than 140 g/km up to and including 155 g/km	20% or €400 whichever is the greater
More than 155 g/km up to and including 170 g/km	24% or €480 whichever is the greater
More than 170 g/km up to and including 190 g/km	28% or €560 whichever is the greater
More than 190 g/km up to and including 225 g/km	32% or €640 whichever is the greater
More than 225 g/km	36% or €720 whichever is the greater

][41]

[(3A) Notwithstanding subsection (3), where the Commissioners are of the opinion that a vehicle has not been registered at the time specified in Regulation 8 of the Vehicle Registration and Taxation Regulations 1992 (S.I. No. 318 of 1992), the amount of vehicle registration tax due and payable in accordance with subsection (3) shall be increased by an amount calculated in accordance with the following formula:

$$A \times P \times N$$

where —

A is the amount of vehicle registration tax calculated in accordance with subsection (3),

P is 0.1 per cent, and

N is the number of days from the date the vehicle should have been registered in accordance with Regulation 8 of the Vehicle Registration and Taxation Regulations 1992 and the date of registration of the vehicle.][42]

[(4) (a) Where a motor-cycle is shown, to the satisfaction of the Commissioners, to be more than 3 months old, the total amount of vehicle registration tax payable in respect of the motor-cycle shall be reduced by reference to its age by the appropriate percentage specified in the Table to this subsection.

(b) In this subsection "**age**", in relation to a motor-cycle, means the time that has elapsed since the date on which the motor-cycle first entered into service.

TABLE

Age of motor-cycle	Percentage by which the amount of vehicle registration tax payable shall be reduced
Over 3 months but not more than 1 year	10%
Over 1 year but not more than 2 years	20%
Over 2 years but not more than 3 years	40%
Over 3 years but not more than 4 years	50%
Over 4 years but not more than 5 years	60%
Over 5 years but not more than 7 years	70%
Over 7 years but not more than 10 years	80%
Over 10 years but not more than 30 years	90%
Over 30 years	100%

][43]

[(5)   Where a registered vehicle which is converted and on which, in a former state, vehicle registration tax or motor vehicle excise duty imposed by the Order of 1979 has been paid, then the amount of vehicle registration tax payable on the vehicle under subsection (3) shall be reduced by -

(a)   in the case of a vehicle in respect of which vehicle registration fax has been so paid, such amount as bears to the amount of the tax paid the same proportion as the open market selling price of the vehicle immediately prior to its conversion bears to the open market selling price of the vehicle at the time of its registration, and

(b)   in the case of a vehicle in respect of which motor vehicle excise duty under the Order of 1979 has been so paid, such amount as bears to the amount of the duty paid the same proportion as the open market selling price of the vehicle immediately prior to its conversion bears to the open market selling price of the vehicle, as determined by the Commissioners, at the time of the charging of the duty.]⁴⁴

[(6)   Where a vehicle is registered without payment of vehicle registration tax under subsection (1), (4) or (5) of section 134 or the tax in respect of the registration has been paid at less than the rate ordinarily chargeable, or has been repaid in whole or in part, under the said subsection (5) and, by reason of a change in the use to which it is put, it is used otherwise than in accordance with the conditions, restrictions or limitations to which the registration without payment of vehicle registration tax was subject, vehicle registration tax shall become due and payable at the time of such change in use at the rate and on the value appropriate to the vehicle at that time unless the Commissioners determine otherwise.]⁴⁵

Chargeable value

133. (1)   Where the rate of vehicle registration tax charged in relation to a category A vehicle or a category B vehicle is calculated by reference to the value of the vehicle, that value shall be taken to be the open market selling price of the vehicle at the time of the charging of the tax thereon.

(2)   (a)   For a new vehicle on sale in the State which is supplied by a manufacturer or sole wholesale distributor, such manufacturer or distributor shall declare to the Commissioners in the prescribed manner [the price, inclusive of all taxes and duties,]⁴⁶ which, in his opinion, a vehicle of that model and specification, including any enhancements or accessories fitted or attached thereto or supplied therewith by such manufacturer or distributor, might reasonably be expected to fetch on a first arm's length sale thereof in the open market in the State by retail.

(b)   A price standing declared for the time being to the Commissioners in accordance with this subsection in relation to a new vehicle shall be deemed to be the open market selling price of each new vehicle of that model and specification.

[...][47]

[(c)   Notwithstanding the provisions of paragraph (b), where a price stands declared for a vehicle in accordance with this subsection which, in the opinion of the Commissioners, is higher or lower than the open market selling price at which a vehicle of that model and specification or a vehicle of a similar type and character is being offered for sale in the State while such price stands declared, the open market selling price may be determined from time to time by the Commissioners for the purposes of this section.][48]

[(d)   Where a manufacturer or sole wholesale distributor fails to make a declaration under paragraph (a) or to make it in the prescribed manner, the open market selling price of the vehicle concemed may be determined [from time to time][49] by the Commissioners for the purposes of this section.][50]

(3)   In this section -

"new vehicle" means a vehicle which is less than 3 months old when reckoned from its first entry into service or which has travelled less than 3,000 kilometres;

["open market selling price" means -

(a)   in the case of a new vehicle referred to in subsection (2), the price as determined by that subsection,

(b)   in the case of any other new vehicle, the price, inclusive of all taxes and duties, which, in the opinion of the Commissioners, would be determined under subsection (2) in relation to that vehicle if it were on sale in the State following supply by a manufacturer or sole wholesale distributor in the State,

(c)   in the case of a vehicle other than a new vehicle, the price, inclusive of all taxes and duties, which, in the opinion of the Commissioners, the vehicle might reasonably be expected to fetch on a first arm's length sale thereof in the State by retail and, in arriving at such price -

(i)   there shall be included in the price, having regard to the model and specification of the vehicle concerned, the value of any enhancements or accessories which at the time of registration are not fitted or attached to the vehicle or sold therewith but which would normally be expected to be fitted or attached thereto or sold therewith unless it is shown to the satisfaction of the Commissioners that, at that time, such enhancements or accessories have not been removed from the vehicle or not sold therewith for the purposes of reducing its open market selling price, and

    (ii)   the value of those enhancements or accessories which would not be taken into account in determining the open market selling price of the vehicle under the provisions of subsection (2) if the vehicle were a new vehicle to which that subsection applied shall be excluded from the price.][51]

Permanent reliefs

134. (1)   A vehicle may, subject to any conditions, restrictions or limitations prescribed by the Minister by regulations made by him under section 141 be registered without payment of vehicle registration tax if the vehicle is -

    (a)   the personal property of a private individual and is being brought permanently into the State by the individual when he is transferring his normal residence from a place outside the State to a place in the State,

    (b)   being brought permanently into the State as part of the capital goods and other equipment of a business undertaking which definitively ceases, its activity outside the State and moves to the State in order to carry on a similar activity there,

    (c)   the personal property of a deceased person and is being brought permanently into the State by a person resident in the State, or a person or body of persons established in the State and engaged in a non-profit making activity, who either acquired by inheritance the ownership or beneficial ownership of such vehicle or is the personal representative resident in the State of the deceased person,

    (d)   given as a gift, in token of friendship or good will by an official body, public authority or group carrying on an activity in the public service or interest, which is located outside the State, to an official body, public authority or group carrying on an activity in the public service or interest, which is located in the State and is approved by the Commissioners for the purposes of this paragraph,

    (e)   for official use by an institution of the European Communities,

(f)   for the personal use of officials or other members of the staff of an institution of the European Communities who transfer their residence to the State to take up a position there with an institution of the European Communities,

(g)   supplied under diplomatic, consular or similar arrangements by virtue of the Diplomatic Relations and Immunities Acts, 1967 and 1976, and orders made thereunder,

[(h)   for official use by the European Foundation for the Improvement of Living and Working Conditions,

(i)   for the personal use of officials or other members of the staff of the European Foundation for the Improvement of Living and Working Conditions, who transfer their residence to the State to take up a position there with the Foundation.]⁵²

(2)   Effect may be given to the provisions of subsection (1) by means of a repayment of vehicle registration tax subject to any conditions the Commissioners see fit to impose.

(3)   The reliefs allowed under the Disabled Drivers (Tax Concessions) Regulations, 1989 (S.I. No.340 of 1989), shall apply with any necessary modifications to vehicle registration tax.

(4)   A vehicle may be registered, subject to such conditions, limitations and restrictions (if any) as the Commissioners may impose, without payment of vehicle registration tax and with the repayment of any such tax paid, where the Commissioners are satisfied that such vehicle is for use -

(i)   in the establishment or maintenance of an international air service using or involving the use of an airport in the State,

(ii)   in the establishment or maintenance of radio or meteorological services or other aids to air navigation ancillary to any such international air service, or

(iii)   for experimental purposes in connection with the establishment or maintenance of any such international air service.

(5)   Whenever the Minister so thinks proper, he may authorise the Commissioners to register a vehicle, subject to such conditions, limitations or restrictions (if any) as they may impose, either without payment of vehicle registration tax or on payment of the tax at less than the rate ordinarily chargeable or, where the said tax has been paid, to repay the tax in whole or in part.

[(6)   When an entry in the register is deleted and the Commissioners are satisfied that the deletion is warranted by exceptional circumstances which arose within 7 working days after the registration of the vehicle concerned and the vehicle had not been the subject of a licence under the Act of 1952, they may, subject to such conditions as they may impose, repay the whole or part of the vehicle registration tax paid on the vehicle concerned.

(7)   Subject to subsection (9), where a person carrying on the business of leasing or hiring vehicles to others or providing instruction in the driving of vehicles, acquires an unregistered category A vehicle or motor-cycle and the acquisition is one in respect of which he is entitled under section 12 of the Value-Added Tax Act, 1972, to a deduction of the value-added tax charged to him in respect of the acquisition, an amount of the vehicle registration tax paid in respect of the vehicle shall be repaid to the person, subject to any prescribed conditions, restrictions and limitations. **[For the avoidance of doubt, the business of hiring vehicles does not include and shall be deemed never to have included the hiring of vehicles that are a supply of the kind specified in paragraph (i)(e) of the First Schedule of the Value-Added Tax Act 1972, in respect of vehicles supplied pursuant to an agreement in accordance with section 3(1)(b) of that Act.]**[53]

(8)   The amount of the repayment of vehicle registration tax to a person under subsection (7) shall be a percentage of such tax paid in respect of the vehicle concerned determined by the formula -

$$\frac{R \times 100}{(R + 100)}$$

where R is the percentage rate of value-added tax chargeable on the acquisition of the vehicle by the person.

(9)   A repayment of vehicle registration tax to a person under subsection (7) shall be made only where an entitlement to a deduction of value added tax charged has accrued to the person upon the acquisition of the vehicle concerned after the 1st day of January, 1993:

Provided that, any value-added tax payable by the person otherwise entitled to the refund of vehicle registration tax provided for under subsection (7) and due by the date of repayment of vehicle registration tax has been paid.

(10)   Nothing in subsection (7) shall authorise more than one repayment of vehicle registration tax in respect of a vehicle.][54]

[(11)   (a)   Subject to the provisions of this section, where an authorised person-

        (i)   has declared a new category A vehicle to the Commissioners for the purposes of registration,

                or

        (ii)   has acquired (whether by purchase or under a lease or otherwise) a new category A vehicle prior to the 1st day of July, 1993,

and the vehicle has been used by him subsequently solely for hiring to others under short-term self-drive contracts, an amount, calculated pursuant to subsection (12), of the vehicle registration tax, or, as the case may be, of the motor vehicle excise duty under the Order of 1979, paid in respect of the vehicle shall, subject to any prescribed conditions, restrictions or limitations, be repaid to the person when he ceases to use the vehicle solely for hiring to others under such contracts.

[(b)   In paragraph (a) 'short-term self-drive contracts' means contracts under which vehicles are hired to persons for the purpose of being driven by them for any term or part of a term which, when added to the term of any such hiring of the same vehicle or any other vehicle to the same person does not exceed 5 weeks in any period of 6 months from the date of the commencement of the last hiring.]⁵⁵

[Provided that for the purposes of subsections (11) to (14) a vehicle shall not include a vehicle hired, lent or otherwise given or arranged by an authorised person as a replacement vehicle for a vehicle either being repaired or due to be repaired by him or on his behalf and not previously declared under subsection (11).]⁵⁶]⁵⁷

[(12)   (a)   The amount (if any) of the repayment to a person under subsection (11) shall be -

(i)   in the case of a vehicle in respect of which vehicle registration tax has been paid, such amount as bears to the amount of the tax paid (less the amount of any repayment paid or due to the person under subsection (7)) the same proportion as the appropriate amount bears to the open market selling price of the vehicle at the time of its registration, and

(ii)   in the case of a vehicle in respect of which motor vehicle excise duty under the Order of 1979 has been paid, such amount as bears to the amount of the duty paid the same proportion as the appropriate amount bears to the open market selling price of the vehicle, as determined by the Commissioners, at the time of the charging of the duty.

(b)   In paragraph (a) "the appropriate amount", in relation to a vehicle, means the amount (if any), determined by the Commissioners, by which the open market selling price of the vehicle has fallen between the time of its registration or, as the case may be, the time of the charging of the excise duty under the Order of 1979 and the time of the cessation, in relation to the vehicle, referred to in subsection (11)(a).]⁵⁷

[(13)   [A repayment to a person under subsection (11) shall not be made-

   (a)   where a vehicle has travelled less than 5,000 miles from the date of its declaration for registration,

   (b)   where a vehicle is removed from hire within 3 months of the date of its declaration for registration,

   (c)   where a vehicle is removed from hire prior to the 31st day of August in the year of its declaration for registration,

   (d)   where a vehicle is not at a premises used by the person for the purpose of carrying on the business of hiring vehicles under short-term self-drive contracts within 10 working days of the date of its declaration for registration,

          where any vehicle registration tax or value-added tax payable by the person by the date of repayment has not been paid, or

   (f)   in respect of a vehicle on which motor vehicle excise duty under the Order of 1979 has been paid prior to the 1st day of January, 1991.]⁵⁸]⁵⁷

(14)   [A repayment under subsection (11) shall be made only in respect of a vehicle as respects which the cessation referred to in subsection (11)(a) occurs on or after the 1st day of September, 1993.]⁵⁷

[[(15)   (a)   **The repayment amount referred to in subsection (11)(a) shall be reduced by 33 per cent for vehicles that are withdrawn from short-term car-hire during the period 1 October 2009 to 30 September 2010.**

         (b)   **The repayment amount referred to in subsection (11)(a) shall be reduced by 66 per cent for vehicles that are withdrawn from short-term car-hire during the period 1 30 September 2011.]⁵⁹]⁵⁷**

[...]⁶⁰]⁶¹

Temporary exemption from registration

[135.   (1)   **A vehicle which is temporarily brought into the State may be exempted by the Commissioners from the requirement to be registered, in such manner and subject to such conditions, restrictions and limitations as the Minister may prescribe by regulations made under section 141(3) if the vehicle is —**

         (a)   **brought into the State by a person established outside the State for such person's private or business use,**

(b) brought into the State by an individual established in the State for such individual's private or business use where such an individual—

(i) is employed by an employer established in another Member State who provides a vehicle as part of their contract of employment, where such vehicle is owned or leased by the employer, or

(ii) is self-employed and has established a legally accountable undertaking in another Member State, whose business is carried on solely or principally in the other Member State, and where the vehicle is a category A vehicle or a motor-cycle, it is used principally for business use in another Member State,

(c) brought into the State solely for the purpose of a competition, exhibition, show, demonstration, or similar purpose and is not intended to be sold or offered for sale in the State and is intended to be taken out of the State on the fulfilment of such purpose, or

(d) designed or specially adapted as professional equipment brought into the State by a person established outside the State for use exclusively by such person or under his or her personal supervision.

(2) A vehicle which is temporarily brought into the State for a period in excess of 42 days (or such longer period as may be prescribed by the Commissioners) may, subject to regulations, be required to be registered in accordance with section 131 without the payment of vehicle registration tax.

(3) In respect of a vehicle to which subsection (2) relates, a statement issued by a competent person under section 131(1)(ba) shall be produced to the Commissioners prior to the registration of the vehicle.

(4) Any fee charged by the competent person for the examination shall be agreed with the Commissioners and shall be paid by the person presenting the vehicle for the pre-registration examination. Such fee shall be credited against any vehicle registration tax subsequently payable by the person so presenting if the vehicle subsequently becomes liable for that tax without the vehicle being permanently removed from the State.

(5) In this section a reference to the temporary importation of a vehicle shall be construed in accordance with Regulation 5 of the Temporary Exemption from Registration of Vehicles Regulations 1993 (S.I. No. 60 of 1993).][62]

Special purpose vehicles

[135A. A special purpose vehicle which is intended for use other than in a public place is exempt from the requirement to be registered unless and until it is required to be the subject of a licence under the Act of 1952.][63]

Repayment of amounts in respect of vehicle registration tax in certain cases

[135B. (1)   The Commissioners may repay to a person an amount of £1,000 in respect of vehicle registration tax paid in respect of a new category A vehicle if -

(a)   the vehicle is first registered during the period from the 1st day of July, 1995 to the [31st day of December, 1997,][64]

(b)   the person becomes registered as the owner of the vehicle at the time when the vehicle is first registered, and

(c)   a category A vehicle owned by the person ("**the scrapped vehicle**") is shown, to the satisfaction of the Revenue Commissioners, to have been scrapped during the period aforesaid and within one month of the date of the first registration of the other vehicle,

(d)   the scrapped vehicle was first registered or recorded, not less than 10 years before the date on which it is scrapped, under section 131 or section 6 of the Roads Act, 1920, or a system for maintaining a record of vehicles and their ownership established by or on behalf of the government of another state, and

(e)   during the whole of the period of 2 years ending on the date aforesaid

(i)   a licence under section 1 of the Act of 1952 taken out by the person was in force in respect of the scrapped vehicle, and

(ii)   an approved policy of insurance referred to in paragraph (a) of section 56(1) of the Road Traffic Act, 1961, and issued to the person, was in force in respect of the scrapped vehicle, or the person was an exempted person within the meaning of section 60 (inserted by section 54 of the Road Traffic Act, 1968) of that Act:

[Provided that for the purposes of paragraphs (c) and (e) any reference to "**the person**" may, in the application of those provisions, be construed by the Commissioners as a reference to the person concerned or to that person's spouse.][65]

(2)   Notwithstanding paragraph (e) of subsection (1), the Commissioners may make a repayment under that subsection in a case where, during a period or periods not exceeding, or

not exceeding in aggregate, 6 months and occurring in, but not including the last day of, the period, as respects the scrapped vehicle concerned, referred to in the said paragraph (e) -

(a)   a licence referred to in that paragraph was not in force, or

(b)   both such a licence and an approved policy of insurance referred to in that paragraph were not in force,

in respect of the scrapped vehicle if, in respect of the period or each period during which such a licence was not in force, a declaration of non-use of the vehicle made before a member of the Garda Síochána and stamped with the appropriate Garda Síochána station stamp was accepted by the licensing authority concerned in respect of the vehicle.

(3)   A vehicle in respect of which a repayment under subsection (1) has been made shall not be disposed of during the period of 6 months from the date of its first registration and, if such a vehicle is so disposed of, the person to whom such a repayment was made shall pay to the Commissioners on the day of the disposal an amount in respect of vehicle registration tax equal to the amount of the repayment.

(4)   An amount due by a person to the Commissioners under subsection (3) may be recovered by them from the person as a simple contract debt in any court of competent jurisdiction.

(5)   In this section -

"**new**" means not used or secondhand;

"**scrapped**", in relation to a vehicle, means subjected to the destruction of the

chassis and the engine of the vehicle.][66]

[(6)   (a)   **Subject to sections 105B, 105C and 105D of the Finance Act 2001 where an authorised person pays an amount of vehicle registration tax in respect of a vehicle which was not due, any repayment of the overpaid amount and interest (if any) payable under section 105D shall, subject to the provisions of this subsection, be made to the authorised person on condition that the authorised person pays the amount of the repayment and interest to the person who was the registered owner of the vehicle at the time of the registration of the vehicle.**

    (b)   (i)   **Where the registered owner of the vehicle at the date of the repayment to the authorised person is the first registered owner the amount of the repayment shall be the amount of the vehicle registration tax overpaid.**

        [(ii)   **Where the first registered owner has disposed of the vehicle prior to the date of the making of the** repayment claim the amount of the repayment shall be limited to an amount calculated as follows:

$$\frac{V \times (OP - S)}{OP}$$

where —

V   is the amount of vehicle registration tax overpaid,

S   is the price, if any, received by the first registered owner at the time of disposal but where S is greater than OP, OP shall be taken as the price received, and

OP   is the price, including all taxes, declared to the Commissioners at the time of first registration of the vehicle.][67]

(c)   For the purpose of paragraph (b) the first registered owner shall as a condition of the repayment present documentary proof to the Commissioners of the disposal of the vehicle and the price (if any) received by that owner in respect of that disposal.

(d)   An authorised person shall be entitled to deduct an amount not more than 10 per cent of the repayment from the payment to the first registered owner of the vehicle to cover the costs of the authorised person in processing the repayment claim.

(e)   Where an authorised person fails to make a payment within 30 days to the first registered owner in accordance with paragraph (a) following payment by the Commissioners of such repayment, any amount unpaid, shall for the purpose of this Act, be treated as if it were vehicle registration tax due by the authorised person on the day following the expiry of the 30 day period.][68]

Remission or repayment in respect of vehicle registration tax on certain hybrid electric vehicles

[135C. (1)   In this section —

'hybrid electric vehicle' means a vehicle that derives its motive power from a combination of an electric motor and an internal combustion engine and is capable of being driven on electric propulsion alone for a material part of its normal driving cycle;

'flexible fuel vehicle' means a vehicle that derives its motive power from an internal combustion engine that is capable of using a blend of ethanol and petrol, where such blend contains a minimum of 85 per cent ethanol;

'electric vehicle' means a vehicle that derives its motive power exclusively from an electric motor;

'electric motorcycle' means a motorcycle that derives its motive power exclusively from an electric motor.

(2)   Where a person first registers a category A vehicle or a category B vehicle during the period from 1 January 2008 to 30 June 2008 and the Commissioners are satisfied that the vehicle is—

    (a)   a series production hybrid electric vehicle, or

    (b)   a series production flexible fuel vehicle,

then the Commissioners may remit or repay to that person 50 per cent of the vehicle registration tax payable or paid in accordance with paragraphs (a), (aa), (b) or (c) of section 132(3).

(3)   (a)   Where a person first registers a category A vehicle or a category B vehicle during the period from 1 July 2008 to 31 December 2010 and the Commissioners are satisfied that the vehicle is—

    (i)   a series production hybrid electric vehicle, or

    (ii)   a series production flexible fuel vehicle,

then the Commissioners may remit or repay to that person up to a maximum amount of €2,500 of the vehicle registration tax payable or paid by reference to the Table to this subsection in accordance with paragraphs (a), (b) or (c) of section 132(3).

    (b)   In this subsection "age", in relation to a vehicle means the time that has elapsed since the date on which the vehicle first entered into service.

TABLE

Age of vehicle	Maximum amount which may be remitted or repaid
New vehicle, first registration	€2,500
Not a new vehicle but less than 2 years	€2,250
2 years or over but less than 3 years	€2,000
3 years or over but less than 4 years	€1,750
4 years or over but less than 5 years	€1,500
5 years or over but less than 6 years	€1,250
6 years or over but less than 7 years	€1,000
7 years or over but less than 8 years	€750

Age of vehicle	Maximum amount which may be remitted or repaid
8 years or over but less than 9 years	€200
9 years or over but less than 10 years	€250
10 years or over	Nil

(4)　　A category A electric vehicle or a category B electric vehicle first registered during the period 1 January 2008 to 31 December 2010 is exempt from vehicle registration tax where the Commissioners are satisfied that such vehicle is a series production electric vehicle.

(5)　　An electric motorcycle first registered during the period 1 January 2008 to 31 December 2010 is exempt from vehicle registration tax where the Commissioners are satisfied that such vehicle is a series production electric motorcycle.][69]

Authorisation of manufacturers, distributors and dealers and periodic payment of duty

136. (1)　　Notwithstanding the provisions of section 131, a person may be authorised by the Commissioners to manufacture, distribute, deal in, deliver, store, repair or modify unregistered vehicles and to convert registered vehicles.

(2)　　A person shall not be authorised under this section unless he appears to the Commissioners to satisfy such requirements as they may think fit to impose.

(3)　　The Commissioners may, at any time for reasonable cause (which shall be stated to the authorised person) and following such notice as is reasonable in the circumstances, revoke an authorisation made under this section or vary its terms.

(4)　　An authorised person shall not deliver, send out or otherwise make available for use an unregistered vehicle other than to another authorised person.

(5)　　An authorised person shall not deliver, send out or otherwise make available for use a vehicle which, but for compliance with this subsection, would be unregistered, to a person who is not an authorised person without first -

(a)　　declaring the prescribed details of the vehicle to the Commissioners in accordance with section 131, and

[(aa)　　ensuring that the identification mark assigned to it under section 131(5) is displayed on the vehicle in the prescribed manner, and][70]

(b)　　paying vehicle registration tax in respect of the registration of the vehicle.

[(6)   For the purposes of subsection (5) the Commissioners may, subject to compliance with such conditions for securing payment as they may think fit to impose, permit payment of vehicle registration tax to be deferred -

(a)   to a day not later than the 15th day of the month following that in which the tax is charged,

or

(b)   in the case of a new category A vehicle purchased by an authorised person carrying on the business of hiring vehicles to others under short-term self-drive contracts (within the meaning of section 134(11)(b)) and intended for use solely for the purposes of such hiring in the course of that business -

(i)   if the tax is charged on or after the 1st day of December in any year and prior to the 1st day of September in the following year, to a day not later than the 15th day of September in the said following year,

or

(ii)   if the tax is charged on or after the 1st day of September in any year and prior to the 1st day of December in that year, to a day not later than the 15th day of December in that year,

or the day of the cessation, in relation to the vehicle, referred to in section 134(1l)(a), whichever is the earlier.]⁷¹

(7)   Notwithstanding the provisions of subsections (4) and (5), the Commissioners may, subject to compliance with such conditions as they may think fit to impose, allow an unregistered vehicle to be delivered by an authorised person for temporary display or exhibition.

[(8)   An unregistered vehicle may not be used in a public place by an authorised person except in the course of the business to which the authorisation under section 136 relates and in accordance with such conditions, restrictions or limitations as may be prescribed.]⁷²

Accountability for unregistered vehicles and converted vehicles

137.   An authorised person shall account to the satisfaction of the Commissioners in the prescribed manner for all unregistered vehicles and converted vehicles received by him or manufactured by him.

Appeals

138.   [...]⁷³

Offences and penalties

139. (1)   It shall be an offence under this subsection for a person, in respect of a vehicle in the State -

(a)   to make a declaration under section 131 which is false or in any material respect misleading or to allow any other person to make such a declaration on his behalf,

[(b)   to be in possession of the vehicle if an identification mark referred to in section 131(6) is not displayed on it or is not displayed on it in the prescribed manner,][74]

[(bb)   if the vehicle is an unregistered vehicle, to use it in a public place in contravention of the prescribed conditions,][75]

(c)   to display an identification mark on the vehicle in contravention of section 131(6),

(d)   to destroy, mutilate, deface, alter, amend or in any other way interfere with the certificate without authorisation from the Commissioners,

(e)   to fail to make a declaration under section 133(2)(a), or to make it in the prescribed manner, when required to do so by the Commissioners, or

(f)   to contravene or fail to comply, whether by act or omission, with any other provision of this Chapter or of regulations under section 141.

(2)   Without prejudice to any other penalty to which he may be liable, any person guilty of an offence under subsection (1) shall be liable on summary conviction to a penalty under the law relating to excise of [€5,000][76].

(3)   It shall be an offence under this subsection for a person, in respect of a vehicle in the State -

(a)   to be in possession of the vehicle if it is unregistered unless he is an authorised person or the vehicle is the subject of an exemption under section 135 for the time being in force and the vehicle is being used in accordance with any conditions, restrictions or limitations referred to in section 135,

(b)   if the vehicle is the subject of an exemption under section 134, to be in possession of the vehicle other than in accordance with any conditions, restrictions or limitations referred to in section 134,

(c)   to issue or to be in possession of a document which purports to be, but is not, a certificate,

(d)   to fail to pay any vehicle registration tax due by him,

(e)   if the vehicle is an unregistered vehicle or a converted vehicle, to fail to account for it in accordance with section 137, [...][77]

[(ee) to be in possession of the vehicle if it is a converted vehicle in relation to which particulars of the conversion have not been declared in accordance with section 131 or a converted vehicle in relation to which particulars of the conversion have been so declared but vehicle registration tax has not been paid on the declaration unless he is an authorised person, or][78]

(f)   if the vehicle is an unregistered vehicle or a converted vehicle in relation to which particulars of the conversion have not been declared in accordance with section 131 or a converted vehicle in relation to which particulars of the conversion have been so declared but vehicle registration tax has not been paid on the declaration, to deliver the vehicle to a person other than an authorised person.

(4)   Without prejudice to any other penalty to which he may be liable, any person guilty of an offence under subsection (3) shall be liable on summary conviction to a penalty under the law relating to excise of [€5,000][76].

[(5) If any person is knowingly concerned in the evasion or the taking of steps for the purposes of the evasion, whether by himself or by another, of vehicle registration tax, he shall be guilty of an offence and shall be liable -

(a)   on summary conviction, to a penalty under the law relating to excise of [€5,000][76] or to imprisonment for a term not exceeding 6 months or to both,

or

(b)   on conviction on indictment, to a penalty, under the law relating to excise, of three times the amount of the vehicle registration tax concerned or [€12,695][79], whichever is the greater, or to imprisonment for a term not exceeding five years or to both.][80]

[(6) A vehicle in respect of which an offence under subsection (3) or (5) was committed shall be liable to forfeiture.][81]

Evidence

140. (1)   In any proceedings for an offence under this Chapter in respect of failure to pay any amount of vehicle registration tax, it shall be presumed until the contraly is shown that the vehicle registration tax in respect of the vehicle to which the charge relates has not been paid.

(2)   A certificate or a document purporting to be signed by an officer of the Commissioners and to contain particulars extracted from

the register or a document purporting to be signed by an officer of the Commissioners and to contain particulars extracted from any other records relating to vehicles shall, without proof of the signature of such officer, or that he was an officer of the Commissioners, be evidence, until the contrary is shown, of the particulars aforesaid stated in the certificate or document.

Regulations

141. (1) (a) The Commissioners may make such regulations as they consider necessary or expedient for the purpose of managing the registration of vehicles and managing, securing and collecting vehicle registration tax.

(b) The Commissioners shall not make regulations for a purpose specified in subsection (3).

(2) In particular, but without prejudice to the generality of subsection (1), regulations under subsection (1) may -

(a) prescribe the method of establishment and maintenance of the register,

(b) prescribe the particulars to be declared to the Commissioners under section 131,

(c) prescribe the manner in which a declaration under section 131 shall be made,

[...]⁸²

(e) prescribe the manner of assigning identification marks under section 131(5),

(f) prescribe the size, shape and character of the identification marks aforesaid and the manner in which they are to be rendered easily distinguishable, whether by night or by day,

(g) require that specified particulars shall be marked on a vehicle and shall be accessible and legible,

(h) prescribe the method of charging, securing and collecting vehicle registration tax,

(i) make provision in relation to the authorisation of persons under section 136,

(j) make provision in relation to the manufacture, storage, conditions of use and disposal of unregistered vehicles and of converted vehicles in respect of which any vehicle registration tax has not been paid,

(k) require an authorised person to keep in a specified manner, and to preserve for a specified period, specified records and accounts relating to the receipt, manufacture, delivery and sale of unregistered or converted vehicles and to allow an officer of the Commissioners, duly authorised by them in that behalf, on production of his authorisation if so requested by any person affected, to inspect and take copies of or extracts from such records and accounts and any other books or documents kept by him relating to any of the matters aforesaid,

(l) require an authorised person to make proper entry with the proper officer of the Commissioners of all premises intended to be used by him in the carrying on of his business and to provide for the method of entry with the said officer,

(m) prescribe the form and contents of declarations under section 133 and the times at which they shall be made, and

[(n) prescribe the manner of accounting for vehicles under section 137,

(o) make provision in relation to the deletion of an entry from the register,

(p) make provision in relation to the establishment and maintenance of the zz register,

(q) specify the fee payable on the assignment of an identification mark under subsection 131(5A),

(r) specify the conditions subject to which unregistered vehicles may be used in a public place by an authorised person,

[(s) make provision (including the prescription of conditions, restrictions and limitations) in relation to [subsections (7) and (11)]^{83} of section 134 and section 135B,]^{84}]^{85}

[(t) prescribe what constitutes permanently fitted equipment for the purposes of the definition of 'motor caravan' in section 130,

(u) prescribe the manner in which the rigid partition which completely and permanently separates the cab from the area designed, constructed or adapted exclusively for the carriage of goods in a crew cab or a pick-up is to be fixed for the purposes of the definition of 'crew cab' and **'pick-up'** in section 130,

(v) prescribe the manner in which the floor length of the area designed, constructed or adapted exclusively for the carriage of goods in a crew cab or a pick-up is to be measured for the purposes of the definition of 'crew cab' and 'pick-up' **[in section 130,]**^{86}]^{87}

[(w) **make provision for matters to be prescribed for the purposes of section 131(1)(ba), and for the purposes of**

section 135, in respect of the pre-registration examination of vehicles.][88]

[(3) The Minister may make such regulations as he considers necessary or expedient for the purpose of giving full effect to sections 134 ([other than subsections (6), (7), and (11)][89]) and 135][90]

[(3A) Without prejudice to the generality of subsection (3), regulations under that subsection may contain such incidental, supplementary and consequential provisions as appear to the Minister to be necessary for the purposes of giving full effect to the Directives, Council Directive 83/182/EEC of 23 April 1983 and Council Directive 83/183/EEC of 23 April 1983.][91]

(4) In particular, but without prejudice to the generality of subsection (3) regulations under subsection (3) may -

(a) prescribe the criteria for eligibility for the remission or repayment of vehicle registration tax,

(b) prescribe the amount of vehicle registration tax that may be remitted or repaid in respect of vehicles or specified vehicles or classes of vehicles,

(c) specify the time limits within which applications to the Commissioners for remission or repayment of vehicle registration tax under section 134 shall be made,

(d) prohibit the grant of such remission or repayment as aforesaid to a person in respect of vehicles in excess of a specified number,

(e) specify the periods during which a vehicle, in respect of which vehicle registration tax has been remitted or repaid, may not be disposed of, hired out or lent, and

(f) provide for such other matters as the Minister considers necessary or expedient for the purposes of giving full effect to this subsection.

(5) Regulations under this Chapter shall be laid before Dáil Éireann as soon as may be after they are made and, if a resolution annulling the regulations is passed by Dáil Éireann within the next 21 days on which Dáil Éireann has sat after the regulations have been laid before it, the regulations shall be annulled accordingly, but without prejudice to the validity of anything previously done thereunder.

Powers of Officers

142. [...][92]

[(3A) (a) The powers conferred on a member of the Garda Síochána by section 103 of the Road Traffic Act, 1961, in relation to the delivery to persons and affixing to vehicles of notices referred to in that section may be exercised by an officer of the Commissioners, duly authorised by them in that behalf, in relation to an offence under section 71 or 73 of the Finance Act, 1976, as if it were an offence to which the said section 103 applies.

(b)   Subsection (5) of the said section 103 shall apply in relation to an offence under the said section 71 or 73 as if it were an offence to which the said section 103 applies.

(c)   Whenever an officer of the Commissioners is exercising a power under the said section 103 conferred by virtue of paragraph (a), he shall, if so requested by any person affected, produce his authorisation to the person.

(d)   Proceedings for an offence specified in a notice under the said section 103 delivered to a person or affixed to a vehicle by an officer of the Commissioners or an offence under subsection (7) of that section in respect of a contravention of subsection (6) of that section in relation to such a notice may be brought and prosecuted by the Commissioners.][93]

[...][92]

Transitional provisions

143. (1)   A vehicle registered by a licensing authority for use in a public place before the 1st day of January, 1993, shall be deemed to be a registered vehicle.

(2)   Any vehicle on which motor vehicle excise duty has been paid, secured, relieved or remitted under the Order of 1979, [or any motor-cycle on which motor-cycle duty has been paid, secured, relieved or remitted under the Order of 1984,][94] before the 1st day of January, 1993, and which is required to be licensed under the Act of 1952 for use in a public place but which has not been so licensed before that date shall be entered in the register without payment of the duty imposed by section 132.

[(3)   A vehicle on which excise duty has been paid, secured, relieved or remitted under the Order of 1979 or the Order of 1984 before the 1st day of January, 1993, and which was not required to be the subject of a licence under the Act of 1952 before that day shall not be required to be entered in the register unless and until it is required to be the subject of such a licence.][95]

Application of enactments

144. The provisions of the statutes which relate to the duties of excise and the management thereof and of any instrument relating to duties of excise made under statute, and not otherwise applied by this Chapter, shall, with any necessary modifications, apply in relation to registration, vehicle registration tax and declarations under section 131(3) as they apply to duties of excise.

Repeal and revocations

[144A. (1)   Section 75 of the Finance Act, 1984, is hereby repealed with effect from the 1st day of January, 1993.

(2)   The Imposition of Duties (No.236)(Excise Duties on Motor Vehicles, Televisions and Gramophone Records) Order, 1979 (S.I. No.57 of 1979), the Imposition of Duties (No.272) (Excise Duties on Motor Vehicles) Order, 1984 (S.I. No.353 of 1984), the Imposition of Duties (No.273)(Excise Duty on Motor-cycles) Order, 1984 (S.I. No.354 of 1984), and the Imposition of Duties (No.279)(Motor Vehicles and Motor-cycles) (Amendment) Order, 1985 (S.I. No.267 of 1985), are hereby revoked with effect from the 1st day of January, 1993.]⁹⁶

Amendments

1   Definition substituted by s115, FA93, w.e.f. 25 March 1993.
2   Substituted by s53, FA93, w.e.f. 17 June 1993.
3   Inserted by s72(a), FA96, w.e.f. 15 May 1996.
4   Definition substituted by s6(a), F(No. 2)A 92, w.e.f. 1 January 1993.
5   Inserted by s101(1)(a)(i), FA03, w.e.f 1 July 2003.
6   Substituted by s101(1)(a)(i), FA03, w.e.f 1 July 2003.
7   Definition substituted by s169 FA01, w.e.f. date of Min. Order.
8   Definition substituted by s6(a), F(No. 2)A 92, w.e.f. 1 January 1993.
9   Definition inserted by s6(a), F(No. 2)A 92, w.e.f. 1 January 1993.
10 Inserted by s6(b), F(No. 2)A 92, w.e.f. 1 January 1993.
11 Definition substituted by s60(a), F(No. 2)A 2008, w.e.f. 24 December 2008.
12 Definition substituted by s101(1)(b), FA03, w.e.f. 1 July 2003.
13 Amended by s6(c), F(No. 2)A 92, w.e.f. 1 January 1993.
14 Substituted by s60(b), F(No. 2)A 2008, w.e.f. 24 December 2008.
15 Substituted by s63, FA07, w.e.f. 2 April 2007.
16 Inserted by s72(d), FA96, w.e.f. 15 May 1996.
17 Definition substituted by s60(c), F(No. 2)A 2008, w.e.f. 24 December 2008.
18 Definition inserted by s101(1)(c), FA03, w.e.f. 1 July 2003.
19 Inserted by s80, FA97, w.e.f. 10 May 1997.
20 Inserted by s99(a), FA00, w.e.f. 23 March 2000.
21 Inserted by s61, F(No. 2)A 2008, w.e.f. 1 January 2010.
22 Inserted by s7(a), F(No. 2)A 92, w.e.f. 1 January 1993.
23 Inserted by s7(b), F(No. 2)A 92, w.e.f. 1 January 1993.
24 Inserted by s7(c), F(No. 2)A 92, w.e.f. 1 January 1993.
25 Substituted by s102(1), FA 03, w.e.f. 28 May 2004.
26 Inserted by s7(d), F(No. 2)A 92, w.e.f. 1 January 1993.
27 Inserted by s7(e), F(No. 2)A 92, w.e.f. 1 January 1993.
28 Subs8 Deleted by s99(b), FA00, w.e.f. 23 March 2000.
29 S131A inserted by s81, FA97, w.e.f. 10 May 1997.
30 Substituted by s8(a), F(No. 2)A 92, w.e.f. 1 January 1993.
31 Substituted by s62(a), F(No. 2)A 2008, w.e.f. 24 December 2008.
32 Substitited by s79(1)(a), FA08, w.e.f. 1 July 2008.
33 Substituted by s240(a), FA01 & sch5, w.e.f. 1 January 2002, previously £100.
34 Substituted by s240(a), FA01 & sch5, w.e.f. 1 January 2002, previously £40.
35 Substituted by s240(a), FA01 & sch5, w.e.f. 1 January 2002, previously £2.
36 Substituted by s85(1)(c)(i), FA94, w.e.f. 27 January 1994.
37 Substituted by s240(a), FA01 & sch5, w.e.f. 1 January 2002, previously £2.
38 Substituted by s240(a), FA01 & sch5, w.e.f. 1 January 2002, previously £1.

39 Substituted by s85(1)(c)(ii), FA94, w.e.f. 27 January 1994.
40 Inserted by s8(b), F(No. 2)A 92, w.e.f. 1 January 1993.
41 Inserted by s79(1)(b), FA08, w.e.f. 1 July 2008.
42 Inserted by s62(b), F(No. 2)A 2008, w.e.f. 24 December 2008.
43 Inserted by s8(b), F(No. 2)A 92, w.e.f. 1 January 1993.
44 Substituted by s97(b), FA95, w.e.f. 2 June 1995.
45 Inserted by s8(b), F(No. 2)A 92, w.e.f. 1 January 1993.
46 Substituted by s9(a)(i), F(No. 2)A 92, w.e.f. 1 January 1992.
47 Proviso deleted by s9(a)(ii), F(No. 2)A 92, w.e.f. 1 January 1992.
48 Substituted by s101(a), FA00, w.e.f. 23 March 2000.
49 Inserted by s101(b), FA00, w.e.f. 23 March 2000.
50 Inserted by s9(a), F(No. 2)A 92, w.e.f. 1 January 1993.
51 Substituted by s9(b), F(No. 2)A 92, w.e.f. 1 January 1992.
52 Inserted by s10(a), F(No. 2)A 92 w.e.f. 1 January 1993.
53 Inserted by s63(1)(a), F(No. 2)A 2008, w.e.f. 24 December 2008.
54 Inserted by s10(b), F(No. 2)A 92 w.e.f. 1 January 1993.
55 Substituted by s63(1)(b), F(No. 2)A 2008, w.e.f. 24 December 2008.
56 Inserted by s81(a), FA98, w.e.f. 27 March 1998.
57 Section to be deleted w.e.f. 1 October 2011 in accordance with s63(2), F(No. 2)A 2008.
58 Substituted by s81(b), FA98, w.e.f. 27 March 1998.
59 Inserted by s63(1)(c), F(No. 2)A 2008, w.e.f. 24 December 2008.
60 Ss134(15) deleted by s104(1), FA03, w.e.f. 1 May 2003.
61 Inserted by s54, FA93, w.e.f. 17 June 1993.
62 Substituted by s64(1), F(No. 2)A 2008, w.e.f. date of Ministerial Order not available at time of print.
63 Inserted by s5(b), F(No. 2)A 92, w.e.f. 1 January 1993.
64 Substituted w.e.f. 20 December,1996.
65 Inserted by s73, FA96, w.e.f. 15 May,1996.
66 Inserted by s98(a), FA95, w.e.f. 1 July 1995.
67 Replaced by s19, FA09, w.e.f. 3 June 2009.
68 Inserted by s65, F(No. 2)A 2008, w.e.f. 24 December 2008.
69 S135C replaced by s81, FA08, w.e.f. 13 March 2008.
70 Inserted by s12(a), F(No. 2)A 92, w.e.f. 1 January 1993.
71 Substituted by s55, FA93, w.e.f. 17 June 1996.
72 Substituted by s12(b), F(No. 2)A 92, w.e.f. 1 January 1993.
73 Repealed by s108, FA95, w.e.f. 1 January 1996 (see replacement provisions s103-109,FA95).
74 Substituted by s13(a),F(No. 2)A 92, w.e.f. 1 January 1993.
75 Inserted by s13(a), F(No. 2)A 92, w.e.f. 1 January 1993.
76 Substituted by s77, FA08, w.e.f. 13 March 2008.
77 Word 'or' deleted by s82(a), FA98, w.e.f. 27 March 1998.
78 Inserted by s82(b), FA98, w.e.f. 27 March 1998.
79 Substituted by s240(a), FA01 & sch5, w.e.f. 1 January 2002, previously £10,000.
80 Substituted by s13(b), F(No. 2)A 92, w.e.f. 1 January 1993.
81 Inserted by s13(b), F(No. 2)A 92, w.e.f. 1 January 1993.
82 Ss2(d) deleted by s53(1)(a)(i),FA04, w.e.f. 30 June 2004.
83 Substituted by s53(1)(a)(ii), FA04, w.e.f. 25 March 2004.
84 Ss2(s) inserted by s74, FA96, w.e.f. 15 May 1996.
85 Ss2(n)-(s) inserted by s14(a), F(No. 2)A 92,w.e.f. 1 January 1993.
86 Substituted by s66, F(No. 2)A , 2008, w.e.f. 24 December 2008.
87 Ss141(2)(t)-(v) inserted by s106, FA03 w.e.f. 28 March 2003.
88 Inserted by s66, F(No. 2)A , 2008, w.e.f. 24 December 2008.
89 Substituted by s53(1)(b), FA04, w.e.f. 25 March 2004.
90 Substituted by s56(b), FA93, w.e.f. 17 June 1996.
91 Inserted by s89, FA06, w.e.f. 31 March 2006.
92 Ss (1),(2),(3) & (4) repealed by s96 & sch6, FA95, w.e.f. 2 June 1995.
93 Inserted by s15,F(No. 2)A 92, w.e.f. 1 January 1993.
94 Substituted by s16(a), F(No. 2)A 92, w.e.f. 1 January 1993.
95 Inserted by s16(b), F(No. 2)A 92, w.e.f. 1 January 1993.
96 Inserted by s16(c), F(No. 2)A 92, w.e.f. 1 January 1993.

Finance Act 2001

(Number 7 of 2001)

Powers of Officers

Interpretation

133. In this Chapter, except where the context otherwise provides, **"officer"** means an officer of the Commissioners authorised by them to exercise the powers conferred on officers by this Chapter.

Power to stop vehicles

134. (1) An officer in uniform may stop any vehicle in order—

[(a)   that such officer, or any officer accompanying such officer, may exercise any power conferred on them by section 135 in relation to excisable products, any other products chargeable with a duty of excise, or any prohibited goods, where there are reasonable grounds to believe that such products or goods are being transported in or on such vehicle, or][1]

(b)   to examine and take samples of mineral oil under section 135(2)(a).

(2)   An officer in uniform or a member of the Garda Síochána may stop any vehicle for any purpose related to vehicle registration tax or the registration of vehicles in any of the registers established and maintained under Chapter IV of Part II of the Finance Act, 1992.

(3)   Any person in charge of a moving vehicle shall, at the request of an officer in uniform or a member of the Garda Síochána, stop such vehicle.

(4)   Any person in charge of a vehicle shall, whether such vehicle has been stopped by an officer or member of the Garda Síochána under this section, or is already stationary, at the request of an officer or member of the Garda Síochána —

(a)   keep such vehicle stationary for such period as is reasonably required to enable an officer or member to exercise any power conferred on such officer or member by section 135, or

(b)   where such vehicle is in the opinion of such officer or member situated in a place unsuitable for the exercise of any power conferred on such officer or member by section 135, take such vehicle or cause it to be taken to such place as such officer or member may consider suitable for the exercise of such power.

Power to examine and search vehicles and to take samples

135. (1)   An officer, on production of the authorisation of such officer if so requested by any person affected, or any officer accompanying such officer, may—

(a)   examine a vehicle,

(b)   carry out such searches of a vehicle as may appear to the officer to be necessary to establish whether—

(i)   anything on or in the vehicle or in any manner attached to the vehicle is liable to forfeiture under the law relating to excise, or

(ii)   any excisable products being transported in or on, or in any manner attached to, the vehicle correspond in every material respect with the description of any such products in a document referred to in paragraph (d)(iii),

(c)   take samples, without payment, of any excisable products in or on, or in any manner attached to the vehicle, and

(d)   question the person in charge of the vehicle in relation to the vehicle or anything on or in or in any manner attached to the vehicle, and require such person—

(i)   to give, within such time and in such form and manner as may be specified by the officer or accompanying officer, all such information in relation to the vehicle as may reasonably be required by the officer or accompanying officer and is in the possession or procurement of such person,

(ii)   within such time and in such manner as may be specified by the officer or accompanying officer, to produce and permit the inspection of and the taking of copies of, or of extracts from, all such records relating to the vehicle and any products being so transported, as are reasonably required by the officer or accompanying officer and are in the possession or procurement of the person, and

(iii)   to produce to the officer or accompanying officer any accompanying document, duty document or exemption certificate accompanying any excisable products being transported in or on, or in any manner attached to, the vehicle.

(2)   An officer, on production of the authorisation of such officer if so requested by any person affected, or a member of the Garda Síochána, may—

(a)   examine and take samples of any mineral oil in any fuel tank or otherwise present on or in any vehicle, or anything attached to any vehicle, for use or capable of being used for combustion in the engine of the vehicle, whether or not the vehicle is attended,

(b)   examine or inspect any vehicle or anything attached to any vehicle for the purposes of paragraph (a),

(c)   question –

(i)   the owner of any vehicle,

(ii)   any person who for the time being stands registered as the owner of any vehicle in any of the registers established and maintained under Chapter IV of Part II of the Finance Act, 1992,

(iii)   any director, manager or principal officer of such owner where the registered owner is not one or more individuals, or

(iv)   the person in charge of any vehicle,

in relation to such mineral oil, and require such owner, person, director, manager or principal officer to give to him or her any information in relation to such mineral oil as may reasonably be required and which is in the possession or procurement of such owner, person, director, manager or principal officer, as the case may be.

Entry and search of premises

136. (1)   An officer may, at all reasonable times, on production of the authorisation of such officer if so requested by any person affected, enter a premises or other place (other than a dwelling) in which –

(a)   the production, processing, holding, storage, keeping, importation, purchase, packaging, offering for sale, sale or disposal of any product referred to in section 97(1) is being or is reasonably believed by the officer to be carried on,

(b)   the manufacture, distribution, storage, repair, modification, importation, dealing, delivery or disposal of mechanically propelled vehicles is being, or is reasonably believed by the officer to be carried on, or

[(bb)   bets liable to betting duty are reasonably believed to be accepted, or][2]

(c)   any records relating to, or reasonably believed by the officer to relate to, the products or activities referred to in paragraphs [(a), (b) and (bb)]³ are being kept or are reasonably believed by the officer to be kept.

(2)   An officer, on production of the authorisation of such officer if so requested by any person affected, or a member of the Garda Síochána, may —

(a)   enter and inspect any premises or other place (other than a dwelling) for the purposes of section 135(2) and bring onto those premises any vehicle being used in the course of his or her duties,

(b)   make such search and investigation of such premises or place as he or she may consider to be proper.

(3)   An officer in or on any premises or place pursuant to subsection (1) may there —

(a)   carry out such search and investigation as such officer may consider to be proper,

(b)   take account of, and without payment, take samples of any product referred to in section 97(1) and of any materials, ingredients and substances used or to be used in the manufacture of such product,

(c)   in relation to any records referred to in subsection (1)(c) —

(i)   search for, inspect and take copies of or extracts from any such records (including, in the case of any information in a non-legible form, a copy of, or an extract from, such information in a permanent legible form),

(ii)   remove and retain such records for such period as may reasonably be required for their further examination, and

(iii)   require any person to produce any such records which are in that person's possession, custody or procurement and in the case of information in a non-legible form, to produce it in a legible form or to reproduce it in a permanent legible form,

(d)   question any person present in relation to —

(i)   any product referred to in subsection (1)(a) or any materials, ingredients or other substances used or intended to be used in the manufacture of such product,

(ii)   any vehicle,

(iii)   any records referred to in subsection (1)(c),

produced or found in or on such premises or place, and such person shall give to such officer all information required of such person which is in his or her possession, custody or procurement.

[(e)   exercise the power of detention provided for under section 140.]⁴

(4)   An officer in or on any premises or place pursuant to this section, or any person accompanying an officer pursuant to subsection (5), may require any person present to give to such officer or such other person his or her name and address.

[(4A)   (a)   Where an officer in or on any premises or place pursuant to this section has reason to believe that any concealed pipe, conveyance, utensil or other equipment is being kept or made use of in or on such premises or place with intent to evade alcohol products tax, then such officer or any person assisting such officer may break open any floor or wall of such premises or place, or any ground in or adjoining it, to search for such concealed pipe, conveyance, utensil or equipment.

     (b)   Where no concealed pipe, conveyance, utensil or other equipment, to which paragraph (a) relates, is found as a result of the breaking open of any floor or wall of any premises or place, then nothing in that paragraph shall be used as a defence in any civil proceedings to a claim arising out of any damage caused by that breaking open.]⁵

(5)   Without prejudice to any power conferred by subsections (1) to (4), a judge of the District Court may, if satisfied on the sworn information of an officer that there are reasonable grounds for suspecting that—

     (a)   anything liable to forfeiture under the law relating to excise, or

     (b)   any records relating to transactions in contravention of the laws relating to excise,

are kept or concealed on or at any premises or place, issue a search warrant.

(6)   A search warrant issued under this section shall be expressed and to operate to authorise a named officer accompanied by such other officers and such other persons as the officer considers necessary, at any time or times within one month of the date of issue of the warrant, to enter (if need be by force) the premises or other place named or specified in the warrant, to search such premises or other place, to examine anything found there, to inspect any record found there and, if there are reasonable grounds for suspecting that anything found there is liable to forfeiture under the law relating to excise, or that a record found there may be required as evidence in proceedings under the

law relating to excise, to detain or seize the thing as liable to forfeiture or, in the case of a record, to detain it for so long as it is reasonably required for such purpose.

General provision concerning samples

137. (1)   The provisions of section 6 of the Customs and Inland Revenue Act, 1888, shall apply to the taking of samples of excisable products, except where section 135(1)(c) or 136(3)(b) applies.

(2)   The provisions of sections 101 and 102 of the Finance Act, 1998, shall apply to samples of excisable products or other samples taken under the laws relating to excise.

Obligation to answer certain questions, in respect of certain tobacco products

138.   An officer or a member of the Garda Síochána may require any person whom such officer or member has reasonable cause to believe to be guilty of an offence under [section 78 of the Finance Act 2005]6 to furnish to such officer or member of the Garda Síochána -

(a)   his or her name, address and date of birth,

(b)   all such information in relation to the tobacco products in question as may be reasonably required by such officer or member and which is in the possession or procurement of the person.

Power of arrest and detention of persons

139. (1)   Where an officer or a member of the Garda Síochána has reasonable grounds to suspect that a person is committing or has committed an offence under-

(a)   section 119,or

(b)   section 102(3) of the Finance Act, 1999,

then such officer or member may arrest such person without warrant.

(2)   (a)   Where an officer has reasonable grounds to believe that a person is committing or has committed an offence under [section 78 of the Finance Act 2005]6 then such officer may detain the person and, as soon as practicable thereafter-

(i)   present the person, or

(ii)   bring and present the person,

to a member of the Garda Síochána.

(b)   Where a member of the Garda Síochána has reasonable grounds to believe-

(i)   that a person is committing or has committed an offence under [section 78 of the Finance Act 2005][6], or

(ii)   in case of a person presented or brought and presented to such member by an officer, that an offence under the said [section 78][6] was or had been committed by the person and the person was duly detained by an officer under paragraph (a) for the offence and was either presented or brought and presented to such member in accordance with that paragraph,

then, such member may arrest the person without warrant.

Detention of goods and vehicles

140. (1)   Where an officer reasonably suspects that any excisable products, or any other goods, are liable to forfeiture under the law relating to excise then —

(a)   all such excisable products or other goods,

(b)   any other thing being made use of in the conveyance of such products or goods, and

(c)   any vehicle in or on which or attached to which in any manner any such excisable products or goods are found,

may be detained by such officer until such examination, enquiries or investigations as may be deemed necessary by such officer or another officer, have been made for the purposes of determining whether or not such products, goods, thing or vehicle are liable to forfeiture.

(2)   Where a member of the Garda Síochána reasonably suspects that any excisable products, other goods or other thing or any vehicle is liable to forfeiture under [section 78 of the Finance Act 2005][6] such products, goods, other thing or vehicle may be detained by such member until such examination, enquiries or investigations as may be deemed necessary by such member or another member, or by an officer, have been made for the purposes of determining whether or not such products, goods, other thing or vehicle are liable to forfeiture.

(3)   Where an officer or a member of the Garda Síochána reasonably suspects —

(a)   that a vehicle has not been registered in any of the registers established and maintained under Chapter IV of Part II of the Finance Act, 1992,

(b)   that a vehicle has been converted (within the meaning of that Chapter) and a declaration in relation to such conversion has not been made under section 131 of the Finance Act, 1992, or

(c)   that vehicle registration tax has not been paid in respect of a vehicle,

then such officer or member may detain such vehicle for such period as is required to carry out such examination, enquiries or investigations as may be deemed necessary by such officer or member to determine to his or her satisfaction whether or not—

(i)   such vehicle has been registered,

(ii)   such declaration has been made, or

(iii)   such vehicle registration tax has been paid.

(4)   When a determination referred to in subsection (1), (2) or (3) has been made in respect of any excisable products, other goods, other thing or a vehicle or on the expiry of a period of one month from the date on which such products, goods, other thing or vehicle were or was detained under that subsection, whichever is the earlier, such products, goods, other thing or vehicle are to be either seized as liable to forfeiture under the Customs Acts or under section 141, or released.

Seizure of goods and vehicles

141. (1) Any goods or vehicles that are liable to forfeiture under the law relating to excise may be seized by an officer.

(2)   Anything liable to forfeiture under [section 78 of the Finance Act 2005][6] may be seized by a member of the Garda Síochána and shall be delivered to an officer.

Notice of seizure

142. (1) Subject to subsection (2), an officer shall give notice of the seizure of anything as liable to forfeiture and of the grounds for seizure to any person who to the officer's knowledge was at the time of the seizure the owner or one of the owners of the thing seized.

(2)   Notice under subsection (1) need not be given under this section to a person if the seizure was made in the presence of the person, the person whose offence or suspected offence occasioned the seizure or in the case of anything seized in any ship or aircraft, in the presence of the master or commander of such ship or aircraft.

(3)   Notice under subsection (1) shall be given in writing and the notice shall include a statement of section 143 and be deemed to have been duly given to the person concerned—

(a)   if it is delivered to the person personally, or

(b)   if it is addressed to the person and left or forwarded by post to the person at the usual or last known place of abode or business of the person or, in the case of a body corporate, at its registered or principal office, or

(c)   if the person has no known address in the State, by publication of notice of the seizure concerned in Iris Oifigiúil.

Notice of claim

143. (1)   A person who claims that anything seized as liable to forfeiture is not so liable (referred to in this section as the **"claimant"**) shall, within one month of the date of the notice of seizure or, where no such notice has been given to the claimant, within one month of the date of the seizure, give notice in writing of such claim to the Commissioners.

(2)   A notice under subsection (1) shall specify the name and address of the claimant and, in the case of a claimant who is outside the State, the name and address of a solicitor in the State who is authorised to accept service of any document required to be served on the claimant and to act on behalf of the claimant.

Power to deal with seizures, before and after condemnation

144. (1)   In this section "claimant" has the same meaning as it has in section 143.

(2)   The Commissioners may, in their discretion, restore anything seized as liable to forfeiture under the law relating to excise, and the Minister for Finance may order such restoration.

(3)   Without prejudice to subsection (2), where a notice relating to the thing seized has been duly given under section 143, the Commissioners may as they think fit and notwithstanding that such thing seized has not yet been condemned —

(a)   if a notice relating to the thing has been duly given under section 143, deliver it up to the claimant on payment to the Commissioners of such sum as they think proper, being a sum not exceeding that which in their opinion represents the value of the thing, including any duty or tax chargeable on it which has not been paid, or

[(b)   if the thing seized is in the opinion of the Commissioners of a perishable or hazardous nature or is tobacco products, sell or destroy it.][7]

(4)   If, where anything is delivered up, sold or destroyed under this section, it is held by the court in proceedings under this section that the thing was not liable to forfeiture at the time of its seizure, the Commissioners shall, subject to any deduction allowed under subsection (5), on demand tender to such claimant —

(a)   an amount equal to any sum paid by the claimant under subsection (2),

(b)   if they have sold the thing, an amount equal to the proceeds of sale, or

(c)   if they have destroyed the thing, an amount equal to the market value of the thing at the time of its seizure.

(5)   Where the amount to be tendered under subsection (4) includes any sum on account of any duty or tax chargeable on the thing which has not been paid before its seizure, the Commissioners may deduct from the amount so much of it as represents the duty or tax.

(6)   If the claimant accepts any amount tendered under subsection (4), such claimant shall not be entitled to maintain proceedings in any court on account of the seizure, detention, sale or destruction of the thing concerned.

(7)   All goods seized by an officer or by a member of the Garda Síochána as liable to forfeiture shall after condemnation of such goods be either—

(a)   sold or destroyed, or

(b)   otherwise disposed of in accordance with regulations made under section 153.

(8)   Notwithstanding any other provision of this Chapter relating to goods seized as liable to forfeiture, an officer who seizes as liable to forfeiture any spirits or any stills, vessels, utensils, wort or other material for manufacturing, distilling or preparing spirits may at the discretion of such officer forthwith spill, break up or destroy any of those goods.

Delegation of powers, functions and duties of Commissioners

[144A.(1)   For the purposes of this Part, other than sections 107 and 153, and subject to the direction and control of the Commissioners, any power, function or duty conferred or imposed on them may, subject to subsection (2), be exercised or performed on their behalf by an officer.

(2)   Any power, function or duty conferred or imposed on the Commissioners by section 109, 112, 113 or 116 may be exercised or performed on their behalf, and subject to their direction and control, by an officer authorised by them in writing for the purposes of the section concerned.][8]

Chapter 5

Miscellaneous

Appeals to Commissioners

145. (1)   Any person who has paid or who, in the opinion of the Commissioners, is liable to pay a duty of excise and is called on by them to pay an amount of such duty may appeal in accordance with this section against the decision concerned in respect of the liability or the amount of the duty.

[(1A)   **No appeal shall lie under this section against an asessment made under section 99A (inserted by section 46 of the Finance (No. 2) Act 2008).]**[9]

(2)   Any person who has claimed or received a repayment of a duty of excise may appeal to the Commissioners against the decision concerned in respect of the amount of such repayment or the refusal of such repayment.

(3)   Any person who is the subject of any of the following acts of the Commissioners:

     (a)   a refusal to approve a person as an authorised warehousekeeper or a premises as a tax warehouse under section 109, or a revocation, under that section, of any such approval that has been granted,

     (b)   a refusal to approve a person as a tax representative under section 113, or a revocation, under that section, of any such approval that has been granted,

     (c)   a refusal to grant registration of a trader under section 116, or a revocation, under that section, of any such registration that has been granted,

     (d)   a decision in relation to the registration of a vehicle, or the amendment of an entry in or the deletion of an entry from, the register referred to in section 131 of the Finance Act, 1992, by the Commissioners, or on their behalf, under that section 131,

     (e)   a determination of an open market selling price of a vehicle under section 133(2) of the Finance Act, 1992, or

     (f)   a granting, refusal or revocation of an authorisation under section 136 of the Finance Act, 1992, or a decision in relation to the arrangements for payment of vehicle registration tax under that section 136,

may appeal against such an act to the Commissioners.

(4)   An appeal under subsection (1), (2) or (3) shall be in writing and shall set forth in detail the grounds of appeal.

(5)   An appeal is to be lodged by the person concerned with the Commissioners within the period of 2 months from the date of —

   (a)   the payment of a duty of excise,

   (b)   the notification by the Commissioners on being called on by them to pay an amount of a duty of excise,

   (c)   the repayment of a duty of excise,

   (d)   the notification by the Commissioners of a refusal of a repayment by them of a duty of excise, or

   (e)   the notification by the Commissioners of the doing by them of an act referred to in subsection (3),

   or within such longer period as the Commissioners may, in exceptional cases, allow.

(6)   An appeal shall, subject to subsection (12), be determined by the Commissioners within a period of 30 days from its lodgement with the Commissioners.

(7)   The Commissioners may appoint one or more of their officers for the purposes of carrying out their functions under this section but no such officer shall determine an appeal under this section in respect of a decision he or she has made.

(8)   The Commissioners shall notify in writing an appellant concerned of their determination of an appeal and the reasons for their determination.

(9)   Where the Commissioners determine on appeal that the amount due is less than the amount paid, they shall repay the amount overpaid to the appellant concerned.

(10)   Where the Commissioners determine on appeal that the amount due is greater than the amount paid, the appellant concerned shall pay the amount underpaid.

(11)   For the purpose of determination of an appeal any goods or vehicles to which the appeal relates are to be produced to the Commissioners for inspection, if so required.

(12)   Where an appeal has been lodged but not determined in accordance with subsection (6) there shall be deemed to have been a determination by the Commissioners on the last day of the period of 30 days from the date the appeal was lodged that the appeal was not upheld but such deeming shall cease to have effect if a determination is subsequently made by the Commissioners before a determination is made by the Appeal Commissioners under section 146 in respect of the matter concerned.

(13)   The provisions of the Customs Acts or of any instruments made under those Acts, in so far as they apply to appeals concerning duties of excise, shall not apply in relation to any amount of

excise duty capable of being the subject of an appeal under this section.

Appeals to Appeal Commissioners

146. [(1) A person who is aggrieved by —

(a) a determination of the Commissioners under section 145, or

(b) an assessment made on that person under section 99A (inserted by section 46 of the Finance (No. 2) Act 2008),

may, in accordance with this section, appeal to the Appeal Commissioners against such determination or assessment, and the appeal is to be heard and determined by the Appeal Commissioners whose determination is final and conclusive unless a case is required to be stated in relation to it for the opinion of the High Court on a point of law.

(2) A person who intends to appeal under this section against a determination of the Commissioners, or against an assessment under section 99A, shall within 30 days of —

(a) the notification of such determination, or the expiry of the time limit for such determination, whichever is the earlier, or

(b) the notice of such assessment,

give notice in writing to the Commissioners of such intention.][10]

(3) Subject to this section —

(a) Part 40, other than sections 942, 943 and (in so far as it relates to those sections) 944 of the Taxes Consolidation Act, 1997, and

(b) section 957 of that Act,

shall, with any necessary modifications, apply as they apply for the purpose of income tax.

(4) (a) Subject to paragraph (c), where a notice or other document which is required or authorised to be served by this section falls to be served on a body corporate, such notice is to be served on the secretary or other officer of the body corporate.

(b) Any notice or other document which is required or authorised by this section —

(i) to be served by the Commissioners or by an appellant may be served by post, and

(ii) in the case of a notice or other document addressed to the Commissioners, shall be addressed and sent to the Revenue Commissioners, Dublin Castle, Dublin 2.

(c)   Any notice or other document which is required or authorised to be served by the Commissioners on an appellant under this section may be sent to the solicitor, accountant or other agent of the appellant and a notice so served is deemed to have been served on the appellant unless the appellant proves to the satisfaction of the Appeal Commissioners, that he or she had, before the notice or other document was served, withdrawn the authority of such solicitor, accountant or other agent to act on his or her behalf.

(5)   Prima facie evidence of any notice given under this section by the Commissioners or by an officer of the Commissioners may be given in any proceedings by production by an officer of the Commissioners of a document purporting to be a copy of the notice and it shall not be necessary to prove the official position of the person by whom the notice purports to be given or, if it is signed, the signature, or that the person signing and giving it was authorised so to do.

Payment of duty pending appeal

147.   Where an appeal has been made under section 145 or 146 in respect of an amount of duty which a person is called on by the Commissioners to pay, such appeal, shall not be determined by the Commissioners or the Appeal Commissioners, as the case may be, unless such amount of duty has been paid.

Exclusion of criminal matters

148.   Where liability for a duty of excise is the subject of criminal proceedings or a decision is pending on whether to initiate criminal proceedings in respect of such liability, then such liability or the amount of such liability or repayment connected with or sought in respect of such liability may not be appealed under section 145 or 146 until the determination of such criminal proceedings or a decision is duly taken not to initiate criminal proceedings.

Amendments

1   Substituted by FA05 s59, w.e.f 25 March 2005
2   Substituted by FA02 s87(a), w.e.f. 25 March 2002
3   Substituted by FA02 s87(b), w.e.f. 25 March 2002
4   Inserted by FA02 s87(c), w.e.f. 25 March 2002
5   Inserted by FA03 s90, w.e.f. 28 March 2003
6   Substituted by FA05 s93, w.e.f. 30 June 2004
7   Substituted by FA07 s57, w.e.f. 2 April 2007
8   Inserted by FA03 s100, w.e.f. 28 March 2003
9   Inserted by F(No. 2)A 08 s46(b), w.e.f. 24 December 2008.
10 Substituted by F(No. 2)A 08 s46(c), w.e.f. 24 December 2008

Finance Act 2006

(Number of 2006)

123. (1) In this section —

"**the Acts**" means —

(a) the Tax Acts,

(b) the Capital Gains Tax Acts,

(c) the Capital Acquisitions Tax Consolidation Act 2003, and the enactments amending or extending that Act,

(d) the Stamp Duties Consolidation Act 1999, and the enactments amending or extending that Act, and

(e) Chapter IV of Part II of the Finance Act 1992,

and any instruments made thereunder;

"**form or other document**" includes a form or other document for use, or capable of use, in a machine readable form.

(2) Where a provision of the Acts requires that a form or other document used for any purpose of the Acts is to be prescribed, authorised or approved by the Revenue Commissioners, such form or other document may be prescribed, authorised or approved by —

(a) a Revenue Commissioner, or

(b) an officer of the Revenue Commissioners not below the grade or rank of Assistant Secretary authorised by them for that purpose.

(3) Nothing in this section shall be read as restricting section 12 of the Interpretation Act 2005.

S.I. No. 318 of 1992
VEHICLE REGISTRATION AND TAXATION REGULATIONS, 1992

The Revenue Commissioners, in exercise of the powers conferred on them by section 141 of the Finance Act, 1992 (No. 9 of 1992), hereby make the following Regulations:

1.   These Regulations may be cited as the Vehicle Registration and Taxation Regulations, 1992.

2.   Regulations 1, 2, 4, 13, 14, 15, 16, 17, 18, 19 and 21 shall come into operation on the 9th day of November, 1992.

3.   Regulations 3, 5, 6, 7, 8, 9, 10, 11, 12 and 20 shall come into operation on the 1st day of January, 1993.

4.   In these Regulations -

   "the Act" means the Finance Act, 1992 (No. 9 of 1992);

   "approved", **"approved of"** and **"prescribed"** mean, respectively, approved, approved of and prescribed by the Commissioners;

   "authorised person", **"certificate"**, **"the Commissioners"**, **"deal"**, **"licensing authority"**, **"the register"** and **"vehicle"** have, respectively, the meanings assigned to them by Chapter IV of Part II of the Act;

   "distributor" means a person who holds an exclusive franchise to bring into the State for sale particular makes and models of vehicles;

   [**"registration number"**, in relation to a vehicle, means the identification mark assigned to the vehicle under section 131(5) of the Act;][1]

   "registration office" means an office established by the Commissioners at which declarations under section 131 of the Act may be made for the purpose of registration;

   "tax" means vehicle registration tax.

5.   The conditions referred to in paragraph (b) of the definition of "category A vehicle" in section 130 of the Act shall be as follows:

   (a)   an opening referred to in subparagraph (ii) of the said paragraph (b) shall be closed and sealed by being completely covered by means of a panel made of rigid metal or other strong, opaque rigid material and fixed permanently in place,

   (b)   (i)   the floor referred to in subparagraph (iv) of the said paragraph (b) shall be constructed of rigid metal, shall be fixed permanently to the sides of the vehicle and shall cover over any area which might be suitable for use as a footwell or seatwell to the rear of the driver's seat so as to render the latter area level with, or generally level with, the remainder of the floor to the rear of the driver's seat, and

(ii)   where the level of a floor complying with subparagraph (a) of this condition is higher than the level of the floor in the area to the front of the vehicle in which the driver is accommodated, the space between the floors shall be sealed off by means of a metal panel or panels fixed permanently to each floor,

and

(c)   in paragraphs (a) and (b) of this Regulation **"fixed permanently"** means secured by means of continuous seam welding, adhesive bonding, spot welding or brazing and, in the case of spot welding, the welds shall be sufficiently close to each other to ensure a satisfactory seal, being normally not more than 40 millimetres apart, and, in the case of adhesive bonding, the bonding agent shall be approved by the Commissioners.

6.   The register shall consist of the declarations for registration, and the declarations made under section 131 of the Act and any other changes to a vehicle for which declarations are required, as accepted by the Commissioners. All information on the register may be recorded on computer, or on such other medium as the Commissioners may determine.

7.   (1)   A declaration under section 131(2)(a) of the Act shall be in the form numbered VRT3, VRT4 or VRT5, as appropriate to the vehicle in question, in the Third, Fourth and Fifth Schedules to these Regulations, or in such other form as the Commissioners may specify and the particulars of the vehicle concerned declared to the Commissioners under the said section 131(2)(a) shall be those required to be given on such of those forms as is appropriate.

    (2)   Where a registered vehicle is converted, the particulars declared to the Commissioners under section 131(3)(a) of the Act shall be as follows:

        the make and model of the vehicle,

        its registration number,

        the number of its seats and windows,

        the cubic capacity of its load space,

        the length of its floor behind the driver's seat, and

        its unladen weight,

and such other particulars, if any, as the Commissioners may specify.

These particulars shall be declared to the Commissioners in such form as they shall decide.

[(3)   For the purposes of the registration of a vehicle, an original declaration in relation to the vehicle signed by the person paying tax on the vehicle or, in the case of a company, signed by a person nominated by the company, shall be presented to a registration office together with any other documents the Commissioners may require to satisfy themselves as to the bona fides of the declaration. In the case of an authorised person, the declaration, duly signed pursuant to this paragraph, in respect of the registration of a new vehicle (other than a vehicle in respect of which an application for repayment under section 134(11) is intended to be made) may be presented by means of a facsimile machine. Where a declaration is presented to a registration office by means of a facsimile machine, the original declaration shall be forwarded to that office by the authorised person concerned not more than 3 working days later.][2]

8.   (1)   A person not being an authorised person who manufactures or brings into the State a vehicle which is not exempt from registration under section 135 of the Act, shall bring the vehicle to a registration office and make a declaration under section 131 of the Act in relation to the vehicle not later than the next working day after its manufacture or arrival in the State or, in the case of a vehicle which requires the making of a customs entry on arrival in the State, not later than the next working day after its release from customs control.

       (2)   However, where the person referred to in paragraph (1) has reasonable cause to believe that the vehicle concerned may qualify for registration without payment of tax, the person shall bring the vehicle to the registration office and make an application to the office for relief under section 134 of the Act. In such a case, the person shall make a declaration under section 131 of the Act not later than one month from the date of the application aforesaid or as soon as may be after receipt of the decision of the Commissioners on the application, if the decision is given during that month, and it the decision allows the application and is given after payment of the tax on the vehicle, the Commissioners shall repay the tax to the person under the said section 134.

9.   (1)   The identification mark assigned by the Commissioners under section 131(5) of the Act to a vehicle entered in the register (in this Regulation referred to as **"the identification mark"**) shall consist of:

            (a)   the third and fourth numerals of the year in which the vehicle is first brought into use,

            (b)   an index mark, as provided for in the table to paragraph 4 of the First Schedule to these Regulations, corresponding to the functional area of the licensing authority in which the owner at the time of registration ordinarily resides,

(c)   a number which when combined with the appropriate numerals and mark aforesaid produces a unique combination,

(d)   in the case of a vehicle which the Commissioners are satisfied was constructed or first brought into use more than 30 years prior to the time of registration, and the person applying for registration so requests, an index mark ZV and a unique number.

(2)   A determination shall be made by the Commissioners for the purposes of this Regulation as to the year in which a vehicle is brought into use and shall take into account any previous registration documents, the distance which the vehicle has travelled, and any other matters which are, in the opinion of the Commissioners, fair and reasonable in the circumstances of the case.

(3)   The numbers referred to in subparagraph (1)(c) of this Regulation shall be assigned sequentially to each index mark, but the Commissioners may omit any numbers from a sequence established under this Regulation.

(4)   The identification mark of a vehicle shall remain assigned to the vehicle and no other such marks shall be assigned to the vehicle save in such circumstances as may be determined by the Commissioners or where the owner of the vehicle requests that the identification mark assigned to a vehicle which reaches 30 years of age be replaced by a mark in the ZV series.

(5)   Where a declaration under section 131 of the Act is made by a person, not being an person, the identification mark of the vehicle concerned shall be displayed thereon as on and from a day not more than 3 working days after the registration of the vehicle.

(6)   The identification mark of a vehicle shall, until the vehicle is scrapped, destroyed or sent permanently out of the State, be exhibited on the vehicle on a rectangular plate or on an unbroken rectangular surface forming part of the vehicle and, in either case, the identification mark shall comply as to lettering, numbering and otherwise, with the provisions set out in the First Schedule to these Regulations.

(7)   Subject to the provisions of subparagraph (8), the identification mark of a vehicle shall be exhibited, in the case of a vehicle which has only one front wheel, on the back of the vehicle and, in the case of any other vehicle, on the front of and on the back of the vehicle in a vertical or nearly vertical position, so that every letter or figure of the identification mark is vertical or nearly vertical

and is easily distinguishable, in the case of the letters and figures placed on the front of the vehicle, from in front of the vehicle and in the case of the letters and figures placed on the back of the vehicle, from behind the vehicle.

(8)   Where one or more trailers of any kind are attached to a vehicle, a duplicate of the identification mark of the vehicle shall be exhibited on the back of the rearmost trailer in the manner that the identification mark is required to be exhibited on the back of the vehicle.

(9)   Figures, letters, designs, ornamentations, fittings or structures shall not be placed on a vehicle or trailer in such a position as to render more difficult the reading or distinguishing of the identification mark or duplicate identification mark of the vehicle or trailer.

10.   The form and contents of a certificate of registration issued under section 131(5) of the Act shall be as set out in the Second Schedule to these Regulations, or in such other form as the Commissioners may specify.

11.   (1)   A certificate shall be sent by post to the person who is named therein as the owner or, at the discretion of the Commissioners in exceptional circumstances, shall be sent by post to the registration office to which the declaration under section 131 of the Act was made for collection by the person aforesaid.

(2)   A certificate of registration shall be signed by an officer of the Commissioners authorised by them in that behalf. The signature may be applied by facsimile, stamp or computer.

(3)   The Commissioners may require the owner of a vehicle to surrender to them a certificate issued in respect of the vehicle in any case where they have reason to believe that the certificate contains particulars which are not correct, and on being so required, the owner of the vehicle shall surrender the certificate to the Commissioners forthwith and the Commissioners shall return the certificate or issue a new certificate or withdraw the certificate if the vehicle is no longer in the State, as appropriate.

[(4)   Upon a change of ownership of a registered vehicle, Part II of the certificate of registration relating to the vehicle shall be sent or given to the new owner and, if the vehicle is not one that is or has been the subject of a licence under section 1 of the Finance (Excise Duties) (Vehicles) Act, 1952 (No. 24 of 1952), either -

(a)   the person disposing of the vehicle shall insert particulars of the change of ownership on the reverse side of Part I of the certificate, detach that Part from the certificate and send or give it to the Central Vehicle Office of the Commissioners at Harbour in the county of Wexford, or

(b)   if the said Part I has previously been detached from the certificate, the person acquiring the vehicle shall insert particulars of the change of ownership on the reverse side of Part II of the certificate, and send or give it to the said Office.][3]

(5)   If a certificate is irretrievably lost or accidentally damaged or defaced, the owner of the vehicle concerned shall immediately inform the Commissioners of the fact and shall furnish a declaration made and subscribed by him in accordance with the Statutory Declarations Act, 1938 (No.37 of 1938), setting out the circumstances of such loss or destruction or defacement and stating (if it be the case) that the certificate has not, to the best of his knowledge and belief, been fraudulently appropriated or used by any person for the purpose of evasion of registration and also stating that the certificate or the portion thereof which has been lost will, if recovered by him, be surrendered by him to the Commissioners.

(6)   Where such a declaration as aforesaid is made to the Commissioners and they are satisfied that the issue of a certificate in place of the original certificate is warranted they shall issue another certificate to the owner, after inspection of the vehicle and on payment of such fee as they may specify. Such a certificate shall have the words "replacement certificate" clearly endorsed thereon.

12.   The frame number and engine number, in the case of a motor-cycle, and the chassis number and engine number, in the case of all other vehicles, shall be exhibited permanently in a legible form and in an accessible position on a vehicle.

13.   (1)   A declaration for the purposes of section 133(2)(a) of the Act shall be made in writing to the Commissioners at least 21 days before the delivery out of the premises of the person making the declaration of a vehicle of the model and specification to which the declaration relates.

(2)   Where a person becomes of opinion that a price declared by him or a predecessor of his under the said section 133(2)(a) will alter, he shall, as soon as may be, furnish particulars in writing of the alteration to the Commissioners.

14.   (1)   An application for an under section 136 of the Act shall be made in writing to the Commissioners and the applicant shall furnish to the Commissioners, for the purposes of the said section, such information as they may reasonably require in such form (if any) as they may specify.

(2)   Where a person becomes aware that information furnished by him under paragraph (1) of this Regulation has ceased to be correct or accurate, whether before or after an authorisation

under the said section 136 has been granted, the person shall, not later than 7 days thereafter, inform the Commissioners in writing of the cesser.

[(3)   The Commissioners shall grant an authorisation under section 136 of the Act only to a person who—

(a)   intends to be actively engaged in a business referred to in subsection (1) of that section at premises occupied by the person and at which such business may legally be carried on,

(b)   is registered under section 9 of the Value-Added Tax Act 1972 for the purpose of carrying on a business referred to in subsection (1) of that section, and

(c)   is, at the time of application for the authorisation, the holder of a current tax clearance certificate issued in accordance with section 1095 of the Taxes Consolidation Act 1997.][4]

[(4)   For the purposes of subsection (3) of section 136 of the Act, reasonable causes in respect of which the Commissioners may, in accordance with that subsection, revoke an authorisation include the following:

(a)   the authorised person ceases to be actively engaged in the business referred to in section 136(1) of the Act or such business has not, within a reasonable period, commenced,

(b)   the authorised person fails to produce a current tax clearance certificate, issued in accordance with section 1095 of the Taxes Consolidation Act 1997, if requested to do so by the Commissioners, or

(c)   records relating to the business are not kept as prescribed by the Commissioners in Regulation 17.][5]

15.   (1)   As soon as may be after bringing a new, unregistered vehicle into the State, an person, being a distributor, shall furnish to the Commissioners particulars of the vehicle[...][6] in such form (if any) as they may specify.

(2)   When an authorised person, being a distributor, delivers a new, unregistered vehicle to another authorised person, he shall give to the last-mentioned person a copy of form VRT3 specified in the Third Schedule or form VRT5 specified in the Fifth Schedule, as may be appropriate, or of such other form as the Commissioners may specify, in which the appropriate part of Part A has been completed by the first-mentioned person.

16.   (1)   An application for permission to defer the payment of tax under section 136(6) of the Act shall be made to the Commissioners in

writing and shall be accompanied with particulars in writing of arrangements for payment of the tax.

(2)   Before such permission as aforesaid is given, the authorised person concerned shall provide such security for the payment of the tax concerned as the Commissioners may determine.

(3)   The Commissioners may vary or revoke such permission as aforesaid and may from time to time require the provision by the person concerned of additional or different security for the payment of the tax concerned.

(4)   Where the day to which, pursuant to the said section 136(6), payment of tax is permitted to be deferred is a Saturday or Sunday or a public holiday, the tax shall be paid on the preceding working day.

17.   (1)   An authorised person shall keep in a permanent form, approved by the Commissioners, records of:

    (a)   all unregistered vehicles received by him or manufactured by him;

    (b)   all additions, accessories or options fitted or attached to or supplied with unregistered vehicles disposed of by him in the course of his business;

    (c)   all registered vehicles which are converted by him;

    (d)   all unregistered vehicles sent out of his premises temporarily for display or exhibition;

    (e)   all unregistered vehicles delivered by him to another person;

    (f)   all unregistered vehicles sent outside the State or sold to a person who is not a resident of the State for use outside the State;

    (g)   all unregistered vehicles disposed of in a manner other than those aforesaid.

(2)   Records kept by an authorised person pursuant to this Regulation and any books, invoices, credit notes, receipts, accounts, vouchers, debit notes, bank statements or other documents whatsoever or data in a computer which relate to the manufacture or receipt by the person of unregistered vehicles, the conversion of registered vehicles or the sale, delivery or other disposal of unregistered vehicles by the person and which are in his possession, custody or procurement and a copy which is in his possession, custody or procurement of any such invoice, credit note, debit note, receipt, account, voucher or other document as aforesaid that has been issued by the person to another person shall be retained in his possession, custody or procurement for a period of 6 years from the date of the latest transaction to which the records or any of the documents relate:

> Provided that this Regulation shall not require the retention of records or documents in respect of which the Commissioners notify the authorised person concerned that retention is not required, nor shall it apply to the books and papers of a company which has been disposed of in accordance with section 305(1) of the Companies Act, 1963 (No. 33 of 1963).

(3)   The records kept pursuant to this Regulation shall, insofar as they relate to a vehicle, contain particulars of the make, model, version, body type, roof type, colours, seats, windows, options concerned and the letters and numbers of the chassis or frame and engine thereof or such of those particulars as are applicable to the vehicle and, insofar as they relate to a transaction referred to in subparagraph (d), (e), (f) or (g) of paragraph (1) of this Regulation, contain particulars of the name and address and the registration number under the Value-Added Tax Acts, 1972 to 1992, where applicable, of the person receiving a vehicle in the transaction.

18.   An authorised person shall, when required to do so by the Commissioners, furnish to them a true and accurate account in such form as the Commissioners may require, in respect of such period as the Commissioners may specify, of -

(a)   all unregistered vehicles received or manufactured by him, and

(b)   all registered vehicles converted by him,

and the account shall identify each vehicle and give particulars of any such vehicles held by him and, in the case of such vehicles disposed of by him, particulars of their disposal.

19.   An authorised person shall, when required to do so by the Commissioners, make proper entry with them of each premises in which he intends to carry on a business referred to in section 136(1) of the Act by identifying each such premises in such manner as the Commissioners may specify and declaring which such business he intends to carry on in the premises.

20.   For the purposes of section 138(7) of the Act, the time limit within which an appellant shall pay an amount of tax underpaid shall be one month from the date of the determination of the relevant appeal by the Commissioners.

21.   Where, as respects any class of persons, the Commissioners so allow and subject to any conditions which they may think fit to impose, compliance, in whole or in part, with any of these Regulations shall not be required.

Given this 26th day of August, 1993.

C.C. McDomhnaill
Revenue Commissioner

Explanatory Note

These Regulations lay down conditions governing the registration of vehicles and the method of securing and collection of vehicle registration tax. They also prescribe the format, dimensions and technical specification of registration plates to be displayed on vehicles, as well as the forms on which declarations for registration must be made.

[FIRST SCHEDULE

Form of Identification Marks

1. The following provisions shall be complied with in respect of identification marks to be exhibited on vehicles entered in the register.

2. The identification mark of a vehicle shall be displayed on a rectangular plate which shall correspond with either Diagram No. 1 or Diagram No. 2 shown below.

Diagram No. 1

Diagram No. 2

3.   (a)   The plate on which an identification mark is exhibited (in this Schedule referred to as "the plate") shall not contain any words, letters, numbers, emblems or other marks of any kind other than those required under this Schedule.

    (b)   The identification mark shall not incorporate the figure nought unless such figure forms part of the identification mark assigned to the vehicle by the Commissioners.

4.   The plate shall exhibit the set out in the Table to this paragraph opposite the mention in the Table of the index mark on the plate, the flag of the European Communities and the letters IRL all of which shall be arranged in conformity with this Schedule.

TABLE

INDEX MARKS AND CORRESPONDING PLACENAMES

Index Mark	Corresponding Placename	index Mark	Corresponding Placename	index Mark	Corresponding Placename
CW	Ceatharlach	L	Luimneach	RN	Ros Comáin
CN	An Cabhán	LS	Laois	SO	Sligeach
CE	An Clár	LM	Liatroim	TN	Tiobraid Arann
C	Corcaigh	LK	Luimneach	TS	Tiobraid Arann
D	Baile Atha Cliath	LD	An Longfort	W	Port Láirge
DL	Dun na nGall	LU	Lú	WD	Port Láirge
G	Gaillimh	MO	Maigh Eo	WH	An Iarmhi
KY	Ciarraí	MH	An Mhí	WX	Loch Garman
KE	Cill Dara	MN	MuiZneachán	WW	Cill Mhantáin
KK	Cill Chainnigh	OY	Uibh Fhailí		

5.   The periphery of the plate shall be marked all around by a black border having a

6.   An identification mark which is exhibited on a metal plate shall be embossed by being raised above the flat surface of the plate and shall form part of the plate.

7.   An identification mark which is exhibited on a plastic plate shall be affixed with an adhesive substance to the rear of the plate and be so affixed that it cannot be readily detached therefrom.

8.   A plate made of plastic shall be constructed of transparent material of at least 2.5 millimetres in thickness.

9.   The identification mark and shall be formed of black characters and shall be exhibited on white reflex reflective material so that the identification mark appears at all times from the front of the plate as black characters on a white background.

10.   The flag of the European Communities shall appear as a circle of twelve gold stars against a blue background (of a shade generally known as

royal blue); the centrepoints of the twelve stars shall form a circle with a radius of 15 millimetres and the straight lines forming the apexes of the stars shall be 4 millimetres in length.

11. The letters IRL shall appear in white letters on the blue background of the flag of the European Communities underneath the circle of stars and each such letter shall have a height of 20 millimetres and a stroke width of 4 millimetres. The total width of the space taken by each of the letters R and L shall be 12 millimetres. The distances between adjoining letters shall be uniform.

12. The blue background and gold stars of the flag of the European Communities and the white letters shall be formed of reflex reflective material.

13. The placename shall appear in black letters above the identification mark and each letter of the placename shall have a height of not less than 12 millimetres and a stroke width of not less than 3 millimetres. The total width of the space taken by each letter (other than the letter I) shall be not less than 9 millimetres. Where an accented vowel occurs in the placename the length accent character shall have a height of 2 millimetres above the letter. The distances between the nearest parts of adjoining letters shall be uniform. Where the placename comprises more than one word the distances between the nearest letters of adjoining words shall be uniform and not less than three times the distance between adjoining letters.

14. The identification mark shall appear in black characters and each letter or figure shall have a height of 70 millimetres and a stroke width of 10 millimetres. The total width of the space taken by each letter or figure (other than the letter "I" or the number "1") shall be not less than 36 millimetres and not more than 50 millimetres. The distances between adjoining letters and adjoining figures shall be uniform and shall be not less than 8 millimetres.

15. The distance between the inner edge of the blue background of the flag of the European Communities and the first letter of the placename shall be equal to the distance between the last letter of the placename and the inner edge of the black border on the right-hand side of the plate and shall be not less than 8 millimetres.

16. In the case of an identification mark which is exhibited on a plate in conformity with Diagram No. 1 shown in paragraph 2 of this Schedule-

    (a)   the external size of the plate shall be 520 in width and 110 millimetres in height;

    (b)   the blue background of the flag of the European Communities shall extend vertically from the inner edge of the black border at the top of the plate to the inner edge of the black border at the bottom of the plate and shall extend horizontally for a distance of 40 from the inner edge of the black border on the left-hand side of the plate;

(c) the distance between the inner edge of the blue background of the flag of the European Communities and the first figure of the identification mark shall be equal to the distance between the last figure of the identification mark and the inner edge of the black border on the right-hand side of the plate and shall be not less than 8 ;

(d) the index mark shall be separated from adjoining figures on each side of the index mark by a hyphen with a stroke width of 10 which shall extend horizontally for a distance of not less than 13 millimetres and not more than 22 millimetres; the distances between each hyphen and the nearest part of any adjoining letter or figure shall be uniform and shall be not less than 10 millimetres;

(e) the margin between the inner edge of the black border at the top of the plate and the nearest part of any letter in the (excluding any length accent) shall be 5 millimetres in height;

(f) the space between the nearest part of any letter of the and any letter or figure of the identification mark shall be not less than 4 millimetres in height;

(g) the space between the nearest part of any letter or figure of the identification mark and the inner edge of the black border at the bottom of the plate shall be not less than 8 millimetres in height.

17. In the case of an identification mark which is exhibited on a plate in conformity with Diagram No. 2 shown in paragraph 2 of this Schedule-

(a) the external size of the plate shall be 340 in width and 220 millimetres in height;

(b) the blue background of the flag of the European Communities shall be located at the top left-hand corner of the plate and shall extend vertically downwards from the inner edge of the black border at the top of the plate for a distance of 100 millimetres and shall extend horizontally from the inner edge of the black border at the left-hand side of the plate for a distance of 40 millimetres;

(c) the distance between the inner edge of the blue background of the flag of the European Communities and the first figure of the identification mark shall be equal to the distance between the last letter of the index mark and the inner edge of the black border on the right-hand side of the plate;

(d) the index mark shall be separated from the figures on the upper line of the identification mark by a hyphen with a stroke width of 10 millimeters which shall extend horizontally for a distance of 22 ; the distance between the hyphen and the nearest part of any adjoining letter or figure shall be uniform and shall be not less than 10 millimetres;

(e)　　the distance between the inner edge of the black border at the left-hand side of the plate and the nearest figure on the lower line of the identification mark shall be equal to the distance between the last figure on that line and the inner edge of the black border at the right-hand side of the plate and shall be not less than 40 ;

(f)　　the margin between the inner edge of the black border at the top of the plate and the nearest part of any letter in the (excluding any length accent) shall be 12 millimetres in height;

(g)　　the space between the nearest part of any letter of the and the nearest part of any character in the upper line of the identification mark shall be not less than 12 millimetres in height;

(h)　　the space between the upper and lower line of the identification mark shall be not less than 12 millimetres in height;

()　　the margin between the lower line of the identification mark and the inner edge of the black border at the bottom of the plate shall be not less than 12 in height.

18.　　In the case of an identification mark exhibited on a bicycle, an invalid carriage or a pedestrian- controlled vehicle:

(a)　　any of the dimensions prescribed in paragraph 5, 10, 11, 13, 14, 15, 16 or 17 of this Schedule may be reduced to an amount which is not less than half of the amount so prescribed, and

(b)　　the plate need not be rectangular provided that the letters and figures thereon comply as nearly as possible with the arrangement shown in Diagram No. I or Diagram No. 2 in paragraph 2 of this Schedule or as described in paragraph 19 of this Schedule, as the case may be.

19.　　In the case of a bicycle, an invalid carriage or a pedestrian-controlled vehicle on which an identification mark is displayed on a plate generally of the type shown in the said Diagram No. 2, if the dimensions of the identification mark or plate are reduced in accordance with paragraph 18 of this Schedule, the identification mark or plate shall not be held to be in contravention of this Schedule solely because:

(a)　　the flag of the European Communities is at the bottom left-hand corner of the plate, and

(b)　　part of the is above the flag of the European Communities.

20.　　In the case of a vehicle which is provided with an indented space to accommodate a registration plate and the size of the space is such that it can accommodate neither a plate of the dimensions prescribed in paragraph 16(a) of this Schedule nor a plate of the dimensions prescribed in paragraph 17(a) of this Schedule, the dimensions prescribed in paragraphs 5, 10, 11, 13, 14, 15, 16 or 17 of this Schedule may be reduced provided that the dimensions as so reduced comply as nearly as possible with the dimensions so prescribed.

21.   An identification mark or plate shall not be held to be in contravention of this Schedule by reason only of failure to comply with the dimensions prescribed in this Schedule provided that:

(a)   in the case of a prescribed dimension which is 70 or less, the difference between the dimension of the identification mark or plate and the prescribed dimensions is not greater than 1 millimetre, and

(b)   in the case of a prescribed dimension which is greater than 70 , the difference between the dimension of the identification mark or plate and the prescribed dimension is not greater than 3 millimetres.

22.   The provisions of paragraphs 2 to 21 of this Schedule shall not apply in the case of a large public service vehicle (within the meaning of the Road Traffic Act, 1961 (No.24 of 1961)) on which an identification mark is so constructed and used that it is illuminated by transparency or translucency and in such a case the characters of the identification mark shall appear white when the mark is so illuminated and shall appear at all other times white against a black background.

23.   The provisions of this Schedule shall be deemed to be complied with in relation to an identification mark which incorporates the index mark if the identification mark exhibited on the vehicle complies with the provisions of Part 1 of the Third Schedule to the Road Vehicles (Registration and Licensing) Regulations, 1982 (S.1. No. 311 of 1982).][7]

[

SECOND SCHEDULE

OWNER   PART I

DOCUMENT NO.

VEHICLE REGISTRATION NO.

If you sell or transfer the vehicle to someone else PRIOR TO FIRST LICENCING (ROAD TAXING) Part I of this document must be completed overleaf, detached and posted (without postage stamp) to the Central Vehicle Office, Freepost, Rosslare Harbour, Co. Wexford. Part II of this document must be handed to the new owner

VEHICLE REGISTRATION CERTIFICATE  PART II

SERIAL NO.

VEHICLE REGISTRATION NO.

This Certificate is issued by the Revenue Commissioners. Officers of the Revenue Commissioners, Members of the Garda Siochana, and Officials of the Motor Tax Office may require you to produce the Certificate at any time.

YOU ARE REQUIRED BY LAW TO NOTIFY THE REVENUE COMMISSIONERS OF CHANGES TO ANY OF THE DETAILS ON THIS DOCUMENT, AS SOON AS THEY OCCUR.

In the event of a change the boxes overleaf should be completed as appropriate. For further information, please telephone your local Vehicle Registration Office or the Central Vehicle Office.

AT EACH CHANGE OF OWNERSHIP, THIS DOCUMENT MUST BE HANDED TO THE NEW OWNER. WHERE THE VEHICLE IS SCRAPPED, DESTROYED OR SENT PERMANENTLY OUT OF THE STATE THIS DOCUMENT SHOULD BE POSTED (without postage stamp) TO THE CENTRAL VEHICLE OFFICE, FREEPOST, ROSSLARE HARBOUR, CO. WEXFORD.

Make:
Model:

Colour(s):
Body Type:

Engine Number:
Engine Type:
Engine Capacity:
Chassis/Frame Number:
Number of Windows:
Number of Seats:

Search Code:
Statistical Code:
Exemption Code:
Vehicle Category:

Date of Registration:
Month and Year of First
Registration or Manufacture:

Document No.:

RESTRICTION (if any)

_____
Authorised Official

NOTIFICATION OF CHANGE OF OWNERSHIP

NAME AND ADDRESS OF PERSON BUYING OR ACQUIRING THE VEHICLE

Surname or Company Name		Joint Owner (where applicable). First Name and Surname	
Title (e.g. Mr., Mrs., Ms., Miss, Rev., Dr., etc.)		Address	
First Name(s)			

I/We declare that ownership of this vehicle was transferred to the new owner mentioned above on the .... day of

.... 19.......

Signature ....   Date ....

NOTIFICATION OF CHANGES: You must notify changes IMMEDIATELY by completing the appropriate section(s) below in BLOCK CAPITAL LETTERS, signing the DECLARATION and sending this document to the Central Vehicle Office, Freepost, Rosslare Harbour, Co. Wexford.

SECTION 1 - CHANGE OF VEHICLE PARTICULARS (if applicable) and date of change   **DD   MM   YEAR**

A. NEW COLOUR (insert new basic colour e.g. red, green, etc.)

B. NEW/REPLACEMENT ENGINE NUMBER

C. NEW/REPLACEMENT ENGINE CAPACITY   D. NEW BODY TYPE *

E. NEW FUEL (e.g. petrol, diesel, etc.)   F. NEW NUMBER OF WINDOWS *   G. NEW NUMBER OF SEATS *

* Declaration Form VRT 6, obtainable from your local Vehicle Registration Office, must also be completed when a change of Tax Category takes place.

SECTION 2 - VEHICLE SCRAPPED, DESTROYED OR SENT PERMANENTLY OUT OF THE STATE (if applicable)

Please tick the appropriate box   scrapped/ destroyed ✓   sent out of the State ✓   and give the date applicable: **DD   MM   YEAR**

SECTION 3 - NOTIFICATION OF CHANGE OF OWNERSHIP - To be completed by the buyer only where change takes place before the vehicle is first licensed for road use. You must send this document to the Central Vehicle Office, Freepost, Rosslare Harbour, Co. Wexford. A new certificate will be issued to you.

Surname or Company Name		Joint Owner (where applicable). First Name and Surname	
Title (e.g. Mr., Mrs., Ms., Miss, Rev., Dr., etc.)		Address	
First Name(s)			

DECLARATION

I/We declare that I/we have checked the information given on this form and that to the best of my/our knowledge it is correct.

Signature   Date

ANY PERSON WHO ALTERS THE PARTICULARS ON THE FRONT OF THIS CERTIFICATE INCURS HEAVY PENALTIES

WARNING: ROAD TAX LIABILITY GENERALLY COMMENCES FROM THE DATE OF REGISTRATION.
PLEASE CONTACT YOUR LOCAL MOTOR TAX OFFICE FOR FURTHER INFORMATION.   ]8

THIRD SCHEDULE

THE REVENUE COMMISSIONERS DUBLIN CASTLE

DECLARATION FOR REGISTRATION OF A NEW VEHICLE (OTHER THAN A MOTOR CYCLE)

BEFORE COMPLETING THIS FORM PLEASE READ NOTES OVERLEAF

Document Number where applicable

A. VEHICLE PARTICULARS

1. Make
2. Model and Version
3. Colour(s)
4. Body Type
5. Engine Type
6. Engine Capacity
7. Chassis No.
8. Engine No.
9. Number of Seats / Windows
10. Unladen Weight (Kgs)
11. Country of Origin
12. Country whence consigned
13. Options/Extras (please tick) yes / no
14. Design Weights (Commercial Vehicles) GVW ___ Kgs / GCW ___ Kgs
15. Axle Weights (Kgs)
16. Statistical Code
17. FOR OFFICIAL USE ONLY — Registration Number and Date of First Registration in the State — Day / Month / Year — Receipt No. (where applicable)
18. Exempt Code
19. S.A.D. No. & month/year (where applicable)

B. OWNER PARTICULARS

20.
SURNAME OR COMPANY NAME
TITLE — e.g. Mr., Mrs., Ms., Miss, Dr., Rev., etc.
FIRST NAME(S)
ADDRESS
TOWN/CITY
COUNTY — T.A.N. (where applicable)
VAT No. IE
21. Enter Index Mark of County/Borough:

VAT: Where VAT is also payable at the time of registration, VAT 4 Form should be completed.

C. REGISTRATION TAX

22. Extras/Options CODES factory fitted or fitted by Distributor (insert value in Box 24 below.)
23. Basic price IR£
24. Options/Extras IR£
25. Declared OMSP IR£
26. Registration Tax Category:
27. Rate of Tax:
28. Method of payment code
29. Registration Tax Payable: IR£

D. ACCOUNTING DETAILS

PAYER DETAILS

30. Name & Address — a. VAT No. — b. T.A.N.

DISTRIBUTOR DETAILS

31. Name of Distributor — a. T.A.N. — b. Invoice Ref.

DEALER DETAILS

32. Name of Dealer — a. T.A.N. — Telephone Number / Fax Number — b. Sales Invoice Ref.

E. PAYER'S DECLARATION

33. I .... (block capitals)
declare that the particulars herein are true and accurate.
Signature .... Date ....

F. FOR INFORMATION PURPOSES ONLY

34. OMSP Standing declared on — Day / Month / Year

Basic price	Options/Extras	Declared OMSP
IR£	IR£	IR£

G. OFFICIAL USE ONLY

35. Officer's Signature and VRO Stamp

Signature ....

NOTES

These NOTES are intended to be an aid to completing the form. In cases of difficulty consult with any official in your local Vehicle Registration Office. The numbers below refer to the corresponding box numbers on the form. In certain boxes codes are required - a comprehensive list of all codes is available from any Vehicle Registration Office. These codes must be inserted - not to do so will result in a delay in your registration. VAT will only be payable at the time of registration where a new vehicle has been acquired in another Member State by a person/company/institution not entitled to a deduction of VAT under section 12 of the VAT Act, 1972.

SECTION A - VEHICLE PARTICULARS

1.   Only the manufacturer's marque is to be inserted here.
3.   Either one colour or the appropriate combination should be entered here + CODE
4.   As appropriate (e.g. saloon, station wagon, horse box, van, omnibus, minibus, open lorry etc.) + CODE
5.   As appropriate (e.g. petrol only, LP Gas only, petrol/LP Gas, diesel, electricity, steam etc.) + CODE
6.   Cubic Centimetres
9.   A window is defined as including a sheet of glass or other material capable of admitting light, whether or not encased in a frame or channel and whether or not forming a door or part of a door, but does not include a windscreen or sunroof.
10-15. inclusive - Complete as appropriate including CODES
16.   This Code will be available from the Central Vehicle Office, Rosslare Harbour.
17.   For official use only. (If you have reserved a number the receipt number should be entered in the sub-box provided - the receipt itself should accompany this application.)
18.   Where you are entitled to an exemption from VRT please insert the appropriate CODE in this box.
19.   Where a Single Administrative Document Number is applicable (i.e. where the vehicle has been entered to Customs) it should be entered here.

SECTION B - OWNER PARTICULARS

20.   As appropriate. If the owner has a VAT number or a Trader Account Number it should be entered in the appropriate box.
21.   A list of these index marks may be obtained at any Vehicle Registration Office.

SECTION C - REGISTRATION TAX

Your vehicle will be classified in either Category A, Category B, Category C or Category D. The Vehicle Registration Tax rate applicable to each of these categories is available from any Vehicle Registration Office.
22.   Complete if appropriate - in this box the CODES referred to are manufacturer/distributor codes.
23.   The basic price is the price as declared to the Commissioners in the prescribed manner by the manufacturer or distributor
24.   Enter value of options/extras here.
25.   The sum of box 23 + box 24
26.   Enter A, B, C or D
27.   The rate or sum appropriate to Category A, B, C or D.
28.   The sum of box 25 x the percentage in box 27 or the specific sum involved. Where you are claiming that your vehicle is exempt from Registration Tax, you must enter the appropriate CODE in box 18.
29.   Payment may be made by cash (including guaranteed cheque and bank draft), deferred (if approved), FACT or Other Public Department.

Payment by	
CASH	A
DEFERRED	E
FACT	D
OPD	J
EXEMPT	X

SECTION D - ACCOUNTING DETAILS

30.   Where the Payer is the same as the individual/company in Section B it is sufficient to note this here.
31-32. Not be completed in cases of registrations by private individuals

SECTION E - PAYER'S DECLARATION

33.   This box should be signed and dated by the person named in box 30 or, in the case of a company, by an authorised person.

SECTION F - FOR INFORMATION PURPOSES ONLY

34.   For distributor use only.

FOURTH SCHEDULE

DECLARATION FOR REGISTRATION OF A USED VEHICLE (OTHER THAN A MOTOR CYCLE)

BEFORE COMPLETING THIS FORM PLEASE READ NOTES OVERLEAF

A. VEHICLE PARTICULARS

1. Make
2. Model and Version
3. Colour(s)
4. Body Type
5. Engine Type   6. Engine Capacity
7. Chassis No.
8. Engine No.
9. Number of Seats / Windows
11. Country of Origin
12. Country whence consigned
16. Statistical Code

17. FOR OFFICIAL USE ONLY

	Day	Month	Year
Registration Number and Date of First Registration in the State			

Receipt No. (where applicable)

18. Exemption Code   19. S.A.D. No. & month/year (where applicable)

B. OWNER PARTICULARS

SURNAME OR COMPANY NAME	
TITLE	e.g. Mr., Mrs., Ms., Miss, Dr., Rev., etc.
FIRST NAME(S)	
ADDRESS	
TOWN/CITY	
COUNTY	T.A.N. (where applicable)
VAT No.	IE

21. Enter Index Mark of County/Borough:

C. ACCOUNTING DETAILS

OWNER DETAILS

22. Name & Address   a. VAT No.
b. T.A.N.

DEALER DETAILS

23. Name of Dealer   a. T.A.N.
Telephone Number   Fax Number   b. Sales invoice no.

D. PREVIOUS REGISTRATIONS

24.

Latest Registration Number	Country of latest registration	Date of latest registration	Country of first registration	Month & year of first registration

E. PAYER'S DECLARATION

25. I _____ (block capitals) declare that the particulars herein are true and accurate.

Signature _____   Date _____

F. OFFICIAL USE ONLY

26. Value as assessed by Revenue Officer

Total OMSP   IR£

27. Registration Tax Category: 28. Rate of Tax: 30. Method of payment code:
29. Registration Tax Payable: IR£

31. OFFICER'S SIGNATURE AND VRO STAMP

Signature

Form VRT 4

NOTES

These NOTES are intended to be an aid to completing the form. In cases of difficulty consult with any official in your local Vehicle Registration Office. The numbers below refer to the corresponding box numbers on the form. In certain boxes codes are required - a comprehensive list of all codes is available from any Vehicle Registration Office.

SECTION A - VEHICLE PARTICULARS

1.　Only the manufacturer's marque is to be inserted here.
3.　Either one colour or the appropriate combination should be entered here + CODE
4.　As appropriate (e.g. saloon, station wagon, horse box, van,omnibus, minibus, open lorry etc.) + CODE
5.　As appropriate (e.g. petrol only, LP Gas only, petrol/LP Gas, diesel, electricity, steam etc.) + CODE
6.　Cubic Centimetres
9.　A window is defined as including a sheet of glass or other material capable of admitting light, whether or not encased in a frame or channel and whether or not forming a door or part of a door, but does not include a windscreen or sunroof.
10-15. Inclusive - Complete as appropriate including CODES
16.　This Code will be available from the Central Vehicle Registration Office, Rosslare Harbour.
17.　For official use only. (If you have reserved a number the receipt number should be entered in the sub-box provided - the receipt itself should accompany this application.)
18.　Where you are entitled to an exemption from VRT please insert the appropriate CODE in this box.
19.　Where a Single Administrative Document Number is applicable (i.e. where the vehicle has been entered to Customs) it should be entered here.

SECTION B - OWNER PARTICULARS

20.　As appropriate. If the owner has a VAT number or a Trader Account Number it should be entered in the appropriate box.
21.　A list of these index marks is available at any Vehicle Registration Office.

SECTION C - REGISTRATION TAX

22-23. Complete if appropriate. Where the Payer is the same as the individual/company in Section B it is sufficient to note this in box 22. Where box 23 does not apply simply note "not applicable" in the box.

SECTION D - PREVIOUS REGISTRATIONS

24.　Complete as appropriate.

SECTION E - PAYER'S DECLARATION

25.　This box should be signed and dated by the person named in box 22 or, in the case of a company, by an authorised person.

FIFTH SCHEDULE

THE REVENUE COMMISSIONERS
DUBLIN CASTLE

DECLARATION FOR REGISTRATION OF A NEW OR USED MOTOR CYCLE

BEFORE COMPLETING THIS FORM PLEASE READ NOTES OVERLEAF

Document Number where applicable

A. VEHICLE PARTICULARS

1. Make
2. Model and Version
3. Colour(s)
4. Body Type
5. Engine Type   6. Engine Capacity
7. Frame No.
8. Engine No.
9. Power/Weight Ratio   10. Unladen Weight (Kgs)
11. Country of Origin   13. Options/Extras (please tick)   yes   no
12. Country whence consigned
14. Maximum Design Speed (Km/hour)
15. Maximum Engine Power (KW)
16. Statistical Code
17. FOR OFFICIAL USE ONLY

Registration Number and Date of First Registration in the State   Day   Month   Year

Receipt No. (where applicable)

18. Exemption Code   19. S.A.D. No. & month/year (where applicable)

B. OWNER PARTICULARS

20.
SURNAME OR COMPANY NAME
TITLE   e.g. Mr., Mrs., Ms., Miss, Dr., Rev., etc.
FIRST NAME(S)
ADDRESS
TOWN/CITY
COUNTY   T.A.N. (where applicable)
VAT No.   IE
21. Enter Index Mark of County/Borough:

VAT: Where VAT is also payable at the time of registration, form VAT 4 should be completed.

C. REGISTRATION TAX

22. Up yo 350c.c. @ IR£ .... per c.c. =
23. Over 350c.c. IR£ .... per c.c. =
25. Method of payment Code
24. Registration Tax Payable: IR£

D. ACCOUNTING DETAILS

PAYER DETAILS

26. Name & Address   a. VAT No.
b. T.A.N

DISTRIBUTOR DETAILS

27. Name of Distributor   a. T.A.N.
b. Invoice Ref.

DEALER DETAILS

28. Name of Dealer   a. T.A.N
Telephone Number   Fax Number   b. Sales Invoice Ref.

D. PREVIOUS REGISTRATIONS

29. THIS SECTION TO BE COMPLETED ONLY FOR USED VEHICLES

Latest Registration/Registration Number	Country of latest registration	Date of latest registration	Country of first registration	Month & Year of Manufacture

---

E. PAYER'S DECLARATION

30. I .... (block capitals)
declare that the particulars herein are true and accurate.

Signature ....   Date ....

G. OFFICIAL USE ONLY

31. OFFICER'S SIGNATURE AND VRO STAMP

.... Signature

Form VRT 5

NOTES

These NOTES are intended to be an aid to completing the form. In cases of difficulty consult with any official in your local Vehicle Registration Office. The numbers below refer to the corresponding box numbers on the form. In certain boxes codes are required - a comprehensive list of all codes is available from any Vehicle Registration Office. These codes must be inserted - not to do so will result in a delay in your registration. VAT will only be payable at the time of registration where a new vehicle has been acquired in another Member State by a person/company/institution not entitled to a deduction of VAT under Section 12 of the VAT Act, 1972.

SECTION A - VEHICLE PARTICULARS

1.   Only the manufacturer's marque is to be inserted here.
3.   Either one colour or the appropriate combination should be entered here + CODE
4.   As appropriate + CODE
5.   As appropriate (e.g. petrol, electricity, etc.) + CODE
6.   Cubic Centimetres.
9.   As appropriate.
10-15. Inclusive - Complete as appropriate including CODES
16. This Code will be available from the Central Vehicle Office, Rosslare Harbour.
17. For official use only. (If you have reserved a number the receipt number should be entered in the sub-box provided - the receipt itself should accompany this application.)
18. Where you are entitled to an exemption from VRT please insert the appropriate CODE in this box.
19. Where a Single Administrative Document Number is applicable (i.e. where the vehicle has been entered to Customs) it should be entered here.

SECTION B - OWNER PARTICULARS

20. As appropriate. If the owner has a VAT number or a Trader Account Number it should be entered in the appropriate box.
21. A list of these index marks is available at any Vehicle Registration Office.

SECTION C - REGISTRATION TAX

22-23. The rates of Vehicle Registration Tax applicable are available from any Vehicle Registration Office.
24. The total resulting from the calculations in boxes 22 and 23. Where you are claiming that your vehicle is exempt from Registration Tax, you must have entered the CODE in box 18.
25. Payment may be made by cash (including guaranteed cheque and bank draft), deferred (if approved), FACT or Other Public Department.

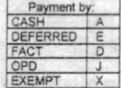

Payment by:	
CASH	A
DEFERRED	E
FACT	D
OPD	J
EXEMPT	X

SECTION D - ACCOUNTING DETAILS

26-28. Complete as appropriate. Where the Payer is the same as the individual/company in Section B it is sufficient to note this in box 26. Where boxes 27 and 28 do not apply simply note "not applicable" in both boxes.

SECTION E - PREVIOUS REGISTRATIONS

Complete this section only where the vehicle is used.

SECTION F - PAYER'S DECLARATION

30. This box should be signed and dated by the person named in box 26 or, in the case of a company, by an authorised person.

Amendments

1   Inserted by reg.12(a), SI No.437 of 1992, w.e.f. 1 January 1993

2   Substituted by reg.8(1)(a), SI No.252 of 1993, w.e.f. 17 June 1993

3   Substituted by reg.8(1)(b), SI No.252 of 1993, w.e.f. 17 June 1993

4   Substituted by r2(a), S.I. No. 576 of 2007, w.e.f. 7 August 2007.

5   Inserted by r2(b) S.I. No. 576 of 2007, w.e.f. 7 August 2007.

6   Words 'in writing' deleted by reg.12(b), SI No.437 of 1992, w.e.f. 1 January 1993

7   First Schedule substituted by SI No.432 of 1999, w.e.f. 22 December 1999

8   Second Schedule substituted by reg.8(1)(c), SI No.252 of 1993, w.e.f. 1 October 1993

S.I. No. 437 of 1992
VEHICLE REGISTRATION AND TAXATION (NO.2)
REGULATIONS, 1992

The Revenue Commissioners, in exercise of the powers conferred on them by section 141 of the Finance Act, 1992, (No. 9 of 1992), as amended by section 14 of the Finance (No.2) Act, 1992 (No.28 of 1992), hereby make the following Regulations:

1.   These Regulations may be cited as the Vehicle Registration and Taxation (No.2) Regulations, 1992.

2.   These Regulations shall come into operation on the 1st day of January, 1993.

3.   In these Regulations -

        "the Act" means the Finance Act, 1992 (No. 9 of 1992), as amended by the Finance (No. 2) Act, 1992, (No. 28 of 1992);

        "the Act of 1952", "authorised person" and "vehicle" have the meanings assigned to them by Chapter IV of Part II of the Act;

        "the Commissioners" means the Revenue Commissioners;

        "tax" means vehicle registration tax;

        "the Regulations" means the Vehicle Registration and Taxation Regulations, 1992 (S.I.No.318 of 1992);

        "the zz register" means the register established under section 131(1)(e) of the Act.

4.   (1)   In this Regulation "the registration body" means the body appointed by the Commissioners by paragraph (9) of this Regulation.

        (2)   The registration body shall, in the performance of its hi nctions under the Act and these Regulations, comply with the instructions of the Commissioners, keep them supplied with up to date copies of the register and furnish them with such extracts from the register as they may request.

        (3)   A person who applies to the registration body under section 131(1)(e) of the Act for the registration of a vehicle in the zz register shall furnish to that body, in the form of the declaration specified in the Schedule to these Regulations, the particulars for which provision is made in the form.

        (4)   The register shall consist of the declarations made by the owners of the vehicles concerned in accordance with paragraph (3), as accepted by the registration body.

        (5)   When declaring a vehicle for registration in the zz register, a person (in this Regulation referred to as "the declarant") shall show, to the satisfaction of the registration body, that he

is a person established outside the State, that the vehicle is in the State temporarily only and solely for the use of persons established outside the State and, as respects the use of the vehicle in a public place, that there is compliance with section 56 of the Road Traffic Act, 1961 (No.24 of 1961).

(6)   Where the registration body is satisfied that a is a person established outside the State and that the vehicle to which his declaration relates qualifies for registration in the zz register, it shall assign an identification mark to the vehicle containing the letters zz and a unique number and shall issue to the declarant -

(a)   a card (referred to subsequently in these Regulations as **"a registration card"**) specifying the identification mark, such particulars of the vehicle as the commissioners may determine, the name and address of the owner of the vehicle and such other (if any) particulars as the Commissioners may determine, and

(b)   2 rectangular plates on which is exhibited the identification mark assigned to the vehicle under this paragraph.

(7)   The identification mark aforesaid shall be displayed on the vehicle in accordance with section 131(1)(h) of the Act by means of the registration plates issued by the registration body under paragraph (6) of this Regulation.

(8)   A registration in the zz register shall be valid for I month from the date of issue. However, where a declarant requires a period of validity of the registration in excess of 1 month, he shall apply in writing to the Commissioners therefore and the Commissioners may extend the period of such validity if they are satisfied that the declarant will continue to remain established outside the State for the period, as extended, of such validity and that the vehicle concerned will not be used by a person established in the State during that period. Where the period of validity of a registration is extended under this paragraph, the Commissioners shall issue to the declarant concerned a document (in these Regulations referred to as **"a confirmation"**) confirming the extension and specifying the period thereof

(9)   The Automobile Association of Ireland is hereby appointed to maintain the zz register on behalf of the Commissioners.

(10)   In this Regulation **"person established outside the State"** means an individual having his normal residence outside the State or a person (other than an individual) having his only or principal place of business outside the State.

(11)   [(a)   In this Regulation **"normal residence"** means the place where a person usually lives, that is to say, where he lives for at least 185 days in each year, because of personal and occupationalties, or, in the case of a person with no

occupational ties, because of personal ties. However, the normal residence of a person whose occupational ties are in a different place from his personal ties, and who consequently lives in turn in different places situated in 2 or more countries shall be regarded as being the place of his personal ties:

Provided that such person returns to the place of his personal ties regularly. This proviso shall not apply if the person is living in a country in order to carry out a task of a definite duration.

A person who lives in a country primarily for the purposes of attending a school or university or other educational or vocational establishment shall not be regarded as having his normal residence in that country.][1]

(b)   Proof of normal residence may be given by means of documents relating to the acquisition of property or to employment or cessation of employment or to other transactions carried out in the course of day to day living and, in addition to or in substitution for the foregoing documents or any of them, any other documentary evidence the Commissioners require or accept.

5.   (1)   The particulars declared to the Commissioners under subsection (2)(c) of section 131 of the Act shall be those specified in Section 1 of the part entitled "Notification of Changes" of the certificate of registration set out in the Second Schedule to the Regulations.

    (2)   A declaration under the said subsection (2)(c) shall be made by completing the said Section 1 and submitting the said certificate to the Commissioners.

6.   (1)   A request under section 131(5A) shall be in writing and shall not be made before the 1st day of November in the year immediately preceding the year in which the vehicle concerned is proposed to be brought into use.

    [(2)   A fee of €1,000 is prescribed for the purpose of section 131 (5A) of the Act][2].

    (3)   A mark assigned under the said section 131(5A) shall not be displayed on the vehicle concerned until it would, but for such assignment, fall to be assigned under Regulation 9(3) of the Regulations.

    [(4)   (a)   The mark assigned to a vehicle under section 131 (5A) shall be cancelled if the owner of the vehicle fails, within a reasonable period, to display that mark when it falls to be assigned under Regulation 9(3) of the Regulations.

        (b)   Where a mark is cancelled pursuant to subparagraph (b), then the fee paid shall not be refunded other than in cases that the Commissioners are satisfied that exceptional circumstances have occurred so as to prevent the person to whom the mark was assigned from using it.

(c)   An application for the purposes of subparagraph (b) shall be made in writing to the Commissioners and shall set out the exceptional circumstances claimed to warrant the repayment. The applicant shall furnish to the Commissioners, if so requested by them, proof to the satisfaction of the Commissioners of those circumstances.][3]

7.   A person who seeks the repayment under section 134(6) of the Act of the tax paid on the registration of a vehicle shall make an application in writing to the Commissioners within 21 days of such registration for the repayment, shall set out in the application the exceptional circumstances claimed to warrant the repayment and shall furnish to the Commissioners, if so requested by them, proof to the satisfaction of the Commissioners of those circumstances.

8.   A person who seeks the repayment under section 134(7) of the Act of any tax paid on the registration of a vehicle shall, if so requested by the Commissioners, furnish to them not later than the 10th day of the month immediately following that in which the vehicle was registered,   such information as they may specify in relation to such of the following matters as they may specify, that is to say, the ownership and use of the vehicle and the source of the moneys used for its acquisition.

9.   The conditions, restrictions and limitations under which an unregistered vehicle may be used in a public place by an person in accordance with section 136(8) of the Act shall be as follows:

(a)   the vehicle shall be used only for the purpose of inspecting or testing it in the course of or following repair of or modification to it, delivering it to an person, driving it to a port or airport or to a place on the land frontier of the State for the purposes of its immediate exportation, demonstrating it to a person who is considering purchasing it or for any other purpose specified by the Commissioners in any particular case,

(b)   the vehicle shall not be used on Sundays or public holidays or before 6.00 a.m. or after 10.00 p.m. on any other day without the permission of the Commissioners,

(c)   the vehicle shall not have more than 3,000 kilometres in the State, and

(d)   the vehicle shall be one to which subsection (6) of section 21 of the Finance (No. 2) Act, 1992 (No.28 of 1992), applies and there shall be exhibited on it in accordance with that section a trade licence issued under that section.

10.   Upon application in writing to the Commissioners in that behalf by the owner of a vehicle and upon furnishing to them such information as

they may reasonably require for the purposes of their functions under this Regulation, the Commissioners may, notwithstanding Regulation 9(6) of the Regulations, if the vehicle is not required to be the subject of a licence under the Act of 1952, issue to such owner a permit in writing authorising (in lieu of complying with the said Regulation 9(6)) the permanent exhibition of the identification mark assigned to the vehicle under section 131(5) of the Act on the chassis or frame of the vehicle in a legible form and in an accessible position.

11.   (1)   An officer of the Commissioners, authorised in writing in that behalf by the Commissioners (upon production of his authorisation if so requested by any person affected), or a member of the Garda Síochána may require the driver of a vehicle exhibiting a registration mark assigned to the vehicle under Regulation 4 of these Regulations or a vehicle to which Regulation 10 applies to produce the registration card relating to the vehicle issued under paragraph (6) of the said Regulation 4 and any confirmation issued under paragraph (8) of the said Regulation 4 in relation to the vehicle or, as the case may be, a permit issued under Regulation 10 of these Regulations in relation to the vehicle and the driver shall comply with the request.

(2)   An officer of the Commissioners in uniform may require the driver of a vehicle exhibiting a registration mark assigned to it under the said Regulation 4 or a vehicle to which the said Regulation 10 applies to stop the vehicle and the driver of the vhicle shall comply with the requirement.

12.   The Regulations are hereby amended -

(a)   in Regulation 4, by the insertion of the following definition after the definition of "distributor":

"'**registration number**', in relation to a vehicle, means the identification mark assigned to the vehicle under section 131(5) of the Act;", and

(b)   in Regulation 15, by the deletion in paragraph (1) of "in writing".

13.   Where, as respects any class of person the Commissioners so allow and subject to any conditions which they may think fit to impose, compliance in whole or in part, with any of these Regulations shall not be required.

GIVEN this 31st day of December, 1992.

D. B. QUIGLEY,
Revenue Commissioner.

Amendments

1   Reg.4(11)(a) substituted by reg.9, Vehicle Registration and Taxation Regulations 1993 ,w.e.f. 17 June 1993
2   Substituted by S.I. 396 of 2008, w.e.f. 7 October 2008 previously €315.
3   Inserted by S.I. 396 of 2008, w.e.f. 7 October 2008

S.I. No. 59 of 1993.
VEHICLE REGISTRATION TAX (PERMANENT RELIEFS) REGULATIONS, 1993.

vehicle Registration Tax (Permanent Reliefs) Regulations, 1993.

I, BERTIE AHERN, Minister for Finance, in exercise of the powers conferred S134 on me by section 141 (3) of the Finance Act, 1992 (No. 9 of 1992), hereby make the following Regulations:

1. These Regulations may be cited as the Vehicle Registration Tax (Permanent Reliefs) Regulations, 1993.

2. These Regulations shall be deemed to have come into operation on the 1st day of January, 1993.

3. (1) In these Regulations -

"**the Act**" means the Finance Act, 1992 (No.9 of 1992);

"**normal residence**" means the place where a person usually lives, that is to say, where he lives for at least 185 days in each year, because of personal and occupational ties, or, in the case of a person with no occupational ties, because of personal ties.

However, the normal residence of a person whose occupational ties are in a different place from his personal ties and who consequently lives in turn in different places situated in 2 or more countries shall be regarded as being the place of his personal ties:

Provided that such person returns to the place of his personal ties regularly. This proviso shall not apply where the person is living in a country in order to carry out a task of a duration of less than one year.

A person who lives in a country primarily for the purposes of attending a school or university or other educational or vocational establishment shall not be regarded as having his normal residence in that country.

"**personal property**" means property for the personal use of the person concerned and his household living with him outside the State but does not include property which by reason of its nature or quantity reflects any commercial interest or is intended to be used for any commercial purpose.

(2) An expression or word used in these Regulations and also used in Chapter IV of Part II of the Act shall, unless the contrary intention appears, have in these Regulations the meaning that it has in that Chapter.

Transfer of residence

4. (1) Subject to paragraph (5), the relief under section 134(1)(a) of the Act shall be granted for any vehicle -

(a)   which is the personal property of an individual transferring his normal residence to the State and which has been in the possession of and used by him outside the State for a period of at least six months before the date on which he ceases to have his normal residence outside the State,

(b)   which has been acquired under the general conditions of taxation in force in the domestic market of a country and which is not the subject, on the grounds of exportation or departure from that country, of any exemption from or any refund of value-added tax, excise duty or any other consumption tax, and

(c)   in respect of which an application for relief, in such form as may be specified by the Commissioners, is made to the Commissioners not later than the next working day following its arrival in the State or, in case the vehicle requires the making of a customs entry on arrival in the State, not later than the next working day after its release from customs control.

(2)   Where a vehicle is -

    (a)   supplied under diplomatic or consular arrangements, or

    (b)   supplied to an international organisation recognised as such by the Minister for Foreign Affairs or to a member of such an organisation within the limits and under the conditions laid down by the international convention establishing the organisation, or by another similar agreement, the conditions specified in paragraph (1)(b) of this Regulation shall be deemed to have been complied with as respects the vehicle and in paragraph (1)(a) of this Regulation the reference to 6 months shall be construed as a reference to 12 months.

(3)   Proof shall be supplied to the Commissioners within one month of the date of the application for the relief aforesaid that the conditions specified in paragraph (1) of this Regulation have been compiled with. The proof shall consist of -

    (a)   a sales invoice, receipt of purchase, or other similar document, which clearly establishes, where relevant, that any value-added tax, excise duty or other consumption tax payable on the vehicle concerned outside the State was paid and not refunded,

    (b)   in relation to the possession of and use of the vehicle by the person concerned for the appropriate period aforesaid, the vehicle registration document and insurance certificates for the vehicle, (c)　　in relation to normal residence outside the State, documents relating to the acquisition of property, or to employment or cessation of employment, or to other transactions carried out in the course of day-to-day living,

(d)　　in relation to the transfer of normal residence to a place in the State, documents relating to the disposal of property in the country of departure and the acquisition of property in the State or to employment (including statements in writing from the person's employer in the State), and

(e)　　evidence of the date on which the vehicle was brought into the State,

and, in addition to the foregoing or in substitution for it or any of it, any other documentary evidence the Commissioners require or accept.

(4)　　A vehicle in respect of which the relief aforesaid is claimed shall be produced to the Commissioners for examination.

(5)　　The relief aforesaid shall not be granted-

(a)　　in respect of a vehicle brought into the State more than 12 months after the transfer of normal residence unless the Commissioners, in their discretion, so decide in any particular case, or

(b)　　in the case of a person who transferred his normal residence from the State to a country outside the State in order to carry out a task of a duration of one year or more and who, upon completion of the task, transfers his normal residence back to the State, in respect of a vehicle in the period of 5 years following the granting of such relief in any particular case or of relief in corresponding circumstances under the provisions that applied in relation to the grant of relief from import taxes by the Commissioners in the case of transfer of residence to the State in force immediately before the 1st day of January, 1993:

Provided that, in the case of a person who commenced so living before the date of the making of these Regulations and who transfers his normal residence to the State after that date on the completion of the task concerned, this paragraph shall not apply in relation to a vehicle brought into the State by him upon such transfer.

(6)　　A vehicle in respect of which the relief aforesaid has been granted shall not be sold or otherwise disposed of, hired out, lent or given as security in the State during the period of 12 months following its registration by the Commissioners unless the vehicle registration tax to which the relief aforesaid relates is paid thereon, except with the prior permission of the Commissioners given on their being satisfied that there are circumstances justifying its non-payment.

(7)   Where a person transferred his residence from the State on or before the date of the making of these Regulations and, on transfer of his residence back to the State, a vehicle of his would, but for the fact that his residence outside the State was not normal residence, have qualified for the relief aforesaid, the Commissioners may grant such relief in respect of the vehicle if the person complies with the other provisions of this Regulation and if he would have, satisfied the provisions in relation to residence outside the State that applied in relation to the grant of relief from import taxes by the Commissioners in the case of the transfer of residence to the State in force immediately before the 1st day of January, 1993.

Transfer of business undertaking

5.   (1)   Subject to paragraph (2), the relief under section 134(1)(b) of the Act shall be granted for any vehicle -

(a)   which has been used in the production process of the business undertaking concerned or, in the case of a service business, directly in the provision of the service, for a period of at least 12 months before the date on which the business undertaking ceased its activity in the country from which it has moved in order to cany on a similar activity in the State,

(b)   which is intended to be used for the same purpose in the State after the transfer of the business undertaking to the State,

(c)   which is brought into the State not later than 12 months after the date on which the undertaking ceased its activities outside the State, and

(d)   in respect of which an application for relief, in such form as may be specified by the Commissioners, is made to the Commissioners not later than the next working day following its arrival in the State or, in case the vehicle requires the making of a customs entry on arrival in the State, not later than the next working day after its release from customs control.

(2)   The relief aforesaid shall not be granted in respect of a vehicle brought into the State by a business undertaking established outside the State the transfer of which to the State is consequent upon or is for the purpose of merging with, or being absorbed by, a business undertaking established in the State, in

circumstances in which a new activity is not, or is not intended to be commenced.

(3)   (a) Proof shall be supplied to the Commissioners within one month of the date of the application for the relief aforesaid that the conditions specified in paragraph (1) of this Regulation have been complied with.

    (b)   The proof referred to in subparagraph (a) of this paragraph shall consist of -

        (i)   in relation to the use of the vehicle concerned for the period aforesaid in the production process aforesaid or in the provision of the service aforesaid, the vehicle registration document and insurance certificates for the vehicle concerned, and

        (ii)   in relation to the cesser aforesaid and the carrying on in the State of an activity similar to the activity aforesaid, documents relating to the disposal of the premises of the business undertaking outside the State, or to the acquisition or construction of permanent business premises in the State, or to any State or local authority approval or consent relating to such acquisition or construction or the carrying on in the State of the activity aforesaid,

        and, in addition to the foregoing or in substitution for it or any of it, any other documentary evidence that the Commissioners may require or accept.

(4)   A vehicle in respect of which the relief aforesaid is claimed shall be produced to the Commissioners for examination.

(5)   A vehicle in respect of which the relief aforesaid has been granted shall not be sold or otherwise disposed of, hired out, lent or given as security in the State during the period of 12 months following its registration by the Commissioners unless the vehicle registration tax to which the relief aforesaid relates is paid thereon, except with the prior permission of the Commissioners given on their being satisfied that there are circumstances justifying its non-payment.

(6)   In special cases, if, in the opinion of the Commissioners, it is justified by the circumstances, the relief aforesaid may be granted notwithstanding the fact that subparagraphs (a) and (c) of paragraph (1) of this Regulation have not been complied with as respects the periods specified in those subparagraphs.

Inheritance

6.   (1)   The relief under section 134(1)(c) of the Act shall be granted for any vehicle

(a)   which was the personal property of the deceased person concerned and is brought into the State not later than 2 years, or such longer period as the Commissioners in their discretion may allow in any particular case, from the date on which the vehicle entered into the possession of the person who acquired it by inheritance or the personal representative of the deceased person takes control of his property,

(b)   in respect of which there is produced to the Commissioners by or on behalf of the person seeking the relief the evidence specified in paragraph (2) of this Regulation and the evidence satisfies the Commissioners that the vehicles qualifies for the relief,

(c)   in respect of which an application for relief, in such form as may be specified by the Commissioners, is made to the Commissioners by a person who, in relation to the deceased person, is a person specified in the said section 134(1)(c) not later than the next working day following its arrival in the State or, in case the vehicle requires the making of a customs entry on arrival in the State, not later than the next working day after its release from customs control.

(2)   The evidence referred to in paragraph (1)(b) of this Regulation shall be supplied to the Commissioners within one month of the date of application for relief and shall consist of-

(a)   evidence of the death of the owner of the vehicle concerned, such as a death certificate or a copy thereof, and

(b)   evidence that the person by or on whose behalf the application for the relief is made is either the person entitled to the ownership of the vehicle under the will or, as the case may be, on the intestacy, of the deceased person or is the personal representative of the deceased person, the evidence being a copy of the will together with proof that the will has been accepted by the appropriate authorities of the place where the deceased person died for the purposes of the administration of his estate or, if the deceased person was intestate as to the vehicle concerned, a declaration issued by a notary or other competent person in the place aforesaid or by a notary in the State that the vehicle was acquired by the person as the beneficiary under the intestacy or as the personal representative of the deceased person, and

(c)   the vehicle registration document,

and, in addition to the foregoing or in substitution for it or any of it, any other documentary evidence the Commissioners may require or accept and, where any such document as aforesaid is in a language other than the English language or the Irish language, a translation thereof into the English language or the Irish language duly certified, to the satisfaction of the Commissioners, to be a true translation.

(3)   A vehicle in respect of which the relief aforesaid is claimed shall be produced to the Commissioners for examination.

Donations by official bodies, public authorities or groups

7.   (1)   The relief under section 134(1) (d) of the Act shall be granted for any vehicle-

(a)   which is not used for commercial purposes,

(b)   where a gift of such a vehicle has not previously been made by the body, authority or group concerned to the body, authority or group concerned or has been made only occasionally, and

(c)   in respect of which an application for relief, in such form as may be specified by the Commissioners, is made to the Commissioners not later than the next working day following its arrival in the State or, in case the vehicle requires the making of a customs entry on arrival in the State, not later than the next working day after its release from customs control.

(2)   Proof shall be supplied to the Commissioners within one month of the date of the application for the relief aforesaid that the conditions specified in subparagraphs (a) and (b) of paragraph (1) of this Regulation have been complied with and the proof shall be in such form as may be specified by the Commissioners.

(3)   A vehicle in respect of which the relief aforesaid is claimed shall be produced to the Commissioners for examination.

Diplomatic and related relief

8.   (1)   The relief under paragraphs (e), (f), (h) (inserted by the Finance (No. 2) Act,1992 (No.28 of 1992)) and (i) (inserted by the said Act) of section 134(1) of the Act shall be granted for -

(a)   not more than one vehicle for the official use of institution of the European Communities or the European Foundation for the improvement of living and working conditions during such period as may be determined by the Commissioners in relation to that case:

Provided that the relief aforesaid may be granted by the Commissioners in respect of additional vehicles in a particular case justified by the circumstances,

(b)   in the case of an official or other member of the staff of an institution of the European Communities or of the European Foundation for the improvement of living and working conditions whose normal residence was not in the State immediately prior to taking up a post with such institution in the State, 2 vehicles which are either brought into or acquired in the State within a period of 12 months of his taking up of the post.

(2)   Where the vehicle concerned is brought into the State, an application for the relief aforesaid, in such form as may be specified by the Commissioners, shall be made to the Commissioners not later than the next working day following its arrival in the State or, in case the vehicle requires the making of a customs entry on arrival in the State, not later than the next working day after its release from customs control. Where the vehicle concerned is acquired in the State, the application aforesaid shall be made before the acquisition of the vehicle.

(3)   A vehicle in respect of which the relief aforesaid has been granted shall not be sold or otherwise disposed of, hired out, lent or given as security in the State during the period of 2 years following its registration by the Commissioners unless the vehicle registration tax to which the relief aforesaid relates is paid thereon, except with the prior permission of the Commissioners given on their being satisfied that there are circumstances justifying its non-payment.

(4)   A vehicle brought into the State in respect of which the relief aforesaid is claimed shall be produced to the Commissioners for examination.

9.   (1)   The relief under section 134(1)(g) of the Act shall be granted -

(a)   in the case of a diplomatic agent accompanied by his spouse, for not more than 2 vehicles for the personal use of the diplomatic agent, his spouse, and family living with him during such period as may be determined by the Commissioners in relation to that case after consultation with the Minister for Foreign Affairs,

(b)   in the case of a diplomatic agent unaccompanied by his spouse, for not more than one vehicle for the personal use of the diplomatic agent during such period as may be determined by the Commissioners in relation to that case after consultation with the Minister for Foreign Affairs:

Provided that the relief aforesaid may be granted in respect of additional vehicles by the Commissioners, in consultation with the Minister for Foreign Affairs, in particular cases justified by the circumstances,

(c)   in the case of a member of the administrative and technical staff of a diplomatic mission, who is neither a national of the State nor a person whose normal residence was in the State immediately prior to his taking up duty in the mission, for one vehicle which is either brought into or acquired in the State within the period of 6 months of his taking up duty in the mission,

(d)   for not more than one vehicle for use as a service car of a diplomatic mission during such period as may be determined by the Commissioners in relation to that case after consultation with the Minister for Foreign Affairs:

Provided that the relief aforesaid may be granted in respect of additional vehicles by the Commissioners, in consultation with the Minister for Foreign Affairs, in particular cases justified by the circumstances.

(2)   Where the vehicle concerned is brought into the State, an application for the relief aforesaid, in such form as may be specified by the Commissioners, shall be made to the Commissioners not later than the next working day following its arrival in the State or, in case the vehicle requires the making of a customs entry on arrival in the State, not later than the next working day after its release from customs control. Where the vehicle concerned is acquired in the State, the application aforesaid shall be made before the acquisition of the vehicle.

(3)   A vehicle in respect of which the relief aforesaid has been granted shall not be sold or otherwise disposed of, hired out, lent or given as security in the State unless the vehicle registration tax to which the relief aforesaid relates is paid thereon, except with the prior permission of the Commissioners given on their being satisfied, in consultation with the Minister for Foreign Affairs, that there are circumstances justifying its non-payment.

(4)   A vehicle brought into the State in respect of which the relief aforesaid is claimed shall be produced to the Commissioners for examination.

(5)   In this Regulation **"diplomatic agent"** and **"member of the administrative and technical staff"** have the meanings assigned to them by Article 1 of the Vienna Convention on Diplomatic Relations done at Vienna on the 18th day of April, 1961, as set out in the First Schedule to the Diplomatic Relations and Immunities Act, 1967 (No.8 of 1967).

Construction

10.   These Regulations shall be construed together with the statutes which relate to the duties of excise and the management of those duties and any instrument relating to the duties of excise and the management of those duties made under statute.

GIVEN under my Official Seal, this 2nd day of March, 1993.

BERTIE AHERN,
Minister for Finance.

Explanatory Note

These Regulations, which are effective from 1 January, 1993 lay down the conditions governing the registration of vehicles without payment of vehicle registration tax where such vehicles are brought permanently into the State-

(a)   in connection with a transfer of normal residence;

(b)   in connection with a transfer of a business activity;

(c)   following acquisition by inheritance;

(d)   as gifts by approved official bodies, public authorities or groups;

(e)   for the use of the European Foundation for the improvement of living and working conditions and the institutions of the EC and their officials, and

(f)   under diplomatic, consular or similar arrangements.

S.I. No. 60 of 1993.
TEMPORARY EXEMPTION FROM REGISTRATION OF VEHICLES REGULATIONS, 1993.

I, BERTIE AHERN, Minister for Finance, in exercise of the powers conferred on me by section 141(3) of the Finance Act, 1992 (No.9 of 1992), hereby make the following Regulations:

1.   These Regulations shall be deemed to have come into operation on the 1st day of January, 1993.

2.   (1)   In these Regulations -

     "the Act" means the Finance Act, 1992 (No. 9 of 1992);

     "business use" means use in the direct exercise of an activity carried on for gain;

     "person established outside the State" means an individual having his normal residence outside the State or a person (other than an individual) having his only or principal place of business outside the State;

     "private use" means use other than business use;

     "transport of goods for the purpose of industry or commerce" does not include -

     (a)   the transport of apparatus for use in the transmission of by sound or television broadcasting or in the making of sound recordings, television films or cinematography films, or

     (b)   transport for a purpose connected solely with an election to Dáil Éireann.

     (2)   (a)   In these Regulations **"normal residence"** means the place where a person usually lives, that is to say, where he lives for at least 185 days in each year, because of personal and occupational ties, or, in the case of a person with no occupational ties, because of personal ties.

     However, the normal residence of a person whose occupational ties are in a different place from his personal ties and who consequently lives in turn in different places situated in 2 or more countries shall be regarded as being the place of this personal ties:

     Provided that such person returns to the place of his personal ties regularly. This proviso shall not apply if the person is living in a country in order to carry out a task of a definite duration.

     A person who lives in a country primarily for the purposes of attending a school or university or other educational or vocational establishment shall not be regarded as having his normal residence in that country.

(b)   Proof of normal residence may be given by means of documents relating to the acquisition of property or to employment of cessation of employment or to other transactions carried out in the course of day to day living and, in addition to or in substitution for the foregoing documents or any of them, any other documentary evidence the Commissioners require or accept.

3.   An expression or word used in these Regulations and also used in Chapter IV of Part II of the Act shall, unless the contrary intentions appears, have in these Regulations the meaning that it has in that Chapter.

4.   (1)   These Regulations shall apply only to a vehicle which has been acquired under the general conditions of taxation in force in the domestic market country and which is not the subject, on the grounds of exportation or departure from that country, of any exemption from or any refund of value-added tax, excise duty or any other consumption tax.

     (2)   Where a vehicle is -

          (a)   supplied under diplomatic or consular arrangements, or

          (b)   supplied to an international organisation recognised as such by the Minister for Foreign Affairs or to a member of such an organisation within the limits and under the conditions laid down by the international convention establishing the organisation or by another similar agreement,

     the conditions specified in paragraph (1) of this Regulation shall be deemed to have been complied with.

     (3)   (a)   The provisions of paragraph (1) of this Regulation shall be presumed to be complied with in relation to a vehicle if the vehicle bears an identification mark of its country of registration (other than a mark assigned to a vehicle temporarily registered),

          (b)   However, in the case of a vehicle registered in a country where the issue of such an identification mark is not conditional upon compliance with the general conditions of taxation in force on the domestic market in that country, the Commissioners may require evidence that any taxes payable there in respect of the vehicle have been paid.

5.   (1)   The exemption under section 135(a) of the Act shall be granted for a period not exceeding 12 months from the date upon which the vehicle concerned was brought into the State or such longer

period as the Commissioners in their discretion may allow in any particular case, if the vehicle -

(a)   is owned by or registered in the name of a person established outside the State,

(b)   is not disposed of or hired out in the State or lent to a person established in the State, and

(c)   whilst in the State, is not driven by a person established in the State save with the permission of the Commissioners.

(2)   When a category A vehicle is temporarily brought into the State for business use, the vehicle shall not be used in the State -

(a)   for the carriage of persons for reward other than persons carried when it entered the State or persons being carried on a journey to a place outside the State, unless such carriage is by law,

(b)   for the transport of goods for the purposes of industry or commerce, between places within the State, whether for reward or not.

(3)   Notwithstanding subparagraph (1)(b), a category A vehicle belonging to a car hire firm established outside the State may, if the vehicle is in the State under a contract, which expired in the State, for the hire of the vehicle -

(a)   be re-hired once only if it is so re-hired to a person established outside the State with a view to its being taken out of the State, or

(b)   be returned by an employee of the car hire firm concerned to the country where the contract was made whether or not the employee is established in the State.

(4)   (a)   Notwithstanding paragraph (1) of this Regulation, where a category A vehicle is registered in another country being the country of normal residence of the user and is used regularly by him for the journey from his residence to his place of work in an undertaking in the State, the period of the exemption under that paragraph shall not be subject to any time limit,

(b)   Notwithstanding the said paragraph (1), where a student residing temporarily in the State primarily for the purpose of pursuing a course of studies uses a category A vehicle in the State and the vehicle is registered outside the State in the country of his normal residence, or (in the case of a vehicle brought into the State before the date of the making of these Regulations by a student who was so residing), in any country outside the State, the exemption referred to in that paragraph shall apply for the period the student remains in the State pursuing such studies.

(5)   The provisions of paragraph (1), (2), (3) and (4) of this regulation shall apply *mutatis mutandis* to a motor-cycle.

6.   (1)   The exemption under subsection (aa) (inserted by the Finance (No.2) Act, 1992 (No.28 of 1992)) of section 135 of the Act shall be granted for a period not exceeding 12 months from the date upon which the vehicle concerned was brought into the State, or such longer period as the Commissioners in their discretion may allow in any particular case, if the vehicle -

(a)   is owned by or registered in the name of a person established outside the State,

(b)   is not driven or used by a person established in the State other than for business use on behalf of a person established outside the State,

(c)   is not disposed of or hired out in the State, or lent to a person established in the State, and

(d)   is not used in the State,

(i)   for the carriage of persons for reward other than persons it carried when it entered the State or persons being carried on a journey to a place outside the State, or

(ii)   for the transport of goods for the purposes of industry or commerce between places within the State, whether for reward or not,

unless such carriage is authorised by law.

(2)   Notwithstanding anything to the contrary in paragraph (1)(c) of this regulation, a vehicle, other than a category A vehicle or a motor-cycle, temporarily brought into the State under a contract for the temporary hire of the vehicle may, with the permission of the Commissioners and subject to such conditions as they may impose, be re-hired once only if it is so re-hired to a person established outside the State and if the re-hiring is effected through a person whose business in the State is or includes the letting out of vehicles for hire and whose only or principal place of business and principal place of residence are in the State.

(3)   Where a vehicle has been re-hired under paragraph (2) of this Regulation, the person to whom the vehicle is re-hired shall as from the date of such re-hiring be deemed for the purpose of these Regulations to be the person who brought the vehicle into the State.

7.   The exemption under section 135(b) of the Act shall be granted, on written application to the Commissioners -

(a)   in case the vehicle concerned is brought into the State as a representative sample of a particular vehicle, to be displayed or used for demonstration with a view to obtaining orders for similar vehicles, of the vehicle -

(i)   is owned by or registered in the name of a person established outside the State,

(ii)   whilst in the State is not put to normal use, except for the purpose of demonstration,

(iii)   is not used for hire or reward,

(iv)   whilst in the State remains the property of a person established outside the State, and

(v)   is intended to be taken out of the State on fulfilment of such purpose,

(b)   in any other case if the vehicle -

(i)   is not intended to be sold or offered for sale in the State,

(ii)   is intended to be taken out of the State on the fulfilment of the purpose specified in the said section 135 (b) for which it was brought into the State, and

(iii)   is being brought into the State by a person whose normal residence is in the State, on provision to the Revenue Commissioners of such security as they may require for the payment of any taxes or duties which, but for this exemption, would be payable in respect of the vehicle on its being so brought into the State.

8.   The exemption under section 135(c) of the Act shall be granted by the Commissioners for a period not exceeding 12 months from the date upon which the vehicle was brought into the State or such longer period as the Commissioners in their discretion may allow in any particular case, if the vehicle -

(a)   is owned by or registered in the name of a person established outside the State,

(b)   whilst in the State remains the property of a person established outside the State, and

(c)   is intended to be taken out of the State.

9.   (1)   an exemption under section 135 of the Act shall cease to have effect upon the expiration of the period fixed by or under these Regulations in relation thereto or if the owner of the vehicle concerned ceases to be established outside the State.

(2)   The documents relating to the ownership, registration or bringing into the State of a vehicle temporarily brought into the State under these Regulations shall be kept with the vehicle when it is in use in and shall be produced at the request of an officer of the

Commissioners, duly by them in that behalf and on production of his authorisation if so requested by any person affected.

10. Nothing in these regulations shall be construed as exempting a person temporarily bringing a vehicle into the State from compliance with any legal requirement, obligation, restriction or prohibition.

11. These Regulations shall be construed together with the statues which relate to the duties of excise and the management of those duties and any instrument relating to the duties of excise and the management of those duties made under statute.

12. The Motor Vehicles (Temporary Importation) Regulations, 1970 (S.I. No.54 of 1970), and the European Communities (Exemption from Import Charges of Certain Vehicles, etc., Temporarily Imported) Regulations, 1983 (S.I. No.422 of 1983), are hereby revoked.

GIVEN under my Official Seal, this 2nd day of March, 1993.

BERTIE AHERN
Minister for Finance.

Explanatory Note

These Regulations, which are effective from 1st January, 1993, prescribe the criteria for eligibility for exemption from the requirement to be registered with the Revenue Commissioners where a vehicle is temporarily brought into the State.

S.I. No. 252 of 1993.
VEHICLE REGISTRATION AND TAXATION REGULATIONS, 1993.

The Revenue Commissioners, in exercise of the powers conferred on them by section 141 Finance Act, 1992 (No.9 of 1992), as amended by section 56 of the Finance Act, 1993 (No.13 of 1993), hereby make the following Regulations.

1.   These Regulations may be cited as the Vehicle Registration and Taxation Regulations, 1993.

2.   These Regulations, other than subparagraphs (b) and (c) of Regulation 8(1) and the Schedule, shall be deemed to have come into operation on 17th day of June, 1993.

3.   In these Regulations-

   "the Act" means the Finance Act, 1992 (No.9 of 1992), as amended by section 56 of the Finance Act, 1993 (No.13 of 1993);

   "the Commissioners" means the Revenue Commissioners;

   "short-term self-drive contracts" has the meaning assigned to it by 134(11)(b) of the Act;

   "tax" means vehicle registration tax.

4.   An authorised person who wishes to obtain a repayment under section 134(11) of the Act in respect of a vehicle registered prior to the 1st day of July, 1993, shall-

   (a)   give particulars of the vehicle to the Commissioners on or before the 6th day of September, 1993, in a form specified by them;

   (b)   furnish with the particulars aforesaid such information and documentation concerning the vehicle and its use since its registration as the Commissioners may reasonably require, (and, if the Commissioners specify a form for this purpose, furnish the particulars in that form);

   (c)   keep in a permanent form, approved by the Commissioners, for a period of 6 years from the date of the latest transaction to which the records or any of the documents relate, detailed records of the use to which the vehicle is put and copies of all contracts under which the vehicle is hired to others from the 1st day of July, 1993, to the time at which the application for the repayment is made, and present them to the Commissioners for inspection when the Commissioners so require;

   (d)   apply to the Commissioners for the repayment within 2 weeks after ceasing to use the vehicle solely for hiring to others under short-term self-drive contracts (and, if the Commissioners specify a form for this purpose, make the application in that form) and supply such documentary evidence concerning the vehicle, including records of its use during the period from the 1st day of July, 1993, to the date of the cessation, as the Commissioners shall require;

(e)   if so requested by the Commissioners, present the vehicle at such office of the Commissioners as they shall nominate, for the purposes of examination.

5.   An person who wishes to obtain a repayment under section 134(11) of the Act in respect of a vehicle registered on or after the 1st day of July, 1993, shall-

(a)   declare the particulars of the vehicle to the Commissioners for registration in a form specified by them;

(b)   at the time of the declaration, give particulars of the vehicle to the Commissioners in a form specified by them;

(c)   keep in a permanent form, approved by the Commissioners, for a period of 6 years from the date of the latest transaction to which the records or any of the documents relate, detailed records of the use to which the vehicle is put since its registration to the time at which the application for the repayment is made and copies of all contracts under which the vehicle is hired to others and present them to the Commissioners for inspection when the Commissioners so require;

(d)   apply to the Commissioners for the repayment within 2 weeks after ceasing to use the vehicle solely for hiring to others under short-term self-drive contracts (and, if the Commissioners specify a form for this purpose, make the application in that form) and supply such documentary evidence concerning the vehicle, including records of its use during the period since its registration to the date of the cessation, as the Commissioners shall require;

(e)   if so requested by the Commissioners, present the vehicle at such office of the Commissioners as they shall nominate, for the purposes of examination.

6.   An authorised person who wishes to obtain a repayment under section 134(15) of the Act in respect of a vehicle or motor-cycle in respect of which tax has been paid prior to the coming into operation of these Regulations and which has been used solely for the purposes of demonstration since its registeration shall-

(a)   give particulars of the vehicle or motor-cycle to the Commissioners on or before the 6th day of September, 1993, in a form specified by them;

(b)   furnish with the particulars aforesaid such information and documentation concerning the vehicle or motor-cycle and its use since its registration as the Commissioners may reasonably require, (and, if the Commissioners specify a form for this purpose, furnish the particulars in that form);

(c) keep in a permanent form, approved by the Commissioners, for a period of 6 years from the date of the latest transaction to which the records or any of the documents relate, detailed records of the use to which the vehicle or motor-cycle from the 1st day of July, 1993, during the remaining period of its use for demonstration purposes and make such records available to the Commissioners on request;

(d) apply to the Commissioners for the repayment within 2 weeks after ceasing to use the vehicle or motor-cycle (and, if the Commissioners specify a form for this purpose, make the application in that form) and supply such documentary evidence concerning the vehicle or motor-cycle, including records of its use during the period from the 1st day of July, 1993, to the date of the disposal, as the Commissioners shall require;

(e) if so requested by the Commissioners, present the vehicle or motor-cycle at such office of the Commissioners as they shall nominate, for the purposes of examination.

7. An authorised person who wishes to obtain a repayment under section 134(15) of the Act in respect of a vehicle or motor-cycle registered on or after the coming into operation of these Regulations, shall-

(a) declare the particulars of the vehicle or motor-cycle to the Commissioners for registration and enter the name and address of the person in the section headed 'owner particulars' on the form in which the declaration is made;

(b) at the time of the declaration, give particulars of the vehicle or motor-cycle to the Commissioners in a form specified by them;

(c) keep in a permanent form, approved by the Commissioners, for a period of 6 years from the date of the latest transaction to which the records or any of the documents relate, detailed records of the use of the vehicle or motor-cycle during the period of its use for demonstration purposes and make such records available to the Commissioners on request;

(d) apply to the Commissioners for the repayment within 2 weeks of the disposal of the vehicle or motor-cycle (and, if the Commissioners specify a form for this purpose, make the application in that form) and supply such documentary evidence concerning the vehicle or motor-cycle, including records of its use during the period since its registration, as the Commissioners shall require;

(e) if so requested by the Commissioners, present the vehicle or motor-cycle at such office of the Commissioners as they shall nominate, for the purposes of examination.

8. (1) The Vehicle Registration and Taxation Regulations, 1992, (S.I. No. 318 of 1992) are hereby amended

(a)   in Regulation 7, by the substitution of the following paragraph for paragraph (3):

"(3) For the purposes of the registration of a vehicle, an original declaration in relation to the vehicle signed by the person paying tax on the vehicle or, in the case of a company, signed by a person nominated by the company, shall be presented to a registration office together with any other documents the Commissioners may require to satisfy themselves as to the bona fides of the declaration. In the case of an authorised person, the declaration, duly signed pursuant to this paragraph, in respect of the registration of a new vehicle (other than a vehicle in respect of which an application for repayment under section 134(11) is intended to be made) may be presented by means of a facsimile machine. Where a declaration is presented to a registration office by means of a facsimile machine, the original declaration shall be forwarded to that office by the authorised person concerned not more than 3 working days later.",

(b)   in Regulation 11, by the substitution of the following paragraph for paragraph (4):

"(4) Upon a change of ownership of a registered vehicle, Part II of the certificate of registration relating to the vehicle shall be sent or given to the new owner and, if the vehicle is not one that is or has been the subject of a licence under section 1 of the Finance (Excise Duties) (Vehicles) Act, 1952 (No. 24 of 1952), either -

    (a)   the person disposing of the vehicle shall insert particulars of the change of ownership on the reverse side of Part I of the certificate, detach that Part from the certificate and send or give it to the Central Vehicle Office of the Commissioners at Harbour in the county of Wexford, or

    (b)   if the said Part I has previously been detached from the certificate, the person acquiring the vehicle shall insert particulars of the change of ownership on the reverse side of Part II of the certificate, and send or give it to the said Office.", and

(c)   by the substitution of the Schedule set out in the Schedule to these Regulations for the Second Schedule.

(2)   Subparagraphs (b) and (c) of paragraph (1) of this Regulation and the Schedule to these Regulations shall come into operation on the 1st day of October, 1993.

9.   The Vehicle Registration and Taxation (No.2) Regulations, 1992, (S.I. No. 437 of 1992) are hereby amended in Regulation 4 (11) by the substitution of the following subparagraph for subparagraph (a):

"(a)   In this Regulation **'normal residence'** means the place where a person usually lives, that is to say, where he lives for at least 185 days in each year, because of personal and occupational ties, or, in the case of a person with no occupational ties, because of personal ties.

However, the normal residence of a person whose occupational ties are in a different place from his personal ties and who consequently lives in turn indifferent places situated in 2 or more countries shall be regarded as being the place of his personal ties:

Provided that such person returns to the place personal ties regularly. This proviso shall not apply if the person is living in a country in order to carry out a task of a definite duration.

A person who lives in a country primarily for the purposes of attending a school or university or other educational or vocational establishment shall not be regarded as having his normal residence in that country.".

10.   Where, as respects any class of person, the Commissioners so allow and subject to any conditions which they may think fit to impose, compliance, in whole or in part, with any of these Regulations shall not be required.

GIVEN this 26th day of August, 1993.

C.C. MacDOMHNAILL,
 Revenue Commissioner.

Explanatory note

These Regulations lay down conditions governing the registration and taxation of vehicles, and should be read together with the Vehicle Registration and Taxation Regulations, 1992, (S.I. No.318 of 1992).

S.I. No. 154 of 1995.
VEHICLE REGISTRATION TAX (REPAYMENTS IN CERTAIN CASES) REGULATIONS, 1995.

The Revenue Commissioners, in exercise of the powers conferred on them by S141 of the Finance Act, 1992 (No.9 of 1992), as amended by section 14 of the Finance (No. 2) Act, 1992 (No. 28 of 1992), section 56 of the Finance Act, 1993, (No. 13 of 1993) and section 98 of the Finance Act, 1995 (No. 8 of 1995), hereby make the following Regulations:

1.   These Regulations may be cited as the Vehicle Registration Tax (Repayment in Certain Cases) Regulations 1995.

2.   These Regulations shall apply to a new category A vehicle to which the principal section relates.

3.   (1)   In these Regulations-

"**the Act of 1992**" means the Finance Act, 1992 (No. 9 of 1992);

"**approved person**" means a person approved by the Commissioners to issue certificates of destruction in accordance with the provisions of Regulation 6;

"**category A vehicle**" has the meaning assigned to it by Chapter IV of Part II of the Act of 1992;

"**certificate of destruction**" means a form provided by the Commissioners on which an approved person may certify' that a vehicle has been scrapped;

"**the Commissioners**" means the Revenue Commissioners;

"licensing authority" has the meaning assigned to it by Chapter IV of Part II of the Act of 1992;

"**new**" and "**scrapped**" have the meanings assigned to them, respectively, by subsection (5) of the principal section and cognate words shall be construed accordingly;

"**officer**" means an officer of the Commissioners;

"**the principal section**" means section 1 35B (inserted by section 98 of the Finance Act, 1995 (No. 8 of 1995)) of the Act of 1992.

(2)   In these Regulations

(a)   a reference to a regulation is to a regulation of these Regulations, and

(b)   a reference to a paragraph is to a paragraph of the provision in which it occurs, unless it is indicated that reference to some other provision is intended.

4.   A person who wishes to apply to the Commissioners for the repayment of vehicle registration tax provided for in the principal section shall -

(a)   complete such form as is issued to him or her for that purpose by the Commissioners,

(b)   certify the particulars shown on that form to be correct, and

(c)   furnish with the completed form the following documents in respect of the scrapped vehicle

     (i)   a certificate of destruction completed by an approved person,

     (ii)   the registration book appropriate to the vehicle,

     (iii)   the licence under section 1 of the Finance (Excise Duties) (Vehicles) Act, 1952 (No. 24 of 1952), appropriate to the vehicle which was in force on the date that the vehicle was scrapped.

     (iv)   the insurance disc within the meaning of the Road Traffic (Insurance Disc) Regulations, 1984 (S.I. No. 355 of 1984), appropriate to the vehicle,

     (v)   a certificate of insurance, within the meaning of subsection (1) of section 56 of the Road Traffic Act, 1961 (No.24 of 1961), which was current immediately prior to the scrapping of the vehicle and such other evidence to the satisfaction of the Commissioners showing that the provisions of the principal section relating to insurance have been complied with:

     Provided that a certificate of insurance will not be required in the case of an exempted person within the meaning of section 60 (inserted by section 54 of the Road Traffic Act, 1968) of the Road Traffic Act, 1961.

5.   For the purposes of paragraph (c) of subsection (I) of the principal section, it shall be taken as showing to the satisfaction of the Commissioners that a vehicle has been scrapped where a person produces to the Commissioners a certificate of destruction issued by an approved person in respect of the said vehicle.

6.   (1)   Any person who wishes to be approved by the Commissioners to issue certificates of destruction shall -

     (a)   apply in writing to the Commissioners to be so approved,

     (b)   furnish such information and allow such inspection of premises as the Commissioners may require in order to satisfy themselves that that person is equipped to scrap vehicles in such a manner that such scrapped vehicles comply with the definition in subsection (5) of the principal section, and

     (c)   undertake to keep at the premises where scrapping is to take place (in this Regulation referred to as an **"approved place"**), or at such other place as the Commissioners may allow, all books, records, invoices, accounts and other documents relating to the receipt, storage and scrapping of vehicles.

(2)   Where the Commissioners are satisfied that a person who has applied to them for approval under paragraph (1) meets the criteria set out in subparagraphs (b) and (c) of that paragraph they shall grant such approval subject to the following conditions:

(a)   the approved person shall keep at the approved place, or such other place as the Commissioners may allow, a record showing in respect of each vehicle to be scrapped -

the date of receipt of the vehicle by the approved person,

the registration number,

(iii)   the chassis number,

(iv)   the engine number,

(v)   the name and address of the registered owner,

(vi)   the date of scrapping, and

(vii)   how the scrapped vehicle was disposed of;

(b)   entries in the record referred to in paragraph (a) shall be made by or under the direction of the approved person before the certificate of destruction to which such entries relate is issued by that approved person;

(c)   an approved person shall retain the record referred to in paragraph (a) for a period of at least 12 months from the date of the last entry therein and shall allow an officer at all reasonable times to inspect and take copies of, or extracts from, the record;

(d)   an approved person shall keep a stock account of all certificate of destruction forms provided to him or her by the Commissioners, store them in a safe and secure place and account for their disposal to the satisfaction of the Commissioners;

(e)   an approved person shall keep at the approved place a true copy of each certificate of destruction issued by him or her and shall produce such copies to an officer when so requested by that officer;

(f)   an approved person shall provide, to the satisfaction of the Commissioners, safe means of access to the approved premises for officers.

GIVEN this 16th day of June, 1995.

D. B. QUIGLEY,
Revenue Commissioner.

Notes

These Regulations, which came into effect on 1 July, 1995 and expired on 31 December, 1997, laid down the conditions governing the issue of certificates of destruction and the issue of repayments under the provisions of section 135B of the Finance Act, 1992, inserted by section 98 of the Finance Act, 1995. Provision was made to repay £1,000 of vehicle registration tax to any person who became the registered owner of a new category A vehicle and who had owned and scrapped a category A vehicle which was at least 10 years old.

S.I. No. 464 of 2002.
TAXES (ELECTRONIC TRANSMISSION OF VEHICLE REGISTRATION RETURNS) (SPECIFIED PROVISIONS AND APPOINTED DAY) ORDER, 2002.

The Revenue Commissioners, in exercise of the powers conferred on them by section 917E (inserted by section 209 of the Finance Act 1999 (No. 2 of 1999)) of the Taxes Consolidation Act 1997 (No. 39 of 1997), order as follows:

1. This Order may be cited as the Taxes (Electronic Transmission of Vehicle Registration Returns)(Specified Provisions and Appointed Day) Order 2002.

2. Each of the Provisions set out in the Schedule to this Order is specified for the purpose of Chapter 6 of Part 38 of the Taxes Consolidation Act 1997.

3. The 4th day of October 2002 is appointed in relation to returns to be made under the provisions specified in Article 2 of this Order.

Schedule

Section 131 (2)(a) of the Finance Act 1992 (No. 9 of 1992).

Section 133 (2)(a) of the Finance Act 1992.

Regulation 13 (2) of the Vehicle Registration and Taxation Regulations 1992 (S.I. No. 318 of 1992).

Regulation 15 of the Vehicle Registration and Taxation Regulations 1992.

GIVEN under my hand,

1 October 2002.
Josephine Feehily,
Revenue Commissioner.

Explanatory Note

This order –

*   applies the legislation governing the electronic filing of tax information to returns of vehicle registration information, and

*   appoints a day, namely, 4 October 2002, in relation to such returns, which ensures that the electronic filing legislation applies to vehicle registration returns which are due to be filed on or after 5 October 2002.

Chapter 6 of Part 38 of the Taxes Consolidation Act 1997 provides the legislative framework whereby tax related information required by law to be provided to the Revenue Commissioners may be supplied electronically. The legislation only applies to information where the provision under which the information is supplied is specified in an order made by the Revenue Commissioners. Where a provision is so specified the legislation applies to information supplied under that provision after the day appointed in the order in relation to the provision concerned. The reason for this procedure is to allow the Revenue Commissioners to manage the roll-out of the system for receiving tax related information electronically. The system will be extended to further informational items as the necessary developmental work in relation to the electronic receipt of particular items is completed.

S.I. No. 249 of 2003.
VEHICLE REGISTRATION TAXATION REGULATIONS, 2003.

The Revenue Commissioners, in exercise of the powers conferred on them by section 141 Finance Act 1992 (No. 9 of 1992) as amended by section 106 Finance Act 2003 (No.3 of 2003), hereby make the following Regulations:

1.   These Regulations may be cited as the Vehicle Registration Tax Regulations 2003.

2.   These Regulations come into operation on 1 July 2003.

3.   In these Regulations–

"**Act of 1992**" means the Finance Act 1992 (No. 9 of 1992);

"**Act of 2003**" means the Finance Act 2003 (No.3 of 2003);

"**innermost**" means that point of a closed rear door or closed tailgate closest to the outermost point of the partition;

"**outermost**" means that point of the partition closest to the rear of a vehicle;

"**partition**" means a permanent rigid structure which completely separates the passenger cab from the goods area of a crew cab or pick-up.

4.   (1)   The partition in a crew cab or pick-up shall be of strong rigid material containing no openings, cut-outs or incisions.

   (2)   For the purposes of —

   (a)   paragraph (i) of the definition of "crew cab" (inserted by paragraph (b) of section 101(1) of the Act of 2003) in section 130 of the Act of 1992, and

   (b)   paragraph (i) of the definition of "pick-up" (inserted by paragraph (c) of section 101(1) of the Act of 2003) in section 130 of the Act of 1992,

   the partition in a crew cab or pick-up shall be fixed permanently to the sides, floor and roof of the vehicle by means of continuous seam welding, adhesive bonding, spot welding or brazing, and —

   (i)   in the case of adhesive bonding, the bonding agent shall be of sufficient strength to bond the partition to the vehicle in order to provide the requisite level of completeness, permanency and rigidity, and

   (ii)   in the case of spot welding, the welds shall be sufficiently close to each other to ensure a satisfactory seal, being not normally more than 40 millimetres apart.

5.   (1)   For the purposes of this Regulation —

"partition reference point" means the point where a vertical line tangential to the outermost point of the partition meets the goods floor;

"rear reference point" means—

(a) where there is a rear door or tailgate, the point where a vertical line tangential to the innermost point of the closed rear door or closed tailgate meets the goods floor and the point is located where the floor is generally level (whether or not corrugated or ribbed) and of consistent width,

(b) where there is a rear door and tailgate or 2 individual rear doors, the point where a vertical line tangential to the innermost point of the closed rear door or closed tailgate nearest the partition meets the goods floor and the point is located where the floor is generally level (whether or not corrugated or ribbed) and of consistent width, and

(c) where there is no rear door or tailgate, the furthest point from the partition reference point, on the rear of the permanent goods floor, excluding any moveable extensions or additions and the point is located where the floor is generally level (whether or not corrugated or ribbed) and of consistent width.

(2) For the purposes of—

(a) paragraph (ii) of the definition of "crew cab" (inserted by paragraph (b) of section 101(1) of the Act of 2003) in section 130 of the Act of 1992, and

(b) paragraph (ii) of the definition of "pick-up" (inserted by paragraph (c) of section 101(1) of the Act of 2003) in section 130 of the Act of 1992,

the floor length of the goods floor in a crew cab or pick-up is the linear measurement of the distance in a straight perpendicular line between –

(i) a straight horizontal line taken through the partition reference point connecting 2 sides, walls or chassis sides of the vehicle, and

(ii) a straight horizontal parallel line taken through the rear reference point connecting 2 sides, walls or chassis sides of the vehicle.

GIVEN on 23 June 2003.

Josephine Feehily,
Revenue Commissioner.

Explanatory Note

(This note is not part of the instrument and does not purport to be a legal interpretation.)

These Regulations prescribe the criteria for the permanent fixing of the rigid partition in crew cabs and pick-up vehicles. They also prescribe the manner in which the cargo area of such vehicles is measured.

(S.I. No. 576 of 2007)
VEHICLE REGISTRATION AND TAXATION (AMENDMENT) REGULATIONS 2007

The Revenue Commissioners, in exercise of the powers conferred on them by section 141 of the Finance Act 1992 (No. 9 of 1992), hereby make the following regulations:

1. These Regulations may be cited as the Vehicle Registration and Taxation (Amendment) Regulations 2007.

2. Regulation 14 of the Vehicle Registration and Taxation Regulations 1992 (S.I. No. 318 of 1992) is amended —

    (a)   by substituting the following for paragraph (3):

    "(3)   The Commissioners shall grant an authorisation under section 136 of the Act only to a person who —

    (a)   intends to be actively engaged in a business referred to in subsection (1) of that section at premises occupied by the person and at which such business may legally be carried on,

    (b)   is registered under section 9 of the Value-Added Tax Act 1972 for the purpose of carrying on a business referred to in subsection (1) of that section, and

    (c)   is, at the time of application for the authorisation, the holder of a current tax clearance certificate issued in accordance with section 1095 of the Taxes Consolidation Act 1997.",

    and

    (b)   by inserting the following after paragraph (3):

    "(4)   For the purposes of subsection (3) of section 136 of the Act, reasonable causes in respect of which the Commissioners may, in accordance with that subsection, revoke an authorisation include the following:

    (a)   the authorised person ceases to be actively engaged in the business referred to in section 136(1) of the Act or such business has not, within a reasonable period, commenced,

    (b)   the authorised person fails to produce a current tax clearance certificate, issued in accordance with section 1095 of the Taxes Consolidation Act 1997, if requested to do so by the Commissioners, or

    (c)   records relating to the business are not kept as prescribed by the Commissioners in Regulation 17.".

GIVEN this 7th day of August 2007.

JOSEPHINE FEEHILY,
Revenue Commissioner.

Explanatory Note

(This note is not part of the instrument and does not purport to be a legal interpretation.)

These Regulations allow the Revenue Commissioners to request a current tax clearance certificate from applicants who are seeking an authorisation under section 136 of the Finance Act 1992.

They also specify some of the cases where, in accordance with section 136(3) of the Finance Act 1992, the Revenue Commissioners may withdraw an existing authorisation under section 136 of that Act. These include cases where the authorised person fails to produce a tax clearance certificate when requested by the Revenue Commissioners, is not actively engaged in the businesses outlined in section 136(1) of the Finance Act 1992 or does not keep records relating to the business in accordance with Regulation 17.

S.I. No. 396 of 2008
VEHICLE REGISTRATION AND TAXATION (AMENDMENT) REGULATIONS 2008

The Revenue Commissioners, in exercise of the powers conferred on them by section 141 of the Finance Act (No. 9 of 1992), hereby make the following regulations:

1.   These Regulations may be cited as the Vehicle Registration and Taxation (Amendment) Regulations 2008.

2.   Regulation 6, of the Vehicle Registration and Taxation (No. 2) Regulations 1992 (S.I. No. 437 of 1992) is amended —

    (a)   by substituting the following for paragraph (2):

        "(2)   A fee of €1,000 is prescribed for the purpose of section 131 (5A) of the Act".

        and

    (b)   by inserting the following paragraph after paragraph (3):

        "(4)   (a)   The mark assigned to a vehicle under section 131 (5A) shall be cancelled if the owner of the vehicle fails, within a reasonable period, to display that mark when it falls to be assigned under Regulation 9(3) of the Regulations.

                (b)   Where a mark is cancelled pursuant to subparagraph (b), then the fee paid shall not be refunded other than in cases that the Commissioners are satisfied that exceptional circumstances have occurred so as to prevent the person to whom the mark was assigned from using it.

                (c)   An application for the purposes of subparagraph (b) shall be made in writing to the Commissioners and shall set out the exceptional circumstances claimed to warrant the repayment. The applicant shall furnish to the Commissioners, if so requested by them, proof to the satisfaction of the Commissioners of those circumstances.".

GIVEN on 7 October 2008

MICHAEL O' GRADY
Minister for Finance.

EXPLANATORY NOTE

(This note is not part of the instrument and does not purport to be a legal interpretation.)

This Regulation increases the fee for reserving an identification mark (registration number) from €315 to €1,000.

The Regulation also states that the Revenue Commissioners will cancel the identification mark (registration number) if it has not been assigned to a vehicle.

Only in exceptional circumstances will a refund be authorised.

Development of the
VAT Acts
1972-2009

DEVELOPMENT OF THE VAT ACTS 1972-2009

Section 1

Value Added Tax Act 1972

Interpretation

1.   (1)   In this Act, save where the context otherwise requires —

"**accountable person**" means a person who is an accountable person in accordance with section 8.

"**Appeal Commissioners**" means persons appointed in accordance with section 156 of the Income Tax Act, 1967, to be Appeal Commissioners for the purposes of the Income Tax Acts;

"**body of persons**" means any body politic, corporate, or collegiate, and any company, partnership, fraternity, fellowship and society of persons, whether corporate or not corporate;

"**business**" includes farming, the promotion of dances and any trade, commerce, manufacture, or any venture or concern in the nature of trade, commerce or manufacture, and any profession or vocation, whether for profit or otherwise;

"**Collector-General**" means the Collector-General appointed under section 162 of the Income Tax Act, 1967;

"**the customs-free airport**" means the land which under the Customs-free Airport Act, 1941, for the time being constitutes the Customs-free airport;

"**development**" in relation to any land, means —

(a)   the construction, demolition, extension, alteration or reconstruction of any building on the land, or

(b)   the carrying out of any engineering or other operation in, on, over or under the land to adapt it for materially altered use,

and "**developed**" shall be construed correspondingly;

"**established**" means having a permanent establishment;

"**exempted activity**" means —

(a)   a delivery of immovable goods in respect of which pursuant to section 4(6) tax is not chargeable, and

(b)   a delivery of any goods or a rendering of any service of a kind specified in the First Schedule or declared by the Minister by order for the time being in force under section 6 to be an exempted activity;

"**goods**" means all movable and immovable objects, but does not include things in action or money and references to goods include references to both new and second-hand goods;

"**harbour authority**" has the meaning assigned to it by section 2 of the Harbours Act, 1946;

"**hire**", in relation to movable goods, includes a letting on any terms including a leasing;

"**hotel**" includes any guest house, holiday hostel, holiday camp, motor hotel, motel, coach hotel, motor inn, motor court, tourist court, caravan park or camping site;

"**immovable goods**" means land;

"**inspector of taxes**" means an inspector of taxes appointed under section 161 of the Income Tax Act, 1967;

"**livestock**" means live cattle, sheep, pigs and horses;

"**local authority**" has the meaning assigned to it by section 2(2) of the Local Government Act, 1941, and includes a health board established under the Health Act, 1970;

"**manufacturer**" means a person who carries on in the State a business of making or assembling goods;

"**the Minister**" means the Minister for Finance;

"**movable goods**" means goods other than immovable goods;

"**permanent establishment**" means any fixed place of business, but does not include a place of business of an agent of a person unless the agent has and habitually exercises general authority to negotiate the terms of and make agreements on behalf of the person or has a stock of goods with which he regularly fulfils on behalf of the person agreements for the supply of goods;

"**registered person**" means a person who is registered in the register maintained under section 9;

"**regulations**" means regulations under section 32;

"**rendering**" in relation to a service, has the meaning assigned to it by section 5;

"**residing**" in relation to an individual, means resident for the purposes of the Income Tax Acts;

"**second-hand**" in relation to goods, means goods which have been used and are not new;

"**secretary**" includes such persons as are mentioned in section 207(2) of the Income Tax Act,

1967, and section 55(1) at the Finance Ace, 1920;

"**the specified day**" means the day appointed by the Minister by order to be the specified day for the purposes of this Act;

"**tax**" means value-added tax chargeable by virtue of this Act;

"**taxable goods**", in relation to any delivery or importation, means goods the delivery of which is not an exempted activity;

"**taxable period**" means a period of two months beginning on the first day of January, March, May, July, September or November;

"**taxable services**" means services the rendering of which is not an exempted activity.

(2) In this Act references to moneys received by a person include references to—

   (a) money lodged or credited to the account of the person in any bank, savings bank, building society, hire purchase finance concern or similar financial concern, and

   (b) money, other than money referred to in paragraph (a), which, under an agreement, other than an agreement providing for discount or a price adjustment made in the ordinary course of business or an arrangement with creditors, has ceased to be due to the person,

   and money lodged or credited to the account of a person as aforesaid shall be deemed to have been received by the person on the date of the making of the lodgement or credit and money which has ceased to be due to a person as aforesaid shall be deemed to have been received by the person on the date of the cesser.

(3) Any reference in this Act to any other enactment shall, except so far as the context otherwise requires, be construed as a reference to that enactment as amended or extended by any subsequent enactment.

(4) In this Act—

   (a) a reference to a section or Schedule is to a section or Schedule of this Act, unless it is indicated that reference to some other enactment is intended, and

   (b) a reference to a subsection, paragraph or subparagraph is to die subsection, paragraph or subparagraph of the provision (including a Schedule) in which the reference occur, unless it is indicated that reference to some other provision is intended.

Finance Act 1973

90.   The Principal Act is hereby amended as specified in column (3) of the Tenth Schedule to this Act.

TENTH SCHEDULE
AMENDMENT OF ENACTMENTS

Number and Year (1)	Short Title (2)	Amendment (3)
No. 22 of 1972	Value-Added Tax Act, 1972	In section 1(1), in the definition of " livestock ", " and pigs " shall be substituted for "pigs and horses"; in the definition of "taxable period", "provided that the taxable period immediately following that commencing on the 1st day of May, 1973, shall be the period commencing on the 1st day of July, 1973, and ending on the 2nd day of September, 1973, and the next succeeding taxable period shall be the period commencing on the 3rd day of September, 1973, and ending on the 31st day of October, 1973 " shall be inserted after " November "; and * in the definition of " manufacturer ", " and, in relation to goods of a kind specified in the Fourth Schedule, includes a person who in the course of business supplies or arranges for the supply of materials to another person for the purpose of having any such goods made or assembled on his behalf by that other or another person " shall be inserted after " goods ".

(With effect from 3 September 1973 except * from 4 August 1973)

Finance Act 1976

61.   In consequence of the amendments specified in sections 53 and 60 and the repeals specified in Part II of the Fifth Schedule, The Principal Act is hereby further amended as specified in Part II of the First Schedule.

PART II
Amendments Consequential on Certain Amendments of
Value-Added Tax Act, 1972

Number and Year (1)	Short Title (2)	Amendment (3)
No. 22 of 1972	Value-Added Tax Act, 1972	In section 1 (1) the following definition shall be inserted:'**fur skin**' means any skin with the fur, hair or wool attached except skin of woolled sheep or lamb;".

(With effect from 1 March 1976)

Value Added Tax (Amendment) Act 1978

2.   Section 1 of the Principal Act is hereby amended by-

(a)   the deletion of the definitions of **"accountable person"** **"established"**, **"manufacturer"**, **"rendering"** and **"residing"**;

(b)   the substitution of **"'establishment'"** for **"'permanent establishment'"** and

(c)   the insertion of the following definitions:

"'agricultural produce' has the meaning assigned to it by section 8;",

"'agricultural service' has the meaning assigned to it by section 8;",

"'Community' means the European Economic Community;",

"'farmer' has the meaning assigned to it by section 8;",

"'flat-rate addition' has the meaning assigned to it by section 12A;",

"'flat-rate farmer' has the meaning assigned to it by section 12A;",

"'supply', in relation to goods, has the meaning assigned to it by section 3 and, in relation to services, has the meaning assigned to it by section 5, and cognate words shall be construed accordingly; and

"'taxable person' has the meaning assigned to it by section 8;".

SECOND SCHEDULE
Consequential Amendments

Reference Number (1)	Existing word or expression (2)	Substituted word or expression (3)	Provision of Principal Act (4)
1	"Delivery"	"Supply"	The definition of "exempted activity", and the definition of "taxable goods" in section 1(1);
2	"Rendering"	"Supply"	The definition of "taxable services" in section 1(1);
12	"delivery of any goods or a rendering of any service"	"supply of any goods or service"	The definition of "exempted activity" in section 1(1).

(With effect from 1 March 1979)

Finance Act 1981

43. Section 1(1) of the Principal Act is hereby amended, with effect as on and from the 1st day of November, 1972, by the insertion in the definition of "development" after "correspondingly" of-

", and

in this definition '**building**' includes, in relation to a transaction, any prefabricated or like structure in respect of which the following conditions are satisfied:

(a) the structure-

    (i) has a rigid roof and one or more rigid walls and, except in the case of a structure used for the cultivation of plants, a floor,

    (ii) is designed so as to provide for human access to, and free movement in, its interior,

    (iii) is for a purpose that does not require that it be mobile or portable, and

    (iv) does not have or contain any aids to mobility or portability,

and

(b) (i) neither the agreement in respect of the transaction nor any other agreement between the parties to that agreement contains a provision relating to the rendering of the structure mobile or portable or the movement or re-location of the structure after its erection, and

    (ii) the person for whom the structure is constructed, extended, altered or reconstructed signs and delivers, at the time of the transaction, to the person who constructed, extended, altered or reconstructed the structure a declaration of his intention to retain it on the site on which it is at that time located".

(With effect from 1 November 1972)

Finance Act 1984

85. Section 1 of the Principal Act is hereby amended-

(a) by the insertion in subsection (1) after the definition of "business" of the following definition:

"'**clothing**' does not include footwear;",

and

(b) by the insertion in the said subsection (1) after the definition of "flat-rate farmer" of the following definition:

"'**footwear**' includes shoes, boots, slippers and the like but does not include stockings, under-stockings, socks, ankle-socks or similar articles or footwear without soles or footwear which is or incorporates skating or swimming equipment;".

(With effect from 1 May 1984)

Finance Act 1986

80. Section 1 of the Principal Act is hereby amended by the insertion in subsection (1) after the definition of "footwear" of the following definition

"'**free port**' means the land declared to be a free port for the purposes of the Free Ports Act, 1986 (No. 6 of 1986), by order made under section 2 of that Act;".

(With effect from 27 May 1986)

S.I. No. 412 of 1986
Imposition of Duties (No 283) (Value-Added Tax) Order 1986

3. Section 1(1) of the Value-Added Tax Act, 1972 is hereby amended by the substitution in the definition of "**livestock**" of ", pigs and deer" for "and pigs".

(With effect from 1 January 1987)

Finance Act 1987

39. (a) Section 1 of the Principal Act is hereby amended by -

   *(i) the substitution in subsection (1) in the definition of "livestock" of ", goats, pigs and deer" for "and pigs", and

   (ii) the insertion in subsection (2) after paragraph (b) of the following:

   "and (c) money, which, in relation to money received by a person from another person, has been deducted in accordance with the provisions of-

   (i)   Chapter III of Part I of the Finance Act, 1987, or

   (ii)   section 17 of the Finance Act, 1970,

   and has thereby ceased to be due to the first-mentioned person by the other person,".

(With effect from 6 June 1987 except * from 9 July 1987)

Finance Act 1988

60. Section 1(2) of the Principal Act is hereby amended by the insertion after paragraph (b) of the following:

"(bb) money due to the person which, in accordance with the provisions of section 73 of the Finance Act, 1988, is paid to the Revenue

Commissioners by another person and has thereby ceased to be
due to the person by that other person, and".

(With effect from 1 October 1988)

Finance Act 1990

98. Section 1 of the Principal Act is hereby amended in subsection (1) by the
insertion in the definition of "**livestock**" of "horses," after "cattle,".

(With effect from 30 May 1990)

Finance Act 1991

77. Section 1 of the Principal Act is hereby amended in subsection (1) by the
deletion of the definition of "hotel".

(With effect from 1 January 1992)

Finance Act 1992

165. Section 1 of the Principal Act is hereby amended-

(a)   in subsection (1):

    (i)   by the insertion after the definition of "exempted activity"
of the following definition:

"'**exportation of goods**' means the exportation of goods
to a destination outside the Community and, where the
context so admits, cognate words shall be construed
accordingly;",

    *(ii)   by the deletion of the definition of "harbour authority",

    (iii)   by the insertion after the definition of "immovable goods"
of the following definition:

"'**importation of goods**' means the importation of
goods from outside the Community into a Member State
either-

(a)   directly, or

(b)   through one or more than one other Member State
where value-added tax referred to in Council
Directive No. 77/388/EEC of 17 May 1977 has
not been chargeable on the goods in such other
Member State or Member States in respect of the
transaction concerned,

and, where the context so admits, cognate words
shall be construed accordingly;",

    (iv)   by the insertion after the definition of "inspector of taxes"
of the following definition:

"'**intra-Community acquisition of goods**' has the
meaning assigned to it by section 3A;",

**(v)   by the insertion after the definition of "the Minister" of the following definition:

"**monthly control statement**' has the meaning assigned to it by section 17;",

(vi)   by the insertion after the definition of "moveable goods" of the following definition:

"**new means of transport**' means motorised land vehicles with an engine cylinder capacity exceeding 48 cubic centimetres or a power exceeding 7.2 kilowatts, vessels exceeding 7.5 metres in length and aircraft with a take-off weight exceeding 1,550 kilogrammes-

(a)   which are intended for the transport of persons or goods, and

(b)   (i)   which were supplied three months or less after the date of first entry into service, or

(ii)   which have travelled 3,000 kilometres or less in the case of land vehicles, sailed for 100 hours or less in the case of vessels or flown for 40 hours or less in the case of aircraft,

other than vessels and aircraft of the kind referred to in paragraph (v) of the Second Schedule;",

(vii)   by the insertion after the definition of "new means of transport of the following definition:

"**a person registered for value-added tax**' means, in relation to another Member State, a person currently issued with an identification number in that State for the purposes of accounting for value-added tax referred to in Council Directive No. 77/388/EEC of 17 May 1977 and, in relation to the State, means a registered person;",

(viii)   by the substitution in the definition of "taxable goods" of "supply, intra-Community acquisition or importation" for "supply or importation",

(ix)   by the substitution in the definition of "taxable services" of "activity;" for "activity", and

(x)   by the insertion after the definition of "taxable services" of the following definition:

"**vessel**', in relation to transport, means a waterborne craft of any type, whether self-propelled or not, and includes a hovercraft.",

and

(b)   by the insertion of the following subsection after subsection (2):

"(2A)   In this Act, save where the context otherwise requires, a reference to the territory of a Member State has the same meaning as it has in Article 3 (inserted by Council Directive No. 91/680/EEC of 16 December 1991 of Council Directive No. 77/388/EEC of 17 May 1977, and references to Member States and cognate references shall be construed accordingly.".

(With effect from 1 January 1993 except: * from 28 May 1992 and ** from 1 November 1992)

S.I. No. 413 of 1992.
European Communities (Value-Added Tax) Regulations, 1992.

4.   Section 1 of the Principal Act is hereby amended in subsection (1) —

(a)   by the substitution of the following definition for the definition of "Community":

"'**Community**', except where the context otherwise requires, has the same meaning as it has in Article 3 of Council Directive No. 77/3881 EEC of 17 May, 1977 (as last amended by council Directive No. 92/111/EEC of 14 December 1992), and cognate references shall be construed accordingly,",

and

(b)   by the insertion after the definition of "**establishment**" of the following definition:

"'**excisable products**' means the products referred to in section 104 of the Finance Act, 1992;".

(With effect from 1 January 1993)

Finance Act 1994

91.   Section 1 of the Principal Act is hereby amended in subsection (1), in subparagraph (b) of the definition of "**new means of transport**" (inserted by the Act of 1992):

(a)   by the substitution of the following clause for clause (i):

"(i)   which in the case of vessels and aircraft were supplied three months or less after the date of first entry into service and in the case of land vehicles were supplied six months or less after the date of first entry into service, or",

and

(b)   by the substitution in clause (ii) of "6,000 kilometres" for "3,000 kilometres-.

(With effect from 1 January 1995)

Finance Act 1995

119. Section 1 of the Principal Act is hereby amended in subsection (1) –

(a) by the insertion after the definition of "agricultural service" (inserted by the Act of 1978) of the following definition:

"'**antiques**' has the meaning assigned to it by section 10A;",

(b) by the insertion after the definition of "Collector-General" of the following definition:

"'**collectors' items**' has the meaning assigned to it by section 10A;",

(c) by the insertion after the definition of "local authority" of the following definition:

"'**margin scheme**' has the meaning assigned to it by section 10A;",

(d) by the substitution of the following definition for the definition of "second-hand":

"'**second-hand goods**' has the meaning assigned to it by section 10A;",

(e) by the insertion after the definition of "tax" of the following definition:

"'**taxable dealer**', in relation to supplies of movable goods other than means of transport, has the meaning assigned to it by section 10A and, in relation to supplies of means of transport, has the meaning assigned to it by section 12B;",

and

(f) by the addition after the definition of "vessel" (inserted by the Act of 1992) of the following definition:

"'**works of art**' has the meaning assigned to it by section 10A.".

(With effect from 1 July 1995)

S.I. No. 363 of 1995.
European Communities (Value-Added Tax) Regulations, 1995.

4. Section 1 of the Principal Act is hereby amended by the insertion after the definition of "Community" of the following definitions:

"'**contractor**', in relation to contract work, means a person who makes or assembles movable goods;

'**contract work**' means the service of handing over by a contractor to another person of movable goods made or assembled by the contractor from goods entrusted to the contractor by that other person, whether or not the contractor has provided any part of the goods used;".

(With effect from 1 January 1996)

Finance Act 1996

88.   Section 1 of the Principal Act is hereby amended in subsection (1)-

*(a)   by the insertion after the definition of "Community" of the following definitions:

"'**contractor**', in relation to contract work, means a person who makes or assembles movable goods;

'**contract work**' means the service of handing over by a contractor to another person of movable goods made or assembled by the contractor from goods entrusted to the contractor by that other person, whether or not the contractor has provided any part of the goods used;",

(b)   by the substitution in the definition of "goods" of "used" for "second-hand",

and

(c)   by the substitution in the definition of "importation of goods" of "the State" for "a Member State".

(With effect from 15 May 1996 except * with effect from 1 January 1996)

Finance Act 1997

96.   Section 1 of the Principal Act is hereby amended in subsection (1)-

(a)   by the insertion after the definition of "Appeal Commissioners" of the following definition:

"'**assignment**', in relation to an interest in immovable goods, means the assignment by a person of that interest in those goods or of any part of those goods to another person:

Provided that where that other person at the time of the assignment retains the reversion on that interest in those goods, that assignment shall be a surrender;",

(b)   by the insertion after the meaning assigned to "supply" of the following definition:

"'**surrender**', in relation to an interest in immovable goods, means the surrender by a person (hereafter referred to in this definition as 'the lessee') of an interest in those goods or any part of those goods to the person (hereafter referred to in this definition as 'the lessor') who at the time of the surrender retains the reversion on the interest in those goods and also includes the abandonment of that interest by the lessee and the failure of the lessee to exercise any option of the type referred to in subsection (1)(b) of section 4 in relation to that interest and surrender of an interest also includes the recovery by the lessor of that interest in those goods by ejectment or forfeiture prior to the date that that interest would, but for its surrender, have expired;",

and

*(c)   by the insertion after the definition of "taxable services" of the following definition:

"'**telecommunications services**' means services relating to the transmission, emission or reception of signals, writing, images and sounds or information of any nature by wire, radio, optical or other electromagnetic systems, including the transfer or assignment of the right to use capacity for such transmission, emission or reception.,".

(With effect from 26 March 1997 except for * with effect from 1 July 1997)

Taxes Consolidation Act 1997

1100. *Schedule 31,* which provides for amendments to other enactments consequential on the passing of this Act, shall apply for the purposes of this Act.

SCHEDULE 31

Consequential Amendments

in the enactments specified in Column (1) of the following Table for the words set out or referred to in Column (2) there shall be substituted the words set out in the corresponding entry in Column (3).

Enactment amended	Words to be replaced	Words to be substituted
(1)	(2)	(3)
The Value-Added Tax Act, 1972:		
section 1, in the definition of "Appeal Commissioners"	section 156 of the Income Tax Act, 1967	section 850 of the Taxes Consolidation Act, 1997
section 1, in the definition of "Collector-General"	section 162 of the Income Tax Act, 1967	section 851 of the Taxes Consolidation Act, 1997
section 1, in the definition of "inspector of taxes"	section 161 of the Income Tax Act, 1967	section 852 of the Taxes Consolidation Act, 1997
section 1, in the definition of "secretary"	section 207(2) of the Income Tax Act, 1967	section 1044(2) of the Taxes Consolidation Act, 1997
section 1(2)(bb)	section 73 of the Finance Act, 1988	section 1002 of the Taxes Consolidation Act, 1997
section 1(2)(c)(i)	Chapter III of Part I of the Finance Act, 1987	Chapter 1 of Part 18 of the Taxes Consolidation Act, 1997
section 1(2)(c)(ii)	section 17 of the Finance Act, 1970	Chapter 2 of Part 18 of the Taxes Consolidation Act, 1997

(With effect from 6 April 1997)

Finance Act 2000

108. Section 1 of the Principal Act is amended by the substitution for the definition of "telecommunications services" of the following:

"'**telecommunications services**' means services relating to the transmission, emission or reception of signals, writing, images and sounds or information of any nature by wire, radio, optical or other electromagnetic systems and includes-

(a)   the related transfer or assignment of the right to use capacity for such transmission, emission or reception, and

(b)   the provision of access to global information networks;".

(With effect from 23 March 2000)

Finance Act 2003

113. Section (1) of the Principal Act is amended in subsection (1) by inserting the following definition after the definition of "development":

" '**electronically supplied services**' includes —

(a)   website supply, web-hosting, distance maintenance of programmes and equipment,

(b)   supply of software and updating of it,

(c)   supply of images, text and information, and making databases available,

(d)   supply of music, films and games, including games of chance and gambling games, and of political, cultural, artistic, sporting, scientific and entertainment broadcasts and events, and

(e)   supply of distance teaching,

and '**electronic service**' shall be construed accordingly, but where the supplier of a service and his or her customer communicates by means of electronic mail, this shall not of itself mean that the service performed is an electronic service;".

(with effect from 1 July 2003)

Finance Act 2004

55. Section 1 of the Principal Act is amended by substituting the following for the definition of "taxable dealer":

"'**taxable dealer**' —

*(a)   in relation to supplies of gas through the natural gas distribution system, or of electricity, has the meaning assigned to it by section 3(6A),

(b)   in relation to supplies of movable goods other than a means of transport, has the meaning assigned to it by section 10A, and

(c)   in relation to supplies of means of transport, has the meaning assigned to it by section 12B;".

(with effect from 25 March 2004 except * with effect from 1 January 2005)

Finance Act 2006

93. (1)   Section 1 of the Principal Act is amended in subsection (1) —

(a)   by inserting the following after the definition of **"agricultural service"**:

"'**ancillary supply**' means a supply, forming part of a composite supply, which is not physically and economically dissociable from a principal supply and is capable of being supplied only in the context of the better enjoyment of that principal supply;",

(b)   by inserting the following after the definition of **"Community"**:

"'**composite supply**' means a supply made by a taxable person to a customer comprising two or more supplies of goods or services or any combination of these, supplied in conjunction with each other, one of which is a principal supply;",

(c)   by inserting the following after the definition of **"importation of goods"**:

"'**individual supply**' means a supply of goods or services which is a constituent part of a multiple supply and which is physically and economically dissociable from the other goods or services forming part of that multiple supply, and is capable of being supplied as a good or service in its own right;",

(d)   by inserting the following after the definition of **"movable goods"**:

"'**multiple supply**' means two or more individual supplies made by a taxable person to a customer where those supplies are made in conjunction with each other for a total consideration covering all those individual supplies, and where those individual supplies do not constitute a composite supply;",

and

(e)   by inserting the following after the definition of **"a person registered for value-added tax"**:

"'**principal supply**' means the supply of goods or services which constitutes the predominant element of a composite supply and to which any other supply forming part of that composite supply is ancillary;".

(with effect from 1 November 2006)

S.I No. 663 of 2006
European Communities (Value-Added Tax) Regulations, 2006

4.   Section 1 of the Principal Act is amended by inserting the following subsection after subsection (2A) (inserted by the Finance Act 1992 (No. 9 of 1992)):

"(2B) In this Act any reference to Council Directive No. 77/388/ EEC (however expressed) or to any Directive amending that Directive shall be read as a reference to Council Directive No. 2006/112/EC of 28 November 2006 and any reference to an Article, paragraph or subparagraph in Council Directive No. 77/388/EEC shall be read as a reference to the corresponding Article, paragraph or subparagraph in accordance with the correlation table in Annex XII to Council Directive No. 2006/ 112/EC of 28 November 2006.".

Finance Act 2007

97.   With effect from 1 January 2007 in each provision of the Principal Act specified in the first column of Schedule 3 for the words set out in the second column of that Schedule at that entry there is substituted the words set out at the corresponding entry in the third column of that Schedule.

Schedule 3
Miscellaneous amendments relating to council directive 2006/112/EC
Amendment of Value-Added Tax Act 1972

Provision of Principal Act	Words to be replaced	Words to be inserted
Section 1(1) in the definition of "Community"	Article 3 of the Council Directive No. 77/388/ EEC of 17 May 1977 (as last amended by Council Directive No. 92/111/EEC of 14 December 1992)	Articles 5 to 8 of Council Directive No. 2006/112/EC of 28 November 2006
Section 1(1) in the definition of "importation of goods"	Council Directive No. 77/388/EEC of 17 May 1977	Council Directive No. 2006/112/EC of 28 November 2006
Section 1(1) in the definition of "a person registered for value added tax"	Council Directive No. 77/388/EEC of 17 May 1977	Council Directive No. 2006/112/EC of 28 November 2006
Section 1(2A)	Article 3 (inserted by Council Directive No. 91/680/EEC of 16 December 1991) of Council Directive No. 77/388/EEC of 17 May 1977	Articles 5 to 8 of the Council Directive No. 2006/112/EC of 28 November 2006

98.   The European Communities (Value-Added Tax) Regulations 2006 (S.I. No. 663 of 2006) shall, with effect from 1 January 2007, be deemed never to have had effect and are revoked.

(With effect from 1 January 2007)

Finance Act 2008

83.   With effect from 1 July 2008 section 1 of the Principal Act is amended in subsection (1) —

(a)   by inserting the following before the meaning assigned to "agricultural produce":

"'**accountable person**' has the meaning assigned to it by section 8;

'**accounting year**' means a period of 12 months ending on 31 December, but if a taxable person customarily makes up accounts for periods of 12 months ending on another fixed date, then, for such a person, a period of 12 months ending on that fixed date;",

(b)   by substituting the following for the definition of "business":

"'**business**' means an economic activity, whatever the purpose or results of that activity, and includes any activity of producers, traders or persons supplying services, including mining and agricultural activities and activities of the professions, and the exploitation of tangible or intangible property for the purposes of obtaining income therefrom on a continuing basis;",

(c)   by inserting the following definition after the definition of "business":

"'**capital goods**' means developed immovable goods and a reference to a capital good includes a reference to any part thereof and the term capital good shall be construed accordingly;",

(d)   by inserting the following definition after the definition of "Community":

"'**completed**', in respect of immovable goods, has the meaning assigned to it by section 4B;",

(e)   by substituting in paragraph (a) of the definition of 'exempted activity' "sections 4(6), 4B(2) and 4C(2)" for "section 4(6)",

(f)   by inserting the following after the definition of "free port":

"'**freehold equivalent interest**' means an interest in immovable goods other than a freehold interest the transfer of which constitutes a supply of goods in accordance with section 3;",

(g)   by inserting the following after the definition of "importation of goods":

"'**independently**', in relation to a taxable person excludes a person who is employed or who is bound to an employer by a contract of employment or by any other legal ties creating the relationship of employer and employee as regards working conditions, remuneration and the employer's liability;",

(h) by inserting the following after the definition of "intra-Community acquisition of goods":

"'**joint option for taxation**' has the meaning assigned to it by section 4B;

'**landlord's option to tax**' has the meaning assigned to it by section 7A;",

(i) by inserting the following after "have expired" in the definition of "surrender":

"but in the case of an interest in immovable goods created on or after 1 July 2008, the failure of the lessee to exercise any option of the type referred to in subsection (1)(b) of section 4 in relation to that interest does not constitute a surrender",

and

(j) by substituting the following for the definition of "taxable person":

"'**taxable person**' means a person who independently carries out any business in the State;".

*141. The enactments specified in Schedule 8 —

(a) are amended to the extent and in the manner specified in paragraphs 1 to 6 of that Schedule, and

(b) apply and come into operation in accordance with paragraph 7 of that Schedule.

Schedule 8
Miscellaneous Technical Amendments in Relation to Tax

3. The Value-Added Tax Act 1972 is amended in accordance with the following provisions:

(a) in section 1(1) —

(i) in the definition of "the customs-free airport" by substituting "Customs-free Airport Act 1947" for "Customs-free Airport Act, 1941",

(ii) by deleting " 'monthly control statement' has the meaning assigned to it by section 17;", and

(iii) in paragraph (c) of the definition of "taxable dealer" by inserting "and in relation to supplies of agricultural machinery, has the meaning assigned to it by section 12C" after "section 12B",

(with effect from 1 July 2008 except * with effect from 13 March 2008)

Finance (No. 2) Act 2008

99. The enactments specified in Schedule 6 –

(a)   are amended to the extent and in the manner specified in paragraphs 1 to 6 of that Schedule, and

(b)   apply and come into operation in accordance with paragraph 7 of that Schedule.

Schedule 6
Miscellaneous Technical Amendments in Relation to Tax

4.   The Value-Added Tax Act 1972 is amended –

(a)   in section 1(1) –

(i)   in the definition of "capital goods" by inserting "and includes refurbishment within the meaning of section 12E," after "immovable goods",

(ii)   in paragraph (a) of the definition of "exempted activity" by substituting "sections 4(6) and 4B(2) and subsections (2) and (6)(b) of section 4C" for "sections 4(6), 4B(2) and 4C(2)", and

(iii)   in the definition of "freehold equivalent interest" by substituting "immovable goods, other than a freehold interest," for "immovable goods other than a freehold interest",

(With effect from 24 December 2008)

Section 2

Value Added Tax Act 1972

Charge of value-added tax

2.   (1)   With effect on and from the specified day a tax, to be called value-added tax, shall, subject to this Act and regulations, be charged, levied and paid-

      (a)   on the delivery of goods and the rendering of services delivered or rendered by an accountable person in the course of business, and

      (b)   on goods imported into the State.

    (2)   In the case of a person authorised in accordance with section 14 to treat the moneys which he has received for the rendering of taxable services or for the delivery of taxable goods and the rendering of taxable services (if any) as the consideration in respect of any such rendering or delivery, subsection (1) shall apply, in relation to any rendering of services or any delivery of goods and rendering of services in respect of which he is so authorised, as if references in that subsection to the delivery of goods or the rendering of services were references to the receipt of moneys in respect of such delivery or rendering, whether the delivery or rendering was or is made or effected before, on or after the said specified day.

(With effect from 1 November 1972)

VAT Amendment Act 1978

3.   Section 2(1) of the Principal Act is hereby amended by the substitution for paragraph (a) of the following paragraph:

    "(a)   on the supply of goods and services effected within the State for consideration by a taxable person in the course or furtherance of any business carried on by him, and".

30.   (1)   The enactment mentioned in column (2) of the First Schedule is hereby repealed to the extent specified in column (3) of that Schedule.

FIRST SCHEDULE
Enactments Repealed

Number and Year (1)	Short Title (2)	Extent of Repeal (3)
No. 22 of 1972	Value-Added Tax Act, 1972.	Section 2 (2).

(With effect from 1 March 1979)

Finance Act 1992

166. Section 2 of the Principal Act is hereby amended by the insertion of the following subsection after subsection (1):

"(1A) Without prejudice to subsection (1), with effect on and from the 1st day of January, 1993, value-added tax shall, subject to this Act and regulations, be charged, levied and paid-

(a) on the intra-Community acquisition of goods, other than new means of transport, effected within the State for consideration by a taxable person, and

(b) on the intra-Community acquisition of new means of transport effected within the State for consideration.".

(With effect from 1 January 1993)

Finance Act 2008

84. Section 2 of the Principal Act is amended with effect from 1 July 2008 in subsection (1) by substituting the following paragraph for paragraph (a):

"(a) on the supply of goods and services effected within the State for consideration by a taxable person acting as such, other than in the course or furtherance of an exempted activity, and".

109. With effect from 1 July 2008 in each provision of the Principal Act specified in the first column of Schedule 4 for the words set out in the second column of that Schedule at that entry (in each place where those words occur in the provision concerned) there is substituted the words set out at the corresponding entry in the third column of that Schedule.

Schedule 4
Miscellaneous Amendments Relating to the Amendment of the Definition of Taxable Person

Amendments to Value-Added Tax Act 1972

Provision of Value-Added Tax Act 1972	Words to be replaced	Words to be inserted
Section 2	a taxable person	an accountable person

(With effect from 1 July 2008)

Section 3
Value Added Tax Act 1972
Delivery of goods

3. (1) In this Act "delivery", in relation to goods, shall include-

    (a) the transfer of ownership of the goods by agreement,

    (b) the handing over of the goods to a person pursuant to an agreement which provides for the renting of the goods for a certain period subject to a condition that ownership of the goods shall be transferred to the person on a date not later than the date of payment of the final sum under the agreement,

    (c) the handing over by a person (in this paragraph referred to as the contractor) to another person of the goods, being goods which he has developed, constructed, manufactured, produced or extracted from goods entrusted to him by that other person for the purpose of any of those operations whether or not the contractor has supplied a part of the goods used,

    (d) the transfer of ownership of the goods pursuant to-

         (i) their acquisition, otherwise than by agreement, by or on behalf of the State or a local authority, or

         (ii) their seizure by any person acting under statutory authority,

    (e) the use by an accountable person for the purposes of his business, other than as stock-in-trade (within the meaning of section 34) of its goods, being goods developed, constructed, manufactured, produced, extracted or imported by him or by another person on his behalf, and

    (f) the appropriation by an accountable person for any purpose other than the purpose of his business of the goods, being goods which were delivered to him, or which were developed, constructed, manufactured, produced, extracted or imported by him in the course of business,

    and cognate words shall be construed accordingly.

    (2) If three or more persons enter into agreements concerning the same goods and fulfil those agreements by a direct delivery of the goods by the first person in the chain of sellers and buyers to the last buyer, then the delivery to such last buyer shall be deemed, for the purposes of this Acts, to constitute a simultaneous delivery by each seller in the chain.

(3)   The sale by auction of goods, being vegetables, fruit, flowers, poultry, eggs or fish shall be deemed, for the purposes of this Act, to constitute a delivery of the goods to and simultaneously by the auctioneer.

(4)   The sale of goods through a person (in this subsection referred to as the agent) who, while purporting to act on his own behalf, concludes agreements in his own name but on the instructions of and for the account of another person shall be deemed, for the purposes of this Act, to constitute a delivery of the goods to and simultaneously by the agent.

(5)   (a)   The transfer of ownership of goods pursuant to a contract of the kind referred to in subsection (1)(b) shall be deemed, for the purposes of this Act, not to be a delivery of the goods.

        (b)   The transfer of ownership of goods-

                (i)   as security for a loan or debt, or

                (ii)   where the goods are held as security for a loan or debt, upon repayment of the loan or debt, or

                (iii)   in connection with the transfer of a business or part thereof to another accountable person,

        shall be deemed, for the purposes of this Act, not to be a delivery of the goods unless the goods are goods of a kind specified in the Fourth Schedule and the delivery of the goods is one in relation to which tax at the rate of 30.26 per cent is chargeable.

(6)   The place where goods are delivered shall be deemed, for the purposes of this Act, to be-

        (a)   in case the delivery of the goods requires their transportation, the place where the transportation begins, and

        (b)   in any other case, the place where the goods are located at the time of the delivery.

(With effect from 1 November 1972)

Finance Act 1973

78.   Section 3 of the Principal Act is hereby amended by the insertion of the following subsection after subsection (1):

        "(1A) Where-

        (a)   goods of a kind specified in paragraph (xii) of the Second Schedule are supplied in a form suitable for human consumption without further preparation,

(b) the supply is made-

  (i) by means of a vending machine, or

  (ii) in the course of operating a hotel, restaurant, cafe, refreshment house, canteen, establishment licensed for the sale of intoxicating liquor, catering business or similar business, or

  (iii) in the course of operating any other business in connection with the carrying on of which facilities are provided for the consumption of the goods supplied, and

(c) apart from this subsection, the supply would constitute a delivery of the goods,

the supply shall, for all the purposes of this Act, be deemed to be a rendering of services and not a delivery of goods.".

90. The Principal Act is hereby amended as specified in column (3) of the Tenth Schedule to this Act.

TENTH SCHEDULE

Amendment of Enactments

Number and Year (1)	Short Title (2)	Amendment (3)
No. 22 of 1972	Value-Added Tax Act, 1972	In section 3, in subsection (1), " subject to subsection (1A)," shall be inserted after "in relation to goods, shall"; and in subsection (5)(b) " for the time being specified in section 11 (1)(c) " shall be substituted for " of 30·26 per cent".

(With effect from 3 September 1973)

Finance Act 1976

51. Section 3 of the Principal Act is hereby amended by the substitution of the following paragraph for paragraph (e) of subsection (1):

  "(e) the application by a person for the purposes of his business of the goods, being goods which were developed, constructed, assembled, manufactured, produced, extracted or imported by him or by another person on his behalf, except where tax chargeable in relation to the goods would, if they had been delivered to the first-mentioned person by an accountable person, be wholly deductible under section 12, and".

*61. In consequence of the amendments specified in sections 53 and 60 and the repeals specified in Part II of the Fifth Schedule, The Principal Act is hereby further amended as specified in Part II of the First Schedule.

PART II

Amendments Consequential on Certain Amendments of Value-Added Tax Act, 1972

Number and Year (1)	Short Title (2)	Amendment (3)
No. 22 of 1972	Value-Added Tax Act, 1972	In section 3(5)(b) "either of the rates" shall be substituted for "the rate".

(With effect from 27 May 1976 except * from 1 March 1976)

Value Added Tax (Amendment) Act 1978

4. Section 3 of the Principal Act is hereby amended-

(a) by the substitution in subsection (1) of "In this Act 'supply', in relation to goods, means-" for "In this Act 'delivery', in relation to goods, shall, subject to subsection (1A), include-", and of the following paragraphs for paragraphs (e) and (f):

"(e) the application (otherwise than by way of disposal to another person) by a person for the purposes of any business carried on by him of the goods, being goods which were developed, constructed, assembled, manufactured, produced, extracted, purchased or imported by him or by another person on his behalf, except where tax chargeable in relation to the application would, if it were charged, be wholly deductible under section 12, and

(f) the appropriation by a taxable person for any purpose other than the purpose of his business or the disposal free of charge of the goods where tax chargeable in relation to the goods-

(i) upon their acquisition by the taxable person, if they had been so acquired, or

(ii) upon their development, construction, assembly, manufacture, production, extraction, importation or application under paragraph (e),

as the case may be, was wholly or partly deductible under section 12,",.

(b) by the substitution of the following subsection for subsection (1A):

"(1A) Anything which is a supply of goods by virtue of paragraph (e) or (f) of subsection (1) shall be deemed, for the purposes of this Act, to have been effected for consideration in the course or furtherance of the business concerned:

Provided, however, that the following shall not be deemed to have been effected for consideration, that is to say:

(a)   a gift of goods made in the course or furtherance of the business (otherwise than as one forming part of a series or succession of gifts made to the same person) the cost of which to the donor does not exceed a sum specified for that purpose in regulations,

(b)   the gift, in reasonable quantity, to the actual or potential customer, of industrial samples in a form not ordinarily available for sale to the public,",

(c)   by the insertion of the following subsection:

"(1B) The provision of electricity, gas and any form of power, heat, refrigeration or ventilation shall be deemed, for the purposes of this Act, to be a supply of goods and not a supply of services.",

and

(d)   by the substitution for subsection (3) of the following subsection:

"(3)   (a)   The supply by auction of goods being-

(i)   livestock, horses, greyhounds, vegetables, fruit, flowers, poultry, eggs or fish, or

(ii)   immovable goods supplied in circums- tances in which tax is not chargeable,

shall be deemed, for the purposes of this Act, to constitute a supply of the goods to and simultaneously by the auctioneer.

(b)   The supply through an estate agent or other agent of-

(i)   livestock, horses or greyhounds, or

(ii)   immovable goods supplied in circumstances in which tax is not chargeable,

shall be deemed, for the purposes of this Act, to constitute a supply of the goods to and simultaneously by the agent.".

30.   (1)   The enactment mentioned in column (2) of the First Schedule is hereby repealed to the extent specified in column (3) of that Schedule.

(2)   In consequence of the amendments of the Principal Act specified
in this Act and of the repeals specified in the First Schedule, the
Principal Act is hereby further amended by the substitution of
the word or expression mentioned in column (3) of the Second
Schedule at any reference number for the word or expression
mentioned in column (2) of that Schedule at that reference
number wherever it occurs in the provision of the Principal
Act mentioned in column (4) of that Schedule at that reference
number.

FIRST SCHEDULE
Enactments Repealed

Number and Year (1)	Short Title (2)	Extent of Repeal (3)
No. 22 of 1972	Value-Added Tax Act, 1972	In paragraph (b) of section 3 (5), the words from "unless the goods" to the end of on paragraph.

SECOND SCHEDULE
Consequential Amendments

Reference Number (1)	Existing word or expression (2)	Substituted word or expression (3)	Provision of Principal Act (4)
1.	"delivery"	"supply"	The definition of "exempted activity", and the definition of "taxable goods" in sections 3(2), 3(4), 3(5)(a), 3(5)(b), 3(6)(a), 3(6)(b)
3.	"delivered"	"supplied"	Sections 3(6)
25.	"accountable person" except where preceded by the word "an"	"taxable person"	Sections 3(5)(b)(iii)
29.	"supplied"	"provided"	section 3(1)(c)

(With effect from 1 March 1979)

Finance Act 1982

75.   Section 3 of the Principal Act is hereby amended by the substitution of
the following subsection for subsection (3):

"(3)   (a)   The supply by auction of livestock, live horses, or live
greyhounds, vegetables, fruit, flowers, poultry, eggs
or fish shall be deemed, for the purposes of this Act, to
constitute a supply of the goods to and simultaneously
by the auctioneer.

(b)   The supply through an agent of livestock, live horses or live greyhounds shall be deemed, for the purposes of this Act, to constitute a supply of the goods to and simultaneously by the agent.".

(With effect from 1 September 1982)

Finance Act 1983

78.   Section 3 of the Principal Act is hereby amended by the insertion after subsection (6) of the following subsection:

"(7)   (i)   Where, in the case of a business carried on, or that has ceased to be carried on, by a taxable person, goods forming part of the assets of the business are, under any power exercisable by another person, including a liquidator and a receiver, disposed of by the other person in or towards the satisfaction of a debt owed by the taxable person, or in the course of the winding-up of a company, they shall be deemed to be supplied by the taxable person in the course or furtherance of his business.

(ii)   A disposal of goods under this subsection shall include any disposal which is deemed to be a supply of immovable goods under section 4(2).".

(With effect from 1 September 1983)

Finance Act 1990

99.   Section 3 of the Principal Act is hereby amended in subsection (3) (inserted by the Finance Act, 1982) by the deletion of ", live horses" from paragraphs (a) and (b).

(With effect from 1 January 1991)

Finance Act 1992

167.   Section 3 of the Principal Act is hereby amended-

(a)   in subsection (1):

(i)   in paragraph (e) (inserted by the Act of 1978):

(I)   by the substitution of ", imported or otherwise acquired" for "or imported, and

(II)   by the deletion of "and",

(ii)   in paragraph (f) (inserted by the Act of 1978):

(I)   by the substitution of the following subparagraph for subparagraph (i):

"(i)   upon their purchase, intra-Community acquisition or importation by the taxable person, or",

(II)   in subparagraph (ii) by the deletion of "importation", and

(III)   by the insertion after "section 12," of "and",

and

(iii)   by the insertion of the following paragraph after paragraph (f)-

"(g)   the transfer by a person of goods from his business in the State to the territory of another Member State for the purposes of his business, other than for the purposes of any of the following:

(i)   the transfer of the goods in question under the circumstances specified in paragraph (b) or (d) of subsection (6),

(ii)   the transfer of the goods referred to in paragraphs (i), (v), (vi) and (x) of the Second Schedule,

(iii)   the transfer of goods for the purpose of having contract work carried out on them,

(iv)   the temporary use of the goods in question in the supply of a service by him in that other Member State,

(v)   the temporary use of the goods in question, for a period not exceeding 24 months, in that other Member State, where the importation into that other Member State of the same goods with a view to their temporary use would be eligible for full exemption from import duties,",

(b)   in subsection (1A) (inserted by the Act of 1978) by the substitution of "(e), (f) or (g)" for "(e) or (f)", and

(c)   by the substitution of the following subsection for subsection 6-

"(6)   The place where goods are supplied shall be deemed, for the purposes of this Act, to be-

(a)   in the case of goods dispatched or transported and to which paragraph (d) does not apply, the place where the dispatch or transportation to the person to whom they are supplied begins,

(b)   in the case of goods which are installed or assembled, with or without a trial run, by or on behalf of the supplier, the place where the goods are installed or assembled,

(c)   in the case of goods not dispatched or transported, the place where the goods are located at the time of supply,

(d)   notwithstanding paragraph (a) or (b), in the case of goods, other than new means of transport, dispatched or transported by or on behalf of the supplier-

(i)   (I)   from the territory of another Member State, or

(II)   from outside the Community through the territory of another Member State into which the said goods have been imported,

to a person who is not a taxable person in the State, or

(ii)   from a taxable person in the State to a person in another Member State who is not registered for value-added tax, the place where the goods are when the dispatch or transportation ends:

Provided that this paragraph shall not apply (unless the supplier, in accordance with regulations, elects that it shall apply) to the supply of goods, other than goods subject to a duty of excise, where the total consideration for such supplies does not exceed or is not likely to exceed-

(A)   in the case of goods to which subparagraph (i) relates, £27,000 in a calendar year, and

(B)   in the case of goods to which subparagraph (ii) relates, the amount specified in the Member State in question in accordance with Article 28b. 13(2) (inserted by Council Directive No. 91/680/EEC of 16 December 1991) of Council Directive No. 77/388/EEC of 17 May 1977.".

(With effect from 1 January 1993)

S.I. No. 413 of 1992.
European Communities (Value-Added Tax) Regulations, 1992.

5.   Section 3 of the Principal Act is hereby amended-

(a)   in paragraph (g) (inserted by the Act of 1992) of subsection (1):

    (i)   by the insertion in subparagraph (i) after "paragraph (b)" of ", (cc)",

    and

    (ii)   by the insertion of the following subparagraph after subparagraph (iii):

        "(iiia) the transfer of goods for the purpose of having a service carried out on them,",

(b)   in subsection (6) (inserted by the Act of 1992):

    (i)   by the addition of the following proviso to paragraph (a):

        "Provided that where the goods are dispatched or transported from a place outside the Community, the place of supply by the person who imports the goods and the place of any subsequent supplies shall be deemed to be where the goods are imported,",

    (ii)   by the insertion of the following paragraph after paragraph (c):

        "(cc)   in the case of goods supplied on board vessels, aircraft or trains during transport, the places of departure and destination of which are within the community, the place where the transport began,",

    and

    (iii)   in paragraph (d):

        (I)   by the deletion in subparagraph (ii) of "a taxable person in", and

        (II)   by the substitution of the following proviso for the proviso to the paragraph:

        "Provided that this paragraph shall not apply to the supply of goods, other than goods subject to a duty of excise, where the total consideration for such supplies does not exceed or is not likely to exceed-

           (A)   in the case of goods to which subparagraph (i) relates, £27,000 in a calendar year, unless the supplier, in accordance with regulations elects that it shall apply, and

(B) in the case of goods to which subparagraph (ii) relates, the amount specified in the Member State in question in accordance with Article 28b. B(2) (inserted by Council Directive No. 91/680/EEC of 16 December 1991) of Council Directive No. 77/388/EEC of 17 May 1977 unless the supplier elects that it shall apply and registers and accounts for value-added tax in that Member State in respect of such supplies.",

and

(c) by the addition of the following subsection after subsection (7) (inserted by the Finance Act, 1983):

"(8) Where a taxable person who is not established in the State makes an intra-Community acquisition of goods in the State and makes a subsequent supply of those goods to a taxable person in the State, the person to whom the supply is made shall be deemed for the purposes of this Act to have made that supply and the intra-Community acquisition shall be disregarded:

Provided that this provision shall only apply where-

(a) the taxable person who is not established in the State has not exercised his option to register in accordance with section 9 by virtue of section 8(3D), and

(b) the person to whom the supply is made is registered in accordance with section 9.".

(With effect from 1 January 1993)

Finance Act 1993

82. Section 3 of the Principal Act is hereby amended in paragraph (g) (inserted by the Act of 1992) of subsection (1) by the insertion after "for the purposes of his business," of "or a transfer of a new means of transport by a person in the State to the territory of another Member State,".

(With effect from 17 June 1993)

Finance Act 1994

92. Section 3 of the Principal Act is hereby amended in subparagraph (ii) of paragraph (g) (inserted by the Act of 1992) of subsection (1) by the insertion after "(va)" of ", (vb)".

(With effect from 23 May 1994)

Finance Act 1995

120.   Section 3 of the Principal Act is hereby amended in subsection (1)-

(a)   by the insertion in paragraph (a) after "by agreement" of "other than the transfer of ownership of the goods to a person supplying financial services of the kind specified in subparagraph (i)(e) of the First Schedule, where those services are supplied as part of an agreement of the kind referred to in paragraph (b) in respect of those goods", and

*(b)   by the insertion of the following paragraph after paragraph (a):

"(aa)   a supply by an auctioneer within the meaning of section 10B or by a taxable dealer,".

(With effect from 2 June 1995 except * from 1 July 1995)

S.I. No. 363 of 1995.
European Communities (Value-Added Tax) Regulations, 1995.

5.   Section 3 of the Principal Act is hereby amended in subsection (1) -

(a)   by the substitution of the following paragraph for paragraph (c):

"(c)   the handing over by a person (in this paragraph referred to as the developer) to another person of immovable goods which have been developed from goods entrusted to the developer by that other person for the purpose of such development, whether or not the developer has supplied any part of the goods used,",

and

(b)   in paragraph (g)-

(i)   by the deletion of subparagraph (iii), and

(ii)   by the addition of the following proviso to subparagraph (iiia):

"Provided that the goods which were so transferred by the person are, after being worked upon, returned to that person in the State,".

(With effect from 1 January 1996)

Finance Act 1996

89.   Section 3 of the Principal Act is hereby amended -

(a)   in subsection (1)-

(i)   by the substitution of the following paragraph for paragraph (aa) (inserted by the Act of 1995):

"(aa)   the sale of movable goods pursuant to a contract under which commission is payable on purchase or sale by an agent or auctioneer who concludes agreements in such agent's or auctioneer's own name but on the instructions of, and for the account of, another person,",

*(ii)   by the substitution of the following paragraph for paragraph (c):

"(c)   the handing over by a person (in this paragraph referred to as the developer) to another person of immovable goods which have been developed from goods entrusted to the developer by that other person for the purpose of such development, whether or not the developer has supplied any part of the goods used,",

and

*(iii) in paragraph (g)-

(I)   by the deletion of subparagraph (iii), and

(II)   by the substitution of the following subparagraph for subparagraph (iiia):

"(iia)   the transfer of goods for the purpose of having a service carried out on them:

Provided that the goods which were so transferred by the person are, after being worked upon, returned to that person in the State,",

(b)   by the deletion of subsection (3) (inserted by the Finance Act, 1982), and

(c)   by the substitution of the following subsection for subsection (4):

"(4)   Where an agent or auctioneer makes a sale of goods in accordance with paragraph (aa) of subsection (1) the transfer of those goods to that agent or auctioneer shall be deemed to be a supply of goods to the agent or auctioneer at the time that that agent or auctioneer makes that sale.".

(With effect from 15 May 1996 except * from 1 January 1996)

Finance Act 1998

105.   Amendment of section 3 (supply of goods) of Principal Act

Section 3 of the Principal Act is hereby amended in subsection (1) by the substitution of the following paragraph for paragraph (f)-

"(f)   the appropriation of goods by a taxable person for any purpose other than the purpose of his business or the disposal of goods free of charge by a taxable person where-

(i)   tax chargeable in relation to those goods-

    (I)   upon their purchase, intra-Community acquisition or importation by the taxable person, or

    (II)   upon their development, construction, assembly, manufacture, production, extraction or application under paragraph (e),

        as the case may be, was wholly or partially deductible under section 12, or

(ii)   the ownership of those goods was transferred to the taxable person in the course of a transfer of a business or part thereof and that transfer of ownership was deemed not to be a supply of goods in accordance with subsection (5)(b), and".

(With effect from 27 March 1998)

Finance Act 1999

120. Section 3 of the Principal Act is hereby amended-

(a)   in paragraph (g) (inserted by the Act of 1992) of subsection (1) by the substitution of the following sub-paragraph for sub-paragraph (ii):

"(ii)   the transfer of goods to another person under the circumstances specified in paragraph (i) of the Second Schedule and the transfer of the goods referred to in paragraphs (v), (va), (vb) and (x) of the Second Schedule,",

(b)   in subsection (5) by the insertion of the following paragraph after paragraph (b):

"(c)   Where a person, in this subsection referred to as an 'owner'-

(i)   supplies financial services of the kind specified in sub-paragraph (i)(e)of the First Schedule in respect of a supply of goods within the meaning of paragraph (b) of subsection (1), being goods which are of such a kind or were used in such circumstances that no part of the tax, if any, chargeable on that supply of those goods was deductible by the person to whom that supply was made, and

(ii)   enforces such owner's right to recover possession of those goods, then the disposal of those goods by such owner shall be deemed for the purposes of this Act not to be a supply of goods.",

and

(c)   in paragraph (A) of the proviso (inserted by the European
       Communities (Value-Added Tax) Regulations, 1992 (S.I. No. 413
       of 1992)) to paragraph (d) of subsection (6) by the substitution of
       "£27,565" for "£27,000".

(With effect from 25 March 1999)

Finance Act 2001

182. Section 3 of the Principal Act is amended in subsection (5)-

(a)   in subparagraph (iii) of paragraph (b) by the insertion after
       "person" of "even if that business or that part thereof had ceased
       trading", and

(b)   by the insertion of the following after paragraph (c) (inserted by
       the Act of 1999):

       "(d)   The disposal of goods by an insurer who has taken
               possession of them from the owner of those goods, in
               this subsection referred to as the "insured", in connection
               with the settlement of a claim under a policy of insurance,
               being goods—

               (a)   in relation to the acquisition of which the insured
                      had borne tax, and

               (b)   which are of such a kind or were used in such
                      circumstances that no part of the tax borne was
                      deductible by the insured,

               shall be deemed for the purposes of this Act not to be a
               supply of goods.".

*240. (1)   (a)   Subject to subsection (2), in each provision specified in
                    column (1) of Schedule 5 for the words or amount set
                    out in column (2) of that Schedule at that entry there
                    shall be substituted the words or amount set out at the
                    corresponding entry in column (3) of that Schedule.

             (b)   Where words are or an amount is mentioned more than
                    once in a provision specified in column (1) of Schedule
                    5, then the substitution provided for by paragraph
                    (a) shall apply as respects those words or that amount
                    to each mention of those words or that amount in that
                    provision.

SCHEDULE 5

PART 4

Value-Added Tax and related matters

Enactment amended (1)	Amount or words to be replaced (2)	Amount or words to be inserted (3)
Value-Added Tax Act, 1972 (No. 22 of 1972) (as amended): section 3(6)(d)(A)	£27,565	€35,000

(With effect from 21 March 2001 except * from 1 January 2002)

Finance Act 2004

56. Section 3 of the Principal Act is amended —

(a)   in subsection (6) (inserted by the Finance Act 1992) by substituting in the proviso to paragraph (d) "such supplies," for "such supplies." and by inserting the following paragraphs after the proviso to paragraph (d):

"(e)   in the case of the supply of gas through the natural gas distribution system, or of electricity, to a taxable dealer, whether in the State, or in another Member State of the Community, or outside the Community, the place where that taxable dealer has established the business concerned or has a fixed establishment for which the goods are supplied, or in the absence of such a place of business or fixed establishment the place where that taxable dealer has a permanent address or usually resides,

(f)   in the case of the supply of gas through the natural gas distribution system, or of electricity, to a customer other than a taxable dealer, the place where that customer has effective use and consumption of those goods; but if all or part of those goods are not consumed by that customer, then the goods not so consumed shall be deemed to have been supplied to that customer and used and consumed by that customer at the place where that customer has established the business concerned or has a fixed establishment for which the goods are supplied or in the absence of such a place of business or fixed establishment, the place where that customer has a permanent address or usually resides,",

and

(b)   by inserting the following after subsection (6):

"(6A) In subsection (6) 'taxable dealer' means a taxable person whose principal business in respect of supplies of gas through the natural gas distribution system, or of electricity, received by that person, is the supply of those goods for consideration in the course or furtherance of business and whose own consumption of those goods is negligible.".

(With effect from 1 January 2005)

Finance Act 2005

99. Section 3 of the Principal Act is amended in subsection (5)(b) by substituting the following for subparagraph (iii)-

"(iii) being the transfer to a taxable person of a totality of assets, or part thereof, of a business even if that business or part thereof had ceased trading, where those transferred assets constitute an undertaking or part of an undertaking capable of being operated on an independent basis,".

(With effect from 25 March 2005)

Finance Act 2007

76. Section 3 of the Principal Act is amended with effect from 1 May 2007 —

(a) in subsection (1)(a) by substituting "including" for "other than",

(b) in subsection (5) —

(i) by inserting in paragraph (a) "by the person supplying financial services of the kind specified in subparagraph (i)(e) of the First Schedule as part of that contract" after "referred to in subsection (1)(b)", and

(ii) in paragraph (c) —

(I) by deleting in subparagraph (i) "being goods which are of such a kind or were used in such circumstances that no part of the tax, if any, chargeable on that supply of those goods was deductible by the person to whom that supply was made," and

(II) by substituting "shall be deemed for the purposes of this Act to be a supply of goods to which paragraph (xxiv) of the First Schedule does not apply" for "shall be deemed for the purposes of this Act not to be a supply of goods".

*97. With effect from 1 January 2007 in each provision of the Principal Act specified in the first column of Schedule 3 for the words set out in the second column of that Schedule at that entry there is substituted the words set out at the corresponding entry in the third column of that Schedule.

Schedule 3
Miscellaneous Amendments Relating To Council Directive 2006/112/EC

Amendment of Value-Added Tax Act 1972

Provision of Principal Act	Words to be replaced	Words to be inserted
Section 3(6)(d)(B)	Article 28b.B(2) (inserted by Council Directive No. 91/680/EEC of 16 December 1991) of Council Directive No. 77/388/EEC of 17 May 1977	Article 34 of Council Directive No. 2006/112/EC of 28 November 2006

(with effect from 1 May 2007 except * with effect from 1 January 2007)

Finance Act 2008

85. With effect from 1 July 2008 section 3 of the Principal Act is amended —

(a)   in subsection (1)(e) by substituting "being movable goods" for "being goods",

(b)   by inserting the following after subsection (1B):

"(1C) For the purposes of this Act in the case of immovable goods 'supply' in relation to goods shall be regarded as including —

(a)   the transfer in substance of the right to dispose of immovable goods as owner or the transfer in substance of the right to dispose of immovable goods, and

(b)   transactions where the holder of an estate or interest in immovable goods enters into a contract or agreement with another person in relation to the creation, establishment, alteration, surrender, relinquishment or termination of rights in respect of those immovable goods, apart from mortgages, and consideration or payments which amount to 50 per cent or more of the open market value of the immovable goods at the time the contract or agreement is concluded are payable pursuant to or associated with the contract or agreement or otherwise either before the making of the contract or agreement or within 5 years of the commencement of such contract or agreement.",

and

(c)   in subsection (8) —

(i)   by substituting "Where a person who is not established in the State makes an intra-Community acquisition of goods in the State and makes a subsequent supply of those goods to an accountable person in the State" for "Where a taxable person who is not established in the State makes an intra-Community acquisition of goods in the State and makes a subsequent supply of those goods to a taxable person in the State", and

(ii)   in paragraph (a) of the proviso by substituting "the person" for "the taxable person".

109.   With effect from 1 July 2008 in each provision of the Principal Act specified in the first column of Schedule 4 for the words set out in the second column of that Schedule at that entry (in each place where those words occur in the provision concerned) there is substituted the words set out at the corresponding entry in the third column of that Schedule.

Schedule 4
Miscellaneous Amendments Relating to the Amendment of the Definition of Taxable Person

Amendments to Value-Added Tax Act 1972

Provision of Value-Added Tax Act 1972	Words to be replaced	Words to be inserted
Section 3(1)(f)	a taxable person	an accountable person
Section 3(1)(f)(i)(I)	the taxable person	the accountable person
Section 3(1)(f)(ii)	the taxable person	the accountable person
Section 3(5)(b)(iii)	a taxable person	an accountable person
Section 3(6)(d)(i)	a taxable person	an accountable person
Section 3(6A)	a taxable person	an accountable person
Section 3(7)(i)	a taxable person	an accountable person
Section 3(7)(i)	the taxable person	the accountable person

(With effect from 1 July 2008)

Finance (No. 2) Act 2008

68.   Section 3 of the Principal Act is amended in subsection (1C) —

(a)   in paragraph (a), by substituting "immovable goods." for "immovable goods, and" and

(b)   by deleting paragraph (b).

(With effect from 24 December 2008)

Section 3A

Finance Act 1992

Intra-Community acquisition of goods

168. The Principal Act is hereby amended by the insertion of the following section after section 3:

"3A. (1)   In this Act **'intra-Community acquisition of goods'** means the acquisition of—

(a)   movable goods, other than new means of transport, supplied by a person registered for value-added tax in a Member State to a person in another Member State (other than an individual who is not a taxable person or who is not entitled to elect to be a taxable person) and which have been dispatched or transported from the territory of a Member State to the territory of another Member State as a result of such supply, or

(b)   new means of transport dispatched or transported from the territory of a Member State to the territory of another Member State.

(2)   (a)   The place where an intra-Community acquisition of goods occurs shall be deemed to be the place where the goods are when the dispatch or transportation ends.

(b)   Without prejudice to paragraph (a), when the person acquiring the goods quotes his value-added tax registration number for the purpose of the acquisition, the place where an intra-Community acquisition of goods occurs shall be deemed to be within the territory of the Member State which issued that registration number.

(3)   For the purposes of this section—

(a)   a supply in the territory of another Member State shall be deemed to have arisen where, under similar circumstances, a supply would have arisen in the State under section 3, and

(b)   a person shall be deemed to be a taxable person or a person who is entitled to elect to be a taxable person in another Member State where, under similar circumstances, the person would be a taxable person or entitled to elect to be a taxable person in the State in accordance with section 8.

(4)   Where goods are dispatched or transported from outside the Community to a person in the State who is not registered for tax and who is not an individual, and value-added tax referred to in Council Directive No. 77/388/EEC of 17 May 1977 is chargeable

on the importation of the said goods into another Member State then, for the purposes of subsection (1), the person shall be deemed to be registered for value-added tax in that other Member State and the goods shall be deemed to have been dispatched or transported from that other Member State.".

(With effect from 1 January 1993)

S.I. No. 413 of 1992.
European Communities (Value-Added Tax) Regulations, 1992.

6.   Section 3A (inserted by the Act of 1992) of the Principal Act is hereby amended —

    (a)   (in paragraph (a) of subsection (1) —

          (i)   (by the insertion after "in a Member State" of "or by a flat-rate farmer in a Member State," and

          (ii)   (by the insertion after "who is not entitled to elect to be a taxable person" of ", unless the said individual carries on an exempted activity",

    (b)   in paragraph (b) of subsection (2) by the insertion after "that registration number" of ", unless the person acquiring the goods can establish that that acquisition has been subject to value-added tax referred to in Council Directive No. 77/388/EEC of 17 May 1977 in accordance with paragraph (a).",

    (c)   in subsection (3) by the insertion of the following paragraphs after paragraph (a):

          "(aa)   an activity in another Member State shall be deemed to be an exempted activity where the same activity, if carried out in the State, would be an exempted activity, and

          (ab)   a person shall be deemed to be a flat-rate farmer in another Member State where, under similar circumstances, the person would be a flat-rate farmer in the State in accordance with section 12A, and",

          and

    (d)   by the addition of the following subsection after subsection (4):

          "(5)   Paragraph (b) of subsection (2) shall not apply where —

          (i)   (a person quotes the registration number assigned to him in accordance with section 9 for the purpose of making an intra-Community acquisition and the goods are dispatched or transported from the territory of a Member State directly to the territory of another Member State, neither of which are the State,

(ii)   (the person makes a subsequent supply of the goods to a person registered for value-added tax in the Member State where the dispatch or transportation ends,

(iii)   (the person issues an invoice in relation to that supply in such form and containing such particulars as would be required in accordance with section 17(1) if he made the supply of the goods in the State to a person registered for value-added tax in another Member State, and containing an explicit reference to the EC simplified triangulation arrangements and indicating that the person in receipt of that supply is liable to account for the value-added tax due in that Member State, and

(iv)   in accordance with regulations, the person includes a reference to the supply in the statement referred to in section 19A as if it were an intra-Community supply for the purposes of that section.".

(With effect from 1 January 1993)

Finance Act 1993

83.   Section 3A (inserted by the Act of 1992) of The Principal Act is hereby amended in subsection (I) —

(a)   by the insertion in paragraph (a) after "a person registered for value-added tax in a Member State "of" or by a person who carries on an exempted activity in a Member State,", and

(b)   by the substitution of the following paragraph for paragraph (b):

"(b)   new means of transport supplied by a person in a Member State to a person in another Member State and which has been dispatched or transported from the territory of a Member State to the territory of another Member State as a result of being so supplied.".

(With effect from 17 June 1993)

Finance Act 1995

121.   Section 3A (inserted by the Act of 1992) of the Principal Act is hereby amended by the insertion of the following subsection after subsection (1):

"(1A)   An intra-Community acquisition of goods shall be deemed not to occur where the supply of those goods is subject to value-added tax referred to in Council Directive No. 77/388/EEC of 17 May 1977 in the Member State of dispatch under the provisions implementing Article 26a or 28o (inserted by Council Directive No. 94/5/EC of 14 February 1994 of that Directive in that Member State.".

(With effect from 1 July 1995)

Finance Act 1997

97. Section 3A (inserted by the Act of 1992) of the Principal Act is hereby amended in paragraph (a) of subsection (1) by the insertion after "supplied by a person registered for value-added tax in a Member State," of "or by a person obliged to be registered for value-added tax in a Member State,".

(With effect from 10 May 1997)

Finance Act 2007

97. With effect from 1 January 2007 in each provision of the Principal Act specified in the first column of Schedule 3 for the words set out in the second column of that Schedule at that entry there is substituted the words set out at the corresponding entry in the third column of that Schedule.

Schedule 3
Miscellaneous Amendments Relating to Council Directive 2006/112/EC

Amendment of Value-Added Tax Act 1972

Provision of Principal Act	Words to be replaced	Words to be inserted
Section 3A(1A)	Council Directive No. 77/388/EEC of 17 May 1977 in the Member State of dispatch under the provisions implementing Article 26a or 28o (inserted by Council Directive No. 94/5/EC of 14 February 1994) of that Directive in that Member State	Council Directive No. 2006/112/ EC of 28 November 2006 in the Member State of dispatch under the provisions implementing Articles 4 and 35, first subparagraph of Article 139(3) and Articles 311 to 341 of that Directive in that Member State
Section 3A(2)(b)	Council Directive No. 77/388/EEC of 17 May 1977	Council Directive No. 2006/112/ EC of 28 November 2006
Section 3A(4)	Council Directive No. 77/388/EEC of 17 May 1977	Council Directive No. 2006/112/ EC of 28 November 2006

Finance Act 2008

109. With effect from 1 July 2008 in each provision of the Principal Act specified in the first column of Schedule 4 for the words set out in the second column of that Schedule at that entry (in each place where those words occur in the provision concerned) there is substituted the words set out at the corresponding entry in the third column of that Schedule.

Schedule 4
Miscellaneous Amendments Relating to the Amendment of the Definition of Taxable Person

Amendments to Value-Added Tax Act 1972

Provision of Value-Added Tax Act 1972	Words to be replaced	Words to be inserted
Section 3A(3)(b)	the person would be a taxable person or entitled to elect to be a taxable person in the State	the person would be an accountable person or entitled to elect to be an accountable person in the State

(With effect from 1 July 2008)

Section 3B

Finance Act 1993

Alcohol Products

84. The Principal Act is hereby amended by the insertion of the following section after section 3A (inserted by the Act of 1992):

> "3B. (1) Where alcohol products are supplied while being held under a duty-suspension arrangement then any such supply effected while the products are held under that arrangement, other than the last such supply in the State, shall be deemed not to be a supply for the purposes of this Act other than for the purposes of section 12 and any previous-
>
>   (a)   intra-Community acquisition, or
>
>   (b)   importation,
>
> of such products shall be disregarded for the purposes of this Act.
>
> (2) Where tax is chargeable on a supply referred to in subsection (1) then, notwithstanding section 19(1), the tax on that supply shall be due at the same time as the duty of excise on the products is due:
>
> Provided that this subsection shall not apply to a supply of the kind referred to in subparagraph (a)(I), (b) or (cc) of paragraph (i) or in paragraph (ia) of the Second Schedule.
>
> (3) Where, other than in the circumstances set out in section 8(2B)(b), a taxable person makes an intra-Community acquisition of alcohol products and by virtue of such acquisition, and in accordance with Chapter II of Part II of the Finance Act, 1992, and any other enactment which is to be construed together with that Chapter, the duty of excise on those products is payable in the State, then, notwithstanding section 19(1A), the tax on the said intra-Community acquisition shall be due at the same time as the duty of excise on the products is due.
>
> (4) Where tax is chargeable on the importation of alcohol products, which are then placed under a duty-suspension arrangement then, notwithstanding section 15(6), the tax on that importation shall be due at the same time as the duty of excise on the products is due.
>
> (5) Notwithstanding subsections (1) and (1A) of section 10 and section 15(3), where the provisions of subsection (2), (3) or (4) apply, the amount on which tax is chargeable

shall include the amount of the duty of excise chargeable on the products on their release for consumption in the State.

(6)   Notwithstanding any other provision to the contrary contained in this Act, where the provisions of subsection (2), (3) or (4) apply then-

(a)   the tax shall be payable at the same time as the duty of excise is payable on the products,

(b)   the provisions of the statutes which relate to the duties of excise and the management thereof and of any instrument relating to duties of excise made under statute, shall, with any necessary modifications and exceptions as may be specified in regulations, apply to such tax as if it were a duty of excise, and

(c)   the person by whom the tax is payable shall complete such form as is provided for the purposes of this subsection by the Revenue Commissioners.

(7)   In this section-

'alcohol products' means the excisable products referred to at subsections (a), (b), (c), (d) and (e) of section 104 of the Finance Act, 1992;

'duty-suspension arrangement' has the meaning assigned to it by section 103 of the Finance Act, 1992. ".

(With effect from 1 August 1993)

Finance Act 2008

109.   With effect from 1 July 2008 in each provision of the Principal Act specified in the first column of Schedule 4 for the words set out in the second column of that Schedule at that entry (in each place where those words occur in the provision concerned) there is substituted the words set out at the corresponding entry in the third column of that Schedule.

Schedule 4
Miscellaneous Amendments Relating to the Amendment of the Definition of Taxable Person

Amendments to Value-Added Tax Act 1972

Provision of Value-Added Tax Act 1972	Words to be replaced	Words to be inserted
Section 3B	a taxable person	an accountable person

*141. The enactments specified in Schedule 8 —

(a)　　are amended to the extent and in the manner specified in paragraphs 1 to 6 of that Schedule, and

(b)　　apply and come into operation in accordance with paragraph 7 of that Schedule.

Schedule 8
Miscellaneous Technical Amendments in Relation to Tax

(b)　　in section 3B —

(i)　　in subsection (1) by substituting "suspension arrangement" for "duty-suspension arrangement",

(ii)　　in subsection (3) by substituting "and in accordance with Chapters 1 and 2 of Part 2 of the Finance Act 2001" for "and in accordance with Chapter II of Part II of the Finance Act, 1992",

(iii)　　in subsection (4) by substituting "suspension arrangement" for "duty-suspension arrangement", and

(iv)　　by substituting the following for subsection (7):

"(7)　　In this section —

'alcohol products' has the same meaning as it has in section 73(1) of the Finance Act 2003;

'suspension arrangement' means an arrangement under which excisable products are produced, processed, held or moved, excise duty being suspended.",

(With effect from 1 July 2008 except * with effect from 13 March 2008)

Section 4

Value Added Tax Act 1972

Special provisions in relation to the delivery of immovable goods

4. (1) (a) This section applies to immovable goods —

      (i) which have been developed by or on behalf of the person delivering them, or

      (ii) in respect of which the person delivering them was, or would, but for the operation of section 3(5) (b)(iii), have been at any time entitled to claim a deduction under section 12 for any tax borne or paid in relation to a delivery or development of them.

    (b) In this section **"interest"**, in relation to immovable goods, means an estate or interest therein which, when it was created, was for a period of at least ten years but does not include a mortgage and a reference to the disposal of an interest includes a reference to the creation of an interest.

(2) Subject to section 2(2), paragraphs (c), (d), (e) and (f) of section 3(1), section 19(2) and subsections (3), (4) and (5), a delivery of immovable goods shall be deemed, for the purposes of this Act, to take place if, but only if, a person having an interest in immovable goods to which this section applies disposes, as regards the whole or any part of those goods, of that interest or of an interest which derives therefrom.

(3) (a) Subject to paragraph (b), where a person having an interest in immovable goods to which this section applies surrenders possession of those goods or of any part thereof in such circumstances that the surrender does not constitute a delivery of the goods for the purposes of subsection (2), the surrender shall be deemed, for the purposes of section 3(1)(f), to be an appropriation of the goods or of the part thereof, as the case may be, for a purpose other than the purpose of his business.

    (b) This subsection shall not apply to-

      (i) any such surrender of possession made in accordance with an agreement for the leasing or letting of the goods if the person surrendering possession is chargeable to tax in respect of the rent or other payment under the agreement, or

      (i) a surrender in connection with a transfer which, in accordance with section 3(5), is declared, for the purposes of this Act, not to be a delivery.

(4)   Where a person having an interest in immovable goods to which this section applies disposes, as regards the whole or any part of those goods, of an interest which derives from that interest in such circumstances that he retains the reversion on the interest disposed of, he shall, in relation to the reversion so retained, be deemed, for the purposes of section 3(1)(f), to have made an appropriation of the goods or of the part thereof, as the case may be, for a purpose other than the purpose of his business.

(5)   Where an accountable person disposes of an interest in immovable goods to which this section applies or carries out any development in relation to such immovable goods and in connection with that disposal or carrying out of development some other person who would not, apart from this subsection, be regarded as an accountable person, disposes of an interest in relation to the goods concerned-

(a)   that other person shall, in relation to the disposal by him, be deemed to be an accountable person, and

(b)   the disposal shall be deemed to be a delivery, made in the course of business, of goods which that other person has developed.

(6)   Notwithstanding anything in this section or in section 2 tax shall not be charged on the delivery of immovable goods-

(a)   in relation to which a right in favour of the person making the delivery to a deduction under section 12 in respect of any tax borne or paid on the delivery or development of the goods did not arise and would not, apart from section 3(5)(b)(iii), have arisen, or

(b)   which had been occupied before the specified day and had not been developed between that date and the date of the delivery.

(7)   The provisions of section 8(3) shall not apply in relation to a person who makes a delivery of goods to which this section applies.

(With effect from 1 November 1972)

Value Added Tax (Amendment) Act 1978

Repeals and consequential amendments

30.   (1)   The enactment mentioned in column (2) of the First Schedule is hereby repealed to the extent specified in column (3) of that Schedule.

(2)   In consequence of the amendments of the Principal Act specified in this Act and of the repeals specified in the First Schedule, the Principal Act is hereby further amended by the substitution of the word or expression mentioned in column (3) of the Second

Schedule at any reference number for the word or expression
mentioned in column (2) of that Schedule at that reference
number wherever it occurs in the provision of the Principal
Act mentioned in column (4) of that Schedule at that reference
number.

FIRST SCHEDULE

Enactments Repealed

Number and Year (1)	Short Title (2)	Extent of Repeal (3)
No. 22 of 1972	Value-Added Tax Act, 1972.	In section 4 (2), the words "section 2(2),"

SECOND SCHEDULE

Consequential Amendments

Reference Number (1)	Existing word or expression (2)	Substituted word or expression (3)	Provision of Principal Act (4)
1	"delivery"	"supply"	The definition of "exempted activity", and the definition of "taxable goods" in section 4(1)(a)(ii), 4(2), 4(3)(a), 4(3)(b)(ii), 4(5)(b), 4(6), 4(7),
5	"delivering"	"supplying"	Sections 4(1)(a)(i) and 4(1)(a)(ii).
26	"an accountable person"	"a taxable person"	Section 4(5)

(With effect from 1 March 1979)

Finance Act 1995

122. Section 4 of the Principal Act is hereby amended-

(a)   by the substitution of the following subsection for subsection
(5):

"(5)   Where a person disposes of an interest in immovable
goods to another person and in connection with that
disposal a taxable person enters into an agreement with
that other person or person connected with that other
person to carry out a development in relation to those
immovable goods, then-

(a)   the person who disposes of the interest in the said
immovable goods shall, in relation to that disposal,
be deemed to be a taxable person,

(b)   the disposal of the interest in the said immovable
goods shall be deemed to be a supply of those

goods made in the course or furtherance of business, and

(c)   the disposal of the interest in the said immovable goods shall, notwithstanding subsection (1), be deemed to be a disposal of an interest in immovable goods to which this section applies.",

and

(b)   by the insertion in paragraph (b) of subsection (6) after "supply" of "other than a supply of immovable goods to which the provisions of subsection (5) apply".

(With effect from 2 June 1995)

Finance Act 1997

98.   Section 4 of the Principal Act is hereby amended-

(a)   in subsection (1):

(i)   by the substitution of the following paragraph for paragraph (b):

"(b)   In this section '**interest**', in relation to immovable goods, means an estate or interest therein which, when it was created was for a period of at least ten years or, if it was for a period of less than ten years, its terms contained an option for the person in whose favour the interest was created to extend it to a period of at least ten years, but does not include a mortgage, and a reference to the disposal of an interest includes a reference to the creation of an interest, and an interval of the type referred to in subsection (2A) shall be deemed to be an interest for the purposes of this section.",

and

(ii)   by the insertion of the following paragraph after paragraph (b):

"(c)   Where an interest is created and, at the date of its creation, its terms contain one or more options for the person in whose favour the interest was so created to extend that interest, then that interest shall be deemed to be for the period from the date of creation of that interest to the date that that interest would expire if those options were so exercised.",

(b)   in subsection (2) by the insertion after "disposes" of "(including by way of surrender or by way of assignment)",

(c)   by the insertion of the following subsections after subsection (2):

"(2A)   Where the surrender of an interest in immovable goods is chargeable to tax, and those goods have not been developed since the date of creation of that interest (hereafter referred to in this subsection as a 'surrendered interest'), and the person to whom the surrendered interest was surrendered subsequently disposes, as regards the whole or any part of those goods, of an interest or of an interest which derives therefrom on a date before the date on which the surrendered interest would, but for its surrender, have expired, then that disposal shall be deemed to be a supply of immovable goods, for the purposes of this Act, and where the interest (hereafter referred to in this section as a 'subsequent interest') disposed of is for a period which extends beyond the date on which the surrendered interest would, but for its surrender, have expired, the disposal of that subsequent interest shall be treated, for the purposes of this Act, as if it were the disposal of an interest for the period equal to the interval between the date of the disposal of the subsequent interest and the date on which the surrendered interest would, but for its surrender, have expired (a period hereafter referred to in this section as an 'interval'), and where such interval is for a period of less than ten years, that disposal shall be treated as a supply of immovable goods to which subsection (6) applies:

Provided that the person, who disposes of a subsequent interest in which the interval is for a period of less than ten years, may opt, subject to and in accordance with regulations, if any, to have that disposal treated as a supply of immovable goods to which subsection (6) does not apply.

(2B)   Where a person disposes of a subsequent interest in such circumstances that such person retains the reversion on the interest disposed of, then-

(a)   if the subsequent interest expires on or after the date on which the surrendered interest which enabled that person to dispose of a subsequent interest (hereafter referred to in this subsection 'as 'the surrendered interest') would, but for its surrender, have expired, the provisions of subsection (4) shall not apply to that reversion;

(b)   if the subsequent interest expires prior to the date on which the surrendered interest would, but for its surrender, have expired, the provisions of subsection (4) shall apply to that reversion and that reversion shall be deemed for the purposes of subsection (4) to be for the period between the date of expiry of the subsequent interest and the date on which the surrendered interest would, but for its surrender, have expired.

(2C) Where the surrender of an interest in immovable goods is chargeable to tax, and those goods have not been developed since that interest was created and the person to whom the interest that was surrendered surrenders possession of those goods or any part thereof, on a date before the date on which the interest that was surrendered would, but for its surrender, have expired, in such circumstances that that surrender of possession does not constitute a supply of goods, that surrender of possession shall be deemed for the purposes of section 3(1)(f), to be an appropriation of the goods or of the part thereof, as the case may be, for a purpose other than the purpose of that person's business except where such surrender of possession is made-

(a) in accordance with an agreement for the leasing or letting of those goods where the person surrendering possession is chargeable to tax in respect of the rent or other payment under the agreement, or

(b) in connection with a transfer which, in accordance with section 3(5), is deemed, for the purposes of this Act, not to be a supply.",

and

(d) by the insertion of the following subsection after subsection (7):

"(8) Where tax is chargeable in relation to a supply of immovable goods which is a surrender of an interest in immovable goods or an assignment of an interest in immovable goods to-

(a) a taxable person,

(b) a Department of State or a local authority, or

(c) a person supplying goods of a kind referred to in paragraph (a) of the definition of 'exempted activity' in section 1 or services of a kind referred to in paragraphs (i), (iv), (ix), (xi), (xia), (xiii) and (xiv) of the First Schedule, in the course or furtherance of business, then, for the purposes of this Act, the person to whom the goods are supplied shall be deemed to supply those goods in the course or furtherance of business and shall be liable to pay the said tax and in that case the person who makes that surrender or assignment shall be deemed not to supply the goods:

Provided that where a Department of State or a local authority is deemed to make a supply under this subsection, an order under subsection (2A)(a) of section 8 shall be deemed to have been made in respect of that supply.".

(With effect from 26 March 1997)

Finance Act 1998

106. Section 4 of the Principal Act is hereby amended by the insertion of the following subsections after subsection (8) (inserted by the Act of 1997):

"(9)   Where a disposal of an interest in immovable goods is chargeable to tax and where those goods have not been developed since the date of the disposal of that interest (hereafter referred to in this subsection as 'the taxable interest') any disposal of an interest in those goods after that date by a person other than the person who acquired the taxable interest shall, for the purposes of this Act, be deemed to be a supply of immovable goods to which subsection (6) applies.

(10)   (a)   Where a disposal of an interest in immovable goods is chargeable to tax and the person who acquires that interest is obliged to pay rent to another person (hereafter referred to in this subsection as 'the landlord') under the terms and conditions laid down in respect of that interest, the landlord-

(i)   shall, notwithstanding the provisions of section 8, be deemed not to be a taxable person in respect of transactions in relation to those immovable goods other than-

(I)   supplies of those immovable goods on which tax is chargeable in accordance with the provisions of this section, or

(II)   supplies of other goods or services effected for consideration by the landlord, or

(III)   post-letting expenses in respect of that interest,

          (ii)   shall not be entitled to deduct tax in respect of transactions in relation to those immovable goods other than-

               (I)   supplies of those immovable goods on which tax is chargeable in accordance with the provisions of this section other than subsection (4), or

               (II)   supplies of other goods or services effected for consideration by the landlord, or

               (III)   post-letting expenses in respect of that interest,

          (iii)   shall be deemed, where that landlord is not the person who made the disposal of the interest, to be a taxable person in respect of post-letting expenses in relation to that interest and shall in relation to those post-letting expenses be entitled to deduct tax, in accordance with section 12, as if those post-letting expenses were for the purposes of the landlord's taxable supplies.

    (b)   For the purposes of this subsection post-letting expenses in relation to an interest in immovable goods are expenses which the landlord incurs-

          (i)   in carrying out services which the landlord is obliged to carry out under the terms and conditions of the written contract entered into on the disposal of the interest which was chargeable to tax but does not include transactions the obligation to perform which is not reflected in the consideration on which tax was charged on the disposal of that interest, or

          (ii)   which directly relate to the collection of rent arising under the contract referred to in subparagraph (i), or

          (iii)   which directly relate to a review of rent where the terms and conditions of the contract referred to in subparagraph (i) provide for such a review, or

          (iv)   which directly relate to the exercise of an option to extend the interest or to exercise a break-clause in relation to that interest where the terms and conditions of the contract referred to in subparagraph (i) provide for such an option or such a break-clause, but do not include any expenses relating to goods or services of the type specified in section 12(3).".

(With effect from 27 March 1998)

Finance Act 2002

99. Section 4 of the Principal Act is amended by the insertion of the following
subsection after subsection (3) —

"(3A) (a) Where a person having an interest in immovable goods to
which this section applies surrenders possession of those
goods or of any part of them by means of a disposal of that
interest or of an interest which derives from that interest,
and where the value of the interest being disposed of is
less than its economic value then for the purposes of this
Act such disposal —

(i) shall be deemed not to be a supply of immovable
goods for the purposes of subsection (2), but

(ii) shall be deemed to be a letting of immovable goods
to which paragraph (iv) of the First Schedule
applies.

(b) This subsection does not apply to the disposal of a
freehold interest.

(c) Where a person establishes to the satisfaction of the
Revenue Commissioners that the value of an interest in
immovable goods being disposed of by such person is
less than the economic value of those immovable goods
because of an unforeseen change in market conditions
affecting the value of that interest since such person
acquired and developed those goods, then the Revenue
Commissioners may determine that that disposal be
treated as a supply of immovable goods for the purposes
of subsection (2).

(d) For the purposes of this subsection —

'**economic value**', in relation to an interest in immovable
goods being disposed of, means the amount on which tax
was chargeable to the person disposing of that interest in
respect of that person's acquisition of that interest and in
respect of any development of those immovable goods
by or on behalf of that person since that acquisition;
but if —

(i) there was no development of those immovable
goods by or on behalf of that person since that
person's acquisition of that interest, and

(ii) that person disposes, including by way of surrender
or assignment, of an interest (in this subsection
referred to as a 'lesser interest') which is derived
from the interest which that person acquired (in
this subsection referred to as a 'greater interest'),
and

(iii) the lesser interest is an interest of not more than 35 years,

then the economic value of the lesser interest shall be deemed to be the amount calculated in accordance with the following formula:

$$E \times \frac{N1}{N2}$$

where –

E   is the economic value of the greater interest,

N1 is the number of full years in the lesser interest, and

N2 is the number of full years in the greater interest, but if the number of full years in the greater interest exceeds 35 or if the greater interest is a freehold interest then N2 shall be deemed to be equal to 35,

but where-

(I) the disposal of the lesser interest is not a disposal by way of surrender or assignment, and

(II) the amount so calculated is less than 75 per cent of the economic value of the greater interest,

then the economic value of the lesser interest shall be deemed to be 75 per cent of the economic value of the greater interest;

'**the value of an interest being disposed of**' means the amount on which tax would be chargeable in accordance with section 10 if that disposal were deemed to be a supply of immovable goods in accordance with subsection (2).".

(With effect from 25 March 2002)

Finance Act 2003

114. Section 4 of the Principal Act is amended in subsection (3A)(d) –

(a)   by substituting "the total amount on which tax was chargeable" for "the amount on which tax was chargeable", and

(b)   by substituting "in respect of or in relation to" for "in respect of" in both places where it occurs.

(With effect from 28 March 2003)

Finance Act 2004

57. Section 4 of the Principal Act is amended by substituting the following for subsection (6) —

"(6)   Notwithstanding anything in this section or in section 2 tax shall not be charged on the supply of immovable goods —

(a)   in relation to which a right in favour of the person making the supply to a deduction under section 12 in respect of any tax borne or paid on the supply or development of the goods did not arise and would not, apart from section 3(5)(b)(iii), have arisen, or

(b)   which had been occupied before the specified day and had not been developed between that date and the date of the supply,

other than a supply of immovable goods to which the provisions of subsection (5) apply.".

(With effect from 4 December 2003)

Finance Act 2005

100. (1)   Section 4 of the Principal Act is amended-

*(a)   in subsection (3)(a), by substituting "Subject to paragraphs (aa) and (b)" for "Subject to paragraph (b)",

*(b)   by inserting the following after paragraph (a) of subsection (3):

"(aa)   Where a person having an interest in immovable goods to which this section applies surrenders possession of those goods or of any part thereof in such circumstances that the surrender does not constitute a supply of the goods for the purposes of subsection (2), the provisions of paragraph (a) shall not apply when this paragraph and paragraph (ab) take effect pursuant to section 100(2) of the Finance Act 2005.

(ab)   Subject to paragraph (b), where a person having an interest in immovable goods to which this section applies surrenders possession of those goods or any part thereof in such circumstances that the surrender does not constitute a supply of the goods for the purposes of subsection (2), that person shall be liable for an amount, in this paragraph referred to as a deductibility adjustment, which shall be payable as if it were tax due by that person in accordance with section 19 for the taxable period in which the surrender occurred, and that deductibility adjustment shall be calculated in accordance with the following formula:

$$\frac{T \times (Y-N)}{Y}$$

where-

T is the amount of tax which the person who surrenders possession of the goods was entitled to deduct in accordance with section 12 in respect of that person's acquisition of the interest in and development of the goods the possession of which is being surrendered,

Y is 20 or, if the interest when it was acquired by the person who surrenders possession of the goods was for a period of less than 20 years, the number of full years in that interest, and

N is the number of full years since that person acquired the interest in the immovable goods being surrendered or, if the goods were developed since that interest was acquired, the number of full years since the most recent development:

but if that N is greater than that Y, such deductibility adjustment shall be deemed to be nil.",

(c) by substituting the following for subsection (6) inserted by the Act of 2004:

"(6) (a) Tax shall not be charged on the supply of immovable goods-

(i) which were used in such circumstances so that the person making the supply had no right to deduction under section 12 in relation to tax borne or paid on the acquisition or development of those goods, or

(ii) which have been occupied before the specified day and had not been developed between that date and the date of the supply.

(b) Paragraph (a) does not apply to a supply of immovable goods, being goods-

(i)   to which subsection 5 applies, or

(ii)   which were acquired by the person making the supply as a result of a transfer in accordance with section 3(5)(b)(iii) and if tax had been chargeable on such transfer the person making the supply would have had a right to deduction under section 12 in relation to such tax.",

(d)   by substituting the following for subsection (8) (inserted by the Finance Act 1997), and subsection (9) (inserted by the Finance Act 1998):

"(8) (a)   Where tax is chargeable in relation to a supply of immovable goods which is a surrender of an interest in immovable goods or an assignment of an interest in immovable goods to-

(i)   a taxable person,

(ii)   a Department of State or a local authority, or

(iii)   a person who supplies immovable goods of a kind referred to in paragraph (a) of the definition of 'exempted activity' in section 1 or services of a kind referred to in paragraphs (i), (iv), (ix), (xi), (xia), (xiii) and (xiv) of the First Schedule, in the course or furtherance of business,

then, the person to whom those goods are supplied shall be accountable for and liable to pay the tax chargeable on that supply and the said tax shall be payable as if it were tax due by that person in accordance with section 19 for the taxable period within which the supply to the person took place and for these purposes the person to whom the goods are supplied shall be a taxable person and the person who made the surrender or assignment shall not be accountable for or liable to pay the said tax.

(b)   Notwithstanding subsection (2A)(a) of section 8, if the supply referred to in paragraph (a) is to a Department of State or a local authority, that Department of State or local authority shall be accountable for and liable to pay the tax referred to in that paragraph.

(c)　(i)　A surrender or assignment of immovable goods referred to in paragraph (a) shall be treated as a supply of goods made by the person to whom the goods are supplied.

(ii)　Upon the surrender or assignment of immovable goods referred to in subparagraph (i), the person who makes the surrender or assignment shall issue a document to the person to whom the surrender or assignment is made indicating the value of the interest being surrendered or assigned and the amount of tax chargeable on that surrender or assignment.

(iii)　For the purposes of section 12, that section shall apply as if this paragraph had not been enacted.

(9)　(a)　Where an interest in immovable goods is created in such circumstances that a reversion on that interest (hereafter referred to in this subsection as a 'reversionary interest') is created and retained, then any subsequent disposal to another person of that reversionary interest or of an interest derived entirely therefrom shall be deemed to be a supply of immovable goods to which subsection (6) applies, provided that, since the date the first-mentioned interest was created, those goods have not been developed by, on behalf of, or to the benefit of, the person making such subsequent disposal: but the provisions of this subsection shall not be construed as applying to a disposal of an interest which includes an interval.

(b)　The Revenue Commissioners may make regulations specifying the circumstances or conditions under which development work on immovable goods is not treated, for the purposes of this subsection, as being on behalf of or to the benefit of a person.".

(2)   Paragraphs (a) and (b) of subsection (1) shall take effect as on and from such day as the Minister for Finance may, by order, appoint.

(With effect from 25 March 2005 except * with effect from 1 May 2005)

Finance Act 2008

*86. Section 4 of the Principal Act is amended by inserting the following after subsection (10):

"(11)   Subject to section 4C the other provisions of this section, apart from subsections (9) and (10), shall not apply as regards—

(a)   a disposal of an interest in immovable goods, or

(b)   a surrender of possession of immovable goods,

which occurs after 1 July 2008. Subsection (9) shall apply only as respects a reversionary interest created prior to 1 July 2008. Subsection (10) shall apply only as respects an interest which is disposed of prior to 1 July 2008.".

109. With effect from 1 July 2008 in each provision of the Principal Act specified in the first column of Schedule 4 for the words set out in the second column of that Schedule at that entry (in each place where those words occur in the provision concerned) there is substituted the words set out at the corresponding entry in the third column of that Schedule.

Schedule 4
Miscellaneous Amendments Relating to the Amendment of the Definition of Taxable Person

Amendments to Value-Added Tax Act 1972

Provision of Value-Added Tax Act 1972	Words to be replaced	Words to be inserted
Section 4(8)	a taxable person	an accountable person
Section 4(10)	a taxable person	an accountable person

(With effect from 1 July 2008 except * with effect from 13 March 2008)

Finance (No. 2) Act 2008

99. The enactments specified in Schedule 6—

(a)   are amended to the extent and in the manner specified in paragraphs 1 to 6 of that Schedule, and

(b)   apply and come into operation in accordance with paragraph 7 of that Schedule.

SCHEDULE 6

Miscellaneous Technical Amendments in Relation to Tax

4.   The Value-Added Tax Act 1972 is amended –

(b)   in section 4(8)(c)(ii) by inserting "This subparagraph shall not apply where the person who makes the surrender or assignment is obliged to issue a document in accordance with section 4C(8)(a) to the person to whom that surrender or assignment is made." After "assignment.",

(With effect from 24 December 2008)

Section 4A

Finance Act 1994

Person liable to pay tax in relation to certain supplies of immovable goods

93.   The Principal Act is hereby amended by the insertion of the following section after section 4:

"4A.   (1)   Subject to the provisions of subsection (3), where tax is chargeable in respect of the letting of immovable goods which is deemed to be a supply of goods in accordance with section 4 and the lessee would, but for the operation of this section, have been entitled to claim a deduction under section 12(1)(a)(i) for all the said tax borne in relation to that supply, the lessor shall not be liable to pay the said tax and, in that case, the lessee shall be liable to pay the said tax as if the lessee had supplied the goods in the course or furtherance of business.

(2)   Where, in relation to a supply, the lessor and the lessee wish the provisions of subsection (1) to apply they shall-

(a)   complete such application form as may be provided by the Revenue Commissioners for that purpose,

(b)   certify the particulars shown on such form to be correct, and

(c)   submit to the Revenue Commissioners the completed and certified application form, together with such further information in support of the application as may be requested by the said Commissioners.

(3)   Where, in relation to a supply of goods referred to in subsection (1), the lessor and lessee have furnished the particulars referred to in subsection (2), the Revenue Commissioners shall, where they are satisfied that it is in order to apply the provisions in subsection (1) in relation to that supply, notify the lessor and the lessee by notice in writing that the provisions of subsection (1) are to be applied in relation to that supply.

(4)   Where the provisions of subsection (1) apply in relation to a supply, the invoice issued by the lessor in accordance with section 17 shall show the following endorsement in lieu of the amount of tax chargeable:

'In accordance with section 4A of the Value-Added Tax Act, 1972, the lessee is liable for the value-added tax of £X.',

and, in that endorsement, the lessor shall substitute the amount of tax chargeable in respect of that supply of goods for '£X'.

(5)   Every notification received by a taxable person, which has been issued to that person by the Revenue Commissioners in accordance with subsection (3), shall be part of the records which that person is required to keep in accordance with section 16.

(6)   For the purposes of this section, and subject to the direction and control of the Revenue Commissioners, any power, function or duty conferred or imposed on them may be exercised or performed on their behalf by an officer of the Revenue Commissioners.

(7)   In this section-

'**lessee**' means the person who receives the goods referred to in subsection (1);

'**lessor**' means the person who supplies the goods referred to in subsection (1).".

(With effect from 7 July 1994)

Finance Act 2001

240. (1)   (a)   Subject to subsection (2), in each provision specified in column (1) of Schedule 5 for the words or amount set out in column (2) of that Schedule at that entry there shall be substituted the words or amount set out at the corresponding entry in column (3) of that Schedule.

(b)   Where words are or an amount is mentioned more than once in a provision specified in column (1) of Schedule 5, then the substitution provided for by paragraph (a) shall apply as respects those words or that amount to each mention of those words or that amount in that provision.

SCHEDULE 5

PART 4

Value-Added Tax and related matters

Enactment amended (1)	Amount or words to be replaced (2)	Amount or words to be inserted (3)
Value-Added Tax Act, 1972 (No. 22 of 1972) (as amended): section 4A(4)	£X	€X

Finance Act 2008

87.   With effect from 1 July 2008 section 4A of the Principal Act is repealed.

(With effect from 1 July 2008)

Section 4B

Finance Act 2008

Supplies of immovable goods

88.   The Principal Act is amended with effect from 1 July 2008 by inserting the following sections before section 5—

"Supplies of immovable goods.

4B.   (1)   In this section—

'**completed**', in respect of immovable goods, means that the development of those goods has reached the state, apart from only such finishing or fitting work that would normally be carried out by or on behalf of the person who will use them, where those goods can effectively be used for purposes for which those goods were designed, and the utility services required for those purposes are connected to those goods;

'**occupied**', in respect of immovable goods, means—

(a)   occupied and fully in use following completion where that use is one for which planning permission for the development of those goods was granted, and

(b)   where those goods are let, occupied and fully in such use by the tenant.

(2)   Subject to subsections (3), (5) and (7), tax is not chargeable on the supply of immovable goods—

(a)   that have not been developed,

(b)   being completed immovable goods, the most recent completion of which occurred more than 5 years prior to that supply, and those goods have not been developed within that 5 year period,

(c)   being completed immovable goods that have not been developed since the most recent completion of those goods, where that supply—

(i)   occurs after the immovable goods have been occupied for an aggregate of at least 24 months following the most recent completion of those goods, and

(ii)   takes place after a previous supply of those goods on which tax was chargeable and that previous supply—

(I)   took place after the most recent completion of those goods, and

(II)   was a transaction between taxable persons who were not connected within the meaning of section 7A,

    (d)   being a building that was completed more than 5 years prior to that supply and on which development was carried out in the 5 years prior to that supply where —

        (i)   such development did not and was not intended to adapt the building for a materially altered use, and

        (ii)   the cost of such development did not exceed 25 per cent of the consideration for that supply,

or

    (e)   being a building that was completed within the 5 years prior to that supply where —

        (i)   the building had been occupied for an aggregate of at least 24 months following that completion,

        (ii)   that supply takes place after a previous supply of the building on which tax was chargeable and that previous supply —

            (I)   took place after that completion of the building, and

            (II)   was a transaction between taxable persons who were not connected within the meaning of section 7A,

and

        (iii)   if any development of that building occurred after that completion —

            (I)   such development did not and was not intended to adapt the building for a materially altered use, and

            (II)   the cost of such development did not exceed 25 per cent of the consideration for that supply.

(3)   Where a person supplies immovable goods to another person and in connection with that supply a taxable person enters into an agreement with that other person or with a person connected with that other person to carry out a development in relation to those immovable goods, then —

    (a)   the person who supplies the goods shall, in relation to that supply, be deemed to be a taxable person,

    (b)   the supply of the said immovable goods shall be deemed to be a supply of those goods to which section 2 applies, and

    (c)   subsection (2) does not apply to that supply.

(4)   Section 8(3) does not apply in relation to a person who makes a supply of immovable goods.

(5)   Where a taxable person supplies immovable goods to another taxable person in circumstances where that supply would otherwise be exempt in accordance with subsection (2) then tax shall, notwithstanding subsection (2), be chargeable on that supply, where the supplier and the taxable person to whom the supply is made enter an agreement in writing to opt to have tax chargeable on that supply (in this Act referred to as a 'joint option for taxation').

(6)   Where a joint option for taxation is exercised in accordance with subsection (5) then –

    (a)   the person to whom the supply is made shall, in relation to that supply, be an accountable person and shall be liable to pay the tax chargeable on that supply as if that person supplied those goods, and

    (b)   the person who made the supply shall not be accountable for or liable to pay the said tax.

(7)   (a)   Where a taxable person supplies immovable goods to another person in circumstances where that supply would otherwise be exempt in accordance with subsection (2), tax shall, notwithstanding subsection (2), be chargeable on that supply where –

        (i)   the immovable goods are buildings designed as or capable of being used as a dwelling,

        (ii)   the person who makes that supply is a person who developed the immovable goods in the course of a business of developing immovable goods or a person connected with that person, within the meaning of section 7A, and

        (iii) the person who developed those immovable goods was entitled to a deduction under section 12 for tax chargeable to that person in respect of that person's acquisition or development of those immovable goods.

    (b)   In the case of a building to which this subsection would apply if the building were supplied by the taxable person at any time during the capital goods scheme adjustment period for that building –

        (i)   section 12E(6) shall not apply, and

        (ii)   notwithstanding section 12E(4) the proportion of total tax incurred that is deductible by that person shall be treated as the initial interval proportion of deductible use.

(With effect from 1 July 2008)

Finance (No. 2) Act 2008

99. The enactments specified in Schedule 6 —

(a) are amended to the extent and in the manner specified in paragraphs 1 to 6 of that Schedule, and

(b) apply and come into operation in accordance with paragraph 7 of that Schedule.

SCHEDULE 6

Miscellaneous Technical Amendments in Relation to Tax

4. The Value-Added Tax Act 1972 is amended —

(c) in section 4B —

(i) in subsection (2) —

(I) by inserting "and section 4C(6)(a)" after "Subject to subsections (3), (5) and (7)",

(II) in paragraph (a), by inserting "within 20 years prior to that supply" after "developed",

(III) in paragraph (c)(ii)(II) by deleting "taxable", and

(IV) in paragraph (e)(ii)(II) by deleting "taxable", and

(ii) in subsection (5) —

(I) by inserting ", subsection (2) or (6)(b) of section 4C" after "subsection (2)" in both places where it occurs, and

(II) by inserting "(no later than the fifteenth day of the month following the month in which that supply occurs)" after "enter an agreement in writing",

(With effect from 24 December 2008)

Section 4C

Finance Act 2008

Transitional measures for supplies of immovable goods.

88. The Principal Act is amended with effect from 1 July 2008 by inserting the following sections before section 5—

4C. (1)   This section applies to—

      (a)   immovable goods which are acquired or developed by a taxable person prior to 1 July 2008 and have not been disposed of by that taxable person prior to that date, until such time as those goods have been disposed of by that taxable person on or after that date, and

      (b)   an interest in immovable goods within the meaning of section 4 other than a freehold interest or a freehold equivalent interest, created by a taxable person prior to 1 July 2008 and held by a taxable person on 1 July 2008.

    (2)   In the case of a supply of immovable goods to which subsection (1)(a) applies, being completed immovable goods within the meaning of section 4B,—

      (a)   where the person supplying those goods had no right to deduction under section 12 in relation to the tax chargeable on the acquisition or development of those goods prior to 1 July 2008, and

      (b)   if any subsequent development of those immovable goods occurs on or after 1 July 2008—

          (i)   that development does not and is not intended to adapt the immovable goods for a materially altered use, and

          (ii)   the cost of that development does not exceed 25 per cent of the consideration for that supply,

          then, subject to section 4B(3), that supply is not chargeable to tax but a joint option for taxation may be exercised in respect of that supply in accordance with section 4B(5) and that tax is payable in accordance with section 4B(6).

    (3)   Where a person referred to in subsection (1)—

      (a)   acquired, developed or has an interest in immovable goods to which this section applies,

      (b)   was entitled to deduct tax, in accordance with section 12 on that person's acquisition or development of those goods, and

      (c)   creates a letting of those immovable goods to which paragraph (iv) of the First Schedule applies, then, that person shall calculate an amount in accordance with the formula in section 4(3)(ab) and that amount shall be payable as if it were tax due by that person in accordance with section 19 for the taxable period in which that letting takes place.

(4)   An assignment or surrender of an interest in immovable goods to which subsection (1)(b) applies is deemed to be a supply of immovable goods for the purposes of this Act for a period of 20 years from the creation of the interest or the most recent assignment or surrender of that interest before 1 July 2008, whichever is the later.

(5)   If a person makes a supply of immovable goods to which this section applies and tax is chargeable on that supply and that person was not entitled to deduct all the tax charged to that person on the acquisition or development of those immovable goods that person shall be entitled to make the appropriate adjustment that would apply under section 12E(7)(a) as if the capital goods scheme applied to that transaction.

(6)   In the case of an assignment or surrender of an interest in immovable goods referred to in subsection (4) —

    (a)   tax shall be chargeable if the person who makes the assignment or surrender was entitled to deduct in accordance with section 12 any of the tax chargeable on the acquisition of that interest, or the development of those immovable goods, and

    (b)   tax shall not be chargeable where the person who makes the assignment or surrender had no right to deduction under section 12 on the acquisition of that interest or the development of those immovable goods, but a joint option for taxation of that assignment or surrender may be exercised.

(7)   (a)   Notwithstanding section 10, the amount on which tax is chargeable on a taxable assignment or surrender to which subsection (6) applies shall be the amount calculated in accordance with the formula in paragraph (b) divided by the rate as specified in section 11(1)(d) expressed in decimal form.

    (b)   The amount of tax due and payable in respect of a taxable assignment or surrender to which subsection (6) applies is an amount calculated in accordance with the following formula:

$$\frac{T \times N}{Y}$$

where —

T   is the total tax incurred referred to in subsection (11)(d),

N   is the number of full intervals plus one, that remain in the adjustment period referred to in subsection (11)(c), at the time of the assignment or surrender,

Y   is the total number of intervals in that adjustment period for the person making the assignment or surrender,

and section 4(8) shall apply to that tax.

(8)   (a)   Where an interest in immovable goods referred to in subsection (6) is assigned or surrendered during the adjustment period and tax is payable in respect of that assignment or surrender, then the person who makes the assignment or surrender shall issue a document to the person to whom the interest is being assigned or surrendered containing the following information:

    (i)   the amount of tax due and payable on that assignment or surrender, and

    (ii)   the number of intervals remaining in the adjustment period.

    (b)   Where paragraph (a) applies, the person to whom the interest is assigned or surrendered shall be a capital goods owner for the purpose of section 12E in respect of the capital good being assigned or surrendered, and shall be subject to the provisions of that section and for this purpose —

    (i)   the adjustment period shall be the period referred to in subsection (11)(c) as correctly specified on the document referred to in paragraph (a),

    (ii)   the total tax incurred shall be the amount of tax referred to in subsection (11)(d) as correctly specified in the document referred to in paragraph (a), and

    (iii)   the initial interval shall be a period of 12 months beginning on the date on which the assignment or surrender occurs.

(9)   (a)   Where a person cancels an election to be an accountable person in accordance with section 8(5A) then, in respect of the immovable goods which were used in supplying the services for which that person made that election, section 12E does not apply if those immovable goods are held by that person on 1 July 2008 and are not further developed after that date.

    (b)   Section 8(5A) does not apply to immovable goods acquired or developed on or after 1 July 2008.

(10)   In the application of section 12E to immovable goods and interests in immovable goods to which this section applies, subsections (4), (5) and (6) of that section shall be disregarded in respect of the person who owns those immovable goods or holds an interest in those immovable goods on 1 July 2008.

(11)   For the purposes of applying section 12E to immovable goods, or interests in immovable goods to which this section applies—

(a)   any interest in immovable goods to which this section applies shall be treated as a capital good,

(b)   any person who has an interest in immovable goods to which this section applies shall be treated as a capital goods owner, but shall not be so treated to the extent that the person has a reversionary interest in those immovable goods if those goods were not developed, by, on behalf of, or to the benefit of that person,

(c)   the period to be treated as the adjustment period in respect of immovable goods to which this section applies is—

(i)   in the case of the acquisition of the freehold interest or freehold equivalent interest in those immovable goods, 20 years from the date of that acquisition,

(ii)   in the case of the creation of an interest in those immovable goods, 20 years or, if the interest when it was created was for a period of less than 20 years, the number of full years in that interest when created, whichever is the shorter, or

(iii)   in the case of the assignment or surrender of an interest in immovable goods the period remaining in that interest at the time of the assignment or surrender of that interest or 20 years, whichever is the shorter,

but where the immovable goods have been developed since the acquisition of those immovable goods or the creation of that interest, 20 years from the date of the most recent development of those goods,

(d)   the amount of tax charged, or the amount of tax that would have been chargeable but for the application of sections 3(5)(b)(iii) or 13A, to the person treated as the capital goods owner on the acquisition of, or the most recent development of, the capital goods shall be treated as the total tax incurred,

(e)   the total tax incurred divided by the number of years in the adjustment period referred to in paragraph (c) shall be treated as the base tax amount,

(f)   each year in the adjustment period   referred to in paragraph (c) shall be treated as an interval,

(g)   the first 12 months of the adjustment period referred to in paragraph (c) shall be treated as the initial interval,

(h)   the second year of the adjustment period referred to in paragraph (c) shall be treated as the second interval,

(i)   each year following the second year in the adjustment period referred to in paragraph (c) shall be treated as a subsequent interval,

(j)   the amount which shall be treated as the total reviewed deductible amount shall be the amount of the total tax incurred as provided for in paragraph (d) less —

    (i)   any amount of the total tax incurred which was charged to the person treated as the capital goods owner but which that owner was not entitled to deduct in accordance with section 12,

    (ii)   any amount accounted for in accordance with section 12D(4) by the person treated as the capital goods owner in respect of a transfer of the goods to that owner prior to 1 July 2008, and

    (iii)   any tax payable in accordance with subsection (3) or section 4(3)(ab) by the person treated as the capital goods owner,

(k)   the amount referred to in paragraph (d) less the amount referred to in paragraph (j) shall be treated as the non-deductible amount,

and for the purposes of applying paragraphs (f), (h) and (i) 'year' means each 12 month period in the adjustment period, the first of which begins on the first day of the initial interval referred to in paragraph (g).

(12)   Where a taxable person acquires immovable goods on or after 1 July 2007, then, notwithstanding subsection (10), section 12E(4) shall apply and, notwithstanding subsection (11)(j), the total reviewed deductible amount shall have the meaning assigned to it by section 12E. However this subsection does not apply where a taxable person has made an adjustment in accordance with section 12(4)(f) in respect of those goods.".

(With effect from 1 July 2008)

Finance (No. 2) Act 2008

99.   The enactments specified in Schedule 6 —

(a)   are amended to the extent and in the manner specified in paragraphs 1 to 6 of that Schedule, and

(b)   apply and come into operation in accordance with paragraph 7 of that Schedule.

SCHEDULE 6

Miscellaneous Technical Amendments in Relation to Tax

4.   The Value-Added Tax Act 1972 is amended—

(d)   in section 4C—

(i)   in subsection (1)—

(I)   in paragraph (a) by inserting ", being completed immovable goods before 1 July 2008," after "prior to 1 July 2008", and

(II)   in paragraph (b)—

(A)   by substituting "section 4," for "section 4", and

(B)   by inserting "and the reversionary interest, within the meaning of section 4(9), on that interest until that interest is surrendered after 1 July 2008" after "held by a taxable person on 1 July 2008",

(ii)   by inserting the following after subsection (1):

"(1A) Where an interest to which subsection (1)(b) applies is surrendered, then, for the purposes of the application of section 12E in respect of the immovable goods concerned—

(a)   the total tax incurred shall include the amount of tax chargeable on the surrender in accordance with subsection (7) and shall not include tax incurred prior to the creation of the surrendered interest, and

(b)   the adjustment period shall consist of the number of intervals specified in subsection (11)(c)(iv) and the initial interval shall begin on the date of that surrender.",

(iii)   in subsection (3)(c) by substituting "makes" for "creates",

(iv)   in subsection (4) by substituting "or the most recent assignment" for "or the most recent assignment or surrender",

(v)   in subsection (7)(b) by inserting "except for the amount of tax charged in respect of any development by the person who makes the assignment or surrender following the acquisition of this interest" after "subsection (11)(d)", (vi)　in subsection (8)(a) –

　　(I)　by inserting "to a taxable person" after "is assigned or surrendered", and

　　(II)　in subparagraph (ii) by inserting "as determined in accordance with subsection (11)(c)(iv)" after "adjustment period",

(vii)　by deleting paragraph (b) of subsection (9),

(viii)　in subsection (10) by inserting "but if that person develops the immovable goods and that development is a refurbishment, within the meaning of section 12E, that is completed on or after 1 July 2008, then these subsections shall not be disregarded in respect of that refurbishment" after "1 July 2008", and

(ix)　in subsection (11) –

　　(I)　by substituting "to immovable goods" for "to immovable goods,",

　　(II)　in paragraph (b) by substituting "developed" for "developed,",

　　(III)　in paragraph (c) –

　　　　(A)　by inserting "or interests in immovable goods" after "in respect of immovable goods",

　　　　(B)　in subparagraph (ii) by substituting "shorter," for "shorter, or",

　　　　(C)　in subparagraph (iii) by inserting "prior to 1 July 2008," after "or surrender of an interest in immovable goods" and by substituting "shorter, or" for "shorter,", and

　　　　(D)　by inserting the following after subparagraph (iii) –

　　　　　　"(iv)　in the case of –

　　　　　　　　(I)　the surrender or first assignment of an interest in immovable goods on or after 1 July 2008, the number of full years remaining in the adjustment period as determined in accordance with subparagraphs (ii) and (iii), plus one, or

　　　　　　　　(II)　the second or subsequent assignment of an interest in immovable goods after

1 July 2008, the number of full intervals remaining in the adjustment period as determined in accordance with clause (I), plus one,

and this number shall thereafter be the number of intervals remaining in the adjustment period,",

(IV)   in paragraph (d) by deleting "the most recent",

(V)   in paragraph (e) by substituting "intervals" for "years",

(VI)   in paragraph (h) by inserting ", but in the case of an interest which is assigned or surrendered on or after 1 July 2008, the second interval of the adjustment period shall have the meaning assigned to it by section 12E" after "second interval", and

(A)   in subparagraph (ii) by substituting "2008," for "2008, and",

(B)   in subparagraph (iii) by substituting "in respect of those capital goods in accordance with section 3(1)(e) or 4(3)(a)" for "in accordance with subsection (3) or section 4(3)(ab)" and by substituting "owner, and" for "owner,", and

(C)   by inserting the following after subparagraph (iii) —

"(iv)   where an adjustment of deductibility has been made in respect of the capital good in accordance with subsection (3) or section 4(3)(ab), the amount 'T' in the formula in section 4(3)(ab),",

(With effect from 24 December 2008)

Section 5

Value Added Tax Act 1972
Rendering of services

5.   (1)   In this Act the **"rendering"**, in relation to a service, means the performance or omission of any act or the toleration of any situation, other than the delivery of goods.

(2)   The rendering of a service by a person for the purposes of any business activity in which he engages shall, subject to regulations, be deemed, for the purposes of this Act, to be the rendering of a service in the course of business.

(3)   The place where a service is rendered shall be deemed, for the purposes of this Act, to be the place where the act is performed or the situation is tolerated or, in the case of the omission of an act, the place where the person responsible for the omission resides or is established:

Provided that in the case of a service rendered by a person who, by virtue of section 8(8), is not an accountable person to an unregistered person residing or established within the State, the following provisions shall apply if the service is rendered for the purposes of any business activities of the unregistered person carried on within the State:

(a)   the service shall be deemed to be rendered at the place where the person to whom it is rendered resides or is established, and

(b)   the person to whom the service is rendered shall, in relation the said service, be an accountable person and shall be accountable for and liable to pay the tax charged under section 2(1)(a) in respect of such rendering.

(4)   (a)   A person who satisfies the Revenue Commissioners-

(i)   that he is engaged in business.

(ii)   that by virtue of section 8(8) he is not an accountable person.

(iii)   that he has suffered tax on services rendered to him within the State for the purposes of the said business, and

(iv)   that the said services were not rendered to him in his capacity as agent for or otherwise on behalf of, and were not used by him in the course of rendering services to, another person residing or established within the State who, if the first-mentioned services had been rendered directly to that other person, would not be entitled to a deduction under section 12 in respect of the tax borne or paid in respect of them.

shall, subject to paragraph (b) and section 20, be entitled to be repaid the tax borne on the services.

(b)   The provisions of section 12(3) shall apply in relation to a computation under this section of the amount of tax repayable to a person as if the person were an accountable person and the computation related to a claim for a deduction under the said section 12.

(5)   (a)   Notwithstanding anything in subsection (1), where the value of movable goods supplied under an agreement for the rendering of services exceeds two-thirds of the total consideration under the agreement for the supply of those goods and the rendering of the services, other than transport services, in relation to them, such consideration shall be deemed, for the purposes of this Act, to be referable solely to the delivery of the goods and tax shall be charged at the appropriate rate or rates specified in section 11 on the basis of any apportionment of such total consideration made in accordance with paragraph (b).

(b)   Where goods of different kinds are supplied under an agreement of the kind referred to in paragraph (a), the amount of the consideration referable to the delivery of goods of each kind shall be ascertained for the purpose of that paragraph by apportioning the total consideration in proportion to the value of the goods of each kind supplied under the agreement.

(With effect from 1 November 1972)

Finance Act 1973

79.   Section 5 of the Principal Act is hereby amended-

(a)   by the substitution for subsection (2) of the following subsection :

"(2)   (a)   Services, whether or not rendered for a consideration or for a separate consideration, which, apart from this subsection, would not be regarded as rendered by a person in the course of business, shall, subject to and to the extent provided by regulations, be regarded as rendered by him in the course of business if they are connected with any business activity in which he engages.

(b)   For the purposes of this subsection and section 32, services shall be regarded as connected with a business activity in which a person engages if he provides facilities for, or contributes in whole or part towards the cost of rendering then.",

and

(b)   by the insertion in subsection (5) after paragraph (b) of the following paragraph :

"(c)   This subsection shall not apply to a supply of goods of a kind specified in paragraph (xii) of the Second Schedule.".

90.   The Principal Act is hereby amended as specified in column (3) of the Tenth Schedule to this Act.

TENTH SCHEDULE
AMENDMENT OF ENACTMENTS

Number and Year (1)	Short Title (2)	Amendment (3)
No. 22 of 1972	Value-Added Tax Act, 1972	In section 5(1), "not being a delivery deemed in accordance with section 3(1A) to be a rendering of services", shall be inserted after "goods".

(With effect from 3 September 1973)

Value Added Tax (Amendment) Act 1978
Supply of services

5.   The following section shall be substituted for section 5 of the Principal Act:

"5.   (1)   In this Act '**supply**', in relation to a service, means the performance or omission of any act or the toleration of any situation other than the supply of goods and other than a transaction specified in section 3(5).

(2)   The provision of food and drink, of a kind specified in paragraph (xii) of the Second Schedule, in a form suitable for human consumption without further preparation-

(a)   by means of a vending machine,

(b)   in the course of operating a hotel, restaurant, cafe, refreshment house, canteen, establishment licensed for the sale for consumption on the premises of intoxicating liquor, catering business or similar business, or

(c)   in the course of operating any other business in connection with the carrying on of which facilities are provided for the consumption of the food or drink supplied,

shall be deemed, for the purposes of this Act, to be a supply of services and not a supply of goods.

(3)   Any of the following shall, if so provided by regulations, and in accordance therewith, be deemed, for the purposes

of this Act, to be a supply of services by a person for consideration in the course or furtherance of his business-

(a)   the use of goods forming part of the assets of his business for purposes other than those of his business,

(b)   the supply by him of services for his own private or personal use and the supply by him of services free of charge for the private or personal use of his staff or for any purposes other than those of his business,

(c)   the supply of services for his own private or personal use or that of his staff, for the supply of which he provides materials or facilities or towards the cost of which he contributes in whole or in part,

(d)   the supply by him of services, other than those referred to in the preceding paragraphs of this subsection, for the purposes of his business except where tax on such services, if it were chargeable, would be wholly deductible under section 12.

(4)   The supply of services through a person (in this subsection referred to as the agent) who, while purporting to act on his own behalf, concludes agreements in his own name but on the instructions of and for the account of another person, shall be deemed, for the purposes of this Act, to constitute a supply of the services to and simultaneously by the agent.

(5)   Subject to subsections (6) and (7), the place where a service is supplied shall be deemed, for the purposes of this Act, to be the place where the person supplying the service has his establishment or (if more than one) the establishment of his which is most concerned with the supply or (if he has no establishment) his usual place of residence.

(6)   (a)   The place of supply of services connected with immovable goods, including the services of estate agents, architects and firms providing on-site supervision in relation to such goods, shall be deemed, for the purposes of this Act, to be the place where the goods are situated.

(b)   Transport services shall be deemed, for the purposes of this Act, to be supplied where the transport takes place.

(c)   The following services shall be deemed, for the purposes of this Act, to be supplied where they are physically performed:

    (i)   cultural, artistic, sporting, scientific, educational, entertainment or similar services.

    (ii)   ancillary transport activities such as loading, unloading and handling,

    (iii)   valuation of movable goods,

    (iv)   work on movable goods,

(d)   The place of supply of services consisting of the hiring out of movable goods (other than means of transport) which are exported by the person from whom they are hired from one member State of the Community with a view to their being used in another such member State shall be deemed, for the purposes of this Act, to be the place of utilisation.

(e)   The place of supply of services of any of the descriptions specified in the Fourth Schedule shall be deemed, for the purposes of this Act, to be-

    (i)   in case they are received, otherwise than for a business purpose, by a person whose usual place of residence is situated outside the Community, the place where he usually resides,

    (ii)   in case they are received by a person who has no establishment in the country in which, but for this subparagraph, the services would be deemed to be supplied and are so received for the purposes of any business carried on by him, the place where he has his establishment or (if more than one) the establishment of his at which or for the purposes of which the services are most directly used or to be used or (if he has no establishment anywhere) the place where he usually resides,

    (iii)   in any other case, the place specified in subsection (5) that is appropriate to the circumstances.

(7)   Provision may be made by regulations for varying, in relation to services generally or of a description specified therein, the rules for determining their place of supply,

and for that purpose the Fourth Schedule may be added to or varied.

(8)   The transfer of the goodwill or other intangible assets of a business, in connection with the transfer of the business or part thereof, to another taxable person shall be deemed, for the purposes of this Act, not to be a supply of services.".

(With effect from 1 March 1979)

Finance Act 1982

76.   Section 5 of the Principal Act is hereby amended by the insertion after subsection (4) of the following subsection-

"(4A)   Where services are supplied by a person and the person is not legally entitled to recover consideration in respect of or in relation to such supply but moneys are received in respect of or in relation to such supply, the services in question shall be deemed, for the purposes of this Act, to have been supplied for consideration and the moneys received shall be deemed to be consideration that the person who supplied the services in question became entitled to receive in respect of or in relation to the supply of those services.".

(With effect from 1 September 1982)

Finance Act 1985

42.   Section 5 (inserted by the Act of 1978) of the Principal Act is hereby amended by the deletion in subsection (6) of paragraph (d).

(With effect from 30 May 1985)

Finance Act 1986

81.   Section 5 (inserted by the Act of 1978) of The Principal Act is hereby amended-

(a)   by the insertion after subsection (3) of the following subsection:

"(3A)   Where a person is in receipt of a service, other than a service specified in the Fourth Schedule, for the purposes of his business and the circumstances are such that value-added tax referred to in Community Council Directive No. 77/388/EEC is not payable on the supply or, if it is payable, is, in accordance with the laws of the country in which the supplier has his establishment, repayable to or deductible by the person, that person shall be deemed, for the purposes of this Act, to have himself supplied the service for consideration in the course or furtherance of his business and shall be liable for tax on the supply except where such tax, if it were chargeable, would be wholly deductible under section 12.",

and

(b)   in subsection (6)-

    (i)   by the insertion after paragraph (c) of the following paragraph:

"(d)   In confirmation of the provisions contained in the Value-Added Tax (Place of Supply of Certain Services) Regulations, 1985 (S.I. No. 343 of 1985), which regulations are hereby revoked, the place of supply of services consisting of the hiring out of movable goods by a person established outside the Community shall be deemed to be the place where the movable goods are, or are to be, effectively used.",

and

    (ii)   by the substitution of the following paragraph for paragraph (e):

"(e)   The place of supply of services of any of the descriptions specified in the Fourth Schedule, with the exception of services of the description specified in paragraph (ia) of the said Schedule supplied by a person who has his establishment outside the Community, shall be deemed, for the purposes of this Act, to be-

    (i)   in case they are received, otherwise than for a business purpose, by a person whose usual place of residence is situated outside the Community, the place where he usually resides,

    (ii)   in case they are received, for the purposes of any business carried on by him, by a person-

        (I)   who has his establishment outside the Community and has not also an establishment in the Community, or

        (II)   who has his establishment in the Community but does not have his establishment or, if he has more than one establishment, his principal establishment in the country in which, but for this subparagraph, the services would be deemed to be supplied,

the place where he has his establishment or, if he has more than one establishment, the establishment of his at which or for the purposes of which the services are most directly used or to be used, as the case may be,

(iii)   in case they are received, for the purposes of any business carried on by him, by a person resident in the Community who has no establishment anywhere, the place where he usually resides,

(iv)   in case they are received by a department of State, by a local authority or by a body established by statute, and are supplied-

(I)   by a person who has his establishment outside the Community and has not also an establishment in the Community, or

(II)   by a person who has his establishment in another Member State of the Community, in circumstances in which value-added tax referred to in Community Council Directive No. 77/388/EEC is not payable in that Member State in respect of the supply,

the State,

(v)   in any other case, the place specified in sub-section (5) that is appropriate to the circumstances.".

(With effect from 27 May 1986)

Finance Act 1989

54.   Section 5 (inserted by the Act of 1978) of The Principal Act is hereby amended by the insertion after subsection (4A) (inserted by the Finance Act, 1982) of the following subsection:

"(4B)   Where a person is indemnified under a policy of insurance in respect of any amount payable in respect of services of a barrister or solicitor, those services shall be deemed, for the purposes of this Act, to be supplied to, and received by, the said person.".

(With effect from 1 March 1989)

Finance Act 1990

100. Section 5 (inserted by the Act of 1978) of The Principal Act is hereby amended in subsection (6)-

(a)   by the addition to clause (II) of subparagraph (ii) of paragraph (e) (inserted by the Act of 1986) of "or" after "supplied,", and

(b)   by the insertion after clause (II) of subparagraph (ii) of paragraph (e) (inserted by the Act of 1986) of the following clause:

"(III)   who has an establishment in the State and his principal establishment in the country in which, but for this subparagraph, the services would be deemed to be supplied,".

(With effect from 30 May 1990)

Finance Act 1992

169. Section 5 (inserted by the Act of 1978) of The Principal Act is hereby amended-

(a)   in subsection (3A) (inserted by the Act of 1986) by the substitution of "specified in paragraphs (f) and (g) of subsection (6) or in the Fourth Schedule" for "specified in the Fourth Schedule",

and

(b)   in subsection (6):

(i)   by the substitution of the following paragraph for paragraph (b):

"(b)   Transport services, with the exception of intra-Community transport of goods, shall be deemed, for the purposes of this Act, to be supplied where the transport takes place.",

(ii)   by the substitution of the following subparagraph for subparagraph (ii) of paragraph (c):

"(ii)   ancillary transport activities such as loading, unloading and handling, with the exception of activities ancillary to the intra-Community transport of goods received by a person registered for value-added tax in any Member State,",

and

(iii)   by the insertion of the following paragraphs after paragraph (e) (inserted by the Act of 1986):

"(f)   The place of supply of the following services received by a person registered for value-added tax in a Member State shall be deemed, for the purposes of this Act, to be within the territory of the Member State that so registered the person for value-added tax, that is to say:

(i)   the intra-Community transport of goods,

(ii)   activities ancillary to the intra-Community transport of goods such as loading, unloading and handling,

(iii)   services of an agent acting in the name and on behalf of another person in the arrangement of services other than those specified in paragraph (vii) of the Fourth Schedule.

(g)   The place of supply of the following services supplied to persons other than those specified in paragraph (f) shall be deemed for the purposes of this Act to be-

(i)   the place of departure in the case of-

(I)   the intra-Community transport of goods,

(II)   services of an agent acting in the name and on behalf of another person in the arrangement of intra-Community transport of goods, and

(ii)   the place where they are physically performed in the case of services of an agent acting in the name and on behalf of another person in the arrangement of services other than those specified in subparagraph (i)(II) of this paragraph and paragraph (vii) of the Fourth Schedule.

(h)   In this subsection-

'**intra-Community transport of goods**' means transport where the place of departure and the place of arrival are situated within the territories of two different Member States;

'**the place of departure**' means the place where the transport of goods actually starts, leaving aside distance actually travelled to the place where the goods are;

'**the place of arrival**' means the place where the transport of goods actually ends.".

(With effect from 1 January 1993)

<h2 style="text-align:center">Finance Act 1995</h2>

123. Section 5 (inserted by the Act of 1978) of the Principal Act is hereby amended in subsection (5) by the insertion after "the service" of "has established his business or".

(With effect from 2 June 1995)

<h2 style="text-align:center">Finance Act 1996</h2>

90. Section 5 (inserted by the Act of 1978) of the Principal Act is hereby amended-

(a)   in paragraph (c) of subsection (6)-

     (i)   by the insertion in subparagraph (iii) after "movable goods" of "except where the provisions of subparagraph (iv) of paragraph (f) apply", and

     (ii)   by the insertion in subparagraph (iv) after "movable goods" of ",including contract work, except where the provisions of subparagraph (iv) of paragraph (f) apply",

and

(b)   in paragraph (f) of subsection (6), by the insertion of the following subparagraph after subparagraph (iii):

"(iv)   valuation of or work on movable goods, including contract work, in cases where the goods are dispatched or transported out of the Member State where the valuation or work was physically carried out.".

(With effect from 1 January 1996)

<h2 style="text-align:center">Finance Act 1997</h2>

99. Section 5 of the Principal Act is hereby amended in subsection (6) by the insertion of the following paragraph after paragraph (d):

"(dd)   Notwithstanding the provisions of subparagraph (v) of paragraph (e), where a person supplies a telecommunications service in the course or furtherance of business from outside the Community to a person in the State who is not a person to whom the provisions of subparagraph (ii), (iii) or (iv) of paragraph (e) apply, the place of supply of that service shall be deemed, for the purposes of this Act, to be the State.".

(With effect from 1 July 1997)

<h2 style="text-align:center">Finance Act 1998</h2>

107. Section 5 of the Principal Act is hereby amended-

(a)   in subsection (6)-

     (i)   by the insertion in paragraph (dd) (inserted by the Act of 1997) after "a telecommunications service" of ", or a telephone card as defined in subsection (6A),",

(ii) by the insertion of the following paragraph after paragraph (dd):

"(ddd) The place of supply of a telecommunications service or of a telephone card as defined in subsection (6A) shall be deemed, for the purposes of this Act, to be the State when that service is supplied by a taxable person from an establishment in the State and it is received, otherwise than for a business purpose, by a person whose usual place of residence is situated outside the Community, and it is effectively used and enjoyed in the State.",

(iii) by the insertion in paragraph (e) (inserted by the Finance Act, 1986) after "specified in the Fourth Schedule" of "with the exception of the supply of services referred to in paragraphs (ddd) and (ee) in the circumstances specified in those paragraphs respectively and", and

(iv) by the insertion of the following paragraph after paragraph (e):

"(ee) The place of supply of services of the description specified in paragraph (v) of the Fourth Schedule shall be deemed, for the purposes of this Act, to be the State, when those services are supplied by a person in the course or furtherance of business established in the State and they are received, otherwise than for a business purpose, by a person whose usual place of residence is situated outside the Community, and they are effectively used and enjoyed in the State.",

and

(b) by the insertion of the following subsection after subsection (6):

"(6A) (a) Subject to paragraph (b), where the supply of a telephone card is taxable within the State and that telephone card is subsequently used outside the Community for the purpose of accessing a telecommunications service, the place of supply of that telecommunications service shall be deemed to be outside the Community and the supplier of that telephone card shall be entitled, in the taxable period within which that supplier acquires proof that that telephone card was so used outside the Community, to a reduction of the tax payable by that supplier in respect of the supply of that telephone card, by an amount calculated in accordance with paragraph (c).

(b)   Where the supply of a telephone card is taxable in the State and the person liable for the tax on that supply is a person referred to in section 8(2)(a) who-

   (i) is not entitled to a deduction, in accordance with section 12, of all of the tax chargeable in respect of that supply, or

   (ii) is entitled to a deduction, in accordance with section 12, of the tax chargeable in respect of that supply because that card was acquired for the purposes of resale,

and that telephone card is subsequently used outside the Community for the purpose of accessing a telecommunications service, the place of supply of that telecommunications service shall be deemed to be outside the Community and the person who is taxable in respect of that supply of that telephone card shall be entitled, in the taxable period within which that person acquires proof that that telephone card was so used outside the Community, to a reduction of the tax payable in respect of that supply of that telephone card to the extent that that telephone card was so used.

(c)   For the purposes of this subsection the amount of the reduction referred to in paragraph (a) shall be calculated as follows:

$$(A - B) \times \frac{C}{C + 100}$$

where –

A   equals the tax inclusive price charged by the supplier for that part of the right contained in the telephone card which was consumed in accessing the telecommunications service which was deemed to be supplied outside the Community,

B   equals the tax inclusive price charged to the supplier for that part of the right contained in the telephone card which was consumed in accessing the telecommunications service which was deemed to be supplied outside the Community, and

C   is the percentage rate of tax chargeable on the supply of the telephone card at the time of that supply by that supplier.

(d)   Where a 'telephone card' is used to access a telecommunications service, the value of the telephone card so used shall, for the purposes of section 10(2), be disregarded.

(e)   In this subsection 'telephone card' means a card or a means other than money which confers a right to access a telecommunications service and for which, when the card or other means is supplied to a person other than for the purposes of resale, the supplier is entitled to a consideration in respect of the supply and for which the user of that card or other means is not liable for any further charge in respect of the receipt of the telecommunications service accessed by means of that card or other means.".

(With effect from 1 May 1998)

Finance Act 1999

121. Section 5 of the Principal Act is hereby amended by the insertion of the following paragraph after paragraph (ddd) (inserted by the Act of 1998) in subsection (6):

"(dddd)   Notwithstanding the provisions of subsection (5), the place of supply of services consisting of the hiring out of means of transport by a person established in the State shall be deemed to be outside the Community where such means of transport are, or are to be, effectively used and enjoyed outside the Community.".

(With effect from 25 March 1999)

Finance Act 2001

183. Section 5 of the Principal Act is amended-

(a)   in subsection (6)(e) by the insertion of the following after subparagraph (iii) (inserted by the Finance Act, 1986):

"(iiia) in case they are received, otherwise than for a business purpose, by a person in the State (referred to in this subparagraph as the 'recipient') and are supplied by a person who has his establishment in another Member State of the Community, in circumstances in which value-added tax referred to in Council Directive No. 77/388/EEC of 17 May 1977 is not payable in that Member State because the recipient held himself out or allowed himself to be held out as a taxable person within the meaning of Article 4 of that Directive in respect of such supplies, the State,",

and

(b)   by the substitution of the following for subsection (8) (inserted by the Act of 1978):

"(8)   (a)   The transfer of goodwill or other intangible assets of a business, in connection with the transfer of the business or part thereof, even if that business or that part thereof had ceased trading, by-

(i)   a taxable person to another taxable person or a flat-rate farmer, or

(ii)   a person who is not a taxable person to another person,

shall be deemed, for the purposes of this Act, not to be a supply of services.

(b)   For the purposes of this subsection, 'taxable person' shall not include a person who is a taxable person solely by virtue of subsections (1A) and (2) of section 8.".

(With effect from 25 March 2001)

Finance Act 2003

115.   Section 5 of the Principal Act is amended in subsection (6) –

(a)   by inserting in paragraph (dd) "or a radio or television broadcasting service," after "subsection (6A),",

(b)   by substituting in paragraph (e) "paragraphs (ddd), (ee) and (eee)" for "paragraphs (ddd) and (ee)", and

(c)   by inserting after paragraph (ee) the following paragraph:

"(eee) The place of supply of services of the description specified in paragraph (iiic) of the Fourth Schedule shall be deemed, for the purposes of this Act, to be the State when those services are supplied from outside the Community in the course or furtherance of business by a person who has an establishment outside the Community and has not also an establishment in the Community and are received, otherwise than for a business purpose, by a person whose usual place of residence is the State.".

(With effect from 1 July 2003)

Finance Act 2005

101.   Section 5 of the Principal Act is amended-

(a)   in subsection (6)-

(i)   by inserting the following after paragraph (ee):

"(eea) Where money transfer services are provided to a person in the State and are effectively used and enjoyed in the State, the place of supply of intermediary services provided in respect of or in relation to such money transfer services to a principal established outside the Community, shall be deemed, for the purposes of this Act, to be the State.",

and

(ii)   in paragraph (eee) (inserted by the Finance Act 2003) by deleting "and has not also an establishment in the Community" after "an establishment outside the Community",

and

(b)   in subsection (8)(a) by inserting "or in connection with a transfer of ownership of goods in accordance with section 3(5)(b)(iii)" after "had ceased trading,".

(With effect from 25 March 2005)

Finance Act 2006

94.   Section 5 of the Principal Act is amended in subsection (3) by substituting the following for paragraphs (a) to (d):

"(a)   the use of goods forming part of the assets of a business —

(i)   for the private use of a taxable person or of such person's staff, or

(ii)   for any purposes other than those of the taxable person's business,

where the tax on such goods is wholly or partly deductible,

(b)   the supply of services carried out free of charge by a taxable person for such person's own private use or that of the staff of such person or for any purposes other than those of such person's business,

(c)   the supply by a taxable person of services for the purposes of such person's business where the tax on such services, were they supplied by another taxable person, would not be wholly deductible.".

(With effect from 31 March 2006)

Finance Act 2007

77.   (1)   Section 5 of the Principal Act is amended in subsection (6) —

*(a)   by deleting paragraph (e)(iv), and

(b)   with effect from 1 January 2008 —

(i)   by substituting the word "intermediary" for "agent" in paragraph (f)(iii) and in subparagraphs (i)(II) and (ii) of paragraph (g), and

(ii)   by inserting the following paragraph after paragraph (g):

"(gg)   Subject to paragraph (f)(iii), the place of supply of services of an intermediary acting in the name and on behalf of another person, other than in cases where that intermediary takes part in the intra-Community transport of goods or in activities ancillary to the intra-Community transport of goods, is the place where the underlying transaction is supplied in accordance with this Act.".

(2)   Subsection (1)(a) comes into operation on such day as the Minister for Finance may by order appoint.

**97. With effect from 1 January 2007 in each provision of the Principal Act specified in the first column of Schedule 3 for the words set out in the second column of that Schedule at that entry there is substituted the words set out at the corresponding entry in the third column of that Schedule.

Schedule 3
Miscellaneous Amendments Relating to Council Directive 2006/112/EC
Amendment of Value-Added Tax Act 1972

Provision of Principal Act	Words to be replaced	Words to be inserted
Section 5(3A)	Community Council Directive No. 77/388/EEC	Council Directive No. 2006/112/EC of 28 November 2006
Section 5(6)(e)(iiia)	Council Directive No. 77/388/EEC of 17 May 1977 is not payable in that Member State because the recipient held himself out or allowed himself to be held out as a taxable person within the meaning of Article 4 of that Directive	Council Directive No. 2006/112/EC of 28 November 2006 is not payable in that Member State because the recipient held himself out or allowed himself to be held out as a taxable person within the meaning of Article 9(1) and Articles 10 to 13 of that Directive
Section 5(6)(e)(iv)(II)	Community Council Directive No. 77/388/EEC	Council Directive No. 2006/112/EC of 28 November 2006

(With effect from 1 January 2008 except * with effect from date of Ministerial Order and ** with effect from 1 January 2007)

Finance Act 2008

89.   With effect from 1 July 2008 section 5 of the Principal Act is amended —

    (a)   in subsection (3)(a) by inserting "other than immovable goods" after "the use of goods", and

    (b)   by inserting the following after subsection (3A):

> "(3B)   The use of immovable goods forming part of the assets of a business —
>
>   (a)   for the private use of an accountable person or of such person's staff, or
>
>   (b)   for any purpose other than those of the accountable person's business,
>
> is a taxable supply of services if —
>
>   (i)   that use occurs during a period of 20 years following the acquisition or development of those goods by the accountable person, and
>
>   (ii)   those goods are treated for tax purposes as forming part of the assets of the business at the time of their acquisition or development.".

109.   With effect from 1 July 2008 in each provision of the Principal Act specified in the first column of Schedule 4 for the words set out in the second column of that Schedule at that entry (in each place where those words occur in the provision concerned) there is substituted the words set out at the corresponding entry in the third column of that Schedule.

Schedule 4
Miscellaneous Amendments Relating to the Amendment of the Definition of Taxable Person

Amendments to Value-Added Tax Act 1972

Provision of Value-Added Tax Act 1972	Words to be replaced	Words to be inserted
Section 5(3)	a taxable person	an accountable person
Section 5(3)	the taxable person's	an accountable person's
Section 5(3)	another taxable person	another accountable person
Section 5(6)(ddd)	a taxable person	an accountable person
Section 5(8)(a)(i)	a taxable person to another taxable person or a flat-rate farmer, or	an accountable person to a taxable person, or
Section 5(8)(a)(ii)	a taxable person	an accountable person
Section 5(8)(b)	'taxable person'	'accountable person'
Section 5(8)(b)	a taxable person	an accountable person

(With effect from 1 July 2008)

Section 5A

Special scheme for electronic services
Finance Act 2003

116. The Principal Act is amended by inserting the following section after section 5:

"5A.   (1)   In this section—

'**electronic services scheme**' means the special arrangements for the taxation of electronically supplied services provided for in Article 26c of Council Directive No. 77/388/EEC of 17 May 1977;

'**EU value-added tax**' means value-added tax referred to in Council Directive No. 77/388/EEC of 17 May 1977 and includes tax within the meaning of section 1;

'**identified person**' has the meaning assigned to it by subsection (5);

'**Member State of consumption**' means the Member State in which the supply of the electronic services takes place according to Article 9(2)(f) of Council Directive No. 77/388/EEC of 17 May 1977;

'**Member State of identification**' means the Member State which the non-established person chooses to contact to state when his or her activity within the Community commences in accordance with the provisions of the electronic services scheme;

'**national tax number**' means a number (whether consisting of either or both numbers and letters) assigned to a non-established person by his or her own national taxation authorities;

'**non-established person**' means a person who has his or her establishment outside the Community and has not also an establishment in the Community and who is not otherwise required to be a person registered for value-added tax within the meaning of section 1;

'**scheme participant**' means a non-established person who supplies electronic services into the Community and who opts to use the electronic services scheme in any Member State;

'**VAT return**' means the statement containing the information necessary to establish the amount of EU value-added tax that has become chargeable in each Member State under the electronic services scheme.

(2)   Subject to and in accordance with the provisions of this section, a non-established person may opt to apply the electronic services scheme to his or her supplies of electronic services to non-taxable persons within the Community.

(3)   The Revenue Commissioners shall set up and maintain a register, referred to in this section as an 'identification register', of non-established persons who are identified in the State for the purposes of the electronic services scheme.

(4)   A non-established person who opts to be identified in the State for the purposes of the electronic services scheme shall inform the Revenue Commissioners by electronic means in a manner specified by them, when his or her taxable activity commences and shall, at the same time, furnish them electronically with the following information—

   (a)   the person's name and postal address,

   (b)   his or her electronic addresses, including website addresses,

   (c)   his or her national tax number, if any, and

   (d)   a statement that the person is not a person registered, or otherwise identified, for value-added tax purposes within the Community.

(5)   Where a person has furnished the particulars required under subsection (4), the Revenue Commissioners shall register that person in accordance with subsection (3), allocate to that person an identification number and notify such person electronically of it, and, for the purposes of this section, a person to whom such an identification number has been allocated shall be referred to as an **'identified person'**.

(6)   An identified person shall, within 20 days immediately following the end of each calendar quarter, furnish by electronic means to the Revenue Commissioners a VAT return, prepared in accordance with, and containing such particulars as are specified in, subsection (7), in respect of supplies made in the Community in that quarter and shall at the same time remit to the Revenue Commissioners, into a bank account designated by them and denominated in euro, the amount of EU value-added tax, if any, payable by such person in respect of such quarter in relation to—

   (a)   supplies made in the State in accordance with section 5(6)(eee), and

(b)   supplies made in other Member States in accordance with the provisions implementing Article 9(2)(f) of Council Directive No. 77/388/ EEC of 17 May 1977 in such other Member States:

but if the identified person has not made any such electronic supplies to non-taxable persons into the Community within a calendar quarter that person shall furnish a nil VAT return in respect of that quarter.

(7)   The VAT return referred to in subsection (6) shall be made in euro and shall contain the following details—

(a)   the person's identification number,

(b)   for each Member State of consumption where EU value-added tax has become due—

(i)   the total value, exclusive of EU value-added tax, of supplies of electronic services for the quarter,

(ii)   the amount of the said value liable to EU value-added tax at the applicable rate, and

(iii)   the amount of EU value-added tax corresponding to the said value at the applicable rate,

and

(c)   the total EU value-added tax due, if any.

(8)   Notwithstanding section 10(9A), where supplies have been made using a currency other than the euro, the exchange rate to be used for the purposes of expressing the corresponding amount in euro on the VAT return shall be that published by the European Central Bank for the last date of the calendar quarter for which the VAT return relates, or, if there is no publication on that date, on the next day of publication.

(9)   Notwithstanding section 12, a scheme participant who supplies services which are deemed in accordance with section 5(6)(eee) to be supplied in the State shall not, in computing the amount of tax payable by him or her in respect of such supplies, be entitled to deduct any tax borne or paid in relation to those supplies but shall be entitled to claim a refund of such tax in accordance with, and using the rules applicable to, Council Directive 86/560/EEC of 17 November 1986, notwithstanding Articles 2(2), 2(3) and 4(2) of that Directive.

(10) A scheme participant who supplies services which are deemed in accordance with section 5(6)(eee) to be supplied in the State shall be deemed to have fulfilled his or her obligations under sections 9, 16 and 19 of this Act if such participant has accounted in full in respect of such supplies in any Member State under the provisions of the electronic services scheme.

(11) For the purposes of this Act, a VAT return required to be furnished in accordance with the electronic services scheme shall, in so far as it relates to supplies made in accordance with section 5(6)(eee), be treated, with any necessary modifications, as if it were a return required to be furnished in accordance with section 19.

(12) (a) An identified person shall—

    (i) keep full and true records of all transactions covered by the electronic services scheme which affect his or her liability to EU value-added tax,

    (ii) make such records available, by electronic means and on request, to the Revenue Commissioners,

    (iii) make such records available, by electronic means and on request, to all Member States of consumption, and

    (iv) notwithstanding section 16, retain such records for each transaction for a period of 10 years from the end of the year when that transaction occurred.

    (b) A scheme participant who is deemed to supply services in the State in accordance with section 5(6)(eee) shall be bound by the requirements of subparagraphs (i), (ii) and (iv) in relation to such supplies.

(13) An identified person shall notify the Revenue Commissioners of any changes in the information submitted under subsection (4) and shall notify them if his or her taxable activity ceases or changes to the extent that such person no longer qualifies for the electronic services scheme. Such notification shall be made electronically.

(14) The Revenue Commissioners shall exclude an identified person from the identification register if—

    (a) they have reasonable grounds to believe that that person's taxable activities have ended, or

        (b)   the identified person –

               (i)   notifies the Revenue Commissioners that he or she no longer supplies electronic services,

               (ii)   no longer fulfils the requirements necessary to be allowed to use the electronic services scheme, or

               (iii)   persistently fails to comply with the provisions of the electronic services scheme.

     (15)   The Revenue Commissioners may make regulations as necessary for the purpose of giving effect to the electronic services scheme.".

(With effect from 1 July 2003)

Finance Act 2007

97.   With effect from 1 January 2007 in each provision of the Principal Act specified in the first column of Schedule 3 for the words set out in the second column of that Schedule at that entry there is substituted the words set out at the corresponding entry in the third column of that Schedule.

Schedule 3
Miscellaneous Amendments Relating To Council Directive 2006/112/EC

Amendment of Value-Added Tax Act 1972

Provision of Principal Act	Words to be replaced	Words to be inserted
Section 5A(1) in the definition of "electronic services scheme"	Article 26c of Council Directive No. 77/388/EEC of 17 May 1977	Articles 358 to 369 of Council Directive No. 2006/112/EC of 28 November 2006
Section 5A(1) in the definition of "EU value-added tax"	Council Directive No. 77/388/EEC of 17 May 1977	Council Directive No. 2006/112/EC of 28 November 2006
Section 5A(1) in the definition of "Member State of consumption"	Article 9(2)(f) of Council Directive No. 77/388/EEC of 17 May 1977	Article 57(1) of Council Directive No. 2006/112/EC of 28 November 2006
Section 5A(6)(b)	Article 9(2)(f) of Council Directive No. 77/388/EEC of 17 May 1977	Article 57(1) of Council Directive No. 2006/112/EC of 28 November 2006

(With effect from 1 January 2007)

Section 6

Value Added Tax Act 1972

Exemptions

6. (1) Tax shall not be chargeable in respect of any exempted activity.

(2) (a) The Minister may by order declare the delivery of goods of any kind or the rendering of a service of any kind to be an exempted activity.

(b) The Minister may by order amend or revoke an order under this subsection, including an order under this paragraph.

(c) An order under this subsection shall be laid before Dáil Éireann as soon as may be after it is made and, if a resolution annulling the order is passed by Dáil Éireann within the next twenty-one days on which Dáil Éireann has sat after the order is laid before it, the order shall be annulled accordingly, but without prejudice to the validity of anything previously done thereunder.

(With effect from 1 November 1972)

Value Added Tax (Amendment) Act 1978

30. (2) In consequence of the amendments of the Principal Act specified in this Act and of the repeals specified in the First Schedule, the Principal Act is hereby further amended by the substitution of the word or expression mentioned in column (3) of the Second Schedule at any reference number for the word or expression mentioned in column (2) of that Schedule at that reference number wherever it occurs in the provision of the Principal Act mentioned in column (4) of that Schedule at that reference number.

SECOND SCHEDULE

Consequential Amendments

Reference Number (1)	Existing word or expression (2)	Substituted word or expression (3)	Provision of Principal Act (4)
15	"delivery of goods of any kind or the rendering of a service"	"supply of goods or services"	Section 6(2)(a)

(With effect from 1 March 1979)

Section 6A

Finance Act 1999

Special scheme for investment gold

122. The Principal Act is hereby amended by the insertion of the following section after section 6:

"6A. (1)   (a)   In this section -

'**intermediary**' means a person who intervenes for another person in a supply of investment gold while acting in the name and for the account of that other person;

'**investment gold**' means-

(i)   gold in the form of-

(I)   a bar, or

(II)   a wafer,

of a weight accepted by a bullion market and of a purity equal to or greater than 995 parts per one thousand parts, and

(ii)   gold coins which-

(I)   are of a purity equal to or greater than 900 parts per one thousand parts,

(II)   are minted after 1800,

(III)   are or have been legal tender in their country of origin, and

(IV)   are normally sold at a price which does not exceed the open market value of the gold contained in the coins by more than 80 per cent.

(b)   For the purposes of the definition of investment gold in paragraph (a), gold coins which are listed in the 'C' series of the Official Journal of the European Communities as fulfilling the criteria referred to in that definition in respect of gold coins shall be deemed to fulfil the said criteria for the whole year for which the list is published.

(2)   The provisions of this section shall apply to-

(a)   investment gold which is represented by securities or represented by certificates for allocated or unallocated gold or traded on gold accounts and including, in particular, gold loans and swaps, involving a right of ownership or a claim in respect of investment gold, and

(b)   transactions concerning investment gold involving futures and forward contracts leading to a transfer of a right of ownership or a claim in respect of investment gold.

(3)   Notwithstanding subsection (1) of section 6, a person who produces investment gold or transforms any gold into investment gold, may, in accordance with conditions set out in regulations, waive such person's right to exemption from tax on a supply of investment gold to another person who is engaged in the supply of goods and services in the course or furtherance of business.

(4)   Where a person waives, in accordance with subsection (3), such person's right to exemption from tax in respect of a supply of investment gold, an intermediary who supplies services in respect of that supply of investment gold may, in accordance with conditions set out in regulations, waive that intermediary's right to exemption from tax in respect of those services.

(5)   (a)   Where a person waives, in accordance with subsection (3), such person's right to exemption from tax in respect of a supply of investment gold, then, for the purposes of this Act, the person to whom the supply of investment gold is made shall, in relation thereto, be a taxable person and be liable to pay the tax chargeable on that supply as if such taxable person had made that supply of investment gold for consideration in the course or furtherance of business and the person who waived the right to exemption in respect of that supply shall not be liable to pay the said tax.

(b)   Where a person is liable for tax in accordance with paragraph (a) in respect of a supply of investment gold, such person shall, notwithstanding the provisions of section 12, be entitled, in computing the amount of tax payable by such person in respect of the taxable period in which that liability to tax arises, to deduct the tax for which such person is liable on that supply, if such person's subsequent supply of that investment gold is exempt from tax.

(6)   (a)   A taxable person may, in computing the amount of tax payable by such person in respect of any taxable period and notwithstanding section 12, deduct-

(i)   the tax charged to such person during that period by other taxable persons by means of invoices, prepared in the manner prescribed by regulations, in respect of supplies of gold to such person,

(ii)   the tax chargeable during that period, being tax for which such person is liable in respect of intra-Community acquisitions of gold, and

(iii)   the tax paid by such person, or deferred, as established from the relevant customs documents kept by such person in accordance with section 16(3) in respect of gold imported by such person

in that period, where that gold is subsequently transformed into investment gold and such person's subsequent supply of that investment gold is exempt from tax.

(b)   A person may claim, in accordance with regulations, a refund of-

(i)   the tax charged to such person on the purchase of gold, other than investment gold, by such person,

(ii)   the tax chargeable to such person on the intra-Community acquisition of gold, other than investment gold, by such person, and

(iii)   the tax paid or deferred on the importation by such person of gold other than investment gold, where that gold is subsequently transformed into investment gold and such person's subsequent supply of that investment gold is exempt from tax.

(7)   (a)   A taxable person may, in computing the amount of tax payable by such person in respect of a taxable period and notwithstanding section 12, deduct the tax charged to such person during that period by other taxable persons by means of invoices, prepared in the manner prescribed by regulations, in respect of the supply to the first-mentioned person of services consisting of a change of form, weight or purity of gold where that person's subsequent supply of that gold is exempt from tax.

(b) A person may claim, in accordance with regulations, a refund of the tax charged to such person in respect of the supply to such person of services consisting of a change of form, weight or purity of gold where such person's subsequent supply of that gold is exempt from tax.

(8) (a) A taxable person who produces investment gold or transforms any gold into investment gold may, in computing the amount of tax payable by such person in respect of a taxable period and notwithstanding section 12, deduct-

  (i) the tax charged to such person during that period by other taxable persons by means of invoices, prepared in the manner prescribed by regulations, in respect of supplies of goods or services to the first-mentioned person,

  (ii) the tax chargeable during that period, being tax for which such person is liable in respect of intra-Community acquisitions of goods, and

  (iii) the tax paid by such person, or deferred, as established from the relevant customs documents kept by such person in accordance with section 16(3) in respect of goods imported by such person in that period, where those goods or services are linked to the production or transformation of that gold, and such person's subsequent supply of that investment gold is exempt from tax.

(b) A person who produces investment gold or transforms any gold into investment gold may claim, in accordance with regulations, a refund of-

  (i) the tax charged to such person on the purchase by such person of goods or services,

  (ii) the tax chargeable to such person on the intra-Community acquisition of goods by such person,

  and

  (iii) the tax paid or deferred by such person on the importation of goods by such person, where those goods or services are linked

to the production or transformation of that gold, and such person's subsequent supply of that gold is exempt from tax.".

(With effect from 1 January 2000)

Finance Act 2000

109. Section 6A (inserted by the Act of 1999) of the Principal Act is amended-

(a) by the substitution in paragraph (a) of subsection (2) of "investment gold, including investment gold which is represented by securities" for "investment gold which is represented by securities",

and

(b) by the insertion of the following subsection after subsection (8):

"(9) Every trader in investment gold shall establish the identity of any person to whom such trader supplies investment gold when the total consideration which such trader is entitled to receive in respect of such supply, or a series of such supplies which are or appear to be linked, amounts to at least 15,000 euros, and such trader shall retain a copy of all documents used to identify the person to whom the investment gold is supplied as if they were records to be kept in accordance with section 16(1A) of this Act.".

(With effect from 23 March 2000)

Finance Act 2008

109. With effect from 1 July 2008 in each provision of the Principal Act specified in the first column of Schedule 4 for the words set out in the second column of that Schedule at that entry (in each place where those words occur in the provision concerned) there is substituted the words set out at the corresponding entry in the third column of that Schedule.

Schedule 4
Miscellaneous Amendments Relating to the Amendment of the Definition of Taxable Person
Amendments to Value-Added Tax Act 1972

Provision of Value-Added Tax Act 1972	Words to be replaced	Words to be inserted
Section 6A	a taxable person	an accountable person
Section 6A	such taxable person	such accountable person
Section 6A	A taxable person	An accountable person
Section 6A	other taxable persons	other accountable persons

(With effect from 1 July 2008)

Section 7

Value Added Tax Act 1972

Waiver of exemption

7. (1) Where, but for the provisions of section 6, tax would be chargeable in respect of the rendering of any of the services specified in paragraphs (iv) and (x) of the First Schedule, a person rendering any such services may, in accordance with regulations, waive his right to exemption from tax in respect thereof. Any such waiver shall extend to all the services specified in the paragraph or paragraphs that the person renders.

(2) A waiver of exemption under subsection (1) shall have effect from the commencement of such taxable period as may be agreed between the person making the waiver and the Revenue Commissioners and shall cease to have effect at the end of the taxable period during which it is cancelled in accordance with subsection (3).

(3) Provision may be made by regulations for the cancellation, at the request of a person, of a waiver made by him under subsection (1) and for the payment by him to the Revenue Commissioners as a condition of cancellation of such sum (if any) as when added to the net total amount of tax (if any) paid by him in accordance with section 19 in relation to do rendering of services by him in the period for which the waiver had effect is equal to the amount of tax repaid to him during such period in respect of tax borne or paid in relation to the rendering of such services.

(4) Where exemption has been waived under subsection (1) in respect of the rendering of any service, tax shall be charged in relation to the person making such waiver during the period for which such waiver has effect as if the service to which the waiver applies was not specified in the First Schedule.

(With effect from 1 November 1972)

Value Added Tax (Amendment) Act 1978

30. (2) In consequence of the amendments of the Principal Act specified in this Act and of the repeals specified in the First Schedule, the Principal Act is hereby further amended by the substitution of the word or expression mentioned in column (3) of the Second Schedule at any reference number for the word or expression mentioned in column (2) of that Schedule at that reference number wherever it occurs in the provision of the Principal Act mentioned in column (4) of that Schedule at that reference number.

SECOND SCHEDULE

Consequential Amendments

Reference Number (1)	Existing word or expression (2)	Substituted word or expression (3)	Provision of Principal Act (4)
2	"rendering"	"supply"	The definition of "taxable services" in sections 7(1) (where the word first occurs), 7(3), 7(4),
6	"rendering"	"supplying"	Section 7(1) (where the word secondly occurs).
8	"renders"	"supplies"	Section 7(1).

Transitional provisions

31. ......

   (2)   In relation to a person who, immediately before the commencement of this Act, was an accountable person-

      (a)   references in subsection (3) of section 7 of the Principal Act to a waiver shall be deemed to include references to a waiver made under subsection (1) of the said section 7 before such commencement,

   ...

      (c)   references in the said subsection (3) of the said section 7 to the supply of services shall be deemed to include references to the rendering of services before such commencement, and

   ...

(With effect from 1 March 1979)

Finance Act 1991

78.   Section 7 of the Principal Act is hereby amended in subsection (1) by the substitution of "to which paragraph (iv) of the First Schedule relates" for "specified in paragraphs (iv) and (x) of the First Schedule" and of "services to which the said paragraph (iv) relates" for "services specified in the paragraph or paragraphs".

(With effect from 1 January 1992)

Finance Act 1997

100.   Section 7 of the Principal Act is hereby amended-

   (a)   by the addition of the following proviso to subsection (1):

      "Provided that where a person waives his right to exemption from tax in respect of the leasing or letting of goods which are subject to an agreement of the type referred to in section 4(2C)(a) then that waiver shall only apply to the supply of services under that agreement.",

and

(b)   by the substitution of the following subsection for subsection (3):

"(3)   Provision may be made by regulations for the cancellation, at the request of a person, of a waiver made by him under subsection (1) and for the payment by him to the Revenue Commissioners as a condition of cancellation of such sum (if any) as when added to the total amount of tax (if any) due by him in accordance with section 19 in relation to the supply of services by him to which the waiver applied is equal to the total of-

(a)   the amount of tax deducted by him in accordance with section 12 in respect of tax borne or paid in relation to the supply of such services,

(b)   the amount of tax that would be deductible by him in accordance with section 12 if tax had been chargeable on the transfer of ownership of goods to him in respect of which the provisions of section 3(5)(b)(iii) were applied, and those goods were used by him in the supply of such services, and

(c)   the amount of tax that would be deductible by him in accordance with section 12 if tax had been chargeable on the supply to him of goods or services in respect of which the provisions of paragraph (via) of the Second Schedule were applied, and those goods or services were used in relation to the supply of services by him to which the waiver applied.".

(With effect from 26 March 1997)

Finance Act 2002

100.   Section 7 of the Principal Act is amended in subsection (1) –

(a)   by renumbering that subsection as paragraph (a) of subsection (1), and

(b)   by inserting the following after paragraph (a):

"(b)   A waiver of exemption from tax under this subsection shall not apply or be extended to any disposal of an interest in immovable goods which is deemed to be a letting of immovable goods to which paragraph (iv) of the First Schedule applies by virtue of section 4(3A)(a)(ii).".

(With effect from 25 March 2002)

Finance Act 2003

117. Section 7 of the Principal Act is amended by inserting the following after paragraph (a) of subsection (3) —

"(aa) the amount of tax deducted by him in accordance with section 12, prior to the commencement of the letting of the immovable goods to which the waiver relates, in respect of or in relation to his acquisition of his interest in, or his development of, those immovable goods,".

(With effect from 28 March 2003)

Finance Act 2007

78. Section 7 of the Principal Act is amended by inserting the following after subsection (1):

"(1A) (a) Notwithstanding subsection (1)(a), a person shall not waive his or her right to exemption from tax on or after the date of passing of the Finance Act 2007 in respect of a letting of immovable goods to which paragraph (iv) of the First Schedule relates which is a letting of all or part of a house, apartment or other similar establishment, to the extent that those immovable goods are used or to be used for residential purposes, including any such letting —

(i) governed by the Residential Tenancies Act 2004,

(ii) governed by the Housing (Rent Books) Regulations 1993 (S.I. No. 146 of 1993),

(iii) governed by section 10 of the Housing Act 1988,

(iv) of a dwelling to which Part II of the Housing (Private Rented Dwellings) Act 1982 applies, or

(v) of accommodation which is provided as a temporary dwelling for emergency residential purposes,

and any waiver of exemption from tax which applies under this section shall not extend to such a letting of immovable goods where those goods are acquired or developed on or after the date of passing of the Finance Act 2007.

(b) For the purpose of applying paragraph (a), immovable goods are considered to be acquired when a person enters into a binding contract in writing for the acquisition of those goods or of an interest in those goods, or for the construction of those goods, and are considered to be developed when an application for planning permission in respect of the development of those goods as a house, apartment or other similar establishment is received by a planning authority.".

(With effect from 2 April 2007)

Finance Act 2008

90.   Section 7 of the Principal Act is amended —

    (a)   by inserting in subsection (3) "or in accordance with section 7B(3)" after "at the request of a person", and

    (b)   by inserting the following after subsection (4):

        "(5)   (a)   No waiver of exemption from tax in accordance with this section shall commence on or after 1 July 2008.

                (b)   Any waiver of exemption from tax which applies under this section shall not extend to any letting of immovable goods where those goods are acquired or developed on or after 1 July 2008.

                (c)   For the purpose of applying paragraph (b), a waiver of exemption, which is in place on 18 February 2008 in respect of the letting of immovable goods which are undergoing development on that day by or on behalf of the person who has that waiver, may extend to a letting of those immovable goods.".

(With effect from 13 March 2008)

Finance Act 2009

21.   Section 7 of the Principal Act is amended —

    (a)   in subsection (3) by substituting "subsection (3), (7) or (9) of section 7B" for "section 7B(3)", and

    (b)   by inserting the following after subsection (5):

        "(6)   Where a person cancelled his or her waiver of exemption before 1 July 2008 then, for the purposes of applying section 12E, the adjustment period (within the meaning of that section or, as the context may require, the period to be treated as the adjustment period in accordance with section 4C(11)) in relation to any capital good the tax chargeable on that person's acquisition or development of which that person was obliged to take into account when that person made that cancellation, shall be treated as if it ended on the date on which that cancellation had effect.".

(With effect from 3 June 2009)

Section 7A

Finance Act 2008

Option to tax lettings of immovable goods

91.   The Principal Act is amended with effect from 1 July 2008 by inserting
the following sections after section 7:

"Option to tax lettings of immovable goods.

7A.   (1)   (a)   Tax shall be chargeable in accordance with this Act
on the supply of a service to which paragraph (iv)
of the First Schedule relates (in this section referred
to as a 'letting') where, subject to subsections (2)
and (4), the supplier (in this section referred to as a
'landlord') opts to make that letting so chargeable,
and a landlord who exercises this option (referred
to in this Act as a 'landlord's option to tax') shall,
notwithstanding section 8(3), be an accountable
person and liable to account for the tax on that
letting in accordance with this Act, and that letting
shall not be a supply to which section 6 applies.

(b)   Where a taxable person is entitled to deduct tax
on the acquisition or development of immovable
goods on the basis that the goods will be used
for the purpose of a letting or lettings in respect
of which a landlord's option to tax will apply,
then—

(i)   that person shall be treated as having exercised
the landlord's option to tax in respect of any
lettings of those immovable goods, and

(ii)   that option shall be deemed to continue in
place until that person makes a letting in
respect of which neither of the conditions of
paragraph (c) are fulfilled.

(c)   A landlord's option to tax in respect of a letting is
exercised by—

(i)   a provision in writing in a letting agreement
between the landlord and the person to whom
the letting is made (in this section referred to as
a 'tenant') that tax is chargeable on the rent, or

(ii)   the issuing by the landlord of a document
to the tenant giving notification that tax is
chargeable on the letting.

(d)   A landlord's option to tax in respect of a letting is terminated —

    (i)   in the case of an option exercised in accordance with paragraph (b), by making a letting of the immovable goods referred to in that paragraph in respect of which neither of the conditions of paragraph (c) are fulfilled,

    (ii)   in the case of an option exercised in accordance with paragraph (c), by —

      (I)   an agreement in writing between the landlord and tenant that the option is terminated and specifying the date of termination, or

      (II)   the delivery to the tenant of a document giving notification that the option has been terminated and specifying the date of termination,

    (iii)   when the landlord and tenant become connected persons,

    (iv)   when a person connected with the landlord commences to occupy the immovable goods that are subject to that letting whether that person occupies those goods by way of letting or otherwise, or

    (v)   when the immovable goods that are subject to that letting are used or to be used for residential purposes within the meaning of subsection (4).

(2)   (a)   A landlord may not opt to tax a letting —

    (i)   subject to paragraph (b), where that landlord and the tenant in respect of that letting are connected persons, or

    (ii)   where the landlord is not connected to the tenant but is connected to any person who occupies the immovable goods that is subject to that letting, whether that person occupies those goods by way of letting or otherwise.

(b)   Paragraph (a)(i) shall not apply where the immovable goods which are the subject of the letting are used for the purposes of supplies or activities which entitle the tenant to deduct at least 90 per cent of the tax chargeable on the letting in accordance with section 12. However, where a landlord has exercised a landlord's option to tax in respect of a letting to which paragraph (a)

(i) would have applied but for this paragraph, paragraph (a)(i) shall apply from the end of the first accounting year in which the goods are used for the purposes of supplies or activities which entitle the tenant to deduct less than 90 per cent of the said tax chargeable.

(3)   (a)   For the purposes of this section any question of whether a person is connected with another person shall be determined in accordance with the following:

(i)   a person is connected with an individual if that person is the individual's spouse, or is a relative, or the spouse of a relative, of the individual or of the individual's spouse,

(ii)   a person is connected with any person with whom he or she is in partnership, and with the spouse or a relative of any individual with whom he or she is in partnership,

(iii)   subject to clauses (IV) and (V) of subparagraph (v), a person is connected with another person if he or she has control over that other person, or if the other person has control over the first-mentioned person, or if both persons are controlled by another person or persons,

(iv)   a body of persons is connected with another person if that person, or persons connected with him or her, have control of that body of persons, or the person and persons connected with him or her together have control of it,

(v)   a body of persons is connected with another body of persons —

(I)   if the same person has control of both or a person has control of one and persons connected with that person or that person and persons connected with that person have control of the other,

(II)   if a group of 2 or more persons has control of each body of persons and the groups either consist of the same persons or could be regarded as consisting of the same persons by treating (in one or more cases) a member of either group as replaced by a person with whom he or she is connected,

(III) if both bodies of persons act in pursuit of a common purpose,

(IV) if any person or any group of persons or groups of persons having a reasonable commonality of identity have or had the means or power, either directly or indirectly, to determine the activities carried on or to be carried on by both bodies of persons, or

(V) if both bodies of persons are under the control of any person or group of persons or groups of persons having a reasonable commonality of identity,

(vi) a person in the capacity as trustee of a settlement is connected with—

(I) any person who in relation to the settlement is a settlor, or

(II) any person who is a beneficiary under the settlement.

(b) In this subsection—

'**control**', in the case of a body corporate or in the case of a partnership, has the meaning assigned to it by section 8(3B);

'**relative**' means a brother, sister, ancestor or lineal descendant.

(4) A landlord's option to tax may not be exercised in respect of all or part of a house or apartment or other similar establishment to the extent that those immovable goods are used or to be used for residential purposes, including any such letting—

(a) governed by the Residential Tenancies Act 2004,

(b) governed by the Housing (Rent Books) Regulations 1993 (S.I. No. 146 of 1993),

(c) governed by section 10 of the Housing Act 1988,

(d) of a dwelling to which Part II of the Housing (Private Rented Dwellings) Act 1982 applies, or

(e) of accommodation which is provided as a temporary dwelling for emergency residential purposes,

and a landlord's option to tax, once exercised, shall immediately cease to have effect to the extent that the immovable goods which are the subject of the letting to which the option applies, come to be used for a residential purpose.

(With effect from 1 July 2008)

Finance (No. 2) Act 2008

69.   Section 7A of the Principal Act is amended —

    (a)   in subsection (1)(d)(iv) —

        (i)   by inserting "the landlord or" after "when", and

        (ii)   by substituting "occupies" for "commences to occupy",
        and

    (b)   in subsection (2) —

        (i)   in paragraph (a) by substituting the following for
        subparagraph (ii):

           "(ii)   where the landlord, whether or not connected to
the tenant, or a person connected to the landlord,
occupies the immovable goods that is subject
to that letting whether that landlord or that
person occupies those goods by way of letting or
otherwise.",

        and

        (ii)   to insert the following after paragraph (b):

           "(c)   Paragraph (a)(ii) and subsection (1)(d)(iv) shall
not apply where the occupant (being any
person including the landlord referred to in that
paragraph or that subsection) uses the immovable
goods which are the subject of the letting for the
purpose of making supplies which entitle that
occupant to deduct, in accordance with section 12,
at least 90 per cent of all tax chargeable in respect
of goods or services used by that occupant for
the purpose of making those supplies. However,
where a landlord has exercised a landlord's option
to tax in respect of a letting to which paragraph
(a)(ii) would have applied but for this paragraph,
paragraph (a)(ii) shall apply from the end of the
first accounting year in which the immovable
goods are used for the purpose of making supplies
which entitle that occupant to deduct less than
90 per cent of the said tax chargeable.".

99.   The enactments specified in Schedule 6 —

    (a)   are amended to the extent and in the manner specified in
paragraphs 1 to 6 of that Schedule, and

    (b)   apply and come into operation in accordance with paragraph 7
of that Schedule.

SCHEDULE 6

Miscellaneous Technical Amendments in Relation to Tax

4.   The Value-Added Tax Act 1972 is amended –

   (e)   in section 7A –

      (i)   in subsection (1)(d)(ii) –

         (I)   in clause (I) by inserting "which shall not be earlier than the date of that agreement" after "the date of termination", and

         (II)   in clause (II) by inserting "which shall not be earlier than the date that notification is received by the tenant" after "the date of termination",

      and

      (ii)   in subsection (2) –

         (I)   in paragraph (a) –

            (A)   by substituting "Subject to paragraphs (b) and (c), a landlord" for "A landlord", and

            (B)   in subparagraph (i) by deleting "subject to paragraph (b),",

         and

         (II)   in paragraph (b) by inserting "and subsection (1) (d)(iii)" after "Paragraph (a)(i)",

(With effect from 24 December 2008)

Section 7B

Finance Act 2008

Transitional measures: waiver of exemption

91.   The Principal Act is amended with effect from 1 July 2008 by inserting the following sections after section 7:

Transitional measures: waiver of exemption.

7B.   (1)   This section applies to an accountable person who had waived his or her right to exemption from tax in accordance with section 7 and who had not cancelled that waiver before 1 July 2008 (hereafter in this section referred to as a **'landlord'**).

(2)   Section 12E does not apply to a landlord to the extent that tax relating to the acquisition or development of immovable goods has been or would be taken into account in calculating, in accordance with section 7(3), the sum, if any, due by that landlord as a condition of the cancellation of a waiver.

(3)   Where a landlord has made a letting and, were that letting not already subject to a waiver, that letting would be one in respect of which the landlord would not, because of the provisions of section 7A(2), be entitled to exercise a landlord's option to tax in accordance with section 7A, then the landlord's waiver of exemption shall, subject to subsection (4), immediately cease to apply to that letting, and —

(a)   that landlord shall pay the amount, as if it were tax due by that person in accordance with section 19 for the taxable period in which the waiver ceases to apply to that letting and the amount shall be the sum, if any, which would be payable in accordance with section 7(3) in respect of the cancellation of a waiver as if that landlord's waiver applied only to the immovable goods or the interest in immovable goods subject to that letting to which the waiver has ceased to apply, and

(b)   the amounts taken into account in calculating that sum, if any, shall be disregarded in any future cancellation of that waiver.

(4)   (a)   Subject to paragraph (c), where a landlord has a letting to which subsection (3) would otherwise apply, the provisions of that subsection shall not apply while, on the basis of the letting agreement in place, the tax that the landlord will be required to account for, in equal amounts for each taxable period, in respect of the letting during the next 12 months is not less than the amount calculated at that time in accordance with the formula in subsection (5).

(b) Where the conditions in paragraph (a) fail to be satisfied because of a variation in the terms of the lease or otherwise or if the tax paid at any time in respect of the letting is less than the tax payable, this subsection shall cease to apply.

(c) This subsection applies to a letting referred to in paragraph (a) —

(i) where a landlord has a waiver in place on 18 February 2008 and —

(I) on 1 July 2008 that letting had been in place since 18 February 2008, or

(II) the immovable goods subject to the letting are owned by that landlord on 18 February 2008 and are in the course of development by or on behalf of that landlord on that day,

or

(ii) where a landlord holds an interest, other than a freehold interest or a freehold equivalent interest in the immovable goods subject to the letting, acquired between 18 February 2008 and 30 June 2008 from a person with whom the landlord is not connected, within the meaning of section 7A, in a transaction which is treated as a supply of goods in accordance with section 4.

(5) The formula to be used for the purposes of subsection (4) is:

$$\frac{A - B}{12 - Y}$$

where —

A is the amount of tax that would be taken into account for the purposes of section 7(3) in respect of the acquisition or development of the immovable goods, if the waiver were being cancelled at the time referred to in subsection (4),

B is the amount of tax chargeable on the consideration by the landlord in respect of the letting of those immovable goods and paid in accordance with section 19 that would be taken into account for the purposes of section 7(3) if the waiver were being cancelled at that time, and if that letting were the only one to which that waiver applied, and

Y   is 11, or the number of full years since the
later of —

(i)   the date of the first letting of those
goods, and

(ii)   the date on which the landlord waived
exemption,

where that number is less than 11 years.".

(With effect from 1 July 2008)

Finance (No. 2) Act 2008

70. Section 7B of the Principal Act is amended by inserting the following
after subsection (5) —

"(6)   Where a landlord has a letting to which subsection (3) or (4)
applies and that landlord becomes a person in a group within
the meaning of section 8(8) on or after 1 July 2008 and the person
to whom that letting is made is a person in that group, then the
person referred to in section 8(8)(a)(i)(I) in respect of that group
shall be liable to pay the amount as specified in subsection (3)(a)
as if it were tax due in accordance with section 19 —

(a)   in the case of a landlord who became a person in that
group before the date of passing of the Finance (No. 2)
Act 2008, in the taxable period in which that Act is
passed, or

(b)   in the case of a landlord who became a person in that
group after the date of passing of the Finance (No. 2) Act
2008, in the taxable period during which that landlord
became a person in that group.".

99. The enactments specified in Schedule 6 —

(a)   are amended to the extent and in the manner specified in
paragraphs 1 to 6 of that Schedule, and

(b)   apply and come into operation in accordance with paragraph 7
of that Schedule.

SCHEDULE 6

Miscellaneous Technical Amendments in Relation to Tax

4. The Value-Added Tax Act 1972 is amended —

(f)   in section 7B(3) by substituting "makes or has made" for "has
made",

(With effect from 24 December 2008)

Finance Act 2009

22.   Section 7B of the Principal Act is amended —

    (a)   by substituting the following for subsection (2):

          "(2)   For the purposes of applying section 12E, the adjustment period (within the meaning of that section or, as the context may require, the period to be treated as the adjustment period in accordance with section 4C(11)) in relation to a capital good the tax chargeable on the landlord's acquisition or development of which that landlord was obliged to take into account when that landlord cancelled his or her waiver of exemption, shall end on the date on which that cancellation had effect.",

    and

    (b)   by inserting the following after subsection (6):

        "(7)   (a)   This subsection applies where —

              (i)   on 1 July 2008 a landlord had an interest in relevant immovable goods,

              (ii)   on the relevant date the landlord did not have an interest in any relevant immovable goods, and

              (iii)   that landlord's waiver of exemption had not been cancelled on or before the relevant date in accordance with section 7 (3).

          (b)   Where this subsection applies —

              (i)   the landlord's waiver of exemption shall be treated as if it were cancelled in accordance with section 7(3) on the date of the passing of the Finance Act 2009, and

              (ii)   that landlord shall pay an amount, being the amount payable in accordance with section 7(3) in respect of the cancellation of that waiver, as if it were tax due by that landlord for the taxable period beginning on 1 May 2009.

        (8)   (a)   This subsection applies where —

              (i)   in the period from 1 July 2008 to the relevant date, a landlord made a supply of relevant immovable goods during the adjustment period (within the meaning of section 12E or, as the context may require, the period to be treated as the adjustment period in accordance with section 4C(11)) in relation to those goods, and

(ii)   tax was not chargeable on that supply.

(b)   Where this subsection applies, then for the purposes of sections 4B(5), 12E(3)(d) and 12E(7)(b) the supply of the relevant immovable goods is treated as if it was made on the date of the passing of the Finance Act 2009.

(c)   Paragraph (b) shall not apply where —

    (i)   the landlord's waiver of exemption has been cancelled in accordance with subsection (7), or

    (ii)   the landlord cancels his or her waiver of exemption in accordance with section 7(3) before 1 July 2009.

(9)   (a)   This subsection applies where —

    (i)   on or after the date of the passing of the Finance Act 2009 a landlord has an interest in relevant immovable goods,

    (ii)   the landlord ceases, whether as a result of disposing of such goods or otherwise, to have an interest in any such goods, and

    (iii)   on the date when that landlord ceases to have any such interest, that landlord's waiver of exemption has not been cancelled in accordance with section 7(3).

(b)   Where this subsection applies —

    (i)   the landlord's waiver of exemption shall be treated as if it were cancelled on the date referred to in paragraph (a)(iii), and

    (ii)   that landlord shall pay an amount, being the amount payable in accordance with section 7(3) in respect of the cancellation of that waiver, as if it were tax due by that landlord for the taxable period in which the waiver of exemption is so treated as cancelled.

(10)   In this section —

'relevant immovable goods' means immovable goods the tax chargeable on the acquisition or development of which a landlord would be obliged to take into account in accordance with section 7(3) in relation to the cancellation of that landlord's waiver of exemption;

'relevant date' means the date immediately before the date of the passing of the Finance Act 2009.".".

(With effect from 3 June 2009)

Section 8

Value Added Tax Act 1972

Accountable persons

8.   (1)   In this section references to a farming business or a fishing business do not include references to-

    (a)   the operation of a nursery or garden for the sale of produce,

    (b)   commercial production of poultry or eggs,

    (c)   fur farming, or

    (d)   fish farming.

(2)   Subject in subsection (3), a person who, otherwise than as the employee of another person, engages in the delivery of taxable goods or the rendering of taxable services in the course of business, whether or two for profit, shall, in addition to the persons referred to in section 4(5), be an accountable person and shall be accountable for and liable to pay the tax charged under section 2(1)(a) in respect of such delivery or rendering. The State and a local authority shall also be deemed, for the purposes of this Act, to be accountable persons in relation to the provision by them of any of the services specified in paragraph (x) of the Second Schedule.

(3)   The following persons shall not, unless they otherwise elect and then only during the period for which such election has effect, be deemed, for the purposes of this Act, to be accountable persons-

    (a)   a person whose deliveries of taxable goods or rendering of taxable services in the course of business consist exclusively of-

        (i)   deliveries of goods of a kind specified in paragraphs (i) to (iv), (vi), subparagraphs (d) and (r) of paragraph (x) and paragraphs (xv),(xxii) and (xxiii) of Part 1 of the Third Schedule which he has produced in the course of a farming business, or caught in the course fishing business,

        (ii)   deliveries of machinery, plant or other equipment which has been used by him in the course of a farming or a fishing business,

        (iii)   rendering of cultivating, fertilising, sowing, harvesting or similar agricultural services, and

        (iv)   deliveries of goods and rendering of services other than those referred to in subparagraphs (i) to (iii) the total consideration for which has not exceeded and is not likely to exceed £1,800 in any period consisting of six consecutive taxable periods:

(b)   (i)   subject to subparagraph (ii), a person for whose delivery of taxable goods and rendering of taxable services the total consideration has not exceeded and is not likely to exceed £2,000 in any taxable period,

      (ii)   subparagraph (i) shall apply if, but only if, not less than 90 per cent of the total consideration referred to therein is derived from the delivery of taxable goods which the person therein referred to has imported or which have been delivered to him by other account able persons an d not less than 50 per cent of such consideration is derived from the delivery of goods and the rendering of services chargeable with tax at the rate of 5.26 per cent;

(c)   (i)   subject to subparagraph (ii), a person for whose delivery of taxable goods and rendering of taxable services the total consideration has not exceeded and is not likely to exceed £1,000 in any taxable period.

      (ii)   subparagraph (i) shall apply if, but only if, not less than 90 per cent of the total consideration referred to therein is derived from the delivery of taxable goods;

      (iii)   a person, other than a person to whom paragraph rendering of taxable services the total consideration has not exceeded and is not likely to exceed £300 in any taxable period.

(4)   Where, by virtue of subsection (3) or (6), a person has not been an accountable person and a change of circumstances occurs which continues beyond the end of the taxable period next after the taxable period or the period referred to in subsection (3)(a)(iv), as the case may be, during which such change occurs whereby he can no longer be deemed, for the purposes of this Act, not to be an accountable person by virtue of either of those subsections, he shall be deemed, for those purpose, to be an accountable person immediately after the end of the first mentioned taxable period.

(5)   Provision may be made by regulation for the cancellation, at the request of a person, of an election made by him under this section and for the payment by him to the Revenue Commissioners of such a sum as a condition of cancellation as when added to the net total amount of tax (if any) paid by him in accordance with section 19 in relation to the delivery of goods or the rendering

of services by him in the period for which the election had effect is equal to the amount of tax repaid to him during such period in respect of tax borne or paid in relation to the delivery of such goods or the rendering of such services.

(6)   An accountable person, other than a person to whom subsection (5) applies, may, in accordance with regulations, at his request, be treated, for the purposes of this Act, as a person who is not an accountable person if-

(a)   he satisfies the Revenue Commissioners that his turnover-

(i)   is permanently of such a character that, in the absence of an election in that behalf, he would not be an accountable person in accordance with the provisions of subsection (3)(a), or

(ii)   has fallen below and remains permanently below such amount as may be appropriate in the particular case having regard to subsection (3)(b), (3)(c) or (3)(d)

and

(b)   he pays to the Revenue Commissioners such a sum as when added to the net total amount of tax (if any) paid by him in accordance with section 19 in relation to the delivery of goods or the rendering of services by him in respect of the period for which he was an accountable person is equal to the amount of tax repaid to him during such period in respect of tax borne or paid in relation to the delivery of such goods or the rendering of such services,

and he shall be treated, for the purposes of this Act, as a person who is not an accountable person immediately after the end of the period in relation to which the provisions of this subsection are complied with by him.

(7)   Where goods are supplied or services are provided by a club or other similar organisation in respect of a payment of money by any of is members, then, for the purposes of this Act-

(a)   the supply of the goods shall be deemed, for the purposes of this Act, to be a delivery of the goods in the course of business, the money shall be deemed, for the said purposes, to be consideration for the delivery and the club or other organisation shall be deemed, for the said purposes, to be the person making the delivery, and

(b)   the provision of the services shall be deemed, for the said purposes, to be a rendering of the services in the course of business.

(8)   Notwithstanding anything in this section a person-

(a)   who does not deliver taxable goods or render taxable services within the State, and

(b)   who is not residing or established in the State,

shall not be an accountable person.

(9)   Provision may be made by regulation whereby, if the Revenue Commissioners are satisfied that the business activities of two or more accountable persons are so interlinked that it would be expedient, in the interests of efficient administration of the tax to do so, then at the request of the accountable persons concerned-

(a)   those activities may be deemed, for the purposes of this Act, to be carried on by up one at to persons and all transactions by or between such persons shall be deemed, for those purposes, to be transactions by that one person and all other rights and obligations under this Act shall be determined accordingly, and

(b)   each such person may be made jointly and severally liable to comply with all the provisions of this Act and regulations (including the provisions requiring the payment of tax) that apply to those persons and subject to the penalties under this Act to which they would be subject if each such person was liable to pay to the Revenue Commissioners the whole of the tax chargeable, apart from regulations under this subsection, in respect of all such persons.

(With effect from 1 November 1972)

Finance Act 1973

90.   The Principal Act is hereby amended as specified in column (3) of the Tenth Schedule to this Act.

TENTH SCHEDULE

Amendment of Enactments

Number and Year (1)	Short Title (2)	Amendment (3)
No. 22 of 1972	Value-Added Tax Act, 1972	In section 8, the following subsection shall be substituted for subsection (1) "(1) In this section references to a farming business do not include references to fur farming."; and in subsection (3), in paragraph (a)(i), "paragraphs (vii), (xii), (xiv) and (xv) of the Second Schedule," shall be inserted after "specified in"; in paragraph (b)(ii) "or which are goods of a kind specified in paragraphs (vi) to (viii) or (xii) to (xv) of the Second Schedule, delivered to him by persons other than accountable persons" shall be inserted after "accountable person"; and "either of the rates for the time being specified in paragraphs (a) or (d) of subsection (1) of section 11" shall be substituted for "the rate of 5.26 per cent."

(With effect from 3 September 1973)

Value-Added Tax (Amendment) Act 1978

6.   Section 8 of the Principal Act is hereby amended by the substitution of the following subsections for subsections (1), (2), (3), (7), (8) and (9):

"(1)   A person who, otherwise than as an employee of another person, engages in the supply, within the State, of taxable goods or services in the course of business shall, in addition to the persons referred to in section 4(5) and subsections (2) and (2A), be a taxable person and shall be accountable for and liable to pay the tax charged in respect of such supply.

(2)   Where by virtue of section 5(6)(e)(ii) a taxable service that, apart from that provision, would be treated as supplied abroad, is deemed to be supplied in the State, the person who receives the service shall, in relation thereto, be a taxable person and be liable to pay the tax charged as if he had himself supplied the service for consideration in the course or furtherance of his business.

(2A)   (a)   The Minister may, following such consultations as he may deem appropriate, by order provide that the State and every local authority shall be taxable persons with respect to specified categories of supplies made by them of goods or services and, accordingly, during the continuance in force of any such order but not otherwise, the State and every local authority shall be accountable for and liable to pay tax in respect of any such supplies made by them as if the supplies had been made in the course of business.

(b) The Minister may by order amend or revoke an order under this subsection, including an order under this paragraph.

(c) An order under this subsection shall be laid before Dáil Éireann as soon as may be after it is made and, if a resolution annulling the order is passed by Dáil Éireann within the next twenty one days on which Dáil Éireann has sat after the order is laid before it, the order shall be annulled accordingly, but without prejudice to the validity of anything previously done thereunder.

(3) The following persons shall not, unless they otherwise elect and then only during the period for which such election has effect, be taxable persons-

(a) a farmer,

(b) a person whose supplies of taxable, goods or services consist exclusively of-

(i) supplies to taxable persons and persons to whom section 13(3) applies of fish (not further processed than gutted, salted and frozen) which he has caught in the course of a sea-fishing business,

(ii) supplies of machinery, plant or other equipment which have been used by him in the course of a sea-fishing business, and

(iii) supplies of goods and services, other than those referred to in subparagraphs (i) and (ii), the total consideration for which has not exceeded and is not likely to exceed £3,000 in any period consisting of 6 consecutive taxable periods,

(c) (i) subject to subparagraph (ii), a person for whose supply of taxable goods and services the total consideration has not exceeded and is not likely to exceed £3,000 in any taxable period,

(ii) subparagraph (i) shall apply if, but only if, not less than 90 per cent of the total consideration referred to therein is derived from the supply of taxable goods which the person has imported or which have been supplied to him by other taxable persons or which, being goods of a kind chargeable with tax at the rate of zero per cent, were supplied to him by persons other than taxable persons and not less than 50 per cent of such consideration is derived from the supply of goods and services chargeable with tax at either of the rates for the time being specified in paragraph (a) or (b) of section 11(1),

(d) (i) subject to subparagraph (ii), a person for whose supply of taxable goods and services the total consideration has not exceeded and is not likely to exceed £1,500 in any taxable period,

(ii) subparagraph (i) shall apply if, but only if, not less than 90 per cent of the total consideration referred to therein is derived from the supply of taxable goods.

(e) a person, other than a person to whom paragraph (a), (b), (c) or (d) applies, for whose supply of taxable goods and services the total consideration has not exceeded and is not likely to exceed £500 in any taxable period.

(7) Where any goods or services are provided by a club or other similar organisation in respect of a payment of money by any of its members, then, for the purposes of this Act, the provision of the goods or services shall be deemed to be a supply by the club or other organisation of the goods or services (as the case may be) in the course or furtherance of a business carried on by it and the money shall be deemed to be consideration for the supply.

(8) Provision may be made by regulations whereby, if the Revenue Commissioners are satisfied that the business activities of two or more taxable persons are so interlinked that it would be expedient, in the interest of efficient administration of the tax to do so, then at the request of the taxable persons concerned-

(a) those activities may be deemed, for the purpose of this Act, to be carried on by any one of the persons and all transactions by or between such persons shall be deemed, for those purposes, to be transactions by that one person and all other rights and obligations under this Act shall be determined accordingly, and

(b) each such person may be made jointly and severally liable to comply with all the provisions of this Act and regulations (including the provisions requiring the payment of tax) that apply to those persons and subject to the penalties under this Act to which they would be subject if each such person was liable to pay to the Revenue Commissioners the whole of the tax chargeable, apart from regulations under this subsection, in respect of all such persons.

(9)   In this Act-

'**agricultural produce**' means, in relation to a farmer, goods, other than live horses and live greyhounds, produced by him in the course of an Annex A activity;

'**agricultural service**' means, in relation to a farmer, any Annex B service supplied by him using his own labour or that of his employees or effected by means of machinery, plant or other equipment normally used for the purposes of an Annex A activity carried on by him;

'**Annex A activity**' means any activity of a description specified in Annex A (which is set out in Part 1 of the Fifth Schedule) of Council Directive No. 77/388/EEC of 17 May, 1977;

'**Annex B service**' means any service of a description specified in Annex B (which is set out in Part II of the Fifth Schedule) of the said Council Directive;

'**farmer**' means a person who engages in at least one Annex A activity and whose supplies of taxable goods and services in the course of business consist exclusively of-

(a)   supplies of agricultural produce,

(b)   supplies of agricultural services,

(c)   supplies of machinery, plant or other equipment which has been used by him for the purposes of an Annex A activity, and

(d)   supplies of goods and services, other than those referred to in paragraphs (a), (b) and (c), the total consideration for which has not exceeded and is not likely to exceed £3,000 in any period consisting of six consecutive taxable periods.".

30.   (2)   In consequence of the amendments of the Principal Act specified in this Act and of the repeals specified in the First Schedule, the Principal Act is hereby further amended by the substitution of the word or expression mentioned in column (3) of the Second Schedule at any reference number for the word or expression mentioned in column (2) of that Schedule at that reference number wherever it occurs in the provision of the Principal Act mentioned in column (4) of that Schedule at that reference number.

SECOND SCHEDULE
Consequential Amendments

Reference Number (1)	Existing word or expression (2)	Substituted word or expression (3)	Provision of Principal Act (4)
9	"delivery of such goods or the rendering of such services"	"supply of such goods and services"	Sections 8(5) and 8(6)(b)
17	"delivery of goods or the rendering of services"	"supply of goods or services"	Sections 8(5), 8(6)(b),
26	"an accountable person"	"a taxable person"	Sections 8(4), 8(6),
36	"subsection (3)(a) (iv)"	"subsection (3)(b)(iii) or (9)"	Section 8(4).
37	"subsection (3)(a)"	"subsection (3) (a) or (b)".	Subsection 8(6)(a)(i).
38	"subsection (3)(b), (3)(c) or (3)(d)"	"subsection (3)(c), (3) (d) or (3)(e)"	Subsection 8(6)(a)(ii).

Transitional provisions

31.   (1)

...

...

(c)   A person who, immediately before the commencement of this Act, was an accountable person and who, upon such commencement, would not, unless he so elected under section 8(3) of the Principal Act, be a taxable person, shall, upon such commencement, be deemed to have so elected and shall be a taxable person until the time when the election is cancelled or he permanently ceases to supply taxable goods and services, whichever is the later.

(2)   In relation to a person who, immediately before the commencement of this Act, was an accountable person-

....

(b)   references in subsection (5) of section 8 of the Principal Act to an election shall be deemed to include references to an election made under subsection (3) of the said section 8,

....

(d)   references in the said subsection (5) and subsection (6)(b) of the said section 8 to the supply of goods or services shall be deemed to include references to the delivery of goods, or the rendering of services, before such commencement.

(With effect from 1 March 1979)

Finance Act 1980

81.   With effect as on and from the 1st day of May, 1980, section 8 of the
Value-Added Tax Act, 1972 (inserted by the Value-Added Tax
(Amendment) Act, 1978), is hereby amended-

(a)   by the substitution of the following paragraph for
paragraph (e) of subsection (3):

"(e)   a person, other than a person to whom paragraph
(a), (b), (c) or (d) applies, for whose supply of
taxable goods and services the total consideration
has not exceeded and is not likely to exceed £3,000
in any period consisting of 6 consecutive taxable
periods",

and

(b)   by the insertion in subsection (4), after "(3)(b)(iii)" of
", (3)(e)" and the substitution of "any one" for "either"
where it occurs in that subsection and the subsection as
so amended is set out in the Table to this section.

TABLE

(4)   Where, by virtue of subsection (3) or (6), a person has not been
a taxable person and a change of circumstances occurs which
continues beyond the end of the taxable period next after the
taxable period or the period referred to in subsection (3)(b)
(iii), (3)(e) or (9), as the case may be, during which such change
occurs whereby he can no longer be deemed, for the purposes
of this Act, not to be a taxable person by virtue of any one of
those subsections, he shall be deemed, for those purposes, to be
a taxable person immediately after the end of the first mentioned
taxable period.

(With effect from 1 May 1980)

Finance (No. 2) Act 1981

11.   Section 8 of the Principal Act is hereby amended-

(a)   in subsection (3) (inserted by the Act of 1978)-

(i)   by the substitution in paragraph (b) of the following
subparagraph for subparagraph (iii):

"(iii)   supplies of goods and services, other than those
referred to in subparagraphs (i) and (ii), the total
consideration for which has not exceeded and is
not likely to exceed £15,000 in any continuous
period of 12 months,",

(ii) by the substitution of the following paragraph for paragraph (c):

"(c) (i) subject to subparagraph (ii), a person for whose supply of taxable goods and services the total consideration has not exceeded and is not likely to exceed £30,000 in any continuous period of 12 months,

(ii) subparagraph (i) shall apply if, but only if, not less than 90 per cent of the total consideration referred to therein is derived from the supply of taxable goods,",

(iii) by the deletion of paragraph (d), and

(iv) by the substitution of the following paragraph for paragraph (e):

"(e) a person, other than a person to whom paragraph (a), (b) or (c) applies, for whose supply of taxable goods and services the total consideration has not exceeded and is not likely to exceed £15,000 in any continuous period of 12 months.",

(b) by the substitution of the following subsection for subsection (4):

"(4) Where, by virtue of subsection (3) or (6), a person has not been a taxable person and a change of circumstances occurs from which it becomes clear that he is likely to become a taxable person, he shall be deemed, for the purposes of this Act, to be a taxable person from the beginning of the taxable period commencing next after such change.",

(c) in subsection (6), by the substitution in paragraph (a) of the following subparagraph for subparagraph (ii):

"(ii) has fallen below and remains permanently below such amount as may be appropriate in the particular case having regard to paragraph (c) or (e) of subsection (3),",

(d) in subsection (8), by the substitution of the following for paragraph (b):

"(b) each such person may be made jointly and severally liable to comply with all the provisions of this Act and regulations (including the provisions requiring the payment of tax) that apply to those persons and subject to the penalties under this Act to which they would be subject if each such person was liable to pay to the Revenue Commissioners the whole of the tax chargeable, apart from regulations under this subsection, in respect of all such persons:

Provided that this subsection shall not apply to business activities consisting of the supply of immovable goods by any such person to any other such person and, where a request is made by such persons pursuant to regulations under this subsection, such business activities shall be treated for the purposes of this Act, as if the request had not been made.",

and

(e)   in subsection (9), by the substitution of the following paragraph for paragraph (d) in the definition of "farmer":

"(d)   supplies of goods and services, other than those referred to in paragraphs (a), (b) and (c), the total consideration for which has not exceeded and is not likely to exceed £15,000 in any continuous period of 12 months.".

Transitional provisions

15.   A person who, immediately before the passing of this Act, was a taxable person and who, upon such passing, would not, unless he so elected under section 8(3) of the Principal Act, be such a person, shall, upon such passing, be deemed to have so elected and shall be a taxable person until the time when the election is cancelled or he permanently ceases to supply taxable goods and services, whichever is the earlier.

(With effect from 20 November 1981)

Finance Act 1982

77.   Section 8 of the Principal Act is hereby amended-

(a)   by the substitution in subsection (3) (inserted by the Act of 1978) of the following paragraph for paragraph (b):

"(b)   a person whose supplies of taxable goods or services consist exclusively of-

(i)   supplies to taxable persons and persons to whom section 13(3) applies of fish (not further processed than gutted, salted and frozen) which he has caught in the course of a sea-fishing business, or

(ii)   supplies of the kind specified in subparagraph (i) and of either or both of the following, that is to say:

(I)   supplies of machinery, plant or equipment which have been used by him in the course of a sea-fishing business, and

(II)   supplies of other goods and services the total consideration for which has not exceeded and is not likely to exceed £15,000 in any continuous period of 12 months.",

(b)   by the insertion after subsection (3) of the following subsection:

"(3A) Where a person who supplies services consisting of the training of horses for racing, the consideration for which has exceeded £15,000 in any continuous period of 12 months, would, but for the supply of such services, be a farmer, he shall be deemed to be a taxable person only in respect of the supply of those services and, in the absence of an election, shall, in relation to the supply of any of the goods and services specified in paragraph (a) and subparagraphs (i) and (iii) of paragraph (b) of the definition of 'farmer' in subsection (9) (inserted by the Act of 1978), be deemed not to be a taxable person. ",

and

(c)   by the substitution in subsection (9) for the definition of "farmer" of the following definition:

"'farmer' means a person who engages in at least one Annex A activity and-

(a)   whose supplies consist exclusively of either or both of the following, that is to say:

(i)   supplies of agricultural produce, or

(ii)   supplies of agricultural services, or

(b)   whose supplies consist exclusively of either or both of the supplies specified in paragraph (a) and of one or more of the following, that is to say:

(i)   supplies of machinery, plant or equipment which has been used by him for the purposes of an Annex A activity,

(ii)   supplies of services consisting of the training of horses for racing the total consideration for which has not exceeded and is not likely to exceed £15,000 in any continuous period of 12 months, or

(iii)   supplies of goods and services, other than those referred to in subparagraphs (i) and (ii) or paragraph (a), the total consideration for which has not exceeded and is not likely to exceed £15,000 in any continuous period of 12 months.".

(With effect from 1 September 1982)

Finance Act 1983

79.   Section 8 of the Principal Act is hereby amended-

(a)   in subsection (3) (inserted by the Act of 1978)-

(i)   in paragraph (b) (inserted by the Act of 1982), by the substitution of "£12,000" for "£15,000",

(ii)   in paragraph (c) (inserted by the Act of 1981), by the substitution of "£25,000" for "£30,000", and

(iii)   in paragraph (e) (inserted by the Act of 1981), by the substitution of "£12,000" for "£15,000",

(b)   in subsection (3A) (inserted by the Act of 1982), by the substitution of "£12,000" for "£15,000", and

(c)   in subsection (9), in the definition of "farmer" (inserted by the Act of 1982), by the substitution of "£12,000" for "£15,000" in each place where it occurs.

(With effect from 1 May 1983)

Finance Act 1984

86.   Section 8 of the Principal Act is hereby amended-

(a)   in subsection (1) (inserted by the Finance Act, 1978) by the insertion after "in the course" of "or furtherance",

(b)   in subsection (3) (inserted by the Finance Act, 1978)-

(i)   in subparagraph (c)(ii) (inserted by the Finance (No. 2) Act, 1981), by the insertion after "taxable goods" of "(not being goods chargeable at either of the rates specified in paragraphs (a) and (c) of subsection (1) of section 11 which were produced or manufactured by him wholly or mainly from materials chargeable at the rate specified in paragraph (b) of that subsection)",

and

(ii)   by the substitution of the following paragraph for paragraph (e) (inserted by the Finance (No. 2) Act, 1981):

"(e) a person, other than a person to whom paragraph (a), (b) or (c) applies, for whose supply of taxable goods and services the total consideration has not exceeded and is not likely to exceed £12,000 in any continuous period of twelve months:

Provided that, where in the case of two or more persons one of whom exercises control over one or more of the other persons, supplies of goods of the same class or of services of the same nature are made by two or more of those persons, the total of the consideration relating to the said supplies shall, for the purposes of the application of paragraphs (c) and (e) in relation to each of the persons aforesaid who made the said supplies be treated as if all of the supplies in question had been made by each of the last-mentioned persons.",

and

(c)   by the insertion after subsection (3A) (inserted by the Finance Act, 1982) of the following subsection:

"(3B) In this section '**control**', in relation to a body corporate, means the power of a person to secure, by means of the holding of shares or the possession of voting power in or in relation to that or any other body corporate, or by virtue of any powers conferred by the articles of association or other document regulating that or any other body corporate, that the affairs of the first-mentioned body corporate are conducted in accordance with the wishes of that person, and, in relation to a partnership, means the right to a share of more than one-half of the assets, or of more than one-half of the income, of the partnership.".

(With effect from 23 May 1984)

Finance Act 1986

82.   Section 8 of the Principal Act is hereby amended by the insertion in subsection (2) (inserted by the Act of 1978) after "section 5(6)(e)(ii)" of ", (iii) or (iv)".

(With effect from 27 May 1986)

Finance Act 1989

55.   Section 8 of the Principal Act is hereby amended-

(a)   in subsection (3) (inserted by the Act of 1978) by the substitution-

(i)   in paragraph (b)(inserted by the Finance Act, 1982) of "£15,000" for "£12,000" (inserted by the Finance Act, 1983),

(ii)   in paragraph (c)(inserted by the Finance (No. 2) Act, 1981) of "£32,000" for "£25,000" (inserted by the Finance Act, 1983),

and

(iii)   in paragraph (e)(inserted by the Finance Act, 1984) of "£15,000" for "£12,000",

(b)   in subsection (3A) (inserted by the Finance Act, 1982), by the substitution of "£15,000" for "£12,000" (inserted by the Finance Act, 1983),

and

(c)   in subsection (9) (inserted by the Act of 1978), in the definition of "farmer" (inserted by the Finance Act, 1982), by the substitution of "£15,000" for "£12,000" (inserted by the Finance Act, 1983) in each place where it occurs.

(With effect from 1 July 1989)

Finance Act 1990

101. Section 8 of the Principal Act is hereby amended in subsection (9) (inserted by the Act of 1978), in the definition of "agricultural produce", by the deletion of "live horses and".

(With effect from 1 January 1991)

Finance Act 1991

79. Section 8 of the Principal Act is hereby amended-

(a)   in subsection (1) (inserted by the Act of 1978) by the substitution of "subsections (2), (2A) and (8)" for "subsections (2) and (2A)",

and

(b)   by the substitution of the following subsection for subsection (8) (inserted by the Act of 1978):

"(8)   (a)   Where the Revenue Commissioners are satisfied that two or more persons established in the State are closely bound by financial, economic and organisational links and that it would be expedient in the interest of efficient administration of the tax to do so then, subject to such conditions as they may impose by regulations, the said Commissioners, for the purpose of this Act, may-

(i)   by notice in writing to each of the persons concerned, deem the activities relating to those links to be carried on by any one of the persons, and all transactions by or between such persons shall be deemed, for that purpose, to be transactions by that one person and all rights and obligations under this Act shall be determined accordingly, and

(ii)   make each such person jointly and severally liable to comply with all the provisions of this Act and regulations (including the provisions requiring the payment of tax) that apply to each of those persons and subject to the penalties under this Act to which they would be subject if each such person was liable to pay to the Revenue Commissioners the whole of the tax chargeable, apart from regulations under this subsection, in respect of each such person:

Provided that this subsection shall not apply in the case of:

(I)   the supply of immovable goods by any such person to any other such person, or

(II)   the transfer of ownership of goods specified in section 3(5)(b)(iii) from any such person to any other such person, except where, apart from the provisions of this subsection, each of the persons whose activities are deemed to be carried on by that one person is a taxable person.

(b)   The Revenue Commissioners may by notice in writing to each of the persons whose activities are, by virtue of a notification issued in accordance with paragraph (a)(i), deemed to be carried on by one of those persons, and as on and from the date specified in the notice (which date shall not be earlier than the date of issue of the notice) cancel the notification under the said paragraph; and as on and from the date specified in the said notice the provisions of the Act and regulations shall apply to all the persons as aforesaid as if a notification under the said paragraph had not been issued, but without prejudice to the liability of any of the persons for tax or penalties in respect of anything done or not done during the period for which the said notification was in force.

(c)   The Revenue Commissioners may, for the purpose of this subsection, deem a person engaged in the supply of non-taxable goods or services in the course or furtherance of business to be a taxable person.".

(With effect from 29 May 1991)

Finance Act 1992

170.   (1)   Section 8 of the Principal Act is hereby amended-

**(a)   in subsection (3) (inserted by the Act of 1978) by the substitution of the following paragraph for paragraph (a):

"(a)   a farmer, for whose supply of agricultural services, other than insemination services, stock-minding or stock-rearing, the total consideration has not exceeded and is not likely to exceed £15,000 in any continuous period of 12 months,",

and

*(b)   by the insertion of the following subsection after subsection (3B) (inserted by the Act of 1984):

"(3C) (a) The licensee of any premises (being premises in respect of which a licence for the sale of intoxicating liquor either on or off those premises was granted) shall be deemed to be the promoter of any dance held, during the subsistence of that licence, on those premises and shall be deemed to have received the total money, excluding tax, paid by those admitted to the dance together with any other consideration received or receivable in connection with the dance.

(b) For the purposes of this subsection 'licensee' means-

(i)   where the licence is held by the nominee of a body corporate, the body corporate, and

(iii) in any other case, the holder of the licence.".

(2)   Section 8 of the Principal Act is hereby further amended-

(a)   in subsection (1) (inserted by the Act of 1978) by the insertion after "subsections" of "(1A),",

(b)   by the insertion of the following subsection after subsection (1):

"(1A) Where a person engages in the intra-Community acquisition of goods he shall be a taxable person and shall be accountable for and liable to pay the tax chargeable.",

(c)   in subsection (2) (inserted by the Act of 1978) by the substitution of "subparagraph (ii), (iii) or (iv) of paragraph (e), or paragraph (f), of subsection (6) of section 5'" for "section 5(6)(e)(ii), (iii) or (iv)",

(d)   by the insertion of the following subsection after subsection (2A) (inserted by the Act of 1978):

"(2B) Notwithstanding the provisions of subsection (1A), an individual who does not engage in the supply of goods or services in the course or furtherance of business shall not be a taxable person in relation to the intra-Community acquisition of goods other than new means of transport:

Provided that an individual who is a taxable person by virtue of subsection (1A) and this subsection, in relation to the intra-Community acquisition of new means of transport, shall be deemed not to be a taxable person for the purposes of registration under section 9.",

(e)   by the substitution of the following subsection for subsection (3) (inserted by the Act of 1978):

"(3)   Notwithstanding the provisions of subsections (1) and (1A), the following persons shall not, unless they otherwise elect and then only during the period for which such election has effect, be taxable persons-

(a)   a farmer, for whose supply of agricultural services, other than insemination services, stock-minding or stock-rearing, the total consideration has not exceeded and is not likely to exceed £15,000 in any continuous period of twelve months,

(b)   a person whose supplies of taxable goods or services consist exclusively of-

(i)   supplies to taxable persons and persons to whom section 13(3) applies of fish (not being at a stage of processing further than that of being gutted, salted and frozen) which he has caught in the course of a sea-fishing business, or

(ii)   supplies of the kind specified in subparagraph (i) and of either or both of the following, that is to say:

(I)   supplies of machinery, plant or equipment which have been used by him in the course of a sea-fishing business, and

(II)   supplies of other goods and services the total consideration for which has not exceeded and is not likely to exceed £15,000 in any continuous period of 12 months,

(c)   (i)   subject to subparagraph (ii), a person for whose supply of taxable goods (other than supplies of the kind specified in section 3(6)(d)(i)) and services the total consideration has not exceeded and is not likely to exceed £32,000 in any continuous period of 12 months,

     (ii)   subparagraph (i) shall apply if, but only if, not less than 90 per cent of the total consideration referred to therein is derived from the supply of taxable goods (not being goods chargeable at any of the rates specified in paragraphs (a), (c), (d) and (e) of subsection (1) of section 11 which were produced or manufactured by him wholly or mainly from materials chargeable at the rate specified in paragraph (b) of that subsection),

(d)   a person for whose intra-Community acquisitions of goods, other than new means of transport and other than goods subject to a duty of excise, the total consideration has not exceeded and is not likely to exceed £32,000 in any continuous period of 12 months,

(e)   a person, other than a person to whom paragraph (a), (b) or (c) applies, for whose supply of taxable goods and services the total consideration has not exceeded and is not likely to exceed £15,000 in any continuous period of twelve months:

Provided that-

(i)   where in the case of two or more persons one of whom exercises control over one or more of the other persons, supplies of goods of the same class or of services of the same nature are made by two or more of those persons, the total of the consideration relating to the said supplies shall, for the purposes of the application of paragraphs (c) and (e) in relation to each of the persons aforesaid who made the said supplies be treated as if all of the supplies in question had been made by each of the last-mentioned persons;

(ii)   in the case of a person specified in paragraph (a), (b), (c) or (e), the total consideration for intra-Community acquisitions of goods, other than new means of transport and other than goods subject to a duty of excise, by him has not exceeded and is not likely to exceed £32,000 in any continuous period of 12 months.",

and

*(f)   by the substitution of the following subsection for subsection (6):

"(6)   A taxable person, other than a person to whom subsection (5) applies, may, in accordance with regulations, be treated, for the purposes of this Act, as a person who is not a taxable person if the Revenue Commissioners are satisfied that, in the absence of an election under subsection (3), he would not be a taxable person.".

(With effect from 1 January 1993 except * from 28 May 1992 and ** from 1 July 1992)

S.I. No. 413 of 1992
European Communities (Value Added Tax) Regulations 1992

7.   Section 8 of the Principal Act is hereby amended-

(a)   in subsection (1A) by the insertion after "goods" of "in the State",

(b)   by the substitution of the following subsection for subsection (2B) (inserted by the Act of 1992):

"(2B)   (a)   Where a person is a taxable person only because of an intra-Community acquisition of a new means of transport, then the person shall not, unless he so elects, be a taxable person for any purposes of this Act with the exception of subsection (4) of section 19.

(b)   Where

(i)   a person is a taxable person only because of an intra-Community acquisition of excisable products, and

(ii) by virtue of this acquisition, and in accordance with Chapter II of Part II of the Finance Act, 1992, and any other enactment which is to be construed together with that Chapter, the duty of excise on those products is payable in the State,

the person shall not, unless he so elects, be a taxable person for any purposes of the Act with the exception of subsection (5) of section 19.",

(c) by the insertion of the following subsection after subsection (3C) (inserted by the Act of 1992):

"(3D) (a) The provisions of paragraphs (b), (c) and (e) of subsection (3) shall not apply to a person who is not established in the State.

(b) A person who is not established in the State shall, unless he opts to register in accordance with section 9, be deemed not to have made an intra-Community acquisition or a supply of those goods in the State where the only supplies by him in the State are in the circumstances set out in section 3(8).",

and

(d) in subsection (8) (inserted by the Finance Act, 1991) by the insertion of the following paragraphs after paragraph I of the proviso to paragraph (a):

"(IA) the requirement to issue an invoice or other document, in accordance with section 17, in respect of supplies to persons other than supplies between persons who are jointly and severally liable to comply with the provisions of this Act in accordance with subparagraph (ii), or

(IB) the requirement to furnish a statement in accordance with section 19A, or".

(With effect from 1 January 1993)

Finance Act 1993

85. Section 8 of the Principal Act is hereby amended-

(a) by the substitution of the following subsection for subsection (1A) (inserted by the Act of 1992):

"(1A) (a) Where a person engages in the intra-Community acquisition of goods in the State in the course or furtherance of business he shall be a taxable person and shall be accountable for and liable to pay the tax chargeable.

(b) Subject to subsection (2), and notwithstanding paragraph (a), a person for whose intra-Community acquisitions of goods (being goods other than new means of transport or goods subject to a duty of excise) the total consideration for which has not exceeded and is not likely to exceed £32,000 in any continuous period of 12 months shall not, unless he otherwise elects and then only during the period for which such election has effect, be a taxable person:

Provided that where the provisions of subsection (1) apply to that person, this paragraph shall not apply unless the provisions of subsection (3) also apply to him.

(c)   A person who is a taxable person by virtue of this subsection and who is a person referred to in paragraph (a) or (b) of subsection (3) shall be deemed to be a taxable person only in respect of-

(i)   intra-Community acquisitions of goods which are made by him, and

(ii)   any services of the kind referred to in subsection (2) which are received by him:

Provided that a person may elect that this paragraph shall not apply to him.

(d)   A person who is a taxable person by virtue of this subsection and who is a person referred to in subsection (M) shall be deemed to be a taxable person only in respect of-

(i)   intra-Community acquisitions of goods which are made by him,

(ii)   racehorse training services which are supplied by him, and

(iii)   any services of the kind referred to in subsection (2) which are received by him:

Provided that a person may elect that this paragraph shall not apply to him.

(e)   For the purposes of this subsection, where an intra-Community acquisition is effected in the State by-

(i)   a Department of State or local authority,

(ii)   a body established by statute, or

(iii)   a person for the purpose of any activity specified in paragraph (vi), (vii), (xxii) or (xxiii) of the First Schedule,

the acquisition shall be deemed to have been effected in the course or furtherance of business.",

(b)   in subsection (2) (inserted by the Act of 1978)-

    (i)   by the transposition of that subsection into paragraph (a) thereof,

    and

    (ii)   by the addition of the following paragraphs:

        "(b)   A person who is a taxable person by virtue of this subsection and who is a person referred to in paragraph (a) or (b) of subsection (3) shall be deemed to be a taxable person only in respect of-

            (i)   any intra-Community acquisitions of goods which are made by him, and

            (ii)   services of the kind referred to in this subsection which are received by him:

        Provided that a person may elect that this paragraph shall not apply to him.

        (c)   A person who is a taxable person by virtue of this subsection and who is a person referred to in subsection (3A) shall be deemed to be a taxable person only in respect of-

            (i)   any intra-Community acquisitions of goods which are made by him,

            (ii)   racehorse training services which are supplied by him, and

            (iii)   services of the kind referred to in this subsection which are received by him:

        Provided that a person may elect that this paragraph shall not apply to him.",

(c)   in subsection (3) (inserted by the Act of 1992)-

    (i)   by the substitution of "Subject to subsections (1A) and (2), and notwithstanding the provisions of subsection (1)" for "Notwithstanding the provisions of subsections (1) and (1A)",

    *(ii)   in subparagraph (ii) of paragraph (c) by the substitution of "paragraphs (a), (c) and (d)" for "paragraphs (a), (c), (d) and (e)",

    (iii)   by the deletion of paragraph (d),

    and

(iv)   in the proviso to the subsection, by the substitution of the following paragraph for paragraph (ii):

"(ii)   the provisions of this subsection shall not apply to a supply of the kind referred to in subsection (2).",

(d)   in subsection (3A) (inserted by the Act of 1982) by the insertion after "the supply of those services" of "and any intra-Community acquisitions of goods made by him and any services of the kind referred to in subsection (2) received by him",

and

(e)   in subsection (5):

(i)   by the insertion after "for which the election had effect is equal to" of "the sum of",

and

(ii)   by the insertion after "such goods or services" of "and the tax deductible under section 12 in respect of intra-Community acquisitions made by him during such period".

(With effect from 17 June 1993 except * from 1 March 1993)

Finance Act 1994

94.   Section 8 of the Principal Act is hereby amended-

*(a)   in subparagraph (iii) of paragraph (e) of subsection (1A) (inserted by the Finance Act, 1993) by the substitution of "specified in the First Schedule" for "specified in paragraph (vi), (vii), (xxii) or (xxiii) of the First Schedule",

(b)   in subsection (3) (inserted by the Act of 1992) by the substitution-

(i)   in paragraph (a) of "£20,000" for "£15,000",

(ii)   in paragraph (b)(ii) of the following clause for clause (II):

"(II)   supplies of other goods and services the total consideration for which is such that such person would not, because of the provisions of paragraph (c) or (e), be a taxable person if such supplies were the only supplies made by such person,",

(iii)   in paragraph (c)(i) of "£40,000" for "£32,000",

and

(iv)   in paragraph (e) of "£20,000" for "£15,000",

(c)   in subsection (3A) (inserted by the Act of 1982) by the substitution of "£20,000" for "£15,000" (inserted by the Act of 1989),

and

(d)   in subsection (9) (inserted by the Act of 1978), in paragraph (b) of the definition of "farmer" (inserted by the Act of 1982)-

    (i)   by the substitution in subparagraph (ii) of "£20,000" for "£15,000" (inserted by the Act of 1989),

and

    (ii)   by the substitution of the following subparagraph for subparagraph (iii):

       "(iii)   supplies of goods and services other than those referred to in subparagraphs (i) and (ii) or paragraph (a), the total consideration for which is such that such person would not, because of the provisions of paragraph (c) or (e) of subsection (3), be a taxable person if such supplies were the only supplies made by such person.".

(With effect from 1 July 1994 except * from 23 May 1994)

Finance Act 1995

124.   Section 8 of the Principal Act is hereby amended-

(a)   in paragraph (a) of subsection (2A) (inserted by the Act of 1978) by the insertion of the following proviso to that paragraph:

"Provided that, where supplies of the kind referred to in, subject to subsection (3E), paragraph (xxiii) of the First Schedule or in paragraph (viic) of the Sixth Schedule are provided by the State or by a local authority, an order under this subsection shall be deemed to have been made in respect of such supplies by the State or by the local authority.",

and

(b)   by the insertion of the following subsection after subsection (3D) (inserted by the European Communities (Value-Added Tax) Regulations, 1992 (S.I. No. 413 of 1992)):

"(3E) (a)   Notwithstanding the provisions of section 6(1) and of subsection (1), and subject to the provisions of subsection (3), where-

    (i)   a person supplies services which are exempt in accordance with section 6 and paragraph (xxiii) of the First Schedule, or

    (ii)   the State or a local authority supplies services of the kind referred to in paragraph (xxiii) of the First Schedule,

then an authorised officer of the Revenue Commissioners shall-

(I)   where such officer is satisfied that such supply of such services has created or is likely to create a distortion of competition such as to place at a disadvantage a commercial enterprise which is a taxable person supplying similar-type services, or

(II) where such officer is satisfied that such supply of such services is managed or administered by or on behalf of another person who has a direct or indirect beneficial interest, either directly or through an intermediary, in the supply of such services,

make a determination in relation to some or all of such supplies as specified in that determination deeming-

(A)   such person, the State or such local authority to be supplying such supplies as specified in that determination in the course or furtherance of business,

(B)   such person, the State or such local authority to be a taxable person in relation to the provision of such supplies as specified in that determination, and

(C)   such supplies as specified in that determination to be taxable supplies to which the rate specified in section 11(1) (d) refers.

(b)   Where a determination is made under paragraph (a), the Revenue Commissioners shall, as soon as may be after the making thereof, issue a notice in writing of that determination to the party concerned, and such determination shall have effect from such date as may be specified in the notice of that determination:

Provided that such determination shall have effect no sooner than the start of the next taxable period following that in which the notice issued.

(c)   Where an authorised officer is satisfied that the conditions that gave rise to the making of a determination under paragraph (a) no longer apply, that officer shall cancel that determination by notice in writing to the party concerned and that cancellation shall have effect from the start of the next taxable period following that in which the notice issued.

(d)   In this subsection 'authorised officer' means an officer of the Revenue Commissioners authorised by them in writing for the purposes of this subsection.".

(With effect from 1 January 1996)

Finance Act 1997

101. Section 8 of the Principal Act is hereby amended in subsection (3)-

(a)   by the substitution of the following paragraph for paragraph (a):

"(a)   a farmer, for whose supply in any continuous period of twelve months of-

(i)   agricultural services, other than insemination services, stock-minding or stock-rearing, the total consideration has not exceeded and is not likely to exceed £20,000, or

(ii)   goods of the type specified in paragraph (xia) of the Sixth Schedule to persons who are not engaged in supplying those goods in the course or furtherance of business, the total consideration has not exceeded and is not likely to exceed £40,000, or

(iii)   services and goods specified in subparagraph (i) and (ii), the total consideration has not exceeded and is not likely to exceed £20,000,",

and

(b)   by the insertion of the following subparagraph after subparagraph (i) in the proviso to the subsection:

"(ia)   where a farmer supplies services or goods of the kind specified in paragraph (a)(i) or (a)(ii), subparagraph (i) of this proviso shall be deemed to apply to those supplies, notwithstanding that the provisions of that subparagraph do not otherwise apply to supplies by a farmer;".

(With effect from 1 September 1997)

Finance Act 1998

108. Section 8 of the Principal Act is hereby amended in subsection (3)-

(a)   in paragraph (a):

       (i)   by the insertion of the following subparagraph after subparagraph (i):

          "(ia)   goods being livestock semen, the total consideration has not exceeded and is not likely to exceed £40,000 and, in calculating that total consideration, supplies of livestock semen to-

            (I)   any other farmer licensed as an artificial insemination centre in accordance with the provisions of the Live Stock (Artificial Insemination) Act, 1947, or

            (II)   a taxable person over whom that farmer exercises control, shall be disregarded, or",

       (ii)   by the substitution in subparagraph (iii) (inserted by the Act of 1997) of "services specified in subparagraph (i) and either or both of goods of the type specified in subparagraph (ia) and goods of the type specified in subparagraph (ii) supplied in the circumstances set out in that subparagraph" for "services and goods specified in subparagraph (i) and (ii)",

       (iii)   by the insertion of "or" at the end of subparagraph (iii), and

       (iv)   by the insertion of the following after subparagraph (iii):

          "(iv)   goods of the type specified in subparagraph (ia) and goods of the type specified in subparagraph (ii) supplied in the circumstances set out in that subparagraph, the total consideration has not exceeded and is not likely to exceed £40,000,",

(b)   in subparagraph (ia) (inserted by the Act of 1997) of the proviso thereto by the insertion after "paragraph (a)(i)" of ", (a)(ia)".

(With effect from 1 July 1998)

Finance Act 1999

123. Section 8 of the Principal Act is hereby amended in sub-paragraph (ia) of paragraph (a) of subsection (3) by the substitution for "livestock", in each place where it occurs, of "bovine".

(With effect from 25 March 1999)

Finance Act 2000

110. Section 8 of the Principal Act is amended-

(a)   in subsection (5):

(i)   by the substitution of "goods or services, other than services of the kind referred to in paragraph (xiii) of the Sixth Schedule," for "such goods or services", and

(ii)   by the substitution of "goods or services, other than services of the kind referred to in paragraph (xiii) of the Sixth Schedule." for "goods or services.",

(b)   by the insertion of the following subsection after subsection (5):

"(5A) (a)   Notwithstanding subsection (5), provision may be made by regulation for the cancellation, by the request of a person who supplies services of the kind referred to in paragraph (xiii) of the Sixth Schedule, of an election made by such person under this section and for the payment by such person to the Revenue Commissioners, in addition to any amount payable in accordance with subsection (5), of such an amount (hereafter referred to in this subsection as the 'cancellation amount'), as shall be determined in accordance with paragraph (b), as a condition of cancellation and the cancellation amount shall be payable as if it were tax due in accordance with section 19 for the taxable period in which the cancellation comes into effect.

(b)   (i) Where the person referred to in paragraph (a)-

(I)   was entitled to deduct tax in accordance with section 12 in respect of the acquisition, purchase or development of immovable goods used by that person in the course of a supply of services of a kind referred to in paragraph (xiii) of the Sixth Schedule, or

(II)   would be entitled to deduct tax in accordance with section 12 in respect of the acquisition, as a result of a transfer to that person, of immovable goods used by that person in the course of a supply of services of a kind referred to in paragraph (xiii) of the Sixth Schedule, if that tax had been chargeable but for the application of the provisions of section 3(5)(b)(iii) on that transfer,

then, in respect of each such acquisition, purchase or development, an amount (hereafter referred to in this subsection as the 'adjustment amount') shall be calculated in accordance with subparagraph (ii) and the cancellation amount shall be the sum of the adjustment amounts so calculated or, if there is only one such adjustment amount, that amount: but if there is no adjustment amount, the cancellation amount is nil.

(ii) The adjustment amount shall be determined by the formula-

$$\frac{A \times (10 - B)}{10}$$

where –

A is –

(I) the amount of tax deductible in respect of the said acquisition, purchase or development of the said immovable goods, or

(II) the amount of tax that would be deductible in respect of the said acquisition of the said immovable goods if the provisions of section 3(5)(b) (iii) had not applied to the transfer of those immovable goods,

and

B is the number of full years for which the said goods were used by the person in the course of the supply of services of a kind referred to in paragraph (xiii) of the Sixth Schedule: but if the said number of full years is in excess of 10, such adjustment amount shall be deemed to be nil.

(c) For the purposes of paragraph (b) a full year shall be any continuous period of 12 months.'',

and

(c)   in subsection (6) (inserted by the Act of 1992) by the insertion after "subsection (5)" of "or subsection (5A)".

(With effect from 23 March 2000)

Finance Act 2001

184. Section 8(2) of the Principal Act is amended in paragraph (a) (inserted by the Finance Act, 1993) by the insertion of ", (iiia)" after "(iii)".

*240. (1)   (a)   Subject to subsection (2), in each provision specified in column (1) of Schedule 5 for the words or amount set out in column (2) of that Schedule at that entry there shall be substituted the words or amount set out at the corresponding entry in column (3) of that Schedule.

(b)   Where words are or an amount is mentioned more than once in a provision specified in column (1) of Schedule 5, then the substitution provided for by paragraph (a) shall apply as respects those words or that amount to each mention of those words or that amount in that provision.

SCHEDULE 5

PART 4

Value-Added Tax and related matters

Enactment amended (1)	Amount or words to be replaced (2)	Amount or words to be inserted (3)
Value-Added Tax Act, 1972 (No. 22 of 1972) (as amended):		
section 8(1A)(b)	£27,565	€35,000
section 8(3)(a)(i)	£32,000	€41,000
section 8(3)(a)(ia)	£20,000	€25,500
section 8(3)(a)(ii)	£40,000	€51,000
section 8(3)(a)(iii)	£40,000	€51,000
section 8(3)(a)(iv)	£20,000	€25,500
section 8(3)(c)(i)	£40,000	€51,000
section 8(3)(e)	£40,000	€51,000
section 8(3A)	£20,000	€25,500
section 8(9)(b)(ii)	£20,000	€25,500
	£20,000	€25,500

(With effect from 21 March 2001 except * from 1 January 2002)

Finance Act 2002

101.- Section 8 of the Principal Act is amended —

(a)   by adding in subsection (1) ", but a person not established in the State who supplies a service in the State in the circumstances set out in subsection (2)(aa) shall not be a taxable person and shall not be accountable for or liable to pay the tax chargeable in respect of such supply" after "in respect of such supply",

(b)   in subsection (2) —

   (i)   by inserting the following after paragraph (a):

      "(aa) Where a person not established in the State supplies a cultural, artistic, entertainment or similar service in the State, then any person, other than a person acting in a private capacity, who receives that service shall —

         (i)   in relation to it, be a taxable person or be deemed to be a taxable person, and

         (ii)   be liable to pay the tax chargeable as if that taxable person had in fact supplied the service for consideration in the course or furtherance of business;

      but where that service is commissioned or procured by a promoter, agent or other person not being a person acting in a private capacity, then that promoter, agent or person shall be deemed to be the person who receives the service.

      (ab) Where the person who receives the services referred to in paragraph (aa) is a body that has received funding from the Arts Council in the 3 years prior to the passing of the Finance Act, 2002, the Revenue Commissioners may, at the request of such body, authorise the application of that paragraph in respect of such services received by that body to be deferred to a time not later than 1 March 2003.",

   and

   (ii)   by inserting the following after paragraph (c):

      "(d)   (i)   Where a person who owns, occupies or controls land (in this subsection referred to as a 'premises provider') allows, in the course or furtherance of business, a person not established in the State to supply goods for consideration in the course or furtherance of business (in this subsection referred to as a 'mobile trader') on that land for a period of less than seven consecutive days, then the premises provider shall, not later than fourteen days before the day when the mobile trader is allowed to supply goods on that land, furnish to the

Revenue Commissioners, at the office of the Revenue Commissioners which would normally deal with the examination of the records kept by the premises provider in accordance with section 16, the following particulars—

(I) the name and address of the mobile trader,

(II) the dates on which the mobile trader intends to supply goods on the premises provider's land,

(III) the address of the land referred to in clause (II), and

(IV) any other information as may be specified in regulations.

(ii) Where a premises provider allows, in the course or furtherance of business, a promoter not established in the State to supply on the premises provider's land a cultural, artistic, entertainment or similar service which in accordance with section (2)(aa) is deemed to be supplied by that promoter, then the premises provider shall, not later than fourteen days before such service is scheduled to begin, furnish to the Revenue Commissioners, at the office of the Revenue Commissioners which would normally deal with the examination of the records kept by the premises provider in accordance with section 16, the following particulars—

(I) the name and address of the promoter,

(II) details, including the dates, duration and venue, of the event or performance commissioned or procured by the promoter in the provision of that service, and

(III) any other information as may be specified in regulations.

(iii) Where a premises provider fails to provide to the Revenue Commissioners true and correct particulars as required in accordance with subparagraph (i) or (ii), then the Revenue Commissioners may, where it appears necessary to them to do so for the protection of the revenue, make such premises provider jointly and severally liable with a mobile trader or promoter, as the case may be, for the tax chargeable in respect of supplies made by that mobile trader or promoter on the premises provider's land, and in those circumstances the Revenue Commissioners shall notify the premises provider in writing accordingly.

(iv)   A premises provider who has been notified in accordance with subparagraph (iii) shall be deemed to be a taxable person and shall be liable to pay the tax referred to in that subparagraph as if it were tax due in accordance with section 19 by the premises provider for the taxable period within which the supplies are made by the mobile trader or promoter, but the premises provider shall not be liable to pay tax referred to in subparagraph (iii) which the Revenue Commissioners are satisfied was accounted for by a mobile trader or promoter.",

and

(c)   in subsection (8) —

(i)   by adding in paragraph (a)(i) "and the persons so notified shall be regarded as being in a group for as long as this paragraph applies to them," after "accordingly,", and

(ii)   by inserting the following after paragraph (c):

"(d)   Where a person in a group (in this subsection referred to as the 'landlord') having acquired an interest in, or developed, immovable goods to which section 4 applies, whether such acquisition or development occurred before or after the landlord became a person in the group, subsequently surrenders possession of those immovable goods, or any part of them, to another person in the group (in this subsection referred to as the 'occupant') where the surrender of possession if it were to a person not in the group would not constitute a supply of immovable goods in accordance with section 4, and either the landlord or the occupant subsequently ceases to be a person in the group (in this subsection referred to as a 'cessation') then, if that landlord does not have a waiver of his or her right to exemption from tax in accordance with section 7 still in effect at the time of the cessation —

(i)   the surrender of possession, or

(ii)   if that landlord surrendered possession of those immovable goods more than once to another person in the group, the first such surrender of possession,

shall be deemed to occur when that first such cessation takes place, but if such a landlord's waiver of his or her right to exemption from tax in accordance with section 7 has been cancelled before a surrender of possession of immovable goods to another person in the group ends, that surrender of possession shall be deemed to take place on the date of the said first such cessation.".

(With effect from 25 March 2002)

Finance Act 2003

118.   Section 8 of the Principal Act is amended —

(a)   in subsection (1) by substituting "goods in the State in the circumstances set out in subsection (1A)(f) or supplies a service in the State in the circumstances set out in subsection (2)(aa)," for "a service in the State in the circumstances set out in subsection (2)(aa)", and

(b)   in subsection (1A) by inserting the following paragraph after paragraph (e) —

"(f)   Where a person not established in the State supplies goods in the State which are installed or assembled, with or without a trial run, by or on behalf of that person, and where the recipient of the supply of those goods is —

(i)   a taxable person,

(ii)   a Department of State or local authority,

(iii)   a body established by statute, or

(iv)   a person who receives that supply for the purpose of any activity specified in the First Schedule,

then that recipient shall in relation to that supply of those goods be a taxable person or be deemed to be a taxable person and shall be liable to pay the tax chargeable as if that recipient supplied those goods in the course or furtherance of business.".

(With effect from 28 March 2003)

Finance Act 2004

58. Section 8 of the Principal Act is amended —

(a)   in subsection (1) (as amended by the Finance Act 2003) by substituting "in paragraph (f) or (g) of subsection (1A)" for "in subsection (1A)(f)", and

(b)   by inserting the following after subsection (1A)(f):

"(g)   Where a taxable person not established in the State supplies gas through the natural gas distribution system, or electricity, to a recipient in the State and where such recipient is —

(i)   a taxable person,

(ii)   a Department of State or local authority,

(iii)   a body established by statute, or

(iv)   a person who receives that supply for the purpose of any activity specified in the First Schedule,

then that recipient shall in relation to that supply be a taxable person or be deemed to be a taxable person and shall be liable to pay the tax chargeable as if that recipient supplied those goods in the course or furtherance of business.".

(With effect from 1 January 2005)

Finance Act 2006

95. Section 8 of the Principal Act is amended —

*(a)   in subsections (3), (3A) and (9), with effect from 1 May 2006, by substituting "€27,500" for "€25,500" and by substituting "€55,000" for "€51,000" wherever it occurs, and

(b)   in subsection (8) paragraph (a) by substituting "where it seems necessary or appropriate to them for the purpose of efficient and effective administration, including collection, of the tax" for "that it would be expedient in the interest of efficient administration of the tax".

(With effect from 31 March 2006 except * with effect from 1 May 2006)

Finance Act 2007

79. Section 8 of the Principal Act is amended —

*(a)   with effect from 1 March 2007 —

(i)   in subsections (3), (3A) and (9), by substituting "€35,000" for "€27,500" in each place it occurs, and

(ii)   in subsection (3) by substituting "€70,000" for "€55,000" in each place it occurs,

and

(b)   in subsection (8) —

(i)   in paragraph (a) —

(I)   by substituting ", established in the State and engaged in the supply of goods or services in the course or furtherance of business," for "established in the State",

(II)   by substituting "for the purpose of this Act, the said Commissioners may, whether following an application on behalf of those persons or otherwise" for "subject to such conditions as they may impose by regulations, the said Commissioners, for the purposes of this Act, may",

(III)   by substituting the following subparagraph for subparagraph (i):

"(i)   by notice in writing to each of those persons deem them to be a single taxable person, referred to in this section as a 'group' and the persons so notified shall then be regarded as being in the group for as long as this paragraph applies to them, but the provisions of section 9 shall apply in respect of each of the members of the group, and —

(I)   one of those persons, who shall be notified accordingly by the Commissioners, shall be responsible for complying with the provisions of this Act in respect of the group, and

(II)   all rights and obligations arising under this Act in respect of the transactions of the group shall be determined accordingly, and",

and

(IV)   in subparagraph (ii) by substituting "make each person in the group" for "make each such person",

(ii)   by deleting paragraph (c), and

(iii)   by inserting the following after paragraph (d) —

"(e)   The Revenue Commissioners may make regulations as seem to them to be necessary for the purposes of this subsection.".

**97. With effect from 1 January 2007 in each provision of the Principal Act specified in the first column of Schedule 3 for the words set out in the second column of that Schedule at that entry there is substituted the words set out at the corresponding entry in the third column of that Schedule.

Schedule 3
Miscellaneous Amendments Relating to Council Directive 2006/112/EC

Amendment of Value-Added Tax Act 1972

Provision of Principal Act	Words to be replaced	Words to be inserted
Section 8(9) in the definition of "Annex A activity"	Annex A (which is set out in Part I of the Fifth Schedule) of Council Directive No. 77/388/EEC of 17 May 1977	Article 295(1) and Annex VII of Council Directive No. 2006/112/EC of 28 November 2006
Section 8(9) in the definition of "Annex B service"	Annex B (which is set out in Part II of the Fifth Schedule) of the said Council Directive	Article 295(1) and Annex VIII of the said Council Directive

(With effect from 2 April 2007, except * with effect from 1 March 2007 ** with effect from 1 January 2007)

Finance Act 2008

92.   Section 8 of the Principal Act is amended —

(a)   by substituting with effect from 1 July 2008 the following for subsection (1):

"(1)   A taxable person who engages in the supply, within the State, of taxable goods or services shall be an accountable person and shall be accountable for and liable to pay the tax charged in respect of such supply. In addition the persons referred to in section 4B(3) and subsections (1A), (2), (2A) and (8) shall be accountable persons. However a person not established in the State who supplies goods in the State only in the circumstances set out in paragraph (f) or (g) of subsection (1A) or supplies a service in the State only in the circumstances set out in subsections (1B) and (2)(aa) shall not be an accountable person.",

(b)   in paragraph (f) of subsection (1A) with effect from 1 July 2008 —

(i)   by deleting subparagraph (iv), and

(ii)   by substituting "an accountable person or be deemed to be an accountable person" for "a taxable person or be deemed to be a taxable person",

(c)   in paragraph (g) of subsection (1A) with effect from 1 July 2008 –

    (i)   by substituting "Where a person" for "Where a taxable person",

    (ii)   by deleting subparagraph (iv), and

    (iii)   by substituting "an accountable person or be deemed to be an accountable person" for "a taxable person or be deemed to be a taxable person",

**(d)   by inserting the following after subsection (1A):

"(1B) (a)   This subsection and sections 12(1)(vc) and 17(1C) shall be construed together with Chapter 2 of Part 18 of the Taxes Consolidation Act 1997.

    (b)   With effect from 1 September 2008 where a principal, other than a principal to whom subparagraphs (ii) or (iii) of section 531(1)(b) of the Taxes Consolidation Act 1997 applies, receives services consisting of construction operations (as defined in paragraphs (a) to (f) of section 530(1) of that Act) from a subcontractor, then that principal shall in relation to that supply be an accountable person or deemed to be an accountable person and shall be liable to pay the tax chargeable as if that principal supplied those services in the course or furtherance of business and the subcontractor shall not be accountable for or liable to pay the said tax in respect of such supplies.

    (c)   This subsection does not apply to services in respect of which the supplier issued or was required to issue an invoice in accordance with section 17 prior to 1 September 2008.",

*(e)   in subsections (3), (3A) and (9) with effect from 1 May 2008 by substituting "€37,500" for "€35,000" and by substituting "€75,000" for "€70,000" wherever it occurs, and

(f)   in subsection (8)(a) with effect from 1 July 2008 by substituting ", at least one of which is a taxable person," for "and engaged in the supply of goods or services in the course or furtherance of business".

109.   With effect from 1 July 2008 in each provision of the Principal Act specified in the first column of Schedule 4 for the words set out in the second column of that Schedule at that entry (in each place where those words occur in the provision concerned) there is substituted the words set out at the corresponding entry in the third column of that Schedule.

Schedule 4
Miscellaneous Amendments Relating to the Amendment of the Definition of Taxable Person

Amendments to Value-Added Tax Act 1972

Provision of Value-Added Tax Act 1972	Words to be replaced	Words to be inserted
Section 8(1A)(a)	a taxable person	an accountable person
Section 8(1A)(b)	a taxable person	an accountable person
Section 8(1A)(c)	a taxable person	an accountable person
Section 8(1A)(d)	a taxable person	an accountable person
Section 8(2)	a taxable person	an accountable person
Section 8(2)	that taxable person	that accountable person
Section 8(2)	the taxable person	the accountable person
Section 8(2A)	be taxable persons	be accountable persons
Section 8(2B)	a taxable person	an accountable person
Section 8(3)	be taxable persons	be accountable persons
Section 8(3)	a taxable person	an accountable person
Section 8(3)	to taxable persons	to accountable persons
Section 8(3)	be a taxable person	be an accountable persons
Section 8(3A)	a taxable person	an accountable person
Section 8(3E)	a taxable person	an accountable person
Section 8(4)	a taxable person	an accountable person
Section 8(6)	A taxable person	An accountable person
Section 8(6)	a taxable person	an accountable person
Section 8(8)(a)(ii)	a taxable person	an accountable person
Section 8(9)	a taxable person	an accountable person

**141. The enactments specified in Schedule 8 —

(a) are amended to the extent and in the manner specified in paragraphs 1 to 6 of that Schedule, and

(b) apply and come into operation in accordance with paragraph 7 of that Schedule.

Schedule 8
Miscellaneous Technical Amendments in Relation to Tax

3. The Value-Added Tax Act 1972 is amended in accordance with the following provisions:

(c) in section 8(2) by deleting paragraph (ab),

(With effect from 1 July 2008 except * with effect from 1 May 2008 and ** with effect from 13 March 2008)

Finance (No. 2) Act 2008

99.   The enactments specified in Schedule 6 —

(a)   are amended to the extent and in the manner specified in paragraphs 1 to 6 of that Schedule, and

(b)   apply and come into operation in accordance with paragraph 7 of that Schedule.

SCHEDULE 6

Miscellaneous Technical Amendments in Relation to Tax

4.   The Value-Added Tax Act 1972 is amended —

(g)   in section 8 —

(i)   in subsection (1B)(b) by inserting "to whom section 531(1) of the Taxes Consolidation Act 1997 applies" after "where a principal",

(ii)   in subsection (5A) by inserting the following after paragraph (c) —

"(d)   This subsection does not apply to immovable goods acquired or developed on or after 1 July 2008.",

and

(iii)   in subsection (8)(d) by inserting "has not exercised the landlord's option to tax in accordance with section 7A in respect of the letting of those immovable goods at the time of the cessation or" after "then, if that landlord",

(With effect from 24 December 2008)

Section 9

Value Added Tax Act 1972
Registration

9. (1) The Revenue Commissioners shall set up and maintain a register of persons who may become or who are accountable persons and shall allot to every such person so registered a registration number and shall cancel such number if the person does not became or ceases to be an accountable person.

    (2) Every person who on the appointed day or on any day thereafter would be an accountable person if tax were chargeable with effect as on and from the appointed day shall, within the period of thirty days beginning on the appointed day or on the day thereafter on which the person first becomes an accountable person or would become such a person if tax were chargeable as aforesaid, furnish in writing to the Revenue Commissioners the particulars specified in regulations an being required for the purpose of registering such person for tax.

    (3) Any person who on the appointed day was registered for the purposes of turnover tax on the basis of particulars furnished in accordance with section 49 (2) of the Finance Act, 1963, shall be deemed, unless he notifies the Revenue Commissioners in writing that he does not wish to be so deemed, to have furnished the particulars required by subsection (2).

    (4) In this section "the appointed day" means the day appointed by the Minister by order to be the appointed day for the purpose of this section.

(With effect from 1 November 1972)

Value Added Tax (Amendment Act) 1978

7. Section 9 of the Principal Act is hereby amended by the substitution of the following subsection for subsection (1):

    "(1) The Revenue Commissioners shall set up and maintain a register of persons who may become or who are taxable persons.".

30. (2) In consequence of the amendments of the Principal Act specified in this Act and of the repeals specified in the First Schedule, the Principal Act is hereby further amended by the substitution of the word or expression mentioned in column (3) of the Second Schedule at any reference number for the word or expression mentioned in column (2) of that Schedule at that reference number wherever it occurs in the provision of the Principal Act mentioned in column (4) of that Schedule at that reference number.

SECOND SCHEDULE

Consequential Amendments

Reference Number (1)	Existing word or expression (2)	Substituted word or expression (3)	Provision of Principal Act (4)
26	"an accountable person"	"a taxable person"	Sections 9(2),

Transitional provisions

31. (1) (a)   The register that, immediately before the commencement of this Act, was the register of persons who may become or who are accountable persons shall, as on and from such commencement, become and be the register of persons who may become or who are taxable persons under section 9 of the Principal Act as amended by this Act and the persons who, immediately before such commencement, were registered in the former register shall, upon such commencement, stand registered in the latter register.

(With effect from 1 March 1979)

Finance Act 1983

80. Section 9 of the Principal Act is hereby amended-

(a)   in subsection (1), by the insertion after "taxable persons" of "or who are persons who dispose of goods which pursuant to section 3(7) are deemed to be supplied by a taxable person in the course or furtherance of his business",

and

(b)   by the insertion after subsection (2) of the following subsection:

"(2A) Every person who disposes of goods which pursuant to section 3(7) are deemed to be supplied by a taxable person in the course or furtherance of his business shall, within fourteen days of such disposal, furnish in writing to the Revenue Commissioners the particulars specified in regulations as being required for the purpose of registering such person for tax.".

(With effect from 1 September 1983)

Finance Act 1992

171. Section 9 of the Principal Act is hereby amended by the insertion of the following subsection after subsection (1) (inserted by the Act of 1978):

"(1A) The Revenue Commissioners shall assign to each person registered in accordance with subsection (1) a registration number.".

(With effect from 28 May 1992)

Finance Act 2008

109. With effect from 1 July 2008 in each provision of the Principal Act specified in the first column of Schedule 4 for the words set out in the second column of that Schedule at that entry (in each place where those words occur in the provision concerned) there is substituted the words set out at the corresponding entry in the third column of that Schedule.

Schedule 4
Miscellaneous Amendments Relating to the Amendment of the Definition of Taxable Person

Amendments to Value-Added Tax Act 1972

Provision of Value-Added Tax Act 1972	Words to be replaced	Words to be inserted
Section 9	are taxable persons	are accountable persons
Section 9	a taxable person	an accountable person

(With effect from 1 July 2008)

Section 10

Value Added Tax Act 1972

Amount on which tax is chargeable

10. (1)   The amount on which tax is chargeable by virtue of section 2(1) (a) shall, subject to this section, be the total consideration which the person delivering goods or rendering services becomes entitled to receive in respect of or in relation to such delivery of goods or rendering of services, including all taxes, commissions, costs and charges whatsoever, but not including value-added tax chargeable in respect of the transaction.

(2)   If the consideration referred to in subsection (1) does not consist of or does not consist wholly of an amount of money, the amount on which tax is chargeable shall, subject to subsection (6), be the total amount of money which might reasonably be expected to be charged if the consideration consisted entirely of an amount of money equal to the open market price:

Provided that in computing the total amount on which tax is chargeable as aforesaid a deduction may be made for the open market price of movable goods given in exchange or part exchange for goods of the same kind.

(3)   Notwithstanding anything in subsection (1) or (2)-

(a)   if for any non-business reason the actual consideration in relation to the delivery of any goods or the rendering of any services is less than that which might reasonably be expected to be received if the consideration were an amount equal to the open market price or there is no consideration, the amount on which tax is chargeable shall be the open market price,

(b)   if the consideration actually received exceeds the amount which the person delivering the goods or rendering the services was entitled to receive, the amount on which tax is chargeable shall be the amount actually received, excluding value-added tax chargeable in respect of the transaction, and

(c)   if, in a case not coming within paragraph (a), the consideration actually received in relation to the delivery of any goods or the rendering of any services is less than the amount on which tax is chargeable or no consideration is actually received, such relief may be given by repayment or otherwise in respect of the deficiency as may be provided for by regulation.

(4)   The amount on which tax is chargeable in relation to deliveries referred to in paragraphs (d)(ii), (e) and (f) of section 3(1) shall be the cost to the person making the delivery of acquiring

or producing the goods excluding the tax which would be deductible under section 12 if the deliveries in question were made in the course of business.

(5)   The amount on which tax is chargeable in respect of the rendering of services referred to in section 5(2) shall be the cost, excluding tax, of providing the services.

(6)   Notwithstanding anything in subsection (2), if the consideration for the delivery of any goods or the rendering of any services consists solely of the surrender of stamps, coupons or other tokens, and the goods or services are of a kind which the person to whom the stamps, coupons or other tokens are surrendered does not deliver or render except in relation to the operation of a scheme under which the said surrender is made, the amount on which tax is chargeable shall be the cost, excluding tax, to the person aforesaid of producing or acquiring the goods or rendering the services, as the case may be.

(7)   The amount on which tax is chargeable by virtue of section 2(1)(a) on the delivery of livestock shall be 19.20 per cent of the total consideration referred to in this subsection (1).

(8)   On the delivery of immovable goods, other than deliveries to which section 4(6) relates, and on the rendering of services consisting of the development of immovable goods, including the installation of fixtures, or the maintenance and repair of those goods-

(a)   the value of any interest in the goods disposed of in connection with the delivery thereof or the rendering of services as aforesaid, shall be included in the consideration.

(b)   if the value of movable goods supplied in pursuance of the agreement for making the delivery aforesaid or rendering any of the services aforesaid does not exceed two-thirds of the total consideration referred to in subsection (1), the amount on which tax is chargeable shall be 60 per cent of such total consideration, and

(c)   (i)   if the value of movable goods supplied under the agreement aforesaid under two-thirds of the total consideration, such consideration shall be deemed, for the purposes of this Act, to be referable solely to the delivery of such goods and tax shall be charged at the appropriate rate or rates specified in section 11 on the basis of any apportionment of such total consideration made in accordance with subparagraph (ii), and

(ii)   where goods of different kinds are supplied under the agreement referred to in subparagraph (i), the amount of the consideration referable to the delivery of goods of each such kind shall be ascertained in the manner specified in section 5(5) (b).

(9)   (a)   The value of any interest in immovable goods shall be the open market price of such interest.

(b)   In this section-

"interest", in relation to immovable goods, and "disposal", in relation to any such interest, shall be construed in accordance with section 4(1), and

"the open market price", in relation to the delivery of any goods or the rendering of any services, means the price, excluding tax, which the goods might reasonably be expected to fetch or which might reasonably be expected to be charged for the services if sold or rendered in the open market at the time of the event in question.

(With effect from 1 November 1972)

Finance Act 1973

90.   The Principal Act is hereby amended as specified in column (3) of the Tenth Schedule to this Act.

TENTH SCHEDULE
Amendment of Enactments

Number and Year (1)	Short Title (2)	Amendment (3)
No. 22 of 1972	Value-Added Tax Act, 1972	In section 10, in subsection (7), " 14.81 " shall be substituted for "19.20"; in subsection (8)(b) "45" shall be substituted for " 60 ".

(With effect from 3 September 1973)

Finance Act 1975

50.   Section 10 of the Value-Added Tax Act, 1972, is hereby amended with effect on and from the 16th day of January, 1975-

(a)   by the insertion, before subsection (3), of the following subsection:

"(2A)   (a)   The amount on which tax is chargeable by virtue of section 2(1)(a) on the delivery of goods of a kind specified in the Fourth Schedule delivered in the circumstances specified in paragraph (b) shall be the open market price.

(b) The circumstances referred to in paragraph (a) in which a delivery is made are-

(i) that the person to whom or to whose order the delivery is made is a body of persons over whom the person making the delivery has control, or the person making the delivery is a body of persons over whom the person to whom or to whose order the delivery is made has control, or both the person making the delivery and the person to whom or to whose order the delivery is made are bodies of persons and some other person has control over both of them,

(ii) that the delivery is made in such circumstances that tax at the rate for the time being specified in section 11(1)(c) is chargeable in relation thereto, and

(iii) that the consideration referred to in subsection (1) is less than the open market price.",

(b) by the insertion, in subsection (3)(c) before "paragraph (a)", of "subsection (2A) or",

and

(c) by the insertion, in subsection (9)(b) before the definition of "the open market price" of the following definition:

"'control', in relation to a body corporate, means the power of a person to secure, by means of the holding of shares or the possession of voting power in or in relation to that or any other body corporate, or by virtue of any powers conferred by the articles of association or other document regulating that or any other body corporate, that the affairs of the first-mentioned body corporate are conducted in accordance with the wishes of that person and, in relation to a partnership, means the right to a share of more than one-half of the assets, or of more than one-half of the income, of the partnership;".

(With effect from 16 January 1975)

Finance Act 1976

52. Section 10 of the Principal Act is hereby amended by the insertion after subsection (6) of the following subsection:

"(6A) (a) In this subsection 'duty' means an excise duty chargeable on the importation, manufacture or production of goods or a customs duty.

(b) The amount on which tax is chargeable on the delivery of goods liable to duty shall, where the delivery is made before the duty falls due be increased by an amount equal to the amount of duty that would be payable in relation to the goods if the duty had become due at the time of the delivery.".

*61. In consequence of the amendments specified in sections 53 and 60 and the repeals specified in Part II of the Fifth Schedule, The Principal Act is hereby further amended as specified in Part II of the First Schedule.

FIRST SCHEDULE
PART II
Amendments Consequential on Certain Amendments of Value Added Tax Act, 1972

Number and Year (1)	Short Title (2)	Amendment (3)
No. 22 of 1972	Value-Added Tax Act, 1972	In section 10(2A)(b)(ii) (inserted by the Finance Act, 1975) "either of the rates" shall be substituted for "the rate". In section 10-(a) in subsection (7), "10 per cent" shall be substituted for "14.81 per cent" (inserted by the Finance Act, 1973), and (b) in subsection (8)(b), "30 per cent." shall be substituted for "45 per cent" (inserted by the Finance Act, 1973).

(With effect from 27 May 1976 except * from 1 March 1976)

Value Added Tax (Amendment) Act 1978

8. The following section shall be substituted for section 10 of the Principal Act:

"10. (1) The amount on which tax is chargeable by virtue of section 2(1)(a) shall, subject to this section, be the total consideration which the person supplying goods or services becomes entitled to receive in respect of or in relation to such supply of goods or services, including all taxes, commissions, costs and charges whatsoever but not including value-added tax chargeable in respect of the supply.

(2) If the consideration referred to in subsection (1) does not consist of or does not consist wholly of an amount of money, the amount on which tax is chargeable shall be the total amount of money which might reasonably be expected to be charged if the consideration consisted entirely of an amount of money equal to the open market price:

Provided that in computing the amount on which tax is chargeable as aforesaid a deduction may be made for the open market price of second-hand movable goods given in exchange or part exchange for goods, whether new or second-hand, of the same kind-

(3) (a) If for any non-business reason the actual consideration in relation to the supply of any goods or services is less than that which might reasonably be expected to be received if the consideration were an amount equal to the open market price or there is no consideration, the amount on which tax is chargeable shall be the open market price.

(b) If the consideration actually received in relation to the supply of any goods or services exceeds the amount which the person supplying the goods or services was entitled to receive, the amount on which tax is chargeable shall be the amount actually received, excluding tax chargeable in respect of the supply.

(c) If, in a case not coming within paragraph (a), the consideration actually received in relation to the supply of any goods or services is less than the amount on which tax is chargeable or no consideration is actually received, such relief may be given by repayment or otherwise in respect of the deficiency as may be provided by regulations.

(4) The amount on which tax is chargeable in relation to a supply of goods referred to in paragraph (d)(ii), (e) or (f) of section 3(1) or a supply of services by virtue of regulations made for the purposes of section 5(3) shall be the cost, excluding tax, of the goods to the person supplying the goods or the cost, excluding tax, of supplying the services, as the case may be.

(5) The amount on which tax is chargeable in relation to services for the tax chargeable on which the recipient is,

by virtue of section 8(2), liable shall be the consideration for which the services were in fact supplied to him.

(6)   Where a right to receive goods or services for an amount stated on any token, stamp, coupon or voucher is granted for a consideration, the consideration shall be disregarded for the purposes of this Act except to the extent (if any) that it exceeds that amount.

(7)   Provision may be made by regulations for the purpose of determining the amount on which tax is chargeable in relation to one or more of the following:

(a)   supplies of goods and services to which an order under section 8(2A) applies,

(b)   supplies of stamps, coupons, tokens or vouchers when supplied as things in action (not being stamps, coupons, tokens or vouchers specified in subsection (6)),

(c)   supplies of goods or services wholly or partly in exchange for stamps, coupons, tokens or vouchers of a kind specified in subsection (6) or paragraph (b),

(d)   supplies deemed, pursuant to subsection (3) or (4) of section 3, to be made to and by the persons therein mentioned,

and such regulations may, in the case of supplies referred to in paragraph (b), provide that the amount on which tax is chargeable shall be nil.

(8)   (a)   Where the value of movable goods (not being goods of a kind specified in paragraph (xii) of the Second Schedule) provided under an agreement for the supply of services exceeds two-thirds of the total consideration under the agreement for the provision of those goods and the supply of the services, other than transport services in relation to them, the consideration shall be deemed to be referable solely to the supply of the goods and tax shall be charged at the appropriate rate or rates specified in section 11 on the basis of any apportionment of the total consideration made in accordance with paragraph (b).

(b)   Where goods of different kinds are provided under an agreement of the kind referred to in paragraph (a), the amount of the consideration referable to the supply of goods of each kind shall be ascertained for the purposes of that paragraph by apportioning the total consideration in proportion to the value of the goods of each kind provided.

(c)   This subsection shall also apply to an agreement for the supply of immovable goods and, accordingly, the references in paragraphs (a) and (b) to an agreement for the supply of services shall be deemed to include a reference to such an agreement.

(9)   (a)   On the supply of immovable goods and on the supply of services consisting of the development of immovable goods, the value of any interest in the goods disposed of in connection with the supply shall be included in the consideration.

(b)   The value of any interest in immovable goods shall be the open market price of such interest.

(10)   In this section-

'**interest**', in relation to immovable goods, and 'disposal', in relation to any such interest, shall be construed in accordance with section 4(1);

'**the open market price**', in relation to the supply of any goods or services, means the price, excluding tax, which the goods might reasonably be expected to fetch or which might reasonably be expected to be charged for the services if sold in the open market at the time of the event in question.".

(With effect from 1 March 1979)

Finance Act 1982

78.   Section 10 (inserted by the Act of 1978) of the Principal Act is hereby amended by the insertion of the following subsection after subsection (4):

"(4A)   Where goods chargeable with a duty of excise are supplied while warehoused, and before payment of the duty, to an unregistered person, the amount on which tax is chargeable in respect of the supply shall be increased by an amount equal to the amount of duty that would be payable in relation to the goods if the duty had become due at the time of the supply.".

(With effect from 1 September 1982)

Finance Act 1992

172.   Section 10 (inserted by the Act of 1978) of The Principal Act is hereby amended-

(a)   by the insertion of the following subsection after subsection (1):

"(1A) The amount on which tax is chargeable on the intra-Community acquisition of goods by virtue of section 2(1A) shall, subject to this section, be the total consideration, including all taxes, commissions, costs and charges whatsoever, but not including value-added tax chargeable, in respect of that acquisition.",

(b)   in subsection (2) by the substitution of "subsections (1) or (1A)" for "subsection (1)",

(c)   in the proviso to subsection (2) by the insertion after "Provided that" of ", as respects subsection (1),",

(d)   by the substitution of the following paragraph for paragraph (a) of subsection (3):

"(a)   If for any non-businesss reason the actual consideration in relation to-

(i)   the supply of any goods or services, or

(ii)   the intra-Community acquisition of goods,

is less than the open market price or there is no consideration, the amount on which tax is chargeable shall be the open market price.",

(e)   in subsection (4) by the substitution of "the person supplying or acquiring the goods" for "the person supplying the goods",

(f)   by the insertion of the following subsection after subsection (4A) (inserted by the Act of 1982):

"(4B) The amount on which tax is chargeable in relation to the supply of goods referred to in section 3(1)(g) shall be the open market price.",

(g)   by the insertion of the following subsection after subsection (5):

"(5A) Where,

(a)   an intra-Community acquisition is deemed to have taken place in the territory of another Member State in accordance with section 3A(2)(a),

(b)   the intra-Community acquisition has been subject to value-added tax, referred to in Council Directive No. 77/388/EEC of 17 May 1977, in that other Member State, and

(c)   the intra-Community acquisition is also deemed to have taken place in the State, in accordance with section 3A(2)(b),

then the consideration for the intra-Community acquisition to which paragraph (c) relates shall be reduced to nil.",

and

(h)   by the insertion in the definition of "the open market price" in subsection (10) after "supply of any goods or services" of "or the intra-Community acquisition of goods".

(With effect from 1 January 1993)

S.I. No. 413 of 1992.
European Communities (Value-Added Tax) Regulations, 1992.

8.   Section 10 (inserted by the Act of 1978) of the Principal Act is hereby amended by the insertion of the following subsection after subsection (9):

"(9A)   In relation to the tax chargeable by virtue of section 2(1)(a) or 2(IA), where an amount is expressed in a currency other than the currency of the State the exchange rate to be used shall be-

(a)   unless paragraph (b) applies, the latest selling rate recorded by the Central Bank of Ireland for the currency in question at the time the tax becomes due,

(b)   where there is an agreement with the Revenue Commissioners for a method to be used in determining the exchange rate, the exchange rate obtained using the said method:

Provided that where paragraph (b) applies the method agreed in accordance with that paragraph shall be applied for all transactions where an amount is expressed in a currency other than that of the State until the agreement to use such method is withdrawn by the Revenue Commissioners.".

(With effect from 1 January 1993)

Finance Act 1993

86.   Section 10 (inserted by the Act of 1978) of The Principal Act is hereby amended in subsection (4A) (inserted by the Act of 1982) by the insertion after "excise" of " other than alcohol products within the meaning of section 3B,".

(With effect from 1 August 1993)

Finance Act 1994

95.   Section 10 of the Principal Act is hereby amended in paragraph (c) of subsection (3) by the insertion of the following proviso to that paragraph:

"Provided that in any event this paragraph shall not apply in the case of the letting of immovable goods which is a taxable supply of goods in accordance with section 4.".

(With effect from 23 May 1994)

Finance Act 1995

125. Section 10 of the Principal Act is hereby amended-

*(a) by the deletion of the proviso to subsection (2),

and

(b) by the insertion of the following subsection after subsection (4B) (inserted by the Act of 1992):

> "(4C) In the case of a supply of goods of the type referred to in section 3(1)(b), where, as part of an agreement of the kind referred to in that provision, the supplier of the goods is also supplying financial services of the kind specified in subparagraph (i) (e) of the First Schedule in respect of those goods, the amount on which tax is chargeable in respect of the supply of the goods in question shall be either-
>
> > (a) the open market price of the goods, or
> >
> > (b) the amount of the total consideration as specified in subsection (1) which the person supplying the goods becomes entitled to receive in respect of or in relation to such supply,
>
> whichever is the greater.".

(With effect from 2 June 1995 except * from 1 July 1995)

Finance Act 1997

102. Section 10 of the Principal Act is hereby amended-

*(a) in subsection (3) by the addition of the following paragraph:

> "(d) If, following the issue of an invoice by a taxable person in respect of a supply of goods or services, the person who issued the invoice allows a reduction or discount in the amount of the consideration due in P respect of that supply, the relief referred to in paragraph (c) shall not be given until the person who issued the invoice issues the credit note required in accordance with the provisions of section 17(3)(b) in respect of that reduction or discount.",

(b) by the addition of the following proviso to subsection (4):

> "Provided that where the supply in question is a supply of immovable goods, (hereafter referred to in this proviso as 'appropriation'), the cost to the person making that appropriation shall include an amount equal to the amount on which tax was chargeable on the supply of those goods to that person, being the last supply of those goods to that person which preceded the appropriation.",

*(c)   in subsection 7-

(i)   in paragraph (c) by the insertion before "supplies" of "subject to subsection (7A),",

and

(ii)   by the deletion of paragraph (d),

*(d)   by the insertion of the following subsection after subsection (7):

"(7A) (a)   Where a supplier sells a voucher to a buyer at a discount and promises to subsequently accept that voucher at its face value in full or part payment of the price of goods purchased by a customer who was not the buyer of the voucher, and who does not normally know the actual price at which the voucher was sold by the supplier, the consideration represented by the voucher shall, subject to regulations, if any, be the sum actually received by the supplier upon the sale of the voucher.

(b)   Paragraph (a) is for the purpose of giving further effect to Article 11A. 1.(a) of Council Directive No. 77/388/EEC of 17 May 1977, and shall be construed accordingly.",

(e)   in subsection (9), by the addition of the following proviso to paragraph (b):

"Provided that where a surrender or an assignment of an interest in immovable goods is a supply of immovable goods which is chargeable to tax, the open market price of such interest shall be determined as if the person who surrendered or assigned that interest were disposing of an interest in those goods which that person had created for the period between the date of the surrender or assignment and the date on which that surrendered or assigned interest would, but for its surrender or assignment, have expired.",

and

(f)   by the substitution of the following subsection for subsection (10):

"(10)   In this section-

'**interest**', in relation to immovable goods, and 'disposal' in relation to any such interest, shall be construed in accordance with section 4(1), provided that for the purposes of determining the open market price of a surrendered or assigned interest in accordance with the proviso to paragraph (b) of subsection (9), an interest in immovable goods shall also mean an estate or interest which, when it was created, was for a period equal to the period referred to in that proviso, regardless of the duration of that period;

'**the open market price**'-

(a)   in relation to the value of an interest in immovable goods which is not a freehold interest, means the price, excluding tax, which the right to receive an unencumbered rent in respect of those goods for the period of the interest would fetch on the open market at the time that that interest is disposed of, and

(b)   in relation to the supply of any other goods or services or the intra-Community acquisition of goods, means the price, excluding tax, which the goods might reasonably be expected to fetch or which might reasonably be expected to be charged for the services if sold in the open market at the time of the event in question;

'**unencumbered rent**', for the purposes of valuing an interest in immovable goods, means the rent at which an interest would be let, if that interest was let on the open market free of restrictive conditions.".

(With effect from 26 March 1997 except * from 10 May 1997)

Finance Act 1998

109. Section 10 of the Principal Act is hereby amended in subsection (6) by the insertion after "goods or services" of ", other than telecommunications services,".

(With effect from 1 May 1998)

Finance Act 1999

124. Section 10 of the Principal Act is hereby amended in subsection (4B) (inserted by the Act of 1992) by the substitution for "open market price" of "cost of the goods to the person making the supply or, in the absence of such a cost, the cost price of similar goods in the State, and where an intra-Community acquisition occurs in the State following a supply of goods in another Member State which, if such supply was carried out in similar circumstances in the State would be a supply of goods in accordance with section 3(1)(g), then the amount on which tax is chargeable in respect of that intra-Community acquisition shall be the cost to the person making the supply in that Member State or, in the absence of a cost to that person, the cost price of similar goods in that other Member State".

(With effect from 25 March 1999)

Finance Act 2002

102. Section 10 of the Principal Act is amended —

    (a)   by substituting in subsection (6) "Subject to subsection (6A), where" for "Where",

    (b)   by inserting the following after subsection (6):

"(6A) Notwithstanding the provisions of subsection (6), where—

    (a)   a supplier—

        (i)   supplies a token, stamp, coupon or voucher, which has an amount stated on it, to a person who acquires it in the course or furtherance of business with a view to resale, and

        (ii)   promises to subsequently accept that token, stamp, coupon or voucher at its face value in full or part payment of the price of goods,

and

    (b)   a person who acquires that token, stamp, coupon or voucher, whether from the supplier referred to in paragraph (a) or from any other person in the course or furtherance of business, supplies it for consideration in the course or furtherance of business,

then in the case of each such supply the consideration received shall not be disregarded for the purposes of this Act and when such token, stamp, coupon or voucher is used in payment or part payment of the price of goods, the face value of it shall, for the purposes of section 10(2), be disregarded.",

and

    (c)   in subsection (7)(c) by inserting "(6A) or" after "subject to subsection".

(With effect from 25 March 2002)

Finance Act 2005

102. Section 10 of the Principal Act is amended in subsection (9) by inserting the following subparagraphs after the proviso to subparagraph (b):

"(c)   Where the Revenue Commissioners wish to ascertain the open market price of an interest in immovable goods, they may authorise a person to inspect the immovable goods and to report to them the open market price of such interest in those goods for the purposes of this Act, and a person having custody or possession of those goods shall permit the person so authorised to inspect the goods at such reasonable times as the Revenue Commissioners consider necessary.

(d)   Where the Revenue Commissioners require a valuation to be made by a person named by them, the costs of such valuation shall be defrayed by the Commissioners.".

(With effect from 25 March 2005)

Finance Act 2006

96.   Section 10 of the Principal Act is amended in subsection (4) —

(a)   by substituting "for the purposes of paragraph (a) or (b) of section 5(3)" for "for the purposes of section 5(3)", and

(b)   by inserting ", and the amount on which tax is chargeable in relation to a supply of services by virtue of regulations made for the purposes of section 5(3)(c) shall be the open market price of the services supplied" after "as the case may be".

(with effect from 31 March 2006)

Finance Act 2007

80.   Section 10 of the Principal Act is amended:

(a)   in subsection (3) —

    (i)   by deleting paragraph (a), and

    (ii)   in paragraph (c) by substituting "subsection (3A)" for "paragraph (a)",

(b)   by inserting the following subsection after subsection (3):

"(3A) (a)   The Revenue Commissioners may, where they consider it necessary or appropriate to do so to ensure the correct collection of the tax, make a determination that the amount on which tax is chargeable on a supply of goods or services is the open market value of that supply, if they are satisfied that the actual consideration in relation to that supply is —

    (i)   lower than the open market value of that supply where the recipient of that supply has no entitlement to deduct tax under section 12, or is not entitled to deduct all of the tax chargeable on that supply, or is a flat-rate farmer,

    (ii)   lower than the open market value of that supply, being an exempted activity, where the supplier engages in the course or furtherance of business in non-deductible supplies or activities as defined in section 12(4)(a), or is a flat-rate farmer, or

(iii) higher than the open market value where the supplier engages in the course or furtherance of business in non-deductible supplies or activities as defined in section 12(4)(a), or is a flat-rate farmer,

and that —

(I) the supplier and the recipient of that supply are persons connected by financial or legal ties, being persons who are party to any agreement, understanding, promise or undertaking whether express or implied and whether or not enforceable or intended to be enforceable by legal proceedings, or

(II) either the supplier or the recipient of that supply exercises control over the other and for this purpose 'control' has the meaning assigned to it by section 8(3B).

(b) A value determined in accordance with this subsection shall be deemed to be the true value of the supply to which it applies, for all the purposes of this Act.

(c) The Revenue Commissioners may make regulations as seem to them to be necessary for the purposes of this subsection.

(d) A determination under this section may be made by an inspector of taxes or such other officer as the Revenue Commissioners may authorise for the purpose.",

and

(c) in subsection (10) by inserting the following after the definition of 'open market price':

"'open market value', in relation to a supply of goods or services, means the total consideration excluding tax that a customer, at a marketing stage which is the same as the stage at which the supply of the goods or services takes place, would reasonably be expected to pay to a supplier at arm's length under conditions of fair competition for a comparable supply of such goods or services;

but if there is no such comparable supply of goods or services then 'open market value' means:

(a)   in respect of a supply of goods, an amount that is not less than the purchase price of the goods or of similar goods or, in the absence of a purchase price, the cost price, determined at the time of supply,

(b)   in respect of a supply of services, an amount that is not less than the full cost to the supplier of providing the service;".

*97.   With effect from 1 January 2007 in each provision of the Principal Act specified in the first column of Schedule 3 for the words set out in the second column of that Schedule at that entry there is substituted the words set out at the corresponding entry in the third column of that Schedule.

Schedule 3
Miscellaneous Amendments Relating to Council Directive 2006/112/EC

Amendment of Value-Added Tax Act 1972

Provision of Principal Act	Words to be replaced	Words to be inserted
Section 10(5A)(b)	Council Directive No. 77/388/EEC of 17 May 1977	Council Directive No. 2006/112/EC of 28 November 2006
Section 10(7A)(b)	Article 11A.1.(a) of Council Directive No. 77/388/EEC of 17 May 1977	Article 73 of Council Directive No. 2006/112/EC of 28 November 2006

(With effect from 2 April 2007 except * with effect from 1 January 2007)

Finance Act 2008

93.   Section 10 of the Principal Act is amended —

(a)   by inserting with effect from 1 July 2008 the following after subsection (4C):

"(4D) (a)   The amount on which tax is chargeable in relation to a supply of services referred to in section 5(3B) in any taxable period shall be an amount equal to one sixth of one twentieth of the cost of the immovable goods used to provide those services, being —

(i)   the amount on which tax was chargeable to the person making the supply in respect of that person's acquisition or development of the immovable goods referred to in section 5(3B), and

(ii)   in the case where section 3(5)(b)(iii) applied to the acquisition of the immovable goods, the amount on which tax would have been chargeable but for the application of that section, adjusted to correctly reflect the proportion of the use of the goods in that period.

(b)   The Revenue Commissioners may make regulations specifying methods which may be used—

(i)   to identify the proportion which correctly reflects the extent to which immovable goods are used for the purposes referred to in section 5(3B), and

(ii)   to calculate the relevant taxable amount or amounts.",

*(b)   in subsection (8) by inserting with effect from 1 September 2008 the following after sub-paragraph (c):

"(d)   This subsection does not apply in respect of a supply of services to which section 8(1B) applies.",

and

(c)   in subsection (9)—

**(i)   by inserting the following after paragraph (b):

"(ba)   Subsections (a) and (b) apply in respect of transactions which take place prior to 1 July 2008.",

and

(ii)   with effect from 1 July 2008 in paragraph (c), by substituting"value"for"price"inbothplaces where it occurs.

109.   With effect from 1 July 2008 in each provision of the Principal Act specified in the first column of Schedule 4 for the words set out in the second column of that Schedule at that entry (in each place where those words occur in the provision concerned) there is substituted the words set out at the corresponding entry in the third column of that Schedule.

Schedule 4
Miscellaneous Amendments Relating to the Amendment of the Definition of Taxable Person

Amendments to Value-Added Tax Act 1972

Provision of Value-Added Tax Act 1972	Words to be replaced	Words to be inserted
Section 10(3)(d)	a taxable persons	an accountable persons

(With effect from 1 July 2008 except * 1 September 2008 and ** with effect from 13 March 2008)

Section 10A

Finance Act 1995

Margin scheme goods

126. The Principal Act is hereby amended by the insertion of the following section after section 10:

"**10A.** (1)   In this section-

'**antiques**' means any of the goods specified in paragraph (xvia) of the Sixth Schedule or in paragraph (iii) of the Eighth Schedule;

'**collectors' items**' means any of the goods specified in paragraph (ii) of the Eighth Schedule;

'**margin scheme**' means the special arrangements for the taxation of supplies of margin scheme goods;

'**margin scheme goods**' means any works of art, collectors' items, antiques or second-hand goods supplied within the Community to a taxable dealer-

(a)   by a person, other than a person referred to in paragraph (c), who was not entitled to deduct, under section 12, any tax in respect of that person's purchase, intra-Community acquisition or importation of those goods:

Provided that person is not a taxable person who acquired those goods from-

(i)   a taxable dealer who applied the margin scheme to the supply of those goods to that taxable person, or

(ii)   an auctioneer within the meaning of section 10B who applied the auction scheme within the meaning of section 10B to the supply of those goods to that taxable person,

or

(b)   by a person in another Member State who was not entitled to deduct, under the provisions implementing Article 17 of Council Directive No. 77/388/EEC of 17 May 1977, in that Member State, any value-added tax referred to in that Directive in respect of that person's purchase, intra-Community acquisition or importation of those goods, or

(c)   by another taxable dealer who has applied the margin scheme to the supply of those goods or applied the provisions implementing Article 26a (inserted by Council Directive No. 94/5/EC of 14 February 1994) of Council Directive No. 77/388/ EEC of 17 May 1977, in another Member State to the supply of those goods;

'**precious metals**' means silver (including silver plated with gold or platinum), gold (including gold plated with platinum), and platinum, and all items which contain any of these metals when the consideration for the supply does not exceed the open market price, as defined in section 10, of the metal concerned;

'**precious stones**' means diamonds, rubies, sapphires and emeralds, whether cut or uncut, when they are not mounted, set or strung;

'**profit margin**' means the profit margin in respect of a supply by a taxable dealer of margin scheme goods and shall be deemed to be inclusive of tax and shall be an amount which is equal to the difference between the taxable dealer's selling price for those goods and the taxable dealer's purchase price for those goods:

Provided that, in respect of that supply, where the purchase price is greater than the selling price, the profit margin shall be deemed to be nil;

'**purchase price**', in relation to an acquisition of margin scheme goods, means the total consideration including all taxes, commissions, costs and charges whatsoever, payable by a taxable dealer to the person from whom that taxable dealer acquired those goods;

'**second-hand goods**' means any tangible movable goods which are suitable for further use either as they are or after repair, other than means of transport, works of art, collectors' items, antiques, precious metals and precious stones;

'**selling price**' means the total consideration which a taxable dealer becomes entitled to receive in respect of or in relation to a supply of margin scheme goods including all taxes, commissions, costs and charges whatsoever and value-added tax, if any, payable in respect of the supply;

'**taxable dealer**' means a taxable person who in the course or furtherance of business, whether acting on that person's own behalf, or on behalf of another person pursuant to a contract under which commission is payable on purchase or sale, purchases or acquires margin scheme goods or the goods referred to in paragraphs (b) and (c) of subsection (4), with a view to resale, or imports the goods referred to in paragraph (a) of subsection (4), with a view to resale, and a person in another Member State shall be deemed to be a taxable dealer where, in similar circumstances, that person would be a taxable dealer in the State under this section;

'**works of art**' means any of the goods specified in paragraph (xvi), or subparagraph (a) of paragraph (xxii), of the Sixth Schedule or in paragraph (i) of the Eighth Schedule.

(2)   Subject to and in accordance with the provisions of this section, a taxable dealer may apply the margin scheme to a supply of margin scheme goods.

(3)   Where the margin scheme is applied to a supply of goods, then notwithstanding section 10, the amount on which tax is chargeable by virtue of section 2(1)(a) on that supply shall be the profit margin less the amount of tax included in the profit margin.

(4)   Subject to such conditions (if any) as may be specified in regulations, a taxable dealer may, notwithstanding subsection (2), opt to apply the margin scheme to all that dealer's supplies of any of the following as if they were margin scheme goods-

(a)   a work of art, collector's item or antique which the taxable dealer imported, or

(b)   a work of art which has been supplied to the taxable dealer by its creator or the creator's successors in title, or

(c)   a work of art which has been supplied to the taxable dealer by a taxable person other than a taxable dealer, where the supply to that dealer is of the type referred to in section 11(1AA)(b)(ii):

Provided that where a taxable dealer so opts in accordance with this subsection, such option shall be for a period of not less than two years from the date when such option was exercised.

(5)   Where a taxable dealer exercises the option in accordance with subsection (4), in respect of the goods specified at paragraph (a) thereto, then notwithstanding the definition of purchase price in subsection (1), the purchase price for the purposes of determining the profit margin in relation to a supply of those goods shall be an amount equal to the value of those goods for the purposes of importation

determined in accordance with section 15 increased by the amount of any tax payable in respect of the importation of those goods.

(6)   Subject to subsection (7) and notwithstanding section 12, a taxable dealer who exercises the option in respect of the supply of the goods specified in subsection (4) shall not be entitled to deduct any tax in respect of the purchase or importation of those goods.

(7)   Where a taxable dealer exercises the option in accordance with subsection (4), that dealer may, notwithstanding the proviso to subsection (4), in respect of any individual supply of the goods specified in subsection (4), opt not to apply the margin scheme to that supply, and in such case the right to deduction of the tax charged on the purchase, intra-Community acquisition or importation of those goods shall, notwithstanding section 12, arise only in the taxable period in which the dealer supplies those goods.

(8)   (a)   Notwithstanding subsection (3), and subject to and in accordance with regulations (if any)-

    (i)   where a taxable dealer acquires low value margin scheme goods in job lots or otherwise, the amount of tax due and payable in respect of that dealer's supplies of low value margin scheme goods shall, in respect of a taxable period, be the amount of tax included in that dealer's aggregate margin, or margins, for that period and the amount of tax in each aggregate margin shall be determined by the formula:

$$\frac{A \times B}{B + 100}$$

where-

A   is the aggregate margin for the taxable period in question, and

B   is the percentage rate of tax chargeable in relation to the supply of those goods, and

    (ii)   where the taxable dealer referred to in paragraph (i) in any taxable period makes supplies which are subject to different rates of tax, that taxable dealer shall calculate separate aggregate margins for that taxable period in respect of the supplies at each of the relevant rates.

(b) Subject to, and in accordance with regulations (if any), where a taxable dealer supplies a low value margin scheme good for an amount in excess of £500 then-

    (i) notwithstanding the definition of low value margin scheme goods in paragraph (c), the supply of that good shall be deemed not to be a supply of a low value margin scheme good,

    (ii) in determining the aggregate margin for the taxable period in which the supply occurs, the taxable dealer shall deduct the purchase price of that good from the sum of the taxable dealer's purchase prices of low value margin scheme goods for that period, and

    (iii) the purchase price of that good shall be used in determining the profit margin in relation to the supply of that good.

(c) In this subsection-

'aggregate margin', in respect of a taxable period, means an amount which is equal to the difference between the taxable dealer's total turnover in that period from supplies of low value margin scheme goods, to which the same rate of tax applies, less the sum of that taxable dealer's purchase prices of low value margin scheme goods to which that rate of tax applies to the supply thereof, in that taxable period:

Provided that where the sum of that dealer's said purchase prices is in excess of the said total turnover, the appropriate aggregate margin shall be deemed to be nil and subject to, and in accordance with, regulations (if any), the amount of the excess shall be carried forward and added to the sum of that dealer's purchase prices for low value margin scheme goods for the purposes of calculating that dealer's appropriate aggregate margin for the immediately following taxable period;

'low value margin scheme goods' means margin scheme goods where the purchase price payable by the dealer for each individual item is less than £500.

(9) Notwithstanding section 17, a taxable dealer shall not, in relation to any supply to which the margin scheme

has been applied, indicate separately the amount of tax chargeable in respect of the supply on any invoice or other document in lieu thereof issued in accordance with that section.

(10)   Where the margin scheme is applied to a supply of goods dispatched or transported from the State to a person registered for value-added tax in another Member State, then notwithstanding paragraph (i)(b) of the Second Schedule, the provisions of section 11(1)(b) shall not apply, unless such goods are of a kind specified elsewhere in the Second Schedule.

(11)   Notwithstanding section 3(6)(d), where the margin scheme is applied to a supply of goods dispatched or transported, the place of supply of those goods shall be deemed to be the place where the dispatch or transportation begins.

(12)   Where a taxable dealer applies the margin scheme to a supply of goods on behalf of another person pursuant to a contract under which commission is payable on purchase or sale, the goods shall be deemed to have been supplied by that other person to the taxable dealer when the said taxable dealer supplies those goods.

(13)   Notwithstanding paragraph (xxiv) of the First Schedule, where a taxable person acquires goods to which the margin scheme has been applied and that person subsequently supplies those goods, the provisions of that paragraph shall not apply to that supply.".

(With effect from 1 July 1995)

Finance Act 1999

125.   Section 10A (inserted by the Act of 1995) of the Principal Act is hereby amended in subsection (1)(a) -

by the substitution of the following definition for the definition of "margin scheme goods":

"'margin scheme goods' means any works of art, collectors' items, antiques or second-hand goods supplied within the Community to a taxable dealer-

(a)   by a person, other than a person referred to in paragraph (c), who was not entitled to deduct, under section 12, any tax in respect of that person's purchase, intra-Community acquisition or importation of those goods:

Provided that person is not a taxable person who acquired those goods from-

(i)   a taxable dealer who applied the margin scheme to the supply of those goods to that taxable person, or

(ii)   an auctioneer within the meaning of section
10B who applied the auction scheme within the
meaning of section 10B to the supply of those
goods to that taxable person,

or

(b)   by a person in another Member State who was not entitled
to deduct, under the provisions implementing Article 17
of Council Directive No. 77/388/EEC of 17 May 1977, in
that Member State, any value-added tax referred to in
that Directive in respect of that person's purchase, intra-
Community acquisition or importation of those goods,
or

(c)   by another taxable dealer who has applied the margin
scheme to the supply of those goods or applied the
provisions implementing Article 26a (inserted by Council
Directive No. 94/5/EC of 14 February 1994) of Council
Directive No. 77/388/EEC of 17 May 1977, in another
Member State to the supply of those goods,

and also includes goods acquired by a taxable dealer as a result of
a disposal of goods by a person to such taxable dealer where that
disposal was deemed not to be a supply of goods in accordance
with section (5)(c).",

and

(b)   in the definition of "second-hand goods" by the insertion after
"means of transport," of "agricultural machinery (within the
meaning of section 12C),".

(With effect from 1 September 1999)

Finance Act 2001

185.   Section 10A (inserted by the Act of 1995) of the Principal Act is amended
in the definition of "margin scheme goods" (inserted by the Act of 1999)
by the substitution of "paragraphs (c) and (d) of subsection (5) of section
3" for "section 3(5)(c)".

*240. (1)   (a)   Subject to subsection (2), in each provision specified in
column (1) of Schedule 5 for the words or amount set
out in column (2) of that Schedule at that entry there
shall be substituted the words or amount set out at the
corresponding entry in column (3) of that Schedule.

(b)   Where words are or an amount is mentioned more than
once in a provision specified in column (1) of Schedule
5, then the substitution provided for by paragraph
(a) shall apply as respects those words or that amount
to each mention of those words or that amount in that
provision.

SCHEDULE 5

PART 4

Value-Added Tax and related matters

Enactment amended (1)	Amount or words to be replaced (2)	Amount or words to be inserted (3)
Value-Added Tax Act, 1972 (No. 22 of 1972) (as amended):		
section 10A(8)(b))	£500	€635
section 10A(8)(c)	£500	€635

(With effect from 21 March 2001 except * from 1 January 2002)

Finance Act 2007

81. Section 10A(1) of the Principal Act is amended with effect from 1 May 2007 in the definition of "margin scheme goods" by substituting "section 3(5)(d)" for "paragraphs (c) and (d) of subsection (5) of section 3".

*97. With effect from 1 January 2007 in each provision of the Principal Act specified in the first column of Schedule 3 for the words set out in the second column of that Schedule at that entry there is substituted the words set out at the corresponding entry in the third column of that Schedule.

Schedule 3
Miscellaneous Amendments Relating to Council Directive 2006/112/EC

Amendment of Value-Added Tax Act 1972

Provision of Principal Act	Words to be replaced	Words to be inserted
Section 10A(1)(b)	Article 17 of Council Directive No. 77/388/EEC of 17 May 1977	Articles 167, 173, 176 and 177 of Council Directive No. 2006/112/EC of 28 November 2006
Section 10A(1)(c)	Article 26a (inserted by Council Directive No. 94/5/EC of 14 February 1994) of Council Directive No. 77/388/EEC of 17 May 1977	Articles 4 and 35, first subparagraph of Article 139(3) and Articles 311 to 325 and 333 to 340 of Council Directive No. 2006/112/EC of 28 November 2006

(with effect from 1 May 2007 except * with effect from 1 January 2007)

Finance Act 2008

109. With effect from 1 July 2008 in each provision of the Principal Act specified in the first column of Schedule 4 for the words set out in the second column of that Schedule at that entry (in each place where those words occur in the provision concerned) there is substituted the words set out at the corresponding entry in the third column of that Schedule.

Schedule 4
Miscellaneous Amendments Relating to the Amendment of the Definition of Taxable Person

Amendments to Value-Added Tax Act 1972

Provision of Value-Added Tax Act 1972	Words to be replaced	Words to be inserted
Section 10A	a taxable person	an accountable person
Section 10A	that taxable person	that accountable person

(With effect from 1 July 2008)

Section 10B

Finance Act 1995

Special scheme for auctioneers

127. The Principal Act is hereby amended by the insertion of the following section after section 10A (inserted by this Part):

"10B. (1)   In this section-

'**auctioneer**' means a taxable person who, in the course or furtherance of business, acting on behalf of another person pursuant to a contract under which commission is payable on purchase or sale, offers tangible movable goods for sale by public auction with a view to handing them over to the highest bidder;

'**auctioneer's margin**' means an amount which is equal to the difference between the total amount, including any taxes, commissions, costs and charges whatsoever, payable by the purchaser to the auctioneer in respect of the auction of auction scheme goods and the amount payable by the auctioneer to the principal in respect of the supply of those goods and shall be deemed to be inclusive of tax;

'**auction scheme**' means the special arrangements for the taxation of supplies of auction scheme goods;

'**auction scheme goods**' means any works of art, collectors' items, antiques or second-hand goods sold by an auctioneer at a public auction while acting on behalf of a principal who is-

(a)   a person, other than a person referred to in paragraph (c), who was not entitled to deduct, under section 12, any tax in respect of that person's purchase, intra-Community acquisition or importation of those goods:

Provided that person is not a taxable person who acquired those goods from-

(i)   an auctioneer who applied the auction scheme to the supply of those goods to that taxable person, or

(ii)   a taxable dealer who applied the margin scheme to the supply of those goods to that taxable person,

or

(b)   a person in another Member State who was not entitled to deduct, under the provisions implementing Article 17 of Council Directive No. 77/388/EEC of 17 May 1977, in that Member State, any value-added tax referred to in that Directive in respect of that person's purchase, intra-Community acquisition or importation of those goods, or

(c)   a taxable dealer who applied the margin scheme to the supply of those goods or applied the provisions implementing Article 26a (inserted by Council Directive No. 94/5/EC of 14 February 1994) of Council Directive No. 77/388/EEC of 17 May 1977, in another Member State to the supply of those goods;

'**principal**' means the person on whose behalf an auctioneer auctions goods;

'**purchaser**' means the person to whom an auctioneer supplies auction scheme goods.

(2)   Subject to and in accordance with the provisions of this section, an auctioneer shall apply the auction scheme to any supply of auction scheme goods.

(3)   Notwithstanding section 10, the amount on which tax is chargeable, by virtue of section 2(1)(a), on a supply by an auctioneer of auction scheme goods shall be the auctioneer's margin less the amount of tax included in that auctioneer's margin.

(4)   Where auction scheme goods are auctioned, the auctioneer shall issue, subject to such conditions (if any) as may be specified in regulations, to both the principal and the purchaser, invoices or documents in lieu thereof setting out the relevant details in respect of the supply of the auction scheme goods.

(5)   Notwithstanding section 17, an auctioneer shall not, in relation to any supply to which the auction scheme has been applied, indicate separately the amount of tax chargeable in respect of the supply on any invoice or other document in lieu thereof issued in accordance with that section.

(6)   Where auction scheme goods are auctioned by an auctioneer on behalf of a principal who is a taxable person, the invoice or document in lieu thereof issued to the principal in accordance with subsection (4) shall be deemed to be an invoice for the purposes of section 17, and the said principal shall be deemed to have issued same.

(7)   Where the auction scheme is applied to a supply of goods dispatched or transported from the State to a person registered for value-added tax in another Member State then, notwithstanding paragraph (i)(b) of the Second Schedule. the provisions of section 11(1)(b) shall not apply, unless such goods are of a kind specified elsewhere in the Second Schedule.

(8)   Notwithstanding section 3(6)(d) where the auction scheme is applied to a supply of goods dispatched or transported, the place of supply of those goods shall be deemed to be the place where the dispatch or transportation begins.

(9)   Where an auctioneer supplies tangible movable goods by public auction, the principal shall be deemed to have made a supply of the auction scheme goods in question to the auctioneer when the said auctioneer sells those goods at a public auction.

(10)   Notwithstanding paragraph (xxiv) of the First Schedule, where a taxable person acquires goods to which the auction scheme has been applied and that person subsequently supplies those goods, the provisions of that paragraph shall not apply to that supply.".

(With effect from 1 July 1995)

Finance Act 1996

91.   Section 10B (inserted by the Act of 1995) of the Principal Act is hereby amended in subsection (9) by the substitution of "auction scheme goods" for "tangible movable goods".

(With effect from 15 May 1996)

Finance Act 1999

126.   Section 10B (inserted by the Act of 1995) of the Principal Act is hereby amended in subsection (1) by the insertion in the definition of "auction scheme goods" of the following paragraph after paragraph (a):

"(aa)   an owner within the meaning of section 3(5)(c) who enforced such owner's right to recover possession of those goods under the circumstances set out in section 3(5)(c), or".

(With effect from 25 March 1999)

Finance Act 2001

186.   Section 10B (inserted by the Act of 1995) of the Principal Act is amended by the insertion of the following after paragraph (aa) (inserted by the Act of 1999):

"(aaa) an insurer within the meaning of section 3(5)(d) (inserted by this Act) who took possession of those goods in connection with the settlement of a claim under a policy of insurance and whose disposal of the goods is deemed not to be a supply of the goods in accordance with section 3(5)(d) (inserted by this Act)".

(With effect from 21 March 2001)

Finance Act 2007

82. Section 10B of the Principal Act is amended with effect from 1 May 2007 by deleting paragraph (aa) of subsection (1).

*97. With effect from 1 January 2007 in each provision of the Principal Act specified in the first column of Schedule 3 for the words set out in the second column of that Schedule at that entry there is substituted the words set out at the corresponding entry in the third column of that Schedule.

Schedule 3
Miscellaneous Amendments Relating to Council Directive 2006/112/EC

Amendment of Value-Added Tax Act 1972

Provision of Principal Act	Words to be replaced	Words to be inserted
Section 10B(1)(b)	Article 17 of Council Directive No. 77/388/EEC of 17 May 1977	Articles 167, 173, 176 and 177 of Council Directive No. 2006/112/EC of 28 November 2006
Section 10B(1)(c)	Article 26a (inserted by Council Directive No. 94/5/EC of 14 February 1994) of Council Directive No. 77/388/EEC of 17 May 1977	Articles 4 and 35, first subparagraph of Article 139(3) and Articles 311 to 325 and 333 to 340 of Council Directive No. 2006/112/EC of 28 November 2006

(With effect from 1 May 2007 except * with effect from 1 January 2007)

Finance Act 2008

109. With effect from 1 July 2008 in each provision of the Principal Act specified in the first column of Schedule 4 for the words set out in the second column of that Schedule at that entry (in each place where those words occur in the provision concerned) there is substituted the words set out at the corresponding entry in the third column of that Schedule.

Schedule 4
Miscellaneous Amendments Relating to the Amendment of the Definition of Taxable Person

Amendments to Value-Added Tax Act 1972

Provision of Value-Added Tax Act 1972	Words to be replaced	Words to be inserted
Section 10B	a taxable person	an accountable person
Section 10B	that taxable person	that accountable person

(With effect from 1 July 2008)

Section 10C

Finance (No. 2) Act 2008

Travel agent's margin scheme

71.   The Principal Act is amended with effect from 1 January 2010 by inserting the following after section 10B:

"10C.   (1)   In this section—

'**bought-in services**' means goods or services which a travel agent purchases for the direct benefit of a traveller from another taxable person or from a person engaged in business outside the State;

'**margin scheme services**' means bought-in services supplied by a travel agent to a traveller;

'**travel agent**' means a taxable person who acts as a principal in the supply to a traveller of margin scheme services, and for the purposes of this section travel agent includes tour operator;

'**travel agent's margin**', in relation to a supply of margin scheme services, means an amount which is calculated in accordance with the following formula:

$$A - B$$

where—

A   is the total consideration which the travel agent becomes entitled to receive in respect of or in relation to that supply of margin scheme services including all taxes, commissions, costs and charges whatsoever and value-added tax payable in respect of that supply, and

B   is the amount payable by the travel agent to a supplier in respect of bought-in services included in that supply of margin scheme services to the traveller, but any bought-in services purchased by the travel agent prior to 1 January 2010 in respect of which that travel agent claims deductibility in accordance with section 12 shall be disregarded in calculating the margin,

and if that B is greater than that A the travel agent's margin in respect of that supply shall be deemed to be nil;

'**travel agent's margin scheme**' means the special arrangements for the taxation of margin scheme services.

(2)   A supply of margin scheme services by a travel agent to a traveller in respect of a journey shall be treated as a single supply.

(3) The place of supply of margin scheme services is the place where a travel agent has established that travel agent's business, but if those services are provided from a fixed establishment of that travel agent located in a place other than the place where that travel agent has established that travel agent's business, the place of supply of those services is the place where that fixed establishment is located.

(4) The travel agent's margin scheme shall apply to the supply of margin scheme services in the State.

(5) Notwithstanding section 10, the amount on which tax is chargeable by virtue of section 2(1)(a) on a supply of margin scheme services shall be the travel agent's margin less the amount of tax included in that margin.

(6) Notwithstanding sections 12 and 13, a travel agent shall not be entitled to a deduction or a refund of tax borne or paid in respect of bought-in services supplied by that travel agent as margin scheme services.

(7) Where a travel agent supplies margin scheme services together with other goods or services to a traveller for a total consideration, then that total consideration shall be apportioned by that travel agent so as to correctly reflect the ratio which the value of those margin scheme services bears to that total consideration, and in that case the proportion of the total consideration relating to the value of the margin scheme services shall be subject to the travel agent's margin scheme.

(8) Margin scheme services shall be treated as intermediary services when the bought-in services are performed outside the Community.

(9) Where a travel agent makes a supply of margin scheme services that includes some services that are treated as intermediary services in accordance with subsection (8), then the total travel agent's margin in respect of that supply shall be apportioned by that travel agent so as to correctly reflect the ratio which the cost to that travel agent of the bought-in services used in the margin scheme services that are treated as intermediary services in that supply bears to the total cost to that travel agent of all bought-in services used in making that supply of margin scheme services.

(10) A travel agent being an accountable person who supplies margin scheme services shall include the tax due on that person's supplies of margin scheme services for a taxable

period in the return that that person is required to furnish in accordance with section 19(3).

(11)   The Revenue Commissioners may make such regulations as they consider necessary for the purposes of the operation of this section including provisions for simplified accounting arrangements.".

(With effect from 1 January 2010)

Section 11

Value Added Tax Act 1972

Rates of tax

11. (1) Tax shall, subject to subsection (2), be charged at whichever of the following rates is appropriate in any particular case-

(a) 5.26 per cent of the appropriate amount of any consideration, other than consideration to which paragraph (b) applies, which relates to the delivery of goods or the rendering of services of a kind specified in the Third Schedule,

(b) 11.11 per cent of the appropriate amount of any consideration which relates to the promotion of dances and the delivery (if any) of goods of a kind specified in the Third Schedule and the rendering (if any) of services which but for this paragraph would be chargeable at the rate of 5.26 per cent delivered or rendered in connection with dances, where payment of the consideration for such delivery or rendering is included in the consideration in respect of admission to the dance or is a condition of admission,

(c) 30.26 per cent of the appropriate amount of any consideration which relates to the delivery of goods of a kind specified in the Fourth Schedule,

(d) zero per cent of the appropriate amount of any consideration which relates to the delivery of any goods in the circumstances specified in paragraph (i) or (v) of the Second Schedule or the delivery of goods of a kind specified in paragraphs (vi) to (viii) of that Schedule or the rendering of services of a kind specified in that Schedule, and

(e) 16.37 per cent of the appropriate amount of any consideration which relates to the delivery of any other goods or the rendering of any other services.

(2) Where goods which are of a kind specified in the Fourth Schedule and which-

(a) were imported, or sold in the State, before the specified day in such circumstances that wholesale tax was chargeable or would have been chargeable if that tax had been in force on the date of the importation or sale, or

(b) were imported or delivered on any previous occasion on or after that date in such circumstances that tax at the rate of 30.26 per cent was chargeable in relation to such importation or delivery, are delivered within the State on or after the specified day by a person other than a manufacturer of goods of the kind so delivered, tax shall be charged at the rate of 5.26 per cent of the appropriate amount of the consideration for such delivery.

(3)   Subject to sections 5(5) and 10(8)(c), where-

(a)   goods of different kinds or services of different kinds or goods, whether or not of different kinds, and services, whether or not of different kinds, are delivered, or rendered, or delivered and rendered, for a consideration that is referable to the transaction as a whole and not separately to the different kinds of goods or goods and services, and

(b)   but for this subsection, tax would fall to be charged at two or more rates in respect of the transaction.

tax shall be chargeable in respect of the transaction at the rate which is the higher or highest rate that, but for this subsection, would be chargeable in relation to any of the goods or services, as the case may be.

(4)   Where goods for the manufacture of which materials have been supplied by or on behalf of any person are delivered by the manufacturer to that person and the rate of tax chargeable in relation to the delivery of the goods exceeds that chargeable in relation to the delivery of the materials, the person who delivers the goods shall be liable, in addition to any other liability imposed on him by this Act, to pay tax on the value of the materials supplied to him, at a rate equivalent to the difference between the two aforementioned rates.

(5)   Where, in relation to an agreement of the kind referred to in section 3(1)(b), the accountable person in respect of the tax chargeable on any portion of the consideration is a person other than the person who delivered the goods to which the agreement relates, the rate of tax at which the said portion of the consideration shall be chargeable shall be the rate applicable to the delivery of the goods in question.

(6)   Where immovable goods consisting of machinery or business installations are let separately from other immovable goods of which they form part, tax shall be chargeable in respect of the transaction at the rate which would be chargeable if it were a hiring of movable goods of the same kind.

(7)   The following provisions shall have effect for the purposes of subsection (1)(b):

(a)   sections 8(3) and 14 shall not apply to a person in so far as he is chargeable with tax at the rate specified in the said subsection (1)(b);

(b)   the **"appropriate amount of any consideration"** shall be the total amount of money, excluding tax, received or receivable from persons admitted to a dance in respect of admission, together with, in case goods are delivered or services are rendered, or both goods are delivered and services are rendered, in connection with the dance, and payment of the consideration therefor is a condition of admission and is not included in the consideration in respect of admission, the total amount of money received or receivable in respect thereof;

(c)   every person who intends to promote a dance or a series of dances shall notify the Revenue Commissioners in accordance with regulations of his intention to do so:

(d)   the proprietor of any premises shall not promote a dance therein, or allow a dance to be promoted therein by any other person, unless he has received notice from the Revenue Commissioners that they have been notified in accordance with paragraph (c);

(e)   paragraphs (a) to (d) and subsection (1)(b) shall not apply in any case in which the number of persons to be admitted to the dance is limited to one hundred and the consideration for admission does not exceed twenty new pence.

(8)   (a)   The Minister may by order declare that the rate at which tax shall be charged on the delivery or the importation of goods of any kind, or on the rendering of services of any kind, shall be a rate specified in subsection (1) which is lower than the rate at which, but for the order, tax would be charged.

(b)   The Minister may by order amend or revoke an order under this subsection, including an order under this paragraph.

(c)   An order under this subsection shall be laid before Dáil Éireann as soon as may be after it has been made and, if a resolution annulling the order is passed by Dáil Éireann within the next twenty-one days on which Dáil Éireann has sat after the order is laid before it, the order shall be annulled accordingly, but without prejudice to the validity of anything previously done thereunder.

(9)   Subject to subsection (7), in this section "appropriate amount of any consideration" means the amount, as ascertained in accordance with section 10, on which tax is chargeable.

(With effect from 1 November 1972)

Finance Act 1973

80.   Section 11 of the Principal Act is hereby amended-

(a)   by the substitution of the following paragraphs for paragraphs (a) and (b) of subsection (1):

"(a)   6.75 per cent of the appropriate amount of any consideration, other than consideration to which paragraph (b) applies, which relates to the delivery of goods of a kind specified in Part I of the Third Schedule or the rendering of services of a kind specified in Part II of that Schedule,

(b)   11.11 per cent of the appropriate amount of any consideration which relates to the promotion of dances and the delivery (if any) of goods of a kind specified in paragraphs (vi) to (viii) and (xii) to (xv) of the Second Schedule or in Part I of the Third Schedule and the rendering (if any) of services which, but for this paragraph, would be chargeable at the rate specified in paragraph (a) delivered or rendered in connection with dances, where payment of the consideration for such delivery or rendering is included in the consideration in respect of admission to the dance or is a condition of admission,",

(b)   by the substitution in subsection (1)(c) of "36.75" for "30.26",

(c)   by the substitution in subsection (1)(e) of "19.50" for "16.37",

(d)   by the insertion of the following subsections after subsection (1):

"(1A)   (a)   The rate at which tax shall be chargeable shall, in relation to tax chargeable under section 2(1)(a), be the rate for the time being in force at the time at which the tax becomes due in accordance with subsection (1) or (2), as may be appropriate, of section 19.

(b)   Goods or services which are specifically excluded from any paragraph of a Schedule shall, unless the contrary intention is expressed, be regarded as excluded from every other paragraph of that Schedule, and shall not be regarded as specified in that Schedule.

(1B)   (a)   On receipt of an application in writing from an accountable person, the Revenue Commissioners shall, in accordance with regulations and after such consultation (if any) as may seem to them to be necessary with such person or body of persons as in their option may be of assistance to them, make a determination concerning-

      (i)   whether an activity of any particular kind carried on by the person is an exempted activity, or

      (ii)   the rate at which tax is chargeable in relation to the delivery by the person of goods of any kind, the delivery of goods in any particular circumstances or the rendering by the person of services of any kind.

(b)   The Revenue Commissioners may, whenever they consider it expedient to do so, in accordance with regulations and after such consultation (if any) as may seem to them to be necessary with such person or body of persons as in their opinion may be of assistance to them, make a determination concerning-

      (i)   whether an activity of any particular kind is an exempted activity, or

      (ii)   the rate at which tax is chargeable in relation to the delivery of goods of any kind, the delivery of goods in any particular circumstances or the rendering of services of any kind.

(c)   A determination under this subsection shall have effect for all the purposes of this Act, in relation to an accountable person who makes an application therefore, as, on and from the date upon which particulars of the determination are communicated to him in accordance with paragraph (e)(i) and, in relation to any other person, as on and from the date of publication of the determination in the *Iris Oifigiúil*.

(d)   The Revenue Commissioners shall not make a determination under this section concerning any matter which has been determined on appeal under this Act or which is for the time being governed by an order under section 6(2) or 11(8), and shall not be required to make such a determination in relation to any of the matters referred to in an application under paragraph (a) if-

      (i)   a previous determination has been published in regard to the matter, or

      (ii)   in their opinion the subject matter of the application is sufficiently free from doubt as not to warrant the making and publication of a determination.

(e)   (i)   A determination under paragraph (a) shall, as soon as may be after the making thereof, be communicated to the person who made the application therefore by the service on him by the Revenue Commissioners of a notice containing particulars of the determination.

(ii)   A determination under paragraph (a) may and a determination under paragraph (b) shall be published in the *Iris Oifigiúil* and, in that event, it shall also be published in at least one daily newspaper published in the State.

(f)   A person, aggrieved by a determination under paragraph (a) made pursuant to an application by him, may, on giving notice in writing to the Revenue Commissioners within the period of twenty-one days beginning on the date of service on him of notice of the determination in accordance with paragraph (e)(i), appeal to the Appeal Commissioners.

(g)   Any accountable person who, in the course of business, delivers goods or renders services of a kind or in circumstances specified in a determination under paragraph (a) or (b) may, on giving notice in writing to the Revenue Commissioners within the period of twenty-one days beginning on the date of the publication of the determination in the *Iris Oifigiúil*, appeal to the Appeal Commissioners.",

(e)   by the insertion of the following subsection after subsection (4):

"(4A)   Where-

(a)   goods of a kind specified in paragraph (xii) of the Second Schedule are used by a person in the course of the rendering by him of taxable services, and

(b)   the goods are supplied by the person to whom the services are rendered or by any other person other than the person by whom the services are rendered,

the person who renders the taxable services shall be deemed to have supplied the goods so used in the course of business and shall be liable, in addition to any other liability imposed on him under this Act, to pay tax on the value of the goods so used at the rate specified in section 11(1)(a).",

and

(f)   by the substitution of the following paragraph for paragraph (a) of subsection (8):

"(a)   The Minister may by order vary the Second or Third Schedules by adding to or deleting therefrom descriptions of goods or services of any kind or by varying any description of goods or services for the time being specified therein, and may, in like manner, vary the Fourth Schedule by deleting therefrom descriptions of goods of any kind or by varying any description of goods for the time being specified therein, but no order shall be made under this section for the purpose of increasing any of the rates of tax or extending the classes of activities or goods in respect of which tax is for the time being chargeable.".

90.   The Principal Act is hereby amended as specified in column (3) of the Tenth Schedule to this Act.

TENTH SCHEDULE
AMENDMENT OF ENACTMENTS

Number and Year (1)	Short Title (2)	Amendment (3)
No. 22 of 1972	Value-Added Tax Act, 1972	In section 11, in subsection (1)(d),", other than consideration to which paragraph (b) applies," shall be inserted after" consideration", "(v) or (xvi)" shall be substituted for "or (v)" and "and (xii) to (xv)" shall be inserted after "(viii)"; in subsection (2), "for the time being specified in subsection (1)(c)" shall be substituted for "of 30.26 per cent" and "for the time being specified in subsection (1)(a) on" shall be substituted for "of 5.26 per cent of"; and in for "of 5.26 per cent of"; and in subsection (3), "paragraph (xvi) of the Second Schedule and paragraph (xxxii) of Part I of the Third Schedule," shall be inserted after "10(8)(c),".

(With effect from 3 September 1973)

Finance Act 1975

51.   Section 11 of the Value-Added Tax Act, 1972, is hereby amended with effect on and from the 16th day of January, 1975-

(a)   by the substitution of the following subsection for subsection (2):

"(2)   Where goods which are of a kind specified in the Fourth Schedule and which-

(a)   were imported, or sold in the State, before the specified day in such circumstances that wholesale

tax was chargeable or would have been chargeable
if that tax had been in force on the date of the
importation or sale, or

(b)   were, on any previous occasion on or after the
specified day, imported by or delivered to a person
other than a manufacturer of goods of the kind
so delivered or imported in such circumstances
that tax at the rate for the time being specified in
subsection (1)

(c)   was chargeable in relation to such importation or
delivery, are delivered within the State on or after
the specified day, tax shall be charged at the rate
for the time being specified in subsection (1)(a) on
the appropriate amount of any consideration for
such delivery.",

and

(b)   by the substitution of the following subsection for subsection
(4):

"(4)   Where goods for the manufacture of which materials
have been supplied by or on behalf of any person are
delivered by the manufacturer to that person and the rate
of tax chargeable in relation to the delivery of the goods
exceeds that which would be chargeable in relation to
a delivery within the State of the materials, the person
who delivers the goods shall, in respect of the delivery
of such goods, be liable, in addition to any other liability
imposed on him by this Act, to pay tax on the value of
the materials supplied to him at a rate equivalent to the
difference between the two aforementioned rates.".

(With effect from 16 January 1975)

Finance Act 1976

53.   Section 11 of the Principal Act is hereby amended-

(a)   by the substitution in subsection (1) of the following paragraph
for paragraph (a) (inserted by the Act of 1973 .

"(a)   10 per cent of the appropriate amount of any consideration
which relates to the delivery of goods of a kind specified
in Part I of the Third Schedule or the rendering of services
of a kind specified in Part II of that Schedule,",

(b)   by the substitution of the following paragraphs for paragraphs
(c), (d) and (e) of subsection (1):

"(c)   (i)   35 per cent of the appropriate amount of any
consideration which relates to the delivery of

goods of a kind specified in Part I of the Fourth Schedule,

(ii)   40 per cent of the appropriate amount of any consideration which relates to the delivery of goods of a kind specified in Part II of the Fourth Schedule,

(d)   zero per cent of the appropriate amount of any consideration which relates to the delivery of any goods in the circumstances specified in paragraph (i), (v) or (xvi) of the Second Schedule or the delivery of goods of a kind specified in paragraphs (vi) to (viii), (xii) to (xv) and (xvii) to (xx) of that Schedule or the rendering of services of a kind specified in that Schedule, and

(e)   20 per cent of the appropriate amount of any consideration which relates to the delivery of any other goods or the rendering of any other services.",

and

(c)   by the substitution of the following subsection for subsection (7)-

"(7)   (a)   Sections 8(3) and 14 shall not apply to a person in so far as he is chargeable with tax in respect of the promotion of a dance, and the promotion of a dance or a series of dances by a person shall be deemed, for the purposes of this Act, to be a separate business carried on by such person.

(b)   Notwithstanding subsection (1) and section 10, tax shall in relation to the promotion of a dance, be charged at the rate specified in subsection (1)(a) on the total amount of money, excluding tax received or receivable from persons admitted to the dance in respect of admission together with the total amount of money (if any), excluding tax, received or receivable in respect of-

(i)   goods of a kind specified in paragraph (e)(i) delivered, or

(ii)   services of a kind specified in paragraph (e)(ii) rendered, in connection with the dance where payment of the consideration in respect thereof is a condition of admission to the dance and is not included in the consideration in respect of admission.

(c)   Every person who intends to promote a dance or a series of dances shall notify the Revenue Commissioners in accordance with regulations of his intention to do so.

(d) The proprietor of any premises shall not propionate a dance therein, or allow a dance to be promoted therein by any other person, unless he has received notice from the Revenue Commissioners that they have been notified in accordance with paragraph (c).

(e) In this subsection-

'the promotion of a dance' includes-

(i) the delivery in connection with the dance of any goods to which, but for this subsection, subsection (1)(a) or subsection (1)(d) would apply where payment of the consideration for such delivery is included in the consideration in respect of admission to the dance or is a condition of admission.

(ii) the rendering in connection with the dance of any services to which, but for this subsection, subsection (1)(a) or subsection (1)(d) would apply where payment of the consideration for such rendering is included in the consideration in respect of admission to the dance or is a condition of admission;

'dance' does not include a dance the number of persons to be admitted to which is limited to one hundred and the consideration for admission to which does not exceed twenty pence.".

61. In consequence of the amendments specified in sections 53 and 60 and the repeals specified in Part II of the Fifth Schedule, The Principal Act is hereby further amended as specified in Part II of the First Schedule.

FIRST SCHEDULE

PART II

Amendments Consequential on Certain Amendments of Value-Added Tax Act, 1972

Number and Year (1)	Short Title (2)	Amendment (3)
No. 22 of 1972	Value-Added Tax Act, 1972.	In section 11- (a) in subsection (2)(b) (inserted by the Finance Act, 1975) "a rate" shall be substituted for "the rate", and (b) in subsection (3), "paragraph (xxix) shall be substituted for "paragraph (xxxii)".

Transitional provisions in respect of motor vehicles

63.   (1)   In this section-

"**qualified vehicles**" means vehicles which, on or before the 29th day of February, 1976, were delivered to or imported by a person other than a manufacturer of goods of the kind so delivered or imported in such circumstances that tax at the rate of 36.75 per cent was chargeable in relation to such delivery or importation;

"**relevant delivery**" means a delivery of any qualified vehicles in such circumstances that, but for this section, tax at the rate of 10 per cent would be chargeable;

"**vehicles**" means goods (other than secondhand goods) of a kind specified in Part I of the Fourth Schedule (inserted by this Act) to The Principal Act.

(2)   During the period which commenced on the 1st day of March, 1976, and ended on the 30th day of April, 1976, notwithstanding the provisions of section 11 of the Principal Act, tax shall, in relation to a relevant delivery, be chargeable and be deemed to have been chargeable at the rate of 6.75 per cent.

(3)   Notwithstanding the provisions of section 12(1) of the Principal Act, the amount deductible by a person under that section in relation to-

(a)   any qualified vehicles, and

(b)   the delivery or importation of any vehicles (not being qualified vehicles) in relation to the consideration for a delivery of which by him tax was charged at the rate of 6.75 per cent,

shall not exceed, in the case of a delivery of such goods to him, 6.75 per cent of the consideration payable by him exclusive of any tax payable in respect of the delivery by the person making the delivery and, in the case of an importation, 6.75 per cent of the value of the goods calculated in accordance with section 15(4) of the said Act.

81.   (1)   The enactment mentioned in column (2) of Part I of the Fifth Schedule to this Act is hereby repealed to the extent specified in column (3) of that Schedule.

(2)   The enactment mentioned in column (2) of Part II of the Fifth Schedule to this Act is hereby repealed to the extent specified in column (3) of that Schedule.

(3)   (a)   Subsection (1) of this section shall be deemed to have come into operation on the 6th day of April, 1976.

(b)   Subsection (2) of this section shall be deemed to have come into operation on the 1st day of March, 1976.

FIFTH SCHEDULE

Enactments Repealed

PART II

No. 22 of 1972	Value-Added Tax Act, 1972	Section 11(1)(b)

(With effect from 1 March 1996)

Value Added Tax (Amendment) Act 1978

9.   Section 11 of the Principal Act is hereby amended by the substitution of the following subsections for subsections (1), (2), (3) and (4A):

"(1)   Tax shall, subject to subsection (2), be charged at whichever of the following rates is appropriate in any particular case-

(a)   10 per cent of the amount on which tax is chargeable in relation to the supply of goods of a kind specified in Part I of the Third Schedule or the supply of services of a kind specified in Part II of that Schedule.

(b)   zero per cent of the amount on which tax is chargeable in relation to the supply of any goods in the circumstances specified in paragraph (i) of the Second Schedule or the supply of goods of a kind specified in paragraphs (v)(a) and (b), (vii), (viii), (x), (xii) to (xv) and (xvii) to (xx) of that Schedule or the supply of services of a kind specified in that Schedule, and

(c)   20 per cent of the amount on which tax is chargeable in relation to the supply of any other goods or services.

(2)   (a)   In relation to the supply of livestock, tax shall be chargeable at the rate specified in subsection (1)(a) on 10 per cent of the total amount on which tax is chargeable and at the rate of zero per cent on the balance of the said total amount.

(b)   On the supply of immovable goods and on the supply of services consisting of the development of immovable goods, or the maintenance and repair of those goods including the installation of fixtures, if the value of movable goods (if any) provided in pursuance of the agreement for making any such supply does not exceed two-thirds of the total amount on which tax is chargeable in respect of the agreement, tax shall be chargeable at the rate specified in subsection (1)(a) on 30 per cent of the total amount on which tax is chargeable and at the rate of zero per cent on the balance of the said total amount.

(3)   Subject to section 10(8), where-

(a)   supplies of different kinds are made for a consideration in money which is referable to all the supplies and not separately to the different kinds of supplies, and

(b)   one or both of the following subparagraphs applies or apply, that is to say-

(i)   but for this subsection, tax would not be chargeable in respect of one or more (but not all) of the supplies,

(ii)   but for this subsection, tax would (apart from subsection (2)) fall to be charged at two or more of the rates specified in subsection (1) in respect of the supplies,

then, unless regulations provide for apportionment of the consideration-

(c)   where subparagraph (i) (but not subparagraph (ii)) of paragraph (b) applies, tax shall be chargeable in respect of all the supplies at the rate specified in subsection (1) appropriate to the supply of taxable goods or services included in the supplies,

(d)   where subparagraph (ii) of paragraph (b) applies (whether alone or with subparagraph (i) of that paragraph), tax shall be chargeable in respect of all the supplies at the higher or highest rate (as the case may be) specified in subsection (1) appropriate to the supply of any taxable goods or services included in the supplies:

Provided that, where goods

(I)   are chargeable with tax at different rates,

(II)   are packaged for sale as a unit, and

(III)   are offered for sale for a consideration in money which is referable to the package as a whole and not to the different kinds of goods included therein,

the inclusion in the package of goods chargeable at a particular rate shall not be taken into account for the purpose of the preceding provisions of this subsection where the total tax-exclusive value of such goods does not exceed 50 per cent of the total tax-exclusive consideration for the package or 5 pence, whichever is the lesser, and, in any such case, the rate of tax chargeable in relation to the package shall be determined by reference to the other goods included therein.

(4A)   Where-

(a)   goods of a kind specified in paragraph (xii) of the Second Schedule are used by a person in the course of the supply by him of taxable services, and

(b)   the goods are provided by or on behalf of the person to whom the services are supplied,

the person who supplies the taxable services shall be liable in respect thereof, in addition to any other liability imposed on him under this Act, to pay tax on the value of the goods so used at the rate specified in section 11(1)(a).".

30.   (1)   The enactment mentioned in column (2) of the First Schedule is hereby repealed to the extent specified in column (3) of that Schedule.

(2)   In consequence of the amendments of the Principal Act specified in this Act and of the repeals specified in the First Schedule, the Principal Act is hereby further amended by the substitution of the word or expression mentioned in column (3) of the Second Schedule at any reference number for the word or expression mentioned in column (2) of that Schedule at that reference number wherever it occurs in the provision of the Principal Act mentioned in column (4) of that Schedule at that reference number.

FIRST SCHEDULE
Enactments Repealed

Number and Year (1)	Short Title (2)	Extent of Repeal (3)
No. 22 of 1972	Value-Added Tax Act, 1972	In section 11(8)(a), the words "and may, in like manner, vary the Fourth Schedule by deleting therefrom descriptions of goods of any kind or by varying any description of goods for the time being specified therein,". Section 11(9).

SECOND SCHEDULE
Consequential Amendments

Reference Number (1)	Existing word or expression (2)	Substituted word or expression (3)	Provision of Principal Act (4)
1	"delivery"	"supply"	The definition of "exempted activity", and the definition of "taxable goods" in sections 11(1B)(a)(ii), 11(1B)(b)(ii), 11(4), 11(5), 11(7)(e)(i),
2	"rendering"	"supply"	The definition of "taxable services" in sections 11(1B)(a)(ii), 11(1B)(b)(ii), 11(7)(e)(ii),
3	"delivered"	"supplied"	Sections 11(4), 11(5), 11(7)(b)(i),
4	"rendered"	"supplied"	Sections 11(7)(b)(ii),
7	"delivers"	"supplies"	Section 11(4).
21	"delivers goods or renders services"	"supplies goods or services"	Section 11(1B)(g),
25	"accountable person" except where preceded by the word "an"	"taxable person"	Sections 11(IB)(g), 11(5), 12(2),
26	"an accountable person"	"a taxable person"	Sections 11(1B)(a), 11(1B)(c),
29	"supplied"	"provided"	section 11(4)
30	"subsection (1) (d)"	"subsection (1) (b)"	Section 11(7)(e)(i), 11(7)(e)(ii).

(With effect from 1 March 1979)

Finance Act 1980

80.   As respects goods supplied or imported, or services supplied, on or after the 1st day of May, 1980-

(a)   section 11(1) (inserted by the Value-Added Tax (Amendment) Act, 1978) of the Value-Added Tax Act, 1972, shall have effect as if the following paragraph were substituted for paragraph (c):

"(c)   25 per cent of the amount on which tax is chargeable in relation to the supply of any goods or services, other than goods or services on which tax is chargeable at either of the rates specified in paragraphs (a) and (b) or which are mentioned in the First Schedule, but including radio receiving sets that are of the domestic or portable type or that are of a type suitable for use in road vehicles, and gramophones, radio-gramophones and record players.",

(With effect from 1 May 1980)

Finance Act (No. 2) 1981

12.   (1)   Section 11 of the Principal Act is hereby amended-

(a)   in subsection (1) (inserted by the Act of 1978), by the substitution in paragraph (a) of "15 per cent" for "10 per cent",

(b)   in subsection (2) (inserted by the Act of 1978), by the substitution in paragraph (b) of "20 per cent" for "30 per cent", and

(c)   by the insertion after the said paragraph (b) of the following paragraph:

"(c)   On the supply of agricultural services consisting of-

(i)   field work, reaping, mowing, threshing, baling, harvesting, sowing and planting;

(ii)   disinfecting and ensilage of agricultural products;

(iii)   destruction of weeds and pests and dusting and spraying of crops and land;

(iv)   lopping, tree felling and similar forestry services,

and

(v)   land drainage and reclamation.

tax shall be chargeable at the rate specified in subsection (1)(a) on 20 per cent of the total amount on which tax is chargeable and at the rate of zero per cent on the balance of the said total amount.".

(2)   This section shall have, and be deemed to have had, effect as on and from the 1st day of September, 1981.

Relief for Hotels, etc.

14.   (1)   In this section "**qualifying service**" means a service consisting of the supply, for the benefit of persons not resident in the State, under an agreement made before the 1st day of January, 1981, of sleeping accommodation, with or without board or of motor cars upon hire, boats upon hire or entertainment, at charges fixed at the time of the making of the agreement, to persons carrying on the business of travel agent, tour operator or the hiring out of motor cars or boats.

(2)   In respect of the taxable periods commencing on the 1st day of September, 1981, and the 1st day of November, 1981,

notwithstanding the provisions of section 11 of the Principal Act (as amended by this Act), tax shall, in relation to the supply of a qualifying service, be chargeable, and be deemed to have been chargeable, at the rate of 10 per cent.

(With effect from 1 September 1981)

Finance Act 1982

79. (1)   Section 11 of the Principal Act is hereby amended-

(a)   in subsection (1) (inserted by the Act of 1978)-

(i)   in paragraph (a), by the substitution of "18 per cent" for "15 per cent" (inserted by the Act of 1981),

(ii)   in paragraph (b), by the substitution of "(xva)" for "(xv)",

and

(iii)   in paragraph (c) (inserted by the Finance Act, 1980), by the substitution of "30 per cent" for "25 per cent" (inserted by the Act of 1981),

(b)   in subsection (2)-

(i)   in paragraph (b) (inserted by the Act of 1978), by the substitution of "16.67 per cent" for "20 per cent" (inserted by the Act of 1981), and

(ii)   in paragraph (c) (inserted by the Act of 1981), by the substitution of "16.67 per cent" for "20 per cent",

and

(iii)   by the insertion after the said paragraph (c) of the following paragraphs:

"(d)   On the supply by an auctioneer, solicitor, estate agent or other agent of services directly related to the supply of immovable goods used for the purposes of an Annex A activity tax shall be chargeable at the rate specified in subsection 5(1)(a) on 16.67 per cent of the total amount on which tax is chargeable and at the rate of zero per cent on the balance of the said total amount.

(e)   On the supply of farm accountancy services or farm management services tax shall be chargeable at the rate specified in subsection (1)(a) on 16.67 per cent of the total amount on which tax is chargeable and at the rate of zero per cent on the balance of the said total amount.".

(2)   This section other than subsection (1)(b)(iii) shall have, and be deemed to have had, effect as on and from the 1st day of May, 1982.

Relief for hotels etc.

90.   (1)   In this section **"qualifying service"** means a service consisting of the supply, for the benefit of persons not resident in the State, under an agreement made before the 1st day of January, 1982, of sleeping accommodation, with or without board, or of motor cars upon hire, boats upon hire or entertainment, at charges fixed at the time of the making of the agreement, to persons carrying on the business of travel agent, tour operator or the hiring out of motor cars or boats.

(2)   In respect of the taxable periods commencing on the 1st day of May, 1982, the 1st day of July, 1982, the 1st day of September, 1982, and the 1st day of November, 1982, notwithstanding the provisions of section 11 of the Principal Act (as amended by this Act), tax shall, in relation to the supply of a qualifying service, be, and be deemed to have been, chargeable, at the rate of 15 per cent.

(With effect from 1 May 1982)

Finance Act 1983

81.   *(1)   Section 11 of the Principal Act is hereby amended-

(a)   in subsection (1)-

(i)   in paragraph (a) (inserted by the Act of 1978), by the substitution of "23 per cent" for "18 per cent" (inserted by the Act of 1982),

and

(ii)   in paragraph (c) (inserted by the Finance Act, 1980), by the substitution of "35 per cent" for "30 per cent" (inserted by the Act of 1982),

and

(b)   in subsection (2)-

(i)   in paragraph (a) (inserted by the Act of 1978), as respects supplies on or after the 1st day of July, 1983, by the substitution of "8.69 per cent" for "10 per cent",

(ii)   in paragraph (b) (inserted by the Act of 1978), by the substitution of "21.74 per cent" for "16.67 per cent" (inserted by the Act of 1982),

         (iii)   in paragraph (c) (inserted by the Act of 1981), by the substitution of "21.74 per cent" for "16.67 per cent" (inserted by the Act of 1982),

         (iv)   in paragraph (d) (inserted by the Act of 1982), by the substitution of "21.74 per cent" for "16.67 per cent",

and

         (v)   in paragraph (e) (inserted by the Act of 1982), by the substitution of "21.74 per cent" for "16.67 per cent".

(2)   section 11 of the Principal Act is hereby further amended-

    (a)   in subsection (1)-

         (i)   by the insertion of the following paragraph after paragraph (a):

             "(aa) 5 per cent of the amount on which tax is chargeable in relation to the supply of goods or services of a kind specified in the Sixth Schedule,",

and

         (ii)   in paragraph (c), by the substitution of "any of the rates specified in paragraphs (a), (aa) and (b)" for "either of the rates specified in paragraphs (a) and (b)",

    (b)   in subsection (2), by the deletion of paragraphs (b), (c), (d) and (e),

    (c)   in subsection (7) (inserted by the Act of 1976), by the insertion in paragraph (e)(i) after "subsection (1)(a)" of "subsection (1)(aa)",

and

    (d)   in subsection (8), by the substitution in paragraph (a) (inserted by the Finance Act, 1973) of "Second, Third or Sixth Schedule" for "Second or Third Schedules".

Relief for hotels etc.

*89. (1)   (a)   In this section "qualifying service" means a service consisting of the supply, for the benefit of persons not resident in the State, under an agreement made before the 1st day of January, 1983, of sleeping accommodation, with or without board, or of motor cars upon hire, boats upon hire or entertainment, at charges fixed at the time of the making of the agreement, to persons carrying on the business of travel agent, tour operator or the hiring out of motor cars or boats.

(b)   In respect of the taxable periods commencing on the 1st day of March, 1983, the 1st day of May, 1983, the 1st day of July, 1983, the 1st day of September, 1983 and the 1st day of November, 1983, notwithstanding the provisions of section 11 of the Principal Act (as amended by this Act), tax shall, in relation to the supply of a qualifying service, be, and be deemed to have been, chargeable at the rate of 18 per cent.

(2)   Notwithstanding the provisions of section 11 of the Principal Act (as amended by this Act), the rate of tax chargeable in relation to the letting of immovable goods specified in paragraph (iv)(b) of the First Schedule to The Principal Act shall be 18 per cent.

(With effect from 1 May 1983 except * from I March 1983)

Finance Act 1984

87.   Section 11 of the Principal Act is hereby amended-

(a)   in subsection (1) (inserted by the Value-Added Tax (Amendment) Act, 1978)-

(i)   by the insertion after paragraph (aa) (inserted by the Act of 1983) of the following paragraph:

"(aaa) 8 per cent of the amount on which tax is chargeable in relation to the supply of goods of a kind specified in the Seventh Schedule,",

and

(ii)   by the insertion in paragraph (c) (inserted by the Finance Act, 1980) after "(aa)" of ",(aaa)",

(b)   in subsection (7) (inserted by the Act of 1976), by the insertion in paragraph (e)(i) after "subsection (1)(aa)" of ",subsection (1)(aaa)",

and

(c)   in subsection (8), by the substitution in paragraph (a) (inserted by the Finance Act, 1973) of "Second, Third, Sixth or Seventh" for "Second, Third or Sixth".

Rate of tax in relation to short-term hiring of certain goods

*96.   Notwithstanding the provisions of section 11 of the Principal Act, the rate of value-added tax chargeable on the following services shall be 18 per cent of the amount in respect of which tax is chargeable in relation to those services:

(a)   the service specified in paragraph (ii) of Part II of the Third Schedule to The Principal Act, and

(b)   the service consisting of the hiring to a person, under an agreement of the kind specified in the said paragraph (ii) of a tent or of a vehicle designed and constructed, or adapted, for the conveyance of persons by road.

(With effect from 1 May 1984 except * from 1 March 1984)

Finance Act 1985

43.   Section 11 of the Principal Act is hereby amended-

(a)   by the substitution of the following subsection for subsection (1) (inserted by the Act of 1978):

"(1)   Tax shall be charged at whichever of the following rates is appropriate in any particular case-

(a)   23 per cent. of the amount on which tax is chargeable in relation to the supply of taxable goods or services, other than goods or services on which tax is chargeable at any of the rates specified in paragraphs (b), (c) and (d),

(b)   zero per cent. of the amount on which tax is chargeable in relation to the supply of any goods in the circumstances specified in paragraph (i) of the Second Schedule or the supply of goods of a kind specified in paragraphs (v), (vii), (viii), (x), (xii) to (xva) and (xvii) to (xx) of that Schedule or the supply of services of a kind specified in that Schedule,

(c)   10 per cent. of the amount on which tax is chargeable in relation to the supply of goods or services of a kind specified in the Sixth Schedule, and

(d)   2.2 per cent of the amount on which tax is chargeable in relation to the supply of livestock",

(b)   by the deletion of subsection (2) (inserted by the Act of 1978),

(c)   in subsection (3) (inserted by the Act of 1978), by the deletion of "(apart from subsection (2))" in paragraph (b) (ii),

(d)   in subsection (7) (inserted by the Act of 1976)-

(i)   by the substitution in paragraph (e)(i) of "taxable goods" for "any goods to which, but for this subsection, subsection (1)(a), subsection (1)(aa), subsection (1)(aaa) or subsection (1)(b) would apply",

and

(ii)   by the substitution in paragraph (e)(ii) of "taxable services" for "any services to which, but for this subsection, subsection (1)(a) or subsection (1)(b) would apply",

and

(e)   in subsection (8), by the substitution in paragraph (a)
        (inserted by the Finance Act, 1973) of "Second or Sixth for
        "Second, Third, Sixth or Seventh".

Repeals

*53. Section 89(2) of the Act of 1983 and section 96 of the Act of 1984 are
hereby repealed.

Deferment of increase in rate of tax (private dwellings)

54.   (1)   For the purposes of this section-

                "**dwelling**" means a house, or an apartment, flat, penthouse or
                similar unit of accommodation;

                "**qualifying supply**" means the supply on or before the 30th day
                of April, 1985, to a person, being an individual acting on his own
                behalf, of a service consisting of the development of immovable
                goods, being the construction of a dwelling designed for the
                private use of, and occupation by, such person, and includes a
                supply of immovable goods to that person on or before the said
                date in connection with the supply of the said service.

        (2)   In this section reference to the construction of a dwelling does not
                include reference to the conversion, reconstruction, alteration or
                enlargement of any existing building or buildings.

        (3)   In respect of the taxable period commencing on the 1st day of
                March, 1985, notwithstanding the provisions of section 11 of the
                Principal Act (as amended by this Act), value-added tax shall, in
                relation to a qualifying supply, be, and be deemed to have been,
                chargeable, at the rate of 5 per cent.

(With effect from 1 March 1985 except * from 1 May 1985)

Finance Act 1986

83.   Section 11 (inserted by the Act of 1978) of The Principal Act is hereby
amended-

        (a)   in subsection 1-

                (i)   in paragraph (a) by the substitution of "5 per cent" for "23
                        per cent",

                and

                (ii)   in paragraph (d) by the substitution of "2.4 per cent" for
                        "2.2 per cent",

        and

        *(b)   in subsection (4A) (inserted by the Finance Act, 1973) by the
                substitution of "section 11(1)(c)" for "section 11(1)(a)".

(With effect from 1 March 1986 except * from 1 July 1986)

Finance Act 1987

40.   Section 11 of the Principal Act is hereby amended in subsection (1) (inserted by the Act of 1985) by the substitution in) paragraph (d) of "1.7 per cent " for "2.4 per cent" (inserted by the Act of 1986).

(With effect from 1 May 1987)

Finance Act 1988

61.   Section 11(1) (inserted by the Finance Act, 1985) of The Principal Act is hereby amended-

(a)   by the insertion in paragraph (a) after "in paragraphs (b)" of ", (bb)",

(b)   by the insertion of the following paragraph after paragraph (b):

"(bb)   5 per cent of the amount on which tax is chargeable in relation to the supply of electricity,",

and

(c)   by the substitution in paragraph (d) of "1.4 per cent" for "1.7 per cent" (inserted by the Finance Act, 1987).

(With effect from 1 March 1988)

Finance Act 1989

56.   Section 11 of the Principal Act is hereby amended in subsection (1) (inserted by the Act of 1985)-

*(a)   by the substitution of the following paragraph for paragraph (bb) (inserted by the Act of 1988):

"(bb)   5 per cent of the amount on which tax is chargeable in relation to the supply of electricity:

Provided that this paragraph shall not apply to the distribution of any electricity where such distribution is wholly or mainly in connection with the distribution of communications signals,",

and

(b)   by the substitution in paragraph (d) of "2 per cent" for "1.4 per cent" (inserted by the Act of 1988).

(With effect from 1 March 1989)

Finance Act 1990

102. Section 11 of the Principal Act is hereby amended in subsection (1) (inserted by the Act of 1985)-

    (a)   in paragraph (a)-

        (i)   by the substitution of "23 per cent" for "25 per cent" (inserted by the Act of 1986),

    and

        (ii)   by the deletion of ", (bb)" (inserted by the Finance Act, 1988),

    (b)   by the deletion of paragraph (bb) (inserted by the Act of 1989),

    and

    (c)   paragraph (d)-

        (i)   by the substitution of "2.3 per cent" for "2 per cent" (inserted by the Act of 1989),

    and

        *(ii)   by the insertion after "livestock" of "and live greyhounds, and to the hire of horses".

(With effect from 1 March 1990 except * from 1 January 1991)

Finance Act 1991

80. Section 11 of the Principal Act is hereby amended-

    (a)   in subsection (1) (inserted by the Act of 1985):

        (i)   in paragraph (a)-

            (I)   by the substitution of "21 per cent" for "23 per cent" (inserted by the Finance Act, 1990),

        and

            (II)   by the insertion after "in paragraphs (b)" of ", (bi)",

        (ii)   by the insertion of the following paragraph after paragraph (b):

            "(bi)   10 per cent of the amount on which tax is chargeable in relation to goods or services of a kind specified in the Third Schedule,",

    and

        (iii)   in paragraph (c), by the substitution of " 12.5 per cent for " 10 per cent",

    and

(b)   in subsection (8), by the substitution in paragraph (a) (inserted by the Finance Act, 1973) of "Second, Third or Sixth Schedule" for "Second or Sixth Schedule".

(With effect from 1 March 1991)

Finance Act 1992

173. (1)   Section 11 of the Principal Act is hereby amended in subsection (1) (inserted by the Act of 1985)-

(a)   by the substitution of the following paragraph for paragraph (c) (as amended by the Act of 1991):

"(c)   (i)   12.5 per cent of the amount on which tax is chargeable in relation to the supply of goods or services of a kind specified in subparagraphs (a) , (aa), (b) and (c) of paragraph (i), paragraphs (xia) to (xif) and paragraphs (xiiif), (xiiih), (xiiij) and (xiv) of the Sixth Schedule,

(ii)   16 per cent of the amount on which tax is chargeable in relation to the supply of goods or services of a kind specified in the Sixth Schedule other than those to which subparagraph (i) of this paragraph relates, and",

and

(b)   by the substitution, in paragraph (d), of "2.7 per cent" for "2.3 per cent" (inserted by the Act of 1990).

*(2)   Section 11 of the Principal Act is hereby further amended-

(a)   by the substitution of the following subsection for subsection (1) (inserted by the Act of 1985):

"(1)   Tax shall be charged, in relation to the supply of taxable goods or services and the importation of goods, at whichever of the following rates is appropriate in any particular case-

(a)   21 per cent of the amount on which tax is chargeable other than in relation to goods or services on which tax is chargeable at any of the rates specified in paragraphs (b), (c), (d), (e) and (f),

(b)   zero per cent of the amount on which tax is chargeable in relation to goods in the circumstances specified in paragraph (i) of the Second Schedule or of goods or services of a kind specified in paragraphs (iii) to (xx) of that Schedule,

(c)   10 per cent of the amount on which tax is chargeable in relation to goods or services of a kind specified in the Third Schedule,

(d)   12.5 per cent of the amount on which tax is chargeable in relation to goods or services of a kind specified in the Sixth Schedule,

(e)   16 per cent of the amount on which tax is chargeable in relation to goods or services of a kind specified in the Seventh Schedule, and

(f)   2.7 per cent of the amount on which tax is chargeable in relation to the supply of livestock and live greyhounds and to the hire of horses.",

(b)   by the deletion of subsection (7) (inserted by the Act of 1976),

and

(c)   in subsection (8), by the substitution in paragraph (a) (inserted by the Act of 1973) of "Second, Third, Sixth or Seventh Schedule" for "Second, Third or Sixth Schedule".

**(3)   Section 11 of the Principal Act is hereby further amended-

(a)   in subsection (1) (inserted by subsection (2) of this section) by the insertion after "taxable goods or services" of ", the intra-Community acquisition of goods",

(b)   by the substitution in subsection (1A)(a) (inserted by the Act of 1973) of "subsection (1)(a) or (1A) of section 2 "for "section 2(1)(a)", and of "subsection (1), (1A) or (2)" for "subsection (1) or (2)",

(c)   in subsection (1B) (inserted by the Act of 1973):

(i)   by the substitution in paragraph (a) of the following subparagraph for subparagraph (ii):

"(ii)   the rate at which tax is chargeable in relation to the supply or intra-Community acquisition by the person of goods of any kind, the supply or intra-Community acquisition of goods in any particular circumstances or the supply by the person of services of any kind.",

        (ii)   by the substitution in paragraph (b) of the following subparagraph for subparagraph (ii):

> "(ii)   the rate at which tax is chargeable in relation to the supply or intra-Community acquisition of goods of any kind, the supply or intra-Community acquisition of goods in any particular circumstances or the supply of services of any kind.",

and

        (iii)   by the substitution in paragraph (g) of "supplies goods or makes an intra-Community acquisition of goods, or supplies services," for "supplies goods or services",

and

    (d)   in subsection (3) (inserted by the Act of 1978):

        (i)   by the insertion after "section 10(8)" of "in relation to supplies of goods and services",

        (ii)   by the insertion after "supplies", in each place where it occurs, of "or intra-Community acquisitions",

        (iii)   by the insertion in paragraph (c) after "supply of taxable goods or services" of ", or intra-Community acquisition of goods,"

and

        (iv)   by the insertion in paragraph (d) after "supply of any taxable goods or services" of ",or any intra-Community acquisition of goods,".

(With effect from 1 March 1992 except * from 28 May 1992 and ** from 1 January 1993)

S.I. No. 413 of 1992.
European Communities (Value-Added Tax) Regulations, 1992.

9.   Section 11 of the Principal Act is hereby amended in subsection (1) (inserted by the Act of 1992) by the insertion in paragraph (b) after "paragraph (i)" of "or (ia)".

(With effect from 1 January 1993)

Finance Act 1993

87.   Section 11 of the Principal Act is hereby amended-

    *(a)   in subsection (1) (inserted by the Act of 1992)- Act.

        (i)   by the deletion in paragraph (a) of ", (e)",

        (ii)   by the insertion in paragraph (d) after "the Sixth Schedule," of "and",

(iii)   by the deletion of paragraph (e),

and

(iv)   by the substitution in paragraph (t) of "2.5 per cent" for "2.7 per cent",

(b)   in subsection (4A) (inserted by the Act of 1978) by the substitution of "section 11(1)(d)" for "section 11(1)(c)",

and

*(c)   in paragraph (a) of subsection (8) (inserted by the Act of 1973) by the substitution of "Second, Third or Sixth Schedule" for "Second, Third, Sixth or Seventh Schedule" (inserted by the Act of 1992).

(With effect from 17 June 1993 except * from 1 March 1993)

Finance Act 1995

128. Section 11 of the Principal Act is hereby amended-

*(a)   by the insertion of the following subsection after subsection (1A):

"(1AA) Notwithstanding subsection (1), tax shall be charged at the rate specified in section 11(1)(d) of the amount on which tax is chargeable in relation to-

(a)   the importation into the State of goods specified in the Eighth Schedule,

(b)   the supply of a work of art of the kind specified in paragraph (i) of the Eighth Schedule, effected-

(i) by its creator or the creator's successors in title, or

(ii) on an occasional basis by a taxable person other than a taxable dealer where-

(I)   that work of art has been imported by the taxable person, or

(II)   that work of art has been supplied to the taxable person by its creator or the creator's successors in title, or

(III)   the tax chargeable in relation to the purchase, intra-Community acquisition or importation of that work of art by the taxable person was wholly deductible under section 12,

and

(c)   the intra-Community acquisition in the State by a taxable person of a work of art of the kind specified in paragraph (i) of the Eighth Schedule where the supply of that work of art to that taxable person which resulted in that intra-Community acquisition is a supply of the type that would be charged at the rate specified in section 11(1)(d) in accordance with paragraph (b), if that supply had occurred within the State.",

and

(b)   by the deletion of subsection (5).

(With effect from 2 June 1995 except * from 1 July 1995)

Finance Act 1996

92.   Section 11 of the Principal Act is hereby amended-

(a)   in subsection (1) (inserted by the Act of 1992) by the substitution in paragraph (f) of "2.8 per cent" for "2.5 per cent" (inserted by the Act of 1993),

and

*(b)   by the insertion of the following subsection after subsection (1AA):

"(1AB)   Notwithstanding subsection (1), the rate at which tax is chargeable on a supply of contract work shall be the rate that would be chargeable if that supply of services were a supply of the goods being handed over by the contractor to the person to whom that supply is made:

Provided that this subsection shall not apply to a supply of contract work in the circumstances specified in paragraph (xvi) of the Second Schedule.".

(With effect from 1 March 1996 except * from 1 January 1996)

Finance Act 1997

103.   Section 11 of the Principal Act is hereby amended-

*(a)   in subsection (1) (inserted by the Act of 1992) by the substitution in paragraph (f) of "3.3 per cent" for "2.8 per cent" (inserted by the Act of 1996),

and

(b)   in the proviso to subsection (3) (inserted by the Act of 1978) by the substitution of "25 pence" for "5 pence".

(With effect from 10 May 1997 except * from 1 March 1997)

Finance Act 1998

110. Section 11 of the Principal Act is hereby amended in subsection (1) (inserted by the Act of 1992) by the substitution in paragraph (f) of "3.6 per cent" for "3.3 per cent" (inserted by the Act of 1997).

(With effect from 1 March 1998)

Finance Act 1999

127. Section 11 of the Principal Act is hereby amended in subsection (1) (inserted by the Act of 1992) by the substitution in paragraph (f) of "4 per cent" for "3.6 per cent" (inserted by the Act of 1998).

(With effect from 1 March 1999)

Finance Act 2000

111. Section 11 of the Principal Act is amended in subsection (1) (inserted by the Act of 1992) by the substitution in paragraph (f) of "4.2 per cent" for "4 per cent" (inserted by the Act of 1999).

(With effect from 1 March 2000)

Finance Act 2001

187. Section 11 of the Principal Act is amended in subsection (1) (inserted by the Finance Act, 1992-

    (a)   by the substitution in paragraph (a) of "20 per cent" for "21 per cent", and

    (b)   by the substitution in paragraph (f) of "4.3 per cent" for "4.2 per cent" (inserted by the Act of 2000).

*240. (1)   (a)   Subject to subsection (2), in each provision specified in column (1) of Schedule 5 for the words or amount set out in column (2) of that Schedule at that entry there shall be substituted the words or amount set out at the corresponding entry in column (3) of that Schedule.

           (b)   Where words are or an amount is mentioned more than once in a provision specified in column (1) of Schedule 5, then the substitution provided for by paragraph (a) shall apply as respects those words or that amount to each mention of those words or that amount in that provision.

SCHEDULE 5

PART 4

Value-Added Tax and related matters

Enactment amended (1)	Amount or words to be replaced (2)	Amount or words to be inserted (3)
Value-Added Tax Act, 1972 (No. 22 of 1972) (as amended): section 11(3)	25 pence	40 cents

(With effect from 1 January 2001 except * from 1 January 2002)

Finance Act 2002

103. Section 11(1)(a) of the Principal Act is amended by substituting "21 per cent" for "20 per cent" (inserted by the Finance Act, 2001).

(With effect from 1 March 2002)

SCHEDULE 6

Miscellaneous Technical Amendments in Relation to Tax

1. The Value-Added Tax Act, 1972, is amended in accordance with the following provisions:

(a) section 11(3) is amended by substituting "40 cent" for "40 cents" (inserted by the Finance Act, 2001),

(With effect from 1 January 2002)

Finance Act 2003

119. Section 11(1)(d) of the Principal Act is amended by substituting "13.5 per cent" for "12.5 per cent".

(With effect from 1 January 2003)

Finance Act 2004

59. Section 11 of the Principal Act is amended in subsection (1)(f) (inserted by the Finance Act 1992) by substituting "4.4 per cent" for "4.3 per cent" (inserted by the Act of 2001).

(With effect from 1 January 2004)

Finance Act 2005

103. With effect from 1 January 2005, section 11 of the Principal Act is amended in subsection (1)(f) (inserted by the Finance Act 1992) by substituting "4.8 per cent" for "4.4 per cent" (inserted by the Act of 2004).

(With effect from 1 January 2005)

Finance Act 2006

97. (1) Section 11 of the Principal Act is amended —

(a) in subsection (1B) by substituting the following for paragraph (c):

"(c) A determination under this subsection shall have effect for all the purposes of this Act —

(i) in relation to a taxable person who makes an application for the determination, as on and from the date which shall be specified for the purpose in the determination communicated to the taxable person in accordance with paragraph (e)(i), and

(ii) in relation to any other person, as on and from the date which shall be specified for the purpose in the determination as published in the Iris Oifigiúil.",

and

*(b) by substituting the following for subsection (3):

"(3) (a) Subject to section 10(8) —

(i) in the case of a composite supply, the tax chargeable on the total consideration which the taxable person is entitled to receive for that composite supply shall be at the rate specified in subsection (1) which is appropriate to the principal supply, but if that principal supply is an exempted activity, tax shall not be chargeable in respect of that composite supply,

(ii) in the case of a multiple supply, the tax chargeable on each individual supply in that multiple supply shall be at the rate specified in subsection (1) appropriate to each such individual supply and, in order to ascertain the taxable amount referable to each individual supply for the purpose of applying the appropriate rate thereto, the total consideration which the taxable person is entitled to receive in respect of that multiple supply shall be apportioned between those individual supplies in a way that correctly reflects the ratio which the value of each such individual supply bears to the total consideration for that multiple supply.

(b) In the case where a person acquires a composite supply or a multiple supply by means of an intra-Community acquisition, the provisions of this subsection shall apply to that acquisition.

(c) The Revenue Commissioners may make regulations as necessary specifying —

    (i)   the circumstances or conditions under which a supply may or may not be treated as an ancillary supply, a composite supply, an individual supply, a multiple supply or a principal supply,

    (ii)   the methods of apportionment which may be applied for the purposes of paragraphs (a) and (b),

    (iii)   a minimum amount, or an element of a supply, which may be disregarded for the purposes of applying this subsection.".

(With effect from 31 March 2006 except * with effect from 1 November 2006)

Finance Act 2007

128. The enactments specified in Schedule 4 —

(a)   are amended to the extent and in the manner specified in paragraphs 1 to 5 of that Schedule, and

(b)   apply and come into operation in accordance with paragraph 6 of that Schedule.

Schedule 4
Miscellaneous Technical Amendments in Relation to Tax

3. The Value-Added Tax Act 1972 is amended in section 11(3)(c)(iii) by substituting "relatively small amount" for "minimum amount".

(With effect from 2 April 2007)

Finance Act 2008

109. With effect from 1 July 2008 in each provision of the Principal Act specified in the first column of Schedule 4 for the words set out in the second column of that Schedule at that entry (in each place where those words occur in the provision concerned) there is substituted the

words set out at the corresponding entry in the third column of that
Schedule.

Schedule 4
Miscellaneous Amendments Relating to the Amendment of the Definition of Taxable Person

Amendments to Value-Added Tax Act 1972

Provision of Value-Added Tax Act 1972	Words to be replaced	Words to be inserted
Section 11(1AA)	a taxable person	an accountable person
Section 11(1AA)	the taxable person	the accountable person
Section 11(1AA)	that taxable person	that accountable person
Section 11(1B)	a taxable person	an accountable person
Section 11(1B)	the taxable person	the accountable person
Section 11(1B)	Any taxable person	Any accountable person
Section 11(3)	the taxable person	the accountable person

(With effect from 1 July 2008)

Finance (No. 2) Act 2008

72.   Section 11 of the Principal Act is amended with effect from
       1 December 2008 in subsection (1)(a) by substituting "21.5 per cent" for
       "21 per cent".

(With effect from 1 December 2008)

Section 12

Value-Added Tax Act 1972

Deduction for tax borne or paid

12. (1) In computing the amount of tax payable by an accountable person in respect of any taxable period there may be deducted-

(a) the tax charged to him during such period by other accountable persons by means of invoices, prepared in the manner prescribed by regulations, in respect of deliveries of goods made or services rendered to him,

(b) the tax charged to him during such period by means of invoices, prepared in the manner prescribed by regulations and issued by persons authorised in accordance with section 13 to issue such invoices, in respect of deliveries of goods made or services rendered to him,

(c) the tax paid by him during such period in respect of goods imported by him,

(d) the tax chargeable during such period in respect of goods used for the purposes of his business and treated as delivered in accordance with section 3(1)(e), and

(e) the tax chargeable during such period in respect of services rendered by him for the purposes of his own business and deemed under section 5(2), for the purposes of this Act, to be rendered in the course of business:

Provided that, in relation to the delivery or importation of any goods of a kind specified in the Fourth Schedule, the amount deductible under this section by a person, other than a manufacturer of goods of the kind so delivered or imported, shall not exceed a sum representing, in the case of delivery of such goods to him, 5.26 per cent of the consideration payable by him, exclusive of the tax payable in respect of the delivery by the person making the delivery or, in the case of an importation, 5.26 per cent of the value of the goods calculated in accordance with section 15(4).

(2) If, in relation to any taxable period, the total amount deductible under this section exceeds the amount which, but for this section, would be payable in respect of such period, the excess shall be repaid to the accountable person.

(3) Notwithstanding anything in subsection (1), a deduction of tax shall not be made if, and to the extent that, such tax relates to-

(a)   the provision of food, drink, accommodation or other personal services for the accountable person, his agents or employees,

(b)   entertainment expenses incurred by the accountable person, his agents or employees,

(c)   the acquisition (including hiring) of motor vehicles of a kind specified in the Fourth Schedule otherwise than as stock-in-trade (within the meaning of section 34) or for the purposes of a business which consists in whole or part of the hiring of such vehicles,

(d)   the purchase of petrol otherwise than as stock-in-trade (within the meaning of the said section 34),

(e)   any activity of the accountable person which is either an exempted activity or is outside the scope of his business.

(4)   Any necessary apportionment between tax which may be deducted in accordance with this section and tax which may not be deducted shall be made in accordance with regulations.

(With effect from 1 November 1972)

Finance Act 1973

81.   Section 12 of the Principal Act is hereby amended-

(a)   by the insertion of the following subsection after subsection 1-

"(1A) (a)   A person who, by election or in accordance with the provisions of section 8(4) is deemed to become an accountable person, shall, in accordance with regulations, be entitled, in computing the amount of tax payable by him in respect of the first taxable period for which he is so deemed to be an accountable person, to treat as tax deductible under subsection (1) such part of the value of the stock-in-trade (within the meaning of section 34) held by him immediately before the commencement of that taxable period as could reasonably be regarded as the amount which he would be entitled to claim under the said subsection (1) if be had been an accountable person at the time of the delivery to him of such stock-in-trade.

(b)   No claim shall lie under this subsection for a deduction for the tax relating to any stock-in-trade (within the meaning of section 34) if, and to the extent that, a deduction under subsection (1) could be claimed apart from this subsection.

(c)   This subsection shall have effect in relation of taxable periods commencing on or after the 3rd day of September, 1973.",

and

(b)   by the deletion in subsection (1) of paragraph (e).

90.   The Principal Act is hereby amended as specified in column (3) of the Tenth Schedule to this Act.

TENTH SCHEDULE
AMENDMENT OF ENACTMENTS

Number and Year (1)	Short Title (2)	Amendment (3)
No. 22 of 1972	Value-Added Tax Act, 1972	In section 12, in subsection (1), " tax at the rate specified in section 11(1)(a) on " shall be substituted for "5.26 per cent of " in both places where it occurs; in subsection (3)(a), " except to the extent that such provision constitutes a rendering of services in respect of which he is accountable for tax " shall be added.

(With effect from 3 September 1973)

Finance Act 1976

54.   Section 12 of the Principal Act is hereby amended by the substitution for paragraph (d) of and the proviso to subsection (1) of the following:

"(d)   the tax chargeable during such period in respect of goods applied for the purposes of his business and treated as delivered in accordance with section 3(1)(e):

Provided that, in relation to-

(i)   the application of any goods of a kind specified in the Fourth Schedule by a person for the purposes of his business and treated as delivered in accordance with section 3(1)(e),

(ii)   the delivery (otherwise than by virtue of section 3(1)(e)) of any goods of a kind specified in the Fourth Schedule delivered to a manufacturer of goods of the kind so delivered, being goods applied by him for the purposes of his business otherwise than as stock-in-trade (within the meaning of section 34), or

(iii)   the delivery (otherwise than by virtue of section 3(1)(e)) or importation of any goods of a kind specified in the Fourth Schedule delivered to or imported by a person other than a manufacturer of goods of the kind so delivered or imported,

the amount deductible under this section by any such person shall not exceed a sum representing tax at the rate for the time being specified in section 11(1)(a) on the amount or value, as the case may be, on which tax was chargeable in respect of the application, delivery or importation in question.".

*81. ......

(2) The enactment mentioned in column (2) of Part II of the Fifth Schedule to this Act is hereby repealed to the extent specified in column (3) of that Schedule.

(3) ...

(b) Subsection (2) of this section shall be deemed to have come into operation on the 1st day of March, 1976.

FIFTH SCHEDULE
ENACTMENTS REPEALED
PART II

No. 22 of 1972	Value Added Tax Act, 1972	Section 12(1)(b)

(With effect from 27 May 1976 except * from 1 March 1976)

Value Added Tax (Amendment) Act 1978

10. Section 12 of the Principal Act is hereby amended by the substitution of the following subsections for subsections (1) and (3):

"(1) In computing the amount of tax payable by a taxable person in respect of a taxable period there may be deducted-

(a) the tax charged to him during the period by other taxable persons by means of invoices, prepared in the manner prescribed by regulations, in respect of supplies of goods or services to him.

(b) the tax paid by him during the period, or payable by him in relation to the period, in respect of goods imported by him,

(c) the tax chargeable during the period in respect of goods applied for the purposes of his business and treated as supplied in accordance with section 3(1)(e),

(d) the tax chargeable during the period in respect of services carried out by him for the purposes of his business and treated as supplied by him for consideration in the course or furtherance of his business in accordance with section 5(3)(d),

(e)   the tax chargeable during the period, being tax for which he is liable by virtue of section 8(2), in respect of services received by him, and

(f)   tax charged to him during the period by means of invoices prepared in the manner prescribed by regulations and issued to him in accordance with section 12A.

(3) (a)   Notwithstanding anything in subsection (1), a deduction of tax under that subsection shall not be made if, and to the extent that, the tax relates to-

(i)   the provision of food or drink, or accommodation or other personal services, for the taxable person, his agents or his employees, except to the extent, if any, that such provision constitutes a supply of services in respect of which he is accountable for tax,

(ii)   entertainment expenses incurred by the taxable person, his agents or his employees.

(iii)   the acquisition (including hiring) of motor vehicles otherwise than as stock-in-trade or for the purposes of a business which consists in whole or part of the hiring of motor vehicles or for use, in a driving school business, for giving driving instruction,

(iv)   the purchase of petrol otherwise than as stock-in-trade, or

(v)   goods or services used by the taxable person for the purposes of an exempted activity (whether carried on in the State or elsewhere) or for purposes other than those of his business.

but subparagraph (v) shall not operate to prevent a deduction of tax if, and to the extent that, the tax relates to goods and services used for the purposes of any of the following activities:

(I)   transport outside the State of passengers and their accompanying baggage,

(II)   services specified in paragraph (i), (xi) or (xii) of the First Schedule, and agency services in regard thereto, supplied outside the Community, and

    (III)   insurance services and the provision of credit, and agency services in regard thereto, directly in connection with the export of goods to a place outside the Community.

  (b)   In paragraph (a) of this subsection **'motor vehicles'** means motor vehicles designed and constructed for the conveyance of persons by road and sports motor vehicles, estate cars, station wagons, motor cycles, motor scooters, mopeds and auto cycles, whether or not designed and constructed for the purpose aforesaid, excluding vehicles designed and constructed for the carriage of more than 16 persons (inclusive of the driver), invalid carriages and other vehicles of a type designed for use by invalids or infirm persons.".

30. ...

  (2)   In consequence of the amendments of the Principal Act specified in this Act and of the repeals specified in the First Schedule, the Principal Act is hereby further amended by the substitution of the word or expression mentioned in column (3) of the Second Schedule at any reference number for the word or expression mentioned in column (2) of that Schedule at that reference number wherever it occurs in the provision of the Principal Act mentioned in column (4) of that Schedule at that reference number.

SECOND SCHEDULE

Consequential Amendments

Reference Number (1)	Existing word or expression (2)	Substituted word or expression (3)	Provision of Principal Act (4)
25	"accountable person" except where preceded by the word "an"	"taxable person"	Section 12(2),
26	"an accountable person"	"a taxable person"	Section 12(1A)(a),

(With effect from 1 March 1979)

Finance Act 1981

44.   Section 12(2) of the Principal Act is hereby amended by the substitution of "refunded to the taxable person in accordance with section 20(1)" for "repaid to the taxable person".

(With effect from 28 May 1981)

Finance Act 1982

80.   Section 12 of the Principal Act is hereby amended-

(a)   in subsection (1) (inserted by the Act of 1978), by the substitution of the following paragraph for paragraph (b):

"(b)   in respect of goods imported by him in the period, the tax paid by him or deferred as established from the relevant customs documents kept by him in accordance with section 16(3),",

and

(b)   in subsection (3) (inserted by the Act of 1978), in subparagraph (v) of paragraph (a), by the insertion after "his business" of "or for activities in relation to which he is, in accordance with section 8(3A), deemed not to be a taxable person".

(With effect from 1 September 1982)

Finance Act 1986

84.   Section 12 of the Principal Act is hereby amended-

(a)   in subsection (1) (inserted by the Act of 1978) by the insertion after paragraph (d)of the following paragraph:

"(dd)   the tax chargeable during the period, being tax for which he is liable by virtue of section 5(3A), in respect of services received by him,"

and

(b)   in subsection (2) by the insertion after "section 20(1)" of ", but subject to section 20(1A)".

(With effect from 27 May 1986)

Finance Act 1987

41.   Section 12 of the Principal Act is hereby amended-

(a)   by the substitution of the following subsection for subsection (1) (inserted by the Act of 1978):

"(1)   (a)   In computing the amount of tax payable by him in respect of a taxable period, a taxable person may, insofar as the goods and services are used by him for the purposes of his taxable supplies or of any of the qualifying activities, deduct-

(i)   the tax charged to him during the period by other taxable persons by means of invoices, prepared in the manner prescribed by regulations, in respect of supplies of goods or services to him,

(ii)   in respect of goods imported by him in the period, the tax paid by him or deferred as established from the relevant customs documents kept by him in accordance with section 16(3),

(iii)   the tax chargeable during the period in respect of goods treated as supplied by him in accordance with section 3(1)(e),

(iv)   the tax chargeable during the period in respect of services treated as supplied by him for consideration in the course or furtherance of his business in accordance with section 5(3)(d),

(v)   the tax chargeable during the period, being tax for which he is liable by virtue of section 5(3A), in respect of services received by him,

(vi)   if so provided by regulations and subject to and in accordance with any such regulations, the amount of tax, as defined, included in the consideration payable for specified second-hand goods or categories of second-hand goods acquired, in circumstances other than those described in the proviso to section 10(2), for resale from a person who is not a taxable person or from a taxable person where the goods were used by the said taxable person for the purposes of a business carried on by him, but in relation to the acquisition or application of which he had borne tax and the goods were of such a kind or were used in such circumstances that no part of the said tax was deductible under this section,

(vii)   the tax chargeable during the period, being tax for which he is liable by virtue of section 8(2), in respect of services received by him, and

(viii)   tax charged to him during the period by means of invoices prepared in the manner prescribed by regulations and issued to him in accordance with section 12A.

(b)   In paragraph (a) '**qualifying activities**' means-

(i)   transport outside the State of passengers and their accompanying baggage,

     (ii) services specified in paragraph (i), (ix) (b), (c) or (d), or (xi), of the First Schedule, supplied-

         (I) outside the Community, or

         (II) directly in connection with the export of goods to a place outside the Community, and

     (iii) supplies of goods or services outside the State which would be taxable supplies if made in the State.",

  (b) in subsection (3)(a) (inserted by the Act of 1978) by-

     (i) the substitution for "in subsection (1), a deduction of tax under that subsection" of "in this section, a deduction of tax under this section",

     (ii) the insertion, after subparagraph (iii), of "or",

    and

     (iii) the deletion of all of that part of the said subsection (3)(a) which follows subparagraph (iv),

    and the said subsection (3)(a), as so amended, is set out in the Table to this paragraph,

TABLE

 (3) (a) Notwithstanding anything in this section, a deduction of tax under this section shall not be made if, and to the extent that, the tax relates to-

     (i) the provision of food or drink, or accommodation or other personal services, for the taxable person, his agents or his employees, except to the extent, if any, that such provision constitutes a supply of services in respect of which he is accountable for tax,

     (ii) entertainment expenses incurred by the taxable person, his agents or his employees,

     (iii) the acquisition (including hiring) of motor vehicles otherwise than as stock-in-trade or for the purposes of a business which consists in whole or part of the hiring of motor vehicles or for use, in a driving school business, for giving driving instruction, or

     (iv) the purchase of petrol otherwise than as stock-in-trade.,

  and

(c)   by the substitution of the following subsection for subsection

"(4)   Where goods or services (not being goods or services on
the acquisition of which a deduction of tax shall not, in
accordance with subsection (3), be made) are used by a
taxable person for the purposes of supplies or activities
in relation to which tax is deductible in accordance
with this section and also for the purposes of other
supplies or activities, such proportion only of tax shall
be deductible as is attributable to those first mentioned
supplies or activities and the said proportion shall be
determined in accordance with regulations.".

(With effect from 1 November 1987)

Finance Act 1991

81.   Section 12 of the Principal Act is hereby amended in paragraph (a)
of subsection (1) (inserted by the Act of 1987) by the insertion of the
following subparagraph after subparagraph (iii):

"(iiia)   the tax charged to him during the period by other taxable persons
in respect of services directly related to the transfer of ownership
of goods specified in section 3(5)(b)(iii),".

(With effect from 29 May 1991)

Finance Act 1992

174.   Section 12 of the Principal Act is hereby amended-

(a)   in subsection (1) (inserted by the Act of 1987) by the insertion
of the following subparagraphs after subparagraph (ii) of
paragraph (a):

"(iia)   subject to such conditions (if any) as may be specified in
regulations, the tax chargeable during the period, being
tax for which he is liable in respect of intra-Community
acquisitions of goods,

(iib)   subject to and in accordance with regulations, in respect
of goods supplied under section 3(1)(g) an amount equal
to any residual tax included in the consideration for the
supply,",

and

(b)   in subsection (3) (inserted by the Act of 1978):

(i)   by the substitution in subparagraph (iii) of paragraph (a)
for "acquisition (including hiring)" of "purchase, hiring,
intra-Community acquisition, or importation",

and

     (ii)   by the insertion in subparagraph (iv) of paragraph (a) after "purchase" of "intra-Community acquisition or importation".

(With effect from 1 January 1993)

S.I. No. 413 of 1992.
European Communities (Value-Added Tax) Regulations, 1992.

10.   Section 12 of the Principal Act is hereby amended in paragraph (b) of subsection (1) (inserted by the Finance Act, 1987)-

    (a)   by the insertion of the following subparagraph after subparagraph (i):

        "(ia)   supplies of goods which, by virtue of section 3(6)(d), are deemed to have taken place in the territory of another Member State:

              Provided that the supplier is registered for value-added tax in that other Member State,",

and

    (b)   by the insertion in subparagraph (iii) after "goods" of "(other than supplies of goods referred to in section 3(6)(d))".

(With effect from 1 January 1993)

Finance Act 1993

88.   Section 12 of the Principal Act is hereby amended in paragraph (a) of sub-section 1:

    *(a)   by the insertion of the following subparagraph after subparagraph (iib) (inserted by the Act of 1992):

        "(iic) subject to such conditions (if any) as may be specified in regulations, in respect of goods referred to in section 313, the tax due in the period in accordance with that section,",

    (b)   by the substitution in subparagraph (viii) of "flat-rate addition, which shall be deemed to be tax," for "tax",

and

    (c)   by the addition of the following proviso to the said paragraph (a):

        "Provided that this paragraph shall not apply to-

        (I)   a taxable person referred to in subsection (1A)(c) or (2)(b) of section 8, or

        (II)   a taxable person referred to in subsection (1A)(d) or (2)(c) of section 8 unless the tax relates to racehorse training services supplied by him.".

(With effect from 17 June 1993 except * from 1 August 1993)

Finance Act 1994

96.   Section 12 of the Principal Act is hereby amended-

    *(a)   in paragraph (a) of subsection (1) by the insertion of the following subparagraph after subparagraph (iiia) (inserted by the Finance Act, 1991):

        "(iiib) the tax chargeable during the period, being tax for which he is liable by virtue of section 4A(1), in respect of goods received by him,",

    and

    (b)   in subsection (3)-

        (i)   in paragraph (a) by the insertion of the following subparagraph after subparagraph (i):

            "(ia)   expenditure incurred by the taxable person on food or drink, or accommodation or other entertainment services, where such expenditure forms all or part of the cost of providing an advertising service in respect of which tax is due and payable by the taxable person,",

        and

        (ii)   by the insertion of the following paragraphs after paragraph (b):

            "(c)   In subparagraph (i) of paragraph (a), reference to the provision of accommodation includes expenditure by the taxable person on a building, including the fitting out of such building, to provide such accommodation.

            (d)   In subparagraph (ii) of paragraph (a), 'entertainment expenses' includes expenditure on a building or facility, including the fitting out of such building or facility, to provide such entertainment.".

(With effect from 23 May 1994 except * from 7 July 1995)

Finance Act 1995

129.   Section 12 of the Principal Act is hereby amended-

    (a)   in paragraph (a) of subsection (1) by the substitution of the following subparagraph for subparagraph (vi):

        "(vi)   subject to and in accordance with regulations (if any), residual tax referred to in section 12B,",

    and

(b)   by the insertion of the following subsection after subsection (3):

"(3A) Notwithstanding anything in this section, where-

(a)   the provisions of subsection (3) or (8) of section 10A or subsection (3) of section 10B have been applied to a supply of goods to a taxable person, or

(b)   a taxable dealer deducts residual tax, in accordance with subsection (1)(a)(vi), in respect of a supply of a means of transport to a taxable person,

that taxable person shall not deduct, in accordance with subsection (1), any tax in relation to the supply to that person.".

(With effect from 1 July 1995)

Finance Act 1996

93.   Section 12 of the Principal Act is hereby amended-

*(a)   in paragraph (a) of subsection (1) by the insertion of the following subparagraph after subparagraph (i):

"(ia)   the amount in respect of tax indicated separately on a document issued during the period in accordance with section 17(1AA) in respect of a supply of goods to him.",

and

(b)   in paragraph (a) of subsection (3) by the deletion of "or" (inserted by the Finance Act, 1987) at the end of subparagraph (iii) and by the insertion of the following subparagraph after subparagraph (iv):

"(iva) the procurement of a supply of contract work where such supply consists of the handing over of goods to which this paragraph applies.".

(With effect from 15 May 1996 except * from 1 July 1996)

Finance Act 1997

104.   Section 12 of the Principal Act is hereby amended in paragraph (a) of subsection (1) by the insertion of the following subparagraphs after subparagraph (iiib):

"(iiic) the tax chargeable during the period, being tax for which he is liable by virtue of section 4(8), in respect of a supply of immovable goods deemed to be supplied by him:

Provided that this subparagraph shall apply only where he would be entitled to a deduction of that tax elsewhere under this subsection if the goods in question were supplied to him by another person and if he had not been deemed to have supplied them in accordance with section 4(8), (iiid)   the tax chargeable to him during the period by other taxable persons in respect of goods or services directly related to a supply of immovable goods which is deemed not to be supplied by him in accordance with section 4(8),".

(With effect from 26 March 1997)

Finance Act 1998

111. Amendment of section 12 (deduction for tax borne or paid) of Principal Act

Section 12 of the Principal Act is hereby amended-

(a)   by the insertion in subsection (1)(b)(iii) after "outside the State" of ", other than services consisting of the hiring out of motor vehicles (as defined in subsection (3)(b)) for utilisation in the State,",

and

(b)   by the substitution in subsection (2) of "sections 20(1A) and 20(5)" for "section 20(1A)".

(With effect from 27 March 1998)

Finance Act 1999

128. Section 12 of the Principal Act is hereby amended by the insertion in paragraph (a) of subsection (1) of-

(a)   the following sub-paragraph after sub-paragraph (iiid) (inserted by the Act of 1997):

"(iiie) the tax chargeable during the period, being tax or which he is liable by virtue of section 6A(5)(a) in respect of investment gold (within the meaning of section 6A) received by him,"

and

(b)   the following sub-paragraph after sub-paragraph (vi) (inserted by the Act of 1995):

"(via) the residual tax referred to in section 12C, being residual tax contained in the price charged to him for the purchase of agricultural machinery (within the meaning of section 12C), by means of invoices issued to him during the period by flat-rate farmers,".

(With effect from 1 January 2000)

Finance Act 2000

112. Section 12 of the Principal Act is amended-

    (a)   by the insertion in paragraph (a) of subsection (1) of the following subparagraph after subparagraph (via) (inserted by the Act of 1999):

        "(vib) the residual tax referred to in section 12C, being residual tax contained in the price charged to the taxable person for the purchase of agricultural machinery (within the meaning of section 12C), by means of documents issued to that person during the period in accordance with section 12C(1B),",

    and

    (b)   by the substitution of the following for subsection (4):

        "(4)   (a)   In this subsection-

            'deductible supplies or activities' means the supply of taxable goods or taxable services, or the carrying out of qualifying activities as defined in subsection (1)(b);

            'dual-use inputs' means goods or services (other than goods or services on the purchase or acquisition of which, by virtue of subsection (3), a deduction of tax shall not be made) which are not used solely for the purposes of either deductible supplies or activities or non-deductible supplies or activities;

            'non-deductible supplies or activities' means the supply of goods or services or the carrying out of activities other than deductible supplies or activities;

            'total supplies and activities' means deductible supplies or activities and non-deductible supplies or activities.

        (b)   Where a taxable person engages in both deductible supplies or activities and non-deductible supplies or activities then, in relation to that person's acquisition of dual-use inputs for the purpose of that person's business for a period, that person shall be entitled to deduct in accordance with subsection (1) only such proportion of tax, borne or payable on that acquisition, which is calculated in accordance with the provisions of this subsection and regulations, as being attributable to that person's deductible supplies or activities and such proportion of tax is, for the purposes of this subsection, referred to as the 'proportion of tax deductible'.

(c) For the purposes of this subsection and regulations, the proportion of tax deductible by a taxable person for a period shall be calculated on any basis which results in a proportion of tax deductible which correctly reflects the extent to which the dual-use inputs are used for the purposes of that person's deductible supplies or activities and has due regard to the range of that person's total supplies and activities.

(d) The proportion of tax deductible may be calculated on the basis of the ratio which the amount of a person's tax-exclusive turnover from deductible supplies or activities for a period bears to the amount of that person's tax-exclusive turnover from total supplies and activities for that period but only if that basis results in a proportion of tax deductible which is in accordance with paragraph (c).

(e) Where it is necessary to do so to ensure that the proportion of tax deductible by a taxable person is in accordance with paragraph (c), a taxable person shall-

(i) calculate a separate proportion of tax deductible for any part of that person's business, or

(ii) exclude, from the calculation of the proportion of tax deductible, amounts of turnover from incidental transactions by that person of the type specified in paragraph (i) of the First Schedule or amounts of turnover from incidental transactions by that person in immovable goods.

(f) The proportion of tax deductible as calculated by a taxable person for a taxable period may be adjusted in accordance with regulations, if, for the accounting period in which the taxable period ends, that proportion does not correctly reflect the extent to which the dual-use inputs are used for the purposes of that person's deductible supplies or activities or does not have due regard to the range of that person's total supplies and activities.".

(With effect from 23 March 2000)

Finance Act 2001

188. Section 12 of the Principal Act is amended-

(a)   by the insertion in paragraph (a) of subsection (1) after "deduct", of ", subject to making any adjustment required in accordance with section 12D,",

(b)   by the insertion in paragraph (b) (inserted by the Finance Act, 1987) of subsection (1) of the following after paragraph (ia):

"(ib)   the operation, in accordance with Commission Regulation (EC) No. 2777/2000 of 18 December 2000, of the Cattle Testing or Purchase for Destruction Scheme, by a body who is a taxable person by virtue of the Value-Added Tax (Agricultural Intervention Agency) Order, 2001 (S.I. No. 11 of 2001).",

and

(c)   by the substitution in paragraph (f) of subsection (4) (inserted by the Act of 2000) of "shall" for "may".

(With effect from 21 March 2001 except * from 8 January 2002)

Finance Act 2002

SCHEDULE 6

Miscellaneous Technical Amendments in Relation to Tax

1.   The Value-Added Tax Act, 1972, is amended in accordance with the following provisions:

(b)   section 12 is amended in subsection (1)(b)(ii) (inserted by the Finance Act, 1987) by deleting "(b), (c) or",

(With effect from 25 March 2002)

Finance Act 2004

60.   Section 12 of the Principal Act is amended in subsection (1)(a) by inserting the following after subparagraph (v):

"(va)   the tax chargeable during the period, being tax for which the taxable person is liable by virtue of section 8(1A)(f) in respect of goods which are installed or assembled; but this subparagraph shall apply only where the taxable person would be entitled to a deduction of that tax elsewhere under this subsection if that tax had been charged to such person by another taxable person,

*(vb)   the tax chargeable during the period, being tax for which the taxable person is liable by virtue of section 8(1A)(g) in respect of the supply to such person of gas through the natural gas distribution network, or of electricity; but this subparagraph shall apply only where the taxable person would be entitled to a

deduction of that tax elsewhere under this subsection if that tax had been charged to such person by another taxable person,".

(With effect from 25 March 2004 except * with effect from 1 January 2005)

Finance Act 2005

104. (1) Section 12 of the Principal Act is amended-

(a) in subsection (1)(a)-

(i) by substituting the following for subparagraph (iiic) (including the proviso to that subparagraph):

"(iiic) the tax chargeable during the period, being tax for which the taxable person is liable by virtue of section 4(8), in respect of a supply to that person of immovable goods,",

and

(ii) by deleting subparagraph (iiid),

and

*(b) by inserting the following after subsection (4)-

"(5) At the time when a person disposes of an interest in immovable goods the possession of which that person had previously surrendered in circumstances where the person had paid a deductibility adjustment in accordance with section 4(3)(ab), that person is entitled to increase the amount of tax deductible for the taxable period within which the disposal is made, by an amount calculated in accordance with the following formula:

$$\frac{T \times (Y-N)}{Y}$$

where-

T is the amount of tax which the person who previously surrendered possession of the goods was entitled to deduct in accordance with this section, prior to that surrender of possession, in respect of that person's acquisition of the interest in and the development of those goods,

Y is 20 or, if the interest when it was acquired by the person who surrendered possession of the goods was for a period of less than 20 years, the number of full years in that interest when it was so acquired, and

> N   is the number of full years since that person
> acquired the interest in the immovable goods
> being disposed of or, if the goods were
> developed since that interest was acquired,
> but before the deductibility adjustment
> in accordance with section 4(3)(ab) was
> payable, the number of full years since that
> development:
>
> but if that N is greater than that Y, such amount
> shall be deemed to be nil.".

(2)   Paragraph (b) of subsection (1) shall take effect as on and
from such a day as the Minister for Finance may, by order,
appoint.

(With effect from 25 March 2005 except * with effect from 1 May 2005)

Finance Act 2006

98.   Section 12 of the Principal Act is amended in subsection (1)(b) —

(a)   by substituting "the Community," for "the Community, and" in
subparagraph (ii)(II), and

(b)   by inserting the following after subparagraph (ii):

> "(iia)   services consisting of the issue of new stocks, new shares,
> new debentures or other new securities by the taxable
> person in so far as such issue is made to raise capital for
> the purposes of the taxable person's taxable supplies,
> and".

(With effect from 31 March 2006)

Finance Act 2007

83.   Section 12 of the Principal Act is amended —

(a)   with effect from 1 May 2007 in subsection (1)(a) by deleting
subparagraph (ia), and

(b)   in subsection (3) —

> *(i)   with effect from 1 July 2007 in paragraph (a) by substituting
> the following for subparagraph (i):
>
> > "(i)   expenditure incurred by the taxable person on
> > food or drink, or accommodation other than
> > qualifying accommodation in connection with
> > attendance at a qualifying conference as defined
> > in paragraph (ca), or other personal services, for
> > the taxable person, the taxable person's agents or
> > employees, except to the extent, if any, that such

expenditure is incurred in relation to a supply of services in respect of which that taxable person is accountable for tax,",

(ii)   with effect from 1 May 2007 in paragraph (a)(iii) by inserting "or for the purpose of the supply thereof by a person supplying financial services of the kind specified in subparagraph (i)(e) of the First Schedule in respect of those motor vehicles as part of an agreement of the kind referred to in section 3(1)(b)" after "stock-in-trade", and

*(iii)   with effect from 1 July 2007 by inserting the following paragraph after paragraph (c):

"(ca)   For the purposes of subparagraph (a)(i) —

'**delegate**' means a taxable person or a taxable person's employee or agent who attends a qualifying conference in the course or furtherance of that taxable person's business;

'**qualifying accommodation**' means the supply to a delegate of a service consisting of the letting of immovable goods or accommodation covered by paragraph (xiii) of the Sixth Schedule, for a maximum period starting from the night prior to the date on which the qualifying conference commences and ending on the date on which the conference concludes;

'**qualifying conference**' means a conference or meeting in the course or furtherance of business organised to cater for 50 or more delegates, which takes place on or after 1 July 2007 at a venue designed and constructed for the purposes of hosting 50 or more delegates and in respect of which the person responsible for organising the conference issues in writing the details of the conference to each taxable person who attends or sends a delegate, and such details shall include —

(i)   the location and dates of the conference,

(ii)   the nature of the business being conducted,

(iii)   the number of delegates for whom the conference is organised, and

(iv)   the name, business address and VAT registration number of the person responsible for organising the conference.".

(With effect from 1 May 2007 except * with effect from 1 July 2007)

Finance Act 2008

94.   Section 12 of the Principal Act is amended—

(a)   in subsection (1)(a)—

(i)   in paragraph (iiic) with effect from 1 July 2008 by substituting "section 4B(6)(a) or 4(8)" for "section 4(8)", and

*(ii) with effect from 1 September 2008 by inserting the following after subparagraph (vb):

"(vc) the tax chargeable during the period, being tax for which the principal is liable by virtue of section 8(1B) in respect of construction operations services received by that principal; but this subparagraph shall apply only where that principal would be entitled to a deduction of that tax elsewhere under this subsection if that tax had been charged to such principal by another accountable person,",

(b)   in subsection (4) with effect from 1 July 2008—

(i)   in paragraph (a) by inserting "movable" after "means" in the definition of "dual-use inputs", and

(ii)   in paragraph (f) by substituting "accounting year" for "accounting period",

and

(c)   with effect from 1 July 2008 by deleting subsection (5).

109. With effect from 1 July 2008 in each provision of the Principal Act specified in the first column of Schedule 4 for the words set out in the second column of that Schedule at that entry (in each place where those words occur in the provision concerned) there is substituted the words set out at the corresponding entry in the third column of that Schedule.

Schedule 4
Miscellaneous Amendments Relating to the Amendment of the Definition of Taxable Person
Amendments to Value-Added Tax Act 1972

Provision of Value-Added Tax Act 1972	Words to be replaced	Words to be inserted
Section 12(1)	a taxable person	an accountable person
Section 12(1)	other taxable persons	other accountable persons
Section 12(1)	the taxable person	the accountable person
Section 12(1)	another taxable person	another accountable person
Section 12(1)	the taxable person's	the accountable person's
Section 12(1A)	a taxable person	an accountable person
Section 12(2)	the taxable person	the accountable person
Section 12(3)(a)	the taxable person	the accountable person
Section 12(3)(a)	the taxable person's	the accountable person's
Section 12(3)(a)	that taxable person	that accountable person
Section 12(3)(c)	the taxable person	the accountable person
Section 12(3A)	that taxable person	that accountable person
Section 12(3A)	a taxable person	an accountable person
Section 12(4)	a taxable person	an accountable person

(With effect from 1 July 2008 except * with effect from 1 September 2008)

Finance (No. 2) Act 2008

73.   Section 12 of the Principal Act is amended —

    (a)   in subsection (1) —

        (i)   in paragraph (a) by deleting "and" in subparagraph (vii), and by substituting "section 12A, and" for "section 12A." in subparagraph (viii),

        (ii)   by inserting the following after subparagraph (viii) of paragraph (a):

        "(ix)   subject to subsection (4) and regulations (if any), 20 per cent of the tax charged to that accountable person in respect of the purchase, hiring, intra-Community acquisition or importation of a qualifying vehicle (within the meaning assigned by paragraph (c)), where that vehicle is used primarily for business purposes, being at least 60 per cent of the use to which that vehicle is put, and where that accountable person subsequently disposes of that vehicle the tax deducted by that person in accordance with this subsection shall be treated as if it was not deductible by that person for the purposes of paragraph (xxiv)(c) of the First Schedule:",

    and

(iii)   by inserting the following after paragraph (b):

"(c)   For the purposes of paragraph (a)(ix) and subsection (4)(ba), a 'qualifying vehicle' means a motor vehicle which, for the purposes of vehicle registration tax is first registered, in accordance with section 131 of Finance Act 1992, on or after 1 January 2009 and has, for the purposes of that registration, a level of CO_2 emissions of less than 156g/km.",

(b)   in subsection (3)(a)(iii) by inserting "subject to subsection (1)(a)(ix)" before "the purchase",

(c)   in subsection (4) by inserting the following after paragraph (b):

"(ba)   For the purposes of this subsection, the reference in paragraph (b) to 'tax, borne or payable' shall, in the case of an acquisition of a qualifying vehicle (within the meaning assigned by subsection (1)(c)) be deemed to be a reference to '20 per cent of the tax, borne or payable'.",

and

(d)   by inserting the following after subsection (4):

"(4A)   (a)   Where an accountable person deducts tax in relation to the purchase, intra-Community acquisition or importation of a qualifying vehicle in accordance with subsection (1)(a)(ix) and that person disposes of that qualifying vehicle within 2 years of that purchase, acquisition or importation, then that person shall be obliged to reduce the amount of the tax deductible by that person for the taxable period in which the vehicle is disposed of by an amount calculated in accordance with the following formula:

$$\frac{TD \times (4-N)}{4}$$

where—

TD   is the amount of tax deducted by that accountable person on the purchase, acquisition or importation of that vehicle, and

N   is a number that is equal to the number of days from the date of purchase, acquisition or importation of the vehicle by that accountable person to the date of disposal by that person, divided by 182 and rounded down to the nearest whole number,

but if that N is greater than 4 then N shall be 4.

(b)   Where an accountable person deducts tax in relation to the purchase, intra-Community acquisition or importation of a qualifying vehicle in accordance with subsection (1)(a)(ix) and the vehicle is subsequently used for less than 60 per cent business purposes in a taxable period, then that person is obliged to reduce the amount of tax deductible by that person for that taxable period by an amount calculated in accordance with the following formula:

$$\frac{TD \times (4-N)}{4}$$

where—

TD   is the amount of tax deducted by that accountable person on the purchase, acquisition or importation of that vehicle, and

N   is a number that is equal to the number of days from the date of purchase, acquisition or importation of the vehicle by that accountable person to the first day of the taxable period in which the vehicle is used for less than 60 per cent business purposes, divided by 182 and rounded down to the nearest whole number,

but if that N is greater than 4 then N shall be 4.".

99.   The enactments specified in Schedule 6—

(a)   are amended to the extent and in the manner specified in paragraphs 1 to 6 of that Schedule, and

(b)   apply and come into operation in accordance with paragraph 7 of that Schedule.

SCHEDULE 6

Miscellaneous Technical Amendments in Relation to Tax

4.   The Value-Added Tax Act 1972 is amended—

(h)   in section 12—

(i)   in subsection (1)(a)(iv) by substituting "section 5(3)(c)" for "section 5(3)(d)", and

(ii)   in subsection (4)(a) in the definition of "dual-use inputs" by inserting ", or services related to the development of immovable goods that are subject to the provisions of section 12E" after "be made",

(With effect from 24 December 2008)

Section 12A

Value Added Tax (Amendment) Act 1978

Special provisions for tax invoiced by flat-rate farmers

11. The following section shall be inserted after section 12 of the Principal Act:

"12A. (1) Where a flat-rate farmer supplies agricultural produce or an agricultural service to a person, the farmer shall, subject to section 17(2), issue to the person an invoice indicating the consideration (exclusive of the flat-rate addition) in respect of the supply and an amount (in this Act referred to as 'a flat-rate addition') equal to 1 per cent of the said consideration (exclusive of the said addition), and the person shall, if he is a taxable person, be entitled to treat the flat-rate addition as tax deductible under section 12 subject, however, to any restrictions imposed by or under subsection (3) or (4) of that section.

(2) In this Act **'flat-rate farmer'** means a farmer who is not a taxable person.".

(With effect from 1 March 1979)

Finance Act (No. 2) 1981

13. (1) Section 12A (inserted by the Act of 1978) of the Principal Act is hereby amended by the substitution in subsection (1) of "1.5 per cent" for "1 per cent", and the said subsection (1), as so amended, is set out in the Table to this section.

TABLE

Where a flat-rate farmer supplies agricultural produce or an agricultural service to a person, the farmer shall, subject to section 17(2), issue to the person an invoice indicating the consideration (exclusive of the flat-rate addition) in respect of the supply and an amount (in this Act referred to as 'a flat-rate addition') equal to 1.5 per cent of the said consideration (exclusive of the said addition), and the person shall, if he is a taxable person, be entitled to treat the flat-rate addition as tax deductible under section 12 subject, however, to any restrictions imposed by or under subsection (3) or (4) of that section.

(2) This section shall have, and be deemed to have had, effect as on and from the 1st day of September, 1981.

(With effect from 1 September 1981)

Finance Act 1982

81. (1) Section 12A of the Principal Act (inserted by the Act of 1978) is hereby amended-

*(a) in subsection (1), by the substitution of "1.8 per cent" for "1.5 per cent" (inserted by the Act of 1981),

and

(b) by the substitution of the following subsection for subsection (2)-

"(2) In this Act **'flat-rate farmer'** means a farmer who is not a taxable person and, in relation to the supplies specified in the definition of 'farmer' in section 8(9), includes a person who in accordance with section 8(3A), is deemed not to be a taxable person.".

(2) Subsection (1)(a) of this section shall have, and be deemed to have had, effect as on and from the 1st day of May, 1982.

(With effect from 1 September 1982 except * from 1 May 1982)

Finance Act 1983

82. Section 12A (inserted by the Act of 1978) of the Principal Act is hereby amended-

(a) as respects supplies on or after the 1st day of March, 1983, by the substitution in subsection (1) of "2.3 per cent" for "1.8 per cent" (inserted by the Act of 1982),

and

(b) as respects supplies on or after the 1st day of July, 1983, by the substitution in the said subsection (1) of "2 per cent" for "2.3 per cent" (inserted by paragraph (a)).

(With effect from 1 March 1983)

Finance Act 1985

44. Section 12A (inserted by the Act of 1978) of The Principal Act is hereby amended by the substitution in subsection (1) of "2.2 per cent" for "2 per cent" (inserted by the Act of 1983).

(With effect from 1 March 1985)

Finance Act 1986

85. Section 12A (inserted by the Act of 1978) of The Principal Act is hereby amended by the substitution of "2.4 per cent" for "2.2 per cent" (inserted by the Act of 1985).

(With effect from 1 March 1986)

Finance Act 1987

42.   Section 12A (inserted by the Act of 1978) of the Principal Act is hereby amended by the substitution in subsection (1) of "1.7 per cent" for "2.4 per cent" (inserted by the Act of 1986).

(With effect from 1 May 1987)

Finance Act 1988

62.   Section 12A (inserted by the Value-Added Tax (Amendment) Act, 1978) of The Principal Act is hereby amended by the substitution in subsection (1) of "1.4 per cent" for "1.7 per cent" (inserted by the Finance Act, 1987).

(With effect from 1 March 1988)

Finance Act 1989

57.   Section 12A (inserted by the Act of 1978) of The Principal Act is hereby amended by the substitution in subsection (1) of "2 per cent" for "1.4 per cent" (inserted by the Act of 1988).

(With effect from 1 March 1989)

Finance Act 1990

103.   Section 12A (inserted by the Act of 1978) of The Principal Act is hereby amended by the substitution in subsection (1) of "2.3 per cent" for "2 per cent" (inserted by the Act of 1989).

(With effect from 1 March 1990)

Finance Act 1992

175.   (1)   Section 12A (inserted by the Act of 1978) of The Principal Act is hereby amended in subsection (1) by the substitution of "2.7 per cent" for "2.3 per cent" (inserted by the Act of 1990).

       *(2)   section 12A of the Principal Act is hereby further amended in subsection (1) by the deletion of ", and the person shall, if he is a taxable person, be entitled to treat the flat-rate addition as tax deductible under section 12 subject, however, to any restrictions imposed by or under subsection (3) or (4) of that section".

(With effect from 1 March 1992 except * from 1 January 1993)

Finance Act 1993

89.   Section 12A (inserted by the Act of 1978) of the Principal Act is hereby amended-

       *(a)   in subsection (1) by the substitution of "2.5 per cent" for "2.7 per cent" (inserted by the Act of 1992),

       and

       (b)   by the substitution of the following subsection for subsection (2):

               "(2)   In this Act 'flat-rate farmer' means

               (a)   a farmer who is not a taxable person,

      (b)   a farmer who is a taxable person referred to in subsection (1A)(c) or (2)(b) of section 8, or

      (c)   a person who, in accordance with section 8(M), is deemed not to be a taxable person in relation to the supplies specified in the definition of 'farmer' in section 8(9).".

(With effect from 17 June 1993 except * from 1 March 1993)

Finance Act 1996

94. Section 12A (inserted by the Act of 1978) of The Principal Act is hereby amended in subsection (1) by the substitution of "2.8 per cent" for "2.5 per cent" (inserted by the Act of 1993).

(With effect from 1 March 1996)

Finance Act 1997

105. Section 12A (inserted by the Act of 1978) of The Principal Act is hereby amended in subsection (1) by the substitution of "3.3 per cent" for "2.8 per cent" (inserted by the Act of 1996).

(With effect from 1 March 1997)

Finance Act 1998

112. Section 12A (inserted by the Value-Added Tax (Amendment) Act, 1978) of the Principal Act is hereby amended in subsection (1) by the substitution of "3.6 per cent" for "3.3 per cent" (inserted by the Act of 1997).

(With effect from 1 March 1998)

Finance Act 1999

129. Section 12A (inserted by the Act of 1978) of the Principal Act is hereby amended in subsection (1) by the substitution of "4 per cent" for "3.6 per cent" (inserted by the Act of 1998).

(With effect from 1 March 1999)

Finance Act 2000

111. Section 12A (inserted by the Act of 1978) of the Principal Act is amended in subsection (1) by the substitution of "4.2 per cent" for "4 per cent" (inserted by the Act of 1999).

(With effect from 1 March 2000)

Finance Act 2001

189. Section 12A (inserted by the Act of 1978) of the Principal Act is amended in subsection (1) by the substitution of "4.3 per cent" for "4.2 per cent" (inserted by the Act of 2000).

(With effect from 1 January 2001)

Finance Act 2004

61. Section 12A (inserted by the Act of 1978) of the Principal Act is amended in subsection (1) by substituting "4.4 per cent" for "4.3 per cent" (inserted by the Act of 2001).

(With effect from 1 January 2004)

Finance Act 2005

105. With effect from 1 January 2005, section 12A (inserted by the Value-Added Tax (Amendment) Act 1978) of the Principal Act is amended in subsection (1) by substituting "4.8 per cent" for "4.4 per cent" (inserted by the Act of 2004).

(With effect from 1 January 2005)

Finance Act 2007

84. With effect from 1 January 2007, section 12A of the Principal Act is amended in subsection (1) by substituting "5.2 per cent" for "4.8 per cent".

(With effect from 1 January 2007)

Finance Act 2008

109. With effect from 1 July 2008 in each provision of the Principal Act specified in the first column of Schedule 4 for the words set out in the second column of that Schedule at that entry (in each place where those words occur in the provision concerned) there is substituted the words set out at the corresponding entry in the third column of that Schedule.

Schedule 4
Miscellaneous Amendments Relating to the Amendment of the Definition of Taxable Person

Amendments to Value-Added Tax Act 1972

Provision of Value-Added Tax Act 1972	Words to be replaced	Words to be inserted
Section 12A	a taxable person	an accountable person

(With effect from 1 July 2008)

Section 12B

Finance Act 1995

Special scheme for means of transport supplied by taxable dealers.

130. The Principal Act is hereby amended by the insertion of the following section after section 12A:

"12B. (1) Where a taxable dealer supplies a means of transport, the residual tax which is deductible in accordance with section 12(1)(a)(vi) shall be deemed to be tax and shall be the amount referred to in subsection (4).

(2) The entitlement to deduct residual tax referred to in subsection (1) shall arise only where a taxable dealer purchases or acquires-

(a) a means of transport from a person, other than a person referred to in subsection (10), who was not entitled to deduct, under section 12, any tax in respect of that person's purchase, intra-Community acquisition or importation of that means of transport, or

(b) a means of transport other than a new means of transport from a person in another Member State who was not entitled to deduct, under the provisions implementing Article 17 of Council Directive No. 77/388/EEC of 17 May 1977 in that Member State, any value-added tax referred to in that Directive in respect of that person's purchase, intra-Community acquisition or importation of that means of transport, or

(c) a means of transport from a taxable person who has exercised the entitlement under section 12(1)(a)(vi) to deduct the residual tax in respect of that person's supply of that means of transport to the said dealer, or

(d) a means of transport other than a new means of transport from a taxable dealer in another Member State who has applied the provisions implementing Article 26a or 28o (inserted by Council Directive No. 94/5/EC of 14 February 1994) of Council Directive No. 77/388/EEC of 17 May 1977 to the supply of that means of transport, in that other Member State.

(3) In this section-

'**taxable dealer**' means a taxable person who in the course or furtherance of business, whether acting on that person's own behalf, or on behalf of another person pursuant to a contract under which commission is payable on purchase or sale, purchases or acquires means of transport as stock-in-trade with a view to resale, and a person in another Member State shall be deemed to be a taxable dealer where, in similar circumstances, that person would be a taxable dealer in the State under this section;

'means of transport' means motorised land vehicles with an engine cylinder capacity exceeding 48 cubic centimetres or a power exceeding 7.2 kilowatts, vessels exceeding 7.5 metres in length and aircraft with a take-off weight exceeding 1,550 kilogrammes, which are intended for the transport of persons or goods, other than vessels and aircraft of the kind referred to in paragraph (v) of the Second Schedule.

(4) The residual tax which may be deducted by a taxable dealer in accordance with section 12(1)(a)(vi) shall be the residual tax deemed to be included in the purchase price payable by such dealer when acquiring a means of transport and shall be determined by the formula-

$$\frac{A \times B}{B + 100}$$

where-

A is the purchase price of the means of transport, and

B is the percentage rate of tax specified-

(a) in section 11(1)(a) where the means of transport is deemed to be supplied within the State to the taxable dealer, or

(b) in provisions implementing Article 12(1) of Council Directive No. 77/388/EEC of 17 May 1977 in another Member State where the means of transport is deemed to be supplied within that Member State to the taxable dealer:

Provided that, subject to subsection (8), where the amount so calculated is in excess of the tax chargeable on the supply by the taxable dealer of the means of transport, the residual tax shall be an amount equal to the amount of tax chargeable on that supply.

(5) Notwithstanding section 17, where a taxable dealer deducts residual tax referred to in subsection (1) in respect of a supply of a means of transport, that dealer shall not indicate separately the amount of tax chargeable in respect of that supply on any invoice or other document issued in lieu thereof in accordance with that section.

(6)   Notwithstanding section 3(6)(d), in the case of a supply of a means of transport which is dispatched or transported and where-

(a)   a taxable dealer deducts residual tax referred to in subsection (1) in respect of the supply of that means of transport, or

(b)   a taxable dealer in another Member State has applied the provisions implementing Article 26a or 28o of Council Directive No. 77/388/EEC of 17 May 1977 in that other Member State, to the supply of that means of transport,

the place of supply shall be deemed to be the place where the dispatch or transportation begins.

(7)   Where a taxable dealer deducts residual tax referred to in subsection (1) in respect of a supply of a means of transport, then, subject to subsection (8), the provisions of section 11(1)(b) shall not apply in respect of that supply.

(8)   Notwithstanding subsection (7), where a taxable dealer deducts residual tax referred to in subsection (1) in respect of the supply of a new means of transport dispatched or transported by the supplier to a person in another Member State, the provisions of section 11(1)(b) shall apply, and in determining the amount of the residual tax in accordance with subsection (4) the proviso to that subsection shall not apply.

(9)   Where a taxable dealer supplies a means of transport on behalf of another person pursuant to a contract under which commission is payable on purchase or sale, the means of transport shall be deemed to have been supplied by that other person to the taxable dealer when the said taxable dealer supplies that means of transport.

(10)   Notwithstanding paragraph (xxiv) of the First Schedule, the provisions of that paragraph shall not apply to-

(a)   a supply by a taxable person of a means of transport, other than a motor vehicle as defined in section 12(3)(b), which that person acquired from a taxable dealer who deducted residual tax in respect of the supply of that means of transport to that person, and

(b)   a supply by a taxable person other than a taxable dealer of a motor vehicle, as defined in section 12(3)(b), which that person acquired as stock-in-trade or for the purposes of a business which consists in whole or part of the hiring of motor vehicles or for use, in a driving school business, for giving driving instruction, from a taxable dealer who deducted residual tax in respect of the supply of that motor vehicle to that person.".

(With effect from 1 July 1995)

Finance Act 1999

130. Section 12B (inserted by the Act of 1995) of the Principal Act is hereby amended-

(a)　　in subsection (2)-

(i)　　by the insertion of "(other than in the circumstances where an owner as referred to in paragraph (c) of subsection (5) of section 3, enforces such owner's right to recover possession of a means of transport)" after "purchases or acquires", and

(ii)　　by the insertion of the following paragraph after paragraph (a):

"(aa)　a means of transport from a person where the disposal of that means of transport by such person to such taxable dealer was deemed not to be a supply of goods in accordance with section 3(5)(c), or",

and

*(b)　　in subsection (3) in the definition of "means of transport" by the insertion after "other than" of "agricultural machinery (within the meaning of section 12C), and".

(With effect from 25 March 1999 except * from 1 September 1999)

Finance Act 2001

190. Section 12B (inserted by the Act of 1995) of the Principal Act is amended in subsection (2)(aa) by the substitution of "paragraphs (c) and (d) of subsection (5) of section 3" for "section 3(5)(c)".

(With effect from 21 March 2001)

Finance Act 2003

120. Section 12B of the Principal Act is amended —

(a)　　in subsection (10), by deleting "and" at the end of paragraph (a), by substituting "of that motor vehicle to that person, and" for "of that motor vehicle to that person." in paragraph (b) and by inserting the following after paragraph (b):

"(c)　a supply by a taxable dealer of a means of transport being a motor vehicle as defined in section 12(3)(b) which has been declared for registration in accordance with section 131 of the Finance Act 1992 on that dealer's own behalf, unless it can be shown to the satisfaction of the Revenue Commissioners that, on the basis of the use to which that means of transport has been put by that taxable dealer, the provisions of subsection (11)(b) should not apply to that supply.",

and

(b)   by inserting the following after subsection (10):

"(11) (a)   Where a means of transport which is a motor vehicle as defined in section 12(3)(b) is declared for registration to the Revenue Commissioners in accordance with section 131 of the Finance Act 1992 by a taxable dealer on that dealer's own behalf and on which deductibility in accordance with section 12 has been claimed by that dealer, then that means of transport shall be treated for the purposes of this Act as if it were removed from stock-in-trade and such removal is deemed to be a supply of that means of transport by that taxable dealer for the purposes of section 3(1)(e).

(b)   At the time when a taxable dealer supplies to another person a means of transport which is deemed to have been supplied in accordance with paragraph (a), then that means of transport is deemed to be re-acquired by that dealer as stock-in-trade and, notwithstanding subsection (2), the taxable dealer is entitled to deduct residual tax referred to in subsection (1) and in that case for the purposes of the formula in subsection (4) the residual tax is calculated as if 'A' were equal to the total of—

(i)   the amount on which tax was chargeable on the supply of that means of transport to the dealer,

(ii)   the tax which was chargeable on the supply referred to at subparagraph (i), and

(iii)   the vehicle registration tax accounted for by that dealer in respect of the registration of that means of transport,

and, apart from the cases provided for in paragraph (c), the amount referred to in subparagraph (i) is the amount on which tax was chargeable on the supply of that means of transport in accordance with section 3(1)(e).

(c)   Where a taxable dealer declares a means of transport for registration in the circumstances described in paragraph (a) but does not claim deductibility in accordance with section 12 in respect of that means of transport, then paragraph (b) applies when that dealer supplies that means of transport to another person.".

(With effect from 1 May 2003)

Finance Act 2007

85.   Section 12B of the Principal Act is amended with effect from 1 May 2007 in subsection (2)(aa) by substituting "section 3(5)(d)" for "paragraphs (c) and (d) of subsection (5) of section 3".

*97.   With effect from 1 January 2007 in each provision of the Principal Act specified in the first column of Schedule 3 for the words set out in the second column of that Schedule at that entry there is substituted the words set out at the corresponding entry in the third column of that Schedule.

Schedule 3
Miscellaneous Amendments Relating to Council Directive 2006/112/EC
Amendment of Value-Added Tax Act 1972

Enactment amended	Words to be replaced	Words to be substituted
Section 12B(2)(b)	Article 17 of Council Directive No. 77/388/EEC of 17 May 1977	Articles 167,173,176 and 177 of Council Directive No. 2006/112/EC of 28 November 2006
Section 12B(2)(d)	Article 26a or 28o (inserted by Council Directive No. 94/5/EC of 14 February 1994) of Council Directive No. 77/388/EEC of 17 May 1977	Articles 4 and 35, first subparagraph of Article 139(3) and Articles 311 to 341 of Council Directive No. 2006/112/EC of 28 November 2006
Section 12B(4) in paragraph (b) of the meaning given to "B"	Article 12(1) of Council Directive No. 77/388/EEC of 17 May 1977	Article 93 of Council Directive No. 2006/112/EC of 28 November 2006
Section 12B(6)(b)	Article 26a or 28o of Council Directive No. 77/388/EEC of 17 May 1977	Articles 4 and 35, first subparagraph of Article 139(3) and Articles 311 to 341 of Council Directive No. 2006/112/EC of 28 November 2006

(With effect from 1 May 2007 except * with effect from 1 January 2007)

Finance Act 2008

95. Section 12B of the Principal Act is amended —

    (a)   in subsection (3) with effect from 1 July 2008 by substituting the following for the definition of "taxable dealer":

        " 'taxable dealer' —

        (a)   means an accountable person who in the course or furtherance of business, whether acting on that person's own behalf, or on behalf of another person pursuant to a contract under which commission is payable on purchase or sale, purchases or acquires means of transport as stock-in-trade with a view to resale, and

        (b)   includes a person supplying financial services of the kind specified in subparagraph (i)(e) of the First Schedule who acquires or purchases means of transport for the purpose of the supply thereof as part of an agreement of the kind referred to in section 3(1)(b),

        and, for the purpose of this interpretation, a person in another Member State shall be deemed to be a taxable dealer where, in similar circumstances, that person would be a taxable dealer in the State under this section;",

        and

    *(b)   in subsection (11)(a) by inserting "and, for the avoidance of doubt, the amount of tax chargeable in respect of that supply is included and was always included in the amount deductible in accordance with paragraph (b) and accordingly is not included and was never included in any amount which the taxable person is entitled to deduct in accordance with section 12(1)(a)(iii)" after "section 3(1)(e)".

109. With effect from 1 July 2008 in each provision of the Principal Act specified in the first column of Schedule 4 for the words set out in the second column of that Schedule at that entry (in each place where those words occur in the provision concerned) there is substituted the words set out at the corresponding entry in the third column of that Schedule.

Schedule 4
Miscellaneous Amendments Relating to the Amendment of the Definition of Taxable Person

Amendments to Value-Added Tax Act 1972

Provision of Value-Added Tax Act 1972	Words to be replaced	Words to be inserted
Section 12B(2)	a taxable person	an accountable person
Section 12B(10)	a taxable person	an accountable person

(With effect from 1 July 2008 except * with effect from 13 March 2008)

Section 12C

Finance Act 1999

Special scheme for agricultural machinery.

131. The Principal Act is hereby amended by the insertion of the following
section after section 12B (inserted by the Act of 1995):

"12C. (1)   A taxable dealer who purchases agricultural machinery
from a flat-rate farmer shall, subject to the provisions
of this section and in accordance with sub-paragraph
(via) of paragraph (a) of subsection (1) of section 12,
be entitled to deduct the residual tax contained in the
price payable by such taxable dealer in respect of that
purchase.

  (2)   A flat-rate farmer who supplies agricultural machinery to
a taxable dealer shall, subject to section 17(2A), issue an
invoice in respect of that supply.

  (3)   The residual tax referred to in subsection (1) shall be
determined by the formula-

$$\frac{A \times B}{B + 100}$$

where

A is the purchase price of the agricultural machinery
payable by the taxable dealer,

and

B is the percentage rate of tax specified in section
11(1)(a).

  (4)   Where a taxable dealer supplies agricultural machinery
in respect of which such dealer was entitled to deduct
residual tax and where the tax chargeable in respect of
that supply is less than the residual tax deducted by that
dealer in respect of the purchase of that machinery, then
the excess of the residual tax over the tax payable on that
supply shall be deemed to be tax chargeable in respect of
that supply.

  (5)   In this section

'agricultural machinery' means machinery or equipment,
other than a motor vehicle as defined in subsection (3)
of section 12, which has been used by a flat-rate farmer
for the purpose of such farmer's Annex A activity in
circumstances where any tax charged on the supply
of that machinery or equipment to that farmer would
have been deductable by such farmer if such farmer had

elected to be a taxable person at the time of that supply of the machinery or equipment to such farmer;

'**taxable dealer**' means a taxable person who in the course or furtherance of business, whether acting on that person's own behalf, or on behalf of another person pursuant to a contract under which commission is payable on purchase or sale, purchases agricultural machinery as stock-in-trade with a view to resale.".

(With effect from 1 September 1999)

Finance Act 2000

114. Section 12C (inserted by the Act of 1999) of the Principal Act is amended by the insertion of the following subsections after subsection (1):

"(1A) A taxable dealer who purchases agricultural machinery from a person where the disposal of that agricultural machinery by such person to such taxable dealer was deemed in accordance with section 3(5)(c) not to be a supply of goods shall, subject to the provisions of this section and in accordance with subparagraph (vib) of paragraph (a) of subsection (1) of section 12, be entitled to deduct the residual tax, determined by the formula in subsection (3), contained in the price payable by such taxable dealer in respect of that purchase.

(1B) A person who disposes of agricultural machinery to a taxable dealer where the disposal of that agricultural machinery by such person to such taxable dealer was deemed in accordance with section 3(5)(c) not to be a supply of goods shall issue a document to the taxable dealer to whom the disposal is made and shall indicate on the document-

(a)   that person's name and address,

(b)   the name and address of the taxable dealer,

(c)   the date of issue of the document,

(d)   a description of the agricultural machinery, including details of the make, model and, where appropriate, the year of manufacture, the engine number and registration number of that machinery,

(e)   the consideration for the disposal of the agricultural machinery,

(f)   confirmation that the disposal is deemed in accordance with section 3(5)(c) not to be a supply of goods, and

(g)   such other particulars as may be specified by regulations, if any.".

(With effect from 23 March 2000)

Finance Act 2002

SCHEDULE 6

Miscellaneous Technical Amendments in Relation to Tax

1.   The Value-Added Tax Act, 1972, is amended in accordance with the following provisions:

(c)   section 12C (inserted by the Finance Act, 1999) is amended in subsections (1A), (1B) and (1B)(f) (inserted by the Finance Act, 2000) by substituting "3(5)(c) or (d)" for "3(5)(c)",

(With effect from 25 March 2002)

Finance Act 2007

86.   Section 12C of the Principal Act is amended in subsections (1A) and (1B) by substituting "section 3(5)(d)" for "section 3(5)(c) or (d)" wherever it occurs.

(With effect from 2 April 2007)

Finance Act 2008

96.   Section 12C of the Principal Act is amended with effect from 1 July 2008 in the definition of "taxable dealer" in subsection (5) by inserting "and includes a person supplying financial services of the kind specified in subparagraph (i)(e) of the First Schedule who purchases agricultural machinery for the purpose of the supply thereof as part of an agreement of the kind referred to in section 3(1)(b)" after "stock-in-trade with a view to resale".

109. With effect from 1 July 2008 in each provision of the Principal Act specified in the first column of Schedule 4 for the words set out in the second column of that Schedule at that entry (in each place where those words occur in the provision concerned) there is substituted the words set out at the corresponding entry in the third column of that Schedule.

Schedule 4
Miscellaneous Amendments Relating to the Amendment of the Definition of Taxable Person

Amendments to Value-Added Tax Act 1972

Provision of Value-Added Tax Act 1972	Words to be replaced	Words to be inserted
Section 12C(5)	a taxable person	an accountable person

(With effect from 1 July 2008)

Section 12D

Finance Act 2001

Adjustment of tax deductible in certain circumstances

191. The Principal Act is amended by the insertion of the following after section 12C-

"12D. (1) For the purposes of this section-

'**full year**' shall be any continuous period of twelve months;

'**interest**' in relation to immovable goods has the meaning assigned to it by section 4.

(2) Where-

(a) a person makes a transfer of an interest in immovable goods in accordance with section 3(5)(b)(iii), and

(b) but for the application of that section, tax would have been chargeable on the transfer, and the person (referred to in this section as a 'transferor') was entitled to deduct part of the tax charged on the most recent purchase or acquisition of an interest in, or the development of, the immovable goods subject to that transfer,

that transferor shall, for the purposes of section 12, be entitled to increase the amount of tax deductible for the taxable period within which the transfer is made by an amount calculated in accordance with the following formula:

$$\frac{(T - TD) \times (Y - N)}{Y}$$

where-

T   is the tax chargeable on that most recent purchase or acquisition of an interest in, or that development of, the immovable goods,

TD is the tax that the transferor was entitled to deduct on that most recent purchase or acquisition of an interest in, or that development of, the immovable goods,

Y   is 20 or, if the interest when it was created in the immovable goods being transferred was for a period of less than 20 years, the number of full years in that interest, and

N   is the number of full years since the interest was created or, if the goods were developed since that interest was created, the number of full years since the most recent development:

but if that N is greater than that Y, such an amount calculated shall be deemed to be nil.

(3)   Where a transferor acquired an interest in immovable goods as a result of a transfer in accordance with section 3(5)(b)(iii) and the transferor did not develop those immovable goods since the acquisition then, for the purposes of subsection (2), the amount by which that transferor shall be entitled to increase the amount of tax deductible, in accordance with section 12, for the taxable period in which the transferor transfers those goods, shall be calculated in accordance with the following formula:

$$\frac{A \times (Y - N)}{Y}$$

where-

A   is the amount which the transferor was required to calculate and reduce his or her deductible amount by, in accordance with subsection (4), when the transferor acquired the interest in those goods,

Y   is 20 or, if the interest when it was created in the immovable goods being transferred was for a period of less than 20 years, the number of full years in that interest, and

N   is the number of full years since the interest was created 15 or, if the goods were developed since that interest was created, the number of full years since the most recent development:

but if that N is greater than that Y, such an amount calculated shall be deemed to be nil.

(4)   Where a person receives an interest in immovable goods as a result of a transfer and the person would not have been entitled to deduct all the tax that would have been chargeable on the transfer but for the application of section 3(5)(b)(iii), that person shall reduce the amount of tax deductible by that person, for the purposes of section 12, for the period within which the transfer was made, by an amount calculated in accordance with the following formula:

$$\frac{(T1 - TD1) \times (Y - N)}{Y}$$

where-

T1   is the amount of tax that would have been chargeable on the transfer if section 3(5)(b)(iii) did not apply,

TD1   is the amount of tax that would have
             been deductible by the transferee if
             section 3(5)(b)(iii) had not applied to
             the transfer,

Y   is 20 or, if the interest when it was created in
       the immovable goods being transferred was
       for a period of less than 20 years, the number
       of full years in that interest, and

N   is the number of full years since the interest was
       created or, if the goods were developed since
       that interest was created, the number of full
       years since the most recent development:

       but if that N is greater than that Y, such an amount
       calculated shall be deemed to be nil.".

(With effect from 21 March 2001)

Finance Act 2002

104. Section 12D of the Principal Act is amended in subsection (4) by
substituting "calculate an amount which shall be payable as if it were
tax due by that person in accordance with section 19 for the taxable
period within which the transfer was made, and that amount shall be
calculated" for "reduce the amount of tax deductible by that person, for
the purposes of section 12, for the period within which the transfer was
made, by an amount calculated".

(With effect from 25 March 2002)

Finance Act 2008

97. Section 12D of the Principal Act is amended by inserting the following
after subsection (4):

"(5)   This section does not apply to a transfer of an interest in
immovable goods which occurs on or after 1 July 2008.".

(With effect from 13 March 2008)

Section 12E

Finance Act 2008

Capital Goods Scheme

98.   The Principal Act is amended with effect from 1 July 2008 by inserting the following section after section 12D:

"12E.   (1)   This section applies to capital goods —

(a)   on the supply or development of which tax was chargeable to a taxable person, or

(b)   on the supply of which tax would have been chargeable to a taxable person but for the application of section 3(5)(b)(iii).

(2)   In this section —

'**adjustment period**', in relation to a capital good, means the period encompassing the number of intervals as provided for in subsection (3)(a) during which adjustments of deductions are required to be made in respect of a capital good;

'**base tax amount**', in relation to a capital good, means the amount calculated by dividing the total tax incurred in relation to that capital good by the number of intervals in the adjustment period applicable to that capital good;

'**capital goods owner**' means —

(a)   except where paragraph (b) applies, a taxable person who incurs expenditure on the acquisition or development of a capital good,

(b)   in the case of a taxable person who is a flat-rate farmer, means a taxable person who incurs expenditure to develop or acquire a capital good other than a building or structure designed and used solely for the purposes of a farming business or for fencing, drainage or reclamation of land, and which has actually been put to use in such business;

'**deductible supplies or activities**' has the meaning assigned to it by section 12(4);

'**initial interval**', in relation to a capital good, means a period of 12 months beginning on the date when a capital good is completed or, in the case of a capital good that is supplied following completion, the initial interval for the recipient of that supply is the 12 month period beginning on the date of that supply;

'**initial interval proportion of deductible use**', in relation to a capital good, means the proportion that correctly reflects the extent to which a capital good is used during the initial interval for the purposes of a capital goods owner's deductible supplies or activities;

'**interval**', in relation to a capital good, means the initial, second or subsequent interval in an adjustment period, whichever is appropriate;

'**interval deductible amount**', in relation to a capital good in respect of the second and each subsequent interval, means the amount calculated by multiplying the base tax amount in relation to that capital good by the proportion of deductible use for that capital good applicable to the relevant interval;

'**non-deductible amount**', in relation to a capital good, means the amount which is the difference between the total tax incurred in relation to that capital good and the total reviewed deductible amount in relation to that capital good;

'**proportion of deductible use**', in relation to a capital good for an interval other than the initial interval, means the proportion that correctly reflects the extent to which a capital good is used during that interval for the purposes of a capital goods owner's deductible supplies or activities;

'**reference deduction amount**', in relation to a capital good, means the amount calculated by dividing the total reviewed deductible amount in relation to that capital good by the number of intervals in the adjustment period applicable to that capital good;

'**refurbishment**' means development on a previously completed building, structure or engineering work;

'**second interval**', in relation to a capital good, means the period beginning on the day following the end of the initial interval in the adjustment period applicable to that capital good and ending on the final day of the accounting year during which the second interval begins;

'**subsequent interval**', in relation to a capital good, means each accounting year of a capital goods owner in the adjustment period applicable to that capital good, which follows the second interval;

'**total reviewed deductible amount**', in relation to a capital good, means the amount calculated by multiplying the total tax incurred in relation to that capital good by the initial interval proportion of deductible use in relation to that capital good;

'**total tax incurred**', in relation to a capital good, has the meaning assigned to it by subsection (3)(b).

(3)   (a)   In relation to a capital good the number of intervals in the adjustment period during which adjustments of deductions are required under this section to be made, is —

    (i)   in the case of refurbishment, 10 intervals,

    (ii)   in the case of a capital good to which paragraph (c) or (d) of subsection (6) applies, the number of full intervals remaining in the adjustment period applicable to that capital good plus one as required to be calculated in accordance with the formula in subsection (7)(b), and

    (iii) in all other cases, 20 intervals.

(b)   In this section 'total tax incurred' in relation to a capital good means —

    (i)   the amount of tax charged to a capital goods owner in respect of that owner's acquisition or development of a capital good,

    (ii)   in the case of a transferee where a transfer of ownership of a capital good to which section 3(5)(b)(iii) applies —

    (I)   where such a transfer would have been a supply but for the application of section 3(5)(b)(iii) and that supply would have been exempt in accordance with section 4B(2), then the total tax incurred that is required to be included in the copy of the capital good record that is required to be furnished by the transferor in accordance with subsection (10), and

    (II)   where such a transfer is not one to which clause (I) applies, then the amount of tax that would have been chargeable on that transfer but for the application of sections 3(5)(b)(iii) and 13A,

and

    (iii) the amount of tax that would have been chargeable, but for the application of section 13A, to a capital goods owner on that owner's acquisition or development of a capital good.

(c)   Where a capital goods owner acquires a capital good —

(i)   by way of a transfer, being a transfer to which section 3(5)(b)(iii) applies other than a transfer to which subsection (10) applies, on which tax would have been chargeable but for the application of section 3(5)(b)(iii), or

(ii)   on the supply or development of which tax was chargeable in accordance with section 13A,

then, for the purposes of this section, that capital goods owner is deemed to have claimed a deduction in accordance with section 12 of the tax that would have been chargeable —

(I)   on the transfer of that capital good but for the application of section 3(5)(b)(iii), less any amount accounted for by that owner in respect of that transfer in accordance with subsection (7)(d), and

(II)   on the supply or development of that capital good but for the application of section 13A.

(d)   Where a capital goods owner supplies or transfers by means of a transfer to which section 3(5)(b)(iii) applies a capital good during the adjustment period then the adjustment period for that capital good for that owner shall end on the date of that supply or transfer.

(4)   (a)   Where the initial interval proportion of deductible use in relation to a capital good differs from the proportion of the total tax incurred in relation to that capital good which was deductible by that owner in accordance with section 12, then that owner shall, at the end of the initial interval, calculate an amount in accordance with the following formula:

$$A - B$$

where —

A   is the amount of the total tax incurred in relation to that capital good which was deductible by that owner in accordance with section 12, and

B   is the total reviewed deductible amount in relation to that capital good.

(b)   Where in accordance with paragraph (a) —

    (i)   A is greater than B, then the amount calculated in accordance with the formula in paragraph (a) shall be payable by that owner as if it were tax due in accordance with section 19 for the taxable period immediately following the end of the initial interval, or

    (ii)   B is greater than A, then that owner is entitled to increase the amount of tax deductible for the purposes of section 12 by the amount calculated in accordance with paragraph (a) for the taxable period immediately following the end of the initial interval.

(c)   Where a capital good is not used during the initial interval then the initial interval proportion of deductible use is the proportion of the total tax incurred that is deductible by the capital goods owner in accordance with section 12.

(5)   (a)   (i)   Subject to subsection (6)(b), where in respect of an interval, other than the initial interval, the proportion of deductible use for that interval in relation to that capital good differs from the initial interval proportion of deductible use in relation to that capital good, then the capital goods owner shall, at the end of that interval, calculate an amount in accordance with the following formula:

$$C - D$$

where —

C   is the reference deduction amount in relation to that capital good, and

D   is the interval deductible amount in relation to that capital good.

(ii)   Where in accordance with subparagraph (i) —

    (I)   C is greater than D, then the amount calculated in accordance with the formula in subparagraph (i) shall be payable by that owner as if it were tax due in accordance with section 19 for the taxable period immediately following the end of that interval, or

    (II)   D is greater than C, then that owner is entitled to increase the amount of tax deductible for the purposes of section 12 by the amount calculated in accordance with the formula in subparagraph (i) for the taxable period immediately following the end of that interval.

(b)   Where for the second or any subsequent interval, a capital good is not used during that interval, the proportion of deductible use in respect of that capital good for that interval shall be the proportion of deductible use for the previous interval.

(6)   (a)   (i)   Where in respect of a capital good for an interval other than the initial interval the proportion of deductible use expressed as a percentage differs by more than 50 percentage points from the initial interval proportion of deductible use expressed as a percentage, then the capital goods owner shall at the end of that interval calculate an amount in accordance with the following formula:

$$(C - D) \times N$$

where—

C   is the reference deduction amount in relation to that capital good,

D   is the interval deductible amount in relation to that capital good, and

N   is the number of full intervals remaining in the adjustment period at the end of that interval plus one.

(ii)   Where in accordance with subparagraph (i)—

(I)   C is greater than D, then the amount calculated in accordance with the formula in subparagraph (i) shall be payable by that owner as if it were tax due in accordance with section 19 for the taxable period immediately following the end of that interval, or

(II)   D is greater than C, then that owner is entitled to increase the amount of tax deductible for the purposes of section 12 by the amount calculated in accordance with the formula in subparagraph (i) for the taxable period immediately following the end of that interval.

(iii)   The provisions of subparagraph (i) shall not apply to a capital good or part thereof that has been subject to the provisions of paragraphs (c) or (d) during the interval to which subparagraph (i) applies.

(iv) Where a capital goods owner is obliged to carry out a calculation referred to in subparagraph (i) in respect of a capital good, then, for the purposes of the remaining intervals in the adjustment period, the proportion of deductible use in relation to that capital good for the interval in respect of which the calculation is required to be made shall be treated as if it were the initial interval proportion of deductible use in relation to that capital good and, until a further calculation is required under subparagraph (i), all other definition amounts shall be calculated accordingly.

(b) Where the provisions of paragraph (a) apply to an interval then the provisions of subsection (5) do not apply to that interval.

(c) Where a capital goods owner who is a landlord in respect of all or part of a capital good terminates his or her landlord's option to tax in accordance with section 7A(1) in respect of any letting of that capital good, then—

(i) that owner is deemed, for the purposes of this section, to have supplied and simultaneously acquired the capital good to which that letting relates,

(ii) that supply shall be deemed to be a supply on which tax is not chargeable and no option to tax that supply in accordance with section 4B(5) shall be permitted on that supply, and

(iii) the capital good acquired shall be treated as a capital good for the purposes of this section and the amount calculated in accordance with subsection (7)(b) on that supply shall be treated as the total tax incurred in relation to that capital good.

(d) Where in respect of a letting of a capital good that is not subject to a landlord's option to tax in accordance with section 7A(1), a landlord subsequently exercises a landlord's option to tax in respect of a letting of that capital good, then—

(i) that landlord is deemed, for the purposes of this section, to have supplied and simultaneously acquired that capital good to which that letting relates,

(ii) that supply shall be deemed to be a supply on which tax is chargeable, and

(iii) the capital good acquired shall be treated as a capital good for the purposes of this section, and—

    (I) the amount calculated in accordance with subsection (7)(a) shall be treated as the total tax incurred in relation to that capital good, and

    (II) the total tax incurred shall be deemed to have been deducted in accordance with section 12 at the time of that supply.

(7)   (a)   Where a capital goods owner supplies a capital good or transfers a capital good, being a transfer to which section 3(5)(b)(iii) applies, other than a transfer to which subsection (10) applies, during the adjustment period in relation to that capital good, and where—

(i) tax is chargeable on that supply, or tax would have been chargeable on that transfer but for the application of section 3(5)(b)(iii), and

(ii) the non-deductible amount in relation to that capital good for that owner is greater than zero or in the case of a supply or transfer during the initial interval, that owner was not entitled to deduct all of the total tax incurred in accordance with section 12,

then that owner is entitled to increase the amount of tax deductible by that owner for the purposes of section 12 for the taxable period in which the supply or transfer occurs, by an amount calculated in accordance with the following formula:

$$\frac{E \times N}{T}$$

where—

E   is the non-deductible amount in relation to that capital good, or in the case of a supply before the end of the initial interval the amount of the total tax incurred in relation to that capital good which was not deductible by that owner in accordance with section 12,

N   is the number of full intervals remaining in the adjustment period in relation to that capital good at the time of supply plus one, and

T   is the total number of intervals in the adjustment period in relation to that capital good.

(b)   Where a capital goods owner supplies a capital good during the adjustment period applicable to that capital good and where tax is not chargeable on the supply and where either —

(i)   the total reviewed deductible amount in relation to that capital good is greater than zero, or

(ii)   in the case of a supply before the end of the initial interval where the amount of the total tax incurred in relation to that capital good which was deductible by that owner in accordance with section 12 is greater than zero,

then that owner shall calculate an amount which shall be payable as if it were tax due in accordance with section 19 for the taxable period in which the supply occurs in accordance with the following formula:

$$\frac{B \times N}{T}$$

where —

B   is the total reviewed deductible amount in relation to that capital good, or, in the case of a supply to which subparagraph (ii) applies, the amount of the total tax incurred in relation to that capital good which that owner claimed as a deduction in accordance with section 12,

N   is the number of full intervals remaining in the adjustment period in relation to that capital good at the time of supply plus one, and

T   is the total number of intervals in the adjustment period in relation to that capital good.

(c)   Where a capital goods owner supplies or transfers, being a transfer to which section 3(5)(b)(iii) applies, part of a capital good during the adjustment period, then for the remainder of the adjustment period applicable to that capital good —

(i)   the total tax incurred,

(ii)   the total reviewed deductible amount, and

(iii) all other definition amounts,

in relation to the remainder of that capital good for that owner shall be adjusted accordingly on a fair and reasonable basis.

(d)   Where a transfer of ownership of a capital good occurs, being a transfer to which section 3(5)(b)(iii) applies, but excluding a transfer to which subsection (10) applies, and where the transferee would not have been entitled to deduct all of the tax that would have been chargeable on that transfer but for the application of section 3(5)(b)(iii), then that transferee shall calculate an amount as follows:

$$F - G$$

where—

F   is the amount of tax that would have been chargeable but for the application of section 3(5)(b)(iii), and

G   is the amount of that tax that would have been deductible in accordance with section 12 by that transferee if section 3(5)(b)(iii) had not applied to that transfer,

and that amount shall be payable by that transferee as if it were tax due in accordance with section 19 for the taxable period in which the transfer occurs and for the purposes of this section that amount shall be deemed to be the amount of the total tax incurred in relation to that capital good that the transferee was not entitled to deduct in accordance with section 12.

(8)   (a)   Where a tenant who has an interest other than a freehold equivalent interest in immovable goods is the capital goods owner in respect of a refurbishment carried out on those immovable goods, assigns or surrenders that interest, then that tenant shall calculate an amount in respect of that capital good which is that refurbishment in accordance with the formula in subsection (7)(b), and that amount shall be payable by that tenant as if it were tax due in accordance with section 19 for the taxable period in which the assignment or surrender occurs.

(b)   Paragraph (a) shall not apply where—

(i)   the total reviewed deductible amount in relation to that capital good is equal to the total tax incurred in relation to that capital good, or in relation to an assignment or surrender that occurs prior to the end of the initial interval in relation to that capital good the tenant was entitled to deduct all of the total tax incurred in accordance with section 12 in relation to that capital good,

(ii) the tenant enters into a written agreement with the person to whom the interest is assigned or surrendered, to the effect that that person shall be responsible for all obligations under this section in relation to the capital good referred to in paragraph (a) from the date of the assignment or surrender of the interest referred to in paragraph (a), as if —

    (I) the total tax incurred and the amount deducted by that tenant in relation to that capital good were the total tax incurred and the amount deducted by the person to whom the interest is assigned or surrendered, and

    (II) any adjustments required to be made under this section by the tenant were made,

and

(iii) the tenant issues a copy of the capital good record in respect of the capital good referred to in paragraph (a) to the person to whom the interest is being assigned or surrendered.

(c)   Where paragraph (b) applies the person to whom the interest is assigned or surrendered shall be responsible for the obligations referred to in paragraph (b)(ii) and shall use the information in the copy of the capital good record issued by the tenant in accordance with paragraph (b)(iii) for the purposes of calculating any tax chargeable or deductible in accordance with this section in respect of that capital good by that person from the date of the assignment or surrender of the interest referred to in paragraph (a).

(d)   Where the capital good is one to which subsection (11) applies paragraphs (a), (b) and (c) shall not apply.

(9)   Where a capital goods owner —

(a)   supplies a capital good during the adjustment period applicable to that capital good, and where tax is chargeable on that supply, or (b)　　transfers, other than a transfer to which subsection (10) applies, a capital good during the adjustment period applicable to that capital good and tax would have been chargeable on that transfer but for the application of section 3(5)(b)(iii),

and where, at the time of that supply or transfer, that owner and the person to whom the capital good is supplied or transferred are connected within the meaning of section 7A, and where —

(i)　　the amount of tax chargeable on the supply of that capital good,

(ii)　　the amount of tax that would have been chargeable on the transfer of that capital good but for the application of section 3(5)(b)(iii), or

(iii)　　the amount of tax that would have been chargeable on the supply but for the application of section 13A,

is less than the amount, hereafter referred to as the "adjustment amount", calculated in accordance with the following formula:

$$\frac{H \times N}{T}$$

where —

H　is the total tax incurred in relation to that capital good for the capital goods owner making the supply or transfer,

N　is the number of full intervals remaining in the adjustment period in relation to that capital good plus one, and

T　is the total number of intervals in the adjustment period in relation to that capital good,

then, that owner shall calculate an amount, which shall be payable by that owner as if it were tax due in accordance with section 19 for the taxable period in which the supply or transfer occurs, in accordance with the following formula:

$$I - J$$

where —

I　is the adjustment amount, and

J　is the amount of tax chargeable on the supply of that capital good, or the amount of tax that would have been chargeable on the transfer of that capital good but for the application of section 3(5)(b)(iii), or the amount of tax that would have been chargeable on the supply but for the application of section 13A.

(10) Where a capital goods owner transfers a capital good, being a transfer to which section 3(5)(b)(iii) applies and that transfer would have been a supply but for the application of section 3(5)(b)(iii), and where such supply would be exempt in accordance with section 4B(2) then—

    (a) the transferor shall issue a copy of the capital good record to the transferee,

    (b) the transferee shall be the successor to the capital goods owner transferring the capital good and shall be responsible for all obligations of that owner under this section from the date of the transfer of that capital good, as if—

        (i) the total tax incurred and the amount deducted by the transferor in relation to that capital good were the total tax incurred and the amount deducted by the transferee, and

        (ii) any adjustments required to be made under this section by the transferor were made,

    and

    (c) that transferee as successor shall use the information in the copy of the capital good record issued by the transferor in accordance with paragraph (a) for the purposes of calculating tax chargeable or deductible by that successor in accordance with this section for the remainder of the adjustment period applicable to that capital good from the date of transfer of that capital good.

(11) If a capital good is destroyed during the adjustment period in relation to that capital good, then no further adjustment under this section shall be made by the capital goods owner in respect of any remaining intervals in the adjustment period in relation to that capital good.

(12) A capital goods owner shall create and maintain a record (in this section referred to as a 'capital good record') in respect of each capital good and that record shall contain sufficient information to determine any adjustments in respect of that capital good required in accordance with this section.

(13) The Revenue Commissioners may make regulations necessary for the purposes of the operation of this section,

in particular in relation to the duration of a subsequent interval where the accounting year of a capital goods owner changes.".

(With effect from 1 July 2008)

Finance (No. 2) Act 2008

99.   The enactments specified in Schedule 6 —

    (a)   are amended to the extent and in the manner specified in paragraphs 1 to 6 of that Schedule, and

    (b)   apply and come into operation in accordance with paragraph 7 of that Schedule.

SCHEDULE 6
Miscellaneous Technical Amendments in Relation to Tax

4.   The Value-Added Tax Act 1972 is amended —

    (i)   in section 12E —

        (i)   in subsection (3)(b)(ii)(I) by substituting "section 4B(2) or subsection (2) or (6)(b) of section 4C" for "section 4B(2)", and

        (ii)   in subsection (10) by substituting "section 4B(2) or subsection (2) or (6)(b) of section 4C" for "section 4B(2)",

(With effect from 24 December 2008)

Section 13

Value-Added Tax Act 1972

Special provisions for tax invoiced by farmers and fishermen.

13. (1) Subject to subsection (2), where a person who carries on the business of farming or fishing and-

(a) who is not an accountable person under the provisions of section 8(3)(a), and

(b) who is not an accountable person by election,

delivers goods or renders services to an accountable person, the first-mentioned person shall, subject to section 17(2), issue to the accountable person an invoice, and the accountable person shall be entitled to treat as tax deductible under section 12 an amount equal to 1 per cent of the consideration stated in the invoice, including any tax stated separately therein.

(2) Subsection (1) shall apply if, but only if-

(a) the goods in question are goods of a kind specified in subparagraph (i) or (ii) of section 8(3)(a) or the services in question are services of a kind specified in subparagraph (iii) of the said section 8(3)(a), and

(b) a deduction could have been claimed under section 12 by the accountable person if such goods or services had been delivered or rendered to him by another accountable person and an invoice charging the appropriate tax had been issued in accordance with regulations.

(3) (a) The Minister may by order vary the percentage of consideration which may, in accordance with subsection (1), be treated as tax deductible under section 12 and may by order make corresponding variations in the percentage of total consideration specified in section 10(7) on which tax is chargeable on the delivery of livestock and in the percentage of value specified in section 15(4)(b) on which tax is chargeable on the importation of livestock.

(b) The Minister may by order amend or revoke an order under this subsection, including this paragraph,

(c) An order under this subsection shall be laid before Dáil Éireann as soon as may be after it has been made and, if a resolution annulling the order is passed by Dáil Éireann within the next twenty-one days on which Dáil Éireann has sat after the order is laid before it, the order shall be annulled accordingly, but without prejudice to the validity of anything previously done thereunder.

(4)   For the purposes of this section "farming or fishing" does not include-

(a)   the operation of a nursery or garden for the sale of produce,

(b)   commercial production of poultry or eggs,

(c)   fur farming, or

(d)   fish farming,

by a person other than a person to whom paragraph (c) or (d) of section 8(3) applies.

(With effect from 1 November 1972)

Finance Act 1973

90.   The Principal Act is hereby amended as specified in column (3) of the Tenth Schedule to this Act.

TENTH SCHEDULE
AMENDMENT OF ENACTMENTS

Number and Year (1)	Short Title (2)	Amendment (3)
No. 22 of 1972	Value-Added Tax Act, 1972	In section 13, in subsection (2)(b)," tax were chargeable in respect of the delivery or rendering " shall be inserted after " another accountable person "; and the following subsection shall be substituted for subsection (4)- "(4) For the purposes of this section farming does not include fur farming by a person other than a person to whom paragraph (c) or (d) of section 8(3) applies "

(With effect from 3 September 1973)

Finance Act 1975

52.   Section 13 of the Value-Added Tax Act, 1972, is hereby amended by the insertion, after subsection (2), of the following subsection:

"(2A)   (a)   With effect on and from the 1st day of March, 1975, notwithstanding any other provision of this Act or of regulations-

(i)   subsection (1) and section 17(2) shall not apply to deliveries of live cattle, and

(ii)   dealers in livestock and auctioneers (including persons operating a livestock mart) shall not be treated as persons required under this section to issue invoices in respect of the delivery of live cattle.

(b)   (i)   This subsection shall expire at the end of the appointed day.

(ii)   in this paragraph 'the appointed day' means the 30th day of June, 1976, or such day before that day as the Minister may specify by order under this paragraph.

(iii)   The reference in paragraph (c) of subsection (3) to an order under that subsection shall be construed as including a reference to an order under this paragraph and paragraph (c) shall have effect accordingly.".

(With effect from 1 March 1975)

Finance Act 1976

81. (1)   The enactment mentioned in column (2) of Part I of the Fifth Schedule to this Act is hereby repealed to the extent specified in column (3) of that Schedule.

(2)   The enactment mentioned in column (2) of Part II of the Fifth Schedule to this Act is hereby repealed to the extent specified in column (3) of that Schedule.

(3)   (a)   Subsection (1) of this section shall be deemed to have come into operation on the 6th day of April, 1976.

(b)   Subsection (2) of this section shall be deemed to have come into operation on the 1st day of March, 1976.

FIFTH SCHEDULE

Enactments Repealed
PART II

| No. 22 of 1972 | Value-Added Tax Act, 1972 | Section 13 |

(With effect from 1 March 1976)

Value Added Tax (Amendment) Act 1978

Remission of tax on goods exported, etc.

12.   The following section shall be inserted after section 12A (inserted by this Act) of the Principal Act:

"13.   (1)   Regulations may make provision for remitting or repaying, subject to such conditions (if any) as may be specified in the regulations or as the Revenue Commissioners may impose, the tax chargeable in respect of the supply of goods, or of such goods as may be specified in the regulations, in cases where the Revenue Commissioners are satisfied-

(a)   that the goods have been or are to be exported,

(b)   that the goods have been shipped on board an aircraft or ship proceeding to a place outside the State,

(c)   that the goods are, or are to be used in, a fishing vessel used or to be used for the purposes of commercial sea fishing.

(2)   Regulations may make provision for remitting or repaying, subject to such conditions (if any) as may be specified in the regulations or as the Revenue Commissioners may impose, the tax chargeable in respect of the supply of all or any one or more (as may be specified in the regulations) of the following services:

(a)   services directly linked to the export of goods or the transit of goods from a place outside the State to another place outside the State,

(b)   the repair, maintenance and hiring of plant or equipment used in a vessel or an aircraft specified in paragraph (v) of the Second Schedule,

(c)   the repair, maintenance and hiring of a vessel used, or of plant or equipment used in a vessel used, for the purposes of commercial sea fishing.

(3)   (a)   The Revenue Commissioners shall, in accordance with regulations, repay to a person to whom this subsection applies, deductible tax chargeable in respect of supplies of goods or services to him or in respect of goods imported by him.

(b)   This subsection applies to a person who shows to the satisfaction of the Revenue Commissioners that he carries on a business outside the State and that he supplies no goods or services in the State.

(c)   In this subsection "**deductible tax**", in relation to a person to whom this subsection applies, means tax chargeable in respect of goods or services used by him for the purposes of any business carried on by him to the extent that such tax would be deductible by him under section 12 if the business were carried on by him within the State but does not include tax chargeable in respect of goods for supply within the State or for hiring out for utilisation within the State.

(4)   Where imported goods chargeable with tax under section 2(1)(b) are supplied while warehoused and before the tax becomes due, the supply shall be disregarded for the purposes of this Act if it is made under an agreement

in writing requiring the purchaser to account for such tax and, in such a case, the purchaser shall be deemed, for the purposes of sections 15 and 27(4), to have imported the goods.

(5)   Where goods chargeable with a duty of excise on their manufacture or production are supplied while warehoused and before payment of the duty, then-

(a)   if there is more than one such supply, any but the last such supply shall be disregarded for the purposes of this Act,

(b)   the amount on which tax is chargeable in relation to such supply or the last such supply (as the case may be) shall be increased by the amount of the duty, and

(c)   the tax chargeable on the supply shall be payable, together with the duty, by the person by whom the duty is paid:

Provided that regulations may-

(a)   make provision for enabling goods which are supplied as aforesaid and are so supplied to a registered person for the purposes of a business carried on by him to be removed from warehouse, subject to such conditions or restrictions as may be specified in the regulations or as the Revenue Commissioners may impose, without payment of the tax on the supply and

(b)   provide that tax be accounted for by him in the return, made by him under section 19(3), in respect of the taxable period during which the goods are so removed.".

(With effect from 1 March 1979)

Finance Act 1982

82.   Section 13 of the Principal Act (inserted by the Act of 1978) is hereby amended by the deletion of subsections (4) and (5).

(With effect from 1 September 1982)

Finance Act 1985

45.   Section 13 (inserted by the Act of 1978) of the Principal Act is hereby amended by the deletion in subsection (3)(c) of "or for hiring out for utilisation within the State".

(With effect from 30 May 1985)

Finance Act 1987

43.   Section 13 (inserted by the Act of 1978) of the Principal Act is hereby
      amended by the insertion in subsection (3)(c) after "within the State",
      where that secondly occurs, of "or in respect of means of transport for
      hiring out for utilisation within the State".

(With effect from 9 July 1987)

Finance Act 1992

176. Section 13 (inserted by the Act of 1978) of The Principal Act is hereby
      amended-

      (a)   in paragraph (c) of subsection (3) by the insertion of "(including
            any flat-rate addition)" after "means tax chargeable",

      (b)   by the insertion of the following subsection after subsection (3):

            "(3A) (a)   The Revenue Commissioners shall, in accordance
                        with regulations, repay to a person to whom this
                        subsection applies the residual tax included in
                        the consideration for supply of a new means of
                        transport, where such new means of transport is
                        subsequently dispatched or transported to another
                        Member State.

                  (b)   This subsection applies to a person not entitled to
                        a deduction under section 12 of the tax borne or
                        paid by him on the purchase, intra-Community
                        acquisition or importation of the goods in
                        question.".

(With effect from 1 January 1993)

Finance Act 1997

106. Section 13 of the Principal Act is hereby amended-

      (a)   by the insertion of the following subsections after subsection (1)

            "(1A) The Revenue Commissioners shall, subject to and in
                  accordance with regulations (if any), allow the application
                  of paragraph (b) of subsection (1) of section 11 (hereafter
                  referred to in this section as 'zero-rating') to-

                  (a)   the supply of a traveller's qualifying goods, and

                  (b)   the supply of services by a VAT refunding agent
                        consisting of the service of repaying the tax
                        claimed by a traveller in relation to the supply of
                        a traveller's qualifying goods or the procurement
                        of the zero-rating of the supply of a traveller's
                        qualifying goods,

                  where they are satisfied that the supplier of the goods or
                  services as the case may be-

(i)   has proof that the goods were exported by or on behalf of the traveller by the last day of the third month following the month in which the supply takes place,

(ii)   repays, within such time limit as may be specified in regulations, any amount of tax paid by the traveller and claimed by that person in respect of goods covered by the provisions of paragraph (i),

(iii)   notifies the traveller in writing of any amount (including the mark-up) charged by the supplier for procuring the repayment of the amount claimed or arranging for the zero-rating of the supply,

(iv)   uses, as the exchange rate in respect of monies being repaid to a traveller in a currency other than the currency of the State, the latest selling rate recorded by the Central Bank of Ireland for the currency in question at the time of the repayment, or where there is an agreement with the Revenue Commissioners for a method to be used in determining the exchange rate, the exchange rate obtained using the said method, and

(v)   has made known to the traveller such details concerning the transaction as may be specified in regulations.

(1B)   Regulations may make provision for the authorisation, subject to certain conditions, of taxable persons or a class of taxable persons for the purposes of zero-rating of the supply of a traveller's qualifying goods or to operate as a VAT refunding agent in the handling of a repayment of tax on the supply of a traveller's qualifying goods and such regulations may provide for the cancellation of such authorisation and matters consequential to such cancellation.

(1C)   A VAT refunding agent acting as such may, in accordance with regulations, treat the tax charged to the traveller on the supply of that traveller's qualifying goods as tax that is deductible by the agent in accordance with paragraph (a) of subsection (1) of section 12, provided that that agent fulfils the conditions set out in subsection (1A) in respect of that supply.",

and

(b) by the insertion of the following subsections after subsection (3A):

"(3B) In this section-

'**traveller**' means a person whose domicile or habitual residence is not situated within the Community and includes a person who is normally resident in the Community but who, at the time of the supply of the goods intends to take up residence outside the Community in the near future and for a period of at least 12 consecutive months;

'**traveller's qualifying goods**' means goods, other than goods transported by the traveller for the equipping, fuelling and provisioning of pleasure boats, private aircraft or other means of transport for private use, which are supplied within the State to a traveller and which are exported by or on behalf of that traveller by the last day of the third month following the month in which the supply takes place;

'**VAT refunding agent**' means a person who supplies services which consist of the procurement of a zero-rating or repayment of tax in relation to supplies of a traveller's qualifying goods.

(3C) For the purposes of this section, and subject to the direction and control of the Revenue Commissioners, any power, function or duty conferred or imposed on them may be exercised or performed on their behalf by an officer of the Revenue Commissioners.".

(With effect from 1 July 1997)

Finance Act 1998

113. Section 13 of the Principal Act is hereby amended in subsection (3)(c) by the substitution of "or in respect of motor vehicles (as defined in section 12(3)(b))" for "or in respect of means of transport".

(With effect from 27 March 1998)

Finance Act 1999

132. Section 13 of the Principal Act is hereby amended in paragraph (iii) of subsection (1A) (inserted by the Act of 1997) by the insertion after "the supply," of "and where an amount so notified is expressed in terms of a percentage or a fraction, such percentage or fraction shall relate to the tax remitted or repayable under this subsection,".

(With effect from 1 May 1999)

Finance Act 2002

105. Section 13 of the Principal Act is amended in subsection (3)(b) by adding "other than services for which in accordance with section 8(2) the person who receives them is solely liable for the tax chargeable" after "in the State".

(With effect from 25 March 2002)

Finance Act 2008

109. With effect from 1 July 2008 in each provision of the Principal Act specified in the first column of Schedule 4 for the words set out in the second column of that Schedule at that entry (in each place where those words occur in the provision concerned) there is substituted the words set out at the corresponding entry in the third column of that Schedule.

Schedule 4
Miscellaneous Amendments Relating to the Amendment of the Definition of Taxable Person

Amendments to Value-Added Tax Act 1972

Provision of Value-Added Tax Act 1972	Words to be replaced	Words to be inserted
Section 13	of taxable persons	of accountable persons

(With effect from 1 July 2008)

Finance (No. 2) Act 2008

99. The enactments specified in Schedule 6 —

(a)   are amended to the extent and in the manner specified in paragraphs 1 to 6 of that Schedule, and

(b)   apply and come into operation in accordance with paragraph 7 of that Schedule.

SCHEDULE 6
Miscellaneous Technical Amendments in Relation to Tax

4.   The Value-Added Tax Act 1972 is amended —

(j)   in section 13(3)(b) by substituting "paragraph (f) or (g) of subsection (1A), or subsection (1B)(b) or (2), of section 8" for "section 8(2)".

(With effect from 24 December 2008)

Section 13A

Finance Act 1993

Supplies to, and intra-Community acquisitions and imports by, certain taxable persons

90. The Principal Act is hereby amended by the insertion of the following section after section 13:

"13A. (1)   For the purposes of this section and paragraph (via) of the Second Schedule-

'authorised person' means a qualifying person who has been authorised in accordance with subsection (3);

'qualifying person' means a taxable person whose turnover from his supplies of goods made in accordance with subparagraph (a) (1) or (b) of paragraph (i) of the Second Schedule amounts to, or is likely to amount to, 75 per cent of his total annual turnover from his supplies of goods and services:

Provided that the turnover from a supply of goods to a taxable person which are subsequently leased back from that person is excluded from the total annual turnover for the purposes of establishing whether the person is a qualifying person;

'qualifying goods' means all taxable goods excluding motor vehicles within the meaning of section 12(3)(b) and petrol;

'qualifying services' means all taxable services excluding the provision of food or drink, accommodation, other personal services, entertainment services or the hire of motor vehicles within the meaning of section 12(3)(b).

(2)   A person who wishes to become an authorised person shall-

(a)   complete such application form as may be provided by the Revenue Commissioners for that purpose,

(b)   certify the particulars shown on such form to be correct, and

(c)   submit to the Revenue Commissioners the completed and certified application form, together with such further information in support of the application as may be requested by them.

(3)   (a)   Where a person has furnished the particulars required under subsection (2), the Revenue

Commissioners shall, where they are satisfied that
he is a qualifying person, issue to that person in
writing an authorisation certifying him to be an
authorised person.

(b)   An authorisation issued in accordance with
paragraph (a) shall be valid for such period as may
be determined by the Revenue Commissioners.

(c)   Where a person who has been authorised in
accordance with paragraph (a) ceases to be a
qualifying person, he shall, by notice in writing,
advise the Revenue Commissioners accordingly
not later than the end of the taxable period during
which he ceased to be a qualifying person.

(d)   The Revenue Commissioners shall, by notice in
writing, cancel an authorisation issued to a person
in accordance with paragraph (a) where they are
satisfied that he is no longer a qualifying person
and such cancellation shall have effect from the
date specified in the notice.

(4)   An authorised person shall furnish a copy of the
authorisation referred to in subsection (3) to each taxable
person in the State who supplies taxable goods or taxable
services to him.

(5)   A taxable person who supplies goods or services in
circumstances where the provisions of paragraph (via)
of the Second Schedule apply, shall, in addition to the
details to be included on each invoice, credit note or
other document required to be issued in accordance with
section 17, include on such invoice, credit note or other
document a reference to the number of the authorisation
issued to the authorised person in accordance with
subsection (3).

(6)   In relation to each consignment of goods to be imported
by an authorised person at the rate specified in section
11(1)(b) by virtue of paragraph (via) of the Second
Schedule the following conditions shall be complied
with:

(a)   a copy of the authorisation referred to at subsection
(3) shall be produced with the relevant customs
entry; and

(b)   the relevant customs entry shall incorporate-

(i)   a declaration by the authorised person, or by
his representative duly authorised in writing
for that purpose, that he is an authorised

person in accordance with this section for the purposes of paragraph (via) of the Second Schedule, and

(ii) a claim for importation at the rate specified in section 11(1)(b).

(7) For the purposes of subsections (1)(a)(ii) and (6)(a) of section 4, the tax charged at the rate specified in section 11(1)(b) by virtue of paragraph (via) of the Second Schedule shall be deemed to be tax which is deductible under section 12.

(8) Where an authorised person is in receipt of a service in respect of which, had the provisions of paragraph (via) of the Second Schedule not applied, tax would have been chargeable at a rate other than the rate specified in section 11(1)(b) and all or part of such tax would not have been deductible by him under section 12, then the authorised person shall, in relation to such service, be liable to pay tax as if he himself had supplied the service for consideration in the course or furtherance of his business to a person who is not an authorised person.

(9) For the purposes of this section, and subject to the direction and control of the Revenue Commissioners, any power, function or duty conferred or imposed on them may be exercised or performed on their behalf by an officer of the Revenue Commissioners.".

(With effect from 1 August 1993)

Finance Act 1996

95. Section 13A (inserted by the Act of 1993) of the Principal Act is hereby amended in subsection (1) by the insertion after "Second Schedule" in the definition of "qualifying person" of ", supplies of contract work where the place of supply is deemed to be a Member State other than the State and supplies of contract work made in accordance with paragraph (xvi) of the Second Schedule".

(With effect from 1 January 1996)

Finance Act 2001

192. Section 13A of the Principal Act (inserted by the Finance Act, 1993) is amended in subsection (1) by the substitution in the definition of "qualifying person" of "subparagraphs (a)(I), (aa), or (b)" for "subparagraph (a)(I) or (b)".

(With effect from 21 March 2001)

Finance Act 2008

109. With effect from 1 July 2008 in each provision of the Principal Act specified in the first column of Schedule 4 for the words set out in the second column of that Schedule at that entry (in each place where those words occur in the provision concerned) there is substituted the words set out at the corresponding entry in the third column of that Schedule.

Schedule 4
Miscellaneous Amendments Relating to the Amendment of the Definition of Taxable Person

Amendments to Value-Added Tax Act 1972

Provision of Value-Added Tax Act 1972	Words to be replaced	Words to be inserted
Section 13A	a taxable person	an accountable person
Section 13A	each taxable person	each accountable person
Section 13A	A taxable person	An accountable person

(With effect from 1 July 2008)

Section 14

Value Added Tax Act 1972
Payment based on cash receipts

14. (1) (a)   A person who satisfies the Revenue Commissioners that, taking one taxable period with another, he derives not less than 90 per cent of the total amount on which, but for this section, tax payable by him would be chargeable by virtue of section 2(1)(a), from the delivery of taxable goods to persons who are not registered persons or the rendering of taxable services to such persons, may, in accordance with regulations, be authorised to treat the moneys which he has received in respect of the delivery of taxable goods or rendering of taxable services as the consideration in respect of such delivery at goods or rendering of services and, during the period during which he is so authorised, references in this Act to consideration shall, in relation to the person so authorised, be construed, for the purposes of section 10(1) as references to moneys which he has actually received.

     (b)   A person, other than a person to whom paragraph (a) applies, may, in accordance with regulations, be authorised to treat the moneys which he has received in respect of the rendering of taxable services as the consideration for the rendering of such services, and during the period during which he is so authorised, references in this Act to consideration shall, in relation to services rendered by the person so authorised, be construed, for the purposes of section 10(1), as references to moneys which he has actually received.

   (2)   Where a person, who for any period of time is authorised under subsection (1) to treat the moneys which he has received for the delivery of goods or the rendering of services as the consideration for such delivery or rendering, ceases to be so authorised or ceases to be an accountable person, his liability for the taxable period in which the cesser occurs shall, in accordance with regulations, be adjusted by reference to the amounts, if any, due to him at the commencement and end of that period of time in respect of such deliveries and such rendering of services.

(With effect from 1 November 1972)

Value Added Tax (Amendment) Act 1978

Determination of tax due by reference to cash receipts

13.   The following section is hereby substituted for section 14 of the Principal Act:

"14.   (1)   (a)   A person who satisfies the Revenue Commissioners that, taking one period with another, he derives not less than 90 per cent of his turnover from the supply of taxable goods or services to persons who are not registered persons may, in accordance with regulations, be authorised to determine the amount of tax which becomes due by him during any taxable period (or part thereof) during which the authorisation has effect by reference to the amount of the moneys which he receives during such taxable period (or part thereof) in respect of supplies, whether made before, on or after the specified day, of taxable goods and services.

(b)   A person, other than a person to whom paragraph (a) applies, may, in accordance with regulations, be authorised to determine the amount of tax referable to taxable services which becomes due by him during any taxable period (or part thereof) during which the authorisation has effect by reference to the amount of the moneys which he receives during such taxable period (or part thereof) in respect of the supply, whether before, on or after the specified day, of taxable services.

(2)   The Revenue Commissioners may, in accordance with regulations, cancel an authorisation under paragraph (a) or (b) of subsection (1), and may, by regulations, exclude from the application of the said paragraphs (a) and (b) any tax due in respect of specified descriptions of supplies of goods or services and any moneys received in respect of such supplies.".

Transitional provisions

31.   (1)   ...

(b)   A person who, immediately before the commencement of this Act, was authorised to treat-

(i)   the moneys which he received in respect of the delivery of taxable goods or rendering of taxable services as the consideration in respect of such delivery of goods or rendering of services,

and

(ii)   the moneys he received in respect of the rendering of taxable services as the consideration for the rendering of such services,

shall he deemed (if he could be so authorised) to have been authorised to determine his tax liability in respect of supplies of goods and services or supplies of services, as the case may be, under section 14 of the Principal Act as amended by this Act.

(With effect from 1 March 1979)

Finance Act 1982

83.   Section 14 of the Principal Act (inserted by the Act of 1978) is hereby amended by the insertion in subsection (1)(b) after "of taxable services" of "(including services which, if they were supplied in such taxable period, would be taxable services)".

(With effect from 1 September 1982)

Finance Act 1992

177. (1)   Section 14 of the Principal Act is hereby amended-

(a)   in subsection 1-

(i)   by the substitution of "taxable supplies" for "the supply of taxable goods or services" and

*(ii)   by the deletion of paragraph (b),

(b)   by the insertion of the following subsection after subsection (1):

"(1A) Where an authorisation to which subsection (1) relates has not been cancelled under subsection (2), then-

(a) the rate of tax due by the person concerned in respect of a supply shall be the rate of tax chargeable at the time the goods or services are supplied,

(b) if tax on a supply has already been due and payable under any other provisions of this Act prior to the issue of such authorisation, tax shall not be due again in respect of any such supply as a result of the application of subsection (1), and

(c) if no tax is due or payable on a supply made prior to the issue of such authorisation, tax shall not be due in respect of any such supply as a result of the application of subsection (1).",

*(c)   in subsection (2) by the deletion of "or (b)", and of "and (b)",

and

(d)   by the insertion of the following subsection after subsection (2):

"(3)   This section shall not apply to tax provided for by subsection (1)(b) of section 2".

*(2)   section 14 of the Principal Act is hereby further amended in subsection (3) (inserted by subsection (1) of this section) by the insertion after "subsection (1)(b)" of "or (1A)".

(With effect from 28 May 1992 except * from 1 January 1993)

Finance Act 1994

97.   Section 14 (inserted by the Act of 1978) of the Principal Act is hereby amended-

(a)   by the substitution of the following subsection for subsection (1):

"(1)   A person who satisfies the Revenue Commissioners that-

(a)   taking one period with another, not less than 90 per cent of such person's turnover is derived from taxable supplies to persons who are not registered persons, or

(b)   the total consideration which such person is entitled to receive in respect of such person's taxable supplies has not exceeded and is not likely to exceed £250,000 in any continuous period of twelve months,

may, in accordance with regulations, be authorised to determine the amount of tax which becomes due by such person during any taxable period (or part thereof) during which the authorisation has effect by reference to the amount of the moneys which such person receives during such taxable period (or part thereof) in respect of taxable supplies.",

and

(b)   in subsection (2)-

(i)   by the deletion of "paragraph (a) of", and

(ii)   by the substitution of "that subsection" for "the said paragraphs (a)".

(With effect from 23 May 1994)

Finance Act 1995

131. Section 14 (inserted by the Act of 1978) of The Principal Act is hereby amended by the insertion of the following subsection after subsection (1A) (inserted by the Act of 1992):

"(1B) (a)   The Minister may, by order-

(i)   increase the amount specified in subsection (1)(b), or

(ii)   where an amount stands specified by virtue of an order under this paragraph, including an order relating to this subparagraph, further increase the amount so specified.

(b)   An order under paragraph (a) shall be laid before Dáil Éireann as soon as may be after it is made and, if a resolution annulling the order is passed by Dáil Éireann within the next twenty-one sitting days on which Dáil Éireann has sat after the order is laid before it, the order shall be annulled accordingly, but without prejudice to the validity of anything previously done thereunder.".

(With effect from 2 June 1995)

S.I. No. 316 of 1997
Value Added Tax (Elegibility to Determine Tax Due by Reference to Moneys Received) Order 1997

1.   This order may be acted as the Value Added Tax (Eligibility to determine tax due by reference to moneys received) Order 1997.

2.   The amount specified in Section 14(1)(b) (inserted by Section 97(a), Finance Act, 1994 (No. 13 of 1994)) of the Value Added Tax Act, 1972 (No. 22 of 1972), is hereby increased to £500,000.

(With effect from 17 July 1997)

Finance Act 2001

240. (1) (a)   Subject to subsection (2), in each provision specified in column (1) of Schedule 5 for the words or amount set out in column (2) of that Schedule at that entry there shall be substituted the words or amount set out at the corresponding entry in column (3) of that Schedule.

(b)   Where words are or an amount is mentioned more than once in a provision specified in column (1) of Schedule 5, then the substitution provided for by paragraph (a) shall apply as respects those words or that amount to each mention of those words or that amount in that provision.

SCHEDULE 5

PART 4

Value-Added Tax and related matters

Enactment amended (1)	Amount or words to be replaced (2)	Amount or words to be inserted (3)
Value-Added Tax Act, 1972 (No. 22 of 1972) (as amended): section 14(1)(b)	£500,000	€635,000

(With effect from 1 January 2002)

Finance Act 2007

87.   Section 14 of the Principal Act is amended with effect from 1 March 2007 in subsection (1) by substituting the following paragraph for paragraph (b):

"(b)   the total consideration which such person is entitled to receive in respect of such person's taxable supplies has not exceeded and is not likely to exceed €1,000,000 in any continuous person of 12 months".

(With effect from 1 March 2007)

Finance Act 2008

99.   Section 14 of the Principal Act is amended by inserting the following after subsection (2):

"(2A)   Where an authorisation has issued to any person in accordance with subsection (1) and that person fails to issue a credit note in accordance with section 17(3)(b) in respect of any supply where the consideration as stated in the invoice issued by that person for that supply is reduced or a discount is allowed, then, at the time when a credit note should have issued in accordance with section 17(7) –

(a)   such tax as is attributable to the reduction or discount shall be treated as being excluded from the application of subsection (1), and

(b)   that person shall be liable for that tax as if it were tax due in accordance with section 19 at that time.".

(With effect from 13 March 2008)

Section 15

Value Added Tax Act 1972

Charge of tax on imported goods

15. (1) Subject to subsection (2), sections 3 to 10, 12, 14, 16 to 19, 21 to 26, 32 to 37, 39, 40 and 42 shall not apply in tax provided for by section 2(1)(b) and, as an and from the specified day that tax shall be charged-

   (a) on goods of a kind specified in Part I of the Third Schedule at the rate of 5.26 per cent of the value of the goods,

   (b) on goods of a kind specified in Fourth Schedule at the rate of 30.26 per cent of the value of the goods, and

   (c) on all other goods at the rate of 16·37 per cent of the value of the goods.

   (2) (a) Subject to paragraph (b), tax as aforesaid shall not be charged on-

      (i) goods imported by a registered person for the purposes of his business, or

      (ii) goods of a kind specified in paragraphs (vi) to (viii) of the Second Schedule or the delivery of which would be an exempted activity.

   (b) Where a person imports goods of a kind specified in the Fourth Schedule, paragraph (a) shall not apply in relation to the goods unless the importer is a manufacturer of goods of the kind imported.

   (3) Subject to the foregoing provisions of this section, the provisions of the Customs Consolidation Act, 1876, and the enactments amending that Act and other enactments relating to customs (but excluding section 11 of the Finance (Miscellaneous Provisions) Act, 1958), shall apply to tax referred to in this section as if it were a duty of customs:

   Provided however that section 6 of the customs and Inland Revenue Act, 1879, and section 25(2) of the Finance Act, 1933, shall so apply only in relation to goods which are being reimported by the person who exports them.

   (4) (a) Subject to paragraph (b), the value of any goods for the purpose of this section shall be their value as ascertained in accordance with section 15 of, and the Third Schedule to, the Finance Act, 1952, increased by the amount of any customs duty payable thereon.

(b)   The value of livestock for the purposes of this section shall be 19.20 per cent of their value as ascertained in accordance with paragraph (a).

(With effect from 1 November 1972)

Finance Act 1973

90.   The Principal Act is hereby amended as specified in column (3) of the Tenth Schedule to this Act.

TENTH SCHEDULE
AMENDMENT OF ENACTMENTS

Number and Year (1)	Short Title (2)	Amendment (3)
No. 22 of 1972	Value-Added Tax Act, 1972	In section 15, in subsection (1), "specified in section 11(1)(a) on " shall be substituted for "of 5.26 per cent of "; " specified in section 11(1)(c) on " shall be substituted for "of 30.26 per cent of ", and " specified in section 11(1)(e) on " shall be substituted for "of 16.37 per cent of "; in subsection (2), " and (xii) to (xv)" shall be inserted after " (viii) " and in subsection (4)(b), " 14.81 " shall be substituted for " 19.20".

(With effect from 3 September 1973)

Finance Act 1976

55.   Section 15 of the Principal Act is hereby amended by the substitution of the following paragraph for paragraph (a) of subsection (4):

"(a)   Subject to paragraph (b), the value of any goods for the purpose of this section shall be their value as ascertained in accordance with Regulation 14 of the European Communities (Customs) Regulations, 1972, increased by the amount of any duty, levy or other tax (excluding value-added tax) payable in relation to their importation.".

*61.   In consequence of the amendments specified in sections 53 and 60 and the repeals specified in Part II of the Fifth Schedule, The Principal Act is hereby further amended as specified in Part II of the First Schedule.

FIRST SCHEDULE
AMENDMENT OF ENACTMENTS
PART II

Amendments Consequential on Certain Amendments of Value-Added Tax Act, 1972

Number and Year (1)	Short Title (2)	Amendment (3)
No. 22 of 1972	Value-Added Tax Act, 1972	In section 15-(a) in subsection (1), the following paragraph shall be substituted for paragraph (b) "(b)(i) on goods of a kind specified in Part I of the Fourth Schedule at the rate specified in section 11(1)(c)(i) on the value of the goods, (ii) Part II of the Fourth Schedule at the rate specified in section 11(1) (c)(ii) on the value of the goods, and" and (b) in subsection (4)(b), "10 per cent" shall be substituted or "14.81 per cent" (inserted by the Finance Act, 1973).

(With effect from 27 May 1976 except * from 1 March 1976)

Value Added tax (Amendment) Act 1978

14.   The following section is hereby substituted for section 15 of the Principal Act:

"15.   (1)   Subject to subsection (2), section 14 shall not apply to tax provided for by section 2(1)(b) and that tax shall be charged-

(a)   on goods of a kind specified in Part I of the Third Schedule at the percentage specified in section 11(1)(a) of the value of the goods.

(b)   on all other goods at the percentage specified in section 11(1)(c) of the value of the goods.

(2)   Tax as aforesaid shall not be charged on goods of a kind specified in paragraphs (xviii), (xx) and (xxi) of the First Schedule and paragraphs (v), (vii), (viii), (x), (xii) to (xv) and (xvii) to (xx) of the Second Schedule.

(3)   The value of imported goods for the purposes of this section shall be their value determined in accordance with the acts for the time being in force adopted by the institutions of the Community relating to the valuation of goods for customs purposes, modified by the substitution of references to the territory of the State for references to the customs territory of the Community, together with any taxes, duties and other charges levied either outside or, by reason of importation, within the State (except value-added tax) on the goods and not included in the determination.

(4)   Notwithstanding subsection (3), the value of imported livestock for the purposes of this section shall be 10 per cent of their value as ascertained in accordance with that subsection.

(5)   The Revenue Commissioners may, in accordance with regulations, remit or repay, if they think fit, the whole or part of the tax chargeable-

   (a)   on the importation of any goods which are shown to their satisfaction to have been previously exported,

   (b)   on the importation of any goods if they are satisfied that the goods have been or are to be re-exported,

   (c)   on the importation of any goods from the customs free airport by an unregistered person who shows to the satisfaction of the Revenue Commissioners that be has already borne tax on the goods.

(6)   Subject to the foregoing provisions of this section, the provisions of the Customs Consolidation Act, 1876, and of other law in force in the State relating to customs shall apply, with such exceptions and modifications (if any) as may be specified in regulations, to tax referred to in this section as if it were a duty of customs.

(7)   Regulations may-

   (a)   make provision for enabling goods imported by registered persons or by such classes of registered persons as may be specified in the regulations for the purposes of a business carried on by them to be delivered or removed, subject to such conditions or restrictions as may be specified in the regulations or as the Revenue Commissioners may impose, without payment of the tax chargeable on the importation, and

   (b)   provide that the tax be accounted for by the persons or classes of persons aforesaid in the return, made by them under section 19(3), in respect of the taxable period during which the goods are so delivered or removed.".

(With effect from 1 March 1979)

Finance Act 1982

84. (1)   Section 15 (inserted by the Act of 1978) of the Principal Act is hereby amended by-

* (a)   the substitution in subsection (2) of "(xva)" for "(xv)", and

(b)   the insertion after subsection (6) of the following subsection:

"(6A) Regulation 26 of the Value- Added Tax Regulations, 1979 (S.I. No. 63 of 1979), is hereby revoked and tax charged under section 2(1)(b) shall, in accordance with the provisions of the Customs Consolidation Act, 1876, and of other law in force in the State relating to customs, as applied to tax by subsection (6) and regulations thereunder, be paid in the manner and at the time that it would have been payable if that regulation had not been made.".

(2)   Subsection (1)(a) shall have, and be deemed to have had, effect as on and from the 1st day of May, 1982.

(With effect from 1 September 1982 except * from 1 May 1982)

Finance Act 1983

83.   Section 15 of the Principal Act is hereby amended-

(a)   in subsection (1), by the insertion after paragraph (a) of the following paragraph:

"(aa) on goods of a kind specified in the Sixth Schedule at the percentage specified in section 11(1)(aa) of the value of the goods, and",

and

(b)   in subsection (4), as respects importations on or after the 1st day of July, 1983, by the substitution of "8.69 per cent" for "10 per cent".

(With effect from 1 July 1983)

Finance Act 1984

88.   Section 15 of the Principal Act is hereby amended by the insertion after paragraph (aa) (inserted by the Act of 1983) of subsection (1) of the following paragraph:

"(aaa) on goods of a kind specified in the Seventh Schedule at the percentage specified in section 11(1)(aaa) of the value of the goods, and".

(With effect from 1 May 1984)

Finance Act 1985

46.   Section 15 (inserted by the Act of 1978) of the Principal Act is hereby amended-

   (a)   by the substitution of the following subsection for subsection (1):

   "(1)   Section 14 shall not apply to tax provided for by section 2(1)(b) and that tax shall, subject to subsection (2), be charged-

   (a)   on goods of a kind specified in the Sixth Schedule at the rate specified in section 11(1)(c) of the value of the goods,

   (b)   on livestock at the rate specified in section 11(1)(d) of the value of the goods, and

   (c)   on all other goods at the rate specified in section 11(1)(a) of the value of the goods.", and

   (b)   by the deletion of subsection (4).

   (With effect from 1 March 1985)

Finance Act 1990

104.   Section 15 (inserted by the Act of 1978) of The Principal Act is hereby amended-

   (a)   by the insertion in paragraph (b) of subsection (1) (inserted by the Act of 1985) after "livestock" of "and live grey hounds", and

   (b)   by the substitution in subsection (2) of "paragraph (xviii)" for "paragraphs (xviii), (xx) and (xxi)".

   (With effect from 1 January 1991)

Finance Act 1991

82.   Section 15 (inserted by the Act of 1978) of The Principal Act is hereby amended in subsection (1) (inserted by the Act of 1985) by the insertion of the following paragraph after paragraph (a):

   "(aa)   on goods of a kind specified in the Third Schedule at the rate specified in section 11(1)(bi) of the value of the goods,".

   (With effect from 1 March 1991)

Finance Act 1992

178. Section 15 (inserted by the Act of 1978) of The Principal Act is hereby amended-

(a)   by the substitution of the following subsection for subsection (1) (inserted by the Act of 1985):

"(1)   Tax shall be charged on the importation of goods at whichever of the rates specified in section 11(1) is the appropriate rate in respect of such goods.",

(b)   by the deletion of subsection (2),

and

(c)   by the insertion of the following subsection after subsection (5):

"(5A)   The Revenue Commissioners shall, in accordance with regulations, repay the tax chargeable on the importation of goods where the goods have been dispatched or transported:

(a)   to another Member State from outside the Community, and

(b)   to a person, other than an individual, who is not registered for value-added tax in that other Member State:

Provided that this subsection shall only apply where it is shown to the satisfaction of the Revenue Commissioners that the goods in question have been subject to value-added tax referred to in Council Directive No. 77/388/EEC of 17 May 1977 in that other Member State.".

(With effect from 28 May 1992)

S.I. No. 363 of 1995.
European Communities (Value-Added Tax) Regulations, 1995.

8.   Section 15 (inserted by the Act of 1978) of the Principal Act is hereby amended in subsection (3) by the insertion after "duties" of ", expenses resulting from the transport of the goods to another place of destination within the Community, if that destination is known at the time of the importation,".

(With effect from 1 January 1996)

Finance Act 1996

96.   Section 15 (inserted by the Act of 1978) of The Principal Act is hereby amended in subsection (3) by the insertion after "duties" of ", expenses resulting from the transport of the goods to another place of destination within the Community, if that destination is known at the time of the importation,".

(With effect from 1 January 1996)

Finance Act 2007

97. With effect from 1 January 2007 in each provision of the Principal Act specified in the first column of Schedule 3 for the words set out in the second column of that Schedule at that entry there is substituted the words set out at the corresponding entry in the third column of that Schedule.

Schedule 3
Miscellaneous Amendments Relating to Council Directive 2006/112/EC

Amendment of Value-Added Tax Act 1972

Provision of Principal Act	Words to be replaced	Words to be inserted
Section 15(5A) proviso	Council Directive No. 77/388/EEC of 17 May 1977	Council Directive No. 2006/112/EC of 28 November 2006

(with effect from 1 January 2007)

Section 15A

S.I. No. 413 of 1992.
European Communities (Value-Added Tax) Regulations, 1992.
Goods in transit

11. The Principal Act is hereby amended by the insertion of the following
     section after section 15:

"15A. (1)   Where-

(a)   goods from another Member State were imported
      into the State on or before the 31st day of December,
      1992, and

(b)   the tax referred to in section 2(1)(b) was not
      chargeable because the goods were, at the time
      of such importation, placed under one of the
      arrangements referred to in subparagraph (b) or
      (c) of paragraph 1 of Article 14, or subparagraph A
      of paragraph 1 of Article 16, of Council Directive
      No. 77/388/EEC of 17 May 1977, and

(c)   the goods are still subject to such an arrangement
      on the 1st day of January, 1993,

then, the provisions in force at the time the goods were
placed under the arrangement shall continue to apply in
relation to those goods until such time as, in accordance
with those provisions, the goods cease to be covered by
those arrangements.

(2)   (a)   Notwithstanding the definition of 'importation
            of goods' in section 1, an importation within the
            meaning of that definition shall be deemed to
            occur in the following cases:

(i)   where goods have been placed under an
       internal Community transit operation in
       another Member State before the 1st day of
       January, 1993, and the operation terminates
       in the State on or after that date;

(ii)   where goods referred to in subsection (1)
       cease to be covered by the arrangements
       referred to in that subsection;

(iii) where goods are returned to the State
       after the 1st day of January, 1993, being
       goods which were exported from the
       State before that date and imported into
       another Member State in accordance with

any of the arrangements referred to in subsection (1)(b).

(b)   In this subsection **'internal Community transit operation'** means the dispatch or transport of goods under cover of the internal Community transit arrangement referred to in paragraph 3 of Article 1 of Council Regulation (EEC) No. 222/77 of 13 December 1976, or under the cover of a T2L or equivalent document provided for in that Regulation and includes the sending of goods by post.

(3)   The tax referred to in section 2(1)(b) shall not be chargeable in the cases referred to in subsection (2) where-

(a)   the goods are dispatched or transported outside the Community,

(b)   the goods are other than a means of transport and are being returned to the State and to the person who exported them from the State, or

(c)   the goods are a means of transport which was acquired or imported before the 1st day of January, 1993, and in respect of which value-added tax referred to in Council Directive No. 77/388/EEC of 17 May 1977 has been paid in a Member State and that value-added tax has not subsequently been refunded because of exportation from that Member State of the means of transport:

Provided that this paragraph shall be deemed to be complied with where it is shown to the satisfaction of the Revenue Commissioners that the first use of the means of transport was prior to the 1st day of January, 1985, or that the tax due does not exceed £100.

(4)   In this section, references to subparagraph (b) or (c) of paragraph 1 of Article 14, and to subparagraph A of paragraph 1 of Article 16, of Council Directive No. 77/388/EEC of 17 May 1977 shall be deemed to be references to those provisions of the Directive immediately prior to their amendment by Council Directive 91/680/EEC of 16 December 1991.".

(With effect from 1 January 1993)

Finance Act 2001

240. (1)   (a)   Subject to subsection (2), in each provision specified in column (1) of Schedule 5 for the words or amount set out in column (2) of that Schedule at that entry there shall be substituted the words or amount set out at the corresponding entry in column (3) of that Schedule.

        (b)   Where words are or an amount is mentioned more than once in a provision specified in column (1) of Schedule 5, then the substitution provided for by paragraph (a) shall apply as respects those words or that amount to each mention of those words or that amount in that provision.

SCHEDULE 5

PART 4

Value-Added Tax and related matters

Enactment amended (1)	Amount or words to be replaced (2)	Amount or words to be inserted (3)
Value-Added Tax Act, 1972 (No. 22 of 1972) (as amended): section 15A(3)(c)	£100	€130

(With effect from 1 January 2002)

Section 15B

S.I. No. 448 of 1994.
European Communities (Value-Added Tax) Regulations, 1994.

Goods in transit (additional provisions)

4. The Principal Act is hereby amended by the insertion of the following section after section 15A:

"Goods in transit (additional provisions)

15B. (1) Where-

    (a) goods from a new Member State were imported into the State on or before the 31st day of December, 1994, and

    (b) the tax referred to in section 2(1)(b) was not chargeable because the goods were, at the time of such importation, placed-

        (i) under an arrangement for temporary importation with total exemption from customs duty, or

        (ii) under one of the arrangements referred to in clauses (a), (b), (c) and (d) of subparagraph B of paragraph 1 of Article 16, of Council Directive No. 77/388/EEC of 17 May 1977, and

    (c) the goods are still subject to such an arrangement on the 1st day of January, 1995,

    then, the provisions in force at the time the goods were placed under that arrangement shall continue to apply until the goods leave that arrangement on or after the 1st day of January, 1995.

  (2) (a) Where-

        (i) goods were placed under the common transit procedure or under another customs transit procedure in a new Member State on or before the 31st day of December, 1994, and

        (ii) those goods have not left the procedure concerned before the 1st day of January, 1995,

        then the provisions in force at the time the goods were placed under that procedure shall continue to apply until the goods leave that procedure on or after the 1st day of January, 1995.

(b)   In this subsection 'common transit procedure' means the procedure approved by the Council of the European Communities by Council Decision No. 87/415/EEC of 15 June 1987(2), approving the Convention done at Interlaken on the 20th day of May, 1987, between the European Community, the Republic of Austria, the Republic of Finland, the Republic of Iceland, the Kingdom of Norway, the Kingdom of Sweden and the Swiss Confederation on a common transit procedure, the text of which is attached to that Council Decision.

(3)   Where goods were in free circulation in a new Member State prior to entry into the State, an importation into the State shall be deemed to occur in the following cases:

(a)   the removal, including irregular removal, within the State of the goods referred to in subsection (1) from the arrangement referred to in subparagraph (i) of paragraph (b) of that subsection;

(b)   the removal, including irregular removal, within the State of the goods referred to in subsection (1) from the arrangement referred to in subparagraph (ii) of paragraph (b) of that subsection;

(c)   the termination within the State of any of the procedures referred to in subsection (2).

(4)   An importation into the State shall be deemed to occur when goods, which were supplied within a new Member State on or before the 31st day of December, 1994, and which were not chargeable to a value-added tax in that new Member State, because of their exportation from that new Member State, are used in the State on or after the 1st day of January, 1995, and have not been imported before that date.

(5)   The tax referred to in section 2(1)(b) shall not be chargeable where-

(a)   the imported goods referred to in subsections (3) and (4) are dispatched or transported outside the enlarged Community,

(b)   the imported goods referred to in paragraph (a) of subsection (3) are other than means of transport and are being returned to the new Member State from which they were exported and to the person who exported them, or

(c)   the imported goods referred to in paragraph (a) of subsection (3) are means of transport which were acquired in or imported into a new Member State before the 1st day of January, 1995 in accordance with the general conditions of taxation in force on the domestic market of that new Member State and which have not been subject by reason of their exportation to any exemption from or refund of a value-added tax in that new Member State:

Provided that this paragraph shall be deemed to be complied with where it is shown to the satisfaction of the Revenue Commissioners that the first use of the means of transport was prior to the 1st day of January, 1987, or that the tax due does not exceed £100.

(6)   The provisions of section 15A shall not apply to goods imported or deemed to be imported from a new Member State

(7)   (a)   In this section-

'**the enlarged Community**' means the Community after the accession of the new Member States;

'**new Member State**' means the Republic of Austria, the Republic of Finland (excluding the Aland Islands) or the Kingdom of Sweden.

(b)   A word or expression that is used in this section and is also used in Council Directive No. 94/76/ EC of 22 December 1994 has, unless the contrary intention appears, the meaning in this section that it has in that Council Directive.".

(With effect from 1 January 1995)

Finance Act 2004

62.   Section 15B (inserted by the European Communities (Value-Added Tax) Regulations 1994 (S.I. 448 of 1994)) of the Principal Act is amended –

(a)   by substituting "before the date of accession" for "on or before the 31st day of December, 1994" in each place where it occurs,

(b)   by substituting "date of accession" for "1st day of January, 1995" in each place where it occurs,

(c)   in subsection (5) by deleting the proviso to paragraph (c),

(d)   by inserting the following after subsection (5):

"(5A) Subsection (5)(c) shall be deemed to be complied with where it is shown to the satisfaction of the Revenue Commissioners that –

(i)   the date of the first use of the means of transport was before 1 January 1987 in the case of means of transport entering the State from the Republic of

Austria, the Republic of Finland (excluding the Åland Islands) or the Kingdom of Sweden,

(ii) the date of the first use of the means of transport was before 1 May 1996 in the case of means of transport entering the State from the Czech Republic, the Republic of Estonia, the Republic of Cyprus, the Republic of Latvia, the Republic of Lithuania, the Republic of Hungary, the Republic of Malta, the Republic of Poland, the Republic of Slovenia or the Slovak Republic, or

(iii) the tax due by reason of the importation does not exceed €130.",

and

(e) in paragraph (7)(a) —

(i) by inserting the following definition before the definition of "the enlarged Community":

" 'date of accession' means 1 January 1995 in respect of the Republic of Austria, the Republic of Finland (excluding the Åland Islands) and the Kingdom of Sweden or 1 May 2004 in respect of the Czech Republic, the Republic of Estonia, the Republic of Cyprus, the Republic of Latvia, the Republic of Lithuania, the Republic of Hungary, the Republic of Malta, the Republic of Poland, the Republic of Slovenia and the Slovak Republic;",

and

(ii) by substituting the following for the definition of "new Member State":

" 'new Member State' means any state referred to in the definition of 'date of accession' with effect from the relevant date.".

(With effect from 1 May 2004)

S.I. No. 663 of 2006
European Communities (Value-Added Tax) Regulations, 2006

5. Section 15B (inserted by the Finance Act 2004 (No. 8 of 2004)) of the Principal Act is amended —

(a) in subsection (5A)-

(i) by substituting "the Slovak Republic," for "the Slovak Republic, or" in subparagraph (ii), and

(ii) by inserting the following after subparagraph (ii):

"(iia)   the date of the first use of the means of transport
was before 1 January 1999 in the case of means of
transport entering the State from the Republic of
Bulgaria or Romania, or",

and

(b)   in the definition of 'date of accession' in subsection (7)(a) by
inserting "or 1 January 2007 in respect of the Republic of Bulgaria
and Romania" after "Slovak Republic"..

Finance Act 2007

88.   With effect from 1 January 2007, section 15B is amended —

(a)   in subsection (5A) —

(i)   by substituting "the Slovak Republic," for "the Slovak
Republic, or" in subparagraph (ii), and

(ii)   by inserting the following after subparagraph (ii):

"(iia)   the date of the first use of the means of transport
was before 1 January 1999 in the case of means of
transport entering the State from the Republic of
Bulgaria or Romania, or",

and

(b)   in the definition of 'date of accession' in subsection (7)(a) by
inserting "or 1 January 2007 in respect of the Republic of Bulgaria
and Romania" after "Slovak Republic".

98.   The European Communities (Value-Added Tax) Regulations 2006
(S.I. No. 663 of 2006) shall, with effect from 1 January 2007, be deemed
never to have had effect and are revoked.

97.   With effect from 1 January 2007 in each provision of the Principal Act
specified in the first column of Schedule 3 for the words set out in the
second column of that Schedule at that entry there is substituted the
words set out at the corresponding entry in the third column of that
Schedule.

Schedule 3
Miscellaneous Amendments Relating To Council Directive 2006/112/EC

Amendment of Value-Added Tax Act 1972

Provision of Principal Act	Words to be replaced	Words to be inserted
Section 15B(1)(b)(ii)	clauses (a), (b), (c) and (d) of subparagraph B of paragraph 1 of Article 16, of Council Directive No. 77/388/EEC of 17 May 1977	Article 156(1) of Council Directive No. 2006/112/ EC of 28 November 2006

(With effect 1 January 2007)

Section 16

Value-Added Tax Act 1972

Duty to keep records

16. (1) Every accountable person shall, in accordance with regulations, keep full and true records of all transactions which affect or may affect his liability to tax.

(2) Every person, other than an accountable person, who delivers goods in the course of business or renders services in the course of business shall keep all invoices issued to him in connection with the delivery of goods or the rendering of services to him for the purpose of such business.

(3) Records and invoices kept by a person pursuant to this section and any books, credit notes, debit notes, receipts, accounts, vouchers, bank statements or other documents whatsoever which relate to the delivery of goods by the person or the rendering of services by the person and are in the power, possession or procurement of the person and, in the case of any such book, invoice, credit note, debit note, receipt, account, voucher or other document which has been issued by the person to another person, any copy thereof which is in the power, possession or procurement of the person shall be retained in his power, possession or procurement for a period of six years from the date of the latest transaction to which the records or invoices or any of the other documents relate:

Provided that this section shall not require the retention of records or invoices or any of the other documents in respect of which the Revenue Commissioners notify the person concerned that retention is not required, nor shall it apply to the books and papers of a company which have been disposed of in accordance with section 305(1) of the Companies Act, 1963.

(With effect from 1 November 1972)

Value-Added Tax (Amendment) Act 1978

30. (1) The enactment mentioned in column (2) of the First Schedule is hereby repealed to the extent specified in column (3) of that Schedule.

(2) In consequence of the amendments of the Principal Act specified in this Act and of the repeals specified in the First Schedule, the Principal Act is hereby further amended by the substitution of the word or expression mentioned in column (3) of the Second Schedule at any reference number for the word or expression mentioned in column (2) of that Schedule at that reference number wherever it occurs in the provision of the Principal Act mentioned in column (4) of that Schedule at that reference number.

<h1 style="text-align:center">SECOND SCHEDULE</h1>
Consequential Amendments

Reference Number (1)	Existing word or expression (2)	Substituted word or expression (3)	Provision of Principal Act (4)
13	"delivery of goods by the person or the rendering of services"	"supply of goods or services	Section 16(3)
17	"delivery of goods or the rendering of services"	"supply of goods or services"	Sections 16(2)
22	"delivers goods in the course of business or renders services in the course of business"	"supplies goods or services in the course or furtherance of any business"	Section 16(2)
25	"accountable person" except where preceded by the word "an"	"taxable person"	Sections 16(1)
26	"an accountable person"	"a taxable person"	Sections 16(2)

(With effect from 1 March 1979)

<h2 style="text-align:center">Finance Act 1982</h2>

85. Section 16 of the Principal Act is hereby amended:

(a)   in subsection (2), by the insertion after "such business" of and, in respect of goods imported by him, copies, stamped on behalf of the Revenue Commissioners, of the relevant customs entries", and

(b)   in subsection (3)-

(i)   by the deletion of "and invoices",

(ii)   by the insertion after "any books" of "invoices, copies, stamped on behalf of the Revenue Commissioners, of customs entries", and

(iii)   by the insertion after "the supply of goods or services" of ", or the importation of goods,",

and the said subsections (other than the proviso to subsection (3)), as so amended, are set out in the Table to this section.

TABLE

(2)   Every person, other than a taxable person, who supplied goods or services in the course or furtherance of any business shall keep all invoices issued to him in connection with the supply of goods or services to him for the purpose of such business

and, in respect of goods imported by him, copies, stamped on behalf of the Revenue Commissioners, of the relevant customs entries.

(3)   Records kept by a person pursuant to this section and any books, invoices, copies, stamped on behalf of the Revenue Commissioners, customs entries, credit notes, debit notes, receipts, accounts, vouchers, bank statements or other documents whatsoever which relate to the supply of goods or services, or the importation of goods, by the person and are in his power, possession or procurement of the person, and in the case of any such book, invoice, credit note, debit note, receipt, account, voucher or other document which has been issued by the person to another person, any copy thereof which is in the power, possession or procurement of the person shall be retained in his power, possession or procurement for a period of six years from the date of the latest transaction to which the records or invoices or any of the other documents relate:

(With effect from 1 September 1982)

Finance Act 1992

179. Section 16 of the Principal Act is hereby amended-

*(a)   in subsection (2) by the deletion of "and, in respect of goods imported by him, copies, stamped on behalf of the Revenue Commissioners, of the relevant customs entries", and

(b)   in subsection 3-

(i)   by the deletion of ", stamped on behalf of the Revenue Commissioners,",

*(ii)   by the insertion, after "the supply of goods or services," of "the intra-Community acquisition of goods,",

**(iii) by the insertion after "invoices," where it first occurs of "monthly control statements,",

**(iv) by the substitution of "records, invoices, monthly control statements" for "records or invoices", and

**(v)   by the insertion after "invoice," of "monthly control statement,".

(With effect from 28 May 1992 except * from 1 January 1993 and ** from 1 November 1992)

Finance Act 1999

133. Section 16 of the Principal Act is hereby amended by the insertion of the following subsection after subsection (1): "(1A) Every person who trades in investment gold (within the meaning of section 6A) shall, in accordance with regulations, keep full and true records of that person's transactions in investment gold.".

(With effect from 1 January 2000)

Finance Act 2003

121. Section 16 of the Principal Act is amended—

(a)   in subsection (3) by inserting ", subject to subsection (4)," after "any copy thereof which is in the power, possession or procurement of the person shall", and

(b)   by inserting the following subsection after subsection (3):

"(4)   Notwithstanding the retention period specified in subsection (3) the following retention periods shall apply:

(a)   where a person acquires or develops immovable goods to which section 4 applies, the period for which that person shall retain records pursuant to this section in relation to that person's acquisition or development of those immovable goods shall be the duration that such person holds a taxable interest in such goods plus a further period of six years,

(b)   where a person exercises a waiver of exemption from tax in accordance with section 7, the period for which that person shall retain records pursuant to this section shall be the duration of the waiver plus a further period of six years.".

(With effect from 28 March 2003)

Finance Act 2007

89. Section 16 of the Principal Act is amended by inserting the following subsection after subsection (2):

"(2A)   (a)   A taxable person who claims a deduction of tax pursuant to section 12 in respect of qualifying accommodation as defined in section 12(3)(ca) shall retain full and true records in relation to the attendance by the delegate at the relevant qualifying conference, including the details referred to in section 12(3)(ca) issued to that taxable person by the person responsible for organising that conference.

(b)   A person responsible for organising a qualifying conference as defined in section 12(3)(ca) and to which section 12(3)(a)(i) relates shall keep full and true records of each such conference organised by that person.".

(With effect 2 April 2007)

Finance Act 2008

100. Section 16 of the Principal Act is amended —

    (a)   in subsection (1) by inserting "and entitlement to deductibility" after "tax", and

    (b)   by inserting the following after subsection (4):

        "(5)   The requirement to keep records in accordance with this section shall apply to records relating to —

            (a)   exercising and terminating a landlord's option to tax,

            (b)   a capital good record referred to in section 12E, and

            (c)   a joint option for taxation.".

*109. With effect from 1 July 2008 in each provision of the Principal Act specified in the first column of Schedule 4 for the words set out in the second column of that Schedule at that entry (in each place where those words occur in the provision concerned) there is substituted the words set out at the corresponding entry in the third column of that Schedule.

Schedule 4
Miscellaneous Amendments Relating to the Amendment of the Definition of Taxable Person

Amendments to Value-Added Tax Act 1972

Provision of Value-Added Tax Act 1972	Words to be replaced	Words to be inserted
Section 16	Every taxable person	Every accountable person
Section 16	a taxable person	an accountable person
Section 16	A taxable person	An accountable person
Section 16	that taxable person	that accountable person

141. The enactments specified in Schedule 8 —

    (a)   are amended to the extent and in the manner specified in paragraphs 1 to 6 of that Schedule, and

    (b)   apply and come into operation in accordance with paragraph 7 of that Schedule.

Schedule 8
Miscellaneous Technical Amendments in Relation to Tax

    (d)   in section 16(3) —

        (i)   by deleting "monthly control statements,",

        (ii)   by deleting "monthly control statement,", and

        (iii)   by deleting "monthly control statements" where it last occurs,

(With effect from 13 March 2008 except * with effect from 1 July 2008)

Section 17

Value Added Tax Act 1972

Invoices

17.　(1)　An accountable person who delivers goods or renders services to another accountable person in such circumstances that tax is chargeable shall issue to that other accountable person in respect of each such delivery of goods or rendering of services an invoice in such form and containing such particulars as may be specified by regulations.

　　　(2)　A person who in accordance with section 13(1) is required to issue an invoice in respect of the delivery of goods or the rendering of services to an accountable person shall, in respect of each delivery of goods or rendering of services of a kind specified in section 13(2), issue an invoice in the form and containing such particulars as may be specified by regulations if, but only if, the following conditions are fulfilled:

　　　　　(a)　the issue of an invoice is requested by the accountable person,

　　　　　(b)　the accountable person supplies the form for the purpose of the invoice and enters the appropriate particulars thereon, and

　　　　　(c)　the accountable person gives to the person by whom the goods are delivered or the services are rendered a copy of the invoice.

　　　(3)　Where, subsequent to the issue of an invoice by a person to an accountable person in accordance with subsection (1), the consideration as stated in the invoice is increased or reduced, or a discount is allowed, whichever of the following provisions is appropriate shall have effect:

　　　　　(a)　if the consideration is increased, the person shall issue to the accountable person another invoice in such form and containing such particulars as may be specified by regulations in respect of such increase,

　　　　　(b)　if the consideration is reduced or a discount is allowed, the person shall issue to the accountable person a document (in this Act referred to as a credit note) containing particulars of the reduction or discount in such form and containing such other particulars as may be specified by regulations, and the amount which the accountable person may deduct under section 12 shall, in accordance with regulations, be reduced by the amount of tax shown on the credit note.

(4)   Where, subsequent to the issue by a person to an accountable person of an invoice in accordance with subsection (2), the consideration as stated on the invoice is increased or reduced, or a discount is allowed, whichever of the following provisions is appropriate shall have effect:

(a)   if the consideration is increased and the conditions specified in subsection (2) are fulfilled in relation to the invoice hereinafter mentioned, the person shall issue to the accountable person another invoice in inspect of the increase in such form and containing such particulars as may be specified by regulations, and

(b)   if the consideration is reduced or a discount is allowed, the accountable person shall amend the invoice by reducing the consideration stated therein by the amount of the reduction or discount and by making, in accordance with regulations, a corresponding reduction in the amount deductible under section 12.

(5)   If an accountable person issues an invoice stating a greater amount of tax than that properly attributable to the consideration stated therein, or issues a credit note stating a lesser amount of tax than that properly attributable to the reduction in consideration or the discount stated therein, he shall be liable to pay to the Revenue Commissioners the excess amount of tax stated in the invoice or the amount of the deficiency of tax stated in the credit note.

(6)   A person who is not a registered person and who, otherwise than as required by section 13, issues an invoice stating an amount of tax shall, in relation to the amount of tax stated, be deemed, for the purposes of this Act, to be an accountable person and shall be liable to pay the amount to the Revenue Commissioners.

(7)   An invoice or credit note shall be issued within such time after the date of delivering goods or rendering services as may be specified by regulations and an amendment of an invoice pursuant to subsection (4)(b) shall be effected within such time as may be specified by regulations.

(8)   Notwithstanding anything in subsection (7), where payment for the delivery of goods or the rendering of services is made to a person, either in full or by instalments, before the delivery or rendering is completed, the person shall issue an invoice in accordance with subsection (1) or subsection (2), as may be appropriate, within such time after the date of actual receipt of the full payment or the instalment as may be specified by regulations.

(9)   (a)   Notwithstanding anything in subsection (3), where, subsequent to the issue to a registered person of an invoice in accordance with subsection (1), the consideration stated

in the invoice is reduced or a discount is allowed in such circumstances that, by agreement between the persons concerned, the amount of tax stated in the invoice is unaltered, paragraph (b) of the said subsection (3) shall not apply in relation to the person by whom the invoice was issued.

(b)   In a case to which paragraph (a) applies-

    (i)   the reduction or discount concerned shall not be taken into account in computing the liability to tax of the person making the reduction or allowing the discount,

    (ii)   subsection (5) shall not apply, and

    (iii)   the amount which the person in whose favour the reduction or discount is made or allowed may deduct in respect of the relevant transaction under section 12 shall not be reduced.

(10)   Where-

(a)   goods are delivered or services are rendered to a registered person by another registered person or goods or services of a kind specified in section 13(2) are delivered or rendered to such a person by a person who is not a registered person but who is required under section 13(1) to issue an invoice to a registered person, and

(b)   the person to whom the goods are delivered or the services are rendered issues to the other person, before the date on which an invoice is issued by that other person, a document (in this Act referred to as a settlement voucher) in such form and containing such particulars as may be specified by regulations, then, for the purposes of this Act-

    (i)   the person who issues the settlement voucher shall, if the person to whom it is issued accepts it, be deemed to have received from the person by whom the voucher was accepted an invoice containing the particulars set out in the voucher, and

    (ii)   the person to whom the settlement voucher is issued shall, if he accepts it, be deemed to have issued to the person to whom the voucher was received an invoice containing the particulars set out in the voucher.

(11)   Where a person who is entitled to receive a credit note under subsection (3)(b) from another person issues to that other person, before the date on which a credit note is issued by that

other person, a document (in this subsection referred to as a debit note) in such form and containing such particulars as may be specified by regulations, then, for the purposes of this Act-

(a) the person who issues the debit note shall, if the person to whom it is issued accepts it, be deemed to have received from the person by whom the note was accepted a credit note containing the particulars set out in such debit note, and

(b) the person to whom such debit note is issued shall, if he accepts it, be deemed to have issued to the person from whom the debit note was received a credit note containing the particulars set out in such debit note.

(12) (a) An accountable person shall-

(i) if requested in writing by another person and if the request states that the other person is entitled to repayment of tax under section 20(3), give to that other person in writing the particulars of the amount at tax chargeable to the accountable person in respect of the delivery by him of the goods specified in the request or of the rendering by him of the services so specified,

(ii) if requested in writing by another person and if the request states that that other person is entitled to repayment of tax under section 5(4), give to that other person in writing the particulars specified in regulations for the purposes of subsection (1) in respect of the services rendered by the accountable person to that other person that are specified in he request, and

(iii) if requested in writing by another person and if the request states that that other person is entitled to repayment of tax under section 20(2), give to that other person in writing the particulars at the amount of tax chargeable to the accountable person in respect of the delivery by him of the radio broadcasting reception apparatus and parts thereof that are specified in the request.

(b) A request under paragraph (a) shall be complied with by the person to whom it is given within thirty days after the date on which the request is received by him.

(With effect from 1 November 1972)

Finance Act 1973

90.   The Principal Act is hereby amended as specified in column (3) of the Tenth Schedule to this Act.

TENTH SCHEDULE
AMENDMENT OF ENACTMENTS

Number and Year (1)	Short Title (2)	Amendment (3)
No. 22 of 1972	Value-Added Tax Act, 1972	In section 17(1), " at any of the rates specified in section 11(1), including the rate of zero per cent," shall be inserted after " chargeable ".

(With effect from 3 September 1973)

Finance Act 1976

81.   (1)   The enactment mentioned in column (2) of Part I of the Fifth Schedule to this Act is hereby repealed to the extent specified in column (3) of that Schedule.

(2)   The enactment mentioned in column (2) of Part II of the Fifth Schedule to this Act is hereby repealed to the extent specified in column (3) of that Schedule.

(3)   (a)   Subsection (1) of this section shall be deemed to have come into operation on the 6th day of April, 1976.

(b)   Subsection (2) of this section shall be deemed to have come into operation on the 1st day of March, 1976.

FIFTH SCHEDULE
ENACTMENTS REPEALED
PART II

No. 22 of 1972	Value-Added Tax Act, 1972.	In section 17
		(a) subsections (2) and (4),
		(b) in subsection (6), the words, "otherwise than as required by section 13,",
		(c) in subsection (7), the words from and an amendment of an invoice to the end of the subsection,
		(d) in subsection (8), the words "or subsection (2), as may be appropriate," and
		(e) in subsection (10) (a), the words from or goods or services to "to a registered person".

(With effect from 1 March 1976)

Value Added Tax (Amendment) Act 1978

15.   Section 17 of the Principal Act is hereby amended-

(a)   by the insertion, after subsection (1), of the following subsection:

"(2)   A flat-rate farmer who, in accordance with section 12A, is required to issue an invoice in respect of the supply of agricultural produce or an agricultural service shall, in respect of each such supply, issue an invoice in the form and containing such particulars (in addition to those specified in the said section 12A) as may be specified by regulations if the following conditions are fulfilled:

(a)   the issue of an invoice is requested by a taxable person,

(b)   the taxable person provides the form for the purpose of the invoice and enters the appropriate particulars thereon, and

(c)   the taxable person gives to the flat-rate farmer a copy of the invoice,

but may issue the invoice if those conditions or any of them are not fulfilled:",

(b)   by the insertion, after subsection (3), of the following subsection:

"(4)   Where subsequent to the issue by a flat-rate farmer of an invoice in accordance with subsection (2), the consideration as stated on the invoice is increased or reduced, or a discount is allowed, whichever of the following provisions is appropriate shall have effect:

(a)   in case the consideration is increased, the flat-rate farmer shall issue another invoice (if the conditions referred to in subsection (2) are fulfilled in relation to it) containing particulars of the increase and of the flat-rate addition appropriate thereto and in such form and containing such other particulars as may be specified by regulations and such other invoice shall be deemed, for the purposes of section 12, to be issued in accordance with section 12A, but the said farmer may issue the invoice if the said conditions or any of them are not fulfilled,

(b)   in case the consideration is reduced or a discount is allowed, the flat-rate farmer shall, if the person to whom the supply was made is a taxable person, issue a document (in this section referred to as 'a farmer credit note') containing particulars of the reduction or discount and in such form and containing such other particulars as may be specified by regulations, and the amount which the taxable person may deduct under section 12 shall, in accordance with regulations, be reduced by an amount equal to the amount of the flat-rate addition appropriate to the amount of the reduction or discount.",

(c)   by the insertion after subsection (6) of the following subsection:

"(6A) (a)   If a person, other than a flat-rate farmer, issues an invoice stating an amount of flat-rate addition, he shall be liable to pay to the Revenue Commissioners as tax the amount of flat-rate addition stated and shall, in relation to such amount, be deemed, for the purposes of this Act, to be a taxable person.

(b)   If a flat-rate farmer issues an invoice stating an amount of flat-rate addition otherwise than in respect of an actual supply of agricultural produce or an agricultural service or in respect of such a supply but stating a greater amount of flat-rate addition than is appropriate to the supply, he shall be liable to pay to the Revenue Commissioners as tax the amount or the excess amount, as the case may be, of the flat-rate addition stated and shall, in relation to such amount or such excess amount, be deemed, for the purposes of this Act, to be a taxable person.

(c)   If a flat-rate farmer, in a case in which he is required to issue a farmer credit note under subsection (4)(b), fails to issue the credit note within the time allowed by regulations or issues a credit note stating a lesser amount of flat-rate addition than is appropriate to the reduction in consideration or the discount, he shall be liable to pay to the Revenue Commissioners as tax the amount of flat-rate addition which should have been stated on the credit note or the amount of the deficiency of flat-rate addition, as the case may be, and shall, in relation to such amount or such deficiency, be deemed, for the purposes of this Act, to be a taxable person.",

(d)   by the insertion in subsection (8), after "subsection (1)" of "or subsection (2), as may be appropriate,",

(e)   by the insertion in subsection (9), after paragraph (a), of the following paragraph-

"(aa)   Paragraph (a) shall not apply where the person who issued the invoice referred to therein was, at the time of its issue, a person authorised, in accordance with section

14(1), to determine his tax liability in respect of supplies of the kind in question by reference to the amount of moneys received.",

(f)   by the insertion in subsection (10)(a) after "another registered person" of "or agricultural produce or agricultural services are supplied to a registered person by a flat-rate farmer",

(g)   by the insertion after subsection (11) of the following subsection:

"(11A) Where a person who is entitled to receive a farmer credit note under subsection (4)(b) from another person issues to that other person, before the date on which a farmer credit note is issued by that other person, a document (in this section referred to as 'a farmer debit note') in such form and containing such particulars as may be specified by regulations, then, for the purposes of this Act-

(a)   the person who issues the debit note shall, if the person to whom it is issued accepts it, be deemed to have received from the person by whom the debit note was accepted a farmer credit note containing the particulars set out in such debit note, and

(b)   the person to whom such debit note is issued shall, if he accepts it, be deemed to have issued to the person from whom the debit note was received a farmer credit note containing the particulars set out in such debit note.",

(h)   by the insertion in subsection (12)(a)(ii) before "services", of "goods or ",

and

(i)   by the insertion of the following subsection after subsection (12):

"(13)   The provisions of this Act (other than this section) relating to credit notes and debit notes issued under subsections (3) and (11), respectively, of this section shall apply in relation to farmer credit notes and farmer debit notes as they apply in relation to the credit notes and debit notes aforesaid.".

30.   (1)   The enactment mentioned in column (2) of the First Schedule is hereby repealed to the extent specified in column (3) of that Schedule.

(2)   In consequence of the amendments of the Principal Act specified in this Act and of the repeals specified in the First Schedule, the Principal Act is hereby further amended by the substitution of the word or expression mentioned in column (3) of the Second

Schedule at any reference number for the word or expression mentioned in column (2) of that Schedule at that reference number wherever it occurs in the provision of the Principal Act mentioned in column (4) of that Schedule at that reference number.

SECOND SCHEDULE
Consequential Amendments

Reference Number (1)	Existing word or expression (2)	Substituted word or expression (3)	Provision of Principal Act (4)
1	"delivery"	"supply"	The definition of "exempted activity", and the definition of "taxable goods" in sections 17(12)(a)(i), 17(12)(a)(iii)
2	"rendering"	"supply"	The definition of "taxable services" in sections 17(12)(a)(i)
4	"rendered"	"supplied"	Sections 17(12)(a)(ii)
10	"delivery of goods or rendering of the service"	"supply of goods or services"	Section 17(1)
16	"delivery or rendering"	"supply"	Sections 17(8)
17	"delivery of goods or the rendering of services"	"supply of goods or services"	Sections 17(8)
20	"delivering goods or rendering services"	"supplying goods or services"	Section 17(7)
21	"delivers goods or renders services"	"supplies goods or services"	Sections 17(1)
23	"goods are delivered or services are rendered"	"goods or services are supplied"	Sections 17(10)(a)
24	"goods are delivered or services are rendered"	"goods or services are supplied"	Sections 17(10)(b)
25	"accountable person" except where preceded by the word "an"	"taxable person"	Sections 17(1), 17(3)(a), 17(3)(b), 17(12)(a)(i), 17(12)(a)(ii), 17(12)(a)(iii).
26	"an accountable person"	"a taxable person"	Sections 17(1), 17(3), 17(5), 17(6), 17(12)(a)
31	"section 5(4)"	"section 13"	Section 17(12)(a)(ii)

(With effect from 1 March 1979)

Finance Act 1986

86.   Section 17 of the Principal Act is hereby amended by the insertion after subsection (1) of the following subsection:

"(1A) (a)   An invoice or other document required to be issued under this section shall, subject to paragraph (b), be deemed to be so issued if the particulars which are required by regulations to be contained in such invoice or other document, as the case may be, are recorded and retained in an electronic data processing system and are transmitted by electronic means without the issue of any invoice or other document.

(b)   An invoice or other document required to be issued under this section shall not be deemed by paragraph (a) to be issued unless the person who is required to issue such invoice or other document, as the case may be, has given to the Revenue Commissioners at least one month's notice in writing that he proposes to keep and retain such records and make such transmissions as are referred to in that paragraph, and he complies with such other conditions as may be specified by regulations.

(c)   A person who receives the transmissions referred to in paragraphs (a) and (b) shall not be deemed to be issued with an invoice or other document, as the case may be, required to be issued under this section unless he has given to the Revenue Commissioners at least one month's notice in writing that he proposes to receive such transmissions, and he complies with such other conditions as may be specified by regulations.".

(With effect from 27 May 1986)

Finance Act 1990

Non-application, for a limited period, of section 17 (invoices) of Principal Act in respect of certain services

105.   In respect of the period from the 1st day of October, 1990, to the 31st day of December, 1990, the provisions of section 17 of the Principal Act shall not apply in the case of the supply of services specified in paragraph (va) (inserted by this Act) of the Sixth Schedule (inserted by the Act of 1985) to The Principal Act.

(With effect from 1 October 1990)

Finance Act 1992

180.   Section 17 of the Principal Act is hereby amended-

(a)   in subsection (1):

(i)   by the insertion after "another taxable person" of "or goods to a person, other than an individual, in another Member State of the Community"

(ii)   by the deletion of ", including the rate of zero per cent,",

and

(iii)   by the substitution of "person" for "other taxable person",

*(b)   in subsection (1A) (inserted by the Act of 1986) by the substitution of the following paragraphs for paragraphs (b) and (c):

"(b)   An invoice or other document required to be issued under this section shall not be deemed by paragraph (a) to be issued unless the person, who is required to issue such invoice or other document, as the case may be, has been authorised by the Revenue Commissioners to issue such invoice or other document to a recipient who has been authorised by the Revenue Commissioners in accordance with paragraph (c), and he complies with such conditions as may be specified by regulations.

(c)   A person who receives the transmissions referred to in paragraphs (a) and (b) shall not be deemed to be issued with an invoice or other document, as the case may be, required to be issued under this section unless he has been authorised in that respect by the Revenue Commissioners and he complies with such conditions as may be specified by regulations.

(d)   The Revenue Commissioners may, in accordance with regulations, cancel an authorisation under paragraph (b) or (c).",

**(c)   by the insertion of the following subsection after subsection (1A) (inserted by the Act of 1986):

"(1B)   A taxable person who supplies goods to another taxable person in such circumstances that tax is chargeable at any of the rates specified in section 11(1) shall issue to that other taxable person a single document (in this Act referred to as a monthly control statement) in respect of all such supplies to that other taxable person during each calendar month, and every such statement shall be in such form, contain such particulars, and be issued within such time as may be specified by regulations:

Provided that this provision shall not apply to taxable persons whose taxable turnover in respect of supplies of goods to other taxable persons has not exceeded £2,000,000 in the previous period of 12 months.",

(d)   in subsection (2) (inserted by the Act of 1978) by the substitution of "purchaser" for "taxable person", in each place where it occurs,

(e)   in subsection 3 -

(i)   by the substitution of "to another person" for "to a taxable person",

> (ii)   in paragraph (a) by the substitution of "to that other person" for "to the taxable person", and
>
> (iii)   in paragraph (b):
>
>> (I)   by the substitution of "to that other person" for "to the taxable person", where it first occurs, and
>>
>> (II)   by the substitution of "and, if that other person is a taxable person, the amount for "and the amount",

(f)   in paragraph (b) of subsection (4) (inserted by the Act of 1978):

> (i)   by the deletion of ", if the person to whom the supply was made is a taxable person," and
>
> (ii)   by the substitution of "and the amount which the person may deduct under section 12 or is entitled to be repaid under section 13 shall," for "and the amount which the taxable person may deduct under section 12 shall,",

(g)   in subsection (8) by the insertion after "supply of goods or services" of ", other than supplies of the kind specified in subparagraph (b) or (c) of paragraph (i) of the Second Schedule,",

and

(h)   in subsection (12):

> (i)   by the insertion of the following paragraph after paragraph (a):
>
>> "(ai)   A flat-rate farmer shall, if requested in writing by another person and if the request states that the other person is entitled to repayment of the flat-rate addition under section 13, give to that other person in writing the particulars specified in regulations for the purpose of subsection (2) in respect of the goods or services supplied by the flat-rate farmer to that other person that are specified in the request.",
>
> and
>
> (ii)   by the insertion in paragraph (b) after "paragraph (a)" of "or (ai)".

(With effect from 1 January 1993 except * from 28 May 1992 and ** from 1 November 1992)

S.I. No. 413 of 1992.
European Communities (Value-Added Tax) Regulations, 1992.

12.   Section 17 of the Principal Act is hereby amended in subsection (1) by the deletion after "to another taxable person or" of "goods".

(With effect from 1 January 1993)

Finance Act 1993

91.   Section 17 of the Principal Act is hereby amended-

(a)   in subsection (1) (inserted by the Act of 1992) by the insertion after "section 11(1)", of "or who supplies goods to a person in another Member State of the Community in the circumstances referred to in section 3(6)(d)(ii),"

and

(b)   by the insertion of the following subsection after subsection (3):

"(3A) Notwithstanding subsections (5) and (9), where a person issues an invoice in accordance with subsection (1) which indicates a rate of tax and subsequent to the issue of that invoice it is established that a lower rate of tax applied, then-

(a)   the amount of consideration stated on that invoice shall be deemed to have been reduced to nil,

(b)   the provisions of subsection (3)(b) shall have effect, and

(c)   following the issue of a credit note in accordance with the provisions of subsection (3)(b), the person shall issue another invoice in accordance with this Act and regulations made thereunder.".

(With effect from 17 June 1993)

Finance Act 1995

132.   Section 17 of the Principal Act is hereby amended by the substitution of the following proviso for the proviso to subsection (1B) (inserted by the Act of 1992):

"Provided that this provision shall not apply-

(a)   to taxable persons whose taxable turnover in respect of supplies of goods to other taxable persons has not exceeded £2,000,000 in the previous period of 12 months, and

(b)   in any event, in respect of all such supplies made in the taxable periods commencing on or after the 1st day of May, 1995.".

(With effect from 2 June 1995)

Finance Act 1996

97.   Section 17 of the Principal Act is hereby amended-

(a)   by the addition of the following proviso to subsection (1):

"Provided that, where goods are supplied in accordance with the terms of paragraph (b) of subsection (1) of section 3, and the ownership of those goods is transferred to a person supplying, in respect of those goods, financial services of the kind specified in subparagraph (e) of paragraph (i) of the First Schedule, the taxable person making the supply of the goods in question shall issue the invoice to the person supplying the said financial services in lieu of the taxable person to whom the supply of the goods is made and that invoice shall include the name and address of the person supplying those financial services.",

(b)   by the insertion of the following subsections after subsection (1A):

"(1AA)   Where the proviso to subsection (1) applies, the person supplying the financial services in question shall issue a document to the person to whom the supply of goods is made and shall indicate thereon-

(a)   the amount which is set out in respect of tax on the invoice issued to the person supplying the financial services in accordance with the said proviso in respect of that supply of goods, and

(b)   such other particulars as are specified by regulations in respect of an invoice issued in accordance with subsection (1).

(1AB)   Where any person issues a document for the purposes of subsection (1AA) that person shall, in respect of the document, be treated as a taxable person for the purposes of sections 16 and 18.",

(c)   by the insertion of the following subsection after subsection (3A):

"(3AB)   Where any person supplying financial services receives a credit note issued under the terms of paragraph (b) of subsection (3) in respect of a supply of goods to which the proviso to subsection (1) applies, that person shall, within seven days of receipt of such credit note, issue to the person to whom the goods in question were supplied, a document corresponding to that credit note indicating such particulars as are specified by regulations in respect of the issue of such credit notes, and the amount which the taxable person to whom the goods were supplied may deduct under section 12 in respect of that supply shall be reduced by the amount in respect of tax shown in the document.",

(d)   by the insertion of the following subsection after subsection (5):

"(5A)   If any person issues a document for the purposes of subsection (1AA) in relation to a supply of goods indicating a greater amount in respect of tax than the amount of tax invoiced in accordance with the proviso to subsection (1) in relation to that supply, that person shall, in relation to that excess, be deemed for the purposes of this Act to be a taxable person and a person to whom subsection (5) applies, and that excess shall be deemed to be tax.",

and

(e)   by the insertion of the following subsection after subsection (7):

"(7A) A document required to be issued in accordance with subsection (1AA) shall be issued within twenty-two days next following the month of supply of the goods.".

(With effect from 1 July 1996)

Finance Act 1999

134. Section 17 of the Principal Act is hereby amended by the insertion of the following subsection after subsection (2) (inserted by the Act of 1978):

"(2A) A flat-rate farmer who, in accordance with section 12C, is required to issue an invoice in respect of a supply of agricultural machinery shall, in respect of each supply, issue an invoice in the form and containing such particulars as may be specified by regulations if the following conditions are fulfilled:

(a)   the issue of the invoice is requested by the taxable dealer,

(b)   the taxable dealer provides the form for the purpose of the invoice and enters the appropriate particulars thereon, and

(c)   the taxable dealer gives to the flat-rate farmer a copy of the invoice,

but may issue the invoice if those conditions or any one of them are not fulfilled.".

(With effect from 1 September 1999)

Finance Act 2000

115. Section 17 of the Principal Act is amended by the insertion in subsection (1AB) (inserted by the Finance Act, 1996) after "sub-section (1AA)" of "or section 12C(1B)".

(With effect from 23 March 2000)

Finance Act 2001

193. Section 17 of the Principal Act is amended-

(a)   by the substitution of the following for subsection (1A) (inserted by the Finance Act, 1986):

"(1A) (a)   An invoice or other document required to be issued by a person under this section shall, subject to paragraph (b), be deemed to be so issued by that person if the particulars which are required by regulations to be contained in such invoice or other document are recorded, retained and transmitted electronically by a system or systems which ensures the integrity of those particulars and the authenticity of their origin, without the issue of any invoice or other document containing those particulars.

(b)   An invoice or other document required to be issued under this section shall not be deemed by paragraph (a) to be so issued unless the person, who is required to issue such invoice or other document, complies with such conditions as are specified by regulations and the system or systems used by that person conforms with such specifications as are required by regulations.

(c)   The person who receives a transmission referred to in paragraph (a) shall not be deemed to be issued with an invoice or other document required to be issued under this section unless the particulars which are required by regulations to be contained in such invoice or other document are received electronically in a system which ensures the integrity of those particulars and the authenticity of their origin and unless the system conforms with such specifications as are required by regulations and that person complies with such conditions as are specified by regulations.",

*(b)   by the insertion of the following after subsection (1AA) (inserted by the Finance Act, 1996):

"(1AAA)   Where a person, referred to in this subsection as the 'owner', supplies financial services of the kind specified in subparagraph (i)(e) of the First Schedule in respect of goods which are supplied within the meaning of section (3)(1)(b), being goods which are handed over from a person in another Member State to a taxable person acting as such in the State, referred to in this subsection as the 'acquirer', then the owner shall issue a document to the acquirer and shall indicate thereon-

(a)   that the acquirer is liable to account for the tax, if any, due in respect of the intra-Community acquisition of those goods, and

(b)   such other particulars as are specified by regulations in respect of an invoice issued in accordance with subsection (1).",

and

*(c)   by the substitution of "subsections (1AA), (1AAA)" for "subsection (1AA)" in subsection (1AB).

(With effect from 21 March 2001 except * from 1 July 2001)

Finance Act 2003

122. Section 17 of the Principal Act is amended –

(a)   by inserting in subsection (1) "or to a Department of State or local authority or to a body established by statute or to a person who carries on an exempted activity" after "who supplies goods or services to another taxable person",

(b)   by deleting in subsection (10)(a) "goods or services are supplied to a registered person by another registered person or",

(c)   by substituting in subsection (10)(b) "agricultural produce" for "goods", and

(d)   by inserting the following after subsection (13):

"(14) (a)   An invoice required under this section to be issued in respect of a supply by a person, in this subsection referred to as the 'supplier', is deemed to be so issued by that supplier if that invoice is drawn up and issued by the person to whom that supply is made, in this subsection referred to as the 'customer', where –

(i)   there is prior agreement between the supplier and the customer that the customer may draw up and issue such invoice,

(ii)   the customer is a person registered for value-added tax,

(iii)   any conditions which are imposed by this Act or by regulations on the supplier in relation to the form, content or issue of the invoice are met by the customer, and

(iv)   agreed procedures are in place for the acceptance by the supplier of the validity of the invoice.

(b)   An invoice, which is deemed to be issued by the supplier in accordance with paragraph (a), is deemed to have been so issued when such invoice is accepted by that supplier in accordance with the agreed procedures referred to in paragraph (a)(iv).

(c)   An invoice required to be issued by a supplier under this section shall be deemed to be so issued by that supplier if —

       (i)   that invoice is issued by a person who acts in the name and on behalf of the supplier, and

       (ii)   any conditions which are imposed by this Act or by regulations on the supplier in relation to the form, content or issue of the invoice are met.

(d)   Any credit note or debit note issued in accordance with this section which amends and refers specifically and unambiguously to an invoice is treated as if it were an invoice for the purposes of this subsection.

(e)   The Revenue Commissioners may make regulations in relation to the conditions applying to invoices covered by this subsection.

(15)   (a)   A person who issues, or is deemed to issue, an invoice under this section shall ensure that —

       (i)   a copy of any invoice issued by such person,

       (ii)   a copy of any invoice deemed to be issued by such person in the circumstances specified in subsection (14), and

       (iii)   any invoice received by such person,

is stored, and for the purposes of section 16(1) the reference to the keeping of full and true records therein shall be construed accordingly in so far as it relates to invoices covered by this section.

(b)   Any invoice not stored by electronic means in a manner which conforms with requirements laid down by the Revenue Commissioners shall be stored within the State, but subject to the agreement of the Revenue Commissioners and any conditions set by them such invoice may be stored outside the State.".

(With effect from 1 January 2004)

Finance Act 2004

63. Section 17 of the Principal Act is amended in subsection (1) by inserting the following after "section 11(1),":

"or who supplies goods or services to a person in another Member State who is liable to pay value-added tax pursuant to Council Directive No. 77/388/EEC of 17 May 1977 on such supply,".

(With effect from 25 March 2004)

Finance Act 2006

127. The enactments specified in Schedule 2—

    (a)   are amended to the extent and in the manner specified in paragraphs 1 to 8 of that Schedule, and

    (b)   apply and come into operation in accordance with paragraph 9 of that Schedule.

Schedule 2

    8.   The Value-Added Tax Act 1972 is amended in sections 17(12)(a)(i) and 17(12)(a)(iii) by substituting "by the taxable person" for "to the taxable person".

(With effect from 31 March 2006)

Finance Act 2007

90. Section 17 of the Principal Act is amended with effect from 1 May 2007—

    (a)   in subsection (1) by deleting the proviso to that subsection,

    (b)   by deleting subsections (1AA), (3AB), (5A) and (7A), and

    (c)   in subsection (1AB) by substituting "for the purposes of subsection (1AAA)" for "for the purposes of subsections (1AA), (1AAA)".

*97. With effect from 1 January 2007 in each provision of the Principal Act specified in the first column of Schedule 3 for the words set out in the second column of that Schedule at that entry there is substituted the words set out at the corresponding entry in the third column of that Schedule.

Schedule 3
Miscellaneous Amendments Relating To Council Directive 2006/112/EC

Amendment of Value-Added Tax Act 1972

Provision of Principal Act	Words to be replaced	Words to be inserted
Section 17(1)	Council Directive No. 77/388/EEC of 17 May 1977	Council Directive No. 2006/112/EC of 28 November 2006

(With effect from 1 May 2007 except * with effect from 1 January 2007)

Finance Act 2008

101. (1)   Section 17 of the Principal Act is amended—

**(a)   by inserting with effect from 1 September 2008 the following before subsection (2):

"(1C)   (a)   Where a subcontractor who is an accountable person supplies a service to which section 8(1B) applies, that subcontractor shall issue a document to the principal indicating—

(i)   that the principal is liable to account for the tax chargeable on that supply, and

(ii)   such other particulars as would be required to be included in that document if that document was an invoice required to be issued in accordance with subsection (1) but excluding the amount of tax payable.

(b)   Where the principal and the subcontractor so agree, the provisions of subsection (14)(a) may apply to this document as if it were an invoice.",

(b)   by deleting with effect from 1 July 2008 subsection (1AAA),

(c)   in subsection (1AB) by substituting with effect from 1 July 2008 "for the purposes of section 12C(1B)" for "for the purposes of subsection (1AAA) or section 12C(1B)",

*(d)   by inserting the following after subsection (3A):

"(3B)   Where, subsequent to the issue of an invoice by a person to another person in accordance with subsection (1) in respect of an amount received by way of a deposit and where section 19(2B) applies, then—

(a)   the amount of the consideration stated on that invoice is deemed to be reduced to nil, and

(b)   the person shall issue to that other person a document to be treated as if it were a credit note containing particulars of the reduction in such form and containing such other particulars as would be required to be included in that document if that document was a credit note, and if that other person is a taxable person the amount which that other person may deduct under section 12 shall be reduced by the amount of tax shown on the document as if that document were a credit note.",

and

*(e)   in subsection (9)(aa) by inserting "in any case where subsection (3B) applies or" after "shall not apply".

(2)   Section 17(3B) (inserted by subsection (1)(d)) is further amended with effect from 1 July 2008 by substituting "an accountable person" for "a taxable person".

109. With effect from 1 July 2008 in each provision of the Principal Act specified in the first column of Schedule 4 for the words set out in the second column of that Schedule at that entry (in each place where those words occur in the provision concerned) there is substituted the words set out at the corresponding entry in the third column of that Schedule.

Schedule 4
Miscellaneous Amendments Relating to the Amendment of the Definition of Taxable Person

Amendments to Value-Added Tax Act 1972

Provision of Value-Added Tax Act 1972	Words to be replaced	Words to be inserted
Section 17	A taxable person	An accountable person
Section 17	another taxable person	another accountable person
Section 17	a taxable person	a accountable person
Section 17	the taxable person	the accountable person

*141. The enactments specified in Schedule 8 —

(a)   are amended to the extent and in the manner specified in paragraphs 1 to 6 of that Schedule, and

(b)   apply and come into operation in accordance with paragraph 7 of that Schedule.

Schedule 8
Miscellaneous Technical Amendments in Relation to Tax

3.   The Value-Added Tax Act 1972 is amended in accordance with the following provisions:

(e)   in section 17 by deleting subsection (1B),

(With effect from 1 July 2008 except * with effect from 13 March 2008 and ** with effect from 1 September 2008)

Section 18

Value Added Tax Act 1972

Inspection and removal of records

18. (1) An authorised officer may, for the purpose of making any enquiry which he considers necessary in relation to liability to tax of any person, enter any premises in which the officer has reason to believe that such person is carrying on business and the officer may request the production of, search for and inspect any books, invoices, credit notes, debit notes, receipts, accounts, bank statements vouchers or other documents whatsoever relating to the delivery of goods or the rendering of services and may remove and retain any such books, invoices credit notes, debit notes, receipts, accounts, vouchers bank statements or other documents for such pedal as may be reasonable for their examination or for the purpose of any proceedings for the recovery of a penalty under this Act.

    (2) Upon request made by an authorised officer at any promises in which a person carries on business, the person, or any person employed by him, shall produce to the authorised officer all books, invoices, credit notes, debit notes, receipts, accounts, vouchers, bank statements or other documents whatsoever relating to the said business which may be in the power, possession or procurement of the person to whom the request is made and shall permit the officer to inspect and remove any documents so produced.

    (3) A person shall not wilfully obstruct or delay an authorised officer in the exercise of his powers under this section.

    (4) Where, in pursuance of this section, an authorised officer enters any premises, carries out any search or requests production of any documents, he shall, on request, show his authorisation for the purpose of this section to the person concerned.

    (5) In this section "**authorised officer**" means an officer of the Revenue Commissioners authorised by them in writing for the purposes of this section.

(With effect from 1 November 1972)

Value Added Tax (Amendment) Act 1978

30. (1) The enactment mentioned in column (2) of the First Schedule is hereby repealed to the extent specified in column (3) of that Schedule.

    (2) In consequence of the amendments of the Principal Act specified in this Act and of the repeals specified in the First Schedule, the Principal Act is hereby further amended by the substitution of the word or expression mentioned in column (3) of the Second

Schedule at any reference number for the word or expression mentioned in column (2) of that Schedule at that reference number wherever it occurs in the provision of the Principal Act mentioned in column (4) of that Schedule at that reference number.

SECOND SCHEDULE

Consequential Amendments

Reference Number (1)	Existing word or expression (2)	Substituted word or expression (3)	Provision of Principal Act (4)
18.	"delivery of goods or the rendering of services"	"the said business"	Section 18(1).

(With effect from 1 March 1979)

Finance Act 1979

48.   Section 18 of the Value-Added Tax Act, 1972, is hereby amended by the substitution of the following subsection for subsection (1):

"(1)   An authorised officer may, for the purpose of making any enquiry which he considers necessary concerning matters relating to liability to tax or repayment of tax in regard to any person, enter any premises in which the officer has reason to believe that such person is carrying on business and the officer may request the production of, search for and inspect any books, invoices, credit notes, debit notes, receipts, accounts, bank statements, vouchers or other documents whatsoever relating to the said business and may remove and retain any such books, invoices, credit notes, debit notes, receipts, accounts, vouchers, bank statements or other documents for such period as may be reasonable for their examination or for the purpose of any proceedings for the recovery of a penalty under this Act."

(With effect from 1 June 1979)

Finance Act 1984

89.   Section 18 of the Principal Act is hereby amended-

(a)   by the substitution of the following subsection for subsection (1):

"(1)   (a)   For the purposes of this Act and regulations, an authorised officer may at all reasonable times enter any premises or place where he has reason to believe that business is carried on or anything is done in connection with business and-

(i)   may require the person carrying on the business, or any person on those premises or in that place who is employed by the person carrying on the business or who is associated with him in the carrying on of the business, to produce any books, records, accounts or other documents relating to the business or to any other business which he has reason to believe may be, or have been, connected with the said business or have, or have had, trading relations with the said business,

(ii)   may, if he has reason to believe that any of the books, records, accounts or other documents, which he has required to be produced to him under the provisions of this subsection have not been so produced, search in those premises or that place for those books, records, accounts or other documents,

(iii)   may, in the case of any such books, records, accounts or other documents produced to or found by him, take copies of or extracts from them and remove and retain them for such period as may be reasonable for their further examination or for the purposes of any proceedings for the recovery of a penalty in relation to tax,

(iv)   may, if he has reason to believe that goods connected with taxable supplies or importations are held on those premises or in that place and that particulars of such goods have not been kept and retained, as required by this Act or by regulations, in the books, records, accounts or other documents of the business or of any other business similarly required to keep and retain particulars of those goods, search those premises or that place for the said goods and, on their discovery, examine and take particulars of them,

(v)   may require the person carrying on the business, or any person on those premises or in that place, who is employed by the person carrying on the business or who is associated with him in the carrying on of the business, to give the authorised officer all reasonable assistance.

(b)   Nothing in this subsection shall be construed as requiring any person carrying on a profession, or any person employed by any person carrying on a profession, to produce to an authorised officer any documents relating to a client, other than such documents as are material to the tax affairs of the person carrying on the profession, and, in particular, he shall not be required to disclose any information or professional advice of a confidential nature given to a client.",

and

(b)   by the deletion of subsection (2).

(With effect from 23 May 1984)

Finance Act 1992

181. Section 18 of the Principal Act is hereby amended-

(a)   in paragraph (a) of subsection 1-

*(i)   by the insertion of the following subparagraph (iia) after subparagraph (ii):

"(iia)   may, if he has reason to believe that a person is carrying or has in his possession any records which may be required as evidence in criminal proceedings in accordance with section 94 (as amended by section 243 of the Finance Act, 1992) of the Finance Act, 1983, in relation to the tax, request the person to produce any such records, and if that person should fail to do so, the authorised officer or a member of the Garda Síochána may search that person:

Provided that-

(A)   the officer or the member of the Garda Síochána conducting the search shall ensure, as far as practicable, that the person understands the reason for the search,

(B)   the search is conducted with due regard to the privacy of that person,

(C)   the person being searched shall not be searched by an officer or member of the Garda Síochána of the opposite sex, and

(D)   the person being searched shall not be requested to remove any clothing other than headgear or a coat, jacket, glove or a similar article of clothing.",

(ii)   by the deletion in paragraph (iii) of "for the recovery of a penalty",

*(iii)   by the insertion in paragraph (iv) after "supplies" of ", intra-Community acquisitions",

(iv)   by the insertion in paragraph (v) after "all reasonable assistance" of ",including providing information and explanations and furnishing documents in connection with the business, as required by the authorised officer",

and

(b)   by the insertion of the following subsections after subsection (1):

"(1A) A taxable person shall, on request from an authorised officer, furnish to that officer, in respect of a specified period, the following information:

(a)   the name and address of each of his customers and the total consideration payable in respect of supplies of goods and services made by him to each customer and the tax thereon, and

(b)   the name, address and registration number of each of his suppliers and the total consideration payable in respect of goods and services supplied to him from each supplier and the tax thereon.

(1B)   In this section '**records**' means any document, or any other written or printed material in any form, including any information stored, maintained or preserved by means of any mechanical or electronic device, whether or not stored, maintained or preserved in a legible form, which a person is required to keep, retain, issue or produce for inspection or which may be inspected under any provision relating to tax.".

(With effect from 28 May 1992 except * from 1 January 1993)

Finance Act 1995

133.   Section 18 of the Principal Act is hereby amended in subsection (1A) (inserted by the Act of 1992), in paragraph (a) by the insertion after "thereon" of "and the value and description of any gifts or promotional items given by him to any person in connection with such supplies or any other payments made by him to any person in connection with such supplies".

(With effect from 2 June 1995)

Taxes Consolidation Act 1997

1100. Schedule 31, which provides for amendments to other enactments consequential on the passing of this Act, shall apply for the purposes of this Act.

SCHEDULE 31

Consequential Amendments

in the enactments specified in Column (1) of the following Table for the words set out or referred to in Column (2) there shall be substituted the words set out in the corresponding entry in Column (3).

Enactment amended (1)	Words to be replaced (2)	Words to be substituted (3)
The Value-Added Tax Act, 1972:		
section 18(1)(a)(iia)	Section 94 (as amended by Section 243 of the Finance Act, 1992) of the Finance Act, 1983	Section 1078 of the Taxes Consolidation Act, 1997

(With effect from 6 April 1997)

Finance Act 2008

109. With effect from 1 July 2008 in each provision of the Principal Act specified in the first column of Schedule 4 for the words set out in the second column of that Schedule at that entry (in each place where those words occur in the provision concerned) there is substituted the words set out at the corresponding entry in the third column of that Schedule.

Schedule 4
Miscellaneous Amendments Relating to the Amendment of the Definition of Taxable Person

Amendments to Value-Added Tax Act 1972

Provision of Value-Added Tax Act 1972	Words to be replaced	Words to be inserted
Section 18	A taxable person	An accountable person

(With effect from 1 July 2008)

Section 19

Value-Added Tax Act 1972

Tax Due and Payable

19. (1) Tax chargeable under section 2(1)(a) shall be due-

(a) in case an invoice is required under section 17 to be issued, at the time of issue of the invoice, or if the invoice is not issued in due time, upon the expiration of the period within which the invoice should have been issued;

(b) in case a person is liable under subsection (5) or (6) of section 17 to pay an amount of tax by reference to an invoice or credit note issued by him, at the time of issue of such invoice or credit note, and

(c) in any other case, at the time the goods are delivered or the services are rendered:

Provided that in relation to any delivery of taxable goods or rendering of taxable services in respect of which the moneys received are authorised in accordance with section 14 to be treated as the consideration for such delivery or rendering-

(i) paragraph (a) shall not apply; and

(ii) the tax chargeable in relation to the delivery of goods or he rendering of services to other persons shall be due when the moneys in respect of such, transactions are received.

(2) Notwithstanding anything in this Act, the tax chargeable under section 2(1)(a) or the relevant part thereof, shall fall due not later than the time when the amount in respect of which it is payable has been received either in full or in part and where the amount is received in full or in part before the delivery of the goods or the rendering of the service to which it relates, a delivery or rendering for a consideration equal to the amount received of such part of the goods or services as is equal in value to the amount received, shall be deemed, for the purposes of this Act, to have taken place at the time of such receipt.

(3) Within nine days immediately after the tenth day of the month immediately following a taxable period, an accountable person shall furnish to the Collector-General a true and correct return prepared in accordance with regulations of the amount of tax which became due under section 2(1)(a) by him during the taxable period and the amount, if any, which may be deducted in accordance with section 12 in computing the amount of tax payable by him in respect of such taxable period and shall due same time remit to the Collector-General the amount of tax, if any, payable by him in respect of such taxable period.

(With effect from 1 November 1972)

Finance Act 1973

82. Section 19 of the Principal Act is hereby amended by the substitution of the following subsection for subsection (3):

"(3)   (a)   Within nine days immediately after the tenth day of the month immediately following a taxable period, an accountable person shall furnish to the Collector-General a true and correct return prepared in accordance with regulations of the amount of tax which became due under section 2(1)(a) by him during the taxable period and the amount, if any, which may be deducted in accordance with section 12 in computing the amount of tax payable by him in respect of such taxable period, and shall at the same time remit to the Collector-General the amount of tax, if any, payable by him in respect of such taxable period.

        (b)   Paragraph (a) shall be construed in relation to the taxable period commencing on the first day of July, 1973, as if the reference therein to nine days immediately after the tenth day of the month immediately following a taxable period were a reference to nine days immediately after the tenth day of the month in which the taxable period ends.".

(With effect from 3 September 1973)

Value Added Tax (Amendment) Act 1978

16. Section 19 of the Principal Act is hereby amended by the substitution of the following subsection for subsection (3):

"(3)   Within 9 days immediately after the tenth day of the month immediately following a taxable period, a taxable person shall furnish to the Collector-General a true and correct return prepared in accordance with regulations of the amount of tax which became due by him during the taxable period, not being tax already paid by him in relation to goods imported by him, and the amount, if any, which may be deducted in accordance with section 12 in computing the amount of tax payable by him in respect of such taxable period and such other particulars as may be specified in regulations, and shall at the same time remit to the Collector-General the amount of tax, if any, payable by him in respect of such taxable period.".

30.   (1)   The enactment mentioned in column (2) of the First Schedule is hereby repealed to the extent specified in column (3) of that Schedule.

      (2)   In consequence of the amendments of the Principal Act specified in this Act and of the repeals specified in the First Schedule, the Principal Act is hereby further amended by the substitution of the word or expression mentioned in column (3) of the Second Schedule at any reference number for the word or expression

mentioned in column (2) of that Schedule at that reference number wherever it occurs in the provision of the Principal Act mentioned in column (4) of that Schedule at that reference number.

FIRST SCHEDULE

Enactments Repealed

Number and Year (1)	Short Title (2)	Extent of Repeal (3)
No. 22 of 1972	Value-Added Tax Act, 1972	The proviso to section 19(1)

SECOND SCHEDULE

Consequential Amendments

Reference Number (1)	Existing word or expression (2)	Substituted word or expression (3)	Provision of Principal Act (4)
11	"delivery of the goods or the rendering of the service"	"supply of the goods or services"	Section 19 (2)
16	"delivery or rendering"	"supply"	Sections 19(2)
24	"goods are delivered or services are rendered"	"goods or services are supplied"	Sections 19(1)(c)

(With effect from 1 March 1979)

Finance Act 1983

84. Section 19 of the Principal Act is hereby amended by the substitution of the following subsection for subsection (3):

"(3) (a) Subject to paragraph (b), a taxable person shall, within 9 days immediately after the tenth day of the month immediately following a taxable period, furnish to the Collector-General a true and correct return prepared in accordance with regulations of the amount of tax which became due by him during the taxable period, not being tax already paid by him in relation to goods imported by him, and the amount, if any, which may be deducted in accordance with section 12 in computing the amount of tax payable by him in respect of such taxable period and such other particulars as may be specified in regulations, and shall at the same time remit to the Collector-General the amount of tax, if any, payable by him in respect of such taxable period.

(b)   A person who disposes of goods which pursuant to section 3(7) are deemed to be supplied by a taxable person in the course or furtherance of his business-

(i)   shall within 9 days immediately after the tenth day of the month immediately following a taxable period furnish to the Collector-General a true and correct return, prepared in accordance with regulations, of the amount of tax which became due by such taxable person in relation to the disposal, and such other particulars as may be specified in regulations, and shall at the same time remit to the Collector-General the amount of tax payable in respect of the taxable period in question,

(ii) shall send to the person whose goods were disposed of a statement containing such particulars as may be specified in regulations, and

(iii) shall treat the said amount of tax as a necessary disbursement out of the proceeds of the disposal.

(c)   The owner of goods which pursuant to section 3(7) are deemed to be supplied by a taxable person in the course or furtherance of his business shall exclude from any return, which he is or, but for this subparagraph, would be, required to furnish under this Act, the tax payable in accordance with paragraph (b).".

(With effect from 1 September 1983)

Finance Act 1989

58.   Section 19 of the Principal Act is hereby amended in subsection (3) (inserted by the Finance Act, 1983) by the insertion after paragraph (a) of the following paragraph:

"(aa) (i)   In this paragraph:

'**accounting period**' means a period, as determined by the Collector-General from time to time in any particular case, consisting of a number of consecutive taxable periods not exceeding six;

'**authorised person**' means a taxable person who has been authorised in writing by the Collector-General for the purposes of this paragraph and 'authorise' and 'authorisation' shall be construed accordingly.

(ii) Notwithstanding the provisions of paragraph (a) -

(I)   the Collector-General may, from time to time, authorise in writing a taxable person for the purposes of this paragraph, unless the taxable person objects in writing to the authorisation,

and

(II) an authorised person may, within nine days immediately after the tenth day of the month immediately following an accounting period furnish to the Collector-General a true and correct return prepared in accordance with regulations of the amount of tax which became due by him during the taxable periods which comprise the accounting period, not being tax already paid by him in relation to goods imported by him, and, the amount, if any, which may be deducted in accordance with section 12 in computing the amount of tax payable by him in respect of such taxable periods and such other particulars as may be specified in regulations, and at the same time remit to the Collector-General any amount of tax payable by him in respect of such taxable periods, and, where the authorised person concerned so furnishes and remits, he shall be deemed to have complied with the provisions of paragraph (a) in relation to the said taxable periods.

(iii) For the purposes of issuing an authorisation to a taxable person, the Collector-General shall, where he considers it appropriate, have regard to the following matters-

(I) he has reasonable grounds to believe that-

(A) the authorisation will not result in a loss of tax, and

(B) the taxable person will meet all his obligations under the authorisation,

and

(II) the taxable person has-

(A) been a registered person during all of the period consisting of the six taxable periods immediately preceding the period in which an authorisation would, if it were issued, have effect, and

(B) complied with the provisions of paragraph (a).

(iv) An authorisation may-

(I) be issued either without conditions or subject to such conditions as the Collector-General, having regard in particular to the considerations mentioned in subparagraph (iii), considers proper and specifies in writing to the taxable person concerned when issuing the authorisation,

(II)   without prejudice to the generality of the foregoing, require an authorised person to remit to the Collector-General, within nine days immediately after the tenth day of the month immediately following each taxable period (other than the final taxable period) which is comprised in an accounting period, such an amount as may be specified by the Collector-General.

(v)   The Collector-General may, by notice in writing, terminate an authorisation and, where a taxable person requests him to do so, he shall terminate the authorisation.

(vi)   For the purposes of terminating an authorisation the Collector-General shall, where he considers it appropriate, have regard to the following matters:

(I)   he has reasonable grounds to believe that the authorisation has resulted or could result in a loss of tax, or

(II)   the taxable person-

(A)   has furnished, or there is furnished on his behalf, any incorrect information for the purposes of the issue to him of an authorisation, or

(B)   has not complied with the provisions of paragraph (a) or of this paragraph, including the conditions, if any, specified by the Collector General under subparagraph (iv) in relation to the issue to him of an authorisation.

(vii)   In relation to any taxable period in respect of which he has not complied with the provisions of paragraph (a), a person whose authorisation is terminated shall be deemed to have complied with paragraph (a) if, within twenty-one days of issue to him of a notice of termination, he furnishes to the Collector-General the return specified in paragraph (a) and at the same time remits to the said Collector-General the amount of tax payable by him in accordance with that paragraph.

(viii) (I) An authorisation shall be deemed to have been terminated by the Collector-General on the date that an authorised person-

(A) ceases to trade (except for the purposes of disposing of the stocks and assets of his business), whether for reasons of insolvency or any other reason,

(B) being a body corporate, goes into liquidation, whether voluntarily or not, or

(C) ceases to be a taxable person or a registered person, dies or becomes bankrupt.

(II) A taxable person to whom this subparagraph relates shall, in relation to any taxable period (or part of a taxable period) comprised in the accounting period which was in operation in his case on the date to which clause (I) of this subparagraph relates, be deemed to have complied with paragraph (a) if he furnishes to the Collector-General the return specified in subparagraph (ii)(II) and at the same time remits to the said Collector-General the amount of tax payable by him for the purposes of that subparagraph as if he were an authorised person whose accounting period ended on the last day of the taxable period during which the termination occurred:

Provided that the personal representative of a person who was an authorised person shall be deemed to be the taxable person concerned.".

(With effect from 24 May 1989)

Finance Act 1992

182. Section 19 of the Principal Act is hereby amended-

(a) by the insertion after subsection (1) of the following subsection:

"(1A) Tax chargeable under section 2(1A) shall be due-

(a) on the fifteenth day of the month following that during which the intra-Community acquisition occurs;

(b) in case an invoice is issued before the date specified in paragraph (a) by the supplier in another Member State to the person acquiring the goods, when that invoice is issued.",

(b) in subsection (2) by the insertion after "section 2(1)(a)" of ",other than tax chargeable in respect of supplies of the kind specified in subparagraph (b) or (c) of paragraph (i) of the Second Schedule,",
and

(c)   by the insertion after subsection (3) (inserted by the Act of 1983) of the following subsection:

"(4)   Notwithstanding subsection (3), where-

(a)   a taxable person makes an intra-Community acquisition of a motor vehicle in respect of which he is not entitled to a deduction of tax under section 12, or

(b)   an individual who is a taxable person in accordance with subsections (1A) and (2B) of section 8 makes an intra-Community acquisition of a new means of transport,

the tax shall be payable, at a time and in a manner to be determined by regulations.".

(With effect from 1 January 1993)

Finance Act 1993

92.   Section 19 of the Principal Act is hereby amended-

(a)   by the insertion of the following proviso to paragraph (a) of subsection (3):

"Provided that-

(a)   where the taxable period is the period ending on the 31st day of December, the amount of tax payable for such period shall be reduced by the amount paid, if any, in accordance with subsection (6)(a) where that amount was due during that taxable period;

(b)   the Revenue Commissioners shall refund the amount of the excess where-

(i)   the taxable period is the period ending on the 31st day of December, and

(ii)   the amount paid in accordance with subsection (6)(a) and which was due during that taxable period exceeds the amount of tax which would be so payable before such reduction.",

*(b)   by the substitution of the following subsection for subsection (4) (inserted by the Act of 1992):

"(4)   (a)   Notwithstanding subsection (3), where-

(i)   a person makes an intra-Community acquisition of a new means of transport, other than a vessel or aircraft, in respect

of which he is not entitled to a deduction
under section 12, then-

(I)   the tax shall be payable at the time
of payment of vehicle registration
tax or, if no vehicle registration tax is
payable, at the time of registration of
the vehicle,

(II) the person shall complete such form
as may be provided by the Revenue
Commissioners for the purpose of
this subsection, and

(III) the provisions relating to recovery
and collection of vehicle registration
tax shall apply, with such exceptions
and modifications (if any) as may be
specified in regulations, to tax referred
to in this subparagraph as if it were
vehicle registration tax,

and

(ii) a person makes an intra-Community
acquisition of a new means of transport
which is a vessel or aircraft, in respect of
which he is not entitled to a deduction
under section 12, then-

(I)   the tax shall be payable at a time and
in a manner to be determined by
regulations, and

(II) the provisions relating to the recovery
and collection of a duty of customs
shall apply, with such exceptions
and modifications (if any) as may be
specified in regulations, to tax referred
to in this subparagraph as if it were a
duty of customs.

(b)   In this subsection-

'**registration of the vehicle**' means the registration
of the vehicle in accordance with section 131 of the
Finance Act, 1992;

'**vehicle registration tax**' means the tax referred to
in section 132 of the Finance Act, 1992.",

and

(c)   by the substitution of the following subsections for subsection (5):

"(5)   Notwithstanding the provisions of subsection (3), where the provisions of section 8(213)(b) apply, the tax shall be payable at the time of payment of the duty of excise on the goods and the provisions relating to recovery and collection of that duty of excise shall apply, with such exceptions and modifications (if any) as may be specified in regulations, to tax referred to in this subsection as if it were that duty of excise.

(6)   (a)   Notwithstanding the provisions of subsection (3), a taxable person shall on the 1st day of December, 1993, and on each 1st day of December thereafter pay to the Collector-General an amount (hereafter referred to in this subsection as the 'advance payment') equal to one-twelfth of the total net tax due by the taxable person for the relevant period:

Provided that as respects any such 1st day of December, this paragraph shall not apply so as to require an advance payment from a taxable person if the total net tax due by the taxable person for the relevant period does not exceed £120,000 (hereafter referred to in this subsection as the 'threshold').

(b)   Where a taxable person is required by the provisions of paragraph (a) to pay an advance payment to the Collector-General by the due date in any year and fails to pay the advance payment by that date, he shall be liable to an additional amount (hereafter referred to in this subsection as the 'surcharge) calculated in accordance with paragraph (d):

Provided that no surcharge shall be payable under this paragraph in respect of a failure to pay the advance payment by the due date where, prior to that date, the taxable person by whom the advance payment is payable enters into an arrangement, by agreement with the Collector-General, which guarantees payment of the advance payment by the immediately following 21st day of December and the taxable person pays the advance payment by that 21st day of December.

(c)   Notwithstanding the provisions of paragraph (b), where a taxable person has complied with the provisions of paragraph (a) as respects any advance payment due by the due date in any year, he shall nevertheless be liable to the surcharge, calculated in accordance with paragraph (d), as if he had not paid the advance payment, if he has failed to pay to the Collector-General-

(i)   any amount of tax payable by him,

(ii)   any amount payable by him pursuant to Chapter IV of Part V of the Income Tax Act, 1967, and the regulations made thereunder, or

(iii)   any amount of employment contributions payable by him under the Social Welfare Acts,

where the date for payment of such amount fell on or before the 21st day of December immediately following the due date, unless any such amount referred to in subparagraph (i), (ii) or (iii) is the subject of an agreed payment arrangement with the Collector-General and the terms of that arrangement have been complied with by the taxable person as of the 21st day of December following the due date:

Provided that where the only amount payable referred to in-

(I)   subparagraph (i) is consequent to an assessment under section 23, or

(II)   subparagraph (ii) or (iii) is consequent to an estimate under section 8 of the Finance Act, 1968,

determined after the 21st day of December immediately following the due date, no surcharge shall be payable under this paragraph where the amount payable referred to in subparagraph (i), (ii) or (iii) is less than 10 per cent of the advance payment due at that due date, or where the Revenue Commissioners consider that, having regard to the circumstances of the case, the adjustment arose from an accidental or genuine misunderstanding or error and should be disregarded for the purposes of the application of the provisions relating to the advance payment and to the application of the surcharge.

(d)   The surcharge referred to in paragraphs (b) and (c) shall be calculated at the rate of 0.25 per cent per day on the amount of the advance payment with effect from and including the due date until the day immediately preceding the day which is-

   (i)   the day on which the advance payment is paid,

   (ii)   the day on which the Collector-General receives a return for the taxable period during which the advance payment is due together with the tax, if any, payable for that period, or

   (iii)   the 20th day of January immediately following the date on which the advance payment is due,

whichever is the earliest:

Provided that the provisions of subparagraph (i) or (ii) shall only apply where the provisions of paragraph (c) do not apply.

(e)   The Revenue Commissioners may, where they consider that an advance payment is payable by a taxable person and where they consider it appropriate to do so, estimate the amount of the advance payment and serve notice on him of the amount so estimated, and the Commissioners may, where they consider it appropriate to do so, vary the amount originally estimated.

(f)   All the provisions of this Act shall apply to an estimate under paragraph (e) as if it were the advance payment and, where at any time after the service of the notice the taxable person declares the actual advance payment, the declared amount shall supersede the estimated amount for the purposes of the application of the provisions of this Act.

(g)   The provisions of this Act in relation to the recovery of tax shall apply to the advance payment and the surcharge as if they were tax.

(h)   (i) The Minister may, as respects any due date, by order

        (I)   increase the threshold to be applied for the purposes of this subsection to that due date, or

        (II)   increase, reduce or revoke an increase in the threshold resulting from any previous order under this subparagraph, including an order relating to this clause:

Provided that where the threshold is so reduced, it shall not be reduced below £120,000.

(ii) An order under subparagraph (i) shall be laid before Dáil Éireann as soon as may be after it is made and, if a resolution annulling the order is passed by Dáil Éireann within the next twenty one sitting days on which Dáil Éireann has sat after the order is laid before it, the order shall be annulled accordingly, but without prejudice to the validity of anything previously done thereunder.

(i) Following payment of the advance payment, any subsequent increase of a taxable person's total net tax, whether by way of assessment or otherwise, for the relevant period shall be disregarded for the purposes of the application of the provisions relating to the advance payment and to the application of the surcharge where-

(i) the effect of such increase is to increase the amount of the advance payment by less than 10 per cent, or

(ii) the Revenue Commissioners consider that, having regard to the circumstances of the case, the adjustment arose from an accidental or genuine misunderstanding or error and should be disregarded for the purposes of the application of the provisions relating to the advance payment and to the application of the surcharge.

(j) For the purposes of this subsection and subject to the direction and control of the Revenue Commissioners, any power, function or duty conferred or imposed on them may be exercised or performed on their behalf by an officer of the Revenue Commissioners.

(k) In this subsection-

'**due date**' means the date on which, in accordance with paragraph (a), the advance payment is due;

'**relevant period**' means, as respects a taxable person in relation to the 1st day of December in any year, the period ending on the 30th day of June in that year and commencing on the 1st day of July in the immediately preceding year:

Provided that where a person became a taxable person in that period, the relevant period shall be deemed to commence on the date on which the person first became a taxable person; 'total net tax' means the total tax payable by the taxable person on supplies, importations and intra-Community acquisitions less the amount which may be deducted by him in accordance with section 12.".

(With effect from 17 June 1993 except * from 1 September 1993)

(S.I. No. 303 of 1993)
VALUE-ADDED TAX (THRESHOLD FOR ADVANCE PAYMENT) ORDER 1993

3.   The threshold to be applied for the purposes of section 19(6) of the Act to the due date which is the 1st day of December, 1993, and to each successive due date thereafter, shall be £300,000.

(With effect from 1 December 1993)

(S.I. No. 342 of 1994)
VALUE-ADDED TAX (THRESHOLD FOR ADVANCE PAYMENT) (AMENDMENT) ORDER 1994

3.   The threshold to be applied for the purposes of section 19(6) of the Act to the due date which is the 10th day of December, 1994, and to each successive due date thereafter, shall be £1,000,000 and, accordingly, for the purposes of section 19(6)(h)(i)(II) of the Act the threshold of £300,000 specified in Article 3 of the Value-Added Tax (Threshold for Advance Payment) Order, 1993 (S.I. No. 303 of 1993), is hereby increased to £1,000,000.

(With effect from 1 December 1994)

Finance Act 1995

134. (1) Section 19 of the Principal Act is hereby amended in the definition of "accounting period" in subparagraph (i) of paragraph (aa) (inserted by the Finance Act, 1989) of subsection (3) by the substitution of the following definition for the definition of "accounting period":

"'**accounting period**' means a period, as determined by the Collector-General from time to time in any particular case, consisting of a number of consecutive taxable periods not exceeding six or such other period not exceeding a continuous period of twelve months as may be specified by the Collector-General:

Provided that-

(I)   where an accounting period begins before the end of a taxable period, the period of time from the beginning of the accounting period to the end of the taxable period during which the accounting period begins shall, for the purposes of this paragraph, be treated as if such period of time were a taxable period, and

(II)   where an accounting period ends after the beginning of a taxable period, the period of time from the beginning of the taxable period during which the accounting period ends to the end of the accounting period shall, for the purposes of this paragraph, be treated as if such period of time were a taxable period,

and any references in this paragraph to a taxable period shall be construed accordingly;".

(2)   Subsection (1) shall take effect as on and from such day or days as the Minister for Finance may by order or orders appoint, either generally or with reference to any particular category of taxable person to whom section 19(3)(aa) of the Value-Added Tax Act, 1972, applies.

(With effect from 1 September 1996)

Finance Act 1997

107.   Section 19 of the Principal Act is hereby amended-

(a)   by the insertion of the following subsection after subsection (2):

"(2A) Where a payment is made prior to the 1st day of July, 1997, in respect of a telecommunications service which is to be supplied by a person in the course or furtherance of business from outside the State on or after that date and the place of supply of that service is deemed by virtue of paragraph (e) of subsection (6) of section 5 to be, at the time of its supply, the State, then that payment shall be deemed, for the purposes of subsection (2), to be made on that date.",

*(b)   by the deletion of the proviso (inserted by the Act of 1993) to paragraph (a) of subsection (3), and

*(c)   by the deletion of subsection (6) (inserted by the Act of 1993).

(With effect from 1 July 1997
except * from 7 November 1996)

Finance Act 1999

135.   Section 19 of the Principal Act is hereby amended in clause (I) of sub-paragraph (i) of paragraph (a) of subsection (4) (inserted by the Finance Act, 1993) by the insertion after "registration of the vehicle" of "or, if

section 131 of the Finance Act, 1992, does not provide for registration of the vehicle, at a time not later than the time when the tax is due in accordance with subsection (1A)".

(With effect from 25 March 1999)

Finance Act 2001

194. Section 19 of the Principal Act is amended in subsection (3)(aa) (inserted by the Finance Act, 1989) –

(a) by the insertion in subparagraph (ii)(II) after "remit to the Collector-General any amount of tax payable by him in respect of such taxable periods," of "and, in the case of an authorised person referred to in subparagraph (iv)(III) that amount shall be the balance of tax remaining to be paid, if any, after deducting from it, the amount of tax paid by him by direct debit in respect of his accounting period,", and

(b) in subparagraph (iv) by the insertion after clause (II) of the following:

"(III) without prejudice to the generality of the fore-going, require an authorised person to agree with the Collector-General a schedule of amounts of money which he undertakes to pay on dates specified by the Collector-General by monthly direct debit from his account with a financial institution and the total of the amounts specified in that schedule shall be that person's best estimate of his total tax liability for his accounting period and he shall review on an on-going basis whether the total of the amounts specified in that schedule is likely to be adequate to cover his actual liability for his accounting period and where this is not the case or is not likely to be the case, he shall agree a revised schedule of amounts with the Collector-General and adjust his monthly direct debit amounts accordingly.".

(With effect from 21 March 2001)

Finance Act 2002

106. Section 19 of the Principal Act is amended –

*(a) in subsection (2) by inserting "However this subsection does not apply to the tax chargeable in respect of supplies of goods or services where tax is due in accordance with paragraph (a) or (b) of subsection (1) by a taxable person who is not authorised under section 14 to account for tax due by reference to the amount of the moneys received during a taxable period or part thereof." after "at the time of such receipt.", and

(b)   by inserting the following after subsection (3)(c):

"(d)   (i)   A return required to be furnished by a taxable person under this subsection may be furnished by the taxable person or another person acting under the taxable person's authority for that purpose and a return purporting to be a return furnished by a person acting under a taxable person's authority shall be deemed to be a return furnished by the taxable person, unless the contrary is proved.

(ii)   Where a return in accordance with paragraph (i) is furnished by a person acting under a taxable person's authority the provisions of any enactment relating to value-added tax shall apply as if it had been furnished by the taxable person.".

SCHEDULE 6

Miscellaneous Technical Amendments in Relation to Tax

1.   The Value-Added Tax Act, 1972, is amended in accordance with the following provisions:

(d)   section 19 is amended in subsection (3)(aa)(vii) by substituting "fourteen" for "twenty-one", and

(With effect from 25 March 2002 except * from 1 May 2002)

Finance Act 2003

123.   Section 19 of the Principal Act is amended by inserting the following after subsection (5):

"(6)   Notwithstanding the provisions of subsection (3), in cases where the provisions of section 5A are applied, the tax shall be payable at the time the VAT return is required to be submitted in accordance with section 5A(6).".

(With effect from 1 July 2003)

Finance Act 2005

106.   Section 19 of the Principal Act is amended-

(a)   in subsection (1)-

(i)   by deleting "and" at the end of paragraph (b), and

(ii)   by inserting the following after paragraph (b):

"(bb)   in the case of continuous supplies being supplies of telecommunications services, electricity, or gas which has the meaning assigned to it in paragraph (i)(c) of the Sixth Schedule, for which a statement of account issues periodically, supplied to a person other than a person to whom an invoice is required under section 17 to be issued, at the time of issue of the statement of account in respect of those supplies, and in this paragraph 'statement of account' means a balancing statement, or a demand for payment which issues at least once every 3 months, and",

and

(b)   in subsection (2) by substituting "paragraph (a), (b) or (bb)" for "paragraph (a) or (b)".

(With effect from 25 March 2005)

Finance Act 2008

*102. Section 19 of the Principal Act is amended by inserting the following after subsection (2A):

"(2B) Where a person accounts in accordance with subsection (3) for tax referred to in subsection (2) on an amount received by way of a deposit from a customer before the supply of the goods or services to which it relates, and—

(a)   that supply does not subsequently take place owing to a cancellation by the customer,

(b)   the cancellation is recorded as such in the books and records of that person,

(c)   the deposit is not refunded to the customer, and

(d)   no other consideration, benefit or supply is provided to the customer by any person in lieu of the refund of that amount,

then, the tax chargeable under section 2(1)(a) shall be reduced in the taxable period in which the cancellation is recorded by the amount of tax accounted for on the deposit.".

109.   With effect from 1 July 2008 in each provision of the Principal Act specified in the first column of Schedule 4 for the words set out in the second column of that Schedule at that entry (in each place where those words occur in the provision concerned) there is substituted the words set out at the corresponding entry in the third column of that Schedule.

Schedule 4
Miscellaneous Amendments Relating to the Amendment of the Definition of Taxable Person

Amendments to Value-Added Tax Act 1972

Provision of Value-Added Tax Act 1972	Words to be replaced	Words to be inserted
Section 19(2)	a taxable person	an accountable person
Section 19(3)(a)	a taxable person	an accountable person
Section 19(3)(aa)(i)	a taxable person	an accountable person
Section 19(3)(aa)(ii)	a taxable person	an accountable person
Section 19(3)(aa)(ii)	the taxable person	the accountable person
Section 19(3)(aa)(iii)	a taxable person	an accountable person
Section 19(3)(aa)(iii)	the taxable person	the accountable person
Section 19(3)(aa)(iv)	the taxable person	the accountable person
Section 19(3)(aa)(v)	a taxable person	an accountable person
Section 19(3)(aa)(vi)	the taxable person	the accountable person
Section 19(3)(aa)(viii)	a taxable person or a registered person	an accountable person
Section 19(3)(aa)(viii)	A taxable person	An accountable person
Section 19(3)(aa)(viii)	the taxable person	the accountable person
Section 19(3)(b)	a taxable person	an accountable person
Section 19(3)(b)	such taxable person	such accountable person
Section 19(3)(c)	a taxable person	an accountable person
Section 19(3)(d)	a taxable person	an accountable person
Section 19(3)(d)	the taxable person	the accountable person
Section 19(3)(d)	the taxable person's	the accountable person's
Section 19(3)(d)	a taxable person's	an accountable person's

(With effect from 1 July 2008 except * with effect from 13 March 2008)

Finance (No. 2) Act 2008

96.   (1)   The enactments specified in Schedule 3 are amended to the extent and in the manner specified in paragraphs 1 and 2 of that Schedule.

      (2)   This section and Schedule 3 have effect as on and from 1 January 2009.

SCHEDULE 3

Miscellaneous Amendments: Incentive to Pay and File Electronically

2.   The Value-Added Tax Act 1972 is amended in section 19 by inserting the following after subsection (3):

"(3A) Where a remittance or, as the case may be, a return and remittance, referred to in paragraph (a), subparagraphs (ii)(II) and (iv)(II) of paragraph (aa) and paragraph (b) of subsection (3) is or are —

(a)   as respects the remittance, made by such electronic means (within the meaning of section 917EA of the Taxes Consolidation Act 1997) as are required by the Revenue Commissioners, and

(b)   as respects the return, made by electronic means and in accordance with Chapter 6 of Part 38 of the Taxes Consolidation Act 1997,

then the said paragraphs (a), (aa) and (b) shall apply and have effect as if '13 days' were substituted for '9 days' or, as the case may be, 'nine days' in each place where it occurs; but where that remittance or return is made after the period provided for in this subsection this Act shall apply and have effect without regard to the provisions of this subsection.".

(With effect from 1 January 2009)

Section 19A

Finance Act 1992

Statement of intra-Community supplies

183. The Principal Act is hereby amended by the insertion of the following section after section 19:

"19A. (1)   Subject to subsections (2) and (3), a taxable person shall by the last day of the month immediately following the end of each calendar quarter, furnish to the Revenue Commissioners a statement of his intra-Community supplies in that quarter prepared in accordance with, and containing such other particulars as may be specified in, regulations.

(2)   The Revenue Commissioners shall, on request, authorise a taxable person to furnish by the last day of each month a statement of his intra-Community supplies in the previous month prepared in accordance with, and containing such other particulars as may be specified in, regulations.

(3)   The Revenue Commissioners may, on request, authorise a taxable person, whose supplies do not exceed or are not likely to exceed, in a calendar year, an amount or amounts specified in regulations, to furnish by the last day of January following that calendar year a statement of such intra-Community supplies prepared in accordance with and containing such other particulars as may be specified in regulations.

(4)   Notwithstanding the provisions of subsections (1), (2) and (3), a taxable person who made no intra-Community supplies in the relevant period, but who was liable to furnish a statement in respect of a previous period, shall, unless authorised by the Revenue Commissioners, furnish to them within the relevant time limit a statement indicating that he made no such supplies in that period.

(5)   The Revenue Commissioners may, in accordance with regulations, cancel an authorisation under subsection (2) or (3).

(6)   In this section '**intra-Community supplies**' means:

(a)   supplies of goods to a person registered for value-added tax in another Member State, and

(b)   transfers of the kind referred to in section 3(1)(g) (iii).".

(With effect from 1 January 1993)

Finance Act 2005

107. Section 19A (inserted by the Finance Act 1992) of the Principal Act is amended by substituting the following for subsection (6):

"(6)   In this section **'intra-Community supplies'** means supplies of goods to a person registered for value-added tax in another Member State.".

(With effect from 25 March 2005)

Finance Act 2008

109. With effect from 1 July 2008 in each provision of the Principal Act specified in the first column of Schedule 4 for the words set out in the second column of that Schedule at that entry (in each place where those words occur in the provision concerned) there is substituted the words set out at the corresponding entry in the third column of that Schedule.

Schedule 4
Miscellaneous Amendments Relating to the Amendment of the Definition of Taxable Person

Amendments to Value-Added Tax Act 1972

Provision of Value-Added Tax Act 1972	Words to be replaced	Words to be inserted
Section 19A	a taxable person	an accountable person

(With effect from 1 July 2008)

Section 19B

Letter of expression of doubt

Finance Act 2002

107. The Principal Act is amended by inserting the following section after section 19A —

"19B. (1) (a) Where a taxable person is in doubt as to the correct application of any enactment relating to value-added tax (in this section referred to as 'the law') to a transaction which could give rise to a liability to tax by that person or affect that person's liability to tax or entitlement to a deduction or refund of tax, then that taxable person may, at the same time as the taxable person furnishes to the Collector-General the return due in accordance with section 19 for the period in which the transaction occurred, lodge a letter of expression of doubt with the Revenue Commissioners at the office of the Revenue Commissioners which would normally deal with the examination of the records kept by that person in accordance with section 16, but this section shall only apply if that return is furnished within the time limits prescribed in section 19.

(b) For the purposes of this section 'letter of expression of doubt' means a communication received in legible form which —

(i) sets out full details of the circumstances of the transaction and makes reference to the provisions of the law giving rise to the doubt,

(ii) identifies the amount of tax in doubt in respect of the taxable period to which the expression of doubt relates,

(iii) is accompanied by supporting documentation as relevant, and

(iv) is clearly identified as a letter of expression of doubt for the purposes of this section,

and reference to an expression of doubt shall be construed accordingly.

(2) Subject to subsection (3), where a return and a letter of expression of doubt relating to a transaction are furnished by a taxable person to the Revenue Commissioners in accordance with this section, the provisions of section 21 shall not apply to any additional liability arising from a

notification to that person by the Revenue Commissioners of the correct application of the law to the said transaction, on condition that such additional liability is accounted for and remitted to the Collector-General by the taxable person as if it were tax due for the taxable period in which the notification is issued.

(3)   Subsection (2) does not apply where the Revenue Commissioners do not accept as genuine an expression of doubt in respect of the application of the law to a transaction, and an expression of doubt shall not be accepted as genuine in particular where the Revenue Commissioners—

(a)   have issued general guidelines concerning the application of the law in similar circumstances,

(b)   are of the opinion that the matter is otherwise sufficiently free from doubt as not to warrant an expression of doubt, or

(c)   are of the opinion that the taxable person was acting with a view to the evasion or avoidance of tax.

(4)   Where the Revenue Commissioners do not accept an expression of doubt as genuine they shall notify the taxable person accordingly, and the taxable person shall account for any tax, which was not correctly accounted for in the return referred to in subsection (1), as tax due for the taxable period in which the transaction occurred, and the provisions of section 21 shall apply accordingly.

(5)   A taxable person who is aggrieved by a decision of the Revenue Commissioners that that person's expression of doubt is not genuine may, by giving notice in writing to the Revenue Commissioners within the period of twenty-one days after the notification of the said decision, require the matter to be referred to the Appeal Commissioners.

(6)   A letter of expression of doubt shall be deemed not to have been made unless its receipt is acknowledged by the Revenue Commissioners and that acknowledgement forms part of the records kept by the taxable person for the purposes of section 16.

(7)   (a)   For the purposes of this section 'taxable person' includes a person who is not a registered person and is in doubt as to whether he or she is a taxable person in respect of a transaction and in that case references to a return and records are to be construed as referring to a return that would be

due under section 19 and records that would be kept for the purposes of section 16, if that person were in fact a taxable person.

(b)   A person whose expression of doubt concerns whether he or she is a taxable person shall lodge that expression of doubt for the purposes of applying subsection (2) not later than the nineteenth day of the month following the taxable period in which the transaction giving rise to the expression of doubt occurred.".

(With effect from 25 March 2002)

Finance Act 2008

109.   With effect from 1 July 2008 in each provision of the Principal Act specified in the first column of Schedule 4 for the words set out in the second column of that Schedule at that entry (in each place where those words occur in the provision concerned) there is substituted the words set out at the corresponding entry in the third column of that Schedule.

Schedule 4
Miscellaneous Amendments Relating to the Amendment of the Definition of Taxable Person

Amendments to Value-Added Tax Act 1972

Provision of Value-Added Tax Act 1972	Words to be replaced	Words to be inserted
Section 19B	a taxable person	an accountable person
Section 19B	that taxable person	that accountable person
Section 19B	the taxable person	the accountable person
Section 19B	A taxable person	An accountable person
Section 19B	'taxable person'	'accountable person'

(With effect from 1 July 2008)

Section 20
Value Added Tax Act 1972
Refund of tax

20. (1)   Where, on a claim made in accordance with regulations, it is shown to the satisfaction of the Revenue Commissioners that, in relation to any taxable period, the amount of tax actually paid to the Collector-General in accordance with section 19 together with the amount of tax which qualified for deduction under section 12 exceeds the tax, if any, which would, properly be payable if no deduction were made under the said section 12, they may refund the excess and may include any interest which has been paid under section 21 in the amount refunded.

      (2)   Notwithstanding anything in this Act, a refund of the tax paid in respect of radio broadcasting reception apparatus and parts thereof belonging to an institution or society may be made to the institution or society if, but only if-

           (a)   in the opinion of the Revenue Commissioners, it has for its primary object the amelioration of the lot of blind persons, and

           (b)   it shows, to the satisfaction of the Revenue Commissioners, that the goods in question are intended for the use of blind persons.

      (3)   (a)   The Minister may by order provide that a person who fulfils to the satisfaction of the Revenue Commissioners such conditions as may be specified in the order in relation to the delivery to such person of goods of a kind specified in the order or the rendering to him of services of a kind so specified shall be entitled to be repaid so much, as is specified in the order, of any tax borne or paid by him in relation to such delivery or rendering as does not qualify for deduction under section 12 in computing his liability to tax.

           (b)   The Minister may by order amend or revoke an order under this subsection, including an order under this paragraph.

           (c)   An order under this subsection shall be laid before Dáil Éireann as soon as may be after it is made and, if a resolution annulling the order is passed by Dáil Éireann within the next twenty-one days on which Dáil Éireann has sat after the order is laid before it, the order shall be annulled accordingly, but without prejudice to the validity of anything previously done thereunder.

(4)   No refund shall be made under this section or under section 5(4) unless the claim is made within the period of ten years from the end of the taxable period to which the claim relates.

(With effect from 1 November 1972)

Value–Added Tax (Amendment) Act 1978

30.   (1)   The enactment mentioned in column (2) of the First Schedule is hereby repealed to the extent specified in column (3) of that Schedule.

(2)   In consequence of the amendments of the Principal Act specified in this Act and of the repeals specified in the First Schedule, the Principal Act is hereby further amended by the substitution of the word or expression mentioned in column (3) of the Second Schedule at any reference number for the word or expression mentioned in column (2) of that Schedule at that reference number wherever it occurs in the provision of the Principal Act mentioned in column (4) of that Schedule at that reference number.

SECOND SCHEDULE
Consequential Amendments

Reference Number (1)	Existing word or expression (2)	Substituted word or expression (3)	Provision of Principal Act (4)
14	"delivery to such person of goods of a kind specified in the order or the rendering to him of services"	"supply to such person of goods or services"	Section 20(3).
16	"delivery or rendering"	"supply"	Section 20(3)(a).
32	"section 5 (4)"	"any other provision of this Act or regulations"	Section 20(4).

(With effect from 1 March 1979)

Finance Act 1981

45.   Section 20 of the Principal Act is hereby amended by the substitution of the following subsection for subsection (1):

"(1)   Where, in relation to a return lodged under section 19 or a claim made in accordance with regulations, it is shown to the satisfaction of the Revenue Commissioners that, as respects any taxable period, the amount of tax, if any, actually paid to the Collector-General in accordance with section 19 together with the amount of tax, if any, which qualified for deduction under section 12 exceeds the tax, if any, which would properly be payable if no deduction were made under the said section 12, they shall refund the amount of the excess less any sums previously refunded under this subsection or repaid under section 12 and may include in the amount refunded any interest which has been paid under section 21.".

(With effect from 28 May 1981)

Finance Act 1986

87.   Section 20 of the Principal Act is hereby amended-

(a)   in subsection (1) by the substitution of "Subject to subsection (1A), where" for "Where",

and

(b)   by the insertion after subsection (1) of the following subsection:

"(1A) The Revenue Commissioners may defer repayment of all or part of any tax refundable to any taxable person under subsection (1) where they are satisfied that the business activities of that taxable person are so interlinked with the business activities of one or more other taxable persons that it would have been expedient to apply the provisions of section 8(8) in relation to all the taxable persons concerned, if the request specified in that section had been made, and any of the said one or more other taxable persons has not furnished all returns and remitted all amounts of tax referred to in section 19(3).".

(With effect from 27 May 1986)

Finance Act 1989

59.   Section 20(3)(as amended by the Act of 1978) of The Principal Act is hereby amended in paragraph (a) by the substitution of "shall, in relation to the supply to such person of goods or services of a kind so specified," for "in relation to the supply to such person of goods or services of a kind so specified shall", and the said paragraph (a), as so amended, is set out in the Table to this section.

TABLE

(3)   (a)   The Minister may by order provide that a person who fulfils to the satisfaction of the Revenue Commissioners such conditions as may be specified in the order shall, in relation to the supply to such person of goods or services of a kind so specified, be entitled to be repaid so much, as is specified in the order, of any tax borne or paid by him in relation to such supply as does not qualify for deduction under section 12 in computing his liability to tax.

(With effect from 1 March 1989)

Finance Act 1991

83. Section 20 of the Principal Act is hereby amended by the substitution of the following subsection for subsection (1A) (inserted by the Act of 1986):

"(1A) Where the Revenue Commissioners apply the provisions of section 8(8) to a number of persons they may defer repayment of all or part of any tax refundable under subsection (1) to any one or more of the said persons prior to the application of those provisions, where any one or more of the said persons have not furnished all returns and remitted all amounts of tax referred to in section 19(3) at the time of such application.".

(With effect from 29 May 1991)

Finance Act 1992

184. (1) Section 20 of the Principal Act is hereby amended-

    (a) in subsection (1) (inserted by the Act of 1981) by the substitution of "Subject to subsections (1A) and (1B)" for "Subject to subsection (1A)",

    (b) by the insertion after subsection (1A) (inserted by the Act of 1991) of the following subsection:

        "(1B) The Revenue Commissioners may, where it appears requisite to them to do so for the protection of the revenue, require as a condition for making a refund in accordance with subsection (1) the giving of security of such amount and in such manner and form as they may determine:

        Provided that the amount of such security shall not, in any particular case, exceed the amount to be refunded.",

    *(c) in subsection (3) by the substitution of the following paragraph for paragraph (a):

        "(a) The Minister may by order provide that a person who fulfils to the satisfaction of the Revenue Commissioners such conditions as may be specified in the order shall be entitled to be repaid so much, as is specified in the order, of any tax borne or paid by him as does not qualify for deduction under section 12.",

    and

    (d) by the insertion of the following subsection after subsection (4):

        "(5) (a) If a person pays an amount of tax which was not properly due by him, he may claim

a refund of the amount and the Revenue
Commissioners shall, subject to the provisions
of this section, refund to him that amount.

(b) It shall be a defence in relation to a claim under
this subsection or under any other provision
of this Act or regulations for a refund that
payment of the refund would unjustly enrich
the claimant.".

(2)   Every order made under Section 20(3)(a) of The Principal
Act which is a subsisting order immediately before the
commencement of this section shall, upon such commencement,
continue in force as if made under the said section 20(3)(a) as
amended by this section.

(With effect from 28 May 1992 except * from 1 January 1993)

Finance Act 1993

93.   Section 20 of the Principal Act is hereby amended in sub-section (1)
(inserted by the Act of 1981) by the insertion of the following proviso to
that subsection:

"Provided that where the taxable period is the period ending on the 31st
day of December in any year, the amount of tax to be refunded shall be
increased by the amount paid, if any, in accordance with paragraph (a)
of subsection (6) of section 19 where that amount was due during that
taxable period.".

(With effect from 17 June 1993)

Finance Act 1995

135. Section 20 of the Principal Act is hereby amended by the insertion of the
following subsection after subsection (5) (inserted by the Act of 1992):

"(6)   Where the Revenue Commissioners refund any amount due
under subsection (1) or subsection (5), they may if they so
determine refund any such amount directly into an account,
specified by the person to whom the amount is due, in a financial
institution.".

(With effect from 2 June 1995)

Finance Act 1997

108. Section 20 of the Principal Act is hereby amended by the deletion of the
proviso to subsection (1) (inserted by the Act of 1993).

(With effect from 7 November 1996)

Finance Act 1998

114. Section 20 of the Principal Act is hereby amended -

(a)   by the substitution of the following subsection for subsection (4):

"(4)   (a)   In relation to any taxable period ending before the 1st day of May, 1998, no refund shall, subject to paragraph (b), be made under this section or any other provision of this Act or regulations unless a claim for that refund is made within the period of ten years from the end of the taxable period to which the claim relates.

(b)   In relation to any taxable period commencing on or after the 1st day of May, 1998, and on or after the 1st day of May, 1999, in relation to any other taxable period, no refund shall be made under this section or under any other provision of this Act or regulations unless a claim for that refund is made within the period of six years from the end of the taxable period to which that claim relates.",

and

(b)   by the substitution of the following subsection for subsection (5) (inserted by the Act of 1992):

"(5)   (a)   Where, due to a mistaken assumption in the operation of the tax, whether that mistaken assumption was made by a taxable person, any other person or the Revenue Commissioners, a person accounts for an amount of tax for which that person was not properly accountable, hereafter referred to in this subsection as the 'overpaid amount', that person may claim a refund of the over-paid amount and the Revenue Commissioners shall, subject to the provisions of this subsection, refund to the claimant the overpaid amount unless that refund would result in the unjust enrichment of the claimant.

(b)   Unjust enrichment of the claimant for the purposes of this section means the refund to a claimant of an overpaid amount or any part of an overpaid amount in circumstances where the cost of such overpaid amount or part thereof was, for practical purposes, passed on by the claimant to other persons in the price charged by the claimant for goods or services supplied by the claimant.

(c)   Where, in relation to any claim under paragraph (a), the Revenue Commissioners have withheld an amount of the overpaid amount claimed under paragraph (a) as it would result in the unjust enrichment of the claimant the Revenue Commissioners shall, notwithstanding the provisions of paragraph (a), refund to the claimant out of the amount withheld, the amount quantified at paragraph (d)(iii) which would appropriately compensate the claimant for any loss of profits due to the mistaken assumption made in the operation of the tax, where the Revenue Commissioners are satisfied that the conditions in paragraph (d) have been met.

(d)   The conditions referred to in paragraph (c), are that the claimant must -

(i)   establish, based on an economic analysis which takes into account the price elasticity of demand of the goods or services supplied by the claimant, that the claimant's business has suffered a loss of turnover due to the mistaken assumption made in the operation of the tax,

(ii)   quantify the extent of that loss,

(iii)   quantify the extent of the claimant's loss of profits due to that loss of turnover.

(e)   Where, in relation to any claim under paragraph (a), the Revenue Commissioners have withheld an amount of the overpaid amount claimed under paragraph (a) as it would result in the unjust enrichment of the claimant the Revenue Commissioners shall, notwithstanding the provisions of paragraph (a), refund to the claimant that part of the withheld amount which the claimant has undertaken to repay to the persons to whom the cost of the overpaid amount was passed on where they are satisfied that the claimant has adequate arrangements in place to identify and repay those persons.

(f)   Where a claimant receives a refund in accordance with paragraph (e) and fails to repay the persons concerned at the latest by the thirtieth day next following the payment by the Revenue Commissioners of that refund, then any amount not so repaid shall, for the purposes of this Act, be treated as if it were tax due by the claimant for the taxable period within which that day falls.".

(With effect from 27 March 1998)

Finance Act 2000

116. Section 20 of the Principal Act is amended-

(a)   by the insertion in subsection (3) of the following paragraph after paragraph (b):

"(bb)   An order under this subsection may, if so expressed, have retrospective effect.",

(b)   by the substitution in subsection (5) of the following paragraph for paragraph (a):

"(a)   Where, due to a mistaken assumption in the operation of the tax, whether that mistaken assumption was made by a taxable person, any other person or the Revenue Commissioners, a person-

(i)   accounted, in a return furnished to the Revenue Commissioners, for an amount of tax for which that person was not properly accountable, or

(ii)   did not, because that person's supplies of goods and services were treated as exempted activities, furnish a return to the Revenue Commissioners and, therefore, did not receive a refund of an amount of tax in accordance with subsection (1), or

(iii)   did not deduct an amount of tax in respect of qualifying activities, as defined in section 12(1)(b), which that person was entitled to deduct,

then, in respect of the total amount of tax referred to in subparagraphs (i), (ii) or (iii) (in this subsection referred to as the 'overpaid amount') that person may claim a refund of the overpaid amount and the Revenue Commissioners shall, subject to the provisions of this subsection, refund to the claimant the overpaid amount unless that refund would result in the unjust enrichment of the claimant.",

(c)   by the substitution in subsection (5)(d)(i) of "a loss of demand for those goods or services, for the period for which the claim is being made", for "a loss of turnover", and

(d)   by the substitution in subsection (5)(d)(iii) of "loss of demand" for "loss of turnover".

(With effect from 23 March 2000)

Finance Act 2003

124. Section 20 of the Principal Act is amended —

(a)   in subsection (4)(a) —

(i)   by substituting "1 May 2003" for "the 1st day of May, 1998", and

(ii)   by substituting "six years" for "ten years",

(b)   in subsection (4)(b) –

(i)   by substituting "1 May 2003" for "the 1st day of May, 1998",

(ii)   by substituting "1 January 2005" for "the 1st day of May, 1999,", and

(iii)   by substituting "four years" for "six years",

(c)   in subsection (5)(e) by inserting "together with any interest payable in accordance with section 21A" after "refund to the claimant that part of the withheld amount", and

(d)   by inserting the following subsection after subsection (6):

"(7)   The Revenue Commissioners shall not refund any amount of tax except as provided for in this Act, or any order or regulation made under this Act.".

(With effect from 1 November 2003)

Finance Act 2008

109.   With effect from 1 July 2008 in each provision of the Principal Act specified in the first column of Schedule 4 for the words set out in the second column of that Schedule at that entry (in each place where those words occur in the provision concerned) there is substituted the words set out at the corresponding entry in the third column of that Schedule.

Schedule 4
Miscellaneous Amendments Relating to the Amendment of the Definition of Taxable Person
Amendments to Value-Added Tax Act 1972

Provision of Value-Added Tax Act 1972	Words to be replaced	Words to be inserted
Section 20	a taxable person	an accountable person

(With effect from 1 July 2008)

Finance (No. 2) Act 2008

74.   Section 20 of the Principal Act is amended –

(a)   in subsection (5)(a) by substituting "unless they determine that the refund of that overpaid amount or part thereof would result in the unjust enrichment of the claimant" for "unless that refund would result in the unjust enrichment of the claimant", and

(b)   by substituting the following for paragraphs (b), (c) and (d) of subsection (5):

"(b)   A person who claims a refund of an overpaid amount under this subsection shall make that claim in writing setting out full details of the circumstances of the case and identifying the overpaid amount in respect of each taxable period to which the claim relates. The claimant shall furnish such relevant documentation to support the claim as the Revenue Commissioners may request.

(c)   (i)   For the purposes of determining whether a refund of an overpaid amount or part there-of would result in the unjust enrichment of a claimant, the Revenue Commissioners shall have regard to —

(I)   the extent to which the cost of the overpaid amount was, for practical purposes, passed on by the claimant to other persons in the price charged by that claimant for goods or services supplied by that claimant,

(II)   any net loss of profits which they have reason to believe, based on their own analysis and on any information that may be provided to them by the claimant, was borne by the claimant due to the mistaken assumption made in the operation of the tax, and

(III)   any other factors that the claimant brings to their attention in this context.

(ii)   The Revenue Commissioners may request from the claimant all reasonable information relating to the circumstances giving rise to the claim as may assist them in reaching a determination for the purposes of subparagraph (i).

(d)   Where, in accordance with paragraph (c), the Revenue Commissioners determine that a refund of an overpaid amount or part thereof would result in the unjust enrichment of a claimant, they shall refund only so much of the overpaid amount as would not result in the unjust enrichment of that claimant.".

(With effect from 24 December 2008)

Section 21

Value Added Tax Act 1972

Interest

21.   (1)   Where any amount of tax becomes payable under section 19(3) and is not paid, simple interest on the amount shall be paid by the accountable person, and such interest shall be calculated from the date on which the amount became payable and at a rate of 1 per cent for each month or part of a month during which the amount remains unpaid:

Provided that if the amount of the interest as so calculated is less than £5, the amount of interest payable shall be £5.

(2)   Subsection (1) shall apply-

(a)   to tax recoverable by virtue of a notice under section 22 as if the tax were tax which the person was liable to pay for the respective taxable period or periods comprised in the notice, and

(b)   to tax recoverable by virtue of a notice under section 23 as if the tax were tax which the person was liable to pay for the taxable period during which the period of fourteen days from the date of the service of the notice expired or the appeal provided for in that section was determined by agreement or otherwise, whichever taxable period is the later.

(With effect from 1 November 1972)

Finance Act 1975

28.   (1)   This section applies to interest chargeable under-

(a)   Section 14 of the Finance Act, 1962,

(b)   Section 129 of the Income Tax Act, 1967,

(c)   Section 550 of the said Income Tax Act, 1967,

(d)   Section 17(6A) of the Finance Act, 1970,

(e)   Sections 20(2) and 50(2) of the Finance Act, 1971, and

(f)   Section 21 of the Value-Added Tax Act, 1972.

(2)   Where any interest to which this section applies is chargeable for any month commencing on or after the 6th day of April, 1975, or any part of such a month, in respect of tax due to be paid or remitted whether before, on or after such date, such interest shall be chargeable at the rate of 1.5 per cent for each month or part of a month instead of at the rate specified in the said sections and those sections shall have effect as if the rate aforesaid were substituted for the rates specified in those sections.

(3)   In this section "tax" means income tax, sur-tax, corporation profits tax or value-added tax, as may be appropriate.

(With effect from 1 May 1975)

Finance Act 1976

56. Section 21 of the Principal Act is hereby amended by the substitution for paragraph (b) of subsection (2) of the following paragraph:

"(b)   to tax recoverable by virtue of a notice under section 23 as if (whether a notice of appeal under that section is received or not) the tax were tax which the person was liable to pay for the taxable period or, as the case may be, the later or latest taxable period included in the period comprised in the notice.".

Priority in bankruptcy and winding-up

62. (1)   There shall be included among the debts which, under section 4 of the Preferential Payments in Bankruptcy (Ireland) Act, 1889, are to be paid in priority to all other debts in the distribution of the property of a person, being a bankrupt, arranging debtor, or person dying insolvent, any tax for which the person is liable in relation to taxable periods which shall have ended within the period of 12 months next before the date on which the order of adjudication of the bankrupt was made, the petition of arrangement of the debtor was filed, or, as the case may be, the person died insolvent and any interest payable by the person under section 21 of the Principal Act.

(2)   (a)   There shall be included among the debts which, under section 285 of the Companies Act, 1963, are to be paid in priority to all other debts in the winding-up of a company any tax for which the company is liable in relation to taxable periods which shall have ended within the period of 12 months next before the relevant date and any interest payable by the company under section 21 of the Principal Act.

(b)   Paragraph (a) shall, for the purposes of section 98 of the Companies Act, 1963, be deemed to be contained in section 285 of that Act.

(c)   In paragraph (a) "the relevant date" has the same meaning as it has in section 285 of the Companies Act, 1963.

(With effect from 27 May 1976)

Finance Act 1978

46. (1)   This section applies to interest chargeable under-

(a)   section 14 of the Finance Act, 1962,

(b)   sections 129 and 550 of the Income Tax Act, 1967,

(c)   section 17(6A) of the Finance Act, 1970,

(d)   sections 20(2) and 50(2) of the Finance Act, 1971,

(e)   section 21 of the Value Added Tax Act, 1972,

(f)   sections 145 and 152 of the Corporation Tax Act, 1976.

(2)   Where any interest to which this section applies is chargeable for any month commencing on or after the date of the passing of this Act, or any part of such a month, in respect of tax due to be paid or remitted whether before, on or after such date, such interest shall, notwithstanding the provisions of section 28 of the Finance Act, 1975, be chargeable at the rate of 1.25 per cent for each month or part of a month instead of at the rate specified in the said sections and those sections shall have effect as if the rate aforesaid were substituted for the rates specified in those sections.

(3)   In this section "tax" means income tax, sur-tax, capital gains tax, corporation profits tax, corporation tax or value-added tax, as may be appropriate.

(With effect from 1 August 1978)

Value–Added Tax (Amendment) Act 1978

30.   (1)   The enactment mentioned in column (2) of the First Schedule is hereby repealed to the extent specified in column (3) of that Schedule.

(2)   In consequence of the amendments of the Principal Act specified in this Act and of the repeals specified in the First Schedule, the Principal Act is hereby further amended by the substitution of the word or expression mentioned in column (3) of the Second Schedule at any reference number for the word or expression mentioned in column (2) of that Schedule at that reference number wherever it occurs in the provision of the Principal Act mentioned in column (4) of that Schedule at that reference number.

SECOND SCHEDULE
Consequential Amendments

Reference Number	Existing word or expression	Substituted word or expression	Provision of Principal Act
25	"accountable person" except where preceded by the word "an"	"taxable person"	Section 21(1).

(With effect from 1 March 1979)

Finance Act 1998

133. Interest on unpaid or overpaid taxes

    (1)   The Taxes Consolidation Act, 1997, is hereby amended

        (a)   in sections 240(3)(a), 531(9) and 991(1) and paragraphs (a) and (b) of section 1080(1), by the substitution of "1 per cent" for "1.25 per cent" in each place where it occurs, and

        (b)   in section 953(7), by the substitution of "0.5 per cent" for "0.6 per cent".

    (2)   The Finance Act, 1983, is hereby amended?

        (a)   in section 105(1), by the substitution of "1 per cent" for "1.25 per cent.", and

        (b)   in section 107(2), notwithstanding Regulation 3 of the Payment of Interest on Overpaid Tax Regulations, 1990 (S.I. No. 176 of 1990), by the substitution of "0.5 per cent" for "1.25 per cent".

    (3)   Section 46 of the Finance Act, 1978, is hereby repealed in so far as it relates to value-added tax.

    (4)   The Capital Acquisitions Tax Act, 1976, is hereby amended-

        (a)   in section 41(2), as construed by reference to section 43 of the Finance Act, 1978, by the substitution of "1 per cent" for "1.25 per cent", and

        (b)   in section 46(1), notwithstanding Regulation 3 of the Payment of Interest on Overpaid Tax Regulations, 1990, by the substitution of "0.5 per cent" for "one per cent".

    (5)   The Wealth Tax Act, 1975, is hereby amended-

        (a)   in section 18(2), by the substitution of "1 per cent" for " 1.5 per cent", and

        (b)   in section 22(2), by the substitution of "0.5 per cent" for "1.5 per cent".

    (6)   This section shall apply as respects interest chargeable or payable under-

        (i)   Sections 240, 531, 953, 991 and 1080 of the Taxes Consolidation Act, 1997,

        (ii)   Sections 105 and 107 of the Finance Act, 1983,

        (iii)   Sections 41 and 46 of the Capital Acquisitions Tax Act, 1976,

        (iv)   Sections 18 and 22 of the Wealth Tax Act, 1975, and

        (v)   Section 21 of the Value-Added Tax Act, 1972,

        for any month, or any part of a month, commencing on or after the date of the passing of this Act, in respect of an amount due to be paid or remitted or an amount due to be repaid or retained, as the case may be, whether before, on or after that date in accordance with those provisions.

(With effect from 27 March 1998)

Finance Act 2001

195. Section 21 of the Principal Act is amended by the insertion of the following after subsection (1):

"(1A) Where the amount of the balance of tax remaining to be paid in accordance with section 19(3)(aa)(ii)(II) by an authorised person referred to in section 19(3)(aa)(iv)(III) (in this subsection referred to as the 'balance') represents more than per cent of the tax which the authorised person became accountable for in respect of his accounting period, then, for the purposes of this subsection, that balance shall be deemed to be payable on a day (in this subsection referred to as the 'accrual day') which is 6 months prior to the final day for the furnishing of a return in accordance with section 19(3)(aa)(ii)(II) and simple interest in accordance with this section shall apply from that accrual day, however, where an authorised person can demonstrate to the satisfaction of the Collector-General that the amount of interest payable on the balance, in accordance with this subsection, is greater than the sum of the amounts of interest which would have been payable in accordance with this section if-

(a) the authorised person was not so authorised,

(b) the person had submitted a return in accordance with section 19(3)(a) for each taxable period comprising the accounting period, and

(c) the amounts which were paid by direct debit during a taxable period are deemed to have been paid on the due date for submission of that return for that taxable period,

then that sum of the amounts of interest is payable.".

*240. (1) (a) Subject to subsection (2), in each provision specified in column (1) of Schedule 5 for the words or amount set out in column (2) of that Schedule at that entry there shall be substituted the words or amount set out at the corresponding entry in column (3) of that Schedule.

(b) Where words are or an amount is mentioned more than once in a provision specified in column (1) of Schedule 5, then the substitution provided for by paragraph (a) shall apply as respects those words or that amount to each mention of those words or that amount in that provision.

SCHEDULE 5

PART 4

Value-Added Tax and related matters

Enactment amended (1)	Amount or words to be replaced (2)	Amount or words to be inserted (3)
Value-Added Tax Act, 1972 (No. 22 of 1972) (as amended): section 21(1)	£5	€6

(With effect from 21 March 2001 except * from 1 January 2002)

Finance Act 2002

108. Section 21 of the Principal Act is amended by substituting the following subsection for subsection (1) —

"(1)   (a)   Where any amount of tax becomes payable under section 19(3) and is not paid, simple interest on the amount shall be paid by the taxable person, and such interest shall be calculated from the date on which the amount became payable and at a rate of 0.0322 per cent for each day or part of a day during which the amount remains unpaid.

       (b)   Where an amount of tax is refunded to a person and where —

            (i)   no amount of tax was properly refundable to that person under section 20(1), or

            (ii)   the amount of tax refunded is greater than the amount properly refundable to that person under section 20(1),

simple interest shall be paid by that person on any amount of tax refunded to that person which was not properly refundable to that person under section 20(1), from the date the refund was made, at the rate of 0.0322 per cent for each day or part of a day during which the person does not correctly account for any such amount refunded which was not properly refundable.".

(With effect from 1 September 2002)

Finance Act 2008

109. With effect from 1 July 2008 in each provision of the Principal Act specified in the first column of Schedule 4 for the words set out in the second column of that Schedule at that entry (in each place where those words occur in the provision concerned) there is substituted the words set out at the corresponding entry in the third column of that Schedule.

Schedule 4
Miscellaneous Amendments Relating to the Amendment of the Definition of Taxable Person

Amendments to Value-Added Tax Act 1972

Provision of Value-Added Tax Act 1972	Words to be replaced	Words to be inserted
Section 21	the taxable person	the accountable person

(With effect from 1 July 2008)

Finance Act 2009

29.   (4)   Section 21(1) of the Value-Added Tax Act 1972 is amended —

    (a)   in paragraph (a) by substituting "0.0274" for "0.0322", and

    (b)   in paragraph (b) by substituting "0.0274" for "0.0322".

(With effect from 1 July 2009)

Section 21A

Interest on refunds of tax

Finance Act 2003

125. The Principal Act is amended by inserting the following section after section 21 —

"21A. (1) For the purposes of this section —

'**claimant**' means a person who submits a valid claim for a refundable amount;

'**overpaid amount**' means an amount which is a refundable amount as a result of a claimant having made a payment of tax;

'**refundable amount**' means an amount which a person is entitled to receive from the Revenue Commissioners in accordance with this Act or any order or regulation made under this Act and which is claimed within the period provided for in subsection 20(4), but such amount does not include interest payable under this section;

'**valid claim**' means a return or a claim, furnished in accordance with this Act or any order or regulation made under it, and which includes all information required by the Revenue Commissioners to establish the refundable amount.

(2) Where a mistaken assumption in the operation of the tax is made by the Revenue Commissioners and as a result a refundable amount is payable to a claimant, interest at the rate set out in subsection (4) or prescribed by order under subsection (7) shall, subject to section 1006A(2A) of the Taxes Consolidation Act 1997, be payable by the Revenue Commissioners on that amount from —

(a) in the case of an overpaid amount, the day that overpaid amount was received by the Revenue Commissioners,

(b) in the case of any other refundable amount, the 19th day of the month following the taxable period in respect of which a claimant would have been entitled to receive a refundable amount but for the mistaken assumption in the operation of the tax by the Revenue Commissioners, but where a return was due in accordance with section 19 from that claimant in respect of that taxable period, the day such return was received, to the day on which the refundable amount is paid by the Revenue Commissioners to the claimant.

(3)   Where, for any reason other than a mistaken assumption in the operation of the tax made by the Revenue Commissioners, a refundable amount is payable to a claimant but is not paid until after the expiry of six months from the day the Revenue Commissioners receive a valid claim for that amount, interest at the rate specified in subsection (4) or prescribed by order under subsection (7) shall, subject to section 1006A(2A) of the Taxes Consolidation Act 1997, be payable by the Revenue Commissioners on that amount from the day on which that six months expires to the day on which the refundable amount is paid by the Revenue Commissioners to the claimant.

(4)   Interest payable in accordance with this section shall be simple interest payable at the rate of 0.011 per cent per day or part of a day, or such other rate as may be prescribed by the Minister for Finance by order under subsection (7).

(5)   Interest shall not be payable if it amounts to less than €10.

(6)   (a)   The Revenue Commissioners shall not pay interest in respect of any amount under this Act except as provided for by this section.

        (b)   This section shall not apply in relation to any refund of tax in respect of which interest is payable under or by virtue of any provision of any other enactment.

(7)   (a)   The Minister for Finance may, from time to time, make an order prescribing a rate for the purposes of subsection (4).

        (b)   Every order made by the Minister for Finance under paragraph (a) shall be laid before Dáil Éireann as soon as may be after it is made and, if a resolution annulling the order is passed by Dáil Éireann within the next 21 days on which Dáil Éireann has sat after the order is laid before it, the order shall be annulled accordingly, but without prejudice to the validity of anything previously done under it.

(8)   The Revenue Commissioners may make regulations as necessary governing the operation of this section.".

(With effect from 1 November 2003)

Finance Act 2007

121. (2)   Subsection (3) of section 21A (inserted by the Finance Act 2003) of the Value-Added Tax Act 1972 is amended by substituting "93 days" for "six months" in both places where it occurs.

(With effect from 2 April 2007)

Section 22

Value Added Tax Act 1972

Estimation of tax due for a taxable period

22. (1)   If within the time prescribed by section 19(3) an accountable person fails to furnish in accordance with the relevant regulation a return of the tax payable by him in respect of any taxable period, then, without prejudice to any other action which may be taken, the Revenue Commissioners may, in accordance with regulations, but subject to section 30, estimate the amount of tax payable by him in respect of that taxable period and serve notice on him of the amount estimated.

(2)   Where a notice is served under subsection (1) on a person, the following provisions shall apply:

(a)   the person may, if he claims that he is not an accountable person, by giving notice in writing to the Revenue Commissioners within the period of twenty-one days from the date of the service of the notice, require the claim to be referred for decision to the Appeal Commissioners and their decision shall, subject to section 25, be final and conclusive,

(b)   on the expiration of the said period, if no such claim is required to be so referred, or if such a claim is required to be so referred, on final determination against the claim, the estimated tax specified in the notice shall be recoverable in the same manner and by the like proceedings as if the person had furnished, within the prescribed period, a true and correct return, in accordance with regulations, for the taxable period to which the estimate relates, showing as due by him such estimated tax.

(c)   if at any time after the service of the notice the person furnishes a return, in accordance with regulations, in respect of the taxable period specified in the notice and pays tax in accordance with the return, together with any interest and costs which may have been incurred in connection with the default, the notice shall, subject to paragraph (d), stand discharged and any excess of tax which may have been paid shall be repaid.

(d)   where action for the recovery of tax specified in a notice under subsection (1), being action by way of the institution of proceedings in any court or the issue of a certificate under section 485 of the income Tax Act, 1967, has been taken, paragraph (c) shall not, unless the Revenue

Commissioners otherwise direct, apply in relation to that notice until the said action has been completed.

(3)   A notice given by the Revenue Commissioners under subsection (1) may extend to two or more taxable periods.

(With effect from 1 November 1972)

Value Added Tax (Amendment) Act 1978

30. (1)   The enactment mentioned in column (2) of the First Schedule is hereby repealed to the extent specified in column (3) of that Schedule.

(2)   In consequence of the amendments of the Principal Act specified in this Act and of the repeals specified in the First Schedule, the Principal Act is hereby further amended by the substitution of the word or expression mentioned in column (3) of the Second Schedule at any reference number for the word or expression mentioned in column (2) of that Schedule at that reference number wherever it occurs in the provision of the Principal Act mentioned in column (4) of that Schedule at that reference number.

SECOND SCHEDULE
Consequential Amendments

Reference Number (1)	Existing word or expression (2)	Substituted word or expression (3)	Provision of Principal Act (4)
26	"an accountable person"	"a taxable person"	Sections 22(1), 22(2)(a)

(With effect from 1 March 1979)

Finance Act 1995

136. Section 22 of the Principal Act is hereby amended in subsection (1) by the insertion of the following proviso to that subsection:

"Provided that where the Revenue Commissioners are satisfied that the amount so estimated is excessive, they may amend the amount so estimated by reducing it and serve notice on the person concerned of the revised amount estimated and such notice shall supersede any previous notice issued under this subsection.".

(With effect from 2 June 1995)

Taxes Consolidation Act 1997

1100. Schedule 30

(**Note** this schedule should have substituted "section 485 of the income Tax Act, 1967 with " section 962 of the Taxes Consolidation Act 1997" in 22(2)(d)).

Finance Act 2000

117.   Section 22 of the Principal Act is amended in subsections (1) and (2) by the substitution of "period" for "taxable period" wherever it occurs.

(With effect from 23 March 2000)

Finance Act 2001

196.   Section 22 of the Principal Act is amended by the substitution in paragraph (a) of subsection (2) of "fourteen" for "twenty-one".

(With effect from 21 March 2001)

Finance Act 2003

126.   Section 22 of the Principal Act is amended by replacing the proviso in subsection (1) with the following:

"Provided that where the Revenue Commissioners are satisfied that—

(a)   the amount so estimated is excessive, they may amend the amount so estimated by reducing it, or

(b)   the amount so estimated is insufficient, they may amend the amount so estimated by increasing it,

then, in either case, they shall serve notice on the person concerned of the revised amount estimated and such notice shall supercede any previous notice issued under this subsection.".

(With effect from 28 March 2003)

Finance Act 2008

109.   With effect from 1 July 2008 in each provision of the Principal Act specified in the first column of Schedule 4 for the words set out in the second column of that Schedule at that entry (in each place where those words occur in the provision concerned) there is substituted the words set out at the corresponding entry in the third column of that Schedule.

Schedule 4
Miscellaneous Amendments Relating to the Amendment of the Definition of Taxable Person

Amendments to Value-Added Tax Act 1972

Provision of Value-Added Tax Act 1972	Words to be replaced	Words to be inserted
Section 22	a taxable person	an accountable person

(With effect from 1 July 2008)

Finance (No. 2) Act 2008

97.   The enactments specified in Schedule 4 are amended to the extent and manner specified in paragraphs 1 to 6 of, and the Table to, that Schedule.

SCHEDULE 4

Provisions Relating to Collection and Recovery of Tax

2.   Each enactment (in this Schedule referred to as the "repealed enactments") mentioned in the second column of Part 1 of the Table to this Schedule is repealed to the extent specified opposite that mentioned in the third column of that Part.

3.   Part 2 of the Table to this Schedule, which provides for amendments to other enactments consequential on this Schedule coming into effect, shall have effect.

4.   Any reference, whether express or implied, in any enactment or document (including the repealed enactments and enactments passed or documents made after this Schedule comes into effect) —

   (a)   to any provision of the repealed enactments, or

   (b)   to things done, or to be done under or for the purposes of any provision of the repealed enactments, shall, if and in so far as the nature of the reference permits, be construed as including, in relation to the times, years or periods, circumstances or purposes in relation to which the corresponding provision of this Schedule applies, a reference to, or as the case may be, to things done or deemed to be done or to be done under or for the purposes of, the corresponding provision.

5.   All documents made or issued under a repealed enactment and in force immediately before this Schedule comes into effect shall continue in force as if made or issued under the provision inserted into the Taxes Consolidation Act 1997 by this Schedule which corresponds to the repealed enactment.

6.   This Schedule comes into effect and applies as respects any tax that becomes due and payable on or after 1 March 2009.

TABLE

PART 1

REPEALS

Number and Year	Short Title	Extent of Repeal
No. 22 of 1972.	Value-Added Tax Act 1972.	In section 22(2)(c) delete ", subject to paragraph (d),". Section 22(2)(d).

(With effect from 1 March 2009)

Section 22A

Finance Act 1999

Generation of estimates and assessments by electronic, photographic or other process

136. The Principal Act is hereby amended by the insertion of the following section after section 22:

"22A. For the purposes of this Act and regulations, where an officer of the Revenue Commissioners nominated in accordance with regulations for the purposes of section 22 or an inspector of taxes or an officer of the Revenue Commissioners authorised for the purposes of section 23, or any other officer of the Revenue Commissioners acting with the knowledge of such nominated officer or such inspector or such authorised officer causes to issue, manually or by any electronic, photographic or other process, a notice of estimation or assessment of tax bearing the name of such nominated officer or such inspector or such authorised officer, that estimate or assessment to which the notice of estimation or assessment of tax relates shall be deemed-

    (a)   in the case of an estimate made under section 22, to have been made by such nominated officer, and

    (b)   in the case of an assessment made under section 23, to have been made by such inspector or such authorised officer, as the case may be, to the best of such inspector's or such authorised officer's opinion.".

(With effect from 25 March 1999)

Section 23

Value-Added Tax Act 1972

Estimation of tax due for any period

23. (1)   Where the Revenue Commissioners have reason to believe that the total amount of tax payable by an accountable person, in relation to any period consisting of one taxable period or of two or more consecutive taxable periods, was greater than the total amount of tax (it any) paid by him in relation to that period, then, without prejudice to any other action which may be taken, they may, in accordance with regulations but subject to section 30, make an estimate in one sum of the total amount of tax which in their opinion should have been paid in respect of the taxable period or periods comprised in such period and may serve a notice on the person specifying-

    (a)   the total amount of tax so estimated.

    (b)   the total amount of tax (if any) paid by the person in relation to the said period, and

    (c)   the balance of tax remaining unpaid.

(2)   Where notice is served on an accountable person under subsection (1), the following provisions shall apply:

    (a)   the person may, if he claims that the total amount of tax or the balance of tax remaining unpaid is excessive, on giving notice in writing to the Revenue Commissioners within the period of twenty one days from the date of the service of the notice, appeal to the Appeal Commissioners,

    (b)   on the expiration of the said period, if no notice of appeal is received or, if notice of appeal is received, on determination of the appeal by agreement or otherwise, the balance of tax remaining unpaid as specified in the notice or the amended balance of tax as determined in relation to the appeal shall become due and payable as if the tax were tax which the person was liable to pay for the taxable period during which the period of fourteen days from the date of the service of the notice under subsection (1) expired or the appeal was determined by agreement or otherwise, whichever taxable period is the later.

(With effect from 1 November 1972)

Value Added Tax (Amendment) Act 1978

17.   The following section shall be substituted for section 23 of the Principal Act:

"(1)   Where, in relation to any period consisting of one taxable period or of two or more consecutive taxable periods, the Revenue Commissioners have reason to believe that an amount of tax is due and payable to them by a person in any of the following circumstances:

(a)   the total amount of tax payable by the person was greater than the total amount of tax (if any) paid by him,

(b)   the total amount of tax refunded to the person in accordance with section 20(1) was greater than the amount (if any) properly refundable to him, or

(c)   an amount of tax is payable by the person and a refund under section 20(1) has been made to the person,

then, without prejudice to any other action which may be taken, they may, in accordance with regulations but subject to section 30, make an estimate in one sum of the total amount of tax which in their opinion should have been paid or the total amount of tax (including a nil amount) which in accordance with section 20(1) should have been refunded, as the case may be, in respect of the taxable period or periods comprised in such period and may serve a notice on the person specifying-

(i)   the total amount of tax so estimated,

(ii)   the total amount of tax (if any) paid by the person or refunded to the person in relation to the said period, and

(iii)   the total amount so due and payable as aforesaid (referred to subsequently in this section as 'the amount due')

(2)   Where notice is served on a person under subsection (1), the following provisions shall apply:

(a)   the person may, if he claims that the amount due is excessive, on giving notice to the Revenue Commissioners within the period of twenty-one days from the date of the service of the notice, appeal to the Appeal Commissioners, and

(b)   on the expiration of the said period, if no notice of appeal is received or, if notice of appeal is received, on determination of the appeal by agreement or otherwise, the amount due or the amended amount due as determined in relation to the appeal, shall become due and payable as if the tax were tax which the person was liable to pay for the taxable period during which the period of fourteen days from the date of the service of the notice under subsection (1) expired or the appeal was determined by agreement or otherwise, whichever taxable period is the later.".

(With effect from 1 March 1979)

Finance Act 1985

47. Section 23 (inserted by the Act of 1978) of the Principal Act is hereby amended-

   (a)   in subsection (1)-

   (i)   by the substitution of "the inspector of taxes, or such other officer as the Revenue Commissioners may authorise to exercise the powers conferred by this section (hereafter referred to in this section as 'other officer'), has reason to believe" for "the Revenue Commissioners have reason to believe",

   (ii)   by the substitution of "the Revenue Commissioners" for "them",

   (iii) by the substitution of "the inspector or other officer may" for "they may", and

   (iv)   by the substitution of "his" for "their", and

   (b)   in subsection (2)(a), by the substitution of "the inspector or other officer" for "the Revenue Commissioners".

(With effect from 30 May 1985)

Finance Act 1992

185. Section 23 of the Principal Act is hereby amended-

   (a)   in subsection (1):

   (i)   by the substitution of "assessment" for "estimate", and

   (ii)   by the substitution of "assessed" for "estimated", and

   (b)   by the insertion of the following subsection after subsection (2):

   "(3)   Where a person appeals an assessment under subsection (1), within the time limits provided for in subsection (2), he shall pay to the Revenue Commissioners the amount which he believes to be due, and if-

   (a)   the amount paid is greater than 80 per cent of the amount of the tax found to be due on the determination of the appeal, and

   (b)   the balance of the amount found to be due on the determination of the appeal is paid within one month of the date of such determination, interest in accordance with section 21 shall not be chargeable from the date of raising of the assessment.".

(With effect from 28 May 1992)

Finance Act 2000

118. Section 23 (inserted by the Act of 1978) of the Principal Act is amended in subsection (1):

(a)   by the deletion of "consisting of one taxable period or of two or more consecutive taxable periods", and

(b)   by the deletion of "the taxable period or periods comprised in".

(With effect from 23 March 2000)

Section 23A
Finance Act 1992
Security to be given by certain taxable persons

186. The Principal Act is hereby amended by the insertion of the following section after section 23:

"23A. (1) The Revenue Commissioners may, where it appears requisite to them to do so for the protection of the revenue, require a taxable person, as a condition of his supplying goods or services under a taxable supply, to give security, or further security, of such amount and in such manner and form as they may determine, for the payment of any tax which is, or may become, due from him from the date of service on him of a notice in writing to that effect.

(2) Where notice is served on a person in accordance with subsection (1) the person may, on giving notice to the Revenue Commissioners within the period of twenty-one days from the date of the service of the notice, appeal the requirement of giving any security under subsection (1) to the Appeal Commissioners.".

(With effect from 28 May 1992)

Finance Act 2008

109. With effect from 1 July 2008 in each provision of the Principal Act specified in the first column of Schedule 4 for the words set out in the second column of that Schedule at that entry (in each place where those words occur in the provision concerned) there is substituted the words set out at the corresponding entry in the third column of that Schedule.

Schedule 4
Miscellaneous Amendments Relating to the Amendment of the Definition of Taxable Person

Amendments to Value-Added Tax Act 1972

Provision of Value-Added Tax Act 1972	Words to be replaced	Words to be inserted
Section 23A	a taxable person	an accountable person

(With effect from 1 July 2008)

Section 24

Value–Added Tax Act 1972

Recovery of tax

24. (1) (a) Without prejudice to any other mode of recovery, the provisions of any enactment relating to the recovery of income tax and the provisions of any rule of court so relating shall apply to the recovery of any tax payable in accordance with this Act and the regulations thereunder as they apply in relation to the recovery of income tax.

(b) In particular and without prejudice to the generality of paragraph (a), that paragraph applies the provisions of sections 480, 485, 486, 487, 488 and 491 of the Income Tax Act, 1967.

(c) Provisions as applied by this section shall so apply subject to any modifications specified by regulations under this Act.

(2) In proceedings instituted under this section or any regulations for the recovery of any amount of tax-

(a) a certificate signed by an officer of the Revenue Commissioners which certifies that a stated amount of tax is due and payable by the defendant shall be evidence, until the contrary is proved, that that amount is so due and payable, and

(b) a certificate certifying as aforesaid and purporting to be signed by an officer of the Revenue Commissioners may be tendered in evidence without proof and shall be deemed, until the contrary is proved, to have been signed by an officer of the Revenue Commissioners.

(3) Any reference in me foregoing subsections to an amount at tax includes a reference to interest payable in the case in question under section 21.

(4) Subject to this section, the rules of the court concerned for the time being applicable to civil proceedings shall apply to proceedings by virtue of this section or any regulation under this Act.

(5) Where an order which was made before the passing of this Act under section 12 of the Court Officers Act, 1945, contains a reference to levy under a certificate issued under section 485 of the Income Tax Act, 1967, that reference shall be construed as including a reference to levy under a certificate issued under the said section 485 as extended by this section.

(With effect from 1 November 1972)

Taxes Consolidation Act 1997

1100. Schedule 31, which provides for amendments to other enactments consequential on the passing of this Act, shall apply for the purposes of this Act.

SCHEDULE 31
Consequential Amendments

In the enactments specified in Column (1) of the following Table for the words set out or referred to in Column (2) there shall be substituted the words set out in the corresponding entry in Column (3).

Enactment amended (1)	Words to be replaced (2)	Words to be substituted (3)
The Value Added Tax Act, 1972:		
section 24(1)(b)	sections 480, 485, 486, 487, 488 and 491 of the Income Tax Act, 1967	Sections 962, 963, 964(1), 966, 967 and 998 of the Taxes Consolidation Act, 1997
section 24(5)	under section 485 of the Income Tax Act, 1967 section 485	under section 962 of the Taxes Consolidation Act, 1997 Section 962

(With effect from 6 April 1997)

Finance Act 2005

108. (1)   Section 24 of the Principal Act is amended in subsection (1)-

(a)   by substituting the following for paragraph (a):

"(a)   Without prejudice to any other mode of recovery, the provisions of any enactment relating to the recovery of income tax and the provisions of any rule of court so relating shall, subject to any necessary modifications, apply to the recovery of any tax payable in accordance with this Act and the regulations thereunder as they apply in relation to the recovery of income tax." ,

and

(b)   by deleting paragraph (c).

(2)   Notwithstanding subsection (1)(b) regulations made under the Principal Act and to which section 24(1)(c) of that Act related shall continue in force and may be amended or revoked accordingly.

(With effect from 25 March 2005)

Finance (No. 2) Act 2008

97. The enactments specified in Schedule 4 are amended to the extent and manner specified in paragraphs 1 to 6 of, and the Table to, that Schedule.

SCHEDULE 4

Provisions Relating to Collection and Recovery of Tax

2. Each enactment (in this Schedule referred to as the "repealed enactments") mentioned in the second column of Part 1 of the Table to this Schedule is repealed to the extent specified opposite that mentioned in the third column of that Part.

3. Part 2 of the Table to this Schedule, which provides for amendments to other enactments consequential on this Schedule coming into effect, shall have effect.

4. Any reference, whether express or implied, in any enactment or document (including the repealed enactments and enactments passed or documents made after this Schedule comes into effect) —

(a)   to any provision of the repealed enactments, or

(b)   to things done, or to be done under or for the purposes of any provision of the repealed enactments, shall, if and in so far as the nature of the reference permits, be construed as including, in relation to the times, years or periods, circumstances or purposes in relation to which the corresponding provision of this Schedule applies, a reference to, or as the case may be, to things done or deemed to be done or to be done under or for the purposes of, the corresponding provision.

5. All documents made or issued under a repealed enactment and in force immediately before this Schedule comes into effect shall continue in force as if made or issued under the provision inserted into the Taxes Consolidation Act 1997 by this Schedule which corresponds to the repealed enactment.

6. This Schedule comes into effect and applies as respects any tax that becomes due and payable on or after 1 March 2009.

TABLE

PART 1

REPEALS

Number and Year	Short Title	Extent of Repeal
No. 22 of 1972	Value-Added Tax Act 1972	Sections 24 and 42

(With effect from 1 March 2009)

Section 25

Value-Added Tax Act 1972

Appeals

25. (1) Any person aggrieved by a determination of the Revenue Commissioners in relation to-

    (a)   a liability to tax under subsection (5) or (6) of section 17,

    (b)   a charge of tax in accordance with regulations, or

    (c)   a claim for repayment of tax,

against which an appeal to the Appeal Commissioners is not otherwise provided for under this Act may, on giving notice in writing to the Revenue Commissioners within twenty-one days after the notification to the person aggrieved of the determination, appeal to the Appeal Commissioners.

(2) The provisions of the Income Tax Acts relating to-

    (a)   the appointment of times and places for the hearing of appeals;

    (b)   the giving of notice to each person who has given notice of appeal of he time and place appointed for the hearing of his appeal;

    (c)   the determination of an appeal by agreement between the appellant and an inspector of taxes or other officer appointed by the Revenue Commissioners in that behalf;

    (d)   the determination of an appeal by the appellant giving notice of his intention not to proceed with the appeal;

    (e)   the hearing and determination of an appeal by the Appeal Commissioners, including the hearing and determination of an appeal by one Appeal Commissioner;

    (f)   the determination of an appeal through the neglect or refusal of a person who has given notice of appeal to attend before the Appeal Commissioners at the time and place appointed;

    (g)   the extension of the time for giving notice of appeal, and he readmission of appeals by the Appeal Commissioners;

    (h)   the rehearing of an appeal by a judge of the Circuit Court and the statement of a case for the opinion of the High Court on a point of law;

    (i)   the payment of tax in accordance with the determination of the Appeal Commissioners notwithstanding that an appeal is required to be reheard by a judge of the Circuit Court or that a case for the opinion of the High Court on a point of law has been required to be stated or is pending;

(j)   the payment of tax which is agreed not to be in dispute in relation to an appeal; and

(k)   the procedures for appeal,

shall, with any necessary modifications, apply to a claim under section 22 or an appeal under section 11(1B) or 23 of this section as if the claim or appeal were an appeal against an assessment to income tax.

(With effect from 1 November 1972)

Finance Act 1973

90.   The Principal Act is hereby amended as specified in column (3) of the Tenth Schedule to this Act.

TENTH SCHEDULE

Amendment of Enactments

Number and Year (1)	Short Title (2)	Amendment (3)
No. 22 of 1972	Value-Added Tax Act, 1972	In section 25(2), "11(1B) or" shall be inserted before "23".

(With effect from 3 September 1973)

Finance Act 1983

85.   Section 25(2) of the Principal Act is hereby amended-

(a)   by the substitution of the following paragraphs for paragraph (f):

"(f)   the determination of an appeal through the failure of a person who has given notice of appeal to attend before the Appeal Commissioners at the time and place appointed;

(ff)   the refusal of an application for the adjournment of any proceedings in relation to an appeal, and the dismissing of an appeal, by the Appeal Commissioners;",

and

(b)   by the substitution of "shall, subject to the modifications set out hereunder and to other necessary modifications, apply to a claim under section 22 or an appeal under section 11(1B) or 23 or this section as if the claim or appeal were an appeal against an assessment to income tax:

(i)   a reference to a year of assessment shall include a reference to the taxable periods concerned,

(ii)   a reference to a return of income shall include a reference to a return required to be made under section 19,

(iii)   a reference to interest shall include a reference to interest payable under section 21"

for the words from paragraph (k) to the end of the section.

(With effect from 8 June 1983)

Finance Act 1991

84.   Section 25 of the Principal Act is hereby amended in subsection (1) by the insertion of the following paragraph after paragraph (a):

"(aa)   the treatment of one or more persons as a single taxable person in accordance with section 8(8),".

(With effect from 29 May 1991)

Finance Act 1992

187.   Section 25 of the Principal Act is hereby amended-

(a)   in subsection (1) by the insertion after paragraph (aa) (inserted by the Act of 1991) of the following paragraph:

"(ab)   the deeming, in accordance with section 37, of a person to have made supplies in the course or furtherance of business,",

and

(b)   in subsection (2) by the substitution of "section 11(1B), 23 or 23A" for "section 11(1B) or 23".

(With effect from 28 May 1992)

Finance Act 1995

137.   Section 25 of the Principal Act is hereby amended-

*(a)   in subsection (1) by the insertion after paragraph (ab) (inserted by the Act of 1992) of the following paragraph:

"(ac)   a determination under section 8(3E),",

and

(b)   by the insertion of the following subsection after subsection (1):

"(1A)   Where a person is aggrieved by a decision of the Revenue Commissioners that such person is not a taxable person then such person may, on giving notice in writing to the Revenue Commissioners within twenty-one days after the notification of that decision to such person, appeal to the Appeal Commissioners.",

and

(c)   in subsection (2) by the insertion after paragraph (d) of the following paragraph:

"(dd)   the refusal of an application for an appeal hearing;".

(With effect from 2 June 1995 except * from 1 January 1996)

Finance Act 1997

109. Section 25(1) of the Principal Act is hereby amended by the insertion of the following paragraph after paragraph (ac):

"(ad)   the refusal of an application for authorisation to operate as a VAT refunding agent (within the meaning assigned by section 13(3B)) or the cancellation of any such authorisation,".

(With effect from 1 July 1997)

Finance Act 1998

134. Appeals

...

(2)   Section 25(2) of the Value-Added Tax Act, 1972, is hereby amended by the insertion of the following paragraph after paragraph (e):

"(ee)   the publication of reports of determinations of the Appeal Commissioners;".

(With effect from 27 March 1998)

Finance Act 2000

119. Section 25 of the Principal Act is amended in clause (i) of subsection (2) by the substitution of "periods" for "taxable periods".

(With effect from 23 March 2000)

Finance Act 2002

109. Section 25 of the Principal Act is amended in subsection (1) —

(a)   by deleting paragraph (ab), and

(b)   by inserting the following after paragraph (ad):

"(ae)   the treatment of a person who allows supplies to be made on land owned, occupied or controlled by that person, as jointly and severally liable with another person, in accordance with section 8(2)(d),

(af)   the application of section 4(3A)(c),".

(With effect from 25 March 2002)

Finance Act 2007

91. Section 25 of the Principal Act is amended —

(a)   in subsection (1)(ac) by inserting "or 10(3A)" after "section 8(3E)", and

(b)   in subsection (2) by deleting paragraph (i).

(With effect from 2 April 2007)

Finance Act 2008

109. With effect from 1 July 2008 in each provision of the Principal Act specified in the first column of Schedule 4 for the words set out in the second column of that Schedule at that entry (in each place where those words occur in the provision concerned) there is substituted the words set out at the corresponding entry in the third column of that Schedule.

Schedule 4
Miscellaneous Amendments Relating to the Amendment of the Definition of Taxable Person

Amendments to Value-Added Tax Act 1972

Provision of Value-Added Tax Act 1972	Words to be replaced	Words to be inserted
Section 25	single taxable person	single accountable person
Section 25	a taxable person	an accountable person

(With effect from 1 July 2008)

Section 26

Value–Added Tax Act 1972

Penalties generally

26. (1)   A person who does not comply with section 9(2), 11(7), 13, 16, 17, 18 or 19 or any provision of regulations in regard to any matter to which the foregoing sections relate shall be liable to a penalty of £20, together with, in the case of a continuing non-compliance, a penalty of the like amount for every day on which the non-compliance is continued.

(2)   A person who is not a registered person and who, on or alter the specified day, otherwise than under and in accordance with section 13, issues an invoice in which an amount of tax is stated shall be liable to a penalty of £20.

(3)   Where a person mentioned in subsection (1) or (2) is a body of persons, the secretary shall be liable to a separate penalty of £20.

(4)   All penalties under this section may, without prejudice to any other method of recovery, be proceeded for and recovered summarily in the same manner as in summary proceedings for recovery of any penalty under any Act relating to the excise, and, notwithstanding section 10(4) of the Petty Sessions (Ireland) Act, 1851, summary proceedings under this section may be instituted within three years from the date of the incurring of the penalty.

(5)   Where-

(a)   a person does not comply with section 9(2), 18(2) or 19(3),

(b)   compliance is required within a particular period, and

(c)   the person continues, during a further period of two or more days, not to furnish the particulars or return concerned or produce for inspection or permit the removal of the documents concerned,

the non-compliance shall be regarded, for the purposes of subsection (1), as a non-compliance continuing on every day, other than the first, of the further period.

(6)   In proceedings for recovery of a penalty under this section-

(a)   a certificate signed by an officer of the Revenue Commissioners which certifies that he has inspected the relevant records of the Revenue Commissioners and that it appears from them that, during a stated period, stated particulars or stated returns were not furnished by the defendant shall be evidence until the contrary is proved that the defendant did not, during that period, furnish the particulars or return,

(b)   a certificate signed by an officer of the Revenue Commissioners which certifies that he has inspected the relevant records of the Revenue Commissioners and that it appears from them that a stated document was duly sent to the defendant on a stated day shall be evidence until the contrary is proved that that person received that document in the ordinary course,

(c)   a certificate signed by an officer of the Revenue Commissioners which certifies that he has inspected the relevant records of the Revenue Commissioners and that it appears from them that a stated notice was not issued by them to the defendant shall be evidence until the contrary is proved that the defendant did not receive the notice in question,

(d)   a certificate certifying as provided form paragraph (a), (b) or (c) and purporting to be signed by an officer of the Revenue Commissioners may be tendered in evidence without proof and shall be deemed, until the contrary is proved, to have been signed by an officer of the Revenue Commissioners.

(7)   Subject to this section, the rules of the court concerned for the time being applicable to civil proceedings shall apply to proceedings pursuant to this section.

(With effect from 1 November 1972)

Finance Act 1973

83.   Section 26 of the Principal Act is hereby amended-

(a)   by the substitution in subsection (1) of "18(2)" for "18",

and

(b)   by the insertion after subsection (3) of the following subsection:

"(3A)   person who does not comply with section 18(3) shall be liable to a penalty of £100.".

(With effect from 3 September 1973)

Finance Act 1976

57.   Section 26 of the Principal Act is hereby amended by the substitution for paragraph (d) of subsection (6) of the following paragraphs:

"(d)   a certificate signed by an officer of the Revenue Commissioners which certifies that he has inspected the relevant records of the Revenue Commissioners and that it appears from them that, during a stated period, the defendant was an accountable person or was a registered person or was not a registered person shall be evidence until the contrary is proved that, during that period, the defendant was an accountable person or was a registered person or was not a registered person, as the case may be,

(e)   a certificate certifying as provided for in paragraph (a), (b), (c) or (d) and purporting to be signed by an officer of the Revenue Commissioners may be tendered in evidence without proof and shall be deemed, until the contrary is proved to have been signed by an officer of the Revenue Commissioners.".

*81. (1)   The enactment mentioned in column (2) of Part I of the Fifth Schedule to this Act is hereby repealed to the extent specified in column (3) of that Schedule.

      (2)   The enactment mentioned in column (2) of Part II of the Fifth Schedule to this Act is hereby repealed to the extent specified in column (3) of that Schedule.

      (3)   (a)   Subsection (1) of this section shall be deemed to have come into operation on the 6th day of April, 1976.

              (b)   Subsection (2) of this section shall be deemed to have come into operation on the 1st day of March, 1976.

FIFTH SCHEDULE
ENACTMENTS REPEALED
PART II

No. 22 of 1972	Value-Added Tax Act, 1972	In section 26 (a) in subsection (1), the numerals "13,", and (b) in subsection (2), the words "otherwise than under and in accordance with section 13,"

(With effect from 27 May 1976 except * from 1 March 1976)

Value Added Tax (Amendment) Act 1978

18.   Section 26 of the Principal Act is hereby amended-

      (a)   by the insertion, in subsection (1) after "11(7),", of "12A,",

      (b)   by the insertion after subsection (2) of the following subsection:

              "(2A) Any person who, otherwise than under and in accordance with section 12A or 17(4), issues an invoice in which an amount of flat-rate addition is stated shall be liable to a penalty of £20.", and

      (c)   by the insertion, in subsection (3), after "(2)" of "or (2A)".

30.   (1)   The enactment mentioned in column (2) of the First Schedule is hereby repealed to the extent specified in column (3) of that Schedule.

(2)   In consequence of the amendments of the Principal Act specified in this Act and of the repeals specified in the First Schedule, the Principal Act is hereby further amended by the substitution of the word or expression mentioned in column (3) of the Second Schedule at any reference number for the word or expression mentioned in column (2) of that Schedule at that reference number wherever it occurs in the provision of the Principal Act mentioned in column (4) of that Schedule at that reference number.

SECOND SCHEDULE
Consequential Amendments

Reference Number	Existing word or expression	Substituted word or expression	Provision of Principal Act
26	"an accountable person"	"a taxable person"	Section 26(6)(d)

(With effect from 1 March 1979)

Finance Act 1982

86.   Section 26 of the Principal Act is hereby amended-

(a)   by the substitution of the following subsection for subsection (1):

"(1)   A person who does not comply with section 9 (2),11 (7), 12A, 16, 17, 18 (2) or 19 or any provision of regulations in regard to any matter to which the foregoing sections relate shall be liable to a penalty of £800.",

(b)   in subsection (2), by the substitution of "£500 for "£20",

(c)   in subsection (2A) (inserted by the Act of 1978), by the substitution of "£500" for "£20",

(d)   in subsection (3), by the substitution of "£500" for "£20",

(e)   in subsection (3A) (inserted by the Finance Act, 1973), by the substitution of "£800" for "£100", and

(f)   by the deletion of subsection (5).

(With effect from 1 September 1982)

Finance Act 1984

90.   Section 26 of the Principal Act is hereby amended, as respects non-compliance occurring on or after the date of passing of this Act-

(a)   in subsection (1), by the deletion of "18 (2)", and

(b)   in subsection (3A), by the substitution of "subsection (3) of section 18 or with a requirement of an authorised officer under that section" for "section 18 (3)".

(With effect from 23 May 1984)

Finance Act 1992

188. Section 26 of the Principal Act is hereby amended-

    (a)   in subsection (1) (inserted by the Act of 1982):

        *(i)   by the substitution of ", 19 or 19A" for "or 19", and

        (ii)   by the substitution of "£1,200" for "£800",

    (b)   in subsection (2) by the substitution of "£750" for "£500",

    (c)   in subsection (2A) (inserted by the Act of 1982) by the substitution of "£750" for "£500",

    (d)   in subsection (3) by the substitution of "£750" for "£500",

    (e)   in subsection (3A) (inserted by the Act of 1973) by the substitution of "£1,000" for "£800", and

    (f)   by the insertion of the following subsection after subsection (3A):

        "(3B) A person who supplies taxable goods or services in contravention of the requirement of security specified in section 23A shall be liable to a penalty of £1,200 in respect of each such supply.".

(With effect from 28 May 1992 except * from 1 January 1993)

Finance Act 2001

240. (1)   (a)   Subject to subsection (2), in each provision specified in column (1) of Schedule 5 for the words or amount set out in column (2) of that Schedule at that entry there shall be substituted the words or amount set out at the corresponding entry in column (3) of that Schedule.

            (b)   Where words are or an amount is mentioned more than once in a provision specified in column (1) of Schedule 5, then the substitution provided for by paragraph (a) shall apply as respects those words or that amount to each mention of those words or that amount in that provision.

SCHEDULE 5

PART 4

Value-Added Tax and related matters

Enactment amended (1)	Amount or words to be replaced (2)	Amount or words to be inserted (3)
Value-Added Tax Act, 1972 (No. 22 of 1972) (as amended):		
section 26(1)	£1,200	€1,520
section 26(2)	£750	€950
section 26(2A)	£750	€950
section 26(3)	£750	€950
section 26(3A)	£1,000	€1,265
section 26(3B)	£1,200	€1,520

(With effect from 1 January 2002)

Finance Act 2005

109. Section 26 of the Principal Act is amended by inserting the following subsection after subsection (3A):

"(3AA) Where a person is authorised in accordance with section 10(9)(c) to inspect any immovable goods for the purpose of reporting to the Revenue Commissioners the open market price of an interest in those goods and the person having custody or possession of those goods prevents such inspection or obstructs the person so authorised in the performance of his or her functions in relation to the inspection, the person so having custody or possession shall be liable to a penalty of €1,265.".

(With effect from 25 March 2005)

Finance Act 2008

103. With effect from 1 July 2008 section 26 of the Principal Act is amended in subsection (3AA) by substituting "open market value" for "open market price".

109. With effect from 1 July 2008 in each provision of the Principal Act specified in the first column of Schedule 4 for the words set out in the second column of that Schedule at that entry (in each place where those words occur in the provision concerned) there is substituted the words set out at the corresponding entry in the third column of that Schedule.

Schedule 4
Miscellaneous Amendments Relating to the Amendment of the Definition of Taxable Person

Amendments to Value-Added Tax Act 1972

Provision of Value-Added Tax Act 1972	Words to be replaced	Words to be inserted
Section 26	a taxable person	an accountable person

(With effect from 1 July 2008)

Finance (No. 2) Act 2008

98. (1)   The enactments specified in Schedule 5 are amended or repealed to the extent and manner specified in that Schedule and, unless the contrary is stated, shall come into effect after the passing of this Act.

SCHEDULE 5
Miscellaneous Amendments in Relation to Penalties

PART 3
Value-Added Tax: Penalties

3.   The Value-Added Tax Act 1972 is amended —

(a)   in section 26 —

(i)   by substituting —

(I)   "€4,000" for "€1,520" in both places where it occurs,

(II)   "€4,000" for "€950" in each place where it occurs, and

(III) "€4,000" for "€1,265" in both places where it occurs,

and

(ii)   by deleting subsections (4), (6) and (7),

(With effect from 24 December 2008)

Section 27

Value–Added Tax Act 1972

Fraudulent returns, etc.

27.   (1)   Where a person fraudulently or negligently, for the purposes of this Act or of regulations, produces, furnishes, gives, sends or otherwise makes use of, any incorrect return, invoice, credit note, debit note, receipt, account, voucher, bank statement, estimate, statement, information, book, document, record or declaration, he shall, subject to subsection (2), be liable to a penalty of-

      (a)   £100, and

      (b)   the amount, or, in the case of fraud, twice the amount of the difference between the amount of tax paid by such person for the period in question and the amount of tax properly payable by him if the said return, invoice, credit note, debit note, receipt, account, voucher, bank statement, estimate, statement, information, book, document, record or declaration had been correct.

   (2)   Where a person mentioned in the foregoing subsection is a body of persons-

      (a)   the reference in paragraph (a) of that subsection to £100 shall be construed as a reference to £500, or, in the case of fraud, £1,000, and

      (b)   the secretary shall be liable to a separate penalty of £100, or, in the case of fraud, £200.

   (3)   Where any such return, invoice, credit note, debit note, receipt, account, voucher, bank statement, estimate, statement, information, book, document, record or declaration as is mentioned in subsection (1) was made or submitted by a person neither fraudulently nor negligently and it comes to his notice (or, if he has died, to the notice of his personal representative) that it was incorrect, then, unless the error is remedied without unreasonable delay, the return, invoice, credit note, debit note, receipt, account, voucher, bank statement, estimate, statement, information, book, document, record or declaration shall be treated for the purposes of this section as having been negligently made or submitted by him.

   (4)   If a person, in a case in which he represents that he is a registered person or is a manufacturer of certain goods or uses a registration number allotted under section 9, improperly procures the importation of goods without payment of tax in circumstances in which tax is chargeable, he shall be liable to a penalty of £500, and, in addition, he shall be liable to pay to the Revenue

Commissioners the amount of any tax which should have been paid on importation.

(5)   A person who fraudulently or negligently-

(a)   issues an invoice in which an amount of tax is stated, in such circumstances that the said amount does not represent the amount of tax which becomes due by him in respect of the transaction to which the invoice relates, or

(b)   issues a credit note showing an amount of tax other than that properly applicable to the transaction to which the credit note relates,

shall be liable to a penalty of £100 in addition to his liability under section 17(5) in respect of the issue of any such invoice or credit note.

(6)   Notwithstanding anything in section 30, proceedings for the recovery of any penalties under this section shall not be out of time by reason that they are commenced after the time allowed by the said section 30.

(7)   For the purposes of this section, any return, invoice, credit note, debit note, receipt, account, voucher, bank statement, estimate, statement, information, book, document, record or declaration submitted on behalf of a person shall be deemed to have been submitted by that person unless he proves that it was submitted without his consent or knowledge.

(8)   Any reference in the foregoing subsections to an amount of tax includes a reference to interest payable in the case in question under section 21.

(With effect from 1 November 1972)

Finance Act 1973

84.   Section 27 of the Principal Act is hereby amended by the substitution of the following subsection for subsection (5).

"(5)   A person who fraudulently or negligently-

(a)   issues an invoice in which an amount of tax is stated, in such circumstances that, apart from his liability under subsection (5) or (6) of section 17, the said amount does not represent the amount of tax (if any) which becomes due by him in respect of the transaction to which the invoice relates, or

(b)   issues a credit note showing an amount of tax other than that properly applicable to the transaction to which the credit note relates, shall be liable to a penalty of-

(i)   £100, and

(ii)   the amount, or, in the case of fraud, twice the amount of his liability under the said subsection (5) or (6), as the case may be, in respect of the issue of any such invoice or credit note.".

(With effect from 3 September 1973)

Value–Added Tax (Amendment) Act 1978

19.   Section 27 of the Principal Act is hereby amended-

(a)   by the substitution of the following subsection for subsection (4):

"(4)   If a person, in a case in which he represents that he is a registered person or that goods imported by him were so imported for the purposes of a business carried on by him, improperly procures the importation of goods without payment of tax in circumstances in which tax is chargeable, he shall be liable to a penalty of £500, and, in addition, he shall be liable to pay to the Revenue Commissioners the amount of any tax that should have been paid on the importation.",

and

(b)   by the insertion of the following subsections after subsection (8):

"(9)   Where, in pursuance of regulations made for the purposes of section 13(1)(a), tax on the supply of any goods has been remitted or repaid and-

(a)   the goods are found in the State after the date on which they were alleged to have been or were to be exported, or

(b)   any condition specified in the regulations or imposed by the Revenue Commissioners is not complied with,

and the presence of the goods in the State after that date or the non-compliance with the condition has not been authorised for the purposes of this subsection by the Revenue Commissioners, the goods shall be liable to forfeiture and the tax which was remitted or repaid shall be charged upon and become payable forthwith by the person to whom the goods were supplied or any person in whose possession the goods are found in the State and the provisions of section 24(1) shall apply accordingly, but the Revenue Commissioners may, if they think fit, waive payment of the whole or part of that tax.

(10)   The provisions of the Customs Acts relating to forfeiture
        and condemnation of goods shall apply to goods liable to
        forfeiture under subsection (9) as if they had become liable
        to forfeiture under those Acts and all powers which may
        be exercised by an officer of Customs and Excise under
        those Acts may be exercised by officers of the Revenue
        Commissioners authorised to exercise those powers for
        the purposes of the said subsection.".

(With effect from 1 March 1979)

Finance Act 1992

189.   Section 27 of the Principal Act is hereby amended-

(a)   in subsection (1):

(i)   by the insertion after "invoice," of "registration number,
       monthly control statement, claim,", and

(ii)   by the substitution of the following paragraph for
       paragraph (b):

"(b)   the amount, or in the case of fraud, twice the
       amount of the difference between-

(i)   the amount of tax properly payable by, or
       refundable to, such person if the said return,
       invoice, registration number, monthly control
       statement, claim, credit note, debit note, receipt,
       account, voucher, bank statement, estimate,
       statement, information, book, document,
       record or declaration had been correct, and

(ii)   the amount of tax (if any) paid, or claimed by
       way of refund.",

(b)   in subsections (3) and (7) by the insertion after "invoice," in each
       place where it occurs, of "registration number, monthly control
       statement, claim,",

*(c)   by the insertion of the following subsection after subsection (9):

"(9A) (1)

       Where goods-

(a)   were supplied at the rate of zero per cent
       subject to the condition that they were to be
       dispatched or transported outside the State in
       accordance with subparagraph (a), (b) or (c) of
       paragraph (i) of the Second Schedule and the
       goods were not so dispatched or transported,

(b)   were acquired without payment of value-
       added tax referred to in Council Directive
       No. 77/388/EEC of 17 May 1977 in another

Member State as a result of the declaration of an incorrect registration number, or

(c) are being supplied by a taxable person who has not complied with the provisions of section 9 (2),

the goods shall be liable to forfeiture.

(2) Whenever an officer authorised by the Revenue Commissioners reasonably suspects that goods are liable to forfeiture in accordance with subsection (1) the goods may be detained by the said officer until such examination, enquiries or investigations as may be deemed necessary by the said officer, or by another authorised officer of the Revenue Commissioners, have been made for the purpose of determining to the satisfaction of either officer whether or not the goods were so supplied or acquired.

(3) When a determination referred to in subsection (2) has been made in respect of any goods, or upon the expiry of a period of two months from the date on which the said goods were detained under the said subsection, whichever is the earlier, the said goods shall be seized as liable to forfeiture or released.",

*(d) in subsection (10) by the substitution of:

(i) "subsection (9) or (9A)" for "subsection (9)", and

(ii) "the said subsections and any provisions in relation to offences under those Acts shall apply, with any necessary modifications, in relation to the said subsections" for "the said subsection",

and

*(e) by the insertion of the following subsection after subsection (10):

"(11) Where an officer authorised by the Revenue Commissioners for the purposes of this subsection or a member of the Garda Síochána has reasonable grounds for suspecting that a criminal offence has been committed under the provisions of section 94 (as amended by section 243 of the Finance Act, 1992) of the Finance Act, 1983, in relation to tax, by a person who is not established in the State, or whom he believes is likely to leave the State, he may arrest that person.".

(With effect from 1 November 1992 except * from 1 January 1993)

Finance Act 1994

98. Section 27 of the Principal Act is hereby amended by the insertion in subsection (9A) (inserted by the Act of 1992) after paragraph (3) of the following:

"(4) For the purposes of subparagraph (b) of paragraph (1), 'the declaration of an incorrect registration number' means-

(a) the declaration by a person of another person's registration number,

(b) the declaration by a person of a number which is not an actual registration number which he purports to be his registration number,

(c) the declaration by a person of a registration number which was obtained from the Revenue Commissioners by supplying incorrect information, or

(d) the declaration by a person of a registration number which was obtained from the Revenue Commissioners for the purposes of acquiring goods without payment of value-added tax referred to in Council Directive No. 77/388/EEC of 17 May, 1977, and not for any bona fide business purpose.".

(With effect from 23 May 1994)

Taxes Consolidation Act 1997

1100. Schedule 31, which provides for amendments to other enactments consequential on the passing of this Act, shall apply for the purposes of this Act.

SCHEDULE 31

Consequential Amendments

In the enactments specified in Column (1) of the following Table for the words set out or referred to in Column (2) there shall be substituted the words set out in the corresponding entry in Column (3).

Enactment amended	Words to be replaced	Words to be substituted
The Value Added Tax Act, 1972:		
Section 27(11)	Section 94 (as amended by section 243 of the Finance Act, 1992) of the Finance Act, 1983	Section 1078 of the Taxes Consolidation Act, 1997

(With effect from 6 April 1997)

Finance Act 2000

120.   Section 27 of the Principal Act is amended by the deletion of subsection (8).

(With effect from 23 March 2000)

Finance Act 2001

197.   Section 27 of the Principal Act is amended-

(a)   by the insertion of the following after subsection (4):

> "(4A) If a person acquires goods without payment of value-added tax (as referred to in Council Directive No. 77/388/EEC of 17 May 1977) in another Member State as a result of the declaration of an incorrect registration number, that person shall be liable to a penalty of £500 and, in addition, that person shall be liable to pay to the Revenue Commissioners an amount equal to the amount of tax which would have been chargeable on an intra-Community acquisition of those goods if that declaration had been the declaration of a correct registration number.",

and

(b)   in subsection (9A)(4) (inserted by the Finance Act, 1994)-

(i)   by the substitution of "For the purposes of this section" for "For the purposes of subparagraph (b) of paragraph (1)",

and

(ii)   by the insertion of the following after subparagraph (b):

> "(bb) the declaration by a person of a registration number which is cancelled,".

*240. (1)   (a)   Subject to subsection (2), in each provision specified in column (1) of Schedule 5 for the words or amount set out in column (2) of that Schedule at that entry there shall be substituted the words or amount set out at the corresponding entry in column (3) of that Schedule.

(b)   Where words are or an amount is mentioned more than once in a provision specified in column (1) of Schedule 5, then the substitution provided for by paragraph (a) shall apply as respects those words or that amount to each mention of those words or that amount in that provision.

SCHEDULE 5

PART 4

Value-Added Tax and related matters

Enactment amended (1)	Amount or words to be replaced (2)	Amount or words to be inserted (3)
Value-Added Tax Act, 1972 (No. 22 of 1972) (as amended):		
section 27(1)(a	£100	€125
section 27(2)(a)	£100	€125
section 27(2)(a)	£500	€630
section 27(2)(a)	£1000	€1,265
section 27(2)(b)	£100	€125
section 27(2)(b)	£200	€250
section 27(4)	£500	€630
section 27(4A)	£500	€630
section 27(5)(b)(i)	£100	€125

(With effect from 21 March 2001 except * from 1 January 2002)

Finance Act 2003

127.   Section 27 of the Principal Act is amended —

(a)   by inserting the following subsection after subsection (1):

"(1A) Where a person fraudulently or negligently fails to comply with a requirement in accordance with this Act or regulations to furnish a return, that person shall be liable to a penalty of —

(a)   €125, and

(b)   the amount, or in the case of fraud twice the amount, of the difference between —

(i)   the amount of tax properly payable by such person if such return had been furnished by that person and that return had been correct, and

(ii)   the amount of tax (if any) paid in respect of the taxable period for which the said return was not furnished.",

and

(b)   in subsection (2) —

(i)   by substituting "subsection (1) or (1A)" for "the foregoing subsection", and

(ii)   by substituting "any reference in those subsections" for "the reference in paragraph (a) of that subsection".

(With effect from 28 March 2003)

Finance Act 2005

110.   Section 27 of the Principal Act is amended-

(a)   in subsection (1)(b) (inserted by the Finance Act 1992) by deleting ", or in the case of fraud, twice the amount",

(b)   in subsection (1A)(b) (inserted by the Finance Act 2003) by deleting ", or in the case of fraud twice the amount,",

(c)   in subsection (5)(ii) (inserted by the Finance Act 1973) by deleting ", or, in the case of fraud, twice the amount".

(With effect from 25 March 2005)

Finance Act 2007

97.   With effect from 1 January 2007 in each provision of the Principal Act specified in the first column of Schedule 3 for the words set out in the second column of that Schedule at that entry there is substituted the words set out at the corresponding entry in the third column of that Schedule.

Schedule 3
Miscellaneous Amendments Relating to Council Directive 2006/112/EC

Amendment of Value-Added Tax Act 1972

Provision of Principal Act	Words to be replaced	Words to be inserted
Section 27(4A)	Council Directive No. 77/388/EEC of 17 May 1977	Council Directive No. 2006/112/EC of 28 November 2006
Section 27(9A)(1)(b)	Council Directive No. 77/388/EEC of 17 May 1977	Council Directive No. 2006/112/EC of 28 November 2006
Section 27(9A)(4)(d)	Council Directive No. 77/388/EEC of 17 May 1977	Council Directive No. 2006/112/EC of 28 November 2006

(With effect from 1 January 2007)

Finance Act 2008

104.   Section 27 of the Principal Act is amended in subsection (9A) —

(a)   in the paragraph numbered (1) —

(i)   by renumbering that paragraph as paragraph (a),

(ii)   by renumbering as subparagraphs (i), (ii) and (iii), respectively, the subparagraphs designated as (a), (b) and (c), and

(iii)   by deleting "or" in subparagraph (ii) (as so renumbered) and by inserting the following after that subparagraph:

"(iia)   were acquired in another Member State and those goods are new means of transport in respect of which the acquirer—

(I)   makes an intra-Community acquisition in the State,

(II)   is not entitled to a deduction under section 12 in respect of the tax chargeable on that acquisition, and

(III) fails to account for the tax due on that acquisition in accordance with section 19,

or",

(b)   in the paragraph numbered (2) —

(I)   by renumbering that paragraph as paragraph (b), and

(II)   by substituting "paragraph (a)" for "subsection (1)",

(c)   in the paragraph numbered (3) —

(I)   by renumbering that paragraph as paragraph (c), and

(II)   by substituting "paragraph (b)" for "subsection (2)",

and

(d)   in the paragraph numbered (4) —

(I)   by renumbering that paragraph as paragraph (d), and

(II)   by renumbering as subparagraphs (i), (ii), (iii), (iv) and (v), respectively, the subparagraphs designated as (a), (b), (bb), (c) and (d).

*109. With effect from 1 July 2008 in each provision of the Principal Act specified in the first column of Schedule 4 for the words set out in the second column of that Schedule at that entry (in each place where those words occur in the provision concerned) there is substituted the words set out at the corresponding entry in the third column of that Schedule.

Schedule 4
Miscellaneous Amendments Relating to the Amendment of the Definition of Taxable Person

Amendments to Value-Added Tax Act 1972

Provision of Value-Added Tax Act 1972	Words to be replaced	Words to be inserted
Section 27	a taxable person	an accountable person

141.   The enactments specified in Schedule 8 –

   (a)   are amended to the extent and in the manner specified in paragraphs 1 to 6 of that Schedule, and

   (b)   apply and come into operation in accordance with paragraph 7 of that Schedule.

Schedule 8
Miscellaneous Technical Amendments in Relation to Tax

3.   The Value-Added Tax Act 1972 is amended in accordance with the following provisions:

   (f)   in section 27 by deleting "monthly control statement," in each place where it occurs,

(With effect from 13 March 2008 except * with effect from 1 July 2008)

Finance (No. 2) Act 2008

98.   (1)   The enactments specified in Schedule 5 are amended or repealed to the extent and manner specified in that Schedule and, unless the contrary is stated, shall come into effect after the passing of this Act.

SCHEDULE 5

Miscellaneous Amendments in Relation to Penalties

PART 3
Value-Added Tax: Penalties

3.   The Value-Added Tax Act 1972 is amended –

   (b)   by deleting section 27,

(With effect from 24 December 2008)

Section 27A

Finance (No. 2) Act 2008

98.   (1)   The enactments specified in Schedule 5 are amended or repealed
to the extent and manner specified in that Schedule and, unless
the contrary is stated, shall come into effect after the passing of
this Act.

SCHEDULE 5

Miscellaneous Amendments in Relation to Penalties

PART 3

Value-Added Tax: Penalties

3.   The Value-Added Tax Act 1972 is amended —

(c)   by inserting the following before section 28:

Section 27A

"Penalty for deliberately or carelessly making incorrect returns, etc.

27A.   (1)   In this section —

'carelessly' means failure to take reasonable care;

'liability to tax' means a liability to the amount of the difference
specified in subsection (11) or (12) arising from any matter
referred to in subsection (2), (3), (5) or (6);

'period' means taxable period, accounting period or other
period, as the context requires;

'prompted qualifying disclosure', in relation to a person, means
a qualifying disclosure that has been made to the Revenue
Commissioners or to a Revenue officer in the period between —

(a)   the date on which a person is notified by a Revenue officer
of the date on which an investigation or inquiry into any
matter occasioning a liability to tax of that person will
start, and

(b)   the date that the investigation or inquiry starts;

'qualifying disclosure', in relation to a person, means —

(a)   in relation to a penalty referred to in subsection (4), a
disclosure that the Revenue Commissioners are satisfied
is a disclosure of complete information in relation to, and
full particulars of, all matters occasioning a liability to
tax that gives rise to a penalty referred to in subsection
(4), and full particulars of all matters occasioning any
liability to tax or duty that gives rise to a penalty referred

to in section 1077E(4) of the Taxes Consolidation Act 1997, section 134A(2) of the Stamp Duties Consolidation Act 1999 and the application of section 1077E(4) of the Taxes Consolidation Act 1997 to the Capital Acquisitions Tax Consolidation Act 2003, and

(b) in relation to a penalty referred to in subsection (7), a disclosure that the Revenue Commissioners are satisfied is a disclosure of complete information in relation to, and full particulars of, all matters occasioning a liability to tax that gives rise to a penalty referred to in subsection (7) for the relevant period,

made in writing to the Revenue Commissioners or to a Revenue officer and signed by or on behalf of that person and that is accompanied by —

(i) a declaration, to the best of that person's knowledge, information and belief, made in writing that all matters contained in the disclosure are correct and complete, and

(ii) a payment of the tax and duty payable in respect of any matter contained in the disclosure and the interest on late payment of that tax and duty;

'**Revenue officer**' means an officer of the Revenue Commissioners;

'**unprompted qualifying disclosure**', in relation to a person, means a qualifying disclosure that the Revenue Commissioners are satisfied has been voluntarily furnished to them —

(a) before an investigation or inquiry had been started by them or by a Revenue officer into any matter occasioning a liability to tax of that person, or

(b) where the person is notified by a Revenue officer of the date on which an investigation or inquiry into any matter occasioning a liability to tax of that person will start, before that notification.

(2) Where a person furnishes a return or makes a claim or declaration for the purposes of this Act or of regulations made under it and, in so doing, the person deliberately, furnishes an incorrect return, or makes an incorrect claim or declaration, then that person shall be liable to a penalty.

(3) Where a person deliberately fails to comply with a requirement in accordance with this Act or regulations to furnish a return, then that person shall be liable to a penalty.

(4) The penalty referred to —

(a) in subsection (2), shall be the amount specified in subsection (11), and

(b)   in subsection (3), shall be the amount specified in subsection (12),

reduced, where the person liable to the penalty cooperated fully with any investigation or inquiry started by the Revenue Commissioners or by a Revenue officer into any matter occasioning a liability to tax of that person, to —

(i)   75 per cent of that amount where paragraph (ii) or (iii) does not apply,

(ii)   50 per cent of that amount where a prompted qualifying disclosure is made by that person, or

(iii)   10 per cent of that amount where an unprompted qualifying disclosure has been made by that person.

(5)   Where a person furnishes a return or makes a claim or declaration for the purposes of this Act or of regulations made under it and, in so doing, the person carelessly, but not deliberately, furnishes an incorrect return or makes an incorrect claim or declaration, then that person shall be liable to a penalty.

(6)   Where a person carelessly but not deliberately fails to comply with a requirement in accordance with this Act or regulations to furnish a return, then that person shall be liable to a penalty.

(7)   (a)   The penalty referred to —

(i)   In subsection (5) shall be the amount specified in subsection (11), and

(ii)   in subsection (6) shall be the amount specified in subsection (12),

reduced to 40 per cent in cases where the excess referred to in subparagraph (I) of paragraph (b) applies and to 20 per cent in other cases.

(b)   Where the person liable to the penalty cooperated fully with any investigation or inquiry started by the Revenue Commissioners or by a Revenue officer into any matter occasioning a liability to tax of that person, the penalty referred to —

(i)   in subsection (5) shall be the amount specified in subsection (11), and

(ii)   in subsection (6) shall be the amount specified in subsection (12),

reduced —

(I)   where the difference referred to in subsection (11) or (12), as the case may be, exceeds 15 per cent of the amount referred to in paragraph (b) of subsection (11) or paragraph (b) of subsection (12), to —

    (A)   30 per cent of that difference where clause (B) or (C) does not apply,

    (B)   20 per cent of that difference where a prompted qualifying disclosure is made by that person, or

    (C)   5 per cent of that difference where an unprompted qualifying disclosure is made by that person,

or

   (II)   where the difference referred to in subsection (11) or (12), as the case may be, does not exceed 15 per cent of the amount referred to in paragraph (b) of subsection (11) or paragraph (b) of subsection (12) to —

    (A)   15 per cent of that difference where clause (B) or (C) does not apply,

    (B)   10 per cent of that difference where a prompted qualifying disclosure is made by that person, or

    (C)   3 per cent of that difference where an unprompted qualifying disclosure is made by that person.

(8)   Where, for the purposes of this Act or of regulations, a person deliberately or carelessly produces, furnishes, gives, sends or otherwise makes use of, any incorrect invoice, registration number, credit note, debit note, receipt, account, voucher, bank statement, estimate, statement, information, book, document or record, then that person shall be liable to —

    (a)   a penalty of €3,000 where that person has acted carelessly, or

    (b)   a penalty of €5,000 where that person has acted deliberately.

(9)   Where any return, claim or declaration as is mentioned in subsection (2) or (5) was furnished or made by a person, neither deliberately nor carelessly, and it comes to that person's notice that it was incorrect, then, unless the error is remedied without unreasonable delay, the return, claim or declaration shall be treated for the purposes of this section as having been deliberately made or submitted by that person.

(10)   Subject to section 1077D(2) of the Taxes Consolidation Act 1997, proceedings or applications for the recovery of any penalty

under this section shall not be out of time by reason that they are commenced after the time allowed by section 30.

(11)   The amount referred to in paragraph (a) of subsection (4) and in paragraph (a)(i) of subsection (7) shall be the difference between—

(a)   the amount of tax (if any) paid or claimed by the person concerned for the relevant period on the basis of the incorrect return, claim or declaration as furnished or otherwise made, and

(b)   the amount properly payable by, or refundable to, that person for that period.

(12)   The amount referred to in paragraph (b) of subsection (4) and in paragraph (b)(ii) of subsection (7) shall be the difference between—

(a)   the amount of tax (if any) paid by that person for the relevant period before the start by the Revenue Commissioners or by any Revenue officer of any inquiry or investigation where the Revenue Commissioners had announced publicly that they had started an inquiry or investigation or where the Revenue Commissioners have, or a Revenue officer has, carried out an inquiry or investigation in respect of any matter that would have been included in the return if the return had been furnished by that person and the return had been correct, and

(b)   the amount of tax properly payable by that person for that period.

(13)   Where a second qualifying disclosure is made by a person within 5 years of such person's first qualifying disclosure, then as regards matters pertaining to that second disclosure—

(a)   in relation to subsection (4)—

(i)   paragraph (ii) shall apply as if '75 per cent' were substituted for '50 per cent', and

(ii)   paragraph (iii) shall apply as if '55 per cent' were substituted for '10 per cent',

and

(b)   in relation to subparagraph (I) of subsection (7)(b)—

(i)   clause (B) shall apply as if '30 per cent' were substituted for '20 per cent', and

(ii)   clause (C) shall apply as if '20 per cent' were substituted for '5 per cent'.

(14)   Where a third or subsequent qualifying disclosure is made by a person within 5 years of such person's second qualifying disclosure, then as regards matters pertaining to that third or subsequent disclosure, as the case may be —

    (a)   the penalty referred to in paragraphs (a) and (b) of subsection (4) shall not be reduced, and

    (b)   the reduction referred to in subparagraph (I) of subsection (7)(b) shall not apply.

(15)   A disclosure in relation to a person shall not be a qualifying disclosure where —

    (a)   before the disclosure is made, a Revenue officer had started an inquiry or investigation into any matter contained in that disclosure and had contacted or notified that person, or a person representing that person, in this regard, or

    (b)   matters contained in the disclosure are matters —

        (i)   that have become known, or are about to become known, to the Revenue Commissioners through their own investigations or through an investigation conducted by a statutory body or agency,

        (ii)   that are within the scope of an inquiry being carried out wholly or partly in public, or

        (iii)   to which the person who made the disclosure is linked, or about to be linked, publicly.

(16)   For the purposes of this section, any return, claim or declaration submitted on behalf of a person shall be deemed to have been submitted by that person unless that person proves that it was submitted without that person's consent or knowledge.

(17)   Where a person mentioned in subsection (2), (3), (5) or (6) is a body of persons the secretary shall be liable to a separate penalty of €1,500 or, in the case of deliberate behaviour, €3,000.

(18)   If a person, in a case in which that person represents that he or she is a registered person or that goods imported by him or her were so imported for the purposes of a business carried on by him or her, improperly procures the importation of goods without payment of tax in circumstances in which tax is chargeable, then that person shall be liable to a penalty of €4,000 and, in addition, that person shall be liable to pay to the Revenue Commissioners the amount of any tax that should have been paid on the importation.

(19)   If a person acquires goods without payment of value-added tax (as referred to in Council Directive No. 2006/112/EC of 28 November 2006) in another Member State as a result of the declaration of an incorrect registration number, that person shall

be liable to a penalty of €4,000 and, in addition, that person shall be liable to pay to the Revenue Commissioners an amount equal to the amount of tax which would have been chargeable on an intra-Community acquisition of those goods if that declaration had been the declaration of a correct registration number.

(20) Where, in pursuance of regulations made for the purposes of section 13(1)(a), tax on the supply of any goods has been remitted or repaid and —

(a) the goods are found in the State after the date on which they were alleged to have been or were to be exported, or

(b) any condition specified in the regulations or imposed by the Revenue Commissioners is not complied with,

and the presence of the goods in the State after that date or the non-compliance with the condition has not been authorised for the purposes of this subsection by the Revenue Commissioners, then the goods shall be liable to forfeiture and the tax which was remitted or repaid shall be charged upon and become payable forthwith by the person to whom the goods were supplied or any person in whose possession the goods are found in the State and the provisions of sections 960I(1), 960J, 960L and 960N of the Taxes Consolidation Act 1997 shall apply accordingly, but the Revenue Commissioners may, if they think fit, waive payment of the whole or part of that tax.

(21) (a) Where goods —

(i) were supplied at the rate of zero per cent subject to the condition that they were to be dispatched or transported outside the State in accordance with subparagraph (a), (b) or (c) of paragraph (i) of the Second Schedule and the goods were not so dispatched or transported,

(ii) were acquired without payment of value-added tax referred to in Council Directive No. 2006/112/EC of 28 November 2006 in another Member State as a result of the declaration of an incorrect registration number,

(iii) were acquired in another Member State and those goods are new means of transport in respect of which the acquirer —

(I) makes an intra-Community acquisition in the State,

(II) is not entitled to a deduction under section 12 in respect of the tax chargeable on that acquisition, and

(III)   fails to account for the tax due on that acquisition in accordance with section 19,

or

(iv)   are being supplied by an accountable person who has not complied with the provisions of section 9(2),

then those goods shall be liable to forfeiture.

(b)   Whenever an officer authorized by the Revenue Commissioners reasonably suspects that goods are liable to forfeiture in accordance with paragraph (a) the goods may be detained by the said officer until such examination, inquiries or investigations as may be deemed necessary by the said officer, or by another authorised officer of the Revenue Commissioners, have been made for the purpose of determining to the satisfaction of either officer whether or not the goods were so supplied or acquired.

(c)   When a determination referred to in paragraph (b) has been made in respect of any goods, or upon the expiry of a period of two months from the date on which the said goods were detained under the said subsection, whichever is the earlier, the said goods shall be seized as liable to forfeiture or released.

(d)   For the purposes of this section 'the declaration of an incorrect registration number' means—

(i)   the declaration by a person of another person's registration number,

(ii)   the declaration by a person of a number which is not an actual registration number which that person purports to be his or her registration number,

(iii)   the declaration by a person of a registration number which is cancelled,

(iv)   the declaration by a person of a registration number which was obtained from the Revenue Commissioners by supplying incorrect information, or

(v)   the declaration by a person of a registration number which was obtained from the Revenue Commissioners for the purposes of acquiring goods without payment of value-added tax referred to in Council Directive No. 2006/112/EC of 28 November 2006, and not for any bona fide business purpose.

(22) The provisions of the Customs Acts relating to forfeiture and condemnation of goods shall apply to goods liable to forfeiture under subsection (20) or (21) as if they had become liable to forfeiture under those Acts and all powers which may be exercised by an officer of Customs and Excise under those Acts may be exercised by officers of the Revenue Commissioners authorised to exercise those powers for the purposes of the said subsections and any provisions in relation to offences under those Acts shall apply, with any necessary modifications, in relation to the said subsections.

(23) Where an officer authorised by the Revenue Commissioners for the purposes of this subsection or a member of the Garda Síochána has reasonable grounds for suspecting that a criminal offence has been committed under the provisions of section 1078 of the Taxes Consolidation Act 1997, in relation to tax, by a person who is not established in the State, or whom that officer believes is likely to leave the State, that officer may arrest that person.

(With effect from 24 December 2008)

Section 28

Value Added Tax Act 1972

Assisting in making incorrect returns, etc.

28.　　Any person who assists in or induces the making or delivery, for the purposes of tax, of any return, invoice, credit note, debit note, receipt, account, voucher, bank statement, estimate, statement, information, book, document, record or declaration which he knows to be incorrect shall be liable to a penalty of £500.

(With effect from 1 November 1972)

Finance Act 1992

190.　Section 28 of the Principal Act is hereby amended-

*(a)　　by the insertion after "invoice," of "monthly control statement, claim,",

and

(b)　　by the substitution of "£750" for "£500".

(With effect from 28 May 1992 except * from 1 November 1992)

Finance Act 2001

240.　(1)　(a)　Subject to subsection (2), in each provision specified in column (1) of Schedule 5 for the words or amount set out in column (2) of that Schedule at that entry there shall be substituted the words or amount set out at the corresponding entry in column (3) of that Schedule.

(b)　Where words are or an amount is mentioned more than once in a provision specified in column (1) of Schedule 5, then the substitution provided for by paragraph (a) shall apply as respects those words or that amount to each mention of those words or that amount in that provision.

SCHEDULE 5

PART 4

Value-Added Tax and related matters

Enactment amended (1)	Amount or words to be replaced (2)	Amount or words to be inserted (3)
Value-Added Tax Act, 1972 (No. 22 of 1972) (as amended): section 28	£750	€950

(With effect from 1 January 2002)

141. The enactments specified in Schedule 8 —

    (a)   are amended to the extent and in the manner specified in paragraphs 1 to 6 of that Schedule, and

    (b)   apply and come into operation in accordance with paragraph 7 of that Schedule.

Schedule 8
Miscellaneous Technical Amendments in Relation to Tax

3. The Value-Added Tax Act 1972 is amended in accordance with the following provisions:

    (g)   in section 28 by deleting "monthly control statement,",

(With effect from 13 March 2008)

Finance (No. 2) Act 2008

98. (1)   The enactments specified in Schedule 5 are amended or repealed to the extent and manner specified in that Schedule and, unless the contrary is stated, shall come into effect after the passing of this Act.

SCHEDULE 5

Miscellaneous Amendments in Relation to Penalties

PART 3
Value-Added Tax: Penalties

3. The Value-Added Tax Act 1972 is amended —

    (d)   in section 28 by substituting "€4,000" for €950",

(With effect from 24 December 2008)

Section 29

Value Added Tax Act 1972

Proceedings in High Court in respect of penalties

29. (1) Without prejudice to any other mode of recovery of a penalty under this Act, an officer of the Revenue Commissioners, authorised by them for the purposes of this subsection, may sue in his own name by civil proceedings for the recovery of the penalty in the High Court as a liquidated sum and the provisions of section 94 of the Courts of Justice Act, 1924, shall apply accordingly.

    (2) If an officer who has commenced proceedings pursuant to this section, or who has continued the proceedings by virtue of this subsection, dies or otherwise ceases for any reason to be an officer authorised for the purposes of subsection (1) of this section-

    (a) the right of such officer to continue the proceedings shall cease and the right to continue them shall vest in such other officer so authorised as may be nominated by the Revenue Commissioners,

    (b) where such other officer is nominated under paragraph (a) of this subsection, he shall be entitled accordingly to be substituted as a party to the proceedings in the place of the first mentioned officer, and

    (c) where an officer is so substituted, he shall give notice in writing of the substitution to the defendant.

    (3) In proceedings pursuant to this section, a certificate signed by a Revenue Commissioner certifying the following facts, namely, that a person is an officer of the Revenue Commissioners and that he has been authorised by them for the purposes of subsection (1), shall be evidence until the contrary is proved of those facts.

    (4) In proceedings pursuant to this section, a certificate signed by a Revenue Commissioner certifying the following facts, namely, that the plaintiff has ceased to be an officer of the Revenue Commissioners authorised by them for the purposes of subsection (1), that another person is an officer of the Revenue Commissioners, that such other person has been authorised by them for the purposes of subsection (1) and that he has been nominated by them in relation to the proceedings, for the purposes of subsection (2), shall be evidence until the contrary is proved of those facts.

    (5) In proceedings pursuant to this section, a certificate certifying the facts referred to in subsection (3) or (4) and purporting to be signed by a Revenue Commissioner may be tendered in evidence

without proof, and shall be deemed, until the contrary is proved, to have been so signed.

(6)   Subject to this section, the rules of the High Court for the time being application to civil proceedings shall apply to proceedings pursuant to this section.

(With effect from 1 November 1972)

Finance Act 2003

128. (1)   Section 29 of the Principal Act is amended—

(a)   in subsection (1), by substituting "for the recovery of the penalty in any court of competent jurisdiction as a liquidated sum, and, where appropriate, section 94 of the Courts of Justice Act 1924 shall apply accordingly." For "for the recovery of the penalty in the High Court as a liquidated sum and the provisions of section 94 of the Courts of Justice Act, 1924, shall apply accordingly.", and

(b)   in subsection (6), by substituting "the rules of court" for "the rules of the High Court".

(2)   Subsection (1) applies as respects civil proceedings commenced on or after the passing of this Act.

(With effect from 28 March 2003)

Finance (No. 2) Act 2008

98. (1)   The enactments specified in Schedule 5 are amended or repealed to the extent and manner specified in that Schedule and, unless the contrary is stated, shall come into effect after the passing of this Act.

SCHEDULE 5

Miscellaneous Amendments in Relation to Penalties

PART 3

Value-Added Tax: Penalties

3.   The Value-Added Tax Act 1972 is amended—

(e)   by deleting section 29, and

(With effect from 24 December 2008)

Section 30

Value Added Tax Act 1972

Time limits

30. (1) Subject to subsection (3) and sections 26 (4) and 27 (6), proceedings for the recovery of any penalty under this Act may be commenced at any time within six years next after the date on which it was incurred.

(2) Where the person who has incurred any penalty has died, any proceedings under this Act which have been or could have been commenced against him may be continued or commenced against his personal representative and any penalty awarded in proceedings so continued or commenced shall be a debt due from and payable out of his estate.

(3) Proceedings commenced by virtue of subsection (2) may be begun at any time not later than three years after the expiration of the year in which the deceased person died in a case in which the grant of probate or letters of administration was made in that year and at any time not lens: than two years after the expiration of the year in which such grant was made in any other case, but the foregoing provisions of this subsection shall have effect subject to the proviso that where the personal representative lodges a corrective affidavit for the purpose of assessment of estate duty after the year in which, the deceased person died, the proceedings may be begun at any time before the expiration of two years next after the end of the year in which the corrective affidavit was lodged.

(4) (a) An estimation of tax under section 22 or 23 may be made at any time not later than ten years after the end of the taxable period to which the estimate relates or, where the period in respect of which the estimate is made consists of two or more taxable periods, after the end of the earlier or earliest taxable period comprised in such period:

Provided that in a case in which any form of fraud or neglect has been committed by or on behalf of any person in connection with or in relation to tax, an estimation as aforesaid may be made at any time for any period for which, by reason of the fraud or neglect, tax would otherwise be lost to the Exchequer.

(b) In this subsection "**neglect**" means negligence or a failure to give any notice, to furnish particulars, to make any return or to produce or furnish any invoice, credit note, debit note, receipt, account, voucher, bank statement, estimate, statement, information, book, document, record or declaration required to be given furnished made or produced by or under this Act or regulations:

Provided that a person shall be deemed not to have failed to do anything required to be done within a limited time if he did it within such further time, if any, as the Revenue Commissioners may have allowed; and where a person had a reasonable excuse for not doing anything required to be done, he shall be deemed not to have failed to do it if he did it without unreasonable delay after the excuse had ceased.

(5)   (a)   Where a person dies, an estimation of tax under section 22 or 23 (as the case may be) may be made on his personal representative for any period for which such an estimation could have been made upon him immediately before his death, or could be made upon him if he were living, in respect of tax which became due by such person before his death, and the amount of tax recoverable under any such estimation shall be a debt due from and payable out of the estate of such person.

(b)   No estimation of tax shall be made by virtue of this subsection later than three years after the expiration of the year in which the deceased person died in a case in which the grant of probate or letters of administration was made in that year and no such estimation shall be made later than two years after the expiration of the year in which such grant was made in any other case, but the foregoing provisions of this paragraph shall have effect subject to the proviso that where the personal representative lodges a corrective affidavit for the purposes of assessment of estate duty after the year in which the deceased person died, such estimation may be made at any time before the expiration of two years after the end of the year in which the corrective affidavit was lodged.

(With effect from 1 November 1972)

Value Added Tax (Amendment) Act 1978

20.   Section 30 of the Principal Act is hereby amended-

(a)   by the substitution of the following subsection for subsection (3):

"(3)   Proceedings may not be commenced by virtue of subsection (2) against the personal representative of a deceased person at a time when, by virtue of paragraph (b) of subsection (5) an estimation of tax may not be made on the said personal representative in respect of tax which became due by such person before his death.",

and

(b)   by the substitution, in subsection (5), of the following paragraph for paragraph (b):

> "(b)   No estimation of tax shall be made by virtue of this subsection later than three years after the expiration of the year in which the deceased person died, in a case in which the grant of probate or letters of administration was made in that year, and no such estimation shall be made later than two years after the expiration of the year in which such grant was made in any other case, but the foregoing provisions of this subsection shall have effect subject to the proviso that where the personal representative-
>
> > (i)   after the year in which the deceased person died, lodges a corrective affidavit for the purposes of assessment of estate duty or delivers an additional affidavit under section 38 of the Capital Acquisitions Tax Act, 1976, or
> >
> > (ii)   is liable to deliver an additional affidavit under the said section 38, has been so notified by the Revenue Commissioners and did not deliver the said additional affidavit in the year in which the deceased person died,
>
> such estimation may be made at any time before the expiration of two years after the end of the year in which the corrective affidavit was lodged or the additional affidavit was or is delivered.".

(With effect from 1 March 1979)

Finance Act 1992

191.   Section 30 of the Principal Act is hereby amended

(a)   by the insertion after "estimation", wherever it occurs, of "or assessment",

(b)   by the insertion after "estimate", wherever it occurs, of "or assessment", and

*(c)   by the insertion in subsection (4)(b) after "invoice," of "monthly control statement,".

(With effect from 28 May 1992 except * from 1 November 1992)

Finance Act 1998

115.   Section 30 of the Principal Act is hereby amended in subsection (4) by the substitution of the following paragraphs for paragraph (a):

> "(a)   (i)   In relation to any taxable period ending before the 1st day of May, 1998, an estimation or assessment of tax under section 22 or 23 may, subject to subparagraph (ii), be made at any time not later than ten years after the end

of the taxable period to which the estimate or assessment relates or, where the period in respect of which the estimate or assessment is made consists of two or more taxable periods, after the end of the earlier or earliest taxable period comprised in such period.

(ii)   In relation to any taxable period commencing on or after the 1st day of May, 1998, and on or after the 1st day of May, 1999, in relation to any other taxable period, an estimation or assessment of tax under section 22 or 23 may be made at any time not later than six years after the end of the taxable period to which the estimate or assessment relates or, where the period in respect of which the estimate or assessment is made consists of two or more taxable periods, after the end of the earlier or earliest taxable period comprised in such period.

(aa)   Notwithstanding paragraphs (a)(i) and (a)(ii) in a case in which any form of fraud or neglect has been committed by or on behalf of any person in connection with or in relation to tax, an estimate or assessment as aforesaid may be made at any time for any period for which, by reason of the fraud or neglect, tax would otherwise be lost to the Exchequer.".

(With effect from 27 March 1998)

Capital Acquisitions Tax Consolidation Act 2003

SCHEDULE 3
CONSEQUENTIAL AMENDMENTS

In the enactments specified in column (1) of the following Table for the words set out or referred to in column (2), there shall be substituted the words set out in the corresponding entry in column (3).

Enactment amended (1)	Words to be replaced (2)	Words to be substituted (3)
Value Added Tax Act, 1972:		
section 30(5)(b)(i)	section 38 of the Capital Acquisitions Tax Act 1976	section 48 of the Capital Acquisitions Tax Consolidation Act 2003
section 30(5)(b)(ii)	section 38	section 48

(With effect from 21 February 2003)

Finance Act 2003

129. Section 30 of the Principal Act is amended –

(a)   in subsection (4)(a)(i) –

(i)   by substituting "1 May 2003" for "the 1st day of May, 1998", and

(ii)   by substituting "six years" for "ten years",

and

(b)   in subsection (4)(a)(ii) —

(i)   by substituting "1 May 2003" for "the 1st day of May, 1998",

(ii)   by substituting "1 January 2005" for "the 1st day of May, 1999,", and

(iii)   by substituting "four years" for "six years".

(With effect from 1 November 2003)

Finance Act 2008

141. The enactments specified in Schedule 8 —

(a)   are amended to the extent and in the manner specified in paragraphs 1 to 6 of that Schedule, and

(b)   apply and come into operation in accordance with paragraph 7 of that Schedule.

Schedule 8
Miscellaneous Technical Amendments in Relation to Tax

3.   The Value-Added Tax Act 1972 is amended in accordance with the following provisions:

(h)   in section 30(4)(b) by deleting "monthly control statement,",

(With effect from 13 March 2008)

Finance (No. 2) Act 2008

98.   (1)   The enactments specified in Schedule 5 are amended or repealed to the extent and manner specified in that Schedule and, unless the contrary is stated, shall come into effect after the passing of this Act.

SCHEDULE 5

Miscellaneous Amendments in Relation to Penalties

PART 3

Value-Added Tax: Penalties

3.   The Value-Added Tax Act 1972 is amended —

(f)   in section 30 by deleting subsections (2) and (3).

(With effect from 24 December 2008)

Section 31

Value Added Tax Act 1972

Application of section 512 of the Income Tax Act, 1967

31. The provisions of section 512 of the Income Tax Act, 1967, shall apply to any penalty incurred under this Act.

(With effect from 1 November 1972)

Taxes Consolidation Act 1997

1100. Schedule 31, which provides for amendments to other enactments consequential on the passing of this Act, shall apply for the purposes of this Act.

SCHEDULE 31
Consequential Amendments

In the enactments specified in Column (1) of the following Table for the words set out or referred to in Column (2) there shall be substituted the words set out in the corresponding entry in Column (3).

Enactment amended (1)	Words to be replaced (2)	Words to be substituted (3)
The Value Added Tax Act, 1972:		
section 31	section 512 of the Tax Act, 1967	section 1065 of the Taxes Consolidation Act, 1997

(With effect from 6 April 1997)

Section 32

Value–Added Tax Act 1972

Regulations

32. (1) The Revenue Commissioners shall make such regulations as seem to them to be necessary for the purpose of giving effect to this Act and of enabling them to discharge their functions thereunder and, without prejudice to the generality of the foregoing, the regulations may make provision in relation to all or any of the following matters-

(a) the manner in which exemption in respect of certain services may be waived under section 7 and any such waiver may be cancelled, and the adjustments, including a charge of tax, which may be made as a condition of any such cancellation;

(b) the treatment under section 5(2) of the rendering of a service by a person for the purpose of a business activity in which he engages as me rendering of such service in the course of business;

(c) the particulars required for registration and the manner in which registration may be effected and cancelled;

(d) the manner in which a person may elect to be an accountable person and any such election may be cancelled, the treatment of an accountable person as a person who is not accountable, and the adjustments, including a charge of tax, which may be made as a condition of any such cancellation or treatment;

(e) the manner in which any amount may be apportioned;

(f) the treatment of portion of the consideration payable to certain farmers and fishermen in respect of goods delivered and services rendered by them as tax that may be deducted under section 12 in computing the amount of tax payable;

(g) the treatment of the total of the moneys actually received by a person in respect of the delivery of goods or the rendering of services as the total of the consideration which he is entitled to receive for such delivery or rendering and the adjustments, including a charge of tax, which may be made when a person becomes liable to account for tax on the basis of moneys received or, having been so liable, ceases to be so liable or ceases to be an accountable person;

(h) the keeping by accountable persons of records and the retention of such records and supporting documents;

(i)   the form of invoice, credit note, debit note and settlement voucher required to be used for the purposes of this Act, the particulars required to be inserted in such documents and the period within which such documents are required to be issued:

(j)   the furnishing of returns and the particulars to be shown thereon;

(k)   the nomination by the Revenue Commissioners of officers to perform any acts and discharge any functions authorised by this Act to be performed or discharged by the Revenue Commissioners;

(l)   the manner in which tax is to be recovered in cases of default of payment;

(m)   the refund of tax in excess of the amount required by law to be borne, or paid to the Revenue Commissioners;

(n)   disclosure to the Revenue Commissioners of such information as they may require for the ascertainment of liability to tax;

(o)   the remission at the discretion of the Revenue Commissioners of small amounts of tax and interest;

(p)   matters consequential on the death of a registered person or his becoming subject to any incapacity;

(q)   service of notices;

(r)   the acceptance of estimates (whether or not subject to subsequent review) of the amount of tax payable or of any amounts relating to such tax;

(s)   the adjustment of the liability of an accountable person who delivers goods or renders services and of the liability of an accountable person to whom goods are delivered or services are rendered where goods are returned, the consideration is reduced, a bad debt is incurred or a discount is allowed;

(t)   the valuation of interests in or over immovable goods;

(u)   the estimation of tax due for a taxable or other period;

(v)   the relief for stock-in-trade held on the specified day;

(w)   the relief of a dealer in livestock from accountability for tax on the delivery by him of any such goods and the treatment of such dealer as a person required under section 13 to issue an invoice in respect of the delivery by him of any such goods; the treatment of a sale by auction by an auctioneer (including a livestock mart) of livestock as a delivery of such goods by a person required under section 13 to issue an invoice in respect of the delivery of such goods;

(x)   the apportionment between tax which may be deducted under section 12 and tax which may not be deducted under that section, the review, by reference to the circumstances obtaining in any period not exceeding one year, of any such apportionment previously made, the charge or repayment of tax consequent on any such review and the furnishing of particulars by an accountable person to the Revenue Commissioners for the purpose of any such review;

(y)   the particulars to be furnished and the manner in which notification is to be given to the Revenue Commissioners by a person who intends to promote a dance, and the manner in which the Revenue Commissioners shall notify the proprietor of any premises in regard to dances proposed to be promoted in such premises.

(2)   Regulations under this section may make different provisions in relation to different cases and may in particular provide for differentiation between different classes of persons affected by this Act and for the adoption of different procedures for any such different classes.

(3)   Every regulation made under this section shall be laid before Dáil Éireann as soon as may be after it is made and, if a resolution annulling the regulation is passed by Dáil Éireann within the next twenty-one days on which Dáil Éireann has sat after the regulation is laid before it, the regulation shall be annulled accordingly, but without prejudice to the validity of anything previously done thereunder.

(With effect from 1 November 1972)

Finance Act 1973

85.   Section 32(1) of the Principal Act is hereby amended by the insertion of the following paragraphs after paragraph (x):

"(xx)   the relief (if any) to be given to an accountable person in respect of tax borne or paid by him on stock-in-trade held by him immediately before the commencement of the first taxable period for which he is deemed to become an accountable person;

(xxx)   the manner in which a determination may be made for the purposes of section 11(1B);".

90.   The Principal Act is hereby amended as specified in column (3) of the Tenth Schedule to this Act.

TENTH SCHEDULE
AMENDMENT OF ENACTMENTS

Number and Year (1)	Short Title (2)	Amendment (3)
No. 22 of 1972	Value-Added Tax Act, 1972	In section 32(1)(b), " by a person of a service which is connected with any " shall be substituted for " of a service by a person for the purpose of a ".

(With effect from 3 September 1973)

Finance Act 1976

58. Section 32 of the Principal Act is hereby amended by the insertion in subsection (1), after paragraph (b), of the following paragraph:

"(uu) the adjustments to be made by an accountable person of any apportionment referred to in paragraph (x) or deduction under section 12 previously made, being adjustments by reference to changes, occurring not later than five years from the end of the taxable period to which the original apportionment or deduction relates, in any of the matters by reference to which the apportionment or deduction was made or allowed, and the determination of the taxable period in and from which or in which any such adjustment is to take effect;".

*81. (1) The enactment mentioned in column (2) of Part I of the Fifth Schedule to this Act is hereby repealed to the extent specified in column (3) of that Schedule.

(2) The enactment mentioned in column (2) of Part II of the Fifth Schedule to this Act is hereby repealed to the extent specified in column (3) of that Schedule.

(3) (a) Subsection (1) of this section shall be deemed to have come into operation on the 6th day of April, 1976.

(b) Subsection (2) of this section shall be deemed to have come into operation on the 1st day of March, 1976.

FIFTH SCHEDULE
ENACTMENTS REPEALED
PART I

No. 22 of 1972	Value Added Tax Act, 1972.	In section 32(1) (a) paragraph (f), and (b) in paragraph (w), the words from" and the treatment" to the end of the paragraph.

(With effect from 27 May 1976 except * 1 March 1976)

Value Added Tax (Amendment) Act 1978

21.   Section 32 of the Principal Act is hereby amended-

(a)   by the substitution in subsection (1) of the following paragraphs for paragraphs (b), (e), (g) and (p):

"(b)   the treatment under section 5(3) of the use and services specified therein as services supplied by a person for consideration in the course of business;

(e)   the manner in which, notwithstanding section 11(3), any amount may be apportioned;

(g)   the determination, under section 14, of a person's tax liability for any period by reference to moneys received and the adjustments, including a charge of tax, which may be made when a person becomes entitled to determine his tax liability in the manner aforesaid or, having been so entitled, ceases to be so entitled, or ceases to be a taxable person;

(p)   matters consequential on the death of a registered person or his becoming subject to any incapacity including the treatment of a person of such class or classes as may be specified in the regulations as a person carrying on the business of the deceased or incapacitated person;",

(b)   by the deletion of paragraph (w) of the said subsection (1),

and

(c)   by the insertion after subsection (2) of the following subsection:

"(2A)   Regulations under this section for the purposes of section 5(7), subsection (1) or (2) of section 13 or subsection (6) or (7) of section 15 shall not be made without the consent of the Minister for Finance.".

(With effect from 1 March 1979)

30.   (1)   ...

(2)   In consequence of the amendments of the Principal Act specified in this Act and of the repeals specified in the First Schedule, the Principal Act is hereby further amended by the substitution of the word or expression mentioned in column (3) of the Second Schedule at any reference number for the word or expression mentioned in column (2) of that Schedule at that reference number wherever it occurs in the provision of the Principal Act mentioned in column (4) of that Schedule at that reference number.

SECOND SCHEDULE
Consequential Amendments

Reference Number (1)	Existing word or expression (2)	Substituted word or expression (3)	Provision of Principal Act (4)
21.	"delivers goods or renders services"	"supplies goods or services"	Section 32(1)(s)
23.	"goods are delivered or services are rendered"	"goods or services are supplied"	Section 32 (1)(s).
26.	"an accountable person"	"a taxable person"	Sections 32(1)(d), 32(1)(s) 32(1 (uu), 32(1)(x), 32(1)(xx),.
27.	"accountable persons"	"taxable persons"	Section 32(1)(h).
28.	"not accountable"	"not a taxable person"	Section 32(1)(d).

(With effect from 1 March 1979)

Finance Act 1984

91.   Section 32 of the Principal Act is hereby amended-

(a)   by the insertion in subsection (1) after paragraph (v) of the following paragraph:

"(w)   the determination of average build for the purposes of paragraph (xvii) of the Second Schedule;",

and

(b)   by the insertion in subsection (2A) after "section 15" of "or in relation to the matter specified in subsection (1)(w)".

(With effect from 1 May 1984)

Finance Act 1985

48.   Section 32 of the Principal Act is hereby amended-

(a)   by the insertion in subsection (1) after paragraph (w) of the following paragraph:

"(ww) the determination of average foot size for the purposes of paragraph (xix) of the Second Schedule;",

and

(b)   by the substitution in subsection (2A) of "matters specified in subsection (1)(w) or (1)(ww)" for "matter specified in subsection (1)(w)".

(With effect from 1 March 1985)

Finance Act 1986

88. Section 32 of the Principal Act is hereby amended-

(a)   in paragraph (h) by the insertion after "documents" of "or other recorded data",

and

(b)   by the substitution of the following paragraph for paragraph (i):

"(i)   the form of invoice, credit note, debit note and settlement voucher, including electronic form, required to be used for the purposes of this Act, the particulars required to be inserted in such documents or electronically recorded and the period within which such documents or electronic data are required to be issued or transmitted and such other conditions in relation to the issue or receipt, in any form, of an invoice, credit note, debit note and settlement voucher as may be imposed by the Revenue Commissioners;".

(With effect from 27 May 1986)

Finance Act 1987

44. Section 32 of the Principal Act is hereby amended by the insertion in subsection (2A) (inserted by the Act of 1978) after "section 5(7),", of "subsection 1(a)(vi) of section 12,".

(With effect from 9 July 1987)

Finance Act 1989

60. Section 32 of the Principal Act is hereby amended in subsection (2A) (inserted by the Act of 1978) by the substitution of ", subsection (6) or (7) of section 15 or paragraph (ia) of the Sixth Schedule" for "or subsection (6) or (7) of section 15".

(With effect from 24 May 1989)

Finance Act 1992

192. Section 32 of the Principal Act is hereby amended in subsection (1):

*(a)   by the insertion of the following paragraphs after paragraph (a):

"(aa)   the deduction of tax chargeable in respect of intra-Community acquisitions;

(ab)   the manner in which residual tax referred to in section 12(1)(a)(iib) may be calculated and deducted;

(ac)   the manner in which residual tax referred to in section 13(3A) may be calculated and repaid;

(ad)   the repayment, in accordance with section 15(5A), of tax chargeable on the importation of goods;

(ae)   the time and manner in which tax shall be payable in respect of the goods referred to in section 19(4);

(af)   the form of statement required to be furnished in accordance with section 19A, the particulars to be specified therein and the amount or amounts to be applied for the purposes of section 19A(3);

(ag)   the supply of goods by tax-free shops in accordance with paragraph (ia) of the Second Schedule;

(ah)   the importation of goods consigned to another Member State in accordance with paragraph (iiib) of the Second Schedule;

(ai)   the circumstances in which a person may elect not to apply the proviso to subsection (6)(d) of section 3;",

and

(b)   by the insertion in paragraph (i) (inserted by the Act of 1978) of "monthly control statement," after "invoice," in each place where it occurs.

(With effect from 1 November 1992 except * from 1 January 1993)

Finance Act 1995

138. Section 32 of the Principal Act is hereby amended in subsection (1) by the insertion of the following paragraphs after paragraph (d):

"(da) the conditions for a taxable dealer to opt to apply the margin scheme to certain supplies in accordance with section 10A(4);

(db)   the determination of the aggregate margin in accordance with section 10A(8);

(dc)   the form of the invoice or other document that shall be issued in accordance with section 10B(4);

(dd)   the manner in which residual tax referred to in section 12(1)(a) (vi) may be deducted;

(de)   the particulars to be furnished in relation to antiques as specified in paragraph (xvia) of the Sixth Schedule or paragraph (iii) of the Eighth Schedule;".

(With effect from 2 June 1995)

Finance Act 1999

137. Section 32 of the Principal Act is hereby amended in subsection (1) by the insertion of the following sub-paragraphs after sub-paragraph (h):

"(ha) the keeping by persons trading in investment gold (within the meaning of section 6A) of records and the retention of such records and supporting documents or other recorded data;

(hb)   the conditions under which a person may waive his right to exemption from tax on the supply of investment gold (within the meaning of section 6A);

(hc)　　the conditions under which an intermediary (within the meaning of section 6A) may waive his right to exemption from tax on his supply of services;

(hd)　　the conditions under which a person may claim a refund of tax in accordance with subsections (6)(b), (7)(b) and (8)(b) of section 6A, and the manner in which such refund may be claimed;".

(With effect from 25 March 1999)

S.I. 196 of 1999
European Communities (Value-Added Tax) Regulations, 1999

3.　　In these Regulations "the Principal Act" means the Value-Added Tax Act, 1972 (No. 22 of 1972).

4.　　Section 32 of the Principal Act is hereby amended in paragraph (ag) (inserted by the Finance Act 1992 (No. 9 of 1992)) of subsection (1) by the deletion of "by tax-free shops".

(With effect from 1 July 1999)

Finance Act 2000

121.　　Section 32 of the Principal Act is amended in paragraph (ag) (inserted by the Act of 1992) of subsection (1) by the deletion of "by tax-free shops".

128.　　The European Communities (Value-Added Tax) Regulations, 1999 (S.I. No. 196 of 1999) shall be deemed to have been revoked with efect from 1 July 1999.

(With effect from 1 July 1999)

Finance Act 2003

130.　　Section 32 of the Principal Act is amended in subsection (1) –

(a)　　by inserting the following after paragraph (b):

"(ba)　the manner in which the electronic services scheme referred to in section 5A shall operate;",

and

(b)　　by inserting the following after paragraph (m):

"(ma)　the conditions governing a person's entitlement to interest in accordance with section 21A;".

(with effect from 1 July 2003 except * with effect from 1 November 2003)

Finance Act 2005

111.　　Section 32 of the Principal Act is amended in subsection (1)-

(a)　　by inserting the following after paragraph (t):

"(ta)　specifying the circumstances or conditions under which development work on immovable goods is not treated as being on behalf of, or to the benefit of, a person;",

(b)   by inserting the following after paragraph (ww):

" (www) the circumstances, terms and conditions under which a letting of immovable goods constitutes a letting in the short-term guest sector or holiday sector, or under which accommodation is or is not holiday accommodation (within the meaning of paragraph (xiii) of the Sixth Schedule);",

and

(c)   in subsection (2A) by substituting "paragraph (w), (ww) or (www) of subsection (1)" for "subsection (1)(w) or (1)(ww)".

(With effect from 25 March 2005)

Finance Act 2006

99. (1)   Section 32 of the Principal Act is amended —

*(a)   by substituting the following for subsection (1)(e):

"(e)   (i)   the manner in which any amount may be apportioned, including the methods of apportionment which may be applied for the purposes of paragraphs (a) and (b) of section 11(3),

(ii)   the circumstances or conditions under which a supply may or may not be treated as an ancillary supply, a composite supply, an individual supply, a multiple supply or a principal supply,

(iii) a relatively small amount, or an element of a supply, which may be disregarded for the purposes of applying section 11(3);",

and

(b)   by inserting the following after subsection (2A):

"(2B) Regulations under this Act may contain such incidental, supplementary and consequential provisions as appear to the Revenue Commissioners to be necessary for the purposes of giving full effect to —

(a)   Council Directive No. 77/388/EEC of 17 May 1977,

(b)   Council Directive No. 79/1072/EEC of 6 December 1979,

(c)   Council Directive No. 86/560/EEC of 17 November 1986.".

(With effect from 31 March 2006 except * with effect from 1 November 2006)

Finance Act 2007

92. Section 32 of the Principal Act is amended in subsection (1) by inserting the following paragraph after paragraph (xxx):

"(xxxx) the making of a determination under section 10(3A);".

*97. With effect from 1 January 2007 in each provision of the Principal Act specified in the first column of Schedule 3 for the words set out in the second column of that Schedule at that entry there is substituted the words set out at the corresponding entry in the third column of that Schedule.

Schedule 3
Miscellaneous Amendments Relating to Council Directive 2006/112/EC

Amendment of Value-Added Tax Act 1972

Provision of Principal Act	Words to be replaced	Words to be inserted
Section 32(2B)(a)	Council Directive No. 77/388/EEC of 17 May 1977	Council Directive No. 2006/112/EC of 28 November 2006

(With effect from 2 April 2007 except * with effect from 1 January 2007)

Finance Act 2008

105. Section 32 of the Principal Act is amended in subsection (1) with effect from 1 July 2008 by inserting the following after paragraph (ta):

"(tb) the operation of the capital goods scheme and in particular the duration of a subsequent interval where the accounting year of a capital goods owner changes;

(tc) the methods which may be used for the purposes of applying section 10(4D);".

109. With effect from 1 July 2008 in each provision of the Principal Act specified in the first column of Schedule 4 for the words set out in the second column of that Schedule at that entry (in each place where those words occur in the provision concerned) there is substituted the words set out at the corresponding entry in the third column of that Schedule.

Schedule 4
Miscellaneous Amendments Relating to the Amendment of the Definition of Taxable Person

Amendments to Value-Added Tax Act 1972

Provision of Value-Added Tax Act 1972	Words to be replaced	Words to be inserted
Section 32	a taxable person	an accountable person
Section 32	by taxable persons	by accountable persons

*141. The enactments specified in Schedule 8 —

(a)   are amended to the extent and in the manner specified in paragraphs 1 to 6 of that Schedule, and

(b)   apply and come into operation in accordance with paragraph 7 of that Schedule.

Schedule 8
Miscellaneous Technical Amendments in Relation to Tax

3.   The Value-Added Tax Act 1972 is amended in accordance with the following provisions:

(i)   in section 32(1)(i) by deleting "monthly control statement," in both places where it occurs,

(With effect from 1 July 2008 except * with effect from 13 March 2008)

Finance (No. 2) Act 2008

75.   Section 32 of the Principal Act is amended in subsection (1) —

(a)   by inserting the following after paragraph (dc):

"(dca) the manner in which the travel agent's margin scheme referred to in section 10C shall operate;",

and

(b)   by inserting the following after paragraph (dd):

"(dda) the manner in which the deduction entitlement referred to in section 12(1)(a)(ix) may be calculated;".

(With effect from 24 December 2008)

Section 33

Value-Added Tax Act 1972

Officer responsible in case of body of persons

33. (1) The secretary or other officer acting as secretary for the time being of any body of persons shall be answerable in addition to the body for doing all such acts as are required to be done by the body under any of the provisions relating to tax.

(2) Every such officer as aforesaid may from time to time retain out of any money coming into his hands, on behalf of the body, so much thereof as is sufficient to pay the tax due by the body and shall be indemnified for all such payments made in pursuance of this section.

(3) Any notice required to be given to a body of persons under any of the provisions relating to tax may be given to the secretary or other acting as secretary for the being of such body.

(4) In this section "**the provisions relating to tax**" means-

(a) the provisions of this Act and regulations, and

(b) the provisions relating to tax of any subsequent Act.

(With effect from 1 November 1972)

Section 34

Value Added Tax Act 1972

Relief for stock-in-trade held on the specified day

34. (1)   In computing the amount of tax payable by an accountable person, the following amounts may, subject to subsections (3) and (4), in addition to the deductions authorised by section 12, be deducted on account of stock-in-trade which has been delivered to, and has not been delivered by, him before the specified day and which is held by him at the commencement of that day, or incorporated in other stock-in-trade held by him at such commencement that is to say:

    (a)   in case the accountable person was, immediately before the specified day, not registered for turnover tax under the provisions of section 49 of the Finance Act, 1963, nor required under the provisions of that section to furnish the particulars specified for registration, and was met registered for wholesale tax under the provisions of section 4 of the Finance (No. 2) Act, 1966, nor required under the provisions of that section to furnish the particulars specified for registration, an amount equal to the sum of the amounts which he would be liable to pay on account of turnover tax and wholesale tax if,

        (i)   he had been accountable for each of those taxes,

        (ii)   he had on the day immediately preceding the specified day sold the whole of his stock-in-trade aforesaid in the course of business to a person who was carrying on the same activities as his own and who had not given him, in accordance with section 50 of the Finance Act, 1963, a statement in writing quoting the turnover tax registration number of the person nor given him, in accordance with section 5 of the Finance (No. 2) Act, 1966, a statement in writing quoting the wholesale tax registration number of the person, and

        (iii)   he had on the said day immediately preceding the specified day received from the person mentioned in subparagraph (ii) payment for the stock-in-trade so deemed to have been sold of an amount equal to the cost to the accountable person of such stock or the market vale thereof, whichever is the lower, and

    (b)   in case, immediately before the specified day the accountable person was registered for turnover tax under the provisions of section 49 of the Finance Act,

1963, or required under the provisions of that section to furnish the particulars specified for registration, but was not registered for wholesale tax under the provisions of section 4 of the Finance (No. 2) Act, 1966, nor required under the provisions of that section to furnish the particulars specified for registration, an amount equal to the amount of wholesale tax which he would be liable to pay if,

(i)   he had been an accountable person for the purposes of wholesale tax,

(ii)   he had on the day immediately preceding the specified day sold the whole of his stock-in-trade aforesaid in the course of business to a person who was carrying on the same activities as his own and who had in accordance with section 50 of the Finance Act, 1963, given him a statement in writing quoting the registration number of the person but had not given him, in accordance with section 5 of the Finance (No. 2) Act, 1966, a statement in writing quoting the wholesale tax registration number of such person, and

(iii) he had on the said day immediately preceding the specified day received from the person mentioned in subparagraph (ii) payment for the stock-in-trade so deemed to have been sold of an amount equal to the cost to the accountable person of such stock or the market value thereof, whichever is the lower.

(2)   Where an accountable person-

(a)   is not such a person as is mentioned in paragraph (a) or (b) of subsection (1) but was such a person at any time during the year ended the day immediately preceding the specified day or

(b)   is such a person as is mentioned in paragraph (a) or (b) of subsection (1) and was such a person during a part of the year ended the day immediately preceding the specified day but was not such a person during another part of that year,

the Revenue Commissioners may allow such deduction or make such restriction in the deduction which would otherwise be allowable as in their opinion is just and reasonable having regard to the nature of the business carried on, the period during the year ended on the day immediately preceding the specified day during which the business was carried on and the period during the said year during which the person was such a person as is mentioned in the said paragraph (a) or (b) of subsection (1).

(3)   A claim for a deduction under this section shall be made in accordance with regulations and the amount authorised to be deducted may be deducted by equal instalments in computing the amount of tax payable in respect of each of the taxable periods beginning on the first day of the first and second taxable periods next following that in which the specified day occurs.

(4)   No deduction shall be granted under this section for any amount which is referable to turnover tax or wholesale tax on immovable goods on the delivery of which tax is, by virtue of section 4(6), not chargeable or to wholesale tax on newspapers or periodicals, second hand goods or any goods of a kind specified in the Fourth Schedule.

(5)   In this section-

'**stock-in-trade**' mean, in relation to any person, goods which are either-

(a)   movable goods of a kind that are delivered by the person in the ordinary course of his business and are actually held for delivery or would be so held if they were mature or if their manufacture, preparation or construction were complete, or

(b)   materials incorporated in incorporated in immovable goods of a kind that are delivered by the person in the ordinary course of his business and that have not been delivered by him since the goods were developed, but are actually held for delivery or would be so held if their development were complete, or

(c)   consumable materials incorporated in immovable goods by the person in the course of a business consisting of the rendering of a service of constructing, repairing, painting or decorating immovable goods where that service has not been completed, or

(d)   materials which have not been incorporated in goods and are such as are used by the person in the manufacture or construction of goods of a kind that are delivered by the person in the ordinary course of his business or, where his ordinary business consists of repairing, painting or decorating goods, are used by him as consumable materials in the course of that business;

materials referred to in paragraph (b) of the paragraph of "stock-in-trade" shall, for the purposes of subsection (1), be regarded as having been delivered to the same extent as the immovable goods into which they have been incorporated can be regarded as having been delivered;

materials referred to in paragraph (c) the definition of "stock-in-trade" shall be regarded as having been delivered to the extent that the service in relation to which they have been used has been rendered;

'**cost**' means, in relation to stock-in-trade, the total of the money payable by the person for the delivery of the stock, including any addition made for turnover tax or wholesale tax, but excluding any discount or allowance deducted or deductible on payment for the stock.

(With effect from 1 November 1972)

Finance Act 1976

59.   Section 34 of the Principal Act is hereby amended by the substitution of the following paragraph for paragraph (a) of subsection (5):

"(a)   movable goods of a kind that are delivered by the person in the ordinary course of his business being goods which are actually held for delivery (otherwise than by virtue of section 3(1) (e)) or which would be so held if they were mature or if their manufacture, preparation or construction were complete, or".

(With effect from 27 May 1976)

Value-Added Tax (Amendment) Act 1978

30.   (1)   The enactment mentioned in column (2) of the First Schedule is hereby repealed to the extent specified in column (3) of that Schedule.

(2)   In consequence of the amendments of the Principal Act specified in this Act and of the repeals specified in the First Schedule, the Principal Act is hereby further amended by the substitution of the word or expression mentioned in column (3) of the Second Schedule at any reference number for the word or expression mentioned in column (2) of that Schedule at that reference number wherever it occurs in the provision of the Principal Act mentioned in column (4) of that Schedule at that reference number.

SECOND SCHEDULE
Consequential Amendments

Reference Number (1)	Existing word or expression (2)	Substituted word or expression (3)	Provision of Principal Act (4)
1.	"delivery"	"supply"	Section 34(5).
2.	"rendering"	"supply"	section 34(5)(c).
3.	"delivered"	"supplied"	Section 34(1) .
4.	"rendered"	"supplied"	Section 34(5).
25.	"accountable person" except where preceded by the word "an"	"taxable person"	Sections 34(1)(a) and 34(1)(b).
26.	"an accountable person"	"a taxable person"	Sections 34(1), 34(2).
33.	"second-hand goods or any goods of a kind specified in the Fourth Schedule"	"or second-hand goods"	Section 34(4).

(With effect from 1 March 1979)

Finance Act 2008

109. With effect from 1 July 2008 in each provision of the Principal Act specified in the first column of Schedule 4 for the words set out in the second column of that Schedule at that entry (in each place where those words occur in the provision concerned) there is substituted the words set out at the corresponding entry in the third column of that Schedule.

Schedule 4
Miscellaneous Amendments Relating to the Amendment of the Definition of Taxable Person

Amendments to Value-Added Tax Act 1972

Provision of Value-Added Tax Act 1972	Words to be replaced	Words to be inserted
Section 34	a taxable person	an accountable person
Section 34	the taxable person	the accountable person

(With effect from 1 July 2008)

Section 35

Value Added Tax Act 1972

Special provisions for adjustment and recovery of consideration

35. (1)   (a)   Notwithstanding the repeal by this Act of the provisions relating to turnover tax and wholesale tax, sums due on account of turnover tax or wholesale tax under a contract entered into before the specified day, together with any additional sums which might be recoverable by virtue of the provisions of section 9 of the Finance (No. 2) Act, 1966, section 7 of the Finance (No. 2) Act, 1968 section 58 of the Finance Act, 1969, section 51 of the Finance Act, 1970, or section 4 of the Finance (No. 2) Act, 1970, shall, in the absence of agreement to the contrary, but subject to subsection (2), be recoverable as if the said provisions relating to turnover tax and wholesale tax had not been repealed.

      (b)   (i)   Subject to subparagraph (ii), where, under an agreement made before the specified day, an accountable person delivers goods or renders services on or after that day in such circumstances that tax is chargeable, the consideration provided for under the agreement shall, in the absence of any agreement to the contrary, be adjusted by excluding therefrom the amount, if any, included on account of turnover tax or wholesale tax or both of those taxes, as the case may be, and including therein an amount equal to the amount of the tax so chargeable, and the consideration as so adjusted shall be deemed to be the consideration provided for under the agreement.

            (ii)   The consideration provided for under an agreement for the delivery of immovable goods or the rendering of a service consisting of a development made before the specified day shall, in the absence of agreement to the contrary, be deemed, for the purposes of this paragraph, to include an amount of turnover tax and wholesale tax combined equal to the amount of tax chargeable in respect of the transaction.

      (c)   Where, under an agreement made before the specified day, a person, other than an accountable person, delivers goods or renders services on or after that day to another person (in this paragraph referred to as the buyer) in such circumstances that the buyer is, or would, if he where an accountable person, be entitled under section 13 to treat as tax deductible under section 12 such amount of the consideration for such delivery or rendering as is specified in subsection (1) of the said section 13, the consideration provided for under the agreement shall, in the absence of agreement to the contrary, be increased by that amount.

(2)   Where, in relation to a delivery of goods or a rendering of services by an accountable person, the person issues an invoice in which the tax chargeable in respect of the transaction is stated separately, he tax so stated shall, for the purpose of its recovery, be deemed to be part of the consideration for the transaction and shall be recoverable accordingly by the person:

Provided that, if the invoice is issued pursuant to section 17(1), this subsection shall not apply unless it is in the form and contains the particulars specified by regulations.

(With effect from 1 November 1972)

Finance Act 1973

86.   Section 35 of the Principal Act is hereby amended by the insertion after subsection (1) of the following subsection:

"(1A) (a)   Where, after the making of an agreement for the delivery of goods or the rendering of services and before the date on which under subsection (1) or (2), as may be appropriate, of section 19 any tax in respect of the transaction would, if the proviso to the said subsection (1) were disregarded, fall due, there is a change in the amount of tax chargeable on the delivery or rendering in question, then, in the absence of agreement to the contrary, there shall be added to or deducted from the total amount of the consideration and any tax stated separately under the agreement an amount equal to the amount of the change in the tax chargeable.

(b)   References in this subsection to a change in the amount of tax chargeable on the delivery of goods or the rendering of services include references to a change to or from a situation in which no tax is being charged on the delivery or rendering.".

(With effect from 3 September 1973)

Finance Act 1976

81. (1) The enactment mentioned in column (2) of Part I of the Fifth Schedule to this Act is hereby repealed to the extent specified in column (3) of that Schedule.

    (2) The enactment mentioned in column (2) of Part II of the Fifth Schedule to this Act is hereby repealed to the extent specified in column (3) of that Schedule.

    (3) (a) Subsection (1) of this section shall be deemed to have come into operation on the 6th day of April, 1976.

        (b) Subsection (2) of this section shall be deemed to have come into operation on the 1st day of March, 1976.

FIFTH SCHEDULE
ENACTMENTS REPEALED
PART II

Number and Year (1)	Short Title (2)	Extent of Repeal (3)
No. 22 of 1972	Value Added Tax Act, 1972.	Section 35 (1) (c).

(With effect from 1 March 1976)

Value Added Tax (Amendment) Act 1978

22. Section 35 of the Principal Act is hereby amended by the addition to the section of the following subsection:

    "(3) (a) Where, under an agreement made before the commencement of section 12A, a flat-rate farmer supplies agricultural produce or an agricultural service after such commencement to any person, the consideration provided for under the agreement shall, in the absence of agreement to the contrary, be increased by an amount equal to the flat-rate addition appropriate to the said consideration.

        (b) Where, in relation to a supply of agricultural produce or an agricultural service by a flat-rate farmer, the flat-rate farmer issues an invoice in which the flat-rate addition is stated separately, the flat-rate addition so stated shall, for the purpose of its recovery, be deemed to be part of the consideration for the transaction and shall be recoverable accordingly by the flat-rate farmer."

30. (1) The enactment mentioned in column (2) of the First Schedule is hereby repealed to the extent specified in column (3) of that Schedule.

(2)   In consequence of the amendments of the Principal Act specified
        in this Act and of the repeals specified in the First Schedule, the
        Principal Act is hereby further amended by the substitution of
        the word or expression mentioned in column (3) of the Second
        Schedule at any reference number for the word or expression
        mentioned in column (2) of that Schedule at that reference
        number wherever it occurs in the provision of the Principal
        Act mentioned in column (4) of that Schedule at that reference
        number.

SECOND SCHEDULE
Consequential Amendments

Reference Number (1)	Existing word or expression (2)	Substituted word or expression (3)	Provision of Principal Act (4)
16	"delivery or rendering"	"supply"	Sections 35(1A)(a) and 35(1A)(b).
17	"delivery of goods or the rendering of services"	"supply of goods or services"	Sections 35(1A)(a) 35(1A)(b).
19	"delivery of goods or a rendering of services"	"supply of goods or services"	Section 35(2).
21	"delivers goods or renders services"	"supplies goods or services"	Section 35(1)(b)(i).
26	"an accountable person"	"a taxable person"	Sections 35(1)(b)(i) and 35(2).
34	"would, if the proviso to the said subsection (1) were disregarded, fall due"	"falls due"	Section 35(1A)(a).

(With effect from 1 March 1979)

Finance Act 2008

109.   With effect from 1 July 2008 in each provision of the Principal Act
        specified in the first column of Schedule 4 for the words set out in
        the second column of that Schedule at that entry (in each place where
        those words occur in the provision concerned) there is substituted the
        words set out at the corresponding entry in the third column of that
        Schedule.

Schedule 4
Miscellaneous Amendments Relating to the Amendment of the Definition of Taxable Person

Amendments to Value-Added Tax Act 1972

Provision of Value-Added Tax Act 1972	Words to be replaced	Words to be inserted
Section 35	a taxable person	an accountable person

(With effect from 1 July 2008)

Section 36

Value Added Tax Act 1972

Special provisions for deliveries made prior to the specified day

36. Notwithstanding anything in this Act, where, in relation to goods of any kind the consideration for the delivery of which would be chargeable at a particular rate if delivered on or after the specified day, the total consideration in respect of deliveries made during, the period of three months ended on the day immediately preceding the specified day by a person, other than a person authorised under section 14 to account for tax in respect of the taxable period commencing on the specified day on the basis of moneys actually received, exceeds by more than 10 per cent the moneys received during that period in respect of sales of goods of that kind, the excess shall, unless the Revenue Commissioners otherwise direct, be deemed, for the purposes of this Act, to be the consideration for the delivery of goods of that kind and the delivery shall be deemed, for those purposes, to have been made on the specified day.

(With effect from 1 November 1972)

Value–Added Tax (Amendment) Act 1978

30. (1)   The enactment mentioned in column (2) of the First Schedule is hereby repealed to the extent specified in column (3) of that Schedule.

FIRST SCHEDULE
Enactments Repealed

Number and Year (1)	Short Title (2)	Extent of Repeal (3)
No. 22 of 1972	Value Added Tax Act, 1972.	Section 36.

(With effect from 1 March 1979)

Section 37

Value-Added Tax Act 1972

Substitution of agent, etc, for person not resident in State.

37.   Where a person who is accountable for any tax, or on whom any duties are imposed by this Act or regulations, is not residing in the State, the Revenue Commissioners may, by notice in writing served on any agent, manager or factor, who is residing in the State and has acted on behalf of that person in the matters by reference to which that person is accountable or those duties are imposed, direct that he shall be substituted for that person as the person accountable for any such tax due in respect of transactions effected after the date of the service of the notice or that he shall be under an obligation to discharge any such duties arising after such date and upon such direction having been served, he shall stand substituted accordingly and shall be subject to the same penalty as if he the person who is accountable for the tax or on whom the duties are imposed.

(With effect from 1 November 1972)

Finance Act 1992

193.   The Principal Act is hereby amended by the substitution of the following section for section 37:

Substitution of certain persons for persons not established in the State

"37.   Where a taxable person not established in the State supplies goods or services, the Revenue Commissioners may, where it appears requisite to them to do so for the protection of the revenue, deem a person who-

(a)   acts or has acted on behalf of the taxable person in relation to such supplies, or

(b)   allows or has allowed such supplies to be made on land owned, occupied or controlled by him,

to have made such supplies in the course or furtherance of business from the date of service on him of a notice in writing to that effect.".

(With effect from 28 May 1992)

Finance Act 2001

198.   Section 37 of the Principal Act is repealed.

(With effect from 1 January 2002)

Section 38

Value Added Tax Act 1972
Extension of certain Acts

38. (1) Section 1 of the Provisional Collection of Taxes Act, 1927, is hereby amended by the insertion of "and value-added tax" before "but no other tax or duty".

(2) Section 1 of the Imposition of Duties Act, 1957, is hereby amended by the insertion in paragraph (gg) (inserted by the Finance Act, 1963) after "turnover tax" of "or value-added tax", but no order shall be made under that Act for the purposes of increasing any of the rates of tax or extending the classes of activities or goods in respect of which tax is for the time being chargeable.

(3) Section 39 of the Inland Revenue Regulation Act, 1890, is hereby amended by the insertion of "value-added tax," before "stamp duties".

(4) The First Schedule to the Stamp Act, 1891, shall have effect as if the following exemption were inserted therein under the heading "Bill of Exchange or Promissory Note":

"Bill drawn on any form supplied by the Revenue Commissioners for the purpose of remitting amounts of value-added tax".

(With effect from 1 November 1972)

Section 39

Value Added Tax Act 1972

Consequential adjustments in regard to capital allowances

39. (1) In computing for any of the purposes of Parts XIII to XVIII inclusive of the Income Tax Act, 1967, or of section 22 of the Finance Act, 1971, the cost to a person of any machinery and plant or the amount of expenditure incurred by him, no account shall be taken of any account included in such cost or expenditure for tax in respect of which the person may claim a deduction under section 12.

(2) In calculating for any of the purposes of Part XVI of the Income Tax Act, 1967, the amount of sale, insurance, salvage or compensation moneys to be taken into account in computing a balancing allowance or balancing charge to be made to or on a person, no account shall be taken of the amount of tax (if any) chargeable to the person in respect of those moneys.

(With effect from 1 November 1972)

Finance Act 1975

29. ...

...

(2) Section 39 of the Value Added Tax Act, 1972, is hereby repealed.

(With effect from 6 April 1975)

Section 40

Value-Added Tax Act 1972

Increase of excise duty on betting

40. The duty on bets imposed by section 24 of the Finance Act, 1926, shall (subject and without prejudice to the provisions of section 20 of the Finance Act, 1931) be charged, levied and paid on bets entered into on or after the specified day at the rate of fifteen per cent of the amount of the bet in lieu of the rate of ten per cent mentioned in section 13 of the Finance Act, 1956.

(With effect from 1 November 1972)

Section 41

Value-Added Tax Act 1972

Repeals

41. Each enactment specified in column (2) of the Fifth Schedule is hereby repealed to the extent specified in column (3) of that Schedule in relation to moneys received on or after the specified day and as on and from the said specified day in relation to goods imported into the State.

FIFTH SCHEDULE
ENACTMENTS REPEALED

Number and Year	Short Title	Extent of Repeal
No. 23 of 1963	Finance Act, 1963	Section 41 and Part VI
No. 22 of 1965	Finance Act, 1965	Part VI
No. 17 of 1966	Finance Act, 1966	Part VI
No. 22 of 1966	Finance (No. 2) Act, 1966	The whole Act
No. 33 of 1968	Finance Act, 1968	Parts V and VI
No. 37 of 1968	Finance Act (No. 2) Act, 1968	Section 6 and 7
No. 21 of 1969	Finance Act, 1969	Parts VII and VIII
No. 14 of 1970	Finance Act, 1970	Part V
No. 25 of 1970	Finance (No. 2) Act, 1970	Sections 3 and 4

(With effect from 1 November 1972)

Section 42

Value Added Tax Act 1972

Collection of tax

42. Tax shall be paid to and collected and levied by the Collector-General.

(With effect from 1 November 1972)

Finance (No. 2) Act 2008

97. The enactments specified in Schedule 4 are amended to the extent and manner specified in paragraphs 1 to 6 of, and the Table to, that Schedule.

SCHEDULE 4

Provisions Relating to Collection and Recovery of Tax

2. Each enactment (in this Schedule referred to as the "repealed enactments") mentioned in the second column of Part 1 of the Table to this Schedule is repealed to the extent specified opposite that mentioned in the third column of that Part.

3. Part 2 of the Table to this Schedule, which provides for amendments to other enactments consequential on this Schedule coming into effect, shall have effect.

4. Any reference, whether express or implied, in any enactment or document (including the repealed enactments and enactments passed or documents made after this Schedule comes into effect) —

(a)   to any provision of the repealed enactments, or

(b)   to things done, or to be done under or for the purposes of any provision of the repealed enactments, shall, if and in so far as the nature of the reference permits, be construed as including, in relation to the times, years or periods, circumstances or purposes in relation to which the corresponding provision of this Schedule applies, a reference to, or as the case may be, to things done or deemed to be done or to be done under or for the purposes of, the corresponding provision.

5. All documents made or issued under a repealed enactment and in force immediately before this Schedule comes into effect shall continue in force as if made or issued under the provision inserted into the Taxes Consolidation Act 1997 by this Schedule which corresponds to the repealed enactment.

6. This Schedule comes into effect and applies as respects any tax that becomes due and payable on or after 1 March 2009.

TABLE

PART 1

REPEALS

Number and Year	Short Title	Extent of Repeal
No. 22 of 1972	Value-Added Tax Act 1972	Sections 24 and 42

(With effect from 1 March 2009)

Section 43

Value Added Tax Act 1972

Care and management of tax

43.   Tax is hereby placed under the care and management of the Revenue Commissioners.

(With effect from 1 November 1972)

Section 44

Value Added Tax Act 1972

Short Title

44.   This Act may be cited as the Value Added Tax Act, 1972.

(With effect from 1 November 1992)

Finance Act 2001

243.   (4)   Part 4 shall be construed together with the Value-Added Tax Acts, 1972 to 2000, and may be cited together therewith as the Value-Added Tax Acts, 1972 to 2001.

(With effect from 21 March 2001)

FIRST SCHEDULE
EXEMPTED ACTIVITIES
Value Added Tax Act 1972

(i) Supply of stocks, shares and other securities;

(ii) supply of unused Irish postal, fiscal or social insurance stamps; or other stamps, coupons or tokens when supplied as things in action for a money consideration which is charged separately from the consideration for any goods or other services supplied in conjunction with the supply of such things in action and which is reasonable having regard to the exchange value of such things in action.

(iii) delivery of water by local authorities;

(iv) letting of immovable goods with the exception of-

    (a) letting of machinery or business installations when let separately from any other immovable goods of which such machinery or installations form part;

    (b) letting in the course of carrying on a hotel business; and

    (c) provision of parking accommodation for vehicles by the operators car parks;

(v) provision of board and lodging otherwise than in the course of carrying on a hotel business;

(vi) services provided by the State or by a local authority other than the construction, repair, maintenance and improvement of roads, harbours and sewerage works;

(vii) services given in return for wages and salaries in respect of which income tax is chargeable under Schedule E of the Income Tax Act, 1967;

(viii) professional services of a medical, dental, optical or educational nature other than services rendered in the course of carrying on a business which consists in whole or in part of selling jobs:

(ix) services rendered by hospitals, nursing homes, schools and similar establishments;

(x) services rendered in the course of their profession by solicitors, accountants, actuaries and veterinary surgeons;

(xi) services rendered in the course of their profession by barristers;

(xii) agency services in regard to-

    (a) the arrangement of passenger transport or accommodation for persons,

(b) the delivery of goods sold by a house agent, or by an auctioneer in such circumstances the goods are not regarded as delivered by the auctioneer,

(c) the collection of debts, rents or insurance premiums, and

(d) the rendering of other exempt services;

(xiii) banking and insurance services;

(xiv) lending money or affording credit otherwise than by means of hire-purchase or credit-sale transactions.

(xv) the national broadcasting and television services, excluding advertising:

(xvi) transport in the State of passengers and their accompanying baggage and the hiring (in this paragraph referred to as the current hiring) to a person of a motor vehicle, designed and constructed for the conveyance of persons by road, under a contract, other than a contract of a kind referred to in section 3(1)(b), for any term or part of a term which when added to the term of any such hiring (whether of the same or another motor vehicle) to the same person during the period of 12 months ending on the date of the commencement of the current hiring does not exceed 5 weeks;

(xvii) betting;

(xviii) the issue of tickets or coupons for the purpose of a lottery;

(xix) admissions to zoological gardens;

(xx) the promotion of and admissions to sporting events, agricultural, commercial or industrial fairs, shows or exhibitions.

(xxi) the collection, storage and supply of human blood;

(xxii) funeral undertaking;

(xxiii) valuation services rendered by an auctioneer, house agent or chartered surveyor.

(With effect from 1 November 1972)

Finance Act 1973

87. The First Schedule to The Principal Act is hereby amended-

(a) by the substitution for paragraph (ix) of the following paragraph:

"(ix) services of a medical or educational nature rendered by hospitals, nursing homes, schools and similar establishments; and catering services rendered-

(a) to patients of a hospital or nursing home in the hospital or nursing home, and

(b) to students of a school in the school;"

and

(b)   by the insertion after paragraph (xxiii) of the following paragraphs:

"(xxiv)   delivery of live horses;

(xxv)   delivery of live greyhounds;

(xxvi)   the natural or artificial insemination of livestock .".

(With effect from 3 September 1973)

Finance Act 1976

60.   The Principal Act is hereby amended by -

(a)   the substitution for the First Schedule thereto of the Schedule contained in Part I of the Table to this section,

TABLE

PART I

FIRST SCHEDULE

Exempted Activities

(i)   Supply of stocks, shares and other securities;

(ii)   supply of unused Irish postal, fiscal or social insurance stamps; or other stamps, coupons or tokens when supplied as things in action for a money consideration which is charged separately from the consideration for any goods or other services supplied in conjunction with the supply of such things in action and which is reasonable having regard to the exchange value of such things in action;

(iii)   delivery of water by local authorities;

(iv)   letting of immovable goods with the exception of-

(a)   letting of machinery or business installations when let separately from any other immovable goods of which such machinery or installations form part,

(b)   letting in the course of carrying on a hotel business, and

(c)   provision of parking accommodation for vehicles by the operators of car parks;

(v)   provision of board and lodging otherwise than in the course of carrying on a hotel business,

(vi)   services provided by the State or by a local authority other than the construction, repair, maintenance and improvement of roads, harbours and sewerage works;

(vii)   services given in return for wages and salaries in respect of which income tax is chargeable under Schedule E of the Income Tax Act, 1967;

(viii) professional services of a medical, dental, optical or educational nature other than services rendered in the course of carrying on a business which consists in whole or in part of selling goods;

(ix)   services of a medical or educational nature rendered by hospitals, nursing homes, schools and similar establishments; and catering services rendered-

    (a)   to patients of a hospital or nursing home in the hospital or nursing home, and

    (b)   to students of a school in the school;

(x)   services rendered in the course of their profession by solicitors, accountants, actuaries and veterinary surgeons;

(xi)   services rendered in the course of their profession by barristers;

(xii)   agency services in regard to-

    (a)   the arrangement of passenger transport or accommodation for persons,

    (b)   the delivery of goods sold by a house agent, or by an auctioneer in such circumstances that the goods are not regarded as delivered by the auctioneer,

    (c)   the collection of debts, rents or insurance premiums, and

    (d)   the rendering of other exempt services;

(xiii) banking and insurance services,

(xiv)   lending money or affording credit otherwise than by means of hire-purchase or credit-sale transactions;

(xv)   the national broadcasting and television services, excluding advertising,

(xvi)   transport in the State of passengers and their accompanying baggage,

(xvii) betting;

(xviii) the issue of tickets or coupons for the purpose of a lottery;

(xix)   admissions to zoological gardens;

(xx)   the promotion of and admissions to sporting events and agricultural, commercial or industrial fairs, shows or exhibitions,

(xxi)   the collection, storage and supply of human blood;

(xxii) funeral undertaking,

(xxiii) valuation services rendered by an auctioneer, house agent or chartered surveyor;

(xxiv) delivery of live horses;

(xxv) delivery of live greyhounds;

(xxvi) the natural or artificial insemination of livestock.

(With effect from 1 March 1976)

Value-Added Tax (Amendment) Act 1978

24. The Principal Act is hereby amended by the substitution of the following Schedule for the First Schedule thereto:

FIRST SCHEDULE
Exempted Activities

(i) supply of stocks, shares or other securities;

(ii) school or university education, and vocational training or retraining (including the supply of goods and services incidental thereto), provided by educational establishments recognised by the State, and education, training or retraining of a similar kind provided by other persons;

(iii) professional services of a medical, dental or optical nature other than services rendered in the course of carrying on a business which consists in whole or in part of selling goods;

(iv) letting of immovable goods with the exception of-

    (a) letting of machinery or business installations when let separately from any other immovable goods of which such machinery or installations form part;

    (b) letting in the course of carrying on a hotel business;

    (c) provision of parking accommodation for vehicles by the operators of car parks; and

    (d) hire of safes;

(v) hospital and medical care or treatment provided by a hospital, nursing home, clinic or similar establishment;

(vi) services for the protection or care of children and young persons, and the provision of goods closely related thereto, provided otherwise than for profit;

(vii) supply of goods and services closely related to welfare and social security by non-profit making organisations;

(viii) services supplied in the course of their profession by barristers;

(ix) agency services in regard to-

(a)   the arrangement of passenger transport or accommodation for persons, and

(b)   the collection of debts, rents or insurance premiums,

(c)   banking and insurance services,

(d)   supply of stocks, shares and other securities,

(e)   the lending of money or affording of credit otherwise than by way of hire-purchase or credit-sale transactions;

(x)   services rendered in the course of their profession by solicitors, accountants, actuaries and veterinary surgeons;

(xi)   banking and insurance services.

(xii)   lending money or affording credit otherwise than by means of hire-purchase or credit-sale transactions;

(xiii)   the national broadcasting and television services, excluding advertising;

(xiv)   transport of passengers and their accompanying baggage;

(xv)   betting;

(xvi)   issue of tickets or coupons for the purpose of a lottery;

(xvii)   promotion of and admissions to sporting events;

(xviii)   collection, storage and supply of human organs, human blood and human milk;

(xix)   funeral undertaking;

(xx)   supply of live horses;

(xxi)   supply of live greyhounds;

(xxii)   supply of services and of goods closely related thereto for the benefit of their members by non-profit making organisations whose aims are primarily of a political, trade union, religious, patriotic, philosophical, philanthropic or civic nature where such supply is made without payment other than the payment of any membership subscription;

(xxiii)   provision of facilities for taking part in sporting and physical education activities, and services closely related thereto, provided for its members by non-profit making organisations;

(xxiv)   supply of goods by a person being goods-

(a)   which were used by him for the purposes of a business carried on by him,

(b)   in relation to the acquisition or application of which he had borne tax, and (c)　which are of such a kind or were used in such circumstances that no part of the said tax was deductible under section 12;

(xxv)　catering services supplied-

(a)　to patients of a hospital or nursing home in the hospital or nursing home, and

(b)　to students of a school in the school.".

(With effect from 1 March 1979)

Finance Act 1980

82.　With effect as on and from the 1st day of July, 1980, the First Schedule to the Value-Added Tax Act, 1972 (inserted by the Value Added Tax (Amendment) Act, 1978) is hereby amended by the substitution of the following paragraph for paragraph (xv):

"(xv)　the acceptance of bets subject to the duty of excise imposed by section 24 of the Finance Act, 1926, and of bets where the event which is the subject of the bet is either a horse race or a greyhound race and the bet is entered into during the meeting at which such race takes place and at the place at which such meeting is held;".

(With effect from 1 July 1980)

Finance Act 1982

87.　The First Schedule to the Principal Act (inserted by the Act of 1978) is hereby amended-

(a)　by the deletion of paragraph (viii),

(b)　by the substitution of the following subparagraph for subparagraph (b) of paragraph (ix):

"(b)　the collection of insurance premiums,",

and

(c)　by the substitution of the following paragraph for paragraph (x):

"(x)　services supplied in the course of their profession by veterinary surgeons;".

(With effect from 1 September 1982)

Finance Act 1985

49.　The First Schedule (inserted by the Act of 1978) to the Principal Act is hereby amended by the insertion, after paragraph (vii), of the following paragraph:

"(viii)　promotion of and admissions to live theatrical or musical performances, including circuses, but not including-

(a)　dances to which section 11(7) relates, or

(b)   performances in conjunction with which facilities are available for the consumption of food or drink during all or part of the performance by persons attending the performance;".

(With effect from 1 May 1985)

Finance Act 1986

89.   The First Schedule (inserted by the Act of 1978) to The Principal Act is hereby amended by the insertion after paragraph (iii) of the following paragraph:

"(iiia)   supply by dental technicians of services of a dental nature and of dentures or other dental prostheses;".

(With effect from 1 July 1986)

Finance Act 1987

45.   The First Schedule (inserted by the Act of 1978) to the Principal Act is hereby amended-

(a)   by the substitution of the following paragraph for paragraph (i):

"(i)   Financial services consisting of-

(a)   the issue, transfer or receipt of, or any dealing in, stocks, shares, debentures and other securities, other than documents establishing title to goods,

(b)   the arranging for, or the underwriting of, an issue specified in subparagraph (a),

(c)   the operation of any current, deposit or savings account,

(d)   the issue, transfer or receipt of, or any dealing in, currency, bank notes and metal coins, in use as legal tender in any country, excluding such bank notes and coins when supplied as investment goods or as collectors' pieces,

(e)   lending money or affording credit otherwise than by means of hire-purchase or credit-sale transactions,

(f)   the granting of, or any dealing in, credit guarantees or any other security for money and the management of credit guarantees by the person who granted the credit,

(g)   the management of a unit trust scheme which is-

      (I)   registered under the Unit Trusts Act, 1972,

      (II)   administered by the holder of an authorisation granted pursuant to the European Communities (Life Assurance) Regulations (S.I. No. 57 of 1984), or by a person who is deemed, pursuant to Article 6 of those Regulations, to be such a holder, the criteria in relation to which are the criteria specified, in relation to an arrangement administered by the holder of a licence under the Insurance Act, 1936, in section 7(4) of the Unit Trusts Act, 1972,

      (III)   established solely for the purposes of superannuation fund schemes or charities, or

      (IV)   determined by the Minister for Finance to be a unit trust scheme to which the provisions of this subparagraph apply;

(h)   services supplied to a person under arrangements which provide for the reimbursement of the person in respect of the supply by him of goods or services in accordance with a credit card, charge card or similar card scheme;",

(b)   in paragraph (ix) by-

    (i)   the deletion in subparagraph (a) of "and",

    (ii)   the substitution of the following subparagraphs for subparagraphs (c), (d) and (e):

      "(c)   insurance services, and

      (d)   services specified in paragraph (i),",

and

    (iii)   the insertion after subparagraph (d) (inserted by this Act) of the following:

"excluding management and safekeeping services in regard to the services specified in paragraph (i)(a), not being services specified in paragraph (i)(g);",

and the said paragraph, as so amended, is set out in the Table to this paragraph,

TABLE

(ix)   agency services in regard to-

      (a)   the arrangement of passenger transport or accommodation for persons,

      (b)   the collection of insurance premiums,

      (c)   insurance services, and

      (d)   services specified in paragraph (i),

excluding management and safekeeping services in regard to the services specified in paragraph (i)(a), not being services specified in paragraph (i)(g);,

(c)   by the deletion in paragraph (xi) of "banking and", and the said paragraph, as so amended, is set out in the Table to this paragraph,

TABLE

(xi)   insurance services;,

and

(d)   by the deletion of paragraphs (xia) (inserted by the Value-Added Tax (Exempted Activities) (No. 1) Order, 1985 (S.I. No. 430 of 1985)) and (xii).

(With effect from 1 November 1987)

Finance Act 1989

61.   The First Schedule (inserted by the Act of 1978) to The Principal Act is hereby amended-

(a)   by the insertion of the following subparagraph after subparagraph (g) of paragraph (i) (inserted by the Finance Act, 1987):

"(gg)   the management of an undertaking which is a collective investment undertaking within the meaning of section 18 of the Finance Act, 1989, other than services specified in subparagraph (g);",

*(b)   by the substitution of the following paragraph for paragraph (iii):

"(iii)   professional services of a medical nature, other than services specified in paragraph (iiib), but excluding such services supplied in the course of carrying on a business which consists in whole or in part of selling goods;",

*(c)   by the insertion after paragraph (iiia) (inserted by the Finance Act, 1986) of the following paragraph:

"(iiib)   professional services of a dental or optical nature;",

and

(d)   by the substitution in paragraph (ix) of "subparagraph (g)or (gg) of paragraph (i)" for "paragraph (i) (g)".

(With effect from 1 July 1989
except * from 1 November 1989)

Finance Act 1990

106.   The First Schedule (inserted by the Act of 1978) to The Principal Act is hereby amended-

(a)   by the insertion in paragraph (ii) after "kind" of ", excluding instruction in the driving of mechanically propelled road vehicles other than vehicles designed or constructed for the conveyance of goods with a capacity of 1.5 tonnes or more,",

(b)   by the insertion after paragraph (viii) (inserted by the Act of 1985) of the following paragraph:

"(viiia) supply of cultural services and of goods closely linked thereto by any cultural body, whether established by or under statute or otherwise, which is recognised as such a body by the Revenue Commissioners for the purposes of this paragraph, not being services to which paragraph (viii) relates;",

*(c)   by the deletion of paragraphs (xx) and (xxi),
and

(d)   by the insertion after paragraph (xxii) of the following paragraph:

"(xxiia) supply of services by an independent group of persons (being a group which is an independent entity established for the purpose of administrative convenience by persons whose activities are exempt from or are not subject to tax) for the purpose of rendering its members the services directly necessary for the exercise of their activities and where the group only recovers from its members the exact reimbursement of each member's share of the joint expenses;".

(With effect from 30 May 1990 except * from 1 January 1991)

Finance Act 1991

85.   The First Schedule (inserted by the Act of 1978) to The Principal Act is hereby amended-

(a)   in paragraph (i) (inserted by the Act of 1987)-

(i)   by the insertion in subparagraph (c)after "account" of and the negotiation of, or any dealings in, payments, transfers, debts, cheques and other negotiable instruments excluding debt collection and factoring",

    (ii)   by the substitution of the following subparagraph for subparagraph (g) (inserted by the Act of 1987):

"(g)   the management of an undertaking which is-

    (I)   a collective investment undertaking within the meaning of section 18 of the Finance Act, 1989, or

    (II)   administered by the holder of an authorisation granted pursuant to the European Communities (Life Assurance) Regulations, 1984 (S.I. No. 57 of 1984), or by a person who is deemed, pursuant to Article 6 of those Regulations, to be such a holder, the criteria in relation to which are the criteria specified in relation to an arrangement administered by the holder of a licence under the Insurance Act, 1936, in section 9(2) of the Unit Trusts Act, 1990, or

    (III)   a unit trust scheme established solely for the purpose of superannuation fund schemes or charities, or

    (IV)   determined by the Minister for Finance to be a collective investment undertaking to which the provisions of this subparagraph apply;",

    (iii)   by the deletion of subparagraph (gg) (inserted by the Finance Act, 1989),

and

    (iv)   by the substitution in paragraph (ix) (inserted by the Act of 1978) of "(g)" for "(g) or (gg)"

*(b)   by the substitution in paragraph (iv) of the following subparagraph for subparagraph (b):

"(b)   letting of the kind to which paragraph (vi) of the Third Schedule refers;",

*(c)   by the deletion of paragraph (x) (inserted by the Finance Act, 1982),

and

*(d)   by the insertion of the following paragraph after paragraph (xi):

"(xia)   public postal services (including the supply of goods and services incidental thereto) supplied by An Post including postmasters, or by persons licensed in accordance with section 73 or subsection (1) of section 111 of the Postal and Telecommunications Services Act, 1983;".

(With effect from 29 May 1991 except * from 1 January 1992)

Finance Act 1992

194. (1)   The First Schedule (inserted by the Act of 1978) to The Principal Act is hereby amended-

*(a)   in paragraph (iv) by the insertion of the following subparagraph after subparagraph (b) (inserted by the Act of 1991):

"(bi) provision of facilities of the kind to which paragraph (viia) of the Sixth Schedule refers,",

(b)   in paragraph (viii) (inserted by the Act of 1985) by the deletion in paragraph (a) of "to which section 11(7) relates",

*(c)   by the substitution of the following paragraph for paragraph (xvii):

"(xvii) promotion of (other than in the course of the provision of facilities of the kind specified in paragraph (viia) of the Sixth Schedule), or the admission of spectators to, sporting events,",

(d)   in paragraph (xviii) by the substitution of ",supply and importation" for "and supply",

and

*(e)   in paragraph (xxiii) by the deletion of "for its members".

(2)   The First Schedule to The Principal Act is hereby further amended-

**(a)   in paragraph (xviii) (as amended by subsection (1) of this section) by the substitution of "supply, intra-Community acquisition or importation" for "supply and importation",

and

**(b)   in paragraph (xxiv) by the insertion of ", other than a supply of goods of a kind specified in section 3(1)(g)," after "supply of goods".

(With effect from 28 May 1992 except * from 1 July 1992 and ** from 1 January 1993)

Finance Act 1993

94.   The First Schedule (inserted by the Act of 1978) to The Principal Act, is hereby amended by the substitution in subparagraph (b) of paragraph (iv) (inserted by the Act of 1991) of "paragraph (ii) of the Third Schedule or paragraph (xiii) of the Sixth Schedule" for "paragraph (vi) of the Third Schedule".

(With effect from 1 March 1993)

Finance Act 1994

99.   The First Schedule (inserted by the Act of 1978) to the Principal Act is hereby amended-

*(a)   in paragraph (ix) by the insertion after "excluding" of "the services of loss adjusters and excluding",

and

(b)   in paragraph (xv) (inserted by the Finance Act, 1980) by the insertion after "the Finance Act, 1926," of "of bets of the kind referred to in section 89 of the Finance Act, 1994,".

(With effect from commencement of section 89 except * from 1 September 1994)

Finance Act 1995

139.   The First Schedule (inserted by the Act of 1978) to the Principal Act is hereby amended-

(a)   in paragraph (i) by the substitution of the following subparagraph for subparagraph (e):

"(e)   the granting and the negotiation of credit and the management of credit by the person granting it,",

and

*(b)   in paragraph (xxiii) by the insertion after "organisations" of "with the exception of facilities to which paragraph (viib) or (viic) of the Sixth Schedule refers".

(With effect from 2 June 1995 except * from 1 January 1996)

Finance Act 1997

110.   The First Schedule (inserted by the Act of 1978) to the Principal Act is hereby amended-

(a)   in paragraph (ii) by the insertion before "school" of "children's or young people's education,", and

(b)   in paragraph (vi) by the insertion after "profit" of the following:

"and the supply of services for the protection or care of children and young persons, and the provision of goods closely related thereto, provided by persons whose activities may be regulated by regulations made under Part VII of the Child Care Act, 1991;".

(With effect from 1 May 1997)

Taxes Consolidation Act 1997

1100. Schedule 31, which provides for amendments to other enactments consequential on the passing of this Act, shall apply for the purposes of this Act.

SCHEDULE 31
CONSEQUENTIAL AMENDMENTS

In the enactments specified in Column (1) of the following Table for the words set out or referred to in Column (2) there shall be substituted the words set out in the corresponding entry in Column (3).

Enactment amended (1)	Words to be replaced (2)	Words to be substituted (3)
The Value Added Tax Act, 1972:		
First Schedule, in paragraph (i)(g)	section 18 of the Finance Act, 1989	Section 734 of the Taxes Consolidation Act, 1997

(With effect from 6 April 1997)

Finance Act 1999

138. The First Schedule (inserted by the Act of 1978) to the Principal Act is hereby amended-

(a) by the insertion in sub-paragraph (g) (inserted by the Finance Act, 1991) of paragraph (i) of the following clause after clause (I):

"(Ia) a special investment scheme within the meaning of section 737 of the Taxes Consolidation Act, 1997, or",

and

(b) by the insertion of the following paragraphs after paragraph (xviii):

"(xviiia) supply, intra-Community acquisition and importation of investment gold (within the meaning of section 6A) other than supplies of investment gold to the Central Bank of Ireland;

(xviiib) supply of services of an intermediary (as defined in section 6A) acting in that capacity;".

(With effect from 25 March 1999)

Finance Act 2000

122. The First Schedule to the Principal Act is amended in paragraph (xv) (inserted by the Finance Act, 1980) by the insertion after "Finance Act, 1994," of "of bets of the kind referred to in section 75 of the Finance Act, 1996,".

(With effect from 23 March 2000)

Finance Act 2001

199.   The First Schedule to the Principal Act is amended-

   *(a)   by the insertion in paragraph (ii) after "(including the supply of goods and services incidental thereto" of ", other than the supply of research services",

   *(b)   by the insertion in paragraph (iv) after "letting of immovable goods" of "(which does not include the service of allowing a person use a toll road or a toll bridge)",

   (c)   by the insertion in paragraph (ix)(a) after "persons," of "and",

   (d)   by the deletion in paragraph (ix) of-

      (i)   subparagraph (b) (inserted by the Finance Act, 1982),

      (ii)   subparagraph (c) (inserted by the Finance Act, 1987), and

      (iii) of the words "the services of loss adjusters and excluding" (inserted by the Finance Act, 1994),

   and

   (e)   by the substitution of the following for paragraph (xi):

      (xi)   insurance and reinsurance transactions, including related services performed by insurance brokers and insurance agents and, for the purposes of this paragraph, 'related services' includes the collection of insurance premiums, the sale of insurance, and claims handling and claims settlement services where the supplier of the insurance services delegates the authority to an agent and is bound by the decision of that agent in relation to that claim;".

(With effect from 1 May 2001 except * from 1 September 2001)

Finance Act 2002

110.   The First Schedule to the Principal Act is amended by inserting the following after paragraph (xv):

"(xva)   The acceptance of totalisator bets —

      (a)   by a person or a body of persons operating under a licence granted under the Totalisator Act, 1929, or

      (b)   by a licensed bookmaker acting in accordance with the provisions of section 19A(a) of the Betting Act, 1931 (inserted by the Horse and Greyhound Racing Act, 2001);".

SCHEDULE 6

Miscellaneous Technical Amendments in Relation to Tax

1.   The Value-Added Tax Act, 1972, is amended in accordance with the following provisions:

(e)   the First Schedule is amended by substituting the following for paragraph (i)(g)(I):

"(i)   (g) (I) a collective investment undertaking as defined in section 172A of the Taxes Consolidation Act, 1997 (as amended by section 59 of the Finance Act, 2000), or".

(With effect from 25 March 2002)

Finance Act 2003

SCHEDULE 6

2.   The Value-Added Tax Act 1972 is amended in paragraph (vi) of the First Schedule by substituting "Part VII or Part VIII of the Child Care Act 1991" for "Part VII of the Child Care Act 1991".

(With effect from 28 March 2003)

Finance Act 2004

64.   The First Schedule to the Principal Act is amended —

(a)   in paragraph (i)(g) (as substituted by the Finance Act 1991) —

(i)   by substituting "the management of an undertaking specified in one of the following clauses, and such management may comprise any of the three functions listed in Annex II to Directive 2001/107/EC of the European Parliament and Council (being the functions included in the activity of collective portfolio management) where those functions are supplied by the person with responsibility for the provision of the functions concerned in respect of the undertaking, and which is — " for "the management of an undertaking which is — ",

(ii)   in clause (IV) by substituting "this subparagraph apply, or" for "this subparagraph apply;", and

(iii)   by inserting the following after clause (IV):

"(V)   an undertaking which is a qualifying company for the purposes of section 110 of the Taxes Consolidation Act 1997;",

*(b)   in paragraph (xxv)(b) by substituting "the school;" for "the school.", and

*(c)   by inserting the following after paragraph (xxv):

"(xxvi) the importation of gas through the natural gas distribution system, or the importation of electricity.".

(With effect from 25 March 2004 except * with effect from 1 January 2005)

Finance Act 2005

112. The First Schedule (inserted by the Value-Added Tax (Amendment) Act 1978) to the Principal Act is amended-

(a) by substituting the following for paragraph (xv) (as inserted by the Finance Act 1980):

"(xv) the acceptance of bets subject to excise duty imposed by section 67 of the Finance Act 2002 and of bets exempted from excise duty by section 68 of the Finance Act 2002;",

(b) by deleting paragraph (xva), and

(c) by inserting in paragraph (xxiv) "a supply of immovable goods to which section 3(1)(c) or 4 relates, or" after "supply of goods other than".

(With effect from 25 March 2005)

Finance Act 2006

100. The First Schedule (inserted by the Value-Added Tax (Amendment) Act 1978) to the Principal Act is amended —

(a) in paragraph (i)(a) by inserting "other than the issue of new stocks, new shares, new debentures or new securities made to raise capital, the" after "the issue,", and

(b) in paragraph (i)(b) by substituting "of stocks, shares, debentures and other securities, other than documents establishing title to goods," for "specified in subparagraph (a),".

(With effect from 31 March 2006)

Finance Act 2007

93. The First Schedule to the Principal Act is amended by inserting the following after paragraph (v):

"(va) services closely related to medical care covered by section 61 or 61A of the Health Act 1970 which are undertaken by or on behalf of the Health Service Executive or by home care providers duly recognised by that Executive under section 61A of that Act;".

(With effect from 2 April 2007)

Finance Act 2008

106. The First Schedule to the Principal Act is amended with effect from 1 July 2008 by deleting "to which section 3(1)(c) or 4 relates," in paragraph (xxiv).

*141.　The enactments specified in Schedule 8 —

> (a)　are amended to the extent and in the manner specified .in paragraphs 1 to 6 of that Schedule, and

> (b)　apply and come into operation in accordance with paragraph 7 of that Schedule.

Schedule 8
Miscellaneous Technical Amendments in Relation to Tax

3.　The Value-Added Tax Act 1972 is amended in accordance with the following provisions:

> (j)　in paragraph (xia) of the First Schedule by substituting "designated persons in accordance with the European Communities (Postal Services) Regulations 2000 (S.I. No. 310 of 2000)" for "persons licensed in accordance with section 73 or subsection (1) of section 111 of the Postal and Telecommunications Services Act, 1983", and

(With effect from 1 July 2008 except * with effect from 13 March 2008)

Finance (No. 2) Act 2008

76.　The First Schedule to the Principal Act is amended with effect from 1 January 2010 by deleting subparagraph (a) of paragraph (ix).

(With effect from 1 January 2010)

SECOND SCHEDULE

GOODS AND SERVICES CHARGEABLE AT THE RATE OF ZERO PER CENT

Value-Added Tax Act 1972

(i)   Goods delivered-

    (a)   outside the State, or

    (b)   inside the State but subject to a condition that they are to be transported directly by or on behalf of the person making the delivery-

        (I)   outside the State, or

        (II)   to a registered person within the customs-free airport;

(ii)   services rendered outside the State;

(iii)   the carriage of goods in the State by or on behalf of a person in execution of a contract to transfer the goods to or from a place outside the State;

(iv)   the provision of docking, landing, loading or unloading facilities, including customs clearance, directly in connection with the disembarkation or embarkation of passengers or the importation or exportation of goods;

(v)   goods delivered on board ships or aircraft going to places outside the State; and the repairing and servicing of ships and aircraft engaged in international commercial transport of passengers and goods;

(vi)   fishing nets, and sections thereof, of a kind commonly used by commercial fishermen for the purposes of their occupation and not commonly used for any other purpose;

(vii)   any feeding stuff (within the meaning of the Fertilisers, Feeding Stuffs and Mineral Mixtures Act, 1955), compound feeding stuff (within the meaning of the said Act) or mineral mixture (within the meaning of the said Act)-

    (a)   which is delivered in units of not less than 10 kilograms and is not packaged, sold or otherwise designated for the use of dogs, cats, cage birds or domestic pets, and

    (b)   the sale or manufacture for sale of which is not prohibited under section 4 or 6 of the said Act;

(viii)   fertiliser (within the meaning of the Fertilisers, Feeding Stuffs and Mineral Mixtures Act, 1955) which is delivered in units of not less than 10 kilograms and the sale or manufacture for sale of which is not prohibited under section 4 or 6 of the said Act;

(ix)   services provided by the Commissioners of Irish Lights in connection with the operation of lightships, lighthouses or other navigational aids; and

(x)   the construction, repair, maintenance and improvement of roads, harbours and sewerage works by the State, local authorities or harbour authorities.

(With effect from 1 November 1972)

Finance Act 1973

88.   The Second Schedule to The Principal Act is hereby amended-

(a)   by the substitution of the following paragraph for paragraph (vii):

"(vii)   animal feeding stuff, excluding feeding stuff which is packaged, sold or otherwise designated for the use of dogs, cats, cage birds or domestic pets;",

and

(b)   by the insertion of the following paragraphs after paragraph (x):

"(xi)   life saving services provided by the Royal National Lifeboat Institution including the organisation and maintenance of the lifeboat service;

(xii)   food and drink of a kind used for human consumption, excluding-

(a)   beverages chargeable with any duty of customs or excise specifically charged on spirits, beer, wine, cider, perry or Irish wine, and preparations thereof,

(b)   other manufactured beverages, including fruit juices and bottled waters, and syrups, concentrates, essences, powders, crystals or other products for the preparation of beverages, but not including-

(I)   tea and preparations thereof,

(II)   cocoa, coffee and chicory and other roasted coffee substitutes, and preparations and extracts thereof,

(III)   preparations and extracts of meat, yeast, egg or milk,

(c)   ice cream, ice lollipops, water ices and similar frozen products, and prepared mixes and powders for making such products,

(d)   (I)   chocolates, sweets and similar confectionery (including drained, glacé or crystallised fruits), biscuits, crackers and wafers of all kinds, and all confectionery and bakery products other than bread,

     (II)   for the purposes of this paragraph "bread" means food for human consumption manufactured by baking dough composed exclusively of a mixture of cereal flour and any one or more of the ingredients mentioned in the following subclauses in quantities not exceeding the limitation, if any, specified for each ingredient-

         (1)   yeast or other leavening or aerating agent, salt, malt extract, milk, water, gluten,

         (2)   fat, sugar and bread improver, subject to the limitation that the weight of any ingredient specified in this subclause shall not exceed 2 per cent of the weight of flour included in the dough,

         (3)   dried fruit, subject to the limitation that the weight thereof shall not exceed 10 per cent of the weight of flour included in the dough,

     other than food packaged for sale as a unit (not being a unit designated as containing only food specifically for babies) containing two or more slices, segments, sections or other similar pieces, having a crust over substantially the whole of their outside surfaces, being a crust formed in the course of baking or toasting,

(e)   any of the following when supplied for human consumption without further preparation, namely, potato crisps, potato sticks, potato chips, potato puffs and similar products made from potato, or from potato flour, or from potato starch, popcorn, and salted or roasted nuts whether or not in shells;

(xiii)   medicine of a kind used for human oral consumption;

(xiv)   medicine of a kind used for animal oral consumption, excluding medicine which is packaged, sold or otherwise designated for the use of dogs, cats, cage birds or domestic pets;

(xv)   seeds, plants, spores, bulbs, tubers, tuberous roots, corms, crowns and rhizomes, of a kind used for sowing in order to produce food;

(xvi)   goods of different kinds which are packaged for sale as a unit (hereinafter in this paragraph referred to as the package) and in relation to which all the following conditions are satisfied-

(a)   the package consists of goods in relation to the delivery of some of which for a separate consideration tax would be chargeable at the rate specified in section 11(1)(d), and in relation to the delivery of the remainder of which for a separate consideration, tax would be chargeable at the rate specified in section 11(1)(e),

(b)   the consideration for delivery is referable to the package as a whole and not to the different kinds of goods included therein, and

(c)   the total tax-exclusive value of the goods included in the package, in relation to the delivery of which for a separate consideration tax would be chargeable at the rate specified in the said section 11(1)(e), does not exceed 50 per cent of the total tax exclusive consideration for the package 2½ new pence, whichever is the lesser.".

(With effect from 3 September 1973)

Finance (No. 2) Act 1975

2.   (1)   The Value-Added Tax Act, 1972, is hereby amended by the addition of the following paragraphs to the Second Schedule-

"(xvii) clothing, including textile handkerchiefs and footwear;

(xviii) fabrics, yarn and thread of a kind normally used in the manufacture of clothing, including elastics, tape and padding materials in the form supplied for the manufacture of clothing;

(xix) sole and upper leather of a kind supplied for the manufacture and repair of footwear, and also soles, heels and insoles of any material;

(xx)   (a)   coal, peat and other solid substances held out for sale solely as fuel,

(b)   gas of a kind used for domestic or industrial heating or lighting, whether in gaseous or liquid form, but not including gas of a kind normally used for welding and cutting metals or gas sold as lighter fuel,

(c)   electricity,

(d)   hydrocarbon oil of a kind used to domestic or industrial heating not being hydrocarbon oil sold for use in internal combustion engines.".

(2)   In consequence of the amendment specified in subsection (1), the Value-Added Tax Act 1972, is hereby further amended as specified in the Schedule to this Act.

(With effect from 30 July 1975)

Finance Act 1976

60. The Principal Act is hereby amended by-

...

(b)   the substitution for the Second Schedule thereto of the Schedule contained in Part II of the said Table,

...

PART II

SECOND SCHEDULE

Goods and Services Chargeable at the Rate of Zero per Cent

(i)   Goods delivered-

(a)   outside the State, or

(b)   inside the State but subject to a condition that they are to be transported directly by or on behalf of the person making the delivery-

(I)   outside the State, or

(II)   to a registered person within the customs free airport;

(ii)   services rendered outside the State;

(iii)   the carriage of goods in the State by or on behalf of a person in execution of a contract to transfer the goods to or from a place outside the State;

(iv)   the provision of docking, landing, loading or unloading facilities, including customs clearance, directly in connection with the disembarkation or embarkation of passengers or the importation or exportation of goods;

(v)   goods delivered on board ships or aircraft going to places outside the State; and the repairing and servicing of ships and aircraft engaged in international commercial transport of passengers and goods;

(vi)   fishing nets, and sections thereof, of a kind commonly used by commercial fishermen for the purposes of their occupation and not commonly used for any other purpose;

(vii)   animal feeding stuff, excluding feeding stuff which is packaged, sold or otherwise designated for the use of dogs, cats, cage birds or domestic pets;

(viii) fertiliser (within the meaning of the Fertilisers, Feeding Stuffs and Mineral Mixtures Act, 1955) which is delivered in units of not less than 10 kilograms and the sale or manufacture for sale of which is not prohibited under section 4 or 6 of the said Act;

(ix)   services provided by the Commissioners of Irish Lights in connection with the operation of lightships, lighthouses or other navigational aids;

(x)   the construction, repair, maintenance and improvement of roads, harbours, and sewerage works by the State, local authorities or harbour authorities;

(xi)   life saving services provided by the Royal National Lifeboat Institution including the organisation and maintenance of the lifeboat service;

(xii)   food and drink of a kind used for human consumption, excluding food and drink specified in paragraph (xv) of the Third Schedule;

(xiii)   medicine of a kind used for human oral consumption;

(xiv)   medicine of a kind used for animal oral consumption, excluding medicine which is packaged, sold or otherwise designated for the use of dogs, cats, cage birds or domestic pets;

(xv)   seeds, plants, trees, spores, bulbs, tubers, tuberous roots, corms, crowns and rhizomes, of a kind used for sowing in order to produce food;

(xvi)   goods of different kinds which are packaged for sale as a unit (hereinafter in this paragraph referred to as the package) and in relation to which all the following conditions are satisfied-

    (a)   the package consists of goods in relation to the delivery of some of which for a separate consideration tax would be chargeable at the rate specified in section 11(1)(d) and, in relation to the delivery of the remainder of which for a separate consideration, tax would be chargeable at the rate specified in section 11(1)(e),

    (b)   the consideration for delivery is referable to the package as a whole and not to the different kinds of goods included therein, and

    (c)   the total tax-exclusive value of the goods included in the package, in relation to the delivery of which for a separate consideration tax would be chargeable at the rate specified in the said section 11(1)(e), does not exceed 50 per cent of the total tax-exclusive consideration for the package or 2 ½ pence, whichever is the lesser;

(xvii)   articles of personal clothing, footwear and textile handkerchiefs, excluding articles of clothing made wholly or partly of fur skin other than garments merely trimmed with fur skin unless the trimming has an area greater than one-fifth of the area of the outside material;

(xviii) fabrics, yarn and thread of a kind normally used in the manufacture of clothing, including elastics, tape and padding materials in the form supplied for the manufacture of clothing;

(xix) sole and upper leather of a kind supplied for the manufacture and repair of footwear, and also soles, heels and insoles of any material;

(xx) (a) coal, peat and other solid substances held out for sale solely as fuel,

(b) gas of a kind used for domestic or industrial heating or lighting, whether in gaseous or liquid form, but not including gas of a kind normally used for welding and cutting metals or gas sold as lighter fuel,

(c) electricity,

(d) hydrocarbon oil of a kind used for domestic or industrial heating excluding gas oil (within the meaning of the Hydrocarbon Oil (Rebated Oil) Regulations, 1961) other than gas oil which has been duly marked in accordance with Regulation 6(2) of the said Regulations.

(With effect from 1 March 1976)

Value Added Tax (Amendment) Act 1978

25.   The Second Schedule to the Principal Act is hereby amended-

(a)   by the substitution of the following paragraph for paragraph (i):

"(i)   Goods supplied-

(a)   subject to a condition that they are to be transported directly by or on behalf of the person making the supply-

(I)   outside the State, or

(II)   to a registered person within the customs-free airport,

or

(b)   by a registered person within the customs-free airport to another registered person;",

(b)   by the substitution for paragraph (v) of the following paragraph:

"(v)   the supply, modification, repair, maintenance and hiring of-

(a)   sea-going vessels of a gross tonnage of more than 15 tons being vessels used or to be used-

    (I)   for the carriage of passengers for reward,

    (II)   for the purposes of a sea fishing business.

    (III)   for other commercial or industrial purposes.

    or

    (IV)   for rescue or assistance at sea, or

(b)   aircraft used or to be used by a transport undertaking operating for reward chiefly on international routes;",

(c)   by the substitution of the following paragraph for paragraph (vi):

    "(vi)   services, supplied by an agent acting in the name and on behalf of another person, in procuring-

        (a)   the export of goods from the State,

        (b)   services specified in paragraphs (iii), (iv), (v) or (x). or

        (c)   the supply of goods or services outside the State;",

(d)   by the substitution of the following paragraph for paragraph (x):

    "(x)   gold supplied to the Central Bank of Ireland;",

and

(e)   by the substitution of the following paragraph for paragraph (xvi):

    "(xvi)   the supply, to a person who has neither an establishment nor his usual place of residence in the State, of work on movable goods acquired within the State, or imported for the purpose of having such mark carried out, and afterwards exported;",

(With effect from 1 March 1979)

30.   (1)   The enactment mentioned in column (2) of the First Schedule is hereby repealed to the extent specified in column (3) of that Schedule.

    (2)   In consequence of the amendments of the Principal Act specified in this Act and of the repeals specified in the First Schedule, the

Principal Act is hereby further amended by the substitution of the word or expression mentioned in column (3) of the Second Schedule at any reference number for the word or expression mentioned in column (2) of that Schedule at that reference number wherever it occurs in the provision of the Principal Act mentioned in column (4) of that Schedule at that reference number.

FIRST SCHEDULE
Enactments Repealed

Number and Year (1)	Short Title (2)	Extent of Repeal (3)
No. 22 of 1972	Value-Added Tax Act, 1972	Paragraph (ii) of the Second schedule

SECOND SCHEDULE
Consequential Amendments

Reference Number (1)	Existing word or expression (2)	Substituted word or expression (3)	Provision of Principal Act (4)
3	"delivered"	"supplied"	Paragraph (viii) of Second Schedule

(With effect from 1 March 1979)

S.I. No. 53 of 1981
Value-Added Tax (Reduction Of Rate) (No. 5) Order, 1981

2.   The Second Schedule (inserted by the Finance Act, 1976 (No. 16 of 1976)) to the Value-Added Tax Act, 1972, shall be varied by the insertion after paragraph (xix) of the following paragraph:

"(xixa) medical equipment and appliances being—

    (a)   invalid carriages, and other vehicles (excluding mechanically propelled road vehicles), of a kind designed for use by invalids or infirm persons,

    (b)   orthopaedic appliances, surgical belts, trusses and the like, deaf aids, and artificial limbs and other artificial parts of the body excluding artificial teeth,

    (c)   walking frames and crutches,

    (d)   parts or accessories suitable for use solely or principally with any of the goods specified in subparagraphs (a), (b) and (c) of this paragraph;".

3.   The Third Schedule (inserted by the Finance Act, 1976) to the Value-Added Tax Act, 1972, shall be varied by—

    (a)   the deletion of subparagraph (c) of paragraph (xvii), and

(b)   the substitution of the following subparagraph for subparagraph
        (*f*) of that paragraph: "(f) artificial teeth, splints and other fracture
        appliances,".

(With effect from 1 March 1981)

Finance Act 1982

88.   (1)   The Second Schedule (inserted by the Act of 1976) to the Principal
                Act is hereby amended-

        (a)   by the substitution of the following subparagraph for
                subparagraph (b) of paragraph (i) (inserted by the Act of
                1978):

                "(b)   by a registered person within the customs-free
                        airport to another registered person within the
                        customs-free airport;",

        and

        *(b)   by the insertion after paragraph (xv) (inserted by the
                Finance Act, 1973) of the following paragraph:

                "(xva) printed books and booklets including atlases but
                        not including newspapers, periodicals, brochures,
                        catalogues, programmes, books of stationery,
                        cheque books, diaries, albums, books of stamps, of
                        tickets or of coupons;".

        (2)   This section, other than subsection (1)(a), shall have, and be
                deemed to have had, effect as on and from the 1st day of May,
                1982.

(With effect from 1 September 1982 except * from 1 May 1982)

Finance Act 1983

86.   The Second Schedule (inserted by the Act of 1976) to the Principal Act
        is hereby amended by the substitution of the following paragraph for
        paragraph (xx):

"(xx)   (a)   electricity,

        (b)   wax candles and night-lights which are white and
                cylindrical, excluding candles and night-lights which are
                decorated, spiralled, tapered or perfumed.".

(With effect from 1 May 1983)

Finance Act 1984

92.   The Second Schedule (inserted by the Act of 1976) to the Principal Act is
        hereby amended-

        (a)   by the substitution for paragraph (xvii) of the following
                paragraph:

"(xvii) articles of children's personal clothing of sizes which do not exceed the sizes of those articles appropriate to children of average build of 10 years of age (a child whose age is 10 years or 10 years and a fraction of a year being taken for the purposes of this paragraph to be a child of 10 years of age), but excluding-

(a)   articles of clothing made wholly or partly of fur skin other than garments merely trimmed with fur skin, unless the trimming has an area greater than one-fifth of the area of the outside material, and

(b)   articles of clothing which are not described, labelled, marked or marketed on the basis of age or size;",

and

(b)   by the substitution for paragraph (xviii) of the following paragraphs:

"(xviii)   sanitary towels and sanitary tampons;

(xviiia)   footwear;".

(With effect from 1 May 1984)

Finance Act 1985

50.   The Second Schedule (inserted by the Act of 1976) to the Principal Act is hereby amended-

(a)   by the substitution of the following paragraph for paragraph (xii):

"(xii)   food and drink of a kind used for human consumption, excluding-

(a)   beverages chargeable with any duty of excise specifically charged on spirits, beer, wine, cider, perry or Irish wine, and preparations thereof,

(b)   other manufactured beverages, including fruit juices and bottled waters, and syrups, concentrates, essences, powders, crystals or other products for the preparation of beverages, but excluding-

(I)   tea and preparations thereof,

(II)   cocoa, coffee and chicory and other roasted coffee substitutes, and preparations and extracts thereof, or

(III) preparations and extracts of meat, yeast, egg or milk,

(c) ice cream, ice lollipops, water ices and similar frozen products, and prepared mixes and, powders for making such products,

(d) (I) chocolates, sweets and similar confectionery (including drained, glacé or crystallised fruits), biscuits, crackers and wafers of all kinds, and all other confectionery and bakery products excluding bread,

(II) in this subparagraph "**bread**" means food for human consumption manufactured by baking dough composed exclusively of a mixture of cereal flour and any one or more of the ingredients mentioned in the following subclauses in quantities not exceeding the limitation, if any, specified for each ingredient-

(1) yeast or other leavening or aerating agent, salt, malt extract, milk, water, gluten,

(2) fat, sugar and bread improver, subject to the limitation that the weight of any ingredient specified in this subclause shall not exceed 2 per cent of the weight of flour included in the dough,

(3) dried fruit, subject to the limitation that the weight thereof shall not exceed 10 per cent of the weight of flour included in the dough,

other than food packaged for sale as a unit (not being a unit designated as containing only food specifically for babies) containing two or more slices, segments, sections or other similar pieces, having a crust over substantially the whole of their outside surfaces, being a crust formed in the course of baking or toasting, and

(e) any of the following when supplied for human consumption without further preparation, namely, potato crisps, potato sticks, potato chips, potato puffs and similar products made from potato, or from potato flour or from potato starch, popcorn, and salted or roasted nuts whether or not in shells;",

and

(b)   by the substitution of the following paragraph for paragraphs (xviiia) (inserted by the Act of 1984) and (xix) (inserted by the Act of 1976):

"(xix) articles of children's personal footwear of sizes which do not exceed the size appropriate to children of average foot size of 10 years of age (a child whose age is 10 years or 10 years and a fraction of a year being taken for the purposes of this paragraph to be a child of 10 years of age), but excluding footwear which is not described, labelled, marked or marketed on the basis of age or size;".

(With effect from 1 May 1985)

Finance Act 1986

90.   The Second Schedule (inserted by the Finance Act, 1976) to The Principal Act is hereby amended-

(a)   in paragraph i-

(i)   by the insertion of the following subparagraph after subparagraph (a):

"(aa)   by a registered person within a free port to another registered person within a free port,",

and

(ii)   by the insertion in subparagraph (b), after "customs-free airport" where that secondly occurs, of "or a free port", and

(b)   in paragraph xii-

(i)   by the insertion after "food and drink of a kind used for human consumption" of ", other than the supply thereof specified in paragraph (xic) of the Sixth Schedule",

and

(ii)   by the deletion in subparagraph (e) of ", potato chips".

(With effect from 1 July 1986)

Finance Act 1987

46.   The Second Schedule (inserted by the Finance Act, 1976) to the Principal Act is hereby amended by the deletion in subparagraph (d)(I) of paragraph (xii) (inserted by the Act of 1985) of "drained,".

(With effect from 1 July 1987)

Finance Act 1988

63.   The Second Schedule (inserted by the Finance Act, 1976) to The Principal
Act is hereby amended by the deletion of paragraph (xx)(a) (inserted by
the Finance Act, 1983).

(With effect from I March 1988)

Finance Act 1989

62.   The Second Schedule (inserted by the Finance Act, 1976) to The
Principal Act is hereby amended by the insertion in subparagraph (b) of
paragraph (xixa) (inserted by the Value-Added Tax (Reduction of Rate)
(No. 5) Order, 1981 (S.I. No. 53 of 1981)), after "teeth", of ", corrective
spectacles and contact lenses".

(With effect from 1 November 1989)

Finance Act 1992

195.   (1)   The Second Schedule (inserted by the Act of 1976) to The
Principal Act is hereby amended-

(a)   by the insertion of the following paragraph after
paragraph (v) (inserted by the Act of 1978):

"(va)   the supply, repair, maintenance and hiring of
equipment incorporated or used in aircraft to which
subparagraph (b) of paragraph (v) relates;", and

(b)   in paragraph (xii) (inserted by the Act of 1985):

(i)   by the substitution of "paragraph (iv) of the
Sixth Schedule" for "paragraph (xic) of the Sixth
Schedule",

**(ii)   by the substitution of the following subparagraph
for subparagraph (b):

"(b)   other beverages, including water and syrups,
concentrates, essences, powders, crystals
or other products for the preparation of
beverages, but not including-

(I)   tea and preparations thereof,

(II)   cocoa, coffee and chicory and other
roasted coffee substitutes, and
preparations and extracts thereof,

(III)   milk and preparations and extracts
thereof, or

(IV)   preparations and extracts of meat,
yeast, or egg,",

*(iii)   by the substitution of the following subparagraph for subparagraph (c):

"(c)   ice cream, ice lollipops, water ices, frozen desserts, frozen yoghurts and similar frozen products, and prepared mixes and powders for making any such product or such similar product,",

*(iv)   in subparagraph (d):

(I)   in clause (I) by the insertion after "bakery products" of ", whether cooked or uncooked,", and

(II)   in clause (II) by the insertion after "in the course of baking" of ", frying", and

*(v)   by the substitution of the following subparagraph for subparagraph (e):

"(e)   any of the following when supplied for human consumption without further preparation, namely-

(I)   potato crisps, potato sticks, potato puffs and similar products made from potato, or from potato flour or from potato starch,

(II)   savoury products made from cereal or grain, or from flour or starch derived from cereal or grain, pork scratchings, and similar products,

(III)   popcorn, and

(IV)   salted or roasted nuts whether or not in shells;".

***(2)   The Second Schedule to The Principal Act is hereby further amended-

(a)   by the substitution of the following paragraphs for paragraph (i) (inserted by the Act of 1985):

"(i)   The supply of goods-

(a)   subject to a condition that they are to be transported directly by or on behalf of the person making the supply-

(I)   outside the Community, or

(II)   to a registered person within the customs-free airport,

(b)   dispatched or transported from the State to a person registered for value-added tax in another Member State,

(c) being new means of transport dispatched or transported directly by or on behalf of the supplier to a person in the territory of another Member State,

(d) by a registered person within a free port to another registered person within a free port,

(e) by a registered person within the customs-free airport to another registered person within the customs-free airport or a free port;

(ia) the supply of goods by tax-free shops, in such amounts and subject to such conditions as may be specified in regulations, to travellers departing the State;",

(b) in paragraph (iii) by the substitution of "outside the Community" for "outside the State",

(c) by the insertion of the following paragraphs after paragraph (iii):

"(iiia) intra-Community transport services involving the carriage of goods to and from the Azores or Madeira;

(iiib) subject to and in accordance with regulations, the importation of goods which, at the time of the said importation, are consigned to another Member State;",

(d) in paragraph (vi) (inserted by the Act of 1978):

(i) by the deletion in subparagraph (a) of "from the State",

(ii) by the insertion in subparagraph (b) of "(iiia)" after "(iii)", and

(iii) by the substitution in subparagraph (c) of "Community" for "State",

and

(e) by the substitution of the following paragraph for paragraph (xvi) (inserted by the Act of 1978):

"(xvi) the supply of services, to a person not established in the Community, consisting of work on movable goods acquired or imported for the purpose of undergoing such work within the Community and subsequently exported;".

(effective from 28 May 1992 except * from 1 July 1992 ** from 1 November 1992 and *** from 1 January 1993)

Finance Act 1993

95.   The Second Schedule (inserted by the Act of 1976) to the Amendment of Principal act is hereby amended -

   (a)   by the insertion of the following paragraph after paragraph (va) (inserted by the Act of 1992):

   "(vb)   the supply of goods for the fuelling and provisioning of sea-going vessels and aircraft of the kind specified in paragraph (v);",

   and

   *(b)   by the insertion of the following paragraph after paragraph (vi) (inserted by the Act of 1978):

   "(via)   subject to and in accordance with section 13A, the supply of qualifying goods and qualifying services to, or the intra-Community acquisition or importation of qualifying goods by, an authorised person in accordance with that section, excluding supplies of goods within the meaning of paragraph (e) or (1) of subsection (1) of section 3;".

(With effect from 17 June except * from 1 August 1993)

Finance Act 1994

100.   The Second Schedule (inserted by the Finance Act, 1976) to The Principal Act is hereby amended by the substitution of the following paragraph for paragraph (ia) (inserted by the Act of 1992):

   "(ia)   subject to such conditions and in such amounts as may be specified in regulations, the supply of goods-

   (a)   to travellers departing the State, in a tax-free shop approved by the Revenue Commissioners, or

   (b)   to travellers on board vessels or aircraft, where the goods are deemed to be supplied in the State in accordance with section 3(6)(cc);".

(With effect from 23 May 1994)

Finance Act 1996

98.   The Second Schedule (inserted by the Finance Act of 1976) to the Principal Act is hereby amended-

   (a)   by the deletion in paragraph (iii) (as amended by the Act of 1992) after "goods to" of "or from",

(b)   by the substitution of the following paragraph for paragraph (xvi) (inserted by the Act of 1992):

"(xvi) the supply of services consisting of work on movable goods acquired or imported for the purpose of undergoing such work within the Community and dispatched or transported out of the Community by or on behalf of the person providing the services",

and

*(c)   by the insertion of the following paragraph after paragraph (xvi) (inserted by paragraph (b)):

"(xvia)the supply of transport services relating to the importation of goods where the value of such services is included in the taxable amount in accordance with section 15(3);".

(With effect from 15 May 1996 except * from 1 January 1996)

Finance Act 1997

111. The Second Schedule to the Principal Act is hereby amended-

(a)   in paragraph (i):

(i)   by the substitution in subparagraph (a) of the following clause for clause (I):

"(I)   outside the Community:

Provided that this subparagraph shall not apply to a supply of goods to a traveller (within the meaning assigned by section 13(3B)) which such traveller exports on behalf of the supplier and such supply shall be deemed to be a supply of the type referred to in subparagraph (f) or", and

(ii)   by the addition of the following subparagraph after subparagraph (e):

"(f)   which are a traveller's qualifying goods (within the meaning assigned by subsection (3B) of section 13), provided that the provisions of subsection (1A) of that section and regulations (if any) made thereunder are complied with;",

and

(b)   by the addition of the following subparagraph after subparagraph (via):

"(vib) the supply of services in procuring a repayment of tax due on the supply of a traveller's qualifying goods (within the meaning assigned by subsection (313) of section 13) or the application of the provisions of subparagraph (i)(t) of this Schedule to that supply of goods, provided that the provisions of subsection (1A) of that section and regulations (if any) made thereunder are complied with;".

(With effect from 1 July 1997)

Taxes Consolidation Act 1997

1100. Schedule 31, which provides for amendments to other enactments consequential on the passing of this Act, shall apply for the purposes of this Act.

SCHEDULE 31
CONSEQUENTIAL AMENDMENTS

In the enactments specified in Column (1) of the following Table for the words set out or referred to in Column (2) there shall be substituted the words set out in the corresponding entry in Column (3).

Enactment amended (1)	Words to be replaced (2)	Words to be substituted (3)
The Value-Added Tax Act, 1972:		
First Schedule, in paragraph (i)(g)	section 18 of the Finance Act, 1989	Section 734 of the Taxes Consolidation Act, 1997

(With effect from 6 April 1997)

Finance Act 1998

116. The Second Schedule to the Principal Act is hereby amended -

(a)   by the insertion of the following paragraph after paragraph (vb) (inserted by the Finance Act, 1993):

"(vc)   the supply of navigation services by the Irish Aviation Authority to meet the needs of aircraft used by a transport undertaking operating for reward chiefly on international routes;",

and

*(b)   by the substitution of the following paragraph for paragraph (xva) (inserted by the Finance Act, 1982):

"(xva) printed books and booklets including atlases but excluding -

(a)   newspapers, periodicals, brochures, catalogues and programmes,

(b)   books of stationery, cheque books and the like,

(c)   diaries, organisers, yearbooks, planners and the like the total area of whose pages consist of 25 per cent or more of blank spaces for the recording of information,

(d)   albums and the like, and

(e)   books of stamps, of tickets or of coupons.".

(With effect from 27 March 1998 except * from 1 May 1998)

Finance Act 1999

139.   The Second Schedule (inserted by the Finance Act, 1976) to the Principal Act is hereby amended in paragraph (i) by the insertion of the following sub-paragraph after sub-paragraph (a):

"(aa)   subject to a condition that they are to be dispatched or transported directly outside the Community by or on behalf of the purchaser of the goods where that purchaser is established outside the State,".

(With effect from 1 July 1999)

S.I. No. 196 of 1999
European Communities (Value-Added Tax) Regulations, 1999

3.   In these regulations "the Principal Act" means the Value-Added Tax Act, 1972 (No. 22 of 1972).

5.   The Second Schedule to the Principal Act is amended-

(a)   by the substitution of the following paragraph for paragraph (ia) (inserted by the Finance Act, 1994):

"(ia)   subject to such conditions and in such amounts as may be specified in regulations,-

(a)   the supply of goods, in a tax-free shop approved by the Revenue Commissioners, to travellers departing the State for a place outside the Community, or

(b)   the supply, other than by means of a vending machine, of food, drink and tobacco products on board a vessel or aircraft to passengers departing the State for another Member State, for consumption on board that vessel or aircraft;",

and

(b)   by the insertion in paragraph (vb) (inserted by the Finance Act, 1993) after "paragraph (v)" of "but not including goods for supply on board such vessels or aircraft to passengers for the purpose of those goods being carried off such vessels or aircraft".

Finance Act 2000

123.   The Second Schedule to the Principal Act is amended-

(a)   by the substitution of the following paragraph for paragraph (ia) (inserted by the Finance Act, 1994):

"(ia)   subject to such conditions and in such amounts as may be specified in regulations,-

(a)   the supply of goods, in a tax-free shop approved by the Revenue Commissioners, to

travellers departing the State for a place outside the Community, or

(b)   the supply, other than by means of a vending machine, of food, drink and tobacco products on board a vessel or aircraft to passengers departing the State for another Member State, for consumption on board that vessel or aircraft;",

(b)   by the insertion in paragraph (vb) (inserted by the Finance Act, 1993) after "paragraph (v)" of "but not including goods for supply on board such vessels or aircraft to passengers for the purpose of those goods being carried off such vessels or aircraft", and

*(c)   by the insertion in subparagraph (a) of paragraph (xva) (inserted by the Finance Act, 1998) after "catalogues" of ", directories".

(With effect from 1 July 1999 except * from 23 March 2000)

128.   The European Communities (Value-Added Tax) Regulations, 1999 (S.I. No. 196 of 1999) shall be deemed to have been revoked with effect from 1 July 1999.

(With effect from 1 July 1999)

Finance Act 2001

200.   The Second Schedule to the Principal Act is amended by the insertion of the following after paragraph (va):

"(vaa)   subject to and in accordance with regulations, if any, the supply, hiring, repair and maintenance of equipment incorporated or for use in sea-going vessels to which subparagraph (a) of paragraph (v) relates;".

(With effect from 1 May 2001)

Finance Act 2007

94.   Second Schedule to the Principal Act is amended:

(a)   by inserting the following after subparagraph (iiib):

"(iiic)   the supply of goods or services to international bodies recognised as such by the public authorities of the host Member State, and to members of such bodies, within the limits and under the conditions laid down by the international conventions establishing the bodies or by the agreements between the headquarters of those bodies and the host Member State of the headquarters;",

(b)   in paragraph (v) by substituting "maintenance, chartering and hiring" for "maintenance and hiring", and

(c)   in subparagraph (b) of paragraph (xii) by substituting "drinking water, juice extracted from, and other drinkable products derived from, fruit or vegetables," for "including water".

(With effect from 2 April 2007)

Finance (No. 2) Act 2008

77.   The Second Schedule to the Principal Act is amended —

*(a)   with effect from 1 January 2010 by inserting the following after paragraph (vib):

"(vic)   services which are treated as intermediary services in accordance with section 10C(8);",

and

(b)   in paragraph (xii) —

     (i)   by substituting the following for clauses (I) and (II) of subparagraph (b):

         "(I)   tea and preparations thereof when supplied in non-drinkable form,

         (II)   cocoa, coffee and chicory and other roasted coffee substitutes, and preparations and extracts thereof, when supplied in non-drinkable form,",

and

     (ii)   by inserting the following after subparagraph (b):

         "(ba)   tea and preparations thereof when supplied in drinkable form,

         (bb)   cocoa, coffee and chicory and other roasted coffee substitutes, and preparations and extracts thereof, when supplied in drinkable form,".

(With effect from 24 December 2008 except *with effect from 1 January 2010)

THIRD SCHEDULE

GOODS CHARGEABLE AT THE RATE OF 5.26 PER CENT

Value Added Tax Act 1972

PART I

(i)   Animal medicine and feeding stuff other than-

    (a)   medicine or feeding stuff which is packaged, sold or otherwise designated for the use of dogs, cats, cage birds or domestic pets, and

    (b)   feeding stuff of a kind specified in paragraph (vii) of the Second Schedule;

(ii)   animal and vegetable produce in an unprocessed state, such as wool, horsehair, bristles, feathers, hides, skins, carcases, roots, plants and cereals,

(iii)   fertiliser other than fertiliser of a kind specified in paragraph (viii) of the Second Schedule;

(iv)   live animals:

(v)   machinery, plant or equipment of a kind commonly used by farmers or fishermen in the State for the purposes of their occupation and not commonly used for any other purpose;

(vi)   seed, plants, trees, spores, bulbs, tubers, tuberous roots, corms, crowns and rhizomes of a kind used for sowing;

(vii)   printed books and booklets;

(viii) newspapers and periodicals;

(ix)   maps, atlases and globes;

(x)   materials commonly used in the construction of buildings (including haybarns, harbours, bridges and roads) being-

    (a)   blocks, beams, piles, pillars, posts, slabs, lintels, cills and members of concrete, whether reinforced or not.

    (b)   cement, concrete, lime, mortar, plaster, stone and bricks,

    (c)   dampcourse felts and other materials normally supplied as dampcourses,

    (d)   earth, sand and gravel,

    (e)   floor and wall tiles of concrete or clay,

    (f)   flue liners and chimney pots,

    (g)   glass in the sheet, but not including mirrors.

    (h)   insulation material in the form of sheets, slabs or rolls.

(i)   nails, screws, bolts, nuts, hinges, locks, fasteners and fittings for doors, windows and tubing,

(j)   paint and distemper,

(k)   plaster board,

(l)   polyethylene film of a kind commonly used by builders or farmers for the purposes of their occupation,

(m)   roofing felts and semi-solid substances used as a substitute for roofing felts,

(n)   roofing tiles, including ridge and hip tiles and slates.

(o)   sheets of metal or of other material, other than glass, not further worked than painted, sprayed or similarly finished,

(p)   steel or aluminium in the form of angles, tees, joists, channels, bars, wire, extrusions or plate, not further worked than galvanised, sprayed, or similarly finished.

(q)   tar, asphalt, bitumen and pitch,

(r)   timber including plywood, blockboard, laminated wood, reconstituted wood and wood veneer sold in the form of planks, sheets or beams and not further worked than sawn lengthwise, planned, moulded, tongued, grooved or v-sheeted,

(s)   tubing and gutters of metal, clay, cement, rubber, plastic or similar material of a kind normally supplied for structural purposes or for use as a conduit for cable, liquids, steam, gases or sewage;

(xi)   clothing, excluding handkerchiefs;

(xii)   fabrics, yarn and thread of a kind normally used in the manufacture of clothing, including elastics, tape and padding materials in the form supplied for the manufacture of clothing;

(xiii)   sole and upper leather of a kind supplied for the manufacture and repair of footwear, and also soles, heels and insoles of any material;

(xiv)   calculating machines, accounting machines, cash registers, postage franking machines and similar machines incorporating a calculating device, automatic data processing machines and units thereof, magnetic and optical readers, machines for transcribing data onto data media in coded form and machines for processing such data, parts suitable for use solely or principally with any of the machines specified in this paragraph;

(xv)   food and drink for human consumption

(xvi)   medicines for human use excluding goods which are, or are described or marketed as, soaps, shampoos, detergents, bleaches, germicides, insecticides, antiseptics or disinfectants;

(xvii)   medical equipment and appliances being-

     (a)   apparatus based on the use of x-rays or of the radiations from radio-active substances (including radiography and radiotherapy apparatus),

     (b)   furniture designed exclusively for medical, dental, surgical, or veterinary use (for example, operating tables and hospital beds with mechanical fittings),

     (c)   invalid carriages, and other vehicles of a kind designed for use by invalids or infirm persons,

     (d)   mechano-therapy appliances, massage apparatus, oxygen therapy apparatus, artificial respiration and similar apparatus and breathing appliances, excluding articles of a kind not designed exclusively for medical use,

     (e)   medical, dental, surgical and veterinary instruments and appliances of a kind used solely in professional practice either to make a diagnosis or to prevent or treat an illness or to operate.

     (f)   orthopaedic appliances, surgical belts, trusses and the like; artificial limbs, eyes, teeth and other artificial parts of the body; deaf aids, splints and other fracture appliances.

     (g)   parts or accessories suitable for use solely or principally with any of the goods in the foregoing subparagraphs of this paragraph,

     (h)   diagnostic reagents,

     (i)   x-ray film, and opacifying preparations for x-ray examinations,

     (j)   wadding, gauze, bandages and similar goods (for example, dressings, adhesive plasters, poultices) and surgical sutures;

(xviii)   railway rolling stock and parts thereof; railway and tramway track fixtures; traffic signalling equipment (including fog signals), railway and tramway track construction material of iron or steel including rails, check-rails, switch blades, crossings (or frogs), crossing pieces, point rods, rack rails, sleepers, fish plates, chairs, chair wedges, sole plates, rail chips, bedplates and ties;

(xix)   mechanically propelled road vehicles, other than vehicles of a land specified in the Fourth Schedule;

(xx)   trailers, excluding caravans, mobile homes and trailer tents;

(xxi) ships, boats or other vessels other than-

> (a) ships, boats or other vessels designed and constructed for the conveyance of passengers and not exceeding one hundred tons gross, and

> (b) sports and pleasure craft of all descriptions including yachts, cabin cruisers, dinghies, canoes, skiffs and racing boats;

(xxii) tobacco;

(xxiii) fuel;

(xxiv) hydrocarbon oils (including greases);

(xxv) tyres, tyre cases, interchangeable tyre treads, inner tubes and tyre flaps, for wheels of all kinds;

(xxvi) spare parts for goods of a kind specified in paragraphs (v) and (xx) and for mechanically propelled road vehicles, bicycles and boats;

(xxvii) bodies and chassis designed for mechanically propelled road vehicles other than for motor vehicles of a kind specified in the Fourth Schedule;

(xxviii) second-hand movable goods, other than goods of a kind specified in the Fourth Schedule;

(xxix) immovable goods;

(xxx) chemicals which are specifically designated for use in agriculture, being seed dressings, herbicides, fungicides, insecticides, rodenticides, verminicides, soil sterilants, growth regulators, disinfectants or dairy detergents, but excluding chemicals which are packaged, sold or otherwise designated for human or domestic use;

(xxxi) goods (other than hand tools) of any of the following descriptions, namely:

> (a) lifting, handling, loading or unloading machinery (for example, lifts, hoists, winches, transporter cranes, jacks and pulley tackle),

(b)   excavating, levelling, boring and extracting machinery for earth, minerals or ores (for example, bulldozers, mechanical shovels, excavators, scrapers, levellers and turf cutters),

(c)   machines designed, constructed and intended for use in spreading or finishing asphalt, bitumen, tar, tarmacadam or concrete,

(d)   works trucks that are mechanically propelled and are of the kind used in factories or warehouses for transport or handling of, goods over short distances, and

(e)   equipment and parts that are specially designed for use with any of the goods specified in subparagraph (a) to (d) and are of a kind not normally used for any other purpose.

PART II

Services Chargeable at the Rate of 5.26 per Cent.

(i)   Services other than the promotion of dances and the hiring or letting of goods;

(ii)   the hiring (in this paragraph referred to as the current hiring) to a person of-

(a)   goods of any kind specified in subparagraph (a) or (b) of paragraph (xxi) of Part I, or

(b)   a caravan, mobile home or trailer tent,

under a contract, other than a contract of a kind referred to in section 3(1)(b) for any term or part of a term which when added to the term of such hiring (whether of the same goods or of other goods of the same kind) to the same person, during the period of 12 months ending on the date of the commencement of the current hiring does not exceed 5 weeks;

(iii)   the hiring of goods of a kind on the delivery of which, if paragraph (xxviii) of Part I of this Schedule were disregarded, tax would be chargeable at the rate of 5.26 per cent;

(iv)   the hiring of goods of a kind specified in the Fourth Schedule;

(v)   the hiring of cinematograph films;

(vi)   the letting of immovable goods.

(With effect from 1 November 1972)

Finance Act 1973

89.   The Third Schedule to The Principal Act is hereby amended-

(a)   by the substitution in Part I of the Schedule of the following paragraph for paragraph (i):

"(i)   Animal medicine excluding medicine-

(a)   of a kind specified in paragraph (xiv) of the Second Schedule, or

(b)   which is packaged, sold or otherwise designated for the use of dogs, cats, cage birds or domestic pets;",

(b)   by the addition to Part I of the Schedule of the following paragraph:

"(xxxii) goods of different kinds which are packaged for sale as a unit (hereinafter in this paragraph referred to as the package) and in relation to which all the following conditions are satisfied:

(a)   the package consists of goods in relation to the delivery of some of which for a separate consideration tax would be chargeable at the rate specified in section 11(1)(a), and in relation to the delivery of the remainder of which for such a consideration, tax would be chargeable at any other rate or rates,

(b)   the consideration for delivery is referable to the package as a whole and not to the different kinds of goods included therein, and

(c)   the total tax-exclusive value of the goods included in the package, in relation to the delivery of which for a separate consideration or separate considerations tax would be chargeable at a rate or rates other than the rate specified in the said section 11(1)(a), does not exceed 50 per cent of the total tax-exclusive consideration for the package or 21/2 new pence, whichever is the lesser,", and

(c)   by the addition to Part II of the Schedule of the following paragraph:

"(vii) the hiring to a person under a contract in writing, other than a contract of a kind referred to in section 3(1)(b), entered into before the 24th day of October, 1972, of movable goods in the possession of the person on the 1st day of November, 1972, of a kind on the delivery of which, if paragraph (xxviii) of Part I of this Schedule were disregarded, tax would be chargeable at the rate specified in section 11(1)(e).".

90. The Principal Act is hereby amended as specified in column (3) of the Tenth Schedule to this Act.

TENTH SCHEDULE

Amendment of Enactments

Number and Year (1)	Short Title (2)	Amendment (3)
No. 22 of 1972	Value-Added Tax Act, 1972	In the Third Schedule, in Part I, "other than horses and greyhounds" shall be added to paragraph (iv); "for a purpose other than the production of food" shall be added to paragraph (vi); "including textile" shall be substituted in paragraph (xi) for "excluding" other than food and drink of a kind specified in paragraph (xii) of the Second Schedule " shall be added to paragraph (xv); and "other than by oral consumption" shall be inserted in paragraph (xvi), after "use".

(With effect from 3 September 1973)

Finance Act 1975

53. The Third Schedule to the Value-Added Tax Act, 1972, is hereby amended by the substitution in paragraph (iii) of Part II of "specified in section 11(1)(a)" for "of 5.26 per cent" and the said paragraph, as so amended, is set out in the Table to this section.

TABLE

(iii)   the hiring of goods of a kind on the delivery of which, if paragraph (xxviii) of Part I of this Schedule were disregarded, tax would be chargeable at the rate specified in section 11(1)(a);

(With effect from 14 May 1975)

Finance Act 1976

60. The Principal Act is hereby amended by-

...

...

(c)   the substitution for the Third Schedule thereto of the Schedule contained in Part Ill of the said Table, and

...

PART III

THIRD SCHEDULE

PART I

Goods Chargeable at the Rate Specified in Section 11(1)(A)

(i)   Animal medicine excluding medicine-

         (a)   of a kind specified in paragraph (xiv) of the Second Schedule, or

         (b)   which is packaged, sold or otherwise designated for the use of dogs, cats, cage birds or domestic pets;

(ii)   animal and vegetable produce in an unprocessed state, such as wool, horsehair, bristles, feathers, hides, skins, carcases, roots, plants and cereals;

(iii)   fertiliser other than fertiliser of a kind specified in paragraph (viii) of the Second Schedule;

(iii)   live animals, other than horses and greyhounds;

(v)   machinery, plant or equipment of a kind commonly used by farmers or fishermen in the State for the purposes of their occupation and not commonly used for any other purpose;

(vi)   seeds, plants, trees, spores, bulbs, tubers, tuberous roots, corms, crowns and rhizomes, of a kind used for sowing for a purpose other than the production of food,

(vii)   printed books and booklets:

(viii)   newspapers and periodicals;

(ix)   maps, atlases and globes,

(x)   materials commonly used in the construction of buildings (including haybarns, harbours, bridges and roads) being-

         (a)   blocks, beams, piles, pillars, posts, slabs, lintels, sills and members of concrete, whether reinforced or not,

         (b)   cement, concrete, lime, mortar, plaster, stone and bricks,

         (c)   dampcourse felts and other materials normally supplied as dampcourses,

         (d)   earth, sand and gravel,

         (e)   floor and wall tiles of concrete or clay,

         (f)   flue liners and chimney pots,

         (g)   glass in the sheet, but not including mirrors,

         (h)   insulation material in the form of sheets, slabs or rolls,

(i)   nails, screws, bolts, nuts, hinges, locks, fasteners; and fittings for doors, windows, tubing and gutters,

(j)   paint and distemper

(k)   plaster board,

(l)   polyethylene film of a kind commonly used by builders or farmers for the purposes of their occupation,

(m)   roofing felts and semi-solid substances used as a substitute for roofing felts,

(n)   roofing tiles, including ridge and hip tiles and slates,

(o)   sheets of metal or of other material, other than glass, not further worked than painted, sprayed or similarly finished,

(p)   steel or aluminium in the form of angles, tees, joists, channels, bars, wire, extrusions or plate, not further worked than galvanised, sprayed or similarly finished,

(q)   tar, asphalt, bitumen and pitch,

(r)   timber, including plywood, blockboard, laminated wood, reconstituted wood and wood veneer sold in the form of planks, sheets or beams and not further worked than sawn lengthwise, planed, moulded, tongued, grooved or v-sheeted,

(s)   tubing and gutters of metal, clay, cement, rubber, plastic or similar material of a kind normally supplied for structural purposes or for use as a conduit for cable, liquids, steam, gases or sewage;

(xi)   goods (other than hand tools) of any of the following descriptions namely:

(a)   lifting, handling, loading or unloading machinery (for example, lifts, hoists, winches, transporter cranes, jacks and pulley tackle),

(b)   excavating, levelling, boring and extracting machinery for earth, minerals or ores (for example, bulldozers, mechanical shovels, excavators, scrapers, levellers and turf cutters),

(c)   machines designed, constructed and intended for use in spreading or finishing asphalt, bitumen, tar, tarmacadam or concrete,

(d)   works trucks that are mechanically propelled and are of the kind used in factories or warehouses for the transport or handling of goods over short distances, and

(e)   equipment and parts that are specially designed for use with any of the goods specified in subparagraphs (a) to (d) and are of a kind not normally used for any other purpose;

(xii)   immovable goods;

(xiii) chemicals which are specifically designated for use in agriculture, being seed dressings, herbicides, fungicides, insecticides, rodenticides, verminicides, soil sterilants, growth regulators, disinfectants or dairy detergents, but excluding chemicals which are packaged, sold or otherwise designated for human or domestic use;

(xiv)   calculating machines, accounting machines, cash registers, postage franking machines and similar machines incorporating a calculating device, automatic data processing machines and units thereof, magnetic and optical readers, machines for transcribing data onto data media in coded form and machines for processing such data, parts suitable for use solely or principally with any of the machines specified in this paragraph;

(xv)   food and drink for human consumption of the following descriptions, that is to say-

    (a)   beverages chargeable with any duty of excise specifically charged on spirits, beer, wine, cider, perry or Irish wine, and preparations thereof,

    (b)   other manufactured beverages, including fruit juices and bottled waters, and syrups, concentrates, essences, powders, crystals or other products for the preparation of beverages, but excluding-

        (I)   tea and preparations thereof,

        (II)   cocoa, coffee and chicory and other roasted coffee substitutes, and preparations and extracts thereof, or

        (III)   preparations and extracts of meat, yeast, egg or milk,

    (c)   ice cream, ice lollipops, water ices and similar frozen products, and prepared mixes and powders for making such products,

    (d)   (I)   chocolates, sweets and similar confectionery (including drained, glacé or crystallised fruits), biscuits, crackers and wafers of all kinds, and all other confectionery and bakery products excluding bread.

        (II)   in this subparagraph "bread" means food for human consumption manufactured by baking dough composed exclusively of a mixture of cereal flour and any one or more of the ingredients mentioned in the following subclauses in quantities not exceeding the limitation if any, specified for each ingredient-

(1) yeast or other leavening or aerating agent, salt, malt extract, milk, water, gluten,

(2) fat, sugar and bread improver, subject to the limitation that the weight of any ingredient specified in this subclause shall not exceed 2 per cent of the weight of flour included in the dough,

(3) dried fruit, subject to the limitation that the weight thereof shall not exceed 10 per cent of the weight of flour included in the dough,

other than food packaged for sale as a unit (not being a unit designated as containing only food specifically for babies) containing two or more slices, segments, sections or other similar pieces, having a crust over substantially the whole of their outside surfaces, being a crust formed in the course of baking or toasting, and

(e)   any of the following when supplied for human consumption without further preparation namely, potato crisps, potato sticks, potato chips, potato puffs and similar products made from potato, or from potato flour or from potato starch, popcorn, and salted or roasted nuts whether or not in shells;

(xvi)   medicines for human use other than by oral consumption, excluding goods which are, or are described or marketed as, soaps, shampoos, detergents, bleaches, germicides, insecticides, antiseptics or disinfectants,

(xvii) medical equipment and appliances being-

(a)   apparatus based on the use of x-rays or of the radiations from radio-active substances (including radiography and radiotherapy apparatus),

(b)   furniture designed exclusively for medical, dental, surgical or veterinary use (for example, operating tables and hospital beds with mechanical fittings),

(c)   invalid carriages and other vehicles of a kind designed for use by invalids or infirm persons.

(d)   mechano-therapy appliances, massage apparatus, oxygen therapy apparatus, artificial respiration and similar apparatus and breathing appliances, excluding articles of a kind not designed exclusively for medical use.

(e)   medical, dental, surgical and veterinary instruments and appliances of a kind used solely in professional practice either to make a diagnosis or to prevent or treat an illness or to operate.

(f)   orthopaedic appliances, surgical belts, trusses and the like, artificial limbs, eyes, teeth and other artificial parts of the body, deaf aids, splints and other fracture appliances,

(g)   parts or accessories suitable for use solely or principally with any of the goods specified in subparagraphs (a) to

(h)   diagnostic reagents.

(i)   x-ray film, and opacifying preparations for x-ray examinations,

(j)   wadding, gauze, bandages and similar goods (for example, dressings, adhesive plasters, poultices) and surgical sutures;

(xviii) railway rolling stock and parts thereof railway and tramway track fixtures, traffic signalling equipment (including fog signals), railway and tramway track construction materials of iron or steel, including rails, check-rails, switch blades, crossings (or frogs), crossing pieces, point rods, rack rails, sleepers, fish plates, chairs, chair wedges, sole plates, rail chips, bedplates and ties;

(xix)   mechanically propelled road vehicles, other than vehicles of a kind specified in Part I of the Fourth Schedule;

(xx)   trailers (excluding caravans, mobile homes and trailer tents),

(xxi)   ships, boats and other vessels excluding-

(a)   ships, boats and other vessels designed and constructed for the conveyance of passengers and not exceeding one hundred tons gross, and

(b)   sports and pleasure craft of all descriptions including yachts, cabin cruisers, dinghies, canoes, skiffs and racing boats;

(xxii) tobacco;

(xxiii) fuel, other than fuel of a kind specified in paragraph (xx) of the Second Schedule;

(xxiv) hydrocarbon oil (including greases), other than hydrocarbon oil of a kind specified in paragraph (xx) of the Second Schedule;

(xxv)   tyres, tyre cases, interchangeable tyre treads, inner tubes and tyre flaps, for wheels of all kinds;

(xxvi)   spare parts for goods of a kind specified in paragraphs (v) and (xx) and for mechanically propelled road vehicles, bicycles and boats;

(xxvii) bodies and chassis designed for mechanically propelled road vehicles other than for motor vehicles of a kind specified in Part I of the Fourth Schedule;

(xxviii) second-hand movable goods, other than goods of a kind specified in the Second Schedule or the Fourth Schedule;

(xxix)   goods of different kinds which are packaged for sale as a unit (hereinafter in this paragraph referred to as the package) and in relation to which all the following conditions are satisfied:

    (a)   the package consists of goods in relation to the delivery of some of which for a separate consideration tax would be chargeable at the rate specified in section 11(1)(a) and, in relation to the delivery of the remainder of which for such a consideration, tax would be chargeable at any other rate or rates,

    (b)   the consideration for delivery is referable to the package as a whole and not to the different kinds of goods included therein, and

    (c)   the total tax-exclusive value of the goods included in the package, in relation to the delivery of which for a separate consideration or separate considerations tax would be chargeable at a rate or rates other than the rate specified in the said section 11(1)(a), does not exceed 50 per cent of the total tax-exclusive consideration for the package or 2 ½ pence, whichever is the lesser.

PART II

Services Chargeable at the Rate Specified in Section 11(1)(A)

(i)   Services other than the hiring or letting of goods;

(ii)   the hiring (in this paragraph referred to as the current hiring) to a person of-

    (a)   goods of a kind described in subparagraph (a) or (b) of paragraph (xxi) of Part I of this Schedule, or

    (b)   a caravan, mobile home or trailer tent,

under an agreement, other than an agreement of the kind referred to in section 3(1)(b), for any term or part of a term which, when added to the term of any such hiring (whether of the same goods or of other goods of the same kind) to the same person during the period of 12 months ending on the date of the commencement of the current hiring, does not exceed 5 weeks;

(iii)   the hiring of goods of a kind on the delivery of which, if paragraph (xxviii) of Part I of this Schedule were disregarded, tax would be chargeable at the rate specified in section 11(1)(a);

(iv)   the hiring of goods of a kind specified in the Fourth Schedule;

(v)   the hiring of cinematograph films,

(vi)   the letting of immovable goods;

(vii)   the hiring to a person under an agreement in writing, other than an agreement of the kind referred to in section 3(1)(b), entered into before the 24th day of October, 1972, of movable goods in the possession of the person on the 1st day of November, 1972, of a kind on the delivery of which, if paragraph (xxviii) of Part I of this Schedule were disregarded, tax would be chargeable at the rate specified in section 11(1)(e);

(viii)   the hiring of goods of a kind specified in paragraph (xvii) of the Second Schedule.

(With effect from 1 March 1976)

Value Added Tax (Amendment) Act 1978

26.   The Third Schedule to the Principal Act is hereby amended-

(a)   by the substitution for paragraph (xix) of the following paragraph:

"(xix) mechanically propelled road vehicles;",

(b)   by the substitution for paragraph (xxi) of the following paragraph:

"(xxi) ships, boats and other vessels excluding-

(a)   ships, boats and other vessels designed and constructed for the conveyance of passengers and not exceeding 15 tons gross,

(b)   sports and pleasure craft of all descriptions including yachts, cabin cruisers, dinghies, canoes, skiffs and racing boats. And

(c)   vessels of a kind specified in paragraph (v)(a) of the Second Schedule;",

(c)   by the substitution for paragraph (xxvii) of the following paragraph:

"(xxvii) bodies and chassis designed for mechanically propelled road vehicles;",

(d)   by the substitution for paragraph (xxviii) of the following paragraph:

"(xxviii) second-hand movable goods other than goods of a kind specified in the Second Schedule;",

and

(e)   by the substitution of the following paragraphs for paragraph (xxix):

"(xxix) radio receiving sets and television receiving sets that are of the domestic or portable type or that are of a type suitable for use in road vehicles;

(xxx)   gramophones, radiogramophones and record players;

(xxxi)   gramophone records.".

(With effect from 1 March 1979)

30.   (1)   The enactment mentioned in column (2) of the First Schedule is hereby repealed to the extent specified in column (3) of that Schedule.

(2)   In consequence of the amendments of the Principal Act specified in this Act and of the repeals specified in the First Schedule, the Principal Act is hereby further amended by the substitution of the word or expression mentioned in column (3) of the Second Schedule at any reference number for the word or expression mentioned in column (2) of that Schedule at that reference number wherever it occurs in the provision of the Principal Act mentioned in column (4) of that Schedule at that reference number.

FIRST SCHEDULE
Enactments Repealed

Number and Year (1)	Short Title (2)	Extent of Repeal (3)
No. 22 of 1972	Value-Added Tax Act, 1972	Paragraph (iv) of Part II of the Third Schedule

SECOND SCHEDULE
Consequential Amendments

Reference Number (1)	Existing word or expression (2)	Substituted word or expression (3)	Provision of Principal Act (4)
35	"section 11(1)(e)"	"section 11(1)(c)"	Paragraph (vii) of Part II of Third Schedule

(With effect from 1 March 1979)

Finance Act 1979

49.   With effect as on and from the 1st day of March, 1979, the rate of value-added tax on radio receiving sets that are of the domestic or portable type or that are of a type suitable for use in road vehicles, and on gramophones, radio-gramophones and record players, shall be increased from 10 per cent. of the amount or value, as the case may be, in respect of which tax is chargeable on those goods to 20 per cent of that amount or value and, accordingly, the Third Schedule to the Value-Added Tax Act, 1972, shall be amended-

    (a)   by the deletion of "radio receiving sets and" in paragraph (xxix), and

    (b)   by the deletion of paragraph (xxx).

(With effect from 1 March 1979)

Finance Act 1982

89.   (1)   Part I of the Third Schedule (inserted by the Act of 1976) to the Principal Act is hereby amended-

    (a)   by the substitution of the following paragraph for paragraph (vii):

"(vii)   printed books and booklets other than-

    (I)   those specified in paragraph (xva) of the Second Schedule to which section 11 applies, and

    (II)   books of stationery, cheque books, diaries, albums and books of stamps, of tickets or of coupons;",

    (b)   by the insertion in paragraph (x) after subparagraph (r) of the following subparagraph:

"(rr)   timber joinery; and doors, door frames, window frames, window panels, staircases and roofing trusses and of any material,",

and

    (c)   by the substitution of the following paragraphs for paragraph (xxxi) (inserted by the Act of 1978):

"(xxxi)gramophone records;

(xxxii) furniture, including sections and parts thereof and furniture in kit form, of the following descriptions, that is to say-

    (a)   beds, including cots and cradles, but not including baby carriages,

    (b)   chairs, stools, kneelers, couches, and similar goods,

(c)   tables, dressing tables, wardrobes, chests of drawers, tallboys, presses, lockers, desks, and similar goods,

(d)   cabinets, including cabinets specially constructed for radios, record players, speakers and television sets,

(e)   playpens, safety screens, shelves, shelving and shelving units, serving trolleys, hat and coat stands, and similar stands,

but not including furniture constructed or adapted for the playing of games or for physical exercise, musical instruments, ornaments, lamps, ash trays, log boxes, coal scuttles and other hearth furniture or furniture which incorporates or is fitted with any machine or appliance;

(xxxiii)(a)   floor coverings, blinds, curtains including curtain materials and parts and accessories for the manufacture of curtains, and similar furnishings, but not including wall or ceiling coverings,

(b)   blankets, mattresses, sheets, pillows and other articles of bed clothing, towels and towelling material,

(c)   carpet wool and canvas,

(d)   fabrics, padding materials, trimming materials, webbing and springs and springing material of a kind normally used in the manufacture of furniture, and

(e)   curtain rails, tracks and pelmets including parts, accessories and curtain cord, parts and accessories for blinds, stair nosings and carpet grips;

(xxxiv)coffins and other goods of a kind commonly used to hold the remains of the dead including materials and accessories commonly used in the manufacture of such goods and not commonly used for any other purposes.".

(2)   This section shall have, and be deemed to have had, effect as and from the 1st day of May, 1982.

(With effect from 1 May 1982)

Finance Act 1983

87.   The Third Schedule (inserted by the Act of 1976) to the Principal Act is hereby amended-

(a)   in Part I-

    (i)   in paragraph (ix), by the deletion of "atlases",

    (ii)   by the deletion of paragraph (xii), and

    (iii)   by the insertion in paragraphs (xxiii) and (xxiv) after "Schedule" of "or paragraph (i) of the Sixth Schedule", and

(b)   in Part II, by the substitution of the following paragraph for paragraph (i):

"(i)   Services other than-

    (a)   the hiring or letting of goods,

    (b)   services of a kind specified in the Sixth Schedule;".

(With effect from 1 May 1983)

Finance Act 1984

93.   The Third Schedule (inserted by the Act of 1976) to the Principal Act is hereby amended-

(a)   in Part I-

    *(i)   by the deletion in paragraph (x)(b) of "concrete,", and

    (ii)   by the insertion in paragraph (xxviii) after "Second" of ",Sixth or Seventh",

and

(b)   in Part II, by the substitution of the following paragraph for paragraph (viii):

"(viii) the hiring of goods specified in paragraphs (xvii) and (xviii) of the Second Schedule and paragraph (i) of the Seventh Schedule.".

(With effect from 1 May 1984 except * from 1 March 1984)

Finance Act 1985

51.   The Principal Act is hereby amended by-

(a)   the deletion of the Third Schedule (inserted by the Act of 1976),

...

...

(With effect from 1 May 1985)

Finance Act 1991

86.   (1)   The Principal Act is hereby amended by the insertion after the Second Schedule (inserted by the Finance Act, 1976) of the following Schedule:

"THIRD SCHEDULE

Goods and Services Chargeable at the Rate Specified in Section 11(1)(bi)

(i)   immovable goods;

(ii)   services, other than services specified in paragraph (xiv) of the Sixth Schedule, consisting of the development of immovable goods and the maintenance and repair of immovable goods including the installation of fixtures, where the value of movable goods (if any) provided in pursuance of an agreement in relation to such services does not exceed two-thirds of the total amount on which tax is chargeable in respect of the agreement;

(iii)   concrete ready to pour;

(iv)   blocks, of concrete, of a kind which comply with the specification contained in the Standard Specification (Concrete Building Blocks) Declaration, 1974 (Irish Standard 20: 1974);

(v)   newspapers and periodicals, normally published at least fortnightly, the contents of each issue of which consist, wholly or mainly, as regards the quantity of printed matter contained in them, of information on the principal current events and topics of general public interest;

(vi)   letting of the kind to which paragraph (iv)(b) of the First Schedule refers;

(vii)   tour guide services;

(viii)   the hiring (in this paragraph referred to as 'the current hiring') to a person of-

    (a)   a vehicle designed and constructed, or adapted, for the conveyance of persons by road,

    (b)   a ship, boat or other vessel designed and constructed for the conveyance of passengers and not exceeding 15 tons gross,

    (c)   a sports or pleasure craft of any description including a yacht, cabin cruiser, dinghy, canoe, skiff or racing boat, or

    (d)   a caravan, mobile home, tent or trailer tent,

under an agreement, other than an agreement of the kind referred to in section 3(1)(b), for any term or part of a term which, when added to the term of any such hiring (whether of the same goods or of other goods of the same kind) to the same person during the period of 12 months ending on the date of the commencement of the current hiring, does not exceed 5 weeks.".

(2)   The Third Schedule (inserted by subsection (1) to The Principal Act) is hereby amended-

   (a)   in paragraph (ii) by the substitution of "paragraph (xiib) (b) or (xiv)" for "paragraph (xiv)", and

   (b)   by the substitution of the following paragraph for paragraph (vi):

   "(vi)   (a)   letting of immovable goods-

             (I)   by a hotel or guesthouse, or by a similar establishment which provides accommodation for visitors or travellers,

             (II)   in a house, apartment or other similar establishment which is advertised or held out as being holiday accommodation or accommodation for visitors or travellers, or

             (III) in a caravan park, camping site or other similar establishment,

       or

       *(b)   the provision of accommodation which is advertised or held out as holiday accommodation in any caravan, mobile home, tent, trailer tent or houseboat.".

(With effect from 1 March 1991 except * from 1 January 1992)

Finance Act 1992

196. The Third Schedule (inserted by the Act of 1991) to The Principal Act is hereby amended-

   (a)   by the substitution in paragraph (ii) of "paragraph (xi) of the Sixth Schedule or paragraph (xi)(b) of the Seventh Schedule" for "paragraphs (xiib)(b) or (xiv) of the Sixth Schedule", and

   *(b)   by the insertion in subparagraph (a) of paragraph (vi) after "goods" of "(other than in the course of the provision of facilities of the kind specified in paragraph (viia) of the Sixth Schedule)".

(With effect from 28 May 1992 except * from 1 July 1992)

Finance Act 1993

96. The Principal Act is hereby amended by the substitution of the following Schedule for the Third Schedule (inserted by the Act of 1991):

"THIRD SCHEDULE

Goods and Services Chargeable at the Rate Specified in Section 11(1)(C).

(i) Immovable goods being a domestic dwelling for which a contract with a private individual has been entered into before the 25th day of February, 1993, for such supply;

(ii) services specified in paragraph (xiii) of the Sixth Schedule, under an agreement made before the 25th day of February, 1993, and at charges fixed at the time of the agreement for such supply;

(iii) services specified in subparagraph (a) of paragraph (xv) of the Sixth Schedule, under an agreement made before the 25th day of February, 1993, and at charges fixed at the time of the agreement for such supply.".

(With effect from 1 March 1993)

FOURTH SCHEDULE

GOODS CHARGEABLE AT THE RATE OF
30.26 PER CENT

Value-Added Tax Act 1972

(i)   Motor vehicles designed and constructed for the conveyance of persons by road including sports motor vehicles, estate cars, station wagons, motor cycles, motor scooters, mopeds and auto cycles, but not including vehicles designed and constructed for the carriage of more that sixteen persons (inclusive of the driver), invalid carriages and other vehicles of a type designed for use by invalids or infirm persons;

(ii)   radio receiving sets and television receiving sets of the domestic or portable type including sets suitable for use in road vehicles;

(iii)   gramophones, radiogramophones, record reproducers;

(iv)   gramophone records.

(With effect from 1 November 1972)

Finance Act 1976

60.   The Principal Act is hereby amended by-

(a)   ...

(b)   ...

(c)   ..., and

(d)   the substitution for the Fourth Schedule thereto of the Schedule contained in Part IV of the said Table.

PART IV

FOURTH SCHEDULE

PART I

Goods Chargeable at the Rate Specified in Section 11(1)(c)(i)

Motor vehicles designed and constructed for the conveyance of persons by road, and sports motor vehicles, estate cars, station wagons, motor cycles, motor scooters, mopeds and auto cycles, whether or not designed and constructed for the purpose aforesaid, excluding vehicles designed and constructed for the carriage of more than sixteen persons (inclusive of the driver), invalid carriages and other vehicles of a type designed for use by invalids or infirm persons.

PART II

Goods Chargeable at the Rate Specified in Section 11(1)(c)(ii)

(i)   Radio receiving sets and television receiving sets which are of the domestic or portable type or which are of a kind suitable for use in road vehicles;

(ii)   gramophones, radiogramophones, record reproducers;

(iii)   gramophone records.

(With effect from 1 March 1976)

Value Added Tax (Amendment) Act 1978

27.   The following Schedule shall be substituted for the Fourth Schedule to the Principal Act:

"FOURTH SCHEDULE

Services that are taxed where received

(i)   Transfers and assignments of copyright, patents, licences, trade marks and similar rights;

(ii)   advertising services:

(iii)   services of consultants, engineers, consultancy bureaux, lawyers, accountants and other similar services, data processing and provision of information (but excluding services connected with immovable goods);

(iv)   acceptance of any obligation to refrain from pursuing or exercising in whole or in part, any business activity or any such rights as are referred to in paragraph (i);

(v)   banking, financial and insurance services (including re-insurance, but not including the provision of safe deposit facilities);

(vi)   the provision of staff;

(vii)   the services of agents who act in the name and for the account of a principal when procuring for him any services specified in paragraphs (i) to (vi).".

(With effect from 1 March 1979)

Finance Act 1985

52.   The Fourth Schedule (inserted by the Act of 1978) to the Principal Act is hereby amended by the insertion, after paragraph (i), of the following paragraph:

"(ia)   hiring out of movable goods other than means of transport;".

(With effect from 30 May 1985)

Finance Act 1997

112.   The Fourth Schedule to the Principal Act is hereby amended by the insertion of the following paragraph after paragraph (iii):

"(iiia)   telecommunications services;".

(With effect from 1 July 1997)

Finance Act 2003

131.   The Fourth Schedule to the Principal Act is amended by inserting the following after paragraph (iiia):

"(iiib)   radio and television broadcasting services;

(iiic)   electronically supplied services;".

(With effect from 1 July 2003)

Finance Act 2004

65.   The Fourth Schedule to the Principal Act is amended —

*(a)   by inserting the following after paragraph (iiic):

"(iiid) the provision of access to, and of transport or transmission through, natural gas and electricity distribution systems and the provision of other directly linked services;",

and

(b)   in paragraph (v) by inserting "and financial fund management functions" after "re-insurance".

(With effect from 25 March 2004 except * with effect from 1 January 2005)

Finance Act 2007

95.   The Fourth Schedule to the Principal Act is amended, with effect from 1 January 2008, by substituting "intermediaries" for "agents" in paragraph (vii).

(With effect from 1 January 2008)

FIFTH SCHEDULE

ENACTMENTS REPEALED

VALUE-ADDED TAX ACT 1972

Number and Year	Short Title	Extent of Repeal
No. 23 of 1963	Finance Act, 1963	Section 41 and Part VI
No. 22 of 1965	Finance Act, 1965	Part VI
No. 17 of 1966	Finance Act, 1966	Part VI
No. 22 of 1966	Finance (No. 2) Act, 1966	The whole Act
No. 33 of 1968	Finance Act, 1968	Parts V and VI
No. 37 of 1968	Finance (No. 2) Act, 1968	Sections 6 and 7
No. 21 of 1969	Finance Act, 1969	Parts VII and VIII
No. 14 of 1970	Finance Act, 1970	Part V
No. 25 of 1970	Finance (No. 2) Act, 1970	Sections 3 and 4

(Effective from 1 November 1972)

Value-Added Tax (Amendment) Act 1978

28. The following Schedule shall be substituted for the Fifth Schedule to the Principal Act:

Section 8 of Principal Act.

"FIFTH SCHEDULE

PART I

Annex A of Council Directive No. 77/388/EEC of 17 May, 1977

LIST OF AGRICULTURAL PRODUCTION ACTIVITIES

I.   CROP PRODUCTION

    1.   General agriculture, including viticulture

    2.   Growing of fruit (including olives) and of vegetables, flowers and ornamental plants, both in the open and under glass

    3.   Production of mushrooms, spices, seeds and propagating materials; nurseries

II. STOCK FARMING TOGETHER WITH CULTIVATION

    1.   General stock farming

    2.   Poultry farming

    3.   Rabbit farming

    4.   Beekeeping

    5.   Silkworm farming

    6.   Snail farming

III.   FORESTRY

IV.   FISHERIES

   1.   Fresh-water fishing

   2.   Fish farming

   3.   Breeding of mussels, oysters and other molluscs and crustaceans

   4.   Frog farming

V.   Where a farmer processes, using means normally employed in an agricultural, forestry or fisheries undertaking, products deriving essentially from his agricultural production, such processing shall also be regarded as agricultural production.

PART II

Annex B of Council Directive No. 77/388/EEC of 17 May, 1977

LIST OF AGRICULTURAL SERVICES

Supplies of agricultural services which normally play a part in agricultural production shall be considered the supply of agricultural services and include the following in particular:

-    field work, reaping and mowing, threshing, baling, collecting, harvesting, sowing and planting

-    packing and preparation for market, for example drying, cleaning, grinding, disinfecting and ensilage of agricultural products

-    storage of agricultural products

-    stock minding, rearing and fattening

-    hiring out, for agricultural purposes, of equipment normally used in agricultural, forestry or fisheries undertakings

-    technical assistance

-    destruction of weeds and pests, dusting and spraying of crops and land

-    operation of irrigation and drainage equipment

-    lopping, tree felling and other forestry services.".

(With effect from 1 March 1979)

Finance Act 2007

97.   With effect from 1 January 2007 in each provision of the Principal Act specified in the first column of Schedule 3 for the words set out in the second column of that Schedule at that entry there is substituted the words set out at the corresponding entry in the third column of that Schedule.

Schedule 3
Miscellaneous Amendments Relating to Council Directive 2006/112/EC

Amendment of Value-Added Tax Act 1972

Provision of Principal Act	Words to be replaced	Words to be inserted
Fifth Schedule Part I Title	PART I Annex A of Council Directive No. 77/388/EEC of 17 May 1977	PART I Article 295(1) and Annex VII of Council Directive No. 2006/112/EC of 28 November 2006
Fifth Schedule Part II Title	PART II Annex B of Council Directive No. 77/388/EEC of 17 May 1977	PART II Article 295(1) and Annex VIII of Council Directive No. 2006/112/EC of 28 November 2006

(With effect from 1 January 2007)

SIXTH SCHEDULE

GOODS AND SERVICES CHARGEABLE AT THE RATE SPECIFIED IN SECTION 11(1)(aa)

Finance Act 1983

88.   The Principal Act is hereby amended by the insertion after the Fifth Schedule of the following Schedule:

"SIXTH SCHEDULE

Goods and Services Chargeable at the Rate Specified in Section 11(1)(aa)

   (i)   (a)   Coal, peat and other solid substances, held out for sale solely as fuel,

            (b)   gas of a kind used for domestic or industrial heating or lighting, whether in gaseous or liquid form, but not including gas of a kind normally used for welding and cutting metals or gas sold as lighter fuel,

            (c)   hydrocarbon oil of a kind used for domestic or industrial heating, excluding gas oil (within the meaning of the Hydrocarbon Oil (Rebated Oil) Regulations, 1961 (S.I. No. 122 of 1961)), other than gas oil which has been duly marked in accordance with Regulation 6(2) of the said Regulations;

   (ii)   immovable goods;

   (iii)   services consisting of the development of immovable goods, and the maintenance and repair of immovable goods including the installation of fixtures, where the value of movable goods (if any) provided in pursuance of an agreement in relation to such services does not exceed two-thirds of the total amount on which tax is chargeable in respect of the agreement;

   (iv)   services, supplied on or after the 1st day of July, 1983, consisting of the repair or maintenance of mechanically propelled land vehicles including self-propelled mobile machinery (other than vehicles and machinery designed, constructed or intended for use on rails) and goods specified in paragraph (v), insofar as it applies to farmers, and paragraph (xx), of Part I of the Third Schedule, including the provision and installation in the course of supplying such services of goods of a kind normally included as parts of such vehicles when supplied new, but excluding-

            (a)   the provision in the course of a repair or maintenance service of accessories, attachments, goods specified in paragraph (xxv) of the said Part I and batteries,

            (b)   the repair and maintenance, whether performed separately or in the course of the repair or maintenance of other goods, of articles which are accessories or attachments or goods specified in the said paragraph (xxv), other than such articles that are of a kind specified in the said paragraph (v), insofar as it applies to farmers, and the said paragraph (xx), and

    (c)   washing, cleaning and polishing;

(v)   agricultural services consisting of-

    (a)   field work, reaping, mowing, threshing, baling, harvesting, sowing and planting,

    (b)   disinfecting and ensilage of agricultural products,

    (c)   destruction of weeds and pests and dusting and spraying of crops and land,

    (d)   lopping, tree felling and similar forestry services, and

    (e)   land drainage and reclamation;

(vi)   services of an auctioneer, solicitor, estate agent or other agent, directly related to the supply of immovable goods used for the purposes of an Annex A activity;

(vii)   farm accountancy or farm management services.".

(With effect from 1 May 1983)

Finance Act 1984

94.   The Sixth Schedule (inserted by the Act of 1983) to the Principal Act is hereby amended-

    (a)   by the insertion after paragraph (ii) of the following paragraph:

        "(iia)   concrete ready to pour;",

and

    (b)   by the insertion after paragraph (iii) of the following paragraph:

        "(iiia) promotion of or admission to live theatrical or musical performances, including circuses, but not including-

        (a)   dances to which section 11(7) relates, or

        (b)   performances in conjunction with which facilities are available for the consumption of food or drink during all or part of the performance by persons attending the performance;".

(With effect from 1 March 1984)

Finance Act 1985

51.   The Principal Act is hereby amended by-

...

...

(c)   the substitution of the following Schedule for the Sixth Schedule
        (inserted by the Act of 1983):

"SIXTH SCHEDULE

Goods and Services Chargeable at the Rate Specified in Section 11(1)(c)

(i)   (a)   Coal, peat and other solid substances held out for sale
                solely as fuel,

        (b)   gas of a kind used for domestic or industrial heating
                or lighting, whether in gaseous or liquid form, but not
                including gas of a kind normally used for welding and
                cutting metals or gas sold as lighter fuel,

        (c)   hydrocarbon oil of a kind used for domestic or industrial
                heating, excluding gas oil (within the meaning of the
                Hydrocarbon Oil (Rebated Oil) Regulations, 1961 (S.I.
                No. 122 of 1961)), other than gas oil which has been duly
                marked in accordance with Regulation 6(2) of the said
                Regulations;

(ii)   immovable goods;

(iii)   services consisting of the development of immovable goods,
        and the maintenance and repair of immovable goods including
        the installation of fixtures, where the value of movable goods
        (if any) provided in pursuance of an agreement in relation to
        such services does not exceed two-thirds of the total amount on
        which tax is chargeable in respect of the agreement;

(iv)   concrete ready to pour;

(v)   blocks, of concrete, of a kind which comply with the specification
        contained in the Standard Specification (Concrete Building
        Blocks) Declaration, 1974 (Irish Standard 20: 1974);

(vi)   articles of personal clothing and textile handkerchiefs,
        excluding-

        (a)   articles of clothing made wholly or partly of fur skin,
                other than garments merely trimmed with fur skin unless
                the trimming has an area greater than one-fifth of the area
                of the outside material, and

        (b)   articles of personal clothing of a kind specified in
                paragraphs (xvii) and (xviii) of the Second Schedule;

(vii)   (a)   fabrics, yarn, thread and leather, of a kind normally used in the manufacture of clothing, including elastics, tapes and padding materials in the form supplied for the manufacture of clothing, and

            (b)   yarn of a kind normally used in the manufacture of clothing fabrics;

(viii)   articles of personal footwear, other than articles of personal footwear of a kind specified in paragraph (xix) of the Second Schedule;

(ix)   sole and upper leather of a kind normally used for the manufacture and repair of footwear, and also soles, heels and insoles of any material;

(x)   (a)   the national daily newspapers published in the State,

            (b)   other newspapers, normally published at least weekly, the format, and the range and nature of the contents of which are similar to those of any newspaper referred to in subparagraph (a);

(xi)   letting of the kind to which paragraph (iv)(b) of the First Schedule refers;

(xii)   the hiring (in this paragraph referred to as 'the current hiring') to a person of-

            (a)   a vehicle designed and constructed, or adapted, for the conveyance of persons by road,

            (b)   a ship, boat or other vessel designed and constructed for the conveyance of passengers and not exceeding 15 tons gross,

            (c)   a sports or pleasure craft of any description including a yacht, cabin cruiser, dinghy, canoe, skiff or racing boat, or

            (d)   a caravan, mobile home, tent or trailer tent,

under an agreement, other than an agreement of the kind referred to in section 3(1)(b), for any term or part of a term which, when added to the term of any such hiring (whether of the same goods or of other goods of the same kind) to the same person during the period of 12 months ending on the date of the commencement of the current hiring, does not exceed 5 weeks;

(xiii)   services consisting of the repair or maintenance of-

            (a)   mechanically propelled land vehicles including self-propelled mobile machinery (other than vehicles and machinery designed, constructed or intended for use on rails),

(b)   machinery, plant or equipment of a kind commonly used by farmers in the State for the purposes of their occupation and not commonly used for any other purpose, or

(c)   trailers (excluding caravans, mobile homes and trailer tents),

including the provision and installation in the course of supplying such services of goods of a kind normally included as parts of such vehicles, machinery, plant, equipment or trailers when supplied new, but excluding-

(I)   the provision in the course of a repair or maintenance service of-

(A)   accessories or attachments,

(B)   tyres, tyre cases, interchangeable tyre treads, inner tubes and tyre flaps, for wheels of all kinds, or

(C)   batteries, and

(II)   the repair or maintenance, whether performed separately or in the course of the repair or maintenance of other goods, of articles which are accessories or attachments or goods specified in clause (1)(B) of this paragraph, other than goods to which clauses (b) and (c) and subclause (1) (c) of this paragraph refer, and

(III)   washing, cleaning and polishing;

(xiv)   agricultural services consisting of-

(a)   field work, reaping, mowing, threshing, baling, harvesting, sowing and planting,

(b)   disinfecting and ensilage of agricultural products,

(c)   destruction of weeds and pests and dusting and spraying of crops and land,

(d)   lopping, tree felling and similar forestry services, and

(e)   land drainage and reclamation;

(xv)   services of an auctioneer, solicitor, estate agent or other agent, directly related to the supply of immovable goods used for the purposes of an Annex A activity;

(xvi)   farm accountancy or farm management services.".

(With effect from 1 May 1985)

Finance Act 1986

91.   The Sixth Schedule (inserted by the Act of 1985) to The Principal Act is hereby amended-

*(a)   by the substitution of the following paragraph for paragraph (x):

"(x)   (a)   newspapers, normally published daily, the contents of each issue of which consist, wholly or mainly, as regards the quantity of printed matter contained in them, of information on the principal current events and topics of general public interest,

(b)   newspapers, normally published at least fortnightly, which are similar in range and nature of contents to any newspaper of a kind specified in subparagraph (a) and are also similar in format to any newspaper published in the State which is of a kind specified in subparagraph (a);",

(b)   by the insertion after paragraph (xi) of the following paragraphs:

"(xia)   the provision of food and drink of a kind specified in paragraph (xii) of the Second Schedule in a form suitable for human consumption without further preparation-

(a)   by means of a vending machine,

(b)   in the course of operating a hotel, restaurant, cafe, refreshment house, canteen, establishment licensed for the sale for consumption on the premises of intoxicating liquor, catering business or similar business, or

(c)   in the course of operating any other business in connection with the carrying on of which facilities are provided for the consumption of the food or drink supplied;

(xib)   the supply, in the course of the provision of a meal, of goods of a kind specified in subparagraph (c), (d) or (e) of paragraph (xii) of the Second Schedule, and fruit juices other than fruit juices chargeable with a duty of excise-

(a)   in the course of operating a hotel, restaurant, cafe, refreshment house, canteen, establishment licensed for the sale for consumption on the premises of intoxicating liquor, catering business or similar business, or

(b)   in the course of operating any other business in connection with the carrying on of which facilities are provided for the consumption of the food or drink supplied;

(xic)   the supply of food and drink (other than beverages specified in subparagraph (a) or (b) of paragraph (xii) of the Second Schedule) which is, or includes, food or drink which-

(a)   has been heated for the purpose of enabling it to be consumed at a temperature above the ambient air temperature, or

(b)   has been retained heated after cooking for the purpose of enabling it to be consumed at a temperature above the ambient air temperature, or

(c)   is supplied, while still warm after cooking, for the purpose of enabling it to be consumed at a temperature above the ambient air temperature,

and is above the ambient air temperature at the time of supply;

(xid)   promotion of and admissions to cinematographic performances;

(xie)   promotion of and admissions to live theatrical or musical performances, excluding-

(a)   dances to which section 11(7) relates, and

(b)   performances specified in paragraph (viii) of the First Schedule;

(xif)   entertainment services, other than dances to which section 11(7) relates and circuses, supplied in fairgrounds by travelling showmen where, in any particular case, the total period spent in any one locality in relation to a series of successive performances does not exceed 19 consecutive days and an interval of at least one month elapses before the next performance in the same locality;",

(c)   by the insertion of the following paragraphs after paragraph (xii):

"(xiia) services consisting of-

(a)   the repair or maintenance of movable goods, or

(b)   the alteration of second-hand movable goods,

other than any such services specified in paragraph (v) or (xvi) of the Second Schedule,

but excluding the provision in the course of any such repair, maintenance or alteration service of-

(I)   accessories, attachments or batteries, or

(II)   tyres, tyre cases, interchangeable tyre treads, inner tubes and tyre flaps, for wheels of all kinds;

(xiib) services consisting of work on immovable goods, other than services consisting of such work specified in paragraph (xiv) and services specified in paragraph (iii);

(xiic) services consisting of the care of the human body, excluding such services specified in the First Schedule, but including services supplied in the course of a health studio business or similar business;",

and

(d) by the deletion of paragraph (xiii).

(With effect from 1 July 1986 except * from 27 May 1986)

Finance Act 1987

47. The Sixth Schedule (inserted by the Act of 1985) to the Principal Act is hereby amended by the insertion-

(a) after paragraph (xif) (inserted by the Act of 1986) of the following paragraph:

"(xig) tour guide services;"

and

(b) after paragraph (xiic) (inserted by the Act of 1986) of the following paragraphs:

"(xiii) the supply to a person of photographic prints (other than goods produced by means of a photocopying process), slides or negatives, which have been produced from goods provided by that person;

(xiiia) goods being-

(a) photographic prints (other than goods produced by means of a photocopying process), mounted or unmounted, but unframed,

(b) slides and negatives, and

(c) cinematographic and video film,

which record particular persons, objects or events, supplied under an agreement to photograph those persons, objects or events;

(xiiib) the supply by a photographer of-

(a) negatives which have been produced from film exposed for the purposes of his business, and

(b) film which has been exposed for the purposes of his business;

(xiiic) photographic prints produced by means of a vending machine which incorporates a camera and developing and printing equipment;

(xiiid) services consisting of-

    (a)　　the editing of photographic, cinematographic and video film, and

    (b)　　microfilming;

(xiiie) agency services in regard to a supply specified in paragraph (xiii);

(xiiif) services consisting of the acceptance for disposal of waste material;

(xiiig) instruction in the driving of mechanically propelled road vehicles, not being education, training or retraining of the kinds specified in paragraph (ii) of the First Schedule;

(xiiih) admissions to exhibitions, of the kind normally held in museums and art galleries, of objects of historical, cultural, artistic or scientific interest;".

(With effect from 1 July 1987)

Finance Act 1989

63. The Sixth Schedule (inserted by the Act of 1985) to The Principal Act is hereby amended-

    (a)　　by the insertion of the following paragraphs after paragraph (i):

"(ia)　every work of art being-

    (a)　　a painting, drawing or pastel, or any combination thereof, executed entirely by hand, excluding hand-decorated manufactured articles and plans and drawings for architectural, engineering, industrial, commercial, topographical or similar purposes.

    (b)　　an original lithograph, engraving, or print, or any combination thereof, produced directly from lithographic stones, plates or other engraved surfaces, which are executed entirely by hand,

    (c)　　an original sculpture or statuary, excluding mass-produced reproductions and works of craftsmanship of a commercial character, or

    (d)　　subject to and in accordance with regulations, an article of furniture, silver, glass or porcelain, whether hand-decorated or not, specified in the said regulations, where it is shown to the satisfaction of the Revenue Commissioners to be more than 100 years old, other than goods specified in subparagraph (a), (b) or (c);

(ib)   literary manuscripts certified by the Director of the National Library as being of major national importance and of either cultural or artistic importance;",

and

*(b)   by the insertion of the following paragraph after paragraph (ix):

"(ixa) corrective spectacles and contact lenses, including parts thereof;".

(With effect from 1 July 1989 except *from 1 November 1989)

Finance Act 1990

107.   The Sixth Schedule (inserted by the Act of 1985) to The Principal Act is hereby amended-

*(a)   by the insertion in paragraph (i), after subparagraph (a), of the following subparagraph:

"(aa)   electricity:

Provided that this subparagraph shall not apply to the distribution of any electricity where such distribution is wholly or mainly in connection with the distribution of communications signals,",

(b)   by the insertion of the following paragraph after paragraph (v):

"(va)   telecommunications services (including the supply of goods and services incidental thereto) supplied by Bord Telecom Éireann or by any person licensed in accordance with subsection (1) of section 111 of the Postal and Telecommunications Services Act, 1983, other than services of the kind specified in paragraph (d), (e) or (f)of subsection (3) of section 87 of the said Act;",

**(c)   by the substitution of the following paragraph for paragraph (x) (inserted by the Act of 1986):

"(x)   newspapers and periodicals, normally published at least fortnightly, the contents of each issue of which consist, wholly or mainly, as regards the quantity of printed matter contained in them, of information on the principal current events and topics of general public interest;",

and

(d)   by the insertion in paragraph (xiiih) (inserted by the Finance Act, 1987) after "interest" of ",not being services of the kind specified in paragraph (viiia) of the First Schedule".

(With effect from 24 May 1990 except * from 1 March 1990 and ** from 1 July 1990)

Finance Act 1991

87.   (1)   The Sixth Schedule (inserted by the Act of 1985) to The Principal Act is hereby amended-

        *(a)   by the deletion of paragraphs (ii), (iii), (iv), (v), (x) (inserted by the Act of 1986), (xi), (xig) (inserted by the Act of 1987) and (xii),

        *(b)   in paragraph (xiib), (inserted by the Act of 1986) by the substitution of "paragraph (ii) of the Third Schedule" for "paragraph (iii)",

        **(c)   by the insertion of the following paragraph after paragraph (xiic) (inserted by the Act of 1986):

           "(xiid) services supplied in the course of their profession by jockeys;",

        ***(d)   by the insertion of the following paragraph after paragraph (xiiih) (inserted by the Act of 1987):

           "(xiiij) services supplied in the course of their profession by veterinary surgeons;",

and

        (e)   in paragraph (xiv), by the deletion of "and" in subparagraph (d) and by the deletion of subparagraph (e).

    (2)   The Sixth Schedule (inserted by the Act of 1985) to The Principal Act is hereby amended by the substitution of the following paragraph for paragraph (xiib) (inserted by the Act of 1986):

        "(xiib) (a) services consisting of work on immovable goods, other than services specified in-

           (i)   subparagraph (b) or paragraph (xiv), or

           (ii)   paragraph (ii) of the Third Schedule, or

        (b)   services consisting of the routine cleaning of immovable goods;".

(With effect from 29 May 1991 except * from 1 March 1991 **from 1 July 1991 and *** from 1 January 1992)

Finance Act 1992

197. *(1)   The Sixth Schedule (inserted by the Act of 1985) to The Principal
Act is hereby amended in paragraph i -

(a)   by the insertion in subparagraph (b) after "not
including" of "gas of a kind specified in subparagraph
(bi),", and

(b)   by the insertion of the following subparagraph after
subparagraph (b):

"(bi)   motor vehicle gas within the meaning of section
42(1) of the Finance Act, 1976,".

(2)   The Principal Act is hereby further amended by the substitution
of the following Schedule for the Sixth Schedule:

"SIXTH SCHEDULE

Goods and Services Chargeable at the Rate Specified in Section 11(1)(d)

(i)   (a)   Coal, peat and other solid substances held out for
sale solely as fuel,

(b)   electricity:
Provided that this subparagraph shall not apply
to the distribution of any electricity where such
distribution is wholly or mainly in connection
with the distribution of communications signals,

(c)   gas of a kind used for domestic or industrial heating
or lighting, whether in gaseous or liquid form, but
not including gas of a kind specified in paragraph
(i) of the Seventh Schedule, gas of a kind normally
used for welding and cutting metals or gas sold as
lighter fuel,

(d)   hydrocarbon oil of a kind used for domestic
or industrial heating, excluding gas oil (within
the meaning of the Hydrocarbon (Heavy) Oil
Regulations, 1989 (ST No. 121 of 1989)), other than
gas oil which has been duly marked in accordance
with Regulation 6(2) of the said Regulations;

(ii)   the provision of food and drink of a kind specified in
paragraph (xii) of the Second Schedule in a form suitable
for human consumption without further preparation-

(a)   by means of a vending machine,

(b)   in the course of operating a hotel, restaurant, cafe,
refreshment house, canteen, establishment licensed
for the sale for consumption on the premises of

             intoxicating liquor, catering business or similar business, or

    (c)   in the course of operating any other business in connection with the carrying on of which facilities are provided for the consumption of the food or drink supplied;

(iii)   the supply, in the course of the provision of a meal, of goods of a kind specified in subparagraph (c), (d) or (e) of paragraph (xii) of the Second Schedule, and fruit juices other than fruit juices chargeable with a duty of excise-

    (a)   in the course of operating a hotel, restaurant, cafe, refreshment house, canteen, establishment licensed for the sale for consumption on the premises of intoxicating liquor, catering business or similar business, or

    (b)   in the course of operating any other business in connection with the carrying on of which facilities are provided for the consumption of the food or drink supplied;

(iv)   the supply of food and drink (other than beverages specified in subparagraph (a) or (b) of paragraph (xii) of the Second Schedule) which is, or includes, food and drink which-

    (a)   has been heated for the purpose of enabling it to be consumed at a temperature above the ambient air temperature, or

    (b)   has been retained heated after cooking for the purpose of enabling it to be consumed at a temperature above the ambient air temperature, or

    (c)   is supplied, while still warm after cooking, for the purpose of enabling it to be consumed at a temperature above the ambient air temperature,

and is above the ambient air temperature at the time of supply;

(v)   promotion of and admissions to cinematographic performances;

(vi)   promotion of and admissions to live theatrical or musical performances, excluding-

    (a)   dances, and

    (b)   performances specified in paragraph (viii) of the First Schedule;

(vii)   entertainment services, other than dances and circuses, supplied in fairgrounds by travelling showmen where, in any particular case, the total period spent in any one locality in relation to a series of successive performances does not exceed 19 consecutive days and an interval of at least one month elapses before the next performance in the same locality;

(viii)   services consisting of the acceptance for disposal of waste material;

(ix)   admissions to exhibitions, of the kind normally held in museums and art galleries, of objects of historical, cultural, artistic or scientific interest, not being services of the kind specified in paragraph (viiia) of the First Schedule;

(x)   services supplied in the course of their profession by veterinary surgeons;

(xi)   agricultural services consisting of-

    (a)   field work, reaping, mowing, threshing, baling, harvesting, sowing and planting,

    (b)   disinfecting and ensilage of agricultural products,

    (c)   destruction of weeds and pests and dusting and spraying of crops and land,

    (d)   lopping, tree felling and similar forestry services.".

**(3)   The Sixth Schedule to The Principal Act (as amended by this Act) is hereby further amended-

    (a)   by the insertion of the following paragraph after paragraph (vii):

    "(viia) the provision by a person other than a non-profit making organisation of facilities for taking part in sporting activities;",

and

    (b)   in paragraph (xi) by the insertion after subparagraph (a) of the following subparagraph:

    "(ai)   stock-minding, stock-rearing, farm relief services and farm advisory services (not being services of the kind specified in paragraph (xxii) of the Seventh Schedule),".

(With effect from 28 May 1992except * from 1 March 1992 and ** from 1 July 1992)

Finance Act 1993

97.   (1)   The Sixth Schedule (inserted by the Act of 1992) to the Principal
              Act is hereby amended-

       (a)   by the substitution in subparagraph (c) of paragraph (i)
              of "motor vehicle gas within the meaning of section 42(1)
              of the Finance Act, 1970 for "gas of a kind specified in
              paragraph (i) of the Seventh Schedule",

       (b)   by the substitution in paragraph (xi) of the following
              subparagraph for subparagraph (d):

              "(d) lopping, tree felling and similar forestry
                    services;",

       (c)   by the insertion of the following paragraphs after
              paragraph (xi):

              "(xii) newspapers and periodicals, normally published
                      at least fortnightly, the contents of each issue of
                      which consist, wholly or mainly, as regards the
                      quantity of printed matter contained in them, of
                      information on the principal current events and
                      topics of general public interest;

              (xiii) (a) letting of immovable goods (other than in the
                          course of the provision of facilities of the kind
                          specified in paragraph (viia))-

                          (I)   by a hotel or guesthouse, or by a
                                 similar establishment which provides
                                 accommodation for visitors or
                                 travellers,

                          (II)   in a house, apartment or other similar
                                 establishment which is advertised
                                 or held out as being holiday
                                 accommodation or accommodation
                                 for visitors or travellers, or

                          (III) in a caravan park, camping site or
                                 other similar establishment,

                          or

                      (b) the provision of accommodation which
                          is advertised or held out as holiday
                          accommodation;

              (xiv)   tour guide services;

(xv)   the hiring (in this paragraph referred to as 'the current hiring') to a person of-

  (a) a vehicle designed and constructed, or adapted, for the conveyance of persons by road,

  (b) a ship, boat or other vessel designed and constructed for the conveyance of passengers and not exceeding 15 tonnes gross,

  (c) a sports or pleasure boat of any description, or

  (d) a caravan, mobile home, tent or trailer tent,

  under an agreement, other than an agreement of the kind referred to in section 3(1)(b), for any term or part of a term which, when added to the term of any such hiring (whether of the same goods or of other goods of the same kind) to the same person during the period of 12 months ending on the date of the commencement of the current hiring, does not exceed 5 weeks;

(xvi) every work of art being-

  (a) a painting, drawing or pastel, or any combination thereof, executed entirely by hand, excluding hand-decorated manufactured articles and plans and drawings for architectural, engineering, industrial, commercial, topographical or similar purposes,

  (b) an original lithograph, engraving, or print, or any combination thereof, produced directly from lithographic stones, plates or other engraved surfaces, which are executed entirely by hand,

  (c) an original sculpture or statuary, excluding mass-produced reproductions and works or craftsmanship of a commercial character, or

  (d) subject to and in accordance with regulations, an article of furniture, silver, glass or porcelain, whether hand-decorated or not, specified in the said regulations, where it is shown to the satisfaction of the Revenue Commissioners to be more than 100 years old, other than goods specified in subparagraph (a), (b) or (c);

(xvii) literary manuscripts certified by the Director of the National Library as being of major national importance and of either cultural or artistic importance;

(xviii) services consisting of-

    (a) the repair or maintenance of movable goods, or

    (b) the alteration of second-hand movable goods, other than such services specified in paragraph (v), (va) or (xvi) of the Second Schedule, but excluding the provision in the course of any such repair, maintenance or alteration service of-

        (I)   accessories, attachments or batteries, or

        (II)   tyres, tyre cases, interchangeable tyre treads, inner tubes and tyre flaps, for wheels of all kinds;

(xix) services consisting of the care of the human body, excluding such services specified in the First Schedule, but including services supplied in the course of a health studio business or similar business;

(xx) services supplied in the course of their profession by jockeys;

(xxi) the supply to a person of photographic prints (other than goods produced by means of a photocopying process), slides or negatives, which have been produced from goods provided by that person;

(xxii) goods being-

    (a) photographic prints (other than goods produced by means of a photocopying process), mounted or unmounted, but unframed,

    (b) slides and negatives, and

    (c) cinematographic and video film,

which record particular persons, objects or events, supplied under an agreement to photograph those persons, objects or events;

(xxiii) the supply by a photographer of-

    (a) negatives which have been produced from film exposed for the purpose of his business, and

(b) film which has been exposed for the purposes of his business;

(xxiv) photographic prints produced by means of a vending machine which incorporates a camera and developing and printing equipment;

(xxv) services consisting of-

(a) the editing of photographic, cinematographic and video film, and

(b) microfilming;

(xxvi) agency services in regard to a supply specified in paragraph (xxi);

(xxvii) instruction in the driving of mechanically propelled road vehicles, not being education, training or retraining of the kinds specified in paragraph (ii) of the First Schedule;

(xxviii) immovable goods;

(xxix) services consisting of the development of immovable goods and work on immovable goods including the installation of fixtures, where the value of movable goods (if any) provided in pursuance of an agreement in relation to such services does not exceed two-thirds of the total amount on which tax is chargeable in respect of the agreement;

(xxx) services consisting of the routine cleaning of immovable goods;

(xxxi) (a) cakes, crackers and wafers and other flour-based bakery products other than those included in paragraph (xii) of the Second Schedule;

(b) biscuits, other than biscuits wholly or partly covered or decorated with chocolate or some other similar product similar in taste and appearance.".

*(2) The Sixth Schedule to The Principal Act is hereby further amended by the substitution of the following paragraphs for paragraph (xxxi) (inserted by this Act):

"(xxxi) food of a kind used for human consumption, other than that included in paragraph (xii) of the Second Schedule, being flour or egg based bakery products including cakes, crackers, wafers and biscuits, but excluding-

(a) wafers and biscuits wholly or partly covered or decorated with chocolate or some other product similar in taste and appearance,

(b) food of a kind specified in subparagraph (c) or (e) (II) of paragraph (xii) of the Second Schedule, and

(c) chocolates, sweets and similar confectionery;

(xxxii) concrete ready to pour;

(xxxiii) blocks, of concrete, of a kind which comply with the specification contained in the Standard Specification (Concrete Building Blocks, Part 1, Normal Density Blocks) Declaration, 1987 (Irish Standard 20: Part 1: 1987).".

(With effect from 1 March 1993 except * from 1 July 1993)

Finance Act 1994

101. The Sixth Schedule (inserted by the Act of 1992) to the Principal Act is hereby amended-

*(a) by the substitution of the following paragraph for paragraph (vii):

"(vii) amusement services of the kind normally supplied in fairgrounds or amusement parks:

Provided that this paragraph shall not apply to-

(I) services consisting of dances,

(II) services consisting of circuses,

(III) services consisting of gaming, as defined in section 2 of the Gaming and Lotteries Act, 1956 (including services provided by means of a gaming machine of the kind referred to in section 43 of the Finance Act, 1975), or

(IV) services provided by means of an amusement machine of the kind referred to in section 120 of the Finance Act, 1992;",

*(b) in paragraph (x) by the insertion after "services" of "of a kind", and

(c) in paragraph (xi) by the substitution in subparagraph (ai) of "(other than farm accountancy or farm management services)" for "(not being services of the kind specified in paragraph (xxii) of the Seventh Schedule)".

(With effect from 23 May 1994 except * from 1 July 1994)

Finance Act 1995

140. The Sixth Schedule (inserted by the Act of 1992) to the Principal Act is hereby amended-

*(a)   by the insertion of the following paragraphs after paragraph (viia) (inserted by the Act of 1992)-

"(viib) the provision by a member-owned golf club of facilities for taking part in golf to any person, other than an individual whose membership subscription to that club at the time the facilities are used by that individual entitles that individual to use such facilities without further charge on at least 200 days (including the day on which such facilities are used by that individual) in a continuous period of twelve months, where the total consideration received by that club for the provisions of such facilities has exceeded or is likely to exceed £20,000 in any continuous period of twelve months and, for the purpose of this paragraph, the provision of facilities for taking part in golf shall not include the provision of facilities for taking part in pitch and putt;

(viic) the provision by a non-profit making organisation, other than an organisation referred to in paragraph (viib), of facilities for taking part in golf to any person where the total consideration received by that organisation for the provision of such facilities has exceeded or is likely to exceed £20,000 in any continuous period of twelve months and, for the purposes of this paragraph, the provision of facilities for taking part in golf shall not include the provision of facilities for taking part in pitch and putt;",

(b)   by the substitution of the following paragraph for paragraph xvi-

"(xvi) a work of art being-

(a)   a painting, drawing or pastel, or any combination thereof, executed entirely by hand, excluding hand-decorated manufactured articles and plans and drawings for architectural, engineering, industrial, commercial, topographical or similar purposes,

(b)   an original lithograph, engraving, or print, or any combination thereof, produced directly from lithographic stones, plates or other engraved surfaces, which are executed entirely by hand, or

(c)   an original sculpture or statuary, excluding mass-produced reproductions and works or craftsmanship of a commercial character, but excluding the supply of such work of art by a taxable dealer in accordance with the provisions of subsection (3) or (8) of section 10A or by an auctioneer within the meaning of section 10B and in accordance with the provisions of subsection (3) of section 10B;",

(c)   by the insertion of the following paragraph after paragraph (xvi)-

(xvia) antiques being, subject to and in accordance with regulations, articles of furniture, silver, glass or porcelain, whether hand-decorated or not, specified in the said regulations, which are shown to the satisfaction of the Revenue Commissioners to be more than 100 years old, other than goods specified in paragraph (xvi), but excluding the supply of such antiques by a taxable dealer in accordance with the provisions of subsection (3) or (8) of section 10A or by an auctioneer within the meaning of section 10B and in accordance with the provisions of subsection (3) of section 10B;",

(d)   in subparagraph (b) of paragraph (xviii) by the substitution of "used" for "second-hand",

(e)   by the insertion of the following paragraph after paragraph (xx)-

"(xxa) greyhound feeding stuff, which is packaged, advertised or held out for sale solely as greyhound feeding stuff, and which is supplied in units of not less than 10 kilograms;",

(f)   in paragraph (xxxii) by the insertion after "pour" of "but excluding the supply of such goods by a taxable dealer in accordance with the provisions of subsection (3) or (8) of section 10A or by an auctioneer within the meaning of section 10B and in accordance with the provisions of subsection (3) of section 1013",

and

(g)   in paragraph (xxxiii) by the insertion after "(Irish Standard 20: Part I: 1987)" of "but excluding the supply of such goods by a taxable dealer in accordance with the provisions of subsection (3) or (8) of section 10A or by an auctioneer within the meaning of section 10B and in accordance with the provisions of subsection (3) of section 1013".

(With effect from 1 July 1995 except * from 1 January 1996)

Finance Act 1996

99.   The Sixth Schedule (inserted by the Act of 1992) to the Principal Act is hereby amended in subparagraph (b) of paragraph (xviii) by the insertion after "other than" of "contract work or".

(With effect from 1 January 1996)

Finance Act 1997

113. The Sixth Schedule (inserted by the Act of 1992) to the Principal Act is hereby amended by the addition of the following paragraph after paragraph (xi):

"(xia) nursery or garden centre stock consisting of live plants, live trees, live shrubs, bulbs, roots and the like, not being of a type specified in paragraph (xv) of the Second Schedule, and cut flowers and ornamental foliage not being artificial or dried flowers or foliage;".

(With effect from 1 September 1997)

Finance Act 1998

117. The Sixth Schedule (inserted by the Act of 1992) to the Principal Act is hereby amended-

    (a)   by the insertion of the following paragraphs after paragraph (xia) (inserted by the Act of 1997):

        *"(xib)   animal insemination services;

        *(xic)   livestock semen;

        (xid)   live poultry and live ostriches;",

and

    (b)   by the substitution of the following paragraph for paragraph (xii):

        "(xii)   printed matter consisting of:

        (a)   newspapers and periodicals;

        (b)   brochures, leaflets and programmes;

        (c)   catalogues, including directories, and similar printed matter;

        (d)   maps, hydrographic and similar charts;

        (e)   printed music other than in book or booklet form;

        but excluding:

        (i)   other printed matter wholly or substantially devoted to advertising,

        (ii)   the goods specified in subparagraphs (b) to (e) of paragraph (xva) of the Second Schedule, and

        (iii)   any other printed matter;".

(With effect from 1 May 1998 except * from 1 July 1998)

Finance Act 2001

240. (1)   (a)   Subject to subsection (2), in each provision specified in column (1) of Schedule 5 for the words or amount set out in column (2) of that Schedule at that entry there shall be substituted the words or amount set out at the corresponding entry in column (3) of that Schedule.

        (b)   Where words are or an amount is mentioned more than once in a provision specified in column (1) of Schedule 5, then the substitution provided for by paragraph (a) shall apply as respects those words or that amount to each mention of those words or that amount in that provision.

SCHEDULE 5

PART 4

Value-Added Tax and related matters

Enactment amended (1)	Amount or words to be replaced (2)	Amount or words to be inserted (3)
Value-Added Tax Act, 1972 (No. 22 of 1972) (as amended): para (viib) of the Sixth Schedule para (viic) of the Sixth Schedule	£20,000 £20,000	25,500 25,500

(With effect from 1 January 2002)

Finance Act 2005

113. The Sixth Schedule (inserted by the Finance Act 1992) to the Principal Act is amended-

    (a)   in paragraph (iv)-

        (i)   by inserting "(other than bread as defined in subparagraph (d), of paragraph (xii) of the Second Schedule)" after "the supply of food",

        (ii)   by substituting in subparagraph (a) "heated, enabling" for "heated for the purpose of enabling",

        (iii)   by substituting in subparagraph (b) "heated after cooking, enabling" for "heated after cooking for the purpose of enabling",

        (iv)   by deleting in subparagraph (c) "for the purpose of", and

        (v)   by substituting "at the time it is provided to the customer" for "at the time of supply",

    and

    *(b)   with effect from 1 July 2005, by substituting the following for paragraph (xiii):

    "(xiii) subject to and in accordance with regulations, if any-

        (a)   the letting of immovable goods (other than in the course of the provision of facilities of the kind specified in paragraph (viia))-

            (I)   in the hotel or guesthouse sector, or

            (II)   being a letting of all or part of a house, apartment or other similar establishment when that letting is provided in the short-term guest sector or holiday sector, or

            (III)   in a caravan park, camping site or other similar establishment,

        or

        (b)   the provision of holiday accommodation;".

(With effect from 25 March 2005 except * with effect from 1 July 2005)

Finance Act 2006

101. With effect from 1 May 2006, the Sixth Schedule to the Principal Act is amended in paragraphs (viib) and (viic) by substituting "€27,500" for "€25,500".

(With effect from 1 May 2006)

Finance Act 2007

96.   The Sixth Schedule to the Principal Act is amended —

   (a)   with effect from 1 March 2007 by substituting "€35,000" for "€27,500", in paragraphs (viib) and (viic), and

   *(b)   with effect from 1 July 2007, by inserting the following after paragraph (xv):

   "(xva) children's car safety seats,".

(With effect from 1 March 2007 except * with effect from 1 May 2007 in accordance with Revenue ebrief 22/2007)

Finance Act 2008

107.   The Sixth Schedule to the Principal Act is amended —

   *(a)   with effect from 1 May 2008 by substituting "€37,500" for "€35,000", in paragraphs (viib) and (viic),

   **(b)   with effect from 1 March 2008 by inserting the following after paragraph (xid):

   "(xie) miscanthus rhizomes, seeds, bulbs, roots and similar goods used for the agricultural production of bio-fuel;",

   and

   (c)   by inserting the following after paragraph (xix):

   "(xixa) non-oral contraceptive products;".

141.   The enactments specified in Schedule 8 —

   (a)   are amended to the extent and in the manner specified in paragraphs 1 to 6 of that Schedule, and

   (b)   apply and come into operation in accordance with paragraph 7 of that Schedule.

Schedule 8
Miscellaneous Technical Amendments in Relation to Tax

3.   The Value-Added Tax Act 1972 is amended in accordance with the following provisions:

   (k)   in paragraph (i)(d) of the Sixth Schedule by substituting "(within the meaning of the Mineral Oil Tax Regulations 2001 (S.I. No. 442 of 2001))" for "(within the meaning of the Hydrocarbon (Heavy) Oil Regulations, 1989 (S.I. No. 121 of 1989))".

(With effect from 13 March 2008 except * with effect from 1 May 2008 and ** with effect from 1 March 2008)

SEVENTH SCHEDULE

GOODS CHARGEABLE AT THE RATE SPECIFIED
IN SECTION 11(1)(aaa)

Finance Act 1984

95.   The Principal Act is hereby amended by the insertion after the Sixth Schedule (inserted by the Act of 1983) of the following Schedule:

"SEVENTH SCHEDULE

Goods Chargeable at the Rate Specified in Section 11(1)(aaa)

(i)   Articles of personal clothing and textile handkerchiefs, excluding-

    (a)   articles of clothing made wholly or partly of fur skin, other than garments merely trimmed with fur skin unless the trimming has an area greater than one-fifth of the area of the outside material, and

    (b)   articles of personal clothing of a kind specified in paragraphs (xvii) and (xviii) of the Second Schedule;

(ii)   (a)   fabrics, yarn, thread and leather, of a kind normally used in the manufacture of clothing, including elastics, tapes and padding materials in the form supplied for the manufacture of clothing, and

    (b)   yarn of a kind normally used in the manufacture of clothing fabrics.".

(With effect from 1 May 1984)

Finance Act 1985

51.   The Principal Act is hereby amended by-

(a)   ...,

(b)   the deletion of the Seventh Schedule (inserted by the Act of 1984), and

(c)   ...:

(With effect from 1 March 1985)

Finance Act 1992

198. The Principal Act is hereby amended by the insertion after the Sixth Schedule (inserted by this Act) of the following Schedule:

"SEVENTH SCHEDULE

Goods and Services Chargeable at the Rate Specified in Section 11(1)(E)

(i)   Motor vehicle gas within the meaning of section 42(1) of the Finance Act, 1976;

(ii)   every work of art being-

     (a)   a painting, drawing or pastel, or any combination thereof, executed entirely by hand, excluding hand-decorated manufactured articles and plans and drawings for architectural, engineering, industrial, commercial, topographical or similar purposes,

     (b)   an original lithograph, engraving, or print, or any combination thereof, produced directly from lithographic stones, plates or other engraved surfaces, which are executed entirely by hand,

     (c)   an original sculpture or statuary, excluding mass-produced reproductions and works or craftsmanship of a commercial character, or

     (d)   subject to and in accordance with regulations, an article of furniture, silver, glass or porcelain, whether hand-decorated or not, specified in the said regulations, where it is shown to the satisfaction of the Revenue Commissioners to be more than 100 years old, other than goods specified in subparagraph (a), (b) or (c);

(iii)   literary manuscripts certified by the Director of the National Library as being of major national importance and of either cultural or artistic importance;

(iv)   telecommunications services (including the supply of goods and services incidental thereto) supplied by Bord Telecom Éireann or by any person licensed in accordance with subsection (1) of section 111 of the Postal and Telecommunications Services Act, 1983, other than services of the kind specified in paragraph (d), (e) or (f) of subsection (3) of section 87 of the said Act;

(v)   articles of personal clothing and textile handkerchiefs, excluding-

     (a)   articles of clothing made wholly or partly of fur skin, other than garments merely trimmed with fur skin unless the trimming has an area greater than one-fifth of the area of the outside material, and

(b)   articles of personal clothing of a kind specified in paragraphs (xvii) and (xviii) of the Second Schedule;

(vi)   (a)   fabrics, yarn, thread and leather, of a kind normally used in the manufacture of clothing, including elastics, tapes and padding materials in the form supplied for the manufacture of clothing, and

(b)   yarn of a kind normally used in the manufacture of clothing fabrics;

(vii)   articles of personal footwear, other than articles of personal footwear of a kind specified in paragraph (xix) of the Second Schedule;

(viii)   sole and upper leather of a kind normally used for the manufacture and repair of footwear, and also soles, heels and insoles of any material;

(ix)   corrective spectacles and contact lenses, including parts thereof;

(x)   services consisting of-

(a)   the repair or maintenance of movable goods, or

(b)   the alteration of second-hand movable goods, other than such services specified in paragraph (v), (va) or (xvi) of the Second Schedule, but excluding the provision in the course of any such repair, maintenance or alteration service of-

(I)   accessories, attachments or batteries, or

(II)   tyres, tyre cases, interchangeable tyre treads, inner tubes and tyre flaps, for wheels of all kinds;

(xi)   (a)   services consisting of work on immovable goods, other than services specified in-

(i)   paragraph (xi) of the Sixth Schedule or subparagraph (b),

(ii)   paragraph (ii) of the Third Schedule,

or

(b)   services consisting of the routine cleaning of immovable goods;

(xii)   services consisting of the care of the human body, excluding such services specified in the First Schedule, but including services supplied in the course of a health studio business or similar business;

(xiii)   services supplied in the course of their profession by jockeys;

(xiv)   the supply to a person of photographic prints (other than goods produced by means of a photocopying process), slides or negatives, which have been produced from goods provided by that person;

(xv)   goods being-

       (a)   photographic prints (other than goods produced by means of a photocopying process), mounted or unmounted, but unframed,

       (b)   slides and negatives, and

       (c)   cinematographic and video film,

which record particular persons, objects or events, supplied under an agreement to photograph those persons, objects or events;

(xvi)   the supply by a photographer of-

       (a)   negatives which have been produced from film exposed for the purpose of his business, and

       (b)   film which has been exposed for the purposes of his business;

(xvii)   photographic prints produced by means of a vending machine which incorporates a camera and developing and printing equipment;

(xviii)   services consisting of-

       (a)   the editing of photographic, cinematographic and video film, and

       (b)   microfilming;

(xix)   agency services in regard to a supply specified in paragraph (xiv);

(xx)   instruction in the driving of mechanically propelled road vehicles, not being education, training or retraining of the kinds specified in paragraph (ii) of the First Schedule;

(xxi)   services of an auctioneer, solicitor, estate agent or other agent, directly related to the supply of immovable goods used for the purposes of an Annex A activity;

(xxii)   farm accountancy or farm management services.".

(With effect from 28 May 1992)

Finance Act 1993

98.   The Seventh Schedule (inserted by the Act of 1992) to the Principal Act is hereby repealed.

(With effect from 1 March 1993)

EIGHTH SCHEDULE
WORKS OF ART, COLLECTORS' ITEMS AND ANTIQUES
CHARGEABLE AT THE RATE SPECIFIED IN SECTION 11(1)(d)
IN THE CIRCUMSTANCES SPECIFIED IN SECTION 11(1AA)

Finance Act 1995

141.   The Principal Act is hereby amended by the addition of the following Schedule:

"EIGHTH SCHEDULE

Works of Art, Collectors' Items and Antiques
Chargeable at the Rate Specified in Section 11(1)(d)
in the Circumstances Specified in Section 11(1AA)

(i)   Works of art:

Every work of art being-

(a)   a picture (other than a painting, drawing or pastel specified in paragraph (xvi) of the Sixth Schedule), collage or similar decorative plaque, executed entirely by hand by an artist, other than-

(I)   plans and drawings for architectural, engineering, industrial, commercial, topographical or similar purposes,

(II)   hand-decorated manufactured articles, and

(III)   theatrical scenery, studio back cloths or the like of painted canvas,

(b)   a sculpture cast the production of which is limited to eight copies and supervised by the artist or by the artist's successors in title provided that, in the case of a statuary cast produced before the 1st day of January, 1989, the limit of eight copies may be exceeded where so determined by the Revenue Commissioners,

(c)   a tapestry or wall textile made by hand from original designs provided by an artist, provided that there are not more than eight copies of each,

(d)   individual pieces of ceramics executed entirely by an artist and signed by the artist,

(e)   enamels on copper, executed entirely by hand, limited to eight numbered copies bearing the signature of the artist or the studio, excluding articles of jewellery, goldsmiths' wares and silversmiths' wares, or

(f)   a photograph taken by an artist, printed by the artist or under the artist's supervision, signed and numbered and limited to 30 copies, all sizes and mounts included, other than photographs specified in paragraph (xxii)(a) of the Sixth Schedule;

(ii)   Collectors' items:

Every collectors' item being one or more-

      (a)   postage or revenue stamps, postmarks, first-day covers, pre-stamped stationery and the like, franked, or if unfranked not being of legal tender and not being intended for use as legal tender, or

      (b)   collections and collectors' pieces of zoological, botanical, mineralogical, anatomical, historical, archaeological, palaeontological, ethnographic or numismatic interest;

(iii)   Antiques:

Every antique being, subject to and in accordance with regulations, one or more goods which are shown to the satisfaction of the Revenue Commissioners to be more than 100 years old, other than goods specified in paragraph (xvi) (xvia) or (xxii)(a) of the Sixth Schedule or in paragraph (i) or (ii) of this Schedule.".

(With effect from 1 July 1995)

COUNCIL DIRECTIVE
2006/112/EC

COUNCIL DIRECTIVE 2006/112/EC

of 28 November 2006

on the common system of value added tax

Official Journal L347, 11/12/2006 p. 01-118

> This Directive is substantially amended by Council Directive 2008/8/EC of 12 February 2008. The amendments are either effective from 1 January 2009, 1 January 2010, 1 January 2011, 1 January 2013 or 1 January 2015. The amendments which are effective from 1 January 2009 have been included within the text of the Directive this year and the 1 January 2010 amendments are detailed in the footnotes to each section. The Articles which will be amended in later years have been highlighted with *.

THE COUNCIL OF THE EUROPEAN UNION,

Having regard to the Treaty establishing the European Community, and in particular Article 93 thereof,

Having regard to the proposal from the Commission,

Having regard to the Opinion of the European Parliament,

Having regard to the Opinion of the European Economic and Social Committee,

Whereas:

(1)   Council Directive 77/388/EEC of 17 May 1977 on the harmonisation of the laws of the Member States relating to turnover taxes — Common system of value added tax: uniform basis of assessment has been significantly amended on several occasions. Now that new amendments are being made to the said Directive, it is desirable, for reasons of clarity and rationalisation that the Directive should be recast.

(2)   The recast text should incorporate all those provisions of Council Directive 67/227/EEC of 11 April 1967 on the harmonisation of legislation of Member States concerning turnover taxes which are still applicable. That Directive should therefore be repealed.

(3)   To ensure that the provisions are presented in a clear and rational manner, consistent with the principle of better regulation, it is appropriate to recast the structure and the wording of the Directive although this will not, in principle, bring about material changes in the existing legislation. A small number of substantive amendments are however inherent to the recasting exercise and should nevertheless be made. Where such changes are made, these are listed exhaustively in the provisions governing transposition and entry into force.

(4)   The attainment of the objective of establishing an internal market presupposes the application in Member States of legislation on turnover taxes that does not distort conditions of competition or hinder the free movement of goods and services. It is therefore necessary to achieve such harmonisation of legislation on turnover taxes by means of a system of value added tax (VAT), such as will eliminate, as far as

possible, factors which may distort conditions of competition, whether at national or Community level.

(5)   A VAT system achieves the highest degree of simplicity and of neutrality when the tax is levied in as general a manner as possible and when its scope covers all stages of production and distribution, as well as the supply of services. It is therefore in the interests of the internal market and of Member States to adopt a common system which also applies to the retail trade.

(6)   It is necessary to proceed by stages, since the harmonisation of turnover taxes leads in Member States to alterations in tax structure and appreciable consequences in the budgetary, economic and social fields.

(7)   The common system of VAT should, even if rates and exemptions are not fully harmonised, result in neutrality in competition, such that within the territory of each Member State similar goods and services bear the same tax burden, whatever the length of the production and distribution chain.

(8)   Pursuant to Council Decision 2000/597/EC, Euratom, of 29 September 2000 on the system of the European Communities' own resources, the budget of the European Communities is to be financed, without prejudice to other revenue, wholly from the Communities' own resources. Those resources are to include those accruing from VAT and obtained through the application of a uniform rate of tax to bases of assessment determined in a uniform manner and in accordance with Community rules.

(9)   It is vital to provide for a transitional period to allow national laws in specified fields to be gradually adapted.

(10)   During this transitional period, intra-Community transactions carried out by taxable persons other than exempt taxable persons should be taxed in the Member State of destination, in accordance with the rates and conditions set by that Member State.

(11)   It is also appropriate that, during that transitional period, intra-Community acquisitions of a certain value, made by exempt persons or by non-taxable legal persons, certain intra-Community distance selling and the supply of new means of transport to individuals or to exempt or non-taxable bodies should also be taxed in the Member State of destination, in accordance with the rates and conditions set by that Member State, in so far as such transactions would, in the absence of special provisions, be likely to cause significant distortion of competition between Member States.

(12)   For reasons connected with their geographic, economic and social situation, certain territories should be excluded from the scope of this Directive.

(13)   In order to enhance the non-discriminatory nature of the tax, the term 'taxable person' should be defined in such a way that the Member States may use it to cover persons who occasionally carry out certain transactions.

(14) The term 'taxable transaction' may lead to difficulties, in particular as regards transactions treated as taxable transactions. Those concepts should therefore be clarified.

(15) With a view to facilitating intra-Community trade in work on movable tangible property, it is appropriate to establish the tax arrangements applicable to such transactions when they are carried out for a customer who is identified for VAT purposes in a Member State other than that in which the transaction is physically carried out.

(16) A transport operation within the territory of a Member State should be treated as the intra-Community transport of goods where it is directly linked to a transport operation carried out between Member States, in order to simplify not only the principles and arrangements for taxing those domestic transport services but also the rules applicable to ancillary services and to services supplied by intermediaries who take part in the supply of the various services.

(17) Determination of the place where taxable transactions are carried out may engender conflicts concerning jurisdiction as between Member States, in particular as regards the supply of goods for assembly or the supply of services. Although the place where a supply of services is carried out should in principle be fixed as the place where the supplier has established his place of business, it should be defined as being in the Member State of the customer, in particular in the case of certain services supplied between taxable persons where the cost of the services is included in the price of the goods.

(18) It is necessary to clarify the definition of the place of taxation of certain transactions carried out on board ships, aircraft or trains in the course of passenger transport within the Community.

(19) Electricity and gas are treated as goods for VAT purposes. It is, however, particularly difficult to determine the place of supply. In order to avoid double taxation or non taxation and to attain a genuine internal market free of barriers linked to the VAT regime, the place of supply of gas through the natural gas distribution system, or of electricity, before the goods reach the final stage of consumption, should therefore be the place where the customer has established his business. The supply of electricity and gas at the final stage, that is to say, from traders and distributors to the final consumer, should be taxed at the place where the customer actually uses and consumes the goods.

(20) In the case of the hiring out of movable tangible property, application of the general rule that supplies of services are taxed in the Member State in which the supplier is established may lead to substantial distortion of competition if the lessor and the lessee are established in different Member States and the rates of taxation in those States differ. It is therefore necessary to establish that the place of supply of a service is the place where the customer has established his business or has a

fixed establishment for which the service has been supplied or, in the absence thereof, the place where he has his permanent address or usually resides.

(21) However, as regards the hiring out of means of transport, it is appropriate, for reasons of control, to apply strictly the general rule, and thus to regard the place where the supplier has established his business as the place of supply.

(22) All telecommunications services consumed within the Community should be taxed to prevent distortion of competition in that field. To that end, telecommunications services supplied to taxable persons established in the Community or to customers established in third countries should, in principle, be taxed at the place where the customer for the services is established. In order to ensure uniform taxation of telecommunications services which are supplied by taxable persons established in third territories or third countries to non-taxable persons established in the Community and which are effectively used and enjoyed in the Community, Member States should, however, provide for the place of supply to be within the Community.

(23) Also to prevent distortions of competition, radio and television broadcasting services and electronically supplied services provided from third territories or third countries to persons established in the Community, or from the Community to customers established in third territories or third countries, should be taxed at the place of establishment of the customer.

(24) The concepts of chargeable event and of the chargeability of VAT should be harmonised if the introduction of the common system of VAT and of any subsequent amendments thereto are to take effect at the same time in all Member States.

(25) The taxable amount should be harmonised so that the application of VAT to taxable transactions leads to comparable results in all the Member States.

(26) To prevent loss of tax revenues through the use of connected parties to derive tax benefits, it should, in specific limited circumstances, be possible for Member States to intervene as regards the taxable amount of supplies of goods or services and intra-Community acquisitions of goods.

(27) In order to combat tax evasion or avoidance, it should be possible for Member States to include within the taxable amount of a transaction which involves the working of investment gold provided by a customer, the value of that investment gold where, by virtue of being worked, the gold loses its status of investment gold. When they apply these measures, Member States should be allowed a certain degree of discretion.

(28) If distortions are to be avoided, the abolition of fiscal controls at frontiers entails, not only a uniform basis of assessment, but also

sufficient alignment as between Member States of a number of rates and rate levels.

(29) The standard rate of VAT in force in the various Member States, combined with the mechanism of the transitional system, ensures that this system functions to an acceptable degree. To prevent divergences in the standard rates of VAT applied by the Member States from leading to structural imbalances in the Community and distortions of competition in some sectors of activity, a minimum standard rate of 15% should be fixed, subject to review.

(30) In order to preserve neutrality of VAT, the rates applied by Member States should be such as to enable, as a general rule, deduction of the VAT applied at the preceding stage.

(31) During the transitional period, certain derogations concerning the number and the level of rates should be possible.

(32) To achieve a better understanding of the impact of reduced rates, it is necessary for the Commission to prepare an assessment report on the impact of reduced rates applied to locally supplied services, notably in terms of job creation, economic growth and the proper functioning of the internal market.

(33) In order to tackle the problem of unemployment, those Member States wishing to do so should be allowed to experiment with the operation and impact, in terms of job creation, of a reduction in the VAT rate applied to labour intensive services. That reduction is also likely to reduce the incentive for the businesses concerned to join or remain in the black economy.

(34) However, such a reduction in the VAT rate is not without risk for the smooth functioning of the internal market and for tax neutrality. Provision should therefore be made for an authorisation procedure to be introduced for a period that is fixed but sufficiently long, so that it is possible to assess the impact of the reduced rates applied to locally supplied services. In order to make sure that such a measure remains verifiable and limited, its scope should be closely defined.

(35) A common list of exemptions should be drawn up so that the Communities' own resources may be collected in a uniform manner in all the Member States.

(36) For the benefit both of the persons liable for payment of VAT and the competent administrative authorities, the methods of applying VAT to certain supplies and intra-Community acquisitions of products subject to excise duty should be aligned with the procedures and obligations concerning the duty to declare in the case of shipment of such products to another Member State laid down in Council Directive 92/12/EEC of 25 February 1992 on the general arrangements for products subject to excise duty and on the holding, movement and monitoring of such products.

(37)   The supply of gas through the natural gas distribution system, and of electricity is taxed at the place of the customer. In order to avoid double taxation, the importation of such products should therefore be exempted from VAT.

(38)   In respect of taxable operations in the domestic market linked to intra-Community trade in goods carried out during the transitional period by taxable persons not established within the territory of the Member State in which the intra-Community acquisition of goods takes place, including chain transactions, it is necessary to provide for simplification measures ensuring equal treatment in all the Member States. To that end, the provisions concerning the taxation system and the person liable for payment of the VAT due in respect of such operations should be harmonised. It is however, necessary to exclude in principle from such arrangements goods that are intended to be supplied at the retail stage.

(39)   The rules governing deductions should be harmonised to the extent that they affect the actual amounts collected. The deductible proportion should be calculated in a similar manner in all the Member States.

(40)   The scheme which allows the adjustment of deductions for capital goods over the lifetime of the asset, according to its actual use, should also be applicable to certain services with the nature of capital goods.

(41)   It is appropriate to specify the persons liable for payment of VAT, particularly in the case of services supplied by a person who is not established in the Member State in which the VAT is due.

(42)   Member States should be able, in specific cases, to designate the recipient of supplies of goods or services as the person liable for payment of VAT. This should assist Member States in simplifying the rules and countering tax evasion and avoidance in identified sectors and on certain types of transactions.

(43)   Member States should be entirely free to designate the person liable for payment of the VAT on importation.

(44)   Member States should be able to provide that someone other than the person liable for payment of VAT is to be held jointly and severally liable for its payment.

(45)   The obligations of taxable persons should be harmonised as far as possible so as to ensure the necessary safeguards for the collection of VAT in a uniform manner in all the Member States.

(46)   The use of electronic invoicing should allow tax authorities to carry out their monitoring activities. It is therefore appropriate, in order to ensure the internal market functions properly, to draw up a list, harmonised at Community level, of the particulars that must appear on invoices and to establish a number of common arrangements governing the use of electronic invoicing and the electronic storage of invoices, as well as for self-billing and the outsourcing of invoicing operations.

(47)   Subject to conditions which they lay down, Member States should allow certain statements and returns to be made by electronic means, and may require that electronic means be used.

(48)   The necessary pursuit of a reduction in the administrative and statistical formalities to be completed by businesses, particularly small and medium-sized enterprises, should be reconciled with the implementation of effective control measures and the need, on both economic and tax grounds, to maintain the quality of Community statistical instruments.

(49)   Member States should be allowed to continue to apply their special schemes for small enterprises, in accordance with common provisions, and with a view to closer harmonisation.

(50)   Member States should remain free to apply a special scheme involving flat rate rebates of input VAT to farmers not covered by the normal scheme. The basic principles of that special scheme should be established and a common method adopted, for the purposes of collecting own resources, for calculating the value added by such farmers.

(51)   It is appropriate to adopt a Community taxation system to be applied to second-hand goods, works of art, antiques and collectors' items, with a view to preventing double taxation and the distortion of competition as between taxable persons.

(52)   The application of the normal VAT rules to gold constitutes a major obstacle to its use for financial investment purposes and therefore justifies the application of a special tax scheme, with a view also to enhancing the international competitiveness of the Community gold market.

(53)   The supply of gold for investment purposes is inherently similar to other financial investments which are exempt from VAT. Consequently, exemption appears to be the most appropriate tax treatment for supplies of investment gold.

(54)   The definition of investment gold should cover gold coins the value of which primarily reflects the price of the gold contained. For reasons of transparency and legal certainty, a yearly list of coins covered by the investment gold scheme should be drawn up, providing security for the operators trading in such coins. That list should be without prejudice to the exemption of coins which are not included in the list but which meet the criteria laid down in this Directive.

(55)   In order to prevent tax evasion while at the same time alleviating the financing burden for the supply of gold of a degree of purity above a certain level, it is justifiable to allow Member States to designate the customer as the person liable for payment of VAT.

(56)   In order to facilitate compliance with fiscal obligations by operators providing electronically supplied services, who are neither established

nor required to be identified for VAT purposes within the Community, a special scheme should be established. Under that scheme it should be possible for any operator supplying such services by electronic means to non-taxable persons within the Community, if he is not otherwise identified for VAT purposes within the Community, to opt for identification in a single Member State.

(57) It is desirable for the provisions concerning radio and television broadcasting and certain electronically supplied services to be put into place on a temporary basis only and to be reviewed in the light of experience within a short period of time.

(58) It is necessary to promote the uniform application of the provisions of this Directive and to that end an advisory committee on value-added tax should be set up to enable the Member States and the Commission to cooperate closely.

(59) Member States should be able, within certain limits and subject to certain conditions, to introduce, or to continue to apply, special measures derogating from this Directive in order to simplify the levying of tax or to prevent certain forms of tax evasion or avoidance.

(60) In order to ensure that a Member State which has submitted a request for derogation is not left in doubt as to what action the Commission plans to take in response, time-limits should be laid down within which the Commission must present to the Council either a proposal for authorisation or a communication setting out its objections.

(61) It is essential to ensure uniform application of the VAT system. Implementing measures are appropriate to realise that aim.

(62) Those measures should, in particular, address the problem of double taxation of cross-border transactions which can occur as the result of divergences between Member States in the application of the rules governing the place where taxable transactions are carried out.

(63) Although the scope of the implementing measures would be limited, those measures would have a budgetary impact which for one or more Member States could be significant. Accordingly, the Council is justified in reserving to itself the right to exercise implementing powers.

(64) In view of their limited scope, the implementing measures should be adopted by the Council acting unanimously on a proposal from the Commission.

(65) Since, for those reasons, the objectives of this Directive cannot be sufficiently achieved by the Member States and can therefore be better achieved by at Community level, the Community may adopt measures, in accordance with the principle of subsidiarity as set out in Article 5 of the Treaty. In accordance with the principle of proportionality, as set out in that Article, this Directive does not go beyond what is necessary in order to achieve those objectives.

(66) The obligation to transpose this Directive into national law should be confined to those provisions which represent a substantive change as compared with the earlier Directives. The obligation to transpose into national law the provisions which are unchanged arises under the earlier Directives.

(67) This Directive should be without prejudice to the obligations of the Member States in relation to the time-limits for transposition into national law of the Directives listed in Annex XI, Part B,

HAS ADOPTED THIS DIRECTIVE:

TABLE OF CONTENTS

TITLE I
SUBJECT MATTER AND SCOPE
Article 1

1. This Directive establishes the common system of value added tax (VAT).

2. The principle of the common system of VAT entails the application to goods and services of a general tax on consumption exactly proportional to the price of the goods and services, however many transactions take place in the production and distribution process before the stage at which the tax is charged.

On each transaction, VAT, calculated on the price of the goods or services at the rate applicable to such goods or services, shall be chargeable after deduction of the amount of VAT borne directly by the various cost components.

The common system of VAT shall be applied up to and including the retail trade stage.

Article 2

s2(1) 1. The following transactions shall be subject to VAT:

s2(1)(a)   (a) the supply of goods for consideration within the territory of a Member State by a taxable person acting as such;

  (b) the intra-Community acquisition of goods for consideration within the territory of a Member State by:

s2(1A)
s2(3A)   (i) a taxable person acting as such, or a non-taxable legal person, where the vendor is a taxable person acting as such who is not eligible for the exemption for small enterprises provided for in Articles 282 to 292 and who is not covered by Articles 33 or 36;

    (ii) in the case of new means of transport, a taxable person, or a non-taxable legal person, whose other acquisitions are not subject to VAT pursuant to Article 3(1), or any other non-taxable person;

    (iii) in the case of products subject to excise duty, where the excise duty on the intra-Community acquisition is chargeable, pursuant to Directive 92/12/EEC, within the territory of the Member State, a taxable person, or a non-taxable legal person, whose other acquisitions are not subject to VAT pursuant to Article 3(1);

s2(1)(a)   (c) the supply of services for consideration within the territory of a Member State by a taxable person acting as such;

s2(1)(b)   (d) the importation of goods.

<table>
<tr><td>1(1)
B(3)</td><td>2</td><td>(a)</td><td>For the purposes of point (ii) of paragraph 1(b), the following shall be regarded as 'means of transport', where they are intended for the transport of persons or goods:</td></tr>
</table>

        (i)   motorised land vehicles the capacity of which exceeds 48 cubic centimetres or the power of which exceeds 7,2 kilowatts;

        (ii)   vessels exceeding 7,5 metres in length, with the exception of vessels used for navigation on the high seas and carrying passengers for reward, and of vessels used for the purposes of commercial, industrial or fishing activities, or for rescue or assistance at sea, or for inshore fishing;

        (iii) aircraft the take-off weight of which exceeds 1 550 kilograms, with the exception of aircraft used by airlines operating for reward chiefly on international routes.

    (b)   These means of transport shall be regarded as 'new' in the cases:

        (i)   of motorised land vehicles, where the supply takes place within six months of the date of first entry into service or where the vehicle has travelled for no more than 6 000 kilometres;

        (ii)   of vessels, where the supply takes place within three months of the date of first entry into service or where the vessel has sailed for no more than 100 hours;

        (iii) of aircraft, where the supply takes place within three months of the date of first entry into service or where the aircraft has flown for no more than 40 hours.

    (c)   Member States shall lay down the conditions under which the facts referred to in point (b) may be regarded as established.

s1(1) 3.   **'Products subject to excise duty'** shall mean energy products, alcohol and alcoholic beverages and manufactured tobacco, as defined by current Community legislation, but not gas supplied through the natural gas distribution system or electricity.

Article 3

1)(g) 1.   By way of derogation from Article 2(1)(b)(i), the following transactions shall not be subject to VAT:

    (a)   the intra-Community acquisition of goods by a taxable person or a non-taxable legal person, where the supply of such goods within the territory of the Member State of acquisition would be exempt pursuant to Articles 148 and 151;

    (b)   the intra-Community acquisition of goods, other than those referred to in point (a) and Article 4, and other than new means of transport or products subject to excise duty, by a taxable person for the purposes of his agricultural, forestry or fisheries business subject to the common flat-rate scheme for farmers, or by a taxable person who carries out only supplies of goods or services in respect of which VAT is not deductible, or by a non-taxable legal person.

2. Point (b) of paragraph 1 shall apply only if the following conditions are met:

(a) during the current calendar year, the total value of intra-Community acquisitions of goods does not exceed a threshold which the Member States shall determine but which may not be less than EUR 10 000 or the equivalent in national currency;

(b) during the previous calendar year, the total value of intra-Community acquisitions of goods did not exceed the threshold provided for in point (a).

The threshold which serves as the reference shall consist of the total value, exclusive of VAT due or paid in the Member State in which dispatch or transport of the goods began, of the intra-Community acquisitions of goods as referred to under point (b) of paragraph 1.

3. Member States shall grant taxable persons and non-taxable legal persons eligible under point (b) of paragraph 1 the right to opt for the general scheme provided for in Article 2(1)(b)(i).

Member States shall lay down the detailed rules for the exercise of the option referred to in the first subparagraph, which shall in any event cover a period of two calendar years.

Article 4

In addition to the transactions referred to in Article 3, the following transactions shall not be subject to VAT:

(a) the intra-Community acquisition of second-hand goods, works of art, collectors' items or antiques, as defined in points (1) to (4) of Article 311(1), where the vendor is a taxable dealer acting as such and VAT has been applied to the goods in the Member State in which their dispatch or transport began, in accordance with the margin scheme provided for in Articles 312 to 325;

(b) the intra-Community acquisition of second-hand means of transport, as defined in Article 327(3), where the vendor is a taxable dealer acting as such and VAT has been applied to the means of transport in the Member State in which their dispatch or transport began, in accordance with the transitional arrangements for second-hand means of transport;

(c) the intra-Community acquisition of second-hand goods, works of art, collectors' items or antiques, as defined in points (1) to (4) of Article 311(1), where the vendor is an organiser of sales by public auction, acting as such, and VAT has been applied to the goods in the Member State in which their dispatch or transport began, in accordance with the special arrangements for sales by public auction.

TITLE II

TERRITORIAL SCOPE

Article 5

s1(1)s1(2A) For the purposes of applying this Directive, the following definitions shall apply:

(1)   '**Community**' and '**territory of the Community**' mean the territories of the Member States as defined in point (2);

(2)   '**Member State**' and '**territory of a Member State**' mean the territory of each Member State of the Community to which the Treaty establishing the European Community is applicable, in accordance with Article 299 of that Treaty, with the exception of any territory referred to in Article 6 of this Directive;

(3)   '**third territories**' means those territories referred to in Article 6;

(4)   '**third country**' means any State or territory to which the Treaty is not applicable.

Article 6

1(2A) 1.   This Directive shall not apply to the following territories forming part of the customs territory of the Community:

(a)   Mount Athos;

(b)   the Canary Islands;

(c)   the French overseas departments;

(d)   the Åland Islands;

(e)   the Channel Islands.

2.   This Directive shall not apply to the following territories not forming part of the customs territory of the Community:

(a)   the Island of Heligoland;

(b)   the territory of Büsingen;

(c)   Ceuta;

(d)   Melilla;

(e)   Livigno;

(f)   Campione d'Italia;

(g)   the Italian waters of Lake Lugano.

Article 7

s1(2A) 1.   In view of the conventions and treaties concluded with France, the United Kingdom and Cyprus respectively, the Principality of Monaco, the Isle of Man and the United Kingdom Sovereign Base Areas of Akrotiri and

Dhekelia shall not be regarded, for the purposes of the application of this Directive, as third countries.

2.   Member States shall take the measures necessary to ensure that transactions originating in or intended for the Principality of Monaco are treated as transactions originating in or intended for France, that transactions originating in or intended for the Isle of Man are treated as transactions originating in or intended for the United Kingdom, and that transactions originating in or intended for the United Kingdom Sovereign Base Areas of Akrotiri and Dhekelia are treated as transactions originating in or intended for Cyprus.

Article 8

If the Commission considers that the provisions laid down in Articles 6 and 7 are no longer justified, particularly in terms of fair competition or own resources, it shall present appropriate proposals to the Council.

TITLE III

TAXABLE PERSONS

Article 9

s1(1) 1.   'Taxable person' shall mean any person who, independently, carries out
s8(1)   in any place any economic activity, whatever the purpose or results of that activity.

Any activity of producers, traders or persons supplying services, including mining and agricultural activities and activities of the professions, shall be regarded as 'economic activity'. The exploitation of tangible or intangible property for the purposes of obtaining income therefrom on a continuing basis shall in particular be regarded as an economic activity.

s8(2B) 2.   In addition to the persons referred to in paragraph 1, any person who, on an occasional basis, supplies a new means of transport, which is dispatched or transported to the customer by the vendor or the customer, or on behalf of the vendor or the customer, to a destination outside the territory of a Member State but within the territory of the Community, shall be regarded as a taxable person.

Article 10

s8(1) The condition in Article 9(1) that the economic activity be conducted 'independently' shall exclude employed and other persons from VAT in so far as they are bound to an employer by a contract of employment or by any other legal ties creating the relationship of employer and employee as regards working conditions, remuneration and the employer's liability.

Article 11

s8(8) After consulting the advisory committee on value added tax (hereafter, the 'VAT Committee'), each Member State may regard as a single taxable person any persons established in the territory of that Member State who, while legally independent, are closely bound to one another by financial, economic and organisational links.

A Member State exercising the option provided for in the first paragraph, may adopt any measures needed to prevent tax evasion or avoidance through the use of this provision.

Article 12

4(2) 1.   Member States may regard as a taxable person anyone who carries out, on an occasional basis, a transaction relating to the activities referred to in the second subparagraph of Article 9(1) and in particular one of the following transactions:

  (a)   the supply, before first occupation, of a building or parts of a building and of the land on which the building stands;

  (b)   the supply of building land.

2.   For the purposes of paragraph 1(a), 'building' shall mean any structure fixed to or in the ground.

Member States may lay down the detailed rules for applying the criterion referred to in paragraph 1(a) to conversions of buildings and may determine what is meant by 'the land on which a building stands'.

Member States may apply criteria other than that of first occupation, such as the period elapsing between the date of completion of the building and the date of first supply, or the period elapsing between the date of first occupation and the date of subsequent supply, provided that those periods do not exceed five years and two years respectively.

3.   For the purposes of paragraph 1(b), '**building land**' shall mean any unimproved or improved land defined as such by the Member States.

Article 13

(2A) 1.   States, regional and local government authorities and other bodies
(3E)   governed by public law shall not be regarded as taxable persons in respect of the activities or transactions in which they engage as public authorities, even where they collect dues, fees, contributions or payments in connection with those activities or transactions.

However, when they engage in such activities or transactions, they shall be regarded as taxable persons in respect of those activities or transactions where their treatment as non-taxable persons would lead to significant distortions of competition.

In any event, bodies governed by public law shall be regarded as taxable persons in respect of the activities listed in Annex I, provided that those activities are not carried out on such a small scale as to be negligible.

2.   Member States may regard activities, exempt under Articles 132, 135, 136, 371, 374 to 377, and Article 378(2), Article 379(2), or Articles 380 to

390, engaged in by bodies governed by public law as activities in which those bodies engage as public authorities.

TITLE IV
TAXABLE TRANSACTIONS

CHAPTER 1

supply of goods
Article 14

s3(1)(e) 1.   **'Supply of goods'** shall mean the transfer of the right to dispose of tangible property as owner.

2.   In addition to the transaction referred to in paragraph 1, each of the following shall be regarded as a supply of goods:

s3(1)(d)   (a)   the transfer, by order made by or in the name of a public authority or in pursuance of the law, of the ownership of property against payment of compensation;

s3(1)(b)   (b)   the actual handing over of goods pursuant to a contract for the hire of goods for a certain period, or for the sale of goods on deferred terms, which provides that in the normal course of events ownership is to pass at the latest upon payment of the final instalment;

s3(1)(aa)   (c)   the transfer of goods pursuant to a contract under which
s3(4)   commission is payable on purchase or sale.

s3(1)(c) 3.   Member States may regard the handing over of certain works of construction as a supply of goods.

Article 15

s3(1B) 1.   Electricity, gas, heat, refrigeration and the like shall be treated as tangible property.

s3(1)(c) 2.   Member States may regard the following as tangible property:
s4(2)

(a)   certain interests in immovable property;

(b)   rights in rem giving the holder thereof a right of use over immovable property;

(c)   shares or interests equivalent to shares giving the holder thereof de jure or de facto rights of ownership or possession over immovable property or part thereof.

Article 16

s3(1)(f) The application by a taxable person of goods forming part of his business assets for his private use or for that of his staff, or their disposal free of charge or, more generally, their application for purposes other than those of his business, shall be treated as a supply of goods for consideration, where the VAT on those goods or the component parts thereof was wholly or partly deductible.

(1A) However, the application of goods for business use as samples or as gifts of small value shall not be treated as a supply of goods for consideration.

Article 17

g) 1.   The transfer by a taxable person of goods forming part of his business assets to another Member State shall be treated as a supply of goods for consideration.

'Transfer to another Member State' shall mean the dispatch or transport of movable tangible property by or on behalf of the taxable person, for the purposes of his business, to a destination outside the territory of the Member State in which the property is located, but within the Community.

2.   The dispatch or transport of goods for the purposes of any of the following transactions shall not be regarded as a transfer to another Member State:

)(g)(i)   (a)   the supply of the goods by the taxable person within the territory of the Member State in which the dispatch or transport ends, in accordance with the conditions laid down in Article 33;

)(g)(i)   (b)   the supply of the goods, for installation or assembly by or on behalf of the supplier, by the taxable person within the territory of the Member State in which dispatch or transport of the goods ends, in accordance with the conditions laid down in Article 36;

)(g)(i)   (c)   the supply of the goods by the taxable person on board a ship, an aircraft or a train in the course of a passenger transport operation, in accordance with the conditions laid down in Article 37;

(d)   the supply of gas through the natural gas distribution system, or of electricity, in accordance with the conditions laid down in Articles 38 and 39;

1)(g)(ii)   (e)   the supply of the goods by the taxable person within the territory of the Member State, in accordance with the conditions laid down in Articles 138, 146, 147, 148, 151 or 152;

1)(g)(iiia)   (f)   the supply of a service performed for the taxable person and consisting of work on the goods in question physically carried out within the territory of the Member State in which dispatch or transport of the goods ends, provided that the goods, after being worked upon, are returned to that taxable person in the Member State from which they were initially dispatched or transported;

3(1)(g)(iv)   (g)   the temporary use of the goods within the territory of the Member State in which dispatch or transport of the goods ends, for the purposes of the supply of services by the taxable person established within the Member State in which dispatch or transport of the goods began;

s3(1)(g)(v) (h) the temporary use of the goods, for a period not exceeding twenty-four months, within the territory of another Member State, in which the importation of the same goods from a third country with a view to their temporary use would be covered by the arrangements for temporary importation with full exemption from import duties.

3.   If one of the conditions governing eligibility under paragraph 2 is no longer met, the goods shall be regarded as having been transferred to another Member State. In such cases, the transfer shall be deemed to take place at the time when that condition ceases to be met.

Article 18

Member States may treat each of the following transactions as a supply of goods for consideration:

s3(1)(e) (a) the application by a taxable person for the purposes of his business of goods produced, constructed, extracted, processed, purchased or imported in the course of such business, where the VAT on such goods, had they been acquired from another taxable person, would not be wholly deductible;

s3(1)(f) (b) the application of goods by a taxable person for the purposes of a non-taxable area of activity, where the VAT on such goods became wholly or partly deductible upon their acquisition or upon their application in accordance with point (a);

s3(7) (c) with the exception of the cases referred to in Article 19, the retention of goods by a taxable person, or by his successors, when he ceases to carry out a taxable economic activity, where the VAT on such goods became wholly or partly deductible upon their acquisition or upon their application in accordance with point (a).

Article 19

3(5)(b)(iii) In the event of a transfer, whether for consideration or not or as a contribution to a company, of a totality of assets or part thereof, Member States may consider that no supply of goods has taken place and that the person to whom the goods are transferred is to be treated as the successor to the transferor.

s12D Member States may, in cases where the recipient is not wholly liable to tax,
s12E(7) take the measures necessary to prevent distortion of competition. They may also adopt any measures needed to prevent tax evasion or avoidance through the use of this Article.

CHAPTER 2

Intra-Community acquisition of goods

Article 20

s1(1) 'Intra-Community acquisition of goods' shall mean the acquisition of the
A(1) right to dispose as owner of movable tangible property dispatched or
transported to the person acquiring the goods, by or on behalf of the vendor
or the person acquiring the goods, in a Member State other than that in
which dispatch or transport of the goods began.

3A(4) Where goods acquired by a non-taxable legal person are dispatched or
transported from a third territory or a third country and imported by
that non-taxable legal person into a Member State other than the Member
State in which dispatch or transport of the goods ends, the goods shall be
regarded as having been dispatched or transported from the Member State
of importation. That Member State shall grant the importer designated
or recognised under Article 201 as liable for payment of VAT a refund of
the VAT paid in respect of the importation of the goods, provided that the
importer establishes that VAT has been applied to his acquisition in the
Member State in which dispatch or transport of the goods ends.

Article 21

The application by a taxable person, for the purposes of his business, of goods
dispatched or transported by or on behalf of that taxable person from another
Member State, within which the goods were produced, extracted, processed,
purchased or acquired within the meaning of Article 2(1)(b), or into which they
were imported by that taxable person for the purposes of his business, shall
be treated as an intra-Community acquisition of goods for consideration.

Article 22

The application by the armed forces of a State party to the North Atlantic
Treaty, for their use or for the use of the civilian staff accompanying them, of
goods which they have not purchased subject to the general rules governing
taxation on the domestic market of a Member State shall be treated as an intra-
Community acquisition of goods for consideration, where the importation of
those goods would not be eligible for the exemption provided for in point (h)
of Article 143.

Article 23

(3)(a) Member States shall take the measures necessary to ensure that a transaction
which would have been classed as a supply of goods if it had been carried out
within their territory by a taxable person acting as such is classed as an intra-
Community acquisition of goods.

CHAPTER 3

Supply of services

Article 24

s5(1) 1. **'Supply of services'** shall mean any transaction which does not constitute a supply of goods.

s1(1) 2. **'Telecommunications services'** shall mean services relating to the transmission, emission or reception of signals, words, images and sounds or information of any nature by wire, radio, optical or other electromagnetic systems, including the related transfer or assignment of the right to use capacity for such transmission, emission or reception, with the inclusion of the provision of access to global information networks.

Article 25

s5(1) A supply of services may consist, inter alia, in one of the following transactions:

    (a)   the assignment of intangible property, whether or not the subject of a document establishing title;

    (b)   the obligation to refrain from an act, or to tolerate an act or situation;

    (c)   the performance of services in pursuance of an order made by or in the name of a public authority or in pursuance of the law.

Article 26

1. Each of the following transactions shall be treated as a supply of services for consideration:

s5(3)(a)   (a)   the use of goods forming part of the assets of a business for the private use of a taxable person or of his staff or, more generally, for purposes other than those of his business, where the VAT on such goods was wholly or partly deductible;

s5(3)(b)   (b)   the supply of services carried out free of charge by a taxable person for his private use or for that of his staff or, more generally, for purposes other than those of his business.

2. Member States may derogate from paragraph 1, provided that such derogation does not lead to distortion of competition.

Article 27

s5(3)(c) In order to prevent distortion of competition and after consulting the VAT Committee, Member States may treat as a supply of services for consideration the supply by a taxable person of a service for the purposes of his business, where the VAT on such a service, were it supplied by another taxable person, would not be wholly deductible.

Article 28

5(4) Where a taxable person acting in his own name but on behalf of another person takes part in a supply of services, he shall be deemed to have received and supplied those services himself.

Article 29

5(8) Article 19 shall apply in like manner to the supply of services.

CHAPTER 4

Importation of goods

Article 30

1(1) **'Importation of goods'** shall mean the entry into the Community of goods which are not in free circulation within the meaning of Article 24 of the Treaty.

In addition to the transaction referred to in the first paragraph, the entry into the Community of goods which are in free circulation, coming from a third territory forming part of the customs territory of the Community, shall be regarded as importation of goods.

TITLE V

PLACE OF TAXABLE TRANSACTIONS

CHAPTER 1

Place of supply of goods

Section 1

Supply of goods without transport

Article 31

6(c) Where goods are not dispatched or transported, the place of supply shall be deemed to be the place where the goods are located at the time when the supply takes place.

Section 2

Supply of goods with transport

Article 32

6(a) Where goods are dispatched or transported by the supplier, or by the customer, or by a third person, the place of supply shall be deemed to be the place where the goods are located at the time when dispatch or transport of the goods to the customer begins.

However, if dispatch or transport of the goods begins in a third territory or third country, both the place of supply by the importer designated or recognised under Article 201 as liable for payment of VAT and the place of any subsequent supply shall be deemed to be within the Member State of importation of the goods.

Article 33

s3(6)(d) 1.   By way of derogation from Article 32, the place of supply of goods dispatched or transported by or on behalf of the supplier from a Member State other than that in which dispatch or transport of the goods ends shall be deemed to be the place where the goods are located at the time when dispatch or transport of the goods to the customer ends, where the following conditions are met:

    (a)   the supply of goods is carried out for a taxable person, or a non-taxable legal person, whose intra-Community acquisitions of goods are not subject to VAT pursuant to Article 3 (1) or for any other non-taxable person;

    (b)   the goods supplied are neither new means of transport nor goods supplied after assembly or installation, with or without a trial run, by or on behalf of the supplier.

2.   Where the goods supplied are dispatched or transported from a third territory or a third country and imported by the supplier into a Member State other than that in which dispatch or transport of the goods to the customer ends, they shall be regarded as having been dispatched or transported from the Member State of importation.

Article 34

s3(6)(d) 1.   Provided the following conditions are met, Article 33 shall not apply to supplies of goods all of which are dispatched or transported to the same Member State, where that Member State is the Member State in which dispatch or transport of the goods ends:

    (a)   the goods supplied are not products subject to excise duty;

    (b)   the total value, exclusive of VAT, of such supplies effected under the conditions laid down in Article 33 within that Member State does not in any one calendar year exceed EUR 100 000 or the equivalent in national currency;

    (c)   the total value, exclusive of VAT, of the supplies of goods, other than products subject to excise duty, effected under the conditions laid down in Article 33 within that Member State did not in the previous calendar year exceed EUR 100 000 or the equivalent in national currency.

2.   The Member State within the territory of which the goods are located at the time when their dispatch or transport to the customer ends may limit the threshold referred to in paragraph 1 to EUR 35 000 or the equivalent in national currency, where that Member State fears that the threshold of EUR 100 000 might cause serious distortion of competition.

Member States which exercise the option under the first subparagraph shall take the measures necessary to inform accordingly the competent public authorities in the Member State in which dispatch or transport of the goods begins.

3. The Commission shall present to the Council at the earliest opportunity a report on the operation of the special EUR 35 000 threshold referred to in paragraph 2, accompanied, if necessary, by appropriate proposals.

4. The Member State within the territory of which the goods are located at the time when their dispatch or transport begins shall grant those taxable persons who carry out supplies of goods eligible under paragraph 1 the right to opt for the place of supply to be determined in accordance with Article 33.

The Member States concerned shall lay down the detailed rules governing the exercise of the option referred to in the first subparagraph, which shall in any event cover two calendar years.

Article 35

Articles 33 and 34 shall not apply to supplies of second-hand goods, works of art, collectors' items or antiques, as defined in points (1) to (4) of Article 311(1), nor to supplies of second-hand means of transport, as defined in Article 327(3), subject to VAT in accordance with the relevant special arrangements.

Article 36

6)(b) Where goods dispatched or transported by the supplier, by the customer or by a third person are installed or assembled, with or without a trial run, by or on behalf of the supplier, the place of supply shall be deemed to be the place where the goods are installed or assembled.

Where the installation or assembly is carried out in a Member State other than that of the supplier, the Member State within the territory of which the installation or assembly is carried out shall take the measures necessary to ensure that there is no double taxation in that Member State.

Section 3

Supply of goods on board ships, aircraft or trains

Article 37

6)(cc) 1. Where goods are supplied on board ships, aircraft or trains during the section of a passenger transport operation effected within the Community, the place of supply shall be deemed to be at the point of departure of the passenger transport operation.

2. For the purposes of paragraph 1, **'section of a passenger transport operation effected within the Community'** shall mean the section of the operation effected, without a stopover outside the Community, between

the point of departure and the point of arrival of the passenger transport operation.

'Point of departure of a passenger transport operation' shall mean the first scheduled point of passenger embarkation within the Community, where applicable after a stopover outside the Community.

'Point of arrival of a passenger transport operation' shall mean the last scheduled point of disembarkation within the Community of passengers who embarked in the Community, where applicable before a stopover outside the Community.

In the case of a return trip, the return leg shall be regarded as a separate transport operation.

3.   The Commission shall, at the earliest opportunity, present to the Council a report, accompanied if necessary by appropriate proposals, on the place of taxation of the supply of goods for consumption on board and the supply of services, including restaurant services, for passengers on board ships, aircraft or trains.

Pending adoption of the proposals referred to in the first subparagraph, Member States may exempt or continue to exempt, with deductibility of the VAT paid at the preceding stage, the supply of goods for consumption on board in respect of which the place of taxation is determined in accordance with paragraph 1.

Section 4

Supply of goods through distribution systems

Article 38

s3(6)(e)   1.   In the case of the supply of gas through the natural gas distribution system, or of electricity, to a taxable dealer, the place of supply shall be deemed to be the place where that taxable dealer has established his business or has a fixed establishment for which the goods are supplied, or, in the absence of such a place of business or fixed establishment, the place where he has his permanent address or usually resides.

s3(6A)   2.   For the purposes of paragraph 1, 'taxable dealer' shall mean a taxable person whose principal activity in respect of purchases of gas or electricity is reselling those products and whose own consumption of those products is negligible.

Article 39

s3(6)(f)   In the case of the supply of gas through the natural gas distribution system, or of electricity, where such a supply is not covered by Article 38, the place of supply shall be deemed to be the place where the customer effectively uses and consumes the goods.

Where all or part of the gas or electricity is not effectively consumed by the customer, those non-consumed goods shall be deemed to have been used and consumed at the place where the customer has established his business or has a fixed establishment for which the goods are supplied. In the absence of such a place of business or fixed establishment, the customer shall be deemed to have used and consumed the goods at the place where he has his permanent address or usually resides.

CHAPTER 2

Place of an intra-Community acquisition of goods

Article 40

(2)(a) The place of an intra-Community acquisition of goods shall be deemed to be the place where dispatch or transport of the goods to the person acquiring them ends.

Article 41

2)(b) Without prejudice to Article 40, the place of an intra-Community acquisition of goods as referred to in Article 2(1)(b)(i) shall be deemed to be within the territory of the Member State which issued the VAT identification number under which the person acquiring the goods made the acquisition, unless the person acquiring the goods establishes that VAT has been applied to that acquisition in accordance with Article 40.

If VAT is applied to the acquisition in accordance with the first paragraph and subsequently applied, pursuant to Article 40, to the acquisition in the Member State in which dispatch or transport of the goods ends, the taxable amount shall be reduced accordingly in the Member State which issued the VAT identification number under which the person acquiring the goods made the acquisition.

Article 42

(5) The first paragraph of Article 41 shall not apply and VAT shall be deemed to have been applied to the intra-Community acquisition of goods in accordance with Article 40 where the following conditions are met:

(a) the person acquiring the goods establishes that he has made the intra-Community acquisition for the purposes of a subsequent supply, within the territory of the Member State identified in accordance with Article 40, for which the person to whom the supply is made has been designated in accordance with Article 197 as liable for payment of VAT;

(b) the person acquiring the goods has satisfied the obligations laid down in Article 265 relating to submission of the recapitulative statement.

CHAPTER 3

Place of supply of services

Section 1

[General rule]¹

[Article 43

s5(5) The place of supply of services shall be deemed to be the place where the supplier has established his business or has a fixed establishment from which the service is supplied, or, in the absence of such a place of business or fixed establishment, the place where he has his permanent address or usually resides.]²

Amendments

1   With effect from 1 January 2010 and in accordance with Art 2(1) of Council Directive 2008/8/EC of 12 February 2008, the title of Section 1 (referring to Art 43) will change from 'General rule' to 'Definitions'.
2   With effect from 1 January 2010 and in accordance with Art 2(1) of Council Directive 2008/8/EC of 12 February 2008, Article 43 will read:

'For the purpose of applying the rules concerning the place of supply of services:
1.   a taxable person who also carries out activities or transactions that are not considered to be taxable supplies of goods or services in accordance with Article 2(1) shall be regarded as a taxable person in respect of all services rendered to him;
2.   a non-taxable legal person who is identified for VAT purposes shall be regarded as a taxable person.'

Section 2

[Particular provisions

Subsection 1

Supply of services by intermediaries]¹

[Article 44

s5(6)(gg) The place of supply of services by an intermediary acting in the name and on behalf of another person, other than those referred to in Articles 50 and 54 and in Article 56(1), shall be the place where the underlying transaction is supplied in accordance with this Directive.

However, where the customer of the services supplied by the intermediary is identified for VAT purposes in a Member State other than that within the territory of which that transaction is carried out, the place of the supply of services by the intermediary shall be deemed to be within the territory of the Member State which issued the customer with the VAT identification number under which the service was rendered to him.]²

Amendments

1   With effect from 1 January 2010 and in accordance with Art 2(1) of Council Directive 2008/8/EC of 12 February 2008, the title of Section 2 will change from 'Particular Provisions, Subsection 1, Supply of services by intermediaries' to 'General Rules'.
2   With effect from 1 January 2010 and in accordance with Art 2(1) of Council Directive 2008/8/EC of 12 February 2008, Art 44 will read:

'The place of supply of services to a taxable person acting as such shall be the place where that person has established his business. However, if those services are provided to a fixed establishment of the taxable person located in a place other than the place where he has established his business, the place of supply of those services shall be the place where that fixed establishment is located. In the absence of such place of establishment or fixed establishment, the place of supply of services shall be the place where the taxable person who receives such services has his permanent address or usually resides.'

[Subsection 2

Supply of services connected with immovable property][1]

[Article 45

5)(a) The place of supply of services connected with immovable property, including the services of estate agents and experts, and services for the preparation and coordination of construction work, such as the services of architects and of firms providing on-site supervision, shall be the place where the property is located.][2]

Amendments

1   With effect from 1 January 2010 and in accordance with Art 2(1) of Council Directive 2008/8/EC of 12 February 2008, the reference to 'Subsection 2' and the subsection title 'Supply of services connected with immovable property' will be deleted.

2   With effect from 1 January 2010 and in accordance with Art 2(1) of Council Directive 2008/8/EC of 12 February 2008, Art 45 will read;

'The place of supply of services to a non-taxable person shall be the place where the supplier has established his business. However, if those services are provided from a fixed establishment of the supplier located in a place other than the place where he has established his business, the place of supply of those services shall be the place where that fixed establishment is located. In the absence of such place of establishment or fixed establishment, the place of supply of services shall be the place where the supplier has his permanent address or usually resides.'

[Subsection 3

Supply of transport][1]

[Article 46

(6)(b) The place of supply of transport other than the intra-Community transport of goods shall be the place where the transport takes place, proportionately in terms of distances covered.][2]

Amendments

1   With effect from 1 January 2010 and in accordance with Art 2(1) of Council Directive 2008/8/EC of 12 February 2008, the reference to 'Subsection 3, Supply of transport' will be replaced by 'Section 3, Particular provisions, Subsection 1, Supply of Services by intermediaries'

2   With effect from 1 January 2010 and in accordance with Art 2(1) of Council Directive 2008/8/EC of 12 February 2008, Art 46 will read:

'The place of supply of services rendered to a non-taxable person by an intermediary acting in the name and on behalf of another person shall be the place where the underlying transaction is supplied in accordance with this Directive.'

[...][1]

[Article 47

(f)(i) The place of supply of intra-Community transport of goods shall be the
(f)(i) place of departure of the transport.

However, where intra-Community transport of goods is supplied to customers identified for VAT purposes in a Member State other than that of the departure of the transport, the place of supply shall be deemed to be within the territory of the Member State which issued the customer with the VAT identification number under which the service was rendered to him.][2]

Amendments
1   With effect from 1 January 2010 and in accordance with Art 2(1) of Council Directive 2008/8/EC of 12 February 2008, the title of Article 47 will read: 'Subsection 2, Supply of services connected with immovable property'.
2   With effect from 1 January 2010 and in accordance with Art 2(1) of Council Directive 2008/8/EC of 12 February 2008, article 47 shall read:

'The place of supply of services connected with immovable property, including the services of experts and estate agents, the provision of accommodation in the hotel sector or in sectors with a similar function, such as holiday camps or sites developed for use as camping sites, the granting of rights to use immovable property and services for the preparation and coordination of construction work, such as the services of architects and of firms providing on-site supervision, shall be the place where the immovable property is located.'

[...][1]

[Article 48

s5(6)(h) 'Intra-Community transport of goods' shall mean any transport of goods in respect of which the place of departure and the place of arrival are situated within the territories of two different Member States.

'Place of departure' shall mean the place where transport of the goods actually begins, irrespective of distances covered in order to reach the place where the goods are located.

'Place of arrival' shall mean the place where transport of the goods actually ends.][2]

Amendments
1   With effect from 1 January 2010 and in accordance with Art 2(1) of Council Directive 2008/8/EC of 12 February 2008, the title to Art 48 shall read; 'Subsection 3, Supply of transport'
2   With effect from 1 January 2010 and in accordance with Art 2(1) of Council Directive 2008/8/EC of 12 February 2008, Art 48 will read:

'The place of supply of passenger transport shall be the place where the transport takes place, proportionate to the distances covered.'

[Article 49

The transport of goods in respect of which the place of departure and the place of arrival are situated within the territory of the same Member State shall be treated as intra-Community transport of goods where such transport is directly linked to transport of goods in respect of which the place of departure and the place of arrival are situated within the territory of two different Member States.][1]

Amendments
1   With effect from 1 January 2010 and in accordance with Art 2(1) of Council Directive 2008/8/EC of 12 February 2008, Art 49 shall read:

'The place of supply of the transport of goods, other than the intra-Community transport of goods, to non-taxable persons shall be the place where the transport takes place, proportionate to the distances covered.'

[Article 50

s5(6)(g)(i)(II) The place of the supply of services by an intermediary, acting in the name and on behalf of another person, where the intermediary takes part in the intra-Community transport of goods, shall be the place of departure of the transport.

However, where the customer of the services supplied by the intermediary is identified for VAT purposes in a Member State other than that of the departure of the transport, the place of the supply of services by the intermediary shall be deemed to be within the territory of the Member State which issued the customer with the VAT identification number under which the service was rendered to him.]¹

Amendments
1   With effect from 1 January 2010 and in accordance with Art 2(1) of Council Directive 2008/8/EC of 12 February 2008, Art 50 will read:

'The place of supply of the intra-Community transport of goods to non-taxable persons shall be the place of departure.'

[Article 51

Member States need not apply VAT to that part of the intra-Community transport of goods taking place over waters which do not form part of the territory of the Community.]¹

Amendments
1   With effect from 1 January 2010 and in accordance with Art 2(1) of Council Directive 2008/8/EC of 12 February 2008, Art 51 will read:

'"Intra-Community transport of goods" shall mean any transport of goods in respect of which the place of departure and the place of arrival are situated within the territories of two different Member States.

"Place of departure" shall mean the place where transport of the goods actually begins, irrespective of distances covered in order to reach the place where the goods are located and "place of arrival" shall mean the place where transport of the goods actually ends.'

[Subsection 4

Supply of cultural and similar services, ancillary transport services or services relating to movable tangible property]¹

[Article 52

5(6)(c) The place of supply of the following services shall be the place where the services are physically carried out:

(a)   cultural, artistic, sporting, scientific, educational, entertainment or similar activities, including the activities of the organisers of such activities and, where appropriate, ancillary services;

(b)   ancillary transport activities, such as loading, unloading, handling and similar activities;

(c)   valuations of movable tangible property or work on such property.]²

Amendments
1   With effect from 1 January 2010 and in accordance with Art 2(1) of Council Directive 2008/8/EC of 12 February 2008, the reference to subsection 4 and the title 'Supply of cultural and similar services, ancilliary transport services or services relating to movable tangible property' is deleted from above Art 52.
2   With effect from 1 January 2010 and in accordance with Art 2(1) of Council Directive 2008/8/EC of 12 February 2008, section 52 will read:

'Member States need not apply VAT to that part of the intra-Community transport of goods to non-taxable persons taking place over waters which do not form part of the territory of the Community.'

[...]¹

*[Article 53

s5(6)(f)(ii) By way of derogation from Article 52(b), the place of supply of services involving activities ancillary to the intra-Community transport of goods, supplied to customers identified for VAT purposes in a Member State other than that in the territory of which the activities are physically carried out, shall be deemed to be within the territory of the Member State which issued the customer with the VAT identification number under which the service was rendered to him.]²

Amendments
1   With effect from 1 January 2010 and in accordance with Art 2(1) of Council Directive 2008/8/EC of 12 February 2008, the title 'Subsection 4, Supply of cultural, artistic, sporting, scientific, educational, entertainment and similar services, ancilliary transport services and valuations of and work on movable property' will be inserted above Art 53.
2   With effect from 1 January 2010 and in accordance with Art 2(1) of Council Directive 2008/8/EC of 12 February 2008, Art 53 shall read:
    'The place of supply of services and ancillary services relating to cultural, artistic, sporting, scientific, educational, entertainment or similar activities, such as fairs and exhibitions, including the supply of services of the organisers of such activities, shall be the place where those activities are physically carried out.'

*[Article 54

s5(6)(g)(ii) The place of the supply of services by an intermediary, acting in the name and on behalf of another person, where the intermediary takes part in the supply of services consisting in activities ancillary to the intra-Community transport of goods, shall be the place where the ancillary activities are physically carried out.

However, where the customer of the services supplied by the intermediary is identified for VAT purposes in a Member State other than that within the territory of which the ancillary activities are physically carried out, the place of supply of services by the intermediary shall be deemed to be within the territory of the Member State which issued the customer with the VAT identification number under which the service was rendered to him.]¹

Amendments
1   With effect from 1 January 2010 and in accordance with Art 2(1) of Council Directive 2008/8/EC of 12 February 2008, Art 54 shall read:
    'The place of supply of the following services to non-taxable persons shall be the place where the services are physically carried out:
    (a) ancillary transport activities such as loading, unloading, handling and similar activities;
    (b) valuations of and work on movable tangible property.'

[...]¹

[Article 55

s5(6)(f)(iv) By way of derogation from Article 52(c), the place of supply of services involving the valuation of movable tangible property or work on such property, supplied to customers identified for VAT purposes in a Member State other than that in the territory of which the services are physically carried out, shall be deemed to be within the territory of the Member State which issued the customer with the VAT identification number under which the service was rendered to him.

The derogation referred to in the first paragraph shall apply only where the goods are dispatched or transported out of the Member State in which the services were physically carried out.][2]

Amendments
1   With effect from 1 January 2010 and in accordance with Art 2(1) of Council Directive 2008/8/EC of 12 February 2008, the title 'Subsection 5, Supply of restaurant and catering services' is inserted above Art 55.
2   With effect from 1 January 2010 and in accordance with Art 2(1) of Council Directive 2008/8/EC of 12 February 2008, Art 55 shall read:
    'The place of supply of restaurant and catering services other than those physically carried out on board ships, aircraft or trains during the section of a passenger transport operation effected within the Community, shall be the place where the services are physically carried out.'

[Subsection 5

Supply of miscellaneous services][1]

*[Article 56

1.   The place of supply of the following services to customers established outside the Community, or to taxable persons established in the Community but not in the same country as the supplier, shall be the place where the customer has established his business or has a fixed establishment for which the service is supplied, or, in the absence of such a place, the place where he has his permanent address or usually resides:

(a)   transfers and assignments of copyrights, patents, licences, trade marks and similar rights;

(b)   advertising services;

(c)   the services of consultants, engineers, consultancy bureaux, lawyers, accountants and other similar services, as well as data processing and the provision of information;

(d)   obligations to refrain from pursuing or exercising, in whole or in part, a business activity or a right referred to in this paragraph;

(e)   banking, financial and insurance transactions, including reinsurance, with the exception of the hire of safes;

(f)   the supply of staff;

(g)   the hiring out of movable tangible property, with the exception of all means of transport;

(h)   the provision of access to, and of transport or transmission through, natural gas and electricity distribution systems and the provision of other services directly linked thereto;

(i)   telecommunications services;

(j)   radio and television broadcasting services;

(k)   electronically supplied services, such as those referred to in Annex II;

(l)   the supply of services by intermediaries, acting in the name and on behalf of other persons, where those intermediaries take part in the supply of the services referred to in this paragraph.

s1(1) 2.   Where the supplier of a service and the customer communicate via electronic mail, that shall not of itself mean that the service supplied is an electronically supplied service for the purposes of point (k) of paragraph 1.

[3.   Points (j) and (k) of paragraph 1 and paragraph 2 shall apply until 31 December 2008.]²]³

Amendments

1   With effect from 1 January 2010 and in accordance with Art 2(1) of Council Directive 2008/8/EC of 12 February 2008, the title above Art 56 will be replaced by 'Subsection 6; Hiring of means of transport'

2   Substituted by Article 1(1) of Council Directive 2008/8/EC of 12 February 2008, (w.e.f. 1 January 2009)

3   With effect from 1 January 2010 and in accordance with Art 2(1) of Council Directive 2008/8/EC of 12 February 2008, Article 56 shall read:

'1.   The place of short-term hiring of a means of transport shall be the place where the means of transport is actually put at the disposal of the customer.

2.   For the purposes of paragraph 1, "short-term" shall mean the continuous possession or use of the means of transport throughout a period of not more than thirty days and, in the case of vessels, not more than ninety days.'

[...]¹

Article 57

s5(6)   1.   Where the services referred to in point (k) of Article 56(1) are supplied
(eee)   to non-taxable persons who are established in a Member State, or who have their permanent address or usually reside in a Member State, by a taxable person who has established his business outside the Community or has a fixed establishment there from which the service is supplied, or who, in the absence of such a place of business or fixed establishment, has his permanent address or usually resides outside the Community, the place of supply shall be the place where the non-taxable person is established, or where he has his permanent address or usually resides.

[2.   Paragraph 1 shall apply until 31 December 2009.]²]³

Amendments

1   With effect from 1 January 2010 and in accordance with Art 2(1) of Council Directive 2008/8/EC of 12 February 2008, the title 'Subsection 7, Supply of restaurant and catering services for consumption on board ships, aircraft or trains' shall be inserted above Art 57.

2   Substituted by Article 1(2) of Council Directive 2008/8/EC of 12 February 2008, (w.e.f. 1 January 2009)

3   With effect from 1 January 2010 and in accordance with Art 2(1) of Council Directive 2008/8/EC of 12 February 2008, Art 56 shall read:

'1.   The place of supply of restaurant and catering services which are physically carried out on board ships, aircraft or trains during the section of a passenger transport operation effected within the Community, shall be at the point of departure of the passenger transport operation.

2.   For the purposes of paragraph 1, "section of a passenger transport operation effected within the Community" shall mean the section of the operation effected, without a stopover outside the Community, between the point of departure and the point of arrival of the passenger transport operation.

"Point of departure of a passenger transport operation" shall mean the first scheduled point of passenger embarkation within the Community, where applicable after a stopover outside the Community.

"Point of arrival of a passenger transport operation" shall mean the last scheduled point of disembarkation within the Community of passengers who embarked in the Community, where applicable before a stopover outside the Community.

In the case of a return trip, the return leg shall be regarded as a separate transport operation.'

[Subsection 6

Criterion of effective use and enjoyment][1]

*[Article 58

(6)(d)
(dd)
In order to avoid double taxation, non-taxation or distortion of competition, Member States may, with regard to the supply of the services referred to in
dd) &
ddd)
Article 56(1) and with regard to the hiring out of means of transport:

(a)   consider the place of supply of any or all of those services, if situated within their territory, as being situated outside the Community, if the effective use and enjoyment of the services takes place outside the Community;

(b)   consider the place of supply of any or all of those services, if situated outside the Community, as being situated within their territory, if the effective use and enjoyment of the services takes place within their territory.

However, this provision shall not apply to the services referred to in point (k) of Article 56(1), where those services are rendered to non-taxable persons.][2]

Amendments

1   With effect from 1 January 2010 and in accordance with Art 2(1) of Council Directive 2008/8/EC of 12 February 2008, the title above Art 58 will change to 'Subsection 8, Supply of electronic services to non-taxable persons'

2   With effect from 1 January 2010 and in accordance with Art 2(1) of Council Directive 2008/8/EC of 12 February 2008, Art 58 will read:

'The place of supply of electronically supplied services, in particular those referred to in Annex II, when supplied to non-taxable persons who are established in a Member State, or who have their permanent address or usually reside in a Member State, by a taxable person who has established his business outside the Community or has a fixed establishment there from which the service is supplied, or who, in the absence of such a place of business or fixed establishment, has his permanent address or usually resides outside the Community, shall be the place where the non-taxable person is established, or where he has his permanent address or usually resides.

Where the supplier of a service and the customer communicate via electronic mail, that shall not of itself mean that the service supplied is an electronically supplied service.'

[...][1]

*[Article 59

s5(6)
(dd)
1.   Member States shall apply Article 58(b) to telecommunications services supplied to non-taxable persons who are established in a Member State, or who have their permanent address or usually reside in a Member State, by a taxable person who has established his business outside the Community or has a fixed establishment there from which the services are supplied, or who, in the absence of such a place of business or fixed establishment, has his permanent address or usually resides outside the Community.

[2.   Until 31 December 2009, Member States shall apply Article 58(b) to radio and television broadcasting services, as referred to in Article 56(1)(j), supplied to non-taxable persons who are established in a Member State, or who have their permanent address or usually reside in a Member State, by a taxable person who has established his business outside the Community or who has a fixed establishment there from which the services are supplied, or who, in the absence of such a place of business or fixed establishment, has his permanent address or usually resides outside the Community.]²]³

Amendments

1 With effect from 1 January 2010 and in accordance with Art 2(1) of Council Directive 2008/8/EC of 12 February 2008, the title 'Subsection 9, Supply of services to non-taxable persons outside the Community' is inserted above Art 59

2 Substituted by Article 1(3) of Council Directive 2008/8/EC of 12 February 2008, (w.e.f. 1 January 2009)

3 With effect from 1 January 2010 and in accordance with Art 2(1) of Council Directive 2008/8/EC of 12 February 2008, Art 59 shall read:

'The place of supply of the following services to a non-taxable person who is established or has his permanent address or usually resides outside the Community, shall be the place where that person is established, has his permanent address or usually resides:

(a) transfers and assignments of copyrights, patents, licences, trade marks and similar rights;

(b) advertising services;

(c) the services of consultants, engineers, consultancy firms, lawyers, accountants and other similar services, as well as data processing and the provision of information;

(d) obligations to refrain from pursuing or exercising, in whole or in part, a business activity or a right referred to in this Article;

(e) banking, financial and insurance transactions including reinsurance, with the exception of the hire of safes;

(f) the supply of staff;

(g) the hiring out of movable tangible property, with the exception of all means of transport;

(h) the provision of access to, and of transport or transmission through, natural gas and electricity distribution systems and the provision of other services directly linked thereto;

(i) telecommunications services;

(j) radio and television broadcasting services;

(k) electronically supplied services, in particular those referred to in Annex II.

Where the supplier of a service and the customer communicate via electronic mail, that shall not of itself mean that the service supplied is an electronically supplied service.'

[...]¹

Amendments

1 With effect from 1 January 2010 and in accordance with Art 2(1) of Council Directive 2008/8/EC of 12 February 2008, Subsection 10, (including Articles 59a and 59b) is inserted and will read as follows:

'**Subsection 10**

Prevention of double taxation or non-taxation

*Article 59a

In order to prevent double taxation, non-taxation or distortion of competition, Member States may, with regard to services the place of supply of which is governed by Articles 44, 45, 56 and 59:

(a) consider the place of supply of any or all of those services, if situated within their territory, as being situated outside the Community if the effective use and enjoyment of the services takes place outside the Community;

(b) consider the place of supply of any or all of those services, if situated outside the Community, as being situated within their territory if the effective use and enjoyment of the services takes place within their territory.

However, this provision shall not apply to the electronically supplied services where those services are rendered to non-taxable persons not established within the Community.

*Article 59b

Member States shall apply Article 59a(b) to telecommunications services and radio and television broadcasting services, as referred to in point (j) of the first paragraph of Article 59, supplied to non-taxable persons who are established in a Member State, or who have their permanent address or usually reside in a Member State, by a taxable person who has established his business outside the Community or has a fixed establishment there from which the services are supplied, or who, in the absence of such a place of business or fixed establishment, has his permanent address or usually resides outside the Community.

CHAPTER 4

Place of importation of goods

Article 60

5(1)
(3)
(6)
(6A)
The place of importation of goods shall be the Member State within whose territory the goods are located when they enter the Community.

Article 61

5(1)
5 (3)
5(6)
5(6A)
By way of derogation from Article 60, where, on entry into the Community, goods which are not in free circulation are placed under one of the arrangements or situations referred to in Article 156, or under temporary importation arrangements with total exemption from import duty, or under external transit arrangements, the place of importation of such goods shall be the Member State within whose territory the goods cease to be covered by those arrangements or situations.

Similarly, where, on entry into the Community, goods which are in free circulation are placed under one of the arrangements or situations referred to in Articles 276 and 277, the place of importation shall be the Member State within whose territory the goods cease to be covered by those arrangements or situations.

TITLE VI

CHARGEABLE EVENT AND CHARGEABILITY OF VAT

CHAPTER 1

General provisions

Article 62

2(1)(a) For the purposes of this Directive:

    (1)   '**chargeable event**' shall mean the occurrence by virtue of which the legal conditions necessary for VAT to become chargeable are fulfilled;

    (2)   VAT shall become '**chargeable**' when the tax authority becomes entitled under the law, at a given moment, to claim the tax from the person liable to pay, even though the time of payment may be deferred.

CHAPTER 2

Supply of goods or services

Article 63

9(1)
The chargeable event shall occur and VAT shall become chargeable when the goods or the services are supplied.

Article 64

(1)(bb) 1.   Where it gives rise to successive statements of account or successive payments, the supply of goods, other than that consisting in the hire of goods for a certain period or the sale of goods on deferred terms, as referred to in point (b) of Article 14(2), or the supply of services shall be regarded as being completed on expiry of the periods to which such statements of account or payments relate.

[2.   Supplies of services for which VAT is payable by the customer pursuant to Article 196, which are supplied continuously over a period of more than one year and which do not give rise to statements of account or payments during that period shall be regarded as being completed on expiry of each calendar year until such time as the supply of services comes to an end.

Member states may provide that, in certain cases other than those referred to in the previous paragraph, the continuous supply of goods or services over a period of time is to be regarded as being completed at least at intervals of one year.].[1]

Amendments
1   Substituted by Art 1(1) of Council Directive 2008/117/EC of 16 December 2008, (w.e.f. 21 January 2009)

Article 65

s19(2) Where a payment is to be made on account before the goods or services are supplied, VAT shall become chargeable on receipt of the payment and on the amount received.

Article 66

s14 By way of derogation from Articles 63, 64 and 65, Member States may provide that VAT is to become chargeable, in respect of certain transactions or certain
s19(1) categories of taxable person at one of the following times:

(a)   no later than the time the invoice is issued;

(b)   no later than the time the payment is received;

(c)   where an invoice is not issued, or is issued late, within a specified period from the date of the chargeable event.

[The derogation provided for in the first paragraph shall not, however, apply to supplies of services in respect of which VAT is payable by the customer pursuant to Article 196.][1]

Amendments
1   Inserted by Art 1(2) of Council Directive 2008/117/EC of 16 December 2008, (w.e.f. 21 January 2009)

Article 67

1.   Where, in accordance with the conditions laid down in Article 138, goods dispatched or transported to a Member State other than that in which dispatch or transport of the goods begins are supplied VAT-exempt or where goods are transferred VAT-exempt to another Member State by a taxable person for the purposes of his business, VAT shall become chargeable on the 15th day of the month following that in which the chargeable event occurs.

2. By way of derogation from paragraph 1, VAT shall become chargeable on issue of the invoice provided for in Article 220, if that invoice is issued before the 15th day of the month following that in which the chargeable event occurs.

CHAPTER 3

Intra-Community acquisition of goods

Article 68

A(1)
(a)
9(1)
The chargeable event shall occur when the intra-Community acquisition of goods is made.

The intra-Community acquisition of goods shall be regarded as being made when the supply of similar goods is regarded as being effected within the territory of the relevant Member State.

Article 69

9(1A)
1. In the case of the intra-Community acquisition of goods, VAT shall become chargeable on the 15th day of the month following that in which the chargeable event occurs.

2. By way of derogation from paragraph 1, VAT shall become chargeable on issue of the invoice provided for in Article 220, if that invoice is issued before the 15th day of the month following that in which the chargeable event occurs.

CHAPTER 4

Importation of goods

Article 70

(6A)
)(b)
(6)
The chargeable event shall occur and VAT shall become chargeable when the goods are imported.

Article 71

s 15
1. Where, on entry into the Community, goods are placed under one of the arrangements or situations referred to in Articles 156, 276 and 277, or under temporary importation arrangements with total exemption from import duty, or under external transit arrangements, the chargeable event shall occur and VAT shall become chargeable only when the goods cease to be covered by those arrangements or situations.

However, where imported goods are subject to customs duties, to agricultural levies or to charges having equivalent effect established under a common policy, the chargeable event shall occur and VAT shall become chargeable when the chargeable event in respect of those duties occurs and those duties become chargeable.

2. Where imported goods are not subject to any of the duties referred to in the second subparagraph of paragraph 1, Member States shall, as regards the chargeable event and the moment when VAT becomes chargeable, apply the provisions in force governing customs duties.

TITLE VII

TAXABLE AMOUNT

CHAPTER 4

Importation Of Goods

Article 72

For the purposes of this Directive, 'open market value' shall mean the full amount that, in order to obtain the goods or services in question at that time, a customer at the same marketing stage at which the supply of goods or services takes place, would have to pay, under conditions of fair competition, to a supplier at arm's length within the territory of the Member State in which the supply is subject to tax.

Where no comparable supply of goods or services can be ascertained, 'open market value' shall mean the following:

(1)   in respect of goods, an amount that is not less than the purchase price of the goods or of similar goods or, in the absence of a purchase price, the cost price, determined at the time of supply;

(2)   in respect of services, an amount that is not less than the full cost to the taxable person of providing the service.

CHAPTER 2

Supply of goods or services

Article 73

s10(1) In respect of the supply of goods or services, other than as referred to in Articles 74 to 77, the taxable amount shall include everything which constitutes consideration obtained or to be obtained by the supplier, in return for the supply, from the customer or a third party, including subsidies directly linked to the price of the supply.

Article 74

s10(4) Where a taxable person applies or disposes of goods forming part of his business assets, or where goods are retained by a taxable person, or by his successors, when his taxable economic activity ceases, as referred to in Articles 16 and 18, the taxable amount shall be the purchase price of the goods or of similar goods or, in the absence of a purchase price, the cost price, determined at the time when the application, disposal or retention takes place.

Article 75

In respect of the supply of services, as referred to in Article 26, where goods forming part of the assets of a business are used for private purposes or services are carried out free of charge, the taxable amount shall be the full cost to the taxable person of providing the services.

Article 76

(1A)
(4B) In respect of the supply of goods consisting in transfer to another Member State, the taxable amount shall be the purchase price of the goods or of similar goods or, in the absence of a purchase price, the cost price, determined at the time the transfer takes place.

Article 77

In respect of the supply by a taxable person of a service for the purposes of his business, as referred to in Article 27, the taxable amount shall be the open market value of the service supplied.

Article 78

(1) The taxable amount shall include the following factors:

(a)   taxes, duties, levies and charges, excluding the VAT itself;

(b)   incidental expenses, such as commission, packing, transport and insurance costs, charged by the supplier to the customer.

For the purposes of point (b) of the first paragraph, Member States may regard expenses covered by a separate agreement as incidental expenses.

Article 79

The taxable amount shall not include the following factors:

(a)   price reductions by way of discount for early payment;

(b)   price discounts and rebates granted to the customer and obtained by him at the time of the supply;

(c)   amounts received by a taxable person from the customer, as repayment of expenditure incurred in the name and on behalf of the customer, and entered in his books in a suspense account.

The taxable person must furnish proof of the actual amount of the expenditure referred to in point (c) of the first paragraph and may not deduct any VAT which may have been charged.

Article 80

(3A) 1.   In order to prevent tax evasion or avoidance, Member States may in any of the following cases take measures to ensure that, in respect of the supply of goods or services involving family or other close personal ties, management, ownership, membership, financial or legal ties as defined by the Member State, the taxable amount is to be the open market value:

(a)   where the consideration is lower than the open market value and the recipient of the supply does not have a full right of deduction under Articles 167 to 171 and Articles 173 to 177;

(b)   where the consideration is lower than the open market value and the supplier does not have a full right of deduction under Articles 167 to 171 and Articles 173 to 177 and the supply is subject to an exemption under Articles 132, 135, 136, 371, 375, 376, 377, 378(2), 379(2) or Articles 380 to 390;

(c)   where the consideration is higher than the open market value and the supplier does not have a full right of deduction under Articles 167 to 171 and Articles 173 to 177.

For the purposes of the first subparagraph, legal ties may include the relationship between an employer and employee or the employee's family, or any other closely connected persons.

2.   Where Member States exercise the option provided for in paragraph 1, they may restrict the categories of suppliers or recipients to whom the measures shall apply.

3.   Member States shall inform the VAT Committee of national legislative measures adopted pursuant to paragraph 1 in so far as these are not measures authorised by the Council prior to 13 August 2006 in accordance with Article 27 (1) to (4) of Directive 77/388/EEC, and which are continued under paragraph 1 of this Article.

Article 81

Member States which, at 1 January 1993, were not availing themselves of the option under Article 98 of applying a reduced rate may, if they avail themselves of the option under Article 89, provide that in respect of the supply of works of art, as referred to in Article 103(2), the taxable amount is to be equal to a fraction of the amount determined in accordance with Articles 73, 74, 76, 78 and 79.

The fraction referred to in the first paragraph shall be determined in such a way that the VAT thus due is equal to at least 5% of the amount determined in accordance with Articles 73, 74, 76, 78 and 79.

Article 82

Member States may provide that, in respect of the supply of goods and services, the taxable amount is to include the value of exempt investment gold within the meaning of Article 346, which has been provided by the customer to be used as basis for working and which as a result, loses its VAT exempt investment gold status when such goods and services are supplied. The value to be used is the open market value of the investment gold at the time that those goods and services are supplied.

CHAPTER 3

Intra-Community acquisition of goods

Article 83

(1A)
(4B)
In respect of the intra-Community acquisition of goods, the taxable amount shall be established on the basis of the same factors as are used in accordance with Chapter 1 to determine the taxable amount for the supply of the same goods within the territory of the Member State concerned. In the case of the transactions, to be treated as intra-Community acquisitions of goods, referred to in Articles 21 and 22, the taxable amount shall be the purchase price of the goods or of similar goods or, in the absence of a purchase price, the cost price, determined at the time of the supply.

Article 84

0(1A)
0(4B)
1. Member States shall take the measures necessary to ensure that the excise duty due from or paid by the person making the intra-Community acquisition of a product subject to excise duty is included in the taxable amount in accordance with point (a) of the first paragraph of Article 78.

2. Where, after the intra-Community acquisition of goods has been made, the person acquiring the goods obtains a refund of the excise duty paid in the Member State in which dispatch or transport of the goods began, the taxable amount shall be reduced accordingly in the Member State in the territory of which the acquisition was made.

CHAPTER 4

Importation of goods

Article 85

s15 In respect of the importation of goods, the taxable amount shall be the value for customs purposes, determined in accordance with the Community provisions in force.

Article 86

s15 1. The taxable amount shall include the following factors, in so far as they are not already included:

(a) taxes, duties, levies and other charges due outside the Member State of importation, and those due by reason of importation, excluding the VAT to be levied;

(b) incidental expenses, such as commission, packing, transport and insurance costs, incurred up to the first place of destination within the territory of the Member State of importation as well as those resulting from transport to another place of destination within the Community, if that other place is known when the chargeable event occurs.

2. For the purposes of point (b) of paragraph 1, 'first place of destination' shall mean the place mentioned on the consignment note or on any other

document under which the goods are imported into the Member State of importation. If no such mention is made, the first place of destination shall be deemed to be the place of the first transfer of cargo in the Member State of importation.

Article 87

s15 The taxable amount shall not include the following factors:

(a)   price reductions by way of discount for early payment;

(b)   price discounts and rebates granted to the customer and obtained by him at the time of importation.

Article 88

s15 Where goods temporarily exported from the Community are reimported after having undergone, outside the Community, repair, processing, adaptation, making up or re-working, Member States shall take steps to ensure that the tax treatment of the goods for VAT purposes is the same as that which would have been applied had the repair, processing, adaptation, making up or re-working been carried out within their territory.

Article 89

s10A Member States which, at 1 January 1993, were not availing themselves of the option under Article 98 of applying a reduced rate may provide that in respect of the importation of works of art, collectors' items and antiques, as defined in points (2), (3) and (4) of Article 311(1), the taxable amount is to be equal to a fraction of the amount determined in accordance with Articles 85, 86 and 87.

The fraction referred to in the first paragraph shall be determined in such a way that the VAT thus due on the importation is equal to at least 5% of the amount determined in accordance with Articles 85, 86 and 87.

CHAPTER 5

Miscellaneous provisions

Article 90

s10(3)(c) 1.   In the case of cancellation, refusal or total or partial non-payment, or where the price is reduced after the supply takes place, the taxable amount shall be reduced accordingly under conditions which shall be determined by the Member States.

2.   In the case of total or partial non-payment, Member States may derogate from paragraph 1.

Article 91

s10(9A) 1.   Where the factors used to determine the taxable amount on importation are expressed in a currency other than that of the Member State in which assessment takes place, the exchange rate shall be determined in accordance with the Community provisions governing the calculation of the value for customs purposes.

2.   Where the factors used to determine the taxable amount of a transaction other than the importation of goods are expressed in a currency other than that of the Member State in which assessment takes place, the exchange rate applicable shall be the latest selling rate recorded, at the time VAT becomes chargeable, on the most representative exchange market or markets of the Member State concerned, or a rate determined by reference to that or those markets, in accordance with the rules laid down by that Member State.

However, for some of the transactions referred to in the first subparagraph or for certain categories of taxable persons, Member States may use the exchange rate determined in accordance with the Community provisions in force governing the calculation of the value for customs purposes.

Article 92

As regards the costs of returnable packing material, Member States may take one of the following measures:

(a)   exclude them from the taxable amount and take the measures necessary to ensure that this amount is adjusted if the packing material is not returned;

(b)   include them in the taxable amount and take the measures necessary to ensure that this amount is adjusted if the packing material is in fact returned.

TITLE VIII

RATES

CHAPTER 1

Application of rates

Article 93

(1A) The rate applicable to taxable transactions shall be that in force at the time of the chargeable event.

However, in the following situations, the rate applicable shall be that in force when VAT becomes chargeable:

(a)   in the cases referred to in Articles 65 and 66;

(b)   in the case of an intra-Community acquisition of goods;

(c)   in the cases, concerning the importation of goods, referred to in the second subparagraph of Article 71(1) and in Article 71(2).

Article 94

s11(1A) 1. The rate applicable to the intra-Community acquisition of goods shall be that applied to the supply of like goods within the territory of the Member State.

s11(1AA) 2. Subject to the option under Article 103(1) of applying a reduced rate to the importation of works of art, collectors' items or antiques, the rate applicable to the importation of goods shall be that applied to the supply of like goods within the territory of the Member State.

Article 95

s 35 Where rates are changed, Member States may, in the cases referred to in Articles 65 and 66, effect adjustments in order to take account of the rate applying at the time when the goods or services were supplied.

Member States may also adopt all appropriate transitional measures.

CHAPTER 2

Structure and level of rates

Section 1

Standard rate

Article 96

s11(1) Member States shall apply a standard rate of VAT, which shall be fixed by each Member State as a percentage of the taxable amount and which shall be the same for the supply of goods and for the supply of services.

Article 97

1. From 1 January 2006 until 31 December 2010, the standard rate may not be less than 15 %.
2. The Council shall decide, in accordance with Article 93 of the Treaty, on the level of the standard rate to be applied after 31 December 2010.

Section 2

Reduced rates
Article 98

1. Member States may apply either one or two reduced rates.

s11(1) 2. The reduced rates shall apply only to supplies of goods or services in the categories set out in Annex III.

[The reduced rates shall not apply to the services referred to in point (k) of Article 56(1).][1]

3.   When applying the reduced rates provided for in paragraph 1 to categories of goods, Member States may use the Combined Nomenclature to establish the precise coverage of the category concerned.

_____
Amendments
1   With effect from 1 January 2010 and in accordance with Art 2(2) of Council Directive 2008/8/EC of 12 February 2008, this subparagraph shall read:
     'The reduced rates shall not apply to electronically supplied services.'

Article 99

1.   The reduced rates shall be fixed as a percentage of the taxable amount, which may not be less than 5%.
2.   Each reduced rate shall be so fixed that the amount of VAT resulting from its application is such that the VAT deductible under Articles 167 to 171 and Articles 173 to 177 can normally be deducted in full.

Article 100

On the basis of a report from the Commission, the Council shall, starting in 1994, review the scope of the reduced rates every two years.

The Council may, in accordance with Article 93 of the Treaty, decide to alter the list of goods and services set out in Annex III.

Article 101

By 30 June 2007 at the latest the Commission shall present to the European Parliament and the Council an overall assessment report on the impact of reduced rates applying to locally supplied services, including restaurant services, notably in terms of job creation, economic growth and the proper functioning of the internal market, based on a study carried out by an independent economic think-tank.

Section 3

Particular provisions

Article 102

s11(1) Member States may apply a reduced rate to the supply of natural gas, of electricity or of district heating, provided that no risk of distortion of competition thereby arises.

Any Member State intending to apply a reduced rate under the first paragraph must, before doing so, inform the Commission accordingly. The Commission shall decide whether or not there is a risk of distortion of competition. If the Commission has not taken that decision within three months of receipt of the information, no risk of distortion of competition shall be deemed to exist.

Article 103

s11(1AA) 1.   Member States may provide that the reduced rate, or one of the reduced rates, which they apply in accordance with Articles 98 and 99 is also to apply to the importation of works of art, collectors' items and antiques, as defined in points (2), (3) and (4) of Article 311(1).

2.   If Member States avail themselves of the option under paragraph 1, they may also apply the reduced rate to the following transactions:

(a)   the supply of works of art, by their creator or his successors in title;

(b)   the supply of works of art, on an occasional basis, by a taxable person other than a taxable dealer, where the works of art have been imported by the taxable person himself, or where they have been supplied to him by their creator or his successors in title, or where they have entitled him to full deduction of VAT.

Article 104

Austria may, in the communes of Jungholz and Mittelberg (Kleines Walsertal), apply a second standard rate which is lower than the corresponding rate applied in the rest of Austria but not less than 15%.

Article 105

Portugal may, in the case of transactions carried out in the autonomous regions of the Azores and Madeira and of direct importation into those regions, apply rates lower than those applying on the mainland.

CHAPTER 3

Temporary provisions for particular labour-intensive services

Article 106

The Council may, acting unanimously on a proposal from the Commission, allow Member States to apply until 31 December 2010 at the latest the reduced rates provided for in Article 98 to services listed in Annex IV.

The reduced rates may be applied to services from no more than two of the categories set out in Annex IV.

In exceptional cases a Member State may be allowed to apply the reduced rates to services from three of those categories.

Article 107

The services referred to in Article 106 must meet the following conditions:

(a)   they must be labour-intensive;

(b)   they must largely be provided direct to final consumers;

(c)   they must be mainly local and not likely to cause distortion of competition.

There must also be a close link between the decrease in prices resulting from the rate reduction and the foreseeable increase in demand and employment. Application of a reduced rate must not prejudice the smooth functioning of the internal market.

Article 108

Any Member State wishing to apply for the first time after 31 December 2005 a reduced rate to one or more of the services referred to in Article 106 pursuant to this Article shall inform the Commission accordingly no later than 31 March 2006. It shall communicate to it before that date all relevant information concerning the new measures it wishes to introduce, in particular the following:

(a)   scope of the measure and detailed description of the services concerned;

(b)   particulars showing that the conditions laid down in Article 107 have been met;

(c)   particulars showing the budgetary cost of the measure envisaged.

CHAPTER 4

Special provisions applying until the adoption of definitive arrangements

Article 109

Pending introduction of the definitive arrangements referred to in Article 402, the provisions laid down in this Chapter shall apply.

Article 110

Member States which, at 1 January 1991, were granting exemptions with deductibility of the VAT paid at the preceding stage or applying reduced rates lower than the minimum laid down in Article 99 may continue to grant those exemptions or apply those reduced rates.

The exemptions and reduced rates referred to in the first paragraph must be in accordance with Community law and must have been adopted for clearly defined social reasons and for the benefit of the final consumer.

Article 111

Subject to the conditions laid down in the second paragraph of Article 110, exemptions with deductibility of the VAT paid at the preceding stage may continue to be granted in the following cases:

(a)   by Finland in respect of the supply of newspapers and periodicals sold by subscription and the printing of publications distributed to the members of corporations for the public good;

(b)   by Sweden in respect of the supply of newspapers, including radio and cassette newspapers for the visually impaired, pharmaceutical products supplied to hospitals or on prescription, and the production of, or other related services concerning, periodicals of non-profit-making organisations.

Article 112

If the provisions of Article 110 cause for Ireland distortion of competition in the supply of energy products for heating and lighting, Ireland may, on specific request, be authorised by the Commission to apply a reduced rate to such supplies, in accordance with Articles 98 and 99.

In the case referred to in the first paragraph, Ireland shall submit a request to the Commission, together with all necessary information. If the Commission has not taken a decision within three months of receiving the request, Ireland shall be deemed to be authorised to apply the reduced rates proposed.

Article 113

Member States which, at 1 January 1991, in accordance with Community law, were granting exemptions with deductibility of the VAT paid at the preceding stage or applying reduced rates lower than the minimum laid down in Article 99, in respect of goods and services other than those specified in Annex III, may apply the reduced rate, or one of the two reduced rates, provided for in Article 98 to the supply of such goods or services.

Article 114

1.   Member States which, on 1 January 1993, were obliged to increase their standard rate in force at 1 January 1991 by more than 2% may apply a reduced rate lower than the minimum laid down in Article 99 to the supply of goods and services in the categories set out in Annex III.

The Member States referred to in the first subparagraph may also apply such a rate to restaurant services, children's clothing, children's footwear and housing.

2.   Member States may not rely on paragraph 1 to introduce exemptions with deductibility of the VAT paid at the preceding stage.

Article 115

Member States which, at 1 January 1991, were applying a reduced rate to restaurant services, children's clothing, children's footwear or housing may continue to apply such a rate to the supply of those goods or services.

Article 116

Portugal may apply one of the two reduced rates provided for in Article 98 to restaurant services, provided that the rate is not lower than 12%.

Article 117

1. For the purposes of applying Article 115, Austria may continue to apply a reduced rate to restaurant services.

2. Austria may apply one of the two reduced rates provided for in Article 98 to the letting of immovable property for residential use, provided that the rate is not lower than 10%.

Article 118

Member States which, at 1 January 1991, were applying a reduced rate to the supply of goods or services other than those specified in Annex III may apply the reduced rate, or one of the two reduced rates, provided for in Article 98 to the supply of those goods or services, provided that the rate is not lower than 12 %.

The first paragraph shall not apply to the supply of second-hand goods, works of art, collectors' items or antiques, as defined in points (1) to (4) of Article 311(1), subject to VAT in accordance with the margin scheme provided for in Articles 312 to 325 or the arrangements for sales by public auction.

Article 119

For the purposes of applying Article 118, Austria may apply a reduced rate to wines produced on an agricultural holding by the producer-farmer, provided that the rate is not lower than 12%.

Article 120

Greece may apply rates up to 30 % lower than the corresponding rates applied in mainland Greece in the departments of Lesbos, Chios, Samos, the Dodecanese and the Cyclades, and on the islands of Thassos, the Northern Sporades, Samothrace and Skiros.

Article 121

Member States which, at 1 January 1993, regarded work under contract as the supply of goods may apply to the delivery of work under contract the rate applicable to the goods obtained after execution of the work under contract.

For the purposes of applying the first paragraph, 'delivery of work under contract' shall mean the handing over by a contractor to his customer of movable property made or assembled by the contractor from materials or objects entrusted to him by the customer for that purpose, whether or not the contractor has provided any part of the materials used.

Article 122

Member States may apply a reduced rate to the supply of live plants and other floricultural products, including bulbs, roots and the like, cut flowers and ornamental foliage, and of wood for use as firewood.

CHAPTER 5

Temporary provisions

[Article 123

The Czech Republic may, until 31 December 2010, continue to apply a reduced rate of not less than 5% to the supply of construction work for residential housing not provided as part of a social policy, excluding building materials.][1]

Amendments
1   Substituted by Art 1(1), Council Directive 2007/75/EC of 20 December 2007, w.e.f. 1 January 2008

[...][1]

Amendments
1   Article 124 deleted by Art 1(2), Council Directive 2007/75/EC of 20 December 2007, w.e.f. 1 January 2008

Article 125

1.   Cyprus may, [until 31 December 2010][1], continue to grant an exemption with deductibility of VAT paid at the preceding stage in respect of the supply of pharmaceuticals and foodstuffs for human consumption, with the exception of ice cream, ice lollies, frozen yoghurt, water ice and similar products and savoury food products (potato crisps/sticks, puffs and similar products packaged for human consumption without further preparation).

2.   Cyprus may continue to apply a reduced rate of not less than 5% to the supply of restaurant services, [until 31 December 2010][1] or until the introduction of definitive arrangements, as referred to in Article 402, whichever is the earlier.

Amendments
1   Substituted by Art 1(3), Council Directive 2007/75/EC of 20 December 2007, w.e.f. 1 January 2008

[...][1]

Amendments
1   Article 126 deleted by Art 1(4), Council Directive 2007/75/EC of 20 December 2007, w.e.f. 1 January 2008

Article 127

Malta may, until [31 December 2010][1], continue to grant an exemption with deductibility of VAT paid at the preceding stage in respect of the supply of foodstuffs for human consumption and pharmaceuticals.

Amendments
1   Substituted by Art 1(5), Council Directive 2007/75/EC of 20 December 2007, w.e.f. 1 January 2008

[Article 128

1.   Poland may, until 31 December 2010, grant an exemption with deductibility of VAT paid at the preceding stage in respect of the supply of certain books and specialist periodicals.

2. Poland may, until 31 December 2010 or until the introduction of definitive arrangements, as referred to in Article 402, whichever is the earlier, continue to apply a reduced rate of not less than 7% to the supply of restaurant services.

3. Poland may, until 31 December 2010, continue to apply a reduced rate of not less than 3% to the supply of foodstuffs as referred to in point (1) of Annex III.

4. Poland may, until 31 December 2010, continue to apply a reduced rate of not less than 7% to the supply of services, not provided as part of a social policy, for construction, renovation and alteration of housing, excluding building materials, and to the supply before first occupation of residential buildings or parts of residential buildings, as referred to in Article 12(1)(a).][1]

Amendments
1 Substituted by Art 1(6), Council Directive 2007/75/EC of 20 December 2007, w.e.f. 1 January 2008

Article 129

1. Slovenia may, [until 31 December 2010][1] or until the introduction of definitive arrangements as referred to in Article 402, whichever is the earlier, continue to apply a reduced rate of not less than 8,5% to the preparation of meals.

2. Slovenia may, [until 31 December 2010][1], continue to apply a reduced rate of not less than 5% to the supply of construction, renovation and maintenance work for residential housing not provided as part of a social policy, excluding building materials.

Amendments
1 Substituted by Art 1(7), Council Directive 2007/75/EC of 20 December 2007, w.e.f. 1 January 2008

[...][1]

Amendments
1 Article 130 deleted by Art 1(2), Council Directive 2007/75/EC of 20 December 2007, w.e.f. 1 January 2008

TITLE IX

EXEMPTIONS

CHAPTER 1
General provisions

Article 131

s56 The exemptions provided for in Chapters 2 to 9 shall apply without prejudice to other Community provisions and in accordance with conditions which the Member States shall lay down for the purposes of ensuring the correct and straightforward application of those exemptions and of preventing any possible evasion, avoidance or abuse.

CHAPTER 2

Exemptions for certain activities in the public interest

Article 132

1.   Member States shall exempt the following transactions:

1st Sch (xia) (a)   the supply by the public postal services of services other than passenger transport and telecommunications services, and the supply of goods incidental thereto;

1st Sch (iii)
1st Sch (iiia)
1st Sch (iiib)
1st Sch (v)
1st Sch (xxv) (b)   hospital and medical care and closely related activities undertaken by bodies governed by public law or, under social conditions comparable with those applicable to bodies governed by public law, by hospitals, centres for medical treatment or diagnosis and

1st Sch (iii)
1st Sch (iiia)   other duly recognised establishments of a similar nature;

1st Sch (iiib)
1st Sch (v) (c)   the provision of medical care in the exercise of the medical and paramedical professions as defined by the Member State concerned;

1st Sch (xviii) (d)   the supply of human organs, blood and milk;

1st Sch (iiia) (e)   the supply of services by dental technicians in their professional capacity and the supply of dental prostheses by dentists and dental technicians;

1st Sch (xxiia) (f)   the supply of services by independent groups of persons, who are carrying on an activity which is exempt from VAT or in relation to which they are not taxable persons, for the purpose of rendering their members the services directly necessary for the exercise of that activity, where those groups merely claim from their members exact reimbursement of their share of the joint expenses, provided that such exemption is not likely to cause distortion of competition;

1st Sch (vii) (g)   the supply of services and of goods closely linked to welfare and social security work, including those supplied by old people's homes, by bodies governed by public law or by other bodies recognised by the Member State concerned as being devoted to social wellbeing;

1st Sch (vi) (h)   the supply of services and of goods closely linked to the protection of children and young persons by bodies governed by public law or by other organisations recognised by the Member State concerned as being devoted to social wellbeing;

1st Sch (ii) (i)   the provision of children's or young people's education, school or university education, vocational training or retraining, including the supply of services and of goods closely related thereto, by bodies governed by public law having such as their aim or by other organisations recognised by the Member State concerned as having similar objects

1st Sch (ii); (j)   tuition given privately by teachers and covering school or university education;

1st Sch (ii)
1st Sch (iii)
1st Sch (vi)
1st Sch (vii)   (k)   the supply of staff by religious or philosophical institutions for the purpose of the activities referred to in points (b), (g), (h) and (i) and with a view to spiritual welfare;

1st Sch (xxii) (l)   the supply of services, and the supply of goods closely linked thereto, to their members in their common interest in return for a subscription fixed in accordance with their rules by non-profit-making organisations with aims of a political, trade-union, religious, patriotic, philosophical, philanthropic or civic nature, provided that this exemption is not likely to cause distortion of competition;

1st Sch (xxiii) (m)   the supply of certain services closely linked to sport or physical education by non-profit-making organisations to persons taking part in sport or physical education;

1st Sch (viiia) (n)   the supply of certain cultural services, and the supply of goods closely linked thereto, by bodies governed by public law or by other cultural bodies recognised by the Member State concerned;

(o)   the supply of services and goods, by organisations whose activities are exempt pursuant to points (b), (g), (h), (i), (l), (m) and (n), in connection with fund-raising events organised exclusively for their own benefit, provided that exemption is not likely to cause distortion of competition;

1st Sch (xiv) (p)   the supply of transport services for sick or injured persons in vehicles specially designed for the purpose, by duly authorised bodies;

1st Sch (xiii) (q)   the activities, other than those of a commercial nature, carried out by public radio and television bodies.

2.   For the purposes of point (o) of paragraph 1, Member States may introduce any restrictions necessary, in particular as regards the number of events or the amount of receipts which give entitlement to exemption.

Article 133

Member States may make the granting to bodies other than those governed by public law of each exemption provided for in points (b), (g), (h), (i), (l), (m) and (n) of Article 132(1) subject in each individual case to one or more of the following conditions:

(a)   the bodies in question must not systematically aim to make a profit, and any surpluses nevertheless arising must not be distributed, but must be assigned to the continuance or improvement of the services supplied;

(b)   those bodies must be managed and administered on an essentially voluntary basis by persons who have no direct or indirect interest, either themselves or through intermediaries, in the results of the activities concerned;

(c)   those bodies must charge prices which are approved by the public authorities or which do not exceed such approved prices or, in respect of those services not subject to approval, prices lower than those charged for similar services by commercial enterprises subject to VAT;

(d)   the exemptions must not be likely to cause distortion of competition to the disadvantage of commercial enterprises subject to VAT.

Member States which, pursuant to Annex E of Directive 77/388/ EEC, on 1 January 1989 applied VAT to the transactions referred to in Article 132(1)(m) and (n) may also apply the conditions provided for in point (d) of the first paragraph when the said supply of goods or services by bodies governed by public law is granted exemption.

Article 134

The supply of goods or services shall not be granted exemption, as provided for in points (b), (g), (h), (i), (l), (m) and (n) of Article 132(1), in the following cases:

(a)   where the supply is not essential to the transactions exempted;

(b)   where the basic purpose of the supply is to obtain additional income for the body in question through transactions which are in direct competition with those of commercial enterprises subject to VAT.

CHAPTER 3

Exemptions for other activities

Article 135

1.   Member States shall exempt the following transactions:

1st Sch (xi) (a)   insurance and reinsurance transactions, including related services performed by insurance brokers and insurance agents;

1st Sch (i)(e) (b)   the granting and the negotiation of credit and the management of credit by the person granting it;

1st Sch (i)(f) (c)   the negotiation of or any dealings in credit guarantees or any other security for money and the management of credit guarantees by the person who is granting the credit;

1st Sch (i)(c) (d)   transactions, including negotiation, concerning deposit and current accounts, payments, transfers, debts, cheques and other negotiable instruments, but excluding debt collection;

1st Sch (i)(d) (e)   transactions, including negotiation, concerning currency, bank notes and coins used as legal tender, with the exception of collectors' items, that is to say, gold, silver or other metal coins or bank notes which are not normally used as legal tender or coins of numismatic interest;

1st Sch (i)(a) (f)   transactions, including negotiation but not management or safekeeping, in shares, interests in companies or associations, debentures and other securities, but excluding documents establishing title to goods, and the rights or securities referred to in Article 15(2);

1st Sch (i)(g) (g)   the management of special investment funds as defined by Member States;

1st Sch (xia) (h)   the supply at face value of postage stamps valid for use for postal services within their respective territory, fiscal stamps and other similar stamps;

1st Sch (xv)
1st Sch (xvi) (i)   betting, lotteries and other forms of gambling, subject to the conditions and limitations laid down by each Member State;

(j)   the supply of a building or parts thereof, and of the land on which it stands, other than the supply referred to in point (a) of Article 12(1);

s4 (k)   the supply of land which has not been built on other than the supply of building land as referred to in point (b) of Article 12(1);

1st Sch (iv) (l)   the leasing or letting of immovable property.

1st Sch (iv) 2.   The following shall be excluded from the exemption provided for in point (l) of paragraph 1:

(a)   the provision of accommodation, as defined in the laws of the Member States, in the hotel sector or in sectors with a similar function, including the provision of accommodation in holiday camps or on sites developed for use as camping sites;

(b)   the letting of premises and sites for the parking of vehicles;

(c)   the letting of permanently installed equipment and machinery;

(d)   the hire of safes.

Member States may apply further exclusions to the scope of the exemption referred to in point (l) of paragraph 1.

Article 136

(xxiv) Member States shall exempt the following transactions:

(a)   the supply of goods used solely for an activity exempted under Articles 132, 135, 371, 375, 376 and 377, Article 378 (2), Article 379(2) and Articles 380 to 390, if those goods have not given rise to deductibility;

(b)   the supply of goods on the acquisition or application of which VAT was not deductible, pursuant to Article 176.

Article 137

s7 1.   Member States may allow taxable persons a right of option for taxation in respect of the following transactions:

(a)   the financial transactions referred to in points (b) to (g) of Article 135(1);

(b)   the supply of a building or of parts thereof, and of the land on which the building stands, other than the supply referred to in point (a) of Article 12(1);

(c)   the supply of land which has not been built on other than the supply of building land referred to in point (b) of Article 12(1);

(d)   the leasing or letting of immovable property.

2.   Member States shall lay down the detailed rules governing exercise of the option under paragraph 1.

Member States may restrict the scope of that right of option.

CHAPTER 4

Exemptions for intra-community transactions

Section 1

Exemptions related to the supply of goods

Article 138

2nd Sch 1.   Member States shall exempt the supply of goods dispatched or
(i)(b)   transported to a destination outside their respective territory but within the Community, by or on behalf of the vendor or the person acquiring the goods, for another taxable person, or for a non-taxable legal person acting as such in a Member State other than that in which dispatch or transport of the goods began.

2.   In addition to the supply of goods referred to in paragraph 1, Member States shall exempt the following transactions:

2nd Sch   (a)   the supply of new means of transport, dispatched or transported
(i)(c)   to the customer at a destination outside their respective territory but within the Community, by or on behalf of the vendor or the customer, for taxable persons, or non-taxable legal persons, whose intra-Community acquisitions of goods are not subject to VAT pursuant to Article 3(1), or for any other non-taxable person;

2nd Sch   (b)   the supply of products subject to excise duty, dispatched or
(i)(cc)   transported to a destination outside their respective territory but within the Community, to the customer, by or on behalf of the vendor or the customer, for taxable persons, or non-taxable legal persons, whose intra-Community acquisitions of goods other than products subject to excise duty are not subject to VAT pursuant to Article 3(1), where those products have been dispatched or

transported in accordance with Article 7(4) and (5) or Article 16 of Directive 92/12/EEC;

(c) the supply of goods, consisting in a transfer to another Member State, which would have been entitled to exemption under paragraph 1 and points (a) and (b) if it had been made on behalf of another taxable person.

Article 139

1. The exemption provided for in Article 138(1) shall not apply to the supply of goods carried out by taxable persons who are covered by the exemption for small enterprises provided for in Articles 282 to 292.

    Nor shall that exemption apply to the supply of goods to taxable persons, or non-taxable legal persons, whose intra-Community acquisitions of goods are not subject to VAT pursuant to Article 3(1).

2. The exemption provided for in Article 138(2)(b) shall not apply to the supply of products subject to excise duty by taxable persons who are covered by the exemption for small enterprises provided for in Articles 282 to 292.

3. The exemption provided for in Article 138(1) and (2)(b) and (c) shall not apply to the supply of goods subject to VAT in accordance with the margin scheme provided for in Articles 312 to 325 or the special arrangements for sales by public auction.

    The exemption provided for in Article 138(1) and (2)(c) shall not apply to the supply of second-hand means of transport, as defined in Article 327(3), subject to VAT in accordance with the transitional arrangements for second-hand means of transport.

Section 2

Exemptions for intra-Community acquisitions of goods

Article 140

3A(3) Member States shall exempt the following transactions:

(a) the intra-Community acquisition of goods the supply of which by taxable persons would in all circumstances be exempt within their respective territory;

(b) the intra-Community acquisition of goods the importation of which would in all circumstances be exempt under points (a), (b) and (c) and (e) to (l) of Article 143;

(c) the intra-Community acquisition of goods where, pursuant to Articles 170 and 171, the person acquiring the goods would in all circumstances be entitled to full reimbursement of the VAT due under Article 2(1)(b).

Article 141

s3A(5)
s8(3D)
(b)
Each Member State shall take specific measures to ensure that VAT is not charged on the intra-Community acquisition of goods within its territory, made in accordance with Article 40, where the following conditions are met:

(a)   the acquisition of goods is made by a taxable person who is not established in the Member State concerned but is identified for VAT purposes in another Member State;

(b)   the acquisition of goods is made for the purposes of the subsequent supply of those goods, in the Member State concerned, by the taxable person referred to in point (a);

(c)   the goods thus acquired by the taxable person referred to in point (a) are directly dispatched or transported, from a Member State other than that in which he is identified for VAT purposes, to the person for whom he is to carry out the subsequent supply;

(d)   the person to whom the subsequent supply is to be made is another taxable person, or a non-taxable legal person, who is identified for VAT purposes in the Member State concerned;

(e)   the person referred to in point (d) has been designated in accordance with Article 197 as liable for payment of the VAT due on the supply carried out by the taxable person who is not established in the Member State in which the tax is due.

Section 3

Exemptions for certain transport services

Article 142

2nd Sch
(iiia)
Member States shall exempt the supply of intra-Community transport of goods to and from the islands making up the autonomous regions of the Azores and Madeira, as well as the supply of transport of goods between those islands.

CHAPTER 5

Exemptions on importation

Article 143

Member States shall exempt the following transactions:

(a)   the final importation of goods of which the supply by a taxable person would in all circumstances be exempt within their respective territory;

(b)   the final importation of goods governed by Council Directives 69/169/ EEC, 83/181/EEC and 2006/79/EC;

(c)   the final importation of goods, in free circulation from a third territory forming part of the Community customs territory, which would be entitled to exemption under point (b) if they had been imported within the meaning of the first paragraph of Article 30;

nd Sch (d)   the importation of goods dispatched or transported from a third
(iiib)   territory or a third country into a Member State other than that in which the dispatch or transport of the goods ends, where the supply of such goods by the importer designated or recognised under Article 201 as liable for payment of VAT is exempt under Article 138;

(e)   the reimportation, by the person who exported them, of goods in the state in which they were exported, where those goods are exempt from customs duties;

(f)   the importation, under diplomatic and consular arrangements, of goods which are exempt from customs duties;

(g)   the importation of goods by international bodies recognised as such by the public authorities of the host Member State, or by members of such bodies, within the limits and under the conditions laid down by the international conventions establishing the bodies or by headquarters agreements;

(h)   the importation of goods, into Member States party to the North Atlantic Treaty, by the armed forces of other States party to that Treaty for the use of those forces or the civilian staff accompanying them or for supplying their messes or canteens where such forces take part in the common defence effort;

(i)   the importation of goods by the armed forces of the United Kingdom stationed in the island of Cyprus pursuant to the Treaty of Establishment concerning the Republic of Cyprus, dated 16 August 1960, which are for the use of those forces or the civilian staff accompanying them or for supplying their messes or canteens;

(j)   the importation into ports, by sea fishing undertakings, of their catches, unprocessed or after undergoing preservation for marketing but before being supplied;

(k)   the importation of gold by central banks;

h (xxvi) (l)   the importation of gas through the natural gas distribution system, or of electricity.

Article 144

Sch (xvia) Member States shall exempt the supply of services relating to the importation of goods where the value of such services is included in the taxable amount in accordance with Article 86(1)(b).

Article 145

1.   The Commission shall, where appropriate, as soon as possible, present to the Council proposals designed to delimit the scope of the

exemptions provided for in Articles 143 and 144 and to lay down the detailed rules for their implementation.

2. Pending the entry into force of the rules referred to in paragraph 1, Member States may maintain their national provisions in force.

Member States may adapt their national provisions so as to minimise distortion of competition and, in particular, to prevent non-taxation or double taxation within the Community.

Member States may use whatever administrative procedures they consider most appropriate to achieve exemption.

3. Member States shall notify to the Commission, which shall inform the other Member States accordingly, the provisions of national law which are in force, in so far as these have not already been notified, and those which they adopt pursuant to paragraph 2.

CHAPTER 6

Exemptions on exportation
Article 146

1. Member States shall exempt the following transactions:

2nd Sch (i)(a)(I) (a) the supply of goods dispatched or transported to a destination outside the Community by or on behalf of the vendor;

2nd Sch (i)(aa) (b) the supply of goods dispatched or transported to a destination outside the Community by or on behalf of a customer not established within their respective territory, with the exception of goods transported by the customer himself for the equipping, fuelling and provisioning of pleasure boats and private aircraft or any other means of transport for private use;

(c) the supply of goods to approved bodies which export them out of the Community as part of their humanitarian, charitable or teaching activities outside the Community;

2nd Sch (xvi) (d) the supply of services consisting in work on movable property acquired or imported for the purpose of undergoing such work within the Community, and dispatched or transported out of the Community by the supplier, by the customer if not established within their respective territory or on behalf of either of them;

(e) the supply of services, including transport and ancillary transactions, but excluding the supply of services exempted in accordance with Articles 132 and 135, where these are directly connected with the exportation or importation of goods covered by Article 61 and Article 157(1)(a).

2. The exemption provided for in point (c) of paragraph 1 may be granted by means of a refund of the VAT.

Article 147

s13 1.   Where the supply of goods referred to in point (b) of Article 146(1) relates to goods to be carried in the personal luggage of travellers, the exemption shall apply only if the following conditions are met:

      (a)   the traveller is not established within the Community;

      (b)   the goods are transported out of the Community before the end of the third month following that in which the supply takes place;

      (c)   the total value of the supply, including VAT, is more than EUR 175 or the equivalent in national currency, fixed annually by applying the conversion rate obtaining on the first working day of October with effect from 1 January of the following year.

However, Member States may exempt a supply with a total value of less than the amount specified in point (c) of the first subparagraph.

    2.   For the purposes of paragraph 1, **'a traveller who is not established within the Community'** shall mean a traveller whose permanent address or habitual residence is not located within the Community. In that case **'permanent address or habitual residence'** means the place entered as such in a passport, identity card or other document recognised as an identity document by the Member State within whose territory the supply takes place.

Proof of exportation shall be furnished by means of the invoice or other document in lieu thereof, endorsed by the customs office of exit from the Community.

Each Member State shall send to the Commission specimens of the stamps it uses for the endorsement referred to in the second subparagraph. The Commission shall forward that information to the tax authorities of the other Member States.

CHAPTER 7

EXEMPTIONS RELATED TO INTERNATIONAL TRANSPORT

Article 148

Member States shall exempt the following transactions:

Sch (vb) (a)   the supply of goods for the fuelling and provisioning of vessels used for navigation on the high seas and carrying passengers for reward or used for the purpose of commercial, industrial or fishing activities, or for rescue or assistance at sea, or for inshore fishing, with the exception, in the case of vessels used for inshore fishing, of ships' provisions;

     (b)   the supply of goods for the fuelling and provisioning of fighting ships, falling within the combined nomenclature (CN) code 8906 10 00, leaving their territory and bound for ports or anchorages outside the Member State concerned;

d Sch (v)(a) (c)   the supply, modification, repair, maintenance, chartering and hiring of the vessels referred to in point (a), and the supply, hiring, repair and maintenance of equipment, including fishing equipment, incorporated or used therein;

nd Sch (iv) (d)   the supply of services other than those referred to in point (c), to meet the direct needs of the vessels referred to in point (a) or of their cargoes;

d Sch (v)(b) (e)   the supply of goods for the fuelling and provisioning of aircraft used by airlines operating for reward chiefly on international routes;

nd Sch (va) (f)   the supply, modification, repair, maintenance, chartering and hiring of the aircraft referred to in point (e), and the supply, hiring, repair and maintenance of equipment incorporated or used therein;

nd Sch (vc) (g)   the supply of services, other than those referred to in point (f), to meet the direct needs of the aircraft referred to in point (e) or of their cargoes.

Article 149

Portugal may treat sea and air transport between the islands making up the autonomous regions of the Azores and Madeira and between those regions and the mainland as international transport.

Article 150

1.   The Commission shall, where appropriate, as soon as possible, present to the Council proposals designed to delimit the scope of the exemptions provided for in Article 148 and to lay down the detailed rules for their implementation.

2.   Pending the entry into force of the provisions referred to in paragraph 1, Member States may limit the scope of the exemptions provided for in points (a) and (b) of Article 148.

CHAPTER 8

Exemptions relating to certain Transactions treated as exports

Article 151

1.   Member States shall exempt the following transactions:

(a)   the supply of goods or services under diplomatic and consular arrangements;

2nd Sch (iiic)   (b)   the supply of goods or services to international bodies recognised as such by the public authorities of the host Member State, and to members of such bodies, within the limits and under the conditions laid down by the international conventions establishing the bodies or by headquarters agreements;

(c)   the supply of goods or services within a Member State which is a party to the North Atlantic Treaty, intended either for the armed forces of other States party to that Treaty for the use of those forces, or of the civilian staff accompanying them, or for supplying their messes or canteens when such forces take part in the common defence effort;

(d)   the supply of goods or services to another Member State, intended for the armed forces of any State which is a party to the North Atlantic Treaty, other than the Member State of destination itself, for the use of those forces, or of the civilian staff accompanying them, or for supplying their messes or canteens when such forces take part in the common defence effort;

(e)   the supply of goods or services to the armed forces of the United Kingdom stationed in the island of Cyprus pursuant to the Treaty of Establishment concerning the Republic of Cyprus, dated 16 August 1960, which are for the use of those forces, or of the civilian staff accompanying them, or for supplying their messes or canteens.

Pending the adoption of common tax rules, the exemptions provided for in the first subparagraph shall be subject to the limitations laid down by the host Member State.

2.   In cases where the goods are not dispatched or transported out of the Member State in which the supply takes place, and in the case of services, the exemption may be granted by means of a refund of the VAT.

Article 152

nd Sch (x)   Member States shall exempt the supply of gold to central banks.

CHAPTER 9

Exemptions for the supply of services by intermediaries

Article 153

d Sch (vi) Member States shall exempt the supply of services by intermediaries, acting in the name and on behalf of another person, where they take part in the transactions referred to in Chapters 6, 7 and 8, or of transactions carried out outside the Community.

The exemption referred to in the first paragraph shall not apply to travel agents who, in the name and on behalf of travellers, supply services which are carried out in other Member States.

CHAPTER 10

Exemptions for transactions relating to international trade
Section 1
Customs warehouses, warehouses other than customs warehouses and similar arrangements
Article 154

For the purposes of this Section, **'warehouses other than customs warehouses'** shall, in the case of products subject to excise duty, mean the places defined as tax warehouses by Article 4(b) of Directive 92/12/EEC and, in the case of products not subject to excise duty, the places defined as such by the Member States.

Article 155

Without prejudice to other Community tax provisions, Member States may, after consulting the VAT Committee, take special measures designed to exempt all or some of the transactions referred to in this Section, provided that those measures are not aimed at final use or consumption and that the amount of VAT due on cessation of the arrangements or situations referred to in this Section corresponds to the amount of tax which would have been due had each of those transactions been taxed within their territory.

Article 156

1.   Member States may exempt the following transactions:

    (a)   the supply of goods which are intended to be presented to customs and, where applicable, placed in temporary storage;

    (b)   the supply of goods which are intended to be placed in a free zone or in a free warehouse;

    (c)   the supply of goods which are intended to be placed under customs warehousing arrangements or inward processing arrangements;

    (d)   the supply of goods which are intended to be admitted into territorial waters in order to be incorporated into drilling or production platforms, for purposes of the construction, repair, maintenance, alteration or fitting-out of such platforms, or to link such drilling or production platforms to the mainland;

    (e)   the supply of goods which are intended to be admitted into territorial waters for the fuelling and provisioning of drilling or production platforms.

2.   The places referred to in paragraph 1 shall be those defined as such by the Community customs provisions in force.

Article 157

1.   Member States may exempt the following transactions:

    (a)   the importation of goods which are intended to be placed under warehousing arrangements other than customs warehousing;

    (b)   the supply of goods which are intended to be placed, within their territory, under warehousing arrangements other than customs warehousing.

2.   Member States may not provide for warehousing arrangements other than customs warehousing for goods which are not subject to excise duty where those goods are intended to be supplied at the retail stage.

Article 158

1.   By way of derogation from Article 157(2), Member States may provide for warehousing arrangements other than customs warehousing in the following cases:

    (a)   where the goods are intended for tax-free shops, for the purposes of the supply of goods to be carried in the personal luggage of travellers taking flights or sea crossings to third territories or third countries, where that supply is exempt pursuant to point (b) of Article 146(1);

    (b)   where the goods are intended for taxable persons, for the purposes of carrying out supplies to travellers on board an aircraft or a ship in the course of a flight or sea crossing where the place of arrival is situated outside the Community;

    (c)   where the goods are intended for taxable persons, for the purposes of carrying out supplies which are exempt from VAT pursuant to Article 151.

2.   Where Member States exercise the option of exemption provided for in point (a) of paragraph 1, they shall take the measures necessary to ensure the correct and straightforward application of this exemption and to prevent any evasion, avoidance or abuse.

3.   For the purposes of point (a) of paragraph 1, 'tax-free shop' shall mean any establishment which is situated within an airport or port and which fulfils the conditions laid down by the competent public authorities.

Article 159

Member States may exempt the supply of services relating to the supply of goods referred to in Article 156, Article 157(1)(b) or Article 158.

Article 160

1.   Member States may exempt the following transactions:

(a)   the supply of goods or services carried out in the locations referred to in Article 156(1), where one of the situations specified therein still applies within their territory;

(b)   the supply of goods or services carried out in the locations referred to in Article 157(1)(b) or Article 158, where one of the situations specified in Article 157(1)(b) or in Article 158 (1) still applies within their territory.

2.   Where Member States exercise the option under point (a) of paragraph 1 in respect of transactions effected in customs warehouses, they shall take the measures necessary to provide for warehousing arrangements other than customs warehousing under which point (b) of paragraph 1 may be applied to the same transactions when they concern goods listed in Annex V and are carried out in warehouses other than customs warehouses.

Article 161

2nd
Sch (i)(d)
2nd
Sch (i)(e)

Member States may exempt supply of the following goods and of services relating thereto:

(a)   the supply of goods referred to in the first paragraph of Article 30 while they remain covered by arrangements for temporary importation with total exemption from import duty or by external transit arrangements;

(b)   the supply of goods referred to in the second paragraph of Article 30 while they remain covered by the internal Community transit procedure referred to in Article 276.

Article 162

Where Member States exercise the option provided for in this Section, they shall take the measures necessary to ensure that the intra-Community acquisition of goods intended to be placed under one of the arrangements or in one of the situations referred to in Article 156, Article 157(1)(b) or Article 158 is covered by the same provisions as the supply of goods carried out within their territory under the same conditions.

Article 163

If the goods cease to be covered by the arrangements or situations referred to in this Section, thus giving rise to importation for the purposes of Article 61, the Member State of importation shall take the measures necessary to prevent double taxation.

Section 2

Transactions exempted with a view to export and in the framework of trade between the Member States

Article 164

s13A 1.   Member States may, after consulting the VAT Committee, exempt the following transactions carried out by, or intended for, a taxable person up to an amount equal to the value of the exports carried out by that person during the preceding 12 months:

    (a)   intra-Community acquisitions of goods made by the taxable person, and imports for and supplies of goods to the taxable person, with a view to their exportation from the Community as they are or after processing;

    (b)   supplies of services linked with the export business of the taxable person.

2.   Where Member States exercise the option of exemption under paragraph 1, they shall, after consulting the VAT Committee, apply that exemption also to transactions relating to supplies carried out by the taxable person, in accordance with the conditions specified in Article 138, up to an amount equal to the value of the supplies carried out by that person, in accordance with the same conditions, during the preceding 12 months.

Article 165

Member States may set a common maximum amount for transactions which they exempt pursuant to Article 164.

Section 3

Provisions common to Sections 1 and 2

Article 166

The Commission shall, where appropriate, as soon as possible, present to the Council proposals concerning common arrangements for applying VAT to the transactions referred to in Sections 1 and 2.

TITLE X

DEDUCTIONS

CHAPTER 1

Origin and scope of right of deduction

Article 167

A right of deduction shall arise at the time the deductible tax becomes chargeable.

Article 168

s12(1)(a) In so far as the goods and services are used for the purposes of the taxed transactions of a taxable person, the taxable person shall be entitled, in the Member State in which he carries out these transactions, to deduct the following from the VAT which he is liable to pay:

(a)   the VAT due or paid in that Member State in respect of supplies to him of goods or services, carried out or to be carried out by another taxable person;

(b)   the VAT due in respect of transactions treated as supplies of goods or services pursuant to Article 18(a) and Article 27;

(c)   the VAT due in respect of intra-Community acquisitions of goods pursuant to Article 2(1)(b)(i);

(d)   the VAT due on transactions treated as intra-Community acquisitions in accordance with Articles 21 and 22;

(e)   the VAT due or paid in respect of the importation of goods into that Member State.

Article 169

s12(1)(b) In addition to the deduction referred to in Article 168, the taxable person shall be entitled to deduct the VAT referred to therein in so far as the goods and services are used for the purposes of the following:

(a)   transactions relating to the activities referred to in the second subparagraph of Article 9(1), carried out outside the Member State in which that tax is due or paid, in respect of which VAT would be deductible if they had been carried out within that Member State;

(b)   transactions which are exempt pursuant to Articles 138, 142 or 144, Articles 146 to 149, Articles 151, 152, 153 or 156, Article 157(1)(b), Articles 158 to 161 or Article 164;

(c)   transactions which are exempt pursuant to points (a) to (f) of Article 135(1), where the customer is established outside the Community or where those transactions relate directly to goods to be exported out of the Community.

Article 170

s13(3) [All taxable persons who, within the meaning of Article 1 of Directive 79/1072/EEC , Article 1 of Directive 86/560/EEC and Article 171 of this Directive, are not established in the Member State in which they purchase goods and services or import goods subject to VAT shall be entitled to obtain a refund of that VAT in so far as the goods and services are used for the purposes of the following:][1]

(a)   transactions referred to in Article 169;

(b)   transactions for which the tax is solely payable by the customer in accordance with Articles 194 to 197 or Article 199.

Amendments
1   With effect from 1 January 2010 and in accordance with Art 2(3) of Council Directive 2008/8/EC of 12 February 2008, this sentence shall read:

'All taxable persons who, within the meaning of Article 1 of Directive 86/560/EEC, Article 2(1) and Article 3 of Directive 2008/9/EC and Article 171 of this Directive, are not established in the Member State in which they purchase goods and services or import goods subject to VAT shall be entitled to obtain a refund of that VAT insofar as the goods and services are used for the purposes of the following:'

Article 171

s13(3) [1.   VAT shall be refunded to taxable persons who are not established in the Member State in which they purchase goods and services or import goods subject to VAT but who are established in another Member State, in accordance with the detailed implementing rules laid down in Directive 79/1072/EEC.][1]

The taxable persons referred to in Article 1 of Directive 79/1072/EEC shall also, for the purposes of applying that Directive, be regarded as taxable persons who are not established in the Member State concerned where, in the Member State in which they purchase goods and services or import goods subject to VAT, they have only carried out the supply of goods or services to a person designated in accordance with Articles 194 to 197 or Article 199 as liable for payment of VAT.

2.   VAT shall be refunded to taxable persons who are not established within the territory of the Community in accordance with the detailed implementing rules laid down in Directive 86/560/EEC.

The taxable persons referred to in Article 1 of Directive 86/560/EEC shall also, for the purposes of applying that Directive, be regarded as taxable persons who are not established in the Community where, in the Member State in which they purchase goods and services or import goods subject to VAT, they have only carried out the supply of goods or services to a person designated in accordance with Articles 194 to 197 or Article 199 as liable for payment of VAT.

3.   [Directives 79/1072/EEC and 86/560/EEC shall not apply to the supply of goods which is, or may be, exempted pursuant to Article 138 where the goods thus supplied are dispatched or transported by or on behalf of the person acquiring the goods.][2]

[...][3]

Amendments
1   With effect from 1 January 2010 and in accordance with Art 2(4) of Council Directive 2008/8/EC of 12 February 2008, this paragraph shall read:

'1.   VAT shall be refunded to taxable persons who are not established in the Member State in which they purchase goods and services or import goods subject to VAT but who are established in another Member State, in accordance with the detailed rules laid down in Directive 2008/9/EC.'

2   With effect from 1 January 2010 and in accordance with Art 2(4) of Council Directive 2008/8/EC of 12 February 2008, paragraph 3 shall read:

'3.   Directive 86/560/EEC shall not apply to:

(a) amounts of VAT which according to the legislation of the Member State of refund have been incorrectly invoiced;
(b) invoiced amounts of VAT in respect of supplies of goods the supply of which is, or may be, exempt pursuant to Article 138 or Article 146(1)(b).'

3 With effect from 1 January 2010 and in accordance with Art 2(5) of Council Directive 2008/8/EC of 12 February 2008, a new article 171a will be inserted and shall read:

'Member States may, instead of granting a refund of VAT pursuant to Directives 86/560/EEC or 2008/9/EC on those supplies of goods or services to a taxable person in respect of which the taxable person is liable to pay the tax in accordance with Articles 194 to 197 or Article 199, allow deduction of this tax pursuant to the procedure laid down in Article 168. The existing restrictions pursuant to Article 2(2) and Article 4(2) of Directive 86/560/EEC may be retained.

To that end, Member States may exclude the taxable person who is liable to pay the tax from the refund procedure pursuant to Directives 86/560/EEC or 2008/9/EC.'

Article 172

1.   Any person who is regarded as a taxable person by reason of the fact that he supplies, on an occasional basis, a new means of transport in accordance with the conditions specified in Article 138(1) and (2)(a) shall, in the Member State in which the supply takes place, be entitled to deduct the VAT included in the purchase price or paid in respect of the importation or the intra-Community acquisition of this means of transport, up to an amount not exceeding the amount of VAT for which he would be liable if the supply were not exempt.

A right of deduction shall arise and may be exercised only at the time of supply of the new means of transport.

2.   Member States shall lay down detailed rules for the implementation of paragraph 1.

CHAPTER 2

Proportional deduction

Article 173

s12(4) 1.   In the case of goods or services used by a taxable person both for transactions in respect of which VAT is deductible pursuant to Articles 168, 169 and 170, and for transactions in respect of which VAT is not deductible, only such proportion of the VAT as is attributable to the former transactions shall be deductible.

The deductible proportion shall be determined, in accordance with Articles 174 and 175, for all the transactions carried out by the taxable person.

2.   Member States may take the following measures:

(a)   authorise the taxable person to determine a proportion for each sector of his business, provided that separate accounts are kept for each sector;

(b)   require the taxable person to determine a proportion for each sector of his business and to keep separate accounts for each sector;

(c)   authorise or require the taxable person to make the deduction on the basis of the use made of all or part of the goods and services;

(d)   authorise or require the taxable person to make the deduction in accordance with the rule laid down in the first subparagraph of paragraph 1, in respect of all goods and services used for all transactions referred to therein;

(e)   provide that, where the VAT which is not deductible by the taxable person is insignificant, it is to be treated as nil.

Article 174

s12(4) 1.   The deductible proportion shall be made up of a fraction comprising the following amounts:

(a)   as numerator, the total amount, exclusive of VAT, of turnover per year attributable to transactions in respect of which VAT is deductible pursuant to Articles 168 and 169;

(b)   as denominator, the total amount, exclusive of VAT, of turnover per year attributable to transactions included in the numerator and to transactions in respect of which VAT is not deductible.

Member States may include in the denominator the amount of subsidies, other than those directly linked to the price of supplies of goods or services referred to in Article 73.

2.   By way of derogation from paragraph 1, the following amounts shall be excluded from the calculation of the deductible proportion:

(a)   the amount of turnover attributable to supplies of capital goods used by the taxable person for the purposes of his business;

(b)   the amount of turnover attributable to incidental real estate and financial transactions;

(c)   the amount of turnover attributable to the transactions specified in points (b) to (g) of Article 135(1) in so far as those transactions are incidental.

3.   Where Member States exercise the option under Article 191 not to require adjustment in respect of capital goods, they may include disposals of capital goods in the calculation of the deductible proportion.

Article 175

2(4)
(1)(x) 1.   The deductible proportion shall be determined on an annual basis, fixed as a percentage and rounded up to a figure not exceeding the next whole number.

2.   The provisional proportion for a year shall be that calculated on the basis of the preceding year's transactions. In the absence of any such transactions to refer to, or where they were insignificant in amount, the deductible proportion shall be estimated provisionally, under the supervision of the tax authorities, by the taxable person on the basis of his own forecasts.

However, Member States may retain the rules in force at 1 January 1979 or, in the case of the Member States which acceded to the Community after that date, on the date of their accession.

3.   Deductions made on the basis of such provisional proportions shall be adjusted when the final proportion is fixed during the following year.

CHAPTER 3

Restrictions on the right of deduction

Article 176

s12(3) The Council, acting unanimously on a proposal from the Commission, shall determine the expenditure in respect of which VAT shall not be deductible. VAT shall in no circumstances be deductible in respect of expenditure which is not strictly business expenditure, such as that on luxuries, amusements or entertainment.

Pending the entry into force of the provisions referred to in the first paragraph, Member States may retain all the exclusions provided for under their national laws at 1 January 1979 or, in the case of the Member States which acceded to the Community after that date, on the date of their accession.

Article 177

After consulting the VAT Committee, each Member State may, for cyclical economic reasons, totally or partly exclude all or some capital goods or other goods from the system of deductions.

In order to maintain identical conditions of competition, Member States may, instead of refusing deduction, tax goods manufactured by the taxable person himself or goods which he has purchased within the Community, or imported, in such a way that the tax does not exceed the amount of VAT which would be charged on the acquisition of similar goods.

CHAPTER 4

Rules governing exercise of the right of deduction

Article 178

In order to exercise the right of deduction, a taxable person must meet the following conditions:

s12(1)(a)(i) (a)   for the purposes of deductions pursuant to Article 168(a), in respect of the supply of goods or services, he must hold an invoice drawn up in accordance with Articles 220 to 236 and Articles 238, 239 and 240;

(b)   for the purposes of deductions pursuant to Article 168(b), in respect of transactions treated as the supply of goods or services, he must comply with the formalities as laid down by each Member State;

(c)   for the purposes of deductions pursuant to Article 168(c), in respect of the intra-Community acquisition of goods, he must set out in the VAT return provided for in Article 250 all the information needed for the amount of the VAT due on his intra-Community acquisitions of goods to be calculated and he must hold an invoice drawn up in accordance with Articles 220 to 236;

(d)   for the purposes of deductions pursuant to Article 168(d), in respect of transactions treated as intra-Community acquisitions of goods, he must complete the formalities as laid down by each Member State;

)(a)(ii) (e)   for the purposes of deductions pursuant to Article 168(e), in respect of the importation of goods, he must hold an import document specifying him as consignee or importer, and stating the amount of VAT due or enabling that amount to be calculated;

(f)   when required to pay VAT as a customer where Articles 194 to 197 or Article 199 apply, he must comply with the formalities as laid down by each Member State.

Article 179

2(1)(a) The taxable person shall make the deduction by subtracting from the total amount of VAT due for a given tax period the total amount of VAT in respect of which, during the same period, the right of deduction has arisen and is exercised in accordance with Article 178.

However, Member States may require that taxable persons who carry out occasional transactions, as defined in Article 12, exercise their right of deduction only at the time of supply.

Article 180

Member States may authorise a taxable person to make a deduction which he has not made in accordance with Articles 178 and 179.

Article 181

Member States may authorise a taxable person who does not hold an invoice drawn up in accordance with Articles 220 to 236 to make the deduction referred to in Article 168(c) in respect of his intra-Community acquisitions of goods.

Article 182

Member States shall determine the conditions and detailed rules for applying Articles 180 and 181.

Article 183

s20(1) Where, for a given tax period, the amount of deductions exceeds the amount
s12(2) of VAT due, the Member States may, in accordance with conditions which they shall determine, either make a refund or carry the excess forward to the following period.

However, Member States may refuse to refund or carry forward if the amount of the excess is insignificant.

CHAPTER 5

Adjustment of deductions

Article 184

s17(3) The initial deduction shall be adjusted where it is higher or lower than that to which the taxable person was entitled.

Article 185

1. Adjustment shall, in particular, be made where, after the VAT return is made, some change occurs in the factors used to determine the amount to be deducted, for example where purchases are cancelled or price reductions are obtained.
2. By way of derogation from paragraph 1, no adjustment shall be made in the case of transactions remaining totally or partially unpaid or in the case of destruction, loss or theft of property duly proved or confirmed, or in the case of goods reserved for the purpose of making gifts of small value or of giving samples, as referred to in Article 16. However, in the case of transactions remaining totally or partially unpaid or in the case of theft, Member States may require adjustment to be made.

Article 186

Member States shall lay down the detailed rules for applying Articles 184 and 185.

Article 187

1. In the case of capital goods, adjustment shall be spread over five years including that in which the goods were acquired or manufactured.

    Member States may, however, base the adjustment on a period of five full years starting from the time at which the goods are first used.

    s12E(3) In the case of immovable property acquired as capital goods, the adjustment period may be extended up to 20 years.
2. The annual adjustment shall be made only in respect of one-fifth of the VAT charged on the capital goods, or, if the adjustment period has been extended, in respect of the corresponding fraction thereof.

    The adjustment referred to in the first subparagraph shall be made on the basis of the variations in the deduction entitlement in subsequent years in relation to that for the year in which the goods were acquired, manufactured or, where applicable, used for the first time.

Article 188

1. If supplied during the adjustment period, capital goods shall be treated as if they had been applied to an economic activity of the taxable person up until expiry of the adjustment period.

    The economic activity shall be presumed to be fully taxed in cases where the supply of the capital goods is taxed.

The economic activity shall be presumed to be fully exempt in cases where the supply of the capital goods is exempt.

2.   The adjustment provided for in paragraph 1 shall be made only once in respect of all the time covered by the adjustment period that remains to run. However, where the supply of capital goods is exempt, Member States may waive the requirement for adjustment in so far as the purchaser is a taxable person using the capital goods in question solely for transactions in respect of which VAT is deductible.

Article 189

2E(2) For the purposes of applying Articles 187 and 188, Member States may take the following measures:

     (a)   define the concept of capital goods;

     (b)   specify the amount of the VAT which is to be taken into consideration for adjustment;

s20(5) (c)   adopt any measures needed to ensure that adjustment does not give rise to any unjustified advantage;

     (d)   permit administrative simplifications.

Article 190

For the purposes of Articles 187, 188, 189 and 191, Member States may regard as capital goods those services which have characteristics similar to those normally attributed to capital goods.

Article 191

If, in any Member State, the practical effect of applying Articles 187 and 188 is negligible, that Member State may, after consulting the VAT Committee, refrain from applying those provisions, having regard to the overall impact of VAT in the Member State concerned and the need for administrative simplification, and provided that no distortion of competition thereby arises.

Article 192

Where a taxable person transfers from being taxed in the normal way to a special scheme or vice versa, Member States may take all measures necessary to ensure that the taxable person does not enjoy unjustified advantage or sustain unjustified harm.

[...][1]

Amendments

1   With effect from 1 January 2010 and in accordance with Art 2(6) of Council Directive 2008/8/EC of 12 February 2008, Art 192a will be inserted and shall read:

'For the purposes of this Section, a taxable person who has a fixed establishment within the territory of the Member State where the tax is due shall be regarded as a taxable person who is not established within that Member State when the following conditions are met:

(a) he makes a taxable supply of goods or of services within the territory of that Member State;

(b) an establishment which the supplier has within the territory of that Member State does not intervene in that supply.'

TITLE XI

OBLIGATIONS OF TAXABLE PERSONS AND CERTAIN NON-TAXABLE PERSONS

CHAPTER 1

Obligation to pay

Section 1

Persons liable for payment of VAT to the tax authorities

Article 193

s8(1) VAT shall be payable by any taxable person carrying out a taxable supply of goods or services, except where it is payable by another person in the cases referred to in Articles 194 to 199 and Article 202.

Article 194

s8(1)(f) 1. Where the taxable supply of goods or services is carried out by a taxable person who is not established in the Member State in which the VAT is due, Member States may provide that the person liable for payment of VAT is the person to whom the goods or services are supplied.

2. Member States shall lay down the conditions for implementation of paragraph 1.

Article 195

s8(1)(g) VAT shall be payable by any person who is identified for VAT purposes in the Member State in which the tax is due and to whom goods are supplied in the circumstances specified in Articles 38 or 39, if the supplies are carried out by a taxable person not established within that Member State.

[Article 196

s8(2) VAT shall be payable by any taxable person to whom the services referred to in Article 56 are supplied or by any person identified for VAT purposes in the Member State in which the tax is due to whom the services referred to in Articles 44, 47, 50, 53, 54 and 55 are supplied, if the services are supplied by a taxable person not established in that Member State.][1]

Amendments

1   With effect from 1 January 2010 and in accordance with Art 2(7) of Council Directive 2008/8/EC of 12 February 2008, this article shall read:

   'VAT shall be payable by any taxable person, or non-taxable legal person identified for VAT purposes, to whom the services referred to in Article 44 are supplied, if the services are supplied by a taxable person not established within the territory of the Member State.'

Article 197

s3(8) 1. VAT shall be payable by the person to whom the goods are supplied when the following conditions are met:

    (a) the taxable transaction is a supply of goods carried out in accordance with the conditions laid down in Article 141;

    (b) the person to whom the goods are supplied is another taxable person, or a non-taxable legal person, identified for VAT purposes in the Member State in which the supply is carried out;

    (c) the invoice issued by the taxable person not established in the Member State of the person to whom the goods are supplied is drawn up in accordance with Articles 220 to 236.

2. Where a tax representative is appointed as the person liable for payment of VAT pursuant to Article 204, Member States may provide for a derogation from paragraph 1 of this Article.

Article 198

s6A 1. Where specific transactions relating to investment gold between a taxable person who is a member of a regulated gold bullion market and another taxable person who is not a member of that market are taxed pursuant to Article 352, Member States shall designate the customer as the person liable for payment of VAT.

If the customer who is not a member of the regulated gold bullion market is a taxable person required to be identified for VAT purposes in the Member State in which the tax is due solely in respect of the transactions referred to in Article 352, the vendor shall fulfil the tax obligations on behalf of the customer, in accordance with the law of that Member State.

2. Where gold material or semi-manufactured products of a purity of 325 thousandths or greater, or investment gold as defined in Article 344(1) is supplied by a taxable person exercising one of the options under Articles 348, 349 and 350, Member States may designate the customer as the person liable for payment of VAT.

3. Member States shall lay down the procedures and conditions for implementation of paragraphs 1 and 2.

Article 199

1. Member States may provide that the person liable for payment of VAT is the taxable person to whom any of the following supplies are made:

    (a) the supply of construction work, including repair, cleaning, maintenance, alteration and demolition services in relation to immovable property, as well as the handing over of construction works regarded as a supply of goods pursuant to Article 14(3);

(b)   the supply of staff engaged in activities covered by point (a);

(c)   the supply of immovable property, as referred to in Article 135(1) (j) and (k), where the supplier has opted for taxation of the supply pursuant to Article 137;

(d)   the supply of used material, used material which cannot be re-used in the same state, scrap, industrial and non industrial waste, recyclable waste, part processed waste and certain goods and services, as listed in Annex VI;

(e)   the supply of goods provided as security by one taxable person to another in execution of that security;

(f)   the supply of goods following the cession of a reservation of ownership to an assignee and the exercising of this right by the assignee;

(g)   the supply of immovable property sold by a judgment debtor in a compulsory sale procedure.

2.   When applying the option provided for in paragraph 1, Member States may specify the supplies of goods and services covered, and the categories of suppliers or recipients to whom these measures may apply.

3.   For the purposes of paragraph 1, Member States may take the following measures:

(a)   provide that a taxable person who also carries out activities or transactions that are not considered to be taxable supplies of goods or services in accordance with Article 2 shall be regarded as a taxable person in respect of supplies received as referred to in paragraph 1 of this Article;

(b)   provide that a non-taxable body governed by public law, shall be regarded as a taxable person in respect of supplies received as referred to in points (e), (f) and (g) of paragraph 1.

4.   Member States shall inform the VAT Committee of national legislative measures adopted pursuant to paragraph 1 in so far as these are not measures authorised by the Council prior to 13 August 2006 in accordance with Article 27(1) to (4) of Directive 77/388/EEC, and which are continued under paragraph 1 of this Article.

Article 200

s8(1A) VAT shall be payable by any person making a taxable intra-Community acquisition of goods.

Article 201

On importation, VAT shall be payable by any person or persons designated or recognised as liable by the Member State of importation.

Article 202

VAT shall be payable by any person who causes goods to cease to be covered by the arrangements or situations listed in Articles 156, 157, 158, 160 and 161.

Article 203

s8(1) VAT shall be payable by any person who enters the VAT on an invoice.

*Article 204

1. Where, pursuant to Articles 193 to 197 and Articles 199 and 200, the person liable for payment of VAT is a taxable person who is not established in the Member State in which the VAT is due, Member States may allow that person to appoint a tax representative as the person liable for payment of the VAT.

    Furthermore, where the taxable transaction is carried out by a taxable person who is not established in the Member State in which the VAT is due and no legal instrument exists, with the country in which that taxable person is established or has his seat, relating to mutual assistance similar in scope to that provided for in Directive 76/308/EEC and Regulation (EC) No 1798/2003, Member States may take measures to provide that the person liable for payment of VAT is to be a tax representative appointed by the non-established taxable person.

    However, Member States may not apply the option referred to in the second subparagraph to a non-established taxable person, within the meaning of point (1) of Article 358, who has opted for the special scheme for electronically supplied services.

2. The option under the first subparagraph of paragraph 1 shall be subject to the conditions and procedures laid down by each Member State.

Article 205

In the situations referred to in Articles 193 to 200 and Articles 202, 203 and 204, Member States may provide that a person other than the person liable for payment of VAT is to be held jointly and severally liable for payment of VAT.

Section 2

Payment arrangements

Article 206

Any taxable person liable for payment of VAT must pay the net amount of the VAT when submitting the VAT return provided for in Article 250. Member States may, however, set a different date for payment of that amount or may require interim payments to be made.

Article 207

Member States shall take the measures necessary to ensure that persons who are regarded as liable for payment of VAT in the stead of a taxable person not established in their respective territory, in accordance with Articles 194 to 197 and Articles 199 and 204, comply with the payment obligations set out in this Section.

Member States shall also take the measures necessary to ensure that those persons who, in accordance with Article 205, are held to be jointly and severally liable for payment of the VAT comply with these payment obligations.

Article 208

s6A Where Member States designate the customer for investment gold as the person liable for payment of VAT pursuant to Article 198(1) or if, in the case of gold material, semi-manufactured products, or investment gold as defined in Article 344(1), they exercise the option provided for in Article 198(2) of designating the customer as the person liable for payment of VAT, they shall take the measures necessary to ensure that he complies with the payment obligations set out in this Section.

Article 209

Member States shall take the measures necessary to ensure that non-taxable legal persons who are liable for payment of VAT due in respect of intra-Community acquisitions of goods, as referred to in Article 2(1)(b)(i), comply with the payment obligations set out in this Section.

Article 210

Member States shall adopt arrangements for payment of VAT on intra-Community acquisitions of new means of transport, as referred to in Article 2(1)(b)(ii), and on intra-Community acquisitions of products subject to excise duty, as referred to in Article 2(1)(b)(iii).

Article 211

s3B(4) Member States shall lay down the detailed rules for payment in respect of the s15 importation of goods.

In particular, Member States may provide that, in the case of the importation of goods by taxable persons or certain categories thereof, or by persons liable for payment of VAT or certain categories thereof, the VAT due by reason of the importation need not be paid at the time of importation, on condition that it is entered as such in the VAT return to be submitted in accordance with Article 250.

Article 212

Member States may release taxable persons from payment of the VAT due where the amount is insignificant.

CHAPTER 2

Identification

Article 213

s9(1) 1. Every taxable person shall state when his activity as a taxable person commences, changes or ceases.

Member States shall allow, and may require, the statement to be made by electronic means, in accordance with conditions which they lay down.

2. Without prejudice to the first subparagraph of paragraph 1, every taxable person or non-taxable legal person who makes intra-Community acquisitions of goods which are not subject to VAT pursuant to Article 3(1) must state that he makes such acquisitions if the conditions, laid down in that provision, for not making such transactions subject to VAT cease to be fulfilled.

Article 214

s9(1A) 1. Member States shall take the measures necessary to ensure that the following persons are identified by means of an individual number:

(a) every taxable person, with the exception of those referred to in Article 9(2), who within their respective territory carries out supplies of goods or services in respect of which VAT is deductible, other than supplies of goods or services in respect of which VAT is payable solely by the customer or the person for whom the goods or services are intended, in accordance with Articles 194 to 197 and Article 199;

(b) every taxable person, or non-taxable legal person, who makes intra-Community acquisitions of goods subject to VAT pursuant to Article 2(1)(b) and every taxable person, or non-taxable legal person, who exercises the option under Article 3(3) of making their intra-Community acquisitions subject to VAT;

(c) every taxable person who, within their respective territory, makes intra-Community acquisitions of goods for the purposes of transactions which relate to the activities referred to in the second subparagraph of Article 9(1) and which are carried out outside that territory.

[...]¹

2. Member States need not identify certain taxable persons who carry out transactions on an occasional basis, as referred to in Article 12.

Amendments

1 With effect from 1 January 2010 and in accordance with Art 2(8) of Council Directive 2008/8/EC of 12 February 2008, the following points shall be added:

'(d)every taxable person who within their respective territory receives services for which he is liable to pay VAT pursuant to Article 196;

(e) every taxable person, established within their respective territory, who supplies services within the territory of another Member State for which VAT is payable solely by the recipient pursuant to Article 196.'

Article 215

Each individual VAT identification number shall have a prefix in accordance with ISO code 3166 — alpha 2 — by which the Member State of issue may be identified.

Nevertheless, Greece may use the prefix 'EL'.

Article 216

Member States shall take the measures necessary to ensure that their identification systems enable the taxable persons referred to in Article 214 to be identified and to ensure the correct application of the transitional arrangements for the taxation of intra-Community transactions, as referred to in Article 402.

CHAPTER 3

Invoicing

Section 1

Definition

Article 217

For the purposes of this Chapter, 'transmission or provision by electronic means' shall mean transmission or provision to the addressee of data using electronic equipment for processing (including digital compression) and storage, and employing wire, radio, optical or other electromagnetic means.

Section 2

Concept of invoice

Article 218

For the purposes of this Directive, Member States shall accept documents or messages on paper or in electronic form as invoices if they meet the conditions laid down in this Chapter.

Article 219

Any document or message that amends and refers specifically and unambiguously to the initial invoice shall be treated as an invoice.

Section 3

Issue of invoices

Article 220

s17(1) Every taxable person shall ensure that, in respect of the following, an invoice is issued, either by himself or by his customer or, in his name and on his behalf, by a third party:

(1)   supplies of goods or services which he has made to another taxable person or to a non-taxable legal person;

(2)   supplies of goods as referred to in Article 33;

(3)   supplies of goods carried out in accordance with the conditions specified in Article 138;

(4)   any payment on account made to him before one of the supplies of goods referred to in points (1), (2) and (3) was carried out;

(5)   any payment on account made to him by another taxable person or non-taxable legal person before the provision of services was completed.

Article 221

1.   Member States may impose on taxable persons an obligation to issue an invoice in respect of supplies of goods or services made in their territory, other than those referred to in Article 220.

Member States may, in respect of the invoices referred to in the first subparagraph, impose fewer obligations than those laid down in Articles 226, 230, 233, 244 and 246.

2.   Member States may release taxable persons from the obligation laid down in Article 220 to issue an invoice in respect of supplies of goods or services which they have made in their territory and which are exempt, with or without deductibility of the VAT paid at the preceding stage, pursuant to Articles 110 and 111, Article 125(1), Article 127, Article 128 (1), Articles 132, 135, 136, 371, 375, 376 and 377, Article 378 (2), Article 379(2) and Articles 380 to 390.

Article 222

Member States may impose time limits on taxable persons for the issue of invoices when supplying goods or services in their territory.

Article 223

In accordance with conditions to be laid down by the Member States in whose territory goods or services are supplied, a summary invoice may be drawn up for several separate supplies of goods or services.

Article 224

s17(14) 1.   Invoices may be drawn up by the customer in respect of the supply to him, by a taxable person, of goods or services, if there is a prior agreement between the two parties and provided that a procedure exists for the acceptance of each invoice by the taxable person supplying the goods or services.

2.   The Member States in whose territory the goods or services are supplied shall determine the terms and conditions of such prior agreements and of the acceptance procedures between the taxable person and the customer.

3.   Member States may impose further conditions on taxable persons supplying goods or services in their territory concerning the issue of

invoices by the customer. They may, in particular, require that such invoices be issued in the name and on behalf of the taxable person.

The conditions referred to in the first subparagraph must always be the same wherever the customer is established.

Article 225

Member States may impose specific conditions on taxable persons supplying goods or services in their territory in cases where the third party, or the customer, who issues invoices is established in a country with which no legal instrument exists relating to mutual assistance similar in scope to that provided for in Directive 76/308/EEC and Regulation (EC) No 1798/2003.

Section 4

Content of invoices

Article 226

Without prejudice to the particular provisions laid down in this Directive, only the following details are required for VAT purposes on invoices issued pursuant to Articles 220 and 221:

(1)   the date of issue;

(2)   a sequential number, based on one or more series, which uniquely identifies the invoice;

(3)   the VAT identification number referred to in Article 214 under which the taxable person supplied the goods or services;

(4)   the customer's VAT identification number, as referred to in Article 214, under which the customer received a supply of goods or services in respect of which he is liable for payment of VAT, or received a supply of goods as referred to in Article 138;

(5)   the full name and address of the taxable person and of the customer;

(6)   the quantity and nature of the goods supplied or the extent and nature of the services rendered;

(7)   the date on which the supply of goods or services was made or completed or the date on which the payment on account referred to in points (4) and (5) of Article 220 was made, in so far as that date can be determined and differs from the date of issue of the invoice;

(8)   the taxable amount per rate or exemption, the unit price exclusive of VAT and any discounts or rebates if they are not included in the unit price;

(9)   the VAT rate applied;

(10)   the VAT amount payable, except where a special arrangement is applied under which, in accordance with this Directive, such a detail is excluded;

(11)   in the case of an exemption or where the customer is liable for payment of VAT, reference to the applicable provision of this Directive, or to the

corresponding national provision, or any other reference indicating that the supply of goods or services is exempt or subject to the reverse charge procedure;

(12)   in the case of the supply of a new means of transport made in accordance with the conditions specified in Article 138(1) and (2)(a), the characteristics as identified in point (b) of Article 2(2);

(13)   where the margin scheme for travel agents is applied, reference to Article 306, or to the corresponding national provisions, or any other reference indicating that the margin scheme has been applied;

(14)   where one of the special arrangements applicable to second-hand goods, works of art, collectors' items and antiques is applied, reference to Articles 313, 326 or 333, or to the corresponding national provisions, or any other reference indicating that one of those arrangements has been applied;

(15)   where the person liable for payment of VAT is a tax representative for the purposes of Article 204, the VAT identification number, referred to in Article 214, of that tax representative, together with his full name and address.

Article 227

Member States may require taxable persons established in their territory and supplying goods or services there to indicate the VAT identification number, referred to in Article 214, of the customer in cases other than those referred to in point (4) of Article 226.

Article 228

Member States in whose territory goods or services are supplied may allow some of the compulsory details to be omitted from documents or messages treated as invoices pursuant to Article 219.

Article 229

Member States shall not require invoices to be signed.

Article 230

The amounts which appear on the invoice may be expressed in any currency, provided that the amount of VAT payable is expressed in the national currency of the Member State in which the supply of goods or services takes place, using the conversion mechanism laid down in Article 91.

Article 231

For control purposes, Member States may require invoices in respect of supplies of goods or services in their territory and invoices received by taxable persons established in their territory to be translated into their national languages.

Section 5

Sending invoices by electronic means

Article 232

s17(1A) Invoices issued pursuant to Section 2 may be sent on paper or, subject to acceptance by the recipient, they may be sent or made available by electronic means.

Article 233

1.   Invoices sent or made available by electronic means shall be accepted by Member States provided that the authenticity of the origin and the integrity of their content are guaranteed by one of the following methods:

   (a)   by means of an advanced electronic signature within the meaning of point (2) of Article 2 of Directive 1999/93/EC of the European Parliament and of the Council of 13 December 1999 on a Community framework for electronic signatures;

   (b)   by means of electronic data interchange (EDI), as defined in Article 2 of Commission Recommendation 1994/820/EC of 19 October 1994 relating to the legal aspects of electronic data interchange, if the agreement relating to the exchange provides for the use of procedures guaranteeing the authenticity of the origin and integrity of the data.

   Invoices may, however, be sent or made available by other electronic means, subject to acceptance by the Member States concerned.

2.   For the purposes of point (a) of the first subparagraph of paragraph 1, Member States may also ask for the advanced electronic signature to be based on a qualified certificate and created by a secure-signature-creation device, within the meaning of points (6) and (10) of Article 2 of Directive 1999/93/EC.

3.   For the purposes of point (b) of the first subparagraph of paragraph 1, Member States may also, subject to conditions which they lay down, require that an additional summary document on paper be sent.

Article 234

Member States may not impose on taxable persons supplying goods or services in their territory any other obligations or formalities relating to the sending or making available of invoices by electronic means.

Article 235

Member States may lay down specific conditions for invoices issued by electronic means in respect of goods or services supplied in their territory from a country with which no legal instrument exists relating to mutual assistance similar in scope to that provided for in Directive 76/308/EEC and Regulation (EC) No 1798/2003.

Article 236

Where batches containing several invoices are sent or made available to the same recipient by electronic means, the details common to the individual invoices may be mentioned only once if, for each invoice, all the information is accessible.

Article 237

The Commission shall present, at the latest on 31 December 2008, a report and, if appropriate, a proposal amending the conditions applicable to electronic invoicing in order to take account of future technological developments in that field.

Section 6

Simplification measures

Article 238

1. After consulting the VAT Committee, Member States may, in accordance with conditions which they may lay down, provide that in the following cases some of the information required under Article 226 and 230, subject to options taken up by Member States under Articles 227, 228 and 231, need not be entered on invoices in respect of supplies of goods or services in their territory:

   (a)   where the amount of the invoice is minor;

   (b)   where commercial or administrative practice in the business sector concerned or the technical conditions under which the invoices are issued make it difficult to comply with all the obligations referred to in Articles 226 and 230.

2. Invoices must, in any event, contain the following information:

   (a)   the date of issue;

   (b)   identification of the taxable person;

   (c)   identification of the type of goods or services supplied;

   (d)   the VAT amount payable or the information needed to calculate it.

3. The simplified arrangements provided for in paragraph 1 may not be applied to the transactions referred to in Articles 20, 21, 22, 33, 36, 138 and 141.

Article 239

In cases where Member States make use of the option under point (b) of the first subparagraph of Article 272(1) of not allocating a VAT identification number to taxable persons who do not carry out any of the transactions referred to in Articles 20, 21, 22, 33, 36, 138 and 141, and where the supplier or the customer has not been allocated an identification number of that type, another number called the tax reference number, as defined by the Member States concerned, shall be entered on the invoice instead.

Article 240

Where the taxable person has been allocated a VAT identification number, the Member States exercising the option under point (b) of the first subparagraph of Article 272(1) may also require the invoice to show the following:

(1)   in respect of the supply of services, as referred to in Articles 44, 47, 50, 53, 54 and 55, and the supply of goods, as referred to in Articles 138 and 141, the VAT identification number and the tax reference number of the supplier;

(2)   in respect of other supplies of goods or services, only the tax reference number of the supplier or only the VAT identification number.

CHAPTER 4

Accounting

Section 1

Definition

Article 241

For the purposes of this Chapter, 'storage of an invoice by electronic means' shall mean storage of data using electronic equipment for processing (including digital compression) and storage, and employing wire, radio, optical or other electromagnetic means.

Section 2

General obligations
Article 242

s16(1) Every taxable person shall keep accounts in sufficient detail for VAT to be applied and its application checked by the tax authorities.

Article 243

1.   Every taxable person shall keep a register of the goods dispatched or transported, by that person or on his behalf, to a destination outside the territory of the Member State of departure but within the Community for the purposes of transactions consisting in work on those goods or their temporary use as referred to in points (f), (g) and (h) of Article 17 (2).

2.   Every taxable person shall keep accounts in sufficient detail to enable the identification of goods dispatched to him from another Member State, by or on behalf of a taxable person identified for VAT purposes in that other Member State, and used for services consisting in valuations of those goods or work on those goods as referred to in point (c) of Article 52.

Section 3

Specific obligations relating to the storage of all invoices
Article 244

$^{6}_{7(15)}$ Every taxable person shall ensure that copies of the invoices issued by himself, or by his customer or, in his name and on his behalf, by a third party, and all the invoices which he has received, are stored.

Article 245

1.   For the purposes of this Directive, the taxable person may decide the place of storage of all invoices provided that he makes the invoices or information stored in accordance with Article 244 available to the competent authorities without undue delay whenever they so request.

2.   Member States may require taxable persons established in their territory to notify them of the place of storage, if it is outside their territory.

Member States may also require taxable persons established in their territory to store within that territory invoices issued by themselves or by their customers or, in their name and on their behalf, by a third party, as well as all the invoices that they have received, when the storage is not by electronic means guaranteeing full online access to the data concerned.

Article 246

The authenticity of the origin and the integrity of the content of the invoices stored, as well as their legibility, must be guaranteed throughout the storage period.

In respect of the invoices referred to in the second subparagraph of Article 233(1), the details they contain may not be altered and must remain legible throughout the storage period.

Article 247

16(3) 1.   Each Member State shall determine the period throughout which taxable persons must ensure the storage of invoices relating to the supply of goods or services in its territory and invoices received by taxable persons established in its territory.

2.   In order to ensure that the conditions laid down in Article 246 are met, the Member State referred to in paragraph 1 may require that invoices be stored in the original form in which they were sent or made available, whether paper or electronic. Additionally, in the case of invoices stored by electronic means, the Member State may require that the data guaranteeing the authenticity of the origin of the invoices and the integrity of their content, as provided for in the first paragraph of Article 246, also be stored.

3.   The Member State referred to in paragraph 1 may lay down specific conditions prohibiting or restricting the storage of invoices in a country with which no legal instrument exists relating to mutual assistance

similar in scope to that provided for in Directive 76/308/EEC and Regulation (EC) No 1798/2003 or to the right referred to in Article 249 to access by electronic means, to download and to use.

Article 248

Member States may, subject to conditions which they lay down, require the storage of invoices received by non-taxable persons.

Section 4

Right of access to invoices stored by electronic means in another Member State

Article 249

Where a taxable person stores invoices which he issues or receives by electronic means guaranteeing online access to the data and where the place of storage is in a Member State other than that in which he is established, the competent authorities in the Member State in which he is established shall, for the purposes of this Directive, have the right to access those invoices by electronic means, to download and to use them, within the limits set by the rules of the Member State in which the taxable person is established and in so far as those authorities require for control purposes.

CHAPTER 5

Returns

Article 250

s19(3) 1.   Every taxable person shall submit a VAT return setting out all the information needed to calculate the tax that has become chargeable and the deductions to be made including, insofar as is necessary for the establishment of the basis of assessment, the total value of the transactions relating to such tax and deductions and the value of any exempt transactions.

2.   Member States shall allow, and may require, the VAT return referred to in paragraph 1 to be submitted by electronic means, in accordance with conditions which they lay down.

Article 251

s19(3) In addition to the information referred to in Article 250, the VAT return covering a given tax period shall show the following:

(a)   the total value, exclusive of VAT, of the supplies of goods referred to in Article 138 in respect of which VAT has become chargeable during this tax period;

(b)   the total value, exclusive of VAT, of the supplies of goods referred to in Articles 33 and 36 carried out within the territory of another Member State, in respect of which VAT has become chargeable during this tax period, where the place where dispatch or transport of the goods began is situated in the Member State in which the return must be submitted;

(c)   the total value, exclusive of VAT, of the intra-Community acquisitions of goods, or transactions treated as such, pursuant to Articles 21 or 22, made in the Member State in which the return must be submitted and in respect of which VAT has become chargeable during this tax period;

(d)   the total value, exclusive of VAT, of the supplies of goods referred to in Articles 33 and 36 carried out in the Member State in which the return must be submitted and in respect of which VAT has become chargeable during this tax period, where the place where dispatch or transport of the goods began is situated within the territory of another Member State;

(e)   the total value, exclusive of VAT, of the supplies of goods carried out in the Member State in which the return must be submitted and in respect of which the taxable person has been designated, in accordance with Article 197, as liable for payment of VAT and in respect of which VAT has become chargeable during this tax period.

Article 252

s19(3) 1.   The VAT return shall be submitted by a deadline to be determined by Member States. That deadline may not be more than two months after the end of each tax period.

2.   The tax period shall be set by each Member State at one month, two months or three months.

Member States may, however, set different tax periods provided that those periods do not exceed one year.

Article 253

Sweden may apply a simplified procedure for small and medium-sized enterprises, whereby taxable persons carrying out only transactions taxable at national level may submit VAT returns three months after the end of the annual direct tax period.

Article 254

In the case of supplies of new means of transport carried out in accordance with the conditions specified in Article 138(2)(a) by a taxable person identified for VAT purposes for a customer not identified for VAT purposes, or by a taxable person as defined in Article 9(2), Member States shall take the measures necessary to ensure that the vendor communicates all the information needed for VAT to be applied and its application checked by the tax authorities.

Article 255

s6A Where Member States designate the customer of investment gold as the person liable for payment of VAT pursuant to Article 198(1) or if, in the case of gold material, semi-manufactured products or investment gold as defined in Article 344(1), they exercise the option provided for in Article 198(2) of designating the customer as the person liable for payment of VAT, they shall take the measures necessary to ensure that he complies with the obligations relating to submission of a VAT return set out in this Chapter.

Article 256

Member States shall take the measures necessary to ensure that persons who are regarded as liable for payment of VAT in the stead of a taxable person not established within their territory, in accordance with Articles 194 to 197 and Article 204, comply with the obligations relating to submission of a VAT return, as laid down in this Chapter.

Article 257

Member States shall take the measures necessary to ensure that non-taxable legal persons who are liable for payment of VAT due in respect of intra-Community acquisitions of goods, as referred to in Article 2(1)(b)(i), comply with the obligations relating to submission of a VAT return, as laid down in this Chapter.

Article 258

Member States shall lay down detailed rules for the submission of VAT returns in respect of intra-Community acquisitions of new means of transport, as referred to in Article 2(1)(b)(ii), and intra-Community acquisitions of products subject to excise duty, as referred to in Article 2(1)(b)(iii).

Article 259

Member States may require persons who make intra-Community acquisitions of new means of transport as referred to in Article 2(1)(b)(ii), to provide, when submitting the VAT return, all the information needed for VAT to be applied and its application checked by the tax authorities.

Article 260

Member States shall lay down detailed rules for the submission of VAT returns in respect of the importation of goods.

Article 261

1.   Member States may require the taxable person to submit a return showing all the particulars specified in Articles 250 and 251 in respect of all transactions carried out in the preceding year. That return shall provide all the information necessary for any adjustments.

2.   Member States shall allow, and may require, the return referred to in paragraph 1 to be submitted by electronic means, in accordance with conditions which they lay down.

CHAPTER 6

Recapitulative statements

[Article 262

s19A Every taxable person identified for VAT purposes shall submit a recapitulative statement of the acquirers identified for VAT purposes to whom he has supplied goods in accordance with the conditions specified in Article 138(1) and (2)(c), and of the persons identified for VAT purposes to whom he has supplied goods which were supplied to him by way of intra-Community acquisitions referred to in Article 42.]¹

Amendments

1 With effect from 1 January 2010 and in accordance with Art 2(9) of Council Directive 2008/8/EC of 12 February 2008, Art 262 shall read:

'Every taxable person identified for VAT purposes shall submit a recapitulative statement of the following:

(a) the acquirers identified for VAT purposes to whom he has supplied goods in accordance with the conditions specified in Article 138(1) and (2)(c);

(b) the persons identified for VAT purposes to whom he has supplied goods which were supplied to him by way of intra-Community acquisitions referred to in Article 42;

(c) the taxable persons, and the non-taxable legal persons identified for VAT purposes, to whom he has supplied services, other than services that are exempted from VAT in the

Member State where the transaction is taxable, and for which the recipient is liable to pay the tax pursuant to Article 196.'

[Article 263

1.   The recapitulative statement shall be drawn up for each calendar month within a period not exceeding one month and in accordance with procedures to be determined by the Member States.

1a.   However, Member States, in accordance with the conditions and limits which they may lay down, may allow taxable persons to submit the recapitulative statement for each calendar quarter within a time limit not exceeding one month from the end of the quarter, where the total quarterly amount, excluding VAT, of the supplies of goods as referred to in Articles 264(1)(d) and 265(1)(c) does not exceed either in respect of the quarter concerned or in respect of any of the previous four quarters the sum of EUR 50 000 or its equivalent in national currency.

The option provided for in the first subparagraph shall cease to be applicable after the end of the month during which the total value, excluding VAT, of the supplies of goods as referred to in Article 264(1)(d) and 265(1)(c) exceeds, in respect of the current quarter, the sum of EUR 50 000 or its equivalent in national currency. In this case, a recapitulative statement shall be drawn up for the month(s) which has (have) elapsed since the beginning of the quarter, within a time limit not exceeding one month.

1b.   Until 31 December 2011, Member States are allowed to set the sum mentioned in paragraph 1a at EUR 100 000 or its equivalent in national currency.

1c.   In the case of supplies of services as referred to in Article 264(1)(d), Member States, in accordance with the conditions and limits which they may lay down, may allow taxable persons to submit the recapitulative statement for each calendar quarter within a time limit not exceeding one month from the end of the quarter.

Member States may, in particular, require the taxable persons who carry out supplies of both goods and services as referred to in Article 264(1)(d) to submit the recapitulative statement in accordance with the deadline resulting from paragraphs 1 to 1b.

2. Member States shall allow, and may require, the recapitulative statement referred to in paragraph 1 to be submitted by electronic file transfer, in accordance with conditions which they lay down.][1]

Amendments

1 Substituted by Art 1(3) of Council Directive 2008/117/EC of 16 December 2008, (w.e.f. 21 January 2009)

Article 264

s19A 1. The recapitulative statement shall set out the following information:

(a) [the VAT identification number of the taxable person in the Member State in which the recapitulative statement must be submitted and under which he has carried out the supply of goods in accordance with the conditions specified in Article 138(1);][1]

(b) [the VAT identification number of the person acquiring the goods in a Member State other than that in which the recapitulative statement must be submitted and under which the goods were supplied to him;][2]

(c) the VAT identification number of the taxable person in the Member State in which the recapitulative statement must be submitted and under which he has carried out a transfer to another Member State, as referred to in Article 138(2)(c), and the number by means of which he is identified in the Member State in which the dispatch or transport ended;

(d) [for each person who acquired goods, the total value of the supplies of goods carried out by the taxable person;][3]

(e) in respect of supplies of goods consisting in transfers to another Member State, as referred to in Article 138(2)(c), the total value of the supplies, determined in accordance with Article 76;

(f) the amounts of adjustments made pursuant to Article 90.

[2. The value referred to in paragraph 1(d) shall be declared for the period of submission established in accordance with Article 263(1) to (1c) during which VAT became chargeable.

The amounts referred to in paragraph 1(f) shall be declared for the period of submission established in accordance with Article 263(1) to

(1c) during which the person acquiring the goods was notified of the adjustment.]⁴

Amendments

1   With effect from 1 January 2010 and in accordance with Art 2(10) of Council Directive 2008/8/EC of 12 February 2008, Art 264(a) shall read:

'the VAT identification number of the taxable person in the Member State in which the recapitulative statement must be submitted and under which he has carried out the supply of goods in accordance with the conditions specified in Article 138(1) and under which he effected taxable supplies of services in accordance with the conditions laid down in Article 44;'

2   With effect from 1 January 2010 and in accordance with Art 2(10) of Council Directive 2008/8/EC of 12 February 2008, Art 264(b) shall read:

'the VAT identification number of the person acquiring the goods or receiving the services in a Member State other than that in which the recapitulative statement must be submitted and under which the goods or services were supplied to him;'

3   With effect from 1 January 2010 and in accordance with Art 2(10) of Council Directive 2008/8/EC of 12 February 2008, Art 264(d) shall read:

'for each person who acquired goods or received services, the total value of the supplies of goods and the total value of the supplies of services carried out by the taxable person;'

4   Substituted by Art 1(4) of Council Directive 2008/117/EC of 16 December 2008, (w.e.f. 21 January 2009)

Article 265

1.   In the case of intra-Community acquisitions of goods, as referred to in Article 42, the taxable person identified for VAT purposes in the Member State which issued him with the VAT identification number under which he made such acquisitions shall set the following information out clearly on the recapitulative statement:

(a)   his VAT identification number in that Member State and under which he made the acquisition and subsequent supply of goods;

(b)   the VAT identification number, in the Member State in which dispatch or transport of the goods ended, of the person to whom the subsequent supply was made by the taxable person;

(c)   for each person to whom the subsequent supply was made, the total value, exclusive of VAT, of the supplies made by the taxable person in the Member State in which dispatch or transport of the goods ended.

[2.   The value referred to in paragraph 1(c) shall be declared for the period of submission established in accordance with Article 263(1) to (1b) during which VAT became chargeable.]¹

Amendments

1   Substituted by Art 1(5) of Council Directive 2008/117/EC of 16 December 2008, (w.e.f. 21 January 2009)

Article 266

By way of derogation from Articles 264 and 265, Member States may provide that additional information is to be given in recapitulative statements.

Article 267

Member States shall take the measures necessary to ensure that those persons who, in accordance with Articles 194 and 204, are regarded as liable for payment of VAT, in the stead of a taxable person who is not established in their territory, comply with the obligation to submit a recapitulative statement as provided for in this Chapter.

Article 268

Member States may require that taxable persons who, in their territory, make intra-Community acquisitions of goods, or transactions treated as such, pursuant to Articles 21 or 22, submit statements giving details of such acquisitions, provided, however, that such statements are not required in respect of a period of less than one month.

Article 269

Acting unanimously on a proposal from the Commission, the Council may authorise any Member State to introduce the special measures provided for in Articles 270 and 271 to simplify the obligation, laid down in this Chapter, to submit a recapitulative statement. Such measures may not jeopardise the proper monitoring of intra-Community transactions.

Article 270

By virtue of the authorisation referred to in Article 269, Member States may permit taxable persons to submit annual recapitulative statements indicating the VAT identification numbers, in another Member State, of the persons to whom those taxable persons have supplied goods in accordance with the conditions specified in Article 138(1) and (2)(c), where the taxable persons meet the following three conditions:

(a)   the total annual value, exclusive of VAT, of their supplies of goods and services does not exceed by more than EUR 35 000, or the equivalent in national currency, the amount of the annual turnover which is used as a reference for application of the exemption for small enterprises provided for in Articles 282 to 292;

(b)   the total annual value, exclusive of VAT, of supplies of goods carried out by them in accordance with the conditions specified in Article 138 does not exceed EUR 15 000 or the equivalent in national currency;

(c)   none of the supplies of goods carried out by them in accordance with the conditions specified in Article 138 is a supply of new means of transport.

Article 271

By virtue of the authorisation referred to in Article 269, Member States which set at over three months the tax period in respect of which taxable persons must submit the VAT return provided for in Article 250 may permit such persons to submit recapitulative statements in respect of the same period where those taxable persons meet the following three conditions:

(a)   the total annual value, exclusive of VAT, of their supplies of goods and services does not exceed EUR 200 000 or the equivalent in national currency;

(b)   the total annual value, exclusive of VAT, of supplies of goods carried out by them in accordance with the conditions specified in Article 138 does not exceed EUR 15 000 or the equivalent in national currency;

(c)   none of the supplies of goods carried out by them in accordance with the conditions specified in Article 138 is a supply of new means of transport.

CHAPTER 7

Miscellaneous provisions

Article 272

s8(3) 1.   Member States may release the following taxable persons from certain or all obligations referred to in Chapters 2 to 6:

(a)   taxable persons whose intra-Community acquisitions of goods are not subject to VAT pursuant to Article 3(1);

(b)   taxable persons carrying out none of the transactions referred to in Articles 20, 21, 22, 33, 36, 138 and 141;

(c)   taxable persons carrying out only supplies of goods or of services which are exempt pursuant to Articles 132, 135 and 136, Articles 146 to 149 and Articles 151, 152 or 153;

(d)   taxable persons covered by the exemption for small enterprises provided for in Articles 282 to 292;

(e)   taxable persons covered by the common flat-rate scheme for farmers.

Member States may not release the taxable persons referred to in point (b) of the first subparagraph from the invoicing obligations laid down in Articles 220 to 236 and Articles 238, 239 and 240.

2.   If Member States exercise the option under point (e) of the first subparagraph of paragraph 1, they shall take the measures necessary to ensure the correct application of the transitional arrangements for the taxation of intra-Community transactions.

3.   Member States may release taxable persons other than those referred to in paragraph 1 from certain of the accounting obligations referred to in Article 242.

Article 273

s18
s21
s22
Member States may impose other obligations which they deem necessary to ensure the correct collection of VAT and to prevent evasion, subject to the requirement of equal treatment as between domestic transactions and transactions carried out between Member States by taxable persons and

provided that such obligations do not, in trade between Member States, give rise to formalities connected with the crossing of frontiers.

The option under the first paragraph may not be relied upon in order to impose additional invoicing obligations over and above those laid down in Chapter 3.

CHAPTER 8

Obligations relating to certain importations and exportations

Section 1

Importation

Article 274

Articles 275, 276 and 277 shall apply to the importation of goods in free circulation which enter the Community from a third territory forming part of the customs territory of the Community.

Article 275

The formalities relating to the importation of the goods referred to in Article 274 shall be the same as those laid down by the Community customs provisions in force for the importation of goods into the customs territory of the Community.

Article 276

Where dispatch or transport of the goods referred to in Article 274 ends at a place situated outside the Member State of their entry into the Community, they shall circulate in the Community under the internal Community transit procedure laid down by the Community customs provisions in force, in so far as they have been the subject of a declaration placing them under that procedure on their entry into the Community.

Article 277

Where, on their entry into the Community, the goods referred to in Article 274 are in one of the situations which would entitle them, if they were imported within the meaning of the first paragraph of Article 30, to be covered by one of the arrangements or situations referred to in Article 156, or by a temporary importation arrangement with full exemption from import duties, Member States shall take the measures necessary to ensure that the goods may remain in the Community under the same conditions as those laid down for the application of those arrangements or situations.

Section 2

Exportation

Article 278

Articles 279 and 280 shall apply to the exportation of goods in free circulation which are dispatched or transported from a Member State to a third territory forming part of the customs territory of the Community.

Article 279

The formalities relating to the exportation of the goods referred to in Article 278 from the territory of the Community shall be the same as those laid down by the Community customs provisions in force for the exportation of goods from the customs territory of the Community.

Article 280

In the case of goods which are temporarily exported from the Community, in order to be reimported, Member States shall take the measures necessary to ensure that, on reimportation into the Community, such goods may be covered by the same provisions as would have applied if they had been temporarily exported from the customs territory of the Community.

TITLE XII

SPECIAL SCHEMES

CHAPTER 1

Special scheme for small enterprises

Section 1

Simplified procedures for charging and collection

Article 281

s8(3) Member States which might encounter difficulties in applying the normal VAT arrangements to small enterprises, by reason of the activities or structure of such enterprises, may, subject to such conditions and limits as they may set, and after consulting the VAT Committee, apply simplified procedures, such as flat-rate schemes, for charging and collecting VAT provided that they do not lead to a reduction thereof.

Section 2

Exemptions or graduated relief

Article 282

s8(3) The exemptions and graduated tax relief provided for in this Section shall apply to the supply of goods and services by small enterprises.

Article 283

s8(3) 1.   The arrangements provided for in this Section shall not apply to the following transactions:

    (a)   transactions carried out on an occasional basis, as referred to in Article 12;

    (b)   supplies of new means of transport carried out in accordance with the conditions specified in Article 138(1) and (2)(a);

(c)   supplies of goods or services carried out by a taxable person who is not established in the Member State in which the VAT is due.

2.   Member States may exclude transactions other than those referred to in paragraph 1 from the arrangements provided for in this Section.

Article 284

s8(3) 1.   Member States which have exercised the option under Article 14 of Council Directive 67/228/EEC of 11 April 1967 on the harmonisation of legislation of Member States concerning turnover taxes — Structure and procedures for application of the common system of value added tax of introducing exemptions or graduated tax relief may retain them, and the arrangements for applying them, if they comply with the VAT rules.

2.   Member States which, at 17 May 1977, exempted taxable persons whose annual turnover was less than the equivalent in national currency of 5000 European units of account at the conversion rate on that date, may raise that ceiling up to EUR 5000.

Member States which applied graduated tax relief may neither raise the ceiling for graduated tax relief nor render the conditions for the granting of it more favourable.

Article 285

Member States which have not exercised the option under Article 14 of Directive 67/228/EEC may exempt taxable persons whose annual turnover is no higher than EUR 5 000 or the equivalent in national currency.

The Member States referred to in the first paragraph may grant graduated tax relief to taxable persons whose annual turnover exceeds the ceiling fixed by them for its application.

Article 286

Member States which, at 17 May 1977, exempted taxable persons whose annual turnover was equal to or higher than the equivalent in national currency of 5 000 European units of account at the conversion rate on that date, may raise that ceiling in order to maintain the value of the exemption in real terms.

Article 287

Member States which acceded after 1 January 1978 may exempt taxable persons whose annual turnover is no higher than the equivalent in national currency of the following amounts at the conversion rate on the day of their accession:

(1)   Greece: 10 000 European units of account;

(2)   Spain: ECU 10 000;

(3)   Portugal: ECU 10 000;

(4)   Austria: ECU 35 000;

(5)   Finland: ECU 10 000;

(6)   Sweden: ECU 10 000;

(7)   Czech Republic: EUR 35 000;

(8)   Estonia: EUR 16 000;

(9)   Cyprus: EUR 15 600;

(10)   Latvia: EUR 17 200;

(11)   Lithuania: EUR 29 000;

(12)   Hungary: EUR 35 000;

(13)   Malta: EUR 37 000 if the economic activity consists principally in the
        supply of goods, EUR 24 300 if the economic activity consists principally
        in the supply of services with a low value added (high inputs), and EUR
        14 600 in other cases, namely supplies of services with a high value
        added (low inputs);

(14)   Poland: EUR 10 000;

(15)   Slovenia: EUR 25 000;

(16)   Slovakia: EUR 35 000.

Article 288

s12(3) The turnover serving as a reference for the purposes of applying the
arrangements provided for in this Section shall consist of the following
amounts, exclusive of VAT:

(1)   the value of supplies of goods and services, in so far as they are taxed;

(2)   the value of transactions which are exempt, with deductibility of
        the VAT paid at the preceding stage, pursuant to Articles 110 or 111,
        Article 125(1), Article 127 or Article 128(1);

(3)   the value of transactions which are exempt pursuant to Articles 146 to
        149 and Articles 151, 152 or 153;

(4)   the value of real estate transactions, financial transactions as referred to
        in points (b) to (g) of Article 135(1), and insurance services, unless those
        transactions are ancillary transactions.

However, disposals of the tangible or intangible capital assets of an enterprise
shall not be taken into account for the purposes of calculating turnover.

Article 289

Taxable persons exempt from VAT shall not be entitled to deduct VAT in
accordance with Articles 167 to 171 and Articles 173 to 177, and may not show
the VAT on their invoices.

Article 290

Taxable persons who are entitled to exemption from VAT may opt either for the normal VAT arrangements or for the simplified procedures provided for in Article 281. In this case, they shall be entitled to any graduated tax relief provided for under national legislation.

Article 291

Subject to the application of Article 281, taxable persons enjoying graduated relief shall be regarded as taxable persons subject to the normal VAT arrangements.

Article 292

The arrangements provided for in this Section shall apply until a date to be fixed by the Council in accordance with Article 93 of the Treaty, which may not be later than that on which the definitive arrangements referred to in Article 402 enter into force.

Section 3

Reporting and review

Article 293

Every four years starting from the adoption of this Directive, the Commission shall present to the Council, on the basis of information obtained from the Member States, a report on the application of this Chapter, together, where appropriate and taking into account the need to ensure the long-term convergence of national regulations, with proposals on the following subjects:

(1)   improvements to the special scheme for small enterprises;

(2)   the adaptation of national systems as regards exemptions and graduated tax relief;

(3)   the adaptation of the ceilings provided for in Section 2.

Article 294

The Council shall decide, in accordance with Article 93 of the Treaty, whether a special scheme for small enterprises is necessary under the definitive arrangements and, if appropriate, shall lay down the common limits and conditions for the implementation of that scheme.

CHAPTER 2

Common flat-rate scheme for farmers

Article 295

s1(1)
s8(9)
s12A

1.   For the purposes of this Chapter, the following definitions shall apply:

(1)   '**farmer**' means any taxable person whose activity is carried out in an agricultural, forestry or fisheries undertaking;

(2)   **'agricultural, forestry or fisheries undertaking'** means an undertaking regarded as such by each Member State within the framework of the production activities listed in Annex VII;

(3)   **'flat-rate farmer'** means any farmer covered by the flat-rate scheme provided for in this Chapter;

(4)   **'agricultural products'** means goods produced by an agricultural, forestry or fisheries undertaking in each Member State as a result of the activities listed in Annex VII;

(5)   **'agricultural services'** means services, and in particular those listed in Annex VIII, supplied by a farmer using his labour force or the equipment normally employed in the agricultural, forestry or fisheries undertaking operated by him and normally playing a part in agricultural production;

(6)   **'input VAT charged'** means the amount of the total VAT attaching to the goods and services purchased by all agricultural, forestry and fisheries undertakings of each Member State subject to the flat-rate scheme where such tax would be deductible in accordance with Articles 167, 168 and 169 and Articles 173 to 177 by a farmer subject to the normal VAT arrangements;

(7)   **'flat-rate compensation percentages'** means the percentages fixed by Member States in accordance with Articles 297, 298 and 299 and applied by them in the cases specified in Article 300 in order to enable flat-rate farmers to offset at a fixed rate the input VAT charged;

(8)   **'flat-rate compensation'** means the amount arrived at by applying the flat-rate compensation percentage to the turnover of the flat-rate farmer in the cases specified in Article 300.

2.   Where a farmer processes, using means normally employed in an agricultural, forestry or fisheries undertaking, products deriving essentially from his agricultural production, such processing activities shall be treated as agricultural production activities, as listed in Annex VII.

Article 296

8(3)(a)   1.   Where the application to farmers of the normal VAT arrangements, or the special scheme provided for in Chapter 1, is likely to give rise to difficulties, Member States may apply to farmers, in accordance with this Chapter, a flat-rate scheme designed to offset the VAT charged on purchases of goods and services made by the flat-rate farmers.

2.   Each Member State may exclude from the flat-rate scheme certain categories of farmers, as well as farmers for whom application of the normal VAT arrangements, or of the simplified procedures provided for in Article 281, is not likely to give rise to administrative difficulties.

3.   Every flat-rate farmer may opt, subject to the rules and conditions to be laid down by each Member State, for application of the normal VAT arrangements or, as the case may be, the simplified procedures provided for in Article 281.

Article 297

s11(1)(f) Member States shall, where necessary, fix the flat-rate compensation percentages. They may fix varying percentages for forestry, for the different sub-divisions of agriculture and for fisheries.

Member States shall notify the Commission of the flat-rate compensation percentages fixed in accordance with the first paragraph before applying them.

Article 298

The flat-rate compensation percentages shall be calculated on the basis of macro-economic statistics for flat-rate farmers alone for the preceding three years.

The percentages may be rounded up or down to the nearest half-point. Member States may also reduce such percentages to a nil rate.

Article 299

The flat-rate compensation percentages may not have the effect of obtaining for flat-rate farmers refunds greater than the input VAT charged.

Article 300

s12A The flat-rate compensation percentages shall be applied to the prices, exclusive of VAT, of the following goods and services:

(1)   agricultural products supplied by flat-rate farmers to taxable persons other than those covered, in the Member State in which these products were supplied, by this flat-rate scheme;

(2)   agricultural products supplied by flat-rate farmers, in accordance with the conditions specified in Article 138, to non-taxable legal persons whose intra-Community acquisitions of goods are subject to VAT, pursuant to Article 2(1)(b), in the Member State in which dispatch or transport of those agricultural products ends;

(3)   agricultural services supplied by flat-rate farmers to taxable persons other than those covered, in the Member State in which these services were supplied, by this flat-rate scheme.

Article 301

s12A 1.   In the case of the supply of agricultural products or agricultural services specified in Article 300, Member States shall provide that the flat-rate compensation is to be paid either by the customer or by the public authorities.

2.   In respect of any supply of agricultural products or agricultural services other than those specified in Article 300, the flat-rate compensation shall be deemed to be paid by the customer.

Article 302

If a flat-rate farmer is entitled to flat-rate compensation, he shall not be entitled to deduction of VAT in respect of activities covered by this flat-rate scheme.

Article 303

1.   Where the taxable customer pays flat-rate compensation pursuant to Article 301(1), he shall be entitled, in accordance with the conditions laid down in Articles 167, 168 and 169 and Articles 173 to 177 and the procedures laid down by the Member States, to deduct the compensation amount from the VAT for which he is liable in the Member State in which his taxed transactions are carried out.

2.   Member States shall refund to the customer the amount of the flat-rate compensation he has paid in respect of any of the following transactions:

(a)   the supply of agricultural products, carried out in accordance with the conditions specified in Article 138, to taxable persons, or to non-taxable legal persons, acting as such in another Member State within the territory of which their intra-Community acquisitions of goods are subject to VAT pursuant to Article 2(1)(b);

(b)   the supply of agricultural products, carried out in accordance with the conditions specified in Articles 146, 147, 148 and 156, Article 157(1)(b) and Articles 158, 160 and 161, to a taxable customer established outside the Community, in so far as the products are used by that customer for the purposes of the transactions referred to in Article 169(a) and (b) or for the purposes of supplies of services which are deemed to take place within the territory of the Member State in which the customer is established and in respect of which VAT is payable solely by the customer pursuant to Article 196;

(c)   the supply of agricultural services to a taxable customer established within the Community but in another Member State or to a taxable customer established outside the Community, in so far as the services are used by the customer for the purposes of the transactions referred to in Article 169(a) and (b) or for the purposes of supplies of services which are deemed to take place within the territory of the Member State in which the customer is established and in respect of which VAT is payable solely by the customer pursuant to Article 196.

3.   Member States shall determine the method by which the refunds provided for in paragraph 2 are to be made. In particular, they may apply the provisions of Directives 79/1072/EEC and 86/560/EEC.

Article 304

Member States shall take all measures necessary to verify payments of flat-rate compensation to flat-rate farmers.

Article 305

Whenever Member States apply this flat-rate scheme, they shall take all measures necessary to ensure that the supply of agricultural products between Member States, carried out in accordance with the conditions specified in Article 33, is always taxed in the same way, whether the supply is effected by a flat-rate farmer or by another taxable person.

CHAPTER 3

Special scheme for travel agents

Article 306

1.   Member States shall apply a special VAT scheme, in accordance with this Chapter, to transactions carried out by travel agents who deal with customers in their own name and use supplies of goods or services provided by other taxable persons, in the provision of travel facilities.

This special scheme shall not apply to travel agents where they act solely as intermediaries and to whom point (c) of the first paragraph of Article 79 applies for the purposes of calculating the taxable amount.

2.   For the purposes of this Chapter, tour operators shall be regarded as travel agents.

Article 307

Transactions made, in accordance with the conditions laid down in Article 306, by the travel agent in respect of a journey shall be regarded as a single service supplied by the travel agent to the traveller.

The single service shall be taxable in the Member State in which the travel agent has established his business or has a fixed establishment from which the travel agent has carried out the supply of services.

Article 308

The taxable amount and the price exclusive of VAT, within the meaning of point (8) of Article 226, in respect of the single service provided by the travel agent shall be the travel agent's margin, that is to say, the difference between the total amount, exclusive of VAT, to be paid by the traveller and the actual cost to the travel agent of supplies of goods or services provided by other taxable persons, where those transactions are for the direct benefit of the traveller.

Article 309

If transactions entrusted by the travel agent to other taxable persons are performed by such persons outside the Community, the supply of services carried out by the travel agent shall be treated as an intermediary activity exempted pursuant to Article 153.

If the transactions are performed both inside and outside the Community, only that part of the travel agent's service relating to transactions outside the Community may be exempted.

Article 310

VAT charged to the travel agent by other taxable persons in respect of transactions which are referred to in Article 307 and which are for the direct benefit of the traveller shall not be deductible or refundable in any Member State.

CHAPTER 4

Special arrangements for second-hand goods, works of art, collectors' items and antiques

Section 1

Definitions

Article 311

s10A(1) 1.   For the purposes of this Chapter, and without prejudice to other Community provisions, the following definitions shall apply:

(1)   '**second-hand goods**' means movable tangible property that is suitable for further use as it is or after repair, other than works of art, collectors' items or antiques and other than precious metals or precious stones as defined by the Member States;

(2)   '**works of art**' means the objects listed in Annex IX, Part A;

(3)   '**collectors' items**' means the objects listed in Annex IX, Part B;

(4)   '**antiques**' means the objects listed in Annex IX, Part C;

(5)   '**taxable dealer**' means any taxable person who, in the course of his economic activity and with a view to resale, purchases, or applies for the purposes of his business, or imports, second-hand goods, works of art, collectors' items or antiques, whether that taxable person is acting for himself or on behalf of another person pursuant to a contract under which commission is payable on purchase or sale;

(6)   '**organiser of a sale by public auction**' means any taxable person who, in the course of his economic activity, offers goods for sale by public auction with a view to handing them over to the highest bidder;

(7)   'principal of an organiser of a sale by public auction' means any person who transmits goods to an organiser of a sale by public auction pursuant to a contract under which commission is payable on a sale.

2.   Member States need not regard as works of art the objects listed in points (5), (6) or (7) of Annex IX, Part A.

3.   The contract under which commission is payable on a sale, referred to in point (7) of paragraph 1, must provide that the organiser of the sale is to put up the goods for public auction in his own name but on behalf of his principal and that he is to hand over the goods, in his own name but on behalf of his principal, to the highest bidder at the public auction.

Section 2

Special arrangements for taxable dealers

Subsection 1

Margin scheme

Article 312

s10A(1) For the purposes of this Subsection, the following definitions shall apply:

(1)   'selling price' means everything which constitutes the consideration obtained or to be obtained by the taxable dealer from the customer or from a third party, including subsidies directly linked to the transaction, taxes, duties, levies and charges and incidental expenses such as commission, packaging, transport and insurance costs charged by the taxable dealer to the customer, but excluding the amounts referred to in Article 79;

(2)   'purchase price' means everything which constitutes the consideration, for the purposes of point (1), obtained or to be obtained from the taxable dealer by his supplier.

Article 313

s10A 1.   In respect of the supply of second-hand goods, works of art, collectors' items or antiques carried out by taxable dealers, Member States shall apply a special scheme for taxing the profit margin made by the taxable dealer, in accordance with the provisions of this Subsection.

2.   Pending introduction of the definitive arrangements referred to in Article 402, the scheme referred to in paragraph 1 of this Article shall not apply to the supply of new means of transport, carried out in accordance with the conditions specified in Article 138(1) and (2)(a).

Article 314

s10A The margin scheme shall apply to the supply by a taxable dealer of second-hand goods, works of art, collectors' items or antiques where those goods have been supplied to him within the Community by one of the following persons:

(a)   a non-taxable person;

(b)   another taxable person, in so far as the supply of goods by that other taxable person is exempt pursuant to Article 136;

(c)   another taxable person, in so far as the supply of goods by that other taxable person is covered by the exemption for small enterprises provided for in Articles 282 to 292 and involves capital goods;

(d)   another taxable dealer, in so far as VAT has been applied to the supply of goods by that other taxable dealer in accordance with this margin scheme.

Article 315

A(1) The taxable amount in respect of the supply of goods as referred to in Article 314 shall be the profit margin made by the taxable dealer, less the amount of VAT relating to the profit margin.

The profit margin of the taxable dealer shall be equal to the difference between the selling price charged by the taxable dealer for the goods and the purchase price.

Article 316

A(4) 1.   Member States shall grant taxable dealers the right to opt for application of the margin scheme to the following transactions:

(a)   the supply of works of art, collectors' items or antiques, which the taxable dealer has imported himself;

(b)   the supply of works of art supplied to the taxable dealer by their creators or their successors in title;

(c)   the supply of works of art supplied to the taxable dealer by a taxable person other than a taxable dealer where the reduced rate has been applied to that supply pursuant to Article 103.

A(5) 2.   Member States shall lay down the detailed rules for exercise of the option provided for in paragraph 1, which shall in any event cover a period of at least two calendar years.

Article 317

A(5) If a taxable dealer exercises the option under Article 316, the taxable amount shall be determined in accordance with Article 315.

In respect of the supply of works of art, collectors' items or antiques which the taxable dealer has imported himself, the purchase price to be taken into account in calculating the profit margin shall be equal to the taxable amount on importation, determined in accordance with Articles 85 to 89, plus the VAT due or paid on importation.

Article 318

s10A(8) 1.   In order to simplify the procedure for collecting the tax and after consulting the VAT Committee, Member States may provide that, for certain transactions or for certain categories of taxable dealers, the taxable amount in respect of supplies of goods subject to the margin scheme is to be determined for each tax period during which the taxable dealer must submit the VAT return referred to in Article 250.

In the event that such provision is made in accordance with the first subparagraph, the taxable amount in respect of supplies of goods to which the same rate of VAT is applied shall be the total profit margin made by the taxable dealer less the amount of VAT relating to that margin.

2.   The total profit margin shall be equal to the difference between the following two amounts:

(a)   the total value of supplies of goods subject to the margin scheme and carried out by the taxable dealer during the tax period covered by the return, that is to say, the total of the selling prices;

(b)   the total value of purchases of goods, as referred to in Article 314, effected by the taxable dealer during the tax period covered by the return, that is to say, the total of the purchase prices.

3.   Member States shall take the measures necessary to ensure that the taxable dealers referred to in paragraph 1 do not enjoy unjustified advantage or sustain unjustified harm.

Article 319

s10A(7) The taxable dealer may apply the normal VAT arrangements to any supply covered by the margin scheme.

Article 320

s10A(7) 1.   Where the taxable dealer applies the normal VAT arrangements to the supply of a work of art, a collectors' item or an antique which he has imported himself, he shall be entitled to deduct from the VAT for which he is liable the VAT due or paid on the import.

Where the taxable dealer applies the normal VAT arrangements to the supply of a work of art supplied to him by its creator, or the creator's successors in title, or by a taxable person other than a taxable dealer, he shall be entitled to deduct from the VAT for which he is liable the VAT due or paid in respect of the work of art supplied to him.

2.   A right of deduction shall arise at the time when the VAT due on the supply in respect of which the taxable dealer opts for application of the normal VAT arrangements becomes chargeable.

Article 321

If carried out in accordance with the conditions specified in Articles 146, 147, 148 or 151, the supply of second-hand goods, works of art, collectors' items or antiques subject to the margin scheme shall be exempt.

Article 322

s10A(6) In so far as goods are used for the purpose of supplies carried out by him and subject to the margin scheme, the taxable dealer may not deduct the following from the VAT for which he is liable:

(a) the VAT due or paid in respect of works of art, collectors' items or antiques which he has imported himself;

(b) the VAT due or paid in respect of works of art which have been, or are to be, supplied to him by their creator or by the creator's successors in title;

(c) the VAT due or paid in respect of works of art which have been, or are to be, supplied to him by a taxable person other than a taxable dealer.

Article 323

s10A(9) Taxable persons may not deduct from the VAT for which they are liable the VAT due or paid in respect of goods which have been, or are to be, supplied to them by a taxable dealer, in so far as the supply of those goods by the taxable dealer is subject to the margin scheme.

Article 324

Where the taxable dealer applies both the normal VAT arrangements and the margin scheme, he must show separately in his accounts the transactions falling under each of those arrangements, in accordance with the rules laid down by the Member States.

Article 325

The taxable dealer may not enter separately on the invoices which he issues the VAT relating to supplies of goods to which he applies the margin scheme.

Subsection 2

Transitional arrangements for second-hand means of transport

Article 326

Member States which, at 31 December 1992, were applying special tax arrangements other than the margin scheme to the supply by taxable dealers of second-hand means of transport may, pending introduction of the definitive arrangements referred to in Article 402, continue to apply those arrangements in so far as they comply with, or are adjusted to comply with, the conditions laid down in this Subsection.

Denmark is authorised to introduce tax arrangements as referred to in the first paragraph.

Article 327

1. These transitional arrangements shall apply to supplies of second-hand means of transport carried out by taxable dealers, and subject to the margin scheme.

2. These transitional arrangements shall not apply to the supply of new means of transport carried out in accordance with the conditions specified in Article 138(1) and (2)(a).

3. For the purposes of paragraph 1, the land vehicles, vessels and aircraft referred to in point (a) of Article 2(2) shall be regarded as 'second-hand means of transport' where they are second-hand goods which do not meet the conditions necessary to be regarded as new means of transport.

Article 328

The VAT due in respect of each supply referred to in Article 327 shall be equal to the amount of VAT that would have been due if that supply had been subject to the normal VAT arrangements, less the amount of VAT regarded as being incorporated by the taxable dealer in the purchase price of the means of transport.

Article 329

The VAT regarded as being incorporated by the taxable dealer in the purchase price of the means of transport shall be calculated in accordance with the following method:

(a) the purchase price to be taken into account shall be the purchase price within the meaning of point (2) of Article 312;

(b) that purchase price paid by the taxable dealer shall be deemed to include the VAT that would have been due if the taxable dealer's supplier had applied the normal VAT arrangements to the supply;

(c) the rate to be taken into account shall be the rate applicable, pursuant to Article 93, in the Member State in the territory of which the place of the supply to the taxable dealer, as determined in accordance with Articles 31 and 32, is deemed to be situated.

Article 330

The VAT due in respect of each supply of means of transport as referred to in Article 327(1), determined in accordance with Article 328, may not be less than the amount of VAT that would be due if that supply were subject to the margin scheme.

Member States may provide that, if the supply is subject to the margin scheme, the margin may not be less than 10% of the selling price within the meaning of point (1) of Article 312.

Article 331

Taxable persons may not deduct from the VAT for which they are liable the VAT due or paid in respect of second-hand means of transport supplied to them by a taxable dealer, in so far as the supply of those goods by the taxable dealer is subject to VAT in accordance with these transitional arrangements.

Article 332

The taxable dealer may not enter separately on the invoices he issues the VAT relating to supplies to which he applies these transitional arrangements.

Section 3

Special arrangements for sales by public auction
Article 333

0B(1) 1.   Member States may, in accordance with the provisions of this Section,
0B(2)   apply special arrangements for taxation of the profit margin made by an organiser of a sale by public auction in respect of the supply of second-hand goods, works of art, collectors' items or antiques by that organiser, acting in his own name and on behalf of the persons referred to in Article 334, pursuant to a contract under which commission is payable on the sale of those goods by public auction.

s10B(1) 2.   The arrangements referred to in paragraph 1 shall not apply to the supply of new means of transport, carried out in accordance with the conditions specified in Article 138(1) and (2)(a).

Article 334

These special arrangements shall apply to supplies carried out by an organiser of a sale by public auction, acting in his own name, on behalf of one of the following persons:

(a)   a non-taxable person;

(b)   another taxable person, in so far as the supply of goods, carried out by that taxable person in accordance with a contract under which commission is payable on a sale, is exempt pursuant to Article 136;

(c)   another taxable person, in so far as the supply of goods, carried out by that taxable person in accordance with a contract under which commission is payable on a sale, is covered by the exemption for small enterprises provided for in Articles 282 to 292 and involves capital goods;

(d)   a taxable dealer, in so far as the supply of goods, carried out by that taxable dealer in accordance with a contract under which commission is payable on a sale, is subject to VAT in accordance with the margin scheme.

Article 335

s10B(9) The supply of goods to a taxable person who is an organiser of sales by public auction shall be regarded as taking place when the sale of those goods by public auction takes place.

Article 336

s10B(3) The taxable amount in respect of each supply of goods referred to in this Section shall be the total amount invoiced in accordance with Article 339 to the purchaser by the organiser of the sale by public auction, less the following:

(a)   the net amount paid or to be paid by the organiser of the sale by public auction to his principal, as determined in accordance with Article 337;

(b)   the amount of the VAT payable by the organiser of the sale by public auction in respect of his supply.

Article 337

The net amount paid or to be paid by the organiser of the sale by public auction to his principal shall be equal to the difference between the auction price of the goods and the amount of the commission obtained or to be obtained by the organiser of the sale by public auction from his principal pursuant to the contract under which commission is payable on the sale.

Article 338

Organisers of sales by public auction who supply goods in accordance with the conditions laid down in Articles 333 and 334 must indicate the following in their accounts, in suspense accounts:

(a)   the amounts obtained or to be obtained from the purchaser of the goods;

(b)   the amounts reimbursed or to be reimbursed to the vendor of the goods.

The amounts referred to in the first paragraph must be duly substantiated.

Article 339

s10B(4) The organiser of the sale by public auction must issue to the purchaser an invoice itemising the following:

(a)   the auction price of the goods;

(b)   taxes, duties, levies and charges;

(c)   incidental expenses, such as commission, packing, transport and insurance costs, charged by the organiser to the purchaser of the goods.

The invoice issued by the organiser of the sale by public auction must not indicate any VAT separately.

Article 340

s10B(4) 1. The organiser of the sale by public auction to whom the goods have been transmitted pursuant to a contract under which commission is payable on a public auction sale must issue a statement to his principal.

The statement issued by the organiser of the sale by public auction must specify separately the amount of the transaction, that is to say, the auction price of the goods less the amount of the commission obtained or to be obtained from the principal.

2. The statement drawn up in accordance with paragraph 1 shall serve as the invoice which the principal, where he is a taxable person, must issue to the organiser of the sale by public auction in accordance with Article 220.

Article 341

Member States which apply the arrangements provided for in this Section shall also apply these arrangements to supplies of second-hand means of transport, as defined in Article 327(3), carried out by an organiser of sales by public auction, acting in his own name, pursuant to a contract under which commission is payable on the sale of those goods by public auction, on behalf of a taxable dealer, in so far as those supplies by that taxable dealer would be subject to VAT in accordance with the transitional arrangements for second-hand means of transport.

Section 4

Measures to prevent distortion of competition and tax evasion

Article 342

Member States may take measures concerning the right of deduction in order to ensure that the taxable dealers covered by special arrangements as provided for in Section 2 do not enjoy unjustified advantage or sustain unjustified harm.

Article 343

Acting unanimously on a proposal from the Commission, the Council may authorise any Member State to introduce special measures to combat tax evasion, pursuant to which the VAT due under the margin scheme may not be less the amount of VAT which would be due if the profit margin were equal to a certain percentage of the selling price.

The percentage of the selling price shall be fixed in the light of the normal profit margins made by economic operators in the sector concerned.

CHAPTER 5

SPECIAL SCHEME FOR INVESTMENT GOLD

Section 1

General provisions

Article 344

s6A 1. For the purposes of this Directive, and without prejudice to other Community provisions, 'investment gold' shall mean:

(1)   gold, in the form of a bar or a wafer of weights accepted by the bullion markets, of a purity equal to or greater than 995 thousandths, whether or not represented by securities;

(2)   gold coins of a purity equal to or greater than 900 thousandths and minted after 1800, which are or have been legal tender in the country of origin, and are normally sold at a price which does not exceed the open market value of the gold contained in the coins by more than 80%.

2.   Member States may exclude from this special scheme small bars or wafers of a weight of 1 g or less.

3.   For the purposes of this Directive, the coins referred to in point (2) of paragraph 1 shall not be regarded as sold for numismatic interest.

Article 345

Starting in 1999, each Member State shall inform the Commission by 1 July each year of the coins meeting the criteria laid down in point (2) of Article 344(1) which are traded in that Member State. The Commission shall, before 1 December each year, publish a comprehensive list of those coins in the 'C' series of the Official Journal of the European Union. Coins included in the published list shall be deemed to fulfil those criteria throughout the year for which the list is published.

Section 2

Exemption from VAT

Article 346

Member States shall exempt from VAT the supply, the intra-Community acquisition and the importation of investment gold, including investment gold represented by certificates for allocated or unallocated gold or traded on gold accounts and including, in particular, gold loans and swaps, involving a right of ownership or claim in respect of investment gold, as well as transactions concerning investment gold involving futures and forward contracts leading to a transfer of right of ownership or claim in respect of investment gold.

Article 347

Member States shall exempt the services of agents who act in the name and on behalf of another person, when they take part in the supply of investment gold for their principal.

Section 3

Taxation option

Article 348

Member States shall allow taxable persons who produce investment gold or transform gold into investment gold the right to opt for the taxation of supplies of investment gold to another taxable person which would otherwise be exempt pursuant to Article 346.

Article 349

1. Member States may allow taxable persons who, in the course of their economic activity, normally supply gold for industrial purposes, the right to opt for the taxation of supplies of gold bars or wafers, as referred to in point (1) of Article 344(1), to another taxable person, which would otherwise be exempt pursuant to Article 346.
2. Member States may restrict the scope of the option provided for in paragraph 1.

Article 350

Where the supplier has exercised the right under Articles 348 and 349 to opt for taxation, Member States shall allow the agent to opt for taxation of the services referred to in Article 347.

Article 351

5A(6) Member States shall lay down detailed rules for the exercise of the options provided for in this Section, and shall inform the Commission accordingly.

Section 4

Transactions on a regulated gold bullion market

Article 352

s6A Each Member State may, after consulting the VAT Committee, apply VAT to specific transactions relating to investment gold which take place in that Member State between taxable persons who are members of a gold bullion market regulated by the Member State concerned or between such a taxable person and another taxable person who is not a member of that market. However, the Member State may not apply VAT to supplies carried out in accordance with the conditions specified in Article 138 or to exports of investment gold.

Article 353

s6A Member States which, pursuant to Article 352, tax transactions between taxable persons who are members of a regulated gold bullion market shall, for the purposes of simplification, authorise suspension of the tax to be collected and relieve taxable persons of the accounting requirements in respect of VAT.

Section 5

Special rights and obligations for traders in investment gold

Article 354

s6A Where his subsequent supply of investment gold is exempt pursuant to this Chapter, the taxable person shall be entitled to deduct the following:

(a) the VAT due or paid in respect of investment gold supplied to him by a person who has exercised the right of option under Articles 348 and 349 or supplied to him in accordance with Section 4;

(b) the VAT due or paid in respect of a supply to him, or in respect of an intra-Community acquisition or importation carried out by him, of gold other than investment gold which is subsequently transformed by him or on his behalf into investment gold;

(c) the VAT due or paid in respect of services supplied to him consisting in a change of form, weight or purity of gold including investment gold.

Article 355

s6A Taxable persons who produce investment gold or transform gold into investment gold shall be entitled to deduct the VAT due or paid by them in respect of the supply, intra-Community acquisition or importation of goods or services linked to the production or transformation of that gold, as if the subsequent supply of the gold exempted pursuant to Article 346 were taxed.

Article 356

s16(1A) 1. Member States shall ensure that traders in investment gold keep, as a minimum, accounts of all substantial transactions in investment gold and keep the documents which enable the customers in such transactions to be identified.

Traders shall keep the information referred to in the first subparagraph for a period of at least five years.

2. Member States may accept equivalent obligations under measures adopted pursuant to other Community legislation, such as Directive 2005/60/EC of the European Parliament and of the Council of 26 October 2005 on the prevention of the use of the financial system for the purpose of money laundering and terrorist financing, to comply with the requirements under paragraph 1.

3. Member States may lay down obligations which are more stringent, in particular as regards the keeping of special records or special accounting requirements.

CHAPTER 6

Special scheme for non-established taxable persons supplying electronic services to non-taxable persons

Section 1

General provisions

*[Article 357

This Chapter shall apply until 31 December 2014.]¹

Amendments

1   Substituted by Article 1(4) of Council Directive 2008/8/EC of 12 February 2008, (w.e.f. 1 January 2009).

*Article 358

5A(1) For the purposes of this Chapter, and without prejudice to other provisions, the following definitions shall apply:

(1)   'non-established taxable person' means a taxable person who has not established his business in the territory of the Community and who has no fixed establishment there and who is not otherwise required to be identified pursuant to Article 214;

[(2)   'electronic services' and 'electronically supplied services' mean the services referred to in point (k) of Article 56(1);]¹

(3)   'Member State of identification' means the Member State which the non-established taxable person chooses to contact to state when his activity as a taxable person within the territory of the Community commences in accordance with the provisions of this Chapter;

(4)   ['Member State of consumption' means the Member State in which, pursuant to Article 57, the supply of the electronic services is deemed to take place;]²

(5)   'VAT return' means the statement containing the information necessary to establish the amount of VAT due in each Member State.

Amendments

1   With effect from 1 January 2010 and in accordance with Art 2(11a) of Council Directive 2008/8/EC of 12 February 2008, Art 358, point 2 shall read:
    '"electronic services" and "electronically supplied services" mean the services referred to in point (k) of the first paragraph of Article 59;'
2   With effect from 1 January 2010 and in accordance with Art 2(11b) of Council Directive 2008/8/EC of 12 February 2008, Art 262 shall read:
    '"Member State of consumption" means the Member State in which, pursuant to Article 58, the supply of the electronic services is deemed to take place;'

Section 2

*Special scheme for electronically supplied services

*Article 359

5A(2) Member States shall permit any non-established taxable person supplying electronic services to a non-taxable person who is established in a Member

State or who has his permanent address or usually resides in a Member State, to use this special scheme. This scheme applies to all electronic services supplied in the Community.

*Article 360

s5A(4) The non-established taxable person shall state to the Member State of identification when he commences or ceases his activity as a taxable person, or changes that activity in such a way that he no longer meets the conditions necessary for use of this special scheme. He shall communicate that information electronically.

*Article 361

s5A(4) 1.   The information which the non-established taxable person must provide to the Member State of identification when he commences a taxable activity shall contain the following details:

(a)   name;

(b)   postal address;

(c)   electronic addresses, including websites;

(d)   national tax number, if any;

(e)   a statement that the person is not identified for VAT purposes within the Community.

2.   The non-established taxable person shall notify the Member State of identification of any changes in the information provided.

*Article 362

s5A(5) The Member State of identification shall allocate to the non-established taxable person an individual VAT identification number and shall notify him of that number by electronic means. On the basis of the information used for that identification, Member States of consumption may have recourse to their own identification systems.

*Article 363

s5A(14) The Member State of identification shall strike the non-established taxable person from the identification register in the following cases:

(a)   if he notifies that Member State that he no longer supplies electronic services;

(b)   if it may otherwise be assumed that his taxable activities have ceased;

(c)   if he no longer meets the conditions necessary for use of this special scheme;

(d)   if he persistently fails to comply with the rules relating to this special scheme.

*Article 364

5A(6) The non-established taxable person shall submit by electronic means to the Member State of identification a VAT return for each calendar quarter, whether or not electronic services have been supplied. The VAT return shall be submitted within 20 days following the end of the tax period covered by the return.

*Article 365

5A(7) The VAT return shall show the identification number and, for each Member State of consumption in which VAT is due, the total value, exclusive of VAT, of supplies of electronic services carried out during the tax period and the total amount of the corresponding VAT. The applicable rates of VAT and the total VAT due must also be indicated on the return.

*Article 366

A(7) 1.   The VAT return shall be made out in euro.
A(8)

Member States which have not adopted the euro may require the VAT return to be made out in their national currency. If the supplies have been made in other currencies, the non-established taxable person shall, for the purposes of completing the VAT return, use the exchange rate applying on the last day of the tax period.

2.   The conversion shall be made by applying the exchange rates published by the European Central Bank for that day, or, if there is no publication on that day, on the next day of publication.

*Article 367

s5A(6) The non-established taxable person shall pay the VAT when submitting the VAT return.

Payment shall be made to a bank account denominated in euro, designated by the Member State of identification. Member States which have not adopted the euro may require payment to be made to a bank account denominated in their own currency.

*Article 368

s5A(9) The non-established taxable person making use of this special scheme may not deduct VAT pursuant to Article 168 of this Directive. Notwithstanding Article 1(1) of Directive 86/560/EEC, the taxable person in question shall be refunded in accordance with the said Directive. Articles 2(2) and (3) and Article 4(2) of Directive 86/560/EEC shall not apply to refunds relating to electronic services covered by this special scheme.

*Article 369

s5A(12) 1.   The non-established taxable person shall keep records of the transactions covered by this special scheme. Those records must be sufficiently detailed to enable the tax authorities of the Member State of consumption to verify that the VAT return is correct.

2.   The records referred to in paragraph 1 must be made available electronically on request to the Member State of identification and to the Member State of consumption.

Those records must be kept for a period of ten years from the end of the year during which the transaction was carried out.

TITLE XIII

DEROGATIONS

CHAPTER 1

Derogations applying until the adoption of definitive arrangements

Section 1

Derogations for States which were members of the Community on 1 January 1978

Article 370

Member States which, at 1 January 1978, taxed the transactions listed in Annex X, Part A, may continue to tax those transactions.

Article 371

Sch (xix)
Sch (xiv)
Member States which, at 1 January 1978, exempted the transactions listed in Annex X, Part B, may continue to exempt those transactions, in accordance with the conditions applying in the Member State concerned on that date.

Article 372

Member States which, at 1 January 1978, applied provisions derogating from the principle of immediate deduction laid down in the first paragraph of Article 179 may continue to apply those provisions.

Article 373

Member States which, at 1 January 1978, applied provisions derogating from Article 28 or from point (c) of the first paragraph of Article 79 may continue to apply those provisions.

Article 374

By way of derogation from Articles 169 and 309, Member States which, at 1 January 1978, exempted, without deductibility of the VAT paid at the preceding stage, the services of travel agents, as referred to in Article 309, may continue to exempt those services. That derogation shall apply also in respect of travel agents acting in the name and on behalf of the traveller.

Section 2

Derogations for States which acceded to the Community after 1 January 1978

Article 375

Greece may continue to exempt the transactions listed in points (2), (8), (9), (11) and (12) of Annex X, Part B, in accordance with the conditions applying in that Member State on 1 January 1987.

Article 376

Spain may continue to exempt the supply of services performed by authors, listed in point (2) of Annex X, Part B, and the transactions listed in points (11) and (12) of Annex X, Part B, in accordance with the conditions applying in that Member State on 1 January 1993.

Article 377

Portugal may continue to exempt the transactions listed in points (2), (4), (7), (9), (10) and (13) of Annex X, Part B, in accordance with the conditions applying in that Member State on 1 January 1989.

Article 378

1. Austria may continue to tax the transactions listed in point (2) of Annex X, Part A.

2. For as long as the same exemptions are applied in any of the Member States which were members of the Community on 31 December 1994, Austria may, in accordance with the conditions applying in that Member State on the date of its accession, continue to exempt the following transactions:

    (a) the transactions listed in points (5) and (9) of Annex X, Part B;

    (b) with deductibility of the VAT paid at the preceding stage, all parts of international passenger transport operations, carried out by air, sea or inland waterway, other than passenger transport operations on Lake Constance.

Article 379

1. Finland may continue to tax the transactions listed in point (2) of Annex X, Part A, for as long as the same transactions are taxed in any of the Member States which were members of the Community on 31 December 1994.

2. Finland may, in accordance with the conditions applying in that Member State on the date of its accession, continue to exempt the supply of services by authors, artists and performers, listed in

point (2) of Annex X, Part B, and the transactions listed in points (5), (9) and (10) of Annex X, Part B, for as long as the same exemptions are applied in any of the Member States which were members of the Community on 31 December 1994.

Article 380

Sweden may, in accordance with the conditions applying in that Member State on the date of its accession, continue to exempt the supply of services by authors, artists and performers, listed in point (2) of Annex X, Part B, and the transactions listed in points (1), (9) and (10) of Annex X, Part B, for as long as the same exemptions are applied in any of the Member States which were members of the Community on 31 December 1994.

Article 381

The Czech Republic may, in accordance with the conditions applying in that Member State on the date of its accession, continue to exempt the international transport of passengers, as referred to in point (10) of Annex X, Part B, for as long as the same exemption is applied in any of the Member States which were members of the Community on 30 April 2004.

Article 382

Estonia may, in accordance with the conditions applying in that Member State on the date of its accession, continue to exempt the international transport of passengers, as referred to in point (10) of Annex X, Part B, for as long as the same exemption is applied in any of the Member States which were members of the Community on 30 April 2004.

Article 383

Cyprus may, in accordance with the conditions applying in that Member State on the date of its accession, continue to exempt the following transactions:

(a)   the supply of building land referred to in point (9) of Annex X, Part B, until 31 December 2007;

(b)   the international transport of passengers, as referred to in point (10) of Annex X, Part B, for as long as the same exemption is applied in any of the Member States which were members of the Community on 30 April 2004.

Article 384

For as long as the same exemptions are applied in any of the Member States which were members of the Community on 30 April 2004, Latvia may, in accordance with the conditions applying in that Member State on the date of its accession, continue to exempt the following transactions:

(a)   the supply of services by authors, artists and performers, as referred to in point (2) of Annex X, Part B;

(b)   the international transport of passengers, as referred to in point (10) of
        Annex X, Part B.

Article 385

Lithuania may, in accordance with the conditions applying in that Member
State on the date of its accession, continue to exempt the international transport
of passengers, as referred to in point (10) of Annex X, Part B, for as long as the
same exemption is applied in any of the Member States which were members
of the Community on 30 April 2004.

Article 386

Hungary may, in accordance with the conditions applying in that Member
State on the date of its accession, continue to exempt the international transport
of passengers, as referred to in point (10) of Annex X, Part B, for as long as the
same exemption is applied in any of the Member States which were members
of the Community on 30 April 2004.

Article 387

For as long as the same exemptions are applied in any of the Member States
which were members of the Community on 30 April 2004, Malta may, in
accordance with the conditions applying in that Member State on the date of
its accession, continue to exempt the following transactions:

(a)   without deductibility of the VAT paid at the preceding stage, the supply
        of water by a body governed by public law, as referred to in point (8) of
        Annex X, Part B;

(b)   without deductibility of the VAT paid at the preceding stage, the supply
        of buildings and building land, as referred to in point (9) of Annex X,
        Part B;

(c)   with deductibility of the VAT paid at the preceding stage, inland passenger
        transport, international passenger transport and domestic inter-island
        sea passenger transport, as referred to in point (10) of Annex X, Part B.

Article 388

Poland may, in accordance with the conditions applying in that Member State
on the date of its accession, continue to exempt the international transport of
passengers, as referred to in point (10) of Annex X, Part B, for as long as the
same exemption is applied in any of the Member States which were members
of the Community on 30 April 2004.

Article 389

Slovenia may, in accordance with the conditions applying in that Member State
on the date of its accession, continue to exempt the international transport of
passengers, as referred to in point (10) of Annex X, Part B, for as long as the
same exemption is applied in any of the Member States which were members
of the Community on 30 April 2004.

Article 390

Slovakia may, in accordance with the conditions applying in that Member State on the date of its accession, continue to exempt the international transport of passengers, as referred to in point (10) of Annex X, Part B, for as long as the same exemption is applied in any of the Member States which were members of the Community on 30 April 2004.

Section 3

Provisions common to Sections 1 and 2

Article 391

s7 Member States which exempt the transactions referred to in Articles 371, 375, 376 or 377, Article 378(2), Article 379(2) or Articles 380 to 390 may grant taxable persons the right to opt for taxation of those transactions.

Article 392

Member States may provide that, in respect of the supply of buildings and building land purchased for the purpose of resale by a taxable person for whom the VAT on the purchase was not deductible, the taxable amount shall be the difference between the selling price and the purchase price.

Article 393

1. With a view to facilitating the transition to the definitive arrangements referred to in Article 402, the Council shall, on the basis of a report from the Commission, review the situation with regard to the derogations provided for in Sections 1 and 2 and shall, acting in accordance with Article 93 of the Treaty decide whether any or all of those derogations is to be abolished.

2. By way of definitive arrangements, passenger transport shall be taxed in the Member State of departure for that part of the journey taking place within the Community, in accordance with the detailed rules to be laid down by the Council, acting in accordance with Article 93 of the Treaty.

CHAPTER 2

Derogations subject to authorisation

Section 1

Simplification measures and measures to prevent tax evasion or avoidance

Article 394

Member States which, at 1 January 1977, applied special measures to simplify the procedure for collecting VAT or to prevent certain forms of tax evasion or avoidance may retain them provided that they have notified the Commission accordingly before 1 January 1978 and that such simplification measures comply with the criterion laid down in the second subparagraph of Article 395(1).

Article 395

1.   The Council, acting unanimously on a proposal from the Commission, may authorise any Member State to introduce special measures for derogation from the provisions of this Directive, in order to simplify the procedure for collecting VAT or to prevent certain forms of tax evasion or avoidance.

Measures intended to simplify the procedure for collecting VAT may not, except to a negligible extent, affect the overall amount of the tax revenue of the Member State collected at the stage of final consumption.

2.   A Member State wishing to introduce the measure referred to in paragraph 1 shall send an application to the Commission and provide it with all the necessary information. If the Commission considers that it does not have all the necessary information, it shall contact the Member State concerned within two months of receipt of the application and specify what additional information is required.

Once the Commission has all the information it considers necessary for appraisal of the request it shall within one month notify the requesting Member State accordingly and it shall transmit the request, in its original language, to the other Member States.

3.   Within three months of giving the notification referred to in the second subparagraph of paragraph 2, the Commission shall present to the Council either an appropriate proposal or, should it object to the derogation requested, a communication setting out its objections.

4.   The procedure laid down in paragraphs 2 and 3 shall, in any event, be completed within eight months of receipt of the application by the Commission.

Section 2

International agreements

Article 396

1.   The Council, acting unanimously on a proposal from the Commission, may authorise any Member State to conclude with a third country or an international body an agreement which may contain derogations from this Directive.

2.   A Member State wishing to conclude an agreement as referred to in paragraph 1 shall send an application to the Commission and provide it with all the necessary information. If the Commission considers that it does not have all the necessary information, it shall contact the Member State concerned within two months of receipt of the application and specify what additional information is required.

Once the Commission has all the information it considers necessary for appraisal of the request it shall within one month notify the requesting Member State accordingly and it shall transmit the request, in its original language, to the other Member States.

3.   Within three months of giving the notification referred to in the second subparagraph of paragraph 2, the Commission shall present to the Council either an appropriate proposal or, should it object to the derogation requested, a communication setting out its objections.

4.   The procedure laid down in paragraphs 2 and 3 shall, in any event, be completed within eight months of receipt of the application by the Commission.

TITLE XIV

MISCELLANEOUS

CHAPTER 1

Implementing measures

Article 397

The Council, acting unanimously on a proposal from the Commission, shall adopt the measures necessary to implement this Directive.

CHAPTER 2

VAT Committee

Article 398

1.   An advisory committee on value added tax, called 'the VAT Committee', is set up.

2.   The VAT Committee shall consist of representatives of the Member States and of the Commission.

The chairman of the Committee shall be a representative of the Commission.

Secretarial services for the Committee shall be provided by the Commission.

3.   The VAT Committee shall adopt its own rules of procedure.

4.   In addition to the points forming the subject of consultation pursuant to this Directive, the VAT Committee shall examine questions raised by its chairman, on his own initiative or at the request of the representative of a Member State, which concern the application of Community provisions on VAT.

CHAPTER 3

Conversion rates

Article 399

Without prejudice to any other particular provisions, the equivalents in national currency of the amounts in euro specified in this Directive shall be determined on the basis of the euro conversion rate applicable on 1 January 1999. Member States having acceded to the European Union after that date, which have not adopted the euro as single currency, shall use the euro conversion rate applicable on the date of their accession.

Article 400

When converting the amounts referred to in Article 399 into national currencies, Member States may adjust the amounts resulting from that conversion either upwards or downwards by up to 10%.

CHAPTER 4

Other taxes, duties and charges

Article 401

Without prejudice to other provisions of Community law, this Directive shall not prevent a Member State from maintaining or introducing taxes on insurance contracts, taxes on betting and gambling, excise duties, stamp duties or, more generally, any taxes, duties or charges which cannot be characterised as turnover taxes, provided that the collecting of those taxes, duties or charges does not give rise, in trade between Member States, to formalities connected with the crossing of frontiers.

TITLE XV

FINAL PROVISIONS

CHAPTER 1

Transitional arrangements for the taxation of trade between Member States

Article 402

1.   The arrangements provided for in this Directive for the taxation of trade between Member States are transitional and shall be replaced by definitive arrangements based in principle on the taxation in the Member State of origin of the supply of goods or services.

2.   Having concluded, upon examination of the report referred to in Article 404, that the conditions for transition to the definitive arrangements are met, the Council shall, acting in accordance with Article 93 of the Treaty, adopt the provisions necessary for the entry into force and for the operation of the definitive arrangements.

Article 403

The Council shall, acting in accordance with Article 93 of the Treaty, adopt Directives appropriate for the purpose of supplementing the common system of VAT and, in particular, for the progressive restriction or the abolition of derogations from that system.

Article 404

Every four years starting from the adoption of this Directive, the Commission shall, on the basis of information obtained from the Member States, present a report to the European Parliament and to the Council on the operation of the common system of VAT in the Member States and, in particular, on the operation of the transitional arrangements for taxing trade between Member States. That report shall be accompanied, where appropriate, by proposals concerning the definitive arrangements.

CHAPTER 2

Transitional measures applicable in the context of accession to the European Union

Article 405

s15B(7)(a) For the purposes of this Chapter, the following definitions shall apply:

(1)   'Community' means the territory of the Community as defined in point (1) of Article 5 before the accession of new Member States;

(2)   'new Member States' means the territory of the Member States which acceded to the European Union after 1 January 1995, as defined for each of those Member States in point (2) of Article 5;

(3)   'enlarged Community' means the territory of the Community as defined in point (1) of Article 5 after the accession of new Member States.

Article 406

The provisions in force at the time the goods were placed under temporary importation arrangements with total exemption from import duty or under one of the arrangements or situations referred to in Article 156, or under similar arrangements or situations in one of the new Member States, shall continue to apply until the goods cease to be covered by these arrangements or situations after the date of accession, where the following conditions are met:

(a)   the goods entered the Community or one of the new Member States before the date of accession;

(b)   the goods were placed, on entry into the Community or one of the new Member States, under these arrangements or situations;

(c)   the goods have not ceased to be covered by these arrangements or situations before the date of accession.

Article 407

The provisions in force at the time the goods were placed under customs transit arrangements shall continue to apply until the goods cease to be covered by these arrangements after the date of accession, where the following conditions are met:

(a)   the goods were placed, before the date of accession, under customs transit arrangements;

(b)   the goods have not ceased to be covered by these arrangements before the date of accession.

Article 408

1.   The following shall be treated as an importation of goods where it is shown that the goods were in free circulation in one of the new Member States or in the Community:

(a)   the removal, including irregular removal, of goods from temporary importation arrangements under which they were placed before the date of accession under the conditions provided for in Article 406;

(b)   the removal, including irregular removal, of goods either from one of the arrangements or situations referred to in Article 156 or from similar arrangements or situations under which they were placed before the date of accession under the conditions provided for in Article 406;

(c)   the cessation of one of the arrangements referred to in Article 407, started before the date of accession in the territory of one of the new Member States, for the purposes of a supply of goods for consideration effected before that date in the territory of that Member State by a taxable person acting as such;

(d)   any irregularity or offence committed during customs transit arrangements started under the conditions referred to in point (c).

2.   In addition to the case referred to in paragraph 1, the use after the date of accession within the territory of a Member State, by a taxable or non-taxable person, of goods supplied to him before the date of accession within the territory of the Community or one of the new Member States shall be treated as an importation of goods where the following conditions are met:

(a)   the supply of those goods has been exempted, or was likely to be exempted, either under points (a) and (b) of Article 146(1) or under a similar provision in the new Member States;

(b)   the goods were not imported into one of the new Member States or into the Community before the date of accession.

Article 409

In the cases referred to in Article 408(1), the place of import within the meaning of Article 61 shall be the Member State within whose territory the goods cease to be covered by the arrangements or situations under which they were placed before the date of accession.

Article 410

1.   By way of derogation from Article 71, the importation of goods within the meaning of Article 408 shall terminate without the occurrence of a chargeable event if one of the following conditions is met:

(a)   the imported goods are dispatched or transported outside the enlarged Community;

(b)   the imported goods within the meaning of Article 408(1) (a) are other than means of transport and are redispatched or transported to the Member State from which they were exported and to the person who exported them;

(c)   the imported goods within the meaning of Article 408(1)(a) are means of transport which were acquired or imported before the date of accession in accordance with the general conditions of taxation in force on the domestic market of one of the new Member States or of one of the Member States of the Community or which have not been subject, by reason of their exportation, to any exemption from, or refund of, VAT.

2.   The condition referred to in paragraph 1(c) shall be deemed to be fulfilled in the following cases:

(a)   when the date of first entry into service of the means of transport was more than eight years before the accession to the European Union.

(b)   when the amount of tax due by reason of the importation is insignificant.

CHAPTER 3

Transposition and entry into force

Article 411

1.   Directive 67/227/EEC and Directive 77/388/EEC are repealed, without prejudice to the obligations of the Member States concerning the time-limits, listed in Annex XI, Part B, for the transposition into national law and the implementation of those Directives.

2.   References to the repealed Directives shall be construed as references to this Directive and shall be read in accordance with the correlation table in Annex XII.

Article 412

1.   Member States shall bring into force the laws, regulations and administrative provisions necessary to comply with Article 2(3), Article 44, Article 59(1), Article 399 and Annex III, point (18) with effect from 1 January 2008. They shall forthwith communicate to the Commission the text of those provisions and a correlation table between those provisions and this Directive.

When Member States adopt those provisions, they shall contain a reference to this Directive or be accompanied by such a reference on the occasion of their official publication. Member States shall determine how such reference is to be made.

2.   Member States shall communicate to the Commission the text of the main provisions of national law which they adopt in the field covered by this Directive.

Article 413

This Directive shall enter into force on 1 January 2007.

Article 414

This Directive is addressed to the Member States.

Done at Brussels, 28 November 2006.

For the Council
The President
E. HEINÄLUOMA

ANNEX I

LIST OF THE ACTIVITIES REFERRED TO IN THE THIRD SUBPARAGRAPH OF ARTICLE 13(1)

(1)   Telecommunications services;

(2)   supply of water, gas, electricity and thermal energy;

(3)   transport of goods;

(4)   port and airport services;

(5)   passenger transport;

(6)   supply of new goods manufactured for sale;

(7)   transactions in respect of agricultural products, carried out by agricultural intervention agencies pursuant to Regulations on the common organisation of the market in those products;

(8)   organisation of trade fairs and exhibitions;

(9)   warehousing;

(10) activities of commercial publicity bodies;

(11) activities of travel agents;

(12) running of staff shops, cooperatives and industrial canteens and similar institutions;

(13) activities carried out by radio and television bodies in so far as these are not exempt pursuant to Article 132(1)(q).

ANNEX II

*[INDICATIVE LIST OF THE ELECTRONICALLY SUPPLIED SERVICES REFERRED TO IN POINT (K) OF ARTICLE 56(1)][1]

s 1(1) (1)   Website supply, web-hosting, distance maintenance of programmes and equipment;

(2)   supply of software and updating thereof;

(3)   supply of images, text and information and making available of databases;

(4)   supply of music, films and games, including games of chance and gambling games, and of political, cultural, artistic, sporting, scientific and entertainment broadcasts and events;

(5)   supply of distance teaching.

Amendments

1   With effect from 1 January 2010 and in accordance with Art 2(12) of Council Directive 2008/8/EC of 12 February 2008, the heading to Annex II shall read:

'INDICATIVE LIST OF THE ELECTRONICALLY SUPPLIED SERVICES REFERRED TO IN ARTICLE 58 AND POINT (K) OF THE FIRST PARAGRAPH OF ARTICLE 59'

ANNEX III

2nd Sch LIST OF SUPPLIES OF GOODS AND SERVICES TO WHICH THE REDUCED RATES REFERRED TO IN ARTICLE 98 MAY BE APPLIED

(1) Foodstuffs (including beverages but excluding alcoholic beverages) for human and animal consumption; live animals, seeds, plants and ingredients normally intended for use in the preparation of foodstuffs; products normally used to supplement foodstuffs or as a substitute for foodstuffs;

(2) supply of water;

(3) pharmaceutical products of a kind normally used for health care, prevention of illnesses and as treatment for medical and veterinary purposes, including products used for contraception and sanitary protection;

(4) medical equipment, aids and other appliances normally intended to alleviate or treat disability, for the exclusive personal use of the disabled, including the repair of such goods, and supply of children's car seats;

(5) transport of passengers and their accompanying luggage;

(6) supply, including on loan by libraries, of books (including brochures, leaflets and similar printed matter, children's picture, drawing or colouring books, music printed or in manuscript form, maps and hydrographic or similar charts), newspapers and periodicals, other than material wholly or predominantly devoted to advertising;

(7) admission to shows, theatres, circuses, fairs, amusement parks, concerts, museums, zoos, cinemas, exhibitions and similar cultural events and facilities;

(8) reception of radio and television broadcasting services;

(9) supply of services by writers, composers and performing artists, or of the royalties due to them;

(10) provision, construction, renovation and alteration of housing, as part of a social policy;

(11) supply of goods and services of a kind normally intended for use in agricultural production but excluding capital goods such as machinery or buildings;

(12) accommodation provided in hotels and similar establishments, including the provision of holiday accommodation and the letting of places on camping or caravan sites;

(13) admission to sporting events;

(14) use of sporting facilities;

(15) supply of goods and services by organisations recognised as being devoted to social wellbeing by Member States and engaged in welfare or social security work, in so far as those transactions are not exempt pursuant to Articles 132, 135 and 136;

(16) supply of services by undertakers and cremation services, and the supply of goods related thereto;

(17) provision of medical and dental care and thermal treatment in so far as those services are not exempt pursuant to points (b) to (e) of Article 132(1);

(18) supply of services provided in connection with street cleaning, refuse collection and waste treatment, other than the supply of such services by bodies referred to in Article 13.

ANNEX IV

LIST OF THE SERVICES REFERRED TO IN ARTICLE 106

(1)   Minor repairing of:

    (a)   bicycles;

    (b)   shoes and leather goods;

    (c)   clothing and household linen (including mending and alteration);

(2)   renovation and repairing of private dwellings, excluding materials which account for a significant part of the value of the service supplied;

(3)   window-cleaning and cleaning in private households;

(4)   domestic care services such as home help and care of the young, elderly, sick or disabled;

(5)   hairdressing.

ANNEX V

CATEGORIES OF GOODS COVERED BY WAREHOUSING ARRANGEMENTS OTHER THAN CUSTOMS WAREHOUSING AS PROVIDED FOR UNDER ARTICLE 160(2)

	CN-code	Description of goods
(1)	0701	Potatoes
(2)	0711 20	Olives
(3)	0801	Coconuts, Brazil nuts and cashew nuts
(4)	0802	Other nuts
(5)	0901 11 00 0901 12 00	Coffee, not roasted
(6)	0902	Tea
(7)	1001 to 1005 1007 to 1008	Cereals
(8)	1006	Husked rice
(9)	1201 to 1207	Grains and oil seeds (including soya beans) and oleaginous fruits
(10)	1507 to 1515	Vegetable oils and fats and their fractions, whether or not refined, but not chemically modified
(11)	1701 11 1701 12	Raw sugar
(12)	1801	Cocoa beans, whole or broken, raw or roasted
(13)	2709 2710 2711 12 2711 13	Mineral oils (including propane and butane; also including crude petroleum oils)
(14)	Chapters 28 and 29	Chemicals in bulk
(15)	4001 4002	Rubber, in primary forms or in plates, sheets or strip
(16)	5101	Wool
(17)	7106	Silver
(18)	7110 11 00 7110 21 00 7110 31 00	Platinum (palladium, rhodium)
(19)	7402 7403 7405 7408	Copper
(20)	7502	Nickel
(21)	7601	Aluminium

	CN-code	Description of goods
(22)	7801	Lead
(23)	7901	Zinc
(24)	8001	Tin
(25)	ex 8112 92 ex 8112 99	Indium

ANNEX VI

LIST OF SUPPLIES OF GOODS AND SERVICES AS REFERRED TO IN POINT (D) OF ARTICLE 199(1)

(1)   Supply of ferrous and non ferrous waste, scrap, and used materials including that of semi-finished products resulting from the processing, manufacturing or melting down of ferrous and non-ferrous metals and their alloys;

(2)   supply of ferrous and non-ferrous semi-processed products and certain associated processing services;

(3)   supply of residues and other recyclable materials consisting of ferrous and non-ferrous metals, their alloys, slag, ash, scale and industrial residues containing metals or their alloys and supply of selection, cutting, fragmenting and pressing services of these products;

(4)   supply of, and certain processing services relating to, ferrous and non-ferrous waste as well as parings, scrap, waste and used and recyclable material consisting of cullet, glass, paper, paperboard and board, rags, bone, leather, imitation leather, parchment, raw hides and skins, tendons and sinews, twine, cordage, rope, cables, rubber and plastic;

(5)   supply of the materials referred to in this annex after processing in the form of cleaning, polishing, selection, cutting, fragmenting, pressing or casting into ingots;

(6)   supply of scrap and waste from the working of base materials.

ANNEX VII

LIST OF THE AGRICULTURAL PRODUCTION ACTIVITIES REFERRED TO IN
POINT (4) OF ARTICLE 295(1)

(1)   Crop production:

    (a)   general agriculture, including viticulture;

    (b)   growing of fruit (including olives) and of vegetables, flowers and ornamental plants, both in the open and under glass;

    (c)   production of mushrooms, spices, seeds and propagating materials;

    (d)   running of nurseries;

(2)   stock farming together with cultivation:

    (a)   general stock farming;

    (b)   poultry farming;

    (c)   rabbit farming;

    (d)   beekeeping;

    (e)   silkworm farming;

    (f)   snail farming;

(3)   forestry;

(4)   fisheries:

    (a)   freshwater fishing;

    (b)   fish farming;

    (c)   breeding of mussels, oysters and other molluscs and crustaceans;

    (d)   frog farming.

ANNEX VIII

5th Sch
PART II
INDICATIVE LIST OF THE AGRICULTURAL SERVICES REFERRED TO IN POINT (5) OF ARTICLE 295(1)

(1) Field work, reaping and mowing, threshing, baling, collecting, harvesting, sowing and planting;

(2) packing and preparation for market, such as drying, cleaning, grinding, disinfecting and ensilage of agricultural products;

(3) storage of agricultural products;

(4) stock minding, rearing and fattening;

(5) hiring out, for agricultural purposes, of equipment normally used in agricultural, forestry or fisheries undertakings;

(6) technical assistance;

(7) destruction of weeds and pests, dusting and spraying of crops and land;

(8) operation of irrigation and drainage equipment;

(9) lopping, tree felling and other forestry services.

ANNEX IX

8th Sch **WORKS OF ART, COLLECTORS' ITEMS AND ANTIQUES, AS REFERRED TO IN POINTS (2), (3) AND (4) OF ARTICLE 311(1)**

PART A

Works of art

(1) Pictures, collages and similar decorative plaques, paintings and drawings, executed entirely by hand by the artist, other than plans and drawings for architectural, engineering, industrial, commercial, topographical or similar purposes, hand-decorated manufactured articles, theatrical scenery, studio back cloths or the like of painted canvas (CN code 9701);

(2) original engravings, prints and lithographs, being impressions produced in limited numbers directly in black and white or in colour of one or of several plates executed entirely by hand by the artist, irrespective of the process or of the material employed, but not including any mechanical or photomechanical process (CN code 9702 00 00);

(3) original sculptures and statuary, in any material, provided that they are executed entirely by the artist; sculpture casts the production of which is limited to eight copies and supervised by the artist or his successors in title (CN code 9703 00 00); on an exceptional basis, in cases determined by the Member States, the limit of eight copies may be exceeded for statuary casts produced before 1 January 1989;

(4) tapestries (CN code 5805 00 00) and wall textiles (CN code 6304 00 00) made by hand from original designs provided by artists, provided that there are not more than eight copies of each;

(5) individual pieces of ceramics executed entirely by the artist and signed by him;

(6) enamels on copper, executed entirely by hand, limited to eight numbered copies bearing the signature of the artist or the studio, excluding articles of jewellery and goldsmiths' and silversmiths' wares;

(7) photographs taken by the artist, printed by him or under his supervision, signed and numbered and limited to 30 copies, all sizes and mounts included.

PART B

Collectors' items

(1) Postage or revenue stamps, postmarks, first-day covers, pre-stamped stationery and the like, used, or if unused not current and not intended to be current (CN code 9704 00 00);

(2) collections and collectors' pieces of zoological, botanical, mineralogical, anatomical, historical, archaeological, palaeontological, ethnographic or numismatic interest (CN code 9705 00 00).

PART C

Antiques

Goods, other than works of art or collectors' items, which are more than 100 years old (CN code 9706 00 00).

ANNEX X

LIST OF TRANSACTIONS COVERED BY THE DEROGATIONS REFERRED TO IN ARTICLES 370 AND 371 AND ARTICLES 375 TO 390

PART A

Transactions which Member States may continue to tax

(1)   The supply of services by dental technicians in their professional capacity and the supply of dental prostheses by dentists and dental technicians;

(2)   the activities of public radio and television bodies other than those of a commercial nature;

(3)   the supply of a building, or parts thereof, or of the land on which it stands, other than as referred to in point (a) of Article 12(1), where carried out by taxable persons who were entitled to deduction of the VAT paid at the preceding stage in respect of the building concerned;

(4)   the supply of the services of travel agents, as referred to in Article 306, and those of travel agents acting in the name and on behalf of the traveller, in relation to journeys outside the Community.

PART B

Transactions which Member States may continue to exempt

(1)   Admission to sporting events;

(2)   the supply of services by authors, artists, performers, lawyers and other members of the liberal professions, other than the medical and paramedical professions, with the exception of the following:

  (a)   assignments of patents, trade marks and other similar rights, and the granting of licences in respect of such rights;

  (b)   work, other than the supply of contract work, on movable tangible property, carried out for a taxable person;

  (c)   services to prepare or coordinate the carrying out of construction work, such as services provided by architects and by firms providing on-site supervision of works;

  (d)   commercial advertising services;

  (e)   transport and storage of goods, and ancillary services;

  (f)   hiring out of movable tangible property to a taxable person;

  (g)   provision of staff to a taxable person;

  (h)   provision of services by consultants, engineers, planning offices and similar services in scientific, economic or technical fields;

(i)   compliance with an obligation to refrain from exercising, in whole or in part, a business activity or a right covered by points (a) to (h) or point (j);

(j)   the services of forwarding agents, brokers, business agents and other independent intermediaries, in so far as they relate to the supply or importation of goods or the supply of services covered by points (a) to (i);

(3)   the supply of telecommunications services, and of goods related thereto, by public postal services;

t Sch (4)   the supply of services by undertakers and cremation services and the supply of goods related thereto;

(5)   transactions carried out by blind persons or by workshops for the blind, provided that those exemptions do not cause significant distortion of competition;

(6)   the supply of goods and services to official bodies responsible for the construction, setting out and maintenance of cemeteries, graves and monuments commemorating the war dead;

(7)   transactions carried out by hospitals not covered by point (b) of Article 132(1);

(8)   the supply of water by a body governed by public law;

(9)   the supply before first occupation of a building, or parts thereof, or of the land on which it stands and the supply of building land, as referred to in Article 12;

st Sch (10)   the transport of passengers and, in so far as the transport of the passengers is exempt, the transport of goods accompanying them, such as luggage or motor vehicles, or the supply of services relating to the transport of passengers;

(11)   the supply, modification, repair, maintenance, chartering and hiring of aircraft used by State institutions, including equipment incorporated or used in such aircraft;

(12)   the supply, modification, repair, maintenance, chartering and hiring of fighting ships;

(13)   the supply of the services of travel agents, as referred to in Article 306, and those of travel agents acting in the name and on behalf of the traveller, in relation to journeys within the Community.

ANNEX XI

PART A

Repealed Directives with their successive amendments

(1)   Directive 67/227/EEC (OJ 71, 14.4.1967, p. 1301)

Directive 77/388/EEC

(2)   Directive 77/388/EEC (OJ L 145, 13.6.1977, p. 1)

Directive 78/583/EEC (OJ L 194, 19.7.1978, p. 16)

Directive 80/368/EEC (OJ L 90, 3.4.1980, p. 41)

Directive 84/386/EEC (OJ L 208, 3.8.1984, p. 58)

Directive 89/465/EEC (OJ L 226, 3.8.1989, p. 21)

Directive 91/680/EEC (OJ L 376, 31.12.1991, p. 1) — (except for Article 2)

Directive 92/77/EEC (OJ L 316, 31.10.1992, p. 1)

Directive 92/111/EEC (OJ L 384, 30.12.1992, p. 47)

Directive 94/4/EC (OJ L 60, 3.3.1994, p. 14) — (only Article 2)

Directive 94/5/EC (OJ L 60, 3.3.1994, p. 16)

Directive 94/76/EC (OJ L 365, 31.12.1994, p. 53)

Directive 95/7/EC (OJ L 102, 5.5.1995, p. 18)

Directive 96/42/EC (OJ L 170, 9.7.1996, p. 34)

Directive 96/95/EC (OJ L 338, 28.12.1996, p. 89)

Directive 98/80/EC (OJ L 281, 17.10.1998, p. 31)

Directive 1999/49/EC (OJ L 139, 2.6.1999, p. 27)

Directive 1999/59/EC (OJ L 162, 26.6.1999, p. 63)

Directive 1999/85/EC (OJ L 277, 28.10.1999, p. 34)

Directive 2000/17/EC (OJ L 84, 5.4.2000, p. 24)

Directive 2000/65/EC (OJ L 269, 21.10.2000, p. 44)

Directive 2001/4/EC (OJ L 22, 24.1.2001, p. 17)

Directive 2001/115/EC (OJ L 15, 17.1.2002, p. 24)

Directive 2002/38/EC (OJ L 128, 15.5.2002, p. 41)

Directive 2002/93/EC (OJ L 331, 7.12.2002, p. 27)

Directive 2003/92/EC (OJ L 260, 11.10.2003, p. 8)

Directive 2004/7/EC (OJ L 27, 30.1.2004, p. 44)

Directive 2004/15/EC (OJ L 52, 21.2.2004, p. 61)

Directive 2004/66/EC (OJ L 168, 1.5.2004, p. 35) — (only Point V of the Annex)

Directive 2005/92/EC (OJ L 345, 28.12.2005, p. 19)

Directive 2006/18/EC (OJ L 51, 22.2.2006, p. 12)

Directive 2006/58/EC (OJ L 174, 28.6.2006, p. 5)

Directive 2006/69/EC (OJ L 221, 12.8.2006, p. 9 — (only Article 1)

Directive 2006/98/EC (OJ L ..., ..., p. ... (*) — (only point 2 of the Annex)

PART B

Time limits for transposition into national law

(referred to in Article 411)

Directive	Deadline for transposition
Directive 67/227/EEC	1 January 1970
Directive 77/388/EEC	1 January 1978
Directive 78/583/EEC	1 January 1979
Directive 80/368/EEC	1 January 1979
Directive 84/386/EEC	1 July 1985
Directive 89/465/EEC	1 January 1990
	1 January 1991
	1 January 1992
	1 January 1993
	1 January 1994 for Portugal
Directive 91/680/EEC	1 January 1993
Directive 92/77/EEC	31 December 1992
Directive 92/111/EEC	1 January 1993
	1 January 1994
	1 October 1993 for Germany
Directive 94/4/EC	1 April 1994
Directive 94/5/EC	1 January 1995
Directive 94/76/EC	1 January 1995
Directive 95/7/EC	1 January 1996
	1 January 1997 for Germany and Luxembourg
Directive 96/42/EC	1 January 1995
Directive 96/95/EC	1 January 1997
Directive 98/80/EC	1 January 2000
Directive 1999/49/EC	1 January 1999
Directive 1999/59/EC	1 January 2000
Directive 1999/85/CE	—
Directive 2000/17/EC	—
Directive 2000/65/EC	31 December 2001
Directive 2001/4/EC	1 January 2001

Directive	Deadline for transposition
Directive 2001/115/EC	1 January 2004
Directive 2002/38/EC	1 July 2003
Directive 2002/93/EC	–
Directive 2003/92/EC	1 January 2005
Directive 2004/7/EC	30 January 2004
Directive 2004/15/EC	–
Directive 2004/66/EC	1 May 2004
Directive 2005/92/EC	1 January 2006
Directive 2006/18/EC	–
Directive 2006/58/EC	1 July 2006
Directive 2006/69/EC	1 January 2008

ANNEX XII

CORRELATION TABLE

Directive 67/227/EEC	Directive 77/388/EEC	Amending Directives	Other Acts	This Directive
Article 1, first paragraph				Article 1(1)
Article 1, second and third paragraphs				—
Article 2, first, second and third paragraphs				Article 1(2), first, second and third subparagraphs
Articles 3, 4 and 6				—
	Article 1			—
	Article 2, point (1)			Article 2(1)(a) and (c)
	Article 2, point (2)			Article 2(1)(d)
	Article 3(1), first indent			Article 5, point (2)
	Article 3(1), second indent			Article 5, point (1)
	Article 3(1), third indent			Article 5, points (3) and (4)
	Article 3(2)			—
	Article 3(3), first subparagraph, first indent			Article 6(2)(a) and (b)
	Article 3(3), first subparagraph, second indent			Article 6(2)(c) and (d)
	Article 3(3), first subparagraph, third indent			Article 6(2)(e), (f) and (g)
	Article 3(3) second subparagraph, first indent			Article 6(1)(b)
	Article 3(3) second subparagraph, second indent			Article 6(1)(c)
	Article 3(3), second subparagraph, third indent			Article 6(1)(a)
	Article 3(4), first subparagraph, first and second indents			Article 7(1)
	Article 3(4), second subparagraph, first second and third indents			Article 7(2)
	Article 3(5)			Article 8
	Article 4(1) and (2)			Article 9(1), first and second subparagraphs
	Article 4(3)(a), first subparagraph, first sentence			Article 12(1)(a)
	Article 4(3)(a), first subparagraph, second sentence			Article 12(2), second subparagraph
	Article 4(3)(a), second subparagraph			Article 12(2), third subparagraph
	Article 4(3)(a), third subparagraph			Article 12(2), first subparagraph

Directive 67/227/EEC	Directive 77/388/EEC	Amending Directives	Other Acts	This Directive
	Article 4(3)(b), first subparagraph			Article 12(1)(b)
	Article 4(3)(b), second subparagraph			Article 12(3)
	Article 4(4), first subparagraph			Article 10
	Article 4(4), second and third subparagraphs			Article 11, first and second paragraphs
	Article 4(5), first, second and third subparagraphs			Article 13(1), first, second and third subparagraphs
	Article 4(5), fourth subparagraph			Article 13(2)
	Article 5(1)			Article 14(1)
	Article 5(2)			Article 15(1)
	Article 5(3)(a), (b) and (c)			Article 15(2)(a), (b) and (c)
	Article 5(4)(a), (b) and (c)			Article 14(2)(a), (b) and (c)
	Article 5(5)			Article 14(3)
	Article 5(6), first and second sentences			Article 16, first and second paragraphs
	Article 5(7)(a), (b) and (c)			Article 18(a), (b) and (c)
	Article 5(8), first sentence			Article 19, first paragraph
	Article 5(8), second and third sentences			Article 19, second paragraph
	Article 6(1), first subparagraph			Article 24(1)
	Article 6(1), second subparagraph, first, second and third indents			Article 25(a), (b) and (c)
	Article 6(2), first subparagraph, points (a) and (b)			Article 26(1)(a) and (b)
	Article 6(2), second subparagraph			Article 26(2)
	Article 6(3)			Article 27
	Article 6(4)			Article 28
	Article 6(5)			Article 29
	Article 7(1)(a) and (b)			Article 30, first and second paragraphs
	Article 7(2)			Article 60
	Article 7(3), first and second subparagraphs			Article 61, first and second paragraphs
	Article 8(1)(a), first sentence			Article 32, first paragraph
	Article 8(1)(a), second and third sentences			Article 36, first and second paragraphs
	Article 8(1)(b)			Article 31
	Article 8(1)(c), first subparagraph Article 37(1)			Article 37(1)

Directive 67/227/EEC	Directive 77/388/EEC	Amending Directives	Other Acts	This Directive
	Article 8(1)(c), second subparagraph, first indent			Article 37(2), first subparagraph
	Article 8(1)(c), second subparagraph, second and third indents			Article 37(2), second and third subparagraphs
	Article 8(1)(c), third subparagraph			Article 37(2), fourth subparagraph
	Article 8(1)(c), fourth subparagraph			Article 37(3), first subparagraph
	Article 8(1)(c), fifth subparagraph			—
	Article 8(1)(c), sixth subparagraph			Article 37(3), second subparagraph
	Article 8(1)(d), first and second subparagraphs			Article 38(1) and (2)
	Article 8(1)(e), first sentence			Article 39, first paragraph
	Article 8(1)(e), second and third sentences			Article 39, second paragraph
	Article 8(2)			Article 32, second paragraph
	Article 9(1)			Article 43
	Article 9(2) introductory sentence			—
	Article 9(2)(a)			Article 45
	Article 9(2)(b)			Article 46
	Article 9(2)(c), first and second indents			Article 52(a) and (b)
	Article 9(2)(c), third and fourth indents			Article 52(c)
	Article 9(2)(e), first to sixth indents			Article 56(1)(a) to (f)
	Article 9(2)(e), seventh indent			Article 56(1)(l)
	Article 9(2)(e), eighth indent			Article 56(1)(g)
	Article 9(2)(e), ninth indent			Article 56(1)(h)
	Article 9(2)(e), tenth indent, first sentence			Article 56(1)(i)
	Article 9(2)(e), tenth indent, second sentence			Article 24(2)
	Article 9(2)(e), tenth indent, third sentence			Article 56(1)(i)
	Article 9(2)(e), eleventh and twelfth indents			Article 56(1)(j) and (k)
	Article 9(2)(f)			Article 57(1)
	Article 9(3)			Article 58, first and second paragraphs
	Article 9(3)(a) and (b)			Article 58, first paragraph, points (a) and (b)
	Article 9(4)			Article 59(1) and (2)
	Article 10(1)(a) and (b)			Article 62, points (1) and (2)

Directive 67/227/EEC	Directive 77/388/EEC	Amending Directives	Other Acts	This Directive
	Article 10(2), first subparagraph, first sentence			Article 63
	Article 10(2), first subparagraph, second and third sentences			Article 64(1) and (2)
	Article 10(2), second subparagraph			Article 65
	Article 10(2), third subparagraph, first, second and third indents			Article 66(a), (b) and (c)
	Article 10(3), first subparagraph, first sentence			Article 70
	Article 10(3), first subparagraph, second sentence			Article 71(1), first subparagraph
	Article 10(3), second subparagraph			Article 71(1), second subparagraph
	Article 10(3), third subparagraph			Article 71(2)
	Article 11(A)(1)(a)			Article 73
	Article 11(A)(1)(b)			Article 74
	Article 11(A)(1)(c)			Article 75
	Article 11(A)(1)(d)			Article 77
	Article 11(A)(2)(a)			Article 78, first paragraph, point (a)
	Article 11(A)(2)(b), first sentence			Article 78, first paragraph, point (b)
	Article 11(A)(2)(b), second sentence			Article 78, second paragraph
	Article 11(A)(3)(a) and (b)			Article 79, first paragraph, points (a) and (b) Article 87(a) and (b)
	Article 11(A)(3)(c), first sentence			Article 79, first paragraph, point (c)
	Article 11(A)(3)(c), second sentence			Article 79, second paragraph
	Article 11(A)(4),first and second subparagraphs			Article 81, first and second paragraphs
	Article 11(A)(5)			Article 82
	Article 11(A)(6), first subparagraph, first and second sentences			Article 80(1), first subparagraph
	Article 11(A)(6), first subparagraph, third sentence			Article 80(1), second subparagraph
	Article 11(A)(6), second subparagraph			Article 80(1), first subparagraph
	Article 11(A)(6), third subparagraph			–Article 80(2)
	Article 11(A)(6), fourth subparagraph			Article 80(3)
	Article 11(A)(7), first and second subparagraphs			Article 72, first and second paragraphs

Directive 67/227/EEC	Directive 77/388/EEC	Amending Directives	Other Acts	This Directive
	Article 11(B)(1)			Article 85
	Article 11(B)(3)(a)			Article 86(1)(a)
	Article 11(B)(3)(b), first subparagraph			Article 86(1)(b)
	Article 11(B)(3)(b), second subparagraph			Article 86(2)
	Article 11(B)(3)(b), third subparagraph			Article 86(1)(b)
	Article 11(B)(4)			Article 87
	Article 11(B)(5)			Article 88
	Article 11(B)(6), first and second subparagraphs			Article 89, first and second paragraphs
	Article 11(C)(1), first and second subparagraphs			Article 90(1) and (2)
	Article 11(C)(2), first subparagraph			Article 91(1)
	Article 11(C)(2), second subparagraph, first and second sentences			Article 91(2), first and second subparagraphs
	Article 11(C)(3), first and second indents			Article 92(a) and (b)
	Article 12(1)			Article 93, first paragraph
	Article 12(1)(a)			Article 93, second paragraph, point (a)
	Article 12(1)(b)			Article 93, second paragraph, point (c)
	Article 12(2), first and second indents			Article 95, first and second paragraphs
	Article 12(3)(a), first subparagraph, first sentence			Article 96
	Article 12(3)(a), first subparagraph, second sentence			Article 97(1)
	Article 12(3)(a), second subparagraph			Article 97(2)
	Article 12(3)(a), third subparagraph, first sentence			Article 98(1)
	Article 12(3)(a), third subparagraph, second sentence			Article 98(2), first subparagraph Article 99(1)
	Article 12(3)(a), fourth subparagraph			Article 98(2), second subparagraph
	Article 12(3)(b), first sentence			Article 102, first paragraph
	Article 12(3)(b), second, third and fourth sentences			Article 102, second paragraph
	Article 12(3)(c), first subparagraph			Article 103(1)
	Article 12(3)(c), second subparagraph, first and second indents			Article 103(2)(a) and (b)

Directive 67/227/EEC	Directive 77/388/EEC	Amending Directives	Other Acts	This Directive
	Article 12(4), first subparagraph			Article 99(2)
	Article 12(4), second subparagraph, first and second sentences			Article 100, first and second paragraphs
	Article 12(4), third subparagraph			Article 101
	Article 12(5)			Article 94(2)
	Article 12(6)			Article 105
	Article 13(A)(1), introductory sentence			Article 131
	Article 13(A)(1)(a) to (n)			Article 132(1)(a) to (n)
	Article 13(A)(1)(o), first sentence			Article 132(1)(o)
	Article 13(A)(1)(o), second sentence			Article 132(2)
	Article 13(A)(1)(p) and (q)			Article 132(1)(p) and (q)
	Article 13(A)(2)(a), first to fourth indents			Article 133(a) to (d)
	Article 13(A)(2)(b), first and second indents			Article 134(a) and (b)
	Article 13(B), introductory sentence			Article 131
	Article 13(B)(a)			Article 135(1)(a)
	Article 13(B)(b), first subparagraph			Article 135(1)(l)
	Article 13(B)(b), first subparagraph, points (1) to (4)			Article 135(2), first subparagraph, points (a) to (d)
	Article 13(B)(b), second subparagraph			Article 135(2), second subparagraph
	Article 13(B)(c)			Article 136(a) and (b)
	Article 13(B)(d)			—
	Article 13(B)(d), points (1) to (5)			Article 135(1)(b) to (f)
	Article 13(B)(d), point (5), first and second indents			Article 135(1)(f)
	Article 13(B)(d), point (6)			Article 135(1)(g)
	Article 13(B)(e) to (h)			Article 135(1)(h) to (k)
	Article 13(C), first subparagraph, point (a)			Article 137(1)(d)
	Article 13(C), first subparagraph, point (b)			Article 137(1)(a), (b) and (c)
	Article 13(C), second subparagraph			Article 137(2), first and second subparagraphs
	Article 14(1), introductory sentence			Article 131
	Article 14(1)(a)			Article 140(a)

Directive 67/227/EEC	Directive 77/388/EEC	Amending Directives	Other Acts	This Directive
	Article 14(1)(d), first and second subparagraphs			Article 143(b) and (c)
	Article 14(1)(e)			Article 143(e)
	Article 14(1)(g), first to fourth indents			Article 143(f) to (i)
	Article 14(1)(h)			Article 143(j)
	Article 14(1)(i)			Article 144
	Article 14(1)(j)			Article 143(k)
	Article 14(1)(k)			Article 143(l)
	Article 14(2), first subparagraph			Article 145(1)
	Article 14(2), second subparagraph, first, second and third indents			Article 145(2), first, second and third subparagraphs
	Article 14(2), third subparagraph			Article 145(3)
	Article 15, introductory sentence			Article 131
	Article 15, point (1)			Article 146(1)(a)
	Article 15, point (2), first subparagraph			Article 146(1)(b)
	Article 15, point (2), second subparagraph, first and second indents			Article 147(1), first subparagraph, points (a) and (b)
	Article 15, point (2), second subparagraph, third indent, first part of the sentence			Article 147(1), first subparagraph, point (c)
	Article 15, point (2), second subparagraph, third indent, second part of the sentence			Article 147(1), second subparagraph
	Article 15, point (2), third subparagraph, first and second indents			Article 147(2), first and second subparagraphs
	Article 15, point (2), fourth subparagraph			Article 147(2), third subparagraph
	Article 15, point (3)			Article 146(1)(d)
	Article 15, point (4), first subparagraph, points (a) and (b)			Article 148(a)
	Article 15, point (4), first subparagraph, point (c)			Article 148(b)
	Article 15, point (4), second subparagraph, first and second sentences			Article 150(1) and (2)
	Article 15, point (5)			Article 148(c)
	Article 15, point (6)			Article 148(f)
	Article 15, point (7)			Article 148(e)
	Article 15, point (8)			Article 148(d)
	Article 15, point (9)			Article 148(g)

Directive 67/227/EEC	Directive 77/388/EEC	Amending Directives	Other Acts	This Directive
	Article 15, point (10), first subparagraph, first to fourth indents			Article 151(1), first subparagraph, points (a) to (d)
	Article 15, point (10), second subparagraph			Article 151(1), second subparagraph
	Article 15, point (10), third subparagraph			Article 151(2)
	Article 15, point (11)			Article 152
	Article 15, point (12), first sentence			Article 146(1)(c)
	Article 15, point (12), second sentence			Article 146(2)
	Article 15, point (13)			Article 146(1)(e)
	Article 15, point (14), first and second subparagraphs			Article 153, first and second paragraphs
	Article 15, point (15)			Article 149
	Article 16(1)			—
	Article 16(2)			Article 164(1)
	Article 16(3)			Article 166
	Article 17(1)			Article 167
	Article 17(2), (3) and (4)			—
	Article 17(5), first and second subparagraphs			Article 173(1), first and second subparagraphs
	Article 17(5), third subparagraph, points (a) to (e)			Article 173(2)(a) to (e)
	Article 17(6)			Article 176
	Article 17(7), first and second sentences			Article 177, first and second paragraphs
	Article 18(1)			—
	Article 18(2), first and second subparagraphs			Article 179, first and second paragraphs
	Article 18(3)			Article 180
	Article 18(4), first and second subparagraphs			Article 183, first and second paragraphs
	Article 19(1), first subparagraph, first indent			Article 174(1), first subparagraph, point (a)
	Article 19(1), first subparagraph, second indent, first sentence			Article 174(1), first subparagraph, point (b)
	Article 19(1), first subparagraph, second indent, second sentence			Article 174(1), second subparagraph
	Article 19(1), second subparagraph			Article 175(1)
	Article 19(2), first sentence			Article 174(2)(a)
	Article 19(2), second sentence			Article 174(2)(a) and (b)

Directive 67/227/EEC	Directive 77/388/EEC	Amending Directives	Other Acts	This Directive
	Article 19(2), third sentence			Article 174(3)
	Article 19(3), first subparagraph, first and second sentences			Article 175(2), first subparagraph
	Article 19(3), first subparagraph, third sentence			Article 175(2), second subparagraph
	Article 19(3), second subparagraph			Article 175(3)
	Article 20(1), introductory sentence			Article 186
	Article 20(1)(a)			Article 184
	Article 20(1)(b), first part of the first sentence			Article 185(1)
	Article 20(1)(b), second part of the first sentence			Article 185(2), first subparagraph
	Article 20(1)(b), second sentence			Article 185(2), second subparagraph
	Article 20(2), first subparagraph, first sentence			Article 187(1), first subparagraph
	Article 20(2), first subparagraph, second and third sentences			Article 187(2), first and second subparagraphs
	Article 20(2), second and third subparagraphs			Article 187(1), second and third subparagraphs
	Article 20(3), first subparagraph, first sentence			Article 188(1), first subparagraph
	Article 20(3), first subparagraph, second sentence			Article 188(1), second and third subparagraphs
	Article 20(3), first subparagraph, third sentence			Article 188(2)
	Article 20(3), second subparagraph			Article 188(2)
	Article 20(4), first subparagraph, first to fourth indents			Article 189(a) to (d)
	Article 20(4), second subparagraph			Article 190
	Article 20(5)			Article 191
	Article 20(6)			Article 192
	Article 21			—
	Article 22			—
	Article 22a			Article 249
	Article 23, first paragraph			Article 211, first paragraph Article 260
	Article 23, second paragraph			Article 211, second paragraph
	Article 24(1)			Article 281
	Article 24(2)			Article 292

Directive 67/227/EEC	Directive 77/388/EEC	Amending Directives	Other Acts	This Directive
	Article 24(2)(a), first subparagraph			Article 284(1)
	Article 24(2)(a), second and third subparagraphs			Article 284(2), first and second subparagraphs
	Article 24(2)(b), first and second sentences			Article 285, first and second paragraphs
	Article 24(2)(c)			Article 286
	Article 24(3), first subparagraph			Article 282
	Article 24(3), second subparagraph, first sentence			Article 283(2)
	Article 24(3), second subparagraph, second sentence			Article 283(1)(a)
	Article 24(4), first subparagraph			Article 288, first paragraph, points (1) to (4)
	Article 24(4), second subparagraph			Article 288, second paragraph
	Article 24(5)			Article 289
	Article 24(6)			Article 290
	Article 24(7)			Article 291
	Article 24(8)(a), (b) and (c)			Article 293, points (1), (2) and (3)
	Article 24(9)			Article 294
	Article 24a, first paragraph, first to twelfth indents			Article 287, points (7) to (16)
	Article 25(1)			Article 296(1)
	Article 25(2), first to eighth indents			Article 295(1), points (1) to (8)
	Article 25(3), first subparagraph, first sentence			Article 297, first paragraph, first sentence and second paragraph
	Article 25(3), first subparagraph, second sentence			Article 298, first paragraph
	Article 25(3), first subparagraph, third sentence			Article 299
	Article 25(3), first subparagraph, fourth and fifth sentences			Article 298, second paragraph
	Article 25(3), second subparagraph			Article 297, first paragraph, second sentence
	Article 25(4), first subparagraph			Article 272(1), first subparagraph, point (e)
	Article 25(5) and (6)			—
	Article 25(7)			Article 304
	Article 25(8)			Article 301(2)
	Article 25(9)			Article 296(2)

Directive 67/227/EEC	Directive 77/388/EEC	Amending Directives	Other Acts	This Directive
	Article 25(10)			Article 296(3)
	Article 25(11) and (12)			–
	Article 26(1) first and second sentences			Article 306(1), first and second subparagraphs
	Article 26(1) third sentence			Article 306(2)
	Article 26(2), first and second sentences			Article 307, first and second paragraphs
	Article 26(2), third sentence			Article 308
	Article 26(3), first and second sentences			Article 309, first and second paragraphs
	Article 26(4)			Article 310
	Article 26a(A)(a), first subparagraph			Article 311(1), point (2)
	Article 26a(A)(a), second subparagraph			Article 311(2)
	Article 26a(A)(b) and (c)			Article 311(1), points (3) and (4)
	Article 26a(A)(d)			Article 311(1), point (1)
	Article 26a(A)(e) and (f)			Article 311(1), points (5) and (6)
	Article 26a(A)(g), introductory sentence			Article 311(1), point (7)
	Article 26a(A)(g), first and second indents			Article 311(3)
	Article 26a(B)(1)			Article 313(1)
	Article 26a(B)(2)			Article 314
	Article 26a(B)(2), first and second indents			Article 314(a) to (d)
	Article 26a(B)(3), first subparagraph, first and second sentences			Article 315, first and second paragraphs
	Article 26a(B)(3), second subparagraph			Article 312
	Article 26a(B)(3), second subparagraph, first and second indents			Article 312, points (1) and (2)
	Article 26a(B)(4), first subparagraph			Article 316(1)
	Article 26a(B)(4), first subparagraph, points (a), (b) and (c)			Article 316(1)(a), (b) and (c)
	Article 26a(B)(4), second subparagraph			Article 316(2)
	Article 26a(B)(4), third subparagraph, first and second sentences			Article 317, first and second paragraphs
	Article 26a(B)(5)			Article 321
	Article 26a(B)(6)			Article 323
	Article 26a(B)(7)			Article 322

Directive 67/227/EEC	Directive 77/388/EEC	Amending Directives	Other Acts	This Directive
	Article 26a(B)(7)(a), (b) and (c)			Article 322(a), (b) and (c)
	Article 26a(B)(8)			Article 324
	Article 26a(B)(9)			Article 325
	Article 26a(B)(10) first and second subparagraphs			Article 318(1), first and second subparagraphs
	Article 26a(B)(10), third subparagraph, first and second indents			Article 318(2)(a) and (b)
	Article 26a(B)(10), fourth subparagraph			Article 318(3)
	Article 26a(B)(11), first subparagraph			Article 319
	Article 26a(B)(11), second subparagraph, point (a)			Article 320(1), first subparagraph
	Article 26a(B)(11), second subparagraph, points (b) and (c)			Article 320(1), second subparagraph
	Article 26a(B)(11), third subparagraph			Article 320(2)
	Article 26a(C)(1), introductory sentence			Article 333(1) Article 334
	Article 26a(C)(1), first to fourth indents			Article 334(a) to (d)
	Article 26a(C)(2), first and second indents			Article 336(a) and (b)
	Article 26a(C)(3)			Article 337
	Article 26a(C)(4), first subparagraph, first, second and third indents			Article 339, first paragraph, points (a), (b) and (c)
	Article 26a(C)(4), second subparagraph			Article 339, second paragraph
	Article 26a(C)(5), first and second subparagraphs			Article 340(1), first and second subparagraphs
	Article 26a(C)(5), third subparagraph			Article 340(2)
	Article 26a(C)(6), first subparagraph, first and second indents			Article 338, first paragraph, points (a) and (b)
	Article 26a(C)(6), second subparagraph			Article 338, second paragraph
	Article 26a(C)(7)			Article 335
	Article 26a(D), introductory sentence			—
	Article 26a(D)(a)			Article 313(2) Article 333(2)
	Article 26a(D)(b)			Article 4(a) and (c)
	Article 26a(D)(c)			Article 35 Article 139(3), first subparagraph

Directive 67/227/EEC	Directive 77/388/EEC	Amending Directives	Other Acts	This Directive
	Article 26b(A), first subparagraph, point (i), first sentence			Article 344(1), point (1)
	Article 26b(A), first subparagraph, point (i), second sentence			Article 344(2)
	Article 26b(A), first subparagraph, point (ii), first to fourth indents			Article 344(1), point (2)
	Article 26b(A), second subparagraph			Article 344(3)
	Article 26b(A), third subparagraph			Article 345
	Article 26b(B), first subparagraph			Article 346
	Article 26b(B), second subparagraph			Article 347
	Article 26b(C), first subparagraph			Article 348
	Article 26b(C), second subparagraph, first and second sentences			Article 349(1) and (2)
	Article 26b(C), third subparagraph			Article 350
	Article 26b(C), fourth subparagraph			Article 351
	Article 26b(D)(1)(a), (b) and (c)			Article 354(a), (b) and (c)
	Article 26b(D)(2)			Article 355
	Article 26b(E), first and second subparagraphs			Article 356(1), first and second subparagraphs
	Article 26b(E), third and fourth subparagraphs			Article 356(2) and (3)
	Article 26b(F), first sentence			Article 198(2) and (3)
	Article 26b(F), second sentence			Articles 208 and 255
	Article 26b(G)(1), first subparagraph			Article 352
	Article 26b(G)(1), second subparagraph			—
	Article 26b(G)(2)(a)			Article 353
	Article 26b(G)(2)(b), first and second sentences			Article 198(1) and (3)
	Article 26c(A)(a) to (e)			Article 358, points (1) to (5)
	Article 26c(B)(1)			Article 359
	Article 26c(B)(2), first subparagraph			Article 360
	Article 26c(B)(2), second subparagraph, first part of the first sentence			Article 361(1)

Directive 67/227/EEC	Directive 77/388/EEC	Amending Directives	Other Acts	This Directive
	Article 26c(B)(2), second subparagraph, second part of the first sentence			Article 361(1)(a) to (e)
	Article 26c(B)(2), second subparagraph, second sentence			Article 361(2)
	Article 26c(B)(3), first and second subparagraphs			Article 362
	Article 26c(B)(4)(a) to (d)			Article 363(a) to (d)
	Article 26c(B)(5), first subparagraph			Article 364
	Article 26c(B)(5), second subparagraph			Article 365
	Article 26c(B)(6), first sentence			Article 366(1), first subparagraph
	Article 26c(B)(6), second and third sentences			Article 366(1), second subparagraph
	Article 26c(B)(6), fourth sentence			Article 366(2)
	Article 26c(B)(7), first sentence			Article 367, first paragraph
	Article 26c(B)(7), second and third sentences			Article 367, second paragraph
	Article 26c(B)(8)			Article 368
	Article 26c(B)(9), first sentence			Article 369(1)
	Article 26c(B)(9), second and third sentences			Article 369(2), first and second subparagraphs
	Article 26c(B)(10)			Article 204(1), third subparagraph
	Article 27(1) first and second sentences			Article 395(1) first and second subparagraphs
	Article 27(2), first and second sentences			Article 395(2), first subparagraphs
	Article 27(2), third sentence			Article 395(2), second subparagraph
	Article 27(3) and (4)			Article 395(3) and (4)
	Article 27(5)			Article 394
	Article 28(1) and (1a)			—
	Article 28(2), introductory sentence			Article 109
	Article 28(2)(a), first subparagraph			Article 110, first and second paragraphs
	Article 28(2)(a), second subparagraph			—
	Article 28(2)(a), third subparagraph, first sentence			Article 112, first paragraph
	Article 28(2)(a), third subparagraph, second and third sentences			Article 112, second paragraph
	Article 28(2)(b)			Article 113

Directive 67/227/EEC	Directive 77/388/EEC	Amending Directives	Other Acts	This Directive
	Article 28(2)(c), first and second sentences			Article 114(1), first and second subparagraphs
	Article 28(2)(c), third sentence			Article 114(2)
	Article 28(2)(d)			Article 115
	Article 28(2)(e), first and second subparagraphs			Article 118, first and second paragraphs
	Article 28(2)(f)			Article 120
	Article 28(2)(g)			—
	Article 28(2)(h), first and second subparagraphs			Article 121, first and second paragraphs
	Article 28(2)(i)			Article 122
	Article 28(2)(j)			Article 117(2)
	Article 28(2)(k)			Article 116
	Article 28(3)(a)			Article 370
	Article 28(3)(b)			Article 371
	Article 28(3)(c)			Article 391
	Article 28(3)(d)			Article 372
	Article 28(3)(e)			Article 373
	Article 28(3)(f)			Article 392
	Article 28(3)(g)			Article 374
	Article 28(3a)			Article 376
	Article 28(4) and (5)			Article 393(1) and (2)
	Article 28(6), first subparagraph, first sentence			Article 106, first and second paragraphs
	Article 28(6), first subparagraph, second sentence			Article 106, third paragraph
	Article 28(6), second subparagraph, points (a), (b) and (c),			Article 107, first paragraph, points (a), (b) and (c)
	Article 28(6), second subparagraph, point (d)			Article 107, second paragraph
	Article 28(6), third subparagraph			Article 107, second paragraph
	Article 28(6), fourth subparagraph, points (a), (b) and (c)			Article 108(a), (b) and (c)
	Article 28(6), fifth and sixth subparagraphs			—
	Article 28a(1), introductory sentence			Article 2(1)
	Article 28a(1)(a), first subparagraph			Article 2(1)(b)(i)
	Article 28a(1)(a), second subparagraph			Article 3(1)

Directive 67/227/EEC	Directive 77/388/EEC	Amending Directives	Other Acts	This Directive
	Article 28a(1)(a), third subparagraph			Article 3(3)
	Article 28a(1)(b)			Article 2(1)(b)(ii)
	Article 28a(1)(c)			Article 2(1)(b)(iii)
	Article 28a(1a)(a)			Article 3(1)(a)
	Article 28a(1a)(b), first subparagraph, first indent			Article 3(1)(b)
	Article 28a(1a)(b), first subparagraph, second and third indents			Article 3(2), first subparagraph, points (a) and (b)
	Article 28a(1a)(b), second subparagraph			Article 3(2), second subparagraph
	Article 28a(2), introductory sentence			—
	Article 28a(2)(a)			Article 2(2), point (a) (i), (ii), and (iii)
	Article 28a(2)(b), first subparagraph			Article 2(2), point (b)
	Article 28a(2)(b), first subparagraph, first and second indents			Article 2(2), point (b) (i), (ii), and (iii)
	Article 28a(2)(b), second subparagraph			Article 2(2), point (c)
	Article 28a(3), first and second subparagraphs			Article 20, first and second paragraphs
	Article 28a(4), first subparagraph			Article 9(2)
	Article 28a(4), second subparagraph, first indent			Article 172(1), second subparagraph
	Article 28a(4), second subparagraph, second indent			Article 172(1), first subparagraph
	Article 28a(4), third subparagraph			Article 172(2)
	Article 28a(5)(b), first subparagraph			Article 17(1), first subparagraph
	Article 28a(5)(b), second subparagraph,			Article 17(1), second subparagraph and (2), introductory sentence
	Article 28a(5)(b), second subparagraph, first indent			Article 17(2)(a) and (b)
	Article 28a(5)(b), second subparagraph, second indent			Article 17(2)(c)
	Article 28a(5)(b), second subparagraph, third indent			Article 17(2)(e)
	Article 28a(5)(b), second subparagraph, fifth, sixth and seventh indents			Article 17(2)(f), (g) and (h)
	Article 28a(5)(b), second subparagraph, eighth indent			Article 17(2)(d)
	Article 28a(5)(b), third subparagraph			Article 17(3)
	Article 28a(6), first subparagraph			Article 21

Directive 67/227/EEC	Directive 77/388/EEC	Amending Directives	Other Acts	This Directive
	Article 28a(6), second subparagraph			Article 22
	Article 28a(7)			Article 23
	Article 28b(A)(1)			Article 40
	Article 28b(A)(2), first and second subparagraphs			Article 41, first and second paragraphs
	Article 28b(A)(2), third subparagraph, first and second indents			Article 42(a) and (b)
	Article 28b(B)(1), first subparagraph, first and second indents			Article 33(1)(a) and (b)
	Article 28b(B)(1), second subparagraph			Article 33(2)
	Article 28b(B)(2), first subparagraph			Article 34(1)(a)
	Article 28b(B)(2), first subparagraph, first and second indents			Article 34(1)(b) and (c)
	Article 28b(B)(2), second subparagraph, first and second sentences			Article 34(2), first and second subparagraphs
	Article 28b(B)(2), third subparagraph, first sentence			Article 34(3)
	Article 28b(B)(2), third subparagraph, second and third sentences			—
	Article 28b(B)(3), first and second subparagraphs			Article 34(4), first and second subparagraphs
	Article 28b(C)(1), first indent, first subparagraph			Article 48, first paragraph
	Article 28b(C)(1), first indent, second subparagraph			Article 49
	Article 28b(C)(1), second and third indents			Article 48, second and third paragraphs
	Article 28b(C)(2) and (3)			Article 47, first and second paragraphs
	Article 28b(C)(4)			Article 51
	Article 28b(D)			Article 53
	Article 28b(E)(1), first and second subparagraphs			Article 50, first and second paragraphs
	Article 28b(E)(2), first and second subparagraphs			Article 54, first and second paragraphs
	Article 28b(E)(3), first and second subparagraphs			Article 44, first and second paragraphs
	Article 28b(F), first and second paragraphs			Article 55, first and second paragraphs
	Article 28c(A), introductory sentence			Article 131
	Article 28c(A)(a), first subparagraph			Article 138(1)

Directive 67/227/EEC	Directive 77/388/EEC	Amending Directives	Other Acts	This Directive
	Article 28c(A)(a), second subparagraph			Article 139(1), first and second subparagraphs
	Article 28c(A)(b)			Article 138(2)(a)
	Article 28c(A)(c), first subparagraph			Article 138(2)(b)
	Article 28c(A)(c), second subparagraph			Article 139(2)
	Article 28c(A)(d)			Article 138(2)(c)
	Article 28c(B), introductory sentence			Articles 131
	Article 28c(B)(a), (b) and (c)			Article 140(a), (b) and (c)
	Article 28c(C)			Article 142
	Article 28c(D), first subparagraph			Article 143(d)
	Article 28c(D), second subparagraph			Article 131
	Article 28c(E), point (1), first indent, replacing Article 16(1)			
	— paragraph 1, first subparagraph			Article 155
	— paragraph 1, first subparagraph, point (A)			Article 157(1)(a)
	— paragraph 1, first subparagraph, point (B), first subparagraph, points (a), (b) and (c)			Article 156(1)(a), (b) and (c)
	— paragraph 1, first subparagraph, point (B), first subparagraph, point (d), first and second indents			Article 156(1)(d) and (e)
	— paragraph 1, first subparagraph, point (B), first subparagraph, point (e), first subparagraph			Article 157(1)(b)
	— paragraph 1, first subparagraph, point (B), first subparagraph, point (e), second subparagraph, first indent			Article 154
	— paragraph 1, first subparagraph, point (B), first subparagraph, point (e), second subparagraph, second indent, first sentence			Article 154
	— paragraph 1, first subparagraph, point (B), first subparagraph, point (e), second subparagraph, second indent, second sentence			Article 157(2)
	— paragraph 1, first subparagraph, point (B), first subparagraph, point (e), third subparagraph, first indent			—

Directive 67/227/EEC	Directive 77/388/EEC	Amending Directives	Other Acts	This Directive
	— paragraph 1, first subparagraph, point (B), first subparagraph, point (e), third subparagraph, second, third and fourth indents			Article 158(1)(a), (b) and (c)
	— paragraph 1, first subparagraph, point (B), second subparagraph			Article 156(2)
	— paragraph 1, first subparagraph, point (C)			Article 159
	— paragraph 1, first subparagraph, point (D), first subparagraph, points (a) and (b)			Article 160(1)(a) and (b)
	— paragraph 1, first subparagraph, point (D), second subparagraph			Articles 160(2)
	— paragraph 1, first subparagraph, point (E), first and second indents			Article 161(a) and (b)
	— paragraph 1, second subparagraph			Article 202
	— paragraph 1, third subparagraph			Article 163
	Article 28c(E), point (1), second indent, inserting paragraph 1a into Article 16			
	— paragraph 1a			Article 162
	Article 28c(E), point (2), first indent, amending Article 16(2)			
	— paragraph 2, first subparagraph			Article 164(1)
	Article 28c(E), point (2), second indent, inserting the second and third subparagraphs into Article 16(2)			
	— paragraph 2, second subparagraph			Article 164(2)
	— paragraph 2, third subparagraph			Article 165
	Article 28c(E), point (3), first to fifth indents			Article 141(a) to (e)
	Article 28d(1), first and second sentences			Article 68, first and second paragraphs
	Article 28d(2) and (3)			Article 69(1) and (2)
	Article 28d(4), first and second subparagraphs			Article 67(1) and (2)
	Article 28e(1), first subparagraph			Article 83
	Article 28e(1), second subparagraph, first and second sentences			Article 84(1) and (2)
	Article 28e(2)			Article 76

Directive 67/227/EEC	Directive 77/388/EEC	Amending Directives	Other Acts	This Directive
	Article 28e(3)			Article 93, second paragraph, point (b)
	Article 28e(4)			Article 94(1)
	Article 28f, point (1) replacing Article 17(2), (3) and (4)			
	— paragraph 2(a)			Article 168(a)
	— paragraph 2(b)			Article 168(e)
	— paragraph 2(c)			Article 168(b) and (d)
	— paragraph 2(d)			Article 168(c)
	— paragraph 3(a), (b) and (c)			Article 169(a), (b) and (c) Article 170(a) and (b)
	— paragraph 4, first subparagraph, first indent			Article 171(1), first subparagraph
	— paragraph 4, first subparagraph, second indent			Article 171(2), first subparagraph
	— paragraph 4, second subparagraph, point (a)			Article 171(1), second subparagraph
	— paragraph 4, second subparagraph, point (b)			Article 171(2), second subparagraph
	— paragraph 4, second subparagraph, point (c)			Article 171(3)
	Article 28f, point (2) replacing Article 18(1)			
	— paragraph 1(a)			Article 178(a)
	— paragraph 1(b)			Article 178(e)
	— paragraph 1(c)			Article 178(b) and (d)
	— paragraph 1(d)			Article 178(f)
	— paragraph 1(e)			Article 178(c)
	Article 28f, point (3) inserting paragraph 3a into Article 18			
	— paragraph 3a, first part of the sentence			Article 181
	— paragraph 3a, second part of the sentence			Article 182
	Article 28g replacing Article 21			
	— paragraph 1(a), first subparagraph			Article 193
	— paragraph 1(a), second subparagraph			Article 194(1) and (2)
	— paragraph 1(b)			Article 196
	— paragraph 1(c), first subparagraph, first, second and third indents			Article 197(1)(a), (b) and (c)
	— paragraph 1(c), second subparagraph			Article 197(2)

Directive 67/227/EEC	Directive 77/388/EEC	Amending Directives	Other Acts	This Directive
	— paragraph 1(d)			Article 203
	— paragraph 1(e)			Article 200
	— paragraph 1(f)			Article 195
	— paragraph 2			—
	— paragraph 2(a), first sentence			Article 204(1), first subparagraph
	— paragraph 2(a), second sentence			Article 204(2)
	— paragraph 2(b)			Article 204(1), second subparagraph
	— paragraph 2(c), first subparagraph			Article 199(1)(a) to (g)
	— paragraph 2(c), second, third and fourth subparagraphs			Article 199(2), (3) and (4)
	— paragraph 3			Article 205
	— paragraph 4			Article 201
	Article 28h replacing Article 22			
	— paragraph 1(a), first and second sentences			Article 213(1), first and second subparagraphs
	— paragraph 1(b)			Article 213(2)
	— paragraph 1(c), first indent, first sentence			Article 214(1)(a)
	— paragraph 1(c), first indent, second sentence			Article 214(2)
	— paragraph 1(c), second and third indents			Article 214(1)(b) and (c)
	— paragraph 1(d), first and second sentences			Article 215, first and second paragraphs
	— paragraph 1(e)			Article 216
	— paragraph 2(a)			Article 242
	— paragraph 2(b), first and second indents			Article 243(1) and (2)
	— paragraph 3(a), first subparagraph, first sentence			Article 220, point (1)
	— paragraph 3(a), first subparagraph, second sentence			Article 220, points (2) and (3)
	— paragraph 3(a), second subparagraph			Article 220, points (4) and (5)
	— paragraph 3(a), third subparagraph, first and second sentences			Article 221(1), first and second subparagraphs
	— paragraph 3(a), fourth subparagraph			Article 221(2)
	— paragraph 3(a), fifth subparagraph, first sentence			Article 219

Directive 67/227/EEC	Directive 77/388/EEC	Amending Directives	Other Acts	This Directive
	— paragraph 3(a), fifth subparagraph, second sentence			Article 228
	— paragraph 3(a), sixth subparagraph			Article 222
	— paragraph 3(a), seventh subparagraph			Article 223
	— paragraph 3(a), eighth subparagraph, first and second sentences			Article 224(1) and (2)
	— paragraph 3(a), ninth subparagraph, first and second sentences			Article 224(3), first subparagraph
	— paragraph 3(a), ninth subparagraph, third sentence			Article 224(3), second subparagraph
	— paragraph 3(a), tenth subparagraph			Article 225
	— paragraph 3(b), first subparagraph, first to twelfth indents			Article 226, points (1) to (12)
	— paragraph 3(b), first subparagraph, thirteenth indent			Article 226, points (13) and (14)
	— paragraph 3(b), first subparagraph, fourteenth indent			Article 226, point (15)
	— paragraph 3(b), second subparagraph			Article 227
	— paragraph 3(b), third subparagraph			Article 229
	— paragraph 3(b), fourth subparagraph			Article 230
	— paragraph 3(b), fifth subparagraph			Article 231
	— paragraph 3(c), first subparagraph			Article 232
	— paragraph 3(c), second subparagraph, introductory sentence			Article 233(1), first subparagraph
	— paragraph 3(c), second subparagraph, first indent, first sentence			Article 233(1), first subparagraph, point (a)
	— paragraph 3(c), second subparagraph, first indent, second sentence			Article 233(2)
	— paragraph 3(c), second subparagraph, second indent, first sentence			Article 233(1), first subparagraph, point (b)
	— paragraph 3(c), second subparagraph, second indent, second sentence			Article 233(3)
	— paragraph 3(c), third subparagraph, first sentence			Article 233(1), second subparagraph
	— paragraph 3(c), third subparagraph, second sentence			Article 237

Directive 67/227/EEC	Directive 77/388/EEC	Amending Directives	Other Acts	This Directive
	— paragraph 3(c), fourth subparagraph, first and second sentences			Article 234
	— paragraph 3(c), fifth subparagraph			Article 235
	— paragraph 3(c), sixth subparagraph			Article 236
	— paragraph 3(d), first subparagraph			Article 244
	— paragraph 3(d), second subparagraph, first sentence			Article 245(1)
	— paragraph 3(d), second subparagraph, second and third sentences			Article 245(2), first and second subparagraphs
	— paragraph 3(d), third subparagraph, first and second sentences			Article 246, first and second paragraphs
	— paragraph 3(d), fourth, fifth and sixth subparagraphs			Article 247(1), (2) and (3)
	— paragraph 3(d), seventh subparagraph			Article 248
	— paragraph 3(e), first subparagraph			Articles 217 and 241
	— paragraph 3(e), second subparagraph			Article 218
	— paragraph 4(a), first and second sentences			Article 252(1)
	— paragraph 4(a), third and fourth sentences			Article 252(2), first and second subparagraphs
	— paragraph 4(a), fifth sentence			Article 250(2)
	— paragraph 4(b)			Article 250(1)
	— paragraph 4(c), first indent, first and second subparagraphs			Article 251(a) and (b)
	— paragraph 4(c), second indent, first subparagraph			Article 251(c)
	— paragraph 4(c), second indent, second subparagraph			Article 251(d) and (e)
	— paragraph 5			Article 206
	— paragraph 6(a), first and second sentences			Article 261(1)
	— paragraph 6(a), third sentence			Article 261(2)
	— paragraph 6(b), first subparagraph			Article 262
	— paragraph 6(b), second subparagraph, first sentence			Article 263(1), first subparagraph
	— paragraph 6(b), second subparagraph, second sentence			Article 263(2)

Directive 67/227/EEC	Directive 77/388/EEC	Amending Directives	Other Acts	This Directive
	− paragraph 6(b), third subparagraph, first and second indents			Article 264(1)(a) and (b)
	− paragraph 6(b), third subparagraph, third indent, first sentence			Article 264(1)(d)
	− paragraph 6(b), third subparagraph, third indent, second sentence			Article 264(2), first subparagraph
	− paragraph 6(b), fourth subparagraph, first indent			Article 264(1)(c) and (e)
	− paragraph 6(b), fourth subparagraph, second indent, first sentence			Article 264(1)(f)
	− paragraph 6(b), fourth subparagraph, second indent, second sentence			Article 264(2), second subparagraph
	− paragraph 6(b), fifth subparagraph, first and second indents			Article 265(1)(a) and (b)
	− paragraph 6(b), fifth subparagraph, third indent, first sentence			Article 265(1)(c)
	− paragraph 6(b), fifth subparagraph, third indent, second sentence			Article 265(2)
	− paragraph 6(c), first indent			Article 263(1), second subparagraph
	− paragraph 6(c), second indent			Article 266
	− paragraph 6(d)			Article 254
	− paragraph 6(e), first subparagraph			Article 268
	− paragraph 6(e), second subparagraph			Article 259
	− paragraph 7, first part of the sentence			Article 207, first paragraph Article 256 Article 267
	− paragraph 7, second part of the sentence			Article 207, second paragraph
	− paragraph 8, first and second subparagraphs			Article 273, first and second paragraphs
	− paragraph 9(a), first subparagraph, first indent			Article 272(1), first subparagraph, point (c)
	− paragraph 9(a), first subparagraph, second indent			Article 272(1), first subparagraph, points (a) and (d)
	− paragraph 9(a), first subparagraph, third indent			Article 272(1), first subparagraph, point (b)
	− paragraph 9(a), second subparagraph			Article 272(1), second subparagraph
	− paragraph 9(b)			Article 272(3)
	− paragraph 9(c)			Article 212

Directive 67/227/EEC	Directive 77/388/EEC	Amending Directives	Other Acts	This Directive
	— paragraph 9(d), first subparagraph, first and second indents			Article 238(1)(a) and (b)
	— paragraph 9(d), second subparagraph, first to fourth indents			Article 238(2)(a) to (d)
	— paragraph 9(d), third subparagraph			Article 238(3)
	— paragraph 9(e), first subparagraph			Article 239
	— paragraph 9(e), second subparagraph, first and second indents			Article 240, points (1) and (2)
	— paragraph 10			Articles 209 and 257
	— paragraph 11			Articles 210 and 258
	— paragraph 12, introductory sentence			Article 269
	— paragraph 12(a), first, second and third indents			Article 270(a), (b) and (c)
	— paragraph 12(b), first, second and third indents			Article 271(a), (b) and (c)
	Article 28i inserting a third subparagraph into Article 24(3)			
	— paragraph 3, third subparagraph			Article 283(1)(b) and (c)
	Article 28j, point (1) inserting a second subparagraph into Article 25(4)			
	— paragraph 4, second subparagraph			Article 272(2)
	Article 28j, point (2) replacing Article 25(5) and (6)			
	— paragraph 5, first subparagraph, points (a), (b) and (c)			Article 300, points (1), (2) and (3)
	— paragraph 5, second subparagraph			Article 302
	— paragraph 6(a), first subparagraph, first sentence			Article 301(1)
	— paragraph 6(a), first subparagraph, second sentence			Article 303(1)
	— paragraph 6(a), second subparagraph, first, second and third indents			Article 303(2)(a), (b) and (c)
	— paragraph 6(a), third subparagraph			Article 303(3)
	— paragraph 6(b)			Article 301(1)
	Article 28j, point (3) inserting a second subparagraph into Article 25(9)			
	— paragraph 9, second subparagraph			Article 305

Directive 67/227/EEC	Directive 77/388/EEC	Amending Directives	Other Acts	This Directive
	Article 28k, point (1), first subparagraph			—
	Article 28k, point (1), second subparagraph, point (a)			Article 158(3)
	Article 28k, point (1), second subparagraph, points (b) and (c)			—
	Article 28k, points (2), (3) and (4)			—
	Article 28k, point (5)			Article 158(2)
	Article 28l, first paragraph			—
	Article 28l, second and third paragraphs			Article 402(1) and (2)
	Article 28l, fourth paragraph			—
	Article 28m			Article 399, first paragraph
	Article 28n			—
	Article 28o(1), introductory sentence			Article 326, first paragraph
	Article 28o(1)(a), first sentence			Article 327(1) and (3)
	Article 28o(1)(a), second sentence			Article 327(2)
	Article 28o(1)(b)			Article 328
	Article 28o(1)(c), first second and third indents			Article 329(a), (b) and (c)
	Article 28o(1)(d), first and second subparagraphs			Article 330, first and second paragraphs
	Article 28o(1)(e)			Article 332
	Article 28o(1)(f)			Article 331
	Article 28o(1)(g)			Article 4(b)
	Article 28o(1)(h)			Article 35 Article 139(3), second subparagraph
	Article 28o(2)			Article 326, second paragraph
	Article 28o(3)			Article 341
	Article 28o(4)			—
	Article 28p(1), first, second and third indents			Article 405, points (1), (2) and (3)
	Article 28p(2)			Article 406
	Article 28p(3), first subparagraph, first and second indents			Article 407(a) and (b)
	Article 28p(3), second subparagraph			—
	Article 28p(4)(a) to (d)			Article 408(1)(a) to (d)
	Article 28p(5), first and second indents			Article 408(2)(a) and (b)

Directive 67/227/EEC	Directive 77/388/EEC	Amending Directives	Other Acts	This Directive
	Article 28p(6)			Article 409
	Article 28p(7), first subparagraph, points (a), (b) and (c)			Article 410(1)(a), (b) and (c)
	Article 28p(7), second subparagraph, first indent			—
	Article 28p(7), second subparagraph, second, third and fourth indents			Article 410(2)(a), (b) and (c)
	Article 29(1) to (4)			Article 398(1) to (4)
	Article 29a			Article 397
	Article 30(1)			Article 396(1)
	Article 30(2), first and second sentences			Article 396(2), first subparagraph
	Article 30(2), third sentence			Article 396(2), second subparagraph
	Article 30(3) and (4)			Article 396(3) and (4)
	Article 31(1)			—
	Article 31(2)			Article 400
	Article 33(1)			Article 401
	Article 33(2)			Article 2(3)
	Article 33a(1), introductory sentence			Article 274
	Article 33a(1)(a)			Article 275
	Article 33a(1)(b)			Article 276
	Article 33a(1)(c)			Article 277
	Article 33a(2), introductory sentence			Article 278
	Article 33a(2)(a)			Article 279
	Article 33a(2)(b)			Article 280
	Article 34			Article 404
	Article 35			Article 403
	Articles 36 and 37			—
	Article 38			Article 414
	Annex A(I)(1) and (2)			Annex VII, point (1)(a) and (b)
	Annex A(I)(3)			Annex VII, points (1)(c) and (d)
	Annex A(II)(1) to (6)			Annex VII, points (2)(a) to (f)
	Annex A(III) and (IV)			Annex VII, points (3) and (4)
	Annex A(IV)(1) to (4)			Annex VII, points (4)(a) to (d)
	Annex A(V)			Article 295(2)
	Annex B, introductory sentence			Article 295(1), point (5)
	Annex B, first to ninth indents			Annex VIII, points (1) to (9)
	Annex C			—
	Annex D(1) to (13)			Annex I, points (1) to (13)

Directive 67/227/EEC	Directive 77/388/EEC	Amending Directives	Other Acts	This Directive
	Annex E(2)			Annex X, Part A, point (1)
	Annex E(7)			Annex X, Part A, point (2)
	Annex E(11)			Annex X, Part A, point (3)
	Annex E(15)			Annex X, Part A, point (4)
	Annex F(1)			Annex X, Part B, point (1)
	Annex F(2)			Annex X, Part B, points (2) (a) to (j)
	Annex F(5) to (8)			Annex X, Part B, points (3) to (6)
	Annex F(10)			Annex X, Part B, point (7)
	Annex F(12)			Annex X, Part B, point (8)
	Annex F(16)			Annex X, Part B, point (9)
	Annex F(17), first and second subparagraphs			Annex X, Part B, point (10)
	Annex F(23)			Annex X, Part B, point (11)
	Annex F(25)			Annex X, Part B, point (12)
	Annex F(27)			Annex X, Part B, point (13)
	Annex G(1) and (2)			Article 391
	Annex H, first paragraph			Article 98(3)
	Annex H, second paragraph, introductory sentence			–
	Annex H, second paragraph, points (1) to (6)			Annex III, points (1) to (6)
	Annex H, second paragraph, point (7), first and second subparagraphs			Annex III, points (7) and (8)
	Annex H, second paragraph, points (8) to (17)			Annex III, points (9) to (18)
	Annex I, introductory sentence			–
	Annex I(a), first to seventh indents			Annex IX, Part A, points (1) to (7)
	Annex I(b), first and second indents			Annex IX, Part B, points (1) and (2)
	Annex I(c)			Annex IX, Part C
	Annex J, introductory sentence			Annex V, introductory sentence
	Annex J			Annex V, points (1) to (25)
	Annex K(1), first, second and third indents			Annex IV, points (1)(a), (b) and (c)
	Annex K(2) to (5)			Annex IV, points (2) to (5)
	Annex L, first paragraph, points (1) to (5)			Annex II, points (1) to (5)
	Annex L, second paragraph			Article 56(2)
	Annex M, points (a) to (f)			Annex VI, points (1) to (6)

Directive 67/227/EEC	Directive 77/388/EEC	Amending Directives	Other Acts	This Directive
		Article 1, point (1), second subparagraph, of Directive 89/465/EEC		Article 133, second paragraph
		Article 2 of Directive 94/5/EC		Article 342
		Article 3, first and second sentences, of Directive 94/5/EC		Article 343, first and second paragraphs
		Article 4 of Directive 2002/38/EC		Article 56(3) Article 57(2) Article 357
		Article 5 of Directive 2002/38/EC		–
			Annex VIII(II), point (2)(a) of the Act of Accession of Greece	Article 287, point (1)
			Annex VIII(II), point (2)(b) of the Act of Accession of Greece	Article 375
			Annex XXXII(IV), point (3) (a), first indent and second indent, first sentence, of the Act of Accession of Spain and Portugal	Article 287, points (2) and (3)
			Annex XXXII(IV), point (3) (b), first subparagraph, of the Act of Accession of Spain and Portugal	Article 377
			Annex XV(IX), point (2)(b), first subparagraph, of the Act of Accession of Austria, Finland and Sweden	Article 104
			Annex XV(IX), point (2)(c), first subparagraph, of the Act of Accession of Austria, Finland and Sweden	Article 287, point (4)
			Annex XV(IX), point (2)(f), first subparagraph, of the Act of Accession of Austria, Finland and Sweden	Article 117(1)
			Annex XV(IX), point (2)(g), first subparagraph, of the Act of Accession of Austria, Finland and Sweden	Article 119
			Annex XV(IX), point (2)(h), first subparagraph, first and second indents, of the Act of Accession of Austria, Finland and Sweden	Article 378(1)
			Annex XV(IX), point (2) (i), first subparagraph, first indent, of the Act of Accession of Austria, Finland and Sweden	–
			Annex XV(IX), point (2)(i), first subparagraph, second and third indents, of the Act of Accession of Austria, Finland and Sweden	Article 378(2)(a) and (b)

Directive 67/227/EEC	Directive 77/388/EEC	Amending Directives	Other Acts	This Directive
			Annex XV(IX), point (2)(j) of the Act of Accession of Austria, Finland and Sweden	Article 287, point (5)
			Annex XV(IX), point (2)(l), first subparagraph, of the Act of Accession of Austria, Finland and Sweden	Article 111(a)
			Annex XV(IX), point (2)(m), first subparagraph, of the Act of Accession of Austria, Finland and Sweden	Article 379(1)
			Annex XV(IX), point (2)(n), first subparagraph, first and second indents, of the Act of Accession of Austria, Finland and Sweden	Article 379(2)
			Annex XV(IX), point (2)(x), first indent, of the Act of Accession of Austria, Finland and Sweden	Article 253
			Annex XV(IX), point (2)(x), second indent, of the Act of Accession of Austria, Finland and Sweden	Article 287, point (6)
			Annex XV(IX), point (2)(z), first subparagraph, of the Act of Accession of Austria, Finland and Sweden	Article 111(b)
			Annex XV(IX), point (2)(aa), first subparagraph, first and second indents, of the Act of Accession of Austria, Finland and Sweden	Article 380
			Protocol No 2 of the Act of Accession of Austria, Finland and Sweden concerning the Åland Islands	Article 6(1)(d)
			Annex V(5), point (1)(a) of the 2003 Act of Accession of the Czech Republic, Estonia, Cyprus, Latvia, Lithuania, Hungary, Malta, Poland Slovenia and Slovakia	Article 123
			Annex V(5), point (1)(b) of the 2003 Act of Accession	Article 381
			Annex VI(7), point (1)(a) of the 2003 Act of Accession	Article 124
			Annex VI(7), point (1)(b) of the 2003 Act of Accession	Article 382
			Annex VII(7), point (1), first and second subparagraphs, of the 2003 Act of Accession	Article 125(1) and (2)
			Annex VII(7), point (1), third subparagraph, of the 2003 Act of Accession	–
			Annex VII(7), point (1), fourth subparagraph, of the 2003 Act of Accession	Article 383(a)

Directive 67/227/EEC	Directive 77/388/EEC	Amending Directives	Other Acts	This Directive
			Annex VII(7), point (1), fifth subparagraph, of the 2003 Act of Accession	–
			Annex VII(7), point (1), sixth subparagraph, of the 2003 Act of Accession	Article 383(b)
			Annex VIII(7), point (1)(a) of the 2003 Act of Accession	–
			Annex VIII(7), point (1)(b), second subparagraph, of the 2003 Act of Accession	Article 384(a)
			Annex VIII(7), point (1), third subparagraph, of the 2003 Act of Accession	Article 384(b)
			Annex IX(8), point (1) of the 2003 Act of Accession	Article 385
			Annex X(7), point (1)(a)(i) and (ii) of the 2003 Act of Accession	Article 126(a) and (b)
			Annex X(7), point (1)(c) of the 2003 Act of Accession	Article 386
			Annex XI(7), point (1) of the 2003 Act of Accession	Article 127
			Annex XI(7), point (2)(a) of the 2003 Act of Accession	Article 387(c)
			Annex XI(7), point (2)(b) of the 2003 Act of Accession	Article 387(a)
			Annex XI(7), point (2)(c) of the 2003 Act of Accession	Article 387(b)
			Annex XII(9), point (1)(a) of the 2003 Act of Accession	Article 128(1) and (2)
			Annex XII(9), point (1)(b) of the 2003 Act of Accession	Article 128(3), (4) and (5)
			Annex XII(9), point (2) of the 2003 Act of Accession	Article 388
			Annex XIII(9), point (1)(a) of the 2003 Act of Accession	Article 129(1) and (2)
			Annex XIII(9), point (1)(b) of the 2003 Act of Accession	Article 389
			Annex XIV(7), first subparagraph, of the 2003 Act of Accession	Article 130(a) and (b)
			Annex XIV(7), second subparagraph, of the 2003 Act of Accession	–
			Annex XIV(7), third subparagraph, of the 2003 Act of Accession	Article 390

Sixth Council

Directive

(repealed by Council Directive
2006/112/EC of 28 November 2006
with effect from 1 January 2007)

SIXTH COUNCIL DIRECTIVE EEC/77/388
of 17 May 1977

SIXTH COUNCIL DIRECTIVE 77/388/EEC

of 17 May 1977

on the harmonisation of the laws of the Member States relating to turnover taxes
- Common system of value added tax: uniform basis of assessment

Official Journal L145, 13/06/1977 p.0001-0040

THE COUNCIL OF THE EUROPEAN COMMUNITIES,

Having regard to the Treaty establishing the European Economic Community, and in particular Articles 99 and 100 thereof,

Having regard to the proposal from the Commission,

Having regard to the opinion of the European Parliament,

Having regard to the opinion of the Economic and Social Committee,

Whereas all Member States have adopted a system of value added tax in accordance with the first and second Council Directives of 11 April 1967 on the harmonization of the laws of the Member States relating to turnover taxes;

Whereas the Decision of 21 April 1970 on the replacement of financial contributions from Member States by the Communities' own resources provides that the budget of the Communities shall, irrespective of other revenue, be financed entirely from the Communities' own resources; whereas these resources are to include those accruing from value added tax and obtained by applying a common rate of tax on a basis of assessment determined in a uniform manner according to Community rules;

Whereas further progress should be made in the effective removal of restrictions on the movement of persons, goods, services and capital and the integration of national economies;

Whereas account should be taken of the objective of abolishing the imposition of tax on the importation and the remission of tax on exportation in trade between Member States; whereas it should be ensured that the common system of turnover taxes is non-discriminatory as regards the origin of goods and services, so that a common market permitting fair competition and resembling a real internal market may ultimately be achieved;

Whereas, to enhance the non-discriminatory nature of the tax, the term `taxable person' must be clarified to enable the Member States to extend it to cover persons who occasionally carry out certain transactions;

Whereas the term `taxable transaction' has led to difficulties, in particular as regards transactions treated as taxable transactions; whereas these concepts must be clarified;

Whereas the determination of the place where taxable transactions are effected has been the subject of conflicts concerning jurisdiction as between Member States, in particular as regards supplies of goods for assembly and the supply of services; whereas although the place where a supply of services is effected should in principle be defined as the place where the person supplying the services has his principal place of business, that place should be defined as being in the country of the person to whom the services are supplied, in particular in the case of certain services supplied between taxable persons where the cost of the services is included in the price of the goods;

Whereas the concepts of chargeable event and of the charge to tax must be harmonized if the introduction and any subsequent alterations of the Community rate are to become operative at the same time in all Member States;

Whereas the taxable base must be harmonized so that the application of the Community rate to taxable transactions leads to comparable results in all the Member States;

Whereas the rates applied by Member States must be such as to allow the normal deduction of the tax applied at the preceding stage;

Whereas a common list of exemptions should be drawn up so that the Communities' own resources may be collected in a uniform manner in all the Member States;

Whereas the rules governing deductions should be harmonized to the extent that they affect the actual amounts collected;

Whereas the deductible proportion should be calculated in a similar manner in all the Member States;

Whereas it should be specified which persons are liable to pay tax, in particular as regards services supplied by a person established in another country;

Whereas the obligations of taxpayers must be harmonized as far as possible so as to ensure the necessary safeguards for the collection of taxes in a uniform manner in all the Member States; whereas taxpayers should, in particular, make a periodic aggregate return of their transactions, relating to both inputs and outputs where this appears necessary for establishing and monitoring the basis of assessment of own resources;

Whereas Member States should nevertheless be able to retain their special schemes for small undertakings, in accordance with common provisions, and with a view to closer harmonization; whereas Member States should remain free to apply a special scheme involving flat rate rebates of input value added tax to farmers not covered by normal schemes; whereas the basic principles of this scheme should be established and a common method adopted for calculating the value added of these farmers for the purposes of collecting own resources;

Whereas the uniform application of the provisions of this Directive should be ensured; whereas to this end a Community procedure for consultation should be laid down; whereas the setting up of a Value Added Tax Committee would enable the Member States and the Commission to cooperate closely;

Whereas Member States should be able, within certain limits and subject to certain conditions, to take or retain special measures derogating from this Directive in order to simplify the levying of tax or to avoid fraud or tax avoidance;

Whereas it might appear appropriate to authorize Member States to conclude with non-member countries or international organizations agreements containing derogations from this Directive;

Whereas it is vital to provide for a transitional period to allow national laws in specified fields to be gradually adapted,

HAS ADOPTED THIS DIRECTIVE:

TITLE I
introductory provisions
Article 1

Member States shall modify their present value added tax systems in accordance with the following Articles.

They shall adopt the necessary laws, regulations and administrative provisions so that the systems as modified enter into force at the earliest opportunity and by 1 January 1978 at the latest.

TITLE II

scope

Article 2

The following shall be subject to value added tax:

a) **1.** The supply of goods or services effected for consideration within the territory of the country by a taxable person acting as such;

b) **2.** The importation of goods.

Case law

British American Tobacco International Ltd, Newman Shipping & Agency Company NV v Belgian State	C435/03	Supply/Theft from tax warehouse
BUPA Hospitals Ltd, Goldsborough Developments Ltd v Commissioners of Customs & Excise	C419/02	Payment on account/Chargeable Event/ Taxable person/Entitlement to VAT recovery
Empresa de Desenvolvimento Mineiro SGPS SA (EDM) and Fazenda Pública	C77/01	Meaning of 'economic activities'/ Meaning of 'incidental financial transactions'/Calculation of deductible proportion
France v Commission	C404/99	Restaurant service charges
Germany v Commission	C287/00	Research activities
Halifax plc, Leeds Permanent Development Services Ltd, County Wide property Investments Ltd v Commissioners of Customs & Excise	C255/02	Economic Activity/Supplies/Abusive practice
Hotel Scandic Gåsabäck AB v Riksskatteverket	C412/03	Application for private use/ Consideration less than cost price
J.C.M Beeher B.V. v Staatssecretaris van Financiën	C124/07	Supply of services relating to insurance transactions/Insurance brokers and insurance agents
KapHag Renditefonds 35 Spreecenter Berlin-Hellersdorf 3. Tranche GbR and Finanzamt Charlottenburg	C442/01	Scope/Admission of member to a partnership
Kennemer Golf & Country Club v Staatssecretaris van Financiën	C174/00	Services connected with the practice of sport/Non-profit-making organisation
Kretztechnik AG, Außenstelle Linz	C465/03	Supply/Share Issue/Admission of company to stock exchange
Levob Verzekeringen BV, OV Bank NV v Staatssecretaris van Financiën	C41/04	Supply and customisation of software
Optigen Ltd, Fulcrum Electronics Ltd, Bond House Systems Ltd v Commissioners of Customs & Excise	C354/03 C355/03 C484/03	Economic activity/Taxable person/ Deduction/Carousel fraud
Town & County Factors Ltd v Customs and Excise	C498/99	Scope/Taxable Amount
University of Huddersfield High Education Corporation v Commissioners of Customs & Excise	C223/03	Economic Activity/Supplies/Abusive practice

TITLE III

territorial application

[Article 3

1. For the purposes of this Directive:

   - `territory of a Member State` shall mean the territory of the country as defined in respect of each Member State in paragraphs 2 and 3,

   - `Community` and `territory of the Community` shall mean the territory of the Member States as defined in respect of each Member State in paragraphs 2 and 3,

   - `third territory` and `third country` shall mean any territory other than those defined in paragraphs 2 and 3 as the territory of a Member State.

2. For the purposes of this Directive, the `territory of the country` shall be the area of application of the Treaty establishing the European Economic Community as defined in respect of each Member State in Article 227.

3. The following territories of individual Member States shall be excluded from the territory of the country:

   - Federal Republic of Germany:

     the Island of Heligoland,

     the territory of Busingen,

   - Kingdom of Spain:

     Ceuta,

     Melilla,

   - Republic of Italy:

     Livigno,

     Campione d'Italia,

     the Italian waters of Lake Lugano.

   The following territories of individual Member States shall also be excluded from the territory of the country:

   - Kingdom of Spain:

     Canary Islands,

   - French Republic:

     the overseas departments,

   - Hellenic Republic:

   - Αγιο Ορος (Mount Athos),

   - Republic of Finland

     Aaland Islands.

[**4.** [By way of derogation from paragraph 1, in view of:

- the conventions and treaties which the Principality of Monaco and the Isle of Man have concluded respectively with the French Republic and the United Kingdom of Great Britain and Northern Ireland,

- the Treaty concerning the Establishment of the Republic of Cyprus,

the Principality of Monaco, the Isle of Man and the United Kingdom Sovereign Base Areas of Akrotiri and Dhekelia shall not be treated for the purpose of the application of this Directive as third territories.][1]

Member States shall take the measures necessary to ensure that transactions originating in or intended for:

- the Principality of Monaco are treated as transactions originating in or intended for the French Republic,

- the Isle of Man are treated as transactions originating in or intended for the United Kingdom of Great Britain and Northern Ireland.][2]

[– the United Kingdom Sovereign Base Areas of Akrotiri and Dhekelia are treated as transactions originating in or intended for the Republic of Cyprus.][3]

5. If the Commission considers that the provisions laid down in paragraphs 3 and 4 are no longer justified, particularly in terms of fair competition or own resources, it shall submit appropriate proposals to the Council.][4]

Amendments
1   Substituted by Protocol No. 3, Part 2, Treaty of Accession, w.e.f. 1 May 2004.
2   Para4 inserted by Art 1, Council Directive 92/111/EEC of 14 December 1992.
3   Inserted by Protocol No. 3, Part 2, Treaty of Accession, w.e.f. 1 May 2004.
4   Art3 substituted by Art 1, Council Directive 91/680/EEC of 16 December 1991, w.e.f. 1 January 1993.

Case law

Berkholz, Gunter v Finanzamt Hamburg - Mitte Altstadt	C168/84	Place of Supply/Gaming Machines on board Ferries
Hamann, Knut v Finanzamt Hamburg Eimsbuttel	C51/88	Yachts/Hire of/Place of Supply
Trans Tirreno Express SpA v Ufficio Provinciale IVA Sassari	C283/84	Transport in International Waters

TITLE IV

taxable persons

Article 4

s8(1) **1.** **'Taxable person'** shall mean any person who independently carries out in any place any economic activity specified in paragraph 2, whatever the purpose or results of that activity.

s1(1) **2.** The economic activities referred to in paragraph 1 shall comprise all activities of producers, traders and persons supplying services including mining and agricultural activities and activities of the professions. The exploitation of tangible or intangible property for the purpose of obtaining income therefrom on a continuing basis shall also be considered an economic activity.

3. Member States may also treat as a taxable person anyone who carries out, on an occasional basis, a transaction relating to the activities referred to in paragraph 2 and in particular one of the following:

s4(2)   (a) the supply before first occupation of buildings or parts of buildings and the land on which they stand; Member States may determine the conditions of application of this criterion to transformations of buildings and the land on which they stand.

Member States may apply criteria other than that of first occupation, such as the period elapsing between the date of completion of the building and the date of first supply or the period elapsing between the date of first occupation and the date of subsequent supply, provided that these periods do not exceed five years and two years respectively.

`A building' shall be taken to mean any structure fixed to or in the ground;

   (b) the supply of building land.

`Building land' shall mean any unimproved or improved land defined as such by the Member States.

s 8(1) **4.** The use of the word `independently' in paragraph 1 shall exclude employed and other persons from the tax insofar as they are bound to an employer by a contract of employment or by any other legal ties creating the relationship of employer and employee as regards working conditions, remuneration and the employer's liability

s 8(8)   Subject to the consultations provided for in Article 29, each Member State may treat as a single taxable person persons established in the territory of the country who, while legally independent, are closely bound to one another by financial, economic and organizational links.

[A Member State exercising the option provided for in the second subparagraph, may adopt any measures needed to prevent tax evasion or avoidance through the use of this provision.][1]

s8(2A)(a) **5.** States, regional and local government authorities and other bodies governed by public law shall not be considered taxable persons in respect of the activities or transactions in which they engage as public authorities, even where they collect dues, fees, contributions or payments in connection with these activities or transactions.

s8(3E) However, when they engage in such activities or transactions, they shall be considered taxable persons in respect of these activities or transactions where treatment as non-taxable persons would lead to significant distortions of competition.

In any case, these bodies shall be considered taxable persons in relation to the activities listed in Annex D, provided they are not carried out on such a small scale as to be negligible.

Member States may consider activities of these bodies which are exempt under Articles 13 or 28 as activities which they engage in as public authorities.

Amendments
1   Inserted by Article 1 (1) Council Directive 2006/69/EC of 24 July 2006 (w.e.f. 13 August 2006).

Case law

Ampliscientifica Srl and Amplifin SpA v Ministero dell'Economia e delle Finanze, Agenzia delle Entrate	C162/07	Taxable persons/Parent companies and subsidiaries
Argos Distributors Ltd v Customs and Excise	C288/94	Taxable Amount/Vouchers
Ayuntamiento de Sevilla v Recaudadores de Tributos de la Zonas Primera & Segunda	C202/90	Taxable persons
Banque Bruxelles Lambert SA v Belgian State	C8/03	Place of supply/Concept of taxable person
BUPA Hospitals Ltd, Goldsborough Developments Ltd v Commissioners of Customs & Excise	C419/02	Payment on account/Chargeable Event/Taxable person/Entitlement to VAT recovery
Camara Municipal do Porto v Fazenda Publica	C446/98	State run car parking
Cibo Participations SA v Directeur régional des impôts du Nord-Pas-de-Calais	C16/00	Holding Coy/Taxable person/ Recovery of VAT
Commune di Carpaneto Piacentino and others v Ufficio Provinciale Imposta sul Valore Aggiunto di Piacenza	C4/89	Taxable Person/Government bodies
Commune di Rivergaro and others v Ufficio Provinciale Imposta sul Valore Aggiunto di Piacenza	C129/88	Taxable Person/Government bodies
Empresa de Desenvolvimento Mineiro SGPS SA (EDM) and Fazenda Pública	C77/01	Meaning of 'economic activities'/ Meaning of 'incidental financial transactions'/Calculation of deductible proportion
Enkler, Renate v Finanzamt Hamburg	C230/94	Taxable person/
FCE Bank plc v Ministero dell' Ecomomia e delle Finanze	C210/04	Concept of taxable person/Fixed establishment
Feuerbestattungsverein Halle eV v Finanzamt Eisleben	C430/04	Private taxable person in competition with public authority
Fini H, I/S v Skatteministeriet	C32/03	Ceased economic activity/Deduction/ Right of
France v European Commission	C50/87	Leased buildings/Deduction/Right of
Halifax plc, Leeds Permanent Development Services Ltd, County Wide property Investments Ltd v Commissioners of Customs & Excise	C255/02	Economic Activity/Supplies/Abusive practice
Harnas and Helm CV v Staatssecretaris van Financien	C80/95	Taxable Person

Heerma J and K. Heerma v Staatssecretaris van Financien	C23/98	Taxable Event/Property let by partner to partnership
Ireland v Commission	C358/97	Toll Roads
Hong Kong Trade Development Council v Staatssecretaris van Financien	C89/81	Government Body/Taxable Person
Intercommunale voor Zeewaterontzilting "Inzo" v Belgium	C110/94	Intending trader/Deduction/Right of
Isle of Wight and Others v The Commisioners for Her Majesty's Revenue and Customs	C288/07	Activities engaged in by bodies governed by public law/Provision of off-street car-parking
Kerrutt and Another v Finanzamt Monchengladbach - Mitte	C73/85	Property/Taxable person/ Undeveloped land
Kollektivavtalsstiftelsen TRR Trygghetsrådet v Skatteverket	C291/07	Place of supply/Consultancy services/ Recipient engaged in economic and non-economic activities
Marktgemeinde Welden v Finanzamt Augsburg - Stadt	C247/95	Tax payable in advance of supply
Netherlands v European Commission	C235/85	Taxable Person/Notaries and Sheriff Officers
Norwich - City of v Customs and Excise	UK Case	Government body/Taxable Person
Optigen Ltd, Fulcrum Electronics Ltd, Bond House Systems Ltd v Commissioners of Customs & Excise	C354/03 C355/03 C484/03	Economic activity/Taxable person/ Deduction/Carousel fraud
Polysar Investments Netherlands BV v Inspecteur der Inveorrechten en Accijnzen	C60/90	Holding Coy/Taxable Person/ Recovery of VAT
Rompelman DA & Rompelman van Deelen EA v Minister van Financien	C268/83	Intending trader/Recovery by
University of Huddersfield High Education Corporation v Commissioners of Customs & Excise	C223/03	Economic Activity/Supplies/Abusive practice
Waterschap Zeeuws Vlaanderen v Staatssecretaris van Financiën	C378/02	Public authority/Supply/Right to adjustment and deduction
Wellcome Trust Ltd v Customs and Excise	C155/94	Taxable person/Shares Deduction/ Right of
Zweckverband zur Trinkwasserversorgung und Abwasserbeseitigung Torgau-Westelbien v Finanzamt Oschatz	C442/05	"Suppy of water" or "Water supply"

TITLE V

taxable transactions

Article 5

Supply of goods

S1(1)
S3(1)(a) **1.** `Supply of goods' shall mean the transfer of the right to dispose of tangible property as owner.

s3(1B) **2.** Electric current, gas, heat, refrigeration and the like shall be considered tangible property.

3. Member States may consider the following to be tangible property:

3(1)(c)
4(2)   (a) certain interests in immovable property;

  (b) rights in rem giving the holder thereof a right of user over immovable property;

  (c) shares or interests equivalent to shares giving the holder thereof de jure or de facto rights of ownership or possession over immovable property or part thereof.

4. The following shall also be considered supplies within the meaning of paragraph 1:

1)(d)   (a) the transfer, by order made by or in the name of a public authority or in pursuance of the law, of the ownership of property against payment of compensation;

1)(b)   (b) the actual handing over of goods, pursuant to a contract for the hire of goods for a certain period or for the sale of goods on deferred terms, which provides that in the normal course of events ownership shall pass at the latest upon payment of the final installment;

s3(1)(aa)
s 3(4)   (c) the transfer of goods pursuant to a contract under which commission is payable on purchase or sale.

(1)(c) **[5.** Member States may consider the handing over of certain works of construction to be supplies within the meaning of paragraph 1.][1]

3(1)(f)
3(1A) **6.** The application by a taxable person of goods forming part of his business assets for his private use or that of his staff, or the disposal thereof free of charge or more generally their application for purposes other than those of his business, where the value added tax on the goods in question or the component parts thereof was wholly or partly deductible, shall be treated as supplies made for consideration. However, applications for the giving of samples or the making of gifts of small value for the purposes of the taxable person's business shall not be so treated.

7. Member States may treat as supplies made for consideration:

s3(1)(e)   (a) the application by a taxable person for the purposes of his business of goods produced, constructed, extracted, processed, purchased or imported in the course of such business, where the value added tax on such goods, had they been acquired from another taxable person, would not be wholly deductible;

s3(1)(f)   (b) the application of goods by a taxable person for the purposes of a non-taxable transaction, where the value added tax on such goods became wholly or partly deductible upon their acquisition or upon their application in accordance with subparagraph (a);

s 3(7)   (c) except in those cases mentioned in paragraph 8, the retention of goods by a taxable person or his successors when he ceases to carry out a taxable economic activity where the value added tax on such goods became wholly or partly deductible upon their acquisition or upon their application in accordance with subparagraph (a).

s3(5)(b) iii,
s5(8) **8.**   In the event of a transfer, whether for consideration or not or as a contribution to a company, of a totality of assets or part thereof, Member States may consider that no supply of goods has taken place and in that event the recipient shall be treated as the successor to the transferor. [Where appropriate, Member States may, in cases where the recipient is not wholly liable to tax, take the measure necessary to prevent distortion of competition. They may also adopt any measures needed to prevent tax evasion or avoidance through the use of this provision.][2]

Amendments
1 Substituted by Art 1(1), Council Directive 95/7/EC of 10 April 1995 w.e.f. 1 January 1996.
2 Substituted by Art 1(2), Council Directive 2006/69/EC of 24 July 2006 w.e.f. 13 August 2006.

Case law

Alfred Benedix Van Tiem v Staatssecretaris van Finan .cien	C186/89	Who is Taxable, Taxable Taxable Event, Rights over land, Lettings, Property,
Auto Lease Holland BV and Bundesamt für Finanzen	C185/01	Place of supply/Refueling of leased vehicle
Brandenstein Klaus v Finauzant Duseldorf - Mettman	C323/99	Self supply
Belgocodex S.A v Belgium	C381/97	Waiver/Property
Careda SA Ferma and Facomara v Administracion General del Estado	C370/95 C371/95 C372/95	Scope of VAT
Coffeeshop Siberie v Staatssecretaris van Financien	C158/98	Sale of drugs/Illegal activities
Commerz Credit Bank AG-Europartner v Finanzamt Saarbrucken	C50/91	Transfer of business
Cooperatieve Vereniging Aardapplenbewaarplaats v Staatssecretaris van Financien - Dutch Potato Case.	C154/80	Consideration for Taxable Event
Cork Communications Limited v Brosnan	Irish	Nature of supply/ Communications or Electricity
De Jong, Pieter v Staatssecretaris van Financien	C20/91	Self Supply/Property/Taxable Amount/ Taxable Event/Deduction,
Far, Miguel Amengual v Amengual Far J	C12/98	Property - Right to waive exemption
France v European Commission	C30/89	Taxable Amount/Own Resources
Goritz Intransco International GmbH v Hauptzollamt Dusseldorf	C292/96	Imports
Hotel Scandic Gåsabäck AB v Riksskatteverket	C412/03	Application for private use/Consideration less than cost price
Kuhne, Heinz v Finanzamt Munchen III	C50/88	Taxable Amount/Self Supply/Car/Taxable Event/Deduction
Mohr, Jurgen v Finanzamt Bad Segeberg	C215/94	Payment to discontinue activity/Taxable Event

Mol v Inspecteur der Invoerrechten en Accijnzen	C269/86	Illegal Sale of Drugs/Taxable Event
Shipping & Forwarding Enterprise Safe BV v Staatssecretaris van Financien	C320/88	Rights over land/Taxable event
Stichting 'Goed Wonen' v Staatssecretaris van Financiën	C326/99	Property/Rights in rem
Stylo Barratt Shoes Ltd v Inspector of Taxes	Irish S.C.	Transfer of a business
Tolsma RJ v Inspecteur der Omzetbelasting Leeuwarden	C16/93	Who is Taxable/Taxable Event/ Consideration
Van Tiem v Staatssecretaris van Financien	C186/89	Who is Taxable/Taxable Event/ Rights over land/Lettings/Property
Vereniging Happy Family Rustenburgerstraat v Inspecteur der Omzetbelasting	C289/86	Illegal Sales
Witzemann, Max v Hauptzollamt Munchen - Mitte	C343/89	Import of counterfeit currency notes
Zita Modes Sàrl and Administration de l'enregistrement et des domaines	C497/01	Transfer of a business

Article 6

Supply of services

s 5(1) **1.** 'Supply of services' shall mean any transaction which does not constitute a supply of goods within the meaning of Article 5. Such transaction may include *inter alia*:

- assignments of intangible property whether or not it is the subject of a document establishing title,
- obligations to refrain from an act or to tolerate an act or situation,
- the performances of services in pursuance of an order made by or in the name of a public authority or in pursuance of the law.

2. The following shall be treated as supplies of services for consideration:

s5(3)(a)   (a) the use of goods forming part of the assets of a business for the private use of the taxable person or of his staff or more generally for purposes other than those of his business where the value added tax on such goods is wholly or partly deductible;

s5(3)(b)   (b) supplies of services carried out free of charge by the taxable person for his own private use or that of his staff or more generally for purposes other than those of his business.

Member States may derogate from the provisions of this paragraph provided that such derogation does not lead to distortion of competition.

3. In order to prevent distortion of competition and subject to the consultations provided for in Article 29, Member States may treat as a supply of services for consideration the supply by a taxable person of a service for the purposes of his undertaking where the value added tax on such a service, had it been supplied by another taxable person, would not be wholly deductible.

s 5(4) **4.** Where a taxable person acting in his own name but on behalf of another takes part in a supply of services, he shall be considered to have received and supplied those services himself.

s 5(8) **5.** Article 5(8) shall apply in like manner to the supply of services.

Case law

Armbrecht, Dieter v Finanzam Uelzen	C291/92	Taxable Event/Property/Self Supply/ Taxable Amount/Deduction
Danfoss and Astra Zeneca v Skatteministeriet	C371/07	Supplies of services carried out free of charge by a taxable person for non-business purposes
Hotel Scandic Gåsabäck AB v Riksskatteverket	C412/03	Application for private use/Consideration less than cost price
Impresa Construziono Comm. Quirino Mazzalai v Ferrovia del Renon SpA	C111/75	Taxable Event/Time of Completed Supply
Levob Verzekeringen BV, OV Bank NV v Staatssecretaris van Financiën	C41/04	Supply and customisation of software
Mohsche, Gerhard v Finanzamt Munchen III	C193/91	Self Supply
Nederlandse Spoorwegen NV V Staatssecretaris van Financien	C126/78	Transport Ancillary Services
Phonographic Performance (Ireland) Ltd v Somers	Ireland IV ITR 314	Taxable Event/Omission of Act Toleration of situation/Equitable Payments
Seeling, Wolfgang v Finanzamt Starnberg	C269/00	Self supply of residential part of property
Town & County Factors Ltd v Customs and Excise	C498/99	Scope/Taxable Amount
W.G. Bradley and Sons v Bourke, Inspector of Taxes	Irish H.C. IV ITR 117	Legal services in insurance

[Article 7

Imports

s1(1) **1.** 'Importation of goods' shall mean:

(a) the entry into the Community of goods which do not fulfill the conditions laid down in Articles 9 and 10 of the Treaty establishing the European Economic Community or, where the goods are covered by the Treaty establishing the European Coal and Steel Community, are not in free circulation;

[(b) the entry into the Community of goods from a third territory, other than the goods covered by (a).][1]

5(1), **2.** The place of import of goods shall be the Member State within the territory
), (6), of which the goods are when they enter the Community.
A)

3. Notwithstanding paragraph 2, where goods referred to in paragraph 1(a) are, on entry into the Community, placed under one of the arrangements referred to in Article 16(1)(B)[(a), (b), (c) and (d)][2] under arrangements for temporary importation with total exemption from import duty or under external transit arrangements, the place of import of such goods shall be the Member State within the territory of which they cease to be covered by these arrangements.

[Similarly, when goods referred to in paragraph 1(b) are placed, on entry into the Community, under one of the procedures referred to in Article 33a(1)(b) or (c), the place of import shall be the Member State within whose territory this procedure ceases to apply.][3]][4]

Amendments
1   Substituted by Art 1(2), Council Directive 92/111/EEC of 14 December 1992, w.e.f. 1 January 1993.
2   Inserted by Art 1(3), Council Directive 92/111/EEC of 14 December 1992, w.e.f. 1 January 1993.
3   Substituted by Art 1(3), Council Directive of 14 December 1992, w.e.f. 1 January 1993.
4   Art7 substituted by Art 1(2), Council Directive 91/680/EEC of 18 December 1991, w.e.f. 1 January 1993.

Case law

Keller Karl v Revenue Commissioners	Irish HC IV ITR 12S	Import of Cars/Taxable amount
Liberexim BV and Staatssecretaris van Financiën	C371/99	Removal of goods from customs supervision
Van der Kooy A.J. v Staatssecretaris van Financiën	C181/97	Import of boat from overseas province

TITLE VI

place of taxable transactions

Article 8

Supply of goods

s 3(6) **1.** The place of supply of goods shall be deemed to be:

(a) in the case of goods dispatched or transported either by the supplier or by the person to whom they are supplied or by a third person: the place where the goods are at the time when dispatch or transport to the person to whom they are supplied begins. Where the goods are installed or assembled, with or without a trial run, by or on behalf of the supplier, the place of supply shall be deemed to be the place where the goods are installed or assembled. In cases where the installation or assembly is carried out [in a Member State other than][1] that of the supplier, [the Member State within the territory of which the installation or assembly is carried out][2] shall take any necessary steps to avoid double taxation in that State;

(b) in the case of goods not dispatched or transported: the place where the goods are when the supply takes place.

[(c) in the case of goods supplied on board ships, aircraft or trains during the part of a transport of passengers effected in the Community: at the point of the departure of the transport of passengers.

For the purposes of applying this provision:

— `part of a transport of passengers effected in the Community' shall mean the part of the transport effected, without a stop in a third territory, between the point of departure and the point of arrival of the transport of passengers,

— `the point of departure of the transport of passengers' shall mean the first point of passenger embarkation foreseen within the Community, where relevant after a leg outside the Community,

— `the point of arrival of the transport of passengers' shall mean the last point of disembarkation of passengers foreseen within the Community of passengers who embarked in the Community, where relevant before a leg outside the Community.

In the case of a return trip, the return leg shall be considered to be a separate transport.

The Commission shall, by 30 June 1993 at the latest, submit to the Council a report accompanied, if necessary, by appropriate proposals on the place of taxation of goods supplied for consumption and services, including restaurant services, provided for passengers on board ships, aircraft or trains.

By 31 December 1993, after consulting the European Parliament, the Council shall take a unanimous decision on the Commission proposal.

Until 31 December 1993, Member States may exempt or continue to exempt goods supplied for consumption on board whose place of taxation is determined in accordance with the above provisions, with the right to deduct the value added tax paid at an earlier stage.][3]

[(d)   in the case of the supply of gas through the natural gas distribution system, or of electricity, to a taxable dealer: the place where that taxable dealer has established his business or has a fixed establishment for which the goods are supplied, or, in the absence of such a place of business or fixed establishment, the place where he has his permanent address or usually resides.

"**Taxable dealer**" for the purposes of this provision means a taxable person whose principal activity in respect of purchases of gas and electricity is reselling such products and whose own consumption of these products is negligible.

[(e)   in the case of the supply of gas through the natural gas distribution system, or of electricity, where such a supply is not covered by point (d): the place where the customer has effective use and consumption of the goods. Where all or part of the goods are not in fact consumed by this customer, these non consumed goods are deemed to have been used and consumed at the place where he has established his business or has a fixed establishment for which the goods are supplied. In the absence of such a place of business or fixed establishment, he is deemed to have used and consumed the goods at the place where he has his permanent address or usually resides.][4]

s3(6)(a) [2.   By way of derogation from paragraph 1(a), where the place of departure of the consignment or transport of goods is in a third territory, the place of supply by the importer as defined in Article 21(2) and the place of any subsequent supplies shall be deemed to be within the Member State of import of the goods.][5]

Amendments
1   Substituted by Art 1(3), Council Directive 91/680/EEC of 16 December 1991, w.e.f. 1 January 1993.
2   Substituted by Art 1(3), Council Directive 91/680/EEC of 16 December 1991, w.e.f. 1 January 1993.
3   Substituted by Art 1(4), Council Directive 92/111/EEC of 14 December 1992, w.e.f. 1 January 1993.
4   Inserted by Art 1(1), Council Directive 2003/92/EC of 7 October 2003, w.e.f. 1 January 2005.
5   Substituted by Art 1(5), Council Directive 91/680/EEC of 16 December 1991, w.e.f. 1 January 1993.

Case law

Aktiebolaget NN v Skatteverket	C111/05	Place of transaction/Supply and installation/Under sea fibre optic cable
Köhler, Antje v Finanzamt Düsseldorf-Nord	C58/04	Supplies on board cruise ships/Stops in a third territory

Article 9
Supply of services

s 5(5) **1.** The place where a service is supplied shall be deemed to be the place where the supplier has established his business or has a fixed establishment from which the service is supplied or, in the absence of such a place of business or fixed establishment, the place where he has his permanent address or usually resides.

2. However:

s5(6)(a)   (a) the place of the supply of services connected with immovable property, including the services of estate agents and experts, and of services for preparing and coordinating construction works, such as the services of architects and of firms providing on-site supervision, shall be the place where the property is situated;

s5(6)(b)
s5(6)(f) ii   (b) the place where transport services are supplied shall be the place where transport takes place, having regard to distances covered;

s5(6)(c)   (c) the place of the supply of services relating to:

  — cultural, artistic, sporting, scientific, educational, entertainment or similar activities, including the activities of the organizers of such activities, and where appropriate, the supply of ancillary services,

  — ancillary transport activities such as loading, unloading, handling and similar activities,

  — valuations of movable tangible property,

  — work on movable tangible property,

  shall be the place where those services are physically carried out;

  (d) [....]¹

s5(6)(e)   (e) the place where the following services are supplied when performed for customers established outside the Community or for taxable persons established in the Community but not in the same country as the supplier, shall be the place where the customer has established his business or has a fixed establishment to which the service is supplied or, in the absence of such a place, the place where he has his permanent address or usually resides:

  — transfers and assignments of copyrights, patents, licences, trade marks and similar rights,

  — advertising services,

  — services of consultants, engineers, consultancy bureaus, lawyers, accountants, and other similar services, as well as data processing and the supplying of information,

  — obligations to refrain from pursuing or exercising, in whole or in part, a business activity or a right referred to in this point (e),

  — banking, financial and insurance transactions including reinsurance, with the exception of the hire of safes,

  — the supply of staff,

– the services of agents who act in the name and for the account of another, when they procure for their principal the services referred to in this point (e),

[– the hiring out of movable tangible property, with the exception of all forms of transport;][2]

[– the provision of access to, and of transport or transmission through, natural gas and electricity distribution systems and the provision of other directly linked services.][3]

[– Telecommunications. Telecommunications services shall be deemed to be services relating to the transmission, emission or reception of signals, writing, images and sounds or information of any nature by wire, radio, optical or other electromagnetic systems, including the related transfer or assignment of the right to use capacity for such transmission, emission or reception. Telecommunications services within the meaning of this provision shall also include provision of access to global information networks[,][4]][5]

[– radio and television broadcasting services,

– electronically supplied services, inter alia, those described in Annex L.][6]

)(eee)   [(f)   the place where services referred to in the last indent of subparagraph (e) are supplied when performed for non-taxable persons who are established, have their permanent address or usually reside in a Member State, by a taxable person who has established his business or has a fixed establishment from which the service is supplied outside the Community or, in the absence of such a place of business or fixed establishment, has his permanent address or usually resides outside the Community, shall be the place where the non-taxable person is established, has his permanent address or usually resides.][6]

5(6)(d), **3.**   [In order to avoid double taxation, non-taxation or the distortion of
1d),   competition, the Member States may, with regard to the supply of services
1dd),   referred to in paragraph 2(e), except for the services referred to in the last
1ddd).   indent when supplied to non-taxable persons, and also with regard to the
                hiring out of forms of transport consider:][4]

(a) the place of supply of services, which under this Article would be situated within the territory of the country, as being situated outside the Community where the effective use and enjoyment of the services take place outside the Community;

(b) the place of supply of services, which under this Article would be situated outside the Community, as being within the territory of the country where the effective use and enjoyment of the services take place within the territory of the country.

5(6)(dd) **[4.**   In the case of telecommunications services and radio and television broadcasting services referred to in paragraph 2(e) when performed for non-taxable persons who are established, have their permanent address or usually reside in a Member State, by a taxable person who has established his business or has a fixed establishment from which the service is supplied outside the Community, or in the absence of such a place of business or fixed establishment, has his permanent address or usually resides outside the Community, Member States shall make use of paragraph 3(b).][4]

Amendments

1   Deleted by Art 1, Council Directive 84/386/EEC of 31 July 1984, w.e.f. 1 July 1985.
2   Inserted by Art 1, Council Directive 84/386/EEC of 31 July 1984, w.e.f. 1 July 1985.
3   Inserted by Art 1(2), Council Directive 2003/92/EC of 7 October, w.e.f. 1 January 2005.
4   Substituted by Art 1, Council Directive 2002/38/EC of 7 May 2002, w.e.f. 15 May 2002.
5   Inserted by Art 1(1), Council Directive 99/59/EC of 17 June 1999, w.e.f. 26 June 1999.
6   Inserted by Art 1, Council Directive 2002/38/EC of 7 May 2002. Amended with effect from 15 May 2002 and provisions applicable from 1 July 2003.

Case law

Aro Lease BV/Inspecteur der Belastingdienst Grote Ondernemingen, Amsterdam	C190/95	Place of Supply/Leasing of means of transport
Banque Bruxelles Lambert SA v Belgian State	C8/03	Place of supply/Concept of taxable person
Berkholz, Gunter v Finanzamt Hamburg Mitte Alstadt	C168/84	Place of Supplies/Gaming Machines on board Ferries
Design Concept SA and Flanders Expo SA	C438/01	Advertising services/supplied indirectly
Dudda, Jurgen v Finanzant Bergisch Gladback	C327/94	Place of Supply
Fischer, Karlheinz v Finanzamt Donaueschingen	C283/95	Arbitrator place of supply
France v European Commission	C68/92	Place of supply Advertising Services
Gillan Beach Ltd v Ministre de l'Économie, des Finances et de l'Industrie	C114/05	Services connected with boat shows/Article 9(2)(c)
Heger Rudi GmbH v Finanzamt Graz - Stadt	C166/05	Place of supply/Transmission of fishing rights
Kollektivavtalsstiftelsen TRR Trygghetsrådet v Skatteverket	C291/07	Place of supply
Leaseplan Luxembourg SA v Belgium	C390/96	Place of Supply
Levob Verzekeringen BV, OV Bank NV v Staatssecretaris van Financiën	C41/04	Supply and customisation of software
Maatschap M.J.M Linthorst, KGP. Pouwels and Scheres v Inspecteur der Belastingdienst/Ondermingen Roermond	C167/95	Place of supply
Madgett (TP) and Baldwin (RM) (T/A Howden Court Hotel) v Customs and Excise	C308/96	Hotel/Tour Operators
RAL (Channel Islands) Ltd and Others v Commissioners of Customs & Excise	C452/03	Slot gaming machines/Place of supply
Reiseburo Binder GmBH v Finanzamt Stuttgart-Korperschaften	C116/96	Place of Supply of Transport Services
Syndicat des Producteurs Independents (SPI) v Ministere de l'economie, des finances et de l'industrie	C108/00	Place of Supply of Advertising Services/Supplied by Third Party
Von Hoffman, Bernd v Finanzamt Trier	C145/96	Arbitrator/Place of Supply

TITLE VII

chargeable event and chargeability of tax

Article 10

1)(a) **1.** (a) **'Chargeable event'** shall mean the occurrence by virtue of which the legal conditions necessary for tax to become chargeable are fulfilled.

s 19 (b) The tax becomes **'chargeable'** when the tax authority becomes entitled under the law at a given moment, to claim the tax from the person liable to pay, notwithstanding that the time of payment may be deferred.

2(1)(a) **2.** The chargeable event shall occur and the tax shall become chargeable when the goods are delivered or the services are performed. Deliveries of goods other than those referred to in Article 5(4)(b) and supplies of services which give rise to successive statements of account or payments shall be regarded as being completed at the time when the periods to which such statements of account or payments pertain expire. [Member States may in certain cases provide that continuous supplies of goods and services which take place over a period of time shall be regarded as being completed at least at intervals of one year.][1]

s 19(2) However, where a payment is to be made on account before the goods are delivered or the services are performed, the tax shall become chargeable on receipt of the payment and on the amount received.

By way of derogation from the above provisions, Member States may provide that the tax shall become chargeable, for certain transactions or for certain categories of taxable person either:

— no later than the issue of the invoice [....][2]; or

— no later than receipt of the price; or

— where an invoice [....][2] is not issued, or is issued late, within a specified period from the date of the chargeable event.

s 15(6) **[3.** The chargeable event shall occur and the tax shall become chargeable when the goods are imported. Where goods are placed under one of the arrangements referred to in Article 7(3) on entry into the Community, the chargeable event shall occur and the tax shall become chargeable only when the goods cease to be covered by these arrangements.

However, where imported goods are subject to customs duties, to agricultural levies or to charges having equivalent effect established under a common policy, the chargeable event shall occur and the tax shall become chargeable when the chargeable event for those Community duties occurs and those duties become chargeable.

Where imported goods are not subject to any of those Community duties, Member States shall apply the provisions in force governing customs duties as regards the occurrence of the chargeable event and the moment when the tax becomes chargeable.][3]

Amendments
1 Inserted by Art 1, Council Directive 2000/65/EC, w.e.f. 17 October 2000.
2 Deleted by Art 4, Council Directive 2001/115/EC of 20 December 2001,(w.e.f. 6 February 2002).
3 Substituted by Art 1(6), Council Directive 91/680/EEC of 16 December 1991, w.e.f. 1 January 1993.

Case law

Balocchi, Maurizio v Ministero delle Finanze dello Stato	C10/92	Payment of VAT before Taxable Event
BUPA Hospitals Ltd, Goldsborough Developments Ltd v Commissioners of Customs & Excise	C419/02	Payment on account/Chargeable Event/Taxable person/Entitlement to VAT recovery
Italittica Spa v Ufficio IVA di Trapani	C144/94	Taxable Event/Receipt of payment
Pezzulo Molini Pastifici Mangimifici Spa v Ministero delle Finanze	C166/94	Payment on default interest on Imports

TITLE VIII

taxable amount

Article 11

s 10

A. Within the territory of the country

1. The taxable amount shall be:

   (a) in respect of supplies of goods and services other than those referred to in (b), (c) and (d) below, everything which constitutes the consideration which has been or is to be obtained by the supplier from the purchaser, the customer or a third party for such supplies including subsidies directly linked to the price of such supplies;

s 10(4)   (b) in respect of supplies referred to in Article 5(6) and (7), the purchase price of the goods or of similar goods or, in the absence of a purchase price, the cost price, determined at the time of supply;

s 10(4)   (c) in respect of supplies referred to in Article 6(2), the full cost to the taxable person of providing the services;

   (d) in respect of supplies referred to in Article 6(3), the open market value of the services supplied.

   [...]¹

s 10(1) 2. The taxable amount shall include:

   (a) taxes, duties, levies and charges, excluding the value added tax itself;

   (b) incidental expenses such as commission, packing, transport and insurance costs charged by the supplier to the purchaser or customer. Expenses covered by a separate agreement may be considered to be incidental expenses by the Member States.

s 10(3) 3. The taxable amount shall not include:

   (a) price reductions by way of discount for early payment;

   (b) price discounts and rebates allowed to the customer and accounted for at the time of the supply;

   (c) the amounts received by a taxable person from his purchaser or customer as repayment for expenses paid out in the name and for the account of the latter and which are entered in his books in a suspense account. The taxable person must furnish proof of the actual amount of this expenditure and may not deduct any tax which may have been charged on these transactions.

[4. By way of derogation from paragraphs 1, 2 and 3, Member States which, on 1 January 1993, did not avail themselves of the option provided for in the third subparagraph of Article 12(3)(a) may, where they avail themselves of the option provided for in Title B(6), provide that, for the transactions referred to in the second subparagraph of Article 12(3)(c), the taxable amount shall be equal to a fraction of the amount determined in accordance with paragraphs 1, 2 and 3.

That fraction shall be determined in such a way that the value added tax thus due is, in any event, equal to at least 5% of the amount determined in accordance with paragraphs 1,2 and 3.][2]

[5. Member States shall have the option of including in the taxable amount in respect of the supply of goods and services, the value of exempt investment gold within the meaning of Article 26b, which has been provided by the customer to be used as a basis for working and which as a result, loses its VAT exempt investment gold status when such goods and services are supplied. The value to be used is the open market value of the investment gold at the time that those goods and services are supplied.

6. In order to prevent tax evasion or avoidance, Member States may take measures to ensure that the taxable amount in respect of a supply of goods or services shall be the open market value. The option shall be applied only in respect of supplies of goods and services involving family or other close personal ties, management, ownership, membership, financial or legal ties as defined by the Member State. For these purposes legal ties may include the relationship between an employer and employee or the employee's family, or any other closely connected persons.

The option in the first subparagraph may apply only in any of the following circumstances:

(a) where the consideration is lower than the open market value and the recipient of the supply does not have a full right of deduction under Article 17;

(b) where the consideration is lower than the open market value and the supplier does not have a full right of deduction under Article 17 and the supply is subject to an exemption under Article 13 or Article 28(3)(b);

(c) where the consideration is higher than the open market value and the supplier does not have a full right of deduction under Article 17.

Member States may restrict the categories of suppliers or recipients to whom the measures in the first and the second subparagraph shall apply.

Member States shall inform the Committee established in accordance with Article 29 of any new national measure adopted pursuant to the provisions of this paragraph.

7. For the purposes of this Directive, "open market value" shall mean the full amount that, in order to obtain the goods or services in question at that time, a customer at the same marketing stage at which the supply of goods or services takes place, would have to pay, under conditions of fair competition, to a supplier at arm's length within the territory of the Member State in which the supply is subject to tax.

Where no comparable supply of goods or services can be ascertained, "open market value" shall mean, in respect of goods, an amount that is not less than the purchase price of the goods or of similar goods or, in the absence of a purchase price, the cost price, determined at the time of supply; in respect of services it shall mean not less than the full cost to the taxable person of providing the service.][3]

s 15

B. Importation of goods

[1. The taxable amount shall be the value for customs purposes, determined in accordance with the Community provisions in force; this shall also apply for the import of goods referred to in Article 7(1)(b).][4]

2. [....][5]

[3. The taxable amount shall include, in so far as they are not already included:

   (a) taxes, duties, levies and other charges due outside the importing Member State and those due by reason of importation, excluding the value added tax to be levied;

   (b) incidental expenses, such as commission, packing, transport and insurance costs, incurred up to the first place of destination within the territory of the importing Member State.

   'First place of destination' shall mean the place mentioned on the consignment note or any other document by means of which the goods are imported into the importing Member State. In the absence of such an indication, the first place of destination shall be taken to be the place of the first transfer of cargo in the importing Member State.

   [The incidental expenses referred to above shall also be included in the taxable amount where they result from transport to an other place of destination within the territory of the Community if that place is known when the chargeable event occurs.][6]][7]

4. The taxable amount shall not include those factors referred to in point A 3(a) and (b).

5. When goods have been temporarily exported [from the Community][8] and are reimported after having undergone [outside the Community][9] repair, processing or adaptation, or after having been made up or reworked [outside the Community][9], [...][10], Member States shall take steps to ensure that the treatment of the goods for value added tax purposes is the same as that which would have applied to the goods in question had the above operations been carried out within the territory of the country.

[6. By way of derogation from paragraphs 1 to 4, Member States which, on 1 January 1993, did not avail themselves of the option provided for in the third subparagraph of Article 12(3)(a) may provide that for imports of the works of art, collectors' items and antiques defined in Article 26a(A) (a), (b) and (c), the taxable amount shall be equal to a fraction of the amount determined in accordance with paragraphs 1 to 4.

   That fraction shall be determined in such a way that the value added tax thus due on the import is, in any event, equal to at least 5% of the amount determined in accordance with paragraphs 1 to 4.][11]

C. Miscellaneous provisions

s10(3)(c) **1.** In the case of cancellation, refusal or total or partial non-payment or where the price is reduced after the supply takes place, the taxable amount shall be reduced accordingly under conditions which shall be determined by the Member States.

However, in the case of total or partial non-payment, Member States may derogate from this rule.

s10(9A) **[2.** Where information for determining the taxable amount on importation is expressed in a currency other than that of the Member State where assessment takes place, the exchange rate shall be determined in accordance with the Community provisions governing the calculation of the value for customs purposes.

Where information for the determination of the taxable amount of a transaction other than an import transaction is expressed in a currency other than that of the Member State where assessment takes place, the exchange rate applicable shall be the latest selling rate recorded, at the time the tax becomes chargeable, on the most representative exchange market or markets of the Member State concerned, or a rate determined by reference to that or those markets, in accordance with the procedures laid down by that Member State. However, for some of those transactions or for certain categories of taxable person, Member States may continue to apply the exchange rate determined in accordance with the Community provisions in force governing the calculation of the value for customs purposes.][12]

3. As regards returnable packing costs, Member States may:

— either exclude them from the taxable amount and take the necessary measures to see that this amount is adjusted if the packing is not returned,

— or include them in the taxable amount and take the necessary measures to see that this amount is adjusted where the packing is in fact returned.

Amendments
1 Deleted by Art 1(3)(a) Council Directive 2006/69/EC of 24 July 2006 w.e.f. 13 August 2006.
2 Inserted by Art 1(1)(a), Council Directive 94/5/EC of 14 February 1994, w.e.f. 1 January 1995.
3 Inserted by Art 1(3)(b) Council Directive 2006/69/EC of 24 July 2006 w.e.f. 13 August 2006.
4 Substituted by Art 1(5), Council Directive 92/111/EEC of 14 December 1992, w.e.f. 1 January 1993.
5 Deleted by Art 1(1)(7)(2nd indent), Council Directive 91/680/EEC of 16 December 1991, w.e.f. 1 January 1993.
6 Substituted by Art 1(1)(2), Council Directive 95/7/EC of 10 April 1995, w.e.f. 1 January 1996.
7 Substituted by Art 1(1)(8), Council Directive 91/680/EEC of 16 December 1991, w.e.f. 1 January 1993.
8 Inserted by Art 1(9), Council Directive 91/680/EEC of 16 December 1991, w.e.f. 1 January 1993.
9 Substituted by Art 1(1)(9), Council Directive 91/680/EEC of 16 December 1991, w.e.f. 1 January 1993.
10 Deleted by Art 1(1)(a), Council Directive 91/680/EEC of 16 December 1991, w.e.f. 1 January 1993.
11 Inserted by Art 1(1)(b), Council Directive 94/5/EC of 14 February 1994, w.e.f. 1 January 1995.
12 Substituted by Art 1(1)(10), Council Directive 91/680/EEC of 16 December 1991, w.e.f. 1 January 1993.

Case law

Baz Bausystem AG v Finanzamt Munchen fur Korperschaften	C222/81	Taxable Amount
Belgium v European Commission	C391/85	Taxable Amount
Bergeres - Becque v Chef de Service Interregional des Douanes Bordeaux	C39/85	Imports/Taxable amount
Bertelsmann AG v Finanzamt Wiedenbrück	C380/99	Taxable amount/Delivery costs of bonuses in kind
Boots Company plc v Customs and Excise	C126/88	Taxable Amount/Vouchers
De Danske Bilimportorer v Skatteministeriet	C98/05	Taxable amount/Registration duty on new motor vehicles
Elida Gibbs Ltd v Customs and Excise	C317/94	Taxable Amount/Discount
Freemans plc v Customs and Excise	C86/99	Taxable amount/Discount accounted for at the time of the supply/Price reduction after the supply takes place
Germany v Commission	C427/98	Taxable amount/Money-off coupons
Glawe Spiel and Unterhaltungsgeraete Aufstellungsgesellschaft mBH and Co. KG v Finanzamt Hamburg Barmbek – Uhlenhorst	C38/93	Taxable Amount
Goldsmith (Jewellers) Ltd v Customs and Excise	C330/95	Taxable Amount
K Line Air Service Europe BV v Eulaerts NV and Belgium	C131/91	Minimum Taxable Amount
Keeping Newcastle Warm Limited v Customs & Excise	C353/00	Taxable amount/Subsidy
Koninklijke Ahold Fiscale eenheid v Staatsecretaris van Financiën	C484/06	Principles of fiscal neutrality and proportionality – Rules concerning rounding of amounts of VAT
Kuwait Petroleum (GB) Ltd v Customs and Excise	C48/97	Taxable Amount/Vouchers
Muys en de Winter's Bouw-en Aannemingsbedrijf BV v Staatssecretaris van Financiën	C281/91	Taxable Amount interest paid to supplier
Naturally Yours Cosmetics Ltd v Customs and Excise	C230/87	Taxable Amount party plan sales
Netherlands v European Commission	C16/84	Taxable Amount/Trade ins
Office des produits wallons ASBL v Belgian State	C184/00	Taxable amount/Subsidies directly linked to the price
Part Service Srl v Ministero dell'Economia e delle Finanze, formerly Ministero delle Finanze	C425/06	Artificial division of the supply into a number of parts/Reduction of the taxable amount/Abusive practice
Primback Ltd v Customs and Excise	C34/99	Taxable Amount
Town & County Factors Ltd v Customs and Excise	C498/99	Scope/Taxable Amount
Yorkshire Co-operatives Ltd v Customs & Excise	C398/99	Reduction Coupons/Taxable amount in hands of retailer

TITLE IX

s 11

rates

Article 12

1. The rate applicable to taxable transactions shall be that in force at the time of the chargeable event. However:

   (a) in the cases provided for in the second and third subparagraphs of Article 10(2), the rate to be used shall be that in force when the tax becomes chargeable;

   (b) [in the cases provided for in the second and third subparagraphs of Article 10(3), the rate applicable shall be that in force at the time when the tax becomes chargeable.][1]

s35(1A) 2. In the event of change in the rates, Member States may:

   — effect adjustments in the cases provided for in paragraph 1(a) in order to take account of the rate applicable at the time when the goods or services were supplied,

   — adopt all appropriate transitional measures.

s11(1) 3. [[(a) The standard rate of value added tax shall be fixed by each Member State as a percentage of the taxable amount and shall be the same for the supply of goods and for the supply of services. From 1 January 2006 until 31 December 2010, the standard rate may not be less than 15%.

   The Council shall decide, in accordance with Article 93 of the Treaty, on the level of the standard rate to be applied after 31 December 2010.][2]

   Member States may also apply either one or two reduced rates. These rates shall be fixed as a percentage of the taxable amount, which may not be less than 5%, and shall apply only to supplies of the categories of goods and services specified in Annex H.][3]

   [The third subparagraph shall not apply to the services referred to in the last indent of Article 9(2)(e).][4]

s11(1) [(b) Member States may apply a reduced rate to supplies of natural gas, electricity and district heating provided that no risk of distortion of competition exists. A Member State intending to apply such a rate must inform the Commission before doing so. The Commission shall give a decision on the existence of a risk of distortion of competition. If the Commission has not taken that decision within three months of the receipt of the information a risk of distortion of competition is deemed not to exist.][5]

s11(1AA) [(c) Member States may provide that the reduced rate, or one of the reduced rates, which they apply in accordance with the third paragraph of (a) shall also apply to imports of works of art, collectors' items and antiques as referred to in Article 26a(A)(a), (b) and (c).

Where they avail themselves of this option, Member States may also apply the reduced rate to supplies of works of art, within the meaning of Article 26a(A)(a):

— effected by their creator or his successors in title,

— effected on an occasional basis by a taxable person other than a taxable dealer, where these works of art have been imported by the taxable person himself or where they have been supplied to him by their creator or his successors in title or where they have entitled him to full deduction of value-added tax.][6]

(d) [....][7]

(e) [....][8]

11(1) 4. [....][9] Each reduced rate shall be so fixed that the amount of value added tax resulting from the application thereof shall be such as in the normal way to permit the deduction therefrom of the whole of the value added tax deductible under the provisions of Article 17.

[On the basis of a report from the Commission, the Council shall, starting in 1994, review the scope of the reduced rates every two years. The Council, acting unanimously on a proposal from the Commission, may decide to alter the list of goods and services in Annex H.][10]

[By 30 June 2007 at the latest the Commission shall present to the European Parliament and the Council an overall assessment report on the impact of reduced rates applying to locally supplied services, including restaurant services, notably in terms of job creation, economic growth and the proper functioning of the internal market, based on a study carried out by an independent economic think-tank.][11]

[5. Subject to paragraph 3(c), the rate applicable on the importation of goods shall be that applied to the supply of like goods within the territory of the country.][12]

[6. The Portuguese Republic may apply to transactions carried out in the autonomous regions of the Azores and Madeira and to direct imports to those regions, reduced rates in comparison to those applying on the mainland.][13]

Amendments
1 Substituted by Art 1(6), Council Directive 92/111/EEC of 14 December 1992, (w.e.f. 1 January 1993).
2 Substituted by Art 1, Council Directive 2005/92/EC of 12 December 2005, (w.e.f. 28 December 2005).
3 Substituted by Art 1, Council Directive 99/49/EC of 25 May 1999, (w.e.f. 1 January 1999).
4 Inserted by Art 1, Council Directive 2002/38/EC of 7 May 2002. Amended with effect from 15 May 2002 and provisions applicable from 1 July 2003.
5 Substituted by Art 1(1)(a), Council Directive 2006/18/EC of 14 February 2006 (w.e.f. 1 January 2006).
6 Substituted by Art 1(2)(a), Council Directive 94/5/EC of 14 February 1994, (w.e.f. 1 January 1995).
7 Deleted by Art 1, Council Directive 96/42/EC of 25 June 1996, (w.e.f. 1 January 1995).
8 Deleted by Art 2, Council Directive 98/80/EC of 12 October 1998, (w.e.f. 17 October 1998).
9 Deleted by Art 1(3), Council Directive 92/77/EEC of 19 October 1992, (w.e.f. 1 January 1993).
10 Inserted by Art 1(3), Council Directive 92/77/EEC of 19 October 1992, (w.e.f. 1 January 1993).
11 Inserted by Art 1(1)(b), Council Directive 2006/18/EC of 14 February 2006 (w.e.f. 1 January 2006).
12 Substituted by Art 1(2)(b), Council Directive 94/5/EC of 14 February 1994, (w.e.f. 1 January 1995).
13 Inserted by Art 26, Annex I, Part V, Point 2, the Act of Accession 1985.

Case law

Cablelink v Inspector of Taxes	Irish S.C. Dec 2003	Separate supplies/Connections services/TV and radio signals
Gmurzynska - Bscher, Krystyna v Oberfinanzdirektion Koln	C231/89	Imports/Rates of VAT
Italy v European Commission	C278/83	Sparkling Wines Excise Duty
Italy v European Commission	C200/85	Imports/Rates
Marks & Spencer plc v The Commissioners for Her Majesty's Revenue and Customs	C309/06	Exemption with refund of tax paid at the preceding stage
Zweckverband zur Trinkwasserversorgung und Abwasserbeseitigung Torgau-Westelbien v Finanzamt Oschatz	C442/05	"Suppy of water" or "Water supply"

TITLE X

exemptions

Article 13

Exemptions within the territory of the country

A. Exemptions for certain activities in the public interest

1. Without prejudice to other Community provisions, Member States shall exempt the following under conditions which they shall lay down for the purpose of ensuring the correct and straightforward application of such exemptions and of preventing any possible evasion, avoidance or abuse:

ˢᵗSch
- (xia)

   (a) the supply by the public postal services of services other than passenger transport and telecommunications services, and the supply of goods incidental thereto;

h
(iiia),
,(v),
/).

   (b) hospital and medical care and closely related activities undertaken by bodies governed by public law or, under social conditions comparable to those applicable to bodies governed by public law, by hospitals, centres for medical treatment or diagnosis and other duly recognized establishments of a similar nature;

Sch
),(iiia),
b),(v),

   (c) the provision of medical care in the exercise of the medical and paramedical professions as defined by the Member State concerned;

Sch
iii),

   (d) supplies of human organs, blood and milk;

Sch
iia)

   (e) services supplied by dental technicians in their professional capacity and dental prostheses supplied by dentists and dental technicians;

Sch
viii)

   (f) services supplied by independent groups of persons whose activities are exempt from or are not subject to value added tax, for the purpose of rendering their members the services directly necessary for the exercise of their activity, where these groups merely claim from their members exact reimbursement of their share of the joint expenses, provided that such exemption is not likely to produce distortion of competition;

1ˢᵗSch
- (vii)

   (g) the supply of services and of goods closely linked to welfare and social security work, including those supplied by old people's homes, by bodies governed by public law or by other organizations recognized as charitable by the Member States concerned;

1ˢᵗSch
- (vi)

   (h) the supply of services and of goods closely linked to the protection of children and young persons by bodies governed by public law or by other organizations recognized as charitable by the Member States concerned;

1ˢᵗSch
- (ii)

   (i) children's or young people's education, school or university education, vocational training or retraining, including the supply of services and of goods closely related thereto, provided by bodies governed by public law having such as their aim or by other organizations defined by the Member States concerned as having similar objects;

1stSch
– (ii)

(j) tuition given privately by teachers and covering school or university education;

1stSch
–(ii),(iii),
(v), (vi).

(k) certain supplies of staff by religious or philosophical institutions for the purpose of subparagraphs (b), (g), (h) and (i) of this Article and with a view to spiritual welfare;

1stSch
– (xxii)

(l) supply of services and goods closely linked thereto for the benefit of their members in return for a subscription fixed in accordance with their rules by non-profit-making organizations with aims of a political, trade-union, religious, patriotic, philosophical, philanthropic or civic nature, provided that this exemption is not likely to cause distortion of competition;

1stSch
– (xxiii)

(m) certain services closely linked to sport or physical education supplied by non-profit-making organizations to persons taking part in sport or physical education;

1stSch
– (viii)
(viiia).

(n) certain cultural services and goods closely linked thereto supplied by bodies governed by public law or by other cultural bodies recognized by the Member State concerned;

(o) the supply of services and goods by organizations whose activities are exempt under the provisions of subparagraphs (b), (g), (h), (i), (l), (m) and (n) above in connection with fund-raising events organized exclusively for their own benefit provided that exemption is not likely to cause distortion of competition. Member States may introduce any necessary restrictions in particular as regards the number of events or the amount of receipts which give entitlement to exemption;

1stSch
– (xiv)

(p) the supply of transport services for sick or injured persons in vehicles specially designed for the purpose by duly authorized bodies;

1stSch
– (xiii)

(q) activities of public radio and television bodies other than those of a commercial nature.

2. (a) Member States may make the granting to bodies other than those governed by public law of each exemption provided for in (1)(b), (g), (h), (i), (l), (m) and (n) of this Article subject in each individual case to one or more of the following conditions:

— they shall not systematically aim to make a profit, but any profits nevertheless arising shall not be distributed but shall be assigned to the continuance or improvement of the services supplied,

— they shall be managed and administered on an essentially voluntary basis by persons who have no direct or indirect interest, either themselves or through intermediaries, in the results of the activities concerned,

— they shall charge prices approved by the public authorities or which do not exceed such approved prices or, in respect of those services not subject to approval, prices lower than those charged for similar services by commercial enterprises subject to value added tax,

— exemption of the services concerned shall not be likely to create distortion of competition such as to place at a disadvantage commercial enterprises liable to value added tax.

(b) The supply of services or goods shall not be granted exemption as provided for in (l)(b), (g), (h), (i), (l), (m) and (n) above if:

— it is not essential to the transactions exempted,

— its basic purpose is to obtain additional income for the organization by carrying out transactions which are in direct competition with those of commercial enterprises liable for value added tax.

B. Other exemptions

Without prejudice to other Community provisions, Member States shall exempt the following under conditions which they shall lay down for the purpose of ensuring the correct and straightforward application of the exemptions and of preventing any possible evasion, avoidance or abuse:

1st Sch
ix),(xi)

(a) insurance and reinsurance transactions, including related services performed by insurance brokers and insurance agents;

(b) the leasing or letting of immovable property excluding:

6th Sch
xiii)(a)

1. the provision of accommodation, as defined in the laws of the Member States, in the hotel sector or in sectors with a similar function, including the provision of accommodation in holiday camps or on sites developed for use as camping sites;

S11(1)

2. the letting of premises and sites for parking vehicles;

3. lettings of permanently installed equipment and machinery;

4. hire of safes.

Member States may apply further exclusions to the scope of this exemption;

1st Sch
-(xxiv)

(c) supplies of goods used wholly for an activity exempted under this Article or under Article 28(3)(b) when these goods have not given rise to the right to deduction, or of goods on the acquisition or production of which, by virtue of Article 17(6), value added tax did not become deductible;

(d) the following transactions:

1st Sch
(i)(e)

1. the granting and the negotiation of credit and the management of credit by the person granting it;

1st Sch
(i)(f)

2. the negotiation of or any dealings in credit guarantees or any other security for money and the management of credit guarantees by the person who is granting the credit;

1st Sch
(i)(c)

3. transactions, including negotiation, concerning deposit and current accounts, payments, transfers, debts, cheques and other negotiable instruments, but excluding debt collection and factoring;

1st Sch
(i)(d)

4. transactions, including negotiation, concerning currency, bank notes and coins used as legal tender, with the exception of collector's items; `collector's items' shall be taken to mean gold, silver or other metal coins or bank notes which are not normally used as legal tender or coins of numismatic interest;

1st Sch
-(xxiv)

5. transactions, including negotiation, excluding management and safekeeping, in shares, interests in companies or associations, debentures and other securities, excluding:

— documents establishing title to goods,

— the rights or securities referred to in Article 5(3);

1st Sch
(i)(g)

6. management of special investment funds as defined by Member States;

1st Sch
(xia)

(e) the supply at face value of postage stamps valid for use for postal services within the territory of the country, fiscal stamps and other similar stamps;

1st Sch
(xv)
(xvi)

(f) betting, lotteries and other forms of gambling, subject to conditions and limitations laid down by each Member State;

S 4

(g) the supply of buildings or parts thereof, and of the land on which they stand, other than as described in Article 4(3)(a);

(h) the supply of land which has not been built on other than building land as described in Article 4(3)(b).

s 7

C. Options

Member States may allow taxpayers a right of option for taxation in cases of:

(a) letting and leasing of immovable property;

(b) the transactions covered in B(d), (g) and (h) above.

Member States may restrict the scope of this right of option and shall fix the details of its use.

Case law

Abbey National plc v Commissioners of Customs & Excise	C169/04	Management of special investment funds/Meaning of 'management'
Akritidis, Savvas v Finanzamt Herne-West	C462/02	Games of chance/Exemption of/ Conditions to/Direct effect
Ambulanter Pflegedienst Kugler GmbH v Finanzamt Fur Korperschafte 1	C141/00	Medical care/Provision by Corporate bodies
Arthur Andersen & Co. Accountants c.s. v Staatssecretaris van Financiën	C472/03	Insurance related services/Back office activities/Exemption of
Assurandør-Societetet, acting on behalf of Taksatorringen and Skatteministeriet	C8/01	Independent groups
Blasi, Elizabeth v Finanzant Munchen	C346/95	Hotel or long term letting
Bulthuis Griffioen W v Inspecteur der Omzetbelasting Zaandam	C453/93	Medical services/Nursing home
Canterbury Hockey Club and Canterbury Ladies Hockey Club v The Commisioners for Her Majesty's Revenue and Customs	C253/07	Services linked to sport
Cantor Fitzgerald International v Commissioners of Customs & Excise	C108/99	Letting of immovable property/Third party taking over lease for consideration

Card Protection Plan Limited v Customs and Excise	C349/96	Composite supply/Insurance
Chassures Bally v Ministry of Finance Belgium	C18/92	Taxable Amount/Credit card transactions
Christoph-Dornier-Stiftung für Klinische Psychologie and Finanzamt Gießen	C45/01	Pscychotherapeutic treatment/Provided by foundation governed by public law
Cibo Participations SA v Directeur régional des impôts du Nord-Pas-de-Calais	C16/00	Holding Coy taxable person/Recovery of VAT
CSC Financial Services Limited (formerly Continuum Europe Ltd.) v Customs and Excise	C235/00	Transactions in securities/Reverse premiums on property
D (a minor) v W (on appeal by Osterreichischer Bundesschatz)	C384/98	Medical expert witnesses
Diagnostiko & Therapeftiko Kentro Athinon-Ygeia AE v Ipourgos Ikonomikon	C394/04 C395/04	Activities closely related to hospital and medical care
d'Ambrumenil, Peter, Dispute Resolution Services Ltd and Commissioners of Customs and Excise	C307/01	Medical services
Diners Club Ltd, The v The Revenue Commissioners	Irish H.C. iii ITR 680	Credit Cards/Exemption
Donner, Andreas Matthias v Netherlands	C39/82	Imports/Exemption
Empresa de Desenvolvimento Mineiro SGPS SA (EDM) and Fazenda Pública	C77/01	Meaning of 'economic activities'/Meaning of 'incidental financial transactions'/ Calculation of deductible proportion
First National Bank of Chicago v Customs and Excise	C172/96	Forex/Exempt
Fonden Marselisborg Lystbådehavn v Skatteministeriet	C428/02	Letting of premises and sites for parking boats/Mooring berths
France v Commission	C76/99	Medical supplies/Taking of samples
Germany v Commission	C287/00	Research activities
Gregg, Jennifer and Mervyn v Customs and Excise	C216/97	Medicine/Nursing home
H.A. Solleveld and JE van den Hout-van Eijnsbergen v Straatssecretaris van Financiën	C443/04 C444/04	Medical care/Paramedical professions/ Definition of
Hoffmann, Matthias	C144/00	Cultural bodies/soloists
Institute of the Motor Industry (the) v Customs and Excise	C149/97	Trade representative body/Taxable Person
Italy v European Commission	C45/95	Outside the scope/Exempt/Supplies where no VAT recovered
J.C.M Beeher B.V. v Staatssecretaris van Financiën	C124/07	Supply of services relating to insurance transactions/Insurance brokers and insurance agents
Jyske Finans A/S v Skatteministeriet	C280/04	Exemption of supplies excluded from the right to deduct/Meaning of taxable dealer
Kennemer Golf & Country Club v Staatssecretaris van Financiën	C174/00	Services connected with the practice of sport/Non-profit-making organisation
Kingscrest Associates Ltd, Montecello Ltd v Commissioners of Customs & Excise	C498/03	Meaning of charitable status
Linneweber, Edith v Finanzamt Gladbeck	C453/02	Games of chance/Exemption of/ Conditions to/Direct effect
Lubbock Fine and Company v Customs and Excise	C63/92	Property/Taxable Event
L.u.P GmbH v Finanzamt Bochum-Mitte	C106/05	Medical care/Conditions for exemption
Maierhofer, Rudolf and Finanzamt Augsburg-Land	C315/00	Letting of immovable property
Mirror Group plc v Customs & Excise	C409/98	Letting of immovable property/ Undertaking to become a tenant
MKG-Kraftfahrzeuge-Factory GmbH and Finanzamt Groß-Gerau	C305/01	Factoring

Sinclair Collis Ltd and Commissioners of Customs and Excise	C275/01	Letting of installed vending
Skandia v Forsakringsaktiebolaget	C240/99	Outsourcing
Spaarkassernes Datacenter v Skatteministeriet	C2/95	Exemption/Outsourcing for bank.
Spain v European Commission	C124/96	Club Membership/Sports
Stichting Central Begeleidingsorgaan voor de Intercollegiale Toetsing	C407/07	Exemptions – Services supplied by independent groups
Stichting 'Goed Wonen' v Staatssecretaris van Financiën	C326/99	Property/Rights in rem
Stichting Kinderopvang Enschede v Staatssecretaris van Financiën	C415/04	Intermediary services linked to welfare, social security work and childcare
Temco Europe SA v Belgian State	C284/03	Licence to occupy
Turn – und Sportunion Waldburg v Finanzlandesdirektion für Oberösterreich	C246/04	Property/Option to tax
United Kingdom v European Commission	C353/85	Who is taxable/Taxable Medicine (Services of practitioners in medical & paramedical professions opticians)
United Utilities plc v Commissioners of Customs & Excise	C89/05	Games of chance/Scope of exemption/ Activity of call centre
Unterpertinger, Margarete and Pensionsversicherungsanstalt der Arbeiter	C212/01	Doctor/expert report
VDP Dental Laboratory NV v Staatssecretaris van Financiën	C401/05	Scope of exemption/Manufacture and repair of dental protheses
Vermietungsgesellschaft Objekt Kirchberg SARL v État du grand-duché de Luxembourg	C269/03	Letting of immovable property/Right of option for taxation

Article 14
Exemptions on importation

1. Without prejudice to other Community provisions, Member States shall exempt the following under conditions which they shall lay down for the purpose of ensuring the correct and straightforward application of such exemption and of preventing any possible evasion, avoidance or abuse:

   (a) final importation of goods of which the supply by a taxable person would in all circumstances be exempted within the country;

   (b) [...][1]

   (c) [...][2]

   (d) final importation of goods qualifying for exemption from customs duties other than as provided for in the Common Customs Tariff [...][3]. However, Member States shall have the option of not granting an exemption where this would be liable to have a serious effect on conditions of competition [...][4],

   [This exemption shall also apply to the import of goods, within the meaning of Article 7(1)(b), which would be capable of benefiting from the exemption set out above if they had been imported within the meaning of Article 7(1)(a);][5]

   (e) reimportation by the person who exported them of goods in the state in which they were exported, where they qualify for exemption from customs duties [...][6],

   (f) [...][7]

   (g) importation of goods:

   — under diplomatic and consular arrangements, which qualify for exemption from customs duties [...],[8]

   — by international organizations recognized as such by the public authorities of the host country, and by members of such organizations, within the limits and under the conditions laid down by the international conventions establishing the organizations or by headquarters agreements,

   — into the territory of Member States which are parties to the North Atlantic Treaty by the armed forces of other States which are parties to that Treaty for the use of such forces or the civilian staff accompanying them or for supplying their messes or canteens where such forces take part in the common defence effort;

   [— the exemptions set out in the third indent shall extend to imports by and supplies of goods and services to the forces of the United Kingdom stationed in the island of Cyprus pursuant to the Treaty of Establishment concerning the Republic of Cyprus, dated 16 August 1960, which are for the use of the forces or the civilian staff accompanying them or for supplying their messes or canteens.][9]

(h) importation into ports by sea fishing undertakings of their catches, unprocessed or after undergoing preservation for marketing but before being supplied;

(i) the supply of services, in connection with the importation of goods where the value of such services is included in the taxable amount in accordance with Article 11B(3)(b);

(j) importation of gold by Central Banks.

[(k) import of gas through the natural gas distribution system, or of electricity.][10]

2. The Commission shall submit to the Council at the earliest opportunity proposals designed to lay down Community tax rules clarifying the scope of the exemptions referred to in paragraph 1 and detailed rules for their implementation.

Until the entry into force of these rules, Member States may:

— maintain their national provisions in force on matters related to the above provisions,

— adapt their national provisions to minimize distortion of competition and in particular the non-imposition or double imposition of value added tax within the Community,

— use whatever administrative procedures they consider most appropriate to achieve exemption.

Member States shall inform the Commission, which shall inform the other Member States, of the measures they have adopted and are adopting pursuant to the preceding provisions.

Amendments
1 Deleted by Art 1(11), Council Directive 91/680/EEC of 16 December 1991, (w.e.f. 1 January 1993).
2 Deleted by Art 1(8), Council Directive 92/111/EEC of 14 December 1992, (w.e.f. 1 January 1993).
3 Deleted by Art 1(11), Council Directive 91/680/EEC of 16 December 1991, (w.e.f. 1 January 1993).
4 Deleted by Art 1(11), Council Directive 91/680/EEC of 16 December 1991, (w.e.f. 1 January 1993).
5 Inserted by Art 1(8), Council Directive 92/111/EEC of 14 December 1992, (w.e.f. 1 January 1993).
6 Deleted by Art 1(11), Council Directive 91/680/EEC of 16 December 1991, (w.e.f. 1 January 1993).
7 Deleted by Art 1(11), Council Directive 91/680/EEC of 16 December 1991, (w.e.f. 1 January 1993).
8 Deleted by Art 1(11), Council Directive 91/680/EEC of 16 December 1991, (w.e.f. 1 January 1993).
9 Inserted by Protocol No. 3, Part 3, Treaty of Accession, w.e.f. 1 May 2004.
10 Inserted by Art 1(3), Council Directive 2003/92/EC of 7 October 2003, (w.e.f. 1 January 2005).

Case law

Abbink, Jan Gerrit	C134/83	Exempted/Imports/Criminal Proceedings
Apple & Pear Development Council v Customs and Excise	C102/86	Taxable person/Trade Association/Voluntary levy
Carciati Giovanni	C833/79	Imports/Value
Denmark v European Commission	C208/88	Travellers allowances
Ireland v European Commission	C158/88	Travellers allowances
Ireland v European Commission	C367/88	Travellers allowances
Profant, Venceslas v Ministere Publique and Ministry of Finance	C249/84	Imports of car to another Member State
Regie Dauphinoise - Cabinet A Forest Sarl v Ministre du Budget and AGFT	C306/94	Apportionment of VAT for recovery
Ryborg NC v Rigsadvoraten	C297/89	Criminal Proceedings/Import of untaxed car

Article 15

[Exemption of exports from the Community and like transactions and international transport][1]

Without prejudice to other Community provisions Member States shall exempt the following under conditions which they shall lay down for the purpose of ensuring the correct and straightforward application of such exemptions and of preventing any evasion, avoidance or abuse:

1. the supply of goods dispatched or transported to a destination outside the Community by or on behalf of the vendor;

2. the supply of goods dispatched or transported to a destination [outside the Community][2] by or on behalf of a purchaser not established within the territory of the country, with the exception of goods transported by the purchaser himself for the equipping, fuelling and provisioning of pleasure boats and private aircraft or any other means of transport for private use.

    [In the case of the supply of goods to be carried in the personal luggage of travellers this exemption shall apply on condition that:

    —   the traveller is not established within the Community;

    —   the goods are transported to a destination outside the Community before the end of the third month following that in which the supply is effected;

    —   the total value of the supply, including value added tax, is more than the equivalent in national currency of ECU 175, fixed in accordance with Article 7(2) of Directive 69/169/EEC; however, Member States may exempt a supply with a total value of less than that amount.

    For the purposes of applying the second subparagraph:

    —   a traveller not established within the Community shall be taken to mean a traveller whose domicile or habitual residence is not situated within the Community. For the purpose of this provision, **"domicile or habitual residence"** shall mean the place entered as such in a passport, identity card or other identity documents which the Member State within whose territory the supply takes place recognizes as valid;

    —   proof of exportation shall be furnished by means of the invoice or other documents in lieu therefore, endorsed by the customs office where the goods left the Community.

    Each Member State shall transmit to the Commission specimens of the stamps it uses for the endorsement referred to in the second indent of the third subparagraph. The Commission shall transmit this information to the tax authorities in the other Member State.][3]

[3. the supply of services consisting of work on movable property acquired or imported for the purpose of undergoing such work within the territory of the Community, and dispatched or transported out of the Community by the person providing the services or by the customer if [not established within the territory of the country][4] or on behalf of either of them;][5]

4. the supply of goods for the fuelling and provisioning of vessels:

(a) used for navigation on the high seas and carrying passengers for reward or used for the purpose of commercial, industrial or fishing activities;

(b) used for rescue or assistance at sea, or for inshore fishing, with the exception, for the latter, of ships' provisions;

(c) of war, as defined in subheading 89.01 A of the Common Customs Tariff, leaving the country and bound for foreign ports or anchorages.

[The Commission shall submit to the Council as soon as possible proposals to establish Community fiscal rules specifying the scope of and practical arrangements for implementing this exemption and the exemptions provided for in (5) to (9). Until these rules come into force, Member States may limit the extent of the exemption provided for in this paragraph.][6]

5. the supply, modification, repair, maintenance, chartering and hiring of the seagoing vessels referred to in paragraph 4(a) and (b) and the supply, hiring, repair and maintenance of equipment - including fishing equipment - incorporated or used therein;

6. the supply, modification, repair, maintenance, chartering and hiring of aircraft used by airlines operating for reward chiefly on international routes, and the supply, hiring, repair and maintenance of equipment incorporated or used therein;

7. the supply of goods for the fuelling and provisioning of aircraft referred to in paragraph 6;

8. the supply of services other than those referred to in paragraph 5, to meet the direct needs of the seagoing vessels referred to in that paragraph or of their cargoes;

9. the supply of services other than those referred to in paragraph 6, to meet the direct needs of aircraft referred to in that paragraph or of their cargoes;

10. supplies of goods and services:

    — under diplomatic and consular arrangements,

    — to international organizations recognized as such by the public authorities of the host country, and to members of such organizations, within the limits and under the conditions laid down by the international conventions establishing the organizations or by headquarters agreements,

    — effected within a Member State which is a party to the North Atlantic Treaty and intended either for the use of the forces of other States which are parties to that Treaty or of the civilian staff accompanying them, or for supplying their messes or canteens which such forces take part in the common defence effort,

    [— to another Member State and intended for the forces of any Member State which is a party to the North Atlantic Treaty, other than the Member State of destination itself, for the use of those forces or of the civilian staff accompanying them, or for supplying their messes or canteens when such forces take part in the common defence effort.][7]

This exemption shall be [subject to [limitations][8] laid down by the host Member State][9] until Community tax rules are adopted.

[In cases where the goods are not dispatched or transported out of the country, and in the case of services, the benefit of the exemption may be given by means of a refund of the tax.][10]

11. supplies of gold to Central Banks;

12. goods supplied to approved bodies which export them [from the Community][11] as part of their humanitarian, charitable or teaching activities [outside the community][12]. This exemption may be implemented by means of a refund of the tax;

[13. the supply of services, including transport and ancillary operations, but excluding the supply of services exempted in accordance with Article 13, where these are directly connected with the export of goods or imports of goods covered by the provisions of Article 7(3) or Article 16(1), Title A;][13]

14. services supplied by brokers and other intermediaries, acting in the name and for account of another person, where they form part of transactions specified in this Article or of transactions carried out [outside the Community][14].

This exemption does not apply to travel agents who supply in the name and for account of the traveller services which are supplied in other Member States.

[15. The Portuguese Republic may treat sea and air transport between the islands making up the autonomous regions of the Azores and Madeira and between those regions and the mainland in the same way as international transport.][15]

Amendments
1 Substituted by Art 1(12), Council Directive 91/680/EEC of 16 December 1991, (w.e.f. 1 January 1993).
2 Substituted by Art 1(13), Council Directive 91/680/EEC of 16 December 1991, (w.e.f. 1 January 1993).
3 Substituted by Art 1(3), Council Directive 95/7/EC of 10 April 1995, (w.e.f. 1 January 1996).
4 Substituted by Art 1(9), Council Directive 92/111/EEC of 14 December 1992, (w.e.f. 1 January 1993).
5 Substituted by Art 1(14), Council Directive 91/680/EEC of 16 December 1991, (w.e.f. 1 January 1993).
6 Substituted by Art 1(9), Council Directive 92/111/EEC of 14 December 1992, (w.e.f. 1 January 1993).
7 Substituted by Art 1(15), Council Directive 91/680/EEC of 16 December 1991, (w.e.f. 1 January 1993).
8 Substituted by Art 1(9), Council Directive 92/111/EEC of 14 December 1992, (w.e.f. 1 January 1993).
9 Substituted by Art 1(16), Council Directive 91/680/EEC of 16 December 1991, (w.e.f. 1 January 1993).
10 Substituted by Art 1(9), Council Directive 92/111/EEC of 14 December 1992, (w.e.f. 1 January 1993).
11 Substituted by Art 1(17), Council Directive 91/680/EEC of 16 December 1991, (w.e.f. 1 January 1993).
12 Substituted by Art 1(17), Council Directive 91/680/EEC of 16 December 1991, (w.e.f. 1 January 1993).
13 Substituted by Art 1(9), Council Directive 92/111/EEC of 14 December 1992, (w.e.f. 1 January 1993).
14 Substituted by Art 1(19), Council Directive 91/680/EEC of 16 December 1991, (w.e.f. 1 January 1993).
15 Inserted by Art 26, Annex I, Part V, Point 2, Act of Accession 1985.

Case law

Cimber Air A/S v Skatteministeriet	C382/02	Aircraft/Exemption/Meaning of 'operating chiefly on international routes'
Elmeka NE v Ipourgos Ikonomikon	C181/04 C182/04 C183/04	Chartering of sea-going vessels/Scope of exemption
Netto Supermarkt GmbH & Co. OHG v Finanzamt Malchin	C271/06	Exports/Conditions for exemption not fulfilled/ Proof of export falsified by the purchaser
Velker International Oil Company NV v Staatssecretaris van Finanzien	C185/89	Provisioning of Ships

Article 16

Special exemptions linked to international goods traffic

[1. Without prejudice to other Community tax provisions, Member States may, subject to the consultations provided for in Article 29, take special measures designed to exempt all or some of the following transactions, provided that they are not aimed at final use and/or consumption and that the amount of value added tax due on cessation of the arrangements on situations referred to at A to E corresponds to the amount of tax which would have been due had each of these transactions been taxed within the territory of the country:

A.   imports of goods which are intended to be placed under warehousing arrangements other than customs;

B.   supplies of goods which are intended to be:

    (a)   produced to customs and, where applicable, placed in temporary storage;

    (b)   placed in a free zone or in a free warehouse;

    (c)   placed under customs warehousing arrangements or inward processing arrangements;

    (d)   admitted into territorial waters:

        —   in order to be incorporated into drilling or production platforms, for purposes of the construction, repair, maintenance, alteration or fitting-out of such platforms, or to link such drilling or production platforms to the mainland,

        —   for the fuelling and provisioning of drilling or production platforms;

    (e)   placed, within the territory of the country, under warehousing arrangements other than customs warehousing.

For the purposes of this Article, warehouses other than customs warehouses shall be taken to be:

    —   for products subject to excise duty, the places defined as tax warehouses for the purposes of Article 4(b) of Council Directive 92/12/EEC;

    —   for goods other than those subject to excise duty, the places defined as such by the Member States. However, Member States may not provide for warehousing arrangements other than customs warehousing where the goods in question are intended to be supplied at the retail stage.

Nevertheless, Member States may provide for such arrangements for goods intended for:

- taxable persons for the purposes of supplies effected under the conditions laid down in Article 28k;

- tax-free shops within the meaning of Article 28k, for the purposes of supplies to travellers taking flights or sea crossing to third countries, where those supplies are exempt pursuant to Article 15;

- taxable persons for the purposes of supplies to travellers on board aircraft or vessels during a flight or sea crossings where the place of arrival is situated outside the Community;

- taxable persons for the purposes of supplies effected free of tax pursuant to Article 15(10).

The places referred to in (a), (b), (c) and (d) shall be as defined by the Community customs provisions in force.

C. supplies of services relating to the supplies of goods referred to in B;

D. supplies of goods and services carried out:

(a) in the places listed in B(a),(b),(c) and (d) and still subject to one of the situations specified therein;

(b) In the places listed in B(e) and still subject, within the territory of the country, to the situation specified therein.

Where they exercise the option provided for in (a) for transactions effected in customs warehouses Member States shall take the measures necessary to ensure that they have defined warehousing arrangements other than customs warehousing which permit the provisions in (b) to be applied to the same transactions concerning goods listed in Annex J which are effected in such warehouses other than customs warehouses;

E. supplies:

- of goods referred to in Article 7(1)(a) still subject to arrangements for temporary importation with total exemption from import duty or external transit arrangements,

- of goods referred to in Article 7(1)(b) still subject to the internal Community transit procedure provided for in Article 33a,

as well as supplies of services related to such supplies.

By way of derogation from the first subparagraph of Article 21(1) (a), the person liable to pay the tax due in accordance with the first subparagraph shall be the person who causes the goods to cease to be covered by the arrangements or situations listed in this paragraph.

When the removal of goods from the arrangements or situations referred to in this paragraph gives rise to importation within the meaning of Article 7(3), the Member State of import shall take the measures necessary to avoid double taxation within the country.][1]

[1a.   Where they exercise the option provided for in paragraph 1, Member States shall take the measures necessary to ensure that intra-Community acquisitions of goods intended to be placed under one of the arrangements or in one of the situations referred to in paragraph 1(B) benefit from the same provisions as supplies of goods effected within the country under the same conditions.][2]

s 13A

2.   Subject to the consultation provided for in Article 29, Member States may opt to exempt intra-Community acquisitions of goods made by a taxable person and imports for and supplies of goods to a taxable person intending to export them [outside the Community][3] as they are or after processing, as well as supplies of services linked with his export business, up to a maximum equal to the value of his exports during the preceding 12 months.

[When they take up this option the Member States shall, subject to the consultation provided for in Article 29, extend the benefit of this exemption to intra-Community acquisitions of goods by a taxable person, imports for and supplies of goods to a taxable person intending to supply them, as they are or after processing, under the conditions laid down in Article 28c(A), as will as supplies of services relating to such supplies, up to a maximum annual to the value of his supplies of goods effected under the conditions laid down in Article 28c(A) during the preceding twelve months.

Member States may set a common maximum amount for transactions which they exempt under the first and second subparagraphs.][4]

3.   The Commission shall submit to the Council at the earliest opportunity proposals concerning common arrangements for applying value added tax to the transactions referred to in paragraphs 1 and 2.

Amendments

1 Substituted by Art 28c(E)(1) (of Sixth Directive) as amended by Art 1(9), Council Directive 95/7/EC of 10 April 1995, (w.e.f. 1 January 1996 except Germany & Lux. From 1 January 1997).

2 Substituted by Art 28c(E)(1) (of Sixth Directive) as amended by Art 1(9), Council Directive 95/7/EC of 10 April 1995, (w.e.f. 1 January 1996 except Germany & Lux. From 1 January 1997).

3 Inserted by Art 28c(E) (of Sixth Directive) as inserted by Art 1(13), Council Directive 92/111/EEC of 14 December 1992, (w.e.f. 1 January 1993).

4 Inserted by Art 28c(E) (of Sixth Directive) as inserted by Art 1(13), Council Directive 92/111/EEC of 14 December 1992, (w.e.f. 1 January 1993).

TITLE XI

deductions

Article 17

Origin and scope of the right to deduct

1. The right to deduct shall arise at the time when the deductible tax becomes chargeable.

[2. In so far as the goods and services are used for the purposes of his taxable transactions, the taxable person shall be entitled to deduct from the tax which he is liable to pay:

   [(a) value added tax due or paid within the territory of the country in respect of goods or services supplied or to be supplied to him by another taxable person;][1]

   (b) value added tax due or paid in respect of imported goods within the territory of the country;

   (c) value added tax due pursuant to Articles 5(7)(a), 6(3) and 28a(6);

   (d) value added tax due pursuant to Article 28a(1)(a).][2]

[3. Member States shall also grant every taxable person the right to the deduction or refund of the value added tax referred to in paragraph 2 in so far as the goods and services are used for the purposes of:

   (a) transactions relating to the economic activities referred to in Article 4(2), carried out in another country, which would be deductible if they had been performed within the territory of the country;

   [(b) transactions which are exempt under Article 14(1)(g) and (i) and under Articles 15, and 16(1)(B) and (C), and paragraph 2][3]

   (c) any of the transactions exempt pursuant to Article 13B(a) and (d)(1) to (5), when the customer is established outside the Community or when those transactions are directly linked with goods to be exported to a country outside the Community.][4]

[4. The refund of value added tax referred to in paragraph 3 shall be effected:

   — to taxable persons who are not established within the territory of the country but who are established in another Member State in accordance with the detailed implementing rules laid down in Directive 79/1072/EEC;

   — to taxable persons who are not established in the territory of the Community, in accordance with the detailed implementing rules laid down in Directive 86/560/EEC.

   [For the purposes of applying the above:

   (a) the taxable persons referred to in Article 1 of Directive 79/1072/EEC shall also be considered for the purposes of applying the said Directive as taxable persons who are not established in the country when, inside the territory of the country, they have only carried out supplies of goods and services to a person who has been designated as the person liable to pay the tax in accordance with [Article 21(1)(a), (1)(c) or (1)(f) or Article 21(2)(c)][5];

(b) the taxable persons referred to in Article 1 of Directive 86/560/EEC shall also be considered for the purposes of applying the said Directive as taxable persons who are not established in the Community when, inside the territory of the country, they have only carried out supplies of goods and services to a person who has been designated as the person liable to pay the tax in accordance with [Article 21(1)(a), or (1)(f) or Article 21(2)(c)][6];

(c) Directives 79/1072/EEC and 86/560/EEC shall not apply to supplies of goods which are, or may be, exempted under Article 28c(A) when the goods supplied are dispatched or transported by the acquirer or for his account.][7]][8]

5. As regards goods and services to be used by a taxable person both for transactions covered by paragraphs 2 and 3, in respect of which value added tax is deductible, and for transactions in respect of which value added tax is not deductible, only such proportion of the value added tax shall be deductible as is attributable to the former transactions.

This proportion shall be determined, in accordance with Article 19, for all the transactions carried out by the taxable person.

However, Member States may:

(a) authorize the taxable person to determine a proportion for each sector of his business, provided that separate accounts are kept for each sector;

(b) compel the taxable person to determine a proportion for each sector of his business and to keep separate accounts for each sector;

(c) authorize or compel the taxable person to make the deduction on the basis of the use of all or part of the goods and services;

(d) authorize or compel the taxable person to make the deduction in accordance with the rule laid down in the first subparagraph, in respect of all goods and services used for all transactions referred to therein;

(e) provide that where the value added tax which is not deductible by the taxable person is insignificant it shall be treated as nil.

6. Before a period of four years at the latest has elapsed from the date of entry into force of this Directive, the Council, acting unanimously on a proposal from the Commission, shall decide what expenditure shall not be eligible for a deduction of value added tax. Value added tax shall in no circumstances be deductible on expenditure which is not strictly business expenditure, such as that on luxuries, amusements or entertainment.

Until the above rules come into force, Member States may retain all the exclusions provided for under their national laws when this Directive comes into force.

7. Subject to the consultation provided for in Article 29, each Member State may, for cyclical economic reasons, totally or partly exclude all or some capital goods or other goods from the system of deductions. To maintain identical conditions of competition, Member States may, instead of refusing deduction, tax the goods manufactured by the taxable person himself or which he has purchased in the country or imported, in such a way that the tax does not exceed the value added tax which would have been charged on the acquisition of similar goods.

Amendments
1   Substituted by Art 28f(1) (Sixth Directive) as amended by Art 1(10), Council Directive 95/7/EC of 10 April 1995, (w.e.f. 25 May 1995).
2   Substituted by Art 28f(1) (Sixth Directive) as inserted by Art 1(22), Council Directive 91/680/EEC of 16 December 1991, (w.e.f. 1 January 1993).
3   Substituted by Protocol No. 3, Part 3, Treaty of Accession, w.e.f. 1 May 2004.
4   Substituted by Art 28f(1) (Sixth Directive) as inserted by Art 1(22), Council Directive 91/680/EEC of 16 December 1991, (w.e.f. 1 January 1993 for transition period specified in Art 28l).
5   Replaced by Art 1(4)(a), Council Directive 2006/69/EC of 24 July 2006 (w.e.f. 13 August 2006).
6   Replaced by Art 1(4)(b) Council Directive 2006/69/EC of 24 July 2006 (w.e.f. 13 August 2006).
7   Inserted by Art 1(18), Council Directive 92/111/EEC of 14 December 1992, (w.e.f. 1 January 1993).
8   Substituted by Art 28f(1) (Sixth Directive) as inserted by Art 1(22), Council Directive 91/680/EEC of 16 December 1991, (w.e.f. 1 January 1993 for transition period specified in Art 28l).

Case law

Ampafrance S.A. v Directeur des Services Fiscaux de Maine-et-Loire	C177/99	Recovery/Entertainment/Restaurant costs
BLP Group v Customs and Excise	C4/94	Shares deduction/Right of
BP Supergas Anonimos Etaira Genik Emporiki Viomichaniki Kai Antiprossopeion v Greece	C62/93	Recovery on imports
Breitsohl, Brigitte v Finanzant Goslar	C400/98	Intending trader
Charles P. and Charles-Tijmens T.S. v Staatssecretaris van Financiën	C434/03	Deduction/Immovable property used for business and private purposes
Cibo Participations SA v Directeur régional des impôts du Nord-Pas-de-Calais	C16/00	Holding Coy/Taxable person/Recovery of VAT
Cookies World Vertriebsgesellschaft mbH iL and Finanzlandesdirektion für Tirol	C155/01	Deduction/Exclusions provided for under national law
Debouche Etienne v Inspecteur der Invoerrechten en Accijinzen Rijswijk	C302/93	Deduction/Right of
Ecotarde SpA v Agenzia delle Entrate – Ufficio di Genova 3	C95/07 – C96/07	Reverse charge procedure/Right to deduct
Empresa de Desenvolvimento Mineiro SGPS SA (EDM) and Fazenda Pública	C77/01	Meaning of 'economic activities'/ Meaning of 'incidental financial transactions'/Calculation of deductible proportion
Erin Executor and Trustee Company Limited t/a IPFPUT v Revenue Commissioners	Irish Supreme Court 363 and 369/1994 ITR Vol II No. 3	Recovery leasehold property
Eurodental Sàrl v Administration de l'enregistrement et des domaines	C240/05	Deduction/Right of/Intra-Community transactions
Faxworld Vorgründungsgesellschaft Peter Hünninghausen und Wolfgang Klein GbR and Finanzamt Offenbach am Main-Land	C137/02	Right to deduct
Fini H, I/S v Skatteministeriet	C32/03	Ceased economic activity/Deduction/ Right of
Floridienne SA v Belgium	C142/99	Recovery/Apportionment/Share dividends to be included

France v Commission	C345/99	Recovery/Limitation to vehicles used exclusively for driving instruction
France v Commission	C40/00	Reintroduction of recovery/Restrictions
France v European Commission	C43/96	Helicopters/Recovery of VAT
France v Commission	C243/03	Deduction/Capital goods financed by subsidies
HE v Bundesfinanzhof (Germany) Finanzamt Bergisch	C25/03	Right to deduct/Use of one room of dwelling for business purposes
"Intiem" Leesportefeuille CV v Staatssecretaris van Financien	C165/86	Deduction/Right of
Investrand BV v Staatssecretaris van Financiën	C435/05	Deduction/Right of
Kittel, Axel v Belgian State and Recolta Recycling SPRL v Belgian State	C439/04 C440/04	Deduction/Carousel Fraud/Void contract
Kretztechnik AG, Außenstelle Linz	C465/03	Supply/Share Issue/Admission of company to stock exchange
Magoora sp. z o. o. v Dyrektor Izby Skrabovej w Krakowie	C414/07	Decuction of VAT on the on the purchase of fuel for certain vehicles irrespective for the purpose for which they are used
Marks and Spencer plc v Customs and Excise	UK - 14692 and 14693 and C62/00	Restriction on Repayments/Unjust enrichment
Metropol Treuhand Wirtschaftstreuhand Gmbh v Finanzlandesdirection fur Steurmark	C409/99	Cars/Recovery
Midland Bank Plc v Customs and Excise	C98/98	Recovery
Netherlands v Commission	C338/98	Cars/Recovery
Optigen Ltd, Fulcrum Electronics Ltd, Bond House Systems Ltd v Commissioners of Customs & Excise	C354/03 C355/03 C484/03	Economic activity/Taxable person/ Deduction/Carousel fraud
Reisdorf, John v Finanzamt Koln-West	C85/95	Deduction
Royscot Leasing Ltd & Others v Customs and Excise	C305/97	Cars/Recovery
Securenta Göttinger Immobilienanlagen und Vermögensmanagement AG v Finanzamt Göttingen	C437/06	Expenditure connected with the issue of shares and atypical silent partnerships/ Apportionment of input VAT according to the economic nature of the activity
Sanofi Winthrop SA v Directeur Service Fiscaux du Val Marne	C181/99	Recovery/Derogation/Proportionality
Spain v Commission	C204/03	Subsidies/Limitation of the right to deduct
Stadler, Michael v Finanzlandesdirektion fur Vorarlberg	C409/99	Cars/Recovery
Terra Baubedarf-Handel GmbH and Finanzamt Osterholz-Scharmbeck	C152/02	Right to deduct/Conditions of exercise
United Kingdom v Commission	C33/03	Fuel costs reimbursed by employer/ Recovery of VAT
Wiley v Revenue Commissioners	Irish Case IV ITR 170	Importation free of Excise Duty

Article 18

Rules governing the exercise of the right to deduct

[1. To exercise his right of deduction, the taxable person must:

    (a) in respect of deductions pursuant to Article 17(2)(a), hold an invoice drawn up in accordance with Article 22(3);

    (b) in respect of deductions pursuant to Article 17(2)(b), hold an import document specifying him as consignee or importer and stating or permitting the calculation of the amount of tax due;

    (c) in respect of deductions pursuant to Article 17(2)(c), comply with the formalities established by each Member State;

    (d) when he is required to pay the tax as a customer or purchaser where [Article 21(1) or Article 21(2)(c)]¹ applies, comply with the formalities laid down by each Member State;

    (e) in respect of deductions pursuant to Article 17(2)(d), set out in the declaration provided for in Article 22(4) all the information needed for the amount of the tax due on his intra-Community acquisitions of goods to be calculated and hold an invoice in accordance with Article 22(3).]²s 12

s12 **2.** The taxable person shall effect the deduction by subtracting from the total amount of value added tax due for a given tax period the total amount of the tax in respect of which, during the same period, the right to deduct has arisen and can be exercised under the provisions of paragraph 1.

However, Member States may require that as regards taxable persons who carry out occasional transactions as defined in Article 4(3), the right to deduct shall be exercised only at the time of the supply.

s 20(1) **3.** Member States shall determine the conditions and procedures whereby a taxable person may be authorized to make a deduction which he has not made in accordance with the provisions of paragraphs 1 and 2.

[**3a.** Member States may authorize a taxable person who does not hold an invoice in accordance with Article 22(3) to make the deduction referred to in Article 17(2)(d); they shall determine the conditions and arrangements for applying this provision.]³

4. Where for a given tax period the amount of authorized deductions exceeds the amount of tax due, the Member States may either make a refund or carry the excess forward to the following period according to conditions which they shall determine.

However, Member States may refuse to refund or carry forward if the amount of the excess is insignificant.

Amendments

1 Substituted by Art 1(5) Council Directive 2006/69/EC of 24 July 2006 (w.e.f 13 August 2006).

2 Substituted by Art 28f(2) (Sixth Directive) as inserted by Art 1(22), Council Directive 91/680/EEC of 16 December 1991, (w.e.f. 1 January 1993 for transition period specified in Art 28l).

3 Substituted by Art 28f(3) (Sixth Directive) as inserted by Art 1(22), Council Directive 91/680/EEC of 16 December 1991, (w.e.f. 1 January 1993 for transition period specified in Art 28l).

Case law

Gerhard Bockemühl and Förvaltnings AB Stenholmen and Riksskatteverket	C90/02	Deduction/obligation to possess invoice/9(2)(e) service
Grendel (R.A.) GmbH v Finanzamt fur Korperschaften, Hamburg	C255/81	Restrictions of repayment/Unjust Enrichment
Italy v European Commission	C104/86	Unjust enrichment
Netherlands v Commission	C338/98	Cars/Recovery
Societe Generales - de Grandes Sources d'eaux Minerales Franciases v Bungessamt Fur Finanzen	C361/96	Recovery
Sosnowska, Alicija v Dyrektor Izby Sakrbowej we Wroclawiu Osrodek Zamiejscowy w Walbrzychu	C25/07	National Legislation determining conditions for repayment of excess VAT
Terra Baubedarf-Handel GmbH and Finanzamt Osterholz-Scharmbeck	C152/02	Right to deduct/Conditions of exercise
United Kingdom v Commission	C33/03	Fuel costs reimbursed by employer/Recovery of VAT
Weissgerber v Finanzamt Neustadt an der Weinstrasse	C207/87	Repayment restriction/Unjust enrichment

s 12(4),
2(1)(x).

Article 19

Calculation of the deductible proportion

1. The proportion deductible under the first subparagraph of Article 17(5) shall be made up of a fraction having:

   - as numerator, the total amount, exclusive of value added tax, of turnover per year attributable to transactions in respect of which value added tax is deductible under Article 17(2) and (3),

   - as denominator, the total amount, exclusive of value added tax, of turnover per year attributable to transactions included in the numerator and to transactions in respect of which value added tax is not deductible. The Member States may also include in the denominator the amount of subsidies, other than those specified in Article 11A(1)(a).

   The proportion shall be determined on an annual basis, fixed as a percentage and rounded up to a figure not exceeding the next unit.

2. By way of derogation from the provisions of paragraph 1, there shall be excluded from the calculation of the deductible proportion, amounts of turnover attributable to the supplies of capital goods used by the taxable person for the purposes of his business. Amounts of turnover attributable to transactions specified in Article 13B(d), insofar as these are incidental transactions, and to incidental real estate and financial transactions shall also be excluded. Where Member States exercise the option provided under Article 20(5) not to require adjustment in respect of capital goods, they may include disposal of capital goods in the calculation of the deductible proportion.

3. The provisional proportion for a year shall be that calculated on the basis of the preceding year's transactions. In the absence of any such transactions to refer to, or where they were insignificant in amount, the deductible proportion shall be estimated provisionally, under supervision of the tax authorities, by the taxable person from his own forecasts. However, Member States may retain their current rules.

   Deductions made on the basis of such provisional proportion shall be adjusted when the final proportion is fixed during the next year.

Case law

António Jorge Lda v Fazenda Pública	C536/03	Dual use inputs/Deductible proportion
Empresa de Desenvolvimento Mineiro SGPS SA (EDM) and Fazenda Pública	C77/01	Meaning of 'economic activities'/Meaning of 'incidental financial transactions'/ Calculation of deductible proportion
Koninklijke Ahold B.V. v Staatsecretaris van Financiën	C484/06	Rules concerning rounding of amounts of VAT
Nordania Finans A/S, BG Factoring A/S v Skatteministeriet	C98/07	Calculation of the deductible proportion/ Exclusion of amounts of turnover attributable to the supplies of capital goods used by the taxable person for the purposes of his business
Royal Bank of Scotland Group plc v Commisioners for Her Majesty's Revenue and Customs	C488/07	Deduction/Goods and services used for both taxable and exempt transactions

| Securenta Göttinger Immobilienanlagen und Vermögensmanagement AG v Finanzamt Göttingen | C437/06 | Expenditure connected with the issue of shares and atypical silent partnerships/ Apportionment of input VAT according to the economic nature of the activity |
| Sofitam SA formerly Satam v Minister responsible for Budget (France) | C333/91 | Holding Coy/Deduction/Right of |

Article 20

Adjustments of deductions

s 17(3) & (4) **1.** The initial deduction shall be adjusted according to the procedures laid down by the Member States, in particular:

    (a) where that deduction was higher or lower than that to which the taxable person was entitled;

    (b) where after the return is made some change occurs in the factors used to determine the amount to be deducted, in particular where purchases are cancelled or price reductions are obtained; however, adjustment shall not be made in cases of transactions remaining totally or partially unpaid and of destruction, loss or theft of property duly proved or confirmed, nor in the case of applications for the purpose of making gifts of small value and giving samples specified in Article 5(6). However, Member States may require adjustment in cases of transactions remaining totally or partially unpaid and of theft.

2. In the case of capital goods, adjustment shall be spread over five years including that in which the goods were acquired or manufactured. The annual adjustment shall be made only in respect of one fifth of the tax imposed on goods. The adjustment shall be made on the basis of the variations in the deduction entitlement in subsequent years in relation to that for the year in which the goods were acquired or manufactured.

By way of derogation from the preceding subparagraph, Member States may base the adjustment on a period of five full years starting from the time at which the goods are first used.

[In the case of immovable property acquired as capital goods, the adjustment period may be extended up to 20 years.][1]

3. In the case of supply during the period of adjustment capital goods shall be regarded as if they had still been applied for business use by the taxable person until expiry of the period of adjustment. Such business activities are presumed to be fully taxed in cases where the delivery of the said goods is taxed; they are presumed to be fully exempt where the delivery is exempt. The adjustment shall be made only once for the whole period of adjustment still to be covered.

However, in the latter case, Member States may waive the requirement for adjustment insofar as the purchaser is a taxable person using the capital goods in question solely for transactions in respect of which value added tax is deductible.

4. For the purposes of applying the provisions of paragraphs 2 and 3, Member States may:

    —   define the concept of capital goods,

    —   indicate the amount of the tax which is to be taken into consideration for adjustment,

    —   adopt any suitable measures with a view to ensuring that adjustment does not involve any unjustified advantage,

    —   permit administrative simplifications.

    [Member States may also apply paragraphs 2 and 3 to services which have characteristics similar to those normally attributed to capital goods.]²

5. If in any Member State the practical effect of applying paragraphs 2 and 3 would be insignificant, that Member State may subject to the consultation provided for in Article 29 forego application of these paragraphs having regard to the need to avoid distortion of competition, the overall tax effect in the Member State concerned and the need for due economy of administration.

6. Where the taxable person transfers from being taxed in the normal way to a special scheme or vice versa, Member States may take all necessary measures to ensure that the taxable person neither benefits nor is prejudiced unjustifiably.

Amendments
1   Substituted by Art 1(4), Council Directive 95/7/EC of 10 April 1996, (w.e.f. 1 January 1996).
2   Inserted by Art 1(6), Council Directive 2006/69/EC of 24 April 2006 (w.e.f. 13 August 2006).

Case law

Genius Holding BV v Staatssecretaris van Financien	C342/87	Deduction/Right of
Ghent Coal Terminal NV v Belgium	C37/95	Deduction/Right of
Jeunehomme, Lea and Societe Anonyme d'Etude et de Gestion Immobiliere "EGI" v Belgium	C123/87 and C330/87	Deduction/Right of
Lennartz v Finanzamt Munchen III	C97/90	Taxable Event/Self Supply/Car Deduction/Taxable Amount
Waterschap Zeeuws Vlaanderen v Staatssecretaris van Financiën	C378/02	Public authority/Supply/Right to adjustment and deduction

TITLE XII

persons liable for payment for tax

[Article 21

Persons liable to pay tax to the authorities

s 8(1) **1.** Under the internal system, the following shall be liable to pay value added
3(8), 37. tax:

[(a) the taxable person carrying out the taxable supply of goods or of services, except for the cases referred to in (b), (c) and (f). Where the taxable supply of goods or of services is effected by a taxable person who is not established within the territory of the country, Member States may, under the conditions determined by them, lay down that the person liable to pay tax is the person for whom the taxable supply of goods or of services is carried out;][1]

(b) taxable persons to whom services covered by Article 9(2)(e) are supplied or persons who are identified for value added tax purposes within the territory of the country to whom services covered by Article 28b(C), (D), (E) and (F) are supplied, if the services are carried out by a taxable person not established within the territory of the country;

(c) the person to whom the supply of goods is made when the following conditions are met:

— the taxable operation is a supply of goods made under the conditions laid down in Article 28c(E)(3),

— the person to whom the supply of goods is made is another taxable person or a non-taxable legal person identified for the purposes of value added tax within the territory of the country,

— the invoice issued by the taxable person not established within the territory of the country conforms to Article 22(3).

However, Member States may provide a derogation from this obligation, where the taxable person who is not established within the territory of the country has appointed a tax representative in that country;

(d) any person who mentions the value added tax on an invoice [....][2];

(e) any person effecting a taxable intra-Community acquisition of goods.

[(f) persons who are identified for value added tax purposes within the territory of the country and to whom goods are supplied under the conditions set out in Article 8(1)(d) or (e), if the supplies are carried out by a taxable person not established within the territory of the country.][1]

2. By way of derogation from the provisions of paragraph 1:

(a) where the person liable to pay tax in accordance with the provisions of paragraph 1 is a taxable person who is not established within the territory of the country, Member States may allow him to appoint a tax representative as the person liable to pay tax. This option shall be subject to conditions and procedures laid down by each Member State;

(b) where the taxable transaction is effected by a taxable person who is not established within the territory of the country and no legal instrument exists, with the country in which that taxable person is established or has his seat, relating to mutual assistance similar in scope to that laid down by Directives 76/308/EEC and 77/799/EEC and by Council Regulation (EEC) No 218/92 of 27 January 1992 on administrative cooperation in the field of indirect taxation (VAT), Member States may take steps to provide that the person liable for payment of the tax shall be a tax representative appointed by the non-established taxable person.

[(c) where the following supplies are carried out, Member States may lay down that the person liable to pay tax is the taxable person to whom those supplies are made:

(i) the supply of construction work, including repair, cleaning, maintenance, alteration and demolition services in relation to immovable property, as well as the handing over of construction works considered to be a supply of goods by virtue of Article 5(5);

(ii) the supply of staff engaged in activities covered by (i);

(iii) the supply of immovable property, as referred to in Article 13(B) (g) and (h), where the supplier has opted for taxation of the supply pursuant to point (C)(b) of that Article;

(iv) the supply of used material, used material which cannot be re-used in the same state, scrap, industrial and non industrial waste, recyclable waste, part processed waste and certain goods and services, as identified in Annex M;

(v) the supply of goods provided as security by one taxable person to another in execution of that security;

(vi) the supply of goods following the cession of the reservation of ownership to an assignee and the exercising of this right by the assignee;

(vii) the supply of immovable property sold by the judgment debtor in a compulsory sale procedure.

For the purposes of this point, Member States may provide that a taxable person who also carries out activities or transactions that are not considered to be taxable supplies of goods or services in accordance with Article 2 shall be deemed to be a taxable person in respect of supplies received as referred to in the first subparagraph. A non-taxable body governed by public law, may be deemed to be a taxable person in respect of supplies received as referred to in (v), (vi) and (vii).

For the purposes of this point, Member States may specify the supplies of goods and services covered, and the categories of suppliers or recipients to whom these measures may apply. They may also limit the application of this measure to some of the supplies of goods and services listed in Annex M.

Member States shall inform the Committee established inaccordance with Article 29 of any new national measure adopted pursuant to the provisions of this point.]³

3. In the situations referred to in paragraphs 1 and 2, Member States may provide that someone other than the person liable for payment of the tax shall be held jointly and severally liable for payment of the tax.

4. On importation, value added tax shall be payable by the person or persons designated or accepted as being liable by the Member State in to which the goods are imported.]⁴

Amendments

1 Amended by Art 28g, as amended by Art 1, Council Directive 2003/92/EC of 7 October 2003, (w.e.f. 1 January 2005).

2 Deleted by Art 28g as amended by Art 4, Council Directive 2001/115/EC of 20 December 2001, (w.e.f. 6 February 2002).

3 Inserted by Art 1(7), Council Directive 2006/69/EC of 24 July 2006 (w.e.f. 13 August 2006).

4 Art 21 substituted by Art 28g as amended by Art 4, Council Directive 00/65/EC of 17 October 2000.

Note

1 Decision 97/510/EEC, derogation, 'Ireland is hereby authorized, from 26 March 1997 until 31 December 2007, to designate the person to whom the supply is made as the person liable to pay the tax where the two following conditions are met:
 - a surrender or assignment of a leasehold interest is treated as a supply of goods made by a lessee,
 - the person acquiring the leasehold interest is a taxable person or a non-taxable legal person.'

Case law

Dimosio, Elliniko and Karageorgou, Maria, Petrova, Katina, and Vlachos, Loukas	C78/02, C79/02 and C80/02	Taxable Person/Erroneous charge of VAT
Ecotarde SpA v Agenzia delle Entrate – Ufficio di Genova 3	C95/07 C96/07	Reverse charge procedure/Right to deduct
Federation of Technological Industries and Others v Customs & Excise	C384/04	Anti-avoidance measures/Persons liable to pay tax
Langhorst, Bernard v Finanzamt Osnabruck - Land	C141/96	Amount of tax payable on credit note issued.
Schmeink and Cofreth AG & Co v Finanzant Borken and Strobel, Manfred v Finanxamt Esslingen	C454/98	Correction of incorrectly issued invoice

TITLE XIII

obligations of persons liable for payment

[Article 22

Obligations under the internal system

9(1) **1.**   [(a) Every taxable person shall state when his activity as a taxable person commences, changes or ceases. Member States shall, subject to conditions which they lay down, allow the taxable person to make such statements by electronic means, and may also require that electronic means are used.]¹

(b) Without prejudice to (a), every taxable person referred to in Article 28a(1)(a), second subparagraph, shall state that he is effecting intra-Community acquisitions of goods when the conditions for application of the derogation provided for in that Article are not fulfilled.

A)   (c) Member States shall take the measures necessary to identify by means of an individual number:

[- Every taxable person, with the exception of those referred to in Article 28a(4), who, within the territory of the country, effects supplies of goods or of services giving him the right of deduction, other than supplies of goods or of services for which tax is payable solely by the customer or the recipient in accordance with Article 21(1)(a), (b), (c) or (f). However, Member States need not identify certain taxable persons referred to in article 4(3),]²

— every taxable person referred to in paragraph 1(b) and every taxable person who exercises the option provided for in the third subparagraph of Article 28a(1)(a).

[- every taxable person who, within the territory of the country, effects intra-Community acquisitions of goods for the purposes of his operations relating to the economic activities referred to in Article 4(2) carried out abroad.]³

(d) Each individual identification number shall have a prefix in accordance with ISO International Standard No. 3166 - alpha 2 - by which the Member State of issue may be identified. [Nevertheless, the Hellenic Republic shall be authorised to use the prefix "EL ".]⁴

(e) Member States shall take the measures necessary to ensure that their identification systems distinguish taxable persons referred to in (c) and to ensure the correct application of the transitional arrangements for the taxation of intra-Community transactions as laid down in this Title.

s 16 **2.**   (a) Every taxable person shall keep accounts in sufficient detail for value added tax to be applied and inspected by the tax authority

[(b) Every taxable person shall keep a register of the goods he has dispatched or transported or which have been dispatched or transported on his behalf out of the territory defined in Article 3 but within the Community for the purposes of the transactions referred to in the fifth, sixth and seventh indents of Article 28a(5)(b).

Every taxable person shall keep sufficiently detailed accounts to permit the identification of goods dispatched to him from another Member State by or on behalf of a taxable person identified for purposes of value added tax in that other Member State, in connection with which a service has been provided pursuant to the third or fourth indent of Article 9(2)(c).][5]

s 17 **[3.**   (a) Every taxable person shall ensure that an invoice is issued, either by himself or by his customer or, in his name and on his behalf, by a third party, in respect of goods or services which he has supplied or rendered to another taxable person or to a non-taxable legal person. Every taxable person shall also ensure that an invoice is issued, either by himself or by his customer or, in his name and on his behalf, by a third party, in respect of the supplies of goods referred to in Article 28b(B)(1) and in respect of goods supplied under the conditions laid down in Article 28c(A).

Every taxable person shall likewise ensure that an invoice is issued, either by himself or by his customer or, in his name and on his behalf, by a third party, in respect of any payment on account made to him before any supplies of goods referred to in the first subparagraph and in respect of any payment on account made to him by another taxable person or non-taxable legal person before the provision of services is completed.

Member States may impose on taxable persons an obligation to issue an invoice in respect of goods or services other than those referred to in the preceding subparagraphs which they have supplied or rendered on their territory. When they do so, Member States may impose fewer obligations in respect of these invoices than those listed under points (b), (c) and (d).

The Member States may release taxable persons from the obligation to issue an invoice in respect of goods or services which they have supplied or rendered in their territory and which are exempt, with or without refund of the tax paid at the preceding stage, pursuant to Article 13, Article 28(2)(a) and Article 28(3)(b).

Any document or message that amends and refers specifically and unambiguously to the initial invoice is to be treated as an invoice. Member States in whose territory goods or services are supplied or rendered may allow some of the obligatory details to be left out of such documents or messages.

Member States may impose time limits for the issue of invoices on taxable persons supplying goods and services in their territory.

Under conditions to be laid down by the Member States in whose territory goods or services are supplied or rendered, a summary invoice may be drawn up for several separate supplies of goods or services.

Invoices may be drawn up by the customer of a taxable person in respect of goods or services supplied or rendered to him by that taxable person, on condition that there is at the outset an agreement between the two parties, and on condition that a procedure exists for the acceptance of each invoice by the taxable person supplying the goods or services. The Member States in whose territory the goods or services are supplied or rendered shall determine the terms and conditions of the agreement and of the acceptance procedures between the taxable person and his customer.

Member States may impose further conditions on the issue of invoices by the customers of taxable persons supplying goods or services on their territory. For example, they may require that such invoices be issued in the name and on behalf of the taxable person. Such conditions must always be the same wherever the customer is established.

Member States may also lay down specific conditions for taxable persons supplying goods or services in their territory in cases where the third party, or the customer, who issues invoices is established in a country with which no legal instrument exists relating to mutual assistance similar in scope to that laid down by Council Directive 76/308/EEC of 15 March 1976 on mutual assistance for the recovery of claims relating to certain levies, duties, taxes and other measures, Council Directive 77/799/EEC of 19 December 1977 concerning mutual assistance by the competent authorities of the Member States in the field of direct and indirect taxation and by Council Regulation (EEC) No 218/92 of 27 January 1992 on administrative cooperation in the field of indirect taxation (VAT).

(b) Without prejudice to the specific arrangements laid down by this Directive, only the following details are required for VAT purposes on invoices issued under the first, second and third subparagraphs of point (a):

— the date of issue;

— a sequential number, based on one or more series, which uniquely identifies the invoice,

— the VAT identification number referred to in paragraph 1(c) under which the taxable person supplied the goods or services;

— where the customer is liable to pay tax on goods supplied or services rendered or has been supplied with goods as referred to in Article 28c(A), the VAT identification number as referred to in paragraph 1(c) under which the goods were supplied or the services rendered to him;

— the full name and address of the taxable person and of his customer;

— the quantity and nature of the goods supplied or the extent and nature of the services rendered;

- the date on which the supply of goods or of services was made or completed or the date on which the payment on account referred to in the second subparagraph of point (a) was made, insofar as that a date can be determined and differs from the date of issue of the invoice;

- the taxable amount per rate or exemption, the unit price exclusive of tax and any discounts or rebates if they are not included in the unit price;

- the VAT rate applied;

- the VAT amount payable, except where a specific arrangement is applied for which this Directive excludes such a detail;

- where an exemption is involved or where the customer is liable to pay the tax, reference to the appropriate provision of this directive, to the corresponding national provision, or to any indication that the supply is exempt or subject to the reverse charge procedure;

- where the intra-Community supply of a new means of transport is involved, the particulars specified in Article 28a(2);

- where the margin scheme is applied, reference to Article 26 or 26a, to the corresponding national provisions, or to any other indication that the margin scheme has been applied;

- where the person liable to pay the tax is a tax representative within the meaning of Article 21(2), the VAT identification number referred to in paragraph 1(c) of that tax representative, together with his full name and address.

Member States may require taxable persons established on their territory and supplying goods or services on their territory to indicate the VAT identification number referred to in paragraph 1(c) of their customer in cases other than those referred to in the fourth indent of the first subparagraph.

Member States shall not require invoices to be signed.

The amounts which appear on the invoice may be expressed in any currency, provided that the amount of tax to be paid is expressed in the national currency of the Member State where the supply of goods or services takes place, using the conversion mechanism laid down in Article 11C(2).

Where necessary for control purposes, Member States may require invoices in respect of goods supplied or services rendered in their territory and invoices received by taxable persons in their territory to be translated into their national languages.

(c) Invoices issued pursuant to point (a) may be sent either on paper or, subject to an acceptance by the customer, by electronic means.

Invoices sent by electronic means shall be accepted by Member States provided that the authenticity of the origin and integrity of the contents are guaranteed:

  — by means of an advanced electronic signature within the meaning of Article 2(2) of Directive 1999/93/EC of the European Parliament and of the Council of 13 December 1999 on a Community framework for electronic signatures; Member States may however ask for the advanced electronic signature to be based on a qualified certificate and created by a secure-signature-creation device, within the meaning of Article 2(6) and (10) of the aforementioned Directive;

  — or by means of electronic data interchange (EDI) as defined in Article 2 of Commission Recommendation 1994/820/EC of 19 October 1994 relating to the legal aspects of electronic data interchange when the agreement relating to the exchange provides for the use of procedures guaranteeing the authenticity of the origin and integrity of the data; however Member States may, subject to conditions which they lay down, require that an additional summary document on paper is necessary.

Invoices may, however, be sent by other electronic means subject to acceptance by the Member State(s) concerned. The Commission will present, at the latest on 31 December 2008, a report, together with a proposal, if appropriate, amending the conditions on electronic invoicing in order to take account of possible future technological developments in this field.

Member States may not impose on taxable persons supplying goods or services in their territory any other obligations or formalities relating to the transmission of invoices by electronic means. However, they may provide, until 31 December 2005, that the use of such a system is to be subject to prior notification.

Member States may lay down specific conditions for invoices issued by electronic means for goods or services supplied in their territory from a country with which no legal instrument exists relating to mutual assistance similar in scope to that laid down by Directives 76/308/EEC and 77/799/EEC and by Regulation (EEC) No 218/92.

When batches containing several invoices are sent to the same recipient by electronic means, the details that are common to the individual invoices may be mentioned only once if, for each invoice, all the information is accessible.

(d) Every taxable person shall ensure that copies of invoices issued by himself, by his customer or, in his name and on his behalf, by a third party, and all the invoices which he has received are stored.

For the purposes of this Directive, the taxable person may decide the place of storage provided that he makes the invoices or information stored there available without undue delay to the competent authorities whenever they so request. Member States may, however, require taxable persons established in their territory to notify them of the place of storage, if it is outside their territory. Member States may, in addition, require taxable persons established in their territory to store within the country invoices issued by themselves or by their customers or, in their name and on their behalf, by a third party, as well as all the invoices which they have received, when the storage is not by electronic means guaranteeing full online access to the data concerned.

The authenticity of the origin and integrity of the content of the invoices, as well as their readability, must be guaranteed throughout the storage period. As regards the invoices referred to in the third subparagraph of point (c), the information they contain may not be altered; it must remain legible throughout the aforementioned period.

The Member States shall determine the period for which taxable persons must store invoices relating to goods or services supplied in their territory and invoices received by taxable persons established in their territory.

In order to ensure that the conditions laid down in the third subparagraph are met, Member States referred to in the fourth subparagraph may require that invoices be stored in the original form in which they were sent, whether paper or electronic. They may also require that when invoices are stored by electronic means, the data guaranteeing the authenticity of the origin and integrity of the content also be stored.

Member States referred to in the fourth subparagraph may impose specific conditions prohibiting or restricting the storage of invoices in a country with which no legal instrument exists relating to mutual assistance similar in scope to that laid down by Directives 76/308/ EEC, 77/799/EEC and by Regulation (EEC) No 218/92 and to the right of access by electronic means, download and use referred to in Article 22a.

Member States may, subject to conditions which they lay down, require the storage of invoices received by non-taxable persons.

(e) For the purposes of points (c) and (d), transmission and storage of invoices "by electronic means" shall mean transmission or making available to the recipient and storage using electronic equipment for processing (including digital compression) and storage of data, and employing wires, radio transmission, optical technologies or other electromagnetic means.

For the purposes of this Directive, Member States shall accept documents or messages in paper or electronic form as invoices if they meet the conditions laid down in this paragraph.][4]

s 19(3) **4.** [(a) Every taxable person shall submit a return by a deadline to be determined by Member States. That deadline may not be more than two months later than the end of each tax period. The tax period shall be fixed by each Member State at one month, two months or a quarter. Member States may, however, set different periods provided that they do not exceed one year. Member States shall, subject to conditions which they lay down, allow the taxable person to make such returns by electronic means, and may also require that electronic means are used.][1]

(b) The return shall set out all the information needed to calculate the tax that has become chargeable and the deductions to be made including, where appropriate, and in so far as it seems necessary for the establishment of the basis of assessment, the total value of the transactions relative to such tax and deductions and the value of any exempt transactions.

(c) The return shall also set out:

— on the one hand, the total value, less value added tax, of the supplies of goods referred to in Article 28c(A) on which tax has become chargeable during the period.

The following shall also be added: the total value, less value added tax, of the supplies of goods referred to in the second sentence of Article 8(1)(a) and in Article 28(b)(B)(1) effected within the territory of another Member State for which tax has become chargeable during the return period where the place of departure of the dispatch or transport of the goods is situated in the territory of the country,

[– on the other hand, the total amount, less value added tax of the intra-Community acquisitions of goods referred to in Article 28a(1) and (6) effected within the territory of the country on which tax has become chargeable.

The following shall also be added: the total value, less value added tax, of the supplies of goods referred to in the second sentence of Article 8(1)(a) and in Article 28(b)(B)(1) effected in the territory of the country on which tax has become chargeable during the return period, where the place of departure of the dispatch or transport of the goods is situated within the territory of another Member State, and the total amount, less value added tax, of the supplies of goods made within the territory of the country for which the taxable person has been designated as the person liable for the tax in accordance with Article 28c(E)(3) and under within the tax has become payable in the course of the period covered by the declaration.]³

19(3)(a) **5.** Every taxable person shall pay the net amount of the value added tax when submitting the regular return. Member States may, however, set a different date for the payment of that amount or may demand an interim payment.

s 19A **6.** [(a) Member States may require a taxable person to submit a statement, including all the particulars specified in paragraph 4, concerning all transactions carried out in the preceding year. That statement shall provide all the information necessary for any adjustments. Member States shall, subject to conditions which they lay down, allow the taxable person to make such statements by electronic means, and may also require that electronic means are used.]¹

[[(b) Every taxable person identified for value added tax purposes shall also submit a recapitulative statement of the acquirers identified for value added tax purposes to whom he has supplied goods under the conditions provided for in Article 28c(A)(a) and (d), and of consignees identified for value added tax purposes in the transactions referred to in the fifth subparagraph.]⁶

[The recapitulative statement shall be drawn up for each calendar quarter within a period and in accordance with procedures to be determined by the Member States, which shall take the measures necessary to ensure that the provisions concerning administrative cooperation in the field of indirect taxation are in any event complied with. Member States shall, subject to conditions which they lay down, allow the taxable person to make such statements by electronic means, and may also require that electronic means are used.]¹

The recapitulative statement shall set out:

— the number by which the taxable person is identified for purposes of value added tax in the territory of the country and under which he effected supplies of goods in the conditions laid down in Article [28c(A)(a)]³,

[— the number by which each person acquiring goods is identified for purposes of value added tax in another Member State and under which the goods were supplied to him,]⁵

— for each person acquiring goods, the total value of the supplies of goods effected by the taxable person. Those amounts shall be declared for the calendar quarter during which the tax became chargeable.

The recapitulative statement shall also set out:

[— for the supplies of goods covered by Article [28c(A)(d)]³, the number by means of which the taxable person is identified for purposes of value added tax in the territory of the country, the number by which he is identified in the Member State of arrival of the dispatch or transport and the total amount of the supplies, determined in accordance with Article 28e(2)]³,

— the amounts of adjustments made under Article 11(C)(1). Those amounts shall be declared for the calendar quarter during which the person acquiring the goods is notified of the adjustment.

[....]⁷

[In the cases set out in the third subparagraph of Article 28b(A)(2), the taxable person identified for value added tax purposes within the territory of the country shall mention in a clear way on the recapitulative statement:

— the number by which he is identified for value added tax purposes within the territory of the country and under which he carried out the intra-Community acquisition and the subsequent supply of goods,

- the number by which, within the territory of the Member State of arrival of the dispatch or transport of the goods, the consignee of the subsequent supply by the taxable person is identified,

- and, for each consignee, the total amount, less value added tax, of the supplies made by the taxable person within the territory of the Member State of arrival of the dispatch or transport of the goods. These amounts shall be declared for the calendar quarter during which the tax became chargeable.]³]⁸

(c) By way of derogation from (b), Member States may:

- require recapitulative statements to be filed on a monthly basis;
- require that recapitulative statements give additional particulars.

(d) In the case of supplies of new means of transport effected under the conditions laid down in Article 28c(A)(b) by a taxable person identified for purposes of value added tax to a purchaser not identified for purposes of value added tax or by a taxable person as defined in Article 28a(4), Member States shall take the measures necessary to ensure that the vendor communicates all the information necessary for value added tax to be applied and inspected by the tax authority.

(e) Member States may require taxable persons who in the territory of the country effect intra-Community acquisitions of goods as defined in Article 28a(1)(a) and (6) to submit statements giving details of such acquisitions provided, however, that such statements may not be required for a period of less than one month.

Member States may also require persons who effect intra-Community acquisitions of new means of transport as defined in Article 28a(1)(b) to provide, when submitting the return referred to in paragraph 4, all the information necessary for value added tax to be applied and inspected by the tax authority.]

[7. Member States shall take the measures necessary to ensure that those persons who, in accordance with Article 21(1) and (2), are considered to be liable to pay the tax instead of a taxable person not established within the territory of the country comply with the obligations relating to declaration and payment set out in this Article; they shall also take the measures necessary to ensure that those persons who, in accordance with Article 21(3), are held to be jointly and severally liable for payment of the tax comply with the obligations relating to payment set out in this Article.]⁹

8. Member States may impose other obligations which they deem necessary for the correct collection of the tax and for the prevention of evasion, subject to the requirement of equal treatment for domestic transactions and transactions carried out between Member States by taxable persons and provided that such obligations do not, in trade between Member States, give rise to formalities connected with the crossing of frontiers.

[The option provided for in the first subparagraph cannot be used to impose additional obligations over and above those laid down in paragraph 3.]⁴

s 19(3)(aa). **9.** (a) Member States may release from certain or all obligations:

- taxable persons carrying out only supplies of goods or of services which are exempt under Articles 13 and 15,

- taxable persons eligible for the exemption from tax provided for in Article 24 and for the derogation provided for in Article 28a(1)(a), second subparagraph,

- taxable persons carrying out none of the transactions referred to in paragraph 4(c).

[Without prejudice to the provisions laid down in point (d), Member States may not, however, release the taxable persons referred to in the third indent from the obligations referred to in Article 22(3).]⁴

(b) Member States may release taxable persons other than those referred to in (a) from certain of the obligations referred to in 2(a).

(c) Member States may release taxable persons from payment of the tax due where the amount involved is insignificant.

[(d) Subject to consultation of the Committee provided for in Article 29 and under the conditions which they may lay down, Member States may provide that invoices in respect of goods supplied or services rendered in their territory do not have to fulfil some of the conditions laid down in paragraph 3(b) in the following cases:

- when the amount of the invoice is minor, or

- when commercial or administrative practice in the business sector concerned or the technical conditions under which the invoices are issued make it difficult to comply with all the requirements referred to in paragraph 3(b).

In any case, these invoices must contain the following:

- the date of issue,

- identification of the taxable person,

- identification of the type of goods supplied or services rendered,

- the tax due or the information needed to calculate it.

- the simplified arrangements provided for in this point may not be applied to transactions referred to in paragraph 4(c).]⁴

[(e) In cases where Member States make use of the option provided for in the third indent of point (a) to refrain from allocating a number as referred to in paragraph 1(c) to taxable persons who do not carry out any of the transactions referred to in paragraph 4(c), and where the supplier or the customer have not been allocated an identification number of this type, the invoice should feature instead another number called the tax reference number, as defined by the Member States concerned.

When the taxable person has been allocated an identification number as referred to in paragraph 1(c), the Member States reh) point 3, the number referred to in paragraph 1(c) and the tax receipt number of the supplier;

— for services rendered referred to in Article 28b(C), (D), (E) and (F) and for the supply of goods referred to in Article 28c(A) and (E) point 3, the number referred to in paragraph 1(c) and the tax receipt number of the supplier;

— for other supplies of goods and services, only the tax reference number of the supplier or only the number referred to in paragraph 1(c).]⁴

s8(1A) **10.** Member States shall take measures to ensure that non-taxable legal
b)&(e) persons who are liable for the tax payable in respect of intra-Community acquisitions of goods covered by the first subparagraph of Article 28a(1)(a) comply with the above obligations relating to declaration and payment and that they are identified by an individual number as defined in paragraph 1(c), (d) and (e).

3B,
2B), **[11.** In the case of intra-Community acquisitions of products subject to
9(4). excise duty referred to in Article 28a(1)(c) as well as]³ in the case of intra-Community acquisitions of new means of transport covered by Article 28a(1)(b), Member States shall adopt arrangements for declaration and subsequent payment.

s19A **12.** Acting unanimously on a proposal from the Commission, the Council may authorize any Member State to introduce particular measures to simplify the statement obligations laid down in paragraph 6(b). Such simplification measures, which shall not jeopardize the proper monitoring of intra-Community transactions, may take the following forms:

(a) Member States may authorize taxable persons who meet the following three conditions to file one-year recapitulative statements indicating the numbers by which the persons to whom those taxable persons have supplied goods under the conditions laid down in Article 28c(A) are identified for purposes of value added tax in other Member States:

— the total annual value, less value added tax, of their supplies of goods or provisions of services, as defined in Articles 5, 6 and 28a(5), does not exceed by more than ECU 35 000 the amount of the annual turnover which is used as a reference for application of the exemption from tax provided for in Article 24,

— the total annual value, less value added tax, of supplies of goods effected by them under the conditions laid down in Article 28c(A) does not exceed the equivalent in national currency of ECU 15 000,

— supplies of goods effected by them under the conditions laid down in Article 28c(A) are other than supplies or new means of transport;

(b) Member States which set at over three months the tax period for which a taxable person must submit the returns provided for in paragraph 4 may authorize such persons to submit recapitulative statements for the same period where those taxable persons meet the following three conditions:

— the overall annual value, less value added tax, of the goods and services they supply, as defined in Articles 5, 6 and 28a(5), does not exceed the equivalent in national currency of ECU 200 000,

— the total annual value, less value added tax, of supplies of goods effected by them under the conditions laid down in Article 28c(A) does not exceed the equivalent in national currency of ECU 15 000,

— supplies of goods effected by them under the conditions provided for in Article 28c(A) are other than supplies of new means of transport][10]

Amendments

1 Substituted by Art 2, Council Directive 2002/38/EC of 7 May 2002 (w.e.f. 15 May 2002).

2 Substituted by Art 1(6), Council Directive 2003/92/EC of 7 October 2003 (w.e.f. 1 January 2005).

3 Inserted by Art 1(20), Council Directive 92/111/EEC of 14 December 1992, (w.e.f. 1 January 1993).

4 Inserted by Art 28h as amended by Art 2, Council Directive 2001/115/EC of 20 December 2001, (w.e.f. 1 January 2004).

5 Inserted by Art 28h (Sixth Directive) as amended by Art 1(12), Council Directive 95/7/EC of 10 April 1995, (w.e.f. 25 May 1995).

6 Substituted by Art 28h (Sixth Directive) as amended by Art 1(12), Council Directive 95/7/EC of 10 April 1995, (w.e.f. 25 May 1995).

7 Para6(b)(5th subpara) deleted by Art 28h (Sixth Directive) as amended by Art 1(12), Council Directive 95/7/EC of 10 April 1995, (w.e.f. 25 May 1995).

8 See note below

9 Amended by Art 28(h) as amended by Art (1), Council Directive 00/65/EC of 17 October 2000.

10 Art22 substituted by Art 28h (Sixth Directive) as amended by Art 1, Council Directive 91/680/EEC of 16 December 1991, (w.e.f. 1 January 1993 for the transitional period specified in Art 28l).

Note

Decision 92/617/EEC derogation, (as amended by Council Decision 00/435/EC) '…, Ireland is hereby authorised, with effect from 1 January 1993 until 31 December 1996 or until the end of the transitional arrangements in the unlikely event that this is later, to introduce particular measures in accordance with subparagraphs (a) and (b) of Article 22 (12), to simplify the obligations laid down in paragraph 6 (b) of Article 22 regarding recapitulative statements.'

Case law

Eismann Alto Adige Srl v Ufficio Imposta sul Valore Aggento di Bolzano	C217/94	Obligations for Payment
Faaborg-Gelting Linien A/S v Finanzamt Flensburg	C231/94	Restaurant services/Place of Supply
Federation of Technological Industries and Others v Customs & Excise	C384/04	Anti-avoidance measures/Persons liable to pay tax
WLD Worldwide Leather Diffusion Ltd v Revenue Commissioners	Irish (1994) ITR 165	Registration/Taxable Person

[Article 22a

Right of access to invoices stored by electronic means in another Member State

When a taxable person stores invoices which he issues or receives by an electronic means guaranteeing online access to the data and when the place of storage is in a Member State other than that in which he is established, the competent authorities in the Member State in which he is established shall have a right, for the purpose of this directive, to access by electronic means, download and use these invoices within the limits set by the regulations of the Member State where the taxable person is established and as far as that State requires for control purposes.][1]

Amendments
1   Inserted by Art 3, Council Directive 2001/115/EC of 20 December 2001, (w.e.f. 1 January 2004).

Article 23

s13A,
3B(4)
& 15

Obligations in respect of imports

As regards imported goods, Member States shall lay down the detailed rules for the making of the declarations and payments.

In particular, Member States may provide that the value added tax payable on importation of goods by taxable persons or persons liable to tax or certain categories of these two need not be paid at the time of importation, on condition that the tax is mentioned as such in a return to be submitted under Article 22(4).

Case law

Drexl, Rainer	C299/86	Imports
Heinonen, Sami	C394/97	Imports/Criminal Proceedings

TITLE XIV

special schemes

Article 24

Special scheme for small undertakings

1. Member States which might encounter difficulties in applying the normal tax scheme to small undertakings by reasons of their activities or structure shall have the option, under such conditions and with such limits as they may set but subject to the consultation provided for in Article 29, of applying simplified procedures such as flat-rate schemes for charging and collecting the tax provided they do not lead to a reduction thereof.

2. Until a date to be fixed by the Council acting unanimously on a proposal from the Commission, but which shall not be later than on which the charging of tax on imports and the remission of tax on exports in trade between the Member States are abolished:

    (a) Member States which have made use of the option under Article 14 of the second Council Directive of 11 April 1967 to introduce exemptions or graduated tax relief may retain them and the arrangements for applying them if they conform with the value added tax system.

    Those Member States which apply an exemption from tax to taxable persons whose annual turnover is less than the equivalent in national currency of 5,000 European Units of Account at the conversion rate of the day on which this Directive is adopted, may increase this exemption up to 5,000 European Units of Account.

    Member States which apply graduated tax relief may neither increase the ceiling of the graduated tax reliefs nor render the conditions for the granting of it more favourable;

    (b) Member States which have not made use of this option may grant an exemption from tax to taxable persons whose annual turnover is at the maximum equal to the equivalent in national currency of 5,000 European Units of Account at the conversion rate of the day on which this Directive is adopted; where appropriate, they may grant graduated tax relief to taxable persons whose annual turnover exceeds the ceiling fixed by the Member States for the application of exemption;

    (c) Member States which apply an exemption from tax to taxable persons whose annual turnover is equal to or higher than the equivalent in national currency of 5,000 European Units of Account at the conversion rate of the day on which this Directive is adopted, may increase it in order to maintain its value in real terms.

3. The concepts of exemption and graduated tax relief shall apply to the supply of goods and services by small undertakings.

    Member States may exclude certain transactions from the arrangements provided for in paragraph 2. The provisions of paragraph 2 shall not, in any case, apply to the transactions referred to in Article 4(3).

[In all circumstances supplies of new means of transport effected under the conditions laid down in Article 28c(A) as well as supplies of goods and services effected by a taxable person who is not established in the territory of the country shall be excluded from the exemption from tax under paragraph 2.][1]

4. The turnover which shall serve as a reference for the purposes of applying the provisions of paragraph 2 shall consist of the amount, exclusive of value added tax, of goods and services supplied as defined in Articles 5 and 6, to the extent that they are taxed, including transactions exempted with refund of tax previously paid in accordance with Article 28(2), and the amount of the transactions exempted pursuant to Article 15, the amount of real property transactions, the financial transactions referred to in Article 13B(d) and insurance services, unless these transactions are ancillary transactions.

   However, disposals of tangible or intangible capital assets of an undertaking shall not be taken into account for the purposes of calculating turnover.

5. Taxable persons exempt from tax shall not be entitled to deduct tax in accordance with the provisions of Article 17, nor to show the tax on their invoices [...][2].

6. Taxable persons eligible for exemption from tax may opt either for the normal value added tax scheme or for the simplified procedures referred to in paragraph 1. In this case they shall be entitled to any graduated tax relief which may be laid down by national legislation.

7. Subject to the application of paragraph 1, taxable persons enjoying graduated relief shall be treated as taxable persons subject to the normal value added tax scheme.

8. At four-yearly intervals, and for the first time on 1 January 1982, and after consultation of the Member States, the Commission shall report to the Council on the application of the provisions of this Article. It shall as far as may be necessary, and taking into account the need to ensure the long-term convergence of national regulations, attach to this report proposals for:

   (a) improvements to be made to the special scheme for small undertakings;

   (b) the adaptation of national systems as regards exemptions and graduated value added tax relief;

   (c) the adaptation of the limit of 5,000 European Units of Account mentioned in paragraph 2.

9. The Council will decide at the appropriate time whether the realization of the objective referred to in Article 4 of the first Council Directive of 11 April 1967 requires the introduction of a special scheme for small undertakings and will, if appropriate, decide on the limits and common implementing conditions of this scheme. Until the introduction of such a scheme, Member States may retain their own special schemes which

they will apply in accordance with the provisions of this Article and of subsequent acts of the Council.

Amendments

1　Inserted by Art 28i (Sixth Directive) w.e.f. 1 January 1993.

2　Deleted by Art 4, Council Directive 2001/115/EC of 20 December 2001, (w.e.f. 6 February 2002).

[Article 24a

In implementing Article 24(2) to (6), the following Member States may grant an exemption from value added tax to taxable persons whose annual turnover is less than the equivalent in national currency at the conversion rate on the date of their accession:

- in the Czech Republic: EUR 35 000;

- in Estonia: EUR 16 000;

- in Cyprus: EUR 15 600;

- in Latvia: EUR 17 200;

- in Lithuania: EUR 29 000;

- in Hungary: EUR 35 000;

- in Malta: EUR 37 000 when the economic activity consists principally in the supply of goods, EUR 24 300 when the economic activity consists principally in the supply of services with a low value added (high inputs), and EUR 14 600 in other cases, namely service providers with a high value added (low inputs);

- in Poland: EUR 10 000;

- in Slovenia: EUR 25 000;

- in Slovakia: EUR 35 000.][1]

Amendments
1 Replaced by Annex V, Point (1)(a), Council Directive 2004/66/EC of 26 April 2004 (w.e.f. 1 May 2004).

Article 25

Common flat-rate scheme for farmers

8(3)(a) **1.** Where the application to farmers of the normal value added tax scheme, or the simplified scheme provided for in Article 24, would give rise to difficulties, Member States may apply to farmers a flat-rate scheme tending to offset the value added tax charged on purchases of goods and services made by the flat-rate farmers pursuant to this Article.

(2). **2.** For the purposes of this Article, the following definitions shall apply:

— `farmer': a taxable person who carries on his activity in one of the undertakings defined below,

— `agricultural, forestry or fisheries undertakings': an undertaking considered to be such by each Member State within the framework of the production activities listed in Annex A,

— `flat-rate farmer': a farmer subject to the flat-rate scheme provided for in paragraphs 3 et seq.,

— `agricultural products': goods produced by an agricultural, forestry or fisheries undertaking in each — Member State as a result of the activities listed in Annex A,

— `agricultural service': any service as set out in Annex B supplied by a farmer using his labour force and/or by means of the equipment normally available on the agricultural, forestry or fisheries undertaking operated by him,

— `value added tax charge on inputs': the amount of the total value added tax attaching to the goods and services purchased by all agricultural, forestry and fisheries undertakings of each Member State subject to the flat-rate scheme where such tax would be deductible under Article 17 by a farmer subject to the normal value added tax scheme,

— `flat-rate compensation percentages': the percentages fixed by Member States in accordance with paragraph 3 and applied by them in the cases specified in paragraph 5 to enable flat-rate farmers to offset at a fixed rate the value added tax charge on inputs,

— `flat-rate compensation': the amount arrived at by applying the flat-rate compensation percentage provided for in paragraph 3 to the turnover of the flat-rate farmer in the cases referred to in paragraph 5.

11(1)(f) **3.** Member States shall fix the flat-rate compensation percentages, where necessary, and shall notify the Commission before applying them. Such percentages shall be based on macro-economic statistics for flat-rate farmers alone for the preceding three years. They may not be used to obtain for flat-rate farmers refunds greater than the value added tax charges on inputs. Member States shall have the option of reducing such percentages to a nil rate. The percentage may be rounded up or down to the nearest half point.

Member States may fix varying flat-rate compensation percentages for forestry, for the different sub-divisions of agriculture and for fisheries.

s 8(3)(a) **4.**   Member States may release flat-rate farmers from the obligations imposed upon taxable persons by Article 22.

[When they exercise this option, Member States shall take the measures necessary to ensure the correct application of the transitional arrangements for the taxation of intra-Community transactions as laid down in Title XVIa.]¹

[**5.**   The flat-rate percentages provided for in paragraph 3 shall be applied to the prices, exclusive of tax, of:

s 11(1)(f)   (a) agricultural products supplied by flat-rate farmers to taxable persons other than those eligible within the territory of the country for the flat-rate scheme provided for in this Article;

(b) agricultural products supplied by flat-rate farmers, under the conditions laid down in Article 28c(A), to non-taxable legal persons not eligible, in the Member State of arrival of the dispatch or transport of the agricultural products thus supplied, for the derogation provided for in Article 28a(1)(a), second subparagraph;

s12A   (c) agricultural services supplied by flat-rate farmers to taxable persons other than those eligible within the territory of the country for the flat-rate scheme provided for in this Article.

This compensation shall exclude any other form of deduction.]²

s12 &12A [**6.**   In the case of supplies of agricultural products and of agricultural services referred to in paragraph 5, Member States shall provide for the flat-rate compensation to be paid either:

(a) by the purchaser or customer. In that event, the taxable purchaser or customer shall be authorized, as provided for in Article 17 and in accordance with the procedures laid down by the Member States, to deduct from the tax for which he is liable within the territory of the country the amount of the flat-rate compensation he has paid to flat-rate farmers.

Member States shall refund to the purchaser or customer the amount of the flat-rate compensation he has paid to flat-rate farmers in respect of any of the following transactions:

— supplies of agricultural products effected under the conditions laid down in Article 28c(A) to taxable persons, or to non-taxable legal persons acting as such in another Member State within which they are not eligible for the derogation provided for in the second subparagraph of Article 28a(1)(a),

— supplies of agricultural products effected under the conditions laid down in Article 15 and in Article 16(1)(B), (D) and (E) to taxable purchasers established outside the Community, provided that the products are used by those purchasers for the purposes of the transactions referred to in Article 17(3)(a) and (b) or for the purposes of services which are deemed to be supplied within the territory of the country and on which tax is payable solely by the customers under Article 21(1)(b),

— supplies of agricultural services to taxable customers established within the Community but in another Member State or to taxable customers established outside the Community, provided that the services are used by those customers for the purposes of the transactions referred to in Article 17(3)(a) and (b) and for the purposes of services which are deemed to be supplied within the territory of the country and on which tax is payable solely by the customers under Article 21(1)(b).

Member States shall determine the method by which the refunds are to be made. In particular, they may apply Article 17(4); or

(b) by the public authorities.][3]

7. Member States shall make all necessary provisions to check properly the payment of the flat-rate compensation to the flat-rate farmers.

s12A 8. As regards all supplies of agricultural products and agricultural services other than those covered by paragraph 5, the flat-rate compensation is deemed to be paid by the purchaser or customer.

(3)(a) 9. Each Member State may exclude from the flat-rate scheme certain categories of farmers and farmers for whom the application of the normal value added tax scheme, or the simplified scheme provided for in Article 24(1), would not give rise to administrative difficulties.

[Whenever they exercise the option provided for in this Article, Member States shall take all measures necessary to ensure that the same method of taxation is applied to supplies of agricultural products effected under the conditions laid down in Article 28b(B)(1), whether the supply is effected by a flat-rate farmer or by a taxable person other than a flat-rate farmer.][4]

(a) 10. Every flat-rate farmer may opt, subject to the rules and conditions to be
(e)   laid down by each Member State, for application of the normal value added tax scheme or, as the case may be, the simplified scheme provided for in Article 24(1).

11. The Commission shall, before the end of the fifth year following the entry into force of this Directive, present to the Council new proposals concerning the application of the value added tax to transactions in respect of agricultural products and services.

12. When they take up the option provided for in this Article the Member States shall fix the uniform basis of assessment of the value added tax in order to apply the scheme of own resources using the common method of calculation in Annex C.

Amendments
1 Inserted by Art 28j(1) (Sixth Directive), w.e.f. 1 January 1993, for the transitional period specified in Art 28l.
2 Inserted by Art 28j(2) (Sixth Directive), w.e.f. 1 January 1993, for the transitional period specified in Art 28l.
3 Inserted by Art 28j(2) (Sixth Directive), w.e.f. 1 January 1993, for the transitional period specified in Art 28l.
4 Inserted by Art 28j(3) (Sixth Directive), w.e.f. 1 January 1993, for the transitional period specified in Art 28l.

Case law
Stadt Sundern v Bundesfinanzhof   C43/04   Flat-rate scheme for farmers/
Finanzamt Arnsberg   Agricultural service

Article 26
Special scheme for travel agents

1. Member States shall apply value added tax to the operations of travel agents in accordance with the provisions of this Article, where the travel agents deal with customers in their own name and use the supplies and services of other taxable persons in the provision of travel facilities. This Article shall not apply to travel agents who are acting only as intermediaries and accounting for tax in accordance with Article 11A(3)(c). In this Article travel agents include tour operators.

2. All transactions performed by the travel agent in respect of a journey shall be treated as a single service supplied by the travel agent to the traveller. It shall be taxable in the Member State in which the travel agent has established his business or has a fixed establishment from which the travel agent has provided the services. The taxable amount and the price exclusive of tax, within the meaning of Article 22(3)(b), in respect of this service shall be the travel agent's margin, that is to say, the difference between the total amount to be paid by the traveller, exclusive of value added tax, and the actual cost to the travel agent of supplies and services provided by other taxable persons where these transactions are for the direct benefit of the traveller.

3. If transactions entrusted by the travel agent to other taxable persons are performed by such persons outside the Community, the travel agent's service shall be treated as an exempted intermediary activity under Article 15(14). Where these transactions are performed both inside and outside the Community, only that part of the travel agent's service relating to transactions outside the Community may be exempted.

4. Tax charged to the travel agent by other taxable persons on the transactions described in paragraph 2 which are for the direct benefit of the traveller, shall not be eligible for deduction or refund in any Member State.

Case law

DFDS A/S v Customs and Excise	C260/95	Travel agent/Taxable Person
First Choice Holidays plc and Commissioners of Customs & Excise	C149/01	Travel Agents/Taxable Amount
Van Ginkel Waddinzveen BV Reis-en Passagebureau van Ginkel BV v Inspecteur der Omzetbelasting	C163/91	Taxable Amount

[Article 26a

Special arrangements applicable to second-hand goods, works of art, collectors' items and antiques

A. Definitions

For the purposes of this Article, and without prejudice to other Community provisions:

(a) **works of art** shall mean the objects referred to in (a) of Annex I.

However, Member States shall have the option of not considering as "works of art" the items mentioned in the final three indents in (a) in Annex I;

(b) **collectors items** shall mean the objects referred to in (b) of Annex I;

(c) **antiques** shall mean the objects referred to in (c) of Annex I;

(d) **second-hand goods** shall mean tangible movable property that is suitable for further use as it is or after repair, other than works of art, collectors' items or antiques and other than precious metals or precious stones as defined by the Member States;

(e) **taxable dealer** shall mean a taxable person who, in the course of his economic activity, purchases or acquires for the purposes of his undertaking, or imports with a view to resale, second-hand goods and/or works of art, collectors' items or antiques, whether that taxable person is acting for himself or on behalf of another person pursuant to a contract under which commission is payable on purchase or sale;

(f) **organizer of a sale by public auction** shall mean any taxable person who, in the course of his economic activity, offers goods for sale by public auction with a view to handing them over to the highest bidder;

(g) **principal of an organizer of a sale by public auction** shall mean any person who transmits goods to an organizer of a sale by public auction under a contract under which commission is payable on a sale subject to the following provisions:

— the organizer of the sale by public auction offers the goods for sale in his own name but on behalf of his principal,

— the organizer of the sale by public auction hands over the goods, in his own name but on behalf of his principal, to the highest bidder at the public auction.

B. Special arrangements for taxable dealers

1. In respect of supplies of second-hand goods, works of art, collectors' items and antiques effected by taxable dealers, Member States shall apply special arrangements for taxing the profit margin made by the taxable dealer, in accordance with the following provisions.

2. The supplies of goods referred to in paragraph 1 shall be supplies, by a taxable dealer, of second-hand goods, works of art, collectors' items or antiques supplied to him within the Community:

- by a non-taxable person, or

- by another taxable person, in so far as the supply of goods by that other taxable person is exempt in accordance with Article 13(B)(c), or

- by another taxable person in so far as the supply of goods by that other taxable person qualifies for the exemption provided for in Article 24 and involves capital assets, or

- by another taxable dealer, in so far as the supply of goods by that other taxable dealer was subject to value added tax in accordance with these special arrangements.

3. The taxable amount of the supplies of goods referred to in paragraph 2 shall be the profit margin made by the taxable dealer, less the amount of value added tax relating to the profit margin. That profit margin shall be equal to the difference between the selling price charged by the taxable dealer for the goods and the purchase price.

For the purposes of this paragraph, the following definitions shall apply:

- **selling price** shall mean everything which constitutes the consideration, which has been, or is to be, obtained by the taxable dealer from the purchaser or a third- party, including subsidies directly linked to that transaction, taxes, duties, levies and charges and incidental expenses such as commission, packaging, transport and insurance costs charged by the taxable dealer to the purchaser but excluding the amounts referred to in Article 11(A)(3),

- **purchase price** shall mean everything which constitutes the consideration defined in the first indent, obtained, or to be obtained, from the taxable dealer by his supplier.

4. Member States shall entitle taxable dealers to opt for application of the special arrangements to supplies of:

(a) works of art, collectors' items or antiques which they have imported themselves;

(b) works of art supplied to them by their creators or their successors in title;

(c) works of art supplied to them by a taxable person other than a taxable dealer where the supply by that other taxable person was subject to the reduced rate pursuant to Article 12(3)(c).

Member States shall determine the detailed rules for exercising this option which shall in any event cover a period at least equal to two calendar years.

If the option is taken up, the taxable amount shall be determined in accordance with paragraph 3. For supplies of works of art, collectors' items or antiques which the taxable dealer has imported himself, the purchase price to be taken into account in calculating the margin shall be equal to the taxable amount on importation, determined in accordance with Article 11(B), plus the value added tax due or paid on importation.

5. Where they are effected in the conditions laid down in Article 15, the supplies of second-hand goods, works of art, collectors' item or antiques subject to the special arrangements for taxing the margin shall be exempt.

6. Taxable persons shall not be entitled to deduct from the tax for which they are liable the value added tax due or paid in respect of goods which have been, or are to be, supplied to them by. a taxable dealer, in so far as the supply of those goods by the taxable dealer is subject to the special arrangements for taxing the margin.

7. In so far as goods are used for the purpose of supplies by him subject to the special arrangements for taxing the margin, the taxable dealer shall not be entitled to deduct from the tax for which he is liable:

    (a) the value added tax due or paid in respect of works of art, collectors' items or antiques which he has imported himself;

    (b) the value added tax due or paid in respect of works of art which have been, or are to be, supplied to him by their creators or their successors in title;

    (c) the value added tax due or paid in respect of works of art which have been, or are to be, supplied to him by a taxable person other than a taxable dealer.

8. Where he is led to apply both the normal arrangements for value added tax and the special arrangements for taxing the margin, the taxable dealer must follow separately in his accounts the transactions falling under each of these arrangements, according to rules laid down by the Member States.

9. The taxable dealer may not indicate separately on the invoices which he issues, [...]¹ tax relating to supplies of goods which he makes subject to the special arrangements for taxing the margin.

10. In order to simplify the procedure for charging the tax and subject to the consultation provided for in Article 29, Member States may provide that, for certain transactions or for certain categories of taxable dealers, the taxable amount of supplies of goods subject to the special arrangements for taxing the margin shall be determined for each tax period during which the taxable dealer must submit the return referred to in Article 22(4).

    In that event, the taxable amount for supplies of goods to which the same rate of value added tax is applied shall be the total margin made by the taxable dealer less the amount of value added tax relating to that margin.

    The total margin shall be equal to the difference between:

    — the total amount of supplies of goods subject to the special arrangements for taxing the margin effected by the taxable dealer during the period; that amount shall be equal to the total selling prices determined in accordance with paragraph 3,

        and

    — the total amount of purchases of goods as referred to in paragraph 2 effected, during that period, by the taxable dealer; that amount shall be equal to the total purchase prices determined in accordance with paragraph 3.

Member States shall take the necessary measures to ensure that the taxable persons concerned do not enjoy unjustified advantages or sustain unjustified loss.

11. The taxable dealer may apply the normal value added tax arrangements to any supply covered by the special arrangements pursuant to paragraph 2 or 4.

Where the taxable dealer applies the normal value added tax arrangements to:

(a) the supply of a work of art, collectors' item or antique which he has imported himself, he shall be entitled to deduct from his tax liability the value added tax due or paid on the import of those goods;

(b) the supply of a work of art supplied to him by its creator or his successors in title, he shall be entitled to deduct from his tax liability the value added tax due or paid for the work of art supplied to him;

(c) the supply of a work of art supplied to him by a taxable person other than a taxable dealer, he shall be entitled to deduct from his tax liability the value added tax due or paid for the work of art supplied to him.

This right to deduct shall arise at the time when the tax due for the supply in respect of which the taxable dealer opts for application of the normal value added tax arrangements become chargeable.

C. Special arrangements for sales by public auction

1. By way of derogation from B, Member States may determine, in accordance with the following provisions, the taxable amount of supplies of second-hand goods, works of art, collectors' items or antiques effected by an organizer of sales by public auction, acting in his own name, pursuant to a contract under which commission is payable on the sale of those goods by public auction, on behalf of:

— a non-taxable person,

or

— another taxable person, in so far as the supply of goods, within the meaning of Article 5(4)(c), by that other taxable person is exempt in accordance with Article 13(B)(c),

or

— another taxable person, in so far as the supply of goods, within the meaning of Article 5(4)(c), by that other taxable person qualifies for the exemption provided for in Article 24 and involves capital assets,

or

— a taxable dealer, in so far as the supply of goods, within the meaning of Article 5(4)(c), by that other taxable dealer,

- is subject to tax in accordance with the special arrangements for taxing the margin provided for in B.

2. The taxable amount of each supply of goods referred to in paragraph 1 shall be the total amount invoiced in accordance with paragraph 4 to the purchaser by the organizer of the sale by public auction, less:

- the net amount paid or to be paid by the organizer of the sale by public auction to his principal, determined in accordance with paragraph 3,

and

- the amount of the tax due by the organizer of the sale by public auction in respect of his supply.

3. The net amount paid or to be paid by the organizer of the sale by public auction to his principal shall be equal to the difference between:

- the price of the goods at public auction,

and

- the amount of the commission obtained or to be obtained by the organizer of the sale by public auction from his principal, under the contract whereby commission is payable on the sale.

4. The organizer of the sale by public auction must issue to the purchaser an invoice [...]² itemizing:

- the auction price of the goods,
- taxes, dues, levies and charges,
- incidental expenses such as commission, packing, transport and insurance costs charged by the organizer to the purchaser of the goods.

That invoice must not indicate any value added tax separately.

5. The organizer of the sale by public auction to whom the goods were transmitted under a contract whereby commission is payable on a public auction sale must issue a statement to his principal.

That statement must itemize the amount of the transaction, i.e. the auction price of the goods less the amount of the commission obtained or to be obtained from the principal.

A statement so drawn up shall serve as the invoice which the principal, where he is a taxable person, must issue to the organizer of the sale by public auction in accordance with Article 22(3).

6. Organizers of sales by public auction who supply goods under the conditions laid down in paragraph 1 must indicate in their accounts, in suspense accounts:

- the amounts obtained or to be obtained from the purchaser of the goods,
- the amount reimbursed or to be reimbursed to the vendor of the goods.

These amounts must be duly substantiated.

7.   The supply of goods to a taxable person who is an organizer of sales by public auction shall be regarded as being effected when the sale of those goods by public auction is itself effected.

D. Transitional arrangements for the taxation of trade between Member States

During the period referred to in Article 281, Member States shall apply the following provisions:

(a) supplies of new means of transport, within the meaning of Article 28a(2), effected within the conditions laid down in Article 28c(A) shall be excluded from the special arrangements provided for in B and C;

(b) by way of derogation from Article 28a(1)(a), intra-Community acquisitions of second-hand goods, works of art, collectors' items or antiques shall not be subject to value added tax where the vendor is a taxable dealer acting as such and the goods acquired have been subject to tax in the Member State of departure of the dispatch or transport, in accordance with the special arrangements for taxing the margin provided for in B, or where the vendor is an organizer of sales by public auction acting as such and the goods acquired have been subject to tax in the Member State of departure of the dispatch or transport, in accordance with the special arrangements provided for in C;

(c) Articles 28b(B) and 28c(A)(a), (c) and (d) shall not apply to supplies of goods subject to value added tax in accordance with either of the special arrangements laid down in B and C.][3]

Amendments
1   Deleted by Art 4, Council Directive 2001/115/EC of 20 December 2001, (w.e.f. 6 February 2002).
2   Deleted by Art 4, Council Directive 2001/115/EC of 20 December 2001, (w.e.f. 6 February 2002).
3   Art26a inserted by Art 1(3), Council Directive 94/5/EC of 14 February 1994.

Case law

Förvaltnings AB Stenholmen and Riksskatteverket	C320/02	Second-hand goods/live animals
Jyske Finans A/S v Skatteministeriet	C280/04	Exemption of supplies excluded from the right to deduct/Meaning of taxable dealer

[Article 26b

Special scheme for investment gold

A. Definition

For the purposes of this Directive, and without prejudice to other Community provisions: `investment gold' shall mean:

(i) gold, in the form of a bar or a wafer of weights accepted by the bullion markets, of a purity equal to or greater than 995 thousandths, whether or not represented by securities. Member States may exclude from the scheme small bars or wafers of a weight of 1 g or less;

(ii) gold coins which:

   — are of a purity equal to or greater than 900 thousandths,

   — are minted after 1800,

   — are or have been legal tender in the country of origin, and

   — are normally sold at a price which does not exceed the open market value of the gold contained in the coins by more than 80 %.

Such coins are not, for the purpose of this Directive, considered to be sold for numismatic interest.

Each Member State shall inform the Commission before 1 July each year, starting in 1999, of the coins meeting these criteria which are traded in that Member State. The Commission shall publish a comprehensive list of these coins in the "C" series of the Official Journal of the European Communities before 1 December each year. Coins included in the published list shall be deemed to fulfill these criteria for the whole year for which the list is published.

B. Special arrangements applicable to investment gold transactions

Member States shall exempt from value added tax the supply, intra-Community acquisition and importation of investment gold, including investment gold represented by certificates for allocated or unallocated gold or traded on gold accounts and including, in particular, gold loans and swaps, involving a right of ownership or claim in respect of investment gold, as well as transactions concerning investment gold involving futures and forward contracts leading to a transfer of right of ownership or claim in respect of investment gold.

Member States shall also exempt services of agents who act in the name and for the account of another when they intervene in the supply of investment gold for their principal.

C. Option to tax

Member States shall allow taxable persons who produce investment gold or transform any gold into investment gold as defined in A a right of option for taxation of supplies of investment gold to another taxable person which would otherwise be exempt under B.

Member States may allow taxable persons, who in their trade normally supply gold for industrial purposes, a right of option for taxation of supplies of investment gold as defined in A(i) to another taxable person, which would otherwise be exempt under B. Member States may restrict the scope of this option. Where the supplier has exercised a right of option for taxation pursuant to the first or second paragraph, Member States shall allow a right of option for taxation for the agent in respect of the services mentioned in the second paragraph of B.

Member States shall specify the details of the use of these options, and shall inform the Commission of the rules of application for the exercise of these options in that Member State.

D. Right of deduction

1. Taxable persons shall be entitled to deduct

    (a) tax due or paid in respect of investment gold supplied to them by a person who has exercised the right of option under C or supplied to them pursuant to the procedure laid down in G;

    (b) tax due or paid in respect of supply to them, or intra-Community acquisition or importation by them, of gold other than investment gold which is subsequently transformed by them or on their behalf into investment gold;

    (c) tax due or paid in respect of services supplied to them consisting of change of form, weight or purity of gold including investment gold,

    if their subsequent supply of this gold is exempt under this Article.

2. Taxable persons who produce investment gold or transform any gold into investment gold, shall be entitled to deduct tax due or paid by them in respect of supplies, or intra-Community acquisition or importation of goods or services linked to the production or transformation of that gold as if their subsequent supply of the gold exempted under this Article were taxable.

E. Special obligations for traders in investment gold

Member States shall, as a minimum, ensure that traders in investment gold keep account of all substantial transactions in investment gold and keep the documentation to allow identification of the customer in such transactions.

Traders shall keep this information for a period of at least five years.

Member States may accept equivalent obligations under measures adopted pursuant to other Community legislation, such as Council Directive 91/308/EEC of 10 June 1991 on prevention of the use of the financial system for the purpose of money laundering, to meet the requirements of the first paragraph.

Member States may lay down stricter obligations, in particular on special record keeping or special accounting requirements.

F. Reverse charge procedure

By way of derogation from Article 21(1)(a), as amended by Article 28g, in the case of supplies of gold material or semi-manufactured products of a purity of 325 thousandths or greater, or supplies of investment gold where an option referred to in C of this Article has been exercised, Member States may designate the purchaser as the person liable to pay the tax, according to the procedures and conditions which they shall lay down. When they exercise this option, Member States shall take the measures necessary to ensure that the person designated as liable for the tax due fulfils the obligations to submit a statement and to pay the tax in accordance with Article 22.

G. Procedure for transactions on a regulated gold bullion market

1. A Member State may, subject to consultation provided for under Article 29, disapply the exemption for investment gold provided for by this special scheme in respect of specific transactions, other than intra-Community supplies or exports, concerning investment gold taking place in that Member State:

   (a) between taxable persons who are members of a bullion market regulated by the Member State concerned, and

   (b) where the transaction is between a member of a bullion market regulated by the Member State concerned and another taxable person who is not a member of that market.

   Under these circumstances, these transactions shall be taxable and the following shall apply.

2. (a) For transactions under 1(a), for the purpose of simplification, the Member State shall authorise suspension of the tax to be collected as well as dispense with the recording requirements of value added tax.

   (b) For transactions under 1(b), the reverse charge procedure under F shall be applicable. Where a non-member of the bullion market would not, other than for these transactions, be liable for registration for VAT in the relevant Member State, the member shall fulfil the fiscal obligations on behalf of the non-member, according to the provisions of that Member State.][1]

Amendments
1   Art26b inserted by Art 1, Council Directive 98/80/EC of 12 October 1998, (w.e.f. 17 October 1998).

Note
   List of gold coins meeting the criteria established in Article 26b(a)(ii) of Council Directive 77/388/EEC of 17 May 1977 as amended by Directive 98/80/EC of 12 October 1998 (special scheme for investment gold)

[**Article 26c**   s5A

Special scheme for non-established taxable persons supplying electronic services to non-taxable persons

A. Definitions

For the purposes of this Article, the following definitions shall apply without prejudice to other Community provisions:

(a) "**non-established taxable person**" means a taxable person who has neither established his business nor has a fixed establishment within the territory of the Community and who is not otherwise required to be identified for tax purposes under Article 22;

(b) "**electronic services**" and "**electronically supplied services**" means those services referred to in the last indent of Article 9(2)(e);

(c) "**Member State of identification**" means the Member State which the non-established taxable person chooses to contact to state when his activity as a taxable person within the territory of the Community commences in accordance with the provisions of this Article;

(d) "**Member State of consumption**" means the Member State in which the supply of the electronic services is deemed to take place according to Article 9(2)(f);

(e) "**value added tax return**" means the statement containing the information necessary to establish the amount of tax that has become chargeable in each Member State.

B. Special scheme for electronically supplied services

1. Member States shall permit a non-established taxable person supplying electronic services to a non-taxable person who is established or has his permanent address or usually resides in a Member State to use a special scheme in accordance with the following provisions. The special scheme shall apply to all those supplies within the Community.

2. The non-established taxable person shall state to the Member State of identification when his activity as a taxable person commences, ceases or changes to the extent that he no longer qualifies for the special scheme. Such a statement shall be made electronically.

   The information from the non-established taxable person to the Member State of identification when his taxable activities commence shall contain the following details for the identification: name, postal address, electronic addresses, including websites, national tax number, if any, and a statement that the person is not identified for value added tax purposes within the Community. The non-established taxable person shall notify the Member State of identification of any changes in the submitted information.

3. The Member State of identification shall identify the non-established taxable person by means of an individual number. Based on the information used for this identification, Member States of consumption may keep their own identification systems.

The Member State of identification shall notify the non-established taxable person by electronic means of the identification number allocated to him.

4. The Member State of identification shall exclude the non-established taxable person from the identification register if:

(a) he notifies that he no longer supplies electronic services, or

(b) it otherwise can be assumed that his taxable activities have ended, or

(c) he no longer fulfils the requirements necessary to be allowed to use the special scheme, or

(d) he persistently fails to comply with the rules concerning the special scheme.

5. The non-established taxable person shall submit by electronic means to the Member State of identification a value added tax return for each calendar quarter whether or not electronic services have been supplied. The return shall be submitted within 20 days following the end of the reporting period to which the return refers.

The value added tax return shall set out the identification number and, for each Member State of consumption where tax has become due, the total value, less value added tax, of supplies of electronic services for the reporting period and total amount of the corresponding tax. The applicable tax rates and the total tax due shall also be indicated.

6. The value added tax return shall be made in euro. Member States which have not adopted the euro may require the tax return to be made in their national currencies. If the supplies have been made in other currencies, the exchange rate valid for the last date of the reporting period shall be used when completing the value added tax return. The exchange shall be done following the exchange rates published by the European Central Bank for that day, or, if there is no publication on that day, on the next day of publication.

7. The non-established taxable person shall pay the value added tax when submitting the return. Payment shall be made to a bank account denominated in euro, designated by the Member State of identification. Member States which have not adopted the euro may require the payment to be made to a bank account denominated in their own currency.

8. Notwithstanding Article 1(1) of Directive 86/560/EEC, the non-established taxable person making use of this special scheme shall, instead of making deductions under Article 17(2)of this Directive, be granted a refund according to Directive 86/560/EEC. Articles 2(2), 2(3) and 4(2) of Directive 86/560/EEC shall not apply to the refund related to electronic supplies covered by this special scheme.

9. The non-established taxable person shall keep records of the transactions covered by this special scheme in sufficient detail to enable the tax administration of the Member State of consumption to determine that the value added tax return referred to in paragraph 5 is correct. These records should be made available electronically on request to the Member State of identification and to the Member State of consumption. These records

shall be maintained for a period of 10 years from the end of the year when the transaction was carried out.

10. Article 21(2)(b) shall not apply to a non-established taxable person who has opted for this special scheme.]¹

Amendments
1 Article 26c inserted by Art 1, Council Directive 2002/38/EC of 7 May 2002. Amended with effect from 15 May 2002 and provisions applicable from 1 July 2003.

TITLE XV

simplification procedures

Article 27

s 3(8),
3A(5)

[1.   The Council, acting unanimously on a proposal from the Commission, may authorise any Member State to introduce special measures for derogation from the provisions of this Directive, in order to simplify the procedure for charging the tax or to prevent certain types of tax evasion or avoidance. Measures intended to simplify the procedure for charging the tax, except to a negligible extent, may not affect the overall amount of the tax revenue of the Member State collected at the stage of final consumption.

2.   A Member State wishing to introduce the measure referred to in paragraph 1 shall send an application to the Commission and provide it with all the necessary information. If the Commission considers that it does not have all the necessary information, it shall contact the Member State concerned within two months of receipt of the application and specify what additional information is required. Once the Commission has all the information it considers necessary for appraisal of the request it shall within one month notify the requesting Member State accordingly and it shall transmit the request, in its original language, to the other Member States.

3.   Within three months of giving the notification referred to in the last sentence of paragraph 2, the Commission shall present to the Council either an appropriate proposal or, should it object to the derogation requested, a communication setting out its objections.

4.   In any event, the procedure set out in paragraphs 2 and 3 shall be completed within eight months of receipt of the application by the Commission.]¹

5.   Those Member States which apply on 1 January 1977 special measures of the type referred to in paragraph 1 above may retain them providing they notify the Commission of them before 1 January 1978 and providing that where such derogations are designed to simplify the procedure for charging tax they conform with the requirement laid down in paragraph 1 above.

Amendments
1   Replaced by Art 1(1), Council Directive 2004/7/EC of 20 January 2004 (w.e.f. 19 February 2004).

Case law

Ampliscientifica Srl and Amplifin SpA v Ministero dell' Economia e delle Finanze, Agenzia delle Entrate	C162/07	Taxable persons/Parent companies and subsidiaries
Direct Cosmetics Ltd (No 1) v Customs & Excise	C5/84	Taxable Amount/party plan selling
Direct Cosmetics Ltd (No 2) v Customs and Excise	C138/86	Taxable Amount/party plan selling
Laughtons Photograph Ltd v Customs and Excise	C139/86	Taxable Amount
Skripalle, Werner v Finanzamt Bergisch Gladback	C63/96	Minimum Taxable Amount
Sosnowska, Alicija v Dyrektor Izby Sakrbowej we Wroclawiu Osrodek Zamiejscowy w Walbrzychu	C25/07	National Legislation determining conditions for repayment of excess VAT

TITLE XVI

transitional provisions

Article 28

1. Any provisions brought into force by the Member States under the provisions of the first four indents of Article 17 of the second Council Directive of 11 April 1967 shall cease to apply, in each Member State, as from the respective dates on which the provisions referred to in the second paragraph of Article 1 of this Directive come into force.

[1a. Until a date which may not be later than 30 June 1999, the United Kingdom of Great Britain and Northern Ireland may, for imports of works of art, collectors' items or antiques which qualified for an exemption on 1 January 1993, apply Article 11(B)(6) in such a way that the value added tax due on importation is, in any event, equal to 2,5% of the amount determined in accordance with Article 11(B)(1) to (4).]¹

s 11(1) [2. Notwithstanding Article 12(3), the following provisions shall apply
2nd &
6th Sch   during the transitional period referred to in Article 28l.

    (a) Exemptions with refund of the tax paid at the preceding stage and reduced rates lower than the minimum rate laid down in Article 12(3) in respect of the reduced rates, which were in force on 1 January 1991 and which are in accordance with Community law, and satisfy the conditions stated in the last indent of Article 17 of the second Council Directive of 11 April 1967 may be maintained.

    Member States shall adopt the measures necessary to ensure the determination of own resources relating to these operations.

    In the event that the provisions of this paragraph create for Ireland distortions of competition in the supply of energy products for heating and lighting, Ireland may, on specific request, be authorized by the Commission to apply a reduced rate to such supplies, in accordance with Article 12(3). In that case, Ireland shall submit its request to the Commission together with all necessary information. If the Commission has not taken a decision within three months of receiving the request, Ireland shall be deemed to be authorized to apply the proposed reduced rates.

    (b) Member States which, at 1 January 1991 in accordance with Community law, applied exemptions with refund of tax paid at the preceding stage, or reduced rates lower than the minimum laid down in Article 12(3) in respect of the reduced rates, to goods and services other than those specified in Annex H, may apply the reduced rate or one of the two reduced rates provided for in Article 12(3) to any such supplies.

    (c) Member States which under the terms of Article 12(3) will be obliged to increase their standard rate as applied at 1 January 1991 by more than 2%, may apply a reduced rate lower than the minimum laid down in Article 12(3) in respect of the reduced rate to supplies of categories of goods and services specified in Annex H. Furthermore, those Member

States may apply such a rate to restaurant services, children's clothing, children's footwear and housing. Member States may not introduce exemptions with refund of the tax at the preceding stage on the basis of this paragraph.

(d) Member States which at 1 January 1991 applied a reduced rate to restaurant services, children's clothing, children's footwear and housing, may continue to apply such a rate to such supplies.

(e) Member States which at 1 January 1991 applied a reduced rate to supplies of goods and services other than those specified in Annex H may apply the reduced rate or one of the two reduced rates provided for in Article 12(3) to such supplies provided that the rate is not lower than 12%.

[This provision may not apply to supplies of second-hand goods, works of art, collectors' items or antiques subject to value added tax in accordance with one of the special arrangements provided for an Article 26a(B) and (C).][2]

(f) The Hellenic Republic may apply VAT rates up to 30% lower than the corresponding rates applied in mainland Greece in the departments of Lesbos, Chios, Samos, the Dodecanese and the Cyclades, and on the following islands in the Aegean: Thasos, Northern Sporades, Samothrace and Skiros.

(g) On the basis of a report from the Commission, the Council shall, before 31 December 1994, re-examine the provisions of subparagraphs (a) to (f) above in relation to the proper functioning of the internal market in particular. In the event of significant distortions of competition arising, the Council, acting unanimously on a proposal from the Commission, shall adopt appropriate measures.

[(h) Member States which, on 1 January 1993, were availing themselves of the option provided for in Article 5(5)(a) as in force on that date, may apply to supplies under a contract to make up work the rate applicable to the goods after making up.

For the purposes of applying this provision, supplies under a contract to make up work shall be deemed to be delivery by a contractor to his customer of movable property made or assembled by the contractor from materials or objects entrusted to him by the customer for this purpose, whether or not the contractor has provided any part of the materials used.][3]][4]

[(i) Member States may apply a reduced rate to supplies of live plants (including bulbs, roots and the like, cut flowers and ornamental foliage) and wood for use as firewood.][5]

[(j) The Republic of Austria may apply one of the two reduced rates provided for in the third subparagraph of Article 12(3)(a) to the letting of immovable property for residential use, provided that the rate is not lower than 10%;

(k) The Portuguese Republic may apply one of the reduced rates provided for in the third subparagraph of Article 12(3)(a) to restaurant services, provided that the rate is not lower than 12%.][6]

1st & **3.** During the transitional period referred to in paragraph 4, Member States
2nd Sch   may:

(a) continue to subject to tax the transactions exempt under Article 13 or 15 set out in Annex E to this Directive;

(b) continue to exempt the activities set out in Annex F under conditions existing in the Member State concerned;

(c) grant to taxable persons the option for taxation of exempt transactions under the conditions set out in Annex G;

(d) continue to apply provisions derogating from the principle of immediate deduction laid down in the first Paragraph of Article 18(2);

(e) continue to apply measures derogating from the provisions of Articles [....],[7] 6(4) and 11A(3)(c);

(f) provide that for supplies of buildings and building land purchased for the purpose of resale by a taxable person for whom tax on the purchase was not deductible, the taxable amount shall be the difference between the selling price and the purchase price;

(g) by way of derogation from Articles 17(3) and 26(3), continue to exempt without repayment of input tax the services of travel agents referred to in Article 26(3). This derogation shall also apply to travel agents acting in the name and on account of the traveller.

[**3a.** Pending a decision by the Council, which, under Article 3 of Directive 89/465/EEC, is to act on the abolition of the transitional derogations provided for in paragraph 3, Spain shall be authorized to exempt the transactions referred to in point 2 of Annex F in respect of services rendered by authors and the transactions referred to in points 23 and 25 of Annex F.][8]

4. The transitional period shall last initially for five years as from January 1, 1978. At the latest six months before the end of this period, and subsequently as necessary, the Council shall review the situation with regard to the derogations set out in paragraph 3 on the basis of a report from the Commission and shall unanimously determine on a proposal from the Commission, whether any or all of these derogations shall be abolished.

5. At the end of the transitional period passenger transport shall be taxed in the country of departure for that part of the journey taking place within the Community according to the detailed rules of procedure to be laid down by the Council acting unanimously on a proposal from the Commission.

[**6.** [The Council, acting unanimously on a proposal from the Commission, may authorise any Member State to apply until 31 December 2010 at the latest the reduced rates provided for in the third subparagraph of Article 12(3)(a) to services listed in a maximum of two of the categories set out in Annex K. In exceptional cases, a Member State may be authorised to apply the reduced rates to services belonging to three of the aforementioned categories.][9]

The services concerned must satisfy the following requirements:

(a) they must be labour intensive;

(b) they must be largely provided direct to final consumers;

(c) they must be mainly local and not likely to create distortions of competition;

(d) there must be a close link between the lower prices resulting from the rate reduction and the foreseeable increase in demand and employment.

The application of a reduced rate must not prejudice the smooth functioning of the internal market.

[Any Member State wishing to apply for the first time after 31 December 2005 a reduced rate to one or more of the services mentioned in the first subparagraph pursuant to this provision shall inform the Commission before 31 March 2006. It shall communicate to it before that date all relevant particulars concerning the new measures it wishes to introduce, and in particular the following:

(a) scope of the measure and detailed description of the services concerned;

(b) particulars showing that the conditions laid down in the second and third subparagraphs have been met;

(c) particulars showing the budgetary cost of the measure envisaged.][10]

Those Member States authorised to apply the reduced rate referred to in the first subparagraph shall, before 1 October 2002, draw up a detailed report containing an overall assessment of the measure's effectiveness in terms notably of job creation and efficiency.

Before 31 December 2002 the Commission shall forward a global evaluation report to the Council and Parliament accompanied, if necessary, by a proposal for appropriate measures for a final decision on the VAT rate applicable to labour-intensive services.][11]

Amendments
1   Para1(a) inserted by Art 1(4), Council Directive 94/5/EC of 14 February 1994.
2   Inserted by Art 1(5), Council Directive 94/5/EC of 14 February 1994.
3   Para2(h) inserted by Art 1(5), Council Directive 95/7/EC of 10 April 1995, (w.e.f. 25 May 1995).
4   Para2 substituted by Art 1(4), Council Directive 92/77/EEC of 19 October 1992, (w.e.f. 1 January 1993).
5   Para2(i) inserted by Art 1(2), Council Directive 96/42/EC of 25 June 1996, (w.e.f. 1 January 1995).
6   Para2(j) & (k) inserted by Art 1, Council Directive 2000/17/EC of 30 March 2000.
7   Deleted by Art 1(8), Council Directive 94/5/EC of 14 February 1994.
8   Para3a inserted by Art 1(21), Council Directive 91/680/EEC of 16 December 1991, (w.e.f. 1 January 1993).
9   Replaced by Art 1(2)(a), Council Directive 2006/18/EC of 14 February 2006 (w.e.f. 1 January 2006).
10 Replaced by Art 1(2)(b), Council Directive 2006/18/EC of 14 February 2006 (w.e.f. 1 January 2006).
11 Para6 inserted by Art 1, Council Directive99/85/EC of 22 October 1999, (w.e.f. 28 October 1999).

Case law

Ideal Tourisme v Belgium	C36/99	Rate of VAT
Marks & Spencer plc v The Commissioners for Her Majesty's Revenue and Customs	C309/06	Exemption with refund of tax paid at the preceding stage
Norbury Developments Ltd v Customs and Excise	C136/97	Exemption/Waiver of/ Immovable property
Talacre Beach Caravan Sales Ltd v Commissioners of Customs & Excise	C251/05	Rate of Tax/Classification of supply/Fitted residential caravans
Victoria Films AS v Riksskatteverket	C134/97	Exemption/Authors/ Temporary Retention of Exemption

[TITLE XVIa

**transitional arrangements for the taxation of
trade between member states]**[1]

[Article 28a

Scope

2(1A), **1.** The following shall also be subject to value added tax:
3A

(a) intra-Community acquisitions of goods for consideration within the territory of the country by a taxable person acting as such or by a non-taxable legal person where the vendor is a taxable person acting as such who is not eligible for the tax exemption provided for in Article 24 and who is not covered by the arrangements laid down in the second sentence of Article 8(1)(a) or in Article 28b(B)(1).

[By way of derogation from the first subparagraph, intra-Community acquisitions of goods made under the conditions set out in paragraph 1a by a taxable person or non-taxable legal person shall not be subject to value added tax.][2]

Member States shall grant taxable persons and non-taxable legal persons eligible under the second subparagraph the right to opt for the general scheme laid down in the first subparagraph. Member States shall determine the detailed rules for the exercise of that option which shall in any case apply for two calendar years;

(b) intra-Community acquisitions of new means of transport effected for consideration within the country by taxable persons or non-taxable legal persons who qualify for the derogation provided for in the second subparagraph of (a) or by any other non-taxable person;

[(c) the intra-Community acquisition of goods which are subject to excise duties effected for consideration within the territory of the country by a taxable person or a non-taxable legal person who qualifies for the derogation referred to in the second subparagraph of point (a), and for which the excise duties become chargeable within the territory of the country pursuant to Directive 92/12/EEC.][3]

nd sch **[1a.** The following shall benefit from the derogation set out in the second
), (va),   subparagraph of paragraph 1(a):
(vb).

(a) intra-Community acquisitions of goods whose supply within the territory of the country would be exempt pursuant to Article 15(4) to (10):

(b) intra-Community acquisitions of goods other than those at (a), made:

— by a taxable person for the purpose of his agricultural, forestry or fisheries undertaking, subject to the flat-rate scheme set out in Article 25, by a taxable person who carries out only supplies of goods or services in respect of which value added tax is not deductible, or by a non-taxable legal person,

— for a total amount not exceeding, during the current calendar year, a threshold which the Member States shall determine but which may not be less than the equivalent in national currency of ECU 10 000, and

- provided that the total amount of intra-Community acquisitions of goods did not, during the previous calendar year, exceed the threshold referred to in the second indent.

The threshold which serves as the reference for the application of the above shall consist of the total amount, exclusive of value added tax due or paid in the Member State from which the goods are dispatched or transported, of intra-Community acquisitions of goods other than new means of transport and other than goods subject to excise duty.][4]

s 1(1) **2.**   For the purposes of this Title:

(a) the following shall be considered as `means of transport': vessels exceeding 7,5 metres in length, aircraft the take-off weight of which exceeds 1 550 kilograms and motorized land vehicles the capacity of which exceeds 48 cubic centimetres or the power of which exceeds 7,2 kilowatts, intended for the transport of persons or goods, except for the vessels and aircraft referred to in Article 15(5) and (6);

[(b) the means of transport referred to in (a) shall not be considered to be "new" where both of the following conditions are simultaneously fulfilled:

- they were supplied more than three months after the date of first entry into service: However, this period shall be increased to six months for the motorized land vehicles defined in (a),

- they have travelled more than 6000 kilometres in the case of land vehicles, sailed for more than 100 hours in the case of vessels, or flown for more than 40 hours in the case of aircraft.

Member States shall lay down the conditions under which the above facts can be regarded as established.][5]

s 3A(1) **3.**   `Intra-Community acquisition of goods' shall mean acquisition of the right to dispose as owner of movable tangible property dispatched or transported to the person acquiring the goods by or on behalf of the vendor or the person acquiring the goods to a Member State other than that from which the goods are dispatched or transported.

s 3A(4)   Where goods acquired by a non-taxable legal person are dispatched or transported from a third territory and imported by that non-taxable legal person into a Member State other than the Member State of arrival of the goods dispatched or transported, the goods shall be deemed to have been dispatched or transported from the Member State of import. That Member State shall grant the importer as defined in Article 21(2) a refund of the value added tax paid in connection with the importation of the goods in so far as the importer establishes that his acquisition was subject to value added tax in the Member State of arrival of the goods dispatched or transported.

3(1)(g), **4.** Any person who from time to time supplies a new means of transport
A(1), 13   under the conditions laid down in Article 28c(A) shall also be regarded
as a taxable person.

The Member State within the territory of which the supply is effected
shall grant the taxable person the right of deduction on the basis of the
following provisions:

— the right of deduction shall arise and may be exercised only at the time
of the supply,

— the taxable person shall be authorized to deduct the value added tax
included in the purchase price or paid on the importation or intra-
Community acquisition of the means of transport, up to an amount
not exceeding the tax for which he would be liable if the supply were
not exempt.

Member States shall lay down detailed rules for the implementation of
these provisions.

3(1)(g), **5.** [The following shall be treated as supplies of goods effected for
5(6)(f).   consideration:][6]

(a) [....][7]

(b) the transfer by a taxable person of goods from his undertaking to
another Member State.

The following shall be regarded as having been transferred to another
Member State: any tangible property dispatched or transported by or on
behalf of the taxable person out of the territory defined in Article 3 but
within the Community for the purposes of his undertaking, other than
the purposes of one of the following transactions:

— the supply of the goods in question by the taxable person within
the territory of the Member State of arrival of the dispatch or
transport under the conditions laid down in the second sentence
of Article 8(1)(a) and in Article 28b(B)(1),

— the supply of the goods in question by the taxable person under
the conditions laid down in Article 8(1)(c),

— the supply of the goods in question by the taxable person within
the territory of the country under the conditions laid down in
Article 15 or in Article 28c(A),

[.....][8]

[- the supply of a service performed for the taxable person and
involving work on the goods in question physically carried out
in the Member State in which the dispatch or transport of the
goods ends, provided that the goods, after being worked upon,
are re-dispatched to that taxable person in the Member State from
which they had initially been dispatched or transported,][9]

— temporary use of the goods in question within the territory of
the Member State of arrival of the dispatch or transport of the
goods for the purposes of the supply of services by the taxable

person established within the territory of the Member State of departure of the dispatch or transport of the goods,

- temporary use of the goods in question, for a period not exceeding 24 months, within the territory of another Member State in which the import of the same goods from a third country with a view to temporary use would be eligible for the arrangements for the temporary importation with full exemption from import duties.

[— the supply of gas through the natural gas distribution system, or of electricity, under the conditions set out in Article 8(1)(d) or (e).][10]

[However, when one of the conditions to which the benefit of the above is subordinated is no longer met, the goods shall be considered as having been transferred to a destination in another Member State. In this case, the transfer is carried out at the moment that the conditions is (sic) no longer met.][11]

6. The intra-Community acquisition of goods for consideration shall include the use by a taxable person for the purposes of his undertaking of goods dispatched or transported by or on behalf of that taxable person from another Member State within the territory of which the goods were produced, extracted, processed, purchased, acquired as defined in paragraph 1 or imported by the taxable person within the framework of his undertaking into that other Member State.

[The following shall also be deemed to be an intra-Community acquisition of goods effected for consideration: the appropriation of goods by the forces of a State party to the North Atlantic Treaty, for their use or for the use of the civilian staff accompanying them, which they have not acquired subject to the general rules governing taxation on the domestic market of one of the Member States, when the importation of these goods could not benefit from the exemption set out in Article 14(1)(g).][12]

s 3A(3) 7. Member States shall take measures to ensure that transactions which would have been classed as `supplies of goods' as defined in paragraph 5 or Article 5 if they had been carried out within the territory of the country by a taxable person acting as such are classed as `intra-Community acquisitions of goods'.][13]

Amendments
1   This title inserted by Art 1(22), Council Directive 91/680/EEC of 16 December 1991.
2   Substituted by Art 1(10), Council Directive 92/111/EEC of 14 December 1992, (w.e.f. 1 January 1993).
3   Inserted by Art 1(10), Council Directive 92/111/EEC of 14 December 1992, (w.e.f. 1 January 1993).
4   Inserted by Art 1(10), Council Directive 92/111/EEC of 14 December 1992, (w.e.f. 1 January 1993).
5   Substituted by Art 1(6), Council Directive 94/5/EC of 14 February 1994.
6   Substituted by Art 1(6), Council Directive 95/7/EC of 10 April 1995, (w.e.f. 25 May 1995).
7   Deleted by Art 1(6), Council Directive 95/7/EC of 10 April 1995, (w.e.f. 25 May 1995).
8   Deleted by Art 1(6), Council Directive 95/7/EC of 10 April 1995, (w.e.f. 25 May 1995).
9   Substituted by Art 1(6), Council Directive 95/7/EC of 10 April 1995, (w.e.f. 25 May 1995).
10 Inserted by Art 1(7), Council Directive 2003/92/EC of 7 October 2003, (w.e.f. 1 January 2005).
11 Inserted by Art 1(10), Council Directive 92/111/EEC of 14 December 1992, (w.e.f. 1 January 1993).
12 Inserted by Art 1(10), Council Directive 92/111/EEC of 14 December 1992, (w.e.f. 1 January 1993).
13 Art28a inserted by Art 1(22), Council Directive 91/680/EEC of 16 December 1991, (w.e.f. 1 January 1993).

[Article 28b

place of transactions

A. Place of the intra-Community acquisition of goods

1. The place of the intra-Community acquisition of goods shall be deemed to be the place where the goods are at the time when dispatch or transport to the person acquiring them ends.

2. Without prejudice to paragraph 1, the place of the intra-Community acquisition of goods referred to in Article 28a(1)(a) shall, however, be deemed to be within the territory of the Member State which issued the value added tax identification number under which the person acquiring the goods made the acquisition, unless the person acquiring the goods establishes that this acquisition has been subject to tax in accordance with paragraph 1.

   If, however, the acquisition is subject to tax in accordance with paragraph 1 in the Member State of arrival of the dispatch or transport of the goods after having been subject to tax in accordance with the first subparagraph, the taxable amount shall be reduced accordingly in the Member State which issued the value added tax identification number under which the person acquiring the goods made the acquisition.

   [For the purposes of applying the first subparagraph, the intra-Community acquisition of goods shall be deemed to have been subject to tax in accordance with paragraph 1 when the following conditions have been met:

   — the acquirer established that he has effected this intra-Community acquisition for the needs of a subsequent supply effected in the Member State referred to in paragraph 1 and for which the consignee has been designated as the person liable for the tax due in accordance with Article 28c(E)(3),

   — the obligations for declaration set out in the last subparagraph of Article 22(6)(b) have been satisfied by the acquirer.][1]

B. Place of supply of goods

1. By way of derogation from Article 8(1)(a) and (2), the place of the supply of goods dispatched or transported by or on behalf of the supplier from a Member State other than that of arrival of the dispatch or transport shall be deemed to be the place where the goods are when dispatch or transport to the purchaser ends, where the following conditions are fulfilled:

   — the supply of goods is effected for a taxable person eligible for the derogation provided for in the second subparagraph of Article 28a(1)(a), for a non-taxable legal person who is eligible for the same derogation or for any other non-taxable person,

   — the supply is of goods other than new means of transport and other than goods supplied after assembly or installation, with or without a trial run, by or on behalf of the supplier.

Where the goods thus supplied are dispatched or transported from a third territory and imported by the supplier into a Member State other than the Member State of arrival of the goods dispatched or transported to the purchaser, they shall be regarded as having been dispatched or transported from the Member State of import.

2. However, where the supply is of goods other than products subject to excise duty, paragraph 1 shall not apply to supplies of goods dispatched or transported to the same Member State of arrival of the dispatch or transport where:

- the total value of such supplies, less value added tax, does not in one calendar year exceed the equivalent in national currency of ECU 100 000, and

- the total value, less value added tax, of the supplies of goods other than products subject to excise duty effected under the conditions laid down in paragraph 1 in the previous calendar year did not exceed the equivalent in national currency of ECU 100 000.

The Member State within the territory of which the goods are when dispatch or transport to the purchaser ends may limit the thresholds referred to above to the equivalent in national currency of ECU 35 000 where that Member State fears that the thresholds of ECU 100 000 referred to above would lead to serious distortions of the conditions of competition. Member States which exercise this option shall take the measures necessary to inform the relevant public authorities in the Member State of dispatch or transport of the goods.

Before 31 December 1994, the Commission shall report to the Council on the operation of the special ECU 35 000 thresholds provided for in the preceding subparagraph. In that report the Commission may inform the Council that the abolition of the special thresholds will not lead to serious distortions of the conditions of competition. Until the Council takes a unanimous decision on a Commission proposal, the preceding subparagraph shall remain in force.

3. The Member State within the territory of which the goods are at the time of departure of the dispatch or transport shall grant those taxable persons who effect supplies of goods eligible under paragraph 2 the right to choose that the place of such supplies shall be determined in accordance with paragraph 1.

The Member States concerned shall determine the detailed rules for the exercise of that option, which shall in any case apply for two calendar years.

5(6) (f)
–(h).

C. Place of the supply of services in the intra-Community transport of goods

1. By way of derogation from Article 9(2)(b), the place of the supply of services in the intra-Community transport of goods shall be determined in accordance with paragraphs 2, 3 and 4. For the purposes of this Title the following definitions shall apply:

— `the intra-Community transport of goods' shall mean transport where the place of departure and the place of arrival are situated within the territories of two different Member States.

[The transport of goods where the place of departure and the place of arrival are situated within the territory of the country shall be treated as intra-Community transport of goods where such transport is directly linked to transport of goods where the place of departure and the place of arrival are situated within the territories of two different Member States;][2]

— `the place of departure' shall mean the place where the transport of goods actually starts, leaving aside distance actually travelled to the place where the goods are,

— `the place of arrival' shall mean the place where the transport of goods actually ends.

2. The place of the supply of services in the intra-Community transport of goods shall be the place of departure.

3. However, by way of derogation from paragraph 2, the place of the supply of services in the intra-Community transport of goods rendered to customers identified for purposes of value added tax in a Member State other than that of the departure of the transport shall be deemed to be within the territory of the Member State which issued the customer with the value added tax identification number under which the service was rendered to him.

4. Member States need not apply the tax to that part of the transport corresponding to journeys made over waters which do not form part of the territory of the Community as defined in Article 3.

s 5(6)
(f) ii

D. Place of the supply of services ancillary to the intra-Community transport of goods

By way of derogation from Article 9(2)(c), the place of the supply of services involving activities ancillary to the intra-Community transport of goods, rendered to customers identified for purposes of value added tax in a Member State other than that within the territory of which the services are physically performed, shall be deemed to be within the territory of the Member State which issued the customer with the value added tax identification number under which the service was rendered to him.

s5(6)
(f), (g)

E. Place of the supply of services rendered by intermediaries

1. By way of derogation from Article 9(1), the place of the supply of services rendered by intermediaries, acting in the name and for the account of other persons, where they form part of the supply of services in the intra-Community transport of goods, shall be the place of departure.

However, where the customer for whom the services rendered by the intermediary are performed is identified for purposes of value added tax in a Member State other than that of the departure of the transport, the place of the supply of services rendered by an intermediary shall be deemed to be within the territory of the Member State which issued the customer with the value added tax identification number under which the service was rendered to him.

2. By way of derogation from Article 9(1), the place of the supply of services rendered by intermediaries acting in the name and for the account of other persons, where they form part of the supply of services the purpose of which is activities ancillary to the intra-Community transport of goods, shall be the place where the ancillary services are physically performed.

However, where the customer of the services rendered by the intermediary is identified for purposes of value added tax in a Member State other than that within the territory of which the ancillary service is physically performed, the place of supply of the services rendered by the intermediary shall be deemed to be within the territory of the Member State which issued the customer with the value added tax identification number under which the service was rendered to him by the intermediary.

3. By way of derogation from Article 9(1), the place of the supply of services rendered by intermediaries acting in the name and for the account of other persons, when such services form part of transactions other than those referred to in paragraph 1 or 2 or in Article 9(2)(e), shall be the place where those transactions are carried out.

However, where the customer is identified for purposes of value added tax in a Member State other than that within the territory of which those transactions are carried out, the place of supply of the services rendered by the intermediary shall be deemed to be within the territory of the Member State which issued the customer with the value added tax identification number under which the service was rendered to him by the intermediary.

s 5(6)(f) iv   **[F. Place of the supply of services in the case of valuations of or work on movable tangible property**

By way of derogation from Article 9(2)(c), the place of the supply of services involving valuations or work on movable tangible property, provided to customers identified for value added tax purposes in a Member State other than the one where those services are physically carried out, shall be deemed to be in the territory of the Member State which issued the customer with the value added tax identification number under which the service was carried out for him.

This derogation shall not apply where the goods are not dispatched or transported out of the Member State where the services were physically carried out.]³]⁴

Amendments
1   Inserted by Art 1(11), Council Directive 92/111/EEC of 14 December 1992, (w.e.f. 1 January 1993).
2   Inserted by Art 1(7), Council Directive 95/7/EC of 10 April 1995, (w.e.f. 25 May 1995).
3   Inserted by Art 1(7), Council Directive 95/7/EC of 10 April 1995, (w.e.f. 25 May 1995).
4   Art28b inserted by Art 1(22), Council Directive 91/680/EEC of 16 December 1991, (w.e.f. 1 January 1993).

Case law
Lipjes, D. and Staatssecretaris van Financiën   C68/03   Services by intermediaries/Place of supply

[Article 28c

Exemptions

A. Exempt supplies of goods

2nd sch

Without prejudice to other Community provisions and subject to conditions which they shall lay down for the purpose of ensuring the correct and straightforward application of the exemptions provided for below and preventing any evasion, avoidance or abuse, Member States shall exempt:

(a) supplies of goods, [as defined in Article 5]¹, dispatched or transported by or on behalf of the vendor or the person acquiring the goods out of the territory referred to in Article 3 but within the Community, effected for another taxable person or a non-taxable legal person acting as such in a Member State other than that of the departure of the dispatch or transport of the goods.

This exemption shall not apply to supplies of goods by taxable persons exempt from tax under Article 24 or to supplies of goods effected for taxable persons or non-taxable legal persons who qualify for the derogation in the second subparagraph of Article 28a(1)(a);

(b) supplies of new means of transport, dispatched or transported to the purchaser by or on behalf of the vendor or the purchaser out of the territory referred to in Article 3 but within the Community, effected for taxable persons or non-taxable legal persons who qualify for the derogation in the second subparagraph of Article 28a(1)(a) or for any other non-taxable person;

[(c) the supply of goods subject to excise duty dispatched or transported to the purchaser, by the vendor, by the purchaser or on his behalf, outside the territory referred to in Article 3 but inside the Community, effected for taxable persons or non-taxable legal persons who qualify for the derogation set out in the second subparagraph of Article 28a(1)(a), when the dispatch or transport of the goods is carried out in accordance with Article 7(4) and (5), or Article 16 of Directive 92/12/EEC.

This exemption shall not apply to supplies of goods subject to excise duty effected by taxable persons who benefit from the exemption from tax set out in Article 24;]²

[(d) the supply of goods, within the meaning of Article 28a(5)(b), which benefit from the exemptions set out above if they have been made on behalf of another taxable person.]³

B. Exempt intra-Community acquisitions of goods

s3A(3)
&11(1)

Without prejudice to other Community provisions and subject to conditions which they shall lay down for the purpose of ensuring the correct and straightforward application of the exemptions provided for below and preventing any evasion, avoidance or abuse, Member States shall exempt:

(a) the intra-Community acquisition of goods the supply of which by taxable persons would in all circumstances be exempt within the territory of the country;

(b) the intra-Community acquisition of goods the importation of which would in all circumstances be exempt under Article 14(1);

(c) the intra-Community acquisition of goods where, pursuant to Article 17(3) and (4), the person acquiring the goods would in all circumstances be entitled to full reimbursement of the value added tax due under Article 28a(1).

2nd sch
-(iiia)

C. Exempt transport services

Member States shall exempt the supply of intra-Community transport services involved in the dispatch or transport of goods to and from the islands making up the autonomous regions of the Azores and Madeira as well as the dispatch or transport of goods between those islands.

2nd sch
-(iiib)

D. Exempt importation of goods

Where goods dispatched or transported from a third territory are imported into a Member State other than that of arrival of the dispatch or transport, Member States shall exempt such imports where the supply of such goods by the importer as defined in Article 21(2) is exempt in accordance with paragraph A.

Member States shall lay down the conditions governing this exemption with a view to ensuring its correct and straightforward application and preventing any evasion, avoidance or abuse.

[E. Other exemptions

[1.   In Article 16:

 − paragraph 1 shall be replaced by the following:

"Without prejudice to other Community tax provisions, Member States may, subject to the consultations provided for in Article 29, take special measures designed to exempt all or some of the following transactions, provided that they are not aimed at final use and/or consumption and that the amount of value added tax due on cessation of the arrangements on situations referred to at A to E corresponds to the amount of tax which would have been due had each of these transactions been taxed within the territory of the country

A. imports of goods which are intended to be placed under warehousing arrangements other than customs;

B. supplies of goods which are intended to be:

(a) produced to customs and, where applicable, placed in temporary storage;

(b) placed in a free zone or in a free warehouse;

(c) placed under customs warehousing arrangements or inward processing arrangements;

(d) admitted into territorial waters:

  — in order to be incorporated into drilling or production platforms, for purposes of the construction, repair, maintenance, alteration or fitting-out of such platforms, or to link such drilling or production platforms to the mainland,

  — for the fuelling and provisioning of drilling or production platforms;

(e) placed, within the territory of the country, under warehousing arrangements other than customs warehousing.

For the purposes of this Article, warehouses other than customs warehouses shall be taken to be:

  — for products subject to excise duty, the places defined as tax warehouses for the purposes of Article 4(b) of Council Directive 92/12/EEC;

  — for goods other than those subject to excise duty, the places defined as such by the Member States. However, Member States may not provide for warehousing arrangements other than customs warehousing where the goods in question are intended to be supplied at the retail stage.

Nevertheless, Member States may provide for such arrangements for goods intended for:

  — taxable persons for the purposes of supplies effected under the conditions laid down in Article 28k;

  — tax-free shops within the meaning of Article 28k, for the purposes of supplies to travellers taking flights or sea crossing to third countries, where those supplies are exempt pursuant to Article 15;

  — taxable persons for the purposes of supplies to travellers on board aircraft or vessels during a flight or sea crossing where the place of arrival is situated outside the Community;

  — taxable persons for the purposes of supplies effected free of tax pursuant to Article 15(10).

The places referred to in (a), (b), (c) and (d) shall be as defined by the Community customs provisions in force.

C. supplies of services relating to the supplies of goods referred to in B;

D. supplies of goods and services carried out:

  (a) in the places listed in B(a),(b),(c) and (d) and still subject to one of the situations specified therein;

  (b) In the places listed in B(e) and still subject , within the territory of the country, to the situation specified therein.

Where they exercise the option provided for in (a) for transactions effected in customs warehouses Member States shall take the measures necessary to ensure that they have defined warehousing arrangements other than customs warehousing which permit the provisions in (b) to be applied to the same transactions concerning goods listed in Annex J which are effected in such warehouses other than customs warehouses;

E. supplies:

  — of goods referred to in Article 7(1)(a) still subject to arrangements for temporary importation with total exemption from import duty or external transit arrangements,

  — of goods referred to in Article 7(1)(b) still subject to the internal Community transit procedure provided for in Article 33a,

as well as supplies of services related to such supplies.

By way of derogation from the first subparagraph of Article 21(1) (a), the person liable to pay the tax due in accordance with the first subparagraph shall be the person who causes the goods to cease to be covered by the arrangements or situations listed in this paragraph.

When the removal of goods from the arrangements or situations referred to in this paragraph gives rise to importation within the meaning of Article 7(3), the Member State of import shall take the measures necessary to avoid double taxation within the country."

— the following paragraph shall be added:

"1a. Where they exercise the option provided for in paragraph 1, Member States shall take the measures necessary to ensure that intra-Community acquisitions of goods intended to be placed under one of the arrangements or in one of the situations referred to in paragraph 1(B) benefit from the same provisions as supplies of goods effected within the country under the same conditions."][4]

2. In Article 16 (2):

— "intra-Community acquisitions of goods made by a taxable person and" shall be added after "may opt to exempt" and "outside the Community" shall be added after "export them",

— the following subparagraphs shall be added:

"When they take up this option the Member States shall, subject to the consultation provided for in Article 29, extend the benefit of this exemption to intra-Community acquisitions of goods by a taxable person, imports for and supplies of goods to a taxable person indenting to supply them, as they are or after processing, under the conditions laid down in Article 28c(A), as will as supplies of services relating to such supplies, up to a maximum annual to the value of his supplies of goods effected under the conditions laid down in Article 28c(A) during the preceding twelve months.

Member States may set a common maximum amount for transactions which they exempt under the first and second subparagraphs."

3. Member States shall take specific measures to ensure that value added tax is not charged on the intra-Community acquisition of goods effected, within the meaning of Article 28b(A)(1), within its territory when the following conditions are met:

- the intra-Community acquisition of goods is effected by a taxable person who is not established in the territory of the country but who is identified for value added tax purposes in another Member State,

- the intra-Community acquisition of goods is effected for the purpose of a subsequent supply of goods made by a taxable person in the territory of the country,

- the goods so acquired by this taxable person are directly dispatched or transported from another Member State than that in which he is identified for value added tax purposes and destined for the person for whom he effects the subsequent supply,

- the person to whom the subsequent supply is made is a taxable person or a non-taxable legal person who is identified for value added tax purposes within the territory of the country,

- the person to whom the subsequent supply is made has been designated in accordance with [Article 21(1)(c)][5] as the person liable for the tax due on the supplies effected by the taxable person not established within the territory of the country.][6][7]

Amendments
1. Substituted by Art 1(8), Council Directive 95/7/EC of 10 April 1995, (w.e.f. 25 May 1995).
2. Art28c(A)(c) substituted by Art 1(12), Council Directive 92/111/EEC of 14 December 1992, (w.e.f. 1 January 1993).
3. Art28c(A)(d) substituted by Art 1(12), Council Directive 92/111/EEC of 14 December 1992, (w.e.f. 1 January 1993).
4. Art28c(E)(1) substituted by Art 1(9), Council Directive 95/7/EC of 10 April 1995, (w.e.f. 1 January 1996).
5. Amended by Art 1(3), Council Directive 00/65/EC of 17 October 2000.
6. Art28c(E) substituted by Art 1(13), Council Directive 92/111/EEC of 14 December 1992, (w.e.f. 1 January 1993).
7. Art28c inserted by Art 1(22), Council Directive 91/680/EEC of 16 December 1991, (w.e.f. 1 January 1993).

Case Law

Collée, Albert v Finanzamt Limburg an der Lahn	C146/05	Intra-Community supply/Refusal of exemption/Belated production of evidence of the supply
Teleos PLC and others v Commissioners of Customs & Excise	C409/04	Intra-Community transactions/Evidence/National measures to combat fraud

[Article 28d
Chargeable event and chargeability of tax

s3A(1),
3A(3)(a)
19(1)

1. The chargeable event shall occur when the intra-Community acquisition of goods is effected. The intra-Community acquisition of goods shall be regarded as being effected when the supply of similar goods is regarded as being effected within the territory of the country.

s 19(1A) **2.** For the intra-Community acquisition of goods, tax shall become chargeable on the 15th day of the month following that during which the chargeable event occurs.

s 19(1A) [**3.** By way of derogation from paragraph 2, tax shall become chargeable on the issue of the invoice [...]¹ provided for in the first subparagraph of Article 22(3)(a) where that invoice [...]¹ is issued to the person acquiring the goods before the fifteenth day of the month following that during which the taxable event occurs.]²

s17(1),
19(1)

4. By way of derogation from Article 10(2) and (3), tax shall become chargeable, for supplies of goods effected under the conditions laid down in Article 28c(A), on the 15th day of the month following that during which the chargeable event occurred.

[However, tax shall become chargeable on the issue of the invoice provided for in the first subparagraph of Article 22(3)(a) [...]¹ serving as invoice where that invoice [...]² is issued before the fifteenth day of the month following that during which the taxable event occurs.]³]⁴

Amendments

1 Deleted by Art 4, Council Directive 2001/115/EC of 20 December 2001, (w.e.f. 6 February 2002).
2 Substituted by Art 1(14) Council Directive 92/111/EEC of 14 December 1992, (w.e.f. 1 January 1993).
3 Substituted by Art 1(14) Council Directive 92/111/EEC of 14 December 1992, (w.e.f. 1 January 1993).
4 Art28d inserted by Art 1(22), Council Directive 91/680/EEC of 16 December 1991, (w.e.f. 1 January 1993).

s 10
s 11

[**Article 28e**

Taxable amount and rate applicable

1. In the case of the intra-Community acquisition of goods, the taxable amount shall be established on the basis of the same elements as those used in accordance with Article 11(A) to determine the taxable amount for supply of the same goods within the territory of the country. [In particular, in the case of the intra-Community acquisition of goods referred to in Article 28a(6), the taxable amount shall be determined in accordance with Article 11(A)(1)(b) and paragraphs 2 and 3.]¹

    Member States shall take the measures necessary to ensure that the excise duty due or paid by the person effecting the intra-Community acquisition of a product subject to excise duty is included in the taxable amount in accordance with Article 11(A)(2)(a).

    [When, after the moment the intra-Community acquisition of goods was effected, the acquirer obtains the refund of excise duties paid in the Member State from which the goods were dispatched or transported, the taxable amount shall be reduced accordingly in the Member State where the intra-Community acquisition took place.]²

[2. For the supply of goods referred to in Article 28c(A)(d), the taxable amount shall be determined in accordance with Article 11(A)(1)(b) and paragraphs 2 and 3.]³

[3.]⁴ The tax rate applicable to the intra-Community acquisition of goods shall be that in force when the tax becomes chargeable.

[4.]⁴ The tax rate applicable to the intra-Community acquisition of goods shall be that applied to the supply of like goods within the territory of the country.]⁵

Amendments
1 Substituted by Art 1(16), Council Directive 92/111/EEC of 14 December 1992, (w.e.f. 1 January 1993).
2 Inserted by Art 1(16), Council Directive 92/111/EEC of 14 December 1992, (w.e.f. 1 January 1993).
3 Inserted by Art 1(17), Council Directive 92/111/EEC of 14 December 1992, (w.e.f. 1 January 1993).
4 Substituted by Art 1(17), Council Directive 92/111/EEC of 14 December 1992, (w.e.f. 1 January 1993).
5 Art28e inserted by Art 1(22), Council Directive 91/680/EEC of 16 December 1991, (w.e.f. 1 January 1993).

[Article 28f

Right of deduction

1. Article 17(2), (3) and (4) shall be replaced by the following:

"2. In so far as the goods and services are used for the purposes of his taxable transactions, the taxable person shall be entitled to deduct from the tax which he is liable to pay:

[(a) value added tax due or paid within the territory of the country in respect of goods or services supplied or to be supplied to him by another taxable person;][1]

(b) value added tax due or paid in respect of imported goods within the territory of the country;

(c) value added tax due pursuant to Articles 5(7)(a), 6(3) and 28a(6);

(d) value added tax due pursuant to Article 28a(1)(a).

3. Member States shall also grant every taxable person the right to the deduction or refund of the value added tax referred to in paragraph 2 in so far as the goods and services are used for the purposes of:

(a) transactions relating to the economic activities referred to in Article 4(2), carried out in another country, which would be deductible if they had been performed within the territory of the country;

[(b) transactions which are exempt pursuant to Article 14(1)(g) and (i), 15, 16(1) (B), (C), (D) or (E) or (2) or 28c (A) and (C).][2];

(c) any of the transactions exempt pursuant to Article 13B(a) and (d)(1) to (5), when the customer is established outside the Community or when those transactions are directly linked with goods to be exported to a country outside the Community.

4. The refund of value added tax referred to in paragraph 3 shall be effected:

— to taxable persons who are not established within the territory of the country but who are established in another Member State in accordance with the detailed implementing rules laid down in Directive 79/1072/EEC;

— to taxable persons who are not established in the territory of the Community, in accordance with the detailed implementing rules laid down in Directive 86/560/EEC.

[For the purposes of applying the above:

(a) the taxable persons referred to in Article 1 of Directive 79/1072/ EEC shall also be considered for the purposes of applying the said Directive as taxable persons who are not established in the country when, inside the territory of the country, they have only carried out supplies of goods and services to a person who has been designated as the person liable to pay the tax in accordance with [Article 21(1)(a), (1)(c) or (1)(f) or Article 21(2)(c)][3]

(b) the taxable persons referred to in Article 1 of Directive 86/560/ EEC shall also be considered for the purposes of applying the said Directive as taxable persons who are not established in the Community when, inside the territory of the country, they have only carried out supplies of goods and services to a person who has been designated as the person liable to pay the tax in accordance with [Article 21(1)(a), (1)(c) or (1)(f) or Article 21(2)(c)][3];

(c) Directives 79/1072/EEC and 86/560/EEC shall not apply to supplies of goods which are, or may be, exempted under Article 28c(A) when the goods supplied are dispatched or transported by the acquirer or for his account.][4]

2. Article 18(1) shall be replaced by the following:

"1.   To exercise his right of deduction, the taxable person must:

(a) in respect of deductions pursuant to Article 17(2)(a), hold an invoice drawn up in accordance with Article 22(3);

(b) in respect of deductions pursuant to Article 17(2)(b), hold an import document specifying him as consignee or importer and stating or permitting the calculation of the amount of tax due;

(c) in respect of deductions pursuant to Article 17(2)(c), comply with the formalities established by each Member State;

(d) when he is required to pay the tax as a customer or purchaser where [Article 21(1) or Article 21(2)(c)][5] applies, comply with the formalities laid down by each Member State;

(e) in respect of deductions pursuant to Article 17(2)(d), set out in the declaration provided for in Article 22(4) all the information needed for the amount of the tax due on his intra-Community acquisitions of goods to be calculated and hold an invoice in accordance with Article 22(3)."

3. The following paragraph shall be inserted in Article 18:

"3a. Member States may authorize a taxable person who does not hold an invoice in accordance with Article 22(3) to make the deduction referred to in Article 17(2)(d); they shall determine the conditions and arrangements for applying this provision."][6]

Amendments
1   Amended by Art 1(10), Council Directive 95/7/EC of 10 April 1995, (w.e.f. 25 May 1995).
2   Amended by Annex V, Point (1)(c), Council Directive 2004/66/EC of 26 April 2004 (w.e.f. 1 May 2004).
3   Amended by Art 1(4), Council Directive 2006/69/EC of 24 July 2006 (w.e.f 13 August 2006).
4   Amended by Art 1(18), Council Directive 92/111/EEC of 14 December 1992, (w.e.f. 1 January 1993).
5   Amended by Art 1(5), Council Directive 2006/69/EC of 24 July 2006 (w.e.f 13 August 2006).
6   Art28f inserted by Art 22, Council Directive 91/680/EEC of 16 December 1991, (w.e.f. 1 January 1993).

[Article 28g

Persons liable for payment of the tax

Article 21 shall be replaced by the following:

["Article 21

Persons liable to pay tax to the authorities

The following shall be liable to pay value added tax:

1. Under the internal system, the following shall be liable to pay value added tax:

   [(a) the taxable person carrying out the taxable supply of goods or of services, except for the cases referred to in (b) and (c) and (f). Where the taxable supply of goods or of services is effected by a taxable person who is not established within the territory of the country, Member States may, under the conditions determined by them, lay down that the person liable to pay tax is the person for whom the taxable supply of goods or of services is carried out;][1]

   (b) taxable persons to whom services covered by Article 9(2)(e) are supplied or persons who are identified for value added tax purposes within the territory of the country to whom services covered by Article 28b(C), (D), (E) and (F) are supplied, if the services are carried out by a taxable person not established within the territory of the country;

   (c) the person to whom the supply of goods is made when the following conditions are met:
   - the taxable operation is a supply of goods made under the conditions laid down in Article 28c(E)(3),
   - the person to whom the supply of goods is made is another taxable person or a non-taxable legal person identified for the purposes of value added tax within the territory of the country,
   - the invoice issued by the taxable person not established within the territory of the country conforms to Article 22(3).

   However, Member States may provide a derogation from this obligation, where the taxable person who is not established within the territory of the country has appointed a tax representative in that country;

   (d) any person who mentions the value added tax on an invoice [...][2];

   (e) any person effecting a taxable intra-Community acquisition of goods.

   (f) persons who are identified for value added tax purposes within the territory of the country and to whom goods are supplied under the conditions set out in Article 8(1)(d) or (e), if the supplies are carried out by a taxable person not established within the territory of the country.][3]

2. By way of derogation from the provisions of paragraph 1:

(a) where the person liable to pay tax in accordance with the provisions of paragraph 1 is a taxable person who is not established within the territory of the country, Member States may allow him to appoint a tax representative as the person liable to pay tax. This option shall be subject to conditions and procedures laid down by each Member State;

(b) where the taxable transaction is effected by a taxable person who is not established within the territory of the country and no legal instrument exists, with the country in which that taxable person is established or has his seat, relating to mutual assistance similar in scope to that laid down by Directives 76/308/EEC and 77/799/EEC and by Council Regulation (EEC) No 218/92 of 27 January 1992 on administrative cooperation in the field of indirect taxation (VAT), Member States may take steps to provide that the person liable for payment of the tax shall be a tax representative appointed by the non-established taxable person.

[(c) where the following supplies are carried out, Member States may lay down that the person liable to pay tax is the taxable person to whom those supplies are made:

(i) the supply of construction work, including repair, cleaning, maintenance, alteration and demolition services in relation to immovable property, as well as the handing over of construction works considered to be a supply of goods by virtue of Article 5(5);

(ii) the supply of staff engaged in activities covered by (i);

(iii) the supply of immovable property, as referred to in Article 13(B)(g) and (h), where the supplier has opted for taxation of the supply pursuant to point (C)(b) of that Article;

(iv) the supply of used material, used material which cannot be re-used in the same state, scrap, industrial and non industrial waste, recyclable waste, part processed waste and certain goods and services, as identified in Annex M;

(v) the supply of goods provided as security by one taxable person to another in execution of that security;

(vi) the supply of goods following the cession of the reservation of ownership to an assignee and the exercising of this right by the assignee;

(vii) the supply of immovable property sold by the judgment debtor in a compulsory sale procedure.

For the purposes of this point, Member States may provide that a taxable person who also carries out activities or transactions that are not considered to be taxable supplies of goods or services in accordance with Article 2 shall be deemed to be a taxable person in respect of supplies received as referred to in the first subparagraph. A non-taxable body governed by public law, may be deemed to be a taxable person in respect of supplies received as referred to in (v), (vi) and (vii).

For the purposes of this point, Member States may specify the supplies of goods and services covered, and the categories of suppliers or recipients to whom these measures may apply. They may also limit the application of this measure to some of the supplies of goods and services listed in Annex M.

Member States shall inform the Committee established in accordance with Article 29 of any new national measure adopted pursuant to the provisions of this point.][4]

3. In the situations referred to in paragraphs 1 and 2, Member States may provide that someone other than the person liable for payment of the tax shall be held jointly and severally liable for payment of the tax.

4. On importation, value added tax shall be payable by the person or persons designated or accepted as being liable by the Member State in to which the goods are imported.][5][6]

Amendments

1 Amended by Art 1(4), Council Directive 2003/92/EC of 7 October 2003, (w.e.f. 1 January 2005).

2 Deleted by Art 4, Council Directive 2001/115/EC of 20 December 2001, (w.e.f. 6 February 2002).

3 Inserted by Art 1(5), Council Directive 2003/92/EC of 7 October 2003, (w.e.f. 1 January 2005).

4 Inserted by Art 1(7), Council Directive 2006/69/EC of 24 July 2006, (w.e.f. 13 August 2006).

5 Amended by Art 1(4), Council Directive 00/65/EC of 17 October 2000.

6 Art28g inserted by Art 1(22), Council Directive 91/680/EEC of 16 December 1991 (w.e.f. 1 January 1993).

[Article 28h

Obligations of persons liable for payment

Article 22 shall be replaced by the following:

"Article 22

Obligations under the internal system

1. [(a) Every taxable person shall state when his activity as a taxable person commences, changes or ceases. Member States shall, subject to conditions which they lay down, allow the taxable person to make such statements by electronic means, and may also require that electronic means are used.]¹

    (b) Without prejudice to (a), every taxable person referred to in Article 28a(1)(a), second subparagraph, shall state that he is effecting intra-Community acquisitions of goods when the conditions for application of the derogation provided for in that Article are not fulfilled.

    (c) Member States shall take the measures necessary to identify by means of an individual number:

    [– Every taxable person, with the exception of those referred to in Article 28a(4), who, within the territory of the country, effects supplies of goods or of services giving him the right of deduction, other than supplies of goods or of services for which tax is payable solely by the customer or the recipient in accordance with Article 21(1)(a), (b), (c) or (f). However, Member States need not identify certain taxable persons referred to in article 4(3),]²

    – every taxable person referred to in paragraph 1(b) and every taxable person who exercises the option provided for in the third subparagraph of Article 28a(1)(a)

    [– every taxable person who, within the territory of the country, effects intra-Community acquisitions of goods for the purposes of his operations relating to the economic activities referred to in Article 4(2) carried out abroad.]³

    (d) Each individual identification number shall have a prefix in accordance with ISO International Standard No. 3166 - alpha 2 - by which the Member State of issue may be identified. [Nevertheless, the Hellenic Republic shall be authorised to use the prefix "EL".]⁴

    (e) Member States shall take the measures necessary to ensure that their identification systems distinguish taxable persons referred to in (c) and to ensure the correct application of the transitional arrangements for the taxation of intra-Community transactions as laid down in this Title.

2. (a) Every taxable person shall keep accounts in sufficient detail for value added tax to be applied and inspected by the tax authority.

    [(b) Every taxable person shall keep a register of the goods he has dispatched or transported or which have been dispatched or transported on his behalf out of the territory defined in Article 3 but within the Community for the purposes of the transactions referred to in the fifth, sixth and seventh indents of Article 28a(5)(b).

Every taxable person shall keep sufficiently detailed accounts to permit the identification of goods dispatched to him from another Member State by or on behalf of a taxable person identified for purposes of value added tax in that other Member State, in connection with which a service has been provided pursuant to the third or fourth indent of Article 9(c);][5]

[3. (a) Every taxable person shall ensure that an invoice is issued, either by himself or by his customer or, in his name and on his behalf, by a third party, in respect of goods or services which he has supplied or rendered to another taxable person or to a non-taxable legal person. Every taxable person shall also ensure that an invoice is issued, either by himself or by his customer or, in his name and on his behalf, by a third party, in respect of the supplies of goods referred to in Article 28b(B)(1) and in respect of goods supplied under the conditions laid down in Article 28c(A).

Every taxable person shall likewise ensure that an invoice is issued, either by himself or by his customer or, in his name and on his behalf, by a third party, in respect of any payment on account made to him before any supplies of goods referred to in the first subparagraph and in respect of any payment on account made to him by another taxable person or non-taxable legal person before the provision of services is completed.

Member States may impose on taxable persons an obligation to issue an invoice in respect of goods or services other than those referred to in the preceding subparagraphs which they have supplied or rendered on their territory. When they do so, Member States may impose fewer obligations in respect of these invoices than those listed under points (b), (c) and (d).

The Member States may release taxable persons from the obligation to issue an invoice in respect of goods or services which they have supplied or rendered in their territory and which are exempt, with or without refund of the tax paid at the preceding stage, pursuant to Article 13, Article 28(2)(a) and Article 28(3)(b).

Any document or message that amends and refers specifically and unambiguously to the initial invoice is to be treated as an invoice. Member States in whose territory goods or services are supplied or rendered may allow some of the obligatory details to be left out of such documents or messages.

Member States may impose time limits for the issue of invoices on taxable persons supplying goods and services in their territory.

Under conditions to be laid down by the Member States in whose territory goods or services are supplied or rendered, a summary invoice may be drawn up for several separate supplies of goods or services.

Invoices may be drawn up by the customer of a taxable person in respect of goods or services supplied or rendered to him by that taxable person, on condition that there is at the outset an agreement between the two parties, and on condition that a procedure exists for the acceptance of each invoice by the taxable person supplying the goods or services. The Member States in whose territory the goods or services are supplied or rendered shall determine the terms and conditions of the agreement and of the acceptance procedures between the taxable person and his customer.

Member States may impose further conditions on the issue of invoices by the customers of taxable persons supplying goods or services on their territory. For example, they may require that such invoices be issued in the name and on behalf of the taxable person. Such conditions must always be the same wherever the customer is established.

Member States may also lay down specific conditions for taxable persons supplying goods or services in their territory in cases where the third party, or the customer, who issues invoices is established in a country with which no legal instrument exists relating to mutual assistance similar in scope to that laid down by Council Directive 76/308/EEC of 15 March 1976 on mutual assistance for the recovery of claims relating to certain levies, duties, taxes and other measures, Council Directive 77/799/EEC of 19 December 1977 concerning mutual assistance by the competent authorities of the Member States in the field of direct and indirect taxation and by Council Regulation (EEC) No 218/92 of 27 January 1992 on administrative cooperation in the field of indirect taxation (VAT).

(b) Without prejudice to the specific arrangements laid down by this Directive, only the following details are required for VAT purposes on invoices issued under the first, second and third subparagraphs of point (a):

— the date of issue;

— a sequential number, based on one or more series, which uniquely identifies the invoice,

— the VAT identification number referred to in paragraph 1(c) under which the taxable person supplied the goods or services;

— where the customer is liable to pay tax on goods supplied or services rendered or has been supplied with goods as referred to in Article 28c(A), the VAT identification number as referred to in paragraph 1(c) under which the goods were supplied or the services rendered to him;

— the full name and address of the taxable person and of his customer;

— the quantity and nature of the goods supplied or the extent and nature of the services rendered;

- the date on which the supply of goods or of services was made or completed or the date on which the payment on account referred to in the second subparagraph of point (a) was made, insofar as that a date can be determined and differs from the date of issue of the invoice;

- the taxable amount per rate or exemption, the unit price exclusive of tax and any discounts or rebates if they are not included in the unit price;

- the VAT rate applied;

- the VAT amount payable, except where a specific arrangement is applied for which this Directive excludes such a detail;

- where an exemption is involved or where the customer is liable to pay the tax, reference to the appropriate provision of this directive, to the corresponding national provision, or to any indication that the supply is exempt or subject to the reverse charge procedure;

- where the intra-Community supply of a new means of transport is involved, the particulars specified in Article 28a(2);

- where the margin scheme is applied, reference to Article 26 or 26a, to the corresponding national provisions, or to any other indication that the margin scheme has been applied;

- where the person liable to pay the tax is a tax representative within the meaning of Article 21(2), the VAT identification number referred to in paragraph 1(c) of that tax representative, together with his full name and address.

Member States may require taxable persons established on their territory and supplying goods or services on their territory to indicate the VAT identification number referred to in paragraph 1(c) of their customer in cases other than those referred to in the fourth indent of the first subparagraph.

Member States shall not require invoices to be signed.

The amounts which appear on the invoice may be expressed in any currency, provided that the amount of tax to be paid is expressed in the national currency of the Member State where the supply of goods or services takes place, using the conversion mechanism laid down in Article 11C(2).

Where necessary for control purposes, Member States may require invoices in respect of goods supplied or services rendered in their territory and invoices received by taxable persons in their territory to be translated into their national languages.

(c) Invoices issued pursuant to point (a) may be sent either on paper or, subject to an acceptance by the customer, by electronic means.

Invoices sent by electronic means shall be accepted by Member States provided that the authenticity of the origin and integrity of the contents are guaranteed:

- by means of an advanced electronic signature within the meaning of Article 2(2) of Directive 1999/93/EC of the European Parliament and of the Council of 13 December 1999 on a Community framework for electronic signatures; Member States may however ask for the advanced electronic signature to be based on a qualified certificate and created by a secure-signature-creation device, within the meaning of Article 2(6) and (10) of the aforementioned Directive;

- or by means of electronic data interchange (EDI) as defined in Article 2 of Commission Recommendation 1994/820/EC of 19 October 1994 relating to the legal aspects of electronic data interchange when the agreement relating to the exchange provides for the use of procedures guaranteeing the authenticity of the origin and integrity of the data; however Member States may, subject to conditions which they lay down, require that an additional summary document on paper is necessary.

Invoices may, however, be sent by other electronic means subject to acceptance by the Member State(s) concerned. The Commission will present, at the latest on 31 December 2008, a report, together with a proposal, if appropriate, amending the conditions on electronic invoicing in order to take account of possible future technological developments in this field.

Member States may not impose on taxable persons supplying goods or services in their territory any other obligations or formalities relating to the transmission of invoices by electronic means. However, they may provide, until 31 December 2005, that the use of such a system is to be subject to prior notification.

Member States may lay down specific conditions for invoices issued by electronic means for goods or services supplied in their territory from a country with which no legal instrument exists relating to mutual assistance similar in scope to that laid down by Directives 76/308/EEC and 77/799/EEC and by Regulation (EEC) No 218/92.

When batches containing several invoices are sent to the same recipient by electronic means, the details that are common to the individual invoices may be mentioned only once if, for each invoice, all the information is accessible.

(d) Every taxable person shall ensure that copies of invoices issued by himself, by his customer or, in his name and on his behalf, by a third party, and all the invoices which he has received are stored.

For the purposes of this Directive, the taxable person may decide the place of storage provided that he makes the invoices or information stored there available without undue delay to the competent authorities whenever they so request. Member States may, however, require taxable persons established in their territory to notify them of the place of storage, if it is outside their territory. Member States may, in addition, require taxable persons established in their territory to store within the country invoices issued by themselves or by their customers or, in their name and on their behalf, by a third party, as well as all the invoices which they have received, when the storage is not by electronic means guaranteeing full on-line access to the data concerned.

The authenticity of the origin and integrity of the content of the invoices, as well as their readability, must be guaranteed throughout the storage period. As regards the invoices referred to in the third subparagraph of point (c), the information they contain may not be altered; it must remain legible throughout the aforementioned period.

The Member States shall determine the period for which taxable persons must store invoices relating to goods or services supplied in their territory and invoices received by taxable persons established in their territory.

In order to ensure that the conditions laid down in the third subparagraph are met, Member States referred to in the fourth subparagraph may require that invoices be stored in the original form in which they were sent, whether paper or electronic. They may also require that when invoices are stored by electronic means, the data guaranteeing the authenticity of the origin and integrity of the content also be stored.

Member States referred to in the fourth subparagraph may impose specific conditions prohibiting or restricting the storage of invoices in a country with which no legal instrument exists relating to mutual assistance similar in scope to that laid down by Directives 76/308/EEC, 77/799/EEC and by Regulation (EEC) No 218/92 and to the right of access by electronic means, download and use referred to in Article 22a.

Member States may, subject to conditions which they lay down, require the storage of invoices received by non-taxable persons.

(e) For the purposes of points (c) and (d), transmission and storage of invoices "by electronic means "shall mean transmission or making available to the recipient and storage using electronic equipment for processing (including digital compression)and storage of data, and employing wires, radio transmission, optical technologies or other electromagnetic means.

For the purposes of this Directive, Member States shall accept documents or messages in paper or electronic form as invoices if they meet the conditions laid down in this paragraph.][4]

4. [(a) Every taxable person shall submit a return by a deadline to be determined by Member States. That deadline may not be more than two months later than the end of each tax period. The tax period shall be fixed by

each Member State at one month, two months or a quarter. Member States may, however, set different periods provided that they do not exceed one year. Member States shall, subject to conditions which they lay down, allow the taxable person to make such returns by electronic means, and may also require that electronic means are used.]¹

(b) The return shall set out all the information needed to calculate the tax that has become chargeable and the deductions to be made including, where appropriate, and in so far as it seems necessary for the establishment of the basis of assessment, the total value of the transactions relative to such tax and deductions and the value of any exempt transactions.

(c) The return shall also set out:

— on the one hand, the total value, less value added tax, of the supplies of goods referred to in Article 28c(A) on which tax has become chargeable during the period.

The following shall also be added: the total value, less value added tax, of the supplies of goods referred to in the second sentence of Article 8(1)(a) and in Article 28(b)(B)(1) effected within the territory of another Member State for which tax has become chargeable during the return period where the place of departure of the dispatch or transport of the goods is situated in the territory of the country,

[— on the other hand, the total amount, less value added tax of the intra-Community acquisitions of goods referred to in Article 28a(1) and (6) effected within the territory of the country on which tax has become chargeable.

The following shall also be added: the total value, less value added tax, of the supplies of goods referred to in the second sentence of Article 8(1)(a) and in Article 28(b)(B)(1) effected in the territory of the country on which tax has become chargeable during the return period, where the place of departure of the dispatch or transport of the goods is situated within the territory of another Member State, and the total amount, less value added tax, of the supplies of goods made within the territory of the country for which the taxable person has been designated as the person liable for the tax in accordance with Article 28c(E)(3) and under within the tax has become payable in the course of the period covered by the declaration.]³

5. Every taxable person shall pay the net amount of the value added tax when submitting the regular return. Member States may, however, set a different date for the payment of that amount or may demand an interim payment.

6. [(a) Member States may require a taxable person to submit a statement, including all the particulars specified in paragraph 4, concerning all transactions carried out in the preceding year. That statement shall provide all the information necessary for any adjustments. Member

States shall, subject to conditions which they lay down, allow the taxable person to make such statements by electronic means, and may also require that electronic means are used.][1]

(b)   [Every taxable person identified for value added tax purposes shall also submit a recapitulative statement of the acquirers identified for value added tax purposes to whom he has supplied goods under the conditions provided for in Article 28c(A)(a) and (d), and of consignees identified for value added tax purposes in the transactions referred to in the fifth subparagraph.][5]

[The recapitulative statement shall be drawn up for each calendar quarter within a period and in accordance with procedures to be determined by the Member States, which shall take the measures necessary to ensure that the provisions concerning administrative cooperation in the field of indirect taxation are in any event complied with. Member States shall, subject to conditions which they lay down, allow the taxable person to make such statements by electronic means, and may also require that electronic means are used.][1]

The recapitulative statement shall set out:

—   the number by which the taxable person is identified for purposes of value added tax in the territory of the country and under which he effected supplies of goods in the conditions laid down in Article [28c(A)(a)][3],

[—   the number by which each person acquiring goods is identified for purposes of value added tax in another Member State and under which the goods were supplied to him,][5]

—   for each person acquiring goods, the total value of the supplies of goods effected by the taxable person. Those amounts shall be declared for the calendar quarter during which the tax became chargeable.

The recapitulative statement shall also set out

[—   for the supplies of goods covered by Article [28c(A)(d)][3], the number by means of which the taxable person is identified for purposes of value added tax in the territory of the country, the number by which he is identified in the Member State of arrival of the dispatch or transport [and the total amount of the supplies, determined in accordance with Article 28e(2)][3]

[—   the amounts of adjustments made under Article 11(C)(1). Those amounts shall be declared for the calendar quarter during which the person acquiring the goods is notified of the adjustment.

[...][5]

[In the cases set out in the third subparagraph of Article 28b(A)(2), the taxable person identified for value added tax purposes within the territory of the country shall mention in a clear way on the recapitulative statement:

- the number by which he is identified for value added tax purposes within the territory of the country and under which he carried out the intra-Community acquisition and the subsequent supply of goods,

- the number by which, within the territory of the Member State of arrival of the dispatch or transport of the goods, the consignee of the subsequent supply by the taxable person is identified,

- and, for each consignee, the total amount, less value added tax, of the supplies made by the taxable person within the territory of the Member State of arrival of the dispatch or transport of the goods. These amounts shall be declared for the calendar quarter during which the tax became chargeable.]³

(c) By way of derogation from (b), Member States may:

- require recapitulative statements to be filed on a monthly basis;

- require that recapitulative statements give additional particulars.

(d) In the case of supplies of new means of transport effected under the conditions laid down in Article 28c(A)(b) by a taxable person identified for purposes of value added tax to a purchaser not identified for purposes of value added tax or by a taxable person as defined in Article 28a(4), Member States shall take the measures necessary to ensure that the vendor communicates all the information necessary for value added tax to be applied and inspected by the tax authority.

(e) Member States may require taxable persons who in the territory of the country effect intra-Community acquisitions of goods as defined in Article 28a(1)(a) and (6) to submit statements giving details of such acquisitions provided, however, that such statements may not be required for a period of less than one month.

Member States may also require persons who effect intra-Community acquisitions of new means of transport as defined in Article 28a(1)(b) to provide, when submitting the return referred to in paragraph 4, all the information necessary for value added tax to be applied and inspected by the tax authority.

[7. Member States shall take the measures necessary to ensure that those persons who, in accordance with Article 21(1) and (2), are considered to be liable to pay the tax instead of a taxable person not established within the territory of the country comply with the obligations relating to declaration and payment set out in this Article; they shall also take the measures necessary to ensure that those persons who, in accordance with Article 21(3), are held to be jointly and severally liable for payment of the tax comply with the obligations relating to payment set out in this Article.]⁶

8. Member States may impose other obligations which they deem necessary for the correct collection of the tax and for the prevention of evasion, subject to the requirement of equal treatment for domestic transactions and transactions carried out between Member States by taxable persons

and provided that such obligations do not, in trade between Member States, give rise to formalities connected with the crossing of frontiers.

[The option provided for in the first subparagraph cannot be used to impose additional obligations over and above those laid down in paragraph 3.][4]

9. (a) Member States may release from certain or all obligations:

— taxable persons carrying out only supplies of goods or of services which are exempt under Articles 13 and 15,

— taxable persons eligible for the exemption from tax provided for in Article 24 and for the derogation provided for in Article 28a(1) (a), second subparagraph,

— taxable persons carrying out none of the transactions referred to in paragraph 4(c).

[Without prejudice to the provisions laid down in point (d), Member States may not, however, release the taxable persons referred to in the third indent from the obligations referred to in Article 22(3).][4]

(b) Member States may release taxable persons other than those referred to in (a) from certain of the obligations referred to in 2(a).

(c) Member States may release taxable persons from payment of the tax due where the amount involved is insignificant.

[(d) Subject to consultation of the Committee provided for in Article 29 and under the conditions which they may lay down, Member States may provide that invoices in respect of goods supplied or services rendered in their territory do not have to fulfil some of the conditions laid down in paragraph 3(b) in the following cases:

— when the amount of the invoice is minor, or

— when commercial or administrative practice in the business sector concerned or the technical conditions under which the invoices are issued make it difficult to comply with all the requirements referred to in paragraph 3(b).

In any case, these invoices must contain the following:

— the date of issue,

— identification of the taxable person,

— identification of the type of goods supplied or services rendered,

— the tax due or the information needed to calculate it.

The simplified arrangements provided for in this point may not be applied to transactions referred to in paragraph 4(c).][4]

[(e) In cases where Member States make use of the option provided for in the third indent of point (a) to refrain from allocating a number as referred to in paragraph 1(c) to taxable persons who do not carry out any of the transactions referred to in paragraph 4(c), and where the supplier or the customer have not been allocated an identification number of this type, the invoice should feature instead another number called the tax reference number, as defined by the Member States concerned.

When the taxable person has been allocated an identification number as referred to in paragraph 1(c), the Member States referred to in the first subparagraph may also require the invoice to show:

- for services rendered referred to in Article 28b(C), (D), (E) and (F) and for the supply of goods referred to in Article 28c(A) and (E) point 3, the number referred to in paragraph 1(c) and the tax reference number of the supplier;

- for other supplies of goods and services, only the tax reference number of the supplier or only the number referred to in paragraph 1(c).][4]

10. Member States shall take measures to ensure that non-taxable legal persons who are liable for the tax payable in respect of intra-Community acquisitions of goods covered by the first subparagraph of Article 28a(1)(a) comply with the above obligations relating to declaration and payment and that they are identified by an individual number as defined in paragraph 1(c), (d) and (e).

[11. In the case of intra-Community acquisitions of products subject to excise duty referred to in Article 28a(1)(c) as well as][3] in the case of intra-Community acquisitions of new means of transport covered by Article 28a(1)(b), Member States shall adopt arrangements for declaration and subsequent payment.

12. Acting unanimously on a proposal from the Commission, the Council may authorize any Member State to introduce particular measures to simplify the statement obligations laid down in paragraph 6(b). Such simplification measures, which shall not jeopardize the proper monitoring of intra-Community transactions, may take the following forms:

(a) Member States may authorize taxable persons who meet the following three conditions to file one-year recapitulative statements indicating the numbers by which the persons to whom those taxable persons have supplied goods under the conditions laid down in Article 28c(A) are identified for purposes of value added tax in other Member States:

- the total annual value, less value added tax, of their supplies of goods or provisions of services, as defined in Articles 5, 6 and 28a(5), does not exceed by more than ECU 35 000 the amount of the annual turnover which is used as a reference for application of the exemption from tax provided for in Article 24,

- the total annual value, less value added tax, of supplies of goods effected by them under the conditions laid down in Article

28c(A) does not exceed the equivalent in national currency of ECU 15 000,

— supplies of goods effected by them under the conditions laid down in Article 28c(A) are other than supplies or new means of transport;

(b) Member States which set at over three months the tax period for which a taxable person must submit the returns provided for in paragraph 4 may authorize such persons to submit recapitulative statements for the same period where those taxable persons meet the following three conditions:

— the overall annual value, less value added tax, of the goods and services they supply, as defined in Articles 5, 6 and 28a(5), does not exceed the equivalent in national currency of ECU 200 000,

— the total annual value, less value added tax, of supplies of goods effected by them under the conditions laid down in Article 28c(A) does not exceed the equivalent in national currency of ECU 15 000,

— supplies of goods effected by them under the conditions provided for in Article 28c(A) are other than — supplies of new means of transport."][7]

Amendments
1 Substituted by Art 2, Council Directive 2002/38/EC of 7 May 2002 (w.e.f. 15 May 2002)
2 Amended by Art 1(6) Council Directive 2003/92/EC of 7 October 2003 (w.e.f. 1 January 2005)
3 Amended by Art 1(20) Council Directive 92/111/EEC of 14 January 1992 (w.e.f. 1 January 1993).
4 Inserted by Art 2, Council Directive 2001/115/EC of 20 December 2001, (w.e.f. 1 January 2004).
5 Amended by Art 1(12), Council Directive 95/7/EC of 10 April 1995, (w.e.f. 25 may 1995).
6 Amended by Art 1(5), Council Directive 00/65/EC of 17 October 2000.
7 Art 28h inserted by Art 1(22), Council Directive 91/680/EEC of 16 December 1991, (w.e.f. 1 January 1993).

[Article 28i

Special scheme for small undertakings

The following subparagraph shall be added to Article 24(3):

["In all circumstances supplies of new means of transport effected under the conditions laid down in Article 28c(A) as well as supplies of goods and services effected by a taxable person who is not established in the territory of the country shall be excluded from the exemption from tax under paragraph 2."][1]][2]

Amendments
1 Amended by Art 1(21), Council Directive 92/111/EEC of 14 December 1992, (w.e.f. 1 January 1993).
2 Art28i inserted by Art 1(22), Council Directive 91/680/EEC of 16 December 1991, (w.e.f. 1 January 1993).

[Article 28j

Common flat-rate scheme for farmers

1. The following subparagraph shall be added to Article 25(4):

"When they exercise this option, Member States shall take the measures necessary to ensure the correct application of the transitional arrangements for the taxation of intra-Community transactions as laid down in Title XVIa."

2. Article 25(5) and (6) shall be replaced by the following:

"5. The flat-rate percentages provided for in paragraph 3 shall be applied to the prices, exclusive of tax, of:

(a) agricultural products supplied by flat-rate farmers to taxable persons other than those eligible within the territory of the country for the flat-rate scheme provided for in this Article;

(b) agricultural products supplied by flat-rate farmers, under the conditions laid down in Article 28c(A), to non-taxable legal persons not eligible, in the Member State of arrival of the dispatch or transport of the agricultural products thus supplied, for the derogation provided for in Article 28a(1)(a), second subparagraph;

(c) agricultural services supplied by flat-rate farmers to taxable persons other than those eligible within the territory of the country for the flat-rate scheme provided for in this Article.

This compensation shall exclude any other form of deduction.

6 In the case of supplies of agricultural products and of agricultural services referred to in paragraph 5, Member States shall provide for the flat-rate compensation to be paid either:

(a) by the purchaser or customer. In that event, the taxable purchaser or customer shall be authorized, as provided for in Article 17 and in accordance with the procedures laid down by the Member States, to deduct from the tax for which he is liable within the territory of the country the amount of the flat-rate compensation he has paid to flat-rate farmers.

Member States shall refund to the purchaser or customer the amount of the flat-rate compensation he has paid to flat-rate farmers in respect of any of the following transactions:

— supplies of agricultural products effected under the conditions laid down in Article 28c(A) to taxable persons, or to non-taxable legal persons acting as such in another Member State within which they are not eligible for the derogation provided for in the second subparagraph of Article 28a(1)(a),

— supplies of agricultural products effected under the conditions laid down in Article 15 and in Article 16(1)(B), (D) and (E)

to taxable purchasers established outside the Community, provided that the products are used by those purchasers for the purposes of the transactions referred to in Article 17(3)(a) and (b) or for the purposes of services which are deemed to be supplied within the territory of the country and on which tax is payable solely by the customers under Article 21(1)(b),

— supplies of agricultural services to taxable customers established within the Community but in another Member State or to taxable customers established outside the Community, provided that the services are used by those customers for the purposes of the transactions referred to in Article 17(3)(a) and (b) and for the purposes of services which are deemed to be supplied within the territory of the country and on which tax is payable solely by the customers under Article 21(1)(b).

Member States shall determine the method by which the refunds are to be made. In particular, they may apply Article 17(4); or

(b) by the public authorities."

3. The following subparagraph shall be added to Article 25(9):

"Whenever they exercise the option provided for in this Article, Member States shall take all measures necessary to ensure that the same method of taxation is applied to supplies of agricultural products effected under the conditions laid down in Article 28b(B)(1), whether the supply is effected by a flat-rate farmer or by a taxable person other than a flat-rate farmer."][1]

Amendments

1   Art28j inserted by Art 1(22), Council Directive 91/680/EEC of 16 December 1991, (w.e.f. 1 January 1993).

[Article 28k

Miscellaneous provisions

The following provisions shall apply until 30 June 1999:

1. Member States may exempt supplies by tax-free shops of goods to be carried away in the personal luggage of travellers taking intra-Community flights or sea crossings to other Member States. For the purposes of this Article:

    (a) `tax-free shop' shall mean any establishment situated within an airport or port which fulfils the conditions laid down by the competent public authorities pursuant, in particular, to paragraph 5;

    (b) `traveller to another Member State' shall mean any passenger holding a transport document for air or sea travel stating that the immediate destination is an airport or port situated in another Member State;

    (c) `intra-Community flight or sea crossing' shall mean any transport, by air or sea, starting within the territory of the country as defined in Article 3, where the actual place of arrival is situated within another Member State.

    Supplies of goods effected by tax-free shops shall include supplies of goods effected on board aircraft or vessels during intra-Community passenger transport.

    This exemption shall also apply to supplies of goods effected by tax-free shops in either of the two Channel tunnel terminals, for passengers holding valid tickets for the journey between those two terminals.

2. Eligibility for the exemption provided for in paragraph 1 shall apply only to supplies of goods:

    [(a) the total value of which per person per journey does not exceed ECU 90.

    By way of derogation from Article 28m, Member States shall determine the equivalent in national currency of the above amount in accordance with Article 7(2) of Directive 69/169/EEC.][1]

    Where the total value of several items or of several supplies of goods per person per journey exceeds those limits, the exemption shall be granted up to those amounts, on the understanding that the value of an item may not be split;

    (b) involving quantities per person per journey not exceeding the limits laid down by the Community provisions in force for the movement of travellers between third countries and the Community.

    The value of supplies of goods effected within the quantitative limits laid down in the previous subparagraph shall not be taken into account for the application of (a).

3. Member States shall grant every taxable person the right to a deduction or refund of the value added tax referred to in Article 17(2) in so far as

the goods and services are used for the purposes of his supplies of goods exempt under this Article.

4.   Member States which exercise the option provided for in Article 16(2) shall also grant eligibility under that provision to imports, intra-Community acquisitions and supplies of goods to a taxable person for the purposes of his supplies of goods exempt pursuant to this Article.

5.   Member States shall take the measures necessary to ensure the correct and straightforward application of the exemptions provided for in this Article and to prevent any evasion, avoidance or abuse.][2]

Amendments
1   Inserted by Art 2, Council Directive 94/4/EC of 14 February 1994, (w.e.f. 3 March 1994).
2   Art28k inserted by Art 1(22), Council Directive 91/680/EEC of 16 December 1991, (w.e.f. 1 January 1993).

[Article 28l

Period of application

The transitional arrangements provided for in this Title shall enter into force on 1 January 1993. Before 31 December 1994 the Commission shall report to the Council on the operation of the transitional arrangements and submit proposals for a definitive system.

The transitional arrangements shall be replaced by a definitive system for the taxation of trade between Member States based in principle on the taxation in the Member State of origin of the goods or services supplied. To that end, after having made a detailed examination of that report and considering that the conditions for transition to the definitive system have been fulfilled satisfactorily, the Council, acting unanimously on a proposal from the Commission and after consulting the European Parliament, shall decide before 31 December 1995 on the arrangements necessary for the entry into force and operation of the definitive system.

The transitional arrangements shall enter into force for a period of four years and shall accordingly apply until 31 December 1996. The period of application of the transitional arrangements shall be extended automatically until the date of entry into force of the definitive system and in any event until the Council has decided on the definitive system.][1]

Amendments
1   Art28l inserted by Art 1(22), Council Directive 91/680/EEC of 16 December 1991, (w.e.f. 1 January 1993).

[Article 28m

Rate of conversion

To determine the equivalents in their national currencies of amounts expressed in ecus in this Title Member States shall use the rate of exchange applicable on 16 December 1991. However, Bulgaria, the Czech Republic, Estonia, Cyprus, Latvia, Lithuania, Hungary, Malta, Poland, Romania, Slovenia and Slovakia shall use the rate of exchange applicable on the date of their accession.][1]

Amendments
1 Art28m substituted by Council Directive 2006/98/EC of 20 November 2006, w.e.f. 1 January 2007.

Note
Council Regulation 2866/98 of 31 December 1998 fixed the conversion rate of the national currencies of the participating Member States irrevocably to the euro.

Council Regulation 1103/97 of 17 June 1997 stated that all references to ecu in EU legislation should now refer to euro, where one euro equals one ecu.

[Article 28n

Transitional measures

1. When goods:

   — entered the territory of the country within the meaning of Article 3 before 1 January 1993,

   and

   — were placed, on entry into the territory of that country, under one of the regimes referred to in Article 14(1)(b) or (c), or Article 16(1)(A),

   and

   — have not left that regime before 1 January 1993, the provisions in force at the moment the goods were placed under that regime shall continue to apply for the period, as determined by those provisions, the goods remain under that regime.

2. The following shall be deemed to be an import of goods within the meaning of Article 7(1):

   (a) the removal, including irregular removal, of goods from the regime referred to in Article 14(1)(c) under which the goods were placed before 1 January 1993 under the conditions set out in paragraph 1;

   (b) the removal, including irregular removal, of goods from the regime referred to in Article 16(1)(A) under which the goods were placed before 1 January 1993 under the conditions set out in paragraph 1;

   (c) the termination of a Community internal transit operation started before 1 January 1993 in the Community for the purpose of supply of goods for consideration made before 1 January 1993 in the Community by a taxable person acting as such;

   (d) the termination of an external transit operation started before 1 January 1993;

   (e) any irregularity of offence committed during an external transit operation started under the conditions set out in (c) or any Community external transit operation referred to in (d);

   (f) the use within the country, by a taxable or non-taxable person, of goods which have been supplied to him, before 1 January 1993, within another Member State, where the following conditions are met:

   — the supply of these goods has been exempted, or was likely to be exempted, pursuant to Article 15(1) and (2),

   — the goods were not imported within the country before 1 January 1993.

   For the purpose of the application of (c), the expression `Community internal transit operation' shall mean the dispatch of transport of goods under the cover of the internal Community transit arrangement or under the cover of a T2 L document or the intra-Community movement carnet, or the sending of goods by post.

3.   In the cases referred to in paragraph 2(a) to (e), the place of import, within the meaning of Article 7(2), shall be the member State within whose territory the goods cease to be covered by the regime under which they were placed before 1 January 1993.

4.   By way of derogation from Article 10(3), the import of the goods within the meaning of paragraph 2 of this Article shall terminate without the occurrence of a chargeable event when:

(a)   the imported goods are dispatched or transported outside the Community within the meaning of Article 3;

or

(b)   the imported goods, within the meaning of paragraph 2(a), are other than a means of transport and are dispatched or transported to the Member State from which they were exported and to the person who exported them;

or

(c)   the imported goods, within the meaning of paragraph 2(a), are means of transport which were acquired or imported before 1 January 1993, in accordance with the general conditions of taxation in force on the domestic market of a Member State, within the meaning of Article 3, and/or have not been subject by reason of their exportation to any exemption from or refund of value added tax.

This condition shall be deemed to be fulfilled when the date of the first use of the means of transport was before 1 January 1985 or when the amount of tax due because of the importation is insignificant.][1]

Amendments
1   Art28n inserted by Art 1(22), Council Directive 92/111/EEC of 14 December 1992, (w.e.f. 1 January 1993).

[TITLE XVIb

transitional provisions applicable in the field of second-hand goods, works of art, collectors' items and antiques

Article 28o

Second-hand goods, works of art, collectors' items, antiques

1. Member States which at 31 December 1992 were applying special tax arrangements other than those provided for in Article 26a(B) to supplies of second-hand means of transport effected by taxable dealers my continue to apply those arrangements during the period referred to in Article 281 in so far as they comply with, or are adjusted to comply with, the following conditions:

    (a) the special arrangements shall apply only to supplies of the means of transport referred to in Article 28a(2)(a) and regarded as second-hand goods within the meaning of Article 26a(A)(d), effected by taxable dealers within the meaning of Article 26a(A)(e), and subject to the special tax arrangements for taxing the margin pursuant to Article 26a(B)(1) and (2). Supplies of new means of transport within the meaning of Article 28a(2)(b) that are carried out under the conditions specified in Article 28c(A) shall be excluded from these special arrangements;

    (b) the tax due in respect of each supply referred to in (a) is equal to the amount of tax that would be due if that supply had been subject to the normal arrangements for value added tax, less the amount of value added tax regarded as being incorporated in the purchase price of the means of transport by the taxable dealer;

    (c) the tax regarded as being incorporated in the purchase price of the means of transport by the taxable dealer shall be calculated according to the following method:

        – the purchase price to be taken into account shall be the purchase price within the meaning of Article 26a(B)(3),

        – that purchase price paid by the taxable dealer shall be deemed to include the tax that would have been due if the taxable dealer's supplier had subjected the supply to the normal value added tax arrangements,

        – the rate to be taken into account shall be the rate applicable within the meaning of Article 12(1), in the Member State within which the place of the supply to the taxable dealer, determined in accordance with Article 8, is deemed to be situated;

    (d) the tax due in respect of each supply as referred to in (a), determined in accordance with the provisions of (b), may not be less than the amount of tax that would be due if that supply had been subject to the special arrangements for taxing the margin in accordance with Article 26a(B)(3).

For the application of the above provisions, the Member States have the option of providing that if the supply had been subject to the special arrangements for taxation of the margin, that margin would not have been less than 10% of the selling price, within the meaning of B(3);

(e) the taxable dealer shall not be entitled to indicate separately on the invoices he issues, [...][1] tax relating to supplies which he is subjecting to the special arrangements;

(f) taxable persons shall not be entitled to deduct from the tax for which they are liable tax due or paid in respect of second-hand means of transport supplied to them by a taxable dealer, in so far as the supply of those goods by the taxable dealer is subject to the tax arrangements in accordance with (a);

(g) by way of derogation from Article 28a(1)(a), intra-Community acquisitions of means of transport are not subject to value added tax where the vendor is a taxable dealer acting as such and the second-hand means of transport acquired has been subject to the tax, in the Member State of departure of the dispatch or transport, in accordance with (a);

(h) Articles 28b(B) and 28c(A)(a) and (d) shall not apply to supplies of second-hand means of transport subject to tax in accordance with (a).

2. By way of derogation from the first sentence of paragraph 1, the Kingdom of Denmark shall be entitled to apply the special tax arrangements laid down in paragraph 1(a) to (h) during the period referred to in Article 281.

3. Where they apply the special arrangements for sales by public auction provided for in Article 26a(C), Member States shall also apply these special arrangements to supplies of second-hand means of transport effected by an organizer of sales by public auction acting in his own name, pursuant to a contract under which commission is payable on the sale of those goods by public auction, on behalf of a taxable dealer, in so far as the supply of the second-hand means of transport, within the meaning of Article 5(4)(c), by that other taxable dealer, is subject to tax in accordance with paragraphs 1 and 2.

4. For supplies by a taxable dealer of works of art, collectors' items or antiques that have been supplied to him under the conditions provided for in Article 26a(B)(2), the Federal Republic of Germany shall be entitled, until 30 June 1999, to provide for the possibility for taxable dealers to apply either the special arrangements for taxable dealers, or the normal VAT arrangements according to the following rules:

(a) for the application of the special arrangements for taxable dealers to these supplies of goods, the taxable amount shall be determined in accordance with Article 11(A)(1), (2) and (3);

(b) in so far as the goods are used for the needs of his operations which are taxed in accordance with (a), the taxable dealer shall be authorized to deduct from the tax for which he is liable:

- the value added tax due or paid for works of art, collectors' items or antiques which are or will be supplied to him by another taxable dealer, where the supply by that other taxable dealer has been taxed in accordance with (a),

- the value added tax deemed to be included in the purchase price of the works of art, collectors' items or antiques which are or will be supplied to him by another taxable dealer, where the supply by that other taxable dealer has been subject to value added tax in accordance with the special arrangements for the taxation of the margin provided for in Article 26a(B), in the Member State within whose territory the place of that supply, determined in accordance with Article 8, is deemed to be situated.

This right to deduct shall arise at the time when the tax due for the supply taxed in accordance with (a) becomes chargeable;

(c) for the application of the provisions laid down in the second indent of (b), the purchase price of the works of art, collectors' items or antiques the supply of which by a taxable dealer is taxed in accordance with (a) shall be determined in accordance with Article 26a(B)(3) and the tax deemed to be included in this purchase price shall be calculated according to the following method:

- the purchase price shall be deemed to include the value added tax that would have been due if the taxable margin made by the supplier had been equal to 20% of the purchase price,

- the rate to be taken into account shall be the rate applicable, within the meaning of Article 12(1), in the Member State within whose territory the place of the supply that is subject to the special arrangements for taxation of the profit margin, determined in accordance with Article 8, is deemed to be situated;

(d) where he applies the normal arrangements for value added tax to the supply of a work of art, collectors' item or antique which has been supplied to him by another taxable dealer and where the goods have been taxed in accordance with (a), the taxable dealer shall be authorized to deduct from his tax liability the value added tax referred to in (b);

(e) the category of rates applicable to these supplies of goods shall be that which was applicable on 1 January 1993;

(f) for the application of the fourth indent of, Article 26a(B)(2), the fourth indent of Article 26a(C)(1) and Article 26a(D)(b) and (c), the supplies of works of art, collectors' items or antiques, taxed in accordance with (a), shall be deemed by Member States to be supplies subject to value added tax in accordance with the special arrangements for taxation of the profit margin provided for in Article 26a(B);

(g) where the supplies of works of art, collectors' items or antiques taxed in accordance with (a) are effected under the conditions provided for in Article 28c(A), the invoice issued in accordance with Article 22(3) shall contain an endorsement indicating that the special taxation arrangements for taxing the margin provided for in Article 28o(4) have been applied.[2]

Amendments
1 Deleted by Art 4, Council directive 201/115/EC of 20 December 2001, (w.e.f. 6 February 2001).
2 Title XVIb and Art 28o Inserted by Art 1(7), Council Directive 94/5/EC of 14 February 1994, (w.e.f. 3 March 1994).

[[TITLE XVIc

Transitional measures applicable in the context of the accession to the European Union of Austria, Finland and Sweden on 1 January 1995, of the Czech Republic, Estonia, Cyprus, Latvia, Lithuania, Hungary, Malta, Poland, Slovenia and Slovakia on 1 May 2004, and of Bulgaria and Romania on 1 January 2007][1]

Article 28p

Transitional measures in the context of the accession

1. For the purposes of applying this Article:

   — `Community' shall mean the territory of the Community as defined in Article 3 before accession,

   [— 'new Member States' shall mean the territory of the Member States acceding to the European Union on 1 January 1995, on 1 May 2004 and on 1 January 2007, as defined for each of those Member States in Article 3 of this Directive,][1]

   — `enlarged Community' shall mean the territory of the Community as defined in Article 3, after accession.

2. When goods:

   — entered the territory of the Community or of one of the new Member States before the date of accession, and

   — were placed, on entry into the territory of the Community or of one of the new Member States, under a temporary admission procedure with full exemption from import duties, under one of the regimes referred to in Article 16(1)(B)(a) to (d) or under a similar regime in one of the new Member States, and

   — have not left that regime before the date of accession,

   the provisions in force at the moment the goods were placed under that regime shall continue to apply until the goods leave this regime, after the date of accession.

3. When goods:

   — were placed, before the date of accession, under the common transit procedure or under another customs transit procedure, and

   — have not left that procedure before the date of accession,

   the provisions in force at the moment the goods were placed under that procedure shall continue to apply until the goods leave this procedure, after the date of accession.

   For the purposes of the first indent, `common transit procedure' shall mean the measures for the transport of goods in transit between the Community and the countries of the European Free Trade Association

(EFTA) and between the EFTA countries themselves, as provided for in the Convention of 20 May 1987 on a common transit procedure.

4. The following shall be deemed to be an importation of goods within the meaning of Article 7(1) where it is shown that the goods were in free circulation in one of the new Member States or in the Community:

    (a) the removal, including irregular removal, of goods from a temporary admission procedure under which they were placed before the date of accession under the conditions set out in paragraph 2;

    (b) the removal, including irregular removal, of goods either from one of the regimes referred to in Article 16(1)(B)(a) to (d) or from a similar regime under which they were placed before the date of accession under the conditions set out in paragraph 2;

    (c) the termination of one of the procedures referred to in paragraph 3 which was started before the date of accession in one of the new Member States for the purposes of a supply of goods for consideration effected before that date in that Member State by a taxable person acting as such;

    (d) any irregularity or offence committed during one of the procedures referred to in paragraph 3 under the conditions set out at (c).

5. The use after the date of accession within a Member State, by a taxable or non-taxable person, of goods supplied to him before the date of accession within the Community or one of the new Member States shall also be deemed to be an importation of goods within the meaning of Article 7(1) where the following conditions are met:

    — the supply of those goods has been exempted, or was likely to be exempted, either under Article 15(1) and (2) or under a similar provision in the new Member States;

    — the goods were not imported into one of the new Member States or into one of the new Member States or into the Community before the date of accession.

6. In the cases referred to in paragraph 4, the place of import within the meaning of Article 7(3) shall be the Member State within whose territory the goods cease to be covered by the regime under which they were placed before the date of accession.

7. By way of derogation from Article 10(3), the importation of goods within the meaning of paragraphs 4 and 5 of this Article shall terminate without the occurrence of a chargeable event when:

    (a) the imported goods are dispatched or transported outside the enlarged Community; or

    (b) he imported goods within the meaning of paragraph 4(a) are other than means of transport and are redispatched or transported to the Member States from which they were exported and to the person who exported them; or

(c)   the imported goods within the meaning of paragraph 4(a) are means of transport which were acquired or imported before the date of accession in accordance with the general conditions of taxation in force on the domestic market of one of the new Member States or of one of the Member States of the Community and/or have not been subject by reason of their exportation to any exemption from or refund of value added tax.

[This condition shall be deemed to be fulfilled in the following cases:

—   when, in respect of Austria, Finland and Sweden, the date of the first use of the means of transport was before 1 January 1987;

—   when, in respect of the Czech Republic, Estonia, Cyprus, Latvia, Lithuania, Hungary, Malta, Poland, Slovenia and Slovakia, the date of the first use of the means of transport was before 1 May 1996;

—   when in respect of Bulgaria and Romania, the date of the first use of the means of transport was before 1 January 1999;

—   when the amount of tax due by reason of the importation is insignificant.][1][2]

Amendments

1   Substituted by Art 1, Council Directive 2006/98/EC of 20 November 2006, w.e.f. 1 January 2007.

2   Title XVIc and Art 28p inserted by Art 1, Council Directive 94/76/EC of 22 December 1994, w.e.f. 1 January 2005.

Title XVII

value added tax committee

Article 29

VAT Committee

1. An Advisory Committee on value added tax, hereinafter called `the Committee', is hereby set up.

2. The Committee shall consist of representatives of the Member States and of the Commission.

   The chairman of the Committee shall be a representative of the Commission.

   Secretarial services for the Committee shall be provided by the Commission.

3. The Committee shall adopt its own rules of procedure.

4. In addition to points subject to the consultation provided for under this Directive, the Committee shall examine questions raised by its chairman, on his own initiative or at the request of the representative of a Member State, which concern the application of the Community provisions on value added tax.

[Article 29a

Implementing measures

The Council, acting unanimously on a proposal from the Commission, shall adopt the measures necessary to implement this Directive.][1]

Amendment
1 Article 29a inserted by Art (1)(2), Council Directive 2004/7/EC of 20 January 2004 (w.e.f. 19 February 2004).

TITLE XVIII

miscellaneous

[Article 30

International Agreements

1. The Council, acting unanimously on a proposal from the Commission, may authorise any Member State to conclude with a third country or an international organisation an agreement which may contain derogations from this Directive.

2. A Member State wishing to conclude such an agreement shall send an application to the Commission and provide it with all the necessary information. If the Commission considers that it does not have all the necessary information, it shall contact the Member State concerned within two months of receipt of the application and specify what additional information is required. Once the Commission has all the information it considers necessary for appraisal of the request it shall within one month notify the requesting Member State accordingly and it shall transmit the request, in its original language, to the other Member States.

3. Within three months of giving the notification referred to in the last sentence of paragraph 2, the Commission shall present to the Council either an appropriate proposal or, should it object to the derogation requested, a communication setting out its objections.

4. In any event, the procedure set out in paragraphs 2 and 3 shall be completed within eight months of receipt of the application by the Commission.][1]

Amendment
1   Article 30 replaced by Art 1(3), Council Directive 2004/7/EC of 20 January 2004 (w.e.f 19 February 2004).

Article 31

Unit of Account

1. The Unit of Account used in this Directive shall be the EUA defined by Decision 75/250/EEC.

2. When converting this Unit of Account into national currencies, Member States shall have the option of rounding the amounts resulting from this conversion either upwards or downwards by up to 10%.

Note

Council Regulation 2866/98 of 31 December 1998 fixed the conversion rate of the national currencies of the participating Member States irrevocably to the euro.

Council Regulation 1103/97 of 17 June 1997 stated that all references to ecu in EU legislation should now refer to euro, where one euro equals one ecu.

Article 32

Second-hand goods

[...][1]

Amendments

1   Deleted by Art 1(9), Council Directive 94/5/EC of 14 February 1994.

Case law

Ireland v European Commission	C17/84	Taxable Amount/Part exchanged goods
Gaston Schul Douane Expediteur BV v Inspecteur Der Invoerrechtenn EN Accijnzen	C15/81	Recovery of VAT on imports of second hand cars
ORO Amsterdam Beheer BV & Concerto BV v Inspecteur der Omzetbelasting Amsterdam	C165/88	Deduction/Right of

[Article 33

Other taxes duties or charges

1. Without prejudice to other Community provisions, in particular those laid down in the Community provisions in force relating to the general arrangements for the holding, movement and monitoring of products subject to excise duty, this Directive shall not prevent a Member State from maintaining or introducing taxes on insurance contracts, taxes on betting and gambling, excise duties, stamp duties and, more generally, any taxes, duties or charges which cannot be characterized as turnover taxes, provided however those taxes, duties or charges do not, in trade between Member States, give rise to formalities connected with the crossing of frontiers.

2. Any reference in this Directive to products subject to excise duty shall apply to the following products as defined by current Community provisions:

    —   mineral oils,

    —   alcohol and alcoholic beverages,

    —   manufactured tobacco.][1]

Amendments
1   Art33 substituted by Art 1(23), Council Directive 91/680/EEC of 16 December 1991, (w.e.f. 1 January 1993).

Case law

Banca Popolare di Cremona Soc. Coop. arl v Agenzia Entrate Ufficio Cremona	C475/03	Definition of 'Turnover taxes'
Beaulande Raymond v Directeur des Services Fiscaux de Nantes	C208/91	Registration tax v VAT
Bergandi, Gabriel v Directeur Generale Des Impots	C252/86	Scope of VAT/State tax on gaming machines
Bozzi Aldo v Cassa Nazionale Di Previdenza ed Assistenza	C347/90	Scope of VAT
Evangelischer Krankenhausverein Wien v Abgabenberufungskommission and Ikera Warenhandelsgesekfschaft mbH v Oberosterreichische Landesregierung	C437/97	Levy
Giant NV v Commune d' Overijse	C109/90	Scope of VAT
GIL Insurance Ltd and others v Commissioners of Customs and Excise	C308/01	Tax on insurance premiums
Lambert and Others v Directeur des Services Fiscaux de L'orne	C317/86	Scope of VAT/State tax on gaming machines
Pelzl Erna v Steiermarkische Landesregierung	C338/97 C344/97 C390/97	Scope of VAT
Rousseau, Wilmot SA v Caisse de Compensation de l'organisation Autunome Nationale de l'Industrie et de Commerce (Organic)	C295/84	Scope of VAT
Spar Osterreichische Warendandels AG v Finanzlandesdirektion Fur Salzburg	C318/96	Scope of VAT/Levy in the nature of VAT/Tax to finance Chambers of Commerce in Austria
Stuag Bau-Aktiengesellschaft v Kartner Landesregierung	C390/97	Levy in nature of VAT
Tulliasiamies and Antti Siilin	C101/00	Nature of VAT/Taxation of imported used cars
Wiener Stadtische Allgemein Versicherungs AG v Tiroler Landesregierung	C344/97	Scope of VAT/Tourism Levy
Wisselink en Co BV v Staatssecretaris van Financien	C93/88 and C94/88	Nature of VAT

[Article 33a

Goods from third territories

1. Goods referred to in Article 7(1)(b) entering the Community from a territory which forms part of the customs territory of the Community but which is considered as a third territory for the purposes of applying this Directive shall be subject to the following provisions:

   (a) the formalities relating to the entry of such goods into the Community shall be the same as those laid down by the Community customs provisions in force for the import of goods into the customs territory of the Community;

   (b) when the place of arrival of the dispatch or transport of these goods is situated outside the Member State where they enter the Community, they shall circulate in the Community under the internal Community transit procedure laid down by the Community customs provisions in force, insofar as they have been the subject of a declaration placing them under this regime when the goods entered the Community;

   (c) when at the moment of their entry into the Community the goods are found to be in one of the situations which would qualify them, if they were imported within the meaning of Article 7(1)(a), to benefit from one of the arrangements referred to in Article 16(1)(B)(a), (b), (c) and (d), or under a temporary arrangement in full exemption from import duties, the Member States shall take measures ensuring that the goods may remain in the Community under the same conditions as those laid down for the application of such arrangements.

2. Goods not referred to in Article 7(1)(a) dispatched or transported from a Member State to a destination in a territory that forms parts of the customs territory of the Community but which is considered as a third territory for the purposes of applying this Directive shall be subject to the following provisions:

   (a) the formalities relating to the export of those goods outside the territory of the Community shall be the same as the Community customs provisions in force in relation to export of goods outside the customs territory of the Community;

   (b) for goods which are temporarily exported outside the Community, in order to be reimported, the Member States shall take the measures necessary to ensure that, on reimportation into the Community, such goods may benefit from the same provisions as if they had been temporarily exported outside the customs territory of the Community.][1]

Amendments
1   Art33a substituted by Art 1(23), Council Directive 92/111/EEC of 14 December 1992, (w.e.f. 1 January 1993).

TITLE XIX

final provisions

Article 34

Reports on the application

For the first time on 1 January 1982 and thereafter every two years, the Commission shall, after consulting the Member States, send the Council a report on the application of the common system of value added tax in the Member States. This report shall be transmitted by the Council to the European Parliament.

Article 35

Parallelism of the VAT systems

At the appropriate time the Council acting unanimously on a proposal from the Commission, after receiving the Opinion of the European Parliament and of the Economic and Social Committee, and in accordance with the interests of the common market, shall adopt further Directives on the common system of value added tax, in particular to restrict progressively or to repeal measures taken by the Member States by way of derogation from the system, in order to achieve complete parallelism of the national value added tax systems and thus permit the attainment of the objective stated in Article 4 of the first Council Directive of 11 April 1967.

Article 36

First Directive

The fourth paragraph of Article 2 and Article 5 of the first Council Directive of 11 April 1967 are repealed.

Article 37

Second Directive

Second Council Directive 67/228/EEC of 11 April 1967 shall cease to have effect in each Member State as from the respective dates on which the provisions of this Directive are brought into application.

Article 38

Addressed to the Member States

This Directive is addressed to the Member States.

Done at Brussels, 17 May 1977.

ANNEX A

list of agricultural production activities

I. CROP PRODUCTION

1. General agriculture, including viticulture.

2. Growing of fruit (including olives) and of vegetables, flowers and ornamental plants, both in the open and under glass.

3. Production of mushrooms, spices, seeds and propagating materials; nurseries.

II. STOCK FARMING TOGETHER WITH CULTIVATION

1. General stock farming

2. Poultry farming

3. Rabbit farming

4. Beekeeping

5. Silkworm farming

6. Snail farming

III. FORESTRY

IV. FISHERIES

1. Fresh water fishing

2. Fish farming

3. Breeding of mussels, oysters and other molluscs and crustaceans

4. Frog farming

V. Where a farmer processes, using means normally employed in an agricultural, forestry or fisheries undertaking, products deriving essentially from his agricultural production, such processing shall also be regarded as agricultural production.

ANNEX B

list of agricultural services

Supplies of agricultural services which normally play a part in agricultural production shall be considered the supply of agricultural services and include the following in particular:

- field work, reaping and mowing, threshing, baling, collecting, harvesting, sowing and planting

- packing and preparation for market, for example drying, cleaning, grinding, disinfecting and ensilage of agricultural products

- storage of agricultural products

- stock minding, rearing and fattening

- hiring out, for agricultural purposes, of equipment normally used in agricultural, forestry or fisheries undertakings

- technical assistance

- destruction of weeds and pests, dusting and spraying of crops and land

- operation of irrigation and drainage equipment

- lopping, tree felling and other forestry services.

ANNEX C

common method of calculation

I. For the purposes of calculating the value added for all agricultural, forestry and fisheries undertakings, the following shall be taken into account exclusive of value added tax:

    1. the value of the total final production including farmers' own consumption of the classes `agricultural products and game' and `wood in the rough' as set out in points IV and V below, plus the output of the processing activities referred to in point V of Annex A;

    2. the value of the total inputs required to achieve the production referred to in 1;

    3. the value of the gross fixed asset formation in connection with the activities listed in Annexes A and B.

II. To determine the deductible taxable inputs and outputs of flat-rate farmers, the inputs and outputs of farmers taxed under the normal value added tax scheme shall be deducted from the national accounts, taking into account the same factors as those in paragraph I.

III. The value added tax for flat-rate farmers is equal to the difference between the value of total final production, exclusive of value added tax, as referred to in point I(1) and the total value of inputs as referred to in point I(2) together with gross fixed-asset formation as referred to in point I(3). All these factors relate to flat-rate farmers only.

IV. AGRICULTURAL PRODUCTS AND GAME

	SOEC Code Number
Cereals (excluding rice)	
Wheat and spelt	10.01.11 1
	10.01.19 1
	-
	-
Durum wheat	10.01.51
	10.01.59
Winter wheat	-
Spring wheat	-
Rye and meslin	
Rye	10.02.00
Winter rye	-
Spring rye	-
Meslin	10.01.11 2
	10.01.19 2
Barley	10.03.10
	10.03.90

Spring barley   -
Winter barley   -

Oats and summer meslin
   Oats   10.04.10
                       10.04.90

   Summer meslin   -

Maize   10.05.01
                       10.05.92

Other cereals (excluding rice)
   Buckwheat   10.07.10
   Millet   10.07.91
   Grain sorghum   10.07.95
   Canary seed   10.07.96
   Cereals, not elsewhere specified (excluding rice)   10.07.99
Rice (in the husk or paddy)   10.06.11

Pulses
   Dried peas and fodder peas   07.05.11
      Dried peas (other than for fodder)   -
      Dried Peas (excluding chick peas)   -
      Chick peas   -
      Fodder peas   -

   Haricot beans, broad and field beans
      Haricot beans   07.05.15
      Broad and field beans   07.05.95

   Other pulses
      Lentils   07.05.91
      Vetches   12.03.31 2
      Lurpins   12.03.49 2
      Dried pulses not elsewhere specified, pulse
      mixtures and cereal and pulse mixtures   07.05.97

Roots (brassicas group for fodder)
Potatoes
   Potatoes (excluding seed potatoes)
      New potatoes   07.01.13
                       07.01.15
      Main crop potatoes   07.01.17
                       07.01.19

   Seed potatoes   07.01.11

Sugar beet   12.04.11

Mangolds and fodder beet; swedes, fodder carrots
and fodder turnips; other roots and fodder brassicas
    Mangolds and foder beet
    Swedes, fodder carrots, fodder turnips   12.10.10
        Swedes
        Fodder carrots, fodder turnips

        Fodder cabbages and kales   12.01.99 2

    Other roots and fodder brassicas
        Jerusalem artichokes   07.06.10
        Sweet potatoes   07.06.50
        Roots and fodder brassicas not elsewhere specified   07.06.30
                                                                                12.10.99 3

Industrial Crops
Oil seeds and oleaginous fruit (excluding olives)
    Colza and rape seed   12.01.91
        Winter colza   -
        Summer colza   -
        Rape   -
    Sunflower seed   12.01.95
    Soya beans   12.01.40
    Castor seed   12.01.50
    Linseed   12.01.61
                                                                            12.01.69

    Sesame, hemp, mustard and poppy seed
        Sesame seed   12.01.97
        Hemp seed   12.01.94
        Mustard seed   12.01.92
        Oil poppy and poppy seed   12.01.93

    Fibre plants
        Flax   54.01.10
        Hemp   57.01.10

Unmanufactured tobacco (including dried cobacco)   12.01.10
                                                                                24.01.90

Hops   12.06.00

Other industrial crops
    Chicory roots   12.05.00
    Medicinal plants, aromatics, spices and plants for
    perfume extraction

Saffron	09.10.31
Caraway	07.01.82

Medicinal plants, aromatics, spices and plants for perfume extraction not elsewhere specified	09.09 (11-13-15-18)
	09.10 (11-20-51-55-71)
	12.07 (10-20-30-40-50
	-60-70-80-91-99)

Fresh vegetables

Cabbages for human consumption

Cauliflowers	07.01.21
	07.01.22

Other cabbages	
Brussels sprouts	07.01.26
White cabbages	07.01.23
Red cabbages	07.01.23
Savoy cabbages	07.01.27 1
Green cabbages	"
Cabbages not elsewhere specified	"

Leaf and stalk vegetables other than cabbages	
Celery and celeriac	07.01.51
	07.01.53
	07.01.97 2
Leeks	07.01.68
Cabbage lettuces	07.01.31
	07.01.33
Endives	07.01.36 1
Spinach	07.01.29
Asparagus	07.01.71
Witloof chicory	07.01.34
Artichokes	07.01.73
Other leaf and stalk vegetables	
Corn salad	07.01.36 2
Cardoons and edible thistle	07.01.37
Fennel	07.01.91
Rhubarb	07.01.97 1
Cress	"
Parsley	"
Broccoli	"
Leaf and stalk vegetables not elsewhere specified	"

Vegetables grown for fruit	
Tomatoes	07.01.75
	07.01.77
Cucumbers and gherkins	07.01.83
	07.01.85

Melons	08.09.10
Aubergines, marrows and pubpkins, courgettes	07.0195
Sweet capsicum	07.01.93
Other vegetables grown for fruit	07.01.97 3

Root and tuber crops	
Kohlrabi	07.01.27 2
Turnips	07.01.54
Carrots	"
Garlic	07.01.67
Onions and shallots	07.01 (62-63-66)
Beetroot (red beet)	07.01.56
Salsify and scorzonera	07.01.59
Other rood and tuber crops (chives, radishes, French turnips, horse radishes)	07.10.59

Pod vegetables	
Green peas	07.01.41
	07.01.43
Beans	07.01.45
	07.01.47
Other pod vegetables	07.01.49
Cultivated mushrooms	07.01.87

Fresh fruit, including citrus fruit (excluding grapes and olives)

Dessert apples and pears	
Dessert apples	08.06 (13-15-17)
Dessert pears	08.06 (36-38)
Cider apples and perry pears	
Cider apples	08.06.11
Perry pears	08.06.32
Stone fruit	
Peaches	08.07.32
Apricots	08.07.10
Cherries	08.07 (51-55)
Plums (including greengages, mirabelles and quetsches)	08.07 (71-75)
Other stone fruit	08.07.90

Nuts	
Walnuts	08.05.31
Hazelnuts	08.05.91
Almonds	08.05.11
	08.05.19
Chestnuts	08.05.50
Other nuts (excluding tropical nuts)	
Pistaches	08.05.70
Nuts not elsewhere specified	08.05.97 1

Other tree fruits

Figs	08.03.10
Quinces	08.06.50
Other tree fruits, not elsewhere specified (excluding tropical fruit)	08.09.90 1
Strawberries	08.08 (11-15)

Berries

Blackcurrants and red currants

Blackcurrants	08.08.41
Redcurrants	08.08.49 1
Raspberries	
Gooseberries	08.08.90 1
Other berries (e.g. cultivated blackberries)	08.09.90 2

Citrus fruit

Oranges	08.02 (21-22-24-27)
Mandarins and clemintines	08.02 (32-36)
Lemons	08.02.50
Grapefruit	08.02.70

Other citrus fruit	08.02.90
Citrons	-
Limes	-
Bergamots	-
Citrus fruit not elsewhere specified	-

Grapes and olives

Grapes

Tablegrapes	08.04 (21-23)
Other grapes (for wine-making, fruit juice production and processing into raisins)	08.04 (25-27)

Olives

Table-olives	07.01.78
Other olives (for olive oil production)	07.01.79
	07.03.13

Other crop products

Fodder crops (1)	12.10.99 1

Nursery products

Fruit trees and bushes	06.02 (19-40-51-55)
Vine slips	06.02 (10-30)
Ornamental trees and shrubs	06.02 (71-75-79-98)
Forest seedlings and cuttings	06.02.60

Vegetable materials used primarily for plaiting

Osier, rushes, rattans	14.01 (11-19-51-59)
Reeds, bamboos	14.01 (31-39)
Other vegetable materials used primarily for plaiting	14.01.90

Flowers, ornamental plants and Christmas trees
    Flower bulbs, corms and tubers   06.01.10
    Ornamental plants   06.01 (31-39)
    Cut flowers, branches and foliage   06.03 (11-15-90)
     06.04 (20-40-50)
    Christmas trees   06.04.90
    Perennial plants   06.02.92

Seeds
    Agricultrual seeds (^{2})   06.02.95
     12.03 (11-19-35-39-
     44-46-84-86-89)
     12.03.31 1
     12.03.49 1
    Flower seeds   12.03.81
    Products gathered in the wild (^{3})   07.01 (88-89)
     08.05.97 2
     08.08.31
     08.08.35
     08.08.49 2
     08.08.90 2
     23.06.10 1

By-products from cultivation of: (^{4})
    Cereals (excluding rice)   12.08 (10-31)
    Rice   12.08.90
     12.09.00
    Pulses   13.03.12
    Root crops   14.02 (10-21-23-25-29)
    Industrial crops   14.03.00
     14.04.00
    Fresh vegetables   14.05 (11-19)
     15.16.10
    Fruit and citrus fruit   23.06.10 2
    Grapes and olives   23.06.30
    Other crops   13.01.00
Crop products not elsewhere specified

Footnotes
1 e.g. hay, clover (excluding brassicas).
2 excluding cereal seeds, rice seeds and seed potatoes
3 e.g. wild mushrooms, cranberries, bilberries, blackberries, wild raspberries, etc.
4 e.g. straw, beet and cabbage tops, pea and bean husks.

Grape must and wine

Grape must	22.05.00
Wine	22.05 (21-25-31-35-41-
	44-45-47-51-57-
	59-61-69)
By-products of wine production (¹)	23.05.00

Footnote

1   e.g. wine lees, argol, etc

Olive oil

Pure olive oil (¹)	15.07.06
Olive oil, unrefined (¹)	15.07 (07-08)
By-products of olive oil extraction (²)	23.04.05

Footnotes

1   The distinction between these two products is based on different methods of processing rather than on different production stages.

2   e.g. olive oil cakes and other residual products of olive oil extraction

---

Cattle

Domestic cattle	01.02 (11-13
	-14-15-17)
Calves	-
Other cattle, less than one year old	-
Heifers	-
Cows	-
Male breeding animals	-
One to two years old	-
More than two years old	-
Cattle for slaughtering and fattening	-
One to two years old	-
More than two years old	-

Pigs

Domestic pigs	01.03 (11-15-17)
Piglets	-
Young pigs	-
Pigs for fattening	-
Sows and gilts for breeding	-
Breeding boars	-

Equines

Horses	01.01 (11-15-19)
Donkeys	01.01.31
Mules and hinnies	01.01.50

Sheep and goats

Domestic sheep	01.04 (11-13)

Domestic goats   01.04.15

Poultry, rabbits, pigeons and other animals
Hens, cocks, cockerels, pullets, chicks   01.05 (10-91)
Ducks   01.05.93
Geese   01.05.95
Turkeys   01.05.97
Guinea fowl   01.05.98
Domestic rabbits   01.06.10
Domestic pigeons   01.06.30

Other animals
   Bees   -
   Silkworms   -
   Animals reared for fur   -
   Snails (excluding sea-snails)   03.03.66
   Animals not elsewhere specified   01.06.99
                                                              02.04.99 1

Game and game meat
   Game (¹)   01.01.39
                                                              01.02.90
                                                              01.03.90
                                                              01.04.90
                                                              01.06.91
   Game meat   02.04.30

Footnote
1 Live game includes only specially reared game and other game kept in captivity.

Milk, untreated
   Cows' milk   -
   Ewes' milk   -
   Goats' milk   -
   Buffalo milk   -

Eggs
Hens' eggs
   Hatching eggs   04.05.12 1
   Other   04.05.14
Other eggs
   Hatching eggs   04.05.12 2
   Other   04.05.16
                                                              04.05.18

Other livestock products
Raw wool (including animal hair (¹))   53.01 (10-20)
                                                              53.02 (93-95)
Honey   04.06.00
Silkworm cocoons   50.01.00

By-products of livestock production (²)   15.15.10

43.01 (10-20-30-90)

Livestock products not elsewhere specified   43.01. (10-20-30-90)

53.02.97

_____

Footnotes

1 If it is a principal product.

2 e.g. skins and animal hair and pelts of slaughtered game, wax, manure, liquid manure

Agricultural services (¹)

_____

Footnote

1 i.e. services which are normally provided by agricultural holdings themselves, e.g. ploughing, mowing and reaping, threshing, tobacco drying, sheep-shearing, care of animals.

Agricultural products almost exclusively imported

Tropical oil seeds and oleaginous fruit

Groundnuts   12.01.11

12.01.15

Copra   12.01.20

Palm nuts and kernels   12.01.30

Cotton seed   12.01.96

Oil seeds and oleaginous fruit not elsewhere specified   12.01.99

Tropical fibre plants

Cotton   55.01.00

Other fibre plants

Manila hemp   57.02.00

Jute   57.03.10

Sisal   57.04.10

Coir   57.04.30

Ramie   54.02.00

Fibre plants, not elsewhere specified   57.04.50

Other tropical plants for industrial use

Coffee   09.01.11

Cocoa   18.01.00

Sugar cane   12.04.30

Tropical fruit

Tropical nuts

Coconuts   08.01.75

Cashew nuts   08.01.77

Brazil nuts   08.01.80

Pecans   08.05.80

Other tropical fruit

Dates   08.01.10

Bananas   08.01. (31-35)

     Pineapples   08.01.50
     Papaws   08.08.50
     Tropical fruit, not elsewhere specified   08.01 (60-99)

     Ivory, unpolished   05.10.00

V. WOOD IN THE ROUGH

Coniferous timber for industrial uses

Coniferous long timber

1   logs

    (1)   fir, spruce, douglas

    (2)   pine, larch

2   mine timber

    (1)   fir, spruce douglas

    (2)   pine, larch

3   other long timber

    (1)   fir, spruce, douglas

    (2)   pine, larch

Coniferous plywood

1   Fir, spruce, douglas

2   Pine, larch

Coniferous firewood

Fir, spruce, douglas

Pine, larch

Leaf-wood for industrial uses

Long timber (leaf-wood)

1   logs

    (1)   oak

    (2)   beech

    (3)   poplar

    (4)   other

2   mine timber

    (1)   oak

    (2)   other

3   other long timber

    (1)   oak

    (2)   beech

    (3)   poplar

    (4)   other

Plywood (leaf)

1   oak

2   beech

3   poplar

4   other

Firewood (leaf)

oak

beech

poplar

other

Forestry services

ANNEX D:

list of activities referred to in the third paragraph of article 4(5)

1. Telecommunications

2. The supply of water, gas, electricity and steam

3. The transport of goods

4. Port and airport services

5. Passenger transport

6. Supply of new goods manufactured for sale

7. The transactions of agricultural intervention agencies in respect of agricultural products carried out pursuant to regulations on the common organization of the market in these products

8. The running of trade fairs and exhibitions

9. Warehousing

10. The activities of commercial publicity bodies

11. The activities of travel agencies

12. The running of staff shops, cooperatives and industrial canteens and similar institutions

13. Transactions other than those specified in Article 13A(1)(q), of radio and television bodies.

ANNEX E

transactions referred to in article 28(3)(a)

1. [....]¹

1ˢᵗ sch 2. Transactions referred to in Article 13A(1)(e)

3. [....]¹

4. [....]¹

5. [....]¹

6. [....]¹

1ˢᵗ sch 7. Transactions referred to in Article 13A(1)(q)

8. [....]¹

9. [....]¹

10. [....]¹

11. Supplies covered by Article 13B(g) in so far as they are made by taxable persons who were entitled to deduction of input tax on the building concerned

12. [....]¹

13. [....]¹

14. [....]¹

1ˢᵗ sch 15. The services of travel agents referred to in Article 26, and those of travel agents acting in the name and on account of the traveller, for journeys outside the Community.

Amendments
1   Abolished by Art 1(1), Council Directive 89/456/EEC of 18 July 1989, (w.e.f. 1 January 1990).

ANNEX F

transactions referred to in article 28(3)(b)

1st sch **1.** Admission to sporting events

2. Services supplied by authors, artists, performers, lawyers and other members of the liberal professions, other than the medical and paramedical professions, in so far as these are not services specified in Annex B to the second Council Directive of 11 April 1967

3. [....]¹

4. [....]²

5. Telecommunications services supplied by public postal services and supplies of goods incidental thereto

8th sch **6.** Services supplied by undertakers and cremation services, together with goods related thereto

7. Transactions carried out by blind persons or workshops for the blind provided these exemptions do not give rise to significant distortion of competition

8. The supply of goods and services to official bodies responsible for the construction, setting out and maintenance of cemeteries, graves and monuments commemorating war dead

9. [....]³

10. Transactions of hospitals not covered by Article 13A(1)(b)

11. [....]⁴

s 8(2A) **12.** The supply of water by public authorities

13. [....]²

14. [....]¹

15. [....]²

s 4 **16.** Supplies of those buildings and land described in Article 4(3)

1st sch 2 **17.** Passenger transport

The transport of goods such as luggage or motor vehicles accompanying passengers and the supply of services related to the transport of passengers, shall only be exempted in so far as the transport of the passengers themselves is exempt

18. [....]¹

19. [....]¹

20. [....]¹

21. [....]¹

22. [....]¹

23. The supply, modification, repair, maintenance, chartering and hiring of aircraft, including equipment incorporated or used therein, used by State institutions

24. [....]²

25. The supply, modification, repair, maintenance, chartering and hiring of warships

26. [....]⁵

1ˢᵗ sch 27. The services of travel agents referred to in Article 26, and those of travel agents acting in the name and on account of the traveller, for journeys within the Community.

Amendments
1. Deleted by Art 1(2), Council Directive 89/456/EECof 18 July 1989 (w.e.f. 1 January 1990).
2. Deleted by Art 1(2), Council Directive 89/456/EECof 18 July 1989 (w.e.f. 1 January 1991).
3. Deleted by Art 1(2), Council Directive 89/456/EECof 18 July 1989 (w.e.f. 1 January 1992).
4. Deleted by Art 1(2), Council Directive 89/456/EECof 18 July 1989 (w.e.f. 1 January 1993).
5. Deleted by Art 1(2), Council Directive 98/80/ECof 12 October 1998 (w.e.f. 17 October 1998).

Case law
Urbing (nee Adam) v Administration de   C267/99   Property agents
l'Enregistrement et des Domaines

ANNEX G

right of option

1. The right of option referred to in Article 28(3)(c) may be granted in the following circumstances:

    (a) in the case of transactions specified in Annex E:

    Member States which already exempt these supplies but also give right of option for taxation may maintain this right of option

    (b) in the case of transactions specified in Annex F:

    Member States which provisionally maintain the right to exempt such supplies may grant taxable persons the right to opt for taxation

2. Member States already granting a right of option for taxation not covered by the provisions of Paragraph 1 above may allow taxpayers exercising it to maintain it until at the latest the end of three years from the date the Directive comes into force.

[ANNEX H

list of supplies of goods and services which may be subject to reduced rates of VAT

In transposing the categories below which refer to goods into national legislation, Member States may use the combined nomenclature to establish the precise coverage of the category concerned.

Category	Description
2nd sch **1.**	Foodstuffs (including beverages but excluding alcoholic beverages) for human and animal consumption; live animals, seeds, plants and ingredients normally intended for use in preparation of foodstuffs; products normally intended to be used to supplement or substitute foodstuffs
2.	Water supplies
2nd sch **3.**	Pharmaceutical products of a kind normally used for health care, prevention of diseases and treatment for medical and veterinary purposes, including products used for contraception and sanitary protection
2nd sch **4.**	Medical equipment, aids and other appliances normally intended to alleviate or treat disability, for the exclusive personal use of the disabled, including the repair of such goods, and children's car seats
1st sch **5.**	Transport of passengers and their accompanying luggage
6.	Supply, including on loan by libraries, of books (including brochures, leaflets and similar printed matter, children's picture, drawing or colouring books, music printed or in manuscript, maps and hydrographic or similar charts), newspapers and periodicals, other than material wholly or substantially devoted to advertising matter
7.	Admissions to shows, theatres, circuses, fairs, amusement parks, concerts, museums, zoos, cinemas, exhibitions and similar cultural events and facilities. Reception of broadcasting services
8.	Services supplied by or royalties due to writers, composers and performing artists
6th sch **9.**	Supply, construction, renovation and alteration of housing provided as part of a social policy
10.	Supplies of goods and services of a kind normally intended for use in agricultural production but excluding capital goods such as machinery or buildings
6th sch **11.**	Accommodation provided by hotels and similar establishments including the provision of holiday accommodation and the letting of camping sites and caravan parks

1st sch **12.**   Admission to sporting events

6th sch **13.**   Use of sporting facilities

1st sch **14.**   Supply of goods and services by organizations recognized as charities by Member States and engaged in welfare or social security work, in so far as these supplies are not exempt under Article 13

1st sch **15.**   Services supplied by undertakers and cremation services, together with the supply of goods related thereto

16.   Provision of medical and dental care as well as thermal treatment in so far as these services are not exempt under Article 13

6th sch **17.**   Services supplied in connection with street cleaning, refuse collection and waste treatment, other than the supply of such services by bodies referred to in Article 4(5)][1]

Amendments

1   Annex H inserted by Art 1(5), Council Directive 92/77/EEC of 19 October 1992, (w.e.f. 1 January 1993).

8th sch

[ANNEX I

works of art, collectors' items and antiques

For the purposes of this Directive:

(a) **"works of art"** shall mean:

— pictures, collages and similar decorative plaques, paintings and drawings, executed entirely by hand by the artist, other than plans and drawings for architectural, engineering, industrial, commercial, topographical or similar purposes, hand-decorated manufactured articles, theatrical scenery, studio back cloths or the like of painted canvas (CN code 9701),

— original engravings, prints and lithographs, being impressions produced in limited numbers directly in black and white or in colour of one or of several plates executed entirely by hand by the artist, irrespective of the process or of the material employed by him, but not including any mechanical or photomechanical process (CN code 9702 00 00),

— original sculptures and statuary, in any material, provided that they are executed entirely by the artist; sculpture casts the production of which is limited to eight copies and supervised by the artist or his successors in title (CN code 97030000); on an exceptional basis, in cases determined by the Member States, the limit of eight copies may be exceeded for statuary casts produced before 1 January 1989,

— tapestries (CN code 5805 00 00) and wall textiles (CN code 6304 00 00) made by hand from original designs provided by artists, provided that there are not more than eight copies of each,

— individual pieces of ceramics executed entirely by the artist and signed by him,

— enamels on copper, executed entirely by hand, limited to eight numbered copies bearing the signature of the artist or the studio, excluding articles of jewelry and goldsmiths' and silversmiths' wares,

— photographs taken by the artist, printed by him or under his supervision, signed and numbered and limited to 30 copies, all sizes and mounts included;

(b) **"collectors' items"** shall mean:

— postage or revenue stamps, postmarks, first-day covers, pre-stamped stationary and the like, franked, or if unfranked not being of legal tender and not being intended for use as legal tender (CN code 9704 00 00),

— collections and collectors' pieces of zoological, botanical, mineralogical, anatomical, historical, archaeological, palaeotological, ethnographic or numismatic interest (CN code 9705 00 00);

(c)   **"antiques"** shall mean objects other than works of art or collectors'
items, which are more than 100 years old (CN code 9706 00 00).][1]

Amendments
1   Annex I inserted by Art 1(10), Council Directive 94/5/EC of 14 February 1994.

[ANNEX J:

DESCRIPTION OF GOODS	CN CODE
Tin	8001
Copper	7402 7403 7405 7408
Zinc	7901
Nickel	7502
Aluminium	7601
Lead	7801
Indium	ex 8112 91 ex 8112 99
Cereals	1001 to 1005 1006: unprocessed rice only 1007 to 1008
Oil seeds and oleaginous fruit Coconuts, Brazil nuts and cashew nut Other nuts Olives	1201 to 1207 0801 0802 0711 20
Grains and seeds (including soya beans)	1201 to 1207
Coffee, not roasted	0901 11 00 0901 12 00
Tea	0902
Cocoa beans, whole or broken, raw or roasted	1801
Raw sugar	1701 11 1701 12
Rubber, in primary forms or in plates, sheets or strip	4001 4002
Wool	5101
Chemicals in bulk	Chapters 28 and 29
Mineral oils (including propane and butane; also including crude petroleum oils)	2709 2710 2711 12 2711 13
Silver	7106
Platinum (Palladium, Rhodium)	7110 11 00 7110 21 00 7110 31 00
Potatoes	0701
Vegetable oils and fats and their fractions, whether or not refined, but not chemically modified	1507 to 1515

]¹

Amendments
1   Annex J inserted by Art 1(13), Council Directive 95/7/EC of 10 April 1995, (w.e.f. 1 January 1995).

[ANNEX K

list of supplies of services referred to in article 28(6)

1. Small services of repairing:
   - bicycles,
   - shoes and leather goods,
   - clothing and household linen (including mending and alteration).

2. Renovation and repairing of private dwellings, excluding materials which form a significant part of the value of the supply.

3. Window cleaning and cleaning in private households.

4. Domestic care services (e.g. home help and care of the young, elderly, sick or disabled).

5. Hairdressing.][1]

Amendments

1   Annex K inserted by Art 1, Council Directive 99/85/EC of 22 October 1999, (w.e.f. 28 October 1999)

[ANNEX L

Illustrative list of electronically supplied services referred to in Article 9(2)(e)

1. Website supply, web-hosting, distance maintenance of programmes and equipment.

2. Supply of software and updating thereof.

3. Supply of images, text and information, and making databases available.

4. Supply of music, films and games, including games of chance and gambling games, and of political, cultural, artistic, sporting, scientific and entertainment broadcasts and events.

5. Supply of distance teaching.

Where the supplier of a service and his customer communicates via electronic mail, this shall not of itself mean that the service performed is an electronic service within the meaning of the last indent of Article 9(2)(e).][1]

Amendments
1   Inserted by Art 1, Council Directive 2002/38/EC of 7 May 2002. Amended with effect from 15 May 2002 and provisions applicable from 1 July 2003.

[ANNEX M

List of supplies of goods and services as referred to in Article 21(2)(c)(iv)

(a) the supply of ferrous and non ferrous waste, scrap, and used materials including that of semi-finished products resulting from the processing, manufacturing or melting down of ferrous and non-ferrous metals and their alloys;

(b) the supply of ferrous and non-ferrous semi-processed products and certain associated processing services;

(c) the supply of residues and other recyclable materials consisting of ferrous and non-ferrous metals, their alloys, slag, ash, scale and industrial residues containing metals or their alloys and the supply of selection, cutting, fragmenting and pressing services for these products;

(d) the supply of, and certain processing services relating to, ferrous and non-ferrous waste as well as parings, scrap, waste and used and recyclable material consisting of cullet, glass, paper, paperboard and board, rags, bone, leather, imitation leather, parchment, raw hides and skins, tendons and sinews, twine, cordage, rope, cables, rubber and plastic;

(e) the supply of the materials referred to in this annex after processing in the form of cleaning, polishing, selection, cutting, fragmenting, pressing or casting into ingots;

(f) the supply of scrap and waste from the working of base materials.][1]

Amendments
1 Inserted by Art 1(8), Council Directive 2006/69/EC of 24 July 2006 (w.e.f. 13 August 2006).

Other European Legislation

- Directives

- Regulations

- Decisions

OTHER EUROPEAN LEGISLATION
DIRECTIVES, REGULATIONS AND DECISIONS

FIRST COUNCIL DIRECTIVE 67/227/EEC

of 11 April 1967

On the harmonisation of legislation of Member States concerning turnover taxes

Official Journal L 71 , 14/04/1967 p. 1301 - 1303

This Directive was repealed by Council Directive 2006/112/EC of 28 November 2006 on the common system of value added tax, with effect from 1 January 2007

THE COUNCIL OF THE EUROPEAN ECONOMIC COMMUNITY,

Having regard to the Treaty establishing the European Economic Community, and in particular Articles 99 and 100 thereof;

Having regard to the proposal from the Commission;

Having regard to the Opinion of the European Parliament;

Having regard to the Opinion of the Economic and Social Committee;

Whereas the main objective of the Treaty is to establish, within the framework of an economic union, a common market within which there is healthy competition and whose characteristics are similar to those of a domestic market;

Whereas the attainment of this objective presupposes the prior application in Member States of legislation concerning turnover taxes such as will not distort conditions of competition or hinder the free movement of goods and services within the common market;

Whereas the legislation at present in force does not meet these requirements; whereas it is therefore in the interest of the common market to achieve such harmonisation of legislation concerning turnover taxes as will eliminate, as far as possible, factors which may distort conditions of competition, whether at national or Community level, and make it possible subsequently to achieve the aim of abolishing the imposition of tax on importation and the remission of tax on exportation in trade between Member States;

Whereas, in the light of the studies made, it has become clear that such harmonisation must result in the abolition of cumulative multi-stage taxes and in the adoption by all Member States of a common system of value added tax;

Whereas a system of value added tax achieves the highest degree of simplicity and of neutrality when the tax is levied in as general a manner as possible and when its scope covers all stages of production and distribution and the provision of services; whereas it is therefore in the interest of the common market and of Member States to adopt a common system which shall also apply to the retail trade;

Whereas, however, the application of that tax to retail trade might in some Member States meet with practical and political difficulties; whereas, therefore, Member States should be permitted, subject to prior consultation, to apply the commom system only up to and including the wholesale trade stage, and to apply, as appropriate, a separate complementary tax at the retail trade stage, or at the preceding stage;

Whereas it is necessary to proceed by stages, since the harmonisation of turnover taxes will lead in Member States to substantial alterations in tax structure and will have appreciable consequences in the budgetary, economic and social fields;

Whereas the replacement of the cumulative multistage tax systems in force in the majority of Member States by the common system of value added tax is bound, even if the rates and exemptions are not harmonised at the same time, to result in neutrality in competition, in that within each country similar goods bear the same tax burden, whatever the length of the production and distribution chain, and that in international trade the amount of the tax burden borne by goods is known so that an exact equalisation of that amount may be ensured; whereas therefore, provision should be made, in the first stage, for adoption by all Member States of the common system of value added tax, without an accompanying harmonisation of rates and exemptions;

Whereas it is not possible to foresee at present how and within what period the harmonisation of turnover taxes can achieve the aim of abolishing the imposition of tax on importation and the remission of tax on exportation in trade between Member States; whereas it is therefore preferable that the second stage and the measures to be taken in respect of that stage should be determined later on the basis of proposals made by the Commission to the Council;

HAS ADOPTED THIS DIRECTIVE:

Article 1

Member States shall replace their present system of turnover taxes by the common system of value added tax defined in Article 2.

In each Member State the legislation to effect this replacement shall be enacted as rapidly as possible, so that it can enter into force on a date to be fixed by the Member State in the light of the conjunctural situation; this date shall not be later than [1 January 1972][1]

From the entry into force of such legislation, the Member State shall not maintain or introduce any measure providing for flat-rate equalisation of turnover taxes on importation or exportation in trade between Member States.

Article 2

The principle of the common system of value added tax involves the application to goods and services of a general tax on consumption exactly proportional to the price of the goods and services, whatever the number of transactions which take place in the production and distribution process before the stage at which tax is charged.

On each transaction, value added tax, calculated on the price of the goods or services at the rate applicable to such goods or services, shall be chargeable after deduction of the amount of value added tax borne directly by the various cost components.

The common system of value added tax shall be applied up to and including the retail trade stage.

[....][2]

Article 3

The Council shall issue, on a proposal from the Commission, a second Directive concerning the structure of, and the procedure for applying, the common system of value added tax.

Article 4

In order to enable the Council to discuss this, and if possible to take decisions before the end of the transitional period, the Commission shall submit to the Council, before the end of 1968, proposals as to how and within what period the harmonisation of turnover taxes can achieve the aim of abolishing the imposition of tax on importation and the remission of tax on exportation in trade between Member States, while ensuring the neutrality of those taxes as regards the origin of the goods or services.

In this connection, particular account shall be taken of the relationship between direct and indirect taxes, which differs in the various Member States; of the effects of an alteration in tax systems on the tax and budget policy of Member States; and of the influence which tax systems have on conditions of competition and on social conditions in the Community.

Article 5

[....]³

Article 6

This Directive is addressed to the Member States.

Done at Brussels, 11 April 1967.

For the Council

The President

R. VAN ELSLANDE

Amendments

1 Substituted by Art 1, Council Directive 69/463/EEC of 1969.
2 Repealed by Art 36, Council Directive 77/388/EEC of 17 May 1977, previously read: `However, until the abolition of the imposition of tax on importation and the remission of tax on exportation in trade between Member States, Member States may, subject to the consultation provided for in Article 5, apply this system only up to and including the wholesale trade stage, and may apply, as appropriate, a separate complementary tax at the retail trade stage or at the preceding stage.'
3 Repealed by Art 36 Council Directive 77/388 of 17 May 1977, previously read: `Should a Member State intend to exercise the power provided for in the last paragraph of Article 2, it shall so inform the Commission in good time, having regard to Article 102 of the Treaty.'

Case law
   Mohr v Finanzamt Bad Segeberg   C215/94   Question of 'consumption'

[COUNCIL DIRECTIVE 76/308/EEC

of 15 March 1976

[on mutual assistance for the recovery of claims relating to certain levies, duties, taxes and other measures][1]

Official Journal L073, 19/03/1976 p.0018-0023

> This Directive was repealed by Council Directive 2008/55/EC of 26 May 2008, with effect from 30 June 2008

This Directive was repealed by Council Directive 2008/55/EC of 26 May 2008 on the common system of value added tax, with effect from 30 June 2008, without prejudice to the obligations of the Member States relating to the time limits for transposition into national law of the Directives set out in Annex I, Part C of Council Directive 2008/55/EC

THE COUNCIL OF THE EUROPEAN COMMUNITIES,

Having regard to the Treaty establishing the European Economic Community, and in particular Article 100 thereof,

Having regard to Council Regulation (EEC) No 729/70 of 21 April 1970 on the financing of the common agricultural policy, as last amended by Regulation (EEC) No 2788/72, and in particular Article 8(3) thereof,

Having regard to the proposal from the Commission,

Having regard to the opinion of the European Parliament,

Having regard to the opinion of the Economic and Social Committee,

Whereas it is not at present possible to enforce in one Member State a claim for recovery substantiated by a document drawn up by the authorities of another Member State;

Whereas the fact that national provisions relating to recovery are applicable only within national territories is in itself an obstacle to the establishment and functioning of the common market;

Whereas this situation prevents Community rules from being fully and fairly applied, particularly in the area of the common agricultural policy, and facilitates fraudulent operations;

Whereas it is therefore necessary to adopt common rules on mutual assistance for recovery;

Whereas these rules must apply both to the recovery of claims resulting from the various measures which form part of the system of total or partial financing of the European Agricultural Guidance and Guarantee Fund and to the recovery of agricultural levies and customs duties within the meaning of Article 2 of Decision 70/243/ECSC, EEC, Euratom of 21 April 1970 on the replacement of financial contributions from Member States by the Communities' own resources, and of Article 128 of the Act of Accession; whereas they must also apply to the recovery of interest and costs incidental to such claims;

Whereas mutual assistance must consist of the following: the requested authority must on the one hand supply the applicant authority with the information which the latter needs in order to recover claims arising in the Member State in which it is situated and notify the debtor of all instruments relating to such claims emanating from that Member State, and on the other hand it must recover, at the request of the applicant authority, the claims arising in the Member State in which the latter is situated;

Whereas these different forms of assistance must be afforded by the requested authority in compliance with the laws, regulations and administrative provisions governing such matters in the Member State in which it is situated;

Whereas it is necessary to lay down the conditions in accordance with which requests for assistance must be drawn up by the applicant authority and to give a limitative definition of the particular circumstances in which the requested authority may refuse assistance in any given case;

Whereas when the requested authority is required to act on behalf of the applicant authority to recover a claim, it must be able, if the provisions in force in the Member State in which it is situated so permit and with the agreement of the applicant authority, to allow the debtor time to pay or authorize payment by instalment; whereas any interest charged on such payment facilities must also be remitted to the Member State in which the applicant authority is situated;

Whereas, upon a reasoned request from the applicant authority, the requested authority must also be able, in so far as the provisions in force in the Member State in which it is situated so permit, to take precautionary measures to guarantee the recovery of claims arising in the applicant Member State; whereas such claims must not however be given any preferential treatment in the Member State in which the requested authority is situated;

Whereas it is possible that during the recovery procedure in the Member State in which the requested authority is situated the claim or the instrument authorizing its enforcement issued in the Member State in which the applicant authority is situated may be contested by the person concerned; whereas it should be laid down in such cases that the person concerned must bring the action contesting the claim before the competent body of the Member State in which the applicant authority is situated and that the requested authority must suspend any enforcement proceedings which it has begun until a decision is taken by the aforementioned body;

Whereas it should be laid down that documents and information communicated in the course of mutual assistance for recovery may not be used for other purposes;

Whereas this Directive should not curtail mutual assistance between particular Member States under bilateral or multilateral agreements or arrangements;

Whereas it is necessary to ensure that mutual assistance functions smoothly and to this end to lay down a Community procedure for determining the detailed rules for the application of such assistance within an appropriate period; whereas it is necessary to set up a committee to organize close and effective collaboration between the Member States and the Commission in this area,

HAS ADOPTED THIS DIRECTIVE:

Article 1

This Directive lays down the rules to be incorporated into the laws, regulations and administrative provisions of the Member States to ensure the recovery in each Member State of the claims referred to in Article 2 which arise in another Member State.

Article 2

[This Directive shall apply to all claims relating to:

   (a) refunds, interventions and other measures forming part of the system of total or partial financing of the European Agricultural Guidance and Guarantee Fund (EAGGF), including sums to be collected in connection with these actions;

   (b) levies and other duties provided for under the common organisation of the market for the sugar sector;

   (c) import duties;

   (d) export duties;

   (e) value added tax;

   (f) excise duties on:

      — manufactured tobacco,

      — alcohol and alcoholic beverages,

      — mineral oils;

   (g) taxes on income and capital;

   (h) taxes on insurance premiums;

   (i) interest, administrative penalties and fines, and costs incidental to the claims referred to in points (a) to (h), with the exclusion of any sanction of a criminal nature as determined by the laws in force in the Member State in which the requested authority is situated.][1]

Article 3

In this Directive:

   — **"applicant authority"** means the competent authority of a Member State which makes a request for assistance concerning a claim referred to in Article 2;

   — **"requested authority"** means the competent authority of a Member State to which a request for assistance is made.

   [— **"import duties"** means customs duties and charges having equivalent effect on imports, and import charges laid down within the framework of the common agricultural policy or in that of specific arrangements applicable to certain goods resulting from the processing of agricultural products,

   — **"export duties"** means customs duties and charges having equivalent effect on exports, and export charges laid down within the framework of the common agricultural policy or in that of specific arrangements applicable to certain goods resulting from the processing of agricultural products,

— "**taxes on income and capital**" means those enumerated in Article 1(3) of Directive 77/799/EEC, read in conjunction with Article 1(4) of that Directive,

— "**taxes on insurance premiums**" means:

in Austria:	(i)	Versicherungssteuer
	(ii)	Feuerschutzsteuer
in Belgium:	(i)	Taxe annuelle sur les contrats d'assurance
	(ii)	Jaarlijkse taks op de verzekeringscontracten
in Germany:	(i)	Versicherungssteuer
	(ii)	Feuerschutzsteuer
in Denmark:	(i)	Afgift af lystfartøjsforsikringer
	(ii)	Afgift af ansvarsforsikringer for motorkøretøjer m.v.
	(iii)	Stempelafgift af forsikringspræmier
in Spain:		Impuesto sobre la prima de seguros
in Greece:	(i)	Φόρος κύκλου εργασιών (Φ.Κ.Ε.)
	(ii)	Τέλη Χαρτοσήμου
in France:	(i)	Taxe sur les conventions d'assurances
in Finland:	(i)	Eräistä vakuutusmaksuista suoritettava vero/skatt på vissa försäkringspremier
	(ii)	Palosuojelumaksu/brandsky -ddsavgift
in Italy:		Imposte sulle assicurazioni private ed i contratti vitalizi di cui alla legge 29.10.1967 No 1216
in Ireland:		levy on insurance premiums
in Luxembourg:	(i)	Impôt sur les assurances
	(ii)	Impôt dans l'interêt du service d'incendie
in the Netherlands:		Assurantiebelasting
in Portugal:		Imposto de selo sobre os prémios de seguros
in Sweden:		none

in the United Kingdom: insurance premium tax (IPT)

[in Malta: Taxxa fuq Dokumenti u Trasferimenti

in Slovenia: (i)   davek od prometa
zavarovalnih poslov

(ii)   požarna taksa]][2]

This Directive shall also apply to claims relating to identical or analogous taxes which supplement or replace the taxes on insurance premiums referred to in the sixth indent. The competent authorities of the Member States shall communicate to each other and to the Commission the dates of entry into force of such taxes."][3]

Article 4

1. At the request of the applicant authority, the requested authority shall provide any information which would be useful to the applicant authority in the recovery of its claim.

   In order to obtain this information, the requested authority shall make use of the powers provided under the laws, regulations or administrative provisions applying to the recovery of similar claims arising in the Member State where that authority is situated.

2. The request for information shall indicate [the name, address and any other relevant information relating to the identification to which the applicant authority normally has access][1] of the person to whom the information to be provided relates and the nature and amount of the claim in respect of which the request is made.

3. The requested authority shall not be obliged to supply information:

   (a) which it would not be able to obtain for the purpose of recovering similar claims arising in the Member State in which it is situated;

   (b) which would disclose any commercial, industrial or professional secrets; or

   (c) the disclosure of which would be liable to prejudice the security of or be contrary to the public policy of the State.

4. The requested authority shall inform the applicant authority of the grounds for refusing a request for information.

Article 5

1. The requested authority shall, at the request of the applicant authority, and in accordance with the rules of law in force for the notification of similar instruments or decisions in the Member State in which the requested authority is situated, notify to the addressee all instruments and decisions, including those of a judicial nature, which emanate from the Member State in which the applicant authority is situated and which relate to a claim and/or to its recovery.

2. The request for notification shall indicate [the name, address and any other relevant information relating to the identification to which the applicant authority normally has access][1] of the addressee concerned, the nature

and the subject of the instrument or decision to be notified, if necessary the name and address of the debtor and the claim to which the instrument or decision relates, and any other useful information.

3. The requested authority shall promptly inform the applicant authority of the action taken on its request for notification and, more especially, of the date on which the instrument or decision was forwarded to the addressee.

Article 6

1. At the request of the applicant authority, the requested authority shall, in accordance with the laws, regulations or administrative provisions applying to the recovery of similar claims arising in the Member State in which the requested authority is situated, recover claims which are the subject of an instrument permitting their enforcement.

2. For this purpose any claim in respect of which a request for recovery has been made shall be treated as a claim of the Member State in which the requested authority is situated, except where Article 12 applies.

Article 7

[1. The request for recovery of a claim which the applicant authority addresses to the requested authority must be accompanied by an official or certified copy of the instrument permitting its enforcement, issued in the Member State in which the applicant authority is situated and, if appropriate, by the original or a certified copy of other documents necessary for recovery.

2. The applicant authority may not make a request for recovery unless:

(a) the claim and/or the instrument permitting its enforcement are not contested in the Member State in which it is situated, except in cases where the second subparagraph of Article 12(2) is applied,

(b) it has, in the Member State in which it is situated, applied appropriate recovery procedures available to it on the basis of the instrument referred to in paragraph 1, and the measures taken will not result in the payment in full of the claim.

3. The request for recovery shall indicate:

(a) the name, address and any other relevant information relating to the identification of the person concerned and/or to the third party holding his or her assets;

(b) the name, address and any other relevant information relating to the identification of the applicant authority;

(c) a reference to the instrument permitting its enforcement issued in the Member State in which the applicant authority is situated;

(d) the nature and the amount of the claim, including the principal, the interest, and any other penalties, fines and costs due indicated in the currencies of the Member States in which both authorities are situated;

(e) the date of notification of the instrument to the addressee by the applicant authority and/or by the requested authority;

(f) the date from which and the period during which enforcement is possible under the laws in force in the Member State in which the applicant authority is situated;

(g) any other relevant information.

4. The request for recovery shall also contain a declaration by the applicant authority confirming that the conditions set out in paragraph 2 have been fulfilled.

5. As soon as any relevant information relating to the matter which gave rise to the request for recovery comes to the knowledge of the applicant authority it shall forward it to the requested authority.][1]

Article 8

[1. The instrument permitting enforcement of the claim shall be directly recognised and automatically treated as an instrument permitting enforcement of a claim of the Member State in which the requested authority is situated.

2. Notwithstanding the first paragraph, the instrument permitting enforcement of the claim may, where appropriate and in accordance with the provisions in force in the Member State in which the requested authority is situated, be accepted as, recognised as, supplemented with, or replaced by an instrument authorising enforcement in the territory of that Member State.

Within three months of the date of receipt of the request for recovery, Member States shall endeavour to complete such acceptance, recognition, supplementing or replacement, except in cases where the third subparagraph is applied. They may not be refused if the instrument permitting enforcement is properly drawn up. The requested authority shall inform the applicant authority of the grounds for exceeding the period of three months.

If any of these formalities should give rise to contestation in connection with the claim and/or the instrument permitting enforcement issued by the applicant authority, Article 12 shall apply.][1]

Article 9

[1. Claims shall be recovered in the currency of the Member State in which the requested authority is situated. The entire amount of the claim that is recovered by the requested authority shall be remitted by the requested authority to the applicant authority.

2. The requested authority may, where the laws, regulations or administrative provisions in force in the Member State in which it is situated so permit, and after consultations with the applicant authority, allow the debtor time to pay or authorise payment by instalment. Any interest charged by the requested authority in respect of such extra time to pay shall also be remitted to the Member State in which the applicant authority is situated.

From the date on which the instrument permitting enforcement of recovery of the claim has been directly recognised or accepted, recognised, supplemented or replaced in accordance with Article 8, interest will be charged for late payment under the laws, regulations and administrative provisions in force in the Member State in which the requested authority is situated and shall also be remitted to the Member State in which the applicant authority is situated.][1]

Article 10

[Notwithstanding Article 6(2), the claims to be recovered shall not necessarily benefit from the privileges accorded to similar claims arising in the Member State in which the requested authority is situated.][1]

Article 11

The requested authority shall inform the applicant authority immediately of the action it has taken on the request for recovery.

Article 12

1. If, in the course of the recovery procedure, the claim and/or the instrument permitting its enforcement issued in the Member State in which the applicant authority is situated are contested by an interested party, the action shall be brought by the latter before the competent body of the Member State in which the applicant authority is situated, in accordance with the laws in force there. This action must be notified by the applicant authority to the requested authority. The party concerned may also notify the requested authority of the action.

2. As soon as the requested authority has received the notification referred to in paragraph 1 either from the applicant authority or from the interested party, it shall suspend the enforcement procedure pending the decision of the body competent in the matter [unless the applicant authority requests otherwise in accordance with the second subparagraph][3]. Should the requested authority deem it necessary, and without prejudice to Article 13, that authority may take precautionary measures to guarantee recovery in so far as the laws or regulations in force in the Member State in which it is situated allow such action for similar claims.

   [Notwithstanding the first subparagraph of paragraph 2, the applicant authority may in accordance with the law, regulations and administrative practices in force in the Member State in which it is situated, request the requested authority to recover a contested claim, in so far as the relevant laws, regulations and administrative practices in force in the Member State in which the requested authority is situated allow such action. If the result of contestation is subsequently favourable to the debtor, the applicant authority shall be liable for the reimbursement of any sums recovered, together with any compensation due, in accordance with the laws in force in the Member State in which the requested authority is situated.][3]

3. Where it is the enforcement measures taken in the Member State in which the requested authority is situated that are being contested the action shall

be brought before the competent body of that Member State in accordance with its laws and regulations.

4. Where the competent body before which the action has been brought in accordance with paragraph 1 is a judicial or administrative tribunal, the decision of that tribunal, in so far as it is favourable to the applicant authority and permits recovery of the claim in the Member State in which the applicant authority is situated shall constitute the "instrument permitting enforcement" within the meaning of Articles 6, 7 and 8 and the recovery of the claim shall proceed on the basis of that decision.

Article 13

On a reasoned request by the applicant authority, the requested authority shall take precautionary measures to ensure recovery of a claim in so far as the laws or regulations in force in the Member State in which it is situated so permit.

In order to give effect to the provisions of the first paragraph, Articles 6, 7(1), (3) and (5), 8, 11, 12 and 14 shall apply *mutatis mutandis*.

Article 14

[The requested authority shall not be obliged:

(a) to grant the assistance provided for in Articles 6 to 13 if recovery of the claim would, because of the situation of the debtor, create serious economic or social difficulties in the Member State in which that authority is situated, in so far as the laws, regulations and administrative practices in force in the Member State in which the requested authority is situated allow such action for similar national claims;

(b) to grant the assistance provided for in Articles 4 to 13, if the initial request under Article 4, 5 or 6 applies to claims more than five years old, dating from the moment the instrument permitting the recovery is established in accordance with the laws, regulations or administrative practices in force in the Member State in which the applicant authority is situated, to the date of the request. However, in cases where the claim or the instrument is contested, the time limit begins from the moment at which the applicant State establishes that the claim or the enforcement order permitting recovery may no longer be contested.][1]

The requested authority shall inform the applicant authority of the grounds for refusing a request for assistance. Such reasoned refusal shall also be communicated to the Commission.

Article 15

1. Questions concerning periods of limitation shall be governed solely by the laws in force in the Member State in which the applicant authority is situated.

2. Steps taken in the recovery of claims by the requested authority in pursuance of a request for assistance, which, if they had been carried out by the applicant authority, would have had the effect of suspending or interrupting the period of limitation according to the laws in force in the

Member State in which the applicant authority is situated, shall be deemed to have been taken in the latter State, in so far as that effect is concerned.

Article 16

Documents and information sent to the requested authority pursuant to this Directive may only be communicated by the latter to:

(a) the person mentioned in the request for assistance;

(b) those persons and authorities responsible for the recovery of the claims, and solely for that purpose;

(c) the judicial authorities dealing with matters concerning the recovery of the claims.

Article 17

Requests for assistance [the instrument permitting the enforcement and other relevant documents][1] shall be accompanied by a translation in the official language, or one of the official languages of the Member State in which the requested authority is situated, without prejudice to the latter authority's right to waive the translation.

Article 18

[1. The requested authority shall recover from the person concerned and retain any costs linked to recovery which it incurs, in accordance with the laws and regulations of the Member State in which it is situated that apply to similar claims.

2. Member States shall renounce all claims on each other for the refund of costs resulting from mutual assistance which they grant each other pursuant to this Directive.

3. Where recovery poses a specific problem, concerns a very large amount in costs or relates to the fight against organised crime, the applicant and requested authorities may agree reimbursement arrangements specific to the cases in question.

4. The Member State in which the applicant authority is situated shall remain liable to the Member State in which the requested authority is situated for any costs and any losses incurred as a result of actions held to be unfounded, as far as either the substance of the claim or the validity of the instrument issued by the applicant authority are concerned.][1]

Article 19

Member States shall provide each other with a list of authorities authorized to make or receive requests for assistance.

Article 20

[1. The Commission shall be assisted by a recovery committee (hereinafter referred to as 'the Committee'), composed of representatives of the Member States and chaired by the representative of the Commission.

2. Where reference is made to this paragraph, Articles 5 and 7 of Decision 1999/468/EC shall apply.

The period referred to in Article 5(6) of Decision 1999/468/EC shall be set at three months.

3.   The Committee shall adopt its own rules of procedure.][1]

Article 21

The committee may examine any matter concerning the application of this Directive raised by its chairman either on his own initiative or at the request of the representative of a Member State.

Article 22

[The detailed rules for implementing Articles 4(2) and (4), 5(2) and (3) and Articles 7, 8, 9, 11, 12(1) and (2), 14, 18(3) and 25 and for determining the means by which communications between the authorities may be transmitted, the rules on conversion, transfer of sums recovered, and the fixing of a minimum amount for claims which may give rise to a request for assistance, shall be adopted in accordance with the procedure laid down in Article 20(2).][1]

Article 23

The provisions of this Directive shall not prevent a greater measure of mutual assistance being afforded either now or in the future by particular Member States under any agreements or arrangements, including those for the notification of legal or extralegal acts.

Article 24

Member States shall bring into force the measures necessary to comply with this Directive not later than 1 January 1978.

Article 25

Each Member State shall inform the Commission of the measures which it has adopted to implement this Directive. The Commission shall forward this information to the other Member States.

[Each Member State shall inform the Commission annually of the number of requests for information, notification and recovery sent and received each year, the amount of the claims involved and the amounts recovered. The Commission shall report biennially to the European Parliament and the Council on the use made of these arrangements and on the results achieved.][3]

Article 26

This Directive is addressed to the Member States.

Done at Brussels, 15 March 1976.

For the Council

The President

R. VOUEL

Amendments
1   Substituted by Art 1, Council Directive 2001/44/EC of 15 June 2001.
2   Inserted by Treaty of Accession to the European Union 2003.
3   Inserted by Art 1, Council Directive 2001/44/EC of 15 June 2001.

[COUNCIL DIRECTIVE 77/799/EEC

of 19 December 1977

concerning mutual assistance by the competent authorities of the Member States in the field of direct taxation and taxation of insurance premiums][1]

Official Journal L 336 , 27/12/1977 p. 0015 - 0020

THE COUNCIL OF THE EUROPEAN COMMUNITIES,

Having regard to the Treaty establishing the European Economic Community, and in particular Article 100 thereof,

Having regard to the proposal from the Commission,

Having regard to the opinion of the European Parliament,

Having regard to the opinion of the Economic and Social Committee,

Whereas practices of tax evasion and tax avoidance extending across the frontiers of Member States lead to budget losses and violations of the principle of fair taxation and are liable to bring about distortions of capital movements and of conditions of competition; whereas they therefore affect the operation of the common market;

Whereas, for these reasons the Council adopted on 10 February 1975 a resolution on the measures to be taken by the Community in order to combat international tax evasion and avoidance;

Whereas the international nature of the problem means that national measures, whose effect does not extend beyond national frontiers, are insufficient; whereas collaboration between administrations on the basis of bilateral agreements is also unable to counter new forms of tax evasion and avoidance, which are increasingly assuming a multinational character;

Whereas collaboration between tax administrations within the Community should therefore be strengthened in accordance with common principles and rules;

Whereas the Member States should, on request, exchange information concerning particular cases; whereas the State so requested should make the necessary enquiries to obtain such information;

Whereas the Member States should exchange, even without any request, any information which appears relevant for the correct assessment of taxes on income and on capital, in particular where there appears to be an artificial transfer of profits between enterprises in different Member States or where such transactions are carried out between enterprises in two Member States through a third country in order to obtain tax advantages, or where tax has been or may be evaded or avoided for any reason whatever;

Whereas it is important that officials of the tax administration of one Member State be allowed to be present in the territory of another Member State if both the States concerned consider it desirable;

Whereas care must be taken to ensure that information provided in the course of such collaboration is not disclosed to unauthorized persons, so that the basic rights of citizens and enterprises are safeguarded; whereas it is therefore necessary that the Member States receiving such information should not use it, without the authorization of the Member State supplying it, other than for the purposes of taxation or to facilitate legal proceedings for failure to observe the tax laws of the receiving State; whereas it is also necessary that the receiving States afford the information the same degree of confidentiality which it enjoyed in the State which provided it, if the latter so requires;

Whereas a Member State which is called upon to carry out enquiries or to provide information shall have the right to refuse to do so where its laws or administrative practices prevent its tax administration from carrying out these enquiries or from collecting or using this information for its own purposes, or where the provision of such information would be contrary to public policy or would lead to the disclosure of a commercial, industrial or professional secret or of a commercial process, or where the Member State for which the information is intended is unable for practical or legal reasons to provide similar information;

Whereas collaboration between the Member States and the Commission is necessary for the permanent study of cooperation procedures and the pooling of experience in the fields considered, and in particular in the field of the artificial transfer of profits within groups of enterprises, with the aim of improving those procedures and of preparing appropriate Community rules,

HAS ADOPTED THIS DIRECTIVE:

Article 1

General provisions

[1. In accordance with the provisions of this Directive the competent authorities of the Member States shall exchange any information that may enable them to effect a correct assessment of taxes on income and on capital, and any information relating to the establishment of taxes on insurance premiums referred to in the sixth indent of Article 3 of Council Directive 76/308/EEC of 15 March 1976 on mutual assistance for the recovery of claims relating to certain levies, duties, taxes and other measures.][1]

2. There shall be regarded as taxes on income and on capital, irrespective of the manner in which they are levied, all taxes imposed on total income, on total capital, or on elements of income or of capital, including taxes on gains from the disposal of movable or immovable property, taxes on the amounts of wages or salaries paid by enterprises, as well as taxes on capital appreciation.

[3. The taxes referred to in paragraph 2 are at present, in particular:

in Belgium:

    Impôt des personnes physiques/Personenbelasting

    Impôt des sociétés/Vennootschapsbelasting

    Impôt des personnes morales/Rechtspersonenbelasting

    Impôt des non-résidents/Belasting der niet-verblijfhouders

in Denmark:

Indkomstskaten til staten

Selsskabsskat

Den kommunale indkomstskat

Den amtskommunale indkomstskat

Folkepensionsbidragene

Sømandsskatten

Den særlige indkomstskat

Kirkeskatten

Formueskatten til staten

Bidrag til dagpengefonden

in Germany:

Einkommensteuer

Körperschaftsteuer

Vermögensteuer

Gewerbesteuer

Grundsteuer

In Greece:

φόρος εισδήματ οςφυσικών προσώπων

φόρος εισδήματ υομικών προσώπων

φόρος ακινήτου περιουσιας

in Spain:

Impuesto sobre la Renta de las Personas Fiscas

Impuesto sobre Sociedades

Impuesto Exraordinairio sobre el Patrimonio de las Personas Fiscas

in France:

Impôt sur le revenu

Impôt sur les sociétés

Taxe professionnelle

Taxe foncière sur les propriétés bâties

Taxe foncière sur les propriétés non bâties

in Ireland:

Income tax

Corporation tax

Capital gains tax

Wealth tax

in Italy:

Imposta sul reddito delle persone fisiche

Imposta sul reddito delle persone giuridiche

Imposta locale sui redditi

in Luxembourg:

Impôt sur le revenu des personnes physiques

Impôt sur le revenu des collectivités

Impôt commercial communal

Impôt sur la fortune

Impôt foncier

in the Netherlands:

Inkomstenbelasting

Vennootschapsbelasting

Vermogensbelasting

in Austria:

Einkommensteuer

Körperschaftsteuer

Grundsteuer

Bodenwertabgabe

Abgabe von land- und forstwirtschaftlichen Betrieben

in Portugal

Contribuição predial

Imposto sobre a indústria agrícola

Contribuição industrial

Imposto de capitas

Imposto profissional

Imposto complementar

Imposto de mais-valias

Imposto sobre o rendimento do petróleo

Os adicionais devidos sobre os impostos precedentes

in Finland

Valtion tuloverot/de statliga inkomstskatterna

Yhteisöjen tulovero/inkomstskatten för samfund

Kunnallisvero/kommunalskatten

Kirkollisvero/kyrkoskatten

Kansaneläkevakuutusmaksu/folkpensionsförsäkringspremien

Sairausvakuutusmaksu/sjukförsäkringspremien

Korkotulon lähdevero/källskatten på ränteinkomst

Rajoitetusti verovelvollisen lähdevero/källskatten för begränsat skattskyldig

Valtion varallisuusvero/den statliga förmögenhetsskatten

Kiinteistövero/fastighetsskatten

in Sweden

Den statliga inkomstskatten

Sjömansskatten

Kupongskatten

Den särskilda inkomstskatten för utomlands bosatta

Den särskilda inkomstskatten för utomlands bosatta artister m.fl.

Den statliga fastighetsskatten

Den kommunala inkomstskatten

Förmögenhetsskatten

in the United Kingdom:

Income tax

Corporation tax

Capital gains tax

Petroleum revenue tax

Development land tax]^2

[in the Czech Republic:

Daně z příjmů

Daň z nemovitostí

Daň dědická, daň darovací a daň z převodu nemovitostí

Daň z přidané hodnoty

Spotřební daně

in Estonia:

    Tulumaks

    Sotsiaalmaks

    Maamaks

in Cyprus:

    Φόρος Εισοδή̃ατος

    Έκτακτη Εισφορά για την Άμυνα της τημοκρατίας

    Φόρος Κεφαλαιουχικών Κερδών

    Φόρος Ακίνητης Ιδιοκτησίας

in Latvia:

    iedzīvotāu ienākuma nodoklis

    nekustamā īpašuma nodoklis

    uzņēmumu ienākuma nodoklis

in Lithuania:

    Gyventojų pajamų mokestis

    Pelno mokestis

    Įmonių ir organizacijų nekilnojamojo turto mokestis

    Žemės mokestis

    Mokestis už valstybinius gamtos išteklius

    Mokestis už aplinkos teršim

    Naftos ir dujų išteklių mokestis

    Paveldimo turto mokestis

in Hungary:

    személyi jövedelemadó

    társasági adó

    osztalékadó

    általános forgalmi adó

    jövedéki adó

    építményadó

    telekadó

in Malta:

    Taxxa fuq l-income

in Poland:

    Podatek dochodowy od osób prawnych

    Podatek dochodowy od osób fizycznych

    Podatek od czynnoœci cywilnoprawnych

in Slovenia:

    Dohodnina

    Davki občanov

    Davek od dobička pravnih oseb

    Posebni davek na bilančno vsoto bank in hranilnic

in Slovakia:

    daň z príjmov fyzických osôb

    daň z príjmov právnických osôb

    daň z dedičstva

    daň z darovania

    daň z prevodu a prechodu nehnutel'ností

    daň z nehnutel'ností

    daň z pridanej hodnoty

    spotrebné dane][3]

[in Bulgaria:

    данък върху доходите на физическите лица

    корпоративен данък

    данъци, удържани при източника

    алтернативни данъци на корпоративния данък

    окончателен годишен (патентен) данък

in Romania:

    impozitul pe venit

    impozitul pe profit

    impozitul pe veniturile obținute din România de nerezidenți

    impozitul pe veniturile microîntreprinderilor

    impozitul pe clădiri

    impozitul pe teren][4]

4. Paragraph 1 shall also apply to any identical or similar taxes imposed subsequently, whether in addition to or in place of the taxes listed in paragraph 3. The competent authorities of the Member States shall inform

one another and the Commission of the date of entry into force of such taxes.

[5. The expression **"competent authority"** means:

in Belgium:

De minister van financiën or an authorized representative

Le ministre des finances or an authorized representative

in Denmark:

Skatteministeren or an authorized representative

in Germany:

Der Bundesminister der Finanzen or an authorized representative

In Greece:

Το Υπουργείο or an authorised representative

in Spain:

El Ministro de Economía y Hacienda or an authorized representative

in France:

Le ministre de l'économie or an authorized representative

in Ireland:

The Revenue Commissioners or their authorized representative

in Italy:

[il Capo del Dipartimento per le Politiche Fiscali or his authorised representatives][5]

in Luxembourg:

Le ministre des finances or an authorized representative

in the Netherlands:

De minister van financiën or an authorized representative

in Austria:

Der Bundesminister für Finanzen or an authorized representative

in Portugal:

O Ministro das Finanças or an authorized representative

in Finland:

Valtiovarainministeriö or an authorized representative

Finansministeriet or an authorized representative

in Sweden:

[Chefen för Finansdepartementet or his authorised representative][5] *in the United Kingdom:*

[The Commissioners of Customs and Excise or an authorised representative for information required concerning taxes on insurance premiums and excise duty.

The Commissioners of Inland Revenue or an authorised representative for all other information.][6][7]

[in the Czech Republic:

Ministr financí or an authorised representative

in Estonia:

Rahandusminister or an authorised representative

in Cyprus:

Υπουργός Οικονομικών or an authorised representative

in Latvia:

Finanšu ministrs or an authorised representative

in Lithuania:

Finansų ministras or an authorised representative

in Hungary:

A pénzügyminiszter or an authorised representative

in Malta:

Il-Ministru responsabbli ghall-Finanzi or an authorised representative

in Poland:

Minister Finansów or an authorised representative

in Slovenia:

Minister za finance or an authorised representative

in Slovakia:

Minister financií or an authorised representative][3]

[in Bulgaria:

Изпълнителният директор на Националната агенция за приходите

in Romania:

Ministerul Finanţelor Publice or an authorised representative][4]

Article 2

Exchange on request

1. The competent authority of a Member State may request the competent authority of another Member State to forward the information referred to in Article 1(1) in a particular case. The competent authority of the requested State need not comply with the request if it appears that the competent authority of the State making the request has not exhausted its own usual sources of information, which it could have utilized, according to the circumstances, to obtain the information requested without running the risk of endangering the attainment of the sought after result.

2. For the purpose of forwarding the information referred to in paragraph 1, the competent authority of the requested Member State shall arrange for the conduct of any enquiries necessary to obtain such information,

    [In order to obtain the information sought, the requested authority or the administrative authority to which it has recourse shall proceed as though acting on its own account or at the request of another authority in its own Member State.][8]

Article 3

Automatic exchange of information

For categories of cases which they shall determine under the consultation procedure laid down in Article 9, the competent authorities of the Member States shall regularly exchange the information referred to in Article 1(1) without prior request.

Article 4

Spontaneous exchange of information

1. The competent authority of a Member State shall without prior request forward the information referred to in Article 1(1), of which it has knowledge, to the competent authority of any other Member State concerned, in the following circumstances:

    (a) the competent authority of the one Member State has grounds for supposing that there may be a loss of tax in the other Member State;

    (b) a person liable to tax obtains a reduction in or an exemption from tax in the one Member State which would give rise to an increase in tax or to liability to tax in the other Member State;

    (c) business dealings between a person liable to tax in a Member State and a person liable to tax in another Member State are conducted through one or more countries in such a way that a saving in tax may result in one or the other Member State or in both;

    (d) the competent authority of a Member State has grounds for supposing that a saving of tax may result from artificial transfers of profits within groups of enterprises;

    (e) information forwarded to the one Member State by the competent authority of the other Member State has enabled information to be obtained which may be relevant in assessing liability to tax in the latter Member State.

2. The competent authorities of the Member States may, under the consultation procedure laid down in Article 9, extend the exchange of information provided for in paragraph 1 to cases other than those specified therein.

3. The competent authorities of the Member States may forward to each other in any other case, without prior request, the information referred to in Article 1 (1) of which they have knowledge.

Article 5

Time limit for forwarding information

The competent authority of a Member State which, under the preceding Articles, is called upon to furnish information, shall forward it as swiftly as possible. If it encounters obstacles in furnishing the information or if it refuses to furnish the information, it shall forthwith inform the requesting authority to this effect, indicating the nature of the obstacles or the reasons for its refusal.

Article 6

Collaboration by officials of the State concerned

For the purpose of applying the preceding provisions, the competent authority of the Member State providing the information and the competent authority of the Member State for which the information is intended may agree, under the consultation procedure laid down in Article 9, to authorize the presence in the first Member State of officials of the tax administration of the other Member State. The details for applying this provision shall be determined under the same procedure.

Article 7

Provisions relating to secrecy

[1. All information made known to a Member State under this Directive shall be kept secret in that State in the same manner as information received under its national legislation. In any case, such information:

- may be made available only to the persons directly involved in the assessment of the tax or in the administrative control of this assessment,

- may be made known only in connection with judicial proceedings or administrative proceedings involving sanctions undertaken with a view to, or relating to, the making or reviewing the tax assessment and only to persons who are directly involved in such proceedings; such information may, however, be disclosed during public hearings or in judgements if the competent authority of the Member State supplying the information raises no objection at the time when it first supplies the information,

- shall in no circumstances be used other than for taxation purposes or in connection with judicial proceedings or administrative proceedings involving sanctions undertaken with a view to, or in relation to, the making or reviewing of the tax assessment.

In addition, Member States may provide for the information referred to in the first subparagraph to be used for assessment of other levies, duties and taxes covered by Article 2 of Directive 76/308/EEC.][5]

2. Paragraph 1 shall not oblige a Member State whose legislation or administrative practice lays down, for domestic purposes, narrower limits than those contained in the provisions of that paragraph, to provide information if the State concerned does not undertake to respect those narrower limits.

3. Notwithstanding paragraph 1, the competent authorities of the Member State providing the information may permit it to be used for other purposes in the requesting State, if, under the legislation of the informing State, the information could, in similar circumstances, be used in the informing State for similar purposes.

4. Where a competent authority of a Member State considers that information which it has received from the competent authority of another Member State is likely to be useful to the competent authority of a third Member State, it may transmit it to the latter competent authority with the agreement of the competent authority which supplied the information.

Article 8

Limits to exchange of information

[1. This Directive does not impose any obligation upon a Member State from which information is requested to carry out inquiries or to communicate information, if it would be contrary to its legislation or administrative practices for the competent authority of that State to conduct such inquiries or to collect the information sought.][5]

2. The provision of information may be refused where it would lead to the disclosure of a commercial, industrial or professional secret or of a commercial process, or of information whose disclosure would be contrary to public policy.

[3. The competent authority of a Member State may decline transmission of information when the Member State requesting it is unable, for reasons of fact or law, to provide the same type of information.][5]

[Article 8a

Notification

1. At the request of the competent authority of a Member State, the competent authority of another Member State shall, in accordance with the rules governing the notification of similar instruments in the requested Member State, notify the addressee of all instruments and decisions which emanate from the administrative authorities of the requesting Member State and concern the application in its territory of legislation on taxes covered by this Directive.

2. Requests for notification shall indicate the subject of the instrument or decision to be notified and shall specify the name and address of the addressee, together with any other information which may facilitate identification of the addressee.

3. The requested authority shall inform the requesting authority immediately of its response to the request for notification and shall notify it, in particular, of the date of notification of the decision or instrument to the addressee.

Article 8b

Simultaneous controls

1. Where the tax situation of one or more persons liable to tax is of common or complementary interest to two or more Member States, those States may agree to conduct simultaneous controls, in their own territory, with a view to exchanging the information thus obtained, whenever they would appear to be more effective than controls conducted by one Member State alone.

2. The competent authority in each Member State shall identify independently the persons liable to tax whom it intends to propose for simultaneous control. It shall notify the respective competent authorities in the other Member States concerned of the cases which, in its view, should be subject to simultaneous control. It shall give reasons for its choice, as far as possible, by providing the information which led to its decision. It shall specify the period of time during which such controls should be conducted.

3. The competent authority of each Member State concerned shall decide whether it wishes to take part in the simultaneous control. On receipt of a proposal for a simultaneous control, the competent authority shall confirm its agreement or communicate its reasoned refusal to its counterpart authority.

4. Each competent authority of the Member States concerned shall appoint a representative with responsibility for supervising and coordinating the control operation.][8]

Article 9

Consultations

1. For the purposes of the implementation of this Directive, consultations shall be held, if necessary in a Committee, between:
   — the competent authorities of the Member States concerned at the request of either, in respect of bilateral questions,
   — the competent authorities of all the Member States and the Commission, at the request of one of those authorities or the Commission, in so far as the matters involved are not solely of bilateral interest.

2. The competent authorities of the Member States may communicate directly with each other. The competent authorities of the Member

States may by mutual agreement permit authorities designated by them to communicate directly with each other in specified cases or in certain categories of cases.

3. Where the competent authorities make arrangements on bilateral matters covered by this Directive other than as regards individual cases, they shall as soon as possible inform the Commission thereof. The Commission shall in turn notify the competent authorities of the other Member States.

Article 10

Pooling of experience

The Member States shall, together with the Commission, constantly monitor the cooperation procedure provided for in this Directive and shall pool their experience, especially in the field of transfer pricing within groups of enterprises, with a view to improving such cooperation and, where appropriate, drawing up a body of rules in the fields concerned.

Article 11

Applicability of wider-ranging provisions of assistance

The foregoing provisions shall not impede the fulfilment of any wider obligations to exchange information which might flow from other legal acts.

Article 12

Final provisions

1. Member States shall bring into force the necessary laws, regulations and administrative provisions in order to comply with this Directive not later than 1 January 1979 and shall forthwith communicate them to the Commission.

2. Member States shall communicate to the Commission the texts of any important provisions of national law which they subsequently adopt in the field covered by this Directive.

Article 13

This Directive is addressed to the Member States.

Done at Brussels, 19 December 1977.

For the Council

The President

G. GEENS

Amendments

1   Replaced by Council Directive 2004/106/EC of 16 November 2004
2   Substituted by the Act of Accession, 1994.
3   Inserted by Treaty of Accession to the European Union 2003
4   Inserted by Council Directive 2006/98/EC of 20 November 2006
5   Substituted by Council Directive 2004/56/EC of 21 April 2004
6   Replaced by Council Directive 2003/93/EC of 7 October 2003
7   Substituted by the Act of Accession, 1994.
8   Inserted by Council Directive 2004/56/EC of 21 April 2004

EIGHTH COUNCIL DIRECTIVE 79/1072/EEC

of 6 December 1979

On the harmonization of the laws of the Member States relating to turnover taxes - Arrangements for the refund of value added tax to taxable persons not established in the territory of the country

Official Journal L 331 , 27/12/1979 p. 0011 - 0019

Repealed by Article 28 of Council Directive 2008/9/EC with effect from 1 January 2010

THE COUNCIL OF THE EUROPEAN COMMUNITIES,

Having regard to the Treaty establishing the European Economic Community,

Having regard to Sixth Council Directive 77/388/EEC of 17 May 1977 on the harmonization of the laws of the Member States relating to turnover taxes - Common system of value added tax (uniform basis of assessment), and particular Article 17(4) thereof,

Having regard to the proposal from the Commission,

Having regard to the opinion of the European Parliament,

Having regard to the opinion of the Economic and Social Committee,

Whereas, pursuant to Article 17(4) of Directive 77/388/EEC, the Council is to adopt Community rules laying down the arrangements governing refunds of value added tax, referred to in paragraph 3 of the said Article, to taxable persons not established in the territory of the country;

Whereas rules are required to ensure that a taxable person established in the territory of one member country can claim for tax which has been invoiced to him in respect of supplies of goods or services in another Member State or which has been paid in respect of imports into that other Member State, thereby avoiding double taxation;

Whereas discrepancies between the arrangements currently in force in Member States, which give rise in some cases to deflection of trade and distortion of competition, should be eliminated;

Whereas the introduction of Community rules in this field will mark progress towards the effective liberalization of the movement of persons, goods and services, thereby helping to complete the process of economic integration;

Whereas such rules must not lead to the treatment of taxable persons differing according to the Member State in the territory of which they are established;

Whereas certain forms of tax evasion or avoidance should be prevented;

Whereas, under Article 17(4) of Directive 77/388/EEC, Member States may refuse the refund or impose supplementary conditions in the case of taxable persons not established in the territory of the Community; whereas steps should, however, also be taken to ensure that such taxable persons are not eligible for refunds on more favourable terms than those provided for in respect of Community taxable persons;

Whereas, initially, only the Community arrangements contained in this Directive should be adopted; whereas these arrangements provide, in particular, that decisions in respect of applications for refund should be notified within six months of the date on which such applications were lodged; whereas refunds should be made within the same period; whereas, for a period of one year from the final date laid down for the implementation of these arrangements, the Italian Republic should be authorized to notify the decisions taken by its competent services with regard to applications lodged by taxable persons not established within its territory and to make the relevant refunds within nine months, in order to enable the Italian Republic to reorganize the system at present in operation, with a view to applying the Community system;

Whereas further arrangements will have to be adopted by the Council to supplement the Community system; whereas, until the latter arrangements enter into force, Member States will refund the tax on the services and the purchases of goods which are not covered by this Directive, in accordance with the arrangements which they adopt pursuant to Article 17(4) of Directive 77/388/EEC,

HAS ADOPTED THIS DIRECTIVE:

Article 1

For the purposes of this Directive, "**a taxable person not established in the territory of the country**" shall mean a person as referred to in Article 4(1) of Directive 77/388/EEC who, during the period referred to in the first and second sentences of the first subparagraph of Article 7(1), has had in that country neither the seat of his economic activity, nor a fixed establishment from which business transactions are effected, nor, if no such seat or fixed establishment exists, his domicile or normal place of residence, and who, during the same period, has supplied no goods or services deemed to have been supplied in that country, with the exception of:

(a) transport services and services ancillary thereto, exempted pursuant to Article 14(1)(i), Article 15 or Article 16(1), B, C and D of Directive 77/388/EEC;

(b) services provided in cases where tax is payable solely by the person to whom they are supplied, pursuant to Article 21(1)(b) of Directive 77/388/EEC.

Article 2

Each Member State shall refund to any taxable person who is not established in the territory of the country but who is established in another Member State, subject to the conditions laid down below, any value added tax charged in respect of services or movable property supplied to him by other taxable persons in the territory of the country or charged in respect of the importation of goods into the country, in so far as such goods and services are used for the purposes of the transactions referred to in Article 17(3)(a) and (b) of Directive 77/388/EEC and of the provision of services referred to in Article 1(b).

Article 3

To qualify for refund, any taxable person as referred to in Article 2 who supplies no goods or services deemed to be supplied in the territory of the country shall:

(a) submit to the competent authority referred to in the first paragraph of Article 9 an application modelled on the specimen contained in Annex A, attaching originals of invoices or import documents. Member States shall make available to applicants an explanatory notice which shall in any event contain the minimum information set out in Annex C;

(b) produce evidence, in the form of a certificate issued by the official authority of the State in which he is established, that he is a taxable person for the purposes of value added tax in that State. However, where the competent authority referred to in the first paragraph of Article 9 already has such evidence in its possession, the taxable person shall not be bound to produce new evidence for a period of one year from the date of issue of the first certificate by the official authority of the State in which he is established. Member States shall not issue certificates to any taxable persons who benefit from tax exemption pursuant to Article 24(2) of Directive 77/388/EEC;

(c) certify by means of a written declaration that he has supplied no goods or services deemed to have been supplied in the territory of the country during the period referred to in the first and second sentences of the first subparagraph of Article 7(1);

(d) undertake to repay any sum collected in error.

Article 4

To be eligible for the refund, any taxable person as referred to in Article 2 who has supplied in the territory of the country no goods or services deemed to have been supplied in the country other than the services referred to in Article 1(a) and (b) shall:

(a) satisfy the requirements laid down in Article 3(a), (b) and (d);

(b) certify by means of a written declaration that, during the period referred to in the first and second sentences of the first subparagraph of Article 7(1), he has supplied no goods or services deemed to have been supplied in the territory of the country other than services referred to in Article 1(a) and (b).

Article 5

For the purposes of this Directive, goods and services in respect of which tax may be refundable shall satisfy the conditions laid down in Article 17 of Directive 77/388/EEC as applicable in the Member State of refund.

This Directive shall not apply to supplies of goods which are, or may by, exempted under item 2 of Article 15 of Directive 77/388/EEC.

Article 6

Member States may not impose on the taxable persons referred to in Article 2 any obligation, in addition to those referred to in Articles 3 and 4, other than the obligation to provide, in specific cases, the information necessary to determine whether the application for refund is justified.

Article 7

1. The application for refund provided for in Articles 3 and 4 shall relate to invoiced purchases of goods or services or to imports made during a period of not less than three months or not more than one calendar year. Applications may, however, relate to a period of less than three months where the period represents the remainder of a calendar year. Such applications may also relate to invoices or import documents not covered by previous applications and concerning transactions completed during the calendar year in question. Applications shall be submitted to the competent authority referred to in the first paragraph of Article 9 within six months of the end of the calendar year in which the tax became chargeable.

    If the application relates to a period of less than one calendar year but not less than three months, the amount for which application is made may not be less than the equivalent in national currency of 200 European units of account; if the application relates to a period of a calendar year or the remainder of a calendar year, the amount may not be less than the equivalent in national currency of 25 European units of account.

2. The European unit of account used shall be that defined in the Financial Regulation of 21 December 1977, as determined on 1 January of the year of the period referred to in the first and second sentences of the first subparagraph of paragraph 1. Member States may round up or down, by up to 10%, the figures resulting from this conversion into national currency.

3. The competent authority referred to in the first paragraph of Article 9 shall stamp each invoice and/or import document to prevent their use for further application and shall return them within one month.

4. Decisions concerning applications for refund shall be announced within six months of the date when the applications, accompanied by all the necessary documents required under this Directive for examination of the application, are submitted to the competent authority referred to in paragraph 3. Refunds shall be made before the end of the above mentioned period, at the applicant's request, in either the Member State of refund or the State in which he is established. In the latter case, the bank charges for the transfer shall be payable by the applicant.

    The grounds for refusal of an application shall be stated. Appeals against such refusals may be made to the competent authorities in the Member State concerned, subject to the same conditions as to form and time limits as those governing claims for refunds made by taxable persons established in the same State.

5. Where a refund has been obtained in a fraudulent or in any other irregular manner, the competent authority referred to in paragraph 3 shall proceed directly to recover the amounts wrongly paid and any penalties imposed, in accordance with the procedure applicable in the Member State concerned, without prejudice to the provisions relating to mutual assistance in the recovery of value added tax.

In the case of fraudulent applications which cannot be made the subject of an administrative penalty, in accordance with national legislation, the Member State concerned may refuse for a maximum period of two years from the date on which the fraudulent application was submitted any further refund to the taxable person concerned. Where an administrative penalty has been imposed but has not been paid, the Member State concerned may suspend any further refund to the taxable person concerned until it has been paid.

Article 8

[...][1]

Refunds may not be granted on terms more favourable than those applied in respect of taxable persons established in the territory of the Community.

Article 9

Member States shall make known, in an appropriate manner, the competent authority to which the application referred to in Article 3(a) and in Article 4(a) are to be submitted.

The certificates referred to in Article 3(b) and in Article 4(a), establishing that the person concerned is a taxable person, shall be modelled on the specimens contained in Annex B.

Article 10

Member States shall bring into force the provisions necessary to comply with this Directive no later than 1 January 1981. This Directive shall apply only to applications for refunds concerning value added tax charged on invoiced purchases of goods or services or in imports made as from that date.

Member States shall communicate to the Commission the texts of the main provisions of national law which they adopt in the field covered by this Directive. The Commission shall inform the other Member States thereof.

Article 11

By away of derogation from Article 7(4), the Italian Republic may, until 1 January 1982, extend the period referred to in this paragraph from six to nine months.

Article 12

Three years after the date referred to in Article 10, the Commission shall, after consulting the Member States, submit a report to the Council on the application of this Directive, and in particular Articles 3, 4 and 7 thereof.

Article 13

This Directive is addressed to the Member States.

Done at Brussels, 6 December 1979.

For the Council

The President

L. PRETI

ANNEX C

Minimum information to be given in explanatory notes

A. The application shall be drawn up on a form printed in one of the official languages of the European Communities. This form shall, however, be completed in the language of the country of refund.

B. The application shall be completed in block capitals and be submitted, by 30 June of the year following that to which the application relates, to the competent authority of the State to which the application is made (see D below).

C. The VAT registration number in the country of refund shall be given, if it is known to the applicant.

[D. The application shall be submitted to the relevant competent authorities, i.e. for:

- Belgium : ...
- Denmark : ...
- Germany : ...
- Greece:...
- Spain: ...
- France : ...
- Ireland : ...
- Italy : ...
- Luxembourg : ...
- the Netherlands : ...
- Austria: ...
- Portugal: ...
- Finland: ...
- Sweden: ...
- the United Kingdom : ...][2]
[- the Czech Republic: Finanční úřad pro Prahu 1
- Estonia: Maksuamet
- Cyprus: Υπουργείο Οικονομικών, Τμήμα Τελωνείων, Υπηρεσία Φ.Π.Α.
- Latvia: Valsts ieņēmumu dienesta Lielo nodokļu maksātāju pārvalde
- Lithuania: Vilniaus apskrities valstybinė mokesčių inspekcija

- Hungary: Adó- és Pénzügyi Ellenőrzési Hivatal
- Malta: Id-Dipartiment tat-Taxxa fuq il-Valur Miżjud fil-Ministeru tal-Finanzi
- Poland: Drugi Urząd Skarbowy Warszawa ródmieście
- Slovenia: Davčni urad Ljubljana
- Slovakia: Daňový úrad Bratislava I']³

[- Bulgaria...
- Romania...]⁴

E. The application shall refer to purchases of goods or services invoiced or to imports made during a period of not less than three months or more than one calendar year. However, it may relate to a period of less than three months where this period represents the remainder of a calendar year. Such an application may also relate to invoices or import documents not covered by previous applications and concerning transactions made during the calendar year in question.

F. In 9(a), the applicant shall describe the nature of the activities for which he has acquired the goods or received the services referred to in the application for refund of the tax (e.g. participation in the International ... Fair, held in ... from ... to ..., stand No ..., or international carriage of goods as from ... to ... on ...).

G. The application shall be accompanied by a certificate issued by the official authority of the State in which the applicant is established and which provides evidence that he is a taxable person for the purposes of value added tax in that State. However, where the competent authority referred to in D above already has such evidence in its possession, the applicant shall not be bound to produce new evidence for a period of one year from the date of issue of the first certificate.

H The application shall be accompanied by the originals of the invoices or import documents showing the amount of value added tax borne by the applicant.

[I. The application may be used for more than one invoice or import document but the total amount of VAT claimed for 19.. may not be less than:

BEF/LUF...

DKK...

DEM...

GRD...

PTE ...

FRF ...

IEP...

ITL...

NLG...

ATS...

ESP...

FIM...

SEK...

GBP...

[CZK...

EEK...

CYP...

LVL...

LTL...

HUF...

MTL...

PLN...

SIT...

SKK...]³

[BGN...

RON...]⁴

if the period to which it relates is less than one calendar year but not less than three months or less than:

BEF/LUF

DKK

DEM

GRD

PTE ...

FRF ...

IEP...

ITL...

NLG...

ATS...

ESP...

FIM...

SEK...

GBP...

[CZK...

EEK...

CYP...

LVL...

LTL...

HUF...

MTL...

PLN...

SIT...

SKK...]³

[BGN...

RON...]⁴

if the period to which it relates is one calendar year or less than three months]⁵.

J.   Exempted transport services are those carried out in connection with the international carriage of goods, including - subject to certain conditions - transport associated with the transit, export or import of goods.

K.   Any refund obtained improperly may render the offender liable to the fines or penalties laid down by the law of the State which has made the refund.

L.   The authority in the country of refund reserves the right to make refunds by cheque or money order addressed to the applicant.

Amendments

1   Deleted by Art 7, Council Directive 86/560/EEC of 17 November 1986, previously read: `In the case of taxable persons not established in the territory of the Community, Member States may refuse refunds or impose special conditions.'

2   Pt D,Annex C substituted by Act of Accession 1994.

3   Inserted by Treaty of Accession to the European Union 2003.

4   Inserted by Art 1 Council Directive 2006/98/EC of 20 November 2006.

5   Pt I,Annex C substituted by Act of Accession 1994.

ELEVENTH COUNCIL DIRECTIVE 80/368/EEC

of 26 March 1980

On the harmonization of the laws of the Member States relating to turnover taxes - exclusion of the French overseas departments from the scope of Directive 77/388/EEC

Official Journal L 090 , 03/04/1980 p. 0041 - 0041

> This Directive was repealed by Council Directive 2006/112/EC of 28 November 2006 on the common system of value added tax, with effect from 1 January 2007

THE COUNCIL OF THE EUROPEAN COMMUNITIES,

Having regard to the Treaty establishing the European Economic Community, and in particular Articles 99 and 100 thereof,

Having regard to the proposal from the Commission,

Whereas the third subparagraph of Article 227(2) of the Treaty requires that the institutions of the Community should, within the framework of the procedures provided for in the Treaty, take care that the economic and social development of the French overseas departments is possible;

Whereas, in accordance with the judgment handed down by the Court of Justice on 10 October 1978 in Case 148/77, the Treaty and secondary legislation apply in the French overseas departments unless a decision is taken by the Community institutions adopting measures particularly suited to the economic and social conditions of those departments;

Whereas, for reasons connected with their geographic, economic and social situation, the French overseas departments should be excluded from the scope of the common system of value added tax as established by Council Directive 77/388/EEC;

Whereas implementation of this Directive does not involve any amendment of the laws of the Member States,

HAS ADOPTED THIS DIRECTIVE:

Article 1

The following indent shall be added to Article 3(2) of Directive 77/388/EEC:

"- French Republic: - the overseas departements."

Article 2

This Directive shall apply with effect from 1 January 1979.

Article 3

This Directive is addressed to the Member States.

Done at Brussels, 26 March 1980.
For the Council

The President
G. MARCORA

COUNCIL DIRECTIVE 83/181/EEC

of 28 March 1983

Determining the scope of Article 14(1)(d) of Directive 77/388/EEC as regards exemption from value added tax on the final importation of certain goods

Official Journal L 105, 23/04/1983 p. 0038 - 0058

THE COUNCIL OF THE EUROPEAN COMMUNITIES,

Having regard to the treaty establishing the European Economic Community, and in particular Articles 99 and 100 thereof;

Having regard to the proposal from the Commission,

Having regard to the opinion of the European Parliament,

Having regard to the opinion of the Economic and Social Committee,

Whereas, pursuant to Article 14(1)(d) of Council Directive 77/388/EEC of 17 May 1977 on the harmonization of the laws of the Member States relating to turnover taxes - common system of value added tax: uniform basis of assessment, Member States shall, without prejudice to other community provisions and under conditions which they shall lay down for the purpose *inter alia* of preventing any possible evasion, avoidance or abuse, exempt final importation of goods qualifying for exemption from customs duties other than as provided for in the common customs tariff or which would qualify therefore if they were imported from a third country;

Whereas, in accordance with Article 14(2) of the above mentioned directive, the Commission is required to submit to the Council proposals designed to lay down Community tax rules clarifying the scope of the exemptions referred to in paragraph 1 of the said article and detailed rules for their implementation;

Whereas, while it is deemed desirable to achieve the greatest possible degree of uniformity between the system for customs duties and that for value added tax, account should be taken, nevertheless, in applying the latter system, of the differences as regards objective and structure between customs duties and value added tax;

Whereas arrangements for value added tax should be introduced that differ according to whether goods are imported from third countries or from other Member States and to the extent necessary to comply with the objectives of tax harmonization; whereas the exemptions on importation can be granted only on condition that they are not liable to affect the conditions of competition on the home market;

Whereas certain reliefs at present applied in the Member States stem from conventions with third countries or with other Member States which, given their purpose, concern only the signatory Member States; whereas it is not expedient to define at community level conditions for granting such reliefs; whereas the Member States concerned need merely be authorized to retain them,

HAS ADOPTED THIS DIRECTIVE:

Article 1

1. The scope of the exemptions from value added tax referred to in article 14(1)(d) of directive 77/388/eec and the rules for their implementation referred to in article 14(2) of that directive shall be defined by this directive. In accordance with the aforesaid article, the member states shall apply the exemptions laid down in this directive under the conditions fixed by them in order to ensure that such exemptions are correctly and simply applied and to prevent any evasion, avoidance or abuses.

2. For the purposes of this directive:

    (a) **"imports"** means imports as defined in article 7 of 77/388/eec and the entry for home use after being subject to one of the systems provided for in article 16 (1) (a) of the said directive or a system of temporary admission or transit;

    (b) **"personal property"** means any property intended for the personal use of the persons concerned or for meeting their household needs.

    The following, in particular, shall constitute "**personal property**":

    — household effects,

    — cycles and motor-cycles, private motor vehicles and their trailers, camping caravans, pleasure craft and private aeroplanes.

    Household provisions appropriate to normal family requirements, household pets and saddle animals shall also constitute "**personal property**".

    The nature or quantity of personal property shall not reflect any commercial interest, nor shall they be intended for an economic activity within the meaning of article 4 of directive 77/388/eec. However, portable instruments of the applied or liberal arts, required by the person concerned for the pursuit of his trade or profession, shall also constitute personal property;

    (c) **"household effects"** means personal effects, household linen and furnishings and items of equipment intended for the personal use of the persons concerned or for meeting their household needs;

    (d) **"alcoholic products"** means products (beer, wine, aperitifs with a wine or alcohol base, brandies, liqueurs and spirituous beverages, etc.) falling within heading nos [22.03 to 22.08][1] of the common customs tariff;

    (e) **"community"** means the territory of the member states where directive 77/388/EEC applies.

TITLE I

importation of personal property belonging to individuals coming from countries situated outside the community

Chapter I

personal property of natural persons transferring their normal place of residence from a third country to the community

Article 2

Subject to articles 3 to 10, exemption from VAT on importation shall be granted on personal property imported by natural persons transferring their normal place of residence from outside the community to a member state of the community.

Article 3

Exemption shall be limited to personal property which:

(a) except in special cases justified by the circumstances, has been in the possession of and, in the case of non-consumable goods, used by the person concerned at his former normal place of residence for a minimum of six months before the date on which he ceases to have his normal place of residence outside the community;

(b) is intended to be used for the same purpose at his new normal place of residence.

The member states may in addition make exemption conditional upon such property having borne, either in the country of origin or in the country of departure, the customs and/or fiscal charges to which it is normally liable.

Article 4

Exemption may be granted only to persons whose normal place of residence has been outside the community for a continuous period of at least 12 months.

However, the competent authorities may grant exceptions to this rule provided that the intention of the person concerned was clearly to reside outside the community for a continuous period of at least 12 months.

Article 5

Exemption shall not be granted in respect of:

(a) alcoholic products;

(b) tobacco or tobacco products;

(c) commercial means of transport;

(d) articles for use in the exercise of a trade or profession, other than portable instruments of the applied or liberal arts.

Vehicles intended for mixed use for commercial or professional purposes may also be excluded from exemption.

Article 6

Except in special cases, exemption shall be granted only in respect of personal property entered for permanent importation within 12 months of the date of establishment, by the person concerned, of his normal place of residence in the member state of importation.

The personal property may be imported in several separate consignments within the period referred to in the preceding paragraph.

Article 7

1. Until 12 months have elapsed from the date of the declaration for its final importation, personal property which has been imported exempt from tax may not be lent, given as security, hired out or transferred, whether for a consideration or free of charge, without prior notification to the competent authorities.

2. Any loan, giving as security, hiring out or transfer before the expiry of the period referred to in paragraph 1 shall entail payment of the relevant value added tax on the goods concerned, at the rate applying on the date of such loan, giving as security, hiring out or transfer, on the basis of the type of goods and the customs value ascertained or accepted on that date by the competent authorities.

Article 8

1. By way of derogation from the first paragraph of article 6, exemption may be granted in respect of personal property permanently imported before the person concerned establishes his normal place of residence in the member state of importation, provided that he undertakes actually to establish his normal place of residence there within a period of six months. Such undertaking shall be accompanied by a security, the form and amount of which shall be determined by the competent authorities.

2. Where use is made of the provisions of paragraph 1, the period laid down in article 3 shall be calculated from the date of importation into the member state concerned.

Article 9

1. Where, owing to occupational commitments, the person concerned leaves the country situated outside the community where he had his normal place of residence without simultaneously establishing his normal place of residence in the territory of a member state, although having the intention of ultimately doing so, the competent authorities may authorize exemption in respect of the personal property which he transfers into the said territory for this purpose.

2. Exemption in respect of the personal property referred to in paragraph 1 shall be granted in accordance with the conditions laid down in articles 2 to 7, on the understanding that:

    (a) the periods laid down in article 3(a) and the first paragraph of article 6 shall be calculated from the date of importation;

(b) the period referred to in article 7(1) shall be calculated from the date when the person concerned actually establishes his normal place of residence in the territory of a member state.

3. Exemption shall also be subject to an undertaking from the person concerned that he will actually establish his normal place of residence in the territory of a member state within a period laid down by the competent authorities in keeping with the circumstances. The latter may require this undertaking to be accompanied by a security, the form and amount of which they shall determine.

Article 10

The competent authorities may derogate from articles 3(a) and (b), 5(c) and (d) and 7 when a person has to transfer his normal place of residence from a country situated outside the community to the territory of a member state as a result of exceptional political circumstances.

Chapter II

goods imported on the occasion of a marriage

Article 11

1. Subject to articles 12 to 15, exemption shall be granted in respect of trousseaux and household effects, whether or not new, belonging to a person transferring his or her normal place of residence from a country outside the community to the territory of a member state on the occasion of his or her marriage.

[2. Exemption shall also be granted in respect of presents customarily given on the occasion of a marriage which are received by a person fulfilling the conditions laid down in paragraph 1 from persons having their normal place of residence in a country situated outside the Community. the exemption shall apply to presents of a unit value of not more than 200 ECU. Member States may, however, grant exemption for more than 200 ECU provided that the value of each exempt present does not exceed 1,000 ECU.][2]

3. The Member State may make exemption of the goods referred to in paragraph 1 conditional on their having borne, either in the country of origin or in the country of departure, the customs and/or fiscal charges to which they are normally liable.

Article 12

The exemption referred to in article 11 may be granted only to persons:

(a) whose normal place of residence has been outside the community for a continuous period of at least 12 months. However, derogations from this rule may be granted provided that the intention of the person concerned was clearly to reside outside the community for a continuous period of at least 12 months;

(b) who produce evidence of their marriage.

Article 13

No exemption shall be granted for alcoholic products, tobacco or tobacco products.

Article 14

1. Save in exceptional circumstances, exemption shall be granted only in respect of goods permanently imported:

   — not earlier than two months before the date fixed for the wedding (in this case exemption may be made subject to the lodging of appropriate security, the form and amount of which shall be determined by the competent authorities), and

   — not later than four months after the date of the wedding.

2. Goods referred to in article 11 may be imported in several separate consignments within the period referred to in paragraph 1.

Article 15

1. Until 12 months have elapsed from the date of the declaration for their final importation, goods which have been imported exempt from tax may not be lent, given as security, hired out or transferred, whether for a consideration or free of charge, without prior notification to the competent authorities.

2. Any loan, giving as security, hiring out or transfer before the expiry of the period referred to in paragraph 1 shall entail payment of the relevant value added tax on the goods concerned, at the rate applying on the date of such loan, giving as security, hiring out or transfer, on the basis of the type of goods and the value ascertained or accepted on that date by the competent authorities.

Chapter III
personal property acquired by inheritance

Article 16

Subject to articles 17 to 19, exemption shall be granted in respect of personal property acquired by inheritance by a natural person having his normal place of residence in a Member State.

Article 17

Exemption shall not be granted in respect of:

   (a) alcoholic products;

   (b) tobacco or tobacco products;

   (c) commercial means of transport;

   (d) articles for use in the exercise of a trade or profession, other than portable instruments of the applied or liberal arts, which were required for the exercise of the trade or profession of the deceased;

   (e) stocks of raw materials and finished or semi-finished products;

(f) livestock and stocks of agricultural products exceeding the quantities appropriate to normal family requirements.

Article 18

1. Exemption shall be granted only in respect of personal property permanently imported not later than two years from the date on which the person becomes entitled to the goods (final settlement of the inheritance).

   However, this period may be extended by the competent authorities on special grounds.

2. The goods may be imported in several separate consignments within the period referred to in paragraph 1.

Article 19

Articles 16 to 18 shall apply *mutatis mutandis* to personal property acquired by inheritance by legal persons engaged in a non-profitmaking activity who are established in the territory of a Member State.

TITLE II

school outfits, scholastic materials and other scholastic household effects

Article 20

1. Exemption shall be granted in respect of outfits, scholastic materials and household effects representing the usual furnishings for a student's room and belonging to pupils or students coming to stay in a Member State for the purposes of studying there and intended for their personal use during the period of their studies.

2. For the purposes of this article:

   (a) pupil or student means any person enrolled in an educational establishment in order to attend full-time the courses offered therein;

   (b) outfit means underwear and household linen as well as clothing, whether or not new;

   (c) scholastic materials means articles and instruments (including calculators and typewriters) normally used by pupils or students for the purposes of their studies.

Article 21

Exemption shall be granted at least once per school year.

TITLE III

imports of negligible value

[Article 22

Goods of a total value not exceeding 10 ECU shall be exempt on admission. Member States may grant exemption for imported goods of a total value of more than 10 ECU but not exceeding 22 ECU.

However, Member States may exclude goods which have been imported on mail order from the exemption provided for in the first sentence of the first subparagraph.][3]

Article 23

Exemption shall not apply to the following:

(a) alcoholic products;

(b) perfumes and toilet waters;

(c) tobacco or tobacco products.

TITLE IV

capital goods and other equipment imported on the transfer of activities

Article 24

1. Without prejudice to the measures in force in the member state with regard to industrial and commercial policy, and subject to articles 25 to 28, Member States may allow exemption, on admission, for imports of capital goods and other equipment belonging to undertakings which definitively cease their activity in the country of departure in order to carry on a similar activity in the member state into which the goods are imported and which, in accordance with article 22(1) of Directive 77/388/EEC, have given advance notice to the competent authorities of the member state of importation of the commencement of such activity.

    Where the undertaking transferred is an agricultural holding, its livestock shall also be exempt on admission.

2. For the purposes of paragraph 1:

    — "**activity**" means an economic activity as referred to in article 4 of Directive 77/388/EEC,

    — "**undertaking**" means an independent economic unit of production or of the service industry.

Article 25

1. The exemption referred to in article 24 shall be limited to capital goods and equipment which:

    (a) except in special cases justified by the circumstances, have actually been used in the undertaking for a minimum of 12 months prior to the date on which the undertaking ceased to operate in the country of departure;

    (b) are intended to be used for the same purposes after the transfer;

    (c) are to be used for the purposes of an activity not exempted under article 13 of Directive 77/388/EEC;

    (d) are appropriate to the nature and size of the undertaking in question.

2. However, Member States may exempt capital goods and equipment imported from another member state by charitable or philanthropic

organizations at the time of the transfer of their principal place of business to the member state of importation.

Such exemption shall, however, be granted only on condition that at the time when they were acquired the capital goods and equipment in question were not exempt under article 15(12) of Directive 77/388/EEC.

3. Pending entry into force of the common rules referred to in the first subparagraph of article 17(6) of Directive 77/388/EEC, member states may exclude from the exemption, in whole or in part, capital goods in respect of which they have availed themselves of the second subparagraph of that paragraph.

Article 26

No exemption shall be granted to undertakings established outside the community and the transfer of which into the territory of a member state is consequent upon or is for the purpose of merging with, or being absorbed by, an undertaking established in the community, without a new activity being set up.

Article 27

No exemption shall be granted for:

(a) means of transport which are not of the nature of instruments of production or of the service industry;

(b) supplies of all kinds intended for human consumption or for animal feed;

(c) fuel and stocks of raw materials or finished or semi-finished products;

(d) livestock in the possession of dealers.

Article 28

Except in special cases justified by the circumstances, the exemption referred to in article 24 shall be granted only in respect of capital goods and other equipment imported before the expiry of a period of 12 months from the date when the undertaking ceased its activities in the country of departure.

TITLE V

importation of certain agricultural products and products intended for agricultural use

Chapter I

products obtained by community farmers on properties located in a state other than the state of importation

Article 29

1. Subject to articles 30 and 31, agricultural, stock-farming, bee-keeping, horticultural and forestry products from properties located in a country adjoining the territory of the member state of importation which are operated by agricultural producers having their principal undertaking in

that member state and adjacent to the country concerned shall be exempt on admission.

2. To be eligible under paragraph 1, stock-farming products must be obtained from animals reared, acquired or imported in accordance with the general tax arrangements applicable in the Member State of importation.

3. Pure-bred horses, not more than six months old and born outside the member state of importation of an animal covered in that state and then exported temporarily to give birth, shall be exempt on admission.

Article 30

Exemption shall be limited to products which have not undergone any treatment other than that which normally follows their harvest or production.

Article 31

Exemption shall be granted only in respect of products imported by the agricultural producer or on his behalf.

Article 32

This chapter shall apply *mutatis mutandis* to the products of fishing or fish-farming activities carried out in the lakes or waterways bordering the territory of the Member State of importation by fishermen established in that member state and to the products of hunting activities carried out on such lakes or waterways by sportsmen established in that Member State.

Chapter II

seeds, fertilizers and products for the treatment of soil and crops

Article 33

Subject to article 34, seeds, fertilizers and products for the treatment of soil and crops, intended for use on property located in a member state adjoining a country situated outside the community or another member state and operated by agricultural producers having their principal undertaking in the said country situated outside the community or member state adjacent to the territory of the member state of importation shall be exempt on admission.

Article 34

1. Exemption shall be limited to the quantities of seeds, fertilizers or other products required for the purpose of operating the property.

2. It shall be granted only for seed, fertilizers or other products introduced directly into the importing member state by the agricultural producer or on his behalf.

3. Member States may make exemption conditional upon the granting of reciprocal treatment.

TITLE VI

importation of therapeutic substances, medicines, laboratory animals and biological or chemical substances

Chapter I

laboratory animals and biological or chemical substances intended for research

Article 35

1. The following shall be exempt on admission:

   (a) animals specially prepared and sent free of charge for laboratory use;

   (b) biological or chemical substances:

   — which are imported free of charge from the territory of another member state, or

   — which are imported from countries outside the community subject to the limits and conditions laid down in [Article 60]⁴ of Council Regulation (EEC) No 918/83 of 28 March 1983 setting up a community system of reliefs from customs duty.

2. The exemption referred to in paragraph 1 shall be limited to animals and biological or chemical substances which are intended for:

   — either public establishments principally engaged in education or scientific research, including those departments of public establishmets which are principally engaged in education or scientific research,

   — or private establishments principally engaged in education or scientific research and authorized by the competent authorities of the member states to receive such articles exempt from tax.

Chapter II

therapeutic substances of human origin and blood-grouping and tissue-typing reagents

Article 36

1. Without prejudice to the exemption provided for in article 14(1)(a) of Directive 77/388/EEC and subject to article 37, the following shall be exempted:

   (a) therapeutic substances of human origin;

   (b) blood-grouping reagents;

   (c) tissue-typing reagents.

2. For the purposes of paragraph 1:

   — "**therapeutic substances of human origin**" means human blood and its derivatives (whole human blood, dried human plasma, human albumin and fixed solutions of human plasma protein, human immunoglobulin and human fibrinogen),

- **"blood-grouping reagents"** means all reagents, whether of human, animal, plant or other origin used for blood-type grouping and for the detection of blood incompatibilities,

- **"tissue-typing reagents"** means all reagents whether of human, animal, plant or other origin used for the determination of human tissue-types.

Article 37

Exemption shall be limited to products which:

(a) are intended for institutions or laboratories approved by the competent authorities, for use exclusively for non-commercial medical or scientific purposes;

(b) are accompanied by a certificate of conformity issued by a duly authorized body in the country of departure;

(c) are in containers bearing a special label identifying them.

Article 38

Exemption shall include the special packaging essential for the transport of therapeutic substances of human origin or blood-grouping or tissue-typing reagents and also any solvents and accessories needed for their use which may be included in the consignments.

[Chapter IIa

Reference substances for the quality control of medical products

Article 38 (a)

Consignments which contain samples of reference substances approved by the World Health Organization for the quality control of materials used in the manufacture of medicinal products and which are addressed to consignees authorized by the competent authorities of the Member States to receive such consignments free of tax shall be exempt on admission.][5]

Chapter III

pharmaceutical products used at international sports events

Article 39

Pharmaceutical products for human or veterinary medical use by persons or animals participating in international sports events shall, within the limits necessary to meet their requirements during their stay in the member state of importation, be exempt on admission.

TITLE VII

goods for charitable or philanthropic organizations

Article 40

Member States may impose a limit on the quantity or value of the goods referred to in Articles 41 to 55, in order to remedy any abuse and to combat major distortions of competition.

Chapter I

goods imported for general purposes

Article 41

1. Subject to articles 42 to 44, the following shall be exempt on admission:

   (a) basic necessities obtained free of charge and imported by state organizations or other charitable or philanthropic organizations approved by the competent authorities for distribution free of charge to needy persons;

   (b) goods of every description sent free of charge, by a person or organization established in a country other than the member state of importation, and without any commercial intent on the part of the sender, to state organizations or other charitable or philanthropic organizations approved by the competent authorities, to be used for fund-raising at occasional charity events for the benefit of needy persons;

   (c) equipment and office materials sent free of charge, by a person or organization established in a country other than the member state of importation, and without any commercial intent on the part of the sender, to charitable or philanthropic organizations approved by the competent authorities, to be used solely for the purpose of meeting their operating needs or carrying out their stated charitable or philanthropic aims.

2. For the purposes of paragraph 1(a) "**basic necessities**" means those goods required to meet the immediate needs of human beings, e.g. food, medicine, clothing and bed-clothes.

Article 42

Exemption shall not be granted in respect of:

   (a) alcoholic products;

   (b) tobacco or tobacco products;

   (c) coffee and tea;

   (d) motor vehicles other than ambulances.

Article 43

Exemption shall be granted only to organizations accounting procedures of which enable the competent authorities to supervise their operations and which offer all the guarantees considered necessary.

Article 44

1. Exempt goods may not be put out by the organization entitled to exemption for loan, hiring out or transfer, whether for a consideration or free of charge, for purposes other than those laid down in article 41(1)(a) and (b), unless the competent authorities have been informed thereof in advance.

2. Should goods and equipment be lent, hired out or transferred to an organization entitled to benefit from exemption pursuant to articles 41 and 43, the exemption shall continue to be granted provided that the latter uses the goods and equipment for purposes which confer the right to such exemption.

In other cases, loan, hiring out or transfer shall be subject to prior payment of value added tax at the rate applying on the date of the loan, hiring out or transfer, on the basis of the type of goods and equipment and the value ascertained or accepted on that date by the competent authorities.

Article 45

1. Organizations referred to in article 41 which cease to fulfil the conditions giving entitlement to exemption, or which are proposing to use goods and equipment exempt on admission for purposes other than those provided for by that article, shall so inform the competent authorities.

2. Goods remaining in the possession of organizations which cease to fulfil the conditions giving entitlement to exemption shall be liable to the relevant import value added tax at the rate applying on the date on which those conditions cease to be fulfilled, on the basis of the type of goods and equipment and the value as ascertained or accepted on that date by the competent authorities.

3. Goods used by the organization benefiting from the exemption for purposes other than those provided for in article 41 shall be liable to the relevant import value added tax at the rate applying on the date on which they are put to another use on the basis of the type of goods and equipment and the value as ascertained on that date by the competent authorities.

Chapter II

Articles imported for the benefit of handicapped persons

Article 46

1. Articles specially designed for the education, employment or social advancement of blind or other physically or mentally handicapped persons shall be exempt on admission where:

(a) they are imported by institutions or organizations that are principally engaged in the education of or the provision of assistance to handicapped persons and are authorized by the competent authorities of the member states to receive such articles exempt from tax; and

(b) they are donated to such institutions or organizations free of charge and with no commercial intent on the part of the donor.

2. Exemption shall apply to specific spare parts, components or accessories specifically for the articles in question and to the tools to be used for the maintenance, checking, calibration and repair of the said articles, provided that such spare parts, components, accessories or tools are imported at the same time as the said articles or, if imported subsequently, that they can be identified as being intended for articles previously exempt on admission or which would be eligible to be so exempt at the time when such entry is

requested for the specific spare parts, components or accessories and tools in question.

3. Articles exempt on admission may not be used for purposes other than the education, employment or social advancement of blind or other handicapped persons.

Article 47

1. Goods exempt on admission may be lent, hired out or transferred, whether for a consideration or free of charge, by the beneficiary institutions or organizations on a non-profitmaking basis to the persons referred to in article 46 with whom they are concerned, without payment of value added tax on importation.

2. No loan, hiring out or transfer may be effected under conditions other than those provided for in paragraph 1 unless the competent authorities have first been informed.

    Should an article be lent, hired out or transferred to an institution or organization itself entitled to benefit from this exemption, the exemption shall continue to be granted, provided the latter uses the article for purposes which confer the right to such exemption.

    In other cases, loan, hiring out or transfer shall be subject to prior payment of value added tax, at the rate applying on the date of the loan, hiring out or transfer, on the basis of the type of goods and the value ascertained or accepted on that date by the competent authorities.

Article 48

1. Institutions or organizations referred to in article 46 which cease to fulfil the conditions giving entitlement to exemption, or which are proposing to use articles exempt on admission for purposes other than those provided for by that article shall so inform the competent authorities.

2. Articles remaining in the possession of institutions or organizations which cease to fulfil the conditions giving entitlement to exemption shall be liable to the relevant import value added tax at the rate applying on the date on which those conditions cease to be fulfilled, on the basis of the type of goods and the value ascertained or accepted on that date by the competent authorities.

3. Articles used by the institution or organization benefiting from the exemption for purposes other than those provided for in article 46 shall be liable to the relevant import value added tax at the rate applying on the date on which they are put to another use on the basis of the type of goods and the value ascertained or accepted on that date by the competent authorities.

Chapter III

goods imported for the benefit of disaster victims

Article 49

1. Subject to articles 50 to 55, goods imported by state organizations or other charitable or philanthropic organizations approved by the competent authorities shall be exempt on admission where they are intended:

    (a) for distribution free of charge to victims of disasters affecting the territory of one or more Member States; or

    (b) to be made available free of charge to the victims of such disasters, while remaining the property of the organizations in question.

2. Goods imported by disaster-relief agencies in order to meet their needs during the period of their activity shall also benefit upon admission from the exemption referred to in paragraph 1 under the same conditions.

Article 50

No exemption shall be granted for materials and equipment intended for rebuilding disaster areas.

Article 51

Granting of the exemption shall be subject to a decision by the Commission, acting at the request of the Member State or states concerned in accordance with an emergency procedure entailing the consultation of the other member states. this decision shall, where necessary, lay down the scope and the conditions of the exemption.

Pending notification of the Commission's decision, Member States affected by a disaster may authorize the suspension of any import value added tax chargeable on goods imported for the purposes described in article 49, subject to an undertaking by the importing organization to pay such tax if exemption is not granted.

Article 52

Exemption shall be granted only to organizations the accounting procedures of which enable the competent authorities to supervise their operations and which offer all the guarantees considered necessary.

Article 53

1. The organizations benefiting from the exemption may not lend, hire out or transfer, whether for a consideration or free of charge, the goods referred to in article 49(1) under conditions other than those laid down in that Article without prior notification thereof to the competent authorities.

2. Should goods be lent, hired out or transferred to an organization itself entitled to benefit from exemption pursuant to Article 49, the exemption shall continue to be granted, provided the latter uses the goods for purposes which confer the right to such exemption.

    In other cases, loan, hiring out or transfer shall be subject to prior payment of value added tax, at the rate applying on the date of the loan, hiring out or transfer, on the basis of the type of goods and the value ascertained or accepted on that date by the competent authorities.

Article 54

1. The goods referred to in Article 49(1)(b), after they cease to be used by disaster victims, may not be lent, hired out or transferred, whether for a consideration or free of charge, unless the competent authorities are notified in advance.

2. Should goods be lent, hired out or transferred to an organization itself entitled to benefit from exemption pursuant to Article 49 or, if appropriate, to an organization entitled to benefit from exemption pursuant to Article 41(1)(a), the exemption shall continue to be granted, provided such organizations use them for purposes which confer the right to such exemption.

    In other cases, loan, hiring out or transfer shall be subject to prior payment of value added tax, at the rate applying on the date of the loan, hiring out or transfer, on the basis of the type of goods and the value ascertained or accepted on that date by the competent authorities.

Article 55

1. Organizations referred to in Article 49 which cease to fulfil the conditions giving entitlement to exemption, or which are proposing to use the goods exempt on admission for purposes other than those provided for by that article shall so inform the competent authorities.

2. In the case of goods remaining in the possession of organizations which cease to fulfil the conditions giving entitlement to exemption, when these are transferred to an organization itself entitled to benefit from exemption pursuant to this chapter or, if appropriate, to an organization entitled to benefit from exemption pursuant to Article 41, the exemption shall continue to be granted, provided the organization uses the goods in question for purposes which confer the right to such exemptions. In other cases, the goods shall be liable to the relevant import value added tax at the rate applying on the date on which those conditions cease to be fulfilled, on the basis of the type of goods and the value ascertained or accepted on that date by the competent authorities.

3. Goods used by the organization benefiting from the exemption for purposes other than those provided for in this chapter shall be liable to the relevant import value added tax at the rate applying on the date on which they are put to another use, on the basis of the type of goods and the value ascertained or accepted on that date by the competent authorities.

TITLE VIII

importation in the context of certain aspects of international relations

Chapter I

honorary decorations or awards

Article 56

On production of satisfactory evidence to the competent authorities by the persons concerned, and provided the operations involved are not in any way of a commercial character, exemption shall be granted in respect of:

(a) decorations conferred by the government of a country other than the Member State of importation on persons whose normal place of residence is in the latter State;

(b) cups, medals and similar articles of an essentially symbolic nature which, having been awarded in a country other than the Member State of importation to persons having their normal place of residence in the latter State as a tribute to their activities in fields such as the arts, the sciences, sport or the public service or in recognition of merit at a particular event, are imported by such persons themselves;

(c) cups, medals and similar articles of an essentially symbolic nature which are given free of charge by authorities or persons established in a country other than the Member State of importation, to be presented in the territory of the latter State for the same purposes as those referred to in (b).

[(d) Awards, trophies and souvenirs of a symbolic nature and of limited value intended for distribution free of charge to persons normally resident in a country other than that of import, at business conferences or similar international events; their nature, unitary value or other features, must not be such as might indicate that they are intended for commercial purposes.][6]

Chapter II

presents received in the context of international relations

Article 57

Without prejudice, where relevant, to the provisions applicable to the international movement of travellers, and subject to articles 58 and 59, exemption shall be granted in respect of goods:

(a) imported by persons who have paid an official visit in a country other than that of their normal residence and who have received such goods on that occasion as gifts from the host authorities;

(b) imported by persons coming to pay an official visit in the Member State of importation and who intend to offer them on that occasion as gifts to the host authorities;

(c) sent as gifts, in token of friendship or goodwill, by an official body, public authority or group carrying on an activity in the public interest which is located in a country other than the Member State of importation, to an official body, public authority or group carrying on an activity in the public interest which is located in the Member State of importation and approved by the competent authorities to receive such goods exempt from tax.

Article 58

No exemption shall be granted for alcoholic products, tobacco or tobacco products.

Article 59

Exemption shall be granted only:

— where the articles intended as gifts are offered on an occasional basis,

— where they do not, by their nature, value or quantity, reflect any commercial interest,

— if they are not used for commercial purposes.

Chapter III

goods to be used by monarchs or heads of state

Article 60

Exemption from tax, within the limits and under the conditions laid down by the competent authorities, shall be granted in respect of:

(a) gifts to reigning monarchs and heads of State;

(b) goods to be used or consumed by reigning monarchs and heads of State of another State, or by persons officially representing them, during their official stay in the Member State of importation. However, exemption may be made subject, by the Member State of importation, to reciprocal treatment.

The provisions of the preceding subparagraph are also applicable to persons enjoying prerogatives at international level analogous to those enjoyed by reigning monarchs or heads of State.

TITLE IX

importation of goods for the promotion of trade

Chapter I

samples of negligible value

Article 61

1. Without prejudice to article 65(1)(a), samples of goods which are of negligible value and which can be used only to solicit orders for goods of the type they represent shall be exempt on admission.

2. The competent authorities may require that certain articles, to qualify for exemption on admission, be rendered permanently unusable by being torn, perforated, or clearly and indelibly marked, or by any other process, provided such operation does not destroy their character as samples.

3. For the purposes of paragraph 1, "**samples of goods**" means any article representing a type of goods whose manner of presentation and quantity, for goods of the same type or quality, rule out its use for any purpose other than that of seeking orders.

Chapter II

printed matter and advertising material

[Article 62

Subject to Article 63, printed advertising matter such as catalogues, price lists, directions for use or brochures shall be exempt on admission provided that they relate to:

(a) goods for sale or hire by a person established outside the Member State of import, or

(b) services offered by a person established in another Member State, or

(c) transport, commercial insurance or banking services offered by a person established in a third country.

Article 63

The exemption referred to in Article 62 shall be limited to printed advertisements which fulfil the following conditions:

(a) printed matter must clearly display the name of the undertaking which produces, sells or hires out the goods, or which offers the services to which it refers;

(b) each consignment must contain no more than one document or a single copy of each document if it is made up of several documents. Consignments comprising several copies of the same document may nevertheless be granted exemption provided their total gross weight does not exceed one kilogram;

(c) printed matter must not be the subject of grouped consignments from the same consignor to the same consignee.

However, the conditions under (b) and (c) shall not apply to printed matter relating to either goods for sale or hire or services offered by a person established in another Member State provided that the printed matter has been imported, and will be distributed, free of charge.][7]

Article 64

Articles for advertising purposes, of no intrinsic commercial value, sent free of charge by suppliers to their customers which, apart from their advertising function, are not capable of being used shall also be exempt on admission.

Chapter III

goods used or consumed at a trade fair or similar event

Article 65

1. Subject to articles 66 to 69, the following shall be exempt on admission:

(a) small representative samples of goods intended for a trade fair or similar event;

(b) goods imported solely in order to be demonstrated or in order to demonstrate machines and apparatus displayed at a trade fair or similar event;

(c) various materials of little value, such as paints, varnishes and wallpaper which are to be used in the building, fitting-out and decoration of temporary stands at a trade fair or similar event, which are destroyed by being used;

(d) printed matter, catalogues, prospectuses, price lists, advertising posters, calendars, whether or not illustrated, unframed photographs and other articles supplied free of charge in order to advertise goods displayed at a trade fair or similar event.

2. For the purposes of paragraph 1, "**trade fair or similar event**" means:

(a) exhibitions, fairs, shows and similar events connected with trade, industry, agriculture or handicrafts;

(b) exhibitions and events held mainly for charitable reasons;

(c) exhibitions and events held mainly for scientific, technical, handicraft, artistic, educational or cultural or sporting reasons, for religious reasons or for reasons of worship, trade union activity or tourism, or in order to promote international understanding;

(d) meetings of representatives of international organizations or collective bodies;

(e) official or commemorative ceremonies and gatherings;

but not exhibitions staged for private purposes in commercial stores or premises to sell goods.

Article 66

The exemption referred to in article 65(1)(a) shall be limited to samples which:

(a) are imported free of charge as such or are obtained at the exhibition from goods imported in bulk;

(b) are exclusively distributed free of charge to the public at the exhibition for use or consumption by the persons to whom they have been offered;

(c) are identifiable as advertising samples of low unitary value;

(d) are not easily marketable and, where appropriate, are packaged in such a way that the quantity of the item involved is lower than the smallest quantity of the same item actually sold on the market;

(e) in the case of foodstuffs and beverages not packaged as mentioned in (d), are consumed on the spot at the exhibition;

(f) in their total value and quantity, are appropriate to the nature of the exhibition, the number of visitors and the extent of the exhibitor's participation.

Article 67

The exemption referred to in article 65(1)(b) shall be limited to goods which are:

(a) consumed or destroyed at the exhibition, and

(b) are appropriate, in their total value and quantity, to the nature of the exhibition, the number of visitors and the extent of the exhibitor's participation.

Article 68

The exemption referred to in article 65(1)(d) shall be limited to printed matter and articles for advertising purposes which:

(a) are intended exclusively to be distributed free of charge to the public at the place where the exhibition is held;

(b) in their total value and quantity, are appropriate to the nature of the exhibition, the number of visitors and the extent of the exhibitor's participation.

Article 69

The exemption referred to in article 65(1)(a) and (b) shall not be granted for

(a) alcoholic products;

(b) tobacco or tobacco products;

(c) fuels, whether solid, liquid or gaseous.

TITLE X
goods imported for examination, analysis or test purposes
Article 70

Subject to articles 71 to 76, goods which are to undergo examination, analysis or tests to determine their composition, quality or other technical characteristics for purposes of information or industrial or commercial research shall be exempt on admission.

Article 71

Without prejudice to article 74, the exemption referred to in article 70 shall be granted only on condition that the goods to be examined, analyzed or tested are completely used up or destroyed in the course of the examination, analysis or testing.

Article 72

No exemption shall be granted in respect of goods used in examination, analysis or tests which in themselves constitute sales promotion operations.

Article 73

Exemption shall be granted only in respect of the quantities of goods which are strictly necessary for the purpose for which they are imported. These quantities shall in each case be determined by the competent authorities, taking into account the said purpose.

Article 74

1. The exemption referred to in article 70 shall cover goods which are not completely used up or destroyed during examination, analysis or testing, provided that the products remaining are, with the agreement and under the supervision of the competent authorities:

   - completely destroyed or rendered commercially valueless on completion of examination, analysis or testing, or
   - surrendered to the state without causing it any expense, where this is possible under national law, or
   - in duly justified circumstances, exported outside the territory of the member state of importation.

2. For the purposes of paragraph 1, **"products remaining"** means products resulting from the examinations, analyses or tests or goods not actually used.

Article 75

Save where article 74(1) is applied, products remaining at the end of the examinations, analyses or tests referred to in article 70 shall be subject to the relevant import value added tax, at the rate applying on the date of completion of the examinations, analyses or tests, on the basis of the type of goods and the value ascertained or accepted on that date by the competent authorities.

However, the interested party may, with the agreement and under the supervision of the competent authorities, convert products remaining to waste or scrap. In this case, the import duties shall be those applying to such waste or scrap at the time of conversion.

Article 76

The period within which the examinations, analyses or tests must be carried out and the administrative formalities to be completed in order to ensure the use of the goods for the purposes intended shall be determined by the competent authorities.

TITLE XI

miscellaneous exemptions

Chapter I

consignments sent to organizations protecting copyrights or industrial and commercial patent rights

Article 77

Trademarks, patterns or designs and their supporting documents, as well as applications for patents for invention or the like, to be submitted to the bodies competent to deal with the protection of copyrights or the protection of industrial or commercial patent rights shall be exempt on admission.

Chapter II

tourist information literature

Article 78

The following shall be exempt on admission:

(a) documentation (leaflets, brochures, books, magazines, guidebooks, posters, whether or not framed, unframed photographs and photographic enlargements, maps, whether or not illustrated, window transparencies, and illustrated calendars) intended to be distributed free of charge and the principal purpose of which is to encourage the public to visit foreign countries, in particular in order to attend cultural, tourist, sporting, religious or trade or professional meetings or events, provided that such literature contains not more than 25% of private commercial advertising and that the general nature of its promotional aims is evident;

(b) foreign hotel lists and yearbooks published by official tourist agencies, or under their auspices, and timetables for foreign transport services, provided that such literature is intended for distribution free of charge and contains not more than 25% of private commercial advertising;

(c) reference material supplied to accredited representatives or correspondents appointed by official national tourist agencies and not intended for distribution, i.e. yearbooks, lists of telephone or telex numbers, hotel lists, fairs catalogues, specimens of craft goods of negligible value, and literature on museums, universities, spas or other similar establishments.

Chapter III

miscellaneous documents and articles

Article 79

The following shall be exempt on admission:

(a) documents sent free of charge to the public services of Member States;

(b) publications of foreign governments and publications of official international bodies intended for distribution without charge;

(c) ballot papers for elections organized by bodies set up in countries other than the Member State of importation;

(d) objects to be submitted as evidence or for like purposes to the courts or other official agencies of the Member States;

(e) specimen signatures and printed circulars concerning signatures sent as part of customary exchanges of information between public services or banking establishments;

(f) official printed matter sent to the central banks of the Member States;

(g) reports, statements, notes, prospectuses, application forms and other documents drawn up by companies with headquarters outside the

Member State of importation and sent to the bearers or subscribers of securities issued by such companies;

(h) recorded media (punched cards, sound recordings, microfilms, etc.) used for the transmission of information sent free of charge to the addressee, in so far as exemption does not give rise to abuses or to major distortions of competition;

(i) files, archives, printed forms and other documents to be used in international meetings, conferences or congresses, and reports on such gatherings;

(j) plans, technical drawings, traced designs, descriptions and other similar documents imported with a view to obtaining or fulfilling orders in a country other than the Member State of importation or to participating in a competition held in that State;

(k) documents to be used in examinations held in the Member State of importation by institutions set up in another country;

(l) printed forms to be used as official documents in the international movement of vehicles or goods, within the framework of international conventions;

(m) printed forms, labels, tickets and similar documents sent by transport undertakings or by undertakings of the hotel industry located in a country other than the Member State of importation to travel agencies set up in that state;

(n) printed forms and tickets, bills of lading, way-bills and other commercial or office documents which have been used;

(o) official printed forms from national or international authorities, and printed matter conforming to international standards sent for distribution by associations of countries other than the Member State of importation to corresponding associations located in that state;

(p) photographs, slides and sterotype mats for photographs, whether or not captioned, sent to press agencies to newspaper or magazine publishers;

(q) articles listed in the Annex to this Directive which are produced by the United Nations or one of its specialized agencies whatever the use for which they are intended;

(r) collectors' pieces and works of art of an educational, scientific or cultural character which are not intended for sale and which are imported by museums, galleries and other institutions approved by the competent authorities of the Member States for the purpose of duty-free admission of these goods. The exemption is granted only on condition that the articles in question are imported free of charge or, if they are imported against payment, that they are not supplied by a taxable person.

[(s) importations of official publications issued under the authority of the country of export, international institutions, regional or local authorities and bodies under public law established in the country of export, and printed matter distributed on the occasion of elections to the European Parliament or on the occasion of national elections in the country in which the printed matter originates by foreign political organizations officially recognized as such in the Member States, insofar as such publications and printed matter have been subject to tax in the country of export and have not benefited from remission of tax on export.][8]

Chapter IV

ancillary materials for the stowage and protection of goods during their transport

Article 80

The various materials such as rope, straw, cloth, paper and cardboard, wood and plastics which are used for the stowage and protection - including heat protection - of goods during their transport to the territory of a Member State, shall be exempt on admission, provided that:

(a) they are not normally re-usable; and

(b) the consideration paid for them forms part of the taxable amount as defined in Article 11 of Directive 77/388/EEC.

Chapter V

litter, fodder and feedingstuffs for animals during their transport

Article 81

Litter, fodder and feedingstuffs of any description put on board the means of transport used to convey animals to the territory of a member state for the purpose of distribution to the said animals during the journey shall be exempt on admission.

Chapter VI

[Fuels and lubricants present in land motor vehicles and special containers][9]

[Article 82

1. Subject to Articles 83, 84 and 85, the following shall be exempt on admission:

(a) fuel contained in the standard tanks of:

— private and commercial motor vehicles and motor cycles;

— special containers;

(b) fuel contained in portable tanks carried by private motor vehicles and motor cycles, up to a maximum of 10 litres per vehicle and without prejudice to national provisions on the holding and transport of fuel.

2. For the purpose of paragraph 1:

(a) 'commercial motor vehicle' means any motorized road vehicle (including tractors with trailers) which, by its type of construction and equipment, is designed for, and capable of, transporting, whether for payment or not:

— more than nine persons including the driver,

— goods,

and any road vehicle for a special purpose other than transport as such;

(b) '**private motor vehicle**' means any motor vehicle not covered by the definition set out in (a);

(c) '**standard tanks**' means:

— the tanks permanently fixed by the manufacturer to all motor vehicles of the same type as the vehicle in question and whose permanent fitting enables fuel to be used directly, both for the purpose of propulsion and, where appropriate, for the operation, during transport, of refrigeration systems and other systems.

Gas tanks fitted to motor vehicles designed for the direct use of gas as a fuel and tanks fitted to ancillary systems with which the vehicle may be equipped shall also be considered to be standard tanks,

— tanks permanently fixed by the manufacturer to all containers of the same type as the container in question and whose permanent fitting enables fuel to be used directly for the operation, during transport, of refrigeration systems and other systems with which special containers are equipped;

(d) '**special container**' means any container fitted with specially designed apparatus for refrigeration systems, oxygenation systems, thermal insulation systems, or other systems.][10]

[Article 83

Member States may limit the application of the exemption for fuel contained in the standard fuel tanks of commercial motor vehicles [and special containers][11]:

(a) when the vehicle comes from a third country, to 200 litres per vehicle and per journey;

(b) when the vehicle comes from another Member State:

— to 200 litres per vehicle and per journey in the case of vehicles designed for, and capable of, the transport, with or without remuneration, of goods,

— to 600 litres per vehicle and per journey in the case of vehicles designed for, and capable of, the transport, with or without remuneration, of more than nine persons, including the driver.

Acting in accordance with the procedures provided for by the Treaty on this point, the Council shall decide, on a proposal from the Commission, before 1 July 1986, on the increase of the quantity of fuel admitted duty-free and contained in the standard fuel tanks of the vehicles referred to in the first indent of (b) of the first subparagraph.'

[(c) to 200 litres per special container and per journey.][12]][13]

Article 84

Member States may limit the amount of fuel exempt on admission in the case of:

[(a) commercial motor vehicles engaged in international transport coming from third countries to their frontier zone, to a maximum depth of 25 kilometres as the crow flies, where such transport consists of journeys made by persons residing in that zone;][14]

(b) private motor vehicles belonging to persons residing in the frontier zone, to a maximum depth of 15 km as the crow flies, contiguous with a third country.

Article 85

Fuel exempt on admission may not be used in a vehicle other than that in which it was imported nor be removed from that vehicle and stored, exept during necessary repairs to that vehicle, or transferred for a consideration or free of charge by the person granted the exemption.

Non-compliance with the preceding paragraph shall give rise to application of the import value added tax relating to the products in question at the rate in force on the date of such non-compliance, on the basis of the type of goods and the value ascertained or accepted on that date by the competent authorities.

Article 86

The exemption referred to in article 82 shall also apply to lubricants carried in motor vehicles and required for their normal operation during the journey in question.

Chapter VII

goods for the construction, upkeep or ornamentation of memorials to, or cemeteries for, war victims

Article 87

Exemption from tax shall be granted in respect of goods imported by organizations authorized for that purpose by the competent authorities, for use in the construction, upkeep or ornamentation of cemeteries and tombs of, and memorials to, war victims of a country other than the Member State of importation who are buried in the latter State.

Chapter VIII

coffins, funerary urns and ornamental funerary articles

Article 88

The following shall be exempt on admission:

(a) coffins containing bodies and urns containing the ashes of deceased persons, as well as the flowers, funeral wreaths and other ornamental objects normally accompanying them;

(b) flowers, wreaths and other ornamental objects brought by persons resident in a member state other than that of importation, attending a funeral or coming to decorate graves in the territory of a member state of importation provided these importations do not reflect, by either their nature or their quantity, any commercial intent.

TITLE XII

general and final provisions

Article 89

Where this directive provides that the granting of an exemption shall be subject to the fulfilment of certain conditions, the person concerned shall, to the satisfaction of the competent authorities, furnish proof that these conditions have been met.

Article 90

1. The exchange value in national currency of the ecu to be taken into consideration for the purposes of this directive shall be fixed once a year. The rates to be applied shall be those obtaining on the first working day in October and shall take effect on 1 January the following year.

2. Member States may round off the amounts in national currency arrived at by converting the amounts in ecu.

3. Member States may continue to apply the amounts of the exemptions in force at the time of the annual adjustment provided for in paragraph 1, if conversion of the amounts of the exemptions expressed in ecu leads, before the rounding-off provided for in paragraph 2, to an alteration of less than 5% in the exemption expressed in national currency [or to a reduction in that exemption][15].

Article 91

No provision of this directive shall prevent Member States from continuing to grant:

(a) the privileges and immunities granted by them under cultural, scientific or technical cooperation agreements concluded between them or with third countries;

(b) the special exemptions justified by the nature of frontier traffic which are granted by them under frontier agreements concluded between them or with countries outside the community.

[(c) exemptions in the context of agreements entered into on the basis of reciprocity with third countries that are Contracting Parties to the Convention on International Civil Aviation (Chicago 1944) for the purpose of implementing Recommended Practices 4.42 and 4.44 in Annex 9 to the Convention (eighth edition, July 1980).][16]

Article 92

Until the establishment of community exemptions upon importation, Member States may retain the exemptions granted to:

(a) merchant-navy seamen;

(b) workers returning to their country after having resided for at least six months outside the importing Member State on account of their occupation.

Article 93

1. Member States shall bring into force the measures necessary to comply with this directive with effect from 1 July 1984.

2. Member States shall inform the Commission of the measures which they adopt to give effect to this Directive, indicating, where the case arises, those measures which they adopt by simple reference to identical provisions of Regulation (EEC) no 918/83.

Article 94

This directive is addressed to the Member States.

Done at Brussels, 28 March 1983.

for the council

The President

J. ERTL

[ANNEX

visual and auditory materials of an educational, scientific or cultural character

CN code	Description
3704 00	Photographic plates, film, paper, paperboard and textiles, exposed but not developed:
ex 3704 00 10	- Plates and film:
	- Cinematograph film, positives, of an educational, scientific or cultural character
ex 3705	Photographic plates and film, exposed and developed, other than cinematograph film:
	- Of an educational, scientific or cultural character
3706	Cinematograph film, exposed and developed, whether or not incorporating sound track or consisting only of sound track:

3706 10	- Of a width of 35 mm or more:
	- - Other:
ex 3706 10 99	- - - Other positives:
	- Newsreels (with or without sound track) depicting events of current news value at the time of importation, and imported up to a limit of two copies of each subject for copying purposes
	- Archival film material (with or without sound track) intended for use in connection with newsreel films
	- Recreational films particularly suited for children and young people
	- Other films of educational, scientific or cultural character
3706 90//	- Other:
	- - Other:
	- - - Other positives:
ex 3706 90 51	- Newsreels (with or without sound track) depicting events of current news value at the time of importation, and imported up to a limit of two copies of each subject for copying purposes
ex 3706 90 91	- Archival film material (with or without sound track) intended for use in connection with newsreel films
ex 3706 90 99	- Recreational films particularly suited for children and young people
	- Other films of educational, scientific or cultural character:
4911	Other printed matter, including printed pictures and photographs:

- Other:

4911 99   - - Other:

ex 4911 99 90   - - - Other:

- Microcards or other information storage media required in computerized information and documentation services of an educational, scientific or cultural character

- Wall charts designed solely for demonstration and education

ex 8524

Records, tapes and other recorded media for sound or other similarly recorded phenomena including matrices and masters for the production of records, but excluding products of Chapter 37:

- Of an educational, scientific or cultural character

ex 9023 00

Instruments, apparatus and models, designed for demonstrational purposes (for example, in education or exhibitions), unsuitable for others uses:

- Patterns, models and wall charts of an educational, scientific or cultural character, designed solely for demonstration and education

- Mock-ups or visualizations of abstract concepts such as molecular structures or mathematical formulae

Various   Holograms for laser projection

Multi-media kits

Materials for programmed instructions, including materials in kit form with the corresponding printed materials][17]

Amendments

1   Substituted by Art 1, Commission Directive of 7 March 1989 (89/219/EEC)
2   Substituted by Art 1(1), Council Directive 88/331/EEC of 13 June 1988.
3   Substituted by Art 1(2), Council Directive 88/331/EEC of 13 June 1988.
4   Substituted by Art 1(3), Council Directive 88/331/EEC of 13 June 1988.
5   Inserted by Art 1(4), Council Directive 88/331/EEC of 13 June 1988.

6　Inserted by Art 1(5), Council Directive 88/331/EEC of 13 June 1988.

7　Art 62-63 substituted by Art 1(6), Council Directive 88/331/EEC of 13 June 1988.

8　Inserted by Art 1(7), Council Directive 88/331/EEC of 13 June 1988.

9　Substituted by Art 1(8), Council Directive 88/331/EEC of 13 June 1988.

10　Substituted by Art 1(9), Council Directive 88/331/EEC of 13 June 1988.

11　Inserted by Art 1(10), Council Directive 88/331/EEC of 13 June 1988.

12　Inserted by Art 1(10), Council Directive 88/331/EEC of 13 June 1988.

13　Art 83 substituted by Art 1, Council Directive 85/346/EEC of 8 July 1985.

14　Substituted by Art 1, Council Directive 85/346/EEC of 8 July 1985.

15　Inserted by Art 1(11), Council Directive 88/331/EEC of 13 June 1988.

16　Inserted by Art 1(12), Council Directive 88/331/EEC of 13 June 1988.

17　Annex replaced by Art 2, Commission Directive 89/219/EEC of 7 March 1989.

COUNCIL DIRECTIVE 83/182/EEC

of 28 March 1983

On tax exemptions within the Community for certain means of transport temporarily imported into one Member State from another

Official Journal L 105 , 23/04/1983 p. 0059 - 0063

Note

This directive ceased to have effect on 31 December 1992, as regards its provisions on VAT, see Art 2(2), Council Directive 91/680/EEC of 16 December 1992.

COUNCIL DIRECTIVE 83/183/EEC

of 28 March 1983

On tax exemptions applicable to permanent imports from a Member State of the personal property of individuals

Official Journal L 105 , 23/04/1983 p. 0064 - 0067

Note

This directive ceased to have effect on 31 December 1992, as regards its provisions on VAT, see Art 2(2), Council Directive 91/680/EEC of 16 December 1992.

TENTH COUNCIL DIRECTIVE 84/386/EEC

of 31 July 1984

On the harmonization of the laws of the Member States relating to turnover taxes, amending Directive 77/388/EEC - Application of value added tax to the hiring out of movable tangible property

Official Journal L 208 , 03/08/1984 p. 0058 - 0058

> This Directive was repealed by Council Directive 2006/112/EC of 28 November 2006 on the common system of value added tax, with effect from 1 January 2007

THE COUNCIL OF THE EUROPEAN COMMUNITIES,

Having regard to the Treaty establishing the European Economic Community, and in particular Articles 99 and 100 thereof,

Having regard to the Sixth Council Directive 77/388/EEC of 17 May 1977 on the harmonization of the laws of the Member States relating to turnover taxes - Common system of value added tax: uniform basis of assessment,

Having regard to the proposal from the Commission,

Having regard to the opinion of the European Parliament,

Having regard to the opinion of the Economic and Social Committee,

Whereas, pursuant to Article 4(2) of the aforementioned Directive, the hiring out of movable tangible property may constitute an economic activity subject to value added tax;

Whereas application of Article 9(1) of the aforementioned Directive to the hiring out of movable tangible property may lead to substantial distortions of competition where the lessor and the lessee are established in different Member States and the rates of taxation in those States differ;

Whereas it is therefore necessary to establish that the place where a service is supplied is the place where the customer has established his business or has a fixed establishment for which the service has been supplied or, in the absence thereof, the place where he has his permanent address or usually resides;

Whereas, however, as regards the hiring out of forms of transport, Article 9(1) should, for reasons of control, be strictly applied, the place where the supplier has established his business being treated as the place of supply of such services,

HAS ADOPTED THIS DIRECTIVE:

Article 1

Directive 77/388/EEC is hereby amended as follows:

1. Article 9(2)(d) is deleted;

2. in Article 9(2)(e) the following indent is added:

   `-   the hiring out of movable tangible property, with the exception of all forms of transport.';

3. in Article 9(3), 'and the hiring out of movable tangible property' is replaced by 'and the hiring out of forms of transport'.

Article 2

1. Member States shall bring into force the measures necessary to comply with this Directive by 1 July 1985.

2. Member States shall inform the Commission of the provisions which they adopt for the purpose of applying this Directive. The Commission shall inform the other Member States thereof.

Article 3

This Directive is addressed to the Member States.

Done at Brussels, 31 July 1984.

For the Council

The President

J. O'KEEFFE

SEVENTEENTH COUNCIL DIRECTIVE 85/362/EEC

of 16 July 1985

On the harmonisation of the laws of the Member States relating to turnover taxes – exemption from value added tax on the temporary importation of goods other than means of transport

Note

This directive ceased to have effect on 31 December 1992 as regards relations between Member States, see preamble, Council Directive 92/111/EEC of 14 December 1992.

THIRTEENTH COUNCIL DIRECTIVE 86/560/EEC

of 17 November 1986

On the harmonization of the laws of the Member States relating to turnover taxes - arrangements for the refund of value added tax to taxable persons not established in Community territory

Official Journal L 326 , 21/11/1986 p. 0040 - 0041

THE COUNCIL OF THE EUROPEAN COMMUNITIES,

Having regard to the Treaty establishing the European Economic Community, and in particular Articles 99 and 100 thereof,

Having regard to the Sixth Council Directive 77/388/EEC of 17 May 1977 on the harmonization of the laws of the Member States relating to turnover taxes - Common system of value added tax: uniform basis of assessment, and in particular Article 17(4) thereof,

Having regard to the proposal from the Commission,

Having regard to the opinion of the European Parliament,

Having regard to the opinion of the Economic and Social Committee,

Whereas Article 8 of Directive 79/1072/EEC on the arrangements for the refund of value added tax to taxable persons not established in the territory of the country provides that in the case of taxable persons not established in the territory of the Community, Member States may refuse refunds or impose special conditions;

Whereas there is a need to ensure the harmonious development of trade relations between the Community and third countries based on the provisions of Directive 79/1072/EEC, while taking account of the varying situations encountered in third countries;

Whereas certain forms of tax evasion or avoidance should be prevented,

HAS ADOPTED THIS DIRECTIVE:

Article 1

For the purposes of this Directive:

1. **'a taxable person not established in the territory of the Community'** shall mean a taxable person as referred to in Article 4(1) of Directive 77/388/ EEC who, during the period referred to in Article 3(1) of this Directive, has had in that territory neither his business nor a fixed establishment from which business transactions are effected, nor, if no such business or fixed establishment exists, his permanent address or usual place of residence, and who, during the same period, has supplied no goods or services deemed to have been supplied in the Member State referred to in Article 2, with the exception of:

   (a) transport services and services ancillary thereto, exempted pursuant to Article 14(1)(i), Article 15 or Article 16(1), B, C and D of Directive 77/388/EEC;

(b) services provided in cases where tax is payable solely by the person to whom they are supplied, pursuant to Article 21(1)(b) of Directive 77/388/EEC;

2. **'Territory of the Community'** shall mean the territories of the Member States in which Directive 77/388/EEC is applicable.

Article 2

1. Without prejudice to Articles 3 and 4, each Member State shall refund to any taxable person not established in the territory of the Community, subject to the conditions set out below, any value added tax charged in respect of services rendered or moveable property supplied to him in the territory or the country by other taxable persons or charged in respect of the importation of goods into the country, in so far as such goods and services are used for the purposes of the transactions referred to in Article 17(3)(a) and (b) of Directive 77/388/EEC or of the provision of services referred to in point 1 (b) of Article 1 of this Directive.

2. Member States may make the refunds referred to in paragraph 1 conditional upon the granting by third States of comparable advantages regarding turnover taxes.

3. Member States may require the appointment of a tax representative.

Article 3

1. The refunds referred to in Article 2(1) shall be granted upon application by the taxable person. Member States shall determine the arrangements for submitting applications, including the time limits for doing so, the period which applications should cover, the authority competent to receive them and the minimum amounts in respect of which applications may be submitted. They shall also determine the arrangements for making refunds, including the time limits for doing so. They shall impose on the applicant such obligations as are necessary to determine whether the application is justified and to prevent fraud, in particular the obligation to provide proof that he is engaged in an economic activity in accordance with Article 4(1) of Directive 77/388/EEC. The applicant must certify, in a written declaration, that, during the period prescribed, he has not carried out any transaction which does not fulfil the conditions laid down in point 1 of Article 1 of this Directive.

2. Refunds may not be granted under conditions more favourable than those applied to Community taxable persons.

Article 4

1. For the purposes of this Directive, eligibility for refunds shall be determined in accordance with Article 17 of Directive 77/388/EEC as applied in the Member State where the refund is paid.

2. Member States may, however, provide for the exclusion of certain expenditure or make refunds subject to additional conditions.

3. This Directive shall not apply to supplies of goods which are or or may be exempted under point 2 of Article 15 of Directive 77/388/EEC.

Article 5

1. Member States shall bring into force the laws, regulations and administrative provisions necessary to comply with this Directive by 1 January 1988 at the latest. This Directive shall apply only to applictions for refunds concerning value added tax charged on purchases of goods or services invoiced or on imports effected on or after that date.

2. Member States shall communicate to the Commission the main provisions of national law which they adopt in the field covered by this Directive and shall inform the Commission of the use they make of the option afforded by Article 2(2). The Commission shall inform the other Member States thereof.

Article 6

Within three years of the date referred to in Article 5, the Commission shall, after consulting the Member States, submit a report to the Council and to the European Parliament on the application of this Directive, particularly as regards the application of Article 2(2).

Article 7

As from the date on which this Directive is implemented, and at all events by the date mentioned in Article 5, the last sentence of Article 17(4) of Directive 77/388/EEC and Article 8 of Directive 79/1072/EEC shall cease to have effect in each Member State.

Article 8

This Directive is addressed to the Member States.

Done at Brussels, 17 November 1986.

For the Council

The President

N. LAWSON

EIGHTEENTH COUNCIL DIRECTIVE 89/465/EEC

of 18 July 1989

On the harmonization of the laws of the Member States relating to turnover taxes - abolition of certain derogations provided for in Article 28(3) of the Sixth Directive, 77/388/EEC

Official Journal L 226 , 03/08/1989 p. 0021 - 0022

> This Directive was repealed by Council Directive 2006/112/EC of 28 November 2006 on the common system of value added tax, with effect from 1 January 2007

THE COUNCIL OF THE EUROPEAN COMMUNITIES,

Having regard to the Treaty establishing the European Economic Community, and in particular Article 99 thereof,

Having regard to the proposal from the Commission,

Having regard to the opinion of the European Parliament,

Having regard to the opinion of the Economic and Social Committee,

Whereas Article 28(3) of the Sixth Council Directive, 77/388/EEC, of 17 May 1977 on the harmonization of the laws of the Member States relating to turnover taxes - Common system of value added tax: uniform basis of assessment, as last amended by the Act of Accession of Spain and Portugal, allows Member States to apply measures derogating from the normal rules of the common system of value added tax during a transitional period; whereas that period was originally fixed at five years; whereas the Council undertook to act, on a proposal from the Commission, before the expiry of that period, on the abolition, where appropriate, of some or all of those derogations;

Whereas many of those derogations give rise, under the Communities' own resources system, to difficulties in calculating the compensation provided for in Council Regulation (EEC, Euratom) No 1553/89 of 29 May 1989 on the definitive uniform arrangements for the collection of own resources accruing from value added tax; whereas, in order to ensure that that system operates more efficiently, there are grounds for abolishing those derogations;

Whereas the abolition of those derogations will also contribute to greater neutrality of the value added tax system at Community level;

Whereas some of the said derogations should be abolished respectively from 1 January 1990, 1 January 1991, 1 January 1992 and 1 January 1993;

Whereas, having regard to the provisions of the Act of Accession, the Portuguese Republic may, until 1 January 1994 at the latest, postpone the abolition of the exemption of the transactions referred to in points 3 and 9 in Annex F to Directive 77/338/EEC;

Whereas it is appropriate that, before 1 January 1991, the Council should, on the basis of a Commission report, review the situation with regard to the other derogations provided for in Article 28(3) of Directive 77/388/EEC, including the one referred to in the second subparagraph of point 1 of Article 1 of this Directive, and that it should take a decision, on a proposal from the Commission, on the abolition of these derogations, bearing in mind any distortion of competition which has resulted from their application or which may arise in connection with the future completion of the internal market,

HAS ADOPTED THIS DIRECTIVE:

Article 1

Directive 77/388/EEC is hereby amended as follows:

1. With effect from 1 January 1990 the transactions referred to in points 1, 3 to 6, 8, 9, 10, 12, 13 and 14 of Annex E shall be abolished.

   Those Member States which, on 1 January 1989, subjected to value added tax the transactions listed in Annex E, points 4 and 5, are authorized to apply the conditions of Article 13A (2) (a), final indent, also to services rendered and goods delivered, as referred to in Article 13A (1) (m) and (n), where such activities are carried out by bodies governed by public law.

2. In Annex F:

   (a) The transactions referred to in points 3, 14 and 18 to 22 shall be abolished with effect from 1 January 1990;

   (b) The transactions referred to in points 4, 13, 15 and 24 shall be abolished with effect from 1 January 1991;

   (c) The transaction referred to in point 9 shall be abolished with effect from 1 January 1992;

   (d) The transaction referred to in point 11 shall be abolished with effect from 1 January 1993.

Article 2

The Portuguese Republic may defer until 1 January 1994 at the latest the dates referred to in Article 1, point 2(a), for the deletion of point 3 from Annex F and in Article 1, point 2(c), for the deletion of point 9 from Annex F.

Article 3

By 1 January 1991 the Council, on the basis of a report from the Commission, shall review the situation with regard to the other derogations laid down in Article 28(3) of Directive 77/388/EEC, including that referred to in the second subparagraph of point 1 of Article 1 of this Directive and, acting on a Commission proposal, shall decide whether these derogations should be abolished, having regard to any distortions of competition which have resulted from their having been applied or which might arise from measures to complete the Internal Market.

Article 4

In respect of the transactions referred to in Article 1, 2 and 3, Member States may take measures concerning deduction of value added tax in order totally or partially to prevent the taxable persons concerned from deriving unwarranted advantages or sustaining unwarranted disadvantages.

Article 5

1. Member States shall take the necessary measures to comply with this Directive not later than the dates laid down in Article 1 and 2.

2. Member States shall inform the Commission of the main provisions of national law which they adopt in the field governed by this Directive.

Article 6

This Directive is addressed to the Member States.

Done at Brussels, 18 July 1989.

For the Council

The President

R. DUMAS

COUNCIL REGULATION 91/3330/EEC

of 7 November 1991

On the statistics relating to the trading of goods between Member States
Official Journal L 316 , 16/11/1991 p. 0001 - 0010

> Repealed by Regulation (EC) No 638/2004 of the European Parliament and of the Council of
> 31 March 2004 on Community statistics relating to the trading of goods between Member
> States and repealing Council Regulation (EEC) No 3330/91, w.e.f. 1 January 2005

THE COUNCIL OF THE EUROPEAN COMMUNITIES,

Having regard to the Treaty establishing the European Economic Community, and in particular Article 100a thereof,

Having regard to the proposal from the Commission,

In cooperation with the European Parliament,

Having regard to the opinion of the Economic and Social Committee,

Whereas abolishing physical barriers between Member States is necessary to complete the internal market; whereas a satisfactory level of information on the trading of goods between Member States should thus be ensured by means other than those involving checks, even indirect ones, at internal frontiers;

Whereas an analysis of the situation of the Community and the Member States after 1992 reveals that a number of specific requirements will persist as regards information on the trading of goods between Member States;

Whereas these requirements are not of a macro-economic nature, unlike those relating, for example, to national accounts or the balance of payments, and many of them cannot be met by means of highly aggregated data alone; whereas matters such as trade policy, sectoral analyses, competition rules, the management and guidance of agriculture and fisheries, regional development, energy projections and the organization of transport must on the contrary be based on statistical documentation providing the most up-to-date, accurate and detailed view of the internal market;

Whereas it is precisely information on the trading of goods between Member States which will contribute to measuring the progress of the internal market, thereby speeding up its completion and consolidating it on a sound basis; whereas this kind of information could prove to be one of the means of assessing the development of economic and social cohesion;

Whereas until the end of 1992 statistics relating to the trading of goods between Member States will benefit from the formalities, documentation and controls which the customs authorities, for their own requirements or for those of other departments, prescribe for consignors and consignees of goods in circulation between Member States, but which will disappear through the elimination of physical frontiers and tax barriers;

Whereas it will consequently be necessary to collect directly from the consignors and consignees the data necessary to compile statistics relating to the trading of goods between Member States, using methods and techniques which will ensure that they are exhaustive, reliable and up to date, without giving rise for the parties concerned, in particular for small and medium-sized businesses, to a burden out of proportion to the results which users of the said statistics can reasonably expect;

Whereas the relevant legislation must henceforth apply to all statistics relating to the trading of goods between Member States, including those statistics which are not to be harmonized or made compulsory by the Community before 1993;

Whereas the statistics relating to the trading of goods between Member States are a function of the movements of goods involved; whereas they may include data on transport, which can be collected simultaneously with the data specific to each of these categories of statistics, thus lightening the overall statistical burden;

Whereas private individuals will derive obvious advantages from the internal market; whereas it is necessary to ensure that these advantages are not diminished in their eyes by requirements for statistical information; whereas the provision of such information would undoubtedly impose an obligation which private individuals would consider inconvenient at the very least and which would be impossible to check on without employing excessive measures; whereas it is therefore reasonable not to regard private individuals as responsible for providing such information, apart from suitable periodic surveys;

Whereas the new collection system to be introduced is to apply to all statistics relating to the trading of goods between Member States; whereas it must therefore be defined first in a general context involving new concepts, particularly as regards the scope, the party responsible for providing the information and the transmission of data;

Whereas the actual concept of the system resides in the use of related administrative networks, and in particular that of the value added tax (VAT) authorities, to provide the statistical services with a minimum degree of indirect verification without thereby increasing the burden on taxpayers; whereas it is nonetheless necessary to avoid confusion arising in the minds of the parties responsible for providing information between their statistical and their tax obligations;

Whereas it is vital to use existing sources to compile basic documentation in each Member State regarding consignors and consignees of goods which are covered by statistics of trade between Member States, so as to identify, in preparation for 1992, the main parties concerned and to develop modern data transmission techniques with their assistance;

Whereas implementation alone will reveal loopholes or weaknesses in the new collection system; whereas improvements and simplifications should be introduced within a reasonable period of time in order to prevent defects from having negative repercussions on the trading of goods between Member States;

Whereas, among the statistics relating to the trading of goods between Member States, statistics of trade between Member States must receive priority, for obvious reasons of importance and continuity; whereas, however, substantial adjustments must be made to these statistics in order to take account of the new conditions on the internal market after 1992;

Whereas it will be necessary to review, inter alia, the definition of their content, the goods classification applicable to them and the list of data to be collected to compile them; whereas it is desirable to adopt forthwith the principle on which the statistical thresholds will operate in order to avoid small and medium-sized businesses incurring expenditure which is disproportionate to overheads;

Whereas the Commission should be assisted by a committee to ensure the regular cooperation of the Member States, in particular to resolve the problems which are bound to arise in connection with information on the trading of goods between Member States following the numerous innovations introduced by the new collection system;

Whereas relevant Community legislation should be supplemented systematically by provisions adopted either by the Council or by the Commission;

Whereas some of the provisions of this Regulation must enter into force without delay so that the Community and its Member States can prepare for the practical consequences which it will entail as from 1 January 1993;

Whereas one of these consequences is that Council Regulation (EEC) No 2954/85 of 22 October 1985 laying down certain measures for the standardization and simplification of the statistics of trade between Member States must be repealed and that Council Regulation (EEC) No 1736/75 of 24 June 1975 on the external trade statistics of the Community and statistics of trade between Member States, as last amended by Regulation (EEC) No 1629/88, will no longer be applicable to statistics relating to the trading of goods between Member States,

HAS ADOPTED THIS REGULATION:

Article 1

The Community and its Member States shall compile statistics relating to the trading of goods between Member States, in accordance with the rules laid down by this Regulation, during the transitional period which shall begin on 1 January 1993 and end on the date of changeover to a unified system of taxation in the Member State of origin.

CHAPTER I

General provisions

Article 2

For the purposes of this Regulation and without prejudice to any individual provisions:

    (a)   '**trading of goods between Member States**' means any movement of goods from one Member State to another;

    (b)   '**goods**' means all movable property, including electric current;

(c)   '**Community goods**' means goods:

-       entirely obtained in the customs territory of the Community, without the addition of goods from non-member countries or territories which are not part of the customs territory of the Community,

-       from countries or territories not forming part of the customs territory of the Community which have been released for free circulation in a Member State,

-       obtained in the customs territory of the Community either from the goods referred to exclusively in the second indent or from the goods referred to in the first and second indents;

(d)   '**non-Community goods**' means goods other than those referred to in (c). Without prejudice to agreements concluded with non-member countries for the implementation of the Community transit arrangements, goods which, while fulfilling the conditions laid down in (c), are reintroduced into the customs territory of the Community after export therefrom are also considered as non-Community goods;

(e)   '**Member State**', when the term is used in the geographical sense, means its statistical territory;

(f)   '**statistical territory of a Member State**' means the territory occupied by that Member State within the statistical territory of the Community, as this latter is defined in Article 3 of Regulation (EEC) No 1736/75;

(g)   '**goods in free movement on the internal market of the Community**' means goods authorized, pursuant to Directive 77/388/EEC, to move from one Member State to another without prior formalities or formalities linked to the crossing of internal frontiers;

(h)   '**private individual**' means any natural person not liable to account for VAT in connection with a given movement of goods.

Article 3

1.   All goods which move from one Member State to another shall be the subject of statistics relating to the trading of goods between Member States.

In addition to the goods which move within the statistical territory of the Community, goods shall be considered as moving from one Member State to another if, in so doing, they cross the external frontier of the Community, whether of not they subsequently enter the territory of a non-member State.

2.   Paragraph 1 shall apply both to non-Community and Community goods, whether or not they are the subject of a commercial transaction.

Article 4

1.   Of the goods referred to in Article 3:

   (a)   transit statistics shall be compiled on those which are transported, with or without transhipment, across a Member State without being stored there for reasons not inherent in their transport;

   (b)   storage statistics shall be compiled on those referred to in Article 2(2) of Regulation (EEC) No 1736/75, as well as those which enter or leave storage facilities determined by the Commission in accordance with Article 30 of this Regulation;

   (c)   statistics of trade between Member States shall be compiled on those which do not meet the conditions of (a) and (b) or which, while meeting either of those conditions, are expressly designated by this Regulation or by the Commission pursuant to Article 30;

   (d)   the Council, on a proposal from the Commission, shall determine the goods that are to be the subject of other statistics relating to the trading of goods between Member States.

2.   Without prejudice to Community provisions on statistical returns in respect of carriage of goods, the data on the movement of goods subject to the statistics referred to in paragraph 1 shall be included, as necessary, in the list of data relating to each of these categories of statistics on the conditions and terms laid down by this Regulation or by the Commission pursuant to Article 30.

Article 5

Without prejudice to Article 15, private individuals shall be exempt from the obligations implied by the preparation of the statistics referred to in Article 4.

This exemption shall also apply to the party responsible for providing information who, being liable to account for VAT, qualifies, in the Member State in which he is responsible for providing information, for one of the special schemes provided for by Articles 24 and 25 of Directive 77/388/EEC. This provision shall be extended, mutatis mutandis, to [legal persons not liable to account for VAT][1] and to [parties liable to account who carry out only transactions not entitling them to any deductions of VAT][2], who, [pursuant to Council Directive 91/680/EEC][3], are not required to submit a tax declaration.

CHAPTER II

Statistical collection system: Intrastat

Article 6

With a view to compiling the statistics relating to the trading of goods between Member States, a statistical collection system shall be set up, hereinafter referred to as the 'Intrastat system'.

Article 7

1. The Intrastat system shall be applied in the Member States whenever they are deemed to be partner countries in the trading of goods between Member States by virtue of paragraph 4.

2. The Intrastat system shall be applied to the goods referred to in Article 3:

    (a)   which are in free movement on the internal market of the Community;

    (b)   which, since they may move on the internal market of the Community only after completion of the formalities prescribed by Community legislation on the circulation of goods, are expressly designated either by this Regulation or by the Commission pursuant to Article 30.

3. The collection of data on the goods referred to in Article 3 to which the Intrastat system does not apply shall be regulated by the Commission pursuant to Article 30 within the framework of the formalities referred to in paragraph 2(b).

4. The Intrastat system shall apply:

    (a)   to statistics of trade between Member States, pursuant to Article 17 to 28;

    (b)   to transit and storage statistics, in accordance with provisions laid down by the Council on a proposal from the Commission pursuant to Article 31.

5. Saving a decision to the contrary by the Council on a proposal from the Commission, in particular pursuant to Article 31, national provisions on the statistics referred to in paragraph 4 of this Article, in so far as they relate to data collection, shall cease to apply after 31 December 1992.

Article 8

Without prejudice to Article 5, the obligation to supply the information required by the Intrastat system shall be incumbent on any natural or legal person who is involved in the trading of goods between Member States.

Among those incurring this obligation, the party responsible for providing information for each category of statistics covered by the Intrastat system shall be designated by the relevant specific provisions.

Article 9

1. The party responsible for providing the information required by the Intrastat system may transfer the task of providing the information to a third party residing in a Member State, but such transfer shall in no way reduce the responsibility of the said party.

    The party responsible for providing information shall provide such third party with all the information necessary to fulfil his obligations as party responsible.

2.   The party responsible for providing information may be required, at the express request of the departments responsible for compiling statistics on the trading of goods between Member States, to notify them that for a given reference period,

-      all the information which is to be the subject of the periodic declaration referred to in Article 13(1) has been provided either by himself or by a third party,

-      he has transferred the task of providing the information required by the Intrastat system to that third party, whom he shall identify.

3.   Paragraph 1 shall not apply:

(a)   in cases where Article 28(4) applies;

(b)   in Member States where the periodic declaration referred to in Article 13 (1) is not distinct from the periodic declaration required for tax purposes and inasmuch as the tax rules in force relating to declaration obligations prevent the transfer referred to in the abovementioned paragraph 1.

4.   The implementing rules for paragraphs 1, 2 and 3 shall be laid down by the Commission in accordance with Article 30.

Article 10

1.   Member States shall take the measures necessary to ensure that those of their departments which are responsible for compiling statistics relating to the trading of goods between Member States have a register of intra-Community operators at their disposal by 1 January 1993.

2.   For the purposes of applying paragraph 1, a list shall be established of upon dispatch the consignors, upon arrival the consignees and where necessary the declarants, within the meaning of Commission Regulation (EEC) No 2792/86, who are involved from 1 January 1991 to 31 December 1992 in trade between Member States.

3.   Paragraph 2 shall not apply in those Member States which take the measures necessary to ensure that their tax authorities have at their disposal, by 1 January 1993 at the latest, a register:

(a)   listing the parties liable to account for VAT who, during the 12 months prior to that date, took part in the trading of goods between Member States, as consignors upon dispatch and as consignees upon arrival;

(b)   intended to list [legal persons not liable to account for VAT][1] and [parties liable to account who carry out only transactions not entitling them to any deductions of VAT][2] who, from that date, carry out their acquisitions, [within the meaning of Council Directive 91/680/EEC][4], in compliance with Article 28(7) of that Directive.

In those Member States, the abovementioned tax authorities shall, in addition to the identification number referred to in paragraph 6, supply the statistical departments referred to in paragraph 1 with the information included in that register which is used to identify those intra-Community operators, under the conditions required for application of this Regulation.

4.   The list of minimum data to be recorded in the register of intra-Community operators in addition to the identification number referred to in paragraph 6 shall be laid down by the Commission pursuant to Article 30.

5.   From 1 January 1993, the register of intra-Community operators shall be managed and updated in the Member States by the relevant departments on the basis of the declarations referred to in Article 13(1) or the lists referred to in Article 11(1), or other administrative sources.

      Where required, the Commission shall draw up, in accordance with Article 30, the other rules relating to the management and updating of the register of intra-Community operators to be applied in the Member States by the relevant departments.

6.   Apart from exceptions which they shall justify to the parties responsible for providing statistical information, the relevant statistical departments shall use in their relations with those parties, and in particular with a view to application of Article 13(1), the identification number allocated to those parties by the tax authorities responsible.

Article 11

1.   The tax authorities responsible in each Member State shall, at least once every three months, furnish the departments in that Member State responsible for compiling statistics relating to the trading of goods between Member States with the lists of those liable to account for VAT who have declared that, during the period in question, they have made acquisitions in other Member States or deliveries to other Member States.

2.   The lists referred to in paragraph 1 shall also include:

      (a)   parties liable to account for VAT who have declared that, during the period in question, they have conducted trading of goods between Member States which, although not resulting from acquisitions or deliveries, must be the subject of a periodic tax declaration;

      (b)   [legal persons not liable to account for VAT][1] and [parties liable to account who carry out only transactions not entitling them to any deduction of VAT][2] who have declared that, during the same period, they have conducted trading of goods between Member States which must be the subject of a periodic tax declaration.

3. The lists shall indicate, for each operator on them, the value of trading of goods between Member States which the operator has mentioned in his periodic tax declaration in accordance with [Directive 91/680/EEC][5].

4. Under restrictive conditions, which the Commission shall determine pursuant to Article 30, each Member State's competent tax authorities shall in addition furnish the departments in that Member State responsible for compiling statistics relating to the trading of goods between Member States, on their own initiative or at the request of the latter, with any information capable of improving the quality of statistics which those liable to account for VAT normally submit to the competent tax authorities to comply with tax requirements.

   The information communicated to them in accordance with the first subparagraph shall be treated by the statistical departments, vis-à-vis third parties, in accordance with the rules applied to it by the tax authorities.

5. Whatever the administrative structure of the Member State, the party responsible for providing statistical information may not be compelled to justify, other than within the limits laid down by paragraph 1, 2 and 3 and by the provisions provided for in paragraph 4, the information he supplies in comparison with the data he communicates to the competent tax authorities.

6. In their relations with persons liable to account for VAT regarding the periodic declaration which such persons must forward to it for tax purposes, the competent tax authorities shall draw attention to the obligations which they may incur as parties responsible for providing the information required by the Intrastat system.

7. For the purpose of applying paragraphs 4 and 6, 'parties liable to account for VAT' shall also mean [legal persons not liable to account for VAT][1] and [parties liable to account who carry out only transactions not entitling them to any deductions of VAT][2] who carry out acquisitions within the meaning of [Directive 91/680/EEC][5].

8. Administrative assistance between national departments of different Member States responsible for compiling statistics relating to the trading of goods between Member States shall, as necessary, be regulated by the Commission pursuant to Article 30.

Article 12

1. The statistical information media required by the Intrastat system shall be set up by the Commission pursuant to Article 30 in respect of each category of statistics relating to the trading of goods between Member States.

2. In order to take account of their particular administrative arrangements, Member States may set up media other than those referred to in paragraph 1, provided that those responsible for providing information may choose which of these media they will use.

Member States exercising this option shall inform the Commission accordingly.

3. Paragraphs 1 and 2 shall not apply:

(a) in cases where Article 28(4) applies:

(b) in Member States where the periodic declaration referred to in Article 13(1) is not distinct from the periodic declaration required for tax purposes and inasmuch as the tax rules in force relating to declaration obligations prevent such application.

Article 13

1. The statistical information required by the Intrastat system shall be covered in periodic declarations to be sent by the party responsible for providing the information to the competent national departments, by deadlines and under conditions which the Commission shall lay down pursuant to Article 30.

2. The Commission shall determine, pursuant to Article 30:

– where not laid down by this Regulation, the reference period applicable to each category of statistics relating to the trading of goods between Member States,

– the procedures for the transmission of the information, especially with a view to making available to the parties responsible for providing information networks of regional data collection offices.

3. The periodic declarations referred to in paragraph 1 or, in any case, the information which they contain shall be retained by the Member States for at least two years following the end of the calendar year of the reference period to which those declarations relate.

Article 14

Failure by any party responsible for providing statistical information to fulfil his obligations under this Regulation shall be liable to the penalties which the Member States shall lay down in accordance with their national provisions.

Article 15

Pursuant to Article 30, periodic surveys may be organized on the trading of goods between Member States by private individuals and on movements of goods or on intra-Community operators excluded from the returns benefitting from simplification measures under specific provisions relating to the various statistics on the trading of goods.

Article 16

The Commission shall report to the European Parliament and the Council in good time on the operation of the Intrastat system for each category of statistics relating to the trading of goods between Member States covered by the Intrastat system, with a view to possible adaptation of the system at the end of the transitional period referred to in Article 1.

CHAPTER III

Statistics on trade between Member States

Article 17

Statistics on trade between Member States shall cover, on the one hand, movements of goods leaving the Member State of dispatch and, on the other, movements of goods entering the Member State of arrival.

Article 18

1. The Member State of dispatch shall be the Member State in which the goods leaving it are the subject of a dispatch.

    '**Dispatch**' shall mean the shipment of goods referred to in paragraph 2 to a destination in another Member State.

2. In a given Member State the following may be the subject of a dispatch:

    (a)   Community goods which, in that Member State:

    -      are not in direct or interrupted transit,

    -      are in direct or interrupted transit, but, having entered that Member State as non-Community goods, have subsequently been released for free circulation there;

    (b)   non-Community goods placed, maintained or obtained in that Member State under inward processing customs arrangements or under arrangements for processing under customs control.

Article 19

The Member State of arrival shall be the Member State in which the goods entering it:

(a)   as Community goods:

-      are not in direct or interrupted transit in that Member State,

-      are in direct or interrupted transit in that Member State but leave it following formalities for export from the statistical territory of the Community;

(b)   as non-Community goods referred to in Article 18(2)(b), are:

(1)   released for free circulation;

(2)   maintained under inward processing customs arrangements or under arrangements for processing under customs control or again made subject to such arrangements.

Article 20

With a view to collecting the data required for the statistics of trade between Member States, the provisions of Chapter II shall be supplemented as follows:

(1)   without prejudice to Article 34, the Intrastat system shall apply to the goods referred to in Articles 18(2)(a) and 19(a);

(2)   the partner countries in trading of goods between Member States within the meaning of Article 7(1) shall be the Member State of dispatch and the Member State of arrival;

(3)   within the Intrastat system, the Member State of dispatch shall be defined as that in which the goods which are dispatched from there to another Member State come under the terms of Article 18(2)(a) [...]⁶;

(4)   within the Intrastat system, the Member State of arrival shall be defined as that in which the goods which enter from another Member State come under the terms of Article 19(a) [...]⁶;

(5)   the party responsible for providing the information referred to in Article 8 shall be the natural or legal person who:

    (a)   [registered for value added tax]⁷ in the Member State of dispatch:

-    has concluded the contract, with the exception of transport contracts, giving rise to the dispatch of goods or, failing this,

-    dispatches or provides for the dispatch of the goods or, failing this,

-    is in possession of the goods which are the subject of the dispatch;

    (b)   [registered for value added tax]⁷ in the Member State of arrival:

-    has concluded the contract, with the expection (*sic*) of transport contracts, giving rise to the delivery of goods or, failing this,

-    takes possession or provides for possession to be taken of the goods or, failing this,

-    is in possession of the goods which are the subject of the delivery;

(6)   the Commission shall adopt the provisions provided for in Article 7(3) in due course;

[(7)   the reference period referred to in the first indent of Article 13(2) shall be:

-    for goods to which the Intrastat system applies, the calendar month during which the value-added tax becomes due on intra-Community deliveries or acquisitions of goods, the movements of which are to be recorded pursuant to this Article; when the period to which the periodic fiscal declaration of a party liable to account for VAT refers does not correspond with a calendar month, quarter, half-year or year, the Member States may adapt the periodicity of the obligations relating to the statistical declarations of that party to the periodicity of his obligations relating to fiscal declarations,

-   for goods to which the Intrastat system does not apply, according to the circumstances:

-   the calendar month during which the goods are either placed or maintained under the inward processing customs procedure (suspension system) or the procedure of processing under customs control or placed in free circulation as a result of one of these procedures,

-   the calendar month during which the goods, circulating between parts of the statistical territory of the Community, at least one of which is not part of the territory of the Community pursuant to Council Directive 77/388/EEC, have been subject to dispatch or arrival procedures.][8]

Article 21

On the statistical data medium to be transmitted to the competent departments:

-   without prejudice to Article 34, goods shall be designated in such a way as to permit easy and precise classification in the finest relevant subdivision of the version of the combined nomenclature in force at the time;

-   the eight-digit code number of the corresponding subdivision of the combined nomenclature shall also be given for each type of goods.

Article 22

1. On the statistical data medium, the Member States shall be described by the alphabetical or numerical codes which the Commission shall determine pursuant to Article 30.

2. Without prejudice to the provisions adopted by the Commission pursuant to Article 30, the parties responsible for providing information shall comply, for the purposes of paragraph 1, with the instructions issued by the competent national departments regarding the compiling of statistics on trade between Member States.

Article 23

1. For each type of goods, the statistical data medium to be transmitted to the competent departments must provide the following data:

    (a)   in the Member State of arrival, the Member State of consignment of the goods, within the meaning of Article 24(1);

    (b)   in the Member State of dispatch, the Member State of destination of the goods, within the meaning of Article 24(2);

    (c)   the quantity of goods, in net mass and supplementary units;

    (d)   the value of the goods;

    (e)   the nature of the transaction;

    (f)   the delivery terms;

    (g)   the presumed mode of transport.

2. Member States may not prescribe that data other than those listed in paragraph 1 be provided on the statistical data medium, except for the following:

    (a)   in the Member State of arrival, the country of origin; however, this item may be required only as allowed by Community law;

    (b)   in the Member State of dispatch, the region of origin; in the Member State of arrival, the region of destination;

    (c)   in the Member State of dispatch, the port or airport of loading; in the Member State of arrival, the port or airport of unloading;

    (d)   in the Member State of dispatch and in the Member State of arrival, the presumed port or airport of transhipment situated in another Member State provided the latter prepares transit statistics;

    (e)   where appropriate, statistical procedure.

3. Insofar as not laid down in this Regulation, the data referred to in paragraphs 1 and 2 and the rules governing their inclusion on the statistical data medium shall be defined by the Commission pursuant to Article 30.

Article 24

1. When, before reaching the Member State of arrival, goods have entered one or more countries in transit and have been subject in those countries to halts or legal operations not inherent in their transport, the Member State of consignment shall be taken to be the last Member State where such halts or legal operations occurred. In other cases, the Member State of consignment shall be the same as the Member State of dispatch.

2.   'Member State of destination' means the last country to which it is
        known, at the time of dispatch, that the goods are to be dispatched.

3.   Notwithstanding Article 23(1)(a), the party responsible for providing
        information in the Member State of arrival may, in the following order:

        -       if he does not know the Member State of consignment, state the
                Member State of dispatch;

        -       if he does not know the Member State of dispatch, state the
                Member State of purchase, within the meaning of paragraph 4.

4.   'The Member State of purchase' means the Member State of residence of
        the contracting partner of the natural or legal person who has concluded
        the contract, with the exception of transport contracts, giving rise to the
        delivery of goods in the Member State of arrival.

Article 25

1.   The Community and the Member States shall compile statistics on trade
        between Member States from the data referred to in Article 23(1).

2.   Member States which do not compile statistics on trade between
        Member States from the data referred to in Article 23(2) shall refrain
        from ordering the collection of such data.

3.   The Community and the Member States shall compile statistics on
        trade between Member States, having regard to such provisions as the
        Commission may adopt pursuant to Article 30 on general and specific
        exemptions and the statistical thresholds.

4.   Any provision which has the effect of excluding goods referred to in
        Articles 18 and 19 from the compilation of the statistics of trade between
        Member States shall suspend the obligation to supply statistical
        information on the goods thus excluded.

Article 26

1.   Member States shall transmit to the Commission their monthly statistics
        on trade between Member States. These statistics shall cover the data
        referred to in Article 23(1).

2.   Where necessary, the procedure for such transmission shall be laid down
        by the Commission pursuant to Article 30.

3.   Data declared confidential by the Member States under the conditions
        referred to in Article 32 shall be transmitted by them in accordance with
        Council Regulation (Euratom, EEC) No 1588/90 of 11 June 1990 on the
        transmission of data subject to statistical confidentiality to the Statistical
        Office of the European Communities.

Article 27

Provisions regarding the simplification of statistical information shall be
adopted by the Council on a proposal from the Commission.

Article 28

1.   For the purposes of this Chapter, statistical thresholds shall be defined as limits expressed in terms of value, at which level the obligations incumbent on parties responsible for providing information shall be suspended or reduced.

     These thresholds shall apply without prejudice to the provisions of Article 15.

2.   The statistical thresholds shall be known as exclusion, assimilation or simplification thresholds.

3.   Exclusion thresholds shall apply to the parties required to provide information referred to in the second subparagraph of Article 5.

     They shall apply in all Member States and shall be determined, by each of the said Member States, in accordance with national tax provisions adopted pursuant to Directive 77/388/EEC.

4.   Assimilation thresholds shall exempt parties required to provide information from having to supply the declarations referred to in Article 13(1); the periodic tax declaration which they make as parties liable to account for VAT, including parties within the meaning of Article 11(7), shall be considered to be the statistical declaration.

     Assimilation thresholds[9] shall apply in all Member States and shall be set, by each of the said Member States, at higher levels than the exclusion thresholds.

[5. Simplification thresholds shall exempt parties required to provide information from the full provisions of Article 23; these parties need only report in the declarations referred to in Article 13(1) a maximum of ten of the finest relevant subheadings of the combined nomenclature that are the most important in terms of value and shall regroup the other products in residual subheadings according to detailed arrangements to be determined by the Commission pursuant to Article 30. For each of the aforementioned subheadings, in addition to the code number referred to in the second indent of Article 21, the Member State of consignment or destination and the value of the goods need to be stated.][9]

     Without prejudice to the first subparagraph of paragraph 9, there shall be applied at the levels determined by paragraph 8 in the Member States whose assimilation thresholds are lower than these levels.

     In Member States whose assimilation thresholds are set at levels equal to or, pursuant to the first subparagraph of paragraph 9, higher than those determined by paragraph 8, simplification thresholds shall be optional.

6.   Assimilation[9] and simplificiation thresholds shall be expressed in annual values of intra-Community trade operations.

     They shall be determined by dispatch or arrival flows.

     They shall apply separately to intra-Community operators at the dispatch stage and to intra-Community operators at the arrival stage.

Without prejudice to paragraph 10, those Member States which elect to use the option set out in the first subparagraph of paragraph 9 may, however, determine the obligations of those responsible for providing the information at both the dispatch and the arrival stages in accordance with the flow for which the annual value of their intra-Community operations is highest.

The assimilation[10] and simplification thresholds may vary from one Member State to another, by product group and by period.

7. With a view to the application of the assimilation and simplification thresholds by the Member States, the Commission shall determine, pursuant to Article 30, the quality requirements which must be met by the statistics compiled by the Member States under Article 25(1).

8. The simplification thresholds shall be set at ECU 100 000 for dispatch and ECU 100 000 for arrival.

Pursuant to Article 30, the Commission may raise the simplification threshold levels, provided that the quality requirements referred to in paragraph 7 above are met.

9. Member States may, provided that the requirements set out in paragraph 7 are met, set their assimilation and simplification thresholds at levels higher than those in paragraph 8. They shall inform the Commission thereof.

Member States may, in order to comply with the requirements set out in paragraph 7, derogate to the extent necessary from the requirements of the second subparagraph of paragraph 5. They shall inform the Commission thereof.

The Commission may ask the Member States to justify the measures which they take by providing it with all appropriate information.

10. If Member States' application of the assimilation[10] and simplification thresholds affects the quality of intra-Community trade statistics, bearing in mind the data supplied by the Member States, or increases the burden on parties required to provide information, such that the objectives of this Regulation are compromised, the Commission shall adopt, pursuant to Article 30, provisions which restore the conditions needed to ensure the required quality or to ease the burden.

CHAPTER IV

Committee on statistics relating to the trading of goods between Member States

Article 29

1. A Committee on the statistics relating to the trading of goods between Member States, hereinafter called 'the Committee', is hereby established. It shall be composed of representatives of the Member States and chaired by a Commission representative.

2.   The Committee shall draw up its rules of procedure.

3.   The Committee may examine any question relating to the implementation of this Regulation raised by its chairman, either on his own initiative or at the request of the representative of a Member State.

Article 30

1.   The provisions required for the implementation of this Regulation shall be adopted according to the procedure laid down in paragraph 2 and 3.

2.   The representative of the Commission shall submit to the committee a draft of the measures to be taken. The Committee shall deliver its opinion on the draft within a time limit which the chairman may lay down according to the urgency of the matter. The opinion shall be delivered by the majority laid down in Article 148(2) of the Treaty in the case of decisions which the Council is required to adopt on a proposal from the Commission. The votes of the representatives of the Member States within the committee shall be weighted in the manner set out in that Article. The chairman shall not vote.

3.   The Commission shall adopt measures which shall apply immediately. However, if these measures are not in accordance with the opinion of the committee, they shall be communicated by the Commission to the Council forthwith.

      In that event, the Commission may defer application of the measures which it has decided for a period of not more than one month from the date of such communication.

      The Council, acting by a qualified majority, may take a different decision within the time limit referred to in the second subparagraph.

CHAPTER V

Final provisions

Article 31

On a proposal from the Commission, the Council shall adopt the provisions necessary to enable the Community or its Member States to compile the statistics other than statistics of trade between Member States referred to in Article 4.

Article 32

1.   On a proposal from the Commission, the Council shall decide on the conditions under which the Member States may declare data compiled in accordance with this Regulation, or the Regulations provided for herein, to be confidential.

2.   Until the conditions referred to in paragraph 1 have been laid down, Member States' provisions on this matter shall apply.

Article 33

The Commission may, by the procedure laid down in Article 30, adapt as necessary the provisions of this Regulation:

-        to the consequences of amendments to Directive 77/388/EEC;

-        to specific movements of goods within the meaning of the statistical regulations of the Community.

Article 34

1.   In respect both of goods subject to the Intrastat system and of other goods, the Commission may, for the purpose of facilitating the task of the parties responsible for providing information, establish in accordance with Article 30 simplified data collection procedures and in particular create the conditions for increased use of automatic data processing and electronic data transmission.

2.   In order to take account of their individual administrative arrangements, Member States may establish simplified procedures other than those referred to in paragraph 1, provided that those responsible for providing information may choose the procedures they will use. Member States exercising this option shall inform the Commission accordingly.

Article 35

This Regulation shall enter into force on the third day following that of its publication in the Official Journal of the European Communities.

Except insofar as they require the Council or the Commission to adopt provisions implementing this Regulation before that date, Article 1 to 9, 11 13(1) and 14 to 27 shall apply as from the date of implementation of Council Regulation (EEC) No 2726/90 of 17 September 1990 on Community transit.

As from the date referred to in the second subparagraph, Regulation (EEC) No 2954/85 shall be repealed and Regulation (EEC) No 1736/75 shall cease to apply to the statistics relating to the trading of goods between Member States to which it was applicable.

This Regulation shall be binding in its entirety and directly applicable in all Member States.

Done at Brussels, 7 November 1991.
For the Council
The President
P. DANKERT

Amendments
1   Substituted by Art 22(2), Council Regulation 92/3046/EEC of 22 October 1992.
2   Substituted by Art 22(2), Council Regulation 92/3046/EEC of 22 October 1992.
3   Substituted by Art 22(1), Council Regulation 92/3046/EEC of 22 October 1992.
4   Substituted by Art 22(1), Council Regulation 92/3046/EEC of 22 October 1992.
5   Substituted by Art 22(1), Council Regulation 92/3046/EEC of 22 October 1992.

6   Deleted by Art 22(1), Council Regulation 92/3046/EEC of 22 October 1992.
7   Substituted by Art 22(3)(a), Council Regulation 92/3046/EEC of 22 October 1992.
8   Substituted by Art 22(3)(b), Council Regulation 92/3046/EEC of 22 October 1992.
9   Substituted by Art 1, Parliament and Council Regulation 1624/2000 of 10 July 2000.

Notes
10 From 1 January 2003 the assimilation thresholds in Ireland are: dispatches €635,000, arrivals €191,000, by
    notice, Iris Oifigiúil, 19 November 2002.

COUNCIL DIRECTIVE 91/680/EEC

of 16 December 1991

Supplementing the common system of value added tax and amending Directive 77/388/EEC with a view to the abolition of fiscal frontiers

Official Journal L 376 , 31/12/1991 p. 0001 - 0019

This Directive (except for Article 2) was repealed by Council Directive 2006/112/EC of 28 November 2006 on the common system of value added tax, with effect from 1 January 2007

THE COUNCIL OF THE EUROPEAN COMMUNITIES,

Having regard to the Treaty establishing the European Economic Community, and in particular Article 99 thereof,

Having regard to the proposal from the Commission,

Having regard to the opinion of the European Parliament,

Having regard to the opinion of the Economic and Social Committee,

Whereas Article 8a of the Treaty defines the internal market as an area without internal frontiers in which the free movement of goods, persons, services and capital is ensured in accordance with the provisions of the Treaty;

Whereas the completion of the internal market requires the elimination of fiscal frontiers between Member States and that to that end the imposition of tax on imports and the remission of tax on exports in trade between Member States be definitively abolished;

Whereas fiscal controls at internal frontiers will be definitively abolished as from 1 January 1993 for all transactions between Member States;

Whereas the imposition of tax on imports and the remission of tax on exports must therefore apply only to transactions with territories excluded from the scope of the common system of value added tax;

Whereas, however, in view of the conventions and treaties applicable to them, transactions originating in or intended for the Principality of Monaco and the Isle of Man must be treated as transactions originating in or intended for the French Republic and the United Kingdom of Great Britain and Northern Ireland respectively;

Whereas the abolition of the principle of the imposition of tax on imports in relations between Member States will make provisions on tax exemptions and duty-free allowances superfluous in relations between Member States; whereas, therefore, those provisions should be repealed and the relevant Directives adapted accordingly;

Whereas the achievement of the objective referred to in Article 4 of the First Council Directive of 11 April 1967, as last amended by the Sixth Directive 77/388/EEC, requires that the taxation of trade between Member States be based on the principle of the taxation in the Member State of origin of goods and services supplied without prejudice, as regards Community trade between taxable persons, to the principle that tax revenue from the imposition of tax at the final consumption stage should accrue to the benefit of the Member State in which that final consumption takes place;

Whereas, however, the determination of the definitive system that will bring about the objectives of the common system of value added tax on goods and services supplied between Member States requires conditions that cannot be completely brought about by 31 December 1992;

Whereas, therefore, provision should be made for a transitional phase, beginning on 1 January 1993 and lasting for a limited period, during which provisions intended to facilitate transition to the definitive system for the taxation of trade between Member States, which continues to be the medium-term objective, will be implemented;

Whereas during the transitional period intra-Community transactions carried out by taxable persons other than exempt taxable persons should be taxed in the Member States of destination, at those Member States' rates and under their conditions;

Whereas intra-Community acquisitions of a certain value by exempt persons or by non-taxable legal persons and certain intra-Community distance selling and supplies of new means of transport to individuals or exempt or non-taxable bodies should also be taxed, during the transitional period, in the Member States of destination, at those Member States' rates and under their conditions, in so far as such transactions would, in the absence of special provisions, be likely to cause significant distortions of competition between Member States;

Whereas the necessary pursuit of a reduction of administrative and statistical formalities for undertakings, particularly small and medium-sized undertakings, must be reconciled with the implementation of effective control measures and the need, on both economic and tax grounds, to maintain the quality of Community statistical instruments;

Whereas advantage must be taken of the transitional period of taxation of intra-Community trade to take measures necessary to deal with both the social repercussions in the sectors affected and the regional difficulties, in frontier regions in particular, that might follow the abolition of the imposition of tax on imports and of the remission of tax on exports in trade between Member States; whereas Member States should therefore be authorized, for a period ending on 30 June 1999, to exempt supplies of goods carried out within specified limits by duty-free shops in the context of air and sea travel between Member States;

Whereas the transitional arrangements will enter into force for four years and will accordingly apply until 31 December 1996; whereas they will be replaced by a definitive system for the taxation of trade between Member States based on the principle of the taxation of goods and services supplied in the Member State of origin, so that the objective referred to in Article 4 of the First Council Directive of 11 April 1967 is achieved;

Whereas to that end the Commission will report to the Council before 31 December 1994 on the operation of the transitional arrangements and make proposals for the details of the definitive system for the taxation of trade between Member States; whereas the Council, considering that the conditions for transition to the definitive system have been fulfilled satisfactorily, will decide before 31 December 1995 on the arrangements necessary for the entry into force and the operation of the definitive system, the transitional arrangements being automatically continued until the entry into force of the definitive system and in any event until the Council has decided on the definitive system;

Whereas, accordingly, Directive 77/388/EEC, as last amended by Directive 89/465/EEC, should be amended,

HAS ADOPTED THIS DIRECTIVE:

Article 1

Note

The various paragraphs of Article 1 made the following amendments to the Sixth Directive: Para(1) substituted Art 3, Sixth Directive: para(2) substituted Art 7, Sixth Directive: para(3) amended Art 8(1)(a), Sixth Directive: para(4) added Art 8(1)(c), Sixth Directive: para(5) substituted Art 8(2), Sixth Directive: para(6) substituted Art 10(3), Sixth Directive: para(7) substituted Art 11B(1) and deleted Art 11B(2), Sixth Directive: para(8) substituted Art 11B(3), Sixth Directive: para(9) amended Art 11(B)(5), Sixth Directive: para(10) substituted Art 11C(2), Sixth Directive: para(11) deleted Art 14(1)(b), Sixth Directive: para(12) substituted heading of Art 15, Sixth Directive: para(13) amended Art 15(1)-(2), Sixth Directive: para(14) substituted Art 15(3), Sixth Directive: para(15) amended Art 15(10), Sixth Directive: para(16) amended Art 15(10), Sixth Directive: para(17) amended Art 15(12), Sixth Directive: para(18) substituted Art 15(13), Sixth Directive: para(19) substituted Art 15(14), Sixth Directive: para(20) substituted Art 16(1A), substituted Art 16(1B), substituted Art 16(1C), substituted Art 16(1D),Sixth Directive: para(21) inserted Art 28(3a), Sixth Directive: para(22) inserted TITLE XVIa,arts28a-m, Sixth Directive: para(23) substituted Art 33, Sixth Directive: para(24) inserted Art 33a, Sixth Directive:

Article 2

1. The following Directives shall cease to have effect on 31 December 1992 as regards relations between Member States:

    Directive 83/181/EEC, as last amended by Directive 89/219/EEC,

    Directive 85/362/EEC.

2. The provisions on value added tax laid down in the following Directive shall cease to have effect on 31 December 1992:

    Directive 74/651/EEC, as last amended by Directive 88/663/EEC,

    Directive 83/182/EEC,

    Directive 83/183/EEC, as amended by Directive 89/604/EEC.

3. The provisions of Directive 69/169/EEC as last amended by Directive 91/191/EEC relating to value added tax shall cease to have effect on 31 December 1992 as regards relations between Member States.

Article 3

1. Member States shall adapt their present value added tax systems to this Directive.

    They shall bring into force such laws, regulations and administrative provisions as are necessary for their arrangements thus adapted to Article 1(1) to (20) and (22) to (24) and 2 of this Directive to enter into force on 1 January 1993.

2. Member States shall inform the Commission of the provisions which they adopt to apply this Directive.

3. Member States shall communicate to the Commission the texts of the provisions of national law which they adopt in the field governed by this Directive.

4. When Member States adopt such measures they shall include a reference to this Directive or shall accompany them by such a reference on the occasion of their official publication.

The manner in which such references shall be made shall be laid down by the Member States.

Article 4

This Directive is addressed to the Member States.

Done at Brussels, 16 December 1991.

For the Council

The President

W. KOK

COUNCIL REGULATION (92/218/EEC)

of 27 January 1992

On administrative cooperation in the field of indirect taxation (VAT)
Official Journal L 024 , 01/02/1992 p. 0001 - 0005

Repealed by Council Regulation (EC) No 1798/2003 of 7 October 2003 on administrative cooperation in the field of value added tax and repealing Regulation (EEC) No 218/92, w.e.f. 1 January 2004

THE COUNCIL OF THE EUROPEAN COMMUNITIES,

Having regard to the Treaty establishing the European Economic Community, and in particular Article 99 thereof,

Having regard to the proposal from the Commission,

Having regard to the opinion of the European Parliament,

Having regard to the opinion of the Economic and Social Committee,

Whereas the establishment of the internal market in accordance with Article 8a of the Treaty requires the creation of an area without internal frontiers in which the free movement of goods, persons, services and capital is ensured; whereas the internal market requires changes in the legislation on value added tax as provided in Article 99 of the Treaty;

Whereas in order to avoid tax revenue losses for Member States the tax harmonization measures taken to complete the internal market and for the transitional period must include the establishment of a common system for the exchange of information on intra-Community transactions between the competent authorities of the Member States;

Whereas in order to permit the abolition of fiscal controls at internal frontiers in accordance with the aims set out in Article 8a of the Treaty the transitional value added tax system introduced by Directive 91/680/EEC, amending Directive 77/388/EEC, must be effectively established without the risk of fraud which might cause distortions of competition;

Whereas this Regulation provides for a common system for the exchange of information on intra-Community transactions, supplementing Directive 77/799/EEC, as last amended by Directive 79/1070/EEC, and intended to serve tax purposes;

Whereas the Member States should provide the Commission with any value added tax information which may be of interest at Community level;

Whereas the establishment of a common system of administrative cooperation may affect individuals' legal positions, in particular because of the exchange of information concerning their tax positions;

Whereas care must be taken to ensure that the provisions concerning the control of indirect taxes are in balance with administrations' needs for effective control and the administrative burdens imposed on taxable persons;

Whereas the operation of such a system requires the establishment of a standing committee on administrative cooperation;

Whereas the Member States and the Commission must establish an effective system for the electronic storage and transmission of certain data for value added tax control purposes;

Whereas care must be taken to ensure that information provided in the course of such collaboration is not disclosed to unauthorized persons, so that the basic rights of citizens and undertakings are safeguarded; whereas it is therefore necessary that an authority receiving such information should not, without the authorization of the authority supplying it, use it for purposes other than taxation or to facilitate legal proceedings for failure to comply with the tax laws of the Member States concerned; whereas the receiving authority must also accord such information the same degree of confidentiality as it enjoyed in the Member State which provided it, if the latter so requires;

Whereas the Member States and the Commission must collaborate on the continuous analysis of cooperation procedures and the pooling of the experience gained in the fields in question, with the aims of improving those procedures and drawing up appropriate Community rules,

HAS ADOPTED THIS REGULATION:

Article 1

This Regulation lays down the ways in which the administrative authorities in the Member States responsible for the application of laws on value added tax shall cooperate with each other and with the Commission to ensure compliance with those laws.

[To that end it lays down procedures for the exchange by electronic means of value added tax information on intra-Community transactions as well as on services supplied electronically in accordance with the special scheme provided for by Article 26c of Directive 77/388/EEC, and also for any subsequent exchange of information and, as far as services covered by that special scheme are concerned, for the transfer of money between Member States' competent authorities.][1]

Article 2

1.   For the purposes of this Regulation:

-     **'competent authority'** shall mean the authority appointed to act as correspondent as defined in paragraph 2,

-     **'applicant authority'** shall mean the competent authority of a Member State which makes a request for assistance,

-     **'requested authority'** shall mean the competent authority of a Member State to which a request for assistance is made,

-     **'person'** shall mean:

-     a natural person,

-     a legal person or,

-     where the possibility is provided for under the legislation in force, an association of persons recognized as having the capacity to perform legal acts but lacking the legal status of a legal person,

-   **'to grant access'** shall mean authorizing access to the relevant electronic data base and providing data by electronic means,

-   **'value added tax identification number'** shall mean the number provided for in with Article 22(1)(c), (d) and (e) of Directive 77/388/EEC,

-   **'intra-Community transactions'** shall mean the intra-Community supply of goods and the intra-Community supply of services as defined in this paragraph,

-   **'intra-Community supply of goods'** shall mean any supply of goods which must be declared in the recapitulative statement provided for in Article 22(6)(b) of Directive 77/388/EEC,

[-   **'intra-Community supply of services"** ' shall mean any supply of services covered by Article 28b (C), (D), (E) or (F) of Directive 77/388/EEC,][1]

-   **'intra-Community acquisition of goods'** shall mean acquisition of the right to dispose as owner of movable tangible property as defined in Article 28a(3) of Directive 77/388/EEC.

2. Each Member State shall notify the other Member States and the Commission of the competent authorities appointed to act as correspondents for the purpose of applying this Regulation. In addition, each Member State shall nominate a central office with principal responsibility for liaison with other Member States in the field of administrative cooperation.

3. The Commission shall publish a list of competent authorities in the *Official Journal of the European Communities* and, where necessary, update it.

TITLE I

Exchange of information - General provisions

Article 3

1. The obligation to give assistance provided for in this Regulation shall not cover the provision of information or documents obtained by the administrative authorities referred to in Article 1 at the request of a judicial authority.

    However, in cases of applications for assistance, such information and documents shall be provided whenever the judicial authority, to which reference must be made, gives its consent.

2. This Regulation shall not restrict the application of provisions of other agreements or instruments relating to cooperation on tax matters.

3.   This Regulation shall not affect the application in the Member States of the rules on mutual assistance in criminal matters.

TITLE II

Exchange of information relating to value added tax in connection with intra-Community transactions

Article 4

1.   The competent authority of each Member State shall maintain an electronic data base in which it shall store and process the information that it collects in accordance with Article 22(6)(b) of Directive 77/388/EEC. To allow the use of this information in the procedures provided for in this Regulation the information shall be stored for at least five years after the end of the calendar year in which access to the information was to be granted. Member States shall ensure that their data bases are kept up to date, complete and accurate. Under the procedure laid down in Article 10 criteria shall be defined to determine what amendments that are not significant, material or useful need not be made.

2.   From the data collected in accordance with paragraph 1, the competent authority of a Member State shall obtain directly and without delay from each Member State, or may have direct access to, the following information:

-    the value added tax identification numbers issued by the Member State receiving the information, and

-    the total value of all intra-Community supplies of goods made to the persons to whom those numbers were issued by all operators identified for the purposes of value added tax in the Member State providing the information; the values shall be expressed in the currency of the Member State providing the information and shall relate to calendar quarters.

3.   From the data collected in accordance with paragraph 1 and solely in order to combat tax fraud, the competent authority of a Member State shall, wherever it considers it necessary for the control of intra-Community acquisitions of goods, obtain directly and without delay, or have direct access to, the following information:

-    the value added tax identification numbers of all persons who have made the supplies referred to in the second indent of paragraph 2, and

-    the total value of such supplies from each such person to each person to whom one of the value added tax identification numbers referred to in the first indent of paragraph 2 has been issued; the values shall be expressed in the currency of the Member State providing the information and shall relate to calendar quarters.

4.   Where the competent authority of a Member State is obliged to grant

access to information under this Article it shall, as regards the information referred to in paragraphs 2 and 3, do so within three months of the end of the calendar quarter to which the information relates. By way of derogation from this rule, where information is added to a data base in the circumstances provided for in paragraph 1, access to such additions shall be granted as quickly as possible and in any event no more than three months after the end of the quarter in which the additional information was collected; the conditions under which access to the corrected information may be granted shall be defined by means of the procedure laid down in Article 10.

5. Where, for purposes of the application of this Article, the competent authorities of the Member States keep information in electronic data bases and exchange such information by electronic means they shall take all measures necessary to ensure compliance with Article 9.

Article 5

1. Where the information provided under Article 4 is insufficient, the competent authority of a Member State may at any time and in specific cases request further information. The requested authority shall provide the information as quickly as possible and in any event no more than three months after receipt of the request.

2. In the circumstances described in paragraph 1 the requested authority shall at least provide the applicant authority with invoice numbers, dates and values in relation to individual transactions between persons in the Member States concerned.

Article 6

1. The competent authority of each Member State shall maintain an electronic data base which shall contain a register of persons to whom value added tax identification numbers have been issued in that Member State.

2. At any time the competent authority of a Member State may obtain directly or have communicated to it, from the data collected in accordance with Article 4 (1), confirmation of the validity of the value added tax identification number under which a person effected or received an intra-Community supply of goods or of services. On specific request the requested authority shall also communicate the date of issue and, where appropriate, the date of cessation of the validity of the value added tax identification number.

3. Where it is so requested a competent authority shall also provide without delay the name and address of the person to whom a number has been issued, provided that such information is not stored by the applicant authority with a view to its possible use at some future time.

[4. The competent authority of each Member State shall ensure that persons involved in the intra-Community supply of goods or of services and persons supplying services referred to in the last indent of Article 9(2)e of

Directive 77/388/EEC are allowed to obtain confirmation of the validity of the value added tax identification number of any specified person. In accordance with the procedure referred to in Article 10, Member States shall, in particular, provide such confirmation by electronic means.][1]

5.   Where, for purposes of the application of this Article, the competent authorities of the Member States keep information in electronic data bases and exchange such information by electronic means they shall take all measures necessary to ensure compliance with Article 9.

TITLE III

Conditions governing the exchange of information

Article 7

1.   A requested authority in one Member State shall provide an applicant authority in another Member State with the information referred to in Article 5(2) provided that:

-       the number and the nature of the requests for information made by the applicant authority within a specific period of time do not impose a disproportionate administrative burden on that requested authority,

-       that applicant authority exhausts the usual sources of information which it can use in the circumstances to obtain the information requested, without running the risk of jeopardizing the achievement of the desired end,

-       that applicant authority requests assistance only if it would be able to provide similar assistance to the applicant authority of another Member State.

In accordance with the procedure laid down in Article 10 and taking into account experience of the new administrative cooperation system during its first year of operation, the Commission shall submit general criteria for the definition of the scope of these commitments before July 1994.

2.   If an applicant authority is unable to comply with the general provisions of paragraph 1 it shall notify the requested authority accordingly without delay, stating its reasons. If a requested authority considers that the general provisions of paragraph 1 are not complied with and that it is therefore not obliged to provide the information, it shall notify the applicant authority accordingly without delay, stating its reasons. The applicant authority and the requested authority shall attempt to reach agreement. If they fail to reach agreement within one month of notification either authority may request that the matter be examined under Article 11.

3.   This Article shall be without prejudice to the application of Directive
       77/799/EEC as regards the exchange of information referred to in
       Article 5(1).

Article 8

In cases of exchanges of information as defined in Article 5, where the national
legislation in force in a Member State provides for notification of the person
concerned of the exchange of information, those provisions may continue to
apply except where their application would prejudice the investigation of tax
evasion in another Member State. In the latter event, at the express request
of the applicant authority, the requested authority shall refrain from such
notification.

Article 9

1.   Any information communicated in whatever form pursuant to this
       Regulation shall be of a confidential nature. It shall be covered by the
       obligation of professional secrecy and shall enjoy the protection extended
       to similar information under both the national law of the Member
       State which received it and the corresponding provisions applicable to
       Community authorities.

       In any case, such information:

       -     may be made available only to the persons directly concerned
             with the bases of assessment, collection or administrative control
             of taxes for the purpose of the assessment of taxes, or to persons
             employed by Community institutions whose duties require that
             they have access to it,

       -     may in addition be used in connection with judicial or
             administrative proceedings that may involve sanctions, initiated
             as a result of infringements of tax law.

2.   By way of derogation from paragraph 1, the competent authority
       of the Member State providing the information shall permit its use
       for other purposes in the Member State of the applicant authority, if,
       under the legislation of the Member State of the requested authority,
       the information could be used in the Member State of the requested
       authority for similar purposes.

3.   Where the applicant authority considers that information which it
       has received from the requested authority is likely to be useful to the
       competent authority of a third Member State, it may transmit it to the
       latter with the agreement of the requested authority.

[TITLE III A

Provisions concerning the special scheme in Article 26c of Directive 77/388/EEC

Article 9a

The following provisions shall apply concerning the special scheme provided for in Article 26c in Directive 77/388/EEC. The definitions contained in point A of that Article shall also apply for the purpose of this Title.

Article 9b

1. The information from the non-established taxable person to the Member State of identification when his activities commences set out in the second subparagraph of Article 26c(B)(2) of Directive 77/388/EEC is to be submitted in an electronic manner. The technical details, including a common electronic message, shall be determined in accordance with the procedure provided for in Article 10.

2. The Member State of identification shall transmit this information by electronic means to the competent authorities of the other Member States within 10 days from the end of the month during which the information was received from the non-established taxable person. In the same manner, the competent authorities of the other Member States shall be informed of the allocated identification number. The technical details, including a common electronic message, by which this information is to be transmitted shall be determined in accordance with the procedure provided for in Article 10.

3. The Member State of identification shall without delay inform by electronic means the competent authorities of the other Members States if a non-established taxable person is excluded from the identification register.

Article 9c

1. The return with the details set out in the second subparagraph of Article 26c(B)(5) of Directive 77/388/EEC is to be submitted in an electronic manner. The technical details, including a common electronic message, shall be determined in accordance with the procedure provided for in Article 10.

2. The Member State of identification shall transmit this information by electronic means to the competent authority of the Member State concerned at the latest 10 days after the end of the month that the return was received. Member States which have required the tax return to be made in a national currency other than euro shall convert the amounts into euro using the exchange rate valid for the last date of the reporting period. The exchange shall be done following the exchange rates published by the European Central Bank for that day, or, if there is no publication on that day, on the next day of publication. The technical details by which this information is to be transmitted shall be determined in accordance with the procedure provided for in Article 10.

3.   The Member State of identification shall transmit by electronic means to the Member State of consumption the information needed to link each payment with a relevant quarterly tax return.

Article 9d

The provisions in Article 4(1) shall apply also to information collected by the Member State of identification in accordance with Article 26c(B)(2) and (5) of Directive 77/388/EEC.

Article 9e

The Member State of identification shall ensure that the amount the non-established taxable person has paid is transferred to the bank account denominated in euro, which has been designated by the Member State of consumption to which the payment is due. Member States which required the payments in a national currency other than euro shall convert the amounts into euro using the exchange rate valid for the last date of the reporting period. The exchange shall be done following the exchange rates published by the European Central Bank for that day, or, if there is no publication on that day, on the next day of publication. The transfer shall take place at the latest 10 days after the end of the month that the payment was received.

If the non-established taxable person does not pay the total tax due, the Member State of identification shall ensure that the payment is transferred to the Member States of consumption in proportion to the tax due in each Member State. The Member State of identification shall inform by electronic means the competent authorities of the Member States of consumption thereof.

Article 9f

1.   Member States shall notify by electronic means the competent authorities of the other Member States of the relevant bank account numbers for receiving payments according to Article 9e.

2.   Member States shall without delay notify by electronic means the competent authorities of the other Member States and the Commission of changes in the standard tax rate.][2]

TITLE IV

Consultation and coordination procedures

Article 10

1.   The Commission shall be assisted by a Standing Committee on Administrative Cooperation in the field of Indirect Taxation, hereinafter referred to as 'the Committee'. It shall consist of representatives of the Member States and have a representative of the Commission as chairman.

2.   The measures required for the application of Articles 4 and 7(1) shall be adopted in accordance with the procedure laid down in paragraphs 3 and 4 of this Article.

3. The Commission representative shall submit to the Committee a draft of the measures to be adopted. The Committee shall deliver its opinion on that draft within a time limit which the chairman may lay down according to the urgency of the matter. The Committee's opinion shall be delivered by a majority, the Member States' votes being weighted in accordance with Article 148(2) of the Treaty. The chairman shall not vote.

4. The Commission shall adopt the measures contemplated where they are in accordance with the Committee's opinion.

Where those measures are not in accordance with the Committee's opinion or if the Committee does not deliver an opinion, the Commission shall without delay submit to the Council a proposal on the measures to be adopted. The Council shall act by a qualified majority.

If within three months of the proposal's being submitted to it the Council has not acted, the proposed measures shall be adopted by the Commission, unless the Council has decided against those measures by a simple majority.

Article 11

The Member States and the Commission shall examine and evaluate the operation of the arrangements for administrative cooperation provided for in this Regulation and the Commission shall pool the Member States' experience, in particular that concerning new means of tax avoidance and evasion, with the aim of improving the operation of those arrangements. To that end the Member States shall also communicate to the Commission any value added tax information on intra-Community transactions that may be of interest at Community level.

Article 12

1. On matters of bilateral interest, the competent authorities of the Member States may communicate directly with each other. The competent authorities of the Member States may by mutual agreement permit authorities designated by them to communicate directly with each other in specified cases or categories of cases.

2. For the purpose of applying this Regulation, Member States shall take all necessary steps to:

    (a) ensure efficient internal co-ordination between the competent authorities referred to in Article 1;

    (b) establish direct co-operation between the authorities specially empowered for the purposes of such co-ordination;

    (c) make suitable arrangements to ensure the smooth operation of the arrangements for the exchange of information provided for in this Regulation.

3. The Commission shall communicate to the competent authority of each Member State, as quickly as possible, any information which it receives and which it is able to supply.

TITLE V

Final provisions

Article 13

[1.   The Commission and the Member States shall ensure that such existing or new communication and information exchange systems which are necessary to provide for the exchanges of information described in Articles 9b and 9c are operational by the date specified in Article 3(1) of Directive 2002/38/EC. The Commission will be responsible for whatever development of the common communication network/common system interface (CCN/CSI) is necessary to permit the exchange of this information between Member States. Member States will be responsible for whatever development of their systems is necessary to permit this information to be exchanged using the CCN/CSI.][3]

[2.][3]   Member States shall waive all claims for the reimbursement of expenses incurred in applying this Regulation except, as appropriate, in respect of fees paid to experts.

Article 14

1.   Every two years after the date of entry into force of this Regulation, the Commission shall report to the European Parliament and the Council on the conditions of application of this Regulation on the basis, in particular, of the continuous monitoring procedures provided for in Article 11.

2.   Member States shall communicate to the Commission the texts of any provisions of national law which they adopt in the field governed by this Regulation.

Article 15

This Regulation shall enter into force on the third day following its publication in the Official Journal of the European Communities.

No exchange of information under this Regulation shall take place before 1 January 1993.

This Regulation shall be binding in its entirety and directly applicable in all Member States.

Done at Brussels, 27 January 1992.
For the Council
The President
A. MARQUES DA CUNHA

Amendments

1   Substituted by Art 1 Council Regulation (EC) No. 792/2002 of 7 May 2002. Amended with effect from 22 May 2002 and provisions applicable from 1 July 2003.

2   Title IIIA inserted by Art 1 Council Regulation (EC) No. 792/2002 of 7 May 2002. Amended with effect from 22 May 2002 and provisions applicable from 1 July 2003.

3   Inserted by Art 1 Council Regulation (EC) No. 792/2002 of 7 May 2002. Amended with effect from 22 May 2002 and provisions applicable from 1 July 2003.

COMMISSION REGULATION (92/2256/EEC)

of 31 July 1992

On statistical thresholds for the statistics on trade between Member States
Official Journal L 219 , 04/08/1992 p. 0040 - 0043

THE COMMISSION OF THE EUROPEAN COMMUNITIES,

Having regard to the Treaty establishing the European Economic Community,

Having regard to Council Regulation (EEC) No 3330/91 of 7 November 1991 on the statistics relating to the trading of goods between Member States, and in particular Article 30 thereof,

Whereas the burden on intra-Community operators must be lightened as much as possible, either by exempting them from statistical obligations or by simplifying procedures;

Whereas this lightening of the burden must be limited only by the demands of statistics of a satisfactory quality, which must consequently be defined by common accord;

Whereas, once this quality has been defined, all the Member States must have their necessary instruments to ensure it, while taking account of their own economic and commercial structure; whereas it is for the Member States themselves to strike the most appropriate balance between lightening of the statistical burden and quality on the basis of the information available to them;

Whereas the information to be analysed by the Member States in order to fix their thresholds differs, particularly as regards coverage, depending on whether they are to be introduced in 1993 or to be adapted as from 1994; whereas a distinction should therefore be drawn between the rules to be followed on one single occasion, as in the first case, and those to be followed each year, as in the second case;

Whereas the obligations of the persons responsible for providing information should be defined in such a way as to take maximum account of their interests, particularly if their intra-Community transactions are expanding;

Whereas the measures provided for in this Regulation are in accordance with the opinion of the Committee on Statistics relating to the trading of goods between Member States,

HAS ADOPTED THIS REGULATION:

Article 1

The Member States shall set annually, in national currency, the assimilation and simplification thresholds referred to in Article 28 of Regulation (EEC) No 3330/91, hereinafter 'the Basic Regulation'. They shall ensure when setting these thresholds that, first, they meet the quality requirements laid down in this Regulation and, secondly, they exploit to the full the ensuing opportunities to relieve the burden on intra-Community operators.

Article 2

For the purposes of this Regulation:

(a)   'error' means the discrepancy between the results obtained with and without application of the thresholds referred to in Article 1; when a correction procedure is applied to the results obtained following application of the thresholds, the error is calculated in relation to the corrected results;

(b)   'total value' means:

- for the introduction of the thresholds in 1993, the value either of the outgoing goods or of the incoming goods, accounted for by intra-Community operators over a period of twelve months,

- for the adjustment of the thresholds from 1994, the value of either of the outgoing goods or of the incoming goods accounted for by intra-Community operators over a twelve-month period, other than those who are exempt under Article 5 of the Basic Regulation;

(c)   'coverage' means in relation to a given total value, the proportionate value of the outgoing goods or of the incoming goods, accounted for by the intra-Community operators who lie above the assimilation threshold.

Article 3

1.   For the introduction of the assimilation thresholds in 1993, the Member States shall meet the following quality requirements:

(a)   Results by goods category

Each Member State shall ensure that the error in annual values does not exceed 5% for 90% of the eight-digit sub-headings of the combined Nomenclature which represent 0,005% or more of the total value of its outgoing or incoming goods.

However, each Member State may raise this quality requirement up to the point that the error in annual values does not exceed 5% for 90% of the eight-digit sub-headings of the Combined Nomenclature which represent 0,001% or more of the total value of its outgoing or incoming goods.

(b)   Results by partner country

Each Member State shall ensure that the error in the annual values of its results by partner country, excluding countries which represent less than 3% of the total value of its outgoing or incoming goods, does not exceed 1%.

(c)   Time series

Each Member State shall ensure that:

-       for 90% of the eight-digit sub-headings of the combined nomenclature which represent the percentage of the total value of its outgoing or incoming goods laid down in point (a), and

-       for 90% of its results by partner country,

The fluctuation over time of the error in annual values will not exceed the limits (L) laid down in the Annex.

If in any Member State applying the requirement leads to an increase in the number of parties responsible for providing information who are required to submit the periodic declaration laid down in Article 13 of the Basic Regulation that is excessive in proportion to the number involved under the more stringent of the other two requirements, the Member State concerned may take steps to reduce the imbalance accordingly. It shall inform the Commission of the action taken.

2.   When a Member State's share of the total value of outgoing or incoming goods in the Community is less than 3%, that Member State may depart from the quality requirements laid down in the first subparagraph of paragraph 1(a) and the first indent of the first subparagraph of paragraph 1(c). In such cases, the 90% and 0,005% shares shall be replaced by 70% and 0,01% respectively.

3.   To meet the quality requirements set out in paragraphs 1 and 2, the Member States shall base the calculation of their thresholds on the results of trade with the other Member States for twelve-month periods prior to the introduction of the thresholds.

For Member States unable to make this calculation because figures are incomplete, the assimilation thresholds shall be fixed at a level not lower than the lowest, nor higher than the highest, thresholds set by the other Member States. However, this provision shall not be binding for Member States which are exempt under paragraph 2.

4.   If, for certain groups of goods, the application of the thresholds calculated in accordance with the provisions of this Article yields results which, mutatis mutandis, fail to meet the quality requirements set out in paragraphs 1 and 2 above, and if the thresholds cannot be lowered without reducing the relief which Article 1 guarantees to intra-Community operators, appropriate measures may be taken, at the initiative of the Commission or the request of a Member State, in accordance with the procedure laid down in Article 30 of the Basic Regulation.

Article 4

For the introduction of the simplification thresholds in 1993, the Member States may set these:

-       at levels above ECU 100 000 pursuant to the first subparagraph of Article 28(9) of the Basic Regulation, provided that they ensure

that at least 95% of the total value of their outgoing or incoming
goods is covered by periodic declarations containing all the
information required under Article 23 of the Basic Regulation,

-       where they are exempt under Article 3(2), at levels below ECU
        100 000 pursuant to the second subparagraph of Article 28(9) of
        the Basic Regulation, to the extent necessary to ensure that at
        least 95% of the total value of their outgoing or incoming goods
        is covered by periodic declarations containing all the information
        required under Article 23 of the Basic Regulation.

Article 5

The information relating to the information of the assimilation and
simplification thresholds in 1993 shall be published not later than 31 August
1992.

Article 6

1.   For the adjustment of the assimilation thresholds from 1994, the quality
        requirements specified in Article 3 shall be regarded as met if the
        coverage is maintained at the level which obtained when the thresholds
        were introduced.

2.   The condition laid down in paragraph 1 shall be met if Member States:

        (a)   calculate their thresholds for the year following the current year
                on the basis of the latest available results for their trade with the
                other Member States over a twelve-month period, and

        (b)   set their thresholds at a level which allows the same coverage
                for the period thus defined as for the period used as a basis for
                calculating their thresholds for the current year.

        Member States shall notify the Commission if they use a different
        method to meet this condition.

3.   Member States may lower their coverage provided that the quality
        requirements laid down in Article 3 continue to be met.

4.   Member States shall calculate adjustments to their assimilation
        thresholds each year. The thresholds shall be adjusted if the adjustment
        involves a change of at least 10% in the threshold values for the current
        year.

Article 7

1.   For the adjustment of the simplification thresholds from 1994, the
        Member States which set these thresholds

        -       at levels higher than the values laid down in by Article 28(8) of
                the Basic Regulation, shall ensure that the condition laid down
                in the first indent of Article 4 of this Regulation is met,

- at levels below these values, since they are exempt pursuant to Article 3(2) above, shall ensure that they comply with the limit laid down in the second indent of Article 4 of this Regulation.

2. To ensure that the condition referred to in the first indent of Article 4 is met or that the limit referred to in the second indent of Article 4 is complied with, it shall be sufficient for Member States to calculate the adjustment of the simplification thresholds using the method laid down in Article 6 (2) for adjusting the assimilation thresholds. Member States shall notify the Commission if they use a different method.

Article 8

The information relating to the adjustment of assimilation and simplification thresholds from 1994 shall be published not later than 31 October of the preceding year.

Article 9

1. Parties responsible for providing information shall be freed from their obligations to the extent allowed by application of the assimilation and simplification thresholds set for a given year, provided they have not exceeded these thresholds during the previous year.

2. For each statistical threshold, the provisions adopted shall apply for the whole year.

   However, if the value of the intra-Community transactions carried out by a party responsible for providing information at some time during the year exceeds the threshold applicable to him, he shall provide information on his intra-Community transactions from the month in which this threshold was exceeded in accordance with the provisions applying to the threshold which becomes applicable. If this provision invovles the transmission of the periodic declarations referred to in Article 13 of the Basic Regulation, the Member States shall lay down the time limit for transmitting these declarations in accordance with their particular administrative arrangements.

Article 10

The Member States shall communicate to the Commission the information regarding the thresholds they have calculated at least two weeks before publication. At the Commission's request, they shall also communicate the information required for assessing these thresholds, both for the period on which their calculation is based and for a given calendar year.

Article 11

This Regulation shall enter into force on the seventh day following its publication in the *Official Journal of the European Communities*.

This Regulation shall be binding in its entirety and directly applicable in all Member States.

Done at Brussels, 31 July 1992.
For the Commission
Henning CHRISTOPHERSEN
Vice-President

ANNEX

(This annex contains the mathematical formulae used to compute the limits referred to in the Regulation).

COUNCIL REGULATION (92/2913/EEC)

of 12 October 1992

Establishing the Community Customs Code
O.J. No L 302 19.10.92

THE COUNCIL OF THE EUROPEAN COMMUNITIES,

Having regard to the Treaty establishing the European Economic Community, and in particular Articles 28, 100a and 113 thereof,

Having regard to the proposal from the Commission,

In cooperation with the European Parliament,

Having regard to the opinion of the Economic and Social Committee,

Whereas the Community is based upon a customs union; whereas it is advisable, in the interests both of Community traders and the customs authorities, to assemble in a code the provisions of customs legislation that are at present contained in a large number of Community regulations and directives; whereas this task is of fundamental importance from the standpoint of the internal market;

Whereas such a Community Customs Code (hereinafter called 'the Code') must incorporate current customs legislation; whereas it is, nevertheless, advisable to amend that legislation in order to make it more consistent, to simplify it and to remedy certain omissions that still exist with a view to adopting complete Community legislation in this area;

Whereas, based on the concept of an internal market, the code must contain the general rules and procedures which ensure the implementation of the tariff and other measures introduced at Community level in connection with trade in goods between the Community and third countries; whereas it must cover, among other things, the implementation of common agricultural and commercial policy measures taking into account the requirements of these common policies;

Whereas it would appear advisable to specify that this Code is applicable without prejudice to specific provisions laid down in other fields; whereas such specific rules may exist or be introduced in the context, inter alia, of legislation relating to agriculture, statistics, commercial policy or own resources;

Whereas, in order to secure a balance between the needs of the customs authorities in regard to ensuring the correct application of customs legislation, on the one hand, and the right of traders to be treated fairly, on the other, the said authorities must be granted, inter alia, extensive powers of control and the said traders a right of appeal; whereas the implementation of a customs appeals system will require the United Kingdom to introduce new administrative procedures which cannot be effected before 1 January 1995;

Whereas in view of the paramount importance of external trade for the Community, customs formalities and controls should be abolished or at least kept to a minimum;

Whereas it is important to guarantee the uniform application of this Code and to provide, to that end, for a Community procedure which enables the procedures for its implementation to be adopted within a suitable time; whereas a Customs Code Committee should be set up in order to ensure close and effective cooperation between the Member States and the Commission in this field;

Whereas in adopting the measures required to implement this Code, the utmost care must be taken to prevent any fraud or irregularity liable to affect adversely the General Budget of the European Communities,

HAS ADOPTED THIS REGULATION:

TITLE I

general provisions

Chapter 1
scope and basic definitions

Article 1

Customs rules shall consist of this Code and the provisions adopted at Community level or nationally to implement them. The Code shall apply, without prejudice to special rules laid down in other fields

- to trade between the Community and third countries,

- to goods covered by the Treaty establishing the European Coal and Steel Community, the Treaty establishing the European Economic Community or the Treaty establishing the European Atomic Energy Community.

Article 2

1. Save as otherwise provided, either under international conventions or customary practices of a limited geographic and economic scope or under autonomous Community measures, Community customs rules shall apply uniformly throughout the customs territory of the Community.

2. Certain provisions of customs rules may also apply outside the customs territory of the Community within the framework of either rules governing specific fields or international conventions.

Article 3

[1. The customs territory of the Community shall comprise:

- the territory of the Kingdom of Belgium,

- the territoy of the Kingdom of Denmark, except the Faroe Islands and Greenland,

- the territory of the Federal Republic of Germany, except the Island of Heligoland and the territory of Buesingen (Treaty of 23

November 1964 between the Federal Republic of Germany and the Swiss Confederation),

- the territory of the Kingdom of Spain, except Ceuta and Melilla,

- the territory of the Hellenic Republic,

- the territory of the French Republic, except the overseas territories and 'collectivités territoriales',

- the territory of Ireland,

- the territory of the Italian Republic, except the municipalities of Livigno and Campione d'Italia and the national waters of Lake Lugano which are between the bank and the political frontier of the area between Ponte Tresa and Porto Ceresio,

- the territory of the Grand Duchy of Luxembourg,

- the territory of the Kingdom of the Netherlands in Europe,

- the territory of the Republic of Austria,

- the territory of the Portuguese Republic,

- the territory of the Republic of Finland, including the Aland Islands, provided a declaration is made in accordance with Article 227(5) of the EC Treaty,

- the territory of the Kingdom of Sweden

the territory of the United Kingdom of Great Britain and Northern Ireland and of the Channel Islands and the Isle of Man;][1]

[- the territory of the Czech Republic,

- the territory of the Republic of Estonia,

- the territory of the Republic of Cyprus,

- the territory of the Republic of Latvia,

- the territory of the Republic of Lithuania,

- the territory of the Republic of Hungary,

- the territory of the Republic of Malta,

- the territory of the Republic of Poland,

- the territory of the Republic of Slovenia,

- the territory of the Slovak Republic][2]

[2.   The following territories situated outside the territory of the Member States shall, taking the conventions and treaties applicable to them into account, be considered to be part of the customs territory of the Community:

(a)   FRANCE

The territory of the principality of Monaco as defined in the Customs Convention signed in Paris on 18 May 1963 (Official Journal of the French Republic of 27 September 1963, p. 8679).

(b)   CYPRUS

The territory of the United Kingdom Sovereign Base Areas of Akrotiri and Dhekelia as defined in the Treaty concerning the Establishment of the Republic of Cyprus, signed in Nicosia on 16 August 1960 (United Kingdom Treaty Series No 4 (1961) Cmnd. 1252)][3]

3.   The customs territory of the Community shall include the territorial waters, the inland maritime waters and the airspace of the Member States, and the territories referred to in paragraph 2, except for the territorial waters, the inland maritime waters and the airspace of those territories which are not part of the customs territory of the Community pursuant to paragraph 1.

Article 4

For the purposes of this Code, the following definitions shall apply:

(1)   '**Person**' means:

-       a natural person,

-       a legal person,

-       where the possibility is provided for under the rules in force, an association of persons recognized as having the capacity to perform legal acts but lacking the legal status of a legal person.

(2)   '**Persons established in the Community**' means:

-       in the case of a natural person, any person who is normally resident there,

-       in the case of a legal person or an association of persons, any person that has in the Community its registered office, central headquarters or a permanent business establishment.

(3)   '**Customs authorities**' means the authorities responsible inter alia for applying customs rules.

(4)   '**Customs office**' means any office at which all or some of the formalities laid down by customs rules may be completed.

[(4a)   '**Customs office of entry**' means the customs office designated by the customs authorities in accordance with the customs rules to which goods brought into the customs territory of the Community must be conveyed without delay and at which they will be subject to appropriate risk-based entry controls;

(4b) **'Customs office of import'** means the customs office designated by the customs authorities in accordance with the customs rules where the formalities for assigning goods brought into the customs territory of the Community to a customs-approved treatment or use, including appropriate risk-based controls, are to be carried out;

(4c) **'Customs office of export'** means the customs office designated by the customs authorities in accordance with the customs rules where the formalities for assigning goods leaving the customs territory of the Community to a customs-approved treatment or use, including appropriate risk-based controls, are to be completed;

(4d) **'Customs office of exit'** means the customs office designated by the customs authorities in accordance with the customs rules to which goods must be presented before they leave the customs territory of the Community and at which they will be subject to customs controls relating to the completion of exit formalities, and appropriate risk-based controls.]⁴

(5) **'Decision'** means any official act by the customs authorities pertaining to customs rules giving a ruling on a particular case, such act having legal effects on one or more specific or identifiable persons; [this term covers inter alia, binding tariff information within the meaning of Article 12.]⁵

(6) **'Customs status'** means the status of goods as Community or non-Community goods.

(7) **'Community goods'** means goods:

[- wholly obtained in the customs territory of the Community under the conditions referred to in Article 23 and not incorporating goods imported from countries or territories not forming part of the customs territory of the Community. Goods obtained from goods placed under a suspensive arrangement shall not be deemed to have Community status in cases of special economic importance determined in accordance with the committee procedure,]⁵;

- imported from countries or territories not forming part of the customs territory of the Community which have been released for free circulation,

- obtained or produced in the customs territory of the Community, either from goods referred to in the second indent alone or from goods referred to in first and second indents.

(8) **'Non-Community goods'** means goods other than those referred to in subparagraph 7.

Without prejudice to Articles 163 and 164, Community goods shall lose their status as such when they are actually removed from the customs territory of the Community.

(9) **'Customs debt'** means the obligation on a person to pay the amount

of the import duties (customs debt on importation) or export duties (customs debt on exportation) which apply to specific goods under the Community provisions in force.

(10) '**Import duties**' means:

-       customs duties and charges having an effect equivalent to customs duties payable on the importation of goods,

-       [...]⁶ import charges introduced under the common agricultural policy or under the specific arrangements applicable to certain goods resulting from the processing of agricultural products.

(11) '**Export duties**' means:

-       customs duties and charges having an effect equivalent to customs duties payable on the exportation of goods,

-       [...]⁷ export charges introduced under the common agricultural policy or under the specific arrangements applicable to certain goods resulting from the processing of agricultural products.

(12) '**Debtor**' means any person liable for payment of a customs debt.

(13) '**Supervision by the customs authorities**' means action taken in general by those authorities with a view to ensuring that customs rules and, where appropriate, other provisions applicable to goods subject to customs supervision are observed.

[(14) '**Customs controls**' means specific acts performed by the customs authorities in order to ensure the correct application of customs rules and other legislation governing the entry, exit, transit, transfer and end-use of goods moved between the customs territory of the Community and third countries and the presence of goods that do not have Community status; such acts may include examining goods, verifying declaration data and the existence and authenticity of electronic or written documents, examining the accounts of undertakings and other records, inspecting means of transport, inspecting luggage and other goods carried by or on persons and carrying out official inquiries and other similar acts.]⁸

(15) '**Customs-approved treatment or use of goods**' means:

(a)   the placing of goods under a customs procedure;

(b)   their entry into a free zone or free warehouse;

(c)   their re-exportation from the customs territory of the Community;

(d)   their destruction;

(e)   their abandonment to the Exchequer.

(16) '**Customs procedure**' means:

(a)   release for free circulation;

(b)   transit;

(c)   customs warehousing;

(d)   inward processing;

(e)   processing under customs control;

(f)   temporary admission;

(g)   outward processing;

(h)   exportation.

(17) '**Customs declaration**' means the act whereby a person indicates in the prescribed form and manner a wish to place goods under a given customs procedure.

(18) '**Declarant**' means the person making the customs declaration in his own name or the person in whose name a customs declaration is made.

(19) '**Presentation of goods to customs**' means the notification to the customs authorities, in the manner laid down, of the arrival of goods at the customs office or at any other place designated or approved by the customs authorities.

(20) '**Release of goods**' means the act whereby the customs authorities make goods available for the purposes stipulated by the customs procedure under which they are placed.

(21) '**Holder of the procedure**' means the person on whose behalf the customs declaration was made or the person to whom the rights and obligations of the abovementioned person in respect of a customs procedure have been transferred.

(22) '**Holder of the authorization**' means the person to whom an authorization has been granted.

(23) '**Provisions in force**' means Community or national provisions.

[(24) **Committee procedure**' means either the procedure referred to in Articles 247 and 247a, or in Articles 248 and 248a.]⁹

[(25) '**Risk**' means the likelihood of an event occurring, in connection with the entry, exit, transit, transfer and end-use of goods moved between the customs territory of the Community and third countries and the presence of goods that do not have Community status, which

—   prevents the correct application of Community or national measures, or

—   compromises the financial interests of the Community and its Member States, or

—   poses a threat to the Community's security and safety, to public health, to the environment or to consumers.

(26) '**Risk management**' means the systematic identification of risk and implementation of all measures necessary for limiting exposure to

risk. This includes activities such as collecting data and information, analysing and assessing risk, prescribing and taking action and regular monitoring and review of the process and its outcomes, based on international, Community and national sources and strategies.][4]

Chapter 2

Sundry general provisions relating in particular to the rights and obligations of persons with regard to customs rules

Section 1

Right of representation

Article 5

1. Under the conditions set out in Article 64(2) and subject to the provisions adopted within the framework of Article 243(2)(b), any person may appoint a representative in his dealings with the customs authorities to perform the acts and formalities laid down by customs rules.

2. Such representation may be:

    - direct, in which case the representative shall act in the name of and on behalf of another person, or

    - indirect, in which case the representatives shall act in his own name but on behalf of another person.

    A Member State may restrict the right to make customs declarations:

    - by direct representation, or

    - by indirect representation, so that the representative must be a customs agent carrying on his business in that country's territory.

3. Save in the cases referred to in Article 64(2)(b) and (3), a representative must be established within the Community.

4. A representative must state that he is acting on behalf of the person represented, specify whether the representation is direct or indirect and be empowered to act as a representative.

    A person who fails to state that he is acting in the name of or on behalf of another person or who states that he is acting in the name of or on behalf of another person without being empowered to do so shall be deemed to be acting in his own name and on his own behalf.

5. The customs authorities may require any person stating that he is acting in the name of or on behalf of another person to produce evidence of his powers to act as a representative.

[Section 1A

Authorised economic operators

Article 5a

1. Customs authorities, if necessary following consultation with other competent authorities, shall grant, subject to the criteria provided for in paragraph 2, the status of "authorised economic operator" to any economic operator established in the customs territory of the Community.

    An authorised economic operator shall benefit from facilitations with regard to customs controls relating to security and safety and/or from simplifications provided for under the customs rules.

    The status of authorised economic operator shall, subject to the rules and conditions laid down in paragraph 2, be recognised by the customs authorities in all Member States, without prejudice to customs controls. Customs authorities shall, on the basis of the recognition of the status of authorised economic operator and provided that the requirements relating to a specific type of simplification provided for in Community customs legislation are fulfilled, authorise the operator to benefit from that simplification.

2. The criteria for granting the status of authorised economic operator shall include:

    —   an appropriate record of compliance with customs requirements,

    —   a satisfactory system of managing commercial and, where appropriate, transport records, which allows appropriate customs controls,

    —   where appropriate, proven financial solvency, and

    —   where applicable, appropriate security and safety standards.

    The committee procedure shall be used to determine the rules:

    —   for granting the status of authorised economic operator,

    —   for granting authorisations for the use of simplifications,

    —   for establishing which customs authority is competent to grant such status and authorisations,

    —   for the type and extent of facilitations that may be granted in respect of customs controls relating to security and safety, taking into account the rules for common risk management,

    —   for consultation with, and provision of information to, other customs authorities;

    and the conditions under which:

    —   an authorisation may be limited to one or more Member States,

—   the status of authorised economic operator may be suspended or withdrawn, and

—   the requirement of being established in the Community may be waived for specific categories of authorised economic operator, taking into account, in particular, international agreements.][10]

Section 2

Decisions relating to the application of customs rules

Article 6

1.   Where a person requests that the customs authorities take a decision relating to the application of customs rules that person shall supply all the information and documents required by those authorities in order to take a decision.

2.   Such decision shall be taken and notified to the applicant at the earliest opportunity.

     Where a request for a decision is made in writing, the decision shall be made within a period laid down in accordance with the existing provisions, starting on the date on which the said request is received by the customs authorities. Such a decision must be notified in writing to the applicant.

     However, that period may be exceeded where the customs authorities are unable to comply with it. In that case, those authorities shall so inform the applicant before the expiry of the abovementioned period, stating the grounds which justify exceeding it and indicating the further period of time which they consider necessary in order to give a ruling on the request.

3.   Decisions adopted by the customs authorities in writing which either reject requests or are detrimental to the persons to whom they are addressed shall set out the grounds on which they are based. They shall refer to the right of appeal provided for in Article 243.

4.   Provision may be made for the first sentence of paragraph 3 to apply likewise to other decisions.

Article 7

Save in the cases provided for in the second subparagraph of Article 244, decisions adopted shall be immediately enforceable by customs authorities.

Article 8

1.   A decision favourable to the person concerned shall be annulled if it was issued on the basis of incorrect or incomplete information and:

     -    the applicant knew or should reasonably have known that the information was incorrect or incomplete, and

- such decision could not have been taken on the basis of correct or complete information.

2. The persons to whom the decision was addressed shall be notified of its annulment.

3. Annulment shall take effect from the date on which the annulled decision was taken.

Article 9

1. A decision favourable to the person concerned, shall be revoked or amended where, in cases other than those referred to in Article 8, one or more of the conditions laid down for its issue were not or are no longer fulfilled.

2. A decision favourable to the person concerned may be revoked where the person to whom it is addressed fails to fulfil an obligation imposed on him under that decision.

3. The person to whom the decision is addressed shall be notified of its revocation or amendment.

4. The revocation or amendment of the decision shall take effect from the date of notification.

However, in exceptional cases where the legitimate interests of the person to whom the decision is addressed so require, the customs authorities may defer the date when revocation or amendment takes effect.

Article 10

Articles 8 and 9 shall be without prejudice to national rules which stipulate that decisions are invalid or become null and void for reasons unconnected with customs legislation.

Section 3
Information

Article 11

1. Any person may request information concerning the application of customs legislation from the customs authorities.

Such a request may be refused where it does not relate to an import or export operation actually envisaged.

2. The information shall be supplied to the applicant free of charge. However, where special costs are incurred by the customs authorities, in particular as a result of analyses or expert reports on goods, or the return of the goods to the applicant, he may be charged the relevant amount.

Article 12

Note
Article 12 is omitted as it refers specifically to Customs Duty.

Section 4

Other provisions

[Article 13

1. Customs authorities may, in accordance with the conditions laid down by the provisions in force, carry out all the controls they deem necessary to ensure that customs rules and other legislation governing the entry, exit, transit, transfer and end-use of goods moved between the customs territory of the Community and third countries and the presence of goods that do not have Community status are correctly applied. Customs controls for the purpose of the correct application of Community legislation may be carried out in a third country where an international agreement provides for this.

2. Customs controls, other than spot-checks, shall be based on risk analysis using automated data processing techniques, with the purpose of identifying and quantifying the risks and developing the necessary measures to assess the risks, on the basis of criteria developed at national, Community and, where available, international level.

    The committee procedure shall be used for determining a common risk management framework, and for establishing common criteria and priority control areas.

    Member States, in cooperation with the Commission, shall establish a computer system for the implementation of risk management.

3. Where controls are performed by authorities other than the customs authorities, such controls shall be performed in close coordination with the customs authorities, wherever possible at the same time and place.

4. In the context of the controls provided for in this Article, customs and other competent authorities, such as veterinary and police authorities, may communicate data received, in connection with the entry, exit, transit, transfer and end-use of goods moved between the customs territory of the Community and third countries and the presence of goods that do not have Community status, between each other and to the customs authorities of the Member States and to the Commission where this is required for the purposes of minimising risk.

    Communication of confidential data to the customs authorities and other bodies (e.g. security agencies) of third countries shall be allowed only in the framework of an international agreement and provided that the data protection provisions in force, in particular Directive 95/46/EC of the European Parliament and of the Council of 24 October 1995 on the protection of individuals with regard to the processing of personal data and on the free movement of such data and Regulation (EC) No 45/2001 of the European Parliament and of the Council of 18 December 2000 on the protection of individuals with regard to the processing of personal data by the Community institutions and bodies and on the free movement of such data are respected.][11]

Article 14

For the purposes of applying customs legislation, any person directly or indirectly involved in the operations concerned for the purposes of trade in goods shall provide the customs authorities with all the requisite documents and information, irrespective of the medium used, and all the requisite assistance at their request and by any time limit prescribed.

[Article 15

All information which is by nature confidential or which is provided on a confidential basis shall be covered by the duty of professional secrecy. It shall not be disclosed by the competent authorities without the express permission of the person or authority providing it. The communication of information shall, however, be permitted where the competent authorities are obliged to do so pursuant to the provisions in force, particularly in connection with legal proceedings. Any disclosure or communication of information shall fully comply with prevailing data protection provisions, in particular Directive 95/46/EC and Regulation (EC) No 45/2001.][12]

Article 16

The persons concerned shall keep the documents referred to in Article 14 for the purposes of [customs controls][13], for the period laid down in the provisions in force and for at least three calendar years, irrespective of the medium used. That period shall run from the end of the year in which:

(a)   in the case of goods released for free circulation in circumstances other than those referred to in (b) or goods declared for export, from the end of the year in which the declarations for release for free circulation or export are accepted;

(b)   in the case of goods released for free circulation at a reduced or zero rate of import duty on account of their end-use, from the end of the year in which they cease to be subject to customs supervision;

(c)   in the case of goods placed under another customs procedure, from the end of the year in which the customs procedure concerned is completed;

(d)   in the case of goods placed in a free zone or free warehouse, from the end of the year on which they leave the undertaking concerned.

Without prejudice to the provisions of Article 221(3), second sentence, where a check carried out by the customs authorities in respect of a customs debt shows that the relevant entry in the accounts has to be corrected, the documents shall be kept beyond the time limit provided for in the first paragraph for a period sufficient to permit the correction to be made and checked.

Article 17

Where a period, date or time limit is laid down pursuant to customs legislation for the purpose of applying legislation, such period shall not be extended and such date or time limit shall not be deferred unless specific provision is made in the legislation concerned.

[Article 18

1.   The value of the ecu in national currencies to be applied for the purposes of determining the tariff classification of goods and import duties shall be fixed once a month. The rates to be used for this conversion shall be those published in the Official Journal of the European Communities on the penultimate working day of the month. Those rates shall apply throughout the following month.

     However, where the rate applicable at the start of the month differs by more than 5 % from that published on the penultimate working day before the 15th of that same month, the latter rate shall apply from the 15th until the end of the month in question.

2.   The value of the ecu in national currencies to be applied within the framework of customs legislation in cases other than those referred to in paragraph 1 shall be fixed once a year. The rates to be used for this conversion shall be those published in the Official Journal of the European Communities on the first working day of October, with effect from 1 January of the following year. If no rate is available for a particular national currency, the rate applicable to that currency shall be that obtaining on the last day for which a rate was published in the Official Journal of the European Communities.

3.   The customs authorities may round up or down the sum resulting from the conversion into their national currency of an amount expressed in ecus for purposes other than determining the tariff classification of goods or import or export duties.

The rounded-off amount may not differ from the original amount by more than 5%. The customs authorities may retain unchanged the national-currency value of an amount expressed in ecus if, at the time of the annual adjustment provided for in paragraph 2, the conversion of that amount, prior to the abovementioned rounding-off, results in a variation of less than 5% in the national-currency value or a reduction in that value.][14]

Article 19

The procedure of the Committee shall be used to determine in which cases and under which conditions the application of customs legislation may be simplified.

TITLE II

factors on the basis of which import duties or export duties and the other measures prescribed in respect of trade in goods are applied

Chapter 1

customs tariff of the european communities and tariff classification of goods

Articles 20 - 26

Note

   Articles 20-26 are omitted as they refer specifically to Customs Duty.

Section 2

Preferential origin of goods

Article 27

The rules on preferential origin shall lay down the conditions governing acquisition of origin which goods must fulfil in order to benefit from the measures referred to in Article 20(3)(d) or (e).

Those rules shall:

(a)   in the case of goods covered by the agreements referred to in Article 20(3)(d), be determined in those agreements;

(b)   in the case of goods benefitting from the preferential tariff measures referred to in Article 20(3)(e), be determined in accordance with the Committee procedure.

Chapter 3

value of goods for customs purposes

Article 28

The provisions of this Chapter shall determine the customs value for the purposes of applying the Customs Tariff of the European Communities and non-tariff measures laid down by Community provisions governing specific fields relating to trade in goods.

Article 29

1.   The customs value of imported goods shall be the transaction value, that is, the price actually paid or payable for the goods when sold for export to the customs territory of the Community, adjusted, where necessary, in accordance with Articles 32 and 33, provided:

(a)   that there are no restrictions as to the disposal or use of the goods by the buyer, other than restrictions which:

| | - | are imposed or required by a law or by the public authorities in the Community, |

         -     limit the geographical area in which the goods may be resold,

or

         -     do not substantially affect the value of the goods;

(b)   that the sale or price is not subject to some condition or consideration for which a value cannot be determined with respect to the goods being valued;

(c)   that no part of the proceeds of any subsequent resale, disposal or use of the goods by the buyer will accrue directly or indirectly to the seller, unless an appropriate adjustment can be made in accordance with Article 32; and

(d)   that the buyer and seller are not related, or, where the buyer and seller are related, that the transaction value is acceptable for customs purposes under paragraph 2.

2.   (a)   In determining whether the transaction value is acceptable for the purposes of paragraph 1, the fact that the buyer and the seller are related shall not in itself be sufficient grounds for regarding the transaction value as unacceptable. Where necessary, the circumstances surrounding the sale shall be examined and the transaction value shall be accepted provided that the relationship did not influence the price. If, in the light of information provided by the declarant or otherwise, the customs authorities have grounds for considering that the relationship influenced the price, they shall communicate their grounds to the declarant and he shall be given a reasonable opportunity to respond. If the declarant so requests, the communication of the grounds shall be in writing.

        (b)   In a sale between related persons, the transaction value shall be accepted and the goods valued in accordance with paragraph 1 wherever the declarant demonstrates that such value closely approximates to one of the following occurring at or about the same time:

            (i)   the transaction value in sales, between buyers and sellers who are not related in any particular case, of identical or similar goods for export to the Community;

            (ii)   the customs value of identical or similar goods, as determined under Article 30(2)(c);

            (iii)   the customs value of identical or similar goods, as determined under Article 30(2)(d).

         In applying the foregoing tests, due account shall be taken of demonstrated differences in commercial levels, quantity levels, the elements enumerated in Article 32 and costs incurred by the seller in sales in which he and the buyer are not related and where such costs are not incurred by the seller in sales in which he and the buyer are related.

(c) The tests set forth in subparagraph (b) are to be used at the initiative of the declarant and only for comparison purposes. Substitute values may not be established under the said subparagraph.

3. (a) The price actually paid or payable is the total payment made or to be made by the buyer to or for the benefit of the seller for the imported goods and includes all payments made or to be made as a condition of sale of the imported goods by the buyer to the seller or by the buyer to a third party to satisfy an obligation of the seller. The payment need not necessarily take the form of a transfer of money. Payment may be made by way of letters of credit or negotiable instrument and may be made directly or indirectly.

(b) Activities, including marketing activities, undertaken by the buyer on his own account, other than those for which an adjustment is provided in Article 32, are not considered to be an indirect payment to the seller, even though they might be regarded as of benefit to the seller or have been undertaken by agreement with the seller, and their cost shall not be added to the price actually paid or payable in determining the customs value of imported goods.

Article 30

1. Where the customs value cannot be determined under Article 29, it is to be determined by proceeding sequentially through subparagraphs (a), (b), (c) and (d) of paragraph 2 to the first subparagraph under which it can be determined, subject to the proviso that the order of application of subparagraphs (c) and (d) shall be reversed if the declarant so requests; it is only when such value cannot be determined under a particular subparagraph that the provisions of the next subparagraph in a sequence established by virtue of this paragraph can be applied.

2. The customs value as determined under this Article shall be:

(a) the transaction value of identical goods sold for export to the Community and exported at or about the same time as the goods being valued;

(b) the transaction value of similar goods sold for export to the Community and exported at or about the same time as the goods being valued;

(c) the value based on the unit price at which the imported goods for identical or similar imported goods are sold within the

Community in the greatest aggregate quantity to persons not related to the sellers;

(d)   the computed value, consisting of the sum of:

   -     the cost or value of materials and fabrication or other processing employed in producing the imported goods,

   -     an amount for profit and general expenses equal to that usually reflected in sales of goods of the same class or kind as the goods being valued which are made by producers in the country of exportation for export to the Community,

   -     the cost or value of the items referred to in Article 32(1)(e).

3.   Any further conditions and rules for the application of paragraph 2 above shall be determined in accordance with the committee procedure.

Article 31

1.   Where the customs value of imported goods cannot be determined under Articles 29 or 30, it shall be determined, on the basis of data available in the Community, using reasonable means consistent with the principles and general provisions of:

   -     the agreement on implementation of Article VII of the General Agreement on Tariffs and Trade, [of 1994,][15]

   -     Article VII of the General Agreement on Tariffs and Trade, [of 1994,][15]

   -     the provisions of this chapter.

2.   No customs value shall be determined under paragraph 1 on the basis of:

(a)   the selling price in the Community of goods produced in the Community;

(b)   a system which provides for the acceptance for customs purposes of the higher of two alternative values;

(c)   the price of goods on the domestic market of the country of exportation;

(d)   the cost of production, other than computed values which have been determined for identical or similar goods in accordance with Article 30(2)(d);

(e)   prices for export to a country not forming part of the customs territory of the Community;

(f)   minimum customs values; or

(g)   arbitrary or fictitious values.

Article 32

1.   In determining the customs value under Article 29, there shall be added to the price actually paid or payable for the imported goods:

(a)   the following, to the extent that they are incurred by the buyer but are not included in the price actually paid or payable for the goods:

(i)   commissions and brokerage, except buying commissions,

(ii)   the cost of containers which are treated as being one, for customs purposes, with the goods in question,

(iii)   the cost of packing, whether for labour or materials;

(b)   the value, apportioned as appropriate, of the following goods and services where supplied directly or indirectly by the buyer free of charge or at reduced cost for use in connection with the production and sale for export of the imported goods, to the extent that such value has not been included in the price actually paid or payable:

(i)   materials, components, parts and similar items incorporated in the imported goods,

(ii)   tools, dies, moulds and similar items used in the production of the imported goods,

(iii)   materials consumed in the production of the imported goods,

(iv)   engineering, development, artwork, design work, and plans and sketches undertaken elsewhere than in the Community and necessary for the production of the imported goods;

(c)   royalties and licence fees related to the goods being valued that the buyer must pay, either directly or indirectly, as a condition of sale of the goods being valued, to the extent that such royalties and fees are not included in the price actually paid or payable;

(d)   the value of any part of the proceeds of any subsequent resale, disposal or use of the imported goods that accrues directly or indirectly to the seller;

(e)   (i)   the cost of transport and insurance of the imported goods, and

(ii)   loading and handling charges associated with the transport of the imported goods

to the place of introduction into the customs territory of the Community.

2.   Additions to the price actually paid or payable shall be made under this Article only on the basis of objective and quantifiable data.

3.   No additions shall be made to the price actually paid or payable in determining the customs value except as provided in this Article.

4.   In this Chapter, the term 'buying commissions' means fees paid by an importer to his agent for the service of representing him in the purchase of the goods being valued.

5.   Notwithstanding paragraph 1(c):

     (a)   charges for the right to reproduce the imported goods in the Community shall not be added to the price actually paid or payable for the imported goods in determining the customs value; and

     (b)   payments made by the buyer for the right to distribute or resell the imported goods shall not be added to the price actually paid or payable for the imported goods if such payments are not a condition of the sale for export to the Community of the goods.

Article 33

1.   Provided that they are shown separately from the price actually paid or payable, the following shall not be included in the customs value:

     (a)   charges for the transport of goods after their arrival at the place of introduction into the customs territory of the Community;

     (b)   charges for construction, erection, assembly, maintenance or technical assistance, undertaken after importation of imported goods such as industrial plant, machinery or equipment;

     (c)   charges for interest under a financing arrangement entered into by the buyer and relating to the purchase of imported goods, irrespective of whether the finance is provided by the seller or another person, provided that the financing arrangement has been made in writing and where required, the buyer can demonstrate that:

          –   such goods are actually sold at the price declared as the price actually paid or payable, and

          –   the claimed rate of interest does not exceed the level for such transactions prevailing in the country where, and at the time when, the finance was provided;

     (d)   charges for the right to reproduce imported goods in the Community;

     (e)   buying commissions;

     (f)   import duties or other charges payable in the Community by reason of the importation or sale of the goods.

Article 34

Specific rules may be laid down in accordance with the procedure of the committee to determine the customs value of carrier media for use in data processing equipment and bearing data or instructions.

Article 35

[Where factors used to determine the customs value of goods are expressed in a currency other than that of the Member State where the valuation is made, the rate of exchange to be used shall be that duly published by the authorities competent in the matter.][9]

Such rate shall reflect as effectively as possible the current value of such currency in commercial transactions in terms of the currency of such Member State and shall apply during such period as may be determined in accordance with the procedure of the committee.

Where such a rate does not exist, the rate of exchange to be used shall be determined in accordance with the procedure of the committee.

Article 36

1. The provisions of this chapter shall be without prejudice to the specific provisions regarding the determination of the value for customs purposes of goods released for free circulation after being assigned a different customs-approved treatment or use.

2. By way of derogation from Articles 29, 30 and 31, the customs value of perishable goods usually delivered on consignment may, at the request of the declarant, be determined under simplified rules drawn up for the whole Community in accordance with the committee procedure.

[Article 36a

1. Goods brought into the customs territory of the Community shall be covered by a summary declaration, with the exception of goods carried on means of transport only passing through the territorial waters or the airspace of the customs territory without a stop within this territory.

2. The summary declaration shall be lodged at the customs office of entry.

   Customs authorities may allow the summary declaration to be lodged at another customs office, provided that this office immediately communicates or makes available electronically the necessary particulars to the customs office of entry.

   Customs authorities may accept, instead of the lodging of the summary declaration, the lodging of a notification and access to the summary declaration data in the economic operator's computer system.

3. The summary declaration shall be lodged before the goods are brought into the customs territory of the Community.

4. The committee procedure shall be used to establish:

- the time limit by which the summary declaration is to be lodged before the goods are brought into the customs territory of the Community,

- the rules for exceptions from, and variations to, the time limit referred to in the first indent, and

- the conditions under which the requirement for a summary declaration may be waived or adapted,

in accordance with the specific circumstances and for particular types of goods traffic, modes of transport and economic operators and where international agreements provide for special security arrangements.

Article 36b

1. The committee procedure shall be used to establish a common data set and format for the summary declaration, containing the particulars necessary for risk analysis and the proper application of customs controls, primarily for security and safety purposes, using, where appropriate, international standards and commercial practices.

2. The summary declaration shall be made using a data processing technique. Commercial, port or transport information may be used, provided that it contains the necessary particulars.

   Customs authorities may accept paper-based summary declarations in exceptional circumstances, provided that they apply the same level of risk management as that applied to summary declarations made using a data processing technique.

3. The summary declaration shall be lodged by the person who brings the goods, or who assumes responsibility for the carriage of the goods into the customs territory of the Community.

4. Notwithstanding the obligation of the person referred to in paragraph 3, the summary declaration may be lodged instead by:

   (a) the person in whose name the person referred to in paragraph 3 acts; or

   (b) any person who is able to present the goods in question or to have them presented to the competent customs authority; or

   (c) a representative of one of the persons referred to in paragraph 3 or points (a) or (b).

5. The person referred to in paragraphs 3 and 4 shall, at his request, be authorised to amend one or more particulars of the summary declaration after it has been lodged. However, no amendment shall be possible after the customs authorities:

   (a) have informed the person who lodged the summary declaration that they intend to examine the goods; or

   (b) have established that the particulars in questions are incorrect; or

(c)   have allowed the removal of the goods.

Article 36c

1.   The customs office of entry may waive the lodging of a summary declaration in respect of goods for which, before expiry of the time limit referred to in Article 36a(3) or (4), a customs declaration is lodged. In such case, the customs declaration shall contain at least the particulars necessary for a summary declaration and, until such time as the former is accepted in accordance with Article 63, it shall have the status of a summary declaration.

      Customs authorities may allow the customs declaration to be lodged at a customs office of import different from the customs office of entry, provided that this office immediately communicates or makes available electronically the necessary particulars to the customs office of entry.

2.   Where the customs declaration is lodged other than by use of data processing technique, the customs authorities shall apply the same level of risk management to the data as that applied to customs declarations made using a data processing technique.][16]

TITLE III

provisions applicable to goods brought into the customs territory of the community until they are assigned a customs-approved treatment or use

Chapter 1

entry of goods into the customs territory of the community

Article 37

1.   Goods brought into the customs territory of the Community shall, from the time of their entry, be subject to customs supervision. They may be subject to [customs controls][17] in accordance with the provisions in force.

2.   They shall remain under such supervision for as long as necessary to determine their customs status, if appropriate, and in the case of non-Community goods and without prejudice to Article 82(1), until their customs status is changed, they enter a free zone or free warehouse or they are re-exported or destroyed in accordance with Article 182.

Article 38

1.   Goods brought into the customs territory of the Community shall be conveyed by the person bringing them into the Community without delay, by the route specified by the customs authorities and in accordance with their instructions, if any:

(a)   to the customs office designated by the customs authorities or to any other place designated or approved by those authorities; or,

(b)   to a free zone, if the goods are to be brought into that free zone direct:

–   by sea or air, or

–   by land without passing through another part of the customs territory of the Community, where the free zone adjoins the land frontier between a Member State and a third country.

2.   Any person who assumes responsibility for the carriage of goods after they have been brought into the customs territory of the Community, inter alia as a result of transhipment, shall become responsible for compliance with the obligation laid down in paragraph 1.

3.   Goods which, although still outside the customs territory of the Community, may be subject to [customs controls by][17] a Member State under the provisions in force, as a result of inter alia an agreement concluded between that Member State and a third country, shall be treated in the same way as goods brought into the customs territory of the Community.

4.   Paragraph 1(a) shall not preclude implementation of any provisions in force with respect to tourist traffic, frontier traffic, postal traffic or traffic of negligible economic importance, on condition that customs supervision and customs control possibilities are not thereby jeopardized.

[5.   Paragraphs 1 to 4 and Articles 36a to 36c and 39 to 53 shall not apply to goods which temporarily leave the customs territory of the Community while moving between two points in that territory by sea or air, provided that the carriage is effected by a direct route and by regular air or shipping services without a stop outside the customs territory of the Community.][18]

6.   Paragraph 1 shall not apply to goods on board vessels or aircraft crossing the territorial sea or airspace of the Member States without having as their destination a port or airport situated in those Member States.

Article 39

1.   Where, by reason of unforeseeable circumstances or force majeure, the obligation laid down in Article 38(1) cannot be complied with, the person bound by that obligation or any other person acting in his place shall inform the customs authorities of the situation without delay. Where the unforeseeable circumstances or force majeure do not result in total loss of the goods, the customs authorities shall also be informed of their precise location.

2.   Where, by reason of unforeseeable circumstances or force majeure, a vessel or aircraft covered by Article 38(6) is forced to put into port or land temporarily in the customs territory of the Community and the obligation laid down in Article 38(1) cannot be complied with, the person bringing the vessel or aircraft into the customs territory of the Community or any other person acting in his place shall inform the customs authorities of the situation without delay.

3. The customs authorities shall determine the measures to be taken in order to permit customs supervision of the goods referred to in paragraph 1 as well as those on board a vessel or aircraft in the circumstances specified in paragraph 2 and to ensure, where appropriate, that they are subsequently conveyed to a customs office or other place designated or approved by the authorities.

Chapter 2

presentation of goods to customs

[Article 40

Goods entering the customs territory of the Community shall be presented to customs by the person who brings them into that territory or, if appropriate, by the person who assumes responsibility for carriage of the goods following such entry, with the exception of goods carried on means of transport only passing through the territorial waters or the airspace of the customs territory of the Community without a stop within this territory. The person presenting the goods shall make a reference to the summary declaration or customs declaration previously lodged in respect of the goods.][19]

Article 41

Article 40 shall not preclude the implementation of rules in force relating to goods:

    (a)   carried by travellers;

    (b)   placed under a customs procedure but not presented to customs.

Article 42

Goods may, once they have been presented to customs, and with the permission of the customs authorities, be examined or samples may be taken, in order that they may be assigned a customs-approved treatment or use. Such permission shall be granted, on request, to the person authorized to assign the goods such treatment or use.

Chapter 3

[Unloading of goods presented to customs][20]

[...][21]

Article 46

1. Goods shall be unloaded or transhipped from the means of transport carrying them solely with the permission of the customs authorities in places designated or approved by those customs authorities.

   However, such permission shall not be required in the event of the imminent danger necessitating the immediate unloading of all or part of the goods. In that case, the customs authorities shall be informed accordingly forthwith.

2. For the purpose of inspecting goods and the means of transport carrying them, the customs authorities may at any time require goods to be unloaded and unpacked.

Article 47

Goods shall not be removed from their original position without the permission of the customs authorities.

Chapter 4

obligation to assign goods presented to customs a customs-approved treatment or use

Article 48

Note

Articles 48-57 are omitted as they refer specifically to Customs Duty.

TITLE IV

customs-approved treatment or use

Chapter 1

General

Article 58

1. Save as otherwise provided, goods may at any time, under the conditions laid down, be assigned any customs-approved treatment or use irrespective of their nature or quantity, or their country of origin, consignment or destination.
2. Paragraph 1 shall not preclude the imposition of prohibitions or restrictions justified on grounds of public morality, public policy or public security, the protection of health and life of humans, animals or plants, the protection of national treasures possessing artistic, historic or archaeological value or the protection of industrial and commercial property.

Chapter 2

customs procedures

Section 1

Placing of goods under a customs procedure

Article 59

1. All goods intended to be placed under a customs procedure shall be covered by a declaration for that customs procedure.

2.   Community goods declared for an export, outward processing, transit or customs warehousing procedure shall be subject to customs supervision from the time of acceptance of the customs declaration until such time as they leave the customs territory of the Community or are destroyed or the customs declaration is invalidated.

Article 60

Insofar as Community customs legislation lays down no rules on the matter, Member States shall determine the competence of the various customs offices situated in their territory, account being taken, where applicable, of the nature of the goods and the customs procedure under which they are to be placed.

Article 61

The customs declaration shall be made:

(a)   in writing; or

(b)   using a data-processing technique where provided for by provisions laid down in accordance with the committee procedure or where authorized by the customs authorities; or

(c)   by means of a normal declaration or any other act whereby the holder of the goods expresses his wish to place them under a customs procedure, where such a possibility is provided for by the rules adopted in accordance with the committee procedure.

A. Declarations in writing

I. Normal procedure

Article 62

1.   Declarations in writing shall be made on a form corresponding to the official specimen prescribed for that purpose. They shall be signed and contain all the particulars necessary for implementation of the provisions governing the customs procedure for which the goods are declared.

2.   The declaration shall be accompanied by all the documents required for implementation of the provisions governing the customs procedure for which the goods are declared.

Article 63

Declarations which comply with the conditions laid down in Article 62 shall be accepted by the customs authorities immediately, provided that the goods to which they refer are presented to customs.

Article 64

1.   Subject to Article 5, a customs declaration may be made by any person

who is able to present the goods in question or to have them presented to the competent customs authority, together with all the documents which are required to be produced for the application of the rules governing the customs procedure in respect of which the goods were declared.

2. However,

    (a) where acceptance of a customs declaration imposes particular obligations on a specific person, the declaration must be made by that person or on his behalf;

    (b) the declarant must be established in the Community.

However, the condition regarding establishment in the Community shall not apply to persons who:

    - make a declaration for transit or temporary importation;

    - declare goods on an occasional basis, provided that the customs authorities consider this to be justified.

3. Paragraph 2(b) shall not preclude the application by the Member States of bilateral agreements concluded with third countries, or customary practices having similar effect, under which nationals of such countries may make customs declarations in the territory of the Member States in question, subject to reciprocity.

Article 65

The declaration shall, at his request, be authorized to amend one or more of the particulars of the declaration after it has been accepted by customs. The amendment shall not have the effect of rendering the declaration applicable to goods other than those it originally covered.

However, no amendment shall be permitted where authorization is requested after the customs authorities:

    (a) have informed the declarant that they intend to examine the goods; or,

    (b) have established that the particulars in question are incorrect; or,

    (c) have released the goods.

Article 66

1. The customs authorities shall, at the request of the declarant, invalidate a declaration already accepted where the declarant furnishes proof that goods were declared in error for the customs procedure covered by that declaration or that, as a result of special circumstances, the placing of the goods under the customs procedure for which they were declared is no longer justified.

Nevertheless, where the customs authorities have informed the declarant of their intention to examine the goods, a request for invalidation of the declaration shall not be accepted until after the examination has taken place.

2.   The declaration shall not be invalidated after the goods have been released, expect in cases defined in accordance with the committee procedure.

3.   Invalidation of the declaration shall be without prejudice to the application of the penal provisions in force.

Article 67

Save as otherwise expressly provided, the date to be used for the purposes of all the provisions governing the customs procedure for which the goods are declared shall be the date of acceptance of the declaration by the customs authorities.

Article 68

For the verification of declarations which they have accepted, the customs authorities may:

(a)   examine the documents covering the declaration and the documents accompanying it. The customs authorities may require the declarant to present other documents for the purpose of verifying the accuracy of the particulars contained in the declaration;

(b)   examine the goods and take samples for analysis or for detailed examination.

Article 69

1.   Transport of the goods to the places where they are to be examined and samples are to be taken, and all the handling necessitated by such examination or taking of samples, shall be carried out by or under the responsibility of the declarant. The costs incurred shall be borne by the declarant.

2.   The declarant shall be entitled to be present when the goods are examined and when samples are taken. Where they deem it appropriate, the customs authorities shall require the declarant to be present or represented when the goods are examined or samples are taken in order to provide them with the assistance necessary to facilitate such examination or taking of samples.

3.   Provided that samples are taken in accordance with the provisions in force, the customs authorities shall not be liable for payment of any compensation in respect thereof but shall bear the costs of their analysis or examination.

Article 70

1.   Where only part of the goods covered by a declaration are examined, the results of the partial examination shall be taken to apply to all the goods covered by that declaration.

However, the declarant may request a further examination of the goods if he considers that the results of the partial examination are not valid as regards the remainder of the goods declared.

2. For the purposes of paragraph 1, where a declaration form covers two or more items, the particulars relating to each item shall be deemed to constitute a separate declaration.

Article 71

1. The results of verifying the declaration shall be used for the purposes of applying the provisions governing the customs procedure under which the goods are placed.

2. Where the declaration is not verified, the provisions referred to in paragraph 1 shall be applied on the basis of the particulars contained in the declaration.

Article 72

1. The customs authorities shall take the measures necessary to identify the goods where identification is required in order to ensure compliance with the conditions governing the customs procedure for which the said goods have been declared.

2. Means of identification affixed to the goods or means of transport shall be removed or destroyed only by the customs authorities or with their permission unless, as a result of unforeseeable circumstances or force majeure, their removal or destruction is essential to ensure the protection of the goods or means of transport.

Article 73

1. Without prejudice to Article 74, where the conditions for placing the goods under the procedure in question are fulfilled and provided the goods are not subject to any prohibitive or restrictive measures, the customs authorities shall release the goods as soon as the particulars in the declaration have been verified or accepted without verification. The same shall apply where such verification cannot be completed within a reasonable period of time and the goods are no longer required to be present for verification purposes.

2. All the goods covered by the same declaration shall be released at the same time.

    For the purposes of this paragraph, where a declaration form covers two or more items, the particulars relating to each item shall be deemed to constitute a separate declaration.

Article 74

1. Where acceptance of a customs declaration gives rise to a customs debt, the goods covered by the declaration shall not be released unless the customs debt has been paid or secured.

However, without prejudice to paragraph 2, this provision shall not apply to the temporary importation procedure with partial relief from import duties.

2. Where, pursuant to the provisions governing the customs procedure for which the goods are declared, the customs authorities require the provision of a security, the said goods shall not be released for the customs procedure in question until such security is provided.

Article 75

Any necessary measures, including confiscation and sale, shall be taken to deal with goods which:

(a)   cannot be released because:

-       it has not been possible to undertake or continue examination of the goods within the period prescribed by the customs authorities for reasons attributable to the declarant; or,

-       the documents which must be produced before the goods can be placed under the customs procedure requested have not been produced; or,

-       payments or security which should have been made or provided in respect of import duties or export duties, as the case may be, have not been made or provided within the period prescribed; or

-       they are subject to bans or restrictions;

(b)   are not removed within a reasonable period after their release.

II. Simplified procedures

Article 76

1. In order to simplify completion of formalities and procedures as far as possible while ensuring that operations are conducted in a proper manner, the customs authorities shall, under conditions laid down in accordance with the committee procedure, grant permission for:

(a)   the declaration referred to in Article 62 to omit certain of the particulars referred to in paragraph 1 of that Article for some of the documents referred to in paragraph 2 of that Article not to be attached thereto;

(b)   a commercial or administrative document, accompanied by request for the goods to be placed under the customs procedure in question, to be lodged in place of the declaration referred to in Article 62;

(c)   the goods to be entered for the procedure in question by means of an entry in the records; in this case, the customs authorities may waive the requirement that the declarant presents the goods to customs.

The simplified declaration, commercial or administrative document or entry in the records must contain at least the particulars necessary for identification of the goods. Where the goods are entered in the records, the date of such entry must be included.

2.   Except in cases to be determined in accordance with the committee procedure, the declarant shall furnish a supplementary declaration which may be of a general, periodic or recapitulative nature.

3.   Supplementary declarations and the simplified declarations referred to in subparagraphs 1(a), (b) and (c), shall be deemed to constitute a single, indivisible instrument taking effect on the date of acceptance of the simplified declarations; in the cases referred to in subparagraph 1(c), entry in the records shall have the same legal force as acceptance of the declaration referred to in Article 62.

4.   Special simplified procedures for the Community transit procedure shall be laid down in accordance with the committee procedure.

B. Other declarations

Article 77

[1.][22] Where the customs declaration is made by means of a data-processing technique within the meaning of Article 61(b), or by an oral declaration or any other act within the meaning of Article 61(c), Articles 62 to 76 shall apply mutatis mutandis without prejudice to the principles set out therein.

[2.   Where the customs declaration is made by means of a data-processing technique, the customs authorities may allow accompanying documents referred to in Article 62(2) not to be lodged with the declaration. In this case the documents shall be kept at the customs authorities' disposal.][22]

C. Post-clearance examination of declarations

Article 78

1.   The customs authorities may, on their own initiative or at the request of the declarant, amend the declaration after release of the goods.

2.   The customs authorities may, after releasing the goods and in order to satisfy themselves as to the accuracy of the particulars contained in the declaration, inspect the commercial documents and data relating to the import or export operations in respect of the goods concerned or to subsequent commercial operations involving those goods. Such inspections may be carried out at the premises of the declarant, of any

other person directly or indirectly involved in the said operations in a business capacity or of any other person in possession of the said document and data for business purposes. Those authorities may also examine the goods where it is still possible for them to be produced.

3. Where revision of the declaration or post-clearance examination indicates that the provisions governing the customs procedure concerned have been applied on the basis of incorrect or incomplete information, the customs authorities shall, in accordance with any provisions laid down, take the measures necessary to regularize the situation, taking account of the new information available to them.

Section 2

Release for free circulation

Article 79

Release for free circulation shall confer on non-Community goods the customs status of Community goods.

It shall entail application of commercial policy measures, completion of the other formalities laid down in respect of the importation of goods and the charging of any duties legally due.

Article 80

1. By way of derogation from Article 67, provided that the import duty chargeable on the goods is one of the duties referred to in the first indent of Article 4(10) and that the rate of duty is reduced after the date of acceptance of the declaration for release for free circulation but before the goods are released, the declarant may request application of the more favourable rate.

2. Paragraph 1 shall not apply where it has not been possible to release the goods for reasons attributable to the declarant alone.

Article 81

Where a consignment is made up of goods falling within different tariff classifications, and dealing with each of those goods in accordance with its tariff classification for the purpose of drawing up the declaration would entail a burden of work and expense disproportionate to the import duties chargeable, the customs authorities may, at the request of the declarant, agree that import duties be charged on the whole consignment on the basis of the tariff classification of the goods which are subject to the highest rate of import duty.

Article 82

1. Where goods are released for free circulation at a reduced or zero rate of duty on account of their end-use, they shall remain under customs supervision. Customs supervision shall end when the conditions laid down for granting such a reduced or zero rate of duty cease to apply,

where the goods are exported or destroyed or where the use of the goods for purposes other than those laid down for the application of the reduced or zero rate of duty is permitted subject to payment of the duties due.

2.   Articles 88 and 90 shall apply mutatis mutandis to the goods referred to in paragraph 1.

Article 83

Goods released for free circulation shall lose their customs status as Community goods where:

(a)   the declaration for release for free circulation is invalidated after release [...][23], or

(b)   the imported duties payable on those goods are repaid or remitted:

-    under the inward processing procedure in the form of the drawback system;

or

-    in respect of defective goods or goods which fail to comply with the terms of the contract, pursuant to Article 238; or

-    in situations of the type referred to in Article 239 where repayment or remission is conditional upon the goods being exported or re-exported or being assigned an equivalent customs-approved treatment or use.

Section 3

Suspensive arrangements and customs procedures with economic impact

A. Provisions common to several procedures

Article 84

1.   In Articles 85 to 90:

(a)   where the term '**procedure**' is used, it is understood as applying, in the case of non-Community goods, to the following arrangements:

-    external transit;

-    customs warehousing;

-    inward processing in the form of a system of suspension;

-    processing]under customs control;

-    temporary importation;

(b)   where the term '**customs procedure with economic impact**' is used, it is understood as applying to the following arrangements:

-     customs warehousing;
-     inward processing;
-     processing under customs control;
-     temporary importation;
-     outward processing.

2.   '**Import goods**' means goods placed under a suspensive procedure and goods which, under the inward processing procedure in the form of the drawback system, have undergone the formalities for release for free circulation and the formalities provided for in Article 125.

3.   '**Goods in the unaltered state**' means import goods which, under the inward processing procedure or the procedures for processing under customs control, have undergone no form of processing.

Article 85

The use of any customs procedure with economic impact shall be conditional upon authorization being issued by the customs authorities.

Article 86

Without prejudice to the additional special conditions governing the procedure in question, the authorization referred to in Article 85 and that referred to in Article 100(1) shall be granted only:

-     to persons who offer every guarantee necessary for the proper conduct of the operations;

-     where the customs authorities can supervise and monitor the procedure without having to introduce administrative arrangements disproportionate to the economic needs involved.

Article 87

1.   The conditions under which the procedure in question is used shall be set out in the authorization.

2.   The holder of the authorization shall notify the customs authorities of all factors arising after the authorization was granted which may influence its continuation or content.

[Article 87a]

In the cases referred to in the second sentence of the first indent of Article 4(7), any products or goods obtained from goods placed under a suspensive arrangement shall be considered as being placed under the same arrangement.][24]

Article 88

The customs authorities may make the placing of goods under a suspensive arrangement conditional upon the provision of security in order to ensure that any customs debt which may be incurred in respect of those goods will be paid.

Special provisions concerning the provision of security may be laid down in the context of a specific suspensive arrangement.

Article 89

1. A suspensive arrangement with economic impact shall be discharged when a new customs-approved treatment or use is assigned either to the goods placed under that arrangement or to compensating or processed products placed under it.

2. The customs authorities shall take all the measures necessary to regularize the position of goods in respect of which a procedure has not been discharged under the conditions prescribed.

Article 90

The rights and obligations of the holder of a customs procedure with economic impact may, on the conditions laid down by the customs authorities, be transferred successively to other persons who fulfil any conditions laid down in order to benefit from the procedure in question.

B. External transit

I. General provisions

Article 91 - 200

Note
Articles 91-200 are omitted as they refer specifically to Customs Duty.

Chapter 2

incurrence of a customs debt

Article 201

1. A customs debt on importation shall be incurred through:

    (a)   the release for free circulation of goods liable to import duties, or

    (b)   the placing of such goods under the temporary importation procedure with partial relief from import duties.

2. A customs debt shall be incurred at the time of acceptance of the customs declaration in question.

3. The debtor shall be the declarant. In the event of indirect representation,

the person on whose behalf the customs declaration is made shall also be a debtor.

Where a customs declaration in respect of one of the procedures referred to in paragraph 1 is drawn up on the basis of information which leads to all or part of the duties legally owed not being collected, the persons who provided the information required to draw up the declaration and who knew, or who ought reasonably to have known that such information was false, may also be considered debtors in accordance with the national provisions in force.

Article 202

1.   A customs debt on importation shall be incurred through:

(a)   the unlawful introduction into the customs territory of the Community of goods liable to import duties, or

(b)   the unlawful introduction into another part of that territory of such goods located in a free zone or free warehouse.

For the purpose of this Article, unlawful introduction means any introduction in violation of the provisions of Articles 38 to 41 and the second indent of Article 177.

2.   The customs debt shall be incurred at the moment when the goods are unlawfully introduced.

3.   The debtors shall be:

-        the person who introduced such goods unlawfully,

-        any persons who participated in the unlawful introduction of the goods and who were aware or should reasonably have been aware that such introduction was unlawful, and

-        any persons who acquired or held the goods in question and who were aware or should reasonably have been aware at the time of acquiring or receiving the goods that they had been introduced unlawfully.

Article 203

1.   A customs debt on importation shall be incurred through:

-        the unlawful removal from customs supervision of goods liable to import duties.

2.   The customs debt shall be incurred at the moment when the goods are removed from customs supervision.

3.   The debtors shall be:

-        the person who removed the goods from customs supervision,

-        any persons who participated in such removal and who were aware or should reasonably have been aware that the goods were being removed from customs supervision,

- any persons who acquired or held the goods in question and who were aware or should reasonably have been aware at the time of acquiring or receiving the goods that they had been removed from customs supervision, and

- where appropriate, the person required to fulfil the obligations arising from temporary storage of the goods or from the use of the customs procedure under which those goods are placed.

Article 204

1. A customs debt on importation shall be incurred through:

    (a)   non-fulfilment of one of the obligations arising, in respect of goods liable to import duties, from their temporary storage or from the use of the customs procedure under which they are placed, or

    (b)   non-compliance with a condition governing the placing of the goods under that procedure or the granting of a reduced or zero rate of import duty by virtue of the end-use of the goods,

    in cases other than those referred to in Article 203 unless it is established that those failures have no significant effect on the correct operation of the temporary storage or customs procedure in question.

2. The customs debt shall be incurred either at the moment when the obligation whose non-fulfilment gives rise to the customs debt ceases to be met or at the moment when the goods are placed under the customs procedure concerned where it is established subsequently that a condition governing the placing of the goods under the said procedure or the granting of a reduced or zero rate of import duty by virtue of the end-use of the goods was not in fact fulfilled.

3. The debtor shall be the person who is required, according to the circumstances, either to fulfil the obligations arising, in respect of goods liable to import duties, from their temporary storage or from the use of the customs procedure under which they have been placed, or to comply with the conditions governing the placing of the goods under that procedure.

Article 205

1. A customs debt on importation shall be incurred through:

    - the consumption or use, in a free zone or a free warehouse, of goods liable to import duties, under conditions other than those laid down by the legislation in force.

    Where goods disappear and where their disappearance cannot be explained to the satisfaction of the customs authorities, those authorities may regard the goods as having been consumed or used in the free zone or the free warehouse.

2.   The debt shall be incurred at the moment when the goods are consumed or are first used under conditions other than those laid down by the legislation in force.

3.   The debtor shall be the person who consumed or used the goods and any persons who participated in such consumption or use and who were aware or should reasonably have been aware that the goods were being consumed or used under conditions other than those laid down by the legislation in force.

Where customs authorities regard goods which have disappeared as having been consumed or used in the free zone or the free warehouse and it is not possible to apply the preceding paragraph, the person liable for payment of the customs debt shall be the last person known to these authorities to have been in possession of the goods.

Article 206

1.   By way of derogation from Articles 202 and 204(1)(a), no customs debt on importation shall be deemed to be incurred in respect of specific goods where the person concerned proves that the non-fulfilment of the obligations which arise from:

-         the provisions of Articles 38 to 41 and the second indent of Article 177, or

-         keeping the goods in question in temporary storage, or

-         the use of the customs procedure under which the goods have been placed,

results from the total destruction or irretrievable loss of the said goods as a result of the actual nature of the goods or unforeseeable circumstances or force majeure, or as a consequence of authorization by the customs authorities.

For the purposes of this paragraph, goods shall be irretrievably lost when they are rendered unusable by any person.

2.   Nor shall a customs debt on importation be deemed to be incurred in respect of goods released for free circulation at a reduced or zero rate of import duty by virtue of their end-use, where such goods are exported or re-exported with the permission of the customs authorities.

Article 207

Where, in accordance with Article 206(1), no customs debt is deemed to be incurred in respect of goods released for free circulation at a reduced or zero rate of import duty on account of their end-use, any scrap or waste resulting from such destruction shall be deemed to be non-Community goods.

Article 208

Where in accordance with Article 203 or 204 a customs debt is incurred in respect of goods released for free circulation at a reduced rate of import duty on account of their end-use, the amount paid when the goods were released for free circulation shall be deducted from the amount of the customs debt.

This provision shall apply mutatis mutandis where a customs debt is incurred in respect of scrap and waste resulting from the destruction of such goods.

Article 209

1. A customs debt on exportation shall be incurred through:
   - the exportation from the customs territory of the Community, under cover of a customs declaration, of goods liable to export duties.
2. The customs debt shall be incurred at the time when such customs declaration is accepted.
3. The debtor shall be the declarant. In the event of indirect representation, the person on whose behalf the declaration is made shall also be a debtor.

Article 210

1. A customs debt on exportation shall be incurred through:
   - the removal from the customs territory of the Community of goods liable to export duties without a customs declaration.
2. The customs debt shall be incurred at the time when the said goods actually leave that territory.
3. The debtor shall be:
   - the person who removed the goods, and
   - any persons who participated in such removal and who were aware or should reasonably have been aware that a customs declaration had not been but should have been lodged.

Article 211

1. A customs debt on exportation shall be incurred through:
   - failure to comply with the conditions under which the goods were allowed to leave the customs territory of the Community with total or partial relief from export duties.
2. The debt shall be incurred at the time when the goods reach a destination other than that for which they were allowed to leave the customs territory of the Community with total or partial relief from export duties or, should the customs authorities be unable to determine that time, the expiry of the time limit set for the production of evidence that the conditions entitling the goods to such relief have been fulfilled.
3. The debtor shall be the declarant. In the event of indirect representation, the person on whose behalf the declaration is made shall also be a debtor.

Article 212

The customs debt referred to in Articles 201 to 205 and 209 to 211 shall be incurred even if it relates to goods subject to measures of prohibition or restriction on importation or exportation of any kind whatsoever. However, no customs debt shall be incurred on the unlawful introduction into the customs territory of the Community of counterfeit currency or of narcotic drugs and psychotropic substances which do not enter into the economic circuit strictly supervised by the competent authorities with a view to their use for medical and scientific purposes. For the purposes of criminal law as applicable to customs offences, the customs debt shall nevertheless be deemed to have been incurred where, under a Member State's criminal law, customs duties provide the basis for determining penalties, or the existence of a customs debt is grounds for taking criminal proceedings.

Article 212a

[Where customs legislation provides for favorable tariff treatment of goods by reason of their nature or end-use or for relief or total or partial exemption from import or export duties pursuant to Articles 21, 82, 145 or 184 to 184, such favorable tariff treatment, relief or exemption shall also apply in cases where a customs debt is incurred pursuant to Articles 202 to 205, 210 or 211, on condition that the behaviour of the person concerned involves neither fraudulent dealing nor obvious negligence and he produces evidence that the other conditions for the application of favourable treatment, relief or exemption have been satisfied.][25]

Article 213

Where several persons are liable for payment of one customs debt, they shall be jointly and severally liable for such debt.

Article 214

1. Save as otherwise expressly provided by this Code and without prejudice to paragraph 2, the amount of the import duty or export duty applicable to goods shall be determined on the basis of the rules of assessment appropriate to those goods at the time when the customs debt in respect of them is incurred.

2. Where it is not possible to determine precisely when the customs debt is incurred, the time to be taken into account in determining the rules of assessment appropriate to the goods concerned shall be the time when the customs authorities conclude that the goods are in a situation in which a customs debt is incurred.

    However, where the information available to the customs authorities enables them to establish that the customs debt was incurred prior to the time when they reached that conclusion, the amount of the import duty or export duty payable on the goods in question shall be determined on the basis of the rules of assessment appropriate to the goods at the earliest time when existence of the customs debt arising from the situation may be established from the information available.

3.   Compensatory interest shall be applied, in the circumstances and under the conditions to be defined in the provisions adopted under the committee procedure, in order to prevent the wrongful acquisition of a financial advantage through deferment of the date on which the customs debt was incurred or entered in the accounts.

[Article 215

1.   A customs debt shall be incurred:
-        at the place where the events from which it arises occur,
-        if it is not possible to determine that place, at the place where the customs authorities conclude that the goods are in a situation in which a customs debt is incurred,
-        if the goods have been entered for a customs procedure which has not been discharged, and the place cannot be determined pursuant to the first or second indent within a period of time determined, if appropriate, in accordance with the committee procedure, at the place where the goods were either placed under the procedure concerned or were introduced into the Community customs territory under that procedure.

2.   Where the information available to the customs authorities enables them to establish that the customs debt was already incurred when the goods were in another place at an earlier date, the customs debt shall be deemed to have been incurred at the place which may be established as the location of the goods at the earliest time when existence of the customs debt may be established.

3.   The customs authorities referred to in Article 217(1) are those of the Member State where the customs debt is incurred or is deemed to have been incurred in accordance with this Article.][26]

[4.   If a customs authority finds that a customs debt has been incurred under Article 202 in another Member State and the amount of that debt is lower than EUR 5 000, the debt shall be deemed to have been incurred in the Member State where the finding was made.][27]

Article 216

1.   In so far as agreements concluded between the Community and certain third countries provide for the granting on importation into those countries of preferential tariff treatment for goods originating in the Community within the meaning of such agreements, on condition that, where they have been obtained under the inward processing procedure, non-Community goods incorporated in the said originating goods are subject to payment of the import duties payable thereon, the validation of the documents necessary to enable such preferential tariff treatment to be obtained in third countries shall cause a customs debt on importation to be incurred.

2.   The moment when such customs debt is incurred shall be deemed to be the moment when the customs authorities accept the export declaration

relating to the goods in question.

3. The debtor shall be the declarant. In the event of indirect representation, the person on whose behalf the declaration is made shall also be a debtor.

4. The amount of the import duties corresponding to this customs debt shall be determined under the same conditions as in the case of a customs debt resulting from the acceptance, on the same date, of the declaration for release for free circulation of the goods concerned for the purpose of terminating the inward processing procedure.

Chapter 3

recovery of the amount of the customs debt

Section 1

Entry in the accounts and communication of the amount of duty to the debtor

Articles 217 - 232

Note

Articles 217-232 are omitted as they refer specifically to Customs Duty.

Chapter 4

extinction of customs debt

Article 233

Without prejudice to the provisions in force relating to the time-barring of a customs debt and non-recovery of such a debt in the event of the legally established insolvency of the debtor, a customs debt shall be extinguished:

(a)   by payment of the amount of duty;

(b)   by remission of the amount of duty;

(c)   where, in respect of goods declared for a customs procedure entailing the obligation to pay duties:

- the customs declaration is invalidated in accordance with Article 66,

- the goods, before their release, are either seized and simultaneously or subsequently confiscated, destroyed on the instructions of the customs authorities, destroyed or abandoned in accordance with Article 182, or destroyed or irretrievably lost as a result of their actual nature or of unforeseeable circumstances or force majeure;

(d)   where goods in respect of which a customs debt is incurred in accordance with Article 202 are seized upon their unlawful introduction and are simultaneously or subsequently confiscated.

In the event of seizure and confiscation, the customs debt shall, nonetheless for the purposes of the criminal law applicable to customs offences, be deemed not to have been extinguished where, under a Member State's criminal law, customs duties provide the basis for determining penalties or the existence of a customs debt is grounds for taking criminal proceedings.

Article 234

A customs debt, as referred to in Article 216, shall also be extinguished where the formalities carried out in order to enable the preferential tariff treatment referred to in Article 216 to be granted are cancelled.

Chapter 5

repayment and remission of duty

Articles 235 - 242

Note

Articles 235-242 are omitted as they refer specifically to Customs Duty..

TITLE VIII
Appeals

Article 243

1. Any person shall have the right to appeal against decisions taken by the customs authorities which relate to the application of customs legislation, and which concern him directly and individually.

   Any person who has applied to the customs authorities for a decision relating to the application of customs legislation and has not obtained a ruling on that request within the period referred to in Article 6(2) shall also be entitled to exercise the right of appeal.

   The appeal must be lodged in the Member State where the decision has been taken or applied for.

2. The right of appeal may be exercised:

   (a) initially, before the customs authorities designated for that purpose by the Member States;

   (b) subsequently, before an independent body, which may be a judicial authority or an equivalent specialized body, according to the provisions in force in the Member States.

Article 244

The lodging of an appeal shall not cause implementation of the disputed decision to be suspended.

The customs authorities shall, however, suspend implementation of such decision in whole or in part where they have good reason to believe that the disputed decision is inconsistent with customs legislation or that irreparable damage is to be feared for the person concerned.

Where the disputed decision has the effect of causing import duties or export duties to be charged, suspension of implementation of that decision shall be subject to the existence or lodging of a security. However, such security need not be required where such a requirement would be likely, owing to the debtor's circumstances, to cause serious economic or social difficulties.

Article 245

The provisions for the implementation of the appeals procedure shall be determined by the Member States.

Article 246

This title shall not apply to appeals lodged with a view to the annulment or revision of a decision taken by the customs authorities on the basis of criminal law.

TITLE IX

final provisions

Chapter 1

customs code committee

[Article 247

The measures necessary for the implementation of this Regulation, including implementation of the Regulation referred to in Article 184, except for Title VIII and subject to Articles 9 and 10 of Regulation (EEC) No 2658/87 and to Article 248 of this Regulation shall be adopted in accordance with the regulatory procedure referred to in Article 247a(2) In compliance with the International commitments entered into by the Community.

Article 247a

1. The Commission shall be assisted by a Customs Code Committee (hereinafter referred to as "the Committee").
2. Where reference is made to this paragraph, Articles 5 and 7 of Decision 1999/468/EC shall apply, having regard to the provisions of Article 8 thereof.

    The period laid down in Article 5(6) of Decision 1999/468/EC shall be set at three months.

    The Committee shall adopt its rules of procedure.

Article 248

The measures necessary for implementing Articles 11, 12 and 21 shall be adopted in accordance with the management procedure referred to In Article 248a(2).

Article 248a

1. The Commission shall be assisted by a Customs Code Committee, hereinafter referred to as "the Committee".

2. Where reference is made to this paragraph, Articles 4 and 7 of Decision 1 999/468/EC shall apply.

    The period laid down in Article 4(3) of Decision 1999/468/EC shall be set at three months.

3. The Committee shall adopt its rules of procedure.

Article 249

The Committee may examine any question concerning customs legislation which is raised by its chairman, either on his own initiative or at the request of a Member State's representative.][28]

Chapter 2

legal effects in a member state of measures taken, documents issued and findings made in another member state

Article 250

Where a customs procedure is used in several Member States,

-   the decisions, identification measures taken or agreed on, and the documents issued by the customs authorities of one Member State shall have the same legal effects in other Member States as such decisions, measures taken and documents issued by the customs authorities of each of those Member States;

-   the findings made at the time controls are carried out by the customs authorities of a Member State shall have the same conclusive force in the other Member States as the findings made by the customs authorities of each of those Member States.

Chapter 3

other final provisions

Article 251

1. The following Regulations and Directives are hereby repealed:

    -   Council Regulation (EEC) No 1224/80 of 28 May 1980 on the valuation of goods for customs purposes (18), as last amended by the Regulation (EEC) No 4046/89;

- Council Regulation (EEC) No 2151/84 of 23 July 1984 on the customs territory of the Community as amended by the Act of Accession of Spain and Portugal;

2. In all Community acts where reference is made to the Regulations or Directives referred to in paragraph 1, that reference shall be deemed to refer to this Code.

Note
  Only repeals within the scope of this book have been included

Article 252

Note
  Articles 252 is omitted as it refer specifically to Customs Duty.

Article 253

This Regulation shall enter into force on the third day following that of its publication in the Official Journal of the European Communities.

It shall apply from 1 January 1994.

Title VIII shall not apply to the United Kingdom until 1 January 1995.

However, Article 161 and, in so far as they concern re-exportation, Articles 182 and 183 shall apply from 1 January 1993. In so far as the said Articles make reference to provisions in this Code and until such time as such provisions enter into force, the references shall be deemed to allude to the corresponding provisions in the Regulations and Directives listed in Article 251.

Before 1 October 1993, the Council shall, on the basis of a Commission progress report on discussions regarding the consequences to be drawn from the monetary conversion rate used for the application of common agricultural policy measures, review the problem of trade in goods between the Member States in the context of the internal market. This report shall be accompanied by Commission proposals if any, on which the Council shall take a decision in accordance with the provisions of the Treaty.

Before 1 January 1998, the Council shall, on the basis of a Commission report, review this Code with a view to making such adaptations as may appear necessary taking into account in particular the achievement of the internal market. This report shall be accompanied by proposals, if any, on which the Council shall take a decision in accordance with the provisions of the Treaty.

This Regulation shall be binding in its entirety and directly applicable in all Member States.

Done at Luxembourg, 12 October 1992.
For the Council
The President
W. WALDEGRAVE

Amendments

1 Substituted by the Fourth Act of Accession 1994.

2 Inserted by Article 20, Annex II, Part 19(A)(I) of the Treaty of Accession to the European Union of 16 April 2003.

3 Substituted by Protocol No. 3, Part 1, Treaty of Accession.

4 Inserted by Art 1(1), Regulation (EC) No 648/2005 of the European Parliament and of the Council of 13 April 2005.

5 Substituted by Art 1(2), Parliament and Council Regulation 82/97 of 19 December 1997.

6 Deleted by Art 1(2)(c), Parliament and Council Regulation 82/97 of 19 December 1997.

7 Deleted by Art 1(2)(d), Parliament and Council Regulation 82/97 of 19 December 1997.

8 Substituted by Art 1(1), Regulation (EC) No 648/2005 of the European Parliament and of the Council of 13 April 2005.

9 Substituted by Art 1, Parliament and Council Regulation 2700/2000 of 16 November 2000.

10 Inserted by Art 1(2), Regulation (EC) No 648/2005 of the European Parliament and of the Council of 13 April 2005.

11 Substituted by Art 1(3), Regulation (EC) No 648/2005 of the European Parliament and of the Council of 13 April 2005.

12 Substituted by Art 1(4), Regulation (EC) No 648/2005 of the European Parliament and of the Council of 13 April 2005.

13 Substituted by Art 1(5), Regulation (EC) No 648/2005 of the European Parliament and of the Council of 13 April 2005.

14 Substituted by Art 1(4) Parliament and Council Regulation 82/97 of 19 December 1997.

15 Inserted by Art 1(6), Parliament and Council Regulation 82/97 of 19 December 1997.

16 Inserted by Art 1(6), Regulation (EC) No 648/2005 of the European Parliament and of the Council of 13 April 2005.

17 Substituted by Art 1(7), Regulation (EC) No 648/2005 of the European Parliament and of the Council of 13 April 2005.

18 Substituted by Art 1(8), Regulation (EC) No 648/2005 of the European Parliament and of the Council of 13 April 2005.

19 Substituted by Art 1(9), Regulation (EC) No 648/2005 of the European Parliament and of the Council of 13 April 2005.

20 Substituted by Art 1(10), Regulation (EC) No 648/2005 of the European Parliament and of the Council of 13 April 2005.

21 Deleted by Art 1(11), Regulation (EC) No 648/2005 of the European Parliament and of the Council of 13 April 2005.

22 Inserted by Art 1, Parliament and Council Regulation 2700/2000 of 16 November 2000.

23 Deleted by Art 1(8), Parliament and Council Regulation 82/97 of 19 December 1997.

24 Inserted by Art 1(9), Parliament and Council Regulation 82/97 of 19 December 1997.

25 Substituted by Art 1(14), Parliament and Council Regulation 2700/2000 of 16 November 2000.

26 Substituted by Art 1(7), Parliament and Council Regulation 955/1999 of 13 April 1999.

27 Inserted by Art 1(15), Parliament and Council Regulation 2700/2000 of 16 November 2000.

28 Substituted by Art 1(19), Parliament and Council Regulation 2700/2000 of 16 November 2000.

COUNCIL DIRECTIVE 92/77/EEC

of 19 October 1992

Supplementing the common system of value added tax and amending Directive
77/388/EEC (approximation of VAT rates)

Official Journal L 316 , 31/10/1992 p. 0001 - 0004

This Directive was repealed` by Council Directive 2006/112/EC of 28 November 2006 on the common system of value added tax, with effect from 1 January 2007

THE COUNCIL OF THE EUROPEAN COMMUNITIES,

Having regard to the Treaty establishing the European Economic Community, and in particular Article 99 thereof,

Having regard to the proposal from the Commission,

Having regard to the opinion of the European Parliament,

Having regard to the opinion of the Economic and Social Committee,

Whereas completing the internal market, which is one of the fundamental objectives of the Community, requires as a first step that fiscal controls at the frontiers be abolished;

Whereas, if distortions are to be avoided, such abolition implies in the case of value added tax, not only a uniform tax base but also a number of rates and rate levels which are sufficiently close as between Member States; whereas it is therefore necessary to amend Directive 77/388/EEC;

Whereas, during the transitional period, certain derogations concerning number and level of rates should be possible,

HAS ADOPTED THIS DIRECTIVE:

Article 1

Directive 77/388/EEC is hereby amended as follows:

1. Article 12(3) is replaced by the following:

    `3. (a) From 1 January 1993 Member States shall apply a standard rate which, until 31 December 1996, may not be less than 15%.

    On the basis of the report on the operation of the transitional arrangements and proposals on the definitive arrangements to be submitted by the Commission pursuant to Article 281 the Council shall decide unanimously before 31 December 1995 on the level of the minimum rate to be applied after 31 December 1996 with regard to the standard rate.

    Member States may also apply either one or two reduced rates. The reduced rates may not be less than 5% and shall only apply to supplies of the categories of goods and services specified in Annex H.

    (b) Member States may apply a reduced rate to supplies of natural gas and electricity provided that no risk of distortion of competition exists. A Member State intending to apply such a rate must, before doing so, inform the Commission. The Commission shall give a decision on the existence of a risk of distortion of competition. If the Commission has not taken that decision within three months of the receipt of the information a risk of distortion of competition is deemed not to exist.

(c) The rules concerning the rates applied to works of art, antiques and collector's items, shall be determined by the directive relating to the special arrangements applicable to second-hand goods, works of art, antiques and collector's items. The Council shall adopt this Directive before 31 December 1992.

(d) The rules concerning the taxation of agricultural outputs other than those falling within category 1 of Annex H shall be decided unanimously by the Council before 31 December 1994 on the basis of a Commission proposal.

Until 31 December 1994, those Member States currently applying a reduced rate may continue to do so; those currently applying a standard rate may not apply a reduced rate. This will allow a two-year postponement of the application of the standard rate.

(e) The rules concerning the regime and the rates applied to gold shall be determined by a directive relating to special arrangements applicable to gold. The Commission shall make such a proposal in time for its adoption by the Council, acting unanimously, before 31 December 1992.

Member States will take all necessary measures to combat fraud in this area from 1 January 1993. These measures may include the introduction of a system of accounting for VAT on supplies of gold between taxable persons in the same Member State which provides for the payment of tax by the buyer on behalf of the seller and a simultaneous right for the buyer to a deduction of the same amount of tax as input tax.';

2. the first sentence of Article 12(4) shall be deleted;

3. the following subparagraph is added to Article 12(4):

`On the basis of a report from the Commission, the Council shall, starting in 1994, review the scope of the reduced rates every two years. The Council, acting unanimously on a proposal from the Commission, may decide to alter the list of goods and services in Annex H.';

4. Article 28(2) is replaced by the following:

`2. Notwithstanding Article 12(3), the following provisions shall apply during the transitional period referred to in Article 281.

(a) Exemptions with refund of the tax paid at the preceding stage and reduced rates lower than the minimum rate laid down in Article 12(3) in respect of the reduced rates, which were in force on 1 January 1991 and which are in accordance with Community law, and satisfy the conditions stated in the last indent of Article

17 of the second Council Directive of 11 April 1967, may be maintained.

Member States shall adopt the measures necessary to ensure the determination of own resources relating to these operations.

In the event that the provisions of this paragraph create for Ireland distortions of competition in the supply of energy products for heating and lighting, Ireland may, on specific request, be authorized by the Commission to apply a reduced rate to such supplies, in accordance with Article 12(3). In that case, Ireland shall submit its request to the Commission together with all necessary information. If the Commission has not taken a decision within three months of receiving the request, Ireland shall be deemed to be authorized to apply the proposed reduced rates.

(b) Member States which, at 1 January 1991 in accordance with Community law, applied exemptions with refund of tax paid at the preceding stage, or reduced rates lower than the minimum laid down in Article 12 (3) in respect of the reduced rates, to goods and services other than those specified in Annex H, may apply the reduced rate or one of the two reduced rates provided for in Article 12(3) to any such supplies.

(c) Member States which under the terms of Article 12(3) will be obliged to increase their standard rate as applied at 1 January 1991 by more than 2%, may apply a reduced rate lower than the minimum laid down in Article 12(3) in respect of the reduced rate to supplies of categories of goods and services specified in Annex H. Furthermore, those Member States may apply such a rate to restaurant services, children's clothing, children's footwear and housing. Member States may not introduce exemptions with refund of the tax at the preceding stage on the basis of this paragraph.

(d) Member States which at 1 January 1991 applied a reduced rate to restaurant services, children's clothing, children's footwear and housing, may continue to apply such a rate to such supplies.

(e) Member States which at 1 January 1991 applied a reduced rate to supplies of goods and services other than those specified in Annex H may apply the reduced rate or one of the two reduced rates provided for in Article 12(3) to such supplies, provided that the rate is not lower than 12%.

(f) The Hellenic Republic may apply VAT rates up to 30% lower than the corresponding rates applied in mainland Greece in the departments of Lesbos, Chios, Samos, the Dodecanese and the Cyclades, and on the following islands in the Aegean: Thasos, Northern Sporades, Samothrace and Skiros.

(g) On the basis of a report from the Commission, the Council shall, before 31 December 1994, reexamine the provisions of subparagraphs (a) to (f) above in relation to the proper functioning of the internal market in particular. In the event of significant distortions of competition arising, the Council, acting unanimously on a proposal from the Commission, shall adopt appropriate measures.';

5.   Annex H in the Annex to this Directive shall be appended.

Article 2

1.   Member States shall bring into force the laws, regulations and adminstrative provisions necessary to comply with this Directive not later than 31 December 1992. They shall forthwith inform the Commission thereof.

When Member States adopt these measures, they shall contain a reference to this Directive or shall be accompanied by such reference on the occasion of their official publication. The methods of making such reference shall be laid down by the Member States.

2.   Member States shall communicate to the Commission the texts of the provisions of national law which they adopt in the field governed by this Directive.

Article 3

This Directive is addressed to the Member States.

Done at Luxembourg, 19 October 1992.
For the Council
The President
J. COPE

`ANNEX H

LIST OF SUPPLIES OF GOODS AND SERVICES WHICH MAY BE SUBJECT TO REDUCED RATES OF VAT

In transposing the categories below which refer to goods into national legislation, Member States may use the combined nomenclature to establish the precise coverage of the category concerned.

Category	Description
1	Foodstuffs (including beverages but excluding alcoholic beverages) for human and animal consumption; live animals, seeds, plants and ingredients normally intended for use in preparation of foodstuffs; products normally intended to be used to supplement or substitute foodstuffs
2	Water supplies
3	Pharmaceutical products of a kind normally used for health care, prevention of diseases and treatment for medical and veterinary purposes, including products used for contraception and sanitary protection
4	Medical equipment, aids and other appliances normally intended to alleviate or treat disability, for the exclusive personal use of the disabled, including the repair of such goods, and children's car seats
5	Transport of passengers and their accompanying luggage
6	Supply, including on loan by libraries, of books (including brochures, leaflets and similar printed matter, children's picture, drawing or colouring books, music printed or in manuscript, maps and hydrographic or similar charts), newspapers and periodicals, other than material wholly or substantially devoted to advertising matter
7	Admissions to shows, theatres, circuses, fairs, amusement parks, concerts, museums, zoos, cinemas, exhibitions and similar cultural events and facilities. Reception of broadcasting services
8	Services supplied by or royalties due to writers, composers and performing artists
9	Supply, construction, renovation and alteration of housing provided as part of a social policy
10	Supplies of goods and services of a kind normally intended for use in agricultural production but excluding capital goods such as machinery or buildings
11	Accommodation provided by hotels and similar establishments including the provision of holiday accomodation and the letting of camping sites and caravan parks
12	Admission to sporting events
13	Use of sporting facilities

14   Supply of goods and services by organizations recognized as charities by Member States and engaged in welfare or social security work, insofar as these supplies are not exempt under Article 13

15   Services supplied by undertakers and cremation services, together with the supply of goods related thereto

16   Provision of medical and dental care as well as thermal treatment in so far as these services are not exempt under Article 13

17   Services supplied in connection with street cleaning, refuse collection and waste treatment, other than the supply of such services by bodies referred to in Article 4(5)'

COMMISSION REGULATION (92/3046/EEC)

of 22 October 1992

Laying down provisions implementing and amending Council Regulation (EEC) No 3330/91 on the statistics relating to the trading of goods between Member States

This Regulation, apart from Article 22, has been repealed by Commission Regulation (EC) No. 1901/2000 with effect from 1 January 2001.

Article 22

1. The references to Directive 77/388/EEC in the Basic Regulation are amended as follows:

    — in the second paragraph of Article 5, 'pursuant to Article 28(7) of the above mentioned Directive' is replaced by 'pursuant to Council Directive 91/680/EEC (1)',

    — in Article 10(3)(b), 'within the meaning of Directive 77/388/EEC, in compliance with Article 28(7) of that Directive' is replaced by 'within the meaning of Directive 91/680/EEC',

    — in Article 11(3) and (7), 'Article 28(7) of Directive 77/388/EEC' is replaced by 'Directive 91/680/EEC',

    — in Article 20, points 3 and 4, 'first indent and - in so far as the provisions of Article 28 (7) of Directive 77/388/EEC apply to them - second indent' is deleted.

2. 'Institutional parties not liable to account for VAT' and 'parties exempt from VAT' which appear in the second paragraph of Article 5, Article 10(3)(6), and Article 11(2)(6) and (7) of the Basic Regulation are replaced respectively by 'legal persons not liable to account for VAT' and 'parties liable to account who carry out only transactions not entitling them to any deduction of VAT'.

3. In Article 20 of the Basic Regulation:

    (a) in point 5(a) and (b), 'residing' is replaced by 'registered for value-added tax';

    (b) point 7 is replaced by the following:

        '(7) the reference period referred to in the first indent of Article 13(2) shall be:

        —for goods to which the Intrastat system applies, the calendar month during which the value-added tax becomes due on intra-Community deliveries or acquisitions of goods, the movements of which are to be recorded pursuant to this Article; when the period to which the periodic fiscal declaration of a party liable to account for VAT refers does not correspond with a calendar month, quarter, half-year or year, the Member States may adapt the periodicity of the obligations relating to the statistical declarations of that party to the periodicity of his obligations relating to fiscal declarations,

— for goods to which the Intrastat system does not apply, according to the circumstances:

— the calendar month during which the goods are either placed or maintained under the inward processing customs procedure (suspension system) or the procedure of processing under customs control or placed in free circulation as a result of one of these procedures,

— the calendar month during which the goods, circulating between parts of the statistical territory of the Community, at least one of which is not part of the territory of the Community pursuant to Council Directive 77/388/EEC, have been subject to dispatch or arrival procedures.'

COMMISSION REGULATION (92/3590/EEC)

of 11 December 1992

Concerning the statistical information media for statistics on trade between Member States

Official Journal L 364 , 12/12/1992 p. 0032 - 0033

Repealed by Commission Regulation (EC) No 1982/2004 of 18 November 2004 implementing Regulation (EC) No 638/2004 of the European Parliament and of the Council on Community statistics relating to the trading of goods between Member States and repealing Commission Regulations (EC) No 1901/2000 and (EEC) No 3590/92, w.e.f 1 January 2005.

THE COMMISSION OF THE EUROPEAN COMMUNITIES,

Having regard to the Treaty establishing the European Economic Community,

Having regard to Council Regulation (EEC) No 3330/91 of 7 November 1991, on the statistics relating to the trading of goods between Member States, as amended by Commission Regulation (EEC) No 3046/92 and in particular Article 12 thereof,

Whereas, in the context of statistics on trade between Member States, it is necessary to adopt standard statistical forms for regular use by the parties responsible for providing information in order to ensure that the declarations required of them adhere to a consistent format, irrespective of the Member State where they are made; whereas the choice accorded to the parties responsible for providing information by Article 12(2) of the abovementioned Regulation is only available if the Commission sets up the appropriate information media; whereas, moreover, certain Member States would rather use Community media than produce national forms of their own;

Whereas it is important to provide the competent authorities with all the technical details required for the printing of these forms;

Whereas it is advisable in order to ensure uniform treatment of the parties responsible for providing information, to contribute towards the cost of these forms; whereas it is necessary to estimate the amount of Community funds required for this; whereas this amount must be in line with the financial perspective set out in the Interinstitutional Agreement of 29 June 1988 on Budgetary Discipline and Improvement of the Budgetary Procedure; whereas, in compliance with this Agreement, the appropriations actually available must be determined in accordance with budgetary procedure;

Whereas it is necessary to take account of other modes of transmitting information, and, in particular, to promote the use of magnetic or electronic information media;

Whereas the measures provided for in this Regulation reflect the opinion of the Committee on Statistics Relating to the Trading of Goods between Member States,

HAS ADOPTED THIS REGULATION:

Article 1

1. With a view to the drawing-up by the Community and its Member States of statistics on trade between the Member States, the statistical information media provided for in Article 12, paragraph 1, of Council Regulation (EEC) No 3330/91, hereafter referred to as 'the basic Regulation', shall be set up in accordance with the provisions of this Regulation.

2. In Member States where no distinction is made between the periodic declaration and the periodic declaration required for tax purposes, the provisions necessary for the setting-up of information media shall, insofar as necessary, be adopted within the framework of Community or national tax regulations, and in conformity with the other implementing provisions of the basic Regulation.

Article 2

Without prejudice to provisions adopted pursuant to Article 34 of the basic Regulation, Intrastat forms N-Dispatch, R-Disaptch and S-Dispatch and N-Arrival, R-Arrival and S-Arrival, specimens of which are annexed to this Regulation, shall be used in conformity with the provisions set out below.

-   Forms N shall be used by parties responsible for providing information who are not subject to the dispensations resulting from the assimilation and simplification thresholds fixed by each Member State, nor to the exemption provided for in the following indent.

-   Forms R shall be used by parties responsible for providing information whom the competent national authorities have exempted from giving a description of the goods.

-   Forms S shall be used by parties responsible for providing information who are subject to the dispensations resulting from the simplification threshold.

Article 3

1. The forms referred to in Article 2 shall consist of a single sheet, which shall be delivered to the competent national authorities.

    The Member States may, however, require parties responsible for providing information to retain a copy in accordance with the instructions of the competent national authorities.

2. The forms shall be printed on paper which is suitable for writing and weighs no less than 70 g/m^2.

    The colour of the paper used shall be white. The colour of the print shall be red. The paper and the print used must meet the technical requirements of optical character recognition (OCR) equipment.

The fields and subdivisions shall be measured horizontally in units of one-tenth of an inch and vertically in units of one-sixth of an inch.

The forms shall measure 210 × 297 mm, subject to maximum tolerances as to length of 5 mm and +8 mm.

3. The conditions under which the forms may be produced using reproduction techniques departing from the provisions of paragraph 2, first and second subparagraphs, shall be determined by the Member States, which shall inform the Commission accordingly.

Article 4

The Member States shall, without charge, supply parties responsible for providing information with the forms reproduced in specimen in the Annex hereto.

The Commission shall contribute annually, at the end of the reporting period, to the costs which the Member States have incurred in printing these forms and distributing them via official postal channels. This contribution shall be calculated in proportion to the number of forms which the parties responsible for providing information have actually transmitted to the competent national authorities during the year in question.

Article 5

Parties responsible for providing information who wish to use magnetic or electronic media shall give prior notice of this intention to the national authorities responsible for compiling statistics on trade between Member States. Parties responsible for providing information shall, in this event, comply with any relevant provisions adopted by the Commission and with any national instructions issued by the abovementioned authorities pursuant to the said provisions, bearing in mind the technical equipment available to them. These instructions shall include in their structuring rules the Cusdec message designed and updated by the United Nations Edifact Board - Message Design Group 3, and shall comply with the provisions relating to the Instat subset of that message, which the Commission shall publish in a user manual.

Article 6

1. In derogation from Article 2, parties responsible for providing information who wish to use as an information medium the statistical forms of the Single Administrative Document as provided for in Council (sic) 717/91 shall comply with the instructions issued by the competent national authorities. The latter shall send a copy of these instructions to the Commission.

2. Member States which set up media other than those provided for in Article 2 or Article 5 above, or paragraph 1 of this Article, shall inform the Commission accordingly in advance. They shall send the Commission an example of such media and/or provide details as to their use.

Article 7

This Regulation shall enter into force on the seventh day following that of its publication in the *Official Journal of the European Communities*.

It shall apply from the date provided for in Article 35, second indent, of the basic Regulation.

This Regulation shall be binding in its entirety and directly applicable in all Member States.

Done at Brussels, 11 December 1992.
For the Commission
Henning CHRISTOPHERSEN
Member of the Commission

COUNCIL DIRECTIVE 92/111/EEC

of 14 December 1992

Amending Directive 77/388/EEC and introducing simplification measures with regard to value added tax

Official Journal L 384 , 30/12/1992 p. 0047 - 0057

> This Directive was repealed by Council Directive 2006/112/EC of 28 November 2006 on the common system of value added tax, with effect from 1 January 2007

THE COUNCIL OF THE EUROPEAN COMMUNITIES,

Having regard to the Treaty establishing the European Economic Community, and in particular Article 99 thereof,

Having regard to the proposal from the Commission,

Having regard to the opinion of the European Parliament,

Having regard to the opinion of the Economic and Social Committee,

Whereas Article 3 of Council Directive 91/680/EEC of 16 December 1991 supplementing the common system of valued added tax and amending Directive 77/388/EEC with a view to the abolition of fiscal frontiers sets 1 January 1993 as the date for the entry into force of these provisions in all the Member States;

Whereas in order to facilitate the application of these provisions and to introduce the simplifications needed, it is necessary to supplement the common system of value added tax, as applicable on 1 January 1993, so as to clarify how the tax shall apply to certain operations carried out with third territories and certain operations carried out inside the Community, as well to define the transitional measures between the provisions in force on 31 December 1992 and those which will enter into force as from 1 January 1993;

Whereas in order to guarantee the neutrality of the common system of turnover tax in respect of the origin of goods, the concept of a third territory and the definition of an import must be supplemented;

Whereas certain territories forming part of the Community customs territory are regarded as third territories for the purposes of applying the common system of value added tax; whereas value added tax is therefore applied to trade between the Member States and those territories according to the same principles as apply to any operation between the Community and third countries; whereas it is necessary to ensure that such trade is subject to fiscal provisions equivalent to those which would be applied to operations carried out under the same conditions with territories which are not part of the Community customs territory; whereas as a result of these provisions the Seventeenth Council Directive 85/362/EEC of 16 July 1985 on the harmonization of the laws of the Member States relating to turnover taxes - Exemption from value added tax on the temporary importation of goods other than means of transport, becomes null and void;

Whereas it is necessary to state exactly how the exemptions relating to certain export operations or equivalent operations will be implemented; whereas it is necessary to adapt the other Directives concerned accordingly;

Whereas it is necessary to clarify the definition of the place of taxation of certain operations carried out on board ships, aircraft or trains transporting passengers inside the Community;

Whereas the transitional arrangements for taxation of trade between the Member States must be supplemented to take account both of the Community provisions relating to excise duties and the need to clarify and simplify the detailed rules for the application of the tax of certain operations which will be carried out between the Member States as from 1 January 1993;

Whereas Council Directive 92/12/EEC of 25 February 1992 on the general arrangements for products subject to excise duty and on the holding, movement and monitoring of such products lays down particular procedures and obligations in relation to declarations in the case of shipments of such products to another Member State; whereas as a result the methods of applying tax to certain supplies and intra-Community acquisitons of products liable to excise duties can be simplified to the benefit both of the persons liable to pay tax and the competent administrations;

Whereas it is necessary to define the scope of the exemptions referred to in Article 28c of Directive 77/388/EEC; whereas it is also necessary to supplement the provisions concerning the chargeability of the tax and the methods of determining the taxable amount of certain intra-Community operations;

Whereas, for taxable operations in the domestic market linked to intra-Community trade in goods which are carried out during the period laid down in Article 28l of Directive 77/388/EEC by taxable persons not established in the Member State referred to in Article 28b(A)(1) of the said Directive, it is necessary to take simplification measures guaranteeing equivalent treatment in all the Member States; whereas to achieve this, the provisions concerning the taxation system and the person liable to tax in respect of such operations must be harmonized;

Whereas in order to take account of the provisions relating to the person liable to pay tax in the domestic market and to avoid certain forms of tax evasion or avoidance, it is necessary to clarify the Community provisions concerning the repayment to taxable persons not established in the country of the value added tax referred to in Article 17(3) of Directive 77/388/EEC as amended by Article 28f of the said Directive;

Whereas the abolition as from 1 January 1993 of tax on imports and tax relief on exports for trade between the Member States makes it necessary to have transitional measures in order to ensure the neutrality of the common system of valued added tax and to avoid situations of double-taxation or non-taxation;

Whereas it is therefore necessary to lay down special provisions for cases where a Community procedure, started before 1 January 1993 for the purposes of a supply effected before that date by a taxable person acting as such in respect of goods dispatched or transported to another Member State, is not completed until after 31 December 1992;

Whereas such provisions should also apply to taxable operations carried out before 1 January 1993 to which particular exemptions were applied which as a result delayed the taxable event;

Whereas it is also necessary to lay down special measures for means of transport which, not having been acquired or imported subject to the general domestic tax conditions of a Member State, have benefited, by the application of national measures, from an exemption from tax because of their temporary import from another Member State;

Whereas the application of these transitional measures, both in relation trade between the Member States and to operations with third territories, presupposes supplementing the definition of the operations to be made subject to taxation as from 1 January 1993 and the clarification for such cases of the concepts of the place of taxation, the taxable event and the chargeability of the tax;

Whereas, on account of the current economic situation, the Kingdom of Spain and the Italian Republic have requested that, as a transitional measure, provisions derogating from the principle of immediate deduction laid down in the frist subparagraph of Article 18(2) of Directive 77/388/EEC be applied; whereas this request should be granted for a period of two years which may not be extended;

Whereas this Directive lays down common provisions for simplifying the treatment of certain intra-Community operations; whereas, in a number of cases, it is for the Member States to determine the conditions for implementing these provisions; whereas certain Member States will not be able to complete the legislative procedure necessary to adapt their legislation on valued added tax within the period laid down; whereas an additional period should therefore be allowed for the implementation of this Directive; whereas a maximum period of twelve months is sufficient for this purpose;

Whereas it is accordingly necessary to amend Directive 77/388/EEC,

HAS ADOPTED THIS DIRECTIVE:

Article 1

Directive 77/388/EEC is hereby amended as follows:

1. Article 3(4) shall be replaced by the following:

    `4. By way of derogation from paragraph 1, in view of the conventions and treaties which they have concluded respectively with the French Republic and the United Kingdom of Great Britain and Northern Ireland, the Principality of Monaco and the Isle of Man shall not be treated for the purposes of the application of this Directive as third territories.

    Member States shall take the measures necessary to ensure that transactions originating in or intended for:

    — the Principality of Monaco are treated as transactions originating in or intended for the French Republic,

     — the Isle of Man are treated as transactions originating in or intended for the United Kingdom of Great Britain and Northern Ireland.';

2. Article 7(1)(b) shall be replaced by the following:

    '(b) the entry into the Community of goods from a third territory, other than the goods covered by (a).';

3. in Article 7(3):

in the first subparagraph `(a), (b), (c) and (d)' shall be added after `Article 16(1)(B)',

the second subparagraph shall be replaced by the following:

'Similarly, when goods referred to in paragraph 1 (b) are placed, on entry into the Community, under one of the procedures referred to in Article 33a (1) (b) or (c), the place of import shall be the Member State within whose territory this procedure ceases to apply.';

4. Article 8(1)(c) shall be replaced by the following:

    '(c) in the case of goods supplied on board ships, aircraft or trains during the part of a transport of passengers effected in the Community: at the point of the departure of the transport of passengers.

    For the purposes of applying this provision:

    — **"part of a transport of passengers effected in the Community"** shall mean the part of the transport effected, without a stop in a third territory, between the point of departure and the point of arrival of the transport of passengers,

    — **"the point of departure of the transport of passengers"** shall mean the first point of passenger embarkation foreseen within the Community, where relevant after a leg outside the Community,

    — **"the point of arrival of the transport of passengers"** shall mean the last point of disembarkation of passengers foreseen within the Community of passengers who embarked in the Community, where relevant before a leg outside the Community.

    In the case of a return trip, the return leg shall be considered to be a separate transport.

    The Commission shall, by 30 June 1993 at the latest, submit to the Council a report accompanied, if necessary, by appropriate proposals on the place of taxation of goods supplied for consumption and services, including restaurant services, provided for passengers on board ships, aircraft or trains.

    By 31 December 1993, after consulting the European Parliament, the Council shall take a unanimous decision on the Commission proposal.

    Until 31 December 1993, Member States may exempt or continue to exempt goods supplied for consumption on board whose place of taxation is determined in accordance with the above provisions, with the right to deduct the value added tax paid at an earlier stage.';

5. Article 11(B)(1) shall be replaced by the following:

'1. The taxable amount shall be the value for customs purposes, determined in accordance with the Community provisions in force; this shall also apply for the import of goods referred to in Article 7(1) (b).';

6. Article 12(1)(b) shall be replaced by the following:

'(b) in the cases provided for in the second and third subparagraphs of Article 10(3), the rate applicable shall be that in force at the time when the tax becomes chargeable.';

7. Article 12(3)(a) shall be replaced by the following:

'3. (a) The standard rate of value added tax shall be fixed by each Member State as a percentage of the taxable amount and shall be the same for the supply of goods and for the supply of services. From 1 January 1993 until 31 December 1996, this percentage may not be less than 15%.

On the basis of the report on the operation of the transitional arrangements and proposals on the definitive arrangements to be submitted by the Commission pursuant to Article 28l, the Council shall decide unanimously before 31 December 1995 on the level of the minimum rate to be applied after 31 December 1996 with regard to the standard rate.

Member States may also apply either one or two reduced rates. These rates shall be fixed as a percentage of the taxable amount which may not be less than 5 % and shall apply only to supplies of the categories of goods and services specified in Annex H.';

8. in Article 14(1):

(c) shall be deleted,

the following shall be added to (d):

'This exemption shall also apply to the import of goods, within the meaning of Article 7(1) (b), which would be capable of benefiting from the exemption set out above if they had been imported within the meaning of Article 7(1)(a).';

9. in Article 15:

the following subparagraphs shall be added to (2):

'The Commission shall submit to the Council as soon as possible proposals to establish Community fiscal rules specifying the scope of and pratical arrangements for implementing this exemption for supplies made at the retail stage of goods to be carried in the personal luggage of travellers. Until these provisions come into force:

- the benefit of the exemption shall be subject to the production of a copy of the invoice or other documents in lieu thereof, endorsed by the customs office where the goods left the Community,

- Member States may set limits in relation to the application of this exemption, may exclude from the benefit of the exemption supplies to travellers whose domicile or habitual residence is situated in the Community and may extend the benefit of the exemption to their residents.

For the purposes of applying the second subparagraph "domicile or habitual residence" means the place entered as such in a passport, identity card or, failing those, other identity documents which the Member State in whose territory the supply takes place recognizes as valid.',

in (3) the words 'established in a third country' shall be replaced by 'not established within the territory of the country',

in (4), the second subparagraph shall be replaced by the following:

'The Commission shall submit to the Council as soon as possible proposals to establish Community fiscal rules specifying the scope of and practical arrangements for implementing this exemption and the exemptions provided for in (5) to (9). Until these rules come into force, Member States may limit the extent of the exemption provided for in this paragraph.',

in the second subparagraph of (10) the words 'conditions and limitations' shall be replaced by 'limitations',

in (10) the third subparagraph shall be replaced by the following:

'In cases where the goods are not dispatched or transported out of the country, and in the case of services, the benefit of the exemption may be given by means of a refund of the tax.',

Point 13 shall be replaced by the following:

'13. The supply of services, including transport and ancillary operations, but excluding the supply of services exempted in accordance with Article 13, where these are directly connected with the export of goods or imports of goods covered by the provisions of Article 7(3) or Article 16(1), Title A;';

10. in Article 28a:

the second subparagraph of paragraph 1(a) shall be replaced by the following:

'By way of derogation from the first subparagraph, intra-Community acquisitions of goods made under ther conditions set out in paragraph 1a by a taxable person or non-taxable legal person shall not be subject to value added tax.',

a new point shall be added as follows to paragraph 1;

'(c) the intra-Community acquisition of goods which are subject to excise duties effected for consideration within the territory of the country by a taxable person or a non-taxable legal person who qualifies for the derogation referred to in the second subparagraph of point (a), and for which the excise duties become chargeable within the territory of the country pursuant to Directive 92/12/EEC'

the following paragraph shall be inserted:

'1a. The following shall benefit from the derogation set out in the second subparagraph of paragraph 1 (a):

(a) intra-Community acquisitions of goods whose supply within the territory of the country would be exempt pursuant to Article 15 (4) to (10);

(b) intra-Community acquisitions of goods other than those at (a), made:

— by a taxable person for the purpose of his agricultural, forestry or fisheries undertaking, subject to the flat-rate scheme set out in Article 25, by a taxable person who carries out only supplies of goods or services in respect of which value added tax is not deductible, or by a non-taxable legal person,

— for a total amount not exceeding, during the current calendar year, a threshold which the Member States shall determine but which may not be less than the equivalent in national currency of ECU 10 000,

and

— provided that the total amount of intra-Community acquisitions of goods did not, during the previous calendar year, exceed the threshold referred to in the second indent.

The threshold which serves as the reference for the application of the above shall consist of the total amount, exclusive of value added tax due or paid in the Member State from which the goods are dispatched or transported, of intra-Community acquisitions of goods other than new means of transport and other than goods subject to excise duty.',

the following subparagraph shall be added to paragraph 5 (b):

'However, when one of the conditions to which the benefit of the above is subordinated is no longer met, the goods shall be considered as having been transferred to a destination in another Member State. In this case, the transfer is carried out at the moment that the conditions is no longer met.',

the following subparagraph shall be added to paragraph 6:

'The following shall also be deemed to be an intra-Community acquisition of goods effected for consideration: the appropriation of goods by the forces of a State party to the North Atlantic Treaty, for their use or for the use of the civilian staff accompanying them, which they have not acquired subject to the general rules governing taxation on the domestic market of one of the Member States, when the importation of these goods could not benefit from the exemption set out in Article 14(1)(g).',

11. in Article 28b(A)(2), the following subparagraph shall be added:

'For the purposes of applying the first subparagraph, the intra-Community acquisition of goods shall be deemed to have been subject to tax in accordance with paragraph 1 when the following conditions have been met:

— the acquirer establishes that he has effected this intra-Community acquisition for the needs of a subsequent supply effected in the Member State referred to in paragraph 1 and for which the consignee has been designated as the person liable for the tax due in accordance with Article 28c(E)(3),

— the obligations for declaration set out in the last subparagraph of Article 22(6)(b) have been satisfied by the acquirer.';

12. in Article 28c (A):

point (c) shall be replaced by the following:

'(c) the supply of goods subject to excise duty dispatched or transported to the purchaser, by the vendor, by the purchaser or on his behalf, outside the territory referred to in Article 3 but inside the Community, effected for taxable persons or non-taxable legal persons who qualify for the derogation set out in the second subparagraph of Article 28a(1)(a), when the dispatch or transport of the goods is carried out in accordance with Article 7(4) and (5), or Article 16 of Directive 92/12/EEC.

This exemption shall not apply to supplies of goods subject to excise duty effected by taxable persons who benefit from the exemption from tax set out in Article 24;',

the following shall be added:

'(d) the supply of goods, within the meaning of Article 28a(5)(b), which benefit from the exemptions set out above if they have been made on behalf of another taxable person.';

13. Article 28c(E) shall be replaced by the following:

`E. Other exemptions

1. The following paragraph shall be added to Article 16:

"1a.When they take up the option provided for in paragraph 1, Member States shall take the measures necessary in order to ensure that the intra-Community acquisitions of goods intended to be placed under one of the regimes or in one of the situations referred to in Article 16(1)(B) benefit from the same provisions as supplies of goods carried out within the territory of the country under the same conditions."

2. In Article 16(2):

"intra-Community acquisitions of goods made by a taxable person and" shall be added after "may opt to exempt" and "outside the Community" shall be added after "export them",

the following subparagraphs shall be added:

"When they take up this option the Member States shall, subject to the consultation provided for in Article 29, extend the benefit of this exemption to intra-Community acquisitions of goods by a taxable person, imports for and supplies of goods to a taxable person intending to supply them, as they are or after processing, under the conditions laid down in Article 28c(A), as well as supplies of services relating to such supplies, up to a maximum equal to the value of his supplies of goods effected under the conditions laid down in Article 28c(A) during the preceding twelve months.

Member States may set a common maximum amount for transactions which they exempt under the first and second subparagraphs."

3. Member States shall take specific measures to ensure that value added tax is not charged on the intra-Community acquisition of goods effected, within the meaning of Article 28b (A) (1), within its territory when the following conditions are met:

— the intra-Community acquisition of goods is effected by a taxable person who is not established in the territory of the country but who is identified for value added tax purposes in another Member State,

— the intra-Community acquisition of goods is effected for the purpose of a subsequent supply of goods made by a taxable person in the territory of the country,

— the goods so acquired by this taxable person are directly dispatched or transported from another Member State than that in which he is identified for value added tax purposes and destined for the person for whom he effects the subsequent supply,

— the person to whom the subsequent supply is made is a taxable person or a non-taxable legal person who is identified for value added tax purposes within the territory of the country,

— the person to whom the subsequent supply is made has been designated in accordance with the third subparagraph of Article 21(1)(a) as the person liable for the tax due on the supplies effected by the taxable person not established within the territory of the country.';

14. Article 28d(3) shall be replaced by the following:

'3. By way of derogation from paragraph 2, tax shall become chargeable on the issue of the invoice or other document serving as invoice provided for in the first subparagraph of Article 22(3)(a) where that invoice or document is issued to the person acquiring the goods before the fifteenth day of the month following that during which the taxable event occurs.';

15. the second subparagraph of Article 28d(4) shall be replaced by the following:

'However, tax shall become chargeable on the issue of the invoice provided for in the first subparagraph of Article 22(3)(a) or other document serving as invoice where that invoice or document is issued before the fifteenth day of the month following that during which the taxable event occurs.';

16. in Article 28e(1):

in the first subparagraph, the second sentence shall be replaced by:

'In particular, in the case of the intra-Community acquisition of goods referred to in Article 28a(6), the taxable amount shall be determined in accordance with Article 11(A)(1)(b) and paragraphs 2 and 3.',

in the second subparagraph, the following sentence shall be added:

'When, after the moment the intra-Community acquisition of goods was effected, the acquirer obtains the refund of excise duties paid in the Member State from which the goods were dispatched or transported, the taxable amount shall be reduced accordingly in the Member State where the intra-Community acquisition took place.';

17. in Article 28e, paragraphs 2 and 3 shall be renumbered 3 and 4 and a new paragraph 2 shall be inserted as follows:

'2. For the supply of goods referred to in Article 28c(A)(d), the taxable amount shall be determined in accordance with Article 11(A)(1)(b) and paragraphs 2 and 3.';

18. in Article 28f:

in Article 17(3)(b), '28c(A)' shall be replaced by '28c(A) and (C)',

the following subparagraph shall be added to Article 17 (4):

'For the purposes of applying the above:

(a) the taxable persons referred to in Article 1 of Directive 79/1072/ EEC shall also be considered for the purposes of applying the said Directive as taxable persons who are not established in the country when, inside the territory of the country, they have only carried out supplies of goods and services to a person who has been designated as the person liable to pay the tax in accordance with Article 21(1)(a);

(b) the taxable persons referred to in Article 1 of Directive 86/560/ EEC shall also be considered for the purposes of applying the said Directive as taxable persons who are not established in the Community when, inside the territory of the country, they have only carried out supplies of goods and services to a person who has been designated as the person liable to pay the tax in accordance with Article 21 (1) (a);

(c) Directives 79/1072/EEC and 86/560/EEC shall not apply to supplies of goods which are, or may be, exempted under Article 28c (A) when the goods supplied are dispatched or transported by the acquirer or for his account.';

19. in Article 28g:

Article 21(1)(a) shall be replaced by the following:

'(a) the taxable person carrying out the taxable supply of goods or of services, other than one of the supplies of services referred to in (b).

Where the taxable supply of goods or of services is effected by a taxable person who is not established within the territory of the country, Member States may adopt arrangements whereby tax is payable by another person. Inter alios a tax representative or the person for whom the taxable supply of goods or of services is carried out may be designated as that other person.

However, the tax is payable by the person to whom the supply of goods is made when the following conditions are met:

— the taxable operation is a supply of goods made under the conditions laid down in paragraph 3 of Title E of Article 28c,

— the person to whom the supply of goods is made is another taxable person or a non-taxable legal person identified for the purposes of value-added tax within the territory of the country,

— the invoice issued by the taxable person not established within the territory of the country conforms to Article 22(3).

However, Member States may provide a derogation from this obligation in the case where the taxable person who is not established within the territory of the country has appointed a tax representative in that country.

Member States may provide that someone other than the taxable person shall be held jointly and severally liable for payment of the tax;';

Article 21(1)(b) shall be replaced by the following:

'(b) persons to whom services covered by Article 9(2)(e) are supplied, or persons, identified for value added tax purposes within the territory of the country, to whom services referred to in Article 28b(C), (D) or (E) are supplied, when the service is carried out by a taxable person established abroad; however, Member States may require that the supplier of the service shall be held jointly and severally liable for payment of the tax;';

20. in Article 28h:

in the first indent of Article 22(1)(c) 'and other than a supply of goods or services to a person who has been designated as the person liable for the tax in accordance with Article 21(1)(a), third paragraph', shall be added after `in accordance with Article 21(1)(b)',

in Article 22(1)(c) the following indent shall be inserted after the second indent:

'- every taxable person who, within the territory of the country, effects intra-Community acquisitions of goods for the purposes of his operations relating to the economic activities referred to in Article 4(2) carried out abroad,';

the following indent shall be added to Article 22(3)(b):

'- where the provisions of Article 28c(E)(3) are applied, an explicit reference to that provision as well as the identification number for value added tax purposes under which the taxable person has carried out the intra-Community acquisition and the subsequent supply of goods and the number by which the person to whom this supply is made is identified for value added tax purposes.',

the second indent of Article 22(4)(c) shall be replaced by the following:

'- on the other hand, the total amount, less value-added tax of the intra-Community acquisitions of goods referred to in Article 28a (1) and (6) effected within the territory of the country on which tax has become chargeable.

The following shall also be added: the total value, less value-added tax, of the supplies of goods referred to in the second sentence of Article 8(1)(a) and in Article 28(b)(B)(1) effected in the territory of the country on which tax has become chargeable during the return period, where the place of departure of the dispatch or transport of the goods is situated within the territory of another Member State, and the total amount, less value-added tax, of the supplies of goods made within the territory of the country for which the taxable person has been designated as the person liable for the tax in accordance with Article 28c(E)(3) and under which the tax has become payable in the course of the period covered by the declaration.',

the first subparagraph of Article 22(6)(b) shall be replaced by the following:

'(b) Every taxable person identified for value-added tax purposes shall also submit a recapitulative statement of the acquirers identified for value-added tax purposes to whom he has supplied goods under the conditions provided for in Article 28c (A) (a) and (d), and of consignees identified for value-added tax purposes in the transactions referred to in the fifth and sixth subparagraphs.',

in the first indent of the third subparagraph of Article 22(6)(b), 'Article 28c(A)' shall be replaced by 'Article 28c(A)(a)',

in the first indent of the fourth subparagraph of Article 22(6 (b) 'Article 28c(A)(c)' shall be replaced by 'Article 28c(A)(d)' and 'and the value of the goods supplied determined in accordance with Article 28e(1)' shall be replaced by 'and the total amount of the supplies, determined in accordance with Article 28e(2).',

in Article 22(6)(b), add the following subparagraph:

'In the cases set out in the third subparagraph of Article 28b(A)(2), the taxable person identified for value added tax purposes within the territory of the country shall mention in a clear way on the recapitulative statement:

— the number by which he is identified for value added tax purposes within the territory of the country and under which he carried out the intra-Community acquisition and the subsequent supply of goods,

— the number by which, within the territory of the Member State of arrival of the dispatch or transport of the goods, the consignee of the subsequent supply by the taxable person is identified,

— and, for each consignee, the total amount, less value added tax, of the supplies made by the taxable person within the territory of the Member State of arrival of the dispatch or transport of the goods. These amounts shall be declared for the calendar quarter during which the tax became chargeable.',

in Article 22(11), the following shall be inserted at the start of the paragraph:

'11. In the case of intra-Community acquisitions of products subject to excise duty referred to in Article 28a(1)(c) as well as';

21. Article 28i shall be replaced by the following:

`Article 28i

Special scheme for small undertakings

The following subparagraph shall be added to Article 24(3):

'In all circumstances supplies of new means of transport effected under the conditions laid down in Article 28c(A) as well as supplies of goods and services effected by a taxable person who is not established in the territory of the country shall be excluded from the exemption from tax under paragraph 2.';'

22. the following Article shall be added:

`Article 28n

Transitional measures

1. When goods:

— entered the territory of the country within the meaning of Article 3 before 1 January 1993,

and

— were placed, on entry into the territory of that country, under one of the regimes referred to in Article 14(1)(b) or (c), or Article 16(1)(A),

and

— have not left that regime before 1 January 1993, the provisions in force at the moment the goods were placed under that regime shall continue to apply for the period, as determined by those provisions, the goods remain under that regime.

2. The following shall be deemed to be an import of goods within the meaning of Article 7 (1):

   (a) the removal, including irregular removal, of goods from the regime referred to in Article 14 (1) (c) under which the goods were placed before 1 January 1993 under the conditions set out in paragraph 1;

   (b) the removal, including irregular removal, of goods from the regime referred to in Article 16 (1) (A) under which the goods were placed before 1 January 1993 under the conditions set out in paragraph 1;

   (c) the termination of a Community internal transit operation started before 1 January 1993 in the Community for the purpose of supply of goods for consideration made before 1 January 1993 in the Community by a taxable person acting as such;

   (d) the termination of an external transit operation started before 1 January 1993;

   (e) any irregularity or offence committed during an external transit operation started under the conditions set out in (c) or any Community external transit operation referred to in (d);

   (f) the use within the country, by a taxable or non-taxable person, of goods which have been supplied to him, before 1 January 1993, within another Member State, where the following conditions are met:

      — the supply of these goods has been exempted, or was likely to be exempted, pursuant to Article 15 (1) and (2),

      — the goods were not imported within the country before 1 January 1993.

   For the purpose of the application of (c), the expression 'Community internal transit operation' shall mean the dispatch or transport of goods under the cover of the internal Community transit arrangement or under the cover of a T2 L document or the intra-Community movement carnet, or the sending of goods by post.

3. In the cases referred to in paragraph 2(a) to (e), the place of import, within the meaning of Article 7(2), shall be the Member

State within whose territory the goods cease to be covered by the regime under which they were placed before 1 January 1993.

4. By way of derogation from Article 10(3), the import of the goods within the meaning of paragraph 2 of this Article shall terminate without the occurrence of a chargeable event when:

   (a) the imported goods are dispatched or transported outside the Community within the meaning of Article 3;

   or

   (b) the imported goods, within the meaning of paragraph 2(a), are other than a means of transport and are dispatched or transported to the Member State from which they were exported and to the person who exported them;

   or

   (c) the imported goods, within the meaning of paragraph 2(a), are means of transport which were acquired or imported before 1 January 1993, in accordance with the general conditions of taxation in force on the domestic market of a Member State, within the meaning of Article 3, and/or have not been subject by reason of their exportation to any exemption from or refund of value added tax.

   This condition shall be deemed to be fulfilled when the date of the first use of the means of transport was before 1 January 1985 or when the amount of tax due because of the importation is insignificant.';

23. Article 33a(1) and (2) shall be replaced by the following:

   '1. Goods referred to in Article 7(1)(b) entering the Community from a territory which forms part of the customs territory of the Community but which is considered as a third territory for the purposes of applying this Directive shall be subject to the following provisions:

   (a) the formalities relating to the entry of such goods into the Community shall be the same as those laid down by the Community customs provisions in force for the import of goods into the customs territory of the Community;

   (b) when the place of arrival of the dispatch or transport of these goods is situated outside the Member State where they enter the Community, they shall circulate in the Community under the internal Community transit procedure laid down by the Community customs provisions in force, insofar as they have been the subject of a declaration placing them under this regime when the goods entered the Community;

   (c) when at the moment of their entry into the Community the goods are found to be in one of the situations which would qualify them, if they were imported within the meaning of Article 7 (1) (a), to benefit from one of the arrangements referred to in Article 16 (1) (B) (a), (b), (c) and (d), or under a temporary arrangement in full exemption from import duties, the Member States shall take measures ensuring that the goods may remain in the Community under the same conditions as those laid down for the application of such arrangements.

2. Goods not referred to in Article 7 (1) (a) dispatched or transported from a Member State to a destination in a territory that forms parts of the customs territory of the Community but which is considered as a third territory for the purposes of applying this Directive shall be subject to the following provisions:

(a) the formalities relating to the export of those goods outside the territory of the Community shall be the same as the Community customs provisions in force in relation to export of goods outside the customs territory of the Community;

(b) for goods which are temporarily exported outside the Community, in order to be reimported, the Member States shall take the measures necessary to ensure that, on reimportation into the Community, such goods may benefit from the same provisions as if they had been temporarily exported outside the customs territory of the Community.';

24. Directive 85/362/EEC shall cease to have effect on 31 December 1992;

25. Article 6 of Directive 69/169/EEC shall be repealed as from 1 January 1993.

Article 2

1. As from 1 January 1993 and for a period of two years, which may not be extended, the Kingdom of Spain and the Italian Republic shall be authorized to apply provisions derogating from the principle of immediate deduction provided for in the first subparagraph of Article 18(2). These provisions may not have the effect of delaying by more than one month the time when the right to deduction, having arisen, may be exercised under Article 18(1).

However, for taxable persons who file the returns provided for in Article 22(4) for quarterly tax periods, the Kingdom of Spain and the Italian Republic shall be authorized to provide that the right to deduction which has come into being which could, under Article 18(1), be exercised in a given quarter, may not be exercised until the following quarter. This provision shall only apply where the Kingdom of Spain or the Italian Republic authorizes such taxable persons to opt for the filing of monthly returns.

2. By way of derogation from the third subparagraph of Article 15(10), the Portuguese Republic, the French Republic, the Kingdom of the Netherlands and the Federal Republic of Germany shall be authorized, in regard to contracts concluded after 31 December 1992, to abolish the repayment, procedure, where it is prohibited by this Directive by 1 October 1993 at the latest.

Article 3

The Council, acting unanimously on a Commission proposal, shall adopt before 30 June 1993, detailed rules for the taxation of chain transactions between taxable persons, so that such rules may enter into force on 1 January 1994.

Article 4

1. The Member States shall adapt their present value added tax system to the provisions of this Directive.

They shall adopt the necessary laws, regulations and administrative provisions for their adapted systems to enter into force 1 January 1993.

Member States may, however, provide that information relating to transactions referred to in the last subparagraph of Article 22 (6) (b) for which the tax becomes payable during the first three calendar months of 1993 must appear at the the latest on the summary statement signed for the second calendar quarter of 1993.

2. By way of derogation from the second subparagraph of paragraph 1, Member States shall be authorized to adopt the necessary laws, regulations and administrative provisions in order to implement by 1 January 1984 at the latest the provisions laid down in the following paragraphs of Article 1:

paragraph 11,

Paragraph 13, insofar as it relates to Article 28c(E)(3);

paragraph 19, insofar as it relates to the third subparagraph of Article 21(1)(a),

paragraph 20, insofar as it relates to obligations in respect of the transactions referred to in the preceding indents.

Member States which, on 1 January 1993, apply measures equivalent to those mentioned above shall adopt the necessary measures to ensure that the principles laid down in Article 22(6) and in current Community provisions on administrative cooperation in the area of indirect taxation are complied with as from 1 January 1993 without fail.

3. By way of derogation from the second subparagraph of paragraph 1, the Federal Repubic of Germany shall be authorized to adopt the necessary laws, regulations and administrative provisions in order to implement by 1 October 1993 at the latest the provisions laid down in Article 1(10) with regard to Article 28a(1a)(a).

4. Member States shall inform the Commission of the provisions which they adopt to apply this Directive.

5. Member States shall communicate the provisions of domestic law which they adopt in the field covered by this Directive to the Commission.

6. When Member States adopt these provisions, they shall contain a reference to this Directive or shall be accompanied by such reference on the occasion of their official publication. The methods of making such a reference shall be laid down by the Member States.

Article 5

This Directive is addressed to the Member States.

Done at Brussels, 14 December 1992.
For the Council
The President
N. LAMONT

COUNCIL DECISION 92/617/EEC

of 21 December 1992

Authorizing Ireland to apply particular measures in accordance with Article 22(12)(a) and (b) of Directive 77/388/EEC

Official Journal L 408 , 31/12/1992 p. 0013 - 0013

THE COUNCIL OF THE EUROPEAN COMMUNITIES,

Having regard to the Treaty establishing the European Economic Community,

Having regard to the Sixth Council Directive, 77/388/EEC, of 17 May 1977 on the harmonization of the laws of the Member States relating to turnover taxes - Common system of value added tax: uniform basis of assessment, and in particular Article 22 thereof.

Having regard to the proposal from the Commission,

Whereas, under Article 22(12) of Directive 77/388/EEC, the Council, acting unanimously on a proposal from the Commission, may authorize any Member State to introduce particular measures to simplify the statement obligations laid down in paragraph 6(b) of Article 22;

Whereas Article 22(12) further stipulates that such simplification measures may not jeopardize the proper monitoring of intra-Community transactions, and may take the forms outlined in subparagraphs (a) and (b) of Article 22(12);

Whereas the Irish Government, by letter received by the Commission on 23 July 1992, has requested authorization for simplification measures which take the form laid down in subparagraphs (a) and (b) of Article 22(12);

Whereas the authorization will be temporary;

Whereas the particular measure will not affect the European Communities' own resources arising from value added tax,

HAS ADOPTED THIS DECISION:

Article 1

As provided for by Article 22(12) of Directive 77/388/EEC, Ireland is hereby authorized, with effect from 1 January 1993 until 31 December 1996 or until the end of the transitional arrangements in the unlikely event that this is later, to introduce particular measures in accordance with subparagraphs (a) and (b) of Article 22(12), to simplify the obligations laid down in paragraph 6(b) of Article 22 regarding recapitulative statements.

Article 2

This Decision is addressed to Ireland.

Done at Brussels, 21 December 1992.
For the Council
The President
D. HURD

COUNCIL REGULATION 93/854/EEC

5th of April 1993

on Transit Statistics Relating to the Trading of Goods between Member States

Official Journal L 90 , 14/4/1993 p. 001 - 004

THE COUNCIL OF THE EUROPEAN COMMUNITIES

Having regard to the Treaty establishing the European Economic Community, and in particular Article 100a thereof.

Having regard to the proposal from the Commission,

In co-operation with the European Parliament,

Having regard to the opinion of the Economic and Social Committee,

Whereas the abolition of customs formalities, controls and documentation for all movements of goods across internal frontiers is necessary for the completion of the internal market;

Whereas, in the Member States, statistics on the trading of goods between Member States resulting from transit movements and movements into and out of warehouses may nevertheless still be needed;

Whereas Council Regulation (EEC) No 3330/91 of 7 November 1991 on the statistics relating to the trading of goods between Member States prohibits the Member States from introducing or maintaining compulsory formalities for the purpose of keeping statistics on transit and storage; whereas it is necessary for that purpose to provide a Community legal base;

Whereas the framework in which the Member States are authorised to organise their statistical surveys on these movements must be determined in order to prevent the burden on those responsible for providing information varying excessively from one Member State to another;

Whereas, within that framework, it is necessary to determine the purpose of transit and storage statistics and the consequences for the collection of information, to ensure that responsibility for collecting that information is directed towards existing administrative sources and to make use of the competent services of the latter to fill any gaps, without increasing the burden on those responsible for providing information;

Whereas that burden must not exceed certain limits, as regards classification, data to be declared or data media;

Whereas it is important that the burden of transit and storage statistics be alleviated, particularly for small and medium-sized enterprises; whereas this should be effected by means of statistical thresholds;

Whereas the Commission must not only adopt provisions implementing this Regulation but must also ensure that other implementing provisions adopted by the Member States do not compromise the alleviation of the burden on those responsible for providing information; whereas the Commission should be assisted in this task by the Committee on Statistics relating to the Trading of Goods between Member States,

HAS ADOPTED THIS REGULATION:

Article 1

1. With a view to compiling transit statistics and storage statistics, Member States may collect data on the trading of goods between Member States, acting in conformity with the rules laid down in this Regulation.

2. Member States which exercise this option shall accordingly inform the Commission.

Article 2

1. For the purposes of this Regulation, the definitions given in Article 2(a), (b), (c), (d), (e) and (f) of Regulation (EEC) No 3330/91 shall apply.

2. For the purpose of this Regulation:

    transit: means the crossing of a given Member State by goods which are being transported between two places situated outside that Member State;

    interrupted transit: means transit during which a break in transport occurs; this also includes transhipment;

    customs warehousing procedure: means the customs warehousing procedure as defined in Articles 1 and 2 of Council Regulation (EEC) No 2503/88 of 25 July 1988 on customs warehouses (OJ L225, 15.8.1988, p 1);

    competent statistical services: means those services in each Member State which are responsible for compiling statistics on the trading of goods between Member States.

Article 3

Of the goods referred to in Article 3 of Regulation (EEC) No 3330/91, data shall be collected for the purpose of compiling statistics on transit through a given Member State on those goods which are in interrupted transit in that Member State, with the exception of goods which having entered that Member State as non-Community goods, have subsequently been put into free circulation there.

Article 4

Of the goods referred to in Article 3 of Regulation (EEC) No 3330/91, data shall be collected for the purpose of compiling storage statistics in a given Member State on:

those which, though the customs warehousing procedure has not terminated, are transferred, within the meaning of Article 20 of Regulation (EEC) No 2503/88, from a customs warehouse situated in that Member State to one situated in another Member State;

those which, though the customs warehousing procedure has not terminated, are transferred, within the meaning of Article 20 of Regulation (EEC) No 2503/88, to a customs warehouse situated in that Member State from a customs warehouse situated in another Member State;

those which are subject to the customs warehousing procedure in that Member State and are sent to another Member State under the procedure for external Community transit;

those which are subject to the customs warehousing procedure in that Member State, having coming from another Member State under the procedure for external Community transit.

Article 5

1. Under conditions which they themselves shall determine, Member States shall authorise those responsible for providing statistical information to use administrative or commercial documents already required for other purposes as the statistical data medium.

   However, with a view to the standardisation of their basic documentation, Member States may establish exclusively statistical media provided that those required to provide statistical information are free to choose which of these media they use.

2. Member States shall inform the Commission of the media which they authorise or establish.

Article 6

1. In a given Member State, the person responsible for providing statistical information as referred to in Article 8 of Regulation (EEC) No 3330/91 shall be the natural or legal person who, engaged in that Member State in the trading of goods between Member States, draws up the administrative or commercial document designated as the statistical data medium pursuant to the first subparagraph of Article 5(1).

   In the absence of such a person and by way of derogation from Article 8 of Regulation (EEC) No 3330/91, each Member State shall designate from among the administrative services to which the document referred to in the first subparagraph is made available, one service which shall provide the information.

2. Member States shall be entitled to proceed in accordance with the second subparagraph of paragraph 1 in order to relieve persons responsible for supplying information of their obligations, in whole or in part.

3. The person or service referred to in paragraph 1 shall confirm to the provisions of this Regulation, the provisions adopted pursuant to Article 30 of Regulation (EEC) No 3330/91 and the measures taken by Member States to implement those provisions.

Article 7

1.   On the statistical data medium to be sent to the competent services:

-    without prejudice to Article 34 of Regulation (EEC) No 3330/91, goods shall be designated according to their usual trade description in sufficiently precise terms to permit their identification and their immediate and unequivocal classification in the most detailed relevant subdivision of the current version of either the classification of the harmonised system for transit statistics or the combined nomenclature for storage statistics, irrespective of the level at which these classifications are applied; however, this provision shall not prevent the Member States applying the standard goods classification for transport statistics - revised (NST/R) instead of the abovementioned classifications, where permissible under the rules governing the medium used.

-    the code number corresponding to the abovementioned nomenclature subdivision may also be required by type of goods.

2.   On the statistical data medium, countries shall be described by the alphabetical or numerical codes laid down in Council Regulation (EEC) No 1736/75 of 24 June 1975 on the external trade statistics of the Community and statistics of trade between Member States (as last amended by Council Regulation 1629/88/EEC;).

For the purposes of the first subparagraph, the parties responsible for providing information shall comply with the instructions issued by the national services competent for compiling statistics on trade between Member States.

Article 8

1.   Member States which compile transit statistics shall determine which of the following data are to be included on the statistical data medium, by type of goods:

(a)   the country of consignment, within the meaning of Article 9;

(b)   the country of destination, within the meaning of Article 9;

(c)   the quantity of goods in gross mass, within the meaning of Article 9;

(d)   the mode of transport in accordance with Article 9(f)(1);

(e)   the place where the interruption in transit took place in accordance with Article 9.

2.   Member States which compile storage statistics shall determine which of the following data are to be included on the statistical data medium, by type of goods:

(a)   the Member State of consignment, in the Member State which the goods enter within the meaning of Article 9;

(b)   the Member State of destination, in the Member State which goods leave within the meaning of Article 9;

(c)   the country of origin, within the meaning of Article 9; however, this item may be required only as allowed by Community law;

(d)   the quantity of goods expressed in gross mass or net mass within the meaning of Article 9 and in supplementary units in accordance with the combined nomenclature, where it is used pursuant to Article 7(1);

(e)   the customs value;

(f)   the presumed mode of transport, in accordance with Article 9(f)(2);

(g)   the region of destination, in the Member State which the goods enter.

3.   In so far as is not laid down in this Regulation, the data referred to in paragraphs 1 and 2 and the rules governing their inclusion on the statistical data medium shall be defined in accordance with the procedure laid down in Article 30 of Regulation (EEC) No 3330/91.

Article 9

For the purpose of applying Article 8:

(a)   country/Member State of consignment: means the last country/ Member State in which the goods were subject to halts or legal operations not inherent in their transport:

(b)   country/Member State of destination: means the last country/ Member State to which it is known, at the time the statistical data medium is drawn up, that the goods are to be sent;

(c)   country of origin: means the country in which the goods originated within the meaning of Council Regulation (EEC) No 802/68 of 27 June 1968 on the common definition of the concept of origin of goods (as last amended by Council Regulation 456/91/EEC;

(d)   gross mass: means the cumulated mass of the goods and all their packaging with the exclusion of the transport equipment, and in particular container;

(e)   net mass: means the mass of the goods, all packaging removed;

(f)   mode of transport: means that actually used

1   before or after the interruption of transit;

2   on entry to or exit from the warehouse.

Modes of transport are as follows:

Code	Designation
1	Sea transport
2	Rail transport
3	Road transport
4	Air transport
5	Post
6	Fixed transport installations
7	Inland waterway transport
8	Self-propelled

If the mode of transport is given as one of those listed under codes 1,2,3,4 or 8, Member States may require that it also be stated whether the goods are transported in containers within the meaning of Article 15(3) of Regulation (EEC) No 1736/75;

(g)   place of interruption of transit: means the port, airport or any other place where transit is interrupted within the meaning of Article 2(2)(b).

Article 10

1.   Where the data referred to in Articles 7 and 8 need not be shown on the administrative or commercial document referred to in the first subparagraph of Article 5(1) for the purposes for which such documents are required, Member States shall instruct the administrative service referred to in the second subparagraph of Article 6(1) to collect them and transmit them to the competent statistical services in accordance with procedures which they shall lay down, bearing in mind the stated requirements of these statistical services.

2.   Without prejudice to the second subparagraph of Article 5(1), Member States shall establish the media to be used by the abovementioned administrative service for transmitting these data.

Article 11

1.   For the purposes of this Regulation, statistical thresholds shall be defined as limits, expressed in gross mass for transit statistics and in terms of value or in mass for storage statistics, below which the obligations on those responsible for providing information are suspended.

2.   The threshold for transit statistics shall be fixed per type of goods at least:

-       50 kg in the case of air transport.

-       1 000 kg for other modes of transport.

3.   The threshold for storage statistics shall be fixed at least ECU 800 per type of goods, irrespective of the mass of the goods, or at least 50 kg per

type of goods in the case of air transport or at least 1 000 kg per type of goods for other modes of transport irrespective of the value of the goods.

Article 12

1. The provisions necessary for implementing this Regulation shall be adopted in accordance with the procedure laid down in Article 30 of Regulation (EEC) No 3330/91.
2. Member States may adopt the provisions required for collecting information in order to compile transit and storage statistics where such provisions are not laid down in this Regulation or adopted in accordance with paragraph 1.

However, if the effect of these national arrangements is to compromise the alleviation of the burden on those responsible for providing information, provisions to restore the conditions for alleviating that burden shall be adopted in accordance with the abovementioned Article.

Article 13

Member States shall communicate to the Commission the measures which they take to implement this Regulation.

Article 14

The Committee on Statistics relating to the Trading of Goods between Member States, set up by Article 29 of Regulation (EEC) No 3330/91, may examine any question, relating to the implementation of this Regulation raised by its chairman, either on his own initiative or at the request of the representative of a Member State.

Article 15

This Regulation shall enter into force on the third day following its publication in the Official Journal of the European Communities.

The Regulation shall remain in force until 31 December 1996. No later than three months before this date, the Commission shall present a report on the application of this Regulation and if necessary put forward a proposal.

This Regulation shall be binding in its entirety and directly applicable in all Member States.

COMMISSION REGULATION (93/2454/EEC)

of 2 July 1993

laying down provisions for the implementation of Council Regulation (EEC) No 2913/92 establishing the Community Customs Code

Official Journal L253, 11/10/1993 p. 0001 - 0533

THE COMMISSION OF THE EUROPEAN COMMUNITIES,

Having regard to the Treaty establishing the European Economic Community,

Having regard to Council Regulation (EEC) No 2913/92 of 12 October 1992 establishing the Community Customs Code, hereinafter referred to as the 'Code', and in particular Article 249 thereof,

Whereas the Code assembled all existing customs legislation in a single legal instrument;

Whereas at the same time the Code made certain modifications to this legislation to make it more coherent, to simplify it and to plug certain loopholes; whereas it therefore constitutes complete Community legislation in this area;

Whereas the same reasons which led to the adoption of the Code apply equally to the customs implementing legislation; whereas it is therefore desirable to bring together in a single regulation those customs implementing provisions which are currently scattered over a large number of Community regulations and directives;

Whereas the implementing code for the Community Customs Code hereby established should set out existing customs implementing rules; whereas it is nevertheless necessary, in the light of experience:

– to make some amendments in order to adapt the said rules to the provisions of the Code,

– to extend the scope of certain provisions which currently apply only to specific customs procedures in order to take account of the Code's comprehensive application,

– to formulate certain rules more precisely in order to achieve greater legal security in their application;

Whereas the changes made relate mainly to the provisions concerning customs debt;

Whereas it is appropriate to limit the application of Article 791 until 1 January 1995 and to review the subject matter in the light of experience gained before that time;

Whereas the measures provided for by this Regulation are in accordance with the opinion of the Customs Code Committee,

HAS ADOPTED THIS REGULATION:

PART I

general implementing provisions

TITLE I

general

Chapter 1

Definitions

Article 1

For the purposes of this Regulation:

1. **Code** means: Council Regulation (EEC) No 2913/92 of 12 October 1992 establishing a Community Customs Code;

[2. **ATA carnet** means: the international customs document for temporary importation established by virtue of the ATA Convention or the Istanbul Convention;][1]

[3. **Committee** means: the Customs Code Committee established by Articles 247a and 248a of the Code;][2]

4. **Customs Cooperation Council** means: the organization set up by the Convention establishing a Customs Cooperation Council, done at Brussels on 15 December 1950;

5. **Particulars required for identification of the goods** means: on the one hand, the particulars used to identify the goods commercially allowing the customs authorities to determine the tariff classification and, on the other hand, the quantity of the goods;

6. **Goods of a non-commercial nature** means: goods whose entry for the customs procedure in question is on an occasional basis and whose nature and quantity indicate that they are intended for the private, personal or family use of the consignees or persons carrying them, or which are clearly intended as gifts;

7. **Commercial policy measures** means: non-tariff measures established, as part of the common commercial policy, in the form of Community provisions governing the import and export of goods, such as surveillance or safeguard measures, quantitative restrictions or limits and import or export prohibitions;

8. **Customs nomenclature** means: one of the nomenclatures referred to in Article 20 (6) of the Code;

9. **Harmonized System** means: the Harmonized Commodity Description and Coding System;

[10. **Treaty** means: the treaty establishing the European Community;][2]

[11. **Istanbul Convention** means: the convention on temporary admission agreed at Istanbul on 26 June 1990.][3]

[12. **Economic operator** means: a person who, in the course of his business, is involved in activities covered by customs legislation.][4]

[13. **Single authorisation** means: an authorisation involving customs administrations in more than one Member State for one of the following procedures:

–   the simplified declaration procedure pursuant to Article 76(1) of the Code, or

–   the local clearance procedure pursuant to Article 76(1) of the Code, or

–   customs procedures with economic impact pursuant to Article 84(1)(b) of the Code, or

–   end-use pursuant to Article 21(1) of the Code.

14.   **Integrated authorisation** means: an authorisation to use more than one of the procedures referred to in point 13; it may take the form of an integrated single authorisation where more than one customs administration is involved.

15.   **Authorising customs authority** means: the customs authority who grants an authorisation.][5]

[Article 1a

For the purpose of applying Articles 291 to 300, the countries of the Benelux Economic Union shall be considered as a single Member State.][6]

Chapter 2

Decisions

Article 2

Where a person making a request for a decision is not in a position to provide all the documents and information necessary to give a ruling, the customs authorities shall provide the documents and information at their disposal.

Article 3

A decision concerning security favourable to a person who has signed an undertaking to pay the sums due at the first written request of the customs authorities, shall be revoked where the said undertaking is not fulfilled.

Article 4

A revocation shall not affect goods which, at the moment of its entry into effect, have already been placed under a procedure by virtue of the revoked authorization.

However, the customs authorities may require that such goods be assigned to a permitted customs-approved treatment or use within the period which they shall set.

[Chapter 3

Data processing techniques

Article 4a

1. Under the conditions and in the manner which they shall determine, and with due regard to the principles laid down by customs rules, the customs authorities may provide that formalities shall be carried out by a data-processing technique. For this purpose:

    –   **"a date-processing technique"** means:

        (a)   the exchange of EDI standard messages with the customs authorities;

        (b)   the introduction of information required for completion of the formalities concerned into customs data-processing systems:

    –   **"EDI"** (Electronic date interchange) means, the transmission of date structured according to agreed message standards, between one computer system and another, by electronic means,

    –   **"standard message"** means a predefined structure recognised for the electronic transmission of data.

2. The condition laid down for carrying out formalities by a data-processing technique shall include inter alia measures for checking the source of data and for protecting date against the risk of unauthorised access, loss alteration or destruction.

Article 4b

Where formalities are carried out by a data-processing technique, the customs authorities shall determine the rules for replacement of the hand-written signature by another technique which may be based on the use of codes.][7]

[Article 4c

For test programmes using data-processing techniques designed to evaluate possible simplifications, the customs authorities may, for the period strictly necessary to carry out the programme, waive the requirement to provide the following information:

(a)   the declaration provided for in Article 178(1);

(b)   by way of derogation from Article 222(1), the particulars relating to certain boxes of the Single Administrative Document which are not necessary for the identification of the goods and which are not the factors on the basis of which import or export duties are applied.

However, the information shall be available on request in the framework of a control operation.

The amount of import duties to be charged in the period covered by a derogation granted pursuant to the first subparagraph shall not be lower than that which would be levied in the absence of a derogation.

Member States wishing to engage in such test programmes shall provide the Commission in advance with full details of the proposed test programme, including its intended duration. They shall also keep the Commission informed of actual implementation and results. The Commission shall inform all the other Member States.][8]

[Chapter 4

Data exchange between customs authorities using information technology and computer networks

Article 4d

1. Without prejudice to any special circumstances and to the provisions of the procedure concerned, which, where appropriate, shall apply *mutatis mutandis*, where electronic systems for the exchange of information relating to a customs procedure or economic operators have been developed by Member States in co-operation with the Commission, the customs authorities shall use such systems for the exchange of information between customs offices concerned.

2. Where the customs offices involved in a procedure are located in different Member States, the messages to be used for the exchange of data shall conform to the structure and particulars defined by the customs authorities in agreement with each other.

Article 4e

1. In addition to the conditions referred to in Article 4a (2), the customs authorities shall establish and maintain adequate security arrangements for the effective, reliable and secure operation of the various systems.

2. To ensure the level of system security provided for in paragraph 1 each input, modification and deletion of data shall be recorded together with information giving the reason for, and exact time of, such processing and identifying the person who carried it out. The original data and any data so processed shall be kept for at least three calendar years from the end of the year to which such data refers, unless otherwise specified.

3. The customs authorities shall monitor security regularly.

4. The customs authorities involved shall inform each other and, where appropriate, the economic operator concerned, of all suspected breaches of security.

Chapter 5

Risk management

Article 4f

1. Customs authorities shall undertake risk management to differentiate between the levels of risk associated with goods subject to customs control or supervision and to determine whether or not, and if so where, the goods will be subject to specific customs controls.

2. The determination of levels of risk shall be based on an assessment of the likelihood of the risk-related event occurring and its impact, should the event actually materialise. The basis for the selection of consignments or declarations to be subject to customs controls shall include a random element.

Article 4g

1. Risk management at Community level, referred to in Article 13(2) of the Code, shall be carried out in accordance with an electronic common risk management framework comprised of the following elements:

    (a) a Community customs risk management system for the implementation of risk management, to be used for the communication among the Member States customs authorities and the Commission of any risk-related information that would help to enhance customs controls;

    (b) common priority control areas;

    (c) common risk criteria and standards for the harmonized application of customs controls in specific cases.

2. Customs authorities shall, using the system referred to in point (a) of paragraph 1, exchange risk-related information in the following circumstances:

    (a) the risks are assessed by a customs authority as significant and requiring customs control and the results of the control establish that the event, as referred to in Article 4(25) of the Code, has occurred;

    (b) the control results do not establish that the event, as referred to in Article 4(25) of the Code, has occurred, but the customs authority concerned considers the threat to present a high risk elsewhere in the Community.

Article 4h

1. Common priority control areas shall cover particular customs-approved treatments or uses, types of goods, traffic routes, modes of transport or economic operators that are to be subject to increased levels of risk analysis and customs controls during a certain period.

2. The application of common priority control areas shall be based upon a common approach to risk analysis and, in order to ensure equivalent levels of customs controls, common risk criteria and standards for the selection of goods or economic operators for control.

3. Customs controls carried out in common priority control areas shall be without prejudice to other controls normally carried out by the customs authorities.

Article 4i

1. The common risk criteria and standards referred to in Article 4g(1)(c) shall include the following elements:

(a) a description of the risk(s);

(b) the factors or indicators of risk to be used to select goods or economic operators for customs control;

(c) the nature of customs controls to be undertaken by the customs authorities;

(d) the duration of the application of the customs controls referred to in point (c).

The information resulting from the application of the elements referred to in the first subparagraph shall be distributed by use of the Community customs risk management system referred to in Article 4g(1)(a). It shall be used by the customs authorities in their risk management systems.

2. Customs authorities shall inform the Commission of the results of customs controls carried out in accordance with paragraph 1.

Article 4j

For the establishment of common priority control areas and the application of common risk criteria and standards account shall be taken of the following elements:

(a) proportionality to the risk;

(b) the urgency of the necessary application of the controls;

(c) probable impact on trade flow, on individual Member States and on control resources.][9]

Note

Articles 4k - 140 are omitted as they refer specifically to Customs Duty.

TITLE V

customs value

Chapter 1

General provisions

Article 141

1.   In applying the provisions of Articles 28 to 36 of the Code and those of this title, Member States shall comply with the provisions set out in Annex 23.

The provisions as set out in the first column of Annex 23 shall be applied in the light of the interpretative note appearing in the second column.

2.   If it is necessary to make reference to generally accepted accounting principles in determining the customs value, the provisions of Annex 24 shall apply.

Article 142

1.   For the purposes of this title:

(a)   **'the Agreement'** means the Agreement on implementation of Article VII of the General Agreement on Tariffs and Trade concluded in the framework of the multilateral trade negotiations of 1973 to 1979 and referred to in the first indent of Article 31 (1) of the Code;

(b)   **'produced goods'** includes goods grown, manufactured and mined;

(c)   **'identical goods'** means goods produced in the same country which are the same in all respects, including physical characteristics, quality and reputation. Minor differences in appearance shall not preclude goods otherwise conforming to the definition from being regarded as identical

(d)   **'similar goods'** means goods produced in the same country which, although not alike in all respects, have like characteristics and like component materials which enable them to perform the same functions and to be commercially interchangeable; the quality of the goods, their reputation and the existence of a trademark are among the factors to be considered in determining whether goods are similar;

(e)   **'goods of the same class or kind'** means goods which fall within a group or range of goods produced by a particular industry or industry sector, and includes identical or similar goods.

2.   **'Identical goods'** and **'similar goods'**, as the case may be, do not include goods which incorporate or reflect engineering, development, artwork,

design work, and plans and sketches for which no adjustment has been made under Article 32(1)(b)(iv) of the Code because such elements were undertaken in the Community.

Article 143

1.   [For the purposes of Title II, Chapter 3 of the Code and of this title, persons shall be deemed to be related only if:][10]

(a)   they are officers or directors of one another's businesses;

(b)   they are legally recognized partners in business;

(c)   they are employer and employee;

(d)   any person directly or indirectly owns, controls or holds 5 % or more of the outstanding voting stock or shares of both of them;

(e)   one of them directly or indirectly controls the other;

(f)   both of them are directly or indirectly controlled by a third person;

(g)   together they directly or indirectly control a third person; or

(h)   they are members of the same family. Persons shall be deemed to be members of the same family only if they stand in any of the following relationships to one another

–   husband and wife,

–   parent and child,

–   brother and sister (whether by whole or half blood),

–   grandparent and grandchild,

–   uncle or aunt and nephew or niece,

–   parent-in-law and son-in-law or daughter-in-law,

–   brother-in-law and sister-in-law.

2.   For the purposes of this title, persons who are associated in business with one another in that one is the sole agent, sole distributor or sole concessionaire, however described, of the other shall be deemed to be related only if they fall within the criteria of paragraph 1.

Article 144

1.   For the purposes of determining customs value under Article 29 of the Code of goods in regard to which the price has not actually been paid at the material time for valuation for customs purposes, the price payable for settlement at the said time shall as a general rule be taken as the basis for customs value.

2.   The Commission and the Member States shall consult within the Committee concerning the application of paragraph 1.

[Article 145

1. Where goods declared for free circulation are part of a larger quantity of the same goods purchased in one transaction, the price actually paid or payable for the purposes of Article 29(1) of the Code shall be that price represented by the proportion of the total price which the quantity so declared bears to the total quantity purchased.

   Apportioning the price actually paid or payable shall also apply in the case of the loss of part of a consignment or when the goods being valued have been damaged before entry into free circulation.

2. After release of the goods for free circulation, an adjustment made by the seller, to the benefit of the buyer, of the price actually paid or payable for the goods may be taken into consideration for the determination of the customs value in accordance with Article 29 of the Code, if it is demonstrated to the satisfaction of the customs authorities that:

   (a) the goods were defective at the moment referred to by Article 67 of the Code;

   (b) the seller made the adjustment in performance of a warranty obligation provided for in the contract of sale, concluded before release for free circulation of the goods;

   (c) the defective nature of the goods has not already been taken into account in the relevant sales contract.

3. The price actually paid or payable for the goods, adjusted in accordance with paragraph 2, may be taken into account only if that adjustment was made within a period of 12 months following the date of acceptance of the declaration for entry to free circulation of the goods.][11]

Article 146

Where the price actually paid or payable for the purposes of Article 29(1) of the Code includes an amount in respect of any internal tax applicable within the country of origin or export in respect of the goods in question, the said amount shall not be incorporated in the customs value provided that it can be demonstrated to the satisfaction of the customs authorities concerned that the goods in question have been or will be relieved therefrom for the benefit of the buyer.

Article 147

1. For the purposes of Article 29 of the Code, the fact that the goods which are the subject of a sale are declared for free circulation shall be regarded as adequate indication that they were sold for export to the customs territory of the Community. [In the case of successive sales before valuation, only the last sale, which led to the introduction of the goods into the customs territory of the Community, or a sake taking place in the customs territory of the Community before entry for free circulation of the goods shall constitute such indication.

Where a price is declared which relates to a sale taking place before the last sale on the basis of which the goods were introduced into the customs territory of the Community, it must be demonstrated to the satisfaction of the customs authorities that this sale of goods took place for export to the customs territory in question.

The provisions of Articles 178 to 181 a shall apply.][12]

2. [...][13], where goods are used in a third country between the time of sale and the time of entry into free circulation the customs value need not be the transaction value.

3. The buyer need satisfy no condition other than that of being a party to the contract of sale.

Article 148

Where, in applying Article 29(1)(b) of the Code, it is established that the sale or price of imported goods is subject to a condition or consideration the value of which can be determined with respect to the goods being valued, such value shall be regarded as an indirect payment by the buyer to the seller and part of the price actually paid or payable provided that the condition or consideration does not relate to either:

(a) an activity to which Article 29(3)(b) of the Code applies; or

(b) a factor in respect of which an addition is to be made to the price actually paid or payable under the provisions of Article 32 of the Code.

Article 149

1. For the purposes of Article 29(3)(b) of the Code, the term 'marketing activities' means all activities relating to advertising and promoting the sale of the goods in question and all activities relating to warranties or guarantees in respect of them.

2. Such activities undertaken by the buyer shall be regarded as having been undertaken on his own account even if they are performed in pursuance of an obligation on the buyer following an agreement with the seller.

Article 150

1. In applying Article 30(2)(a) of the Code (the transaction value of identical goods), the customs value shall be determined by reference to the transaction value of identical goods in a sale at the same commercial level and in substantially the same quantity as the goods being valued. Where no such sale is found, the transaction value of identical goods sold at a different commercial level and/or in different quantities, adjusted to take account of differences attributable to commercial level and/or to quantity, shall be used, provided that such adjustments can be made on the basis of demonstrated evidence which clearly establishes the reasonableness and accuracy of the adjustment, whether the adjustment leads to an increase or a decrease in the value.

2.   Where the costs and charges referred to in Article 32(1)(e) of the Code are included in the transaction value, an adjustment shall be made to take account of significant differences in such costs and charges between the imported goods and the identical goods in question arising from differences in distances and modes of transport.

3.   If, in applying this Article, more than one transaction value of identical goods is found, the lowest such value shall be used to determine the customs value of the imported goods.

4.   In applying this Article, a transaction value for goods produced by a different person shall be taken into account only when no transaction value can be found under paragraph 1 for identical goods produced by the same person as the goods being valued.

5.   For the purposes of this Article, the transaction value of identical imported goods means a customs value previously determined under Article 29 of the Code, adjusted as provided for in paragraphs 1(b) and 2 of this Article.

Article 151

1.   In applying Article 30(2)(b) of the Code (the transaction value of similar goods), the customs value shall be determined by reference to the transaction value of similar goods in a sale at the same commercial level and in substantially the same quantity as the goods being valued.

Where no such sale is found, the transaction value of similar goods sold at a different commercial level and/or in different quantities, adjusted to take account of differences attributable to commercial level and/or to quantity, shall be used, provided that such adjustments can be made on the basis of demonstrated evidence which clearly establishes the reasonableness and accuracy of the adjustment, whether the adjustment leads to an increase or a decrease in the value.

2.   Where the costs and charges referred to in Article 32(1)(e) of the Code are included in the transaction value, an adjustment shall be made to take account of significant differences in such costs and charges between the imported goods and the similar goods in question arising from differences in distances and modes of transport.

3.   If, in applying this Article, more than one transaction value of similar goods is found, the lowest such value shall be used to determine the customs value for the imported goods.

4.   In applying this Article, a transaction value for goods produced by a different person shall be taken into account only when no transaction value can be found under paragraph 1 for similar goods produced by the same person as the goods being valued.

5.   For the purposes of this Article, the transaction value of similar imported goods means a customs value previously determined under Article 29 of the Code, adjusted as provided for in paragraphs 1(b) and 2 of this Article.

Article 152

1.   (a)   If the imported goods or identical or similar imported goods are sold in the Community in the condition as imported, the customs value of imported goods, determined in accordance with Article 30(2)(c) of the Code, shall be based on the unit price at which the imported goods or identical or similar imported goods are so sold in the greatest aggregate quantity, at or about the time of the importation of the goods being valued, to persons who are not related to the persons from whom they buy such goods, subject to deductions for the following:

   (i)   either the commissions usually paid or agreed to be paid or the additions usually made for profit and general expenses (including the direct and indirect costs of marketing the goods in question) in connection with sales in the Community of imported goods of the same class or kind;

   (ii)   the usual costs of transport and insurance and associated costs incurred within the Community;

   (iii) the import duties and other charges payable in the Community by reason of the importation or sale of the goods.

   (b)   If neither the imported goods nor identical nor similar imported goods are sold at or about the time of importation of the goods being valued, the customs value of imported goods determined under this Article shall, subject otherwise to the provisions of paragraph 1(a), be based on the unit price at which the imported goods or identical or similar imported goods are sold in the Community in the condition as imported at the earliest date after the importation of the goods being valued but before the expiration of 90 days after such importation.

2.   If neither the imported goods nor identical nor similar imported goods are sold in the Community in the condition as imported, then, if the importer so requests, the customs value shall be based on the unit price at which the imported goods, after further processing, are sold in the greatest aggregate quantity to persons in the Community who are not related to the persons from whom they buy such goods, due allowance being made for the value added by such processing and the deductions provided for in paragraph 1(a).

3.   For the purposes of this Article, the unit price at which imported goods are sold in the greatest aggregate quantity is the price at which the greatest number of units is sold in sales to persons who are not related to the persons from whom they buy such goods at the first commercial level after importation at which such sales take place.

4.   Any sale in the Community to a person who supplies directly or indirectly free of charge or at reduced cost for use in connection with the

production and sale for export of the imported goods any of the elements specified in Article 32(1)(b) of the Code should not be taken into account in establishing the unit price for the purposes of this Article.

5. For the purposes of paragraph 1(b), the 'earliest date' shall be the date by which sales of the imported goods or of identical or similar imported goods are made in sufficient quantity to establish the unit price.

Article 153

1. In applying Article 30(2)(d) of the Code (computed value), the customs authorities may not require or compel any person not resident in the Community to produce for examination, or to allow access to, any account or other record for the purposes of determining this value.

    However, information supplied by the producer of the goods for the purposes of determining the customs value under this Article may be verified in a non-Community country by the customs authorities of a Member State with the agreement of the producer and provided that such authorities give sufficient advance notice to the authorities of the country in question and the latter do not object to the investigation.

2. The cost or value of materials and fabrication referred to in the first indent of Article 30(2)(d) of the Code shall include the cost of elements specified in Article 32(1)(a)(ii) and (iii) of the Code.

    It shall also include the value, duly apportioned, of any product or service specified in Article 32(1)(b) of the Code which has been supplied directly or indirectly by the buyer for use in connection with the production of the imported goods. The value of the elements specified in Article 32(1)(b)(iv) of the Code which are undertaken in the Community shall be included only to the extent that such elements are charged to the producer.

3. Where information other than that supplied by or on behalf of the producer is used for the purposes of determining a computed value, the customs authorities shall inform the declarant, if the latter so requests, of the source of such information, the data used and the calculations based on such data, subject to Article 15 of the Code.

4. The 'general expenses' referred to in the second indent of Article 30(2)(d) of the Code, cover the direct and indirect costs of producing and selling the goods for export which are not included under the first indent of Article 30(2)(d) of the Code.

Article 154

Where containers referred to in Article 32(1)(a)(ii) of the Code are to be the subject of repeated importations, their cost shall, at the request of the declarant, be apportioned, as appropriate, in accordance with generally accepted accounting principles.

Article 155

For the purposes of Article 32(1)(b)(iv) of the Code, the cost of research and preliminary design sketches is not to be included in the customs value.

Article 156

Article 33(c) of the Code shall apply mutatis mutandis where the customs value is determined by applying a method other than the transaction value.

Article 156a

1. The customs authorities may, at the request of the person concerned, authorize:

    –   by derogation from Article 32 (2) of the Code, certain elements which are to be added to the price actually paid or payable, although not quantifiable at the time of incurrence of the customs debt,

    –   by derogation from Article 33 of the Code, certain charges which are not to be included in the customs value, in cases where the amounts relating to such elements are not shown separately at the time of incurrence of the customs debt,

    to be determined on the basis of appropriate and specific criteria.

    In such cases, the declared customs value is not to be considered as provisional within the meaning of the second indent of Article 254.

2. The authorization shall be granted under the following conditions:

    (a)   the carrying out of the procedures provided for by Article 259 would, in the circumstances, represent disproportionate administrative costs;

    (b)   recourse to an application of Articles 30 and 31 of the Code appears to be inappropriate in the particular circumstances;

    (c)   there are valid reasons for considering that the amount of import duties to be charged in the period covered by the authorization will not be lower than that which would be levied in the absence of an authorization;

    (d)   competitive conditions amongst operators are not distorted.][14]

Chapter 2

Provisions concerning royalties and licence fees

Article 157

1. For the purposes of Article 32(1)(c) of the Code, royalties and licence fees shall be taken to mean in particular payment for the use of rights relating:

- to the manufacture of imported goods (in particular, patents, designs, models and manufacturing know-how), or

- to the sale for exportation of imported goods (in particular, trade marks, registered designs), or

- to the use or resale of imported goods (in particular, copyright, manufacturing processes inseparably embodied in the imported goods).

2.   Without prejudice to Article 32(5) of the Code, when the customs value of imported goods is determined under the provisions of Article 29 of the Code, a royalty or licence fee shall be added to the price actually paid or payable only when this payment:

- is related to the goods being valued, and

- constitutes a condition of sale of those goods.

Article 158

1.   When the imported goods are only an ingredient or component of goods manufactured in the Community, an adjustment to the price actually paid or payable for the imported goods shall only be made when the royalty or licence fee relates to those goods.

2.   Where goods are imported in an unassembled state or only have to undergo minor processing before resale, such as diluting or packing, this shall not prevent a royalty or licence fee from being considered related to the imported goods.

3.   If royalties or licence fees relate partly to the imported goods and partly to other ingredients or component parts added to the goods after their importation, or to post-importation activities or services, an appropriate apportionment shall be made only on the basis of objective and quantifiable data, in accordance with the interpretative note to Article 32(2) of the Code in Annex 23.

Article 159

A royalty or licence fee in respect of the right to use a trade mark is only to be added to the price actually paid or payable for the imported goods where:

- the royalty or licence fee refers to goods which are resold in the same state or which are subject only to minor processing after importation,

- the goods are marketed under the trade mark, affixed before or after importation, for which the royalty or licence fee is paid, and

- the buyer is not free to obtain such goods from other suppliers unrelated to the seller.

Article 160

When the buyer pays royalties or licence fees to a third party, the conditions provided for in Article 157(2) shall not be considered as met unless the seller or a person related to him requires the buyer to make that payment.

Article 161

Where the method of calculation of the amount of a royalty or licence fee derives from the price of the imported goods, it may be assumed in the absence of evidence to the contrary that the payment of that royalty or licence fee is related to the goods to be valued.

However, where the amount of a royalty or licence fee is calculated regardless of the price of the imported goods, the payment of that royalty or licence fee may nevertheless be related to the goods to be valued.

Article 162

In applying Article 32(1)(c) of the Code, the country of residence of the recipient of the payment of the royalty or licence fee shall not be a material consideration.

Chapter 3

Provisions concerning the place of introduction into the Community

Article 163

1.   For the purposes of Article 32(1)(e) and Article 33(a) of the Code, the place of introduction into the customs territory of the Community shall be:

   (a)   for goods carried by sea, the port of unloading, or the port of transhipment, subject to transhipment being certified by the customs authorities of that port;

   (b)   for goods carried by sea and then, without transhipment, by inland waterway, the first port where unloading can take place either at the mouth of the river or canal or further inland, subject to proof being furnished to the customs office that the freight to the port of unloading is higher than that to the first port;

   (c)   for goods carried by rail, inland waterway, or road, the place where the first customs office is situated;

   (d)   for goods carried by other means, the place where the land frontier of the customs territory of the Community is crossed.

[2.   The customs value of goods introduced into the customs territory of the Community and then carried to a destination in another part of that territory through the territories of Belarus, Bulgaria, Russia, Romania, Switzerland, Bosnia and Herzegovina, Croatia, the Federal Republic of Yugoslavia or the former Yugoslav Republic of Macedonia shall be determined by reference to the first place of introduction into the customs territory of the Community, provided that goods are carried direct through the territories of those countries by a usual route across such territory to the place of destination.][15]

3. The customs value of goods introduced into the customs territory of the Community and then carried by sea to a destination in another part of that territory shall be determined by reference to the first place of introduction into the customs territory of the Community, provided the goods are carried direct by a usual route to the place of destination.

[4. Paragraphs 2 and 3 of this Article shall also apply where the goods have been unloaded, transhipped or temporarily immobilised in the territories of Belarus, Bulgaria, Russia, Romania, Switzerland, Bosnia and Herzegovina, Croatia, the Federal Republic of Yugoslavia or the former Yugoslav Republic of Macedonia for reasons related solely to their transport.][15]

5. For goods introduced into the customs territory of the Community and carried directly from one of the French overseas departments to another part of the customs territory of the Community or vice versa, the place of introduction to be taken into consideration shall be the place referred to in paragraphs 1 and 2 situated in that part of the customs territory of the Community from which the goods came, if they were unloaded or transhipped there and this was certified by the customs authorities.

6. When the conditions specified at paragraphs 2, 3 and 5 are not fulfilled, the place of introduction to be taken into consideration shall be the place specified in paragraph 1 situated in that part of the customs territory of the Community to which the goods are consigned.

Chapter 4

Provisions concerning transport costs

Article 164

In applying Article 32(1)(e) and 33(a) of the Code:

(a) where goods are carried by the same mode of transport to a point beyond the place of introduction into the customs territory of the Community, transport costs shall be assessed in proportion to the distance covered outside and inside the customs territory of the Community, unless evidence is produced to the customs authorities to show the costs that would have been incurred under a general compulsory schedule of freight rates for the carriage of the goods to the place of introduction into the customs territory of the Community;

(b) where goods are invoiced at a uniform free domicile price which corresponds to the price at the place of introduction, transport costs within the Community shall not be deducted from that price. However, such deduction shall be allowed if evidence is produced to the customs authorities that the free-frontier price would be lower than the uniform free domicile price;

(c)   where transport is free or provided by the buyer, transport costs to the place of introduction, calculated in accordance with the schedule of freight rates normally applied for the same modes of transport, shall be included in the customs value.

Article 165

1.   All postal charges levied up to the place of destination in respect of goods sent by post shall be included in the customs value of these goods, with the exception of any supplementary postal charge levied in the country of importation.

2.   No adjustment to the declared value shall, however, be made in respect of such charges in determining the value of consignments of a non-commercial nature.

3.   Paragraphs 1 and 2 are not applicable to goods carried by the express postal services known as EMS-Datapost (in Denmark, EMS-Jetpost, in Germany, EMS-Kurierpostsendungen, in Italy, CAI-Post).

Article 166

The air transport costs to be included in the customs value of goods shall be determined by applying the rules and percentages shown in Annex 25.

[...][16]

Chapter 6
Provisions concerning rates of exchange

Article 168

For the purposes of Articles 169 to 171 of this chapter:

(a)   **'rate recorded'** shall mean:

    –   the latest selling rate of exchange recorded for commercial transactions on the most representative exchange market or markets of the Member State concerned, or

    –   some other description of a rate of exchange so recorded and designated by the Member State as the 'rate recorded' provided that it reflects as effectively as possible the current value of the currency in question in commercial transactions;

(b)   **'published'** shall mean made generally known in a manner designated by the Member State concerned;

(c)   **'currency'** shall mean any monetary unit used as a means of settlement between monetary authorities or on the international market.

Article 169

1.   Where factors used to determine the customs value of goods are expressed at the time when that value is determined in a currency other

than that of the Member State where the valuation is made, the rate of exchange to be used to determine that value in terms of the currency of the Member State concerned shall be the rate recorded on the second-last Wednesday of a month and published on that or the following day.

2. The rate recorded on the second-last Wednesday of a month shall be used during the following calendar month unless it is superseded by a rate established under Article 171.

3. Where a rate of exchange is not recorded on the second-last Wednesday indicated in paragraph 1, or, if recorded, is not published on that or the following day, the last rate recorded for the currency in question published within the preceding 14 days shall be deemed to be the rate recorded on that Wednesday.

Article 170

Where a rate of exchange cannot be established under the provisions of Article 169, the rate of exchange to be used for the application of Article 35 of the Code shall be designated by the Member State concerned and shall reflect as effectively as possible the current value of the currency in question in commercial transactions in terms of the currency of that Member State.

Article 171

1. Where a rate of exchange recorded on the last Wednesday of a month and published on that or the following day differs by 5 % or more from the rate established in accordance with Article 169 for entry into use the following month, it shall replace the latter rate from the first Wednesday of that month as the rate to be applied for the application of Article 35 of the Code.

2. Where in the course of a period of application as referred to in the preceding provisions, a rate of exchange recorded on a Wednesday and published on that or the following day differs by 5 % or more from the rate being used in accordance with this Chapter, it shall replace the latter rate and enter into use on the Wednesday following as the rate to be used for the application of Article 35 of the Code. The replacement rate shall remain in use for the remainder of the current month, provided that this rate is not superseded due to operation of the provisions of the first sentence of this paragraph.

3. Where, in a Member State, a rate of exchange is not recorded on a Wednesday or, if recorded, is not published on that or the following day, the rate recorded shall, for the application in that Member State of paragraphs 1 and 2, be the rate most recently recorded and published prior to that Wednesday.

Article 172

When the customs authorities of a Member State authorize a declarant to furnish or supply at a later date certain details concerning the declaration for free circulation of the goods in the form of a periodic declaration, this authorization may, at the declarant's request, provide that a single rate be used for conversion into that Member State's currency of elements forming part of the customs value as expressed in a particular currency. In this case, the rate to be used shall be the rate, established in accordance with this Chapter, which is applicable on the first day of the period covered by the declaration in question.

Chapter 7

Simplified procedures for certain perishable goods

Article 173

1. For the purpose of determining the customs value of products referred to in Annex 26, the Commission shall establish for each classification heading a unit value per 100 kg net expressed in the currencies of the Member States.

    The unit values shall apply for periods of 14 days, each period beginning on a Friday.

2. Unit values shall be established on the basis of the following elements, which are to be supplied to the Commission by Member States, in relation to each classification heading:

    (a)   the average free-at-frontier unit price, not cleared through customs, expressed in the currency of the Member State in question per 100 kg net and calculated on the basis of prices for undamaged goods in the marketing centres referred to in Annex 27 during the reference period referred to in Article 174(1);

    (b)   the quantities entered into free circulation over the period of a calendar year with payment of import duties.

3. The average free-at-frontier unit price, not cleared through customs, shall be calculated on the basis of the gross proceeds of sales made between importers and wholesalers. However, in the case of the London, Milan and Rungis marketing centres the gross proceeds shall be those recorded at the commercial level at which those goods are most commonly sold at those centres.

    There shall be deducted from the figures so arrived at:

    –   a marketing margin of 15 % for the marketing centres of London, Milan and Rungis and of 8 % for the other marketing centres,

    –   costs of transport and insurance within the customs territory,

    –   a standard amount of ECU 5 representing all the other costs which are not to be included in the customs value. This amount shall be converted into the currencies of the Member States on the basis of the latest rates in force established in accordance with Article 18 of the Code,

    –   import duties and other charges which are not to be included in the customs value.

4.   The Member States may fix standard amounts for deduction in respect of transport and insurance costs in accordance with paragraph 3. Such standard amounts and the methods for calculating them shall be made known to the Commission immediately.

Article 174

1.   The reference period for calculating the average unit prices referred to in Article 173(2)(a) shall be the period of 14 days ending on the Thursday preceding the week during which new unit values are to be established.

2.   Average unit prices shall be notified by Member States not later than 12 noon on the Monday of the week during which unit values are established pursuant to Article 173. If that day is a non-working day, notification shall be made on the working day immediately preceding that day.

3.   The quantities entered into free circulation during a calendar year for each classification heading shall be notified to the Commission by all Member States before 15 June in the following year.

Article 175

1.   The unit values referred to in Article 173(1) shall be established by the Commission on alternate Tuesdays on the basis of the weighted average of the average unit prices referred to in Article 173(2)(a) in relation to the quantities referred to in Article 173(2)(b).

2.   For the purpose of determining the weighted average, each average unit price as referred to in Article 173(2)(a) shall be converted into ecu on the basis of the last conversion rates determined by the Commission and published in the Official Journal of the European Communities prior to the week during which the unit values are to be established. The same conversion rates shall be applied in converting the unit values so obtained back into the currencies of the Member States.

3.   The last published unit values shall remain applicable until new values are published. However, in the case of major fluctuations in price in one or more Member States, as a result, for example, of an interruption in the continuity of imports of a particular product, new unit values may be determined on the basis of actual prices at the time of fixing those values.

Article 176

1.   Consignments which at the material time for valuation for customs purposes contain not less than 5% of produce unfit in its unaltered state for human consumption or the value of which has depreciated by not less than 20 % in relation to average market prices for sound produce, shall be treated as damaged.

2.   Consignments which are damaged may be valued:

–   either, after sorting, by application of unit values to the sound portion, the damaged portion being destroyed under customs supervision, or

–   by application of unit values established for the sound produce after deduction from the weight of the consignment of a percentage equal to the percentage assessed as damaged by a sworn expert and accepted by the customs authorities, or

–   by application of unit values established for the sound produce reduced by the percentage assessed as damaged by a sworn expert and accepted by the customs authorities.

Article 177

1.   In declaring or causing to be declared the customs value of one or more products which he imports by reference to the unit values established in accordance with this Chapter, the person concerned joins the simplified procedure system for the current calendar year in respect of the product or products in question.

2.   If subsequently the person concerned requires the use of a method other than the simplified procedures for the customs valuation of one or more of the products he imports, the customs authorities of the Member State concerned shall be entitled to notify him that he will not be allowed to benefit from the simplified procedures for the remainder of the current calendar year in regard to the product or products concerned; this exclusion can be extended for the following calendar year. Such notified exclusion shall be communicated without delay to the Commission, which shall in turn immediately inform the customs authorities of the other Member States.

Chapter 8
Declarations of particulars and documents to be furnished

Article 178

1.   Where it is necessary to establish a customs value for the purposes of Articles 28 to 36 of the Code, a declaration of particulars relating to customs value (value declaration) shall accompany the customs entry made in respect of the imported goods. The value declaration shall be drawn up on a form D.V. 1 corresponding to the specimen in Annex 28, supplemented where appropriate by one or more forms D.V. 1 bis corresponding to the specimen in Annex 29.

[2.   The value declaration provided for in paragraph 1 shall be made only by a person established in the Community and in possession of the relevant facts.

The second indent of Article 64(2)(b) and Article 64(3) of the Code shall apply *mutatis mutandis*.][17]

3.   The customs authorities may waive the requirement of a declaration on the form referred to in paragraph 1 where the customs value of the goods in question cannot be determined under the provisions of Article 29 of the Code. In such cases the person referred to in paragraph 2 shall furnish or cause to be furnished to the customs authorities such other information as may be requested for the purposes of determining the customs value under another Article of the said Code; and such other information shall be supplied in such form and manner as may be prescribed by the customs authorities.

4.   The lodging with a customs office of a declaration required by paragraph 1 shall, without prejudice to the possible application of penal provisions, be equivalent to the engagement of responsibility by the person referred to in paragraph 2 in respect of:

–   the accuracy and completeness of the particulars given in the declaration,

–   the authenticity of the documents produced in support of these particulars, and

–   the supply of any additional information or document necessary to establish the customs value of the goods.

5.   This Article shall not apply in respect of goods for which the customs value is determined under the simplified procedure system established in accordance with the provisions of Articles 173 to 177.

Article 179

1.   Except where it is essential for the correct application of import duties, the customs authorities shall waive the requirement of all or part of the declaration provided for in Article 178(1):

(a)   where the customs value of the imported goods in a consignment does not exceed [EUR 10 000][18], provided that they do not constitute split or multiple consignments from the same consignor to the same consignee; or

(b)   where the importations involved are of a non-commercial nature; or

(c)   where the submission of the particulars in question is not necessary for the application of the Customs Tariff of the European Communities or where the customs duties provided for in the Tariff are not chargeable pursuant to specific customs provisions.

2.   The amount in ecu referred to in paragraph 1(a) shall be converted in accordance with Article 18 of the Code. The customs authorities may round-off upwards or downwards the sum arrived at after conversion. The customs authorities may maintain unamended the exchange value in national currency of the amount determined in ecu if, at the time of the annual adjustment provided for in Article 18 of the Code, the

conversion of this amount, before the rounding-off provided for in this paragraph, leads to an alteration of less than 5 % in the exchange value expressed in national currency or to a reduction thereof.

3. In the case of continuing traffic in goods supplied by the same seller to the same buyer under the same commercial conditions, the customs authorities may waive the requirement that all particulars under Article 178(1) be furnished in support of each customs declaration, but shall require them whenever the circumstances change and at least once every three years.

4. A waiver granted under this Article may be withdrawn and the submission of a D.V. 1 may be required where it is found that a condition necessary to qualify for that waiver was not or is no longer met.

Article 180

Where computerized systems are used, or where the goods concerned are the subject of a general, periodic or recapitulative declaration, the customs authorities may authorize variations in the form of presentation of data required for the determination of customs value.

Article 181

1. The person referred to in Article 178(2) shall furnish the customs authorities with a copy of the invoice on the basis of which the value of the imported goods is declared. Where the customs value is declared in writing this copy shall be retained by the customs authorities.

2. In the case of written declarations of the customs value, when the invoice for the imported goods is made out to a person established in a Member State other than that in which the customs value is declared, the declarant shall furnish the customs authorities with two copies of the invoice. One of these copies shall be retained by the customs authorities; the other, bearing the stamp of the office in question and the serial number of the declaration at the said customs office shall be returned to the declarant for forwarding to the person to whom the invoice is made out.

3. The customs authorities may extend the provisions of paragraph 2 to cases where the person to whom the invoice is made out is established in the Member State in which the customs value is declared.

[Article 181a

1. The customs authorities need not determine the customs valuation of imported goods on the basis of the transaction value method if, in accordance with the procedure set out in paragraph 2, they are not satisfied, on the basis of reasonable doubts, that that the declared value represents the total amount paid or payable as referred to in Article 29 of the Code.

2. Where the customs authorities have the doubts described in paragraph 1 they may ask for additional information in accordance with article 178(4).

If those doubts continue, the customs authorities must, before reaching a final decision, notify the person concerned, in writing if requested, of the grounds for those doubts and provide him with a reasonable opportunity to respond. A final decision and the grounds therefor shall be communicated in writing to the person concerned.][19]

TITLE VI

introduction of goods into the customs territory

Chapter 1

Examination of the goods and taking of samples by the person concerned

Article 182

Note

Articles 182 - 197 have been omitted as they refer specifically to Customs Duty.

TITLE VII

customs declarations - normal procedure

Chapter 1

Customs declarations in writing

Section 1

General provisions

Article 198

1. Where a customs declaration covers two or more articles, the particulars relating to each article shall be regarded as constituting a separate declaration.

2. Component parts of industrial plant coming under a single CN Code shall be regarded as constituting a single item of goods.

Article 199

[1. Without prejudice to the possible application of penal provisions, the lodging of a declaration signed by the declarant or his representative with a customs office or a transit declaration lodged using electronic data-processing techniques shall render the declarant or his representative responsible under the provisions in force for:

— the accuracy of the information given in the declaration,

— the authenticity of the documents presented, and

— compliance with all the obligations relating to the entry of the goods in question under the procedure concerned.

2.   Where the declarant uses data-processing systems to produce his customs declarations, including transit declarations made in accordance with Article 353(2)(b), the customs authorities may provide that the handwritten signature may be replaced by another identification technique which may be based on the use of codes. This facility shall be granted only if the technical and administrative conditions laid down by the customs authorities are complied with.

The customs authorities may also provide that declarations, including transit declarations made in accordance with Article 353(2)(b) produced using customs data-processing systems, may be directly authenticated by those systems, in place of the manual or mechanical application of the customs office stamp and the signature of the competent official.][20]

3.   Under the conditions and in the manner which they shall determine, the customs authorities may allow some of the particulars of the written declaration referred to in Annex 37 to be replaced by sending these particulars to the customs office designated for that purpose by electronic means, where appropriate in coded form.][21]

Article 200

Documents accompanying a declaration shall be kept by the customs authorities unless the said authorities provide otherwise or unless the declarant requires them for other operations. In the latter case the customs authorities shall take the necessary steps to ensure that the documents in question cannot subsequently be used except in respect of the quantity or value of goods for which they remain valid.

[Article 201

1.   The customs declaration shall be lodged at one of the following customs offices:

   (a)   the customs office responsible for the place where the goods were or are to be presented to customs in accordance with the customs rules;

   (b)   the customs office responsible for supervising the place where the exporter is established or where the goods are packed or loaded for export shipment, except in cases provided for in Articles 789, 790, 791 and 794.

The customs declaration may be lodged as soon as the goods are presented or available to the customs authorities for control.

2.   The customs authorities may allow the customs declaration to be lodged before the declarant is in a position to present the goods, or make them available for control, at the customs office where the customs declaration is lodged or at another customs office or place designated by the customs authorities.

The customs authorities may set a time limit, to be determined according to the circumstances, within which the goods shall be presented or made available. If the goods are not presented or made available within this time limit, the customs declaration shall be deemed not to have been lodged.

The customs declaration may be accepted only after the goods in question have been presented to the customs authorities or have, to the satisfaction of the customs authorities, been made available for control.][22]

[3.   The customs authorities may allow the customs declaration to be lodged at a customs office different from the one where the goods are presented or will be presented or made available for control, provided that one of the following conditions is fulfilled:

      (a)   the customs offices referred to in the introductory phrase are in the same Member State;

      (b)   the goods are to be placed under a customs procedure by the holder of a single authorisation for the simplified declaration or the local clearance procedure.][23]

Article 202

1.   The declaration shall be lodged with the competent customs office during the days and hours appointed for opening.

      However, the customs authorities may, at the request of the declarant and at his expense, authorize the declaration to be lodged outside the appointed days and hours.

2.   Any declaration lodged with the officials of a customs office in any other place duly designated for that purpose by agreement between the customs authorities and the person concerned shall be considered to have been lodged in the said office.

[3.   The transit declaration shall be lodged and goods shall be presented at the office of departure during the days and hours established by the customs authorities.

      The office of departure may, at the request and expense of the principal, allow the goods to be presented in another place.][24]

[Article 203

1.   The date of acceptance of the declaration shall be noted thereon.

2.   The Community transit declaration shall be accepted and registered by the office of departure during the days and hours established by the customs authorities.][25]

Article 204

The customs authorities may allow or require the corrections referred to in Article 65 of the Code to be made by the lodging of a new declaration intended to replace the original declaration. In that event, the relevant date for determination of any duties payable and for the application of any other provisions governing the customs procedure in question shall be the date of the acceptance of the original declaration.

Section 2

Forms to be used

Article 205

1. The official model for written declarations to customs by the normal procedure, for the purposes of placing goods under a customs procedure or re-exporting them in accordance with Article 182(3) of the Code, shall be the Single Administrative Document.

2. Other forms may be used for this purpose where the provisions of the customs procedure in question permit.

3. The provisions of paragraphs 1 and 2 shall not preclude:

    –   waiver of the written declaration prescribed in Articles 225 to 236 for release for free circulation, export or temporary importation,

    –   waiver by the Member States of the form referred to in paragraph where the special provisions laid down in Articles 237 and 238 with regard to consignments by letter or parcel-post apply,

    –   use of special forms to facilitate the declaration in specific cases, where the customs authorites so permit,

    –   waiver by the Member States of the form referred to in paragraph 1 in the case of existing or future agreements or arrangements concluded between the administrations of two or more Member States with a view to greater simplification of formalities in all or part of the trade between those Member States,

    [– use, by persons concerned, of loading lists for the completion of Community transit formalities in the case of consignments composed of more than one kind of goods, where Article 353(2) and Article 441 are applied,

    –   printing declarations for export, import and for transit where Article 353(2) is applied and documents certifying the Community status of goods not being moved under the internal Community transit procedure by means of official or private-sector data processing systems, if necessary on plain paper, on conditions laid down by the Member States.][26]

    –   provision by the Member States to the effect that where a computerized declaration-processing system is used, the declaration, within the meaning of paragraph 1, may take the form of the Single Administrative Document printed out by that system.

4. [...][27]

5.   Where in Community legislation, reference is made to an export, re-export or import declaration or a declaration placing goods under another customs procedure, Member States may not require any administrative documents other than those which are:

—   expressly created by Community acts or provided for by such acts,

—   required under the terms of international conventions compatible with the Treaty,

—   required from operators to enable them to qualify, at their request, for an advantage or specific facility,

—   required, with due regard for the provisions of the Treaty, for the implementation of specific regulations which cannot be implemented solely by the use of the document referred to in paragraph 1.

Article 206

The Single Administrative Document form shall, where necessary, also be used during the transitional period laid down in the Act of Accession of Spain and Portugal in connection with trade between the Community as constituted on 31 December 1985 and Spain or Portugal and between those two last-mentioned Member States in goods still liable to certain customs duties and charges having equivalent effect or which remain subject to other measures laid down by the Act of Accession.

For the purposes of the first paragraph, copy 2 or where applicable copy 7 of the forms used for trade with Spain and Portugal or trade between those Member States shall be destroyed.

It shall also be used in trade in Community goods between parts of the customs territory of the Community to which the provisions of Council Directive 77/388/EEC apply and parts of that territory where those provisions do not apply, or in trade between parts of that territory where those provisions do not apply.

Article 207

Without prejudice to Article 205(3), the customs administrations of the Member States may in general, for the purpose of completing export or import formalities, dispense with the production of one or more copies of the Single Administrative Document intended for use by the authorities of that Member State, provided that the information in question is available on other media.

Article 208

1.   The Single Administrative Document shall be presented in subsets containing the number of copies required for the completion of formalities relating to the customs procedure under which the goods are to be placed.

[2.   Where the Community transit procedure or the common transit procedure is preceded or followed by another customs procedure, a subset containing the number of copies required for the completion of formalities relating to the transit procedure where Article 353(2) is applied and the preceding or following procedure may be presented.][28]

3.   The subsets referred to in paragraphs 1 and 2 shall be taken from:

    –   either the full set of eight copies, in accordance with the specimen contained in Annex 31,

    –   or, particularly in the event of production by means of a computerized system for processing declarations, two successive sets of four copies, in accordance with the specimen contained in Annex 32.

4.   Without prejudice to Articles 205(3), 222 to 224 or 254 to 289, the declaration forms may be supplemented, where appropriate, by one or more continuation forms presented in subsets containing the declaration copies needed to complete the formalities relating to the customs procedure under which the goods are to be placed. Those copies needed in order to complete the formalities relating to preceding or subsequent customs procedures may be attached where appropriate.

    The continuation subsets shall be taken from:

    –   either a set of eight copies, in accordance with the specimen contained in Annex 33,

    –   or two sets of our copies, in accordance with the specimen contained in Annex 34.

    The continuation forms shall be an integral part of the Single Administrative Document to which they relate.

5.   By way of derogation from paragraph 4, the customs authorities may provide that continuation forms shall not be used where a computerized system is used to produce such declarations.

Article 209

1.   Where Article 208(2) is applied, each party involved shall be liable only as regards the particulars relating to the procedure for which he applied as declarant, principal or as the representative of one of these.

2.   For the purposes of paragraph 1, where the declarant uses a Single Administrative Document issued during the preceding customs procedure, he shall be required, prior to lodging his declaration, to verify the accuracy of the existing particulars for the boxes for which he is responsible and their applicability to the goods in question and the procedure applied for, and to supplement them as necessary.

In the cases referred to in the first subparagraph, the declarant shall immediately inform the customs office where the declaration is lodged of any discrepancy found between the goods in question and the existing particulars. In this case the declarant shall then draw up his declaration on fresh copies of the Single Administrative Document.

Article 210

Where the Single Administrative Document is used to cover several successive customs procedures, the customs authorities shall satisfy themselves that the particulars given in the declarations relating to the various procedures in question all agree.

Article 211

The declaration must be drawn up in one of the official languages of the Community which is acceptable to the customs authorities of the Member State where the formalities are carried out.

If necessary, the customs authorities of the Member State of destination may require from the declarant or his representative in that Member State a translation of the declaration into the official language or one of the official languages of the latter. The translation shall replace the corresponding particulars in the declaration in question.

By way of derogation from the preceding subparagraph, the declaration shall be drawn up in an official language of the Community acceptable to the Member State of destination in all cases where the declaration in the latter Member State is made on copies other than those initially presented to the customs office of the Member State of departure.

Article 212

1.   The Single Administrative Document must be completed in accordance with the explanatory note in Annex 37 and any additional rules laid down in other Community legislation.

[Where a customs declaration is used as an entry summary declaration, in accordance with Article 36c(1) of the Code, that declaration shall, in addition to the particulars required for the specific procedure set out in Annex 37, include the particulars for an entry summary declaration set out in Annex 30A.][29]

2.   The customs authorities shall ensure that users have ready access to copies of the explanatory note referred to in paragraph 1.

3.   The customs administrations of each Member State may, if necessary, supplement the explanatory note.

[4.   The Member States shall notify the Commission of the list of particulars they require for each of the procedures referred to in Annex 37. The Commission shall publish the list of those particulars.][30]

Article 213

The codes to be used in completing the forms referred to in Article 205(1) are listed in Annex 38.

[The Member States shall notify the Commission of the list of national codes used for boxes 37 (second subdivision), 44 and 47 (first subdivision). The Commission shall publish the list of those codes.][31]

Article 214

In cases where the rules require supplementary copies of the form referred to in Article 205(1), the declarant may use additional sheets or photocopies of the said form for this purpose.

Such additional sheets or photocopies must be signed by the declarant, presented to the customs authorities and endorsed by the latter under the same conditions as the Single Administrative Document. They shall be accepted by the customs authorities as if they were original documents provided that their quality and legibility are considered satisfactory by the said authorities.

Article 215

1. The forms referred to in Article 205(1) shall be printed on self-copying paper dressed for writing purposes and weighing at least 40 g/m². The paper must be sufficiently opaque for the information on one side not to affect the legibility of the information on the other side and its strength should be such that in normal use it does not easily tear or crease.

   [The paper shall be white for all copies. However, on the copies used for Community transit in accordance with Article 353(2), boxes 1 (first and third subdivisions), 2, 3, 4, 5, 6, 8, 15, 17, 18, 19, 21, 25, 27, 31, 32, 33 (first subdivision on the left), 35, 38, 40, 44, 50, 51, 52, 53, 55 and 56 shall have a green background.

   The forms shall be printed in green ink.][32]

2. The boxes are based on a unit of measurement of one tenth of an inch horizontally and one sixth of an inch vertically. The subdivisions are based on a unit of measurement of one-tenth of an inch horizontally.

3. A colour marking of the different copies shall be effected in the following manner:

   (a) on forms conforming to the specimens shown in Annexes 31 and 33:

   – copies 1, 2, 3 and 5 shall have at the right hand edge a continuous margin, coloured respectively red, green, yellow and blue,

   – copies 4, 6, 7 and 8 shall have at the right hand edge a broken margin coloured respectively blue, red, green and yellow;

   (b) on forms conforming to the specimens shown in Annexes 32 and 34, copies 1/6, 2/7, 3/8 and 4/5 shall have at the right hand edge a continuous margin and to the right of this a broken margin coloured respectively red, green, yellow and blue.

The width of these margins shall be approximately 3 mm. The broken margin shall comprise a series of squares with a side measurement of 3 mm each one separated by 3 mm.

4. The copies on which the particulars contained in the forms shown in Annexes 31 and 33 must appear by a self-copying process are shown in Annex 35.

The copies on which the particulars contained in the forms shown in Annexes 32 and 34 must appear by a self-copying process are shown in Annex 36.

5. The forms shall measure 210 × 297 mm with a maximum tolerance as to length of 5 mm less and 8 mm more.

6. The customs administrations of the Member States may require that the forms show the name and address of the printer or a mark enabling the printer to be identified. They may also make the printing of the forms conditional on prior technical approval.

Section 3

Particulars required according to the customs procedure concerned

[Article 216

The list of boxes to be used for declarations for placing goods under a particular customs procedure using the single administrative document is set out in Annex 37.][33]

[Where a customs declaration is required for goods to be brought out of the customs territory of the Community, in accordance with Article 182b of the Code, that declaration shall, in addition to the particulars required for the specific procedure set out Annex 37, include the particulars for an exit summary declaration set out in Annex 30A.][34]

Article 217

The particulars required when one of the forms referred to in Article 205(2) is used depend on the form in question. They shall be supplemented where appropriate by the provisions relating to the customs procedure in question.

Section 4

Documents to accompany the customs declaration

Article 218

1. The following documents shall accompany the customs declaration for release for free circulation:

   (a) the invoice on the basis of which the customs value of the goods is declared, as required under Article 181;

   (b) where it is required under Article 178, the declaration of particulars for the assessment of the customs value of the goods declared, drawn up in accordance with the conditions laid down in the said Article;

(c)   the documents required for the application of preferential tariff arrangements or other measures derogating from the legal rules applicable to the goods declared;

(d)   all other documents required for the application of the provisions governing the release for free circulation of the goods declared.

2.   The customs authorities may require transport documents or documents relating to the previous customs procedure, as appropriate, to be produced when the declaration is lodged.

Where a single item is presented in two or more packages, they may also require the production of a packing list or equivalent document indicating the contents of each package.

[3.   Where goods qualify for the flat rate of duty referred to in Section II (D) of the preliminary provisions of the combined nomenclature or where goods qualify for relief from import duties, the documents referred to in paragraph 1 (a), (b) and (c) need not be required unless the customs authorities consider it necessary for the purposes of applying the provisions governing the release of the goods in question for free circulation.][35]

Article 219

[1.   The goods that are the subject of the transit declaration shall be presented together with the transport document.

The office of departure may waive the requirement to produce this document when the customs formalities are completed, on condition that the document is kept at its disposal.

However, the transport document shall be presented at the request of the customs authorities or any other competent authority in the course of transport.][36]

2.   Without prejudice to any applicable simplification measures, the customs document of export/dispatch or re-exportation of the goods from the customs territory of the Community or any document of equivalent effect shall be presented to the office of departure with the transit declaration to which it relates.

3.   The customs authorities may, where appropriate, require production of the document relating to the preceding customs procedure.

[Article 220

1.   Without prejudice to specific provisions, the documents to accompany the declaration of entry for a customs procedure with economic impact, shall be as follows:

(a)   for the customs warehousing procedure:

–   type D; the documents laid down in Article 218 (1) (a) and (b),

–   other than type D; no documents;

(b)   for the inward-processing procedure

–   drawback system; the documents laid down in Article 218 (1),

–   suspension system; the documents laid down in Article 218 (1) (a) and (b),

and, where appropriate, the written authorization for the customs procedure in question or a copy of the application for authorization where [Article 508(1)][37] applies;

(c)   for processing under customs control the documents laid down in Article 218 (1) (a) and (b), and, where appropriate, the written authorisation for the customs procedure in question [or a copy of the application for authorisation where Article 508(1) applies][38];

(d)   for the temporary importation procedure:

–   with partial relief from import duties; the documents laid down in Article 218 (1),

–   with total relief from import duties; the documents laid down in Article 218 (1) (a) and (b),

and, where appropriate, the written authorisation for the customs procedure in question [or a copy of the application for authorisation where Article 508(1) applies][38];

(e)   for the outward-processing procedures, the documents laid down in Article 221 (1) and, where appropriate, the written authorization of the procedure or a copy of the application for authorization where [Article 508(1)][37] applies.

2.   Article 218 (2) shall apply to declarations of entry for any customs procedure with economic impact.

3.   The customs authorities may allow the written authorization of the procedure or a copy of the application for authorization to be kept at their disposal instead of accompanying the declaration.][39]

Article 221

1.   The export or re-export declaration shall be accompanied by all documents necessary for the correct application of export duties and of the provisions governing the export of the goods in question.

2.   Article 218(2) shall apply to export or re-export declarations.

Chapter 2

[Customs declarations made using a data-processing technique

Article 222

1. Where the customs declaration is made by a data-processing technique, the particulars of the written declaration referred to in Annex 37 shall be replaced by sending to the customs office designated for that purpose, with a view to their processing by computer, data in codified form, or data made out in any other form specified by the customs authorities and corresponding to the particulars required for written declarations.

2. A customs declaration made by EDI shall be considered to have been lodged when the EDI message is received by the customs authorities. Acceptance of a customs declaration made by EDI shall be communicated to the declarant by means of a response message containing at least the identification details of the message received and/or the registration number of the customs declaration and the date of acceptance.

3. Where the customs declaration is made by EDI, the customs authorities shall lay down the rules for implementing the provisions laid down in Article 247.

4. Where the customs declaration is made by EDI, the release of the goods shall be notified to the declarant, indicating at least the identification details of the declaration and the date of release.

5. Where the particulars of the customs declaration are introduced into customs data-processing systems, paragraphs 2, 3 and 4 shall apply mutatis mutandis.

Article 223

Where a paper copy of the customs declaration is required for the completion of other formalities, this shall, at the request of the declarant, be produced and authenticated, either by the customs office concerned, or in accordance with the second subparagraph of Article 199(2).

Article 224

Under the conditions and in the manner which they shall determine, the customs authorities may authorise the documents required for the entry of goods for a customs procedure to be made out and transmitted by electronic means.][40]

Chapter 3

Customs declarations made orally or by any other act

Section 1

Oral declarations

Article 225

Customs declarations may be made orally for the release for free circulation of the following goods:

(a)   goods of a non-commercial nature:

–   contained in travellers' personal luggage, or

–   sent to private individuals, or

–   in other cases of negligible importance, where this is authorized by the customs authorities;

(b)   goods of a commercial nature provided:

–   the total value per consignment and per declarant does not exceed the statistical threshold laid down in the Community provisions in force, and

–   the consignment is not part of a regular series of similar consignments, and

–   the goods are not being carried by an independent carrier as part of a larger freight movement;

(c)   the goods referred to in Article 229, where these qualify for relief as returned goods;

(d)   the goods referred to in Article 230(b) and (c).

Article 226

Customs declarations may be made orally for the export of:

(a)   goods of a non-commercial nature:

–   contained in travellers' personal luggage, or

–   sent by private individuals;

(b)   the goods referred to in Article 225(b);

(c)   the goods referred to in Article 231(b) and (c);

(d)   other goods in cases of negligible economic importance, where this is authorized by the customs authorities.

Article 227

1.   The customs authorities may provide that Articles 225 and 226 shall not apply where the person clearing the goods is acting on behalf of another person in his capacity as customs agent.

2.   Where the customs authorities are not satisfied that the particulars declared are accurate or that they are complete, they may require a written declaration.

Article 228

Where goods declared to customs orally in accordance with Articles 225 and 226 are subject to import or export duty the customs authorities shall issue a receipt to the person concerned against payment of the duty owing.

[The receipt shall include at least the following information:

(a)   a description of the goods which is sufficiently precise to enable them to be identified; this may include the tariff heading;

(b)   the invoice value and/or quantity of the goods, as appropriate;

(c)   a breakdown of the charges collected;

(d)   the date on which it was made out;

(e)   the name of the authority which issued it.

The Member States shall inform the Commission of any standard receipts introduced pursuant to this Article. The Commission shall forward any such information to the other Member States.][41]

Article 229

1.   Customs declarations may be made orally for the temporary importation of the following goods, in accordance with the conditions laid down in [Article 497(3), second subparagraph][42]:

[(a)   [–   animals for transhumance or grazing or for the performance of work or transport and other goods satisfying the conditions laid down in Article 567(b), second subparagraph, point (a),

          –   packings referred to in Article 571(a), bearing the permanent, indelible markings of a person established outside the customs territory of the Community,][42]

          –   radio and television production and broadcasting equipment and vehicles specially adapted for use for the above purpose and their equipment imported by public or private organizations establised outside the customs territory of the Community and approved by the customs authorities issuing the authorization for the procedure to import such equipment and vehicles,

          –   instruments and apparatus necessary for doctors to provide assistance for patients awaiting an organ transplant pursuant to [Article 569][42];

(b)   the goods referred to in Article 232;

(c)   other goods, where this is authorized by the customs authorities.

2.   The goods referred to in paragraph 1 may also be the subject of an oral declaration for re-exportation discharging a temporary importation procedure.

Section 2

Customs declarations made by any other act

Article 230

The following, where not expressly declared to customs, shall be considered to have been declared for release for free circulation by the act referred to in Article 233:

(a)   goods of a non-commercial nature contained in travellers' personal luggage entitled to relief either under Chapter I, Title XI of Council Regulation (EEC) No 918/83, or as returned goods;

(b)   goods entitled to relief under Chapter I, Titles IX and X of Council Regulation (EEC) No 918/83;

(c)   means of transport entitled to relief as returned goods;

(d)   goods imported in the context of traffic of negligible importance and exempted from the requirement to be conveyed to a customs office in accordance with Article 38(4) of the Code, provided they are not subject to import duty.

Article 231

The following, where not expressly declared to customs, shall be considered to have been declared for export by the act referred to in Article 233(b):

(a)   goods of a non-commercial nature not liable for export duty contained in travellers' personal luggage;

(b)   means of transport registered in the customs territory of the Community and intended to be re-imported;

(c)   goods referred to in Chapter II of Council Regulation (EEC) No 918/83;

(d)   other goods in cases of negligible economic importance, where this is authorized by the customs authorities.

Article 232

[1.   The following, where not declared to customs in writing or orally, shall be considered to have been declared for temporary importation by the act referred to in Article 233, subject to Article 579:

(a)   personal effects and goods for sports purposes imported by travellers in accordance with Article 563;

(b)   the means of transport referred to in Articles 556 to 561;

(c)   welfare materials for seafarers used on a vessel engaged in international maritime traffic pursuant to Article 564(a).][43]

2.   Where they are not declared to customs in writing or orally, the goods referred to in paragraph 1 shall be considered to have been declared for re-exportation discharging the temporary importation procedure by the act referred to in Article 233.

Article 233

[1.][44] For the purposes of Articles 230 to 232, the act which is considered to be a customs declaration may take the following forms:

(a)   in the case of goods conveyed to a customs office or to any other place designated or approved in accordance with Article 38(1)(a) of the Code:

- going through the green or 'nothing to declare' channel in customs offices where the two-channel system is in operation,

- going through a customs office which does not operate the two-channel system without spontaneously making a customs declaration;

- affixing a 'nothing to declare' sticker or customs declaration disc to the windscreen of passenger vehicles where this possibility is provided for in national provisions;

(b)   in the case of exemption from the obligation to convey goods to customs in accordance with the provisions implementing Article 38(4) of the Code, in the case of export in accordance with Article 231 and in the case of re-exportation in accordance with Article 232(2)

- the sole act of crossing the frontier of the customs territory of the Community.

[2.   Where goods covered by point (a) of Article 230, point (a) of Article 231, point (a) of Article 232(1) or Article 232(2) contained in a passenger's baggage are carried by rail unaccompanied by the passenger and are declared to customs without the passenger being present in person the document referred to in Annex 38a may be used within the terms and limitations set out in it][45]

Article 234

1.   Where the conditions of Articles 230 to 232 are fulfilled, the goods shall be considered to have been presented to customs within the meaning of Article 63 of the Code, the declaration to have been accepted and release to have been granted, at the time when the act referred to in Article 233 is carried out.

2.   Where a check reveals that the act referred to in Article 233 has been carried out but the goods imported or taken out do not fulfil the

conditions in Articles 230 to 232, the goods concerned shall be considered to have been imported or exported unlawfully.

Section 3

Provisions common to Sections 1 and 2

Article 235

The provisions of Articles 225 to 232 shall not apply to goods in respect of which the payment of refunds or other amounts or the repayment of duties is sought, or which are subject to a prohibition or restriction or to any other special formality.

Article 236

For the purposes of Sections 1 and 2, 'traveller' means:

A.   on import:

     1.   any person temporarily entering the customs territory of the Community, not normally resident there, and

     2.   any person returning to the customs territory of the Community where he is normally resident, after having been temporarily in a third country;

B.   on export:

     1.   any person temporarily leaving the customs territory of the Community where he is normally resident, and

     2.   any person leaving the customs territory of the Community after a temporary stay, not normally resident there.

Section 4

Postal traffic

Article 237

1.   The following postal consignments shall be considered to have been declared to customs:

     A.   for release for free circulation:

        (a)   at the time when they are introduced into the customs territory of the Community:

           –   postcards and letters containing personal messages only,

           –   braille letters,

           –   printed matter not liable for import duties, and

           –   all other consignments sent by letter or parcel post which are exempt from the obligation to be conveyed to customs in accordance with provisions pursuant to Article 38(4) of the Code;

(b)   at the time when they are presented to customs:

–   consignments sent by letter or parcel post other than those referred to at (a), provided they are accompanied by a [CN22][46] and/or [CN23][46] declaration;

B.   for export:

(a)   at the time when they are accepted by the postal authorities, in the case of consignments by letter and parcel post which are not liable to export duties;

(b)   at the time of their presentation to customs, in the case of consignments sent by letter or parcel post which are liable to export duties, provided they are accompanied by a [CN22][46] and/or a [CN23][46] declaration.

2.   The consignee, in the cases referred to in paragraph 1A, and the consignor, in the cases referred to in paragraph 1B, shall be considered to be the declarant and, where applicable, the debtor. The customs authorities may provide that the postal administration shall be considered as the declarant and, where applicable, as the debtor.

3.   For the purposes of paragraph 1, goods not liable to duty shall be considered to have been presented to customs within the meaning of Article 63 of the Code, the customs declaration to have been accepted and release granted:

(a)   in the case of imports, when the goods are delivered to the consignee;

(b)   in the case of exports, when the goods are accepted by the postal authorities.

4.   Where a consignment sent by letter or parcel post which is not exempt from the obligation to be conveyed to customs in accordance with provisions pursuant to Article 38(4) of the Code is presented without a [CN22][46] and/or [CN23][46] declaration or where such declaration is incomplete, the customs authorities shall determine the form in which the customs declaration is to be made or supplemented.

Note

Articles 238 - 856 have been omitted as they refer specifically to Customs Duty.

PART IV

customs debt

TITLE I

Security

Article 857

1. The types of security other than cash deposits or guarantors, within the meaning of Articles 193, 194 and 195 of the Code, and the cash deposit or the submission of securities for which Member States may opt even if they do not comply with the conditions laid down in Article 194(1) of the Code, shall be as follows:

   (a) the creation of a mortgage, a charge on land, an antichresis or other right deemed equivalent to a right pertaining to immovable property;

   (b) the cession of a claim, the pledging, with or without surrendering possession, of goods, securities or claims or, in particular, a savings bank book or entry in the national debt register;

   (c) the assumption of joint contractual liability for the full amount of the debt by a third party approved for that purpose by the customs authorities and, in particular, the lodging of a bill of exchange the payment of which is guaranteed by such third party;

   (d) a cash deposit or security deemed equivalent thereto in a currency other than that of the Member State in which the security is given;

   (e) participation, subject to payment of a contribution, in a general guarantee scheme administered by the customs authorities.

2. The circumstances in which and the conditions under which recourse may be had to the types of security referred to in paragraph 1 shall be determined by the customs authorities.

Article 858

Where security is given by making a cash deposit, no interest thereon shall be payable by the customs authorities.

TITLE II

incurrence of the debt

Chapter 1

Failures which have no significant effect on the operation of temporary storage or of the customs procedure

Article 859

The following failures shall be considered to have no significant effect on the correct operation of the temporary storage or customs procedure in question within the meaning of Article 204(1) of the Code, provided:

– they do not constitute an attempt to remove the goods unlawfully from customs supervision,

– they do not imply obvious negligence on the part of the person concerned, and

– all the formalities necessary to regularize the situation of the goods are subsequently carried out:

1.   exceeding the time limit allowed for assignment of the goods to one of the customs-approved treatments or uses provided for under the temporary storage or customs procedure in question, where the time limit would have been extended had an extension been applied for in time;

[2.   in the case of goods placed under a transit procedure, failure to fulfil one of the obligations entailed by the use of that procedure, where the following conditions are fulfilled:

    (a)   the goods entered for the procedure were actually presented intact at the office of destination;

    (b)   the office of destination has been able to ensure that the goods were assigned a customs-approved treatment or use or were placed in temporary storage at the end of the transit operation;

    (c)   where the time limit set under Article 356 has not been complied with and paragraph 3 of that Article does not apply, the goods have nevertheless been presented at the office of destination within a reasonable time.][47]

3.   in the case of goods placed in temporary storage or under the customs warehousing procedure, handling not authorized in advance by the customs authorities, provided such handling would have been authorized if applied for;

4.   in the case of goods placed under the temporary importation procedure, use of the goods otherwise than as provided for in the authorization, provided such use would have been authorized under that procedure if applied for;

5.   in the case of goods in temporary storage or placed under a customs procedure, unauthorized movement of the goods, provided the goods can be presented to the customs authorities at their request;

[6.   In the case of goods in temporary storage or entered for a customs procedure, removal of the goods from the customs territory of the Community or their introduction into a free zone of control type I within the meaning of Article 799 or into a free warehouse without completion of the necessary formalities;][48]

[7.   in the case of goods or products physically transferred within the meaning of Articles 296, 297 or 511, failure to fulfil one of the conditions under which the transfer takes place, where the following conditions are fulfilled:

        (a)   the person concerned can demonstrate, to the satisfaction of the customs authorities, that the goods or products arrived at the specified premises or destination and, in cases of transfer based on Articles 296, 297, 512(2) or 513, that the goods or products have been duly entered in the records of the specified premises or destination, where those Articles require such entry in the records;

        (b)   where a time limit set in the authorisation was not observed, the goods or products nevertheless arrived at the specified premises or destination within a reasonable time.][47]

[8.   in the case of goods eligible on release for free circulation for the total or partial relief from import duties referred to in Article 145 of the Code, the existence of one of the situations referred to in Article 204 (1) (a) or (b) of the Code while the goods concerned are in temporary storage or under another customs procedure before being released for free circulation;

[9.   in the framework of inward processing and processing under customs control, exceeding the time-limit allowed for submission of the bill of discharge, provided the limit would have been extended had an extension been applied for in time;][48]][49]

[10.   exceeding the time-limit allowed for temporary removal from a customs warehouse, provided the limit would have been extended had an extension been applied for in time.][50]

Article 860

The customs authorities shall consider a customs debt to have been incurred under Article 204(1) of the Code unless the person who would be the debtor establishes that the conditions set out in Article 859 are fulfilled.

Article 861

The fact that the failures referred to in Article 859 do not give rise to a customs debt shall not preclude the application of provisions of criminal law in force or of provisions allowing cancellation and withdrawal of authorizations issued under the customs procedure in question.

Chapter 2

Natural wastage

Article 862

1. For the purposes of Article 206 of the Code, the customs authorities shall, at the request of the person concerned, take account of the quantities missing wherever it can be shown that the losses observed result solely from the nature of the goods and not from any negligence or manipulation on the part of that person.

2. In particular, negligence or manipulation shall mean any failure to observe the rules for transporting, storing, handling, working or processing the goods in question imposed by the customs authorities or by normal practice.

Article 863

The customs authorities may waive the obligation for the person concerned to show that the goods were irretrievably lost for reasons inherent in their nature where they are satisfied that there is no other explanation for the loss.

Article 864

The national provisions in force in the Member States concerning standard rates for irretrievable loss due to the nature of the goods themselves shall be applied where the person concerned fails to show that the real loss exceeds that calculated by application of the standard rate for the goods in question.

[Chapter 3

Goods in special situations][51]

Article 865

The presentation of a customs declaration for the goods in question, or any other act having the same legal effects, and the production of a document for endorsement by the competent authorities, shall be considered as removal of goods from customs supervision within the meaning of Article 203(1) of the Code, where these acts have the effect of wrongly conferring on them the customs status of Community goods.

[However, in the case of airline companies authorised to use a simplified transit procedure with the use of an electronic manifest, the goods shall not be considered to have been removed from customs supervision if, at the initiative or on behalf of the person concerned, they are treated in accordance with their status as non-Community goods before the customs authorities find the existence of an irregular situation and if the behaviour of the person concerned does not suggest any fraudulent dealing.][52]

Article 866

Without prejudice to the provisions laid down concerning prohibitions or restrictions which may be applicable to the goods in question, where a customs debt on importation is incurred pursuant to Articles 202, 203, 204 or 205 of the Code and the import duties have been paid, those goods shall be deemed to be Community goods without the need for a declaration for entry into free circulation.

Article 867

The confiscation of goods pursuant to Article 233(c) and (d) of the Code shall not affect the customs status of the goods in question.

[Article 867a]

1. Non-Community goods which have been abandoned to the Exchequer or seized or confiscated shall be considered to have been entered for the customs warehousing procedure.

2. The goods referred to in paragraph 1 may be sold by the customs authorities only on the condition that the buyer immediately carries out the formalities to assign them a customs-approved treatment or use.

   Where the sale is at a price inclusive of import duties, the sale shall be considered as equivalent to release for free circulation, and the customs authorities themselves shall calculate the duties and enter them in the accounts.

   In these cases, the sale shall be conducted according to the procedures in force in the Member States.

3. Where the administration decides to deal with the goods referred to in paragraph otherwise than by sale, it shall immediately carry out the formalities to assign them one of the customs-approved treatments or uses laid down in Article 4(15)(a), (b), (c) and (d) of the code.][53]

Note

   Articles 868 - 912g have been omitted as they refer specifically to Customs Duty.

PART V

final provisions

Article 913

The following Regulation and Directives shall be repealed:

- Commission Regulation (EEC) No 1494/80 of 11 June 1980 on interpretative notes and generally accepted accounting principles for the purposes of customs value

- Commission Regulation (EEC) No 1495/80 of 11 June 1980 implementing certain provisions of Council Regulation (EEC) No 1224/80 on the valuation of goods for customs purposes, as last amended by Regulation (EEC) No 558/91

- Commission Regulation (EEC) No 1496/80 of 11 June 1980 on the declaration of particulars relating to customs value and on documents to be furnished, as last amended by Regulation (EEC) No 979/93

- Commission Regulation (EEC) No 3177/80 of 5 December 1980 on the place of introduction to be taken into consideration in applying Article 14(2) of Council Regulation (EEC) No 1224/80 on the valuation of goods for customs purposes, as last amended by Regulation (EEC) No 2779/90

- Commission Regulation (EEC) No 3179/80 of 5 December 1980 on postal charges to be taken into consideration when determining the customs value of goods sent by post, as last amended by Regulation (EEC) No 1264/90

- Commission Regulation (EEC) No 1577/81 of 12 June 1981 establishing a system of simplified procedures for the determination of the customs value of certain perishable goods, as last amended by Regulation (EEC) No 3334/90

- Commission Regulation (EEC) No 3158/83 of 9 November 1983 on the incidence of royalties and licence fees in customs value

- Commission Regulation (EEC) No 1766/85 of 27 June 1985 on the rates of exchange to be used in the determination of customs value, as last amended by Regulation (EEC) No 593/91

- Commission Regulation (EEC) No 3903/92 of 21 December 1992 on air transport costs

Article 914

References to the provisions repealed shall be understood as referring to this Regulation.

Article 915

This Regulation shall enter into force on the third day following its publication in the *Official Journal of the European Communities*.

It shall apply from 1 January 1994.

...

This Regulation shall be binding in its entirety and directly applicable in all Member States.

Done at Brussels, 2 July 1993.
For the Commission
Christiane SCRIVENER
Member of the Commission

Note

    Words omitted are outside the scope of this book

ANNEX 23

Interpretative Notes on Customs Value

First column	*Second column*
Reference to provisions of the Customs Code	*Notes*

Article 29(1)

The price actually paid or payable refers to the price for the imported goods. Thus the flow of dividends or other payments from the buyer to the seller that do not relate to the imported goods are not part of the customs value.

Article 29(1)(a)third indent

An example of such restriction would be the case where a seller requires a buyer of automobiles not to sell or exhibit them prior to a fixed date which represents the beginning of a model year.

Article 29(1)(b)

Some examples of this include:

(a)   the seller establishes the price of the imported goods on condition that the buyer will also buy other goods in specified quantities;

(b)   the price of the imported goods is dependent upon the price or prices at which the buyer of the imported goods sells other goods to the seller of the imported goods;

(c)   the price is established on the basis of a form of payment extraneous to the imported goods, such as where the imported goods are semi-finished goods which have been provided by the seller on condition that he will receive a specified quantity of the finished goods.

However, conditions or considerations relating to the production or marketing of the imported goods shall not result in rejection of the transaction value. For example, the fact that the buyer furnishes the seller with engineering and plans undertaken in the country of importation shall not result in rejection of the transaction value for the purposes of Article 29(1).

Article 29(2)

1.   Paragraphs 2(a) and (b) provide different means of establishing the acceptability of a transaction value.

2.   Paragraph 2(a) provides that where the buyer and the seller are related, the circumstances surrounding the sale shall be accepted as the customs value provided that the relationship did not influence the price. It is not intended

that there should be an examination of the circumstances in all cases where the buyer and the seller are related. Such examination will only be required where there are doubts About the acceptability if the price. Where the customs authorities have no doubts about the acceptability of the price, it should be accepted without requesting further information from the declarant. For example, the relationship, or it may already have detailed information concerning the buyer and the seller and may already be satisfied from such examination or information that the relationship did not influence the price.

3. Where the customs authorities are unable to accept the transaction value without further inquiry, it should give the declarant an opportunity to supply further detailed information as may be necessary to enable to examine the circumstances surrounding the sale. In this context, the customs authorities should be prepared to examine relevant aspects of the transaction, including the way in which the buyer and seller organise their commercial relations and the way in which the price in question was arrived at, in order to determine whether the relationship influenced the price. Where it can be shown the buyer and seller, although related, this would demonstrate that the price had not been influenced by the relationship. As an example of this, if the price had been settled in a manner consistent with the normal pricing practices of the industry in question or with the way the seller settles prices for sales to buyers who are not related to him, this would demonstrate that the price had not been influenced by the relationship. As a further example where it is shown that the price is adequate to ensure recovery of all costs plus a profit which is representative for the firm's overall profit realised over a representative period of time (e.g. on an annual basis) in sales of goods of the same class of kind, this would demonstrate that the price had not been influenced.

4. Paragraph 2(b) provides an opportunity for the declarant to demonstrate that the transaction value closely approximates to a "test" value previously accepted by the custom authorities already have sufficient information to be satisfied, without further detailed inquiries, that one of the tests provided in paragraph (2)(b) has been met, there is no reason for them to require the declarant to demonstrate that the test can be met.

Article 29(2)(b)

A number of factors must be taken into consideration in determining whether one value "closely approximates" to another value. These factors include the nature of the imported goods, the nature of the industry itself, the season in which the goods are imported, and, whether the difference in values is commercially significant. Since these factors may vary from case to case, it would be impossible to apply a uniform standard such as a fixed percentage, in each case. For example, a small difference in value in a case involving one type of goods could be unacceptable while a large difference in a case determining whether the transaction value closely approximates to the "test" values set forth in Article 29(2)(b).

Article 29(3)(a)

An example of an indirect payment would be the settlement by the buyer, whether in whole or in part, of a debt owed by the seller.

Article 30(2)(a), (b)

1. In applying these provision, the customs authorities shall, whether possible, use a sale of identical or similar goods, as appropriate, at the same commercial level and in substantially the same quantity as the goods being valued. Where no such sale is found, a sale of identical or similar goods, as appropriate, that takes place under any one of the following three conditions may be used:

(a) a sale at the same commercial level but in a different quantity;

(b) a sale at a different commercial level but in substantially the same quality; or

(c) a sale at a different commercial level and in a different quantity

2. Having found a sale under any of these three conditions adjustments will then be made, as the case may be, for:

(a)   quantity factors only:

(b)   commercial level factors only: or

(c)   both commercial level and quantity factors

3.   The expression "and/or" allows the flexibility to use the sales and make the necessary adjustments in any one of the three conditions described above.

4.   A condition for adjustment because of different commercial levels or different quantities in that such adjustment, whether it leads to an increase or a decrease in value, be made only on the basis of demonstrated evidence that clearly established the reasonableness and accuracy if the adjustment e.g. valid price lists containing prices referring to different levels or different quantities. As an example of this, if the imported goods being valued consist of a shipment of 10 units and the only identical or similar imported goods, as appropriate, for which a transaction value exists involved a sale of 500 units, and it is recognised that the seller grants quantity discounts, the required adjustment may be accomplished by restoring to the seller's price list and using that price applicable to a sale of 10 units. This does not require that a sale had to have been made in quantities of 10 as long as the price list has been established as being bona fide through sales at other quantities. In the absence of such an objective measure, however, the determination of a customs value under the provisions of Article 30(2)(a) and (b) is note appropriate.

Article 30(2)(d)   1.   As a general rule, customs value is determined under these provisions on the basis of information readily available in the Community.. In order to determine a computed value, however, it may be necessary to examine the costs of producing the goods being valued and other information which has to be obtained from outside the Community. Furthermore, in most cases the producer of the goods will be outside the jurisdiction of the authorities of the Member States. The use of the computed value method will generally be limited to those cases where the buyer and seller are related, and the producer is prepared to supply to the authorities of the country of importation the necessary costings and to provide facilities for any subsequent verification which may be necessary costings and to provide facilities for any subsequent verification which may be necessary.

2. The "cost or value" referred to in Article 30(2)(d), first indent, is to be determined on the basis of information relating to the production of the goods being valued supplies by or on behalf of the producer. It is to be based upon the commercial accounts of the producer, provided that such accounts are consistent with the generally accepted accounting principles applied in the country where the goods are produced.

3. The amount for profit and general expenses referred to in Article 30(2)(d), second indent, is to be determined on the basis of information supplied by or on behalf of the producer unless his figures are inconsistent with those usually reflected in sales of the goods of the same class or kind as the goods being valued which are made by producers in the country of exportation for export to the county of importation.

4. No cost or value of the elements referred to in this Article shall be counted twice in determining the computed value.

5. It should be noted in this context that the "amount for profit and general expenses" has to be taken as a whole. It follows that if, in any particular case, the producer's profit figure is low and his general expenses are high, his profit and general expenses taken together may nevertheless be consistent with that usually reflected in sales of goods of the same class or kind. Such a determination might occur, for example of a product were being launched in the Community and the producer accepted a nil or low profit to offset high general expenses associated with the launch. Where the producer can demonstrate that he is taking a low profit on his ales of the imported goods because of particular commercial circumstances, his actual profit figures should be taken into account provided that he has valid commercial reasons to justify them and his pricing policy reflects usual pricing policies in the branch of industry concerned. Such a situation might occur, for

example, where producers have been forced to lower prices temporarily because of an unforeseeable drop in demand or where they sell goods to complement a range of goods being produced in the country of importation and accept a low profit to maintain competitively. Where the producer's own figures for profit and general expenses are not consistent with those usually reflected ion sales of goods of the same class or kind as the goods being valued which are made by producers in the country of exportation for export to the country of importation, the amount for profit and general expenses may be based upon relevant information other than that supplied by or on behalf of the producer of the goods.

6. Whether certain goods are "of the same class or kind" as other goods must be determined on a case-by-case basis with reference to the circumstances involved. In determining the usual profits and general expenses under the provisions of Article 30(2)(d), sales for export to the country of importation of the narrowest group or range of goods, which includes the goods being valued, for which the necessary information can be provided, should be examined. For the purposes of Article 30(2)(d), "goods of the same class or kind" must be from the same country as the goods being valued.

Article 31(1)

1. Customs values determined under the provisions of Article 31(1) should, to the greatest extent possible, be based on previously determined customs values.

2. The methods of valuation to be employed under Article 31(1) should be those laid down in Articles 29 and 30(2), but a reasonable flexibility in the application of such methods would be in conformity with the aims and provisions of Article 31(1).

3. Some examples of reasonable flexibility are as follows:

(a) Identical goods - the requirement that the identical goods should be exported at or about the same time as the goods being valued could be flexibility interpreted; identical imported goods produced in a country other than the country of exportation of the goods being valued could be the basis for customs valuation; customs values of identical imported goods already determined under the provisions of Article 30(2)(c) and (d) could be used.

(b) Similar goods - the requirement that the similar goods should be exported at or about the same time as the goods being valued could be flexibility interpreted; similar imported goods produced in a country other that the country of exportation of the goods being valued could be the basis for customs valuations; customs values of similar imported goods already determined under the provisions of Article 30(2)(c) and (d) could be used.

(c) Deductive method - the requirement that the goods shall have been sold in the "condition as imported" in Article 152(1)(a) could be flexibly interpreted the "90 days" requirement could be administered flexibly.

Article 32(1)(b)(ii)   1.   There are two factors involved in the apportionment of the elements specified in Article 32(1)(b)(ii) to the imported goods - the value of the element itself and the way in which that value is to be apportioned to the imported goods. The apportionment of these elements should be made in a reasonable manner appropriate to the circumstances and in accordance with generally accepted accounting principles.

2.   Concerning the value of the element, if the buyer acquires the element form a seller not related to him at a given cost, the value of the element is that cost. If the element was produced by the buyer or by a person related to him, its value would be the cost of producing it. If the element had been previously used by the buyer, regardless of whether it had been acquired or produced by him, the original cost of acquisition or production would have to be adjusted downwards to reflect its use in order to arrive at the value of the element.

3. Once a value had been determined for the element, it is necessary to apportion that value to the imported goods. Various possibilities exist. For example, the value might be apportioned to the first shipment, if the buyer wished to pay duty on the entire value at one time. As another example, he may request that the value be apportioned over the number of units produced up to the time of the first shipments. As a further example, he may request that the value be apportioned over the entire anticipated production where contracts of firm commitments exist for the production. The method of apportionment used will depend upon the documentation provided by the buyer.

4. As an illustration of the above, a buyer provides the producer with a mould to be used in the production of the imported goods and contracts with him to buy 10,000 units. by the time of arrival of the first shipment of 1,000 units, the producer has already produced 4,000 units. The buyer may request the customs authorities to apportion the value of the mould over 1,000, 4,000 or 10,000 units.

Article 32(1)(b)(iv)

1. Additions for the elements specified in Article 32(1)(b)(iv) should be based on objective and quantifiable data. In order to minimise the burden for both the declarant and customs authorities in determining the values to be added, data readily available in the buyers commercial record system should be used in so far as possible.

2. For those elements supplied by the buyer which were purchased or leased by the buyer, the addition would be the cost of the purchase or the lease. No addition shall be made for those elements available in the public domain, other than the cost of obtaining copies of them.

3. The ease with which it may be possible to calculate the values to be added will depend on a particular firm's structure and management practice, as well as its accounting methods.

4. For example, it is possible that a firm which imports a variety of products from several countries maintains the records of its design centre outside the country of importation

5.   in such a way as to show accurately the costs attributable to a given product. In such cases, a direct adjustment may appropriately be made under the provisions of Article 32.

5.   In another case, a firm may carry the cost of the design centre outside the country of importation as a general overhead expense without allocation to specific products. In this instance, an appropriate adjustment could be made under the provisions of Article 32 with respect to the imported goods by apportioning total design centre costs over total production benefiting form the design centre and adding such apportioned cost on a unit basis to imports.

6.   Variations in the above circumstances will, of course, require different factors to be considered in determining the proper method of allocation.

7.   In cases where the production of the element in question involves a number of countries and over a period of time, the adjustment should be limited to the value actually added to that element outside the country of importation.

Article 32(1)(c)   The royalties and licence fees referred to in Article 21(1)(c) may include, among other things, payments in respect of patents, trademarks and copyrights.

Article 32(2)   Where objective and quantifiable data do note exist with regard to the additions required to be made under the provisions of Article 32, the transaction value cannot be determined under the provisions of Article 29. As an illustration of this, a royalty is paid on the basis of the price in a sale in the importing country of a litre of a particular product that was imported by the kilogram and made up into a solution after importation. If the royalty is based partially on the imported goods and partially on other factors which have nothing to do with the imported goods (such as when the imported goods are mixed with domestic ingredients and are no longer separately identifiable, or when the royalty cannot be distinguished from a special financial arrangements between the buyer and the seller), it would be inappropriate to attempt to make an addition for the royalty. However, if the amount of this royalty is based only on the imported goods and can be readily quantified, an addition to the price actually paid or payable can be made.

Article 143(1)(e)

One person shall be deemed to control another when the former is legally or operationally in a position to exercise restraint or direction over the latter.

Article 152(1)(a)(i)

1. The words "profit and general expenses" should be taken as a whole. The figure for the purposes of this deduction should be determined on the basis of information supplied by the declarant unless his figures are inconsistent with those obtaining in sales in the country of importation of imported goods of the same class or kind. Where the declarant's figures are inconsistent with such figures, the amount for profit and general expenses may be based upon relevant information other than that supplied by the declarant.

2. In determining either the commissions or the usual profits and general expenses under this provision, the question whether certain goods are of the same class or kind as other goods must be determined on a case-by-case basis by reference to the circumstances involved. Sales in the country of importation of the narrowest group or range of imported goods of the same class or kind, which includes the goods being valued, for which the necessary information can be provided, should be examined. For the purposes of this provision, "goods of the same class or kind" includes goods imported from the same country as the goods being valued as well as goods imported from other countries.

Article 152(2)

1. Where this method of valuation is used, deductions made for the value added by further processing shall be based on objective and quantifiable data relating to the cost of work. Accepted industry formulas, recipes, methods of construction, and other industry practices would form the basis of the calculations.

2. This method of valuation would normally not be applicable when, as a result of the further processing, the imported goods lose their identity. However, there can be instances where, although the identity of the imported goods is lost, the value added by the processing can be determined accurately without unreasonable difficulty.

On the other hand, there can also be instances where the imported goods maintain their identity but form such a minor element in the goods sold in the country of importation that the use of this valuation method would be unjustified. In view of the above, each situation of this type must be considered on a case-by-case basis.

Article 152(3)

1.   As an example of this, goods are sold from a price list which grants favourable unit prices for purchases made in larger quantities.

Sale of quantity	Unit price	Number of sales	Total quantity sold at each price
One to 10 units	100	10 sales of five units	65
		Five sales of three units	
11 to 25 units	95	Five sales of 11 units	55
Over 25 units	90	One sale of 30 units	80
		One sale of 50 units	

The greatest number of units sold at a price is 80; therefore, the unit price in the greatest aggregate quantity is 90.

2.   As another example of this, two sales occur. In the first sale 500 units are sold at a price of 95 currency units each.

In the second sale 400 units are sold at the price of 90 currency units each. In this example, the greatest number of units sold at a particular price is 500; therefore, the unit price in the greatest aggregate quantity is 95.

3.   A third example would be the following situation where various quantities are sold at various prices.

(a) Sales

Sale quantity	Unit price
40 units	100
30 units	90
15 units	100
50 units	95
25 units	105
35 units	90
5 units	100

(b) Total

95	90
50	95
60	100
25	105

In this example, the greatest number of units sold at a particular price is 65; therefore, the unit price in the greatest aggregate quantity is 90.

ANNEX 24

Application of generally accepted accounting principles for the determination of Customs Value

1. "Generally accepted accounting principles" refers to the recognised consensus or substantial authoritative support within a country at a particular time as to which economic resources and obligations should be recorded as assets and liabilities, which changes in assets and liabilities should be recorded, how the assets and liabilities and changes in them should be measured, what information should be disclosed and how it should be disclosed, and which financial statements should be prepared. These standards may be broad guidelines of general application as well as detailed practices and procedures.

2. For the purposes of the application of the customs valuation provisions, the customs administration concerned shall utilise information prepared in a manner consistent with generally accepted accounting principles in the country which is appropriate for the Article in question. For example, the determination of usual profit and general expenses under the provisions of Article 152(1)(a)(i) of this Regulation would be carried out utilising information prepared in a manner consistent with generally accepted accounting principles of the country of importation. On the other hand, the determination of usual profit and general expenses under the provisions of Article 30(2)(d) of the Code would be carried out utilising information prepared in a manner consistent with generally accepted accounting principles of the country of production. As a further example, the determination of an element provided for the Article 32(1)(b)(ii) of the Code undertaken in the country of importation would be carried out utilising information in a manner consistent with the generally accepted accounting principles of that country.

[ANNEX 25

Air transport costs to be included in the customs value

1.   The following table shows:

    (a)   third countries listed by continents and zones (column 1).

    (b)   the percentages which represent the part of the air transport costs from a given third country to the EC to be included in the customs value (column 2).

2.   When goods are shipped from countries or from airports not included in the following table, other than the airports referred to in paragraph 3, the percentage given for the airport nearest to that of departure shall be taken.

3.   As regards the French overseas departments of Guadeloupe, Guyana, Martinique and Reunion, of which territories the airports are not included in the table, the following rules shall apply:

    (a)   for goods shipped direct to those departments from third countries, the whole of the air transport cost is to be included in the customs value;

    (b)   for goods shipped to the European part of the Community from third countries and transhipped or unloaded in one of those departments, only the air transport costs which would have been incurred for carrying the goods only as far as the place of transhipment or unloading are to be included in the customs value;

    (c)   for goods shipped to those departments from third countries and transhipped or unloaded in an airport in the European part of the Community, the air transport costs to be included in the customs value are those which result from the application of the percentages given in the following table to the costs which would have been incurred for carrying the goods from the airport of departure to the airport of transhipment or unloading.

The transhipment or unloading shall be certified by an appropriate endorsement by the customs authorities on the air waybill or other air transport document, with the official stamp of the office concerned; failing this certification the provisions of the last subparagraph of Article 163(6) of this Regulation shall apply.

1	2
Zone (country) of departure (third country)	Percentages of the air transport costs to be included in the customs value for zone of arrival EC
America	
Zone A **Canada:** Gander, Halifax, Moncton, Montreal, Ottawa, Quebec, Toronto, (other airports see zone B) **Greenland** **United States of America:** Akron, Albany, Atlanta, Baltimore, Boston, Buffalo, Charleston, Chicago, Cincinati, Columbus, Detroit, Indianapolis, Jacksonville, Kansas City, Lexington, Louisville, Memphis, Milwaukee, Minneapolis, Nashville, New Orleans, NewYork, Philadelphia, Pittsburg, St Louis, Washington DC, (other airports see zones B and C)	70
Zone B **Canada:** Edmonton, Vancouver, Winnipeg, (other airports see zone A) **United States of America:** Albuquerque, Austin, Billings, Dallas, Denver, Houston, Las Vegas, Los Angeles, Miami, Oklahoma, Phoenix, Portland, Puerto Rico, Salt Lake City, San Francisco, Seattle, (other airports see zones A and C) **Central America** (all countries) **South America** (all countries)	78
Zone C **United States of America:** Anchorage, Fairbanks, Honolulu, Juneau, (other airports see zones A and B)	89
Africa	
Zone D Algeria, Egypt, Libya, Morocco, Tunisia	33

Zone E Benin, Burkina Faso, Cameroon, Cape Verde, Central African Republic, Chad, Côte d'Ivoire, Djibouti, Ethiopia, Gambia, Ghana, Guinea, Guinea-Bissau, Liberia, Mali, Mauritania, Niger, Nigeria, Senegal, Sierra Leone, Sudan, Togo	50
Zone F Burundi, Democratic Republic of Congo, Congo (Brazzaville), Equatorial Guinea, Gabon, Kenya, Rwanda, São Tomé and Principe, Seychelles, Somalia, St. Helena, Tanzania, Uganda	61
Zone G Angola, Botswana, Comoros, Lesotho, Madagascar, Malawi, Mauritius, Mozambique, Namibia, Republic of South Africa, Swaziland, Zambia, Zimbabwe	74
Asia	
Zone H Armenia, Azerbaijan, Georgia, Iran, Iraq, Israel, Jordan, Kuwait, Lebanon, Syria	27
Zone I Bahrain, Muscat and Oman, Qatar, Saudi Arabia, United Arab Emirates, Yemen (Arab Republic)	43
Zone J Afghanistan, Bangladesh, Bhutan, India, Nepal, Pakistan	46
Zone K Kazakhstan, Kyrgyzstan, Tajikistan, Turkmenistan, Uzbekistan, Russia: Novosibirsk, Omsk, Perm, Sverdlovsk, (other airports see zones L, M, and O)	57
Zone L Brunei, China, Indonesia, Kampuchea, Laos, Macao, Malaysia, Maldives, Mongolia, Myanmar, Philippines, Singapore, Sri Lanka, Taiwan, Thailand, Vietnam Russia: Irkutsk, Kirensk, Krasnoyarsk, (other airports see zones K, M and O)	70
Zone M Japan, Korea (North), Korea (South) Russia: Khabarovsk, Vladivostok, (other airports see zones K, L and O)	83

Australia and Oceania	
Zone N Australia and Oceania	79
Europe	
Zone O Iceland, Russia: Gorky, Kuibishev, Moscow, Orel, Rostov, Volgograd, Voronej, (other airports see zones K, L and M), Ukraine	30
Zone P Albania, Belarus, Bosnia-Herzegovina, Bulgaria, Faroe Islands, Former Yugoslav Republic of Macedonia, Moldova, Norway, Romania, Serbia and Montenegro, Turkey	15
Zone Q Croatia, Switzerland	5][54]

Amendments

1 Substituted by Art 1(1)(a), Commission Regulation (EC) No 1762/95 of 19 July 1995
2 Substituted by Art 1(1) Commission Regulation (EC) No 444/2002 of 11 March 2002
3 Inserted by Art 1(1)(b), Commission Regulation (EC) No 1762/95 of 19 July 1995
4 Inserted by Art 1(1), Commission Regulation (EC) No 1875/2006 of 18 December 2006
5 Inserted by Art 1(1) Commission Regulation (EC) No 1192/2008 of 17 November 2008
6 Substituted by Art 1(1) Commission Regulation (EC) No 1602/2000 of 24 July 2000
7 Inserted by Art 1(2) Commission Regulation (EC) No 3665/93 of 21 December 1993
8 Inserted by Art 1(1) Commission Regulation (EC) No 2787/2000 of 15 December 2000
9 Inserted by Art 1(2), Commission Regulation (EC) No 1875/2006 of 18 December 2006
10 Inserted by Art 1(8) Commission Regulation (EC) No 46/1999 of 8 January 1999
11 Substituted by Art 1(6) Commission Regulation (EC) No 444/2002 of 11 March 2002
12 Substituted by Art 1(2)(a), Commission Regulation (EC) No 1762/95 of 19 July 1995
13 Deleted by Art 1(2)(b), Commission Regulation (EC) No 1762/95 of 19 July 1995
14 Inserted by Art 1(1) Commission Regulation (EC) No 1676/96 of 30 July 1996
15 Substituted by Article 20, Annex II, Part 19, Treaty of Accession to the European Union 2003 of 16 April 2003
16 Chapter 5 of Title V of Part I deleted by Art 1(7) Commission Regulation (EC) No 444/2002 of 11 March 2002
17 Substituted by Art 1(1) Commission Regulation (EC) No 1677/98 of 29 July 1998
18 Substituted by Art 1(8) Commission Regulation (EC) No 444/2002 of 11 March 2002
19 Inserted by Art 1(9) Commission Regulation (EC) No 3254/94 of 19 December 1994
20 Substituted by Art 1(3) Commission Regulation (EC) No 1192/2008 of 17 November 2008
21 Inserted by Art 1(11), Commission Regulation (EC) No 3665/93 of 21 December 1993
22 Substituted by Art 1(17), Commission Regulation (EC) No 1875/2006 of 18 December 2006
23 Inserted by Art 1(4) Commission Regulation (EC) No 1192/2008 of 17 November 2008
24 Inserted by Art 1(5) Commission Regulation (EC) No 1192/2008 of 17 November 2008
25 Inserted by Art 1(6) Commission Regulation (EC) No 1192/2008 of 17 November 2008
26 Substituted by Art 1(7) Commission Regulation (EC) No 1192/2008 of 17 November 2008
27 Deleted by Art 1(12), Commission Regulation (EC) No 3665/93 of 21 December 1993
28 Substituted by Art 1(8) Commission Regulation (EC) No 1192/2008 of 17 November 2008
29 Inserted by Art 1(18), Commission Regulation (EC) No 1875/2006 of 18 December 2006
30 Inserted by Art 1(3), Commission Regulation (EC) No 2286/2003 of 18 December 2003
31 Inserted by Art 1(4), Commission Regulation (EC) No 2286/2003 of 18 December 2003
32 Substituted by Art 1(9) Commission Regulation (EC) No 1192/2008 of 17 November 2008

33 Substituted by Art 1(5), Commission Regulation (EC) No 2286/2003 of 18 December 2003
34 Inserted by Art 1(19), Commission Regulation (EC) No 1875/2006 of 18 December 2006
35 Inserted by Art 1(1) Commission Regulation (EC) No 482/96 of 19 March 1996
36 Substituted by Art 1(10) Commission Regulation (EC) No 1192/2008 of 17 November 2008
37 Substituted by Art 1(1) Commission Regulation (EC) No 993/2001 of 4 May 2001
38 Inserted by Art 1(1) Commission Regulation (EC) No 993/2001 of 4 May 2001
39 Substituted by Art 1(3), Commission Regulation (EC) No 12/97 of 18 December 1996
40 Substituted by Art 1(13) Commission Regulation (EC) No 3665/93 of 21 December 1993
41 Inserted by Art 1(4) Commission Regulation (EC) No 12/97 of 18 December 1996
42 Substituted by Art 1(2) Commission Regulation (EC) No 993/2001 of 4 May 2001
43 Substituted by Art 1(3) Commission Regulation (EC) No 993/2001 of 4 May 2001
44 Inserted by Art 1(3)(a), Commission Regulation (EC) No 1762/95 of 19 July 1995
45 Inserted by Art 1(3)(b), Commission Regulation (EC) No 1762/95 of 19 July 1995
46 Substituted by Art 1(6) Commission Regulation (EC) No 1602/2000 of 24 July 2000
47 Substituted by Art 1(22) Commission Regulation (EC) No 444/2002 of 11 March 2002
48 Substituted by Art 1(30) Commission Regulation (EC) No 993/2001 of 4 May 2001
49 Inserted by Art 1(11) Commission Regulation (EC) No 1427/97 of 23 July 1997
50 Inserted by Art 1(30) Commission Regulation (EC) No 993/2001 of 4 May 2001
51 Substituted by Art 1(68), Commission Regulation (EC) No 3665/93/EEC of 21 December 1993
52 Inserted by Art 1(4) of Commission Regulation (EC) No 1677/98 of 29 July 1998
53 Inserted by Art 1(69) Commission Regulation (EC) No 3665/93 of 21 December 1993
54 Annex 25 replaced by Art 1(29) and Annex III, Commission Regulation (EC) No 881/2003 of 21 May 2003

COUNCIL DIRECTIVE 94/4/EC

of 14 February 1994

Amending Directives 69/169/EEC and 77/388/EEC and increasing the level of allowances for travellers from third countries and the limits on tax-free purchases in intra-Community travel

Official Journal L 060 , 03/03/1994 p. 0014 - 0015

THE COUNCIL OF THE EUROPEAN UNION,

Having regard to the Treaty establishing the European Community, and in particular Article 99 thereof,

Having regard to the proposal from the Commission,

Having regard to the opinion of the European Parliament,

Having regard to the opinion of the Economic and Social Committee,

Whereas Article 1(1) of Council Directive 69/169/EEC of 28 May 1969 on the harmonization of provisions laid down by law, regulation or administrative action relating to exemption from turnover tax and excise duty on imports in international travel provides for allowances in respect of goods contained in the personal luggage of travellers coming from third countries on condition that such imports have no commercial character;

Whereas the total value of the goods eligible for this exemption may not exceed ECU 45 per person; whereas, in accordance with Article 1(2) of Directive 69/169/EEC, Member States may reduce the allowance to ECU 23 for travellers under 15 years of age;

Whereas account must be taken of measures in favour of travellers recommended by specialized international organizations, in particular the measures contained in Annex F.3 to the International Convention on the Simplification and Harmonization of Customs Procedures;

Whereas these objectives could be attained by increasing the allowances;

Whereas it is necessary to provide, for a limited period, a derogation for Germany, taking into account the economic difficulties likely to be caused by the amount of the allowances, particularly as regards travellers entering the territory of that Member State by land frontiers linking Germany to countries other than Member States and the EFTA members or by means of coastal navigation coming from the said countries;

Whereas there are special links between continental Spain and the Canary Islands, Ceuta and Melilla;

Whereas it is necessary to ensure, during the period when these sales are authorized pursuant to the provisions of Article 28k of Council Directive 77/388/EEC of 17 May 1977 on the harmonization of the laws of the Member States relating to turnover taxes - Common system of value added tax: uniform basis of assessment, that the real value of goods likely to be sold in tax-free shops to travellers on intra-Community flights or sea crossings is maintained,

HAS ADOPTED THIS DIRECTIVE:

Article 1

Directive 69/169/EEC is hereby amended as follows:

1. in Article 1(1), `ECU 45' shall be replaced by `ECU 175';

2. in Article 1(2), `ECU 23' shall be replaced by `ECU 90';

3. Article 7b shall be replaced by the following:

"Article 7b

1. By way of derogation from Article 1 (1), Spain is hereby authorized to apply, until 31 December 2000, an allowance of ECU 600 for imports of the goods in question by travellers coming from the Canary Islands, Ceuta and Melilla who enter the territory of Spain as definied in Article 3 (2) and (3) of Directive 77/388/EEC.

2. By way of derogation from Article 1(2), Spain shall have the option of reducing that allowance to ECU 150 for travellers under 15 years of age."

[Article 2

In Article 28k of Directive 77/388/EEC, the first subparagraph of point 2(a) shall be replaced by the following:

> "(a)the total value of which per person per journey does not exceed ECU 90.

> By way of derogation from Article 28m, Member States shall determine the equivalent in national currency of the above amount in accordance with Article 7(2) of Directive 69/169/EEC."][1]

Article 3

1. Member States shall bring into force the provisions necessary to comply with this Directive by 1 April 1994 at the latest. They shall forthwith inform the Commission thereof.

   When Member States adopt these provisions, they shall contain a reference to this Directive or shall be accompanied by such reference on the occasion of their official publication. The methods of making such a reference shall be laid down by the Member States.

2. By way of derogation from paragraph 1, the Federal Republic of Germany shall be authorized to bring into force the measures necessary to comply with this Directive by 1 January 1998 at the latest for goods imported by travellers entering German territory by a land frontier linking Germany to countries other than Member States and the EFTA members or by means of coastal navigation coming from the said countries.

3. Member States shall communicate to the Commission the text of the provisions of domestic law which they adopt in the field covered by this Directive.

Article 4

This Directive shall enter into force on the day of its publication in the Official Journal of the European Communities.

Article 5

This Directive is addressed to the Member States.

Done at Brussels, 14 February 1994.

For the Council

The President

Y. PAPANTONIOU

Amendments

1   Repealed by Council Directive 2006/112/EC of 28 November 2006 on the common system of value added
    tax, with effect from 1 January 2007

COUNCIL DIRECTIVE 94/5/EC

of 14 February 1994

Supplementing the common system of value added tax and amending Directive 77/388/EEC - special arrangements applicable to second-hand goods, works of art, collectors' items and antiques

Official Journal L 060 , 03/03/1994 p. 0016 - 0024

This Directive was repealed by Council Directive 2006/112/EC of 28 November 2006 on the common system of value added tax, with effect from 1 January 2007

THE COUNCIL OF THE EUROPEAN UNION,

Having regard to the Treaty establishing the European Community, and in particular Article 99 thereof,

Having regard to the proposal from the Commission,

Having regard to the opinion of the European Parliament,

Having regard to the opinion of the Economic and Social Committee,

Whereas, in accordance with Article 32 of the Sixth Council Directive 77/388/EEC of 17 May 1977 on the harmonization of the laws of the Member States relating to turnover taxes - Common system of value added tax: uniform basis of assessment, the Council is to adopt a Community taxation system to be applied to used goods, works of art, antiques and collectors' items;

Whereas the present situation, in the absence of Community legislation, continues to be marked by the application of very different systems which cause distortion of competition and deflection of trade both internally and between Member States; whereas these differences also include a lack of harmonization in the levying of the own resources of the Community; whereas consequently it is necessary to bring this situation to an end as soon as possible;

Whereas the Court of Justice has, in a number of judgments, noted the need to attain a degree of harmonization which allows double taxation in intra-Community trade to be avoided;

Whereas it is essential to provide, in specific areas, for transitional measures enabling legislation to be gradually adapted;

Whereas, within the internal market, the satisfactory operation of the value added tax mechanisms means that Community rules with the purpose of avoiding double taxation and distortion of competition between taxable persons must be adopted;

Whereas it is accordingly necessary to amend Directive 77/388/EEC,

HAS ADOPTED THIS DIRECTIVE:

Article 1

Directive 77/388/EEC is hereby amended as follows:

1. in Article 11

(a) the following paragraph shall be added to Title A:

"4. By way of derogation from paragraphs 1, 2 and 3, Member States which, on 1 January 1993, did not avail themselves of the option provided for in the third subparagraph of Article 12(3)(a) may, where they avail themselves of the option provided for in Title B (6), provide that, for the transactions referred to in the second subparagraph of Article 12(3)(c), the taxable amount shall be equal to a fraction of the amount determined in accordance with paragraphs 1, 2 and 3.

That fraction shall be determined in such a way that the value added tax thus due is, in any event, equal to at least 5% of the amount determined in accordance with paragraphs 1, 2 and 3.";

(b) the following paragraph shall be added to Title B:

"6. By way of derogation from paragraphs 1 to 4, Member States which, on 1 January 1993, did not avail themselves of the option provided for in the third subparagraph of Article 12 (3) (a) may provide that for imports of the works of art, collectors' items and antiques defined in Article 26a (A) (a), (b) and (c), the taxable amount shall be equal to a fraction of the amount determined in accordance with paragraphs 1 to 4.

That fraction shall be determined in such a way that the value added tax thus due on the import is, in any event, equal to at least 5 % of the amount determined in accordance with paragraphs 1 to 4.";

2. in Article 12:

(a) paragraph 3(c) shall be replaced by the following:

"(c) Member States may provide that the reduced rate, or one of the reduced rates, which they apply in accordance with the third paragraph of (a) shall also apply to imports of works of art, collectors' items and antiques as referred to in Article 26a (A) (a), (b) and (c).

Where they avail themselves of this option, Member States may also apply the reduced rate to supplies of works of art, within the meaning of Article 26a (A) (a):

— effected by their creator or his successors in title,

— effected on an occasional basis by a taxable person other than a taxable dealer, where these works of art have been imported by the taxable person himself or where they have been supplied to him by their creator or his successors in title or where they have entitled him to full deduction of value-added tax.";

(b) paragraph 5 shall be replaced by the following:

"5. Subject to paragraph 3(c), the rate applicable on the importation of goods shall be that applied to the supply of like goods within the territory of the country.";

3. the following Article shall be inserted:

"Article 26a

Special arrangements applicable to second-hand goods, works of art, collectors' items and antiques

A. Definitions

For the purposes of this Article, and without prejudice to other Community provisions:

  (a) works of art shall mean the objects referred to in (a) of Annex I.

   However, Member States shall have the option of not considering as "works of art" the items mentioned in the final three indents in (a) in Annex I;

  (b) collectors items shall mean the objects referred to in (b) of Annex I;

  (c) antiques shall mean the objects referred to in (c) of Annex I;

  (d) second-hand goods shall mean tangible movable property that is suitable for further use as it is or after repair, other than works of art, collectors' items or antiques and other than precious metals or precious stones as defined by the Member States;

  (e) taxable dealer shall mean a taxable person who, in the course of his economic activity, purchases or acquires for the purposes of his undertaking, or imports with a view to resale, second-hand goods and/or works of art, collectors' items or antiques, whether that taxable person is acting for himself or on behalf of another person pursuant to a contract under which commission is payable on purchase or sale;

  (f) organizer of a sale by public auction shall mean any taxable person who, in the course of his economic activity, offers goods for sale by public auction with a view to handing them over to the highest bidder;

  (g) principal of an organizer of a sale by public auction shall mean any person who transmits goods to an organizer of a sale by public auction under a contract under which commission is payable on a sale subject to the following provisions:

   — the organizer of the sale by public auction offers the goods for sale in his own name but on behalf of his principal,

   — the organizer of the sale by public auction hands over the goods, in his own name but on behalf of his principal, to the highest bidder at the public auction.

B. Special arrangements for taxable dealers

1. In respect of supplies of second-hand goods, works of art, collectors' items and antiques effected by taxable dealers, Member States shall apply special arrangements for taxing the profit margin made by the taxable dealer, in accordance with the following provisions.

2. The supplies of goods referred to in paragraph 1 shall be supplies, by a taxable dealer, of second-hand goods, works of art, collectors' items or antiques supplied to him within the Community:

    — by a non-taxable person,

        or

    — by another taxable person, in so far as the supply of goods by that other taxable person is exempt in accordance with Article 13(B)(c),

        or

    — by another taxable person in so far as the supply of goods by that other taxable person qualifies for the exemption provided for in Article 24 and involves capital assets,

        or

    — by another taxable dealer, in so far as the supply of goods by that other taxable dealer was subject to value added tax in accordance with these special arrangements.

3. The taxable amount of the supplies of goods referred to in paragraph 2 shall be the profit margin made by the taxable dealer, less the amount of value added tax relating to the profit margin. That profit margin shall be equal to the difference between the selling price charged by the taxable dealer for the goods and the purchase price.

    For the purposes of this paragraph, the following definitions shall apply:

    — selling price shall mean everything which constitutes the consideration, which has been, or is to be, obtained by the taxable dealer from the purchaser or a third party, including subsidies directly linked to that transaction, taxes, duties, levies and charges and incidental expenses such as commission, packaging, transport and insurance costs charged by the taxable dealer to the purchaser but excluding the amounts referred to in Article 11(A)(3),

    — purchase price shall mean everything which constitutes the consideration defined in the first indent, obtained, or to be obtained, from the taxable dealer by his supplier.

4. Member States shall entitle taxable dealers to opt for application of the special arrangements to supplies of:

    (a) works of art, collectors' items or antiques which they have imported themselves;

    (b) works of art supplied to them by their creators or their successors in title;

    (c) works of art supplied to them by a taxable person other than a taxable dealer where the supply by that other taxable person was subject to the reduced rate pursuant to Article 12(3)(c).

    Member States shall determine the detailed rules for exercising this option which shall in any event cover a period at least equal to two calendar years.

If the option is taken up, the taxable amount shall be determined in accordance with paragraph 3. For supplies of works of art, collectors' items or antiques which the taxable dealer has imported himself, the purchase price to be taken into account in calculating the margin shall be equal to the taxable amount on importation, determined in accordance with Article 11 (B), plus the value added tax due or paid on importation.

5. Where they are effected in the conditions laid down in Article 15, the supplies of second-hand goods, works of art, collectors' item or antiques subject to the special arrangements for taxing the margin shall be exempt.

6. Taxable persons shall not be entitled to deduct from the tax for which they are liable the value added tax due or paid in respect of goods which have been, or are to be, supplied to them by a taxable dealer, in so far as the supply of those goods by the taxable dealer is subject to the special arrangements for taxing the margin.

7. In so far as goods are used for the purpose of supplies by him subject to the special arrangements for taxing the margin, the taxable dealer shall not be entitled to deduct from the tax for which he is liable:

   (a) the value added tax due or paid in respect of works af art, collectors' items or antiques which he has imported himself;

   (b) the value added tax due or paid in respect of works of art which have been, or are to be, supplied to him by their creators or their successors in title;

   (c) the value added tax due or paid in respect of works of art which have been, or are to be, supplied to him by a taxable person other than a taxable dealer.

8. Where he is led to apply both the normal arrangements for value added tax and the special arrangements for taxing the margin, the taxable dealer must follow separately in his accounts the transactions falling under each of these arrangements, according to rules laid down by the Member States,

9. The taxable dealer may not indicate separately on the invoices which he issues, or on any other document serving as an invoice, tax relating to supplies of goods which he makes subject to the special arrangements for taxing the margin.

10. In order to simplify the procedure for charging the tax and subject to the consultation provided for in Article 29, Member States may provide that, for certain transactions or for certain categories of taxable dealers, the taxable amount of supplies of goods subject to the special arrangements for taxing the margin shall be determined for each tax period during which the taxable dealer must submit the return referred to in Article 22 (4).

In that event, the taxable amount for supplies of goods to which the same rate of value added tax is applied shall be the total margin made by the taxable dealer less the amount of value added tax relating to that margin.

The total margin shall be equal to the difference between:

— the total amount of supplies of goods subject to the special arrangements for taxing the margin effected by the taxable dealer during the period; that amount shall be equal to the total selling prices determined in accordance with paragraph 3, and

— the total amount of purchases of goods as referred to in paragraph 2 effected, during that period, by the taxable dealer; that amount shall be equal to the total purchase prices determined in accordance with paragraph 3.

— Member States shall take the necessary measures to ensure that the taxable persons concerned do not enjoy unjustfied advantages or sustain unjustified loss.

11. The taxable dealer may apply the normal value added tax arrangements to any supply covered by the special arrangements pursuant to paragraph 2 or 4.

Where the taxable dealer applies the normal value added tax arrangements to:

(a) the supply of a work of art, collectors' item or antique which he has imported himself, he shall be entitled to deduct from his tax liability the value added tax due or paid on the import of those goods;

(b) the supply of a work of art supplied to him by its creator or his successors in title, he shall be entitled to deduct from his tax liability the value added tax due or paid for the work of art supplied to him;

(c) the supply of a work of art supplied to him by a taxable person other than a taxable dealer, he shall be entitled to deduct from his tax liability the value added tax due or paid for the work of art supplied to him.

This right to deduct shall arise at the time when the tax due for the supply in respect of which the taxable dealer opts for application of the normal value added tax arrangements become chargeable.

C. Special arrangements for sales by public auction

1. By way of derogation from B, Member States may determine, in accordance with the following provisions, the taxable amount of supplies of second-hand goods, works of art, collectors' items or antiques effected by an organizer of sales by public auction, acting in his own name, pursuant to a contract under which commission is payable on the sale of those goods by public auction, on behalf of:

— a non-taxable person,

or

— another taxable person, in so far as the supply of goods, within the meaning of Article 5(4)(c), by that other taxable person is exempt in accordance with Article 13(B)(c),

or

- another taxable person, in so far as the supply of goods, within the meaning of Article 5(4)(c), by that other taxable person qualifies for the exemption provided for in Article 24 and involves capital assets,

  or

- a taxable dealer, in so far as the supply of goods, within the meaning of Article 5(4)(c), by that other taxable dealer, is subject to tax in accordance with the special arrangements for taxing the margin provided for in B.

2. The taxable amount of each supply of goods referred to in paragraph 1 shall be the total amount invoiced in accordance with paragraph 4 to the purchaser by the organizer of the sale by public auction, less:

- the net amount paid or to be paid by the organizer of the sale by public auction to his principal, determined in accordance with paragraph 3, and

- the amount of the tax due by the organizer of the sale by public auction in respect of his supply.

3. The net amount paid or to be paid by the organizer of the sale by public auction to his principal shall be equal to the difference between:

- the price of the goods at public auction, and

- the amount of the commission obtained or to be obtained by the organizer of the sale by public auction from his principal, under the contract whereby commission is payable on the sale.

4. The organizer of the sale by public auction must issue to the purchaser an invoice or a document in lieu itemizing:

- the auction price of the goods,

- taxes, dues, levies and charges,

- incidental expenses such as commission, packing, transport and insurance costs charged by the organizer to the purchaser of the goods.

   That invoice must not indicate any value added tax separately.

5. The organizer of the sale by public auction to whom the goods were transmitted under a contract whereby commission is payable on a public auction sale must issue a statement to his principal.

   That statement must itemize the amount of the transaction, i.e. the auction price of the goods less the amount of the commission obtained or to be obtained from the principal.

   A statement so drawn up shall serve as the invoice which the principal, where he is a taxable person, must issue to the organizer of the sale by public auction in accordance with Article 22(3).

6. Organizers of sales by public auction who supply goods under the conditions laid down in paragraph 1 must indicate in their accounts, in suspense accounts:

- the amounts obtained or to be obtained from the purchaser of the goods,

— the amount reimbursed or to be reimbursed to the vendor of the goods.

These amounts must be duly substantiated.

7. The supply of goods to a taxable person who is an organizer of sales by public auction shall be regarded as being effected when the sale of those goods by public auction is itself effected.

D. Transitional arrangements for the taxation of trade between Member States

During the period referred to in Article 28l, Member States shall apply the following provisions:

(a) supplies of new means of transport, within the meaning of Article 28a(2), effected within the conditions laid down in Article 28c(A) shall be excluded from the special arrangements provided for in B and C;

(b) by way of derogation from Article 28a(1)(a), intra-Community acquisitions of second-hand goods, works of art, collectors' items or antiques shall not be subject to value added tax where the vendor is a taxable dealer acting as such and the goods acquired have been subject to tax in the Member State of departure of the dispatch or transport, in accordance with the special arrangements for taxing the margin provided for in B, or where the vendor is an organizer of sales by public auction acting as such and the goods acquired have been subject to tax in the Member State of departure of the dispatch or transport, in accordance with the special arrangements provided for in C;

(c) Articles 28b (B) and 28c(A)(a), (c) and (d) shall not apply to supplies of goods subject to value added tax in accordance with either of the special arrangements laid down in B and C.";

4. the following paragraph shall be inserted in Article 28:

"1a.Until a date which may not be later than 30 June 1999, the United Kingdom of Great Britain and Northern Ireland may, for imports of works of art, collectors' items or antiques which qualified for an exemption on 1 January 1993, apply Article 11(B)(6) in such a way that the value added tax due on importation is, in any event, equal to 2,5% of the amount determined in accordance with Article 11(B)(1) to (4).";

5. the following subparagraph shall be added to Article 28(2)(e):

"This provision may not apply to supplies of second-hand goods, works of art, collectors' items or antiques subject to value added tax in accordance with one of the special arrangements provided for an Article 26a(B) and (C).";

6. Article 28a(2)(b) shall be amended as follows:

"(b)the means of transport referred to in (a) shall not be considered to be "new" where both of the following conditions are simultaneously fulfilled:

— they were supplied more than three months after the date of first entry into service. However, this period shall be increased to six months for the motorized land vehicles defined in (a),

— they have travelled more than 6 000 kilometres in the case of land vehicles, sailed for more than 100 hours in the case of vessels, or flown for more than 40 hours in the case of aircraft.

Member States shall lay down the conditions under which the above facts can be regarded as established.";

7. the following Title and Article shall be inserted:

"TITLE XVIb

TRANSITIONAL PROVISIONS APPLICABLE IN THE FIELD OF SECOND-HAND GOODS, WORKS OF ART, COLLECTORS' ITEMS AND ANTIQUES

Article 28o

1. Member States which at 31 December 1992 were applying special tax arrangements other than those provided for in Article 26a (B) to supplies of second-hand means of transport effected by taxable dealers my continue to apply those arrangements during the period referred to in Article 28l in so far as they comply with, or are adjusted to comply with, the following conditions:

(a) the special arrangements shall apply only to supplies of the means of transport referred to in Article 28a(2)(a) and regarded as second-hand goods within the meaning of Article 26a(A)(d), effected by taxable dealers within the meaning of Article 26a(A)(e), and subject to the special tax arrangements for taxing the margin pursuant to Article 26a(B)(1) and (2). Supplies of new means of transport within the meaning of Article 28a(2)(b) that are carried out under the conditions specified in

Article 28c(A) shall be excluded from these special arrangements;

(b) the tax due in respect of each supply referred to in (a) is equal to the amount of tax that would be due if that supply had been subject to the normal arrangements for value added tax, less the amount of value added tax regarded as being incorporated in the purchase price of the means of transport by the taxable dealer;

(c) the tax regarded as being incorporated in the purchase price of the means of transport by the taxable dealer shall be calculated according to the following method:

— the purchase price to be taken into account shall be the purchase price within the meaning of Article 26a (B) (3),

— that purchase price paid by the taxable dealer shall be deemed to include the tax that would have been due if the taxable dealer's supplier had subjected the supply to the normal value added tax arrangements,

— the rate to be taken into account shall be the rate applicable within the meaning of Article 12(1), in the Member State within which the place of the supply to the taxable dealer, determined in accordance with Article 8, is deemed to be situated;

(d) the tax due in respect of each supply as referred to in (a), determined in accordance with the provisions of (b), may not be less than the amount of tax that would be due if that supply had been subject to the special arrangements for taxing the margin in accordance with Article 26a(B) (3).

For the application of the above provisions, the Member States have the option of providing that if the supply had been subject to the special arrangements for taxation of the margin, that margin would not have been less than 10 % of the selling price, within the meaning of B(3);

(e) the taxable dealer shall not be entitled to indicate separately on the invoices he issues, or on any other document in lieu, tax relating to supplies which he is subjecting to the special arrangements;

(f) taxable persons shall not be entitled to deduct from the tax for which they are liable tax due or paid in respect of second-hand means of transport supplied to them by a taxable dealer, in so far as the supply of those goods by the taxable dealer is subject to the tax arrangements in accordance with (a);

(g) by way of derogation from Article 28a(1)(a), intra-Community acquisitions of means of transport are not subject to value added tax where the vendor is a taxable dealer acting as such and the second-hand means of transport acquired has been subject to the tax, in the Member State of departure of the dispatch or transport, in accordance with (a);

(h) Articles 28b(B) and 28c(A)(a) and (d) shall not apply to supplies of second-hand means of transport subject to tax in accordance with (a).

2. By way of derogation from the first sentence of paragraph 1, the Kingdom of Denmark shall be entitled to apply the special tax arrangements laid down in paragraph 1(a) to (h) during the period referred to in Article 28l.

3. Where they apply the special arrangements for sales by public auction provided for in Article 26a (C), Member States shall also apply these special arrangements to supplies of second-hand means of transport effected by an organizer of sales by public auction acting in his own name, pursuant to a contract under which commission is payable on the sale of those goods by public auction, on behalf of a taxable dealer, in so far as the supply of the second-hand means of transport, within the meaning of Article 5(4)(c), by that other taxable dealer, is subject to tax in accordance with paragraphs 1 and 2.

4. For supplies by a taxable dealer of works of art, collectors' items or antiques that have been supplied to him under the conditions provided for in Article 26a(B)(2), the Federal Republic of Germany shall be entitled, until 30 June 1999, to provide for the possibility for taxable dealers to

apply either the special arrangements for taxable dealers, or the normal VAT arrangements according to the following rules:

(a) for the application of the special arrangements for taxable dealers to these supplies of goods, the taxable amount shall be determined in accordance with Article 11(A)(1), (2) and (3);

(b) in so far as the goods are used for the needs of his operations which are taxed in accordance with (a), the taxable dealer shall be authorized to deduct from the tax for which he is liable:

— the value added tax due or paid for works of art, collectors' items or antiques which are or will be supplied to him by another taxable dealer, where the supply by that other taxable dealer has been taxed in accordance with (a),

— the value added tax deemed to be included in the purchase price of the works of art, collectors' items or antiques which are or will be supplied to him by another taxable dealer, where the supply by that other taxable dealer has been subject to value added tax in accordance with the special arrangements for the taxation of the margin provided for in Article 26a(B), in the Member State within whose territory the place of that supply, determined in accordance with Article 8, is deemed to be situated.

This right to deduct shall arise at the time when the tax due for te supply taxed in accordance with (a) becomes chargeable;

(c) for the application of the provisions laid down in the second indent of (b), the purchase price of the works of art, collectors' items or antiques the supply of which by a taxable dealer is taxed in accordance with (a) shall be determined in accordance with Article 26a(B)(3) and the tax deemed to be included in this purchase price shall be calculated according to the following method:

— the purchase price shall be deemed to include the value added tax that would have been due if the taxable margin made by the supplier had been equal to 20 % of the purchase price,

— the rate to be taken into account shall be the rate applicable, within the meaning of Article 12(1), in the Member State within whose territory the place of the supply that is subject to the special arrangements for taxation of the profit margin, determined in accordance with Article 8, is deemed to be situated;

(d) where he applies the normal arrangements for value added tax to the supply of a work of art, collectors' item or antique which has been supplied to him by another taxable dealer and where the goods have been taxed in accordance with (a), the taxable dealer shall be authorized to deduct from his tax liability the value added tax referred to in (b);

(e) the category of rates applicable to these supplies of goods shall be that which was applicable on 1 January 1993;

(f) for the application of the fourth indent of Article 26a(B)(2), the fourth indent of Article 26a(C)(1) and Article 26a(D)(b) and (c), the supplies of works of art, collectors' items or antiques, taxed in accordance with (a), shall be deemed by Member States to be supplies subject to value added tax in accordance with the special arrangements for taxation of the profit margin provided for in Article 26a(B);

(g) where the supplies of works of art, collectors' items or antiques taxed in accordance with (a) are effected under the conditions provided for in Article 28c(A), the invoice issued in accordance with Article 22(3) shall contain an endorsement indicating that the special taxation arrangements for taxing the margin provided for in Article 28o(4) have been applied.";

8. the derogation provided for in Article 28(3)(e) relating to Article 5(4)(c) shall be deleted;

9. Article 32 shall be deleted;

10. the Annex to this Directive shall be added as Annex I.

Article 2

Member States may take measures concerning the right to deduct value added tax in order to avoid the taxable dealers concerned enjoying unjustified advantages or sustaining unjustified loss.

Article 3

Acting unanimously on a proposal from the Commission, the Council may authorize any Member State to introduce particular measures for the purpose of combating fraud, by providing that the tax due in application of the arrangements for taxing the profit margin provided for in Article 26a(B) cannot be less than the amount of tax which would be due if the profit margin were equal to a certain percentage of the selling price. This percentage shall be fixed taking into account the normal profit margins realized by economic operators in the sector concerned.

Article 4

1. Member States shall adapt their present value added tax system to this Directive.

They shall bring into force such laws, regulations and administrative provisions as are necessary for their system thus adapted to enter into force on 1 January 1995 at the latest.

2. Member States shall inform the Commission of the provisions which they adopt to apply this Directive.

3. Member States shall communicate to the Commission the provisions of national law which they adopt in the field covered by this Directive.

4. When Member States adopt such provisions, they shall contain a reference to this Directive or be accompanied by such reference on the occasion of their official publication. The methods of making such a reference shall be laid down by the Member States.

Article 5

This Directive is addressed to the Member States.

Done at Brussels, 14 February 1994.

For the Council

The President

Y. PAPANTONIOU

ANNEX I

WORKS OF ART, COLLECTORS' ITEMS AND ANTIQUES

For the purposes of this Directive:

(a) **"works of art"** shall mean:

— pictures, collages and similar decorative plaques, paintings and drawings, executed entirely by hand by the artist, other than plans and drawings for architectural, engineering, industrial, commercial, topographical or similar purposes, hand-decorated manufactured articles, theatrical scenery, studio back cloths or the like of painted canvas (CN code 9701),

— original engravings, prints and lithographs, being impressions produced in limited numbers directly in black and white or in colour of one or of several plates executed entirely by hand by the artist, irrespective of the process or of the material employed by him, but not including any mechanical or photomechanical process (CN code 9702 00 00),

— original sculptures and statuary, in any material, provided that they are executed entirely by the artist; sculpture casts the production of which is limited to eight copies and supervised by the artist or his successors in title (CN code 9703 00 00); on an exceptional basis, in cases determined by the Member States, the limit of eight copies may be exceeded for statuary casts produced before 1 January 1989,

— tapestries (CN code 5805 00 00) and wall textiles (CN code 6304 00 00) made by hand from original designs provided by artists, provided that there are not more than eight copies of each,

— individual pieces of ceramics executed entirely by the artist and signed by him,

— enamels on copper, executed entirely by hand, limited to eight numbered copies bearing the signature of the artist or the studio, excluding articles of jewellery and goldsmiths' and silversmiths' wares,

— photographs taken by the artist, printed by him or under his supervision, signed and numbered and limited to 30 copies, all sizes and mounts included;

(b) **"collectors' items"** shall mean:

— postage or revenue stamps, postmarks, first-day covers, pre-stamped stationery and the like, franked, or if unfranked not being of legal tender and not being intended for use as legal tender (CN code 9704 00 00),

— collections and collectors' pieces of zoological, botanical, mineralogical, anatomical, historical, archaeological, palaetological, ethnographic or numismatic interest (CN code 9705 00 00);

(c) **"antiques"** shall mean objects other than works of art or collectors' items, which are more than 100 years old (CN code 9706 00 00).'

COUNCIL DIRECTIVE 94/76/EC

of 22 December 1994

Amending Directive 77/388/EEC by the introduction of transitional measures applicable, in the context of the enlargement of the European Union on 1 January 1995, as regards value added tax

Official Journal L 365 , 31/12/1994 p. 0053 - 0055

This Directive was repealed by Council Directive 2006/112/EC of 28 November 2006 on the common system of value added tax, with effect from 1 January 2007

THE COUNCIL OF THE EUROPEAN UNION,

Having regard to the 1994 Accession Treaty, and in particular Articles 2 and 3 thereof, and the 1994 act of Accession, and in particular Article 169 thereof,

Having regard to the proposal from the Commission,

Whereas, subject to the special provisions set out in Chapter IX of Annex XV to the Act of Accession, the common system of value added tax is to apply to the new Member States as from the date on which the Accession Treaty enters into force;

Whereas, as a result of the abolition on that date of the imposition of tax on importation and remission of tax on exportation in trade between the Community as constituted at present and the new Member States, and between the new Member States themselves, transitional measures are necessary to safeguard the neutrality of the common system of value added tax and prevent situations of double taxation or non-taxation;

Whereas such measures must, in this respect, meet concerns akin to those that led to the measures adopted on completion of the internal market on 1 January 1993, and in particular the provisions of Article 28n of Council Directive 77/388/EEC of 17 May 1977 on the harmonization of the laws of the Member States relating to turn-over taxes - Common system of value added tax: uniform basis of assessment;

Whereas, in the customs sphere, goods will be deemed to be in free circulation in the enlarged Community where it is shown that they were in free circulation in the current Community or in one of the new Member States at the time of accession; whereas conclusions should be drawn from this, particularly for Article 7(1) and (3) and Article 10(3) of Directive 77/388/EEC;

Whereas it is necessary in particular to cover situations in which goods have been placed, prior to accession, under one of the arrangements referred to in Article 16(1)(B)(a) to (d), under a temporary admission procedure with full exemption from import duties or under a similar procedure in the new Member States;

Whereas it is also necessary to lay down specific arrangements for cases where a special procedure (export or transit), initiated prior to the entry into force of the Accession Treaty in the framework of trade between the current Community and the new Member States and between those Member States

for the purposes of a supply effected prior to that date by a taxable person acting as such, is not terminated until after the date of accession,

HAS ADOPTED THIS DIRECTIVE:

Article 1

In Directive 77/388/EEC, the following Title and Article shall be inserted:

"TITLE XVIc

Transitional measures applicable in the context of the accession to the European Union of Austria, Finland and Sweden

28p

1. For the purpose of applying this Article:

    — `Community' shall mean the territory of the Community as defined in Article 3 before accession,

    — `new Member States' shall mean the territory of the Member States acceding to the European Union by the Treaty signed on 24 June 1994, as defined for each of those Member States in Article 3 of this Directive,

    — `enlarged Community' shall mean the territory of the Community as defined in Article 3, after accession.

2. When goods:

    — entered the territory of the Community or of one of the new Member States before the date of accession, and

    — were placed, on entry into the territory of the Community or of one of the new Member States, under a temporary admission procedure with full exemption from import duties, under one of the regimes referred to in Article 16(1)(B)(a) to (d) or under a similar regime in one of the new Member States, and

    — have not left that regime before the date of accession,

    the provisions in force at the moment the goods were placed under that regime shall continue to apply until the goods leave this regime, after the date of accession.

3. When goods:

    — were placed, before the date of accession, under the common transit procedure or under another customs transit procedure, and

    — have not left that procedure before the date of accession,

    the provisions in force at the moment the goods were placed under that procedure shall continue to apply until the goods leave this procedure, after the date of accession.

    For the purposes of the first indent, `common transit procedure' shall mean the measures for the transport of goods in transit between the Community and the countries of the European Free Trade Association (EFTA) and between the EFTA countries themselves, as provided for in the Convention of 20 May 1987 on a common transit procedure.

4. The following shall be deemed to be an importation of goods within the meaning of Article 7(1) where it is shown that the goods were in free circulation in one of the new Member States or in the Community:

    (a) the removal, including irregular removal, of goods from a temporary admission procedure under which they were placed before the date of accession under the conditions set out in paragraph 2;

    (b) the removal, including irregular removal, of goods either from one of the regimes referred to in Article 16(1)(B)(a) to (d) or from a similar regime under which they were placed before the date of accession under the conditions set out in paragraph 2;

    (c) the termination of one of the procedures referred to in paragraph 3 which was started before the date of accession in one of new Member States for the purposes of a supply of goods for consideration effected before that date in that Member State by a taxable person acting as such;

    (d) any irregularity or offence committed during one of the procedures referred to in paragraph 3 under the conditions set out at (c).

5. The use after the date of accession within a Member State, by a taxable or non-taxable person, of goods supplied to him before the date of accession within the Community or one of the new Member States shall also be deemed to be an importation of goods within the meaning of Article 7(1) where the following conditions are met:

    — the supply of those goods has been exempted, or was likely to be exempted, either under Article 15(1) and (2) or under a similar provision in the new Member States,

    — the goods were not imported into one of the new Member States or into the Community before the date of accession.

6. In the cases referred to in paragraph 4, the place of import within the meaning of Article 7(3) shall be the Member State within whose territory the goods cease to be covered by the regime under which they were placed before the date of accession.

7. By way of derogation from Article 10(3), the importation of goods within the meaning of paragraphs 4 and 5 of this Article shall terminate without the occurrence of a chargeable event when:

    (a) the imported goods are dispatched or transported outside the enlarged Community; or

    (b) the imported goods within the meaning of paragraph 4(a) are other than means of transport and are redispatched or transported to the Member State from which they were exported and to the person who exported them; or

    (c) the imported goods within the meaning of paragraph 4(a) are means of transport which were acquired or imported before the date of accession in accordance with the general conditions of taxation in force on the domestic market of one of the new Member States or of one of the Member States of the Community and/or have not been subject, by reason of their exportation, to any exemption from, or refund of, value added tax.

This condition shall be deemed to be fulfilled when the date of the first use of the means of transport was before 1 January 1987 or when the amount of tax due by reason of the importation is insignificant."

Article 2

1. Subject to the entry into force of the 1994 Accession Treaty, Member States shall bring into force the laws, regulations and administrative provisions necessary to comply with this Directive on the date of entry into force of this Directive. They shall forthwith inform the Commission thereof.

   When Member States adopt those provisions, they shall contain a reference to this Directive or shall be accompanied by such reference on the occasion of their official publication. The methods of making such a reference shall be laid down by the Member States.

2. Member States shall communicate to the Commission the provisions of domestic law which they adopt in the field covered by this Directive.

Article 3

This Directive shall enter into force on the same date as the 1994 Accession Treaty.

Article 4

This Directive is addressed to the Member States.

Done at Brussels, 22 December 1994.

For the Council The President

H. SEEHOFER

COUNCIL DIRECTIVE 95/7/EC

of 10 April 1995

Amending Directive 77/388/EEC and introducing new simplification measures with regard to value added tax - scope of certain exemptions and practical arrangements for implementing them

Official Journal L 102 , 05/05/1995 p. 0018 - 0024

This Directive was repealed by Council Directive 2006/112/EC of 28 November 2006 on the common system of value added tax, with effect from 1 January 2007

THE COUNCIL OF THE EUROPEAN UNION,

Having regard to the Treaty establishing the European Community, and in particular Article 99 thereof,

Having regard to the proposal from the Commission,

Having regard to the opinion of the European Parliament,

Having regard to the opinion of the Economic and Social Committee,

Whereas the operation of the internal market can be improved by introducing common rules clarifying the scope of, and arrangements for, applying some of the exemptions provided for in Articles 14(1), 15, point 2, and 16(1) of the Sixth Council Directive 77/388/EEC of 17 May 1977 on the harmonization of the laws of the Member States relating to turnover taxes - common system of value added tax: uniform basis of assessment; whereas the introduction of such common rules is provided for by the aforesaid Directive, and in particular Articles 14(2) and 16(3) thereof;

Whereas Article 3 of Council Directive 92/111/EEC of 14 December 1992 amending Directive 77/388/EEC and introducing simplification measures with regard to value added tax provides for the adoption of special rules for the taxation of chain transactions between taxable persons; whereas such rules must ensure not only compliance with the principle of neutrality of the common system of value added tax as regards the origin of goods and services but also compliance with the choices made as to the principles governing value added tax and its monitoring arrangements during the transitional period;

Whereas it is appropriate to include in the taxable amount on importation all ancillary costs arising from the transport of goods to any place of destination in the Community since that place is known at the time the importation is carried out; whereas, as a result, the supplies of services in question enjoy the exemptions provided for in Article 14(1)(i) of Directive 77/388/EEC;

Whereas Article 15(2) of that Directive provides that the Commission shall submit to the Council proposals to establish Community tax rules specifying the scope of, and practical arrangements for implementing, the export exemptions applicable to supplies of goods carried in the personal luggage of travellers;

Whereas it is appropriate that the period serving as a basis for calculating the adjustments provided for by Article 20(2) of the said Directive should be extended up to 20 years by Member States for immovable property acquired as capital goods, bearing in mind the duration of their economic life;

Whereas Member States should be enabled to maintain the rate applicable to goods after making up work which they carried out under a contract to make up work on 1 January 1993;

Whereas the rules governing territorial application and the tax arrangements applicable in the field of intra-Community goods-transport services function in a simple and satisfactory manner for both traders and the authorities in the Member States;

Whereas, by treating a transport operation within a Member State as an intra-Community goods-transport operation where it is directly linked to a transport operation between Member States, it is possible to simplify not only the principles and arrangements for taxing those domestic transport services but also the rules applicable to ancillary services and to services supplied by intermediaries involved in the supply of these various services;

Whereas the qualification of certain works on movable property as work carried out under a contract to make up work is a source of difficulty and should be eliminated;

Whereas, with a view to facilitating intra-Community trade in the field of work on movable tangible property, the tax arrangements applicable for these transactions should be modified when they are carried out for a person who is identified for value added tax purposes in a Member State other than that of their physical execution;

Whereas Article 16(1)(B) to (E) of the said Directive, taken together in particular with Article 22(9) concerning release from obligations, makes it possible to overcome the difficulties encountered by traders participating in transaction chains involving goods placed and kept under warehousing arrangements;

Whereas it is necessary in this connection to ensure that the tax treatment applied to supplies of goods and the provision of services relating to certain of the goods which may be placed under customs warehousing arrangements can also be applied to the same transactions involving goods placed under warehousing arrangements other than customs warehousing;

Whereas these transactions concern principally raw materials and other goods negotiated on international forward markets; whereas a list of the goods covered by these provisions should be drawn up;

Whereas, subject to consultation of the Committee on Value Added Tax, the Member States are responsible for defining those warehousing arrangements other than customs warehousing; whereas it is necessary nevertheless to exclude in principle from such arrangements goods that are intended to be supplied at the retail stage;

Whereas it is necessary to clarify some of the rules for applying tax when goods cease to be covered by the arrangements provided for in Article 16(1) (B) to (E) of the said Directive, particularly as regards the person liable for payment of the tax due;

Whereas it is necessary to clarify the scope of those provisions of Article 17(2) (a) of the said Directive that are applicable during the transitional period referred to in Article 28l;

Whereas it is accordingly necessary to amend Directive 77/388/EEC,

HAS ADOPTED THIS DIRECTIVE:

Article 1

Directive 77/388/EEC is hereby amended as follows:

1. Article 5(5) shall be replaced by the following:

    "5. Member States may consider the handing over of certain works of construction to be supplies within the meaning of paragraph 1.";

2. Article 11(B)(3)(b), third subparagraph, shall be replaced by the following:

    "The incidental expenses referred to above shall also be included in the taxable amount where they result from transport to another place of destination within the territory of the Community if that place is known when the chargeable event occurs";

3. Article 15(2), second and third subparagraphs, shall be replaced by the following three subparagraphs:

    "In the case of the supply of goods to be carried in the personal luggage of travellers, this exemption shall apply on condition that:

    — the traveller is not established within the Community,

    — the goods are transported to a destination outside the Community before the end of the third month following that in which the supply is effected,

    — the total value of the supply, including value added tax, is more than the equivalent in national currency of ECU 175, fixed in accordance with Article 7(2) of Directive 69/169/EEC;

    however, Member States may exempt a supply with a total value of less than that amount.

    For the purposes of applying the second subparagraph:

    — a traveller not established within the Community shall be taken to mean a traveller whose domicile or habitual residence is not situated within the Community. For the purposes of this provision, "**domicile or habitual residence**" shall mean the place entered as such in a passport, identity card or other identity documents which the Member State within whose territory the supply takes place recognizes as valid,

    — proof of exportation shall be furnished by means of the invoice or other document in lieu thereof, endorsed by the customs office where the goods left the Community.

    Each Member State shall transmit to the Commission specimens of the stamps it uses for the endorsement referred to in the second indent of the third subparagraph. The Commission shall transmit this information to the tax authorities in the other Member States.";

4.   in Article 20(2), the last subparagraph shall be replaced by the following:

"In the case of immovable property acquired as capital goods, the adjustment period may be extended up to 20 years.";

5.   in Article 28(2), the following point shall be added:

"(h) Member States which, on 1 January 1993, were availing themselves of the option provided for in Article 5(5)(a) as in force on that date, may apply to supplies under a contract to make up work the rate applicable to the goods after making up.

For the purposes of applying this provision, supplies under a contract to make up work shall be deemed to be delivery by a contractor to his customer of movable property made or assembled by the contractor from materials or objects entrusted to him by the customer for this purpose, whether or not the contractor has provided any part of the materials used.";

6.   Article 28(a)(5) shall be amended as follows:

the introductory sentence shall be replaced by the following:

"The following shall be treated as supplies of goods effected for consideration:",

(a) shall be deleted,

the fourth indent in the second subparagraph of (b) shall be deleted,

the fifth indent in the second subparagraph of (b) shall be replaced by the following:

"- the supply of a service performed for the taxable person and involving work on the goods in question physically carried out in the Member State in which the dispatch or transport of the goods ends, provided that the goods, after being worked upon, are re-dispatched to that taxable person in the Member State from which they had initially been dispatched or transported";

7.   Article 28b shall be amended as follows:

in the first indent of C(1), the comma shall be replaced by a full stop and the following subparagraph shall be added:

"The transport of goods where the place of departure and the place of arrival are situated within the territory of the country shall be treated as intra-Community transport of goods where such transport is directly linked to transport of goods where the place of departure and the place of arrival are situated within the territories of two different Member States;",

the following section shall be added:

"F. Place of the supply of services in the case of valuations of or work on movable tangible property By way of derogation from Article 9 (2) (c), the place of the supply of services involving valuations or work on movable tangible property, provided to customers identified for value added tax purposes in a Member State other than the one where those services are physically carried out, shall be deemed to be in the territory of the Member State which issued the customer with the value added tax identification number under which the service was carried out for him.

This derogation shall not apply where the goods are not dispatched or transported out of the Member State where the services were physically carried out.";

8. in the first subparagraph of Article 28c(A)(a), "as defined in Articles 5 and 28a(5)(a)" shall be replaced by `as defined in Article 5';

9. Article 28c(E)(1) shall be replaced by the following:

"1. In Article 16:

— paragraph 1 shall be replaced by the following:

"1. Without prejudice to other Community tax provisions, Member States may, subject to the consultations provided for in Article 29, take special measures designed to exempt all or some of the following transactions, provided that they are not aimed at final use and/or consumption and that the amount of value added tax due on cessation of the arrangements on situations referred to at A to E corresponds to the amount of tax which would have been due had each of these transactions been taxed within the territory of the country:

A. imports of goods which are intended to be placed under warehousing arrangements other than customs;

B. supplies of goods which are intended to be:

(a) produced to customs and, where applicable, placed in temporary storage;

(b) placed in a free zone or in a free warehouse

(c) placed under customs warehousing arrangements or inward processing arrangements;

(d) admitted into territorial waters:

in order to be incorporated into drilling or production platforms, for purposes of the construction, repair, maintenance, alteration or fitting-out of such platforms, or to link such drilling or production platforms to the mainland,

for the fuelling and provisioning of drilling or production platforms;

(e) placed, within the territory of the country, under warehousing arrangements other than customs warehousing.

For the purposes of this Article, warehouses other than customs warehouses shall be taken to be:

for products subject to excise duty, the places defined as tax warehouses for the purposes of Article 4 (b) of Directive 92/12/EEC,

for goods other than those subject to excise duty, the places defined as such by the Member States. However, Member States may not provide for warehousing arrangements other than customs warehousing where the goods in question are intended to be supplied at the retail stage.

Nevertheless, Member States may provide for such arrangements for goods intended for:

taxable persons for the purposes of supplies effected under the conditions laid down in Article 28k,

tax-free shops within the meaning of Article 28k, for the purposes of supplies to travellers taking flights or sea crossings to third countries, where those supplies are exempt pursuant to Article 15,

taxable persons for the purposes of supplies to travellers on board aircraft or vessels during a flight or sea crossing where the place of arrival is situated outside the Community,

taxable persons for the purposes of supplies effected free of tax pursuant to Article 15, point 10.

The places referred to in (a), (b), (c) and (d) shall be as defined by the Community customs provisions in force;

C. supplies of services relating to the supplies of goods referred to in B;

D. supplies of goods and of services carried out:

(a) in the places listed in B(a), (b), (c) and (d) and still subject to one of the situations specified therein;

(b) in the places listed in B(e) and still subject, within the territory of the country, to the situation specified therein.

Where they exercise the option provided for in (a) for transactions effected in customs warehouses, Member States shall take the measures necessary to ensure that they have defined warehousing arrangements other than customs warehousing which permit the provisions in (b) to be applied to the same transactions concerning goods listed in Annex J which are efected in such warehouses other than customs warehouses;

E. supplies:

– of goods referred to in Article 7(1)(a) still subject to arrangements for temporary importation with total exemption from import duty or to external transit arrangements,

         – of goods referred to in Article 7(1)(b) still subject to the internal Community transit procedure provided for in Article 33a,

as well as supplies of services relating to such supplies.

By way of derogation from the first subparagraph of Article 21(1)(a), the person liable to pay the tax due in accordance with the first subparagraph shall be the person who causes the goods to cease to be covered by the arrangements or situations listed in this paragraph.

When the removal of goods from the arrangements or situations referred to in this paragraph gives rise to importation within the meaning of Article 7(3), the Member State of import shall take the measures necessary to avoid double taxation within the country.",

the following paragraph shall be added:

"1a.Where they exercise the option provided for in paragraph 1, Member States shall take the measures necessary to ensure that intra-Community acquisitions of goods intended to be placed under one of the arrangements or in one of the situations referred to in paragraph 1(B) benefit from the same provisions as supplies of goods effected within the country under the same conditions."";

10. in Article 28f(1), Article 17(2)(a) shall be replaced by the following:

"(a)value added tax due or paid within the territory of the country in respect of goods or services supplied or to be supplied to him by another taxable person;";

11. in Article 28g, Article 21(1)(b) shall be replaced by the following:

"(b)persons to whom services covered by Article 9 (2) (e) are supplied or persons who are identified for value added tax purposes within the territory of the country to whom services covered by Article 28b, (C), (D), (E) and (F) are supplied, if the services are carried out by a taxable person established abroad; however, Member States may require that the supplier of services shall be held jointly and severally liable for payment of the tax;";

12. Article 28h shall be amended as follows:

Article 22 (2), (b) shall be replaced by the following:

"(b)Every taxable person shall keep a register of the goods he has dispatched or transported or which have been dispatched or transported on his behalf out of the territory defined in Article 3 but within the Community for the purposes of the transactions referred to in the fifth, sixth and seventh indents of Article 28a(5)(b).

Every taxable person shall keep sufficiently detailed accounts to permit the identification of goods dispatched to him from another Member State by or on behalf of a taxable person identified for purposes of value added tax in that other Member State, in connection with which a service has been provided pursuant to the third or fourth indent of Article 9(2)(c);", the first indent of the second subparagraph of Article 22(3)(b) shall be replaced by the following:

"- in the case of the transactions referred to in Article 28b(C), (D), (E) and (F), the number by which the taxable person is identified in the territory of the country and the number by which the customer is identified and under which the service has been rendered to him.",

the first subparagraph of Article 22(6)(b) shall be replaced by the following:

"Every taxable person identified for value added tax purposes shall also submit a recapitulative statement of the acquirers identified for value added tax purposes to whom he has supplied goods under the conditions provided for in Article 28c(A) (a) and (d), and of consignees identified for value added tax purposes in the transactions referred to in the fifth subparagraph.",

the second indent of the third subparagraph of Article 22(6)(b) shall be replaced by the following:

"- the number by which each person acquiring goods is identified for purposes of value added tax in another Member State and under which the goods were supplied to him,",

the fifth subparagraph of Article 22 (6) (b) shall be deleted;

13. Annex J which appears in the Annex to this Directive shall be added.

Article 2

1. Member States shall bring into force the laws, regulations and administrative provisions necessary to comply with this Directive on 1 January 1996. They shall forthwith inform the Commission thereof.

When Member States adopt these measures, they shall contain a reference to this Directive or shall be accompanied by such reference on the occasion of their official publication. The methods of making such reference shall be laid down by Member States.

2. By way of derogation from the first subparagraph of paragraph 1, Member States may take measures by way of law, regulation or administrative action in order to bring the provisions in Article 1(3), (4) and (9) into force not later than 1 January 1996.

However, the Federal Republic of Germany and the Grand Duchy of Luxembourg are authorized to take measures by way of law, regulation or administrative action in order to apply the provisions in Article 1(9) not later than 1 January 1997.

3. Member States shall communicate to the Commission the text of the provisions of national law which they adopt in the field governed by this Directive.

Article 3

This Directive shall enter into force on the 20th day following its publication in the *Official Journal of the European Communities*.

Article 4

This Directive is addressed to the Member States.

Done at Luxembourg, 10 April 1995.

For the Council The President

A. JUPPÉ

ANNEX J:

DESCRIPTION OF GOODS	CN CODE
Tin	8001
Copper	7402 7403 7405 7408
Zinc	7901
Nickel	7502
Aluminium	7601
Lead	7801
Indium	ex 8112 91 ex 8112 99
Cereals	1001 to 1005 1006: unprocessed rice only 1007 to 1008
Oil seeds and oleaginous fruit Coconuts, Brazil nuts and cashew nut Other nuts Olives	1201 to 1207 0801 0802 0711 20
Grains and seeds (including soya beans)	1201 to 1207
Coffee, not roasted	0901 11 00 0901 12 00
Tea	0902
Cocoa beans, whole or broken, raw or roasted	1801
Raw sugar	1701 11 1701 12
Rubber, in primary forms or in plates, sheets or strip	4001 4002
Wool	5101
Chemicals in bulk	Chapters 28 and 29
Mineral oils (including propane and butane; also including crude petroleum oils)	2709 2710 2711 12 2711 13
Silver	7106
Platinum (Palladium, Rhodium)	7110 11 00 7110 21 00 7110 31 00
Potatoes	0701
Vegetable oils and fats and their fractions, whether or not refined, but not chemically modified	1507 to 1515

COUNCIL DIRECTIVE 96/42/EC

of 25 June 1996

amending Directive 77/388/EEC on the common system of value added tax

Official Journal L 170 , 09/07/1996 p. 0034 - 0034

> This Directive was repealed by Council Directive 2006/112/EC of 28 November 2006 on the common system of value added tax, with effect from 1 January 2007

THE COUNCIL OF THE EUROPEAN UNION,

Having regard to the Treaty establishing the European Community, and in particular Article 99 thereof,

Having regard to the proposal from the Commission,

Having regard to the opinion of the European Parliament,

Having regard to the opinion of the Economic and Social Committee,

Whereas Article 12(3)(d) of Directive 77/388/EEC lays down that the rules concerning the taxation of agricultural outputs other than those falling within category 1 of Annex H are to be decided unanimously by the Council before 31 December 1994 on a proposal from the Commission; whereas, until that date, those Member States which had already been applying a reduced rate might continue to do so while those applying a standard rate could not apply a reduced rate; whereas that allowed a two-year postponement in the application of the standard rate;

Whereas experience has shown that the structural imbalance in the VAT rates applicable by Member States to agricultural outputs of the floricultural and horticultural sectors has led to reported cases of fraudulent activities; whereas that structural imbalance is a direct result of the application of Article 12(3)(d) and should be redressed accordingly;

Whereas the most appropriate solution would be to extend to all Member States, on a transitional basis, the option of applying a reduced rate to supplies of agricultural outputs of the floricultural and horticultural sectors and of wood used as firewood,

HAS ADOPTED THIS DIRECTIVE:

Article 1

Directive 77/388/EEC is hereby amended as follows:

1. Article 12(3)(d) shall be deleted;

2. the following shall be inserted in Article 28(2):

    "(i) Member States may apply a reduced rate to supplies of live plants (including bulbs, roots and the like, cut flowers and ornamental foliage) and wood for use as firewood."

Article 2

Member States shall communicate to the Commission the text of the provisions of domestic law which they adopt in the field covered by this Directive.

Article 3

This Directive shall apply from 1 January 1995.

Article 4

This Directive is addressed to the Member States.

Done at Luxembourg, 25 June 1996.
For the Council
The President
M. PINTO

COUNCIL REGULATION (EC) NO 1103/97

of 17 June 1997

on certain provisions relating to the introduction of the euro

Official Journal L 162 , 19/06/1997 p. 0001 - 0003

THE COUNCIL OF THE EUROPEAN UNION,

Having regard to the Treaty establishing the European Community, and in particular Article 235 thereof,

Having regard to the proposal of the Commission,

Having regard to the opinion of the European Parliament,

Having regard to the opinion of the European Monetary Institute,

(1)   Whereas, at its meeting held in Madrid on 15 and 16 December 1995, the European Council confirmed that the third stage of Economic and Monetary Union will start on 1 January 1999 as laid down in Article 109j (4) of the Treaty; whereas the Member States which will adopt the euro as the single currency in accordance with the Treaty will be defined for the purposes of this Regulation as the 'participating Member States';

(2)   Whereas, at the meeting of the European Council in Madrid, the decision was taken that the term 'ECU' used by the Treaty to refer to the European currency unit is a generic term; whereas the Governments of the fifteen Member States have achieved the common agreement that this decision is the agreed and definitive interpretation of the relevant Treaty provisions; whereas the name given to the European currency shall be the 'euro'; whereas the euro as the currency of the participating Member States will be divided into one hundred sub-units with the name 'cent'; whereas the European Council furthermore considered that the name of the single currency must be the same in all the official languages of the European Union, taking into account the existence of different alphabets;

(3)   Whereas a Regulation on the introduction of the euro will be adopted by the Council on the basis of the third sentence of Article 109l(4) of the Treaty as soon as the participating Member States are known in order to define the legal framework of the euro; whereas the Council, when acting at the starting date of the third stage in accordance with the first sentence of Article 109l (4) of the Treaty, shall adopt the irrevocably fixed conversion rates;

(4)   Whereas it is necessary, in the course of the operation of the common market and for the changeover to the single currency, to provide legal certainty for citizens and firms in all Member States on certain provisions relating to the introduction of the euro well before the entry into the third stage; whereas this legal certainty at an early stage will allow preparations by citizens and firms to proceed under good conditions;

(5)   Whereas the third sentence of Article 109l (4) of the Treaty, which allows the Council, acting with the unanimity of participating Member States,

to take other measures necessary for the rapid introduction of the single currency is available as a legal basis only when it has been confirmed, in accordance with Article 109j (4) of the Treaty, which Member States fulfil the necessary conditions for the adoption of a single currency; whereas it is therefore necessary to have recourse to Article 235 of the Treaty as a legal basis for those provisions where there is an urgent need for legal certainty; whereas therefore this Regulation and the aforesaid Regulation on the introduction of the euro will together provide the legal framework for the euro, the principles of which legal framework were agreed by the European Council in Madrid; whereas the introduction of the euro concerns day-to-day operations of the whole population in participating Member States; whereas measures other than those in this Regulation and in the Regulation which will be adopted under the third sentence of Article 109l (4) of the Treaty should be examined to ensure a balanced changeover, in particular for consumers;

(6)   Whereas the ECU as referred to in Article 109g of the Treaty and as defined in Council Regulation (EC) No 3320/94 of 22 December 1994 on the consolidation of the existing Community legislation on the definition of the ECU following the entry into force of the Treaty on European Union will cease to be defined as a basket of component currencies on 1 January 1999 and the euro will become a currency in its own right; whereas the decision of the Council regarding the adoption of the conversion rates shall not in itself modify the external value of the ECU; whereas this means that one ECU in its composition as a basket of component currencies will become one euro; whereas Regulation (EC) No 3320/94 therefore becomes obsolete and should be repealed; whereas for references in legal instruments to the ECU, parties shall be presumed to have agreed to refer to the ECU as referred to in Article 109g of the Treaty and as defined in the aforesaid Regulation; whereas such presumption should be rebuttable taking into account the intentions of the parties;

(7)   Whereas it is a generally accepted principle of law that the continuity of contracts and other legal instruments is not affected by the introduction of a new currency; whereas the principle of freedom of contract has to be respected; whereas the principle of continuity should be compatible with anything which parties might have agreed with reference to the introduction of the euro; whereas, in order to reinforce legal certainty and clarity, it is appropriate explicitly to confirm that the principle of continuity of contracts and other legal instruments shall apply between the former national currencies and the euro and between the ECU as referred to in Article 109g of the Treaty and as defined in Regulation (EC) No 3320/94 and the euro; whereas this implies, in particular, that in the case of fixed interest rate instruments the introduction of the euro does not alter the nominal interest rate payable by the debtor; whereas the provisions on continuity can fulfil their objective to provide legal certainty and transparency to economic agents, in particular for consumers, only if they enter into force as soon as possible;

(8)   Whereas the introduction of the euro constitutes a change in the monetary law of each participating Member State; whereas the recognition of the monetary law of a State is a universally accepted principle; whereas the explicit confirmation of the principle of continuity should lead to the recognition of continuity of contracts and other legal instruments in the jurisdictions of third countries;

(9)   Whereas the term 'contract' used for the definition of legal instruments is meant to include all types of contracts, irrespective of the way in which they are concluded;

(10)   Whereas the Council, when acting in accordance with the first sentence of Article 109l(4) of the Treaty, shall define the conversion rates of the euro in terms of each of the national currencies of the participating Member States; whereas these conversion rates should be used for any conversion between the euro and the national currency units or between the national currency units; whereas for any conversion between national currency units, a fixed algorithm should define the result; whereas the use of inverse rates for conversion would imply rounding of rates and could result in significant inaccuracies, notably if large amounts are involved;

(11)   Whereas the introduction of the euro requires the rounding of monetary amounts; where

       as an early indication of rules for rounding is necessary in the course of the operation of the common market and to allow a timely preparation and a smooth transition to Economic and Monetary Union; whereas these rules do not affect any rounding practice, convention or national provisions providing a higher degree of accuracy for intermediate computations;

(12)   Whereas, in order to achieve a high degree of accuracy in conversion operations, the conversion rates should be defined with six significant figures; whereas a rate with six significant figures means a rate which, counted from the left and starting by the first non-zero figure, has six figures,

HAS ADOPTED THIS REGULATION:

Article 1

For the purpose of this Regulation:

-    '**legal instruments**' shall mean legislative and statutory provisions, acts of administration, judicial decisions, contracts, unilateral legal acts, payment instruments other than banknotes and coins, and other instruments with legal effect,

-    '**participating Member States**' shall mean those Member States which adopt the single currency in accordance with the Treaty,

-    '**conversion rates**' shall mean the irrevocably fixed conversion rates which the Council adopts in accordance with the first sentence of Article 109l(4) of the Treaty, [or in accordance with the fifth paragraph of that article][1]

- **'national currency units'** shall mean the units of the currencies of participating Member States, as those units are defined on the day before the start of the third stage of Economic and Monetary Union, [or, as the case may be, on the day before the euro is substituted for the currency of a Member State which adopts the euro at a later date][2]

- **'euro unit'** shall mean the unit of the single currency as defined in the Regulation on the introduction of the euro which will enter into force at the starting date of the third stage of Economic and Monetary Union.

Article 2

1. Every reference in a legal instrument to the ECU, as referred to in Article 109g of the Treaty and as defined in Regulation (EC) No 3320/94, shall be replaced by a reference to the euro at a rate of one euro to one ECU. References in a legal instrument to the ECU without such a definition shall be presumed, such presumption being rebuttable taking into account the intentions of the parties, to be references to the ECU as referred to in Article 109g of the Treaty and as defined in Regulation (EC) No 3320/94.

2. Regulation (EC) No 3320/94 is hereby repealed.

3. This Article shall apply as from 1 January 1999 in accordance with the decision pursuant to Article 109j(4) of the Treaty.

Article 3

The introduction of the euro shall not have the effect of altering any term of a legal instrument or of discharging or excusing performance under any legal instrument, nor give a party the right unilaterally to alter or terminate such an instrument. This provision is subject to anything which parties may have agreed.

Article 4

1. The conversion rates shall be adopted as one euro expressed in terms of each of the national currencies of the participating Member States. They shall be adopted with six significant figures.

2. The conversion rates shall not be rounded or truncated when making conversions.

3. The conversion rates shall be used for conversions either way between the euro unit and the national currency units. Inverse rates derived from the conversion rates shall not be used.

4. Monetary amounts to be converted from one national currency unit into another shall first be converted into a monetary amount expressed in the

euro unit, which amount may be rounded to not less than three decimals and shall then be converted into the other national currency unit. No alternative method of calculation may be used unless it produces the same results.

Article 5

Monetary amounts to be paid or accounted for when a rounding takes place after a conversion into the euro unit pursuant to Article 4 shall be rounded up or down to the nearest cent.

Monetary amounts to be paid or accounted for which are converted into a national currency unit shall be rounded up or down to the nearest sub-unit or in the absence of a sub-unit to the nearest unit, or according to national law or practice to a multiple or fraction of the sub-unit or unit of the national currency unit. If the application of the conversion rate gives a result which is exactly half-way, the sum shall be rounded up.

Article 6

This Regulation shall enter into force on the day following that of its publication in the Official Journal of the European Communities.

This Regulation shall be binding in its entirety and directly applicable in all Member States.

Done at Luxembourg, 17 June 1997.
For the Council
The President
A. JORRITSMA-LEBBINK

Amendments
1   Inserted by Council Regulation 2595/2000 of 27 November 2000 (w.e.f 1 January 2001)
2   Inserted by Council Regulation 2595/2000 of 27 November 2000 (w.e.f 1 January 2001)

COUNCIL DECISION 97/510/EC

of 24 July 1997

Authorizing Ireland to apply a measure derogating from Article 21 of the Sixth Directive (77/388/EEC) on the harmonization of the laws of the Member States relating to turnover taxes

Official Journal L 214 , 06/08/1997 p. 0037 - 0038

THE COUNCIL OF THE EUROPEAN UNION,

Having regard to the Treaty establishing the European Community,

Having regard to the Sixth Council Directive (77/388/EEC) of 17 May 1977 on the harmonization of the laws of the Member States relating to turnover taxes - Common system of value added tax: uniform basis of assessment, and in particular Article 27 thereof,

Having regard to the proposal from the Commission,

Whereas, under the terms of Article 27(1) of Directive 77/388/EEC, the Council, acting unanimously on a proposal from the Commission, may authorize any Member State to introduce special measures for derogation from the provisions of that Directive in order to simplify the procedure for charging the tax or to prevent certain types of tax evasion or avoidance;

Whereas, by registered letter to the Commission dated 5 February 1997, Ireland requested authorization to introduce a measure derogating from Article 21(1) of Directive 77/388/EEC;

Whereas, in accordance with Article 27(3) of Directive 77/388/EEC, the other Member States were informed on 4 March 1997 of the request made by Ireland;

Whereas Ireland operates a specific system of applying VAT to property based, on the one hand, on the option under Article 5(3) of Directive 77/388/EEC to treat the supply of certain interests (i.e. a lease of 10 years or more) in immovable property as a supply of goods and, on the other hand, on a derogation authorized under Article 27(5) to treat the granting of such an interest by a lessor as a disposal of the lessor's entire interest in the property;

Whereas Community law gives Member States a great deal of discretion in determining the VAT treatment to be applied to immovable goods, and its transposition has led to considerable variations in the national laws applied in this field;

Whereas avoidance schemes have been set up, based on the use of surrender, including by way of abandonment of a leasehold interest or assignment of a leasehold interest, which result in the avoidance of the VAT where the ultimate acquirer of the property is not entitled to a full deduction of VAT;

Whereas it is also necessary to extend the derogation to the surrender or assignment of a leasehold interest to a taxable person having full right of deduction, as the surrender or the assignment of a leasehold interest will often arise due to financial difficulties of the lessee;

Whereas the measure envisaged is a derogation from Article 21(1)(a) of Directive 77/388/EEC, whereby the person liable for the tax is the taxable person who carries out the taxable transaction;

Whereas the derogation provides that, where a surrender or assignment of a lease-hold interest is a taxable supply of goods, the person acquiring the interest is liable for the payment of the tax if that person is a taxable person or a non-taxable legal person;

Whereas this derogation should ensure a better functioning of the current VAT regime applied by Ireland on immovable goods;

Whereas, given the limited scope of the derogation, the special measure is proportionate to the aim pursued;

Whereas there exists a serious risk that use of the said VAT avoidance scheme will increase in the period between the request for a derogation and the authorization thereof; whereas at the latest since the publication on 26 March 1997 of the draft legislation which is the subject of the present request for a derogation, suppliers, lessors and lessees of property have no longer had a legitimate expectation of the continuation of the Irish legislation in force before that date; whereas it is therefore appropriate to authorize the derogation to take effect from 26 March 1997;

Whereas the Commission adopted on 10 July 1996 a work programme based on a step-by-step approach for progressing towards a new common system of VAT;

Whereas the tax treatment of immovable goods is an important issue to be reviewed in this programme;

Whereas the last package of proposals is to be put forward by mid-1999 and, in order to permit an evaluation of the coherence of the derogation with the global approach of the new common VAT system, the authorization is granted until 31 December 1999;

Whereas the derogation does not have a negative impact on the own resources of the European Communities accruing from VAT,

HAS ADOPTED THIS DECISION:

Article 1

By way of derogation from Article 21(1)(a) of Directive 77/388/EEC, Ireland is hereby authorized, from 26 March 1997 until [31 December 2007][1], to designate the person to whom the supply is made as the person liable to pay the tax where the two following conditions are met:

— a surrender or assignment of a leasehold interest is treated as a supply of goods made by a lessee,

— the person acquiring the leasehold interest is a taxable person or a non-taxable legal person.

Article 2

This Decision is addressed to Ireland.

Done at Brussels, 24 July 1997.
For the Council
The President
M. FISCHBACH

Amendments
1   Art 1 amended by Council Decision 857 of 2003, previously 31 December, 2003.

COUNCIL DIRECTIVE 98/80/EC

of 12 October 1998

Supplementing the common system of value added tax and amending Directive 77/388/EEC - special scheme for investment gold

Official Journal L 281 , 17/10/1998 p. 0031 - 0034

> This Directive was repealed by Council Directive 2006/112/EC of 28 November 2006 on the common system of value added tax, with effect from 1 January 2007

THE COUNCIL OF THE EUROPEAN UNION,

Having regard to the Treaty establishing the European Community and in particular Article 99 thereof,

Having regard to the proposal from the Commission,

Having regard to the opinion of the European Parliament,

Having regard to the opinion of the Economic and Social Committee,

Whereas, under the sixth Council Directive 77/388/EEC of 17 May 1977 on the harmonisation of the laws of the Member States relating to turnover taxes - common system of value added tax: uniform basis of assessment transactions concerning gold are in principle taxable although, on the basis of the transitional derogation provided for in Article 28(3) in conjunction with point 26 of Annex F to the said Directive, Member States may continue to exempt transactions concerning gold other than gold for industrial use; whereas the application by some Member States of that transitional derogation is the cause of a certain distortion of competition;

Whereas gold does not only serve as an input for production but is also acquired for investment purposes; whereas the application of the normal tax rules constitutes a major obstacle to its use for financial investment purposes and therefore justifies the application of a specific tax scheme for investment gold; whereas such a scheme should also enhance the international competitiveness of the Community gold market;

Whereas supplies of gold for investments purposes are similar in nature to other financial investments often exempted from tax under the current rules of the sixth Directive, and therefore exemption from tax appears to be the most appropriate tax treatment for supplies of investment gold;

Whereas the definition of investment gold should only comprise forms and weights of gold of very high purity as traded in the bullion markets and gold coins the value of which primarily reflects its gold price; whereas, in the case of gold coins, for reasons of transparency, a yearly list of qualifying coins should be drawn up providing security for the operators trading in such coins; whereas the legal security of traders demands that coins included in this list be deemed to fulfil the criteria for exemption of this Directive for the whole year for which the list is valid; whereas such list will be without prejudice to the exemption, on a case-by-case basis, of coins, including newly minted coins which are not included in the list but which meet the criteria laid down in this Directive;

Whereas since a tax exemption does, in principle, not allow for the deduction of input tax while tax on the value of the gold may be charged on previous operations, the deduction of such input tax should be allowed in order to guarantee the advantages of the special scheme and to avoid distortions of competition with regard to imported investment gold;

Whereas the possibility of using gold for both industrial and investment purposes requires the possibility for operators to opt for normal taxation where their activity consists either in the producing of investment gold or transformation of any gold into investment gold, or in the wholesale of such gold when they supply in their normal trade gold for industrial purposes;

Whereas the dual use of gold may offer new opportunities for tax fraud and tax evasion that will require effective control measures to be taken by Member States; whereas a common standard of minimum obligations in accounting and documentation to be held by the operators is therefore desirable although, where this information does already exist pursuant to other Community legislation, a Member State may consider these requirements to be met;

Whereas experience has shown that, with regard to most supplies of gold of more than a certain purity the application of a reverse charge mechanism can help to prevent tax fraud while at the same time alleviating the financing charge for the operation; whereas it is justified to allow Member States to use such mechanism; whereas for importation of gold Article 23 of the Sixth Directive allows, in a similar way, that tax is not paid at the moment of importation provided it is mentioned in the declaration pursuant to Article 22(4) of that Directive;

Whereas transactions carried out on a bullion market regulated by a Member State require further simplifications in their tax treatment because of the huge number and the speed of such operations; whereas Member States are allowed to disapply the special scheme, to suspend tax collection and to dispense with recording requirements;

Whereas since the new tax scheme will replace existing provisions under Article 12(3)(e) and point 26 of Annex F of the Sixth Directive, these provisions should be deleted,

HAS ADOPTED THIS DIRECTIVE:

Article 1

The following Article 26b shall be added to Directive 77/388/EEC:

"Article 26b

Special scheme for investment gold

A. Definition

For the purposes of this Directive, and without prejudice to other Community provisions: `investment gold' shall mean:

(i) gold, in the form of a bar or a wafer of weights accepted by the bullion markets, of a purity equal to or greater than 995 thousandths, whether or not represented by securities. Member States may exclude from the scheme small bars or wafers of a weight of 1 g or less;

  (ii) gold coins which:

      — are of a purity equal to or greater than 900 thousandths,

      — are minted after 1800,

      — are or have been legal tender in the country of origin, and

      — are normally sold at a price which does not exceed the open market value of the gold contained in the coins by more than 80 %.

Such coins are not, for the purpose of this Directive, considered to be sold for numismatic interest.

Each Member State shall inform the Commission before 1 July each year, starting in 1999, of the coins meeting these criteria which are traded in that Member State. The Commission shall publish a comprehensive list of these coins in the "C" series of the Official Journal of the European Communities before 1 December each year. Coins included in the published list shall be deemed to fulfil these criteria for the whole year for which the list is published.

B. Special arrangements applicable to investment gold transactions

Member States shall exempt from value added tax the supply, intra-Community acquisition and importation of investment gold, including investment gold represented by certificates for allocated or unallocated gold or traded on gold accounts and including, in particular, gold loans and swaps, involving a right of ownership or claim in respect of investment gold, as well as transactions concerning investment gold involving futures and forward contracts leading to a transfer of right of ownership or claim in respect of investment gold.

Member States shall also exempt services of agents who act in the name and for the account of another when they intervene in the supply of investment gold for their principal.

C. Option to tax

Member States shall allow taxable persons who produce investment gold or transform any gold into investment gold as defined in A a right of option for taxation of supplies of investment gold to another taxable person which would otherwise be exempt under B.

Member States may allow taxable persons, who in their trade normally supply gold for industrial purposes, a right of option for taxation of supplies of investment gold as defined in A(i) to another taxable person, which would otherwise be exempt under B. Member States may restrict the scope of this option.

Where the supplier has exercised a right of option for taxation pursuant to the first or second paragraph, Member States shall allow a right of option for taxation for the agent in respect of the services mentioned in the second paragraph of B.

Member States shall specify the details of the use of these options, and shall inform the Commission of the rules of application for the exercise of these options in that Member State.

D. Right of deduction

1. Taxable persons shall be entitled to deduct

    (a) tax due or paid in respect of investment gold supplied to them by a person who has exercised the right of option under C or supplied to them pursuant to the procedure laid down in G;

    (b) tax due or paid in respect of supply to them, or intra-Community acquisition or importation by them, of gold other than investment gold which is subsequently transformed by them or on their behalf into investment gold

    (c) tax due or paid in respect of services supplied to them consisting of change of form, weight or purity of gold including investment gold,

    if their subsequent supply of this gold is exempt under this Article.

2. Taxable persons who produce investment gold or transform any gold into investment gold, shall be entitled to deduct tax due or paid by them in respect of supplies, or intra-Community acquisition or importation of goods or services linked to the production or transformation of that gold as if their subsequent supply of the gold exempted under this Article were taxable.

E. Special obligations for traders in investment gold

Member States shall, as a minimum, ensure that traders in investment gold keep account of all substantial transactions in investment gold and keep the documentation to allow identification of the customer in such transactions.

Traders shall keep this information for a period of at least five years.

Member States may accept equivalent obligations under measures adopted pursuant to other Community legislation, such as Council Directive 91/308/EEC of 10 June 1991 on prevention of the use of the financial system for the purpose of money laundering, to meet the requirements of the first paragraph.

Member States may lay down stricter obligations, in particular on special record keeping or special accounting requirements.

F. Reverse charge procedure

By way of derogation from Article 21(1)(a), as amended by Article 28g, in the case of supplies of gold material or semi-manufactured products of a purity of 325 thousandths or greater, or supplies of investment gold where an option referred to in C of this Article has been exercised, Member States may designate the purchaser as the person liable to pay the tax, according to the procedures and conditions which they shall lay down. When they exercise this option, Member States shall take the measures necessary to ensure that the person designated as liable for the tax due fulfils the obligations to submit a statement and to pay the tax in accordance with Article 22.

G. Procedure for transactions on a regulated gold bullion market

1. A Member State may, subject to consultation provided for under Article 29, disapply the exemption for investment gold provided for by this special scheme in respect of specific transactions, other than intra-Community supplies or exports, concerning investment gold taking place in that Member State:

   (a) between taxable persons who are members of a bullion market regulated by the Member State concerned, and

   (b) where the transaction is between a member of a bullion market regulated by the Member State concerned and another taxable person who is not a member of that market.

   Under these circumstances, these transactions shall be taxable and the following shall apply.

2. (a) For transactions under 1(a), for the purpose of simplification, the Member State shall authorise suspension of the tax to be collected as well as dispense with the recording requirements of value added tax.

   (b) For transactions under 1(b), the reverse charge procedure under F shall be applicable. Where a non-member of the bullion market would not, other than for these transactions, be liable for registration for VAT in the relevant Member State, the member shall fulfil the fiscal obligations on behalf of the non-member, according to the provisions of that Member State."

Article 2

Article 12(3)(e) and point 26 of Annex F to Directive 77/388/EEC shall be deleted.

Article 3

1. Member States shall bring into force the laws, regulations and administrative provisions necessary to comply with this Directive on 1 January 2000. They shall forthwith inform the Commission thereof.

   When Member States adopt these measures, they shall contain a reference to this Directive or shall be accompanied by such reference on the occasion of their official publication. The methods of making such reference shall be laid down by the Member States.

2. Member States shall communicate to the Commission the text of the provisions of domestic law which they adopt in the field governed by this Directive.

Article 4

This Directive shall enter into force on the day of its publication in the Official Journal of the European Communities.

Article 5

This Directive is addressed to the Member States.

Done at Luxembourg, 12 October 1998.

For the Council

The President

R. EDLINGER

COUNCIL REGULATION (EC) No 98/974

of 3 May 1998

on the introduction of the euro

Official Journal L 139, 11/05/1998 p. 0001-0005

THE COUNCIL OF THE EUROPEAN UNION,

Having regard to the Treaty establishing the European Community, and in particular Article 109l(4), third sentence thereof,

Having regard to the proposal from the Commission,

Having regard to the opinion of the European Monetary Institute,

Having regard to the opinion of the European Parliament,

(1)   Whereas this Regulation defines monetary law provisions of the Member States which have adopted the euro; whereas provisions on continuity of contracts, the replacement of references to the ecu in legal instruments by references to the euro and rounding have already been laid down in Council Regulation (EC) No 1103/97 of 17 June 1997 on certain provisions relating to the introduction of the euro; whereas the introduction of the euro concerns day-to-day operations of the whole population in participating Member States; whereas measures other than those in this Regulation and in Regulation (EC) No 1103/97 should be examined to ensure a balanced changeover, in particular for consumers;

(2)   Whereas, at the meeting of the European Council in Madrid on 15 and 16 December 1995, the decision was taken that the term 'ecu' used by the Treaty to refer to the European currency unit is a generic term; whereas the Governments of the 15 Member States have reached the common agreement that this decision is the agreed and definitive interpretation of the relevant Treaty provisions; whereas the name given to the European currency shall be the 'euro'; whereas the euro as the currency of the participating Member States shall be divided into one hundred sub-units with the name 'cent'; whereas the definition of the name 'cent' does not prevent the use of variants of this term in common usage in the Member States; whereas the European Council furthermore considered that the name of the single currency must be the same in all the official languages of the European Union, taking into account the existence of different alphabets;

(3)   Whereas the Council when acting in accordance with the third sentence of Article 109l(4) of the Treaty shall take the measures necessary for the rapid introduction of the euro other than the adoption of the conversion rates;

(4)   Whereas whenever under Article 109k(2) of the Treaty a Member State becomes a participating Member State, the Council shall according to Article 109l(5) of the Treaty take the other measures necessary for the

rapid introduction of the euro as the single currency of this Member State;

(5)   Whereas according to the first sentence of Article 109l(4) of the Treaty the Council shall at the starting date of the third stage adopt the conversion rates at which the currencies of the participating Member States shall be irrevocably fixed and at which irrevocably fixed rate the euro shall be substituted for these currencies;

(6)   Whereas given the absence of exchange rate risk either between the euro unit and the national currency units or between these national currency units, legislative provisions should be interpreted accordingly;

(7)   Whereas the term 'contract' used for the definition of legal instruments is meant to include all types of contracts, irrespective of the way in which they are concluded;

(8)   Whereas in order to prepare a smooth changeover to the euro a transitional period is needed between the substitution of the euro for the currencies of the participating Member States and the introduction of euro banknotes and coins; whereas during this period the national currency units will be defined as sub-divisions of the euro; whereas thereby a legal equivalence is established between the euro unit and the national currency units;

(9)   Whereas in accordance with Article 109g of the Treaty and with Regulation (EC) No 1103/97, the euro will replace the ECU as from 1 January 1999 as the unit of account of the institutions of the European Communities; whereas the euro should also be the unit of account of the European Central Bank (ECB) and of the central banks of the participating Member States; whereas, in line with the Madrid conclusions, monetary policy operations will be carried out in the euro unit by the European System of Central Banks (ESCB); whereas this does not prevent national central banks from keeping accounts in their national currency unit during the transitional period, in particular for their staff and for public administrations;

(10)   Whereas each participating Member State may allow the full use of the euro unit in its territory during the transitional period;

(11)   Whereas during the transitional period contracts, national laws and other legal instruments can be drawn up validly in the euro unit or in the national currency unit; whereas during this period, nothing in this Regulation should affect the validity of any reference to a national currency unit in any legal instrument;

(12)   Whereas, unless agreed otherwise, economic agents have to respect the denomination of a legal instrument in the performance of all acts to be carried out under that instrument;

(13)   Whereas the euro unit and the national currency units are units of the same currency; whereas it should be ensured that payments inside a participating Member State by crediting an account can be made either in the euro unit or the respective national currency unit; whereas the

provisions on payments by crediting an account should also apply to those cross-border payments, which are denominated in the euro unit or the national currency unit of the account of the creditor; whereas it is necessary to ensure the smooth functioning of payment systems by laying down provisions dealing with the crediting of accounts by payment instruments credited through those systems; whereas the provisions on payments by crediting an account should not imply that financial intermediaries are obliged to make available either other payment facilities or products denominated in any particular unit of the euro; whereas the provisions on payments by crediting an account do not prohibit financial intermediaries from coordinating the introduction of payment facilities denominated in the euro unit which rely on a common technical infrastructure during the transitional period;

(14) Whereas in accordance with the conclusions reached by the European Council at its meeting held in Madrid, new tradeable public debt will be issued in the euro unit by the participating Member States as from 1 January 1999; whereas it is desirable to allow issuers of debt to redenominate outstanding debt in the euro unit; whereas the provisions on redenomination should be such that they can also be applied in the jurisdictions of third countries; whereas issuers should be enabled to redenominate outstanding debt if the debt is denominated in a national currency unit of a Member State which has redenominated part or all of the outstanding debt of its general government; whereas these provisions do not address the introduction of additional measures to amend the terms of outstanding debt to alter, among other things, the nominal amount of outstanding debt, these being matters subject to relevant national law; whereas it is desirable to allow Member States to take appropriate measures for changing the unit of account of the operating procedures of organised markets;

(15) Whereas further action at the Community level may also be necessary to clarify the effect of the introduction of the euro on the application of existing provisions of Community law, in particular concerning netting, set-off and techniques of similar effect;

(16) Whereas any obligation to use the euro unit can only be imposed on the basis of Community legislation; whereas in transactions with the public sector participating Member States may allow the use of the euro unit; whereas in accordance with the reference scenario decided by the European Council at its meeting held in Madrid, the Community legislation laying down the time frame for the generalisation of the use of the euro unit might leave some freedom to individual Member States;

(17) Whereas in accordance with Article 105a of the Treaty the Council may adopt measures to harmonise the denominations and technical specifications of all coins;

(18) Whereas banknotes and coins need adequate protection against counterfeiting;

(19) Whereas banknotes and coins denominated in the national currency units lose their status of legal tender at the latest six months after the end of the transitional period; whereas limitations on payments in notes and coins, established by Member States for public reasons, are not incompatible with the status of legal tender of euro banknotes and coins, provided that other lawful means for the settlement of monetary debts are available;

(20) Whereas as from the end of the transitional period references in legal instruments existing at the end of the transitional period will have to be read as references to the euro unit according to the respective conversion rates; whereas a physical redenomination of existing legal instruments is therefore not necessary to achieve this result; whereas the rounding rules defined in Regulation (EC) No 1103/97 shall also apply to the conversions to be made at the end of the transitional period or after the transitional period; whereas for reasons of clarity it may be desirable that the physical redenomination will take place as soon as appropriate;

(21) Whereas paragraph 2 of Protocol 11 on certain provisions relating to the United Kingdom of Great Britain and Northern Ireland stipulates that, inter alia, paragraph 5 of that Protocol shall have effect if the United Kingdom notifies the Council that it does not intend to move to the third stage; whereas the United Kingdom gave notice to the Council on 30 October 1997 that it does not intend to move to the third stage; whereas paragraph 5 stipulates that, inter alia, Article 109l(4) of the Treaty shall not apply to the United Kingdom;

(22) Whereas Denmark, referring to paragraph 1 of Protocol 12 on certain provisions relating to Denmark has notified, in the context of the Edinburgh decision of 12 December 1992, that it will not participate in the third stage; whereas, therefore, in accordance with paragraph 2 of the said Protocol, all Articles and provisions of the Treaty and the Statute of the ESCB referring to a derogation shall be applicable to Denmark;

(23) Whereas, in accordance with Article 109l(4) of the Treaty, the single currency will be introduced only in the Member States without a derogation;

(24) Whereas this Regulation, therefore, shall be applicable pursuant to Article 189 of the Treaty, subject to Protocols 11 and 12 and Article 109k(1),

HAS ADOPTED THIS REGULATION:

PART I

definitions

[Article 1

For the purpose of this Regulation:

(a) **"participating Member States"** shall mean the Member States listed in the table in the Annex;

(b) **"legal instruments"** shall mean legislative and statutory provisions, acts of administration, judicial decisions, contracts, unilateral legal acts, payment instruments other than banknotes and coins, and other instruments with legal effect;

(c) **"conversion rate"** shall mean the irrevocably fixed conversion rate adopted for the currency of each participating Member State by the Council in accordance with the first sentence of Article 123(4) of the Treaty or with paragraph 5 of that Article;

(d) **"euro adoption date"** shall mean either the date on which the respective Member State enters the third stage under Article 121(3) of the Treaty or the date on which the abrogation of the respective Member State's derogation under Article 122(2) of the Treaty enters into force, as the case may be;

(e) **"cash changeover date"** shall mean the date on which euro banknotes and coins acquire the status of legal tender in a given participating Member State;

(f) **"euro unit"** shall mean the currency unit as referred to in the second sentence of Article 2;

(g) **"national currency units"** shall mean the units of the currency of a participating Member State, as those units are defined on the day before the adoption of the euro in that Member State;

(h) **"transitional period"** shall mean a period of three years at the most beginning at 00.00 hours on the euro adoption date and ending at 00.00 hours on the cash changeover date;

(i) **"phasing-out period"** shall mean a period of one year at the most beginning on the euro adoption date, which can only apply to Member States where the euro adoption date and the cash changeover date fall on the same day;

(j) **"redenominate"** shall mean changing the unit in which the amount of outstanding debt is stated from a national currency unit to the euro unit, but which does not have through the act of redenomination the effect of altering any other term of the debt, this being a matter subject to relevant national law;

(k) **"credit institutions"** shall mean credit institutions as defined in Article 1(1) of Directive 2000/12/EC of the European Parliament and of the

Council of 20 March 2000 relating to the taking up and pursuit of the business of credit institutions. For the purpose of this Regulation, the institutions listed in Article 2(3) of that Directive with the exception of post office giro institutions shall not be considered as credit institutions.][1]

[Article 1a

The euro adoption date, the cash changeover date, and the phasing-out period, if applicable, for each participating Member State shall be as set out in the Annex.][2]

PART II
substitution of the euro for the currencies of the participating member states

[Article 2

With effect from the respective euro adoption dates, the currency of the participating Member States shall be the euro. The currency unit shall be one euro. One euro shall be divided into one hundred cent.][3]

Article 3

The euro shall be substituted for the currency of each participating Member State at the conversion rate.

Article 4

The euro shall be the unit of account of the European Central Bank (ECB) and of the central banks of the participating Member States.

PART III
transitional provisions

Article 5

Articles 6, 7, 8 and 9 shall apply during the transitional period.

Article 6

1. The euro shall also be divided into the national currency units according to the conversion rates. Any subdivision thereof shall be maintained. Subject to the provisions of this Regulation the monetary law of the participating Member States shall continue to apply.

2. Where in a legal instrument reference is made to a national currency unit, this reference shall be as valid as if reference were made to the euro unit according to the conversion rates.

Article 7

The substitution of the euro for the currency of each participating Member State shall not in itself have the effect of altering the denomination of legal instruments in existence on the date of substitution.

Article 8

1. Acts to be performed under legal instruments stipulating the use of or denominated in a national currency unit shall be performed in that national currency unit. Acts to be performed under legal instruments stipulating the use of or denominated in the euro unit shall be performed in that unit.

2. The provisions of paragraph 1 are subject to anything which parties may have agreed.

3. Notwithstanding the provisions of paragraph 1, any amount denominated either in the euro unit or in the national currency unit of a given participating Member State and payable within that Member State by crediting an account of the creditor, can be paid by the debtor either in the euro unit or in that national currency unit. The amount shall be credited to the account of the creditor in the denomination of his account, with any conversion being effected at the conversion rates.

4. Notwithstanding the provisions of paragraph 1, each participating Member State may take measures which may be necessary in order to:

   - redenominate in the euro unit outstanding debt issued by that Member State's general government, as defined in the European system of integrated accounts, denominated in its national currency unit and issued under its own law. If a Member State has taken such a measure, issuers may redenominate in the euro unit debt denominated in that Member State's national currency unit unless redenomination is expressly excluded by the terms of the contract; this provision shall apply to debt issued by the general government of a Member State as well as to bonds and other forms of securitised debt negotiable in the capital markets, and to money market instruments, issued by other debtors,

   - enable the change of the unit of account of their operating procedures from a national currency unit to the euro unit by:

   (a) markets for the regular exchange, clearing and settlement of any instrument listed in section B of the Annex to Council Directive 93/22/EEC of 10 May 1993 on investment services in the securities field and of commodities; and

   (b) systems for the regular exchange, clearing and settlement of payments.

5. Provisions other than those of paragraph 4 imposing the use of the euro unit may only be adopted by the participating Member States in

accordance with any time-frame laid down by Community legislation.

6. National legal provisions of participating Member States which permit or impose netting, set-off or techniques with similar effects shall apply to monetary obligations, irrespective of their currency denomination, if that denomination is in the euro unit or in a national currency unit, with any conversion being effected at the conversion rates.

[Article 9

Banknotes and coins denominated in a national currency unit shall retain their status as legal tender within their territorial limits as from the day before the euro adoption date in the participating Member State concerned.][4]

[Article 9a

The following shall apply in a Member State with a "phasing-out" period. In legal instruments created during the phasing-out period and to be performed in that Member State, reference may continue to be made to the national currency unit. These references shall be read as references to the euro unit according to the respective conversion rates. Without prejudice to Article 15, the acts performed under these legal instruments shall be performed only in the euro unit. The rounding rules laid down in Regulation (EC) No 1103/97 shall apply.

TheMemberStateconcernedshalllimittheapplicationofthefirstsubparagraph to certain types of legal instrument, or to legal instruments adopted in certain fields.

The Member State concerned may shorten the period.][5]

PART IV
euro banknotes and coins
[Article 10

With effect from the respective cash changeover dates, the ECB and the central banks of the participating Member States shall put into circulation banknotes denominated in euro in the participating Member States.

Without prejudice to Article 15, these banknotes denominated in euro shall be the only banknotes which have the status of legal tender in participating Member States.

Article 11

With effect from the respective cash changeover date, the participating Member States shall issue coins denominated in euro or in cent and complying with the denominations and technical specifications which the Council may lay down in accordance with the second sentence of Article 106(2) of the Treaty. Without prejudice to Article 15 and to the provisions of any agreement under Article 111(3) of the Treaty concerning monetary matters, those coins shall be the only coins which have the status of legal tender in participating Member

States. Except for the issuing authority and for those persons specifically designated by the national legislation of the issuing Member State, no party shall be obliged to accept more than 50 coins in any single payment.][6]

Article 12

Participating Member States shall ensure adequate sanctions against counterfeiting and falsification of euro banknotes and coins.

PART V
final provisions

[Article 13

Articles 10, 11, 14, 15 and 16 shall apply with effect from the respective cash changeover date in each participating Member State.

Article 14

Where, in legal instruments existing on the day before the cash changeover date, reference is made to the national currency units, these references shall be read as references to the euro unit according to the respective conversion rates. The rounding rules laid down in Regulation (EC) No 1103/97 shall apply.][7]

Article 15

1. Banknotes and coins denominated in a national currency unit as referred to in Article 6(1) shall remain legal tender within their territorial limits until six months [from the respective cash changeover date][8] at the latest; this period may be shortened by national law.

2. Each participating Member State may, for a period of up to six months [from the respective cash changeover date][8], lay down rules for the use of the banknotes and coins denominated in its national currency unit as referred to in Article 6(1) and take any measures necessary to facilitate their withdrawal.

[3. During the period referred to in paragraph 1, credit institutions in participating Member States adopting the euro after 1 January 2002 shall exchange their customers' banknotes and coins denominated in the national currency unit of that Member State for banknotes and coins in euro, free of charge, up to a ceiling which may be set by national law. Credit institutions may require that notice be given if the amount to be exchanged exceeds a ceiling set by national law or, in the absence of such provisions, by themselves and corresponding to a household amount.

The credit institutions referred to in the first subparagraph shall exchange banknotes and coins denominated in the national currency unit of that Member State of persons other than their customers, free of charge up to a ceiling set by national law or, in the absence of such provisions, by themselves.

National law may limit the obligation under the preceding two subparagraphs to specific types of credit institutions. National law may also extend this obligation upon other persons.][9]

Article 16

In accordance with the laws or practices of participating Member States, the respective issuers of banknotes and coins shall continue to accept, against euro at the conversion rate, the banknotes and coins previously issued by them.

PART VI

entry into force Article 17

This Regulation shall enter into force on 1 January 1999.

This Regulation shall be binding in its entirety and directly applicable in all Member States, in accordance with the Treaty, subject to Protocols 11 and 12 and Article 109k(1).

Done at Brussels, 3 May 1998.
For the Council The President

G. BROWN

[ANNEX

Member State	Euro adoption date	Cash changeover date	Member State with a "phasing-out" period
Belgium	1 January 1999	1 January 2002	n/a
Germany	1 January 1999	1 January 2002	n/a
Greece	1 January 2001	1 January 2002	n/a
Spain	1 January 1999	1 January 2002	n/a
France	1 January 1999	1 January 2002	n/a
Ireland	1 January 1999	1 January 2002	n/a
Italy	1 January 1999	1 January 2002	n/a
[Cyprus	1 January 2008	1 January 2008	No][11]
Luxembourg	1 January 1999	1 January 2002	n/a
[Malta	1 January 2008	1 January 2008	No][12]
Netherlands	1 January 1999	1 January 2002	n/a
Austria	1 January 1999	1 January 2002	n/a
Portugal	1 January 1999	1 January 2002	n/a
[Slovenia	1 January 2007	1 January 2007	No][10]
[Slovakia	1 January 2009	1 January 2009	No][14]
Finland	1 January 1999	1 January 2002	n/a

][13]

Amendments

1   Article 1 replaced by Art 1(1) Council Regulation (EC) No 2169/2005 of 21 December 2005
2   Article 1a inserted by Art 1(2) Council Regulation (EC) No 2169/2005 of 21 December 2005
3   Article 2 replaced by Art 1(3) Council Regulation (EC) No 2169/2005 of 21 December 2005
4   Article 9 replaced by Art 1(4) Council Regulation (EC) No 2169/2005 of 21 December 2005
5   Article 9a inserted by Art 1(5) Council Regulation (EC) No 2169/2005 of 21 December 2005

6 Articles 10 and 11 replaced by Art 1(6) Council Regulation (EC) No 2169/2005 of 21 December 2005
7 Articles 13 and 14 replaced by Art 1(7) Council Regulation (EC) No 2169/2005 of 21 December 2005
8 Article 15 amended by Art 1(8)(a) Council Regulation (EC) No 2169/2005 of 21 December 2005
9 Article 15(3) inserted by Art 1(8)(b) Council Regulation (EC) No 2169/2005 of 21 December 2005
10 Inserted by Art 1 Council Regulation (EC) No 1647/2006 of 7 November 2006
11 Inserted by Art 1 Council Regulation (EC) No 834/2007 of 10 July 2007
12 Inserted by Art 1 Council Regulation (EC) No 836/2007 of 10 July 2007
13 Annex replaced by Art 1(9) Council Regulation (EC) No 2169/2005 of 21 December 2005
14 Inserted by Art 1 Council Regulation (EC) No 693/2008 of 8 July 2008

COUNCIL REGULATION (EC) No 98/2866

of 31 December 1998

on the conversion rates between the euro and the currencies of the Member States adopting the euro

Official Journal L 359 , 31/12/1998 p. 0001-0002

THE COUNCIL OF THE EUROPEAN UNION,

Having regard to the Treaty establishing the European Community, and in particular Article 109l(4), first sentence thereof,

Having regard to the proposal from the Commission,

Having regard to the opinion of the European Central Bank,

(1)　Whereas according to Article 109j(4) of the Treaty, the third stage of Economic and Monetary Union shall start on 1 January 1999; whereas the Council, meeting in the composition of Heads of State or Government, has confirmed on 3 May 1998 that Belgium, Germany, Spain, France, Ireland, Italy, Luxembourg, the Netherlands, Austria, Portugal and Finland fulfil the necessary conditions for the adoption of a single currency on 1 January 1999;

(2)　Whereas according to Council Regulation (EC) No 974/98 of 3 May 1998 on the introduction of the euro, the euro shall be the currency of the Member States which adopt the single currency as from 1 January 1999; whereas the introduction of the euro requires the adoption of the conversion rates at which the euro will be substituted for the national currencies and at which rates the euro will be divided into national currency units; whereas the conversion rates in Article 1 are the conversion rates referred to in the third indent of Article 1 of Regulation (EC) No 974/98;

(3)　Whereas according to Council Regulation (EC) No 1103/97 of 17 June 1997 on certain provisions relating to the introduction of the euro, every reference to the ECU in a legal instrument shall be replaced by a reference to the euro at a rate of one euro to one ECU; whereas Article 109l(4), second sentence, of the Treaty, provides that the adoption of the conversion rates shall by itself not modify the external value of the ECU; whereas this is ensured by adopting as the conversion rates, the exchange rates against the ECU of the currencies of the Member States adopting the euro, as calculated by the Commission on 31 December 1998 according to the established procedure for the calculation of the daily official ECU rates;

(4)　Whereas the Ministers of the Member States adopting the euro as their single currency, the Governors of the Central Banks of these Member States, the Commission and the European Monetary Institute/ the European Central Bank, have issued two Communiqués on the determination and on the adoption of the irrevocable conversion rates for the euro dated 3 May 1998 and 26 September 1998, respectively;

(5)   Whereas Regulation (EC) No 1103/97 stipulates that the conversion rates
        shall be adopted as one euro expressed in terms of each of the national
        currencies of the Member States adopting the euro; whereas in order to
        ensure a high degree of accuracy, these rates will be adopted with six
        significant figures and no inverse rates nor bilateral rates between the
        currencies of the Member States adopting the euro will be defined,

HAS ADOPTED THIS REGULATION:

Article 1

The irrevocably fixed conversion rates between the euro and the currencies of
the Member States adopting the euro are:

1 euro =	40,3399 Belgian francs
=	1,95583 German marks
[=	340,750 Greek drachma][1]
=	166,386 Spanish pesetas
=	6,55957 French francs
=	0,787564 Irish pounds
=	1,936,27 Italian lire
[=	0,585274 Cyprus pounds][2]
=	40,3399 Luxembourg francs
[=	0,429300 Maltese liras][3]
=	2,20371 Dutch guilders
=	13,7603 Austrian schillings
=	200,482 Portuguese escudos
[=	239,640 Slovenian tolars][4]
[=	30,1260 Slovak korunas][5]
=	5,94573 Finnish marks.

Article 2

This Regulation shall enter into force on 1 January 1999.

This Regulation shall be binding in its entirety and directly applicable in all
Member States.

Done at Brussels, 31 December 1998.
For the Council
The President
R. EDLINGER

Amendments
1   Inserted by Council Regulation 1478/2000 of 19 June 2000 (w.e.f. 1 January 2001)
2   Inserted by Council Regulation (EC) No 1135/2007 of 10 July 2007 (w.e.f. 1 January 2008)
3   Inserted by Council Regulation (EC) No 1134/2007 of 10 July 2007 (w.e.f. 1 January 2008
4   Inserted by Council Regulation 1086/2006 of 11 July 2006 (w.e.f. 1 January 2007)
5   Inserted by Council Regulation 694/2008 (w.e.f. 1 January 2009)

COUNCIL DIRECTIVE 1999/49/EC

of 25 May 1999

Amending, with regard to the level of the standard rate, Directive 77/388/EEC

on the common system of value added tax

Official Journal L 139 , 02/06/1999 p. 0027 - 0028

> This Directive was repealed by Council Directive 2006/112/EC of 28 November 2006 on the common system of value added tax, with effect from 1 January 2007

THE COUNCIL OF THE EUROPEAN UNION,

Having regard to the Treaty establishing the European Community, and in particular Article 93 thereof,

Having regard to the proposal from the Commission,

Having regard to the opinion of the European Parliament,

Having regard to the opinion of the Economic and Social Committee,

(1) Whereas Article 12(3)(a) of sixth Council Directive 77/388/EEC of 17 May 1977 on the harmonisation of the laws of the Member States relating to turnover taxes - Common system of value added tax: uniform basis of assessment(4), lays down that the Council shall decide on the level of the standard rate to be applied after 31 December 1998; whereas the standard rate of value added tax is fixed by each Member State as a percentage of the taxable amount and is the same for the supply of goods and for the supply of services; whereas from 1 January 1993 until 31 December 1998, this percentage may not be less than 15%;

(2) Whereas experience has shown that the standard rate of value added tax currently in force in the various Member States, combined with the mechanism of the transitional system, have ensured that this transitional system has functioned satisfactorily; whereas it seems therefore appropriate, with regard to the standard rate, to maintain the current level of the minimum rate for a further period of time;

(3) Whereas, however, the Commission report on rates highlighted the fact that distortions of competition exist and are likely to be accentuated by the introduction of the single currency; whereas the period of application of the standard rate should be limited to two years in order to enable the Council at a later stage to decide on the levels of both the standard rate and reduced rate or rates,

HAS ADOPTED THIS DIRECTIVE:

Article 1

Article 12(3)(a) of Directive 77/388/EEC shall be replaced by the following:

"(a) The standard rate of value added tax shall be fixed by each Member State as a percentage of the taxable amount and shall be the same for the supply of goods and for the supply of services. From 1 January 1999 until 31 December 2000, this percentage may not be less than 15%.

On a proposal from the Commission and after consulting the European Parliament and the Economic and Social Committee, the Council shall decide unanimously on the level of the standard rate to be applied after 31 December 2000.

Member States may also apply either one or two reduced rates. These rates shall be fixed as a percentage of the taxable amount, which may not be less than 5%, and shall apply only to supplies of the categories of goods and services specified in Annex H."

Article 2

1. Member States shall bring into force the laws, regulations and administrative provisions necessary to comply with this Directive by 1 January 1999 at the latest. They shall forthwith inform the Commission thereof.

   When Member States adopt these measures, they shall contain a reference to this Directive or shall be accompanied by such reference at the time of their official publication. The methods of making such a reference shall be laid down by the Member States.

2. Member States shall communicate to the Commission the text of the provisions of domestic law which they adopt in the field covered by this Directive.

Article 3

This Directive shall enter into force on the day of its publication in the Official Journal of the European Communities.

It shall apply from 1 January 1999.

Article 4

This Directive is addressed to the Member States.

Done at Brussels, 25 May 1999.

For the Council

The President

H. EICHEL

COUNCIL DIRECTIVE 1999/59/EC

of 17 June 1999

Amending Directive 77/388/EEC as regards the value added tax arrangements
applicable to telecommunications services

Official Journal L 162 , 26/06/1999 p. 0063 - 0064

This Directive was repealed by Council Directive 2006/112/EC of 28 November 2006 on the common system of value added tax, with effect from 1 January 2007

THE COUNCIL OF THE EUROPEAN UNION,

Having regard to the Treaty establishing the European Community, and in particular Article 93 thereof,

Having regard to the proposal from the Commission,

Having regard to the Opinion of the European Parliament,

Having regard to the Opinion of the Economic and Social Committee,

Whereas:

(1) Article 14 of the Treaty defines the internal market as comprising an area without internal frontiers in which the free movement of goods, persons, services and capital is ensured in accordance with the provisions of the Treaty;

(2) the rules currently applicable to VAT on telecommunications services under Article 9 of the Sixth Council Directive (77/388/EEC) of 17 May 1977 on the harmonisation of the laws of the Member States relating to turnover taxes - Common system of value added tax: uniform basis of assessment are inadequate for taxing all such services consumed within the Community and for preventing distortions of competition in this area;

(3) in the interests of the proper functioning of the internal market, such distortions should be eliminated and new harmonised rules introduced for this type of activity;

(4) action should be taken to ensure, in particular, that telecommunications services used by customers established in the Community are taxed in the Community;

(5) to this end, telecommunications services supplied to taxable persons established in the Community or to recipients established in third countries should, in principle, be taxed at the place of the recipient of the services;

(6) in order to ensure uniform taxation of telecommunications services supplied by taxable persons established in third countries to non-taxable persons established in the Community which are effectively used or enjoyed in the Community, Member States should make use of the provisions of Article 9(3)(b) of Directive 77/388/EEC on changing the place of supply; whereas, however, Article 9(3) of that Directive may remain applicable

where corresponding telecommunications services are supplied to other recipients in the Community;

(7) for the purpose of establishing a special rule for determining the place of supply of telecommunications services, such services need to be defined; such definition should draw on definitions already adopted at international level, which include international telephone call routing and termination services and access to global information networks;

(8) taxation at the place of the recipient of the services also means that taxable persons will not have to have recourse to the procedures under Directives 79/1072/EEC and 86/560/EEC; the new rules for determining the place of supply should not mean that foreign taxable persons have to be identified for tax purposes in another State; this will be achieved by making it compulsory for the recipient of the services to be liable for the tax, provided that recipient is a taxable person;

(9) Directive 77/388/EEC should be amended accordingly,

HAS ADOPTED THIS DIRECTIVE:

Article 1

Directive 77/388/EEC is hereby amended as follows:

1. At the end of Article 9(2)(e), the full stop shall be replaced by a semicolon and the following new indent shall be added:

   "- Telecommunications. Telecommunications services shall be deemed to be services relating to the transmission, emission or reception of signals, writing, images and sounds or information of any nature by wire, radio, optical or other electromagnetic systems, including the related transfer or assignment of the right to use capacity for such transmission, emission or reception. Telecommunications services within the meaning of this provision shall also include provision of access to global information networks."

2. The following paragraph 4 shall be added after Article 9(3):

   "4. In the case of telecommunications services referred to in paragraph 2(e) supplied by a taxable person established outside the Community to non-taxable persons established inside the Community, Member States shall make use of paragraph 3(b)."

3. Article 21(1)(b) shall be replaced by the following:

   "(b) taxable persons to whom services covered by Article 9(2)(e) are supplied or persons who are identified for value added tax purposes within the territory of the country to whom services covered by Article 28b(C), (D), (E) and (F) are supplied, if the services are carried out by a taxable person established abroad; however, Member States may require that the supplier of services shall be held jointly and severally liable for payment of the tax;"

Article 2

1. Member States shall adopt the laws, regulations and administrative provisions necessary to comply with this Directive by 1 January 2000. They shall inform the Commission thereof.

   When Member States adopt these measures, they shall contain a reference to this Directive or shall be accompanied by such reference at the time of their official publication. The methods of making such reference shall be laid down by the Member States.

2. Member States shall communicate to the Commission the text of the provisions of domestic law which they adopt in the field covered by this Directive.

Article 3

This Directive shall enter into force on the day of its publication in the Official Journal of the European Communities.

Article 4

This Directive is addressed to the Member States.

Done at Luxembourg, 17 June 1999.

For the Council

The President

F. MÜNTEFERING

COUNCIL DIRECTIVE 1999/85/EC

of 22 October 1999

Amending Directive 77/388/EEC as regards the possibility of applying on an experiment basis a reduced VAT rate on labour-intensive services

Official Journal L 277 , 28/10/1999 p. 0034 - 0036

This Directive was repealed by Council Directive 2006/112/EC of 28 November 2006 on the common system of value added tax, with effect from 1 January 2007

THE COUNCIL OF THE EUROPEAN UNION,

Having regard to the Treaty establishing the European Community, and in particular Article 93 thereof,

Having regard to the proposal from the Commission,

Having regard to the opinion of the European Parliament,

Having regard to the opinion of the Economic and Social Committee,

Whereas:

(1) Article 12(3)(a) of Council Directive 77/388/EEC of 17 May 1977 on the harmonisation of the laws of the Member States relating to turnover taxes - common system of value added tax: uniform basis of assessment(4) provides that the Member States may apply either one or two reduced rates only to supplies of goods and services of the categories specified in Annex H to Directive 77/388/EEC;

(2) however, the problem of unemployment is so serious that those Member States wishing to do so should be allowed to experiment with the operation and impact, in terms of job creation, of a reduction in the VAT rate on labour-intensive services which are not currently listed in Annex H;

(3) this reduced VAT rate is likely to reduce the incentive for the businesses concerned to join or remain in the black economy;

(4) however, the introduction of a targeted reduction in the VAT rate could have a negative impact on the smooth functioning of the internal market and on tax neutrality; provision should therefore be made for an authorisation procedure to be introduced for a full and clearly defined three-year period and for the scope of this measure to be made subject to strict conditions so that it remains verifiable and limited;

(5) in view of the experimental nature of the measure, a detailed assessment of its impact in terms of job creation and efficiency should be carried out by the Member States which implement it and by the Commission;

(6) the measure should be strictly limited in time and should end by 31 December 2002 at the latest;

(7) implementation of this Directive does not involve any amendment of the laws of the Member States,

HAS ADOPTED THIS DIRECTIVE:

Article 1

Directive 77/388/EEC is hereby amended as follows:

1. the following paragraph shall be added to Article 28:

    "6. The Council, acting unanimously on a proposal from the Commission, may authorise any Member State to apply for a maximum period of three years between 1 January 2000 and 31 December 2002 the reduced rates provided for in the third subparagraph of Article 12(3)(a) to services listed in as maximum of two of the categories set out in Annex K. In exceptional cases a Member State may be authorised to apply the reduced rate to services in three of the abovementioned categories.

    The services concerned must satisfy the following requirements:

    (a) they must be labour-intensive;

    (b) they must be largely provided direct to final consumers;

    (c) they must be mainly local and not likely to create distortions of competition;

    (d) there must be a close link between the lower prices resulting from the rate reduction and the foreseeable increase in demand and employment.

    The application of a reduced rate must not prejudice the smooth functioning of the internal market.

    Any Member State wishing to introduce the measure provided for in the first subparagraph shall inform the Commission before 1 November 1999 and shall provide it before that date with all relevant particulars, and in particular the following:

    (a) scope of the measure and detailed description of the services concerned;

    (b) particulars showing that the conditions laid down in the second and third subparagraphs have been met;

    (c) particulars showing the budgetary cost of the measure envisaged.

    Those Member States authorised to apply the reduced rate referred to in the first subparagraph shall, before 1 October 2002, draw up a detailed report containing an overall assessment of the measure's effectiveness in terms notably of job creation and efficiency.

    Before 31 December 2002 the Commission shall forward a global evaluation report to the Council and Parliament accompanied, if necessary, by a proposal for appropriate measures for a final decision on the VAT rate applicable to labour-intensive services."

2. A new Annex K shall be added as set out in the Annex to this Directive.

Article 2

This Directive shall enter into force on the day of its publication in the Official Journal of the European Communities.

Article 3

This Directive is addressed to the Member States.

Done at Luxembourg, 22 October 1999.
For the Council
The President
S. MÖNKÄRE

ANNEX

"ANNEX K

List of supplies of services referred to in Article 28(6)

1. Small services of repairing:

   − bicycles,

   − clothing and household linen (including mending and alteration).

2. Renovation and repairing of private dwellings, excluding materials which form a significant part of the value of the supply.

3. Window cleaning and cleaning in private households.

4. Domestic care services (e.g. home help and care of the young, elderly, sick or disabled).

5. Hairdressing."

COUNCIL DIRECTIVE 2000/17/EC

of 30 March 2000

amending Directive 77/388/EEC on the common system of value added tax - transitional provisions granted to the Republic of Austria and the Portuguese Republic

Official Journal L 084, 05/04/2000 p. 0024 - 0025

> This Directive was repealed by Council Directive 2006/112/EC of 28 November 2006 on the common system of value added tax, with effect from 1 January 2007

THE COUNCIL OF THE EUROPEAN UNION,

Having regard to the Treaty establishing the European Community, and in particular Article 93 thereof,

Having regard to the proposal from the Community,

Having regard to the opinion of the European Parliament,

Having regard to the opinion of the Economic and Social Committee,

Whereas:

(1) Point 2(e) of Part IX "Taxation" of Annex XV to the 1994 Act of Accession authorised the Republic of Austria to derogate from Article 28(2) of sixth Council Directive 77/388/EEC of 17 May 1977 on the harmonisation of the laws of the Member States relating to turnover taxes - common system of value added tax: uniform basis of assessment, (hereinafter referred to as the "sixth VAT Directive") and to apply a reduced rate to the letting of immovable property for residential use until 31 December 1998, provided that the rate was not lower than 10 %.

(2) Under Article 13(B)(b) of the sixth VAT Directive, the letting of immovable property for residential use in Austria has been exempt from VAT since 1 January 1999 without the right to deduct input tax. However, under Article 13(C)(a) of that Directive, Austria may allow taxpayers the right to opt for taxation. In that case, the normal VAT rate and the normal rules for the right to deduction apply.

(3) The Republic of Austria considers that the measure is still essential, mainly because the transitional VAT regime is still in force and the situation has not really changed since the negotiation of the 1994 Act of Accession.

(4) The Republic of Austria also considers that dispensing with the reduced rate of 10 % would inevitably lead to an increase in the price of immovable property rental for the final consumer.

(5) The Portuguese Republic applied a reduced rate of 8 % to restaurant services as at 1 January 1991. Under Article 28(2)(d) of the sixth VAT Directive, Portugal was permitted to continue applying that rate. However, after a comprehensive amendment of the rates and for

political and budgetary reasons, restaurant services were made subject to the normal rate from 1992.

(6)   The Portuguese Republic wishes to reintroduce a reduced rate on these services on the basis that maintaining the normal rate had adverse consequences, in particular job losses and an increase in undeclared employment, and that application of the normal rate increased the price of restaurant services for the final consumer.

(7)   As the derogations in question concern supplies of services within a single Member State, the risk of distortion of competition can be considered non-existent.

(8)   In these circumstances, return to the previous situation may be considered for both the Republic of Austria and the Portuguese Republic, provided that application of the derogations is limited to the transitional period referred to in Article 281 of the sixth VAT Directive. However, the Republic of Austria must take the necessary steps to ensure that the reduced rate has no adverse effects on the European Communities' own resources accruing from VAT, the basis of assessment for which must be reconstituted in accordance with Regulation (EEC, Euratom) No 1553/89,

HAS ADOPTED THIS DIRECTIVE:

Article 1

The following points shall be added to Article 28(2) of the sixth VAT Directive:

"j)   the Republic of Austria may apply one of the two reduced rates provided for in the third subparagraph of Article 12(3)(a) to the letting of immovable property for residential use, provided that the rate is not lower than 10 %;

k)   the Portuguese Republic may apply one of the two reduced rates provided for in the third subparagraph of Article 12(3)(a) to restaurant services, provided that the rate is not lower than 12 %."

Article 2

1.   The Member States referred to in Article 1 shall bring into force the laws, regulations and administrative provisions necessary to comply with this Directive. They shall forthwith inform the Commission thereof.

When the Member States adopt these measures, they shall contain a reference to this Directive or shall be accompanied by such a reference on the occasion of their official publication. The methods for making such a reference shall be laid down by the Member States.

2.   The Member States referred to in Article 1 shall communicate to the Commission the text of the provisions of national law which they adopt in the field governed by this Directive.

Article 3

This Directive shall enter into force on the day of its publication in the Official Journal of the European Communities.

It shall apply as from 1 January 1999 until the end of the transitional period referred to in Article 281 of the sixth VAT Directive.

Article 4

This Directive is addressed to the Member States.

Done at Brussels, 30 March 2000.

For the Council
The President
J. Sócrates

COMMISSION REGULATION (EC) No 2000/1901

of 7 September 2000

laying down certain provisions for the implementation of Council Regulation (EEC) No 3330/91 on the statistics relating to the trading of goods between Member States

Official Journal L228, 08/09/2000 p. 0028 - 0049

> Repealed by Commission Regulation (EC) No 1982/2004 of 18 November 2004 implementing Regulation (EC) No 638/2004 of the European Parliament and of the Council on Community statistics relating to the trading of goods between Member States and repealing Commission Regulations (EC) No 1901/2000 and (EEC) No 3590/92, w.e.f 1 January 2005.

THE COMMISSION OF THE EUROPEAN COMMUNITIES,

Having regard to the Treaty establishing the European Community,

Having regard to Council Regulation (EEC) No 3330/91 of 7 November 1991 on the statistics relating to the trading of goods between Member States, as last amended by European Parliament and Council Regulation (EQ No 1624/2000, and in particular Article 30 thereof,

Whereas:

(1)   Commission Regulation (EEC) No 3046/92 laying down provisions implementing and amending Regulation (EEC) No 3330/91, as last amended by Regulation (EQ No 2535/98, has been substantially amended on several occasions.

(2)   Commission Regulations (EEC) No 2256/92, (EC) No 1125/94 and (EC) No 2820/94 lay down additional provisions for the implementation of Regulation (EEC) No 3330/91, concerning in particular statistical thresholds, deadlines for forwarding results, and threshold values for individual transactions in the context of statistics relating to trade between Member States.

(3)   When further amendments are made to Regulation (EEC) No 3046/92, the relevant regulations should be drawn up in such a way which lightens the burden on enterprises and administrations affected by these regulations.

(4)   With a view to establishing the statistics relating to the trading of goods between Member States, the field of application of the Intrastat system should be precisely defined in relation to both the goods to be included and those to be excluded.

(5)   The date from which the intra-Community operator is in practice to comply with his obligations to supply information must be determined and the extent of the obligations of the third party to whom the party responsible for providing the information may. transfer that task should be defined.

(6)   Certain rules to be complied with by the departments concerned must be specified in detail in particular to allow efficient management of the registers of intra-Community operators.

(7)   A key element of the Intrastat system consists in the use of value added tax information on Intra-Community transactions. In order to ensure that the exhaustiveness of the statistics can be checked, it is appropriate to specify in a restrictive manner the information which may be passed between the administrative authorities in the Member States responsible for the application of laws on value added tax and those responsible for the establishment of statistics relating to the trading of goods between Member States.

(8)   The burden on intra-Community operators must be lightened as much as possible, either by exempting them from statistical obligations or by simplifying procedures. This lightening of the burden must be limited only by the demands of statistics of a satisfactory quality, which must consequently be defined. All the Member States must have the instruments needed to ensure quality, while taking into account their own economic and commercial structure.

(9)   There is a need to specify the way in which the thresholds applying to certain data will be calculated. For the statistical procedure, this information needs to be distinguished from the procedure used for the statistical and tax declarations.

(10)   Despite the existence of statistical thresholds, there remain parties responsible for providing information effecting a large number of low-value transactions who are obliged to communicate these in the greatest detail, an obligation which represents a burden out of all proportion to the usefulness of the information thus obtained. It is necessary to reduce the burden.

(11)   A list should be drawn up of the goods to be excluded from the statistical returns relating to the trading of goods.

(12)   The data to be reported and the arrangements for reporting such data should be defined in more detail.

(13)   Of the units of quantity, net mass, in kilograms, is the main indicator and should in principle be mentioned for every type of goods. However, for certain products, it is not the most appropriate unit of measurement. The party responsible for providing information should therefore be exempted from indicating net mass in such cases.

(14)   Specific movements of goods may account for a substantial share of the statistics on the trading of goods between Member States. The absence of harmonised provisions at Community level is prejudicial to the comparability of statistics between Member States. Wherever possible, harmonisation of statistical legislation in the field of specific movements should be improved by complying with the relevant international recommendations.

(15) In order to ensure that Community statistics on trade between the Member States are complied regularly and within a reasonable time, the Member States must forward their results according to a common timetable. A distinction must be made between overall results and detailed results in order to ensure optimum satisfaction of user needs and take account of data collection and processing requirements.

(16) The measures provided for in this Regulation are in accordance with the Opinion of the Committee on the Statistics relating to the trading of goods between Member States.

HAS ADOPTED THIS REGULATION

TITLE I

GENERAL PROVISIONS

CHAPTER 1

GENERAL CONSIDERATIONS

Article 1

With a view to establishing the statistics relating to the trading of goods between Member States, the Community and its Member States shall apply Regulation (EEC) No 3330/91, hereinafter referred to as 'the Basic Regulation', in accordance with the rules laid down in this Regulation.

Article 2

The Intrastat system shall apply also to the products referred to in Article 3(1) of Council Directive 92112/EEC regardless of the form and content of the document accompanying them, when they move between the territories of the Member States.

Article 3

1.   The Intrastat system shall not apply:

(a)   to goods placed or obtained under the inward processing customs procedure (suspension system) or the procedure of processing under customs control;

(b)   to goods circulating between parts of the statistical territory of the Community, at least one of which is not part of the territory of the Community pursuant to Council Directive 77/388/EEC

However, without prejudice to customs regulations, provisions of this Regulation shall apply to these goods except Articles 2,4,5,8 to 20,24(l), (2) (except indent 3), (3) and (4), and 28, 29,30 and 47.

2.   The Member States shall be responsible for collecting data on the goods referred to in paragraph 1 on the basis of the customs procedures applicable to such goods.

3.   If the statistical copy of the Single Administrative Document containing the data listed in Article 23(1) and (2) of the Basic Regulation is not available, the customs departments shall send the relevant statistical departments a periodic list of those same data by type of goods at lease once a month, in accordance with the arrangements agreed upon by the said departments.

CHAPTER 2

INFORMATION PROVIDERS AND REGISTERS

Article 4

1.   Any natural or legal person carrying out an intra-Community operation for the first time, whether the goods are arriving or being dispatched, shall become responsible for providing the required information within the meaning of Article 20(5) of the Basic Regulation.

2.   The party referred to in paragraph 1 shall provide the data on his intra-Community operations via the periodic declarations referred to in Article 13 of the Basic Regulation as from the month during which the assimilation threshold is exceeded, in accordance with the provisions relating to the threshold which become applicable to him.

3.   When the VAT registration number of a party responsible for providing the information is amended as a result of a change of ownership, name, address, legal status or similar change which does not affect his intra-Community operations to a significant extent, the rule defined in paragraph I need not be applied to the party in question at the time of the change. It shall remain subject 'to the statistical obligations to which it was subject before the change.

Article 5

1.   The third party referred to in Article 9(1) of the Basic Regulation is hereinafter referred to as 'the declaring third party'.

2.   The declaring third party shall provide the competent national departments with the following information:

    (a)   in accordance with Article 6(1), the information necessary:

        — to identify himself,

        — to identify each of the parties responsible for providing the information who have transferred this task to him;

    (b)   for each of the parties responsible for providing information, the data required by the Basic Regulation and In implementation thereof.

Article 6

1.   The information necessary to identify an intra-Community operator within the meaning of Article 10 of the Basic Regulation shall be the following:

- full name of the person or firm,

- full address including post code,

- under the circumstances laid down in Article 10(6) of the Basic Regulation, the VAT registration number.

However, the statistical departments referred to in Article 10(1) of the Basic Regulation may dispense with one or more of the above mentioned items of information or, under circumstances to be determined by them, exempt the intra-Community operators from providing them.

In the Member States referred to in Article 10(3) of the Basic Regulation, the information which serves to identify an intra-Community operator shall be supplied to the abovementioned statistical departments by the tax authorities referred to in the said Article as and when it becomes available to the latter, unless there is an agreement to the contrary between the departments concerned.

2. The minimum list of data to be recorded in the register of intra-Community operators, within the meaning of Article 10 of the Basic Regulation, shall contain, for each intra-Community operator, the following:

(a) the year and month of entry in the register;

(a) the information necessary to identify the operator as laid down in paragraph 1;

(b) where applicable, whether the operator is a party responsible for providing information or a declaring third party, upon either consignment or receipt;

(c) in the case of a party responsible for providing information, the total value of his intra-Community operations, by month and by flow, together with the value referred to in Article 11(3) of the Basic Regulation. However, this information need not be recorded if the checking of the information recorded as statistics using the information referred to in Article 11(3) of the Basic Regulation and the functioning of the statistical thresholds referred to in Article 28 of the said Regulation are organised separately from the management of the register of intra-Community operators.

The competent national departments may record other data in the register in accordance with their requirements.

Article 7

With a view to Implementing Article 10(6) of the Basic Regulation, the case where responsibility for the information, for given operations, lies not with the operator as a legal entity per se but with a constituent part of this entity such as a branch office, a kind or activity unit or local unit, may be considered a justified exception.

Article 8

1. In the lists referred to in Article 11(1) of the Basic Regulation, the tax authorities responsible shall mention intra-Community operators who, as a result of a scission, merger or cessation of activity during the period under review, will no longer appear on the said lists.

2. The provision of information of a fiscal nature referred to in Article 11 (4) of the Basic Regulation by a Member State's administrative authorities responsible for the application of laws on value added tax to the departments in that Member State responsible for compiling statistics relating to the trading of goods between Member States is limited to information which those liable to account for VAT are required to provide in accordance with Article 22 of Directive 77/388/EEC.

Article 9

1. The party responsible for providing information shall transmit the data required under the Basic Regulation and in implementation thereof:

    (a)   in accordance with the Community provision in force;

    (b)   direct to the competent national departments or via the collection offices which the Member States have set up for this or for other statistical or administrative purposes;

    (c)   for a given reference period, at his discretion:

    – either by means of a single declaration, within a time limit which the competent national departments shall lay down in their instructions to the parties responsible for providing information,

    – or by means of several part-declarations. In this case, the competent national departments may require agreement to be reached with them on the frequency of transmission and deadlines, but the last part-declaration must be transmitted within the time limit laid down under the first indent above.

2. By way of derogation from paragraph 1, a party responsible for providing information who benefits from exemption by virtue of application of the assimilation threshold provided for in Article 28(4) of the Basic Regulation must, when transmitting the information, conform only to the regulations of the tax authorities responsible.

3. Pursuant to Article 34 of the Basic Regulation, the provisions of this Article relating to the periodicity of the declaration shall not prevent the conclusion of an agreement providing for the supply of data in real time, when the data are transmitted electronically.

4. By way of derogation to paragraph 1 above, in those Member States where the periodic statistical declaration is the same as the periodic tax declaration, the provisions relating to the transmission of the statistical declaration shall be drawn up in line with Community or national tax regulations.

CHAPTER 3

STATISTICAL THRESHOLDS AND EXEMPTIONS

Section 1

Overall functioning of thresholds

Article 10

The Member States shall set annually the assimilation and simplification thresholds referred to in Article 28 of the Basic Regulation. They shall ensure when setting these thresholds that, first, they meet the quality requirements laid down in this chapter and, secondly, they exploit to the full the ensuing opportunities to relieve the burden on intra-Community operators.

Article 11

For the purposes of this section:

(a) **'error'** means the discrepancy between the results obtained with and without application of the thresholds referred to in Article 10. When a correction procedure is applied to the results obtained following application of the thresholds, the error is calculated in relation to the corrected results;

(b) **'total value'** means, for the purposes of threshold adjustment, the value of either of the outgoing goods or of the incoming goods accounted for by intra-Community operators over a 12-month period, other than those who are exempt under Article 5 of the Basic Regulation;

(c) **'coverage'** means, in relation to a given total value, the proportionate value of the outgoing goods or of the incoming goods accounted for by the intra-Community operators who lie above the assimilation threshold.

Article 12

1. The assimilation thresholds set by the Member States shall meet the following quality requirements:

　　(a) Results by goods category

　　　　Each Member State shall ensure that the error in annual values does not exceed 5 % for 90 % of the eight-digit sub-headings of the Combined Nomenclature which represent 0.005 % or more of the total value of its outgoing or incoming goods.

　　　　However, each Member State may raise this quality requirement up to the point that the error in annual values does not exceed 5% for 90% of the eight-digit sub-headings of the Combined Nomenclature which represent 0.001% or more of the total value of its outgoing or incoming goods.

　　(b) Results by partner country

　　　　Each Member State shall ensure that the error in the annual values of its results by partner country, excluding countries which represent less than 3% of the total value of its outgoing or incoming goods, does not exceed 1%.

2. When a Member State's share of the total value of outgoing or incoming goods in the Community is less than 3%, that Member State may depart from the quality requirements laid down in the first subparagraph of paragraph 1(a). In such cases, the 90% and 0.005% shares shall be replaced by 70% and 0.01% respectively.

3. To meet the quality requirements set out in paragraphs 1 and 2, the Member States shall base the calculation of their thresholds on the results of trade with the other Member States for 12-month periods prior to the introduction of the thresholds.

For Member States unable to make this calculation because figures are incomplete, the assimilation thresholds shall be fixed at a level not lower than the lowest, nor higher than the highest, thresholds set by the other Member States. However, this provision shall not be binding for Member States which are exempt under paragraph 2.

4. If, for certain groups of goods., the application of the thresholds calculated in accordance with the provisions of this Article yields results which, *mutatis mutandis*, fail to meet the quality requirements set out in paragraphs 1 and 2, and if the thresholds cannot be lowered without reducing the relief which Article 10 guarantees to intra-Community operators, appropriate measures may be taken, at the initiative of the Commission or the request of a Member State, in accordance with the procedure laid down in Article 30 of the Basic Regulation.

Article 13

1. For the introduction of the simplification thresholds, the Member States may set these:

   — at levels above EUR 100 000 pursuant to the first subparagraph of Article 28(9) of the Basic Regulation, provided that they ensure that at least 95% of the total value of their outgoing or incoming goods is covered by periodic declarations containing all the information required under Article 23 of the Basic Regulation,

   — where they are exempt under Article 12(2), at levels below EUR 100,000 pursuant to the second subparagraph of Article 28(9) of the Basic Regulation, to the extent necessary to ensure that at least 95% of the total value of their outgoing or incoming goods is covered by periodic declarations containing all the information required under Article 23 of the Basic Regulation.

2. The party responsible for providing information according to the simplified rules of Article 28(5) of the Basic Regulation, shall report in the declaration a maximum of ten of the finest relevant subheadings of the Combined Nomenclature that are the most important in terms of value for the period covered by the declaration. For the residual products the code 9950 00 00 shall be used.

Article 14

1.   For the adjustment of the assimilation thresholds, the quality requirements specified in Article 12 shall be regarded as met if the coverage is maintained at the level obtained when the thresholds were introduced.

2.   The condition laid down in paragraph 1 shall be met if Member States:

   (a)   calculate their thresholds for the year following the current year on the basis of the latest available results for their trade with the other Member States over a 12 month period.

   (b)   set their thresholds at a level which allows the same coverage for the period thus defined as for the period used as a basis for calculating their thresholds for the current year.

   Member States shall notify the Commission if they use a different method, to meet this condition.

3.   Member States may lower their coverage provided that the quality requirements laid down in Article 12 continue to be met.

4.   Member States shall calculate adjustments to their assimilation thresholds each year. The thresholds shall be adjusted if the adjustment involves a change of at least 10% in the threshold values for the current year.

Article 15

1.   For the adjustment of the simplification thresholds, the Member States who set these:

   — at levels higher than the values laid down in by Article 28(8) of the Basic Regulation, shall ensure that the condition laid down in the first indent of Article 13(1) of this Regulation is met,

   — at levels below these values, since they are exempt pursuant to Article 12(2) above, shall ensure that they comply with the limit laid. down in the second indent of Article 13 of this Regulation.

2.   To ensure that the condition referred to in the first indent of Article 13(1) is met or that the limit referred to in the second indent of Article 13(1) is complied with, it shall be sufficient for Member States to calculate the adjustment of the simplification thresholds using the method laid down in Article 14(2) for adjusting the assimilation thresholds. Member States shall notify the Commission if they use a different method.

Article 16

The information relating to the adjustment of assimilation and simplification thresholds shall be published not later than 31 October of the preceding year.

Article 17

1.   Parties responsible for providing information shall be freed from their obligations to the extent allowed by application of the assimilation and

simplification thresholds set out for a given year, provided they have not exceeded these thresholds during the previous year.

2.   For each statistical threshold, the provisions adopted shall apply for the whole year.

However, if the value of the intra-Community transactions carried out by a party responsible for providing information at some time during the year exceeds the threshold applicable to him, he shall provide information on his intra-Community transactions from the month in which this threshold was exceeded in accordance with the provisions applying to the threshold which becomes applicable. If this provision involves the transmission of the periodic declarations referred to in Article 13 of the Basic Regulation, the Member States shall lay down the time limit for transmitting these declarations in accordance with their particular administrative arrangements.

Article 18

The Member States shall communicate to the Commission the information regarding the thresholds they have calculated at least two weeks before publication. At the Commission's request, they shall also communicate the information required for assessing these thresholds, both for the period on which their calculation is based and for a given calendar year.

Section 2
Specific thresholds and exemptions
Article 19

For the implementation of Article 24(3) of this Regulation and Article 23(3) of the Basic Regulation, Member States shall set separate thresholds for arrivals and dispatches at such values that at least 95% of information providers are exempted from the requirement to provide the 'statistical value', 'delivery terms', 'mode of transport' and 'statistical procedure' data.

As far as the 'statistical value' is concerned, the Member States shall ensure that at least 70% of the total value of their dispatches or arrivals is covered. The limit of 95% of information providers may be lowered to 90% if the coverage rate of 70% of the total value of their dispatches or, arrivals is not reached.

The Member States shall calculate these limits from the last available results for their trade with the other Member States over a 12-month period.

The information relating to the introduction of these thresholds shall be published not later than 31 October 2000.

Member States may adjust their thresholds every calendar year provided that the quality requirement laid down in this Article continue to be met. The Member States concerned shall publish the information relating to the adjustment of the thresholds not later than 31 October of the preceding year.

Article 20

1.   A threshold value for individual transactions may be applied under conditions defined in paragraphs 2 and 3. Without prejudice to paragraph 2, this threshold shall give the parties responsible for providing information the option of entering all transactions whose value is below this threshold under a global heading of the Combined Nomenclature, in which case the application of Article 23 of the Basic Regulation shall be limited to the provision of the following data:

— in the case of arrivals, the Member State of dispatch,

— in the case of dispatches, the Member State of consignment.

— the value of the goods.

The global heading referred to in paragraph 1 shall be identified by CN code 9950 00 00.

For the purposes of this Article, **'transaction'** means any operation described under Article 25(1)(a) of this Regulation.

The threshold for each transaction shall be EUR 100.

2.   In the context of this Article, Member States may refuse or limit application of the option provided for in paragraph I if they consider that the aim of maintaining a satisfactory quality of statistical information overrides the desirability of reducing the reporting burden.

3.   Member States may require parties responsible for providing information to ask the national department responsible for compiling statistics on the trading of goods between Member States, in advance, to be allowed to make use of the option referred to in paragraph 1.

4.   When requested to do so by the Commission, Member States shall transmit such information as is necessary for monitoring the application of this Regulation.

Article 21

Data relating to the goods listed in Annex I shall be excluded from compilation and, consequently, pursuant to Article 25(4) of the Basic Regulation, from collection.

CHAPTER 4

STATISTICAL DATA

Article 22

In the medium for the information, the Member States whose statistical territory is described in the nomenclature of countries adopted each year pursuant to Article 9(1) of Council Regulation (EC) No. 1172/95 shall be designated by the following codes:

[Belgium	BE or 017
Czech Republic	CZ or 061
Denmark	DK or 008
Germany	DE or 004
Estonia	EE or 053
Greece	GR or 009
Spain	ES or 011
France	FR or 001
Ireland	IE or 007
Italy	IT or 005
Cyprus	CY or 600
Latvia	LV or 054
Lithuania	LT or 055
Luxembourg	LU or 018
Hungary	HU or 064
Malta	MT or 046
Netherlands	NL or 003
Austria	AT or 038
Poland	PL or 060
Portugal	PT or 010
Slovenia	SI or 091
Slovakia	SK or 063
Finland	FI or 032
Sweden	SE or 030
United Kingdom	GB or 006][1]

Article 23

When the quantity of goods to be mentioned on the data medium is determined:

(a)   **'net mass'** means the actual mass of the good excluding all packaging. It shall be given in kilograms. However, the specification of net mass for the subheadings of the combined nomenclature set out in Annex II shall be optional for the parties responsible for providing information. In order to inform the party responsible for providing the information about possible updates of the annex, resulting from the annual changes in the Combined Nomenclature, an explanatory note will be published in the Official Journal of the European Communities (C series);

(b)   **'supplementary units'** means the units measuring quantity, other than the units measuring mass expressed in kilograms. They must be mentioned in accordance with the information set out in the current version of the Combined Nomenclature, opposite the subheadings concerned, the list of which is published in Part I 'Preliminary provisions' of the said nomenclature.

Article 24

1. The value of the goods referred to in Article 23(1)(d) of the Basic Regulation shall be reported in the statistical information medium on the conditions defined in paragraphs 2 and 3.

2. The value of the goods to be reported in the 'invoiced amount' field in the statistical information medium shall be the taxable amount to be determined for taxation purposes in accordance with Directive 77/388/EEC. For products subject to excise duties, however, the amount of these duties should be excluded from the value of the goods.

    Whenever the taxable amount does not have to be declared for taxation purposes, the value of the goods to be reported shall correspond to the invoice value, excluding VAT, or, failing this, to an amount which would have been invoiced in the event of any sale or purchase.

    In the case of work under contract, the value of the goods to be reported, with a view to and following such operations, shall be the total amount to be invoiced in the event of any sale or purchase.

3. The statistical value of the goods, as defined in paragraph S, shall also be reported in the field provided to this end in the statistical information medium by information providers whose annual arrivals or dispatches exceed the limits set by each Member State, in accordance with Article 19.

4. By way of derogation to paragraph 3, the Member States may exempt information providers from reporting the statistical value of goods.

    In this case, the Member States concerned shall calculate the statistical value of goods, as defined in paragraph 5, by kinds of goods.

5. The statistical value shall be based on the goods reported by the information providers pursuant to paragraph 2. It shall include only incidental expenses, such as transport and insurance costs, referring to the part of the route which:

    — for dispatches, is within the statistical territory of the Member State of dispatch,

    — for arrivals, is outside the statistical territory of the Member State of arrival.

6. The value of the goods defined in the preceding paragraphs shall be expressed in the national currency, whereupon the exchange rate to be applied shall be:

    — that applicable for determining the taxable amount for taxation purposes, when this is established,

    — otherwise, the official rate of exchange at the time of completing the declaration or that applicable to calculating the value for customs purposes, in the absence of any special provisions decided by the Member States.

7. In accordance with Article 26 of the Basic Regulation, the value of the goods given in the results to be transmitted to the Commission shall be the statistical value defined in paragraph 5.

8. At the Commission's request, the Member States shall provide it with the information enabling it to assess the application of paragraph 3.

Article 25

1. For the purposes of this Chapter,

    (a) **'transaction'** shall mean any operation, whether commercial or not, which leads to a movement of goods covered by statistics on the trading of goods between Member States;

    (b) **'nature of the transaction'** means all those characteristic which distinguish one transaction from another.

2. A distinction shall be made between transactions which differ in nature, in accordance with the list in Annex III.

    The nature of the transaction shall be specified, on the information medium, by the code number corresponding to the appropriate category of column A in the above mentioned list.

    Within the limits of the list referred to in paragraph 2, the Member States may prescribe the collection of data on the nature of the transaction up to the level which they use for the collection of data on trade third countries, regardless of whether they collect them in this connection as data on the nature of the transaction or as data on customs procedures.

Article 26

1   **'Country of origin'** shall mean the country where the goods originate.

    Goods which are entirely obtained in a country originate in 'that country.

    An item in the production of which two or more countries are involved originates in the country where the last significant processing or working, economically justified and carried out in an enterprise equipped for this purpose and leading to the manufacture of a new product or representing an important stage of manufacture, takes place.

2   The country of origin is designated by the code assigned it in the current version of the nomenclature of countries discussed in Article 9 of Regulation (EC) No 1172/95, as last amended by Council Regulation (EC) No 374/98.

Article 27

1   **'Region of origin'** shall mean the region of the Member State of dispatch where the foods were produced or were erected, assembled, processed, repaired or maintained. Failing this, the region of origin shall be replaced either by the region where the commercial process took place or by the region where the goods were dispatched.

2.   **'Region of destination'** shall mean the region of the Member States of arrival where the goods are to be consumed or erected, assembled, processed, repaired or maintained. Failing this, the region of destination shall be replaced either by the region where the commercial process is totake place or by the region to which the goods are to be dispatched.

3.   Each Member State exercising the option provided for in Article 23 (2) (b) of the Basic Regulation shall draw up a list of its regions and determine the code, which shall have a maximum of two characters, by which those regions shall be indicated on the information medium.

Article 28

1   For the purposes of this Regulation, **'delivery terms'** shall mean those provisions of the sales contract which lay down the obligations, of the seller and the buyer respectively, in accordance with the Incoterms of the International Chamber of Commerce listed in Annex IV.

2.   Within the limits in Article 19 and those of the list referred to in paragraph 1, Member States may prescribe that data on delivery terms be collected on the information medium and shall give details of how they are to be mentioned.

Article 29

1.   'Presumed mode of transport' shall indicate, upon dispatch, the mode of transport determined by the active means of transport by which the goods are presumed to be going to leave the statistical territory of the Member State of dispatch and, upon arrival, the mode of transport determined by the active means of transport by which the goods are presumed to have entered the statistical territory of the Member State of arrival.

2.   Within the limits set in Article 19, the modes of transport to be mentioned on the information medium are as follows:

Code	Title
1	Sea transport
2	Rail transport
3	Road transport
4	Air transport
S	Postal consignment
7	Fixed transport installations
8	Inland waterway transport
9	Own propulsion

The mode of transport shall be designated on the said medium by the corresponding code number.

Article 30

1.   **'Statistical procedure'** shall mean the category of dispatch or arrival which is not adequately referred to in column A or column B of the list of transactions in Annex III.

2.   Within the limits set in Article 19, Member States may prescribe that data on statistical procedures be collected on the information medium and shall give details of how they are to be reported.

TITLE II
SPECIAL PROVISIONS
CHAPTER 1
DEFINITION OF SPECIFIC MOVEMENT AND
GENERAL CONSIDERATIONS
Article 31

1.   The 'specific movements of goods' referred to in Article 33 of the Basic Regulation have specific features which have some significance for the interpretation of the information and stem, either from the movement as such, from the nature of the goods, from the transaction which results in the movement of the goods or from the information provider.

2.   Specific movements of goods are as follows: industrial plants;

vessels and aircraft, as defined in Chapter 3;

     (a)   industrial plants;

     (b)   vessels and aircraft, as defined in Chapter 3;

     (c)   sea products;

     (d)   ships' and aircraft's stores and supplies;

     (e)   staggered consignments;

     (f)   military goods;

     (g)   offshore installations;

     (h)   spacecraft and spacecraft launchers;

     (i)   motor vehicle and aircraft parts;

     (j)   waste products.

3.   Subject to contrary provision in this Regulation or in the absence of provisions laid down in accordance with Article 30 of the Basic Regulation, specific movements shall be mentioned according to the relevant national provisions.

4.   Without prejudice to Article 13 of the Basic Regulation, the Member States shall adopt the appropriate provisions in order to apply this Title and may use, if necessary, statistical sources other than those laid down by Commission Regulation (EEC) No 3590/92.

CHAPTER 2

INDUSTRIAL PLANTS

Article 32

1. **'Complete industrial plant'** means a combination of machines, apparatus, appliances, equipment, instruments and materials, hereinafter referred to as 'component. parts', which fall under various headings of the Harmonised System classification and which are designed to function together as a large-scale unit to produce goods or provide services.

    All other goods which are used in constructing a complete industrial plant may be treated as component parts thereof, provided they are not excluded from the statistical compilation by virtue of the Basic Regulation.

2. A simplified declaration procedure may be used for recording arrivals or dispatches of complete industrial plants. Those responsible for supplying the statistical information shall be authorised, at their request, to use such simplified procedure in accordance with the conditions laid down in this section.

3. The simplified procedure may be applied only to complete industrial plants, the total statistical value of each of which exceeds EUR 1.5 million, unless they are complete industrial plants for re-use.

    The total value of an industrial plant is calculated by adding the respective statistical values of its component parts and the respective statistical values of the goods referred to in the second subparagraph of paragraph 1. The value to be taken into account is the invoice value of the good or, if this is not available, the amount which would be invoiced in the event of a sale or purchase.

Article 33

1. For the purposes of this chapter, component parts falling within a given chapter shall be classified under the relevant complete industrial plant subheading of Chapter 98 unless the competent department referred to in Article 35 requires the goods to be classified, in Chapter 98, under the relevant complete industrial plant subheadings of the Harmonised System classification headings, or requires the provisions of paragraph 2 to be applied.

    However, the simplified procedure shall not prevent the competent department from classifying certain component parts under the relevant Combined Nomenclature subheadings within the meaning of Article 1(2)(b) of Council Regulation (EEC) No 2658/87

2. Where the competent department referred to in paragraph I considers the value of the items of complete industrial plants to be too low to justify recording them under the complete industrial plant subheadings of the relevant chapters, specific complete industrial plant subheadings, as provided for in the Combined Nomenclature, shall apply.

Article 34

In accordance with the Combined Nomenclature, the code numbers for complete industrial plant subheadings shall be composed in conformity with the following rules.

1. The code shall comprise eight digits.

2. The first two digits shall be 9 and 8 respectively.

3. The third digit, which shall serve to identify complete industrial plant, shall be 8

4. The fourth digit shall vary from 0 to 9 according to the main economic activity carried out by the complete industrial plant and in accordance with the classification given:

Code	Economic Activities
0	Energy (including production and distribution of steam and hot water)
1	Extraction of non-energy-producing minerals (including preparation of metalliferous ores and peat extraction); manufacture of non-metallic mineral products including manufacture of glass and glassware)
2	Iron and steel industry; manufacture of metal articles (excluding mechanical engineering and construction of means of transport)
3	Mechanical engineering and construction of means of transport; instrument engineering
4	Chemical industry (including man-made fibres industry); rubber and plastics industry
5	Food, drink and tobacco industry
6	Textile, leather, footwear and clothing industry
7	Timber and paper industry (including printing and publishing): manufacturing industries not classified elsewhere
8	Transport (excluding services connected with transport, services of travel agents, freightbrokers and other agents facilitating the transport of passengers or goods, storage and warehousing) and communications
9	Collection, purification and distribution of water; services connected with transport; economic activities not classified elsewhere.

5. The fifth and sixth digits shall correspond to the number of the chapter of the Combined Nomenclature to which the complete industrial plant subheading relates. However, for the purposes of Article 33(2), these fifth and sixth digits shall be 9.

6. For complete industrial plant subheadings which are situated:

    — at Combined Nomenclature chapter level, the seventh and eighth digits shall be 0,

    — at Harmonised System heading level, the seventh and eighth digits shall correspond to the third and fourth digits of that heading.

7. The competent department referred to in Article 33(2) shall prescribe the designation and the Combined Nomenclature code number to be used in the statistical information medium to identify the component parts of a complete industrial plant.

Article 35

1.   Those responsible for supplying statistical information may not we the simplified declaration procedure without the prior authorisation of the department responsible for compiling statistics on trade between Member States in accordance with the detailed rules which each Member State shall lay down within the framework of this chapter.

2.   In the case of a complete industrial plant whose component parts are traded by several Member States, authorisation to use the simplified declaration procedure shall be given by each Member State for the flows which concern it.

CHAPTER 3

VESSELS AND AIRCRAFT

Article 36

For the purposes of this chapter,

(a)   **'vessels'** means the vessels used for sea transport, referred to in Additional Notes 1 and 2 of Chapter 89 of the Combined Nomenclature, and warships;

(b)   **'aircraft'** means aeroplanes falling within CN code 8802 for civilian use, provided they are used by an airline, or for military use;

(c)   **'ownership of a vessel or an aircraft'** means the fact of a physical or legal person's registration as owner of a vessel or an aircraft;

(d)   **'partner country'** means:

    — on arrival, the Member State of construction if the vessel or aircraft is new and has been constructed in the Community. In other cases, it shall mean the Member State where the natural or legal person transferring the ownership of the vessel or aircraft is established,

    — on dispatch, the Member State where the natural or legal person to whom the ownership of the vessel or aircraft is transferred is established.

Article 37

1.   In a given Member State, statistics on trade between Member States, and transmission of results to the Commission, shall cover.

    (a)   the transfer of ownership of a vessel or aircraft from a natural or legal person established in one Member State to a natural or legal person established in this Member State. This transaction shall be treated as an arrival;

    (b)   the transfer of ownership of a vessel or aircraft from a natural or legal person established in this Member State to a natural or legal person established in another Member State. This transaction shall be treated as a dispatch.

If the vessel or aircraft is new the dispatch is recorded in the Member State of construction;

(c)   the dispatch or arrival of a vessel or aircraft pending or following work under contract.

2.   The monthly returns on the transactions referred to in paragraph 1(a) and (b), which are transmitted to the Commission by the Member States, shall include the following data:

(a)   the code corresponding to the subdivision of the product classification, referred to in Article 21 of the Basic Regulation;

(b)   the code of the partner Member State;

(c)   the quantity, as number of items and in any other supplementary units laid down in the nomenclature, for vessels. and the quantity, in net mass and in supplementary units, for aircraft;

(d)   the statistical value.

CHAPTER 4

SHIPS' AND AIRCRAFT'S STORES AND SUPPLIES

Article 38

For the purposes of this chapter,

— **'ships'** and **'aircraft's stores'** means the various products for consumption by the crew and passengers of vessels or aircraft,

— **'ships'** and **'aircraft's supplies'** means the products for the operation of the engines, machines and other equipment on vessels or aircraft, such as fuel, oil and lubricants,

— **'vessels or aircraft from another Member State'** for a given Member State, as opposed to a **'national'** vessel or aircraft, means those vessels or aircraft for which the natural or legal person responsible for their commercial use is established in another Member State.

Article 39

1.   In a given Member State, statistics on trade between Member States, and transmission of results to the Commission, shall cover:

(a)   any delivery of ships' and aircraft's stores and supplies to vessels or aircraft from another Member State, which are stationed in a port or airport of the reporting Member State, provided that they are Community goods or non-Community goods which have been placed under inward processing customs arrangements or under arrangements for processing under customs control. This operation shall be treated as a dispatch;

(b)   any direct delivery of ships' and aircraft's stores and supplies from another Member State to national vessels or aircraft which are stationed in a port or airport. of the reporting Member State. This operation shall be treated as an arrival.

2. The monthly returns on the operations referred to in paragraph 1(a), which are transmitted by the Member States to the Commission, shall include the following data:

   (a) the product code, according to the following simplified coding as a minimum:

      — 9930 24 00: goods from Chapters 1 to 24 of the Harmonised System,

      — 9930 27 00: goods from Chapter 27 of the Harmonised System,

      — 9930 99 00: goods classified elsewhere;

   (b) the specific country code QR (or 951);

   (c) the quantity in net mass;

   (d) the statistical value.

CHAPTER 5

STAGGERED CONSIGNMENTS

Article 40

For the purposes of this chapter, **'staggered consignments'** mean arrivals or dispatches of components of complete goods in a disassembled state over several reporting periods for commercial or transport-related reasons.

Article 41

In the monthly returns transmitted to the Commission by the Member States, data on arrivals and dispatches of staggered consignments shall be reported once only, i.e. in the month of arrival or dispatch of the last consignment, with an indication of the full value of the complete assembled good and using the classification code for that good.

CHAPTER 6

MILITARY GOODS

Article 42

1. Statistics on the trading of goods between Member States, and transmission of results to the Commission, shall cover dispatches and arrivals of goods intended for military use in compliance with the definition in force in the Member States.

2. The monthly returns covering the operations referred to in paragraph 1, which are transmitted to the Commission by the Member States, shall include the following data;

   (a) the code corresponding to the subdivision of the product classification referred to in Article 21 of the Basic Regulation;

   (b) the code of the partner Member State;

(c)   the quantity in net mass and, where appropriate, in supplementary units;

(d)   the statistical value.

3.   In the Member States unable to apply the provisions of paragraph 2 owing to military secrecy, appropriate measures shall be taken to ensure that at a minimum the statistical value of the dispatches and arrivals of goods intended for military used are included in the monthly returns transmitted to the Commission.

CHAPTER 7

OFFSHORE INSTALLATIONS

Article 43

1.   For the purposes of this chapter, **'offshore installations'** means the equipment and devices installed in the high sea in order to search for and exploit mineral resources.

2.   **'Foreign' installations,** as opposed to **'national' installations,** mean those installations for which the natural or legal person responsible for their commercial use is established in another Member State.

Article 44

1.   In a given Member State, statistics on trade between Member States, and transmission of results to the Commission, shall cover:

(a)   the delivery of goods to a national installation, directly from another Member State or from a foreign installation. This operation. shall be treated as an arrival;

(b)   the delivery of goods from a national installation to another Member State or to a foreign installation. This operation shall be treated as a dispatch;

(c)   the arrival of goods from a foreign installation on the statistical territory of this Member State;

(d)   the dispatch of goods to a foreign installation from the statistical territory of this Member State.

2.   The monthly returns covering the operations referred to in paragraph 1, which are transmitted to the Commission by the Member States, shall include the following data:

(a)   the code corresponding to the subdivision of the product classification referred to in Article 21 of the Basic Regulation.

However, without prejudice to the Customs Regulations, if the goods are those referred to in Article 38, the Member States shall have the option of using the simplified codes set out in Article 39(2)(a);

(b)   the code of the partner Member State.

However, without prejudice to the Customs Regulations, in the case of goods coming from or destined for installations, the partner country shall be the country where the natural or legal person responsible for the commercial use of the installation in question is established. Where this information is not available, code QV (or 959) shall be used;

(c)   the quantity in net mass;

(d)   the statistical value.

CHAPTER 8

SPACECRAFT

Article 45

For the purposes of this Chapter,

(a)   **'spacecraft'** means craft such as satellites which travel in space outside the earth's atmosphere;

(b)   **'ownership of a spacecraft'** means the fact of a natural or legal persons registration as owner of a spacecraft.

Article 46

1.   Statistics on trade between Member States, and transmission of results to the Commission, shall cover:

(a)   the dispatch or arrival of a spacecraft pending or following work under contract;

(b)   the launch into space of a spacecraft which was the subject of a transfer of ownership between two natural or legal persons established in different Member States. This operation is recorded:

— as a dispatch in the Member State of construction of the finished spacecraft,

— as an arrival in the Member State where the new owner is established;

(c)   the transfer of ownership of a spacecraft, in orbit, between two natural or legal persons established in different Member States. This operation is recorded:

— as a dispatch in the Member State where the former owner is established,

— as an arrival in the Member State where the new owner is established.

2.   The monthly returns on the operations referred to in Article 1(b) and (c), which are transmitted to the Commission by the Member States, shall include the following data:

(a)   the code corresponding to the subdivision of the product classification referred to in Article 21 of the Basic Regulation;

(b)   the code of the partner Member State.

For the dispatches referred to in paragraph 1(b) and (c), the partner Member State is the country in which the natural or legal person to whom ownership of the spacecraft is transferred is established.

For the arrivals referred to in paragraph 1(b), the partner Member State is the country of construction of the finished spacecraft.

For the arrivals referred to in paragraph 1(c), the partner Member State is the country where the natural or legal persons transferring ownership of the spacecraft is established;

(c)   the quantity in net mass and in supplementary units;

(d)   the statistical value.

For the arrivals referred to in paragraph 1(b), the statistical value includes the transport and insurance costs connected with conveyance to the launch base and the space journey.

CHAPTER 9

OTHER PROVISIONS

Article 47

[Those Member States wishing to have more detailed information than that resulting from the application of Article 21 of the basis Regulation may, by way of derogation from that Article, organise the collection of that information.][2]

Those Member States exercising that option shall notify the Commission that they are doing so. At the same time, they shall state the reasons for their decision, supply the list of relevant Combined Nomenclature subheadings and describe the collection method they are using.

TITLE III

FINAL PROVISIONS

Article 48

The Member States shall forward to the Commission (Eurostat) the monthly results of their statistics on trade between the Member States, compiled in accordance with the Basic Regulation, no later than:

— eight weeks after the end of the reference month in the case of the total values, broken down by the Member State of destination on dispatch and the Member State of consignment on arrival,

— 10 weeks after the end of the reference month in the case of detailed results which present all the data referred to in Article 23(1) of the Basic Regulation.

Article 49

1. Regulation (EEC) No 3046/92, with the exception of Article 22, and the regulations amending it, Regulation (EEC) No 2256/92 and Regulations (EC) No 1125/94 and No 2820/94 are repealed effective from 1 January 2001.

2. References to the repealed Regulations shall be deemed to refer to this Regulation and read according to the correspondence table in Annex V.

Article 50

This Regulation shall enter into force on the 20th day following its publication in the Official Journal of the European Communities.

It shall apply from 1 January 2001.

This Regulation shall be binding in its entirety and directly applicable in all Member States.

Done at Brussels, 7 September 2000.
For the Commission
Pedro SOLBES MIRA
Member of the Commission

ANNEX I

List of exemptions referred to in Article 21

Data shall not be required for the following goods:

(a)   means of payment which are legal tender, and securities;

(b)   monetary gold;

(c)   emergency aid for disaster areas;

(d)   because of the diplomatic or similar nature of their intended use:

      1.   goods benefiting from diplomatic and consular or similar immunity;

      2.   gifts to a head of state or to members of a government or parliament;

      3.   items being circulated within the framework of administrative mutual aid;

(e)   provided that the trade is temporary;

      1.   goods intended for fairs and exhibitions;

      2.   theatrical scenery;

      3.   merry-go-rounds and other fairgrounds attractions;

      4.   professional equipment within the meaning of the International Convention of 8 June 1968;

      5.   cinematographic films;

      6.   apparatus and equipment for experimental purposes:

      7.   animals for show, breeding, racing, etc.;

      8.   commercial samples;

      9.   means of transport, containers and equipment connected with transport;

      10.   goods for the repair of the means of transport, containers and related transport equipment and parts replaced during the repairs

      11.   packaging

      12.   goods on hire;

      13.   plant and equipment for civil engineering works;

      14.   goods destined for examination, analysis or test purposes;

(f)   provided that they are not the subject of a commercial transaction:

      1.   decorations, honorary distinctions and prizes, commemorative badges and medals:

2.　　travel equipment, provisions and other items, including sports equipment, intended for personal use or consumption which accompany, precede or follow the traveller;

3.　　bridal outfits, items involved in moving house, or heirlooms;

4.　　coffins, funerary urns, ornamental funerary articles and items for the upkeep of graves and funeral monuments;

5.　　printed advertising material, instructions for use, price lists and other advertising items;

6.　　goods which have become unusable, or which cannot be used for industrial purposes;

7.　　ballast;

8.　　postage stamps;

9.　　pharmaceutical products used at international sporting events;

(g)　products used as part of exceptional common measures for the protection of persons or of the environment;

(h)　goods which are the subject of non-commercial traffic between persons resident in the adjacent zone of the Member States (frontier traffic); products obtained by agricultural producers on properties located outside, but adjacent to, the statistical territory within which they have their principal undertaking;

(i)　goods leaving a given statistical territory to return after crossing a foreign territory, either directly, or with halts inherent in the transport;

(j)　goods dispatched to national armed forces stationed outside the statistical territory as well as goods received from another Member State which had been conveyed outside the statistical territory by the national armed forces, as well as goods acquired or disposed of on the statistical territory of a Member State by the armed forces of another Member State which are stationed there;

(k)　goods used as carriers of Information such as floppy disks, computer tapes, films, plans, audio and videotapes, CD-ROMs which are traded in order to provide information, where developed to order for a particular client or where they are not the subject of a commercial transaction, as well as goods which complement a previous delivery, e.g. an update, and for which the consignee is not invoiced:

(l)　satellite launchers,

　　　— on dispatch and on arrival pending launching into space,

　　　— at the time of launching into space.

[ANNEX II

List of Combined Nomenclature subheadings
referred to in Article 23(a)

0105 11 11	2204 21 62	2204 29 71	5702 20 00
0105 11 19	2204 21 66	2204 29 72	5702 31 00
0105 11 91	2204 21 67	2204 29 75	5702 32 00
0105 11 99	2204 21 68	2204 29 81	5702 39 10
0105 12 00	2204 21 69	2204 29 82	5702 39 90
0105 19 20	2204 21 71	2204 29 83	5702 41 00
0105 19 90	2204 21 74	2204 29 84	5702 42 00
0407 00 11	2204 21 76	2204 29 87	5702 49 10
2202 10 00	2204 21 77	2204 29 88	5702 49 90
2202 90 10	2204 21 78	2204 29 89	5702 51 00
2202 90 91	2204 21 79	2204 29 91	5702 52 00
2202 90 95	2204 21 80	2204 29 92	5702 59 00
2202 90 99	2204 21 81	2204 29 93	5702 91 00
2203 00 01	2204 21 82	2204 29 94	5702 92 00
2203 00 09	2204 21 83	2204 29 95	5702 99 00
2203 00 10	2204 21 84	2204 29 96	5703 10 00
2204 10 11	2204 21 87	2204 29 97	5703 20 11
2204 10 19	2204 21 88	2204 29 98	5703 20 19
2204 10 91	2204 21 89	2204 29 99	5703 20 91
2204 10 99	2204 21 91	2205 10 10	5703 20 99
2204 21 10	2204 21 92	2205 10 90	5703 30 11
2204 21 11	2204 21 93	2205 90 10	5703 30 19
2204 21 12	2204 21 94	2205 90 90	5703 30 51
2204 21 13	2204 21 95	2206 00 10	5703 30 59
2204 21 17	2204 21 96	2206 00 31	5703 30 91
2204 21 18	2204 21 97	2206 00 39	5703 30 99
2204 21 19	2204 21 98	2206 00 51	5703 90 00
2204 21 22	2204 21 99	2206 00 59	5704 10 00
2204 21 24	2204 29 10	2206 00 81	5704 90 00
2204 21 26	2204 29 12	2207 10 00	5705 00 10
2204 21 27	2204 29 13	2207 20 00	5705 00 30
2204 21 28	2204 29 17	2209 00 99	5705 00 90
2204 21 32	2204 29 18	2716 00 00	6101 10 10
2204 21 34	2204 29 42	3702 51 00	6101 10 90
2204 21 36	2204 29 43	3702 53 00	6101 20 10
2204 21 37	2204 29 44	3702 54 10	6101 20 90
2204 21 38	2204 29 46	3702 54 90	6101 30 10
2204 21 42	2204 29 47	5701 10 10	6101 30 90
2204 21 43	2204 29 48	5701 10 91	6101 90 10
2204 21 44	2204 29 58	5701 10 93	6101 90 90
2204 21 46	2204 29 62	5701 10 99	6102 10 10
2204 21 47	2204 29 64	5701 90 10	6102 10 90
2204 21 48	2204 29 65	5701 90 90	6102 20 10

6102 20 90	6104 61 90	6109 90 30	6211 43 42
6102 30 10	6104 62 10	6109 90 90	6212 10 10
6102 30 90	6104 62 90	6110 11 10	6212 10 90
6102 90 10	6104 63 10	6110 11 30	6212 20 00
6102 90 90	6104 63 90	6110 11 90	6212 30 00
6103 11 00	6104 69 10	6110 12 10	6401 10 10
6103 12 00	6104 69 91	6110 12 90	6401 10 90
6103 19 00	6104 69 99	6110 19 10	6401 91 10
6103 21 00	6105 10 00	6110 19 90	6401 91 90
6103 22 00	6105 20 10	6110 20 10	6401 92 10
6103 23 00	6105 20 90	6110 20 91	6401 92 90
6103 29 00	6105 90 10	6110 20 99	6401 99 10
6103 31 00	6105 90 90	6110 30 10	6401 99 90
6103 32 00	6106 10 00	6110 30 91	6402 12 10
6103 33 00	6106 20 00	6110 30 99	6402 12 90
6103 39 00	6106 9010	6110 90 10	6402 19 00
6103 41 10	6106 90 30	6110 90 90	6402 20 00
6103 41 90	6106 90 50	6112 11 00	6402 30 00
6103 42 10	6106 90 90	6112 12 00	6402 91 00
6103 42 90	6107 11 00	6112 19 00	6402 99 10
6103 43 10	6107 12 00	6112 31 10	6402 99 31
6103 43 90	6107 19 00	6112 31 90	6402 99 39
6103 49 10	6107 21 00	6112 3910	6402 99 50
6103 49 91	6107 22 00	6112 39 90	6402 99 91
6103 49 99	6107 29 00	6112 41 10	6402 99 93
6104 11 00	6107 91 10	6112 41 90	6402 99 96
6104 12 00	6107 91 90	6112 49 10	6402 99 98
6104 13 00	6107 92 00	6112 49 90	6403 12 00
6104 19 00	6107 99 00	6115 11 00	6403 19 00
6104 21 00	6108 11 00	6115 12 00	6403 20 00
6104 22 00	6108 19 00	6115 19 00	6403 30 00
6104 23 00	6108 21 00	6210 20 00	6403 40 00
6104 29 00	6108 22 00	6210 30 00	6403 51 11
6104 31 00	6108 29 00	6211 11 00	6403 51 15
6104 32 00	6108 31 10	6211 12 00	6403 51 19
6104 33 00	6108 31 90	6211 20 00	6403 51 91
6104 39 00	6108 32 11	6211 32 31	6403 51 95
6104 41 00	6108 32 19	6211 32 41	6403 51 99
6104 42 00	6108 32 90	6211 32 42	6403 59 11
6104 43 00	6108 39 00	6211 33 31	6403 59 31
6104 44 00	6108 91 10	6211 33 41	6403 59 35
6104 49 00	6108 91 90	6211 33 42	6403 59 39
6104 51 00	6108 92 00	6211 42 31	6403 59 50
6104 52 00	6108 99 10	6211 42 41	6403 59 91
6104 53 00	6108 99 90	6211 42 42	6403 59 95
6104 59 00	6109 10 00	6211 43 31	6403 59 99
6104 61 10	6109 90 10	6211 43 41	6403 91 11

6403 91 13	7108 13 80	8539 29 30	8542 21 83
6403 91 16	7108 20 00	8539 29 92	8542 21 85
6403 91 18	7110 11 00	8539 29 98	8542 21 99
6403 91 91	7110 19 10	8539 31 10	8542 29 10
6403 91 93	7110 19 80	8539 31 90	8542 29 20
6403 91 96	7110 21 00	8539 32 10	8542 29 90
6403 91 98	7110 29 00	8539 32 50	8903 91 10
6403 99 11	7110 31 00	8539 32 90	8903 91 91
6403 99 31	7110 39 00	8539 39 00	8903 91 93
6403 99 33	7110 41 00	8539 41 00	8903 91 99
6403 99 36	7110 49 00	8539 4910	8903 92 10
6403 99 38	7116 10 00	8539 49 30	8903 92 91
6403 99 50	7116 20 11	8540 11 11	8903 92 99
6403 99 91	7116 20 19	8540 11 13	8903 99 10
6403 99 93	7116 20 90	8540 11 15	8903 99 91
6403 99 96	8504 10 10	8540 11 19	8903 99 99
6403 99 98	8504 10 91	8540 11 91	9001 30 00
6404 11 00	8504 10 99	8540 11 99	9001 40 20
6404 19 10	8504 21 00	8540 12 00	9001 40 41
6404 19 90	8504 22 10	8540 20 10	9001 40 49
6404 20 10	8504 22 90	8540 20 80	9001 40 80
6404 20 90	8504 23 00	8540 40 00	9001 50 20
6405 10 10	8504 31 10	8540 50 00	9001 50 41
6405 10 90	8504 31 31	8540 71 00	9001 50 49
6405 20 10	8504 31 39	8540 72 00	9001 50 80
6405 20 91	8504 31 90	8540 79 00	9003 11 00
6405 20 99	8504 32 10	8540 81 00	9003 19 10
6405 90 10	8504 32 30	8540 89 00	9003 19 30
6405 90 90	8504 32 90	8542 21 01	9003 19 90
7101 10 00	8504 33 10	8542 21 05	9006 53 10
7101 21 00	8504 33 90	8542 21 11	9006 53 90
7101 22 00	8504 34 00	8542 21 13	9202 10 10
7103 91 00	8504 40 10	8542 21 15	9202 10 90
7103 99 00	8504 40 20	8542 21 17	9202 90 10
7104 10 00	8504 40 50	8542 21 20	9202 90 30
7104 20 00	8504 40 93	8542 21 25	9202 90 90
7104 90 00	8504 50 10	8542 21 31	9203 00 90
7105 10 00	8518 21 90	8542 21 33	9204 10 00
7105 90 00	8518 22 90	8542 21 35	9204 20 00
7106 10 00	8518 29 20	8542 21 37	9205 10 00
7106 91 10	8518 29 80	8542 21 39	9207 90 10][3]
7106 91 90	8539 10 10	8542 21 45	
7106 92 20	8539 10 90	8542 21 50	
7106 92 80	8539 21 30	8542 21 69	
7108 11 00	8539 21 92	8542 21 71	
7108 12 00	8539 21 98	8542 21 73	
7108 13 10	8539 22 10	8542 21 81	

ANNEX III

List of transactions referred to in Article 25(2)

A	B
1. Transaction involving actual or intended transfer of ownership against compensation (financial or otherwise) (except the transactions listed under 2, 7,8)0 0(3)	1. Outright/purchase/sale (^{2}) 2. Supply for sale on approval or after trial, for consignment 3. Barter trade (compensation in kind) 4. Personal purchases by travellers 5. Financial leasing (hire purchase) (^{3})
2. Return of goods after registration of the original transaction under cod 1 (^{4}); replacement of goods free of charge (^{4})	1. Return of goods 2. Replacement for returned goods 3. Replacement (e.g. under warranty) for goods not being returned.
3. Transactions (not temporary) involving transfer of ownership but without compensation (financial or other)	1. Goods delivered under aid programmes operated or financed partly or wholly by the European Community. 2. Other general government aid deliveries. 3. Other aid deliveries (individuals, non-governmental organisations) 4. Others
4. Operations with a view to processing under contract (^{5}) or repair (^{6}) (except those recorded under 7)	1. Processing under contract 2. Repair and maintenance against payment 3. Repair and maintenance free of charge
5. Operations following processing under contract (^{5}) or repair (^{6}) (except those recorded under 7)	1. Processing under contract 2. Repair and maintenance against payment 3. Repair and maintenance free of charge
6. Transactions not involving transfer of ownership, e.g. hire, loan, operational leasing (^{6}) and other temporary uses (^{8}), except processing under contract or repair (delivery or return)	1. Hire, loan, operational leasing 2. Other goods for temporary use
7. Operations under joint defence projects or other joint intergovernmental production programmes (e.g. Airbus)	
8. Supply of building materials and equipment for works that are part of a general construction or engineering contract(^{9})	
9. Other transactions	

(1) This item covers most dispatches and arrivals, i.e. transactions in respect of which:
  - ownership is transferred from resident to non-resident, and
  - payment or compensation in kind is or will be made.

It should be noted that this also applies to goods sent between related enterprises or from/to central distribution depots, even if no immediate payment is made.

(2) Including spare parts and other replacements made against payment.

(3) Including financial leasing: the lease instalments are calculated in such a way as to cover all or virtually all of the value of the goods. The risks and rewards of ownership are transferred to the lessee. At the end of the contract the lessee becomes the legal owner of the goods.

(4) Return and replacement dispatches of goods originally recorded under items 3 to 9 of column A should be registered under the corresponding items.

(5) Processing operations (whether or not under customs supervision) should be recorded under items 4 and 5 of column A. Processing activities on processor's own account are not covered by this item; they should be registered under item 1 of column A.

(6) Repair entails the restoration of goods to their original function; this may involve some rebuilding or enhancements.

(7) Operational leasing; leasing contracts other than financial leasing (see note (3)).

(8) This item covers goods that are exported/imported with the intention of subsequent re-import/re-export without any change of ownership taking place.

(9) The transaction recorded under item 8 of column A involve only goods which are not separately invoiced, but for which a single invoice covers the total value of the works. Where this is not the case, the transactions should be recorded under item 1.

ANNEX IV

List of delivery terms referred to in Article 28

First sub-box	Meaning	Place to be indicated (1)
Incoterm code	Incoterm ICC/ECE Geneva	
EXW	ex-works	location of works
FCA	free carrier	...agreed place
FAS	free alongside ship	agreed port of loading
FOB	free on board	agreed port of loading
CFR	cost and freight (C & F)	agreed port of destination
CIF	cost, insurance and freight	agreed port of destination
CPT	carriage paid to	agreed place of destination
CIP	carriage and insurance paid to	agreed place of destination
DAF	delivery at frontier	agreed place of delivery at frontier
DES	delivered ex-ship	agreed port of destination
DEQ	delivered ex-quay	after customs clearance, agreed port
DDU	delivered duty unpaid	agreed place of delivery in importing country
DDP	delivered duty paid	agreed place of delivery in importing country
XXX	delivery terms other than the above	precise statement of terms specified in the contract (1)
(1) Provide details in box 6 if necessary (Intrastat N Form only).		

Second sub-box

1. place located in the territory of the Member State concerned

2. place located in another Member State

3. other (place located outside the Community).

ANNEX V

Table of correspondences between the Articles of this Regulation and the Articles of the repealed regulations

Regulation Articles	Reference Articles
Article 1	Article 1 of Regulation (EEC) No 3046/92
Article 2	Article 2(2) of Regulation (EEC) No 3046/92
Article 3	Article 3 of Regulation (EEC) No 3046/92 (amended)
Article 4	Article 4 of Regulation (EEC) No 3046/92
Article 5	Article 5 of Regulation (EEC) No 3046/92
Article 6	Article 6 of Regulation (EEC No 3046/92
Article 7	Article 7 of Regulation (EEC) No 3046/92
Article 8	Article 8 of Regulation (EEC) No 3046/92
Article 9	Article 9 of Regulation (EEC) No 3046/92
Article 10	Article 1 of Regulation (EEC) No 2256/92
Article 11	Article 2 of Regulation (EEC) No 2256/92
Article 12	Article 3 of Regulation (EEC) No 2256/92 (amended)
Article 13	Article 4 of Regulation (EEC) No 2256/92 (amended)
Article 14	Article 6 of Regulation (EEC) No 2256/92
Article 15	Article 7 of Regulation (EEC) No 2256/92
Article 16	Article 8 of Regulation (EEC) No 2256/92
Article 17	Article 9 of Regulation (EEC) No 2256/92
Article 18	Article 10 of Regulation (EEC) No 2256/92
Article 19	(New)
Article 20	Articles 1 & 2 of Regulation (EC) No 2820/94 (amended)
Article 21	Article 20 of Regulation (EEC) No 3046/92
Article 22	Article 10 of Regulation (EEC) No 3046/92 (amended)
Article 23	Article 11 of Regulation (EEC) No 3046/92 (amended)
Article 24	Article 12 of Regulation (EEC) No 3046/92 (amended)
Article 25	Article 13 of Regulation (EEC) No 3046/92
Article 26	Article 16 of Regulation (EEC) No 3046/92
Article 27	Article 17 of Regulation (EEC) No 3046/92
Article 28	Article 14(1) & (2) of Regulation (EEC) No 3046/92 (amended)
Article 29	Article 15 of Regulation (EEC) No 3046/92 (amended)
Article 30	Article 19 of Regulation (EEC) No 3046/92 (amended)
Articles 31 to 46	(New Articles)
Article 47	Article 21(3) of Regulation (EEC) No 3046/92
Article 48	Article 1 of Regulation (EC) No 1125/94
Article 49 and 50	(New Articles)

Amendments

1   Substituted by Treaty of Accession to the European Union 2003
2   Substituted by Commission Regulation (EC) No 1835/2002 of 15 October 2002
3   Substituted by Commission Regulation (EC) No 2150/2001 of 31 October 2001

COUNCIL DIRECTIVE 2000/65/EC

of 17 October 2000

amending Directive 77/388/EEC as regards the determination of the person liable for payment of value added tax

Official Journal L269, 21/10/2000 p. 0044 - 0046

This Directive was repealed by Council Directive 2006/112/EC of 28 November 2006 on the common system of value added tax, with effect from 1 January 2007

THE COUNCIL OF THE EUROPEAN UNION,

Having regard to the Treaty establishing the European Community, and in particular Article 93 thereof,

Having regard to the proposal from the Commission,

Having regard to the opinion of the European Parliament,

Having regard to the opinion of the Economic and Social Committee,

Whereas:

(1) The present rules laid down by Article 21 of sixth Council Directive 77/388/EEC of 17 May 1977 on the harmonisation of the laws of the Member States relating to turnover taxes - Common system of value added tax: uniform basis of assessment, as regards the determination of the person liable for payment of the tax, create serious problems for business and, in particular, for the smallest businesses.

(2) Council Directive 76/308/EEC of 15 March 1976 on mutual assistance for the recovery of claims resulting from operations forming part of the system of financing the European Agricultural Guidance and Guarantee Fund and of the agricultural levies and customs duties, Council Directive 77/799/EEC of 19 December 1977 concerning mutual assistance by the competent authorities of the Member States in the field of direct taxation and Council Regulation (EEC) No 218/92 of 27 January 1992 on administrative cooperation in the field of indirect taxation (VAT) organise mutual assistance between the Member States as regards the correct establishment of VAT and its recovery.

(3) The Commission report on the second phase of the SLIM (simpler legislation for the internal market) project recommends a study of the possibilities and different ways of reforming the tax representation system laid down by Article 21 of Directive 77/388/EEC.

(4) The only change which can in fact substantially simplify the common system of VAT in general and the determination of the person liable for payment of the tax in particular is no longer to allow Member States the option of requiring the appointment of a tax representative.

(5) Therefore, the appointment of a tax representative should in future only be a option for non-established taxable persons.

(6) Under Article 22 of Directive 77/388/EEC, Member States may impose directly on non-established taxable persons the same obligations as those

which apply to established taxable persons, including those which may be laid down under Article 22(8).

(7) Where non-established taxable persons are nationals of countries with which no legal instrument exists which organises mutual assistance similar to that laid down within the Community, it will be possible for the Member States to continue to require such non-established taxable persons to designate a tax representative to be the person liable for payment of the tax in their stead or to designate an agent.

(8) Member States will continue to be entirely free to designate the person liable for payment of the tax on importation.

(9) Member States may continue to provide that someone other than the person liable for payment of the tax shall be held jointly and severally liable for payment of the tax.

(10) Article 10 of Directive 77/388/EEC should also be clarified in order to prevent certain cases of tax avoidance in the case of continuous supplies.

(11) Directive 77/388/EEC should therefore be amended accordingly,

HAS ADOPTED THIS DIRECTIVE:

Article 1

Directive 77/388/EEC is hereby amended as follows:

1. In the first subparagraph of Article 10(2), after the second sentence, the following sentence shall be inserted:

   'Member States may in certain cases provide that continuous supplies of goods and services which take place over a period of time shall be regarded as being completed at least at intervals of one year.'

2. In Article 28f(1) (which amends Article 17(2), (3) and (4) of the same Directive), in Article 17(4)(a), the terms 'Article 21(1)(a)' shall be replaced by 'Article 21(1)(a) and (c)'.

3. In the fifth indent of Article 28c(E) 'Other Exemptions' (3), the terms 'the third subparagraph of Article 21(1)(a)' shall be replaced by 'Article 21(1) (c)'.

4. In Article 28g (which replaces Article 21 of the same Directive), Article 21 shall be replaced by the following:

'Article 21

Persons liable for payment for tax

1. Under the internal system, the following shall be liable to pay value added tax:

(a) the taxable person carrying out the taxable supply of goods or of services, except for the cases referred to in (b) and (c).

Where the taxable supply of goods or of services is effected by a taxable person who is not established within the territory of the country, Member States may, under conditions determined by them, lay down that the person liable to pay tax is the person for whom the taxable supply of goods or of services is carried out;

(b) taxable persons to whom services covered by Article 9(2)(e) are supplied or persons who are identified for value added tax purposes within the territory of the country to whom services covered by Article 28b(C), (D), (E) and (F) are supplied, if the services are carried out by a taxable person not established within the territory of the country;

(c) the person to whom the supply of goods is made when the following conditions are met:

— the taxable operation is a supply of goods made under the conditions laid down in Article 28c(E)(3),

— the person to whom the supply of goods is made is another taxable person or a non -taxable legal person identified for the purposes of value added tax within the territory of the country,

— the invoice issued by the taxable person not established within the territory of the country conforms to Article 22(3).

However, Member States may provide a derogation from this obligation, where the taxable person who is not established within the territory of the country has appointed a tax representative in that country;

(d) any person who mentions the value added tax on an invoice or other document serving as invoice;

(e) any person effecting a taxable intra-Community acquisition of goods.

2. By way of derogation from the provisions of paragraph 1:

(a) where the person liable to pay tax in accordance with the provisions of paragraph 1 is a taxable person who is not established within the territory of the country, Member States may allow him to appoint a tax representative as the person liable to pay tax. This option shall be subject to conditions and procedures laid down by each Member State;

(b) where the taxable transaction is effected by a taxable person who is not established within the territory of the country and no legal instrument exists, with the country in which that taxable person is established or has his seat, relating to mutual assistance similar in scope to that laid down by Directives 76/308/EEC and 77/799/EEC and by Council Regulation (EEC) No 218/92 of 27 January 1992 on administrative cooperation in the field of indirect taxation (VAT), Member States may take steps to provide that the person liable for payment of the tax shall be a tax representative appointed by the non-established taxable person.

3. In the situations referred to in paragraphs 1 and 2, Member States may provide that someone other than the person liable for payment of the tax shall be held jointly and severally liable for payment of the tax.

4. On importation, value added tax shall be payable by the person or persons designated or accepted as being liable by the Member State in to which the goods are imported.

5. In Article 28h (which replaces Article 22 of the same Directive), Article 22 shall be amended as follows:

    (a) In paragraph 1(c) the first indent shall be replaced by the following:

    '- every taxable person, with the exception of those referred to in Article 28a(4), who within the territory of the country effects supplies of goods or of services giving him the right of deduction, other than supplies of goods or of services for which tax is payable solely by the customer or the recipient in accordance with Article 21(1)(a), (b) or (c). However, Member States need not identify certain taxable persons referred to in Article 4(3);'

    (b) Paragraph 7 shall be replaced by the following:

    '7. Member States shall take the measures necessary to ensure that those persons who, in accordance with Article 21(1) and (2), are considered to be liable to pay the tax instead of a taxable person not established within the territory of the country comply with the obligations relating to declaration and payment set out in this Article; they shall also take the measures necessary to ensure that those persons who, in accordance with Article 21(3), are held to be jointly and severally liable for payment of the tax comply with the obligations relating to payment set out in this Article.'

6. Throughout the Directive, notwithstanding points 2, 3 and 5 of this Article, the terms 'Article 21(2)' shall be replaced by 'Article 21(4)'.

Article 2

1. Member States shall bring into force the laws, regulations and administrative provisions necessary to comply with this Directive not later than 31 December 2001. They shall forthwith inform the Commission thereof.

    When Member States adopt these measures, they shall contain a reference to this Directive or shall be accompanied by such reference on the occasion of their official publication. The methods of making such a reference shall be laid down by the Member States.

2. Member States shall communicate to the Commission the text of the provisions of national law which they adopt in the field governed by this Directive and a table correlating the provisions of this Directive with the provisions of national law.

Article 3

This Directive shall enter into force on the day of its publication in the Official Journal of the European Communities.

Article 4

This Directive is addressed to the Member States.

Done at Luxembourg, 17 October 2000.

For the Council
The President

L. FABIUS

COUNCIL DIRECTIVE 2001/4/EC[1]

of 19 January 2001

amending the sixth Directive (77/388/EEC) on the common system of value added tax, with regard to the length of time during which the minimum standard rate is to be applied

Official Journal L22, 24/1/2001 p. 17 - 17

> This Directive was repealed by Council Directive 2006/112/EC of 28 November 2006 on the common system of value added tax, with effect from 1 January 2007

THE COUNCIL OF THE EUROPEAN UNION,

Having regard to the Treaty establishing the European Community, and in particular Article 93 thereof,

Having regard to the proposal from the Commission,

Having regard to the opinion of the European Parliament,

Having regard to the opinion of the Economic and Social

Committee,

Whereas:

(1)   Article 12(3)(a)of the sixth Council Directive (77/388/EEC) of 17 May 1977 on the harmonisation of the laws of the Member States relating to turnover taxes - Common system of value added tax: uniform basis of assessment, hereinafter referred to as the sixth VAT Directive, lays down that the Council is to decide on the level of the standard rate applicable after 31 December 2000.

(2)   While the standard rate of value added tax currently in force in the various Member States, combined with the mechanism of the transitional system, has ensured that this system has functioned to an acceptable degree, it is nonetheless important to prevent a growing divergence in the standard rates of VAT applied by the Member States from leading to structural imbalances in the Community and distortions of competition in some sectors of activity, at least in the period in which a new VAT strategy is being implemented to simplify and modernise current Community legislation on VAT, as set out in the Commission Communication of 7 June 2000.

(3)   It is therefore appropriate to maintain the current minimum standard rate at 15% for a further period long enough to allow the strategy for simplification and modernisation to be implemented,

HAS ADOPTED THIS DIRECTIVE:

Article 1

The first and second subparagraphs of Article 12(3)(a) of the sixth VAT Directive shall be replaced by the following:

'3   (a)   The standard rate of value added tax shall be fixed by each
             Member State as a percentage of the taxable amount and shall be
             the same for the supply of goods and for the supply of services.
             From 1 January 2001 to 31 December 2005, this percentage may
             not be less than 15%.

             On a proposal from the Commission and after consulting the
             European Parliament and the Economic and Social Committee,
             the Council shall decide unanimously on the level of the standard
             rate to be applied after 31 December 2005.'

Article 2

1.   Member States shall bring into force the laws,regulations and
     administrative provisions necessary to comply with this Directive
     before 1 January 2001. They shall forthwith inform the Commission
     thereof. When Member States adopt these measures, they shall contain a
     reference to this Directive or shall be accompanied by such reference on
     the occasion of their official publication. The methods of making such
     reference shall be laid down by Member States.

2.   Member States shall communicate to the Commission the text of the
     provisions of national law which they adopt in the field covered by this
     Directive.

Article 3

This Directive shall enter into force on the third day following that of its
publication in the Official Journal of the European Communities. It shall
apply from 1 January 2001.

Article 4

This Directive is addressed to the Member States.
Done at Brussels, 19 January 2001.
For the Council

The President
B.RINGHOLM

Amendments
1 Corrigendum to Council Directive 2001/41/EC of 19 January 2001 amending the sixth Directive (77/388/
   EEC) on the common system of value added tax, with regard to the length of time during which the
   minimum standard rate is to be applied
   (Official Journal of the European Communities L 22 of 24 January 2001)

   In the contents, on the second page of the cover, and on page 17,in the title:

   for:'2001/41/EC ',
   read:'2001/4/EC '.

COUNCIL DIRECTIVE 2001/44/EC

of 15 June 2001

amending Directive 76/308/EEC on mutual assistance for the recovery of claims resulting from operations forming part of the system of financing the European Agricultural Guidance and Guarantee Fund, and of agricultural levies and customs duties and in respect of value added tax and certain excise duties

Official journal L175, 28/6/2001, p. 17-20

THE COUNCIL OF THE EUROPEAN UNION,

Having regard to the Treaty establishing the European Community, and in particular Articles 93 and 94 thereof,

Having regard to the proposal from the Commission,

Having regard to the opinion of the European Parliament,

Having regard to the opinion of the Economic and Social Committee,

Whereas:

(1) The existing arrangements for mutual assistance for recovery set out in Directive 76/308/EEC should be modified to meet the threat to the financial interests of the Community and the Member States and to the internal market posed by the development of fraud.

(2) In the context of the internal market, Community and national financial interests, which are increasingly threatened by fraud, must be protected so as to safeguard better the competitiveness and fiscal neutrality of the internal market.

(3) In order to safeguard better the financial interests of the Member States and the neutrality of the internal market, claims relating to certain taxes on income and capital and taxes on insurance premiums should be added to the scope of the mutual assistance provided for by Directive 76/308/EEC.

(4) In order to permit more efficient and effective recovery of claims in respect of which a request for recovery has been made, the instrument permitting enforcement of the claim should, in principle, be treated as an instrument of the Member State in which the requested authority is situated.

(5) The use of mutual assistance for recovery cannot, save in exceptional circumstances, be based on financial benefits or an interest in the results obtained, but Member States should be able to agree the reimbursement arrangements when recovery poses a specific problem.

(6) The measures necessary for the implementation of this Directive should be adopted in accordance with Council Decision 1999/468/EC of 28 June 1999 laying down the procedures for the exercise of implementing powers conferred on the Commission.

(7) Directive 76/308/EEC should therefore be amended accordingly,

HAS ADOPTED THIS DIRECTIVE:

Article 1

Directive 76/308/EEC is hereby amended as follows:

1. The title shall be replaced by the following:

    "Council Directive 76/308/EEC of 15 March 1976 on mutual assistance for the recovery of claims relating to certain levies, duties, taxes and other measures."

2. Article 2 shall be replaced by the following:

    "Article 2

    This Directive shall apply to all claims relating to:

    (a) refunds, interventions and other measures forming part of the system of total or partial financing of the European Agricultural Guidance and Guarantee Fund (EAGGF), including sums to be collected in connection with these actions;

    (b) levies and other duties provided for under the common organisation of the market for the sugar sector;

    (c) import duties;

    (d) export duties;

    (e) value added tax;

    (f) excise duties on:
    — manufactured tobacco,

    — alcohol and alcoholic beverages,

    — mineral oils;

    (g) taxes on income and capital;

    (h) taxes on insurance premiums;

    (i) interest, administrative penalties and fines, and costs incidental to the claims referred to in points (a) to (h), with the exclusion of any sanction of a criminal nature as determined by the laws in force in the Member State in which the requested authority is situated."

3. In Article 3, the following indents shall be added:
    "   — 'import duties' means customs duties and charges having equivalent effect on imports, and import charges laid down within the framework of the common agricultural policy or in that of specific arrangements applicable to certain goods resulting from the processing of agricultural products,

        — 'export duties' means customs duties and charges having equivalent effect on exports, and export charges laid down within the framework of the common agricultural policy or in that of specific arrangements applicable to certain goods resulting from the processing of agricultural products,

— 'taxes on income and capital' means those enumerated in Article 1(3) of Directive 77/799/EEC, read in conjunction with Article 1(4) of that Directive,

— 'taxes on insurance premiums' means:

in Austria:	(i)	Versicherungssteuer
	(ii)	Feuerschutzsteuer
in Belgium:	(i)	Taxe annuelle sur les contrats d'assurance
	(ii)	Jaarlijkse taks op de verzekeringscontracten
in Germany:	(i)	Versicherungssteuer
	(ii)	Feuerschutzsteuer
in Denmark:	(i)	Afgift af lystfartøjsforsikringer
	(ii)	Afgift af ansvarsforsikringer for motorkøretøjer m.v.
	(iii)	Stempelafgift af forsikringspræmier
in Spain:		Impuesto sobre la prima de seguros
in Greece:	(i)	Φόρος κύκλου εργασιών (Φ.Κ.Ε.)
	(ii)	Τέλη Χαρτοσήμου
in France:	(i)	Taxe sur les conventions d'assurances
in Finland:	(i)	Eräistä vakuutusmaksuista suoritettava vero/skatt på vissa försäkringspremier
	(ii)	Palosuojelumaksu/ brandskyddsavgift
in Italy:		Imposte sulle assicurazioni private ed i contratti vitalizi di cui alla legge 29.10.1967 No 1216
in Ireland:		levy on insurance premiums
in Luxembourg:	(i)	Impôt sur les assurances
	(ii)	Impôt dans l'interêt du service d'incendie
in the Netherlands:		Assurantiebelasting

in Portugal:	Imposto de selo sobre os prémios de seguros
in Sweden:	none
in the United Kingdom:	insurance premium tax (IPT)

This Directive shall also apply to claims relating to identical or analogous taxes which supplement or replace the taxes on insurance premiums referred to in the sixth indent. The competent authorities of the Member States shall communicate to each other and to the Commission the dates of entry into force of such taxes.

4. In Article 4(2), the words "the name and address" shall be replaced by: "the name, address and any other relevant information relating to the identification to which the applicant authority normally has access".

5. In Article 5(2) the words "the name and address" shall be replaced by: "the name, address and any other relevant information relating to the identification to which the applicant authority normally has access".

6. Articles 7, 8, 9 and 10 shall be replaced by the following:

"Article 7

1. The request for recovery of a claim which the applicant authority addresses to the requested authority must be accompanied by an official or certified copy of the instrument permitting its enforcement, issued in the Member State in which the applicant authority is situated and, if appropriate, by the original or a certified copy of other documents necessary for recovery.

2. The applicant authority may not make a request for recovery unless:

(a) the claim and/or the instrument permitting its enforcement are not contested in the Member State in which it is situated, except in cases where the second subparagraph of Article 12(2) is applied,

(b) it has, in the Member State in which it is situated, applied appropriate recovery procedures available to it on the basis of the instrument referred to in paragraph 1, and the measures taken will not result in the payment in full of the claim.

3. The request for recovery shall indicate:

(a) the name, address and any other relevant information relating to the identification of the person concerned and/or to the third party holding his or her assets;

(b) the name, address and any other relevant information relating to the identification of the applicant authority;

(c) a reference to the instrument permitting its enforcement issued in the Member State in which the applicant authority is situated;

(d) the nature and the amount of the claim, including the principal, the interest, and any other penalties, fines and costs due indicated in the currencies of the Member States in which both authorities are situated;

(e) the date of notification of the instrument to the addressee by the applicant authority and/or by the requested authority;

(f) the date from which and the period during which enforcement is possible under the laws in force in the Member State in which the applicant authority is situated;

(g) any other relevant information.

4. The request for recovery shall also contain a declaration by the applicant authority confirming that the conditions set out in paragraph 2 have been fulfilled.

5. As soon as any relevant information relating to the matter which gave rise to the request for recovery comes to the knowledge of the applicant authority it shall forward it to the requested authority.

Article 8

1. The instrument permitting enforcement of the claim shall be directly recognised and automatically treated as an instrument permitting enforcement of a claim of the Member State in which the requested authority is situated.

2. Notwithstanding the first paragraph, the instrument permitting enforcement of the claim may, where appropriate and in accordance with the provisions in force in the Member State in which the requested authority is situated, be accepted as, recognised as, supplemented with, or replaced by an instrument authorising enforcement in the territory of that Member State.

Within three months of the date of receipt of the request for recovery, Member States shall endeavour to complete such acceptance, recognition, supplementing or replacement, except in cases where the third subparagraph is applied. They may not be refused if the instrument permitting enforcement is properly drawn up. The requested authority shall inform the applicant authority of the grounds for exceeding the period of three months.

If any of these formalities should give rise to contestation in connection with the claim and/or the instrument permitting enforcement issued by the applicant authority, Article 12 shall apply.

Article 9

1. Claims shall be recovered in the currency of the Member State in which the requested authority is situated. The entire amount of the claim that is recovered by the requested authority shall be remitted by the requested authority to the applicant authority.

2. The requested authority may, where the laws, regulations or administrative provisions in force in the Member State in which it is situated so permit, and after consultations with the applicant authority, allow the debtor time to pay or authorise payment by instalment. Any

interest charged by the requested authority in respect of such extra time to pay shall also be remitted to the Member State in which the applicant authority is situated.

From the date on which the instrument permitting enforcement of recovery of the claim has been directly recognised or accepted, recognised, supplemented or replaced in accordance with Article 8, interest will be charged for late payment under the laws, regulations and administrative provisions in force in the Member State in which the requested authority is situated and shall also be remitted to the Member State in which the applicant authority is situated.

Article 10

Notwithstanding Article 6(2), the claims to be recovered shall not necessarily benefit from the privileges accorded to similar claims arising in the Member State in which the requested authority is situated."

7. Article 12(2) shall be amended as follows:

(a) The following shall be added to the first sentence: "unless the applicant authority requests otherwise in accordance with the second subparagraph";

(b) the following subparagraph shall be added:

"Notwithstanding the first subparagraph of paragraph 2, the applicant authority may in accordance with the law, regulations and administrative practices in force in the Member State in which it is situated, request the requested authority to recover a contested claim, in so far as the relevant laws, regulations and administrative practices in force in the Member State in which the requested authority is situated allow such action. If the result of contestation is subsequently favourable to the debtor, the applicant authority shall be liable for the reimbursement of any sums recovered, together with any compensation due, in accordance with the laws in force in the Member State in which the requested authority is situated."

8. In Article 14, the first paragraph, shall be replaced by the following:

"The requested authority shall not be obliged:

(a) to grant the assistance provided for in Articles 6 to 13 if recovery of the claim would, because of the situation of the debtor, create serious economic or social difficulties in the Member State in which that authority is situated, in so far as the laws, regulations and administrative practices in force in the Member State in which the requested authority is situated allow such action for similar national claims;

(b) to grant the assistance provided for in Articles 4 to 13, if the initial request under Article 4, 5 or 6 applies to claims more than five years old, dating from the moment the instrument permitting the recovery is established in accordance with the laws, regulations or administrative practices in force in the Member State in which the applicant authority is situated, to the date of the request. However, in cases where the claim or the instrument is contested, the time limit begins from the moment at which the applicant State establishes that the claim or the enforcement order permitting recovery may no longer be contested."

9. In Article 17, the words "and relevant documents" shall be replaced by: "the instrument J permitting the enforcement and other relevant documents".

10. Article 18 shall be replaced by the following:

"Article 18

1. The requested authority shall recover from the person concerned and retain any costs linked to recovery which it incurs, in accordance with the laws and regulations of the Member State in which it is situated that apply to similar claims.

2. Member States shall renounce all claims on each other for the refund of costs resulting from mutual assistance which they grant each other pursuant to this Directive.

3. Where recovery poses a specific problem, concerns a very large amount in costs or relates to the fight against organised crime, the applicant and requested authorities may agree reimbursement arrangements specific to the cases in question.

4. The Member State in which the applicant authority is situated shall remain liable to the Member State in which the requested authority is situated for any costs and any losses incurred as a result of actions held to be unfounded, as far as either the substance of the claim or the validity of the instrument issued by the applicant authority are concerned."

11. Article 20 shall be replaced by the following:

"Article 20

1. The Commission shall be assisted by a recovery committee (hereinafter referred to as 'the Committee'), composed of representatives of the Member States and chaired by the representative of the Commission.

2. Where reference is made to this paragraph, Articles 5 and 7 of Decision 1999/468/EC shall apply.

    The period referred to in Article 5(6) of Decision 1999/468/EC shall be set at three months.

3. The Committee shall adopt its own rules of procedure."

12. Article 22 shall be replaced by the following:

"Article 22

The detailed rules for implementing Articles 4(2) and (4), 5(2) and (3) and Articles 7, 8, 9, 11, 12(1) and (2), 14, 18(3) and 25 and for determining the means by which communications between the authorities may be transmitted, the rules on conversion, transfer of sums recovered, and the fixing of a minimum amount for claims which may give rise to a request for assistance, shall be adopted in accordance with the procedure laid down in Article 20(2)."

13. The following paragraph shall be added to Article 25:

"Each Member State shall inform the Commission annually of the number of requests for information, notification and recovery sent and received each year, the amount of the claims involved and the amounts recovered. The Commission shall report biennially to the European Parliament and the Council on the use made of these arrangements and on the results achieved."

Article 2

1. Member States shall bring into force the laws, regulations and administrative provisions necessary to comply with this Directive not later than 30 June 2002. They shall forthwith inform the Commission thereof.

   When Member States adopt these measures, they shall contain a reference to this Directive or shall be accompanied by such reference on the occasion of their official publication. The methods of making such reference shall be laid down by Member States.

2. Member States shall communicate to the Commission the text of the main provisions of national law which they adopt in the field covered by this Directive together with a table showing how the provisions of this Directive correspond to the national provisions adopted.

Article 3

This Directive shall enter into force on the 20th day following its publication in the Official Journal of the European Communities.

Article 4

This Directive is addressed to the Member States.

Done at Göteborg, 15 June 2001.

For the Council
The President
B. Ringholm

COUNCIL DIRECTIVE 2001/115/EC

of 20 December 2001

amending Directive 77/388/EEC with a view to simplifying, modernising and harmonising the conditions laid down for invoicing in respect of value added tax

Official Journal L15, 17/1/2002 p. 24 - 28

> This Directive was repealed by Council Directive 2006/112/EC of 28 November 2006 on the common system of value added tax, with effect from 1 January 2007

THE COUNCIL OF THE EUROPEAN UNION,

Having regard to the Treaty establishing the European Community, and in particular Article 93 thereof,

Having regard to the proposal from the Commission,

Having regard to the opinion of the European Parliament,

Having regard to the opinion of the Economic and Social Committee,

Whereas:

(1)   The current conditions laid down for invoicing and listed under Article 22(3),in the version given in Article 28h of the Sixth Council Directive 77/388/EEC of 17 May 1977 on the harmonisation of the laws of the Member States relating to turnover taxes — Common system of value added tax: uniform basis of assessment, are relatively few in number, thus leaving it to the Member States to define the most important such conditions. At the same time, the conditions are no longer appropriate given the development of new invoicing technologies and methods.

(2)   The Commission report on the second phase of the SLIM exercise (Simpler Legislation for the Single Market) recommended that a study be carried out to determine what details should be required for VAT purposes when drawing up an invoice and what the legal and technical requirements are as regards electronic invoicing.

(3)   The conclusions of the Ecofin Council of June 1998 underlined the fact that the development of electronic commerce has made it necessary to establish a legal framework for the use of electronic invoicing to enable tax administrations to continue to perform their controls.

(4)   It is therefore necessary, in order to ensure that the internal market functions properly, to draw up a list, harmonised at Community level, of the particulars that must appear on invoices for the purposes of value added tax and to establish a number of common arrangements governing the use of electronic invoicing and the electronic storage of invoices, as well as for self-billing and the outsourcing of invoicing operations.

(5)   Lastly, the storage of invoices should comply with the conditions laid down by Directive 95/46/EC of the European Parliament and of the

Council of 24 October 1995 on the protection of individuals with regard to the processing of personal data and on the free movement of such data.

(6) Since the introduction of the transitional VAT arrangements in 1993, Greece has adopted the prefix EL rather than the prefix GR laid down in the ISO International Standard No 3166 —alpha 2 referred to in Article 22(1)(d). Given the consequences of amending the prefix in all the Member States, it is important to lay down an exception for Greece providing that the ISO Standard does not apply in Greece.

(7) Directive 77/388/EEC should therefore be amended accordingly,

HAS ADOPTED THIS DIRECTIVE:

Article 1

Directive 77/388/EEC is hereby amended in accordance with the following Articles.

Article 2

At Article 28h (which replaces Article 22 of the same Directive), Article 22 shall be amended as follows:

1. The following sentence shall be added to paragraph 1(d):

'Nevertheless, the Hellenic Republic shall be authorised to use the prefix "EL".'

2. Paragraph 3 shall be replaced by the following:

'3 (a) Every taxable person shall ensure that an invoice is issued, either by himself or by his customer or, in his name and on his behalf, by a third party, in respect of goods or services which he has supplied or rendered to another taxable person or to a non-taxable legal person. Every taxable person shall also ensure that an invoice is issued, either by himself or by his customer or, in his name and on his behalf, by a third party, in respect of the supplies of goods referred to in Article 28b(B)(1) and in respect of goods supplied under the conditions laid down in Article 28c(A).

Every taxable person shall likewise ensure that an invoice is issued, either by himself or by his customer or, in his name and on his behalf, by a third party, in respect of any payment on account made to him before any supplies of goods referred to in the first subparagraph and in respect of any payment on account made to him by another taxable person or non-taxable legal person before the provision of services is completed.

Member States may impose on taxable persons an obligation to issue an invoice in respect of goods or services other than those referred to in the preceding subparagraphs which they have supplied or rendered on their territory. When they do so, Member States may impose fewer obligations in respect of these invoices than those listed under points (b), (c) and (d).

The Member States may release taxable persons from the obligation to issue an invoice in respect of goods or services which they have supplied or rendered in their territory and which are exempt, with or without refund of the tax paid at the preceding stage, pursuant to Article 13, Article 28(2)(a) and Article 28(3)(b).

Any document or message that amends and refers specifically and unambiguously to the initial invoice is to be treated as an invoice. Member States in whose territory goods or services are supplied or rendered may allow some of the obligatory details to be left out of such documents or messages.

Member States may impose time limits for the issue of invoices on taxable persons supplying goods and services in their territory.

Under conditions to be laid down by the Member States in whose territory goods or services are supplied or rendered, a summary invoice may be drawn up for several separate supplies of goods or services.

Invoices may be drawn up by the customer of a taxable person in respect of goods or services supplied or rendered to him by that taxable person, on condition that there is at the outset an agreement between the two parties, and on condition that a procedure exists for the acceptance of each invoice by the taxable person supplying the goods or services. The Member States in whose territory the goods or services are supplied or rendered shall determine the terms and conditions of the agreement and of the acceptance procedures between the taxable person and his customer.

Member States may impose further conditions on the issue of invoices by the customers of taxable persons supplying goods or services on their territory. For example, they may require that such invoices be issued in the name and on behalf of the taxable person. Such conditions must always be the same wherever the customer is established.

Member States may also lay down specific conditions for taxable persons supplying goods or services in their territory in cases where the third party, or the customer, who issues invoices is established in a country with which no legal instrument exists relating to mutual assistance similar in scope to that laid down by Council Directive 76/308/EEC of 15 March 1976 on mutual assistance for the recovery of claims relating to certain levies, duties, taxes and other measures, Council Directive 77/799/EEC of 19 December 1977 concerning mutual assistance by the competent authorities of the Member States in the field of direct and indirect taxation and by Council Regulation (EEC) No 218/92 of 27 January 1992 on administrative cooperation in the field of indirect taxation (VAT).

(b) Without prejudice to the specific arrangements laid down by this Directive, only the following details are required for VAT purposes on invoices issued under the first, second and third subparagraphs of point (a):

— the date of issue;

— a sequential number, based on one or more series, which uniquely identifies the invoice,

— the VAT identification number referred to in paragraph 1(c) under which the taxable person supplied the goods or services;

— where the customer is liable to pay tax on goods supplied or services rendered or has been supplied with goods as referred to in Article 28c(A), the VAT identification number as referred to in paragraph 1(c) under which the goods were supplied or the services rendered to him;

— the full name and address of the taxable person and of his customer;

— the quantity and nature of the goods supplied or the extent and nature of the services rendered;

— the date on which the supply of goods or of services was made or completed or the date on which the payment on account referred to in the second subparagraph of point (a) was made, insofar as that a date can be determined and differs from the date of issue of the invoice;

— the taxable amount per rate or exemption, the unit price exclusive of tax and any discounts or rebates if they are not included in the unit price;

— the VAT rate applied;

— the VAT amount payable, except where a specific arrangement is applied for which this Directive excludes such a detail;

— where an exemption is involved or where the customer is liable to pay the tax, reference to the appropriate provision of this directive, to the corresponding national provision, or to any indication that the supply is exempt or subject to the reverse charge procedure;

— where the intra-Community supply of a new means of transport is involved, the particulars specified in Article 28a(2);

— where the margin scheme is applied, reference to Article 26 or 26a, to the corresponding national provisions, or to any other indication that the margin scheme has been applied;

— where the person liable to pay the tax is a tax representative within the meaning of Article 21(2), the VAT identification number referred to in paragraph 1(c) of that tax representative, together with his full name and address.

Member States may require taxable persons established on their territory and supplying goods or services on their territory to indicate the VAT identification number referred to in paragraph 1(c) of their customer in cases other than those referred to in the fourth indent of the first subparagraph.

Member States shall not require invoices to be signed.

The amounts which appear on the invoice may be expressed in any currency, provided that the amount of tax to be paid is expressed in the national currency of the Member State where the supply of goods or services takes place, using the conversion mechanism laid down in Article 11C(2).

Where necessary for control purposes, Member States may require invoices in respect of goods supplied or services rendered in their territory and invoices received by taxable persons in their territory to be translated into their national languages.

(c) Invoices issued pursuant to point (a) may be sent either on paper or, subject to an acceptance by the customer, by electronic means.

Invoices sent by electronic means shall be accepted by Member States provided that the authenticity of the origin and integrity of the contents are guaranteed:

— by means of an advanced electronic signature within the meaning of Article 2(2) of Directive 1999/93/EC of the European Parliament and of the Council of 13 December 1999 on a Community framework for electronic signatures; Member States may however ask for the advanced electronic signature to be based on a qualified certificate and created by a secure-signature-creation device, within the meaning of Article 2(6) and (10) of the aforementioned Directive;

— or by means of electronic data interchange (EDI) as defined in Article 2 of Commission Recommendation 1994/820/EC of 19 October 1994 relating to the legal aspects of electronic data interchange when the agreement relating to the exchange provides for the use of procedures guaranteeing the authenticity of the origin and integrity of the data; however Member States may, subject to conditions which they lay down, require that an additional summary document on paper is necessary.

Invoices may, however, be sent by other electronic means subject to acceptance by the Member State(s) concerned. The Commission will present, at the latest on 31 December 2008, a report, together with a proposal, if appropriate, amending the conditions on electronic invoicing in order to take account of possible future technological developments in this field.

Member States may not impose on taxable persons supplying goods or services in their territory any other obligations or formalities relating to the transmission of invoices by electronic means. However, they may provide, until 31 December 2005, that the use of such a system is to be subject to prior notification.

Member States may lay down specific conditions for invoices issued by electronic means for goods or services supplied in their territory from a country with which no legal instrument exists relating to mutual assistance similar in scope to that laid down by Directives 76/308/EEC and 77/799/EEC and by Regulation (EEC) No 218/92.

When batches containing several invoices are sent to the same recipient by electronic means, the details that are common to the individual invoices may be mentioned only once if, for each invoice, all the information is accessible.

(d) Every taxable person shall ensure that copies of invoices issued by himself, by his customer or, in his name and on his behalf, by a third party, and all the invoices which he has received are stored.

For the purposes of this Directive, the taxable person may decide the place of storage provided that he makes the invoices or information stored there available without undue delay to the competent authorities whenever they so request. Member States may, however, require taxable persons established in their territory to notify them of the place of storage, if it is outside their territory. Member States may, in addition, require taxable persons established in their territory to store within the country invoices issued by themselves or by their customers or, in their name and on their behalf, by a third party, as well as all the invoices which they have received, when the storage is not by electronic means guaranteeing full on-line access to the data concerned.

The authenticity of the origin and integrity of the content of the invoices, as well as their readability, must be guaranteed throughout the storage period. As regards the invoices referred to in the third subparagraph of point (c), the information they contain may not be altered; it must remain legible throughout the aforementioned period.

The Member States shall determine the period for which taxable persons must store invoices relating to goods or services supplied in their territory and invoices received by taxable persons established in their territory.

In order to ensure that the conditions laid down in the third subparagraph are met, Member States referred to in the fourth subparagraph may require that invoices be stored in the original form in which they were sent, whether paper or electronic. They may also require that when invoices are stored by electronic means, the data guaranteeing the authenticity of the origin and integrity of the content also be stored.

Member States referred to in the fourth subparagraph may impose specific conditions prohibiting or restricting the storage of invoices in a country with which no legal instrument exists relating to mutual assistance similar in scope to that laid down by Directives

76/308/EEC, 77/799/EEC and by Regulation (EEC) No 218/92 and to the right of access by electronic means, download and use referred to in Article 22a.

Member States may, subject to conditions which they lay down, require the storage of invoices received by non-taxable persons.

(e) For the purposes of points (c) and (d), transmission and storage of invoices "by electronic means "shall mean transmission or making available to the recipient and storage using electronic equipment for processing (including digital compression) and storage of data, and employing wires, radio transmission, optical technologies or other electromagnetic means.

For the purposes of this Directive, Member States shall accept documents or messages in paper or electronic form as invoices if they meet the conditions laid down in this paragraph.

3. The following subparagraph shall be added to paragraph 8:

'The option provided for in the first subparagraph cannot be used to impose additional obligations over and above those laid down in paragraph 3.'

4. The following subparagraph shall be added to paragraph 9(a):

'Without prejudice to the provisions laid down in point (d), Member States may not, however, release the taxable persons referred to in the third indent from the obligations referred to in Article 22(3).'

5. The following point shall be added to paragraph 9:

'(d) Subject to consultation of the Committee provided for in Article 29 and under the conditions which they may lay down, Member States may provide that invoices in respect of goods supplied or services rendered in their territory do not have to fulfil some of the conditions laid down in paragraph 3(b) in the following cases:

— when the amount of the invoice is minor, or

— when commercial or administrative practice in the business sector concerned or the technical conditions under which the invoices are issued make it difficult to comply with all the requirements referred to in paragraph 3(b).

In any case, these invoices must contain the following:

— the date of issue,

— identification of the taxable person,

— identification of the type of goods supplied or services rendered,

— the tax due or the information needed to calculate it.

The simplified arrangements provided for in this point may not be applied to transactions referred to in paragraph 4(c).'

6. The following point shall be added to paragraph 9:

'(e) In cases where Member States make use of the option provided for in the third indent of point (a) to refrain from allocating a number as referred to in paragraph 1(c) to taxable persons who do not carry out any of the transactions referred to in paragraph 4(c), and where the supplier or the customer have not been allocated an identification number of this type, the invoice should feature instead another number called the tax reference number, as defined by the Member States concerned.

When the taxable person has been allocated an identification number as referred to in paragraph 1(c), the Member States referred to in the first subparagraph may also require the invoice to show:

— for services rendered referred to in Article 28b(C), (D), (E) and (F) and for the supplies of goods referred to in Article 28c(A) and (E) point 3, the number referred to in paragraph 1(c) and the tax reference number of the supplier;

— for other supplies of goods and services, only the tax reference number of the supplier or only the number referred to in paragraph 1(c).'

Article 3

The following Article shall be inserted:

'Article 22a

Right of access to invoices stored by electronic means in another Member State

When a taxable person stores invoices which he issues or receives by an electronic means guaranteeing on-line access to the data and when the place of storage is in a Member State other than that in which he is established, the competent authorities in the Member State in which he is established shall have a right, for the purpose of this directive, to access by electronic means, download and use these invoices within the limits set by the regulations of the Member State where the taxable person is established and as far as that State requires for control purposes.'

Article 4

1. The words 'or of the document serving as invoice' shall be deleted from the first and third indents of the third subparagraph of Article 10(2).

2. The words 'or on any other documents serving as invoices' shall be deleted from Article 24(5) and the words 'or on any other document serving as an invoice' shall be deleted from Article 26a(B), point 9.

3. The words 'or a document in lieu' shall be deleted from point 4 of Article 26a(C).

4. The words 'or other document serving as invoice' and 'or document' shall be deleted from Article 28d(3) and from the second subparagraph of Article 28d(4).

5. In Article 28g (which replaces Article 21 of the same Directive), Article 21 shall be amended as follows:

    — The words 'or other document serving as invoice ' shall be deleted from paragraph 1(d).

6. The words 'or on any other document in lieu 'shall be deleted from Article 28o(1)(e).

Article 5

Member States shall bring into force the laws, regulations and administrative provisions necessary to comply with this Directive with effect from 1 January 2004. They shall forthwith inform the Commission thereof.

When Member States adopt these measures, they shall contain a reference to this Directive or shall be accompanied by such a reference on the occasion of their official publication. The methods of making such a reference shall be laid down by the Member States.

Article 6

This Directive shall enter into force on the 20th day following that of its publication in the Official Journal of the European Communities.

Article 7

This Directive is addressed to the Member States.

Done at Brussels, 20 December 2001.

For the Council

The President

C. PICQUÉ

COUNCIL DIRECTIVE 2002/38/EC

of 7 May 2002

amending and amending temporarily Directive 77/388/EEC as regards the value added tax arrangements applicable to radio and television broadcasting services and certain electronically supplied services

Official Journal L128, 15/5/2002, p. 41-44

> This Directive was repealed by Council Directive 2006/112/EC of 28 November on the common system of Value Added Tax, with effect from 1 January 2007

THE COUNCIL OF THE EUROPEAN UNION,

Having regard to the Treaty establishing the European Community, and in particular Article 93 thereof,

Having regard to the proposal from the Commission,

Having regard to the opinion of the European Parliament,

Having regard to the opinion of the Economic and Social Committee,

Whereas:

(1)   The rules currently applicable to VAT on radio and television broadcasting services and on electronically supplied services, under Article 9 of the sixth Council Directive 77/388/EEC of 17 May 1977 on the harmonisation of the laws of the Member States relating to turnover taxes — Common system of value added tax: uniform basis of assessment, are inadequate for taxing such services consumed within the Community and for preventing distortions of competition in this area.

(2)   In the interests of the proper functioning of the internal market, such distortions should be eliminated and new harmonised rules introduced for this type of activity. Action should be taken to ensure, in particular, that such services where effected for consideration and consumed by customers established in the Community are taxed in the Community and are not taxed if consumed outside the Community.

(3)   To this end, radio and television broadcasting services and electronically supplied services provided from third countries to persons established in the Community or from the Community to recipients established in third countries should be taxed at the place of the recipient of the services.

(4)   To define electronically supplied services, examples of such services should be included in an annex to the Directive.

(5)   To facilitate compliance with fiscal obligations by operators providing electronically supplied services, who are neither established nor required to be identified for tax purposes within the Community, a special scheme should be established. In applying this scheme any operator supplying such services by electronic means to non-taxable persons within the Community, may, if he is not otherwise identified

for tax purposes within the Community, opt for identification in a single Member State.

(6)   The non-established operator wishing to benefit from the special scheme should comply with the requirements laid down therein, and with any relevant existing provision in the Member State where the services are consumed.

(7)   The Member State of identification must under certain conditions be able to exclude a non-established operator from the special scheme.

(8)   Where the non-established operator opts for the special scheme, any input value added tax that he has paid with respect to goods and services used by him for the purpose of his taxed activities falling under the special scheme, should be refunded by the Member State where the input value added tax was paid, in accordance with the arrangements of the thirteenth Council Directive 86/560/EEC of 17 November 1986 on the harmonisation of the laws of the Member States relating to turn over taxes — arrangements for the refund of value added tax to taxable persons not established in Community territory. The optional restrictions for refund in Article 2(2) and (3) and Article 4(2) of the same Directive should not be applied.

(9)   Subject to conditions which they lay down, Member States should allow certain statements and returns to be made by electronic means, and may also require that electronic means are used.

(10)   Those provisions pertaining to the introduction of electronic tax returns and statements should be adopted on a permanent basis. It is desirable to adopt all other provisions for a temporary period of three years which may be extended for practical reasons but should, in any event, based on experience, be reviewed within three years from 1 July 2003.

(11)   Directive 77/388/EEC should therefore be amended accordingly,

HAS ADOPTED THIS DIRECTIVE:

Article 1

Directive 77/388/EEC is hereby temporarily amended as follows:

1.   in Article 9:

     (a)   in paragraph (2)(e), a comma shall replace the final full stop and the following indents shall be added:

             —   radio and television broadcasting services,

             —   electronically supplied services, *inter alia*, those described in Annex L.'

     (b)   in paragraph 2, the following point shall be added:

             '(f)   the place where services referred to in the last indent of subparagraph (e) are supplied when performed for non-taxable persons who are established, have their permanent address or usually reside in a Member State, by a taxable person who has established his business or has a fixed establishment from which the service is supplied outside the Community or, in the absence of such a place of business or fixed establishment, has his permanent address or usually resides outside the Community, shall be the place where the non-taxable person is established, has his permanent address or usually resides.'

(c)   in paragraph 3, the introductory phrase shall be replaced by the following:

'3.   In order to avoid double taxation non-taxation or the distortion of competition, the Member States may, with regard to the supply of services referred to in paragraph 2(e), except for the services referred to in the last indent when supplied to non-taxable persons, and also with regard to the hiring out of forms of transport consider:'

(d)   paragraph 4 shall be amended as follows:

'4.   In the case of telecommunications services and radio and television broadcasting services referred to in paragraph 2(e) when performed for non-taxable persons who are established, have their permanent address or usually reside in a Member State, by a taxable person who has established his business or has a fixed establishment from which the service is supplied outside the Community, or in the absence of such a place of business or fixed establishment, has his permanent address or usually resides outside the Community, Member States shall make use of paragraph 3(b).'

2.   in Article 12(3)(a), the following fourth subparagraph shall be added:

'The third subparagraph shall not apply to the services referred to in the last indent of Article 9(2)(e).'

3.   the following Article shall be added:

'Article 26c

Special scheme for non-established taxable persons supplying electronic services to non-taxable persons

A. Definitions

For the purposes of this Article, the following definitions shall apply without prejudice to other Community provisions:

(a)   "**non-established taxable person**" means a taxable person who has neither established his business nor has a fixed establishment within the territory of the Community and who is not otherwise required to be identified for tax purposes under Article 22;

(b)   "**electronic services**" and "**electronically supplied services**" means those services referred to in the last indent of Article 9(2)(e);

(c)   "**Member State of identification**" means the Member State which the non-established taxable person chooses to contact to state when his activity as a taxable person within the territory of the Community commences in accordance with the provisions of this Article;

(d)   "**Member State of consumption**" means the Member State in which the supply of the electronic services is deemed to take place according to Article 9(2)(f);

(e)   "**value added tax return**" means the statement containing the information necessary to establish the amount of tax that has become chargeable in each Member State.

B. Special scheme for electronically supplied services

1.   Member States shall permit a non-established taxable person supplying electronic services to a non-taxable person who is established or has his permanent address or usually resides in a Member State to use a special scheme in accordance with the following provisions. The special scheme shall apply to all those supplies within the Community.

2.   The non-established taxable person shall state to the Member State of identification when his activity as a taxable person commences, ceases or changes to the extent that he no longer qualifies for the special scheme. Such a statement shall be made electronically.

The information from the non-established taxable person to the Member State of identification when his taxable activities commence shall contain the following details for the identification: name, postal address, electronic addresses, including websites, national tax number, if any, and a statement that the person is not identified for value added tax purposes within the Community. The non-established taxable person shall notify the Member State of identification of any changes in the submitted information.

3.   The Member State of identification shall identify the non-established taxable person by means of an individual number. Based on the information used for this identification, Member States of consumption may keep their own identification systems.

The Member State of identification shall notify the non-established taxable person by electronic means of the identification number allocated to him.

4.   The Member State of identification shall exclude the non-established taxable person from the identification register if:

(a)   he notifies that he no longer supplies electronic services, or

(b)   it otherwise can be assumed that his taxable activities have ended, or

(c)   he no longer fulfils the requirements necessary to be allowed to use the special scheme, or

(d)   he persistently fails to comply with the rules concerning the special scheme.

5.   The non-established taxable person shall submit by electronic means to the Member State of identification a value added tax return for each calendar quarter whether or not electronic services have been supplied. The return shall be submitted within 20 days following the end of the reporting period to which the return refers.

The value added tax return shall set out the identification number and, for each Member State of consumption where tax has become due, the total value, less value added tax, of supplies of electronic services for the reporting period and total amount of the corresponding tax. The applicable tax rates and the total tax due shall also be indicated.

6.   The value added tax return shall be made in euro. Member States which have not adopted the euro may require the tax return to be made in their national currencies. If the supplies have been made in other currencies, the exchange rate valid for the last date of the reporting period shall be used when completing the value added tax return. The exchange shall be done following the exchange rates published by the European Central Bank for that day, or, if there is no publication on that day, on the next day of publication.

7.   The non-established taxable person shall pay the value added tax when submitting the return. Payment shall be made to a bank account denominated in euro, designated by the Member State of identification. Member States which have not adopted the euro may require the payment to be made to a bank account denominated in their own currency.

8.   Notwithstanding Article 1(1) of Directive 86/560/EEC, the non-established taxable person making use of this special scheme shall, instead of making deductions under Article 17(2) of this Directive, be granted a refund according to Directive 86/560/EEC. Articles 2(2), 2(3) and 4(2) of Directive 86/560/EEC shall not apply to the refund related to electronic supplies covered by this special scheme.

9.   The non-established taxable person shall keep records of the transactions covered by this special scheme in sufficient detail to enable the tax administration of the Member State of consumption to determine that the value added tax return referred to in paragraph 5 is correct. These records should be made available electronically on request to the Member State of identification and to the Member State of consumption. These records shall be maintained for a period of 10 years from the end of the year when the transaction was carried out.

10.   Article 21(2)(b) shall not apply to a non-established taxable person who
       has opted for this special scheme.'

Article 2

Article 22, contained in Article 28h of Directive 77/388/EEC, is hereby
amended as follows:

1.   in paragraph 1, point (a) shall be replaced by the following:

      '(a)   Every taxable person shall state when his activity as a taxable
               person commences, changes or ceases. Member States shall,
               subject to conditions which they lay down, allow the taxable
               person to make such statements by electronic means, and may
               also require that electronic means are used.'

2.   in paragraph 4, point (a) shall be replaced by the following:

      '(a)   Every taxable person shall submit a return by a deadline to be
               determined by Member States. That deadline may not be more
               than two months later than the end of each tax period. The tax
               period shall be fixed by each Member State at one month, two
               months or a quarter. Member States may, however, set different
               periods provided that they do not exceed one year. Member
               States shall, subject to conditions which they lay down, allow the
               taxable person to make such returns by electronic means, and
               may also require that electronic means are used.'

3.   in paragraph 6, point (a) shall be replaced by the following:

      '(a)   Member States may require a taxable person to submit a statement,
               including all the particulars specified in paragraph 4, concerning
               all transactions carried out in the preceding year. That statement
               shall provide all the information necessary for any adjustments.
               Member States shall, subject to conditions which they lay down,
               allow the taxable person to make such statements by electronic
               means, and may also require that electronic means are used.'

4.   in paragraph 6, the second paragraph in point (b) shall be replaced by:

      'The recapitulative statement shall be drawn up for each calendar quarter
      within a period and in accordance with procedures to be determined by
      the Member States, which shall take the measures necessary to ensure
      that the provisions concerning administrative cooperation in the field of
      indirect taxation are in any event complied with. Member States shall,
      subject to conditions which they lay down, allow the taxable person to
      make such statements by electronic means, and may also require that
      electronic means are used.'

Article 3

1. Member States shall bring into force the laws, regulations and administrative provisions necessary to comply with this Directive on 1 July 2003.They shall forthwith inform the Commission thereof.

    When Member States adopt these measures, they shall contain a reference to this Directive or shall be accompanied by such reference on the occasion of their official publication. Member States shall determine how such reference is to be made.

2. Member States shall communicate to the Commission the text of the provisions of domestic law which they adopt in the field covered by this Directive.

[Article 4

Article 1 shall apply until 31 December 2006.][1]

Article 5

The Council, on the basis of a report from the Commission, shall review the provisions of Article 1 of this Directive before 30 June 2006 and shall either, acting in accordance with Article 93 of the Treaty, adopt measures on an appropriate electronic mechanism on a non-discriminatory basis for charging, declaring, collecting and allocating tax revenue on electronically supplied services with taxation in the place of consumption or, if considered necessary for practical reasons, acting unanimously on the basis of a proposal from the Commission, extend the period mentioned in Article 4.

Article 6

This Directive shall enter into force on the day of its publication in the Official Journal of the European Communities.

Article 7

This Directive is addressed to the Member States.

Done at Brussels, 7 May 2002.

For the Council
The President
R. DE RATO Y FIGAREDO

ANNEX

'ANNEX L

Illustrative list of electronically supplied services referred to in Article 9(2)(e)

1. Website supply, web-hosting, distance maintenance of programmes and equipment.

2. Supply of software and updating thereof.

3. Supply of images, text and information, and making databases available.

4. Supply of music, films and games, including games of chance and gambling games, and of political, cultural, artistic, sporting, scientific and entertainment broadcasts and events.

5. Supply of distance teaching.

Where the supplier of a service and his customer communicates via electronic mail, this shall not of itself mean that the service performed is an electronic service within the meaning of the last indent of Article 9(2)(e).'

_____

Amendments
1   Substituted by Art 1 Council Directive 2006/58/EC of 27 June 2006, w.e.f. 28 June 2006

COUNCIL REGULATION (EC) No 792/2002

of 7 May 2002

amending temporarily Regulation (EEC) No 218/92 on administrative cooperation in the field of indirect taxation (VAT) as regards additional measures regarding electronic commerce

Official Journal L128, 15/5/2002, p. 0001 - 0003

THE COUNCIL OF THE EUROPEAN UNION,

Having regard to the Treaty establishing the European Community, and in particular Article 93 thereof,

Having regard to the proposal from the Commission,

Having regard to the opinion of the European Parliament,

Having regard to the opinion of the Economic and Social Committee,

Whereas:

(1) Council Directive 2002/38/EC of 7 May 2002 amending and amending temporarily Directive 77/388/EEC as regards the value added tax arrangements applicable to radio and television broadcasting services and certain electronically supplied services provides for the framework for taxing electronic supplies in the Community by taxable persons who are neither established nor required to be identified for tax purposes within the Community.

(2) The Member State of consumption has primary responsibility for assuring the compliance with their obligations by non-established suppliers. To this end, the information necessary to operate the special scheme for electronically supplied services that is provided for in Article 26c of sixth Council Directive 77/388/EEC of 17 May 1977 on the harmonisation of the laws of the Member States relating to turnover taxes — Common system of value added tax: uniform basis of assessment must be transmitted to those Member States.

(3) It is necessary to provide that the value added tax due in respect of such supplies transferred to accounts designated by the Member States of consumption.

(4) The rules laid down in Directive 77/388/EEC require the non-established taxable person supplying services referred to in the last indent of Article 9(2)e of the Directive to charge VAT to his customer, established or resident in the Community, unless he is satisfied that his customer is a taxable person. The special scheme provided for in Article 26c of the Directive applies only for services provided to non-taxable persons established or resident in the Community. It is thus clear that the non-established taxable person needs certain information about his customer.

(5) To this end, use could in most cases be made of the facility that is available in Member States in the form of electronic databases which

contain a register of persons to whom value added tax identification numbers have been issued in that Member State.

(6)   It is accordingly necessary to extend the common system for the exchange of certain information on intra-Community transaction provided for in Article 6 of Regulation (EEC) No 218/92.

(7)   The provisions of the Regulation should operate for a temporary period of three years which may be extended for practical reasons and Regulation (EEC) No 218/92 should therefore be temporarily amended accordingly,

HAS ADOPTED THIS REGULATION:

Article 1

Regulation (EEC) No 218/92 is hereby temporarily amended:

1.   the second paragraph of Article 1 shall be replaced by the following:

'To that end it lays down procedures for the exchange by electronic means of value added tax information on intra-Community transactions as well as on services supplied electronically in accordance with the special scheme provided for by Article 26c of Directive 77/388/EEC, and also for any subsequent exchange of information and, as far as services covered by that special scheme are concerned, for the transfer of money between Member States' competent authorities.';

2.   in Article 2(1), the ninth indent shall be replaced by the following:

'   —   "**intra-Community supply of services**"shall mean any supply of services covered by Article 28b (C), (D), (E)or (F)of Directive 77/388/EEC,';

3.   in Article 6, paragraph 4 shall be replaced by the following:

'4.   The competent authority of each Member State shall ensure that persons involved in the intra-Community supply of goods or of services and persons supplying services referred to in the last indent of Article 9(2)e of Directive 77/388/EEC are allowed to obtain confirmation of the validity of the value added tax identification number of any specified person. In accordance with the procedure referred to in Article 10, Member States shall, in particular, provide such confirmation by electronic means.';

4.   the following Title shall be added:

'TITLE III A

Provisions concerning the special scheme in Article 26c of Directive 77/388/EEC

Article 9a

The following provisions shall apply concerning the special scheme provided for in Article 26c in Directive 77/388/EEC.The definitions contained in point A of that Article shall also apply for the purpose of this Title.

Article 9b

1.   The information from the non-established taxable person to the Member State of identification when his activities commences set out in the second subparagraph of Article 26c(B)(2) of Directive 77/388/EEC is to be submitted in an electronic manner. The technical details, including a common electronic message, shall be determined in accordance with the procedure provided for in Article 10.

2.   The Member State of identification shall transmit this information by electronic means to the competent authorities of the other Member States within 10 days from the end of the month during which the information was received from the non-established taxable person. In the same manner, the competent authorities of the other Member States shall be informed of the allocated identification number. The technical details, including a common electronic message, by which this information is to be transmitted shall be determined in accordance with the procedure provided for in Article 10.

3.   The Member State of identification shall without delay inform by electronic means the competent authorities of the other Members States if a non-established taxable person is excluded from the identification register.

Article 9c

1.   The return with the details set out in the second subparagraph of Article 26c(B)(5)of Directive 77/388/EEC is to be submitted in an electronic manner. The technical details, including a common electronic message, shall be determined in accordance with the procedure provided for in Article 10.

2.   The Member State of identification shall transmit this information by electronic means to the competent authority of the Member State concerned at the latest 10 days after the end of the month that the return was received. Member States which have required the tax return to be made in a national currency other than euro shall convert the amounts into euro using the exchange rate valid for the last date of the reporting period. The exchange shall be done following the exchange rates published by the European Central Bank for that day, or, if there is no publication on that day, on the next day of publication. The technical details by which this information is to be transmitted shall be determined in accordance with the procedure provided for in Article 10.

3.   The Member State of identification shall transmit by electronic means to the Member State of consumption the information needed to link each payment with a relevant quarterly tax return.

Article 9d

The provisions in Article 4(1) shall apply also to information collected by the Member State of identification in accordance with Article 26c(B) (2) and (5)of Directive 77/388/EEC.

Article 9e

The Member State of identification shall ensure that the amount the non-established taxable person has paid is transferred to the bank account denominated in euro, which has been designated by the Member State of consumption to which the payment is due. Member States which required the payments in a national currency other than euro shall convert the amounts into euro using the exchange rate valid for the last date of the reporting period. The exchange shall be done following the exchange rates published by the European Central Bank for that day, or, if there is no publication on that day, on the next day of publication. The transfer shall take place at the latest 10 days after the end of the month that the payment was received.

If the non-established taxable person does not pay the total tax due, the Member State of identification shall ensure that the payment is transferred to the Member States of consumption in proportion to the tax due in each Member State. The Member State of identification shall inform by electronic means the competent authorities of the Member States of consumption thereof.

Article 9f

1. Member States shall notify by electronic means the competent authorities of the other Member States of the relevant bank account numbers for receiving payments according to Article 9e.

2. Member States shall without delay notify by electronic means the competent authorities of the other Member States and the Commission of changes in the standard tax rate.';

5. in Article 13 the present text shall be renumbered as paragraph 2 and a new paragraph 1 shall be inserted as follows:

    '1. The Commission and the Member States shall ensure that such existing or new communication and information exchange systems which are necessary to provide for the exchanges of information described in Articles 9b and 9c are operational by the date specified in Article 3(1) of Directive 2002/38/EC. The Commission will be responsible for whatever development of the common communication network/common system interface (CCN/CSI) is necessary to permit the exchange of this information between Member States. Member States will be responsible for whatever development of their systems is necessary to permit this information to be exchanged using the CCN/CSI.'

Article 2

Article 1 shall apply for a period provided for in Article 4 of Directive 2002/38/EC.

No exchange of information under this Regulation shall take place before 1 July 2003.

Article 3

This Regulation shall enter into force on the seventh day following its publication in the Official Journal of the European Communities.

This Regulation shall be binding in its entirety and directly applicable in all Member States.

Done at Brussels, 7 May 2002.

For the Council
The President

R.DE RATO Y FIGAREDO

COUNCIL DIRECTIVE 2002/93/EC

of 3 December 2002

amending Directive 77/388/EEC to extend the facility allowing Member States to apply reduced rates of VAT to certain labour-intensive services

Official Journal L331, 07/12/2002 p. 0027

> This Directive was repealed by Council Directive 2006/112/EC of 28 November 2006 on the common system of value added tax, with effect from 1 January 2007

THE COUNCIL OF THE EUROPEAN UNION,

Having regard to the Treaty establishing the European Community, and in particular Article 93 thereof,

Having regard to the proposal from the Commission,

Having regard to the opinion of the European Parliament,

Having regard to the opinion of the Economic and Social Committee,

Whereas:

(1) Article 28(6) of Council Directive 77/388/EC of 17 May 1977 on the harmonisation of the laws of the Member States relating to turnover taxes - common system of value added tax: uniform basis of assessment, allows the reduced rates provided for in the third subparagraph of Article 12(3)(a) also to be applied to the labour-intensive services listed in the categories set out in Annex K to that Directive for a maximum period of three years from 1 January 2000 to 31 December 2002.

(2) Council Decision 2000/185/EC of 28 February 2000 authorising Member States to apply a reduced rate of VAT to certain labour-intensive services in accordance with the procedure provided for in Article 28(6) of Directive 77/388/EEC authorised certain Member States to apply, up to 31 December 2002, a reduced rate of VAT to those labour-intensive services for which they had submitted an application.

(3) Based on the reports to be drawn up by 1 October 2002 by the Member States that have applied such reduced rates, the Commission is required to submit a global evaluation report to the Council and the European Parliament by 31 December 2002, accompanied if necessary by a proposal for a final decision on the rate to be applied to labour-intensive services.

(4) In view of the time needed to produce a thorough global evaluation of such reports to extend the maximum period of application set for this measure in Directive 77/388/EEC.

(5) Directive 77/388/EEC should therefore be amended accordingly,

HAS ADOPTED THIS DIRECTIVE:

Article 1

In the first subparagraph of Article 28(6) of Directive 77/388/EEC the words 'three years between 1 January 2000 and 31 December 2002' shall be replaced by the words 'four years between 1 January 2000 and 31 December 2003'.

Article 2

This Directive shall enter into force on the day of its publication in the Official Journal of the European Communities.

Article 3

This Directive is addressed to the Member States.

Done at Brussels, 3 December 2002.

For the Council
The President

T.PEDERSEN

COMMISSION DIRECTIVE 2002/94/EC

of 9 December 2002

laying down detailed rules for implementing certain provisions of Council Directive 76/308/EEC on mutual assistance for the recovery of claims relating to certain levies, duties, taxes and other measures

Official Journal L337, 13/12/2002, p. 41 - 54

> This Directive was repealed by Commission Regulation (EC) No 1179/2008 of 28 November 2008, with effect from 1 January 2009

THE COMMISSION OF THE EUROPEAN COMMUNITIES,

Having regard to the Treaty establishing the European Community,

Having regard to Council Directive 76/308/EEC of 15 March 1976 on mutual assistance for the recovery of claims relating to certain levies, duties, taxes and other measures, as last amended by Directive 2001/44/EC, and in particular Article 22 thereof,

Whereas:

(1)   The system of mutual assistance between the competent authorities of Member States, as set out in Directive 76/308/EEC, has been amended as regards the information to be supplied to the applicant authority, the notification of the addressee concerning the applicable instruments and decisions, the adoption of precautionary measures, and the recovery by the requested authority of claims on behalf of the applicant authority.

(2)   As regards each of those aspects, therefore, Commission Directive 77/794/EEC of 4 November 1977 laying down detailed rules for implementing certain provisions of Directive 76/308/EEC on mutual assistance for the recovery of claims resulting from operations forming part of the system of financing the European Agricultural Guidance and Guarantee Fund, and of agricultural levies and customs duties, and in respect of value added tax, as last amended by Directive 86/489/EEC, should be amended accordingly.

(3)   Furthermore, detailed rules should be laid down concerning the means by which communications between authorities may be transmitted.

(4)   In the interests of clarity, Directive 77/794/EEC should be replaced.

(5)   The measures provided for in this Directive are in accordance with the opinion of the Committee on Recovery,

HAS ADOPTED THIS DIRECTIVE:

CHAPTER I

GENERAL PROVISIONS

Article 1

This Directive lays down the detailed rules for implementing Article 4(2) and (4), Article 5(2) and (3), Article 7, Article 8, Article 9, Article 11, Article 12(1) and (2), Article 14, Article 18(3) and Article 25 of Directive 76/308/EEC.

It also lays down the detailed rules on conversion, transfer of sums recovered, the fixing of a minimum amount for claims which may give rise to a request for assistance, as well as the means by which communications between authorities may be transmitted.

Article 2

For the purposes of this Directive:

1. transmission 'by electronic means' shall mean transmission using electronic equipment for processing (including digital compression) of data and employing wires, radio transmission, optical technologies or other electromagnetic means;

2. 'CCN/CSI' network shall mean the common platform based on the Common Communication Network (CCN) and Common System Interface (CSI), developed by the Community to ensure all transmissions by electronic means between competent authorities in the area of Customs and Taxation.

CHAPTER II

REQUESTS FOR INFORMATION

Article 3

The request for information referred to in Article 4 of Directive 76/308/EEC shall be made out in writing in accordance with the model in Annex I to this Directive. If the request cannot be transmitted by electronic means, it shall bear the official stamp of the applicant authority and shall be signed by an official thereof duly authorised to make such a request.

Where a similar request has been addressed to any other authority, the applicant authority shall indicate in its request for information the name of that authority.

Article 4

The request for information may relate to:

1. the debtor;

2. any person liable for settlement of the claim under the law in force in the Member State in which the applicant authority is situated (hereinafter 'the Member State of the applicant authority');

3.   any third party holding assets belonging to one of the persons mentioned under point 1 or 2.

Article 5

1.   The requested authority shall acknowledge receipt of the request for information in writing as soon as possible and in any event within seven days of such receipt.

2.   Immediately upon receipt of the request the requested authority shall, where appropriate, ask the applicant authority to provide any additional information necessary. The applicant authority shall provide all additional necessary information to which it normally has access.

Article 6

1.   The requested authority shall transmit each item of requested information to the applicant authority as and when it is obtained.

2.   Where all or some of the requested information cannot be obtained within a reasonable time, having regard to the particular case, the requested authority shall so inform the applicant authority, indicating the reasons therefor.

In any event, at the end of six months from the date of acknowledgement of receipt of the request, the requested authority shall inform the applicant authority of the outcome of the investigations which it has conducted in order to obtain the information requested.

In the light of the information received from the requested authority, the applicant authority may request the latter to continue its investigations. That request shall be made in writing within two months of the receipt of the notification of the outcome of the investigations carried out by the requested authority, and shall be treated by the requested authority in accordance with the provisions applying to the initial request.

Article 7

If the requested authority decides not to comply with the request for information, it shall notify the applicant authority in writing of the reasons for the refusal to comply with the request, specifying the provisions of Article 4 of Directive 76/308/EEC on which it relies. Such notification shall be given by the requested authority as soon as it has taken its decision and in any event within three months of the date of the acknowledgement of the receipt of the request.

Article 8

The applicant authority may at any time withdraw the request for information which it has sent to the requested authority. The decision to withdraw shall be transmitted to the requested authority in writing.

CHAPTER III

REQUESTS FOR NOTIFICATION

Article 9

The request for notification referred to in Article 5 of Directive 76/308/EEC shall be made out in writing in duplicate in accordance with the model in Annex II to this Directive. The said request shall bear the official stamp of the applicant authority and shall be signed by an official thereof duly authorised to make such a request.

Two copies of the instrument or decision, notification of which is requested, shall be attached to the request.

Article 10

The request for notification may relate to any natural or legal person who, in accordance with the law in force in the Member State of the applicant authority, is required to be informed of any instrument or decision which concerns that person.

In so far as such is not indicated in the instrument or decision of which notification is requested, the request for notification shall refer to the rules in force in the Member State of the applicant authority governing the procedure for contestation of the claim or for its recovery.

Article 11

1. The requested authority shall acknowledge receipt of the request for notification in writing as soon as possible and in any event within seven days of such receipt.

    Immediately upon receipt of the request for notification, the requested authority shall take the necessary measures to effect notification in accordance with the law in force in the Member State in which it is situated.

    If necessary, but without jeopardising the final date for notification indicated in the request for notification, the requested authority shall ask the applicant authority to provide additional information.

    The applicant authority shall provide all additional information to which it normally has access.

    The requested authority shall in any event not question the validity of the instrument or decision of which notification is requested.

2. The requested authority shall inform the applicant authority of the date of notification as soon as this has been effected, by returning to it one of the copies of the request with the certificate on the reverse side duly completed.

CHAPTER IV

REQUESTS FOR RECOVERY OR FOR PRECAUTIONARY MEASURES

Article 12

1. Requests for recovery or for precautionary measures referred to in Articles 6 and 13 respectively of Directive 76/308/EEC shall be made out in writing in accordance with the model in Annex III to this Directive.

   Such requests, which shall include a declaration that the conditions laid down in Directive 76/308/EEC for initiating the mutual assistance procedure have been fulfilled, shall bear the official stamp of the applicant authority and shall be signed by an official thereof duly authorised to make such a request.

2. The instrument permitting enforcement shall accompany the request for recovery or for precautionary measures. A single instrument may be issued in respect of several claims where they concern one and the same person.

   For the purposes of Articles 13 to 20 of this Directive, all claims covered by the same instrument permitting enforcement shall be deemed to constitute a single claim.

Article 13

Requests for recovery or for precautionary measures may relate to any person referred to in Article 4.

Article 14

1. If the currency of the Member State of the requested authority is different from the currency of the Member State of the applicant authority, the applicant authority shall express the amount of the claim to be recovered in both currencies.

2. The rate of exchange to be used for the purposes of paragraph 1 shall be the latest selling rate recorded on the most representative exchange market or markets of the Member State of the applicant authority on the date when the request for recovery is signed.

Article 15

1. The requested authority shall, in writing, as soon as possible and in any event within seven days of receipt of the request for recovery or for precautionary measures:

   (a)   acknowledge receipt of the request;

   (b)   ask the applicant authority to complete the request if it does not contain the information or other particulars mentioned in Article 7 of Directive 76/308/EEC.

   The applicant authority shall provide all information to which it has access.

2.   If the requested authority does not take the requisite action within the three-month period laid down in Article 8 of Directive 76/308/EEC, it shall, as soon as possible and in any event within seven days of the expiry of that period, inform the applicant authority in writing of the grounds for its failure to comply with the time limit.

Article 16

Where, within a reasonable time having regard to the particular case, all or part of the claim cannot be recovered or precautionary measures cannot be taken, the requested authority shall so inform the applicant authority, indicating the reasons therefor.

No later than at the end of each six-month period following the date of acknowledgement of the receipt of the request, the requested authority shall inform the applicant authority of the state of progress or the outcome of the procedure for recovery or for precautionary measures.

In the light of the information received from the requested authority, the applicant authority may request the latter to re-open the procedure for recovery or for precautionary measures. That request shall be made in writing within two months of the receipt of the notification of the outcome of that procedure, and shall be treated by the requested authority in accordance with the provisions applying to the initial request.

Article 17

1.   Any action contesting the claim or the instrument permitting its enforcement which is taken in the Member State of the applicant authority shall be notified to the requested authority in writing by the applicant authority immediately after the latter has been informed of such action.

2.   If the laws, regulations and administrative practices in force in the Member State of the requested authority do not permit precautionary measures or the recovery requested under the second subparagraph of Article 12(2) of Directive 76/308/EEC, the requested authority shall notify the applicant authority to that effect as soon as possible and in any event within one month of the receipt of the notification referred to in paragraph 1.

3.   Any action which is taken in the Member State of the requested authority for reimbursement of sums recovered or for compensation in relation to recovery of contested claims under the second subparagraph of Article 12(2) of Directive 76/308/EEC shall be notified to the applicant authority in writing by the requested authority immediately after the latter has been informed of such action.

     The requested authority shall as far as possible involve the applicant authority in the procedures for settling the amount to be reimbursed and the compensation due. Upon a reasoned request from the requested authority, the applicant authority shall transfer the sums reimbursed and the compensation paid within two months of the receipt of that request.

Article 18

1. If the request for recovery or for precautionary measures becomes devoid of purpose as a result of payment of the claim or of its cancellation or for any other reason, the applicant authority shall immediately inform the requested authority in writing so that the latter may stop any action which it has undertaken.

2. Where the amount of the claim which is the subject of the request for recovery or for precautionary measures is adjusted for any reason, the applicant authority shall immediately inform the requested authority in writing, and if necessary issue a new instrument permitting enforcement.

3. If the adjustment entails a reduction in the amount of the claim, the requested authority shall continue the action which it has undertaken with a view to recovery or to the taking of precautionary measures, but that action shall be limited to the amount still outstanding.

    If, at the time when the requested authority is informed of the reduction in the amount of the claim, an amount exceeding the amount still outstanding has already been recovered by it but the transfer procedure referred to in Article 19 has not yet been initiated, the requested authority shall repay the amount overpaid to the person entitled thereto.

4. If the adjustment entails an increase in the amount of the claim, the applicant authority shall as soon as possible address to the requested authority an additional request for recovery or for precautionary measures.

    That additional request shall, as far as possible, be dealt with by the requested authority at the same time as the original request from the applicant authority. Where, in view of the state of progress of the existing procedure, consolidation of the additional request with the original request is not possible, the requested authority shall be required to comply with the additional request only if it concerns an amount not less than that referred to in Article 25(2).

5. In order to convert the adjusted amount of the claim into the currency of the Member State of the requested authority, the applicant authority shall use the exchange rate used in its original request.

Article 19

Any sum recovered by the requested authority, including, where applicable, the interest referred to in Article 9(2) of Directive 76/308/EEC, shall be transferred to the applicant authority in the currency of the Member State of the requested authority. The transfer shall take place within one month of the date on which recovery was effected.

The competent authorities of the Member States may agree different arrangements for the transfer of amounts below the threshold referred to in Article 25(2) of this Directive.

Article 20

Irrespective of any amounts collected by the requested authority by way of the interest referred to in Article 9(2) of Directive 76/308/EEC, the claim shall be deemed to have been recovered in proportion to the recovery of the amount expressed in the national currency of the Member State of the requested authority, on the basis of the exchange rate referred to in Article 14(2) of this Directive.

CHAPTER V

TRANSMISSION OF COMMUNICATIONS

Article 21

1.   All information communicated in writing pursuant to this Directive shall, as far as possible, be transmitted only by electronic means, except for:

   (a)   the request for notification referred to in Article 5 of Directive 76/308/EEC and the instrument or decision of which notification is requested;

   (b)   requests for recovery or for precautionary measures referred to in Articles 6 and 13 respectively of Directive 76/308/EEC, and the instrument permitting enforcement.

2.   The competent authorities of the Member States may agree to waive the communication on paper of the requests and instruments specified in paragraph 1.

Article 22

Each Member State shall designate a central office with principal responsibility for communication by electronic means with other Member States. That office shall be connected to the CCN/CSI network.

Where several authorities are appointed in a Member State for the purpose of applying this Directive, the central office shall be responsible for the forwarding of all communication by electronic means between those authorities and the central offices of other Member States.

Article 23

1.   Where the competent authorities of the Member States store information in electronic data bases and exchange such information by electronic means, they shall take all measures necessary to ensure that any information communicated in whatever form pursuant to this Directive is treated as confidential.

   It shall be covered by the obligation of professional secrecy and shall enjoy the protection extended to similar information under the national law of the Member State which received it.

2.   The information referred to in paragraph 1 may be made available only to the persons and authorities referred to in Article 16 of Directive 76/308/EEC.

Such information may be used in connection with judicial or administrative proceedings initiated for the recovery of levies, duties, taxes and other measures referred to in Article 2 of Directive 76/308/EEC.

Persons duly accredited by the Security Accreditation Authority of the European Commission may have access to this information only in so far as is necessary for the care, maintenance and development of the CCN/CSI network.

3.   Where the competent authorities of the Member States communicate by electronic means, they shall take all measures necessary to ensure that all communications are duly authorised.

Article 24

Information and other particulars communicated by the requested authority to the applicant authority shall be conveyed in the official language or one of the official languages of the Member State of the requested authority or in another language agreed between the applicant and requested authorities.

CHAPTER VI

ELIGIBILITY AND REFUSAL OF REQUESTS FOR ASSISTANCE

Article 25

1.   A request for assistance may be made by the applicant authority in respect of either a single claim or several claims where those are recoverable from one and the same person.

2.   No request for assistance may be made if the total amount of the relevant claim or claims listed in Article 2 of Directive 76/308/EEC is less than EUR1500.

Article 26

If the requested authority decides, pursuant to the first paragraph of Article 14 of Directive 76/308/EEC, to refuse a request for assistance, it shall notify the applicant authority in writing of the reasons for the refusal. Such notification shall be given by the requested authority as soon as it has taken its decision and in any event within three months of the date of receipt of the request for assistance.

CHAPTER VII

REIMBURSEMENT ARRANGEMENTS

Article 27

Each Member State shall appoint at least one official duly authorised to agree reimbursement arrangements under Article 18(3) of Directive 76/308/EEC.

Article 28

1. If the requested authority decides to request reimbursement arrangements it shall notify the applicant authority in writing of the reasons for its view that recovery of the claim poses a specific problem, entails very high costs or relates to the fight against organised crime.

   The requested authority shall append a detailed estimate of the costs for which it requests reimbursement by the applicant authority.

2. The applicant authority shall acknowledge receipt of the request for reimbursement arrangements in writing as soon as possible and in any event within seven days of receipt.

   Within two months of the date of acknowledgement of receipt of the said request, the applicant authority shall inform the requested authority whether and to what extent it agrees with the proposed reimbursement arrangements.

3. If no agreement is reached between the applicant and requested authority with respect to reimbursement arrangements, the requested authority shall continue recovery procedures in the normal way.

CHAPTER VIII

FINAL PROVISIONS

Article 29

Each Member State shall inform the Commission before 15 March each year, as far as possible by electronic means, of the use made of the procedures laid down in Directive 76/308/EEC and of the results achieved in the previous calendar year, in accordance with the model in Annex IV to this Directive.

Article 30

The Member States shall bring into force the laws, regulations and administrative provisions necessary to comply with this Directive by 30 April 2003 at the latest. They shall forthwith inform the Commission thereof.

When Member States adopt those provisions, they shall contain a reference to this Directive or be accompanied by such a reference on the occasion of their official publication. Member States shall determine how such reference is to be made.

Article 31

The Commission shall communicate to the other Member States the measures which each Member State takes for implementing this Directive.

Each Member State shall notify the other Member States and the Commission of the name and address of the competent authorities for the purpose of applying this Directive, as well as of the officials authorised to agree arrangements under Article 18(3) of Directive 76/308/EEC.

Article 32

Directive 77/794/EEC is hereby repealed.

References to the repealed Directive shall be construed as references to this Directive.

Article 33

This Directive shall enter into force on the 20th day following that of its publication in the Official Journal of the European Communities.

Article 34

This Directive is addressed to the Member States.

Done at Brussels, 9 December 2002.

For the Commission

Frederik BOLKESTEIN
Member of the Commission

ANNEX I

Model for the request for information referred to in Article 4 of Directive 76/308/EEC

DIRECTIVE 76/308/EEC

(Article 4)

(Description of the applicant authority, address, telephone, fax and bank account number, etc.)

(Name, e-mail address, telephone, fax and language skills of the official dealing with the request)

....

(Place and date of sending request)

....

(File reference of applicant authority)

To:	(Space reserved for the authority to whom the request is sent)
....	
(Name of the authority to whom the request is sent, Post Box, place etc.)	
....	
....	

REQUEST FOR INFORMATION

I, the undersigned ....,
(Name and official capacity)

acting as the agent duly authorised by the applicant authority indicated above, hereby request the following information to be obtained in accordance with Article 4 of Directive 76/308/EEC:

Information relating to the person concerned (¹)		
(a) For natural persons:	Name:	
	Date and place of birth:	
For legal entities:	Legal status:	Company name:
Address (known/assumed (*)):		
Principal debtor /Co-debtor /Third party holding assets (*):		
(b) Name of the principal debtor if different from person concerned:		
Address (known/assumed (*)):		
(c) Other relevant information concerning the above persons:		

Information relating to the claim(s)

— Amount: Principal:　　　Interests:　　　　　Costs:　　　　　　　Penalties:

— Exact nature of the claim(s):

— Final date permitting recovery:

— Other information:

Other requested authorities:

Information requested

(Signature)

(Official stamp)

(*) Delete as appropriate.
(¹) Natural or legal person.

ANNEX II

Model for the request for notification referred to in Article 5 of Directive 76/308/EEC

DIRECTIVE 76/308/EEC

(Article 5)

(Description of the applicant authority, address, telephone, fax and
bank account number, etc.)

(Name, e-mail address, telephone, fax and language skills of the
official dealing with the request)

....
(Place and date of sending request)

....
(File reference of applicant authority)

To: (Name of the authority to whom the request is sent, Post Box,
place etc.)

....

(Space reserved for the authority to whom the request is sent)

REQUEST FOR NOTIFICATION

I, the undersigned ....
(Name and official capacity)

acting as the agent duly authorised by the applicant authority indicated above, hereby request notification, pursuant to Article 5 of Directive 76/308/EEC, of the following instrument/decision (*):

Information relating to the person concerned ([1])
(a) For natural persons: Name: Date and place of birth: For legal entities: Legal status: Company name: Address (known/assumed (*)):   Principal debtor/Co-debtor /Third party holding assets (*)   (b) Name of the principal debtor if different from person concerned: Address (known/assumed (*)):   (c) Other relevant information concerning the above persons:

Information relating to the claim(s)
— Nature and subject of the instrument (or decision) to be notified: — Amount (inclusive of interest, penalties and costs):   — Exact nature of the claim(s):   — Final date for notification: — Other information: ....   (Signature) (Official stamp)

(*) Delete as appropriate.
([1]) Natural or legal person.

CERTIFICATE

The undersigned hereby certifies:

— that the instrument/decision (*) attached to the request overleaf has been notified to the addressee referred to in the said request dated .... The notification was made in the following manner (¹):

— that the instrument/decision (*) attached to the request overleaf was not able to be notified to the addressee referred to in the said request for the following reasons (*):

....
(Date)

....
(Signature)

(Official stamp)

(*) Delete as appropriate.
(¹) Indicate exactly whether the notification was made to the addressee in person or by another procedure.

ANNEX III

Model for the requests for recovery or for precautionary measures referred to in Articles 6 and 13 of Directive 76/308/EEC

DIRECTIVE 76/308/EEC

(Articles 6 to 13)

(Description of the applicant authority, address, telephone, fax and bank account number, etc.)

(Name, e-mail address, telephone, fax and language skills of the official dealing with the request)

....
(Place and date of sending request)

....
(File reference of applicant authority)

To

....

(Name of the authority to whom the request is sent, Post Box, place etc.)

....

....

(Space reserved for the authority to whom the request is sent)

REQUEST FOR RECOVERY/PRECAUTIONARY MEASURES TO BE TAKEN

I, the undersigned ....,
(Name and official capacity)

acting as the agent duly authorised by the applicant authority indicated above, hereby request:

— recovery of the following claim(s) covered by the attached unit of execution pursuant to Article 7 of Directive 76/308/EEC; the conditions of Article 7(2)(a) and (b) are satisfied (*)

— precautionary measures to be taken, pursuant to Article 13 of Directive 76/308/EEC, in respect of the person mentioned below concerning the claim(s) covered by the attached unit of execution; I attach hereto a statement of the reason for this request (*).

Please remit the entire amount of the claim recovered to:

....
(Bank account number)

....
(Name and address of the account holder)

....
(Payment reference)

Payment by instalment is: acceptable without further consultation/only acceptable after consultation/not acceptable (*)

....
(Signature)

(Official stamp)

Information relating to the person concerned (¹)

(a) For natural persons: Name:

                                 Date and place of birth:

   For legal entities: Legal status: Company name:

   Address (known/assumed (*)):

   Principal debtor/Co-debtor/Third party holding assets (*)

(b) Name of the principal debtor if different from person concerned:

   Address (known/assumed (*)):

(c) If relevant: assets of the debtor held by a third party:

(d) Other relevant information:

   (Detailed description of all other relevant information known about the above persons)

(*) Delete as appropriate.
(¹) Natural or legal person.

Information relating to the claim(s)

(Rate of exchange used:)

Exact nature of the claim(s) (Article 2 points (a) to (h) Directive 76/308/EEC)	Amount of principal (²) (³)	Amount of administrative penalties and fines (²) (³)	Amount of interest up to the date of signature of this document (²) (³)	Amount of the costs up to the date of signature of this document (²) (³)	Total amount of the claim (³)	Date on which enforcement becomes possible	Date of notification of the instrument to the addressee	Period of limitation	Reference to the instrument permitting the enforcement	Details of other documents attached

Other information

(²) Where the unit of execution is general, indicate the amounts of the different claims.
(³) Amount expressed in the currency of the requested authority and of the applicant authority.

ANNEX IV

DIRECTIVE 76/308/EEC
(Article 25)

Model for the Communication from the Member States to the Commission referred to in Article 25 of Directive 76/308/EEC

Requests for mutual assistance on recovery of claims sent and received by .... in the year ....

Member State	Requests for information		Requests for notification		Requests for recovery							
					Requests sent				Requests received			
	Number received	Number sent	Number received	Number sent	Number	Amount of the claims involved	Amounts of the claims recovered for requests made during the year (X)		Number	Amount of the claims involved	Amounts of the claims recovered for requests made during the year (X)	
							Amount	Year			Amount	Year
Belgique/België												
България												
Česká Republika												
Danmark												
Deutschland												
Eesti												
Ελλάδα												
España												
France												
Ireland												
Italia												
Κύπρος												
Latvija												
Lietuva												
Luxembourg												
Magyarország												
Luxembourg												
Malta												
Nederland												
Österreich												
Polska												
Portugal												
România												
Slovenija												
Slovensko												
Suomi/Finland												
Sverige												
United Kingdom												

COUNCIL REGULATION (EC) No 1798/2003

of 7 October 2003

on administrative cooperation in the field of value added tax and repealing Regulation (EEC) No 218/92

Official Journal L264, 15/10/2003, p. 1 - 11

> Council Regulations (EC) No 143/2008 and (EC) No 37/2009 amend various articles contained in this Regulation with effect from 1 January 2010 and 1 January 2015. The articles which will be amended are highlighted with* and those amendments effective from 1 January 2010 are detailed in the footnotes to each section.

THE COUNCIL OF THE EUROPEAN UNION,

Having regard to the Treaty establishing the European Community, and in particular Article 93 thereof,

Having regard to the proposal from the Commission,

Having regard to the opinion of the European Parliament,

Having regard to the opinion of the European Economic and Social Committee,

Whereas:

(1)   Tax evasion and tax avoidance extending across the frontiers of Member States lead to budget losses and violations of the principle of fair taxation and are liable to bring about distortions of capital movements and of the conditions of competition. They therefore affect the operation of the internal market.

(2)   Combating value added tax (VAT) evasion calls for close cooperation between the administrative authorities in each Member State responsible for the application of the provisions in that field.

(3)   The tax harmonisation measures taken to complete the internal market should therefore include the establishment of a common system for the exchange of information between the Member States whereby the Member States' administrative authorities are to assist each other and cooperate with the Commission in order to ensure the proper application of VAT on supplies of goods and services, intra-Community acquisition of goods and importation of goods.

(4)   Electronic storage and transmission of certain data for VAT control purposes is indispensable for the proper functioning of the VAT system.

(5)   The conditions for the exchange of, and direct access of Member States to, electronically stored data in each Member State should be clearly defined. Operators should have access to certain of such data where required for the fulfilment of their obligations.

(6)   The Member State of consumption has primary responsibility for assuring that non-established suppliers comply with their obligations. To this end, the application of the temporary special scheme for electronically supplied services that is provided for in Article 26c of Sixth Council Directive

77/388/EEC of 17 May 1977 on the harmonisation of the laws of Member States relating to turnover taxes, Common system of value added tax: uniform basis of assessment, requires the definition of rules concerning the provision of information and transfer of money between the Member State of identification and the Member State of consumption.

(7)   Council Regulation (EEC) No 218/92 of 27 January 1992 on administrative cooperation in the field of indirect taxation (VAT) established in this respect a system of close cooperation amongst the Member States' administrative authorities and between those authorities and the Commission.

(8)   Regulation (EEC) No 218/92 supplements Council Directive 77/799/ EEC of 19 December 1977 concerning mutual assistance by the competent authorities of the Member States in the field of direct and indirect taxation.

(9)   Those two legal instruments have proved to be effective but are no longer able to meet the new requirements of administrative cooperation resulting from the ever closer integration of economies within the internal market.

(10)   The existence of two separate instruments for cooperation on VAT has, moreover, hampered effective cooperation between tax administrations.

(11)   The rights and obligations of all parties concerned are currently ill-defined. Clearer and binding rules governing cooperation between Member States are therefore necessary.

(12)   There is not enough direct contact between local or national anti-fraud offices, with communication between central liaison offices being the rule. This leads to inefficiency, under-use of the arrangements for administrative cooperation and delays in communication. Provision should therefore be made to bring about more direct contacts between services with a view to making cooperation more efficient and faster.

(13)   Cooperation is also not intensive enough, in that, apart from the VAT information exchange system (VIES), there are not enough automatic or spontaneous exchanges of information between Member States. Exchanges of information between the respective administrations as well as between administrations and the Commission should be made more intensive and swifter in order to combat fraud more effectively.

(14)   The provisions on VAT administrative cooperation of Regulation (EEC) No 218/92 and of Directive 77/799/EEC should therefore be joined and strengthened. For reasons of clarity this should be done in a single new instrument which replaces Regulation (EEC) No 218/92.

(15)   This Regulation should not affect other Community measures which contribute to combating VAT fraud.

(16)   For the purposes of this Regulation, it is appropriate to consider limitations of certain rights and obligations laid down by Directive 95/46/EC of the European Parliament and of the Council of 24 October

1995 on the protection of individuals with regard to the processing of personal data and on the free movement of such data in order to safeguard the interests referred to in Article 13(1)(e) of that Directive.

(17) The measures necessary for the implementation of this Regulation should be adopted in accordance with Council Decision 1999/468/EC of 28 June 1999 laying down the procedures for the exercise of implementing powers conferred on the Commission.

(18) This Regulation respects the fundamental rights and observes the principles which are recognised in particular by the Charter of Fundamental Rights of the European Union,

HAS ADOPTED THIS REGULATION:

CHAPTER I

GENERAL PROVISIONS

*Article 1

1. This Regulation lays down the conditions under which the administrative authorities in the Member States responsible for the application of the laws on VAT on supplies of goods and services, intra-Community acquisition of goods and importation of goods are to cooperate with each other and with the Commission to ensure compliance with those laws.

    To that end, it lays down rules and procedures to enable the competent authorities of the Member States to cooperate and to exchange with each other any information that may help them to effect a correct assessment of VAT.

    This Regulation also lays down rules and procedures for the exchange of certain information by electronic means, in particular as regards VAT on intra-Community transactions.

    [For the period provided for in Article 4 of Directive 2002/38/EC, it also lays down rules and procedures for the exchange by electronic means of value added tax information on services supplied electronically in accordance with the special scheme provided for in Article 26c of Directive 77/388/EEC, and also for any subsequent exchange of information and, as far as services covered by that special scheme are concerned, for the transfer of money between Member States' competent authorities.]¹

2. This Regulation shall not affect the application in the Member States of the rules on mutual assistance in criminal matters.

Amendments

1   With effect from 1 January 2010 and in accordance with Art 1(1), Council Regulation (EC) No 143/2008 of 12 February 2008, this subparagraph will read: 'For the period provided for in Article 357 of Council Directive 2006/112/EC of 28 November 2006 on the common system of value added tax, it also lays down rules and procedures for the exchange by electronic means of value added tax information on services supplied electronically in accordance with the special scheme provided for in Chapter 6 of Title XII of that Directive and also for any subsequent exchange of information and, as far as services covered by that special scheme are concerned, for the transfer of money between Member States' competent authorities.'

*Article 2

For the purposes of this Regulation:

1.   'competent authority of a Member State', means:

—   in Belgium: Le ministre des finances
      De Minister van financiën,

[—   in the Czech Republic:
      Ministerstvo financí][1]

—   in Denmark:
      Skatteministeren,

—   in Germany:
      Bundesministerium der Finanzen,

[—   in Estonia:
      Maksuamet][1]

—   in Greece:
      Υπουργειο Οικονομίας και Οικονομικω,

—   in Spain:
      El Secretario de Estado de Hacienda,

—   in France:
      le ministre de l'économie,des finances et de l'industrie,

—   in Ireland:
      The Revenue Commissioners,

—   in Italy:
      il Capo del Dipartimento delle Politiche Fiscali,

[—   in Cyprus:
      Υπουργός Οικονομικών ή εξουσιοδοτημένος αντιπρόσωπος
      του,

—   in Latvia:
      Valsts ieðçmumu dienests,

—   in Lithuania:
      Valstybinë mokesèiø inspekcija prie Finans ø ministerijos,][1]

—   in Luxembourg:
      L'Administration de l'Enregistrement et des Domaines,

[—   in Hungary:
      Adó- és Pénzügyi Ellenõrzési Hivatal Központi Kapcsolattartó
      Irodája,

—   in Malta:
      Dipartiment tat-Taxxa fuq il-Valur Miżjud fil-Ministeru tal-
      Finanzi u Affarijiet Ekonomici,'][1]

—   in the Netherlands:
      De minister van Financiën,

—   in Austria:
      Bundesminister für Finanzen,

[—   in Poland:
Minister Finansów][2]

—   in Portugal:
O Ministro das Finanças,

[—   in Slovenia:
Ministrstvo za finance,

—   in Slovakia:
Ministerstvo financií][2]

—   in Finland:
Valtiovarainministeriö
Finansministeriet,

—   in Sweden:
Chefen för Finansdepartementet,

—   in the United Kingdom:
The Commissioners of Customs and Excise;

2.   'central liaison office', means the office which has been designated under Article 3(2) with principal responsibility for contacts with other Member States in the field of administrative cooperation;

3.   'liaison department', means any office other than the central liaison office with a specific territorial competence or a specialised operational responsibility which has been designated by the competent authority pursuant to Article 3(3) to exchange directly information on the basis of this Regulation;

4.   'competent official', means any official who can directly exchange information on the basis of this Regulation for which he has been authorised pursuant to Article 3(4);

5.   'requesting authority', means the central liaison office, a liaison department or any competent official of a Member State who makes a request for assistance on behalf of the competent authority;

6.   'requested authority', means the central liaison office, a liaison department or any competent official of a Member State who receives a request for assistance on behalf of the competent authority;

7.   'intra-Community transactions', means the intra-Community supply of goods or services;

8.   ['intra-Community supply of goods', means any supply of goods which must be declared in the recapitulative statement provided for in Article 22(6)(b) of Directive 77/388/EEC;][2]

9.   ['intra-Community supply of services', means any supply of services covered by Article 28b(C), (D), (E) and (F) of Directive 77/388/EEC;][3]

10.   ['intra-Community acquisition of goods', means acquisition of the right to dispose as owner of movable tangible property under Article 28a(3) of Directive 77/388/EEC;][4]

11. ['VAT identification number', means the number provided for in Article 22(1)(c), (d) and (e) of Directive 77/388/EEC;][5]

12. 'administrative enquiry', means all the controls, checks and other action taken by Member States in the performance of their duties with a view to ensuring proper application of VAT legislation;

13. 'automatic exchange', means the systematic communication of predefined information to another Member State, without prior request, at pre-established regular intervals;

14. 'structured automatic exchange', means the systematic communication of predefined information to another Member State, without prior request, as and when that information becomes available;

15. 'spontaneous exchange', means the irregular communication without prior request of information to another Member State;

16. 'person', means:

    (a)   a natural person;

    (b)   a legal person; or

    (c)   where the legislation in force so provides, an association of persons recognised as having the capacity to perform legal acts but lacking the legal status of a legal person;

17. 'to grant access', means to authorise access to the relevant electronic database and to obtain data by electronic means;

18. 'by electronic means', means using electronic equipment for the processing (including digital compression) and storage of data, and employing wires, radio transmission, optical technologies or other electromagnetic means;

19. 'CCN/CSI network', means the common platform based on the common communication network (CCN) and common system interface (CSI), developed by the Community to ensure all transmissions by electronic means between competent authorities in the area of customs and taxation.

Amendments
1   Inserted by Council Regulation (EC) No 885/2004 of 26 April 2004
2   With effect from 1 January 2010 and in accordance with Art 1(2), Council Regulation (EC) No 143/2008 of 12 February 2008, point 8 will read '"intra-Community supply of goods" means any supply of goods which must be declared in the recapitulative statement provided for in Article 262 of Directive 2006/112/EC;'
3   With effect from 1 January 2010 and in accordance with Art 1(2), Council Regulation (EC) No 143/2008 of 12 February 2008, point 9 will read: '"intra-Community supply of services" means any supply of services which must be declared in the recapitulative statement provided for in Article 262 of Directive 2006/112/EC;'
4   With effect from 1 January 2010 and in accordance with Art 1(2), Council Regulation (EC) No 143/2008 of 12 February 2008, point 10 will read: "intra-Community acquisition of goods" means the acquisition of the right under Article 20 of Directive 2006/112/EC to dispose as owner of moveable tangible property;'
5   With effect from 1 January 2010 and in accordance with Art 1(2), Council Regulation (EC) No 143/2008 of 12 February 2008, point 11 will read: '"VAT identification number" means the number provided for in Articles 214, 215 and 216 of Directive 2006/112/EC;'

Article 3

1. The competent authorities referred to in point 1 of Article 2 are the authorities in whose name this Regulation is to be applied, whether directly or by delegation.

2. Each Member State shall designate a single central liaison office to which principal responsibility shall be delegated for contacts with other Member States in the field of administrative cooperation. It shall inform the Commission and the other Member States thereof.

3. The competent authority of each Member State may designate liaison departments. The central liaison office shall be responsible for keeping the list of those departments up to date and making it available to the central liaison offices of the other Member States concerned.

4. The competent authority of each Member State may in addition designate, under the conditions laid down by it, competent officials who can directly exchange information on the basis of this Regulation. When it does so, it may limit the scope of such designation. The central liaison office shall be responsible for keeping the list of those officials up to date and making it available to the central liaison offices of the other Member States concerned.

5. The officials exchanging information under Articles 11 and 13 shall in any case be deemed to be competent officials for this purpose, in accordance with conditions laid down by the competent authorities.

6. Where a liaison department or a competent official sends or receives a request or a reply to a request for assistance, it shall inform the central liaison office of its Member State under the conditions laid down by the latter.

7. Where a liaison department or a competent official receives a request for assistance requiring action outside its territorial or operational area, it shall forward such request without delay to the central liaison office of its Member State and inform the requesting authority thereof. In such a case, the period laid down in Article 8 shall start the day after the request for assistance has been forwarded to the central liaison office.

Article 4

1. The obligation to give assistance as provided for in this Regulation shall not cover the provision of information or documents obtained by the administrative authorities referred to in Article 1 acting with the authorisation or at the request of the judicial authority.

2. However, where a competent authority has the powers in accordance with national law to communicate the information referred to in paragraph 1, it may be communicated as a part of the administrative cooperation provided for in this Regulation. Any such communication must have the prior authorisation of the judicial authority if the necessity of such authorisation derives from national law.

CHAPTER II

EXCHANGE OF INFORMATION ON REQUEST

Section 1

Request for information and for administrative enquiries

*Article 5

1. At the request of the requesting authority, the requested authority shall communicate the information referred to in Article 1, including any information relating to a specific case or cases.

2. For the purpose of forwarding the information referred to in paragraph 1, the requested authority shall arrange for the conduct of any administrative enquiries necessary to obtain such information.

3. The request referred to in paragraph 1 may contain a reasoned request for a specific administrative enquiry. If the Member State takes the view that no administrative enquiry is necessary, it shall immediately inform the requesting authority of the reasons thereof.

4. In order to obtain the information sought or to conduct the administrative enquiry requested, the requested authority or the administrative authority to which it has recourse shall proceed as though acting on its own account or at the request of another authority in its own Member State.

Article 6

Requests for information and for administrative enquiries pursuant to Article 5 shall, as far as possible, be sent using a standard form adopted in accordance with the procedure referred to in Article 44(2).

Article 7

1. At the request of the requesting authority, the requested authority shall communicate to it any pertinent information it obtains or has in its possession as well as the results of administrative enquiries, in the form of reports, statements and any other documents, or certified true copies or extracts thereof.

2. Original documents shall be provided only where this is not contrary to the provisions in force in the Member State in which the requested authority is established.

Section 2

Time limit for providing information

Article 8

The requested authority shall provide the information referred to in Articles 5 and 7 as quickly as possible and no later than three months following the date of receipt of the request.

However, where the requested authority is already in possession of that information, the time limit shall be reduced to a maximum period of one month.

Article 9

In certain special categories of cases, time limits different from the ones provided for in Article 8 may be agreed between the requested and the requesting authorities.

Article 10

Where the requested authority is unable to respond to the request by the deadline, it shall inform the requesting authority in writing forthwith of the reasons for its failure to do so, and when it considers it would be likely to be able to respond.

Section 3

Presence in administrative offices and participation in administrative enquiries

Article 11

1. By agreement between the requesting authority and the requested authority and in accordance with the arrangements laid down by the latter, officials authorised by the requesting authority may, with a view to exchanging the information referred to in Article 1, be present in the offices where the administrative authorities of the Member State in which the requested authority is established carry out their duties. Where the requested information is contained in documentation to which the officials of the requested authority have access, the officials of the requesting authority shall be given copies of the documentation containing the requested information.

2. By agreement between the requesting authority and the requested authority, and in accordance with the arrangements laid down by the latter, officials designated by the requesting authority may, with a view to exchanging the information referred to in Article 1, be present during the administrative enquiries. Administrative enquiries shall be carried out exclusively by the officials of the requested authority. The requesting authority's officials shall not exercise the powers of inspection conferred on officials of the requested authority. They may, however, have access to the same premises and documents as the latter, through their intermediary and for the sole purpose of the administrative enquiry being carried out.

3. The officials of the requesting authority present in another Member State in accordance with paragraphs 1 and 2 must at all times be able to produce written authority stating their identity and their official capacity.

Section 4

Simultaneous controls

Article 12

With a view to exchanging the information referred to in Article 1, two or more Member States may agree to conduct simultaneous controls, in their own territory, of the tax situation of one or more taxable persons who are of common or complementary interest, whenever such controls would appear to be more effective than controls carried out by only one Member State.

Article 13

1. A Member State shall identify independently the taxable persons whom it intends to propose for a simultaneous control. The competent authority of that Member State shall notify the competent authority in the other Member States concerned of the cases proposed for simultaneous controls. It shall give reasons for its choice, as far as possible, by providing the information which led to its decision. It shall specify the period of time during which such controls should be conducted.

2. The Member States concerned shall then decide whether they wish to take part in the simultaneous controls. On receipt of a proposal for a simultaneous control, the competent authority of the Member State shall confirm its agreement or communicate its reasoned refusal to its counterpart authority.

3. Each competent authority of the Member States concerned shall appoint a representative to be responsible for supervising and coordinating the control operation.

CHAPTER III

REQUEST FOR ADMINISTRATIVE NOTIFICATION

Article 14

The requested authority shall, at the request of the requesting authority and in accordance with the rules governing the notification of similar instruments in the Member State in which it is established, notify the addressee of all instruments and decisions which emanate from the administrative authorities and concern the application of VAT legislation in the territory of the Member State in which the requesting authority is established.

Article 15

Requests for notification, mentioning the subject of the instrument or decision to be notified, shall indicate the name, address and any other relevant information for identifying the addressee.

Article 16

The requested authority shall inform the requesting authority immediately of its response to the request for notification and notify it, in particular, of the date of notification of the decision or instrument to the addressee.

CHAPTER IV

EXCHANGE OF INFORMATION WITHOUT PRIOR REQUEST

*Article 17

Without prejudice to the provisions of Chapters V and VI, the competent authority of each Member State shall, by automatic or structured automatic exchange, forward the information referred to in Article 1 to the competent authority of any other Member State concerned, in the following cases:

1. where taxation is deemed to take place in the Member State of destination and the effectiveness of the control system necessarily depends on the information provided by the Member State of origin;

2. where a Member State has grounds to believe that a breach of VAT legislation has been committed or is likely to have been committed in the other Member State;

3. where there is a risk of tax loss in the other Member State.

*Article 18

The following shall be determined in accordance with the procedure referred to in Article 44(2):

1. the exact categories of information to be exchanged;

2. the frequency of the exchanges;

3. the practical arrangements for the exchange of information.

Each Member State shall determine whether it will take part in the exchange of a particular category of information, as well as whether it will do so in an automatic or structured automatic way.

Article 19

The competent authorities of the Member States may, in any case by spontaneous exchange, forward to each other, any information referred to in Article 1 of which they are aware.

Article 20

Member States shall take the necessary administrative and organisational measures to facilitate the exchanges provided for in this Chapter.

Article 21

A Member State cannot be obliged, for the purposes of implementing the provisions of this Chapter, to impose new obligations on persons liable for VAT with a view to collecting information nor to bear disproportionate administrative burdens.

CHAPTER V

STORAGE AND EXCHANGE OF INFORMATION SPECIFIC TO INTRA-COMMUNITY TRANSACTIONS

*Article 22

1. [Each Member State shall maintain an electronic database in which it shall store and process the information that it collects in accordance with Article 22(6)(b) in the version given in Article 28h of Directive 77/388/EEC.]¹

    To enable that information to be used in the procedures provided for in this Regulation, the information shall be stored for at least five years from the end of the calendar year in which access to the information is to be granted.

2. Member States shall ensure that their databases are kept up to date, and are complete and accurate.

    Criteria shall be defined, in accordance with the procedure referred to in Article 44(2), to determine which changes are not pertinent, essential or useful and therefore need not be made.

Amendments
1   With effect from 1 January 2010 and in accordance with Art 1(3), Council Regulation (EC) No 143/2008 of 12 February 2008, this subparagraph will read: 'Each Member State shall maintain an electronic database in which it stores and processes the information which it collects pursuant to Chapter 6 of Title XI of Directive 2006/112/EC.'

*Article 23

On the basis of the data stored in accordance with Article 22, the competent authority of a Member State shall have communicated to it automatically and without delay by any other Member State the following information, to which it may also have direct access:

1. VAT identification numbers issued by the Member State receiving the information;

2. [the total value of all intra-Community supplies of goods to persons holding a VAT identification number by all operators identified for the purposes of VAT in the Member State providing the information.]¹

[The values referred to in point 2 shall be expressed in the currency of the Member State providing the information and shall relate to calendar quarters.]²

Amendments
1   With effect from 1 January 2010 and in accordance with Art 1(4), Council Regulation (EC) No 143/2008 of 12 February 2008, point 2 will read: 'the total value of all intra-Community supplies of goods and the total value of all intra-Community supplies of services to persons holding a VAT identification number by all operators identified for the purposes of VAT in the Member State providing the information.'
2   With effect from 1 January 2010 and in accordance with Art 1(1), Council Regulation (EC) No 37/2009, this paragraph shall read: 'The values referred to in point 2 of the first paragraph shall be expressed in the currency of the Member State providing the information and shall relate to the periods for submission of the recapitulative statements specific to each taxable person which are established in accordance with Article 263 of Directive 2006/112/EC.'

*Article 24

[On the basis of the data stored in accordance with Article 22 and solely in order to prevent a breach of VAT legislation, the competent authority of a Member State shall, wherever it considers it necessary for the control of intra-Community acquisitions of goods, obtain directly and without delay, or have direct access to by electronic means, any of the following information:

1.　　the VAT identification numbers of the persons who effected the supplies referred to in point 2 of Article 23; and

2.　　the total value of such supplies from each such person to each person holding a VAT identification number referred to in point 1 of Article 23.][1]

[The values referred to in point 2 shall be expressed in the currency of the Member State providing the information and shall relate to calendar quarters.][2]

Amendments

1　With effect from 1 January 2010 and in accordance with Art 1(5), Council Regulation (EC) No 143/2008 of 12 February 2008, this paragraph will read:'On the basis of the data stored in accordance with Article 22 and solely in order to prevent a breach of VAT legislation, the competent authority of a Member State shall, wherever it considers it necessary for the control of intra-Community acquisitions of goods or intra-Community supplies of services taxable in its territory, obtain directly and without delay, or have direct access to by electronic means, any of the following information:

　1. the VAT identification numbers of the persons who carried out the supplies of goods and services referred to in point 2 of the first paragraph of Article 23;
　2. the total value of supplies of goods and services from each such person to each person holding a VAT identification number referred to in point 1 of the first paragraph of Article 23.'

2　With effect from 1 January 2010 and in accordance with Art 1(2), Council Regulation (EC) No 37/2009, this paragraph shall read: 'The values referred to in point 2 of the first paragraph shall be expressed in the currency of the Member State providing the information and shall relate to the periods for submission of the recapitulative statements specific to each taxable person which are established in accordance with Article 263 of Directive 2006/112/EC.'

Article 25

1.　　[Where the competent authority of a Member State is obliged to grant access to information under Articles 23 and 24, it shall do so as soon as possible and within three months at the latest of the end of the calendar quarter to which the information relates.

2.　　By way of derogation from paragraph 1, where information is added to a database in the circumstances provided for in Article 22, access to such additional information shall be granted as quickly as possible and no later than three months from the end of the quarter in which it was collected.][1]

3.　　The conditions under which access to the corrected information may be granted shall be laid down in accordance with the procedure referred to in Article 44(2).

Amendments

1　With effect from 1 January 2010 and in accordance with Art 1(3), Council Regulation (EC) No 37/2009, Article 25(1) and (2) shall read:

　'1. Where the competent authority of a Member State is obliged to grant access to information under Articles 23 and 24, it shall do so as soon as possible and, at the latest, within one month of the end of the period to which the information relates.
　2. By way of derogation from paragraph 1, where information is added to a database in the circumstances provided for in Article 22, access to such additional information shall be granted as quickly as possible and no later than one month after the end of the period in which it was collected.'

Article 26

Where, for the purposes of Articles 22 to 25, the competent authorities of the Member States store information in electronic databases and exchange such information by electronic means, they shall take all measures necessary to ensure compliance with Article 41.

*Article 27

1. Each Member State shall maintain an electronic database containing a register of persons to whom VAT identification numbers have been issued in that Member State.

2. At any time the competent authority of a Member State may obtain directly or have communicated to it, from the data stored in accordance with Article 22, confirmation of the validity of the VAT identification number under which a person has effected or received an intra-Community supply of goods or services.

    On specific request, the requested authority shall also communicate the date of issue and, where appropriate, the expiry date of the VAT identification number.

3. On request, the competent authority shall also provide without delay the name and address of the person to whom the number has been issued, provided that such information is not stored by the requesting authority with a view to possible use at some future time.

4. [The competent authorities of each Member State shall ensure that persons involved in the intra-Community supply of goods or of services and, for the period provided for in Article 4 of Directive 2002/38/EC, persons supplying services referred to in the last indent of Article 9(2) e of Directive 77/388/EEC are allowed to obtain confirmation of the validity of the VAT identification number of any specified person.

    For the period provided for in Article 4 of Directive 2002/38/EC Member States shall, in particular, provide such confirmation by electronic means in accordance with the procedure referred to in Article 44(2).][1]

5. Where, for the purposes of paragraphs 1 to 4, the competent authorities of the Member States store information in electronic databases and exchange such information by electronic means, they shall take all measures necessary to ensure compliance with Article 41.

Amendments
1   With effect from 1 January 2010 and in accordance with Art 1(6), Council Regulation (EC) No 143/2008 of 12 February 2008, Article 27(4) will read: 'The competent authorities of each Member State shall ensure that persons involved in the intra-Community supply of goods or of services and, for the period provided for in Article 357 of Directive 2006/112/EC, non-established taxable persons supplying electronically supplied services, in particular those referred to in Annex II of that Directive, are allowed to obtain confirmation of the validity of the VAT identification number of any specified person. During the period provided for in Article 357 of Directive 2006/112/EC, the Member States shall provide such confirmation by electronic means in accordance with the procedure referred to in Article 44(2) of this Regulation.'

CHAPTER VI

*[PROVISIONS CONCERNING THE SPECIAL SCHEME IN ARTICLE 26C OF DIRECTIVE 77/388/EEC][1]

Amendments
1   With effect from 1 January 2010 and in accordance with Art 1(7), Council Regulation (EC) No 143/2008 of 12 February 2008, the heading of Chapter VI point will read: 'PROVISIONS CONCERNING THE SPECIAL SCHEME IN CHAPTER 6 OF TITLE XII OF DIRECTIVE 2006/112/EC'

*Article 28

[The following provisions shall apply concerning the special scheme provided for in Article 26c in Directive 77/388/EEC. The definitions contained in point A of that Article shall also apply for the purpose of this Chapter.][1]

Amendments
1   With effect from 1 January 2010 and in accordance with Art 1(8), Council Regulation (EC) No 143/2008 of 12 February 2008, Art 28 will read: 'The following provisions shall apply concerning the special scheme provided for in Chapter 6 of Title XII of Directive 2006/112/EC. The definitions contained in Article 358 of that Directive shall also apply for the purpose of this Chapter.'

*Article 29

1.   [The information from the non-established taxable person to the Member State of identification when his activities commence set out in the second subparagraph of Article 26c(B)(2) of Directive 77/388/EEC is to be submitted in an electronic manner. The technical details, including a common electronic message, shall be determined in accordance with the procedure provided for in Article 44(2).][1]

2.   The Member State of identification shall transmit this information by electronic means to the competent authorities of the other Member States within 10 days from the end of the month during which the information was received from the non-established taxable person. In the same manner the competent authorities of the other Member States shall be informed of the allocated identification number. The technical details, including a common electronic message, by which this information is to be transmitted, shall be determined in accordance with the procedure provided for in Article 44(2).

3.   The Member State of identification shall without delay inform by electronic means the competent authorities of the other Members States if a non-established taxable person is excluded from the identification register.

Amendments
1   With effect from 1 January 2010 and in accordance with Art 1(9), Council Regulation (EC) No 143/2008 of 12 February 2008, Art 29(1) will read: 'The information provided by the taxable person not established in the Community to the Member State of identification when his activities commence pursuant to Article 361 of Directive 2006/112/EC shall be submitted in an electronic manner. The technical details, including a common electronic message, shall be determined in accordance with the procedure provided for in Article 44(2) of this Regulation.'

*Article 30

[The return with the details set out in the second subparagraph of Article 26c(B) (5) of Directive 77/388/EEC is to be submitted in an electronic manner. The technical details, including a common electronic message, shall be determined in accordance with the procedure provided for in Article 44(2).][1]

The Member State of identification shall transmit this information by electronic means to the competent authority of the Member State concerned at the latest 10 days after the end of the month that the return was received. Member States which have required the tax return to be made in a national currency other than euro, shall convert the amounts into euro using the exchange rate valid for the last date of the reporting period. The exchange shall be done following the exchange rates published by the European Central Bank for that day, or, if there is no publication on that day, on the next day of publication. The technical details by which this information is to be transmitted shall be determined in accordance with the procedure provided for in Article 44(2).

The Member State of identification shall transmit by electronic means to the Member State of consumption the information needed to link each payment with a relevant quarterly tax return.

Amendments
1   With effect from 1 January 2010 and in accordance with Art 1(10), Council Regulation (EC) No 143/2008 of 12 February 2008, this paragraph will read: 'The return with the details set out in Article 365 of Directive 2006/112/EC is to be submitted in an electronic manner. The technical details, including a common electronic message, shall be determined in accordance with the procedure provided for in Article 44(2) of this Regulation.'

*Article 31

[The provisions in Article 22 shall apply also to information collected by the Member State of identification in accordance with Article 26c(B)(2) and (5) of Directive 77/388/EEC.][1]

Amendments
1   With effect from 1 January 2010 and in accordance with Art 1(11), Council Regulation (EC) No 143/2008 of 12 February 2008, Art 31 will read: 'The provisions in Article 22 of this Regulation shall apply also to information collected by the Member State of identification in accordance with Articles 360, 361, 364 and 365 of Directive 2006/112/EC.'

*Article 32

The Member State of identification shall ensure that the amount the non-established taxable person has paid is transferred to the bank account denominated in euro, which has been designated by the Member State of consumption to which the payment is due. Member States which required the payments in a national currency other than euro, shall convert the amounts into euro using the exchange rate valid for the last date of the reporting period. The exchange shall be done following the exchange rates published by the European Central Bank for that day, or, if there is no publication on that day, on the next day of publication. The transfer shall take place at the latest 10 days after the end of the month that the payment was received.

If the non-established taxable person does not pay the total tax due, the Member State of identification shall ensure that the payment is transferred to the Member States of consumption in proportion to the tax due in each Member State. The Member State of identification shall inform by electronic means the competent authorities of the Member States of consumption thereof.

Article 33

Member States shall notify by electronic means the competent authorities of the other Member States of the relevant bank account numbers for receiving payments according to Article 32.

Member States shall without delay notify by electronic means the competent authorities of the other Member States and the Commission of changes in the standard tax rate.

*Article 34

[Articles 28 to 33 shall apply for a period provided for in Article 4 of Directive 2002/38/EC.]¹

Amendments
1　With effect from 1 January 2010 and in accordance with Art 1(12), Council Regulation (EC) No 143/2008 of 12 February 2008, Article 34 will read: 'Articles 28 to 33 of this Regulation shall apply for the period provided for in Article 357 of Directive 2006/112/EC.'

*[........]¹

Amendments
1　With effect from 1 January 2010 and in accordance with Art 1(13), Council Regulation (EC) No 143/2008 of 12 February 2008, a new chapter, VIa 'PROVISIONS CONCERNING THE EXCHANGE AND CONSERVATION OF INFORMATION IN THE CONTEXT OF THE PROCEDURE PROVIDED FOR IN DIRECTIVE 2008/9/EC' will be inserted. This chapter will read:

Article 34a

1.　Where the competent authority of the Member State of establishment receives an application for refund of value added tax under Article 5 of Directive 2008/9/EC of 12 February 2008 laying down detailed rules for the refund of value added tax, provided for in Directive 2006/112/EC, to taxable persons not established in the Member State of refund but established in another Member State and Article 18 of that Directive is not applicable, it shall, within 15 calendar days of its receipt and by electronic means, forward the application to the competent authorities of each Member State of refund concerned with confirmation that the applicant as defined in Article 2(5) of Directive 2008/9/EC is a taxable person for the purposes of value added tax and that the identification or registration number given by this person is valid for the refund period.

2.　The competent authorities of each Member State of refund shall notify by electronic means the competent authorities of the other Member States of any information required by them under Article 9(2) of Directive 2008/9/EC. The technical details, including a common electronic message by which this information is to be transmitted, shall be determined in accordance with the procedure provided for in Article 44(2) of this Regulation.

3.　The competent authorities of each Member State of refund shall notify by electronic means the competent authorities of the other Member States if they want to make use of the option to require the applicant to provide the description of business activity by harmonized codes as referred to in Article 11 of Directive 2008/9/EC.

The harmonised codes referred to in the first subparagraph shall be determined in accordance with the procedure provided for in Article 44(2) of this Regulation on the basis of the NACE classification established by Regulation (EEC) No 3037/90.

CHAPTER VII

RELATIONS WITH THE COMMISSION

Article 35

1.　The Member States and the Commission shall examine and evaluate how the arrangements for administrative cooperation provided for in this Regulation are working. The Commission shall pool the Member States' experience with the aim of improving the operation of those arrangements.

2.   The Member States shall communicate to the Commission any available information relevant to their application of this Regulation.

3.   A list of statistical data needed for evaluation of this Regulation shall be determined in accordance with the procedure referred to in Article 44(2). The Member States shall communicate these data to the Commission in so far as they are available and the communication is not likely to involve administrative burdens which would be unjustified.

4.   With a view to evaluating the effectiveness of this system of administrative cooperation in combating tax evasion and tax avoidance, Member States may communicate to the Commission any other information referred to in Article 1.

5.   The Commission shall forward the information referred to in paragraphs 2, 3 and 4 to the other Member States concerned.

CHAPTER VIII

RELATIONS WITH THIRD COUNTRIES

Article 36

1.   When the competent authority of a Member State receives information from a third country, that authority may pass the information on to the competent authorities of Member States which might be interested in it and, in any event, to all those which request it, in so far as permitted by assistance arrangements with that particular third country.

2.   Provided the third country concerned has given an undertaking to provide the assistance required to gather evidence of the irregular nature of transactions which appear to contravene VAT legislation, information obtained under this Regulation may be communicated to that third country, with the consent of the competent authorities which supplied the information, in accordance with their domestic provisions applying to the communication of personal data to third countries.

CHAPTER IX

CONDITIONS GOVERNING THE EXCHANGE OF INFORMATION

Article 37

Information communicated pursuant to this Regulation shall, as far as possible, be provided by electronic means under arrangements to be adopted in accordance with the procedure referred to in Article 44(2).

Article 38

Requests for assistance, including requests for notification, and attached documents may be made in any language agreed between the requested and requesting authority. The said requests shall only be accompanied by a translation into the official language or one of the official languages of the

Member State in which the requested authority is established, in special cases when the requested authority gives a reason for asking for such a translation.

*Article 39

For the period provided for in Article 4 of Directive 2002/38/EC, the Commission and the Member States shall ensure that such existing or new communication and information exchange systems which are necessary to provide for the exchanges of information described in Articles 29 and 30 are operational. The Commission will be responsible for whatever development of the common communication network/common system interface (CCN/ CSI) is necessary to permit the exchange of this information between Member States. Member States will be responsible for whatever development of their systems is necessary to permit this information to be exchanged using the CCN/CSI.[1]

Member States shall waive all claims for the reimbursement of expenses incurred in applying this Regulation except, where appropriate, in respect of fees paid to experts.

Amendments

1   With effect from 1 January 2010 and in accordance with Art 1(14), Council Regulation (EC) No 143/2008 of 12 February 2008, this paragraph will read: 'For the period provided for in Article 357 of Directive 2006/112/ EC, the Commission and the Member States shall ensure that such existing or new communication and information exchange systems which are necessary to provide for the exchanges of information described in Articles 29 and 30 of this Regulation are operational. The Commission will be responsible for whatever development of the common communication network/common system interface (CCN/CSI) is necessary to permit the exchange of this information between Member States. Member States will be responsible for whatever development of their systems is necessary to permit this information to be exchanged using the CCN/CSI.'

Article 40

1.   The requested authority in one Member State shall provide a requesting authority in another Member State with the information referred to in Article 1 provided that:

   (a)   the number and the nature of the requests for information made by the requesting authority within a specific period do not impose a disproportionate administrative burden on that requested authority;

   (b)   that requesting authority has exhausted the usual sources of information which it could have used in the circumstances to obtain the information requested, without running the risk of jeopardising the achievement of the desired end.

2.   This Regulation shall impose no obligation to have enquiries carried out or to provide information if the laws or administrative practices of the Member State which would have to supply the information do not authorise the Member State to carry out those enquiries or collect or use that information for that Member State's own purposes.

3.   The competent authority of a Member State may refuse to provide information where the Member State concerned is unable, for legal reasons, to provide similar information. The Commission shall be informed of the grounds of the refusal by the requested Member State.

4. The provision of information may be refused where it would lead to the disclosure of a commercial, industrial or professional secret or of a commercial process, or of information whose disclosure would be contrary to public policy.

5. The requested authority shall inform the requesting authority of the grounds for refusing a request for assistance.

6. A minimum threshold triggering a request for assistance may be adopted in accordance with the procedure referred to in Article 44(2).

Article 41

1. Information communicated in any form pursuant to this Regulation shall be covered by the obligation of official secrecy and enjoy the protection extended to similar information under both the national law of the Member State which received it and the corresponding provisions applicable to Community authorities.

   Such information may be used for the purpose of establishing the assessment base or the collection or administrative control of tax for the purpose of establishing the assessment base.

   The information may also be used for the assessment of other levies, duties, and taxes covered by Article 2 of Council Directive 76/308/EEC of 15 March 1976 on mutual assistance for the recovery of claims relating to certain levies, duties, taxes and other measures.

   In addition, it may be used in connection with judicial proceedings that may involve penalties, initiated as a result of infringements of tax law without prejudice to the general rules and legal provisions governing the rights of defendants and witnesses in such proceedings.

2. Persons duly accredited by the Security Accreditation Authority of the European Commission may have access to this information only in so far as it is necessary for care, maintenance and development of the CCN/CSI network.

3. By way of derogation from paragraph 1, the competent authority of the Member State providing the information shall permit its use for other purposes in the Member State of the requesting authority, if, under the legislation of the Member State of the requested authority, the information can be used for similar purposes.

4. Where the requesting authority considers that information it has received from the requested authority is likely to be useful to the competent authority of a third Member State, it may transmit it to the latter authority. It shall inform the requested authority thereof in advance. The requested authority may require that the transmission of the information to a third party be subject to its prior agreement.

5. Member States shall, for the purpose of the correct application of this Regulation, restrict the scope of the obligations and rights provided for in Article 10, Article 11(1), Articles 12 and 21 of Directive 95/46/EC

to the extent required in order to safeguard the interests referred to in Article 13(e) of that Directive.

Article 42

Reports, statements and any other documents, or certified true copies or extracts thereof, obtained by the staff of the requested authority and communicated to the requesting authority under the assistance provided for by this Regulation may be invoked as evidence by the competent bodies of the Member State of the requesting authority on the same basis as similar documents provided by another authority of that country.

Article 43

1. For the purpose of applying this Regulation, Member States shall take all necessary measures to:

    (a)   ensure effective internal coordination between the competent authorities referred to in Article 3;

    (b)   establish direct cooperation between the authorities authorised for the purposes of such coordination;

    (c)   ensure the smooth operation of the information exchange arrangements provided for in this Regulation.

2. The Commission shall communicate to each Member State, as quickly as possible, any information which it receives and which it is able to provide.

CHAPTER X

GENERAL AND FINAL PROVISIONS

Article 44

1. The Commission shall be assisted by the Standing Committee on Administrative Cooperation, (hereinafter referred to as the Committee).

2. Where reference is made to this paragraph, Articles 5 and 7 of Decision 1999/468/EC shall apply, having regard to the provisions of Article 8 thereof.

    The period laid down in Article 5(6) of Decision 1999/468/EC shall be set at three months.

3. The Committee shall adopt its rules of procedure.

Article 45

1. Every three years from the date of entry into force of this Regulation, the Commission shall report to the European Parliament and the Council on the application of this Regulation.

2. Member States shall communicate to the Commission the text of any provisions of national law, which they adopt in the field covered by this Regulation.

Article 46

1. The provisions of this Regulation shall be without prejudice to the fulfilment of any wider obligations in relation to mutual assistance ensuing from other legal acts, including bilateral or multilateral agreements.

2. Where the Member States conclude bilateral arrangements on matters covered by this Regulation other than to deal with individual cases, they shall inform the Commission without delay. The Commission shall in turn inform the other Member States.

Article 47

Regulation (EEC) No 218/92 is hereby repealed.

References made to the repealed Regulation shall be construed as references to this Regulation.

Article 48

This Regulation shall enter into force on 1 January 2004.

This Regulation shall be binding in its entirety and directly applicable in all Member States.

Done at Luxembourg, 7 October 2003.

For the Council
The President

G. TREMONTI

COUNCIL DIRECTIVE 2003/92/EC

of 7 October 2003

amending Directive 77/388/EEC as regards the rules on the place of supply of gas and electricity

Official Journal L260, 11/10/2003, p.8 - 9

THE COUNCIL OF THE EUROPEAN UNION,

This Directive was repealed by Council Directive 2006/112/EC of 28 November 2006 on the common system of value added tax, with effect from 1 January 2007

Having regard to the Treaty establishing the European Community, and in particular Article 93 thereof,

Having regard to the proposal from the Commission,

Having regard to the opinion of the European Parliament,

Having regard to the opinion of the European Economic and Social Committee,

Whereas:

(1) Increasing liberalisation of the gas and electricity sector, aimed at completing the internal market for electricity and natural gas, has revealed a need to review the current VAT rules on the place of supply of those goods, set out in the Sixth Council Directive 77/388/EEC of 17 May 1977 on the harmonisation of the laws of the Member States relating to turnover taxes — Common system of value added tax: uniform basis of assessment, in order to modernise and simplify the operation of the VAT system within the context of the internal market, a strategy to which the Commission is committed.

(2) Electricity and gas are treated as goods for VAT purposes, and, accordingly, the place of their supply with respect to cross-border transactions has to be determined in accordance with Article 8 of Directive 77/388/EEC. However, since electricity and gas are difficult to track physically it is particularly difficult to determine the place of supply under the current rules.

(3) In order to attain a real internal market for electricity and gas without VAT obstacles, the place of supply of gas through the natural gas distribution system and of electricity, before the goods reach the final stage of consumption, should be determined to be the place where the customer has established his business.

(4) The supply of electricity and gas in the final stage, from traders and distributors to final consumer, should be taxed at the place where the customer has effective use and consumption of the goods, in order to ensure that taxation takes place in the country where actual consumption takes place. This is normally the place where the meter of the customer is located.

(5)   Electricity and gas are supplied through distribution networks, to which network operators provide access. In order to avoid double or non-taxation, it is necessary to harmonise the rules governing the place of supply of the transmission and transportation services. Access to and use of the distribution systems and the provision of other services directly linked to these services should therefore be added to the list of specific instances set out in Article 9, paragraph 2(e) of Directive 77/388/EEC.

(6)   The import of gas through the natural gas distribution system, or of electricity, should be exempted in order to avoid double taxation.

(7)   Those changes in the rules governing the place of supply of gas through the natural gas distribution system, or of electricity, should be combined with a compulsory reverse charge when the customer is a person identified for VAT purposes.

(8)   Directive 77/388/EEC should therefore be amended accordingly,

HAS ADOPTED THIS DIRECTIVE:

Article 1

Directive 77/388/EEC is hereby amended as follows:

1.   in Article 8(1), the following points are added:

'(d)   in the case of the supply of gas through the natural gas distribution system, or of electricity, to a taxable dealer: the place where that taxable dealer has established his business or has a fixed establishment for which the goods are supplied, or, in the absence of such a place of business or fixed establishment, the place where he has his permanent address or usually resides.

"Taxable dealer" for the purposes of this provision means a taxable person whose principal activity in respect of purchases of gas and electricity is reselling such products and whose own consumption of these products is negligible.

(e)   in the case of the supply of gas through the natural gas distribution system, or of electricity, where such a supply is not covered by point (d): the place where the customer has effective use and consumption of the goods. Where all or part of the goods are not in fact consumed by this customer, these non consumed goods are deemed to have been used and consumed at the place where he has established his business or has a fixed establishment for which the goods are supplied. In the absence of such a place of business or fixed establishment, he is deemed to have used and consumed the goods at the place where he has his permanent address or usually resides.';

2.   in Article 9(2)(e), the following indent is inserted after the eighth indent:

'—   the provision of access to, and of transport or transmission through, natural gas and electricity distribution systems and the provision of other directly linked services.';

3.   in Article 14(1), the following point is added:

'(k)   import of gas through the natural gas distribution system, or of electricity.';

4.   Article 21(1)(a), in the version set out in Article 28g, is replaced by the following:

'(a)   the taxable person carrying out the taxable supply of goods or of services, except for the cases referred to in (b), (c) and (f). Where the taxable supply of goods or of services is effected by a taxable person who is not established within the territory of the country, Member States may, under the conditions determined by them, lay down that the person liable to pay tax is the person for whom the taxable supply of goods or of services is carried out;'

5.   in Article 21(1), in the version set out in Article 28g, the following point is added:

'(f)   persons who are identified for value added tax purposes within the territory of the country and to whom goods are supplied under the conditions set out in Article 8(1)(d) or (e), if the supplies are carried out by a taxable person not established within the territory of the country.';

6.   in Article 22(1)(c), in the version set out in Article 28h, the first indent is replaced by the following:

'—   Every taxable person, with the exception of those referred to in Article 28a(4), who, within the territory of the country, effects supplies of goods or of services giving him the right of deduction, other than supplies of goods or of services for which tax is payable solely by the customer or the recipient in accordance with Article 21(1)(a), (b), (c) or (f). However, Member States need not identify certain taxable persons referred to in article 4(3),';

7.   in Article 28a(5)(b) the following indent is added:

'—   the supply of gas through the natural gas distribution system, or of electricity, under the conditions set out in Article 8(1)(d) or (e).'

Article 2

Member States shall bring into force the laws, regulations and administrative provisions necessary to comply with this Directive on 1 January 2005. They shall forthwith inform the Commission thereof. When Member States adopt those provisions, they shall contain a reference to this Directive or be accompanied by such a reference on the occasion of their official publication. The methods of making such reference shall be laid down by Member States.

Article 3

This Directive shall enter into force on the day of its publication in the Official Journal of the European Union.

Article 4

This Directive is addressed to the Member States.

Done at Luxembourg, 7 October 2003.

For the Council
The President

G. TREMONTI

COUNCIL DIRECTIVE 2003/93/EC

of 7 October 2003

amending Council Directive 77/799/EEC concerning mutual assistance by the competent authorities of the Member States in the field of direct and indirect taxation

Official Journal L264, 15/10/2003, p.23-24

THE COUNCIL OF THE EUROPEAN UNION,

Having regard to the Treaty establishing the European Community, and in particular Articles 93 and 94 thereof,

Having regard to the proposal from the Commission,

Having regard to the opinion of the European Parliament,
Having regard to the opinion of the European Economic and Social Committee,

Whereas:

(1)   In order to combat value added tax (VAT) evasion it is necessary to strengthen cooperation between tax administrations within the Community and between the latter and the Commission in accordance with common principles.

(2)   To that end, Council Regulation (EEC) No 218/92, which supplemented, as regards VAT, the system of cooperation established by Council Directive 77/799/EEC of 19 December 1977 concerning mutual assistance by the competent authorities of the Member States in the field of direct and indirect taxation, has been replaced by Council Regulation (EC) No 1798/2003 of 7 October 2003 on administrative cooperation in the field of value added tax and repealing Regulation (EEC) No 218/92. The latter Regulation sets out all the provisions relating to administrative cooperation in the field of VAT, with the exception of mutual assistance as provided for by Council Directive 76/308/EEC of 15 March 1976 on mutual assistance for the recovery of claims relating to certain levies, duties, taxes and other measures.

(3)   The scope of mutual assistance laid down by Directive 77/799/EEC must be extended to taxation of the insurance premiums referred to in Directive 76/308/EEC so as to better protect the financial interests of the Member States and the neutrality of the internal market.

(4)   Directive 77/799/EEC should therefore be amended accordingly,

HAS ADOPTED THIS DIRECTIVE:

Article 1

Directive 77/799/EEC is hereby amended as follows:

1.   the title shall be replaced by the following:

'Council Directive 77/799/EEC of 19 December 1977 concerning mutual assistance by the competent authorities of the Member States in the field of direct taxation, certain excise duties and taxation of insurance premium';

2. in Article 1(1), the first indent shall be replaced by the following:

'—   taxation of insurance premiums referred to in the sixth indent of Article 3 of Council Directive 76/308/EEC,';

2(a) in Article 1(5), the wording under the heading 'in the United Kingdom' shall be replaced by the following:

'The Commissioners of Customs and Excise or an authorised representative for information required concerning taxes on insurance premiums and excise duty.

The Commissioners of Inland Revenue or an authorised representative for all other information.';

2(b) in Article 1(5) the wording under 'in Italy' shall be replaced by the following:

'Il ministro dell'economia e delle finanze or an authorised representative.'

3. Article 7(1), shall replaced by the following:

'1.   All information made known to a Member State under this Directive shall be kept secret in that State in the same manner as information received under its national legislation. In any case, such information:

—   may be made available only to the persons directly involved in the assessment of the tax or in the administrative control of this assessment,

—   may be made known only in connection with judicial proceedings or administrative proceedings involving sanctions undertaken with a view to, or relating to, the making or reviewing the tax assessment and only to persons who are directly involved in such proceedings; such information may, however, be disclosed during public hearings or in judgements if the competent authority of the Member State supplying the information raises no objection,

—   shall in no circumstances be used other than for taxation purposes or in connection with judicial proceedings or administrative proceedings involving sanctions undertaken with a view to, or in relation to, the making or reviewing of the tax assessment.

In addition, Member States may provide for the information referred to in the first subparagraph to be used for assessment of other levies, duties and taxes covered by Article 2 of Directive 76/308/EEC.

Article 2

References made to Directive 77/799/EEC in relation to value added tax (VAT) shall be construed as references to Regulation (EC) No 1798/2003.

Article 3

1. Member States shall bring into force the laws, regulations and administrative provisions necessary to comply with this Directive on 31 December 2003. They shall forthwith inform the Commission thereof.

2. When Member States adopt those provisions, they shall contain a reference to this Directive or shall be accompanied by such a reference on the occasion of their official publication. Member States shall determine how such reference is to be made.

Article 4

This Directive shall enter into force on the day of its publication in the Official Journal of the European Union.

Article 5

This Directive is addressed to the Member States.
Done at Luxembourg, 7 October 2003.

For the Council
The President

G. TREMONTI

COUNCIL DECISION

of 25 November 2003

amending Decision 97/510/EC authorising Ireland to apply a measure derogating from Article 21 of the Sixth Directive (77/388/EEC) on the harmonisation of the laws of the Member States relating to turnover taxes

Official Journal L324, 11/12/2003, p. 36

THE COUNCIL OF THE EUROPEAN UNION,

Having regard to the Treaty establishing the European Community,

Having regard to the Sixth Council Directive (77/388/EEC) of 17 May 1977 on the harmonisation of the laws of the Member States relating to turnover taxes — Common system of value added tax: uniform basis of assessment, and in particular Article 27(1) thereof,

Having regard to the proposal from the Commission,

Whereas:

(1) By letter received by the Secretariat-General of the Commission on 4 July 2003, Ireland requested the extension of Decision 97/510/EC authorising it to apply a measure derogating from Article 21 of the Sixth Directive which enables it to combat tax evasion and tax fraud in the real-estate sector until 31 December 2007.

(2) The matters of law and of fact which justified the application of the special measures in question have not changed and still pertain.

(3) The authorisation should therefore be extended until 31 December 2007.

(4) The derogation in question has no impact on the European Communities' own resources from valued added tax,

HAS ADOPTED THIS DIRECTIVE:

Article 1

In Article 1 of Decision 97/510/EC, '31 December 2003' shall be replaced by '31 December 2007'.

Article 2

This Decision is addressed to Ireland.

Done at Brussels, 10 February 2004.

For the Council
The President

G. TREMONTI

COUNCIL DIRECTIVE 2004/7/EC

of 20 January 2004

amending Directive 77/388/EEC concerning the common system of value added tax, as regards conferment of implementing powers and the procedure for adopting derogations

> This Directive was repealed by Council Directive 2006/112/EC of 28 November 2006 on the common system of value added tax, with effect from 1 January 2007

THE COUNCIL OF THE EUROPEAN UNION,

Having regard to the Treaty establishing the European Community, and in particular Article 93 thereof,

Having regard to the proposal from the Commission,

Having regard to the opinion of the European Parliament,

Having regard to the opinion of the European Economic and Social Committee,

Whereas:

(1) Articles 27 and 30 of Council Directive 77/388/EEC of 17 May 1977 on the harmonisation of the laws of the Member States relating to turnover taxes — Common system of value added tax: uniform basis of assessment, lay down procedures that may result in the tacit approval of derogations by the Council.

(2) In the interests of transparency and legal certainty, it is preferable to ensure that every derogation authorised under Article 27 or Article 30 of Directive 77/388/EEC takes the form of an explicit decision adopted by the Council acting on a proposal from the Commission.

(3) The possibility of tacit approval by the Council on the expiry of a given period should therefore be removed.

(4) In order to ensure that a Member State which has submitted a request for derogation is not left in doubt as to what action the Commission plans to take in response, time limits should be laid down within which the Commission must present to the Council either a proposal for authorisation or a communication setting out its objections.

(5) In order to enable Member States to follow more closely the processing of their requests, the Commission should be required, once it has all the information it considers necessary for appraising a request, to notify the requesting Member State accordingly and transmit the request, in its original language, to the other Member States.

(6) In the second sentence of paragraph 1 of Article 27 of Directive 77/388/EEC it is emphasised that the assessment of the negligible extent of the effect of the simplification measure on the amount of tax due at the final consumption stage is made in a global manner by reference to

macroeconomic forecasts relating to the likely impact of the measure on the Community's own resources provided from VAT.

(7)   In the absence of any mechanism for the adoption of binding measures to govern the implementation of Directive 77/388/EEC, the application of rules laid down in that Directive varies from one Member State to another.

(8)   In order to improve the functioning of the internal market, it is essential to ensure more uniform application of the current VAT system. The introduction of a procedure for the adoption of measures to ensure the correct implementation of existing rules would represent a major step forward in that respect.

(9)   Those measures should, in particular, address the problem of double taxation of cross-border transactions which can occur as the result of divergences between Member States in the application of the provisions of Directive 77/388/EEC governing the place of supply.

(10) However, the scope of each implementing measure should remain limited since, albeit designed to clarify a provision laid down in Directive 77/388/EEC, it could never derogate from such a provision.

(11) Although the scope of the implementing measures would be limited, those measures would have a budgetary impact which for one or more Member States could be significant.

(12) The impact of such measures on the budgets of Member States justifies the Council reserving the right to exercise powers for the implementation of Directive 77/388/EEC itself.

(13) Given the restricted scope of the measures envisaged, measures implementing Directive 77/388/EEC should be adopted by the Council acting unanimously on a proposal from the Commission.

(14) Since, for those reasons, the objectives of this Directive cannot be sufficiently achieved by the Member States acting alone and can therefore be better achieved at Community level, the Community may adopt measures in accordance with the principle of subsidiarity as set out in Article 5 of the Treaty. In accordance with the principle of proportionality, as set out in that Article, this Directive does not go beyond what is necessary in order to achieve those objectives.

(15) Directive 77/388/EEC should therefore be amended accordingly,

HAS ADOPTED THIS DIRECTIVE:

Article 1

Directive 77/388/EEC is amended as follows:

1.   In Article 27, paragraphs 1, 2, 3 and 4 shall be replaced by the following:

      '1.   The Council, acting unanimously on a proposal from the Commission, may authorise any Member State to introduce special measures for derogation from the provisions of this

Directive, in order to simplify the procedure for charging the tax or to prevent certain types of tax evasion or avoidance. Measures intended to simplify the procedure for charging the tax, except to a negligible extent, may not affect the overall amount of the tax revenue of the Member State collected at the stage of final consumption.

2.   A Member State wishing to introduce the measure referred to in paragraph 1 shall send an application to the Commission and provide it with all the necessary information. If the Commission considers that it does not have all the necessary information, it shall contact the Member State concerned within two months of receipt of the application and specify what additional information is required. Once the Commission has all the information it considers necessary for appraisal of the request it shall within one month notify the requesting Member State accordingly and it shall transmit the request, in its original language, to the other Member States.

3.   Within three months of giving the notification referred to in the last sentence of paragraph 2, the Commission shall present to the Council either an appropriate proposal or, should it object to the derogation requested, a communication setting out its objections.

4.   In any event, the procedure set out in paragraphs 2 and 3 shall be completed within eight months of receipt of the application by the Commission.'

2.   In Title XVII, the following Article 29a shall be inserted:

'Article 29a

Implementing measures

The Council, acting unanimously on a proposal from the Commission, shall adopt the measures necessary to implement this Directive.'

3.   Article 30 shall be replaced by the following:

'Article 30

International agreements

1.   The Council, acting unanimously on a proposal from the Commission, may authorise any Member State to conclude with a third country or an international organisation an agreement which may contain derogations from this Directive.

2.   A Member State wishing to conclude such an agreement shall send an application to the Commission and provide it with all the necessary information. If the Commission considers that it does not have all the necessary information, it shall contact the Member State concerned within two months of receipt of the application and specify what additional information

is required. Once the Commission has all the information it considers necessary for appraisal of the request it shall within one month notify the requesting Member State accordingly and it shall transmit the request, in its original language, to the other Member States.

3.   Within three months of giving the notification referred to in the last sentence of paragraph 2, the Commission shall present to the Council either an appropriate proposal or, should it object to the derogation requested, a communication setting out its objections.

4.   In any event, the procedure set out in paragraphs 2 and 3 shall be completed within eight months of receipt of the application by the Commission.'

Article 2

This Directive shall enter into force on the 20th day following its publication in the *Official Journal of the European Union*.

Article 3

This Directive is addressed to the Member States.
Done at Brussels, 20 January 2004.

For the Council
The President

C. McCREEVY

COUNCIL DIRECTIVE 2004/15/EC

of 10 February 2004

amending Directive 77/388/EEC to extend the facility allowing Member States to apply reduced rates of VAT to certain labour-intensive services

Official Journal L52, 21/2/2004, p. 61 - 61

This Directive was repealed by Council Directive 2006/112/EC of 28 November 2006 on the common system of value added tax, with effect from 1 January 2007

THE COUNCIL OF THE EUROPEAN UNION,

Having regard to the Treaty establishing the European Community, and in particular Article 93 thereof,

Having regard to the proposal from the Commission,

Having regard to the opinion of the European Parliament,

Having regard to the opinion of the European Economic and Social Committee,

Whereas:

(1)   Article 28(6) of Council Directive 77/388/EEC of 17 May 1977 on the harmonisation of the laws of the Member States relating to turnover taxes — common system of value added tax: uniform basis of assessment, allows the reduced rates provided for in the third subparagraph of Article 12(3)(a) also to be applied to the labour-intensive services listed in the categories set out in Annex K to that Directive for a maximum period of four years from 1 January 2000 to 31 December 2003.

(2)   Council Decision 2000/185/EC of 28 February 2000 authorising Member States to apply a reduced rate of VAT to certain labour-intensive services in accordance with the procedure provided for in Article 28(6) of Directive 77/388/EEC, authorised certain Member States to apply a reduced rate of VAT to those labour intensive services for which they had submitted an application up to 31 December 2003.

(3)   On the basis of the assessment reports submitted by the Member States that have applied the reduced rate, the Commission submitted its global evaluation report on 2 June 2003.

(4)   In line with its strategy to improve the operation of the VAT system within the context of the internal market, the Commission adopted a proposal for a general review of the reduced rates of VAT to simplify and rationalise them.

(5)   Since the Council has not reached an agreement on the content of the proposal, it should be given the necessary time to do so, in order to avoid legal uncertainty from 1 January 2004 the maximum period of application set for this measure in Directive 77/388/EEC should therefore be extended.

(6)   In order to ensure the continuous application of Article 28(6) of Directive 77/388/EEC, provision should be made for this Directive to apply retroactively.

(7)   Implementation of this Directive in no way implies change in the legislative provisions of Member States.

(8)   Decision 77/388/EEC should be amended accordingly,

HAS ADOPTED THIS DIRECTIVE:

Article 1

In the first subparagraph of Article 28(6) of Directive 77/388/EEC the words 'four years between 1 January 2000 and 31 December 2003' shall be replaced by the words 'six years between 1 January 2000 and 31 December 2005'.

Article 2

This Directive shall enter into force on the day of its adoption.
It shall apply from 1 January 2004.

Article 3

This Directive is addressed to the Member States.
Done at Brussels, 10 February 2004.

For the Council
The President

C. McCREEVY

REGULATION (EC) No 638/2004 OF THE EUROPEAN PARLIAMENT AND OF THE COUNCIL

of 31 March 2004

on Community statistics relating to the trading of goods between Member States and repealing Council Regulation (EEC) No 3330/91

Official Journal L102, 07.04.2004, p. 01 – 08

THE EUROPEAN PARLIAMENT AND THE COUNCIL OF THE EUROPEAN UNION,

Having regard to the Treaty establishing the European Community, and in particular Article 285(1) thereof,

Having regard to the proposal from the Commission,

Having regard to the opinion of the European Economic and Social Committee,

Acting in accordance with the procedure laid down in Article 251 of the Treaty,

Whereas:

(1) Council Regulation (EEC) No 3330/91 of 7 November 1991 on the statistics relating to the trading of goods between Member States introduced a completely new system of data collection, which has been simplified on two occasions. In order to improve the transparency of this system and to make it easier to understand, Regulation (EEC) No 3330/91 should be replaced by this Regulation.

(2) This system should be retained, as a sufficiently detailed level of statistical information is still required for the Community policies involved in the development of the internal market and for Community enterprises to analyse their specific markets. Aggregated data also need to be available quickly in order to analyse the development of the Economic and Monetary Union. Member States should have the possibility of collecting information which meets their specific needs.

(3) There is, however, a need to improve the wording of the rules on compiling statistics relating to the trading of goods between Member States so that they can be more easily understood by the companies responsible for providing the data, the national services collecting the data and users.

(4) A system of thresholds should be retained, but in a simplified form, in order to provide a satisfactory response to users' needs whilst reducing the burden of response on the parties responsible for providing statistical information, particularly small and medium-sized enterprises.

(5) A close link should be maintained between the system for collecting statistical information and the fiscal formalities which exist in the context of trade of goods between Member States. This link makes it possible, in particular, to check the quality of the information collected.

(6)   The quality of the statistical information produced, its evaluation by means of common indicators and transparency in this field are important objectives, which call for regulation at Community level.

(7)   Since the objective of the planned action, namely the creation of a common legal framework for the systematic production of Community statistics relating to the trading of goods between Member States, cannot be sufficiently achieved at national level and can be better achieved at Community level, the Community may adopt measures, in accordance with the principle of subsidiarity as set out in Article 5 of the Treaty. In accordance with the principle of proportionality, as set out in that Article, this Regulation does not go beyond what is required to achieve this objective.

(8)   Council Regulation (EC) No 322/97 of 17 February 1997 on Community statistics provides a reference framework for this Regulation. However, the very detailed level of information in the field of statistics relating to the trading of goods requires specific rules with regard to confidentiality.

(9)   It is important to ensure the uniform application of this Regulation and, in order to do so, to make provision for a Community procedure to help determine the implementing arrangements within an appropriate timescale and to make the necessary technical adaptations.

(10)   The measures necessary for implementation of this Regulation should be adopted in accordance with Council Decision 1999/468/EC of 28 June 1999 laying down the procedures for the exercise of implementing powers conferred on the Commission,

HAVE ADOPTED THIS REGULATION:

Article 1

Subject matter

This Regulation establishes a common framework for the systematic production of Community statistics relating to the trading of goods between Member States.

Article 2

Definitions

For the purpose of this Regulation, the following definitions shall apply:

(a)   '**goods**': all movable property, including electric current;

(b)   '**specific goods or movements**': goods or movements which, by their very nature, call for specific provisions, and in particular industrial plants, vessels and aircraft, sea products, goods delivered to vessels and aircraft, staggered consignments, military goods, goods to or from offshore installations, spacecraft, motor vehicle and aircraft parts and waste products;

(c)   **'national authorities'**: national statistical institutes and other bodies responsible in each Member State for producing Community statistics relating to the trading of goods between Member States;

(d)   **'Community goods'**:

    (i)   goods entirely obtained in the customs territory of the Community, without addition of goods from third countries or territories which are not part of the customs territory of the Community;

    (ii)   goods from third countries or territories which are not part of the customs territory of the Community, which have been released for free circulation in a Member State;

    (iii)   goods obtained in the customs territory of the Community either from the goods referred to exclusively in point (ii) or from the goods referred to in points (i) and (ii);

(e)   **'Member State of dispatch'**: the Member State as defined by its statistical territory from which goods are dispatched to a destination in another Member State;

(f)   **'Member State of arrival'**: the Member State as defined by its statistical territory in which goods arrive from another Member State;

(g)   **'goods in simple circulation between Member States'**: Community goods dispatched from one Member State to another, which, on the way to the Member State of destination, travel directly through another Member State or stop for reasons related only to the transport of the goods.

Article 3

Scope

1.   Statistics relating to the trading of goods between Member States shall cover dispatches and arrivals of goods.

2.   Dispatches shall cover the following goods leaving the Member State of dispatch for a destination in another Member State:

    (a)   Community goods, except goods which are in simple circulation between Member States;

    (b)   goods placed in the Member State of dispatch under the inward processing customs procedure or the processing under customs control procedure.

3.   Arrivals shall cover the following goods entering the Member State of arrival, which were initially dispatched from another Member State:

    (a)   Community goods, except goods which are in simple circulation between Member States;

    (b)   goods formerly placed in the Member State of dispatch according to the inward processing customs procedure or the processing according to customs control procedure, which are maintained according to the inward processing customs procedure or the processing according to customs control procedure or released for free circulation in the Member State of arrival.

4.   Different or specific rules, to be determined in accordance with the procedure referred to in Article 14(2), may apply to specific goods or movements.

5.   Some goods, a list of which shall be drawn up in accordance with the procedure referred to in Article 14(2), shall be excluded from the statistics for methodological reasons.

Article 4

Statistical territory

1.   The statistical territory of the Member States shall correspond to their customs territory as defined in Article 3 of Council Regulation (EEC) No 2913/92 of 12 October 1992 establishing the Community Customs Code.

2.   By way of derogation from paragraph 1, the statistical territory of Germany shall include Heligoland.

Article 5

Data sources

1.   A specific data collection system, hereinafter referred to as the 'Intrastat' system, shall apply for the provision of the statistical information on dispatches and arrivals of Community goods which are not the subject of a single administrative document for customs or fiscal purposes.

2.   The statistical information on dispatches and arrivals of other goods shall be provided directly by customs to the national authorities, at least once a month.

3.   For specific goods or movements, sources of information other than the Intrastat system or customs declarations may be used.

4.   Each Member State shall organise the way Intrastat data is supplied by the parties responsible for providing information. To facilitate the task of these parties, the conditions for increased use of automatic data processing and electronic data transmission shall be promoted by the Commission (Eurostat) and the Member States.

Article 6

Reference period

1.   The reference period for the information to be provided in accordance with Article 5 shall be the calendar month of dispatch or arrival of the goods.

2.   The reference period may be adapted to take into account the linkage with value added tax (VAT) and customs obligations, pursuant to

provisions adopted in accordance with the procedure referred to in Article 14(2).

Article 7
Parties responsible for providing information

1. The parties responsible for providing the information for the Intrastat system shall be:

    (a)   the natural or legal person registered for VAT in the Member State of dispatch who:

    　　　(i)   has concluded the contract, with the exception of transport contracts, giving rise to the dispatch of goods or, failing that,

    　　　(ii)   dispatches or provides for the dispatch of the goods or, failing that,

    　　　(iii)   is in possession of the goods which are the subject of the dispatch;

    (b)   the natural or legal person registered for VAT in the Member State of arrival who:

    　　　(i)   has concluded the contract, with the exception of transport contracts, giving rise to the delivery of goods or, failing that,

    　　　(ii)   takes delivery or provides for delivery of the goods or, failing that,

    　　　(iii)   is in possession of the goods which are the subject of the delivery.

2. The parties responsible for providing information may transfer the task to a third party, but such transfer shall in no way reduce the responsibility of the said party.

3. Failure by any party responsible for providing information to fulfil his/her obligations under this Regulation shall render him/her liable to the penalties which the Member States shall lay down.

Article 8
Registers

1. National authorities shall set up and manage a register of intra-Community operators containing at least the consignors, upon dispatch, and the consignees, upon arrival.

2. In order to identify the parties responsible for providing information referred to in Article 7 and to check the information which is provided, the tax administration responsible in each Member State shall furnish the national authority:

(a)   at least once a month, with the lists of natural or legal persons who have declared that, during the period in question, they have supplied goods to other Member States or acquired goods from other Member States. The lists shall show the total values of the goods declared by each natural or legal person for fiscal purposes;

(b)   on its own initiative or at the request of the national authority, with any information provided for fiscal purposes which could improve the quality of statistics.

The arrangements for the communication of the information shall be determined in accordance with the procedure referred to in Article 14(2).

This information shall be treated by the national authority in accordance with the rules applied to it by the tax administration.

3.   The tax administration shall bring to the attention of VAT-registered traders the obligations which they may incur as parties responsible for providing the information required by Intrastat.

Article 9
Intrastat information to be collected

1.   The following information shall be collected by the national authorities:

(a)   the identification number allocated to the party responsible for providing information in accordance with Article 22(1)(c) of the Sixth Council Directive 77/388/EEC of 17 May 1977 on the harmonisation of the laws of the Member States relating to turnover taxes — common system of value added tax: uniform basis of assessment, in the version given in Article 28h thereof;

(b)   the reference period;

(c)   the flow (arrival, dispatch);

(d)   the commodity, identified by the eight-digit code of the Combined Nomenclature as defined in Council Regulation (EEC) No 2658/87 of 23 July 1987 on the tariff and statistical nomenclature and on the Common Customs Tariff;

(e)   the partner Member State;

(f)   the value of the goods;

(g)   the quantity of the goods;

(h)   the nature of the transaction.

Definitions of the statistical data referred to in points (e) to (h) are given in the Annex. Where necessary, the arrangements for the collection of this information, particularly the codes to be employed, shall be determined in accordance with the procedure referred to in Article 14(2).

2.   Member States may also collect additional information, for example:

(a)   the identification of the goods, at a more detailed level than the Combined Nomenclature;

(b)   the country of origin, on arrival;

(c)   the region of origin, on dispatch, and the region of destination, on arrival;

(d)   the delivery terms;

(e)   the mode of transport;

(f)   the statistical procedure.

Definitions of the statistical data referred to in points (b) to (f) are given in the Annex. Where necessary, the arrangements for the collection of this information, particularly the codes to be employed, shall be determined in accordance with the procedure referred to in Article 14(2).

Article 10
Simplification within the Intrastat system

1.   In order to satisfy users' needs for statistical information without imposing excessive burdens on economic operators, Member States shall define each year thresholds expressed in annual values of intra-Community trade, below which parties are exempted from providing any Intrastat information or may provide simplified information.[1]

2.   The thresholds shall be defined by each Member State, separately for arrivals and dispatches.

3.   For defining thresholds below which parties are exempted from providing any Intrastat information, Member States shall ensure that information referred to in Article 9(1), first subparagraph, points (a) to (f), made available by the parties responsible for providing information, is such that at least 97 % of the relevant Member State's total trade expressed in value is covered.

4.   Member States may define other thresholds below which parties may benefit from the following simplification:

(a)   exemption from providing information about the quantity of the goods;

(b)   exemption from providing information about the nature of the transaction;

(c)   possibility of reporting a maximum of 10 of the detailed relevant subheadings of the Combined Nomenclature, that are the most used in terms of value, and regrouping the other products in accordance with rules determined in accordance with the procedure referred to in Article 14(2).

Every Member State applying these thresholds shall ensure that the trade of these parties shall amount to a maximum of 6 % of its total trade.

5. Member States may, under certain conditions, which meet quality requirements and which shall be defined in accordance with the procedure referred to in Article 14(2), simplify the information to be provided for small individual transactions.

6. The information on the thresholds applied by the Member States shall be sent to the Commission (Eurostat) no later than 31 October of the year preceding the year to which they apply.

Article 11

Statistical confidentiality

Where the parties who have provided information so request, the national authorities shall decide whether statistical results which make it possible indirectly to identify the said provider(s) are to be disseminated or are to be amended in such a way that their dissemination does not prejudice statistical confidentiality.

Article 12

Transmission of data to the Commission

1. Member States shall transmit to the Commission (Eurostat) the monthly results of their statistics relating to the trading of goods between Member States no later than:

    (a) 40 calendar days after the end of the reference month for the aggregated data to be defined in accordance with the procedure referred to in Article 14(2);

    (b) 70 calendar days after the end of the reference month in the case of detailed results including the information referred to in Article 9(1), first subparagraph, points (b) to (h).

    As regards the value of the goods, the results shall include the statistical value only, as defined in the Annex.

    Member States shall transmit to the Commission (Eurostat) the data which are confidential.

2. Member States shall provide the Commission (Eurostat) with monthly results which cover their total trade in goods by using estimates, where necessary.

3. Member States shall transmit the data to the Commission (Eurostat) in electronic form, in accordance with an interchange standard. The practical arrangements for the transmission of data shall be determined in accordance with the procedure referred to in Article 14(2).

Article 13

Quality

1. Member States shall take all measures necessary to ensure the quality of the data transmitted according to the quality indicators and standards in force.

2.   Member States shall present to the Commission (Eurostat) a yearly report on the quality of the data transmitted.

3.   The indicators and standards enabling the quality of the data to be assessed, the structure of the quality reports to be presented by the Member States and any measures necessary for assessing or improving the quality of the data shall be determined in accordance with the procedure referred to in Article 14(2).

Article 14

Committee procedure

1.   The Commission shall be assisted by a Committee for the statistics on the trading of goods between Member States.

2.   Where reference is made to this paragraph, Articles 5 and 7 of Decision 1999/468/EC shall apply, having regard to the provisions of Article 8 thereof.

     The period laid down in Article 5(6) of Decision 1999/468/EC shall be set at three months.

3.   The Committee shall adopt its Rules of Procedure.

Article 15

Repeal

1.   Regulation (EEC) No 3330/91 is hereby repealed.

2.   References to the repealed regulation shall be construed as being made to this Regulation.

Article 16

Entry into force

This Regulation shall enter into force on the 20th day following that of its publication in the Official Journal of the European Union.

It shall apply from 1 January 2005.

This Regulation shall be binding in its entirety and directly applicable in all Member States.

Done at Strasbourg, 31 March 2004.

For the European Parliament
The President

P. COX

For the Council
The President

D. ROCHE

ANNEX

DEFINITIONS OF STATISTICAL DATA

1. **Partner Member State**

   (a)   The partner Member State is the Member State of consignment, on arrival. This means the presumed Member State of dispatch in cases where goods enter directly from another Member State. Where, before reaching the Member State of arrival, goods have entered one or more Member States in transit and have been subject in those States to halts or legal operations not inherent in their transport (e.g. change of ownership), the Member State of consignment shall be taken as the last Member State where such halts or operations occurred.

   (b)   The partner Member State is the Member State of destination, on dispatch. This means the last Member State to which it is known, at the time of dispatch, that the goods are to be dispatched.

2. **Quantity of the goods**

   The quantity of the goods can be expressed in two ways:

   (a)   the net mass, which means the actual mass of the goods excluding all packaging;

   (b)   the supplementary units, which mean the possible units measuring quantity other than net mass, as detailed in the annual Commission regulation updating the Combined Nomenclature.

3. **Value of the goods**

   The value of the goods can be expressed in two ways:

   (a)   the taxable amount, which is the value to be determined for taxation purposes in accordance with Directive 77/388/EEC;

   (b)   the statistical value, which is the value calculated at the national borders of the Member States. It includes only incidental expenses (freight, insurance) incurred, in the case of dispatches, in the part of the journey located on the territory of the Member State of dispatch and, in the case of arrivals, in the part of the journey located outside the territory of the Member State of arrival. It is said to be a fob value (free on board) for dispatches, and a cif value (cost, insurance, freight) for arrivals.

4. **Nature of the transaction**

   The nature of transaction means the different characteristics (purchase/sale, work under contract, etc.) which are deemed to be useful in distinguishing one transaction from another.

5. Country of origin

(a) The country of origin, on arrivals only, means the country where the goods originate.

(b) Goods which are wholly obtained or produced in a country originate in that country.

(c) Goods whose production involved more than one country shall be deemed to originate in the country where they underwent their last, substantial, economically justified processing or working in a company equipped for that purpose, resulting in the manufacture of a new product or representing an important stage of manufacture.

6. Region of origin or destination

(a) The region of origin, on dispatch, means the region of the Member State of dispatch where the goods were produced or were erected, assembled, processed, repaired or maintained; failing that, the region of origin is the region where the goods were dispatched, or, failing that, the region where the commercial process took place.

(b) The region of destination, on arrival, means the region of the Member State of arrival where the goods are to be consumed or erected, assembled, processed, repaired or maintained; failing that, the region of destination is the region to which the goods are to be dispatched, or, failing that, the region where the commercial process is to take place.

7. Delivery terms

The delivery terms mean those provisions of the sales contract which lay down the obligations of the seller and the buyer respectively, in accordance with the Incoterms of the International Chamber of Commerce (cif, fob, etc.).

8. Mode of transport

The mode of transport is determined by the active means of transport by which the goods are presumed to be going to leave the statistical territory of the Member State of dispatch, on dispatch, and by the active means of transport by which the goods are presumed to have entered the statistical territory of the Member State of arrival, on arrival.

9. Statistical procedure

The statistical procedure means the different characteristics which are deemed to be useful in distinguishing different types of arrivals/dispatches for statistical purposes.

Notes

From 1 January 2003 the assimilation thresholds in Ireland are: dispatches €635,000, arrivals €191,000, by notice, Iris Oifigiúil, 19 November 2002.

COMMISSION DIRECTIVE 2004/79/EC

of 4 March 2004

adapting Directive 2002/94/EC, in the field of taxation, by reason of the accession of the Czech Republic, Estonia, Cyprus, Latvia, Lithuania, Hungary, Malta, Poland, Slovenia and Slovakia

THE COMMISSION OF THE EUROPEAN COMMUNITIES,

Having regard to the Treaty of Accession of the Czech Republic, Estonia, Cyprus, Latvia, Lithuania, Hungary, Malta, Poland, Slovenia and Slovakia, and in particular Article 2(3) thereof,

Having regard to the Act of Accession of the Czech Republic, Estonia, Cyprus, Latvia, Lithuania, Hungary, Malta, Poland, Slovenia and Slovakia, and in particular Article 57(1) thereof,

Whereas:

(1)   For certain acts which remain valid beyond 1 May 2004, and require adaptation by reason of accession, the necessary adaptations were not provided for in the 2003 Act of Accession, or were provided for but need further adaptations. All these adaptations need to be adopted before accession so as to be applicable as from accession.

(2)   Pursuant to Article 57(2) of the Act of Accession, such adaptations are to be adopted by the Commission in all cases where the Commission adopted the original act.

(3)   Commission Directive 2002/94/EC should therefore be amended accordingly,

HAS ADOPTED THIS DIRECTIVE:

Article 1

Directive 2002/94/EC is amended as set out in the Annex.

Article 2

Member States shall bring into force the laws, regulations and administrative provisions necessary to comply with this Directive by the date of accession at the latest. They shall forthwith communicate to the Commission the text of those provisions and a correlation table between those provisions and this Directive.

When Member States adopt those provisions, they shall contain a reference to this Directive or be accompanied by such a reference on the occasion of their official publication. Member States shall determine how such reference is to be made.

Article 3

This Directive shall enter into force subject to, and as from the date of, the entry into force of the Treaty of Accession of the Czech Republic, Estonia, Cyprus, Latvia, Lithuania, Hungary, Malta, Poland, Slovenia and Slovakia.

Article 4

This Directive is addressed to the Member States.

Done at Brussels, 4 March 2004.

For the Commission
Günter VERHEUGEN

Member of the Commission

ANNEX

TAXATION

Commission Directive 2002/94/EC of 9 December 2002 laying down detailed rules for implementing certain provisions of Council Directive 76/308/EEC on mutual assistance for the recovery of claims relating to certain levies, duties, taxes and other measures.

In Annex IV, the left column under 'Member State' is replaced by the following:

— 'Belgique/België
— Česká Republika
— Danmark
— Deutschland
— Eesti
— Ελλάδα
— España
— France
— Ireland
— Italia
— Κύπρος
— Latvija
— Lietuva
— Luxembourg
— Magyarország
— Malta
— Nederland
— Österreich
— Polska
— Portugal
— Slovenija
— Slovensko
— Finland/Suomi
— Sverige
— United Kingdom'

COUNCIL DIRECTIVE 2004/56/EC

of 21 April 2004

amending Directive 77/799/EEC concerning mutual assistance by the competent authorities of the Member States in the field of direct taxation, certain excise duties and taxation of insurance premiums

THE COUNCIL OF THE EUROPEAN UNION,

Having regard to the Treaty establishing the European Community, and in particular Articles 93 and 94 thereof,

Having regard to the proposal from the Commission,

Having regard to the opinion of the European Parliament,

Having regard to the opinion of the European Economic and Social Committee,

Whereas:

(1)   Council Directive 77/799/EEC of 19 December 1977 concerning mutual assistance by the competent authorities of the Member States in the field of direct taxation, certain excise duties and taxation of insurance premiums established the ground rules for administrative cooperation and the exchange of information between Member States in order to detect and prevent tax evasion and tax fraud and to enable Member States to carry out a correct tax assessment. It is essential to improve, expand and modernise those rules.

(2)   When a Member State conducts enquiries in order to obtain the information necessary to respond to a request for assistance, that State should be regarded as acting on its own account; in that way, there will only be one set of rules applying to the information-gathering process and the investigation will not be undermined by delays.

(3)   It is inappropriate, if the fight against tax fraud is to be effective, that a Member State which has received information from another Member State should subsequently have to request permission to disclose the information in public hearings or judgements.

(4)   It should be made clear that a Member State is not under any obligation to carry out enquiries in order to obtain the information necessary to respond to a request for assistance where either its legislation or administrative practices do not permit its competent authority to conduct enquiries or to collect such information.

(5)   It should be possible for the competent authority of a Member State to refuse information or assistance when the requesting Member State is not in a position to supply the same type of information, whether for reasons of fact or of law.

(6)   In view of the legal requirement in certain Member States that a taxpayer be notified of decisions and instruments concerning his tax liability and of the ensuing difficulties for the tax authorities, including cases where the taxpayer has relocated to another Member State, it is desirable that,

in such circumstances, the tax authorities should be able to call upon the assistance of the competent authorities of the Member State to which the taxpayer has relocated.

(7) Since the tax situation of one or more persons liable to tax established in several Member States often is of common or complementary interest, it should be made possible for simultaneous controls to be carried out to such persons by two or more Member States, by mutual agreement and on a voluntary basis, whenever such controls appear to be more effective than controls carried out by only one Member State.

(8) The Commission submitted its proposal for a Directive on the basis of Article 95 of the Treaty. The Council, taking the view that the proposal for a Directive related to the harmonisation of legislation in the field of both direct and indirect taxation and that the act should therefore be adopted on the basis of Articles 93 and 94 of the Treaty, consulted the European Parliament by letter dated 12 November 2003 informing it of the Council's intention of changing the legal basis.

(9) Directive 77/799/EEC should therefore be amended accordingly,

HAS ADOPTED THIS DIRECTIVE:

Article 1

Directive 77/799/EEC is hereby amended as follows:

1. Article 1(5) shall be amended as follows:

   (a) the wording under 'in Italy' shall be replaced by the following:

   'il Capo del Dipartimento per le Politiche Fiscali or his authorised representatives'

   (b) the wording under 'in Sweden' shall be replaced by the following:

   'Chefen för Finansdepartementet or his authorised representative'

2. in Article 2(2), the following subparagraph shall be added:

   'In order to obtain the information sought, the requested authority or the administrative authority to which it has recourse shall proceed as though acting on its own account or at the request of another authority in its own Member State.'

3. Article 7(1) shall be replaced by the following:

   '1. All information made known to a Member State under this Directive shall be kept secret in that State in the same manner as information received under its national legislation. In any case, such information:

   — may be made available only to the persons directly involved in the assessment of the tax or in the administrative control of this assessment,

— may be made known only in connection with judicial proceedings or administrative proceedings involving sanctions undertaken with a view to, or relating to, the making or reviewing the tax assessment and only to persons who are directly involved in such proceedings; such information may, however, be disclosed during public hearings or in judgements if the competent authority of the Member State supplying the information raises no objection at the time when it first supplies the information,

— shall in no circumstances be used other than for taxation purposes or in connection with judicial proceedings or administrative proceedings involving sanctions undertaken with a view to, or in relation to, the making or reviewing of the tax assessment.

In addition, Member States may provide for the information referred to in the first subparagraph to be used for assessment of other levies, duties and taxes covered by Article 2 of Directive 76/308/EEC.

4.   Article 8 shall be amended as follows:

(a)   paragraph 1 shall be replaced by the following:

'1.   This Directive does not impose any obligation upon a Member State from which information is requested to carry out inquiries or to communicate information, if it would be contrary to its legislation or administrative practices for the competent authority of that State to conduct such inquiries or to collect the information sought.'

(b)   paragraph 3 shall be replaced by the following:

'3.   The competent authority of a Member State may decline transmission of information when the Member State requesting it is unable, for reasons of fact or law, to provide the same type of information.'

5.   the following Articles shall be inserted:

'Article 8a

Notification

1.   At the request of the competent authority of a Member State, the competent authority of another Member State shall, in accordance with the rules governing the notification of similar instruments in the requested Member State, notify the addressee of all instruments and decisions which emanate from the administrative authorities of the requesting Member State and concern the application in its territory of legislation on taxes covered by this Directive.

2.   Requests for notification shall indicate the subject of the instrument or decision to be notified and shall specify the name and address of the addressee, together with any other information which may facilitate identification of the addressee.

3.   The requested authority shall inform the requesting authority immediately of its response to the request for notification and shall notify it, in particular, of the date of notification of the decision or instrument to the addressee.

Article 8b

Simultaneous controls

1.   Where the tax situation of one or more persons liable to tax is of common or complementary interest to two or more Member States, those States may agree to conduct simultaneous controls, in their own territory, with a view to exchanging the information thus obtained, whenever they would appear to be more effective than controls conducted by one Member State alone.

2.   The competent authority in each Member State shall identify independently the persons liable to tax whom it intends to propose for simultaneous control. It shall notify the respective competent authorities in the other Member States concerned of the cases which, in its view, should be subject to simultaneous control. It shall give reasons for its choice, as far as possible, by providing the information which led to its decision. It shall specify the period of time during which such controls should be conducted.

3.   The competent authority of each Member State concerned shall decide whether it wishes to take part in the simultaneous control. On receipt of a proposal for a simultaneous control, the competent authority shall confirm its agreement or communicate its reasoned refusal to its counterpart authority.

4.   Each competent authority of the Member States concerned shall appoint a representative with responsibility for supervising and coordinating the control operation.'

Article 2

Member States shall bring into force the laws, regulations and administrative provisions necessary to comply with this Directive before 1 January 2005. They shall forthwith communicate to the Commission the text of those provisions and a correlation table between those provisions and this Directive.

When Member States adopt these measures, they shall contain a reference to this Directive or shall be accompanied by such a reference on the occasion of their official publication. The methods of making such reference shall be laid down by Member States.

Article 3

This Directive shall enter into force on the day of its publication in the Official Journal of the European Union.

Article 4

This Directive is addressed to the Member States.

Done at Luxembourg, 21 April 2004.
For the Council
The President

J. WALSH

COUNCIL DIRECTIVE 2004/66/EC

of 26 April 2004

adapting Directives 1999/45/EC, 2002/83/EC, 2003/37/EC and 2003/59/EC of the European Parliament and of the Council and Council Directives 77/388/EEC, 91/414/EEC, 96/26/EC, 2003/48/EC and 2003/49/EC, in the fields of free movement of goods, freedom to provide services, agriculture, transport policy and taxation, by reason of the accession of the Czech Republic, Estonia, Cyprus, Latvia, Lithuania, Hungary, Malta, Poland, Slovenia and Slovakia

---

Point V of the Annex to this Directive was repealed by Council Directive 2006/112/EC of 28 November 2006 on the common system of value added tax, with effect from 1 January 2007

THE COUNCIL OF THE EUROPEAN UNION,

Having regard to the Treaty establishing the European Community,

Having regard to the Treaty on the accession of the Czech Republic, the Republic of Estonia, the Republic of Cyprus, the Republic of Latvia, the Republic of Lithuania, the Republic of Hungary, the Republic of Malta, the Republic of Poland, the Republic of Slovenia and the Slovak Republic to the European Union (hereinafter referred to as the 'Treaty of Accession'), and in particular Article 2(3) thereof,

Having regard to the Act of Accession of the Czech Republic, the Republic of Estonia, the Republic of Cyprus, the Republic of Latvia, the Republic of Lithuania, the Republic of Hungary, the Republic of Malta, the Republic of Poland, the Republic of Slovenia and the Slovak Republic and the adjustments to the Treaties on which the European Union is founded (hereinafter referred to as the 'Act of Accession'), and in particular Article 57 thereof,

Having regard to the proposal from the Commission,

Whereas:

(1) For certain acts which remain valid beyond 1 May 2004 and require adaptation by reason of accession, the necessary adaptations were not provided for in the Act of Accession, or were provided for but need further adaptation. All these adaptations need to be adopted before accession so as to be applicable as from accession.

(2) Pursuant to Article 57(2) of the Act of Accession, such adaptations are to be adopted by the Council in all cases where the Council alone or jointly with the European Parliament adopted the original act.

(3) Directives 1999/45/EC, 2002/83/EC, 2003/37/EC and 2003/59/EC of the European Parliament and of the Council and Council Directives 77/388/EEC, 91/414/EEC, 96/26/EC, 2003/48/EC and 2003/49/EC should therefore be amended accordingly,

HAS ADOPTED THIS DIRECTIVE:

Article 1

Directives 1999/45/EC, 2002/83/EC, 2003/37/EC, 2003/59/EC, 77/388/ EEC, 91/414/EEC, 96/26/EC, 2003/48/EC and 2003/49/EC are amended as set out in the Annex of this Directive.

Article 2

Member States shall bring into force the laws, regulations and administrative provisions necessary to comply with this Directive by the date of entry into force of the Treaty of Accession. As regards the provisions of this Directive adapting Directive 91/414/EC as amended, as well as Directives 2002/83/ EC, 2003/37/EC and 2003/59/EC, the date of transposition shall be that laid down therein. Member States shall forthwith submit the text of the provisions transposing this Directive to the Commission, with a table setting out their correlation with the specific provisions of this Directive.

When Member States adopt those provisions, they shall contain a reference to this Directive or be accompanied by such a reference on the occasion of their official publication. The methods of making such reference shall be laid down by Member States.

Article 3

This Directive shall enter into force only subject to and on the date of the entry into force of the Treaty of Accession.

Article 4

This Directive is addressed to the Member States.

Done at Brussels, 26 April 2004.
For the Council
The President

B. COWEN

ANNEX

V. TAXATION

1. Sixth Council Directive 77/388/EEC of 17 May 1977 on the harmonisation of the laws of the Member States relating to turnover taxes — Common system of value added tax: uniform basis of assessment.

   (a) Article 24 bis is replaced by the following:

   'Article 24a

   In implementing Article 24(2) to (6), the following Member States may grant an exemption from value added tax to taxable persons whose annual turnover is less than the equivalent in national currency at the conversion rate on the date of their accession:

   — in the Czech Republic: EUR 35 000;

- in Estonia: EUR 16 000;
- in Cyprus: EUR 15 600;
- in Latvia: EUR 17 200;
- in Lithuania: EUR 29 000;
- in Hungary: EUR 35 000;
- in Malta: EUR 37 000 when the economic activity consists principally in the supply of goods, EUR 24 300 when the economic activity consists principally in the supply of services with a low value added (high inputs), and EUR 14 600 in other cases, namely service providers with a high value added (low inputs);
- in Poland: EUR 10 000;
- in Slovenia: EUR 25 000;
- in Slovakia: EUR 35 000.'

(b) Article 28m is replaced by the following:

'Article 28m

Rate of conversion

To determine the equivalents in their national currencies of amounts expressed in ecus in this Title Member States shall use the rate of exchange applicable on 16 December 1991. However, the Czech Republic, Estonia, Cyprus, Latvia, Lithuania, Hungary, Malta, Poland, Slovenia and Slovakia shall use the rate of exchange applicable on the date of their accession.'.

(c) Article 17(3)(b), in the version set out in Article 28f(1), is replaced by the following:

'(b) transactions which are exempt pursuant to Article 14(1)(g) and (i), 15, 16(1) (B), (C), (D) or (E) or (2) or 28c (A) and (C).'.

Note:
Annex I – IV and Annex V (2) and (3) have been omitted as they do not refer to VAT

COUNCIL REGULATION (EC) No 885/2004

of 26 April 2004

adapting Regulation (EC) No 2003/2003 of the European Parliament and of the Council, Council Regulations (EC) No 1334/2000, (EC) No 2157/2001, (EC) No 152/2002, (EC) No 1499/2002, (EC) No 1500/2003 and (EC) No 1798/2003, Decisions No 1719/1999/EC, No 1720/1999/EC, No 253/2000/EC, No 508/2000/EC, No 1031/2000/EC, No 163/2001/EC, No 2235/2002/EC and No 291/2003/EC of the European Parliament and of the Council, and Council Decisions 1999/382/EC, 2000/821/EC, 2003/17/EC and 2003/893/EC in the fields of free movement of goods, company law, agriculture, taxation, education and training, culture and audiovisual policy and external relations, by reason of the accession of the Czech Republic, Estonia, Cyprus, Latvia, Lithuania, Hungary, Malta, Poland, Slovenia and Slovakia

THE COUNCIL OF THE EUROPEAN UNION,

Having regard to the Treaty establishing the European Community,

Having regard to the Treaty on the accession of the Czech Republic, the Republic of Estonia, the Republic of Cyprus, the Republic of Latvia, the Republic of Lithuania, the Republic of Hungary, the Republic of Malta, the Republic of Poland, the Republic of Slovenia and the Slovak Republic to the European Union (hereinafter referred to as the 'Treaty of Accession'), and in particular Article 2(3) thereof,

Having regard to the Act concerning the conditions of accession of the Czech Republic, the Republic of Estonia, the Republic of Cyprus, the Republic of Latvia, the Republic of Lithuania, the Republic of Hungary, the Republic of Malta, the Republic of Poland, the Republic of Slovenia and the Slovak Republic and the adjustments to the Treaties on which the European Union is founded (hereinafter referred to as the 'Act of Accession'), and in particular Article 57 thereof,

Having regard to the proposal from the Commission,

Whereas:

(1) For certain acts which remain valid beyond 1 May 2004 and require adaptation by reason of accession, the necessary adaptations were not provided for in the Act of Accession, or were provided for but need further adaptation. All these adaptations need to be adopted before accession so as to be applicable as from accession.

(2) Pursuant to Article 57(2) of the Act of Accession, such adaptations are to be adopted by the Council in all cases where the Council alone or jointly with the European Parliament adopted the original act.

(3) Regulation (EC) No 2003/2003 of the European Parliament and of the Council, Council Regulations (EC) No 1334/2000, (EC) No 2157/2001, (EC) No 152/2002, (EC) No 1499/2002, (EC) No 1500/2003 and (EC) No 1798/2003, Decisions No 1719/1999/EC, No 1720/1999/EC, No 253/2000/EC, No 508/2000/EC, No 1031/2000/EC, No 163/2001/EC, No 2235/2002/EC and No 291/2003/EC of the European Parliament

and of the Council, and Council Decisions 1999/382/EC, 2000/821/ EC, 2003/17/EC and 2003/893/EC should therefore be amended accordingly,

HAS ADOPTED THIS REGULATION:

Article 1

Regulations (EC) No 2003/2003, (EC) No 1334/2000, (EC) No 2157/2001, (EC) No 152/2002, (EC) No 1499/2002, (EC) No 1500/2003, and (EC) No 1798/2003 and Decisions No 1719/1999/EC, No 1720/1999/EC, No 253/2000/EC, No 508/2000/EC, No 1031/2000/EC, No 163/2001/EC, No 2235/2002/EC, No 291/2003/EC, 1999/382/EC, 2000/821/EC, 2003/17/EC and 2003/893/EC are amended as set out in the Annex of this Regulation.

Article 2

This Regulation shall enter into force only subject to and on the date of the entry into force of the Treaty of Accession.

This Regulation shall be binding in its entirety and directly applicable in all Member States.

Done at Brussels, 26 April 2004.

For the Council
The President

B. COWEN

ANNEX

IV. TAXATION

1. Decision No 2235/2002/EC of the European Parliament and of the Council of 3 December 2002 adopting a Community programme to improve the operation of taxation systems in the internal market (Fiscalis programme 2003-2007).

    Article 4(b) is replaced by the following:

    '(b)   Turkey, on the basis of bilateral agreements on this matter concluded with this country.'

2. Council Regulation (EC) No 1798/2003 of 7 October 2003 on administrative cooperation in the field of value added tax and repealing Regulation (EEC) No 218/92.

    In Article 2(1), the following is inserted between the entries for Belgium and Denmark:

    '—   in the

            Czech Republic:
            Ministerstvo financí,'

    and, between the entries for Germany and Greece:

'—   in Estonia:
        Maksuamet,'

and between the entries for Italy and Luxembourg:

'—   in Cyprus:
        Υπουρός Οικονομικών ήεξουσιοτημένος αντιπρόσωπος του,

—   in Latvia:
        Valsts ieņēmumu dienests,

—   in Lithuania:
        Valstybinė mokesčių inspekcija prie Finansø ministerijos,'

and between the entries for Luxembourg and the Netherlands:

'—   in Hungary:
        Adó- és Pénzügyi Ellenőrzési Hivatal Központi Kapcsolattartó
        Irodája,

—   in Malta:
        Dipartiment tat-Taxxa fuq il-Valur Mi¿jud fil-Ministeru tal-
        Finanzi u Affarijiet Ekonomici,'

and between the entries for Austria and Portugal:

'—   in Poland:
        Minister Finansów,'

and between the entries for Portugal and Finland:

'—   in Slovenia:
        Ministrstvo za finance,

—   in Slovakia:
        Ministerstvo financií'.

_____
Note:
Annex I – III and V – VII have been omitted as they do not refer to VAT

Council Regulation (EC) No 866/2004

of 29 April 2004

on a regime under Article 2 of Protocol 10 to the Act of Accession

Official Journal L206, 09/06/2004 p.0051-0056

THE COUNCIL OF THE EUROPEAN UNION,

Having regard to Protocol 10 on Cyprus to the Act concerning the conditions of accession of the Czech Republic, the Republic of Estonia, the Republic of Cyprus, the Republic of Latvia, the Republic of Lithuania, the Republic of Hungary, the Republic of Malta, the Republic of Poland, the Republic of Slovenia and the Slovak Republic and the adjustments to the Treaties on which the European Union is founded, and in particular Article 2 thereof,

Having regard to Protocol 3 on the Sovereign Base Areas of the United Kingdom of Great Britain and Northern Ireland in Cyprus to the said Act of Accession, and in particular Article 6 thereof,

Having regard to the proposal from the Commission,

Whereas:

(1) The European Council has repeatedly underlined its strong preference for accession by a reunited Cyprus. Regrettably, a comprehensive settlement has not yet been reached. In conformity with paragraph 12 of the conclusions of the European Council in Copenhagen, the Council on 26 April 2004 outlined its position on the current situation on the island.

(2) Pending a settlement, the application of the acquis upon accession has therefore been suspended pursuant to Article 1(1) of Protocol 10, in the areas of the Republic of Cyprus in which the Government of the Republic of Cyprus does not exercise effective control.

(3) Pursuant to Article 2(1) of Protocol 10, this suspension makes it necessary to provide for the terms under which the relevant provisions of EU law shall apply to the line between the abovementioned areas and those areas in which the Government of the Republic of Cyprus exercises effective control. In order to ensure the effectiveness of these rules, their application has to be extended to the boundary between the areas in which the Government of the Republic of Cyprus does not exercise effective control and the Eastern Sovereign Base Area of the United Kingdom of Great Britain and Northern Ireland.

(4) Since the abovementioned line does not constitute an external border of the EU, special rules concerning the crossing of goods, services and persons need to be established, the prime responsibility for which belongs to the Republic of Cyprus. As the abovementioned areas are temporarily outside the customs and fiscal territory of the Community and outside the area of freedom, justice and security, the special rules should secure an equivalent standard of protection of the security of the EU with regard to illegal immigration and threats to public order, and of its economic interests as far as the movement of goods is concerned.

Until sufficient information is available with regard to the state of animal health in the abovementioned areas, the movement of animals and animal products will be prohibited.

(5) Article 3 of Protocol 10 explicitly states that measures promoting economic development in the abovementioned areas are not precluded by the suspension of the acquis. This regulation is intended to facilitate trade and other links between the abovementioned areas and those areas in which the Government of the Republic of Cyprus exercises effective control, whilst ensuring that appropriate standards of protection are maintained as set out above.

(6) Regarding persons, the policy of the Government of the Republic of Cyprus currently allows the crossing of the line by all citizens of the Republic, EU citizens and third country nationals who are legally residing in the northern part of Cyprus, and by all EU citizens and third country nationals who entered the island through the Government Controlled Areas.

(7) While taking into account the legitimate concerns of the Government of the Republic of Cyprus, it is necessary to enable EU citizens to exercise their rights of free movement within the EU and set the minimum rules for carrying out checks on persons at the line and to ensure the effective surveillance of it, in order to combat the illegal immigration of third country nationals as well as any threat to public security and public policy. It is also necessary to define the conditions under which third country nationals are allowed to cross the line.

(8) Regarding checks on persons, this Regulation should not affect the provisions laid down in Protocol 3, and in particular Article 8 thereof.

(9) This Regulation does not affect in any way the mandate of the United Nations in the buffer zone.

(10) Since any change in the policy of the Government of the Republic of Cyprus with regard to the line may pose problems of compatibility with the rules established by this Regulation, such changes should be notified to the Commission, prior to their entry into force, in order to allow it to take the appropriate initiatives so as to avoid inconsistencies.

(11) The Commission should also be allowed to amend Annexes I, and II to this Regulation with a view to responding to changes which may occur and require immediate action,

HAS ADOPTED THIS REGULATION:

TITLE I

GENERAL PROVISIONS

Article 1

Definitions

For the purpose of this Regulation the following definitions shall apply:

1.   the term 'line' means:

    (a)   for the purpose of checks on persons, as defined in Article 2, the line between the areas under the effective control of the Government of the Republic of Cyprus and those areas in which the Government of the Republic of Cyprus does not exercise effective control;

    (b)   for the purpose of checks on goods, as defined in Article 4, the line between the areas in which the Government of the Republic of Cyprus does not exercise effective control and both those areas in which the Government of the Republic of Cyprus exercises effective control and the Eastern Sovereign Base Area of the United Kingdom of Great Britain and Northern Ireland;

2.   the term 'third-country national' means any person who is not a citizen of the Union within the meaning of Article 17(1) of the EC Treaty.

References in this Regulation to areas in which the Government of the Republic of Cyprus does not exercise effective control are to areas within the Republic of Cyprus only.

TITLE II

CROSSING OF PERSONS

Article 2

Check on Persons

1.   The Republic of Cyprus shall carry out checks on all persons crossing the line with the aim to combat illegal immigration of third-country nationals and to detect and prevent any threat to public security and public policy. Such checks shall also be carried out on vehicles and objects in the possession of persons crossing the line.

2.   All persons shall undergo at least one such check in order to establish their identity.

3.   Third-country nationals shall only be allowed to cross the line provided they:

    (a)   possess either a residence permit issued by the Republic of Cyprus or a valid travel document and, if required, a valid visa for the Republic of Cyprus, and

    (b)   do not represent a threat to public policy or public security.

4.   The line shall be crossed only at crossing points authorised by the competent authorities of the Republic of Cyprus. A list of these crossing points is laid down in Annex I.

5.   Checks on persons at the boundary between the Eastern Sovereign Base Area and the areas not under effective control of the Government of the Republic of Cyprus shall be carried out in accordance with Article 5(2) of Protocol 3 to the Act of Accession.

Article 3

Surveillance of the line

Effective surveillance shall be carried out by the Republic of Cyprus all along the line, in such a way as to discourage people from circumventing checks at the crossing points referred to in Article 2(4).

TITLE III

CROSSING OF GOODS

Article 4

Treatment of goods arriving from the areas not under the effective control of the Government of the Republic of Cyprus

1. Without prejudice to Article 6, goods may be introduced in the areas under the effective control of the Government of the Republic of Cyprus, on condition that they are wholly obtained in the areas not under effective control of the Government of the Republic of Cyprus or have undergone their last, substantial, economically justified processing or working in an undertaking equipped for that purpose in the areas not under the effective control of the Government of the Republic of Cyprus within the meaning of Articles 23 and 24 of Council Regulation (EEC) No 2913/92.

2. These goods shall not be subject to customs duties or charges having equivalent effect, nor to a customs declaration, provided that they are not eligible for export refunds or intervention measures. In order to ensure effective controls, the quantities crossing the line shall be registered.

3. The goods shall cross the line only at the crossing points listed in Annex I and the crossing points of Pergamos and Strovilia under the authority of the Eastern Sovereign Base Area.

4. The goods shall be subject to the requirements and undergo the checks as required by Community legislation as set out in Annex II.

5. Goods shall be accompanied by a document issued by the Turkish Cypriot Chamber of Commerce, duly authorised for that purpose by the Commission in agreement with the Government of the Republic of Cyprus, or by another body so authorised in agreement with the latter. The Turkish Cypriot Chamber of Commerce or other duly authorised body will maintain records of all such documents issued to enable the Commission to monitor the type and volume of goods crossing the line as well as their compliance with the provisions of this Article.

6. After the goods have crossed the line into the areas under the effective control of the Government of the Republic of Cyprus, the competent authorities of the Republic of Cyprus shall check the authenticity of the document referred to in paragraph 5 and whether it corresponds with the consignment.

7.   The Republic of Cyprus shall treat the goods referred to in paragraph 1 as not being imported within the meaning of Article 7(1) of Council Directive 77/388/EEC and Article 5 of Council Directive 92/12/EEC, provided the goods are destined for consumption in the Republic of Cyprus.

8.   Paragraph 7 shall not have any effect on the European Communities' own resources accruing from VAT.

9.   The movement of live animals and animal products across the line shall be prohibited.

10.   The authorities of the Eastern Sovereign Base Area may maintain the traditional supply of the Turkish Cypriot population of the village of Pyla with goods coming from the areas which are not under the effective control of the Government of the Republic of Cyprus. They shall strictly supervise the quantities and nature of the goods in view of their destination.

11.   Goods complying with the conditions set out in paragraphs 1 to 10 shall have the status of Community goods, within the meaning of Article 4(7) of Regulation (EEC) No 2913/92.

12.   This Article shall apply immediately as from 1 May 2004 to goods wholly obtained in the areas not under the effective control of the Government of the Republic of Cyprus and complying with Annex II. In respect of other goods, the full implementation of this Article shall be subject to specific rules that take full account of the particular situation in the island of Cyprus on the basis of a Commission decision to be adopted as soon as possible and at the latest within two months of the adoption of this Regulation. For such purpose, the Commission shall be assisted by a Committee and Articles 3 and 7 of Council Decision 1999/468/EC shall apply.

Article 5

Goods sent to the areas not under the effective control of the Government of the Republic of Cyprus

1.   Goods which are allowed to cross the line shall not be subject to export formalities. However, the necessary equivalent documentation shall be provided, in full respect of Cypriot internal legislation, by the authorities of the Republic of Cyprus upon request.

2.   No export refund shall be paid for agricultural and processed agricultural goods when crossing the line.

3.   The supply of goods shall not be exempt under Article 15(1) and (2) of Directive 77/388/EEC.

4.   The movement of goods, the removal or export of which from the customs territory of the Community is prohibited or subject to authorisation, restrictions, duties or other charges on export by Community law, shall be prohibited.

Article 6

Facilities for persons crossing the line

Council Directive 69/169/EEC shall not apply, but goods contained in the personal luggage of persons crossing the line, including a maximum of 20 cigarettes and 1/4 litre of spirits, shall be exempt from turnover tax and excise duty provided they have no commercial character and their total value does not exceed EUR 30 per person. Exemptions from turnover tax and excise duty on tobacco products and alcoholic beverages shall not be granted to persons crossing the line under 17 years of age.

TITLE IV

SERVICES

Article 7

Taxation

To the extent that services are supplied across the line to and from persons established or having their permanent address or usual residence in the areas of the Republic of Cyprus which are not under the effective control of the Government of the Republic of Cyprus, these services shall for VAT purposes be deemed to have been supplied or received by persons established or having their permanent address or usual residence in the areas of the Republic of Cyprus under the effective control of the Government of the Republic of Cyprus.

TITLE V

FINAL PROVISIONS

Article 8

Implementation

The authorities of the Republic of Cyprus and the authorities of the Eastern Sovereign Base Area in Cyprus shall take all appropriate measures in order to ensure full compliance with the provisions of this Regulation and to prevent any circumvention of them.

Article 9

Adaptation of Annexes

The Commission may, in agreement with the Government of Cyprus amend the Annexes to this Regulation. Prior to amending the Annexes, the Commission shall consult the Turkish Cypriot Chamber of Commerce or other body duly authorized by the Government of the Republic of Cyprus as referred to in Article 4(5), as well as the United Kingdom if the Sovereign Base Areas are affected. When amending Annex II the Commission shall follow the appropriate procedure referred to in the relevant Community legislation relating to the matter being amended.

Article 10

Change of policy

Any change in the policy of the Government of the Republic of Cyprus on crossings of persons or goods shall only become effective after the proposed changes have been notified to the Commission and the Commission has not objected to these changes within one month. If appropriate, and after consultation with the United Kingdom if the Sovereign Base Areas are affected, the Commission may propose modifications to this Regulation in order to secure compatibility of national and EU rules applicable to the line.

Article 11

Review and monitoring of the Regulation

1. Without prejudice to Article 4(12), the Commission shall report to the Council on an annual basis, starting not later than one year after the date of entry into force of this Regulation, on the implementation of the Regulation and the situation resulting from its application, attaching to this report suitable proposals for amendments if necessary.

2. The Commission shall examine in particular the application of Article 4 of this Regulation and the patterns of trade between the areas under the effective control of the Government of the Republic of Cyprus and the areas not under its effective control, including the volume and value of trade and products traded.

3. Any Member State may request the Council to invite the Commission to examine and report back to it within a specified time frame on any matter of concern arising from the application of this Regulation.

4. In the event of an emergency creating a threat or risk to public or animal and plant health, the appropriate procedures as set out in EU legislation in Annex II shall apply. In the event of other emergencies or where other irregularities or exceptional circumstances arise which require immediate action, the Commission may in consultation with the Government of the Republic of Cyprus apply forthwith such measures as are strictly necessary to remedy the situation. The measures taken shall be referred to the Council within 10 working days. The Council may, acting by qualified majority vote, amend, modify or annul the measures taken by the Commission within 21 working days from the date of receipt of notification from the Commission.

5. Any Member State may invite the Commission to provide details of the volume, value and products crossing the line to the appropriate standing or management committee, provided it gives one month's notice of its request.

Article 12

Entry into force

This Regulation shall enter into force on the day of accession of Cyprus to the European Union.
This Regulation shall be binding in its entirety and directly applicable in all Member States.

Done at Luxembourg, 29 April 2004.

For the Council

The President

M. McDOWELL

[ANNEX I

List of crossing points referred to in Article 2(4)

- Agios Dhometios
- Astromeritis — Zodhia
- Kato Pyrgos — Karavostasi
- Kato Pyrgos — Kokkina
- Kokkina — Pachyammos
- Ledra Palace
- Ledra Street][1]

ANNEX II

Requirements and checks referred to in Article 4(4)

- Veterinary, phytosanitary and food safety requirements and checks as set out in measures adopted pursuant to Article 37 (former Article 43) and/or Article 152(4)(b) of the EC Treaty. In particular, relevant plants, plant products and other objects shall have undergone phytosanitary checks by duly authorised experts to verify that the provisions of EU phytosanitary legislation (Council Directive 2000/29/EC) are complied with before they cross the line to the areas under the effective control of the Republic of Cyprus.

Amendments
1   Annex 1 replaced by Commission Regulation (EC) No 1283/2005 of 3 August 2005

COMMISSION REGULATION (EC) No 1925/2004

of 29 October 2004

Laying down detailed rules for implementing certain provisions of Council Regulation (EC) No 1798/2003 concerning administrative cooperation in the field of value-added tax

Official Journal L331, 05/11/2004 p.0013-0018

THE COMMISSION OF THE EUROPEAN COMMUNITIES,

Having regard to the Treaty establishing the European Community,

Having regard to Council Regulation (EC) No 1798/2003 of 7 October 2003 on administrative cooperation in the field of value-added tax and repealing Regulation (EEC) No 218/92 and, in particular Articles 18, 35 and 37 thereof,

Whereas:

(1)   The provisions on VAT administrative cooperation laid down in Regulation (EEC) No 218/92 and Council Directive 77/799/EEC of 19 December 1977 concerning mutual assistance by the competent authorities of the Member States in the field of direct taxation, certain excise duties and taxation of insurance premiums have been merged and strengthened in Regulation (EC) No 1798/2003.

(2)   It is necessary to specify the exact categories of information to be exchanged without prior request, as well as the frequency with which those exchanges are to be made, and the relevant practical arrangements.

(3)   Arrangements should be laid down for the provision of information communicated pursuant to Regulation (EC) No 1798/2003 by electronic means.

(4)   Finally, it is necessary to establish a list of the statistical data needed for the evaluation of Regulation (EC) No 1798/2003.

(5)   The measures provided for in this Regulation are in accordance with the opinion of the Standing Committee on Administrative Cooperation,

HAS ADOPTED THIS REGULATION:

Article 1

Subject matter

This Regulation lays down detailed rules for implementing Articles 18, 35 and 37 of Regulation (EC) No 1798/2003.

Article 2

Definitions

For the purposes of this Regulation:

1.   'missing trader' shall mean a trader registered as a taxable person for VAT purposes who, potentially with a fraudulent intent, acquires or

purports to acquire goods or services without payment of VAT and supplies these goods or services with VAT, but does not remit the VAT due to the appropriate national authority.

2.   'to hijack a VAT registration' shall mean to use another trader's VAT registration number illicitly.

Article 3

Categories of information to be exchanged without prior request

The categories of information to be the subject of automatic or structured automatic exchange, in accordance with Article 17 of Regulation (EC) No 1798/2003, shall be the following:

1.   information on non-established traders;

2.   information on new means of transport;

3.   information concerning distance selling not subject to VAT in the Member State of origin;

4.   information concerning intra-Community transactions presumed to be irregular;

5.   information on (potential) 'missing traders'.

Article 4

Subcategories of information to be exchanged without prior request

1.   In respect of non-established traders the information shall relate to the following:

    (a)   the allocation of VAT identification numbers to taxable persons established in another Member State;

    (b)   VAT refunds to taxable persons not established in the territory of the country, pursuant to Council Directive 79/1072/EEC.

2.   In respect of new means of transport, the information shall relate to the following:

    (a)   supplies exempted in accordance with Article 28c(A)(b) of Council Directive 77/388/EEC, of new means of transport as defined in Article 28a(2), by persons regarded as taxable persons pursuant to Article 28a(4) who are registered for VAT;

    (b)   supplies exempted in accordance with Article 28c(A)(b) of Directive 77/388/EEC, of new vessels and aircraft as defined in Article 28a(2), by taxable persons registered for VAT, other than those mentioned under point (a), to persons not registered for VAT;

    (c)   supplies exempted in accordance with Article 28c(A)(b) of Directive 77/388/EEC, of new motorised land vehicles as defined in Article 28a(2), by taxable persons registered for VAT, other than those mentioned under point (a), to persons not registered for VAT.

3.   In respect of distance selling not subject to VAT in the Member State of origin, the information shall relate to the following:

(a)   supplies above the threshold provided for in Article 28b(B)(2) of Directive 77/388/EEC;

(b)   supplies below the threshold provided for in Article 28b(B)(2) of Directive 77/388/EEC, where the taxable person opts for taxation in the Member State of destination in accordance with Article 28b(B)(3) of that Directive.

4.   In respect of intra-Community transactions presumed to be irregular, the information shall relate to the following:

(a)   supplies in cases where it is certain that the value of intra-Community supplies notified under the VAT Information exchange system (VIES) varies significantly from the value of the corresponding intra-Community acquisitions reported;

(b)   intra-Community supplies of goods not exempted from VAT in accordance with Article 28c(A) of Directive 77/388/EEC to a taxable person established in another Member State.

5.   In respect of (potential) 'missing traders', the information shall relate to the following:

(a)   taxable persons for whom a VAT identification number has been cancelled or is no longer valid due to an absence or simulation of economic activity, and who have made intra-Community transactions;

(b)   taxable persons who are (potential) 'missing traders' but whose VAT identification number has not been cancelled;

(c)   taxable persons who carry out intra-Community supplies and their customers in other Member States in cases where the customer is a (potential) 'missing trader' or uses a 'hijacked VAT registration'.

Article 5
Notification of participation in the exchange of information

Each Member State shall notify the Commission in writing, within three months from the entry into force of this Regulation, of its decision, taken in accordance with the second paragraph of Article 18 of Regulation (EC) No 1798/2003, as to whether it is going to take part in the exchange of a particular category or subcategory of information referred to in Articles 3 and 4 and, if so, whether it is going to do so in an automatic or structured automatic way. The Commission shall inform the other Member States accordingly.

A Member State which subsequently modifies the categories or subcategories of information which it exchanges or the way in which it takes part in the exchange of information shall notify the Commission accordingly in writing. The Commission shall inform the other Member States accordingly.

Article 6

Frequency of the transmission of the information

In cases where the automatic exchange system is being used, the information shall be provided in accordance with the following timetable:

(a) at the latest within three months of the end of the calendar year in which that information has become available, with regard to the categories referred to in Article 3(1) and (3);

(b) at the latest within three months of the end of the calendar quarter during which that information has become available, with regard to the categories referred to in Article 3(2).

Information concerning the categories referred to in Article 3(4) and (5) shall be provided as soon as it becomes available.

Article 7

Transmission of communications

1. All information communicated in writing pursuant to Article 37 of Regulation (EC) No 1798/2003 shall, as far as possible, be transmitted only by electronic means via the CCN/CSI network, with the exception of the following:

    (a) the request for notification referred to in Article 14 of Regulation (EC) No 1798/2003 and the instrument or decision of which notification is requested;

    (b) original documents provided pursuant to Article 7 of Regulation (EC) No 1798/2003.

2. The competent authorities of the Member States may agree to waive the communication on paper of the information specified in points (a) and (b) of paragraph 1.

Article 8

Evaluation

The arrangements for administrative cooperation shall be evaluated in accordance with Article 35(1) of Regulation (EC) No 1798/2003, at three-yearly intervals with effect from the entry into force of this Regulation.

Article 9

Statistical data

The list of statistical data referred to in Article 35(3) of Regulation (EC) No 1798/2003 is set out in the Annex.

Each Member State shall, before 30 April each year and as far as possible by electronic means, communicate to the Commission those statistical data, using the model set out in this Annex.

Article 10

Communication of national measures

Member States shall communicate to the Commission the text of any laws, regulations or administrative provisions which they apply in the field covered by this Regulation.

The Commission shall communicate those measures to the other Member States.

Article 11

Entry into force

This Regulation shall enter into force on the twentieth day following that of its publication in the Official Journal of the European Union.

This Regulation shall be binding in its entirety and directly applicable in all Member States.

Done at Brussels, 29 October 2004.

For the Commission

Frederik BOLKESTEIN

Member of the Commission

ANNEX

Model for the communication from the Member States to the Commission referred to in Article 35(3) of Regulation (EC) No 1798/2003

Member State:

Calendar year:

Part A: statistics per Member State:

	Requests for information (Article 5)		Late replies from other Member States (Article 8(1))	Early replies from other Member States (Article 8(2))	Article 10 notifications	Requests for notification (Articles 14 to 16)	
	Number received (Box No 1)	Number sent (Box No 2)	Number of times for which the three month deadline has passed (Box No 3)	Number of times for which the one month deadline has been respected (Box No 4)	Number received (Box No 5)	Number of requests received (Box No 6)	Number of requests sent (Box No 7)
Belgium							
Czech Republic							
Denmark							
Germany							
Estonia							
Greece							
Spain							
France							
Ireland							
Italy							
Cyprus							
Latvia							
Lithuania							
Luxembourg							
Hungary							
Malta							
The Netherlands							
Austria							
Poland							
Portugal							
Slovenia							
Slovak Republic							
Finland							
Sweden							
United Kingdom							

Part B: Other global statistics:

Statistics on traders	
Number of traders identified for VAT that have declared intra-Community acquisitions (Box No 8)	
Number of traders identified for VAT that have reported intra-Community supplies in the quarterly statements (Box No 9)	
Statistics on controls and enquiries	
Number of simultaneous controls organised (Articles 12 and 13) (Box No 10)	
Number of simultaneous controls in which the Member State has participated (Articles 12 and 13) (Box No 11)	
Number of administrative enquiries requested (Article 5(3)) (Box No 12)	
Number of administrative enquiries carried out following a request from another Member State (Article 5(3)) (Box No 13)	
Statistics on information without request	
Number of information exchanges sent without request (Articles 17 to 21) (Box No 14)	
Statistics on VIES	
Percentage of cases where customers' VAT identification numbers did not correspond to construction rules (incorrect lines/total of all lines) at the date when data were captured (Box No 15)	
Number of VAT numbers in the O_MCTL messages received (Box No 16)	

EXPLANATORY NOTES:

Part A. Statistics to be broken down by Member State

Box Nos 1
and 2:

What should be reported here is the number of requests sent or received during the calendar year from each Member State. A request shall be considered to be sent or received only when all accompanying attachments are also sent or received. All requests should be reported even if they are not sent from the Central Liaison Office itself.

Box No 3:

What should be counted here is the number of times the three months deadline has passed during the reporting year, even if the request was sent during the preceding year or even if the reply is still not sent by the end of the reporting year. In case such a reply is still not sent after another year, it should not be counted a second time when submitting the figures for the following reporting period.

Box No 4:

What should be counted here is the number of times a reply is received from a particular Member State, when the request was made less than one month before. Replies to requests sent during the previous year should be counted but not replies received the following year to requests made during the reporting period.

Box No 5:

What should be reported here is the number of Article 10 notifications received during the reporting year.

Box Nos 6
and 7:

What should be reported here is the number of requests sent or received during the calendar year from each Member State. A request shall be considered to be sent or received only when all accompanying attachments are also sent or received.

Part B. Statistics to be reported globally, without any breakdown per Member State

Box Nos 8
and 9:

What should be reported here is the total number of national traders who declared having made such transactions at least once in the reporting period.

Box Nos 10
and 11:

The figures reported here should include those controls that are financed out of the fiscalis 2003-2007 programme but also all other controls (including purely bilateral controls). Simultaneous controls shall be reported within the year during which the notification provided for in Article 13 is done.

Box Nos 12 and 13	Those controls shall be reported within the year during which the request provided for in Article 5(3) is done.
Box No 14:	What should be reported here is the number of information exchanges sent during the calendar year without any request. This includes spontaneous, automatic and structured automatic information.

COUNCIL DIRECTIVE 2004/106/EC

of 16 November 2004

amending Directives 77/799/EEC concerning mutual assistance by the competent authorities of the Member States in the field of direct taxation, certain excise duties and taxation of insurance premiums and 92/12/EEC on the general arrangements for products subject to excise duty and on the holding, movement and monitoring of such products

Official Journal L359, 04/12/2004 p.0030-0031

THE COUNCIL OF THE EUROPEAN UNION,

Having regard to the Treaty establishing the European Community, and in particular Article 93 thereof,

Having regard to the proposal from the Commission,

Having regard to the opinion of the European Parliament,

Having regard to the opinion of the European Economic and Social Committee,

Whereas:

(1) Closer cooperation between Community tax authorities and between the latter and the Commission based on common principles is required to effectively combat excise duty fraud.

(2) Regulation (EC) No 2073/2004 of the European Parliament and of the Council of 16 November 2004 on administrative cooperation in the field of excise duties incorporates all the provisions designed to facilitate administrative cooperation in the field of excise duties contained in Directives 77/799/EEC and 92/12/EEC with the exception of mutual assistance provided for by Council Directive 76/308/EEC of 15 March 1976 on mutual assistance for the recovery of claims relating to certain levies, duties, taxes and other measures.

(3) Council Directive 2004/56/EC amending Directive 77/799/EEC requires Member States to bring into force the laws, regulations and administrative provisions necessary to comply with it before 1 January 2005. These provisions apply in the field of direct taxation, certain excise duties and taxation of insurance premiums. Since the Directive 77/799/EEC will not apply to excise duties, pursuant to this Directive, as from 1 July 2005, it is not appropriate that Member States be required to adopt provisions which are bound to cease to apply within a short time. Therefore, it is necessary to allow Member States not to adopt the provisions necessary to comply with Directive 2004/56/EC concerning excise duties, without prejudice to the obligation to adopt such provisions in respect of other taxes to which Directive 77/799/EC applies.

(4) Directives 77/799/EEC and 92/12/EEC should therefore be amended accordingly,

HAS ADOPTED THIS DIRECTIVE:

Article 1

Directive 77/799/EEC is hereby amended as follows:

1.　　the title shall be replaced by the following title:

'Council Directive 77/799/EEC of 19 December 1977 concerning mutual assistance by the competent authorities of the Member States in the field of direct taxation and taxation of insurance premiums';

2.　　paragraph 1 of Article 1 shall be replaced by the following:

'1.　　In accordance with the provisions of this Directive the competent authorities of the Member States shall exchange any information that may enable them to effect a correct assessment of taxes on income and on capital, and any information relating to the establishment of taxes on insurance premiums referred to in the sixth indent of Article 3 of Council Directive 76/308/EEC of 15 March 1976 on mutual assistance for the recovery of claims relating to certain levies, duties, taxes and other measures.

Article 2

Directive 92/12/EEC is hereby amended as follows:

1.　　Article 15a shall be deleted;

2.　　Article 15b shall be deleted;

3.　　Article 19(6) shall be deleted.

Article 3

References to Directive 77/799/EEC in respect of excise duties shall be construed as being made to Regulation (EC) No 2073/2004.

References to Directive 92/12/EEC in respect of administrative cooperation in the field of excise duties shall be construed as being made to Regulation (EC) No 2073/2004.

Article 4

1.　　Member States shall bring into force the laws, regulations and administrative provisions necessary to comply with this Directive before 30 June 2005. They shall forthwith inform the Commission thereof.

They shall apply these provisions from 1 July 2005.

When Member States adopt these measures, they shall contain a reference to this Directive or be accompanied by such reference on the occasion of their official publication. The methods of making such reference shall be laid down by Member States.

2.　　Member States shall communicate to the Commission the text of the provisions of national law which they adopt in the field covered by this Directive.

3.   By way of derogation from Article 2 of Directive 2004/56/EC, Member States are not obliged to adopt and apply the provisions needed to comply with Directive 2004/56/EC in respect of excise duties.

Article 5

This Directive shall enter into force on the twentieth day following its publication in the Official Journal of the European Union.

Article 6

This Directive is addressed to the Member States.

Done at Brussels, 16 November 2004.

For the Council

The President

G. ZALM

COMMISSION REGULATION (EC) No 1982/2004

of 18 November 2004

implementing Regulation (EC) No 638/2004 of the European Parliament and of the Council on Community statistics relating to the trading of goods between Member States and repealing Commission Regulations (EC) No 1901/2000 and (EEC) No 3590/92

THE COMMISSION OF THE EUROPEAN COMMUNITIES,

Having regard to the Treaty establishing the European Community,

Having regard to Regulation (EC) No 638/2004 of the European Parliament and of the Council of 31 March 2004 on Community statistics relating to the trading of goods between Member States and in particular Articles 3(4) and (5), 6(2), 8(2), 9, 10, 12 and 13(3) thereof,

Whereas:

(1) Statistics relating to the trading of goods between Member States are based on the Regulation (EC) No 638/2004 of the European Parliament and of the Council which reconsiders the statistical provisions with a view to improving transparency and facilitating comprehension and which is adapted to meet current data requirements. Particular implementation arrangements are assigned to the Commission in accordance with Article 14(2) of the said Regulation. Therefore it is necessary to adopt a new Commission Regulation which should refer in a restrictive manner to the assigned responsibility and specify the implementing provisions. Commission Regulations (EC) No 1901/2000 of 7 September 2000 laying down certain provisions for the implementation of Council Regulation (EEC) No 3330/91 on the statistics relating to the trading of goods between Member States and (EEC) No 3590/92 of 11 December 1992 concerning the statistical information media for statistics on trade between Member States should therefore be repealed.

(2) For methodological reasons a number of types of goods and movements should be exempted. It is necessary to draw up a comprehensive list of those goods to be excluded from the statistics to be sent to the Commission (Eurostat).

(3) Goods are to be included in trade statistics at the time when they enter or leave the statistical territory of a country. However, special arrangements are needed when data collection takes account of fiscal and customs procedures.

(4) A link between value added tax information and Intrastat declarations should be maintained in order to check the quality of the collected information. It is appropriate to determine the information to be transmitted by the national tax administration to the national authorities responsible for statistics.

(5)   Common definitions and concepts should apply to data collected within the Intrastat system in order to facilitate a harmonised application of the system.

(6)   With a view to transparency and equal treatment of the companies, harmonised and accurate provisions should be applied for the setting up of thresholds.

(7)   Appropriate provisions have to be determined for some specific goods and movements in order to ensure that the necessary information is collected in a harmonized way.

(8)   Common and appropriate timetables as well as provisions on adjustments and revisions have to be included in order to satisfy users' needs for timely and comparable figures.

(9)   A regular assessment of the system is planned in order to improve the data quality and ensure the transparency of the functioning of the system.

(10)   The measures provided for in this Regulation are in accordance with the opinion of the Committee on the statistics relating to the trading of goods between Member States,

HAS ADOPTED THIS REGULATION:

CHAPTER 1

GENERAL PROVISIONS

Article 1

Subject matter

This Regulation sets up the necessary measures for implementing Regulation (EC) No 638/2004 of the European Parliament and of the Council.

Article 2

Excluded goods

The goods listed in Annex I to this Regulation shall be excluded from statistics relating to the trading of goods between Member States to be transmitted to the Commission (Eurostat).

Article 3

Period of reference

1.   Member States may adapt the period of reference for Community goods on which VAT becomes chargeable on intra-Community acquisitions according to Article 6(2) of Regulation (EC) No 638/2004.

The reference period may then be defined as the calendar month during which the chargeable event occurs.

2.   Member States may adapt the period of reference where the Customs declaration is used in support of the information according to Article 6(2) of Regulation (EC) No 638/2004.

The reference period may then be defined as the calendar month during which the declaration is accepted by Customs.

CHAPTER 2

COMMUNICATION OF INFORMATION BY THE TAX ADMINISTRATION

Article 4

1.   The parties responsible for providing the information for the Intrastat System have the obligation to prove, at the request of the national authority, the correctness of the provided statistical information.

2.   The obligation according to paragraph 1 is limited to data which the provider of statistical information has to deliver to the competent tax administration in connection with his or her intra-Community movements of goods.

Article 5

1.   The tax administration responsible in each Member State shall provide to the national authorities the following information in order to identify the persons who have declared goods for fiscal purposes:

(a)   full name of the natural or legal person;

(b)   full address including post code;

(c)   identification number according to Article 9(1)(a) of Regulation (EC) No 638/2004.

2.   The tax administration responsible in each Member State shall provide to the national authorities for each natural or legal person in accordance with Directive 77/388/EEC:

(a)   the taxable amount of intra-Community acquisitions and deliveries of goods;

(b)   the tax period.

Article 6

The additional information referred to in Article 8(2)(b) of Regulation (EC) No 638/2004 concerns at least the national VIES data (VAT Information Exchange System data).

CHAPTER 3

COLLECTION OF INTRASTAT INFORMATION

Article 7

Partner Member State and country of origin

The partner Member States and where collected, the country of origin shall be reported according to the version of the nomenclature of countries and territories in force.

Article 8

Value of the goods

1. The value of the goods shall be the taxable amount which is the value to be determined for taxation purposes in accordance with Directive 77/388/EEC.

    For products subject to duties, the amount of these duties shall be excluded.

    Whenever the taxable amount does not have to be declared for taxation purposes, a positive value has to be reported which shall correspond to the invoice value, excluding VAT, or, failing this, to an amount which would have been invoiced in the event of any sale or purchase.

    In the case of processing, the value to be collected, with a view to and following such operations, shall be the total amount which would be invoiced in case of sale or purchase.

2. Additionally, Member States may also collect the statistical value of the goods, as defined in the Annex to Regulation (EC) No 638/2004, from part of the providers of information whose trade shall amount to a maximum of 70 % of the relevant Member State's total trade expressed in value.

3. The value of the goods defined in paragraphs 1 and 2 shall be expressed in the national currency. The exchange rate to be applied shall be:

    (a) the rate of exchange applicable for determining the taxable amount for taxation purposes, when this is established; or

    (b) the official rate of exchange at the time of completing the declaration or that applicable to calculating the value for customs purposes, in the absence of any special provisions decided by the Member States.

Article 9

Quantity of the goods

1. The net mass shall be given in kilograms. However, the specification of net mass for the subheadings of the Combined Nomenclature hereinafter referred to as 'CN' as established by Council Regulation (EEC) No 2658/87 set out in Annex II to this Regulation shall not be requested from the parties responsible for providing information.

2. The supplementary units shall be mentioned in accordance with the information set out in Council Regulation (EEC) No 2658/87, opposite the subheadings concerned, the list of which is published in Part I 'Preliminary provisions' of the said Regulation.

Article 10

Nature of transaction

The nature of transaction shall be reported according to the codes specified in the list of Annex III to this Regulation. Member States shall apply the codes of column A or a combination of the code numbers in column A and their subdivisions in column B indicated in this list.

Article 11

Delivery terms

Member States which collect the delivery terms according to Article 9(2)(d) of Regulation (EC) No 638/2004 may use the codes specified in Annex IV to this Regulation.

Article 12

Mode of transport

Member States which collect the mode of transport according to Article 9(2) (e) of Regulation (EC) No 638/2004 may use the codes specified in Annex V to this Regulation.

CHAPTER 4

SIMPLIFICATION WITHIN INTRASTAT

Article 13

1. Member States shall calculate their thresholds for the year following the current calendar year on the basis of the latest available results for their trade with other Member States over a period of at least 12 months. The provisions adopted at the start of a year shall apply for the whole year.

2. The value of the trade of a party responsible for providing information is considered to be above the thresholds:

    (a) when the value of trade with other Member States during the previous year exceeds the applicable thresholds, or

(b)   when the cumulative value of trade with other Member States since the beginning of the year of application exceeds the applicable thresholds. In that case, information shall be provided from the month in which thresholds are exceeded.

3.   Parties responsible for providing information according to the simplified rules of Article 10(4)(c) of Regulation (EC) No 638/2004 shall use the code 9950 00 00 for reporting the residual products.

4.   For individual transactions whose value is less than EUR 200, the parties responsible for providing information may report the following simplified information:

-    the product code 9950 00 00,

-    the partner Member State,

-    the value of the goods.

National authorities:

(a)   may refuse or limit application of this simplification if they consider that the aim of maintaining a satisfactory quality of statistical information overrides the desirability of reducing the reporting burden;

(b)   may require parties responsible for providing information to ask in advance to be allowed to make use of the simplification.

CHAPTER 5

RULES CONCERNING SPECIFIC GOODS AND MOVEMENTS

Article 14

In addition to the provisions of the Regulation (EC) No 638/2004, specific goods and movements shall be subject to the rules set out in this Chapter for data to be transmitted to the Commission (Eurostat).

Article 15

Industrial plant

1.   For the purpose of this Article:

(a)   'industrial plant' is a combination of machines, apparatus, appliances, equipment, instruments and materials which together make up large-scale, stationary units producing goods or providing services;

(b)   'component part' means a delivery for an industrial plant which is made up of goods which all belong to the same chapter of the CN.

2.   Statistics on trade between Member States may cover only dispatches and arrivals of component parts used for the construction of industrial plants or the re-use of industrial plants.

3.   Member States applying paragraph 2 may apply the following particular provisions on condition that the overall statistical value of a given industrial plant exceeds 3 million EUR, unless they are complete industrial plants for re-use:

    (a)   The commodity codes shall be composed as follows:

        -    the first four digits shall be 9880,

        -    the fifth and the sixth digits shall correspond to the CN chapter to which the goods of the component part belong,

        -    the seventh and the eighth digits shall be 0.

    (b)   The quantity shall be optional.

Article 16

Staggered consignments

1.   For the purpose of this Article 'staggered consignments' means the delivery of components of a complete item in an unassembled or disassembled state which are shipped during more than one reference period for commercial or transport-related reasons.

2.   Member States shall transmit data on arrivals or dispatches of staggered consignments only once, in the month that the last consignment arrives or is dispatched.

Article 17

Vessels and aircraft

1.   For the purposes of this Article:

    (a)   'vessel' means a vessel used for sea transport, referred to in Additional Notes 1 and 2 of Chapter 89 of the CN, and warships;

    (b)   'aircraft' means aeroplanes falling within CN code 8802 for civilian use, provided they are used by an airline, or for military use;

    (c)   'ownership of a vessel or aircraft' means the fact of a natural or legal person's registration as owner of a vessel or an aircraft.

2.   Statistics relating to the trading of goods between Member States on vessels and aircraft shall cover only the following dispatches and arrivals:

    (a)   the transfer of ownership of a vessel or aircraft, from a natural or legal person established in another Member State to a natural or legal person established in the reporting Member State. This transaction shall be treated as an arrival;

    (b)   the transfer of ownership of a vessel or aircraft from a natural or legal person established in the reporting Member State to a natural or legal person established in another Member State. This transaction shall be treated as a dispatch.

If the vessel or aircraft is new the dispatch is recorded in the Member State of construction;

(c)   the dispatches and arrivals of vessels or aircraft pending or following processing under contract as defined in Annex III, footnote (e).

3.   Member States shall apply the following specific provisions on statistics relating to the trading of goods between Member States:

(a)   the quantity shall be expressed in number of items and any other supplementary units laid down in the CN, for vessels, and in net mass and supplementary units, for aircraft;

(b)   the statistical value shall be the total amount which would be invoiced -transport and insurance costs being excluded - in case of sale or purchase of the whole vessel or aircraft;

(c)   the partner Member State for the reporting Member State shall be:

-       the Member State of construction, on arrival in the case of new vessel or aircraft constructed in the European Union,

-       in the other cases the partner Member State shall be the Member State where the natural or legal person transferring the ownership of the vessel or aircraft is established, on arrival, or the natural or legal person to whom the ownership of the vessel or aircraft is transferred, on dispatch.

(d)   the reference period for arrivals and dispatches referred to in paragraphs 2(a) and (b) shall be the month where the transfer of ownership takes place.

4.   Provided that there is no conflict with other national or Community legislation, national authorities responsible for Intrastat shall have access to additional data sources other than those of the Intrastat System or the Single Administrative Document for customs or fiscal purposes which they may need to apply this Article.

Article 18

Motor vehicle and aircraft parts

Member States may apply simplified national provisions for motor vehicle and aircraft parts, provided that they keep the Commission (Eurostat) informed on their particular practice before application.

Article 19

Goods delivered to vessels and aircraft

1. For the purposes of this Article:

    (a)   'delivery of goods to vessels and aircraft' means the delivery of products for the crew and passengers, and for the operation of the engines, machines and other equipment of vessels or aircraft;

    (b)   vessels or aircraft shall be deemed to belong to the Member State in which the vessel or aircraft is registered.

2. Statistics relating to the trading of goods between Member States shall cover only dispatches of goods delivered on the territory of the reporting Member State to vessels and aircraft belonging to another Member State. Dispatches shall cover all goods defined in Article 3(2)(a) and (b) of Regulation (EC) No 638/2004.

3. Member States shall use the following commodity codes for goods delivered to vessels and aircraft:

    -    9930 24 00: goods from CN chapters 1 to 24,

    -    9930 27 00: goods from CN chapter 27,

    -    9930 99 00: goods classified elsewhere.

The transmission of data on the quantity is optional. However, the data on net mass shall be transmitted on goods belonging to chapter 27.

In addition, the simplified partner country code 'QR' may be used.

Article 20

Offshore installations

1. For the purposes of this Article:

    (a)   'offshore installation' means the equipment and devices installed and stationary in the sea outside the statistical territory of any given country;

    (b)   these offshore installations shall be deemed to belong to that Member State in which the natural or legal person responsible for their commercial use is established.

2. Statistics relating to the trading of goods between Member States shall cover dispatches and arrivals of goods delivered to and from these offshore installations.

3. Member States shall use the following commodity codes for goods destined for the operators of the offshore installation or for the operation of the engines, machines and other equipment of the offshore installation:

    -    9931 24 00: goods from the CN chapters 1 to 24,

    -    9931 27 00: goods from CN Chapter 27,

- 9931 99 00: goods classified elsewhere.

The transmission of data on the quantity is optional. However, the data on net mass shall be transmitted on goods belonging to chapter 27.

The simplified partner country code 'QV' may be used.

Article 21

Sea products

1. For the purposes of this Article:

    (a) 'sea products' means fishery products, minerals, salvage and all other products which have not yet been landed by sea going vessels;

    (b) sea products shall be deemed to belong to that Member State where the vessel, which is carrying out the capturing, is registered.

2. Statistics relating to the trading of goods between Member States shall cover the following dispatches and arrivals:

    (a) arrivals when sea products are landed in the reporting Member State's ports or acquired by vessels registered in the reporting Member State from a vessel registered in another Member State;

    (b) dispatches when sea products are landed in another Member State's ports or acquired by vessels registered in another Member State from a vessel registered in the reporting Member State.

3. The partner Member State shall be, on arrival, the Member State where the vessel, which is carrying out the capturing, is registered and, on dispatch, the Member State where the sea product is landed or the vessel acquiring the sea product is registered.

4. Provided that there is no conflict with other national or Community legislation, national authorities responsible for Intrastat shall have access to additional data sources other than those of the Intrastat System or the Single Administrative Document for customs or fiscal purposes which they may need to apply this Article.

Article 22

Spacecraft

1. For the purposes of this Article, 'spacecraft' means vehicles which are able to travel outside the earth's atmosphere.

2. Statistics relating to the trading of goods between Member States shall cover the following dispatches and arrivals of spacecraft:

    (a) the dispatch or arrival of a spacecraft pending or following processing under contract as defined in Annex III footnote (e) to this Regulation;

(b)   the launching into space of a spacecraft which was the subject of a transfer of ownership between two natural or legal persons established in different Member States is to be considered:

  (i)   as a dispatch in the Member State of construction of the finished spacecraft,

  (ii)   as an arrival in the Member State where the new owner is established.

3.   The following specific provisions shall apply to the statistics referred to in paragraph 2(b):

(a)   the data on the statistical value shall be defined as the value of the spacecraft ex-works in accordance with the delivery terms specified in Annex IV to this Regulation.

(b)   The data on the partner Member State shall be the Member State of construction of the finished spacecraft, on arrival, and the Member State where the new owner is established, on dispatch.

4.   Provided that there is no conflict with other national or Community legislation, national authorities responsible for Intrastat shall have access to additional data sources other than those of the Intrastat System or the Single Administrative Document for customs or fiscal purposes which they may need to apply this Article.

Article 23

Electricity

1.   Statistics relating to the trading of goods between Member States shall cover dispatches and arrivals of electricity.

2.   Provided that there is no conflict with other national or Community legislation, national authorities responsible for Intrastat shall have access to additional data sources other than those of the Intrastat System or the Single Administrative Document for customs or fiscal purposes which they may need to transmit data on the trading of electricity between Member States to the Commission (Eurostat).

3.   The statistical value transmitted to the Commission (Eurostat) may be based on estimates. Member States have to inform the Commission (Eurostat) on the methodology used for the estimate before application.

Article 24

Military goods

1.   Statistics relating to the trading of goods between Member States shall cover dispatches and arrivals of goods intended for military use.

2.   Member States may transmit less detailed information than indicated in Article 9(1) points (b) to (h) of Regulation (EC) No 638/2004 when the information falls under military secrecy in compliance with the definitions in force in the Member States. However, as a minimum, data

on the total monthly statistical value of the dispatches and arrivals shall be transmitted to the Commission (Eurostat).

CHAPTER 6

DATA TRANSMISSION TO EUROSTAT

Article 25

1. Aggregated results referred to in Article 12(1)(a) of Regulation (EC) No 638/2004 are defined, for each flow, as the total value of the trade with other Member States. In addition, Member States belonging to the euro area shall provide a breakdown of their trade outside the euro area by products according to Sections of the Standard International Trade Classification, Revision 3.

2. Member States shall take all necessary measures to ensure that the collection of trade data from companies above the threshold of 97 % is exhaustive.

3. Adjustments made in application of Article 12 of Regulation (EC) No 638/2004 shall be transmitted to Eurostat with at least a breakdown by partner country and commodity code at two digit level of the CN.

4. As regards the statistical value of the goods, Member States shall estimate this value, where not collected.

5. Member States having adapted the reference period according to Article 3(1) shall ensure that monthly results are transmitted to the Commission (Eurostat), using estimates if necessary, when the reference period for fiscal purposes does not correspond with a calendar month.

6. Member States shall transmit data declared confidential to the Commission (Eurostat) so that they may be published at least under the original first two-digits of the CN code if the confidentiality is thereby assured.

7. When monthly results already transmitted to the Commission (Eurostat) are subject to revisions, Member States shall transmit revised results no later than in the month following the availability of revised data.

CHAPTER 7

QUALITY REPORT

Article 26

1. Member States shall supply the Commission (Eurostat) no later than 10 months following the calendar year with a quality report containing all information that it requests to assess the quality of the data transmitted.

2. The quality report aims at covering quality of statistics with reference to the following dimensions:

    - relevance of statistical concepts,

- accuracy of estimates,

- timeliness in transmission of results to the Commission (Eurostat),

- accessibility and clarity of the information,

- comparability of statistics,

- coherence,

- completeness.

3.   The quality indicators are defined in Annex VI to this Regulation.

CHAPTER 8

FINAL PROVISIONS

Article 27

Regulation (EC) No 1901/2000 and Regulation (EEC) No 3590/92 are hereby repealed with effect from 1 January 2005.

Article 28

This Regulation shall enter into force on the twentieth day following its publication in the Official Journal of the European Union.

It shall apply from 1 January 2005.

This Regulation shall be binding in its entirety and directly applicable in all Member States.

Done at Brussels, 18 November 2004.

For the Commission

Joaquín ALMUNIA

Member of the Commission

ANNEX I

List of goods excluded from statistics relating to the trading of goods between Member States to be transmitted to the Commission (Eurostat)

(a)   means of payment which are legal tender and securities

(b)   monetary gold

(c)   emergency aid for disaster areas

(d)   goods benefiting from diplomatic, consular or similar immunity

(e)   goods for and following temporary use, provided all the following conditions are met:

    1.   no processing is planned or made

    2.   the expected duration of the temporary use is not longer than 24 months

    3.   the dispatch/arrival has not to be declared as a delivery/ acquisition for VAT purposes

(f)   goods used as carriers of information such as floppy disks, computer tapes, films, plans, audio and videotapes, CDROMs with stored computer software, where developed to order for a particular client or where they are not subject of a commercial transaction, as well as complements for a previous delivery e.g. updates for which the consignee is not invoiced.

(g)   provided that they are not the subject of a commercial transaction:

    1.   advertising material

    2.   commercial samples

(h)   goods for and after repair and the associated replacement parts. A repair entails the restoration of goods to their original function or condition. The objective of the operation is simply to maintain the goods in working order; this may involve some rebuilding or enhancements but does not change the nature of the goods in any way

(i)   goods dispatched to national armed forces stationed outside the statistical territory and goods received from another Member State which had been conveyed outside the statistical territory by the national armed forces, as well as goods acquired or disposed of on the statistical territory of a Member State by the armed forces of another Member State which are stationed there

(j)   spacecraft launchers, on dispatch and on arrival pending launching into space, and at the time of launching into space

(k)   sales of new means of transport by natural or legal persons liable to VAT to private individuals from other Member States

ANNEX II

List of CN subheadings referred to Article 9(1)

0105 11 11	2204 21 69	2204 29 88	5703 10 00
0105 11 19	2204 21 71	2204 29 89	5703 20 11
0105 11 91	2204 21 74	2204 29 91	5703 20 19
0105 11 99	2204 21 76	2204 29 92	5703 20 91
0105 12 00	2204 21 77	2204 29 94	5703 20 99
0105 19 20	2204 21 78	2204 29 95	5703 30 11
0105 19 90	2204 21 79	2204 29 96	5703 30 19
0407 00 11	2204 21 80	2204 29 98	5703 30 81
2202 10 00	2204 21 81	2204 29 99	5703 30 89
2202 90 10	2204 21 82	2205 10 10	5703 90 10
2202 90 91	2204 21 83	2205 10 90	5703 90 90
2202 90 95	2204 21 84	2205 90 10	5704 10 00
2202 90 99	2204 21 85	2205 90 90	5704 90 00
2203 00 01	2204 21 87	2206 00 10	5705 00 10
2203 00 09	2204 21 88	2206 00 31	5705 00 30
2203 00 10	2204 21 89	2206 00 39	5705 00 90
2204 10 11	2204 21 91	2206 00 51	6101 10 10
2204 10 19	2204 21 92	2206 00 59	6101 10 90
2204 10 91	2204 21 94	2206 00 81	6101 20 10
2204 10 99	2204 21 95	2207 10 00	6101 20 90
2204 21 10	2204 21 96	2207 20 00	6101 30 10
2204 21 11	2204 21 98	2209 00 99	6101 30 90
2204 21 13	2204 21 99	2716 00 00	6101 90 10
2204 21 13	2204 29 10	3702 51 00	6101 90 90
2204 21 17	2204 29 11	3702 53 00	6102 10 10
2204 21 18	2204 29 12	3702 54 10	6102 10 90
2204 21 19	2204 29 13	3702 54 90	6102 20 10
2204 21 22	2204 29 17	5701 10 10	6102 20 90
2204 21 23	2204 29 18	5701 10 90	6102 30 10
2204 21 24	2204 29 42	5701 90 10	6102 30 90
2204 21 26	2204 29 43	5701 90 90	6102 90 10
2204 21 27	2204 29 44	5702 20 00	6102 90 90
2204 21 28	2204 29 46	5702 31 10	6103 11 00
2204 21 32	2204 29 47	5702 31 80	6103 12 00
2204 21 34	2204 29 48	5702 32 10	6103 19 00
2204 21 36	2204 29 58	5702 32 90	6103 21 00
2204 21 37	2204 29 62	5702 39 00	6103 22 00
2204 21 38	2204 29 64	5702 41 00	6103 23 00
2204 21 42	2204 29 65	5702 42 00	6103 29 00
2204 21 43	2204 29 71	5702 49 00	6103 31 00
2204 21 44	2204 29 72	5702 51 00	6103 32 00
2204 21 46	2204 29 75	5702 52 10	6103 33 00
2204 21 47	2204 29 77	5702 52 90	6103 39 00
2204 21 48	2204 29 78	5702 59 00	6103 41 00
2204 21 62	2204 29 82	5702 91 00	6103 42 00
2204 21 66	2204 29 83	5702 92 10	6103 43 00
2204 21 67	2204 29 84	5702 92 90	6103 49 00
2204 21 68	2204 29 87	5702 99 00	6104 11 00

6104 12 00	6108 91 00	6211 43 42	6403 99 11
6104 13 00	6108 92 00	6212 10 10	6403 99 31
6104 19 00	6108 99 00	6212 10 90	6403 99 33
6104 21 00	6109 10 00	6212 20 00	6403 99 36
6104 22 00	6109 90 10	6212 30 00	6403 99 38
6104 23 00	6109 90 30	6401 10 10	6403 99 50
6104 29 00	6109 90 90	6401 10 90	6403 99 91
6104 31 00	6110 11 10	6401 91 00	6403 99 93
6104 32 00	6110 11 30	6401 92 10	6403 99 96
6104 33 00	6110 11 90	6401 92 90	6403 99 98
6104 39 00	6110 12 10	6401 99 00	6404 11 00
6104 41 00	6110 12 90	6402 12 10	6404 19 10
6104 42 00	6110 19 10	6402 12 90	6404 19 90
6104 43 00	6110 19 90	6402 19 00	6404 20 10
6104 44 00	6110 20 10	6402 20 00	6404 20 90
6104 49 00	6110 20 91	6402 30 00	6405 10 00
6104 51 00	6110 20 99	6402 91 00	6405 20 10
6104 52 00	6110 30 10	6402 99 10	6405 20 91
6104 53 00	6110 30 91	6402 99 31	6405 20 99
6104 59 00	6110 30 99	6402 99 39	6405 90 10
6104 61 00	6110 90 10	6402 99 50	6405 90 90
6104 62 00	6110 90 90	6402 99 91	7101 10 00
6104 63 00	6112 11 00	6402 99 93	7101 21 00
6104 69 00	6112 12 00	6402 99 96	7101 22 00
6105 10 00	6112 19 00	6402 99 98	7103 91 00
6105 20 10	6112 31 10	6403 12 00	7103 99 00
6105 20 90	6112 31 90	6403 19 00	7104 10 00
6105 90 10	6112 39 10	6403 20 00	7104 20 00
6105 90 90	6112 39 90	6403 30 00	7104 90 00
6106 10 00	6112 41 10	6403 40 00	7105 10 00
6106 20 00	6112 41 90	6403 51 11	7105 90 00
6106 90 10	6112 49 10	6403 51 15	7106 10 00
6106 90 30	6112 49 90	6403 51 19	7106 91 10
6106 90 50	6115 11 00	6403 51 91	7106 91 90
6106 90 90	6115 12 00	6403 51 95	7106 92 20
6107 11 00	6115 19 00	6403 51 99	7106 92 80
6107 12 00	6210 20 00	6403 59 11	7108 11 00
6107 19 00	6210 30 00	6403 59 31	7108 12 00
6107 21 00	6211 11 00	6403 59 35	7108 13 10
6107 22 00	6211 12 00	6403 59 39	7108 13 80
6107 29 00	6211 20 00	6403 59 50	7108 20 00
6107 91 00	6211 32 31	6403 59 91	7110 11 00
6107 92 00	6211 32 41	6403 59 95	7110 19 10
6107 99 00	6211 32 42	6403 59 99	7110 19 80
6108 11 00	6211 33 31	6403 91 11	7110 21 00
6108 19 00	6211 33 41	6403 91 13	7110 29 00
6108 21 00	6211 33 42	6403 91 16	7110 31 00
6108 22 00	6211 42 31	6403 91 18	7110 39 00
6108 29 00	6211 42 41	6403 91 91	7110 41 00
6108 31 00	6211 42 42	6403 91 93	7110 49 00
6108 32 00	6211 43 31	6403 91 96	7116 10 00
6108 39 00	6211 43 41	6403 91 98	7116 20 11

7116 20 19	8540 12 00	9001 50 80
7116 20 90	8540 20 10	9003 11 00
8504 10 10	8540 20 80	9003 19 10
8504 10 91	8540 40 00	9003 19 30
8504 10 99	8540 50 00	9003 19 90
8504 21 00	8540 71 00	9006 53 10
8504 22 10	8540 72 00	9006 53 90
8504 22 90	8540 79 00	9202 10 10
8504 23 00	8540 81 00	9202 10 90
8504 31 10	8540 89 00	9202 90 30
8504 31 31	8542 21 01	9202 90 80
8504 31 39	8542 21 05	9204 10 00
8504 31 90	8542 21 11	9204 20 00
8504 32 10	8542 21 13	9205 10 00
8504 32 30	8542 21 15	9207 90 10
8504 32 90	8542 21 17	
8504 33 10	8542 21 20	
8504 33 90	8542 21 25	
8504 34 00	8542 21 31	
8504 40 10	8542 21 33	
8504 40 20	8542 21 35	
8504 40 50	8542 21 37	
8504 40 93	8542 21 39	
8504 50 10	8542 21 45	
8518 21 90	8542 21 50	
8518 22 90	8542 21 69	
8518 29 20	8542 21 71	
8518 29 80	8542 21 73	
8539 10 10	8542 21 81	
8539 10 90	8542 21 83	
8539 21 30	8542 21 85	
8539 21 92	8542 21 99	
8539 21 98	8542 29 10	
8539 22 10	8542 29 20	
8539 29 30	8542 29 90	
8539 29 92	8903 91 10	
8539 29 98	8903 91 92	
8539 31 10	8903 91 99	
8539 31 90	8903 92 10	
8539 32 10	8903 92 91	
8539 32 50	8903 92 99	
8539 32 90	8903 99 10	
8539 39 00	8903 99 91	
8539 41 00	8903 99 99	
8539 49 10	9001 30 00	
8539 49 30	9001 40 20	
8540 11 11	9001 40 41	
8540 11 13	9001 40 49	
8540 11 15	9001 40 80	
8540 11 19	9001 50 20	
8540 11 91	9001 50 41	
8540 11 99	9001 50 49	

ANNEX III

Coding of the nature of transaction

A	B
1 Transactions involving actual or intended transfer of ownership against compensation (financial or otherwise) (except the transactions listed under 2, 7 and 8) (^{a}) (^{b}) (^{c})	1 Outright/purchase/sale (^{b}) 2 Supply for sale on approval or after trial, for consignment or with the intermediation of a commission agent 3 Barter trade (compensation in kind) 4 Purchases by private individuals 5 Financial leasing (hire-purchase) (^{c})
2 Return of goods after registration of the original transaction under code 1 (^{d}); replacement of goods free of charge (^{d})	1 Return of goods 2 Replacement for returned goods 3 Replacement (e.g. under warranty) for goods not being returned
3 Transactions (not temporary) involving transfer of ownership but without compensation (financial or other)	1 Goods delivered under aid programmes operated or financed partly or wholly by the European Community 2 Other general government aid deliveries 3 Other aid deliveries (individuals, non-governmental organisations) 4 Others
4 Operations with a view to processing under contract (^{e}) (except those recorded under 7)	
5 Operations following processing under contract (^{e}) (except those recorded under 7)	
6 Particular transactions coded for national purposes (^{f})	

7 Operations under joint defence projects or other joint intergovernmental production programs	
8 Supply of building materials and equipment for works that are part of a general construction or engineering contract (^{8})	
9 Other transactions	

(a) This item covers most dispatches and arrivals, i.e. transactions in respect of which:
- ownership is transferred from resident to non-resident, and
- payment or compensation in kind is or will be made.

It should be noted that this also applies to goods sent between related enterprises or from/to central distribution depots, even if no immediate payment is made.

(b) Including spare parts and other replacements made against payment.

(c) Including financial leasing: the lease instalments are calculated in such a way as to cover all or virtually all of the value of the goods. The risks and rewards of ownership are transferred to the lessee. At the end of the contract the lessee becomes the legal owner of the goods.

(d) Return and replacement dispatches of goods originally recorded under items 3 to 9 of column A should be registered under the corresponding items.

(e) Processing covers operations (transformation, construction, assembling, enhancement, renovation...) with the objective of producing a new or really improved item. This does not necessarily involve a change in the product classification. Processing activities on a processor's own account are not covered by this item and should be registered under item 1 of column A.

Goods for or following processing have to be recorded as arrivals and dispatches.

However, a repair should not be recorded under this position. A repair entails the restoration of goods to their original function or condition. The objective of the operation is simply to maintain the goods in working order; this may involve some rebuilding or enhancements but does not change the nature of the goods in anyway.Goods for and after repair are excluded from statistics relating to the trading of goods between Member States to be transmitted to the Commission (Eurostat) (see Annex I (h)).

(f) Transactions recorded under this position could be: transactions not involving transfer of ownership e.g. repair, hire, loan, operational leasing and other temporary uses less than two years, except processing under contract (delivery or return). Transactions recorded with this code shall not be transmitted to the Commission (Eurostat).

(g) The transactions recorded under item 8 of column A involve only goods which are not separately invoiced, but for which a single invoice covers the total value of the works. Where this is not the case, the transactions should be recorded under item 1.

ANNEX IV

Coding of delivery terms

	Meaning	Place to be indicated, when required
Incoterm Code	Incoterm ICC/ECE Geneva	
EXW	ex-works	location of works
FCA	free carrier	agreed place
FAS	free alongside ship	agreed port of loading
FOB	free on board	agreed port of loading
CFR	cost and freight (C&F)	agreed port of destination
CIF	cost, insurance and freight	agreed port of destination
CPT	carriage paid to	agreed place of destination
CIP	carriage and insurance paid to	agreed place of destination
DAF	delivered at frontier	agreed place of delivery at frontier
DES	delivered ex-ship	agreed port of destination
DEQ	delivered ex-quay	after customs clearance, agreed port
DDU	delivered duty unpaid	agreed place of destination in arriving country
DDP	delivered duty paid	agreed place of delivery in arriving country
XXX	delivery terms other than the above	precise statement of terms specified in the contract

Additional information (when required):

1. place located in the territory of the Member State concerned
2. place located in another Member State
3. other (place located outside the Community)

ANNEX V

Coding of mode of transport

Code	Title
1	Sea transport
2	Rail transport
3	Road transport
4	Air transport
5	Postal consignment
7	Fixed transport installations
8	Inland waterway transport
9	Own propulsion

ANNEX VI

Quality indicators

The information on the quality of the data provided by the Member States shall be based on a common set of quality indicators and the necessary descriptive metadata.

1. **Relevance** of statistical concepts means that the data meet users' needs.

2. **Accuracy** is one of the main needs of users. It can be assessed by indicators made up as follows:

    (a) *Thresholds*

         (i)   member States shall report the levels of current threshold.

         (ii)   in order to monitor the levels at which thresholds have been set, Member States shall report:

                -    the coverage rate (%), expressed in terms of value, of trade above the exemption threshold.

         (iii) in order to monitor the impact of the thresholds, Member States shall report:

                -    the method of adjustment used to estimate trade below the thresholds,

                -    the share (%) of estimated trade below the thresholds.

    (b) *Non-response*

         In order to assess the level of non-response, Member States shall report:

         -    the method of adjustment used to estimate missing trade,

         -    the share (%) of values estimated for missing trade.

    (c) *Statistical value*

         In order to assess the impact of calculating the statistical value, Member States shall report:

         -    the methodology used to calculate the statistical value,

         -    the quantitative impact of calculating the statistical value.

    (d) *Revisions*

         In order to assess the impact of the revisions procedures, Member States shall report:

         -    a description of the revision policy,

         -    the change (%) of the total trade value between the first results and the last available results.

(e)   *Confidentiality*

In order to assess the impact of confidential trade, Member States shall report:

- a description of confidentiality rules,

- the share (%) of confidential trade expressed in value terms,

- the number of product codes within the CN affected by confidentiality.

(f)   *Other links to accuracy*

Other indicators are useful for assessing the quality of data, so Member States shall include the following in the quality report:

- description of control procedures,

- monthly average number of lines in the declarations,

- number of PSIs (Providers of Statistical Information),

- % of electronic declarations,

- % of values declared electronically.

3.   **Timeliness** shall be assessed by Eurostat by calculating the average time between the end of the reference month and transmission of the data to Eurostat, as follows:

- annual average delay (+ X days) or advance (- Y days) in the transmission of aggregate results, in calendar days, with reference to the legal deadline.

- annual average delay (+ X days) or advance (- Y days) in the transmission of detailed results, in calendar days, with reference to the legal deadline.

4.   **Accessibility** to users gives value to statistical data, which is increased if the data are readily available in formats required by users. **Clarity** of the data available depends on the assistance provided in using and interpreting the statistics and on the available comments and analysis of results.

Consequently, Member States shall include in the quality report the media used to disseminate external trade statistics and references to further information that can assist the users of the statistics (e.g. methodological information, previous or similar publications, etc.).

5.   **Comparability** aims at measuring the impact of differences in applied statistical concepts and definitions when statistics are compared between geographical areas, non-geographical domains, or reference periods.

The use of differing concepts and definitions in Member States may affect comparability in foreign trade statistics (*comparability over space*).

To evaluate the impact, Member States shall report mirror exercises conducted by them and the investigation of asymmetry carried out if the mirror effect becomes significant.

Comparability over time is another important aspect of quality. Member States shall report any changes to definitions, coverage or methods that will have an impact on continuity.

6. **Coherence** is defined by how well sets of statistics can be used together. Apart from External Trade Statistics, information on external trade can be found in National Accounts, Business Statistics and Balance of Payments.

    In this context, Member States shall report any information concerning the coherence of foreign trade statistics and statistics originating from other sources.

7. **Completeness** refers to the fact that the themes for which statistics are available reflect the needs and the priorities expressed by users of the European Statistical System.

COMMISSION REGULATION (EC) No 601/2005

of 18 April 2005

amending Annex I to Council Regulation (EC) No 866/2004 on a regime under Article 2 of Protocol No 10 to the Act of Accession

Official Journal L99, 19.04.2005, p.10 - 10

THE COMMISSION OF THE EUROPEAN COMMUNITIES,

Having regard to the Treaty establishing the European Community,

Having regard to Protocol No 10 on Cyprus to the Act concerning the conditions of accession of the Czech Republic, the Republic of Estonia, the Republic of Cyprus, the Republic of Latvia, the Republic of Lithuania, the Republic of Hungary, the Republic of Malta, the Republic of Poland, the Republic of Slovenia and the Slovak Republic and the adjustments to the Treaties on which the European Union is founded,

Having regard to Council Regulation (EC) No 866/2004 of 29 April 2004 on a regime under Article 2 of Protocol No 10 to the Act of Accession, and in particular Article 9 thereof,

Whereas:

(1)   Annex I to Regulation (EC) No 866/2004 lays down a list of crossing points at which persons and goods may cross the line between the areas under the effective control of the Government of the Republic of Cyprus and those areas in which the Government of the Republic of Cyprus does not exercise effective control.

(2)   Following agreement on the opening of new crossing points in Zodia and Ledra Street, it is necessary to adapt Annex I.

(3)   The Government of the Republic of Cyprus gave its agreement to this adaptation.

(4)   The Turkish Cypriot Chamber of Commerce was consulted on this matter,

HAS ADOPTED THIS REGULATION:

Article 1

Annex I to Regulation (EC) No 866/2004 is replaced by the following:

'ANNEX I

List of crossing points referred to in Article 2(4)

-    Agios Dhometios

-    Ledra Palace

-    Ledra Street

-    Zodia.'

Article 2

This Regulation shall enter into force on the third day following its publication in the Official Journal of the European Union.

This Regulation shall be binding in its entirety and directly applicable in all Member States.

Done at Brussels, 18 April 2005.

For the Commission

Olli REHN

Member of the Commission

REGULATION (EC) No 648/2005 OF THE EUROPEAN PARLIAMENT AND OF THE COUNCIL

of 13 April 2005

amending Council Regulation (EEC) No 2913/92 establishing the Community Customs Code

Official Journal L117, 04/05/2005, p. 0013 - 0019

THE EUROPEAN PARLIAMENT AND THE COUNCIL OF THE EUROPEAN UNION,

Having regard to the Treaty establishing the European Community, and in particular Articles 26, 95, 133 and 135 thereof,

Having regard to the proposal from the Commission,

Having regard to the opinion of the European Economic and Social Committee,

Acting in accordance with the procedure laid down in Article 251 of the Treaty,

Whereas:

(1) Council Regulation (EEC) No 2913/92 lays down the rules for the customs treatment of goods that are imported or to be exported.

(2) It is necessary to establish an equivalent level of protection in customs controls for goods brought into or out of the customs territory of the Community. In order to achieve this objective, it is necessary to establish an equivalent level of customs controls in the Community and to ensure a harmonised application of customs controls by the Member States, which have principal responsibility for applying these controls. Such controls should be based upon commonly agreed standards and risk criteria for the selection of goods and economic operators in order to minimise the risks to the Community and its citizens and to the Community's trading partners. Member States and the Commission should therefore introduce a Community-wide risk management framework to support a common approach so that priorities are set effectively and resources are allocated efficiently with the aim of maintaining a proper balance between customs controls and the facilitation of legitimate trade. Such a framework should also provide for common criteria and harmonised requirements for authorised economic operators and ensure a harmonised application of such criteria and requirements. The establishment of a risk management framework common to all Member States should not prevent Member States from controlling goods by spot-checks.

(3) Member States should grant the status of authorised economic operator to any economic operator that meets common criteria relating to the operator's control systems, financial solvency and compliance record. The status of authorised economic operator, once granted by one Member State, should be recognised by the other Member States, but does not confer the right to benefit automatically in the other Member States from

simplifications provided for in the customs rules. However, the other Member States should allow the use of simplifications by authorised economic operators provided they meet all the specific requirements for use of the particular simplifications. In considering a request to use simplifications, the other Member States need not repeat the evaluation of the operator's control systems, financial solvency or compliance record, which will already have been completed by the Member State that granted the operator the status of authorised economic operator, but should ensure that any other specific requirements for use of the particular simplification are met. The use of simplifications in other Member States may also be coordinated by agreement between the customs authorities concerned.

(4) Simplifications under the customs rules should continue to be without prejudice to customs controls as defined within the Community Customs Code, notably relating to safety and security. Such controls are the responsibility of the customs authorities and, while the status of authorised economic operator should be recognised by those authorities as a factor during risk analysis and in the granting of any facilitation to the economic operator with regard to controls relating to safety and security, the right to control should remain.

(5) Risk-related information on import and export goods should be shared between the competent authorities of the Member States and the Commission. To this end, a common, secure system should be set up, enabling the competent authorities to access, transfer and exchange this information in a timely and effective manner. Such information may also be shared with third countries where an international agreement so provides.

(6) The conditions under which information provided by economic operators to customs may be disclosed to other authorities in the same Member State, other Member States, to the Commission, or to authorities in third countries should be specified. For this purpose, it should be clearly indicated that Directive 95/46/EC of the European Parliament and of the Council of 24 October 1995 on the protection of individuals with regard to the processing of personal data and on the free movement of such data and Regulation (EC) No 45/2001 of the European Parliament and of the Council of 18 December 2000 on the protection of individuals with regard to the processing of personal data by the Community institutions and bodies and on the free movement of such data apply to the processing of personal data by the competent authorities as well as by any other authority receiving data pursuant to the Community Customs Code.

(7) In order to allow for appropriate risk-based controls, it is necessary to establish the requirement of pre-arrival or pre-departure information for all goods brought into or out of the customs territory of the Community, except for goods passing through by air or ship without a stop within this territory. Such information should be available before the goods are brought into or out of the customs territory of the Community. Different

timeframes and rules may be set according to the type of goods, of transport or of economic operator or where international agreements provide for special security arrangements. In order to avoid security loopholes, this requirement should also be introduced with regard to goods brought into or out of a free zone.

(8) Regulation (EEC) No 2913/92 should therefore be amended accordingly,

HAVE ADOPTED THIS REGULATION

Article 1

Regulation (EEC) No 2913/92 is hereby amended as follows:

1.   Article 4 shall be amended as follows:

  —   the following points shall be inserted:

'(4a) "Customs office of entry" means the customs office designated by the customs authorities in accordance with the customs rules to which goods brought into the customs territory of the Community must be conveyed without delay and at which they will be subject to appropriate risk-based entry controls;

(4b) "Customs office of import" means the customs office designated by the customs authorities in accordance with the customs rules where the formalities for assigning goods brought into the customs territory of the Community to a customs-approved treatment or use, including appropriate risk-based controls, are to be carried out;

(4c) "Customs office of export" means the customs office designated by the customs authorities in accordance with the customs rules where the formalities for assigning goods leaving the customs territory of the Community to a customs-approved treatment or use, including appropriate risk-based controls, are to be completed;

(4d) "Customs office of exit" means the customs office designated by the customs authorities in accordance with the customs rules to which goods must be presented before they leave the customs territory of the Community and at which they will be subject to customs controls relating to the completion of exit formalities, and appropriate risk-based controls.';

  —   point 14 shall be replaced by the following:

'(14) "Customs controls" means specific acts performed by the customs authorities in order to ensure the correct application of customs rules and other legislation governing the entry, exit, transit, transfer and end-use of goods moved between the customs territory of the Community and third countries and the presence of goods that do not have Community status; such acts may include examining goods, verifying declaration data and the existence and authenticity of electronic or written documents, examining the accounts of undertakings and other records, inspecting means of transport, inspecting luggage and other goods carried by or on persons and carrying out official inquiries and other similar acts.';

— The following points shall be added:

'(25) "Risk" means the likelihood of an event occurring, in connection with the entry, exit, transit, transfer and end-use of goods moved between the customs territory of the Community and third countries and the presence of goods that do not have Community status, which

- prevents the correct application of Community or national measures, or

- compromises the financial interests of the Community and its Member States, or

- poses a threat to the Community's security and safety, to public health, to the environment or to consumers.

(26) "Risk management" means the systematic identification of risk and implementation of all measures necessary for limiting exposure to risk. This includes activities such as collecting data and information, analysing and assessing risk, prescribing and taking action and regular monitoring and review of the process and its outcomes, based on international, Community and national sources and strategies.';

2. the following Section and Article shall be inserted:

'Section 1A

Authorised economic operators

Article 5a

1. Customs authorities, if necessary following consultation with other competent authorities, shall grant, subject to the criteria provided for in paragraph 2, the status of "authorised economic operator" to any economic operator established in the customs territory of the Community.

An authorised economic operator shall benefit from facilitations with regard to customs controls relating to security and safety and/or from simplifications provided for under the customs rules.

The status of authorised economic operator shall, subject to the rules and conditions laid down in paragraph 2, be recognised by the customs authorities in all Member States, without prejudice to customs controls. Customs authorities shall, on the basis of the recognition of the status of authorised economic operator and provided that the requirements relating to a specific type of simplification provided for in Community customs legislation are fulfilled, authorise the operator to benefit from that simplification.

2.   The criteria for granting the status of authorised economic operator shall include:

-       an appropriate record of compliance with customs requirements,

-       a satisfactory system of managing commercial and, where appropriate, transport records, which allows appropriate customs controls,

-       where appropriate, proven financial solvency, and

-       where applicable, appropriate security and safety standards.

The committee procedure shall be used to determine the rules:

-       for granting the status of authorised economic operator,

-       for granting authorisations for the use of simplifications,

-       for establishing which customs authority is competent to grant such status and authorisations,

-       for the type and extent of facilitations that may be granted in respect of customs controls relating to security and safety, taking into account the rules for common risk management,

-       for consultation with, and provision of information to, other customs authorities;

and the conditions under which:

-       an authorisation may be limited to one or more Member States,

-       the status of authorised economic operator may be suspended or withdrawn, and

-       the requirement of being established in the Community may be waived for specific categories of authorised economic operator, taking into account, in particular, international agreements.';

3.   Article 13 shall be replaced by the following:

'Article 13

1. Customs authorities may, in accordance with the conditions laid down by the provisions in force, carry out all the controls they deem necessary to ensure that customs rules and other legislation governing the entry, exit, transit, transfer and end-use of goods moved between the customs territory of the Community and third countries and the presence of goods that do not have Community status are correctly applied. Customs controls for the purpose of the correct application of Community legislation may be carried out in a third country where an international agreement provides for this.

2. Customs controls, other than spot-checks, shall be based on risk analysis using automated data processing techniques, with the purpose of identifying and quantifying the risks and developing the necessary measures to assess the risks, on the basis of criteria developed at national, Community and, where available, international level.

   The committee procedure shall be used for determining a common risk management framework, and for establishing common criteria and priority control areas.

   Member States, in cooperation with the Commission, shall establish a computer system for the implementation of risk management.

3. Where controls are performed by authorities other than the customs authorities, such controls shall be performed in close coordination with the customs authorities, wherever possible at the same time and place.

4. In the context of the controls provided for in this Article, customs and other competent authorities, such as veterinary and police authorities, may communicate data received, in connection with the entry, exit, transit, transfer and end-use of goods moved between the customs territory of the Community and third countries and the presence of goods that do not have Community status, between each other and to the customs authorities of the Member States and to the Commission where this is required for the purposes of minimising risk.

   Communication of confidential data to the customs authorities and other bodies (e.g. security agencies) of third countries shall be allowed only in the framework of an international agreement and provided that the data protection provisions in force, in particular Directive 95/46/EC of the European Parliament and of the Council of 24 October 1995 on the protection of individuals with regard to the processing of personal data and on the free movement of such data and Regulation (EC) No 45/2001 of the European Parliament and of the Council of 18 December 2000 on the protection of individuals with regard to the processing of personal data by the Community institutions and bodies and on the free movement of such data are respected.

4.   Article 15 shall be replaced by the following:

'Article 15

All information which is by nature confidential or which is provided on a confidential basis shall be covered by the duty of professional secrecy. It shall not be disclosed by the competent authorities without the express permission of the person or authority providing it. The communication of information shall, however, be permitted where the competent authorities are obliged to do so pursuant to the provisions in force, particularly in connection with legal proceedings. Any disclosure or communication of information shall fully comply with prevailing data protection provisions, in particular Directive 95/46/EC and Regulation (EC) No 45/2001.';

5.   in Article 16 'control by the customs authorities' shall be replaced by 'customs controls';

6.   the following Articles shall be inserted under Chapter 1 of Title III:

'Article 36a

1.   Goods brought into the customs territory of the Community shall be covered by a summary declaration, with the exception of goods carried on means of transport only passing through the territorial waters or the airspace of the customs territory without a stop within this territory.

2.   The summary declaration shall be lodged at the customs office of entry.

Customs authorities may allow the summary declaration to be lodged at another customs office, provided that this office immediately communicates or makes available electronically the necessary particulars to the customs office of entry.

Customs authorities may accept, instead of the lodging of the summary declaration, the lodging of a notification and access to the summary declaration data in the economic operator's computer system.

3.   The summary declaration shall be lodged before the goods are brought into the customs territory of the Community.

4.   The committee procedure shall be used to establish:

-    the time limit by which the summary declaration is to be lodged before the goods are brought into the customs territory of the Community,

-    the rules for exceptions from, and variations to, the time limit referred to in the first indent, and

- the conditions under which the requirement for a summary declaration may be waived or adapted,

in accordance with the specific circumstances and for particular types of goods traffic, modes of transport and economic operators and where international agreements provide for special security arrangements.

Article 36b

1. The committee procedure shall be used to establish a common data set and format for the summary declaration, containing the particulars necessary for risk analysis and the proper application of customs controls, primarily for security and safety purposes, using, where appropriate, international standards and commercial practices.

2. The summary declaration shall be made using a data processing technique. Commercial, port or transport information may be used, provided that it contains the necessary particulars.

   Customs authorities may accept paper-based summary declarations in exceptional circumstances, provided that they apply the same level of risk management as that applied to summary declarations made using a data processing technique.

3. The summary declaration shall be lodged by the person who brings the goods, or who assumes responsibility for the carriage of the goods into the customs territory of the Community.

4. Notwithstanding the obligation of the person referred to in paragraph 3, the summary declaration may be lodged instead by:

   (a) the person in whose name the person referred to in paragraph 3 acts; or

   (b) any person who is able to present the goods in question or to have them presented to the competent customs authority; or

   (c) a representative of one of the persons referred to in paragraph 3 or points (a) or (b).

5. The person referred to in paragraphs 3 and 4 shall, at his request, be authorised to amend one or more particulars of the summary declaration after it has been lodged. However, no amendment shall be possible after the customs authorities:

   (a) have informed the person who lodged the summary declaration that they intend to examine the goods; or

   (b) have established that the particulars in questions are incorrect; or

   (c) have allowed the removal of the goods.

Article 36c

1.   The customs office of entry may waive the lodging of a summary declaration in respect of goods for which, before expiry of the time limit referred to in Article 36a(3) or (4), a customs declaration is lodged. In such case, the customs declaration shall contain at least the particulars necessary for a summary declaration and, until such time as the former is accepted in accordance with Article 63, it shall have the status of a summary declaration.

Customs authorities may allow the customs declaration to be lodged at a customs office of import different from the customs office of entry, provided that this office immediately communicates or makes available electronically the necessary particulars to the customs office of entry.

2.   Where the customs declaration is lodged other than by use of data processing technique, the customs authorities shall apply the same level of risk management to the data as that applied to customs declarations made using a data processing technique.';

7.   in Article 37(1) 'control by the customs authority' shall be replaced by 'customs controls' and in Article 38(3) 'the control of the customs authority of' shall be replaced by 'customs controls by';

8.   Article 38(5) shall be replaced by the following:

'5.   Paragraphs 1 to 4 and Articles 36a to 36c and 39 to 53 shall not apply to goods which temporarily leave the customs territory of the Community while moving between two points in that territory by sea or air, provided that the carriage is effected by a direct route and by regular air or shipping services without a stop outside the customs territory of the Community.';

9.   Article 40 shall be replaced by the following:

'Article 40

Goods entering the customs territory of the Community shall be presented to customs by the person who brings them into that territory or, if appropriate, by the person who assumes responsibility for carriage of the goods following such entry, with the exception of goods carried on means of transport only passing through the territorial waters or the airspace of the customs territory of the Community without a stop within this territory. The person presenting the goods shall make a reference to the summary declaration or customs declaration previously lodged in respect of the goods.';

10.   in Title III, Chapter 3 shall be re-titled 'Unloading of goods presented to customs';

11.   Articles 43 to 45 shall be deleted;

12.   Article 170(2) shall be replaced by the following:

'2.   Goods shall be presented to the customs authorities and undergo the prescribed customs formalities where:

   (a)   they have been placed under a customs procedure which is discharged when they enter a free zone or free warehouse; however, where the customs procedure in question permits exemption from the obligation to present goods, such presentation shall not be required;

   (b)   they have been placed in a free zone or free warehouse on the basis of a decision to grant repayment or remission of import duties;

   (c)   they qualify for the measures referred to in Article 166(b);

   (d)   they enter a free zone or free warehouse directly from outside the customs territory of the Community.';

13.   Article 176(2) shall be replaced by the following:

   '2.   Where goods are transhipped within a free zone, the records relating to the operation shall be kept at the disposal of the customs authorities. The short-term storage of goods in connection with such transhipment shall be considered to be an integral part of the operation.

   For goods brought into a free zone directly from outside the customs territory of the Community or out of a free zone directly leaving the customs territory of the Community, a summary declaration shall be lodged in accordance with Articles 36a to 36c or 182a to 182d, as appropriate.';

14.   Article 181 shall be replaced by the following:

'Article 181

The customs authorities shall satisfy themselves that the rules governing exportation, outward processing, re-exportation, suspensive procedures or the internal transit procedure, as well as the provisions of Title V, are respected where goods are to leave the customs territory of the Community from a free zone or free warehouse.';

15.   in Article 182(3), first sentence, 'Re-exportation or' shall be deleted;

16.   under Title V (Goods leaving the customs territory of the Community) the following Articles shall be inserted:

'Article 182a

1.   Goods leaving the customs territory of the Community, with the exception of goods carried on means of transport only passing through the territorial waters or the airspace of the customs territory without a stop within this territory, shall be covered either by a customs declaration or, where a customs declaration is not required, a summary declaration.

2.   The committee procedure shall be used to establish:

-        the time limit by which the customs declaration or a summary declaration is to be lodged at the customs office of export before the goods are brought out of the customs territory of the Community,

-        the rules for exceptions from and variations to the time limit referred to above,

-        the conditions under which the requirement for a summary declaration may be waived or adapted, and

-        the cases in which and the conditions under which goods leaving the customs territory of the Community are not subject to either a customs declaration or a summary declaration,

in accordance with the specific circumstances and for particular types of goods traffic, modes of transport and economic operators and where international agreements provide for special security arrangements.

Article 182b

1.   Where goods leaving the customs territory of the Community are assigned to a customs approved treatment or use for the purpose of which a customs declaration is required under the customs rules, this customs declaration shall be lodged at the customs office of export before the goods are to be brought out of the customs territory of the Community.

2.   Where the customs office of export is different from the customs office of exit, the customs office of export shall immediately communicate or make available electronically the necessary particulars to the customs office of exit.

3.   The customs declaration shall contain at least the particulars necessary for the summary declaration referred to in Article 182d(1).

4.   Where the customs declaration is made other than by use of a data processing technique, the customs authorities shall apply the same level of risk management to the data as that applied to customs declarations made using a data processing technique.

Article 182c

1.   Where goods leaving the customs territory of the Community are not assigned to a customs approved treatment or use for which a customs declaration is required, a summary declaration shall be lodged at the customs office of exit before the goods are to be brought out of the customs territory of the Community.

2.   Customs authorities may allow the summary declaration to be lodged at another customs office, provided that this office

immediately communicates or makes available electronically the necessary particulars to the customs office of exit.

3. Customs authorities may accept, instead of the lodging of a summary declaration, the lodging of a notification and access to the summary declaration data in the economic operator's computer system.

Article 182d

1. The committee procedure shall be used to establish a common data set and format for the summary declaration, containing the particulars necessary for risk analysis and the proper application of customs controls, primarily for security and safety purposes, using, where appropriate, international standards and commercial practices.

2. The summary declaration shall be made using a data processing technique. Commercial, port or transport information may be used, provided that it contains the necessary particulars.

    Customs authorities may accept paper-based summary declarations in exceptional circumstances, provided that they apply the same level of risk management as that applied to summary declarations made using a data processing technique.

3. The summary declaration shall be lodged by:

    (a) the person who brings the goods, or who assumes responsibility for the carriage of the goods, out of the customs territory of the Community; or

    (b) any person who is able to present the goods in question or to have them presented to the competent customs authority; or

    (c) a representative of one of the persons referred to in points (a) or (b).

4. The person referred to in paragraph 3 shall, at his request, be authorised to amend one or more particulars of the summary declaration after it has been lodged. However, no amendment shall be possible after the customs authorities:

    (a) have informed the person who lodged the summary declaration that they intend to examine the goods; or

    (b) have established that the particulars in questions are incorrect; or

    (c) have allowed the removal of the goods.'

Article 2

This Regulation shall enter into force on the seventh day following its publication in the *Official Journal of the European Union*.

Article 5a(2), Article 13(2) 2nd subparagraph, Article 36a(4), Article 36b(1), Article 182a(2) and Article 182d(1) shall be applicable from 11 May 2005.

All other provisions shall be applicable once the implementing provisions on the basis of the Articles referred to in the second subparagraph have entered into force. However, electronic declaration and automated systems for the implementation of risk management and for the electronic exchange of data between customs offices of entry, import, export and exit, as stipulated in Articles 13, 36a, 36b, 36c, 182b, 182c and 182d, shall be in place three years after these Articles have become applicable.

Not later than two years after these Articles have become applicable, the Commission shall evaluate any request from Member States for an extension of the three-year period referred to in the third subparagraph for electronic declaration and automated systems for the implementation of risk management and for the electronic exchange of data between customs offices. The Commission shall submit a report to the European Parliament and to the Council and propose, where appropriate, an extension of the three-year period referred to in the third subparagraph.

This Regulation shall be binding in its entirety and directly applicable in all Member States.

Done at Strasbourg, 13 April 2005.
For the European Parliament
The President
J. P. BORRELL FONTELLES
For the Council
The President
N. SCHMIT

COMMISSION REGULATION (EC) No 750/2005

of 18 May 2005

on the nomenclature of countries and territories for the external trade statistics of the Community and statistics of trade between Member States

Official Journal L 126, 19/05/2005, p. 0012 - 0021

THE COMMISSION OF THE EUROPEAN COMMUNITIES,

Having regard to the Treaty establishing the European Community,
Having regard to Council Regulation (EC) No 1172/95 of 22 May 1995 relating to the trading of goods by the Community and its Member States with non-member countries, and in particular Article 9 thereof,

Whereas:

(1)   Commission Regulation (EC) No 2081/2003 of 27 November 2003 on the nomenclature of countries and territories for the external trade statistics of the Community and statistics of trade between Member States set out the version valid on 1 January 2004.

(2)   The alphabetical coding of countries and territories is based on the ISO alpha standard 2 in force as far as it is compatible with the requirements of Community legislation.

(3)   It is necessary to identify separately Serbia, Montenegro and Kosovo (as defined by United Nations Security Council Resolution 1244 of 10 June 1999) for the management of agreements concluded between the European Community and some of those territories on trade in textile products. As well, the conditions laid down in the relevant Community provisions regarding the declaration of the origin of the goods in trade with non-members countries require the creation of a specific code for determining the Community origin of goods.

(4)   It is therefore appropriate to draw up a new version of this nomenclature that takes into account those new items as well as changes affecting some codes.

(5)   It is preferable to provide for a transition period to allow certain Member States to adapt to the amendments made to the Community legislation regarding the end of the use of numerical codes; it is essential for purposes of simplification for this transition period to end when the provisions revising the rules on the Single Administrative Document come into force.

(6)   The measures provided for in this Regulation are in accordance with the opinion of the Committee on Statistics relating to the Trading of Goods with Non-Member Countries,

HAS ADOPTED THIS REGULATION:

Article 1

The version valid from 1 June 2005 of the nomenclature of countries and territories for the external trade statistics of the Community and statistics of trade between Member States is set out in the Annex hereto.

Article 2

This Regulation shall enter into force on 1 June 2005.

However, the Member States may use the three-digit numeric codes also shown in the Annex to the Regulation until the provisions revising Annexes 37 and 38 of Commission Regulation (EEC) No 2454/93 come into force.

This Regulation shall be binding in its entirely and directly applicable in all Member States.

Done at Brussels, 18 May 2005.

For the Commission
Joaquín ALMUNIA
Member of the Commission

ANNEX

NOMENCLATURE OF COUNTRIES AND TERRITORIES FOR THE EXTERNAL TRADE STATISTICS OF THE COMMUNITY AND STATISTICS OF TRADE BETWEEN MEMBER STATES

(Version valid with effect from 1 June 2005)

Code			
Alphabetical	Numerical	Text	Description
AD	(043)	Andorra	
AE	(647)	United Arab Emirates	Abu Dhabi, Ajman, Dubai, Fujairah, Ras al Khaimah, Sharjah and Umm al Qaiwain
AF	(660)	Afghanistan	
AG	(459)	Antigua and Barbuda	
AI	(446)	Anguilla	
AL	(070)	Albania	
AM	(077)	Armenia	
AN	(478)	Netherlands Antilles	Bonaire, Curaçao, Saba, St Eustatius and southern part of St Martin
AO	(330)	Angola	Including Cabinda

Code		Text	Description
Alphabetical	**Numerical**		
AQ	(891)	Antarctica	Territory south of 60° south latitude; not including the French Southern Territories (TF), Bouvet Island (BV), South Georgia and South Sandwich Islands (GS)
AR	(528)	Argentina	
AS	(830)	American Samoa	
AT	(038)	Austria	
AU	(800)	Australia	
AW	(474)	Aruba	
AZ	(078)	Azerbaijan	
BA	(093)	Bosnia and Herzegovina	
BB	(469)	Barbados	
BD	(666)	Bangladesh	
BE	(017)	Belgium	
BF	(236)	Burkina Faso	
BG	(068)	Bulgaria	
BH	(640)	Bahrain	
BI	(328)	Burundi	
BJ	(284)	Benin	
BM	(413)	Bermuda	
BN	(703)	Brunei Darussalam	Often referred to as Brunei
BO	(516)	Bolivia	
BR	(508)	Brazil	
BS	(453)	Bahamas	
BT	(675)	Bhutan	
BV	(892)	Bouvet Island	
BW	(391)	Botswana	
BY	(073)	Belarus	Often referred to as Belorussia
BZ	(421)	Belize	
CA	(404)	Canada	

Code			
Alphabetical	Numerical	Text	Description
CC	(833)	Cocos Islands (or Keeling Islands)	
CD	(322)	Congo, Democratic Republic of	Formerly Zaire
CF	(306)	Central African Republic	
CG	(318)	Congo	
CH	(039)	Switzerland	Including the German territory of Büsingen and the Italian municipality of Campione d'Italia
CI	(272)	Côte d'Ivoire	Often referred to as Ivory Coast
CK	(837)	Cook Islands	
CL	(512)	Chile	
CM	(302)	Cameroon	
CN	(720)	China, People's Republic of	Often referred to as China
CO	(480)	Colombia	
CR	(436)	Costa Rica	
CU	(448)	Cuba	
CV	(247)	Cape Verde	
CX	(834)	Christmas Island	
CY	(600)	Cyprus	
CZ	(061)	Czech Republic	
DE	(004)	Germany	Including the island of Heligoland; excluding the territory of Büsingen
DJ	(338)	Djibouti	
DK	(008)	Denmark	
DM	(460)	Dominica	
DO	(456)	Dominican Republic	
DZ	(208)	Algeria	
EC	(500)	Ecuador	Including Galápagos Islands
EE	(053)	Estonia	
EG	(220)	Egypt	

Code			
Alphabetical	**Numerical**	**Text**	**Description**
ER	(336)	Eritrea	
ES	(011)	Spain	Including Balearic Islands and Canary Islands; excluding Ceuta and Melilla
ET	(334)	Ethiopia	
FI	(032)	Finland	Including Åland Islands
FJ	(815)	Fiji	
FK	(529)	Falkland Islands	
FM	(823)	Micronesia, Federated States of	Chuuk, Kosrae, Pohnpei and Yap
FO	(041)	Faroe Islands	
FR	(001)	France	Including Monaco and the French overseas departments (French Guiana, Guadeloupe, Martinique and Réunion)
GA	(314)	Gabon	
GB	(006)	United Kingdom	Great Britain, Northern Ireland, Channel Islands and Isle of Man
GD	(473)	Grenada	Including Southern Grenadines
GE	(076)	Georgia	
GH	(276)	Ghana	
GI	(044)	Gibraltar	
GL	(406)	Greenland	
GM	(252)	Gambia	
GN	(260)	Guinea	
GQ	(310)	Equatorial Guinea	
GR	(009)	Greece	
GS	(893)	South Georgia and South Sandwich Islands	
GT	(416)	Guatemala	
GU	(831)	Guam	
GW	(257)	Guinea-Bissau	

Code			
Alphabetical	**Numerical**	**Text**	**Description**
GY	(488)	Guyana	
HK	(740)	Hong Kong	Hong Kong Special Administrative Region of the People's Republic of China
HM	(835)	Heard Island and McDonald Islands	
HN	(424)	Honduras	Including Swan Islands
HR	(092)	Croatia	
HT	(452)	Haiti	
HU	(064)	Hungary	
ID	(700)	Indonesia	
IE	(007)	Ireland	
IL	(624)	Israel	
IN	(664)	India	
IO	(357)	British Indian Ocean Territory	Chagos Archipelago
IQ	(612)	Iraq	
IR	(616)	Iran, Islamic Republic of	
IS	(024)	Iceland	
IT	(005)	Italy	Including Livigno; excluding the municipality of Campione d'Italia
JM	(464)	Jamaica	
JO	(628)	Jordan	
JP	(732)	Japan	
KE	(346)	Kenya	
KG	(083)	Kyrgyz, Republic	
KH	(696)	Cambodia	
KI	(812)	Kiribati	
KM	(375)	Comoros	Anjouan, Grande Comore and Mohéli
KN	(449)	St Kitts and Nevis	
KP	(724)	Korea, Democratic People's Republic of	Often referred to as North Korea

Code		Text	Description
Alphabetical	Numerical		
KR	(728)	Korea, Republic of	Often referred to as South Korea
KW	(636)	Kuwait	
KY	(463)	Cayman Islands	
KZ	(079)	Kazakhstan	
LA	(684)	Lao People's Democratic Republic	Often referred to as Laos
LB	(604)	Lebanon	
LC	(465)	St Lucia	
LI	(037)	Liechtenstein	
LK	(669)	Sri Lanka	
LR	(268)	Liberia	
LS	(395)	Lesotho	
LT	(055)	Lithuania	
LU	(018)	Luxembourg	
LV	(054)	Latvia	
LY	(216)	Libyan Arab Jamahiriya	Often referred to as Libya
MA	(204)	Morocco	
MD	(074)	Moldova, Republic of	
MG	(370)	Madagascar	
MH	(824)	Marshall Islands	
MK[1]	(096)	Former Yugoslav Republic of Macedonia	
ML	(232)	Mali	
MM	(676)	Myanmar	Often referred to as Burma
MN	(716)	Mongolia	
MO	(743)	Macao	Special Administrative Region of the People's Republic of China
MP	(820)	Northern Mariana Islands	
MR	(228)	Mauritania	
MS	(470)	Montserrat	

Code			
Alphabetical	Numerical	Text	Description
MT	(046)	Malta	Including Gozo and Comino
MU	(373)	Mauritius	Mauritius, Rodrigues Island, Agalega Islands and Cargados Carajos Shoals (St Brandon Islands)
MV	(667)	Maldives	
MW	(386)	Malawi	
MX	(412)	Mexico	
MY	(701)	Malaysia	Peninsular Malaysia and Eastern Malaysia (Labuan, Sabah and Sarawak)
MZ	(366)	Mozambique	
NA	(389)	Namibia	
NC	(809)	New Caledonia	Including Loyalty Islands (Lifou, Maré and Ouvéa)
NE	(240)	Niger	
NF	(836)	Norfolk Island	
NG	(288)	Nigeria	
NI	(432)	Nicaragua	Including Corn Islands
NL	(003)	Netherlands	
NO	(028)	Norway	Including Svalbard Archipelago and Jan Mayen Island
NP	(672)	Nepal	
NR	(803)	Nauru	
NU	(838)	Niue	
NZ	(804)	New Zealand	Excluding Ross Dependency (Antarctica)
OM	(649)	Oman	
PA	(442)	Panama	Including former Canal Zone
PE	(504)	Peru	
PF	(822)	French Polynesia	Marquesas Islands, Society Islands (including Tahiti), Tuamotu Islands, Gambier Islands and Austral Islands. Also Clipperton Island

Code			
Alphabetical	**Numerical**	**Text**	**Description**
PG	(801)	Papua New Guinea	Eastern part of New Guinea; Bismarck Archipelago (including New Britain, New Ireland, Lavongai (New Hanover) and Admiralty Islands); Northern Solomon Islands (Bougainville and Buka); Trobriand Islands, Woodlark Island; d'Entrecasteaux Islands and Louisiade Archipelago
PH	(708)	Philippines	
PK	(662)	Pakistan	
PL	(060)	Poland	
PM	(408)	St Pierre and Miquelon	
PN	(813)	Pitcairn	Including the Ducie, Henderson and Oeno Islands
PS	(625)	Occupied Palestinian Territory	West Bank (including East Jerusalem) and Gaza Strip
PT	(010)	Portugal	Including Azores and Madeira
PW	(825)	Palau	
PY	(520)	Paraguay	
QA	(644)	Qatar	
RO	(066)	Romania	
RU	(075)	Russian Federation	Often referred to as Russia
RW	(324)	Rwanda	
SA	(632)	Saudi Arabia	
SB	(806)	Solomon Islands	
SC	(355)	Seychelles	Mahé Island, Praslin Island, La Digue, Frégate and Silhouette; Amirante Islands (including Desroches, Alphonse, Platte and Coëtivy); Farquhar Islands (including Providence); Aldabra Islands and Cosmoledo Islands

Code			
Alphabetical	Numerical	Text	Description
SD	(224)	Sudan	
SE	(030)	Sweden	
SG	(706)	Singapore	
SH	(329)	Saint Helena	Including Ascension Island and Tristan da Cunha Islands
SI	(091)	Slovenia	
SK	(063)	Slovakia	
SL	(264)	Sierra Leone	
SM	(047)	San Marino	
SN	(248)	Senegal	
SO	(342)	Somalia	
SR	(492)	Suriname	
ST	(311)	Sao Tome and Principe	
SV	(428)	El Salvador	
SY	(608)	Syrian Arab Republic	Often referred to as Syria
SZ	(393)	Swaziland	
TC	(454)	Turks and Caicos Islands	
TD	(244)	Chad	
TF	(894)	French Southern Territories	Including Kerguélen Islands, Amsterdam Island, Saint-Paul Island, Crozet Archipelago
TG	(280)	Togo	
TH	(680)	Thailand	
TJ	(082)	Tajikistan	
TK	(839)	Tokelau	
TL	(626)	Timor-Leste	
TM	(080)	Turkmenistan	
TN	(212)	Tunisia	
TO	(817)	Tonga	
TR	(052)	Turkey	
TT	(472)	Trinidad and Tobago	
TV	(807)	Tuvalu	

| Code | | Text | Description |
Alphabetical	Numerical		
TW	(736)	Taiwan	Separate customs territory of Taiwan, Penghu, Kinmen and Matsu
TZ	(352)	Tanzania, United Republic of	Tanganyika, Zanzibar Island and Pemba
UA	(072)	Ukraine	
UG	(350)	Uganda	
UM	(832)	United States Minor Outlying Islands	Including Baker Island, Howland Island, Jarvis Island, Johnston Atoll, Kingman Reef, Midway Islands, Navassa Island, Palmyra Atoll and Wake Island
US	(400)	United States	Including Puerto Rico
UY	(524)	Uruguay	
UZ	(081)	Uzbekistan	
VA	(045)	Holy See (Vatican City State)	
VC	(467)	St Vincent and the Grenadines	
VE	(484)	Venezuela	
VG	(468)	Virgin Islands, British	
VI	(457)	Virgin Islands, U.S.	
VN	(690)	Vietnam	
VU	(816)	Vanuatu	
WF	(811)	Wallis and Futuna	Including Alofi Island
WS	(819)	Samoa	Formerly known as Western Samoa
XC	(021)	Ceuta	
XK	(095)	Kosovo	As defined by United Nations Security Council Resolution 1244 of 10 June 1999
XL	(023)	Melilla	Including Peñón de Vélez de la Gomera, Peñón de Alhucemas and Chafarinas Islands
XM	(097)	Montenegro	

Code			
Alphabetical	Numerical	Text	Description
XS	(098)	Serbia	
YE	(653)	Yemen	Formerly North Yemen and South Yemen
YT	(377)	Mayotte	Grande-Terre and Pamandzi
ZA	(388)	South Africa	
ZM	(378)	Zambia	
ZW	(382)	Zimbabwe	

Miscellaneous

Code			
Alphabetical	Numerical	Text	Description
EU	(999)	European Community	Code reserved, in trade with non-member countries, for the declaration of the origin of goods according to the conditions laid down in the relevant Community provisions. Code not to be used for statistical purposes
QQ or	(950)	Stores and provisions	Optional heading
QR	(951)	Stores and provisions within the framework of intra-Community trade	Optional heading
QS	(952)	Stores and provisions within the framework of trade with third countries	Optional heading
QU or	(958)	Countries and territories not specified	Optional heading
QV	(959)	Countries and territories not specified in the framework of intra-Community trade	Optional heading
QW	(960)	Countries and territories not specified within the framework of trade with third countries	Optional heading

Code		Text	Description
Alphabetical	**Numerical**		
QX or	(977)	Countries and territories not specified for commercial or military reasons	Optional heading
QY	(978)	Countries and territories not specified for commercial or military reasons in the framework of intra-Community trade	Optional heading
QZ	(979)	Countries and territories not specified for commercial or military reasons in the framework of trade with third countries	Optional heading

[1] Provisional Code that does not affect the definitive denomination of the country to be attributed after the conclusion of the negotiations currently taking place in the United Nations.

COMMISSION REGULATION (EC) No 1283/2005

of 3 August 2005

amending Annex I to Council Regulation (EC) No 866/2004 on a regime under Article 2 of Protocol No 10 to the Act of Accession

Official Journal L 203, 04/08/2005, p. 0008 - 0008

THE COMMISSION OF THE EUROPEAN COMMUNITIES,

Having regard to the Treaty establishing the European Community,

Having regard to Protocol No 10 on Cyprus to the Act concerning the conditions of accession of the Czech Republic, the Republic of Estonia, the Republic of Cyprus, the Republic of Latvia, the Republic of Lithuania, the Republic of Hungary, the Republic of Malta, the Republic of Poland, the Republic of Slovenia and the Slovak Republic and the adjustments to the Treaties on which the European Union is founded,

Having regard to Council Regulation (EC) No 866/2004 of 29 April 2004 on a regime under Article 2 of Protocol No 10 to the Act of Accession, and in particular Article 9 thereof,

Whereas:

(1) Annex I to Council Regulation (EC) No 866/2004 lays down a list of crossing points at which persons and goods may cross the line between the areas under the effective control of the Government of the Republic of Cyprus and those areas in which the Government of the Republic of Cyprus does not exercise effective control.

(2) Following agreement on the opening of new crossing points in Kato Pyrgos and Kokkina, it is necessary to adapt Annex I.

(3) The Government of the Republic of Cyprus gave its agreement to this adaptation.

(4) The Turkish Cypriot Chamber of Commerce was consulted on this matter,

HAS ADOPTED THIS REGULATION:

Article 1

Annex I to Regulation (EC) No 866/2004 is replaced by the following:

'ANNEX I

List of crossing points referred to in Article 2(4)

— Agios Dhometios

— Astromeritis — Zodhia

— Kato Pyrgos — Karavostasi

— Kato Pyrgos — Kokkina

— Kokkina — Pachyammos

- Ledra Palace

- Ledra Street'.

Article 2

This Regulation shall enter into force on the third day following that of its publication in the *Official Journal of the European Union*.

This Regulation shall be binding in its entirety and directly applicable in all Member States.

Done at Brussels, 3 August 2005.
For the Commission
Olli REHN
Member of the Commission

COUNCIL REGULATION (EC) No 1777/2005

of 17 October 2005

laying down implementing measures for Directive 77/388/EEC on the common system of value added tax

Official Journal L 288, 29/10/2005, p. 0001 - 0009

THE COUNCIL OF THE EUROPEAN UNION,

Having regard to the Treaty establishing the European Community,

Having regard to the Sixth Council Directive 77/388/EEC of 17 May 1977 on the harmonisation of the laws of the Member States relating to turnover taxes — Common system of value added tax: uniform basis of assessment, hereinafter referred to as 'Directive 77/388/EEC', and in particular Article 29a thereof,

Having regard to the proposal from the Commission,

Whereas:

(1) Directive 77/388/EEC contains rules on value added tax which, in some cases, are subject to interpretation by the Member States. The adoption of common provisions implementing Directive 77/388/EEC should ensure that application of the value added tax system complies more fully with the objective of the internal market, in cases where divergences in application have arisen or may arise which are incompatible with the proper functioning of the said market. These implementing measures are legally binding only from the date of the entry into force of this Regulation and are without prejudice to the validity of the legislation and interpretation previously adopted by the Member States.

(2) It is necessary for the achievement of the basic objective of ensuring a more uniform application of the current value added tax system to lay down rules implementing Directive 77/388/EEC, in particular in respect of taxable persons, the supply of goods and services, and the place of their supply. In accordance with the principle of proportionality as set out in the third subparagraph of Article 5 of the Treaty, this Regulation does not go beyond what is necessary in order to achieve the objective pursued. Since it is binding and directly applicable in all Member States, uniformity of application will be best ensured by a Regulation.

(3) These implementing provisions contain specific rules in response to selective questions of application and are designed to bring uniform treatment throughout the Community to those specific circumstances only. They are therefore not conclusive for other cases and, in view of their formulation, are to be applied restrictively.

(4) The further integration of the internal market has led to an increased need for cooperation by economic operators established in different Member States across internal borders and the development of European economic interest groupings (EEIGs), constituted in accordance with Regulation (EEC) No 2137/85, it should therefore be provided that such

EEIGs are also taxable persons where they supply goods or services for consideration.

(5) The sale of an option as a financial instrument should be treated as a supply of services separate from the underlying transactions to which the option relates.

(6) It is necessary, on the one hand, to establish that a transaction which consists solely of assembling the various parts of a machine provided by a customer must be considered as a supply of services, and, on the other hand, to establish the place of such supply.

(7) Where various services supplied in the framework of organising a funeral form a part of a single service, the rule on the place of supply should also be determined.

(8) Certain specific services such as the assignment of television broadcasting rights in respect of football matches, the translation of texts, services for claiming value added tax refunds, certain services as an agent, the hiring of means of transport and certain electronic services involve cross-border scenarios or even the participation of economic operators established in third countries. The place of supply of these services needs to be clearly determined in order to create greater legal certainty. It should be noted that the services identified as electronic services or otherwise do not constitute a definitive, exhaustive list.

(9) In certain specific circumstances a credit or debit card handling fee which is paid in connection with a transaction should not reduce the taxable amount for the latter.

(10) Vocational training or retraining should include instruction relating directly to a trade or profession as well as any instruction aimed at acquiring or updating knowledge for vocational purposes, regardless of the duration of a course.

(11) 'Platinum nobles' should be treated as being excluded from the exemptions for currency, bank notes and coins.

(12) Goods transported outside the Community by the purchaser thereof and used for the equipping, fuelling or provisioning of means of transport used for nonbusiness purposes by persons other than natural persons, such as bodies governed by public law and associations, should be excluded from the exemption for export transactions.

(13) To guarantee uniform administrative practices for the calculation of the minimum value for exemption on exportation of goods carried in the personal luggage of travellers, the provisions on such calculations should be harmonised.

(14) Electronic import documents should also be admitted to exercise the right to deduct, where they fulfil the same requirements as paper-based documents.

(15) Weights for investment gold which are definitely accepted by the bullion market should be named and a common date for establishing the value

of gold coins be determined to ensure equal treatment of economic operators.

(16) The special scheme for taxable persons not established in the Community, supplying electronic services to nontaxable persons established or resident within the Community is subject to certain conditions. Where those conditions are no longer fulfilled, the consequences thereof should, in particular, be made clear.

(17) In the case of intra-Community acquisition of goods, the right of the Member State of acquisition to tax the acquisition should remain unaffected by the value added tax treatment of the transaction in other Member States.

(18) Rules should be established to ensure the uniform treatment of supplies of goods once a supplier has exceeded the distance selling threshold for supplies to another Member State,

HAS ADOPTED THIS REGULATION:

CHAPTER I

SUBJECT MATTER

Article 1

This Regulation lays down measures for the implementation of Articles 4, 6, 9, 11, 13, 15, 18, 26b, 26c, 28a and 28b of Directive 77/388/EEC, and of Annex L thereto.

CHAPTER II

TAXABLE PERSONS AND TAXABLE TRANSACTIONS

SECTION 1

(Article 4 of Directive 77/388/EEC)

Article 2

A European Economic Interest Grouping (EEIG) constituted in accordance with Regulation (EEC) No 2137/85 which supplies goods or services for consideration to its members or to third parties shall be a taxable person within the meaning of Article 4(1) of Directive 77/388/EEC.

SECTION 2

(Article 6 of Directive 77/388/EEC)

Article 3

1. The sale of an option, where such a sale is a transaction within the scope of point (5) of Article 13(B)(d) of Directive 77/388/EEC, shall be a supply of services within the meaning of Article 6(1) of that Directive. That supply of services shall be distinct from the underlying operations to which the services relate.

2.   Where a taxable person only assembles the different parts of a machine all of which were provided to him by his customer, that transaction shall be a supply of services within the meaning of Article 6(1) of Directive 77/388/EEC.

CHAPTER III

PLACE OF TAXABLE TRANSACTIONS

SECTION 1

(Article 9(1) of Directive 77/388/EEC)

Article 4

Insofar as they constitute a single service, services supplied in the framework of organising a funeral shall fall within the scope of Article 9(1) of Directive 77/388/EEC.

SECTION 2

(Article 9(2) of Directive 77/388/EEC)

Article 5

Except where the goods being assembled become part of immovable property, the place of the supply of services specified in Article 3(2) of this Regulation shall be established in accordance with Article 9(2)(c) or Article 28b(F) of Directive 77/388/EEC.

Article 6

The service of translation of texts shall be covered by Article 9(2)(e) of Directive 77/388/EEC.

Article 7

Where a body established in a third country assigns television broadcasting rights in respect of football matches to taxable persons established in the Community, that transaction shall be covered by the first indent of Article 9(2)(e) of Directive 77/388/EEC.

Article 8

The supply of services which consist in applying for or receiving refunds under Directive 79/1072/EEC shall be covered by the third indent of Article 9(2)(e) of Directive 77/388/EEC.

Article 9

The supply of services of agents as referred to in the seventh indent of Article 9(2)(e) of Directive 77/388/EEC shall cover the services of agents acting in the name and for the account of the recipient of the service procured and services performed by the agents acting in the name and for the account of the provider of the service procured.

Article 10

Trailers and semi-trailers, as well as railway wagons, shall be forms of transport for the purposes of the eighth indent of Article 9(2)(e) of Directive 77/388/EEC.

Article 11

1.   'Electronically supplied services' as referred to in the 12th indent of Article 9(2)(e) of Directive 77/388/EEC and in Annex L to Directive 77/388/EEC shall include services which are delivered over the Internet or an electronic network and the nature of which renders their supply essentially automated and involving minimal human intervention, and in the absence of information technology is impossible to ensure.

2.   The following services, in particular, shall, where delivered over the Internet or an electronic network, be covered by paragraph 1:

    (a)   the supply of digitised products generally, including software and changes to or upgrades of software;

    (b)   services providing or supporting a business or personal presence on an electronic network such as a website or a webpage;

    (c)   services automatically generated from a computer via the Internet or an electronic network, in response to specific data input by the recipient;

    (d)   the transfer for consideration of the right to put goods or services up for sale on an Internet site operating as an online market on which potential buyers make their bids by an automated procedure and on which the parties are notified of a sale by electronic mail automatically generated from a computer;

    (e)   Internet Service Packages (ISP) of information in which the telecommunications component forms an ancillary and subordinate part (i.e. packages going beyond mere Internet access and including other elements such as content pages giving access to news, weather or travel reports; playgrounds; website hosting; access to online debates etc.);

    (f)   the services listed in Annex I.

Article 12

The following, in particular, shall not be covered by the 12th indent of Article 9(2)(e) of Directive 77/388/EEC:

1.   radio and television broadcasting services as referred to in the 11th indent of Article 9(2)(e) of Directive 77/388/EEC;

2.   telecommunications services, within the meaning of the 10th indent of Article 9(2)(e) of Directive 77/388/EEC;

3.   supplies of the following goods and services:

    (a)   goods, where the order and processing is done electronically;

(b)   CD-ROMs, floppy disks and similar tangible media;

(c)   printed matter, such as books, newsletters, newspapers or journals;

(d)   CDs, audio cassettes;

(e)   video cassettes, DVDs;

(f)   games on a CD-ROM;

(g)   services of professionals such as lawyers and financial consultants, who advise clients by e-mail;

(h)   teaching services, where the course content is delivered by a teacher over the Internet or an electronic network, (namely via a remote link);

(i)   offline physical repair services of computer equipment;

(j)   offline data warehousing services;

(k)   advertising services, in particular as in newspapers, on posters and on television;

(l)   telephone helpdesk services;

(m)   teaching services purely involving correspondence courses, such as postal courses;

(n)   conventional auctioneers' services reliant on direct human intervention, irrespective of how bids are made;

(o)   telephone services with a video component, otherwise known as videophone services;

(p)   access to the Internet and World Wide Web;

(q)   telephone services provided through the Internet.

CHAPTER IV

TAXABLE AMOUNT

(Article 11 of Directive 77/388/EEC)

Article 13

Where a supplier of goods or services, as a condition of accepting payment by credit or debit card, requires the customer to pay an amount to himself or another undertaking, and where the total price payable by that customer is unaffected irrespective of how payment is accepted, that amount shall constitute an integral part of the taxable amount for the supply of the goods or services, under Article 11 of Directive 77/388/EEC.

CHAPTER V

EXEMPTIONS

SECTION 1

(Article 13 of Directive 77/388/EEC)

Article 14

Vocational training or retraining services provided under the conditions set out in Article 13(A)(1)(i) of Directive 77/388/EEC shall include instruction relating directly to a trade or profession as well as any instruction aimed at acquiring or updating knowledge for vocational purposes. The duration of a vocational training or retraining course shall be irrelevant for this purpose.

Article 15

The exemption referred to in Article 13(B)(d)(4) of Directive 77/388/EEC shall not apply to platinum nobles.

SECTION 2

(Article 15 of directive 77/388/EEC)

Article 16

'Means of transport for private use' as referred to in the first subparagraph of Article 15(2) of Directive 77/388/EEC shall include means of transport used for non-business purposes by persons other than natural persons, such as bodies governed by public law within the meaning of Article 4(5) of that Directive and associations.

Article 17

In order to determine whether the threshold set by a Member State in accordance with the third indent of the second subparagraph of Article 15(2) of Directive 77/388/EEC has been exceeded, the calculation shall be based on the invoice value. The aggregate value of several goods may be used only if all those goods are included on the same invoice issued by the same taxable person supplying goods to the same customer.

CHAPTER VI

DEDUCTIONS

(Article 18 of Directive 77/388/EEC)

Article 18

Where the importing Member State has introduced an electronic system for completing customs formalities, the expression 'import document' as referred to in Article 18(1)(b) of Directive 77/388/EEC shall cover electronic versions of such documents, provided that they allow for the exercise of the right of deduction to be checked.

CHAPTER VII

SPECIAL SCHEMES

(Articles 26b and 26c of Directive 77/388/EEC)

Article 19

1.   'Weights accepted by the bullion markets' as referred to in Article 26b(A) (i), first paragraph, of Directive 77/388/EEC shall at least cover the units and the weights traded as set out in Annex II to this Regulation.

2.   For the purposes of establishing the list referred to in the third subparagraph of Article 26b(A) of Directive 77/388/EEC, 'price' and 'open market value' as referred to in the fourth indent of point (ii) of the first subparagraph shall be the price and open market value on 1 April of each year. If 1 April does not fall on a day on which those values are fixed, the values of the next day on which they are fixed shall be used.

Article 20

1.   Where, in the course of a calendar quarter, a non-established taxable person using the special scheme provided for in Article 26c(B) of Directive 77/388/EEC meets at least one of the criteria for exclusion laid down in Article 26c(B)(4), the Member State of identification shall exclude that non-established taxable person from the special scheme. In such cases the non-established taxable person may subsequently be excluded from the special scheme at any time during that quarter.

    In respect of electronic services supplied prior to exclusion but during the calendar quarter in which exclusion occurs, the non-established taxable person shall submit a return for the entire quarter in accordance with Article 26c(B)(5) of Directive 77/388/EEC. The requirement to submit this return shall have no effect on the requirement, if any, to register under the normal rules in a Member State.

2.   A Member State of identification which receives a payment in excess of that resulting from the return submitted under Article 26c(B)(5) of Directive 77/388/EEC shall reimburse the overpaid amount directly to the taxable person concerned.

    Where the Member State of identification has received an amount pursuant to a return subsequently found to be incorrect, and that Member State has already distributed that amount among the Member States of consumption, those Member States shall directly reimburse the overpayment to the non-established taxable person and inform the Member State of identification of the adjustment to be made.

3.   Any return period (quarter) within the meaning of Article 26c(B)(5) of Directive 77/388/EEC shall be a separate return period.

    Once a return under Article 26c(B)(5) of Directive 77/388/EEC has been rendered, any subsequent changes to the figures contained therein may be made only by means of an amendment to that return and not by an adjustment to a subsequent return.

Amounts of value added tax paid under Article 26c(B)(7) of Directive 77/388/EEC shall be specific to that return. Any subsequent amendments to the amounts paid may be effected only by reference to that return and may not be allocated to another return, or adjusted on a subsequent return.

4.   Amounts on value added tax returns made under the special scheme provided for in Article 26c(B) of Directive 77/388/EEC shall not be rounded up or down to the nearest whole monetary unit. The exact amount of value added tax shall be reported and remitted.

CHAPTER VIII

TRANSITIONAL MEASURES

(Articles 28a and 28b of Directive 77/388/EEC)

Article 21

Where an intra-Community acquisition of goods within the meaning of Article 28a of Directive 77/388/EEC has taken place, the Member State in which the dispatch or transport ends shall exercise its power of taxation irrespective of the VAT treatment applied to the transaction in the Member State in which the dispatch or transport began.

Any request by a supplier of goods for a correction in the tax invoiced by him and reported by him to the Member State where the dispatch or transport of the goods began shall be treated by that State in accordance with its own domestic rules.

Article 22

Where in the course of a calendar year the threshold applied by a Member State in accordance with Article 28b(B)(2) of Directive 77/388/EEC is exceeded, Article 28b(B) of that Directive shall not modify the place of supplies of goods other than products subject to excise duty carried out in the course of the same calendar year which are made before the threshold applied by the Member State for the calendar year then current is exceeded provided that the supplier:

(a)   has not exercised the option under Article 28b(B)(3) of that Directive and

(b)   did not exceed the threshold in the course of the preceding calendar year.

However, Article 28b(B) of Directive 77/388/EEC shall modify the place of the following supplies to the Member State in which the dispatch or transport ends:

(a)   the supply by which the threshold applied by the Member State for the calendar year then current was exceeded in the course of the same calendar year;

(b)   any subsequent supplies within that Member State in that calendar year;

(c)   supplies within that Member State in the calendar year following the calendar year in which the event referred to in point (a) occurred.

CHAPTER IX

FINAL PROVISIONS

Article 23

This Regulation shall enter into force on 1 July 2006.

Article 13 shall be applicable from 1 January 2006.

This Regulation shall be binding in its entirety and directly applicable in all Member States.

Done at Luxembourg, 17 October 2005.

For the Council
The President
M. BECKETT

ANNEX I

Article 11 of this Regulation

1.   Item 1 of Annex L to Directive 77/388/EEC

    (a)   Website hosting and webpage hosting

    (b)   Automated, online and distance maintenance of programmes

    (c)   Remote systems administration

    (d)   Online data warehousing where specific data is stored and retrieved electronically

    (e)   Online supply of on-demand disc space.

2.   Item 2 of Annex L to Directive 77/388/EEC

    (a)   Accessing or downloading software (including procurement/ accountancy programmes and anti-virus software) plus updates

    (b)   Software to block banner adverts showing, otherwise known as Bannerblockers

    (c)   Download drivers, such as software that interfaces computers with peripheral equipment (such as printers)

    (d)   Online automated installation of filters on websites

    (e)   Online automated installation of firewalls.

3.   Item 3 of Annex L to Directive 77/388/EEC

    (a)   Accessing or downloading desktop themes

(b)   Accessing or downloading photographic or pictorial images or screensavers

(c)   The digitised content of books and other electronic publications

(d)   Subscription to online newspapers and journals

(e)   Weblogs and website statistics

(f)   Online news, traffic information and weather reports

(g)   Online information generated automatically by software from specific data input by the customer, such as legal and financial data, (in particular such data as continually updated stock market data, in real time)

(h)   The provision of advertising space including banner ads on a website/web page

(i)   Use of search engines and Internet directories.

4.   Item 4 of Annex L to Directive 77/388/EEC

(a)   Accessing or downloading of music on to computers and mobile phones

(b)   Accessing or downloading of jingles, excerpts, ringtones, or other sounds

(c)   Accessing or downloading of films

(d)   Downloading of music on to computers and mobile phones

(e)   Accessing automated online games which are dependent on the Internet, or other similar electronic networks, where players are geographically remote from one another.

5.   Item 5 of Annex L to Directive 77/388/EEC

(a)   Automated distance teaching dependent on the Internet or similar electronic network to function and the supply of which requires limited or no human intervention, including virtual classrooms, except where the Internet or similar electronic network is used as a tool simply for communication between the teacher and student

(b)   Workbooks completed by pupils online and marked automatically, without human intervention.

ANNEX II

Article 19 of this Regulation

Unit	Weights traded
Kg	12,5/1
Gram	500/250/100/50/20/10/5/2,5/2
Ounce (1 oz = 31,1035 g)	100/10/5/1/½/¼
Tael (1 tael = 1,193 oz.) [1]	10/5/1
Tola (10 tolas = 3,75 oz.) [2]	10

[1] Tael = a traditional Chinese unit of weight. The nominal fineness of a Hong Kong tael bar is 990 but in Taiwan 5 and 10 tael bars can be 999,9 fineness.

[2] Tola = a traditional Indian unit of weight for gold. The most popular sized bar is 10 tola, 999 fineness.

COUNCIL DIRECTIVE 2005/92/EC

of 12 December 2005

amending Directive 77/388/EEC with regard to the length of time during which the minimum standard rate of VAT is to be applied

Official Journal L345, 28.12.2005, p. 19 - 20

> This Directive was repealed by Council Directive 2006/112/EC of 28 November 2006 on the common system of value added tax, with effect from 1 January 2007

THE COUNCIL OF THE EUROPEAN UNION,

Having regard to the Treaty establishing the European Community, and in particular Article 93 thereof,

Having regard to the proposal from the Commission,

Having regard to the opinion of the European Parliament,

Having regard to the opinion of the European Economic and Social Committee,

Whereas:

(1) The second subparagraph of Article 12(3)(a) of the sixth Council Directive 77/388/EEC of 17 May 1977 on the harmonisation of the laws of the Member States relating to turnover taxes — Common system of value added tax: uniform basis of assessment, lays down that the Council shall decide on the level of the standard rate to be applied after 31 December 2005.

(2) The standard rate of value added tax (VAT) currently in force in the various Member States, combined with the mechanisms of the transitional system, has ensured that this system has functioned to an acceptable degree. It is nonetheless important to prevent a growing divergence in the standard rates of VAT applied by the Member States from leading to structural imbalances within the Community and distortions of competition in some sectors of activity.

(3) It is therefore appropriate to maintain the minimum standard rate at 15 % for a further period long enough to cover the ongoing implementation of the strategy to simplify and modernise current Community legislation on VAT.

(4) Directive 77/388/EEC should be amended accordingly,

HAS ADOPTED THIS DIRECTIVE:

Article 1

The first and second subparagraphs of Article 12(3)(a) of Directive 77/388/EEC shall be replaced by the following:

'The standard rate of value added tax shall be fixed by each Member State as a percentage of the taxable amount and shall be the same for the supply of goods and for the supply of services. From 1 January 2006 until 31 December 2010, the standard rate may not be less than 15 %.

The Council shall decide, in accordance with Article 93 of the Treaty, on the level of the standard rate to be applied after 31 December 2010.'

Article 2

1.   Member States shall bring into force the laws, regulations and administrative provisions necessary to comply with this Directive with effect from 1 January 2006. They shall forthwith inform the Commission thereof.

2.   When Member States adopt the measures, they shall contain a reference to this Directive or shall be accompanied by such a reference on the occasion of their official publication. The methods of making such reference shall be laid down by Member States.

3.   Member States shall communicate to the Commission the text of the provisions of national law which they adopt in the field covered by this Directive.

Article 3

This Directive shall enter into force on the day of its publication in the Official Journal of the European Union.

Article 4

This Directive is addressed to the Member States.

Done at Brussels, 12 December 2005.

For the Council
The President
J. STRAW

COUNCIL REGULATION (EC) No 2169/2005

of 21 December 2005

amending Regulation (EC) No 974/98 on the introduction of the euro

Official Journal L346, 29.12.2005, p. 01 - 05

THE COUNCIL OF THE EUROPEAN UNION,

Having regard to the Treaty establishing the European Community, and in particular to the third sentence of Article 123(4) thereof,

Having regard to the proposal from the Commission,

Having regard to the Opinion of the European Parliament,

Having regard to the Opinion of the European Central Bank,

Whereas:

(1) Council Regulation (EC) No 974/98 of 3 May 1998 on the introduction of the euro provides for the substitution of the euro for the currencies of the Member States which fulfilled the necessary conditions for the adoption of the single currency at the time when the Community entered the third stage of economic and monetary union. That Regulation also includes rules which apply to the national currency units of these Member States during the transitional period ending on 31 December 2001, and rules on banknotes and coins.

(2) Council Regulation (EC) No 2596/2000 amended Regulation (EC) No 974/98 to provide for the substitution of the euro for the currency of Greece.

(3) Regulation (EC) No 974/98 sets out a timetable for transition to the euro in the Member States currently participating. In order to provide clarity and certainty with regard to the rules governing the introduction of the euro in other Member States, it is necessary to lay down general provisions specifying how the various periods in the transition to the euro are to be determined in the future.

(4) It is appropriate to provide for a list of participating Member States which may be extended when further Member States adopt the euro as the single currency.

(5) In order to prepare a smooth changeover to the euro, Regulation (EC) No 974/98 provides for a transitional period between the substitution of the euro for the currencies of the participating Member States and the introduction of euro banknotes and coins. The transitional period should last three years at the most, but should be as short as possible.

(6) The transitional period can be reduced to zero, in which case the euro adoption date and the cash changeover date fall on the same day, if a Member State considers that a longer transitional period is not necessary. In that case, euro banknotes and coins will become legal tender in that Member State on the euro adoption date. However, it should be possible for such a Member State to benefit from a 'phasing-out' period of one year, during which it would be possible to continue to

make reference to the national currency unit in new legal instruments. This would give economic actors in such a Member State more time to adapt to the introduction of the euro and therefore ease the transition.

(7)   It should be possible for the general public to exchange banknotes and coins denominated in the national currency unit for euro banknotes and coins free of charge during the dual circulation period, subject to certain ceilings.

(8)   Regulation (EC) No 974/98 should therefore be amended accordingly,

HAS ADOPTED THIS REGULATION:

Article 1

Regulation (EC) No 974/98 is hereby amended as follows:

1.   Article 1 shall be replaced by the following:

'Article 1

For the purpose of this Regulation:

(a)   **"participating Member States"** shall mean the Member States listed in the table in the Annex;

(b)   **"legal instruments"** shall mean legislative and statutory provisions, acts of administration, judicial decisions, contracts, unilateral legal acts, payment instruments other than banknotes and coins, and other instruments with legal effect;

(c)   **"conversion rate"** shall mean the irrevocably fixed conversion rate adopted for the currency of each participating Member State by the Council in accordance with the first sentence of Article 123(4) of the Treaty or with paragraph 5 of that Article;

(d)   **"euro adoption date"** shall mean either the date on which the respective Member State enters the third stage under Article 121(3) of the Treaty or the date on which the abrogation of the respective Member State's derogation under Article 122(2) of the Treaty enters into force, as the case may be;

(e)   **"cash changeover date"** shall mean the date on which euro banknotes and coins acquire the status of legal tender in a given participating Member State;

(f)   **"euro unit"** shall mean the currency unit as referred to in the second sentence of Article 2;

(g)   **"national currency units"** shall mean the units of the currency of a participating Member State, as those units are defined on the day before the adoption of the euro in that Member State;

(h)   **"transitional period"** shall mean a period of three years at the most beginning at 00.00 hours on the euro adoption date and ending at 00.00 hours on the cash changeover date;

(i)   **"phasing-out period"** shall mean a period of one year at the most beginning on the euro adoption date, which can only apply to Member States where the euro adoption date and the cash changeover date fall on the same day;

(j)   **"redenominate"** shall mean changing the unit in which the amount of outstanding debt is stated from a national currency unit to the euro unit, but which does not have through the act of redenomination the effect of altering any other term of the debt, this being a matter subject to relevant national law;

(k)   **"credit institutions"** shall mean credit institutions as defined in Article 1(1) of Directive 2000/12/EC of the European Parliament and of the Council of 20 March 2000 relating to the taking up and pursuit of the business of credit institutions. For the purpose of this Regulation, the institutions listed in Article 2(3) of that Directive with the exception of post office giro institutions shall not be considered as credit institutions.

2.   the following Article shall be inserted:

'Article 1a

The euro adoption date, the cash changeover date, and the phasing-out period, if applicable, for each participating Member State shall be as set out in the Annex.';

3.   Article 2 shall be replaced by the following:

'Article 2

With effect from the respective euro adoption dates, the currency of the participating Member States shall be the euro. The currency unit shall be one euro. One euro shall be divided into one hundred cent.';

4.   Article 9 shall be replaced by the following:

'Article 9

Banknotes and coins denominated in a national currency unit shall retain their status as legal tender within their territorial limits as from the day before the euro adoption date in the participating Member State concerned.';

5.   the following Article shall be inserted:

'Article 9a

The following shall apply in a Member State with a "phasing-out" period. In legal instruments created during the phasing-out period and to be performed in that Member State, reference may continue to be made to the national currency unit. These references shall be read as references to the euro unit according to the respective conversion rates. Without prejudice to Article 15, the acts performed under these legal instruments shall be performed only in the euro unit. The rounding rules laid down in Regulation (EC) No 1103/97 shall apply.

The Member State concerned shall limit the application of the first subparagraph to certain types of legal instrument, or to legal instruments adopted in certain fields.

The Member State concerned may shorten the period.';

6.   Articles 10 and 11 shall be replaced by the following:

'*Article 10*

With effect from the respective cash changeover dates, the ECB and the central banks of the participating Member States shall put into circulation banknotes denominated in euro in the participating Member States.

Without prejudice to Article 15, these banknotes denominated in euro shall be the only banknotes which have the status of legal tender in participating Member States.

Article 11

With effect from the respective cash changeover date, the participating Member States shall issue coins denominated in euro or in cent and complying with the denominations and technical specifications which the Council may lay down in accordance with the second sentence of Article 106(2) of the Treaty. Without prejudice to Article 15 and to the provisions of any agreement under Article 111(3) of the Treaty concerning monetary matters, those coins shall be the only coins which have the status of legal tender in participating Member States. Except for the issuing authority and for those persons specifically designated by the national legislation of the issuing Member State, no party shall be obliged to accept more than 50 coins in any single payment.';

7.   Articles 13 and 14 shall be replaced by the following:

'*Article 13*

Articles 10, 11, 14, 15 and 16 shall apply with effect from the respective cash changeover date in each participating Member State.

Article 14

Where, in legal instruments existing on the day before the cash changeover date, reference is made to the national currency units, these references shall be read as references to the euro unit according to the respective conversion rates. The rounding rules laid down in Regulation (EC) No 1103/97 shall apply.';

8.   Article 15 shall be amended as follows:

(a)   in paragraphs 1 and 2, the words 'after the end of the transitional period' shall be replaced by the words 'from the respective cash changeover date.';

(b)   the following paragraph shall be added:

'3.   During the period referred to in paragraph 1, credit institutions in participating Member States adopting the euro after 1 January 2002 shall exchange their customers' banknotes and coins denominated in the national currency unit of that Member State for banknotes and coins in euro, free of charge, up to a ceiling which may be set by national law. Credit institutions may require that notice be given if the amount to be exchanged exceeds a ceiling set by national law or, in the absence of such provisions, by themselves and corresponding to a household amount.

The credit institutions referred to in the first subparagraph shall exchange banknotes and coins denominated in the national currency unit of that Member State of persons other than their customers, free of charge up to a ceiling set by national law or, in the absence of such provisions, by themselves.

National law may limit the obligation under the preceding two subparagraphs to specific types of credit institutions. National law may also extend this obligation upon other persons.';

9.   the text appearing in the Annex to this Regulation shall be added as an Annex.

Article 2

This Regulation shall enter into force on the twentieth day following that of its publication in the Official Journal of the European Union.

This Regulation shall be binding in its entirety and directly applicable in the Member States in accordance with the Treaty establishing the European Community, subject to Protocols 25 and 26 to, and Article 122(1) of, the Treaty.

Done at Brussels, 21 December 2005.

For the Council
The President
B. BRADSHAW

ANNEX

'ANNEX

Member State	Euro adoption date	Cash changeover date	Member State with a "phasing-out" period
Belgium	1 January 1999	1 January 2002	n/a
Germany	1 January 1999	1 January 2002	n/a
Greece	1 January 2001	1 January 2002	n/a
Spain	1 January 1999	1 January 2002	n/a
France	1 January 1999	1 January 2002	n/a
Ireland	1 January 1999	1 January 2002	n/a
Italy	1 January 1999	1 January 2002	n/a
Luxembourg	1 January 1999	1 January 2002	n/a
Netherlands	1 January 1999	1 January 2002	n/a
Austria	1 January 1999	1 January 2002	n/a
Portugal	1 January 1999	1 January 2002	n/a
Finland	1 January 1999	1 January 2002	n/a

COUNCIL DIRECTIVE 2006/18/EC

of 14 February 2006

amending Directive 77/388/EEC with regard to reduced rates of value added tax

Official Journal L51, 22.02.2006, p. 12 - 13

This Directive was repealed by Council Directive 2006/112/EC of 28 November 2006 on the common system of value added tax, with effect from 1 January 2007

THE COUNCIL OF THE EUROPEAN UNION,

Having regard to the Treaty establishing the European Community, and in particular Article 93 thereof,

Having regard to the proposal from the Commission,

Having regard to the opinion of the European Parliament,

Having regard to the opinion of the European Economic and Social Committee,

Whereas:

(1)   The possibility of applying a reduced rate of value added tax should be granted in respect of supplies of district heating as for supplies of natural gas and electricity, for which the possibility of applying a reduced rate is already allowed in Sixth Council Directive 77/388/EEC of 17 May 1977 on the harmonisation of the laws of the Member States relating to turnover taxes — Common system of value added tax: uniform basis of assessment.

(2)   To achieve a better understanding of the impact of reduced rates, it is necessary for the Commission to prepare an assessment report on the impact of reduced rates applied to locally supplied services, notably in terms of job creation, economic growth and the proper functioning of the internal market.

(3)   The experiment of reduced rates for labour-intensive services should therefore be extended until 31 December 2010 and it should also be made possible for all Member States to take part in it under the same conditions.

(4)   Accordingly, Member States wishing to avail themselves, for the first time, of the option provided for in Article 28(6) of Directive 77/388/EEC and those wishing to amend the list of services to which they have applied the said provision in the past should submit a request to the Commission, together with the relevant particulars for the purpose of assessment. Such prior assessment by the Commission does not appear necessary where Member States have previously benefited from an authorisation and submitted a report on the matter to the Commission.

(5)   To ensure legal continuity, this Directive should be applicable as from 1 January 2006.

(6)   Implementation of this Directive in no way implies change in the legislative provisions of Member States,

HAS ADOPTED THIS DIRECTIVE:

Article 1

Directive 77/388/EEC is hereby amended as follows:

1.   Article 12 shall be amended as follows:

(a)   paragraph 3(b) shall be replaced by the following:

'(b)   Member States may apply a reduced rate to supplies of natural gas, electricity and district heating provided that no risk of distortion of competition exists. A Member State intending to apply such a rate must inform the Commission before doing so. The Commission shall give a decision on the existence of a risk of distortion of competition. If the Commission has not taken that decision within three months of the receipt of the information a risk of distortion of competition is deemed not to exist.';

(b)   in paragraph 4, the following subparagraph shall be inserted:

'By 30 June 2007 at the latest the Commission shall present to the European Parliament and the Council an overall assessment report on the impact of reduced rates applying to locally supplied services, including restaurant services, notably in terms of job creation, economic growth and the proper functioning of the internal market, based on a study carried out by an independent economic think-tank.';

2.   Article 28(6) shall be amended as follows:

(a)   the first subparagraph shall be replaced by the following:

'The Council, acting unanimously on a proposal from the Commission, may authorise any Member State to apply until 31 December 2010 at the latest the reduced rates provided for in the third subparagraph of Article 12(3)(a) to services listed in a maximum of two of the categories set out in Annex K. In exceptional cases, a Member State may be authorised to apply the reduced rates to services belonging to three of the aforementioned categories.';

(b)   the fourth subparagraph shall be replaced by the following:

'Any Member State wishing to apply for the first time after 31 December 2005 a reduced rate to one or more of the services mentioned in the first subparagraph pursuant to this provision shall inform the Commission before 31 March 2006. It shall communicate to it before that date all relevant particulars concerning the new measures it wishes to introduce, and in particular the following:

(a) scope of the measure and detailed description of the services concerned;

(b) particulars showing that the conditions laid down in the second and third subparagraphs have been met;

(c) particulars showing the budgetary cost of the measure envisaged.'

Article 2

This Directive shall enter into force on the day of its publication in the *Official Journal of the European Union.*

It shall be applicable as from 1 January 2006.

Article 3

This Directive is addressed to the Member States.

Done at Brussels, 14 February 2006.

For the Council
The President
K.-H. GRASSER

COUNCIL DIRECTIVE 2006/58/EC

of 27 June 2006

amending Council Directive 2002/38/EC as regards the period of application of the value added tax arrangements applicable to radio and television broadcasting services and certain electronically supplied services

Official Journal L 174, 28/06/2006, p.5-6

This Directive was repealed by Council Directive 2006/112/EC of 28 November on the common system of Value Added Tax, with effect from 1 January 2007.

THE COUNCIL OF THE EUROPEAN UNION,

Having regard to the Treaty establishing the European Community,

Having regard to Council Directive 2002/38/EC of 7 May 2002 amending and amending temporarily Directive 77/388/EEC as regards the value added tax arrangements applicable to radio and television broadcasting services and certain electronically supplied services, and in particular Article 5 thereof,

Having regard to the proposal from the Commission,

Whereas:

(1)   The review provided for in Article 5 of Council Directive 2002/38/EC has been carried out.

(2)   It appears from that review that the provisions of Article 1 of Directive 2002/38/EC have operated in a satisfactory manner and have achieved their objective.

(3)   On 29 December 2003 the Commission presented a proposal for a Directive on the place of supply between taxable persons, which was amended by its proposal of 22 July 2005 in order to include supplies by taxable persons to non-taxable customers. Under the amended proposal all broadcasting and electronically supplied services will be taxed at the place of consumption.

(4)   On 4 November 2004 the Commission presented a proposal for a Directive on the simplification of VAT obligations which will provide for a more general electronic mechanism than that provided for in Council Directive 2002/38/EC in order to facilitate compliance with fiscal obligations with respect to cross-border services.

(5)   Although significant progress has been made with a view to the adoption, on the basis of the said legislative proposals, of the necessary broader measures which will replace the measures contained in Article 1 of Directive 2002/38/EC, it has not been possible to adopt the former before the expiry of the latter on 30 June 2006.

(6)   In the light of the adoption of such broadened measures in the short or medium term, and of the findings of the abovementioned review procedure, it is appropriate that, in the interests of the proper functioning of the internal market and in order to ensure the continued elimination of distortion, the provisions applicable to radio and television broadcasting services and certain electronically supplied services as provided for in Article 1 of Directive 2002/38/EC should continue to apply until 31 December 2006.

(7)   Article 5 of Directive 2002/38/EC provides for such extension for practical reasons by the Council, acting unanimously on the basis of a proposal from the Commission.

(8)   Directive 2002/38/EC should therefore be amended accordingly.

(9)   Given the urgency of the matter, in order to avoid a legal gap, it is imperative to grant an exception to the six-week period mentioned in point I(3) of the Protocol on the role of national Parliaments in the European Union, annexed to the Treaty on European Union and to the Treaties establishing the European Communities,

HAS ADOPTED THIS DIRECTIVE:

Article 1

Article 4 of Directive 2002/38/EC shall be replaced by the following:

'*Article 4*

Article 1 shall apply until 31 December 2006'.

Article 2

1.   Member States shall bring into force the laws, regulations and administrative provisions necessary to comply with this Directive with effect from 1 July 2006. They shall forthwith communicate to the Commission the text of those provisions.

When Member States adopt those provisions, they shall contain a reference to this Directive or be accompanied by such a reference on the occasion of their official publication. The methods of making such reference shall be laid down by Member States.

2.   Member States shall communicate to the Commission the text of the main provisions of national law which they adopt in the field covered by this Directive.

Article 3

This Directive shall enter into force on the day of its publication in the *Official Journal of the European Union.*

Article 4

This Directive is addressed to the Member States.

Done at Luxembourg, 27 June 2006.

For the Council
The President
J. PRÖLL

COUNCIL DIRECTIVE 2006/69/EC

of 24 July 2006

amending Directive 77/388/EEC as regards certain measures to simplify the procedure for charging value added tax and to assist in countering tax evasion or avoidance, and repealing certain Decisions granting derogations

Official Journal L221 of 12.08.2006, p.009 - 14

THE COUNCIL OF THE EUROPEAN UNION,

Having regard to the Treaty establishing the European Community, and in particular Article 93 thereof,

Having regard to the proposal from the Commission,

Having regard to the opinion of the European Parliament,

Having regard to the opinion of the European Economic and Social Committee,

Whereas:

(1) In order to combat tax evasion or avoidance and to simplify the procedure for charging value added tax, certain derogations covering similar problems were granted under varying terms to individual Member States by the Council pursuant to Article 27(1) of Sixth Council Directive 77/388/EEC of 17 May 1977 on the harmonisation of the laws of the Member States relating to turnover taxes — Common system of value added tax: uniform basis of assessment. A solution to the said problems should be made available to all Member States through incorporation into that Directive. Those measures should be proportionate and limited to countering the problem concerned. Given that the Member States have different needs, that incorporation should be limited to extending the option of adopting the rules concerned to all Member States, as and when the need arises.

(2) Member States should be able to take action to ensure that measures provided for in Directive 77/388/EEC relating to the taxable person and the transfer of a business as a going concern are not being exploited to evade and avoid tax.

(3) It should be possible for Member States to intervene as regards the value of supplies and acquisitions in specific limited circumstances, to ensure that there is no loss of tax through the use of connected parties to derive tax benefits.

(4) It should be possible for Member States to include, within the taxable amount of a transaction which involves the working of investment gold provided by a customer, the value of that investment gold where, by virtue of being worked, the gold loses its status of investment gold.

(5) It should be emphasised that certain services with the nature of capital items may be included in the scheme which allows the adjustment of deductions for capital items over the lifetime of the asset, according to its actual use.

(6)   Member States should be able, in specific cases, to designate the recipient of supplies as the person responsible for paying and accounting for value added tax. This should assist Member States in simplifying the rules and countering tax evasion and avoidance in identified sectors and on certain types of transactions.

(7)   Directive 77/388/EEC should therefore be amended accordingly.

(8)   Consequently, Member States should not be able to continue to avail themselves of individual derogations granted to them by certain Council Decisions adopted pursuant to Article 27(1) of Directive 77/388/EEC and which are covered by the provisions in this Directive. The Decisions concerned should therefore be explicitly repealed. This Directive should not affect measures applied by Member States pursuant to Article 27(5) of Directive 77/388/EEC; nor should it affect derogations which have been granted pursuant to Article 27(1) of that Directive and which have not been repealed by this Directive.

(9)   The application of certain provisions in this Directive should be optional and they should allow Member States a certain degree of discretion. Where appropriate for reasons of transparency, it should be provided that Member States should inform the other Member States through the Advisory Committee on value added tax established under Article 29 of Directive 77/388/EEC of any national law adopted pursuant to those provisions. Such information should not be necessary with respect to national measures taken under a Decision which is repealed by this Directive, or which expires at the date of this Directive's entry into force, but which a Member State continues to apply under the provisions of this Directive,

HAS ADOPTED THIS DIRECTIVE:

[Article 1

Directive 77/388/EEC is amended as follows:

1.   In Article 4(4), the following subparagraph shall be added:

'A Member State exercising the option provided for in the second subparagraph, may adopt any measures needed to prevent tax evasion or avoidance through the use of this provision.'.

2.   In Article 5(8) the second sentence shall be replaced by the following:

'Where appropriate, Member States may, in cases where the recipient is not wholly liable to tax, take the measures necessary to prevent distortion of competition. They may also adopt any measures needed to prevent tax evasion or avoidance through the use of this provision.'.

3.   Article 11(A) shall be amended as follows:

(a)   in paragraph (1)(d) the second subparagraph shall be deleted;

(b)   the following paragraphs shall be added:

'5.   Member States shall have the option of including in the taxable amount in respect of the supply of goods and services, the value of exempt investment gold within the meaning of Article 26b, which has been provided by the customer to be used as a basis for working and which as a result, loses its VAT exempt investment gold status when such goods and services are supplied. The value to be used is the open market value of the investment gold at the time that those goods and services are supplied.

6.   In order to prevent tax evasion or avoidance, Member States may take measures to ensure that the taxable amount in respect of a supply of goods or services shall be the open market value. The option shall be applied only in respect of supplies of goods and services involving family or other close personal ties, management, ownership, membership, financial or legal ties as defined by the Member State. For these purposes legal ties may include the relationship between an employer and employee or the employee's family, or any other closely connected persons.

The option in the first subparagraph may apply only in any of the following circumstances:

(a)   where the consideration is lower than the open market value and the recipient of the supply does not have a full right of deduction under Article 17;

(b)   where the consideration is lower than the open market value and the supplier does not have a full right of deduction under Article 17 and the supply is subject to an exemption under Article 13 or Article 28(3)(b);

(c)   where the consideration is higher than the open market value and the supplier does not have a full right of deduction under Article 17.

Member States may restrict the categories of suppliers or recipients to whom the measures in the first and the second subparagraph shall apply.

Member States shall inform the Committee established in accordance with Article 29 of any new national measure adopted pursuant to the provisions of this paragraph.

7.   For the purposes of this Directive, "open market value" shall mean the full amount that, in order to obtain the goods or services in question at that time, a customer at the same marketing stage at which the supply of goods or services takes place, would have to pay, under conditions

of fair competition, to a supplier at arm's length within the territory of the Member State in which the supply is subject to tax.

Where no comparable supply of goods or services can be ascertained, "open market value" shall mean, in respect of goods, an amount that is not less than the purchase price of the goods or of similar goods or, in the absence of a purchase price, the cost price, determined at the time of supply; in respect of services it shall mean not less than the full cost to the taxable person of providing the service.'.

4.   Article 17(4), in the version set out in Article 28f(1), shall be amended as follows:

(a)   in point (a) of the second subparagraph 'Article 21(1)(a) and (c)' shall be replaced by 'Article 21(1)(a), (1)(c) or (1)(f) or Article 21(2)(c)';

(b)   in point (b) of the second subparagraph 'Article 21(1)(a)' shall be replaced by 'Article 21(1)(a), or (1)(f) or Article 21(2)(c)'.

5.   In Article 18(1)(d), in the version set out in Article 28f(2), 'Article 21(1)' shall be replaced by 'Article 21(1) or Article 21(2)(c)'.

6.   In Article 20(4), the following subparagraph shall be added:

'Member States may also apply paragraphs 2 and 3 to services which have characteristics similar to those normally attributed to capital goods.'.

7.   In Article 21(2), in the version set out in Article 28g, the following point shall be added:

'(c)   where the following supplies are carried out, Member States may lay down that the person liable to pay tax is the taxable person to whom those supplies are made:

(i)   the supply of construction work, including repair, cleaning, maintenance, alteration and demolition services in relation to immovable property, as well as the handing over of construction works considered to be a supply of goods by virtue of Article 5(5);

(ii)   the supply of staff engaged in activities covered by (i);

(iii)   the supply of immovable property, as referred to in Article 13(B)(g) and (h), where the supplier has opted for taxation of the supply pursuant to point (C)(b) of that Article;

(iv)   the supply of used material, used material which cannot be re-used in the same state, scrap, industrial and non industrial waste, recyclable waste, part processed waste and certain goods and services, as identified in Annex M;

(v)   the supply of goods provided as security by one taxable person to another in execution of that security;

(vi)   the supply of goods following the cession of the reservation of ownership to an assignee and the exercising of this right by the assignee;

(vii)   the supply of immovable property sold by the judgment debtor in a compulsory sale procedure.

For the purposes of this point, Member States may provide that a taxable person who also carries out activities or transactions that are not considered to be taxable supplies of goods or services in accordance with Article 2 shall be deemed to be a taxable person in respect of supplies received as referred to in the first subparagraph. A non-taxable body governed by public law, may be deemed to be a taxable person in respect of supplies received as referred to in (v), (vi) and (vii).

For the purposes of this point, Member States may specify the supplies of goods and services covered, and the categories of suppliers or recipients to whom these measures may apply. They may also limit the application of this measure to some of the supplies of goods and services listed in Annex M.

Member States shall inform the Committee established in accordance with Article 29 of any new national measure adopted pursuant to the provisions of this point.'.

8.   Annex M set out in Annex I to this Directive shall be added.]¹

Article 2

Decisions listed in Annex II of this Directive shall be repealed with effect from 1 January 2008.

Article 3

Member States shall bring into force the laws, regulations and administrative provisions necessary to comply with this Directive.

They shall apply the provisions necessary to comply with Article 1(3), as concerns a new Article 11A(7) of Directive 77/388/EEC, and with Article 1(4), as concerns the reference in Article 17(4) points (a) and (b) of Directive 77/388/EEC in the version set out in Article 28f(1) to Article 21(1)(f) of that Directive, from 1 January 2008 at the latest.

When Member States adopt provisions under this Directive, they shall forthwith communicate to the Commission the text of those provisions, which shall contain a reference to this Directive or shall be accompanied by such a reference on the occasion of their official publication. The methods of making such reference shall be laid down by Member States.

Article 4

This Directive shall enter into force on the day following that of its publication in the *Official Journal of the European Union*.

Article 5

This Directive is addressed to the Member States.

Done at Brussels, 24 July 2006.

For the Council
The President
K. RAJAMÄKI

ANNEX I

'ANNEX M

List of supplies of goods and services as referred to in Article 21(2)(c)(iv)

(a)   the supply of ferrous and non ferrous waste, scrap, and used materials including that of semi-finished products resulting from the processing, manufacturing or melting down of ferrous and non-ferrous metals and their alloys;

(b)   the supply of ferrous and non-ferrous semi-processed products and certain associated processing services;

(c)   the supply of residues and other recyclable materials consisting of ferrous and non-ferrous metals, their alloys, slag, ash, scale and industrial residues containing metals or their alloys and the supply of selection, cutting, fragmenting and pressing services for these products;

(d)   the supply of, and certain processing services relating to, ferrous and non-ferrous waste as well as parings, scrap, waste and used and recyclable material consisting of cullet, glass, paper, paperboard and board, rags, bone, leather, imitation leather, parchment, raw hides and skins, tendons and sinews, twine, cordage, rope, cables, rubber and plastic;

(e)   the supply of the materials referred to in this annex after processing in the form of cleaning, polishing, selection, cutting, fragmenting, pressing or casting into ingots;

(f)   the supply of scrap and waste from the working of base materials.'

ANNEX II

List of Decisions under Article 27 of Directive 77/388/EEC repealed by this Directive

The Council Decision deemed to have been adopted on 15 April 1984 authorising the United Kingdom to apply a measure derogating from the Sixth Directive with a view to avoiding certain types of fraud or tax evasion on supplies of gold, gold coins and gold scrap between taxable persons by a special tax accounting scheme.

The Council Decision deemed to have been adopted on 11 April 1987 authorising the United Kingdom to apply a measure derogating from Article 11 of Directive 77/388/EEC.

Council Decision 88/498/EEC authorising the Kingdom of the Netherlands to apply a measure derogating from Article 21(1)(a) of Directive 77/388/EEC.

A Council Decision deemed to have been adopted on 18 February 1997 under the procedure contained in Article 27(4) of Directive 77/388/EEC in its version of 17 May 1977 authorising the Republic of France to apply a measure derogating from Articles 2 and 10 of Directive 77/388/EEC. This decision follows notification of the request to Member States on 18 December 1996.

Council Decision 98/23/EC authorising the United Kingdom to extend application of a measure derogating from Article 28e(1) of Directive 77/388/ EEC.

Council Decision 2002/439/EC authorising Germany to apply a measure derogating from Article 21 of Directive 77/388/EEC.

Council Decision 2002/880/EC authorising Austria to apply a measure derogating from Article 21 of Directive 77/388/EEC.

Council Decision 2004/290/EC authorising Germany to apply a measure derogating from Article 21 of Directive 77/388/EEC.

Council Decision 2004/736/EC authorising the United Kingdom to introduce a special measure derogating from Article 11 of Directive 77/388/EEC.

Council Decision 2004/758/EC authorising Austria to apply a measure derogating from Article 21 of Directive 77/388/EEC.

Amendments
1   Article 1 repealed by Council Directive 2006/112/EC of 28 November 2006, w.e.f. 1 January 2007.

COUNCIL DIRECTIVE 2006/79/EC

of 5 October 2006

on the exemption from taxes of imports of small consignments of goods of a non-commercial character from third countries

Official Journal L286, 17.10.2006, p.15 - 18

THE COUNCIL OF THE EUROPEAN UNION,

Having regard to the Treaty establishing the European Community, and in particular Article 93 thereof,

Having regard to the proposal from the Commission,

Having regard to the opinion of the European Parliament,

Having regard to the opinion of the European Economic and Social Committee,

Whereas:

(1) Council Directive 78/1035/EEC of 19 December 1978 on the exemption from taxes of imports of small consignments of goods of a non-commercial character from third countries has been substantially amended several times. In the interests of clarity and rationality, the said Directive should be codified.

(2) Provision should be made for the exemption from turnover taxes and excise duties of imports of small consignments of goods of a non-commercial character from third countries.

(3) To that end the limits within which such exemption is to be applied should, for practical reasons, be as far as possible the same as those laid down for the Community arrangements for exemption from customs duties in Council Regulation (EEC) No 918/83 of 28 March 1983 setting up a Community system of reliefs from customs duty.

(4) It is necessary to set special limits for certain products because of the high level of taxation to which they are at present subject in the Member States.

(5) This Directive should be without prejudice to the obligations of the Member States relating to the time-limits for transposition into national law of the Directives set out in Annex I, Part B,

HAS ADOPTED THIS DIRECTIVE:

Article 1

1. Goods in small consignments of a non-commercial character sent from a third country by private persons to other private persons in a Member State shall be exempt on importation from turnover tax and excise duty.

2. For the purposes of paragraph 1, 'small consignments of a non-commercial character' shall mean consignments which:

(a) are of an occasional nature;

(b)   contain only goods intended for the personal or family use of the consignees, the nature and quantity of which do not indicate that they are being imported for any commercial purpose;

(c)   contain goods with a total value not exceeding EUR 45;

(d)   are sent by the sender to the consignee without payment of any kind.

Article 2

1.   Article I shall apply to the goods listed below subject to the following quantitative limits:

(a)   tobacco products

    (i)   50 cigarettes,

    or

    (ii)   25 cigarillos (cigars of a maximum weight of three grams each),

    or

    (iii)   10 cigars,

    or

    (iv)   50 grams of smoking tobacco;

(b)   alcohol and alcoholic beverages:

    (i)   distilled beverages and spirits of an alcoholic strength exceeding 22 % vol.; undenatured ethyl alcohol of 80 % vol. and over: one standard bottle (up to 1 litre),

    or

    (ii)   distilled beverages and spirits, and aperitifs with a wine or alcohol base, tafia, saké or similar beverages of an alcoholic strength of 22 % vol. or less; sparkling wines, fortified wines: one standard bottle (up to 1 litre),

    or

    (iii)   still wines: two litres;

(c)   perfumes: 50 grams,

    or

toilet waters: 0,25 litre or eight ounces;

(d)   coffee: 500 grams,

    or

coffee extracts and essences: 200 grams;

(e)   tea: 100 grams,

or

tea extracts and essences: 40 grams.

2.   Member States shall have the right to reduce the quantities of the products referred to in paragraph 1 eligible for exemption from turnover tax and excise duties, or to abolish exemption for such products altogether.

Article 3

Any goods listed in Article 2 which are contained in a small consignment of a non-commercial character in quantities exceeding those laid down in the said Article shall be excluded in their entirety from exemption.

Article 4

1.   The euro equivalent in national currency which shall apply for the implementation of this Directive shall be fixed once a year. The rates applicable shall be those obtaining on the first working day of October with effect from 1 January of the following year.

2.   Member States may round off the amounts in national currency resulting from the conversion of the amounts in euros provided for in Article 1(2), provided such rounding-off does not exceed EUR 2.

3.   Member States may maintain the amount of the exemption in force at the time of the annual adjustment provided for in paragraph 1 if, prior to the rounding-off provided for in paragraph 2, conversion of the amount of the exemption expressed in euros would result in a change of less than 5 % in the exemption expressed in national currency.

Article 5

Member States shall communicate to the Commission the text of the main provisions of national law which they adopt in the field covered by this Directive. The Commission shall inform the other Member States thereof.

Article 6

Directive 78/1035/EEC shall be repealed, without prejudice to the obligations of the Member States relating to the time-limits for transposition into national law of the Directives set out in Annex I, Part B.

References to the repealed Directive shall be construed as references to this Directive and shall be read in accordance with the correlation table in Annex II.

Article 7

This Directive shall enter into force on the 20th day following its publication in the *Official Journal of the European Union*.

Article 8

This Directive is addressed to the Member States.

Done at Brussels, 19 December 2006.

For the Council
The President
K. RAJAMÄKI

ANNEX I

PART A

Repealed Directive with its successive amendments

Council Directive 78/1035/EEC
(OJ L 366, 28.12.1978, p. 34)

Council Directive 81/933/EEC - only Article 2
(OJ L 338, 25.11.1981, p. 24)

Council Directive 85/576/EEC
(OJ L 372, 31.12.1985, p. 30)

PART B

Time-limits for transposition into national law

(referred to in Article 6)

Directive	Time-limit for transposition
78/1035/EEC	1 January 1979
81/933/EEC	31 December 1981
85/576/EEC	30 June 1986

CORRELATION TABLE

Directive 78/1035/EEC	This Directive
Article 1(1)	Article 1(1)
Article 1(2), first indent	Article 1(2)(a)
Article 1(2), second indent	Article 1(2)(b)
Article 1(2), third indent	Article 1(2)(c)
Article 1(2), fourth indent	Article 1(2)(d)
Article 2(1)(a), from '50 cigarettes' to '50 grams of smoking tobacco'	Article 2(1)(a)(i) to (iv)
Article 2(1)(b)	Article 2(1)(b)
Article 2(1)(b), first indent	Article 2(1)(b)(i)
Article 2(1)(b), second indent	Article 2(1)(b)(ii)
Article 2(1)(b), third indent	Article 2(1)(b)(iii)
Article 2(1)(c), (d) and (e)	Article 2(1)(c), (d) and (e)
Article 2(2)	Article 2(2)

Directive 78/1035/EEC	This Directive
Article 2(3)	—
Article 3	Article 3
Article 4(1)	—
Article 4(2)	Article 4(1)
Article 4(3)	Article 4(2)
Article 4(4)	Article 4(3)
Article 5(1)	—
Article 5(2)	Article 5
—	Article 6
—	Article 7
Article 6	Article 8
—	Annex I
—	Annex II

COUNCIL DIRECTIVE 2006/84/EC

of 23 October 2006

adapting Directive 2002/94/EC laying down detailed rules for implementing certain provisions of Council Directive 76/308/EEC on mutual assistance for the recovery of claims relating to certain levies, duties, taxes and other measures, by reason of the accession of Bulgaria and Romania

Official Journal L362, 20/12/2006 p. 99 - 100

THE COMMISSION OF THE EUROPEAN COMMUNITIES,

Having regard to the Treaty of Accession of Bulgaria and Romania, and in particular Article 4(3) thereof,

Having regard to the Act of Accession of Bulgaria and Romania, and in particular Article 56 thereof,

Whereas:

(1)   Pursuant to Article 56 of the Act of Accession, where acts which remain valid beyond 1 January 2007 require adaptation by reason of accession, and the necessary adaptations have not been provided for in the Act of Accession or its Annexes, the necessary adaptations are to be adopted by the Commission in all cases where the Commission adopted the original act.

(2)   The Final Act of the Conference which drew up the Treaty of Accession indicated that the High Contracting Parties had reached political agreement on a set of adaptations to acts adopted by the Institutions required by reason of accession and invited the Council and the Commission to adopt these adaptations before accession, completed and updated where necessary to take account of the evolution of the law of the Union.

(3)   Commission Directive 2002/94/EC of 9 December 2002 laying down detailed rules for implementing certain provisions of Council Directive 76/308/EEC on mutual assistance for the recovery of claims relating to certain levies, duties, taxes and other measures should therefore be amended accordingly,

HAS ADOPTED THIS DIRECTIVE:

Article 1

Directive 2002/94/EC is amended as set out in the Annex.

Article 2

1.   Member States shall adopt and publish, by the date of accession of Bulgaria and Romania to the European Union at the latest, the laws, regulations and administrative provisions necessary to comply with this Directive. They shall forthwith communicate to the Commission the text of those provisions and a correlation table between those provisions and this Directive.

They shall apply those provisions from the date of accession of Bulgaria and Romania to the European Union.

When Member States adopt those provisions, they shall contain a reference to this Directive or be accompanied by such a reference on the occasion of their official publication. Member States shall determine how such reference is to be made.

2.   Member States shall communicate to the Commission the text of the main provisions of national law which they adopt in the fields covered by this Directive.

Article 3

This Directive shall enter into force subject to, and on the date of, the entry into force of the Treaty of Accession of Bulgaria and Romania.

Article 4

This Directive is addressed to the Member States.

Done at Brussels, 23 October 2006.

For the Commission
Olli REHN
Member of the Commission

ANNEX

TAXATION

32002 L 0094: Commission Directive 2002/94/EC of 9 December 2002 laying down detailed rules for implementing certain provisions of Council Directive 76/308/EEC on mutual assistance for the recovery of claims relating to certain levies, duties, taxes and other measures (OJ L 337, 13.12.2002, p. 41), as amended by:

— 32004 L 0079: Commission Directive 2004/79/EC of 4.3.2004 (OJ L 168, 1.5.2004, p. 68).

In Annex IV, the left column under 'Member State' is replaced by the following:

'Belgique/België
България
Česká Republika
Danmark
Deutschland
Eesti
Ελλάδα
España
France
Ireland
Italia
Κύπρος
Latvija

Lietuva
Luxembourg
Magyarország
Malta
Nederland
Österreich
Polska
Portugal
România
Slovenija
Slovensko
Suomi/Finland
Sverige
United Kingdom'.

COUNCIL DIRECTIVE 2006/138/EC

of 19 December 2006

amending Directive 2006/112/EC on the common system of value added tax as regards the period of application of the value added tax arrangements applicable to radio and television broadcasting services and certain electronically supplied services

Official Journal L 384, 29/12/2006 p 0092 - 0093

THE COUNCIL OF THE EUROPEAN UNION,

Having regard to the Treaty establishing the European Community, and in particular Article 93 thereof,

Having regard to the proposal from the Commission,

Having regard to the opinion of the European Parliament,

Having regard to the opinion of the European Economic and Social Committee,

Whereas:

(1)   The temporary value added tax arrangements of Directive 77/388/EEC applicable for radio and television broadcasting services and certain electronically supplied services were extended until 31 December 2006 by Council Directive 2006/58/EC of 27 June 2006 amending Council Directive 2002/38/EC as regards the period of application of the value added tax arrangements applicable to radio and television broadcasting services and certain electronically supplied services.

(2)   It has not yet been possible to adopt provisions on the place of supply of services and on a more general electronic mechanism. Considering that the legal situation and the facts which justified the extension until 31 December 2006 have not changed and that to avoid a temporary gap in the value added tax arrangements for radio and television broadcasting services and certain electronically supplied services, those arrangements should continue to apply until 31 December 2008.

(3)   Council Directive 2006/112/EC of 28 November 2006 on the common system of value added tax, which has recast Directive 77/388/EEC, should therefore be amended accordingly.

(4)   Given the urgency of the matter, in order to avoid a legal gap, it is imperative to grant an exception to the six-week period mentioned in point I(3) of the Protocol on the role of national Parliaments in the European Union, annexed to the Treaty on European Union and to the Treaties establishing the European Communities,

HAS ADOPTED THIS DIRECTIVE:

Article 1

Directive 2006/112/EC is hereby amended as follows:

1.   in Article 56, paragraph 3 shall be replaced by the following:

'3.   Points (j) and (k) of paragraph 1 and paragraph 2 shall apply until 31 December 2008.';

2.   in Article 57, paragraph 2 shall be replaced by the following:

'2.   Paragraph 1 shall apply until 31 December 2008.';

3.   in Article 59, paragraph 2 shall be replaced by the following:

'2.   Until 31 December 2008, Member States shall apply Article 58(b) to radio and television broadcasting services, as referred to in point (j) of Article 56(1), supplied to nontaxable persons who are established in a Member State, or who have their permanent address or usually reside in a Member State, by a taxable person who has established his business outside the Community or who has a fixed establishment there from which the services are supplied, or who, in the absence of such a place of business or fixed establishment, has his permanent address or usually resides outside the Community.';

4.   Article 357 shall be replaced by the following:

'Article 357

This Chapter shall apply until 31 December 2008.'

Article 2

1.   Member States shall bring into force the laws, regulations and administrative provisions necessary to comply with this Directive with effect from 1 January 2007. They shall forthwith communicate to the Commission the text of those provisions

When Member States adopt these measures, they shall contain a reference to this Directive or be accompanied by such a reference on the occasion of their official publication. The methods of making such reference shall be laid down by Member States.

2.   Member States shall communicate to the Commission the text of the main provisions of national law which they adopt in the field covered by this Directive.

Article 3

This Directive shall enter into force on the day of its publication in the *Official Journal of the European Union.*

It shall apply from 1 January 2007.

Article 4

This Directive is addressed to the Member States.

Done at Brussels, 19 December 2006.

For the Council
The President
J. KORKEAOJA

COUNCIL DIRECTIVE 2007/75/EC

of 20 December 2007

amending Directive 2006/112/EC with regard to certain temporary provisions concerning rates of value added tax

Official Journal L346, 29/12/2007, p. 13 - 14

THE COUNCIL OF THE EUROPEAN UNION,

Having regard to the Treaty establishing the European Community, and in particular Article 93 thereof,

Having regard to the proposal from the Commission,

Having regard to the Opinion of the European Parliament,

Having regard to the Opinion of the European Economic and Social Committee,

Whereas:

(1)   Council Directive 2006/112/EC of 28 November 2006 on the common system of value added tax provides for certain derogations with respect to VAT rates. Some of the derogations expire on a fixed date, while others last until the adoption of definitive arrangements.

(2)   The derogations with respect to VAT rates provided for by Directive 2006/112/EC in conformity with the 2003 Act of Accession, and which allow for the smooth adaptation of the economies of certain new Member States to the internal market, have a fixed date and expire shortly.

(3)   A number of these new Member States have expressed their wish to apply the derogations from which they thus benefit for a further period.

(4)   In view of the pending debate on the use of reduced rates and the legislative proposal to be presented by the Commission, it is appropriate to extend certain derogations until the end of 2010, the date to which the experiment on the application of a reduced rate to labour-intensive services has been extended.

(5)   Directive 2006/112/EC should therefore be amended accordingly,

HAS ADOPTED THIS DIRECTIVE:

Article 1

With effect from 1 January 2008, Directive 2006/112/EC is hereby amended as follows:

1.   Article 123 shall be replaced by the following:

'Article 123

The Czech Republic may, until 31 December 2010, continue to apply a reduced rate of not less than 5 % to the supply of construction work for residential housing not provided as part of a social policy, excluding building materials.';

2.   Article 124 shall be deleted;

3.   in Article 125(1) and (2), the words 'until 31 December 2007' shall be replaced by 'until 31 December 2010';

4.   Article 126 shall be deleted;

5.   in Article 127, '1 January 2010' shall be replaced by '31 December 2010';

6.   Article 128 shall be replaced by the following:

'Article 128

1.   Poland may, until 31 December 2010, grant an exemption with deductibility of VAT paid at the preceding stage in respect of the supply of certain books and specialist periodicals.

2.   Poland may, until 31 December 2010 or until the introduction of definitive arrangements, as referred to in Article 402, whichever is the earlier, continue to apply a reduced rate of not less than 7 % to the supply of restaurant services.

3.   Poland may, until 31 December 2010, continue to apply a reduced rate of not less than 3 % to the supply of foodstuffs as referred to in point (1) of Annex III.

4.   Poland may, until 31 December 2010, continue to apply a reduced rate of not less than 7 % to the supply of services, not provided as part of a social policy, for construction, renovation and alteration of housing, excluding building materials, and to the supply before first occupation of residential buildings or parts of residential buildings, as referred to in Article 12(1)(a).';

7.   in Article 129(1) and (2), the words 'until 31 December 2007' shall be replaced by 'until 31 December 2010';

8.   Article 130 shall be deleted.

Article 2

Member States shall communicate to the Commission the text of the provisions of national law which they adopt in the field covered by this Directive.

Article 3

This Directive shall enter into force on the day of its publication in the Official Journal of the European Union.

Article 4

This Directive is addressed to the Member States.

Done at Brussels, 20 December 2007.

For the Council

The President
F. NUNES CORREIA

COUNCIL DIRECTIVE 2008/8/EC

of 12 February 2008

amending Directive 2006/112/EC as regards the place of supply of services

Official Journal L 44, 20/2/2008, p. 11–22

THE COUNCIL OF THE EUROPEAN UNION,

Having regard to the Treaty establishing the European Community, and in particular Article 93 thereof,

Having regard to the proposal from the Commission,

Having regard to the opinion of the European Parliament,

Having regard to the opinion of the European Economic and Social Committee,

Whereas:

(1) The realisation of the internal market, globalisation, deregulation and technology change have all combined to create enormous changes in the volume and pattern of trade in services. It is increasingly possible for a number of services to be supplied at a distance. In response, piece meal steps have been taken to address this over the years and many defined services are in fact at present taxed on the basis of the destination principle.

(2) The proper functioning of the internal market requires the amendment of Council Directive 2006/112/EC of 28 November 2006 on the common system of value added tax as regards the place of supply of services, following the Commission's strategy of modernisation and simplification of the operation of the common VAT system.

(3) For all supplies of services the place of taxation should, in principle, be the place where the actual consumption takes place. If the general rule for the place of supply of services were to be altered in this way, certain exceptions to this general rule would still be necessary for both administrative and policy reasons.

(4) For supplies of services to taxable persons, the general rule with respect to the place of supply of services should be based on the place where the recipient is established, rather than where the supplier is established. For the purposes of rules determining the place of supply of services and to minimise burdens on business, taxable persons who also have non-taxable activities should be treated as taxable for all services rendered to them. Similarly, non-taxable legal persons who are identified for VAT purposes should be regarded as taxable persons. These provisions, in accordance with normal rules, should not extend to supplies of services received by a taxable person for his own personal use or that of his staff.

(5) Where services are supplied to non-taxable persons, the general rule should continue to be that the place of supply of services is the place where the supplier has established his business.

(6)   In certain circumstances, the general rules as regards the place of supply of services for both taxable and non- taxable persons are not applicable and specified exclusions should apply instead. These exclusions should be largely based on existing criteria and reflect the principle of taxation at the place of consumption, while not imposing disproportionate administrative burdens upon certain traders.

(7)   Where a taxable person receives services from a person not established in the same Member State, the reverse charge mechanism should be obligatory in certain cases, meaning that the taxable person should self-assess the appropriate amount of VAT on the acquired service.

(8)   To simplify the obligations on businesses engaging in activities in Member States where they are not estab lished, a scheme should be set up enabling them to have a single point of electronic contact for VAT identi fication and declaration. Until such a scheme is estab lished, use should be made of the scheme introduced to facilitate compliance with fiscal obligations by taxable persons not established within the Community.

(9)   In order to further the correct application of this Directive every taxable person identified for VAT purposes should submit a recapitulative statement of the taxable persons and the non-taxable legal persons identified for VAT purposes to whom he has supplied taxable services which fall under the reverse charge mechanism.

(10)   Some of the changes made to the place of supply of services could have a considerable impact on the budget of Member States. To ensure a smooth transition these changes should be introduced over time.

(11)   In accordance with point 34 of the Interinstitutional Agreement on better law-making Member States are encouraged to draw up, for themselves and in the interests of the Community, their own tables illustrating, as far as possible, the correlation between this Directive and the transposition measures, and to make them public.

(12)   Directive 2006/112/EC should therefore be amended accordingly,

HAS ADOPTED THIS DIRECTIVE:

Article 1

From 1 January 2009, Directive 2006/112/EC is hereby amended as follows:

1.   in Article 56, paragraph 3 shall be replaced by the following:

'3. Points (j) and (k) of paragraph 1 and paragraph 2 shall apply until 31 December 2009.';

2.   in Article 57, paragraph 2 shall be replaced by the following: '2. Paragraph 1 shall apply until 31 December 2009.';

3.   in Article 59, paragraph 2 shall be replaced by the following:

'2. Until 31 December 2009, Member States shall apply Article 58(b) to radio and television broadcasting services, as referred to in Article 56(1) (j), supplied to non-taxable persons who are established in a Member State, or who have their permanent address or usually reside in a Member State, by a taxable person who has established his business outside the Community or who has a fixed establishment there from which the services are supplied, or who, in the absence of such a place of business or fixed establishment, has his permanent address or usually resides outside the Community.';

4.   Article 357 shall be replaced by the following:

'Article 357

This Chapter shall apply until 31 December 2014.'.

Article 2

From 1 January 2010, Directive 2006/112/EC is hereby amended as follows:

1.   Chapter 3 of Title V shall be replaced by the following:

'CHAPTER 3

Place of supply of services

Section 1

Definitions

Article 43

For the purpose of applying the rules concerning the place of supply of services:

1.   a taxable person who also carries out activities or transactions that are not considered to be taxable supplies of goods or services in accordance with Article 2(1) shall be regarded as a taxable person in respect of all services rendered to him;

2.   a non-taxable legal person who is identified for VAT purposes shall be regarded as a taxable person.

Section 2

General rules

Article 44

The place of supply of services to a taxable person acting as such shall be the place where that person has established his business. However, if those services are provided to a fixed establishment of the taxable person located in a place other than the place where he has established his business, the place of supply of those services shall be the place where that fixed establishment is located. In the absence of such place of establishment or fixed establishment, the place of supply of services shall be the place where the taxable person who receives such services has his permanent address or usually resides.

Article 45

The place of supply of services to a non-taxable person shall be the place where the supplier has established his business. However, if those services are provided from a fixed establishment of the supplier located in a place other than the place where he has established his business, the place of supply of those services shall be the place where that fixed establishment is located. In the absence of such place of establishment or fixed establishment, the place of supply of services shall be the place where the supplier has his permanent address or usually resides.

Section 3

Particular provisions

Subsection 1

Supply of services by intermediaries

Article 46

The place of supply of services rendered to a non-taxable person by an intermediary acting in the name and on behalf of another person shall be the place where the underlying transaction is supplied in accordance with this Directive.

Subsection 2

Supply of services connected with immovable property

Article 47

The place of supply of services connected with immovable property, including the services of experts and estate agents, the provision of accommodation in the hotel sector or in sectors with a similar function, such as holiday camps or sites developed for use as camping sites, the granting of rights to use immovable property and services for the preparation and coordination of construction work, such as the services of architects and of firms providing on-site supervision, shall be the place where the immovable property is located.

Subsection 3

Supply of transport

Article 48

The place of supply of passenger transport shall be the place where the transport takes place, proportionate to the distances covered.

Article 49

The place of supply of the transport of goods, other than the intra-Community transport of goods, to non-taxable persons shall be the place where the transport takes place, proportionate to the distances covered.

Article 50

The place of supply of the intra-Community transport of goods to non-taxable persons shall be the place of departure.

Article 51

"Intra-Community transport of goods" shall mean any transport of goods in respect of which the place of departure and the place of arrival are situated within the territories of two different Member States.

"Place of departure" shall mean the place where transport of the goods actually begins, irrespective of distances covered in order to reach the place where the goods are located and "place of arrival" shall mean the place where transport of the goods actually ends.

Article 52

Member States need not apply VAT to that part of the intra-Community transport of goods to non-taxable persons taking place over waters which do not form part of the territory of the Community.

Subsection 4

Supply of cultural, artistic, sporting, scientific, educational, entertainment and similar services, ancillary transport services and valuations of and work on movable property

Article 53

The place of supply of services and ancillary services relating to cultural, artistic, sporting, scientific, educational, entertainment or similar activities, such as fairs and exhibitions, including the supply of services of the organisers of such activities, shall be the place where those activities are physically carried out.

Article 54

The place of supply of the following services to non-taxable persons shall be the place where the services are physically carried out:

(a)   ancillary transport activities such as loading, unloading, handling and similar activities;

(b)   valuations of and work on movable tangible property.

Subsection 5

Supply of restaurant and catering services

Article 55

The place of supply of restaurant and catering services other than those physically carried out on board ships, aircraft or trains during the section of a passenger transport operation effected within the Community, shall be the place where the services are physically carried out.

Subsection 6

Hiring of means of transport

Article 56

1. The place of short-term hiring of a means of transport shall be the place where the means of transport is actually put at the disposal of the customer.

2. For the purposes of paragraph 1, "short-term" shall mean the continuous possession or use of the means of transport throughout a period of not more than thirty days and, in the case of vessels, not more than ninety days.

Subsection 7

Supply of restaurant and catering services for consumption on board ships, aircraft or trains

Article 57

1. The place of supply of restaurant and catering services which are physically carried out on board ships, aircraft or trains during the section of a passenger transport operation effected within the Community, shall be at the point of departure of the passenger transport operation.

2. For the purposes of paragraph 1, "section of a passenger transport operation effected within the Community" shall mean the section of the operation effected, without a stopover outside the Community, between the point of departure and the point of arrival of the passenger transport operation.

    "Point of departure of a passenger transport operation" shall mean the first scheduled point of passenger embarkation within the Community, where applicable after a stopover outside the Community.

    "Point of arrival of a passenger transport operation" shall mean the last scheduled point of disembarkation within the Community of passengers who embarked in the Community, where applicable before a stopover outside the Community. In the case of a return trip, the return leg shall be regarded as a separate transport operation.

Subsection 8

Supply of electronic services to non-taxable persons

Article 58

The place of supply of electronically supplied services, in particular those referred to in Annex II, when supplied to non-taxable persons who are established in a Member State, or who have their permanent address or usually reside in a Member State, by a taxable person who has established his business outside the Community or has a fixed establishment there from which the service is supplied, or who, in the absence of such a place of business or fixed establishment, has his permanent address or usually resides outside the Community, shall be the place where the non-taxable person is established, or where he has his permanent address or usually resides.

Where the supplier of a service and the customer communicate via electronic mail, that shall not of itself mean that the service supplied is an electronically supplied service.

Subsection 9

Supply of services to non-taxable persons outside the Community

Article 59

The place of supply of the following services to a non-taxable person who is established or has his permanent address or usually resides outside the Community, shall be the place where that person is established, has his permanent address or usually resides:

(a)   transfers and assignments of copyrights, patents, licences, trade marks and similar rights;

(b)   advertising services;

(c)   the services of consultants, engineers, consultancy firms, lawyers, accountants and other similar services, as well as data processing and the provision of information;

(d)   obligations to refrain from pursuing or exercising, in whole or in part, a business activity or a right referred to in this Article;

(e)   banking, financial and insurance transactions including reinsurance, with the exception of the hire of safes;

(f)   the supply of staff;

(g)   the hiring out of movable tangible property, with the exception of all means of transport;

(h)   the provision of access to, and of transport or transmission through, natural gas and electricity distribution systems and the provision of other services directly linked thereto;

(i)   telecommunications services;

(j)   radio and television broadcasting services;

(k)   electronically supplied services, in particular those referred to in Annex II.

Where the supplier of a service and the customer communicate via electronic mail, that shall not of itself mean that the service supplied is an electronically supplied service.

Subsection 1 0

Prevention of double taxation or non-taxation

Article 59a

In order to prevent double taxation, non-taxation or distortion of competition, Member States may, with regard to services the place of supply of which is governed by Articles 44, 45, 56 and 59:

(a)   consider the place of supply of any or all of those services, if situated within their territory, as being situated outside the Community if the effective use and enjoyment of the services takes place outside the Community;

(b)   consider the place of supply of any or all of those services, if situated outside the Community, as being situated within their territory if the effective use and enjoyment of the services takes place within their territory.

However, this provision shall not apply to the electronically supplied services where those services are rendered to non-taxable persons not established within the Community.

Article 59b

Member States shall apply Article 59a(b) to telecommunications services and radio and television broadcasting services, as referred to in point (j) of the first paragraph of Article 59, supplied to non-taxable persons who are established in a Member State, or who have their permanent address or usually reside in a Member State, by a taxable person who has established his business outside the Community or has a fixed establishment there from which the services are supplied, or who, in the absence of such a place of business or fixed establishment, has his permanent address or usually resides outside the Community.';

2.   in Article 98(2), the second subparagraph shall be replaced by the following:

'The reduced rates shall not apply to electronically supplied services.';

3.   the introductory sentence of Article 170 shall be replaced by the following:

All taxable persons who, within the meaning of Article 1 of Directive 86/560/EEC, Article 2(1) and Article 3 of Directive 2008/9/EC and Article 171 of this Directive, are not established in the Member State in which they purchase goods and services or import goods subject to VAT shall be entitled to obtain a refund of that VAT insofar as the goods and services are used for the purposes of the following:

4.   Article 171 shall be amended as follows:

(a)   paragraph 1 shall be replaced by the following:

'1.   VAT shall be refunded to taxable persons who are not established in the Member State in which they purchase goods and services or import goods subject to VAT but who are established in another Member State, in accordance with the detailed rules laid down in Directive 2008/9/EC.';

(b)   paragraph 3 shall be replaced by the following:

'3.   Directive 86/560/EEC shall not apply to:

(a)   amounts of VAT which according to the legislation of the Member State of refund have been incor rectly invoiced;

(b)   invoiced amounts of VAT in respect of supplies of goods the supply of which is, or may be, exempt pursuant to Article 138 or Article 146(1)(b).';

5.   the following Article 171a shall be inserted:

'Article 171a

Member States may, instead of granting a refund of VAT pursuant to Directives 86/560/EEC or 2008/9/EC on those supplies of goods or services to a taxable person in respect of which the taxable person is liable to pay the tax in accordance with Articles 194 to 197 or Article 199, allow deduction of this tax pursuant to the procedure laid down in Article 168. The existing restrictions pursuant to Article 2(2) and Article 4(2) of Directive 86/560/ EEC may be retained.

To that end, Member States may exclude the taxable person who is liable to pay the tax from the refund procedure pursuant to Directives 86/560/ EEC or 2008/9/EC.';

6.   in Section 1 of Chapter 1 of Title XI, the following Article 192a shall be inserted:

'Article 192a

For the purposes of this Section, a taxable person who has a fixed establishment within the territory of the Member State where the tax is due shall be regarded as a taxable person who is not established within that Member State when the following conditions are met:

(a)   he makes a taxable supply of goods or of services within the territory of that Member State;

(b)   an establishment which the supplier has within the territory of that Member State does not intervene in that supply.';

7.   Article 196 shall be replaced by the following:

Article 196

VAT shall be payable by any taxable person, or non-taxable legal person identified for VAT purposes, to whom the services referred to in Article 44 are supplied, if the services are supplied by a taxable person not established within the territory of the Member State.';

8.   in Article 214, the following points shall be added:

     '(d)   every taxable person who within their respective territory receives services for which he is liable to pay VAT pursuant to Article 196;

     (e)   every taxable person, established within their respective territory, who supplies services within the territory of another Member State for which VAT is payable solely by the recipient pursuant to Article 196.';

9.   Article 262 shall be replaced by the following:

Article 262

Every taxable person identified for VAT purposes shall submit a recapitulative statement of the following:

     (a)   the acquirers identified for VAT purposes to whom he has supplied goods in accordance with the conditions specified in Article 138(1) and (2)(c);

     (b)   the persons identified for VAT purposes to whom he has supplied goods which were supplied to him by way of intra-Community acquisitions referred to in Article 42;

     (c)   the taxable persons, and the non-taxable legal persons identified for VAT purposes, to whom he has supplied services, other than services that are exempted from VAT in the Member State where the transaction is taxable, and for which the recipient is liable to pay the tax pursuant to Article 196.';

10.   in Article 264, paragraph 1 shall be amended as follows:

     (a)   points (a) and (b) shall be replaced by the following:

          '(a)   the VAT identification number of the taxable person in the Member State in which the recapitulative statement must be submitted and under which he has carried out the supply of goods in accordance with the conditions specified in Article 138(1) and under which he effected taxable supplies of services in accordance with the conditions laid down in Article 44;

          (b)   the VAT identification number of the person acquiring the goods or receiving the services in a Member State other than that in which the recapitulative statement must be submitted and under which the goods or services were supplied to him;';

(b)   point (d) shall be replaced by the following:

'(d)   for each person who acquired goods or received services, the total value of the supplies of goods and the total value of the supplies of services carried out by the taxable person;';

11.   Article 358 shall be amended as follows:

(a)   point (2) shall be replaced by the following:

'(2)   "electronic services" and "electronically supplied services" mean the services referred to in point (k) of the first paragraph of Article 59;';

(b)   point (4) shall be replaced by the following:

'(4)   "Member State of consumption" means the Member State in which, pursuant to Article 58, the supply of the electronic services is deemed to take place;';

12.   in Annex II, the heading shall be replaced by the following:

INDICATIVE LIST OF THE ELECTRONICALLY SUPPLIED SERVICES REFERRED TO IN ARTICLE 58 AND POINT (K) OF THE FIRST PARAGRAPH OF ARTICLE 59'.

Article 3

From 1 January 2011, Articles 53 and 54 of Directive 2006/112/EC shall be replaced by the following:

'Article 53

The place of supply of services in respect of admission to cultural, artistic, sporting, scientific, educational, entertainment or similar events, such as fairs and exhibitions, and of ancillary services related to the admission, supplied to a taxable person, shall be the place where those events actually take place.

Article 54

1.   The place of supply of services and ancillary services, relating to cultural, artistic, sporting, scientific, educational, entertainment or similar activities, such as fairs and exhibitions, including the supply of services of the organisers of such activities, supplied to a non-taxable person shall be the place where those activities actually take place.

2.   The place of supply of the following services to a non- taxable person shall be the place where the services are physically carried out:

(a)   ancillary transport activities such as loading, unloading, handling and similar activities;

(b)   valuations of and work on movable tangible property.'.

Article 4

From 1 January 2013, Article 56(2) of Directive 2006/112/EC shall be replaced by the following:

'2.   The place of hiring, other than short-term hiring, of a means of transport to a non-taxable person shall be the place where the customer is established, has his permanent address or usually resides.

However, the place of hiring a pleasure boat to a non-taxable person, other than short-term hiring, shall be the place where the pleasure boat is actually put at the disposal of the customer, where this service is actually provided by the supplier from his place of business or a fixed establishment situated in that place.

3.   For the purposes of paragraphs 1 and 2, "short-term" shall mean the continuous possession or use of the means of transport throughout a period of not more than thirty days and, in the case of vessels, not more than 90 days.'.

Article 5

From 1 January 2015, Directive 2006/112/EC is hereby amended as follows:

1.   in Section 3 of Chapter 3 of Title V, Subsection 8 shall be replaced by the following:

'Subsection 8

Supply of telecommunications, broadcasting and electronic services
to non-taxable persons

Article 58

The place of supply of the following services to a non-taxable person shall be the place where that person is established, has his permanent address or usually resides:

(a)   telecommunications services;

(b)   radio and television broadcasting services;

(c)   electronically supplied services, in particular those referred to in Annex II.

Where the supplier of a service and the customer communicate via electronic mail, that shall not of itself mean that the service supplied is an electronically supplied service.';

2.   in Article 59, points (i), (j) and (k) of the first paragraph and the second paragraph shall be deleted;

3.   Article 59a shall be replaced by the following:

'Article 59a

In order to prevent double taxation, non-taxation or distortion of competition, Member States may, with regard to services the place of supply of which is governed by Articles 44, 45, 56, 58 and 59:

(a)   consider the place of supply of any or all of those services, if situated within their territory, as being situated outside the Community if the effective use and enjoyment of the services takes place outside the Community;

(b)   consider the place of supply of any or all of those services, if situated outside the Community, as being situated within their territory if the effective use and enjoyment of the services takes place within their territory.';

4.   Article 59b shall be deleted;

5.   in Article 204(1), the third subparagraph shall be replaced by the following:

'However, Member States may not apply the option referred to in the second subparagraph to a taxable person not established within the Community, within the meaning of point (1) of Article 358a, who has opted for the special scheme for telecommunications, broadcasting or electronic services.';

6.   in Title XII, the heading of Chapter 6 shall be replaced by the following:

'Special schemes for non-established taxable persons supplying telecommunications services, broadcasting services or electronic services to non-taxable persons.';

7.   Article 357 shall be deleted;

8.   Article 358 shall be replaced by the following:

'Article 358

For the purposes of this Chapter, and without prejudice to other Community provisions, the following definitions shall apply:

1.   "telecommunications services" and "broadcasting services" mean the services referred to in points (a) and (b) of the first paragraph of Article 58;

2.   "electronic services" and "electronically supplied services" mean the services referred to in point (c) of the first paragraph of Article 58;

3.   "Member State of consumption" means the Member State in which the supply of the telecommunications, broadcasting or electronic services is deemed to take place according to Article 58;

4.   "VAT return" means the statement containing the information necessary to establish the amount of VAT due in each Member State.';

9. in Chapter 6 of Title XII, the heading of Section 2 shall be replaced by the following:

'Special scheme for telecommunications, broadcasting or electronic services supplied by taxable persons not established within the Community';

10. in Section 2 of Chapter 6 of Title XII, the following Article shall be inserted:

Article 358a

For the purposes of this Section, and without prejudice to other Community provisions, the following definitions shall apply:

1.   "taxable person not established within the Community" means a taxable person who has not established his business in the territory of the Community and who has no fixed establishment there and who is not otherwise required to be identified for VAT purposes;

2.   "Member State of identification" means the Member State which the taxable person not established within the Community chooses to contact to state when his activity as a taxable person within the territory of the Community commences in accordance with the provisions of this Section.';

11. Articles 359 to 365 shall be replaced by the following:

'Article 359

Member States shall permit any taxable person not established within the Community supplying telecommunications, broadcasting or electronic services to a non-taxable person who is established in a Member State or has his permanent address or usually resides in a Member State, to use this special scheme. This scheme applies to all those services supplied within the Community.

Article 360

The taxable person not established within the Community shall state to the Member State of identification when he commences or ceases his activity as a taxable person, or changes that activity in such a way that he no longer meets the conditions necessary for use of this special scheme. He shall communicate that information electronically.

Article 361

1.   The information which the taxable person not established within the Community must provide to the Member State of identification when he commences a taxable activity shall contain the following details:

(a)   name;

(b)   postal address;

(c)   electronic addresses, including websites;

(d)   national tax number, if any;

(e)   a statement that the person is not identified for VAT purposes within the Community.

2.   The taxable person not established within in the Community shall notify the Member State of identification of any changes in the information provided.

Article 362

The Member State of identification shall allocate to the taxable person not established within the Community an individual VAT identification number and shall notify him of that number by electronic means. On the basis of the information used for that identification, Member States of consumption may have recourse to their own identification systems.

Article 363

The Member State of identification shall delete the taxable person not established within the Community from the identification register in the following cases:

(a)   if he notifies that Member State that he no longer supplies telecommunications, broadcasting or electronic services;

(b)   if it may otherwise be assumed that his taxable activities have ceased;

(c)   if he no longer meets the conditions necessary for use of this special scheme;

(d)   if he persistently fails to comply with the rules relating to this special scheme.

Article 364

The taxable person not established within the Community shall submit by electronic means to the Member State of identification a VAT return for each calendar quarter, whether or not telecommunications, broadcasting or electronic services have been supplied. The VAT return shall be submitted within 20 days following the end of the tax period covered by the return.

Article 365

The VAT return shall show the identification number and, for each Member State of consumption in which VAT is due, the total value, exclusive of VAT, of supplies of telecommunications, broadcasting and electronic services carried out during the tax period and total amount per rate of the corresponding VAT. The applicable rates of VAT and the total VAT due must also be indicated on the return.';

12. Article 366(1) shall be replaced by the following:

'1. The VAT return shall be made out in euro.

Member States which have not adopted the euro may require the VAT return to be made out in their national currency. If the supplies have been made in other currencies, the taxable person not established within the Community shall, for the purposes of completing the VAT return, use the exchange rate applying on the last day of the tax period.';

13. Articles 367 and 368 shall be replaced by the following:

'Article 367

The taxable person not established within the Community shall pay the VAT, making reference to the relevant VAT return, when submitting the VAT return, at the latest, however, at the expiry of the deadline by which the return must be submitted.

Payment shall be made to a bank account denominated in euro, designated by the Member State of identification. Member States which have not adopted the euro may require the payment to be made to a bank account denominated in their own currency.

Article 368

The taxable person not established within the Community making use of this special scheme may not deduct VAT pursuant to Article 168 of this Directive. Notwithstanding Article 1(1) of Directive 86/560/EEC, the taxable person in question shall be refunded in accordance with the said Directive. Articles 2(2) and (3) and Article 4(2) of Directive 86/560/EEC shall not apply to refunds relating to telecommunications, broadcasting or electronic services covered by this special scheme.';

14. Article 369(1) shall be replaced by the following:

'1. The taxable person not established within the Community shall keep records of the transactions covered by this special scheme. Those records must be sufficiently detailed to enable the tax authorities of the Member State of consumption to verify that the VAT return is correct.';

15. in Chapter 6 of Title XII, the following Section shall be inserted:

'Section 3

Special scheme for telecommunications, broadcasting or electronic services supplied by taxable persons established within the Community but not in the Member State of consumption

Article 369a

For the purposes of this Section, and without prejudice to other Community provisions, the following definitions shall apply:

1. "taxable person not established in the Member State of consumption" means a taxable person who has estab lished his business in the territory of the Community or has a fixed establishment there but has not established his business and has no fixed establishment within the territory of the Member State of consumption;

2. "Member State of identification" means the Member State in the territory of which the taxable person has established his business or, if he has not established his business in the Community, where he has a fixed estab lishment.

Where a taxable person has not established his business in the Community, but has more than one fixed establishment therein, the Member State of identification shall be the Member State with a fixed establishment where that taxable person indicates that he will make use of this special scheme. The taxable person shall be bound by this decision for the calendar year concerned and the two calendar years following.

Article 369b

Member States shall permit any taxable person not established in the Member State of consumption supplying telecommunications, broadcasting or electronic services to a non-taxable person who is established or has his permanent address or usually resides in that Member State, to use this special scheme. This special scheme applies to all those services supplied in the Community.

Article 369c

The taxable person not established in the Member State of consumption shall state to the Member State of identification when he commences and ceases his taxable activities covered by this special scheme, or changes those activities in such a way that he no longer meets the conditions necessary for use of this special scheme. He shall communicate that information electronically.

Article 369d

A taxable person making use of this special scheme shall, for the taxable transactions carried out under this scheme, be identified for VAT purposes in the Member State of identification only. For that purpose the Member State shall use the individual VAT identification number already allocated to the taxable person in respect of his obligations under the internal system.

On the basis of the information used for that identification, Member States of consumption may have recourse to their own identification systems.

Article 369e

The Member State of identification shall exclude the taxable person not established in the Member State of consumption from this special scheme in any of the following cases:

(a)   if he notifies that he no longer supplies telecommuni cations, broadcasting or electronic services;

(b)   if it may otherwise be assumed that his taxable activities covered by this special scheme have ceased;

(c)   if he no longer meets the conditions necessary for use of this special scheme;

(d)   if he persistently fails to comply with the rules relating to this special scheme.

Article 369f

The taxable person not established in the Member State of consumption shall submit by electronic means to the Member State of identification a VAT return for each calendar quarter, whether or not telecommunications, broadcasting or electronic services have been supplied. The VAT return shall be submitted within 20 days following the end of the tax period covered by the return.

Article 369g

The VAT return shall show the identification number referred to in Article 369d and, for each Member State of consumption in which VAT is due, the total value, exclusive of VAT, of supplies of telecommunications, broadcasting or electronic services carried out during the tax period and the total amount per rate of the corresponding VAT. The applicable rates of VAT and the total VAT due must also be indicated on the return.

Where the taxable person has one or more fixed establishments, other than that in the Member State of identification, from which the services are supplied, the VAT return shall in addition to the information referred to in the first paragraph include the total value of supplies of telecommunications, broadcasting or electronic services covered by this special scheme, for each Member State in which he has an establishment, together with the individual VAT identification number or the tax reference number of this establishment, broken down by Member State of consumption.

Article 369h

1. The VAT return shall be made out in euro.

    Member States which have not adopted the euro may require the VAT return to be made out in their national currency. If the supplies have been made in other currencies, the taxable person not established in the Member State of consumption shall, for the purposes of completing the VAT return, use the exchange rate applying on the last date of the tax period.

2. The conversion shall be made by applying the exchange rates published by the European Central Bank for that day, or, if there is no publication on that day, on the next day of publication.

Article 369i

The taxable person not established in the Member State of consumption shall pay the VAT, making reference to the relevant VAT return, when submitting the VAT return, at the latest, however, at the expiry of the deadline by which the return must be submitted.

Payment shall be made to a bank account denominated in euro, designated by the Member State of identification. Member States which have not adopted the euro may require the payment to be made to a bank account denominated in their own currency.

Article 369j

The taxable person not established in the Member State of consumption making use of this special scheme may not, in respect of his taxable activities covered by this scheme, deduct VAT pursuant to Article 168 of this Directive. Notwithstanding Article 2(1) and Article 3 of Directive 2008/9/EC, the taxable person in question shall be refunded in accordance with the said Directive.

If the taxable person not established in the Member State of consumption making use of this special scheme also carries out in the Member State of consumption activities not covered by this scheme in respect of which he is obliged to be registered for VAT purposes, he shall deduct VAT in respect of his taxable activities which are covered by this scheme in the VAT return to be submitted pursuant to Article 250.

Article 369k

1. The taxable person not established in the Member State of consumption shall keep records of the transactions covered by this special scheme. Those records must be sufficiently detailed to enable the tax authorities of the Member State of consumption to verify that the VAT return is correct.

2. The records referred to in paragraph 1 must be made available electronically on request to the Member State of consumption and to the Member State of identification.

Those records must be kept for a period of 10 years from 31 December of the year during which the transaction was carried out.';

16.   in Annex II, the heading shall be replaced by the following:

INDICATIVE LIST OF THE ELECTRONICALLY SUPPLIED SERVICES REFERRED TO IN POINT (C) OF THE FIRST PARAGRAPH OF ARTICLE 58'.

Article 6

The Commission shall, by 31 December 2014, submit a report on the feasibility of applying efficiently the rule laid down in Article 5 for the supply of telecommunications services, radio and television broadcasting services and electronically supplied services to non-taxable persons and on the question whether that rule still corresponds to the general policy at that time concerning the place of supply of services.

Article 7

1.   Member States shall bring into force the laws, regulations and administrative provisions necessary to comply with Articles 1 to 5 of this Directive from the respective dates provided for in those provisions.

They shall forthwith inform the Commission thereof. When Member States adopt these provisions, they shall contain a reference to this Directive or be accompanied by such a reference on the occasion of their official publication. The methods of making such reference shall be laid down by Member States.

2.   Member States shall communicate to the Commission the text of the main provisions of national law which they adopt in the field covered by this Directive.

Article 8

This Directive shall enter into force on the day of its publication in the *Official Journal of the European Union*.

Article 9

This Directive is addressed to the Member States.

Done at Brussels, 12 February 2008.

For the Council
The President
A. BAJUK

COUNCIL DIRECTIVE 2008/9/EEC

of 12 February 2008

laying down detailed rules for the refund of value added tax, provided for in Directive 2006/112/EC, to taxable persons not established in the Member State of refund but established in another Member State

Official Journal L 44, 20/2/2008, p. 23–28

THE COUNCIL OF THE EUROPEAN UNION,

Having regard to the Treaty establishing the European Community, and in particular Article 93 thereof,

Having regard to the proposal from the Commission,

Having regard to the opinion of the European Parliament,

Having regard to the opinion of the European Economic and Social Committee,

Whereas:

(1) Considerable problems are posed, both for the administrative authorities of Member States and for businesses, by the implementing rules laid down by Council Directive 79/1072/EEC of 6 December 1979 on the harmonisation of the laws of the Member States relating to turnover taxes - Arrangements for the refund of value added tax to taxable persons not established in the territory of the country.

(2) The arrangements laid down in that Directive should be amended in respect of the period within which decisions concerning applications for refund are notified to businesses. At the same time, it should be laid down that businesses too must provide responses within specified periods. In addition, the procedure should be simplified and modernised by allowing for the use of modern technologies.

(3) The new procedure should enhance the position of businesses since the Member States shall be liable to pay interest if the refund is made late and the right of appeal by businesses will be strengthened.

(4) For clarity and better reading purposes, the provision concerning the application of Directive 79/1072/EEC, previously contained in Council Directive 2006/112/EC of 28 November 2006 on the common system of value added tax, should now be integrated in this Directive.

(5) Since the objectives of this Directive cannot be sufficiently achieved by the Member States and can therefore, by reason of the scale of the action, be better achieved at Community level, the Community may adopt measures, in accordance with the principle of subsidiarity as set out in Article 5 of the Treaty. In accordance with the principle of proportionality, as set out in that Article, this Directive does not go beyond what is necessary in order to achieve those objectives.

(6) In accordance with point 34 of the Interinstitutional Agreement on better law-making, Member States are encouraged to draw up, for themselves and in the interests of the Community, their own tables

illustrating, as far as possible, the correlation between this Directive and the transposition measures, and to make them public.

(7)   In the interest of clarity, Directive 79/1072/EEC should therefore be repealed, subject to the necessary transitional measures with respect to refund applications introduced before 1 January 2010,

HAS ADOPTED THIS DIRECTIVE:

Article 1

This Directive lays down the detailed rules for the refund of value added tax (VAT), provided for in Article 170 of Directive 2006/112/EC, to taxable persons not established in the Member State of refund, who meet the conditions laid down in Article 3.

Article 2

For the purposes of this Directive, the following definitions shall apply:

1.   'taxable person not established in the Member State of refund' means a taxable person within the meaning of Article 9(1) of Directive 2006/112/EC who is not established in the Member State of refund but established in the territory of another Member State;

2.   'Member State of refund' means the Member State in which the VAT was charged to the taxable person not established in the Member State of refund in respect of goods or services supplied to him by other taxable persons in that Member State or in respect of the importation of goods into that Member State;

3.   'refund period' means the period mentioned in Article 16 covered by the refund application;

4.   'refund application' means the application for refund of VAT charged in the Member State of refund to the taxable person not established in the Member State of refund in respect of goods or services supplied to him by other taxable persons in that Member State or in respect of the importation of goods into that Member State;

5.   'applicant' means the taxable person not established in the Member State of refund making the refund application.

Article 3

This Directive shall apply to any taxable person not established in the Member State of refund who meets the following conditions:

(a)   during the refund period, he has not had in the Member State of refund, the seat of his economic activity, or a fixed establishment from which business transactions were effected, or, if no such seat or fixed establishment existed, his domicile or normal place of residence;

(b)   during the refund period, he has not supplied any goods or services deemed to have been supplied in the Member State of refund, with the exception of the following transactions:

  (i)   the supply of transport services and services ancillary thereto, exempted pursuant to Articles 144, 146, 148, 149, 151, 153, 159 or 160 of Directive 2006/112/EC;

  (ii)   the supply of goods and services to a person who is liable for payment of VAT in accordance with Articles 194 to 197 and Article 199 of Directive 2006/112/EC.

Article 4

This Directive shall not apply to:

(a)   amounts of VAT which, according to the legislation of the Member State of refund, have been incorrectly invoiced;

(b)   amounts of VAT which have been invoiced in respect of supplies of goods the supply of which is, or may be, exempt under Article 138 or Article 146(1)(b) of Directive 2006/112/EC.

Article 5

Each Member State shall refund to any taxable person not established in the Member State of refund any VAT charged in respect of goods or services supplied to him by other taxable persons in that Member State or in respect of the importation of goods into that Member State, insofar as such goods and services are used for the purposes of the following transactions:

(a)   transactions referred to in Article 169(a) and (b) of Directive 2006/112/EC;

(b)   transactions to a person who is liable for payment of VAT in accordance with Articles 194 to 197 and Article 199 of Directive 2006/112/EC as applied in the Member State of refund.

Without prejudice to Article 6, for the purposes of this Directive, entitlement to an input tax refund shall be determined pursuant to Directive 2006/112/EC as applied in the Member State of refund.

Article 6

To be eligible for a refund in the Member State of refund, a taxable person not established in the Member State of refund has to carry out transactions giving rise to a right of deduction in the Member State of establishment.

When a taxable person not established in the Member State of refund carries out in the Member State in which he is established both transactions giving rise to a right of deduction and transactions not giving rise to a right of deduction in that Member State, only such proportion of the VAT which is refundable in accordance with Article 5 may be refunded by the Member State of refund as is attributable to the former transactions in accordance with Article 173 of Directive 2006/112/EC as applied by the Member State of establishment.

Article 7

To obtain a refund of VAT in the Member State of refund, the taxable person not established in the Member State of refund shall address an electronic refund application to that Member State and submit it to the Member State in which he is established via the electronic portal set up by that Member State.

Article 8

1. The refund application shall contain the following information:

    (a) the applicant's name and full address;

    (b) an address for contact by electronic means;

    (c) a description of the applicant's business activity for which the goods and services are acquired;

    (d) the refund period covered by the application;

    (e) a declaration by the applicant that he has supplied no goods and services deemed to have been supplied in the Member State of refund during the refund period, with the exception of transactions referred to in points (i) and (ii) of Article 3(b);

    (f) the applicant's VAT identification number or tax reference number;

    (g) bank account details including BAN and BIC codes.

2. In addition to the information specified in paragraph 1, the refund application shall set out, for each Member State of refund and for each invoice or importation document, the following details:

    (a) name and full address of the supplier;

    (b) except in the case of importation, the VAT identification number or tax reference number of the supplier, as allocated by the Member State of refund in accordance with the provisions of Articles 239 and 240 of Directive 2006/112/EC;

    (c) except in the case of importation, the prefix of the Member State of refund in accordance with Article 215 of Directive 2006/112/EC;

    (d) date and number of the invoice or importation document;

    (e) taxable amount and amount of VAT expressed in the currency of the Member State of refund;

    (f) the amount of deductible VAT calculated in accordance with Article 5 and the second paragraph of Article 6 expressed in the currency of the Member State of refund;

    (g) where applicable, the deductible proportion calculated in accordance with Article 6, expressed as a percentage;

    (h) nature of the goods and services acquired, described according to the codes in Article 9.

Article 9

1.   In the refund application, the nature of the goods and services acquired shall be described by the following codes:

     1   = fuel;

     2   = hiring of means of transport;

     3   = expenditure relating to means of transport (other than the goods and services referred to under codes 1 and 2);

     4   = road tolls and road user charge;

     5   = travel expenses, such as taxi fares, public transport fares;

     6   = accommodation;

     7   = food, drink and restaurant services;

     8   = admissions to fairs and exhibitions;

     9   = expenditure on luxuries, amusements and entertainment;

     10   = other.

     If code 10 is used, the nature of the goods and services supplied shall be indicated.

2.   The Member State of refund may require the applicant to provide additional electronic coded information as regards each code set out in paragraph 1 to the extent that such information is necessary because of any restrictions on the right of deduction under Directive 2006/112/EC, as applicable in the Member State of refund or for the implementation of a relevant derogation received by the Member State of refund under Articles 395 or 396 of that Directive.

Article 10

Without prejudice to requests for information under Article 20, the Member State of refund may require the applicant to submit by electronic means a copy of the invoice or importation document with the refund application where the taxable amount on an invoice or importation document is EUR 1 000 or more or the equivalent in national currency. Where the invoice concerns fuel, the threshold is EUR 250 or the equivalent in national currency.

Article 11

The Member State of refund may require the applicant to provide a description of his business activity by using the harmonised codes determined in accordance with the second subparagraph of Article 34a(3) of Council Regulation (EC) No 1798/2003.

Article 12

The Member State of refund may specify which language or languages shall be used by the applicant for the provision of information in the refund application or of possible additional information.

Article 13

If subsequent to the submission of the refund application the deductible proportion is adjusted pursuant to Article 175 of Directive 2006/112/EC, the applicant shall make a correction to the amount applied for or already refunded.

The correction shall be made in a refund application during the calendar year following the refund period in question or, if the applicant makes no refund applications during that calendar year, by submitting a separate declaration via the electronic portal established by the Member State of establishment.

Article 14

1. The refund application shall relate to the following:

    (a)   the purchase of goods or services which was invoiced during the refund period, provided that the VAT became chargeable before or at the time of the invoicing, or in respect of which the VAT became chargeable during the refund period, provided that the purchase was invoiced before the tax became chargeable;

    (b)   the importation of goods during the refund period.

2. In addition to the transactions referred to in paragraph 1, the refund application may relate to invoices or import documents not covered by previous refund applications and concerning transactions completed during the calendar year in question.

Article 15

1. The refund application shall be submitted to the Member State of establishment at the latest on 30 September of the calendar year following the refund period. The application shall be considered submitted only if the applicant has filled in all the information required under Articles 8, 9 and 11.

2. The Member State of establishment shall send the applicant an electronic confirmation of receipt without delay.

Article 16

The refund period shall not be more than one calendar year or less than three calendar months. Refund applications may, however, relate to a period of less than three months where the period represents the remainder of a calendar year.

Article 17

If the refund application relates to a refund period of less than one calendar year but not less than three months, the amount of VAT for which a refund is applied for may not be less than €400 or the equivalent in national currency.

If the refund application relates to a refund period of a calendar year or the remainder of a calendar year, the amount of VAT may not be less than €50 or the equivalent in national currency.

Article 18

1. The Member State of establishment shall not forward the application to the Member State of refund where, during the refund period, any of the following circumstances apply to the applicant in the Member State of establishment:

   (a) he is not a taxable person for VAT purposes;

   (b) he carries out only supplies of goods or of services which are exempt without deductibility of the VAT paid at the preceding stage pursuant to Articles 132, 135, 136, 371, Articles 374 to 377, Article 378(2)(a), Article 379(2) or Articles 380 to 390 of Directive 2006/112/EC or provisions providing for identical exemptions contained in the 2005 Act of Accession;

   (c) he is covered by the exemption for small enterprises provided for in Articles 284, 285, 286 and 287 of Directive 2006/112/EC;

   (d) he is covered by the common flat-rate scheme for farmers provided for in Articles 296 to 305 of Directive 2006/112/EC.

2. The Member State of establishment shall notify the applicant by electronic means of the decision it has taken pursuant to paragraph 1.

Article 19

1. The Member State of refund shall notify the applicant without delay, by electronic means, of the date on which it received the application.

2. The Member State of refund shall notify the applicant of its decision to approve or refuse the refund application within four months of its receipt by that Member State.

Article 20

1. Where the Member State of refund considers that it does not have all the relevant information on which to make a decision in respect of the whole or part of the refund application, it may request, by electronic means, additional information, in particular from the applicant or from the competent authorities of the Member State of establishment, within the four month period referred to in Article 19(2). Where the additional information is requested from someone other than the applicant or a competent authority of a Member State, the request shall be made by

electronic means only if such means are available to the recipient of the request.

If necessary, the Member State of refund may request further additional information.

The information requested in accordance with this paragraph may include the submission of the original or a copy of the relevant invoice or import document where the Member State of refund has reasonable doubts regarding the validity or accuracy of a particular claim. In that case, the thresholds mentioned in Article 10 shall not apply.

2. The Member State of refund shall be provided with the information requested under paragraph 1 within one month of the date on which the request reaches the person to whom it is addressed.

Article 21

Where the Member State of refund requests additional information, it shall notify the applicant of its decision to approve or refuse the refund application within two months of receiving the requested information or, if it has not received a reply to its request, within two months of expiry of the time limit laid down in Article 20(2). However, the period available for the decision in respect of the whole or part of the refund application shall always be at least six months from the date of receipt of the application by the Member State of refund.

Where the Member State of refund requests further additional information, it shall notify the applicant of its decision in respect of the whole or part of the refund application within eight months of receipt of the application by that Member State.

Article 22

1. Where the refund application is approved, refunds of the approved amount shall be paid by the Member State of refund at the latest within 10 working days of the expiry of the deadline referred to in Article 19(2) or, where additional or further additional information has been requested, the deadlines referred to in Article 21.

2. The refund shall be paid in the Member State of refund or, at the applicant's request, in any other Member State. In the latter case, any bank charges for the transfer shall be deducted by the Member State of refund from the amount to be paid to the applicant.

Article 23

1. Where the refund application is refused in whole or in part, the grounds for refusal shall be notified by the Member State of refund to the applicant together with the decision.

2. Appeals against decisions to refuse a refund application may be made by the applicant to the competent authorities of the Member State of refund in the forms and within the time limits laid down for appeals in

the case of refund applications from persons who are established in that Member State.

If, under the law of the Member State of refund, failure to take a decision on a refund application within the time limits specified in this Directive is not regarded either as approval or as refusal, any administrative or judicial procedures which are available in that situation to taxable persons established in that Member State shall be equally available to the applicant. If no such procedures are available, failure to take a decision on a refund application within these time limits shall mean that the application is deemed to be rejected.

Article 24

1. Where a refund has been obtained in a fraudulent way or otherwise incorrectly, the competent authority in the Member State of refund shall proceed directly to recover the amounts wrongly paid and any penalties and interest imposed in accordance with the procedure applicable in the Member State of refund, without prejudice to the provisions on mutual assistance for the recovery of VAT.

2. Where an administrative penalty or interest has been imposed but has not been paid, the Member State of refund may suspend any further refund to the taxable person concerned up to the unpaid amount.

Article 25

The Member State of refund shall take into account as a decrease or increase of the amount of the refund any correction made concerning a previous refund application in accordance with Article 13 or, where a separate declaration is submitted, in the form of separate payment or recovery.

Article 26

Interest shall be due to the applicant by the Member State of refund on the amount of the refund to be paid if the refund is paid after the last date of payment pursuant to Article 22(1).

If the applicant does not submit the additional or further additional information requested to the Member State of refund within the specified time limit, the first paragraph shall not apply. It shall also not apply until the documents to be submitted electronically pursuant to Article 10 have been received by the Member State of refund.

Article 27

1. Interest shall be calculated from the day following the last day for payment of the refund pursuant to Article 22(1) until the day the refund is actually paid.

2. Interest rates shall be equal to the interest rate applicable with respect to refunds of VAT to taxable persons established in the Member State of refund under the national law of that Member State.

If no interest is payable under national law in respect of refunds to established taxable persons, the interest payable shall be equal to the interest or equivalent charge which is applied by the Member State of refund in respect of late payments of VAT by taxable persons.

Article 28

1.   This Directive shall apply to refund applications submitted after 31 December 2009.

2.   Directive 79/1072/EEC shall be repealed with effect from 1 January 2010. However, its provisions shall continue to apply to refund applications submitted before 1 January 2010.

References to the repealed Directive shall be construed as references to this Directive except for refund applications submitted before 1 January 2010.

Article 29

1.   Member States shall bring into force the laws, regulations and administrative provisions necessary to comply with this Directive with effect from 1 January 2010. They shall forthwith inform the Commission thereof.

When such provisions are adopted by Member States, they shall contain a reference to this Directive or be accompanied by such reference on the occasion of their official publication. The methods of making such reference shall be laid down by Member States.

2.   Member States shall communicate to the Commission the text of the main provisions of national law which they adopt in the field covered by this Directive.

Article 30

This Directive shall enter into force on the day of its publication in the *Official Journal of the European Union.*

Article 31

This Directive is addressed to the Member States.

Done at Brussels, 12 February 2008.

For the Council
The President
A. BAJUK

COUNCIL REGULATION (EC) No 143/2008

of 12 February 2008

amending Regulation (EC) No 1798/2003 as regards the introduction of administrative cooperation and the exchange of information concerning the rules relating to the place of supply of services, the special schemes and the refund procedure for value added tax

Official Journal L 44, 20/2/2008, p. 01–06

THE COUNCIL OF THE EUROPEAN UNION,

Having regard to the Treaty establishing the European Community, and in particular Article 93 thereof,

Having regard to the proposal from the Commission,

Having regard to the opinion of the European Parliament,

Having regard to the opinion of the European Economic and Social Committee,

Whereas:

(1)   The amendments introduced with regard to the place of supply of services by Council Directive 2008/8/EC of 12 February 2008 amending Directive 2006/112/EC as regards the place of supply of services mean that services to taxable persons are supplied principally where the recipient is established. Where the supplier and the recipient of the services are established in different Member States, the reverse charge mechanism will be applicable more frequently than hitherto.

(2)   To ensure the proper application of value added tax (VAT) on services which are subject to the reverse charge mechanism, the data collected by the Member State of the supplier should be communicated to the Member State where the recipient is established. Council Regulation (EC) No 1798/2003 of 7 October 2003 on administrative cooperation in the field of value added tax should provide for such communication.

(3)   Directive 2008/8/EC also extends the scope of the special scheme for electronic services supplied by taxable persons not established within the Community.

(4)   Council Directive 2008/9/EC of 12 February 2008 laying down detailed rules for the refund of value added tax, provided for in Directive 2006/112/EC, to taxable persons not established in the Member State of refund but in another Member State simplifies the refund procedure for VAT in a Member State in which the taxable person concerned is not identified for VAT purposes.

(5)   The extension of the scope of the special scheme and the amendments to the refund procedure for taxable persons not established in the Member State of refund mean that the Member States concerned will need to exchange considerably more information. The required exchange of information should not make any excessive administrative demands on the Member State concerned. This exchange of information should

thus take place electronically under existing systems for exchanging information.

(6) Regulation (EC) No 1798/2003 should therefore be amended accordingly,

HAS ADOPTED THIS REGULATION:

Article 1

From 1 January 2010, Regulation (EC) No 1798/2003 is hereby amended as follows:

1. in Article 1(1), the fourth subparagraph shall be replaced by the following:

    'For the period provided for in Article 357 of Council Directive 2006/112/EC of 28 November 2006 on the common system of value added tax, it also lays down rules and procedures for the exchange by electronic means of value added tax information on services supplied electronically in accordance with the special scheme provided for in Chapter 6 of Title XII of that Directive and also for any subsequent exchange of information and, as far as services covered by that special scheme are concerned, for the transfer of money between Member States' competent authorities.

2. in Article 2, points 8 to 11 shall be replaced by the following:

    '8.   "intra-Community supply of goods" means any supply of goods which must be declared in the recapitulative statement provided for in Article 262 of Directive 2006/112/EC;

    9.   "intra-Community supply of services" means any supply of services which must be declared in the recapitulative statement provided for in Article 262 of Directive 2006/112/EC;

    10.   "intra-Community acquisition of goods" means the acquisition of the right under Article 20 of Directive 2006/112/EC to dispose as owner of moveable tangible property;

    11.   "VAT identification number" means the number provided for in Articles 214, 215 and 216 of Directive 2006/112/EC;';

3. in Article 22(1), the first subparagraph shall be replaced by the following:

    '1.   Each Member State shall maintain an electronic database in which it stores and processes the information which it collects pursuant to Chapter 6 of Title XI of Directive 2006/112/EC.';

4. in the first paragraph of Article 23, point 2 shall be replaced by the following:

    '2.   the total value of all intra-Community supplies of goods and the total value of all intra-Community supplies of services to persons holding a VAT identification number by all operators identified for the purposes of VAT in the Member State providing the information.';

5. in Article 24, the first paragraph shall be replaced by the following:

    'On the basis of the data stored in accordance with Article 22 and solely in order to prevent a breach of VAT legislation, the competent authority of a Member State shall, wherever it considers it necessary for the control of intra-Community acquisitions of goods or intra-Community supplies of services taxable in its territory, obtain directly and without delay, or have direct access to by electronic means, any of the following information:

    1. the VAT identification numbers of the persons who carried out the supplies of goods and services referred to in point 2 of the first paragraph of Article 23;

    2. the total value of supplies of goods and services from each such person to each person holding a VAT identification number referred to in point 1 of the first paragraph of Article 23.';

6. Article 27(4) shall be replaced by the following:

    '4. The competent authorities of each Member State shall ensure that persons involved in the intra-Community supply of goods or of services and, for the period provided for in Article 357 of Directive 2006/112/EC, non-established taxable persons supplying electronically supplied services, in particular those referred to in Annex II of that Directive, are allowed to obtain confirmation of the validity of the VAT identification number of any specified person.

    During the period provided for in Article 357 of Directive 2006/112/EC, the Member States shall provide such confirmation by electronic means in accordance with the procedure referred to in Article 44(2) of this Regulation.';

7. the heading of Chapter VI shall be replaced by the following:

    'PROVISIONS CONCERNING THE SPECIAL SCHEME IN CHAPTER 6 OF TITLE XII OF DIRECTIVE 2006/112/EC';

8. Article 28 shall be replaced by the following:

    'Article 28

    The following provisions shall apply concerning the special scheme provided for in Chapter 6 of Title XII of Directive 2006/112/EC. The definitions contained in Article 358 of that Directive shall also apply for the purpose of this Chapter.';

9.   Article 29(1) shall be replaced by the following:

'1.   The information provided by the taxable person not established in the Community to the Member State of identification when his activities commence pursuant to Article 361 of Directive 2006/112/EC shall be submitted in an electronic manner. The technical details, including a common electronic message, shall be determined in accordance with the procedure provided for in Article 44(2) of this Regulation.';

10.   in Article 30, the first paragraph shall be replaced by the following:

'The return with the details set out in Article 365 of Directive 2006/112/EC is to be submitted in an electronic manner. The technical details, including a common electronic message, shall be determined in accordance with the procedure provided for in Article 44(2) of this Regulation.';

11.   Article 31 shall be replaced by the following:

'Article 31

The provisions in Article 22 of this Regulation shall apply also to information collected by the Member State of identification in accordance with Articles 360, 361, 364 and 365 of Directive 2006/112/EC.';

12.   Article 34 shall be replaced by the following:

Article 34

Articles 28 to 33 of this Regulation shall apply for the period provided for in Article 357 of Directive 2006/112/EC.';

13.   the following Chapter VIa shall be inserted:

'CHAPTER 6a

PROVISIONS CONCERNING THE EXCHANGE AND CONSER-VATION OF INFORMATION IN THE CONTEXT OF THE PROCEDURE PROVIDED FOR IN DIRECTIVE 2008/9/EC

Article 34a

1.   Where the competent authority of the Member State of establishment receives an application for refund of value added tax under Article 5 of Directive 2008/9/EC of 12 February 2008 laying down detailed rules for the refund of value added tax, provided for in Directive 2006/112/EC, to taxable persons not established in the Member State of refund but established in another Member State and Article 18 of that Directive is not applicable, it shall, within 15 calendar days of its receipt and by electronic means, forward the application to the competent authorities of each Member State of refund concerned with

confirmation that the applicant as defined in Article 2(5) of Directive 2008/9/EC is a taxable person for the purposes of value added tax and that the identification or registration number given by this person is valid for the refund period.

2.   The competent authorities of each Member State of refund shall notify by electronic means the competent authorities of the other Member States of any information required by them under Article 9(2) of Directive 2008/9/EC. The technical details, including a common electronic message by which this information is to be transmitted, shall be determined in accordance with the procedure provided for in Article 44(2) of this Regulation.

3.   The competent authorities of each Member State of refund shall notify by electronic means the competent authorities of the other Member States if they want to make use of the option to require the applicant to provide the description of business activity by harmonised codes as referred to in Article 11 of Directive 2008/9/ EC.

The harmonised codes referred to in the first subparagraph shall be determined in accordance with the procedure provided for in Article 44(2) of this Regulation on the basis of the NACE classification established by Regulation (EEC) No 3037/90.

14.   in Article 39, the first paragraph shall be replaced by the following:

'For the period provided for in Article 357 of Directive 2006/112/EC, the Commission and the Member States shall ensure that such existing or new communication and information exchange systems which are necessary to provide for the exchanges of information described in Articles 29 and 30 of this Regulation are operational. The Commission will be responsible for whatever development of the common communication network/common system interface (CCN/CSI) is necessary to permit the exchange of this information between Member States. Member States will be responsible for whatever development of their systems is necessary to permit this information to be exchanged using the CCN/CSI.'.

Article 2

From 1 January 2015, Regulation (EC) No 1798/2003 is hereby amended as follows:

1.   in Article 1(1), the fourth subparagraph shall be replaced by the following:

'This Regulation also lays down rules and procedures for the exchange by electronic means of value added tax information on services in accordance with the special schemes provided for in Chapter 6 of Title XII of Directive 2006/112/EC and also for any subsequent exchange of information and, as far as services covered by those special schemes are concerned, for the transfer of money between Member States' competent authorities.';

2.   in Article 2, the sole paragraph shall be numbered '1' and the following paragraph shall be added:

'2.   The definitions contained in Articles 358, 358a and 369a of Directive 2006/112/EC shall also apply for the purposes of this Regulation.';

3.   in Article 5, paragraph 3 shall be replaced by the following:

'3.   The request referred to in paragraph 1 may contain a reasoned request for a specific administrative enquiry. If the Member State takes the view that no administrative enquiry is necessary, it shall immediately inform the requesting authority of the reasons thereof.

Notwithstanding the first subparagraph and without prejudice to Article 40 of this Regulation, an enquiry into the amounts declared by a taxable person in connection with the supply of telecommunications services, broadcasting services and electronically supplied services which are taxable in the Member State in which the requesting authority is situated and for which the taxable person makes use or opts not to make use of the special scheme provided for in Section 3 of Chapter 6 of Title XII of Directive 2006/112/EC, may only be refused by the requested authority if information on the same taxable person obtained in an administrative enquiry held less than two years previously, has already been supplied to the requesting authority.

However, with respect to the requests referred to in the second subparagraph made by the requesting authority and assessed by the requested authority in conformity with a Statement of Best Practices concerning the interaction of this paragraph and Article 40(1) to be adopted in accordance with the procedure referred to in Article 44(2), a Member State which refuses to hold an administrative enquiry on the basis of Article 40 shall provide to the requesting authority the dates and values of any relevant supplies made over the last two years by the taxable person in the Member State of the requesting authority.';

4.   in Article 17, the following paragraph shall be added:

'For the purposes of the first paragraph, each Member State of establishment shall cooperate with each Member State of consumption so as to make it possible to ascertain whether the taxable persons established on its territory declare and pay correctly the VAT due with regard to telecommunications services, broadcasting services and electronically supplied services for which the taxable person makes use or opts not to make use of the special scheme provided for in Section 3 of Chapter 6 of Title XII of Directive 2006/112/EC. The Member State of establishment shall inform the Member State of consumption of any discrepancies of which it becomes aware.';

5.   in Article 18, the second paragraph shall be replaced by the following:

'Each Member State shall determine whether it will take part in the exchange of a particular category of information, as well as whether it will do so in an automatic or structured automatic way. However, each Member State shall take part in exchanges of the information available to it with regard to telecommunications services, broadcasting services and electronically supplied services for which the taxable person makes use or opts not to make use of the special scheme provided for in Section 3 of Chapter 6 of Title XII of Directive 2006/112/EC.';

6.   Article 27(4) shall be replaced by the following:

'4.   The competent authorities of each Member State shall ensure that persons involved in the intra-Community supply of goods or of services and non-established taxable persons supplying telecommunication services, broadcasting services and electronically supplied services, in particular those referred to in Annex II of Directive 2006/112/EC, are allowed to obtain confirmation of the validity of the VAT identification number of any specified person.

The Member States shall provide such confirmation by electronic means in accordance with the procedure referred to in Article 44(2) of this Regulation.';

7.   the heading of Chapter VI shall be replaced by the following:

'PROVISIONS CONCERNING THE SPECIAL SCHEMES IN CHAPTER 6 OF TITLE XII OF DIRECTIVE 2006/112/EC';

8.   Article 28 shall be replaced by the following:

'Article 28

The following provisions shall apply concerning the special schemes provided for in Chapter 6 of Title XII of Directive 2006/112/EC.';

9.   Article 29 shall be replaced by the following:

'Article 29

1.   The information provided by the taxable person not established in the Community to the Member State of identification when his activities commence pursuant to Article 361 of Directive 2006/112/EC shall be submitted in an electronic manner. The technical details, including a common electronic message, shall be determined in accordance with the procedure provided for in Article 44(2) of this Regulation.

2.   The Member State of identification shall transmit the information referred to in paragraph 1 by electronic means to the competent authorities of the other Member States within 10 days from the end of the month during which the information was received

from the taxable person not established within the Community. Similar details for the identification of the taxable person applying the special scheme under Article 369b of Directive 2006/112/EC shall be transmitted within 10 days from the end of the month during which the taxable person stated that his taxable activities under that scheme commenced. In the same manner the competent authorities of the other Member States shall be informed of the allocated identification number.

The technical details, including a common electronic message, by which this information is to be transmitted, shall be determined in accordance with the procedure provided for in Article 44(2) of this Regulation.

3.   The Member State of identification shall without delay inform by electronic means the competent authorities of the other Member States if a taxable person not established in the Community or a taxable person not established in the Member State of consumption is excluded from the special scheme.';

10.   in Article 30, the first and second paragraphs shall be replaced by the following:

'The return with the details set out in Articles 365 and 369g of Directive 2006/112/EC is to be submitted in an electronic manner. The technical details, including a common electronic message, shall be determined in accordance with the procedure provided for in Article 44(2) of this Regulation.

The Member State of identification shall transmit this information by electronic means to the competent authority of the Member State of consumption concerned at the latest 10 days after the end of the month in which the return was received. The information provided for in the second paragraph of Article 369g of Directive 2006/112/EC shall also be transmitted to the competent authority of the Member State of establishment concerned. Member States which have required the tax return to be made in a national currency other that euro, shall convert the amounts into euro using the exchange rate valid for the last date of the reporting period. The exchange shall be done following the exchange rates published by the European Central Bank for that day, or, if there is no publication on that day, on the next day of publication. The technical details by which this information is to be transmitted shall be determined in accordance with the procedure provided for in Article 44(2) of this Regulation.';

11.   Article 31 shall be replaced by the following:

'Article 31

The provisions in Article 22 of this Regulation shall apply also to information collected by the Member State of identification in accordance with Articles 360, 361, 364, 365, 369c, 369f and 369g of Directive 2006/112/EC.';

12.   in Article 32, the following paragraph shall be added:

'Concerning the payments to be transferred to the Member State of consumption in accordance with the special scheme provided for in Section 3 of Chapter 6 of Title XII of Directive 2006/112/EC, the Member State of identification shall, of the amounts referred to in the first and second paragraphs, be entitled to retain:

(a)   from 1 January 2015 until 31 December 2016 — 30%,

(b)   from 1 January 2017 until 31 December 2018 — 15%,

(c)   from 1 January 2019 — 0 %.';

13.   Article 34 shall be deleted;

14.   in Article 39, the first paragraph shall be replaced by the following:

'The Commission and the Member States shall ensure that such existing or new communication and information exchange systems which are necessary to provide for the exchanges of information described in Articles 29 and 30 are operational. The Commission will be responsible for whatever development of the common communication network/common system interface (CCN/CSI) is necessary to permit the exchange of this information between Member States. Member States will be responsible for whatever development of their systems is necessary to permit this information to be exchanged using the CCN/CSI.'.

Article 3

This Regulation shall enter into force on the day of its publication in the *Official Journal of the European Union.*

Articles 1 and 2 shall apply from the following dates:

(a)   Article 1, from 1 January 2010;

(b)   Article 2, from 1 January 2015.

This Regulation shall be binding in its entirety and directly applicable in all Member States.

Done at Brussels, 12 February 2008.

For the Council
The President
A. BAJUK

COUNCIL DIRECTIVE 2008/55/EC

of 26 May 2008

on mutual assistance for the recovery of claims relating to certain levies, duties, taxes and other measures

Official Journal L 150, 10/6/2008, p. 28-38

THE COUNCIL OF THE EUROPEAN UNION,

Having regard to the Treaty establishing the European Community, and in particular Articles 93 and 94 thereof,

Having regard to the proposal from the Commission,

Having regard to the opinion of the European Parliament,

Having regard to the opinion of the European Economic and Social Committee,

Whereas:

(1)   Council Directive 76/308/EEC of 15 March 1976 on mutual assistance for the recovery of claims relating to certain levies, duties, taxes and other measures has been substantially amended several times. In the interests of clarity and rationality the said Directive should be codified.

(2)   The fact that national provisions relating to recovery are applicable only within national territories is in itself an obstacle to the functioning of the internal market. This situation prevents Community rules from being fully and fairly applied, particularly in the area of the common agricultural policy, and facilitates fraudulent operations.

(3)   It is necessary to meet the threat to the financial interests of the Community and the Member States and to the internal market posed by the development of fraud so as to safeguard better the competitiveness and fiscal neutrality of the internal market.

(4)   It is therefore necessary to adopt common rules on mutual assistance for recovery.

(5)   These rules should apply to the recovery of claims resulting from the various measures which form part of the system of total or partial financing of the European Agricultural Guarantee Fund and the European Agricultural Fund for Rural Development, to the recovery of levies and other duties and import and export duties, valued added tax and harmonised excise duties (manufactured tobacco, alcohol and alcoholic beverages and mineral oils), as well as of taxes on income, on capital and on insurance premiums. They should also apply to the recovery of interest, administrative penalties and fines, with the exclusion of any sanction of a criminal nature, and costs incidental to such claims.

(6)   Mutual assistance should consist of the following: the requested authority should on the one hand supply the applicant authority with

the information which the latter needs in order to recover claims arising in the Member State in which it is situated and notify the debtor of all instruments relating to such claims emanating from that Member State, and on the other hand it should recover, at the request of the applicant authority, the claims arising in the Member State in which the latter is situated.

(7)   These different forms of assistance should be afforded by the requested authority in compliance with the laws, regulations and administrative provisions governing such matters in the Member State in which it is situated.

(8)   It is necessary to lay down the conditions in accordance with which requests for assistance must be drawn up by the applicant authority and to give a limitative definition of the particular circumstances in which the requested authority may refuse assistance in any given case.

(9)   In order to permit more efficient and effective recovery of claims in respect of which a request for recovery has been made, the instrument permitting enforcement of the claim should, in principle, be treated as an instrument of the Member State in which the requested authority is situated.

(10) When the requested authority is required to act on behalf of the applicant authority to recover a claim, it should be able, if the provisions in force in the Member State in which it is situated so permit and with the agreement of the applicant authority, to allow the debtor time to pay or authorise payment by instalment. Any interest charged on such payment facilities should also be remitted to the Member State in which the applicant authority is situated.

(11) Upon a reasoned request from the applicant authority, the requested authority should also be able, in so far as the provisions in force in the Member State in which it is situated so permit, to take precautionary measures to guarantee the recovery of claims arising in the applicant Member State. Such claims should not necessarily benefit from the privileges accorded to similar claims arising in the Member State in which the requested authority is situated.

(12) During the recovery procedure in the Member State in which the requested authority is situated the claim or the instrument authorising its enforcement issued in the Member State in which the applicant authority is situated may be contested by the person concerned. It should be laid down in such cases that the person concerned must bring the action contesting the claim before the competent body of the Member State in which the applicant authority is situated and that the requested authority must suspend, unless the applicant authority requests otherwise, any enforcement proceedings which it has begun until a decision is taken by the aforementioned body.

(13) It should be laid down that documents and information communicated in the course of mutual assistance for recovery may not be used for other purposes.

(14) The use of mutual assistance for recovery cannot, save in exceptional circumstances, be based on financial benefits or an interest in the results obtained, but Member States should be able to agree the reimbursement arrangements when recovery poses a specific problem.

(15) This Directive should not curtail mutual assistance between particular Member States under bilateral or multilateral agreements or arrangements.

(16) The measures necessary for the implementation of this Directive should be adopted in accordance with Council Decision 1999/468/EC of 28 June 1999 laying down the procedures for the exercise of implementing powers conferred on the Commission.

(17) This Directive should be without prejudice to the obligations of the Member States relating to the time-limits for transposition into national law of the Directives set out in Annex I, Part C,

HAS ADOPTED THIS DIRECTIVE:

Article 1

This Directive lays down the rules to be incorporated into the laws, regulations and administrative provisions of the Member States to ensure the recovery in each Member State of the claims referred to in Article 2 which arise in another Member State.

Article 2

This Directive shall apply to all claims relating to:

(a)   refunds, interventions and other measures forming part of the system of total or partial financing of the European Agricultural Guarantee Fund (EAGF) and the European Agricultural Fund for Rural Development (EAFRD), including sums to be collected in connection with these actions;

(b)   levies and other duties provided for under the common organisation of the market for the sugar sector;

(c)   import duties;

(d)   export duties;

(e)   value added tax;

(f)   excise duties on:

    (i)   manufactured tobacco,

    (ii)   alcohol and alcoholic beverages,

    (iii) mineral oils;

(g)   taxes on income and capital;

(h)   taxes on insurance premiums;

(i)   interest, administrative penalties and fines, and costs incidental to the claims referred to in points (a) to (h), with the exclusion of any sanction of a criminal nature as determined by the laws in force in the Member State in which the requested authority is situated.

It shall also apply to claims relating to taxes which are identical or analogous to the taxes on insurance premiums referred to in Article 3(6) which supplement or replace them. The competent authorities of the Member States shall communicate to each other and to the Commission the dates of entry into force of such taxes.

Article 3

For the purposes of this Directive:

1.   'applicant authority' means the competent authority of a Member State which makes a request for assistance concerning a claim referred to in Article 2;

2.   'requested authority' means the competent authority of a Member State to which a request for assistance is made;

3.   'import duties' means customs duties and charges having equivalent effect on imports, and import charges laid down within the framework of the common agricultural policy or in that of specific arrangements applicable to certain goods resulting from the processing of agricultural products;

4.   'export duties' means customs duties and charges having equivalent effect on exports, and export charges laid down within the framework of the common agricultural policy or in that of specific arrangements applicable to certain goods resulting from the processing of agricultural products;

5.   'taxes on income and capital' means those enumerated in Article 1(3) of Council Directive (77/799/EEC) of 19 December 1977 concerning mutual assistance by the competent authorities of the Member States in the field of direct taxation and taxation of insurance premiums, read in conjunction with Article 1 of that Directive;

6.   'taxes on insurance premiums' means:

(a) in Belgium:	(i)	taxe annuelle sur les contrats d'assurance,
	(ii)	Jaarlijkse taks op de verzekeringscontracten;
(b) in Denmark:	(i)	afgift af lystfartøjsforsikringer,
	(ii)	afgift af ansvarsforsikringer for motorkøretøjer m.v.,
	(iii)	stempelafgift af forsikringspræmier;
(c) in Germany:	(i)	Versicherungssteuer,
	(ii)	Feuerschutzsteuer;

(d) in Greece:	(i)	Φòρος κύκλου εργασιών (Φ.Κ.Ε.),
	(ii)	Τέλη Χαρτοσήμου;
(e) in Spain:		Impuesto sobre las primas de seguros;
(f) in France:		taxe sur les conventions d'assurances;
(g) in Ireland:		levy on insurance premiums;
(h) in Italy:		imposte sulle assicurazioni private ed i contratti vitalizi di cui alla legge 29.10.1967 No 1216;
(i) in Luxembourg:	(i)	impôt sur les assurances,
	(ii)	impôt dans l'interêt du service d'incendie;
(j) in Malta:		taxxa fuq dokumenti u trasferimenti;
(k) in the Netherlands:		assurantiebelasting;
(l) in Austria:	(i)	Versicherungssteuer,
	(ii)	Feuerschutzsteuer;
(m) in Portugal:		imposto de selo sobre os prémios de seguros;
(n) in Slovenia:	(i)	davek od promenta zavarovalnih poslov,
	(ii)	požarna taksa;
(o) in Finland:	(i)	eräistä vakuutusmaksuista suoritettava vero/skatt på vissa försäkringspremier,
	(ii)	palosuojelumaksu/brandskyddsavgift;
(p) in the United Kingdom:		insurance premium tax (IPT).

Article 4

1. At the request of the applicant authority, the requested authority shall provide any information which would be useful to the applicant authority in the recovery of its claim.

   In order to obtain this information, the requested authority shall make use of the powers provided under the laws, regulations or administrative provisions applying to the recovery of similar claims arising in the Member State where that authority is situated.

2. The request for information shall indicate the name and address of the person to whom the information to be provided relates and any other relevant information relating to the identification to which the applicant authority normally has access and the nature and amount of the claim in respect of which the request is made.

3. The requested authority shall not be obliged to supply information:

   (a) which it would not be able to obtain for the purpose of recovering similar claims arising in the Member State in which it is situated;

   (b) which would disclose any commercial, industrial or professional secrets; or

(c) the disclosure of which would be liable to prejudice the security of or be contrary to the public policy of the State.

4. The requested authority shall inform the applicant authority of the grounds for refusing a request for information.

Article 5

1. The requested authority shall, at the request of the applicant authority, and in accordance with the rules of law in force for the notification of similar instruments or decisions in the Member State in which the requested authority is situated, notify to the addressee all instruments and decisions, including those of a judicial nature, which emanate from the Member State in which the applicant authority is situated and which relate to a claim and/or to its recovery.

2. The request for notification shall indicate the name and address of the addressee concerned and any other relevant information relating to the identification to which the applicant authority normally has access, the nature and the subject of the instrument or decision to be notified, if necessary the name, and address of the debtor and any other relevant information relating to the identification to which the applicant authority normally has access and the claim to which the instrument or decision relates, and any other useful information.

3. The requested authority shall promptly inform the applicant authority of the action taken on its request for notification and, more especially, of the date on which the instrument or decision was forwarded to the addressee.

Article 6

At the request of the applicant authority, the requested authority shall, in accordance with the laws, regulations or administrative provisions applying to the recovery of similar claims arising in the Member State in which the requested authority is situated, recover claims which are the subject of an instrument permitting their enforcement.

For this purpose any claim in respect of which a request for recovery has been made shall be treated as a claim of the Member State in which the requested authority is situated, except where Article 12 applies.

Article 7

1. The request for recovery of a claim which the applicant authority addresses to the requested authority shall be accompanied by an official or certified copy of the instrument permitting its enforcement, issued in the Member State in which the applicant authority is situated and, if appropriate, by the original or a certified copy of other documents necessary for recovery.

2. The applicant authority may not make a request for recovery unless:

(a) the claim and/or the instrument permitting its enforcement are not contested in the Member State in which it is situated, except in cases where the second subparagraph of Article 12(2) applies;

(b) it has, in the Member State in which it is situated, applied appropriate recovery procedures available to it on the basis of the instrument referred to in paragraph 1, and the measures taken will not result in the payment in full of the claim.

3. The request for recovery shall indicate:

(a) the name, address and any other relevant information relating to the identification of the person concerned and/or to the third party holding his or her assets;

(b) the name, address and any other relevant information relating to the identification of the applicant authority;

(c) a reference to the instrument permitting its enforcement issued in the Member State in which the applicant authority is situated;

(d) the nature and the amount of the claim, including the principal, the interest, and any other penalties, fines and costs due indicated in the currencies of the Member States in which both authorities are situated;

(e) the date of notification of the instrument to the addressee by the applicant authority and/or by the requested authority;

(f) the date from which and the period during which enforcement is possible under the laws in force in the Member State in which the applicant authority is situated;

(g) any other relevant information.

The request for recovery shall also contain a declaration by the applicant authority confirming that the conditions set out in paragraph 2 have been fulfilled.

4. As soon as any relevant information relating to the matter which gave rise to the request for recovery comes to the knowledge of the applicant authority it shall forward it to the requested authority.

Article 8

The instrument permitting enforcement of the claim shall be directly recognised and automatically treated as an instrument permitting enforcement of a claim of the Member State in which the requested authority is situated.

Notwithstanding the first paragraph, the instrument permitting enforcement of the claim may, where appropriate and in accordance with the provisions in force in the Member State in which the requested authority is situated, be accepted as, recognised as, supplemented with, or replaced by an instrument authorising enforcement in the territory of that Member State.

Within three months of the date of receipt of the request for recovery, Member States shall endeavour to complete such acceptance, recognition, supplementing or replacement, except in cases referred to in the fourth paragraph. These formalities may not be refused if the instrument permitting enforcement is properly drawn up. The requested authority shall inform the applicant authority of the grounds for exceeding the period of three months.

If any of these formalities should give rise to contestation in connection with the claim or the instrument permitting enforcement issued by the applicant authority, Article 12 shall apply.

Article 9

1. Claims shall be recovered in the currency of the Member State in which the requested authority is situated. The entire amount of the claim that is recovered by the requested authority shall be remitted by the requested authority to the applicant authority.

2. The requested authority may, where the laws, regulations or administrative provisions in force in the Member State in which it is situated so permit, and after consultations with the applicant authority, allow the debtor time to pay or authorise payment by instalment. Any interest charged by the requested authority in respect of such extra time to pay shall also be remitted to the Member State in which the applicant authority is situated.

From the date on which the instrument permitting enforcement of recovery of the claim has been directly recognised in accordance with the first paragraph of Article 8 or accepted, recognised, supplemented or replaced in accordance with the second paragraph of Article 8, interest will be charged for late payment under the laws, regulations and administrative provisions in force in the Member State in which the requested authority is situated and shall also be remitted to the Member State in which the applicant authority is situated.

Article 10

Notwithstanding the second paragraph of Article 6, the claims to be recovered shall not necessarily benefit from the privileges accorded to similar claims arising in the Member State in which the requested authority is situated.

Article 11

The requested authority shall inform the applicant authority immediately of the action it has taken on the request for recovery.

Article 12

1. If, in the course of the recovery procedure, the claim and/or the instrument permitting its enforcement issued in the Member State in which the applicant authority is situated are contested by an interested party, the action shall be brought by the latter before the competent body of the Member State in which the applicant authority is situated, in accordance with the laws in force there. This action shall be notified by the applicant authority to the requested authority. The party concerned may also notify the requested authority of the action.

2. As soon as the requested authority has received the notification referred to in paragraph 1 either from the applicant authority or from the interested party, it shall suspend the enforcement procedure pending the decision of the body competent in the matter, unless the applicant authority requests otherwise in accordance with the second subparagraph of this paragraph. Should the requested authority deem it necessary, and without prejudice to Article 13, that authority may take precautionary measures to guarantee

recovery in so far as the laws or regulations in force in the Member State in which it is situated allow such action for similar claims.

The applicant authority may, in accordance with the law, regulations and administrative practices in force in the Member State in which it is situated, request the requested authority to recover a contested claim, in so far as the relevant laws, regulations and administrative practices in force in the Member State in which the requested authority is situated allow such action. If the result of contestation is subsequently favourable to the debtor, the applicant authority shall be liable for the reimbursement of any sums recovered, together with any compensation due, in accordance with the laws in force in the Member State in which the requested authority is situated.

3. Where it is the enforcement measures taken in the Member State in which the requested authority is situated that are being contested the action shall be brought before the competent body of that Member State in accordance with its laws and regulations.

4. Where the competent body before which the action has been brought in accordance with paragraph 1 is a judicial or administrative tribunal, the decision of that tribunal, in so far as it is favourable to the applicant authority and permits recovery of the claim in the Member State in which the applicant authority is situated, shall constitute the 'instrument permitting enforcement' referred to in Articles 6, 7 and 8 and the recovery of the claim shall proceed on the basis of that decision.

Article 13

On a reasoned request by the applicant authority, the requested authority shall take precautionary measures to ensure recovery of a claim in so far as the laws or regulations in force in the Member State in which it is situated so permit.

In order to give effect to the provisions of the first paragraph, Articles 6, 7(1), (3) and (4), 8, 11, 12 and 14 shall apply *mutatis mutandis*.

Article 14

The requested authority shall not be obliged:

(a) to grant the assistance provided for in Articles 6 to 13 if recovery of the claim would, because of the situation of the debtor, create serious economic or social difficulties in the Member State in which that authority is situated, in so far as the laws, regulations and administrative practices in force in the Member State in which the requested authority is situated allow such action for similar national claims;

(b) to grant the assistance provided for in Articles 4 to 13, if the initial request under Articles 4, 5 or 6 applies to claims more than five years old, dating from the moment the instrument permitting the recovery is established in accordance with the laws, regulations or administrative practices in force in the Member State in which the applicant authority is situated, to the date of the request. However, in cases where the claim or the instrument is contested, the time-limit begins from the moment at which the applicant State establishes that the claim or the instrument permitting recovery may no longer be contested.

The requested authority shall inform the applicant authority of the grounds for refusing a request for assistance. Such reasoned refusal shall also be communicated to the Commission.

Article 15

1. Questions concerning periods of limitation shall be governed solely by the laws in force in the Member State in which the applicant authority is situated.

2. Steps taken in the recovery of claims by the requested authority in pursuance of a request for assistance, which, if they had been carried out by the applicant authority, would have had the effect of suspending or interrupting the period of limitation according to the laws in force in the Member State in which the applicant authority is situated, shall be deemed to have been taken in the latter State, in so far as that effect is concerned.

Article 16

Documents and information sent to the requested authority pursuant to this Directive may only be communicated by the latter to:

(a) the person mentioned in the request for assistance;

(b) those persons and authorities responsible for the recovery of the claims, and solely for that purpose;

(c) the judicial authorities dealing with matters concerning the recovery of the claims.

Article 17

Requests for assistance, the instrument permitting the enforcement and other relevant documents shall be accompanied by a translation in the official language, or one of the official languages of the Member State in which the requested authority is situated, without prejudice to the latter authority's right to waive the translation.

Article 18

1. The requested authority shall recover from the person concerned and retain any costs linked to recovery which it incurs, in accordance with the laws and regulations of the Member State in which it is situated that apply to similar claims.

2. Member States shall renounce all claims on each other for the refund of costs resulting from mutual assistance which they grant each other pursuant to this Directive.

3. Where recovery poses a specific problem, concerns a very large amount in costs or relates to the fight against organised crime, the applicant and requested authorities may agree reimbursement arrangements specific to the cases in question.

4. The Member State in which the applicant authority is situated shall remain liable to the Member State in which the requested authority is situated for any costs and any losses incurred as a result of actions held to

be unfounded, as far as either the substance of the claim or the validity of the instrument issued by the applicant authority are concerned.

Article 19

Member States shall provide each other with a list of authorities authorised to make or receive requests for assistance.

Article 20

1. The Commission shall be assisted by the recovery committee (hereinafter referred to as the Committee).

2. Where reference is made to this paragraph, Articles 5 and 7 of Decision 1999/468/EC shall apply.

The period referred to in Article 5(6) of Decision 1999/468/EC shall be set at three months.

Article 21

The Committee may examine any matter concerning the application of this Directive raised by its chairman either on his own initiative or at the request of the representative of a Member State.

Article 22

The detailed rules for implementing Articles 4(2) and (4), 5(2) and (3) and Articles 7, 8, 9, 11, 12(1) and (2), 14, 18(3) and 24 and for determining the means by which communications between the authorities may be transmitted, the rules on conversion, transfer of sums recovered, and the fixing of a minimum amount for claims which may give rise to a request for assistance, shall be adopted in accordance with the procedure referred to in Article 20(2).

Article 23

This Directive shall not prevent a greater measure of mutual assistance being afforded either now or in the future by particular Member States under any agreements or arrangements, including those for the notification of legal or extra-legal acts.

Article 24

Each Member State shall inform the Commission of the measures which it has adopted to implement this Directive.

The Commission shall forward this information to the other Member States.

Each Member State shall inform the Commission annually of the number of requests for information, notification and recovery sent and received each year, the amount of the claims involved and the amounts recovered.

The Commission shall report biennially to the European Parliament and the Council on the application of these arrangements and on the results achieved.

Article 25

Directive 76/308/EEC, as amended by the acts listed in Annex I, Parts A and B, is repealed, without prejudice to the obligations of the Member States relating to the time-limits for transposition into national law of the Directives set out in Annex I, Part C.

References to the repealed Directive shall be construed as references to this Directive and shall be read in accordance with the correlation table in Annex II.

Article 26

This Directive shall enter into force on the 20th day following its publication in the *Official Journal of the European Union*.

Article 27

This Directive is addressed to the Member States.

Done at Brussels, 26 May 2008.

For the Council

The President

D. RUPEL

ANNEX I

PART A

Repealed Directive with its successive amendments
(referred to in Article 25)

Directive 76/308/EEC
(OJ L 73, 19.3.1976, p. 18).

Directive 79/1071/EEC
(OJ L 331, 27.12.1979, p. 10).

Directive 92/12/EEC   Only Article 30a
(OJ L 76, 23.3.1992, p. 1).

Directive 92/108/EEC   Only Article 1, point 9
(OJ L 390, 31.12.1992, p. 124).

Directive 2001/44/EC
(OJ L 175, 28.6.2001, p. 17)

PART B

Amended acts which are not repealed

1979 Act of Accession

1985 Act of Accession

1994 Act of Accession

2003 Act of Accession

PART C

List of time-limits for transposition into national law
(referred to in Article 25)

Directive	Time-limit for transposition
76/308/EEC	1 January 1978
79/1071/EEC	1 January 1981
92/12/EEC	1 January 1993[(1)]
92/108/EEC	31 December 1992
2001/44/EC	30 June 2002

(1) With regard to Article 9(3) the Kingdom of Denmark is authorised to introduce
the laws, regulations and administrative provisions required for complying
with this provisions by 1 January 1993 at the latest.

ANNEX II

Correlation table

Directive 76/308/EEC	This Directive
Article 1	Article 1
Article 2, introductory wording, points (a) to (e)	Article 2, first paragraph, points (a) to (e)
Article 2, introductory wording, point (f) first, second and third indents	Article 2, first paragraph, point (f)(i), (ii) and (iii)
Article 2, introductory wording, points (g) to (i)	Article 2, first paragraph, points (g) to (i)
Article 3, first paragraph, first to fifth indents	Article 3, first paragraph, points (1) to (5)
Article 3, sixth indent, first paragraph, point (a)	Article 3(6)(l)
Article 3, sixth indent, first paragraph, point (b)	Article 3(6)(a)
Article 3, sixth indent, first paragraph, point (c)	Article 3(6)(c)
Article 3, sixth indent, first paragraph, point (d)	Article 3(6)(b)
Article 3, sixth indent, first paragraph, point (e)	Article 3(6)(e)
Article 3, sixth indent, first paragraph, point (f)	Article 3(6)(d)
Article 3, sixth indent, first paragraph, point (g)	Article 3(6)(f)
Article 3, sixth indent, first paragraph, point (h)	Article 3(6)(o)
Article 3, sixth indent, first paragraph, point (i)	Article 3(6)(h)
Article 3, sixth indent, first paragraph, point (j)	Article 3(6)(g)
Article 3, sixth indent, first paragraph, point (k)	Article 3(6)(i)
Article 3, sixth indent, first paragraph, point (l)	Article 3(6)(k)
Article 3, sixth indent, first paragraph, point (m)	Article 3(6)(m)
Article 3, sixth indent, first paragraph, point (n)	—
Article 3, sixth indent, first paragraph, point (o)	Article 3(6)(p)

Directive 76/308/EEC	This Directive
Article 3, sixth indent, first paragraph, point (p)	Article 3(6)(j)
Article 3, sixth indent, first paragraph, point (q)	Article 3(6)(n)
Article 3, sixth indent, second paragraph	Article 2, second paragraph
Articles 4 and 5	Articles 4 and 5
Article 6(1)	Article 6 first paragraph
Article 6(2)	Article 6 second paragraph
Article 7(1) and (2)	Article 7(1) and (2)
Article 7(3)	Article 7(3), first subparagraph
Article 7(4)	Article 7(3), second subparagraph
Article 7(5)	Article 7(4)
Article 8(1)	Article 8, first paragraph
Article 8(2), first, second and third paragraphs	Article 8, second, third and fourth paragraphs
Articles 9 to 19	Articles 9 to 19
Article 20(1) and (2)	Article 20(1) and (2)
Article 20(3)	—
Articles 21, 22 and 23	Articles 21, 22 and 23
Article 24	—
Article 25, first paragraph, first and second sentences	Article 24, first and second paragraphs
Article 25, first paragraph, first and second sentences	Article 24, second and third paragraphs
Article 26	Article 27
—	Annex I
—	Annex II

COMMISSION REGULATION (EC) No 1179/2008

of 28 November 2008

laying down detailed rules for implementing certain provisions of Council Directive 2008/55/EC on mutual assistance for the recovery of claims relating to certain levies, duties, taxes and other measures

Official Journal L 319, 29/11/2008, p. 21-43

THE COMMISSION OF THE EUROPEAN COMMUNITIES,

Having regard to the Treaty establishing the European Community,

Having regard to Council Directive 2008/55/EC of 26 May 2008 on mutual assistance for the recovery of claims relating to certain levies, duties, taxes and other measures, and in particular Article 22 thereof,

Whereas:

(1)   Detailed rules for implementing certain provisions of Directive 2008/55/EC are laid down in Commission Directive 2002/94/EC. However, experience has shown that, a Directive, due to its legal nature, is not the most efficient legal instrument to fully achieve the purpose of a uniform procedure for mutual assistance. Therefore, it is appropriate to replace that Directive by a Regulation.

(2)   In order to facilitate the exchange of information between the competent authorities of the Member States, all assistance requests and all accompanying documents and information should, as far as possible, be communicated by electronic means.

(3)   In order to ensure that appropriate data and information are transmitted, models of forms for requests for mutual assistance among national authorities of the Member States should be established. It should be possible to update the structure and the lay-out of the electronic forms without amending the models in order to adapt those forms to the requirements and possibilities of the electronic communication system, provided that the requests contain the set of data and information required.

(4)   In order to enable the Commission to evaluate the effect and efficiency of the procedures laid down in Directive 2008/55/EC on a regular basis, it is appropriate to set out certain information to be communicated to the Commission by the Member States every year.

(5)   The measures provided for in this Regulation are in accordance with the opinion of the Committee on Recovery,

HAS ADOPTED THIS REGULATION:

Chapter I

General provisions

Article 1

This Regulation lays down the detailed rules for implementing Article 4(2) and (4), Article 5(2) and (3), Article 7, Article 8, Article 9, Article 11, Article 12(1) and (2), Article 14, Article 18(3) and Article 24 of Directive 2008/55/EC.

It also lays down the detailed rules on conversion, transfer of sums recovered, the fixing of a minimum amount for claims which may give rise to a request for assistance, as well as the means by which communications between authorities may be transmitted.

Article 2

For the purposes of this Regulation, the following definitions shall apply:

1. transmission 'by electronic means' means transmission using electronic equipment for processing, including digital compression, of data and employing wires, radio transmission, optical technologies or other electromagnetic means;

2. 'CCN/CSI network' means the common platform based on the Common Communication Network (CCN) and Common System Interface (CSI), developed by the Community to ensure all transmissions by electronic means between competent authorities in the area of Customs and Taxation.

Chapter II

Requests for information

Article 3

The request for information referred to in Article 4 of Directive 2008/55/EC shall comprise the set of data and information contained in the model of the form set out in Annex I to this Regulation.

Where a similar request has been addressed to any other authority, the applicant authority shall indicate in its request for information the name of that authority.

Article 4

The request for information may relate to any of the following:

1. the debtor;

2. any person liable for settlement of the claim under the law in force in the Member State in which the applicant authority is situated (hereinafter 'the Member State of the applicant authority');

3. any third party holding assets belonging to one of the persons mentioned under points (1) or (2).

Article 5

1. The requested authority shall acknowledge receipt of the request for information as soon as possible and in any event within seven days of such receipt.

2. Immediately upon receipt of the request the requested authority shall, where appropriate, ask the applicant authority to provide any additional information necessary. The applicant authority shall provide all additional necessary information to which it normally has access.

Article 6

1. The requested authority shall transmit each item of requested information to the applicant authority as and when it is obtained.

2. Where all or some of the requested information cannot be obtained within a reasonable time, having regard to the particular case, the requested authority shall so inform the applicant authority, indicating the reasons therefore.

In any event, at the end of six months from the date of acknowledgement of receipt of the request, the requested authority shall inform the applicant authority of the outcome of the investigations which it has conducted in order to obtain the information requested.

In the light of the information received from the requested authority, the applicant authority may request the latter to continue its investigation. That request shall be made within two months of the receipt of the notification of the outcome of the investigations carried out by the requested authority, and shall be treated by the requested authority in accordance with the provisions applying to the initial request.

Article 7

If the requested authority decides not to comply with the request for information, it shall notify the applicant authority of the reasons for the refusal to comply with the request, specifying the provisions of Article 4 of Directive 2008/55/EC on which it relies. Such notification shall be given by the requested authority as soon as it has taken its decision and in any event within three months of the date of the acknowledgement of the receipt of the request.

Article 8

The applicant authority may at any time withdraw the request for information which it has sent to the requested authority. The decision to withdraw shall be transmitted to the requested authority.

Chapter III

Requests for notification

Article 9

The request for notification referred to in Article 5 of Directive 2008/55/EC shall comprise the set of data and information contained in the model of the form set out in Annex II to this Regulation.

The original or a certified copy of the instrument or decision, notification of which is requested, shall be attached to the request.

Article 10

The request for notification may relate to any natural or legal person who, in accordance with the law in force in the Member State of the applicant authority, is required to be informed of any instrument or decision which concerns that person.

In so far as such is not indicated in the instrument or decision of which notification is requested, the request for notification shall refer to the rules in force in the Member State of the applicant authority governing the procedure for contestation of the claim or for its recovery.

Article 11

1. The requested authority shall acknowledge receipt of the request for notification as soon as possible and in any event within seven days of such receipt.

    Immediately upon receipt of the request for notification, the requested authority shall take the necessary measures to effect notification in accordance with the law in force in the Member State in which it is situated.

    If necessary, but without jeopardising the final date for notification indicated in the request for notification, the requested authority shall ask the applicant authority to provide additional information.

    The applicant authority shall provide all additional information to which it normally has access.

2. The requested authority shall inform the applicant authority of the date of notification as soon as this has been effected, by certifying the notification in the request form returned to the applicant authority.

Chapter IV

Requests for recovery or for precautionary measures

Article 12

1. Requests for recovery or for precautionary measures referred to in Articles 6 and 13 respectively of Directive 2008/55/EC shall comprise the set of data and information contained in the model of the form set out in Annex III to this Regulation.

    Such requests shall include a declaration that the conditions laid down in Directive 2008/55/EC for initiating the mutual assistance procedure have been fulfilled.

2. The original or a certified copy of the instrument permitting enforcement shall accompany the request for recovery or for precautionary measures. A single instrument may be issued in respect of several claims where they concern one and the same person.

    For the purposes of Articles 13 to 20 of this Regulation, all claims covered by the same instrument permitting enforcement shall be deemed to constitute a single claim.

Article 13

Requests for recovery or for precautionary measures may relate to any person referred to in Article 4.

Article 14

1. If the currency of the Member State of the requested authority is different from the currency of the Member State of the applicant authority, the applicant authority shall express the amount of the claim to be recovered in both currencies.

2. The rate of exchange to be used for the purposes of paragraph 1 shall be the latest selling rate recorded on the most representative exchange market or markets of the Member State of the applicant authority on the date when the request for recovery is sent.

Article 15

1. The requested authority shall, as soon as possible and in any event within seven days of receipt of the request for recovery or for precautionary measures:

    (a)   acknowledge receipt of the request;

    (b)   ask the applicant authority to complete the request if it does not contain the information or other particulars mentioned in Article 7 of Directive 2008/55/EC.

2.   If the requested authority does not take the requisite action within the three-month period laid down in Article 8 of Directive 2008/55/EC, it shall, as soon as possible and in any event within seven days of the expiry of that period, inform the applicant authority of the grounds for its failure to comply with the time limit.

Article 16

Where, within a reasonable time having regard to the particular case, all or part of the claim cannot be recovered or precautionary measures cannot be taken, the requested authority shall so inform the applicant authority, indicating the reasons therefore.

No later than at the end of each six-month period following the date of acknowledgement of the receipt of the request, the requested authority shall inform the applicant authority of the state of progress or the outcome of the procedure for recovery or for precautionary measures.

In the light of the information received from the requested authority, the applicant authority may request the latter to re-open the procedure for recovery or for precautionary measures. That request shall be made within two months of the receipt of the notification of the outcome of that procedure, and shall be treated by the requested authority in accordance with the provisions applying to the initial request.

Article 17

1.   Any action contesting the claim or the instrument permitting its enforcement which is taken in the Member State of the applicant authority shall be notified to the requested authority by the applicant authority immediately after the latter has been informed of such action.

2.   If the laws, regulations and administrative practices in force in the Member State of the requested authority do not permit precautionary measures or the recovery requested under the second subparagraph of Article 12(2) of Directive 2008/55/EC, the requested authority shall notify the applicant authority to that effect as soon as possible and in any event within one month of the receipt of the notification referred to in paragraph 1.

3.   Any action which is taken in the Member State of the requested authority for reimbursement of sums recovered or for compensation in relation to recovery of contested claims under the second subparagraph of Article 12(2) of Directive 2008/55/EC shall be notified to the applicant authority by the requested authority immediately after the latter has been informed of such action.

The requested authority shall as far as possible involve the applicant authority in the procedures for settling the amount to be reimbursed and the compensation due. Upon a reasoned request from the requested authority, the applicant authority shall transfer the sums reimbursed and the compensation paid within two months of the receipt of that request.

Article 18

1. If the request for recovery or for precautionary measures becomes devoid of purpose as a result of payment of the claim or of its cancellation or for any other reason, the applicant authority shall immediately inform the requested authority so that the latter may stop any action which it has undertaken.

2. Where the amount of the claim which is the subject of the request for recovery or for precautionary measures is adjusted for any reason, the applicant authority shall inform the requested authority, and if necessary issue a new instrument permitting enforcement.

3. If the adjustment entails a reduction in the amount of the claim, the requested authority shall continue the action which it has undertaken with a view to recovery or to the taking of precautionary measures, but that action shall be limited to the amount still outstanding.

   If, at the time when the requested authority is informed of the reduction in the amount of the claim, an amount exceeding the amount still outstanding has already been recovered by it but the transfer procedure referred to in Article 19 has not yet been initiated, the requested authority shall repay the amount overpaid to the person entitled thereto.

4. If the adjustment entails an increase in the amount of the claim, the applicant authority shall as soon as possible address to the requested authority an additional request for recovery or for precautionary measures.

   That additional request shall, as far as possible, be dealt with by the requested authority at the same time as the original request from the applicant authority. Where, in view of the state of progress of the existing procedure, consolidation of the additional request with the original request is not possible, the requested authority shall be required to comply with the additional request only if it concerns an amount not less than that referred to in Article 25(2).

5. In order to convert the adjusted amount of the claim into the currency of the Member State of the requested authority, the applicant authority shall use the exchange rate used in its original request.

Article 19

Any sum recovered by the requested authority, including, where applicable, the interest referred to in Article 9(2) of Directive 2008/55/EC, shall be transferred to the applicant authority in the currency of the Member State of the requested authority. The transfer shall take place within one month of the date on which recovery was effected.

The competent authorities of the Member States may agree different arrangements for the transfer of amounts below the threshold referred to in Article 25(2) of this Regulation.

Article 20

Irrespective of any amounts collected by the requested authority by way of the interest referred to in Article 9(2) of Directive 2008/55/EC, the claim shall be deemed to have been recovered in proportion to the recovery of the amount expressed in the national currency of the Member State of the requested authority, on the basis of the exchange rate referred to in Article 14(2) of this Regulation.

Chapter V

Transmission of communications

Article 21

1. All assistance requests, instruments permitting enforcement and copies of these instruments, and any other accompanying documents, as well as any other information communicated with regard to these requests shall, as far as possible, be transmitted by electronic means, via the CCN/CSI network.

    Such documents transmitted in electronic form or print outs thereof shall be deemed to have the same legal effect as documents transmitted by post.

2. If the applicant authority sends a copy of the instrument permitting enforcement or of any other document, it shall certify the conformity of this copy with the original, by stating in this copy, in the official language or one of the official languages of the Member State in which it is situated, the words 'certified a true copy', the name of the certifying official and the date of this certification.

3. If requests for mutual assistance are transmitted by electronic means, the structure and the lay-out of the models referred to in the first paragraph of Article 3, the first paragraph of Article 9 and in Article 12(1) may be adapted to the requirements and possibilities of the electronic communication system, provided that the content of information is not altered.

4. If a request cannot be transmitted by electronic means, it shall be transmitted by post. In that case, the request shall be signed by an official of the applicant authority, duly authorised to make such a request.

Article 22

Each Member State shall designate a central office with principal responsibility for communication by electronic means with other Member States. That office shall be connected to the CCN/CSI network.

Where several authorities are appointed in a Member State for the purpose of applying this Regulation, the central office shall be responsible for the forwarding of all communication by electronic means between those authorities and the central offices of other Member States.

Article 23

1. Where the competent authorities of the Member States store information in electronic data bases and exchange such information by electronic means, they shall take all measures necessary to ensure that any information communicated in whatever form pursuant to this Regulation is treated as confidential.

   It shall be covered by the obligation of professional secrecy and shall enjoy the protection extended to similar information under the national law of the Member State which received it.

2. The information referred to in paragraph 1 may be made available only to the persons and authorities referred to in Article 16 of Directive 2008/55/EC.

   Such information may be used in connection with judicial or administrative proceedings initiated for the recovery of levies, duties, taxes and other measures referred to in Article 2 of Directive 2008/55/EC.

   Persons duly accredited by the Security Accreditation Authority of the European Commission may have access to this information only in so far as is necessary for the care, maintenance and development of the CCN/CSI network.

3. Where the competent authorities of the Member States communicate by electronic means, they shall take all measures necessary to ensure that all communications are duly authorised.

Article 24

Information and other particulars communicated by the requested authority to the applicant authority shall be conveyed in the official language or one of the official languages of the Member State of the requested authority or in another language agreed between the applicant and requested authorities.

Chapter VI

Eligibility and refusal of requests for assistance

Article 25

1. A request for assistance may be made by the applicant authority in respect of either a single claim or several claims where those are recoverable from one and the same person.

2. No request for assistance may be made if the total amount of the relevant claim or claims listed in Article 2 of Directive 2008/55/EC is less than EUR 1 500.

Article 26

If the requested authority decides, pursuant to the first paragraph of Article 14 of Directive 2008/55/EC, to refuse a request for assistance, it shall notify the applicant authority of the reasons for the refusal. Such notification shall be given by the requested authority as soon as it has taken its decision and in any event within three months of the date of receipt of the request for assistance.

Chapter VII

Reimbursement arrangements

Article 27

Each Member State shall appoint at least one official duly authorised to agree reimbursement arrangements under Article 18(3) of Directive 2008/55/EC.

Article 28

1.　If the requested authority decides to request reimbursement arrangements it shall notify the applicant authority of the reasons for its view that recovery of the claim poses a specific problem, entails very high costs or relates to the fight against organised crime.

　　The requested authority shall append a detailed estimate of the costs for which it requests reimbursement by the applicant authority.

2.　The applicant authority shall acknowledge receipt of the request for reimbursement arrangements as soon as possible and in any event within seven days of receipt.

　　Within two months of the date of acknowledgement of receipt of the said request, the applicant authority shall inform the requested authority whether and to what extent it agrees with the proposed reimbursement arrangements.

3.　If no agreement is reached between the applicant and requested authority with respect to reimbursement arrangements, the requested authority shall continue recovery procedures in the normal way.

Chapter VIII

Final provisions

Article 29

Each Member State shall inform the Commission before 15 March each year, as far as possible by electronic means, of the use made of the procedures laid down in Directive 2008/55/EC and of the results achieved in the previous calendar year.

The communication of that information shall comprise the elements contained in the model of the form set out in Annex IV to this Regulation.

Communication of any additional information, relating to the nature of the claims for which recovery assistance was requested or granted, shall comprise the elements contained in the model of the form set out in Annex V to this Regulation.

Article 30

Each Member State shall notify the other Member States and the Commission of the name and address of the competent authorities for the purpose of applying this Regulation, as well as of the officials authorised to agree arrangements under Article 18(3) of Directive 2008/55/EC.

Article 31

Directive 2002/94/EC is hereby repealed.

The references to that Directive shall be construed as references to this Regulation.

Article 32

This Regulation shall enter into force on 1 January 2009.

This Regulation shall be binding in its entirety and directly applicable in all Member States.

Done at Brussels, 28 November 2008.

For the Commission
László KOVÁCS
Member of the Commission

ANNEX I

Reference (*): AA_RA_aaaaaaaaaaaa_rrrrrrrrrrrr_20YYMMDD_x(xxx)_RI

(*) Reference number:

— AA: ISO code of the Member State (MS) of the applicant authority

— RA: ISO code of the MS of the requested authority

— aaaaaaaaaaaa: reference number (alphanumeric) of the applicant authority

— rrrrrrrrrrrr: reference number (alphanumeric) of the requested authority

— 20YYMMDD: date on which the initial request is sent (Year, Month, Date)

— x(xxx): indicates the nature of the claim (to be understood in accordance with Article 2 of Directive 2008/55/EC):

    — a: agricultural levies (see Article 2(a))

    — b: sugar levies (see Article 2(b))

    — c: import duties (see Article 2(c))

    — d: export duties (see Article 2(d))

    — e: value added tax (see Article 2(e))

    — f: excise duties (see Article 2(f))

    — g: taxes on income and capital (see Article 2(g))

    — h: taxes on insurance premiums (see Article 2(h))

    Example: 'cef' = import duties + value added tax + excise duties

    Note: the request must be filled out in accordance with the competence of the requested authority!

— RI = request for information (RN = request for notification; RR = request for recovery and/or precautionary measures)

(*) Instructions on how to fill out this form:

— Within each box of this form, please click on the appropriate □.

— Within each box, the underlined parts must be filled out.

— The other data should be provided if available. Providing the maximum information will help the requested authority to send a better or faster response.

REQUEST FOR INFORMATION
Based on Article 4 of Directive 2008/55/EC

1. MEMBER STATE OF THE APPLICANT AUTHORITY	
A. Applicant authority Country: Name: Telephone: Name of the official dealing with the request:	**B. Office initiating the request** Name: Address: Postcode: Town: Telephone: E-mail: Reference of the file: Name of the official dealing with the request:

2. MEMBER STATE OF THE REQUESTED AUTHORITY	
A. Requested authority Country: Name: Telephone: Name of the official dealing with the request:	**B. Office handling the request** Name: Address: Postcode: Town: Telephone: E-mail: Reference of the file: Name of the official dealing with the request:

3. CONFIRMATION CONCERNING THE FULFILMENT OF THE CONDITIONS FOR REQUESTING ASSISTANCE

A. Age of the claim(s)

This request concerns a claim (claims) which, at the date of the initial request for assistance, is (are):

☐ not more than 5 years old,

☐ more than 5 years old,

dating from the moment the instrument permitting the recovery was established (for contested claims or instruments: from the moment at which the claim or the instrument may no longer be contested) (Article 14(b) of Directive 2008/55/EC).

☐ For claims of more than 5 years old: This request is based on the following circumstances: **Common language or translation required**

☐ This request is connected with the request of 20YY/MM/DD, which was processed by the requested authority under reference number:

B. Amount of the claim(s)

The total amount of all claim(s) (inclusive of interest, penalties and costs) is (in currencies of both Member States):

4. INFORMATION RELATING TO THE REQUEST MADE

A. Other requested authorities:

☐ A similar request is sent to the following competent authority(ies) within the Member State of the requested authority:

☐ A similar request is sent to the following competent authority(ies) within the following Member State(s):

B. Non-disclosure of this request to the person concerned

☐ I, applicant authority, ask the requested authority not to inform the person(s) concerned about this request.

5. INFORMATION RELATING TO THE PERSON CONCERNED

A. Information is requested with regard to:

☐ *For natural persons:*
First name(s):
Surname:
Maiden name (name at birth):
Date of birth:
Place of birth:
VAT number:
Tax Identification Number:
Other identification data:

☐ *Or for legal entities:*
Company name:
Legal status:
VAT number:
Tax Identification Number:
Other identification data:

B. Address of this person/legal entity: ☐ known — ☐ assumed

Street and number:
Details of address:
Postcode and town:
Country:

C. Liability

1. **The person concerned is:**
   - ☐ the principal debtor (Article 4(1) of this Regulation)
   - ☐ co-debtor (Article 4(2) of this Regulation)
   - ☐ a third party holding assets (Article 4(3) of this Regulation)

2. **Principal debtor if different from person concerned:**

   ☐ *For natural persons:*
   First name(s):
   Surname:

   ☐ *Or for legal entities:*
   Company name:
   Legal status:

   Address: ☐ known — ☐ assumed
   Street and number:
   Details of address:
   Postcode and town:
   Country:

3. **If relevant: assets of the debtor held by a third party: Common language or translation required**

D. Other relevant information concerning the above persons: Common language or translation required

6. INFORMATION REQUESTED

- ☐ Information about the identity of the person concerned (for natural persons: full name, date and place of birth; for legal entities: company name and legal status)
- ☐ Information about the address
- ☐ Information about the income and assets for recovery
- ☐ Other: **Common language or translation required**

7. FOLLOW-UP OF THE REQUEST FOR INFORMATION

Date	No	Message	Applicant authority	Requested authority
	A	On receipt of the request:		
YY/MM/DD	0 ☐	I, requested authority, acknowledge receipt of the request.		
YY/MM/DD	1 ☐	I, requested authority, do not have competence for any of the taxes to which the request relates.		
YY/MM/DD	2 ☐ ☐	I, requested authority, do not provide assistance for claims **a** which are more than 5 years old (Article 14(b) of Directiv 2008/55/EC). **b** of which the total amount is less than EUR 1 500 (Article 25(2) of this Regulation).		
YY/MM/DD	3 ☐	I, requested authority, invite the applicant authority to complete the request with the following additional information: **Common language or translation required**		
YY/MM/DD	4 ☐ ☐	I, applicant authority, **a** provide on request the following additional information: **Common language or translation required** **b** I am not able to provide the requested additional information (because: **Common language or translation required**)		
YY/MM/DD	5 ☐	I, requested authority, acknowledge receipt of the additional information and am now in a position to proceed		

	B At any time, but at the latest within six months from the date of receipt of the request:
	6 I, requested authority:

YY/MM/DD	☐ cannot provide the information within six months.
	    (☐ I have asked information from other public bodies)
	    (☐ I have asked information from a third party)
	    (☐ I am arranging a personal call)
	    (☐ other reason: **Common language or translation required**)

YY/MM/DD	☐ transmit the following part of the requested information:

YY/MM/DD	☐ Transmit all (or the final part of) the requested information:
	☐ **a** identity confirmed
	☐ **b** address confirmed
	☐ **c** Following data about the identity of the person concerned have changed (or are added):
	    For natural persons:
	    ☐ First name(s):
	    ☐ Surname:
	    ☐ Maiden name:
	    ☐ Date of birth:
	    ☐ Place of birth:
	    For legal entities:
	    ☐ Legal Status:
	    ☐ Company name:
	☐ **d** Following address data have changed (or are added):
	    ☐ Street and number:
	    ☐ Details of address:
	    ☐ Postcode and town:
	    ☐ Country:
	    ☐ Telephone:
	    ☐ Fax:
	    ☐ E-mail:
	☐ **e** Financial situation
	    ☐ Employment details: ☐ Employee — ☐ Self-employed — ☐ Unemployed
	    ☐ It seems that the person concerned has no means to settle the debt/no assets to cover recovery
	      ☐ Person concerned is bankrupt/insolvent:
	      — Date of order:
	      — Date of release:
	      — Liquidators details:
	       ... Name:
	       ... Street and number:
	       ... Details of address:
	       ... Postcode and town:
	       ... Country:
	    ☐ It seems that the person concerned has:
	      ☐ limited means to partially settle the debt
	      ☐ sufficient means/assets for recovery
	    ☐ Comments: **Common language or translation required**
	☐ **f** I recommend proceeding with recovery procedures
	☐ **g** I recommend not proceeding with recovery procedures
	☐ **h** Debt disputed
	    ☐ person concerned has been advised to contest the claim in the Member State of the applicant authority
	    ☐ references of the dispute, if available:
	    ☐ further details attached
	☐ **i** Debtor deceased on YYYY/MM/DD
	☐ **j** Name and address of heirs/will executor:
	☐ **k** Other comments: **Common language or translation required**

YY/MM/DD	**7** The requested information cannot be obtained because: ☐ **a** person concerned is not known. ☐ **b** insufficient data for identification of person concerned. ☐ **c** person concerned has moved away, address unknown. ☐ **d** other reason: **Common language or translation required**
YY/MM/DD	**8** I, requested authority, refuse to comply with the request for the following reason: ☐ **a** I am not able to obtain this information for the purpose of recovering similar national claims. ☐ **b** this would disclose a commercial, industrial or professional secret. ☐ **c** the disclosure of this information would be liable to prejudice the security or be contrary to the public policy of the State.
YY/MM/DD	**9** I, applicant authority, ☐ withdraw my request for information.

ANNEX II

Reference (*): AA_RA_aaaaaaaaaaaa_rrrrrrrrrrrr_20YYMMDD_x(xxx)_RN

(*) Reference number:

— AA: ISO code of the Member State (MS) of the applicant authority

— RA: ISO code of the MS of the requested authority

— aaaaaaaaaaaa: reference number (alphanumeric) of the applicant authority

— rrrrrrrrrrrr: reference number (alphanumeric) of the requested authority

— 20YYMMDD: date on which the initial request is sent (Year, Month, Date)

— x(xxx): indicates the nature of the claim (to be understood in accordance with Article 2 of Directive 2008/55/EC):

    — a: agricultural levies (see Article 2(a))

    — b: sugar levies (see Article 2(b))

    — c: import duties (see Article 2(c))

    — d: export duties (see Article 2(d))

    — e: value added tax (see Article 2(e))

    — f: excise duties (see Article 2(f))

    — g: taxes on income and capital (see Article 2(g))

    — h: taxes on insurance premiums (see Article 2(h))

    Example: 'cef' = import duties + value added tax + excise duties

    Note: the request must be filled out in accordance with the competence of the requested authority!

— RN = request for notification (RI = request for information; RR = request for recovery and/or precautionary measures)

(*) Instructions on how to fill out this form:

— Within each box of this form, please click on the appropriate ☐.

— Within each box, the underlined parts must be filled out.

— The other data should be provided if available. Providing the maximum information will help the requested authority to send a better or faster response.

REQUEST FOR NOTIFICATION
Based on Article 5 of Directive 2008/55/EC

1. MEMBER STATE OF THE APPLICANT AUTHORITY	
A. Applicant authority Country: Name: Telephone: Name of the official dealing with the request:	**B. Office initiating the request** Name: Address: Postcode: Town: Telephone: E-mail: Reference of the file: Name of the official dealing with the request:

2. MEMBER STATE OF THE REQUESTED AUTHORITY	
A. Requested authority Country: Name: Telephone: Name of the official dealing with the request:	**B. Office handling the request** Name: Address: Postcode: Town: Telephone: E-mail: Reference of the file: Name of the official dealing with the request:

---

3. CONFIRMATION CONCERNING THE FULFILMENT OF THE CONDITIONS FOR REQUESTING ASSISTANCE

A. Age of the claim(s)

This request concerns a claim (claims) which, at the date of the initial request for assistance, is (are):

☐ not more than 5 years old,

☐ more than 5 years old,

dating from the moment the instrument permitting the recovery was established (for contested claims or instruments: from the moment at which the claim or the instrument may no longer be contested) (Article 14(b) of Directive 2008/55/EC).

☐ For claims of more than 5 years old: This request is based on the following circumstances: **Common language or translation required**

☐ This request is connected with the request of 20YY/MM/DD, which was processed by the requested authority under reference number:

B. Amount of the claim(s)

The total amount of all claim(s)(inclusive of interest, penalties and costs) is (in currencies of both Member States) is:

4. INFORMATION RELATING TO THE PERSON CONCERNED

A. This request is made in relation to:

☐ *For natural persons:*
First name(s):
Surname:
Maiden name (name at birth):
Date of birth:
Place of birth:
VAT number:
Tax Identification Number:
Other identification data:

☐ *Or for legal entities:*
Company name:
Legal status:
VAT number:
Tax Identification Number:
Other identification data:

B. Address of this person/legal entity: ☐ known — ☐ assumed

Street and number:
Details of address:
Postcode and town:
Country:

C. Liability:

1. **The person concerned is:**
   ☐ the principal debtor (Article 4(1) of this Regulation)
   ☐ co-debtor (Article 4(2) of this Regulation)
   ☐ a third party holding assets (Article 4(3) of this Regulation)

2. **Principal debtor if different from person concerned:**
   ☐ *For natural persons:*
   First name(s):
   Surname:
   ☐ *Or for legal entities:*
   Company name:
   Legal status:
   Address: ☐ known — ☐ assumed
   Street and number:
   Details of address:
   Postcode and town:
   Country:

D. Other relevant information concerning the above persons: Common language or translation required

5. NOTIFICATION REQUESTED

A. Identification of the document(s) attached (example: reference, date, title, ...):

B. Final date for notification of these documents (if necessary): 20YY/MM/DD

C. Other comments: **Common language or translation required**

6. FOLLOW-UP OF THE REQUEST FOR NOTIFICATION

Date	No	Message	Applicant authority	Requested authority
YY/MM/DD	0 ☐	I, requested authority, acknowledge receipt of the request.		
YY/MM/DD	1 ☐	I, requested authority, do not have competence for any of the taxes to which the request relates.		
YY/MM/DD	2 ☐ ☐	I, requested authority, do not provide assistance for claims **a** which are more than 5 years old (Article 14(b) of Directive 2008/55/EC). **b** of which the total amount is less than EUR 1 500 (Article 25(2) of this Regulation).		
YY/MM/DD	3 ☐	I, requested authority, invite the applicant authority to complete the request with the following additional information:		
YY/MM/DD	4 ☐ ☐	I, applicant authority, **a** provide on request the following additional information: **Common language or translation required** **b** I am not able to provide the requested additional information (because: **Common language or translation required**)		
YY/MM/DD	5 ☐	I, requested authority, acknowledge receipt of the additional information and am now in a position to proceed.		
YY/MM/DD	6 ☐	I, requested authority, certify: **a** that the above-mentioned document(s) [see box 5.A.] has (have) been notified to the natural person/legal entity referred to in Box 4, with legal effect according to the national legislation of the Member State of the requested authority, on 20YY/MM/DD. The notification was made in the following manner: ☐ to the addressee in person ☐ by mail ☐ by registered mail ☐ by bailiff ☐ by another procedure ☐ **b** that the above-mentioned document(s) could not be notified to the person concerned for the following reasons: ☐ addressee(s) not known ☐ addressee(s) deceased ☐ addressee(s) has (have) left the Member State. New address: ☐ other: **Common language or translation required**		
YY/MM/DD	7 ☐	I, applicant authority, withdraw my request for information.		

ANNEX III

Reference (*): AA_RA_aaaaaaaaaaaa_rrrrrrrrrrr_20YYMMDD_x(xxx)_RR

(*) **Reference number:**

— AA: ISO code of the Member State (MS) of the applicant authority

— RA: ISO code of the MS of the requested authority

— aaaaaaaaaaaa: reference number (alphanumeric) of the applicant authority

— rrrrrrrrrrr: reference number (alphanumeric) of the requested authority

— 20YYMMDD: date on which the initial request is sent (Year, Month, Date)

— x(xxx): indicates the nature of the claim (to be understood in accordance with Article 2 of Directive 2008/55/EC):

    — a: agricultural levies (see Article 2(a))

    — b: sugar levies (see Article 2(b))

    — c: import duties (see Article 2(c))

    — d: export duties (see Article 2(d))

    — e: value added tax (see Article 2(e))

    — f: excise duties (see Article 2(f))

    — g: taxes on income and capital (see Article 2(g))

    — h: taxes on insurance premiums (see Article 2(h))

    Example: 'cef' = import duties + value added tax + excise duties

    Note: the request must be filled out in accordance with the competence of the requested authority!

— RR = request for recovery/and or precautionary measures (RI = request for information; RN = request for notification)

(*) **Instructions on how to fill out this form:**

— Within each box of this form, please click on the appropriate ☐.

— Within each box, <u>the underlined parts</u> must be filled out.

— The other data should be provided if available. Providing the maximum information will help the requested authority to send a better or faster response.

REQUEST FOR ☐ RECOVERY MEASURES
Based on Article 6 of Directive 2008/55/EC
AND/OR ☐ PRECAUTIONARY MEASURES
Based on Article 13 of Directive 2008/55/EC

1. MEMBER STATE OF THE APPLICANT AUTHORITY

A. **Applicant authority**	B. **Office initiating the request**
<u>Country:</u> <u>Name:</u> Telephone: Name of the official dealing with the request:	Name: Address: Postcode: Town: Telephone: E-mail: Reference of the file: Name of the official dealing with the request:

2. MEMBER STATE OF THE REQUESTED AUTHORITY

A. **Requested authority**	B. **Office handling the request**
<u>Country:</u> <u>Name:</u> Telephone: Name of the official dealing with the request:	Name: Address: Postcode: Town: Telephone: E-mail: Reference of the file: Name of the official dealing with the request:

3. INFORMATION CONCERNING CONDITIONS FULFILLED (IN SO FAR AS REQUIRED)

☐ This request concerns a claim (claims) which, at the date of the initial request for assistance, is (are):

     ☐ not more than 5 years old,

     ☐ more than 5 years old,

dating from the moment the instrument permitting the recovery was established (for contested claims or instruments: from the moment at which the claim or the instrument may no longer be contested) (Article 14(b) of Directive 2008/55/EC).

☐ For claims of more than 5 years old: This request is based on the following circumstances: **Common language or translation required**

☐ This request is connected with the request of 20YY/MM/DD, which was processed by the requested authority under reference number:

☐ The total amount of all claim(s)(inclusive of interest, penalties and costs) is not less than EUR 1 500.

☐ The claim(s) is (are) the subject of an instrument permitting the enforcement (see attached document) (Article 7(1) of Directive 2008/55/EC).

☐ The claim(s) is (are) not contested (Article 7(2)(a) and Article 12(2) of Directive 2008/55/EC).

☐ The claim(s) may no longer be contested by an administrative appeal/by an appeal to the courts (Article 7(2)(a) and Article 12(2) of Directive 2008/55/EC).

☐ The claim(s) is (are) contested but the laws, regulations and administrative practices in force in the State of the applicant authority allow recovery of a contested claim (Article 12(2) of Directive 2008/55/EC).

☐ Appropriate recovery procedures have been applied in the Member State of the applicant authority but will not result in the payment in full of the claim (Article 7(2)(b) of Directive 2008/55/EC).

4. INFORMATION CONCERNING THE REQUEST(S) MADE

☐ A similar request is sent to the following competent authority(ies) within the Member State of the requested authority:

☐ A similar request is sent to the following competent authority(ies) within the following Member State(s):

☐ I request not to inform the debtor/other person concerned before the precautionary measures have been taken.

☐ Identification of the document(s) attached (example: reference, date, title, ...)

5. PAYMENT INSTRUCTIONS

A. Please remit the amount of the claim recovered to:

     — Bank account number (IBAN):

     — Bank identification code (BIC):

     — Name of the bank:

     — Name of the account holder:

     — Address of the account holder:

     — Payment reference to be used at the transfer of the money:

B. Payment by instalment is:

     ☐ acceptable without further consultation

     ☐ only acceptable after consultation (Please use box 7, point 18 for this consultation)

     ☐ not acceptable

---

6. INFORMATION RELATING TO THE PERSON CONCERNED

A. **Recovery/precautionary measures are requested with regard to:**

☐ *For natural persons:*

First name(s):

Surname:

Maiden name (name at birth):

Date of birth:

Place of birth:

VAT number:

Tax Identification Number:

Other identification data:

☐ *Or for legal entities:*

Legal status:

Company name:

VAT number:

Tax Identification Number:

Other identification data:

B. **Address of this person/legal entity:** ☐ known — ☐ assumed

Street and number:

Details of address:

Postcode and town:

Country:

C. **Liability:**

1. **The person concerned is:**

   ☐ the principal debtor (Article 4(1) of this Regulation)

   ☐ co-debtor (Article 4(2) of this Regulation)

   ☐ a third party holding assets (Article 4(3) of this Regulation)

2. **Principal debtor if different from person concerned:**

   ☐ *For natural persons:*

   First name(s):

   Surname:

   ☐ *Or for legal entities:*

   Legal status:

   Company name:

   Address: ☐ known — ☐ assumed

   Street and number:

   Details of address:

   Postcode and town:

   Country:

3. **If relevant: assets of the debtor held by a third party: Common language or translation required**

D. **Other relevant information concerning the above persons: Common language or translation required**

7. FOLLOW-UP OF THE REQUEST FOR RECOVERY AND/OR PRECAUTIONARY MEASURES

Date	No	Message	Applicant authority	Requested authority
	A	**On receipt of the request**		
YY/MM/DD	0	I, requested authority,		
	☐	acknowledge receipt of the request (Article 15(1)(a) of this Regulation).		
YY/MM/DD	1	I, requested authority, do not have competence for		
	☐	a the tax(es) to which your request relates.		
	☐	b the following tax(es) of your request (indicate the letter):		
YY/MM/DD	2	I, requested authority, do not provide assistance for claims		
	☐	a which are more than 5 years old (Article 14(b) of Directive 2008/55/EC).		
	☐	b Of which the total amount is less than EUR 1 500 (Article 25(2) of this Regulation).		
YY/MM/DD	3	I, requested authority, will not take the requested action(s), for the following reasons:		
	☐	a my national legislation and practice does not allow recovery measures for claims that are contested.		
	☐	b my national legislation and practice does not allow precautionary measures for claims that are contested.		
YY/MM/DD	4	I, requested authority,		
	☐	invite the applicant authority to complete the request with the following additional information: **Common language or translation required**		
YY/MM/DD	5	I, applicant authority,		
	☐	a provide on request the following additional information:		
	☐	b am not able to provide the requested additional information (because: **Common language or translation required**)		
YY/MM/DD	6 ☐	I, requested authority, acknowledge receipt of the additional information and am now in a position to proceed.		
	B	**Immediately when the action is taken and at the latest at the end of each period of six months from the date of the receipt of the request.**		
	7	I, requested authority, have conducted the following procedures for recovery and/or precautionary measures:		
YY/MM/DD	☐	a I established contact with the debtor and requested payment on 20YY/MM/DD.		
YY/MM/DD	☐	b I am negotiating payment by instalment.		
YY/MM/DD	☐	c I have commenced enforcement procedures on 20YY/MM/DD. The following actions have been taken: **Common language or translation required**		
	☐	d I have commenced precautionary measures on 20YY/MM/DD. The following actions have been taken: **Common language or translation required**		
	☐	e I, requested authority, ask to be informed whether the measures which I have taken (described under point c and/or d above) have interrupted or suspended the time limit for recovery and, if so, what the new time limit is.		
YY/MM/DD	8 ☐	Procedures are still going on. I, requested authority, will inform applicant authority when changes occur.		
YY/MM/DD	9 ☐	I, applicant authority, confirm that, as a result of the action mentioned under point 7, the time limit has been changed. The new time limit is indicated in box 8.		

	C **At any time**
YY/MM/DD	**10** I, requested authority, inform the applicant authority that:
	☐ **a** the claim has been fully recovered on 20YY/MM/DD
	— of which the following amount (indicate the currency of the Member State of the requested authority) relates to the claim as mentioned in the request:
	— of which the following amount relates to the interest charged under the laws of the Member State of the requested authority (in accordance with Article 9(2) of Directive 2008/55/EC):
YY/MM/DD	☐ **b** the claim has been partly recovered on 20YY/MM/DD.
	— for the amount of (indicate the currency of the Member State of the requested authority):
	— of which the following amount relates to the claim as mentioned in the request:
	— of which the following amount relates to the interest charged under the laws of the Member State of the requested authority (in accordance with Article 9(2) of Directive 2008/55/EC):
	☐ I will take no further action.
	☐ I will continue recovery procedures.
YY/MM/DD	☐ **c** precautionary measures have been taken.
	(The requested authority is invited to indicate the nature of these measures: **Common language or translation required**)
YY/MM/DD	☐ **d** the following payment by instalment has been agreed:
YY/MM/DD	**11** I, requested authority, confirm that all or part of the claim could not be recovered/precautionary measures will not be taken, and the case will be closed because:
	☐ **a1** The person concerned is not known.
	☐ **a2** The person concerned is known, but moved to:
	☐ **a3** The person concerned is known, but moved to an unknown address.
	☐ **b** The person concerned is deceased on YYYY/MM/DD.
	☐ **c** Debtor/co-debtor is insolvent.
	☐ **d** Debtor/co-debtor is bankrupt and the claim has been lodged.
	Date of order: 20YY/MM/DD — Date of release: 20YY/MM/DD
	☐ **e** Debtor/co-debtor is bankrupt/no recovery possible
	☐ **f** Others: **Common language or translation required**
YY/MM/DD	**12** I, applicant authority, confirm that the case is closed. ☐
YY/MM/DD	**13** I, requested authority, inform the applicant authority that I have received notification that an action has been launched contesting the claim or the instrument permitting its enforcement and will suspend enforcement procedures. ☐ Further,
	☐ **a** I have taken precautionary measures to ensure recovery of the claim on 20YY/MM/DD.
	☐ **b** I ask the applicant authority to inform me whether I should recover the claim.
	☐ **c** I inform the applicant authority that the laws, regulations and administrative practices in force in the Member State in which I am situated do not permit (continued) recovery of the claim as long as it is contested.
YY/MM/DD	**14** I, applicant authority, having been informed that an action has been launched contesting the claim or the instrument permitting its enforcement,
	☐ **a** ask the requested authority to suspend any action which it has undertaken.
	☐ **b** ask the requested authority to take precautionary measures to ensure recovery of the claim.
	☐ **c** ask the requested authority to (continue to) recover the claim.

YY/MM/DD	**15**	I, requested authority, inform the applicant authority that:
	☐ a	the laws, regulations and administrative practices in force in the Member State in which I am situated do not permit the action requested:
		☐ under point 14(b).
		☐ under point 14(c).
	☐ b	I, requested authority, inform the applicant authority that I will proceed in accordance with the request mentioned
		☐ under point 14(a).
		☐ under point 14(b).
		☐ under point 14(c).
YY/MM/DD	**16**	I, applicant authority,
	☐ a	amend the request for recovery/precautionary measures as mentioned in the revised box 8 'Information relating to the claim(s)',
		☐ in accordance with the decision about the contested claim, delivered on 20YY/MM/DD by the body competent in this matter;
		☐ because part of the claim was paid directly to the applicant authority;
		☐ for another reason: **Common language or translation required**
	☐ b	ask the requested authority to resume enforcement procedures since the contestation was not favourable to the debtor (decision of the body competent in this matter of 20YY/MM/DD).
YY/MM/DD	**17**	I, applicant authority, withdraw this request for recovery/precautionary measures because:
	☐ a	the amount was paid directly to the applicant authority.
	☐ b	the time limit for recovery action has elapsed.
	☐ c	the claim(s) has (have) been annulled by a national court or by an administrative body.
	☐ d	the instrument permitting enforcement has been annulled.
	☐ e	other reason: **Common language or translation required**
	D	**Other**
YY/MM/DD	**18**	Other: **Common language or translation required** (Please start each comment by indicating the date)
	☐	

8. INFORMATION RELATING TO THE CLAIM(S)
☐ initial claim(s), for which the request for mutual assistance was sent on 20YY/MM/DD.
☐ revised claim on the decision of an administrative body or a court of 20YY/MM/DD.
☐ revised claim because partial payment was made directly to the applicant authority.

Currency of the Applicant Authority (AA):
Currency of the Requested Authority (RA):
Exchange rate used:

Identification of the claim (¹)	Principal amount (²) (³)	Amount of administrative penalties and fines (²) (³)	Amount of interest up to date of the request (²) (³)	Amount of the costs up to date of the request (²) (³)	Total amount of the claim (²) (³)	Date on which enforcement becomes possible	Last day of the limitation period
Ref.: Nature: Name: Period: Date establishment: 20YY/MM/DD Date notification: 20YY/MM/DD	Currency AA: Currency RA:	Currency AA: Currency RA:	Currency AA: Currency RA:	Currency AA: Currency RA:	Currency AA: Currency RA:	20YY/MM/DD	20YY/MM/DD
Ref.: Nature: Name: Period: Date establishment: 20YY/MM/DD Date notification: 20YY/MM/DD	Currency AA: Currency RA:	Currency AA: Currency RA:	Currency AA: Currency RA:	Currency AA: Currency RA:	Currency AA: Currency RA:	20YY/MM/DD	20YY/MM/DD
Ref.: Nature: Name: Period: Date establishment: 20YY/MM/DD Date notification: 20YY/MM/DD	Currency AA: Currency RA:	Currency AA: Currency RA:	Currency AA: Currency RA:	Currency AA: Currency RA:	Currency AA: Currency RA:	20YY/MM/DD	20YY/MM/DD
Ref.: Nature: Name: Period: Date establishment: 20YY/MM/DD Date notification: 20YY/MM/DD	Currency AA: Currency RA:	Currency AA: Currency RA:	Currency AA: Currency RA:	Currency AA: Currency RA:	Currency AA: Currency RA:	20YY/MM/DD	20YY/MM/DD

Overall total amount of the claims: in the currency of the AA: .... — in the currency of the RA: .... — in EUR: ....

Other information: **Common language or translation required**

(¹) For each claim: reference number; nature of the claim (Article 2 points (a) to (h) of Directive 2008/55/EC; name of the tax concerned in the Member State of the AA; date of establishment of the claim; date of notification (see Article 7(3)(e) of Directive 2008/55/EC).
(²) Amounts should preferably be specified for each claim separately.
(³) Amounts expressed in the currency of the Member State of the applicant authority and of the Member State of the requested authority.

ANNEX IV

Model A for the communication of statistics on the use of the mutual recovery assistance — general information

Requests for mutual assistance on recovery of claims received and sent by:

Member State	Requests for Information		Requests for notification		In the year:										
					Requests received from:				Requests for recovery						
												Requests sent to:			
							amounts of the claims recovered for requests made during the year (¹)						amounts of the claims recovered for requests made during the year (¹)	
	number received from:	number sent to:	number received from:	number sent to:	number	amount of the claims involved	amount in EUR (²)	year	number	amount of the claims involved	amount in EUR (²)	year	number	amount of the claims involved	amount in EUR (²)	year
BE — België/Belgique															
BG — България (Bulgaria)															
CZ — Česká Republika															
DK — Danmark															
DE — Deutschland															
IE — Ireland															
EE — Eesti															
EL — Ελλάδα (Ellas)															
ES — España															
FR — France															
IT — Italia															
CY — Κύπρος (Kypros)															
LV — Latvija															
LT — Lietuva															
LU — Luxembourg															
HU — Magyarország															
MT — Malta															
NL — Nederland															
AT — Österreich															
PL — Polska															
PT — Portugal															
RO — România															
SI — Slovenija															
SK — Slovensko															
FI — Suomi/Finland															
SE — Sverige															
UK — United Kingdom															
Total	0	0	0	0	0	0	0		0	0	0		0	0	0	

(¹) Please split the total amounts recovered according to the year of request to which they relate.

(²) Effectively recovered (no amounts for which precautionary measures have been taken or deferred payment has been agreed).

(³) These amounts also include any debt, for which mutual assistance has been requested, paid directly by the debtor to the requesting Member State.

ANNEX V

Model B for the communication of statistics on the use of mutual recovery assistance — information on the nature of the claims

Requests for recovery sent or received by:	In the year:			
Nature of the claims concerned	requests sent		requests received	
	amount of the claims involved	amounts of the claims recovered ([7])	amount of the claims involved	amounts of the claims recovered ([8])
claims of Article 2(a) to (d) of Directive 2008/55/EC ([1]) ([6])				
claims of Article 2(e) of Directive 2008/55/EC ([2]) ([6])				
claims of Article 2(f) of Directive 2008/55/EC ([3]) ([6])				
claims of Article 2(g) of Directive 2008/55/EC ([4]) ([6])				
claims of Article 2(h) of Directive 2008/55/EC ([5]) ([6])				
Total	0	0	0	0

([1]) Agricultural and sugar levies, import and export duties.
([2]) VAT.
([3]) Excise duties.
([4]) Taxes on income and capital.
([5]) Taxes on insurance premiums.
([6]) Including interest, administrative penalties and fines, and costs.
([7]) These amounts also include any debt, for which mutual assistance has been requested, paid directly by the debtor to the requesting Member State.
([8]) Effectively recovered (no amounts for which precautionary measures have been taken or deferred payment has been agreed).

COUNCIL DIRECTIVE 2008/117/EC

of 16 December 2008

amending Directive 2006/112/EC on the common system of value added tax to combat tax evasion connected with intra-Community transactions

Official Journal L14, 20/01/2009 p. 7 - 9

THE COUNCIL OF THE EUROPEAN UNION,

Having regard to the Treaty establishing the European Community, and in particular Article 93 thereof,

Having regard to the proposal from the Commission,

Having regard to the opinion of the European Parliament,

Having regard to the opinion of the European Economic and Social Committee,

Whereas:

(1) The evasion of value added tax (VAT) has a significant impact on the Member States' tax revenue and distorts economic activity in the single market by creating unjustified flows of goods and by placing goods on the market at abnormally low prices.

(2) The shortcomings of the intra-Community VAT arrangements, and in particular the system for the exchange of information on supplies of goods within the Community, as laid down by Council Directive 2006/112/EC, are one of the causes of this tax evasion. In particular, the time that elapses between a transaction and the corresponding exchange of information under the VAT information exchange system is an obstacle to the effective use of that information to tackle fraud.

(3) In order to combat VAT evasion effectively, it is necessary for the administration of the Member State in which the VAT is chargeable to receive information on intra-Community supplies of goods within a deadline not exceeding one month.

(4) In order for the cross-checking of information to be useful for combating fraud, intra-Community transactions should be declared for the same tax period by both the supplier and the purchaser or customer.

(5) In view of changes in the business environment and operative tools, it is desirable to ensure that these declarations can be made by simple electronic procedures in order to reduce the administrative burden to a minimum.

(6) In order to preserve the balance between the Community's objectives in combating tax evasion and reducing the administrative burden on economic operators, Member States should be allowed to authorise operators to submit on a quarterly basis the recapitulative statements concerning intra-Community supplies of goods where their amount is not significant. It is appropriate that Member States wishing to organise a

progressive entry into application of this proposal could, on a transitory basis, set this amount at a higher level. Likewise, Member States should be allowed to authorise operators to submit the information on intra-Community supplies of services on a quarterly basis.

(7)   The impact of the speeding-up of the exchange of information on Member States' ability to combat VAT fraud as well as the option mechanisms should be assessed by the Commission after one year of application of the new measures, in particular with a view to determine whether these option mechanisms should be maintained.

(8)   Since the objectives of the proposed action to tackle VAT evasion cannot be sufficiently achieved by the Member States, whose action in the matter depends on information collected by the other Member States, and can therefore, by reason of the need to involve all Member States, be better achieved at Community level, the Community may adopt measures in accordance with the principle of subsidiarity, as set out in Article 5 of the Treaty. In accordance with the principle of proportionality, as set out in that Article, this Directive does not go beyond what is necessary in order to achieve those objectives.

(9)   Directive 2006/112/EC should therefore be amended accordingly.

(10)   In accordance with point 34 of the Interinstitutional Agreement on better law-making, Member States are encouraged to draw up, for themselves and in the interest of the Community, their own tables, which will, as far as possible, illustrate the correlation between this Directive and their transposition measures, and to make them public,

HAS ADOPTED THIS DIRECTIVE:

Article 1

Directive 2006/112/EC is hereby amended as follows:

1.   Article 64(2) shall be replaced by the following:

'2.   Supplies of services for which VAT is payable by the customer pursuant to Article 196, which are supplied continuously over a period of more than one year and which do not give rise to statements of account or payments during that period shall be regarded as being completed on expiry of each calendar year until such time as the supply of services comes to an end.

Member States may provide that, in certain cases other than those referred to in the previous paragraph, the continuous supply of goods or services over a period of time is to be regarded as being completed at least at intervals of one year.';

2.   in Article 66, the following subparagraph shall be added:

'The derogation provided for in the first paragraph shall not, however, apply to supplies of services in respect of which VAT is payable by the customer pursuant to Article 196.';

3.   Article 263 shall be replaced by the following:

'Article 263

1.   The recapitulative statement shall be drawn up for each calendar month within a period not exceeding one month and in accordance with procedures to be determined by the Member States.

1a.   However, Member States, in accordance with the conditions and limits which they may lay down, may allow taxable persons to submit the recapitulative statement for each calendar quarter within a time limit not exceeding one month from the end of the quarter, where the total quarterly amount, excluding VAT, of the supplies of goods as referred to in Articles 264(1)(d) and 265(1)(c) does not exceed either in respect of the quarter concerned or in respect of any of the previous four quarters the sum of EUR 50 000 or its equivalent in national currency.

The option provided for in the first subparagraph shall cease to be applicable after the end of the month during which the total value, excluding VAT, of the supplies of goods as referred to in Article 264(1)(d) and 265(1)(c) exceeds, in respect of the current quarter, the sum of EUR 50 000 or its equivalent in national currency. In this case, a recapitulative statement shall be drawn up for the month(s) which has (have) elapsed since the beginning of the quarter, within a time limit not exceeding one month.

1b.   Until 31 December 2011, Member States are allowed to set the sum mentioned in paragraph 1a at EUR 100 000 or its equivalent in national currency.

1c.   In the case of supplies of services as referred to in Article 264(1)(d), Member States, in accordance with the conditions and limits which they may lay down, may allow taxable persons to submit the recapitulative statement for each calendar quarter within a time limit not exceeding one month from the end of the quarter.

Member States may, in particular, require the taxable persons who carry out supplies of both goods and services as referred to in Article 264(1)(d) to submit the recapitulative statement in accordance with the deadline resulting from paragraphs 1 to 1b.

2.   Member States shall allow, and may require, the recapitulative statement referred to in paragraph 1 to be submitted by electronic file transfer, in accordance with conditions which they lay down.';

4.   Article 264(2) shall be replaced by the following:

'2.   The value referred to in paragraph 1(d) shall be declared for the period of submission established in accordance with Article 263(1) to (1c) during which VAT became chargeable.

The amounts referred to in paragraph 1(f) shall be declared for the period of submission established in accordance with Article 263(1) to (1c) during which the person acquiring the goods was notified of the adjustment.';

5.   Article 265(2) shall be replaced by the following:

'2.   The value referred to in paragraph 1(c) shall be declared for the period of submission established in accordance with Article 263(1) to (1b) during which VAT became chargeable.'.

Article 2

On the basis of information provided by the Member States, the Commission shall present, no later than 30 June 2011, a report assessing the impact of Article 263(1) of Directive 2006/112/EC on Member States' ability to fight against VAT fraud connected with intra-Community supplies of goods and services as well as the usefulness of the options provided for in Article 263(1a) to (1c), as well as, depending on the conclusions of the report, the appropriate proposals.

Article 3

1.   Member States shall bring into force the laws, regulations and administrative provisions necessary to comply with this Directive with effect from 1 January 2010. They shall forthwith communicate to the Commission the text of those provisions and a correlation table between those provisions and this Directive.

When Member States adopt those provisions, they shall contain a reference to this Directive or be accompanied by such a reference on the occasion of their official publication. Member States shall determine how such reference is to be made.

2.   Member States shall communicate to the Commission the text of the main provisions of national law which they adopt in the field covered by this Directive.

Article 4

This Directive shall enter into force on the day following its publication in the *Official Journal of the European Union*.

Article 5

This Directive is addressed to the Member States.

Done at Brussels, 16 December 2008.

For the Council

The President

R. BACHELOT-NARQUIN

COUNCIL REGULATION (EC) No 37/2009

of 16 December 2008

amending Regulation (EC) No 1798/2003 on administrative cooperation in the field of value added tax, in order to combat tax evasion connected with intra-Community transactions

Official Journal L14, 20/01/2009 p. 1 - 2

THE COUNCIL OF THE EUROPEAN UNION,

Having regard to the Treaty establishing the European Community, and in particular Article 93 thereof,

Having regard to the proposal from the Commission,

Having regard to the opinion of the European Parliament,

Having regard to the opinion of the European Economic and Social Committee,

Whereas:

(1) To combat VAT evasion more effectively, it is imperative that the Member States collect and exchange information on intra-Community transactions as rapidly as possible. A period of one month is the most appropriate response to this need, taking account of businesses' accounting and financial periods and the objectives of reducing the administrative burden on businesses.

(2) In view of the amendments to the period for declaring intra-Community transactions made by Council Directive 2008/117/EC of 16 December 2008 amending Directive 2006/112/EC on the common system of value added tax to combat tax evasion connected with intra-Community transactions, it is necessary to amend the references to that period in Council Regulation (EC) No 1798/2003.

(3) Since the objectives of the proposed action to tackle VAT evasion cannot be sufficiently achieved by the Member States, whose action in the matter depends on information collected by the other Member States, and can therefore, by reason of the need to involve all Member States, be better achieved at Community level, the Community may adopt measures, in accordance with the principle of subsidiarity, as set out in Article 5 of the Treaty. In accordance with the principle of proportionality, as set out in that Article, this Regulation does not go beyond what is necessary in order to achieve those objectives.

(4) Since the amendments contained in this Regulation are necessary to adapt Regulation (EC) No 1798/2003 to the measures provided for in Directive 2008/117/EC, with which the Member States have to comply by 1 January 2010, this Regulation must enter into force on the same date.

(5) Regulation (EC) No 1798/2003 should therefore be amended accordingly,

HAS ADOPTED THIS REGULATION:

Article 1

Regulation (EC) No 1798/2003 is hereby amended as follows:

1. in Article 23, the second paragraph shall be replaced by the following:

    'The values referred to in point 2 of the first paragraph shall be expressed in the currency of the Member State providing the information and shall relate to the periods for submission of the recapitulative statements specific to each taxable person which are established in accordance with Article 263 of Directive 2006/112/EC.';

2. In Article 24, the second paragraph shall be replaced by the following:

    'The values referred to in point 2 of the first paragraph shall be expressed in the currency of the Member State providing the information and shall relate to the periods for submission of the recapitulative statements specific to each taxable person which are established in accordance with Article 263 of Directive 2006/112/EC.';

3. Article 25(1) and (2) shall be replaced by the following:

    '1. Where the competent authority of a Member State is obliged to grant access to information under Articles 23 and 24, it shall do so as soon as possible and, at the latest, within one month of the end of the period to which the information relates.

    2. By way of derogation from paragraph 1, where information is added to a database in the circumstances provided for in Article 22, access to such additional information shall be granted as quickly as possible and no later than one month after the end of the period in which it was collected.'.

Article 2

This Regulation shall enter into force on 1 January 2010.

This Regulation shall be binding in its entirety and directly applicable in all Member States.

Done at Brussels, 16 December 2008.

For the Council

The President

R. BACHELOT-NARQUIN

(2) Regulation (EC) No 1798/2003 should, therefore, be amended accordingly.

HAS ADOPTED THIS REGULATION:

Article 1

Regulation (EC) No 1798/2003 is hereby amended as follows:

1. In Article 23, the second paragraph shall be replaced by the following:

'The values referred to in point 2 of the first paragraph shall be expressed in the currency of the Member State providing the information and shall relate to the periods for submission of the recapitulative statements specific to each taxable person which are established in accordance with Article 263 of Directive 2006/112/EC.'

2. In Article 24, the second paragraph shall be replaced by the following:

'The values referred to in point 2 of the first paragraph shall be expressed in the currency of the Member State providing the information and shall relate to the periods for submission of the recapitulative statements specific to each taxable person which are established in accordance with Article 263 of Directive 2006/112/EC.'

Article 25(1) and (2) shall be replaced by the following:

1. Where the competent authority of a Member State is obliged to grant access to information under Articles 23 and 24, it shall do so as soon as possible and, at the latest, within one month of the end of the period to which the information relate.

2. By way of derogation from paragraph 1, where information is added to a database in the circumstances provided for in Article 22, access to such additional information shall be granted as quickly as possible and no later than one month after the end of the period in which it was collected.

Article 2

This Regulation shall enter into force on 1 January 2010.

This Regulation shall be binding in its entirety and directly applicable in all Member States.

Done at Brussels, 16 December 2008.

For the Council
The President
R. BACHELOT-NARQUIN

DEVELOPMENT OF COUNCIL DIRECTIVE 2006/112/EC

DEVELOPMENT OF COUNCIL DIRECTIVE
2006/112/EC

COUNCIL DIRECTIVE 2006/112/EC

of 28 November 2006

on the common system of value added tax

THE COUNCIL OF THE EUROPEAN UNION,

Having regard to the Treaty establishing the European Community, and in particular Article 93 thereof,

Having regard to the proposal from the Commission, Having regard to the Opinion of the European Parliament, Having regard to the Opinion of the European Economic and Social Committee,

Whereas:

(1)   Council Directive 77/388/EEC of 17 May 1977 on the harmonisation of the laws of the Member States relating to turnover taxes — Common system of value added tax: uniform basis of assessment has been significantly amended on several occasions. Now that new amendments are being made to the said Directive, it is desirable, for reasons of clarity and rationalisation that the Directive should be recast.

(2)   The recast text should incorporate all those provisions of Council Directive 67/227/EEC of 11 April 1967 on the harmonisation of legislation of Member States concerning turnover taxes which are still applicable. That Directive should therefore be repealed.

(3)   To ensure that the provisions are presented in a clear and rational manner, consistent with the principle of better regulation, it is appropriate to recast the structure and the wording of the Directive although this will not, in principle, bring about material changes in the existing legislation. A small number of substantive amendments are however inherent to the recasting exercise and should nevertheless be made. Where such changes are made, these are listed exhaustively in the provisions governing transposition and entry into force.

(4)   The attainment of the objective of establishing an internal market presupposes the application in Member States of legislation on turnover taxes that does not distort conditions of competition or hinder the free movement of goods and services. It is therefore necessary to achieve such harmonisation of legislation on turnover taxes by means of a system of value added tax (VAT), such as will eliminate, as far as possible, factors which may distort conditions of competition, whether at national or Community level.

(5)   A VAT system achieves the highest degree of simplicity and of neutrality when the tax is levied in as general a manner as possible and when its scope covers all stages of production and distribution, as well as the supply of services. It is therefore in the interests of the internal market and of Member States to adopt a common system which also applies to the retail trade.

(6)   It is necessary to proceed by stages, since the harmonisation of turnover taxes leads in Member States to alterations in tax structure and appreciable consequences in the budgetary, economic and social fields.

(7)   The common system of VAT should, even if rates and exemptions are not fully harmonised, result in neutrality in competition, such that within the territory of each Member State similar goods and services bear the same tax burden, whatever the length of the production and distribution chain.

(8)   Pursuant to Council Decision 2000/597/EC, Euratom, of 29 September 2000 on the system of the European Communities' own resources, the budget of the European Communities is to be financed, without prejudice to other revenue, wholly from the Communities' own resources. Those resources are to include those accruing from VAT and obtained through the application of a uniform rate of tax to bases of assessment determined in a uniform manner and in accordance with Community rules.

(9)   It is vital to provide for a transitional period to allow national laws in specified fields to be gradually adapted.

(10)   During this transitional period, intra-Community transactions carried out by taxable persons other than exempt taxable persons should be taxed in the Member State of destination, in accordance with the rates and conditions set by that Member State.

(11)   It is also appropriate that, during that transitional period, intra-Community acquisitions of a certain value, made by exempt persons or by non-taxable legal persons, certain intra-Community distance selling and the supply of new means of transport to individuals or to exempt or non-taxable bodies should also be taxed in the Member State of destination, in accordance with the rates and conditions set by that Member State, in so far as such transactions would, in the absence of special provisions, be likely to cause significant distortion of competition between Member States.

(12)   For reasons connected with their geographic, economic and social situation, certain territories should be excluded from the scope of this Directive.

(13)   In order to enhance the non-discriminatory nature of the tax, the term 'taxable person' should be defined in such a way that the Member States may use it to cover persons who occasionally carry out certain transactions.

(14)   The term 'taxable transaction' may lead to difficulties, in particular as regards transactions treated as taxable transactions. Those concepts should therefore be clarified.

(15)   With a view to facilitating intra-Community trade in work on movable tangible property, it is appropriate to establish the tax arrangements applicable to such transactions when they are carried out for a customer who is identified for VAT purposes in a Member State other than that in which the transaction is physically carried out.

(16) A transport operation within the territory of a Member State should be treated as the intra-Community transport of goods where it is directly linked to a transport operation carried out between Member States, in order to simplify not only the principles and arrangements for taxing those domestic transport services but also the rules applicable to ancillary services and to services supplied by intermediaries who take part in the supply of the various services.

(17) Determination of the place where taxable transactions are carried out may engender conflicts concerning jurisdiction as between Member States, in particular as regards the supply of goods for assembly or the supply of services. Although the place where a supply of services is carried out should in principle be fixed as the place where the supplier has established his place of business, it should be defined as being in the Member State of the customer, in particular in the case of certain services supplied between taxable persons where the cost of the services is included in the price of the goods.

(18) It is necessary to clarify the definition of the place of taxation of certain transactions carried out on board ships, aircraft or trains in the course of passenger transport within the Community.

(19) Electricity and gas are treated as goods for VAT purposes. It is, however, particularly difficult to determine the place of supply. In order to avoid double taxation or non taxation and to attain a genuine internal market free of barriers linked to the VAT regime, the place of supply of gas through the natural gas distribution system, or of electricity, before the goods reach the final stage of consumption, should therefore be the place where the customer has established his business. The supply of electricity and gas at the final stage, that is to say, from traders and distributors to the final consumer, should be taxed at the place where the customer actually uses and consumes the goods.

(20) In the case of the hiring out of movable tangible property, application of the general rule that supplies of services are taxed in the Member State in which the supplier is established may lead to substantial distortion of competition if the lessor and the lessee are established in different Member States and the rates of taxation in those States differ. It is therefore necessary to establish that the place of supply of a service is the place where the customer has established his business or has a fixed establishment for which the service has been supplied or, in the absence thereof, the place where he has his permanent address or usually resides.

(21) However, as regards the hiring out of means of transport, it is appropriate, for reasons of control, to apply strictly the general rule, and thus to regard the place where the supplier has established his business as the place of supply.

(22) All telecommunications services consumed within the Community should be taxed to prevent distortion of competition in that field. To that end, telecommunications services supplied to taxable persons

established in the Community or to customers established in third countries should, in principle, be taxed at the place where the customer for the services is established. In order to ensure uniform taxation of telecommunications services which are supplied by taxable persons established in third territories or third countries to non-taxable persons established in the Community and which are effectively used and enjoyed in the Community, Member States should, however, provide for the place of supply to be within the Community.

(23) Also to prevent distortions of competition, radio and television broadcasting services and electronically supplied services provided from third territories or third countries to persons established in the Community, or from the Community to customers established in third territories or third countries, should be taxed at the place of establishment of the customer.

(24) The concepts of chargeable event and of the chargeability of VAT should be harmonised if the introduction of the common system of VAT and of any subsequent amendments thereto are to take effect at the same time in all Member States.

(25) The taxable amount should be harmonised so that the application of VAT to taxable transactions leads to comparable results in all the Member States.

(26) To prevent loss of tax revenues through the use of connected parties to derive tax benefits, it should, in specific limited circumstances, be possible for Member States to intervene as regards the taxable amount of supplies of goods or services and intra-Community acquisitions of goods.

(27) In order to combat tax evasion or avoidance, it should be possible for Member States to include within the taxable amount of a transaction which involves the working of investment gold provided by a customer, the value of that investment gold where, by virtue of being worked, the gold loses its status of investment gold. When they apply these measures, Member States should be allowed a certain degree of discretion.

(28) If distortions are to be avoided, the abolition of fiscal controls at frontiers entails, not only a uniform basis of assessment, but also sufficient alignment as between Member States of a number of rates and rate levels.

(29) The standard rate of VAT in force in the various Member States, combined with the mechanism of the transitional system, ensures that this system functions to an acceptable degree. To prevent divergences in the standard rates of VAT applied by the Member States from leading to structural imbalances in the Community and distortions of competition in some sectors of activity, a minimum standard rate of 15% should be fixed, subject to review.

(30) In order to preserve neutrality of VAT, the rates applied by Member States should be such as to enable, as a general rule, deduction of the VAT applied at the preceding stage.

(31) During the transitional period, certain derogations concerning the number and the level of rates should be possible.

(32) To achieve a better understanding of the impact of reduced rates, it is necessary for the Commission to prepare an assessment report on the impact of reduced rates applied to locally supplied services, notably in terms of job creation, economic growth and the proper functioning of the internal market.

(33) In order to tackle the problem of unemployment, those Member States wishing to do so should be allowed to experiment with the operation and impact, in terms of job creation, of a reduction in the VAT rate applied to labour intensive services. That reduction is also likely to reduce the incentive for the businesses concerned to join or remain in the black economy.

(34) However, such a reduction in the VAT rate is not without risk for the smooth functioning of the internal market and for tax neutrality. Provision should therefore be made for an authorisation procedure to be introduced for a period that is fixed but sufficiently long, so that it is possible to assess the impact of the reduced rates applied to locally supplied services. In order to make sure that such a measure remains verifiable and limited, its scope should be closely defined.

(35) A common list of exemptions should be drawn up so that the Communities' own resources may be collected in a uniform manner in all the Member States.

(36) For the benefit both of the persons liable for payment of VAT and the competent administrative authorities, the methods of applying VAT to certain supplies and intra-Community acquisitions of products subject to excise duty should be aligned with the procedures and obligations concerning the duty to declare in the case of shipment of such products to another Member State laid down in Council Directive 92/12/EEC of 25 February 1992 on the general arrangements for products subject to excise duty and on the holding, movement and monitoring of such products.

(37) The supply of gas through the natural gas distribution system, and of electricity is taxed at the place of the customer. In order to avoid double taxation, the importation of such products should therefore be exempted from VAT.

(38) In respect of taxable operations in the domestic market linked to intra-Community trade in goods carried out during the transitional period by taxable persons not established within the territory of the Member State in which the intra-Community acquisition of goods takes place, including chain transactions, it is necessary to provide for simplification measures ensuring equal treatment in all the Member States. To that

end, the provisions concerning the taxation system and the person liable for payment of the VAT due in respect of such operations should be harmonised. It is however, necessary to exclude in principle from such arrangements goods that are intended to be supplied at the retail stage.

(39) The rules governing deductions should be harmonised to the extent that they affect the actual amounts collected. The deductible proportion should be calculated in a similar manner in all the Member States.

(40) The scheme which allows the adjustment of deductions for capital goods over the lifetime of the asset, according to its actual use, should also be applicable to certain services with the nature of capital goods.

(41) It is appropriate to specify the persons liable for payment of VAT, particularly in the case of services supplied by a person who is not established in the Member State in which the VAT is due.

(42) Member States should be able, in specific cases, to designate the recipient of supplies of goods or services as the person liable for payment of VAT. This should assist Member States in simplifying the rules and countering tax evasion and avoidance in identified sectors and on certain types of transactions.

(43) Member States should be entirely free to designate the person liable for payment of the VAT on importation.

(44) Member States should be able to provide that someone other than the person liable for payment of VAT is to be held jointly and severally liable for its payment.

(45) The obligations of taxable persons should be harmonised as far as possible so as to ensure the necessary safeguards for the collection of VAT in a uniform manner in all the Member States.

(46) The use of electronic invoicing should allow tax authorities to carry out their monitoring activities. It is therefore appropriate, in order to ensure the internal market functions properly, to draw up a list, harmonised at Community level, of the particulars that must appear on invoices and to establish a number of common arrangements governing the use of electronic invoicing and the electronic storage of invoices, as well as for self-billing and the outsourcing of invoicing operations.

(47) Subject to conditions which they lay down, Member States should allow certain statements and returns to be made by electronic means, and may require that electronic means be used.

(48) The necessary pursuit of a reduction in the administrative and statistical formalities to be completed by businesses, particularly small and medium-sized enterprises, should be reconciled with the implementation of effective control measures and the need, on both economic and tax grounds, to maintain the quality of Community statistical instruments.

(49) Member States should be allowed to continue to apply their special schemes for small enterprises, in accordance with common provisions, and with a view to closer harmonisation.

(50) Member States should remain free to apply a special scheme involving flat rate rebates of input VAT to farmers not covered by the normal scheme. The basic principles of that special scheme should be established and a common method adopted, for the purposes of collecting own resources, for calculating the value added by such farmers.

(51) It is appropriate to adopt a Community taxation system to be applied to second-hand goods, works of art, antiques and collectors' items, with a view to preventing double taxation and the distortion of competition as between taxable persons.

(52) The application of the normal VAT rules to gold constitutes a major obstacle to its use for financial investment purposes and therefore justifies the application of a special tax scheme, with a view also to enhancing the international competitiveness of the Community gold market.

(53) The supply of gold for investment purposes is inherently similar to other financial investments which are exempt from VAT. Consequently, exemption appears to be the most appropriate tax treatment for supplies of investment gold.

(54) The definition of investment gold should cover gold coins the value of which primarily reflects the price of the gold contained. For reasons of transparency and legal certainty, a yearly list of coins covered by the investment gold scheme should be drawn up, providing security for the operators trading in such coins. That list should be without prejudice to the exemption of coins which are not included in the list but which meet the criteria laid down in this Directive.

(55) In order to prevent tax evasion while at the same time alleviating the financing burden for the supply of gold of a degree of purity above a certain level, it is justifiable to allow Member States to designate the customer as the person liable for payment of VAT.

(56) In order to facilitate compliance with fiscal obligations by operators providing electronically supplied services, who are neither established nor required to be identified for VAT purposes within the Community, a special scheme should be established. Under that scheme it should be possible for any operator supplying such services by electronic means to non-taxable persons within the Community, if he is not otherwise identified for VAT purposes within the Community, to opt for identification in a single Member State.

(57) It is desirable for the provisions concerning radio and television broadcasting and certain electronically supplied services to be put into place on a temporary basis only and to be reviewed in the light of experience within a short period of time.

(58) It is necessary to promote the uniform application of the provisions of this Directive and to that end an advisory committee on value-added tax should be set up to enable the Member States and the Commission to cooperate closely.

(59) Member States should be able, within certain limits and subject to certain conditions, to introduce, or to continue to apply, special measures derogating from this Directive in order to simplify the levying of tax or to prevent certain forms of tax evasion or avoidance.

(60) In order to ensure that a Member State which has submitted a request for derogation is not left in doubt as to what action the Commission plans to take in response, time-limits should be laid down within which the Commission must present to the Council either a proposal for authorisation or a communication setting out its objections.

(61) It is essential to ensure uniform application of the VAT system. Implementing measures are appropriate to realise that aim.

(62) Those measures should, in particular, address the problem of double taxation of cross-border transactions which can occur as the result of divergences between Member States in the application of the rules governing the place where taxable transactions are carried out.

(63) Although the scope of the implementing measures would be limited, those measures would have a budgetary impact which for one or more Member States could be significant. Accordingly, the Council is justified in reserving to itself the right to exercise implementing powers.

(64) In view of their limited scope, the implementing measures should be adopted by the Council acting unanimously on a proposal from the Commission.

(65) Since, for those reasons, the objectives of this Directive cannot be sufficiently achieved by the Member States and can therefore be better achieved by at Community level, the Community may adopt measures, in accordance with the principle of subsidiarity as set out in Article 5 of the Treaty. In accordance with the principle of proportionality, as set out in that Article, this Directive does not go beyond what is necessary in order to achieve those objectives.

(66) The obligation to transpose this Directive into national law should be confined to those provisions which represent a substantive change as compared with the earlier Directives. The obligation to transpose into national law the provisions which are unchanged arises under the earlier Directives.

(67) This Directive should be without prejudice to the obligations of the Member States in relation to the time-limits for transposition into national law of the Directives listed in Annex XI, Part B,

HAS ADOPTED THIS DIRECTIVE:

Article 56

Subsection 5
Supply of miscellaneous service

Article 56

1. The place of supply of the following services to customers established outside the Community, or to taxable persons established in the Community but not in the same country as the supplier, shall be the place where the customer has established his business or has a fixed establishment for which the service is supplied, or, in the absence of such a place, the place where he has his permanent address or usually resides:

    (a) transfers and assignments of copyrights, patents, licences, trade marks and similar rights;

    (b) advertising services;

    (c) the services of consultants, engineers, consultancy bureaux, lawyers, accountants and other similar services, as well as data processing and the provision of information;

    (d) obligations to refrain from pursuing or exercising, in whole or in part, a business activity or a right referred to in this paragraph;

    (e) banking, financial and insurance transactions, including reinsurance, with the exception of the hire of safes;

    (f) the supply of staff;

    (g) the hiring out of movable tangible property, with the exception of all means of transport;

    (h) the provision of access to, and of transport or transmission through, natural gas and electricity distribution systems and the provision of other services directly linked thereto;

    (i) telecommunications services;

    (j) radio and television broadcasting services;

    (k) electronically supplied services, such as those referred to in Annex II;

    (l) the supply of services by intermediaries, acting in the name and on behalf of other persons, where those intermediaries take part in the supply of the services referred to in this paragraph.

2. Where the supplier of a service and the customer communicate via electronic mail, that shall not of itself mean that the service supplied is an electronically supplied service for the purposes of point (k) of paragraph 1.

3. Points (j) and (k) of paragraph 1 and paragraph 2 shall apply until 31 December 2006.

COUNCIL DIRECTIVE 2006/138/EC

of 19 December 2006

amending Directive 2006/112/EC on the common system of value added tax as regards the period of application of the value added tax arrangements applicable to radio and television broadcasting services and certain electronically supplied services

Article 1

Directive 2006/112/EC is hereby amended as follows:

1.   in Article 56, paragraph 3 shall be replaced by the following:

'3.   Points (j) and (k) of paragraph 1 and paragraph 2 shall apply until 31 December 2008.';

This amendment must be read in conjunction with the Preamble to Council Directive 2006/138/EC

COUNCIL DIRECTIVE 2008/8/EC

of 12 February 2008

amending Directive 2006/112/EC as regards the place of supply of services

Article 1

From 1 January 2009, Directive 2006/112/EC is hereby amended as follows:

1.   in Article 56, paragraph 3 shall be replaced by the following:

'3.   Points (j) and (k) of paragraph 1 and paragraph 2 shall apply until 31 December 2009.';

This amendment must be read in conjunction with the Preamble to Council Directive 2008/8/EC

Article 57

1. Where the services referred to in point (k) of Article 56(1) are supplied to non-taxable persons who are established in a Member State, or who have their permanent address or usually reside in a Member State, by a taxable person who has established his business outside the Community or has a fixed establishment there from which the service is supplied, or who, in the absence of such a place of business or fixed establishment, has his permanent address or usually resides outside the Community, the place of supply shall be the place where the non-taxable person is established, or where he has his permanent address or usually resides.

2. Paragraph 1 shall apply until 31 December 2006.

COUNCIL DIRECTIVE 2006/138/EC

of 19 December 2006

amending Directive 2006/112/EC on the common system of value added tax as regards the period of application of the value added tax arrangements applicable to radio and television broadcasting services and certain electronically supplied services

Article 1

Directive 2006/112/EC is hereby amended as follows:

2. in Article 57, paragraph 2 shall be replaced by the following:

    '2. Paragraph 1 shall apply until 31 December 2008.';

This amendment must be read in conjunction with the Preamble to Council Directive 2006/138/EC

COUNCIL DIRECTIVE 2008/8/EC

of 12 February 2008

amending Directive 2006/112/EC as regards the place of supply of services

Article 1

From 1 January 2009, Directive 2006/112/EC is hereby amended as follows:

2. in Article 57, paragraph 2 shall be replaced by the following:

    '2. Paragraph 1 shall apply until 31 December 2009.';

This amendment must be read in conjunction with the Preamble to Council Directive 2008/8/EC

Article 59

1.   Member States shall apply Article 58(b) to telecommunications services supplied to non-taxable persons who are established in a Member State, or who have their permanent address or usually reside in a Member State, by a taxable person who has established his business outside the Community or has a fixed establishment there from which the services are supplied, or who, in the absence of such a place of business or fixed establishment, has his permanent address or usually resides outside the Community.

2.   Until 31 December 2006, Member States shall apply Article 58(b) to radio and television broadcasting services, as referred to in point (j) of Article 56(1), supplied to non-taxable persons who are established in a Member State, or who have their permanent address or usually reside in a Member State, by a taxable person who has established his business outside the Community or who has a fixed establishment there from which the services are supplied, or who, in the absence of such a place of business or fixed establishment, has his permanent address or usually resides outside the Community.

COUNCIL DIRECTIVE 2006/138/EC

of 19 December 2006

amending Directive 2006/112/EC on the common system of value added tax as regards the period of application of the value added tax arrangements applicable to radio and television broadcasting services and certain electronically supplied services

Article 1

Directive 2006/112/EC is hereby amended as follows:

3.   in Article 59, paragraph 2 shall be replaced by the following:

      '2.   Until 31 December 2008, Member States shall apply Article 58(b) to radio and television broadcasting services, as referred to in point (j) of Article 56(1), supplied to non-taxable persons who are established in a Member State, or who have their permanent address or usually reside in a Member State, by a taxable person who has established his business outside the Community or who has a fixed establishment there from which the services are supplied, or who, in the absence of such a place of business or fixed establishment, has his permanent address or usually resides outside the Community.';

This amendment must be read in conjunction with the Preamble to Council Directive 2006/138/EC

COUNCIL DIRECTIVE 2008/8/EC

of 12 February 2008

amending Directive 2006/112/EC as regards the place of supply of services

Article 1

From 1 January 2009, Directive 2006/112/EC is hereby amended as follows:

3. in Article 59, paragraph 2 shall be replaced by the following:

'2. Until 31 December 2009, Member States shall apply Article 58(b) to radio and television broadcasting services, as referred to in Article 56(1)(j), supplied to non-taxable persons who are established in a Member State, or who have their permanent address or usually reside in a Member State, by a taxable person who has established his business outside the Community or who has a fixed establishment there from which the services are supplied, or who, in the absence of such a place of business or fixed establishment, has his permanent address or usually resides outside the Community.';

This amendment must be read in conjunction with the Preamble to Council Directive 2008/8/EC

Article 64

TITLE VI

CHARGEABLE EVENT AND CHARGEABILITY OF VAT

CHAPTER 2

Supply of goods or services

Article 64

1. Where it gives rise to successive statements of account or successive payments, the supply of goods, other than that consisting in the hire of goods for a certain period or the sale of goods on deferred terms, as referred to in point (b) of Article 14 (2), or the supply of services shall be regarded as being completed on expiry of the periods to which such statements of account or payments relate.

2. Member States may provide that, in certain cases, the continuous supply of goods or services over a period of time is to be regarded as being completed at least at intervals of one year.

COUNCIL DIRECTIVE 2008/117/EC

of 16 December 2008

amending Directive 2006/112/EC on the common system of value added tax to combat tax evasion connected with intra-Community transactions

Article 1

Directive 2006/112/EC is hereby amended as follows:

1. Article 64(2) shall be replaced by the following:

    '2. Supplies of services for which VAT is payable by the customer pursuant to Article 196, which are supplied continuously over a period of more than one year and which do not give rise to statements of account or payments during that period shall be regarded as being completed on expiry of each calendar year until such time as the supply of services comes to an end.

    Member States may provide that, in certain cases other than those referred to in the previous paragraph, the continuous supply of goods or services over a period of time is to be regarded as being completed at least at intervals of one year.';

This amendment must be read in conjunction with the Preamble to Council Directive 2008/117/EC

Article 66

By way of derogation from Articles 63, 64 and 65, Member States may provide that VAT is to become chargeable, in respect of certain transactions or certain categories of taxable person at one of the following times:

(a)   no later than the time the invoice is issued;

(b)   no later than the time the payment is received;

(c)   where an invoice is not issued, or is issued late, within a specified period from the date of the chargeable event.

COUNCIL DIRECTIVE 2008/117/EC

of 16 December 2008

amending Directive 2006/112/EC on the common system of value added tax to combat tax evasion connected with intra-Community transactions

Article 1

Directive 2006/112/EC is hereby amended as follows:

2.   in Article 66, the following subparagraph shall be added:

'The derogation provided for in the first paragraph shall not, however, apply to supplies of services in respect of which VAT is payable by the customer pursuant to Article 196.';

This amendment must be read in conjunction with the Preamble to Council Directive 2008/117/EC

Article 123

The Czech Republic may, until 31 December 2007, continue to apply a reduced rate of not less than 5 % to the following transactions:

(a)   the supply of heat energy used by households and small entrepreneurs who are not subject to VAT for heating and the production of hot water, excluding raw materials used to generate heat energy;

(b)   the supply of construction work for residential housing not provided as part of a social policy, excluding building materials.

COUNCIL DIRECTIVE 2007/75/EC

of 20 December 2007

amending Directive 2006/112/EC with regard to certain temporary provisions concerning rates of value added tax

With effect from 1 January 2008, Directive 2006/112/EC is hereby amended as follows:

1.   Article 123 shall be replaced by the following:

'Article 123

The Czech Republic may, until 31 December 2010, continue to apply a reduced rate of not less than 5 % to the supply of construction work for residential housing not provided as part of a social policy, excluding building materials.';

This amendment must be read in conjunction with the Preamble to Council Directive 2007/75/EC

Article 124

Estonia may, until 30 June 2007, continue to apply a reduced rate of not less than 5% to the supply of heating sold to natural persons, housing associations, apartment associations, churches, congregations, and institutions or bodies financed from the State, rural municipality or city budget, as well as to the supply of peat, fuel briquettes, coal and firewood to natural persons.

COUNCIL DIRECTIVE 2007/75/EC
of 20 December 2007

amending Directive 2006/112/EC with regard to certain temporary provisions concerning rates of value added tax

With effect from 1 January 2008, Directive 2006/112/EC is hereby amended as follows:

2.   Article 124 shall be deleted;

This amendment must be read in conjunction with the Preamble to Council Directive 2007/75/EC

Article 125

1.   Cyprus may, until 31 December 2007, continue to grant an exemption with deductibility of VAT paid at the preceding stage in respect of the supply of pharmaceuticals and foodstuffs for human consumption, with the exception of ice cream, ice lollies, frozen yoghurt, water ice and similar products and savoury food products (potato crisps/sticks, puffs and similar products packaged for human consumption without further preparation).

2.   Cyprus may continue to apply a reduced rate of not less than 5 % to the supply of restaurant services, until 31 December 2007 or until the introduction of definitive arrangements, as referred to in Article 402, whichever is the earlier.

COUNCIL DIRECTIVE 2007/75/EC

of 20 December 2007

amending Directive 2006/112/EC with regard to certain temporary provisions concerning rates of value added tax

With effect from 1 January 2008, Directive 2006/112/EC is hereby amended as follows:

3.   in Article 125(1) and (2), the words 'until 31 December 2007' shall be replaced by 'until 31 December 2010';

This amendment must be read in conjunction with the Preamble to Council Directive 2007/75/EC

Article 126

Hungary may continue to apply a reduced rate of not less than 12 % to the following transactions:

(a)   the supply of coal, coal-brick and coke, firewood and charcoal, and the supply of district heating services, until 31 December 2007;

(b)   the supply of restaurant services and of foodstuffs sold on similar premises, until 31 December 2007 or until the introduction of definitive arrangements, as referred to in Article 402, whichever is the earlier.

COUNCIL DIRECTIVE 2007/75/EC

of 20 December 2007

amending Directive 2006/112/EC with regard to certain temporary provisions concerning rates of value added tax

With effect from 1 January 2008, Directive 2006/112/EC is hereby amended as follows:

4.   Article 126 shall be deleted;

This amendment must be read in conjunction with the Preamble to Council Directive 2007/75/EC

Article 127

Malta may, until 1 January 2010, continue to grant an exemption with deductibility of VAT paid at the preceding stage in respect of the supply of foodstuffs for human consumption and pharmaceuticals.

COUNCIL DIRECTIVE 2007/75/EC

of 20 December 2007

amending Directive 2006/112/EC with regard to certain temporary provisions concerning rates of value added tax

With effect from 1 January 2008, Directive 2006/112/EC is hereby amended as follows:

5.   in Article 127, '1 January 2010' shall be replaced by '31 December 2010';

This amendment must be read in conjunction with the Preamble to Council Directive 2007/75/EC

Article 128

1. Poland may, until 31 December 2007 grant an exemption with deductibility of VAT paid at the preceding stage in respect of the supply of certain books and specialist periodicals.

2. Poland may, until 31 December 2007 or until the introduction of definitive arrangements, as referred to in Article 402, whichever is the earlier, continue to apply a reduced rate of not less than 7% to the supply of restaurant services.

3. Poland may, until 30 April 2008, continue to apply a reduced rate of not less than 3 % to the supply of foodstuffs as referred to in point (1) of Annex III.

4. Poland may, until 30 April 2008, continue to apply a reduced rate of not less than 3 % to the supply of goods and services of a kind normally intended for use in agricultural production, but excluding capital goods such as machinery or buildings, as referred to in point (11) of Annex III.

5. Poland may, until 31 December 2007, continue to apply a reduced rate of not less than 7% to the supply of services, not provided as part of a social policy, for construction, renovation and alteration of housing, excluding building materials, and to the supply before first occupation of residential buildings or parts of residential buildings, as referred to in point (a) of Article 12(1).

COUNCIL DIRECTIVE 2007/75/EC

of 20 December 2007

amending Directive 2006/112/EC with regard to certain temporary provisions concerning rates of value added tax

With effect from 1 January 2008, Directive 2006/112/EC is hereby amended as follows:

6. Article 128 shall be replaced by the following:

'Article 128

1. Poland may, until 31 December 2010, grant an exemption with deductibility of VAT paid at the preceding stage in respect of the supply of certain books and specialist periodicals.

2. Poland may, until 31 December 2010 or until the introduction of definitive arrangements, as referred to in Article 402, whichever is the earlier, continue to apply a reduced rate of not less than 7 % to the supply of restaurant services.

3. Poland may, until 31 December 2010, continue to apply a reduced rate of not less than 3 % to the supply of foodstuffs as referred to in point (1) of Annex III.

4.   Poland may, until 31 December 2010, continue to apply a reduced rate of not less than 7 % to the supply of services, not provided as part of a social policy, for construction, renovation and alteration of housing, excluding building materials, and to the supply before first occupation of residential buildings or parts of residential buildings, as referred to in Article 12(1)(a).';

This amendment must be read in conjunction with the Preamble to Council Directive 2007/75/EC

Article 129

1. Slovenia may, until 31 December 2007 or until the introduction of definitive arrangements as referred to in Article 402, whichever is the earlier, continue to apply a reduced rate of not less than 8,5 % to the preparation of meals.

2. Slovenia may, until 31 December 2007, continue to apply a reduced rate of not less than 5 % to the supply of construction, renovation and maintenance work for residential housing not provided as part of a social policy, excluding building materials.

COUNCIL DIRECTIVE 2007/75/EC

of 20 December 2007

amending Directive 2006/112/EC with regard to certain temporary provisions concerning rates of value added tax

With effect from 1 January 2008, Directive 2006/112/EC is hereby amended as follows:

7. in Article 129(1) and (2), the words 'until 31 December 2007' shall be replaced by 'until 31 December 2010';

This amendment must be read in conjunction with the Preamble to Council Directive 2007/75/EC

Article 130

Slovakia may continue to apply a reduced rate of not less than 5 % to the following transactions:

(a)   the supply of construction work for residential housing not provided as part of a social policy, excluding building materials, until 31 December 2007;

(b)   the supply of heat energy used by private households and small entrepreneurs who are not subject to VAT for heating and the production of hot water, excluding raw materials used to generate heat energy, until 31 December 2008.

COUNCIL DIRECTIVE 2007/75/EC

of 20 December 2007

amending Directive 2006/112/EC with regard to certain temporary provisions concerning rates of value added tax

With effect from 1 January 2008, Directive 2006/112/EC is hereby amended as follows:

8.   Article 130 shall be deleted.

This amendment must be read in conjunction with the Preamble to Council Directive 2007/75/EC

Article 263

1. The recapitulative statement shall be drawn up for each calendar quarter within a period and in accordance with procedures to be determined by the Member States. Member States may, however, provide that recapitulative statements are to be submitted on a monthly basis.

2. Member States shall allow, and may require, the recapitulative statements referred to in paragraph 1 to be submitted by electronic means, in accordance with conditions which they lay down.

COUNCIL DIRECTIVE 2008/117/EC
of 16 December 2008

amending Directive 2006/112/EC on the common system of value added tax to combat tax evasion connected with intra-Community transactions

Article 1

Directive 2006/112/EC is hereby amended as follows:

3. Article 263 shall be replaced by the following:

'Article 263

   1.   The recapitulative statement shall be drawn up for each calendar month within a period not exceeding one month and in accordance with procedures to be determined by the Member States.

  1a.   However, Member States, in accordance with the conditions and limits which they may lay down, may allow taxable persons to submit the recapitulative statement for each calendar quarter within a time limit not exceeding one month from the end of the quarter, where the total quarterly amount, excluding VAT, of the supplies of goods as referred to in Articles 264(1)(d) and 265(1)(c) does not exceed either in respect of the quarter concerned or in respect of any of the previous four quarters the sum of EUR 50 000 or its equivalent in national currency.

       The option provided for in the first subparagraph shall cease to be applicable after the end of the month during which the total value, excluding VAT, of the supplies of goods as referred to in Article 264(1)(d) and 265(1)(c) exceeds, in respect of the current quarter, the sum of EUR 50 000 or its equivalent in national currency. In this case, a recapitulative statement shall be drawn up for the month(s) which has (have) elapsed since the beginning of the quarter, within a time limit not exceeding one month.

  1b.   Until 31 December 2011, Member States are allowed to set the sum mentioned in paragraph 1a at EUR 100 000 or its equivalent in national currency.

1c.   In the case of supplies of services as referred to in Article 264(1) (d), Member States, in accordance with the conditions and limits which they may lay down, may allow taxable persons to submit the recapitulative statement for each calendar quarter within a time limit not exceeding one month from the end of the quarter.

Member States may, in particular, require the taxable persons who carry out supplies of both goods and services as referred to in Article 264(1)(d) to submit the recapitulative statement in accordance with the deadline resulting from paragraphs 1 to 1b.

2.   Member States shall allow, and may require, the recapitulative statement referred to in paragraph 1 to be submitted by electronic file transfer, in accordance with conditions which they lay down.';

This amendment must be read in conjunction with the Preamble to Council Directive 2008/117/EC

Article 264

1. The recapitulative statement shall set out the following information:

    (a) the VAT identification number of the taxable person in the Member State in which the recapitulative statement must be submitted and under which he has carried out the supply of goods in accordance with the conditions specified in Article 138(1);

    (b) the VAT identification number of the person acquiring the goods in a Member State other than that in which the recapitulative statement must be submitted and under which the goods were supplied to him;

    (c) the VAT identification number of the taxable person in the Member State in which the recapitulative statement must be submitted and under which he has carried out a transfer to another Member State, as referred to in Article 138(2)(c), and the number by means of which he is identified in the Member State in which the dispatch or transport ended;

    (d) for each person who acquired goods, the total value of the supplies of goods carried out by the taxable person;

    (e) in respect of supplies of goods consisting in transfers to another Member State, as referred to in Article 138(2)(c), the total value of the supplies, determined in accordance with Article 76;

    (f) the amounts of adjustments made pursuant to Article 90.

2. The value referred to in point (d) of paragraph 1 shall be declared for the calendar quarter during which VAT became chargeable.

    The amounts referred to in point (f) of paragraph 1 shall be declared for the calendar quarter during which the person acquiring the goods was notified of the adjustment.

COUNCIL DIRECTIVE 2008/117/EC

of 16 December 2008

amending Directive 2006/112/EC on the common system of value added tax to combat tax evasion connected with intra-Community transactions

Article 1

Directive 2006/112/EC is hereby amended as follows:

4. Article 264(2) shall be replaced by the following:

    '2. The value referred to in paragraph 1(d) shall be declared for the period of submission established in accordance with Article 263(1) to (1c) during which VAT became chargeable.

    The amounts referred to in paragraph 1(f) shall be declared for the period of submission established in accordance with Article 263(1) to (1c) during which the person acquiring the goods was notified of the adjustment.';

This amendment must be read in conjunction with the Preamble to Council Directive 2008/117/EC

Article 265

1. In the case of intra-Community acquisitions of goods, as referred to in Article 42, the taxable person identified for VAT purposes in the Member State which issued him with the VAT identification number under which he made such acquisitions shall set the following information out clearly on the recapitulative statement:

    (a)   his VAT identification number in that Member State and under which he made the acquisition and subsequent supply of goods;

    (b)   the VAT identification number, in the Member State in which dispatch or transport of the goods ended, of the person to whom the subsequent supply was made by the taxable person;

    (c)   for each person to whom the subsequent supply was made, the total value, exclusive of VAT, of the supplies made by the taxable person in the Member State in which dispatch or transport of the goods ended.

2. The value referred to in point (c) of paragraph 1 shall be declared for the calendar quarter during which VAT became chargeable.

COUNCIL DIRECTIVE 2008/117/EC

of 16 December 2008

amending Directive 2006/112/EC on the common system of value added tax to combat tax evasion connected with intra-Community transactions

Article 1

Directive 2006/112/EC is hereby amended as follows:

5. Article 265(2) shall be replaced by the following:

    '2.   The value referred to in paragraph 1(c) shall be declared for the period of submission established in accordance with Article 263(1) to (1b) during which VAT became chargeable.'.

This amendment must be read in conjunction with the Preamble to Council Directive 2008/117/EC

Article 357

TITLE XII

SPECIAL SCHEMES

CHAPTER 6

Special scheme for non-established taxable persons supplying electronic services to non-taxable persons

Section 1

General provisions

Article 357

This Chapter shall apply until 31 December 2006.

COUNCIL DIRECTIVE 2006/138/EC

of 19 December 2006

amending Directive 2006/112/EC on the common system of value added tax as regards the period of application of the value added tax arrangements applicable to radio and television broadcasting services and certain electronically supplied services

Article 1

Directive 2006/112/EC is hereby amended as follows:

4.   Article 357 shall be replaced by the following:

'Article 357

This Chapter shall apply until 31 December 2008.'

This amendment must be read in conjunction with the Preamble to Council Directive 2006/138/EC

COUNCIL DIRECTIVE 2008/8/EC

of 12 February 2008

amending Directive 2006/112/EC as regards the place of supply of services

Article 1

From 1 January 2009, Directive 2006/112/EC is hereby amended as follows:

4.   Article 357 shall be replaced by the following:

'Article 357

This Chapter shall apply until 31 December 2014.'.

This amendment must be read in conjunction with the Preamble to Council Directive 2008/8/EC

VALUE-ADDED TAX (VAT)
(EXEMPT INVESTMENT GOLD)

List of gold coins meeting the criteria established in Article 344(1), point (2) of the Council Directive 2006/112/EC (Special scheme for investment gold)

Valid for the year 2009

EXPLANATORY NOTE

(a) This list reflects the contributions sent by Member States to the Commission within the deadline set by Article 345 of the Council Directive 2006/112/EC of 28 November 2006 on the Common System of Value Added Tax.

(b) The coins included in this list are considered to fulfil the criteria of Article 344 and therefore will be treated as investment gold in those Member States. As a result their supply is exempt from VAT for the whole of the 2009 calendar year.

(c) The exemption will apply to all issues of the given coin in this list, except to issues of coins with a purity lower than 900 thousandths fine.

(d) However, if a coin does not appear in this list, its supply will still be exempt where the coin meets the criteria for the exemption laid down in the VAT Directive.

(e) The list is in alphabetical order, by names of countries and denominations of coins. Within the same category of coins, the listing follows the increasing value of the currency.

(f) In the list the denomination of the coins reflects the currency shown on the coins. However, where the currency on the coins is not shown in roman script, where possible, its denomination in the list is shown in parenthesis.

COUNTRY OF ISSUE & DENOMINATION OF THE COINS

AFGHANISTAN	**AUSTRALIA**
(20 AFGHANI)	5 DOLLARS
10 000 AFGHANI	15 DOLLARS
(1/2 AMANI)	25 DOLLARS
(1 AMANI)	50 DOLLARS
(2 AMANI)	100 DOLLARS
(4 GRAMS)	150 DOLLARS
(8 GRAMS)	200 DOLLARS
1 TILLA	250 DOLLARS
2 TILLAS	500 DOLLARS
	1 000 DOLLARS
ALBANIA	2 500 DOLLARS
20 LEKE	3 000 DOLLARS
50 LEKE	10 000 DOLLARS
100 LEKE	1/2 SOVEREIGN (= 1/2 POUND)
200 LEKE	1 SOVEREIGN (= 1 POUND)
500 LEKE	
	AUSTRIA
ALDERNEY	10 CORONA (= 10 KRONEN)
5 POUNDS	20 CORONA (= 20 KRONEN)
25 POUNDS	100 CORONA (= 100 KRONEN)
1 000 POUNDS	1 DUCAT
	(4 DUCATS)
ANDORRA	10 EURO
50 DINERS	25 EURO
100 DINERS	50 EURO
250 DINERS	100 EURO
1 SOVEREIGN	4 FLORIN = 10 FRANCS (= 4 GULDEN)
	8 FLORIN = 20 FRANCS (= 8 GULDEN)
ANGUILLA	25 SCHILLING
5 DOLLARS	100 SCHILLING
10 DOLLARS	200 SCHILLING
20 DOLLARS	500 SCHILLING
100 DOLLARS	1 000 SCHILLING
	2 000 SCHILLING
ARGENTINA	
1 ARGENTINO	**BAHAMAS**
	10 DOLLARS
ARUBA	20 DOLLARS
10 FLORIN	25 DOLLARS
25 FLORIN	50 DOLLARS
	100 DOLLARS

150 DOLLARS	**BRAZIL**
200 DOLLARS	300 CRUZEIROS
250 DOLLARS	(4 000 REIS)
2 500 DOLLARS	(5 000 REIS)
	(6 400 REIS)
BELGIUM	(10 000 REIS)
10 ECU	(20 000 REIS)
25 ECU	
50 ECU	**BRITISH VIRGIN ISLANDS**
100 ECU	100 DOLLARS
50 EURO GOLD	
100 EURO	**BULGARIA**
5 000 FRANCS	10 LEVA
	20 LEVA
BELIZE	100 LEVA
25 DOLLARS	
50 DOLLARS	**BURUNDI**
100 DOLLARS	10 FRANCS
250 DOLLARS	25 FRANCS
	50 FRANCS
BERMUDA	100 FRANCS
10 DOLLARS	
25 DOLLARS	**CANADA**
30 DOLLARS	1 DOLLAR
50 DOLLARS	2 DOLLARS
60 DOLLARS	5 DOLLARS
100 DOLLARS	10 DOLLARS
200 DOLLARS	20 DOLLARS
250 DOLLARS	50 DOLLARS
	100 DOLLARS
BHUTAN	175 DOLLARS
1 SERTUM	200 DOLLARS
2 SERTUMS	350 DOLLARS
5 SERTUMS	1 SOVEREIGN
BOLIVIA	**CAYMAN ISLANDS**
4 000 PESOS BOLIVIANOS	25 DOLLARS
	50 DOLLARS
BOTSWANA	100 DOLLARS
5 PULA	250 DOLLARS
150 PULA	
10 THEBE	**CHAD**
	3 000 FRANCS
	5 000 FRANCS

10 000 FRANCS	
20 000 FRANCS	
CHILE	
2 PESOS	
5 PESOS	
10 PESOS	
20 PESOS	
50 PESOS	
100 PESOS	
200 PESOS	
CHINA	
5/20 YUAN (1/20 oz)	
10/50 YUAN (1/10 oz)	
50/200 YUAN (1/2 oz)	
100/500 YUAN (1 oz)	
5 (YUAN)	
10 (YUAN)	
20 (YUAN)	
25 (YUAN)	
50 (YUAN)	
100 (YUAN)	
150 (YUAN)	
200 (YUAN)	
250 (YUAN)	
300 (YUAN)	
400 (YUAN)	
450 (YUAN)	
500 (YUAN)	
1 000 (YUAN)	
COLOMBIA	
1 PESO	
2 PESOS	
2 1/2 PESOS	
5 PESOS	
10 PESOS	
20 PESOS	
100 PESOS	
200 PESOS	
300 PESOS	
500 PESOS	
1 000 PESOS	

1 500 PESOS	
2 000 PESOS	
15 000 PESOS	
CONGO	
10 FRANCS	
20 FRANCS	
25 FRANCS	
50 FRANCS	
100 FRANCS	
COOK ISLANDS	
100 DOLLARS	
200 DOLLARS	
250 DOLLARS	
COSTA RICA	
5 COLONES	
10 COLONES	
20 COLONES	
50 COLONES	
100 COLONES	
200 COLONES	
1 500 COLONES	
5 000 COLONES	
25 000 COLONES	
CUBA	
4 PESOS	
5 PESOS	
10 PESOS	
20 PESOS	
50 PESOS	
100 PESOS	
CYPRUS	
50 POUNDS	
CZECH REPUBLIC	
1 000 KORUN (1 000 Kč)	
2 000 KORUN (2 000 Kč)	
2 500 KORUN (2 500 Kč)	
5 000 KORUN (5 000 Kč)	
10 000 KORUN (10 000 Kč)	

CZECHOSLOVAKIA	250 DOLLARS
1 DUKÁT	
2 DUKÁT	**FINLAND**
5 DUKÁT	100 EUROA
10 DUKÁT	
	FRANCE
DENMARK	1/4 EURO
20 KRONER	10 EURO
	20 EURO
DOMINICAN REPUBLIC	50 EURO
30 PESOS	5 FRANCS
100 PESOS	10 FRANCS
200 PESOS	40 FRANCS
250 PESOS	50 FRANCS
	100 FRANCS
ECUADOR	500 FRANCS
1 CONDOR	655,97 FRANCS
10 SUCRES	
	GABON
EL SALVADOR	10 FRANCS
25 COLONES	25 FRANCS
50 COLONES	50 FRANCS
100 COLONES	100 FRANCS
200 COLONES	1 000 FRANCS
250 COLONES	3 000 FRANCS
	5 000 FRANCS
EQUATORIAL GUINEA	10 000 FRANCS
250 PESETAS	20 000 FRANCS
500 PESETAS	
750 PESETAS	**GAMBIA**
1 000 PESETAS	200 DALASIS
5 000 PESETAS	500 DALASIS
	1 000 DALASIS
ETHIOPIA	
400 BIRR	**GIBRALTAR**
600 BIRR	1/25 CROWN
10 (DOLLARS)	1/10 CROWN
20 (DOLLARS)	1/5 CROWN
50 (DOLLARS)	1/2 CROWN
100 (DOLLARS)	1 CROWN
200 (DOLLARS)	2 CROWNS
	50 PENCE
FIJI	1 POUND
200 DOLLARS	5 POUNDS

3535

25 POUNDS	
50 POUNDS	
100 POUNDS	
1/25 ROYAL	
1/10 ROYAL	
1/5 ROYAL	
1/2 ROYAL	
1 ROYAL	

GUATAMALA

5 QUETZALES
10 QUETZALES
20 QUETZALES

GUERNSEY

1 POUND
5 POUNDS
10 POUNDS
25 POUNDS
50 POUNDS
100 POUNDS

GUINEA

1 000 FRANCS
2 000 FRANCS
5 000 FRANCS
10 000 FRANCS

HAITI

20 GOURDES
50 GOURDES
100 GOURDES
200 GOURDES
500 GOURDES
1 000 GOURDES

HONDURAS

200 LEMPIRAS
500 LEMPIRAS

HONG KONG

1 000 DOLLARS

HUNGARY

1 DUKAT
4 FORINT = 10 FRANCS
8 FORINT = 20 FRANCS
50 FORINT
100 FORINT
200 FORINT
500 FORINT
1 000 FORINT
5 000 FORINT
10 000 FORINT
20 000 FORINT
50 000 FORINT
100 000 FORINT
20 KORONA
100 KORONA

ICELAND

500 KRONUR
10 000 KRONUR

INDIA

1 MOHUR
15 RUPEES
1 SOVEREIGN

INDONESIA

2 000 RUPIAH
5 000 RUPIAH
10 000 RUPIAH
20 000 RUPIAH
25 000 RUPIAH
100 000 RUPIAH
200 000 RUPIAH

IRAN

(1/2 AZADI)
(1 AZADI)
(1/4 PAHLAVI)
(1/2 PAHLAVI)
(1 PAHLAVI)
(2 1/2 PAHLAVI)
(5 PAHLAVI)

(10 PAHLAVI)	1 000 LIROT
500 RIALS	5 000 LIROT
750 RIALS	5 NEW SHEQALIM
1 000 RIALS	10 NEW SHEQALIM
2 000 RIALS	20 NEW SHEQALIM
50 POUND	5 SHEQALIM
	10 SHEQALIM
IRAQ	500 SHEQEL
(5 DINARS)	
(50 DINARS)	**IVORY COAST**
(100 DINARS)	10 FRANCS
	25 FRANCS
ISLE OF MAN	50 FRANCS
1/20 ANGEL	100 FRANCS
1/10 ANGEL	
1/4 ANGEL	**JAMAICA**
1/2 ANGEL	100 DOLLARS
1 ANGEL	250 DOLLARS
5 ANGEL	
10 ANGEL	**JERSEY**
15 ANGEL	1 POUND
20 ANGEL	2 POUNDS
1/25 CROWN	5 POUNDS
1/10 CROWN	10 POUNDS
1/5 CROWN	20 POUNDS
1/2 CROWN	25 POUNDS
1 CROWN	50 POUNDS
50 PENCE	100 POUNDS
1 POUND	1 SOVEREIGN
2 POUNDS	
5 POUNDS	**JORDAN**
50 POUNDS	2 DINARS
(1/2 SOVEREIGN)	5 DINARS
(1 SOVEREIGN)	10 DINARS
(2 SOVEREIGNS)	25 DINARS
(5 SOVEREIGNS)	50 DINARS
	60 DINARS
ISRAEL	
20 LIROT	**KATANGA**
50 LIROT	5 FRANCS
100 LIROT	
200 LIROT	**KENYA**
500 LIROT	100 SHILLINGS

250 SHILLINGS	
500 SHILLINGS	
KIRIBATI	
150 DOLLARS	
LATVIA	
100 LATU	
LESOTHO	
1 LOTI	
2 MALOTI	
4 MALOTI	
10 MALOTI	
20 MALOTI	
50 MALOTI	
100 MALOTI	
250 MALOTI	
500 MALOTI	
LIBERIA	
12 DOLLARS	
20 DOLLARS	
25 DOLLARS	
30 DOLLARS	
50 DOLLARS	
100 DOLLARS	
200 DOLLARS	
250 DOLLARS	
500 DOLLARS	
2 500 DOLLARS	
LUXEMBOURG	
5 EURO	
10 EURO	
20 FRANCS	
40 FRANCS	
MACAU	
250 PATACAS	
500 PATACAS	
1 000 PATACAS	
10 000 PATACAS	

MALAWI	
250 KWACHA	
MALAYSIA	
100 RINGGIT	
200 RINGGIT	
250 RINGGIT	
500 RINGGIT	
MALI	
10 FRANCS	
25 FRANCS	
50 FRANCS	
100 FRANCS	
MALTA	
5 (LIRI)	
10 (LIRI)	
20 (LIRI)	
25 (LIRI)	
50 (LIRI)	
100 (LIRI)	
25 LM	
50 EURO	
MARSHALL ISLANDS	
20 DOLLARS	
50 DOLLARS	
200 DOLLARS	
MAURITIUS	
100 RUPEES	
200 RUPEES	
250 RUPEES	
500 RUPEES	
1 000 RUPEES	
MEXICO	
2 PESOS	
2 1/2 PESOS	
5 PESOS	
10 PESOS	
20 PESOS	
50 PESOS	

250 PESOS	
500 PESOS	
1 000 PESOS	
2 000 PESOS	
1/20 ONZA	
1/10 ONZA	
1/4 ONZA	
1/2 ONZA	
1 ONZA	
MONACO	
100 FRANCS	
200 FRANCS	
10 EURO	
20 EURO	
100 EURO	
MONGOLIA	
750 (TUGRIK)	
1 000 (TUGRIK)	
NEPAL	
1 ASARPHI	
1 000 RUPEES	
NETHERLANDS	
(1 DUKAAT)	
(2 DUKAAT)	
1 GULDEN	
5 GULDEN	
10 EURO	
20 EURO	
50 EURO	
NETHERLANDS ANTILLES	
5 GULDEN	
10 GULDEN	
50 GULDEN	
100 GULDEN	
300 GULDEN	
NEW ZEALAND	
10 DOLLARS	
150 DOLLARS	

NICARAGUA	
50 CORDOBAS	
NIGER	
10 FRANCS	
25 FRANCS	
50 FRANCS	
100 FRANCS	
NORWAY	
1 500 KRONER	
OMAN	
25 BAISA	
50 BAISA	
100 BAISA	
1/4 OMANI RIAL	
1/2 OMANI RIAL	
OMANI RIAL	
5 OMANI RIALS	
10 OMANI RIALS	
15 OMANI RIALS	
20 OMANI RIALS	
25 OMANI RIALS	
75 OMANI RIALS	
PAKISTAN	
3 000 RUPEES	
PANAMA	
100 BALBOAS	
500 BALBOAS	
PAPUA NEW GUINEA	
100 KINA	
PERU	
1/5 LIBRA	
1/2 LIBRA	
1 LIBRA	
5 SOLES	
10 SOLES	
20 SOLES	

50 SOLES	
100 SOLES	
PHILIPPINES	
1 000 PISO	
1 500 PISO	
5 000 PISO	
POLAND	
50 ZLOTY (Golden Eagle)	
100 ZLOTY (Golden Eagle)	
100 ZLOTY	
200 ZLOTY (Golden Eagle)	
200 ZLOTY	
500 ZLOTY (Golden Eagle)	
PORTUGAL	
1 ESCUDO	
100 ESCUDOS	
200 ESCUDOS	
500 ESCUDOS	
10 000 REIS	
5 EURO	
8 EURO	
RHODESIA	
10 SHILLINGS	
1 POUND	
5 POUNDS	
RUSSIA	
25 ROUBLES	
50 ROUBLES	
100 ROUBLES	
200 ROUBLES	
1 000 ROUBLES	
10 000 ROUBLES	
RWANDA	
10 FRANCS	
25 FRANCS	
50 FRANCS	
100 FRANCS	

SAN MARINO	
1 SCUDO	
2 SCUDI	
5 SCUDI	
10 SCUDI	
20 EURO	
50 EURO	
SAUDI ARABIA	
1 GUINEA (= 1 SAUDI POUND)	
SENEGAL	
10 FRANCS	
25 FRANCS	
50 FRANCS	
100 FRANCS	
250 FRANCS	
500 FRANCS	
1 000 FRANCS	
2 500 FRANCS	
SERBIA	
10 DINARA	
20 DINARA	
SEYCHELLES	
1 000 RUPEES	
1 500 RUPEES	
SIERRA LEONE	
1/4 GOLDE	
1/2 GOLDE	
1 GOLDE	
5 GOLDE	
10 GOLDE	
1 LEONE	
20 DOLLARS	
50 DOLLARS	
100 DOLLARS	
250 DOLLARS	
500 DOLLARS	
2 500 DOLLARS	

SINGAPORE		1 oz NATURA	
1 DOLLAR		1/10 PROTEA	
2 DOLLARS		1 PROTEA	
5 DOLLARS		1/2 POND	
10 DOLLARS		1 POND	
20 DOLLARS		1 RAND	
25 DOLLARS		2 RAND	
50 DOLLARS		5 RAND	
100 DOLLARS		25 RAND	
150 DOLLARS		1/2 SOVEREIGN (= 1/2 POUND)	
250 DOLLARS		1 SOVEREIGN (= 1 POUND)	
500 DOLLARS			
		SOUTH KOREA	
SLOVENIA		2 500 WON	
2 500 TOLARS		20 000 WON	
5 000 TOLARS		25 000 WON	
20 000 TOLARS		30 000 WON	
25 000 TOLARS		50 000 WON	
100 EURO			
180 EURO		**SPAIN**	
		2 (ESCUDOS)	
SOLOMON ISLANDS		10 (ESCUDOS)	
10 DOLLARS		10 PESETAS	
25 DOLLARS		20 PESETAS	
50 DOLLARS		5 000 PESETAS	
100 DOLLARS		10 000 PESETAS	
		20 000 PESETAS	
SOMALIA		40 000 PESETAS	
20 SHILLINGS		80 000 PESETAS	
50 SHILLINGS		200 EURO	
100 SHILLINGS		400 EURO	
200 SHILLINGS			
500 SHILLINGS		**SUDAN**	
1 500 SHILLINGS		25 POUNDS	
		50 POUNDS	
SOUTH AFRICA		100 POUNDS	
1/10 KRUGERRAND			
1/4 KRUGERRAND		**SURINAM**	
1/2 KRUGERRAND		100 GULDEN	
1 KRUGERRAND			
1/10 oz NATURA		**SWAZILAND**	
1/4 oz NATURA		2 EMALANGENI	
1/2 oz NATURA		5 EMALANGENI	

10 EMALANGENI	
20 EMALANGENI	
25 EMALANGENI	
50 EMALANGENI	
100 EMALAGENI	
250 EMALAGENI	
1 LILANGENI	
SWEDEN	
20 KRONOR	
1 000 KRONOR	
2 000 KRONOR	
SWITZERLAND	
50 FRANCS	
100 FRANCS	
SYRIA	
(1/2 POUND)	
(1 POUND)	
TANZANIA	
1 500 SHILINGI	
2 000 SHILINGI	
THAILAND	
(150 BAHT)	
(300 BAHT)	
(400 BAHT)	
(600 BAHT)	
(800 BAHT)	
(1 500 BAHT)	
(2 500 BAHT)	
(3 000 BAHT)	
(4 000 BAHT)	
(5 000 BAHT)	
(6 000 BAHT)	
TONGA	
1/2 HAU	
1 HAU	
5 HAU	
1/4 KOULA	

1/2 KOULA	
1 KOULA	
TUNISIA	
2 DINARS	
5 DINARS	
10 DINARS	
20 DINARS	
40 DINARS	
75 DINARS	
10 FRANCS	
20 FRANCS	
100 FRANCS	
5 PIASTRES	
TURKEY	
(25 KURUSH) (= 25 PIASTRES)	
(50 KURUSH) (= 50 PIASTRES)	
(250 KURUSH) (= 250 PIASTRES)	
(500 KURUSH) (= 500 PIASTRES)	
1/2 LIRA	
1 LIRA	
500 LIRA	
1 000 LIRA	
10 000 LIRA	
50 000 LIRA	
100 000 LIRA	
200 000 LIRA	
1 000 000 LIRA	
60 000 000 LIRA	
TURKS & CAICOS ISLANDS	
100 CROWNS	
TUVALU	
50 DOLLARS	
UGANDA	
50 SHILLINGS	
100 SHILLINGS	
500 SHILLINGS	
1 000 SHILLINGS	

UNITED ARAB EMIRATES
(500 DIRHAMS)
(750 DIRHAMS)
(1 000 DIRHAMS)

UNITED KINGDOM
(1/3 GUINEA)
(1/2 GUINEA)
50 PENCE
2 POUNDS
5 POUNDS
10 POUNDS
25 POUNDS
50 POUNDS
100 POUNDS
(1/2 SOVEREIGN) (= 1/2 POUND)
(2 SOVEREIGNS)
(5 SOVEREIGNS)

URUGUAY
5 000 NUEVO PESOS
20 000 NUEVO PESOS
5 PESOS

USA
10 DOLLARS (AMERICAN EAGLE)
1 DOLLAR
2,5 DOLLARS
5 DOLLARS
20 DOLLARS
25 DOLLARS
50 DOLLARS

VATICAN
10 LIRE GOLD
20 LIRE

100 LIRE GOLD
20 EURO
50 EURO

VENEZUELA
(10 BOLIVARES)
(20 BOLIVARES)
(100 BOLIVARES)
1 000 BOLIVARES
3 000 BOLIVARES
5 000 BOLIVARES
10 000 BOLIVARES
5 VENEZOLANOS

WESTERN SAMOA
50 TALA
100 TALA

YUGOSLAVIA
1 DUCAT
4 DUCATS
20 DINARA
100 DINARA
200 DINARA
500 DINARA
1 000 DINARA
1 500 DINARA
2 000 DINARA
2 500 DINARA
5 000 DINARA

ZAIRE
100 ZAIRES

ZAMBIA
250 KWACHA

Glossary of Terms

Accountable Person

Any person who supplies or intends to supply taxable goods or services in the course or furtherance of business is an accountable person. In some circumstances there are de minimus limits and accountable persons are only those persons making (or intending to make) supplies above these limits.

As in other fields of taxation, the word 'person' does not refer simply to individuals but also to trustees, partnerships, companies and public corporations. In some countries it also applies to local authorities in certain circumstances.

Acquisition - intra-Community goods transaction within the European Union

Acquisition of the right to dispose as owner of movable tangible property dispatched or transported to the person acquiring the goods by or on behalf of the vendor or the person acquiring the goods to a Member State other than that from which the goods are dispatched or transported.

Appeals

A taxable person may appeal to the courts to arbitrate in certain disputes between the person and Revenue authorities, for example, additional tax imposed by the authorities, refusal by the authorities to repay tax which has been overpaid and formal interpretation by the authorities, etc. In some countries an appeal must first be heard by an independent arbitrator before going to court.

Normally there is a very short time limit within which the aggrieved person may lodge written notice of appeal.

Chain Transactions

Several entrepreneurs/taxable persons may enter into subsequent transactions, involving the same goods. Each person within the chain is then deemed to have made a supply, even if the actual ownership is transferred directly from the first to the last recipient in the chain.

In some countries-special rules apply to determine the place of supply of the goods involved in chain transactions.

Consideration

That which is given in exchange for the supply and on which the charge to tax is based. It may take the form of money, barter, or the performance of some service, the release from an obligation, etc.

Where goods or services are supplied for a consideration which does not wholly consist of money, the amount on which tax is chargeable is usually the open market value of the goods or services supplied.

When there is no consideration in any form there is no liability to VAT for services, (but supplies of goods may be deemed to be taxable supplies whether or not made for a consideration) and generally there is no entitlement to a credit for related input tax.

Even if there is no consideration in any form, goods and services used for the entrepreneur's non-taxable activities may be liable to VAT in certain circumstances.

Convention

A convention is an international agreement between the Member States aimed at securing for the benefit of their nationals one of the objects listed under Article 220 of the Treaty. It has to be ratified by all the member states before it comes into effect.

In the field of taxation, Council directives are the norm, with limited exceptions.

Decision

A decision is binding on those to whom it is addressed. Decisions may be addressed to individuals, Member States or Community institutions.

Recommendations and opinions are two other forms of EEC instrument, but these have no legal effect.

Deferred accounting system

Under the deferred accounting system VAT is due at the time of removal of the goods from the port, or is payable by direct debit to the importer's bank account after the removal (ie on the fifteenth day of the month following the removal). The importer needs an appropriate guarantee.

Delivery

Delivery means the time at which the transfer of ownership of the goods occurs, thus triggering the liability to VAT. Transfer of ownership generally coincides with the handing over of the goods.

Directive

A directive, while binding on each member state as to the result to be achieved, leaves to national authorities the form and methods of implementation. Unlike a regulation, a directive does not have legal effect until it is implemented by a member state. However, if a directive is not implemented by the date laid down, it may confer on individuals rights which are enforceable by the national courts.

Distance sales

A distance sale (within the European Union) is one in which goods are sold to an unregistered person in a different Member State to that of the seller and the goods are transported by or on behalf of the seller to the customer's country.

EEC

The European Economic Community (EEC) was one of three European Communities. Where general reference is made to the European Communities, as distinct from the EEC, this is abbreviated to EC and is often referred to as the Community. Since the Treaty on European Union the Union is referred to as the EU.

Election to be subject to VAT

A person who makes taxable supplies but who does not qualify to be registered for VAT because his turnover is below the registration threshold together with farmers and fishermen'may elect to be subject to VAT so also may farmers and fishermen.

EFTA countries

The countries belonging to the European Free Trade Association (EFTA) are Iceland, Norway and Switzerland.

Entrepreneur

Anyone, other than employees, independently conducting a trade, business or liberal profession will generally qualify as an entrepreneur.

One can be an entrepreneur whatever the form of trade or business. It therefore includes individuals, companies, trustees, partnerships, public corporations, local authorities, etc. An entrepreneur will be considered a taxable person if he makes taxable supplies.

EU

European Union (see EEC)

Euro €

This is the name for the European currency unit, which is common currency in the 'euro zone' countries. It was previously known as the ECU (european currency unit) and prior to that the EUA (european unit of account) The-unit of account was previously used to determine Member States' contributions to the budget. In April 1975 the ECU was introduced.

The national currencies of the Member States in the 'euro-zone' have been fixed irrevocably to the Euro by Council Regulation (EC) No 2866/98 and Council Regulation (EC) No. 1478/2000 as follows:

1 euro	=	40,3399	Belgian francs
	=	1,95583	German marks
	=	340,750	Greek Drachma
	=	166,386	Spanish pesetas
	=	6,55957	French francs
	=	0,787564	Irish pounds
	=	1,936,27	Italian lire
	=	0,585274	Cyprus pounds
	=	40,3399	Luxembourg francs
	=	0,429300	Maltese liras
	=	2,20371	Dutch guilders
	=	13,7603	Austrian schillings
	=	200,482	Portuguese escudos
	=	239,640	Slovenian tolars
	=	30,1260	Slovak korunas
	=	5,94573	Finnish marks

Exempt

This term normally denotes supplies which are not liable to VAT. However, in some countries certain supplies may be exempt with credit or exempt without credit for input tax.

Exemption with credit for input tax

This applies to supplies, such as exports, international transport, etc where output tax is not chargeable but the supplier is entitled to recover input tax subject to local regulations. This is similar to zero-rating in many countries.

Exemption without credit for input tax

This applies to supplies which are specifically excluded from the charge to tax by local legislation. Persons making such supplies are not entitled to recover any related input tax.

They are, in effect, regarded as the end users.

Exports

Means the exportation of goods to a destination outside the European Union. For example goods shipped from Ireland to Peru.

Imported services

Services received from outside a country are sometimes referred to as imported services. Their liability to VAT depends on the place of supply as defined and they may sometimes give rise to the reverse charge mechanism.

Imports

Means the importation of goods from outside the European Union into Ireland either

(a)   directly, or

(b)   through one or more than one other Member State where VAT has not been charged in the other Member State(s).

It is important to note that the importation of a good gives rise to a charge to VAT. The VAT is charged by Customs & Excise when the goods arrive in the country.

Inclusive/Exclusive

The words inclusive and exclusive are simply used to describe whether the price of a good or service is including or excluding the VAT element of the price.

Inclusive means the price quoted is the gross price (net price + VAT).

Exclusive means the price quoted is the net price only.

When an unregistered person (private individual) considers buying an item he is interested in the inclusive cost.

However when a registered person (shopkeeper) considers buying an item for his business use he is interested in the exclusive price as he is entitled to claim back the VAT he pays out on buying the item.

Interest - commercial

Interest charged by suppliers is regarded as taxable when it is related to the late payment of taxable supplies.

Interest - financial

Interest charged for loans granted by banks or financial institutions, or by suppliers independently from the supply of goods or services, is not taxable.

Input tax

Input tax is VAT incurred by a person on the importation, acquisition or purchase of goods and services. It can be offset against output tax or refunded if in excess of output tax when it is attributable to the provision of taxable goods and services. The recovery of VAT is limited in the case of partial exemption and in respect of certain specific items.

Non-taxable Supply of Goods

The following transactions are not supplied under the Act:

1. Transfer of ownership of goods as a security for a loan or debt or the handing back of such goods on repayment of the loan or debt

2. Transfer of business of part of a business from one taxable person to another

3. Gifts of goods made in the course of furtherance of a business providing the cost of the goods to the donor does not exceed €20. For example a grocer gives a customer a bottle of whiskey as a gift at Christmas valued at €15 pounds, this is not a taxable supply. However if the gift was valued at €30 VAT inclusive the gift is a taxable supply with a VAT liability of €5.30.

4. Gifts of industrial samples in reasonable quantities to potential customers providing the samples are in form not ordinarily available for sale to the public. For example shampoo sachets delivered door to door as a marketing ploy.

OJ

OJ is a reference to the *Official Journal of the European Communities*. The OJ is the publication in which certain regulations and directives must be published. Adopted legislation is published in the 'L' series, proposals in the 'C' series. References to the OJ in this report refer to the number of the publication and the year, e.g. OJ L145/77 therefore signifies journal number 145 in the L series of 1977.

Objections/claims

In order to obtain a reduction or a repayment of VAT wrongly assessed, an entrepreneur must file a formal request to the local tax authorities. Objections have to be submitted within certain time limits which differ from country to country. It is only after the tax authorities have made their decision that it can be appealed before the courts (see also 'Appeals').

Partial exemption

A taxable person who supplies goods and services some of which are taxable and some exempt is regarded as 'partially exempt'. In such circumstances input tax is generally only recoverable where it was paid on the purchase, acquisition or importation of goods or services which are attributable to the taxable business. Where tax was suffered on goods or importations which were used for both taxable and non-taxable purposes only a proportion of such input VAT may be recovered.

Place of supply of Goods

As Irish VAT liability only applies to supplies in Ireland it is important to be able to identify when a supply is made here.

Most supplies are covered by the rule that the place where goods are located at the time of supply is the place of supply.

However while most supplies would be covered by this rule there are special rules for dealing with certain supplies involving transportation or assembly of the goods.

Where goods are transported (other than Distance Sales) the place of supply is where the transport begins. However there is a provision that where the goods are transported from outside the European Union, the place of supply by the person who imports the goods and the place of any subsequent supplies shall be deemed to where the goods are imported.

In the case of goods being supplied and installed or assembled by or on behalf of the supplier, the place of supply is where the goods are installed or assembled.

In the case of goods supplied on board vessels, aircraft or trains during transport, the places of departure and destination of which are within the European Union, the place of supply is where the transport began.

Where goods (other than new means of transport) are transported by or on behalf of the supplier (i.e. Distance sales)

(1) (a) from the territory of another Member State, or

(b) from outside the European Union through the territory of another Member State into which the goods have been imported.

to a person who is not a taxable person in the State, or

(2) from the State to a person in another Member State who is not registered for VAT,

the place where the goods are when the transportation ends.

Place of Supply of Services

For most services there is little difficulty in determining the place of their supply. For example, the services of cinemas, restaurants, hairdressers, etc. are supplied where the business is situated.

However the situation is not always as simple. In order to avoid double taxation or non-taxation, rules have been drawn up relating to the place where services are to be treated as supplied.

General Rule

The general rule is that the service is taxable where the supplier is established.

Similarly, the place of supply of repair services is also the place where the repair is carried out.

Property

The place where services connected with immovable property are supplied is the place where the property is situated.

Services supplied in connection with property situated outside the State are not therefore liable to Irish VAT. The services may, however, be liable to VAT in the other country.

Transport And Related Ancillary Services

These services, whether in relation to goods or passengers, are in most cases treated as being supplied where the transport takes place.

However, special rules relate to the transport of goods between EU Member States.

Cultural, Artistic, Sporting, Scientific, Educational Or Entertainment Services

The place where these services are supplied for VAT purposes is the place where they are physically performed.

Fourth Schedule Services

The services affected are;

(a) Transfers and assignments of copyrights, patents, licences, trade marks and similar rights

(b) Hiring out of movable goods other than means of transport

(c) Advertising services

(d) Services of consultants, engineers, constancy bureaux, lawyers, accountants and other similar services, data processing and provision of information (but excluding services connected with immovable goods)

(e) Acceptance of any obligation to refrain from pursuing or exercising in whole or in part, any business activity or any such rights as are referred to in paragraph (a)

(f) Banking, financial and insurance services (excluding re-insurance, but not including the provision of safe deposit facilities)

(g) The provision of staff

(h) The services of intermediaries who act in the name and for the account of a principle when procuring any services specified above.

(i) Telecommunications services

(j) The provision of access to, and of transport or transmission through, natural gas and electricity distribution systems and the provision of other directly linked services.

When Fourth Schedule Services are received for a business purpose in this State from abroad the place of supply is deemed to be in this State and it is the recipient who is liable for payment of VAT.

This provision means that even persons engaged in "VAT-exempt" activities e.g. insurance, banking, stockbroking and bookmaking, who are not registered for VAT in respect of their normal supplies are obliged to register and account for VAT in respect of Fourth Schedule services received from abroad.

Similarly when such services are supplied from a business in the State to a person in another Member State of the European Union for the purpose of his business then Irish VAT is not chargeable on the supply.

The VAT is charged in the State where the recipient has his place of establishment. Services supplied for non-business purposes in another Member State do attract Irish VAT. Services supplied to non-EU countries are not liable for Irish VAT whether for business or private use.

The purpose of the provisions dealing with Fourth Schedule services is to avoid unfair competition within the European Union.

Postponed accounting system

Under the postponed accounting system, entrepreneurs/taxable persons in some countries may import goods without payment of VAT at the point of entry, but may defer payment until the next periodic VAT return.

Provided the importer is not exempt or partially exempt (ie he is fully taxable and thus entitled to a credit for input tax), no VAT will actually become payable.

Special application must be made to the tax authorities for permission to use the postponed accounting system and there are certain conditions which must be met. Normally only resident entrepreneurs qualify for the system.

Real estate/real property/immovable properties

These terms apply to land and buildings.

Registered person

A taxable person who has complied with the obligation to register with the tax authorities is a registered person. Not every taxable person is obliged to register for VAT because of de minimus limits or special regimes (for example, for farmers and fishermen).

Some taxable persons who are not required to register may do so voluntarily and in some countries persons supplying certain exempt services or goods may also register voluntarily.

Normally a taxable person is registered only once in respect of all his business activities, but in some countries it is possible to register separate parts or divisions of the same business.

Regulation (European Council/Commission)

A regulation is general in application and normally directly binds all the Member States from the date of its adoption as if it were a national law. No implementing legislation is required. National laws conflicting with an EEC regulation are overridden.

Reverse charge mechanism

In certain cases liability to the tax shifts from the supplier to the recipient. This is achieved by deeming the recipient to be the supplier as if he had supplied the service to himself. He is also entitled to treat the deemed supply as a purchase. If the recipient is fully taxable there will normally not be any additional tax payable, but if he is exempt or partially exempt some of the VAT payable may not be recoverable.

This mechanism is applied differently in many countries. In the Netherlands, it also concerns goods and services provided in the Netherlands by foreign non-resident entrepreneurs. In Ireland, the United Kingdom and France it only concerns the supply of specified services imported by resident entrepreneurs.

Sixth Council Directive

The central VAT text to which reference is frequently made is the sixth VAT directive. Its full title is the 'Sixth Council Directive 77/388/EEC on the harmonisation of the laws of the Member States relating to turnover taxes - Common system of value added tax: uniform basis of assessment'. The Sixth Directive was repealed by Council Directive No. 2006/112/EC of 28 November 2006, with effect from 1 January 2007.

Taxes and duties

Value added tax is a multi-stage consumption tax where tax paid (VAT) by traders on their purchases is generally refunded so that the trader effectively pays tax only on the value he has added to the product. Such a tax is a multi-stage non-cumulative tax because the tax paid at a previous stage in the chain does not cumulate.

Cascade tax is one where no credit is given to traders for tax paid on the purchase of their inputs. Such a tax is therefore a multi-stage cumulative tax. Herein lies the main difference from VAT.

Excise duties are the most commonly applied selective consumption taxes. The 'major excises are levied on drinking, smoking and motoring, although a wide range of other selective excises are applied. Excise duties are major revenue earners but can also be used, inter alia, to discourage certain forms of consumption or to implement the 'polluter pays' principle.

Taxable person

Any person (i.e. individual, trustee, partnership, company etc.) who independently carries out any business in the State is a taxable person.

Taxable Supply of Goods

A taxable supply of goods means the normal transfer of ownership of goods by one person to another and includes the supply of goods at the zero rate. It takes place in any of the following circumstances:

(1)   When ownership of goods is transferred by agreement

(2)   When goods are handed over under a hire-purchase or leasing agreement

(3)   When a contractor hands over to a customer goods which he has made up from materials supplied to him in whole or in part by the customer

(4)   When a person appropriates to a private or exempt use goods or materials which he has himself processed, purchased or imported

(5)   When goods are seized by a sheriff or other person acting under legal authority

(6)   The supply of electricity, gas and any form of power, heat, refrigeration or ventilation

(7)   When goods are transferred from a persons business in the State to another Member State for the purpose of his business or the transfer of a new means of transport by a person in the State to the territory of another Member State

(8)   With effect 1/1/93 the intra-Community acquisition of goods by business persons VAT free is a taxable supply

Some points in connection with the above should be noted:

1.   The supply of ready to eat zero-rated food by a catering business -hotel, cafe, canteen etc., is a service not a supply of goods

2.   Supply of goods under a hire-purchase agreement is not a service but a taxable supply of the goods in question but the handing over of the goods at the termination of the agreement is not a supply

3.   For example, a manufacturer constructs an exhibition stand from materials supplied by a customer. The effect is the same as if the customer had bought the stand without supplying any of the materials.

4.   Where a builder builds a house for his own use, there is a taxable supply

5.   It is as if the taxable person had sold the goods and paid the sheriff. It is an anti-evasion clause to ensure that the final purchaser has paid tax on the goods

Taxable Supply of Services

For VAT purposes a service is any commercial activity other than a supply of goods. Typical services include the services of caterers, mechanics, plumbers, accountants, solicitors, consultants, etc. and the hiring or leasing of goods. Services also include refraining, for a consideration, from doing something and the granting and surrendering of a right.

Trader

A registered person is often referred to as a trader.

Transfer of business

The sale of the assets and liabilities of a business by one taxable person to another is not regarded as a taxable supply in most countries. Normally input tax suffered in connection with such a transfer is recoverable.

In some countries all of the business must be sold as a going concern; in others the sale of part of a business which is not a going concern may also qualify as a non-taxable supply.

Waiver of exemption

In some countries, persons supplying certain exempt services and goods may elect to charge VAT on the supply and thus become taxable persons in respect of that supply. Such action will generally entitle them to a credit for input tax. In some countries it is referred to as 'opting to tax'.

Zero rate

In some countries the rate of tax applicable to some taxable supplies, such as exports, foods, etc, is zero. Because the supply is liable to VAT, the supplier is entitled to recovery of input tax subject to local regulations. It is similar to the term 'exemption with credit' used in some other countries.

In some countries all of the business must be sold as a going concern. In others, the sale of part of a business which is not a going concern may also qualify as a non-taxable supply.

Waiver of exemption

In some countries a person supplying certain exempt services and goods may elect to charge VAT on their supply and must treat the taxable persons in respect of that supply. Such election will generally entitle them to a credit for input tax. In some countries it is referred to as 'opting to tax'.

Zero rate

In some countries the rate of tax applicable to comparable supplies, such as... foods, are... zero. Because the supply is liable to VAT the supplier is entitled to recover... or input tax subject to local regulations. It is similar to the term 'exemption with credit' used in some other countries.

LAW OF VALUE ADDED TAX

INDEX TO PROVISIONS